PRENTICE HALL

Social
Studies

The
quality
choice
for
today's
classrooms

TEACHER'S EDITION

PRENTICE HALL

AMERICA
PATHWAYS
TO THE
PRESENT

With Integrated Technology
• Videodiscs
• Videotapes
• Interactive Software
• Internet Activities
• CD-ROMs

Prentice Hall
can help you
build a bridge.

The only U.S. History Program that creates a bridge to today.

America: Pathways to the Present ©1998

The Student Edition starts with a simple idea: history is not predictable.

History's decision makers—whether famous or ordinary citizens—never knew how things were going to turn out. But the consequences of their decisions helped determine how we arrived where we are today. Tracing these pathways makes students active participants in the unfolding of history.

In developing the narrative for each chapter, the authors utilized the concept of the "big idea." The "big idea" organizes and focuses the chapter, helping students better see the connections between the diverse peoples and stories of a period.

Students' understanding is strengthened by focusing on turning points in history, events that changed the course of history and have lasting impact on our contemporary lives.

A Teacher's Edition that organizes and focuses instruction.

Every historical period is a complex web of events, influences, and relationships. But in each era there is a main trend, a big idea, that can be used pedagogically to cut through the clutter and help students understand, focus, and master this important subject matter.

Each chapter of the Teacher's Edition is "jump started" by discussing the relevance of the big idea that organizes chapter content. The lesson plan that follows is structured around that big idea, too.

Our Teacher's Edition employs a wraparound style in which comments, answers to questions, program resources, and background notes occur when you need them. It is the teaching equivalent of perfect timing.

Teaching Resources based on real-world strategies.

Arranged on a chapter-by-chapter basis, the extensive Teaching Resources package combines everything you need in one place. We provide you with every bit of mortar and steel you need to build a bridge to your students. The *Social Studies Educator's Handbook* series provides information on educational issues with strategies tested by teachers in actual classrooms.

The Transparencies recognize that *some* students learn better visually.

The visual medium of the transparencies is perfect for showing historical change. For example, you can use **Pathways'** set of overlay transparencies to follow the evolution of a theme across the span of U.S. History.

Multimedia Resources that recognize your need for flexibility.

Prentice Hall's award-winning original multimedia package is specifically designed to work simultaneously with this new U.S. History program. Finally you will have the opportunity to merge print and media together easily. For those who have access to videotape, videodisc, or computer equipment, **Pathways** provides this optional level of integrated classroom technology. Also available are CD-ROMs, Internet activities, additional videotapes and videodiscs— with point-of-use correlations.

In addition, you can take advantage of our:

• Computer Test Bank (Macintosh and Windows)
• Social Studies Update
• Guided Reading Audiotapes (Spanish and English)
• *Our Times, Multimedia Encyclopedia of the 20th Century* CD-ROM
• *Resource Pro*™ CD-ROM

" One of our biggest challenges is to get kids to realize that history is meaningful. . . .
Many students think, 'What do I need this for?' "
— *Indiana United States history teacher*

Pathways Makes History Relevant . . .

1 Through a Dramatic Narrative

Political and Social History. *America: Pathways to the Present* offers a balance of political and social history, telling the stories of key people and events as well as capturing what life was like for ordinary Americans. *(See the Table of Contents, pages vi–1.)*

> H undreds of bodies of our brave boys lie on Hill 212, captured with such a brave loss of blood. . . .

Primary Sources. Primary sources and first-person accounts are interspersed throughout the narrative, adding a human face to far-off events. *(See pages 114, 273, 345, and 561 for examples.)*

 SOURCE READINGS

America: Pathways to the Present ends each unit with Source Readings—a collection of primary sources and literature that relates to chapter content. *(See pages 1 and 2 for a complete list.)*

 **In Depth**
Multicultural Perspectives

America: Pathways to the Present reflects the multicultural nature of United States history, recognizing that diversity has given the United States its special character. In-Depth notes in the **Teacher's Edition** offer additional information for teachers to share with students. *(For examples in the Student Edition, see pages 79, 86, 361, 711, 831, and 838. For examples in the Teacher's Edition, see pages 76, 112, 291, and 709.)*

2 By Looking In Depth at Pivotal Moments in Our Past

 TURNING POINTS

Certain events—turning points— have shifted the direction of American society and had immediate consequences on political, economic, and social life. Each of these turning points also had a lasting impact that can still be felt today. *(See pages 256, 402, 629, and 803 for examples.)*

 RESOURCE DIRECTORY

In the **Teaching Resources** box you will find extension activities that further explore the lasting impact of each "Turning Point" event.

 Videodiscs/Videotapes

Visions of America, the program's award-winning multimedia component, includes "Turning Point" stories that dramatize the "Turning Points" with archival footage. In addition, *Visions of America* includes "Roundtable Discussions" in which historians debate and discuss the turning point's meaning. Barcodes in the **Teacher's Edition** correlate videodisc segments to **Student Edition** content.

3 By Encouraging Students to Become Active Learners

MAKING CONNECTIONS

Questions in the middle of each section ask students to connect what they have just read with something they read earlier or with something in their own lives. *(See pages 139, 216, 220, and 437 for examples.)*

4 By Emphasizing Decision Making

History might not have Happened This Way

"History Might Not Have Happened This Way" features focus on key decisions, exploring the background of the decision makers, both famous and ordinary, and the consequences of their decisions. By emphasizing that people's decisions influence the course of history, students come to see that they, too, can play a part in shaping the present and future. *(See pages 52, 134, 486, 764, and 928 for examples.)*

 ## RESOURCE DIRECTORY

In the **Teaching Resources** box are decision-making extension activities that focus on a contemporary decision related to each "History Might Not Have Happened This Way" topic in the **Student Edition**.

Computer Software

Visions of America includes a software game that allows students to explore pivotal decisions in United States history.

5 By Appealing to Today's Visual Learners

  ## Maps, Graphs, Charts and Tables

The **Student Edition** includes maps, graphs, charts, tables, and graphic organizers designed to meet the needs of visual learners. These illustrations, along with photographs, provide opportunities for visual learners to study U.S. history. *(See pages 140, 207, 219, 283, and 693 for examples.)*

 ## Teaching Resources

"Visual Learning Activities" in the **Teaching Resources** utilize cartoons, advertisements, posters, and photographs to illustrate main ideas, summarize chapter content, and spark discussion. *(See pages 27 and 28 of the Unit 1 folder in the Teaching Resources for examples.)*

 ## Transparencies

A collection of 170 color overhead transparencies with lesson suggestions includes fine art, maps, charts, tables, political cartoons, and photographs—to help you teach and enrich main ideas. *(See the Transparency Sampler in the Teaching Resources box.)*

 ## American Album

Pictorial essays in each unit teach history through artifacts from the exhibitions and collections of the Smithsonian Institution's National Museum of American History. *(See pages 68, 238, 356, and 714 for examples.)*

 ## Videodiscs/Videotapes

Visions of America videodiscs and videotapes include video montages, "Scenes of an Era," for each unit that capture students' interest with sounds and images as exciting as music videos.

"Here's what matters to me: What has the publisher done to help me cut down on planning time? I want to spend my time teaching—not hunting and gathering."

— *Virginia United States history teacher*

Pathways Makes Instruction Manageable . . .

1 By Focusing on Big Ideas

THE BIG IDEA

Every chapter in *America: Pathways to the Present* was written with a "big idea" in mind. These big ideas help students focus on key ideas in United States history to see how we as a nation got where we are today. To help manage instruction, lesson plans in the **Teacher's Edition** are structured around the big ideas. Before each chapter, a graphic organizer in the **Teacher's Edition** highlights the chapter's big idea and shows how each section of the chapter relates to it. *(See pages 12B and 38B for examples.)*

 ## Connecting to the Big Idea

At the beginning of each section in the **Teacher's Edition** is a suggestion for "Connecting to the Big Idea" to help you focus instruction. *(See page 14 for an example.)* Concluding the section is a suggestion for "Reinforcing the Big Idea" to help you close instruction. *(See page 20 for an example.)* In addition, the **Teaching Resources** includes an alternate lesson plan, "Demonstrating the Big Idea," for every chapter. *(See pages 1, 6, 11, and 16 of the Alternate Lesson Plans folder in the **Teaching Resources** box for examples.)*

2 By Addressing the Needs of Different Types of Learners

Instructional Options. *America: Pathways to the Present* offers a variety of instructional options. In the **Teacher's Edition** you will find a modified Madeline Hunter—Focus, Instruct, Assess, Close—lesson plan in the side columns. *(See pages 14–20 of the **Teacher's Edition** for an example.)* In addition, in the **Teaching Resources**, each section has an alternate lesson plan in one of three categories: Critical Thinking, Cooperative Learning, and Learning Styles. *(See pages 2, 3, 4, and 5 of the Unit 1 folder in the **Teaching Resources** for examples.)*

Assessment Options. In the **Teaching Resources** box you will find traditional methods of assessment, such as chapter and unit tests, as well as information about the Computer Test Bank.

 ## Alternative Assessment

Because many teachers are becoming interested in alternative methods of assessment, the **Teacher's Edition** of *America: Pathways to the Present* offers an alternative assessment activity for every chapter, including suggestions for setting up, monitoring, and evaluating each activity. *(See pages 13, 26, and 37 in the **Teacher's Edition** for examples.)*

RESOURCE DIRECTORY

A separate handbook in the **Teaching Resources** box discusses how to construct alternative assessments such as portfolio and performance assessments for your United States history classes. It also provides scoring rubrics and evaluation forms for both students and teachers.

3 By Organizing Teaching Resources Chapter by Chapter

Unit Folders

America: Pathways to the Present **Teaching Resources** are organized the way you teach — chapter by chapter, arranged in unit folders. All core resources for the chapter are housed in a convenient file folder, eliminating the need for "hunting and gathering." Complete topic-by-topic index is included.

4 By Offering Technology Options That Fit Your Requirements

Multimedia

Visions of America, the award-winning multimedia component custom-made for *America: Pathways to the Present*, is a flexible technology package of videodiscs, videotapes, and software.

United States History Video Collection with videodiscs and videotapes, including a Spanish-language track. Collection spans the nation's history from the beginnings to modern times.

Internet activities for students in the **Student Edition** and additional activities in the **Teacher's Edition.**

Our Times*, *Multimedia Encyclopedia of the 20th Century CD-ROM provides students with access to one of the world's best encylopedias and an interactive way of learning about the pivotal events of the twentieth century.

Decision America videodiscs and videotapes help students in understanding and analyzing contemporary issues.

RESOURCE PRO The entire **Teaching Resources** on CD-ROM includes the program overview, Planning Express to organize and customize your lessons, and the Test Bank.

5 By Clearly Referencing All Program Resources at Point of Use

RESOURCE DIRECTORY

Block Scheduling *America: Pathways to the Present* **Teacher's Edition, Teaching Resources, American History Block Scheduling Support** provides block scheduling options, teacher-developed models, sample unit lessons, and a 40-folder interdisciplinary support box for extended class schedules.

America: Pathways to the Present **Teacher's Edition** brings all these resources together. The **Teaching Resources** includes the Social Studies Educator's Handbooks on trends of interest—from Block Scheduling to Using the Internet. In the Resource Directory at the bottom of each page all program resources—activity sheets, transparencies, and multimedia—are referenced at the point of use. It's the teaching equivalent of perfect timing. *(See pages 12–35 for examples.)*

PRENTICE HALL

AMERICA

PATHWAYS
— TO THE —
PRESENT

Program Reviewers and Advisers

Teacher Reviewers

Pamela Lee Gray
Foothill High School
Tustin, California

Cherlynn Renner
Muncie Central High School
Muncie, Indiana

Phillip James
Lincoln-Sudbury Regional High School
Sudbury, Massachusetts

Jerome L. Ruderman
Social Studies Department Head
Frankford High School
Philadelphia, Pennsylvania

Block Scheduling

Michael Rettig
Assistant Professor of Education
James Madison University
Harrisonburg, Virginia

Judith Cannizzaro
K–12 Social Studies Supervisor
Nashville, Tennessee

Alternative Assessment

Hannah Kruglanski
Director of Curriculum and Assessment
Edunetics Corporation
Arlington, Virginia

Photo Credits
Page T10 *Stone axes* Richard Alexander Cooke III; **T11** *Student at archeological dig* Courtesy, Shaun P. Bresnahan; **T11** *Pueblo bowl* Eric Long, Smithsonian Institution, Courtesy of the Museum of Indian Arts and Culture, Laboratory of Anthropology Collection, Santa Fe; **T17** *Classroom* Ken Karp; **T18** *Disks* David Dennis/Tom Stack & Associates; **T19** *Monitor* Ken O'Donoghue; **T19** *Computer screen image* James Karales; **T19** *Student at computer* FPG International

PRENTICE HALL
Simon & Schuster Education Group
A VIACOM COMPANY

ISBN 0-13-432402-1

1 2 3 4 5 6 7 8 9   02 01 00 99 98

HISTORY EDUCATOR'S HANDBOOK

Making History Relevant

Shaun Bresnahan was voted National Social Studies Teacher of the Year in 1992. He has been teaching United States history in Belchertown, Massachusetts, for thirty years.

RELEVANCE: The Ultimate Challenge

by Shaun Bresnahan

If there is one single challenge that history teachers face continually, it is the challenge of making history relevant to our students. Every year we find it getting harder and harder. We are often asked what spells we use to entice our students to learn. What do we do to challenge our students' intellectual curiosity, encourage self-motivation, and foster critical thinking skills? Each and every one of you has your own methods and ideas. There is no one magical method or technique waiting to be discovered in some dusty tome. I'd like to share with you some of the ways that I try to meet the challenge and teach United States history to my high school class.

Meeting the Challenge

Over the last thirty years, I have designed activities that use a discovery approach to education. I have found that one of the most accessible routes to participation in the study of history is through the study of material culture. The study of material culture, or artifact analysis, has been a tool in anthropology and archeology for some time now. By examining objects from the past, students take on the roles of researcher, archeologist, and detective. They explore not only the physical remains of past societies but also the thoughts and feelings of people in the period they are studying. Primary sources abound in the form of architecture, music, tools, and toys; and they can be found in every town and community throughout the country. Artifacts in all forms, from a bowl or button to a computer or church window, offer students a glimpse of the past, a puzzle to solve, and a problem to analyze in their continuing efforts to bridge the historical past and connect it to their own lives.

Here are some of the strategies that I use to make history meaningful to my students and to teach them the critical thinking and evaluative skills that are so necessary in the world today.

Role-Play

I walk into the classroom and say, "I pledge you, I pledge myself, to a new deal for the American public." Or I bring in an apple, write on the chalkboard, "There were 6,000 apple sellers in New York City in 1931," and recite a song, "I don't want your millions, mister. I don't want your diamond ring. All I want is the right to live, mister. Give me back my job again." "Who are these characters?" I ask my students. "What are they talking about, and why?" I stay in character and answer students' questions.

Artifact Analysis

When examining the cultural diversity of the indigenous peoples of the Atlantic World, I conduct a simulated archeological dig. Using a soccer or baseball field, I section off the field into a number of "sites" and cover each one with a plastic trash bag. On top of each trash bag are artifacts representing cultures we studied in class. These include vegetables, broken pottery, pictures of Native American masks, animal skins, and burnt ash. Students probe and investigate a number of sites and reconstruct information from that period. During the course of the archeological dig, students participate in games, listen to music, and eat foods that represent the cultures being studied. I've done this activity in my classroom on a smaller scale covering almost every time period in United States history.

History Alive

I have my students choose a time period, event, or society that they would like to explore in greater detail. Then they re-create that time or event by using primary source documents, artifacts, and role-playing. The history of our local community has always been a favorite topic. I have used our high school gym to stage the re-creation of our community as it was two hundred years ago. Through dance, music, art, and a little carpentry, students become members of our eighteenth-century town. This is the stuff that cultural history is made of. Students soon begin to discover what makes history; they personalize it, and they undertake the reassembling of history in order to bring it to life.

The Mystery of History

Not all my classes are devoted to creating Federalist villages or archeological digs. I have students focus on how a particular event in history has influenced their lives. Or I ask them to consider what their lives might have been like if the incident had happened differently. How might our societies have been affected? Why did the participants in a particular historical event make the decisions they did? The process of answering these questions helps students understand that history is not, as they often think, a predetermined straight line connecting the past to the present. The people involved in an event did not know how things would turn out. As students come to recognize the uncertain and dramatic quality of the past for those who lived through it, they can begin to see that they, too, are participants in history.

These strategies may not cast a magic spell. But I do believe that they arouse curiosity. They prompt students to be active in learning history, convey to them that their decisions, too, play a part in determining how the present will be remembered, and above all give them a sense that history is a great adventure.

Artifacts—from a bowl or button to a computer or church window—offer students a glimpse of the past, a puzzle to solve, and a problem to analyze in their continuing efforts to bridge the historical past and connect it to their own lives.

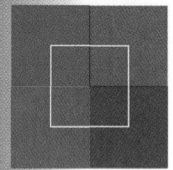

Block Scheduling

Michael Rettig, Assistant Professor of Education
James Madison University, Harrisonburg, Virginia

Judith Cannizzaro, K–12 Social Studies
Supervisor, Nashville, Tennessee

D uring the past ten years, American schools have been experimenting with a new kind of organization known as block scheduling. These schools have shifted from the traditional school day, organized into six, seven, or eight single class periods, to "block" schedules, in which students take fewer classes of longer duration daily.

Why Block Scheduling?

Teachers who are adopting block scheduling hope to ease a number of problems that they associate with the traditional school day. By introducing block scheduling, they say, schools will:

- Reduce the number of students teachers must interact with each day and/or each term.

- Reduce the number of courses teachers must prepare for each day and/or each term.

- Reduce the number of classes that students attend and prepare for each day and/or each term.

- Provide teachers with blocks of teaching time that allow and encourage the use of active teaching strategies and greater student involvement.

- Give teachers more planning time.

- Provide students with variable amounts of time for learning, without lowering standards and without penalizing those who need more or less time to learn.

- Reduce the number of class changes and the discipline problems that go along with them.

- Give teachers the time to deal with discipline problems as they arise.

Going "On the Block"

Block scheduling can take a variety of forms. Some of the most popular forms are outlined below. It is important to select the one that is suitable for your school situation before going "on the block."

- **Intensive Block** Students on an intensive block schedule concentrate on one or two subjects at a time. The classic intensive block is the trimester plan, which has students completing two courses in 60 days, then moving on to two different courses. Advocates like the intensive block because they can concentrate on fewer students at a time. Critics, however, worry about students who transfer to or from schools on traditional schedules.

- **4x4 Block** Sometimes called the accelerated block, the 4x4 block allows students to take four subjects each semester in blocks of 85 to 100 minutes each. Because of the accelerated pace, students complete a year's work in a single semester. Again, many teachers and students are enthusiastic, but midyear transfers are difficult.

- **A/B Plan** This model is often called the alternating day schedule or block 8 because students attend eight blocks of classes over a two-day period. A variation is to schedule six blocks over two days. The A/B Plan makes transfers easier because students complete courses at about the same pace as students on a traditional schedule.

■ **Modified Block** Many different plans go by this name. At some schools, a modified block combines a 4x4 block four days a week with a traditional seven- or eight-period Friday devoted to electives. At others, students take two block courses and three single-period classes each day. The block courses end after a semester, but the single-period classes continue all year to accommodate music, foreign languages, and other courses that benefit from daily sessions.

"The 4x4 block allows students to take four subjects each semester in blocks of 85 to 100 minutes each. . . . Many teachers and students are enthusiastic, but midyear transfers are difficult."

■ **Other Options** The scheduling options multiply when schools combine various block modifications with different ways of dividing up the school year. One option is a 75-75-30 plan used in an Ohio school. The students have two 75-day block-scheduled semesters. Then, near the end of April, when "school's a bear," they get a fresh start with a short semester in which teachers offer specialty courses in their subject areas. Another variation is a 75-30-75 plan that would offer these courses midyear, the way many colleges do.

From Theory to Practice
America: Pathways to the Present

Student Edition
■ provides hands-on activities appropriate for block schedules in Historian's Toolbox, Time and Place, History Might Not Have Happened This Way, and Turning Points features.
■ features Making Connections activities in each chapter review—including Evaluating Primary Sources, Understanding the Visuals, and Writing About the Chapter—that encourage analysis and presentation.

Teacher's Edition
■ presents a wide range of Alternative Assessment activities that are appropriate for block schedules.
■ offers a cooperative learning lesson idea for each section of the Student Edition. These lesson ideas address differences in learning styles and help develop the group interaction and student-directed learning that is an important goal of block scheduling.

Teaching Resources
■ presents thematic units in the Local History Resources file that are suitable for use in extended class periods.
■ includes a broad variety of Alternate Lesson Plans that are useful for block schedules.
■ features a wide range of multimedia materials, including the *Visions of America* videodiscs and videotapes, and *Resource Pro*™ CD-ROM. These materials, plus full-color atlas and fine art transparencies, can be used to introduce a lesson segment, serve as a transition from one part of a lesson to another, or provide the focus of a wrap-up activity in a block schedule. They can also be useful in student projects and presentations.

American History Block Scheduling Support
■ offers 40 separate folders on key topics in American history, complete with primary source, literature, biography, geography and history, and debating activities.
■ provides classroom-tested sample unit lesson plans designed for teaching in a block.

Dr. Slavin has authored or co-authored more than 140 articles and 14 books, including *Cooperative Learning: Theory, Research, and Practice* (Prentice Hall, 1990); *Educational Psychology: Theory and Practice* (Allyn & Bacon, 1994); *Effective Programs for Students at Risk* (Allyn & Bacon, 1989); *Preventing Early School Failure* (Allyn & Bacon, 1994); and *School and Classroom Organization* (Erlbaum, 1989).

Cooperative Learning

Prentice Hall Interviews Robert Slavin

Cooperative learning is being used now more than ever before. But what is cooperative learning, and why should you incorporate it into your classroom activities?

For a clearer picture, we talked with Dr. Robert E. Slavin, Director of the Early and Elementary School Program at the Center for Research on Effective Schooling for Disadvantaged Students at the Johns Hopkins University Center for Social Organization of Schools. He is one of the nation's leading researchers on the use of cooperative learning in the classroom.

Q What are we talking about when we say "cooperative learning"?

A Cooperative learning actually refers to a wide range of different methods. What is common to all of them is the idea that kids of the same age are working together to help each other learn.

Q How does that happen? How does cooperative learning reinforce or expand learning?

A One of the things that cooperative learning does is motivate students to be concerned about each other's learning, so that students feel that their peers are supporting their learning efforts.

Another benefit is that students, in the process of discussing material presented by the teacher, get to voice their own current understanding. This helps them because people learn by teaching. Cooperative learning also helps kids by filling in gaps in their understanding. Explaining ideas to each other helps kids grasp ideas that they may have only dimly understood at the end of the teacher's lesson.

Q Why should cooperative learning be used in the classroom? For example, what are its benefits?

A The main benefit of cooperative learning is that it improves student achievement. Many studies that have compared it to traditional learning have found that cooperative learning improves the achievement of high, average, and low achievers in many different circumstances.

Cooperative learning also fosters improved intergroup relations, including acceptance of mainstreamed academically handicapped kids. Since kids enjoy working cooperatively, they feel good about a class in which they are able to work together in this way.

Q What is the ideal group size?

A Four is an ideal group size. It allows for activities in pairs and activities as a total team.

Q How should groups be assigned?

A They should be assigned by the teacher. Have a high and a low achiever and a couple of average achievers in each group. Be sure that there's some kind of balance of sex and ethnicity. Take into account which kids are likely to work together—you know, which kids were dating but have now broken up and the personalities involved.

Q What are some specific ways cooperative learning can be used in the social studies classroom?

A There are many forms of cooperative learning that have been successfully used. It is important to use the right methods for the objective being pursued. For example, one method is for students to study together to make sure that everyone has learned a given body of knowledge. Students are then quizzed on the material, and groups earn certificates based on the average of the quiz scores. This is excellent for teaching facts and concepts of history, geography, and economics. Another method, well adapted to learning from texts, requires each student in a group to become an expert on some aspect of a text and to meet with experts from other groups. The experts return to their groups and teach their groupmates what they have learned. A third method involves students working together on group projects, each student being responsible for one portion of the project. The chosen method should include some evaluation of students' individual work and evaluation of the project based on the performance of all group members.

Q How can cooperative learning be structured so that one student doesn't do all the work?

A The group has to work to earn certificates or some recognition based on the learning of all its members. What this means is that the only way for the group to succeed is if everybody learns. There's no way that one student can do all the work. You rarely want to give the group a single activity that everyone has to do, because then it *is* possible for one student to do all the work.

Q You've said that group success should depend on individual learning. How does that work?

A The success of the group must be dependent on the individual learning of each student. There must be something that can be traced back to each person. For example, teams might earn certificates if the average score on quizzes or essays completed individually by all group members is higher than 80 percent. The idea here is that if students want their groups to succeed, they need to do a good job of teaching each other, of making sure that every group member has learned.

Q Some people are opposed to using rewards and certificates. How do you feel about that?

A There are some kinds of objectives for which they may not be necessary, such as composition, because kids enjoy that anyway; but for most school subjects, some kind of a group reward is necessary. It doesn't have to be big, just something to communicate to the kids that the activity is important. Without that, the students don't see as clearly the need to help each other. There has to be something that they're trying to work toward as a group. However, simple recognition is often enough.

Q How often should cooperative learning be used?

A It should be used pretty extensively. Even when you're using cooperative learning, the kids are not working in groups all day or all the time. There's a cycle of activities that includes instruction, individual assessment, and may include some individual work. There are many classrooms where cooperative learning is used all year. But it also makes sense to use it for shorter periods, as long as

you're not using it on, say, every other Thursday when it's raining. It's important to use it consistently for a period of time, maybe six weeks, rather than to do it just from time to time.

Q Should the groups be constant over that period?

A Yes. A group should stay together for about six weeks. There is a major benefit to having a group that kids can identify with and think is important. If you're changing groups every day, that's not going to happen.

America: Pathways to the Present provides teachers with many cooperative learning resources. The **Teacher's Edition** wraparound includes a cooperative learning activity for every chapter. The **Teaching Resources** package contains an Alternate Lesson Plans folder offering a number of cooperative learning lesson plans.

How It Works	
Group Size	4–5 students
Group Make-Up	Combination of high, average, and low achievers, with a balance of sex, ethnicity, and personalities.
Duration of Groups	Change after about six weeks.
Frequency of Use	As often as practical; consistency is important.
Accountability	Group success should depend on individual learning—measured by one evaluation, or by improvement over time.
Recognition	Something small to show that group success is valued—praise and public recognition are often enough; bonus points or small prizes such as stickers or pins are good, too.

Deborah Larson taught social studies and English for thirteen years. She is now Director of Instruction for McFarland Community Schools, Wisconsin.

Accommodating Individual Learning Styles

by Deborah K. Larson

The task of accommodating a broad range of student abilities, interests, and needs is greater than ever before. This essay is designed to help you meet the task of creating a learning environment in which all students can thrive.

Each student has a personal set of strategies for taking in, storing, and retrieving information. In some cases the strategy is easily observable, such as in the behavior of good spellers. When in doubt, they may close their eyes or write the word on a scrap of paper in order to visualize the word. In other cases, however, the strategy isn't quite so easy to see. Therefore, teachers should use a screening tool to help students determine whether their preferred learning style is *visual, auditory,* or *tactile/kinesthetic.* Most of these diagnostic instruments are checklists and take only a few minutes to administer and interpret.

Some learners have a very strong preference for a specific learning style, while others use a more balanced combination. The ideal situation exists when a student knows his or her strength, employs a variety of strategies to maximize that strength, and has the ability to tap into other styles as well. To increase student achievement, many of the alternate lesson plans in the **Teaching Resources** for *America: Pathways to the Present* target specific learning styles. Each of the alternate lesson plans is described in the Resource Directory at the bottom of the **Teacher's Edition** pages.

THE MAIN TYPES OF LEARNING STYLES

The Visual Learner

Visual learners enjoy reading and writing. Strong visual learners are able to reconstruct a mental image of the information when attempting to remember something. They benefit by highlighting text as they read, recopying their notes, creating graphic organizers, making lists, and viewing all sorts of visual stimuli—including graphs, charts, works of art, political cartoons, comics, and videotapes.

The Auditory Learner

Auditory learners retain information they have heard better than information they have only read. Strong auditory learners learn best by listening intently; and they may resist the distraction of taking notes. They benefit from listening to videotapes, television or audiotapes; reading or chanting aloud when studying; interviewing people; studying with others and discussing their notes; and repeating information aloud after hearing it.

The Tactile/Kinesthetic Learner

Tactile/kinesthetic learners are sensitive to touch. In many classrooms they are the most neglected group of learners, for their preferred strategies are usually incorporated in active, hands-on projects and go beyond reading, writing, discussing, and listening. They like to handle, manipulate, and change their environment. Frequently, they are good at building things and may show talent for movement, dance, or athletics. They benefit from constructing models, finding and examining artifacts, sketching and drawing, physically enacting an event through role-playing, visiting a place they're learning about (or constructing a model of it), moving around while studying, and solving problems with objects that they can move, such as maps cut out as puzzles and games that require moving pieces.

Projects

Undertaking projects, a common practice in many social studies classes, offers a practical means for tailoring the curriculum to individual learning styles and for making history meaningful and immediate. Complex projects and activities usually require the application of many skills and present opportunities for students to exercise a degree of choice. Projects give students chances to act as historians, anthropologists, sociologists, economists, and geographers by collecting and analyzing data (including primary sources and artifacts), interviewing, debating, constructing models, and creating maps and other graphics. The Resource Directory in the **Teacher's Edition**, the enrichment activities in the wraparound, the Teacher-to-Teacher Activity Network folder, and the Alternate Lesson Plans folder in the **Teaching Resources** are rich sources of strategies and activities based on actual classroom experiences that can be adapted to suit specific classes or individuals.

The Role of the Arts

Art, music, drama, and literature are powerful sources for making history come alive and for giving students a forum for individual expression. Visual learners can interpret and personalize an event through art, literature, and film. Through drama and music, auditory learners connect with a historical event in a way that it is impossible for them to do through text alone. Drama and other forms of role-playing, finding and interviewing real people, and constructing dioramas and other models are all activities that help tactile/kinesthetic learners absorb difficult concepts and enable them to share their special talents.

For those who have access to videotape, videodisc, and computer equipment, *America: Pathways to the Present*'s multimedia resource package, *Visions of America*, combines motion, sound, photography, graphics, and text to immerse students in a period, theme, or topic. Each of the ten textbook units has a video montage, and the "Turning Points" examined in the text are also extended through video presentations.

"We're given only one textbook and we're given twenty-five abilities. We often encounter four or five different learning styles . . ."

Classroom teacher in Detroit, Michigan

Group Work

Teachers who frequently use cooperative learning strategies are adept at structuring groups in a variety of ways. One consideration in setting up a group can be the learning styles of the participants. A variety of styles within a group will broaden the outlook and lead to a richer end product. The combining of students' learning styles in cooperative learning groups teaches students to appreciate the differing talents of their classmates and challenges them to build on their strengths and strengthen their weaknesses. For example, the most verbal student should not always be the one to speak for the group, and the best reader should not always be the one to search for information or interpret a chart. The activities in *America: Pathways to the Present* frequently suggest group discussion, analysis, or problem solving and offer many opportunities to use cooperative learning skills.

For alternate lesson plans that address different learning styles, please see the Alternate Lesson Plans folder in your **Teaching Resources** package.

Alan November is a social studies teacher and national technology consultant. He advises for the Glenbrook High Schools in Illinois.

Technology in the Classroom

by Alan November

Our society has a great capacity to invent new products to make our lives more productive and entertaining, and easier to manage. The classroom is no exception. In the last few years, we have seen the introduction there of the computer, the VCR, the videodisc player, the CD-ROM drive, and access to the World Wide Web on the Internet. All these devices help teachers and students do their work better. The new technologies also offer us another, perhaps greater, benefit—a new ability to innovate, to explore, and to create new learning opportunities for teachers and students.

Applying Technology

When a new technology is introduced, we often end up using it in ways that were not imagined by its inventor. The application of technology is constantly changing. For example, when Alexander Graham Bell set out to design the telephone he thought he was designing a tool to help deaf people communicate. Instead, most of us now have phones and use them for calling our friends and relatives or accessing computer networks. As time goes on, new uses for the phone are still evolving.

Similarly, the first computer software programs for the schools were electronic workbooks—more, better, and faster ways to "drill and kill." The first software also offered us familiar but easier ways to administer, grade, and record the results for traditional tests. Today we see new computer programs that offer simulations, explorations, innovative ways to collect and store information, and student authoring systems. Eventually, new computer programs may be introduced that are as different from the first software as the modern telecommunications network is from Bell's original telephone.

These examples illustrate that there are two ways to think about applying any technology. One is *automating*; the other can be called *informatting*.

Automating

The first stage of thinking about applying technology is to improve current reality, or to automate. When you automate, you look at what is currently happening at school or at home and you apply technology to make things easier to do or more comfortable, cheaper, or faster.

Let's apply the concept of automation to something familiar—the refrigerator. We can add a water cooler, an ice maker, and a defroster. Automating these features saves us time. Now, we don't need to store containers of water, fill and empty ice cube trays, or chip ice away.

Informatting

What if we built a kitchen network around our refrigerator that could monitor all the nutrient and calorie information in our foods? We could add a barcode reader to the inside of the refrigerator that automatically reads nutrient information on all the foods we put in. The data could be stored in a kitchen computer. We then would have an accurate record of the nutrient and calorie flow into our bodies. We could use this information to lead healthier lives.

This refrigerator has added more than convenience. It is now providing a health service. Typically, informatting leads to new roles for old inventions and new roles for the people using them.

The Difference Between Automating and Informatting

The difference between automating and informatting is a difference in how we think. The first requires knowledge about the current situation; the second requires the ability to make connections between activities—connections that currently do not exist. When we automate, we keep the same relationships and jobs. When we informat, there can be changes in relationships and jobs.

In our refrigerator example, when we informat the kitchen, the repair person's job changes significantly. He or she is still required to use a dolly to move the refrigerator, but now he or she must also know something about computers. The repair person learns a whole new set of skills. The end user's, or eater's, role in this situation also changes. The user can use the informatted refrigerator to lead a healthier life.

How do we know if a system has been automated or informatted? There is one critical question that needs to be asked: Have the roles changed? In an automated system, the roles do not change. We use new technology to do what we have always done, but better. In an informatted system, new roles are created and skills need to be learned. Informatting means that many more of us—like the repair person—will need to develop more complex problem-solving skills.

New Uses for Technology in the Schools

In the classroom, we have used the overhead projector, the slide projector, the filmstrip, the VCR, the CD-ROM drive, the computer, and the videodisc player. In an automated classroom, you would use a videodisc player, for example, as a presentation tool. Students would still receive information, conduct research, and present reports in much the same way as they have always done. In this example, the videodisc becomes a powerful automation tool and the classroom has more interesting visual elements. The roles of you and your students stay the same, with improvement in learning.

Using technology in the classroom might also change the roles of teachers and students in the following ways:
- Students would have a sense of owning and defining problems rather than just being given assignments.
- The teacher becomes a facilitator for students who are learning new skills.
- Students would work in teams with other students, members of the community, and even people from around the world across electronic networks.
- Students' success could be assessed in new ways.
- Students with different skill levels could successfully pursue projects at their own pace and level of sophistication.
- Students would become experienced problem solvers.

As educators, we have options. We can create new and innovative learning opportunities for students. With technology we have a new, powerful tool that enables our students to become critical thinkers, better problem solvers, and producers of useful information products.

America: Pathways to the Present offers integrated multimedia packages in videodisc and videotape formats such as *Visions of America*, *United States History Video Collection*, and *Decision America*. It also offers CD-ROMs such as *Our Times* for student use and *Resource Pro™* for teacher use. In addition, Internet activities are provided in both the **Teaching Resources** in Using the Internet folder and the **Teacher's Edition** wraparound.

Hannah Kruglanski is currently the Director of Curriculum and Assessment, Edunetics Corporation, Arlington, Virginia.

H. Kruglanski

New Trends in Assessment

by Hannah Kruglanski

When closely examining alternative assessments—tests that differ from the traditional multiple-choice, true-false, and matching assessments—social studies teachers usually find them both familiar and unfamiliar. The essays, presentations, constructions, and portfolios used in alternative assessments seem familiar because they have long been a part of the social studies classroom. They appear unfamiliar primarily because teachers are asked to use these activities in unaccustomed ways.

The Importance of Testing

We know that tests play a major role in the lives of students—and teachers. Tests signal to students what is important; students then make adjustments in their efforts to get the best possible grades. Tests determine students' placement in programs and "track" future schooling paths. Test scores affect schools as well by indicating the quality of programs to district administrators and legislators. Furthermore, tests communicate educational standards and signal to the community—students, teachers, and parents—what the community considers important to teach and to learn.

Too often the tests used in our schools reward only the memorization of facts. Thus, students gear their learning and teachers focus their instruction on the bits of information needed for the test. If we choose to emphasize reasoning, problem solving, and application of knowledge over memorization, we need to provide assessments that measure these outcomes and foster their learning. This goal—improving critical thinking and the ability to apply knowledge—is why the new forms of assessment are important.

What Is Alternative Assessment?

All forms of alternative assessments require students to construct answers, generate information, or create products in response to test assignments. They tap higher-order thinking skills and challenge students to apply their knowledge in problem-solving situations that foster active learning. The various forms of alternative assessments foster conceptual understanding and the making of connections to students' own lives. They frequently mirror the processes of learning by asking students to reflect on their work, periodically assess their own knowledge, and seek feedback from peers and experts. Alternative assessments allow for a broader, more comprehensive measurement of diverse learning experiences than do the limited responses to standardized tests.

Teachers do not need to throw out traditional tests when adopting alternative assessments. For subjects such as geography, where the amassing of a knowledge base is an important instructional outcome, traditional tests offer a good measurement of this outcome. However, students need to learn how to evaluate the knowledge they acquire—to apply it, to use it to solve problems, and to link that new knowledge to their old knowledge and their lives. Alternative assessments provide a means for meeting these goals.

How to Carry Out Alternative Assessments

The most frequently used forms are performance, portfolio, essay, and exhibition assessments. Examining performance assessment and portfolio assessment in more detail will provide examples of how to carry out alternative assessments in the classroom.

Performance Assessment

This method consists of open-ended and multistep tasks that are designed to demonstrate how students can apply and use their learning in solving problems and making decisions. The tasks usually reflect authentic, or real-life, problems and issues. They focus on the "big ideas," or important concepts. Student responses could be in the form of written or oral presentations or in a visual form such as videotapes or posters.

Social studies performance assessments could require students to analyze an issue, form an opinion, debate various points of view, or consider causes and effects.

Performance assessment tasks link students' prior knowledge and provide opportunities for new connections to be made. Although tasks do not target facts or formulas, students are still expected to use and apply knowledge of facts when appropriate.

Portfolio Assessment

This assessment tool is designed to measure growth in student performance over time by keeping a systematic record of progress as demonstrated in samples of students' work. Before students begin assembling their portfolios, teachers should determine:

♦ *Its Purpose*—Will it be used for instruction, assessment, or both?

♦ *How It Will Be Used*—Will it be the sole measurement of students' work for that course? Will it be used for the entire year or for a specific time period?

♦ *Criteria for Selection of Items*—Will it be the students' best work, their typical work, or an assortment of their work?

♦ *Ownership*—Who decides what goes in the portfolio—the teacher, the student, or both?

♦ *Scoring Criteria*—Will the entire portfolio, the separate components, or a composite be scored?

Once these decisions have been made, the teacher should next focus on the contents of the portfolios. A valid portfolio includes a variety of evidence and a range of students' work. Evidence in a portfolio needs to relate directly to the outcomes it is intended to measure. Use the following guidelines to help ensure that portfolios meet those criteria:

♦ *Work Biographies*—To demonstrate student development, collect samples of students' work from different points in time but on a specific topic or type of activity. For example, several drafts of a writing assignment constitute a work biography.

♦ *Range of Work*—To demonstrate growth, collect samples across different types of work. For example, work in different areas of social studies constitutes a range of work.

♦ *Self-Assessment*—To show changes in students' awareness about their performance and perspective in relation to their previous work, collect evidence that shows how students react to the contents of their own portfolios.

Scoring Alternative Assessments

Alternative assessments are scored in a way that reflects the desired outcomes and are closely linked with instruction. The procedure for scoring involves developing a rubric—a pre-established criterion for a scoring scale and sample performances to illustrate each point on the scale. To begin developing the rubric, the teacher explains the characteristics of an outstanding performance; this is the top scoring point. The teacher then spells out the criteria for an unacceptable or limited performance; this is the bottom point on the scale. Generally, the rubric contains two scoring points between unacceptable and outstanding—one for an acceptable performance and one for an extensive or commendable performance.

There are several methods of scoring—the two major strategies being holistic and analytic.

♦ *Holistic Scoring*—This strategy rates a task on one criterion and a single score is given for the overall quality of the task. It provides general information about the performance.

♦ *Analytic Scoring*—This strategy rates the task by multiple criteria. Scores are given for each criterion. They reflect the relative contribution of each criterion and can provide a diagnosis of the performance.

♦ *Modified Holistic Scoring*—This strategy combines elements from holistic and analytic scoring. A single score is given, but the relative contribution of each criterion can be isolated.

The **Teacher's Edition** of *America: Pathways to the Present* provides alternative assessment project strategies for each chapter in the wraparound. For more in-depth information on scoring criteria, strategies for alternative methods of assessment, as well as sample evaluation forms for teachers and student self-evaluation, see the Alternative Assessment folder in the **Teaching Resources**.

Themes in American History
A Development Guide

Themes show relevance: This guide presents the scope and sequence for the ten key themes developed in *America: Pathways to the Present*. These themes are introduced and explained in the Prologue, and are also highlighted in every unit opener. The themes are also addressed in the Teacher's Edition, the Teaching Resources, in the multimedia packages including *Visions of America* videotapes and videodiscs, *Our Times Multimedia Encyclopedia of the 20th Century* CD-ROM, *Decision America* videodiscs and videotapes, *Resource Pro*™ CD-ROM, and color transparencies. The following charts identify their special treatment throughout the entire *America: Pathways to the Present* student textbook.

Reform Movements

Student Text
Pathways to the Future p. 982
Minimum Wage and the Role of Government, p. 999

Turning Points
The Lasting Impact of Women in Public Life, p. 262; The Lasting Impact of the Great Strikes, p. 408; The Lasting Impact of the Nineteenth Amendment, p. 544; The Lasting Impact of Nonviolent Confrontation, p. 808

Links Across Time
Divided Reform Movements, p. 251; Protecting Workers from Their Workplace, p. 529; Equal Rights Movements, p. 816; Native American Pride and Sports Team Names, p. 837

History Might Not Have Happened This Way
The Dred Scott Decision, p. 316; The Decision to Rule Against Women's Suffrage, p. 486; The Decision to Lock the Doors at the Triangle Shirtwaist Company, p. 532; The Decision to Integrate Major League Baseball, p. 764

Time And Place
Routes to Freedom, p. 254; After Silent Spring, p. 844

Historian's Toolbox
Formulating Questions, p. 248; Reading a Political Cartoon, p. 481; Testing Conclusions, p. 538; Using Autobiography and Biography, p. 802; Recognizing Bias, p. 830

Literature and Primary Source Readings

Values

Student Text
Pathways to the Future p. 982
Immigration and the Golden Door, p. 984; Gun Control and Crime, p. 992

Turning Points
The Lasting Impact of the Election of 1800, p. 166; The Lasting Impact of the Atom Bomb, p. 686; The Lasting Impact of Nonviolent Confrontation, p. 808; The Lasting Impact of the Year 1968, p. 884

Links Across Time
Preserving the Environment, p. 19; Boycotting for Change, p. 107; The Final Solution and Ethnic Cleansing, p. 675; Equal Rights Movements, p. 816

History Might Not Have Happened This Way
The Decision to Move Native Americans West, p. 234; The Decision to Integrate Major League Baseball, p. 764; The Decision to Reveal the Effects of Agent Orange, p. 928

American Album
The First Encounters, p. 68; Personal Legacy, p. 874

Time And Place
Routes to Freedom, p. 254; After Silent Spring, p. 844

Historian's Toolbox
Recognizing Bias, p. 830; Recognizing Ideologies, p. 922

Literature and Primary Source Readings

Economics

Student Text
Pathways to the Future p. 982
Minimum Wage and the Role of Government, p. 999; Entitlements: Rethinking Government Guarantees, p. 1006; The United States in the Western Hemisphere, p. 1015

Turning Points
The Lasting Impact of Women on Public Life, p. 262; The Lasting Impact of Great Strikes, p. 408

Links Across Time
Boycotting for Change, p. 107; Picking Cotton: Humans vs. Machines, p. 302; Putting People to Work, p. 641

History Might Not Have Happened This Way
The Decision to Use Enslaved Africans for Labor, p. 52; The Decision to Lock the Doors at the Triangle Shirtwaist Company, p. 532

American Album
Engines of Change, p. 238; From Field to Factory, p. 574; The Information Age, p. 980

Time And Place
The End of the Open Range, p. 426; The Black Blizzards, p. 618; The Suburban Explosion, p. 752; The Rise of the Sunbelt, p. 954

Historian's Toolbox
Interpreting an Economic Activity Chart, p. 78; Drawing Conclusions, p. 433; Predicting Consequences, p. 977

Literature and Primary Source Readings

Technology

Student Text
Pathways to the Future p. 982
The United States in the Western Hemisphere, p. 1015; Technology and You in the Next Century, p. 1034

Turning Points
The Lasting Impact of the Atomic Bomb, p. 686

Links Across Time
Navigating the Ocean, p. 33; Time and Its Measure, p. 82; New Ways to Communicate, p. 390; Irrigation Then and Now, p. 423; The Incredible Shrinking Computer, p. 744

History Might Not Have Happened This Way
Kennedy's Decision to Send an American to the Moon, p. 782

American Album
Engines of Change, p. 238; The Information Age, p. 980

Time And Place
The Building of the Panama Canal, p. 512; After Silent Spring, p. 844

Historian's Toolbox
Demonstrating Reasoned Judgement, p. 944

Literature and Primary Source Readings

Environment

Student Text
Pathways to the Future p. 982
Minimum Wage and the Role of Government, p. 999; Entitlements: Rethinking Government Guarantees, p. 1006; The United States in the Western Hemisphere, p. 1015

Turning Points
The Lasting Impact of Women on Public Life, p. 262; The Lasting Impact of Great Strikes, p. 408

Links Across Time
Boycotting for Change, p. 107; Picking Cotton: Humans vs. Machines, p. 302; Putting People to Work, p. 641

History Might Not Have Happened This Way
The Decision to Use Enslaved Africans for Labor, p. 52; The Decision to Lock the Doors at the Triangle Shirtwaist Company, p. 532

American Album
Engines of Change, p. 238; From Field to Factory, p. 574; The Information Age, p. 980

Time And Place
The End of the Open Range, p. 426; The Black Blizzards, p. 618; The Suburban Explosion, p. 752; The Rise of the Sunbelt, p. 954

Historian's Toolbox
Interpreting an Economic Activity Chart, p. 78; Drawing Conclusions, p. 433; Predicting Consequences, p. 977

Literature and Primary Source Readings

Diversity

Student Text
Pathways to the Future p. 982
Immigration and the Golden Door, p. 984

Turning Points
The Lasting Impact of King Philip's War, p. 64; The Lasting Impact of Women in Public Life, p. 262; The Lasting Impact of Nonviolent Confrontation, p. 808

Links Across Time
The Pueblo Influence on Architecture, p. 44; Lincoln's Call Is Repeated, p. 349; The "Final Solution" and "Ethnic Cleansing," p. 675; Native American Pride and Sports Team Names, p. 837

History Might Not Have Happened This Way
The Decision to Move Native Americans West, p. 234; The Decision to Restrict Immigration, p. 584; The Decision to Integrate Major League Baseball, p. 764

American Album
First Encounters, p. 68; From Field to Factory, p. 574

Time And Place
Two Settlement Patterns, p. 92; Routes to Freedom, p. 254

Historian's Toolbox
Reading Tables and Analyzing Statistics, p. 459; Recognizing Bias, p. 830; Predicting Consequences, p. 977; Reading a Political Cartoon, p. 481; Using Autobiography and Biography, p. 802

Literature and Primary Source Readings

Unity and Conflict

Student Text
Pathways to the Future p. 982
Gun Control and Crime, p. 992; Entitlements: Rethinking Government Guarantees, p. 1006

Turning Points
The Lasting Impact of the Election of 1800, p. 166; The Lasting Impact of Women in Public Life, p. 262; The Lasting Impact of the Great Strikes, p. 408; The Lasting Impact of the Nineteenth Amendment, p. 544; The Lasting Impact of Nonviolent Confrontation, p. 808

Links Across Time
Boycotting for Change, p. 107; Political Parties Then and Now, p. 160; Divided Reform Movements, p. 252; Protecting Workers from Their Workplace, p. 529; Equal Rights Movements, p. 816

History Might Not Have Happened This Way
The Decision to Reject the Articles of Confederation, p. 134; The Dred Scott Decision, p. 316; The Decision to Rule Against Women's Suffrage, p. 486; The Decision to Integrate Major League Baseball, p. 764

American Album
After the Revolution, p. 108; From Field to Factory, p. 574

Time And Place
Two Settlement Patterns in the Colonies, p. 92

Historian's Toolbox
Expressing Problems Clearly, p. 108; Identifying Central Issues, p. 143; Making Comparisons, p. 161; Identifying Alternatives, p. 554; Checking Consistency, p. 862

Literature and Primary Source Readings

Themes in American History
A Development Guide (continued)

American Culture

Student Text
Pathways to the Future p. 982
Immigration and the Golden Door, p. 984; Technology and You in the Next Century, p. 1034

Turning Points
The Lasting Impact of King Philip's War, p. 64; The Lasting Impact of the Year 1968, p. 884

Links Across Time
The Pueblo Influence on Architecture, p. 44; New Ways to Communicate, p. 390; Entertaining a Changing Nation, p. 474; Women's Fashions, p. 593; Music: The Sound of Rebellion, p. 865

History Might Not Have Happened This Way
The Decision to Integrate Major League Baseball, p. 764; Kennedy's Decision to Send an American to the Moon, p. -782

American Album
The Growth of Sports, p. 490; The Jazz Age, p. 606; Personal Legacy, p. 874

Time And Place
Moving the East to the West, p. 172; After Silent Spring, p. 844

Historian's Toolbox
Identifying Assumptions, p. 705; Using Artifacts, p. 212; Analyzing Tombstones, p. 285; Reading a Political Cartoon, p. 481; Examining Photographs, p. 681; Evaluating Magazine Advertisements, p. 747; Using Autobiography and Biography, p. 802

Literature and Primary Source Readings

American Democracy

Student Text
Pathways to the Future p. 982
Gun Control and Crime, p. 992; Minimum Wage and the Role of Government, p. 999

Turning Points
The Lasting Impact of the Election of 1800, p. 166; The Lasting Impact of Women in Public Life, p. 262; The Lasting Impact of the Great Strikes, p. 408; The Lasting Impact of the Nineteenth Amendment, p. 544; The Lasting Impact of the Election of 1932, p. 634

Links Across Time
Political Parties Then and Now, p. 160; Divided Reform Movements, p. 251; Lincoln's Call Is Repeated, p. 349; The Hunt for Witches and Communists, p. 736; Equal Rights Movements, p. 816

History Might Not Have Happened This Way
The Decision to Reject the Articles of Confederation, p. 134; The Dred Scott Decision, p. 316; The Decision to Rule Against Women's Suffrage, p. 486

Time And Place
Routes to Freedom, p. 254

Historian's Toolbox
Expressing Problems Clearly, p. 108; Identifying Central Issues, p. 143; Making Comparisons, p. 161; Determining Relevance, p. 229; Identifying Alternatives, p. 554; Distinguishing Fact from Fiction, p. 652; Analyzing Political Speeches, p. 310

Literature and Primary Source Readings

The U.S. and the World

Student Text
Pathways to the Future p. 982
The United States in the Western Hemisphere, p. 1015; Foreign Policy After the Cold War, p. 1024

Turning Points
The Lasting Impact of the Atomic Bomb, p. 686; The Lasting Impact of the Year 1968, p. 884

Links Across Time
Making the World Safe for Democracy, p. 557; The "Final Solution" and "Ethnic Cleansing," p. 675; Taking Care of the Troops, p. 698; Intervention in Latin America, p. 786; The Wall: Its Rise and Fall, p. 954; Sarajevo Then and Now, p. 967

History Might Not Have Happened This Way
The Decision to Use Africans for Labor, p. 52; The Decision to Restrict Immigration, p. 584; The Decision to Reveal the Effects of Agent Orange, p. 928

American Album
Bringing the War Home, p. 714

Time And Place
The Building of the Panama Canal, p. 512; Routes to Freedom, p. 254

Historian's Toolbox
Using a Time Zone Map, p. 506; Expressing Problems Clearly, p. 108; Identifying Alternatives, p. 554; Recognizing Cause and Effect, p. 722; Checking Consistency, p. 862; Recognizing Ideologies, p. 922

Literature and Primary Source Readings

Critical Thinking: Correlation Guide

America: Pathways to the Present teaches, reinforces, and applies seventeen types of critical thinking skills, which are listed in the table below. Each critical thinking skill is taught in the "Historian's Toolbox" feature in the **Student Edition** and is reinforced and applied through questions and activities in the **Student Edition**, **Teacher's Edition**, and **Teaching Resources**. The page numbers in the chart list where these critical thinking skills are covered in each of the three components. (ALP denotes Alternate Lesson Plan.)

SKILL	STUDENT EDITION on pages	TEACHER'S EDITION on pages	TEACHING RESOURCES on pages
Expressing problems clearly To succinctly describe a complex situation or body of information	37, 108, 236, 243, 251, 263, 267, 268, 350, 396, 489, 513, 571, 583, 635, 689, 719, 721, 727, 738, 759, 840, 873, 909, 912, 943, 946, 961	37, 48, 90, 103, 108, 116, 215, 236, 251, 263, 267, 268, 298, 303, 311, 318, 350, 396, 429, 435, 469, 478, 482, 489, 513, 569, 571, 583, 635, 688, 709, 719, 720, 726, 734, 738, 759, 837, 838, 840, 873, 909, 919, 943, 967	Unit 1: 52, 68, 103, 106, 124, 139, 142 Unit 2: 36 Unit 3: 21, 109, 112 Unit 4: 62, 106 Unit 5: 74 Unit 6: 33 Unit 8: 25, 145 Unit 9: 20 Unit 10: 71, 133 Unit 11: 17, 44
Identifying central issues To identify the main ideas in a piece of information	51, 88, 100, 114, 123, 160, 195, 228, 247, 310, 319, 332, 340, 345, 353, 355, 368, 401, 425, 485, 505, 511, 517, 526, 531, 543, 546, 547, 573, 617, 625, 646, 657, 681, 721, 781, 829, 843, 883, 931, 957, 979, 1005	22, 32, 46, 50, 86, 88, 100, 114, 123, 153, 159, 169, 190, 195, 228, 245, 246, 310, 314, 319, 321, 332, 340, 344, 345, 353, 355, 368, 400, 424, 444, 485, 501, 505, 510, 516, 525, 531, 542, 546, 547, 573, 602, 613, 625, 627, 646, 656, 681, 718, 720, 780, 812, 828, 843, 883, 931, 950, 957, 960, 968, 972, 979	Unit 1: 8, 10, 12, 14, 15, 29, 30, 32, 33, 41, 43, 45, 66, 67, 69, 70, 71, 78, 82, 84, 88, 92, 101, 102, 104, 105, 113, 115, 117, 119, 134, 135, 136, 137, 138, 140, 141, 142, 143, 144 Unit 2: 8, 10, 12, 14, 31, 32, 33, 34, 35, 36, 44, 46, 48, 50, 52, 60, 71, 72, 73, 74, 75, 83, 85, 87, 89, 104, 105, 107, 108, 110, 111, 113, 114 Unit 3: 9, 11, 13, 15, 17, 34, 35, 36, 37, 38, 39, 46, 47, 48, 50, 52, 71, 72, 73, 74, 75, 83, 85, 87, 89, 104, 105, 107, 108, 110, 111, 113, 114, 115 Unit 4: (ALP 59), 8, 10, 12, 14, 43, 45, 47, 49, 59, 69, 70, 72, 73, 80, 82, 84, 86, 88, 92, 102, 103, 104, 105 Unit 5: 8, 10, 14, 31, 33, 52, 69, 70, 71, 72, 73, 74, 81, 83, 85, 87, 99, 102, 103, 105, 106, 114, 116, 118, 120, 137, 138 Unit 6: 8, 10, 12, 14, 31, 49, 68, 69, 70, 71, 72, 81, 83, 85, 87, 89, 93, 95, 104, 105, 107, 109, 113, 114, 115 Unit 7: 9, 11, 13, 15, 17, 34, 35, 36, 37, 38, 39, 47, 76, 77, 78, 79, 85, 87, 89, 104, 105, 107, 108, 110, 111, 113, 114, 115 Unit 8: (ALP 124, 128), 8, 10, 12, 14, 31, 32, 33, 34, 35, 36, 43, 45, 47, 49, 64, 65, 66, 67, 68, 69, 76, 78, 80, 82, 88, 97, 98, 99, 100, 101, 102, 109, 111, 113, 115,

SKILL	STUDENT EDITION on pages	TEACHER'S EDITION on pages	TEACHING RESOURCES on pages
Identifying central issues (continued)			134, 135, 137, 138, 140, 141, 142, 143, 144, 145 Unit 9: (ALP 151), 7, 9, 11, 28, 29, 31, 32, 40, 42, 44, 63, 64, 65, 66, 67, 68, 75, 77, 79, 81, 89, 99, 101, 102, 103, 111, 113, 115, 117, 119, 128, 135, 136, 137 Unit 10: 8, 10, 12, 31, 32, 33, 34, 35, 36, 43, 47, 66, 67, 68, 70, 71, 78, 80, 82, 84, 95, 102, 103, 104, 105, 112, 114, 116, 131, 132, 133, 134, 135, 136 Unit 11: 9, 10, 18, 19, 27, 28, 36, 37, 45, 46, 54, 55, 63
Making comparisons To identify how different ideas, objects, historic figures, or situations are alike and/or different	20, 36, 45, 47, 50, 56, 58, 61, 67, 79, 88, 93, 95, 123, 159, 161, 171, 174, 177, 192, 200, 205, 206, 220, 224, 225, 228, 229, 237, 252, 261, 269, 279, 282, 289, 291, 310, 319, 351, 381, 409, 411, 450, 465, 480, 489, 504, 511, 513, 517, 545, 565, 570, 593, 597, 622, 643, 658, 659, 673, 679, 713, 721, 738, 739, 751, 767, 786, 791, 792, 793, 805, 820, 826, 840, 855, 857, 887, 921, 935, 937, 938, 939, 948, 957, 970, 971, 1014	15, 18, 20, 25, 28, 36, 45, 47, 48, 50, 56, 58, 61, 67, 73, 79, 80, 86, 87, 93, 94, 156, 159, 161, 171, 174 176, 187, 192, 200, 205, 206, 220, 223, 224, 225, 226, 228, 236, 243, 252, 257, 259, 261, 265, 269, 270, 272, 274, 279, 280, 282, 289, 298, 310, 319, 351, 378, 381, 393, 404, 409, 410, 417, 420, 450, 461, 465, 473, 475, 480, 483, 488, 497, 502, 504, 510, 511, 513, 514, 517, 523, 540, 545, 565, 570, 592, 593, 597, 606, 621, 622, 630, 643, 658, 665, 673, 679, 713, 716, 719, 720, 724, 730, 738, 739, 742, 751, 754, 755, 761, 766, 770, 786, 790, 792, 793, 805, 824, 826, 827, 840, 855, 857, 861, 871, 882, 878, 887, 921, 922, 935, 939, 940, 945, 957, 971	Unit 1: (ALP 12), 23, 24, 31, 34, 60, 63, 71, 86, 90, 92, 103, 106, 121, 136, 139, 142 Unit 2: 27, 33, 36, 61, 76, 95 Unit 3: (ALP 40), 36, 39, 73, 100 Unit 4: 73, 99, 103 Unit 5: 19, 20, 22, 23, 54, 71, 74, 94, 124, 133, 139, 142 Unit 6: (ALP 92), 16, 20, 36, 70, 112, 115 Unit 7: (ALP 108), 20, 32, 36, 39, 93, 103, 112, 115 Unit 8: (ALP 138), 33, 36, 63, 106, 107, 139 Unit 9: (ALP 149), 17, 84, 100, 136, 139 Unit 10: (ALP 173), 18, 30, 103, 125 Unit 11: 19, 39
Determining relevance To decide if and how events, situations, or items are related to one another	25, 37, 59, 67, 86, 95, 101, 107, 181, 191, 197, 206, 207, 229, 242, 259, 261, 330, 335, 391, 439, 447, 455, 458, 465, 469, 485, 512, 515, 531, 533, 556, 558, 567, 596, 618, 624, 636, 637, 708, 732, 736, 763, 780, 781, 783, 793, 817, 829, 847, 861, 864, 871, 891, 902, 916, 917, 941, 957, 962, 965, 979	12, 15, 25, 37, 38, 59, 67, 70, 94, 96, 101, 106, 145, 154, 178, 181, 196, 206, 207, 212, 219, 229, 240, 242, 259, 260, 269, 272, 296, 307, 322, 324, 330, 335, 384, 389, 390, 399, 404, 412, 439, 440, 447, 455, 458, 465, 466, 469, 485, 494, 512, 515, 520, 531, 533, 556, 558, 567, 587, 592, 596, 597, 623, 636, 638, 708, 731, 736, 748, 763, 773, 780, 781, 783, 793, 817, 824, 828, 861, 864, 871, 882, 891, 902, 916, 917, 924, 953, 962, 965	Unit 1: 13, 20, 57, 97, 98 106 Unit 2: 22, 57, 58, 68, 112 Unit 3: (ALP 52), 20, 24, 58, 95 Unit 4: 18, 20 Unit 5: (ALP 72), 18 Unit 6: (ALP 96), 36, 91, 106 Unit 7: 30, 76 Unit 8: 102, 125, 142 Unit 9: (ALP 143), 15, 17, 25, 27, 94, 139 Unit 10: (ALP 167), 30, 68, 71, 98, 103, 125, 136 Unit 11: 23, 44, 54, 98
Formulating questions To create questions that seek answers to specific objectives and lead to a deeper understanding of an issue	26, 177, 201, 248, 355, 439, 465, 516, 590, 628, 676, 687, 695, 809, 821, 873, 949	26, 27, 55, 60, 62, 80, 147, 177, 201, 202, 230, 233, 248, 249, 277, 303, 355, 366, 439, 465, 472, 516, 561, 590, 628, 647, 675, 687, 695, 696, 756, 781, 809, 821, 836, 840, 873, 916, 938, 949, 960	Unit 1: (ALP 3) Unit 2: (ALP 25), 33, 115 Unit 3: 61 Unit 5: 60, 71, 126 Unit 6: 18, 73, 90 Unit 7: (ALP 115), 90 Unit 9: 25, 57 Unit 10: 57, 106 Unit 11: (ALP 182), 28

SKILL	STUDENT EDITION on pages	TEACHER'S EDITION on pages	TEACHING RESOURCES on pages
Distinguishing fact from opinion To separate those statements that can be proven to be true from those that reflect a personal viewpoint	48, 90, 95, 111, 167, 288, 451, 519, 651, 652, 680, 710, 725, 751, 821, 830, 868, 965	21, 35, 48, 90, 95, 111, 167, 451, 579, 650, 652, 680, 709, 710, 725, 751, 821, 868	Unit 1: (ALP 9) Unit 5: 36 Unit 6: 106 Unit 7: 94 Unit 8: 28, 122, 123 Unit 10: 52, 88 Unit 11: 28, 44
Checking consistency To compare two or more items or ideas and determine whether they agree or disagree with each other	30, 63, 121, 151, 197, 301, 302, 317, 379, 437, 528, 553, 560, 569, 573, 632, 651, 853, 862, 931	30, 63, 120, 121, 151, 196, 300, 302, 317, 379, 437, 528, 553, 560, 569, 573, 632, 650, 678, 679, 853, 862, 931	Unit 1: (ALP 3), 31, 125, 136, 142 Unit 6: 33, 112 Unit 7: 79, 109 Unit 8: 69, 99, 136 Unit 9: 30, 33, 124 Unit 10: 33, 53 Unit 11: 34
Distinguishing false from accurate images To examine a widely held belief about a person, place, or thing and determine whether or not the belief is based in fact	35, 237, 347, 355, 417, 421, 437, 439, 480, 605, 625, 632, 689, 861, 905, 1002	34, 236, 293, 347, 355, 417, 421, 437, 439, 480, 605, 625, 633, 688, 861, 905	Unit 2: 109 Unit 3: 36, 65, 68 Unit 4: 54 Unit 6: 59, 109 Unit 7: 64, 76, 79 Unit 8: 58, 66, 89 Unit 9: 85, 100 Unit 10: 17 Unit 11: 26
Identifying assumptions To recognize unstated beliefs that may underlie a statement, action, or event	67, 111, 183, 217, 221, 269, 284, 397, 411, 432, 458, 465, 517, 535, 617, 699, 705, 713, 737, 829, 866, 885, 914, 979, 1008	67, 111, 153, 183, 221, 269, 284, 397, 411, 432, 458, 465, 497, 517, 535, 617, 699, 705, 713, 731, 828, 866, 914, 962, 979	Unit 1: 22, 73, 87, 100 Unit 3: 90, 97 Unit 4: 17, 22, 70 Unit 5: (ALP 85), 17, 134 Unit 7: 28, 39, 60, 79, 106 Unit 8: 51, 99, 128, 131 Unit 9: 33, 89, 136, 139 Unit 10: (ALP 163), 125, 133 Unit 11: 26, 27, 37, 53
Recognizing bias To identify a stated or unstated viewpoint or slant that is designed to promote one set of beliefs	284, 336, 379, 395, 399, 407, 421, 446, 453, 458, 475, 595, 649, 699, 704, 747, 757, 830, 835, 974	173, 284, 336, 379, 395, 399, 407, 420, 421, 437, 446, 452, 458, 474, 540, 595, 699, 704, 709, 747, 757, 830, 834, 941	Unit 1: (ALP 18), 18, 126, 129 Unit 2: 27, 62, 97, 100 Unit 5: 63, 71, 139 Unit 6: (ALP 90), 36, 54, 109 Unit 7: 39, 101 Unit 8: 19, 20, 61 Unit 9: 88, 90 Unit 11: 44
Recognizing ideologies To identify underlying beliefs from actions or statements	53, 83, 95, 165, 179, 231, 321, 375, 381, 405, 421, 430, 461, 526, 543, 567, 573, 594, 601, 605, 659, 759, 789, 798, 845, 859, 922, 936, 973, 998, 1019	53, 83, 94, 165, 179, 231, 232, 293, 321, 374, 381, 405, 421, 430, 444, 461, 525, 528, 542, 567, 573, 594, 601, 605, 658, 759, 789, 798, 810, 845, 859, 922, 939, 946, 951, 973	Unit 1: 16, 18, 56, 62, 122, Unit 3: 23, 57, 62, 69, 76 Unit 5: 89, 129 Unit 7: 36, 95, 112 Unit 8: (ALP 132), 17, 62, 95, 102, 121, 136 Unit 9: 121 Unit 10: (ALP 172), 33, 56, 87, 92, 103, 106 Unit 11: 17, 53
Drawing conclusions To find an answer or to form an opinion based on available information	18, 24, 44, 99, 103, 110, 123, 192, 244, 253, 304, 328, 331, 368, 372, 373, 375, 376, 381, 405, 419, 432, 433, 459, 465, 476, 481, 489, 497, 499, 510, 519, 543, 547, 551, 552, 565, 590, 646, 666, 667, 671, 693, 702, 720, 721, 739, 750, 767, 775, 787, 807, 815, 819, 847, 882, 898, 926, 946, 970, 971, 993	16, 21, 23, 24, 44, 74, 99, 110, 123, 128, 139, 163, 193, 204, 216, 221, 253, 304, 328, 331, 376, 381, 388, 405, 419, 424, 431, 433, 456, 459, 462, 465, 475, 481, 488, 497, 499, 510, 519, 535, 547, 551, 552, 565, 582, 590, 601, 611, 645, 666, 667, 671, 684, 693, 702, 720, 721, 739, 750, 766, 775, 787, 807, 815, 819, 833, 847, 882, 898, 926, 946, 962, 970	Unit 1: 31, 34, 53, 56 Unit 2: 70, 73, 103, 115 Unit 3: 36, 39, 60, 109, 115 Unit 4: 85, 98, 103 Unit 5: 33, 36, 59, 101, 123 Unit 6: 22, 103, 112, 115 Unit 7: 21, 61, 71, 76, 106, Unit 8: (ALP 139), 56, 83, Unit 9: 24, 125 Unit 10: (ALP 165), 28, 60, 90, 91, 106, 117, 122 Unit 11: 17, 35, 98

SKILL	STUDENT EDITION on pages	TEACHER'S EDITION on pages	TEACHING RESOURCES on pages
Recognizing cause and effect To examine how one event or idea causes other events or ideas to occur	20, 26, 35, 36, 45, 62, 63, 91, 95, 104, 107, 121, 181, 207, 228, 253, 263, 269, 355, 391, 389, 411, 446, 487, 519, 537, 572, 573, 599, 617, 637, 686, 689, 698, 711, 714, 722, 727, 745, 746, 809, 820, 843, 883, 927, 938, 955, 962, 970, 1038	12, 20, 28, 36, 44, 62, 63, 91, 95, 99, 104, 107, 120, 180, 207, 228, 253, 263, 269, 290, 355, 390, 398, 411, 420, 423, 446, 487, 497, 519, 537, 572, 573, 581, 589, 599, 617, 621, 636, 686, 689, 694, 696, 698, 710, 714, 722, 726, 745, 752, 809, 820, 843, 883, 897, 927, 938, 955, 962, 970	Unit 1: 15, 114, 120, 145 Unit 2: (ALP 31), 17, 84, 98, 106, 109, 115 Unit 4: 18, 53, 73 Unit 5: (ALP 76), 33, 56, 84, 107, 115, 128, 139 Unit 6: (ALP 103), 28, 70, 112, 115 Unit 7: (ALP 106), 12, 27, 36 Unit 8: 33, 66, 69, 87, 94, 102, 119, 136, 139, 142 Unit 9: (ALP 156), 19, 80, 100, 136 Unit 10: (ALP 170), 36, 79, 133 Unit 11: 17, 45, 62
Predicting consequences To determine the likely effect of an event or action on the outcome of future events or actions	37, 43, 77, 105, 188, 207, 217, 235, 275, 323, 370, 395, 403, 471, 585, 637, 667, 703, 713, 753, 765, 767, 793, 957, 976, 977	37, 41, 43, 60, 77, 105, 183, 188, 207, 217, 235, 265, 274, 322, 370, 395, 403, 471, 585, 592, 600, 636, 667, 683, 703, 713, 753, 765, 767, 793, 858, 878, 905, 951, 976, 977	Unit 1: 98 Unit 2: (ALP 29), 28, 64, 94 Unit 4: (ALP 62), 55, 70, 73 Unit 5: 24, 55 Unit 6: 62, 96, 109 Unit 7: (ALP 113), 31 Unit 8: 22, 36, 59, 84, 86 Unit 9: 14, 95, 128, 130 Unit 10: 22, 36, 121 Unit 11: (ALP 185), 46, 62
Identifying alternatives To identify one or more methods to achieve a goal or solve a problem; to recognize the possibility of other goals	65, 123, 309, 554, 558, 619, 685, 739, 821, 909, 976, 1023, 1043	52, 61, 65, 123, 153, 175, 293, 309, 402, 415, 554, 558, 619, 685, 739, 786, 821, 850, 892, 909, 917, 951	Unit 1: 51, 55 Unit 3: (ALP 46), 25, 90 Unit 4: 18, 95 Unit 5: (ALP 87), 36, 121, 142 Unit 6: 73, 98 Unit 8: (ALP 125), 36, 55 Unit 9: 21, 120 Unit 10: 55, 120 Unit 11: 64
Testing conclusions To examine a conclusion and determine whether or not it is supported by known facts	142, 315, 339, 361, 380, 431, 463, 488, 531, 538, 669, 681, 774, 829, 852, 905, 931	21, 32, 64, 141, 194, 315, 338, 339, 361, 380, 431, 463, 488, 531, 538, 556, 669, 681, 754, 774, 824, 829, 852, 905, 931	Unit 1: 34, 103, 136 Unit 2: (ALP 36), 24 Unit 4: (ALP 67) Unit 5: (ALP 82), 51, 88, 104 Unit 6: 17, 58, 106 Unit 7: 25, 90, 112 Unit 8: 18, 120, 139, 145 Unit 9: (ALP 160), 103 Unit 10: 68, 71 Unit 11: 10, 36, 63
Demonstrating reasoned judgment To present evidence or reasoning that supports a given opinion or statement	30, 57, 79, 80, 123, 194, 207, 223, 229, 236, 255, 267, 287, 313, 322, 365, 381, 475, 519, 547, 551, 557, 563, 594, 603, 605, 625, 649, 659, 685, 767, 774, 790, 791, 799, 801, 812, 814, 842, 852, 873, 895, 896, 905, 912, 931, 944, 955, 957, 985, 996, 1026	15, 30, 41, 57, 72, 79, 80, 98, 123, 150, 194, 198, 207, 223, 227, 229, 237, 255, 256, 267, 236, 272, 286, 287, 298, 313, 322, 365, 377, 381, 393, 454, 475, 507, 515, 519, 547, 550, 557, 563, 564, 580, 592, 593, 603, 605, 610, 615, 625, 649, 658, 666, 685, 718, 743, 760, 766, 777, 781, 790, 791, 799, 801, 804, 814, 824, 841, 842, 847, 852, 854, 864, 878, 895, 896, 905, 912, 924, 931, 944, 945, 953, 955, 957, 996, 1026	Unit 1: 16, 24, 68, 71, 95, 131, 139, 145 Unit 2: 23, 33, 76, 91, 112 Unit 3: 31, 36, 39, 60, 76, 106, Unit 4: 65, 70, 103, 106 Unit 5: 107, 142 Unit 6: 65, 115 Unit 7: (ALP 119), 23, 115 Unit 8: (ALP 129), 33, 50, 66, 69, 99 Unit 9: (ALP 151), 30, 33, 54, 103 Unit 10: 30, 33, 36, 91, 136 Unit 11: 17, 34

Daily Pacing Guide

The following pacing guide shows how the units and chapters of *America: Pathways to the Present* can be adapted to fit your specific course focus and time constraints. The guide is based on 36 weeks or 180 days.

Unit 1 Origins of a New Society to 1783

	U.S. History Survey (days)	Twentieth-Century U.S. History (days)	U.S. History and the Constitution (days)
Chapter 1 Three Cultures Collide, Before and After the 1400s			
Section 1 The Native American World	1	.5	.5
Section 2 The European World	1	.5	.5
Section 3 The World of the West Africans	1	.5	.5
Section 4 The Atlantic World Is Born	1	.5	.5
Chapter 2 European Settlement and Native American Resistance, 1519 – 1689			
Section 1 Spanish and Native American Interaction	1	.5	.5
Section 2 A Colony in the Chesapeake Bay Area	1	.5	1
Section 3 Europeans and Native Americans in the Northeast	1	.5	.5
Section 4 King Philip's War: A Turning Point in History	1	.5	1
Chapter 3 The Maturing of Colonial Societies, 1689 – 1754			
Section 1 An Empire and Its Colonies	1	1	1
Section 2 Life in Colonial America	.5	.5	.5
Section 3 African Americans in the Colonies	1	1	1
Section 4 Emerging Tensions	.5	.5	.5
Chapter 4 The American Revolution, 1754 – 1783			
Section 1 The French and Indian War Challenges Colonial Thinking	.5	.5	1
Section 2 The Issues That Led to the War for Independence	.5	.5	2
Section 3 The Ideas That Led to the War for Independence	1.5	1	2
Section 4 The War for Independence	1.5	1	2
Total weeks for unit	**3 weeks**	**2 weeks**	**3 weeks**

Unit 2 Balancing Liberty and Order, 1781 – 1830

	U.S. History Survey (days)	Twentieth-Century U.S. History (days)	U.S. History and the Constitution (days)
Chapter 5 The Constitution of the United States, 1781 – 1789			
Section 1 Government by the States	1	1	5
Section 2 The Constitutional Convention	1	1	5
Section 3 Ratifying the Constitution	1.5	1	5
Section 4 The New Government	1.5	1	5
Chapter 6 The Origins of American Politics, 1789 – 1820			
Section 1 Liberty Versus Order in the 1790s	1	.5	2
Section 2 The Election of 1800: A Turning Point in History	1.5	1	2
Section 3 The Jefferson Administration	1	.5	2
Section 4 Native American Politics	1	.5	2
Section 5 War, Panic, and Uneasy Compromise	.5	.5	2
Chapter 7 Life in the New Nation, 1783 – 1830			
Section 1 Migrating Multitudes	1.5	1	1.5
Section 2 The Spirit of Improvement	1.5	1	1.5
Section 3 Shifting Social Relationships	1	.5	1
Section 4 The Democratization of American Religion	1	.5	1
Total weeks for unit	**3 weeks**	**2 weeks**	**7 weeks**

Unit 3 An Emerging New Nation, 1800 – 1860	U.S. History Survey (days)	Twentieth-Century U.S. History (days)	U.S. History and the Constitution (days)
Chapter 8 The Market Revolution, 1815 – 1845			
Section 1 Changing Households and New Markets	1	1	1
Section 2 The Northern Section	1	.5	1
Section 3 The Southern Section	1	.5	1
Section 4 The Second American Party System	1	.5	1
Section 5 The Age of Jackson	1	.5	1
Chapter 9 Religion and Reform, 1815 – 1860			
Section 1 Middle-Class Reform	1	.5	.5
Section 2 The Antislavery Movement	1.5	1.5	1
Section 3 Women in the Public Sphere: A Turning Point in History	1.5	1.5	1
Section 4 Reform Efforts Highlight Cultural Divisions	1	.5	.5
Chapter 10 Beyond the Mississippi, 1800 – 1860			
Section 1 The Native Americans of the Plains	1.5	.5	.5
Section 2 Hispanic North America	1	1	.5
Section 3 Trails to the West	1	.5	.5
Section 4 Conquest of a Continent	1.5	1	.5
Total weeks for unit	**3 weeks**	**2 weeks**	**2 weeks**

Unit 4 Division and Uneasy Reunion, 1848 – 1877

	U.S. History Survey (days)	Twentieth-Century U.S. History (days)	U.S. History and the Constitution (days)
Chapter 11 The Coming of the Civil War, 1848 – 1861			
Section 1 Two Nations?	1	.5	2.5
Section 2 New Political Parties	1.5	1	2.5
Section 3 The System Fails	1.5	1	2.5
Section 4 A Nation Divided Against Itself	1	.5	2.5
Chapter 12 The Civil War, 1861 – 1865			
Section 1 The First Two Years of the Civil War	1.5	1	1
Section 2 War Brings Change	1.5	1	1
Section 3 Turning Point: The Siege of Vicksburg	1	.5	.5
Section 4 A New Birth of Freedom	1	.5	.5
Chapter 13 Reconstruction, 1863 – 1877			
Section 1 The Meaning of Freedom	1	1	3
Section 2 Three Plans for Reconstruction	1.5	1	3
Section 3 Reconstruction in the South	1.5	1	3
Section 4 The Retreat from Reconstruction in the North	1	1	3
Total weeks for unit	**3 weeks**	**2 weeks**	**5 weeks**

Unit 5 Expansion: Rewards and Costs, 1860 – 1920

	U.S. History Survey (days)	Twentieth-Century U.S. History (days)	U.S. History and the Constitution (days)
Chapter 14 The Expansion of American Industry, 1865 – 1900			
Section 1 A Technological Revolution	1	1.5	.5
Section 2 The Growth of Big Business	1	1	.5
Section 3 Industrialization and Workers	1	1	.5
Section 4 The Great Strikes: A Turning Point in History	1	1.5	.5
Chapter 15 Looking to the West, 1860 – 1900			
Section 1 Moving West	.5	1	.5
Section 2 The Conquest of the Native Americans	1	1	.5
Section 3 Modernization, Mining, and Ranching	1	1	.5
Section 4 Populism	1	1	1
Section 5 Frontier Myths	.5	1	.5
Chapter 16 Politics, Immigration, and Urban Life, 1877 – 1920			
Section 1 Politics in the Gilded Age	.5	1.5	.5
Section 2 People on the Move	.5	1.5	.5
Section 3 The Challenge of the Cities	1	1	.5
Section 4 Ideas for Reform	1	1	.5
Chapter 17 Cultural and Social Transformations, 1870 – 1915			
Section 1 The Expansion of Education	1	1	.5
Section 2 Recreation for the Masses	1	1	.5
Section 3 The World of Jim Crow	1	1.5	1
Section 4 The Woman Question	1	1.5	1
Total weeks for unit	**3 weeks**	**4 weeks**	**2 weeks**

Unit 6 The United States on the Brink of Change, 1890 – 1920

	U.S. History Survey (days)	Twentieth-Century U.S. History (days)	U.S. History and the Constitution (days)
Chapter 18 Becoming a World Power, 1890 – 1913			
Section 1 The Pressure to Expand	1	1	1
Section 2 Foreign Entanglements, War, and Annexations	1	2	1
Section 3 A Forceful Diplomacy	2	1	1
Section 4 The People's Response to Imperialism	1	1	1
Chapter 19 The Era of Progressive Reform, 1890 – 1920			
Section 1 The Origins of Progressivism	1	1	1
Section 2 Progressivism: Its Legislative Impact	2	1	1.5
Section 3 Progressivism: Its Impact on National Politics	1	1	1.5
Section 4 Suffrage at Last: A Turning Point in History	1	2	2
Chapter 20 The World War I Era, 1914 – 1920			
Section 1 The Road to War	1	1	1
Section 2 The United States Declares War	1	1	1
Section 3 Americans on the European Front	1	1	1
Section 4 On the Home Front	1	1	1
Section 5 Global Peacemaker	1	1	1
Total weeks for unit	**3 weeks**	**3 weeks**	**3 weeks**

Unit 7 Boom Times to Hard Times, 1919 – 1938

	U.S. History Survey (days)	Twentieth-Century U.S. History (days)	U.S. History and the Constitution (days)
Chapter 21 A Stormy Era, 1919 – 1929			
Section 1 Postwar Adjustments	1	1	.5
Section 2 Social and Political Developments	2	2	1
Section 3 New Manners, New Morals	1	1	.5
Section 4 Creating a Shared Culture	1	2	.5
Section 5 Stemming the Tide of Change	2	1	.5
Chapter 22 Crash and Depression, 1929 – 1933			
Section 1 The Economy in the Late 1920s	1	1	.5
Section 2 The Stock Market Crash	2	1	.5
Section 3 Social Effects of the Depression	1	2	.5
Section 4 Surviving the Great Depression	1	1	.5
Section 5 The Election of 1932: A Turning Point in History	2	2	1
Chapter 23 The New Deal, 1933 – 1938			
Section 1 Forging a New Deal	2	2	3
Section 2 The New Deal's Critics	2	2	3
Section 3 Enduring Legacies of the New Deal	2	2	3
Total weeks for unit	**4 weeks**	**4 weeks**	**3 weeks**

Unit 8 Hot and Cold War, 1939 – 1960

	U.S. History Survey (days)	Twentieth-Century U.S. History (days)	U.S. History and the Constitution (days)
Chapter 24 World War II, 1939 – 1945			
Section 1 Prelude to War	1.5	2	1
Section 2 The Military Struggle	1	1.5	.5
Section 3 Americans on the Battle Fronts	1	1.5	.5
Section 4 Dropping the Atomic Bomb: A Turning Point in History	1.5	2	1
Chapter 25 World War II at Home, 1941 – 1945			
Section 1 The Shift to Wartime Production	1	1	.5
Section 2 Daily Life on the Home Front	1	1	.5
Section 3 Women and the War	1	1	.5
Section 4 The Struggle for Justice at Home	2	2	.5
Chapter 26 The Cold War and American Society, 1945 – 1960			
Section 1 Origins of the Cold War	1	2	.5
Section 2 Containment	1.5	2	.5
Section 3 The Cold War in Asia, the Middle East, and Latin America	1	2	.5
Section 4 The Cold War in the United States	1.5	2	.5
Chapter 27 The Postwar Years at Home, 1945 – 1960			
Section 1 The Postwar Economy	1.5	1.5	1
Section 2 The Mood of the 1950s	1.5	1	1
Section 3 Domestic Politics and Policy	1	1	.5
Section 4 The Continuing Struggle for Equality	1	1.5	.5
Total weeks for unit	**4 weeks**	**5 weeks**	**2 weeks**

Unit 9 The Upheaval of the Sixties, 1960 – 1975

	U.S. History Survey (days)	Twentieth-Century U.S. History (days)	U.S. History and the Constitution (days)
Chapter 28 The Kennedy and Johnson Years, 1960 – 1968			
Section 1 The New Frontier	1.5	1	1
Section 2 The Great Society	1.5	1	1
Section 3 Foreign Policy in the 1960s	2	2	1
Chapter 29 The Civil Rights Movement, 1960 – 1968			
Section 1 Leaders and Strategies	2	2	2
Section 2 Nonviolent Confrontation: A Turning Point in History	1	2	2
Section 3 The Political Response	1	2	1.5
Section 4 The Challenge of Black Power	1	2	1
Chapter 30 Continuing Social Revolution, 1960 – 1975			
Section 1 The Women's Movement	1.5	1	2
Section 2 Ethnic Minorities Seek Equality	1	1	2
Section 3 Native American Struggles	1	1	1
Section 4 Environmental and Consumer Movements	1.5	1	1
Chapter 31 The Vietnam War and American Society, 1960 – 1975			
Section 1 The War in the 1960s	1	1	1
Section 2 The Brutality of the War	1	2	.5
Section 3 Student Protest	1	2	1
Section 4 The Counterculture	1	2	1
Section 5 The End of the War	1	2	1
Total weeks for unit	**4 weeks**	**5 weeks**	**4 weeks**

Unit 10 Continuity and Change, 1968 – Present

	U.S. History Survey (days)	Twentieth-Century U.S. History (days)	U.S. History and the Constitution (days)
Chapter 32 The Nixon Years, 1968 – 1974			
Section 1 1968: A Turning Point in History	2	1.5	1.5
Section 2 The Nixon Administration	1	1.5	1.5
Section 3 Nixon's Foreign Policy	1	1	2
Section 4 The Watergate Scandal	1	2	2
Chapter 33 The Post-Watergate Period, 1974 – 1980			
Section 1 The Ford Administration	1	1	.5
Section 2 The Carter Transition	1	1	.5
Section 3 Carter's Foreign Policy	1	2	.5
Section 4 Carter's Domestic Problems	1	2	.5
Chapter 34 The Conservative Revolution, 1980 – 1992			
Section 1 Roots of the New Conservatism	1	1.5	.5
Section 2 The Reagan Revolution	1	1.5	.5
Section 3 Reagan's Second Term	1	1	.5
Section 4 The Bush Presidency	2	1	.5
Chapter 35 Entering a New Era, 1992 – Present			
Section 1 The Clinton Presidency	2	2	1.5
Section 2 The United States in a New World	2	3	1.5
Section 3 Twenty-First Century Americans	2	3	1
Total weeks for unit	**4 weeks**	**5 weeks**	**3 weeks**

	U.S. History Survey (days)	Twentieth-Century U.S. History (days)	U.S. History and the Constitution (days)
Unit 11 Pathways to the Future			
Chapter 36 Immigration and the Golden Door	1	1	1
Chapter 37 Gun Control and Crime	1	1	1
Chapter 38 Minimum Wage and the Role of Government	1	1	1
Chapter 39 Entitlements: Rethinking Government Guarantees	2	2	2
Chapter 40 The United States in the Western Hemisphere	2	2	2
Chapter 41 Foreign Policy After the Cold War	1	1	1
Chapter 42 Technology and You in the Next Century	2	2	2
Total weeks for unit	**2 weeks**	**2 weeks**	**2 weeks**

PRENTICE HALL

AMERICA

PATHWAYS
—TO THE—
PRESENT

Comprehensive Index with Teaching Resources and Additional Activities. See pages 1152–1178.

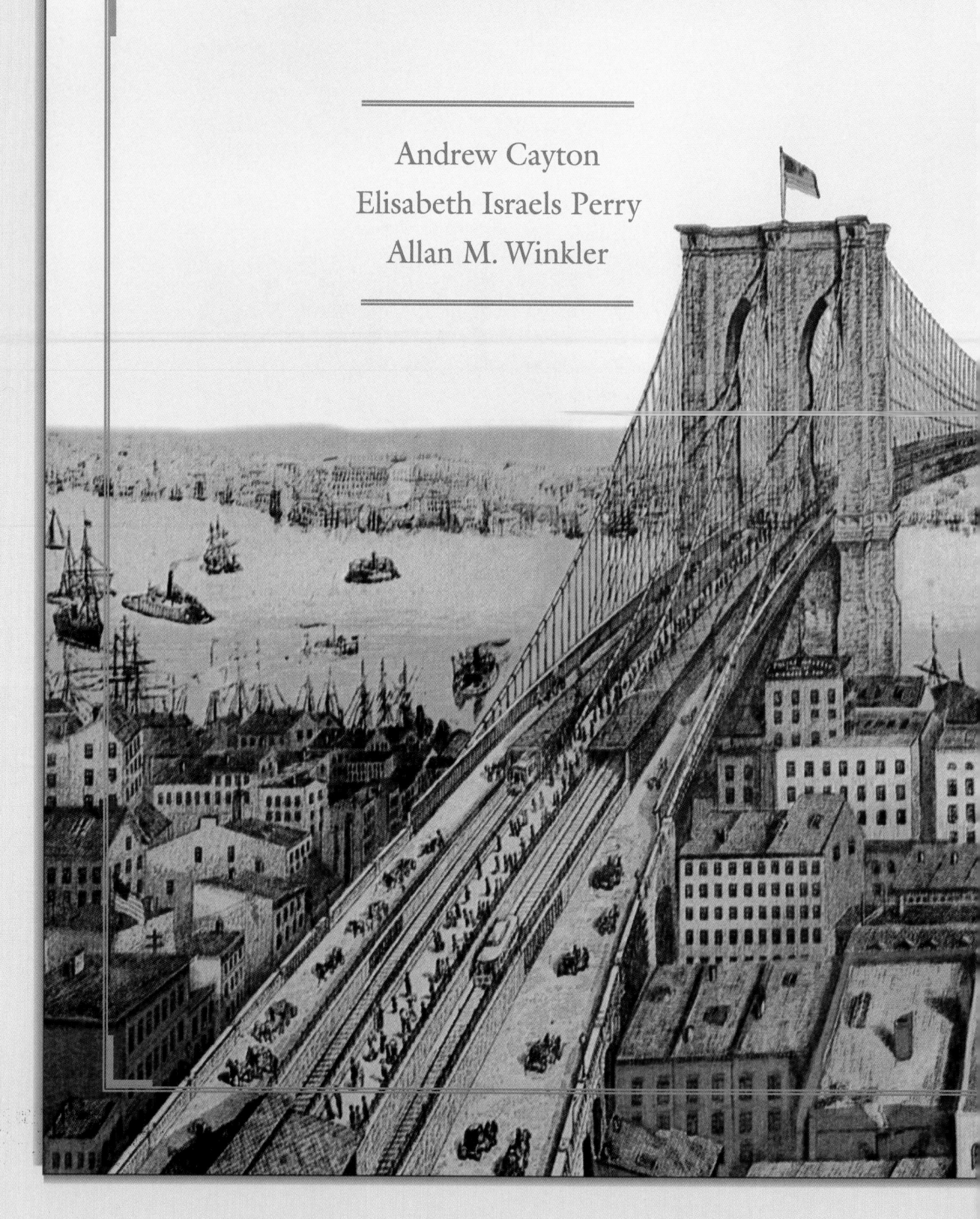

Andrew Cayton
Elisabeth Israels Perry
Allan M. Winkler

AMERICA

PATHWAYS
—TO THE—
PRESENT

THE TRIBUNE

PRENTICE HALL
NEEDHAM, MASSACHUSETTS

About the Authors

Andrew Cayton, Ph.D.

Andrew Cayton is Professor of History at Miami University in Oxford, Ohio. Born in Cincinnati, Ohio, he is the grandson of a high school history teacher. Dr. Cayton received his B.A. with high honors from the University of Virginia and his M.A. and Ph.D. from Brown University.

Dr. Cayton is an early American historian, whose specialization is political and social history. He is the author of *The Frontier Republic: Ideology and Politics in the Ohio Country, 1780–1825* and coauthor of *The Midwest and the Nation: Rethinking the History of an American Region.* His most recent book is *Frontier Indiana.*

Dr. Cayton received the 1993 Outstanding Teacher Award from the Ohio Academy of History and the 1992 Distinguished Educator Award from the College of Arts and Sciences at Miami University. He lives in Oxford, Ohio, with his wife, Mary Kupiec Cayton, and daughters, Elizabeth and Hannah.

Elisabeth Israels Perry, Ph.D.

Elisabeth Israels Perry directs the Masters Program in Women's History at Sarah Lawrence College, in Bronxville, New York. She previously taught U.S. women's history at Vanderbilt University, in Nashville, Tennessee. She received her B.A. and Ph.D. in history from the University of California at Los Angeles.

Dr. Perry's period of specialization is the late nineteenth and early twentieth centuries. Her greatest scholarly interests are women's history, reform movements, and issues of citizenship and identity in U.S. history. She is the author of *Belle Moskowitz: Feminine Politics and the Exercise of Power in the Age of Alfred E. Smith* and *Women in Action: Rebels and Reformers, 1920–1980.* She coedited *The Challenge of Feminist Biography: Writing the Lives of Modern American Women.*

Dr. Perry has received major grants from Fulbright, the National Endowment for the Humanities, and the American Council of Learned Societies. She has directed four NEH Summer Seminars for secondary school teachers and led numerous curriculum enrichment workshops for teachers of history and literature across the country.

Allan M. Winkler, Ph.D.

Allan M. Winkler is Professor of History at Miami University of Ohio. He received his B.A. from Harvard University, his M.A. from Columbia University, and his Ph.D. from Yale University.

Dr. Winkler's specialization is twentieth-century social and political history. He is the author of eight books, including *The Politics of Propaganda: The Office of War Information, 1942–1945; Modern America: The United States from the Second World War to the Present; The Recent Past: Readings on America Since World War II;* and *Home Front U.S.A.: America During World War II.* His most recent book, published in 1993, is *Life Under a Cloud: American Anxiety About the Atom.*

Dr. Winkler began his teaching career in the Peace Corps in the Philippines, where he worked at the elementary and secondary level as well as at the college level. He has taught at Yale University, the University of Oregon, and the University of Nairobi, in Kenya. He has also held the Bicentennial Chair in American Studies in Helsinki, Finland and the John Adams Chair in American Civilization in Amsterdam, in the Netherlands.

 PRENTICE HALL
Simon & Schuster Education Group
A VIACOM COMPANY

ISBN 0-13-432345-9

1 2 3 4 5 6 7 8 9   02 01 00 99 98 97

Program Reviewers

Teacher Advisory Panel

David Bardos
Carmel High School
Carmel, Indiana

Alfred B. Cate, Jr.
Central High School
Memphis, Tennessee

Elsie E. Clark
Johnson High School
Savannah, Georgia

Janet K. Chandler
Hamilton Southeastern High School
Fishers, Indiana

Vern Cobb
Okemos High School
Okemos, Michigan

Bernard Crispin
Connersville High School
Connersville, Indiana

Alice D'Addario
Walt Whitman High School
Huntington Station, New York

Richard Di Giacomo
Yerba Buena High School
San Jose, California

James Fogarty
Arroyo Grande High School
Arroyo Grande, California

Pamela Gray
Sonora High School
Fullerton School District, California

Paula M. Hanzel
Johnson High School West Campus
Sacramento, California

Richard Hart
El Cajon High School
El Cajon, California

Robert Hasty
Lawrence Central High School
Indianapolis, Indiana

Rosemary Hess
John Adams High School
South Bend, Indiana

Richard Hryniewicki
Cudahy High School
Cudahy, Wisconsin

Phillip James
Lincoln-Sudbury High School
Sudbury, Massachusetts

Gary L. Kelly
Novi High School
Novi, Michigan

Ronald Maggiano
West Springfield High School
Springfield, Virginia

Steve McClung
Santa Teresa High School
San Jose, California

Ellen Oicles
Piedmont Hills High School
San Jose, California

Preston G. Proctor
Monroe Central High School
Parker City, Indiana

Cherlynn Renner
Muncie Central High School
Muncie, Indiana

Wayne D. Rice
Carlsbad High School
Carlsbad, California

Ed Robinson
Tulare Western High School
Tulare, California

Jane Rotsko
Ipswich High School
Ipswich, Massachusetts

Jerome L. Ruderman
Frankford High School
Philadelphia, Pennsylvania

Kerry Steed
Ponderosa High School
Shingle Springs, California

George A. Stewart
Hoffman Estates High School
Hoffman Estates, Illinois

Walter T. Thurnau
Southwestern Central High School
Jamestown, New York

Dennis E. Wallace
Pendleton Heights High School
Pendleton, Indiana

Donald S. Winters
Davis High School
Davis, California

Ruth Writer
Buchanan High School
Buchanan, Michigan

v

CONTENTS

TABLE OF CONTENTS

TABLE OF CONTENTS

TABLE OF CONTENTS

ix

OVER ★ THERE

TABLE OF CONTENTS

TABLE OF CONTENTS

TABLE OF CONTENTS

TABLE OF CONTENTS

TABLE OF CONTENTS

TABLE OF CONTENTS

xix

TABLE OF CONTENTS

History might not have Happened This Way

Examples of how decision makers—both political leaders and ordinary citizens—shaped history

American Album

Artifacts from the exhibitions and collections at the Smithsonian Institution National Museum of American History

105-horsepower, six-cylinder engine

One of four Lewis machine guns

One of two 57-mm pedestal-mounted guns

Armor plating

Driver

Commander

Pressed steel track plate

HISTORIAN'S TOOLBOX

Step-by-step skill lessons to help understand and practice
important skills needed to study history

SOURCE READINGS
Connections to Literature

A collection of literature and primary source readings that provide thoughtful insights into our nation's history

Maps

Graphs, Charts, and Tables

Households with Radios, 1920-1930

Year	Number of Households with Radio Sets
1920	20,000
1922	60,000
1924	1,250,000
1926	4,500,000
1928	8,000,000
1930	13,750,000

Source: *Historical Statistics of the United States*

TABLE OF CONTENTS

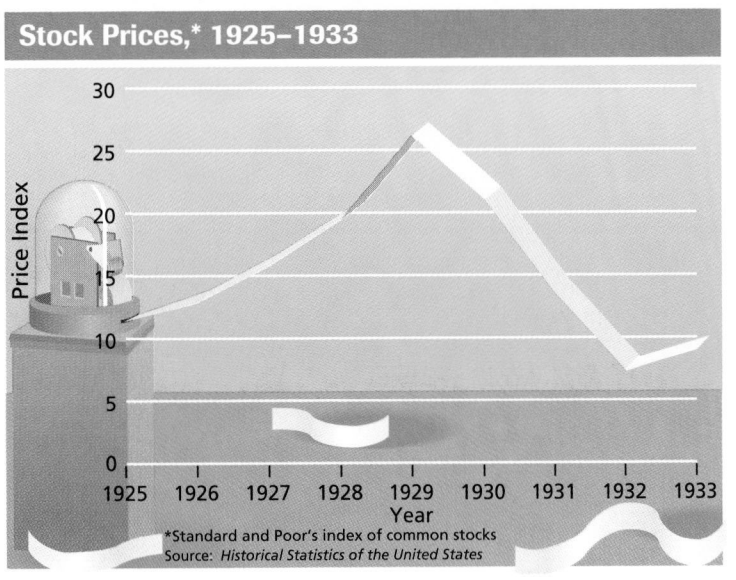

Stock Prices,* 1925–1933

Price Index

*Standard and Poor's index of common stocks
Source: *Historical Statistics of the United States*

Why Study History?

I know no way of judging the future but by the past.
—Patrick Henry, 1775

History Is Everyone's Story

American history is not only the story of famous heroes but also that of ordinary people. Remarkable leaders like Washington and Lincoln have guided the country well in times of crisis, while other men and women have been outstanding in business, science, and education. But America's greatness also rests on the hard work and dedicated effort of countless others, like this veteran coming home from Vietnam. Since the country began, they have plowed the fields, built the cities, raised the families, fought the wars, and done all the everyday things that add up to a country's history. While we may never know all their names, we know these people's stories—because they are our story, too.

The Present Is Linked to the Past

Throughout history, Americans have looked for new frontiers. Pioneers pushed westward into unknown territory, across rugged mountains and wide prairies. They built new towns and added new states to the nation. The frontier spirit has stayed with us, giving Americans a strong sense of energy, personal freedom, and individualism. More recently, Americans have looked toward farther frontiers, pioneering in space with the first moon landing and probes to distant planets.

If we forget what we did, we won't know who we are.
—Ronald Reagan, 1989

History Is Unpredictable

You might mistakenly think of history as a collection of cut-and-dried facts—names, dates, laws, statistics. But in fact, history is full of unexpected twists and turns, situations that could easily have turned out differently and so changed the course of many people's lives. The Pilgrims' first landfall in America, for instance, was due to a storm that blew their ship off course. President Harry Truman's election victory in 1948 was an upset that surprised almost everyone. Like many other events, it showed that history is never predictable and often has surprise endings.

Real People Change the Course of History

History is not only about yesterday's events—it is about today's headlines and tomorrow's news. As you are reading this, someone in the United States is taking an action that could change history. That person may not be famous or powerful, but may be just an ordinary citizen, like one of the students at a 1963 sit-in to desegregate a lunch counter. Ordinary people from many different backgrounds—like you and your friends and neighbors—are the people who really write history. And that is one answer to the question, Why study history? Because you are a part of it.

Themes in American History

M uch of what you learn about American history can be better understood if you view events as part of a larger pattern. The themes listed on page 9 apply to all periods of American history and can help you link events across time.

Americans have met challenges throughout their history. They have faced revolution, civil war, economic catastrophe, world wars, and divisive conflicts in faraway countries. They have been able to overcome obstacles because of the enduring values that link past generations to the present. (Above) Raising the flag atop Mount Suribachi on the Pacific island of Iwo Jima during World War II. (Top right) Vietnam Veterans Memorial, Washington, D.C.

REFORM MOVEMENTS

People in the United States have frequently taken action in grass-roots movements to right perceived wrongs and to secure improvements in the quality of life.

VALUES

A variety of religious, ethical, and moral beliefs have propelled and guided the quest of Americans for a just and ordered society.

ECONOMICS

Americans have searched for new and better ways to make a living and have struggled to define government's role in this pursuit.

TECHNOLOGY

Americans' ability to develop new skills and tools and to increase their knowledge of the physical world has greatly affected the way they live and work, and has led to a high standard of living.

ENVIRONMENT

The geography and available resources of the continent have affected the actions of Americans. Similarly, the actions of Americans have affected the environment and physical landscape.

DIVERSITY

The United States throughout its history has been made up of a gathering of many peoples from throughout the world. Americans have both benefited from and encountered problems with this diversity.

UNITY AND CONFLICT

Americans have developed unique political systems and laws that affirm a shared commitment to certain goals, such as individual rights and equality. Nevertheless, groups with differing views on how to achieve these goals have sometimes clashed.

AMERICAN CULTURE

In every period of their history, Americans gave special expression to their views in forms such as art, literature, films, music, manners, and morals.

AMERICAN DEMOCRACY

The concepts of democratic representation, equality under the law, and freedom from discrimination have been gradually broad-ened to include previously excluded groups.

THE UNITED STATES AND THE WORLD

America's relationships with other countries have been influenced at different times by a sense of mission, by values, and by self-interest.

Origins of a New Society to 1783

Introducing the Unit

Interpreting the Visual The first encounter between Europeans and Native Americans marked the beginning of a new society, created from the mingling of three cultures and three histories: Native American, African, and European. As the proverb on page 10 reminds us, it is essential to understand the story of that encounter.

From the start, Europeans were fascinated by Native Americans. They interpreted the scanty information they received about the inhabitants of the Americas according to images and patterns familiar to them. The painting shown here is one such interpretation.

Divide the class into small groups. Ask each group to read the caption and answer the following questions about the painting shown on pages 10–11:
● What event is portrayed in the picture? Where was the painter when the event occurred?
● Which group dominates the picture?
● What adjectives might the painter have used to describe Native Americans?
● Who saw this painting when it was completed? What incorrect impressions did it give them?
● How might a Native American artist have portrayed this event?

Establishing Chronology This unit describes the creation of a new, American society. Beginning with an overview of the Native American, African, and European worlds before the 1400s, the unit relates how these worlds encountered one another in the first European settlements in the Americas during the 1500s and 1600s. It ends by describing how in the 1700s, the British colonies sought independence.

Origins of a New Society To 1783

"A people without a history
is like wind on the buffalo grass."
—Proverb, Teton Sioux

*T*his Sioux proverb reminds us of how important it is to be aware of our past. To understand the early history of the United States, it is essential to know something about the past of not one but three peoples: Native Americans, Africans, and Europeans. The rich and varied histories of these groups shaped the growth and direction of the Americas. When the colonists overthrew British rule in the American Revolution, the new nation they created was already a society of people from different parts of the world.

RESOURCE DIRECTORY

Teaching Resources

📄 **Local History Activity** "Publick Times in Colonial Williamsburg" and the Local Focus research topic suggestions, found in the Local History Resources folder, pp. 3–5, are designed to help students understand how history affects all lives.

★ **Themes in American History Posters** Wall-size, illustrated posters, found in the Teaching Resources package, illustrate the four unit themes.

📄 **Unit Test** Forms A and B are found in the Unit 1 folder, pp. 140–145.

"Europeans Encountering Indians," artist unknown, was painted around 1700. From the strengths of such diverse peoples, a new society emerged.

Media and Technology

Visions of America: Scenes of an Era To introduce students to the main idea and events covered in this unit, play "Scenes of an Era: Origins of a New Society" (length: 2.5 minutes). This selection can be located on side 1 of the videodiscs. This selection can also be located on videotape 1. Lesson plans for "Scenes of an Era" can be found in the Visions of America Guidebook.

Using Multimedia Technology This folder contains instructional tools and strategies for using technology in the classroom.

Transparency Binder Contains full-color transparencies with lesson suggestions. From a large collection divided into twelve categories, specific transparencies are referenced throughout the chapters at appropriate points of use. For this unit, see American Photo, B-1; Our Multicultural Heritage, C-1; Time Lines, E-1 and E-2; Links Across Time, J-1; Political Cartoon, K-1; and Historical Maps, L-1.

Themes in American History

Teachers may wish to discuss specific historical events in the context of historical themes. Here are four suggestions for Unit 1.

Diversity *Throughout its history America has been made up of a gathering of many peoples from throughout the world. Americans have both benefited from and encountered problems with this diversity.*

● Native American groups in North America differed greatly from one another in most aspects of their culture.

● European colonization and the importation of slaves from Africa brought peoples from three continents together in North America.

Values *A variety of religious, ethical, and moral beliefs have propelled and guided the quest of Americans for a just and ordered society.*

● Religious beliefs played a major role in the founding and governing of the American colonies.

● Social rank was of primary importance in colonial society, which was based on a firm belief in the inequality of people.

Economics *Americans have searched for new and better ways to make a living and have struggled to define government's role in this pursuit.*

● The competition among European countries for trading partners led directly to European settlement in North America.

● The economic theory of mercantilism altered trade and political relationships between Britain and its colonies and contributed to calls for independence.

The United States and the World

America's relationships with other countries have been influenced at different times by a sense of mission, by values, and by self-interest.

● European colonists brought devastating diseases and wars to Native Americans.

● American colonists grew increasingly independent of their European roots and eventually sought complete independence through a rebellion.

Chapter 1 Three Cultures Collide
Before and After the 1400s

📁 Teaching Resources (See Unit 1 Folder)

	Instruction	Enrichment
Section 1 **The Native American World** (pp. 14–20)	Reproducible Lesson Plan, p. 3 Alternate Lesson Plan, p. 2 Guided Reading and Review, p. 7 Quiz, p. 8	Literature Activity, Corn Mother, p. 25–26 Critical Thinking Activity, Determining Relevance, p. 20 Historian's Toolbox Activity, Using Artifacts, p. 19
Section 2 **The European World** (pp. 22–26)	Reproducible Lesson Plan, p. 4 Alternate Lesson Plan, p. 3 Guided Reading and Review, p. 9 Quiz, p. 10	American Profiles Activity, Isabella I, Queen of Castile, p. 16 Literature Activity, The Koran, p. 24 Visual Learning Activity, Mapmakers, p. 27
Section 3 **The World of the West Africans** (pp. 27–30)	Reproducible Lesson Plan, p. 5 Alternate Lesson Plan, p. 4 Guided Reading and Review, p. 11 Quiz, p. 12	American Profiles Activity, Askia Muhammad, p. 15 Visual Learning Activity, Slave Factories, p. 28 Primary Source Activity, The Portuguese in West Africa, p. 23
Section 4 **The Atlantic World Is Born** (pp. 31–35)	Reproducible Lesson Plan, p. 6 Alternate Lesson Plan, p. 5 Guided Reading and Review, p. 13 Quiz, p. 14 Chapter Test, Forms A & B, pp. 29–34	Primary Source Activity, Europeans Encounter Native Americans, pp. 21–22 Viewpoints Activity, On Celebrating Columbus Day, pp. 17–18

📁 Additional Chapter Resources

Resource Organizer, p. 2
Alternate Lesson Plan, p. 1
Answer Keys, pp. 146–160

Bibliography

For the Teacher
Kopper, Philip, and the editors of Smithsonian Books. *The Smithsonian Book of North American Indians Before the Coming of the Europeans.* Smithsonian Books, 1986. (Well-illustrated overview of environments and cultures of Native American groups in North America.)
Thornton, John. *Africa and Africans in the Making of the Atlantic World, 1400–1680.* Cambridge University Press, 1992.

Prentice Hall Literature Excerpts from *The American Experience,* 1994, including Columbus, Christopher. *Journal of the First Voyage to America.*

Media and Technology

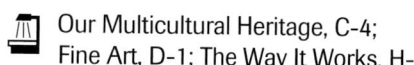 Our Multicultural Heritage, C-4; Fine Art, D-1; The Way It Works, H-1

 Cause and Effect, F-1

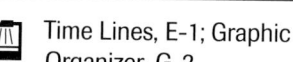 Time Lines, E-1; Graphic Organizer, G-2

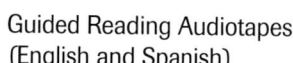 Guided Reading Audiotapes (English and Spanish)

 Computer Test Bank

For the Student

Digging Up America's Past: North America Before Columbus. National Geographic Society. Filmstrip.

Davidson, Basil, and editors of Time-Life Books. *African Kingdoms.* Time-Life, 1966. (Well illustrated.)

Morison, Samuel Eliot. *Admiral of the Ocean Sea: A Life of Christopher Columbus.* Little, Brown, 1942. (Focuses on Columbus the mariner.)

THE BIG IDEA

The Big Idea for the chapter and how the main ideas in each section relate to the Big Idea are graphically displayed below. Comprehension of this chapter's Big Idea is critical to students' understanding of United States history and how we as a nation got where we are today.

CHAPTER 1

Five hundred years ago, frequent contacts began among Native Americans, Europeans, and West Africans on the shores of North America. The resulting conflicts and interactions among these rich but different cultures had far-reaching effects, sometimes tragic and destructive, for the people of these three worlds.

SECTION 1

The Native American world of the 1400s was a place of many flourishing, though contrasting, societies.

SECTION 2

Spurred by a hunger for trade and wealth, and helped by advances in technology and navigation, Renaissance Europe was ready for a new era of discovery and expansion.

SECTION 3

West Africa in the 1400s was a land of rich and powerful trading kingdoms, with strong societies and a tradition of religion and learning.

SECTION 4

The first voyage of Columbus began centuries of interactions among Native Americans, Europeans, and Africans within the Atlantic World. These contacts brought an exchange of goods and ideas but led to the spread of diseases and the growth of the slave trade.

The Relevance of the Big Idea

Five hundred years ago in North America, three different cultures—Native American, European, and West African—came into contact and conflict. The results of their interactions were felt by people on all three continents.

Discuss with students other areas in the world where different cultures are or have recently been in conflict, such as the former Yugoslavia, the Middle East, or central Africa. You might use photos and articles to provide background and engage students' interest. What do they see as likely causes of such conflicts? (*Longstanding ethnic/ religious differences and prejudices, competition for territory and resources, etc.*) Discuss how people might avoid cultural conflicts.

In Depth

Global Connections

Finding a fast sea route to Asia was a top priority for most European explorers in the 1400s and 1500s. After Columbus's voyages, many believed that Asia still lay only a short distance beyond the western coast of North America. They thought that they had only to find a water passage through the continent to reach it. Great rivers leading inland, such as the St. Lawrence and the Hudson, raised the hopes of many explorers. Even when Balboa sighted the Pacific Ocean in 1513, no one had any idea of the distance across it. It was the first circumnavigation of the globe, by Magellan's expedition in 1519–22, that gave an accurate idea of the distance across the Pacific Ocean.

Three Cultures Collide
Before and After the 1400s

*F*ive hundred years ago, a few frail ships crossing the waters of the Atlantic Ocean brought Europeans to Native American shores. Africans torn from their homelands soon followed. At that time regular contact—often violent and darkened by misunderstanding—began among the three cultures. What does that encounter mean to us? It is the beginning of an answer to pressing questions: Who are we? Where have we come from? Where are we going?

Events in the United States

800–1000
Navahos migrate to the Southwest from the fringes of North America.

1000 Norse voyagers under Ericsson land on the coast of North America.

| 800 | 900 | 1000 | 1100 | 1200 |

Events in the World

1096 European Christians set out on the First Crusade to capture Palestine from the Muslims.

▶ RESOURCE DIRECTORY

Teaching Resources

Alternate Lesson Plan: Demonstrating the Big Idea found in the Alternate Lesson Plans folder, p. 1, provides a lesson strategy designed to instruct students about the Big Idea that the collision of three cultures set the course of the Americas after 1492.

Alternative Assessment Handbook provides information, guidance, and strategies for alternative methods of assessment. It includes an essay on new trends in assessment, guidance, and strategies for developing performance tasks and portfolios, scoring rubrics, and sample evaluation forms.

Pages 14–20

The Native American World

"Flourishing variety"—this phrase sums up the world of the Native Americans in the 1400s. America was a land of contrasting societies long before these native cultures encountered those of the Europeans and Africans.

Pages 22–26

The European World

Europeans approached the 1400s with an ever-increasing hunger for trade and wealth. Armed with technological innovations, they were ready for a new era of discovery and expansion.

Pages 27–30

The World of the West Africans

A land of powerful kingdoms, ancient learning, great religions, and the wealth of thriving trade—such was Africa by the end of the 1400s.

Pages 31–35

The Atlantic World Is Born

The voyage of an Italian navigator was the prelude to centuries of trade, cultural exchange, and conflict among Native Americans, Europeans, and Africans.

		Late 1400s *Ozette village destroyed by a mudslide.* *• Etowah population reaches its peak.*	*1513 The Calusas of Florida drive off Spanish explorer Poncé de León.*	*1540 Spanish explorer Coronado introduces horses and pigs into the Southwest.*
	1327 The Aztecs establish Mexico City.			
1300	**1400**	**1500**		**1600**
1271 Marco Polo journeys to China.	*1350s Due to the plague, life expectancy in Europe drops to eighteen years.*	*1492 Columbus sails from Spain and lands on islands in the Caribbean.*	*1538 Ten years after being forced from power, Askia Muhammed, ruler of Songhai, dies.*	

Alternative Assessment

As an ongoing chapter project, students can simulate the early interactions between the three Atlantic cultures. To prepare, they will divide into three groups, acting as advisers to one of these leaders: the head of a Native American town on the coast of North America (Northeast or Southeast), the king of a West African kingdom, the captain of a European ship. One member will later act as team spokesperson.

In preparation for an expected meeting with each of the other two groups, each group works up a "position paper"—a list of questions or points to guide their first meeting. It should cover these points:

● Who are these people? Why are they here?

● What do they want from us? Are they a threat to us? Are we a threat to them?

● What do we know about other cultures? How can that help us in meeting these people?

● What things are important to this group—land, gold, power?

Student work will be assessed according to the following criteria:

● **Unacceptable** Activity not attempted; performance does not demonstrate an understanding of the issues.

● **Limited/Acceptable** Performance demonstrates a partial understanding of the issues and adequate preparation.

● **Extensive/Commendable** Performance demonstrates thorough research, a clear understanding of the issues, and thoughtful preparation.

● **Extraordinary/Outstanding** Performance demonstrates imagination, insight into the issues, and original thought and creativity.

For information and guidance on alternative assessment trends and strategies, see the Alternative Assessment Handbook in the Resource Directory on page 12.

The Native American World

SECTION 1

The Native American World

The Native American World

1. FOCUS

Connecting to the Big Idea

See page 12B. Explain to students that the Native American world—the first of the three cultures that met in North America—included a diversity of peoples. Across the continent, these different groups established kinship networks, traded with other groups, and observed religious beliefs and ceremonies. Ask students what factors influenced this cultural diversity.

Objectives

● Understand that people have lived throughout North and South America for thousands of years.
● Describe the regional variations among Native American cultures as evidence of diversity.
● Identify the social, religious, and political functions served by the family in Native American culture.
● Explain the importance of trade among the peoples of North America.

Bellringer

Ask students to name any Native American groups that are familiar to them from movies, television, reading, or local influences (such as geographical names). Ask them to recall any facts they know about the group, such as their location or way of life. Students can locate these groups on the map of Native American groups on page 16.

Reading Strategy

Reading for Evidence Ask students to locate evidence showing why the Native American world in the 1400s could be described as both "flourishing" and "varied." Ask them to make a note of one fact about each regional culture indicating how it differed from others.

SECTION PREVIEW

"Flourishing variety"—this phrase sums up the world of the Native Americans in the 1400s. America was a land of contrasting societies long before these native cultures encountered those of the Europeans and Africans.

Key Concepts
• North and South America have been populated for tens of thousands of years.
• By the 1400s, North America was inhabited by diverse cultural groups who adapted their way of life to the variations of the land and climate in which they lived.
• Among Native Americans, families served social, religious, and political functions.
• Age-old Native American trade routes crisscrossed North America by the 1400s.

Native American artists in what is now Gallatin County, Kentucky, sculpted in stone the spare, crisp lines and curves of this face.

Key Terms, People, and Places
kinship network, clan, division of labor, oral tradition

Before Europeans or Africans ever reached North or South America, hundreds of societies already populated the American land. The people who made up those societies, and Americans descended from them, are today generally called Native Americans. Native Americans developed their own ways of life over the course of thousands of years. During that time, few of them ever came into contact with people from other continents. This section examines some patterns of early Native American life that would play an important role once Native Americans, Europeans, and Africans—the three Atlantic cultures—finally made contact with one another.

The Ancient Roots of Native American Culture

No one knows exactly when people first came to the Americas. Among many other ancient traces, they left fingerprints in mud in New Mexico that hardened 28,000 years ago, baskets in Pennsylvania that may be 19,000 years old, and weapons in Alaska that may have been chipped from stone 12,000 years ago. Archaeologists think that the first Americans may have arrived even earlier than this evidence suggests—as much as 40,000 years ago. At that time, the level of the world's oceans was low, and people could walk from Asia to what is now Alaska over a "land bridge."

Some archaeologists also suggest that separate waves of migrating people may have come across the land bridge from Asia at different times. As they moved southward from Alaska, the groups dispersed. Settling into different regions, from the Arctic Circle to the southernmost tip of South America, these separate groups developed distinct languages and customs.

By the late 1400s, when the encounter among the Atlantic cultures began, some eight to ten million people may have lived in what is now the United States. Some scholars contest these figures, claiming that as few as 700,000 to 800,000 Native Americans lived in the continental United States before contact across the Atlantic began. The map on page 16 shows that whatever the size of this population, it included a broad variety of distinct groups.

Native Americans Adapted to Land and Climate

The North American environment varies drastically from region to region. It includes the surf-swept beaches of the West Coast, the windy plains of the Midwest, and the rocky

---

 RESOURCE DIRECTORY

Teaching Resources

Reproducible Lesson Plan found in the Unit 1 folder, p. 3, provides a summary of the Section 1 lesson plan content.

Alternate Lesson Plan: Learning Styles found in the Alternate Lesson Plans folder, p. 2, is especially effective for visual learners and designed to help students create a diagram or poster on Native American societies.

Guided Reading and Review found in the Unit 1 folder, p. 7, provides a structure for reading and mastering the key concepts and reviewing the key terms for Section 1. (Guided Practice)

coast of New England. Since the people who first inhabited this land adapted their way of life to fit their local environment, their cultures also varied from place to place.

The North On the coastal fringes of North America lived two northern peoples, the Inuit and Aleut. They were skilled at hunting on ice and snow, on shores and plains mild in summer and bitter in winter. Other northern groups such as the Koyukon and Ingalik were nomadic. They moved their homes as they hunted, fished, and gathered food in huge forests and along the shores of lakes and waterways.

The Northwest Coast Waterways were also the primary source of food for Native Americans of the Northwest Coast. Here rivers, fed by rainfall that could be twice as heavy as the average elsewhere in North America, poured into a teeming ocean fishing ground. The Coos, Coast Salish, Makah, and others in the Northwest developed a remarkable fishing and food storage technology. It allowed them to harvest and preserve a seemingly inexhaustible wealth of food, including seal, salmon, and euluchon—a fish so rich in oil that when dried it could be burned as a candle.

California South along the coast from the fishing people lies what is now the state of California. During the 1400s, only about 300,000 people lived in its mountains and broad valleys, including the Chumash, Yurok, Serrano, and other people. They spoke more than a hundred variations of twenty basic languages, and they generally lived in small bands. Depending on their location, they might eat deep-sea fish, acorns from mountain oaks, or beans from a desert scrub known as mesquite.

The Plateau Inland from the Northwest Coast, between the Cascade Mountains and the Rockies, stretches a plateau of dry plains crisscrossed by rivers. Dozens of groups in this area—including the Chinook and Cayuse—fished the rivers for salmon and dug in the plains for edible roots. They often built villages that looked down from high riverbanks and dominated the waters below.

The Great Basin The map on page 16 shows the Great Basin, a region that also lies between two mountain ranges: the Sierra Nevada and the Rockies. Here in this mostly dry land, food was scarce. Most people in this region—including the Paiute, Ute, and Shoshoni—lived in small groups. Members of a group worked together hunting and gathering food—which included everything from roots and pine nuts to rabbits and insects.

The Southwest As little as four inches of rain falls annually in some parts of the Southwest region, which lies south of the Great Basin. Some groups here—the Hopi and Zuni are examples—lived settled lives and developed farming techniques to suit the dry environment. Others, such as the Apache, were nomadic. The Navaho moved to this region from the North, adapting their way of life as they did so. As a rule, Native Americans in the Southwest lived in large groups. For example, the people later known by their Spanish name, Pueblo ("town"), lived in complexes of hundreds of rooms that resemble today's apartment houses.

The Plains In villages along the rivers that drain the central area of the continent, the Mandans,

Using Historical Evidence Two families of the Nootka people of the Northwest Coast prepare fish in this 1784 engraving. *Describe Nootka technology as it appears in the illustration.*

Activity

(The clock icon indicates an activity that can be successfully conducted within a class period. Each chapter has at least one such activity.)

Teaching Heterogeneous Groups

So that all students grasp the idea that *where* we live influences *how* we live, brainstorm a list of categories that help define people's lifestyle. (Kinds of housing, clothing, foods, leisure activities, etc.) Divide students into groups representing the different geographic regions discussed in this section. Using the categories they listed, each group is to make a Where We Live/How We Live chart for the Native Americans of their region. "Where We Live" should include climate, vegetation, and other geographic factors. **LEP**

Enrichment

Much of what we know about earlier Native American cultures comes from the work of archaeologists and anthropologists. Have students choose one Native American group—perhaps one with a connection to your community—and find out what has been discovered about its history and way of life. What is its status today?

Caption Answer to …

 Interpreting Maps

The north; the cold climate in this region deterred settlement by large numbers of Native Americans.

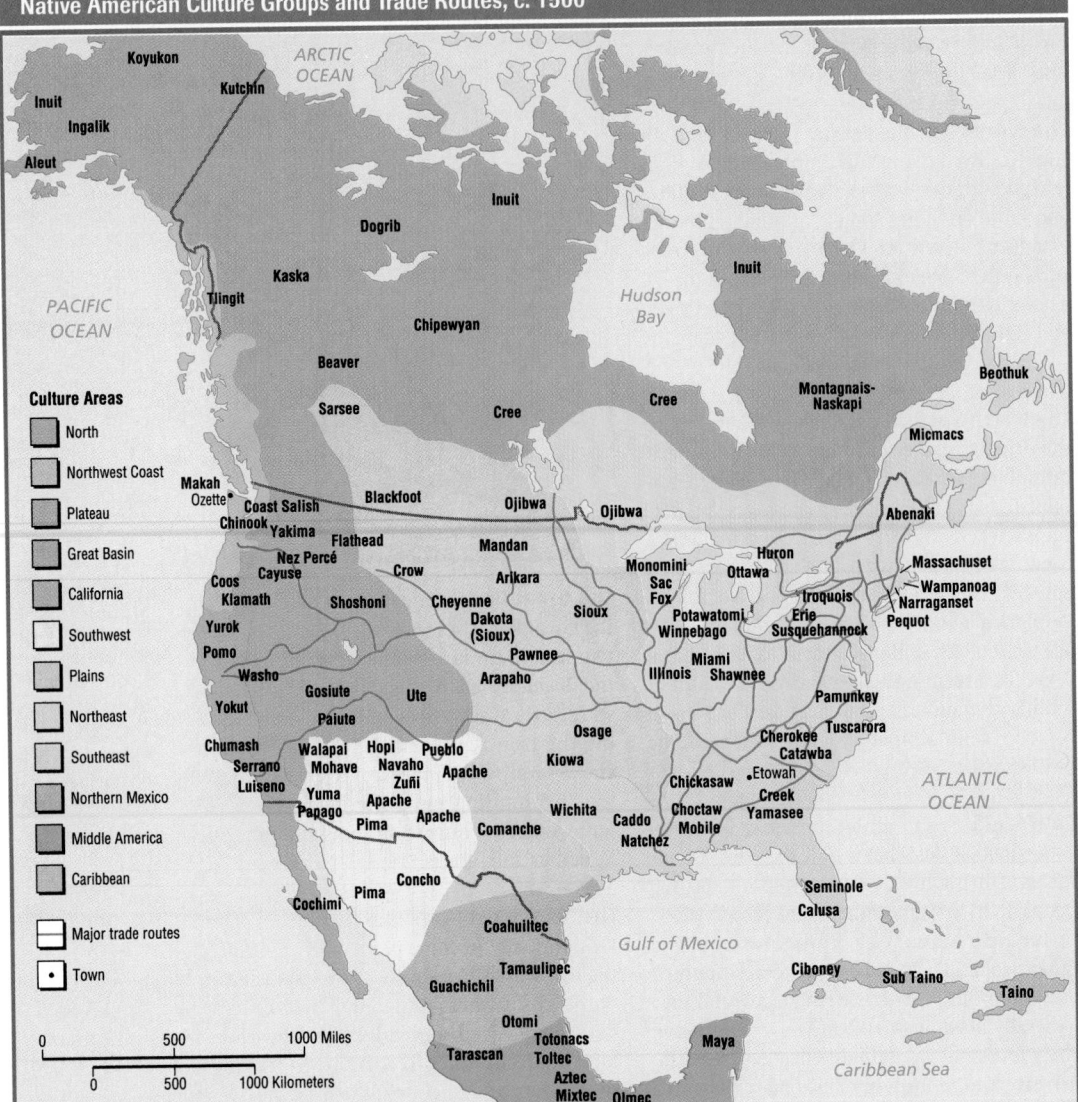

Native American Culture Groups and Trade Routes, c. 1500

Culture Areas
- North
- Northwest Coast
- Plateau
- Great Basin
- California
- Southwest
- Plains
- Northeast
- Southeast
- Northern Mexico
- Middle America
- Caribbean
- Major trade routes
- Town

 Geography and History: Interpreting Maps
The map shows only some of the groups thriving in North America in the 1400s. The trade routes, too, are only a selection; nearly any waterway or path served as a potential path for trade. *In which region is a small number of culture groups spread out over a large area? Why?*

the Wichita, the Pawnee, and other groups planted corn, beans and squash. They also ranged great distances on foot, hunting the vast herds of buffalo that grazed on the Plains. They used the buffalo to fulfill many of their needs, from food to clothing and shelter.

The Northeast Extensive woodlands and ample rainfall influenced the way of life of the Native Americans in the Northeast. Generally, these people gathered wild plants, hunted, and grew crops such as corn, beans and squash. They also fished bodies of water, whether local

▶ RESOURCE DIRECTORY

Teaching Resources

⭐ **Critical Thinking Activity** Determining Relevance: Solving an Archaeological Puzzle, found in the Unit 1 folder, p. 20, is designed to help students apply this skill by analyzing a tool of Neanderthal, or Stone Age, times.

trout streams, glacial lakes, or the Atlantic Ocean. In several groups—the Seneca and the Lenape, for example—women managed the dwelling and the garden clearings around it, and men hunted deer, bear, moose, and other game in the woods.

The Southeast From mountains to swamp to seacoast, the Southeast varied—and cultures in the region varied in response. Like the Northeast, the Southeast was mostly wooded, and its inhabitants depended on growing corn and hunting. They knew what plants to use to make almost anything, from rope to medicine, clothing, or even poison to catch fish.

One group in the Southeast, the Natchez of the lower Mississippi, preserved the way of life of the Mississippian culture, which around 1300 had stretched from Louisiana to Wisconsin. Several thousand people lived in each Natchez town. The towns boasted great temples on raised mounds and hundreds of individual houses. The Creek and the Cherokee, like several other groups to the east of the Natchez, built similar communities. The pyramid of the Cherokee town of Etowah in Georgia was over 60 feet high; on its crest stood wooden temples, and marble statues have been found in its ruins.

The Social Organization of Native Americans

No matter how Native Americans adapted to their environment, they generally looked to the family to fulfill many of their social needs. Their families provided them with many of the services we expect today from governments, churches, and private organizations. Such services included medical care, child care, settlement of disputes, and education.

For the Native American the family was made up of more than just parents and children. Instead, it was a **kinship network**—a group of relatives, or kin, such as parents, children, grandparents, aunts, uncles, cousins, and those who had married into the family.

One kind of kinship network is today referred to as a **clan**. A clan was formed of groups of families who were all descended from a common ancestor. The Lenape people of the mid-Atlantic seaboard had at least three clans. The diagram below illustrates how Lenape clans gathered to-gether for ceremonies that had social, religious, and political significance. Native American groups across the continent—from the Lenape to the Makahs of the Northwest Coast— lived in societies based on kinship networks.

Native Americans in Oklahoma used these stone axes in ceremonies.

Central post This post was a symbolic link to the sky, home of the Creator.

Carvings These carvings represented twelve sky spirits.

Entry at east This entry symbolized birth.

Oval Floor The shape represented the back of the turtle that was believed to form the earth.

Wolf clan

Drummers

Turtle clan

Turkey clan

Circle of men

Circle of women

Exit at west This exit symbolized death.

In a ceremony of prayer, chanting, and dance, clans of the Lenape gave thanks to the Creator. The longhouse and everything in it reflected the Lenape view of relationships in the universe. For example, men sat within a circle of women, who headed the clans.

Media and Technology

Transparencies
Our Multicultural Heritage, C-4; Fine Art, D-1; The Way It Works, H-1

In Depth

Then and Now

A new interest in and respect for Native American cultures has developed in recent years. One result is the establishment of a new museum in the Smithsonian Institution complex—the National Museum of the American Indian (NMAI). The new museum will be built on the last open site on the Mall in Washington, D.C., east of the National Air and Space Museum. Native Americans have played major roles in creating the museum's collections and displays of artifacts, with sensitivity to tribal feelings. They have also been leaders of the group planning the architecture and landscaping, whose design reflects the symbolic importance of the circle and other traditional Native values. Construction was scheduled to begin in 1998; in the meantime, a small collection opened in New York City.

In Depth

Did You Know?

Changes in the language of the Navaho people dramatically demonstrate how culture and environment interact. The Navaho once lived in eastern Alaska, where they adapted to snow and cold by gathering wild food and hunting. Later they migrated to the more temperate Southwest, where they grew corn as a basic food. The Navaho chose the corn plant as a symbol of life and incorporated it into their religious beliefs and creation stories. Because they needed a word for *seed*, they adapted their old word for *snowflake*.

The People of Ozette

Sometime in the late 1400s, the Native American village of **Ozette**, at the foot of a steep hill on the coast of what is now Washington state, met an unexpected end. Soaked by heavy rains, the hillside over the village gave way. Thousands of tons of mud swept over the village, instantly burying its houses. Most of its inhabitants, who were Makahs, escaped. Ozette became a time capsule of life among the Makahs 500 years ago.

The site lay hidden until 1970, when archaeologists began painstakingly washing away the hardened mud. Although their labor was agonizingly slow—it lasted for over a decade—the 80,000 artifacts they uncovered allowed them to reconstruct the life of the buried village.

This Makah whaler with harpoon and floats was photographed c. 1901. Archaeologists at Ozette unearthed the figure shown cradled in a shell.

The Houses of Ozette The largest artifacts archaeologists recovered were the houses of Ozette— designed much like present-day wood-frame houses. To build them, the Makahs first raised a heavy framework of logs. Then they covered the framework with wide planks split from cedar trees. The roof, also planked with cedar, included sections that could be opened to let the smoke of cooking fires out of the interior.

Inside the house, carved animal designs painted with bold colors brightened the walls. Around the wooden floor of the central area, the Makahs set up separate spaces for sleeping and for cooking food over individual fires. Smaller family units—parents and children— lived within these partitioned spaces. The

illustration on page 15 of the Nootkan house provides an example of a similar living arrangement. Together, all the people in the house made up a kinship network. The typical kinship network at Ozette required a house that might be 65 feet long and 35 feet wide.

The Daily Life of the People of Ozette Like others of the Northwest Coast, the people of Ozette took advantage of the rich fishing resources of the region—whales and salmon, as well as clams, mussels, and other shellfish. They preserved fish by hanging them from the rafters of their houses to dry in the smoke.

Gathering food inevitably took the Makahs away from the house. Some of this work was divided between men and women: men caught whales, seals, and fish, which women cleaned and filleted. Women also gathered shellfish, crabs, and other foods from the shore. In this **division of labor**, or the way tasks are assigned, both men and women worked hard, although with different purposes and sometimes in different places. Both men and women, however, shared an overriding goal: to produce the food, clothing, and shelter necessary for the survival of the family.

MAKING CONNECTIONS

Is labor divided between men and women in our society? Explain your answer.

The Religious Life of Native Americans

As the illustration of the Lenape gathering on page 17 demonstrates, family and clan frequently joined together in ceremonial celebrations. According to the Native American view, the most powerful forces in the world were spiritual. In that view, to exercise any influence over nature or other people, humans had to perform ceremonies that recognized the power of those spiritual forces.

Like Africans and Europeans, Native Americans also believed that misfortunes, such as military defeat, disease, or bad harvests, happened to people who ignored rituals. For this reason, whether they were planting crops, choosing a mate, or burying their dead, Native Americans strictly followed traditional rituals. Failure to do so was an invitation to disaster.

To preserve their essential spiritual beliefs, Native Americans relied on **oral traditions**. That means they passed on their history and beliefs from generation to generation by word of mouth. Old people told young people stories, songs, and instructions for ceremonies, and the young as they grew old retold this lore to their children. As one Cherokee leader explained in 1751, "My tongue is my pen and my mouth my paper." Native American oral tradition is still alive today, although much of it was lost in the upheaval that followed the meeting of the Atlantic cultures.

A Pattern of Interaction: Peaceful Trade

All Native American groups, no matter how large or small, traded food or goods within their group and outside it. They traded not only for items they needed or wanted, but also to demonstrate hospitality and friendliness. Even basic economic transactions had social importance, because sharing was a sign of respect. Such trading customs began thousands of years before the arrival of Europeans and Africans and continued long afterward. A French priest, Father Joseph François Lafitau, noted in 1724 that the Native Americans

> have traded with each other from time immemorial. . . . The feasts and dances which they have when they go to deal with other tribes make their trade an agreeable diversion. . . . Their way of engaging in trade is by an exchange of gifts.

By the 1400s, trading routes had criss-crossed the American continents for thousands of years. The Inuit traded copper from the Copper River in southern Alaska for sharks' teeth collected by Native Americans living at the mouth of the Columbia River in Washington. Shells harvested by the Northwest Coast groups found their way to central California and North Dakota. The Mohave of the Great Basin bartered with people on the coast of California and then traded coastal goods to the Pueblo in what is now Arizona. Rocky Mountain groups took obsidian, a volcanic glass, eastward into Ohio. The Iroquois east of the Great Lakes bartered with groups from

1650   1700   1750   1800   **Links Across Time**   1850   1900   1950   2000

Preserving the Environment

In 1963, Stewart Udall, then secretary of the interior, noted, "It is ironical that today the conservation movement finds itself turning back to ancient Indian land ideas, to the Indian understanding that we are not outside nature, but of it."

Udall was referring to the body of Native American beliefs that was characterized by an intimate relationship with nature and a great respect for all life. To the native people who held these convictions, the world was a community in which the spirits that inhabited all forms of life were connected. In that web of life, humans were of equal, but not superior, stature. Bedagi, or Big Thunder, of the Wabanakis Nation said, "The Great Spirit is our father, but the earth is our mother. She nourishes us." The Lakota holy man and philosopher, Black Elk, expressed a similar belief when he asked, "Is not the sky a father and earth a mother and are not all living things, with feet and wings or roots their children?"

To the Native American, each form of life had a function to carry out to maintain the balance of nature. A deer or bear killed for food was fulfilling its function to help people survive. Similarly, it was the duty of the birch tree to provide the bark for a canoe or shelter. All living things eventually returned to the land. There, souls mingled with soil to feed the roots of emerging plants and trees—and a new cycle of life began. **What actions have government or individuals taken in recent years to preserve the connection between humans and the environment?**

In Depth

Biography

Contemporary Native Americans continue the storytelling tradition. Writer Louise Erdrich (b. 1954) is a member of the Turtle Mountain group of Chippewa and grew up in North Dakota, where her grandparents lived on a reservation. Her poetry, stories, and novels draw on her Native American heritage. Speaking of how she began her career, Erdrich said, "My father used to give me a nickel for every story I wrote." Her novel *Love Medicine* won the National Book Critics' Circle Award in 1984. In 1991 Erdrich and her husband, Michael Dorris, co-wrote *The Crown of Columbus,* a modern Native American perspective on American history.

Section 1 Review Answers

1. (a) kinship network, see p. 17, (b) clan, see p. 17, (c) division of labor, see p. 18, (d) oral tradition, see p. 19.

2. Evidence includes fingerprints in mud in New Mexico that hardened 28,000 years ago, baskets in Pennsylvania that may be 19,000 years old, and weapons in Alaska that may have been chipped from stone 12,000 years ago.

3. Students might choose from groups living in the North, the Northwest Coast, California, the Plateau, the Great Basin, the Southwest, the Plains, the Northeast, and the Southeast. For each group, students should describe the environment and how it affected the group's way of life.

4. Trade brought Native Americans goods they wanted or needed, and it also allowed them to demonstrate hospitality and friendliness.

5. Possible answer: Diversity probably encouraged trade, because groups with different ways of life and different resources to draw on would acquire or produce things that other groups did not have.

Reteach

Have students create a chart that allows them visually to compare the Native American groups in different regions, using these criteria: social organization and kinship patterns, food supply, religious beliefs and observations, trading patterns.

Reinforcing the Big Idea

Fifteenth-century North America was home to a diverse group of flourishing Native American cultures, which also shared common traits. The next section describes the diversity of European nations and cultures in the 1400s and explains the motivations that sent European explorers to make contact with other cultures.

Minnesota to get stone for tobacco pipes. Other Northeast Woodland people traded tobacco itself, as well as corn and flint. In the Southeast, Native Americans traded salt and copper from the Appalachian Mountains.

Although Native Americans used natural trade routes such as the Mississippi River and the Great Lakes, they also built a network of trading paths. One, from central Connecticut to what is now Providence, Rhode Island, had been so well worn by Native American travelers that by the 1600s it was two feet below the level of the surrounding land. These routes often led to centers where Native Americans held trade gatherings during the summer. At the Dalles, a site on the Columbia River in Oregon, the Chinook people caught and dried salmon and traded it to visiting groups. At an annual summer fair on Kotzebue Sound in Alaska, inland groups swapped clothing, jadeite stone and red ocher (used as makeup) for sealskins and seal oil offered by coastal groups. These numerous examples offer only a glimpse of the complex trade networks of North America. As a result of thousands of years of trade, those networks stretched not only from end to end but even past what is now the United States—into Canada, Mexico, and beyond.

This neck ornament, found inland at the town of Etowah in Georgia, is made of shell, a sure sign that it was a trade item from a distant seacoast.

The Native American View of Land Use

Native Americans might give away possessions as gifts, but they never traded land. In their view, the land could not be owned. They believed that people had a right to use land and could grant others the right to use it too. But to sell land outright, as people in other countries did at the time and as we do today, was unthinkable to Native Americans.

Altering the land so that it would no longer support their way of life was also unthinkable to Native Americans. However, Native Americans did modify their environment, sometimes extensively. For example, they sometimes burned forest underbrush to improve hunting. Despite this alteration of their environment, their religious beliefs taught that the land, like all of nature, deserved respect.

Chief Joseph, a leader of the Nez Percé people in the late 1800s, expressed the age-old Native American view:

> The country was made without lines of demarcation [boundary lines], *and it is no man's business to divide it. . . . The earth and myself are of one mind. The measure of the land and the measure of our bodies are the same. . . . I never said the land was mine to do with it as I chose. The one who has the right to dispose of it is the one who has created it.* ★

As you will see in the next section, Europeans had different ideas about land ownership. For Europeans, owning land meant being wealthy and having power. In spite of this and other differences between Native American and European cultures, the next section shows that Europeans, like Native Americans, were busy trading, worshipping, and working to keep their families alive.

SECTION 1 REVIEW

Key Terms, People, and Places
1. Define (a) kinship network, (b) clan, (c) division of labor, (d) oral tradition.

Key Concepts
2. What evidence shows that Native Americans have lived in the Americas for tens of thousands of years?
3. Give three examples of cultural groups in North America, and explain how they adapted to their environment.
4. What purposes did trade serve among Native Americans?

Critical Thinking
5. **Drawing Conclusions** Do you think that the diversity of Native American groups encouraged or discouraged trade? Explain your answer.

 RESOURCE DIRECTORY

Teaching Resources

 Literature Activity "Corn Mother," found in the Unit 1 folder, pp. 25–26, uses a Penobscot folktale to portray the Native American view of how to use the land.

 Quiz found in the Unit 1 folder, p. 8, covers the main ideas in this section as well as the key terms.

Using Artifacts

Artifacts—objects made by humans such as tools, weapons, pottery, or jewelry—provide information about people and events of the past. When researching information about a historical period, development, or event, historians use artifacts as one type of evidence that helps to piece together the past.

Many experts think that it is probable that separate waves of migrants came to North America from Asia at different times, as many as 40,000 years ago. This theory is one of several about the first human inhabitants of the Americas. Another theory proposes that humans first entered North America around 12,000 years ago in a single migration from Asia into what is now Alaska. A growing body of historical evidence seems to support the multiple migration theory, however.

Any historical evidence must be analyzed carefully to determine whether it supports or refutes a particular theory. To evaluate the artifacts and excerpt below, use the following steps.

1. Identify the nature of the artifacts. Read the excerpt, examine the photograph of the artifact, and answer the following questions.
(a) What type of artifact was found?
(b) What were the artifacts probably used for? (c) Why was it important to be certain about their age?

2. Determine what facts are known about the artifacts.
(a) Who found the artifacts?
(b) Where were they found?
(c) About how old are they?
(d) How do they compare to other artifacts of this type?

3. Determine whether the available facts support a given theory. To help decide whether the archaeologists' theory of migration is based on fact, answer the following questions.
(a) What theory do they propose?
(b) Which facts support their theory?
(c) Do the facts support any other possible theories? Explain. (d) What conclusions can be drawn about the artifacts and their makers?

The often-challenged theory that humans first entered the New World around twelve thousand years ago in a single migration from Asia into Alaska has taken another blow. Two archaeologists say that they have found evidence of two different cultures coexisting in Alaska between eleven thousand and twelve thousand years ago. . . .

The new find consists of several flint spear points and other stone tools found atop a small mesa that looks out over a vast plain where bison and mammoths would have roamed. "It was a hunting lookout," says Michael Kunz, an archaeologist with the Bureau of Land Management who discovered the site in 1978 when surveying Alaska's North Slope before it was opened to oil drillers.

The age of the stone weapons has only just been established by radiocarbon dating of charcoal found with them. . . . What makes the spear points remarkable is that they resemble "Paleoindian" [early American hunting people]

weapons common in the lower forty-eight states.

Yet nothing like a Paleoindian weapon had been found in Alaska in a context that could be reliably dated [until now]. Instead, the state's only other culture of comparable antiquity, called the Nenana complex, made use of very different forms of stone tools. When the various tool types made by cultures differ significantly, archaeologists tend to think the peoples who made them belonged to different cultures.

Richard Reanier, a University of Washington archaeologist who is collaborating with Kunz, says it is possible that the Paleoindian weapon style originated in Asia and came with the migrants; but no such points have been found in Asia. He says it also is possible that the style originated in Alaska and spread into the rest of North America.

Excerpt from Boyce Rensberger, "Pointing to a Shift in Migration Theories," *The Washington Post National Weekly Edition*, April 5–11, 1993, p. 38.

21

Historian's Toolbox Activity Using Artifacts, found in the Unit 1 folder, p. 19, takes students 2,000 years into the future to enhance their understanding of the science of archeology.

Historical Evidence
Using Artifacts

Focus Evaluate artifacts and use them to evaluate a historical theory.

Instruct Show students a mysterious object, such as a toast gripper or a small spring from a toy. Brainstorm to deduce as many facts as possible about the item by asking questions such as the following: What is it made of? Does that tell you anything about how old it is? Does it show wear? What kind of wear? Does the wear tell you anything about how it may have been used? Have you ever seen anything like this? What was it used for? What does it tell you about the people who made it or used it?

List conclusions about the artifact and its maker on the board. Ask students if any of the conclusions listed require additional evidence. What sort of evidence would support those conclusions?

Extend See the Historian's Toolbox Activity in the Resource Directory below.

Answers

1. (a) Several flint spear points and other stone tools. (b) Probably used for hunting. (c) The age of artifacts is a reliable indicator of a time when humans lived at that site.

2. (a) Two archeologists. (b) In Alaska's North Slope. (c) Between 11,000 and 12,000 years old. (d) They are different from other stone tools previously found in Alaska. They resemble Paleoindian weapons common in the lower forty-eight states.

3. (a) The archeologists propose that two different cultures lived in Alaska at the same time between 11,000 and 12,000 years ago. (b) The fact that two different forms of stone tools were found. (c) Other theories are that the Paleoindian style originated in Asia and came with the migrants, or that the style originated in Alaska and spread to the rest of North America. (d) A group of hunting people lived in Alaska between 11,000 and 12,000 years ago and that they were probably culturally different from those who lived in other parts of North America.

SECTION 2

The European World

1. FOCUS

Connecting to the Big Idea

See page 12B. Explain to students that the people of Europe in the 1400s were ready to expand and explore, leading to encounters with other cultures, especially those of the Atlantic World. Have students think about what factors in European society influenced and motivated this era of discovery and expansion.

Objectives

• Explain how the Crusades and the Renaissance increased Europeans' thirst for knowledge about the rest of the world.
• Trace the development of trade with Asia and its consequences for Europe.
• Identify the technological advances that helped spur the European voyages of exploration.

Bellringer

Ask students to make a list of the major nations of western Europe today. Which of them do they think were important in the fifteenth century? Then ask students to underline the names of nations that they believe made contact with the Native American cultures in North America. They can change or revise their lists as they complete the chapter.

Reading Strategy

Reinforcing Key Ideas Point out that a variety of different factors motivated and made possible the voyages of discovery that brought Europeans to the Americas. Ask students to take note of each of these factors as they read the section and to notice how the reasons interacted.

To illuminate, or illustrate, a manuscript such as this one was a long, painstaking process undertaken by Christian monks and nuns. The subject matter of such manuscripts was often religious. Christian illuminators believed their illustrations had to match the beauty of the pages' content.

SECTION PREVIEW

Europeans approached the 1400s with an ever-increasing hunger for trade and wealth. Armed with technological innovations, they were ready for a new era of discovery and expansion.

Key Concepts
• The Crusades and the Renaissance gave Europeans a thirst for knowledge, especially knowledge about lands to the East.
• As Europeans clamored for Asian products, merchants and monarchs searched for better trade routes to Asia.
• Technological advances helped make possible long sea voyages of exploration.

Key Terms, People, and Places
feudalism, hierarchy, Islam, Renaissance; Marco Polo, Isabella

By the 1400s, the stage was set for contact among three mighty cultures: European, African, and American. Europeans took the lead, partly because of their technology. By the end of the 1400s, they had seaworthy ships in which they could sail great distances and return safely with their cargoes. Gunpowder, invented by the Chinese but known to Europe since the fourteenth century, gave Europeans an advantage in warfare. Printing with movable type had been invented only in the 1440s. By about 1500, twenty million books had already been printed—evidence of the revolution in communication taking place in Europe.

Yet these technologies alone did not enable Europeans to cross the oceans and reach Africa and the Americas. One aim in particular motivated them: the desire to win wealth through trade. Their trade, however, was very different from Native American trade, and arose in a very different kind of society.

Europe Looks Outward

For hundreds of years, starting about A.D. 500, much of European society had been organized in a system based on land and war. At the bottom level of society lived people called serfs, who owned no land. Instead, they were bound by tradition to live on land owned by a local lord. The serfs farmed the land on which they lived, and gave part of their crops to their lord. In return, the lord protected them in case of attack.

Lords themselves traditionally were the servants of a more powerful person: another lord, or perhaps a king or queen. As the serfs owed crops to their lord, so the lord owed loyalty to his superior in wartime. In return, the lord received a gift of land called a fief. This system of duties and exchanges based on land, war, and tradition was called **feudalism**. It was an inward-looking system: based heavily on local relationships. The experiences and interests of feudal Europeans did not extend much further than the lands on which they lived.

A World of Ordered Levels Religion was a crucial ingredient of the glue that held the feudal society together. A mostly Christian people, Europeans believed that everything, from the universe to the average household, was part of a **hierarchy**. The world hierarchy, which scholars of the time called the Great Chain of Being, stretched from God to humans, from humans to animals, and from animals through plants, down to stones and other lifeless matter. A later English immigrant to the Americas named

▶ RESOURCE DIRECTORY

Teaching Resources

Reproducible Lesson Plan found in the Unit 1 folder, p. 4, provides a summary of the Section 2 lesson plan content.

Alternate Lesson Plan: Critical Thinking Formulating Questions, found in the Alternate Lesson Plans folder, p. 3, is designed to enhance students' application of this skill by writing questions to the key concepts in the section.

Guided Reading and Review found in the Unit 1 folder, p. 9, provides a structure for reading and mastering the key concepts and reviewing the key terms for Section 2. (Guided Practice)

★ **Literature Activity** The Koran, found in the Unit 1 folder, p. 24, is designed to enhance students' understanding of Islam through an excerpt from the Koran.

John Winthrop described the human part of this chain:

> G od Almighty in his most holy and wise providence . . . so disposed of the condition of mankind, as in all times some must be rich, some poor some high and eminent in power and dignity; others mean [lowly] and in subjection.
>
> *The Model of Christian Charity,* 1630

Because of their faith in the Great Chain of Being, Europeans believed that trying to change one's place in society meant disobeying God's will. Not wanting to incur the wrath of God, few people tried to change their status within the feudal society. The basic hierarchy of feudalism remained intact for hundreds of years.

The Crusades As the year 1000 passed, however, the European world entered an era of great change. One of the most important instruments of change was religion. Though it was a powerful force for tradition, Christianity now forced Europeans to pay more attention to the world around them.

⭐ Between 622 and 632, a faith called **Islam**, inspired by the teachings of the prophet Muhammad, had arisen in Arabia. Starting in 700, followers of Islam, known as Muslims, had spread their faith over much of the Mediterranean world, including the city of Jerusalem.

For centuries, Muslims and Christians shared Jerusalem, which is a holy city for both religions. But when a new wave of Muslim invaders from Turkey took over Jerusalem around 1000, that era of tolerance ended. Europeans began to hear reports of Christians being tortured and killed, their churches turned into

Using Historical Evidence Europeans loved the Asian spices that the Crusaders brought back to Europe. Merchants like the ones shown here sold the spices—which included cinnamon, pepper, and cloves—in marketplaces like this one. *What do you think were the consequences of European demand for Asian products?*

Islamic mosques. In 1096, in an effort to reclaim their holy land, Christians from Europe began to travel to what is now Israel, Jordan, and neighboring areas—an area then called Palestine—to fight the Turks. These holy wars, which lasted for about 150 years, were called the Crusades.

Trade with Asia The Europeans who fought in the Crusades did not accomplish their goal—their holy land ultimately remained in Muslim hands—but they changed their world nonetheless. Those who returned to Europe often brought back with them Asian products such as spices, perfumes, and exotic fabrics. European consumers were intrigued and impressed with these new items, and clamored for more of them.

To meet this new demand, European merchants began to trade with merchants in south-

Caption Answer to ...

Using Historical Evidence

Merchants like the ones in the painting began to set up trade routes to Asia, so they could buy Asian products and then sell them at a profit to European consumers.

2. INSTRUCT

Explain/Discuss

To give students unfamiliar with world history a better grasp of these events, you may want to reproduce the lower part of the timeline on pages 12–13 on the chalkboard. Have students suggest other events discussed in this section to add to the timeline (for example, the voyages of Dias and da Gama). Encourage them to discuss the cause-effect relationships among events.

Discuss how the "world view" of some Europeans changed radically from the feudal era to the age of the Crusades and the Renaissance. Ask students whether they think all levels of European society shared in this changing viewpoint. Have them consider why the development of a middle class of merchants and craftspeople was significant.

Analyze

Have students locate England, France, Portugal, and Castile (Spain) on the map on page 24. Ask why these nations were likely to lead in developing a trans-Atlantic trade.

Activity

(The clock icon indicates an activity that can be successfully conducted within a class period. Each chapter has at least one such activity.)

Cooperative Learning

Time: One class period.
Activity: Research the nations of Europe in the late 1400s.
Grouping: Groups of four students. Three are to do research as "experts"; the fourth acts as the recorder/spokesperson.
Purpose: Have each group research one of the following states of Europe in this period: Portugal, France, England, Castile and Aragon, Holy Roman Empire, Naples. One student in each group should research the government, economy, or culture of the chosen country. The fourth person in the group will collect the data, record it on a chart, and present it in class.
Outcome: Students will gain a "snapshot" view of the political, economic, and cultural aspects of major European nations in the late 1400s.

Enrichment

Ask students to choose one person important in European history at this time and research his or her biography. They may choose either a person mentioned in the chapter, such as Marco Polo or Isabella, or another influential figure.

Caption Answer to ...

 Interpreting Maps

Islam

---

western Asia. In 1271, merchants Maffeo and Niccolo Polo and Niccolo's son **Marco Polo** left their native Venice on a journey that would expand Europe's sphere of knowledge and interest even farther east. After traveling for three years, they arrived at the court of Kublai Khan, the emperor of China. The Polos remained in China as Kublai Khan's guests for the next 17 years. After the family's return to Venice, Marco Polo produced a description of his experiences that sent European merchants hurrying to set up trading expeditions to eastern Asia. Soon, trade routes sprouted from Europe to China and India, where merchants bartered for the hugely profitable silks, spices, and gold that Asian markets had to offer.

A Changing World

Trade with Asia brought more to Europe than consumer goods, however. Starting with the Crusades, travelers to southwestern Asia often returned to Europe with books by Muslim scholars. The books included both information gathered in the Muslim world and knowledge from the world of the ancient Greeks and Romans. This influx of information helped to spark one of the greatest fires ever to engulf the continent of Europe: the intellectual fire of the **Renaissance**.

The Renaissance The word "renaissance" means "rebirth." The European Renaissance, which started around 1300, was the rebirth of a quest for knowledge. One major part of this quest was a revival of scholarly interest in the workings of the physical world. Since the fall of Rome in 476, European scholars had most often studied the spiritual world of religion. Now, inspired by the texts of the Muslims and

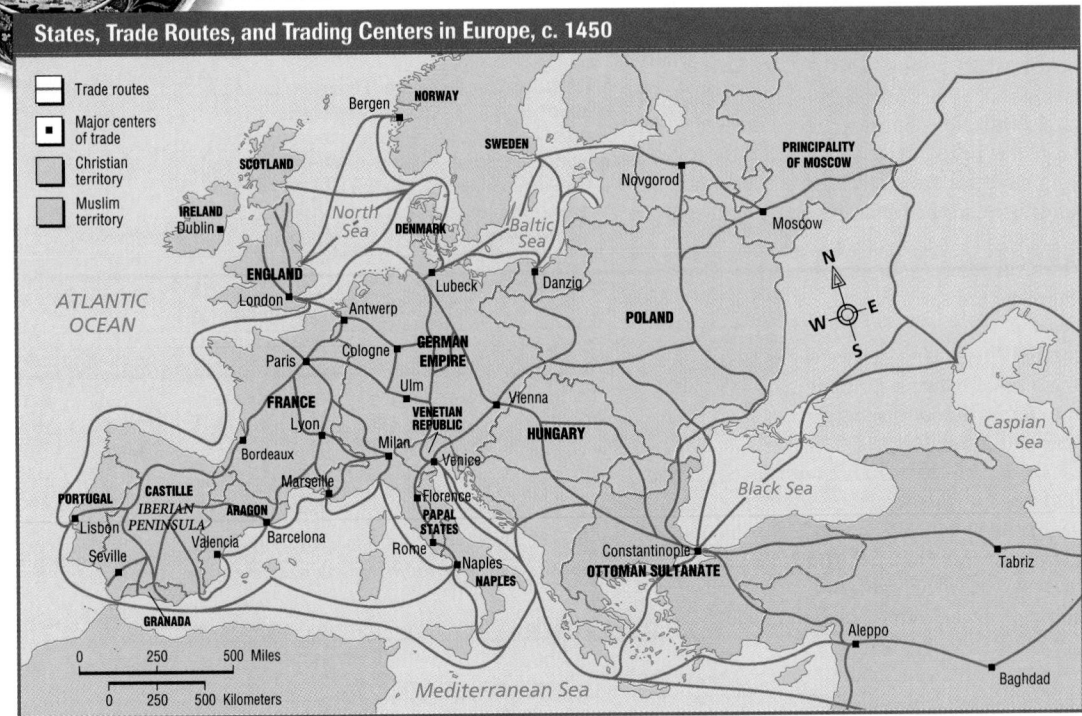

States, Trade Routes, and Trading Centers in Europe, c. 1450

Trade routes
Major centers of trade
Christian territory
Muslim territory

Geography and History: Interpreting Maps ⭐
Europe at this time was divided into numerous states, which vied for control of the limited trade and land available on the continent. One key to power was trade outside of Europe; soon, another key would be conquest. Above left: This plate was made in 1507 as a trade item. *What religion challenged Christianity in the region around the Mediterranean Sea?*

▶ RESOURCE DIRECTORY

⭐ **Visual Learning Activity** Mapmakers, found in the Unit 1 folder, p. 27, promotes students' understanding of Renaissance art and of how maps were made in the age of exploration.

the ancient Greeks and Romans, European scholars began to look critically at the world around them. Many studied the sciences, especially mathematics, a discipline in which Muslim scholars had made great advances.

The most revolutionary aspect of the Renaissance, however, was the rebirth of a spirit of inquiry. For more than 100 years, despite the Crusades and the growth of Asian trade, most Europeans had been preoccupied with mere survival. Years of plague and starvation that began in the mid-1300s had ravaged the continent. Few Europeans were prepared to question their fate. As the plague began to lose its grip, people began to ask questions about the things they saw and heard. This new spirit of questioning would eventually lead Europeans across the Atlantic Ocean and around the globe.

Political Change While Europe's leading thinkers were busy studying their world, Europe's political leaders were starting to consolidate their power over the world around them. The system of local rulers that had been common during the feudal era gradually began to give way in the 1400s. In its place, kings and queens started to organize some of the modern nation-states of Europe that we know today. For the first time, Europeans thought of themselves as members of nations such as France, England, and Portugal.

The Nations of Europe Compete in Trade A growing middle class made up of merchants and craftspeople provided economic support for the new nations. These people produced and exchanged goods for money. Just as China and India produced certain goods for sale, so the nations of Europe were known for certain products. England, for example, shipped lead and tin from its mines, and hides, wool, honey, and butter from its farms. English craftspeople added value to raw materials by turning them into more finished goods. Increasingly, traders shipped out woolen cloth produced by English spinners and weavers instead of raw wool. During the two centuries after 1350, the percentage of total wool exports shipped in the form of cloth surged from 4 percent to 60 percent.

In the bustling ports of Spain, France, and Portugal, English traders exchanged their goods for wines, fruit, silk, spices, silver, and gold. But as European trade continued to expand, nations faced economic competition with one another. An anonymous English poet lamented:

> *O ther lands advanced be, And buy and sell among us free … French ware hither is brought, And English handcraft goeth to naught.*

This fierce competition illustrates a crucial difference between the way Europeans and Native Americans conducted trade. Unlike Native Americans, Europeans tended to see trade as a simple material exchange that did not create further social obligations between people. As in the case of many other differences between cultures, neither view was right or wrong. In this particular case, however, the difference would lead to bitter misunderstandings when Europeans finally crossed the Atlantic.

MAKING CONNECTIONS

What evidence do you see in your own life of nations competing for trade?

The Age of Discovery Begins

By the 1400s, access to Asian goods was the key to profitable trade in Europe. At the start of the century, the only trade routes to Asia were over land. Trading expeditions took a long time—remember the Polos' three-year trip to China—and they were often attacked by bandits. Europeans who could find a faster route to Asia that avoided the

In medieval European universities, many students studied religious subjects. During the Renaissance, more scholars began to study the physical world.

Media and Technology

Transparency
Cause and Effect, F-1

Answer to …

MAKING CONNECTIONS

Answers will vary but students may be aware of the competition between American and foreign manufacturers, especially Asian nations. They may mention the large number of imported products in use, such as electronics and clothing, which are sometimes less expensive than American-made goods.

3. ASSESS

Section 2 Review Answers

1. (a) feudalism, see p. 22, (b) hierarchy, see p. 22

2. (a) Islam, see p. 23, (b) Marco Polo, see p. 23, (c) Renaissance, see p. 24, (d) Isabella, see p. 26

3. Europeans returning from the Crusades brought back Asian products, such as spices, perfume, and exotic fabrics, which European consumers wanted. Crusaders also brought back books of Muslim and classical scholarship.

In Depth

Biography

Between 1480 and 1780, European voyagers explored all the seas in the world except for the polar regions, giving this period the name, "Age of Discovery." In Spain's search for new land and markets, Vasco Nuñez de Balboa (1475–1519) became the first European to see the Pacific Ocean. Balboa came to the Americas in 1500 and settled on Hispaniola. Later he traveled to what is now Panama. Looking for gold, in 1513 Balboa led an expedition across the Isthmus of Panama to the western coast, where he climbed a mountain ridge and saw the great ocean. He named it the Sea of the South (Mar del Sur), since he thought it was south of Asia. In fact, it was near the site of the present-day Panama Canal.

4. The trip was long and dangerous.

5. Instruments such as the compass, astrolabe, and quadrant allowed sailors to determine direction and location and so travel out of sight of land. The caravel could sail both with and against the wind, which made navigating much easier.

6. Students might answer this "chicken-or-egg" question by suggesting that technology, trade, and exploration all probably served to spur the others.

Reteach

Have students imagine that they are European merchants who want royal support for voyages of exploration. Ask them to list reasons they would give to persuade the monarch that such voyages will benefit the state.

Alternative Assessment

Mid-Point Monitoring

Ask students if they have
- Assigned roles within their team
- Made notes of questions in preparation for writing their "position paper"
- Looked at comparisons and interactions between each group

4. CLOSE

Reinforcing the Big Idea

Europeans were to be the prime movers in the coming encounters and conflicts of the three cultures in the Atlantic World. Their eagerness for trade and wealth, helped by new technology, spurred them to travel across the world.

The statue that decorates Queen Isabella's tomb shows her praying. She and her husband, King Ferdinand, wanted to expand Christianity as well as trade.

perils of the roads would greatly increase their nation's profits.

Seafaring Technology The fastest route from Europe to Asia was by sea. However, before the 1400s, Europeans did not have the technology to explore such a sea route to Asia. Sailors on ships could not calculate their position if they were out of sight of land, and their ships couldn't reliably sail against the wind. Sailors were understandably wary of venturing too far out to sea; they were never sure that they could find their way home.

With the help of instruments developed by Renaissance scholars, however, long-range sea travel finally became possible. With a compass, sailors could determine direction even when neither the coast nor the sun was visible. With an astrolabe, captains could use the stars to find their ships' location. And with a quadrant, they could use the sun or the stars to figure out their ships' position on a map. With these new tools, the search for a sea route to Asia was nearly ready to begin.

Portugal Takes to the Seas Portugal took an early lead in the Age of Discovery. In 1418, Prince Henry of Portugal, later called Prince Henry the Navigator, established a navigation school at Sagres, on the southwestern tip of Portugal. There, his mariners developed another crucial piece of technology: a new kind of ship, called a caravel, which could sail both with and against the wind. In 1488, a Sagres-trained navigator, Bartolomeu Dias, rounded the southernmost cape of Africa, the Cape of Good Hope. Nine years later, another Portuguese mariner, Vasco da Gama, sailed from Portugal to India. The first sea route from Europe to Asia had officially been explored.

The Christian Monarchs No sooner had Portugal established itself on the seas than it had a rival: the kingdom of Castile, which was located on the Iberian peninsula in the region now known as Spain. The ruler of Castile, Queen **Isabella**, and her husband, King Ferdinand, ruler of another Iberian nation called Aragon, were devout Christians. For 700 years, the Christian nations of Castile and Aragon had been at war with a third Iberian nation, the Muslim kingdom of Granada. In 1492, Granada fell to Christian forces.

Isabella was not content with military victory, however. Her goal was religious unity: she wanted all of her subjects to embrace Christianity. As her nation's navigators began to challenge Portugal on the high seas, Isabella recognized an opportunity. Castile's ships could carry more than marketable goods. They could also carry with them the teachings of Christianity.

When Europeans first encountered the Americas, Christians such as Isabella would seize eagerly upon the possibility of expanding their religion there, even as they sought opportunities to enrich themselves in trade. Meanwhile, they already were coming into contact with another of the cultures on the shores of the Atlantic—the culture of West Africa.

SECTION 2 REVIEW

Key Terms, People, and Places
1. Define (a) feudalism, (b) hierarchy.
2. Identify (a) Islam, (b) Marco Polo, (c) the Renaissance, (d) Isabella.

Key Concepts
3. How did the Crusades spark European interest in Asia?
4. Why did European traders find the land routes to Asia unsatisfactory?

5. Explain how technological advances made long-distance sea voyages possible.

Critical Thinking
6. **Recognizing Cause and Effect** Do you think that the urge to trade and explore led to new technology, or did new technology encourage trade and exploration?

RESOURCE DIRECTORY

Teaching Resources

American Profiles Activity found in the Unit 1 folder, p. 16, profiles Isabella I, Queen of Castile, who backed the voyages of Christopher Columbus for the glory of Spain.

Quiz found in the Unit 1 folder, p. 10, covers the main ideas in this section as well as the key terms.

The World of the West Africans

SECTION 3

The World of the West Africans

SECTION PREVIEW

A land of powerful kingdoms, ancient learning, great religions, and the wealth of thriving trade—such was Africa by the end of the 1400s.

Key Concepts
- The forest kingdoms of West Africa were complex and wealthy cultures.
- West Africa had an extensive trading system extending from the Guinea coast to North Africa.
- The Songhai Empire interacted with other lands through trade and participation in Islamic culture.

Key Terms, People, and Places
lineage, Koran; Askia Muhammad; Guinea, Benin, Songhai

The Atlantic Ocean that washed against the Americas and Europe broke also on the shores of Africa. It surged into tangled deltas and met great rivers like the Niger pouring forth from the dense rain forest. During the 1400s, the Atlantic was already a highway over which Europeans traveled to reach Africa and the world of well-ordered kingdoms that lay beyond its coast.

The Forest Kingdoms

As the map on page 29 shows, the region where European and African cultures came into contact along the Atlantic coast stretched from Morocco in the north through the Congo River in the south. In the center of this long swath was the area of heaviest interaction, generally called **Guinea.** In the 1400s, Guinea was home to three energetic forest kingdoms: Oyo, Ife, and **Benin.**

A Wealthy State The people of the Guinea kingdoms passed on their culture from genera-

tion to generation through oral traditions, and "wrote" about their culture by creating works of art. In Benin, artists left a record of their society in a series of bronze plaques that once decorated the palace of the king, or Oba. From a central city, also called Benin, the Oba ruled all of the surrounding forest land, waging war, directing agriculture, and regulating trade through administrators.

Trade was vital to Benin. Like North America and Europe, Africa at this time had a network of trade routes that linked its many societies. Benin merchants traded farm products, works of art, and goods forged from African iron, which was probably superior to any in the world at that time.

Wealth from Benin's trade supported its capital, a city of striking size. One Portuguese who visited Benin several times reported:

This city is about a league [three miles] *long from gate to gate; it has no wall but is surrounded by a large moat, very wide and deep, which suffices for its defense.... Its houses are made of mud walls covered with palm leaves.*
Duarte Pacheco Pereira, 1505

A Society Based on Lineage Most societies in Guinea were made up of people who lived in towns and supported themselves primarily through farming. As in the Americas, kinship networks were the major social units in this part of Africa. When people in a kinship network trace their line of origin from a common ancestor, the kinship network is called a **lineage.** (Native American clans were a form of lineage group.) Usually, most of the people in a town in Guinea belonged to the same lineage. Even in larger urban areas, people probably lived close to their families, since their

The Baule people of Guinea made this pendant, over three inches long, from the gold for which their region of Africa was well known.

---

1. FOCUS

Connecting to the Big Idea

See page 12B. Explain that the first interactions between European and African cultures came in the 1400s along the coast of West Africa. These would lead to later interactions in the Americas. At the time, the great kingdoms of West Africa had prosperous, complex cultures. Have students think about what those cultures were like and what factors influenced the relationships that developed with European cultures.

Objectives
- Locate and identify the forest kingdoms of Guinea and describe their societies.
- Describe the trading system among the West African kingdoms.
- Explain how Songhai interacted with other regions through trade and through its position as a center of Islamic culture.

Bellringer

Ask students to list as many facts as they can about the continent of Africa—names of countries, rivers, and other geographical features; impressions of people; languages and culture. You may want to display a map of Africa and point out the both the places they name and those mentioned in this section.

Reading Strategy

Question Writing As preparation for reading the section, ask students to scan the main headings and subheadings and then turn each subheading into a who, what, when, or why/how question. As they read, they should find the answers to their questions.

Explain/Discuss

Have students locate Songhai and Benin on the map on page 29 and notice the trade routes in this part of Africa. What kinds of items were traded? How did trade make Songhai and its ruler wealthy?

Point out that trade often brings new ideas and technology as well as goods to buy and sell. Discuss with students how Islam was brought to Songhai. In what ways did it set Songhai apart from other cultures in West Africa at the time?

Analyze

Have students examine how slavery became part of the African trading system. You may want to prompt discussion with questions such as: Why was human labor scarce in Africa? How was this different from the situation in Europe?

Answer to ...

MAKING CONNECTIONS

Answers will vary but may focus, for instance, on how a current popular song might be perceived in the future. Encourage students to realize that each work of art carries with it a message about the time in which it was produced.

The Oba, attended by servants holding symbols of power, is offered trade goods by Portuguese traders (background) in a bronze plaque of the 1500s.

lineage provided them with social support when they needed it.

The ruling classes in this region of Africa were generally groups of people who shared a lineage, or family tie. The rulers dealt with their people primarily through local headmen, who usually were also the heads of extended families.

Religious Belief in Guinea The people of Guinea held religious beliefs that varied considerably from one group to another. However, they generally shared the belief that a Supreme Being created other, lesser gods or spirits. These spirits inhabited everything, from animals to trees and stones. The people of Guinea believed that humans, too, were living spirits both before and after death. In short, the world was full of spirits of all kinds. Like Native Americans and Europeans, Africans believed that the goodwill of more-than-human forces must be won through prayer and ceremony.

MAKING CONNECTIONS

Part of the reason we know about life in Benin is that its people passed on their knowledge in works of art. What would your favorite works of art, music, or writing tell people who live after you about your life and times?

A Golden Empire South of the Sahara

Beyond the coastal forests, in the grasslands south of the Sahara, lay **Songhai,** an empire that in the late 1400s was one of the largest in the world. Songhai lay between the forest kingdoms and lands in North Africa. As a result of its location, Songhai played a major part in the flow of trade in West Africa in the late 1400s and early 1500s—the period when European

traders were beginning to link up with the West African trading network.

Trade with the Forest Kingdoms and North Africa Leo Africanus was an Arab born in Granada who visited Songhai at this time. Africanus enthused about Songhai's trading power, saying, "It is a wonder to see what plentie of Merchandize is daily brought hither and how costly and sumptious all things be." Songhai's traders obtained goods such as gold and ivory from the forest kingdoms. The forests also supplied another popular trade item, kola nuts, used to flavor a beverage that was the first version of the colas people drink today. The traders carried these goods north across Songhai, paying heavy fees to Songhai's ruler, and then continued on across the Sahara in caravans of as many as 12,000 camels. On their return trip from North Africa, Songhai's traders brought books, paper, weapons, cloth, horses, and salt.

Songhai's Government The person who profited most from this trade was **Askia Muhammad,** the ruler of Songhai. One writer who saw Askia at his court in the city of Timbuktu marveled: "The rich king of Tombuto [Timbuktu] hath many plates and scepters of gold, some whereof weigh 1300 pounds. . . . He keeps a magnificent and well furnished court." ✪

Yet Askia's empire was not all glittering show. Said another African writer: "He was obeyed with as much docility [willing obedience] on the farther limits of the empire as he was in his own palace, and there reigned everywhere great plenty and absolute peace."

The map on page 29 shows that the farther limits of Askia's empire extended across much of western Africa. To rule over this domain, Askia directed a highly developed, hierarchical system of paid officials. They administered laws, kept the peace, collected taxes, and monitored diplomatic exchanges with other nations of the world. Under Askia's direction, they ran a sophisticated banking system. They also oversaw great royal estates that produced food or manufactured goods.

RESOURCE DIRECTORY ✪

Teaching Resources

✪ **American Profiles Activity** found in the Unit 1 folder, p. 15, profiles Askia Muhammad, the brilliant ruler of the West African kingdom of Songhai.

Visual Learning Activity Slave Factories, found in the Unit 1 folder, p. 28, is designed to enhance students' understanding of slavery through an illustration of a West African slave "factory."

Learning and Islam Askia Muhammad loved making money, but he also loved knowledge. At Timbuktu, a world-renowned center of learning, some 150 schools served a population of 100,000. Other Songhai cities—Gao, Walata, and Jenné—boasted centers of scholarship as well. About Timbuktu, Leo Africanus observed:

A great store of doctors, judges, priests, and other learned men . . . are bountifully maintained at the King's cost and charges. And hither are brought diverse manuscripts or written books out of Barbarie [foreign lands] which are sold for more money than any other merchandise.
The History and Description of Africa,
c. 1526

The major curriculum in Timbuktu was the **Koran,** the holy book of Islam. Islam had reached Songhai by trade and by invasion from the north; with the new religion came knowledge of Arabic, the original language of the Koran. Thousands of African Muslims found that practicing the rituals of Islam gave great meaning to their lives. In the 1400s, however, both Islam and Arabic were still foreign to much of West Africa. The majority of the population, especially outside the cities, held beliefs like those of the people in Guinea.

Slavery in Africa

⭐ As in some parts of Europe and North America, a more grim kind of trade could be found in Africa as well. This was trade in human life—in the form of people kidnapped from one region of Africa to another and enslaved. In a sense, the entire trading system was built on slaves. Not only were slaves sold as goods themselves, but they also produced or gathered many of the other goods that were exchanged. Slaves also carried goods through parts of West Africa where animals were not an effective means of transport.

The Origin of Slavery in Africa Africans, like Europeans, believed in the private ownership of goods and property, but they differed from Europeans in their attitudes toward land and

people. Land was not in short supply in Africa, as it was in Europe, where scarcity made land the basis of wealth. Thus in Africa, no one could become wealthy and powerful by claiming a large area of land, because land was so abundant.

What was scarce in Africa—and therefore highly valued—was labor. Agricultural work was difficult at best in the tropical climate. Evidence suggests that due to disease and other

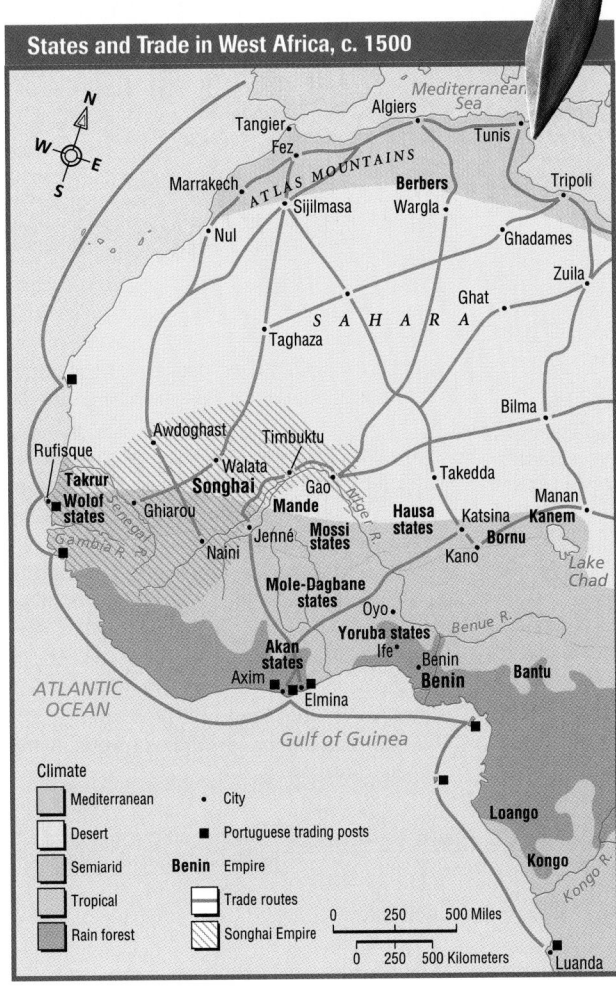

States and Trade in West Africa, c. 1500

Climate
- Mediterranean
- Desert
- Semiarid
- Tropical
- Rain forest

- • City
- ■ Portuguese trading posts
- **Benin** Empire
- Trade routes
- Songhai Empire

Geography and History: Interpreting Maps
States both large and small were involved in the trade that moved goods through Songhai and then across Africa. Above: This ivory spoon was carved in Benin and traded to the Portuguese. *Besides the overland routes shown here, what major path might traders have taken from the coast to Songhai?*

Enrichment
Have students use current travel guides and almanacs, along with information from tourist bureaus, to prepare an itinerary for a present-day traveler to West Africa. Itineraries might include visits to major cities, archaeological sites, and scenic or historic places.

Activity
(The clock icon indicates an activity that can be successfully conducted within a class period. Each chapter has at least one such activity.)
Teaching Heterogeneous Groups
To help students better understand trade in West Africa, have them trace the route of an imaginary trader going from Benin to Songhai to North Africa. Using the map on page 29, they will answer these questions: What direction will the trader travel from Benin to Songhai? About how far is it from the city of Benin to Timbuktu? From Timbuktu to Fez in North Africa? What kind of terrain will the trader have to cross? **LEP**

Caption Answer to . . .
🌍 **Interpreting Maps**

The Niger River, which flows between Benin and Songhai.

3. ASSESS

Section 3 Review Answers

1. (a) lineage, see p. 27, (b) Koran, see p. 29.

2. Askia Muhammad, see p. 28.

3. (a) Guinea, see p. 27, (b) Benin, see p. 27, (c) Songhai, see p. 28.

4. Complexity: elaborate works of art, strong ruler, centralized government, regulation of trade, knowledge of metalworking (bronze, iron). Wealth: farm products, other trade goods, impressive capital city.

5. Songhai traders obtained goods from the forest kingdoms and traded them with North Africa. Songhai's ruler collected fees from traders crossing his territory.

6. In Europe, where land was scarce, land ownership brought wealth and power. Large landowners were Europe's political and social leaders. In West Africa, there was no shortage of land, so control or ownership of land did not affect status. But people were scarce and lifespans short; command of a large labor force was the key to wealth and power.

Reteach

Have students write "Forest Kingdoms" and "Songhai" as headings on a piece of paper. Ask them to write details under each heading to support the statement that the West African kingdoms were rich and well-organized.

4. CLOSE

Reinforcing the Big Idea

Students should keep in mind what they have learned about the highly organized and complex cultures of West Africa, with their rich trade and centers of learning. In the next section students will discover how these people became a part of the newly created Atlantic World.

An engraving from the 1800s captures a moment repeated countless times through the centuries: a caravan arrives at the city of Timbuktu.

factors, the average lifespan was no more than a few decades. For this reason, a leader's power rested on the number of people he ruled rather than the amount of land he controlled.

Who Was Enslaved? In response to the combination of a shortage of labor and an excess of land, Africans had followed a course adopted by other peoples throughout history—they developed the institution of slavery. During the 1400s, enslaved people also could be found in some European lands, including Spain and Portugal, and in some Native American societies. In Africa, people who had been cut off from their lineage were those most likely to be enslaved. They included prisoners of war (probably the greatest source), as well as orphans, criminals, or other people torn from their homes or rejected by society. Generally, slaves were adopted into existing kinship networks.

⭐ In their new lineages, enslaved people filled a wide variety of positions. Women slaves were highly valued because they could bear children that would increase the size of the lineage and because women did most of the farming. Enslaved men were soldiers and administrators, although men, too, labored in the fields. Thus, enslaved people played a major role in African life. After they encountered Europeans, Africans would also be forced to go to the Americas, where they would take part in creating new societies.

SECTION 3 REVIEW

Key Terms, People, and Places
1. Define (a) lineage, (b) Koran.
2. Identify Askia Muhammad.
3. Identify (a) Guinea, (b) Benin, (c) Songhai.

Key Concepts
4. Give evidence to show that Benin was a complex and wealthy kingdom.

5. What role did Songhai have in the West African trading network?

Critical Thinking
6. **Making Comparisons** Compare the European view of land ownership to the African view of land ownership. How did those points of view affect the societies of Europe and West Africa?

 RESOURCE DIRECTORY

Teaching Resources

⭐ **Primary Source Activity** The Portuguese in West Africa, found in the Unit 1 folder, p. 23, uses a chronicle written in the mid-1400s to present the reasons Portugal explored West Africa.

Quiz found in the Unit 1 folder, p. 12, covers the main ideas in this section as well as the key terms.

The Atlantic World Is Born

SECTION PREVIEW

The voyage of an Italian navigator was the prelude to centuries of trade, cultural exchange, and tragic conflict among Native Americans, Europeans, and Africans.

Key Concepts

- Contact between Europeans, Africans, and Native Americans led to a vast global interchange of people, animals, goods, ideas, technology, and disease.
- Europeans competed among themselves to claim land in the Americas.
- Millions of West Africans were transported against their will to the Americas.

Key Terms, People, and Places

Columbian Exchange; Christopher Columbus

S hortly before sunrise on Friday, August 3, 1492, three ships set sail from the seaport of Palos, in the Spanish kingdom of Castile. Before the crews lay the ocean and a great enterprise—"The Enterprise of the Indies," as their commander called it—the challenge of finding a new route to the Indies, or Asia.

A Voyage of Encounter

The expedition was Spanish, but its commander, **Christopher Columbus**, was not. He had been born into a family of wool-weavers in Genoa, Italy. Stubborn and moody, he had devoted most of his forty-one years to mastering the craft of navigation and to trying to persuade European monarchs to give him financing for this very voyage.

Going West to Reach the East Not until January 1492 had Isabella, Queen of Castile, finally granted Columbus his wish. Dubbing him High Admiral of the Ocean Sea, Isabella autho-

rized him to make contact with the people of "the lands of India." As the admiral later explained, Isabella and her husband, King Ferdinand, had "ordained that [Columbus] should not go eastward by land in the usual manner but by the western way which no one about whom we have positive information has ever followed."

Columbus knew that the earth was a sphere. As daunting as the trip was, he was not afraid of falling off the planet when he sailed westward, as later legend suggested. However, Columbus was gambling when he assumed he could reach the Indies, or Asia, by sailing west across the vast expanse of the ocean. It was a gamble he would have lost, because he had underestimated the size of the planet. The expedition had neither food nor water enough to sail all the way to Asia.

The Encounter Begins Fortunately for Columbus and his crew, in mid-October he reached the islands of the Caribbean Sea and the Native Americans on them, the Tainos. The Tainos greeted the newcomers with gifts—much astonishing Columbus, who was not familiar with the Native American view of trade as an exchange of gifts. In 1493 Columbus wrote about the Tainos to Isabella and Ferdinand:

They are so ingenuous [innocent] and free with all they have, that no one would believe it who has not seen it; of anything that they possess, if it be asked of them, they never say no; on the contrary, they invite you to share it and show as much love as if their hearts went with it.

Christopher Columbus believed that he could reach Asia in a few weeks by sailing west from Europe.

📄 **Reproducible Lesson Plan** found in the Unit 1 folder, p. 6, provides a summary of the Section 4 lesson plan content.

📄 **Alternate Lesson Plan: Learning Styles** found in the Alternate Lesson Plans folder, p. 5, especially effective for visual learners, is designed to help students create a diagram on the European–Native American exchange of cultures.

📄 **Guided Reading and Review** found in the Unit 1 folder, p. 13, provides a structure for reading and mastering the key concepts and reviewing the key terms for Section 4. (Guided Practice)

Connecting to the Big Idea

See page 12B. Discuss with students how the voyage of Columbus from Spain to the Caribbean, in a sense, created what is termed the Atlantic World. The three cultures of that world—Native American, European, African—began centuries of interaction, which brought great changes. Ask students how those changes affected each culture.

Objectives

● Understand the nature and variety of interchanges that occurred within the Atlantic World.
● Describe the competition among European nations for land in the Americas.
● Explain why the interaction in the Atlantic World led to slavery for millions of Africans.

Bellringer

Ask students to recall whatever facts or stories they know about the first voyage of Columbus. What if he had not made the journey? Do students think that interaction within the Atlantic World was inevitable, considering what they have learned about Europeans' motivations and technology?

Reading Strategy

Reinforcing the Key Idea Tell students that in this section they will read about the early interactions among the three cultures of the Atlantic World and the major consequences. As they read, they should take notes about the effects of the interaction on the people of each of the three cultures.

2. INSTRUCT

Explain/Discuss

Point out to students that the Atlantic World was based on elements from all three interacting cultures—Native American, West African, and European—although historically it appears that the Europeans were the dominant element. Ask them to suggest ways in which the other cultures influenced and contributed to the interchange.

Discuss with students the three reasons Europeans had for wanting to conquer the Americas *(land, resources for trade, conversion to Christianity)*. Ask how technology and disease helped them succeed.

Activity

Conducting a Debate

Divide the class into groups to debate the following statement: Resolved, that the only people to benefit from the development of the Atlantic World were the wealthy and powerful of Europe. Let students in a group work together to brainstorm and list reasons that either support or refute the proposition. One volunteer from each group should present the group's position.

Answer to ...

MAKING CONNECTIONS

Answers will vary: some students may point out continuing close ties between the United States and Europe (such as NATO) as well as the family ties that link many Americans with Africa or Europe; others may think that there is now more of a "Global World," including Asia and involving the same kinds of cultural clashes, exchanges, and blendings of populations.

Whales and flying fish, suggesting the hazards of the Atlantic, alarm the crew of a lively Portuguese caravel in this painting from 1594.

Columbus's voyage was significant because it was one of encounter, not discovery. After all, the Americas had long since been known to others, the Native Americans. In fact, Columbus was not even the first European to land in the Americas. Norse voyagers, led by Leif Ericsson, claimed that distinction around 1000, when they set up a small, short-lived settlement on what is now Newfoundland.

Still, Columbus's journey marked the beginning of an entirely new era in European and American history: an era of transatlantic communication, trade, and exploitation. Columbus himself never realized exactly what he had begun. Even after Isabella financed him for three more trips to the Caribbean, in 1493, 1498, and 1502, he refused to admit that he had encountered an entirely new continent. Through the end of his life, Columbus was sure that he had reached "the Indies," islands off the southeast coast of Asia.

Other people in Columbus's time realized that those "Indies" were not part of Asia at all. In 1499, a merchant from Florence named Amerigo Vespucci made the first of two voyages to the Caribbean. After having sailed along the coast of South America, Vespucci suggested that the lands he had seen might be a continent previously unknown to Europeans, "what we may rightly call a New World." A French mapmaker named Waldseemüller read Vespucci's account and took it to heart. In 1507, he printed the first map showing the continents of the "New World" as separate from Asia. He named the unfamiliar lands "America," after Amerigo Vespucci.

Thus, with Columbus's crossing in 1492, a regular, permanent exchange began among the people of the Atlantic World—the Americas, Africa, and Europe. Known as the **Columbian Exchange**, this was an interaction that involved people, animals, goods, ideas, technology and even disease.

MAKING CONNECTIONS

Is it still accurate to speak of an Atlantic World today? Why or why not?

The Impact of the Encounter on the Native Americans: Disease

For the people of the early Atlantic World, life expectancy was much lower than it is today. In their era, minor illnesses or wounds could suddenly become fatal due to poor hygiene and medical practices. Exchange across the Atlantic only made this problem worse. It brought together people who had been isolated from one another and had no resistance to one another's diseases.

Diseases Strike Native Americans Europeans had already experienced a severe decline in their population due to plague and other diseases. They brought a similar disaster to the American continents. Passing germs through even the most casual contact, explorers and soldiers infected Native Americans with smallpox, typhus, measles, and other deadly diseases.

Once Europeans reached the Americas, disease spread ahead of them, carried by the extensive Native American trading system. Inca Garcilaso, the son of a Native American woman and a Spanish captain, described what explorers found in 1540 when they first reached Talomeca, a town of the Creek Native American group in what is now Georgia.

The Castilians found the town of Talomeco without any people at all, because [of] the recent pestilence [disease]. . . [Near] the rich temple, it is said they found four longhouses filled with bodies from the plague.

The Impact of the Encounter on Europeans: Struggle and Exchange

Europeans were unaware that they were passing on disease to the Native Americans. Instead, many Europeans believed that the "pestilence" that was ravaging the Native American population was a sign that God intended Europeans to conquer the Americas. And conquest was exactly what Europeans planned, for three reasons. The first was to obtain land, which was scarce in Europe. The second was to convert the vast natural resources of the Americas into goods that could be traded. The third reason was to "bring to the worship of [Christ] and the profession of the Catholic faith [the] residents and inhabitants" of the Americas, in the words of Pope Alexander VI in 1493.

A Native American in Mexico drew this picture of a victim of smallpox comforted by a healer. The squiggle symbolizes spoken words.

Links Across Time

1650　1700　1750　1800　1850　1900　1950　2000

Navigating the Ocean

Early sailors sighted the sun on an astrolabe to find their latitude (above). Today they rely on a geopositioning instrument that reads signals from satellites to give a ship's position by night or day (left). *What advantage does the new technology offer?*

Enrichment

Ask students to choose one of the food or animal products involved in the Columbian Exchange (see chart on page 34) and research the effects its importation had on people and society in the lands where it was taken. Possibilities: corn or potatoes in European diet and cuisine; manioc and peanuts in Africa or Asia; wheat in the Americas; the horse in Native American culture; quinine or cocoa in Europe.

Answer to ...

Links Across Time

It lets sailors find their position at night or on days when the sun is not visible.

In Depth

Interdisciplinary

Educated Europeans in the 1400s accepted the calculations made by the Greek scholar Eratosthenes (3rd century B.C.). Measuring differences in the lengths of shadows, he had estimated the circumference of the earth at what would be calculated today as 25,000 miles. What educated people feared about sailing west, therefore, was not falling off the edge of the world, but having to travel too long without fresh water and food before reaching Asia. Columbus took a calculated risk because he believed the less accurate figures of the later scientist Ptolemy of Alexandria (A.D. 100s), who estimated that the world was only 18,000 miles around. When Columbus reached the islands of the Caribbean, he named them the West Indies, believing they lay off the coast of Asia. He died without understanding that he had encountered a separate landmass.

Section 4 Review Answers

1. Columbian Exchange, see p. 32.

2. Christopher Columbus, see p. 31.

3. Native Americans had no resistance to the diseases; diseases were carried from group to group by way of widespread trading routes.

4. European nations began to compete for resources and land; the Treaty of Tordesillas was intended to split the Americas between Spain and Portugal; new foods, such as potatoes and corn, fed poorer Europeans; gold and silver from the Americas made Europe's economy the richest on earth.

5. Europeans in the Americas were growing labor-intensive crops such as sugar and wanted to use West Africans as laborers.

6. Answers will vary but possibilities include diseases, gold and silver, wheat, the potato, and firearms.

Caption Answer to ...

 Interpreting Charts

Toward the Americas.

 In Depth

Multicultural Perspectives

Medieval Muslim scholars, working in centers such as Baghdad, made significant contributions in the sciences, medicine, and mathematics. Until the seventeenth century, Arab textbooks on diseases and diagnoses were considered the best in their fields. Muslims established one of the first systems of medical training, including exams for doctors and pharmacists. In chemistry, Muslim scientists invented the beakers and crystallizing dishes still used in laboratories today.

Competing for Empire At the urging of Pope Alexander, in 1494 Portugal and Spain agreed to the Treaty of Tordesillas. Under the treaty, any lands not already claimed by other Christians would be divided between the two countries by an invisible line around the world called the Line of Demarcation. Spain was to rule over lands west of the line, including most of the Americas. Portugal was left with control over the rest, including Brazil and the sea route around Africa.

For centuries, Spain and Portugal were able to control much of the regions they claimed. Soon, however, the people of other nations grew eager for a share of the wealth. France, England, and the Netherlands began to move into North America in the 1500s and 1600s (Chapter 2). ✪

The Exchange of Cultures The culture that Europeans brought to the Americas included languages, laws, and customs. Europeans also introduced crops, such as wheat, and domesticated animals, such as the cow and the horse. Settlers brought European technologies, including the firearm and the wheel.

As the chart at left shows, however, exchange across the Atlantic was not one-sided. One American plant, the potato, quickly became the new food of the poor in Europe, bringing an end to the repeated famines Europeans had suffered. Another, manioc, became the chief food throughout much of Africa.

Europe's wealthy also benefited from the exchange. In the first century after Columbus's voyage, the amount of gold and silver in Europe's economy increased eight times over, boosted by ore from the mines of the Americas.

The Impact of the Encounter on Africans: Slavery

Europeans needed a large amount of labor to exploit the natural resources of the Americas. They turned to West Africa to supply that labor. West Africans soon were swept into their own encounter with the Americas, suffering violence and displacement for centuries after Columbus's voyage.

Europeans Enter the African Slave Trade Regular interaction between Europeans and Africans had begun even before the voyage of Columbus. Throughout the late 1400s, the Portuguese had been moving down the West African coast in search of new markets. They built a string of small forts along the coast, where they traded with the Africans. The Portuguese found that from Songhai to the forest kingdoms, West Africans had a well-developed economy, and could control European trade within their countries.

For years, Europeans were primarily interested in exchanging their goods with West Africans for gold. As time went on, Europeans realized that they could take advantage of

The Columbian Exchange

From the Americas to Europe, Africa, and Asia

maize
potato
sweet potato
beans
manioc
peanut
squashes
pumpkin
papaya
guava
avocado
pineapple
tomato
chile pepper
cocoa
quinine

wheat
sugar
banana
rice
grape (wine)
olive oil
bluegrass
daisy
dandelions
horse
pig
cattle
goat
sheep
chicken
guinea hen
mule
smallpox
measles
typhus

From Europe, Africa, and Asia to the Americas

 Interpreting Charts
Exchanges across the Atlantic went both ways and included valued crops, domesticated animals, and diseases. *In which direction did the listed diseases move?*

▶ RESOURCE DIRECTORY

Teaching Resources

✪ **Primary Source Activity** Europeans Encounter Native Americans, found in the Unit 1 folder, pp. 21–22, contrasts the views of Christopher Columbus with those of Spanish nobleman Juan Gines de Sepulveda to illustrate the thinking of the day.

another valuable resource: the West Africans themselves. European slave traders began to supply the labor needed in the Americas by tapping into the existing West African slave trade. As early as the 1400s, European slave traders began to set up slave trading stations on the West African coast.

The Growth of the Slave Trade Facts and figures on the impact of slavery on West Africa remain a matter of controversy. Some researchers estimate that during the 1500s some 275,000 West Africans were transported involuntarily across the Atlantic Ocean. By contrast, they say, the 1700s saw 6,050,000 transported. Estimates of the total number of West Africans abducted from their homeland and taken to North and South America range from 9,300,000 to 11,500,000 or more.

Mere numbers, however, cannot portray the full horror of slavery for West Africans. Slavery had existed in Africa before the encounter of the Atlantic cultures, but Europeans gave it a very different face. Slavery in Africa was based on the belief that people who had been enslaved were inferior to their masters because they were not connected with their master's lineage. However, among Africans (and Native Americans), captives taken in war might later be adopted into a lineage and regain at least some freedom. Such adoption shows that the basic humanity of enslaved people was recognized in Africa. By contrast, most Europeans at that time believed that people of races other than their own were inferior by nature. Because slavery in the Americas was based on race, enslavement there usually

Viewpoints
On Celebrating Columbus Day

In 1992, many Americans celebrated the five hundredth anniversary of Columbus's historic voyage. But some Americans questioned whether honoring Columbus was appropriate. *Compare and contrast the "Columbus" described in the following statements.*

Against Honoring Columbus

"Columbus came here, however, not to trade, but to conquer; he came to enrich himself and enslave his captives. . . . Columbus was a man of his time. . . . Columbus is neither hero nor villain, but rather a symbol of a world forevermore transformed."

David Archambault, president of the American Indian College Fund, from a speech given April 6, 1992

For Honoring Columbus

"Columbus . . . changed the world by . . . his 'discovery,' or 'encounter' or 'exchange.' Whichever [term] you select, it does not diminish the remarkable achievements of Christopher Columbus [who is] a hero not only for his times but our times as well."

Donald J. Senese, former Assistant Secretary of Education, from a speech given October 18, 1992

offered enslaved people no hope of regaining their freedom.

In the aftermath of the encounter across the Atlantic Ocean, vast changes tested the ways of life and the values of people on four continents. Out of that collision the society of the United States would eventually emerge—a society struggling to understand cultural differences that had their origin on separate continents hundreds of years ago.

SECTION 4 REVIEW

Key Terms, People, and Places
1. Define Columbian Exchange.
2. Identify Christopher Columbus.

Key Concepts
3. Why did European diseases spread so rapidly among the Native Americans?
4. What changes did contact with the Americas bring to Europe?

5. For what purpose did Europeans enslave West Africans?

Critical Thinking
6. **Demonstrating Reasoned Judgment** Of all the new things that Native Americans and Europeans exchanged, which do you think had the most far-reaching consequences? Explain your answer.

Viewpoints Activity On Celebrating Columbus Day, found in the Unit 1 folder, pp. 17–18, provides additional viewpoints and perspectives on Christopher Columbus and the spirit of the times.

Quiz found in the Unit 1 folder, p. 14, covers the main ideas in this section as well as the key terms.

Chapter Test Forms A and B are found in the Unit 1 folder, pp. 29–34.

Answer Keys found in the Unit 1 folder, pp. 146–160, provide answers to all student activities.

Media and Technology

Transparencies
Time Lines, E-1; Graphic Organizer, G-2

Guided Reading Audiotapes
(English and Spanish)

Computer Test Bank

Archambault paints Columbus as a conqueror who came to America to enrich himself and enslave Native Americans. He says Columbus is "neither hero nor villain." Senese claims, on the contrary, that Columbus is a hero—a remarkable person of remarkable achievements. Both speakers agree that Columbus changed the world. For a more thorough examination of the debate on celebrating Columbus Day, see the Resource Directory below.

Reteach

Ask students to use or trace an outline map of the world and draw lines to represent the major interactions among the three cultures of the Atlantic World. Have them use symbols or icons to show the major items that were interchanged: foods and crops; animals; diseases; slaves; gold and silver.

4. CLOSE

Reinforcing the Big Idea

Encounters among the different cultures of Native Americans, Europeans, and West Africans led to interactions that created the Atlantic World. The resulting conflicts and interchanges among the three cultures had lasting impacts on three continents and still influence people today.

Chapter Review Answers

Understanding Key Terms, People, and Places

Terms
Students should refer to the definitions of the key terms in the chapter to write sentences that show the relation of each word to the cultures of the Native Americans, the Europeans, the West Africans, or to the Atlantic World in the 1400s.

Matching
1. Koran
2. lineage or clan
3. oral tradition
4. Renaissance
5. division of labor

True or False
1. true
2. false, Songhai
3. false, the Columbian Exchange
4. true
5. false, Christopher Columbus

Reviewing Main Ideas
1. They walked across a "land bridge" connecting Asia with what is now Alaska.
2. Their cultures were influenced by the environment—the land and climate—in which they lived.
3. They provided medical care, child care, settlement of disputes, education, and a structure within which to practice their religion.
4. They used natural routes, such as the Mississippi River and the Great Lakes, as well as a network of trading paths.
5. Factors included the Crusades, which introduced Europeans to exotic products as well as Muslim scholarship; consumer demand for the new Asian products; and Marco Polo's tales of his experiences in China.
6. Asian goods brought large profits to European merchants, but the early land routes between Asia and Europe were long and dangerous. Finding a new route to Asian markets would mean greater profit.
7. Portugal's Prince Henry the Navigator set up a navigation school at Sagres, where sailors learned to use new tools such as the astrolabe, quadrant, and caravel. With these tools, a Portuguese mariner, Vasco da Gama, sailed from Portugal around Africa to India, thus opening the first sea route to Asia.
8. The forest kingdoms produced farm products, works of art, forged iron, gold, ivory, and kola nuts. Traders carried the goods across the Sahara to North Africa,

CHAPTER 1

Chapter Review

Understanding Key Terms, People, and Places

Key Terms
1. kinship network
2. clan
3. division of labor
4. oral tradition
5. feudalism
6. hierarchy
7. Islam
8. Renaissance
9. lineage
10. Koran
11. Columbian Exchange

People
12. Marco Polo
13. Isabella
14. Askia Muhammad
15. Christopher Columbus

Places
16. Guinea
17. Benin
18. Songhai

Terms For each term above, write a sentence that explains its relation to the cultures of the Native Americans, the Europeans, the West Africans, or to the Atlantic World in the 1400s.

Matching Review the key terms in the list above. If you are not sure of a term's meaning, review its definition in the chapter. Then choose a term from the list that best matches each description below.
1. the holy book of Islam
2. a group of people who trace their line of origin from a common ancestor
3. passing on history and beliefs by word of mouth
4. the rebirth of a quest for knowledge in Europe
5. the way tasks are assigned

True or False Determine whether each statement is true or false. If it is true, write "true." If it is false, change the underlined person or place to make the statement true.
1. The region of <u>Guinea</u> included three kingdoms: Oyo, Ife, and Benin.
2. Located in the grasslands south of the Sahara, <u>Benin</u> was one of the largest empires in the world during the 1400s.
3. The interaction among Native American, European, and African cultures during the 1400s and 1500s was called <u>feudalism</u>.
4. One goal of <u>Isabella and Ferdinand</u> was for all of their subjects to embrace Christianity.
5. <u>Marco Polo</u> sailed from Europe to the Caribbean Sea in 1492.

Reviewing Main Ideas

Section 1 (pp. 14–20)
1. According to archaeologists, how and from where did the first people arrive in the Americas?
2. Why did Native American cultures vary from region to region?
3. What religious and social services did Native Americans' families provide for their members?
4. What routes did Native Americans use for trading?

Section 2 (pp. 22–26)
5. What factors sparked Europeans' interest in Asia after the year 1000?
6. Why were European merchants eager to find new ways to reach Asian markets?
7. How did Portugal take the lead in the quest for easier access to Asian goods?

Section 3 (pp. 27–30)
8. What goods did the forest kingdoms of West Africa produce, and where and for what were those goods traded?
9. How did Songhai's location make it a major participant in West African trade?
10. Who were the people most likely to be enslaved in West Africa?

Section 4 (pp. 31–35)
11. In what ways did Columbus's voyage begin a new era in European and American history?
12. What was the significance of the Treaty of Tordesillas?
13. How did attitudes toward slavery differ among Africans and Europeans?

where they were traded for books, paper, weapons, cloth, horses, and salt.

9. Songhai lay between the forest kingdoms, with their extensive trading networks, and North Africa.

10. People who had been cut off from their lineage—prisoners of war, orphans, and criminals—were those most likely to be enslaved.

11. It began an era of transatlantic communication, trade, and exploitation and set up a permanent exchange (the Columbian Exchange) of goods, people, ideas, and diseases in a new Atlantic World.

12. Under the terms of the treaty, any land not already claimed by other Christians would be divided between Spain and Portugal by an invisible line around the world. Spain's share included most of the

Americas; Portugal's included Brazil and the sea route around Africa.

13. Among Africans, slaves could be adopted into a lineage and regain some freedoms, a practice that recognized the basic humanity of enslaved people. Europeans, who considered other races inferior, based slavery on race, thus making it a permanent condition.

Thinking Critically

1. **Identifying Assumptions** When Columbus met the Tainos, he described them as "ingenuous and free with all they have…of anything that they possess, if it be asked of them…they invite you to share it…." How does this description reflect a misunderstanding of Native American views on trade?

2. **Predicting Consequences** How might the history of the Atlantic World have changed if the Christians and Muslims had successfully negotiated a peaceful settlement to their dispute over Jerusalem instead of taking up arms against each other?

3. **Expressing Problems Clearly** The birth of the Atlantic World represented the collision of three distinct cultures. What values, beliefs, and customs differed among the three cultures? Choose one way in which the three cultures differed, and explain why this difference might have led to misunderstanding and conflict.

Making Connections

1. **Evaluating Primary Sources** Review the primary source excerpt on page 25. What does the English merchant's statement reveal about the economic and political conditions in Europe at this time?

2. **Understanding the Visuals** Write a paragraph explaining why the illustrations on pages 23 and 30 deal with the same theme. How do the maps on pages 24 and 29 relate to that theme?

3. **Writing About the Chapter** Imagine that you are traveling in the Atlantic World around the time of Columbus's voyage. Write several journal entries in which you describe your observations of the Native Americans, the Europeans, or the Africans you meet. First, decide which region you will "visit" and which traditions, adaptations to the environment, and lifestyles you wish to describe. Then write a draft of the journal entries in which you note your observations. Revise your entries, making certain that your descriptions are clear and accurate. Proofread your entries and draft a final copy.

4. **Using the Graphic Organizer** This graphic organizer uses a web to compare and contrast characteristics of Native American, European, and African societies. (a) Using the right side of the graphic organizer, summarize the view of land held by each society. (b) Using the left side, explain the way each society was organized. (c) Working on a separate sheet of paper, create your own web to compare and contrast Native Americans, Europeans, and Africans in terms of religion and trade.

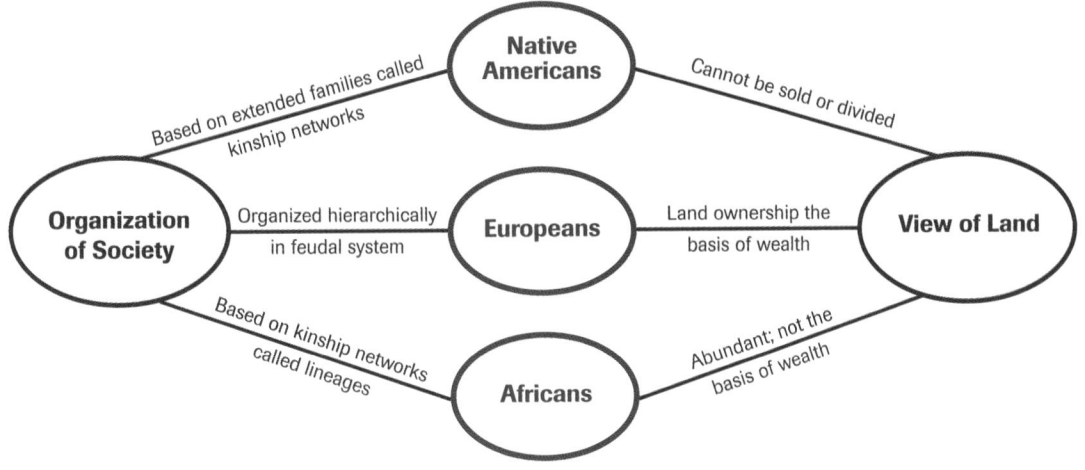

Thinking Critically

1. Columbus came from a European culture, in which trade was a simple economic transaction. He did not understand that, in Native American cultures, trade was more than a mere exchange of goods, but a demonstration of hospitality, friendliness, or respect.

2. The Crusades might not have taken place, which could have had several important consequences. Europeans might have been slower to develop a taste for Asian products. Without consumer demand, merchants might not have sought a sea route to Asia, and the technology for long-distance sea travel might have developed more slowly, delaying Columbus's voyage and the encounter of Atlantic cultures. With-out the ideas and information provided by Muslim scholars, the Renaissance might not have occurred when it did.

3. Possible answers: different views toward trade, slavery, religious and spiritual beliefs, and land use; as an example of possible consequences, different views of land use might lead to a clash over land itself.

Making Connections

1. People in Europe at this time thought of themselves as members of nations such as England and France; those nations were also in a state of economic competition.

2. The painting on page 23 shows a European marketplace, where goods from Asia were traded for goods from Europe. The engraving on page 30 shows a caravan arriving at Timbuktu, presumably carrying goods from other parts of the world to North Africa. The maps on pages 24 and 29 show the trade routes by which the merchants in both illustrations would have carried the goods they are selling.

3. Journal entries should demonstrate an understanding of the writing process as well as the characteristics of the culture about which they choose to write.

4. (a) Native Americans viewed land as something that could be used but not owned and, therefore, not sold. Europeans associated land ownership with wealth. Land was so abundant in Africa that it was not a basis of wealth. (b) Native American societies were organized around families, or kinship networks; European societies were organized hierarchically, according to the feudal system; African societies were organized around kinship networks called lineages. (c) Students' webs should reflect an understanding of the role of religion and trade in each of the three cultures.

Alternative Assessment

Final Evaluation

Allow student teams to conduct simulations in class. Use the following criteria to evaluate student performances:

● Adequate preparation
● Thoughtfulness of presentation
● Evidence of creativity
● Evidence of sensitivity regarding issues

Encourage students to include written projects in their portfolios.

Chapter 2 European Settlement and Native American Resistance 1519–1689

📁 Teaching Resources (See Unit 1 Folder)

	Instruction	Enrichment
Section 1 **Spanish and Native American Interaction** (pp. 40–45)	Reproducible Lesson Plan, p. 36 Alternate Lesson Plan, p. 7 Guided Reading and Review, p. 40 Quiz, p. 41	American Profiles Activity, Bartolomé de Las Casas, p. 52 American Profiles Activity, Popé, Medicine Man of the Pueblos, p. 53
Section 2 **A Colony in the Chesapeake Bay Area** (pp. 46–51)	Reproducible Lesson Plan, p. 37 Alternate Lesson Plan, p. 8 Guided Reading and Review, p. 42 Quiz, p. 43	Critical Thinking Activity, Determining Relevance, p. 57 Viewpoints Activity, On Life in Jamestown, pp. 54–55 Primary Source Activity, Cultural Clashes in the Virginia Colony, pp. 58–59 Literature Activity, The Fate of an Indentured Servant, p. 61 History Might Not . . . Activity, The Decision to Use Enslaved Africans for Labor, pp. 50–51
Section 3 **Europeans and Native Americans in the Northeast** (pp. 54–58)	Reproducible Lesson Plan, p. 38 Alternate Lesson Plan, p. 9 Guided Reading and Review, p. 44 Quiz, p. 45	Primary Source Activity, Native American Customs, p. 60 Visual Learning Activity, The Pequot War, p. 65 Literature Activity, Puritan Poetry, pp. 62–63 Historian's Toolbox Activity, Using Time Lines, p. 56
Section 4 **King Philip's War: A Turning Point in History** (pp. 60–63)	Reproducible Lesson Plan, p. 39 Alternate Lesson Plan, p. 10 Guided Reading and Review, p. 46 Quiz, p. 47 Chapter Test, Forms A & B, pp. 66–71	Visual Learning Activity, A Lasting Stereotype, p. 64 Turning Point Extension Activity, The Lasting Impact of King Philip's War, pp. 48–49

📁 Additional Chapter Resources

Resource Organizer, p. 35
Alternate Lesson Plan p. 6
Answer Keys, pp. 140–160

Bibliography

For the Teacher
Catton, Bruce. *The Bold and Magnificent Dream: America's Founding Years, 1492–1815.* Doubleday, 1978. (Account of the nation's history from colonial settlement to the early years of independence.)

Prentice Hall Literature Excerpts from *The American Experience,* 1994, including "Native American Voices" and "Explorers."

Media and Technology

 Critical Thinking, I-4

 Visions of America: History Might Not Have Happened This Way Game

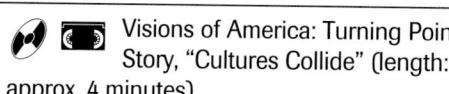 Visions of America: Turning Point Story, "Cultures Collide" (length: approx. 4 minutes)

 Visions of America: Roundtable Discussion on "Cultures Collide"

 Graphic Organizer, G-3

 Guided Reading Audiotapes (English and Spanish)

 Computer Test Bank

For the Student

Irving, Washington. "Philip of Pakanoket." In *Rip Van Winkle, The Legend of Sleepy Hollow and Other Stories.* Easton Press, 1967. (A moving account of King Philip's War.)

THE BIG IDEA

The Big Idea for the chapter and how the main ideas in each section relate to the Big Idea are graphically displayed below. Comprehension of this chapter's Big Idea is critical to students' understanding of United States history and how we as a nation got where we are today.

CHAPTER 2

Each group of Europeans in North America during the sixteenth and seventeenth centuries formed a distinct society, and each group disrupted the Native American societies it encountered. By the end of the seventeenth century, Native American resistance in New England finally gave way to a single dominant group—the English.

SECTION 1

By the 1550s, the Spanish had well-established colonies in the Americas. Strong Native American resistance in New Mexico and Florida forced the Spanish to limit their settlements there.

SECTION 2

The Virginia Colony of the English almost failed, but eventually did grow into a planter society dominated by a few rich gentlemen.

SECTION 3

In the Northeast, French and Dutch settlers based their colonies on trade with Native Americans. English Puritans created a well-ordered, prosperous society, intolerant of religious dissension.

SECTION 4

In 1675 Native Americans fought a disastrous war against English settlers that finally broke the strength of the Native Americans in New England.

European Settlement and Native American Resistance
1519–1689

 The Relevance of the Big Idea

The European encounters with the Native Americans in the sixteenth century have a modern parallel in the fate of the three thousand Native Americans of the Kaypo group in the Amazon Basin. The Kaypo live in a government reserve the size of Maryland, but the boundaries of their reserve have never been marked on the ground, and the discovery of gold on the fringes of their reservation has brought intruders and pollution into their area. The Kaypo themselves hunger for the goods of the modern world but they do not want to lose their lands. Discuss what the Kaypo and the government officials who try to protect their way of life can learn from the history of early European settlement in the Americas.

 In Depth

Global Connections

In the late 1500s, an undeclared war developed between Catholic Spain, the most powerful nation in Europe, and Protestant England. English "sea dogs" scoured the Atlantic Ocean pirating Spanish treasure ships from the Americas. In 1588, King Philip II of Spain responded by sending a huge fleet, known as the Armada, against England. Though the English navy was outnumbered, it won a stunning victory. Spain's dominance of Europe was shattered.

European Settlement and Native American Resistance
1519–1689

When Europeans migrated to North America, each nationality—Spanish, English, French, and Dutch—had its own distinctive way of settling in the land and interacting with Native Americans. As a result, each of the European societies that emerged in North America was unique. During the years that these societies were forming, Native Americans and Europeans alternately dominated and resisted one another. Gradually, however, Europeans began to take control.

Events in the United States				
1513 Spanish explorer Ponce de León lands in Florida.	1535 Spaniard Hernán Cortés explores lower peninsula of California.	1565 Spain establishes the settlement of St. Augustine in Florida.	1598 Spain claims territory of New Mexico.

1510	1530	1550	1570	1590

 Events in the World

	1519 Cortés arrives in Mexico to conquer the Aztec empire.	1533 Spaniard Francisco Pizarro completes conquest of Inca empire.		1591 End of the Songhai empire in West Africa.

 RESOURCE DIRECTORY

Teaching Resources

Alternate Lesson Plan: Demonstrating the Big Idea found in the Alternate Lesson Plans folder, p. 6, provides a lesson strategy designed to instruct students in the Big Idea that each different group of colonizing Europeans had a unique pattern of interacting with the Native Americans.

Alternative Assessment Handbook provides information, guidance, and strategies for alternative methods of assessment. It includes an essay on new trends in assessment, guidance and strategies for developing performance tasks and portfolios, scoring rubrics, and sample evaluation forms.

Pages 40–45
Spanish and Native American Interaction

After the collision of the Atlantic cultures, the Spanish quickly pushed their way into Native American lands. In Florida and New Mexico, however, Native Americans resisted and eventually forced the Spanish to adjust the goals of their invasion.

 Pages 46–51
A Colony in the Chesapeake Bay Area

Due to hunger, disease, and determined Native American resistance, the Virginia colony nearly failed. Tobacco saved the colony, but created a society in which a few gentlemen dominated everyone else.

 Pages 54–58
Europeans and Native Americans in the Northeast

The French and Dutch disturbed Native American societies in the Northeast indirectly by exploiting their trading system. By contrast, the Puritans of New England directly challenged Native Americans by trying to completely remake their culture and environment.

 Pages 60–63
King Philip's War: A Turning Point in History

Faced with the destruction of their way of life, Native Americans in New England fought back against English settlers in 1675. The war only shattered the strength of Native Americans and settlers alike, however.

Pages 64–65
The Lasting Impact of King Philip's War

1607 Britain establishes first successful colony at Jamestown.	1622 Native Americans attempt to drive English settlers from Virginia.	1637 Anne Hutchinson is called to trial in Boston and banished from the colony.		1680 Pueblo people expel the Spanish from New Mexico.
1610	**1630**	**1650**	**1670**	**1690**
1603 William Shakespeare publishes Hamlet.		1648 The Taj Mahal is completed in India.		1689 Peter the Great becomes czar of Russia.

Media and Technology

 Transparency
The Way It Works, H-2

Alternative Assessment

As an ongoing chapter project, students, in a small group, can role-play settlers in one of the new colonies. The purpose is to have students discuss how their country of origin, their view of the land, and the changes they have experienced have impacted their lives. Students need to research the period, apparel, language of the time and colony, and habits and values of particular settlers. The "settlers" in each group should answer the following questions from "visitors from outside":
● What country did you come from? Why did you come? Are you doing what you came to do? Do you own property? Will you be able to own property at some point?
● Who governs your settlement?
● How do settlers here support themselves? Who does the work?
● How do you think the Native Americans view your settlement?

Explain that finished projects will be assessed according to the following standards:
● **Unacceptable** Projects are not completed, or fail to meet requirements outlined.
● **Limited/Acceptable** Students provide basic, accurate information from the textbook only.
● **Extensive/Commendable** Students demonstrate use of outside research and can provide detailed information about the period.
● **Extraordinary/Outstanding** Projects are based on extensive research. Students role-play well-defined, believable characters, consistent with historical research. They may have created a believable environment through costumes and props.

For information and guidance on alternative assessment strategies, see the Alternative Assessment Handbook in the Resource Directory on page 38.

Spanish and Native American Interaction

Spanish and Native American Interaction

1. FOCUS

Connecting to the Big Idea

See page 38B. Explain that the Spanish, the first Europeans to invade the Americas, forced Native Americans to participate in the culture they created. Native American resistance in New Mexico and Florida compelled the Spanish to change their plans for those areas. Ask students what the culture created by the combination of Spanish and Native American elements was like. How did Native Americans resist the Spanish?

Objectives

● Trace the Spanish pattern of conquest and describe the culture that resulted in their settlements.
● Give reasons for the creation of Spanish outposts in Florida and New Mexico.
● Describe Native American resistance to the Spanish in New Mexico and Florida and describe how the Spanish settlement pattern changed in response to it.

In Depth

Multicultural Perspectives

Europeans adopted many Native American words to describe some of the animals and plants they found in the Americas, including *caribou*, *skunk*, *maize*, *avocado*, and *tapioca*. The English colonists had already picked up several Native American words that had entered English via Spanish, such as the Mayan *cigar* and the Taino *potato*.

SECTION PREVIEW

After the collision of the Atlantic cultures, the Spanish quickly pushed their way into Native American lands. In Florida and New Mexico, however, Native Americans resisted and eventually forced the Spanish to adjust the goals of their invasion.

Key Concepts
• Following the pattern of conquest they had established in Europe, the Spanish forced Native Americans to participate in the culture they introduced into the Americas. The result was a culture that combined Spanish and Native American elements.
• The Spanish established outposts in Florida and New Mexico to protect their treasure fleets and spread Christianity.
• Native Americans experienced some success in resisting the Spanish in New Mexico and Florida.

Key Terms, People, and Places
conquistador, hidalgo, colony, *encomienda* system, presidio, *congregacion;* Popé

A silent witness to the Spanish attempt to conquer Florida, this soldier's helmet was lost in the 1500s at Palm Beach and discovered in recent times.

A fter the American, European, and African cultures collided in the 1400s, the Spanish were the first to invade the Americas. The way they treated Native Americans there was based on their long experience with violent conquest in their own land.

The Spanish Pattern of Conquest

Christians in Spain fought Muslims for seven hundred years in the *reconquista*—an effort to expel followers of Islam from the Iberian peninsula. The *reconquista* determined how the Spanish would treat the people it encountered in the Americas. In other words, it created a pattern of conquest.

How the Pattern Was Established As Spanish Christians had gradually moved into Muslim lands on the Iberian peninsula over the centuries, Christians and Muslims began to live next to each other. The two groups traded with one another, intermarried, and borrowed from one another's cultures. For this reason, the Spanish **conquistadores,** or conquerors, expected the outcome of conquest to be a culture that had elements of both their own culture and the conquered culture. To their minds, the Spanish elements of the new culture would be superior. One example of this blending of cultures can be seen in Mexico, Central America, and South America today. In much of this region, Spanish is the official language, even though most of the population have Native American ancestors.

The *reconquista* established three reasons for conquest. For centuries, young Spanish gentlemen, or **hidalgos,** had led expeditions against Muslims in order to spread the Christian religion, to loot Muslim cities for wealth, and to win fame for their exploits—in short, for God, gold, and glory. These same motives led them to the shores of the Americas—and perhaps the love of gold most of all. One conquistador, the thirty-four-year-old Hernán Cortés, spoke for many when he said in 1519: "I and my companions suffer from a disease of the heart which can be cured only by gold."

How the Pattern Was Applied In search of such wealth, between 1519 and 1521 Cortés led about six hundred men in the conquest of a vast Native American empire ruled by the Aztec

---

RESOURCE DIRECTORY

Teaching Resources

Reproducible Lesson Plan found in the Unit 1 folder, p. 36, provides a summary of the Section 1 lesson plan content.

Alternate Lesson Plan: Cooperative Learning found in the Alternate Lesson Plans folder, p. 7, is designed to help groups of students to examine and describe Spanish and Native American interaction.

Guided Reading and Review found in the Unit 1 folder, p. 40, provides a structure for reading and mastering the key concepts and reviewing the key terms for Section 1. (Guided Practice)

European Exploration of the Americas, 1492–1682

Exploration sponsored by:
- Spain
- Portugal
- England
- France

Geography and History: Interpreting Maps
For more than a century after Columbus's voyage, explorers sailed for any power that would sponsor them. Cabot and Verrazano were Italian, and Hudson was English. Estevanico was originally a slave of African descent, later freed to explore the Southwest. *What nations sponsored Cabot, Verrazano, Hudson, and Estevanico?*

people in Mexico. The Aztec capital, Tenochtitlán, had 250,000 inhabitants; it was one of the world's largest urban centers. From this splendid city in the mountains of Mexico, the Aztecs governed 20 million people, a population twice the size of that of all Spain at that time.

In 1532, Francisco Pizarro and approximately 170 men conquered another empire, that of the Incas, centered in what is now Peru in South America. In both cases, the Spanish would not have won without the help of Native American allies, or without smallpox and measles epidemics that killed millions of Native Americans.

By the 1550s, the Spanish controlled well-established **colonies.** Colonies are land areas settled by immigrants who continue to be the subjects of their parent country. These Spanish colonies formed a large empire on the islands of the Caribbean Sea, and in Mexico, Central America, and South America. After they had

plundered the riches of the great cities of the Aztecs and Incas, the Spanish used enslaved Native Americans and Africans to take vast amounts of silver and gold from the mountains of Mexico and Peru.

While acquiring this wealth, the Spanish conquistadores ruthlessly destroyed much of the culture they found in the Americas. They did not try to replace it completely, however, by driving out the Native Americans. Instead, they attempted to force Native Americans into Spanish culture. One method the Spanish employed to accomplish this was known as the ***encomienda* system.** Under this system, Native Americans were required to farm, ranch, or mine for the profit of an individual Spaniard. In return, the Spaniard was supposed to see to their well-being. The *encomienda* system was a version of the social system of Europe, where the wealthy controlled land worked by the poor.

Bellringer
Ask students to consider what might happen if a new teacher took over their history class at midsemester, abandoning all the things they liked about the class and establishing expectations and evaluations totally unfamiliar to them.

Reading Strategy
Reading for Evidence Ask students to look for evidence as they read to support the statement that the Spanish pattern of conquest in the present-day United States differed from the pattern in the rest of the Spanish Empire in the Americas.

Caption Answer to ...

 Interpreting Maps

England, France, England, and Spain, respectively.

In Depth
Interdisciplinary

The economic system set up by the Spanish in Latin America—the *encomienda* system—was based on the labor of a specific population and depended upon nearly absolute control of that labor. The *encomienda* system enslaved the native peoples until most had died of disease or ill treatment. Examples of similar systems include the plantation system of the American South before the Civil War. (See Chapter 8.)

Explain/Discuss

Remind students that European Christians thought it was their duty to spread their religion throughout the world. Discuss how this belief affected the dealings of the Spanish with Native Americans. Ask students to compare the pattern of conquest applied in other parts of the Spanish Empire with the pattern that emerged in New Mexico in the 1700s. How did the Spanish relax their religious demands?

Discuss with students why the Spanish wanted the Native Americans to work for them. Ask students to describe the *encomienda* system and compare it to the Native American way of life.

Analyze

Analyze the role of geography in the Spanish settlement of North America. Why were the North American settlements less important to the Spanish than their other settlements?

Caption Answer to ...

 Interpreting Maps

No settlement shown is farther north than about 35° N latitude.

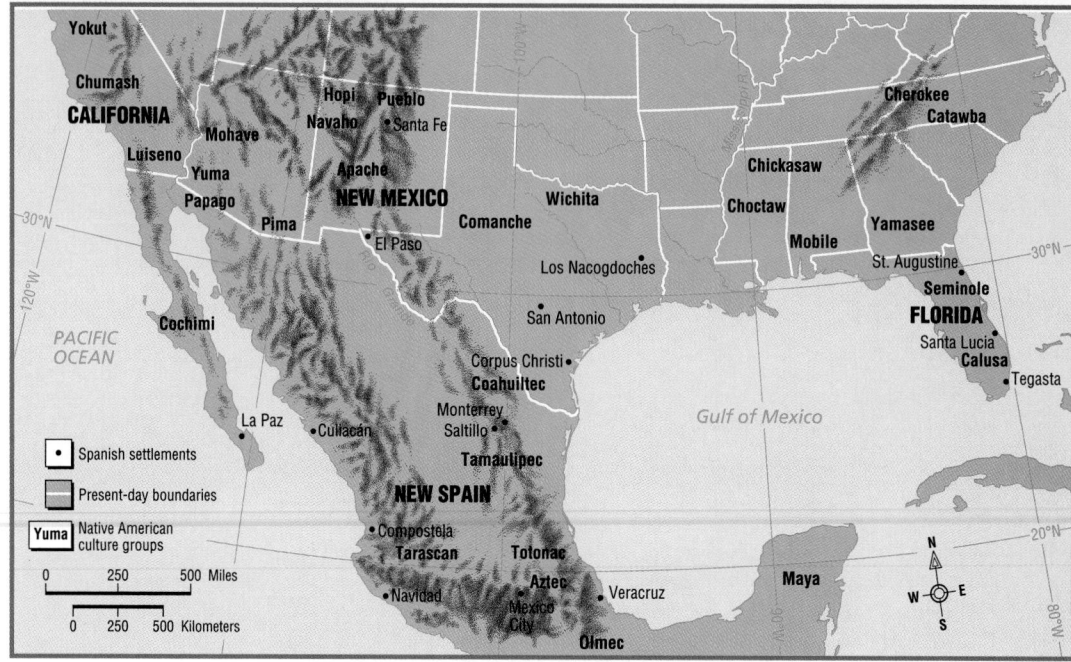

Spanish Settlements and Native American Groups in the South, 1500s–1600s

Yokut
Chumash
CALIFORNIA
Mohave
Luiseno
Yuma
Papago
Pima
Hopi
Navaho
Pueblo
• Santa Fe
Apache
NEW MEXICO
• El Paso
Cochimi
La Paz
• Culiacán
Wichita
Comanche
Los Nacogdoches
San Antonio
Corpus Christi •
Coahuiltec
Monterrey
Saltillo •
Tamaulipec
NEW SPAIN
• Compostela
Tarascan
• Navidad
Totonac
Aztec
Mexico City
• Veracruz
Olmec
Chickasaw
Choctaw
Mobile
Cherokee
Catawba
Yamasee
St. Augustine •
Seminole
FLORIDA
Santa Lucia •
Calusa
• Tegasta
Maya
Gulf of Mexico
PACIFIC OCEAN

• Spanish settlements
Present-day boundaries
Yuma Native American culture groups

0 250 500 Miles
0 250 500 Kilometers

N / S / E / W compass

Geography and History: Interpreting Maps
An adviser to the Spanish king in the 1500s remarked: "It is towards the south, not towards the frozen north, that those who seek their fortune should bend their way; for everything at the equator is rich." *Cite evidence from the map to show that Spanish settlers followed this policy.*

Spanish Settlements in What Is Now the United States

Within decades of Columbus's first voyage, Spanish explorers mapped and studied the land and peoples in the southeastern and southwestern parts of what would become the United States. In 1513, for instance, the Spanish explorer Ponce de León encountered the land he named Florida. In 1535, Cortés came upon the lower peninsula of California, which he named after a legendary island. The map on page 41 shows the routes of the major European explorers during this early period of colliding cultures. Because the region did not offer much in riches or agricultural possibilities, however, by far the greatest part of the 450,000 immigrants from Spain before 1650 did not come to the lands that are now the United States, but to more southern parts of the Americas.

Spanish Defensive Bases By 1550, the Spanish government felt the need to protect the northern border of its Mexican empire from other Europeans. It also wanted to safeguard the fleets that sailed from Cuba to Spain loaded with silver and gold from the Americas. Because these fleets sailed northward along the Gulf Stream, a powerful current that crosses the Atlantic, the Spanish were particularly concerned with building settlements to serve as defensive bases along the southeast coast of North America. Several of these bases are shown in the map above.

In 1565, Pedro Menendez de Aviles, a conquistador, established the settlement of St. Augustine in Florida for this purpose. In the next few years, he built half-a-dozen other outposts. But the Spanish commitment to these forts was small, and they rarely survived for very long. Only St. Augustine survived from this first wave of Spanish settlement in Florida.

▶ RESOURCE DIRECTORY

Teaching Resources

⭐ 📁 **American Profiles Activity** found in the Unit 1 folder, p. 52, profiles Bartolomé de Las Casas, a sixteenth-century Dominican priest who spoke out against Spain's treatment of Native Americans.

The Spanish also turned their attention to the West. They hoped to extend the mining industry of Mexico into what is now the Southwest of the United States. In January 1598, the conquistador Juan de Oñate and about 400 men, women, and children claimed an area they called New Mexico and established several forts in the region. (Spanish New Mexico included parts of what is now Arizona and Texas. See the map on page 42.) Meanwhile, the Spanish had begun to take a closer look at California in the hopes of keeping it from European rivals who might interfere with their trade across the Pacific.

How Well Did the Settlements Succeed?
The settlements that dotted the south and west were really just forts, or **presidios,** manned by a few soldiers. But the survival of these Spanish outposts was due not to the soldiers, but to the faith of a few dozen Franciscans. These priests, members of a Catholic order dedicated to the work of St. Francis of Assisi, settled throughout Florida and New Mexico. They established dozens of missions—headquarters for their work of converting Native Americans to Christianity. In addition to converting Native Americans, they also wanted to make them follow European customs. With the help of soldiers, they forced the Native Americans into settled villages, or **congregacions,** where they would farm and worship like Catholic Europeans.

In 1634, one missionary, Fray Alonso de Benavides, reported cheerfully that many Native Americans

are now converted, baptized, and very well ministered to. . . . The whole land is dotted with churches, convents, and crosses along the roads. The people are so well taught that they now live like perfect Christians.

MAKING CONNECTIONS

The Spanish combined force and persuasion to settle Native Americans in *congregacions.* How would you expect the Native Americans to react? Read on to find out what happened.

Native American Resistance to the Spanish

While zealous priests such as Benavides might sometimes feel they were achieving their goals, overall they found less success than they desired. Some Native Americans, particularly nomadic groups like the Apache of the Southwest, refused to cooperate with the Spanish at all. Even those who did so resisted Spanish exploitation time after time. Such resistance broke out as early as 1597 and occasionally throughout the 1600s. ✪

Conflict in New Mexico Native American fighting against the Spanish was generally disorganized. But in New Mexico, following years of drought that weakened Spanish power, the Pueblo people united and expelled the Spanish in what is called the Revolt of 1680.

In the early 1500s, around 248,000 Pueblo Indians lived in New Mexico. They first came in contact with the Spanish when conquistadores under Franciso Vasquez de Coronado entered the region in 1540 to 1541. The conquistadores were disappointed by the lack of great riches in the area, however, and did not stay long.

La V.ᵐ Maria de Iesus de Agreda Predicando á los Chichimecos del Nuebo mexico.

Using Historical Evidence In this symbolic woodcut from 1631, María de Agreda, a Franciscan nun, preaches to Native Americans. *How has the Spanish artist used his art to promote his view of contact between the cultures?*

Activity
Cooperative Learning

Time: One class period.
Activity: Produce a guidebook-style description for a first-time visitor to New Mexico today.
Grouping: Groups of four to six students.
Purpose: The group will produce a guide that locates and describes a site in present-day New Mexico and provides an understanding of the interaction between Spanish and Native American cultures. An example is the village of Isleta, a surviving Native American village rebuilt after its destruction during the revolt of 1680. Groups should consult references such as travel guides, atlases, and historical maps such as those produced by *National Geographic* magazine.
Roles: Students should assign themselves the following roles: researcher, cartographer, writer, editor, publisher, and reader.
Outcome: Students will understand how specific sites in New Mexico reveal the way in which Native American and Spanish cultures interacted.

Answer to . . .

MAKING CONNECTIONS

Answers should suggest that Native Americans would most likely resist the imposition of Spanish culture in the move to *congregacions.*

Caption Answer to . . .

Using Historical Evidence

The artist has made Agreda large and detailed, the center of the picture, suggesting the superiority of her religion; the Native Americans are shown as diminutive and stereotyped worshipers.

Enrichment

Ask students to report on selected aspects of the Aztec, Maya, or Inca cultures. For example, students might report on topics such as language, archeological sites, sculpture and metal working, government, or building and construction.

Answer to ...

Links Across Time

Modern architects have adopted Pueblo designs because they recognize that Pueblo houses meet today's needs. Using local materials and few windows—to shield people from the desert heat—is energy efficient.

3. ASSESS

Section 1 Review Answers

1. (a) conquistador, see p. 40, (b) hidalgo, see p. 40, (c) colony, see p. 41, (d) *congregacion*, see p. 43, (e) presidio, see p. 43

2. Popé , see p. 44

3. The Spanish pattern of conquest involved a forced blending of cultures. Following the example of the *reconquista,* the Spanish government authorized individual hidalgos to act in the name of the Spanish Crown and the Catholic Church, raiding lands for God, gold, and glory.

4. Under the *encomienda* system, Native Americans were required to labor at farming, ranching, or mining for the profit of an individual Spaniard, who was supposed to see to their well-being in return.

5. The Native Americans adopted only those parts of Christianity they chose, and then only on their own terms. In New Mexico, they gathered forces and expelled the Spanish and their religion.

The Pueblo Influence on Architecture

When the Spanish first explored the Southwest, they heard tales of cities of gold—probably Pueblo towns like the one at left. Formed of sandstone blocks covered with mud (adobe), their thick walls with few windows shielded the Pueblo from the desert heat. Today, recognizing the true "gold" of the Pueblo tradition, architects use similar designs in modern buildings (above). **Why have modern architects adopted Pueblo designs?**

Spanish soldiers returned to the land of the Pueblo in 1598. This time they established outposts along the Rio Grande, including a capital at Santa Fe in 1610. As was typical on the northern border of the Spanish empire, the true European conquistadores were Franciscan friars. They claimed thousands of converts among the Native Americans. Recent historians believe, however, that the Spanish hold over the vast majority of the Pueblo was weak. They suggest that Pueblo Christians accepted the Franciscans' ways because the friars controlled valuable tools and equipment and offered protection from other Native Americans within the walls of the missions.

Nothing testifies to the weakness of the Spanish hold on the Pueblo of New Mexico better than the success of the Revolt of 1680. By the 1670s, widespread sickness and drought had reduced the Pueblo population to 17,000 people. Seeking to reverse this decline, the Pueblo began to turn back to their traditional religious practices, which the Spanish denounced as witchcraft and tried to stamp out. Then a brilliant medicine man named **Popé** rallied the disheartened Pueblos and some Apaches and organized a full-scale revolt. Popé blamed the Spanish for all the Native Americans' miseries. One Pueblo witness, Jeronimo, later reported Popé's claim that when the Europeans were gone the Pueblo

would gather large crops of grain, maize [corn] *with large and thick ears, many bundles of cotton, many calabashes* [squash] *and watermelons.*

In August 1680, the 2,350 Spaniards in New Mexico suddenly were confronted with a well-coordinated revolt by more than 8,000 warriors. The Native Americans killed 21 of 33 priests and 375 colonists, destroyed missions, and drove the Spanish out of Santa Fe. By early September, around 1500 Spaniards and some 500 Pueblo and Apache slaves—the sole survivors of the revolt—gathered near El Paso.

Meanwhile, Popé and his followers ruthlessly destroyed all signs of Christianity and European culture. The Pueblo took ritual baths to cleanse themselves of their experience with the Christian religion. The ancient ways of the Pueblo were reborn.

▶ RESOURCE DIRECTORY

Teaching Resources

American Profiles Activity Popé, Medicine Man of the Pueblos, found in the Unit 1 folder, p. 53, illustrates Pueblo attachment to ancient beliefs and traditions through the biography of a medicine man.

The clash between the Catholic and Native American beliefs is clear from the report of one Spaniard, Antonio de Otermín. He rephrased in his own words the statement of a captured Native American resister:

H*e declared that the resentment which all the Indians have in their hearts has been so strong, from the time this kingdom was discovered, because the [priests] and the [other] Spaniards took away their [religion]; that they have inherited successively from their old men the things pertaining to their ancient customs; and that he has heard this resentment spoken of since he was of an age to understand.*

The Pueblo struggle of 1680 was one of the most successful Native American wars of resistance in North American history. It took the Spanish years to reestablish themselves along the Rio Grande. They did not retake Santa Fe until 1696. During this time, however, the Pueblo still declined rapidly in number, under increasing attack by the neighboring Apache and Navaho people. By 1706, the Pueblo population had shrunk to only 9,000. In the 1700s they accepted Spanish rule to gain protection.

In forming this new connection, however, both sides compromised. The Pueblo became Catholics who continued to practice traditional rituals. They acknowledged Spanish authority, but governed their own local affairs. The *encomienda* system was abolished altogether. Ultimately, the Spanish and Pueblo forged a new bond in which their dependence on each other overcame mutual distrust.

Native American Resistance in Florida In Florida, similar Native American rebellions occurred in the late 1600s, as the Spanish were trying once again to establish presidios. Some Native Americans also combined forces with the English, who were at war with Spain at that time. With Native American assistance, the English mounted several crushing attacks on Spanish presidios in Florida from their own colony in South Carolina.

This combined resistance of the English and the Native Americans caused the Spanish to limit their settlement efforts. By 1706, the only remaining Spanish settlements in Florida were St. Augustine and two newer presidios, San Marcos de Apalachee and Pensacola.

Like the Spanish, the English who fought them also had serious difficulties starting colonies in the lands north of Mexico. To one problem—how to make their colonies profitable—they found an unexpected solution. It came in the form of a weed.

Anticipating continued conquest, the Spanish motto from a book of 1599 reads: "By the sword and the compass, more and more and more and more." The Spanish, however, suffered numerous setbacks on the northern border of their empire.

SECTION 1 REVIEW

Key Terms, People, and Places
1. Define (a) conquistador, (b) hidalgo, (c) colony, (d) *congregacion,* (e) presidio.
2. Identify Popé.

Key Concepts
3. Describe the Spanish pattern of conquest in Europe and the Americas.
4. What was the *encomienda* system?

5. What was the effect of Native American resistance in New Mexico and in Florida?

Critical Thinking
6. **Making Comparisons** Compare the quotation of Fray Alonso de Benavides with the quotation on page 45 describing the reaction of the Native Americans to the Spanish attempt to convert them to Christianity.

Quiz found in the Unit 1 folder, p. 41, covers the main ideas in this section as well as the key terms.

6. Answers may suggest that Benavides assumes that he is replacing false beliefs with true beliefs; he assumes that the values and religion chosen by others cannot have meaning if they do not mirror his own beliefs. The Native American suggests that his people have not been converted at all, that they have been passing on ancient customs from generation to generation, and that all Native Americans harbor a deep resentment against the Spanish.

Reteach

Ask students to write the date 1680 in the center of a piece of paper and identify the event that happened in that year in New Mexico. Then have students write a brief description to the left of the date of the Spanish *encomienda* system as it was applied in South and Central America, and a brief description to the right of the date of how the Spanish modified the *encomienda* system in New Mexico after the Revolt of 1680.

4. CLOSE

Reinforcing the Big Idea

The Spanish imposed a pattern of conquest designed to bring them wealth and convert the Native Americans to Christianity. In the more scattered Spanish settlements in what is now the southwestern United States, the pattern was loosened as a result of Native American resistance. The next section describes the settlement pattern established by the English in their first colonies in North America.

A Colony in the Chesapeake Bay Area

A Colony in the Chesapeake Bay Area

1. FOCUS

Connecting to the Big Idea

See page 38B. Explain that in its early days the Virginia Colony nearly failed, and many of its first settlers died. The discovery of a popular kind of tobacco ensured the colony's future, led to its domination by a few rich planters, and to the use of enslaved Africans as laborers. Ask students what patterns of conquest and settlement were at work in Virginia.

Objectives

● Describe how the English attempted to transform the land and the Native American cultures as they settled in North America.
● Identify the early problems of the Virginia Colony.
● Explain the effect of Native American resistance on English settlement.
● Identify Bacon's Rebellion and describe its short- and long-term results.

Bellringer

Ask students to think about why people want to own things such as land and other forms of property. What image does ownership convey?

Reading Strategy

Reinforcing Key Ideas Ask students to note this sentence on page 51: "The Chesapeake Bay area altered dramatically during the 1600s." Ask students to list and briefly describe the changes discussed in this section.

SECTION PREVIEW

Due to hunger, disease, and determined Native American resistance, the Virginia colony nearly failed. Tobacco saved the colony, but created a society in which a few gentlemen dominated everyone else.

Europeans used tampers like this to pack their pipes with the tobacco that became a boom crop in the Chesapeake region.

Key Concepts

• When the English conquered and settled in the Americas, they attempted to transform completely the land and the Native American cultures in it.
• During its first years, the Virginia Colony struggled with severe problems and nearly failed.
• The Native Americans of the Chesapeake Bay area resisted English settlement, but were sharply reduced in number during the 1600s.
• Bacon's Rebellion confirmed that wealthy landholders would continue to hold power over those who owned less land or no land at all.

Key Terms, People, and Places

Reformation, joint-stock company, indentured servant, enclosure movement; Powhatan, John Smith; Jamestown

In the race to exploit the possibilities of the Atlantic World after the voyage of Columbus, the Spanish were soon far ahead. Other European nations tried to catch up, in the hope that they too could reap wealth as great as the riches of Mexico and Peru. These nations developed different patterns of conquest and settlement, based not only on their past experiences, but also on what they found in the Americas.

The English Pattern of Conquest

The English based their pattern of conquest on their experiences in Ireland, the island nation off their western coast. For centuries, English rulers had been trying to assert control in this neighboring land, and the Irish people had steadily resisted.

A new complication arose in the early 1500s, when a powerful religious movement, the **Reformation,** brought bitter divisions to Europe. During the Reformation, a new Christian faith, called Protestantism, developed in protest against what was seen as the corruption and inadequacy of the Catholic church. Nations rapidly took sides as Catholic or Protestant. These hostile feelings followed Europeans to the Americas. They were part of the reason the Protestant English raided the Florida settlements of Catholic Spain.

Because the English were Protestant and the Irish were Catholic, the Reformation also heightened the conflict between the English and the Irish. During the 1500s and 1600s, England made Ireland its first overseas colony, and English settlers poured onto the island. The English put down Irish resistance to this invasion with stern measures, repeatedly taking land away from the native Irish.

During this colonizing effort, the English developed a harsh attitude toward conquered peoples. In their experience, it was best to remake completely any culture they conquered. They did not practice the forced blending of European and Native American societies that was taking place across the Atlantic in the colonies of the Spanish. For the English, conquest would be all—or nothing. This is one reason why people descended from Native Americans make up only a small part of the population of the United States today.

RESOURCE DIRECTORY

Teaching Resources

Reproducible Lesson Plan found in the Unit 1 folder, p. 37, provides a summary of the Section 2 lesson plan content.

Alternate Lesson Plan: Learning Styles found in the Alternate Lesson Plans folder, p. 8, is especially effective for visual learners and is designed to help students create a poster or graphic organizer illustrating conditions in the early English settlements.

Guided Reading and Review found in the Unit 1 folder, p. 42, provides a structure for reading and mastering the key concepts and reviewing the key terms for Section 2. (Guided Practice)

Critical Thinking Activity Determining Relevance: Native American Words, found in the Unit 1 folder, p. 57, is designed to help students apply this skill by making a chart of Native American words.

MAKING CONNECTIONS

The Spanish pattern of conquest influenced the composition of the current population of Mexico, Central America, and South America. How is this different from the way the English pattern of conquest influenced the composition of the current population of the United States?

Roanoke: A Disastrous Beginning

The English began their entrance into the American world in the 1560s and 1570s, led by men such as Sir Francis Drake. Acting as privateers, which are pirates operating under the authority of their government, these English adventurers raided Spanish fleets, eager for a share in the silver and gold from the mountains of Mexico and Peru.

By the 1580s, the English were ready to establish a permanent position in the Americas. In particular, they were looking for places to serve as bases for raids on the Spanish and for further exploration. In 1587, the thirty-one-year-old favorite of Queen Elizabeth, Sir Walter Raleigh, financed the establishment of one such base on Roanoke Island, one of a chain of islands called the Outer Banks that runs along the coast of what is now North Carolina.

This first attempt at an English colony was a disaster, for reasons that are still a mystery. Its settlers vanished completely; a relief expedition in 1590 found only empty buildings. On a doorpost was carved the only clue to the fate of the settlers—the word *Croatoan*, an early form of the name of a nearby Native American group, the Croatans. The English may well have been adopted by the Croatan people: even today forty-one of the settlers' family names continue in use among the Croatan people.

The Jamestown Settlement

After the Roanoke disaster, about twenty years passed before the English tried to settle on the Atlantic Coast of North America. In 1607 they established a settlement in a mosquito-infested swamp 60 miles from the mouth of the James River in the Chesapeake Bay region. (See map on page 50.) They called the new village **Jamestown** in honor of their king, James I. The land itself they called Virginia, after their last ruler, Elizabeth, who had never married and bore the title "the Virgin Queen." The 104 adventurers who started the colony were shareholders in the Virginia Company, a **joint-stock company** established in London in 1606.

Joint-stock companies like the Virginia Company were organized by investors, or

Using Historical Evidence
Jamestown was founded at the water's edge. *How does the town reflect the English pattern of settlement? What advantages and disadvantages did the location offer?*

Media and Technology

 Transparency
Critical Thinking, I-4

Answer to ...

MAKING CONNECTIONS

People descended from Native Americans make up a large part of the population in Mexico and lands to the south; by contrast, descendants of Native Americans make up only a tiny part of the population of the United States.

Caption Answer to ...

Using Historical Evidence

Settlers building the town attempted to reconstruct the landscape by building according to English notions. The location offered the advantage of easy access by water for ships from England; this access was a disadvantage, however, when enemies made use of it. The location was also too wet, promoting sickness among the colonists.

In Depth

Did You Know?

Sir Francis Drake, one of the boldest of the English pirates, or "sea dogs," made an especially daring raid on Spanish ships in 1573. Aided by escaped African slaves, he and his crew stole the yearly silver shipment being carried from Peru to Spain over the Isthmus of Panama. Four years later, Drake followed Magellan's route around the world, raiding Spanish settlements on the Pacific coast of South America along the way.

Possible answers: The reports came from people who had not been to Jamestown, or from people who could profit from sending people to Jamestown. For a more thorough examination of life in the English settlements, see the Resource Directory below.

2. INSTRUCT

Discuss

Ask students to compare the English pattern of conquest with that of the Spanish. How did the English and Spanish attitudes toward Native Americans differ? How did the attitude of the English affect the manner in which they interacted with Native Americans in terms of labor, trade, or social life? Encourage students to speculate about the fate of the Roanoke settlers. Ask students what evidence would be needed to prove or disprove any of their hypotheses.

Discuss the problems of the early settlement. How did the settlers eventually solve the problems of hunger, disease, and strained relations with Native Americans? How did tobacco solve some problems and create others?

Analyze

Analyze the role of tobacco, relations with Native Americans, and the dissatisfactions of indentured servants in the decision to buy enslaved West Africans to work in Virginia. Which factor was probably most significant?

Activity

Debate

Have pairs of students improvise a debate between William Berkeley and Nathaniel Bacon about Bacon's reasons for rebelling and his plans for the western lands of the colony. Each pair of students should take a point and illustrate it through argument.

Viewpoints
On Life in Jamestown

Many of the settlers of Jamestown left England having been led to believe that the colonies offered wealth and an easy life for a gentleman. The realities of settlement life soon overwhelmed those dreams. *Why would the English in London have described America in such positive terms?*

Dreams of Riches

"I tell thee golde is more plentifull there than copper is with us . . . Why man all their dripping pans and their chamber pottes are pure golde; . . . and as for rubies and diamonds, they goe forth on holy dayes and gather 'hem by the seashore to hang on their children's coates and sticke in their cappes."
— Description of Virginia from *Eastward Ho!*,
a popular London play, 1605

Realities of Jamestown

"Of five hundred within six months after Captain Smith's departure, there remained not past sixtie men, women and children, most miserable and poore creatures; and those were preserved for the most part, by roots, herbes, acornes, walnuts, berries, now and then a little fish . . . yea even the skinnes of our horses. . . . [S]o great was our famine, that a Savage [Native American] we slew and buried, the poorer sorte took him up againe and eat him . . . . [I]t were too vile to say, and scarce to be beleeved, what we endured."
— A survivor's record of the Starving Time
in Jamestown, October 1609 to March 1610

shareholders, who each contributed money to the costs of an enterprise, and expected a share of the profit. Most of the investors in the Virginia Company remained in England. But young men could earn a share by simply paying their way to Virginia. At first the colony was made up exclusively of men; women and children eventually followed.

Native American Reaction The Virginia Company had plans for a permanent colony. In fact, the English had high hopes about their ability to live peacefully with the Native Americans in the Chesapeake Bay area while at the same time exploiting Native American labor and wealth. The Native Americans, however, had no intention of being exploited. Shortly after the arrival of the English, about two hundred Native Americans attacked them. Only an English cannon forced them to retreat.

About eight thousand Native Americans lived in the Chesapeake region. Most of them recognized the authority of one powerful group, the Pamunkey people. They particularly honored the Pamunkey leader, **Powhatan,** paying him tribute—a kind of regular tax—in skins, beads, and food. Within weeks of the first attack on the English, several Englishmen traveled to neighboring Native American villages to offer tribute of their own and to persuade the Native Americans that their intentions in settling in the area were good.

Powhatan had every reason to distrust those intentions. The Spanish had captured Powhatan's brother, Opechancanough, in the 1560s. Opechancanough had visited Spain twice, lived for a time in the capital of Spanish Mexico, and accompanied Spanish expeditions to the Chesapeake area. In 1570 he returned to the Pamunkey people.

During these years with the Spanish, Opechancanough came to know and despise the goals of European settlers. Doubtless he and Powhatan understood well that the settlement was a threat to their people's way of life.

The Settler's Hardships In spite of mutual suspicion, after initial conflicts both sides tried to keep the peace that developed between them. The settlers had a powerful motive for doing so, for Jamestown was very nearly a complete disaster like Roanoke. In its first decade, starvation was common; the settlers even resorted to cannibalism. One particularly difficult period from October 1609 to March 1610 was remembered as the Starving Time. If the Native Americans had not given the English timely assistance in the form of food and water, the settlement surely would have died out.

Disease, too, struck the English hard. Because they lived near and drew their water from swamps and pools of standing water where disease-carrying mosquitos bred, the colonists suffered from dysentery, typhus, and malaria. By 1624, of the approximately 6,000 Europeans who had migrated to Virginia over the preceding sixteen years, only about 1,300 remained alive.

RESOURCE DIRECTORY

Teaching Resources

Viewpoints Activity On Life in Jamestown, found in the Unit 1 folder, pp. 54–55, provides additional viewpoints and perspectives on survival in the Jamestown settlement.

Primary Source Activity Cultural Clashes in the Virginia Colony, found in the Unit 1 folder, pp. 58–59, uses passages written by settlers John Smith and Edward Waterhouse and a speech by Wahunsonacock (also called Powhatan), leader of the Pamunkey, to illustrate the deterioration in relations between settlers and Native Americans.

The Reasons Behind Jamestown's Hardships
In part, Jamestown's misfortunes were the fault of the Virginia Company, which was poorly managed. In 1618, under the direction of the treasurer, Sir Edmund Sandys, the stockholders attempted to save the situation by creating a government in Virginia to deal directly with local issues. This government, the House of Burgesses, was the first English assembly of representatives in the colonies. But these and other measures were too little, too late. In 1624 King James dissolved the bankrupt Virginia Company and assumed personal responsibility for the colony.

The near-failure of Jamestown also resulted from the unrealistic expectations of many of its early settlers. The adventurers had migrated to Virginia to become wealthy by living off the work of others. In Europe wealthy landowners did little physical work. When men who were or wanted to be gentlemen came to Virginia, their leader, **John Smith,** found it difficult to get them to do any work at all. Even when they were starving, many men simply refused to compromise their image of themselves as gentlemen by growing corn. In 1608 Smith warned them:

Y*ou must obey this now for a law, that he that will not work shall not eat . . . for the labors of thirty or forty honest and industrious men shall not be consumed to maintain a hundred and fifty idle loiterers.*

Relations Between Native Americans and the English Although the Native Americans did help the English in their difficulties, tensions persisted. Incidents of violence occurred side-by-side with regular trade. Exchanges begun on both sides with good intentions could become angry confrontations in a matter of minutes through simple misunderstandings. Indeed, the failure of each group to understand the culture of the other prevented any lasting cooperation between English and Native Americans. The English, for example, who considered farming to be the work of men and hunting an idle sport, mocked Native American men for "making" women work in the fields while they hunted. On the other hand, the English obsession with building sturdy houses and fully covering their bodies

seemed ridiculous to Native Americans accustomed to the warm climate of the Chesapeake.

In March 1622, relations between Native Americans and the English broke down altogether. Opechancanough planned and led a brilliantly coordinated surprise attack on Jamestown designed to wipe out the English. It was only partially successful. Still, 347 of the English lost their lives—more than 10 percent of the population of the settlement at that time. Within days, the settlers killed as many or more Native Americans in retaliation.

Powhatan's people mounted their last major act of armed resistance against the English in the Chesapeake in 1644. It failed. During the attack, Opechancanough, still active and defiant at nearly 100 years of age, was shot through the back in the streets of Jamestown. Two years later, the Native Americans agreed to pay tribute to the English in return for a guarantee of some land. By 1669, however, there were only two thousand Native Americans left in the Chesapeake region.

The Tobacco Colony

During the early years of their settlement, only one thing saved the Virginia colonists from failing altogether: growing tobacco for sale. When the Virginian John Rolfe developed a new, milder variety of this weed in 1613, tobacco quickly became a hit in Europe. Because it caused a sensation of "besottedness," or drunkenness, they called tobacco the "sot-weed."

Tobacco soon became the foundation of the colony's economy. In 1616, Virginians sent 2,500 pounds of the weed to England; by 1640,

An engraving published in England in 1619 promised potential immigrants leisurely hunting and fishing as well as abundant food in Virginia.

Enrichment
Ask students to create an advertisement designed to attract young Englishmen and women to indenture themselves for passage to the Virginia Colony. Students should review the section for information about conditions in England before deciding how best to "sell" Virginia to the English.

In Depth

Did You Know?

John Smith's iron will and his ability to make friends with the Native Americans was crucial to the success of the small Jamestown settlement. According to legend, Smith was saved from execution at the hands of Powhatan's warriors by the chief's young daughter, Pocahontas. She also brought food to the hungry settlers and was, according to Smith, "the instrument to preserve this Colony from death, famine, and utter confusion." Later Pocahontas married settler John Rolfe, and the two of them took Virginia's first tobacco crop to London.

Interpreting Maps

Roanoke was on an island exposed to the Atlantic Ocean; Jamestown was farther inland, on the James River.

3. ASSESS

Section 2 Review Answers

1. (a) Reformation, see p. 46, (b) joint-stock company, see p. 47, (c) indentured servant, see p. 50, (d) enclosure movement, see p. 50

2. (a) Powhatan, see p. 48, (b) John Smith, see p. 49

3. The English conquered and settled by remaking any culture they conquered rather than forcing it to blend with their own.

4. The Virginia Colony suffered from starvation, disease, poor management, the unrealistic expectations on the part of many early settlers, and constant tension between Native Americans and settlers.

5. Bacon felt that the government composed of newly rich planters acted in conspiracy against the best interests of the public.

6. Answers may suggest that Europeans primarily expected wealth from their settlements in North America. Many also moved to North America to spread the Christian religion or to escape economic conditions brought on by the enclosure movement.

Jamestown and Roanoke Colonies, 1580–1680

Geography and History: Interpreting Maps The Chesapeake Bay area was the first foothold of English settlers on Native American soil. *How did the location of Roanoke differ from the location of Jamestown?*

Virginia and its neighboring colony Maryland (established in 1632 by English Catholics) were sending home 3 million pounds a year.

In order to cash in on the tobacco boom, settlers moved out from Jamestown in the 1610s and 1620s. The gentlemen who owned land established plantations—large farms—along the rivers so that they could grow and transport tobacco more easily. So important was the sot-weed that it became the currency of the colony: people used tobacco leaves like paper money.

Indentured Servants Supply Labor To produce tobacco, planters needed people to work the fields. During the first sixty years after the founding of the colony, they turned primarily to **indentured servants** from England. These were people who had to work for a master for a period of time, usually seven years, under a contract called an indenture. In return for their work, their master paid the cost of their voyage to Virginia and gave them food and shelter. Some indentures promised a piece of land to the servant at the end of the indenture period. Historians

The labor of indentured servants included bundling and packing dried tobacco leaves.

estimate that between 100,000 and 150,000 men and women came as servants to work in the fields of Virginia and Maryland during the 1600s. Most of them were eighteen to twenty-two years of age, unmarried, and poor. ★

Why did these young people take the risk of living in a land that was strange to them? The answer lies in changes taking place in England. The country had recovered from its earlier population decline. During the late 1500s and early 1600s England had more people than it could support. Landowners had found that they could make more money from raising livestock than they could collecting rents from tenant farmers. The landowners forced their tenants to leave and turned fields into pasture, or enclosed them. Many people in Europe lost their homes as a result of this **enclosure movement.** Thus, England was swarming with young people in search of food and work. Called "masterless" men and women because they did not have a master, or employer, they had few other choices besides signing indentures to work for land in Virginia. Why not take a risk in a colony when you had nothing to lose, either there or at home?

Few of the indentured servants lived long enough to claim their land at the end of their service. Exposure to the climate and diseases of the Chesapeake Bay killed them in horrendous numbers. Typical was the complaint of Richard Frethorne, who wrote to his parents in England in 1623, begging them to save him. As Frethorne reported it, one of his fellow Jamestown residents

marveled that you would send me a servant to the [Virginia] Company. He sayeth I had been better knocked on the head, and Indeed so I find it now to my great grief and misery, and saith, that if you love me you will redeem me [pay off the indenture] suddenly [at once], for which I do entreat and beg.

Just as discouraging was the fact that it became harder to make a fortune after the first years of the tobacco boom. Early and wealthy settlers had taken the most fertile and easily accessible land. Property far from water was virtually worthless because transporting crops by land was too expensive.

▶ RESOURCE DIRECTORY

Teaching Resources

★ **Literature Activity** "The Fate of an Indentured Servant," found in the Unit 1 folder, p. 61, uses Englishman James Revel's poem to illustrate the harsh life of indentured servitude.

Bacon's Rebellion In the 1600s, life in the Chesapeake Bay area was brutal and short. Over time, however, as the settlers adjusted to the climate and as the Native Americans were pushed farther west, some wealthier men survived and then thrived as dominant planters. They grew huge amounts of tobacco and plowed the profits into buying more land and servants.

A governor appointed by the English king served the interests of this new class of rich planters. Eventually both the rich planters and the government failed to respond to the needs of the less powerful in Virginia society. On the western frontier of Virginia, the zone of interaction where the land controlled by European settlers pressed against land still controlled by Native Americans, violent conflicts continued throughout the 1600s. In 1676 one planter, Nathaniel Bacon, raised an unauthorized force to drive the Native Americans farther west and take their land. He and his followers were frustrated because the best tobacco land had been already taken by the wealthy.

The Virginia governor William Berkeley gathered an army to stop Bacon. When this happened, Bacon changed his plans and attacked Jamestown instead. The colonial government, as well as the English king Charles II, was horrified to see this group of disgruntled planters win the support of large numbers of indentured servants who also wanted a chance for wealth. In a manifesto, or statement of intent, Bacon branded the government of newly rich planters a "cabal," or secret conspiracy, acting against the best interests of the public.

For several months the government and the rebels struggled for control of the colony. Only Bacon's sudden death by dysentery cut short one of America's earliest violent protest movements. The "cabal" Bacon detested remained in power, and the English king reasserted government control over the colony.

Thus, in both Virginia and Maryland, power remained in the hands of a small group of planters who owned the best land and occupied the seats of government. In the aftermath of Bacon's Rebellion, this elite group grew even stronger. Those in power saw that they needed a more controllable source of labor—human beings who would never be allowed a chance to achieve their freedom, own a piece of land, or challenge the government. They wanted enslaved people instead of indentured servants. Accordingly they began to buy enslaved West Africans brought across the Atlantic Ocean by slave traders. As discussed in Chapter 3, these enslaved Africans had a major effect on the culture and economy of the Southern Colonies, beginning in the 1700s.

The Chesapeake Bay area altered dramatically during the 1600s. It changed from a land of thriving Native American villages to one of increasingly wealthy English settlements. Instead of being a region where Native Americans lived off a broad variety of natural wealth, it became a region where the wealth of the English settlers was built on one crop—the tobacco weed. As the next section shows, Europeans moving into Native American land in northern regions would choose other resources on which to build new wealth for themselves.

Nathaniel Bacon, shown above, declared that he meant "not only to ruin . . . all Indians in General but all Manner of Trade and Commerce with them."

SECTION 2 REVIEW

Key Terms, People, and Places
1. Define (a) Reformation, (b) joint-stock company, (c) indentured servant, (d) enclosure movement.
2. Identify (a) Powhatan, (b) John Smith.

Key Concepts
3. Describe the English pattern of conquest and settlement.

4. Why did the Virginia Colony nearly fail?
5. Why did Bacon and his followers turn against the government of Virginia?

Critical Thinking
6. **Identifying Central Issues** North America was a difficult, dangerous place for both the Spanish and the English. Why did they want to move there?

Quiz found in the Unit 1 folder, p. 43, covers the main ideas in this section as well as the key terms.

The Decision to Use Enslaved Africans for Labor

Focus Few decisions have affected the history of the United States as completely as the decision to use enslaved Africans for labor in the Virginia Colony. This was not a decision made once by a central authority. In the late 1600s, individual planters in the Chesapeake Bay area chose to buy enslaved Africans. Their decisions contributed to a number of future events that shaped the country. This decision about labor changed the population and culture of our country, led us into a Civil War, a period of bitter Reconstruction, and an ongoing movement for civil rights that spread from African Americans to other groups in our society. Students are asked to evaluate the decision to purchase enslaved Africans and to recognize some of the assumptions of the planters who made it.

Instruct Tell students that the first Africans in the Virginia Colony were treated as indentured servants, in part because they had Spanish names and were thought to have been baptized into Christianity.

As you read the following list of factors, ask students to indicate to what extent they think each added to the likelihood of establishing slavery:

• West Africans did not speak English.
• West Africans were immune to European diseases.
• West Africans could survive in semi-tropical climates.
• It cost less to purchase and support enslaved Africans than to bring indentured servants from England.
• American colonists did not respect Africans or their culture.

Ask students to explain their reasoning.

Extend You might ask students to propose alternatives to using enslaved Africans in the Virginia colony. What other crops might they have planted? What else could they have done with the land?

The Decision to Use Enslaved Africans for Labor

Time Frame:	Mid to late 1600s
Place:	The Chesapeake Bay area
Key People:	English gentlemen planters
Situation:	In the 1600s, planters in the Chesapeake Bay searched for a steady source of labor to work their fields. Their decision about where to obtain that labor would have a profound effect on the future United States.

To English colonists in early Virginia, the possibilities for making money seemed almost limitless. They had nearly all of what we now call the three factors of production. Backers in England had put up one of these factors, the investment money, or capital, needed to begin the settlement. Virginia offered the second, abundant land. Only one factor was missing: someone to do the work of clearing forests, plowing fields, and harvesting crops.

Labor Options

As gentlemen, the planters had no intention of performing physical labor, since in the social structure with which they were familiar, such labor was a badge of lower social status. They wanted to create a society in which they could live off the labor of others.

Nor did the planters consider simply hiring workers, the way we would today. The notion of laborers working for a certain number of hours for a wage is a fairly modern one. People in the 1600s generally did not view labor itself as something that could be bought or sold.

What other choices did the planters have? In the beginning, they planned to use Native Americans. They knew that the Spanish had successfully forced Native Americans to work in mines to the south. Moreover, Native Americans already were living in Virginia and

knew the land and climate. The English had great confidence in their ability to persuade Native Americans to work for them in exchange for the advantages offered by the supposedly superior civilization of Europe.

Another potential source of labor was indentured servants from England. They proved inexpensive, because disease and grim working conditions killed close to two thirds of them before they could take possession of the land promised in their indentures.

Planters discovered a third option when a ship landed a group of enslaved Africans in Jamestown in 1619, an event that is depicted in the painting below. But it was not an option they seized on immediately. Forty years later, fewer than 1,700 Africans lived in Virginia and Maryland; sixty years later, in the 1680s, Africans totaled only around 4,000.

Weighing the Choices

The decision about which form of labor to use was not made suddenly and dramatically. Over the decades the choice grew clear. Native Americans demonstrated by an active resistance that they would have no part in the plans of the English. Moreover, European disease soon severely reduced Native American populations, conclusively canceling that option.

▶ RESOURCE DIRECTORY

Teaching Resources

History Might Not . . . Activity The Decision to Use Enslaved Africans for Labor, found in the Unit 1 folder, pp. 50–51, helps students understand the long-term repercussions of colonial economic decisions.

At first, English landowners clearly preferred the second option—English indentured servants. Indentured labor cost landowners little, especially if the servants died young. Furthermore, indentured servants already shared the language and customs of the planters. By contrast, enslaved Africans were expensive to purchase and came from a culture unfamiliar to the English. For this reason slavery contributed such a small part to the Chesapeake labor force that the practice was not legally recognized until 1661.

In the last few decades of the 1600s, however, English gentlemen began to buy large numbers of slaves from Africa. By 1700, there were 20,000 enslaved Africans in Virginia. Another 100,000 were imported by 1750. What brought about this reversal in established practice? Why did so many individual planters make the conscious decision, at approximately the same time, to replace indentured servants with enslaved Africans?

Part of the answer is strictly economic. By the middle of the 1600s, better diets and improved working conditions meant that white servants were living longer—and demanding their promised 50 acres. The high early death rate that had made indentured servitude cheaper than slavery was disappearing. At the same time, many planters were increasingly able to afford enslaved Africans. It became cheaper to buy and support an African laborer for the duration of his or her lifetime than it was to support an indentured servant for seven years and then give him 50 acres.

Part of the reason for the shift was political. Bacon's Rebellion revealed the tensions between rich planters in the Chesapeake area and those who were less fortunate. The gentry began to see enslaved Africans as a more stable and less unruly source of labor than indentured servants.

GOALS	Find a cheap and reliable source of labor to exploit the natural resources of the Chesapeake Bay area.		
POSSIBLE ACTIONS	Use Native Americans	Use English indentured servants	Use enslaved Africans
ADVANTAGES/ DISADVANTAGES	• Difficulty in obtaining and controlling laborers due to resistance • Failure of labor supply due to decrease in Native American population	• In the early and mid 1600s, low cost of labor due to short life of indentured servants; need for constant supply because of high death rate • Ease of communication and interaction due to shared language and customs • In the late 1600s, increased cost due to increased life span • Possible political disturbances	• In the late 1600s, a lower cost than indentured servants to obtain and maintain • Steady supply due to immunity to European disease and hardiness to warm climate • Problems in communication and interaction due to language and customs different from English

They imagined enslaved people simply would become a permanent part of the lower order in the hierarchical society of the colonies. Their assumption was that Africans would never expect their freedom, would never expect any land, and would never expect to have any say in running the colony.

During the 1700s, slavery became well established throughout the English colonies. It had never been inevitable, however. It was a deliberate choice among three options made by powerful men in order to secure their economic and political position.

EVALUATING DECISIONS

1. Why were planters forced to give up the idea of using Native Americans for labor?
2. Why did planters in the Chesapeake Bay area prefer indentured labor in the early years?

Critical Thinking

3. **Recognizing Ideologies** Summarize the key assumptions made by wealthy planters in deciding to use African labor.

Media and Technology

Visions of America: History Might Not Have Happened This Way Game
To encourage students to explore pivotal moments in United States history, have students use the Visions of America software. Refer to the Visions of America Guidebook for viewing objectives, activities, game instructions, and discussion questions.

Answers

1. Native Americans resisted English attempts to use their labor. They were also severely reduced in number by European diseases.

2. Indentured labor was cheaper than slave labor, and indentured servants understood the language and customs of the planters.

3. Answers should include mention of the planters' basic assumption that others should provide them with a living; that Native Americans would benefit from the supposedly superior culture of Europe; and that Africans would take their place in the established hierarchy without protest.

SECTION 3

Europeans and Native Americans in the Northeast

Connecting to the Big Idea

See page 38B. Point out that French, Dutch, and English settlers all established settlements in the Northeast. Ask students how these groups interacted with the Native Americans in the territories they claimed.

Objectives

● Demonstrate that the French and Dutch colonies were based on trade with Native Americans.
● Describe how the fur trade caused war and shifts in power among Native Americans of the Northeast.
● Explain why the Puritans came to North America and describe how they treated those with differing viewpoints.

In Depth

Biography

Jacques Marquette (1637–1675), was sent to the French colonies in North America by the Jesuits. He befriended the Native Americans with whom he lived and quickly learned several of their languages. In 1672, Marquette joined fur trader Louis Jolliet and five traders in mapping a route down the Wisconsin River into the Mississippi River. Marquette and Jolliet sought precious metals as well as a water passage to the Pacific Ocean. When Native Americans told them that the Mississippi emptied into the Gulf of Mexico, not to the west or to the east, they returned north. Marquette and Jolliet are believed to have been the first Europeans to explore the upper Mississippi and parts of Illinois and Wisconsin.

SECTION PREVIEW

The French and Dutch disturbed Native American societies in the Northeast indirectly by exploiting their trading system. By contrast, the Puritans of New England directly challenged Native Americans by trying to completely remake their culture and environment.

Key Concepts

• The French and Dutch colonies, penetrating far into the interior along rivers, were based on trade with Native American groups.
• The fur trade caused war and shifts in regional power among Native Americans of the Northeast.
• The Puritans came to North America to escape religious persecution and build a new society, but they themselves could not accept differing viewpoints.

Key Terms, People, and Places

Great Migration, religious toleration; Samuel de Champlain, Puritans

The English in Plymouth wore shoes like these reproductions as they worked to turn the forests of New England into fields.

T he English were not the only Europeans interested in establishing settlements on the east coast of North America. The French had been exploring the Northeast for decades, looking for trading opportunities. The Dutch soon followed.

The Fur Trade

French settlement enjoyed long-term success only in the north, along what is now the St. Lawrence River in Canada. In 1608, a French explorer, **Samuel de Champlain,** founded the town of Quebec. Perched on heights above a narrow stretch of the St. Lawrence, Quebec was a prime location for a settlement. Not only could traders ship goods easily up and down the river, French soldiers also could readily spot anyone approaching and defend against them.

Champlain was the agent of a French joint-stock company, the Company of New France. His ultimate goal, like that of Columbus, was to find a navigable waterway in order to "reach easily the Kingdom of China and the East Indies, whence great riches could be drawn." But the St. Lawrence River was no route to China—it was a dead end for shipping, and the French could find no precious metals in the wild land of "New France."

The French Pattern of Interaction in North America The St. Lawrence River served another purpose, however. Unable to uncover riches like those the Spanish had found in Central and South America, the French, like the English in Virginia, sought another way to make a profit. They found it in the fur trade. Deer and beaver skins became their tobacco. But the fur trade did not require elaborate farms or towns. Rather, it depended on forming trading ties to Native American hunters and trappers, on leaving the forests and streams that formed the animals' natural habitats alone, and on shipping over natural water routes.

By the late 1600s, New France was essentially a long, narrow colony extending far into the interior of what is now Canada, along the St. Lawrence and the Great Lakes. (See the map on page 55.) French colonists were few in number, in part because France was generally prosperous at this time. Almost all of the colonists were men. They tended to congregate in towns such as Quebec and Montreal. Many acted as traders operating between the Native Americans who trapped animals for their skins and European merchants who resold the skins to be

---

RESOURCE DIRECTORY

Teaching Resources

Reproducible Lesson Plan found in the Unit 1 folder, p. 38, provides a summary of the Section 3 lesson plan content.

Alternate Lesson Plan: Critical Thinking Activity Distinguishing Fact from Opinion, found in the Alternate Lesson Plans folder, p. 9, is designed to enhance students' application of this skill by identifying facts and opinions in the textbook and their own writing.

Guided Reading and Review found in the Unit 1 folder, p. 44, provides a structure for reading and mastering the key concepts and reviewing the key terms for Section 3. (Guided Practice)

Primary Source Activity Native American Customs, found in the Unit 1 folder, p. 60, uses an excerpt from settler John Lawson's *History of North Carolina* (1709) to enhance students' understanding of Native American traditions.

made into hats and other items. Because the French depended on Native American trapping, Native Americans in areas of French contact remained more powerful than those in Virginia.

The Dutch Pattern of Interaction The Dutch, from the Netherlands, had a similar experience in the Northeast. In 1621 they had formed the Dutch West India Company to develop trading opportunities in the Americas. From the beginning, the company envisioned its colony of New Netherlands as a commercial outpost. Dutch settlers established New Amsterdam (now New York City) in 1626 to control the fur trade along the Hudson River. Later, Fort Orange (Albany), founded in 1624, became the center of the trade with the Native Americans.

The Dutch established connections with Native American trade in much the same way the Europeans linked up with existing trade in West Africa. The Dutch were less interested in conquering Native Americans or in transforming the countryside than in simply obtaining furs by trade. As the Dutchman Adriaen Van der Donck pointed out in 1655:

> The country is well calculated [well formed] *and possesses the necessaries for a profitable trade. First, it is a fine fruitful country. Secondly, it has fine navigable rivers extending far inland, by which the productions of the country can be brought to places of traffic. The Indians, without our labour or trouble, bring to us their fur trade, worth tons of gold, which may be increased, and is like goods found.*

Native Americans Interact with Europeans in the Fur Trade The fur trade tied the Native Americans of the Northeast into the commerce of the Atlantic World. They produced furs for European markets and became eager consumers of European goods, including guns, cloth, and jewelry. In New France, they interacted with Catholic missionaries, adopting and adapting Catholic rituals as they saw fit.

Along with new ways of trading and worshiping, the Europeans also brought the ravages of disease to the Native Americans. Because it was a Native American custom in the Northeast

to capture members of other groups to adopt into shrinking lineages, wars grew more common as disease took its toll. Native American groups also fought one another over hunting grounds, since the number of furs they took determined how much of the new trade they could control.

One group, the Iroquois, was particularly successful at both war and trade. They lived in what is now New York state between the Hudson River and Lake Erie. In the mid- to late 1600s, the Iroquois engaged in a series of struggles called the Beaver Wars. In the end, they pushed

Wampum belts, made of beads of shell, served as currency in the trade between Native Americans and Europeans. This one belonged to an Iroquois.

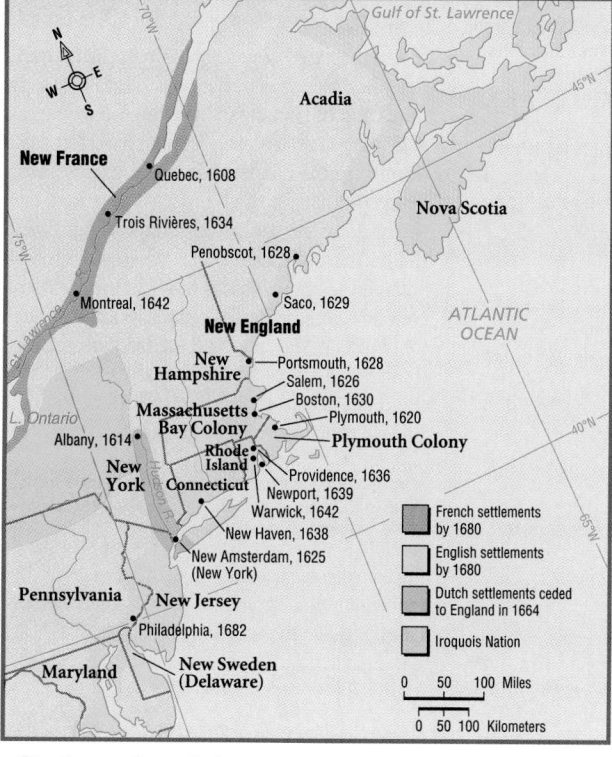

Northeast and Middle Colonies Before 1680

Legend:
- French settlements by 1680
- English settlements by 1680
- Dutch settlements ceded to England in 1664
- Iroquois Nation

0   50   100 Miles
0 50 100 Kilometers

Geography and History: Interpreting Maps
Native Americans and Europeans quickly became dependent upon one another. While Native Americans controlled vast stretches of woodland, European settlement was at first limited to coastal and river areas. *How did the location of the Iroquois help make them powerful?*

Explain/Discuss

Lead a discussion comparing the aims of the three groups of colonists in the Northeast. Why were the French in New France? the Dutch in New Netherlands? the Puritans in Massachusetts Bay?

Ask students to discuss why the French and Dutch had reasonably good relations with Native Americans, while the Puritans provoked resentment. What unintended harm did Europeans bring to Native American societies?

Answer to . . .

MAKING CONNECTIONS

In both West Africa and North America, European trade led to warfare and a decrease in and displacement of populations. Encourage students to compare the effects of European trade at these opposite ends of the Atlantic World.

In Depth

Interdisciplinary

Laws of every society reflect the attitude of its members. The early colonists were no exception. For example, in South Carolina in the seventeenth century, stealing someone else's slave was punishable by death; killing a slave was punishable by a fine. No one could sell or give a good hoe or a good dog to Native Americans in Virginia in 1619. Here are some examples of early Puritan laws:

• No garment could be made with short sleeves "whereby the nakedness of the arm may be discovered." (Massachusetts, 1639)

• No worldly labor, games, hunting, shooting, horse racing, or social gatherings were permitted on Sunday. (New York, 1685)

By the time this painting was made, about 1650, the English had taken New Amsterdam from the Dutch, renaming it New York.

the Hurons and other Native American groups out of their homelands to an area west of the Great Lakes.

As the map on page 55 shows, the Iroquois occupied the area between the French to the north and the Dutch and the English to the east and south. The Iroquois were in a perfect position to tip the balance of power among European colonists in the Northeast. For instance, the Iroquois were allies of both the English and the Dutch even after 1633, when the English entered the region that is now Connecticut and New York and began to compete with the Dutch for control of the area. And the Iroquois retained their powerful position into the early 1700s, finding it easy to accept the transition when the English took over New Netherlands completely.

MAKING CONNECTIONS

In what ways was the impact of European trading on West Africa similar to the impact of the French and Dutch fur trade on Native American culture in North America?

Puritans in New England

In 1630, while the French and Dutch were building trade links with Native Americans, the **Great Migration**—a wave of English migration across the Atlantic Ocean—began to reach the shores of New England. Immigrants had come to New England before then—the most familiar today is the group known as the Pilgrims, who settled at Plymouth, Massachusetts, in 1620. The Pilgrims, however, numbered only 102 people when they landed. By contrast, a total of one thousand settlers braved the Atlantic crossing in 1630 to found the new Massachusetts Bay Colony. By 1643 the colony's population had increased to 16,000 people living in twenty towns, including its capital, Boston.

These colonists left England for many reasons. Sometimes they desired to improve their financial circumstances. More often, however, they longed for a new form of society and feared religious persecution, or harassment, in England.

Most of these people were **Puritans,** members of the Protestant Church of England who wanted to reform, or purify, the Protestant church from within. They disliked the Church of England's reliance on a hierarchy of bishops, highly decorated churches, and elaborate worship ceremonies. They preferred to study the Bible, listen to sermons, and closely examine their lives and their world for clues to God's will.

They found one such hint of God's plan in the social unrest and economic depression of England in the early 1600s, which was the result of many causes, including population growth. To the Puritans, this unrest proved that England had fallen from God's favor, and suggested that they must create a totally new society.

RESOURCE DIRECTORY

Teaching Resources

⭐ **Visual Learning Activity** The Pequot War, found in the Unit 1 folder, p. 65, presents a drawing from 1638 that will enhance students' understanding of the settlers' battle with the Pequots of Connecticut.

⭐ **Literature Activity** Puritan Poetry, found in the Unit 1 folder, pp. 62–63, enriches students' understanding of Puritan beliefs by contrasting the poems of Anne Bradstreet and Edward Taylor.

The Transformation of New England

To accomplish their goals, some Puritans migrated to New England and transformed its landscape. They replaced forests with fields, cultivated wheat, barley, and corn, and raised domestic animals like cows and pigs rather than relying on wild deer or beaver. One settler, Samuel Maverick, commented in 1660 that

I n the year 1626 or thereabouts, there was not a Neat Beast [cow] Horse or sheep in the Country and a very few Goats or hogs, and now it is a wonder to see the great herds of Cattle belonging to every Town.

✪ Not only did the Puritans try to transform the land, they also attempted to remake Native Americans in their own image. They convinced about one thousand Native Americans to adopt Puritan religious beliefs and customs and live in fourteen "praying towns." But these English versions of *congregacions* only scrambled the self-image of Native Americans. In the praying towns, for example, Native American men were forced to farm—a task that in their society was defined as belonging to women.

The Puritan Community The term *Puritan* has come to be associated with cheerlessness and hypocritical morality. Contrary to this inaccurate image, Puritans were people capable of affection and merriment as well as religious devotion. They did, however, insist that social order begins with personal order.

Puritans generally migrated as traditional households. They frowned on people who wanted to live alone. Similarly, they insisted that everyone in a community attend the same church and pay taxes to support it. Well-ordered families in well-ordered towns in well-ordered colonies: that was the Puritan ideal. ✪

John Winthrop, governor of the colony of Massachusetts, summarized the attitude of New England settlers in a speech of 1630. To succeed, he said,

W e must be knit together in this work, as one man. We must entertain each other in brotherly affection. . . . We must

Using Historical Evidence David, Joanna, and Abigail Mason posed for this portrait about 1670. Like other Puritan children, they could expect to live twice as long as children in colonies where life was harder. *What evidence of prosperity do you see in this painting?*

delight in each other; make other's conditions our own; rejoice together, mourn together, labor and suffer together. . . . For we must consider that we shall be as a city upon a hill. The eyes of all people are upon us.

In many ways, the New England settlers were successful. They worked hard, took care of themselves, and lived long lives. Children born there had at least double the life expectancy of someone in Virginia. By 1700, the region was home to over 93,000 people living relatively comfortable lives. But the society they created was not as ordered as they had hoped. Dissent soon intruded on their "city upon a hill."

As part of their attempt to control their community, Puritans passed laws against clothing like these gloves, worn by a Massachusetts governor.

Dissent from the Community The Puritans did not believe in the principle of **religious toleration**—the idea that people of different religions should live in peace together. They had come from England in part because they were unable to tolerate other religious beliefs. It was not surprising,

Analyze

Have students consider the concept of "balance of power" and how the Iroquois used it to deal with the European settlements in their area.

Activity
Teaching Heterogeneous Groups

The new settlers' choice of primary occupation and industry influenced their relationship with Native Americans. For example, because the French were trapping and trading fur, an activity the Native Americans also pursued, they experienced fewer conflicts with the Native Americans than did the English, whose agricultural settlements interrupted the Native American way of life. Have groups of four students choose an industry to be introduced into their community and list three ways it would alter their present way of life. You might want to create a list of industries, similar to and different from those already in your community, for students to choose from.

LEP

Enrichment

Ask students to research and report on the Iroquois League, or Iroquois Confederacy, specifically its origin and effect on Iroquois life.

Caption Answer to ...

Using Historical Evidence

Well-made clothing, probably of expensive cloth; accessories, such as the cane and jewelry.

3. ASSESS

Section 3 Review Answers

1. (a) Great Migration, see p. 56, (b) religious toleration, see p. 57

2. (a) Samuel de Champlain, see p. 54, (b) Puritans, see p. 56

3. The French and Dutch depended heavily on the fur trade, which required furs to be shipped from the interior of the continent over natural water transport routes.

4. The Iroquois occupied the area between the French to the north and the Dutch and English to the east and south. Because of this location, they were able to control the fur trade and choose their trading partners from among their European neighbors.

5. Some Puritans were drawn to New England by a desire to improve their financial circumstances. More often, however, they were driven by a longing for a new form of society and a fear of religious persecution, or harrassment, in England.

6. Rather than adopting the Spanish practice of forcing Native Americans to blend with their culture, the French chose to live in exclusively French colonies. Like the Spanish, the French established religious missions in their colonies.

Reteach

Ask students to imagine that they are writing a feature article for a European newspaper in the 1600s. Ask them to write at least three questions for interviews with a typical fur trader from New France, a merchant from New Netherlands, a Puritan farmer from Massachusetts Bay Colony, and an Iroquois leader. At least one question for each subject should focus on the future of the European settlements.

4. CLOSE

Reinforcing the Big Idea

The French, Dutch, and English created different types of settlements in the Northeast. The Dutch and French exploited the trading system of the Native Americans, while the English tried to transform Native Americans and their culture. The next section describes how the expression of Native American resistance in King Philip's War marked a turning point in history.

---

then, that they punished dissidents—people who disagree with a political or religious system. One such dissident, Roger Williams, was forced to move out of Massachusetts in 1635; he founded what is now Rhode Island, which soon became a center for religious exiles. A few dissidents were hanged, including Mary Dyer, a Quaker woman who had continued to preach in the colony after she was legally banished. Similar suspicion led the Puritans to hang fourteen women and five men for witchcraft in Salem, Massachusetts, in 1692. But the Puritans saw one of the greatest threats to their community not in other religious groups or in witchcraft, but in a dissident Puritan, Anne Hutchinson.

This engraving from the 1800s captures the calm defiance of Anne Hutchinson asserting her right to worship as she saw fit.

AMERICAN PROFILES
Anne Hutchinson

Born in England in 1591, Anne Marbury married a wealthy merchant named William Hutchinson in 1612 and bore fourteen children (twelve of whom survived infancy) over the three decades of their marriage. In 1634, the Hutchinson household—a wealthy, stable unit—migrated to Boston to escape heavy taxation in England and join others of the Puritan religion.

Before she left England, Hutchinson had become a devout follower of the Reverend John Cotton, who preached that the congregation of a church should control it, not leaders appointed by the king and the church hierarchy. Soon Hutchinson went beyond Cotton's position. She saw little sense in obeying the authority of the church if she felt it was in conflict with her

understanding of what God wanted her to do. In her Boston home, critics of the government of Massachusetts governor John Winthrop gathered, as did groups of women interested in studying the Bible. The Puritan authorities felt threatened by these activities and called Hutchinson to trial in November 1637 to explain her actions.

Hutchinson skillfully defended herself with references to law and scripture. She proved to be more than a match for her chief accuser and judge, the learned Governor Winthrop. Still, the judges objected to her claim that her own relationship with God could override the authority of Puritan laws and leaders. The court, declaring Hutchinson "unfit for our society," banished her from the colony.

Early the next year, the Hutchinsons left for land on Narragansett Bay in what is now Rhode Island. In 1642, after the death of her husband, Hutchinson and her remaining family moved on to New Netherlands, where the Dutch promised religious tolerance. In the early fall of 1643, she and her family were killed, victims in a war between the Dutch and Native Americans on Long Island.

Thus Anne Hutchinson, though originally part of their own culture, proved intolerable to the Puritans. If the Puritans could not endure her different ideas, how could they learn to live with those among them who belonged to a different culture, the Native Americans? As the next section shows, the clash between Puritan and Native American ways of life soon went beyond accusations, trials, and exile. It became open warfare.

SECTION 3 REVIEW

Key Terms, People, and Places
1. Define (a) Great Migration, (b) religious toleration.
2. Identify (a) Samuel de Champlain, (b) Puritans.

Key Concepts
3. Why did the French and Dutch depend heavily on the rivers of the Northeast?
4. Explain how the Iroquois were able to tip the

balance of power in the Northeast.
5. Why did the Puritans migrate from England to the Northeast?

Critical Thinking
6. **Making Comparisons** How did the French pattern of interacting with Native Americans differ from the Spanish pattern? How was it similar?

RESOURCE DIRECTORY

Teaching Resources

Quiz found in the Unit 1 folder, p. 45, covers the main ideas in this section as well as the key terms.

Using Time Lines

Time lines are visual presentations of events in the order they occurred. When studying history, seeing events set out in chronological order can help you understand the events and their relationship to each other.

In the seventeenth century, Europe's major powers were greatly interested in North America. By the early 1600s, the Spanish, English, French, and Dutch were scrambling to establish colonies there and fighting to secure their claims against rivals—both European and Native American.

The two time lines below set out in chronological order several events that occurred during this period. The upper one, a standard time line, covers major events within a broad time frame. The condensed time line, the lower of the two, works something like a microscope. It magnifies a short time segment from the standard time line and deals with just one subject—in this case, the French explorer Samuel de Champlain.

Practice using and comparing the two types of time lines by following these steps.

1. Identify the time period covered by each time line. Study the time lines to discover the span of history each covers. (a) What are the earliest and the latest dates shown on the standard time line? (b) How many years are covered by the standard time line? (c) What are the earliest and the latest dates on the condensed time line? (d) How many years does the condensed time line cover?

2. Determine how each time line has been divided. Time lines are divided into equal periods of time, such as 10-year, 25-year, or 100-year intervals. (a) Study the dates on the standard time line below. Into what intervals is this time line divided? (b) Into what intervals is the condensed time line divided?

3. Study the time lines to see whether events might be related. Explore the possible relationship between events on the two time lines. (a) When did hostilities between the French and the Iroquois begin? (b) How long did the hostilities last? (c) What events on the time lines help explain why the Dutch and English settlers both allied themselves with the Iroquois?

Historian's Toolbox Activity Using Time Lines, found in the Unit 1 folder, p. 56, uses a time line of significant events during the cold war (1945–1992), to assist students in the application of the skill, and serves as a guide to international relations today.

King Philip's War: A Turning Point in History

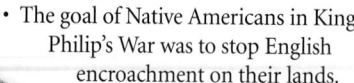

King Philip's War: A Turning Point in History

1. FOCUS

Connecting to the Big Idea

See page 38B. Explain that in 1675, Native Americans in New England fought back against English settlers in King Philip's War. Ask students what the results of the war were for settlers and for Native Americans.

Objectives

● Define the goal of Native Americans in King Philip's War as the cessation of English encroachment on their lands.
● Describe the terror and violence of King Philip's War.
● Identify the major result of the war as an end to the equal balance of power between Native Americans and English settlers.

Bellringer

Propose the following hypothetical situation: Students from another part of the community suddenly arrive at your school and take over the cafeteria, classrooms, library, gymnasium, and so on. Ask students to think about how they would react to such encroachment. Then ask students how the encroachment of English colonists might have affected relations between them and the Native Americans.

Reading Strategy

Question Writing Ask students to turn each of the section's headings and subheadings into a question. Have them then skim the text to answer these questions before reading the section.

SECTION PREVIEW

Faced with the destruction of their way of life, Native Americans in New England fought back against English settlers in 1675. The war only shattered the strength of Native Americans and settlers alike, however.

Key Concepts

• The goal of Native Americans in King Philip's War was to stop English encroachment on their lands.
• King Philip's War brought terror and violence to both Native Americans and the English.
• The conflict put a permanent end to an equal balance of power between Native Americans and English settlers.

Key Terms, People, and Places
sachem; Metacom

Native Americans fought on both sides in the war that sprang up in 1675. This medal was presented to those who helped the English.

Thursday, June 24, 1675, was a day of prayer for the people of Swansea, in the Plymouth Colony of Massachusetts. They had gathered in the Baptist church in the center of their village, hoping that prayer would avert a war between the English settlers and their Native American neighbors, the Wampanoags. But even while they prayed, war was beginning not far away.

On one of the Swansea farms an old man and a boy had discovered some Wampanoags of the Pokanoket group killing the cows in their pasture. The boy took up a musket and fired on the Pokanokets, fatally wounding one. The death of this man, though it must have been tragic to his people, was also a good omen to them. The shamans, or wise ones, of the Wampanoags had foretold that the Native

Americans could succeed in a war against the English only if their enemy fired the first shot.

The Origins of the War

Why had relations between English settlers and Native Americans broken into open hostilities? Many of the settlers at the time blamed one man. His Native American name was **Metacom,** but he has been known in American history by the name the settlers gave him, King Philip; the war itself has become known as King Philip's War. Metacom did not cause the war, however. Although he bore some responsibility for the fighting, he was acting as the leader of a threatened people.

Trade Brings a Balance Like many Native Americans of the 1600s, Metacom had spent much of his life moving between Native American and white society. He was the son of Massasoit, a **sachem,** or leader, of the Pokanokets, who had helped the Pilgrims of Plymouth Colony survive in the first years of settlement. In the years that followed, the Pokanokets and other Native Americans traded furs and skins for English goods and wampum—strings of beads that served as a form of money.

Trade could not erase the basic tension between the two groups. Most Puritans could scarcely see Native Americans as anything but evil savages, whom they believed might well be in league with the devil. Native Americans had a similarly negative view of the Puritans. Furthermore, the Native Americans also were increasingly unhappy with the growing numbers of Europeans on their land and the rapid spread of their settlements.

The Balance Tilts The peace remained uneasy until, in the 1670s, it finally came to an end. By

---

▶ **RESOURCE DIRECTORY**

Teaching Resources

Reproducible Lesson Plan found in the Unit 1 folder, p. 39, provides a summary of the Section 4 lesson plan content.

Alternate Lesson Plan: Cooperative Learning found in the Alternate Lesson Plans folder, p. 10, is designed to guide groups of students in a discussion of King Philip's War.

Guided Reading and Review found in the Unit 1 folder, p. 46, provides a structure for reading and mastering the key concepts and reviewing the key terms for Section 4. (Guided Practice)

that time some 45,000 English people were living in about ninety towns in the New England area; they were destroying forests, putting up fences, and creating pastures for their cattle. All of these actions threatened the livelihood of the Native Americans. The Native American groups in the Northeast, many of whom belonged to the Algonquian culture like the Wampanoags, lived by hunting game, gathering plants for food, and growing crops. This way of life required sixteen to twenty times as much land per person as the way of life practiced by Puritan farmers. The growing Puritan population was quickly making life more difficult for Native Americans.

"You know," recalled Miantonomo, sachem of the Narraganset people, in 1642,

O ur fathers had plenty of deer and skins, our plains were full of deer, as also our woods, and of turkies, and our coves full of fish and fowl. But these English having gotten our land, they with scythes cut down the grass, and with axes fell the trees; their cows and horse eat the grass, and their hogs spoil our clam banks, and we shall be starved.

Metacom himself expressed his people's dilemma eloquently in a speech he was reported to have made in 1675, at a peace conference held in Rhode Island about a week before the war broke out:

T he English who came first to this country were but an handful of people, forlorn, poor and distressed. My father was then sachem, he relieved their distresses in the most kind and hospitable manner. He gave them land to plant and build upon . . . they flourished and increased. By various means they got possession of a great part of his territory. But he still remained their friend till he died. My elder brother became sachem. . . . He was seized and confined and thereby thrown into illness and died. Soon after I became sachem they disarmed all my people . . . their land was taken. But [only] a small part of the dominion [territory] of my ancestors remains. I am determined not to live [that is, not to simply keep on living] until I have no country.

Using Historical Evidence The motto on the seal of the Massachusetts Bay Colony, designed in 1629, shows an imaginary Native American asking Puritans to come over and help his people become Christians. The seal reflects the Puritans' belief that they should convert Native Americans to Christianity. *How did the relationship between Puritans and Native Americans change between 1629 and 1675?*

MAKING CONNECTIONS

As you read in Section 2, the English enclosure movement had changed the use of land in England, creating masses of homeless and unemployed people. Compare this to the effect of English land use on the Native Americans.

The Course of the War

Minor disagreements between Metacom and Plymouth lit the fuse of war in the spring of 1675. Rallying Native Americans throughout southern New England, the Wampanoags aggressively defended their threatened way of life—much as the Pueblos were doing in the Southwest and the Pamunkeys had done in the Virginia colony.

Mutual Destruction For over a year after that June day at Swansea, Metacom and his people struck the English severely. His allies included groups from Rhode Island to Maine—the Narraganset, Nipmuck, Piscataqua, Kennebec, Ammoscoggin, Pequaket, Ossipee, and many smaller groups. Native American warriors

2. INSTRUCT

Explain/Discuss

Discuss with students the difficulty of a life such as Metacom's, moving between two very different societies that were basically at odds. Ask why Metacom gave up trying to maintain peace. What were the long-term causes of the war?

Students might work in groups to brainstorm possible solutions to the conflicts between the Native Americans and the English. Why were the English not interested in finding such solutions?

Caption Answer to . . .

Using Historical Evidence

Between 1629 and 1675, the relationship changed from one of trade and an uneasy peace to one of open warfare.

Answer to . . .

MAKING CONNECTIONS

The effect in North America was similar—here the Native Americans were displaced and deprived of their customary means of living in the area.

In Depth

Historical Misconceptions

A popular perception was that Europeans were more "civilized" than Native Americans. After all, the Europeans had guns, sailing ships, and the ability to read and write. Yet in colonial North America, few Native Americans lingered long in European cultures. In contrast, many captured Europeans actually preferred to continue living among Native Americans rather than return to white society. Recorded comments of "white Indians" suggest that they enjoyed the kinship networks and valued the social equality of Native American societies.

Media and Technology

 Visions of America: Turning Point Story To enhance students' understanding of the Turning Point topic, play "Cultures Collide," a story about the contemporary resonances of King Philip's War (length: approximately 4 minutes). This selection can be located on side 1 of the videodiscs. This selection can also be located on videotape 1. Lesson plans for Turning Point stories can be found in the Visions of America Guidebook.

Visions of America: Roundtable Discussion To introduce students to different and differing viewpoints on the Turning Point topic, play all or part of the Roundtable Discussion on "Cultures Collide," remarks by respected historians and social commentators. This selection can be found on side 1 of the videodiscs. This selection can also be located on videotape 1.

Analyze

Ask students how the war ended. Why did Metacom lose the support of some of his followers? Why did the English settlers remain unified?

Activity

Conducting an Interview

Ask students to stage an interview with Metacom in the style of *Meet the Press*. Ask students to write two or three questions for Metacom about King Philip's War. Ask for volunteers to take turns answering in the role of Metacom.

Enrichment

Ask students to read Mary Rowlandson's account of her capture by Native Americans during King Philip's War. Ask students to report on Rowlandson's experiences and on her assumptions about her captors and her life as a Puritan woman. (See page 72.)

Caption Answer to . . .

 Interpreting Maps

It would make surprise attacks easier and defense in general more difficult.

In Depth

Then and Now

By 1675, tuberculosis and smallpox had reduced the southern New England population of Native Americans to about 20,000—against the approximately 50,000 settlers who had displaced them. This put the Native Americans at a disadvantage before King Philip's War had even begun, and one present-day writer regards King Philip's defeat as "America's first war of ethnic cleansing." Today, there are approximately 12,000 Wampanoag living in Massachusetts—many on Cape Cod and on the Gay Head reservation on Martha's Vineyard.

---

destroyed 17 towns, attacked 52 others, and killed close to 2,000 Europeans. In addition, they ruined fields, slaughtered cattle, and kidnapped dozens of people.

At one point during the winter, the Native Americans were operating within 16 miles of Boston. After burning the town of Medfield, they nailed this notice on a post:

> *K*now by this paper, that the Indians whom thou hast provoked to wrath and anger, will war these 21 years if you will. There are many Indians yett. We come three hundred at this time. You must consider the Indians lost nothing but their life: you must lose your fair houses and cattle.

Soon, however, the English went on the offensive, destroying villages and killing or wounding around four thousand Native Americans. They also captured men, women, and children and sold them into slavery in the West Indies. In proportion to the number of people involved and their possessions, no war in American history cost more in lives and property than King Philip's. Unspeakable brutalities were committed on both sides. ⭐

The Settlers Gain the Upper Hand Although in the beginning the destruction was mutual, as time went on the sheer numbers of the English began to prevail. While the English settlers were united by common language and customs, Metacom was having difficulty keeping his loose alliance of Native American groups together. Furthermore, in a twist that was typical of the shifting power alignments during these early years of interaction between Europeans and Native Americans, the English were able to enlist other Native Americans on their side.

The decisive blow came from the west. Metacom traveled with four hundred men to the Hudson River Valley to obtain weapons and to recruit other Native American allies. The Mohawks of the area, however, were more interested in protecting their trade with New

King Philip's War, 1675–1676

Geography and History: Interpreting Maps
Attacks on English settlements during King Philip's War are well recorded in history; the exact locations of Native American villages attacked by English settlers are in many cases unclear. It is known, however, that Native Americans and settlers lived close to one another within the region. *How would the lack of separate regions of control make the war more costly for both sides?*

▶ RESOURCE DIRECTORY

Teaching Resources

⭐ **Visual Learning Activity** A Lasting Stereotype, found in the Unit 1 folder, p. 64, enriches the section content with a colonial drawing of Chief Joseph Brant.

This incident at Hadley, Massachusetts, is one of the legends that grew up around King Philip's War. Supposedly William Goffe, a Puritan hero and fugitive from England, came out of hiding to lead the English against attacking Native Americans. Whether the story is true or not, the engraving reflects the equal nature of the struggle.

York than they were in helping the Native Americans of southern New England. Encouraged by Governor Edmund Andros of New York, Mohawk warriors staged a surprise attack on Metacom's camp, killing over 350 of his men.

In July the English forces hit Metacom hard once more in another camp in Massachusetts. Although the leader escaped, the settlers captured his wife, Wootonekanuska, along with their son, and sold them into slavery (probably in the West Indies). Cotton Mather, a Puritan minister, gloated:

It must be as bitter as death to him to lose his wife and only son, for the Indians are marvelously fond and affectionate toward their children.

Legend has it that when Metacom heard the news he exclaimed, "My heart breaks. Now I am ready to die."

The End of the War

It was dawn of an August day in 1676 when a force of English and Native Americans caught up with Metacom near Mount Hope, Rhode Island. He leapt from his sleeping place and tried to escape, but a shot in the heart brought him down. His enemies then cut off his head and, as was the custom in executions of the time, divided his body into quarters.

The head was sent to Plymouth Colony where the residents publicly displayed it for decades. From his pulpit, Cotton Mather boasted: "God hath sent us the head of Leviathan [a monster] for a feast."

Even after the death of Metacom, the Native Americans' armed struggle against the New England colonies continued for nearly a year in northern New England. When hostilities finally ended, the Puritans' conquest of the region was virtually complete.

SECTION 4 REVIEW

Key Terms, People, and Places
1. Define sachem.
2. Identify Metacom.

Key Concepts
3. What was the goal of Native Americans in King Philip's War?
4. Give three reasons why English settlers won the war.

5. What permanent effect did King Philip's War have on interaction between settlers and Native Americans in New England?

Critical Thinking
6. **Checking Consistency** If the land of New England was able to support so many Europeans, why could it not also support the less numerous Native Americans?

 Quiz found in the Unit 1 folder, p. 47, covers the main ideas in this section as well as the key terms.

 Chapter Test Forms A and B are found in the Unit 1 folder, pp. 66–71.

 Answer Keys found in the Unit 1 folder, pp. 140–160, provide answers to all student activities.

Media and Technology

Transparency
Graphic Organizer, G-3

Guided Reading Audiotape
(English and Spanish)

Computer Test Bank

The Lasting Impact of King Philip's War

Focus King Philip's War weakened both the English and the Native Americans. The war was costly both in lives and property. It also cost both sides in ways that can scarcely be measured. What did New England and our whole country lose in King Philip's War?

Instruct Ask students to evaluate the suffering of both sides after the war. Do students feel one side suffered more than the other? Why?

Ask for volunteers to list the short-term and long-term results of King Philip's War on the chalkboard. Ask students to evaluate these results in terms of their importance to the nation as a whole. Can students identify any of the results as having worldwide importance?

Discuss with students the way in which the story of King Philip's War came to be taught in school. Whose version of the story did most Americans learn? Why was the other side not heard? How do students think Americans came to learn the other side?

Extend Ask students to explore common stereotypes of Native Americans by analyzing and evaluating an old "western" film or by reviewing a book that portrays the conflict between Native Americans and settlers as "savages versus good guys." Ask students to use their knowledge of Native American lifestyles to point out the film's or book's inaccuracies.

The Lasting Impact of King Philip's War

Although King Philip's War ended over three hundred years ago, its aftereffects have rippled through the centuries to our own time. Indeed, these consequences were more like shock waves than mere ripples.

Native American Losses

The immediate cost on the side of the Native Americans was huge. More than half of their population in New England was wiped out. Many died of starvation in the upheaval of the times, if they were not massacred outright or sold into slavery. The Algonquian culture group of southern New England nearly vanished—including the Wampanoags, Nipmucks, and Narragansets.

Without these vital Native American groups, New England became English in fact as well as in name. Furthermore, by robbing later generations of an Algonquian contribution, King Philip's War left American culture poorer in ways that cannot be counted or understood; for when a people and a culture are lost, their absence is heard only as a silence in history.

A Disaster for New England

After King Philip's War, Native Americans were no longer integral to New England society and commerce, as they had been before 1675. Instead, the colonists became dominant. Their unequal position in the region came at great cost, however.

Economic Costs So staggering was the population loss and displacement in New England that even twenty years after the war, all the towns burned by

1775 This painting shows Revere's ride, which was part of the American fight for independence, after years of relying on Britain's protection.

1700	1750	1800

1700s Metacom becomes a stereotype—the grim Native American warrior.

RESOURCE DIRECTORY

Teaching Resources

Turning Point Extension Activity The Lasting Impact of King Philip's War, found in the Unit 1 folder, pp. 48–49, extends students' understanding of the wars between Native Americans and settlers and of the inevitable shift of power in favor of the settlers.

Philip and his allies had still not been reoccupied. Lost people also meant fewer laborers and a failure of economic growth. Crops destroyed, houses torched, tools and goods stolen and displaced—all were further factors in slow recovery after the war. In fact, as a result of New England's war losses, income per person in the region did not surpass the prewar level for over 140 years.

Political Costs These economic injuries crippled New England. Independent before the war, it now became dependent on the support of its mother country. As New Englanders looked to England for leadership and financial assistance, the stresses and strains began that would contribute to the onset of the American Revolution (see Chapter 4).

Scars on a Common Society

In an effort to justify themselves after the war, Puritans promoted the image of the Native American as violent and bloodthirsty. This image became a lasting stereotype during this period.

It was not until the 1800s that people began to consider the Native American point of view. A critic of one of the older histories wrote in 1814:

The events of the war are transmitted to us by a worthy clergyman of the time [Cotton Mather], who dwells with horror and indignation on every hostile act of the Indians, however justifiable, whilst he mentions with applause the most sanguinary [bloody] atrocities of the whites. Philip is reviled as a murderer and a traitor without considering that he was a true-born prince gallantly fighting at the head of his subjects to avenge the wrongs of his family, to retrieve the tottering power of his line [lineage], and to deliver his native land from the oppression of usurping strangers.

Washington Irving, author and critic

In many ways, this stereotype of the cruel Native American was the worst legacy of the war. It was one among several factors that prevented European Americans from forming a truly mutual society with Native Americans.

REVIEWING THE FACTS

1. What permanent losses did King Philip's War inflict on Native Americans?
2. What was the war's long-term political effect?

Critical Thinking
3. **Identifying Alternatives** Philip and English settlers tried to settle their differences at a peace conference shortly before the war. If they had succeeded in doing so, how might that have changed history?

1930s Artist Thomas Hart Benton portrays Metacom as a romanticized dreamer.

1900   1950   2000

1871 Congress ends the process of making treaties with Native Americans; conflict over western lands continues.

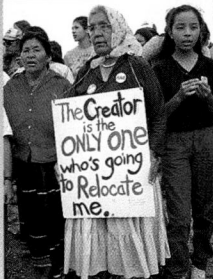

1986 Over 300 years after King Philip's War, relocation of Native Americans continues in the Navaho and Hopi reservations.

Answers

1. More than half of their population in New England was wiped out. Many died of starvation in the upheaval of the times, if they were not massacred outright or sold into slavery. The Algonquin culture group of southern New England essentially vanished. Native Americans were also denied a place as equals in the society of European Americans, because the war perpetuated a stereotype of Native Americans as cruel.

2. Independent before the war, New England became dependent on the support of its mother country. As New Englanders looked to England for leadership and financial assistance, so began the stresses and strains that would ultimately lead to the American Revolution.

3. Students may suggest that an alternative to the war was for English settlers to develop respect for Native American land use—blending Native American practices with their own rather than remaking the environment to resemble England. Such a course of action might have resulted in a more mutual society than was subsequently achieved.

Chapter Review Answers

Understanding Key Terms, People, and Places

Terms
Students should refer to the definitions of the key terms in the chapter to write sentences that show the relation of each word to the interaction between Europeans and Native Americans or to the colonization of the Americas.

True or False
1. false, enclosure movement
2. false, sachem
3. false, hidalgos
4. true
5. false, Great Migration

Matching
1. Popé
2. Samuel de Champlain
3. Metacom
4. Powhatan

Reviewing Main Ideas

1. The *reconquista* established a pattern of conquest and determined how the Spanish would treat people in the Americas. When Spanish Christians moved into Muslim lands in Europe, the two groups traded, intermarried, and borrowed each other's customs. The Spanish expected the outcome of conquest in America to involve a merging of cultures, but with the Spanish culture dominant.

2. The Franciscans were a powerful presence; they established missions to convert Native Americans to Christianity and make them conform to European customs.

3. In 1680, a Pueblo medicine man named Popé organized a successful revolt against the Spanish, whom he blamed for widespread sickness and drought. After the war, it took the Spanish years to reestablish themselves along the Rio Grande.

4. Because of his contact with the Spanish, Powhatan's brother, Opechancanough, had come to despise the goals of European settlers.

5. The English considered farming to be the work of men and hunting an idle sport; in Native American culture, the women farmed while the men hunted. The sturdy houses and fully covered bodies of the English, however, seemed ridiculous to Native Americans accustomed to the Chesapeake's mild climate.

Chapter Review

Understanding Key Terms, People, and Places

Key Terms
1. conquistador
2. hidalgo
3. colony
4. *encomienda* system
5. presidio
6. *congregacion*
7. Reformation
8. joint-stock company
9. indentured servant
10. enclosure movement
11. Great Migration
12. religious toleration
13. sachem

People
14. Popé
15. Powhatan
16. John Smith
17. Samuel de Champlain
18. Puritans
19. Metacom

Places
20. Jamestown

Terms For each term above, write a sentence that explains its relation to the interaction between Europeans and Native Americans or to the colonization of the Americas.

True or False Determine whether each statement is true or false. If it is true, write "true." If it is false, change the underlined term to make the statement true.
1. As a result of the <u>encomienda</u> system, landowners forced their tenants to leave and turned the fields into pasture.
2. Metacom was the son of Massasoit, a <u>conquistador</u> who helped the Pilgrims survive the first few years in Plymouth Colony.
3. For centuries, Spanish <u>indentured servants</u> looted Muslim cities.
4. The settlers who started Virginia were investors in a <u>joint-stock company</u> called the Virginia Company.
5. A group of one thousand settlers who came to Massachusetts in 1630 began the <u>Reformation</u>.

Matching Review the key people in the list above. If you are not sure of the significance of a person, review it in the chapter. Then choose a name from the list that best matches each description below.
1. the leader of the Pueblo Revolt against the Spanish in 1680
2. the French explorer who founded the town of Quebec
3. the leader who was called King Philip by the English settlers in New England
4. the Pamunkey leader who collected tribute from Native Americans in the Chesapeake region

Reviewing Main Ideas

Section 1 (pp. 40–45)
1. How did the *reconquista* influence the way the Spanish treated people in the Americas?
2. What was the role of the Franciscans in helping the Spanish outposts to succeed?
3. Describe the Pueblo Revolt of 1680.

Section 2 (pp. 46–51)
4. Why did Powhatan distrust the English settlers?
5. What cultural misunderstandings contributed to the tensions between English settlers and Native Americans?
6. Explain how a small number of wealthy landowners came to dominate the Virginia colony.

Section 3 (pp. 54–58)
7. Why was Quebec an ideal location for a settlement?
8. Give two reasons why war became more common among Native Americans of the Northeast.
9. How did the Puritans differ from other Protestants in England?

Section 4 (pp. 60–63)
10. How did Puritans and Native Americans view one another before King Philip's War?
11. According to the text, did the Native Americans or the English cause more destruction? Give examples to support your answer.
12. How did the Mohawks help tip the balance of power in favor of the English?

---

6. As Virginia became a tobacco colony, the gentlemen who owned land established huge plantations along the rivers, forcing the many indentured servants from England to work their fields. After the first boom, it became harder to establish a plantation because the best land was already taken.

7. Because of its location on heights above the St. Lawrence, traders could ship goods up and down the river, and soldiers could readily spot advancing enemies.

8. As European disease took its toll on the Native American population, rivalries developed over adopting captives into shrinking lineages. Native American groups also fought over hunting grounds, since the number of furs they took determined how much trade they controlled.

9. The Puritans disliked English Protestantism's reliance on a hierarchy of bishops, highly decorated churches, and elaborate worship ceremonies. They preferred to study the Bible, listen to sermons, and examine their lives and surroundings for clues to God's will.

1. **Making Comparisons** How did the first English, Dutch, and French settlements differ in their impact on the land?
2. **Identifying Assumptions** Recent historians sometimes offer points of view that differ from the ideas of contemporary observers. For example, what the Spanish called rebellions by Native Americans, modern historians call armed struggles for liberation. What assumptions underlie each of these terms?
3. **Determining Relevance** In the Atlantic World, events on one continent might affect events on other continents in unpredictable ways. What effect did Bacon's Rebellion have on West Africa?

1. **Evaluating Primary Sources** Review the second primary source excerpt on page 57. Observe both the quotation's language and its message. Why would the ideals expressed in this speech contribute to the success of the New England settlers?
2. **Understanding the Visuals** The picture on page 47 shows the sharp contrast between the land settled by the English and the land as yet unsettled by them. Describe the difference.
3. **Writing About the Chapter** Imagine that you have a chance to interview one of the following people: a Spanish conquistador, a Franciscan priest in Florida or New Mexico, Powhatan, a survivor of the first years of Jamestown, a Puritan recently arrived in Massachusetts, Anne Hutchinson, or Metacom. First, make a list of questions you would like to ask.

Next, review the chapter for information to help clarify your character's background. Then write a draft of your character's answers. Revise your interview, making sure that it provides insight into your character and his or her beliefs and struggles. Proofread your interview and draft a final copy.

4. **Using the Graphic Organizer** This graphic organizer uses a tree map to describe patterns of conquest in North America. (a) The graphic organizer shows that the French and Dutch pattern was determined in North America. Where were the Spanish and English patterns determined? (b) What reason for conquest or move for migration is common to all three patterns? (c) On a separate sheet of paper, create your own graphic organizer to describe the Revolt of 1680 and King Philip's War.

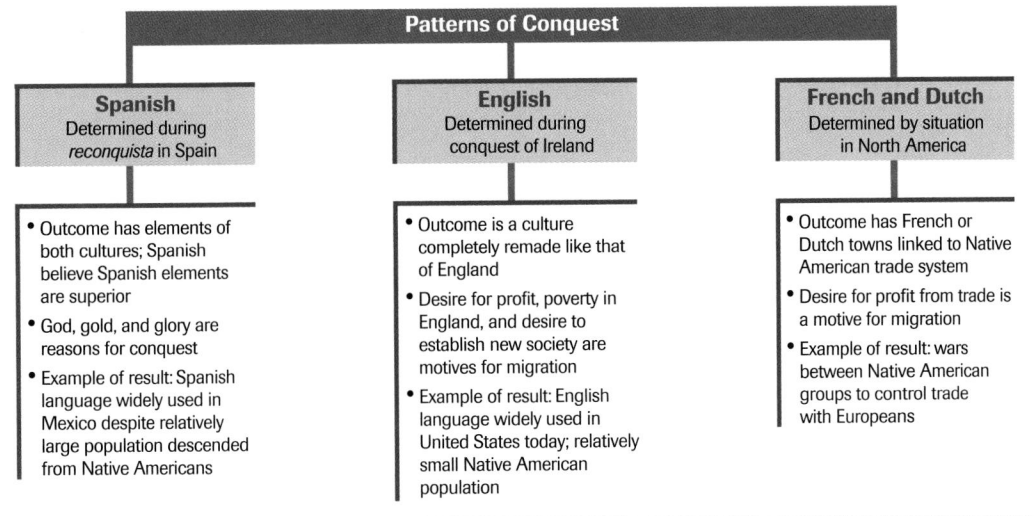

Patterns of Conquest

Spanish	English	French and Dutch
Determined during *reconquista* in Spain	Determined during conquest of Ireland	Determined by situation in North America
• Outcome has elements of both cultures; Spanish believe Spanish elements are superior	• Outcome is a culture completely remade like that of England	• Outcome has French or Dutch towns linked to Native American trade system
• God, gold, and glory are reasons for conquest	• Desire for profit, poverty in England, and desire to establish new society are motives for migration	• Desire for profit from trade is a motive for migration
• Example of result: Spanish language widely used in Mexico despite relatively large population descended from Native Americans	• Example of result: English language widely used in United States today; relatively small Native American population	• Example of result: wars between Native American groups to control trade with Europeans

10. Most Puritans viewed Native Americans as evil savages. Native Americans had a similarly negative view of the Puritans.

11. According to the text, both sides caused equal destruction. Examples include the following: In King Philip's War, Native American warriors destroyed seventeen towns and killed almost two thousand Europeans. They ruined fields and slaughtered cattle. The English destroyed villages; killed or wounded four thousand Native Americans; and captured men, women, and children and sold them into slavery.

12. The Mohawks were more interested in preserving their trade with New York than in helping the Native Americans of New England. They were therefore willing to stage a surprise attack on Metacom's camp.

Thinking Critically

1. The French and Dutch trappers and traders depended on leaving the animals' natural habitats alone and on shipping over natural transportation routes. The English, on the other hand, made a much greater impact on the land—constructing towns, building fences, and raising livestock.

2. The term *rebellion* implies simply a resistance to authority, which the Spanish would have seen as legitimate authority. The phrase "armed struggle for liberation" clearly assumes the legitimacy of the Native Americans' desire to free themselves from Spanish domination.

3. Bacon's Rebellion persuaded planters in North America to turn to slavery. The increased slave trade caused disruptions in West Africa, including war and displacement of population.

Making Connections

1. The speech urges the settlers to work together as a caring community to achieve common goals. It also appeals to their sense of honor by stating that the people of Massachusetts are an example to the rest of the world. Students may point out that the parallel phrasing ("We must...") reinforces the inspirational quality of the message.

2. The settled land has fewer trees; it has houses, fortifications, and shows evidence of activity such as farming.

3. Students should use details in the chapter as well as their imaginations to provide both a context for and information about the character they have chosen. For example, a Puritan might be asked about her reasons for leaving England, her religious and social beliefs, her hopes for the future of the colony, and her views of the Native Americans who share the nearby land.

4. (a) The Spanish and English patterns were determined in Europe. (b) Gold or profit. (c) Students' graphic organizers should indicate differences between the two conflicts in motivation and outcome, as well as other characteristics.

 ## Alternative Assessment

Final Evaluation
Use the following guidelines to evaluate projects:

● **Evidence of outside research** To what extent did students use materials outside the textbook to support their understanding of colonial life?

● **Evidence of comprehension** To what extent did students demonstrate an understanding of life in the early settlements?

● **Evidence of cooperation** To what extent did the efforts of the group enhance the results of the project?

Review with students the mission of the *conquistadores:* to force the Native Americans, including the Pueblos, to adopt the religion, customs, and practices of their Spanish culture. Recall the efforts of the Pueblo people to maintain their own cultural identity. Ask students to cite evidence of the Pueblos' persistence and success in preserving their own culture. (*Revolt of 1680, led by Popé.*) Remind students that this was one of the most successful Native American wars of resistance. In addition to temporarily destroying all signs of Christianity and European culture, it served as a rebirth of ancient Pueblo rituals.

Ask students to examine the examples of Pueblo artifacts presented in the American Album display. Ask what aspects of Pueblo culture are familiar to them. (*Responses will vary by where students live, as well as by their individual experiences.*) Ask students to read the captions and discuss the significance of each artifact for the Pueblo lifestyle, religion, and culture.

Students may note that what eventually evolved was a blending of the Spanish and Native American cultures. One example is the word *pueblo* itself; a Spanish word meaning "town" that is used to refer to both the people and their villages.

You might encourage interested students to research Pueblo life today. Topics for research include working pueblos in New Mexico, such as the Taos Pueblo; pottery making and weaving, for which the Pueblo are so well known; or the ancient rituals associated with religious ceremonies, such as the kachina dance in which people dress up to represent the spirits of earth, sky, and water.

FIRST ENCOUNTERS

The Pueblo people of what is today New Mexico first met Hispanic settlers in 1598. Some in the diverse group of settlers came from Spain. Others came from Mexico and had mixed Spanish and Native American ancestry; a few had African ancestors. As with other encounters between Native Americans and settlers, intolerance and misunderstanding led to conflict and violence. The Pueblo people fought hard against the Spanish to maintain their own cultural identity. *What aspects of Pueblo culture are familiar to you?*

▲ BOWL, MADE AROUND 1500 The Pueblo traded the goods they made, such as this bowl, with peoples from as far away as the coast of California. In return they received a wide range of goods, such as shells, corals, and baskets. The arrival of Europeans disrupted trade among Native Americans and dramatically changed their economy.

◄ SANTA CLARA PUEBLO, ABOUT 1900 The pueblo in the picture retains many features of pueblos built centuries earlier. Stone or adobe houses are grouped around small plazas. Within each plaza is a *kiva*, or ceremonial chamber, that has special significance for different groups within the pueblo.

◄ STORAGE JAR, AROUND 1840
Pottery making was a family activity with special meaning. Mothers and aunts taught children distinctive family styles of making and decorating pottery. Family members created the pots for daily or ceremonial use or traded them to other Native American and Hispanic villagers.

◄ ROCK PAINTING, BEFORE 1700 The Pueblo people staged a revolt in 1680 that drove the Spanish out of New Mexico for twelve years. This painting of a missionary pierced by a lance depicts the revolt and the ongoing conflict between the Pueblo people and the Spanish.

▲ MISSION BELL, ABOUT 1800 The mission bell was a symbol of the life imposed on the Pueblo Indians by the Spanish. The ringing bell guided the highly structured day of work, meals, instruction, and prayer.

▼ RIO GRANDE BLANKET, ABOUT 1880 Blankets of the Pueblo show the influences of both Hispanic and Native American culture.

▲ ARCHANGEL ST. MICHAEL, ABOUT 1775 This Spanish sculpture was made for the church at Zuni Pueblo. While many Native Americans accepted Catholicism, they rarely gave up their traditional beliefs; some Pueblo never converted. The Pueblo and the Spanish soon learned to be more tolerant of each other's culture and religion. Catholic and native religious ways existed side by side.

Chapter 3 The Maturing of Colonial Societies
1689–1754

📁 Teaching Resources (See Unit 1 Folder)

	Instruction	Enrichment
Section 1 **An Empire and Its Colonies** (pp. 72–77)	Reproducible Lesson Plan, p. 73 Alternate Lesson Plan, p. 12 Guided Reading and Review, p. 77 Quiz, p. 78	Literature Activity, The Captivity of Mary Rowlandson, pp. 97–98 American Profiles Activity, Hannah Callowhill Penn, p. 87 Historian's Toolbox Activity, Interpreting an Economic Activity Map, p. 91
Section 2 **Life in Colonial America** (pp. 79–83)	Reproducible Lesson Plan, p. 74 Alternate Lesson Plan, p. 13 Guided Reading and Review, p. 79 Quiz, p. 80	Visual Learning Activity, The First American Schoolbook, p. 100 Literature Activity, As Poor Richard Says, p. 96 Primary Source Activity, A Marriage Agreement, p. 93 Critical Thinking Activity, Identifying Central Issues, p. 92
Section 3 **African Americans in the Colonies** (pp. 84–88)	Reproducible Lesson Plan, p. 75 Alternate Lesson Plan, p. 14 Guided Reading and Review, p. 81 Quiz, p. 82	Visual Learning Activity, Education as a Step Toward Freedom, p. 99
Section 4 **Emerging Tensions** (pp. 89–91)	Reproducible Lesson Plan, p. 76 Alternate Lesson Plan, p. 15 Guided Reading and Review, p. 83 Quiz, p. 84 Chapter Test, Forms A & B, pp. 101–106	Viewpoints Activity, On Expansion into Native American Lands, pp. 89–90 American Profiles Activity, Jonathan Edwards, p. 88 Primary Source Activity, The Great Awakening, pp. 94–95 Time and Place Activity, Changing Economic Patterns in the South, pp. 85–86

📁 Additional Chapter Resources

Resource Organizer, p. 72
Alternate Lesson Plan, p. 11
Answer Keys, pp. 146–160

Bibliography

For the Teacher

Heimert, Alan E., and Perry Miller, eds. *Great Awakening: Documents Illustrating the Crisis and Its Consequences.* Bobbs, 1967. (Primary source material.)

Kaplan, Sidney, and Emma Nagrady Kaplan. *The Black Presence in the Era of the American Revolution.* University of Massachusetts, 1989. (Includes a chapter on the founders of the African Baptist and African Methodist churches.)

Prentice Hall Literature Excerpts from *The American Experience,* 1994, including Edwards, Jonathan. "Sinners in the Hands of an Angry God," from Faust, Clarence H., and Thomas H. Johnson. *Jonathan Edwards: Representative Selections.* Hill and Wang, 1935.

THE BIG IDEA

The Big Idea for the chapter and how the main ideas in each section relate to the Big Idea are graphically displayed below. Comprehension of this chapter's Big Idea is critical to students' understanding of United States history and how we as a nation got where we are today.

Media and Technology

 Time Lines, E-2; Historical Maps, L-1

 Our Multicultural Heritage, C-6; Fine Art, D-3; The Way It Works, H-3

 Our Multicultural Heritage, C-1

 Graphic Organizer, G-5

 Guided Reading Audiotapes (English and Spanish)

 Computer Test Bank

For the Student

Colonial America. C.A.I. Software. Video. (Narrated by eminent historian Henry Steele Commager. Focuses on the Pilgrims' search for freedom of religion.)

Hawthorne, Nathaniel. *The Scarlet Letter.* Silver Burdett Classics, 1985. (A famous novel that draws on sin and guilt in Puritan New England.)

Williams, Selma R. *Demeter's Daughters: The Women Who Founded America, 1587–1792.* Atheneum, 1976. (Discusses the roles, rights, and responsibilities of colonial women.)

CHAPTER 3

The years up to 1754 were a defining period for the American colonies. Varied landforms and climate, a steady stream of immigrants from different regions of the world, and England's own colonial policy of salutary neglect all gave rise to a future hallmark of America: diversity of belief, economy, and people. The American cultural landscape became one defined by distinct and often separate cultures and societies. A spirit of independence spread among the colonists during this period, but it wasn't just independence from England—it was also from each other.

SECTION 1

During the mid-1600s and early 1700s, England paid little attention to its colonies, other than to take their raw materials and sell them finished goods. Perhaps because of this salutary neglect, the colonies grew and thrived.

SECTION 2

Colonial society was organized into a hierarchy. At the top were the wealthy landowners who held most of the power. They were almost always white men. Although women had little legal power, their work was vital to the success of the colonies.

SECTION 3

Enslaved African Americans had no rights at all in colonial America. Conditions for enslaved people varied from region to region in the colonies.

SECTION 4

Patterns of western expansion reflected ethnic divisions in society and further hampered relations with Native Americans. Religious upheaval brought new tensions to the colonies, increasing the threat to social and political order.

The Maturing of Colonial Societies
1689–1754

The Relevance of the Big Idea

During the years 1689–1754, no single society emerged to characterize "the American people." From an economic point of view, diversity helped support colonial society. The small farming and seafaring New England colonies, the commercial Middle colonies, and the agricultural Southern colonies all contributed to growth and prosperity. Colonial society, however, was defined by intolerance, strong class and ethnic distinctions, and inequality among races.

Point out that throughout American history phrases such as *melting pot* have been used to characterize the association of diverse cultures in our society. Words such as *assimilation* and *integration* have been used to promote policies of race relations. Discuss with students how they view American society today. Is it a land where diverse cultures together form a unique whole or where they simply coexist side by side?

In Depth

Global Connections

By the mid-1500s, Spanish rule stretched from Florida to California across the southern part of what is today the United States. In all of the Spanish, as in the English, colonies, the death rate of Native Americans was high enough to be described by some scholars as genocide. Between 1519 and 1605, for example, the Native American population of Mexico and Central America fell from about 25 million to 1 million—they were replaced by slaves from Africa.

The Maturing of Colonial Societies
1689–1754

The scene: The thirteen colonies of Great Britain on the Atlantic coast of North America, in the years between 1689 and 1754. Settlers from Britain, the Netherlands, Sweden, and other European nations, along with enslaved Africans, were finding ways to make a living and live with one another. As they did so, distinct colonial societies emerged. They were not societies that valued or expected equality—instead, the colonists accepted the ideas that power belonged solely to those who owned land and that owning land was a right reserved for only a few.

Events in the United States

1689 New England colonists rebel against Governor Andros.	1702 The colony of Delaware is established.	1712 Enslaved Africans rebel in New York City.

1684	1691	1698	1705	1712

Events in the World

1689 Parliament replaces King James II with William and Mary in the Glorious Revolution.	1700 The Native American population of Central and South America has dropped from 50 million to 4 million.	1707 Last Mogul ruler dies, leaving India weak and divided.	1713 Treaty of Utrecht ends war between France and England.

RESOURCE DIRECTORY

Teaching Resources

Alternate Lesson Plan: Demonstrating the Big Idea found in the Alternate Lesson Plans folder, p. 11, provides a lesson strategy to instruct students in the Big Idea that as the North American colonies grew and matured, they developed new political roles, and distinctive economic and social relationships.

Alternative Assessment Handbook provides information, guidance, and strategies for alternative methods of assessment. It includes an essay on new trends in assessment, guidance and strategies for developing performance tasks and portfolios, scoring rubrics, and sample evaluation forms.

Pages 72–77

An Empire and Its Colonies

For England in the mid-1600s and early 1700s, the colonies were a reliable source of raw materials and a prime place to sell English goods. Like healthy seedlings thriving without a gardener's care, the colonies eventually grew and prospered with little direct interference from the English government.

Pages 79–83

Life in Colonial America

It is a principle of American government today that all people are created equal. When the American colonists in the 1700s considered that idea, however, they found it truly revolutionary. Colonial American society was fundamentally unequal, a world of ranks and privileges that favored the few over the many.

Pages 84–88

African Americans in the Colonies

By 1760, about 325,800 people of African descent lived in the thirteen colonies, nearly all of them enslaved. Although they had no rights in the highly unequal world of colonial America, African Americans actively shaped society from very early times.

Pages 89–91

Emerging Tensions

In the mid-1700s, some colonial Americans began to look westward for more territory, while others challenged the social and political order in a "great awakening" of religious feeling. As a result, new tensions pulled at the fabric of colonial society.

	1730 Enslaved Africans make up 60 percent of the population of South Carolina.	**1734** Revival led by Jonathan Edwards and others brings the Great Awakening to New England.	**1740s** Eliza Pinckney promotes growth of indigo as a cash crop in the South.	**1750** Number of enslaved African Americans in the colonies passes 236,000.

1719	1726	1733	1740	1747	1754

	1726 Gulliver's Travels, *by Jonathan Swift, is published.*	**1736** First successful operation for appendicitis performed.	**1754** First woman doctor graduates from a German university.

An Empire and Its Colonies

SECTION 1

An Empire and Its Colonies

1. FOCUS

Connecting to the Big Idea

See page 70B. Explain that the relationship between England and its colonies in the late 1600s and early 1700s was generally peaceful but distant. Ask students why England purposely neglected its colonies. How did the colonies develop into prosperous but distinct regions?

Objectives

- Define *mercantilism* and explain its consequences for the colonies.
- Explain why England chose to neglect its colonies.
- Identify and describe the economies and societies of the three colonial regions.

Bellringer

Ask students to define the term *empire* as broadly as they can. Encourage students to think about why a country would want an empire. What obligations and responsibilities does an empire bring with it?

Reading Strategy

Reading for Evidence Ask students to find evidence as they read the section to support the statement on page 72 that "... the colonies eventually grew and prospered with little direct interference from the English government."

SECTION PREVIEW

For England in the mid-1600s and early 1700s, the colonies were a reliable source of raw materials and a prime place to sell English goods. Like healthy seedlings thriving without a gardener's care, the colonies eventually grew and prospered with little direct interference from the English government.

Key Concepts

- Although England flirted with the idea of strictly regulating its colonies in order to increase its power and wealth, on the whole it let them develop on their own in the early 1700s.
- As they grew, the colonies in each region developed very different economies and societies.

Key Terms, People, and Places

mercantilism, balance of trade, salutary neglect, Fall Line, triangular trade

Playing their part in trade by buying finished goods from the parent country, customers in the colonies ordered English cloth from this sample book.

I n the late 1600s and early 1700s, England prized its cluster of colonies on the Atlantic coast of North America for two reasons: the colonies were suppliers of food and raw materials, such as tobacco, rice, and lumber, and they were avid buyers of English goods. Although King Philip's War had a long-term impact on New England, especially on Massachusetts, its effect on other colonies was limited, and even New England recovered and grew. Because the colonists were in general loyal to their parent country, England got what it wanted from its colonies—raw materials and a place to sell its goods—by leaving them alone.

Events in England, 1640–1660

During the years from 1640 to 1660, England had another reason for its hands-off approach to the colonies. In the 1640s, tensions that had long simmered in England boiled over in a full-scale civil war. The nation became so preoccupied with conflicts within its own borders that it could pay little attention to its North American colonies.

Two opponents faced off in the clash: King Charles I and Parliament, England's governing body. Parliament, made up of representatives, had the power to make laws and approve new taxes. Many of its members believed that Charles was a corrupt man intent upon limiting the power of English property owners.

After defeating the king's army in a series of battles, Parliament ordered the execution of Charles in January 1649. Until his death in 1658, Oliver Cromwell, the commander of the Parliamentary armies, governed England under the title "Lord Protector." In 1660, after decades of upheaval, Parliament recognized the need for stability and restored Charles II, the exiled son of the executed king, to the throne.

Mercantilism and its Consequences

Before 1650, the people of England were too busy pursuing—and beheading—their king to be concerned with a cluster of small colonies on the other side of the Atlantic. Then England's priorities changed.

A New Theory Takes Hold By 1650, many nations in western Europe were working to improve their economies, spurred on by a new theory called **mercantilism.** This economic theory, when put into practice, was meant to increase a nation's wealth and, with it, its power. This theory had several key elements. It held that a country should try to get and keep as much bullion, or gold and silver, as possible. For England, France, and other countries without mines like those Spain controlled in the Americas, the only way to obtain more bullion was to have a favorable **balance of trade**—that

▶ RESOURCE DIRECTORY

Teaching Resources

Reproducible Lesson Plan found in the Unit 1 folder, p. 73, provides a summary of the Section 1 lesson plan content.

Alternate Lesson Plan: Critical Thinking Making Comparisons, found in the Alternate Lesson Plans folder, p. 12, helps students apply this critical thinking skill, using physical maps and creating economic activity charts of the early colonies.

Guided Reading and Review found in the Unit 1 folder, p. 77, provides a structure for reading and mastering the key concepts and reviewing the key terms for Section 1. (Guided Practice)

Literature Activity The Captivity of Mary Rowlandson, found in the Unit 1 folder, pp. 97–98, uses excerpts from a narrative of one woman's experience during King Philip's War to show some of the prevailing attitudes of the times.

is, to export more goods than were imported. Mercantilist Thomas Mun, writing in 1664, explained the theory this way:

As the treasure [money] *which is brought into the Realm by the balance of our foreign trade is that money which only does abide with us, and by which we are enriched; so by . . . money thus gotten (and no otherwise) do our Lands improve.*

To boost its balance of trade, mercantilists believed, a nation should have colonies where it could buy raw materials and sell products. The colonies should not be allowed to sell products to other nations or even to manufacture goods. The right to make goods for sale was reserved exclusively for the parent country, since manufacturing was a major source of profit. And in order to maintain control over trade and to increase its profit, the parent country required colonies to use its ships to transport raw materials, not their own.

Mercantilism Influences Trade Laws The new theory appealed to English rulers. They came to realize that colonies could provide raw materials, such as tobacco, furs, and perhaps gold, for England to sell to other countries. Furthermore, the colonies could buy England's manufactured goods—for example, its glass, china, and books. This exchange would greatly improve England's balance of trade. Consequently, English leaders decided that it was necessary to have as many colonies as possible and to control colonial trade in order to provide the maximum profit to England.

In 1660 Charles II approved a stronger version of a previous law called the Navigation Act. Together with other legislation, the Navigation Act required the colonies to sell certain goods, including sugar, tobacco, and cotton, only to

England. Moreover, if colonists wanted to sell anything to people in other parts of the world, they had to take the crop or product to England first and pay a duty, or tax, on it; and by law they had to use English ships for all their trade.

Mercantilism Influences War and Politics The effect of mercantilism on the Atlantic World as a whole was that more and more, France, Spain, the Netherlands, and England went to war with each other over territory and trade routes rather than over religion. In the 1500s, for example, Protestant England's major enemy had been Catholic Spain. But from 1652 to 1654, and again from 1665 to 1667, the English fought wars against the Protestant Dutch over control of trade and land in North America. To eliminate the Dutch as a major trade rival in North America, the English conquered the Dutch colony of New Netherland in 1664, renaming it New York in honor of James, Duke of York and brother to King Charles II.

During the next two decades, Charles II and James tried a variety of means to increase their authority over the colonies. Their actions reached a climax in the mid-1680s when James, now king, attempted to take direct control over New York and the New England colonies by

The colonies supplied England with food and raw materials. This detail from a map of 1751 shows tobacco being loaded at a southern dock for shipment to England.

2. INSTRUCT

Explain/Discuss
Underline for students the basic goal of mercantilism: to accumulate as much gold and silver as possible, using foreign trade and colonies to accomplish this task. Discuss England's single-minded economic approach to its colonies. Ask students to explain the purpose of the Navigation Act. (*To bring in more money to the English treasury.*) Why did England adopt a colonial policy of salutary neglect in the 1700s? (*The colonies were benefiting the treasury without large expenditures.*)

Using physical and climate maps, discuss some of the geographical features that helped the colonies to grow into distinct regions. For example, ask students to trace the long rivers of the Southern Colonies and compare them to the rivers of New England. Point out the sea islands and coastal marshes of South Carolina and Georgia, where rice grew well. Compare and contrast the climate of the Middle Colonies with that of the New England Colonies.

Analyze
Analyze the role of the Middle Colonies as a region of tolerance and neutrality between the Anglican plantation colonies of the South and the Puritan colonies of New England. How did the Middle Colonies also take a middle ground in matters of religion and immigration?

Divide the class into teams of students and assign each team one of the following nations: Portugal, France, Spain, England, the Netherlands. Tell students that they will play a game in which the object is to identify as many raw materials as possible that their country may acquire from its colonies in the year 1650. Groups may use a historical atlas and other reference materials to identify their country's colonies and spheres of influence. For each raw material acquired from a colony, a team can score one point. The same item may be imported from more than one colony. The group with the highest number of points wins.

Answer to ...

MAKING CONNECTIONS

Possible answers: Colonists might develop independent institutions and a tradition of operating without interference, making it difficult for the British to assert their authority when they wished to do so.

In Depth

Historical Misconceptions

The Puritans' control over religious affairs in their own colony was amply demonstrated at the Salem witch trials. Accusations were used to punish people who deviated from the established social norms. Historian John Demos, in a study of witchcraft in colonial New England, found that women accused of being witches were most likely to be middle-aged (forty to sixty), married but without children, of low social status, and involved in medical care such as midwifery. Without question, the trials at Salem were extraordinary in their ferocity, but belief in witchcraft went well beyond either religion or the hysteria of a particular time and place.

creating the Dominion of New England. This action abolished colonial legislatures within the Dominion and replaced them with a governor and a council appointed by the king.

The Colonists Rebel Colonists up and down the Atlantic seaboard deeply resented James' grab for power in the Northeast. Edmund Andros, appointed governor of the Dominion by James, made matters worse. He collected taxes without the approval of either the king or the colonists and demanded payment of an annual land tax. He also declared a policy of religious toleration. The Puritans felt these heavy-handed actions were a blow both to their freedom from English influence and to their tight control over religious affairs in their own colony.

Meanwhile, James II was rapidly making enemies in England. News reached North

America in the spring of 1689 that Parliament had replaced James with his daughter Mary and her husband William of Orange, a change of rulers known as the Glorious Revolution. New England citizens promptly held their own mini-rebellion against the Andros government; Bostonians imprisoned Governor Andros and his associates. In response to this colonial protest, William and Mary dissolved the Dominion of New England and reestablished the colonies that James had abolished.

This portrait of James II appears on the handwritten document that created the short-lived Dominion of New England.

Britain's Colonial Policy in the 1700s

In the early 1700s, after Charles and James, the British government rarely tried to interfere directly in the affairs of its colonies. It allowed legislative bodies, such as the House of Burgesses in Virginia or assemblies in other colonies, to gain extensive power over local affairs. Most of these colonial assemblies consisted of an upper house of prominent colonists appointed by the king and a lower house elected by voting landowners. Even in colonies owned by the king in the manner described in

the chart on page 76, laws could not go into effect without the consent of the free men of the colony or their chosen representatives.

Why did the British government allow its colonies such freedom in governing themselves—far more than was found in Spanish or French colonies? Part of the answer lies in the English traditions of strong local government and weak central power; part of it in the fact that the British government lacked the resources and the bureaucracy to enforce its wishes. Then, too, colonists recognized the authority of the king and Parliament without being forced to; most were proud to be British subjects.

Finally, the economy and the politics of the colonists served the interests of Great Britain very well. The British realized that the most salutary, or beneficial, policy was to neglect their colonies. Thus later historians would call British colonial policy during the early 1700s **salutary neglect.** In the early 1700s, Great Britain neglected its trade regulations, such as the Navigation Act, because neglect served its economic interests better than strict enforcement. The colonies prospered, as did their trade with Britain, without much government interference. Meanwhile, the colonies developed ways of governing themselves that were largely their own, and the British government did not have to expend money and soldiers it did not have on enforcing its laws.

MAKING CONNECTIONS

Can you think of ways in which the policy of salutary neglect might backfire on the British and harm their interests in the colonies?

The Expanding and Diverse Economies of the Colonies

The economic foundations of American society were in place by the early 1700s. While the Spanish colonies continued to rely on mining silver and growing sugar, and New France still focused on the fur trade, the British regions of eastern North America—the Southern, Middle, and New England colonies—developed diverse economies.

For the most part, English-speaking settlements continued to hug the Atlantic and the deep rivers that empty into it, as shown on the map on page 77. Most commerce took place on water; it was simply too expensive and too difficult to carry crops and goods long distances over land. Even water traffic on rivers, however, was blocked at the waterfalls and rapids of the **Fall Line**, where the inland hills meet the coastal plain. Roads were little more than footpaths or rutted trails. It was not until the middle of the 1700s that settlers began to move more than a hundred miles into the interior in great numbers. Until then, the Atlantic Ocean remained so vital to travel that there was generally more contact between Boston and London than between Boston and Virginia.

Staple Crops in the Southern Colonies In the Southern Colonies—Virginia, Maryland, South Carolina, North Carolina, and Georgia—the economy was based on growing crops that were in constant demand. Such crops are called staples. In Virginia and North Carolina, the staple crop was tobacco; in the warm and wet coastal regions of South Carolina and Georgia, it was rice. In the early 1730s, these two colonies were exporting 16.8 million pounds of rice per year; by 1770, the number was 76.9 million. Meanwhile, the number of pounds of tobacco exported per year by Virginia, Maryland, and Delaware rose from 32 million in 1700 to 83.8 million in 1770.

Throughout the Southern Colonies, enslaved Africans supplied most of the labor on tobacco and rice plantations. Virginia planters began to purchase large numbers of Africans in the mid-1600s. In 1650, Africans in Virginia numbered only about 500, which accounted for 3 percent of the colony's population. By 1700, enslaved Africans totaled 16,000, or 28 percent of the colony. About 1750, the figure was 40 percent. In South Carolina, Africans outnumbered Europeans throughout the 1700s. In 1730, for example, 60 percent of South Carolina's population was of African heritage.

To produce staple crops, planters needed huge amounts of land and labor but very little else. As a result, the Southern Colonies remained a region of plantations strung out along rivers and coastlines. Except for the cities of Charles Town (Charleston), South Carolina, and Williamsburg, Virginia, the South had few towns and only a small group of people who could be called merchants.

A Mixture in the Middle Colonies From Maryland north to New York, the economy of the Middle Colonies was a mixture of farming and commerce. The length of the Delaware and Hudson rivers and the tributaries that fed them allowed colonists to move into the interior and establish farms on rich, fertile soil. There they specialized in growing grains, including wheat, barley, and rye. This kind of farming was very profitable. Eastern Pennsylvania, full of such farms, was called "the best poor man's country in the world."

But commerce was just as important as agriculture in the Middle Colonies. New York and Philadelphia were already among the largest cities in North America. Home to growing numbers of merchants, traders, and artisans—craftspeople such as printers, bakers, and furniture makers—the streets of these cities teemed with people in the business of buying and selling goods.

In these ports, ships arrived regularly from all over the Atlantic World, carrying immigrants as well as merchandise. Philadelphia became the

The lawmaking assemblies of the colonies—like the Virginia House of Burgesses shown here—continued the English tradition of strong local authority.

In Depth

Did You Know?

By the 1700s, it was said that in the colony of Virginia "the Establishment is indeed Tobacco," because this staple was the crop around which much of Virginia's economy revolved. Clergymen, for example, were paid in tobacco rather than in hard currency. In 1695, the annual salary of a clergyman was legally fixed at 16,000 pounds of tobacco, and the money value of the minister's salary depended solely on the quality of the local crop. Ministers, often recruited from England, were more easily lured to the colony by offers from regions growing the higher-priced "Sweet Scented" tobacco.

Interpreting Tables

One pattern is the prevalence of religious reasons for settlement in the New England Colonies; another is the prevalence of trade in New England and the Middle Colonies.

3. ASSESS

Section 1 Review Answers

1. (a) mercantilism, see p. 72, (b) balance of trade, see p. 72, (c) salutary neglect, see p. 74, (d) Fall Line, see p. 75, (e) triangular trade, see p. 77

2. The Navigation Act required the colonists to sell certain goods only to England; to ship any crop they wished to sell anywhere in the world to England first and pay a duty on it; and to use only English ships for their trade.

3. The British had a tradition of strong local government and weak central power; they lacked the resources and the bureaucracy to enforce their wishes overseas; most colonists recognized the authority of the crown and Parliament without being forced to; and the economy and politics of the colonies served the interests of Great Britain very well the way they were.

 In Depth

Multicultural Perspectives

More than a thousand important bodies of water in the United States still bear Native American names, from the Kennebec River in Maine to the Potomac River in Virginia and Maryland; from Massachusetts Bay (which gave its name to the state) to the Mississippi River and beyond.

The Colonies in America, 1607–1776

Colony	European Settlement	Reason for Settlement	Leaders	Charter[1]	Economic Activities
NEW ENGLAND COLONIES					
Massachusetts Plymouth (1620–1691) **Massachusetts Bay Colony (1630–1691)**	1620	Escape religious persecution Establish a Puritan commonwealth	William Bradford John Winthrop	Mayflower Compact 1620–1621; joint-stock 1621–1691 Joint-stock 1630–1684; royal 1684–1691 Two colonies merged in 1691; royal 1691	Fishing, lumber, shipbuilding, triangular trade, rum, whaling
New Hampshire **Exeter (1638)**	1623	Profit from trade and fishing Escape religious persecution	Benning Wentworth; John Wentworth John Wheelwright	Proprietary 1622–1641; joint-stock (part of Massachusetts)1641–1679; royal 1679–1776	Trade, fishing
Connecticut	1636	Establish a Puritan settlement; establish a fur trade route	Thomas Hooker	Self-governing 1636–1662; royal 1662–1776	Triangular trade
Rhode Island[2]	1636	Escape religious intolerance of Massachusetts Bay	Roger Williams	Self-governing 1636–1644; joint-stock 1644–1663; royal 1663–1776	Shipping, livestock, agriculture
MIDDLE COLONIES					
New York[3]	1625	Expansion	James, Duke of York; Richard Nicolls; Thomas Dongan; John Montgomerie	Colony of Dutch West Indian Co. 1625–1664; proprietary (English) 1664–1685; royal 1685–1776	Wheat, milling, lumber, furs, sugar refining, distilling, shipbuilding, trade
Delaware[4]	1638	Trade	Johan Printz; Johan Rising William Penn	Proprietary (Swedish) 1638–1682; part of Penn. (proprietary) 1682–1704; royal 1704–1776	Trade, farming
New Jersey	1664	Trading post; refuge for Quakers from England	John Berkeley; John Carteret	Proprietary 1664–1702; royal 1702–1776	Trade, farming
Pennsylvania[5]	1637	Establish a Quaker colony, tolerance of religion	William Penn	Proprietary 1681–1692; royal 1692–1694; proprietary 1694–1776	Trade, farming
SOUTHERN COLONIES					
Virginia	1607	Search for gold, English outpost against Spain	John Smith; John Rolfe; Thomas Dale	Joint-stock 1607–1624; royal 1625–1776	Tobacco
Maryland	1632	Establish a Catholic settlement; escape religious persecution	George Calvert (Lord Baltimore); Cecilius Calvert	Proprietary 1632–1691; royal 1691–1716; proprietary 1716–1776	Tobacco
The Carolinas North Carolina (1712) South Carolina (1712)	1663	Land wealth, refuge for small farmers; strengthen English possessions in the Americas	William Berkeley; Anthony Ashley-Cooper; John Locke	Proprietary 1712–1729; royal 1729–1776 Proprietary 1670–1719; royal 1719–1776	Ship supplies, rice, indigo, tobacco
Georgia[6]	1732	Settlement for debtors; buffer Carolinas from Spanish Florida	James Oglethorpe	Proprietary 1732–1752; royal 1752–1776	Rice, indigo, lumber, beef, pork, ship supplies, trade

[1] Corporate colonies were organized by a joint-stock company, or corporation, for the benefit of shareholders. Such colonies could only be formed when the English king issued a charter, or certificate of his approval. In a royal colony, a governor appointed by the king served as its chief official, though a colonial assembly approved laws before they could go into effect. Self-governing colonies were independent of the king or a corporation. Proprietary colonies were granted by the king to a proprietor, or owner, whether one person or a small group of people.
[2] The four original settlements of Providence, Portsmouth, Warwick, and Newport created a united government in 1647 under the name "Providence Plantations."
[3] Called New Netherland until 1664 when the English took it over from the Dutch.
[4] Settled in 1638 by Swedes and called New Sweden. Seized by Dutch in 1655 and became part of New Netherland. Conquered by English in 1664.
[5] First settled by Swedes in 1637. Part of New Sweden until 1665, when seized by Dutch and became part of New Netherland. Conquered by English in 1664.
[6] Originally part of South Carolina.

 Interpreting Tables

Each of the thirteen colonies developed different characteristics because of their differing economic activities, government structures, reasons for settlement, and variations in the ethnic groups in each region. One clear regional pattern is the growing of tobacco and rice in the Southern Colonies. *What other regional patterns can you find in the chart?*

▶ RESOURCE DIRECTORY

Teaching Resources

⭐ **American Profiles Activity** found in the Unit 1 folder, p. 87, profiles Hannah Callowhill Penn, who ran her husband's proprietary colony of Pennsylvania during his illness and after his death.

major port of entry for Germans and Scots-Irish people coming to North America as indentured servants. (Scots-Irish were Scots who had settled in northern Ireland.) The populations of both the colony of New York and the colony of Pennsylvania were ethnically diverse. They included English, Dutch, French, Scots, Irish, Scots-Irish, Germans, Swedes, Portuguese, Welsh, Africans, and Native Americans. No wonder a traveler in the late 1750s despaired of ever discovering "any precise or determinate character" in the population of New York—it was made up of "different nations, different languages, and different religions." In contrast, most of the residents of Massachusetts were still of English descent, and almost everyone in the South was either of African or of English descent.

Agriculture and Trade in New England In the 1700s, the New England Colonies were a region of small, relatively self-sufficient farms and of towns dependent on long-distance trade. Unlike the merchants of Philadelphia and New York, those in Boston, Salem, and Newport, Rhode Island, did not rely heavily on local crops for their commerce. Instead, they had long since developed a business of carrying crops and goods from one place to another—a "carrying trade." They might haul china, books, and cloth from England to the West Indies in the Caribbean Sea; transport sugar back to New England, where it was usually distilled into rum; trade rum and firearms for slaves in West Africa; and then carry slaves to the West Indies for more sugar. This trade between three points in the Atlantic World—the Americas, Europe, and Africa—was called the **triangular trade.**

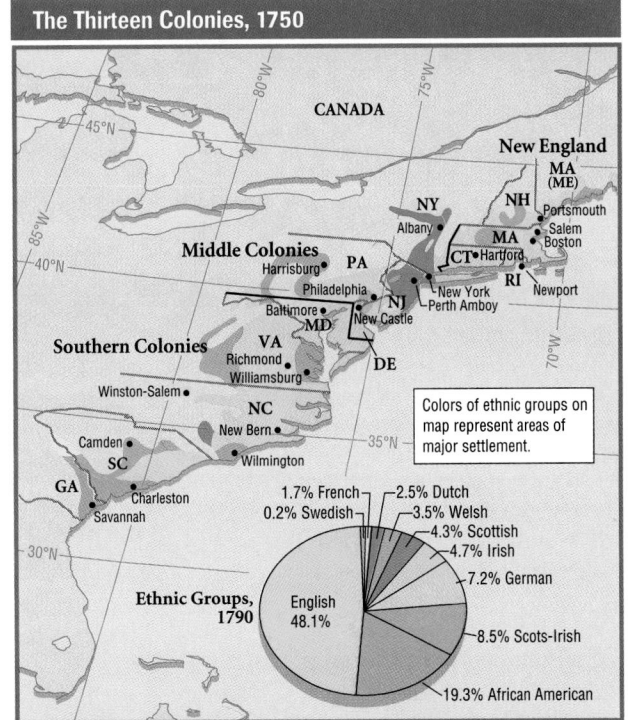

The Thirteen Colonies, 1750

Colors of ethnic groups on map represent areas of major settlement.

Ethnic Groups, 1790

- English 48.1%
- 1.7% French
- 0.2% Swedish
- 2.5% Dutch
- 3.5% Welsh
- 4.3% Scottish
- 4.7% Irish
- 7.2% German
- 8.5% Scots-Irish
- 19.3% African American

 Geography and History: Interpreting Maps
English settlements in North America in the 1700s generally clung to the Eastern seaboard and its rivers. In this narrow band, however, lived a wide variety of ethnic groups. *Which was the largest group after the English?*

The diverse economies of the Southern, Middle, and New England colonies might lead to the expectation of vast differences in culture. Americans from South Carolina to New England had much in common, however, as the next section shows.

 SECTION 1 REVIEW

Key Terms, People, and Places
1. Define (a) mercantilism, (b) balance of trade, (c) salutary neglect, (d) Fall Line, (e) triangular trade.

Key Concepts
2. Describe three ways in which England tried to control its colonies with the Navigation Act.
3. Give four reasons why the British were able to neglect their colonies in the 1700s.

4. Describe the economies of the Southern Colonies, the Middle Colonies, and the New England Colonies.

Critical Thinking
5. **Predicting Consequences** How might the growth of the American colonies have been affected if the British had strictly enforced the Navigation Act of 1660?

Quiz found in the Unit 1 folder, p. 78, covers the main ideas in this section as well as the key terms.

Media and Technology

Transparencies
Time Lines, E-2; Historical Maps, L-1

---

4. The Southern Colonies had economies based on staple crops and African American labor; the Middle Colonies had mixed economies based on commerce and agriculture; the New England Colonies had economies based on self-sufficient farms and a long-distance carrying trade.

5. Possible answers: The economic growth of the colonies might have been hampered by the need to pay duties in England, as well as to transport all goods there first. For example, the triangular trade would have been much more difficult if the Navigation Act had been enforced.

Caption Answer to ...

 Interpreting Maps

African Americans

Reteach
Ask students to imagine that they are advisers to the king of England in 1700. They must report to the king on the economic condition of the colonies. First they must describe the current English policy toward the colonies, next report on its success, and then describe the economies of the three colonial regions.

4. CLOSE

Reinforcing the Big Idea
By the early 1700s, England had adopted a policy of salutary neglect under which the colonies prospered and developed distinct regional differences. The next section describes the social structure of the colonies.

TOOLBOX

Geography

Interpreting an Economic Activity Map

Focus Identify the purpose of an economic activity map, interpret its symbols, and analyze the relationships indicated by the information displayed.

Instruct Ask students to define the term *region* as it is used by geographers and historians. *(A group of places bound together by one or more similar characteristics.)* Ask students what on the map justifies classifying the colonies into three regions. *(The symbols and color-coded key indicate the distinct economic activities of each region.)*

Ask students to find current economic activity maps in a geography textbook or encyclopedia showing the same regions. Ask students to compare the maps and name at least three things in each area that have changed.

Extend See Historian's Toolbox Activity in the Resource Directory below.

Answers

1. (a) general farming (b) fishing and whaling (c) North Carolina (d) general farming

2. (a) Southern Colonies (b) Lumber production enabled the New England Colonies to build ships that could be used for fishing and whaling. (c) New York and Georgia appear to have provided the best opportunities for raising livestock.

GEOGRAPHY	GRAPHS & CHARTS	HISTORIAN'S TOOLBOX	CRITICAL THINKING	HISTORICAL EVIDENCE

Interpreting an Economic Activity Map

An economic activity map shows how the land in a particular region is used and helps demonstrate the ways that geography can influence historical events and developments. Economic activity maps also illustrate ways in which regions are similar or different.

Often a region's economic activity is related to its natural resources and climate. For example, mining can take place only in regions where enough minerals are present to make this activity profitable. By the mid-1700s, clear patterns of economic activity were emerging among the British colonies in North America. This map uses symbols and a color-coded key to communicate basic information about land use in the colonies.

Use the following steps to analyze the economic activity map.

1. Identify the variety of economic activities shown. Use the map and key to answer the following questions. (a) What was the major economic activity in Delaware? (b) What were the major economic activities north of Massachusetts? (c) Which colony produced tobacco, rice, and indigo? (d) According to the map, what economic activity supported residents of Pennsylvania and New Jersey?

2. Look for relationships or patterns among the colonies and their economic activities. (a) As shown on the map, was farmland more extensive in the Southern or the New England colonies? (b) What other economic activities in the New England Colonies encouraged shipbuilding? (c) If you had been a livestock herder in Britain planning to move to the colonies, which of the American colonies do you think would have offered you the most opportunity for making a living?

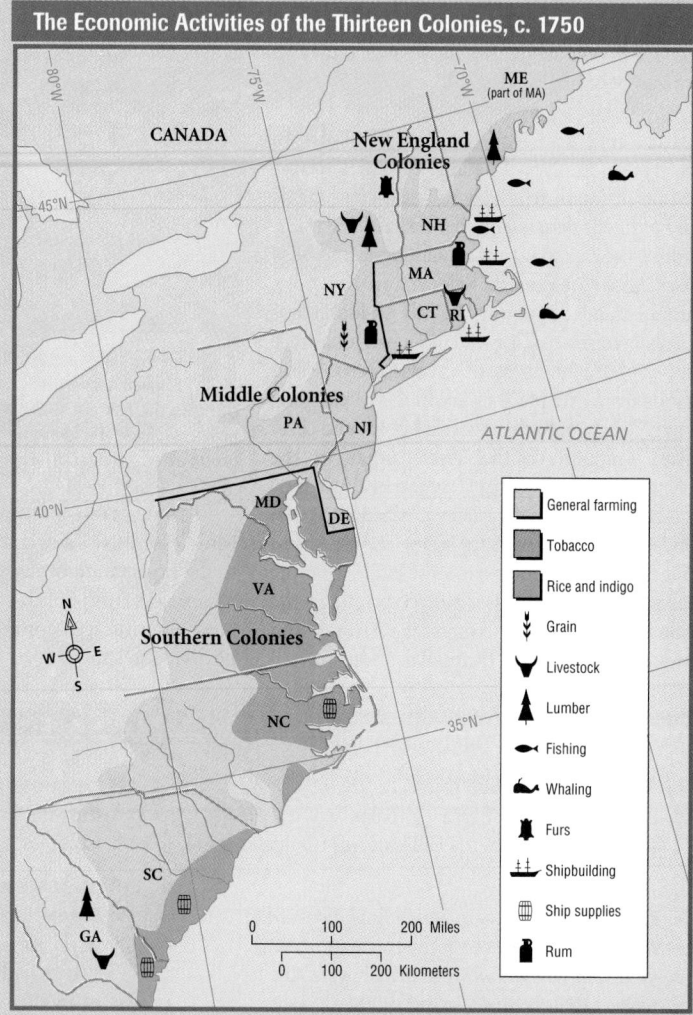

The Economic Activities of the Thirteen Colonies, c. 1750

Key:
- General farming
- Tobacco
- Rice and indigo
- Grain
- Livestock
- Lumber
- Fishing
- Whaling
- Furs
- Shipbuilding
- Ship supplies
- Rum

RESOURCE DIRECTORY

Teaching Resources

Historian's Toolbox Activity Interpreting an Economic Activity Map, found in the Unit 1 folder, p. 91, is designed to enhance students' skills in analyzing and understanding land use maps.

Life in Colonial America

SECTION PREVIEW

It is a principle of American government today that all people are created equal. When the American colonists in the 1700s considered that idea, however, they found it truly revolutionary. Colonial American society was fundamentally unequal, a world of ranks and privileges that favored the few over the many.

Key Concepts

- Colonial Americans organized their society according to a belief in inequality.
- A small group of white, upper-class men dominated colonial American society.
- Although women had little power, colonial society could not have functioned without their contributions.
- Except for the few at the top of the social scale, the lives of most people in colonial America were defined by work.

Key Terms, People, and Places

gentry, cousinocracy; William Byrd, Benjamin Franklin, Eliza Lucas Pinckney

B ased on what you already know about the American past, you could probably make some accurate statements about what life was like in the thirteen colonies. For example, many people relied primarily on their own labor or on slave labor for food, clothing, and shelter. You might guess that their society operated on a principle of equality very different from the one that we strive to live by today.

In general, colonial American society was dedicated to the belief that people were not equal. Almost all Americans of European descent, for example, accepted slavery as a normal part of life. Nearly all colonists also assumed that women were not equal to men. Some may not have liked these assumptions, but colonial society offered little opportunity for debate over such issues. In the words of one New Englander, "ranks and degrees" were as much a part of this world as "Mountains and Plains, Hills and Vallies."

Colonial clothes, houses, and manners offer the best evidence of this belief in inequality. **Gentry,** or men and women wealthy enough to afford others to work for them, set themselves apart by their clothing: wigs, silk stockings, lace cuffs, and the latest fashions in suits, dresses, and hats. Ordinary people wore plain breeches and shirts or dresses. Wigs were an unmistakable sign of status, power, and wealth. Looking back on his boyhood as the son of a farmer-artisan in the 1730s, the Reverend Mr. Devereux Jarratt of Virginia wrote in his autobiography:

HAIR POWDER
Of the firſt Quality,
Manufactured and Sold by
HUGH HENRY,
No. 38, Chſnut-ſtreet,
PHILADELPHIA:
Where Merchants, Captains
and Dealers may be ſupplied
on the ſhorteſt Notice.
☞ Starch put up for Exportation.

A periwig, *in those days, was a distinguishing badge of* gentle folk—*and when I saw a man riding the road, near our house, with a wig on, it would so alarm my fears . . . that, I dare say, I would run off as for my life.*

"Gentle folk," a colonial term for the gentry class that so alarmed Jarratt, were the most important members of colonial society; to be considered "gentle," one had to be wealthy. For English colonists, the foundation of real wealth was land. Although adult, single women and free African Americans could legally own land, almost all landowners were white men.

In the unequal society of the colonies, a white wig, or hair powdered to look like one, was the hallmark of a gentleman.

MAKING CONNECTIONS

You have read that equality is a principle of our government today. Has that made our society more equal than colonial society? Give evidence to support your opinion.

1. FOCUS

Connecting to the Big Idea

See page 70B. Point out that the colonists created a hierarchical society of many levels. Ask students who held power in colonial America. What governed the lives of most people?

Objectives

- Define the fundamental belief in inequality that governed the way colonists organized their society.
- Identify the group that dominated colonial American society.
- Describe the position of women in colonial society and explain why that society could not have functioned without their contributions.
- Define the role of work in most colonists' lives.

Bellringer

Write the words Ladies and Gentlemen on the chalkboard. Ask students what associations come to mind when they hear this phrase. How do the images of ladies and gentlemen during colonial times compare with those of today?

Answer to ...

MAKING CONNECTIONS

Answers may cite evidence of continuing inequality, or stress that much of the inequality accepted in colonial times—the superior position of men and the wealthy, for instance—is no longer widely considered acceptable.

📄 **Reproducible Lesson Plan** found in the Unit 1 folder, p. 74, provides a summary of the Section 2 lesson plan content.

📄 **Alternate Lesson Plan: Learning Styles** found in the Alternate Lesson Plans folder, p. 13, is especially effective for visual learners and is designed to help students understand the nature of work in the colonial period.

📄 **Guided Reading and Review** found in the Unit 1 folder, p. 79, provides a structure for reading and mastering the key concepts and reviewing the key terms for Section 2. (Guided Practice)

Question Writing Have students skim the section and read each of the headings and subheadings. Ask students to turn each heading into a question. Then have students jot down answers to the questions they have created as they read.

2. INSTRUCT

Explain/Discuss

Explain to students that colonial society was basically unequal. Ask students to describe the gentry and to identify the symbols that signified their class. Ask students why the gentry were considered "gentle folk." You might want to recall students' associations from the Bellringer activity and compare colonial society with society today.

Discuss with students the lives, rights, and duties of colonial women. Ask what right single women possessed that married women and underage daughters with living fathers did not. (*The right to conduct business.*)

Discuss how work in colonial times differed from work today.

Analyze

Analyze Benjamin Franklin's image of himself as a gentleman. How did he compromise his career and potential contributions to society by maintaining this status?

Caption Answer to ...

Using Historical Evidence

Their clothing is very elaborate; it includes stockings and lace. The man may be wearing a wig.

A Society Dominated by Landowning Men

From New Hampshire to the Carolinas and Georgia, colonial American society rested on a foundation of inequality. In each colony, a small group of landowning men dominated politics. Lawyers, planters, and merchants held most of the seats in the colonial assemblies, or lawmaking bodies. Landowning gentry often were related to one another by blood or marriage. For example, approximately a hundred families ran the colony of Virginia, forming what some historians have called a **"cousinocracy."**

Using Historical Evidence The gentle class had the leisure time to spend on perfecting elaborate social graces. The marks beneath the feet of these dancers record the complex steps they had to learn to participate in the dances of their time. *How does their clothing indicate that the dancers belong to the gentle class?*

In the early 1700s, gentry devoted much of their time to displaying their status and perfecting their "gentle" manners. To impress others, they had mansions and townhouses built for themselves. They stocked these houses with fine china, silver, and furniture, as well as portraits of themselves wearing their daily finery: silk stockings, wigs, and lace made in Europe. To refine their own manners, they eagerly read newspapers and books from England; to refine those of their sons, they sent the boys to expensive schools. They were people of leisure; they supervised, but they did not actually perform physical labor.

We know from *The Diary, and Life, of William Byrd II of Virginia, 1674–1744* that gentlemen tried to live their lives according to a refined, well-mannered routine. **William Byrd** owned several plantations in the colony of Virginia; at his home plantation lived several dozen slaves, including five or six house servants. In his diary, Byrd relates that every day he read Greek or Latin, said his prayers, and "danced his dance" (performed a series of exercises) in the garden of his home. Byrd rarely varied from these regular habits. Although he did have to keep an eye on his plantations, which involved care and mental work, such labor was not the focus of his life. Like many other colonial gentlemen, Byrd wished to demonstrate to the world his refinement and self-control and to prove that he deserved the respect of others.

Gentlemen such as Byrd did, in fact, receive the respect they sought—in North America. When they traveled to Europe, however, people often ignored or scorned them. No matter how much colonial gentlemen worked at their manners and their language, Europeans always seemed to perceive them as unsophisticated and clumsy. American gentry were in the curious position of being very important in America and very unimportant in Europe. This perception lasted into the late 1700s, when **Benjamin Franklin,** a Philadelphia printer and a leading statesman in America, created a stir in France by simply giving the French what they expected. He wore a coonskin cap, dressed in plain clothes, and acted like a country bumpkin. The French adored him.

▶ RESOURCE DIRECTORY

Teaching Resources

Visual Learning Activity The First American Schoolbook, found in the Unit 1 folder, p. 100, encourages students to consider the similarities and differences between colonial and present-day education.

Literature Activity As Poor Richard Says, found in the Unit 1 folder, p. 96, uses maxims published by Benjamin Franklin in *Poor Richard's Almanac* to reflect the concerns and humor of this well-known colonist.

Primary Source Activity A Marriage Agreement, found in the Unit 1 folder, p. 93, illustrates issues of family life as well as the nature of legal arrangements in the colonies.

Using Historical Evidence Prudence Punderson, a Connecticut housewife, created this symbolic view in needlework of the life of a colonial woman. The symbols, from right to left, indicate birth, work, and death. *What three symbols would you choose to sum up your own life? How do they differ from the symbols Punderson chose?*

Still, even Franklin spent most of his life trying to win acceptance as a gentleman. After his successful career as a printer, Franklin retired when he was only in his early forties. Why? He preferred the status of gentleman to making more money. And he could not be a gentleman as long as he worked as a printer. In retirement, Franklin did the "work" of an important man of leisure; he dabbled in science and politics and spent much of his time in Europe. He also wrote his famous *Autobiography,* which was full of rules for controlling oneself and behaving in a respectable manner.

Women in Colonial America

⭐ This overriding belief in inequality defined the status of colonial women, including the wives and daughters of gentlemen. Most women, either as underage daughters or as wives, were legally the dependents of men. Since these women had no legal or political standing, they could not own property. Without property, they could never be independent, and thus they could not vote or hold office or serve on a jury. Even adult, single women—widows, for instance, who took ownership of land from their late husbands—did not have any political rights, although they could conduct business.

The Legal Situation Under English common law, a woman was under her husband's control. She had no identity of her own. According to the English writer William Blackstone in his influential *Commentaries on the Laws of England,* published in the 1760s,

> By marriage, the husband and wife are one person in law; that is, the very being or legal existence of the woman is suspended during the marriage, or at least is incorporated and consolidated into that of the husband; under whose wing, protection, and cover, she performs everything.

Within the households of colonial America, husbands exercised nearly unlimited power.

Answer to ...

Links Across Time

Answers will vary but may include the following: Clocks make life simpler because they are a dependable way to schedule our work and social appointments; clocks make life more complex because we have to learn to live by them, whereas before timepieces, people lived life more at the pace of nature.

3. ASSESS

Section 2 Review Answers

1. (a) gentry, see p. 79, (b) cousinocracy, see p. 80

2. (a) William Byrd, see p. 80, (b) Benjamin Franklin, see p. 80, (c) Eliza Lucas Pinckney, see p. 82

3. Colonial American society was based on a belief in inequality. It continued the hierarchical society that had originated in Europe, in which most power was held by white, upper-class men who owned land.

4. The gentry devoted much of their time to displaying their status and perfecting their "gentle" manners. They built mansions and townhouses stocked with fine china, silver, furniture, and portraits. They read newspapers and books from England and sent their sons to expensive schools.

5. Women took chief responsibility for the tasks that kept a household operating, such as cooking, gardening, washing, spinning cloth, cleaning, and sewing; they supported one another by

---

English law, for example, permitted men to beat their wives without fear of prosecution. Divorces, although legal, were rare. Ironically, the easiest place to obtain a divorce was Puritan New England. The Puritans were so concerned about order and stability that they preferred to allow a bad marriage to end rather than let it continue to create disorder among them.

Women's Duties In practice, however, men and women depended heavily on one another. In colonial America, women juggled a number of duties that contributed to the well-being of the household and also of the community. Women took chief responsibility for the tasks that kept a household operating, such as cooking, gardening, washing, spinning cloth, cleaning, and sewing. They supported one another by helping in childbirth, sharing equipment and tools, and applying community pressure on offenders in cases of domestic abuse. Women also assisted in whatever work their husbands did, from planting crops to managing the business affairs of the family. And they trained their daughters in the traditional responsibilities of women. ✪

By pumping the pedal under this spinning wheel, a housewife turned bobbins that drew flax into linen thread.

Women sometimes took on these multiple duties before marriage. One example is **Eliza Lucas Pinckney** of South Carolina, who as a teenager managed her father's plantations in the late 1730s and early 1740s. This responsibility fell to Pinckney because, as she wrote to a friend, "Mama's bad state of health prevents her going thro' any fatigue," and her father, the governor of the Caribbean island of Antigua, was usually absent. As she wrote to her friend:

I have the business of 3 plantations to transact, which requires much writing and more business and fatigue of other sorts than you can imagine, but lest you should imagine it too burdensome to a girl at my early time of life, give me leave to assure you I think myself happy that I can be useful to so good a father.

Pinckney was more than just a stand-in for her father. She was one of the people responsible for promoting the growing of indigo, a type of plant used in making a blue dye for cloth, which became a major staple crop in South Carolina.

In spite of their hard work and dedication, women remained legally inferior to men. They might argue with their fathers or unite with their neighbors to expose an abusive husband. But women almost never directly challenged the patriarchal order of colonial society.

| 1650 | 1700 | 1750 | 1800 | **Links Across Time** | 1850 | 1900 | 1950 | 2000 |

Time and Its Measure

In the 1700s, only very wealthy people owned clocks. Clocks were unnecessary for others because most people were task- rather than time-oriented. This means they performed a task when it needed to be done and worked for as long as necessary. Sometimes—for example, at harvest time—they worked intensively from dawn until dusk; at other times, they might have comparatively little to do. Because work schedules often revolved around variations in the seasons and the amount of available daylight, day was for labor, night was for rest.

In the late twentieth century, people awaken, not with the crow of roosters at daybreak, but with alarm clocks. From one end of the day to the other, clocks dictate many of our daily activities: when we wake up, go to work or school, eat our meals, attend meetings and movies, watch the evening news, and go to sleep, to name just a few. The modern world of schedules, appointments, and international communications demands a commonly accepted, accurate measurement of time. *Do you think that clocks make life simpler or more complex?*

▶ RESOURCE DIRECTORY

Teaching Resources

✪ **Critical Thinking Activity** Identifying Central Issues: The Status of Colonial Women, found in the Unit 1 folder, p. 92, is designed to help students apply this skill by answering questions summarizing excerpts from several colonial authors.

The Nature of Work in Colonial America

While the few at the top of the social scale were learning and putting into practice their refined manners, most people in colonial American society were working. By the mid-1700s, life was better for most Europeans in North America than it would have been in Europe; they ate better, lived longer, and had more children to help them with their work. Still, whether they were skilled artisans in cities or small farmers in the countryside, they had to labor very hard to keep themselves and their families alive.

Everyone in a household—husbands, wives, children, and servants—worked to maintain the household by producing food and goods. In fact, the basic goal of the household was to maintain itself. While men grew crops or made goods such as shoes, guns, or candles, the rest of the household was equally busy. Many women sewed and spun cloth, made butter, and tended small gardens and animals. Children helped both parents from an early age. Almost all work was performed in or around the home; the separation between work and home with which we are familiar today did not develop until the 1800s. Even artisans worked out of shops in the front of their houses. And both farmers and artisans worked on different time schedules than we do now.

Because people worked when they needed to and for as long as a task required, little in the way of organized leisure time was available. It is no coincidence that professional sports teams appeared in the 1800s when people began to work regular hours and had predictable amounts

A woman's work might last from dawn to dusk or even longer. In this engraving a woman tends a vegetable garden with her daughters.

of free time. In the colonial period, people amused themselves at festivals and special occasions, such as days when court was in session.

Colonial American households, particularly those in the Southern and Middle colonies, included Africans who had been sold into slavery. As part of colonial America, Africans were active participants in creating colonial society, as is discussed in the next section.

In her free time, a colonial girl might play with this doll made of corn husks.

SECTION 2 REVIEW

Key Terms, People, and Places
1. Define (a) gentry, (b) cousinocracy.
2. Identify (a) William Byrd, (b) Benjamin Franklin, (c) Eliza Lucas Pinckney.

Key Concepts
3. Describe the fundamental belief on which colonial American society was based and its effect.

4. Describe how colonial gentry lived.
5. What duties did women perform in colonial America?

Critical Thinking
6. **Recognizing Ideologies** Eliza Lucas Pinckney wrote that she was happy just to be of use to her father. What does this suggest about her attitude toward herself?

Quiz found in the Unit 1 folder, p. 80, covers the main ideas in this section as well as the key terms.

Media and Technology

Transparency
The Way It Works, H-3

---

helping in childbirth, sharing equipment and tools, and applying community pressure on offenders in cases of domestic abuse; they assisted in whatever work their husbands did, from planting crops to managing the business affairs of the family; and they trained their daughters in the traditional responsibilities of women.

6. Answers may suggest that Pinckney had an underlying belief that her father was more valuable than she was.

Reteach

Ask students to correct any of the following incorrect statements.
● The most powerful people in the English colonies were bankers, because they controlled the money supply.
● Any woman could own land in the colonies, but only unmarried women without fathers could vote.
● Most colonists did not work hard.
● Colonial women had few rights.
● Any colonists could become one of the gentry.

Alternative Assessment

Mid-Point Monitoring
Ask students if they have
● Chosen a format for their projects
● Begun their outside research
● Started drafting portions of their project

4. CLOSE

Reinforcing the Big Idea

Colonial society was organized hierarchically; white, upper-class landowners ranked highest. The lives of most colonists were governed by the need to work. The next section describes the lives and work of those at the bottom rung of the colonial hierarchy—enslaved Africans and African Americans.

SECTION 3

African Americans in the Colonies

African Americans in the Colonies

Connecting to the Big Idea

See page 70B. Point out that about 20 percent of the colonists were Africans or of African descent. Ask students what their lives were like. What contributions did Africans make to society?

Objectives

- Describe how enslaved Africans came to the colonies.
- Explain why people of African descent enslaved in South Carolina and Georgia were able to preserve many of their cultural traditions.
- Describe the unique culture created by African Americans in Virginia and Maryland.
- Explain why the lives of African Americans in the New England and Middle colonies were varied.

Bellringer

Ask students to think about the concept of *family.* What makes up a family? What needs do families fill in people's lives? How has the disintegration of many families affected American society today?

Continuing traditions established in Africa, enslaved African Americans made and played this banjo and fiddle in North America.

SECTION PREVIEW

By 1760, about 325,800 people of African descent lived in the thirteen colonies, nearly all of them enslaved. Although they had no rights in the highly unequal world of colonial America, African Americans actively shaped society from very early times.

Key Concepts

- Slave traders removed Africans from their homelands by force and transported them across the Atlantic Ocean.
- People of African descent enslaved in South Carolina and Georgia were especially successful in preserving many of their cultural traditions.
- African Americans in Virginia and Maryland created a unique blend of European and African cultures and established stable family systems.
- The lives of African Americans in the New England and Middle colonies varied like the economies they supported with their labor.

Key Terms, People, and Places

Middle Passage, low country

Not counting Native Americans, about one out of every five people living in British North America by the middle of the 1700s was of African descent. As in the case of all immigrants, the experiences of African Americans in the colonies varied depending on where they lived.

Although there was no typical African American experience in the colonies, for many African men, women, and children, interaction with colonial society began when they were uprooted from their homeland and sold into slavery. One African who later told his story from the beginning was Olaudah Equiano.

AMERICAN PROFILES

Olaudah Equiano

Olaudah Equiano was born around 1745 in the country of Benin. He wrote in his autobiography decades later that the land of his youth was "uncommonly rich and fruitful" and "a nation of dancers, musicians and poets." As a child, he learned "the art of war" and proudly wore "the emblems of a warrior" made by his mother. When Equiano was ten, his world was shattered. Two men and a woman kidnapped him and one of his sisters while their parents were working. Separated from his sister, Equiano was enslaved to a series of African masters. About six months after he was kidnapped, Equiano found himself facing a still greater trial. Taken to the coast, he was sold again and put aboard a British slave ship bound for the Americas. In his autobiography, he wrote:

> The first object which saluted my eyes when I arrived on the coast was the sea, and a slave ship which was then riding at anchor and waiting for its cargo. These filled me with astonishment, which was soon converted into terror when I was carried on board. . . . Indeed such were the horrors of my views and fears at the moment that, if ten thousand worlds had been my own, I would have freely parted with them all to have exchanged my condition with that of the meanest [lowest] slave in my own country.
>
> *Equiano's Travels,* 1789

During the **Middle Passage,** the name given to the part of the triangular trade that went between Africa and the Americas bearing enslaved Africans, Equiano witnessed many scenes of brutality. Although historians differ on the actual figures, from 10 to 40 percent of the Africans on a slave ship might perish in a

▶ RESOURCE DIRECTORY

Teaching Resources

Reproducible Lesson Plan found in the Unit 1 folder, p. 75, provides a summary of the Section 3 lesson plan content.

Alternate Lesson Plan: Learning Styles found in the Alternate Lesson Plans folder, p. 14, is particularly helpful for auditory learners, as it guides students through a discussion and oral presentation of the slave experience in colonial times.

Guided Reading and Review found in the Unit 1 folder, p. 81, provides a structure for reading and mastering the key concepts and reviewing the key terms for Section 3. (Guided Practice)

"No eye pities; no hand helps," said a slaver describing the condition of his human cargo. An eyewitness painted this scene aboard a slave ship in 1846.

Reading Strategy

Reinforcing Key Ideas Point out the following regions on an outline map of the colonies: South Carolina and Georgia, Virginia and Maryland, the New England and Middle colonies. Have students take notes as they read about the lives of enslaved Africans and their descendants in each of the regions.

crossing. Sick with fear about where they were being taken, they were forced to endure chains, heat, disease, and the overpowering odor caused by the lack of sanitation and their cramped, stuffy quarters. As Equiano wrote, "Many a time we were near suffocation from the want of fresh air, which we were often without for whole days together." Conditions were so grim on Equiano's voyage that two people committed suicide; a third was prevented from doing so and then whipped.

Occasionally enslaved Africans physically resisted during the Middle Passage by staging what the slavers called "mutinies." The heavily armed and manned slave ships were evidence that the slavers lived in continual fear of Africans striking out for their freedom. No mutiny took place aboard Equiano's ship, although statistics about the British slave trade show that a rebellion occurred every two years on the average. Many of these were successful.

Equiano's ship finally arrived at a port on the island of Barbados, in the West Indies, where the crew put up the Africans for sale at a public auction. Most went to work and die in the sugar plantations of the West Indies. Equiano noted how the sale separated families, leaving people grief-stricken and alone.

In this manner, without scruple, are relations and friends separated, most of them never to see each other again. I remember in the vessel in which I was brought over, in the men's apartment there were several brothers who, in the sale, were sold in different lots; and it was very moving on this occasion to see and hear their cries at parting. O, ye nominal Christians [Christians in name only]! might not an African ask you, Learned you this from your God, who says unto you, Do unto all men as you would men should do unto you?

Treating humans as property led to unspeakable cruelties. This branding iron was used to mark an owner's initials on enslaved Africans.

In 1766 Equiano was taken to Virginia, where he was eventually able to buy his freedom. Migrating to Great Britain, he found work as a barber and a personal servant and became active in the antislavery movement.

Equiano's case was unusual. Relatively few enslaved Africans ever regained their freedom. The very uniqueness of his story illustrates, however, how the experiences of Africans varied

In Depth

Then and Now

Enslaved Africans brought with them to the United States the ancient tradition of storytelling. Alex Haley, who grew up listening to his grandmother's stories about an African ancestor, Kunta Kinte, journeyed to West Africa to research his family's origins. The trip led Haley to write his best-selling novel, *Roots*, which was viewed by a record 130 million people when it was dramatized for television in 1977. *Roots* awakened a popular interest in African American history and culture and, by the 1980s, in fiction written by African Americans. In 1993, Toni Morrison, whose works include the Pulitzer Prize–winning novel *Beloved*, was awarded the Nobel Prize in Literature and became the first African American to be so honored.

Discuss

Discuss with students why slave traders treated Africans so poorly. Compare the lives of enslaved Africans and their descendants in the southern coastal colonies, Virginia and Maryland, and the New England and Middle colonies. Ask students whether the owners of rice and indigo plantations consciously allowed enslaved Africans to maintain some of their traditions. What factors enabled them to maintain a language with roots in Africa, for example? Ask students to consider why the lives of enslaved African Americans were most varied in the New England and Middle colonies.

Analyze

Ask students why the revolts of enslaved African Americans were unsuccessful. What factors worked against them?

Answer to ...

MAKING CONNECTIONS

Answers may cite negotiations between individuals such as parents and children and between groups such as corporate managers and labor unions.

In Depth

Biography

Paul Cuffe (1759–1817), the son of an ex-slave father and a Native American mother, went to sea at sixteen. He became a successful shipowner, hiring only African American crews. Cuffe, who joined the Quakers in 1808, became convinced that African Americans should resettle in Africa. In 1811 he took the first African American recruits to Africa. He died before he could carry out his plans to settle many more African Americans in their land of origin.

This authentic watercolor painted on a South Carolina plantation in the late 1700s documents a dance form and musical instruments that have been linked to the Yoruba people of West Africa.

greatly in colonial times. Slavery was legal everywhere, but the number of enslaved people in each region and the kind of labor they performed made for significant differences in African American life from one place to another. African Americans, moreover, not only survived slavery but preserved and adapted elements of their original cultures. Through the process of negotiation that occurs in all human relationships, they were often able to better their situations—even in spite of the intentions of their masters.

MAKING CONNECTIONS

Give examples of negotiation in society today, both between individuals and between groups.

Africans in South Carolina and Georgia

Much of the seaboard region of South Carolina and Georgia is formed by a coastal plain called **low country.** Planters found the low country excellent for the cultivation of rice and indigo. Enslaved people there labored under particularly brutal conditions. Charles Ball, an African American observer whose account was published in 1836, describes the situation as it had existed for well over a century:

> *The general features of slavery are the same every where; but the utmost rigor of the system, is only to be met with on the cotton plantations of Carolina and Georgia, or in the rice fields which skirt the deep swamps and morasses of the southern rivers.*

By contrast, North Carolina was more suited to tobacco farming, and so the lives of enslaved people in that colony were similar to the lives of African Americans in the other tobacco colonies, Virginia and Maryland.

African Americans in South Carolina and Georgia made up the majority of the population, and they generally had regular contact with only a handful of colonists. As a result, they were able to exercise greater control over their day-to-day existence than those enslaved in other colonies and to preserve many of their cultural traditions. Many had come to South Carolina and Georgia directly from Africa. They still practiced the crafts of their homeland, such as basket weaving and pottery, and they continued making the music they loved and telling

RESOURCE DIRECTORY

the stories their parents and grandparents had passed down to them. In some cases, they kept their culture alive in their speech. The most well-known example is the Gullah language, a combination of English and African. As late as the 1940s, speakers of Gullah were using four thousand words from the languages of more than twenty-one separate groups in West Africa. African Americans even preserved the African manner of burial.

Strong African kinship networks helped people not only survive slavery but also preserve their traditions. Family relationships remained of supreme importance. When they had no relatives or only a few, enslaved Africans created new relationships with one another by acting as substitute kin. In these relationships, people behaved as if they were brothers or sisters or aunts or uncles, though in fact they were not.

The skills and knowledge that African Americans brought with them to South Carolina and Georgia also profoundly affected the lives of their masters. African Americans had superior knowledge of cattle herding and fishing, as well as great skill in the use of semi-tropical herbs. Because many had grown rice extensively in their homelands, they generally had vital, practical know-how about its cultivation. Without this knowledge, to say nothing of African American labor, it is doubtful that the colonies that came to depend on rice as a staple could have survived.

In these and many other ways, the African American majority in South Carolina and Georgia made the best of a horrible situation. Forced to come to North America, they found strength in each other's company and in the memory of their African origins. In the low-lying areas along the South Carolina and Georgia coasts, Africans worked not only to raise rice but to make the environment as much their own as their masters'.

Africans in Virginia and Maryland

The way enslaved people lived in Virginia and Maryland differed sharply from the way of life of African Americans in South Carolina and Georgia, in three ways. First, enslaved people in Virginia and Maryland made up a

minority rather than a majority of the population and relatively few had come directly from Africa. Second, the work they performed was different. Cultivating tobacco, the major crop, did not take as much time as growing rice, so slaveowners put enslaved African Americans to work at a variety of other tasks. And third, African Americans in Virginia and Maryland had more regular contact with European Americans. The result was greater integration of European American and African American cultures than in South Carolina and Georgia.

Virginia planters could not afford to buy many slaves, so they encouraged enslaved African Americans to raise families. Thus colonists in Virginia and Maryland tended to allow fuller development of African American family and community life than those colonists from the rice plantations of the low country. It was economically advantageous for tobacco planters to allow such social interaction.

In the latter half of the 1700s, African Americans in Virginia and Maryland laid the foundation for stable family units and blended the customs of African and European origin. They mingled the African and the European in everything from food and clothes to religion. Meanwhile, some enslaved men in Virginia worked away from plantations as artisans or laborers in Richmond and other towns. As long as they sent back a percentage of their wages to the plantations, they lived relatively independent of their master's control. They were, however, still subject to harsh laws that controlled what they could do, and their children were born enslaved.

Slavery in New England and the Middle Colonies

About 400,000 African Americans lived in the Southern Colonies by the late 1700s, compared to about 50,000 in the New England and Middle colonies combined. The lives and work of African Africans in these colonies north of Maryland reflected the region's mixed economy and its varied ways of life. They had considerably more freedom to choose their occupations than did African Americans in the Southern Colonies.

Activity
Cooperative Learning

Time: One class period.
Activity: Create a quilt, based on facts about the lives of African Americans.
Grouping: Groups of four students.
Purpose: Research and design a colonial quilt with at least eight pieces of colored paper or fabric. On each piece, have students write and illustrate one aspect of the African American experience, including facts about the passage to the colonies, life in different regions of the colonies, and attempts to revolt.
Roles: Researchers, designers, writers, illustrators.
Outcome: Students will describe circumstances under which African Americans arrived and survived in the colonies.

Enrichment

Ask students to prepare a report about the steps involved in growing and preparing rice and indigo.

3. ASSESS

Section 3 Review Answers

1. (a) Middle Passage, see p. 84, (b) low country, see p. 86

2. Their responses ranged from suicide to open rebellion.

3. In South Carolina and Georgia, Africans formed the majority of the population and had fewer direct contacts with Europeans. They retained some control over their daily lives and preserved more African cultural traditions. In Virginia and Maryland, Africans were a significant minority; and few came directly from Africa. They were also employed in a greater variety of tasks and had more regular interaction with Europeans.

4. Most African Americans in the north worked on farms; in the forests as lumberjacks; or on the seacoast as dockworkers, merchant sailors, fisherman, whalers, and privateers. Others worked in cities, manufacturing and trading, or as domestic servants in the homes of wealthy families.

5. Answers should state that in general the African American family survived under the enormous pressures produced by slavery. For example, many families were torn apart when transported from Africa. Families did, however, adapt to circumstances, as can be seen in South Carolina and Georgia, where substitute kin were employed. Virginia and Maryland, which encouraged the development of the African American family for economic reasons, were exceptions.

Caption Answer to ...

 Interpreting Tables

The Southern Colonies.

Reteach

Write the following geographical areas on the chalkboard: South Carolina and Georgia, Virginia and Maryland, the New England and Middle colonies. Ask students to match each statement to the appropriate region.

• Enslaved African Americans worked as shipbuilders, sailors, dockworkers, and privateers.
• Torn from their own families, enslaved Africans formed new families by acting as substitute kin.
• Planters in these colonies encouraged enslaved African Americans to raise families.

4. CLOSE

 Reinforcing the Big Idea

African Americans played an important role in the development of American society, despite the fact that they came to the colonies in slavery. The next section describes how western expansion and religious tension affected colonial society.

Estimated African Population of the Colonies, 1690–1750

Year	New England Colonies	Middle Colonies	Southern Colonies
1690	905	2,472	13,307
1700	1,680	3,361	22,476
1710	2,585	6,218	36,063
1720	3,956	10,825	54,058
1730	6,118	11,683	73,220
1740	8,541	16,452	125,031
1750	10,982	20,736	204,702

Source: *Historical Statistics of the United States*

Interpreting Tables
The growth in the number of African Americans, although relatively small in the 1600s, jumped considerably in the early 1700s. *In which group of colonies did the number of African Americans increase most sharply?*

This doll—perhaps made by an African American for one of his or her children—was found in the attic walls of an old house.

Throughout the 1700s, most African Americans in the north worked on farms, either in the fields or as cooks, housekeepers, personal servants, or artisans. They also worked in the forests as lumberjacks. Because shipbuilding and shipping were major economic activities in the New England and Middle colonies, some African American men worked along the seacoast. As dockworkers, merchant sailors, fisherman, whalers, and privateers, their labor contributed to the growth of the Atlantic economy. Others, men and women, worked in cities, in manufacturing and trading or as servants in the homes of wealthy families.

Laws and Revolts

⭐ Beginning about 1680, all the colonies passed laws controlling the activities of African Americans. Generally, enslaved African Americans could not go aboard ships or ferries or leave the town limits without a written pass; in some colonies they were forbidden to gather even for a dance. Punishment by whipping, banishment to the West Indies, and death were the norm for crimes ranging from owning hogs and carrying canes to disturbing the peace and striking a white person. In New York, for instance, any African American found traveling alone more than 40 miles from Albany could be put to death. In Virginia, runaways caught at night were by law supposed to be cut into pieces. Many of these laws also were applied to free African Americans and to Native Americans.

Harsh conditions sparked forceful resistance. In New York City, where the population in 1740 was 16 percent African American, brutal laws were passed to control African Americans. These led to rebellions in 1708, 1712, and 1741. After the rebellion of 1741, thirteen African Americans were burned alive in punishment. In the colonies as a whole, African Americans undertook about forty-seven documented revolts during the sixty years from 1740 to 1800.

Thus slavery became part of the new kind of society that grew up in North America, built on inequality but also built, as all societies are, on relationships between ordinary people. The next section shows how new tensions would emerge in that society during the 1700s, due to western expansion and religious upheaval.

SECTION 3 REVIEW

Key Terms, People, and Places
1. Define (a) Middle Passage, (b) low country.

Key Concepts
2. How did African Americans respond to conditions on the Middle Passage?
3. In general, how did the lives of enslaved Africans in Virginia and Maryland differ from the lives of those in South Carolina and Georgia?
4. How were enslaved people generally employed in the New England Colonies?

Critical Thinking
5. **Identifying Central Issues** How was the African American family in the 1700s affected by slavery?

▶ RESOURCE DIRECTORY

Teaching Resources

⭐ **Visual Learning Activity** Education as a Step Toward Freedom, found in the Unit 1 folder, p. 99, is designed to promote students' understanding of differing views on slavery in the colonies.

Quiz found in the Unit 1 folder, p. 82, covers the main ideas in this section as well as the key terms.

Emerging Tensions

SECTION 4

SECTION PREVIEW

In the mid-1700s, some colonial Americans began to look westward for more territory, while others challenged the social and political order in a "great awakening" of religious feeling. As a result, new tensions pulled at the fabric of colonial society.

Key Concepts
- During the mid-1750s, British settlers moved beyond the confines of the thirteen colonies.
- As British settlers migrated west, tension increased among Native Americans, the French, and the British, as all competed for the same territory.
- A religious movement called the Great Awakening indirectly challenged the fundamental colonial belief in inequality.

Key Terms, People, and Places
Great Awakening; forks of the Ohio River

B y the mid-1700s, the British colonies in North America were economic successes. Colonial settlers, with the forced cooperation of enslaved African Americans, had transformed the Atlantic colonies into a world of prosperous farms, towns, and plantations. The success of the colonies came with a price, however. The growth of the colonies, both in population and territory, created new problems and revived old ones.

Western Expansion

Though it may be hard to believe, by the mid-1700s British colonists felt crowded, especially in New England. According to English custom, fathers tried to provide their sons with land; New Englanders now found it increasingly difficult to do so. Since maintaining a family required about 45 acres and since Americans were having many children, there was simply not enough accessible and fertile land to go around.

This apparent shortage of land worried many Americans, and appeared to be increasing tensions between parents and children. Why should sons labor for a household that could give them very little in return? In addition, as writers such as Benjamin Franklin feared, a land shortage would make it more difficult for American men to secure their independence by owning private property. Could the colonies survive if they remained cramped along the Atlantic Ocean?

For many colonists, the answer was clearly no. By the middle of the 1700s, European settlers were moving into the interior of North America. Scots-Irish and Germans settled central Pennsylvania and the Shenandoah Valley of Virginia. Farther to the north, people were spreading into the Mohawk River valley in New York and the Connecticut River valley in what is now Vermont. They were migrating in search of land on which they could stake their independence and maintain their households.

Two forces created tension in the 1700s: the westward push of European settlers and an effort to rediscover the meaning of Christianity.

Native American and French Reaction

Just ahead of the English migrants were Native Americans, including the Delaware and the Shawnee. They were moving west, too. Though heavily involved in trade with the Europeans, they preferred forest life to farm life. By the mid-1700s, disease and war over trade had taken a toll on Native American cultures; the Iroquois, for example, were no longer as strong militarily as they had been in the 1600s. Native Americans nonetheless

Reproducible Lesson Plan found in the Unit 1 folder, p. 76, provides a summary of the Section 4 lesson plan content.

Alternate Lesson Plan: Learning Styles found in the Alternate Lesson Plans folder, p. 15, is designed to encourage students to identify and depict elements of English colonial expansion and is especially useful for visual learners.

Guided Reading and Review found in the Unit 1 folder, p. 83, provides a structure for reading and mastering the key concepts and reviewing the key terms for Section 4. (Guided Practice)

1. FOCUS

Connecting to the Big Idea

See page 70B. Explain that by the mid-1700s, conflicts emerged in colonial society. Ask what tensions were aroused by the desire of colonists to move westward. How did a revival of religious feeling indirectly challenge colonial society and British government?

Objectives
- Explain why British settlers moved beyond the confines of the thirteen colonies.
- Delineate the tensions created among Native Americans, the French, and the British as settlers migrated west.
- Describe how the Great Awakening indirectly challenged the colonial belief in inequality.

Bellringer

Ask students to think about what land ownership signifies. What are the reasons for wanting land today? What were they in colonial times?

Reading Strategy

Predicting Content Read aloud the following sentence from page 89: "The growth of the colonies, both in population and territory, created new problems and revived old ones." Ask students to skim Section 4 and predict the two major types of problems described in the section. When they have finished reading, ask students to test their predictions against the actual text.

Answer to ...
Viewpoints

Canassatego values the land as the life-giving force of his people and laments the fact that white settlers are running roughshod over it. The governor of Pennsylvania values the land only in terms of financial gain. For a more thorough examination of expansion into Native American lands, see the Resource Directory below.

Answer to ...

Answers should suggest a conflict among the French, British, and Native Americans for control of the Ohio River valley.

2. INSTRUCT

Explain/Discuss

Review the reasons that the French and Native Americans did not welcome English settlers onto their lands. How did settlers disrupt the lives of Native Americans? How did British settlement affect the fur trade of the French?

Ask students to explain how religion helped to maintain order. How did the preachers of the Great Awakening stress the importance of each person? Ask students why the Great Awakening threatened order.

Analyze

Ask students to consider how the growing distance from the frontier to the centers of colonial government contributed to the increasing independence of the pioneer settlers.

Enrichment

In 1768 or 1769, Charles Woodmason, an Anglican clergyman, said:
" . . .They [the wandering clergy of the Great Awakening] are continually ranging from River to River. . . . The wont is, That they don't all agree in one Tune. For one sings this Doctrine, and the next a different—So

Viewpoints
On Expansion into Native American Lands

The selections below are speeches made during negotiations over the English purchase of Native American lands in Pennsylvania. *How does each of the speakers below describe the value of the land?*

Against Expansion

"We know our Lands are now become more valuable. The white People think we do not know their Value; but we are sensible [aware] that the Land is everlasting, and the few Goods we receive for it are soon worn out and gone. . . . Besides, we are not well used [treated] with respect to the lands still unsold by us. Your people daily settle on these lands, and spoil our hunting. . . . Your horses and cows have eaten the grass our deer used to feed on."

Canassatego, Iroquois leader, July 7, 1742

For Expansion

"It is very true that lands are of late becoming more valuable; but what raises their value? Is it not entirely owing to the industry and labor used by the white people in their cultivation and improvement? Had not they come among you, these lands would have been of no use to you, any further than to maintain you. . . . The value of the land is no more than it is worth in money."

Governor of Pennsylvania, July 7, 1742

remained powerful players in the development of American colonial society. And they remained adept at playing on the rivalry between the French in Canada and the British in New York and Pennsylvania.

The relentless intrusion of the English alarmed the French as well as the Native Americans. By the early 1750s, it was clear that some kind of explosion was rapidly approaching. The most likely setting was western Pennsylvania. There the interests of the colonies of Pennsylvania and Virginia were in conflict with both the Native Americans and the French. Whoever controlled the **forks of the Ohio River,** the place where the Allegheny and Monongahela rivers meet to form the Ohio, would have a considerable strategic advantage over everyone else.

The paragraph you have just read uses foreshadowing, a writing technique that hints at future events or developments. What kind of event do you think is being foreshadowed here?

Religious Tensions Within the Colonies

While tensions built along the outer edges of the British colonies, unrest was also increasing within them. Nowhere was this more obvious than in colonial religious life.

While the British colonies were overwhelmingly Protestant (aside from a few Jews in cities and some Catholics in Maryland), no particular group of Protestants was more powerful than any other. Southern planters and northern merchants and professionals tended to belong to the Church of England. Most New Englanders were either Congregationalists or Presbyterians. Quakers were strong in Pennsylvania, as were Lutherans and Mennonites. The Dutch Reformed Church was thriving in the colony of New York.

In the early 1700s, many ministers, particularly Congregationalists, believed that the colonists had fallen away from the faith of their Puritan ancestors. In the 1730s and 1740s, they led a series of revivals that especially touched women of all ages and young men. This revival of religious feeling is now known as the **Great Awakening.**

⭐ The purpose of the preachers who brought about the Great Awakening was to remind people of the power of God and—at least in the beginning—of the authority of their ministers. In a well-known fiery sermon, "Sinners in the Hands of an Angry God," revivalist Jonathan Edwards appealed to the individuals in his congregation in Northampton, Massachusetts:

O sinner! Consider the fearful danger you are in: it is a great furnace of wrath, a wide and bottomless pit, full of the fire of wrath, that you are held over in the hand of that God, whose wrath is provoked and incensed as much against you, as

RESOURCE DIRECTORY

Teaching Resources

Viewpoints Activity On Expansion into Native American Lands, found in the Unit 1 folder, pp. 89–90, provides additional quotes to extend students' understanding of colonial expansion.

⭐ **American Profiles Activity** found in the Unit 1 folder, p. 88, profiles Jonathan Edwards, a fiery preacher who ushered the Great Awakening into New England.

⭐ **Primary Source Activity** The Great Awakening, found in the Unit 1 folder, pp. 94–95, uses an account by Benjamin Franklin and the text of a sermon by Jonathan Edwards to help students understand the phenomenon of the Great Awakening.

against many of the damned in hell. You hang by a slender thread.

As time went on, however, the Great Awakening did more than revive people's religious conviction. It energized them to speak for themselves and to reject the traditional authority of ministers and books. As George Whitefield, one of the most famous and popular revivalists, said,

The Generality of Preachers talk of an unknown, unfelt Christ. And the Reason why Congregations have been so dead, is because dead Men preach to them.

People flocked not to the established ministers but to wandering preachers, often poorly educated, who told of the ability of all people to have a personal relationship with Jesus Christ. According to these preachers, the infinitely great power of God did not put Him beyond the reach of ordinary people. The message these ministers spread was that faith and sincerity were the major requirements needed to understand the Gospel.

Proof of the new religious independence brought about by the Great Awakening can be seen in the shift of many people in New England to the Baptist faith in the 1740s and 1750s, and in the South, to both the Baptist and the Methodist churches. The appeal of these two particular churches lay in their emotionalism and their celebration of ordinary people.

⭐ The impact of the Great Awakening on society at large was no less significant than the turmoil it brought to religious life in the colonies. Methodists and Baptists tended to be

people at the middle or bottom of the colonial hierarchy. When they claimed that every individual could act on his or her own faith and did not have to rely on a minister or other authority in spiritual matters, they were indirectly attacking the fundamental notion that some people are better and more important than others.

In the end, the Great Awakening became a challenge to the social and political order of British North America. If ordinary people could figure out how to worship God on their own, couldn't they figure out how to govern themselves as well?

Known for their "pathetical," or emotional, style, preachers such as George Whitefield (left) encouraged ordinary people to believe that they, too, could reach out to God.

"The bow of God's wrath is bent, and the arrow made ready on the string." Such was the warning of God's power contained throughout Jonathan Edwards's fiery sermon.

SECTION 4 REVIEW

Key Terms, People, and Places
1. Define Great Awakening.
2. Identify the forks of the Ohio River.

Key Concepts
3. Why was it increasingly necessary for British colonists to expand westward in the mid-1700s?
4. How did Native Americans and the French react to westward expansion by British settlers?

5. Why was the Great Awakening an indirect challenge to the hierarchical social order of the British colonies?

Critical Thinking
6. **Recognizing Cause and Effect** What effect did the European custom of giving land to sons have on Native Americans like Canassatego, quoted in the "Viewpoints" on page 90?

 Quiz found in the Unit 1 folder, p. 84, covers the main ideas in this section as well as the key terms.

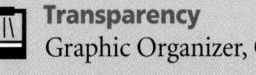 **Chapter Test** Forms A and B are found in the Unit 1 folder, pp. 101–106.

 Answer Keys found in the Unit 1 folder, pp. 146–160, provide answers to all student activities.

Media and Technology

📖 **Transparency**
Graphic Organizer, G-5

🎧 **Guided Reading Audiotapes**
(English and Spanish)

📖 **Computer Test Bank**

---

that Peoples Brains are turn'd and bewilder'd."

Ask students to comment on Woodmason's stand in the ferment created by the Great Awakening.

3. ASSESS

Section 4 Review Answers
1. Great Awakening, see p. 90
2. the forks of the Ohio River, see p. 90
3. They believed that there was not enough land for them to maintain independent families.
4. They were alarmed by the expansion; it became clear that some kind of explosion was likely, probably at the forks of the Ohio River.
5. It raised the question whether ordinary people, if they could worship God on their own, could also figure out how to govern themselves.
6. This custom had the indirect effect of depriving Native Americans of their land.

Reteach

Each sentence below describes a development in colonial society. Ask students to explain why each development caused tension in colonial society.
● Settlers moved into the interior of North America.
● Many colonists followed the preachers of the Great Awakening rather than the ministers of the established churches.

4. CLOSE

 Reinforcing the Big Idea

The westward movement and the doctrines of equality taught by preachers of the Great Awakening created tensions in colonial society and set the stage for greater conflicts to come.

Two Settlement Patterns in the Colonies

Focus Colonists from England created and maintained colonies in New England and in Pennsylvania. They were rapidly joined by settlers from other parts of Europe. The result was two unique places: places that were not only not like England but also quite unlike each other.

In this section students will analyze some of the factors that made New England so distinct from Pennsylvania. **Instruct** Ask students how they could tell if they were flying over New England or over Pennsylvania—solely from the aerial view. Ask students what clues they would look for from the plane. (*The ocean, formation of shoreline, hills, mountains, rivers, cities.*) Then tell students that they might have been able to notice the difference between colonial New England and colonial Pennsylvania from the air.

Divide the class into small groups, assigning each group either New England or Pennsylvania. Tell each group to use physical and historical maps of the colonies to create a description of their assigned colony in 1750— from the air. Have students first decide on three or four landmarks or cities to use as anchors for their descriptions and then determine where to begin and end their description. Suggest that students use the information in the feature about the types and sizes of towns and farms.

After students have presented and discussed their bird's-eye views, ask them to analyze the advantages each mode of settlement gave its colonists. In New England, people moved into new territory as a group starting a town. How did this help the colonists survive? (*Security from attack, ability to help one another quickly.*) How did the pattern of large farms help the settlers of Pennsylvania? (*It provided ample crops to feed the settlers.*)

Two Settlement Patterns in the Colonies

By 1750, several distinct settlement regions had emerged in colonial North America. What human and physical geographic characteristics distinguished these regions?

Many regions of the New England and Middle colonies were settled at roughly the same time. Yet each region was unique, and even the casual traveler could tell one place from the other. Two regions in particular had different physical landscapes—New England and, in the Middle Colonies, Pennsylvania. But physical appearance was not the only feature that distinguished these places, as the maps at right show. The human imprint placed on the land by the people who settled it was equally, or more, distinctive.

Place: Settlement Patterns Form Unique Geographic Signatures

Every place differs from others in its physical and human characteristics. An important human characteristic of a place is the way it has been settled. How was the land divided? How were towns set up? What were the most important ways of making a living in the region? What cultural traditions did the people bring from their old homes? The answers to these questions give a clearer picture of each region and help to distinguish each one from the others.

> The Puritans valued both family and church and thus created settlements rooted in community and faith.

New England

The character of the New England colonies was strongly influenced by the Puritan settlers who first came to Massachusetts in 1620. The Puritans valued both family and church and thus created settlements rooted in community and faith. They had come to America to escape persecution and to worship according to their beliefs. But they were intolerant of others who believed in a different form of worship and excluded them from their communities.

Typically, an immigrating Puritan group was granted a town by the colonial legislature. A town was a piece of land about 6 square miles in size, usually divided into 36 lots. The group would establish a village near the center of the town where the meetinghouse or church, the public school, and other public buildings were located. Each family in the group received a house lot in the village, some acres to farm in the town lands nearby, and the right to use any of the town's common land.

Puritan settlements of this sort were first established in the area around Boston, Massachusetts, and the lower Connecticut River valley. The map of Sudbury shows the typical settlement characteristics of New England by 1750: a homogeneous population, one in which nearly all members had a common origin; clusters of closely linked towns with small family farms; and village centers typically built around a piece of public, or common, land and dominated by a single church.

Pennsylvania

In 1681 William Penn, a Quaker, received a huge land grant from King Charles II of England on

RESOURCE DIRECTORY

Teaching Resources

Time and Place Activity Changing Economic Patterns in the South, found in the Unit 1 folder, pp. 85–86, uses regional maps to chart the evolution of the southern economy between the Civil War and 1980.

Fields held in common

House

Town Pound
North Field
Meetinghouse
Pond
Mill Pond
Cart Path
Mill Rd.
Schoolhouse
Mill
Great River Meadow
Cow Common

Sudbury

0   1/4   1/2 Mile
0   1/4   1/2 Kilometer

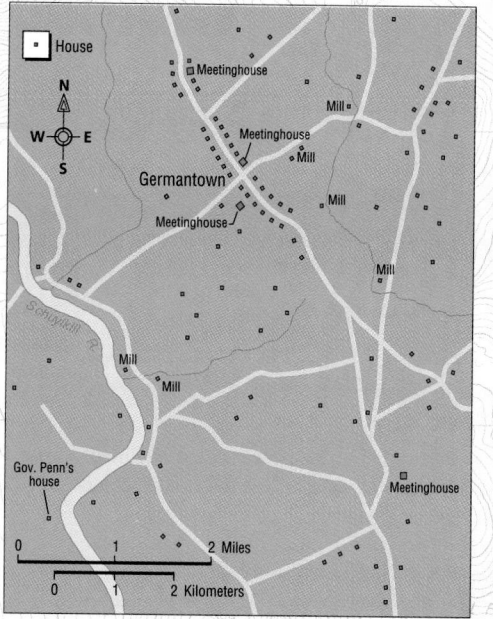

House

Meetinghouse
Mill
Meetinghouse
Mill
Germantown
Meetinghouse
Mill
Schuylkill R.
Mill
Mill
Mill
Gov. Penn's house
Meetinghouse

0   1   2 Miles
0   1   2 Kilometers

the west side of the lower Delaware River. Penn founded Pennsylvania, or "Penn's Woods," which he saw as a "Holy Experiment," a mecca of religious tolerance and social equality. Penn negotiated land treaties with Native Americans and then brought over the first of many Quaker settlers from England.

The Quakers were a religious group who fled persecution in England, as had the Puritans before them. Unlike the Puritans, however, the Quakers valued individuality and practiced tolerance for others. Soon, Pennsylvania drew Quakers from Wales, Germany, and other American colonies. Many gravitated to Philadelphia, the fast-growing city that was the nucleus of the colony; others came to farm the rich lands in the Great Valley to the west of Philadelphia.

The colony started recruiting non-Quakers who were interested in cheap land and religious tolerance. The German Lutherans, Scots-Irish Presbyterians, and Swiss Mennonites tended to settle on family farms some distance apart in the southeastern region of the colony. As the map of Germantown shows, the few large villages and towns that dotted the region differed in one important way from New

England towns—they featured churches or meetinghouses of several different Christian groups.

By 1750 Pennsylvania had developed a character that was marked by prosperity, attitudes of individualism and religious tolerance, and by the cultural diversity resulting from the intermingling of several ethnic groups. The colony differed greatly from Puritan New England, where the population was homogeneous, more rooted in the doctrines of a single church, and less tolerant of religious variation of any kind.

GEOGRAPHIC CONNECTIONS

1. Explain how the Puritan settlers influenced the character of the New England colonies.
2. What was the main difference between the New England and Pennsylvania colonies?

Critical Thinking

3. **Making Comparisons** Based on their different religious beliefs, how might the colonists in New England and Pennsylvania have differed in their attitudes toward Native Americans?

Chapter Review Answers

Understanding Key Terms, People, and Places

Terms
Students should refer to the definitions of key terms in the chapter to create sentences that show an understanding of their relation to England and its colonies or to life in colonial America.

True or False
1. false, the Great Awakening
2. true
3. false, mercantilism
4. false, Middle Passage

Matching
1. William Byrd
2. Eliza Lucas Pinckney
3. Benjamin Franklin

Reviewing Main Ideas

1. The colonies supplied England with food and raw materials and were enthusiastic buyers of English goods.

2. Relying on the policy of salutary neglect, Parliament rarely tried to interfere in the affairs of the colonies.

3. New Englanders shipped goods such as china, books, and cloth from England to the West Indies, transported sugar from the West Indies to New England to distill into rum, traded rum and firearms for slaves in West Africa, then carried slaves to the West Indies to trade for more sugar.

4. Most colonists accepted slavery as a normal part of life. Most also assumed that women were not equal to men. In addition, the landed gentry set themselves apart from ordinary people by their superior clothes, houses, and manners.

5. Although under English common law women had few powers and no personal identity, in reality men and women depended heavily on each other to maintain the household and the community.

6. Because so much work was required to maintain a household, work was the central focus in most people's lives.

7. Equiano's case was unusual because he eventually gained his freedom.

8. African Americans made up the majority of the population in these colonies, had mostly come directly from Africa, generally had little contact with colonists, and were able to preserve their kinship networks.

9. Enslaved people in Virginia and Maryland had regular contact with white Americans.

CHAPTER 3
Chapter Review

Understanding Key Terms, People, and Places

Key Terms
1. mercantilism
2. balance of trade
3. salutary neglect
4. Fall Line
5. triangular trade
6. gentry
7. cousinocracy
8. Middle Passage
9. low country
10. Great Awakening

People
11. William Byrd
12. Benjamin Franklin
13. Eliza Lucas Pinckney

Places
14. forks of the Ohio River

Terms For each term above, write a sentence that explains its relation to England and its colonies or to life in colonial America.

True or False Determine whether each statement is true or false. If it is true, write "true." If it is false, change the underlined term to make the statement true.
1. The revival of religious feeling in the 1730s and 1740s was called <u>mercantilism</u>.
2. Because so many landowners were related, some colonies were run by a <u>cousinocracy</u>.
3. The theory of <u>salutary neglect</u> held that a country should try to get and keep as much wealth as possible.
4. On the part of the triangular trade called the <u>Great Awakening</u>, African slaves were transported to the Americas.

Matching Review the key people in the list above. If you are not sure of a person's significance, review his or her importance in the chapter. Then choose a name from the list that best matches each description below.
1. the Virginia gentleman who kept a diary of his daily routine
2. the South Carolina teenager who managed three plantations
3. a Philadelphia printer, leading statesman, and gentleman

Reviewing Main Ideas

Section 1 (pp. 72–77)
1. Why was the relationship between England and the colonies prosperous for both sides?
2. What was the British government's policy toward the colonies after the rule of King James had ended?
3. Describe the system of triangular trade used by New Englanders in the 1700s.

Section 2 (pp. 79–83)
4. Give evidence to support the statement that colonial Americans organized their society according to a fundamental belief in inequality.
5. How did the legal status of women differ from their actual importance in colonial society?
6. Describe the importance of work in colonial America.

Section 3 (pp. 84–88)
7. What was unusual about Olaudah Equiano's story compared to that of other slaves in the colonies?

8. Give four reasons why African Americans in South Carolina and Georgia were able to preserve many of their cultural traditions.
9. What factor contributed to the integration of European American and African American cultures in Virginia and Maryland?
10. How did the employment of enslaved African Americans in the New England and Middle colonies reflect the geography and economy of the North?

Section 4 (pp. 89–91)
11. Aside from needing land for farming, why did American men fear a land shortage?
12. Why was western Pennsylvania a likely hot spot for confrontation between the French, English, and Native Americans?
13. What attracted people to wandering preachers during the Great Awakening?

---

10. In the North, slaves worked in the forests and on the seacoast. Others worked in manufacturing or as domestic servants.

11. A land shortage would make it more difficult to achieve personal independence by owning private property.

12. In western Pennsylvania, the English colonists came into conflict with both Native Americans and the French over land and the strategically important forks of the Ohio River.

13. The wandering preachers spread the message that God was not beyond the reach of ordinary people and that faith and sincerity were the major requirements for salvation.

Thinking Critically

1. The British in the 1600s felt that nations should have colonies and had a right to exploit them for wealth.

2. Answers will vary. Students may note that although American society today is far more egalitarian than in colonial times, it is not classless. Dress is less of an indicator of wealth than in the past, but wealth and power still often overlap.

3. Instead of devoting himself to work, Franklin aspired to being a member of the gentry by undertaking a variety of other pursuits. His *Poor Richard's Almanac* reflects the gentleman's ideal of living an orderly and self-disciplined life.

Thinking Critically

1. **Recognizing Ideologies** Today many people consider it wrong for a nation to have colonies. How does this view of colonies contrast with that held by the British in the 1600s?
2. **Making Comparisons** During the 1700s, the gentry—the wealthiest, most influential people in society—set themselves apart from other people by their clothes, houses, and manners. Is there a gentry class in the United States today? If so, does this group set itself apart by its dress, manners, and possessions?
3. **Determining Relevance** In what ways was Benjamin Franklin a typical man of his times?
4. **Distinguishing Fact from Opinion** Is the quotation from George Whitefield on page 91 fact or opinion? Explain your reasoning.

Making Connections

1. **Evaluating Primary Sources** Review the primary source excerpt on page 85. What does the quotation reveal about the way slave dealers viewed the African people they had brought to the Americas?
2. **Understanding the Visuals** Examine the picture on page 75. What is one indication that some of the members of the legislative assembly in the picture are gentry?
3. **Writing About the Chapter** Write a diary entry from the point of view of one of the following people in colonial America: (a) a member of the gentry, (b) an African American slave, (c) a woman, (d) an ordinary worker. First, make a list of the ways in which you might spend a typical day. Note any feelings you might have toward the way you spend your day, as well as reasons for why you live as you do. Next,

write a draft of your entry, in which you explain your typical day in as much detail as possible. Revise your entry, making sure that your details reflect the times in which your character is writing. Proofread your entry and draft a final copy.
4. **Using the Graphic Organizer** This graphic organizer uses a multi-flow map to organize the causes and effects of England's policy of salutary neglect toward its colonies. (a) Economic benefit appears as both a cause and an effect in the graphic organizer. Explain. (b) Give two reasons why the colonies were able to govern themselves to a large extent. (c) On a separate sheet of paper, create your own graphic organizer showing the causes and effects of the Great Awakening, using this graphic organizer as an example.

4. The quotation is an expression of opinion. Whitefield is making a value judgment concerning other preachers and congregations.

Making Connections

1. Slave dealers did not view Africans as people with feelings and family ties like themselves, but as commodities.
2. The man leading the assembly is wearing a wig, the hallmark of the gentry class.
3. Answers will vary. Students' diary entries should reveal a grasp of their character's station in colonial society and the expectations surrounding that station.

4. (a) The more the colonies prospered, the more they benefited England and the more England could afford to leave them alone. Thus cause and effect were circular. (b) The English government was preoccupied with a civil war, and the colonists had a tradition of strong local government, which they applied to self-rule. (c) Students' graphic organizers should indicate the main cause of the Great Awakening: the revival of religious feeling and a personal relationship with God. The main effect was that people began to question authority when they realized that they could interpret the Bible by themselves.

Chapter 4 The American Revolution
1754–1783

📁 Teaching Resources (See Unit 1 Folder)

	Instruction	Enrichment
Section 1 **The French and Indian War Challenges Colonial Thinking** (pp. 98–101)	Reproducible Lesson Plan, p. 108 Alternate Lesson Plan, p. 17 Guided Reading and Review, p. 112 Quiz, p. 113	Primary Source Activity, Braddock's Defeat, p. 126
Section 2 **The Issues That Led to the War for Independence** (pp. 102–107)	Reproducible Lesson Plan, p. 109 Alternate Lesson Plan, p. 18 Guided Reading and Review, p. 114 Quiz, p. 115	American Profiles Activity, Pontiac, Chief of the Ottawa, p. 120 Visual Learning Activity, The American Rattlesnake, p. 133 Visual Learning Activity, Boycotting Tea, p. 132 Historian's Toolbox Activity, Expressing Problems Clearly, p. 124
Section 3 **The Ideas That Led to the War for Independence** (pp. 109–114)	Reproducible Lesson Plan, p. 110 Alternate Lesson Plan, p. 19 Guided Reading and Review, p. 116 Quiz, p. 117	Literature Activity, To the King, p. 129 Literature Activity, Common Sense, pp. 130–131 Viewpoints Activity, On Rule by the People, pp. 122–123
Section 4 **The War for Independence** (pp. 115–121)	Reproducible Lesson Plan, p. 111 Alternate Lesson Plan, p. 20 Guided Reading and Review, p. 118 Quiz, p. 119 Chapter Test, Forms A & B, pp. 134–139	Critical Thinking Activity, Checking Consistency, p. 125 American Profiles Activity, Deborah Sampson Gannett, p. 121 Primary Source Activity, War Diary of Margaret Hill Morris, pp. 127–128

📁 Additional Chapter Resources

Resource Organizer, p. 107
Alternate Lesson Plan, p. 16
Answer Keys, pp. 146–159

Bibliography

For the Teacher

Harling, Frederick, and Martin Kaufman, eds. *The Ethnic Contribution to the American Revolution.* Historical Journal of Western Massachusetts, 1976. (Documents illustrating the contributions to the Revolution made by various minority groups.)

Kristol, Irving, Martin Diamond, and G. Warren Nutter. *The American Revolution: Three Views.* American Brands, 1975. (Three perspectives on the notion of revolution as applied to the War for Independence.)

Smith, Page. *A New Age Now Begins: A People's History of the American Revolution.* McGraw-Hill, 1976. (Fast-paced, comprehensive account of the Revolutionary period.)

Prentice Hall Literature Excerpts from *The American Experience,* 1994, "The Revolutionary Period, 1750–1800," including Henry, Patrick. "Speech in the Virginia Convention."

Media and Technology

 Critical Thinking, I-10; The Way It Works, H-4

 Cause and Effect, F-2

 Fine Art, D-4, D-5; Graphic Organizer, G-2

 Guided Reading Audiotapes (English and Spanish)

 Computer Test Bank

For the Student

America. Part 4, *Inventing a Nation.* Time-Life. Filmstrip. (Alistair Cooke investigates the Independence Hall debates.)

Lagguth, A. J. *Patriots: The Men Who Started the American Revolution.* Simon & Schuster, 1988. (Well-illustrated biographical sketches of some of the most important male figures of the Revolution.)

Meltzer, Milton. *The American Revolutionaries: A History in Their Own Words.* Crowell, 1987. (Includes an exchange of letters between Abigail and John Adams.)

THE BIG IDEA

The Big Idea for the chapter and how the main ideas in each section relate to the Big Idea are graphically displayed below. Comprehension of this chapter's Big Idea is critical to students' understanding of United States history and how we as a nation got where we are today.

CHAPTER 4

The American Revolution was more than a war for independence. The struggle reflected the development of a unique American identity that was fueled by colonists' personal definitions of democracy and equality. This new consciousness inspired a war that led to independence from Great Britain and the creation of a radically new society.

SECTION 1

The French and Indian War made many colonists aware of how different they were from the British and challenged them to establish an identity independent from their parent country.

SECTION 2

Many colonists were deeply angered by British attempts to make them pay taxes, which they felt robbed them of their personal liberty and reduced them to slavery.

SECTION 3

Important new beliefs, including the ideas that men were born equal and could rule themselves, helped fuel the War for Independence.

SECTION 4

The War for Independence established the American colonies' independence from Great Britain and laid the foundation for a new society based on principles of equality and democracy.

The American Revolution
1754–1783

The Relevance of the Big Idea

Before the American Revolution, the thought of establishing a society based on the principles of liberty, equality, and the pursuit of happiness was almost unimaginable. At that time, most people in the world were governed by some form of absolute ruler. But even as the rhetoric of the Revolution was being written down, it became clear that the founding fathers did not necessarily equate principles with actions. Liberty and equality were neither guaranteed nor universally enjoyed. The application of such principles to all groups in society would be gradual and ongoing throughout American history.

Ask students to provide examples from their own experiences or knowledge of history in which principles have not been practiced.

In Depth

Global Connections

By the mid-eighteenth century, Britain and France had emerged as the two main contenders in the struggle for world empire. Their rivalry dominated the Seven Years' War (1756–1763), a global conflict involving nine European nations that was fought in Europe, Asia, and North America. In North America it was known as the French and Indian War. In the end, the British were victorious in India and, with the help of American colonists, in North America, thus gaining an empire and moving into a position of global supremacy.

The American Revolution
1754–1783

*S*truggling for their rights and protesting against what they saw as British wrongs, colonists in the Americas demanded and won their independence from Great Britain. The firestorm of revolution that swept the colonies was sparked by particular issues and fueled by powerful ideas. Those ideas changed more than just the public, male world of politics; they transformed virtually every aspect of American society by creating a nation committed, at least in theory, to democracy and equality.

Events in the United States

	1754 The French and Indian War begins.	**1759** The British defeat the French at Quebec.	**1763** Pontiac's Rebellion breaks out between the Native Americans and the British.	**1766** Colonists riot to protest the Stamp Act.	**1770** The Boston Massacre increases British-colonial tensions.
	1754	1758	1762	1766	1770

Events in the World

1756 The French and Indian War spreads to Europe.	**1762** Catherine the Great becomes ruler of Russia.	**1769** Scotland's James Watt makes a steam engine capable of running other machines.

▶ RESOURCE DIRECTORY

Teaching Resources

Alternate Lesson Plan: Demonstrating the Big Idea found in the Alternate Lesson Plans folder, p. 16, provides a lesson strategy to instruct students about the Big Idea that a unique American identity developed among the colonists, fueled by a greater sense of democracy and equality than the British had.

Alternative Assessment Handbook provides information, guidance, and strategies for alternative methods of assessment. It includes an essay on new trends in assessment, guidance and strategies for developing performance tasks and portfolios, scoring rubrics, and sample evaluation forms.

1776 The War for Independence rages.
• The Continental Congress signs the Declaration of Independence.

1781 British general Lord Cornwallis surrenders at Yorktown.

1783 The Treaty of Paris grants the colonies official independence.

1774	1778	1782	1786	1790	1794

1778 English explorer James Cook lands on Hawaii.

1789 The French Revolution begins, taking its inspiration from the American Revolution.

Alternative Assessment

As an ongoing chapter project, have students assume the role of adviser to King George III on colonial affairs and conduct an investigation into the unrest in the American colonies. Encourage students to collect information and analyze its significance in terms of its threat to Great Britain's authority. Presentations should contain a minimum of three of the following sources:

• Copies of political pamphlets outlining radical beliefs
• Letters to British citizens from relatives in the colonies with information about the political mood of the colonies
• Reports from British spies on rebel activities and rebel leaders
• Maps showing areas of rebel activity, such as towns with militias, and specific locations of weapon storehouses
• Interviews with high-ranking British officers regarding the political situation in the colonies

Explain that projects will be evaluated according to the following guidelines:

• **Unacceptable** Project is not attempted or fails to meet basic requirements.
• **Limited/Acceptable** Assignments are completed and an attempt is made to understand and interpret the data in terms of its seriousness to Great Britain.
• **Extensive/Commendable** Assignments are completed, the data is plausibly interpreted, and the seriousness of its implications is well judged.
• **Extraordinary/Outstanding** More than three sources are used to compile data which is thoroughly interpreted, and specific pieces are assessed for their relative importance to Great Britain's position.

For information and guidance on alternative assessment trends and strategies, see the Alternative Assessment Handbook in the Resource Directory on page 96.

The French and Indian War Challenges Colonial Thinking

SECTION 1

1. FOCUS

Connecting to the Big Idea

See page 96B. Explain to students that the French and Indian War marked a turning point in the relationship between the American colonists and Great Britain. It showed the colonists more and more clearly that they had their own, distinctly American identity. Ask students to describe that unique identity.

Objectives

● Explain how the French and Indian War made Americans aware of how different they were from the British.
● Describe the strategy the British used to win the French and Indian War.

Bellringer

Ask students to explain why relationships between teenagers and their parents are often difficult. What types of issues are the source of such conflict?

Reading Strategy

Reading for Evidence Ask students to find evidence, as they read, to support the statement on page 98 that "many colonists began to see themselves as different from the British troops they fought beside."

SECTION 1

The French and Indian War Challenges Colonial Thinking

SECTION PREVIEW

During their long war against the French and Native Americans, many colonists began to see themselves as different from the British troops they fought beside. The war challenged them to rethink their traditional relationship with their parent country—and to decide ultimately that the relationship had to change.

Key Concepts
• During the French and Indian War, Americans became increasingly aware of how different they were from the British.
• The British won the French and Indian War by capturing key towns and forts first in the east and the west, and then in the center of the long line of towns and forts by which the French controlled the territory of New France.

Key Terms, People, and Places
American Revolution, War for Independence, French and Indian War; minutemen, George Washington

When the British and Americans fought against the French and their Native American allies, this horn served a soldier both as a container for gunpowder and as a map of wilderness forts.

B y two o'clock in the morning on April 19, 1775, about 130 men had made their way to the green in the center of Lexington, Massachusetts. They were **minutemen**—local residents organized as a defensive force who had pledged to respond in a matter of minutes when called to action. For some time they simply stood around on the green, waiting for the British force that was to march through Lexington on its way to destroy a store of military supplies in neighboring Concord. Before the British appeared, some of the minutemen grew tired and bored and went home; others headed for a nearby tavern.

Toward dawn, a scout roused the seventy men remaining on or near the green. They took up positions in a double file. Captain John Parker, their forty-five-year-old leader, warned them to "let the troops pass by, and don't molest them, without they begin first." The colonists had no plans to stop the British—their presence on the green was only meant as a protest.

Within fifteen minutes, Major John Pitcairn led between 700 and 800 British regulars into Lexington, outnumbering the minutemen ten times over. Pitcairn took a position behind the Americans and ordered them to give up their guns. Captain Parker told his men to go home. Some began to leave; others stood their ground.

Exactly what happened next will never be known. Both British and Americans denied shooting at each other first. In any case, the British soldiers were soon firing into the American ranks and using their bayonets. Within minutes, eight dead Americans lay on Lexington Green and another nine were wounded. The victorious British regrouped and marched on toward Concord.

This brief encounter was the beginning of an eight-year war between the British government and thirteen of its North American colonies. To win their independence, the colonies would organize themselves into a loose confederation called the United States of America. The war and the political and social changes that accompanied it are called the **American Revolution.** The war itself is called the **War for Independence.**

But before you read about the Revolution, you must first understand why the Americans rebelled. What motivated several dozen farmers and artisans to stand on a green in the middle of the night and defy the authority of their king? Why were so many colonists, who were

---

 RESOURCE DIRECTORY

Teaching Resources

Reproducible Lesson Plan found in the Unit 1 folder, p. 108, provides a summary of the Section 1 lesson plan content.

Alternate Lesson Plan: Learning Styles found in the Alternate Lesson Plans folder, p. 17, helps students explain the strategies and describe the effects of the war by creating a chart and is especially useful for visual or tactile learners.

 Guided Reading and Review found in the Unit 1 folder, p. 112, provides a structure for reading and mastering the key concepts and reviewing the key terms for Section 1. (Guided Practice)

perhaps the least taxed, most prosperous, and freest people in the world, willing to risk everything in a revolution?

These questions have several answers. One is that in response to British actions during the 1750s and 1760s, many colonists began to think of themselves as different and separate from the British.

The French and Indian War

In 1754, over twenty years before the clash at Lexington, an inexperienced, twenty-one-year-old officer from Virginia led a small force of colonists and Native Americans to the forks of the Ohio. In this strategic location, mentioned in Chapter 3, the French had built Fort Duquesne to control the upper Ohio River valley. The force of colonists had been sent by the

governor of Virginia, who wanted to protect Virginia's claim to the area.

After ambushing a scouting party and killing ten of the French, the officer and his men retreated about 60 miles and hastily built an outpost, which they named Fort Necessity. The French soon caught up with them, surrounded their fort, and forced them to surrender. In the end, the colonists had to make their way back to Virginia in disgrace. The expedition was not a promising start for the officer in charge, **George Washington,** a man who would one day be remembered for his leadership.

French and Native Americans Take the Lead
George Washington's unsuccessful military expedition was the first skirmish of a major war that lasted until 1763. Called the **French and Indian War** because the British and their colonists

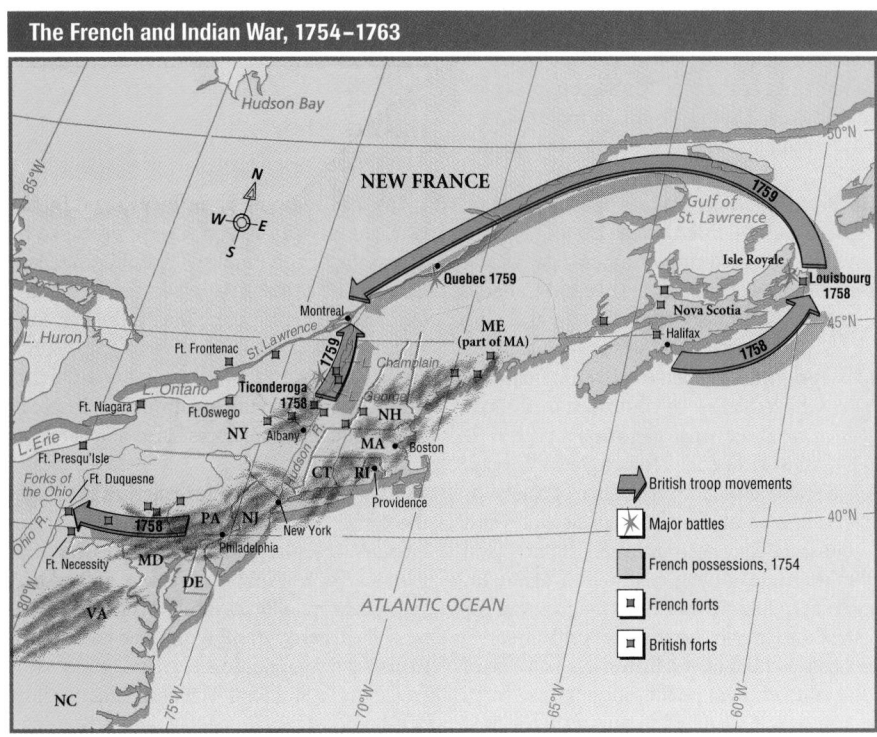

The French and Indian War, 1754–1763

Geography and History: Interpreting Maps
The three main thrusts of British strategy are shown here. In 1758, British forces struck in two directions—at French strongholds in the west and against Louisbourg in the east. Finally, in 1759, they attacked Quebec and Montreal. *Why was it necessary to capture Louisbourg before attacking Quebec?*

2. INSTRUCT

Explain/Discuss
Review with students the relationship between the colonists and Great Britain before and during the French and Indian War. How did Americans feel about this relationship?

Discuss the war against the French and Native Americans. Ask students to describe the respective roles of the colonists and the Native Americans. What strategy did the British use to win the war?

Analyze
Have students analyze the effect of the French and Indian War on the future of the colonies. In what ways did the war challenge colonists to rethink their relationship with Great Britain?

Activity
Cooperative Learning
Time: One class period.
Activity: Enact a gathering in a tavern.
Grouping: Groups of six to eight students.
Purpose: In order to show how the French and Indian War brought the British and the colonists into contact with one another, have students enact a discussion in a tavern on a given topic from the viewpoint of either British soldiers or colonists. Possible topics include life in Britain compared with life in the colonies, British mercantile policy, or the conduct of the French and Indian War.
Roles: British soldiers (officers and enlisted men) or colonists.
Outcome: Students will appreciate the differences between the British and the colonists and understand better the tensions that developed as a result.

Caption Answer to ...

 Interpreting Maps

To gain access to the St. Lawrence River.

Ask students to research one of the major battles of the French and Indian War, such as those at Fort Duquesne, Fort Niagara, Fort Necessity, or Fort Ticonderoga. Have students diagram the battle they study.

Answer to ...

Answers should summarize the main trends of this period: initial Native American dominance, followed by a time of equilibrium and relatively equal conflict between Native Americans and European settlers, then a time of European dominance, and finally, British dominance in North America north of New Spain.

In Depth

Interdisciplinary

"Listen my children and you shall hear
Of the midnight ride of Paul Revere. . . ."

Thus begins "Paul Revere's Ride" by Henry Wadsworth Longfellow, one of the most popular American poets of the nineteenth century. Before the poem's publication in 1863, Revere and his now-famous ride were virtually unknown, but Longfellow's romanticized account soon made the patriot's name a household word all over America. Longfellow's poetry, which includes "The Song of Hiawatha," remains the source of some of America's most lasting legends.

waged it against the French and their Native American allies, it was the final struggle among the British, the French, and the Native Americans for control of eastern North America. While Native Americans fought on both sides, many tended to ally themselves with the French in the beginning. They saw the French as less likely to disrupt their way of life, not only because fewer French had come to North America, but also because the French were not trying to transform Native American lands into another Europe.

⭐ Until late in 1758, the French and Native Americans took the lead in the fighting. Their most impressive victory came in 1755, again near the forks of the Ohio River. On July 9, some 200 Frenchmen and 600 Native Americans surprised 1,460 British troops led by Major General Edward Braddock. In a three-hour battle, they killed or wounded two thirds of the British. Among the wounded, and soon to die, was Braddock, who had arrogantly insisted that he knew best how to wage a war even in unfamiliar surroundings. He had refused to listen to the warnings of the plucky officer in his colonial forces, the same Virginian major whose misadventure had signaled the start of the war.

The British Win the War In 1758, better-prepared and better-led British troops began to move in overwhelming numbers against the French in western Pennsylvania and Canada. The British strategy called first for attacking both the eastern and western limits of the long line of forts and settlements by which the French controlled their territory, as shown on the map on page 99. It called second for a force to break through the center of the French line of control at Lake Champlain and to press on toward Quebec. They accomplished the first goal by taking Louisbourg on the gulf of the St. Lawrence in July 1758 and Fort Duquesne at the forks of the Ohio in November. (Fort Duquesne, renamed Fort Pitt after a British leader, William Pitt, eventually became Pittsburgh.)

The second goal had to wait until the next year, 1759, which proved decisive. The French were on the defensive. More important, the Iroquois, still playing the Europeans off against each other, decided the French position was

Many Native Americans joined the British against the French in 1759. This medal was issued by Britain after the war to confirm the new alliance.

hopeless and began to actively support the British. The French abandoned their forts on Lakes George and Champlain in New York and retreated to Canada. After a three-month siege, British general James Wolfe led his troops by night over a goat path up the steep heights of the city of Quebec. There his men defeated the enemy and forced the surrender of the capital city of New France.

With the fall of Quebec, the war was virtually over. In the Treaty of Paris, signed in 1763, the French turned over all of Canada to the British. A century and a half after the founding of Jamestown and Quebec, the British were the only Europeans governing the American continent outside New Spain.

MAKING CONNECTIONS

Describe in two sentences how the Atlantic World changed from the founding of Jamestown to the end of the French and Indian War.

The War Shows the Colonists They Are Different from the British

At the beginning of the French and Indian War, colonists in America were proud to be part of the British Empire. They did experience occasional problems: trade between the colonies and Britain sometimes caused tension, and individual colonists traveling in Britain often were treated with contempt. On the whole, however, the relationship between Britain and its colonies was harmonious.

The War Changes the Interaction Between the British and the Colonists The French and Indian War severely strained British-American relations. For example, the arrogance of Braddock and other royal officers insulted colonial gentlemen like George Washington. The behavior of British troops, moreover, struck many New Englanders as immoral. Their bad language horrified men who believed that God determined the outcome of individual events depending on the piety, or religious sincerity, of those involved. One New Englander, surgeon Caleb Rea, wrote of British troops in New York in 1758:

▶ RESOURCE DIRECTORY

Teaching Resources

⭐ 📁 **Primary Source Activity** Braddock's Defeat, found in the Unit 1 folder, p. 126, focuses on Benjamin Franklin's account of the disastrous defeat of British General Braddock's forces in the French and Indian War.

I can't but remark, and that with regret, the horrid cursing and swearing there is in the camp, more especially among the regulars. And as a moral cause I can't but charge [blame] our defeat on this sin, which so prevails even among the chief commanders.

During the war, the presence of large numbers of British troops forcibly reminded the Americans that they were merely colonists. When the British dealt with colonial governments and merchants in a high-handed manner, it seemed to the Americans that the British considered them inferior.

For their part, the British denounced the colonists as uncooperative and unwilling to spend money when money was needed. A British general, Lord Loudon, complained in 1756 that Americans had unreasonable expectations. The colonists, he said, had

assumed to themselves, what they call Rights and Privileges, totally unknown in the Mother Country. . . . They will give you, not one Shilling, to carry on the War; they will give you no one thing, but for double the Money it ought to cost. . . . I hope a time will come, that with a little Sweet and a little Sour [that is, with rewards and threats], *they may be brought about.*

The Colonists' Self-Image Changes Loudon was too optimistic. The colonists would never be "brought about," or persuaded to be content with their inferior position. Slowly but surely, they were beginning to view what had seemed like embarrassing faults as praiseworthy qualities. Americans knew they were less formal

than the British; but that did not mean they were fools. Rather, Americans saw their simplicity as a reflection of their status as a people with a superior sense of right and wrong, who could be confident of having God on their side. They increasingly saw the British as a corrupt and degenerate people who had fallen from the path of righteousness. Thus when the armed clash between Britain and the colonies began in 1775, the portion of the American population that openly rebelled—perhaps a third—felt morally justified in doing so.

At the end of the French and Indian War, Americans felt they had every right to be treated like full-fledged citizens of a great empire. As the next section will show, however, during the 1760s the British demonstrated that they had no intention of treating their colonists as citizens equal to those in Britain. And that, too, like the colonists' belief that they were morally superior to the British, would send dozens of minutemen to Lexington Green in the middle of an April night in 1775.

Using Historical Evidence By distorting space and time, the painter of this view of the British attack on Quebec was able to illustrate several events at once. *What British actions are shown?*

SECTION 1 REVIEW

Key Terms, People, and Places
1. Define (a) American Revolution, (b) War for Independence, (c) French and Indian War.
2. Identify (a) minutemen, (b) George Washington.

Key Concepts
3. What was the basic British strategy for winning the French and Indian War?

4. How did the self-image of Americans change during the French and Indian War?

Critical Thinking
5. **Determining Relevance** How might the belief of Americans that they were different from the British lead them to demand self-government?

Quiz found in the Unit 1 folder, p. 113, covers the main ideas in this section as well as the key terms.

3. ASSESS

Section 1 Review Answers
1. (a) American Revolution, see p. 98, (b) War for Independence, see p. 98, (c) French and Indian War, see p. 99

2. (a) minutemen, see p. 98, (b) George Washington, see p. 99

3. The British strategy was to attack New France at both ends (the mouth of the St. Lawrence River and Fort Duquesne) and in the middle (through Lake Champlain).

4. Americans came to believe that they were different from the British, that they had many praiseworthy qualities, and that they were morally superior to the British.

5. The belief of Americans in their difference from the British might persuade them that the British government was not able to appreciate their concerns.

Reteach

Ask students to list important events of the French and Indian War and ways in which the war brought to light the colonists' differences from the British.

4. CLOSE

Reinforcing the Big Idea

The French and Indian War made the colonists realize that they were different from the British. They were proud of their unique identity and unwilling to give up control over their own destiny. The next section describes issues of conflict between the colonists and the British government.

The Issues That Led to the War for Independence

SECTION 2

The Issues That Led to the War for Independence

1. FOCUS

Connecting to the Big Idea

See page 96B. Tell students that the French and Indian War left Great Britain heavily in debt. In order to increase tax revenues, Great Britain tried to tighten its control over the colonies. The colonists resisted fiercely. Ask students what events caused Americans to think that their freedom was threatened.

Objectives

● Describe how British policy toward the colonists changed during the 1760s.

● Explain why the colonists protested the Stamp Act.

● Describe the series of events between 1763 and 1775 that led Americans to believe they were being deprived of their rights.

Bellringer

Ask students to jot down a list of items that the state and/or federal government singles out for taxes. Ask students if they think these taxes are fair or unfair and whether they feel that they restrict individual freedom in any way.

Reading Strategy

Reinforcing Key Ideas Ask students to note this sentence on page 105: "By 1770, growing numbers of Americans were convinced that British politicians were engaged in nothing less than a deliberate plot to rob them of their personal independence through taxation." As they read, students should list and briefly describe specific British actions that led so many Americans to feel this way.

SECTION PREVIEW

Under the pressure of new debts from the war against the French, the British government tried to make its colonies pay what it cost to govern and protect them. In doing so, the British sparked deep anger and resentment among many colonists, who thought they were being treated like enslaved people rather than free men and women.

Key Concepts

• During the 1760s, the British changed their policy to ensure that colonists shared in the cost of running the colonies.

• The colonists protested the Stamp Act because they believed their interests had not been represented when Parliament approved the tax.

• The pattern of events between 1763 and 1775 led many Americans to believe the British were using taxation as an excuse to deprive Americans of their rights.

Key Terms, People, and Places

depression, Pontiac's Rebellion, Proclamation of 1763, Stamp Act, boycott, Boston Tea Party, Intolerable Acts; King George III

Colonists who poured their tea from this pot bolstered their resistance to the Stamp Act, a British tax law that led to the War for Independence.

I n the 1760s the British government began to interfere more directly than ever before in the economic and political affairs of its colonies. From the point of view of the British, they were doing nothing wrong. After all, according to the theory of mercantilism, the colonies existed to serve the interests of the parent country.

Furthermore, in protecting Americans with troops and ships during the French and Indian War, Great Britain had built up huge debts. It only made sense that the colonists should pay their share of the cost of running the Empire so that Britain could pay off those debts. Besides, the British knew that the colonists were well off; their collective standard of living was higher than any in Europe. Britain, in particular, was in the midst of a serious **depression,** or economic slump.

For years, the British had been working to improve the operation of the entire Empire in accordance with mercantilist theory. In the process, they had drafted plans for more regulation of the colonies. Now the British government put those plans into effect. Virtually no one expected any colonial resistance; indeed, British politicians were too worried about problems in Britain even to consider the possibility of protest in the colonies.

British Colonial Policy Changes

In 1763 George Grenville, the chief minister under the British king, **George III,** began a series of changes in British policy designed to deal with debts from the French and Indian War. In early 1764, under Grenville's leadership, the British Parliament passed the Sugar Act. The act lowered the existing tax on molasses in order to encourage the colonists to buy more, which would result in more tax money for Britain. Up to this time, the British had only taxed the colonists as a way of controlling trade, and they had largely ignored violations of the existing tax law. With the passage of the Sugar Act, they began taxing the colonists with the specific intention of increasing the British treasury with tax money. Even more worrisome for the colonists was the fact that the British would not be lax about enforcing the act, as they had been with previous laws. Instead they would closely regulate American trade in order to collect their money. No longer would the British practice

▶ RESOURCE DIRECTORY

Teaching Resources

Reproducible Lesson Plan found in the Unit 1 folder, p. 109, provides a summary of the Section 2 lesson plan content.

Alternate Lesson Plan: Critical Thinking Recognizing Bias, found in the Alternate Lesson Plans folder, p. 18, helps students to recognize bias clearly by writing editorials on a prewar event from the British and American perspectives.

Guided Reading and Review found in the Unit 1 folder, p. 114, provides a structure for reading and mastering the key concepts and reviewing the key terms for Section 2. (Guided Practice)

American Profiles Activity found in the Unit 1 folder, p. 120, profiles Pontiac, chief of the Ottawa and head of a Native American confederation that, both on its own and with French allies, fought the spread of the British colonies.

salutary neglect of their colonies. Now they would deliberately interfere in local matters, disrupting old traditions and accepted customs.

Grenville's government also dealt with another serious problem. After the French and Indian War, the social ties that Native Americans in the Great Lakes area had developed with the French were broken. These ties included the exchange of vital gifts such as tools and gunpowder. The British, in an attempt to control the Native Americans, refused to continue the trade. Responding to this change in their situation, and foreseeing continued British expansion into their lands, the Ottawa, Potawatomi, and Huron in the Great Lakes region rose against British rule. The British called the resulting series of struggles **Pontiac's Rebellion,** after an Ottawa sachem involved in the warfare. During the conflict, Native Americans captured several British forts, but neither side could defeat the other. By 1764 both sides were keeping an uneasy truce. ✪

Meanwhile, in response to this conflict, the British Parliament passed the **Proclamation of 1763.** It closed the trans-Appalachian region, the area shown on the map at right between the crest of the Appalachian Mountains and the Mississippi River, to all settlement by colonists. Parliament reasoned that if there were no settlers in the region, no money would be required to protect them.

Like the Native Americans of the Great Lakes region, colonists who were involved in overseas commerce were upset by Britain's disturbance of long-established trading patterns. This group, which included tobacco and rice planters as well as northern merchants, was especially displeased with the Sugar Act. Other colonists did not like the limits placed on western expansion by the Proclamation of 1763. The growing anger over British government actions finally exploded in 1765 after Parliament's passage of the Stamp Act.

The Stamp Act Crisis

Grenville intended the **Stamp Act** in part to raise money for the defense and support of the American colonies. It required that all legal documents and printed materials—newspapers, for example—should have an attached paper stamp bought from the government. The stamp simply showed that a required fee had been paid. The modern practice of putting a paper stamp on a piece of mail is similar.

Grenville consulted with agents of the colonies and gave them time to suggest alternatives. His consideration for colonial feelings won him no friends, however. News of the Stamp Act created a firestorm of protest in the colonies. Merchants and artisans joined together to **boycott** British goods, or refuse to buy them as a means of protest. Colonial legislatures met to argue that they were freeborn Englishmen and Parliament could not tax them without their consent. They had no representatives in Parliament, they pointed out, and so Parliament had no right to decide what kind of taxes they should pay. In other words, there should be no taxation without representation.

In the Virginia House of Burgesses in May 1765, a young lawyer named Patrick Henry spoke passionately about American liberty. No genuine account of this speech has survived, but an anonymous French traveler who witnessed the debate reported what happened after Henry spoke.

Caught in a clash between cultures, two white children taken prisoner during Pontiac's Rebellion are reluctant to leave their Native American captors.

Land Claims After 1763

Geography and History: Interpreting Maps
The Proclamation of 1763 prohibited white settlement west of a line through the Appalachian Mountains. *Besides American colonists, what other groups claimed the trans-Appalachian region as of 1763?*

Media and Technology

Transparency
Critical Thinking, I-10

2. INSTRUCT

Explain/Discuss
Review British policy toward the colonies up until the 1760s. Ask why Great Britain felt justified in exerting more political and economic control over the colonies after the French and Indian War. Why did the colonists react so strongly?

Discuss the growing tension between the colonists and Great Britain. Ask why the passage of the Sugar Act was significant. Why did the Stamp Act inspire such strong American protest? What measures led Americans to believe that the British were trying to take away their freedom?

Caption Answer to . . .

🌐 **Interpreting Maps**

British, Native Americans

In Depth

Did You Know?

Women played a central role in the movement to boycott British goods. Instead of tea, Patriot women served coffee and herbal brews. Refusing to buy British cotton, they dressed themselves and their families in homespun. At times women took more direct action. One Boston man described a "Female Riot" in which a large mob of women attacked a merchant who was overcharging for coffee, "and demanded the Keys to his Store, which he refusing to deliver, they immediately placed him in a Cart and threatened to Cart him out of Town . . . ."

Have students analyze the American colonists' growing resentment of British authority. Have students explain the words *enslavement* and *slaves* as Americans like John Dickinson defined them. Why had many Americans come to take their freedom so seriously that they were willing to risk death for it?

Caption Answer to ...

 Interpreting Charts

1766, 1767, 1768; answers may also include 1770.

 Activity

Teaching Heterogeneous Groups

To demonstrate the British policy of forcing the colonists to share in the cost of running the colonies, (and the colonists' reaction to it), have students list their most cherished privileges at home. Responses may include using the phone, driving the family car, watching TV, and so on. Then announce that students will be taxed for such privileges. Divide the class into two groups—parents (Tories) and students (Colonists). Have the groups informally debate this new taxation policy.

Enrichment

Tell students it was a Bostonian named Samuel Adams who coined the name "Boston Massacre" to refer to the confrontation between British troops and colonists on March 5, 1770. Have them research the role this leading patriot played in events leading up to the War for Independence.

Colonists saw the "cursed stamp" as a symbol of enslavement to the British crown.

The speaker of the house rose and said, He, the last that stood up had spoke treason, and was sorry to see that not one of the members of the house was loyal enough to stop him, before he had gone so far, upon which the same member stood up again (his name is Henry) and said that if he had affronted [insulted] the speaker, or the house, he was ready to ask pardon, and he would show his loyalty to his majesty King George the Third, at the expense of the last drop of his blood, but what he had said must be attributed to the interest of his country's dying liberty, which he had at heart.

Patrick Henry's attitude was typical. Although Americans everywhere were proclaiming their loyalty to King George, they were also demanding their rights as his subjects.

In October, a gathering of delegates from several colonies—the Stamp Act Congress—met in New York to make the same point. The Stamp Act Congress informed King George

that it is inseparably essential to the Freedom of a People, and the undoubted Right of Englishmen, that no taxes be imposed on them, but with their own Consent, given personally, or by their representatives.

★ Some colonists did not limit their protests to words. In several cities, groups of people attacked officials who defended British policy. A mob broke into the Boston home of one such official, Massachusetts lieutenant governor Thomas Hutchinson, while his family was eating supper. They ransacked the house, stealing furniture, china, silver, money, and books. According to Hutchinson, they "emptied the house of every thing whatsoever except a part of the kitchen furniture, not leaving a single book or paper in it." As the

Interpreting Charts

In the time line below, events before the War for Independence are charted as cause and effect. They combine to form a series of provocations and tragic miscommunications on both sides. *In what years did delayed effects of the Quartering Act occur?*

1764	1765	1766	1767	1768	1769

Some events are shown out of order within their proper year to clarify cause and effect.

1764
Parliament passes and strictly enforces **the Sugar Act** to raise money to pay for the cost of administering the colonies.

Colonists respond with written protests, occasional boycotts, and cries of **"No taxation without representation."**

1765
The Stamp Act requires the purchase of tax stamps, which are to be attached to all printed goods.

Colonists protest violently. Delegates of nine colonies meet in New York as **the Stamp Act Congress** and prepare a Declaration of Rights and Grievances. **Boycott** of British goods begins.

The Quartering Act requires the colonies to quarter, or provide food and lodging for, British soldiers.

Most colonial legislatures refuse to pay for supplies required by the Quartering Act.

1766
The Stamp Act is repealed at the urging of British merchants, who are feeling the effects of colonial boycotts.
The Declaratory Act reminds colonists that Britain keeps the right to make laws in the colonies.

Even though colonists rejoice at the repeal of the Stamp Act, they continue to resist other British-imposed laws like the Quartering Act.

1767
The Townshend Duties require colonies to pay minor import duties on tea, glass, lead, oil, paper, and painter's colors.

John Dickinson encourages protests against the Townshend Duties by writing the first of twelve "Letters from a Farmer in Pennsylvania," which are published in all but four of the colonies' newspapers. **Colonies boycott British imports again,** cutting trade in half.

The **New York Assembly is suspended** for the colony's refusal to comply fully with Quartering Act.

1768
The British government orders troops to be stationed in Boston to enforce the Townshend Duties.

Boston colonists refuse to quarter British troops.

1769
The British governor of Virginia dissolves the Virginia Assembly for its resolution against British taxes and other protests.

Virginia, Maryland, and South Carolina agree not to import certain British goods.

| British Action |
| Colonial Action |

JOIN OR DIE

 RESOURCE DIRECTORY

Teaching Resources

Visual Learning Activity The American Rattlesnake, found in the Unit 1 folder, p. 133, uses a cartoon depicting the rebellious colonies as a rattlesnake to emphasize the seriousness and strength of the colonists' position.

sun rose the next morning, men were still trying to remove the roof.

British merchants, too, howled in protest as they saw their trade with the colonies threatened by the boycott. In the face of such a torrent of opposition and the virtual refusal of colonists to buy the stamps, Parliament backed down. Grenville was forced from power, and new leaders repealed the Stamp Act in 1766.

MAKING CONNECTIONS

How would you expect the colonists to react if the British tried again to tax them? Read on to find out.

The Colonists Resist "Slavery"

The triumphant colonists quieted down. But the issues raised by the Stamp Act would not go away. Could Parliament tax Americans without representation in Parliament? Did the rights English law gave to free men in England also belong to free men in the American colonies?

In 1767 Parliament reasserted its authority by placing taxes on certain imported goods, including lead, glass, and tea. The Townshend Duties, named after the chief British financial official, Charles Townshend, also provoked protests and a boycott. Once again, Parliament eventually backed down, repealing all the taxes in 1770—all the taxes, that is, except for one that Parliament kept to save its pride: the tax on tea. As a result, tea became a symbol of British injustice, and many Americans refused to drink it.

A Conspiracy? By 1770, growing numbers of Americans were convinced that British politicians were engaged in nothing less than a deliberate plot to rob them of their personal independence through taxation. Protest groups that had formed throughout the colonies during the Stamp Act crisis—"Sons of Liberty" and "Daughters of Liberty"—complained that the British were taxing them in order to take away

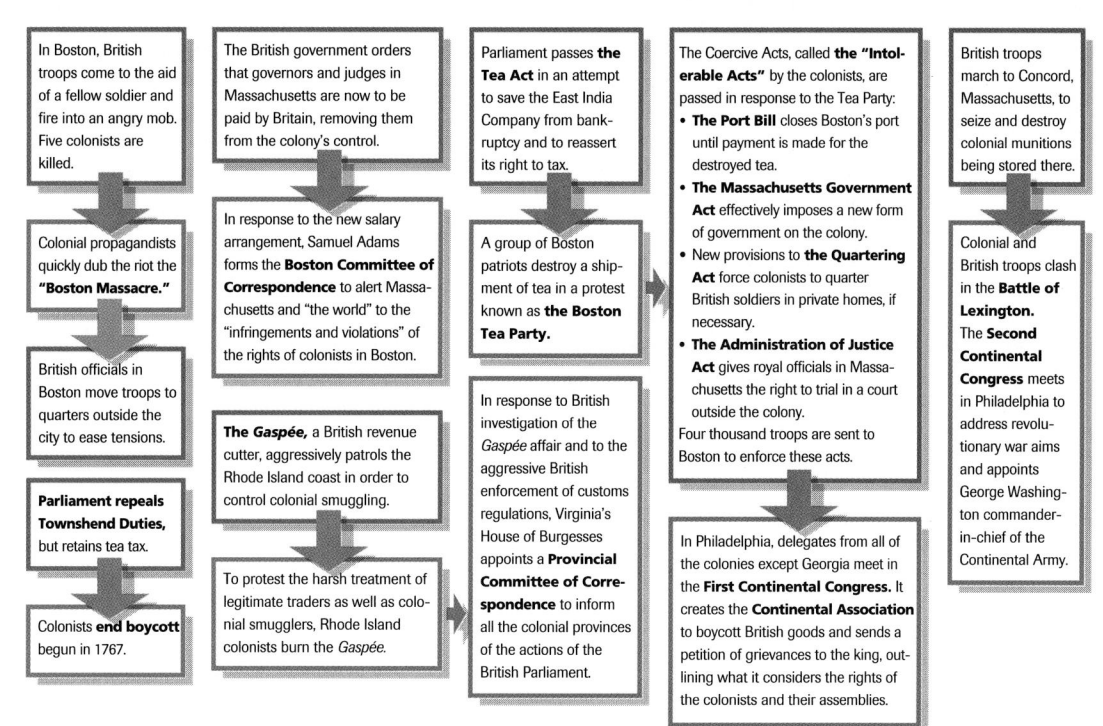

1770

In Boston, British troops come to the aid of a fellow soldier and fire into an angry mob. Five colonists are killed.

Colonial propagandists quickly dub the riot the **"Boston Massacre."**

British officials in Boston move troops to quarters outside the city to ease tensions.

Parliament repeals Townshend Duties, but retains tea tax.

Colonists **end boycott** begun in 1767.

1772

The British government orders that governors and judges in Massachusetts are now to be paid by Britain, removing them from the colony's control.

In response to the new salary arrangement, Samuel Adams forms the **Boston Committee of Correspondence** to alert Massachusetts and "the world" to the "infringements and violations" of the rights of colonists in Boston.

The Gaspée, a British revenue cutter, aggressively patrols the Rhode Island coast in order to control colonial smuggling.

To protest the harsh treatment of legitimate traders as well as colonial smugglers, Rhode Island colonists burn the *Gaspée.*

1773

Parliament passes **the Tea Act** in an attempt to save the East India Company from bankruptcy and to reassert its right to tax.

A group of Boston patriots destroy a shipment of tea in a protest known as **the Boston Tea Party.**

In response to British investigation of the *Gaspée* affair and to the aggressive British enforcement of customs regulations, Virginia's House of Burgesses appoints a **Provincial Committee of Correspondence** to inform all the colonial provinces of the actions of the British Parliament.

1774

The Coercive Acts, called **the "Intolerable Acts"** by the colonists, are passed in response to the Tea Party:
- **The Port Bill** closes Boston's port until payment is made for the destroyed tea.
- **The Massachusetts Government Act** effectively imposes a new form of government on the colony.
- New provisions to **the Quartering Act** force colonists to quarter British soldiers in private homes, if necessary.
- **The Administration of Justice Act** gives royal officials in Massachusetts the right to trial in a court outside the colony.

Four thousand troops are sent to Boston to enforce these acts.

In Philadelphia, delegates from all of the colonies except Georgia meet in the **First Continental Congress.** It creates the **Continental Association** to boycott British goods and sends a petition of grievances to the king, outlining what it considers the rights of the colonists and their assemblies.

1775

British troops march to Concord, Massachusetts, to seize and destroy colonial munitions being stored there.

Colonial and British troops clash in the **Battle of Lexington.** The **Second Continental Congress** meets in Philadelphia to address revolutionary war aims and appoints George Washington commander-in-chief of the Continental Army.

In Depth

Did You Know?

The goods on which the Townshend Acts placed small customs duties—including paper and paint—were valued imports from Britain. Chancellor of the Exchequer Charles Townshend insisted that the duties were merely regulations of trade and, he argued, the colonists had agreed such regulation was within Parliament's rights. But the colonists saw the acts for what they were: taxes to raise money for England, not duties to control trade. The Townshend Duties encouraged the colonists to manufacture goods themselves rather than import them from England. Suddenly it became more fashionable to use colonial-made goods than English luxury goods.

2 A mob, drawn by news of trouble, floods into the street from a nearby square.

3 Responding to a call for help, a British captain brings seven soldiers from headquarters.

4 Attacked by the mob, soldiers fire on citizens, killing five.

1 Boys throw ice at a sentry guarding the Customs House.

Paul Revere, a silversmith and Patriot, used the so-called Boston Massacre as the subject of anti-British propaganda (left). His engraving shows the end result—troops firing on citizens—but omits the events leading up to the shooting (above). A handful of soldiers attacked by hundreds of angry citizens fired without orders; they and their commanding officer were charged with murder but later acquitted.

Section 2 Review Answers

1. (a) depression, see p. 102, (b) Pontiac's Rebellion, see p. 103, (c) Proclamation of 1763, see p. 103, (d) Stamp Act, see p. 103, (e) boycott, see p. 103, (f) Boston Tea Party, see p. 106, (g) Intolerable Acts , see p. 107

2. King George III, see p. 102

3. The British abandoned the policy of salutary neglect in the early 1760s because of the huge debt accumulated during the French and Indian War and a widespread feeling that the prosperous colonists (who had benefited most from the war) could and should help pay for their own protection and government.

4. Such actions include the occupation of Boston, the Boston Massacre, and a series of controversies that arose between the British and individual colonies.

5. They did not want to be taxed without representation in Parliament. They wanted to be treated like full members of the British empire, with all the rights and privileges of that status.

6. Answers should suggest that the American colonists would act in the same way whether or not the conspiracy was real.

In Depth

Then and Now

Although tea, coffee, and chocolate were all introduced to North America in the seventeenth century, by the 1770s tea was the most popular nonalcoholic drink in the colonies. With the imposition of the tea tax and the Boston Tea Party, however, Americans developed a taste for coffee, a preference that is still apparent. Today the United States consumes about 70 percent of the world's coffee crop, an average of 15 to 16 pounds of coffee per person a year, or three cups of coffee a day.

their property, and make them into what amounted to slaves. This was something many people, whether gentlemen, farmers, or artisans, believed they simply could not tolerate. In the words of John Dickinson, a Pennsylvania lawyer,

> T hose who are taxed *without their own consent, expressed by themselves or their representatives, are* slaves. We are taxed *without our own consent, expressed by ourselves or our representatives.* We *are therefore—SLAVES.*

Other events seemed to confirm the conspiracy. British troops occupied Boston in the late 1760s to protect officials enforcing the Townshend Duties. Tensions between soldiers and townspeople exploded in the Boston Massacre on March 5, 1770. An African American, Crispus Attucks, and four other colonists were killed. In addition, a series of controversies soon arose between the British and individual colonies. Taken together, all these challenges suggested to the Americans that they were facing a serious threat to their lives and property.

The Dispute over Freedom In 1773 the British government announced that it was going to sell millions of pounds of tea at discounted rates directly to the American public. To the colonists, the move seemed a way of trying to buy their acceptance of the detested tea tax. In harbors up and down the Atlantic seaboard, ships loaded with tea were turned away. Some residents of Boston, in a protest now known as the **Boston Tea Party,** threw the cargoes of several ships into the harbor. ★

Losing all patience, Parliament passed the Coercive Acts in 1774 to punish the colony of Massachusetts. Among other things, these

RESOURCE DIRECTORY

Teaching Resources

★ **Visual Learning Activity** Boycotting Tea, found in the Unit 1 folder, p. 132, focuses on the symbolic importance of the British Tea Act and the subsequent colonial boycott of British tea.

Boicotting for Change

When colonists successfully organized boycotts to protest the Stamp Act and the Townshend Duties, they proved that, as consumers, citizens have the power to use economic pressure to effect political change. Americans have used the same tactic ever since.

In December 1955, Rosa Parks, an African American, refused to give up her seat on a Montgomery bus to a white passenger, as required by Alabama state law. She was

promptly arrested. Angered by the treatment Parks had received and the law that required her to relinquish her seat, the African American community in Montgomery refused to use the bus system. After 381 days the Supreme Court ruled that segregation on buses was illegal. Not only did the ruling grant African Americans their right to equal treatment, but in an ironic twist, it saved the bus company, which had been about to go bankrupt.

In a similar protest in 1966, Mexican American labor leader César Chávez organized a nationwide boycott of California grapes. The growers had refused to negotiate with the newly formed farm worker's union led by Chávez. The boycott finally ended four years later, when growers signed agreements with the United Farm Workers, granting them better pay and working conditions. ***What factors contribute to making boycotts successful?***

---

acts—called the **Intolerable Acts** by colonists everywhere—virtually shut down individual town governments and the colonial legislature. These strong measures only confirmed American suspicions that the British were moving to take away their freedoms.

Local Committees of Correspondence, groups formed to coordinate protest throughout the colonies, met to elect delegates to the First Continental Congress. The delegates discussed the proper reaction to the Coercive Acts. Their efforts to find a peaceful solution failed. In July 1775, after the war had erupted at Concord and Lexington, the Second Continental Congress agreed to a statement they called *A Declaration of the Causes and Necessities of Taking Up Arms.*

It stated that the members were "resolved to die Free men rather than live Slaves."

The Continental Congress was only putting into words the belief that had brought the farmers and artisans of eastern Massachusetts to the green at Lexington that April. It was the conviction of the Congress and the minutemen alike that at some point they had to take a stand against the pattern of enslavement they saw in the actions of the British, whom they perceived as corrupt, immoral, and power hungry. They did not consider themselves radicals or revolutionaries; they were simply protecting their way of life, their land, and their households. As the next section shows, however, their protest against British laws soon ignited other challenges to authority.

SECTION 2 REVIEW

Key Terms, People, and Places
1. Define (a) depression, (b) Pontiac's Rebellion, (c) Proclamation of 1763, (d) Stamp Act, (e) boycott, (f) Boston Tea Party, (g) Intolerable Acts.
2. Identify King George III.

Key Concepts
3. Why did the British abandon the policy of salutary neglect in the early 1760s?
4. Describe three British actions the colonists inter-

preted as signs of a British intention to take away their liberty.
5. Why did many colonists react so strongly to the Stamp Act?

Critical Thinking
6. **Determining Relevance** By 1770 many Americans thought the British were trying to take away their freedoms. Did it matter whether or not they were right? Explain your thinking.

 Quiz found in the Unit 1 folder, p. 115, covers the main ideas in this section as well as the key terms.

Media and Technology

 Transparency
The Way It Works, H-4

Answer to ...

Links Across Time

Possible answers: widespread support; publicity; willingness to continue the boycott for a long time, if necessary.

Reteach
Have students make a list of British actions, beginning with the Sugar Act in 1764 and ending with the Intolerable Acts, that led to the War for Independence. Next to each action students should write one sentence describing its immediate effect.

 Alternative Assessment

Mid-Point Monitoring
Ask students if they have
● Selected the activities they will include in their project
● Begun to research the issues for each

 4. CLOSE

Reinforcing the Big Idea
As Great Britain tried to increase its authority over the American colonies, the colonists became convinced that the British were trying to take away their liberty. Americans decided at the Second Continental Congress that war against the British was their only option if they wanted to keep their freedom. The next section describes the ideas that led to the War for Independence.

TOOLBOX

Critical Thinking
Expressing Problems Clearly

Focus Clearly express the dispute between supporters of the Stamp Act and its opponents.

Instruct Provide students with the following facts: (1) Most Patriot politicians had never lobbied to send representatives to the British parliament. (2) Americans were being treated no differently than their British counterparts in being taxed without representation, since a majority of British adult males were not entitled to vote because they did not own enough property.

Ask students how this information might change their perception of the dispute between supporters and opponents of the Stamp Act.

Extend See Historian's Toolbox Activity in the Resource Directory below.

Answers

1. (a) The tax imposed under the Stamp Act was not legal. (b) To be considered British subjects, the American colonists must share in the payment of Britain's tax burden.

2. (a) To keep the colonists from being subjected to a tax that violated their rights as British citizens. (b) Colonists to acknowledge Parliament's authority and pay a fair share of Britain's taxes.

3. (a) No. This characterization is essentially an interpretation of the problem. (b) Excerpt A: The characterization of the situation as a calamity and the feelings of concern and alarming apprehension; the reference to a "fiction of law." Excerpt B: the statement about squandering away blood and treasure in the colonies' defense.

4. The Stamp Act's supporters wanted the colonists to recognize the authority of Parliament and abide by its resolutions. They wanted the colonists to pay the taxes imposed by the Stamp Act and to acknowledge fairness. Opponents wanted the Stamp Act nullified in recognition of the fact that it was imposed illegally, and in violation of the colonists' rights as British subjects.

Expressing Problems Clearly

The ability to express a problem clearly means being able to describe the nature of a situation or a question that is difficult, puzzling, or open to debate. When you express a problem clearly, you are taking the first step toward understanding and solving it.

Following Parliament's passage of the Stamp Act in 1765, articles like those excerpted on this page appeared in American and British newspapers.

Use the following steps to practice expressing problems clearly.

1. Analyze the information. When you are confronted with a problem, study the information involved. Read excerpts A and B. (a) What was the nature of the case made by the American colonist in excerpt A? (b) What information was given by the British writer in excerpt B?

2. Identify the basic concepts involved. Problems usually arise out of a specific set of circumstances. However, they often revolve around a general principle, such as fairness. To identify this concept, try to express the problem in terms of what each side wants for itself. (a) What benefit did the American writer want to achieve for the colonists? (b) What did the British writer want?

3. Identify the function of the supporting details. In any problem, details often are presented that may

not be basic to the problem itself. (a) The British writer characterizes the colonists' opposition to an act of Parliament as "an alarming crisis." Is this a basic part of the problem? Why or why not? (b) What other details in these excerpts did not relate to the basic issue of disagreement?

4. Express the problem clearly. Now that you have identified the main area of dispute and stripped away irrelevant details, you are ready to express the problem clearly. How would you describe the dispute between the British supporters of the Stamp Act and its American opponents?

A *"In all the calamities which have ever befallen this country, we have never felt so great a concern, or such alarming apprehensions, as on this occasion. . . . We [find] this tax to be unconstitutional. We have always understood it to be a grand and fundamental principle of the [British] constitution, that no freeman should be subject to any tax to which he has not given his own consent, in person or by proxy [representation]. And . . . that no freeman can be separated from his property but by his own act or fault. We take it clearly, therefore, to be inconsistent with the spirit of the . . . principles of the British constitution, that we should be subject to any tax imposed by the British Parliament; because we are not represented in that assembly in any sense, unless it be by a fiction of law."*
John Adams, *Instructions of the Town of Braintree Massachusetts on the Stamp Act*, October 14, 1765

B *"The question now is, Whether those American subjects are, or are not, bound by the resolutions of a British parliament? If they are not, they are entirely a separate people from us. On the other hand, if the people of America are bound by the proceedings of the English legislature, . . . [then] the present crisis . . . is really an alarming one. The people of the colonies know very well that the taxes of the Mother country are every day increasing; and can they expect that no addition whatsoever will be made to theirs? . . . In assisting the colonies we had an eye to our own interest. It would be ridiculous otherwise to squander away our blood and our treasure in their defense. But surely the benefit was mutual; and consequently the disadvantage [of taxes] should be mutual too."*
"William Pym" to the *London General Evening Post*, August 20, 1765, reprinted in the *Newport Mercury*, October 28, 1765

 RESOURCE DIRECTORY

Teaching Resources

Historian's Toolbox Activity Expressing Problems Clearly, found in the Unit 1 folder, p. 124, helps students apply this skill by examining various opinions about the issue of increased taxes.

The Ideas That Led to the War for Independence

SECTION PREVIEW

The War for Independence did not arise solely because of events and issues like the Stamp Act; new beliefs fueled the war as well. Those new beliefs—that people were born equal and that they could rule themselves—encouraged all kinds of challenges to authority in the 1770s and 1780s.

Key Concepts

- Writings of the 1770s established new and radical principles of freedom and equality in American government and society.
- Enslaved African Americans pointed out that they too had the right to be free.
- As a result of the Revolution, many women began to question patriarchy as well as government by kings.

Key Terms, People, and Places

natural rights, social contract, popular sovereignty, Declaration of Independence; Thomas Paine, Thomas Jefferson, Abigail Adams

---

F rom the beginning, the American Revolution was more than a rebellion or a war for independence. The Revolution itself began long before the war and continued long after the war had ended. It announced the creation of a new society committed to such powerful ideas as equality and democracy. Although the immediate accomplishment of the Revolution was simply to preserve the power of white men of the "gentle" class, its long-term significance lay in changing people's thinking about the world. As this section shows, during the time of the Revolution, Americans acquired the habit of challenging authority and asserting their rights—a habit they have never lost. ✪

Two Documents Develop Democratic Ideas

One of the chief documents that expressed and developed the ideas of the Revolution was *Common Sense*, published in 1776. Written by **Thomas Paine,** a recent immigrant from England, this pamphlet sold around 150,000 copies, or about one for every eight white men in the colonies. While the average political pamphlet in the 1700s sold a few hundred copies, mostly to gentlemen, Paine's words reached hundreds of thousands of readers of all social classes.

Paine was an artisan with little formal education. The plain, direct style in which he chose to write *Common Sense* suggested that anyone could understand the issues involved in the conflict between the colonies and Great Britain. Paine avoided the references to Greek and Latin literature that were common in writing at that time. Instead he bolstered his points with references to the Bible, with which most people were familiar.

Common Sense was democratic in substance as well as in style. It was a direct assault on the whole idea of government by kings and aristocrats. What good were kings? asked

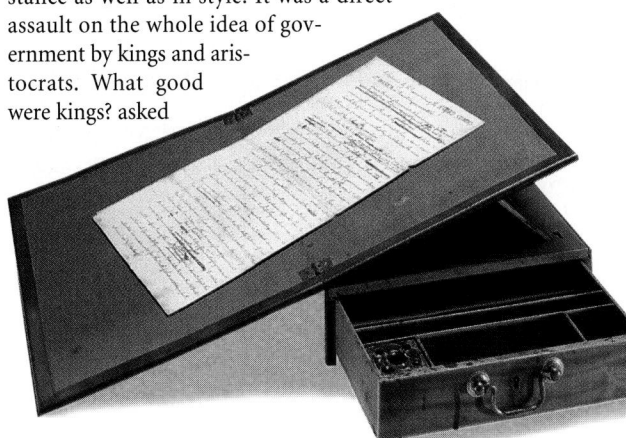

Thomas Jefferson wrote the Declaration of Independence at this desk, built to his own design.

---

1. FOCUS

Connecting to the Big Idea

See page 96B. Tell students that the War for Independence was fueled by more than British actions. Powerful new ideas inspired Americans to challenge authority in hopes of creating a completely different kind of society. Ask students what these new ideas were.

Objectives

- Describe the ideas contained in *Common Sense* and the Declaration of Independence.
- Identify how African Americans used the ideas of the Revolution to seek freedom.
- Explain why women began to question patriarchy and rule by kings.

Bellringer

Write the word *idealistic* on the chalkboard. Ask students to briefly define the word and list some attributes of an idealistic person.

Reading Strategy

Structured Overview Point out the heading on page 109, Two Documents Develop Democratic Ideas. Have students scan that section for subheadings and note details that relate to the documents' ideas.

📄 **Reproducible Lesson Plan** found in the Unit 1 folder, p. 110, provides a summary of the Section 3 lesson plan content.

📄 **Alternate Lesson Plan: Learning Styles** found in the Alternate Lesson Plan folder, p. 19, helps clarify the ideas in the section through the creation of a graphic organizer and is particularly effective for visual learners.

📄 **Guided Reading and Review** found in the Unit 1 folder, p. 116, provides a structure for reading and mastering the key concepts and reviewing the key terms for Section 3. (Guided Practice)

✪ 📄 **Literature Activity** To the King, found in the Unit 1 folder, p. 129, uses a Phillis Wheatley poem to illustrate popular colonial sentiment toward King George III in prerevolutionary times.

Explain/Discuss

Explain to students that ideas played an important role in the War for Independence. Ask students to discuss the war in terms of the ideas of thinkers like Thomas Paine and Thomas Jefferson. Why might these men be considered idealists? You might want to refer to the attributes students listed in the Bellringer activity.

Discuss with students how the ideas that fueled the War for Independence also helped create a new society. Ask why *Common Sense* was important to the development of democracy. What important political ideas of foreign thinkers provided the foundation for the Declaration of Independence? What enduring principles of American government and society are included in it?

Caption Answer to ...

Using Historical Evidence

He changed it to "for one people"; it better balances the phrase "with another" and emphasizes the unity of the colonies.

In Depth

Interdisciplinary

Long before he became the elder statesman of the American Revolution, Ben Franklin was a scientist whose experiments involving electricity brought him fame in British and European scientific circles. His now legendary experiment of flying a kite in a thunderstorm proved that lightning is a form of electricity. He also observed "the wonderful effect of pointed bodies, both in *drawing off* and *throwing off* the electrical fire," which led him to invent the lightning rod in 1752, a thoroughly practical application of knowledge that typified Franklin's scientific attitude.

Paine bluntly. "Of more worth is one honest man to society, and in the sight of God," he said, "than all the crowned ruffians that ever lived." ★

Drafting a Declaration The other great democratic document of 1776 was written not by an artisan, but by **Thomas Jefferson,** an American aristocrat, or member of the gentle class. In June 1776, after the colonies had been at war with Britain for over a year, the Continental Congress decided that it was high time to issue a statement declaring that the colonies were cutting their ties with their parent country. Congress appointed a committee of five to write the declaration: the tall, redheaded Virginian planter, Jefferson; John Adams, a Boston lawyer; Robert Sherman, a judge from Connecticut; Robert Livingston, the lawyer son of a wealthy New York family; and the ever-useful Benjamin Franklin of Philadelphia. The committee depended upon Jefferson to compose the first draft, even though at thirty-three he was

Using Historical Evidence The Declaration of Independence, said Thomas Jefferson (above), was "an expression of the American mind." The suggestions of other members of the drafting committee are marked on his first draft. *How did Jefferson correct the phrase "for a people"? Why did he make this change?*

the youngest among them by far. So successful was he that his fellow committee members proposed very few changes.

Jefferson divided his argument into four sections. The first was a preamble, or introduction, in which he explained the purpose of the declaration. The second was an explanation of the political ideas behind the document. For this part, Jefferson drew largely on a theory of government devised by earlier European political thinkers, including the Englishman John Locke. These theorists believed that people had **natural rights**—rights that belonged to them simply because they were human, not because kings or governments had granted these rights to them. According to this theory, originally people had been completely free of government. In order to gain increased safety and comfort, they had joined together in a community. They had then given certain individuals the power to govern the community, forming a **social contract.** If a ruler failed to act in the best interests of those he governed, he was breaking the social

RESOURCE DIRECTORY

Teaching Resources

★ **Literature Activity** *Common Sense,* found in the Unit 1 folder, pp. 130–131, uses excerpts from Thomas Paine's famous pamphlet to enhance students' understanding of the pro-independence faction's arguments.

contract. In that case, the people had the right to revolt against his unjust rule and choose a new form of government.

Because the second section is based on this theory, it is sometimes referred to as the "Declaration of Natural Rights." In it Jefferson wrote that governments get their power from "the consent of the governed," implying that ordinary people can and should govern themselves. This idea is now called **popular sovereignty**, although the term did not come into use until later.

Following the statement of natural rights was a third section that spelled out the wrongs the colonists believed had been committed by the British king. "The history of the present King of Great Britain is a history of repeated injuries," wrote Jefferson, "all having in direct object the establishment of an absolute Tyranny."

Jefferson concluded his document with a fourth section titled "Resolution of Independence by the United States." In it he wrote "these United Colonies . . . are and of Right ought to be Free and Independent States." For the entire work he chose the unifying title *A Declaration by the Representatives of the United States of America*. We now call the document the **Declaration of Independence.**

What the Declaration Accomplished The committee presented the Continental Congress with the completed declaration on July 1. The delegates attending at that time did not reach agreement to approve the document until July 2. All thirteen colonies were not officially represented, however, and so the debate was taken up again two days later. After further discussion, a paragraph condemning King George for allowing the sale of slaves in the colonies was removed; both northern and southern slaveholders objected to it. Other changes were made as well. It was not until July 4—the date now celebrated as Independence Day—that all thirteen colonies joined in accepting the declaration. With that vote, they ceased being colonies and officially became a new nation, the United States.

But the Declaration achieved more than just proclaiming the existence of the United States of America. It also announced the basic principles of American government and soci-

ety. According to the Declaration, Americans held certain "truths to be self-evident." One of these truths was the idea of popular sovereignty. Another was the simple but powerful idea that "all men are created equal."

Jefferson, like most members of the Continental Congress, had no intention of surrendering power to people who were not like him. Though he condemned slavery in theory, he was a slaveholder himself, and he could not have imagined a society in which African Americans were treated as his equals. Nor could he have understood how women might share in the rights and responsibilities of government. The "Founding Fathers"—the men who approved the Declaration and those who later created the federal government—were just that: patriarchs, heads of households with many dependents. When they talked about equality and popular sovereignty, they meant equality

Viewpoints Activity On Rule by the People, found in the Unit 1 folder, pp. 122–123, uses a 1774 newspaper article and a 1775 parliamentary speech to illustrate both sides of the debate over how the colonies should be governed.

Media and Technology

Transparency
Cause and Effect, F-2

Viewpoints
On Rule by the People

As the colonies neared the brink of conflict with Britain, some voices urged independence and others called for reconciliation. One issue that separated the two sides was the question of whether or not people were capable of ruling themselves. *What are the assumptions behind each writer's statement?*

For Rule by the People

"The American Congress derives all its power, wisdom, and justice, not from scrolls of parchment signed by kings but from the people. A more august [respectable] and a more equitable legislative body never existed in any quarter of the globe. It is founded upon the principles of the most perfect liberty. A free man, in honoring and obeying the Congress, honors and obeys himself."

Anonymous newspaper editorial, November 14, 1774

Against Rule by the People

"Suppose we were to revolt from Great Britain, declare ourselves independent, and set up a republic of our own—what would be the consequence? I stand aghast at the prospect; my blood runs chill when I think of the calamities, the complicated evils that must ensue, and may be clearly seen—it is impossible for any man to foresee them all. "

Rev. Charles Inglis, *The True Interest of America*, 1776

Analyze

Have students analyze the impact of the ideas behind the War for Independence on the development of democracy in the United States. Why were the beliefs that all people were born equal and that they were capable of ruling themselves considered radical in the 1770s? What was the long-term significance of the Revolution?

Answer to . . .

 Viewpoints

The anonymous writer of the newspaper editorial assumes that freedom will bring wise and legitimate rule; Rev. Charles Inglis assumes that freedom from monarchical rule will bring disaster. For a more thorough examination of popular sovereignty, see the Resource Directory below.

 In Depth

Biography

Elizabeth Freeman (1744–1829) was a Massachusetts slave who in 1781 sued for her freedom under the new state constitution that declared all people "free and equal" under the law. Represented by a lawyer, she won her case and went free, setting a legal precedent that would help to end slavery in Massachusetts. Freeman, who lived into her eighties, became widely admired. Her lawyer once said of her, "Having known this woman, I cannot believe in the moral or physical inferiority of the race to which she belonged."

Teaching Heterogeneous Groups

The colonists described a government by popular sovereignty. To demonstrate this departure from royal sovereignty, divide students into two groups, representing two countries. Assign government by royal sovereignty to one country and a system of popular sovereignty to the other. Announce that it would be desirable to ban hats in both countries. Have students demonstrate how the matter would be resolved according to the governance of each country. **LEP**

Answer to ...

MAKING CONNECTIONS

Students may argue that ordinary people do run their own government through representatives, or point out that interest groups wield power and influence over government unmatched by the ordinary citizen.

In Depth

Multicultural Perspectives

The poet Phillis Wheatley, considered the first important African American writer, was brought to Boston on a slave ship in 1761 while still a child. Something of a prodigy, she studied English, Latin, the Bible, and poetry; and she published her first poem at the age of fourteen. Wheatley was a Patriot, admired by Washington, Franklin, and Hancock, and she wrote several poems on patriotic themes. Her only book of poems, however, *Poems on Various Subjects, Moral and Religious,* published in England in 1773, was decidedly apolitical.

and sovereignty for gentlemen of property and high standing in society. But once these ideas were let loose, neither the Founders nor later generations of white men could control them.

Together the Declaration of Independence and *Common Sense* defined the basic principles of the new American nation. The United States was to be a nation in which ordinary citizens would run their own government. Furthermore, both documents also attacked the age-old notion that some people were better than others simply because of the circumstances of their birth. People born rich or in long-established families, for instance, should have no more rights than people born poor or of unknown parents. As the later history of the United States shows, the idea that all people were equal—and thus should have equal rights—would prove a very contagious idea indeed. In many ways, we are still discovering the full meaning of the Declaration of Independence.

The Great Seal of the United States promised a *novus ordo seclorum*—"a new order for the ages"—echoing the belief of Americans that the Revolution had begun a new era of human liberty.

MAKING CONNECTIONS

Do you think the United States today is a nation in which ordinary citizens run their own government? Explain your thinking.

Liberty Begins to Catch On

An exhilarating sense of liberation swept over most Americans in the 1770s. Many felt free of the past, free to experiment and change. They were creating "a new order for the ages"—a motto that eventually became a part of the Great Seal of the United States. In this new social order, women, Native Americans, and African Americans would not have equality or liberty for some time to come. Those ideas, however, were beginning to take hold.

Few Changes in Status To be sure, no one but white men gained much legal and political power from the Revolution. For Native Americans, also involved in the fighting between American rebels and British troops, the Revolution was largely a disaster. The Iroquois suffered heavily during the war and were essentially pushed out of western New York and destroyed as a military power.

Women saw no major change in their status. In New Jersey, some women were granted the right to vote for about two decades. There seems to have been an increase in divorces initiated by women, possibly demonstrating increased assertiveness. But on balance women had no more political or legal power after the Revolution than they had before it.

On paper, the Revolution did not improve conditions for African Americans either. It is true that most northern states abolished slavery in the late 1700s and early 1800s; but these states simultaneously passed laws severely restricting the rights of African Americans. In the South, if the Revolution brought about any change in slavery at all, that change was only a tightening of slavery. Confronted with the idea that all people are created equal, slaveholders were faced with the choice of giving up slavery or insisting that African Americans were not people like everyone else. They enacted laws restricting the movement as well as the educational and religious activity of enslaved people. On the national level, the United States forbade the establishment of slavery north of the Ohio River in the Northwest Ordinance of 1787, but this was intended more to exclude slave labor than to free African Americans. And as the next chapter shows, when the document that established the federal government was written in 1787, it suggested that an enslaved person was only three fifths of a human being.

Laying the Basis for Future Change In spite of these indications that change would be slow, the ideas of the Revolution did have a long-term impact on the status of African Americans and women, if not Native Americans. For example, African Americans repeatedly pointed out in legal actions the contradiction of fighting a war against political slavery while still practicing racial slavery. In asking the

Massachusetts legislature to free them, four enslaved men invoked the revolutionary spirit of the times as early as 1773.

> *We expect great things from men who have made such a noble stand against the designs of their fellow-men to enslave them. . . . The divine spirit of freedom, seems to fire every humane breast on this continent . . . We cannot but expect your house will . . . give us that ample relief which, as men, we have a natural right to.*
> Peter Bestes, Sambo Freeman,
> Felix Holbrook, Chester Joie

Similarly, Lemuel Haynes, a minuteman and mulatto (a person of mixed European and African heritage), issued an attack on slavery in 1776. Titled *Liberty Further Extended*, it contained a direct quotation from the Declaration of Independence in support of freedom for African Americans:

> *We hold these truths to be self-evident, that all men are created Equal, that they are Endowed By their Creator with Certain unalienable rights, that among these are Life, Liberty, and the pursuit of happyness.*

Through these and other efforts, African Americans made white Americans aware that fighting to avoid their own enslavement—while at the same time enslaving others—was illogical. As time would show, this new awareness would never fade away.

Like African Americans, women shared in the revolutionary experience. The challenging of authority, the questioning of traditional social relationships, and the asserting of the "rights of man" had a tremendous influence on them as well. Many people began to talk openly about the status of women. One of those who did so was **Abigail Adams.**

AMERICAN PROFILES

Abigail Adams

Born on November 22, 1744, Abigail Smith grew up in a Massachusetts household. Abigail's youth was a comfortable one; she devoted much of her time to religion and reading. Shortly before her twentieth birthday, Abigail married twenty-nine-year-old John Adams. Abigail's marriage decided the shape of her life. She entered her husband's household, and following the laws and customs of the time, she became subject to his authority.

In the 1770s, John Adams became one of the leaders of the opposition to British colonial policy. By the time he joined Jefferson on the committee that wrote the Declaration of Independence, Adams already had earned a reputation as a stubborn and outspoken lawyer. While Abigail remained shut off from the public debate because she was a woman, she did not hesitate to express her opinions to her husband. Abigail saw the Revolution as an opportunity for Americans to rethink domestic as well as public relationships.

Several months before the signing of the Declaration of Independence, Abigail sent a letter to John, who was attending the Continental Congress.

> *I long to hear that you have declared an independency—and by the way in the new Code of Laws which I suppose it will be necessary for you to make I desire you would Remember the Ladies, and be more generous and favorable to them than your ancestors. Do not put such unlimited power into the hands of the Husbands. Remember all Men would be tyrants if they could. If particular care and attention is not paid to the Ladies we are determined to foment [stir up] a Rebellion, and will not hold ourselves bound by any Laws in which we have no voice, or Representation.*

Part of Abigail's intention was to tease John by implying that he was included in her negative representation of husbands. The two had an affectionate relationship and truly respected

Abigail Adams advised her husband to "Remember the Ladies" when declaring independence for the new nation.

Enrichment

Invite students to go back in time to the 1770s and hold an informal debate over the question of whether or not people are capable of self-rule. Suggest that different students assume the role of an artisan, farmer, African American, woman, gentleman member of the "leisure" class, British supporter, or other individual from the revolutionary period. Have students do research to prepare for their role in the debate.

In Depth

Multicultural Perspectives

In 1767 a Caribbean landowner traveled to London with his slave, Jonathan Strong, and, in a fit of rage, he beat Strong viciously. Strong was found and befriended by a white Englishman, Granville Sharp, who helped him to escape. In 1772 Sharp took the issue of slavery before the British Lord Chief Justice who ruled, "Is not a Negro a Man? . . . As soon as any slave sets foot on English soil he shall be free." Sharp also helped organize the British Anti-Slavery Movement. In 1807 Parliament voted to halt Britain's slave trade, but it did not end slavery in British colonies.

Section 3 Review Answers

1. (a) natural rights, see p. 110,
(b) social contract, see p. 110,
(c) popular sovereignty, see p. 111,
(d) Declaration of Independence,
see p. 111

2. (a) Thomas Paine, see p. 109,
(b) Thomas Jefferson, see p. 110,
(c) Abigail Adams, see p. 113

3. Paine attacked the whole idea of government by kings and aristocrats.

4. They used the principles of the American Revolution to make white Americans aware that fighting to avoid slavery while owning slaves was a contradiction in terms.

5. She wanted men to give up "the harsh title of Master for the more tender and endearing one of Friend."

6. Students' responses should demonstrate an understanding of the beliefs held by most people in 1776, as well as an awareness of how Americans' beliefs have changed over time.

Reteach

Have students work as a group to outline the key ideas contained in *Common Sense* and the Declaration of Independence.

4. CLOSE

Reinforcing the Big Idea

The beliefs that people were born equal and that they could rule themselves took a passionate hold on colonial thinking. The ideals of equality and liberty for all people encouraged Americans to rebel against Great Britain in the hope of creating a new society. In the next section, students will read about the War for Independence.

each other. She was serious, however, in her complaints about how men in general treated women. As she explained, she wanted husbands to change their relationships with their wives by giving up "the harsh title of Master for the more tender and endearing one of Friend." She employed the very language that John and other men were using against Great Britain to suggest that it was time to rethink the old relationship between men and women.

John Adams did not attempt to follow through on Abigail's request. But his reply demonstrates that the talk of liberty was everywhere in North America in the late 1700s.

In an illustration from a magazine of 1792, a woman offers a declaration of the rights of women to a figure representing Liberty.

As to your extraordinary Code of Laws, I cannot but laugh. We have been told that our Struggle has loosened the bands of Government every where. That Children and Apprentices were disobedient—that schools and Colleges were grown turbulent—that Indians slighted their Guardians and Negroes grew insolent to their Masters. But your Letter was the first Intimation [hint] *that another Tribe more numerous and powerful than all the rest were grown discontented.*— This is rather too coarse a Compliment but you are so saucy [bold], *I won't blot it out.*

The humor and friendship that lighted Abigail and John's letters remained a part of their marriage through bad times and good, until her death in 1818. Together they weathered the War for Independence and eventually became the first presidential couple to live in the White House.

Abigail Adams was not the only woman of her time to question a society in which women could be beaten by husbands, in which they seldom owned property, and in which it was assumed they had no opinion in public affairs. For example, in an essay directed to men in *The Massachusetts Magazine* in 1790, writer Judith Sargeant Murray declared:

Yes, ye lordly, ye haughty sex, our souls are by nature equal *to yours; the same breath of God animates, enlivens, and invigorates us.*

Even if it would take decades or centuries to do anything about the inequality of women, the Revolution made that inequality an issue.

Abigail Adam's questioning of the existing order was part of the revolution begun by men such as Jefferson and Paine when they attacked the sovereignty of kings, denounced tyranny, and declared the basic equality of men. The next section shows that before any Americans could enjoy the fruits of that revolution, they had a difficult war to win.

SECTION 3 REVIEW

Key Terms, People, and Places
1. Define (a) natural rights, (b) social contract, (c) popular sovereignty, (d) Declaration of Independence.
2. Identify (a) Thomas Paine, (b) Thomas Jefferson, (c) Abigail Adams.

Key Concepts
3. What ideas did Thomas Paine attack in *Common Sense?*
4. How did African Americans use the principles of the American Revolution to begin changing white Americans' view of slavery?
5. How did Abigail Adams want men to change their relationship to women?

Critical Thinking
6. **Identifying Central Issues** Why did Americans in 1776 neither grant freedom to enslaved African Americans nor make women legally equal to men?

RESOURCE DIRECTORY

Teaching Resources

Quiz found in the Unit 1 folder, p.117, covers the main ideas in this section as well as the key terms.

The War for Independence

SECTION PREVIEW

Americans won their independence militarily by outlasting the British in one of the longest and costliest wars in American history. It was a true people's war—though not all the American people fought on the same side.

Key Concepts

- Despite the size and experience of the British military, the British did not have a superior position at the start of the war any more than the Americans did.
- The forces of the United States continued to fight against the British despite repeated losses.
- The Americans, with the help of the French, ended the war by trapping Cornwallis's army at Yorktown.
- Many American groups, including Native Americans and African Americans, experienced violence and hardship during the war.

Key Terms, People, and Places

Treaty of Paris, inflation; Patriots, Loyalists, Tories, Marquis de Lafayette, Baron von Steuben

As important as all the talk of self-government was, it would remain only talk if Americans could not win their independence. The British were not willing to let thirteen colonies go their way without a fight, especially when those colonies were prosperous. It took the Americans eight years, from 1775 to 1783, to accomplish their goal of freedom. Not only was the War for Independence the longest war in United States history after the Vietnam War, but it was the only one to be fought throughout the entire nation.

Advantages and Disadvantages

After scattering the rebels—or **Patriots,** as the Americans preferred to call themselves—

from Lexington Green on April 19, 1775, the British forces continued on to Concord. (See Section 1.) There they fulfilled their mission by burning some rebel war supplies. As the British returned to Boston, however, Patriots from nearby towns gathered along the route and sniped at them from behind stone walls and other cover by the roadside. The easy British victory at dawn had become an exhausting and costly defeat by evening, as the British tallied 273 wounded or killed, compared to only 95 Patriots. ✪

Still, the British had several reasons for believing that they would easily crush the rebellion in their American colonies. After all, Great Britain was the most powerful nation on earth. It had the richest economy, the largest navy, and an experienced and confident military. Almost a decade earlier, its armies and ships had defeated France in North America and Europe and added India as well as Canada to its Empire.

American Disadvantages The Americans, on the other hand, had no navy, no army, and no real government. They were not only disorganized, they were divided by state, by region, and by differing political goals. They even were split along racial lines. In the South, the British offered freedom to enslaved African Americans who would fight against the rebels. Throughout the colonies, Native Americans were outraged by American attacks against them and believed that their best interests lay in supporting the British, who were trying to prevent settlement in the West.

Furthermore, a great many colonists, called **Loyalists**—or **Tories,** after the majority party in Britain's Parliament—preferred to remain loyal to King George, even if they disagreed with the policies of his officials. John Adams estimated that one third of Americans were rebels, one third Tories, and one third neither. Tories tended

In a gesture symbolizing America's self-reliance, George Washington, the commander of the United States forces, declined to accept these elegant silver pistols captured from British Major John Pitcairn.

1. FOCUS

Connecting to the Big Idea

See page 96B. Explain to students that the War for Independence was a long and costly war that caused people great hardship. In the end, Americans won their independence from Great Britain. Ask students why the Americans were victorious.

Objectives

- Explain why neither the British nor the Americans had an advantage over the other at the start of the war.
- Describe how American forces continued to fight despite repeated losses.
- Explain how American forces, with the help of the French, finally ended the war.
- Identify how the war affected Native Americans and African Americans.

Bellringer

Ask students if they can recall a time in their life when they felt hopelessly defeated but kept going in spite of their feelings and were eventually successful. What techniques did they use to boost their morale?

Reading Strategy

Predicting Content Ask students to skim Section 4, list the main headings and subheadings, and write a sentence or phrase to predict the content listed under each one. When they have finished reading Section 4, ask them to review their predictions and test them against the actual text.

Reproducible Lesson Plan found in the Unit 1 folder, p. 111, provides a summary of the Section 4 lesson plan content.

Alternate Lesson Plan: Learning Styles found in the Alternate Lesson Plan folder, p. 20, especially useful for kinesthetic or auditory learners, provides a strategy to help students identify and explain the key battles of the War for Independence.

Guided Reading and Review found in the Unit 1 folder, p. 118, provides a structure for reading and mastering the key concepts and reviewing the key terms for Section 4. (Guided Practice)

✪ **Critical Thinking Activity** Checking Consistency: Lexington and Concord, found in the Unit 1 folder, p. 125, helps students apply this skill by presenting two differing accounts of which side fired the first shot of the Revolutionary War.

Explain/Discuss

Explain to students that Americans made great sacrifices during the long, hard, and costly war. Why were they willing to sacrifice so much?

Discuss the course of the war, and ask why it took the colonists so long to win. What kinds of hardships did Americans suffer during the war? How did they finally win?

Analyze

Have students analyze why the war can be considered "a people's war." Why did so many different kinds of people become involved? What might African Americans have hoped to gain by participating in it? Why do you suppose so many Americans sided with the British?

In Depth

Historical Misconceptions

The first major conflict of the Revolutionary War, and one that has become synonymous with the fight for American independence, is the Battle of Bunker Hill. The battle, however, was actually fought a few thousand feet away from Bunker Hill, at a mound known as Breed's Hill. Though colonial officers were ordered to fortify Bunker Hill against possible British attack in an effort to control Boston Harbor, the officers, for reasons still unknown, fortified Breed's Hill. Today, Breed's Hill is known as Bunker Hill, and the original site of Bunker Hill has houses built on it.

A minuteman using shoot-and-run tactics killed the British officer who carried this sword during the retreat from the Battle of Concord on April 19, 1776.

to be either merchants or well-established people with connections to the British government. They might also be freed slaves, Scots-Irish people in the backcountry, and other people who preferred to be ruled by the British rather than by colonial gentlemen. About 80,000 people left the United States during the war rather than give up their allegiance to the British Crown.

British Disadvantages The British had their own problems, however. The war was not popular in Great Britain. Many of the British resented paying taxes to fight the war and sympathized with the Americans. In addition, the British had to fight against an enemy that was thousands of miles away across an ocean, spread out over a huge territory, difficult to identify, and without any visible organization that could be attacked. As Americans would discover two centuries later in Vietnam, winning battles and having superiority in training are not enough when your opponent constantly shifts ground—and will not give up.

The Battle of Bunker Hill

The British began the war assuming that they could crush the rebellion by simply "showing the flag." They would remind people in New England of the power and authority of their government. They would intimidate them into surrender. The best example of this strategy was the battle for Breed's Hill near Boston in June 1775. (It has come to be called the Battle of Bunker Hill, after a nearby hill.)

After pursuing the British on their return from Concord in April, the Patriots—a varied group of white and African American artisans, farmers, and others—had surrounded Boston. But they were so disorganized that they could not agree on what to do next; in fact, they were unable to feed themselves and keep their camps around Boston in order.

Meanwhile, the British under General Thomas Gage sat in Boston, well supplied and protected by the British navy in the harbor. In early June, the Americans extended their lines north of Boston to the hills in Charlestown. General Gage decided to take

advantage of this move to overawe the rebels and send them home. He ordered a massive frontal assault by some 2,200 troops on the Patriot camp at the top of Breed's Hill.

After landing by ship, the British had to march uphill for about a mile. They began their attack at about 3 P.M. on a sunny day. It was a magnificent sight. Hundreds of soldiers in scarlet coats moved forward up the slope, accompanied by drums and bagpipes and carrying battle flags in an impressive display of discipline and power.

When the British neared the American line, the rebels fired a ragged but deadly volley into their ranks. Without cover on the open hillside, the British were an easy target for this withering fire. Their proud army staggered and retreated. According to one anonymous Englishman,

> *Our light-infantry were served up in companies against the grass fence* [a defensive barrier], *without being able to penetrate. . . . Most of our grenadiers and light-infantry . . . lost three fourths, and many nine tenths of their men. Some had only eight or nine men a company* [about 100 men] *left; some only three, four, and five.*

Embarrassed but still determined, the British troops attacked again. Again, the rebels stopped them. Again, the British attacked. This time the rebels, out of ammunition, retreated in disarray. The British troops, having picked their way through the bodies of dozens of wounded and dead comrades, overran the American position and took the hill.

The Battle of Bunker Hill was a British victory. But it came at too high a price. Of the 2,200 men Gage sent into battle that day, 226 were killed and another 828 were wounded. In other words, the number of casualties, or dead and wounded combined, was close to 50 percent, more than the British could bear. Above all, the battle demonstrated that the Americans would not be intimidated easily.

In early July, the general appointed by Congress, George Washington, assumed command of the American troops and brought greater discipline to the army. The siege of Boston continued throughout the fall and winter until the

 RESOURCE DIRECTORY

Americans dragged cannon they had captured in New York into position on the hills south of Boston. Faced with the possibility of deadly bombardment, the new British general, William Howe, evacuated Boston on March 17, 1776.

MAKING CONNECTIONS

Even in this early period of the war, the British and Americans constantly alternated between attacking and retreating. As you read on, notice how this general pattern continues. Who would be most likely to win such a war, and why?

War for Morale, 1776 to 1778

The British fleet took General Howe, his army, and thousands of Loyalists to Halifax, Nova Scotia, where they regrouped. In late summer, Howe launched an attack on New York City. The British had decided to concentrate on the Middle Colonies because the population of those colonies included more Tories, who could support them. In a series of large and small battles, Howe trounced Washington's poorly trained, poorly equipped, and poorly organized army.

An American volunteer, Michael Graham, later recalled one of these battles in August 1776.

I t is impossible for me to describe the confusion and horror of the scene that ensued: the artillery flying with the chains [of the gun carriages] over the horses' backs, our men running in almost every direction, and run which way they would, they were almost sure to meet the British. . . . And the enemy huzzahing when they took prisoners made it truly a day of distress to the Americans.

The Crisis By October the British had captured New York City and driven Washington's army all the way to Pennsylvania. Men were deserting Washington in droves; between the summer and winter of 1776, Washington's army shrank from 20,000 to about 6,000. The entire cause was on the verge of collapse.

In December 1776, Thomas Paine issued a paper he called *The Crisis*, which began with these words:

T hese are the times that try men's souls. The summer soldier and the sunshine patriot will, in this crisis, shrink from the service of their country; but he that stands it NOW, deserves the love and thanks of man and woman. Tyranny, like hell, is not easily conquered; yet we have this consolation with us, that the harder the conflict, the more glorious the triumph. What we obtain too cheap, we esteem [value] too lightly: It is dearness [expensiveness] only that gives every thing its value.

The Surprise Attack on Trenton Although the "summer soldiers" may have deserted, Washington still had some Patriots to form an army that next winter. He had the daring to put them to good use, too, as he broke the rules of

In a costly attempt to overawe American forces, waves of British troops climb Breed's Hill toward the waiting enemy.

Media and Technology

Transparencies
Fine Art, D-4, D-5

Caption Answer to ...

 Interpreting Maps

1775: Concord, Lexington, Bunker Hill, Ticonderoga; 1777: Germantown, Brandywine; 1781: Cowpens, Guilford Court House, Yorktown.

war by ordering a surprise attack on the enemy in their winter quarters. On Christmas Eve, 1776, Massachusetts fishermen rowed Washington and 2,400 men across the Delaware River to New Jersey. At dawn, they attacked Trenton, as shown on the map below, and captured the mercenaries, or hired soldiers, whom Great Britain had brought from the German state of Hesse; a few days later, the Patriots fought a small battle at Princeton. Then Washington retreated to Pennsylvania.

The significance of Trenton was immense, as it boosted American morale and persuaded many of Washington's soldiers to re-enlist. It was hardly a great military victory—in fact, Washington lost most of the battles he fought during the war. He was, however, a great leader. He inspired people to follow him, and he recognized when to act boldly and decisively. Furthermore, he gradually came to understand that winning individual battles meant little compared to just hanging on and being ready to strike when the British made a mistake. Despite all the victories the British won in 1776, they could not win the war because they could not put Washington out of business.

The War for Independence, 1775–1781

Geography and History: Interpreting Maps
Because the movements of United States forces were so often a reaction to British advances or retreats, only British movements are shown here. The major battles of the early part of the war took place in the North, but the focus shifted gradually southward. *Locate battles that took place in 1775, 1777, and 1781.*

In Depth

Did You Know?

The Journal of Nicholas Cresswell, 1774–1777 chronicles the travels of a young English Loyalist who said of Trenton: "Six weeks ago . . . [the Americans thought] all was gone, all was lost. But now the scale is turned and Washington's name is extolled to the clouds. Alexander, Pompey, and Hannibal were but pygmy Generals, in comparison with the magnanimous Washington. Poor General Howe is ridiculed in all companies and all my countrymen abused. I am obliged to hear this daily and dare not speak a word in their favor. It is the damned Hessians that has caused this, curse the scoundrel that first thought of sending them here."

The War Turns at Saratoga The next summer brought only mixed success for the Americans. Howe brushed aside Washington's army and captured the American capital of Philadelphia. But at Saratoga in upstate New York, a hastily organized army of Americans defeated a British army moving south from Canada in October 1777. Many historians call this victory the turning point of the war, for it convinced many people that the Americans would win if they could just hold on.

Among those persuaded was the French government. At the urging of Ambassador Benjamin Franklin, the French joined sides with the Americans. Not only did this mean money and supplies, it also meant that the British had to protect themselves in Europe. The French officer the **Marquis de Lafayette,** who fought alongside the Americans, later persuaded the French to assist with an army of 6,000 men.

Another European was also vital to the American cause: the Prussian officer **Baron von Steuben.** During a bitter winter at Valley Forge, Pennsylvania, he drilled Washington's troops and wrote a book of regulations that brought much-needed discipline to the Continental Army.

In the same year, 1778, the British abandoned Philadelphia and marched back across New Jersey toward New York City. At Monmouth Court House in New Jersey, Washington's army, now better equipped and better trained, caught up with the rear guard of the British and fought them to a standstill. After years of disorganization, the American army now had the discipline that made it a unit fit to be reckoned with.

Fighting the War to an End

While they continued to occupy New York, the British turned their primary attention to the South. There they hoped to demoralize the Americans by freeing slaves and laying waste the countryside. In 1780 the British captured Charleston, South Carolina. They then used the city as a base of operations, winning several battles.

The war, always an ugly business, was especially vicious in the South. Most of the southern war was fought by Americans against Americans, as Tories and Patriots clashed. At the battle of King's Mountain in South Carolina in 1780, where the Tories suffered a defeat, all the combatants were Americans. Elsewhere in the western part of the South, other Patriot forces dealt the British several losses.

Meanwhile, the British general Lord Cornwallis marched from South Carolina toward New York. Harassed but not defeated by small American armies commanded by Nathanael Greene and the Marquis de Lafayette, Cornwallis decided to transport his army to New York by ship in the summer of 1781. Marching his forces to the Virginia coast, he took up a position at Yorktown, near the point where the York River enters the Chesapeake Bay.

Washington, who was in camp near New York City, again acted boldly; he left the middle states and moved his army quickly south. There, together with the recently arrived French army, he laid siege to Yorktown in September. Luckily for the Americans, a French fleet turned back a British fleet off the coast of Virginia, and Cornwallis was trapped by a force twice the size of his own. On October 19, 1781, he had the "mortification," as he put it in a later letter to his superior, of surrendering his army to Washington and the French.

As the war moved into the southern states, it became increasingly hard fought. The commander of the British troops in this cavalry skirmish, Colonel Banastre Tarleton, was known as "the Butcher" for killing his prisoners.

In Depth

Interdisciplinary

From the beginning of the war, geography helped the American cause by making it impossible for Britain to control the American seacoast. Blockade-running colonists needed to go no farther than the Caribbean to beat the blockade and find a market. Since the trade winds from Europe led directly to the Caribbean islands, many other countries found them an ideal location for trading with America. The neutral port of the Dutch-held island St. Eustasius was especially crowded with American ships, where traders could buy anything from tea to gunpowder, guns to sugar. In 1780, the admiral of the British fleet wrote, "this rock of only six miles in length and three in breadth has done more harm than all the arms of her most potent enemies, and alone supported the infamous American rebellion."

A wife of one of the American soldiers, Sarah Osborn, was present at the surrender. Over fifty years later, she recalled that the British forces

This woodcut was published in 1779 with a poem in which a Daughter of Liberty described civilian hardships during the War for Independence.

> marched out beating and playing a melancholy [sad] tune, their drums covered with black handkerchiefs and their fifes with black ribbons tied around them, into an old field and there grounded their arms and then returned into town again to await their destiny.

The "melancholy tune" the British played was a song popular at the time called "The World Turned Upside Down." And that it was; the world would never be the same again. Faced with rising opposition at home, a new British government began negotiations that resulted in the signing of the **Treaty of Paris** in September 1783. Under this treaty, George III was no longer sovereign, or ruler, in his thirteen former colonies. Instead, the people were sovereign, although exactly which people that meant and how they would rule remained to be determined. In any case, it was not just white men, but all kinds of people who had fought the War for Independence.

A People's War

The British lost their colonies because Americans—or at least some Americans—had the determination to outlast them, even in the face of repeated military defeats. Like all wars, the War for Independence affected many people. Perhaps 200,000 men or more served at one time or another in the American cause.

The American Soldier's Experience Most of the fighting was carried out by young, relatively poor men. They and their officers were paid badly, if at all, and poorly fed and clothed. Washington wrote: "You might have tracked the army . . . to Valley Forge by the blood of their feet." In 1780 a soldier named Joseph Plumb Martin described their situation:

> The men were . . . exasperated [irritated] beyond endurance; they could

not stand it any longer. . . . What was to be done? Here was the army starved and naked, and there their country sitting still and expecting the army to do notable things while fainting from sheer starvation.

Occasionally their various frustrations boiled over into unrest, as in the case of the brief mutiny in January 1781 by a unit known as the Pennsylvania Line.

African American men—about five thousand of them—also experienced the life of a soldier, in the fighting on both sides. Women, too, both white and African American, served the cause they believed in, whether rebel or Tory. Many followed husbands, lovers, or fathers into battle, cared for them, and nursed them. These women formed an unofficial but vital part of the army, which could not have functioned without them. And a few actually fought side by side with men. The most famous was Deborah Sampson, who disguised herself as a man, took the name Robert Shurtleff, and served in the Continental Army from May 1782 to October 1783. Her husband later became the only man to be granted a pension as the "widow" of a veteran.

The Civilian Experience of the War The war affected civilians too. The British navy blockaded the seacoast and severely disrupted American commerce. Measured in the British monetary unit of pounds sterling, the combined value of American imports and exports fell from about £4,600,000 in 1775 to £200,000 in 1777. Exports of tobacco and rice in particular fell markedly. Occupation by British soldiers damaged cities such as New York. In fact, half of the 21,000 people who lived in New York before the war left the city.

Nearly everyone felt the pinch during the war. Often needed goods were scarce. Even when goods were available, it was not always possible to purchase them, due to **inflation,** or a steady increase in prices over a period of time that reduces people's ability to buy goods. In Massachusetts, for example, the price of a bushel of corn rose from less than one dollar in 1777 to almost eighty dollars in 1779. Congress issued paper money (called Continental

In Depth

Multicultural Perspectives

African American Patriots, both free and enslaved, were first encouraged to enlist in the Continental Army. Nonetheless, in a move designed to appease the Southern Colonies, the Continental Congress banned all African American enlistments in October, 1775. The British then offered freedom to slaves who would fight for them. So many slaves responded that General Washington decided to allow the reenlistment of free blacks who had already served. Only gradually, however, as the manpower shortage became acute, did the Continental Army readmit slaves into its ranks.

RESOURCE DIRECTORY

Teaching Resources

American Profiles Activity found in the Unit 1 folder, p. 121, profiles Deborah Sampson Gannett, a Massachusetts woman who defied the social conventions of her time by enlisting in the Continental Army dressed as a man.

Primary Source Activity War Diary of Margaret Hill Morris, found in the Unit 1 folder, pp. 127–128, recounts a colonial woman's reactions to the advance of British troops toward her Pennsylvania town.

dollars) to pay for military expenses. But inflation soon made the money of little value. In 1777 it took three Continental dollars to equal one dollar in gold; by 1778, it took seven; one hundred in 1780; and almost a hundred and fifty in 1781. This decline in value gave rise to the expression "not worth a Continental." In the long run, the War for Independence stimulated economic development. But its short-term impact was harsh. ⭐

The Native American Experience of the War
Not all of the pain of the war was economic. In the middle and southern states especially, rebels and Tories treated each other savagely; they harassed each other, destroyed property, and killed hundreds of people. But the group most hurt by the war was the Native American population. At first, the Iroquois tried to stay out of what Mohawk sachem Little Abraham called "a family affair" between Britain and its colonies. The war, however, provided an excuse for Americans on the New York frontier to settle the question of control in the region. Angered by American attacks on their villages, the Iroquois joined the British in 1777. Under the able leadership of another Mohawk sachem, Joseph Brant, they launched several devastating raids in New York and Pennsylvania. In 1779, Americans under

Despite the brilliant leadership of Joseph Brant (above) and others, Native Americans suffered great hardships during the long war.

the command of General John Sullivan retaliated with raids of their own. Meanwhile, in the South, Virginians and Carolinians sent repeated expeditions to attack the Cherokee for supporting the British. For most Native Americans, the American victory in 1783 was a serious blow, the meaning of which would only become clear in the next two to three decades.

The War for Independence was a long and brutal war, complete with betrayals and corruption, torture and terrible violence. But it confirmed the commitment of many white Americans to the cause of independence. Now that they had won, however, they faced the difficult challenge of defining exactly what their victory meant.

Georgia's Nancy Hart was said to have shot one of the six Tories who broke into her home, wounded another, and held the rest prisoner until her husband returned— to help her hang them.

SECTION 4 REVIEW

Key Terms, People, and Places
1. Define (a) Treaty of Paris, (b) inflation.
2. Identify (a) Patriots, (b) Loyalists, (c) Tories, (d) Marquis de Lafayette, (e) Baron von Steuben.

Key Concepts
3. Give two advantages and two disadvantages of the British at the beginning of the War for Independence.

4. Explain how the victory at Saratoga led to final victory at Yorktown.
5. What was the overall effect of the war on Native Americans?

Critical Thinking
6. **Checking Consistency** Analyze George Washington's qualities of leadership.

 Quiz found in the Unit 1 folder, p. 119, covers the main ideas in this section as well as the key terms.

 Chapter Test Forms A and B are found in the Unit 1 folder, pp. 134–139.

 Answer Keys found in the Unit 1 folder, pp. 146–159, provide answers to all student activities.

Media and Technology

 Transparency
Graphic Organizer, G-2

Guided Reading Audiotapes
(English and Spanish)

 Computer Test Bank

---

3. ASSESS

Section 4 Review Answers
1. (a) Treaty of Paris, see p. 120, (b) inflation, see p. 120

2. (a) Patriots, see p. 115, (b) Loyalists, see p. 115, (c) Tories, see p. 115, (d) Marquis de Lafayette, see p. 119, (e) Baron von Steuben, see p. 119

3. Possible answers: Among its advantages, Great Britain was the most powerful nation on earth; it had the world's largest navy and an experienced military. Among the disadvantages of the British, many resented paying taxes to fight the war, and they had to fight against an enemy that was thousands of miles away.

4. The American victory convinced the French that the Americans might be able to win the war. The French then provided troops and supplies to the American forces, making possible the final success at Yorktown.

5. For most Native Americans, the American victory in 1783 was a serious blow.

6. Washington was not a great general, because he lost most of the battles he fought during the war. He was, however, a great leader, because he inspired people to follow him and recognized when the time had come to act boldly and decisively.

Reteach
Have students make a list of the major battles between the British and the Americans and indicate beside each entry who won. Then have them write one or two sentences summarizing the reasons for the Americans' final victory.

4. CLOSE

Reinforcing the Big Idea
Now that Americans had won their independence, they faced the challenge of establishing a new society based on their ideals.

Chapter Review Answers

Understanding Key Terms, People, and Places

Terms
Students should refer to the definitions of the key terms in the chapter to write sentences that show the relation of each word to the War for Independence.

Word Relationships
1. (c) does not belong. The Treaty of Paris ended the War for Independence, which along with its accompanying social and political changes is also known as the American Revolution. Pontiac's War followed the French and Indian War and resulted from the British refusal to continue trade with Native Americans.

2. (b) does not belong. Popular sovereignty and the social contract are important ideas in the Declaration of Independence. Inflation refers to rising prices.

3. (a) does not belong. The expense of the French and Indian War and depression in Britain caused the British to pass laws such as the Stamp Act to raise money. The Treaty of Paris stated that George III was no longer sovereign in the thirteen colonies.

4. (d) does not belong. The Proclamation of 1763, the Intolerable Acts, and the Stamp Act were British laws that angered the colonists. Natural rights are the rights that people are born with rather than those granted by a king or government.

True or False
1. false, Thomas Paine
2. false, minutemen
3. true
4. false, Baron von Steuben

Reviewing Main Ideas

1. They attacked the eastern and western limits of the French territory, breaking through the center of the French line of control at Lake Champlain and pressing on toward Quebec.

2. Once the French were on the defensive, the Iroquois actively began to support the British. The French then retreated into Canada, and the British were able to capture Quebec.

3. The colonists were exposed to large numbers of British troops. The troops behaved in ways that seemed to the colonists arrogant and unprincipled.

4. The British passed the Sugar Act, the Proclamation of 1763, the Stamp Act; they closely regulated colonial trade.

Chapter Review

Understanding Key Terms, People, and Places

Key Terms
1. American Revolution
2. War for Independence
3. French and Indian War
4. depression
5. Pontiac's Rebellion
6. Proclamation of 1763
7. Stamp Act
8. boycott
9. Boston Tea Party
10. Intolerable Acts
11. natural rights
12. social contract
13. popular sovereignty
14. Declaration of Independence
15. Treaty of Paris
16. inflation

People
17. minutemen
18. George Washington
19. King George III
20. Thomas Paine
21. Thomas Jefferson
22. Abigail Adams
23. Patriots
24. Loyalists
25. Tories
26. Marquis de Lafayette
27. Baron von Steuben

Terms For each term above, write a sentence that explains its relation to the War for Independence.

Word Relationships Three of the terms in each of the following sets of terms are related. Choose the term that does not belong and explain why it does not belong.
1. (a) American Revolution, (b) Treaty of Paris, (c) Pontiac's Rebellion, (d) War for Independence
2. (a) social contract, (b) inflation, (c) Declaration of Independence, (d) popular sovereignty
3. (a) Treaty of Paris, (b) Stamp Act, (c) depression, (d) French and Indian War
4. (a) Proclamation of 1763, (b) Intolerable Acts, (c) Stamp Act, (d) natural rights

True or False Determine whether each statement is true or false. If it is true, write "true." If it is false, change the underlined name to make the statement true.
1. Baron von Steuben wrote a pamphlet called *Common Sense* in which he examined new ideas about freedom and government.
2. Organized as a defensive force of local residents, Tories pledged to respond quickly when called to action.
3. On one of his first missions, George Washington retreated from Fort Necessity in disgrace.
4. The Prussian officer Thomas Jefferson brought discipline to Washington's army at Valley Forge.

Reviewing Main Ideas

Section 1 (pp. 98–101)
1. What strategy did the British use to win the French and Indian War?
2. What events proved decisive to British victory in the French and Indian War?
3. Why did the French and Indian War lead to a new awareness of the colonists' differences from the British?

Section 2 (pp. 102–107)
4. What new policies did the British begin during the 1760s?
5. What actions did the colonists take to protest the Stamp Act?
6. Describe the effect of the Intolerable Acts on the colonists' perception of the British.

Section 3 (pp. 109–114)
7. What basic principles were defined in the pamphlet *Common Sense* and the Declaration of Independence?
8. What short-term and long-term effects did the Revolution have on African Americans?
9. What does the profile of Abigail Adams reveal about the impact of the Revolution on American women?

Section 4 (pp. 115–121)
10. What were some of the disadvantages that Americans had to face at the beginning of the Revolution?
11. What did the Battle of Bunker Hill and the attack on Trenton demonstrate about American troops?
12. How did the French help the Americans win the war?
13. What groups were most severely affected by the war?

---

5. Delegates from several colonies—the Stamp Act Congress—gathered in New York to declare that their rights as British subjects had been violated. Other colonists forced stamp distributors to resign and attacked officials who supported the policy.

6. The Intolerable Acts seemed to confirm the colonists' suspicions that the British intended to take away their freedoms.

7. *Common Sense* and the Declaration of Independence expounded the principles of freedom and equality in American government and society.

8. In the short term, the Revolution did little to help African Americans achieve freedom and equality. But it made whites aware of the contradiction between fighting for liberty and practicing slavery.

9. The profile of Abigail Adams shows that women begin to question their inequality.

10. The Americans had no organized military and no real government. African Americans and Native Americans had no incentives to fight the British. Also, many colonists remained loyal to King George.

11. The Battle of Bunker Hill demonstrated that American troops could not be easily intimidated and would continue to fight even if the odds were against them. Trenton showed that at least some Americans would continue fighting despite losses; it also demonstrated the Americans' daring.

1. **Demonstrating Reasoned Judgment** The colonists resented the restrictions that the British placed on their freedoms. On what grounds would you feel justified in rebelling against government restrictions?

2. **Identifying Alternatives** In America today the media—television in particular—significantly influence public opinion. In the absence of television in the late 1700s, newspapers, pamphlets, and documents like the Declaration of Independence informed and incited the colonists. Do you think the Revolution would have taken place without these writings? Explain your reasoning.

3. **Identifying Central Issues** On page 112, you read that "In many ways, we are still discovering the full meaning of the Declaration of Independence." Do you agree with this statement? Explain your answer.

4. **Drawing Conclusions** You have read that after their defeat at Yorktown, the British played a song called "The World Turned Upside Down." In what ways was this an appropriate title for the times?

1. **Evaluating Primary Sources** Review the first primary source excerpt on page 113. Do the speakers have a logical argument? If so, why did it take almost another century before slavery was actually abolished?

2. **Understanding the Visuals** Explain what changes should be made to Revere's drawing of the Boston Massacre on page 106 to make it reflect events more accurately.

3. **Writing About the Chapter** It is 1776. You are writing a letter to your cousin in England explaining why you support, or do not support, the colonists' decision to rebel against Britain. First, list what you see as the reasons for your support or lack of support. Mention any ways in which you can sympathize with the other side's point of view. Then write a draft of your letter in which you explain your position. Revise your letter, making sure that each idea is expressed clearly. Proofread your letter and draft a final copy.

4. **Using the Graphic Organizer** This graphic organizer uses a double web to compare and contrast British and American self-images during the French and Indian War. (a) What did the British and the Americans have in common? (b) How did their views of one another contribute to the American Revolution? (c) On a separate sheet of paper, create your own graphic organizer comparing and contrasting the advantages and disadvantages of the British and Americans at the start of the War for Independence.

12. The French offered money, supplies, troops, and the assistance of the Marquis de Lafayette. At Yorktown, the French turned back a British fleet off the coast of Virginia, trapping Cornwallis.

13. Young, poor men, including African Americans, did most of the fighting. Many women accompanied them. Native Americans suffered the most because, hoping to keep control of their lands, they sided with the British.

Thinking Critically

1. Answers should center on restrictions that are arbitrary and unnecessary. Most students will feel that rebellion against unnecessary restrictions can be justified.

2. Answers should show an awareness that the Revolution was provoked not only by specific actions like the Stamp Act but also by the spread of new beliefs about freedom and equality. These beliefs were explained in the writings that circulated among the colonists before and during the Revolution.

3. Answers should indicate that the United States is still struggling with issues of equality for all of its people, notably minorities and women.

4. The world must have felt turned upside down for the British, who entered the war feeling that their superior strength could easily put down the colonists' rebellion. The outcome of the Revolution also upset the British belief in an unchanging hierarchy. In addition, this song symbolizes the fact that many groups, including women and African Americans, who took up the ideas of the American Revolution, would not earlier have spoken out for these ideas.

Making Connections

1. The speakers' argument that those who oppose political slavery should also oppose racial slavery is entirely logical. However, custom, economics, and prejudice proved stronger than logic for the next hundred years.

2. Answers should stress that the soldiers were under attack by an unruly crowd and were actually acting defensively, rather than offensively, as Revere's engraving suggests.

3. Letters should reflect an understanding of the British policies that led to the Revolution and of the colonists' new ideas about freedom and equality.

4. (a) Both the British and the Americans took pride in the empire and were allied against the French. (b) The British attitude contributed to the war by treating the colonists as inferior; the colonists' view contributed by discouraging reconciliation. (c) Students' graphic organizers should reflect an understanding of the advantages and disadvantages of both sides in the war.

 ## Alternative Assessment

Final Evaluation
Use the following criteria to evaluate student projects:
- **Evidence of mastery of content** To what extent do projects demonstrate knowledge and understanding of chapter content?
- **Evidence of thoughtfulness** To what extent do projects demonstrate King George III's perspective regarding colonial affairs?
- **Evidence of outside research** To what extent do projects demonstrate students' outside research?

UNIT 2

Introducing the Unit

Interpreting the Visual American artists waged their own "American Revolution," finding subjects and styles that suited their new nation rather than copying European subjects and imitating European styles.

German-born John Lewis Krimmel (1729–1821) was one painter who found his subjects in American places and American types. In the painting shown on pages 124–125, Krimmel depicts the American enthusiasm for politics.

Divide the class into small groups. The members of each group should take turns writing one sentence that describes Krimmel's painting until they have exhausted their ideas. Have a volunteer from each group read the collective description to the class. Then ask the class to find evidence in the picture of Krimmel's opinion of democracy in Philadelphia. What do students think Krimmel would include in an election day painting today?

Establishing Chronology Tell students that this unit covers the forty-nine years from 1781 to 1830. In those tumultuous years, thirteen rebellious colonies won a war, ratified a Constitution, established an American style of politics, and created a strong federal nation reaching to the Mississippi River.

Balancing Liberty and Order
1781–1830

"The American war is over, but this is far from being the case with the American Revolution."

—Benjamin Rush, 1783

Achieving a workable balance between liberty and order has never been easy, as Patriot Benjamin Rush well understood. The central government created by the Articles of Confederation granted liberty but did not achieve order. Amid alarming signs of disorder in the young nation, fifty-five of the most distinguished citizens of the day met in Philadelphia in the hot summer of 1787 to discuss the crisis. They crafted the United States Constitution, which, in the decades after its adoption, attempted to balance Americans' desire for both liberty and order.

▶ RESOURCE DIRECTORY

Teaching Resources

 Local History Activity "When Washington Was a Wilderness" and the Local Focus research topic suggestions, found in the Local History Resources folder, pp. 6–8, are designed to help students understand how history affects all lives.

★ **Themes in American History Posters** Wall-size, illustrated posters, found in the Teaching Resources package, illustrate the four unit themes.

Unit Test Forms A and B are found in the Unit 2 folder, pp. 110–115.

The excitement of government by the people is captured in this 1815 painting of Independence Hall, titled "Election Day in Philadelphia," by John L. Krimmel.

Media and Technology

Visions of America: Scenes of an Era To introduce students to the main idea and events covered in this unit, play "Scenes of an Era: Balancing Liberty and Order" (length: 2.5 minutes). This selection can be located on side 1 of the videodiscs. This selection can also be located on videotape 1. Lesson plans for "Scenes of an Era" can be found in the Visions of America Guidebook.

Using Multimedia Technology This folder contains instructional tools and strategies for using technology in the classroom.

Transparency Binder Contains full-color transparencies with lesson suggestions. From a large collection divided into twelve categories, specific transparencies are referenced throughout the chapters at appropriate points of use. For this unit, see American Photo, B-2; Fine Art, D-6; The Way It Works, H-6; Links Across Time, J-2; and Political Cartoon, K-2.

Themes in American History

Teachers may wish to discuss specific historical events in the context of historical themes. Here are four suggestions for Unit 2.

Technology *Americans' ability to develop new skills and tools and to increase their knowledge of the physical world has greatly affected the way they live and work, and has led to a high standard of living.*

● The Industrial Revolution led to vast improvements in transportation, communications, and industry.
● In the early 1800s the American people developed a strong belief in the power of science and invention to bring about social progress and improve material wealth.

Environment *The geography and available resources of the continent have affected the actions of Americans. Similarly, the actions of Americans have affected the environment and physical landscape.*

● The Louisiana Purchase doubled the size of the United States and gave the nation control of America's interior waterways.
● The invention of the steamboat and the construction of canals connected the East Coast with lands west of the Appalachians.

American Democracy *The concepts of democratic representation, equality under the law, and freedom from discrimination have been gradually broadened to include previously excluded groups.*

● The Constitution called for a representative government with some restrictions limiting the power of the people.
● The peaceful transfer of power to an opposition party after the election of 1800 was a major test of American constitutional government.

American Culture *In every period of their history, Americans gave special expression to their views through art, literature, films, music, manners, and morals.*

● Many more Americans learned to read and write, and Americans began to see education as the key to individual success and national stability and prosperity.

Chapter 5 The Constitution of the United States
1781–1789

📁 **Teaching Resources** (See Unit 2 Folder)

	Instruction	Enrichment
Section 1 **Government by the States** (pp. 128–133)	Reproducible Lesson Plan, p. 3 Alternate Lesson Plan, p. 22 Guided Reading and Review, p. 7 Quiz, p. 8	Viewpoints Activity, On the United States as an Independent Nation, pp. 19–20 American Profiles Activity, Daniel Shays, p. 17 Literature Activity, The Contrast, pp. 26–27 History Might Not . . . Activity, Redistributing Government Power, pp. 15–16
Section 2 **The Constitutional Convention** (pp. 136–142)	Reproducible Lesson Plan, p. 4 Alternate Lesson Plan, p. 23 Guided Reading and Review, p. 9 Quiz, p. 10	Literature Activity, On America, p. 28 Primary Source Activity, Hamilton and Jefferson, p. 23 Critical Thinking Activity, Determining Relevance, p. 22 Historian's Toolbox Activity, Identifying Central Issues, p. 21
Section 3 **Ratifying the Constitution** (pp. 144–147)	Reproducible Lesson Plan, p. 5 Alternate Lesson Plan, p. 24 Guided Reading and Review, p. 11 Quiz, p. 12	Primary Source Activity, A Department of Peace, p. 25 Visual Learning Activity, The First United States Coins, p. 29
Section 4 **The New Government** (pp. 148–151)	Reproducible Lesson Plan, p. 6 Alternate Lesson Plan, p. 25 Guided Reading and Review, p. 13 Quiz, p. 14 Chapter Test, Forms A & B, pp. 31–36	Visual Learning Activity, A Portrait of a President, p. 30 Primary Source Activity, Meeting President and Mrs. Washington, p. 24 American Profiles Activity, Benjamin Banneker, p. 18

📁 **Additional Chapter Resources**

Resource Organizer, p. 2
Alternate Lesson Plan, p. 21
Answer Keys pp. 116–125

Bibliography

For the Teacher
DePauw, Linda Grant. *Founding Mothers: Women in America in the Revolutionary Era.* Houghton Mifflin, 1975. (Narrative accounts of women's contributions during the revolutionary period.)

Lessons on the Federalist Papers: Supplement to High School Courses in American History, Government and Civics. Organization of American Historians, 1987. (Core concepts from the *Federalist* papers such as the separation of powers, limited government, and the rights of individuals. Ten lessons.)

Prentice Hall Literature Excerpts from *The American Experience,* 1994, including Wheatley, Phillis. "To His Excellency, General Washington," from *The Poems of Phillis Wheatley.* University of North Carolina Press, 1966.

Media and Technology

 Visions of America: History Might Not Have Happened This Way Game

 Critical Thinking, I-6; The Way It Works, H-5

 Graphic Organizer, G-1

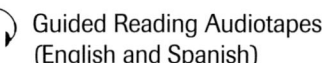 Guided Reading Audiotapes (English and Spanish)

Computer Test Bank

For the Student

Bowen, Catherine D. *Miracle at Philadelphia: The Story of the Constitution, May to September, 1787.* Little, Brown, 1986.

Lindop, Edmund. *Birth of the Constitution.* Enslow, 1987. (An easy-to-read description of the Constitutional Convention, including the text of the Constitution and the amendments.)

America: A Personal History of the United States, No. 4—Inventing a Nation. 16mm, 52 minutes. Time-Life Films, 1972. Color film. (An investigation of the Independence Hall debates, narrated by Alistair Cooke.)

THE BIG IDEA

The Big Idea for the chapter and how the main ideas in each section relate to the Big Idea are graphically displayed below. Comprehension of this chapter's Big Idea is critical to students' understanding of United States history and how we as a nation got where we are today.

CHAPTER 5

A group of powerful men succeeded in writing and winning approval of the federal Constitution and in establishing a powerful central government. The conflict generated by their efforts resulted in safeguards in the form of the Bill of Rights to protect Americans' liberty from government infringement.

SECTION 1

Many Americans were happy with the country's highly democratic government after the War for Independence; but economic and political problems caused other Americans to worry that the nation would be destroyed if the national government was not strengthened.

SECTION 2

Delegates gathered at the Constitutional Convention to restructure the country's government. After a great deal of compromise, they came up with a new plan for government that blended popular sovereignty with a strong national government.

SECTION 3

Many Americans opposed the Constitution because they were afraid it meant the end of liberty, and it was narrowly ratified when the Federalists agreed to add the Bill of Rights.

SECTION 4

With the framework for the new government finally in place, Federalists set about making their vision of a great "republican empire" come true.

The Constitution of the United States
1781–1789

The Relevance of the Big Idea

The struggle to resolve the two points of view that led to the creation of the Constitution—a plan for government combining strong national powers with a respect for and protection of individual liberty—is debated even after more than two hundred years. Issues such as gun control, states' rights regarding death penalties, seat-belt laws, and reproductive rights are all part of the same debate.

Discuss with students that many people feel that institutions have too much power over individuals. Have students generate a list of possible institutions, such as school, family, and clubs or other organizations to which they may belong, and explain how they feel about the level of power of those institutions.

In Depth

Global Connections

After the success of the American Revolution, many British people blamed King George III, whose irascible nature and inability to compromise, they felt, provoked the American colonies to rebel. Also, the aftermath of the war with America left the British economy severely strained. Within a few years, however, the British economy greatly improved, as trade with the United States became a more lucrative enterprise than it had ever been between Britain and its American colonies.

The Constitution of The United States
1781–1789

Concerned about disorder among the people and worried about the stability of the new nation, a group of well-educated, well-organized men worked in the 1780s to save the United States. They succeeded in writing and winning approval of the Constitution and in establishing a powerful central government. By century's end a new capital, a symbol of their hopes for an American empire, was rising on the banks of the Potomac River.

Events in the United States

1781 The Articles of Confederation are approved.

1783 George Washington resigns as commander of the American army.

1781	1782	1783	1784	1785

Events in the World

1783 Simón Bolívar, later hero of South American war for independence, is born in Venezuela.

1785 Edmund Cartwright invents the power loom in Britain.

RESOURCE DIRECTORY

Teaching Resources

Alternate Lesson Plan: Demonstrating the Big Idea found in the Alternate Lesson Plans folder, p. 21, provides a lesson strategy to instruct students about the big idea that the United States Constitution was the result of much conflict and debate between the powerful men of the time.

Alternative Assessment Handbook provides information, guidance, and strategies for alternative methods of assessment. It includes an essay on new trends in assessment, guidance and strategies for developing performance tasks and portfolios, scoring rubrics, and sample evaluation forms.

Pages 128–133
Government by the States

Many Americans were pleased with the highly democratic state and national governments created during the American Revolution. But a sizable number of citizens, worried that there was too much social disorder in the new nation, lobbied hard for a stronger national government.

Pages 136–142
The Constitutional Convention

During the long summer of 1787, delegates to a convention in Philadelphia fashioned a Constitution that forever sealed the people's right to direct their government—with some restrictions.

Pages 144–147
Ratifying the Constitution

With a combination of political skill and persuasive argument, the Federalists managed to win narrow approval of the Constitution. Their key concession to their opponents was the Bill of Rights.

Pages 148–151
The New Government

In the first years under the Constitution, Federalists labored to make the United States government as impressive as possible. They chose talented officials, opted for high ceremony, and made plans for an elaborate national capital.

1786 The Annapolis Convention takes place.

1787 The Constitutional Convention is held in Philadelphia.
• Shays's Rebellion begins.

1788 The Constitution is approved by the states and goes into effect.

1789 George Washington becomes the first President of the United States.

1790 Rhode Island becomes the last of the original 13 states to ratify the Constitution.

1791 The Bill of Rights is ratified and becomes part of the Constitution.

1786	1787	1788	1789	1790	1791

1787 Turkey declares war on Russia.

1789 The French Revolution begins.

1791 Austrian composer Wolfgang Amadeus Mozart dies.
• Haitians revolt against French rule.

Government by the States

Connecting to the Big Idea

See page 126B. Explain to students that the years after the War for Independence were difficult ones for the United States. The new country was disorganized and suffered from economic and political problems. Some Americans, known as Nationalists, began to demand a stronger national government. Ask students why the Nationalists felt that a stronger national government would be beneficial.

Objectives

● Describe government in the United States before 1788.
● Explain why the Nationalists believed there should be a strong national government.
● Explain the reaction of the Nationalists to Shays's Rebellion.

Bellringer

Ask students on what occasions, or for what reasons, people turn to the federal government. For example, why do people expect the federal government to help after natural disasters?

Answer to ...

MAKING CONNECTIONS

Answers may suggest that a dictatorship might be able to decree solutions to some problems, if it was so inclined, whereas the conflicting interests represented in a democracy often hinder decision and swift action. Dictatorships, however, often bring problems of reduced personal freedom, police terror, and increased inequalities between classes.

Government by the States

SECTION PREVIEW

Many Americans were pleased with the highly democratic state and national governments created during the American Revolution. But a sizable number of citizens, worried that there was too much social disorder in the new nation, lobbied hard for a stronger national government.

A testimony to changed attitudes, this bowl made by diehard revolutionary Paul Revere honors a general who crushed a rebellion against increased taxes in 1787.

Key Concepts

• Before 1788 the national government was weak and the state constitutions were powerful.
• The Nationalists believed that the new nation's many problems could only be solved by a strong national government.
• Shays's Rebellion persuaded many that the United States was on the brink of dangerous disorder.

Key Terms, People, and Places

confederation, Articles of Confederation, legislative branch, executive branch, judicial branch, unicameral legislature, bicameral legislature; Nationalists

O n December 23, 1783, a month after watching the British army leave New York forever, George Washington performed perhaps the most remarkable act of his life: he voluntarily gave up power. Having helped Americans achieve their freedom from a king, he did not want to become another ruler over them. In an act of formal resignation that astonished the world, he gave up his commission as commander of the American army.

Washington's resignation highlighted a new dilemma for the American people. Could they enjoy their freedom without the strong, unified, national government symbolized by Washington's leadership? Could they keep their new liberty and maintain order at the same time? In short, what kind of government should a free people have?

MAKING CONNECTIONS

Would a dictatorship—the very government Washington was afraid of creating—be able to solve the problems of the United States today more easily than a democracy? Explain.

Government in the Early United States

George Washington had become powerful in large part because a single military authority was needed to win the War for Independence. The Congress that approved the Declaration of Independence in 1776 was nothing more than a loose collection of representatives from thirteen separate states. Almost no one imagined creating a powerful national government. After all, Americans were rebelling against an imperial government that had tried repeatedly to strengthen its power over them.

Instead, many people saw Congress as only a necessary wartime inconvenience. The white men who had a voice in government thought of themselves as citizens of individual states rather than as citizens of a nation. It is significant that in referring to the United States, most Americans in those times wrote "the united States are" rather than "the United States is," as people do today. They believed that the nation as a whole was less important than its thirteen parts. It was not a nation as much as it was a **confederation**—an alliance of states formed to coordinate their defense and their relations with foreign governments.

The Articles of Confederation To govern the United States, the Continental Congress created a set of laws called the **Articles of Confederation.** Although written in 1776, the Articles were not approved until 1781. Under the Articles, the government consisted of a legislature, or group of representatives from the states who gathered

RESOURCE DIRECTORY

Teaching Resources

Reproducible Lesson Plan found in the Unit 2 folder, p. 3, provides a summary of the Section 1 lesson plan content.

Alternate Lesson Plan: Learning Styles found in the Alternate Lesson Plans folder, p. 22, helps students chart the weaknesses of the Articles of Confederation and is especially useful for visual learners.

Guided Reading and Review found in the Unit 2 folder, p. 7, provides a structure for reading and mastering the key concepts and reviewing the key terms for Section 1. (Guided Practice)

Both the stern general and his officers were overcome by emotion on the day Washington left the army. With his resignation, the nation was left without strong leadership.

to conduct business. The gathering of the legislature was called a Congress. This Continental Congress passed laws and tried to make sure they were enforced. Thus it combined the functions of a **legislative branch**—the part that makes laws—and an **executive branch,** the part that executes or puts into action the laws passed by a legislature. The Articles made no attempt to create a **judicial branch,** the part of government that judges whether laws have been broken; that job was left to the states.

Under the Articles, states could send as many representatives to Congress as they wished. But each state had only one vote in Congress. It took nine votes, not just a simple majority, to pass any measure dealing with money and unanimous approval to amend or change the Articles. Congress also did not have the power to tax—a serious disadvantage that forced the national government to beg funds from the states. Nor did Congress have any coercive power, the power to force the states to do what it wanted.

These and other defects in the Articles made the United States government weak. But that was exactly what most Americans wanted their national government to be. As late as 1783, the author of the Declaration of Independence, Thomas Jefferson, put forth the argument that "the constant session [meeting] of Congress cannot be necessary in time of peace." Congressional representatives, Jefferson stated, should "separate and return to [their] respective states, leaving only a Committee of the states, [and thus] destroy the strange idea of their being a permanent body."

State Constitutions

Far more important than the Articles in the country's early years were the individual state constitutions—the sets of laws that established the governments of the states. Not every state adopted a new constitution during the Revolution, but most did. The most revolutionary was the

Weaknesses in the Articles of Confederation

- One vote for each state, regardless of size
- Congress powerless to impose and collect taxes or duties
- Congress powerless to regulate foreign and interstate commerce
- No separate executive to enforce acts of Congress
- No national court system to interpret laws
- Amendment only with consent of all the states
- A 9/13 majority required to pass laws
- Articles only a "firm league of friendship"

 Interpreting Tables
The weaknesses of the Articles aroused concern both at home and abroad. "All respect for our government is annihilated [destroyed]," Thomas Jefferson reported from France. "The present is justly considered an alarming crisis," added an observer in the states. *Choose one weakness listed in the chart and explain why it would hurt the nation.*

Reading Strategy

Question Writing Have students read the section's main headings. Then ask students to write a question about each heading and to look for the answers to their questions as they read.

2. INSTRUCT

Discuss

Review with students the ideas that fueled the American Revolution. Ask them to explain how the government of the United States before 1788 reflected these ideas. Why were many Americans happy with a weak national government?

Discuss the problems faced by the United States after the War for Independence. What role did government play in these problems? What were the defects of the Articles of Confederation? Why were some Americans critical of the new state constitutions? What kind of government did the Nationalists propose? Why?

Analyze

Have students analyze the Nationalists' desire for a strong central government. Why do you think well-educated and prominent American gentlemen were generally in favor of a more powerful national government, while less privileged Americans were content with the highly democratic way the new nation was governed? Why did the Nationalists, who were themselves revolutionaries, feel so threatened by Shays's Rebellion?

Caption Answer to ...

Interpreting Tables

Possible answer: The lack of power to regulate commerce would result in conflicting regulations by different states and an inability to respond when foreign nations heavily taxed American imports.

Teaching Heterogeneous Groups

In 1776, a loose confederation of thirteen states met to establish the Articles of Confederation. This attempt to centralize government was resisted by state governments. To demonstrate this struggle, divide the class into thirteen "states," each of which should write its own constitution of three laws. Then have each state send a representative to the "First Continental Congress" to establish ten federal laws that do not conflict with their state constitutions.

Enrichment

Historians have sometimes described the participants in Shays's Rebellion as "rabble." Yet, out of those indicted for treason as a result of the uprising, a number were referred to in court records as "gentlemen." Have students research the social backgrounds and characters of the leaders of the rebellion.

In Depth

Then and Now

In 1786, the United States' national debt totaled over $50 million. The debt forced state governments to print cheap paper money to allow people to repay their loans. In 1992, the national debt was over $4 trillion, and some economists estimate that by the year 2000 the deficit will reach $13 trillion, more than 260,000 times what it was a little more than two hundred years ago.

Pennsylvania Constitution of 1776. Under this state constitution, all white men twenty-one or older who paid taxes—not just gentlemen—were allowed to vote. In itself this was a radical innovation.

The writers of the Pennsylvania constitution went still further, however. They took care to make the legislature the most powerful part of the government, because the legislature was the body most directly responsible to the people. The representatives in the legislature were very responsive to the people's wishes, since they stood for election every year. Their terms of office—like those of officers in the executive branch—were limited, so that no one could hold power too long. Furthermore, the representatives served in a **unicameral legislature**—that is, a legislature with just one house, or group of representatives. No other house balanced its power, as is the case in a **bicameral legislature,** a legislature with two houses. Thus the voters of Pennsylvania had great control over their own government. This was a truly radical government structure in a time when most nations were still ruled by kings and queens.

While other state constitutions did not go as far as Pennsylvania's, most made popular sovereignty a central principle of government. The men who wrote these early constitutions believed it was more important to protect the people from their government than it was to protect the government from the people.

Are you in debt? Print money to pay your bills. Many states resorted to this tactic during the War for Independence and the years afterward.

Criticism of the New Constitutions

Some Americans did not like either the Articles of Confederation or the new state constitutions. Their numbers increased as the years passed. More and more gentlemen worried that the American Revolution had given too much power to the "people"—in other words, those who were not of their own class. As a general rule, democracy involves more conflict of opinion and apparent disorder than other systems of government, and these critics worried that such freedom was incompatible with an orderly, smoothly functioning society.

They had plenty of disorder to point to. By 1786, three years after Washington's resignation, the nation still owed about $50 million—a huge sum at that time—to foreign countries and to its own citizens for the expenses of the War for Independence. Debt everywhere was such a problem that some state governments were distributing cheap paper money to help their citizens pay off their loans. This was creating economic chaos.

All the states were desperately looking for ways to raise money. States with good seaports heavily taxed goods bound for neighboring states—whose citizens were outraged at the taxes. Land sales also became an issue. In the Treaty of Paris in 1783, the United States had gained political control over the vast area between the Appalachian Mountains and the Mississippi River. The states, disregarding the rights of Native Americans in the territory, quarreled bitterly among themselves over which should be able to profit by the sale of this land.

A considerable number of American gentlemen believed that much of this disorder had arisen because the people had too much power in their state legislatures. As noble as this kind of democracy might be, these critics thought, it was not always the best way to run a government or a society.

The Nationalists Fear That the Government Is Too Weak By the early 1780s, a group of men called **Nationalists** were working to make the national government stronger, so that it could counterbalance what they saw as the unpredictable behavior of the states. The Nationalists were former military officers, members of Congress, merchants, planters, and lawyers, and many whose names are now familiar: George Washington, Benjamin Franklin, James Madison, and Alexander Hamilton.

In the 1780s, Nationalists expressed their views about the dangers of a weak national government and too much democracy both in private correspondence and in letters written for publication in newspapers. They pointed out that Congress sometimes did not have enough members in attendance to do anything. They warned that the lack of a national court system and national economic policies would create tension and chaos. They feared that the United States would not command respect from the rest of the world and that Americans would be treated badly abroad.

Most of all, however, they worried that Americans' fondness for challenging authority and for asserting individual rights was getting out of hand. For this reason, the Nationalists called the years from 1781 to 1787 the Critical Period—which they perceived as a time of social disorder and indecision about how to govern the new nation. Fisher Ames of Massachusetts put it this way:

> *Every man of sense must be convinced that our disturbances have arisen more from the want of* [government] *power than the abuse of it.*

Most Americans did not agree with this view. The new state constitutions and the Articles of Confederation were doing exactly what they were supposed to be doing: keeping government close to the people. So what if government was disorderly? So what if mistakes were made? Better to have mistakes under the government of the people than efficiency under the rule of tyrants. Besides, Congress under the Articles had won the War for Independence and worked out a treaty with Great Britain. Those were no small accomplishments.

The Nationalists Argue from History
Because the Nationalists, a relatively small group, were generally successful men with a standing in society that they wanted to protect, some historians have concluded that they were essentially looking after their own interests when they called for a stronger national government. To a certain extent, that is exactly what they were doing. But they were also well educated in European history. They knew that nearly every European nation of any size that had tried a republican government—a government of the people—had failed, ending in chaos and then tyranny. This had happened to the Roman Republic, over 1800 years before their time; it might, the Nationalists reasoned, happen to the United States as well. They believed history had demonstrated that people were not naturally wise enough to have so much power over their own affairs. Concluded George Washington as he surveyed what he considered the disorder of the times: "We have . . . had too good an opinion of human nature in forming our confederation."

The Nationalists See America as a Model
Finally, the Nationalists agreed with Thomas Paine that America was a model for the world. It would be irresponsible, they believed, to allow the nation to fall into disagreement and

Though the Revolution was over, many Americans were still challenging authority. In this engraving, a crowd puts an end to a county meeting by throwing a government official into a brook.

In Depth

Then and Now

In 1787, rumors circulating about the drafting of a constitution were met with fear by many American citizens. The new government, it was said, would have powers to tax and regulate their lives. The discussion of federalism did not end with the Founding Fathers. In the late 1980s a senator joked that, "There are two ways to empty a room in Washington: Hold a fund-raiser for a defeated candidate or a debate on federalism."

Andrew Burnaby, the British clergyman, is concerned that the colonists, coming from different parts of Europe with varying customs and religions, could never become unified into a stable political entity. He is, in fact, predicting how regional differences would eventually lead the country into civil war. For a more thorough examination of American independence, see the Resource Directory below.

In Depth

Did You Know?

About Shays's Rebellion George Washington said to James Madison, "If there exists not a power to check them, what security has a man for life, liberty, or property?" Thomas Jefferson, on the other hand, saw it differently: "A little revolution now and then is a good thing; the tree of liberty must be refreshed from time to time with the blood of patriots and tyrants."

Viewpoints
On the United States as an Independent Nation

Long before what the Nationalists called the Critical Period, the question of the United States' future was debated on both sides of the Atlantic. **What major concern is expressed in the British viewpoint below?**

European Opinion

"*I [see] insurmountable causes for weakness that will prevent America from being a powerful state. . . . In short, such is the difference of character, manners, religion and interest of the different colonies that if they were left to themselves, there would soon be a civil war from one end of the continent to another.*"
Andrew Burnaby, British clergyman, in *Burnaby's Travels Through North America*, 1775

Colonial Opinion

"*Let us view [America] as it now is—AN INDEPENDENT STATE that has taken an equal station amid the nations of the earth. . . . It is a vitality [living thing] liable, indeed, to many disorders, many dangerous diseases; but it is young and strong, and will struggle . . . against those evils and surmount them. . . . Its strength will grow with its years.*"
Thomas Pownall, former governor of Massachusetts, in *The New Relation Between the Old and the New World*, 1780

violence. If they did, wrote Englishman Richard Price in 1785,

> the fairest experiment ever tried in human affairs will miscarry; and . . . a REVOLUTION which had revived the hopes of good men and promised an opening to better times, will become a discouragement to all future efforts in favor of liberty, and prove only an opening to a new scene of human degeneracy and misery.

Indeed, as you have seen, it was Washington's profound understanding of history and his regard for this greater cause that led him to give up his command to civilian authorities so promptly. He did not want to play the role of Julius Caesar of ancient Rome—a general who became a symbol of tyranny by replacing a republican government with a dictatorship.

Shays's Rebellion

In 1786, Nationalists managed to arrange a meeting of the representatives of the states in Annapolis, Maryland, to discuss the economic problems caused by the Articles of Confederation. But only twelve delegates from five states attended. There simply was not much interest in revising the Articles. All that the Nationalist leaders could obtain was a promise to try again. They called for another meeting in Philadelphia in the summer of 1787.

Between the time of the convention in Annapolis and that in Philadelphia, dramatic changes occurred—including the outbreak of armed rebellion in Massachusetts. The uprising became known as Shays's Rebellion after its leader, Captain Daniel Shays, a veteran of the War for Independence. ⬤

The Causes of the Rebellion At its root, Shays's Rebellion was a struggle over debts and taxes. In the 1780s, Massachusetts was in a serious economic depression, yet it owed money both to private lenders and to the national government for the expenses of the War for Independence. In 1786 the legislature voted the heaviest direct tax in the history of Massachusetts to that time. Furthermore, the legislature decreed that the tax had to be paid in specie, or gold or silver coin, which was scarce, rather than in paper money. In taxing their citizens so heavily, public officials were driven by a desire to honor the state's debts and by pressure from merchants to whom much of the money was owed.

Already suffering hard times, citizens now had to come up with specie to pay heavy taxes. Many refused to do so, and the rebellion was under way. Throughout rural areas of Massachusetts, but especially in the west, citizens drove off tax collectors and protested the new taxes with petitions and public meetings. When the courts rejected their petitions, the rebels closed them down. Crowds of protesters reacted violently when the state legislature refused to repeal the taxes.

Historians argue about exactly who supported the rebellion. In fact, people often chose sides for purely personal or local reasons. Still,

RESOURCE DIRECTORY

Teaching Resources

Viewpoints Activity On the United States as an Independent Nation, found in the Unit 2 folder, pp. 19–20, uses opposing European views of the United States' likelihood of long-term survival to help students understand the challenges that the nation faced in its infancy.

⬤ **American Profiles Activity** found in the Unit 2 folder, p. 17, profiles Captain Daniel Shays, leader of the influential Shays's Rebellion against the Massachusetts state government.

⬤ **Literature Activity** *The Contrast*, found in the Unit 2 folder, pp. 26–27, uses Royall Tyler's social comedy to help students understand some contemporary views of Shays's Rebellion.

it is safe to say that in Shays's Rebellion many citizens were reacting violently to the direct interference of merchants and politicians in their lives. They were very mindful that part of the reason they had fought the American Revolution was to keep a distant government from imposing taxes after an expensive war. Unlike the government and the merchants they fought, they believed that the growth of state power was a bad development. ⭐

The Aftermath of the Rebellion Even in this case of open rebellion, Congress could only look on helplessly, unable to provide any assistance. It had no money to raise an army and no way to force the states to give it money. Finally the government of Massachusetts managed to gather an army and send it to the western part of the state, where it dispersed the rebels in January 1787. The unrest soon quieted down. Many rebels and their families left Massachusetts for Vermont, New York, or Ohio.

The significance of Shays's Rebellion lived on, however. This significance was twofold. From the perspective of the rebels, the rebellion demonstrated a continuing commitment to defy the authority of any government when that government acted against the people's wishes. From the perspective of the Nationalists, Shays's Rebellion was an example of the kind of civil unrest that was coming if they did not act soon. It confirmed their worst fears that Americans would sacrifice social order for individual liberty. A Pennsylvania doctor, Benjamin Rush, wrote after Shays's Rebellion:

The same enthusiasm now pervades all classes in favor of government that actuated us [put us in action] in favor of liberty in the years 1774 and 1775.

The rebellion did indeed convince many well-educated and prominent Americans that they had to act. In May 1787, delegates began to arrive in Philadelphia—in a trickle at first, but after a week or so in sufficient number to begin the business at hand. In the words of one key participant, James Madison, that business was to "decide forever the fate of republican government."

Liberty and order clashed in Shays's Rebellion, as protesters—shown here blocking a courthouse—refused to pay taxes, and the government insisted that laws be obeyed.

SECTION 1 REVIEW

Key Terms, People, and Places
1. Define (a) confederation, (b) Articles of Confederation, (c) legislative branch, (d) executive branch, (e) judicial branch, (f) unicameral legislature, (g) bicameral legislature.
2. Identify Nationalists.

Key Concepts
3. What were three weaknesses of the Articles of Confederation?

4. Why did the Nationalists call the years between 1781 and 1787 the Critical Period?
5. What is the twofold significance of Shays's Rebellion?

Critical Thinking
6. **Checking Consistency** Why did the Nationalists believe that disorder during Shays's Rebellion was not justified, although disorder was justified during the American Revolution?

Quiz found in the Unit 2 folder, p. 8, covers the main ideas in this section as well as the key terms.

3. ASSESS

Section 1 Review Answers
1. (a) confederation, see p. 128, (b) Articles of Confederation, see p. 128, (c) legislative branch, see p. 129, (d) executive branch, see page 129, (e) judicial branch, see p. 129, (f) unicameral legislature, see p. 130, (g) bicameral legislature, see p. 130

2. Nationalists, see pp. 130–131

3. The executive and legislative functions were combined. There was no judicial branch. Amending the Articles required unanimous approval. Congress had no coercive power and no power to tax.

4. The Nationalists considered these years a time of social disorder and indecision about how to govern the new nation.

5. From the perspective of the rebels, the rebellion was significant because it demonstrated a continuing commitment to defy the authority of any government that acted against the people's wishes. From the perspective of the Nationalists, Shays's Rebellion confirmed their worst fears that Americans would sacrifice social order for individual liberty.

6. Answers should state that the Nationalists believed that disorder in the name of liberty was no longer allowed once liberty from Great Britain had been achieved.

Reteach

Have students create a time line of the events discussed in this section that led to the Constitutional Convention.

4. CLOSE

Reinforcing the Big Idea

After the War for Independence, the United States suffered severe political and economic problems. To save the new nation, a small group of Americans made plans to restructure the government. The next section describes the Constitutional Convention.

The Decision to Reject the Articles of Confederation

Focus The Nationalists' decision to reject the Articles of Confederation completely rather than amending them resulted in a drastic change in the way the United States was governed. Students are asked to evaluate the Nationalists' rejection and to examine alternatives.

Instruct Review with students the text of the Articles of Confederation. To check student understanding of the division of power between the states and the federal government as outlined in the Articles, ask students to list the powers assigned to the states and those given to the federal government. Have students explain in what ways the federal government was structurally weak.

Review the debate over whether the Articles should be amended or abandoned. Ask students to role-play Nationalists debating this question.

Extend To extend this activity, have students assume that the Articles were amended so that the states retained all powers but granted the federal government the power to direct the economy and to raise money for national needs. Ask students to read Amendments 11–26 of the Constitution and describe some ways in which the United States might have become a very different place had the Articles remained the basis for United States government.

might not have
History Happened This Way
Key Decisions and Decision Makers

The Decision to Reject the Articles of Confederation

Time Frame:	1786–1787
Place:	The Continental Congress
Key People:	James Madison, Charles Pinckney
Situation:	The Nationalists, led by James Madison of Virginia, considered whether to amend or reject the Articles of Confederation before the Continental Congress ever took up the debate. The behind-the-scenes decision of these influential men played a pivotal part in the final decision made by the convention as a whole.

In May 1786, Charles Pinckney of South Carolina called upon the Continental Congress to reform the federal government. The Congress, he insisted, should either call a national convention to make a thorough change in the way the nation was governed or it should ask the states to increase the power of Congress under the Articles of Confederation. By the time Pinckney made his proposal, most members of the Continental Congress had come to agree that something had to be done. If Congress was going to pay the nation's debts or direct the emerging national economy, it had to have more power. The question in Congress was not so much whether a change in the shape of government was necessary, but how to go about achieving that change.

Two Options: Reform or "Revolution"

Some members of the Continental Congress wanted simply to amend, or make specific changes in, the Articles of Confederation. In the summer of 1786, in response to Pinckney's suggestion, Congress debated seven amendments designed to make "the federal government adequate to the ends for which it was instituted." These amendments would have made it easier for Congress to direct the economy and to raise money for national needs.

Yet, in a move that was to have a major impact on the events to come, Congress never sent the proposed amendments to the states. Historians suspect that it failed to do so because some very influential delegates, such as James Madison of Virginia, already had decided that complete reform was the best option. In order for any change to be made to the Articles, all thirteen states had to agree. This made revision of the Articles likely to be unsuccessful, since at least one state would be bound to resist any given amendment. Instead, why not offer reform on a grand scale? What Madison and his friends had in mind was no less than another revolution.

Weighing the Options

Why did Nationalists such as Madison push for such a stark, dramatic choice? Why did they not throw all their considerable talents and energies into strengthening the national government through amendments to the Articles of Confederation? The answer reveals that the Nationalists considered thoroughly the possible results of their decision either to support amendment of the Articles or to start over completely.

In large part, their decision to reject the Articles completely was political. These Nationalists were hardheaded and practical. They knew from their reading of

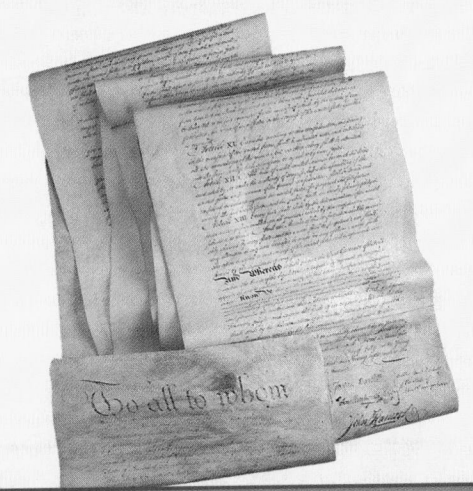

▶ RESOURCE DIRECTORY

Teaching Resources

History Might Not . . . Activity
Decision Making: Redistributing Government Power, found in the Unit 2 folder, pp. 15–16, provides a structure for groups of students to examine the issues of President Nixon's "New Federalism" and make decisions on how to put such a policy into practice.

GOAL				
	Strengthen the federal government			
POSSIBLE ACTIONS	**Try to amend the Articles of Confederation**		**Adopt a completely new framework for the national government**	
POSSIBLE RESULTS	• One state alone can prevent any particular reform. • Some improvements can be made if the states are willing to accept limited reforms. • If the states remain more powerful than the national government, the United	States might be unable to pay its debts, negotiate treaties, keep the peace, protect its frontiers, or promote trade in the nation as a whole. • Those who fear a strong national government will be less likely to block changes.	• This is an all-or-nothing strategy. If it proves unsuccessful, all reforms will be defeated. • Some states might reject the new government and leave the union. • If the strategy is successful, the United States will be	able to pay its debts and deal effectively with other nations; it will have more control over the states and its citizens.

history and their personal experience that people tend to argue endlessly over details. They also believed that discussing specific amendments would probably degenerate into a fight among groups with special interests. If that happened, they would not be able to take advantage of the general sense among leading Americans that the Articles of Confederation should be reformed.

The Nationalists who sided with Madison also knew that it was extremely difficult to win the unanimous consent of the legislatures of the thirteen states, as required to amend the Articles. In the early 1780s, Congress had tried to convince the states to adopt the Impost of 1781, a tax on imported goods. Twelve states had approved; but Rhode Island had lived up to the reputation it had at that time as a maverick, and had said no. The impost had failed. It was a lesson that Madison and other reformers took to heart.

Instead of proposing individual amendments, these reformers chose to act in a way that demonstrated their vision of a new direction for the United States. When they arrived at the Convention in 1787 they would propose sweeping, stunning changes in the entire structure of the government of the United States. They foresaw that convincing people that a completely new government was needed would be easier than convincing them to accept specific amendments to the old government.

But even if they did propose a grand new plan, wouldn't they run the same danger that one state legislature would be able to prevent any change? They considered this possibility. By working in a national convention, however, rather than in the Continental Congress, the reformers would be able to bypass the rules for changing the government under the Articles. They would not ask state legislatures to approve their work; instead they would turn to special conventions elected to consider the new form of government. And they would make sure that the approval of only nine states was required for the new government to become a reality.

Despite the work of Madison and his supporters, by the time the Nationalists arrived at the Convention in the summer of 1787 no formal decision had been made by the Congress at large as to whether the Articles should be amended or abandoned. Many of the delegates to the convention still felt that only amendments were necessary. The clash between the two options would continue, in one form or another, through a good part of that fateful summer.

EVALUATING DECISIONS

1. Why was it such a difficult task to amend the Articles of Confederation?
2. What kind of power did Congress want from the states? Why?

Critical Thinking

3. **Identifying Alternatives** Write one amendment that would have helped provide the Continental Congress with the kind of power it needed.

Media and Technology

Visions of America: History Might Not Have Happened This Way Game

To encourage students to explore pivotal moments in United States history, have students use the Visions of America software. Refer to the Visions of America Guidebook for viewing objectives, activities, game instructions, and discussion questions.

Answers

1. It was necessary to have the unanimous approval of all thirteen states.

2. Congress wanted the power to raise money and regulate economic activities, in order to pay off the nation's debt and direct the economy.

3. Answers should reflect an understanding of the difficulties the nation was having under the Articles, as discussed in Section 1.

SECTION 2

The Constitutional Convention

Connecting to the Big Idea

See page 126B. Explain that restructuring the United States government was a difficult task. Delegates to the Constitutional Convention struggled over the issue of how much power should remain with the states and how much should be given to the national government. Ask students how the new government was structured.

Objectives

● Describe James Madison's contributions to the Constitutional Convention.

● Explain the debate over how states would be represented in the legislature.

● Describe how the Constitution blended popular sovereignty with restrictions that limited the power of the people.

Bellringer

Ask students to define the word *compromise* and recall a time in their life when they compromised about an important issue.

Reading Strategy

Structured Overview Ask students to write the following section headings on a piece of paper: James Madison, Divisions and Compromises at the Convention, The Outlines of the New Government. Have students scan the section for subheadings under each heading and fill in details from the text as they read.

SECTION PREVIEW

During the long summer of 1787, delegates to a convention in Philadelphia fashioned a Constitution that forever sealed the people's right to direct their government—with some restrictions.

Key Concepts

• James Madison was a central figure in the gathering of Nationalists at the Constitutional Convention.

• A key question in the debate about the new government was whether each state would have equal representation in the legislature or whether larger states would have more power than smaller states.

• The founders of the Constitution blended popular sovereignty with restrictions that limited the power of the people.

Key Terms, People, and Places
Virginia Plan, veto, New Jersey Plan, Great Compromise, Three-fifths Compromise, separation of powers, system of checks and balances, Electoral College; James Madison

During the Constitutional Convention, Benjamin Franklin often wondered if the decoration on the chair in which Washington sat represented a sunset or a sunrise—and whether the convention would be an end or a new beginning for the United States.

T he delegates to the convention in the summer of 1787—that is, most of them—did not leave Philadelphia until they had written a new set of rules by which the nation was to be governed, rules which today Americans refer to simply as the Constitution. It begins with this Preamble:

W e the People of the United States, in Order to form a more perfect Union, establish Justice, insure domestic Tranquility, provide for the common defence, promote

the general Welfare, and secure the Blessings of Liberty to ourselves and our Posterity, do ordain and establish this Constitution for the United States of America.

Over the years, Americans have come to see the first three words of the Constitution, "We the People," as the most important. Everything else in the document follows from the basic assumption that in the United States the people will govern themselves.

The men who wrote the Constitution, however, were not as interested in protecting popular sovereignty as they were in restraining it. Notice that among their purposes they listed forming "a more perfect union," because the union of states was far from perfect. They wanted to "insure domestic tranquility," or peace within the nation, because Shays's Rebellion had shown how weak the safeguards of tranquility were. Finally, they wanted "to secure the blessings of liberty" for themselves and for those who would come after them, because they were afraid they might lose their liberty if chaos broke out.

The Constitutional Convention was by no means a gathering to make the final refinement of a successful government; instead it was a rescue mission for one that might well be failing. According to the most influential member of the convention, **James Madison,** the idea was to find a way to "at once support . . . the national authority, and leave in force the local authorities" only to the extent that the local authorities could be useful without interfering with the national government.

AMERICAN PROFILES

James Madison

Madison, like many of the fifty-five men who attended the convention in Philadelphia during the summer of 1787, was a relatively

RESOURCE DIRECTORY

Teaching Resources

Reproducible Lesson Plan found in the Unit 2 folder, p. 4, provides a summary of the Section 2 lesson plan content.

Alternate Lesson Plan: Learning Styles found in the Alternate Lesson Plans folder, p. 23, is especially effective for kinesthetic learners and helps students create presentations on issues of debate at the Constitutional Convention.

Guided Reading and Review found in the Unit 2 folder, p. 9, provides a structure for reading and mastering the key concepts and reviewing the key terms for Section 2. (Guided Practice)

young man. He was only thirty-seven; half of the delegates were over forty-two. Aside from being gentlemen of about the same age, the delegates had little in common. They were from a wide variety of backgrounds. A few were very rich, but some had no more than a comfortable living. Many were well educated and familiar with the theories of European political thinkers. Few, however, had spent as much time on the specifics of a possible government as had Madison. In his home at the foot of the Blue Ridge Mountains he spent evening after evening poring over books of history, government, and law. By the time of the convention, Madison had already invested a year of thought in the form of new government.

James Madison (above) looked like a boy even at age thirty-seven. The Nationalist Fisher Ames described him as "little and ordinary," but added, "his language is very pure . . . and to the point."

The "Father of the Constitution," as Madison came to be called, grew up on a plantation in Orange County, Virginia, where he studied European political thought under a Scottish tutor. Although Madison was an unassuming man, he always retained something of an intellectual edge over his peers due to natural inclination and his intensive training.

Madison's studies of philosophy had led him to believe that people are naturally selfish creatures driven by powerful emotions and personal interests. That did not mean there was no hope for order in society, however. European theorists had argued that through proper government, humans could take control of themselves and their world and improve the condition of both. Constitutions established political structures that encouraged the best in people while restraining their worst tendencies. A dream of devising just such a constitution was exactly what would bring James Madison to the Philadelphia Convention.

Even after he entered public life, Madison was never comfortable with crowds and their politics. He did not marry until he was forty-three, but when he did he found a good match in the lively and cheerful Dolley Todd, a twenty-six-year-old widow. They were happily married for forty-two years.

Supporting his life of productive leisure and domestic happiness, however, were several dozen enslaved people. Madison, like many of the Framers of the Constitution who owned slaves, considered slavery immoral. And like them, he was unable to bring himself to do anything about this contradiction. Madison knew that if he had been born a slave, he could not have become a successful public man. He would not have had the opportunity to accomplish what he did in the Virginia legislature and at the Continental Congress, or the convention itself.

Madison made it his business to attend every meeting of the convention. During these sessions, he could be seen busily taking the notes that later would become our best record of the proceedings. The delegates were intentionally secretive; they allowed no reporters to attend and kept silent when questioned by outsiders. They even posted sentries to keep curious onlookers away from the windows of the room where they met. Only in secrecy, they believed, could they speak their minds freely.

Inside that room, the Assembly Room of the Pennsylvania State House (now called Independence Hall), was a colorful and exciting scene. There sat the members of the Convention, representing every state except Rhode Island, which had declined to send delegates. All the summer long, the members came to Philadelphia and went away again; never were the full fifty-five participants present at once. They stayed until family or business called them home—or until the sweltering heat of the city summer, with its smell and its infinite number of flies, drove them away.

2. INSTRUCT

Explain/Discuss
Explain to students that although delegates to the Constitutional Convention shared the same basic beliefs about government, crafting a workable and lasting national government was an arduous process of debate and compromise. Ask students why compromise was so important to the successful outcome of the convention.

Discuss the divisive issues and important compromises of the Constitutional Convention. Encourage discussion with questions such as the following: What was the major division at the Constitutional Convention? What role did James Madison play at the convention? How did the Virginia Plan differ from the New Jersey Plan? What was the Great Compromise? the Three-fifths Compromise?

Analyze
Have students analyze the Constitution and the new government it created. How did the Constitution combine popular sovereignty with a strong national government? Why did delegates to the convention impose limits on presidential power? Are there problems today that the Constitution fails to address?

Activity

An Eyewitness Account

Ask students to imagine that they have found a spot where they can observe the proceedings at the Constitutional Convention unnoticed. Have them write a description of the event.

Enrichment

Some historians have suggested that, to a degree, delegates to the Constitutional Convention created the Constitution to protect their own financial interests. Other historians reject the idea that the delegates put self-interest ahead of principle. Ask students to research the life of one delegate to the convention and write a short paper discussing his motives for taking part in the convention.

Divisions and Compromises at the Convention

⭐ The major division at the Constitutional Convention in 1787 was between those who wanted to abandon the Articles of Confederation and those who merely wanted to amend them. Nearly everyone agreed on the need for a stronger national government, but some saw no need to start from scratch. Madison and others who wanted truly significant changes were able to dominate the proceedings by bringing a plan with them. Their **Virginia Plan** became the focus of discussion against which all other ideas were weighed.

The Convention Is Divided The Virginia Plan called for the creation of a bicameral, or two-house, national legislature. Each state would send representatives in proportion to the number of its citizens. A state with a large population would have more representatives in both houses than a state with a small population—and thus have more voting power in the legislature. The proposed government would also have an executive branch and a judicial branch, as well as the right to tax its citizens, thus correcting serious shortcomings of the Articles of Confederation. It would also have the power to **veto,** or overturn, any act of a state legislature—an idea that frightened some because it would give the national government greater power than the states. ⭐

Opponents of the Virginia Plan, many of whom were from smaller states, were afraid they would have no power in the new government. So they proposed an alternative, the **New Jersey Plan.** Like the Virginia Plan, this plan would give Congress the power to tax and would create executive and judicial branches. It preserved a feature of the Articles of Confederation that the big states did not like, however: every state would continue to have an equal vote in a unicameral Congress, no matter how large the state population. The New Jersey Plan ensured that the states would remain the most powerful governments in America.

The Convention Compromises On July 2, the convention voted on whether representation in the legislature should be based on population. The vote was split and the convention deadlocked. For a while, matters seemed hopeless. Then, over a period of several days, a solution emerged, one that is now called the **Great Compromise.** The legislative branch would be made up of two houses, as called for in the Virginia Plan. But in one house—the House of Representatives—each state would have a number of representatives that corresponded to the size of its population. In the other house, the Senate, every state would have an equal number of representatives.

An observer noted that the streets outside the Pennsylvania State House during the convention were filled with people of "every rank and condition in life, from the highest to the lowest, male and female, of every age and every color. . . . There seemed to be some of every nation under heaven."

As they signed the Constitution on September 17, 1787, the delegates put an end to the divisions of opinion that had made the work of the convention difficult.

The Great Compromise, approved on July 16, included the answer to another crucial question. How should the enslaved people who were so numerous in the southern states be counted? If they were all included in the count of the general population, the southern states would have great power in the House of Representatives. If they were not counted at all, the southern states would be weak in the House. The delegates adopted a formula that became known as the **Three-fifths Compromise.** Under this plan, all enslaved people would be counted, but then the total would be multiplied by three fifths.

The Three-fifths Compromise did not mean that enslaved African Americans would be allowed to vote, however, or that their interests would be represented in Congress. They, like Native Americans, were excluded from participating in the government, although in this early period some free African Americans in some states could vote.

Although many features of Madison's plan survived these compromises, the delegates never went as far in strengthening the national government as Madison would have liked. For example, they refused to give Congress the right to veto state legislation. So upset with such revisions was Alexander Hamilton, a key Nationalist delegate from New York, that he left the convention. Madison, too, was disappointed, but he stayed in Philadelphia.

MAKING CONNECTIONS

Slavery became an increasingly divisive issue in the United States, eventually becoming one of the causes of the Civil War—a period when the Constitution failed to hold the nation together. What problems do we face today that the Founders were unable to foresee?

The Outlines of the New Government

After further debate over the exact provisions of the Constitution, the convention turned the document over to a Committee on Style on September 9. It then approved the final draft on September 17, 1787. Although the delegates provided a way to change the Constitution,

Answer to ...

MAKING CONNECTIONS

Possible answers: widespread violence, conflict over social issues such as prayer in schools, and foreign ownership of American businesses.

In Depth

Multicultural Perspectives

That slaves, indentured servants, women, Native Americans, and men without land were not protected under the Constitution was forcefully pointed out by Charles Beard (1874–1948). In *An Economic Interpretation of the Constitution* (1913) he reviewed the backgrounds of the fifty-five white men who drew up the Constitution in 1787. Finding most of them to be wealthy landowners, Beard stirred passions pro and con by suggesting that they established a system of government to protect their own economic interests.

Caption Answer to ...

Interpreting Charts

It appoints federal judges and grants pardons to federal offenders.

The American System of Checks and Balances

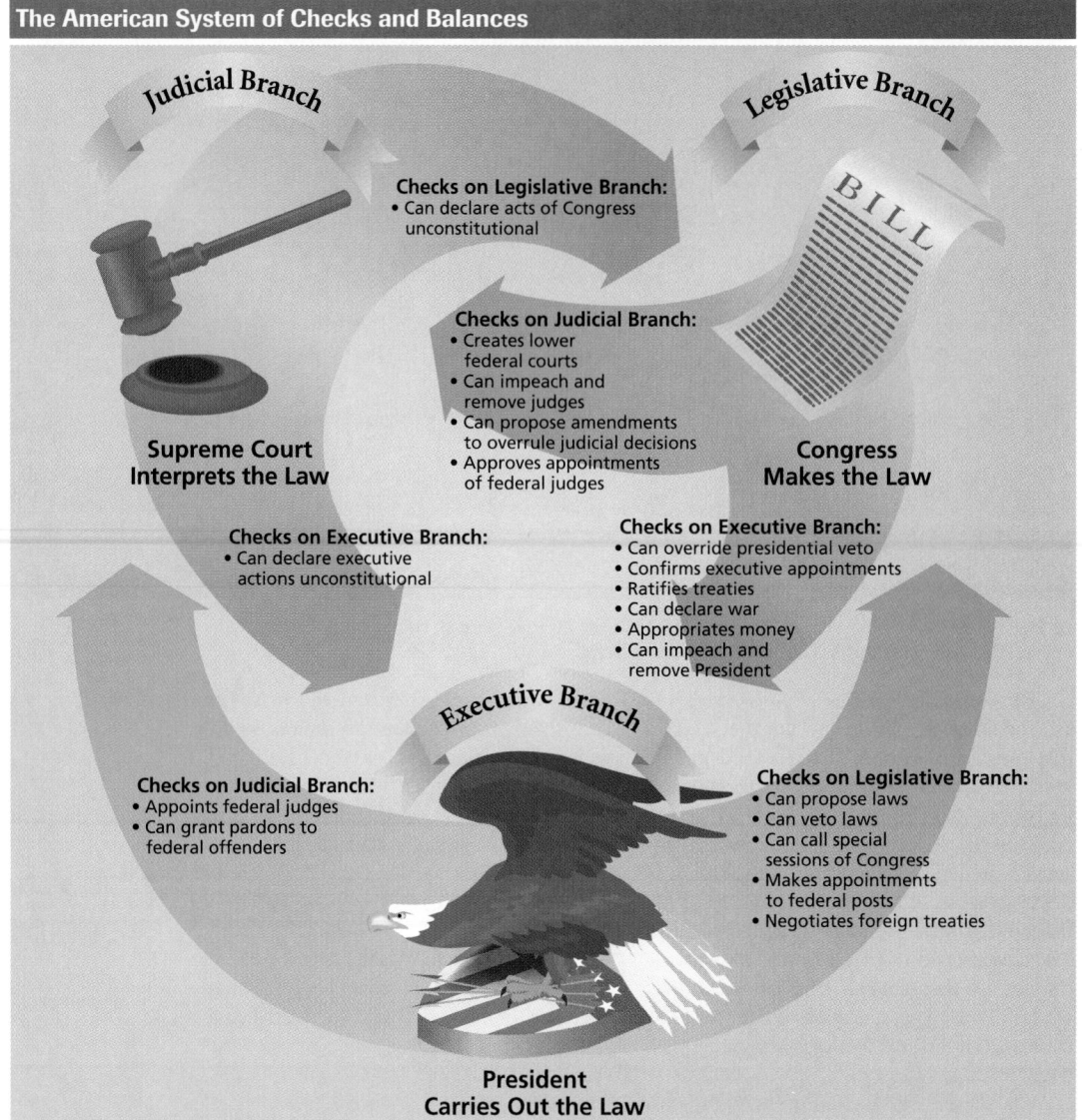

Judicial Branch

Checks on Legislative Branch:
• Can declare acts of Congress unconstitutional

Checks on Judicial Branch:
• Creates lower federal courts
• Can impeach and remove judges
• Can propose amendments to overrule judicial decisions
• Approves appointments of federal judges

Supreme Court Interprets the Law

Checks on Executive Branch:
• Can declare executive actions unconstitutional

Legislative Branch

Congress Makes the Law

Checks on Executive Branch:
• Can override presidential veto
• Confirms executive appointments
• Ratifies treaties
• Can declare war
• Appropriates money
• Can impeach and remove President

Executive Branch

Checks on Judicial Branch:
• Appoints federal judges
• Can grant pardons to federal offenders

Checks on Legislative Branch:
• Can propose laws
• Can veto laws
• Can call special sessions of Congress
• Makes appointments to federal posts
• Negotiates foreign treaties

President Carries Out the Law

Interpreting Charts
"You must first enable the government to control the governed," wrote Madison, "and in the next place, oblige it to control itself." The control Madison meant is found in the system of checks and balances in the Constitution. *How does the executive branch check the judicial branch?*

which has been amended twenty-seven times, this written plan of government has remained basically the same for over two hundred years.

The delegates created what some began to call a federal government, in which power was shared among state and national authorities.

The Constitution called for a **separation of powers** among the three branches. That is, powers of government at the national level would be divided among legislative, executive, and judicial branches. In addition, each branch would be able to check, or stop, the others in

RESOURCE DIRECTORY

Teaching Resources

Critical Thinking Activity Determining Relevance: Checks and Balances, found in the Unit 2 folder, p. 22, enhances students' understanding of complex issues through identification of relationships.

certain ways. For instance, the President, as the head of the executive branch, could veto acts of Congress. This executive power was balanced, however, by Congress's power to overturn the veto with a two-thirds vote of both houses. This government structure is known today as the **system of checks and balances,** illustrated in the chart on page 140.

The New Congress By dividing power between the state and national governments and among the three branches of the national government, the delegates had ingeniously constructed a government that both preserved and limited popular sovereignty. A comparison of the House of Representatives and the Senate further demonstrates their aims.

Because voting in the House of Representatives was based on population, the House was the part of government most directly responsible to the people. Therefore, its members were all to be chosen every two years. If the people wished, they could change the membership of the House quickly.

They could not do the same with the Senate. According to the process outlined in the Constitution (later changed), members of state legislatures would elect senators for six-year terms. Only one third of the Senate would come up for reelection every two years. Thus it was harder for the people to have a direct and sudden impact on the membership of the Senate.

Why did the convention make the Senate more removed from the people? The authors of the Constitution felt that in this way the Senate would be less likely to follow the whims of the crowd. Because no law could be passed unless approved by this more elite body of representatives, the people could not force the passage of bad laws. Furthermore, the writers of the Constitution wanted to make sure that the Senate could be trusted with certain powers, such as giving advice and consent to the President, a responsibility they did not grant to the House of Representatives. They did, however, decide that bills about raising and spending money should be introduced in the House of Representatives alone, because the large states were afraid of losing their influence over money matters.

The House of Representatives and the Senate, when combined as the Congress of the United States, became the most powerful legislative body in the nation. Only the Congress could coin money, deal with other nations, declare war, raise an army, provide for a navy, and regulate commerce. In a sweeping statement now known as the Elastic Clause because it fits so many situations, the Constitution declares that the Congress can

make all Laws which shall be necessary and proper for carrying into Execution the foregoing Powers, and all other Powers vested by this Constitution in the Government of the United States, or in any Department or Officer thereof.

Article 1, Section 8, Clause 18

The President of the United States The Constitution created a strong executive officer, the President of the United States. His term was to be only four years, but he could be reelected as many times as the people wished.

Again, the writers of the Constitution placed a shield between the government and the people by making the election of the President complicated. Voters were to choose electors to do their electing for them. Each state would have as many electoral votes as it had members of Congress. Whoever received the majority of the votes in the meeting of the electors—the **Electoral College**—would become President.

Members of the convention knew that George Washington was likely to be the nation's first President. They believed, however, that it would be difficult for presidential candidates after him to win the required majority—Washington was unique in being popular nationally. Thus the convention provided for the House of Representatives to be the final decision makers. If the Electoral College failed to produce a clear majority for one candidate, the choice would go to the House of Representatives. There each state would have one vote, and the representatives would continue to vote until one of the candidates received a majority.

The Electoral College was a device to allow the people to feel as if they were participating in the choice of their President, while ensuring that

Media and Technology

Transparencies
Critical Thinking, I-6; The Way It Works, H-5

Section 2 Review Answers

1.(a) veto, see p. 138, (b) the Great Compromise, see p. 138, (c) Three-fifths Compromise, see page 139, (d) system of checks and balances, see p. 141, (e) Electoral College, see p. 141

2. James Madison, see p. 136

3. Madison's studies of philosophy had led him to believe that people are naturally selfish creatures driven by powerful emotions. That did not mean that there was no hope for order in society, however. European theorists had argued that through proper government, humans could take control of themselves and their world and improve the condition of both. Constitutions established political structures that encouraged the best in people while restraining their worst tendencies.

4. The Virginia Plan called for the creation of a bicameral national legislature. Each state would send representatives in proportion to the number of its citizens. The New Jersey plan proposed a unicameral legislature in which every state would continue to have an equal vote.

5. They made the election of the President complex. Voters were to choose electors to do their electing for them. Each state would have as many electoral votes as it had members of Congress. Whoever received a majority of the votes in the meeting of the electors—the Electoral College—would become President.

6. Possible answers: the possibility of amending the Constitution, the elastic clause, and the purposeful absence of specifics on the judicial branch.

Reteach

Tell students that the Constitution has often been called a "bundle of compromises." Ask them to identify specific examples of compromise as outlined in the section.

The Framers expected that Washington would be the only future candidate for President who would be nationally known and thus able to be elected by a clear majority of the voters.

electors or members of Congress would make the actual selection. Or so the writers of the Constitution thought. As it turned out, a deadlock of the electors has only occurred twice in American his-

tory—in the elections of 1800 and 1824. But in 1787 many assumed that it would happen often.

The Constitution gave the President enormous powers. He was to be commander-in-chief of the armed forces. In the system of checks and balances, he also had the power to veto acts of Congress.

Federal Courts The President, again with the advice and consent of the Senate, would also choose judges for the national court system. These judges would hold office for life, as long as they did not act dishonorably. The choice of judges was one step removed from the people—that is, the President, indirectly chosen by the people, chose the judges. In addition, removing judges was made difficult so that the people could not directly control them. Although the Constitution called for one Supreme Court and several lesser ones, the details were left purposely vague. In later years, Congress developed the court system to fit the nation's needs.

This, then, was the outline of the new government as set forth in the Constitution, completed by the delegates in three months of intense work during the summer of 1787. They agreed to submit their new document to state conventions for approval rather than directly to the people. And they required the approval of only nine of thirteen states to make the Constitution legal. Supporters of the new Constitution knew that winning approval for it would not be easy. The following section tells the story of their struggle to make sure that the document they had crafted in debate and compromise became the law of the land.

SECTION 2 REVIEW

Key Terms, People, and Places

1. Define (a) veto, (b) the Great Compromise, (c) Three-fifths Compromise, (d) system of checks and balances, (e) Electoral College.
2. Identify James Madison.

Key Concepts

3. Describe James Madison's view of government.
4. What were the differences between the Virginia Plan and the New Jersey Plan?

5. How did the authors of the Constitution keep the people from directly electing the President?

Critical Thinking

6. **Testing Conclusions** A commentator in the late 1800s said that in making the Constitution, the Founders built "a machine that would go of itself." Cite some features of the structure of the Constitution that have made it adaptable to the changing needs of the nation.

RESOURCE DIRECTORY

Teaching Resources

Quiz found in the Unit 2 folder, p. 10, covers the main ideas in this section as well as the key terms.

Identifying Central Issues

I dentifying central issues means recognizing the problems at the core of a piece of information. Usually, all the problems a writer discusses are connected in some way with the central issues. Thus it is vital to be able to recognize central issues—and to be able to judge them without being swayed by the way they are expressed.

The excerpt below is part of an article that appeared in a newspaper in Rhode Island, the only state that did not send delegates to the Constitutional Convention. It is a parable—a story in which a lesson is set forth in symbols. In a parable, the symbols are chosen specifically to influence the reader's understanding of the central issues being discussed.

First read the excerpt and then use the following steps to identify the story's central issues.

1. Identify the subject of the excerpt. Refer to the excerpt to answer these questions. (a) What is the subject of the excerpt? (b) On what date did the parable appear in the newspaper? (c) Given the subject and the date of the excerpt, to what historical period or event do you think the writer of the parable is referring?

2. Examine the excerpt to determine the meaning of its symbols. A symbol is something that stands for or suggests something else. Review the excerpt then answer these questions. (a) Who or what do you think

the parents and the sons in the parable represent? (b) What historical period or event is represented by the events in the parable that occur between the building of the house and the addition to the house? (c) Who or what do you think the three rooms of the dwelling represent? (d) Who or what do you think the "thirteenth son" represents?

3. Summarize the message or main idea and identify the central issue of the excerpt. (a) What central issue does the excerpt from a 1787 newspaper article address? (b) Explain how the parable illustrates this point. (c) What point does the parable make about the consequences of failing to participate in a common effort?

Philadelphia, August 25, 1787

The conduct of the United States, with respect to their governments, may be illustrated by the following story:—An old man arrived, after a long and dangerous voyage, upon the coast of America, with a family consisting of a wife, a few choice old servants, and *thirteen* sons. As soon as they landed, they joined and built a large and commodious dwelling-house, where they lived in safety for several years. The sons, however, grew weary of the company of their parents, and each of them built a cabin for himself, at a distance from the family mansion-house. They had not lived long in this way, before they began to suffer many difficulties and wants. . . . At last *twelve* of them met by agreement upon a plain, and agreed to petition their father to be admitted again under his protection. The venerable [honorable] old man opened his doors to them, and they again became members of his family. They first joined in repairing and fortifying the old mansion-house. They, moreover, added *two* more rooms to it, for the separate use of the old man and his wife, in order thereby to preserve their dignity and authority. From this time the whole family became respectable, happy, and prosperous . . . .

The *thirteenth* son, who refused to accompany his brothers to his father's house, after living a miserable life . . . by himself in the woods, was found *hanging* . . . to the limb of a tree near his cabin.

—*Providence Gazette and Country Journal,* Vol. 24 (Saturday, September 8, 1787), p. 2

Historian's Toolbox Activity Identifying Central Issues: Statehood for Washington, D.C., found in the Unit 2 folder, p. 21, encourages students to apply this skill in writing a parable to reflect the political status of the District of Columbia.

Ratifying the Constitution

SECTION 3

Ratifying the Constitution

1. FOCUS

Connecting to the Big Idea

See page 126B. Explain to students that at the time the Constitution was written it was a highly controversial document. The Anti-Federalists, representing a significant number of Americans, were afraid that it meant the end of liberty. The Constitution was approved by only a narrow margin. Ask how the Federalists finally managed to get the Constitution ratified.

Objectives

- State the Federalists' argument in favor of the Constitution.
- Explain why the Anti-Federalists opposed the Constitution.
- State why the Bill of Rights was created.

Bellringer

Ask students if they think the United States government infringes too much on individual liberty. Possible examples of infringement include taxes or military service. Have them justify their answers.

Reading Strategy

Question Writing Ask students to scan the section, and create *who*, *what*, *when*, *where*, and *why* questions for the text. Have them exchange papers and answer the questions as they read.

SECTION PREVIEW

With a combination of political skill and persuasive argument, the Federalists managed to win narrow approval of the Constitution. Their key concession to their opponents was the Bill of Rights.

As the debate on the new Constitution spread across the land, its supporters rallied around a new symbol—a ship with full sails, ready to ride the winds of the future.

Key Concepts

- The Federalists based their argument in favor of the Constitution on the nation's need for a strong, energetic government.
- The Anti-Federalists feared strong government under the proposed Constitution more than they feared the direct rule of the people.
- The Bill of Rights was designed to protect Americans against the power of the national government.

Key Terms, People, and Places

faction, ratify, Bill of Rights; Federalists, Anti-Federalists

---

Today, many Americans seem to assume that approval of the Constitution was a foregone conclusion. In actuality, the proposed government was highly controversial. Had the Constitution been put to a vote in 1787, it is extremely doubtful that a majority of Americans would have voted for it.

Federalists: For the Constitution

Supporters of the Constitution were called **Federalists** because they stood for a strong federal government. They had all been Nationalists, but not all Nationalists were now Federalists. The Federalist leaders included Washington, Madison, and Alexander Hamilton of New York—the man who had left the Convention in disgust, but now had decided to throw his

support behind the Constitution. Federalists argued that even if there were problems with the document, it had to be approved.

The most influential statement of their reasoning was a series of eighty-five essays now called *The Federalist,* published in a New York City newspaper. The authors were Hamilton, Madison, and John Jay, a Nationalist from New York. The purpose of *The Federalist* essays was simply to convince the members of the New York state convention to agree to the Constitution.

In the papers, Hamilton and Madison explained the need for the Constitution and how the federal government would work. They called for "a republican empire." In the 1700s the word *republican* did not refer to a political party. It referred to a government by the people. Because most previous empires had been governed by lone rulers, an empire governed by the people was a striking idea.

Indeed, because the country was so big, wrote Madison in *The Federalist* Number Ten, no one **faction**—what we call a "special interest group" today—would be able to control the government. Instead, the United States would referee the conflict of interests that could not be avoided in a democracy. Madison argued that the strength of the federal system was not in preventing regional or economic or religious interests from fighting with each other, but in keeping any one of them from getting the upper hand for long. Without the Constitution, argued the Federalists, the United States would degenerate into anarchy—lack of government—and civil war.

Anti-Federalists: Against the Constitution

By contrast with the Federalists, the opponents of the Constitution, who were called **Anti-Federalists,** were certain that the new government would be the death of American liberty. They were led by older revolutionary

---

RESOURCE DIRECTORY

Teaching Resources

Reproducible Lesson Plan found in the Unit 2 folder, p. 5, provides a summary of the Section 3 lesson plan content.

Alternate Lesson Plan: Learning Styles found in the Alternate Lesson Plans folder, p. 24, uses a talk show format to help students understand and participate in the constitutional debate, and is particularly useful for auditory learners.

Guided Reading and Review found in the Unit 2 folder, p. 11, provides a structure for reading and mastering the key concepts and reviewing the key terms for Section 3. (Guided Practice)

figures, such as Patrick Henry of Virginia, and had widespread support in the areas that had less commerce, particularly the lands distant from the Atlantic Ocean and major rivers. People in these areas had less need for the leadership and laws of a strong national government.

The Anti-Federalists condemned the Constitution as a betrayal of the American Revolution. What was the President but a king? Had people fought and died in the long war against Great Britain to create a faraway government that could tax them and regulate their affairs even more than the British had ever attempted to do?

While the Federalists feared the people more than government, the Anti-Federalists feared government more than the people. Many objected not only to the presidency, but to the new federal court system. They also worried that those governments closest to the people—the local and state governments—would be crushed by this new giant of a federal government.

How the Federalists Won Ratification

Most Americans probably agreed with the Anti-Federalists. But the Federalists had several advantages in their campaign for ratification of the Constitution. First, they played on the feeling of many that the Articles of Confederation needed to be reformed. Second, they made the Anti-Federalists look as if they were merely negative critics with no constructive plan of their own to offer. Third, the Federalists were a well-organized *national* group in regular contact with each other. The Anti-Federalists tended to be men with only local and state power who could not coordinate their activities on the national level. Fourth, the Federalists had George Washington.

It is easy to dismiss the influence of one man. But the fact that so many people admired and trusted Washington was of critical importance. Everyone expected him to be the first President, and that made them more willing to accept the idea of the new government. They knew he was a leader; he had proved that in a long war, despite repeated defeat and discouragement. More significant, he had given up his power at the end of the war, demonstrating his willingness to act within the law.

For the Constitution to replace the Articles of Confederation, nine states had to **ratify,** or approve, it. Several states—Delaware, New Jersey, and Connecticut—ratified it quickly. They were relatively small states and their citizens expected advantages in being part of a large federal structure. Georgia, too, approved the Constitution promptly. The Georgians feared a war with Native Americans and wanted a national government to ensure they would have federal help. In Pennsylvania, conservatives had won power and were revising the state constitution of 1776; they readily agreed to the new federal government. These states acted in December 1787 and January 1788. Then Massachusetts narrowly voted to ratify. Maryland and South Carolina soon fell into line. The honor of being the ninth state went to New Hampshire, although the Federalists there had to delay the vote until they had a majority.

Even with the approval of nine states, everyone knew the new nation would not be able to succeed unless the highly populated states of Virginia and New York joined in. Loud debates and shady maneuvers during the summer of 1788 produced Federalist victories by slim margins in the voting in both these key states. North Carolina had rejected the Constitution but finally reversed itself and agreed to ratify it in November 1789. In May 1790 Rhode Island similarly reversed an earlier vote of rejection and became the last of the original thirteen states to say yes.

The Bill of Rights

The states did adopt the Constitution—but the voting was close, and they might easily have rejected it. What turned the tide in close states like

Caption Answer to ...

Using Historical Evidence

Alexander Hamilton

Activity

Teaching Heterogeneous Groups

Two years after writing the Constitution, state representatives met again to amend it with the Bill of Rights in order to protect individual freedoms. Divide students into groups and ask each group to propose amendments to protect student rights within the school, using the language and form of the Bill of Rights. Have a representative from each group present its "bill of rights" to the class.

Enrichment

The idea of individual liberties had long been developing in Europe. Ask students to research the ideas behind the French Revolution of 1789 and identify similarities to ideas of freedom found in the Bill of Rights.

3. ASSESS

Section 3 Review Answers

1. (a) faction, see p. 144, (b) ratify, see p. 145, (c) Bill of Rights, see p. 146

2. (a) Federalists, see p. 144, (b) Anti-Federalists, see p. 144

3. Anti-Federalists believed that the Constitution was a betrayal of the Revolution, that the President would be just another king, and that the government would tax them and regulate their affairs even more than the British had proposed.

4. They played on the widespread agreement that there was a need for reform of the Articles of Confederation. They kept their opponents on the defensive, making them look as if they were merely negative critics with no constructive plan of their own to offer. The Federalists were a well-organized national group in regular contact with each other. The Anti-Federalists tended to be men with only local and state power. The Federalists had the prestige of George Washington's support.

Using Historical Evidence In a celebration of a successful conclusion to a hard ratification fight in a key state, the federal ship sailed through the streets of New York. *In this engraving, which Federalist is identified with the success of ratification?*

Nine states had to approve the new Constitution before it became law. This cartoon shows the states as pillars, with nine upright and a tenth being raised.

Massachusetts, Virginia, and New York? While the persuasive skills of men such as Madison and Hamilton had an impact, by far the most important factor was the Federalist offer to adopt immediately several changes in the Constitution. Congress proposed them in September 1789. And in December 1791 the resulting ten amendments became part of the document. They are known today as the **Bill of Rights.**

The Argument Against the Bill of Rights Most Federalists saw no need for these amendments. Members of the Constitutional Convention had talked about protecting freedom of speech, the press, and religion. But they decided such provisions were unnecessary, largely because they were establishing a government of, for, and by the people. Under the Constitution, the people and the government were the same. So why did the people need to protect their rights from themselves? In *The Federalist* Number 84, Hamilton quoted the Preamble of the Constitution and argued that under the proposed new system "the people surrender nothing"—that is, they keep all power for themselves. "Here is a better recognition of popular rights," he asserted, than any added list of rights. Most Americans, however, did not buy this clever argument.

The Argument for the Bill of Rights To many Americans, the new federal government seemed a potentially tyrannical force in their lives. They wanted protection from it. Thomas Jefferson, who generally approved of the Constitution, urged Madison to agree to explicit protection for freedom of religion and of the press as well as from armies and unjust courts.

United we stand—Divided we fall

> A bill of rights is what the people are entitled to against every government on earth . . . and what no government should refuse, or rest on inference [leave unstated].

⭐ So strong was the Anti-Federalist demand for a Bill of Rights that Madison and other Federalists gave in to it. In fact, it was this concession of the Federalists—their agreement to amend the Constitution to protect certain basic freedoms—that was the key to their victory. Without the promise of a Bill of Rights, several states probably would not have ratified the Constitution.

Thus the Bill of Rights, the most significant guarantee of individual freedoms to American citizens, came about in part because Federalist leaders traded it for approval of the Constitution. These ten amendments, shown in the

RESOURCE DIRECTORY

Teaching Resources

⭐ **Primary Source Activity** A Department of Peace, found in the Unit 2 folder, p. 25, uses an excerpt from Benjamin Rush's "Plan of a Peace-Office for the United States" to help show the ideals people had for the development of their new country.

⭐ **Visual Learning Activity** The First United States Coins, found in the Unit 2 folder, p. 29, displays the design of the first coin minted as United States currency.

The Bill of Rights

1st Amendment	Guarantees freedom of religion, speech, press, assembly, and petition
2nd Amendment	Guarantees the individual states the right to maintain a militia
3rd Amendment	Restricts the manner in which the federal government may house troops in the homes of citizens
4th Amendment	Protects individuals against unreasonable searches and seizures
5th Amendment	Provides that a person can be tried for a serious federal crime only if he or she has been accused of that crime by a grand jury; protects individuals against self-incrimination and against being tried twice for the same crime; prohibits unfair, arbitrary actions by the federal government; prohibits the federal government from taking private property for public use without paying a fair price for the property taken
6th Amendment	Guarantees persons accused of crime the right to a swift and fair trial
7th Amendment	Guarantees the right to a jury trial in cases of civil suits heard in federal courts
8th Amendment	Protects against cruel and unusual punishment and excessive bail
9th Amendment	Establishes that the people have rights beyond those stated in the Constitution
10th Amendment	Establishes that all powers not guaranteed to the federal government and not prohibited to the states are held by each of the states, or the people of each state

Interpreting Tables
The Bill of Rights was intended to protect Americans from the powerful government the Constitution created. The Third Amendment, for instance, ensured that the government could not put citizens on trial without a jury drawn from the people themselves. *Which amendment protects the people from government interference in their religion?*

table above, protect Americans from their government.

Jefferson wished the Bill of Rights had been more explicit in protecting the rights of citizens. For instance, he wanted it to specify the number of days a person could be held under arrest without a trial. He also believed it was important to ensure that the army would disband immediately after its service. But even

as it was written, the Bill of Rights became the foundation of American liberty. If the Anti-Federalists lost the war over ratification, they nonetheless won a major victory for freedom in the process.

 The Bill of Rights was one of the first items on the agenda of the new government. A truly new government Americans made of it, too, as the next section shows.

SECTION 3 REVIEW

Key Terms, People, and Places
1. Define (a) faction, (b) ratify, (c) Bill of Rights.
2. Identify (a) Federalists, (b) Anti-Federalists.

Key Concepts
3. Explain why Anti-Federalists objected to the Constitution.
4. What advantages did the Federalists have in their efforts to win approval of the Constitution?

5. Why did Federalists think the Bill of Rights was unnecessary?

Critical Thinking
6. **Formulating Questions** If you had been trying to decide whether to ratify the Constitution, what questions would you have asked the Federalists? Explain how the questions you suggest reveal your view of government.

Quiz found in the Unit 2 folder, p. 12, covers the main ideas in this section as well as the key terms.

---

5. The Federalists believed they were establishing a government of, for, and by the people. Under the Constitution, the people and the government were the same. The people therefore would not need to protect their rights from themselves.

6. Possible questions: Why do the people not elect the President directly? What guarantee do the people have that the legislature will not pass laws that restrict their liberties, such as freedom of the press and freedom to worship as they please? What guarantee do the people have that the courts that Congress creates will not be cruel and unfair? Answers should also note that the questions reveal the same concerns the Federalists and Anti-Federalists had about the conflict between liberty and order.

Caption Answer to ...

 Interpreting Tables

The First Amendment.

Reteach

Have students create a chart with the column headings Federalists and Anti-Federalists. Under each heading have students list the relative positions of each, and the milestones in the ratification process.

4. CLOSE

Reinforcing the Big Idea

With the ratification of the Constitution, the United States created a truly new government that combined a powerful central government with a respect for individual liberty. In the next section, students will read about the leaders and policies of the new government.

The New Government

1. FOCUS

Connecting to the Big Idea

See page 126B. Explain to students that with the ratification of the Constitution, the work of strengthening the central government had only just begun. Now the Federalists had to get down to the business of making the new plan work. Ask how they did this.

Objectives

● Describe the political differences between Thomas Jefferson and Alexander Hamilton.
● Explain how the government under George Washington tried to make the new government impressive.
● Show how Washington, D.C., fulfilled the Federalist dream of an imposing capital of the United States.

Bellringer

Ask students to recall magazine, newspaper, or television pictures of Washington, D.C. What are their impressions of the capital?

Reading Strategy

Reading for Evidence Ask students to find evidence as they read the section that the government under Washington was either sensitive or insensitive to the American need for a government that was both powerful and democratic.

The New Government

SECTION PREVIEW

In the first years under the Constitution, Federalists labored to make the United States government as impressive as possible. They chose talented officials, opted for high ceremony, and made plans for an elaborate national capital.

Key Concepts

• Washington chose as two of his key officials Jefferson and Hamilton—men who had very different views of the role of government.
• The first Congress and the executive branch under Washington tried to set an impressive tone for the new government.
• Washington, D. C., is the product of Federalist dreams for an imposing capital for the "republican empire" of the United States.

Key Terms, People, and Places

cabinet, administration; Alexander Hamilton; District of Columbia, Washington

A souvenir of the first presidential inauguration proclaims: "Deafness to the ears and silence to the tongue that will utter a calumny [insult] against the immortal Washington."

I n the elections that took place in the fall of 1788, most of those elected to Congress were Federalists. George Washington of Virginia and John Adams of Massachusetts were chosen as President and Vice President. The selection of Washington was unanimous. But the work of strengthening the government had only just begun.

Few groups have ever had grander plans for the United States than the Federalists. Having created a Constitution to secure the republic from too much influence by the people at large, they moved to make their vision of a great "republican empire" come true.

The Leaders of the New Republic

Washington became President in New York City on April 30, 1789. He was dressed in a brown broadcloth suit made in Hartford, Connecticut, and white silk stockings. His hair was freshly powdered. A committee of newly elected members of Congress escorted him to Federal Hall. There, on a small porch in front of thousands of people crowding nearby streets and rooftops, he took the oath of office and kissed a Bible. The crowd roared their approval. "Never," wrote a French ambassador,

has sovereign reigned more completely in the hearts of his subjects than did Washington in those of his fellow-citizens. . . . He has the soul, look and figure of a hero united in him.

In addition to great popularity, Washington also had formidable tasks. The United States had a huge debt, no permanent capital, and no federal officers beyond the elected members of Congress and the President and Vice President. Immediately, Washington began to appoint officials, including the **cabinet**—the heads of the major departments of the executive branch. For attorney general, he chose Edmund Randolph of Virginia; for secretary of war, the able Henry Knox. The choices to head the state and treasury departments were even more crucial.

Secretary of State Thomas Jefferson
Washington chose Thomas Jefferson to be secretary of state—the official who would manage the nation's relations with other countries. Jefferson was not particularly well known in 1789, despite the fact that he had been the principal author of the Declaration of Independence. Jefferson had been the American ambassador to France from 1785 to 1789, in touch with events in the United States only through correspondence with friends like James Madison. Though in France when the Constitution was drafted and adopted, Jefferson supported the Constitution and the addition of the Bill of Rights. Jefferson would one day become the third President of the United States.

▶ RESOURCE DIRECTORY

Teaching Resources

Reproducible Lesson Plan found in the Unit 2 folder, p. 6, provides a summary of the Section 4 lesson plan content.

Alternate Lesson Plan: Critical Thinking Formulating Questions, found in the Alternate Lesson Plans folder, p. 25, helps students apply this skill by identifying the nation's early leaders and their concerns.

Guided Reading and Review found in the Unit 2 folder, p. 13, provides a structure for reading and mastering the key concepts and reviewing the key terms for Section 4. (Guided Practice)

Visual Learning Activity A Portrait of a President, found in the Unit 2 folder, p. 30, uses a 1789 print of George Washington, surrounded by symbols of the United States, to illustrate some images and ideals prevalent at that time.

Many years later, when John F. Kennedy was hosting a supper at the White House for Nobel Prize winners, the President joked that his guests were the greatest gathering of talent ever to dine in the building, except when Thomas Jefferson ate there by himself. He *was* a man of many talents. Not only a planter, lawyer, and diplomat, Jefferson was also a violinist and an inventor. Perhaps his greatest passion was architecture. Jefferson built several homes for himself. The most famous was Monticello, an intricately planned house on a small mountain outside of Charlottesville, Virginia.

Jefferson had a passionate commitment to human rights—and yet he owned slaves. Jefferson well knew that slavery was wrong. Few white planters wrote more eloquently about it as a moral evil; and yet he could never bring himself to free more than a few slaves. As a planter, his livelihood depended on their labor. He would not discard his prejudices and risk losing the personal comfort that slave labor brought him, even for the principle of democratic equality.

Washington chose Jefferson to be secretary of state because he had experience dealing with France, still the closest ally of the new republic. But in the bargain he also got a man who would become one of the President's most ardent critics. While Jefferson approved of the Constitution, he never trusted the new government.

Treasury Secretary Alexander Hamilton
Like Jefferson, Treasury Secretary **Alexander Hamilton** was relatively young (only thirty-four) and intellectually brilliant. The son of a West Indies planter, Hamilton was raised by aunts and then sent to King's College (now Columbia University) in New York City. By his early twenties, Hamilton was already writing political pamphlets and seeking power.

He soon displayed a talent for making himself indispensable to powerful people. As an officer in the United States Army during the War for Independence, Hamilton became an aide and private secretary to General Washington.

Now Washington entrusted the young Hamilton with control of the largest department in the government and with responsibility

for finding a way to pay off the huge debt the nation still owed from the War for Independence. In contrast to Jefferson, who never really trusted government and remained idealistic about the people, Hamilton was a practical fellow who believed that governmental power, properly used, could accomplish great things. He had every intention of making his time in the federal government an active one.

Jefferson and Hamilton were on a collision course. But in the first months, even years, of the new government, matters went fairly smoothly. The adoption of the Constitution occurred at the same time as a general recovery from the economic problems brought on by the war. Americans were happy to have the question of their national government resolved. They were eager to move on to other things.

Formalities of the New Government

During the first four years of Washington's **administration,** or term in office, the government was preoccupied with matters both large and small. Washington and his officials were doing things no one else had done before. No one knew exactly what the Supreme Court was supposed to do. No one knew exactly how

With enthusiastic hopes for their new government, Americans cheered the inauguration of Washington on April 29, 1789.

2. INSTRUCT

Explain/Discuss
Explain to students that although the Constitution provided a framework for the new government, it had never before been implemented. Washington and the members of Congress were charting completely new territory when they took office. Ask students what were the unique challenges faced by the first government of the United States.

Discuss the new government with students in terms of its grand designs. Ask questions such as the following: How did Washington choose his cabinet members? Was there provision for a cabinet in the Constitution? What impression did government officials hope to give the people about the government? What elements of design made the new capital a symbol of a powerful national government?

In Depth

Biography

As a young twenty-nine-year-old adviser to General George Washington, Alexander Hamilton (1755–1804) saw the need for a strong central government to unify the thirteen states. He insisted that the states convene at a larger meeting to discuss the matter—the successful Constitutional Convention of 1787. As an army captain who helped turn back British General Cornwallis at Yorktown, a prominent attorney, and a political theorist who wrote most of the influential *Federalist* papers, Hamilton was one of the fathers of the republic. He died in 1804 in a dramatic duel with political rival Aaron Burr.

Have students analyze the Federalists' vision of a great "republican empire" as it was realized during Washington's presidency. What fueled the Federalist dreams for a government characterized by ceremony and grandeur?

Answer to ...

MAKING CONNECTIONS

Answers will vary.

Caption Answer to ...

Using Historical Evidence

The grandness and formality shown represent exactly what the Federalists wanted in their new government.

Activity

Cooperative Learning

Time: One class period.
Activity: Designing a capital.
Grouping: Four to six students.
Purpose: The Federalists commissioned the French architect Pierre L'Enfant to design Washington, D.C., as a city that would symbolize a strong republic with noble roots. He produced a magnificent city plan, with classical buildings and broad boulevards radiating outward from the center of government. Have students design a capital that reflects the Anti-Federalist view of government.
Roles: Building architects, landscape architects, artists, contractors.
Outcome: Students will understand how the design of Washington, D.C., reflects the philosophy of government of the early Federalists.

Enrichment

Just as the role of women has changed since the American Revolution, so has the position of the President's wife. Ask students to compare the role Martha Washington played to the role of a modern First Lady, such as Hillary Rodham Clinton.

Using Historical Evidence This painting of a reception during the Washington administration is titled "The Republican Court." *How does the scene reflect Federalist plans for the new government?*

The campaign buttons of modern times are the offspring of these buttons commemorating Washington's inauguration.

Congress and the President should deal with each other.

Typical of this sense of newness and experimentation was the debate in the Senate over what to call the President. Should something like "Your Majesty" be used? Or would "Mr. Washington" be more appropriate? A Senate committee recommended "His Highness the President of the United States of America and Protector of the Rights of the Same." The House of Representative refused to endorse that title, however, and the issue died. Today we simply use the more democratic form of address: "Mr. President." ✪

President Washington was doing what he could to make his government impressive. His appearance and personality helped. Washington was tall (over six feet) and physically imposing, especially on horseback. He was also solemn and reserved, a very private man. During the Constitutional Convention, some members had dared Gouverneur Morris of Pennsylvania to put his hand on Washington's shoulder. According to an account of the incident,

> Washington withdrew his hand, stepped suddenly back, [and] fixed his eye on Morris for several minutes with an angry frown, until the latter retreated abashed, and sought refuge in the crowd.

The President lived in a formal, if not extravagant, manner, believing that it was necessary to command the respect of the citizens of the United States as well as the rest of the world. Soldiers escorted his carriage, which was pulled by six horses. He and his wife Martha held regular Friday afternoon parties, or levees, to entertain government officials and ambassadors. Every year, government officials celebrated the President's birthday with elaborate ceremonies and pageantry. To many, such parties and ceremonies made Washington seem like a king with a court.

Odd as such controversy over presidential behavior may seem, it reveals just how experimental the new republic was. Americans were sailing on uncharted waters. No wonder they found it difficult to balance the need to make their government appear both powerful and democratic at the same time. In fact, only a few American Presidents have succeeded in this balancing act.

MAKING CONNECTIONS

Too much ceremony in government can result in an expensive spectacle that only irritates taxpayers. Does government ceremony today, such as the inauguration of the President, impress you or strike you as excessive? Explain your reaction.

Planning a Capital City

The efforts to make the new government awe inspiring went beyond recruiting talented officials and holding formal ceremonies. The United States needed an impressive capital, too. It got one, as a result of the Residence Act of 1790, which specified that the capital would be a 10-square-mile tract of land on the Potomac River near Washington's home at Mount Vernon. ✪ This federally governed area was to be called by the grand name of the **District of Columbia**. (The name **Washington** was not used for the capital city itself until 1799, after President Washington had died.) On Jefferson's recommendation, George Washington appointed an African American mathematician and inventor, Benjamin Banneker, to the

RESOURCE DIRECTORY

Teaching Resources

✪ **Primary Source Activity** Meeting President and Mrs. Washington, found in the Unit 2 folder, p. 24, provides a personal viewpoint on George and Martha Washington.

✪ **American Profiles Activity** found in the Unit 2 folder, p. 18, profiles Benjamin Banneker, an African American member of the team that surveyed the land prior to construction of the nation's capital.

Changes to the Capitol

The Capitol in 1800 was no more than one wing in a muddy wilderness (left). Today, with two wings and a dome, the Capitol dominates the Washington skyline (above). *Describe in your own words the impression the Capitol gives today.*

commission in charge of surveying the city. Pierre Charles L'Enfant, a French artist and architect who had fought for the United States during the War for Independence, developed the city plan. L'Enfant designed a capital with broad streets, public walks, a mansion for the President, a pedestrian mall, and the Capitol. Although the federal government moved to the District in 1800, it took decades longer to realize the L'Enfant plan in its entirety.

Washington, D.C., with its great boulevards, marble buildings in the Roman style, and public monuments, is the most obvious legacy of the Federalists' grand plans for the United States. They meant to display the power and majesty of their new national government. Washington, D.C., was the symbol of the strong federal government they had lobbied for throughout the 1780s and outlined in the Constitution.

Some Americans, however, found the Federalists' interest in ceremony and grandeur disturbing, not to mention expensive. And in the 1790s, they would unite in growing numbers behind Secretary of State Thomas Jefferson to protect what they believed was the true legacy of the American Revolution—liberty.

SECTION 4 REVIEW

Key Terms, People, and Places
1. Define (a) cabinet, (b) administration.
2. Identify Alexander Hamilton.
3. Identify (a) District of Columbia, (b) Washington.

Key Concepts
4. How did Jefferson and Hamilton differ?
5. Why did Washington promote formality in his administration?

6. What impression were the Federalists hoping for when they approved L'Enfant's design for Washington, D.C.?

Critical Thinking
7. **Checking Consistency** In an empire, a central government has control over extensive territory and many different peoples. How might an empire be inconsistent with the ideal of popular sovereignty?

 Quiz found in the Unit 2 folder, p. 14, covers the main ideas in this section as well as the key terms.

 Chapter Test Forms A and B are found in the Unit 2 folder, pp. 31–36.

 Answer Keys found in the Unit 2 folder, pp. 116–125, provide answers to all student activities.

Media and Technology

Transparency Graphic Organizer, G-1

Guided Reading Audiotapes (English and Spanish)

Computer Test Bank

---

3. **ASSESS**

Section 4 Review Answers
1. (a) cabinet, see p. 148, (b) administration, see p. 149
2. Alexander Hamilton, see p. 149
3. (a) District of Columbia, see p. 150, (b) Washington, see p. 150
4. Jefferson was a temperamental idealist, a man of many talents who, despite his slaveholding, possessed an abiding faith in liberty and progress; he trusted the people more than government. Just as brilliant in his own way, Hamilton was far more pragmatic and focused than Jefferson. A man who had advanced by attaching himself to important figures, he preferred structure and order to liberty and freedom.
5. He believed that it was necessary to set the proper tone for his government, one that would command the respect of the citizens of the United States as well as the rest of the world.
6. They were hoping to display the power and majesty of their new national government.
7. Answers should point out that an empire is inconsistent with the idea of rule by the people insofar as it does not necessarily give the people a voice in the central government.

Reteach
Have students write two paragraphs summarizing Section 4, in which they leave important ideas, key terms, people, or places blank. When summaries are complete, have pairs of students exchange papers and fill in the missing words.

4. **CLOSE**

 Reinforcing the Big Idea
Federalists worked hard in the first few years under the Constitution to make the United States government as impressive as possible. A growing number of Americans were disturbed by their taste for ceremony and expensive displays of power. They worried that the real ideals of the Revolution were being lost.

Chapter Review

Understanding Key Terms, People, and Places

Terms

Students should refer to the definitions of the key terms in the chapter to write sentences that show the relation of each word to the Constitutional Convention of 1787, ratification of the Constitution, or the United States government in its first years.

Matching

1. Great Compromise
2. legislative branch
3. cabinet
4. Bill of Rights

True or False

1. false, Anti-Federalists
2. true
3. true

Reviewing Main Ideas

1. Congress before 1788 was only a loose collection of separate states; people in fact wrote "the United States are" rather than "the United States is." Congress did not have the power to force the states to do what it wanted.

2. The Nationalists wanted to make the United States government stronger and avoid too much democracy, which they felt led to disorder.

3. Shays's Rebellion convinced many people of the necessity of attending the Philadelphia Convention in order to avoid the civil unrest that the rebellion seemed to foreshadow.

4. Madison envisioned a constitution that would encourage the best in people while restraining their tendencies toward selfishness.

5. The Great Compromise provided for a bicameral legislature; in one house each state would have a number of votes based on the size of its population, while in the other house each state would have an equal number of votes.

6. The Constitution limits popular sovereignty by dividing power between the state and national governments and among the three branches of the national government; it also gives the Electoral College the final say in a presidential election in case of a deadlock.

7. The Federalists feared that without the Constitution, the country would degenerate into anarchy and civil war.

Key Terms

1. confederation
2. Articles of Confederation
3. legislative branch
4. executive branch
5. judicial branch
6. unicameral legislature
7. bicameral legislature
8. Virginia Plan
9. veto
10. New Jersey Plan
11. Great Compromise
12. Three-fifths Compromise
13. separation of powers
14. system of checks and balances
15. Electoral College
16. faction
17. ratify
18. Bill of Rights
19. cabinet
20. administration

People

21. Nationalists
22. James Madison
23. Federalists
24. Anti-Federalists
25. Alexander Hamilton

Places

26. District of Columbia
27. Washington

Terms For each term above, write a sentence that explains its relation to events leading to the Constitutional Convention of 1787, ratification of the Constitution, or the United States government in its first years.

Matching Review the key terms in the list above. If you are not sure of a term's meaning, review its definition in the chapter. Then choose a term from the list that best matches each description below.

1. the solution to the issue of whether representation in the legislature should be based on population
2. the part of government that makes laws
3. the heads of the major departments of the executive branch
4. the ten amendments that became part of the Constitution in 1791

True or False Determine whether each statement is true or false. If it is true, write "true." If it is false, change the underlined name to make the statement true.

1. Federalists opposed the Constitution as a betrayal of the American Revolution.
2. By the time the Constitutional Convention took place, James Madison had already devised a plan for a new Constitution.
3. Alexander Hamilton believed that government power could accomplish great things if used properly.

Reviewing Main Ideas

Section 1 (pp. 128–133)

1. Give evidence to prove that before 1788 the national government was weak while the state governments were powerful.
2. What were the goals of the Nationalists?
3. What effect did Shays's Rebellion have on the 1787 Philadelphia Convention?

Section 2 (pp. 136–142)

4. Describe the kind of constitution that James Madison envisioned when he came to Philadelphia.
5. How was the question of whether larger states would have more power than smaller ones finally resolved?
6. How does the Constitution limit popular sovereignty?

Section 3 (pp. 144–147)

7. Why did the Federalists support the Constitution?
8. Explain the following statement: "While the Federalists feared people more than government, the Anti-Federalists feared government more than people."

Section 4 (pp. 148–151)

9. Which cabinet member became a critic of the new government, Alexander Hamilton or Thomas Jefferson? Explain your answer.
10. Describe the tone that President Washington set for the new government.
11. What features of Washington, D.C., suggest the power and dignity of the federal government?

8. The Federalists' greatest fear was that democracy would lead to anarchy; the Anti-Federalists' greatest fear was that a more powerful government would mean the end of American liberty.

9. Thomas Jefferson. He distrusted government and did not want it to become too powerful.

10. Washington set a tone of formality and dignity.

11. Features that suggest power and dignity include the city's great boulevards, marble buildings in the Roman style, and public monuments.

Thinking Critically

1. The Three-fifths Compromise suggested that the Framers thought that African American slaves counted for less than other citizens.

2. Answers will vary. Students' responses should discuss the advantages and disadvantages of a strong central government.

3. Answers will vary. Some students may choose to preserve the grandeur of the capital as it is now, believing that government must remain formal and dignified in order to be respected. Others may opt for a less formal style, believing that government should reflect the styles of the people whom the government represents.

Thinking Critically

1. **Identifying Assumptions** What did the Three-fifths Compromise suggest about how the Framers of the Constitution viewed enslaved African Americans?
2. **Identifying Central Issues** Imagine that you had been a delegate to the Constitutional Convention. Would you have been a Federalist or an Anti-Federalist? Explain your choice.
3. **Identifying Alternatives** If you were commissioned to design a new United States capital, how would it be similar to or different from L'Enfant's plans for Washington, D.C.? Explain your thinking.

Making Connections

1. **Evaluating Primary Sources** Review the primary source excerpt on page 132. What sentiment is the speaker expressing? How did sentiments such as this help to bring about the Philadelphia Convention?
2. **Understanding the Visuals** Contrast the painting of Washington's resignation on page 129 with the description of Washington's character on page 150. Does the painting support Washington's reputation as a reserved man? Explain your answer.
3. **Writing About the Chapter** The year is 1789. Write a letter to one of the Framers in which you express your opinion on the Constitution. First, create a list of what you see as the positive aspects of the document. Then, list the negative features. Note any suggestions you have for improvements. Next, write a draft of your letter in which you offer your ideas. Revise your letter, making certain that each idea is clearly explained. Proofread your letter and draft a final copy.
4. **Using the Graphic Organizer** This graphic organizer uses a tree map to organize information about reasons for the Constitutional Convention. (a) How is the problem of a weak Continental Congress related to Shays's Rebellion? (b) What was the main source of tension between the states? (c) On a separate sheet of paper, create your own tree map about the new government in the first years after the Constitution was written, using this graphic organizer as an example.

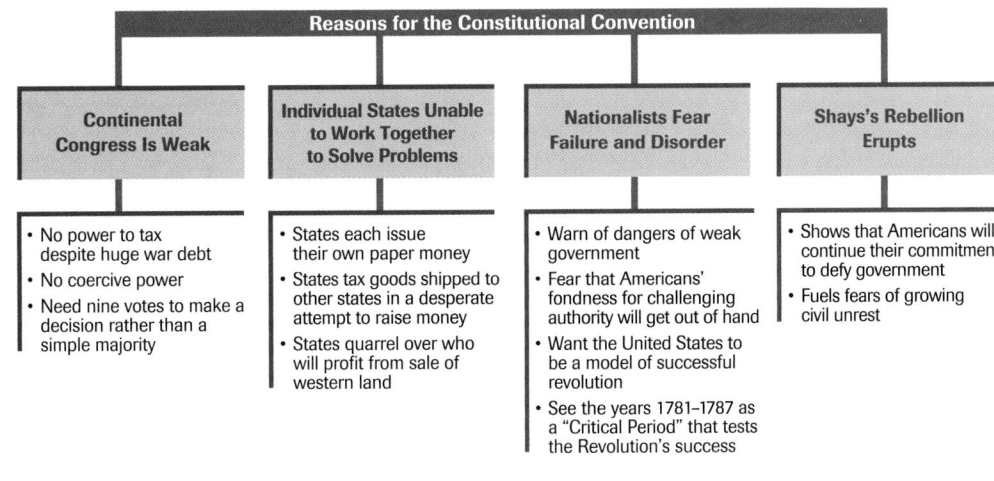

Reasons for the Constitutional Convention

Continental Congress Is Weak	Individual States Unable to Work Together to Solve Problems	Nationalists Fear Failure and Disorder	Shays's Rebellion Erupts
• No power to tax despite huge war debt • No coercive power • Need nine votes to make a decision rather than a simple majority	• States each issue their own paper money • States tax goods shipped to other states in a desperate attempt to raise money • States quarrel over who will profit from sale of western land	• Warn of dangers of weak government • Fear that Americans' fondness for challenging authority will get out of hand • Want the United States to be a model of successful revolution • See the years 1781–1787 as a "Critical Period" that tests the Revolution's success	• Shows that Americans will continue their commitment to defy government • Fuels fears of growing civil unrest

4. (a) Because the Continental Congress had no coercive power, it was unable to gather troops to put down the rebellion. (b) The main source of tension between the states was vying for ways to raise money. (c) Students' graphic organizers should include information about Jefferson and Hamilton, the tone of the new administration, and the planning of Washington, D.C.

 Alternative Assessment

Final Evaluation

Use the following guidelines to evaluate student projects:

● **Evidence of thoughtfulness** Do the projects include the main topics from the chapter?

● **Evidence of outside research** To what extent did students use outside research materials for their project?

● **Evidence of synthesis** Do projects demonstrate that students understand how topics are related?

● **Communication style** Do the projects convey their purpose to an audience in a clear, appealing way?

Allow interested students to present their finished projects to the class.

Making Connections

1. This quotation reveals the belief that the United States had a responsibility to act as an example to other countries around the world and to be sure it succeeded so that other would-be democracies would be inspired. Such sentiments helped to bring about the Philadelphia Convention, because those who held these beliefs saw the disorder and disagreements taking place in the new nation under the Articles of Confederation as a threat to the success of the United States. To fulfill their obligation to other nations, the national government had to be fashioned in such a way that it would not fail.

2. The painting indicates that although Washington appeared reserved, according to this painter he was capable of feeling and exhibiting strong emotion.

3. Students' responses should take into account such issues as fair representation, whether or not the Constitution grants the states and the national government too much or too little power, and the wisdom of the elastic clause, the amendments procedure, and the Electoral College.

Chapter 6 The Origins of American Politics
1789–1820

📁 Teaching Resources (See Unit 2 Folder)

	Instruction	Enrichment

Section 1
Liberty Versus Order in the 1790s
(pp. 156–160)
	Reproducible Lesson Plan, p. 38
	Alternate Lesson Plan, p. 27
	Guided Reading and Review, p. 43
	Quiz, p. 44
		Literature Activity, American Literature,
		  pp. 66–68
		Critical Thinking Activity, Recognizing Bias,
		  p. 62
		Historian's Toolbox Activity, Making
		  Comparisons, p. 61

Section 2
The Election of 1800: A Turning Point in History
(pp. 162–165)
	Reproducible Lesson Plan, p. 39
	Alternate Lesson Plan, p. 28
	Guided Reading and Review, p. 45
	Quiz, p. 46
		American Profiles Activity, Noah Webster,
		  p. 57
		Turning Points Extension Activity, The Lasting
		  Impact of the Election of 1800, pp. 53–54

Section 3
The Jefferson Administration
(pp. 168–171)
	Reproducible Lesson Plan, p. 40
	Alternate Lesson Plan, p. 29
	Guided Reading and Review, p. 47
	Quiz, p. 48
		Visual Learning Activity, Honoring Thomas
		  Jefferson, p. 69
		Primary Source Activity, Napoleon Sells
		  Louisiana, pp. 63–64
		Time and Place Activity, Moving the City to the
		  Country, pp. 55–56

Section 4 **Native American Politics** (pp. 174–177)	Reproducible Lesson Plan, p. 41 Alternate Lesson Plan, p. 30 Guided Reading and Review, p. 49 Quiz, p. 50	Primary Source Activity, Native American Politics, p. 65

Section 5
War, Panic, and Uneasy Compromise
(pp. 178–181)
	Reproducible Lesson Plan, p. 42
	Alternate Lesson Plan, p. 31
	Guided Reading and Review, p. 51
	Quiz, p. 52
	Chapter Test, Forms A & B, pp. 71–76
		American Profiles Activity, Francis Scott Key,
		  p. 58
		Viewpoints Activity, For and Against the War
		  of 1812, pp. 59–60
		Visual Learning Activity, The Present State of
		  Our Country, p. 70

📁 Additional Chapter Resources

Resource Organizer, p. 37
Alternate Lesson Plan, p. 26
Answer Keys, pp. 116–125

Bibliography

For the Teacher

Boorstin, D. *The Lost World of Thomas Jefferson.* University of Chicago Press, 1981. (An acclaimed re-creation of the Jeffersonian world view.)

Kutler, Stanley I., ed. *John Marshall.* Prentice Hall, 1972. (Selected essays by Marshall's contemporaries and others assessing the famous Chief Justice's place in history.)

Prentice Hall Literature Excerpts from *The American Experience,* 1994, including Jean de Crèvecoeur, Michel-Guillaume. *Letters from an American Farmer.* Reprint of 1782 edition, Reprint Services, 1990.

The Big Idea for the chapter and how the main ideas in each section relate to the Big Idea are graphically displayed below. Comprehension of this chapter's Big Idea is critical to students' understanding of United States history and how we as a nation got where we are today.

CHAPTER 6

In the years following the ratification of the Constitution, American leaders fought passionately over the formation of the new government. Some groups that were not represented in the legislatures, including Native Americans and African Americans, tried to acquire or maintain liberty by other means. Only for a brief period following the War of 1812 did the new nation enjoy prosperity and political harmony.

SECTION 1

Two political parties quickly formed in the new nation: the Federalists, who favored a strong central government; and the Democrats, who wanted to guarantee individual liberty.

SECTION 2

In the rancorous election of 1800, Thomas Jefferson was elected President, and for the first time political power was transferred peacefully between opposing parties.

SECTION 3

As President, Jefferson tried to reduce the influence of the national government. However, he used the government's power to extend United States territory and to restrict trade with other nations.

SECTION 4

Alarmed by the westward expansion of the United States, Native Americans responded in various ways, attempting to maintain some control over their lands and their lives.

SECTION 5

The United States fought Great Britain in the War of 1812. A sudden depression dampened the good feelings that followed the war. The Missouri Compromise resolved, for a time, the differences between North and South over limits to slavery.

Media and Technology

 Visions of America: Turning Point Story, "Natural Aristocracy" (length: approx. 4 minutes)

 Visions of America: Roundtable Discussion on "Natural Aristocracy"

 Critical Thinking, I-14; Historical Maps, L-2

 Fine Art, D-2

 Graphic Organizer, G-3

 Guided Reading Audiotapes (English and Spanish)

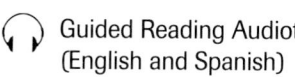 Computer Test Bank

For the Student

Electing the President. Encyclopedia Britannica. Film/Video. (The development of the electoral process from the beginning of the Republic to the present.)

Meltzer, Milton. *American Politics: How It Really Works.* William Morrow, 1989. (Study of the American political process at the local, state, and federal levels.)

154B

The Relevance of the Big Idea

In 1799 an Englishman traveling through the United States commented on the conversations he heard in taverns and inns: "It is scarcely possible for a dozen Americans to sit together without quarreling about politics." Americans are still arguing about politics and the roles political parties play. Some Americans think that the two-party system is on its way out.

Discuss with students why some Americans look toward minor parties. A case in point might be the 1992 presidential election, in which H. Ross Perot, an independent candidate, won almost 20 percent of the vote. Are minor parties "spoilers," unable to win a major election, or are they able to clarify the views of the front-runners?

The arguments about minor parties will continue, much as they did in the early years of the nation.

In Depth

Global Connections

In the wake of the French Revolution in 1789, France hoped to spread republican fervor. The first ambassador of the French Republic, Edmond Genêt, arrived in 1793 urging the United States to join France in war against Britain. He went as far as to arm ships himself, threatening the neutrality declared by Washington. Resentment against Genêt's intrusion solidified support for the anti-French Federalists, and weakened the position of Jeffersonian Republicans, who had championed the French cause.

CHAPTER 6

The Origins of American Politics
1789–1820

*P*olitics—the business of getting, keeping, and exercising power—took more than one form in the early republic. People who had a say in government focused on how much power the national government should have and slowly organized themselves into what amounted to political parties. Those who felt shut out of electoral politics, whether white, African American, or Native American, tended to rely on ways of expressing themselves that were outside the system—including rebellion.

Events in the United States		1790s Native Americans form alliances to resist encroachment onto their land.	1794 The Whiskey Rebellion is crushed, establishing the strength of the federal government.		1800 Gabriel Prosser leads a group of African Americans in an uprising against slavery.	
	1789	1792	1795	1798	1801	
Events in the World	1789 The people of France start the French Revolution.	1791 Haitians revolt against French rule.		1796 British physician Edward Jenner introduces a vaccination against smallpox.	1799 The discovery of the Rosetta Stone in Egypt makes deciphering of hieroglyphics possible.	1802 Nguy Anh unites country in and calls it Vietnam.

▶ RESOURCE DIRECTORY

Teaching Resources

Alternate Lesson Plan: Demonstrating the Big Idea found in the Alternate Lesson Plans folder, p. 26, provides a lesson strategy to instruct students about the Big Idea that the early nineteenth century was an era fraught with both domestic and international conflict for the United States.

Alternative Assessment Handbook provides information, guidance, and strategies for alternative methods of assessment. It includes an essay on new trends in assessment, guidance and strategies for developing performance tasks and portfolios, scoring rubrics, and sample evaluation forms.

Pages 156–160
Liberty Versus Order in the 1790s
While Federalists focused on the need for social order, the newly emerging Jeffersonian Republicans placed their priority on defending liberty.

Pages 162–165
The Election of 1800: A Turning Point in History
With the election of 1800, American leaders peacefully accomplished the nation's first transfer of power from one party to another, a victory for democratic government.

Pages 166–167
The Lasting Impact of the Election of 1800

Pages 168–171
The Jefferson Administration
Jefferson succeeded in reversing much of the Federalist program, yet demonstrated the government's power when he restricted the nation's trade with other countries.

Pages 174–177
Native American Politics
As the United States continued to expand onto their land, Native Americans responded in various ways, from acceptance to armed resistance.

Pages 178–181
War, Panic, and Uneasy Compromise
Prosperity and political harmony followed the War of 1812—until depression and controversy raised storm clouds on the horizon.

1803 The Louisiana Purchase doubles the size of the United States.		1811 The Battle of Tippecanoe in Indiana rages between Native Americans and European settlers.	1814 The Treaty of Ghent is signed, ending the War of 1812 between Americans and British.		1820 The Missouri Compromise forbids slavery in certain areas of the United States.
1804	**1807**	**1810**	**1813**	**1816**	**1819**
			1813 Simón Bolívar leads Venezuela to independence.		

Media and Technology

Transparency
Time Lines, E-3

As an ongoing chapter project, students can create an "administration in review" paper or pamphlet for the administration of one of the following Presidents: Adams, Jefferson, or Madison. Student projects should include information about the goals, successes, and failures of that administration. They should compare or contrast their chosen President's philosophy upon taking office with what he actually achieved in office. Students may include research on relevant topics such as the President's family, background, and other events of interest occurring at the time, including the fashions of the day.

Explain that finished projects will be assessed according to the following standards:

● **Unacceptable** Projects are not attempted or fail to meet requirements outlined.

● **Limited/Acceptable** Projects are based on material from the textbook and outline the important successes and failures of the administration.

● **Extensive/Commendable** Projects include all important successes and failures of the administration and show evidence of some outside research.

● **Extraordinary/Outstanding** Projects include detailed analysis of the successes and failures of the administration and show evidence of extensive research.

For information and guidance on alternative assessment trends and strategies, see the Alternative Assessment Handbook in the Resource Organizer on page 154.

Liberty Versus Order in the 1790s

SECTION 1

1. FOCUS

Connecting to the Big Idea

See page 154B. As the Federalists tried to institute their vision of the American government, their opponents organized to stop them, creating a new political party in the process. Ask what were the major differences between the Federalist party and their opposition, the Jeffersonian Republicans (Democrats).

Objectives

● Explain how the national government won support by assuming the debts of the states.

● Present the objections to the Federalist financial programs.

● Explain how the conflict between liberty and order in the French Revolution was reflected in American politics.

● Cite the government's reaction to the Whiskey Rebellion as evidence that it was willing to enforce the law.

Bellringer

Ask students if they consider themselves Republicans, Democrats, Independents, or members of a minor political party. Have them define the different political goals of these parties.

Reading Strategy

Reinforcing Key Ideas Ask students to imagine that they are television newscasters preparing a segment on the political differences between Alexander Hamilton and the Federalists and Thomas Jefferson and his supporters. Ask students to take notes on the two parties and the differences between them as they read the section.

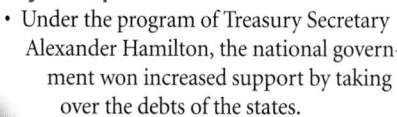

SECTION PREVIEW

While Federalists focused on the need for social order, the newly emerging Jeffersonian Republicans placed their priority on defending liberty.

Key Concepts

• Under the program of Treasury Secretary Alexander Hamilton, the national government won increased support by taking over the debts of the states.

   • Opponents of the Federalist programs objected to the interference of the national government in their lives.

   • The conflict between liberty and order in the French Revolution was reflected in the division of American politics in the 1790s.

   • The government's reaction to the Whiskey Rebellion demonstrated its willingness to enforce the law.

Key Terms, People, and Places

political party, first American party system, excise, tariff, French Revolution, Whiskey Rebellion, precedent; Jeffersonian Republicans

Alexander Hamilton participated in framing the Constitution, argued eloquently for ratification, and crafted a brilliant plan to use the young nation's debts as a source of strength.

T oday politics in the United States is dominated by two major **political parties.** These are groups actively involved in the political process of the nation, which run candidates for offices in order to control government policies. One party is the Republican party; the other is the Democratic party. The Republican party came into being in the 1850s, but the first form of the Democratic party—one of the oldest continuous political parties in the world—became active in the United States in the 1790s.

When Thomas Jefferson and other critics of George Washington's administration formed the alliance of widely different people that later became the Democratic party, they did not intend to create a permanent party at all. In

fact, they saw parties as evidence of social chaos and moral decay, because struggles between parties have led to civil war frequently throughout history. Originally these critics were called Republicans or Democratic Republicans because they stood for a more democratic republic. To avoid confusing them with the modern Republican party, historians call them **Jeffersonian Republicans.** This group, along with the Federalists, formed what today is known as the **first American party system.**

The Division of Views in the United States

Secretary of the Treasury Alexander Hamilton summarized the differences between Federalists and Jeffersonian Republicans in 1792.

O *ne side* [the Jeffersonians] *appears to believe that there is a serious plot to overturn the State governments and substitute a monarchy to the present republican system. The other side* [the Federalists] *firmly believes that there is a serious plot to overturn the general government and elevate the separate powers of the States upon its ruins.*

To this statement Hamilton added, "Both sides may be equally wrong." Only a few Federalists—and they did not include Washington or Hamilton—wanted to restore monarchy in the United States; most were deeply committed to the new republic. And virtually all of the Jeffersonian Republicans accepted the national government created by the Constitution.

Hamilton's Program

Secretary Hamilton was a keen supporter of strong national power. He had little faith in the people. The Constitution, he believed, was not enough in itself to preserve the new nation. In

RESOURCE DIRECTORY

Teaching Resources

Reproducible Lesson Plan found in the Unit 2 folder, p. 38, provides a summary of the Section 1 lesson plan content.

Alternate Lesson Plan: Learning Styles found in the Alternate Lesson Plans folder, p. 27, provides a structure for students to compare the viewpoints of Jefferson and Hamilton, and is particularly effective for auditory learners.

Guided Reading and Review found in the Unit 2 folder, p. 43, provides a structure for reading and mastering the key concepts and reviewing the key terms for Section 1. (Guided Practice)

his view, the government had to expand its role and actively direct the development of the economy and society of the United States.

To this end, Hamilton proposed a complicated plan. In 1790, after months of deadlock and debate, Hamilton narrowly won congressional approval for the national government to take on the debts incurred by the states during the War for Independence. This decision may seem strange at first. The United States already had a huge debt of about $50 million. Why would the government want to add to this burden?

The Reasons Behind Hamilton's Program
The answer is simpler than one might think. Most of the state and national debt was owed to European banks and American merchants and speculators, or people who take a financial risk in the hope of future profit. Hamilton knew that these creditors, or lenders, were interested in keeping alive and well whatever government owed them money. If the states owed them money, Hamilton reasoned, they would care about the states. But if the United States owed them the money, they would be less interested in the individual states and more concerned with the future of the United States as a whole.

But why would creditors go along with this plan? Because Hamilton outlined a regular budget and set up a regular payment scheme. Two measures would help to raise money to pay off the debts. In 1791 Congress made whiskey the target of a new **excise,** which is a tax on something manufactured within a country. Furthermore, in 1792, Congress created a tax on foreign goods imported into the country, a type of tax called a **tariff.** Most of the money raised by these two taxes went to pay the expenses of the government, such as the salaries of officials. But Hamilton also put some of it into a special fund used to pay creditors a little money every year. He did not intend to pay them off right away; if he did, they would have no reason to care what happened to the United States. Instead, the government paid them interest—a percentage of the money they were owed. To handle these complicated financial matters, Congress also established the Bank of the United States in 1791.

Hamilton thus transformed the debts of all American governments into what amounted to

Triumph Government; perish all its enemies...
Trectors be warned; justice though slow is sure.

a long-term investment in the United States government. The national debt had been a weakness in the 1780s. Now, even though it totaled over $80 million, it had become a source of strength.

Opposition to Hamilton's Plan Many Americans did not like Hamilton's plan. Among them were slaveholders, planters, commercial farmers, and people distant from urban areas. They objected to the interference of the national government in local and state affairs. They thought the United States had no business regulating the economy. And they disliked taxes.

To the opponents of the Washington administration, Hamilton's policy of taxation and regulation seemed similar to the one the British had proposed in the 1760s. Coupled with the elegant style of Washington's presidency, the Federalist program smacked of aristocracy and monarchy, an all-out assault on the hard-won liberty of the American people.

Secretary of State Jefferson had fierce arguments with Hamilton over the treasury secretary's plans. President Washington usually sided with Hamilton, and Jefferson increasingly found himself the odd man out in the President's cabinet. At the end of 1793, he formally resigned. From his home at Monticello, however, Jefferson remained involved by corresponding with other critics of Hamilton's plans, including

Dragging at the wheels of the Federalist carriage, Jefferson and others of his party oppose Washington's administration in this cartoon from the 1790s.

2. INSTRUCT

Explain/Discuss
Explain to students that although the Federalists had a substantial majority in both houses of Congress during its first session, there were strong regional differences within the party. New Englanders, for example, opposed tariffs because of the amount of goods, especially molasses for rum manufacture, that they imported.

Ask students to determine how much of Hamilton's and Jefferson's respective policies can be deduced from the following information: Hamilton favored Great Britain and industry, while Jefferson favored France and rural life. Ask which of the two supported tariffs, a national bank, and the Jay Treaty.

Analyze
Ask students to consider why the young United States was more inclined to favor France than Great Britain. Then ask them to analyze the case for going to war against Great Britain, against France, or for remaining neutral.

In Depth
Interdisciplinary
The federal government may manipulate money in order to produce a desired economic effect within the American economy. In the 1790s the government sought to pay off war debts from the Revolution completely; by assuming the debts of the states, it aimed to restore national credit, create wealth, and promote new business. During the Great Depression the government, following Keynesian economics, purposely ran up large deficits to get money into circulation, promote private spending, and hasten the return of prosperity. (See Chapter 22, pages 630–632.)

Assign volunteers one of the following roles: a farmer from western Pennsylvania, a French revolutionary, a Dutch banker, John Adams, John Marshall, the wife of a Virginia tobacco planter, a wealthy Boston merchant, or a tavern keeper from upper New York state. Ask students to state their point of view (Federalist or Jeffersonian), giving two reasons in support of their chosen party.

Enrichment

Tell students that in 1969, President Richard Nixon announced a new policy that he called the "New Federalism." Ask students to write a description based on what they have learned about Federalist beliefs and programs, of what such a policy might entail. Students might also research and report on the "New Federalism."

Caption Answer to ...

 Interpreting Tables

They favored a strict interpretation of the constitutional powers of Congress.

Federalists vs. Jeffersonian Republicans	
Federalists	**Jeffersonian Republicans**
Example: Hamilton	**Example: Jefferson**
Typical view of Constitution: • loose • favored a strong central government • favored a national bank	**Typical view of Constitution:** • strict • favored weak central government • opposed a national bank
Favored using national debt to establish credit	Favored paying off national debt
For protective tariffs	Against protective tariffs
Pro-business	Pro-agriculture
For strong standing armies and navies	Against large standing armies and navies
Believed political power should rest with wealthy, educated men	Believed that common men should hold political power
Pro-British	Pro-French
Members were generally businessmen from the commercial Northeast	Members were diverse, including slaveholders frightened of a strong national government, urban artisans upset with pro-British foreign policy, and commercial farmers opposed to national taxes and regulation

Interpreting Tables
The Federalists thought the Constitution should be considered a loose framework on which to build the nation. Thus they felt Congress could create a national bank, even though the Constitution does not explicitly give Congress the power to do so. *Why did Jeffersonian Republicans oppose the national bank?*

one of the congressional delegates from Virginia, James Madison.

Some historians describe the difference between Jefferson and Hamilton in terms of their construction, or view of, the Constitution. Jefferson favored a strict construction. He believed that the government should not do anything—such as start a national bank—that was not granted to it as a specific power in the Constitution. Hamilton preferred a loose construction. He thought the Constitution was only a loose framework of laws on which Congress could build the nation as it saw fit. The table above outlines the two philosophies.

The differences between the two men went deeper than this, however. Jefferson believed that Hamilton and his Federalist allies were betraying the American Revolution. They were, he told Thomas Paine in 1792, "a sect preaching up and pouting after an English constitu-

tion of king, lords, & commons." Jefferson had more faith in the people than in their government. He took pride in not being one of those men who preferred "the calm of despotism [tyranny] to the boisterous sea of liberty." ◆

The French Revolution

That "boisterous sea" threw a tidal wave over France in 1789, when the people of France started the **French Revolution.** According to their public declaration, the revolution was committed to "liberty, fraternity, and equality." By the early 1790s, disagreement over how to make these ideals reality led not to fraternity, or brotherhood, but to a prolonged period of violence called the Reign of Terror. During this time, thousands of people, including King Louis XVI and Queen Marie Antoinette, were executed by the revolutionary government.

Frightened that the lower classes in their own nations might also revolt, European governments, led by that of Great Britain, rallied against the French. The French fought back. In 1793 a full-scale war broke out, beginning a series of conflicts called the Wars of the French Revolution, which continued off and on until 1815.

The issue of the French Revolution sharply divided Americans. Federalists tended to oppose it, seeing it as an example of a democratic revolution gone wrong. "Behold France," wrote the committed Federalist Fisher Ames, "an open hell, still ringing with agonies and blasphemies [offenses against God], still smoking with sufferings and crimes, in which we see . . . perhaps our future state."

The Jeffersonians, meanwhile, generally embraced the French Revolution as an extension of the American Revolution. Though disturbed by its excesses, they applauded its rejection of government by kings and its acceptance of republican government. Even during the Reign of Terror, Jefferson said that he "would have seen half the earth desolated" rather than see the French Revolution fail. ◆

While Americans debated the French Revolution, the outbreak of the war between Britain and France created more immediate practical problems. Even if Americans sympathized with the French, they had to face the fact that the

▶ RESOURCE DIRECTORY ◆

Teaching Resources

◆ **Literature Activity** American Literature, found in the Unit 2 folder, pp. 66–68, uses excerpts from Washington Irving's *Rip Van Winkle, The Sketch Book,* and *The Legend of Sleepy Hollow* to enrich students' understanding of early American themes and settings.

◆ **Critical Thinking Activity** Recognizing Bias: The Seeds of Nationalism, found in the Unit 2 folder, p. 62, is designed to help students apply this skill by analyzing a patriotic song written in the 1800s.

British navy dominated the oceans. What course should the United States take? The nation could not afford to offend the British, but there was little sentiment for abandoning the French, who had contributed to the success of the War for Independence. The most sensible strategy was to remain neutral. But the United States's far-flung commerce made that almost impossible.

Federalists Respond to Popular Resistance

Meanwhile, resistance to Hamilton's economic program grew beyond the small group of men involved in national politics. In western Pennsylvania and other frontier areas, many people refused to pay the excise tax on whiskey. Whiskey was of critical importance to their economy. It was not just a traditional beverage—it was one of the only products farmers could make out of corn that could be transported to market without spoiling. Whiskey was so indispensable that it was even used as a kind of currency, like tobacco leaves in colonial Virginia. In 1794 opposition to the whiskey tax was so strong that western Pennsylvania appeared to be in a state of rebellion against the authority of the United States.

This **Whiskey Rebellion** followed the tradition of the Stamp Act and Shays's Rebellion. The rebels closed courts and harassed tax collectors. But President Washington and Secretary Hamilton were determined to crush resistance. They saw the rebellion as an opportunity to demonstrate the power of the United States government. Hamilton himself declared that a government can never be said to be established until it has proved itself by exerting its military force.

In the summer of 1794, Washington gathered an army of over 12,000 men. General "Light Horse Harry" Lee, accompanied by Hamilton himself, led them to the Pittsburgh area. The rebellion soon dissolved. Thousands of uniformed men marching across the Appalachian Mountains had demonstrated to both American citizens and the rest of the world the

ability of the United States to force its citizens to obey its laws.

MAKING CONNECTIONS

Contrast the response of the national government during the Whiskey Rebellion with its response during Shays's Rebellion. What accounts for the difference?

About the time of the Whiskey Rebellion, farmers' protests against Federalist economic plans included this rough drawing. It shows a government agent collecting taxes—in the form of two kegs of whiskey.

The forces sent against the Whiskey Rebellion were awe-inspiring. Two days after Washington had reviewed the gathered troops, shown in the painting above, Hamilton wrote to his wife: "There is not the least appearance of opposition."

Emergence of the Jeffersonians

In 1794 the debate over whether the United States should be neutral in the war between Great Britain and France rose to a fever pitch. Washington and Hamilton decided to reach an agreement with Great Britain, believing that the long-term interests of the United States would be served better by an alliance with Britain than with France. John Jay, Chief Justice of the Supreme Court, went to London and negotiated the Jay Treaty, the effect of which was to commit the United States to favoring the British over the French in commercial and diplomatic matters.

3. ASSESS

Section 1 Review Answers

1. (a) political party, see p. 156, (b) first American party system, see p. 156, (c) excise, see p. 157, (d) tariff, see p. 157, (e) French Revolution, see p. 158, (f) Whiskey Rebellion, see p. 159, (g) precedent, see p. 160

2. Jeffersonian Republicans, see p. 156

3. The goal of Hamilton's financial program was to strengthen outside support for the national government by having it assume the states' war debts, thus transforming the debt into a long-term investment in the United States.

4. Many Americans—slaveholders, planters, commercial farmers, and people distant from urban areas—did not like Hamilton's plans because they objected to the interference of the national government in local and state affairs. They thought the United States had no business regulating the economy, and they disliked taxes.

5. Federalists tended to oppose the French Revolution, seeing it as an example of a democratic revolution gone wrong. The Jeffersonians generally embraced the French Revolution as an extension of the American Revolution. They applauded its rejection of government by kings and its acceptance of republican government.

6. The federal government demonstrated its power and its willingness to use that power against those who defied federal laws. Hamilton had stated that a government can never be said to be established until it has shown its power by exerting its military force.

7. The French Revolution reflected the deep division in the United States between those who favored a strong national government that could impose and maintain order and those who were willing to accept more disorder for the sake of continued liberty from taxes and other forms of strong national control.

Answer to ...

Possible answers: budget issues; how much to spend on defense; whether to trim or expand social programs; whether to legislate in favor of hand-gun control, abortion rights, or environmental protection; how best to foster economic growth; how to reform health care.

Reteach

Ask students to mark with the letter *H* each statement that correctly identifies one of Alexander Hamilton's beliefs or policies.
- Hamilton believed that national government should have strong powers.
- Hamilton had little faith in the people's ability to make good decisions.
- Hamilton wanted the individual states to pay their debts.
- Hamilton did not want the government to impose taxes on its citizens.
- Hamilton thought that the national debt could be a source of strength.

4. CLOSE

Reinforcing the Big Idea

Hamilton, Jefferson, and their respective followers disagreed about the amount of power the national government should have, about taxes and regulation, and about whether the United States should ally itself with France or with Great Britain. Many people believed that the hard-fought election of 1800, described in the next section, would determine the nation's future.

| 1650 | 1700 | 1750 | 1800 | **Links Across Time** | 1850 | 1900 | 1950 | 2000 |

Political Parties Then and Now

During the first years of the new nation, observers such as George Washington were alarmed at the formation of political parties. In his Farewell Address of 1796, Washington warned that the party system "agitates the Community with ill-founded jealousies and false alarms, kindles the animosity of one part against another, [and] foments [stirs up] occasional riot and insurrection." Today, however, people accept political parties as a traditional part of American life. What accounts for this change of outlook?

Part of the answer is that the two major parties of today are very different from parties in Washington's time. The Jeffersonian Republicans and the Federalists mainly clashed over the principles under which the new government would operate. In contrast, the Republicans and Democrats of today share many of the same general principles and beliefs on which American government is based. That is, the Republican and Democratic parties are not primarily principle oriented. Instead, the two major parties are mainly concerned with running the government through the winning of elections, and so are election oriented. *What are some of the political issues that divide the two major parties today?*

The Jay Treaty unleashed a storm of controversy throughout the United States. Many Americans saw it as a betrayal of revolutionary ideals, a sell-out to the hated British. Despite the fury of the opposition, however, Congress ratified the treaty.

The Federalists had established their economic program, suppressed the Whiskey Rebellion, and allied the nation with Great Britain. But in so doing, they had lost the support of a great many Americans. As early as 1793, artisans and professional men were forming what were called Democratic Societies to oppose the Federalists. Meanwhile, Jefferson, Madison, and various state leaders were furiously promoting resistance to the Federalists in letters to one another; some also were encouraging newspaper attacks on the Washington administration.

In the midst of this storm of bitter feelings, President Washington chose not to run for a third term. He thus set a **precedent**—a custom followed in later times though not a written law. Washington's precedent was followed until 1940, when President Franklin D. Roosevelt ran for a third term.

Washington's Vice President, John Adams, ran for President against Thomas Jefferson in 1796. Adams gained a majority of electoral votes; Jefferson finished second. In accordance with the election system established by the Constitution, Jefferson became the new Vice President. President Washington left office in a bit of a huff, warning the nation about the dangers of factionalism—the struggle between factions, or parties. As the next section shows, his warning came none too soon.

SECTION 1 REVIEW

Key Terms, People, and Places
1. Define (a) political party, (b) first American party system, (c) excise, (d) tariff, (e) French Revolution, (f) Whiskey Rebellion, (g) precedent.
2. Identify Jeffersonian Republicans.

Key Concepts
3. What was the major goal of Hamilton's financial program?

4. Who opposed the Federalists, and why?
5. What view did the political parties in the United States take of the French Revolution?
6. What did the federal government demonstrate in its reaction to the Whiskey Rebellion?

Critical Thinking
7. **Identifying Central Issues** Why did the French Revolution divide Americans so sharply?

RESOURCE DIRECTORY

Teaching Resources

Quiz found in the Unit 2 folder, p. 44, covers the main ideas in this section as well as the key terms.

Making Comparisons

Making comparisons means examining two or more ideas, objects, events, or people to discover ways that they are alike and ways they are different. When studying history, being able to make comparisons allows you to evaluate more fully historical periods and specific events or viewpoints.

One way to evaluate an event, idea, or historical period is to compare the views that different people have about it. At right are excerpts from an article by James Madison that appeared in the *National Gazette*, an Anti-Federalist newspaper, and from a statement by Robert Goodloe Harper, a Federalist. Use the following steps to compare their points of view.

1. Identify the basis on which you will make the comparison. It is not possible to compare two or more items that are fundamentally different. Making a comparison is possible only when items share a common concept or characteristic. Read the excerpts below, then answer the following questions. (a) What subject do the statements have in common? (b) When was each statement written? (c) What purpose would a comparison of these statements serve?

2. Determine the ways in which the statements are alike. Making comparisons includes finding similarities between two or more items. Are the statements below similar in their views on the potential value or potential harm of political parties? If so, in what ways are they similar?

3. Determine the ways in which the statements are different. Making comparisons also includes finding any differences that may exist between items. In what fundamental ways do the statements below differ from one another in their views about political parties?

4. Summarize and evaluate your comparison of the statements. Complete the comparison based on similarities and differences. (a) Why does Robert Goodloe Harper view political parties as beneficial? (b) How does Madison imply that parties are a negative influence on government? (c) In your opinion, which statement more accurately describes the state of political parties today?

James Madison

"In every political society, parties are unavoidable. A difference of interests, real or supposed, is the most natural and fruitful source of them. The great object should be to combat the evil: (1) by establishing a political equality among all; (2) by withholding unnecessary opportunities from a few to increase the equality of property . . . ; (3) by the silent operation of laws, which, without violating the rights of property, reduce extreme wealth toward a state of mediocrity [averageness] and raise extreme [poverty] toward a state of comfort; (4) by abstaining from measures which . . . favor one interest at the expense of another; (5) by making one party a check on the other. . . . If this is not the language of reason it is that of republicanism."

From "Parties," by James Madison, in the *National Gazette*, January 23, 1792

Robert Goodloe Harper

"While opposite parties in the Government . . . [struggle] for pre-eminence, they . . . [are] like persons engaged in an exhibition before the public, who are obliged to display superior merit and superior excellence in order to gain the prize. The public is the judge . . . and that party which possesses power must employ it properly, must conduct the government wisely, in order to insure public [approval] and retain their power. In this [competition], while the two parties draw different ways, a middle course is produced generally conformable to public good."

From Robert Goodloe Harper, January 1798, *Annals of Congress*, Fifth Congress, 2d session

---

Historian's Toolbox Activity Making Comparisons: Political Parties, found in the Unit 2 folder, p. 61, helps students compare the relative strengths of present and past political parties.

Critical Thinking

Making Comparisons

Focus Compare historical statements presenting different sides of an issue to learn more about the period and the reasons for people's actions.

Instruct After students have read the selections and worked through the questions, ask them to look for examples of two or more statements about the same topic in newspapers, magazines, or newsletters. Ask students to clip or photocopy the quotations and bring them to class. Display the pairs of statements on a bulletin board, point out grounds for comparison and contrast, and discuss possible evaluations of the statements.

Extend See Historian's Toolbox Activity in the Resource Directory below.

Answers

1. (a) Both statements express views on political parties. (b) Madison, 1792; Harper, 1798. (c) A comparison could clarify some of the positive and negative aspects of political parties from the perspective of individuals who were involved in the debate at the time.

2. The statements are similar in that they both admit that political parties are an inevitable part of American politics.

3. Madison thinks that political parties are unavoidable, but ultimately harmful. Harper thinks that political parties will have a positive effect on government.

4. (a) Harper believes that, in order to gain the public's confidence and retain the public's approval, the party in power will act in ways that display excellence and merit and select a moderate course for the country. (b) Madison writes that "the great object should be to combat the evil," the "evil" being political parties. (c) Possible answers: Political parties today display behavior such as Harper describes during political campaigns; in office, however, they act just as Madison fears.

The Election of 1800: A Turning Point in History

SECTION 2

1. FOCUS

Connecting to the Big Idea

See page 154B. Although the election of 1800 was bitter and raucous, power was peacefully transferred from the Federalists to the Jeffersonians. Ask students to describe how this was accomplished.

Objectives

● Describe the Federalist laws that restricted freedoms and explain the Jeffersonian reaction to those laws.
● Identify Gabriel Prosser and describe his revolt.
● Identify the result of the election of 1800 and explain the significance of the transfer of power from one party to another.

Bellringer

Ask students to rate (on a scale of 1–5, with 1 being the lowest possible score) the importance of the following conditions to presidential campaigns: length of the campaign, honesty of the campaign, relevance of issues raised during the campaign.

Reading Strategy

Predicting Content Have students predict before they read the section who won the election of 1800. Ask them to check their prediction as they read the section.

The Election of 1800: A Turning Point in History

SECTION PREVIEW

With the election of 1800, American leaders peacefully accomplished the nation's first transfer of power from one party to another, a victory for democratic government.

In 1800, during widespread enthusiasm over a turn away from Federalism and back to the republican principles of 1776, an unknown artist painted Liberty feeding the American eagle.

Key Concepts

• Spurred on by a fear of war, the Federalists passed laws restricting freedoms—and the Jeffersonians reacted angrily.
• Gabriel Prosser, with other African Americans, planned a revolt to win freedom for enslaved people in Virginia.
• White American men had the option of voting to determine their political future, and they exercised it in 1800 by electing Jefferson.

Key Terms, People, and Places

XYZ Affair, Alien and Sedition Acts of 1798; Gabriel Prosser, midnight judges

---

From the beginning of the Adams administration, the United States began to drift toward war with France. Hoping to settle disagreements over the Jay Treaty, shipping, and other issues, Adams sent officials to Paris to negotiate with the revolutionary government. The French met them not with diplomats, however, but with secret agents, later identified only as X, Y, and Z, who asked for a bribe of $250,000 and a loan to the French of $10 million. Though such a request was common practice in European diplomacy, it outraged Americans and became notorious as the **XYZ Affair.** The slogan "Millions for defense, but not one cent for tribute" rang out in the United States. By 1798 France and the United States were involved in what amounted to an undeclared war, firing on and seizing one another's ships on the high seas.

The Federalists Act and the Jeffersonians React

The Federalists took advantage of the war crisis to press even stronger measures through Congress. Among these were an increase in the size of the army, higher taxes to support the army and navy, and the **Alien and Sedition Acts of 1798.** Under the Alien Act, the President gained the right to imprison or deport citizens of other countries residing in the United States. Under the Sedition Act, persons who wrote, published, or said anything "of a false, scandalous, and malicious" nature against the government of the United States or its agents were subject to heavy fines and imprisonment. In other words, it was against the law to criticize government officials unless you could prove everything you said. The Federalists used the Sedition Act to muzzle their critics.

Jefferson and Madison responded to these actions with the Virginia and Kentucky resolutions. Adopted by the legislatures of those two states, in essence these resolutions argued that the people, acting through their states, had the right to judge whether federal laws agreed with the Constitution. Neither Virginia nor Kentucky tried to enforce these laws, but their defiance of federal power was clear enough.

Both Federalists and Jeffersonian Republicans were angry by the late 1790s. Congressmen were physically assaulting each other in the House of Representatives. Crowds taunted President Adams, forcing him to enter the presidential

---

RESOURCE DIRECTORY

Teaching Resources

Reproducible Lesson Plan found in the Unit 2 folder, p. 39, provides a summary of the Section 2 lesson plan content.

Alternate Lesson Plan: Learning Styles found in the Alternate Lesson Plans folder, p. 28, guides pairs of students in preparing campaign materials for Adams or Jefferson, and helps students—particularly

visual or auditory learners—understand the importance of the election of 1800.

Guided Reading and Review found in the Unit 2 folder, p. 45, provides a structure for reading and mastering the key concepts and reviewing the key terms for Section 2. (Guided Practice)

residence in Philadelphia through the back door. In Virginia, Jeffersonians drank a toast calling for "a speedy death to General Washington."

As the presidential election loomed, many people believed that the future of the nation was at stake. Would the nation tilt toward what Jefferson called "the Spirit of 1776," the ideal of liberty found in the Declaration of Independence, or toward the Spirit of 1787, the emphasis on order stated in the Constitution? Before the election took place, however, another event in the summer of 1800 demonstrated the limits of the gains made in the American Revolution.

Gabriel Prosser's Rebellion

Although barred from any participation in the emerging political system, enslaved African Americans embraced the discussion of liberty all around them. After all, no Americans had a better appreciation of the importance of human rights than those who were enslaved.

In the area around Richmond, Virginia, a blacksmith named **Gabriel Prosser** and several other enslaved people planned a revolution of their own, later called Gabriel's Rebellion. They elected Prosser as their leader and planned to lead the enslaved in an overthrow of their white masters. One rebel stated: "I will fight for my freedom as long as I have breath, and that is as much as any man can do."

The plan called for about two hundred men to take over Richmond, terrorize its inhabitants into submission, capture arms, and take Governor James Monroe as a hostage. The goal was simple and straightforward—freedom. Recalled Prosser's coconspirator, Ben Woolfolk: "All the whites were to be massacred, except the Quakers, the Methodists, and the Frenchmen, and they were to be spared on account . . . of their being friendly to liberty."

But Prosser's small-scale revolution failed. Betrayed by a deserter and hampered by torrential rains, the rebels were caught and tried by the Commonwealth of Virginia. At least twenty of them, including Prosser, were executed. At the trial, one defendant said, "I have adventured my life in endeavoring to obtain the liberty of my countrymen, and am a willing sacrifice to their cause."

DOCUMENTS RESPECTING THE INSURRECTION OF THE SLAVES.

— (CONTINUED.) —

Communications of Ben, alias Ben Woodfork.

The first time I ever heard of this conspiracy was from Mrs. Anne Smith's George. The second person that gave me information was Samuel, alias Samuel Bird, the property of Mrs. Jane Clark. They asked me last night to come over to their houses on a Friday

Using Historical Evidence In meetings at night, Gabriel Prosser encouraged his followers to adopt the ideas about liberty that had sparked the American Revolution. *Based on Woolfolk's statement, given in this 1803 account, where did he meet the other members of the conspiracy?*

MAKING CONNECTIONS

The Jeffersonian Republicans, although defenders of liberty, largely ignored the issues raised by Prosser's rebellion. In what way was the attitude of the Jeffersonians a continuation of the original Spirit of 1776?

The Election of 1800

By contrast with enslaved African Americans, in 1800 many white male Americans had the option of resolving at the ballot box the issue of their own political revolt against the Federalists. Rather than relying on violence to make their point, as they had in the American Revolution, citizens turned the presidential election into a decision on the nature of their government as a whole. It was as clear a choice about governmental direction as Americans have ever made.

Who Won and Who Lost The loser was President John Adams. In a way, the defeat was an

2. INSTRUCT

Explain/Discuss

Explain that Jefferson called the election of 1800 "as real a revolution in the principles of our government as that of 1776 was in its form." The Federalists moved out and the Jeffersonians moved in.

Ask students to summarize the reasons behind the Federalist Alien and Sedition Acts and the effects of those laws. Then have them describe the Jeffersonian response to the acts.

Discuss the reasons for Prosser's revolt. Ask students to think about and list reasons why Prosser failed.

Caption Answer to . . .

Using Historical Evidence

At the homes of Mrs. Anne Smith and Mrs. Jane Clark.

Answer to . . .

MAKING CONNECTIONS

The original Spirit of 1776 called for liberty for a particular group: white males. In ignoring the issues raised by Prosser's Rebellion, Jeffersonian Republicans demonstrated that they still had not come to see the ideas of the Declaration of Independence as applying to all groups within the nation.

Media and Technology

Visions of America: Turning Point Story To enhance students' understanding of the Turning Point topic in this section, play "Natural Aristocracy," a story about party politics prior to the election of 1800 (length: approximately 4 minutes). This selection can be located on side 1 of the videodiscs. This selection can also be located on videotape 1. Lesson plans for Turning Point stories can be found in the Visions of America Guidebook.

Visions of America: Roundtable Discussion To introduce students to different and differing viewpoints on the Turning Point topic in this section, play all or part of the Roundtable Discussion on "Natural Aristocracy," remarks by respected historians and social commentators. This selection can be located on side 1 of the videodiscs. This selection can also be located on videotape 1.

Analyze

Tell students that Adams won all electoral votes of the New England states. The Federalists took the southern votes. Ask students to speculate about the meaning and future effects of such sectional division.

Activity

Cooperative Learning

Time: One class period.
Activity: Simulate live television coverage of the House balloting for President during the election of 1800.
Grouping: Four to six students.
Purpose: To re-create the tension and impact of the balloting for President in the House of Representatives, reporters should interview Jefferson, Hamilton, and members of the House.
Roles: Reporters, members of the House, Jefferson, Hamilton, a producer.
Outcome: Students will identify key issues of the election of 1800 through interviews with Jefferson, Hamilton, and members of the House.

In Depth

Historical Misconceptions

It is often assumed that because women could not vote (except in New Jersey for a couple of decades after the American Revolution), they had no interest in politics. But diaries and letters of middle-class women in the early 1800s reveal strong opinions about the struggles of the Federalists and the Jeffersonian Republicans. Rosalie Siters Calvert of Maryland wrote: "Our politics are going badly. Jacobinism and democracy increase every day. [President Jefferson] really is a fool, full of vanity and desire to pass himself off as a philosopher and a great man."

During the presidential campaign of 1800, each side attacked the other bitterly. In this Federalist cartoon, Jefferson is about to destroy the Constitution and lead the nation into violence like that of the French (Gallic) Revolution. God, detecting the crime, sends a Federalist eagle to save the nation.

unfair judgment on his abilities. Adams was more devoted to public service and, some historians believe, more personally honest than most Presidents. Rising above Federalist hostility to France, he had sent a second diplomatic mission to that country in 1799, which had cooled tensions considerably. Like most decisive Presidents, however, Adams failed to appease his critics and angered many of his supporters.

John Adams (above), an outspoken and decisive Federalist President, was driven out of office after only one term when the Federalists and Jeffersonian Republicans clashed in the election of 1800.

The winner was Thomas Jefferson. By 1800 Jefferson was the acknowledged leader of those who preferred local to national government and who believed it was better to risk too much liberty than suffer from too much government. Jefferson always denied that he was a politician; he never saw himself as working to build a permanent political party. Nevertheless, that is exactly what he did.

The Election Process The personal attacks and negative campaigning of elections today are nothing new. The election of 1800

was truly a nasty campaign. Jeffersonian newspapers accused Adams of being a monarchist, a terrible insult at the time. Federalists, on the other hand, asserted that Jefferson was a godless man who would lead the United States into chaos. ✪

Jefferson won the popular vote in balloting that took place in December 1800. He was unable to get a majority in the Electoral College, however. Despite the fact that the Jeffersonians had won most of the seats in the new Congress, the old House of Representatives—mostly Federalist—had to decide who would be President. Even before the voting began in the House on February 11, 1801, it was clear that no candidate could get a majority immediately.

Although the political system was controlled by men, women watched the drawn-out voting process with equal interest. The wife of Representative Craik of Maryland told him bluntly that she would divorce him if he did not cast his vote for Jefferson. Margaret Bayard Smith, the wife of a newspaper editor, later described both the scene at the Capitol and her own feelings as she awaited the news:

I t was an awful crisis. The people, who with such an overwhelming majority had declared their will, would never peaceably have allowed the man of their choice to be set aside. . . . A civil war must have taken place. . . . Crowds . . . from the adjacent county and cities thronged to the seat of government and hung like a thunder cloud over the Capitol. . . . That night I never lay down or closed my eyes. As the hour drew near its close, my heart would almost audibly beat.

On February 17, only a few days before the end of Adams's term, the House of Representatives finally elected Jefferson as the third President of the United States on the thirty-sixth ballot. Wrote Margaret Smith: "The dark and threatening cloud which had hung over the political horizon rolled harmlessly away."

Federalist Salvage Efforts After the election, it was clear that the Federalists would control neither the executive branch nor the legislative

RESOURCE DIRECTORY

Teaching Resources

✪ 📄 **American Profiles Activity** found in the Unit 2 folder, p. 57, profiles Noah Webster, an active Federalist who compiled a comprehensive dictionary of American English in 1828.

branch. Before he left office, John Adams acted to save some power for the Federalists in the judicial branch. With the help of Federalists in Congress, Adams reduced the size of the Supreme Court to five members and chose many federal judges, known as the **midnight judges** because they were selected at the very end of the presidential term. These Federalist appointees would hold office long after Adams's term ran out—in fact, for as long as they lived. The most important of them was John Marshall of Virginia, a Federalist who despised Jefferson; he became Chief Justice of the Supreme Court. After signing these appointments, President Adams left Washington, D.C., in disgust, refusing to be present at Jefferson's inauguration.

New Jersey law allowed women to vote until 1808. During the crucial election of 1800, they helped Jefferson win the state and sent a full slate of Jeffersonian Republicans to Congress. When the election had to be decided in the House of Representatives, New Jersey was one of eight states that stood by Jefferson throughout the balloting.

A Revolution Without Violence

Washington, D.C., in 1801 seemed very much like the Federalists' plans in general: grand and unfinished. The new capital designed by L'Enfant with broad boulevards and Roman buildings was little more than a swamp with muddy, rutted roads and half-completed structures. Here, on March 4, 1801, Thomas Jefferson took the oath of office administered by Adams's appointee, Chief Justice Marshall.

With this inauguration, the Federalist leaders of the young republic proved that they could do what so many leaders in other times and places have found so difficult. Although few on either side could forget their bitter disagreements and personal hatreds, the Federalists did step down and let the Jeffersonian Republicans take over. Whether they stood for the Spirit of 1776 or the Spirit of 1787, Americans had proved that they could transfer power from one party to another—and do it peacefully.

SECTION 2 REVIEW

Key Terms, People, and Places
1. Define (a) XYZ Affair, (b) Alien and Sedition Acts.
2. Identify (a) Gabriel Prosser, (b) midnight judges.

Key Concepts
3. What principle did the Virginia and Kentucky resolutions endorse, and why were they passed?
4. What did Gabriel's Rebellion have in common with the American Revolution?

5. Why was the election of 1800 a turning point in the history of the United States?

Critical Thinking
6. **Recognizing Ideologies** How does the Sedition Act reflect the Federalists' position in the controversy between those who favored liberty and those who favored order?

 Quiz found in the Unit 2 folder, p. 46, covers the main ideas in this section as well as the key terms.

Enrichment
Ask students to write a short biography of Aaron Burr. Have them research his fascinating career, including his role in the election of 1800.

3. ASSESS

Section 2 Review Answers
1. (a) XYZ Affair, see p. 162, (b) Alien and Sedition Acts of 1798, see p. 162

2. (a) Gabriel Prosser, see p. 163, (b) midnight judges, see p. 165

3. They argued that the people, acting through their states, had the right to judge whether federal laws agreed with the Constitution. They were passed in response to Federalist laws restricting the right to free speech.

4. As in the American Revolution, people acted not just for themselves but for posterity. Men organized and voted in the name of liberty.

5. The election of 1800 was a significant victory for the political system that was emerging in the United States. Rather than relying on violence to make their point, citizens turned the presidential election into a decision on the very nature of their government.

6. It was a clear statement that the overall good of the national government was of more importance to the Federalists than the right of the individual to speak freely.

Reteach
Ask students to answer each of the following questions:
- Who were the candidates in the election of 1800?
- What parties did they represent?
- Who won the election?
- Why was the election significant?

4. CLOSE

Reinforcing the Big Idea

The bitter and closely contested election of 1800 showed that power could peacefully pass from one party to another. In the next section, students will learn how President Jefferson performed in office.

The Lasting Impact of the Election of 1800

Focus: The election of 1800 was the first in which two strong political factions opposed each other. Although some predicted that the result of the election of 1800 would be civil war rather than a new President, Jefferson finally did become the new chief executive, marking the defeat of the Federalists and the rise of the Jeffersonians. What has been the lasting impact of the election of 1800?

Instruct Tell students that during the election of 1800, one pamphlet put out by the Jeffersonians asked, "Is it not high time for a CHANGE?" Although we are used to the challenging party insisting on the value of change from the incumbent party, in 1800 the idea of such a change was unprecedented.

Ask students how the peaceful transfer of power allowed politics to flourish. Once the voters and the nation's leaders showed that they could use ballots and abide by their results, dissent became less charged.

Ask students to use a list of Presidents to count how many times the nation has transferred the office of President from one political party to another.

Discuss with students what might have happened if the Federalists had somehow managed to invalidate the election results or rig the election to remain in power. What options would have been open to anti-Federalists to remove them from office? Would there have been an election of 1804?

Extend Ask students to create a political cartoon about the election of 1800. The cartoon may support either Adams or Jefferson or may celebrate the peaceful transfer of power from one party to another.

The Lasting Impact of the Election of 1800

What were the long-term consequences when the Jeffersonian Republicans won the election of 1800 and took office? The answer lies in the peaceful transfer of power from one group to another and the gradual understanding that diversity could strengthen, rather than destroy, the nation.

The Transfer of Power

The real winner of the election of 1800 was the Constitution of the United States, simply because it survived. As late as February 16, several representatives were heard to proclaim they would "go without a constitution and take the risk of civil war" rather than vote for "such a wretch as Jefferson." The governors of Virginia and Pennsylvania, both Jeffersonians, were on alert, probably intending to respond with troops if the Federalists acted against the will of the people. Had that happened, it is impossible to know what the consequences would have been on the United States of today.

Jefferson himself described the crisis and its significance in a letter shortly after his election.

We can no longer say there is nothing new under the sun. For this whole chapter in the history of man is new. . . . The order & good sense displayed in this recovery from delusion, and in the momentous crisis which lately arose, really bespeak a strength of character in our nation which augurs well [foretells a good future] for the duration of our Republic; & I am much better satisfied now of its stability than I was before it was tried.

With this example of a peaceful exchange of power to look back upon, American democracy gained a maturity that today we take for granted.

1800 Despite Federalists' fears, "Mad Tom" Jefferson does not pull down the federal government, as this cartoon predicts.

1880s–1890s Candidates for President continue to broaden their appeal to the people.

1800	1840	1880

1824 A smooth transfer of power occurs even though the House of Representatives elects John Quincy Adams as President in defiance of the popular vote for Andrew Jackson.

RESOURCE DIRECTORY

Teaching Resources

Turning Points Extension Activity
The Lasting Impact of the Election of 1800, found in the Unit 2 folder, pp. 53–54, allows students to discover the relevance of the principles of order and liberty in their lives through a mock council election and debate.

A Political Revolution

Another consequence of the election was that the nation turned from the Federalist interest in order to the Jeffersonian insistence upon liberty. In later years, Jefferson called the election of 1800 "as real a revolution in the principles of our government as that of 1776 was in its form."

The Federalists, too, felt the force of the change. A Federalist newspaper in Boston printed this obituary notice in a black border:

> *YESTERDAY EXPIRED*
> *Deeply regretted by MILLIONS of grateful*
> *Americans,*
> *And by all GOOD MEN,*
> *The Federal Administration*
> *of the*
> *GOVERNMENT of the* United States

A Lesson in Party Politics

The contest between liberty and order would later resume, but first another party besides that of the Federalists would have to arise. Although the Federalists attempted a comeback in the next few

1941 *Demonstrating continued national unity despite party differences, Congress approves President Roosevelt's call for a declaration of war.*

elections, they had little chance of success. As the observer Noah Webster remarked at the time, "They have attempted to resist the force of current public opinion, instead of falling into the current with a view to direct it." The long-term result? Never again would a political party hope to gain power by telling the people it was wiser than they were. From then to modern times, politicians have appealed to the people, no matter whose interests they actually represented.

It can be argued that the most enduring change brought by the election of 1800 was the one that was slowest to take effect. Gradually, as the decades passed, Americans would take to heart the lesson of the election—learning that differences of opinion would not destroy the nation, and that no matter what politics Americans profess, they are still Americans united under the Constitution. As Jefferson himself said in his inaugural address,

> *Every difference of opinion is not a difference of principle. . . . We are all republicans; we are all federalists.*

REVIEWING THE FACTS

1. What was the "real winner" of the election of 1800?
2. How did the failure of the Federalists influence later politics?

Critical Thinking

3. **Distinguishing Fact from Opinion** When Jefferson called the election of 1800 a revolution, was he stating a fact or voicing an opinion? Explain your reasoning.

1920 1960 2000

1992 *The forty-second change of Presidents follows the pattern for a smooth transition set after the election of 1800.*

TURNING POINTS

Answers

1. The "real winner" of the election of 1800 was the Constitution of the United States, simply because it survived.

2. Never again would a political party hope to gain power by telling the people it was wiser than they were.

3. Answers should recognize that Jefferson was stating his opinion; others might not see the transfer of power from Federalists to Jeffersonian Republicans as deserving of such an extreme statement.

SECTION 3

1. FOCUS

Connecting to the Big Idea

See page 154B. Although President Jefferson was able to carry out much of his agenda to reduce the influence of the national government on the lives of Americans, he was also willing to use his powers as President and even to expand them. Ask for what purposes Jefferson used the powers of government.

Objectives

● Describe how Jefferson reduced the influence of government during his first term.
● Explain how the Supreme Court gained the vital power of judicial review.
● Identify the territory purchased from France with Jefferson's authorization.
● Explain why Jefferson outlawed trade with Great Britain and France in 1807.

Bellringer

Have students consider the following question: Under what circumstances might reversing one's opinion be a sign of flexibility and strength? When might sticking to an opinion be a sign of weakness?

Reading Strategy

Predicting Content Write the section headings on the chalkboard. Ask students to think of at least two questions about each heading and to look for answers to their questions as they read.

The Jefferson Administration

SECTION PREVIEW

Jefferson succeeded in reversing much of the Federalist program, yet demonstrated the government's power when he restricted the nation's trade with other countries.

Key Concepts

• Jefferson's program of reducing the power of the national government made him highly popular at first.
• During the Jefferson administration, the Supreme Court gained the vital new power of reviewing laws to make sure that they did not conflict with the Constitution.
• Jefferson set the stage for future expansion with a new federal land policy and the purchase of a huge amount of western land from France.
• In 1807 Jefferson outlawed trade with France and Britain to punish those countries for their warlike actions.

Although Jefferson's morning clothes may not seem casual by the standard of today's fashions, in the early 1800s they made a powerful statement against formality, as did his administration in general.

Key Terms, People, and Places

Marbury v. *Madison*, judicial review, Louisiana Purchase, Embargo of 1807; John Marshall; Northwest Territory

---

O ne day during Jefferson's first term, the ambassador of King George III, dressed in a fancy uniform and driven in a coach, visited the President for the first time to present his credentials. When the ambassador's servant knocked on the door of the White House, who should answer it but President Jefferson himself, wearing his casual morning clothes and shabby slippers. What was the reason behind this striking informality? Thomas Jefferson was as cultured a man as ever resided in the White House. By

personally answering the door, without attention to customary procedure, he was purposely demonstrating the democratic style of his new government. The President, Jefferson believed, was simply the first among equals, only temporarily the most important of his fellow citizens. ⊙

Jefferson's Program at Home

Thomas Jefferson entered office with a straightforward agenda. His goal was to reduce the influence of the national government in the lives of the American people. Jefferson believed that "the sum of good government" was

a wise and frugal [minimal] Government, which shall restrain men from injuring one another, shall leave them otherwise free to regulate their own pursuits of industry and improvement, and shall not take from the mouth of labor the bread it has earned.

Domestic Politics To accomplish these goals, Jefferson reversed much of what the Federalists had done, starting with matters of presidential style. He refused to deliver speeches to Congress, claiming that to do so would seem too much like the act of a king. And he finally resolved a question that had troubled Congress—what to call the President—by asking to be addressed simply as "Mr. President."

Of course, Jefferson's effect on government, like that of Washington and Hamilton, went beyond style. Together with Congress, he reduced the amount of taxes paid by the American people and severely cut the size of the federal bureaucracy and the armed forces. The attorney general, for instance, was not even allowed a clerk; the army was reduced from 12,000 soldiers to only 3,000. Jefferson's goal was to stop the national government from being an intimidating presence in people's lives.

▶ RESOURCE DIRECTORY

Teaching Resources

▢ **Reproducible Lesson Plan** found in the Unit 2 folder, p. 40, provides a summary of the Section 3 lesson plan content.

▢ **Alternate Lesson Plan: Critical Thinking** Predicting Consequences, found in the Alternate Lesson Plans folder, p. 29, enhances students' ability to use this skill by charting Jefferson's foreign and domestic policies and their consequences.

▢ **Guided Reading and Review** found in the Unit 2 folder, p. 47, provides a structure for reading and mastering the key concepts and reviewing the key terms for Section 3. (Guided Practice)

⊙ ▢ **Visual Learning Activity** Honoring Thomas Jefferson, found in the Unit 2 folder, p. 69, features a picture of Thomas Jefferson's monument, which reveals the accomplishments for which Jefferson most wanted to be remembered.

Still, Jefferson did not intend to destroy the government created by the Constitution, or even to undo all the acts of the Federalists. For example, he let the Bank of the United States created by Hamilton continue to function, knowing that its twenty-year term would run out in 1811.

Jefferson's program made him an immensely popular President during his first term. In 1804, when he overwhelmingly won reelection, he even received the electoral votes of the staunchly Federalist state of Massachusetts. Indeed, the Federalists seemed to be disappearing. Many were older men who simply abandoned politics and retired to private life.

Jefferson was lucky as well as popular. His biggest rivals were his ambitious Vice President, Aaron Burr, and Alexander Hamilton, now a lawyer in New York. In the summer of 1804, Burr killed Hamilton in a duel. With one shot, Burr removed the leader of the Federalists and made himself a criminal. Although he was never tried, and even continued to preside over the Senate after the duel, Burr was never again a serious challenge to Jefferson.

Judicial Review The most controversial part of Jefferson's first term was his relationship with the judicial branch, particularly the Supreme Court. The Constitution had left the organization and role of this branch of government extremely vague. Congress had filled in some of the details with the Judiciary Act of 1789 and the Judiciary Act of 1801. But the role of the judges was not entirely clear. Believing that Federalist judges were thwarting the will of the people who had voted to change their government in 1800, the Jefferson administration tried to block the action of the courts by various means. This campaign largely failed, however.

The case of *Marbury* v. *Madison* arose out of just such an attempt to block the activities of Federalist judges. President Adams had appointed William Marbury a justice of the peace for the District of Columbia just before he left office. But Secretary of State James Madison, under orders from President Jefferson, never delivered Marbury's commission, the official papers giving Marbury his authority. Marbury sued Madison, demanding that the Supreme Court order the secretary of state to let him take

his office. According to the Judiciary Act of 1789, the Court had the power to do this. But the Chief Justice, **John Marshall,** ruled that it was against the Constitution for the Supreme Court to give this order to the executive branch. In other words, Marshall declared part of the Judiciary Act of 1789 unconstitutional—the first time a federal court had been so bold.

Marshall knew that as a practical matter he could not force Madison to deliver the commission. But he was cleverly able to gain power for the Court out of a case that might otherwise only have confirmed the Court's weakness. His decision upheld the Jefferson administration but established the power of **judicial review,** under which federal courts review laws and if necessary declare them unconstitutional. Though today this is a vital power of the judicial branch, the principle of judicial review is not clearly stated anywhere in the Constitution.

MAKING CONNECTIONS

Judicial review protects the people from unconstitutional laws made by Congress and the President. Explain the position Jeffersonian Republicans would be likely to take on this principle.

Jefferson's Program in the West

In the early 1800s, the Jeffersonian Republicans used the power of the national government to aid the expansion of the United States into the Native American lands of the trans-Appalachian West.

Creating States on the Frontier The United States had developed a national policy regarding this region even before taking possession of it. The Land Ordinance of 1785 provided for the regular survey and sale of Native American land northwest of the Ohio River, called the **Northwest Territory,** or the Old Northwest, to distinguish it from the present-day Northwest. (See "Time and Place: Moving the East to the West," pages 172–173.) The Northwest Ordinance of 1787 established a process by which

John Marshall (above) was the Chief Justice of the Supreme Court for thirty-four years, handing down decisions in 1,106 cases. One observer said that Marshall could understand a case with "a single glance of his mind."

2. INSTRUCT

Discuss

Discuss the ways in which Jefferson was able to reduce the influence of the national government. Why were those steps almost guaranteed to make him popular with voters?

Now ask students to list the ways in which Jefferson used and expanded the power of the national government. Ask students to state in their own words Jefferson's dilemma concerning the Louisiana Purchase.

Discuss the reasons for the failure of the Embargo of 1807. Ask students why Jefferson wanted the embargo. Why were Britain and France largely unaffected by it?

Answer to ...

MAKING CONNECTIONS

Jeffersonian Republicans would probably have favored judicial review, thinking it would limit the number of laws imposed on citizens and also tend to reinforce a strict construction of the Constitution. It can be argued, however, that Jeffersonian Republicans would see judicial review as the tool of an unelected branch of government, contradicting the Constitution's guarantee of representative government.

In Depth

Biography

Chief Justice John Marshall (1755–1855) was licensed to practice law by his cousin Thomas Jefferson. But Marshall, stating a firm belief in "a more efficient and better organized general government," embarked upon a lifelong crusade against the Jeffersonian cause of states' rights. One hundred years after his death, a scholar said that Marshall "embodied in his career clear proof that ours is a government of men, not of laws."

Ask why the power of the Supreme Court to judge a law's constitutionality is important to the United States system of government. How does this power help the Supreme Court to check the power of Congress?

Activity

Presenting a Monologue

Ask students to write or prepare to deliver a brief monologue on the final outcome of *Marbury* v. *Madison* by one of the following figures in the case: President Jefferson, Chief Justice Marshall, potential judge William Marbury, Secretary of State Madison.

Enrichment

Jefferson commissioned Lewis and Clark to explore and map the Louisiana Territory. Ask students to research and report on the instructions Jefferson gave to the two explorers and to map the route they took.

Caption Answer to ...

 Interpreting Maps

The Missouri, the Platte, the Arkansas, the Red.

3. ASSESS

Section 3 Review Answers

1. (a) Louisiana Purchase, see p. 170, (b) Embargo of 1807, see p. 170

2. John Marshall, see p. 169

3. Northwest Territory, see p. 169

4. Jefferson reversed much of what the Federalists had done. He refused to deliver speeches to Congress and asked to be addressed as "Mr. President." He reduced taxes and severely cut the size of the federal bureaucracy, including the army and navy.

5. Judicial review refers to the power of the federal courts to declare laws unconstitutional. It was established by the Supreme Court in *Marbury* v. *Madison.*

territories, as lands in the West were called, could become states.

The Jeffersonians sped the development of the frontier through a new federal land policy. Under the Land Act of 1800, Americans were able to get land in relatively small parcels and on credit. Federal land offices appeared across the West, making easier the transfer of land from the United States government to its citizens.

The Louisiana Purchase To develop the West, the Mississippi River, a vital trade route, had to be kept open. But the French had taken over much of the Spanish land in the West and controlled the mouth of the Mississippi at New Orleans. In 1803 Jefferson sent James Monroe to Paris to buy the city of New Orleans from the French government. The French, however, offered to sell not just New Orleans, but French claims to the vast area of Native American land shown on the map below. ⭐

When Jefferson heard of the French proposal, he was at first troubled because the Constitution did not allow for purchase of new lands beyond the Mississippi River. He over-

came his doubts, however, and urged Congress to complete the sale. Although the **Louisiana Purchase** dramatically increased the national debt, it also doubled the size of United States claims with the stroke of a pen.

Jefferson's Foreign Policy

During Jefferson's first term, a brief peace settled on European nations. Although Jefferson would have preferred to keep the United States completely out of European affairs, Americans simply were trading too much with Europeans for him to do so.

The Jay Treaty, under which the United States favored trade with Great Britain, expired in 1805. By then, Europeans were back at war with each other. French warships began harassing American ships trading with Britain, and British ships interfered with American ships trading with France. The British also impressed, or kidnapped, American sailors to serve in their navy. In 1807 a British ship, the *Leopard*, attacked the U.S.S. *Chesapeake*, inflicted twenty-one casualties, and boarded it to search for deserters from His Majesty's navy.

Jefferson, like other Americans, was outraged by these acts and believed that they should not go unpunished. At his insistence, Congress passed the **Embargo of 1807,** halting all commerce with Europeans. Refusing to use military force—both on principle and because the United States had no real navy—Jefferson instead tried economic pressure to force both the British and the French to back off. The idea was that Americans would not trade with either of them until they behaved in a more civilized fashion. The embargo, or restriction on trade with other countries, hurt Britain, but that nation's economy and trade had grown too strong and diverse to be severely injured by such a boycott. The French, too, were largely unaffected.

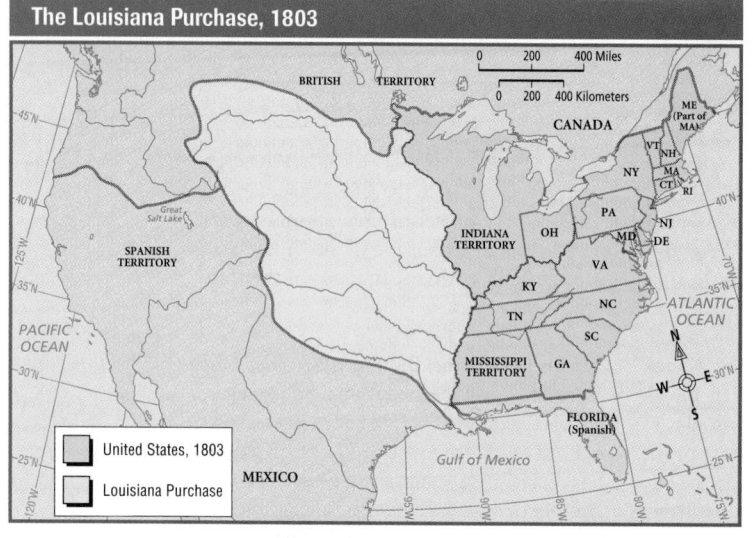

The Louisiana Purchase, 1803

United States, 1803

Louisiana Purchase

Geography and History: Interpreting Maps
By purchasing Louisiana, the United States asserted a claim to a huge portion of Native American land in North America. The Louisiana Purchase included not only land, however, but a vast natural highway system: the many rivers that drain into the Mississippi. *Identify three such rivers.*

▶ RESOURCE DIRECTORY

Teaching Resources

⭐ **Primary Source Activity** Napoleon Sells Louisiana, found in the Unit 2 folder, pp. 63–64, includes excerpts from Lucien Bonaparte's *Memoires* to give insight into the Louisiana Purchase.

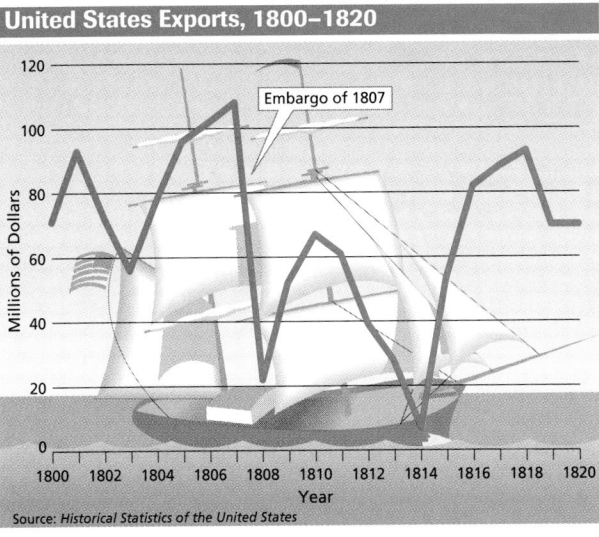

United States Exports, 1800–1820

Embargo of 1807

Source: *Historical Statistics of the United States*

Interpreting Graphs
The Embargo of 1807 sharply cut United States export trade. *What was the level of trade before the embargo? What was the level of trade after the embargo? Did export trade return to its pre-embargo high during the period covered by the graph? Before the embargo, what was the general trend in exports during the Jefferson administration?*

During the Embargo of 1807, smuggling increased dramatically. In the cartoon below, a smuggler is being caught by the turtle Ograbme —"Embargo" spelled backwards. In a later cartoon on the same theme, however, the turtle nabbed Jefferson's successor, President James Madison.

Many Americans, on the other hand, hated the embargo—particularly New Englanders who made their living through trade. They now smuggled goods to Great Britain and other countries in defiance of the President and Congress. With the authority of the national government at stake, Jefferson had no alternative but to use his little gunboat navy and federal agents to enforce the law. In some ways, the enforcement of the embargo was Jefferson's version of the suppression of the Whiskey Rebellion.

Jefferson's general political success ended with the embargo. Many Americans despised the direct interference of the national government in the economy. Federalists exploited this anger, and the party enjoyed a revival. While Jefferson was able to see his secretary of state, James Madison, elected President in 1808, he retired to Monticello an unpopular figure. Neither Jefferson nor Madison could resolve the nation's differences with two major powers that soon would make war on the United States—the Native Americans in the West, and the British to the east.

SECTION 3 REVIEW

Key Terms, People, and Places
1. Define (a) Louisiana Purchase, (b) Embargo of 1807.
2. Identify John Marshall.
3. Identify Northwest Territory.

Key Concepts
4. Describe the changes Jefferson made in the effect of government on the people.
5. What is judicial review, and how was it established?

6. In what ways did the national government influence the development of the trans-Appalachian West?
7. Why was Jefferson unpopular when he left office?

Critical Thinking
8. **Making Comparisons** How was the enforcement of the Embargo of 1807 like the suppression of the Whiskey Rebellion?

Quiz found in the Unit 2 folder, p. 48, covers the main ideas in this section as well as the key terms.

Media and Technology

Transparency
Historical Maps, L-2

---

6. The Northwest Ordinance of 1787 established the process by which territories could become states. Under the Land Act of 1800, Americans were able to get land in relatively small parcels and on credit. The Louisiana Purchase doubled the size of the United States.

7. Jefferson became unpopular because of his foreign policy. Many Americans, particularly New Englanders who made their living through trade, hated the embargo against the British and French. In addition, many Americans despised the direct interference of the national government in the economy.

8. Possible answers: Both the Whiskey Rebellion and resistance to the embargo were expressions of popular outrage over government interference in the lives of ordinary citizens, suppression of which required the use of the national government's superior firepower.

Caption Answer to ...

Interpreting Graphs

1807: $108 million; 1808: $22 million; no; the trend was a rising one.

Reteach
Ask students to rewrite each of the following incorrect statements.
• Jefferson was able to purchase Louisiana from France because the Constitution gives the President the power to acquire territory.
• Jefferson convinced Congress to outlaw all trade with Europeans to keep Americans from attacking French and British ships.

4. CLOSE

Reinforcing the Big Idea
While Jefferson was successful in undoing some of the Federalists' programs, he also used the power of his office to make the Louisiana Purchase and to restrict trade with European countries. The next section discusses Native American resistance to the expansion of the United States into their territory.

Moving the East to the West

Focus In this section students will examine how the location of Marietta, Ohio, the first settlement in the western lands of the United States, contributed to its success, and how the characteristics of the New Englanders who built the new town endured.

Instruct Ask students if any of them have lived in, or visited, another part of the country. Discuss the types of distinct differences that exist between their former and present communities. Ask students what might account for such differences.

Before students read the feature, you might want to review the descriptions of New England society and New England towns given in Chapter 2. Point out that in some ways, Marietta became just like a New England town.

Explain that Marietta was the first of a number of Ohio towns begun by New Englanders. As a first step, prospective settlers formed covenants with one another that resembled those made by their ancestors upon first reaching the shores of Massachusetts. The New England settlers of Oberlin, Ohio, for example, pledged one another to "a life of simplicity, to special devotion to church and school, and to earnest labor in the missionary cause." (Quoted in Smith, Page. *The Shaping of America, A People's History of the Young Republic,* Vol. 3. McGraw-Hill, 1980, p. 735.) Similarly, when twenty-four members of the Congregational Church of Granville, Massachusetts, decided to emigrate to Ohio, they first signed a covenant. They took a minister and church deacons to what became Granville, Ohio.

Like Granville, many towns in Ohio were named for New England towns (which, of course, may have been named for places in England). Ask students to use road maps (or other detailed maps) of New England and Ohio to find other place names in Ohio that seem to be based on place names in New England. Students can then consult a geographical atlas to find out

Moving the East to the West

Marietta, Ohio, was the first major United States settlement on the western frontier. How did settlers go about remaking the wilderness of Ohio into the kind of land they knew?

After the American Revolution, the Continental Congress gained control of the vast lands between the Appalachian Mountains and the Mississippi River. Eager to pay off its war debts, Congress cast about for a systematic way to sell the public lands northwest of the Ohio River—the land known as the Northwest Territory, shown in the map on page 173. The success of the first settlement on western lands depended on three geographical factors: the location of the land chosen, the imprint of humans on the land, and the characteristics humans brought to the place.

Location

The Appalachian Mountains had always formed a barrier between the original British colonies and the land to the west. By the time of the American Revolution, however, settlers had pierced this barrier by making use of military roads that linked Pennsylvania with the Ohio River.

For this reason, Congress chose a tract of land on the Ohio River as the first to be sold in the Northwest Territory. (The area labeled "Area of First Survey" on the map on page 173 is part of that tract, which totaled about 5 million acres.) The Ohio Company—the organization that bought the land—quickly founded the town of Marietta where the Muskingum River flows into the Ohio River. Marietta grew rapidly because it was a magnet for new settlers. Furthermore, the town was a jumping-off point to lands farther west and so carried on a thriving trade with travelers.

Between 1788 and 1790 alone, nearly nine hundred boats carrying a total of twenty thousand settlers passed along Marietta's shores on their way west.

The Human Imprint on the Land

Under the terms of the Land Ordinance of 1785, western lands had to be surveyed according to a particular system before they could be sold. This system was based on principles used in laying out New England towns. (See "Time and Place: Two Settlement Patterns in the Colonies," pages 92–93.)

The survey system had a tremendous impact on the geography of the West, because it was adopted, with modifications, throughout that region.

The major unit of this system was the township, which was a square, six miles on a side and thirty-six square miles in area. Under the survey system, townships were to be measured off in tiers from an intersecting Principal Meridian and Base Line. Every other township was to be subdivided into thirty-six lots (now called sections), each lot being a square mile (640 acres) in size, with lot number 16 set aside for maintaining a public school in the township. Lots were to be the smallest sized unit offered for sale, and the minimum price was to be $1.00 per acre. The idea was that lots could be purchased by individual farmers who could afford them, and undivided townships might be purchased by groups wishing to start communities in the New England tradition, or by people pooling their resources to acquire a township for division into individual farm units.

Marietta became a pocket of New England beliefs and attitudes in the Northwest Territory.

▶ RESOURCE DIRECTORY

Teaching Resources

Time and Place Activity Moving the City to the Country, found in the Unit 2 folder, pp. 55–56, focuses on the city of Reston, Virginia, a modern example of planned community development.

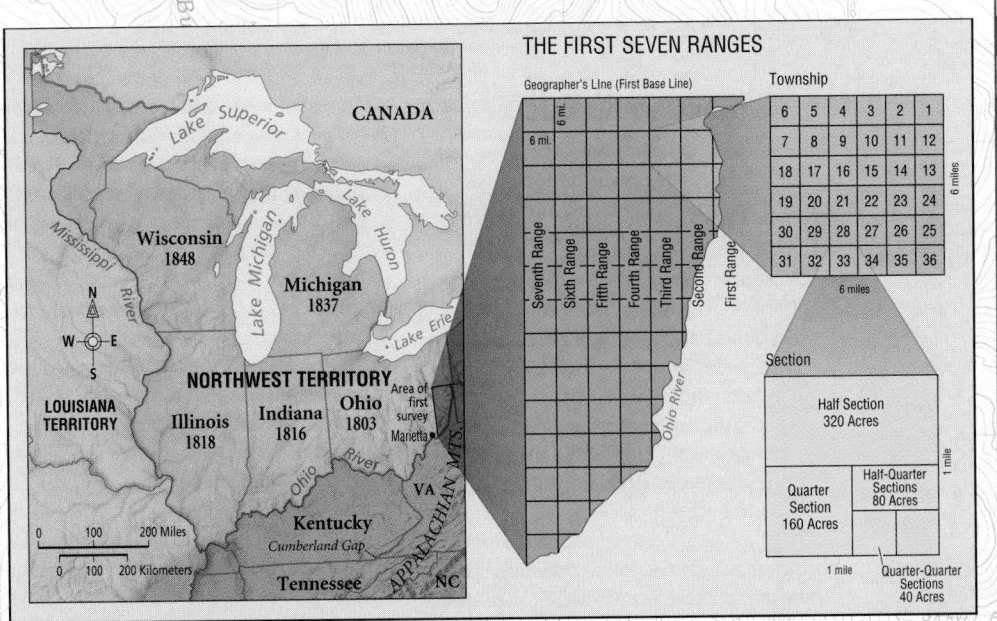

THE FIRST SEVEN RANGES

Geographer's Line (First Base Line)

Township

6	5	4	3	2	1
7	8	9	10	11	12
18	17	16	15	14	13
19	20	21	22	23	24
30	29	28	27	26	25
31	32	33	34	35	36

6 miles

Section

Half Section
320 Acres

Quarter Section
160 Acres

Half-Quarter Sections
80 Acres

1 mile

Quarter-Quarter Sections
40 Acres

Seventh Range, Sixth Range, Fifth Range, Fourth Range, Third Range, Second Range, First Range

Ohio River

CANADA

Lake Superior

Lake Michigan

Lake Huron

Lake Erie

Wisconsin 1848

Michigan 1837

Mississippi River

NORTHWEST TERRITORY

Illinois 1818

Indiana 1816

Ohio 1803

Area of first survey

Marietta

LOUISIANA TERRITORY

Ohio River

Kentucky

Cumberland Gap

Tennessee

VA

NC

APPALACHIAN MTS.

0   100   200 Miles
0   100   200 Kilometers

Human Characteristics of Place

The type of people who settle a place may largely determine whether the settlement will succeed. Even the word *frontier* brings to mind colorful figures who seem larger than life. White settlement west of the Appalachians, however, owed more to land companies and those who founded them. The Ohio Company was started by speculators—investors who hoped to resell the land for a profit. But they were not just little-known business people. "No colony in America," declared George Washington of the first settlement, "was ever settled under such favorable [sponsorship]. . . . Information, property, and strength will be its characteristics. I know many of the settlers personally, and there never were men better calculated to promote the welfare of such a community."

Although the character of the founders of the Ohio Company was vital in its success, they might well have come from any part of the United States, north or south. As it happened, they were New Englanders and persuaded people from that region to move to Ohio with them. And this New England background distinguished the place from surrounding territory settled by people from other parts of the United States. Marietta became a pocket of New England beliefs and attitudes in the Northwest Territory. This is reflected in the voting patterns of the settlers and their descendants in national elections until well into the nineteenth century. Marietta's residents voted as New Englanders did, rather than as did the inhabitants of the surrounding areas of Ohio and Kentucky. The human characteristics of the original settlement—like its location and the human imprint left by land division—endured into modern times.

GEOGRAPHIC CONNECTIONS

1. How did the location of the Ohio Company land contribute to its success?
2. How did settlers in the Ohio Company land affect the way the West was settled?

Critical Thinking

3. **Recognizing Bias** Is there anything in Washington's statement about the prospects of Marietta to suggest that his assessment might not have been an objective one?

when the Ohio towns were founded. If they were established in the late 1700s or early 1800s, they may indeed have been named by emigrating New Englanders.

The Marietta region of Ohio and the Western Reserve region, which was heavily populated by emigrants from Connecticut, voted with New England on many matters, especially against any extension of slavery. In many presidential elections, the Marietta and Western Reserve regions supported candidates other than those favored by the rest of the state.

Tell students that Congress applied the principles of the Northwest Ordinance to other areas of the growing United States. Britain also adopted these policies in Canada, Australia, and New Zealand.

Extend Ask students to suppose that a small group of settlers from their community is emigrating to an undeveloped, extremely isolated section of Alaska. Ask each student to make a list of at least ten major principles or institutions that they would expect to see replicated in the new settlement.

Answers

1. Part of the reason for the settlement's success was that the land was located on one of the major routes west, and western settlement began in earnest during this time.

2. Settlers of the Ohio Company land came from New England and established a land survey system based on the New England town and on the principle that only surveyed land would be granted to settlers. This system was then used throughout the West.

3. Washington's statement, "I know many of the settlers personally. . ." suggests that his assessment was not entirely objective.

1. FOCUS

Connecting to the Big Idea

See page 154B. As settlers from the United States continued to move into Native American lands, different groups tried to deal with the United States in different ways. Ask what those ways were. How successful were they?

Objectives

- Explain why the Native Americans of the eastern United States were in a weakened condition in the late 1790s.
- Compare the options for dealing with white society proposed by Little Turtle and Handsome Lake.
- Describe how Tenskwatawa and Tecumseh tried to maintain Native American independence.

Bellringer

Ask students to define the terms *accommodation* and *assimilation*. Ask students when they have accommodated to the wishes of a stronger power, such as the rules of an institution, or tried to become assimilated into a new group.

Reading Strategy

Reinforcing Key Ideas List the names Little Turtle, Handsome Lake, Tenskwatawa, and Tecumseh on the chalkboard. Ask students to take notes on the ways each of these leaders tried to deal with the encroachment of white society on Native American territory.

Answer to ...

MAKING CONNECTIONS

Answers should indicate the change from a large population of different groups to a drastically reduced population being pushed westward by white settlement.

Native American Politics

SECTION PREVIEW

As the United States continued to expand onto their land, Native Americans responded in various ways, from acceptance to armed resistance.

Key Concepts

- Due to prolonged disease, war, and loss of their lands, Native Americans of the eastern United States were in a weakened condition in the late 1790s.
  - While Little Turtle proposed participation in white society, Handsome Lake called for blending the Christian religion with traditional beliefs.
- Tenskwatawa and Tecumseh urged spiritual purity and military action to maintain Native American independence from white culture.

Key Terms, People, and Places

reservation, assimilation, pan-Indian movement, Battle of Tippecanoe; Little Turtle, Handsome Lake, Tenskwatawa, Tecumseh

During the 1800s, many Native Americans called for a return to the religious purity of their ancestors. This animal-skin rattle was used in Native American religious ceremonies in the 1700s.

Throughout the first century of United States history, Native Americans experienced a continuous invasion of their lands by settlers from the United States. The early years—the 1780s, 1790s, and the years of Jefferson's administration—were no exception.

The Background: War in the Old Northwest

The War for Independence had broken the power of the Iroquois nations in the North and beaten back the Cherokee in the South. In the 1780s Native Americans were in a state of disarray, unable to agree on a unified strategy for dealing with ever-encroaching settlers from the United States.

In the early 1790s, however, many Miami, Delaware, Shawnee, and others came together and created a sizeable resistance to American expansion. Assisted by the British in Canada and led by warriors such as **Little Turtle** and Blue Jacket, they smashed a United States army at Miamitown (now Fort Wayne, Indiana) in 1790. Then they overran an expedition commanded by Northwest Territory governor Arthur St. Clair, inflicting one of the biggest defeats ever suffered by a United States army.

The Native American alliance, however, soon was deserted by the British. Worse still, they now faced a tougher foe in General "Mad Anthony" Wayne, who trained and equipped a new national force, the Legion of the United States. In 1794 Wayne led the Legion to victory over the Native Americans at the Battle of Fallen Timbers in what is now northwestern Ohio. As a result of this battle, in the next year the Miami, Delaware, Shawnee, and other Native Americans were forced to accept the Treaty of Greenville, in which they lost the southern two thirds of Ohio. The treaty also compelled them to acknowledge that the Ohio River was no longer a permanent boundary between their lands and lands settled by Americans of European descent.

From New York to Indiana to Mississippi, Native Americans ended the 1700s in a demoralized condition. Still weakened by occasional epidemics and decades of war, many Native Americans increasingly turned to alcohol as a means of escape from their pain.

MAKING CONNECTIONS

Compare the situation of Native Americans in the eastern United States at the end of the 1700s with their situation before the opening of the Atlantic World.

Political Movements and Choices

In the early 1800s, several Native American leaders proposed different ways to deal with the

---

▶ RESOURCE DIRECTORY

Teaching Resources

📁 **Reproducible Lesson Plan** found in the Unit 2 folder, p. 41, provides a summary of the Section 4 lesson plan content.

📁 **Alternate Lesson Plan: Cooperative Learning** found in the Alternate Lesson Plans folder, p. 30, guides groups of students in a speechwriting activity to explain and describe Native Americans' varied responses to their situation.

📄 **Guided Reading and Review** found in the Unit 2 folder, p. 49, provides a structure for reading and mastering the key concepts and reviewing the key terms for Section 4. (Guided Practice)

United States. The options they suggested included accommodation, or acceptance of another way of life, religious revitalization, and military and political alliance.

Little Turtle Tries Accommodation Some Native Americans followed the path of Little Turtle, a Miami. A brilliant military leader who had engineered the great victories of the early 1790s, Little Turtle made peace with the white settlers. He lived in northern Indiana on annual payments from the government, traveled to Philadelphia and Washington to visit with federal officials, and adopted some of the customs and clothes of Americans of European descent. After devoting much of his life to fighting the Americans, Little Turtle accepted defeat and made the best of the situation.

Handsome Lake Offers Another Path Meanwhile, in western New York **Handsome Lake,** a Seneca, offered a middle course. Handsome Lake had fought with the British against the Americans during the War for Independence. Later, he had suffered the humiliation of being confined to a **reservation,** an area where Native Americans were forced to live after losing their homelands. At times, he was overcome with depression and drinking. But one day in 1799, while lying in a trancelike state, Handsome Lake had a vision of a new life for his people. He began to call for a revitalization of Seneca culture that would blend traditional beliefs and customs with those of Americans of European descent.

Handsome Lake preached that the end of the world was near. He urged Native Americans to prepare for this disaster by giving more attention to traditional rituals and abandoning alcohol and war. Handsome Lake enjoyed great popularity for several years, and his teachings helped to stabilize Seneca society. While holding on to age-old beliefs, Handsome Lake and his followers adopted European American notions about land, agriculture, and family life. If Little Turtle's way was acceptance, Handsome Lake's was acceptance on Native American terms. As he told President Jefferson:

O ur lands are decaying because we do not think on the Great Spirit, but we

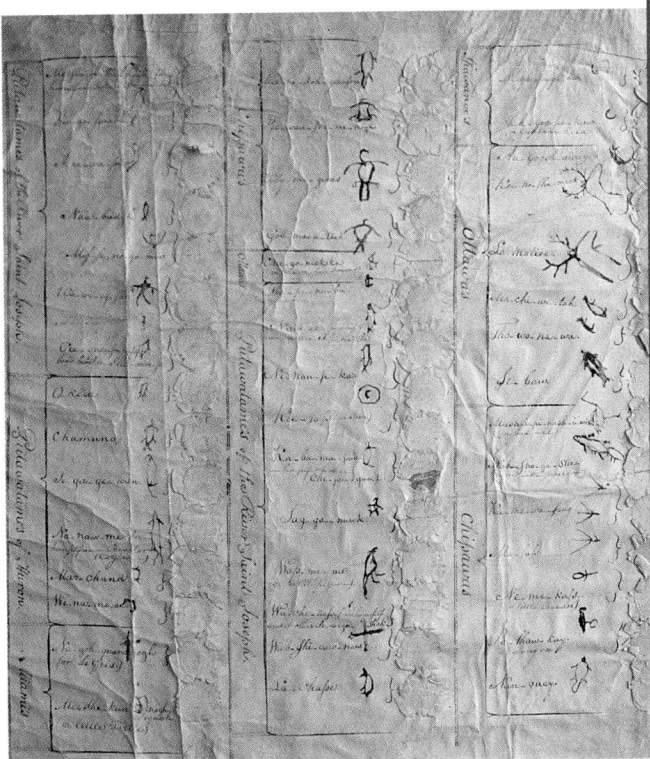

Using Historical Evidence Forced to sign away their rights to Ohio in the Treaty of Greenville (above), Native Americans made their mark beside the English spelling of their names. *What Native American groups are identified in the vertical headings?*

are now going to renew our Minds and think on the great Being who made us all. . . . Dear Brother, the Lord has confidence in your people as well as ours, provided we can settle all our Business.

Tenskwatawa Calls for Cooperation In Indiana another prophet arose, among the Shawnee, Delaware, and Miami. **Tenskwatawa,** also known simply as "the Prophet," called for total rejection of society based on European values and a return to traditional Native American ways. He was against **assimilation,** the process by which people of one culture merge into and become indistinguishable from the people of another culture. In one of Tenskwatawa's visions, the Master of Life revealed that he had not created European Americans:

Media and Technology

 **Transparency**
Fine Art, D-2

Explain/Discuss

Explain why it was difficult for Native American groups to adopt a united policy for dealing with the United States—groups spoke different languages, observed different customs, and some had been enemies for generations.

Discuss the Native American leaders Little Turtle, Handsome Lake, Tenskwatawa, and Tecumseh. Ask students to identify the group each leader belonged to and highlight the suggestions of each for dealing with the United States.

Analyze

In 1810, Tecumseh replied to an attempt by William Henry Harrison to have him cede lands in the Ohio Country to the United States: "Why not sell the air, the clouds, and the great sea, as well as the earth?" Ask students how a negotiator with Harrison might have replied to Tecumseh. In what other ways might the United States have dealt with the Native American claims to western lands?

Caption Answer to . . .

Using Historical Evidence

Shawanoes (Shawnee), Ottawas (Ottawa), Chipawas (Chippewa), Putawatames (Potawatomi), Putawatames of the River St. Joseph, Putawatames of Huron, Miamis (Miami).

 In Depth

Multicultural Perspectives

Over two centuries before the Articles of Confederation, the Native American Iroquois nation forged the first viable confederate government in North America. The Iroquois Confederacy (or League) united five Native American groups in the area of today's New York state into a defensive alliance, much like the Articles.

Activity

Teaching Heterogeneous Groups

While Jeffersonian Republicans were struggling to maintain their liberty from the national government, Native Americans were fighting to remain free from the encroachment of settlers on their land. Divide students into three groups and have each group prepare a short skit demonstrating the three ways in which Native Americans reacted to European settlers. The Little Turtle group should demonstrate a policy of accommodation, the Handsome Lake group give an example of blending, and the Tenskwatawa group demonstrate military and political alliance.

Enrichment

Ask students to research and report on the conscious decision of the Cherokee to assimilate and adopt much of the civilization of their white United States neighbors, including their system of government, language, and forms of agriculture.

3. ASSESS

Section 4 Review Answers

1. (a) reservation, see p. 175, (b) assimilation, see p. 175, (c) pan-Indian movement, see p. 176, (d) Battle of Tippecanoe, see p. 177

2. (a) Little Turtle, see p. 174, (b) Handsome Lake, see p. 175, (c) Tenskwatawa, see p. 175, (d) Tecumseh, see p. 176

3. Native Americans were generally demoralized in the late 1790s due to prolonged disease, war, and continuing loss of their lands.

4. Handsome Lake called for a revitalization of Seneca culture that would blend traditional beliefs and customs with those of European Americans. Tenskwatawa called for total rejection of European society and a return to traditional Native American ways.

*T*hey are not my children, but the children of the Evil Spirit. . . . They grew from the scum of the great Water when it was troubled by the Evil Spirit. And the froth was driven into the Woods by a strong east wind. They are numerous but I hate them. They are unjust. They have taken away your lands, which were not made for them.

Like Handsome Lake, Tenskwatawa argued that part of the blame for the desperate situation of Native Americans lay with themselves. He said that one reason they had lost so much was because they had forgotten to honor their traditions; any path to revitalization had to begin with renewed respect for Native American culture. He warned that they must stop drinking and fighting among themselves before they could deal with the threat posed by settlers from the United States.

In 1808 Tenskwatawa established Prophetstown on the Wabash River (near present-day Lafayette, Indiana). In the years following, hundreds of Native Americans from all over the region came to this center to follow Tenskwatawa's visions. He offered them a sense of dignity and the promise of social stability. He also adopted an increasingly militant attitude toward the United States and its officials. In this he was aided by his older brother, **Tecumseh.**

The Shawnee prophet, Tenskwatawa (right), called on his followers to return to their ancient ways and obey the Master of Life, who had told him: "If you Indians will do everything which I have told you, I will overturn the land, so that all the white people will be covered and you alone shall inhabit the land."

AMERICAN PROFILES

Tecumseh

Born in 1768, Tecumseh had earned a reputation as a talented war chief by the early 1800s. He had fought against the United States in the 1780s and 1790s, refusing to participate in the negotiations that led to the Treaty of Greenville in 1795. In the early 1800s, he welcomed his younger brother's visions and shared his yearning for spiritual renewal.

⭐ Tecumseh was interested in what historians have called a **pan-Indian movement,** one that would transcend local and group differences among Native Americans. He believed that the only hope Native Americans had of resisting the expansion of the United States was a combination of spiritual renewal and political unity.

The Shawnee brothers demonstrated their power by rallying opposition to the Treaty of Fort Wayne. In this treaty, negotiated in 1809 by William Henry Harrison, governor of what was then the Indiana Territory, Native Americans gave up much of south-central Indiana. Like many treaties and settlements with Native Americans before and since, it made use of a legal trick to take their land. Because Native Americans in each group held their land in common, they all had to agree before the status of the land could change. In practice, such group consent to give up land was difficult or impossible to achieve. Government officials would find a few individuals who could be persuaded to sign away their people's land. They would then ignore protests from the rest of the group. In August 1810, Tecumseh and several dozen warriors met with Governor Harrison in the territorial capitol of Vincennes to protest such a trick. Said Tecumseh:

*T*his land that was sold and the goods that was given for it was only done by a few. . . . If you continue to purchase of them it will produce war among the different tribes and at last I do not know what will be the consequence to the white people.

Governor Harrison took the warning and moved first, while Tecumseh was in Alabama

▶ RESOURCE DIRECTORY

Teaching Resources

⭐ 📄 **Primary Source Activity** Native American Politics, found in the Unit 2 folder, p. 65, uses excerpts from journals, letters, and speeches of both Native American and United States leaders to illustrate the pros and cons of westward expansion.

and Mississippi trying to get the Choctaw and the Creek to join in the pan-Indian resistance. Harrison marched north from Vincennes to Prophetstown with roughly one thousand militia and soldiers.

Just before sunrise on November 7, 1811, after a day of negotiations, Tenskwatawa sent between six hundred and eight hundred warriors to attack Harrison and his men. The **Battle of Tippecanoe** lasted about two hours. Tactically, it was a draw. But, Tippecanoe was a disaster for Tenskwatawa and Tecumseh in the long run. The battle shattered Native American morale and eroded confidence in the leadership of Tenskwatawa. Within a couple of days of the battle, Harrison burned an abandoned Prophetstown to the ground.

Native American military resistance was not over, however. Tecumseh soon rallied warriors to fight alongside the British in Canada against United States troops in the war described in Section 5. He died from a gunshot wound to the chest in the Battle of the Thames in Ontario, Canada, on October 5, 1813. In that encounter, Harrison and several thousand United States soldiers overwhelmed several hundred British and Native Americans.

Little more than one month before, Tecumseh had replied to a British officer's talk of retreat with defiance. He had chosen his path and it was resistance. He would take it where it led him. He was not going to give up his ideals or surrender. Amid the heartfelt war cries of his followers, Tecumseh announced to the officer:

Y ou have got the arms and ammunition which our great father sent for his red children. If you have an idea of going away, give them to us, and you may go and welcome. As for us, our lives are in the hands of the Great Spirit. We are determined to defend our lands, and if it be his will we wish to leave our bones upon them.

Although Tecumseh and his brother did not accomplish their objectives, they left a vital legacy of defiance of invasion and respect for themselves, their people, and their culture. In later years, they would be a model for Native Americans reclaiming their traditions.

William Henry Harrison reported that Tecumseh (center) wished to "form a combination of all the Indian Tribes . . . to put a stop to the encroachments of the white people." The warclub above belonged to Tecumseh's followers.

5. Along with his brother Tecumseh, Tenskwatawa established Prophetstown. He gave back dignity to the hundreds of Native Americans who came there from all over the region, as well as offering them the promise of social stability. Although Tecumseh and his brother did not accomplish their goals, they left a vital legacy of defiance and respect for themselves, their people, and their culture. In later years, they became models for Native Americans desiring to reclaim their traditions.

6. Possible questions: What response do you believe Native Americans should make to white settlement in their lands? Why are Native Americans unable to stop white encroachment? How does the Master of Life feel about white settlement?

Reteach

Identify the Native American leader whose ideas for dealing with the United States are summarized in each of the following statements:
- We must renew ourselves spiritually, unite politically, and oppose any more loss of our lands.
- We must revitalize our culture, blending our beliefs with those of Americans of European descent. We must abandon alcohol and war.
- We must make peace with the United States and make the best of our situation.

Alternative Assessment

Mid-Point Monitoring
Ask students if they have
- Started taking notes on the successes and failures of the presidential administrations
- Begun their outside research

Quiz found in the Unit 2 folder, p. 50, covers the main ideas in this section as well as the key terms.

SECTION 4 REVIEW

Key Terms, People, and Places
1. Define (a) reservation, (b) assimilation, (c) pan-Indian movement, (d) Battle of Tippecanoe.
2. Identify (a) Little Turtle, (b) Handsome Lake, (c) Tenskwatawa, (d) Tecumseh.

Key Concepts
3. Why were Native Americans in a weakened condition by the end of the 1700s?

4. How did the paths proposed by Handsome Lake and Tenskwatawa differ?
5. What did Tecumseh and Tenskwatawa accomplish?

Critical Thinking
6. **Formulating Questions** What questions might a Native American in the early 1800s have asked of Tenskwatawa in trying to understand his views?

 CLOSE

 Reinforcing the Big Idea

Native American leaders responded in different ways to the relentless encroachment of the white settlers on their land. Tecumseh fought for the British during the War of 1812, described in the next section.

War, Panic, and Uneasy Compromise

SECTION 5

War, Panic, and Uneasy Compromise

1. FOCUS

Connecting to the Big Idea

See page 154B. In 1812, Congress declared war on Great Britain, a war that ended because both sides eventually decided that they did not want to fight any longer. Ask how the nation responded when the initial postwar period of prosperity was followed by a period of severe economic depression. How did the debate over admitting Missouri to the Union open up a debate over slavery?

Objectives

● Describe the course of the War of 1812.

● Explain why the Battle of New Orleans cheered Americans and made Andrew Jackson a national hero.

● Explain why the depression of 1819 persuaded many Americans to consider ways the government could guide the economy.

● Describe the debate over the admission of Missouri to the Union and outline the provisions of the Missouri Compromise.

Bellringer

Ask students to think of times when they have had to compromise. When is compromise necessary? What elements are required for a compromise to work?

Reading Strategy

Structured Overview Ask students to write the main section headings on a piece of paper. Have students then scan the section and note the subheadings under each of the headings. Ask them to fill in details from the text as they read.

SECTION PREVIEW

Prosperity and political harmony followed the War of 1812—until depression and controversy raised storm clouds on the horizon.

A new war with Britain brought the humiliation of defeat and the pride of resistance. This "star-spangled banner" inspired the national anthem as it flew bravely through a British attack on Baltimore in 1814.

Key Concepts

• In the War of 1812 the United States proved a poor match for its powerful opponent, Great Britain.

• The Battle of New Orleans belatedly cheered Americans and created a new national hero.

• A sudden and severe depression in 1819 persuaded many Americans to consider ways the government could guide the economy.

• North and South differed sharply over whether slavery should be legal in a new state, Missouri, but eventually reached a compromise.

Key Terms, People, and Places

Hartford Convention, Treaty of Ghent, Battle of New Orleans, Panic of 1819, Missouri Compromise; Andrew Jackson

---

G reat Britain, at war with France since 1803, had continually interfered with United States shipping and encouraged Native Americans to resist the settlement of the West. In June 1812, Congress, fed up with British harassment and urged on by President Madison, declared war on Britain.

A War of Mixed Success and Humiliation

In many ways, the declaration of war was a foolhardy action. The United States had only a small army and navy and no foreign assistance. The nation would have to deal not only with the powerful British, but with Native Americans to the north and south who were angered by western expansion.

The Land War Despite these disadvantages, United States planners expected to strike a swift, damaging blow to the enemy by pushing into Canada and conquering that vast British territory. To their surprise, United States invasion forces—poorly equipped and led—were beaten by the British in the summer of 1812.

The United States did manage some victories on land. William Henry Harrison defeated the British and Native Americans, including Tecumseh's forces, at the Battle of the Thames in October 1813. **Andrew Jackson,** a general who like Harrison would later be President of the United States, won out over Native Americans at Horseshoe Bend in Alabama in March 1814. But these modest successes were not about to convince a great power like Britain to give up.

The War on Water On inland waters and on the high seas, where British ships outnumbered American vessels by about twenty to one, Americans at first performed surprisingly well. The United States had a half-dozen frigates, or medium-sized warships, that won several lone duels with British warships. American privateers captured over a thousand British ships. And in the summer of 1813, Master Commandant Oliver Hazard Perry defeated a British flotilla on Lake Erie, enabling the United States to control that lake and protect a vital stretch of its northern border. Eventually, however, the superiority of the British navy began to have an effect. The British blockaded the American coast, strangling trade and putting a stop to the bravado of United States frigates.

In 1814 the British ended a difficult and dangerous war they had been fighting against the French emperor Napoleon in Europe. They

---

 RESOURCE DIRECTORY

Teaching Resources

Reproducible Lesson Plan found in the Unit 2 folder, p. 42, provides a summary of the Section 5 lesson plan content.

Alternate Lesson Plan: Critical Thinking Recognizing Cause and Effect, found in the Alternate Lesson Plans folder, p. 31, helps students apply this skill in examining the War of 1812, the Panic of 1819, and the Missouri Compromise.

Guided Reading and Review found in the Unit 2 folder, p. 51, provides a structure for reading and mastering the key concepts and reviewing the key terms for Section 5. (Guided Practice)

American Profiles Activity found in the Unit 2 folder, p. 58, profiles Francis Scott Key, who wrote "The Star Spangled Banner" after witnessing the battle of Fort McHenry.

then turned their attention to teaching the upstart United States a lesson. Reversing American strategy, some 14,000 British troops tried to invade the United States from Canada in the late summer of 1814. To the surprise of the British, however, a greatly outnumbered American force drove them back across the border.

By contrast, the British ships that arrived in Chesapeake Bay at about the same time scored a major success. About 4,000 enemy troops disembarked and descended on Washington, D.C., meeting little serious opposition. On August 24, President James Madison and his wife, Dolley Madison, were warned of the approach of the British and fled. Toward evening, the enemy entered the capital and started fires that consumed the city. Even the Capitol and the White House were gutted by flames.

⭐ Ironically, it was this humiliating, one-sided campaign in the Chesapeake Bay area that gave the United States its national anthem. Lawyer Francis Scott Key wrote "The Star-Spangled Banner" after watching the British bombard Fort McHenry at the entrance to Baltimore harbor. He knew the fort remained unconquered because

the rockets' red glare,
the bombs bursting in air,
gave proof through the night that our flag
was still there.

Opinion Is Divided Not all Americans felt as patriotic about the War of 1812 as did Francis Scott Key. In December 1814, New Englanders, who had suffered tremendous losses in trade, sent delegates to Hartford, Connecticut, to consider the possibility of leaving the nation. In the end, the **Hartford Convention** called only for constitutional amendments to increase New England's political power. ⭐

Meanwhile, both the British and the Americans had recognized that this was a war no one wanted. On December 24, 1814, representatives of the two nations met in Belgium and signed the **Treaty of Ghent**, ending the War of 1812. All the old boundaries between the United States and British territory in North America were restored.

Viewpoints
For and Against the War of 1812

The War of 1812 was promoted by the War Hawks, a group of politicians mostly from the landlocked states of the South and West who were eager to see the United States expand into Canada. Their opponents, mostly from New England and the Middle Atlantic states, feared Britain would attack the coast and cut off shipping. *To what fear does each speaker appeal?*

For War with Britain
"We shall drive the British from our continent—they will no longer have an opportunity of intriguing [conspiring] with our Indian neighbors, and setting on the ruthless savage to tomahawk our women and children."
Representative Felix Grundy of Kentucky, December 1811

Against War with Britain
"It was our own thirst for territory, our own want of moderation that had driven these sons of nature [Native Americans] to desperation, of which we felt the effects. . . . Go! March to Canada! . . . . The coast is to be left defenseless, while men of the interior are reveling in conquest and spoil."
Representative John Randolph of Virginia, December 1811

The Battle of New Orleans

Although fighting was officially ended by the Treaty of Ghent, the greatest victory for the United States came after the treaty was signed. This final twist to a strange war was the result of the slow communication of the times.

On December 23, a British force of 11,000 men tried to take New Orleans from the south. General Andrew Jackson and 4,500 soldiers and volunteers from all over the Mississippi Valley, including two battalions of free African Americans, defended the city.

On January 8, the overconfident British, fresh from victories over the French in Europe, foolishly threw their troops against the Americans' well-protected positions. Without cover, the advancing British were easy targets for American gunners. The battle was finished in just over an hour; in fact, most of the shooting took place in about twenty minutes. The British suffered 2,036 casualties; the Americans, 21. Although the **Battle of New Orleans** was the

📘 **Viewpoints Activity** For and Against the War of 1812, found in the Unit 2 folder, pp. 59–60, presents quotations from government leaders and journalists to further illustrate the debate over starting a war with Britain.

⭐ 📘 **Visual Learning Activity** "The Present State of Our Country," found in the Unit 2 folder, p. 70, uses a political cartoon to demonstrate the conflict many people felt over the possible war against Britain.

Explain/Discuss

Discuss the reasons for the United States' declaration of war on Great Britain. Ask students to identify what the United States hoped to gain and what it actually accomplished.

Ask students to suggest ways in which the government might have regulated the economy to prevent the depression of 1819. Ask students to consider how economic hardship increased feelings of sectionalism at the expense of national unity.

Analyze

Ask whether the Missouri Compromise was a solution or a return to the status quo on the issue of slavery. Ask how those who opposed slavery as a moral evil probably reacted to the Missouri Compromise.

Answer to . . .

Viewpoints

Grundy appeals to Americans' fear that the British will persuade Native Americans to attack settlements along the interior frontier. Randolph touches on the fear that the British might attack coastal cities. For a more thorough examination of the War of 1812, see the Resource Directory below.

In Depth

Then and Now

An intense spirit of nationalism ensued after both the American Revolution and the War of 1812. This unifying spirit, which usually accompanies times of conflict, was conspicuously absent during the Vietnam War in the 1960s and 1970s. Many citizens protested openly against the war on a grand scale, and many refused to join the armed forces. (See Chapter 31, pages 854–861.)

Activity

Simulating the Missouri Compromise

Have students use historical atlases to identify the twenty-two states in the Union before the admission of Missouri and Maine and to note the free and slave states. Ask students to suggest why the balance in the Senate between slave and free states was so important.

Enrichment

Ask students to choose a topic related to the War of 1812 to research and report on, such as the defeat of the *Guerrière* and the *Java* by the *Constitution* ("Old Ironsides"), the Battle of Put-in-Bay and Commodore Oliver Perry, the writing of "The Star-Spangled Banner" and its subsequent adoption as the national anthem, the Battle of Plattsburg, or the role of pirate Jean Laffite in the Battle of New Orleans.

3. ASSESS

Section 5 Review Answers

1. (a) Hartford Convention, see p. 179, (b) Treaty of Ghent, see p. 179, (c) Battle of New Orleans, see p. 179, (d) Panic of 1819, see p. 180, (e) Missouri Compromise, see p. 181

2. Andrew Jackson, see p. 178

3. British interference with American trade overseas and some desire to expand U.S. territory into Canada led the United States into war. The United States had only a tiny army and navy, no foreign assistance, and a powerful opponent.

This exaggerated painting highlights the new hero that the Battle of New Orleans gave to the United States: Andrew Jackson, shown riding a white horse.

result of a British blunder, it was a remarkable victory. It made Jackson a national hero and finally gave the American people something to crow about.

Post-War Boom and Panic

In 1815 the United States entered a period of growth and prosperity. The prevailing mood was now one of national pride. Jefferson's ally, James Monroe, the former governor of Virginia, easily won election as the fifth President of the United States in 1816. The Federalist party, never very strong after the election of 1800, disappeared as a national political force.

Congress, in an attempt to deal with financial problems resulting from the war, created the Second Bank of the United States in 1816. Encouraged by abundant credit from this bank and others, as well as by federal land laws, Americans began moving westward at an incredible rate. The United States sold them hundreds of thousands of acres of land, from Indiana to Louisiana. Meanwhile, American ships were busy carrying agricultural products and other goods to Europe. Everything seemed to be going well.

Then, in 1819, the first great depression in the history of the United States struck the nation. Known as the **Panic of 1819,** it began across the Atlantic when London banks demanded that banks in the United States pay money owed to them. These United States banks in turn demanded back money that they had loaned to the American public. Americans who had borrowed too much in the days of easy loans after 1815 were financially ruined.

The collapse of the economic system was startling. It was not just that many people were thrown out of work or lost their property. Many had never reckoned with the possibility that economic expansion might have limits. Even today, the United States economy alternates between periods of prosperity and periods of depression—a boom-and-bust economic cycle. Although they had experienced hard times before, Americans had thought their economic problems were over for good. Shocked by the Panic of 1819, many began to think about ways of reforming the government to improve the performance of the economy.

MAKING CONNECTIONS

What part of the boom-and-bust cycle is the nation in now? How are the government and the public responding?

The Missouri Compromise

Still another dark cloud appeared on the horizon in 1819, as Congress took up the question of the admission of the state of Missouri to the United States. The Ordinance of 1787 had established that no state northwest of the Ohio River could be a slave state—a state where slavery was legal. But because Missouri was not northwest of the Ohio River, it was not covered by this definition. Several members of Congress from the North objected to admitting Missouri as a slave state. They were not simply concerned about the liberty of African Americans;

RESOURCE DIRECTORY

Teaching Resources

they worried that another slave state might increase the power of the southern states in the national government. Members of Congress from the South replied that the national government had no business dictating to states what they could and could not do. They feared that if the United States could forbid slavery in Missouri, it could do so elsewhere.

After months of bitter debate, Congress reached what is now called the **Missouri Compromise,** which was signed into law in 1820. Slavery would be permitted in Missouri; at the same time, Maine was carved out of what had been northern Massachusetts and admitted to the union as a free, or nonslave, state. This arrangement would balance power in the Senate between North and South. Furthermore, Congress agreed that as the United States expanded westward, states north of 36° 30' N latitude would be free states, and states south of that line would be slave states, as the map above shows.

By the mid-1820s, both the Panic of 1819 and the Missouri controversy had faded from public attention. The economy had recovered and politicians agreed to avoid the divisive issue of slavery. But the economic and moral questions raised by these events were not going to go away.

To Thomas Jefferson, still a keen observer of the national scene, the Missouri controversy sounded "like a fire bell in the night" and "filled [him] with terror." Could the United States survive ongoing struggles over questions of economic and racial justice and the power of the national government? As Jefferson had written earlier about the existence of slavery in a democratic republic:

> I tremble for my country when I reflect that God is just: that his justice cannot sleep for ever.

The Missouri Compromise, 1820

 OREGON COUNTRY
(Occupied by U.S. and Great Britain)

CANADA

Unorganized Territory

MICH. TERR.

36°30' N
Missouri Compromise Line

ARK. TERR.

PACIFIC OCEAN

MEXICO

ATLANTIC OCEAN

ME VT NH MA NY RI CT NJ PA DE MD IL IN OH VA MO KY NC TN SC MS AL GA LA FLA. TERR.

States formed by Missouri Compromise

Free states and territories closed to slavery

Slave states and territories open to slavery

0 150 300 Miles
0 150 300 Kilometers

 Geography and History: Interpreting Maps
Under the terms of the Missouri Compromise, a new free state, Maine, was carved out of Massachusetts to balance the new slave state, Missouri. Congress also agreed that in the future, only states south of 36° 30' N latitude would be slave states. Southerners figured that cotton would not grow north of this line. *Which would cover more land under the compromise, the new free states or the new slave states?*

SECTION 5 REVIEW

Key Terms, People, and Places
1. Define (a) Hartford Convention, (b) Treaty of Ghent, (c) Battle of New Orleans, (d) Panic of 1819, (e) Missouri Compromise.
2. Identify Andrew Jackson.

Key Concepts
3. What caused the War of 1812 and why did the United States fail to achieve overall success during it?

4. Why was the Battle of New Orleans so encouraging to Americans?
5. How did the Panic of 1819 affect the way Americans thought of the role of government?

Critical Thinking
6. **Determining Relevance** Now that you have read about how difficult the War of 1812 was for the United States, comment on the importance of French help during the War for Independence.

 Quiz found in the Unit 2 folder, p. 52, covers the main ideas in this section as well as the key terms.

 Chapter Test Forms A and B are found in the Unit 2 folder, pp. 71–76.

 Answer Keys found in the Unit 2 folder, pp. 116–125, provides answers to all student activities.

Media and Technology

Transparency
Graphic Organizer, G-3

Guided Reading Audiotapes
(English and Spanish)

Computer Test Bank

---

4. The Battle of New Orleans, a devastating loss for the British, gave Americans something to crow about after years of unsatisfactory successes and embarrassing defeats.

5. The Panic of 1819 encouraged Americans to consider how to reform the economy and how the government could prevent the suffering brought on by a nationwide depression.

6. Answers should state that though the circumstances were different, the failure of the United States to achieve victory during the War of 1812 suggests that the help of the French was of great consequence in the war that had taken place thirty years earlier.

Reteach

Ask students to correct any of the following statements that are incorrect:
● Before the War of 1812, the United States thought that its large army and navy would easily defeat the smaller forces of the British.
● The Battle of New Orleans tipped the balance of the war in favor of the Americans.
● The War of 1812 was followed by a period of national pride and prosperity.
● The Missouri Compromise brought Missouri into the Union as a slave state but forbade slavery in all future states.

Caption Answer to ...

 Interpreting Maps

The new free states.

4. CLOSE

Reinforcing the Big Idea
The War of 1812 was mostly a series of discouraging losses for the United States, yet it was followed by a period of national pride and prosperity. Economic depression and controversy over slavery soon dampened the nation's political good feelings.

Understanding Key Terms, People, and Places

Terms

Students should refer to the definitions of the key terms in the chapter to write sentences that show the relation of each word to the origins of American politics, events in Native American politics, or conflicts with France and Britain from 1789 to 1820.

Word Relationships

1. (d) does not belong. In order to raise money to pay foreign creditors, Congress created tariffs on foreign goods and an excise tax on whiskey, an action that led to the Whiskey Rebellion. The Battle of Tippecanoe was fought between Native Americans and government troops in 1811.

2. (c) does not belong. Reservation, assimilation, and the pan-Indian movement are all associated with Native American issues. The Panic of 1819 occurred when European creditors called in their debts.

3. (a) does not belong. The Hartford Convention was convened because New Englanders had suffered tremendous losses as a result of the War of 1812, the Treaty of Ghent ended the war, and the Battle of New Orleans was a major victory for the United States. The Missouri Compromise temporarily settled the question of whether slavery would be allowed in Missouri.

4. (b) does not belong. The XYZ Affair, the French Revolution, and the Louisiana Purchase are all associated with France and U.S.–France relations. *Marbury* v. *Madison* established the principle of judicial review.

5. (c) does not belong. Judicial review, political party, and precedent are all associated with development of the new government. The Embargo of 1807 was Jefferson's attempt to place economic pressure on Britain and France.

True or False

1. false, John Marshall's
2. false, Jeffersonian Republicans
3. true
4. false, Andrew Jackson

Reviewing Main Ideas

1. Hamilton transformed the debts of all the states into a long-term investment in the United States government for the country's creditors.

2. They saw it as an example of a democratic revolution gone wrong.

Chapter Review

Understanding Key Terms, People, and Places

Key Terms
1. political party
2. first American party system
3. excise
4. tariff
5. French Revolution
6. Whiskey Rebellion
7. precedent
8. XYZ Affair
9. Alien and Sedition Acts of 1798
10. *Marbury* v. *Madison*
11. judicial review
12. Louisiana Purchase
13. Embargo of 1807
14. reservation
15. assimilation
16. pan-Indian movement
17. Battle of Tippecanoe
18. Hartford Convention
19. Treaty of Ghent
20. Battle of New Orleans
21. Panic of 1819
22. Missouri Compromise

People
23. Jeffersonian Republicans
24. Gabriel Prosser
25. midnight judges
26. John Marshall
27. Little Turtle
28. Handsome Lake
29. Tenskwatawa
30. Tecumseh
31. Andrew Jackson

Places
32. Northwest Territory

Terms For each term above, write a sentence that explains its relation to American politics, Native Americans, or conflicts with France and Britain from 1789 to 1820.

Word Relationships Three of the terms in each of the following sets of terms are related. Choose the term that does not belong and explain why it does not belong.
1. (a) excise, (b) tariff, (c) Whiskey Rebellion, (d) Battle of Tippecanoe
2. (a) reservation, (b) assimilation, (c) Panic of 1819, (d) pan-Indian movement
3. (a) Missouri Compromise, (b) Treaty of Ghent, (c) Hartford Convention, (d) Battle of New Orleans
4. (a) XYZ Affair, (b) *Marbury* v. *Madison,* (c) French Revolution, (d) Louisiana Purchase
5. (a) judicial review, (b) political party, (c) Embargo of 1807, (c) precedent

True or False Determine whether each statement is true or false. If it is true, write "true." If it is false, change the underlined name to make the statement true.
1. Andrew Jackson's decision in *Marbury* v. *Madison* established the power of the federal courts to review laws to see if they conflict with the Constitution.
2. Historians call the critics of George Washington's administration midnight judges.
3. Tenskwatawa opposed assimilation and called for cooperation among Native Americans.
4. Gabriel Prosser was a hero of the Battle of New Orleans and a future President.

Reviewing Main Ideas

Section 1 (pp. 156–160)
1. How was Alexander Hamilton able to change the national debt from a weakness to a strength?
2. Why was the federal government determined to crush the Whiskey Rebellion?

Section 2 (pp. 162–165)
3. What measures did the Federalists take in response to the undeclared war with France in the late 1790s?
4. What was the goal of Gabriel Prosser's Rebellion?

Section 3 (pp. 168–171)
5. What new power did the Supreme Court acquire under the Jefferson administration?

6. What was the effect of the Louisiana Purchase on the westward expansion of the United States?

Section 4 (pp. 174–177)
7. How did the boundaries of Native American lands change during the 1790s?
8. Explain Tenskwatawa's and Tecumseh's beliefs about the path that Native Americans should follow.
9. What compromise did Handsome Lake offer?

Section 5 (pp. 178–181)
10. What disadvantages did the United States face during the War of 1812?
11. Explain the issues of the Missouri Compromise.

---

3. The Federalists increased the size of the army, raised taxes, and passed the Alien and Sedition Acts of 1798, which restricted freedoms.

4. The goal of Gabriel's Rebellion was freedom from slavery.

5. The Court acquired the power of judicial review, i.e., the power by which federal courts review laws through specific cases in court and if necessary declare them unconstitutional.

6. The Louisiana Purchase allowed westward expansion all the way to Oregon.

7. As a result of the Treaty of Greenville, Native Americans lost the southern two thirds of Ohio and were forced to acknowledge that the Ohio River was no longer a permanent boundary for their lands.

8. They rejected assimilation and called for a return to traditional Native American ways.

9. Handsome Lake urged his followers to adopt some European notions while holding on to age-old Seneca beliefs.

10. The United States had only a small army and navy and no foreign assistance; it also had to fight Native Americans as well as the British.

11. The Missouri Compromise arose over the question of slavery in the new state of Missouri; it was designed to preserve the balance in the Senate between free and slave states so as not to increase unfairly the power of the southern states.

Thinking Critically

1. Identifying Assumptions Today we expect a peaceful transfer of power when Americans vote to change political parties in a presidential election. Why were people unable to make this assumption in the election of 1800?

2. Predicting Consequences Thomas Jefferson said that the Missouri Compromise "filled [him] with terror." Why might Jefferson have viewed the compromise with such foreboding?

Making Connections

1. Evaluating Primary Sources Review Jefferson's primary source quotation on the top of page 158. Do you think that a French revolutionary in the late 1700s would have preferred "the calm of despotism to the boisterous sea of liberty"? A citizen of the former Soviet Union in the early 1990s?

2. Understanding the Visuals Examine the graph on page 171. Using your knowledge of the chapter, explain the drop in trade that ended in 1814.

3. Writing About the Chapter The election of 1800 is rapidly approaching. Write a letter to the editor of your local newspaper explaining why you plan to vote for Thomas Jefferson or for John Adams. First, create a list of what you see as the reasons for supporting your candidate. List the reasons why you oppose the other candidate. Note the direction you would like to see the nation take during the next

presidential term, and explain why your candidate is the best person to lead the country in that direction. Next, write a draft of your letter in which you explain your reasons for supporting your candidate. Revise your letter, making certain that each reason is clearly explained. Proofread your letter and draft a final copy.

4. Using the Graphic Organizer This graphic organizer uses a tree map to organize information about problems and choices in the early nation. (a) What problems did the three groups represented in the graphic organizer face during the period from 1789 to 1820? (b) What did the Whiskey Rebels, Gabriel Prosser, and Tecumseh have in common? (c) On a separate sheet of paper, create your own graphic organizer about Jefferson's presidency, using this graphic organizer as an example.

4. (a) Conflict between liberty and order (white Americans), enslavement (African Americans), and loss of control over their lands (Native Americans). (b) They all tried armed resistance as a solution to their problems. (c) Students' graphic organizers should mention the reduction in the federal government, Jefferson's clash with the judicial branch, the Louisiana Purchase, and the Embargo of 1807.

Alternative Assessment

Final Evaluation

Use the following guidelines to evaluate student projects:

- **Evidence of mastery of content** To what extent do pamphlets show knowledge and understanding of chapter content?
- **Evidence of thoughtfulness** To what extent do pamphlets show understanding of the importance and significance of particular events?
- **Evidence of outside research** To what extent do projects use materials and information from outside sources?

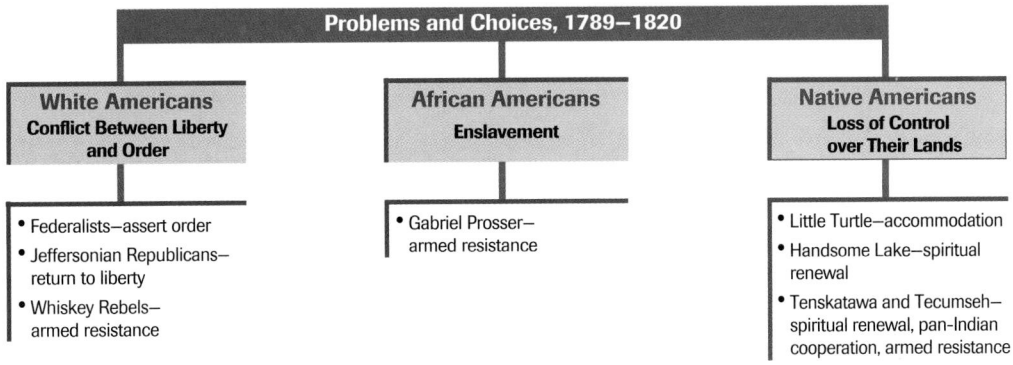

Problems and Choices, 1789–1820

White Americans
Conflict Between Liberty and Order
- Federalists—assert order
- Jeffersonian Republicans—return to liberty
- Whiskey Rebels—armed resistance

African Americans
Enslavement
- Gabriel Prosser—armed resistance

Native Americans
Loss of Control over Their Lands
- Little Turtle—accommodation
- Handsome Lake—spiritual renewal
- Tenskatawa and Tecumseh—spiritual renewal, pan-Indian cooperation, armed resistance

Thinking Critically

1. The election of 1800 was the first time that the United States had experienced a change in power. Under European monarchies, such changes had often been accompanied by violence. Americans were therefore unsure whether a peaceful transfer of power could actually be accomplished.

2. Jefferson sensed that the Missouri Compromise was only a temporary measure that did not solve the moral question surrounding the institution of slavery. He knew that a real resolution of the issue would threaten the very fabric of the nation.

Making Connections

1. A French revolutionary would have preferred liberty to despotism because the purpose of the French Revolution was to overthrow the tyranny of the monarchy. The opinion among citizens of the former Soviet Union may be mixed. While many people are relieved to be free of the tyranny of communism, freedom has also led to economic collapse and political chaos.

2. Answers should indicate an understanding that the War of 1812 and the Treaty of Ghent affected the drop in exports.

Chapter 7 Life in the New Nation
1783–1830

📁 Teaching Resources (See Unit 2 Folder)

	Instruction	Enrichment

Section 1
Migrating Multitudes
(pp. 186–191)
	Reproducible Lesson Plan, p. 78
	Alternate Lesson Plan, p. 33
	Guided Reading and Review, p. 82
	Quiz, p. 83
		Critical Thinking Activity, Making
		  Comparisons, p. 95
		Primary Source Activity, Moving West,
		  pp. 96–97
		Literature Activity, The Pioneers, pp. 99–100
		Historian's Toolbox Activity, Using Population
		  Density Maps, p. 94

Section 2
The Spirit of Improvement
(pp. 193–197)
	Reproducible Lesson Plan, p. 79
	Alternate Lesson Plan, p. 34
	Guided Reading and Review, p. 84
	Quiz, p. 85
		American Profiles Activity, Catherine Littlefield
		  Greene, p. 90
		Viewpoints Activity, On Educating the People,
		  pp. 92–93
		Literature Activity, The Natural World, p. 101
		American Profiles Activity, Anne Newport
		  Royall, p. 91

Section 3 **Shifting Social Relationships** (pp. 198–201)	Reproducible Lesson Plan, p. 80 Alternate Lesson Plan, p. 35 Guided Reading and Review, p. 86 Quiz, p. 87	Visual Learning Activity, Do They Miss Me at Home? p. 102 Visual Learning Activity, Married Mum? p. 103
Section 4 **The Democratization of American** **Religion** (pp. 202–205)	Reproducible Lesson Plan, p. 81 Alternate Lesson Plan, p. 36 Guided Reading and Review, p. 88 Quiz, p. 89 Chapter Test, Forms A & B, pp. 104–109	Primary Source Activity, The American Spirit, p. 98

📁 Additional Chapter Resources

Resource Organizer, p. 77
Alternate Lesson Plan, p. 32
Answer Keys, pp. 116–125

Bibliography

For the Teacher
Cott, Nancy F. *The Bonds of Womanhood: "Woman's Sphere"*
  in New England, 1780–1835. Yale University Press, 1977.
  (Covers different perspectives of women's lives of the
  period.)
Walker, Juliet E. K. *Free Frank: A Black Pioneer on the*
  Antebellum Frontier. University of Kentucky Press, 1983.
  (An account of an African American couple who worked to
  buy their own freedom and that of their family members.)

Prentice Hall Literature Excerpts from *The American*
  Experience, 1994, including Irving, Washington. "The Devil
  and Tom Walker," from *Tales of a Traveler.* Hall, 1987.

THE BIG IDEA

The Big Idea for the chapter and how the main ideas in each section relate to the Big Idea are graphically displayed below. Comprehension of this chapter's Big Idea is critical to students' understanding of United States history and how we as a nation got where we are today.

Media and Technology

 Critical Thinking, I-3; Our Multicultural Heritage, C-10; Fine Art, D-6

 The Way It Works, H-6, H-7

 Our Multicultural Heritage, C-7; Graphic Organizer, G-3

 Guided Reading Audiotapes (English and Spanish)

 Computer Test Bank

For the Student

Green, Constance. *Eli Whitney and the Birth of American Technology.* Scott Foresman, 1956. (Comprehensive study of the technological revolution.)

Inventions in America's Growth, Part 1, 1750–1850. Film/Video. Coronet Films. (Includes the effects of the cotton gin, steamboat, locomotive, and telegraph.)

Irving, Washington. *The Sketch Book of Geoffrey Crayton.* Penguin, 1988. (Published in 1824, the novel that made Rip Van Winkle and Ichabod Crane unforgettable American characters.)

CHAPTER 7

The original thirteen states had only a fraction of the population of the twenty-four states in the Union by 1830. The dramatic population growth and movement, as well as new technology, brought both opportunities and uncertainties to the people of the new republic. Americans responded to the changes with growing confidence in material progress and religious salvation.

SECTION 1

In the early republic, Americans of both European and African descent crossed the physical divide of the Appalachians, putting new pressure on the declining Native American population.

SECTION 2

Many Americans believed that the American Revolution marked a new era of invention, social progress, and material improvements that would bring dramatic changes to their lives.

SECTION 3

From duels to courtship, American social relationships and the rules that governed them were changing.

SECTION 4

A Second Great Awakening stirred a new spirit of equality and democracy in American religious denominations.

Life in the New Nation
1783–1830

The Relevance of the Big Idea

The settlers' feelings combined a sense of anticipation of new opportunities ahead with trepidation about the rapid changes affecting American families and society.

Ask students which of them have experienced a move—to a new school or a new town—that they thought would bring improvement in their lives. Discuss their sense of anticipation about the impending change. Were they excited? Were they at the same time frightened?

Life in the New Nation
1783–1830

Change, change, change! During the early republic, the nation grew dramatically, and its jostling, young population faced new challenges on every side. Settlers streamed over the Appalachians, joining to create new states, but finding too that their new society was one of loneliness and uncertainty. Many Americans were buoyed up by a sense that they could improve their lives— whether through new, profitable technology or through a fresh awakening of their spiritual life.

In Depth

Global Connections

In the early 1800s, a strong national spirit governed relations between the United States and Europe. In 1819, Spain sold all of Florida for $5 million and gave up its claim to the Pacific Northwest. Secretary of State John Quincy Adams was disappointed not to gain Texas as well. The absorption of all North America by the United States, he said in 1819, was "as much a law of nature . . . as that the Mississippi should flow to the sea."

Events in the United States

1787 The Northwest Ordinance makes slavery illegal north of the Ohio River.

1793 Eli Whitney invents the cotton gin.

1783	1788	1793	1798	1803

Events in the World

1784 The British government assumes control of the East India Company.

1792 Denmark becomes the first nation to abolish the slave trade.

1805 Modern day Egypt is founded.

RESOURCE DIRECTORY

Teaching Resources

Alternate Lesson Plan: Demonstrating the Big Idea found in the Alternate Lesson Plans folder, p. 32, is an alternate lesson strategy to instruct students about the Big Idea that during this period Americans developed an increasing belief that their lives would be improved through technology, education, and religion.

Alternative Assessment Handbook provides information, guidance, and strategies for alternative methods of assessment. It includes an essay on new trends in assessment, guidance and strategies for developing performance tasks and portfolios, scoring rubrics, and sample evaluation forms.

Pages 186–191

Migrating Multitudes

In the early republic, a young and dynamic population of Americans of both European and African descent migrated west over the barrier of the Appalachians and in a few decades settled the Ohio and Mississippi valleys and the Gulf Coast. Meanwhile, Native American populations, still declining in number, were also on the move.

 Pages 193–197

The Spirit of Improvement

Many Americans believed that the American Revolution had ushered in a new era—a time to experiment and invent new and better ways to do old tasks. They were confident they could bring social progress and dramatic material improvements to their lives.

 Pages 198–201

Shifting Social Relationships

Men meeting in a duel at dawn or couples courting at dusk were all dealing as well as they could with a time of change, in which Americans searched—sometimes with violence and sometimes with affection—for new rules to guide their social relationships.

 Pages 202–205

The Democratization of American Religion

Americans stirred by the Second Great Awakening believed that in the search for religious salvation, all people were equal. Joining Methodist and other popular churches, they found a new form of fulfillment in the democratic community of their fellow believers.

1807 Robert Fulton proves that boats can be driven by steam power.

1810s A Second Great Awakening revives religion in the United States.

1819 The Adams-Onís Treaty transfers ownership of Florida from Spain to the United States.

1825 The Erie Canal is completed and opened to traffic.

1829 The Cherokee declare themselves an independent nation.

| 1808 | 1813 | 1818 | 1823 | 1828 |

1815 Brazil declares its independence. • Napoleon is defeated at Waterloo.

1824 Simón Bolívar becomes emperor of Peru.

1830 The military in Warsaw, Poland, revolts against Russian rule.

Media and Technology

 Transparency
Time Lines, E-3

 Alternative Assessment

As an ongoing chapter project, students can create a work of historical fiction—a short story, a play or skit, or an episode of a TV drama—that looks at life in an American town in about 1830. The dramatization can span a day, a week, or a longer time period. The content should depict family life, society, and the impact of migration, technology, and religion on the town. The setting should be clearly described and identified as being either east or west of the Appalachians. Students may choose to tell the story through a narrator, an omniscient writer, or a citizen of the town. More ambitious works will incorporate outside research to create a more accurate contemporary atmosphere.

Explain that projects will be evaluated according to the following guidelines:

● **Unacceptable** Project is not attempted or fails to meet the requirements outlined.

● **Limited/Acceptable** Project gives an accurate picture of some social aspects of American life in the 1830s.

● **Extensive/Commendable** Project integrates the required criteria into a work that is accurate and lively.

● **Extraordinary/Outstanding** Project shows evidence of outside research in an integrated, accurate, and lively presentation.

For more information and guidance on alternative assessment trends and strategies, see the Alternative Assessment Handbook in the Resource Directory on page 184.

SECTION 1

Migrating Multitudes

1. FOCUS

Connecting to the Big Idea

See page 184B. Tell students that a young, energetic generation of Americans of both European and African heritage scaled the Appalachian barrier during this period and moved into the river valleys from the Ohio to the mouth of the Mississippi. Ask what effect this migration had on the original inhabitants of these regions.

Objectives

● Characterize the population of the United States between 1780 and 1830.
● Describe the settling of the trans-Appalachian region.
● Describe the role of African Americans in United States territorial expansion.
● Analyze the effects of westward migration on Native Americans.

Bellringer

Tell students that in 1810 only one-seventh of the American population of 7.2 million lived west of the Alleghenies; by 1840 more than a third of 17.2 million Americans lived there. Then ask students to consider the impact of such rapid population growth on the country.

Reading Strategy

Predicting Content Have students read the headings in Section 1 and write a sentence or two predicting the outcome of the section. When they have finished reading, ask them to check the accuracy of their predictions.

SECTION PREVIEW

In the early republic, a young and dynamic population of Americans of both European and African descent migrated west over the barrier of the Appalachians and in a few decades settled the Ohio and Mississippi valleys and the Gulf Coast. Meanwhile, Native American populations, still declining in number, were also on the move.

Key Concepts
• The population of the United States in the period between 1780 and 1830 was young, doubling every twenty years, and constantly in motion.
• Americans settled and transformed the trans-Appalachian region of the United States with unprecedented speed and thoroughness.
• Although most were enslaved, African Americans were key participants in the territorial expansion of the United States.
• Native Americans were also migrants, but their population was declining instead of increasing like the population of other Americans.

Key Terms, People, and Places
Adams-Onís Treaty, black codes; persister

The main reason that the United States grew explosively during its early years was that Americans had so many babies. One of them lay in this cradle about 1800.

 A certain baby, given the name Frank, was born enslaved in South Carolina in 1777. Seventy-seven years later, in 1854, he died a free man in Illinois under the name Free Frank. His migration from the East Coast to the western region of the expanding United States parallels the movement of thousands of other Americans during this time.

Frank's mother was Juda, a West African woman, and his father was probably George McWhorter, her Scots-Irish owner. Without the opportunity to participate in revolutionary activities like fighting battles and writing constitutions, Free Frank no doubt spent his early life doing chores and working in the fields.

In 1795, when Frank was eighteen years old, George McWhorter moved to Pulaski County, Kentucky. There McWhorter and his four enslaved workers cleared land and planted crops. The next year, Frank met and courted Lucy, a twenty-five-year-old woman belonging to the Denham family. Although Frank and Lucy shared a love that would keep them together for fifty-five years, they could not legally marry because they were enslaved.

Frank and Lucy, however, were married in their own ceremony in 1799. A daughter named after Frank's mother, Juda, was born in 1800. Lucy bore sixteen more children over the next three decades. Of them, only six would survive to adulthood, and only four would be born free.

Capitalizing on Frank's talents, George McWhorter rented his slave labor to others in the early 1800s. So profitable was Frank's work that even after McWhorter moved to Tennessee in 1810, Frank stayed behind to run the farm and hire out his own time, sending McWhorter an annual payment.

More important, Frank earned money for himself, planning to buy his freedom and that of his family. To do this, he opened his own business preparing saltpeter, which was the principal ingredient in gunpowder. Because the United States was at war between 1812 and 1815, the production of saltpeter was highly profitable.

By 1817 Frank had earned the $800 necessary to purchase freedom for Lucy. She was freed first, so that all their future children would be free. Moreover, Lucy could now apply

▶ RESOURCE DIRECTORY

Teaching Resources

📄 **Reproducible Lesson Plan** found in the Unit 2 folder, p. 78, provides a summary of the Section 1 lesson plan content.

📄 **Alternate Lesson Plan: Learning Styles** found in the Alternate Lesson Plans folder, p. 33, provides a strategy, especially effective for auditory learners, to help students discuss the experiences of many groups of people during the westward migration.

📄 **Guided Reading and Review** found in the Unit 2 folder, p. 82, provides a structure for reading and mastering the key concepts and reviewing the key terms for Section 1. (Guided Practice)

⭐📄 **Critical Thinking Activity** Making Comparisons: Population Boom, found in the Unit 2 folder, p. 95, allows students to apply the skill by analyzing census data from 1790 to 1830.

the money she made in spinning, weaving, and knitting to buying freedom for other members of the family. Frank also expanded his business interests and bought over 700 acres of land. In 1819 the couple had the $800 necessary to buy Frank's freedom.

Frank—now Free Frank—and Lucy were eventually able to buy the freedom of two sons, two daughters, one daughter-in-law, four grandsons, three granddaughters, and two great-grandchildren. The total cost was $16,000. This sum represented an enormous amount of work in a time when the yearly income of the average American worker was under $100.

In 1830 Free Frank moved across the Ohio River into the free state of Illinois. There he purchased land and founded the town of New Philadelphia. In 1839 Frank and Lucy were formally married in Illinois. When asked whether he would love, cherish, and support Lucy, Free Frank replied: "Why, God bless your soul! I've done that thing for the last 40 years." Free Frank died in New Philadelphia in 1854. Lucy lived until 1870, long enough to see the end of slavery in the United States.

The success of Free Frank and Lucy in buying their freedom and achieving a comfortable existence in a free state was very unusual for enslaved African Americans. But in several ways Frank and Lucy were typical of most Americans in the new nation: they repeatedly moved farther west, they worked hard at making money, they tried to gain control over their own lives, and they had a large family.

This painting of Lucy was copied from a photograph taken in 1870.

A Young and Growing Nation

⭐ The population of the United States grew explosively during the period before 1830, as the graph at right shows. About 2.7 million people lived in the original thirteen states in 1780. By 1830, there were 12 million people in 24 states. During the 1780s, the population increased by more than 40 percent, the greatest increase by percentage in the country's history. The number of Americans was roughly doubling about every twenty years. Had the population continued to grow at this rate, more than a billion people would live in the United States today, about four times its actual population. In fact, population growth in this country in the first half of the 1800s was more than double that of any other place in the world.

Most of this increase was the result of reproduction, not immigration. Like Lucy and Free Frank, Americans were having lots of babies. In the early 1800s, there were hundreds of thousands of immigrants from Europe and Africa. But they amounted to no more than 10 percent of the population growth.

Between 1800 and 1849, the average woman had 4.9 children. And this high number of births occurred despite a trend toward birth control among white couples. So strong

It may have been a homesick sailor who carved this whale tooth in 1834. He showed what was on his mind: a scene of family life in the young United States.

United States Population Growth, 1780–1830

Number of Persons (in thousands) — Legend: Total, White, African American

Years: 1780*, 1790, 1800, 1810, 1820, 1830

*Estimated
Source: *Historical Statistics of the United States*

 Interpreting Graphs
The census, a national head count taken every ten years, recorded the startling population growth of the United States. *Which group grew more rapidly, white or African American? About how much did the total population increase between 1780 and 1830?*

Media and Technology

📽 **Transparency**
Critical Thinking, I-3

Discuss
Call students' attention to the quotations on page 188. How could it be said that "Old America seems to be breaking up?" What was the "Old America" to which Morris Birkbeck referred? What ideals, concerns, and dreams caused this upheaval?

Ask students how Free Frank's life parallels the movement of thousands of other Americans during the settlement of trans-Appalachia. Have them compare his experience with that of other African Americans at the time.

Analyze
Ask students why people were so willing to endure the hardships and heartbreaks of moving west. What motivated them? Compare the motives of whites, African Americans (free and enslaved), and Native Americans. Why are people today willing to undergo the hardships of relocation? Are there opportunities today that resemble those of the frontiers of the 1800s?

Caption Answer to ...

📊 **Interpreting Graphs**

The white population grew more rapidly; by about 9 or 10 million.

Teaching Heterogeneous Groups
Between 1780 and 1830 the population of the United States was rapidly growing and constantly in motion. To demonstrate a contrast and/or similarity to this period of migration, have students map the movement of their own families. Depending on class population, students' maps will either reflect or contrast with the migration period of the early republic. **LEP**

Enrichment

Have students write a short biography of Cherokee leader John Ross. Encourage them to research the traditions and changes in the society in which he grew up.

Answer to ...

Links Across Time

Possible answer: An older population means increased spending for health care, pensions, and retirement housing.

---

was this trend that advertisements relating to birth control occupied one eighth of the space in American newspapers by the middle of the 1800s.

Although African Americans continued to have many children, the white population grew a good deal faster. The result was that the percentage of Americans who were African began to fall from a high of 20 percent in 1790. The percentage continued to decline even after the 1870s, when white women were only bearing an average of 2.8 children. By the early 1900s, only 10 percent of Americans were of African American descent.

No matter what their heritage, most Americans in the new nation were under the age of twenty-one. In 1820 the median age of Americans was about seventeen. This means that there were as many people under the age of seventeen as there were over that age.

With a dynamic and youthful population, the United States was full of energy. People cherished all kinds of dreams for their families and hopes for the future. Everywhere men and women planned for a better tomorrow. There was a sense of anticipation in the air, the belief that somehow people who worked hard and were patient would achieve exactly what they wanted. The place to achieve their dreams, many Americans felt, was west of the Appalachian mountains.

The Settlement of Trans-Appalachia

Starting in the 1770s, Americans of both European and African descent migrated over the Appalachians into the Ohio, Mississippi, Tennessee, and Cumberland river valleys. In a matter of years, cities developed at key points such as Cincinnati, St. Louis, Memphis, and Chicago. Territories became states, and farms and plantations appeared in place of forests and meadows. As Morris Birkbeck, a traveler who described his journey over the Appalachians, wrote in the spring of 1817:

Old America seems to be breaking up, and moving westward. We are seldom out of sight, as we travel on this grand track towards the Ohio, of family groups behind, and before us, some with a view to a particular spot, close to a brother perhaps, or a friend who has gone before, and reported well of the country.

In 1787, when the United States Constitution was being written, only a few hundred Europeans were living north of the Ohio River. By 1830 there were hundreds of thousands of Americans of European and African descent living in the three states and two territories in the region. Ohio had close to a million residents, Indiana almost 350,000, and Illinois over 150,000.

| 1650 | 1700 | 1750 | 1800 | **Links Across Time** | 1850 | 1900 | 1950 | 2000 |

The Graying of America

Historians use median age to give people a sense of how old or how young a nation's population is as a whole. The *median* is the middle point of a set of data. Therefore, if the nation's median age is, for example, 16.7, exactly half of the nation's population is older than 16.7 years old and half is younger than 16.7 years. The higher the median age, the older the population.

Except for a slight decline between 1950 and 1970, the median age of the American population has been increasing decade by decade since 1820. In that year, the median age was 16.7. In 1870, the median age was 20.2; in 1920 it was 25.3. In 1990 the Bureau of the Census reported a median age of 33.

Census bureau projections show that median age will continue to rise. The projected median age for the year 2020 is 40.2. What accounts for this so-called graying of America? A decline in the birth rate since 1965 is one major factor. An increased life expectancy for older Americans is another. Unlike the Americans of the 1800s, Americans today generally choose to have few children and can expect to live at least into their 70s. *In what ways might an increasingly older population affect government spending?*

 RESOURCE DIRECTORY

Teaching Resources

Primary Source Activity Moving West, found in the Unit 2 folder, pp. 96–97, uses excerpts from artist John James Audubon's *Audubon's America*, to help students visualize the life of a Kentucky settler.

Most of these people had migrated down the Ohio River from western Pennsylvania and Virginia or northward from Kentucky and Tennessee. They usually traveled as families. Typically, men would go west to look for a good location and then return to gather the members and possessions of their households.

⭐ South of the Ohio River, Kentucky and Tennessee also had hundreds of thousands of people by 1830. Along the coast of the Gulf of Mexico, Alabama was home to more than 300,000 people, while Louisiana's population exceeded 215,000 and Mississippi's 130,000. To the west of Kentucky, the new slave state of Missouri had more than 140,000 residents.

Daniel Boone is probably the most well-known of the trans-Appalachia pioneers. In 1775, working for a land company interested in opening up the bluegrass region of central Kentucky to white settlement, Boone and a group of men cut the Wilderness Road through the Cumberland Gap of the Appalachian Mountains. Many of the people who migrated into trans-Appalachia traveled along this road, which began in eastern Tennessee and ended in present-day Louisville, Kentucky. One of the most prominent citizens of the Ohio Valley, Boone was a member of the Virginia legislature, a land speculator, and a tavern keeper as well as a hunter and a trapper. Staying close to the front lines of American expansion, Boone moved to Missouri in 1799. He died there in 1820. Twenty-five years later, Kentucky reclaimed the remains of its most famous citizen and reburied them in Frankfort.

The history of Florida demonstrates the relentless speed of American expansion. In 1810 Florida was under Spanish control; the estimated population was 11,000. In 1819 the **Adams-Onís Treaty,** negotiated by Secretary of State John Quincy Adams and Spain's Don Luis de Onís, transferred Florida to the United States. During the 1820s, Americans of European and African descent moved into the territory, raising the

population to almost 35,000 by 1830 and close to 55,500 by 1840. Five years later, Florida became a state.

Like Free Frank and Lucy's family, migrants often stayed in one place only a short period of time. Families seemed to be constantly on the go, moving west or south in search of better and cheaper land. Nearly everywhere, however, small groups of families, whom historians call **persisters,** took up permanent residence and became a core population in an area. They were surrounded by a changing horde of people who stayed in one place for only a few years.

African American Pioneers

As the experience of Free Frank and Lucy shows, not all of these migrants were of European heritage. One recent historian has estimated that owners forcibly relocated some 98,000 enslaved African Americans from Virginia and Maryland between 1790 and 1810. When the people brought directly from Africa or from the West Indies are added in, some 194,000 African Americans were among the multitudes of people who settled Kentucky, Tennessee, and the Gulf Coast states. Another 144,000 followed between 1810 and 1820.

Enslaved couples were not always able to keep their families together, because slaveholders were not legally obligated to respect slave

Using Historical Evidence Starting a new home in Ohio was tough work for most of the nearly 1 million people who settled there by 1830. *What tasks are shown in the picture above?*

Caption Answer to ...

Using Historical Evidence

Clearing land, building a house, cooking over an open fire, gathering firewood, tending horses.

In Depth

Multicultural Perspectives

As early as 1651, an African American couple were landowners in Virginia. Anthony and Mary Johnson had been indentured servants. After earning their freedom in 1651, the Johnsons began planting corn and tobacco on their own land. They prospered until a fire destroyed their home and forced them to seek tax relief from the courts. On reviewing the Johnsons' hardship, the court ruled that they no longer had to pay taxes.

Media and Technology

Transparencies
Our Multicultural Heritage, C-10; Fine Art, D-6

The region had originally been populated or settled by Native Americans; later population and settlement of the region thus can accurately be referred to as a repopulation or resettlement.

3. ASSESS

Section 1 Review Answers

1. (a) Adams-Onís Treaty, see p. 189, (b) black codes, see p. 190

2. persister, see p. 189

3. Frank, like other Americans of the time, migrated westward repeatedly, worked hard at making money, tried to gain control over his own life, and had a large family. Since most enslaved African Americans could not profit from their own labor, few were able to buy their freedom and improve their lots by moving west.

4. The trans-Appalachia area, including the Ohio, Mississippi, Tennessee, and Cumberland river valleys.

In Depth

Historical Misconceptions

No image is more associated with American history than that of the move westward toward the frontier—perpetuated in popular stories and films as the triumph of cowboys over Native Americans, of settlers over hunters. Now some claim that the very word *frontier* masks the facts of European conquest and exploitation of Native Americans. Some historians are sympathetic to such criticism and would like to redefine the term. Historian Richard White, for example, describes the frontier as a zone, a middle ground, a place of relatively equal interaction among different peoples where no particular group is dominant.

marriages. Migration, too, often pulled African American families apart. A husband or wife might be sold to another slaveholder at a great distance or forced to migrate with another master to a far-away state or territory.

North of the Ohio River, slavery was technically illegal, in accordance with the Northwest Ordinance of 1787. But laws called **black codes** kept African Americans there under the authority of white Americans. Indentured servitude, too, was used as a means to exploit African American labor without resorting to enslavement.

More powerful than the willingness to exploit African Americans, however, was the prejudice that led new settlers to try to keep African Americans out of their territories and states altogether. Many Americans of European descent living in Ohio, Indiana, and Illinois did not want African Americans in their states, not only because of bias, but because of their fear that African Americans would take up land and take away jobs. As a result, stiff requirements for African American settlers kept the African American population north of the Ohio River very small. In Illinois, for example, one requirement for taking up residence called for African Americans to post a $1,000 security bond unless they owned land.

Hundreds of thousands of enslaved African Americans settled in the West with their owners. This sketch by Louis Miller shows a group on the march from Virginia to Tennessee.

MAKING CONNECTIONS

The migration into the trans-Appalachian region has been called a repopulation or resettlement. Why?

Native American Migration and Adjustment

Native Americans, too, were migrating during this period. In most cases, their movements were involuntary. The map on page 191 shows how the treaties signed by Native Americans gradually transferred their land to the United States government. The loss of their homelands forced Native Americans to undertake long and perilous journeys to new areas west of the Mississippi River.

No matter where Native Americans lived, their numbers continued to decline. As had been true for three hundred years, the main cause was disease transmitted by contacts with Europeans. Epidemics regularly devastated villages both east and west of the Mississippi River.

Most whites were hostile to Native Americans. But a handful of missionaries and government officials worked to convert them to Christianity and educate them in European ways. Congress even appropriated $20,000 in 1793 to teach Native Americans how to read and write and how to grow crops. However well-intentioned, these efforts required Native Americans to renounce their cultures and become like Americans of European descent in their daily lives as well as in their religion.

Many Native Americans, under the leadership of men like Tecumseh and Tenskwatawa, actively resisted European cultural as well as military dominance. A major exception were the Cherokee who lived in eastern Tennessee, western North Carolina, and northern Georgia. Under the leadership of men of mixed Native American and European American heritage, such as John Ross, the Cherokee adopted a policy of accommodation. They devised legal and political systems that blended Cherokee and European traditions and in 1827 declared themselves an independent nation. Meanwhile, many Cherokee adopted the notion of private property and became farmers and artisans. The 15,000 Cherokee owned 22,000 cattle, 1,300 enslaved African Americans, 31 mills for grinding flour, 10 sawmills, 8 cotton gins, and 18 schools. They also published their own newspaper using an alphabet invented by one of their

▶ RESOURCE DIRECTORY

Teaching Resources

⭐ 📄 **Literature Activity** The Pioneers, found in the Unit 2 folder, pp. 99–100, uses James Fenimore Cooper's *The Pioneers* to reveal the changing attitudes of frontier Americans during the early 1800s.

Native American Land Transfer Before 1850

Native American land cessions
- Land ceded before 1784
- Land ceded 1784–1819
- Land ceded 1820–1834
- Land ceded 1835–1850
- Reservations established by 1850

 Geography and History: Interpreting Maps
A map can only hint at the hardship and turmoil that being forced to move meant to Native Americans. For instance, the Seminole people fought valiantly against United States troops well into the 1840s to avoid being removed from their homeland. Some remain there even today. *Where is the Seminole homeland?*

leaders, Sequoyah. Cultural accommodation by the Cherokee did not make white Americans less hungry for Cherokee land, however, a problem that soon would lead to trouble.

⭐ Turmoil and change—not only for Native American society, but for American society as a whole—was inevitable. In less than half a century, Americans had conquered and settled the region from western Florida to southern Wisconsin. In 1775 the future United States had been a series of British colonies hugging the Atlantic Coast and the rivers of eastern North America. By 1830 the nation was a dynamic and aggressive land filled with millions of young, restless, and ambitious people, many of whom were sure they could change their world for the better.

SECTION 1 REVIEW

Key Terms, People, and Places
1. Define (a) Adams-Onís Treaty, (b) black codes.
2. Identify persister.

Key Concepts
3. How was Free Frank's life typical of American life in the new nation? How was it not typical of the lives of enslaved African Americans?
4. What area did Americans settle in the early 1800s?

5. What was the main cause of the great increase in the United States population before 1830?
6. How did the Cherokee react to continued American expansion and population growth?

Critical Thinking
7. **Determining Relevance** Would a young population be more inclined to migrate than an older population? Explain your thinking.

📄 **Quiz** found in the Unit 2 folder, p. 83, covers the main ideas in this section as well as the key terms.

---

5. Some immigration and the continued importation of slaves fueled population growth. But by far the most important factor was the high number of births. The average woman had 4.9 children in the early 1800s. American society was reproducing itself naturally.

6. They adopted a policy of accommodation, which included adopting some European political and economic practices, as well as becoming a nation of farm and artisan families.

7. Possible answers: Older people might be less inclined to embark on the difficult undertaking of migration. Older people have already had children if they are going to do so, so they do not need to migrate for additional land. Younger people may migrate to find land because land in settled areas is unavailable or too expensive.

Reteach
Ask students to make a chart entitled Migration, with the subheadings Who, Where, and Why. Have them add details under each subheading, using information from the section.

Caption Answer to ...

 Interpreting Maps

Florida

4. CLOSE

Reinforcing the Big Idea
A young, restless United States population was on the move in the early republic. As described in the next section, this energy would also be expressed in efforts to become an educated, disciplined, and technological society.

Geography

Using Population Density Maps

Focus Analyze and draw conclusions from a population density map.

Instruct Review the concept of population density by asking (1) Is your school in a densely populated region? (2) Is your county or township densely populated? (3) What parts of your state are more densely populated than other areas? Then have students read the text on this page and follow the steps outlined.

Extend See Historian's Toolbox Activity in the Resource Directory below.

Answers

1. (a) A range of population densities, or the number of persons per square mile. (b) Darkest: a population density of 90 or more persons per square mile; lightest: a population density of two or fewer persons per square mile. (c) No. Although Rhode Island had more people per square mile than any other state, it was also the smallest state in terms of total land area.

2. (a) 1790 map: Massachusetts, Rhode Island, Connecticut, New York, Pennsylvania, New Jersey, Virginia; 1830 map: Maine, New Hampshire, Massachusetts, Rhode Island, Connecticut, New York, Pennsylvania, New Jersey, Virginia, Ohio, Indiana, Kentucky, Tennessee. (b) New York, Pennsylvania, Ohio, Indiana, Kentucky, Tennessee, Louisiana, Alabama, and Georgia. (c) Differences: In 1790 settlement patterns were largely confined to the Atlantic coastal region. By 1830 settlement had expanded inland on a massive scale to the northwest, west, and southwest. Similarities: In both 1790 and 1830, the most densely populated areas were in the North. Southern regions remained far less densely populated than the northern regions.

3. (a) The South remained less densely populated than the North, because its economy remained based almost wholly in agriculture. Large tracts of land were taken up with crops—not people. The North's economy was more diversified. (b) Rivers, because the land around them was often fertile and the rivers themselves could be used to transport goods to market. Mountain ranges probably discouraged settlement, because their rugged terrain would have been difficult to farm.

Using Population Density Maps

Figures for population density indicate the average number of people living in a given area—usually a square mile or square kilometer. Population density maps can show density for a small area, such as a city, or a very large area, such as a continent or the entire world. Overall patterns of human settlement at a particular period of time also can be shown on a population density map. The population density maps on this page, for example, provide a broad picture of the number and distribution of European and African American people living in the United States at two different points in time—1790 and 1830. These maps are based on United States census counts, which at that time did not include Native Americans. Use the following steps to read and analyze the population density maps below.

1. Determine what information the maps provide. To interpret the population data, first look at the map key and then at the maps. (a) What kind of information is represented by the color-coded key on the map? (b) What do the darkest and lightest colors on the key represent? (c) You can tell at a glance that Rhode Island was the most densely populated state in 1790. Do you think that it also had the largest total population of any state? Explain.

2. Analyze population density patterns. Study the maps and answer the following questions. (a) Which states on each map included population densities of 45 or more people per square mile? (b) Which states experienced the greatest and most widespread increase in population density between 1790 and 1830? (c) What differences and similarities are apparent in the human settlement patterns in the United States in 1790 and 1830?

3. Study the maps to draw conclusions. Relate what you know from your reading to what you see on the maps. (a) What economic factors do you think accounted for the difference between the population densities of the North and South, both in 1790 and in 1830? (b) What geographical factors probably contributed to the overall pattern of settlement in 1830? Explain.

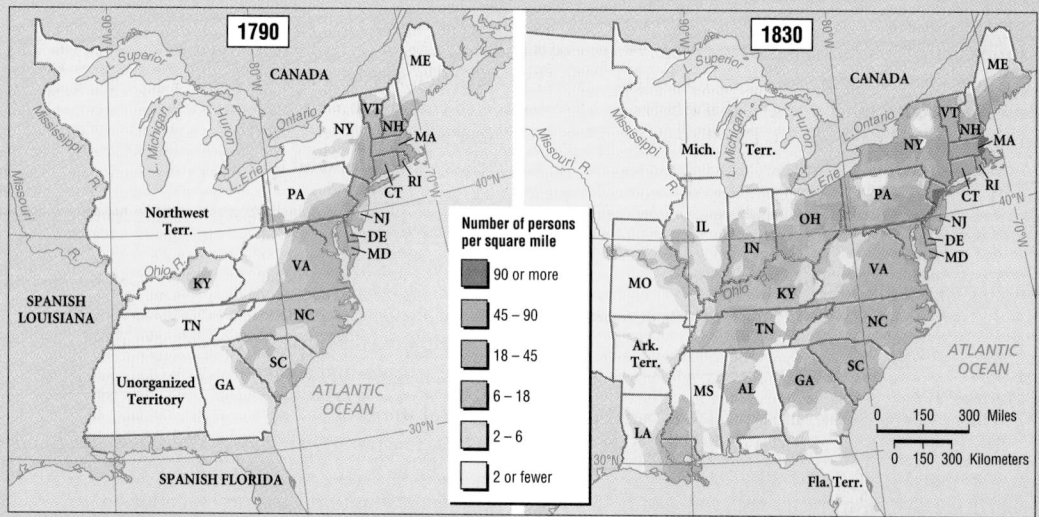

RESOURCE DIRECTORY

Teaching Resources

 Historian's Toolbox Activity Using Population Density Maps, found in the Unit 2 folder, p. 94, provides an opportunity to extend the lesson with a 1990 population density map of the western United States.

The Spirit of Improvement

SECTION 2

The Spirit of Improvement

SECTION PREVIEW

Many Americans believed that the American Revolution had ushered in a new era—a time to experiment and invent new and better ways to do old tasks. They were confident they could bring social progress and dramatic material improvements to their lives.

Key Concepts

• Many leading Americans emphasized that education was the key to making the United States into a stable and prosperous nation.
• Middle-class women gained status in a new role as "republican" mothers and wives.
• Inventions such as the cotton gin and improvements in transportation allowed rapid economic development, while a revolution in communication changed the social and political life of the new nation.

Key Terms, People, and Places

republican women, Industrial Revolution, system of interchangeable parts; Noah Webster, Samuel Slater, Eli Whitney

I n the 1780s, Americans believed that liberty would do more than free people from kings; it would allow them to improve the general condition of humankind. They organized dozens of societies dedicated to the improvement of the human condition—groups opposed to slavery, groups to improve jails, and groups to establish libraries. Despite the political squabbles of the period, a sense of anticipation and excitement about the possibilities of the future infected much of the population.

Science Lights a New Path

In Europe, the Enlightenment—an expansion of thought both about scientific and social issues in the 1700s—inspired a deep interest in the advancement of science and learning in the United States. This interest was shared by many well-educated Americans in the early republic, both men and women. Mercy Otis Warren wrote a history of the American Revolution. Benjamin Rush led a revolution in American medicine and wrote extensively on everything from agriculture to politics. The African American Benjamin Banneker, who had helped survey the nation's capital, was also a mathematician and printer. Among other things, he published a popular almanac.

Charles Willson Peale, yet another believer in the power of improvement, was an artist, a scientist, and an inventor. Born in Philadelphia, Peale started as a saddler and clock repairman and became an accomplished portrait painter. Like many other Americans of the time, Peale believed that people could find order in the natural world. To do so, they had to observe everything and record all the information they possibly could. Explained Peale in 1800:

Hoping that Americans would expand their minds as they expanded the nation, in 1839 the American Society for the Diffusion of Useful Knowledge published a traveling library (above) for settlers in the West. Below is a ticket to Charles Willson Peale's museum, which he ran to teach Americans how to read from the book of nature.

> The comfort, happiness, and support of all ranks, depend on their knowledge of nature. . . . In short, it is a source from which man is taught to know himself: whose lessons teach him to bear with patience, or to alleviate [lighten], the various sufferings to which human beings are liable.

Reproducible Lesson Plan found in the Unit 2 folder, p. 79, provides a summary of the Section 2 lesson plan content.

Alternate Lesson Plan: Cooperative Learning found in the Alternate Lesson Plans folder, p. 34, guides groups of students in compiling and presenting information about the material changes of the era and the social effects of those changes.

Guided Reading and Review found in the Unit 2 folder, p. 84, provides a structure for reading and mastering the key concepts and reviewing the key terms for Section 2. (Guided Practice)

1. FOCUS

Connecting to the Big Idea

See page 184B. To many Americans, the Revolution seemed to mark a new era of experimentation and invention. Ask students what kinds of social change this new attitude brought about.

Objectives

● Explain why education grew in importance in the early republic.
● Characterize the ideal "republican" woman of the early 1800s.
● Explain how technology changed the economic, social, and political life of the new nation.

Bellringer

Have students list ways in which they or other people try to change either their own lives or society in general. Do people always respond favorably to efforts toward change? Why or why not?

Reading Strategy

Reinforcing Key Ideas As they read, students should look for evidence of the "spirit of improvement" during the late 1700s and early 1800s, listing specific ways in which Americans tried to make their lives and their society better.

Answers will vary, but students should cite clear examples in support of their stated viewpoint.

2. INSTRUCT

Explain/Discuss

Point out to students that the ideas of rapid change, progress, and improvement of humankind are concepts most Americans take for granted today. This was not always the case, but after the Revolutionary War, a sense of new possibilities began to take hold among the nation's citizens. Discuss what caused this change in people's thinking. How did society's values change? What was the connection between changes in people's attitudes and changes in technology?

Analyze

Ask students why it could be said that the country became more united at the end of the 1700s and in the early 1800s. Have them consider the effect of ideas as well as technology.

In Depth

Biography

Emma Willard (1787–1870), a champion of women's rights, proposed "a Plan for Improving Female Education" in 1819 to widen women's access to knowledge and to end misconceptions about the ability of women to handle such "masculine" subjects as mathematics and philosophy. She put her plan into action in 1821 when she founded the Troy Female Seminary, one of the first women's colleges in the United States.

MAKING CONNECTIONS

Many Americans still believe in the power of science and technology to improve their lives. Do you? Explain why or why not, giving examples to prove your point.

Education as a Key to Success

In the colonial period, most of the schools and the handful of colleges that existed had been reserved for a few gentlemen. But in the new, democratic, enlightened American republic, many men and women began to insist that if the people were to govern the United States, they needed the benefits of education.

Noah Webster, who lived from 1758 to 1843, devoted much of his life to stressing the importance of a standard national language and to promoting education. When we refer to "Webster's" today, we are referring to a dictionary written according to his model. In 1790 Webster wrote:

> *Americans, unshackle your minds, and act like independent beings. . . . You have an empire to raise and support by your exertions, and a national character to establish and extend by your wisdom and virtues. To effect these great objects, it is necessary to frame a liberal plan of policy, and build it on a broad system of education.*

Many state constitutions called for public support of education, but few governments did much about it. The major exception was Massachusetts. In 1789 the Massachusetts legislature required towns to hire and pay the wages of college-educated schoolteachers. Their idealistic and nearly impossible task was to teach students

The spirit of improvement in the early republic called for better education. Here, women study music and geography at a school for young ladies about 1810.

---

the principles of piety, justice, and a sacred regard to truth, love to their country, . . . sobriety, industry and frugality, chastity, moderation and temperance, and those other virtues which are the ornament of human society, and the basis upon which the Republican Constitution is structured.

Outside of New England, support for public education rarely went beyond such fancy talk. Most Americans were not willing to pay taxes to support public schools. Rural people in particular expected their children to learn the skills they needed in life by working in the home. Consequently, the schools of this time—or academies, as they were often called—were mostly private.

Republican Women

In the late 1700s, the vast majority of these academies were exclusively for boys. In 1780 there were twice as many literate men as women in New England. But this gap narrowed over the next fifty years, as ideas about women changed.

In the early 1800s, many Americans started to see that educated women were crucial to the success of the nation. It was not just that they thought that women should know how to read and write. They also believed women should learn how to be genteel, or refined, and moral creatures; they should have discipline and self-restraint. The assumption was that women would serve society primarily as mothers and wives and in related fields, such as teaching. They would be **republican women,** or women fitted to make a contribution to the success of the new republic. As such, they needed to become models of quiet virtue. By the early 1800s, local academies were adding "female departments" to help girls learn the self-restraint necessary to become republican mothers and wives.

Miss P. W. Jackson was a graduate of a women's academy in Connecticut. In an observation made in 1809, she described her belief that the education of women was vital.

> *A woman who is skilled in every useful art, who practices every domestic virtue*

RESOURCE DIRECTORY

Teaching Resources

⭐ **American Profiles Activity** found in the Unit 2 folder, p. 90, profiles Catherine Littlefield Greene, who supported and encouraged Eli Whitney in his invention of the cotton gin.

. . . may, by her precept [direction] and example, inspire her brothers, her husband, or her sons, with such a love of virtue, such just ideas of the true value of civil liberty . . . that future heroes and statesmen, when arrived at the summit of military or political fame, shall exaltingly declare, it is to my mother I owe this elevation.

The message for young middle-class women in the Northeast was mixed. They were to be educated because they were important to the success of the nation as a whole, but their role was only a supporting one. With their virtue, according to the theory, they would support and encourage men to do great things.

Practical Improvements

While people—both men and women—were working to improve society, they also gave thought to increasing their own economic profit. As the United States expanded in the early republic, people came up with all kinds of money-making inventions and schemes.

A Revolution Encourages Inventions Many of the inventions stemmed from a development in Britain known as the **Industrial Revolution.** This revolution was a major change in the economy due to the increased use of machines powered by sources other than humans or animals. The British jealously guarded this new technology, making it against the law for anyone knowledgeable in the design of industrial machines to emigrate to another country.

In 1789, however, an English textile worker named **Samuel Slater** defied British law and brought the Industrial Revolution to the United States. Working from memory alone, he duplicated British machinery that quickly and efficiently spun cotton fibers into thread. Slater's water-powered spinning mill at Pawtucket, Rhode Island, was only the first of many. Throughout the 1790s and into the 1800s, New Englanders were building mills at the many waterfalls of their region.

⭐ The boom in milling cotton was fed by another new invention, the cotton gin. Devised by New Englander **Eli Whitney** while visiting a

Viewpoints
On Educating The People

Many people in the early 1800s agreed that education of the general public was crucial to gaining the knowledge that would improve the world. Few, however, were willing to pay the extra taxes such education would require. Each of the writers below is stating an opinion on this subject. *Summarize the viewpoint of each writer.*

Against Free Public Education
"I hope you do not conceive it at all necessary that everybody should be able to read, write, and cipher [solve math problems]. If one is to keep a store or a school, or to be a lawyer or physician, such branches may perhaps, be taught him. . . . But if he is to be a plain farmer, or a mechanic, they are of no manner of use, but rather a detriment."

Anonymous letter to the North Carolina state legislature, November 1829

For Free Public Education
"In a republic, the people constitute the government. . . . They frame the laws and create the institutions that promote their happiness or produce their destruction. If they be wise and intelligent, no laws but what are just and equal will receive their . . . [votes]. If they be ignorant and capricious [flighty], they will be deceived by mistaken or designing rulers into the support of laws that are unequal and unjust."

From a report of a workingmen's committee in Philadelphia, March 1830

Georgia plantation in 1793, the gin easily separated the seeds from cotton fiber. A worker could clean 1 pound of cotton per day without a gin; with a gin operated by water power, he could clean 1,000 pounds. Profit per pound of cotton skyrocketed, and with it the amount of cotton planted for harvest. The bales of cotton produced in the South rose from 6,000 in 1792 to 146,000 by 1805 and 334,378 by 1820. As profits grew, so did the demand for slave labor. The cotton gin, shown on page 196, was largely responsible for the continued growth and economic success of the slave labor system. It also fed the southern fever to move to undeveloped lands in the West, where sure wealth was the reward of anyone who put large acreage into producing cotton.

📄 **Viewpoints Activity** On Educating the People, found in the Unit 2 folder, pp. 92–93, provides further material on the debate over public education.

Answer to . . .
Viewpoints

The first writer is against free public education, claiming that people need only education specific to their own trades and professions. The second writer, in favor of free public education, feels that an informed and educated population is essential to the success of a republic, since the people constitute the government. For a more thorough examination of public education, see the Resource Directory below.

Activity
Creating a Poster
Have each student construct a poster entitled "New Types of Freedom." Posters should use text and drawings to illustrate how, after obtaining political freedom from Britain, Americans gained freedom from other types of "tyranny." **LEP**

Enrichment
Students can write a short essay on the "republican" woman, addressing the following questions: In what ways did this new image of women represent both progress and restriction? Why might some women have found it difficult to embody this new ideal?

Section 2 Review Answers

1. See page 196. Each part of a product is made to an exact standard so that it is interchangeable with the same part on other products of the same kind.

2. (a) Noah Webster, see p. 194, (b) Samuel Slater, see p. 195, (c) Eli Whitney, see p. 195

3. While Peale hoped to make money, he and other Americans in the late 1700s strongly believed that human beings could understand and thereby control their natural environment.

4. As wives, mothers, teachers of children, and models of virtue, educated women were seen as vital to the success of the nation. Their roles were seen as supporting the work of husbands, brothers, and sons.

5. Slater's re-creation of British textile machinery vastly increased production capacity. This expansion inspired many American inventions, such as the cotton gin and steam power, and launched the American Industrial Revolution.

6. Newspapers made information available to large numbers of people cheaply and relatively quickly. No longer was access to information about the world limited to a few privileged merchants, lawyers, and planters. Ordinary people now had easy access to information.

7. Possible answers: Differences are due to the widespread belief held by Americans in the early republic that they could change, order, and improve society; in contrast, goals for education today are more limited.

Reteach

Ask students to list the changes highlighted in this section in the following categories: science, self-improvement, technology, and communication.

Another change, too, contributed to the Industrial Revolution in the United States. This was the **system of interchangeable parts.** In colonial times, a worker made each part for a product one at a time. After he had assembled the product, he started over. Each part was slightly different and could not be interchanged or swapped with the parts from another product. Under the new system of interchangeable parts, each part of a product was made to an exact standard so that it could be interchanged with others like it. The system allowed workers to assemble products speedily. Eli Whitney is often credited with inventing the system of interchangeable parts in the 1790s, but it had been in use in Europe a decade earlier.

Steam Power Although inventors had once been limited to natural power from wind and falling water, now they no longer had to depend on those sources alone. The Industrial Revolution expanded rapidly as inventors increasingly exploited steam power. Robert Fulton proved that a ship could be driven by a steam engine when his 160-ton *Clermont* plied the Hudson River in 1807. In 1811 the *New Orleans* successfully navigated the Ohio and Mississippi rivers from Pittsburgh to New Orleans. The great advantage of the steamboat was that it could go upriver, against the current. By the 1820s, dozens of steamboats were on American rivers, reducing the costs of transportation and commerce.

People today are so used to rapid travel that they may find it hard to understand the significance of the steamboat. Before this invention, the speed at which humans could travel had not changed much in centuries. In the 1700s it still took as long to travel from Rome to London as it had taken in the time of the Roman Empire. Now the steam engine created a revolution in transportation. Soon it would be adapted for travel on land—by railroads—and for use as a power source by factories and mills.

Canals People were not only overcoming river currents; they were creating their own rivers in the form of canals. Waterways were still the cheapest and fastest means to carry people and goods over long distances. If rapids or waterfalls interrupted the easy flow of commerce, or if moving goods from one river to another was vital, the solution was to build a canal. In the early 1800s, as the map on page 197 shows, there was a virtual frenzy of canal building, much of it by states, some by private investors.

In the 1830s, states such as Ohio and Indiana borrowed millions of dollars to build canals to connect the Great Lakes and the Ohio River. The canal with the greatest impact, however, was the Erie Canal, which opened in 1825. Built by the state of New York, this 363-mile ditch linked the Hudson River and Lake Erie. But it affected an even wider area. The Erie Canal led to the settlement and development of the entire Great Lakes region. Farmers could now ship their products to markets as far away as New York City and beyond. The canal linked the economies and to some extent the destinies of the mid-Atlantic states and the Great Lakes region.

A Communication Revolution

⭐ After steamboats and canals, perhaps the most dramatic impact on the nation came from improvements in the means of spreading information. Here the federal government took the lead. There were only 75 post offices in the United States in 1790; by 1830 there were 8,450. Regular mail delivery made communication with distant places more efficient than ever

Planters had been looking for a way to clean the seeds from the short-fiber cotton that grew well in the South, and Eli Whitney's cotton gin filled that need.

5 The **clearer** brushes clean cotton fibers off the cylinder.

2 The **movable bar** forces raw cotton against the grate.

1 The **hopper** holds raw cotton.

6 The **clearer compartment** catches cleaned cotton.

3 The cotton seeds are too large to pass through the **grate**.

4 Teeth on the **cylinder** catch cotton fibers and pull them through the grate. Cotton seeds

▶ RESOURCE DIRECTORY

Teaching Resources

⭐ **Literature Activity** The Natural World, found in the Unit 2 folder, p. 101, uses William Cullen Bryant's "Inscription for the Entrance to a Wood" to reveal how this poet and journalist viewed nature.

⭐ **American Profiles Activity** found in the Unit 2 folder, p. 91, profiles Anne Newport Royall, considered to be the first female American journalist.

before. It also created a national network of information, since the mail also carried newspapers, magazines, and books.

An explosion also occurred in the amount of printed material available in the United States after the Revolution. In the colonial era, only a few newspapers had been published, in the major seaport cities. Generally, only white gentlemen living in these few places were able to read newspapers or to buy them on a regular basis, and so they had a monopoly on information. The ordinary person depended on word of mouth.

In the early republic, however, enterprising people hauled printing presses all over the United States. They had only to set up shop near a post office and a seat of government, and they were in business overnight. By the 1820s, more than five hundred newspapers and periodicals of all sorts were being published in the new nation.

 Newspapers and magazines now made information available to large numbers of people. Newspapers were to the early 1800s what television was to the late 1900s. The way Americans experienced their world would never be the same again. As a Massachusetts minister, William Bentley, observed in 1816,

the great number of newspapers put in circulation every incident which is raised in every local situation . . . so not a fire, an accident, a fear or a hope but it flies quickly throughout the union.

Thus newspapers and magazines helped to make American society more democratic. They also brought a kind of human contact to people trying to find their way through the new form American society had taken: the world of strangers described in the next section.

Growth of Canals by 1850

0   150   300 Miles
0   150   300 Kilometers

Canals built by 1825
Canals built 1826–1840
Canals built 1841–1850

Geography and History: Interpreting Maps
Americans built canals with great enthusiasm during the early 1800s. During the celebration that marked the opening of the Erie Canal, the governor of New York poured water into the Atlantic Ocean from the keg at right. *By what year was the Erie Canal open?*

SECTION 2 REVIEW

Key Terms, People, and Places
1. Define system of interchangeable parts.
2. Identify (a) Noah Webster, (b) Samuel Slater, (c) Eli Whitney.

Key Concepts
3. Why was Charles Willson Peale typical of his times?
4. Why did people in the new nation decide that the education of women was vital?
5. Explain how the Industrial Revolution in Britain affected the United States.
6. What effect did the increase in the numbers of newspapers have on the United States?

Critical Thinking
7. **Checking Consistency** Create a list of the goals of your school system as you see them. Compare it with the list developed by the Massachusetts legislature (page 194). Explain any differences between your list and the legislature's list.

Quiz found in the Unit 2 folder, p. 85, covers the main ideas in this section as well as the key terms.

Media and Technology

Transparencies
The Way It Works, H-6, H-7

Alternative Assessment

Mid-Point Monitoring
Ask students if they have
● Determined the location for their fictional American town
● Decided on a point of view from which the story will be told
● Constructed a rough outline for the plot that includes at least some of the key people or elements

4. CLOSE

Reinforcing the Big Idea

The postrevolutionary period marked a time of invention, social progress, and material improvement. These changes, however, also brought uncertainty for many Americans. The next section describes the search for new rules to guide social relationships.

1. FOCUS

Connecting to the Big Idea

See page 184B. In a changing America, the rules of society began to change, too. Ask why these shifts occurred and how they affected people's behavior.

Objectives

● Explain why America as an early republic was a nation of strangers.
● Describe how social rules changed for the younger generation.
● Contrast marriage considerations among wealthy whites with those that influenced the lower classes and enslaved African Americans.

Bellringer

Ask students how many of their families have moved from another state or country, and how many think that they will move to another state if they leave home. Then ask how many would still leave if they knew that in doing so they would probably never see their families again.

Reading Strategy

Reading for Evidence Ask students to find specific examples to support the statement on page 198 that ". . . rapid population growth, territorial expansion, and improvements . . . created an entirely new set of challenges that people had not anticipated."

SECTION 3

Shifting Social Relationships

SECTION PREVIEW

Men meeting in a duel at dawn or couples courting at dusk were all dealing as well as they could with a time of change, in which Americans searched—sometimes with violence and sometimes with affection—for new rules to guide their social relationships.

Key Concepts

- Population growth and migration made the early republic a nation of strangers, where people looked for new ways of judging others.
- Young people increasingly asserted themselves and considered their own wishes rather than those of their parents when determining whom they would marry.
- Among the lower classes and enslaved African Americans, marriage was heavily influenced by practical considerations.

Key Terms, People, and Places
Susanna Haswell Rowson

In the changing world of the 1800s, people took increased care in choosing a marriage partner. This wreath was worn by Lucy B. Marsh when she married Hiliah Hawks in 1827.

L iving in a world of rapid population growth, territorial expansion, and improvements was sometimes exciting. But it also created an entirely new set of challenges that people had not anticipated.

The technological changes of the early republic sparked high hopes for a rapid improvement in conditions. Many people, however, were left disappointed. Just as the success of Lucy and Free Frank was unusual among African Americans, it was highly unusual for Americans of European descent to become wealthy as well. Attempts at creating businesses resulted in far more failures than successes. Measured against the new, boundless opportunities promised by improving technology and commerce, even a little success was not enough. Some historians

believe that suicide and drunkenness became more common in this period, in part because so many people felt disappointed. The increase in suicide and the use of alcohol, however, may also have resulted from a new kind of loneliness.

A World of Strangers

⭐ The explosive expansion of American society put a tremendous strain on people. Colonial Americans had moved around, but in the early republic, migration occurred on a scale previously unknown. When sons and daughters left Massachusetts or other eastern states for Ohio, they had little hope of seeing their families again. Thus white middle-class Americans began to consider their relationships with nonrelatives to be as vital as those with kin. In a world of strangers, friendship became a significant social relationship. To be sure, friendship was nothing new. But now it was becoming the primary link between people, replacing more than supplementing family ties.

Without family ties, people had to rely on strangers. They had to know whom they could trust. And judging a stranger required knowing what class he or she belonged to. Colonial Americans had known a person's social class from social cues such as wigs and clothes, manners and speech. These cues were backed up by local knowledge: in the society of colonial times, which was centered in small cities or villages, people in a given area knew almost all its inhabitants and their status. But in a nation doubling in territory and population, in which people were constantly moving about, a stranger's place in society was unclear. The old cues could not be counted on. Likewise, people found their own standing in society might be called into question.

Defending One's Honor One response to the new uncertainty in society was for a man to defend to the death his "honor," or reputation for courage and honesty. Such fanatical

---

 RESOURCE DIRECTORY

Teaching Resources

Reproducible Lesson Plan found in the Unit 2 folder, p. 80, provides a summary of the Section 3 lesson plan content.

Alternate Lesson Plan: Learning Styles found in the Alternate Lesson Plans folder, p. 35, is especially helpful for visual learners and encourages students to describe the changing social relationships of the time and examine the causes for the changes.

Guided Reading and Review found in the Unit 2 folder, p. 86, provides a structure for reading and mastering the key concepts and reviewing the key terms for Section 3. (Guided Practice)

⭐ **Visual Learning Activity** "Do They Miss Me at Home?" found in the Unit 2 folder, p. 102, uses a songsheet from the early 1800s to illustrate the great social changes that occurred as a result of westward migration.

concern about honor had a long tradition that began in Europe. When their honor was challenged, gentlemen in Europe and colonial America had defended themselves in duels, in which one man challenged another to a fight with swords or pistols according to well-known rules. But in the early American republic, all kinds of men, gentlemen or not, took up this tradition and defended their honor in formal duels or free-for-all fights.

Andrew Jackson, the hero of the Battle of New Orleans and President of the United States from 1829 to 1837, avidly pursued this tradition. Jackson was an orphan from a poor family, and thus not genuinely a gentleman at all. Yet on various occasions in the late 1790s and early 1800s, he defended his honor with a walking stick, a horsewhip, and a .70-caliber pistol. In one formal duel in 1806, he took the bullet of Tennessee's most deadly duelist in his chest and then calmly killed his opponent.

Successful defense of one's honor was no guarantee of a pure character. Jackson had a reputation as "the most roaring, rollicking, game-cocking, horse-racing, card-playing, mischievous fellow . . . the head of rowdies." Some historians believe that the increase in dueling and other forms of violence was partly due to heavy drinking. Their theory is supported by evidence that during the early republic, more alcohol was consumed per person than at any other time in American history.

Courtship Women, too, had to deal with uncertainty about others in the rapidly changing world of the early republic. One of the few major decisions in her life that a young middle-class woman had some control over was the question of whom she would marry. It was vital that she know the man with whom she was to begin a lifelong relationship.

Previously, people had found partners among those with whom they were familiar; often fathers chose spouses for their children. Now all that had changed. Partly in the spirit of democratic revolution, partly in response to the weakening of parental authority brought about by the expansion of the United States, young couples were increasingly making their own decisions about marriage.

Women looking for guidance in this new world of choice found it in books. Some turned to advice manuals, but moralizing novels were more popular. Ancestor of the modern romance novel, this type of book usually told the story of an innocent young woman whose life was ruined because she ignored the advice of her parents and fell in love with a man simply because he was charming or good-looking. Steady, sober men might not seem attractive at first, admitted the writers, but because of their strength of character, such men would be responsible providers for wives and children over the long term.

By far the most popular of these works was the 1794 novel *Charlotte Temple* by **Susanna Haswell Rowson.** Having married a completely irresponsible man, Rowson was forced to support her family as a writer and headmistress of an academy for young women. *Charlotte Temple* tells the sad tale of a fifteen-year-old girl carried off by a handsome man in a splendid military uniform, who soon abandons her. Penniless and desperate, Charlotte bears the child that results from this affair and then dies in the arms of her forgiving father, who arrives just in time to care for his grandchild. The moral of the story is that appearances do not provide enough clues to the character of a potential partner. One chapter title in the book, a quote from Shakespeare, sums up Rowson's message: "A Man May Smile, and Smile, and Be a Villain." Rowson wrote:

In the upheaval of society in the early republic, Americans took up the old European custom of dueling to prove their honor. Andrew Jackson owned this set of saw-handled dueling pistols.

Visual Learning Activity "Married Mum?" found in the Unit 2 folder, p. 103, uses a humorous cartoon to describe the social lifestyles on the western frontier during the 1780s.

2. INSTRUCT

Explain/Discuss

Discuss with students how the expansion of society and the mobility of the population put a strain on Americans in the early 1800s. Ask how the "rules" of American society changed as a result. How would these changes be exciting? How would they be frightening? What kinds of behavior seemed to reflect people's fears?

Analyze

Ask students why men were willing to risk their lives in duels. How did duels improve the status of men in their own eyes and in the eyes of others?

Activity

Teaching Heterogeneous Groups
Constant migration turned the early republic into a nation of strangers. To ease their loneliness, many Americans turned to church and social organizations to establish relationships, social contact, and a sense of community. To demonstrate the importance of community and social relationships, have students identify the community of which they feel a part. These could be neighborhoods, schools, religious groups, clubs, or their town or city. Ask what needs are filled by their community and what qualities members have in common. The information might be recorded on a class chart.

Enrichment

Students can choose either marriage or defending one's honor as the topic for a short paper in which they compare and contrast customs in the early republic with customs today.

Possible answers: There is less emphasis today on dating as a means to finding a marriage partner at a young age; dating is less formal today; many students go out in groups rather than just as couples.

3. ASSESS

Section 3 Review Answers

1. Susanna Haswell Rowson, see p. 199

2. Rapid improvements raised expectations, leaving many disappointed. Migration also led to loneliness because family ties were broken.

3. Jackson, although only dubiously a gentleman, was involved in numerous duels, including one in which he killed Tennessee's most successful duelist. One reason for the increase in dueling at this time was that cues that determined position had become blurred as a result of migration and expansion.

4. Because of the population mobility during this period, a woman was less likely to know much about the status and family background of a potential partner; the courtship became an opportunity to get to know him better before making a final commitment.

In Depth

Did You Know?

For women in the 1800s, marriage meant the loss of their legal rights. When feminist Lucy Stone agreed to marry Henry Blackwell in 1865, the following protest against the existing marriage laws was read at their wedding: "We protest . . . against those laws which give to the husband:
(1) The custody of the wife's person. (2) The exclusive control and guardianship of their children.
(3) The sole ownership of her personal [property], and use of her real estate . . . ."

This little tale . . . may . . . be of service to some who are so unfortunate as to have neither friends to advise, or understanding to direct them, through the various and unexpected evils that attend a young and unprotected woman in her first entrance into life.

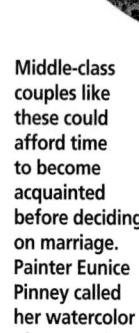

Middle-class couples like these could afford time to become acquainted before deciding on marriage. Painter Eunice Pinney called her watercolor *The Courtship*.

As middle-class women exercised more power in their choice of spouses, they became increasingly cautious about romantic relationships. In the early republic, many delayed marriage for as long as possible. They also used long engagements to learn the true character of their prospective husbands. Since falling in love might well cloud a person's judgment, anyone considering marriage needed time to think carefully before taking such a step. A definite trend emerged: men and women devoted a prolonged period, known as courtship, to getting acquainted and negotiating the terms of their future life together before they finally and formally committed themselves to marriage.

Consider, for example, the proposal of Zadoc Long, a twenty-four-year-old storekeeper in Buckfield, Maine. After a year of courtship, he asked Julia Davis to be his wife. His offer—which was accepted—sounds like a response to a long list of demands presented during intense negotiations.

I feel sad when I don't see you. Be married, why won't you? And come to live with me. I will make you as happy as I can. You shall not be obliged to work hard; and when you are tired, you may lie in my lap, and I will sing you to rest. . . . I will play a tune upon the violin as often as you ask and as well as I can; and leave off smoking, if you say so. . . . I would be always very kind to you, I think,

because I love you so well. I will not make you bring in wood and water, or feed the pig, or milk the cow, or go to the neighbors to borrow milk. Will you be married?

MAKING CONNECTIONS

How did courtship in the early republic differ from dating today?

Marriage in the Lower Classes

Middle-class men and women had the time and the standard of living needed to support long engagements, during which they sounded out one another's commitment and character. For working-class and enslaved women, long courtships were an unaffordable luxury. But they, too, exercised a great deal of independence in choosing husbands, although their courtships tended to be more practical than romantic.

Young working women and men in New York and other cities had to act quickly when courting one another. Their parents were rarely able or willing to support them past the first dozen years of life. Establishing households was for them less a matter of affection than of necessity. This is not to say that husbands and wives in the lower classes did not love one another. Certainly many of them did. But for them, marriage was first of all a union of two people who would share the obligations of having children and supporting a household.

Among enslaved women and men, freedom in choosing a marriage partner was common, if only because slave marriages were not recognized by the law and thus owners often did not bother to interfere in them. Furthermore, marriage between enslaved African Americans often required a great commitment simply to keep a family together. An enslaved husband and wife living on separate plantations might travel for miles several nights a week to be with each other. For these reasons, African Americans generally remained extremely loyal not just to their spouses but to their children as well.

The freedom working-class and enslaved women had in choosing their marriage partners was viewed with disapproval by women of

RESOURCE DIRECTORY

Teaching Resources

Using Historical Evidence Whether rushed or carefully considered, courtship led to the marriages that were building the new nation. *Country Wedding,* a painting of about 1819, gently pokes fun at young love and informal country life. *Describe the activities of the participants in the wedding.*

the middle class. Middle-class women were increasingly emphasizing their personal virtue as republican women. To them, the rapidly formed marriages of the lower classes seemed a result of "passion," or lack of self-control. They did not understand that their lower-class counterparts were not "fallen" women, that is, lacking in self-control or virtue. Women of the lower classes were simply driven by the neces-

sity of forming bonds to survive in a rapidly changing world.

As the next section shows, during the early republic, women of both the lower class and the middle class looked increasingly to religion to help them make sense of the sweeping changes in their lives. Like other Americans of the time, they believed that they could improve their spiritual as well as their material circumstances.

SECTION 3 REVIEW

Key Terms, People, and Places
1. Identify Susanna Haswell Rowson.

Key Concepts
2. Give two possible causes for the increase in suicide and alcohol abuse that some historians detect in the early republic.
3. How is Andrew Jackson's career an example of the social uncertainty of the United States in the early decades of the 1800s?

4. Why did courtships gain in importance during the early republic?
5. Why did enslaved men and women have some freedom in choosing a marriage partner?

Critical Thinking
6. **Formulating Questions** Imagine you were asked to advise two young people of the early republic who were considering marriage. What questions would you suggest they ask each other?

Quiz found in the Unit 2 folder, p. 87, covers the main ideas in this section as well as the key terms.

5. Slave marriages were not recognized by the law and thus masters often did not bother to interfere in them.

6. Possible questions: Have you been married before? What are your interests? How large a family do you consider ideal? Do you either anticipate or object to migration to another place?

Reteach

Ask students to use the information from the section to describe the social problems faced by each of the following groups of people: men; upper-class and lower-class women; enslaved African Americans.

Caption Answer to ...

Using Historical Evidence

The couple being married are absorbed in the process, as is the minister marrying them; the children in the foreground are involved in their own game; the woman wiping her eyes seems to be enjoying the consolation of the man beside her; several other occupants of the room are paying little or no attention to the wedding.

4. CLOSE

Reinforcing the Big Idea

In a nation of strangers, the rules governing social behavior caused uncertainty for many Americans. The next section describes the comfort and sense of purpose many found in rising egalitarian religious denominations during this period.

1. FOCUS

Connecting to the Big Idea

See page 184B. A Second Great Awakening stirred Americans to the belief that all people were equal in the search for salvation. Ask students in what ways that belief was fulfilled.

Objectives

● Describe how the idea of religious equality was practiced.
● Analyze why women in particular were attracted to the Second Great Awakening.
● Trace the development of the African Methodist Episcopal Church.

Bellringer

Write the word *evangelist* on the chalkboard and ask students to define it. Then ask students to think about what draws people to evangelism. Ask who are some of today's evangelists and where they can be seen.

Reading Strategy

Question Writing Ask students to skim the section, noting the headings and subheadings. Then have them turn the headings into questions and answer the questions as they read the section.

The Democratization of American Religion

SECTION 4

SECTION PREVIEW

Americans stirred by the Second Great Awakening believed that in the search for religious salvation, all people were equal. Joining Methodist and other popular churches, they found a new form of fulfillment in the democratic community of their fellow believers.

Key Concepts

• Camp meetings and other revival practices allowed anyone to participate and experience salvation if they chose to do so. Religion thus became more democratic.

• Women in particular found in the Second Great Awakening a focus for community life and a means of achieving power in society.

• The African Methodist Episcopal Church became popular with African Americans by offering an emotional religious experience in a setting free from white prejudice and restraint.

This lantern lit the way to a meeting at a religious camp during the great reawakening of religious life that took place during the early 1800s.

Key Terms, People, and Places
denomination, Second Great Awakening, evangelical movement; Richard Allen

The Bill of Rights established the separation of churches and the national government in American society. Some churches still had state ties, however. The Congregational churches, which were the descendants of the Puritan churches, received support from New England states well into the 1800s. But there was a growing sense everywhere that church and state should be separate. This view was not surprising, considering that as early as 1790, when the first census was taken, only about one out of ten Americans was a member of a church.

Those Americans who did attend church had many different ways of worshipping. Christianity dominated, but within that religion, a growing number of different subgroups, or **denominations,** were evolving. Many of them emphasized voluntary participation and the ability of all people to find salvation without the aid of educated ministers or fancy churches.

The Second Great Awakening

In the early 1800s, a new wave of religious revivals called the **Second Great Awakening** swept the United States. Like the First Great Awakening in the 1730s and 1740s, this revival was an **evangelical movement,** stressing preaching instead of rituals, and emphasizing that people could be saved for a happy life after death if they believed in Christ and the Bible. This evangelical movement was highly democratic—its members believed that anyone could participate and experience salvation if he or she chose to do so. Beginning in Kentucky and Tennessee, the Second Great Awakening attracted large numbers of people searching for meaning and community in a constantly shifting world of strangers and migration.

Camp meetings were the hallmark of the Awakening. These revival gatherings were like huge democratic fairs, in which what mattered was not who you were, but how deeply you felt your faith. One participant, William Thacher, described a meeting in New Haven, Connecticut, in 1804:

> The power increased during the whole meeting. . . . Triumphing, . . . weeping, people falling, the voice of joy and sorrow mingling, prayer, praise, and shouting, shouting, shouting filled the groves around.

RESOURCE DIRECTORY

Teaching Resources

Reproducible Lesson Plan found in the Unit 2 folder, p. 81, provides a summary of the Section 4 lesson plan content.

Alternate Lesson Plan: Critical Thinking Testing Conclusions, found in the Alternate Lesson Plans folder, p. 36, provides an alternate strategy to enhance students' understanding of the characteristics of the Second Great Awakening.

Guided Reading and Review found in the Unit 2 folder, p. 88, provides a structure for reading and mastering the key concepts and reviewing the key terms for Section 4. (Guided Practice)

Methodists and Mormons Among the denominations that experienced the most growth during the Second Great Awakening were Baptists, Methodists, and Disciples of Christ. Methodists in particular attracted large numbers of converts in the late 1700s and early 1800s. With a well-developed organization and an insistence on the idea that anyone could achieve salvation, Methodists grew into one of the largest Christian denominations in the United States in the 1800s.

Distinctively American religions, such as the Disciples of Christ and the Mormons, or Church of the Latter Day Saints, appeared for the first time in this period. The Disciples were strongest in Kentucky, emphasizing simple worship by equals. The Mormons took root in upstate New York. *The Book of Mormon*, which founder Joseph Smith claimed to have translated from gold plates he had found, foretold that God would soon restore a truer, simpler church, freed from the shackles of ministers—and He would do so not in the far away Holy Land, but in North America.

Women and the Awakening Women and children were the main participants in the religious awakening of the early 1800s. The Great Awakening may have appealed to them in part because it was a form of community, attracting those who were lonely and unhappy in new surroundings or on the frontier.

Within the new church community, women organized sewing circles and women's auxiliaries, or clubs. They also formed local and regional reform societies to help widows and orphans, to convert people to Christianity, and to improve the conditions of mothers. Typical was the Female Missionary Society, founded in 1814 in Oneida County, New York, to encourage revivalism. Members of local chapters wrote to one another, exchanging what they called "heartfelt communications of hope, joy, and gratitude." In a world of strangers, they were particularly grateful for the company of "beloved sisters" who shared their religious views.

In addition to participating in this enlarged community, women exercised increasing power over the selection of ministers within the churches. The successful minister was generally one who consulted frequently with the women in his congregation. For the most part, women themselves did not preach or take public leadership roles. An exception was the charismatic

Using Historical Evidence Camp meetings were a scene of excitement and energy. *Describe the reactions of the crowd to the speaker at this meeting.*

2. INSTRUCT

Discuss

Discuss the political and social conditions that made the United States ripe for the Second Great Awakening in the early 1800s. In what ways did the new religious denominations of this period reflect a truly American outlook? Why did the Great Awakening hold particular appeal for women?

Analyze

During the Second Great Awakening, events such as revival meetings attracted large numbers of people searching for meaning. Ask students to describe the feelings an American might have experienced attending a revival meeting for the first time.

Caption Answer to ...

Using Historical Evidence

Some are fainting or otherwise showing signs of being carried away; others are more interested in the crowd than the speaker; still others are paying little attention at all.

In Depth

Then and Now

Mormons were cruelly persecuted for their beliefs—particularly the practice of polygamy. However, the Mormon church renounced polygamy in 1890, after the Supreme Court found it illegal. Now 80 percent of the more than five million Mormons worldwide live in the United States. Mormons run a vast network of worship, education, and charitable activities from their headquarters in Salt Lake City, Utah. (See Chapter 10, page 289.)

MAKING CONNECTIONS

Students may cite work in religious organizations, school clubs, or committees, but may also note that the means open to them are often limited.

Activity

Cooperative Learning

Time: One class period.

Activity: Reenact the confrontation at the St. George Methodist Church in Philadelphia in 1792. Students should prepare scripts for their skits or perform them as improvisational role-plays. It is important that they include the feelings and reactions of the African Americans at the St. George Methodist Church and explain why the African Americans formed their own congregation under Richard Allen.

Grouping: Groups of six students.

Purpose: To role-play the event that led African Americans, led by Richard Allen, to organize the African Methodist Episcopal Church.

Roles: Richard Allen, white and African American church members.

Outcome: Students will identify issues of religious conflict and understand how tension between white Methodists and African Americans led to the organization of a new denomination.

Enrichment

Ask students to create pamphlets advertising an upcoming revival meeting of the period. Encourage them to consider what features would have encouraged people of the time to participate.

African American woman Jarena Lee, who frequently addressed African American congregations in the Philadelphia area.

Evangelical religion energized women living in the changing world of the early republic. Through religion, women shared a sense of spiritual equality with men, even if their political power was limited. Religious work gave them wide outlets for their talents, offering an opportunity to influence the moral development of their communities.

MAKING CONNECTIONS

What means are available to you to influence the morals generally held in your community?

African Americans and Democratic Religion

In the 1700s, Methodist and other evangelical congregations had been largely multiracial. During the American Revolution, Americans of both European and African heritage often worshiped God together. Indeed, American Protestantism owed a great deal to African religious traditions, such as the call-and-response, in which the congregation responded as a whole to a statement made by one member.

In many communities of enslaved people, a rich combination of Christian and African

Richard Allen (right) had a profound belief that religion belonged to the people, not to church ministers. "The plain and simple gospel," he wrote, "suits best for any people; for the unlearned can understand, and the learned are sure to understand."

spiritual traditions was emerging. Along the coast of South Carolina, enslaved African Americans transformed Christian worship services into a mutual activity of both preachers and congregations. When they incorporated their own traditional African beliefs, such as the belief in possession by spirits, they gave an entirely new dimension to the worship.

Enslaved people also adopted Christian ideas and stories that condemned their bondage and offered some hope of rescue. African American hymns, or spirituals, became powerful testaments to the confidence of enslaved people that some day, in heaven if not on earth, they would be liberated. When they sang of crossing the River Jordan, which in the Bible was the border of the Promised Land, they were referring to more than religious salvation—they were talking about their own hunger to be free.

Although some white Methodists and others in the late 1700s did attack slavery, most whites were uncomfortable with multiracial worship, especially as African Americans became more assertive about sharing in democratic liberty. In the North, this tension soon produced another distinctively American denomination, the African Methodist Episcopal Church (AME), founded by **Richard Allen,** a brilliant African American minister.

AMERICAN PROFILES

Richard Allen

Born enslaved in Philadelphia, Pennsylvania, in 1760, Allen had grown up on a farm in Delaware. He became a devout Methodist and impressed his owner so much with the sincerity of his belief that his owner not only became a Methodist but also allowed Allen and his family to buy their freedom.

The self-educated and charismatic Allen was a popular preacher throughout the Delaware River Valley. Like other African Americans, he favored Methodism because it was straightforward, dramatic, direct—and democratic. According to John Thompson, an enslaved African American in Maryland in the early 1800s, when the Methodist religion was first preached among enslaved people

▶ RESOURCE DIRECTORY

Teaching Resources

⭐ **Primary Source Activity** The American Spirit, found in the Unit 2 folder, p. 98, uses the impressions of two European travelers to show the accomplishments of the new republic and its hopes for the future.

the new doctrine produced great consternation [worry] among the slaveholders. It was something which they could not understand. It brought glad tidings to the poor bondman; it bound up the broken-hearted; it opened the prison doors to them that were bound, and let the captive go free.

In the mid-1780s, Allen moved to Philadelphia. There, encouraged by white Methodists, he spoke regularly at St. George Methodist Church. Eventually, his forceful presence attracted so many African Americans to the church that its white members grew alarmed. During worship one Sunday in 1792, whites ordered the African Americans to leave the main floor and sit in the gallery. The African Americans refused. Under Allen's leadership, many joined in the organization of a new church. African Americans in other cities soon formed their own churches as well. In 1816, sixteen congregations joined to form the African Methodist Episcopal Church and elected Allen as their first bishop. When he died in 1831, his legacy included 86 churches with 7,954 members and $125,000 worth of property. Allen himself had asserted when forming the church:

Our only design is to secure to ourselves our rights and privileges, to regulate our own affairs, temporal [worldly] and spiritual, the same as if we were white people.

Like other Americans, great numbers of African Americans turned to evangelical religion in the early republic because they believed their souls were at risk; their faith was profound and genuine. But Methodism and other Protestant denominations also offered the framework of community and assurance that what mattered in the United States was not wealth or education or color, but what Martin Luther King, Jr., would later call "the content of one's character."

The democratic power of evangelical Christianity was enormous. This power did not overcome prejudice based on race or establish real equality. Still, revivals reinforced in the field of religion what the American Revolution had begun in the world of politics. Though the United States was far from achieving full social equality and popular sovereignty, there was no getting away from the fact that Americans were defining themselves as a nation in those very terms. ✪

Richard Allen was a key figure in organizing African American churches in the early republic. One such church, the Bethel Church of Baltimore (above), celebrated its good relationship with the minister of a neighboring white congregation in 1845.

SECTION 4 REVIEW

Key Terms, People, and Places
1. Define (a) denomination, (b) Second Great Awakening, (c) evangelical movement.
2. Identify Richard Allen.

Key Concepts
3. Why was the Second Great Awakening democratic?
4. Why were women in particular attracted to the churches that became popular during the Second Great Awakening?
5. Why did Richard Allen favor Methodism?

Critical Thinking
6. **Making Comparisons** Compare and contrast the First Great Awakening and the Second Great Awakening.

---

3. ASSESS

Section 4 Review Answers

1. (a) denomination, see p. 202, (b) Second Great Awakening, see p. 202, (c) evangelical movement, see p. 202

2. Richard Allen, see p. 204

3. Its members believed that anyone could participate and experience salvation if he or she chose to do so.

4. The churches were a form of community, attracting women who were lonely and unhappy in new surroundings or on the frontier.

5. Allen viewed Methodism as straightforward, dramatic, direct, and democratic.

6. Possible answers: The First Great Awakening (of the 1730s and 1740s) energized people to reject the traditional authorities of ministers and books; the Second Great Awakening (in the early 1800s) likewise promised salvation to anyone who was willing to believe in the authority of Christ and the Bible. Both democratized religion, although the Second Great Awakening carried this trend further.

Reteach

Ask students to list the ways in which the Second Great Awakening affected women and African Americans.

4. CLOSE

 Reinforcing the Big Idea

The Second Great Awakening was a religious movement based on the principle that all people were equally entitled to salvation. New Christian denominations arose during this period, attracting many women and African Americans as followers.

Chapter Review Answers

Understanding Key Terms, People, and Places

Terms
Students should refer to the definitions of the key terms in the chapter to write sentences that show the relation of each word to life in the United States during the era of the new republic.

Matching
1. persisters
2. black codes
3. Second Great Awakening
4. Adams-Onís Treaty
5. denomination

True or False
1. false, Samuel Slater
2. true
3. false, Richard Allen

Reviewing Main Ideas

1. The American population was young and doubled in size about every twenty years.

2. Americans repopulated North America with relentless speed.

3. Although most African Americans were enslaved or forced into subordination by black codes, they participated in the development of the region by clearing the land and supporting homesteads in countless ways.

4. Most of the Native American migrations were undertaken involuntarily, imposed by treaties with the United States.

5. They organized societies dedicated to improving conditions for humankind, gathered information on many subjects, and became deeply interested in the advancement of science and learning.

6. People considered education extremely important and began to insist that it be made more widely available, to both men and women.

7. Republican women wanted to contribute to the success of the new republic by controlling destructive emotions and becoming models of quiet virtue.

8. The cotton gin was largely responsible for the continued growth of the institution of slavery, because as profits from cotton grew, the demand for slave labor increased.

Chapter Review

Understanding Key Terms, People, and Places

Key Terms
1. Adams-Onís Treaty
2. black codes
3. republican women
4. Industrial Revolution
5. system of interchangeable parts
6. denomination
7. Second Great Awakening
8. evangelical movement

People
9. persister

10. Noah Webster
11. Samuel Slater
12. Eli Whitney
13. Susanna Haswell Rowson
14. Richard Allen

Terms For each term above, write a sentence that explains its relation to life in the early United States.

Matching Review the key terms in the list above. If you are not sure of a term's meaning, review its definition in the chapter. Then choose a term from the list that best matches each description below.
1. a person who took up permanent residence in the West or South
2. laws that kept African Americans under the authority of someone else
3. a new wave of religious revivals that swept the United States in the early 1800s
4. the agreement that transferred the territory of Florida to the United States
5. a subgroup of a religion

True or False Determine whether each statement is true or false. If it is true, write "true." If it is false, change the underlined name to make the statement true.
1. <u>Richard Allen</u> duplicated British machinery that quickly spun cotton fibers into thread.
2. <u>Susanna Haswell Rowson's</u> novel about a fifteen-year-old girl carried off by a handsome man warned young women to make practical choices about whom they married.
3. The African Methodist Episcopal Church was founded by <u>Noah Webster</u>, a brilliant African American minister.

Reviewing Main Ideas

Section 1 (pp. 186–191)
1. Describe the general age of the population of the United States between 1780 and 1830 and how fast it doubled in size.
2. What was the result of Americans catching "Alabama Fever" and similar "diseases"?
3. How did African Americans participate in the development of the trans-Appalachian region?
4. How were the migrations of Native Americans different from those of people of European descent?

Section 2 (pp. 193–197)
5. How did Americans express their belief in their ability to improve the world?
6. Describe the attitude toward education in the early republic.
7. What were the goals of republican women?

8. What was the effect of the cotton gin on slavery?

Section 3 (pp. 198–201)
9. Why did Americans need to look for new social rules during the early years of the republic?
10. What circumstances allowed young people to make a greater number of their own choices?
11. How did marriage for working-class and enslaved women differ from marriage for middle-class women?

Section 4 (pp. 202–205)
12. What attracted Americans to the Second Great Awakening?
13. Why did women organize sewing circles and other societies as part of the evangelical movement?
14. What was distinctive about the African Methodist Episcopal Church?

9. Americans needed new social rules because migration and expansion were occurring on a scale previously unknown. Friendship replaced family ties as the primary link between people and, in this new unstructured world of strangers, old cues as to a person's status could no longer be trusted.

10. Young people were able to make more decisions partly because of the new spirit of democracy and partly because of the weakening of parental authority brought about by the population's extraordinary mobility.

11. Long courtships in which a man and woman could judge each other's commitment and character were an unaffordable luxury for working class and enslaved women.

12. Many people were attracted by the democratic nature of the movement. Living in a constantly shifting world of strangers and migration, they were also attracted to the movement's promise of meaning and community.

13. Women were seeking a sense of community; they also wanted to influence the moral development of their communities.

14. It offered African Americans an emotional, democratic way to worship, separate from white prejudices.

Thinking Critically

1. **Recognizing Cause and Effect** How did ideals initiated by the American Revolution continue to influence social developments in the early republic?
2. **Determining Relevance** During the early republic, rapid population growth and constant migration created a nation of strangers. Are we a nation of strangers today?
3. **Demonstrating Reasoned Judgment** Imagine living in an era before daily postal service and the widespread availability of newspapers and magazines (and with no telephones, televisions, or radios). How would your daily life be different from what it is today?
4. **Predicting Consequences** You have read that the population of the United States doubled every twenty years during the era of the new republic. What might be the effects on your town or city if its population doubled in the next twenty years?

Making Connections

1. **Evaluating Primary Sources** Review the primary source excerpt on page 188. Create five questions you might ask Morris Birkbeck to better understand the experience of the travelers who migrated across the Appalachians during the early republic.
2. **Understanding the Visuals** Describe in your own words how the cotton gin on page 196 operates.
3. **Writing About the Chapter** It is 1830, and you are visiting the United States from abroad. You have visited once before, in 1783. Write a letter to your family at home describing the changes that you observe in American society. Create a list of the changes that you have observed between the two visits, as well as the things that have remained the same. Next, divide your lists into categories, such as "changes in the role of women," "new inventions," and "life for African Americans." Write a draft of your letter in which you compare your observations from your two visits, organized according to the categories you have chosen. Revise your letter, making certain that each idea is clearly explained. Proofread your letter and draft a final copy.
4. **Using the Graphic Organizer** This graphic organizer uses a tree map to organize information about the ways in which Americans joined in the spirit of improvement during the era after the American Revolution. (a) Name a common theme found in the first three branches of the tree map. (b) What items on the graphic organizer affected the nation's economy? (c) On a separate sheet of paper, create your own graphic organizer about the shifting social relationships in the new republic, using this graphic organizer as an example.

The Spirit of Improvement in the New Nation

Faith in Human Ability to Improve the World	Education Seen as Key to Stability and Prosperity	Women Achieve New Status as Republican Wives and Mothers	Inventions and Improvements Lead to Rapid Economic Growth	Revolution in Communication
• Societies founded to improve human condition • Deep interest in science and learning	• Insistence on wide availability of education • Noah Webster stresses the importance of standardized language • Education is publicly supported in Massachusetts	• Americans realize that educating women is key to nation's success • Republican women contribute to success of republic by providing moral models	• Technology for cotton spinning machines copied from England • Cotton gin • Steam power • Canals	• Regular mail delivery • Explosive growth in number of newspapers and magazines

Thinking Critically

1. The ideal of democracy manifested itself in the evangelical movement, and the ideal of beginning a new era was seen in new inventions and faith in human progress.

2. Answers will vary. Students should recognize that although population growth and migration have slowed significantly, many people today are separated from their families. Many people also still move frequently and are searching for a sense of connection among strangers.

3. Answers will vary. Students should recognize the isolation that they would experience without these forms of communication, as well as the much slower pace of life that would result.

4. Answers will vary. Students should cite the need for more schools, jobs, housing and increased city services; strain on public resources in many regions; and expansion of markets for other goods and services.

Making Connections

1. Possible questions: Why did you decide to migrate? What aspects of your life in the East were you most willing to leave behind? What are you expecting to find when you reach your destination? Do you plan to settle permanently in one place or to continue westward? If you have a family, did you travel west alone first to look for a good location before you brought your family across the mountains?

2. Answers will vary but should mention what the cotton gin does and some of the steps involved.

3. Students' letters should show an understanding of the social and technological developments that took place during the early years of the republic.

4. (a) Education or learning. (b) Answers may include education, inventions, and improvements. (c) Students' graphic organizers should show attitudes toward courtship and marriage among the middle class, working class, and African Americans, as well as the effects of population growth and migration.

 Alternative Assessment

Final Evaluation

Use the following guidelines to evaluate student projects:

• **Evidence of thoughtfulness** Do projects include the main ideas from the chapter?

• **Evidence of outside research** To what extent do projects present outside research?

• **Evidence of synthesis** Do projects demonstrate that students understand how topics are related?

• **Communication style** Do projects convey their purpose to an audience in a clear, appealing way?

207

American Album
Artifacts from Exhibitions and Collections
at the Smithsonian Institution
National Museum of American History

American Album

Ask students to scan the American Album display, After the Revolution. Point out the gridiron on page 209 and read about its function. Then ask students what the word *gridiron* has to do with the sport of football. *(It refers to the playing field, which has lines every ten yards.)* Ask students to speculate how the word came to be used to describe the playing field.

Ask students to study the other artifacts and read the accompanying captions. Using the images as a basis for discussion, ask students what the artifacts reveal about the working life of early Americans. Note the images that indicate the work that young people performed.

Ask students to note the picture and caption for the "freedom suit." Ask what a young man who completed job training today might receive instead of a suit of clothes.

To connect the artifact display to the chapter content, have students look again at the engraving in the bottom right corner. Ask volunteers what *venerate* means *(revere, respect, honor)* and what "venerate the plough" might mean. Why might this engraving be considered a romanticized depiction of farm life? What impact did this idealized view of farming have on the settlement of the United States?

Ask students to list the chores that they and other family members have to do around the house. Do any of them sew, care for animals, or tend a garden? Have volunteers read their lists and compare and contrast their chores with those of people in the early republic. What artifacts and symbols would they use in a display depicting life in the 1990s?

After the Revolution

Life was not the same for everyone following the Revolution. How people lived their life varied depending on where they lived, their wealth, their ethnic background, their gender, and whether they were free or enslaved. This diversity can be seen in the familiar objects of everyday life. *What do these objects tell you about people's lives?*

◀ LIBERTY JUG This practical creamware jug celebrates the nation by listing the populations of the new American states.

◀ BLACKSMITH'S ANVIL AND HAMMER Most everyday objects were handmade by artisans using fairly simple tools, such as an anvil and hammer. A blacksmith heated metal until it was glowing and soft, then shaped it with a hammer on the anvil.

▼ GRAVESTONES These matching stones mark the graves of a husband and wife who were born in Africa. Brought to America to work as slaves, they eventually purchased their own freedom.

◄ GRIDIRON One of the most common household objects, a gridiron was used to broil foods over coals in an open fireplace. Almost all cooking utensils were designed for use in a fireplace.

► SAMPLER A sampler recorded the decorative stitches learned by well-off young girls. Poor girls used sewing to earn money for the family.

▲ DAIRYING This engraving titled "Straining and Skimming" shows an idealized view of two women preparing dairy products from whole milk.

◄ FREEDOM SUIT A young man learned a craft by apprenticing to a master craftsman. Because apprentices were bound for years to one master, the new clothes that some received at the end of training were called a "freedom suit."

◄ NATIVE AMERCAN OBJECTS This cradle board and dolls were made by Iroquois people, a group in upstate New York. White settlers overran most of the Iroquois lands shortly after the Revolution.

► RESPECT FOR THE LAND This engraving from an 1876 magazine shows the popular link between American liberty and hardworking farmers.

VENERATE THE PLOUGH

An Emerging New Nation
1800–1860

UNIT 3

An Emerging New Nation
1800–1860

Introducing the Unit

Interpreting the Visual The Erie Canal was one of the wonders of the young nation: a marvelous work of engineering and an effective means of opening the interior of the nation. The mayor of New York City, Dewitt Clinton, an outspoken booster of the canal, proclaimed that it would create "the greatest inland trade ever witnessed."

As de Tocqueville noted, Americans were energetic, enthusiastic, and proud of their achievements. Like the artist who painted the scene of Lockport reproduced on pages 210–211, they enjoyed the vitality and excitement of their growing nation.

Ask students what the name *Lockport* tells them about the village. Ask them to locate the five locks in the painting and to explain how they worked. Ask half the class to find out how many people live in Lockport today and the other half to locate Lockport on a map.

Establishing Chronology This unit describes the economic, social, and geographic changes in the nation in the six decades from 1800 to 1860. Tell students that those and other changes occurred simultaneously and that some continued through the Civil War. By 1860, however, the nation's attention was fixed on the increasing conflict between North and South.

"America is a land of wonders, in which everything is in constant motion and every change seems an improvement."

—Alexis de Tocqueville, 1835

As the nation began to take shape in the early 1800s, the United States did indeed seem a "land of wonders." The appearance of textile mills in New England signaled the first stirrings of industrialization. Small towns blossomed into bustling urban centers. A growing network of roads, canals, and railroad lines created a new sense of unity. Some citizens poured their energies into social reform movements. Others joined the surge of migration to newly acquired territories in California and Oregon. While the United States expanded from sea to sea, the economic and political focus of the nation gradually shifted from the local to the national level.

▶ RESOURCE DIRECTORY

Teaching Resources

📁 **Local History Activity** "Student Life at Boston High, 1820s Style" and the Local Focus research topic suggestions, found in the Local History Resources folder, pp. 9–11, are designed to help students understand how history affects all lives.

★ **Themes in American History Posters** Wall-size, illustrated posters, found in the Teaching Resources package, illustrate the four unit themes.

📁 **Unit Test** Forms A and B are found in the Unit 3 folder, pp. 110–115.

Lockport, New York, painted in 1836 by an unknown artist, owed its very existence to the Erie Canal. The town arose from a "rattlesnake-infested wilderness" when the canal opened in 1825.

Teachers may wish to discuss specific historical events in the context of historical themes. Here are four suggestions for Unit 3.

Reform Movements *People in the United States have frequently taken action in grass roots movements to right perceived wrongs and to secure improvements in the quality of life.*

● Middle-class reform movements pressed for public education, temperance, and other moral improvements.

● The antislavery and the women's rights movements brought many women and African Americans into the public sphere.

Technology *Americans' ability to develop new skills and tools and to increase their knowledge of the physical world has greatly affected the way they live and work, and has led to a high standard of living.*

● Increasingly, the purchase of goods made in factories removed the need for families to make most of what they used.

● The creation of markets and capital accumulation sparked industrial growth and the development of new technologies.

Unity and Conflict *Americans have developed unique political systems and laws that affirm a shared commitment to certain goals, such as individual rights and equality. Nevertheless, groups with differing views on how to achieve these goals have often clashed.*

● The federal government removed most Native Americans from their lands east of the Mississippi River.

American Democracy *The concepts of democratic representation, equality under the law, and freedom from discrimination have been gradually broadened to include previously excluded groups.*

● Jackson won the presidency in 1828 as a champion of the common man and an opponent of a strong central government.

● A movement for extending women's rights and including women in the political process emerged in the 1840s.

Media and Technology

Visions of America: Scenes of an Era To introduce students to the main idea and events covered in this unit, play "Scenes of an Era: An Emerging New Nation" (length: 2.5 minutes). This selection can be located on side 1 of the videodiscs. This selection can also be located on videotape 2. Lesson plans for "Scenes of an Era" can be found in the Visions of America Guidebook.

Using Multimedia Technology This folder contains instructional tools and strategies for using technology in the classroom.

Transparency Binder Contains full-color transparencies with lesson suggestions. From a large collection divided into twelve categories, specific transparencies are referenced throughout the chapters at appropriate points of use. For this unit, see American Photo, B-3; Fine Art, D-8; Links Across Time, J-3; Political Cartoon, K-3; and Historical Maps, L-2.

Chapter 8 The Market Revolution
1815–1845

📁 **Teaching Resources** (See Unit 3 Folder)

	Instruction	**Enrichment**
Section 1 **Changing Households and New Markets** (pp. 214–217)	Reproducible Lesson Plan, p. 3 Alternate Lesson Plan, p. 38 Guided Reading and Review, p. 8 Quiz, p. 9	Literature Activity, The Life of Washington, pp. 29–30 American Profiles Activity, Sarah Todd Astor, p. 20 Literature Activity, Preacher to the World, p. 31
Section 2 **The Northern Section** (pp. 218–221)	Reproducible Lesson Plan, p. 4 Alternate Lesson Plan, p. 39 Guided Reading and Review, p. 10 Quiz, p. 11	Primary Source Activity, New England Mill Women, pp. 26–27
Section 3 **The Southern Section** (pp. 222–225)	Reproducible Lesson Plan, p. 5 Alternate Lesson Plan, p. 40 Guided Reading and Review, p. 12 Quiz, p. 13	Viewpoints Activity, On Slavery, pp. 22–23 Critical Thinking Activity, Identifying Alternatives, p. 25
Section 4 **The Second American Party System** (pp. 226–228)	Reproducible Lesson Plan, p. 6 Alternate Lesson Plan, p. 41 Guided Reading and Review, p. 14 Quiz, p. 15	Visual Learning Activity, The Jackson Ticket, p. 32 Primary Source Activity, President Jackson's Inauguration, p. 28 Historian's Toolbox Activity, Determining Relevance, p. 24
Section 5 **The Age of Jackson** (pp. 230–233)	Reproducible Lesson Plan, p. 7 Alternate Lesson Plan, p. 42 Guided Reading and Review, p. 16 Quiz, p. 17 Chapter Test, Forms A & B, pp. 34–39	American Profiles Activity, Sequoyah, p. 21 Visual Learning Activity, The Presidential Campaign of 1840, p. 33 History Might Not . . . Activity, Native American Fishing Rights on Trial, pp. 18–19

📁 **Additional Chapter Resources**

Resource Organizer, p. 2
Alternate Lesson Plan, p. 37
Answer Keys, pp. 116–125

Bibliography

For the Teacher
Lerner, Gerda. *Black Women in White America: A Documentary History.* Vintage, 1972. (Collection of primary and secondary source accounts.)
Wertheimer, Barbara M. *We Were There: The Story of Working Women in America.* Pantheon, 1977. (Includes white and African American women in the early nineteenth century.)

Prentice Hall Literature Excerpts from *The American Experience,* 1994, including Douglass, Frederick. *My Bondage and My Freedom.* Johnson Publishing edition of the 1855 autobiography.

THE BIG IDEA

The Big Idea for the chapter and how the main ideas in each section relate to the Big Idea are graphically displayed below. Comprehension of this chapter's Big Idea is critical to students' understanding of United States history and how we as a nation got where we are today.

Media and Technology

 Our Multicultural Heritage, C-8

 Geographic Setting, M-2, M-3; The Way It Works, H-8

 Geographic Setting, M-4; Critical Thinking, I-15

 Visions of America: History Might Not Have Happened This Way Game

 Graphic Organizer, G-1

 Guided Reading Audiotapes (English and Spanish)

 Computer Test Bank

For the Student

Coit, Margaret Louise. *Andrew Jackson.* Grey Castle, 1990. (A biography of the seventh President, recommended for students.)

Ehle, John. *Trail of Tears: The Rise and Fall of the Cherokee Nation.* Anchor, 1988. (Compact account of the forced removal of the Cherokee.)

CHAPTER 8

During the first half of the 1800s, expanding markets and thriving industries and businesses transformed American life. The Market Revolution, as this transformation was called, made the making of money the chief goal of most American men. The change also created divisions between the poor and the wealthy, and between those in different regions of the country.

SECTION 1

The Market Revolution changed the way Americans conducted their economic lives—what they produced, how they sold goods, and why they bought what they did.

SECTION 2

In the Northeast, new industries developed to supply the needs of expanding cities. The growing cities also increased the numbers of wealthy and poor people.

SECTION 3

The South developed a thriving economy based on commercial agriculture and supported by the labor of enslaved African Americans.

SECTION 4

The Market Revolution brought economic issues to the forefront of American government and created a deep split in politics, which led to the second American party system and the election of Andrew Jackson as President in 1828.

SECTION 5

As President, Andrew Jackson worked to clear a path to success for white men. His support of the spoils system further contributed to his image as the champion of the common man.

The Market Revolution
1815–1845

CHAPTER 8

The Market Revolution
1815–1845

The Relevance of the Big Idea

In the first half of the 1800s the United States economy underwent a significant transformation that affected virtually all aspects of American life. In the 1990s, Americans are again finding their lives affected by dramatic economic changes.

Discuss with students the fact that to save money, more and more companies are decentralizing their operations and cutting down on full-time employees. Instead, they are hiring contractors on a job-by-job basis to work from their homes using computers, telephones, fax machines, and modems. Ask students how they think these new work patterns are changing the relationship between work and home.

*D*uring the first half of the 1800s, a revolution transformed the way Americans worked, lived, and bought and sold products. The resulting new market for goods created thriving industries and booming businesses. It swept people from the countryside into the cities. It cut deep divisions between the poor and the well-to-do and between different regions of the nation. Most of all, this change in the market made making money—preferably, lots of money—acceptable as a goal of life in the United States.

In Depth

Global Connections

The economic and territorial growth of the United States relied heavily on a sophisticated banking system, similar in structure to the one that had been established in the United Kingdom. The Rothschild family of financiers had funded Britain's war against Napoleon by making it possible for the British government to raise money by selling securities. The United States government applied the same principle; and between 1816 and 1821 it raised sufficient funds to create six new states, equal in size to six countries in Europe.

Events in the United States				
	1819 The Panic of 1819 throws the nation into a severe depression.		**1826** Thomas Jefferson and John Adams both die on July 4, the fiftieth anniversary of the Declaration of Independence.	**1828** Andrew Jackson wins the presidency.
1815	**1820**	**1825**		**1830**

Events in the World			
1815 Napoleon is defeated at the Battle of Waterloo.	**1819** Carlsbad Decrees suppress freedom of speech in Germany.	**1822** Brazil gains independence from Portugal.	

▶ RESOURCE DIRECTORY

Teaching Resources

Alternate Lesson Plan: Demonstrating the Big Idea found in the Alternate Lesson Plans folder, p. 36, provides a lesson strategy to instruct students about the Big Idea that expanding markets and thriving industries turned the focus of American life to making money, and accentuated differences between regions and classes of people.

Alternative Assessment Handbook provides information, guidance, and strategies for alternative methods of assessment. It includes an essay on new trends in assessment, guidance and strategies for developing performance tasks and portfolios, scoring rubrics, and sample evaluation forms.

Pages 214–217

Changing Households and New Markets

In colonial times, people had focused on how to keep their households operating. For many people in the early republic, that focus gave way to a determination to make money—as much and as quickly as possible.

Pages 218–221

The Northern Section

The North remained largely a land of farmers, now producing cash crops for the city market. But northern cities were growing rapidly. New divisions in society opened between rich and poor as well as between employers and workers.

Pages 222–225

The Southern Section

The South as a whole was devoted to commercial agriculture, with few cities. The largest part of the region's wealth was built on a peculiar relationship between capitalists and their workers—slavery.

Pages 226–228

The Second American Party System

The Market Revolution created a deep split in United States politics. While some called for the national government to take a strong role in building the economy, others argued that the government had no business taking such an active role in economic development.

Pages 230–233

The Age of Jackson

During his presidency, Andrew Jackson became the symbol for an age in which Americans first began to believe that elected officials should act according to the views of the voters.

1831 Nat Turner leads a rebellion in Virginia.

1837 The United States government forces the Cherokee to move west.

1840 New England mills produce 323 million yards of cotton cloth.

1850 The population of New York City reaches half a million.

| 1835 | 1840 | 1845 | 1850 | 1855 |

1835 English becomes the language of government in India.

1839 The Opium War begins in China.
• The first photographs are taken in France and Britain.

1844 The Young Men's Christian Association (YMCA) is founded in Great Britain.

1848 Nationalist revolutions break out in Europe.
• German Karl Marx publishes The Communist Manifesto.

Alternative Assessment

As an ongoing chapter project, students can imagine themselves owning one of the country's earliest advertising agencies in the mid-1800s and prepare a presentation designed to attract a potential client who manufactures an important consumer product. The objective is to illustrate the transformation of the American economy between the years 1815 and 1845.

Projects may include any of the following suggestions:

● Graphs showing statistics on income, population, and spending patterns for the North and the South, with economic projections about the future

● Graphic illustrations of the new American lifestyle

● Simulated or actual statements from business and political leaders about the flourishing economy

● Simulated newspaper clippings about the new American economy, including portraits of successful entrepreneurs and industrialists

Explain that projects will be evaluated according to the following guidelines:

● **Unacceptable** Projects are not attempted or fail to meet requirements outlined.

● **Limited/Acceptable** Projects attempt to show the causes and effects of the changes, as well as connections among economic issues of the time.

● **Extensive/Commendable** Projects show the causes and effects of the changes, as well as connections among issues of the time.

● **Extraordinary/Outstanding** Projects clearly show causes, effects, and connections, as well as successfully relating the material to the needs of the client.

Students may choose to include finished projects in their portfolios.

For information and guidance on alternative assessment trends and strategies, see the Alternative Assessment Handbook in the Resource Directory on page 212.

Changing Households and New Markets

SECTION 1

Changing Households and New Markets

1. FOCUS

Connecting to the Big Idea

See page 212B. Explain to students that the American economy underwent a fundamental change in the early 1800s that affected how Americans lived their lives. Ask how these changes altered the focus of American life.

Objectives

● Explain how the meaning of work changed during this period.
● Explain how the growing power of banks reflected the increasing dependence of Americans on credit and money.
● Describe the effect of increased manufacturing on the household economy.

Bellringer

Ask students whether they have ever come up with a plan for making money, such as taking on a paper route or selling T-shirts they've designed, and, if so, ask them to describe its success or failure.

Reading Strategy

Reading for Evidence Ask students to look for evidence as they read the section that in the early 1800s American men began to "devote themselves to the business of making money," as stated on page 214.

In the early 1800s the banking industry was a powerful force that helped bring changes to the way things were made and sold. One such change—illustrated on this bank note—was that people began to work for a living outside their homes.

SECTION PREVIEW

In colonial times, people had focused on how to keep their households operating. For many people in the early republic, that focus gave way to a determination to make money—as much and as quickly as possible.

Key Concepts

• During this period, the meaning of work changed. Instead of an activity that kept households running, labor became something to be bought and sold.
• The growing power of banks reflected the increasing importance of credit and money.
• As manufacturing increased, more and more households purchased goods that once had been produced in the household.

Key Terms, People, and Places

Market Revolution, entrepreneur, capitalism, capital, household economy, commodity, centralize

W ith a growing population, expanding territory, and constantly improving transportation and communication, the United States in the early 1800s was experiencing a vast change and increase in its market for goods. Americans purchased more and more goods, rather than making those goods themselves. And rather than trading one kind of goods for another, Americans used money—both cash and credit—to get what they needed. This change in the way people made, bought, and sold goods is now called the **Market Revolution.**

⭐ With enormous enthusiasm, American men during this period began to devote themselves to the business of making money. Everywhere, north and south, they went in pursuit of what they called "the main chance"—their opportunity to strike it rich. Among the most successful of these go-getters was the industrialist Samuel Slater.

AMERICAN PROFILES

Samuel Slater

Samuel Slater arrived in New York City in November 1789 with a head full of technological information. He had been born in Derbyshire, England, in 1768, the son of farmers. Slater's father died when Slater was 14. Before his death, his father arranged for Slater to become an apprentice to Jedediah Strutt. As an apprentice, Samuel Slater spent almost seven years learning a trade from Strutt.

Strutt was a pioneer in the development of English cotton mills, or textile factories. Other men, including Richard Arkwright, James Hargreaves, and Samuel Compton, had developed new water-powered machines that spun cotton fibers into thread. Slater worked in Strutt's mills as a manager. Supervising laborers, he learned how the machinery operated and how it was built and repaired. When Slater's apprenticeship ended, he decided to migrate to the United States. He hoped that his experience and knowledge would help him make a lot of money in the new nation, where textile technology was not as advanced as it was in England.

▶ RESOURCE DIRECTORY

Teaching Resources

Reproducible Lesson Plan found in the Unit 3 folder, p. 3, provides a summary of the Section 1 lesson plan content.

Alternate Lesson Plan: Learning Styles found in the Alternate Lesson Plans folder, p. 38, guides students in creating a graphic organizer to identify characteristics of the Market Revolution, and is especially effective for visual learners.

Guided Reading and Review found in the Unit 3 folder, p. 8, provides a structure for reading and mastering the key concepts and reviewing the key terms for Section 1. (Guided Practice)

⭐ **Literature Activity** The Life of Washington, found in the Unit 3 folder, pp. 29–30, presents the work of another colonial entrepreneur, Mason Weems, and encourages students to understand the intent of Weems when he wrote his largely fabricated biography of George Washington.

It was illegal for either textile workers or information about textile machinery to leave England. So Slater had to travel in disguise and memorize as much of the workings of English textile machinery as he could. In 1790, he agreed to build cotton-spinning machines for a textile business in Providence, Rhode Island. Athough the machinery was complicated, Slater reproduced it by memory alone. He soon became a partner in this business. In 1793, Slater and his partners built a mill in Pawtucket, Rhode Island. They chose the spot because of a waterfall in a river, which produced the power to operate the mill.

Samuel Slater was a pioneer in the nation's cotton textile industry.

In 1798, Slater and his wife's father and brothers established Samuel Slater and Company. The new firm made its own machines and built another mill in Pawtucket. Within a few years, Slater was expanding his operations throughout New England. When he died in 1835, he owned all or part of thirteen textile mills. His business made him a rich man by the standards of the time. In 1829, forty years after he had arrived in the United States, Slater estimated his worth at between $800,000 and $1 million.

Other men eager to get rich quickly copied Slater's methods. By 1814, there were about 240 mills operating in the United States, most of them in Pennsylvania, New York, and New England.

More than hard work and a good memory made Slater wealthy. He took advantage of the potential of the young United States. The United States was producing more and more cotton to meet the needs of a growing population and it had many rivers with waterfalls. No wonder Slater succeeded. He gave Americans exactly what they needed when they needed it.

The Nature of Work Changes

Samuel Slater was a businessman who devoted his life to finding that competitive edge that would bring him a profit. This type of person—known as an **entrepreneur**—was becoming much more common in the United States at that time. An entrepreneur is someone who takes on business risks for the sake of profit. Entrepreneurs thrived in the economic system beginning to flourish during this time. In this system, known as **capitalism,** manufacturing is controlled by private corporations and by individuals competing for profit. This system takes its name from the term *capital*. **Capital** is a supply of wealth that can be used to produce goods and make money. Capitalism was not new, strictly speaking, but during the early 1800s, it rapidly expanded. And as it did so, the nature of work itself began to change. ★

The Household Economy Declines In the 1600s and 1700s, the **household economy** had dominated North American life outside the major seaports. In this type of economy, people's business consists of simply keeping their households running. Colonial Americans grew their own food and made their own clothes, soap, and other necessities. Their goal was not to get rich but to have enough property to be able to live comfortably and independently.

To be sure, most Americans in the 1600s and 1700s sold products—from extra crops to eggs to cloth; and many bought items they could not make for themselves, such as books and glass. But such buying and selling did not dominate their lives. Work was something done for and within the household. It was not at that time a **commodity,** something to be bought and sold.

When most Americans work today, they are essentially selling their time and labor. Their employers buy their services. To a great extent, the idea of selling labor in order to earn money dates from the early nineteenth century. As more and more people moved and then moved again, as the United States became a nation of strangers, Americans changed their economic habits. Whether they labored in workshops, mills, or offices, people started to work for a specific number of hours each day and for a specific amount of money.

As time passed, families produced fewer and fewer of the things they needed; instead, they bought those items from stores or other individuals. By 1830, goods such as soap and

★ **American Profiles Activity** found in the Unit 3 folder, p. 20, profiles Sarah Todd Astor, whom many consider to have been the entrepreneurial power behind her husband, fur magnate John Jacob Astor.

Discuss

Review the characteristics of the American economy during colonial times. Ask what factors led to economic change during the early 1800s.

Discuss the expansion of capitalism and the changes it created. Ask students to describe the Market Revolution. How did the relationship between Americans and their work change as a result of the Market Revolution? What role did banks play in fueling the new economy? Why is Mason Weems an appropriate symbol of his time?

Analyze

Have students analyze how the Market Revolution affected American society. How did it alter both the role of the family within society and relationships within the family? What impact do you think it had on the status of women?

Activity

Cooperative Learning

Time: One class period.

Activity: Devise a plan for convincing Americans to buy a factory-made household item.

Grouping: Groups of four students.

Purpose: Through the efforts of entrepreneurs, products that were traditionally made in the household began to be manufactured in factories in the early 1800s. Have groups select a household product from the early 1800s and devise a scheme to persuade Americans to purchase it.

Roles: Entrepreneurs.

Outcome: Students will portray the effects of manufactured goods on the household economy.

Enrichment

Before the Market Revolution, specialized goods, such as clocks and guns, were made by skilled craftspeople. Ask students to research the accomplishments of Eli Terry, Eli Whitney, and Samuel Colt and to explain in a short paper why it might be said that the achievements of these entrepreneurs brought to an end the era of craftsmanship.

Answer to ...

Links Across Time

The new jobs allow people to participate in the increased productivity of the centralized workplace while enjoying the advantages of working in the home, including more flexible hours and the possibility of providing more care and attention to other family members as necessary.

Answer to ...

MAKING CONNECTIONS

Students may describe items that would be eliminated because they could not be made at home. They might also focus on the change in lifestyle that would occur if basic needs were supplied by home production rather than by making money to purchase goods.

Changing the Workplace

When entrepreneurs centralized work during the early 1800s, they drastically changed the way most Americans spent their days. Rather than working at home or on the farm to keep their households running, people increasingly reported to a factory or mill each day where they labored in exchange for a wage.

Today, the workplace for the majority of American workers is neither the factory nor the farm, but the office. A small but increasing number of these office workers, however, are opting to turn back time. Instead of leaving their homes for the workplace each day, they are working for their employers at home—or telecommuting—as part of what some people describe as "a work-at-home revolt." Personal computers, modems, FAX machines, answering machines, and copiers are only some of the high-tech tools that permit workers to perform their jobs from their homes. Today it is estimated that 3 to 6 million people telecommute at least one day a week. That number is expected to increase to some 25 million by the year 2000. *What features of the household economy of the 1700s and the market economy of the 1800s are combined in the new work-at-home jobs?*

clothes were commonly made outside the homes where they were used. The people who made goods—whether in their own homes, in workshops, or in factories—were not the same as the people who used them.

Centralizing Work Making goods in workshops and factories was a logical development of changes in the way things were made. Increasingly entrepreneurs would **centralize** manufacturing by making all tasks involved in producing something happen in one place. Centralizing work dramatically increased production. One centralized industry in New England, the cloth-making mills, produced 4 million yards of cotton cloth in 1817; by 1840 the amount was 323 million yards. Often, however, entrepreneurs hired noncentralized workers—women working at home—to cut and sew the cloth into clothing.

MAKING CONNECTIONS

How would our lives in the United States today be different if households still produced most of what they needed?

Banks Spark Economic Growth

The Market Revolution brought new businesses to the forefront of American life. Banks quickly rose to the top as the most influential of the new organizations, because they provided the credit and the cash necessary for entrepreneurs to buy land or to invest in moneymaking schemes.

The first real banks appeared in the United States in the 1780s and 1790s. By the 1830s, hundreds of them had cropped up. Banks could be found in remote rural areas as well as in the middle of cities. Some Americans favored them because banks meant money, available to borrow. Others saw banks as the source of the problems that came with debt and economic depression.

Banks generally were started by groups of private investors. Although states had to give banks legal standing by issuing each of them a charter, they did not strictly control the banks. As a result, many banks made bad loans—loans to people who could not repay them—and most banks did not have additional money on hand to back up their transactions. Still, as long as they had the confidence of their customers, banks sparked economic growth by putting money into people's pockets.

Money in the early republic was not what it is today. The United States government did not issue paper money. Most people preferred to deal in specie, or coin, mainly of gold or silver. Specie was scarce, however, and difficult to carry around. The most common form of money was bank notes—pieces of paper that

RESOURCE DIRECTORY

Teaching Resources

⭐ **Literature Activity** *Preacher to the World,* found in the Unit 3 folder, p. 31, features excerpts from the journals of Ralph Waldo Emerson to give students a glimpse of other reactions to American materialism.

banks issued to their customers, who then used the notes to pay for goods and services. Similar to modern-day checks, bank notes were promises to pay specie on demand. The problem with these notes was that their value was unpredictable. Imagine selling something and receiving in payment a $100 check that might really be worth anything from $50 to $200, depending on the time and place you tried to cash it.

Despite the shortcomings of their notes, banks fueled the development of the American economy. They provided the loans that allowed Americans to buy millions of acres of federal land in the West and to invest in various money-making schemes. Although people continued to rely on money borrowed from private individuals, they turned increasingly to banks. And banks—because they tended to act together—caused wild economic booms and severe depressions such as the Panic of 1819.

Americans Learn to Buy

As the Market Revolution continued, Americans began to buy more and more goods. In colonial America, only the houses of the wealthiest planters and merchants had been full of goods. But in the 1800s, the relatively simple homes of the 1700s gave way to much more elaborately decorated and furnished homes. In many ways, families were defined more by what they bought than what they sold.

By the middle of the 1800s, the homes of middle-class Americans were positively cluttered with purchased items. Middle-class families bought reproductions of paintings to hang on their walls; china and silverware to eat with; fine materials and silks to make clothing; and more

expensive furniture. Parlors—rooms similar to modern living rooms—became a necessity in every home. Families entertained guests in their parlors, which were filled with knick knacks and furniture, in order to display their good taste and material comfort. When they did not have guests in the house, many people preferred to spend time in their kitchens. How could anyone relax in chilly parlors stuffed with goods?

Some Americans avoided or resisted the Market Revolution. But whether they liked it or not, Americans were affected by a growing acceptance of the idea that making money was a good thing. This straightforward pursuit of capital set Americans of the 1800s apart from their colonial ancestors.

A general commitment to capitalism did not mean economic development was the same everywhere, however. By the 1830s, different sections of the United States were developing in different ways. In particular, the economy and societies of the North and South were growing more and more distinct.

Using Historical Evidence The well-to-do city merchant and his wife who posed for the painting from which this 1843 engraving was taken wanted to be shown in their "best room"—the parlor. *What objects in the engraving reveal the new American passion for buying goods?*

SECTION 1 REVIEW

Key Terms, People, and Places
1. Define (a) Market Revolution, (b) entrepreneur, (c) capitalism, (d) capital, (e) household economy, (f) commodity, (g) centralize.

Key Concepts
2. What was the impact of the Market Revolution on households?

3. What positive effect and what negative effect did banks have on the United States between 1815 and 1845?
4. What changes did increased purchasing of goods bring to American homes?

Critical Thinking
5. **Predicting Consequences** How might bringing workers into one central place affect family life?

Quiz found in the Unit 3 folder, p. 9, covers the main ideas in this section as well as the key terms.

Media and Technology

Transparency
Our Multicultural Heritage, C-8

Caption Answer to ...

Using Historical Evidence
The extensive library, carpets, lamp, and other ornate furnishings.

3. ASSESS

Section 1 Review Answers

1. (a) Market Revolution, see p. 214, (b) entrepreneur, see p. 215, (c) capitalism, see p. 215, (d) capital, see p. 215, (e) household economy, see p. 215, (f) commodity, see p. 215, (g) centralize, see p. 216

2. Families began to produce fewer and fewer of the things they needed; instead, they bought those items from stores or other individuals.

3. Banks fueled the development of the American economy by providing loans that allowed people to buy land and investments. Banks were also the source of problems that came with debt and depression.

4. Homes became much more elaborately decorated and furnished as Americans purchased items such as china, paintings, and silverware.

5. It is likely that family life would suffer because workers had to work away from their homes and families; family members would spend less time together.

Reteach

Ask students to use the following key terms, people, and places in a short essay describing how the American economy changed in the early 1800s: Market Revolution, entrepreneur, capitalism, capital, household economy, commodity, centralize, Mason Weems.

4. CLOSE

Reinforcing the Big Idea
The Market Revolution radically altered life throughout the United States. The next section explains how this revolution affected the northern region of the country.

SECTION 2

The Northern Section

1. FOCUS

Connecting to the Big Idea

See page 212B. Point out that the Market Revolution affected regions of the country in different ways. Although most northerners remained farmers, the region underwent significant economic and social changes. Ask what these changes were.

Objectives

- Explain how farmers in the Old Northwest encouraged both the growth of cities and developed an increasingly complicated system for supplying them with food.
- Describe how goods were produced in the Northeast.
- Explain the effects of the rapid growth of cities and industries in the Northeast.
- Describe the importance of the early labor movement.

Bellringer

Ask students to list the pros and cons of living in a large city. As students share their lists with the class, make a composite list on the chalkboard.

Reading Strategy

Predicting Content Ask students to skim Section 2, listing the main headings and the subheadings, and to write a sentence or phrase under each heading that predicts the content of that section. When they have finished reading, ask students to test their predictions against the actual text.

SECTION PREVIEW

The North remained largely a land of farmers, now producing cash crops for the city market. But northern cities were growing rapidly. New divisions in society opened between rich and poor as well as between employers and workers.

Key Concepts

- Farmers in the Old Northwest encouraged both the growth of cities and an increasingly complicated system for supplying them with farm goods.
- In the Northeast, workshops and factories manufactured the goods households were no longer producing.
- The rapid growth of cities and industries created poverty, divided people by class, and strained the resources of cities.
- The early labor movement demonstrated that workers were aware of their ability to resist poor wages and working conditions.

Key Terms, People, and Places

section, capitalist; Northeast, Old Northwest

A woman going to work in one of the busy mills of the North carried her noonday meal in this tin and wood lunch pail.

I n the early 1800s, Americans became more and more aware that their nation was divided into **sections,** regions distinguished from one another by economic and cultural differences. The two main sections during this period were the North and the South.

The North itself was made up of two parts. One was the **Northeast,** composed of New England, New York, New Jersey, and Pennsylvania—an area that had once been the New England and Middle colonies. The other was the region north and west of the Ohio River, called the **Old Northwest** to distinguish it from the Northwest of today. It included land that is now Ohio, Indiana, Illinois, Michigan, Wisconsin, and part of Minnesota.

The Old Northwest

In the Old Northwest, farmers produced large quantities of corn, wheat, and other grains for sale as far away as Europe. Mostly they worked with the assistance of family members or young men hired to help out during harvests.

Grains were profitable crops, but they tended to spoil. Farmers had to deliver them to market quickly or turn them into a product that would not go bad. For example, corn could be used to raise pigs. Pigs could then be slaughtered and sold not just for meat, but also for fat—which was used to make soap—and bristles, which were useful in brushes. Similarly, wheat and other crops could be fed to cattle. Farm families also sold wheat, oats, barley, and corn to brewers and distillers, who transformed these crops into beer and whiskey, products that were easy to store and transport.

To process and market farm products, farmers depended on urban centers and specialized personnel, including bankers, operators of slaughterhouses and distilleries, and merchants. From Pennsylvania west into Iowa, small towns dotted the landscape, ringing the central urban areas they supplied, such as Cincinnati, St. Louis, and later Chicago. The reputations of these cities reflected their primary business. Cincinnati, for example, was known as "Porkopolis." Some 162,000 hogs were slaughtered there in 1835.

In the early 1800s, farmers sent flour, meal, pork products, whiskey, and other products by river to New Orleans to be sold in the islands of the Caribbean Sea, the eastern United States, and Europe. The market for these goods expanded even more during the 1820s and 1830s, when canals created an economic lifeline through the Great Lakes to New York City.

The Mills of the Northeast

The pork, beef, and beer of the Old Northwest were sold into a market where many

---

RESOURCE DIRECTORY

Teaching Resources

Reproducible Lesson Plan found in the Unit 3 folder, p. 4, provides a summary of the Section 2 lesson plan content.

Alternate Lesson Plan: Critical Thinking Identifying Cause and Effect, found in the Alternate Lesson Plans folder, p. 39, provides a strategy for pairs of students to apply this skill and find links among causal relationships they identify.

Guided Reading and Review found in the Unit 3 folder, p. 10, provides a structure for reading and mastering the key concepts and reviewing the key terms for Section 2. (Guided Practice)

Primary Source Activity New England Mill Women, found in the Unit 3 folder, pp. 26–27, uses a discussion between two Lowell, Massachusetts, millworkers to examine the pros and cons of factory life.

---

people no longer raised their own food. Although most people in the Northeast still lived on farms, many others now worked in the factories supplying the cloth, shoes, and other goods that households had once made for themselves.

After the War of 1812, businessmen in Boston financed huge new mills with water-driven power looms in Waltham and Lowell, Massachusetts. To operate these mills, they hired young unmarried women from New England farms, promising them a regulated and moral environment as well as a predictable income. The women were generally pleased to be able to earn money to put aside before they married, and they enjoyed the company of others their age. They made about $3.25 for a seventy-three-hour week in the 1830s; after deducting $1.25 for room and board, the average woman made about $2.00 per week. Part of the reason the mill owners hired women laborers was because they could be persuaded to work for about half the pay that men would have demanded. Women made up the bulk of factory employees until the 1840s, when immigrant Irish men, unable to find better-paying jobs, took their places.

 Woman millworkers usually lived in boarding houses run by the mill owners. Six days a week, twelve hours a day, from dawn till seven at night, they tended the grinding, clattering machines. In the evening they might attend lectures or classes, or gather in sewing or reading circles. Although the work was boring, the women valued the strong friendships they developed with their co-workers. One millworker recalled her work in the mill:

> There was a great deal of play mixed with it. We were not occupied more than half the time. The intervals were spent frolicking around among the spinning frames, teasing and talking to the older girls, or entertaining ourselves with games and stories in a corner.

Into the Cities

The Northeast was full of young people looking for work. Unable to support themselves as farmers in the Northeast, where the population had outgrown the available land, some went west. But thousands went to cities. In 1810 only about 6 percent of Americans lived in cities. By 1840, 12 percent lived in cities, an increase shown in the graph on page 220.

Clean, cheap power drove the textile mills of New England. Though at first mill builders relied on a system of huge wooden gears to harness river power, they soon adopted the system of belts shown here. On the first floor, cotton was spun into thread; on the second, thread was woven into cloth; on the third, the cloth was dressed or finished.

Labels on image: Overhead shaft · Dressers · Looms · Main shaft · Spinning frames · Main drum · Mill wheel · Water flow

2. INSTRUCT

Discuss

Discuss the changes brought about by the Market Revolution in the Old Northwest and in the Northeast. Ask how farmers in the Northwest contributed to the growth of cities in the Northeast. How did the changing nature of work affect the entire way of life in northern cities? What problems resulted in the cities of the Northeast?

Analyze

Have students analyze the plight of American factory workers and mill workers in the first half of the 1800s. Why did they feel that they had little power to change their working conditions?

In Depth

Did You Know?

Desperate economic conditions in New York City, where fifty thousand people—about one third of the working population—were unemployed, resulted in the Flour Riot of 1837. The New York *Commercial Register* reported on the riot: "Barrels of flour, by dozens, fifties and hundreds were tumbled into the street . . . thrown in rapid succession from the windows. . . . [And] numbers of women were engaged . . . filling . . . their aprons, with flour, and making off with it."

Activity

Role-Play: Workers' Complaints
Assume the role of a worker who is trying to persuade his co-workers to strike, while students role-play the following: a male worker with a large family and a sick wife at home; an unmarried woman with no children; a woman with a large family and no husband; and a young, unmarried male. Ask students to explain their reasons for wanting or not wanting to strike. **LEP**

Enrichment

Ask students to research and report on the development of the canal system that began in the 1820s, particularly the construction of the Erie Canal. Have them include a map of the canal with their report.

Caption Answer to ...

 Interpreting Graphs

1830: about 1,100,000; 1850: about 3,500,000; increase: about 2,400,000.

Answer to ...

MAKING CONNECTIONS

Answers may cite features mentioned in the text. Some services, such as welfare, sewer, and fire services, have improved.

In Depth

Then and Now

The growth of cities meant segregation of economic classes. Many members of the middle class chose to live far away from their places of work. Residing some distance from the downtown urban areas, lawyers, managers, and merchants commuted into town to work. In the 1990s, most members of the middle and upper class live in suburbs. (See Chapter 27, Section 2.)

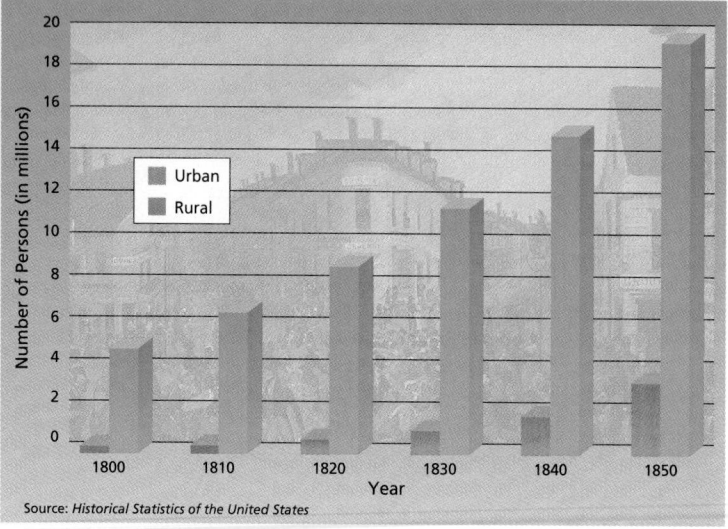

Urban and Rural Populations of the United States, 1800–1850

Source: *Historical Statistics of the United States*

 Interpreting Graphs
The scene in the background of this graph is the Five Points area of Manhattan about 1830. *How many Americans lived in cities in 1830? In 1850? What was the increase in urban population during the years 1830 to 1850?*

The largest cities in colonial North America had had no more than 30,000 residents. By contrast, in the early United States, the population of New York City (meaning Manhattan only) increased sharply—from about 33,000 in 1790 to about 124,000 in 1820, and then to about 516,000 by 1850. The population of Boston and Philadelphia also took off, as did that of smaller places such as Baltimore.

Work had changed in the northern cities, and with it an entire way of life. Colonial households had been more than the homes of families; they had also served as schools, hospitals, welfare centers, and support agencies. Many Americans may not realize that the government services of today were first established to help fill the gap left when the household lost importance. As the household economy broke down, people no longer supplied the same care to their families within the home. Men, and women as well in many cases, no longer worked in the household, and older members of the family often lived alone. Thus, the residents of northern cities were largely on their own, without households to support them in times of trouble.

In the cities, the growing number of poor people were concentrated in areas where housing was cheap. The Five Points area in lower Manhattan, for example, was notorious for its tenements by the 1830s. Two decades later, a group of middle-class Methodist women described Five Points as

miserable-looking buildings, liquor-stores innumerable, neglected children by scores, playing in rags and dirt, squalid-looking women, brutal men with black eyes and disfigured faces proclaiming drunken brawls and fearful violence.

Cities were simply unable to handle the tremendous increase in their population. They lacked sewage systems and reliable supplies of fresh water. Police and fire services were primitive at best. When disease struck, disaster followed. In 1832 and 1833, cholera, a disease carried by contaminated water, swept along the rivers and canals of the United States, leaving thousands dead or weakened in its wake.

MAKING CONNECTIONS

Are the problems of cities in the early 1800s similar to those of cities today? If so, how?

Owners and Workers Clash

Owners of factories and businessmen in general began to see the relationship between themselves and their employees in strictly economic terms. As **capitalists,** they supplied the capital that built the factory or started the business. They then paid for the labor of the people who worked for them. Beyond that, the employees were on their own. The Lowell mill owners were the exception. Most employers believed that if workers lived in poor housing, had little to eat, or dressed in rags, it was of no

▶ RESOURCE DIRECTORY

Teaching Resources

concern to the employer. In a society where buying and selling goods and labor determined so much, human welfare mattered little.

Workers Resist Workers had a different viewpoint. Work was no longer a rewarding focus of personal life, as it had been for most colonial Americans. People looked instead for increased wealth to take the place of that reward. A group of craftworkers in Philadelphia in 1827 announced their firm belief that

> all who toil have a natural and unalienable right to reap the fruits of their own industry; and that they who by labor (the only source) are the authors [creators] of every comfort, convenience and luxury, are in justice entitled to an equal participation . . . in . . . the richest and choicest [comforts] of them all.

Rather than attacking capitalism itself, workers focused on problems that arose in their specific situations, including long hours and low wages. In 1834, for example, one out of every six women in Lowell went on strike when employers announced a 15 percent wage cut in response to poor sales.

Such strikes were the only real weapon workers had. They had become an American tradition as early as the 1700s, when sailors and dockworkers went on strike. Shoemakers also made use of the tactic in the first decade of the 1800s. But between 1834 and 1836, 168 strikes took place in the United States, mainly for shorter hours and higher pay.

In 1834, during this period of intense labor activity, the first national labor organization, the National Trades Union (NTU), was formed. Close to 300,000 people belonged to the NTU and other unions in the 1830s, a large number for that period. The early flowering of unions was short-lived, however, and was killed by economic depression and court rulings that outlawed labor organizations.

Labor and Pride Despite its shortcomings, the early labor movement revealed the deep dissatisfaction of many workers and their willingness to do something about it. Lowell mill worker Harriet Robinson recalled her response when some women hesitated to strike during an 1836 protest against wage cuts.

> Not one of them having the courage to lead off, I . . . became impatient and started on ahead, saying, with childish bravado, "I don't care what you do, I am going to turn out [strike], whether any one else does or not"; and I marched out, and was followed by the others. As I looked back at the long line that followed me, I was more proud than I have ever been since at any success I may have achieved.

In time the labor movement would build on the pride of people such as Robinson. The stage was set for labor activity. By the 1840s, the North had a booming and complex economy. It was increasingly a region of cities and towns, banks and factories, a place with growing tensions between middle- and working-class people. More and more, the market linked people together or pushed them apart. The market was redefining northern society.

SECTION 2 REVIEW

Key Terms, People, and Places
1. Define (a) section, (b) capitalist.
2. Identify (a) Northeast, (b) Old Northwest.

Key Concepts
3. How did agriculture in the Old Northwest encourage the growth of cities?
4. Why did young, unmarried women make up the majority of workers in the first mills in the Northeast?

5. Why were conditions so bad for poor people in the cities of the Northeast in the early 1800s?
6. What did the early labor movement reveal about workers?

Critical Thinking
7. **Identifying Assumptions** Why is it necessary to know the economic class of the people describing the Five Points area in the quotation on page 220?

Quiz found in the Unit 3 folder, p. 11, covers the main ideas in this section as well as the key terms.

1. FOCUS

Connecting to the Big Idea

See page 212B. Explain that most of the southern region's economy centered on commercial agriculture. Yet the South was still a dynamic, capitalist society. Ask what made its economy flourish.

Objectives

● Explain how agriculture in the South was different from agriculture in the North.
● Describe how slave owners viewed enslaved people.
● Describe the ways in which enslaved people resisted slave holders.

Bellringer

Ask students to describe a southern or a northern accent. Next ask them to explain the phrase *regional difference.* Then ask students what regional differences exist between the North and the South today.

Reading Strategy

Structured Overview Ask students to write the following headings on a piece of paper: The Cotton Kingdom, The Slavery System, and Enslaved African Americans Resist. Have students fill in details from the text under the appropriate heading as they read.

The Southern Section

SECTION PREVIEW

The South as a whole was devoted to commercial agriculture, with few cities. The largest part of the region's wealth was built on a peculiar relationship between capitalists and their workers—slavery.

Key Concepts
• Like the North, the South was a dynamic, capitalist society, but its staple crops required little processing or handling before they were shipped directly to markets outside of the South.
  • Slave owners looked upon enslaved people as property and exploited their labor in order to make money.
  • Enslaved people occasionally rebelled as a group, but most resistance consisted of small rebellions in daily relationships.

Key Terms, People, and Places
Denmark Vesey, Nat Turner; South

Even free African Americans were closely controlled in the South. In Charleston, South Carolina, they were required to wear this badge, decorated with a kind of cap that traditionally stood for liberty.

L ike the North, the **South** remained overwhelmingly agricultural. The area considered the South consisted of what is now Delaware, Maryland, Virginia, West Virginia, North Carolina, South Carolina, Georgia, Kentucky, Tennessee, Alabama, Mississippi, Louisiana, and Arkansas. Its primary products were staple crops such as cotton, tobacco, sugar, and rice. Cotton especially was immensely profitable, by far the most valuable single product of the United States in the 1800s. No wonder southerners commonly remarked, "Cotton is king."

The Cotton Kingdom

Most of the staple crops of the South did not require the same kind of processing that was needed to transport the grains of the Old Northwest long distances. Properly cared for, cotton and tobacco would not spoil before they reached distant markets in the Northeast and Europe. In 1860 King Cotton made up two thirds of the total value of American exports; tobacco made up one tenth.

A Dynamic Farm Economy The South had an economy not unlike that of a colony. Its residents produced staple crops and raw materials that were processed and sold elsewhere. They did not develop as many towns and industries as did northerners. The region remained one of farms and open countryside. In the mid-1800s, travelers were struck by how empty the region seemed compared to the increasingly crowded and bustling North.

Yet the South had as active an economy as any part of the United States. White southern men saw in cotton what Parson Weems saw in his biography of George Washington—a ticket to wealth. Southern farmers and planters were just as much developers and entrepreneurs as the factory owners and business people of the North.

Southern Cities Although it was not as town-centered as the North, the South did have cities. New Orleans in Louisiana, Charleston in South Carolina, and Richmond in Virginia had many of the same problems that troubled New York City and Boston. Southern cities, however, were fewer in number, smaller in population, and were growing more slowly. They served the needs of plantations.

The southern cities were also home to large numbers of free African Americans. By 1850, of the 3.7 million African Americans in the United States, 12 percent were free. Some lived in the North, but most resided in southern cities or rural areas away from the large plantations. Generally, free African Americans were older and better educated than enslaved African Americans.

RESOURCE DIRECTORY

Teaching Resources

Reproducible Lesson Plan found in the Unit 3 folder, p. 5, provides a summary of the Section 3 lesson plan content.

Alternate Lesson Plan: Critical Thinking Making Comparisons, found in the Alternate Lesson Plans folder, p. 40, helps students summarize the differences between the economies of the South and North.

Guided Reading and Review found in the Unit 3 folder, p. 12, provides a structure for reading and mastering the key concepts and reviewing the key terms for Section 3. (Guided Practice)

Whether in the North or South, free blacks were usually very poor. Excluded from better-paying jobs, they worked as laborers, servants, cooks, laundresses, and barbers. And although they had their freedom, they enjoyed almost none of the privileges of American citizenship. They could not vote or hold office, for example.

MAKING CONNECTIONS

You have read that the economy of the South was like that of a colony. Was the economy of the North also like that of a colony? Explain your response.

The Slavery System

A planter had to have three things in order to profit from growing cotton, tobacco, sugar, and other agricultural products. The first was land—lots of it. The second was relatively easy and inexpensive access to markets. This requirement meant that the most profitable plantations were located along rivers. Finally, white southerners needed labor to grow crops such as cotton. Enslaved African Americans often supplied this labor.

Most white southerners did not own enslaved people. In 1830, slaveholders made up only 36 percent of the white population. All the same, because of their wealth, slaveholders did possess great influence in politics, society, and of course, the economy. And the South would have been very poor without the African American workers who built its economy. They made up more than half of the population of South Carolina and Mississippi in 1860, and two fifths of the population in Florida, Georgia, Alabama, and Louisiana.

Life on Small and Large Farms The life of enslaved Americans varied depending on circumstances. The typical slaveholder owned only a few African Americans. On small farms, enslaved people often worked side by side with their owners and their families. They sometimes ate together and slept in the same house. Close personal relationships sometimes developed; but, just as often, enslaved workers endured all

manner of cruelties without a larger community to turn to for support and protection.

Most enslaved Americans, however, did not live on small farms. Because a few white men owned most of the enslaved people of the South, most enslaved African Americans lived on plantations. There they had the benefits of a sizeable community of people, usually including twenty or more African Americans. But plantation life had serious drawbacks in contrast to life on a small farm. Labor could be harsher, for example. Plantation workers frequently toiled in gangs under the supervision of foremen and slave drivers.

For enslaved women in particular, life could be extremely difficult. In addition to bearing and caring for their own children and taking care of their households, they cooked and served food, cleaned houses and clothes, and labored in the fields. Especially hard work was required of them at harvest time in the late summer and fall. In addition to the drudgery of plantation life, they also had to endure rape or the threat of rape by slave owners.

Slavery as an Economic Relationship
Whether enslaved people lived closely with their owners or not, their relationship was always affected by the fact that slavery was based on economics. Owners exploited enslaved humans in order to get work done; they saw enslaved

Using Historical Evidence Five generations of an African American family—all enslaved—posed for this photograph outside their plantation home in 1862. *Describe their living conditions. Could this photograph be used as evidence of conditions during the 1840s? Explain your thinking.*

Media and Technology

 Transparency
Geographic Setting, M-4

Answer to ...

MAKING CONNECTIONS

No. The economy of the North did not depend upon producing staple crops and raw materials that were processed and sold elsewhere; it produced many goods, such as cotton cloth, that were sold both within its own market and overseas.

Caption Answer to ...

Using Historical Evidence

Answers may mention disrepair of building, dirt yard, lack of shoes. Answers may suggest that the photograph may be taken as an accurate indicator of living conditions in the 1840s.

2. **INSTRUCT**

Discuss

Discuss the South's economy. Ask how agriculture in the South differed from agriculture in the North. In what ways were southern planters and farmers as capitalistic as their northern counterparts? How did the Market Revolution affect the South differently than it did the North?

 In Depth

Historical Misconceptions

A common misconception is that the South had its own economic system, including slavery, and the North had nothing to do with it. "With us every branch and pursuit of life, every trade, profession, and occupation, is dependent upon the North," an Alabama newspaper complained. "In northern vessels [the southerner's] products are carried to market, his cotton is ginned in northern gins, his sugar is crushed and preserved by northern machinery; his rivers are navigated by northern steamboats. . . and a Yankee clock sits upon his mantelpiece."

Viewpoints

Dew states that enslaved people cannot grasp the concept of liberty; Bibb makes it clear that he understands and treasures his freedom very well. For a more thorough examination of the slavery issue, see the Resource Directory below.

Analyze

Have students analyze the role enslaved people played in the southern economy. Would commercial agriculture as practiced in the South have been possible without slavery?

Activity

Teaching Heterogeneous Groups
Economic differences between the North and South in the first half of the 1800s eventually led to civil war. So that students can explore the different regional lifestyles, divide the class into four groups: two groups to represent northern factory owners and factory workers and two groups to represent southern plantation owners and enslaved people. Have each group write a description of a day in the life of its assigned characters. Then integrate the groups and have students discuss how they want their daily lives to change.

Enrichment

One of the products of the plantation system was the "southern gentleman" who was characterized by a unique style of behavior called chivalry after the medieval code of knights and ladies. Ask students to work in groups to research this southern tradition. Have them write and produce a short skit illustrating the spirit of chivalry.

Viewpoints
On Slavery

Because the economy of the South depended on slave labor, southerners began to defend the institution against a growing antislavery movement. *In the quotations below, how does the viewpoint of the formerly enslaved man conflict with the southerner's viewpoint?*

In Defense of Slavery

"A merrier being does not exist on the face of the globe than the Negro slave of the United States. They are happy and contented, and the master is much less cruel than is generally imagined. Why then . . . should we attempt to disturb his contentment by planting in his mind a vain and indefinite desire for liberty—something which he cannot understand?"
Professor Thomas R. Dew, William and Mary College, address to the Virginia legislature, 1832

In Opposition to Slavery

"I thank God I am not property now, but am regarded as a man like yourself. . . . You may perhaps think hard of us for running away from slavery, but as for myself, I have but one apology to make for it, which is this: I have only to regret that I did not start at an early period."
Henry Bibb, who escaped from slavery with his family, in a letter to his former master, 1844

shoot me. I asked for leave to shake hands with her, which he refused, but said I might stand at a distance and talk with her. My heart was so full that I could say very little. . . . I have never seen or heard from her that day to this. I loved her as I love my life.

Enslaved African Americans Resist

Like working-class people in the North, enslaved people in the South fought back on occasion. One open resistance in the early 1820s was led by **Denmark Vesey,** an African American in Charleston, South Carolina. Having bought his freedom with a lottery jackpot, he supported himself as a carpenter. A preacher at the local African Methodist Episcopal Church, Vesey was well read and determined in his principles. He quoted the Declaration of Independence and the Bible in his arguments against slavery. He was impatient with African Americans who would not stand up to whites. According to the report of his conspiracy, when he saw an enslaved person step aside to allow a white man to pass him on the street, Vesey

would rebuke him, and observe that all men were born equal, and that he was surprised that anyone would degrade himself by such conduct; that he would never cringe to the whites, nor ought anyone who had the feelings of a man. When answered, We are slaves, he would sarcastically and indignantly reply, "You deserve to remain slaves."

Vesey and several allies, including the African-born Gullah Jack, planned to take over Charleston in July 1822. About eighty participants were to act in six units arranged by African origins.

But, like Gabriel Prosser in 1800, Vesey was betrayed by some of his followers. The governor of South Carolina called out five companies of troops in June and the rebellion was smashed before it could get started. Before the end of the summer, thirty-five African Americans were hanged, including Vesey, and another thirty-seven were banished from South Carolina.

Nat Turner, a well-educated, thirty-one-year-old African American preacher who

people as property that performed labor. In a bill of sale from 1811, an enslaved woman named Eve and her child, at a price of $156.00, are listed between a plow for $1.60 and "Eight Fancy Chairs" for $9.25. Such treatment of humans as property was the essence of slavery.

Or consider the situation of one enslaved man, Moses Grandy. He happened to be standing in the street when he saw his wife go by in a group of enslaved people who had been sold to a slaveholder named Rogerson. Grandy later recalled:

M r. Rogerson was with them on his horse, armed with pistols. I said to him, "For God's sake, have you bought my wife?" He said he had: when I asked him what she had done, he said she had done nothing, but that her master wanted money. He drew out a pistol and said that if I went near the wagon on which she was, he would

RESOURCE DIRECTORY

Teaching Resources

Viewpoints Activity On Slavery, found in the Unit 3 folder, pp. 22–23, provides extended quotations from both sides of the debate over slavery in the early nineteenth century.

Critical Thinking Activity Identifying Alternatives: Reacting to Slave Uprisings, found in the Unit 3 folder, p. 25, allows students to apply this skill by assuming the role of a Virginia legislator after Nat Turner's slave rebellion.

believed he acted with divine inspiration, also planned a rebellion. In 1831 he led about seventy enslaved people in southeastern Virginia in an uprising. The rebels killed fifty-five whites. Eventually, local militia captured most of the rebels. The state of Virginia hanged about twenty of them, including Turner. Crowds of frightened and angry whites rioted and slaughtered about a hundred African American bystanders who had no part in the plot.

The aborted Vesey and Turner rebellions led to harsher slave laws. Virginia and North Carolina passed laws against teaching enslaved people to read. Criticizing slavery in speech or writing was forbidden. Whites throughout the South were extremely frightened of possible rebellions. In South Carolina, Edwin C. Holland, who wrote in defense of the South in 1822, claimed that

> NEGROES are truly the Jacobins [revolutionaries] of the country . . . they are the anarchists and the domestic enemy; the common enemy of civilized society, and the barbarians who would, IF THEY COULD, become the DESTROYERS of our race.

Contrary to the picture Holland painted of the South, rebellions of enslaved people in the region were rare. More commonly, enslaved people resisted slavery in less dramatic fashion. Some ran away, though when caught, they might be forcibly returned. Others refused to work at the pace established by their owners, pretending not to hear or understand. Yet another form of resistance was stealing or destroying property.

Though slavery was based on a need for labor, like the relationship between entrepreneurs and workers in the North, it obviously encouraged different attitudes toward labor. The separation between work and home transforming the North did not occur in the South because most people, enslaved or not, continued to work at or near home. Thus the Market Revolution took different forms in the North and South. Both regions were active, expanding capitalistic societies. But the North was a world of farms and cities, banks and factories, while the South was a world of farms and plantations producing cotton and other staples. The North adopted new technologies eagerly, the South more slowly. These differences laid the foundation for serious conflict in the 1850s and 1860s.

An eclipse of the sun in 1831, claimed enslaved African American Nat Turner, was a sign that "I should arise and prepare myself, and slay my enemies with their own weapons." This etching depicts his capture.

SECTION 3 REVIEW

Key Terms, People, and Places
1. Identify (a) Denmark Vesey, (b) Nat Turner.
2. Identify the South.

Key Concepts
3. Explain why, despite the South's use of slave rather than free labor, that region can be considered as capitalist as the North.

4. Describe the slaveholders' view of their relationship with enslaved people.

Critical Thinking
5. **Making Comparisons** How was the relationship between slave owners and enslaved people in the South similar to the relationship between employers and workers in the North? How was it different?

 Quiz found in the Unit 3 folder, p. 13, covers the main ideas in this section as well as the key terms.

Media and Technology

 Transparency
Critical Thinking, I-15

---

3. ASSESS

Section 3 Review Answers

1. (a) Denmark Vesey, see p. 224, (b) Nat Turner, see p. 224

2. the South, see p. 222

3. Southern planters and farmers were just as much developers and entrepreneurs as were the factory owners and businesspeople of the North.

4. Slaveholders viewed their relationship with enslaved people as purely economic. They saw enslaved people as property that performed labor.

5. The relationship between millworkers and mill owners and between slaveholders and enslaved people was purely economic—human welfare mattered little. The lives of enslaved people were much harsher than those of millworkers. Enslaved people were not free to leave their employers; runaways were often forcibly returned to their owners.

Reteach

Ask students to write two one-paragraph summaries of the South's economy—one from the perspective of a plantation owner and the other from the perspective of an enslaved African American.

Alternative Assessment

Mid-Point Monitoring
Ask students if they have
- Chosen the format for their project
- Outlined the main ideas
- Begun outside research

4. CLOSE

Reinforcing the Big Idea

The Market Revolution created deep divisions between the North and the South. Although no less dynamic, the South's economy was very different from that of the North. The next section describes another split caused by the Market Revolution—the division in United States politics.

SECTION 4

The Second American Party System

Connecting to the Big Idea

See page 212B. The Market Revolution pushed economic forces to the forefront of American politics and created a deep split. Ask what role this division played in creating the second American party system.

Objectives

- Explain how Andrew Jackson lost the 1824 presidential election to John Quincy Adams even though Jackson won the popular vote.
- Describe how National Republicans and Jacksonian Democrats viewed the role of national government in United States economic development.

Bellringer

Ask students to write a statement indicating their position on an issue such as raising the legal driving age or imposing a town curfew for teenagers. Ask how students might organize to support their position.

Reading Strategy

Relating to Topic Have students answer the following question as they read: What were the political differences between the Democratic and the National Republican parties, and what role did these differences play in getting candidates elected to office?

Discuss

Ask students how Jackson's defeat in 1824 contributed to the development of the second American party system. What role did the National Republicans believe the government should play in the national economy? What position did Jacksonian Democrats take regarding this issue?

SECTION PREVIEW

The Market Revolution created a deep split in United States politics. While some called for the national government to take a strong role in building the economy, others argued that the government had no business taking such an active role in economic development.

Key Concepts

- In a race among several accomplished candidates for President in 1824, Andrew Jackson won the popular vote, but John Quincy Adams became President.
- National Republicans such as John Quincy Adams and Henry Clay argued that government power should be used to promote economic development. Jacksonian Democrats strongly opposed this role for the national government.

Key Terms, People, and Places

Monroe Doctrine, American System, second American party system; John Quincy Adams, John C. Calhoun, Henry Clay, National Republicans, Jacksonian Democrats

A new clash between political parties began in the election of 1824. During the campaign, supporters of candidate John Quincy Adams distributed this decorated box.

O
n July 4, 1826—the fiftieth anniversary of the Declaration of Independence—Thomas Jefferson and John Adams both died. This remarkable coincidence was just one among many signs that the generation that had brought the United States into being no longer was leading administrations and holding membership in Congress. Two years before, in 1824, James Monroe had ended his second term in office. In 1824, for the first time in the brief history of the nation, none of the presidential candidates could boast of having been a leader during the Revolution.

The Election of 1824

The four main candidates in the election of 1824 were John Quincy Adams of Massachusetts, John C. Calhoun of South Carolina, Henry Clay of Kentucky, and Andrew Jackson of Tennessee.

The Accomplishments of Adams The son of Abigail and John Adams, **John Quincy Adams** had become a Jeffersonian Republican nearly twenty years earlier when he was a senator. He had made his reputation as a diplomat, a role that suited him. While he was well educated and highly ethical, he was also considered to be cold and formal. While serving as secretary of state under Monroe, he had negotiated the Adams-Onís Treaty of 1819, by which the United States acquired Florida from Spain.

Another legacy of Adams's diplomatic career was the **Monroe Doctrine** of 1823, which Adams largely wrote. During the 1820s, every Spanish colony in the Western Hemisphere except Cuba and Puerto Rico had won its independence. The Monroe Doctrine warned European governments to stay out of the Americas and allow the new nations to develop on their own.

But neither the government nor the merchants of the United States had any intention of leaving the former Spanish colonies alone. The new countries possessed huge markets that attracted Americans. Moreover, the United States did not have the armed forces necessary to make the Monroe Doctrine anything but a paper declaration of policy. Still, the policy was a bold one for a young nation whose Capitol had been burned to the ground by a foreign army only a decade earlier. And much of the credit went to John Quincy Adams.

Calhoun and Clay: South and West Born in South Carolina, **John C. Calhoun** had served in the United States Congress and as Monroe's secretary of war. A brilliant man, Calhoun had

---

RESOURCE DIRECTORY

Teaching Resources

Reproducible Lesson Plan found in the Unit 3 folder, p. 6, provides a summary of the Section 4 lesson plan content.

Alternate Lesson Plan: Cooperative Learning found in the Alternate Lesson Plans folder, p. 41, provides a strategy for groups of students to prepare an oral presentation representing the views of a political party in the election of 1824.

Guided Reading and Review found in the Unit 3 folder, p. 14, provides a structure for reading and mastering the key concepts and reviewing the key terms for Section 4. (Guided Practice)

been an early supporter of national economic policies. But in the 1820s, he was beginning to shift toward defending southern sectional interests, which required protection of both slavery and the agricultural exports the slavery system produced, especially cotton. He withdrew from the race when he saw a chance to become Vice President. Besides, another candidate, William H. Crawford of Georgia, was already representing southern interests.

Henry Clay, a former speaker of the House of Representatives and a United States senator from Kentucky, was the most dynamic and colorful politician of his generation. "Harry of the West," as he was called, was a slaveholder and a man of great passions. He wanted to be President, and he was willing to make a political deal if it would improve his chances at a later time.

Jackson's Candidacy Catches Fire Finally, there was the wild card—Andrew Jackson. Jackson had served in the Senate in the 1790s and was a wealthy plantation owner near Nashville, Tennessee. Yet his fame rested not on these eminent positions in government or society, but mainly on military exploits like his victory at New Orleans in 1815. Jackson's iron will and his impulsive, passionate personality made him enormously popular. Those same characteristics also worried many people who saw him as a poorly educated and ill-tempered military chieftain.

As 1824 progressed, Jackson's candidacy caught fire. Like Jefferson, Jackson believed in the common people, whose support he rapidly gained. The general won the majority of the people's votes, but neither he nor any other candidate received a majority of votes in the Electoral College. Thus the House of Representatives had to choose a President from among the top vote-getters. That left Jackson and Adams as the main rivals—and Adams won a majority of votes in the House.

But Jackson and his followers believed that Adams's victory was the result of what they called "a corrupt bargain" with Clay. They charged that Clay, in return for giving Kentucky's votes to Adams, had been given the post of secretary of state. Adams and Clay both denied the accusation, but a great many Americans believed it.

Jackson Forever!
The Hero of Two Wars and of Or'eans!
The Man of the People!
HE WHO COULD NOT BARTER NOR BARGAIN FOR THE
PRESIDENCY!
Who, although " *A Military Chieftain*," valued the purity of Elections and of the Electors, MORE than the Office of PRESIDENT itself! Although the greatest in the gift of his countrymen, and the highest in point of dignity of any in the world,
BECAUSE
It should be derived from the
PEOPLE!
No Gag Laws! No Black Cockades! No Reign of Terror! No Standing Army or Navy Officers, when under the pay of Government, to browbeat, or
KNOCK DOWN
Old Revolutionary Characters, or our Representatives while in the discharge of their duty. To the Polls then, and vote for those who will support
OLD HICKORY
AND THE ELECTORAL LAW.

Using Historical Evidence This poster praises Andrew "Old Hickory" Jackson for honoring the constitutional election system in 1824 even though it cost him the presidency. *How does the poster describe Andrew Jackson?*

MAKING CONNECTIONS

In the election of 1824, the candidate chosen by the majority of American voters was denied the presidency. Such a result is still possible today. Do you think the Constitution should be changed so this can no longer happen? Why or why not?

Two New Parties Face Off

While Jackson plotted to get his revenge in the next election, President Adams and Secretary of State Clay tried to establish a federal policy of actively intervening in the economy of the nation. In 1825, Adams said:

> *The spirit of improvement is abroad upon the earth. . . . Let us not be unmindful that liberty is power; and that the tenure [holding] of power by man is . . . upon condition that it shall be exercised . . . to improve the condition of himself and his fellowmen.*

To Improve the Nation Simply put, Adams believed that the national government should take the lead in developing the economy. The new administration was proposing what Secretary Clay called an **American System.** Under this system the government would support

Caption Answer to . . .

Using Historical Evidence

As "The Hero of Two Wars and of [New] Orleans" and as "The Man of the People."

Answer to . . .

MAKING CONNECTIONS

Changing the Electoral College is a fairly complex issue with many pros and cons; students may support either the principle of majority vote by the people or the existing Electoral College system.

Analyze

Analyze the role of specific economic interests in the second American party system. How does the debate over the role of the national government in the economy continue in politics today?

Activity

Creating a Campaign Slogan
Ask students to create a campaign slogan for the 1828 election for either John Quincy Adams or Andrew Jackson, based on the candidate's view of the role of government in the economy. **LEP**

Enrichment

Ask students to research campaign strategy, and use the information to plan a campaign for Andrew Jackson in the 1828 election.

Interpreting Tables

The National Republicans wanted the federal government to support such improvements; the Jacksonian Democrats wanted the individual states to be responsible for them.

3. ASSESS

Section 4 Review Answers

1. (a) Monroe Doctrine, see p. 226, (b) American System, see p. 227, (c) second American party system, see p. 228

2. (a) John Quincy Adams, see p. 226, (b) John C. Calhoun, see p. 226, (c) Henry Clay, see p. 227

3. Although Jackson won the majority of the popular vote, Adams won the majority of votes in the House.

4. National Republicans believed that government should take the lead in developing the American economy. Jacksonian Democrats believed that they were being true to the Jeffersonian commitment to minimal government.

5. According to the social contract theory of government, those who govern hold power in order to serve the needs of the governed. Adams was suggesting that those in power had an obligation to improve the lives of those they governed.

Reteach

Ask students to supply the most important details for each of these topics: Jackson's defeat in the election of 1824, the American System, the second American party system, National Republicans, Jacksonian Democrats.

4. CLOSE

 Reinforcing the Big Idea

The Market Revolution created a split in American politics that resulted in the development of two distinct parties. In 1828, the people elected Andrew Jackson as their new leader. The next section deals with Jackson's term in office.

Second American Party System

National Republicans/Whigs	Jacksonian Democrats
Example: John Quincy Adams	Example: Andrew Jackson
Federal government should take a leadership role	Federal government should remain as inactive as possible
Federal government should support internal improvements, such as roads and bridges	The individual states should be responsible for internal improvements
For national bank	Against national bank
Tended to be middle-class or well-established Protestants	Tended to be ambitious slave-holders, small farmers, non-Protestants, and working class

Interpreting Tables
Both National Republicans and Jacksonian Democrats agreed on the goals of the American system, but disagreed on how to reach those goals. *How did each party want to bring about internal improvements?*

internal improvements, including roads, canals, bridges, lighthouses, universities, and many other projects. The purpose of the improvements was to encourage the development of American industries. In addition, the government would put a high tariff, or import tax, on goods brought into the United States. This tariff would make foreign goods more expensive and encourage Americans to buy goods manufactured in the United States.

⭐ **The Election of 1828** Few politicians quarreled with the goal of making American industries stronger. But many believed, as did Andrew Jackson, that the United States government had no business taking such an active role in the economic development of the nation. They argued that Americans wanted the national government to leave them alone, and that society and the economy

actually would work better without government interference.

Both Jackson and Adams had once been Jeffersonian Republicans, the party that had quarreled with Federalists, largely over constitutional issues. Now the stupendous changes of the Market Revolution were pushing economic issues to the forefront of the debate, and once again politicians were choosing sides.

The supporters of Adams and Clay began to call themselves **National Republicans.** They believed they were true to the Jeffersonian spirit of improvement. The followers of Jackson called themselves Democrats, a shortened form of Democrat-Republicans, the old name of the Jeffersonian Republicans. Historians often refer to them as **Jacksonian Democrats.** Members of this party believed that they were true to the Jeffersonian commitment to frugal, or minimal, government. This new face-off in politics, in which the National Republicans challenged the Jacksonian Democrats, is now known as the **second American party system.** It is summarized in the table on this page.

Some clever state politicians, including New York senator Martin Van Buren, agreed with Jackson's opposition to a powerful national government. They joined together in supporting Jackson when the election of 1828 rolled around. In this election, voters realized that their choice would determine the role the national government would play in their lives. As a result, more than twice as many men voted in 1828 than had voted in 1824, and most of these new voters threw their support to the man of the people, Andrew Jackson. With this sizable following, Jackson trounced Adams. ⭐

SECTION 4 REVIEW

Key Terms, People, and Places
1. Define (a) Monroe Doctrine, (b) American System, (c) second American party system.
2. Identify (a) John Quincy Adams, (b) John C. Calhoun, (c) Henry Clay.

Key Concepts
3. Why did Adams become President in 1824 rather than Jackson?

4. What was the main difference in outlook between National Republicans and Jacksonian Democrats?

Critical Thinking
5. **Recognizing Cause and Effect** John Quincy Adams said that people hold power on the condition that they use it to improve the lives of others. What does this idea have in common with the notion of the social contract discussed in Chapter 4, Section 3?

 RESOURCE DIRECTORY

Teaching Resources

⭐ **Visual Learning Activity** The Jackson Ticket, found in the Unit 3 folder, p. 32, uses election tickets from 1828 to show the images used to win support for the Democratic candidates.

⭐ **Primary Source Activity** President Jackson's Inauguration, found in the Unit 3 folder, p. 28, describes the inaugural festivities of "the People's President" through a letter written by an astonished witness, Mrs. S. H. Smith.

Quiz found in the Unit 3 folder, p. 15, covers the main ideas in this section as well as the key terms.

Determining Relevance

Determining relevance means discovering whether a logical connection exists between one item of information and another. If relevance does exist, you can use one item to learn about the other. For instance, you have seen that the Market Revolution led to increased opportunities for making money. You have also seen that a new political party system developed in the 1820s because politicians and voters were keenly interested in the role government should play in improving ways to make money. So you know that the Market Revolution is relevant to an understanding of American politics during this period.

Use the tables on this page and the following steps to practice determining the relevance of different pieces of information.

1. Identify the main purpose of each table. Study each table, including titles and headings. (a) What purpose does Table A serve? (b) What is the purpose of Table B? (c) What is the purpose of Table C?

2. Determine the relevance of the tables. Examine each table in the light of a specific need. (a) Imagine you want to find out how people who favored slavery voted in 1828. Which tables would be relevant? (b) Imagine you want to know which candidates in 1824 favored tariffs. Which tables would be most relevant? (c) Imagine you have used Table A to find the total votes cast for Jackson and Adams

in 1828. Now, however, you want to know how each section of the country voted in that election. Which table would now be relevant to your needs?

3. Use your understanding of the relevance of the tables to support an observation. (a) Using the relevant tables, support the statement that western states tended to be against the national bank. (b) Generally speaking, northerners favored the American System of tariffs and internal improvements more than southerners because the North had more industry. Explain how the tables support this generalization. (c) Imagine that you want to demonstrate to someone that in an election the popular vote is often closer than the vote in the Electoral College. Explain how the tables could be used to demonstrate this.

A. Presidential Elections, 1824 and 1828

| Year | Candidate | Political Party | Votes Cast | | |
			Popular	Electoral	House of Representatives
1824	John Quincy Adams	No distinct party designations	108,740	84	13
	Andrew Jackson		153,544	99	7
	Henry Clay		47,136	37	0
	W. H. Crawford		46,618	41	4
1828	Andrew Jackson	Democratic	647,826	178	No vote needed
	John Quincy Adams	National Republican	508,064	83	

Source: *World Almanac & Book of Facts, 1993; Historical Statistics of the United States*

B. State Electoral Votes Cast for President, 1828

| | Slave States | | Free States | | |
	South	West	North	West	Total
Number of States	9	3	9	3	24
Number of Electoral Votes	86	28	123	24	261
Number of Democratic Electoral Votes	77	28	49	24	178
Number of National Republican Electoral Votes	9	0	74	0	83

Source: *Historical Statistics of the United States*

C. Candidate Profiles

Issue	Adams	Jackson
Slavery	Against	For
National Bank	For	Against
Protective Tariffs	For	Generally against
Federally Funded Internal Improvements	For	Against
Voting Rights for Propertyless Workers	Against	For

Historian's Toolbox Activity Determining Relevance, found in the Unit 3 folder, p. 24, uses tables of party affiliation and opinion from the 1990s to provide further practice with this skill.

The Age of Jackson

SECTION 5

The Age of Jackson

1. FOCUS

Connecting to the Big Idea

See page 212B. Explain to students that Andrew Jackson's term in office was marked by a commitment to minimize the role of national government in an effort to clear a path to success for the ordinary white male citizen. Ask what events characterized Jackson's two terms in office.

Objectives

- Explain the significance of Jackson's veto of the rechartering of the Second Bank of the United States.
- Explain why Jackson opposed South Carolina's attempt to strike down a federal law.
- Describe Jackson's response to the Cherokee when the state of Georgia seized their land.
- Describe the influence of economic issues after the Age of Jackson.

Bellringer

Ask students to recall a recent President whose personality played a major role in his popularity and to explain what it was about his personality that the public found so appealing.

Reading Strategy

Writing Questions Ask students to skim the section and turn each subheading into a question beginning with *who, what, when, where, how,* or *why.* Have students answer the questions as they read the section.

SECTION PREVIEW

During his presidency, Andrew Jackson became the symbol for an age in which Americans first began to believe that elected officials should act according to the views of the voters.

Key Concepts

- In 1832 Jackson vetoed the rechartering of the Second Bank of the United States.
- Despite his opposition to a strong national government, Jackson opposed one state's attempt to strike down a federal law.
- Jackson refused to support the Cherokee when the state of Georgia seized their land.
- After the Age of Jackson, economic issues continued to shape the clash between political parties.

Key Terms, People, and Places

Maysville Road Veto, patronage, spoils system, *McCulloch* v. *Maryland,* Tariff of Abominations, nullification, secede, Trail of Tears, Panic of 1837; Whigs

A navy ship bore this figurehead of Andrew Jackson in 1834. In an action typical of the strong political feelings of the time, someone sawed off the head soon after the carving was fastened in place.

L ike Jefferson, Andrew Jackson tried *not* to do much as President. He used his veto power to keep the government as inactive as possible, rejecting more acts of Congress than the six previous Presidents combined. Typical was the **Maysville Road Veto** of 1830. Congress had voted money to build a road from the Ohio River at Maysville across Kentucky to Lexington, but Jackson vetoed the bill. He did not object to the road; he just thought the state of Kentucky, not the national government, should build it.

Jackson Defends the Spoils System

For many years, victorious office seekers had appointed their friends and supporters to public office in their administrations. This practice, known as **patronage,** became official when Andrew Jackson took office. He dismissed more than two hundred previous presidential appointees and nearly two thousand other officeholders and replaced them with Jacksonian Democrats.

Patronage under Jackson became known as the **spoils system.** In this case, the spoils, or booty taken from a conquered enemy, were government jobs for party supporters. Jackson defended the system on the grounds that any intelligent person could perform the duties required and that "rotation in office" would prevent a small group from controlling the government. His support for the spoils system contributed to Jackson's image as the champion of the common man.

The Bank War

The defining moment of Jackson's presidency came in 1832. The President had a deep personal hatred of the Bank of the United States. He had lost money to the first bank in the 1790s, and he had never agreed with the establishment of the second bank in 1816. Like many Americans, Jackson believed the Bank of the United States was a "monster" institution. He held it responsible for the Panic of 1819 and the hard times that had followed.

Under law, the Bank of the United States could only operate until 1836, unless Congress extended the life of the bank by issuing it a new charter. Supporters of the bank, including Senator Henry Clay, Senator Daniel Webster of Massachusetts, and the president of the bank, Nicholas Biddle, decided to recharter it four years early, partly to embarrass Jackson. They expected that he would offend his followers by allowing the bank to continue.

The Bank of the United States already had survived one challenge. In a complicated scheme to hinder the bank, the state of Maryland had tried unsuccessfully to make the bank pay a tax, and then imposed a large penalty when it failed

---

RESOURCE DIRECTORY

Teaching Resources

Reproducible Lesson Plan found in the Unit 3 folder, p. 7, provides a summary of the Section 5 lesson plan content.

Alternate Lesson Plan: Learning Styles found in the Alternate Lesson Plans folder, p. 42, is designed to help students develop criteria and assess the presidency of Andrew Jackson and is particularly helpful for visual or auditory learners.

Guided Reading and Review found in the Unit 3 folder, p. 16, provides a structure for reading and mastering the key concepts and reviewing the key terms for Section 5. (Guided Practice)

to do so. The national government claimed the fine was illegal, and the dispute reached the Supreme Court in 1819. In ***McCulloch v. Maryland,*** Chief Justice John Marshall went to the heart of the issue by declaring the fine illegal and the bank itself constitutional. The powers of the federal government were greater than those spelled out in the Constitution, Marshall said. He based his argument on Article I, Section 8, which states that Congress has the right "to make all laws necessary and proper" for carrying out the powers granted it under the Constitution. Thus Congress had the power to create such a bank if it wished. Furthermore, Chief Justice Marshall stressed that because the national government had created the bank, no state had the power to tax it. "The power to tax is the power to destroy," he pointed out. No state could destroy by taxes what the federal government under the Constitution had created.

In 1832 the supporters of the Bank of the United States acted without understanding the popularity of the President or the unpopularity of the bank. Jackson vetoed the act of Congress that rechartered the bank, dooming it to close in 1836. The President justified his action as a protection of the rights of ordinary citizens. In a lengthy veto message, he attacked the bank as a tool of greedy aristocrats:

I t is to be regretted that the rich and powerful too often bend the acts of government to their selfish purposes. Distinctions in society will always exist under every just government . . . but when the laws undertake . . . to make the rich richer and the potent more powerful, the humble members of society—the farmers, mechanics, and laborers—who have neither the time nor the means of securing like favors to themselves, have a right to complain of the injustice of their Government.

The National Republicans thought they could use the issue of Jackson's veto against him in the election of 1832. They changed their name to the **Whigs,** after the party in the British Parliament that had opposed the king during the 1700s, and ran Henry Clay for President. Criticizing Jackson's veto, however, was a mistaken strategy. As in 1828, Jackson won the election by a huge margin.

MAKING CONNECTIONS

What were the National Republicans trying to say about Jackson by calling themselves Whigs?

In Depth

Biography

Born to privilege and power, Nicholas Biddle (1786–1844) led the attempt to recharter the Bank of the United States in 1832. After reelection, a furious Jackson ordered all government deposits removed from the bank. Biddle then refused to extend credit for existing loans and withdrew credit for new loans. Jackson blamed the ensuing economic downturn on Biddle, whose supporters claimed that he "used the great power of the institution effectively to serve the financial needs of a growing country."

Analyze

Ask students to analyze Jackson's presidency in terms of the Market Revolution. How did his actions, including the relocation of thousands of Cherokee and other Native Americans, reflect the ideals of the Market Revolution? Why might it be said that Jackson embodied the best and the worst of the capitalist spirit?

 Activity

Creating Political Cartoons

Ask students to create an editorial cartoon for or against one of the following policies:

● Jackson institutionalizes the spoils system (champion of the common man or despotic politician).

● The Bank War (an eye for an eye or for the good of the nation).

● The Trail of Tears (in the name of progress or a cruel exile).

Enrichment

Ask students to research the civilization of the Cherokee or Seminole people, especially their cultural contributions and important leaders.

The Nullification Crisis

During his second administration, Jackson proved equal to yet another challenge. Supporters of the American System had passed the Tariff of 1828, which put a high tax on imports in order to encourage manufacturing within the United States. Most manufacturers, however, were in the North, and southerners did not like paying higher prices for goods to help northerners make a profit. They called the Tariff of 1828 the **Tariff of Abominations,** after the term *abomination* used in the Bible for something especially horrible or monstrous. In 1832, after passage of yet another tariff act, South Carolina declared the tariffs "null, void, and no law, nor binding upon this State, its officers or citizens." In doing so, it raised the question of **nullification:** did a state have the right to nullify, or declare illegal, a law passed by Congress? South Carolina also went further by threatening to **secede,** or withdraw, from the United States if its nullification was not respected.

You might expect that Jackson would be sympathetic to South Carolina. After all, he was a supporter of "negative" government, or using government power to protect the people from the government itself. He had put federal power to work attacking politicians he considered

The issue of nullification burst on the national scene in 1830, in a debate on the subject between Massachusetts senator Daniel Webster (standing) and South Carolina senator Robert Hayne (seated, hands before him). Webster rejected nullification, claiming it would make the Constitution "a rope of sand" that would not hold the states together.

corrupt and laws that he thought would prevent the people from fully enjoying their liberty. Thus he had acted to destroy the Bank of the United States. Furthermore, he understood southern issues; he was a slaveholder himself. Yet South Carolina's nullification outraged him.

Why would a believer in negative government take offense when a state asserted its rights? The explanation of this seeming contradiction is simple. President Jackson believed that in defying the laws of the United States, South Carolina was defying the will of the people. That he would never allow.

At Jackson's urging, Congress passed the Force Bill in 1833, which compelled the state of South Carolina to collect the Tariff Act duties. The President threatened to send 50,000 troops to the defiant state. But Henry Clay engineered a compromise that ended the crisis. Congress reduced some of the import duties, and South Carolina cancelled its Nullification Act—although as an act of continued defiance it nullified the Force Bill at the same time.

The Trail of Tears

President Jackson also used federal power negatively to support the relocation of the Cherokee, Choctaw, Creek, Chickasaw, and Seminole peoples to what is now Oklahoma. He had a deep prejudice against Native Americans and believed that they would prevent white people from moving west and opening up land for cotton production.

⭐ Many Americans shared Jackson's prejudice against Native Americans. In 1829 Georgia seized Cherokee land for cotton growers. After appealing to the United States Senate with little result, the Cherokee appealed directly to the American people in 1830. In that appeal, the Cherokee said:

> The people of the United States will have the fairness to reflect, that all the treaties between them and the Cherokee were made . . . for the benefit, of the whites. . . . We wish to remain on the land of our fathers. We have a perfect and original right to remain without interruption. . . . The treaties with us and laws of the United States made in pursuance of treaties, guaranty our

residence. . . . *It cannot be that the community we are addressing, remarkable for its intelligence and religious sensibilities, and preeminent* [admired] *for its devotion to the rights of man, will lay aside this appeal.*

Two years later, Chief Justice Marshall, in the case *Worcester* v. *Georgia,* ruled that Georgia's action was unconstitutional and should not be allowed. But Jackson and Georgia ignored the Supreme Court, which had no power to enforce its decision. In 1837 and 1838, the United States Army gathered about fifteen thousand Cherokee and forced them to migrate west.

On this nightmare journey, which the Cherokee called the **Trail of Tears,** about one out of every four Cherokees died of exposure or disease. In an added outrage, the $6 million spent by the federal government to relocate the Cherokee was charged against the $9 million that the Cherokee had been forced to accept for their lands.

The Age of Jackson Ends

Jackson's presidency was marked by his strong personality, unsinkable courage—and his quick temper. To many Americans, he seemed a larger-than-life figure, a tough, stubborn man who embodied the spirit of the frontier.

After two terms, Andrew Jackson left the presidency. The next President, Martin Van Buren, whom Jackson had supported as a candidate, was not as popular as the general. The **Panic of 1837** struck during his term. In this severe depression, caused in part by the end of the national bank, thousands of people lost their

jobs and poverty grew worse in American cities.

When the next election year arrived in 1840, the depression was still dragging on. The Whigs did what they could to imitate the Democrats. They chose William Henry Harrison as their candidate for President, a military hero like Jackson. They boasted that Harrison, too, was a plain man of the people, and that he had lived in a log cabin. In fact, he was the son of an aristocratic family and had grown up in a mansion. It was a fierce campaign, and over 80 percent of eligible voters cast ballots. Many voted in hopes that a change might end the depression.

Harrison defeated President Van Buren, only to be defeated in turn by illness. He caught a cold while giving a lengthy inaugural speech and died of pneumonia a month later. Vice President John Tyler, who took over as President, was more of a Jacksonian Democrat than a Whig, and his term was largely one of fruitless quarreling between the parties.

Much as Whigs and Jacksonians quarreled, however, they almost all agreed that an essential ingredient of American liberty was the right to compete and to make money. Politicians argued about the effects and the course of the Market Revolution. But rare was the political leader who did not believe that it had brought unparalleled economic and social progress to the United States of America.

William Henry Harrison was known as "Tippecanoe" because he had fought in the battle by that name. Whigs in 1840 campaigned for him and running mate John Tyler with the slogan "Tippecanoe and Tyler too."

SECTION 5 REVIEW

Key Terms, People, and Places
1. Define (a) Maysville Road Veto, (b) patronage, (c) spoils system, (d) *McCulloch* v. *Maryland,* (e) Tariff of Abominations, (f) nullification, (g) secede, (h) Trail of Tears, (i) Panic of 1837.
2. Identify the Whigs.

Key Concepts
3. Why did Jackson veto the rechartering of the Second Bank of the United States ?

4. Why did Jackson oppose nullification?
5. Why did Jackson fail to support the Cherokee when Georgia took their land?
6. Why did Martin Van Buren lose the election of 1840?

Critical Thinking
7. **Formulating Questions** What questions would you have asked a politician during the Age of Jackson to determine whether he was a Whig or a Jacksonian Democrat?

The Decision to Move Native Americans West

Focus The decision of Andrew Jackson's administration to remove the Cherokee, Creek, Choctaw, Chickasaw, and Seminole so that their homelands could be opened up for development provides a vivid example of how Jackson looked out for the interests of white men at the expense of other groups. Students are asked to evaluate this decision to allow the forcible removal of Native Americans in the 1830s.

Instruct To make sure that students understand what options were available to the federal government in dealing with the land conflict between the Native Americans and whites, ask students to summarize the different courses of action the government might have taken and list them on the chalkboard.

To check student understanding of these options, ask which of the suggested solutions would be favored by each of the following individuals:

• A Seminole chief

• A southern plantation owner anxious to expand his holdings, whose land was adjacent to Cherokee land

• A small Georgia farmer with a great fear of Native Americans who thought southerners should be left alone to take care of the Native American "problem" themselves

• A southern senator who resented the Native Americans' autonomy from state government

Review with students Andrew Jackson's choice to support the Indian Removal Act of 1830. Ask students why he made this choice.

Extend To extend the activity, have students investigate the current population figures, location, and lifestyle of the descendants of Native Americans who lost their southern homelands, as well as their feelings about their Native American identity.

The Decision To Move Native Americans West

Time Frame:	1827 to 1830
Place:	Washington, D.C.
Key People:	Native Americans, President Andrew Jackson
Situation:	In the late 1820s, the federal government had to decide how to deal with growing pressure from white settlers who wanted to take land from Native Americans in the South.

I n the 1820s, about 60,000 Cherokee, Creek, Choctaw, Chickasaw, and Seminole occupied approximately 100 million acres between North Carolina and Mississippi. After decades of trading and fighting, most had come to accept a way of life like that of whites. For many, the crops they grew, the style of clothes they wore, and the homes they built were the same as those of other white Americans.

But whites were not prepared to accept Native Americans as neighbors. When they looked at the vast Native American homelands, whites imagined them as profitable cotton fields. In Georgia in 1827, and later in Alabama and Mississippi, white citizens began to act through their state governments to extend state control over Native American land, though they had no legal right to do so. Their intent was to drive Native Americans off the land. In turn, Native Americans responded with legal action to stop them. The federal government now had to make a deci-

sion about whether to intervene in the dispute, and if so, how.

The Federal Government's Options

One option of the federal government was to protect the right of Native Americans to keep their land. In addition to Native Americans, some whites—including missionaries—supported this choice.

Another possibility was that the federal government should stay out of the dispute between Native Americans and the states. People who were generally against federal interference in state matters took this view.

Under a third option, the federal government could work out a compromise between the states and Native Americans. Native Americans would then keep their lands but become subject to state laws.

The fourth possible course of action was for the government to join the states in actively removing Native Americans from land east of the Mississippi River. That was exactly what many southerners wanted the government to do.

RESOURCE DIRECTORY

History Might Not . . . Activity Native American Fishing Rights on Trial, found in the Unit 3 folder, pp. 18–19, focuses on a legal battle in the late 1960s, which resulted from Native American demands that the U. S. government honor rights granted to them by the Medicine Creek Treaty of 1854.

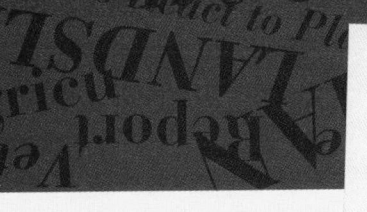

Weighing the Choices

The job of deciding which of these choices to take fell to Andrew Jackson when he was elected President in 1828. As an officer in the military during the War of 1812, he had fought the Seminole in Florida, proving himself their bitter enemy. Protecting the land rights of Native Americans in the South was not an option he would have considered for long, if at all.

Yet from a modern point of view, this option is an obvious first choice. In taking this course, the federal government would demonstrate that it was committed to such basic rights as the right to own property and the right to the full protection of the law. But these rights had never been clearly granted to Native Americans, and Jackson was more interested in establishing the rights of whites. Besides, this option would fuel a debate that would rage for years.

Staying out of the dispute—the second option—was also open to Jackson. It would surely result in bloodshed, however. And the President would be admitting that the federal government could not control the states. As Jackson later proved in the crisis over nullification in 1833, he would not allow the states to defy the will of the nation as a whole. Not taking any action at all would set a poor precedent in cases where the federal government was called upon to act against defiant states.

The third option, working out a compromise between Native Americans and the states, is another choice that today might seem attractive in theory. Native Americans would then have been able to keep their land. But because Native Americans would have to own the land as individuals, rather than in common, it would be easier for whites to take it away from them through legal tricks.

To Jackson, the option of working out a compromise was not attractive because in fact he did not want Native

GOAL	Resolve the struggle for southern lands between whites and Native Americans			
POSSIBLE ACTIONS	**Allow Native Americans to keep their lands**	**Stay out of the dispute**	**Work out a compromise**	**Remove Native Americans**
PROS AND CONS	• The United States would demonstrate that its commitment to such basic rights as property and due process of law was not limited to white males • Legal disputes might continue for decades	• Dispute might become violent • National government would be admitting that it could not control the states • Would set a poor precedent in cases where groups were looking for federal protection	• Native Americans would keep their land, but would have to own it as private property • Whites might simply find other ways to seize Native American land	• Would open millions of acres for immediate economic development • Would eliminate possibility of endless legal battles and possible violence • Would cause untold suffering to Native Americans

Americans to keep their land. As a planter and southerner, he wanted to open millions of acres for development.

Therefore President Jackson took the fourth option. He proposed that the Native Americans should be given land west of the Mississippi in an unequal exchange for their land east of that river. His idea provoked a stormy debate in Congress. Southerners won congressional approval for the Indian Removal Act of 1830 by a narrow margin. Under this act, and later acts and treaties, the Jackson administration would force Native Americans to exchange their 100 million acres of immensely valuable land in the east for 32 million acres in what is now Oklahoma.

EVALUATING DECISIONS

1. What group wanted the federal government to stay out of the dispute?
2. Give at least two reasons that Andrew Jackson decided against protecting Native American land rights.

Critical Thinking

3. **Predicting Consequences** How might the decision of Congress have been affected if Native Americans had been able to vote?

Media and Technology

Visions of America: History Might Not Have Happened This Way Game

To encourage students to explore pivotal moments in United States history, have students use the Visions of America software. Refer to the Visions of America Guidebook for viewing objectives, activities, game instructions, and discussion questions.

Understanding Key Terms, People, and Places

Terms
Students should refer to the definitions of the key terms in the chapter to write sentences that show the relation of each word to the Market Revolution or to the Age of Jackson.

Matching
1. capital
2. Monroe Doctrine
3. spoils system
4. nullification
5. commodity

True or False
1. false, John Quincy Adams
2. false, Old Northwest
3. true

Reviewing Main Ideas

1. Work changed from being an activity centered on keeping the household running to something that could be bought and sold.

2. Banks provided the credit and cash necessary for entrepreneurs to invest or to buy land.

3. Products included flour, meal, pork products, and whiskey.

4. Manufacturers were supplying the goods that households had traditionally supplied for themselves.

5. Rapid urban growth resulted in poverty, class division, and strains on resources.

6. Factory owners treated workers as a commodity; workers rebelled against long hours and low wages.

7. Southerners produced staple crops and raw materials that were processed and sold elsewhere; they also did not develop as many towns or industries as northerners.

8. Harsher slave laws were passed, including laws against teaching slaves to read and against criticizing slavery in speech or writing. People became more fearful of slave rebellions.

9. The four candidates were John Quincy Adams, John C. Calhoun, Henry Clay, and Andrew Jackson.

10. The Adams administration wanted the national government to encourage the development of American industry.

11. Jackson's veto was a victory for those who opposed a strong national government.

Chapter Review

Understanding Key Terms, People, and Places

Key Terms
1. Market Revolution
2. entrepreneur
3. capitalism
4. capital
5. household economy
6. commodity
7. centralize
8. section
9. capitalist
10. Monroe Doctrine
11. American System
12. second American party system
13. Maysville Road Veto
14. patronage
15. spoils system
16. *McCulloch* v. *Maryland*
17. Tariff of Abominations
18. nullification
19. secede
20. Trail of Tears
21. Panic of 1837

People
22. Denmark Vesey
23. Nat Turner
24. John Quincy Adams
25. John C. Calhoun
26. Henry Clay
27. National Republicans
28. Jacksonian Democrats
29. Whigs

Places
30. Northeast
31. Old Northwest
32. South

Terms For each term above, write a sentence that explains its relation to the Market Revolution or to the Age of Jackson.

Matching Review the key terms in the list above. If you are not sure of a term's meaning, review its definition in the chapter. Then choose a term from the list that best matches each description below.
1. a supply of wealth that can be used to produce goods
2. a warning to European governments to stay out of the Americas
3. the name that was first applied to the practice of patronage under Andrew Jackson
4. a state's declaration of the illegality of a federal law
5. something that can be bought and sold

True or False Determine whether each statement is true or false. If it is true, write "true." If it is false, change the underlined name to make the statement true.
1. Henry Clay deserved much of the credit for the Monroe Doctrine.
2. The North was divided into two sections: the Northeast and the states that had once been the New England and Middle colonies.
3. Jacksonian Democrats believed in minimal government.

Reviewing Main Ideas

Section 1 (pp. 214–217)
1. How did the meaning of work change during the first half of the 1800s?
2. Why were there more banks in 1830 than in 1780?

Section 2 (pp. 218–221)
3. What products did the farmers of the Old Northwest produce in the early 1800s?
4. What did the growth of factories and textile mills suggest about the role of the household?
5. Describe the effects of the rapid growth of cities.
6. Why did factory owners and workers clash during the early 1800s?

Section 3 (pp. 222–225)
7. Why was the South like a colony?

8. What were the results of the rebellions led by Denmark Vesey and Nat Turner?

Section 4 (pp. 226–228)
9. Who were the four main candidates in the election of 1824?
10. What was the main goal of the Adams administration?

Section 5 (pp. 230–233)
11. What was the importance of Jackson's veto of the rechartering of the Second Bank of the United States?
12. Why might one expect Jackson to be sympathetic to South Carolina's attempt to nullify federal tariffs?
13. Briefly describe the situation that led to the Trail of Tears.

---

12. Jackson supported "negative government" and opposed laws that he thought would curtail liberty; he was also a slave owner. He was outraged at South Carolina's nullification, however, because he believed that the state was defying the will of the people.

13. In 1829 Georgia seized Cherokee land for cotton growers. Jackson, ignoring the Supreme Court's decision that Georgia's action was unconstitutional, sent the United States Army to force about fifteen thousand Cherokee to move west.

Thinking Critically

1. Answers will vary. Students may point out that although work today is very much a commodity, people still hope to derive personal satisfaction from their work.

2. Answers will vary but should take into account Jackson's philosophy of limited government as well as his actions in vetoing the Second Bank of the United States, opposing South Carolina's attempt at striking down federal tariffs, and supporting Georgia's seizure of Cherokee land.

3. There were few actual open rebellions; most enslaved people rebelled in more subtle ways, such as working slowly or stealing.

Final Evaluation
Use the following guidelines to evaluate student projects:
● **Evidence of thoughtfulness** Did students include the main topics relative to this project from the chapter?
● **Evidence of outside research** To what extent did students use outside research materials for their projects?
● **Evidence of synthesis** Do projects demonstrate that students understand how topics are related?
● **Communication style** Do the projects convey their purpose to an audience in a clear, appealing way?

Thinking Critically

1. **Making Comparisons** During the early 1800s, work changed from an activity that kept one's household running to a commodity to be bought and sold. How do people view work today?
2. **Demonstrating Reasoned Judgment** President Jackson was a man of definite opinions and policies. Based on your reading of the chapter, what is your opinion of his administration?
3. **Distinguishing False from Accurate Images** After the rebellions led by Denmark Vesey and Nat Turner, white people throughout the South became very frightened. Was this fear unjustified?

Making Connections

1. **Evaluating Primary Sources** Review the primary source excerpt on page 231. Give evidence from the quotation that Jackson deserved his reputation as a "man of the people."
2. **Understanding the Visuals** Compare the pictures on page 222 and on page 114. What common element do you find? Do you think someone who has to wear an identification badge is truly free?
3. **Writing About the Chapter** Imagine that you are a man or woman living in colonial times, and you are suddenly transported to the Age of Jackson. Write a letter to your family in which you describe the changes you observe in the nation's economy and society. First, make a list of your observations about life during the Age of Jackson. Note any similarities between the two eras. Next, write a draft of your letter in which you summarize your observations. Revise your letter, making sure that you have used sufficient detail to support your conclusions. Proofread your letter and draft a final copy.
4. **Using the Graphic Organizer** This graphic organizer uses a web to organize information about the Market Revolution. Webs often can describe the attributes of a historical era. In this web, dotted lines show connections among these attributes. (a) Explain the connection between the development of centralized work and the decline of the household economy. (b) Create your own web map about Section 2, using this graphic organizer as an example.

To engage students in the content of the section, ask the following question: What items would you or your parents include on a wish list of new products on the market that you would like to own?

List students' suggestions on the chalkboard, noting next to each product whether it is used mainly for work, daily life, or entertainment or recreation. Repeat these steps for the items shown in the American Album display. Then compare the two lists and discuss the ways in which work and nonwork activities have changed during the last 150 years.

In order to connect this activity to the chapter content, ask students what products today help people work more efficiently. Contrast those items with inventions that spurred the Market Revolution. Then ask students how they think the appearance of new consumer goods might have affected people's attitudes toward spending and saving.

ENGINES OF CHANGE

America's Industrial and Market Revolution produced much more than new machines and new sources of power. It created new methods for organizing work as well as for buying and selling consumer goods. As a result of these changes, the United States in the 1800s changed from a country of farmers and artisans to an urban, industrial nation. *How do you think each product shown here differed from the products that people had used before?*

▲ THE JOHN BULL The Camden & Amboy Railroad imported this locomotive from England in 1831. Over the next few years, mechanics at the railroad changed almost every part. Engineers added front guide wheels that moved independently to keep the train from going off the track. They also added a cab, bell, whistle, headlight, and iron wheels.

◄ COLT REVOLVER Samuel Colt patented his revolving pistol in 1836. Later models were made using the "American system of manufacture" with interchangeable parts, division of labor, and special-purpose tools. The revolver had a single barrel and six chambers in a small, revolving cylinder.

► SAFE LOCK Inventors improved almost every product during the Industrial Revolution. This patented safe lock is one of hundreds of new lock patents.

► SEWING CLAMP Manufactured items did not always lose their homemade look. This ornate device combined pincushions with a clamp to hold one end of a piece of fabric to a table.

► HARVESTING MACHINE This model shows the reaper invented by Cyrus McCormick in 1831. McCormick built a factory in Chicago in 1847 and used many new marketing methods to sell his product. These methods included testimonials, demonstrations, guarantees, and easy-payment plans.

▼ OFFICE SAFE Financing, management, and record keeping became increasingly important as businesses grew. The office safe became a symbol of the new forms of business organization that developed.

CONSUMER GOODS New methods of manufacture during America's Industrial Revolution allowed companies to produce goods in large quantities. The level (above) and adjustable wrench (below) were typical of new consumer items that became available in the mid-1800s.

Chapter 9 Religion and Reform
1815–1860

📁 **Teaching Resources** (See Unit 3 Folder)

	Instruction	Enrichment
Section 1 **Middle-Class Reform** (pp. 242–247)	Reproducible Lesson Plan, p. 41 Alternate Lesson Plan, p. 44 Guided Reading and Review, p. 45 Quiz, p. 46	Critical Thinking Activity, Recognizing Ideologies, p. 62 Primary Source Activity, Protecting Society's Outcasts, pp. 63–64 Visual Learning Activity, Utopian Communities, p. 69 Historian's Toolbox Activity, Formulating Questions, p. 61
Section 2 **The Antislavery Movement** (pp. 249–253)	Reproducible Lesson Plan, p. 42 Alternate Lesson Plan, p. 45 Guided Reading and Review, p. 47 Quiz, p. 48	Visual Learning Activity, Countrymen in Chains, p. 70 American Profiles Activity, William Lloyd Garrison, p. 57 Literature Activity, Life as a Freeman, pp. 67–68 Time and Place Activity, The Sanctuary Movement in the United States, pp. 55–56
Section 3 **Women in the Public Sphere:** **A Turning Point in History** (pp. 256–261)	Reproducible Lesson Plan, p. 43 Alternate Lesson Plan, p. 46 Guided Reading and Review, p. 49 Quiz, p. 50	Literature Activity, Advice on Marriage, p. 66 American Profiles Activity, Maria Mitchell, p. 58 Turning Points Extension Activity, The Lasting Impact of Women in Public Life, pp. 53–54
Section 4 **Reform Efforts Highlight** **Cultural Divisions** (pp. 264–267)	Reproducible Lesson Plan, p. 44 Alternate Lesson Plan, p. 47 Guided Reading and Review, p. 51 Quiz, p. 52 Chapter Test, Forms A & B, pp. 71–76	Primary Source Activity, Plantation Life, p. 65 Viewpoints Activity, On Southern and Northern Women, pp. 59–60

📁 **Additional Chapter Resources**

Resource Organizer, p. 40
Alternate Lesson Plan, p. 43
Answer Keys, pp. 116–125

Bibliography

For the Teacher
Blockson, Charles L. *The Underground Railroad: First-Person Narratives of Escape to Freedom in the North.* Prentice Hall, 1987. (Including accounts of Tubman, Douglass, and Truth.)
McLoughlin, William G. *Revivals, Awakenings, and Reform: An Essay on Religion and Social Change in America, 1607–1977.* Princeton University Press, 1980. (A study of religion in the American experience.)

Prentice Hall Literature Excerpts from *The American Experience,* 1994, including Emerson, Ralph Waldo. *Nature.* Beacon, 1989 and *Self-Reliance.* Peter Pauper, 1967.

The Big Idea for the chapter and how the main ideas in each section relate to the Big Idea are graphically displayed below. Comprehension of this chapter's Big Idea is critical to students' understanding of United States history and how we as a nation got where we are today.

Media and Technology

 Critical Thinking, I-11

 Our Multicultural Heritage, C-5

 Visions of America: Turning Point Story, "Speak Out" (length: approx. 4 minutes)

 Visions of America: Roundtable Discussion on "Speak Out"

 Our Multicultural Heritage, C-13 Graphic Organizer, G-5

 Guided Reading Audiotapes (English and Spanish)

 Computer Test Bank

For the Student

Fitzgerald, Frances. *Cities on a Hill.* Simon & Schuster, 1986. (Compact history of America's utopian communities.)

Scott, John Anthony. *Woman Against Slavery: The Story of Harriet Beecher Stowe.* Crowell, 1978.

Styron, William. *The Confessions of Nat Turner.* Random, 1967. (A blending of fact and fiction on the famous slave uprising.)

CHAPTER 9

The young republic sped through rapid social change in the early 1800s—change that brought not only new benefits but also new regional and cultural tensions. A growing and dynamic reform movement urged Americans to seek both personal and social improvements, shaping society and the nation for generations to come.

SECTION 1

Middle-class Americans took aim at the problems resulting from rapid social change.

SECTION 2

As an antislavery movement of whites and free blacks gained strength, it caused divisions throughout United States society.

SECTION 3

Participation in the antislavery movement inspired many women to consider their own role in society and to press for new freedoms.

SECTION 4

The efforts of middle-class reformers stirred resentment among Americans of other regional and economic groups and intensified cultural divisions.

Religion and Reform
1815–1860

Religion and Reform
1815–1860

Although the rapid transformation of the United States in the early 1800s benefited the young republic in a number of ways, it also created new tensions and exaggerated old problems in American society. Inspired by religious revivals that emphasized the importance of character and the possibility of personal change, many Americans participated in a variety of reform movements during this era. Largely urban, northern, and middle-class in character, these movements tackled the serious social problems of the day but contributed to growing divisions between North and South.

Events in the United States				
1817 The American Colonization Society forms to return African Americans to Africa.	**1821** The nation's first public high school opens in Massachusetts.	**1825** Scottish social reformer Robert Owen founds utopian community of New Harmony, Indiana.	**1831** Abolitionist William Lloyd Garrison founds The Liberator, an antislavery newspaper.

| | 1815 | 1820 | 1825 | 1830 | 1835 |

Events in the World

| **1816** Argentina declares its independence. | **1822** The American Colonization Society founds the West African nation of Liberia. | **1830** Greece becomes an independent state. |

The Relevance of the Big Idea

The pace of social change is always too fast for some people, too slow for others. In the early 1800s, some Americans sought major reforms in their society, while others strongly resisted change. The struggle between the forces for and against change continues—and varies from community to community. Issues such as environmental regulation, education, and health concerns are debated, and sometimes fought over violently, in the 1990s.

Ask students to identify current social problems that have been brought about by new technology or other rapid changes. Then discuss how these problems pit people in various regions or cultures against one another. Ask students to consider why people often respond adversely to change.

In Depth

Global Connections

A French nobleman, Alexis de Tocqueville, wrote what is considered one of the most influential political treatises in American history. Based upon his travels in the 1830s, discussions with prominent Americans, and readings, *Democracy in America* examines in great detail and scope the contemporary status and prospects of the American economy and political system, as well as the influence of democracy on manners, religion, science, and art.

▶ RESOURCE DIRECTORY

Teaching Resources

📄 **Alternate Lesson Plan: Demonstrating the Big Idea** found in the Alternate Lesson Plans folder, p. 43, provides a lesson strategy to instruct students about the Big Idea that the young republic experienced rapid social change in the early 1800s.

📄 **Alternative Assessment Handbook** provides information, guidance, and strategies for alternative methods of assessment. It includes an essay on new trends in assessment, guidance and strategies for developing performance tasks and portfolios, scoring rubrics, and sample evaluation forms.

Pages 242–247
Middle-Class Reform

Dismayed by a wide variety of social problems that accompanied the nation's rapid growth, middle-class Americans banded together in the mid-1800s in an effort to improve life in the United States.

Pages 249–253
The Antislavery Movement

Started by a group of free African Americans and whites, the antislavery movement gained momentum in the 1830s. The debate over ending slavery not only caused divisions among reformers themselves but also created steadily increasing tensions between the North and South.

Pages 256–261
Women In the Public Sphere:
A Turning Point in History

Although middle-class women were expected to devote their energies to home, family, and community in the early 1800s, many women were not content with this work. Their participation in the antislavery movement led to the birth of a women's rights movement in the 1840s.

Pages 262–263
The Lasting Impact of Women In the Public Sphere

Pages 264–267
Reform Efforts Highlight Cultural Divisions

Not all Americans embraced the crusades of northern middle-class reformers. Working-class people and southerners, in particular, resented interfering reformers who told them how to live their lives.

1841 Catharine Beecher publishes *A Treatise on Domestic Economy.*

1848 Lucretia Mott and Elizabeth Cady Stanton organize the Seneca Falls convention on women's rights.

1851 Maine bans the manufacture and sale of all alcoholic beverages.

1861 Kansas becomes a state.

1865 Maria Mitchell becomes the first professor of astronomy at Vassar College.

1840	1845	1850	1855	1860	1865

1840 Female delegates are excluded from the World Anti-Slavery Convention in London.

1845 Irish potato famine spurs immigration to the United States.

1850 The Taiping Rebellion begins in China.

1854 Charles Dickens publishes *Hard Times.*

Media and Technology

Transparency
Time Lines, E-4

Middle-Class Reform

SECTION 1

Middle-Class Reform

1. FOCUS

Connecting to the Big Idea

See page 240B. Many Americans were concerned about the problems that accompanied the growth and development of the United States. Ask students how Americans reacted to these problems.

Objectives

● Characterize the reformers' view of the relationship between the individual and society.

● List the major reforms attempted during the mid-1800s.

● Describe the attempts by some Americans to form ideal societies.

Bellringer

Ask students to describe their ideal society. Would it have rules and standards? If so, what kind? What kinds of values might it seek to promote among its members?

Reading Strategy

Predicting Content Ask students to read the first paragraph on page 242 and predict what steps Americans took in response to society's growing ills. Have students check the accuracy of their predictions as they read the section.

Caption Answer to ...

 Interpreting Tables

Railroads made it easier to travel to new territories and also brought new businesses to remote areas, thus stimulating territorial economies and encouraging their growth.

SECTION PREVIEW

Dismayed by a wide variety of social problems that accompanied the nation's rapid growth, middle-class Americans banded together in the mid-1800s in an effort to improve life in the United States.

Key Concepts

• Middle-class reformers believed that improving individual character was the first step in improving society as a whole.

• Reformers advocated a wide variety of social reforms.

• Some Americans attempted to create perfect societies on a small scale by forming ideal communities.

Key Terms, People, and Places

Transcendentalism, temperance movement, prohibition, compulsory education, utopian community; Charles Grandison Finney, Lyman Beecher, Henry David Thoreau, Horace Mann, Dorothea Dix

A student's reward for high academic achievement in the 1840s was often a colorful certificate like the one pictured above.

A s the United States moved through the early decades of the 1800s, new industries arose, towns grew into cities, railroads and canals crisscrossed the countryside, and immigrants poured in from Ireland, Germany, and Scandinavia. At the same time, Americans in both the North and South pushed westward, expanding the nation's boundaries and adding fifteen new states to the young republic between 1800 and 1850, as the table at right shows. Along with economic growth, geographic expansion, and a skyrocketing increase in population came growing pains in the forms of greater urban poverty, widespread drinking, and calls for a system of basic education. Disturbed by these and other social problems, some Americans—mainly urban, middle-class northerners—set out to do something about them.

Religion Prompts Reform

The evangelical ministers of the Second Great Awakening preached that humans have the power to choose, just as they have the power to accept Jesus Christ as their savior. Unlike the Puritans, these evangelical Protestants did not believe that people's lives were predetermined by God, nor that the world was a rigid hierarchy of orders and ranks. Although they did view God as all-powerful, they also believed that he allowed humans to choose their own destinies. Successful people, in their view, were people with "character," or the ability to exercise self-control and follow God's laws.

Religious Revivals Perhaps the most successful of the revivalists of the Second Great

Admission of States, 1800–1850

State	Year of Admission
Ohio	1803
Louisiana	1812
Indiana	1816
Mississippi	1817
Illinois	1818
Alabama	1819
Maine	1820
Missouri	1821
Arkansas	1836
Michigan	1837
Florida	1845
Texas	1845
Iowa	1846
Wisconsin	1848
California	1850

Interpreting Tables
The combined impact of rapid population growth and westward expansion resulted in the admission of these new states. *How might the growth of the railroads have contributed to the admission of new states to the Union?*

RESOURCE DIRECTORY

Teaching Resources

Reproducible Lesson Plan found in the Unit 3 folder, p. 41, provides a summary of the Section 1 lesson plan content.

Alternate Lesson Plan: Learning Styles found in the Alternate Lesson Plans folder, p. 44, is designed to help groups of students prepare speeches on one of the reform movements of the era, and is especially useful for auditory learners.

Guided Reading and Review found in the Unit 3 folder, p. 45, provides a structure for reading and mastering the key concepts and reviewing the key terms for Section 1. (Guided Practice)

Critical Thinking Activity Recognizing Ideologies: Transcendentalism, found in the Unit 3 folder, p. 62, helps students identify a writer's or speaker's point of view by analyzing an excerpt from Henry David Thoreau's "Higher Laws."

Awakening was **Charles Grandison Finney.** Finney was a tall, well-built man with a great deal of energy. Trained as a lawyer, he became a Presbyterian minister after a powerful conversion experience. In his sermons, Finney repeatedly emphasized the importance of individual conversion, of personal choice in religious beliefs.

Another important revivalist was **Lyman Beecher.** The son of a blacksmith, Beecher attended Yale University and became a popular preacher in Boston. In 1832 he moved to Cincinnati to become president of the Lane Theological Seminary.

Beecher and other revivalists feared that "the vast extent of territory, our numerous and increasing population, . . . diversity of local interests, the power of selfishness, and the fury of sectional jealousy and hate" threatened the future of the United States. How, they wondered, could such a huge, loosely organized nation survive the rapid and far-reaching changes of the Market Revolution?

Many revivalists concluded that the answer to the question of national salvation lay in the work of individual salvation. In other words, they believed that good people would make a good country. By emphasizing individual self-improvement and the possibility of progress, this kind of evangelical revivalism inspired reform-minded Americans and nurtured reform movements in the 1830s and 1840s.

MAKING CONNECTIONS

The evangelical Protestant Christianity of the 1830s and 1840s proved to be an inspiration for many reformers of that era. By contrast, in what sense do you think the Puritanism of the colonial era discouraged its followers from becoming reformers?

The Transcendentalist Belief in Human Progress

One group that grew out of the Second Great Awakening found its inspiration in an intellectual and philosophical movement known as **Transcendentalism.** Relatively few in number—and centered mainly in New England—

the Transcendentalists believed that the most important truths in life went beyond, or "transcended," human understanding. Although the Transcendentalists rejected traditional forms of religion, such as evangelical Protestantism, they did share the evangelicals' belief that humans have control over their fate and have a responsibility to find their own path to a meaningful life.
⭐ Because Transcendentalism prized individual intuition, self-reliance, and the questioning of authority, it is not surprising that many Transcendentalists were active reformers. This dedication to reform is apparent in the works of Ralph Waldo Emerson, who once wrote: "What is man born for but to be a Reformer, a Reformer of what man has made. . . ?" One of Emerson's neighbors and fellow Transcendentalists, **Henry David Thoreau,** is best known for his book *Walden, or Life in the Woods.* Published in 1854, the book is a description of his two years of solitary life at Walden Pond near Concord, Massachusetts. Thoreau is also famous for writing his influential *Essay on the Duty of Civil Disobedience* and for having gone to jail to protest the 1846 Mexican War.

The Temperance Movement

Americans in the early 1800s liked to drink alcoholic beverages. At almost every social and

This painting of a baptism ceremony captures the emotional intensity of a typical religious revival during the Second Great Awakening.

Media and Technology

 Transparency
Critical Thinking, I-11

Explain/Discuss

Explain to students that social reformers could be categorized as those who wanted to get away from society's ills and those who wanted to change them. Ask students to identify people or groups of people who fall into each category. What values or ideas do these people all share?

Analyze

Ask students to analyze utopian communities and to consider why they failed. What steps might these communities have taken to conquer their problems?

Answer to ...

MAKING CONNECTIONS

The Puritan doctrine of predetermination did not encourage a belief in the possibility of human progress or self-improvement. In addition, the Puritans' emphasis on hierarchy and rank discouraged people from challenging authority.

Cooperative Learning

Time: One class period.
Activity: Create a political platform.
Grouping: Groups of three students.
Purpose: Have students imagine that they are starting a new political party of the late twentieth century called the Reform party. Ask them to draft a document stating the key positions and goals of their party.
Roles: Transcendentalist, prohibitionist, education reformer.
Outcome: Students will write position statements, evaluate them, rank them in importance, and combine them into a party platform.

Enrichment

Ask students to research the history of United States prisons, exploring the criminal justice system in the early 1800s, prison conditions, and efforts toward reform.

Caption Answer to ...

 Interpreting Tables

Per capita consumption dropped sharply as the temperance movement began to take effect.

In Depth

Did You Know?

In the early 1800s patriotic songs, such as the hymn *America,* written by Samuel Francis Smith, became part of the effort to create model citizens. The hymn was first sung in 1831 at an Independence Day celebration to the melody of the British national anthem, *God Save the Queen (King).* The song became popular in the North during the Civil War and is one of the most frequently sung patriotic songs in the United States.

---

political event, they drank—and drank heartily. In fact, Americans were drinking more alcoholic beverages per person during this period than at any other time in American history. So common was drinking that the Greene and Delaware Moral Society warned in 1815 that the United States was "actually threatened with becoming a nation of drunkards."

Middle-class reformers opposed anything that weakened self-control. In their eyes, drinking alcohol meant losing control. Because drunken men sometimes would become violent with their wives and children, many women reformers saw drinking as a threat to family life.

These reformers started a campaign against alcohol, known as the **temperance movement.** The movement became the first and most widespread middle-class reform movement of the era. Between 1815 and the 1840s, thousands of local temperance societies appeared. By 1834 the American Temperance Society boasted 7,000 local organizations with 1,250,000 members. Their mission was to improve people's lives by eliminating all alcoholic consumption.

Temperance societies relied primarily on persuasion. Members urged people to take pledges to abstain from alcohol. The societies also lobbied distillers and distributors of alcohol, established alcohol-free hotels and boat lines, encouraged employers to require their workers to sign antidrinking pledges, and worked for political candidates who promised to ban the sale of alcohol.

Maine became the first state to ban the manufacture and sale of all alcoholic beverages in 1851. Although several other states passed similar **prohibition** laws around this time, the protests of brewers, distillers, and other citizens soon led to the repeal of most of these laws.

Despite these setbacks, the temperance movement did have a significant impact on Americans' drinking habits. Between the 1830s and the 1860s, the per capita, or per person, consumption of distilled spirits in the United States dropped dramatically, as the table below shows.

Middle-class reformers promoted temperance both as an economic measure—because it reduced employee absenteeism—and as a health measure. Above all, they stressed its moral and social benefits. Temperate Americans were Americans in control of themselves, Americans free to develop their character and contribute to their nation. A thirty-three-year-old lawyer named Abraham Lincoln illustrated this viewpoint clearly when he spoke in Springfield, Illinois, in 1842. After equating the temperance revolution with the American Revolution, Lincoln looked forward to the

> *happy day when . . . the victory shall be complete—when there shall be neither a slave nor a drunkard on the earth. . . . How nobly distinguished that people who shall have planted and nurtured to maturity both the political and moral freedom of their species.*

Improving Public Education

Although the reformers of the early 1800s stressed the improvement of individual character, many of them came to believe that the social institutions of the United States needed reforming as well. Of particular concern to them was the lack of good public education in the nation. Public education was necessary, they argued, both to provide a democracy with literate, informed voters and to instill the kind of solid moral values that would help shape model citizens.

Before the early 1800s, Americans had not placed a high priority on public education. Even in New England, where colonial laws had required towns to provide elementary schools, support for public education had declined. Many school buildings were old, textbooks and other materials were scarce, and the quality of teaching was generally inadequate. The situation was even worse in the Middle Atlantic states and the South, due partly to geographic reasons. Because many people in these regions lived on isolated farms separated

Alcohol Consumption in the United States, 1800–1860

Year	Gallons Consumed Per Capita
1800	6.6
1810	7.1
1820	6.8
1830	7.1
1840	3.1
1850	1.8
1860	2.1

Source: *The Alcoholic Republic: An American Tradition,* by W. J. Rorabaugh

Interpreting Tables
Per capita, or per person, consumption of alcohol in the United States is shown on this table. *What evidence of the impact of the temperance movement does this table illustrate?*

by poor roads, the community commitment needed to maintain a public school system was often lacking.

Pressure for Reform Beginning in the 1820s, many working-class and middle-class citizens began demanding tax-supported schools in order to improve the quality of their children's lives. They immediately ran into strong opposition. Some taxpayers who had no children, or who sent their children to private schools, objected to supporting public schools that they did not use. Many parents opposed the idea of government taking away some of their control over their children. Families that depended on their children's labor to make ends meet were particularly upset by the idea of **compulsory education** that required children to attend school until a certain age.

Despite this opposition, the movement for educational reform gained strength in the 1830s. The movement owed much of its eventual success to **Horace Mann,** a Massachusetts lawyer who became that state's first secretary of the Board of Education in 1837. Mann rejected complaints against school taxes. Why, he argued, should not governments use their power to fight poverty and allow people to acquire knowledge? Mann believed in "the absolute right to an education of every human being that comes into the world."

Under Mann's leadership, Massachusetts pioneered school reform. He began a system of graded schools, uniform curricula, and teacher training. Using Massachusetts as a model, educational reformers led movements to establish public schools in other states. By the 1850s most northern states had established free public elementary schools.

The opportunity to receive a free high school education also expanded during these decades, though much more slowly. Massachusetts established the nation's first public high school in 1821. By 1860 the number of public high schools in the United States had risen to three hundred. Because most young people still had to leave school at an early age to work, however, a high school education remained the exception rather than the norm at this time.

Teaching Character Like other middle-class reformers of his time, Horace Mann had a particular kind of education in mind, an education that promoted self-discipline and good citizenship. In Mann's day, public schools taught students more than reading, writing, and arithmetic. They also taught—or tried to teach—character. Students learned how to behave, stand in line and wait their turn, deal with each other politely, and respect authority. They learned manners, and they learned how to speak and write in a uniform, respectable fashion.

The textbooks students used promoted evangelical Protestant values. By far the most famous were the readers put together by William Holmes McGuffey. *McGuffey's Readers* instructed students in morality as well as reading, emphasizing such basic values as thrift, obedience, honesty, and temperance. For example, following a moralistic tale about a man who ruined his life through drinking, an 1857 *McGuffey's Reader* included the following questions: "How did intemperance take possession of him? Why was he unsuccessful, do you suppose, in his resistance to intemperate habits?"

Limitations of Reform Despite some impressive achievements, the impact of educational reform on the nation was uneven. Although most northern states provided free public elementary education by the 1850s, progress toward this goal lagged far behind in the South. In addition, access to public education tended to be better in urban than in rural areas.

Even where public schools did exist, some groups remained blocked from using them. Girls, for example, often were discouraged from attending school, particularly if they wished to continue their education after learning to read and write. More frequently, towns and cities barred free African Americans from

This 1857 photograph shows a class at a school in Massachusetts. Teachers of the time tended toward strict discipline and drill to teach their students.

In Depth

Then and Now

In the 1990s there are more women than men in both undergraduate institutions and graduate schools in the United States. Yet, in early 1994, the Gender Equity in Education Act was introduced in Congress. It calls for educators to treat the sexes equally from kindergarten through twelfth grade, supports textbooks that eliminate sexist assumptions, and allows federal funding for such instruction. Supporters of the bill cite factors like females' lower scores on national achievement tests, and the channeling of males and females into gender-oriented roles as reasons for the necessity of such a bill. "Last year there were 18,000 boys eligible for National Merit Scholarships," said Elizabeth T. Kennan, president of Mount Holyoke College, and a supporter of the bill. "And there were only 8,000 girls. So something is happening, and I think it needs to be urgently addressed."

Section 1 Review Answers

1. (a) Transcendentalism, see p. 243, (b) temperance movement, see p. 244, (c) prohibition, see p. 244, (d) compulsory education, see p. 245, (e) utopian community, see p. 247

2. (a) Charles Grandison Finney, see p. 243, (b) Lyman Beecher, see p. 243, (c) Henry David Thoreau, see p. 243, (d) Horace Mann, see p. 245, (e) Dorothea Dix, see p. 246

3. People with good character were people who had voluntarily decided to control their passions and behave in a respectable fashion. Many middle-class Americans believed that individual character was the key to social order in a democratic society. People had to choose to be good.

4. Middle-class people (professionals, merchants, skilled laborers, and their families) were attracted by the emphasis on human beings' power both to choose salvation and to be better people.

5. Drunkenness was the extreme example of what they were trying to stop: people without control over themselves. A drunkard was an irresponsible, passionate person.

6. The desire to create a perfect or ideal society, rather than simply to reform one small piece of a large, imperfect society.

7. The members of many of these movements were motivated by deeply held religious beliefs. In addition, these movements were inspired by a faith in progress, a commitment to democratic ideals, and a belief in the idea that the improvement of individual character can lead to the improvement of national character. A majority of the participants in all of these reform movements were white, middle-class, and Protestant.

Caption Answer to ...

 Interpreting Graphs

Probably white males.

School* Enrollment, 1840–1870

2+2=4

Number of Students (in millions)

Year: 1840, 1850, 1860, 1870

*Primary, secondary, higher
Source: *American Education, The National Experience, 1783–1876,* by Lawrence A. Cremin

Interpreting Graphs
Thanks to the efforts of Horace Mann and other educational reformers, school enrollment in the United States increased rapidly in the mid-1800s. *What group do you think is most represented by these figures?*

entering local public schools. In places where African Americans could attend public schools, such as Boston and New York, black students often were segregated in inferior schools.

Opportunities for women and African Americans in higher education were even more limited. Although sixteen states funded some kind of higher education by 1860, few students at these schools were female or African American. Several private colleges, such as Oberlin, Amherst, and Dartmouth, did open their doors to a small number of African American students, and three black colleges—Avery, Lincoln, and Wilberforce—were founded during this period. In addition, Oberlin, Grinnell, and several other private colleges were coeducational. For the most part, however, white males were the only students welcome at public universities.

Prison Inmates and the Mentally Ill

In the early 1800s, many states had built prisons to house those who had committed crimes. These institutions reflected a shift away from the idea that people were incapable of improvement and toward a belief that human progress was possible. Rather than punishing criminals by

"I come to present the strong claims of suffering humanity," wrote Dorothea Dix in her report to the Massachusetts legislature.

branding them or putting them on display in public stocks, the states isolated them in institutions for a period of years. By leading regular, disciplined lives and having time to reflect on their sins, the theory went, they might reform themselves and become law-abiding citizens.

By the time a Boston schoolteacher named **Dorothea Dix** visited a Massachusetts jail in 1841, the idealism that had led to prisons had given way to a nightmare. Dix discovered men and women, young and old, sane and insane, first-time offenders and hardened criminals all crowded together in deplorable conditions. Many of the inmates she met were dressed in rags, poorly fed, and living in unheated cells.

Shocked, Dix spent the next two years visiting every prison and poorhouse in Massachusetts. In the report she prepared for the Massachusetts legislature, Dix related in vivid detail the appalling conditions and mistreatment she had witnessed. Her powerful testimony convinced Massachusetts lawmakers to pass legislation to improve conditions in prisons and poorhouses. Dix also persuaded them to establish a separate public institution for the mentally ill, arguing that "To confine the insane to persons whose education and habits do not qualify them for this charge is to condemn them to mental death."

As a result of Dix's campaign to have the mentally ill treated as patients rather than criminals, fifteen states established special hospitals for the mentally ill. Dix even persuaded the United States Congress to pass a bill providing federal land grants for more such hospitals, although President Franklin Pierce later vetoed this legislation because he did not believe the federal government should be involved in the business of social welfare. Few individual reformers in United States history have been as effective as Dix.

Utopian Communities

Profound faith in God, self-improvement, and progress led

RESOURCE DIRECTORY

Teaching Resources

Primary Source Activity Protecting Society's Outcasts, found in the Unit 3 folder, pp. 63–64, highlights the inhumane treatment of prisoners and the insane through an excerpt from Dorothea Dix's testimony to the Massachusetts legislature.

Visual Learning Activity Utopian Communities, found in the Unit 3 folder, p. 69, uses the title page from Robert Owen's *The Crisis* to describe the unhappiness that Owen felt about the state of society in the early 1800s.

some reformers to dream about **utopian communities**—small societies that would achieve perfection in social and political conditions. Many of these reformers were uncomfortable with the impact that capitalism and the Industrial Revolution were having on American life. As a result of their efforts, more than one hundred utopian communities, most of which lasted for only a short period of time, were established in the United States during the first half of the 1800s. ★

Among the most famous of these communities was New Harmony, Indiana, founded in 1825 by Scottish industrialist and social reformer Robert Owen. Owen envisioned a town in which well-educated and hardworking people would share property in common and live in harmony. After only a few years, however, the experiment fell victim to laziness, selfishness, and infighting. Other short-lived attempts to found utopian communities included the Transcendentalist-inspired Brook Farm in Boston and the Oneida Community near Syracuse in New York state.

Most utopian communities were religiously oriented. Examples include the Zoar in Ohio, the Amana Colony in Iowa, and the Ephrata Cloister in Pennsylvania. Far more numerous were the Shakers, who wished to isolate themselves from a society they viewed as corrupt, while emphasizing simplicity and equality among women and men.

The attempt to found ideal communities represents the most extreme example of the

reforming impulse that affected so many Americans in the early decades of the 1800s. Inspired by a mixture of religious beliefs and faith in the possibility of individual progress, many middle-class reformers of this era concentrated on trying to improve people's characters, hoping that in the process they also could improve the moral life of the nation. Other reformers grew more intent on making changes in society, as they became increasingly aware of the gap between the nation's democratic ideals and the reality of American life. Nowhere was that gap wider than over the issue of slavery, as the next section shows.

This 1844 painting of Brook Farm conveys the sense of peace and perfection that were the goals of most utopian communities.

SECTION 1 REVIEW

Key Terms, People, and Places
1. Define (a) Transcendentalism, (b) temperance movement, (c) prohibition, (d) compulsory education, (e) utopian community.
2. Identify (a) Charles Grandison Finney, (b) Lyman Beecher, (c) Henry David Thoreau, (d) Horace Mann, (e) Dorothea Dix.

Key Concepts
3. Why did reformers of the early 1800s place so much emphasis on individual character?

4. To whom did the religious revivals of the 1820s and 1830s appeal the most?
5. Why did reformers of this period concentrate so much attention on temperance?
6. What motivated some reformers to establish utopian communities during this era?

Critical Thinking
7. **Identifying Central Issues** What did the various middle-class reform movements of the early 1800s have in common?

Quiz found in the Unit 3 folder, p. 46, covers the main ideas in this section as well as the key terms.

Reteach
Have students review the key facts about middle-class reform by answering these questions:
● *Who* were the reformers?
● *What* did they try to accomplish?
● *When* did the reform movement take hold?
● *Where* did many of the reforms occur?
● *Why* did reformers think change was necessary?
● *How* did reformers bring about change?

4. **CLOSE**

Reinforcing the Big Idea
Social reformers attempted to remedy problems brought about by the nation's rapid growth. One of the main problems reformers tackled was slavery. The next section describes the antislavery movement in the 1830s.

Critical Thinking

Formulating Questions

Focus Analyze a reading selection using questions that demonstrate critical thinking skills.

Instruct Explain to students that just as detectives ask thoughtful questions and make careful observations when attempting to solve a crime, readers need to ask careful questions about a selection. Only then can they determine what kind of information is available from the passage and whether or not the information is reliable.

Extend See Historian's Toolbox Activity in the Resource Directory below.

Answers

1. Possible questions: (a) Why is intemperance a scourge? What is the scourge of intemperance? How bad is the scourge of intemperance? What forms does the scourge of intemperance take? (b) What proofs are offered that intemperance is a scourge? What are the supposed effects of this scourge?

2. Possible questions: (a) and (b) What problems does intemperance create? What sources does the writer use for his facts? How knowledgeable is he likely to be about the facts? How reliable might his reporting be?

3. Possible questions: (a) Who is the writer? For what purpose has he written the piece? (b) How honest is the writer? How likely is he to color the facts to make his point?

Formulating Questions

An important aspect of the critical thinking process is being able to formulate questions as you read. Asking questions about what you read helps you to focus on the facts. It also helps you learn where these facts came from, how reliable they are, and what their significance is. Finally, asking questions helps you recognize the writer's point of view. In short, formulating questions helps you gain insight into the material you read and sharpens your understanding of that material.

To formulate good questions, keep in mind the question words used by reporters: *Who? What? When? Where? Why?* and *How?* The first four words help you gather the basic facts. The last two help you to interpret those facts.

Use the following steps to formulate questions about the excerpt below from an 1830s temperance speech.

1. Identify the topic and the speaker. To guide your reading, first think of a question about the topic of the material. Sometimes you can do this by rephrasing the title in the form of a question. (a) The title of this excerpt is "The Scourge of Intemperance." *Scourge* is another word for the cause of serious trouble. What question can you formulate by rephrasing the title of the excerpt to focus on what the writer's premise, or basic hypothesis, is? (b) What questions would you like to see answered about this premise?

2. Locate the major points. To discover how the writer is going to support his or her premise, skim the first paragraph to get a sense of the problem areas the writer identifies and the sources he uses to support his facts. (a) What questions can you formulate to help you identify the problem areas? (b) What questions can you formulate to focus on the writer's sources of information and their reliability?

3. Identify the writer's point of view. Use the information you have about the writer, the source of the excerpt, and the purpose of the excerpt to help you identify "where the writer is coming from." (a) What questions can you formulate to determine the writer's point of view on the topic? (b) What questions can you formulate to determine how the writer's viewpoint affects the reliability of the proof he offers?

The Scourge of Intemperance

What are the statistics of [intemperance]? Ask the records of madhouses and they will answer that one-third of all their wretched inmates were sent there by intemperance. Ask the keepers of our prisons and they will testify that, with scarcely an exception, their horrible population is from the schools of intemperance. Ask the history of the 200,000 paupers now burdening the hands of public charity and you will find that two-thirds of them have been the victims, directly or indirectly, of intemperance. Inquire at the gates of death and you will learn that no less than 30,000 souls are annually passed for the judgment bar of God, driven there by intemperance.

How many slaves [to intemperance] are at present among us? . . . They are estimated at 480,000! And what does the nation pay for the honor and happiness of this whole system of ruin? Five times as much every year as for the annual support of its whole system of government. These are truths, so often published, so widely sanctioned [approved], so generally received, and so little doubted, that we need not detail the particulars by which they are made out.

—Bishop Charles P. McIlvaine, Protestant Episcopal Church,
Tracts of the American Tract Society, c. 1835

 RESOURCE DIRECTORY

Teaching Resources

Historian's Toolbox Activity Formulating Questions, found in the Unit 3 folder, p. 61, provides further practice in applying this skill with an excerpt from the report to Congress on smoking and health.

The Antislavery Movement

SECTION PREVIEW

Started by a group of free African Americans and whites, the antislavery movement gained momentum in the 1830s. The debate over ending slavery not only caused divisions among reformers themselves but also created steadily increasing tensions between the North and South.

Key Concepts

- Free African Americans, at the forefront of the antislavery movement, began to demand both an end to slavery and an equal place in society during the early 1800s.
- In the late 1830s and the 1840s, serious divisions appeared in the antislavery movement, some reflecting racial tensions and others concerning politics and tactics.
- The movement increasingly divided the North and South over the issue of slavery.

Key Terms, People, and Places

abolition, emancipation, colonization, underground railroad, gag rule; David Walker, William Lloyd Garrison, Frederick Douglass, Harriet Tubman; Liberia

T he best known and most controversial of the many reform movements that sprang up between 1820 and 1860 was the **abolition**, or antislavery, movement. No other reform movement of this era did more to create public debate and stir strong emotions than did abolitionism. In the process, the antislavery movement also contributed to increasing tensions between North and South.

The Roots of Abolitionism

The movement against slavery did not spring up overnight. Even during colonial times, a few Americans in both the North and the South spoke out against slavery. In several cases, enslaved persons petitioned colonial legislatures for their freedom—without success.

The ideas loosed by the American Revolution caught on in many quarters of the nation, and soon after, opposition to slavery grew more visible. During the late 1700s, several antislavery societies formed in the North, while abolitionist newspapers appeared in both the North and the South. At the same time, northern states—starting with Vermont in 1777—passed laws that gradually abolished slavery. ✪

At first, most antislavery activists favored a moderate approach. One of the most important of these early abolitionists was Benjamin Lundy, a Quaker who founded an antislavery newspaper in Ohio in the 1820s. Lundy used his newspaper, *The Genius of Universal Emancipation,* to advocate a gradual program for the **emancipation,** or freeing, of enslaved persons. He favored stopping the spread of slavery to new states and ending the slave trade within the United States as first steps toward full emancipation.

Free blacks had actively opposed slavery long before white reformers became involved in the abolitionist movement. By the end of the 1820s, nearly fifty African American antislavery groups had formed throughout the nation.

One Proposal: Colonization

In the early 1800s, some abolitionists became enthusiastic about **colonization,** a program to return free blacks and emancipated slaves to Africa. Convinced that African Americans would never achieve full participation in American society, these antislavery advocates founded the American Colonization Society in

This fringed banner celebrates the founding of William Lloyd Garrison's famous antislavery newspaper, *The Liberator.*

Connecting to the Big Idea

See page 240B. Explain that African Americans and whites made up a growing antislavery movement in the 1830s. The slavery debate created tensions within both the nation and the abolition movement itself. Ask students to describe the nature of the divisions within the movement.

Objectives

- Describe the role of African Americans in the antislavery movement.
- Trace the development of divisions within the antislavery movement.
- Explain why the antislavery movement caused political tension between North and South.

Bellringer

Ask students for what act the biblical Moses is most remembered. How do they think the name "Black Moses" might apply to Harriet Tubman? Ask them to explain what they think the nickname means.

Reading Strategy

Question Writing Ask students to reformulate the section headings and subheadings as questions and to write answers to those questions as they read.

Reproducible Lesson Plan found in the Unit 3 folder, p. 42, provides a summary of the Section 2 lesson plan content.

Alternate Lesson Plan: Cooperative Learning found in the Alternate Lesson Plans folder, p. 45, guides groups of students in producing an abolitionist newspaper article or graphic to show the goals and tactics, as well as the disagreements, of the antislavery movement.

Guided Reading and Review found in the Unit 3 folder, p. 47, provides a structure for reading and mastering the key concepts and reviewing the key terms for Section 2. (Guided Practice)

Visual Learning Activity Countrymen in Chains, found in the Unit 3 folder, p. 70, uses a popular abolitionist poster to illustrate the sentiment against slavery.

Explain/Discuss

Explain to students that the idea of African Americans going to settle in Africa has surfaced at various times, even in this century. Discuss why the abolition movement was not, technically, a "back to Africa" movement. Ask students to identify some of the arguments for and against abolition. What were people's motives for supporting or rejecting abolition? Do students themselves think it was a good idea? For whom?

Analyze

Ask students to identify people or groups of people who favored immediate abolition, gradual abolition, and the continuation of slavery, respectively. Then have them analyze which approach they think would have been best for the nation and why.

Caption Answer to ...

 Interpreting Graphs

The enslaved population rose more rapidly.

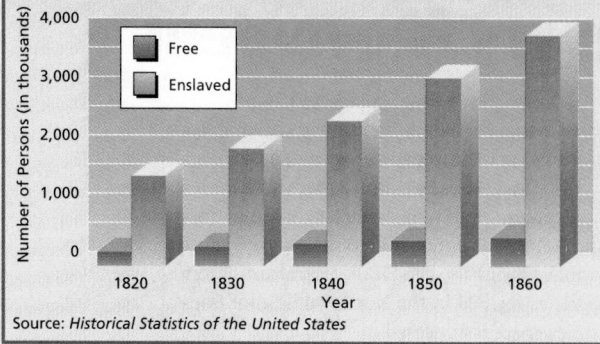

Free and Enslaved African American Population, 1820–1860

Number of Persons (in thousands): 4,000 / 3,000 / 2,000 / 1,000 / 0

Legend: ■ Free □ Enslaved

Years: 1820, 1830, 1840, 1850, 1860

Source: *Historical Statistics of the United States*

Interpreting Graphs
The population of both free and enslaved African Americans rose sharply in the early 1800s. *Which rose more rapidly?*

1817. To pursue their plan of colonization, the society established the West African country of **Liberia** in 1822.

Although most of those who founded the American Colonization Society believed that slavery was wrong, they did not necessarily believe in equality. Many were eager to rid the United States of both slavery *and* African Americans. The society also attracted the support of some southern planters who saw colonization as a way to eliminate the threat of "troublesome" free African Americans who they feared might encourage enslaved persons to seek their freedom.

Although a free African American named Paul Cuffe had been one of the originators of the idea of colonization, the plan offended most African Americans. They were interested in improving their lives in the land they considered their home, the United States, not moving to a continent they had never seen. At an 1817 meeting in Philadelphia, three thousand free African Americans shouted their opposition to such schemes with a roar that threatened to "bring down the walls of the building."

Thanks largely to such opposition, colonization was a resounding failure. As of 1831, only about 1,400 free and once-enslaved African Americans had migrated to Liberia. By that time, both African American and white abolitionists were adopting a more aggressive tone in their fight against slavery.

Calls for Immediate Abolition

Most African Americans wanted to end slavery immediately. In 1829 a forty-four-year-old free African American named **David Walker** captured their sentiments in his *Appeal to the Colored Citizens of the World.*

Walker's essay was an eloquent and angry denunciation of slavery and the nation that tolerated it. He did not mince words. White Americans had made African Americans into "the most wretched, degraded and abject set of beings that ever lived since the world began. . . ." Throwing the words of the Declaration of Independence in the faces of whites, Walker not only demanded equality but also spoke of the right of revolution.

Walker wanted neither charity nor condescension, but to be treated as a human entitled to the opportunities the United States had to offer. He hoped that white people would cooperate so that all Americans could "live in peace and happiness together." But if they would not listen, he warned, then "We must and shall be free . . . in spite of" them, "for America is as much our country, as it is yours."

Radical Abolitionism Although David Walker died in the streets of Boston in 1830, possibly murdered by poison, his *Appeal* marked a shift in the antislavery movement to a more aggressive tone and approach. During the 1830s, many African American and white members of the movement embraced this more militant form of abolitionism. One of the most famous of the radical abolitionists was a white Bostonian named **William Lloyd Garrison,** who in 1831 began publishing *The Liberator,* an antislavery newspaper supported largely by free African Americans. Garrison denounced moderation in the fight against slavery. To the world, he proclaimed his commitment to ending slavery:

> I am in earnest— I will not equivocate—I will not excuse—I will not retreat a single inch—AND I WILL BE HEARD. ✪

With the support of both white and African American abolitionists, Garrison also founded

---

 RESOURCE DIRECTORY

Teaching Resources

✪ **American Profiles Activity** found in the Unit 3 folder, p. 57, profiles William Lloyd Garrison, known as the conscience of the abolitionist movement.

✪ **Literature Activity** Life as a Freeman, found in the Unit 3 folder, pp. 67–68, presents a passage from *Narrative of the Life of Frederick Douglass* to give insight into the views of this prominent African American abolitionist.

the American Anti-Slavery Society in 1833. As the decade progressed, more middle-class northern whites became sympathetic to the cause of the immediate abolition of slavery. By 1835 the American Anti-Slavery Society had some 1,000 local chapters with roughly 150,000 members. With agents traveling throughout the North, the society also distributed more than one million antislavery tracts, or informational pamphlets, per year.

⭐ One of the most influential members of the American Anti-Slavery Society—and probably the most important African American abolitionist—was a self-educated man named **Frederick Douglass**. Born in Maryland around 1817, Douglass spent the first twenty-one years of his life in slavery before escaping to the North in 1838. After settling in New Bedford, Massachusetts, Douglass became a full-time agent for the American Anti-Slavery Society. Douglass condemned slavery in eloquent speeches that he delivered in both the United States and Great Britain.

Tensions Among Abolitionists

Given the intense passions stirred by the issue of slavery and the fierce commitment of many abolitionists, it is not surprising that divisions appeared in the antislavery movement. One of the first splits occurred over the question

of women's participation in the American Anti-Slavery Society. When Garrison insisted that female abolitionists such as Sarah and Angelina Grimké be allowed to speak at antislavery meetings, some members who objected to women's involvement in public political gatherings withdrew from the society.

Garrison also alienated members over the issue of political action. Because he believed that the Constitution supported slavery, Garrison thought that any attempt to achieve emancipation through the political process—that is, by passing new laws—was pointless. Abolitionists who disagreed, such as Arthur and Lewis Tappan, broke with Garrison to pursue a course of political action. Together with former slave owner and abolitionist James Birney, the Tappans formed the Liberty party in 1840 to put pressure on professional politicians to get someone sympathetic to their cause elected. Although the Liberty party received only a fraction of the presidential vote in 1840 and in 1844, it stole enough support from the Whig party in such

Once enslaved, Frederick Douglass often denounced the "murderous traffic" of the slave trade in his abolitionist speeches.

| 1650 | 1700 | 1750 | 1800 | | 1850 | 1900 | 1950 | 2000 |

Links Across Time

Divided Reform Movements

While the antislavery movement was gaining momentum in the 1830s and 1840s, its members were becoming increasingly divided on a variety of issues. Abolitionists did not speak with a single voice but represented a wide variety of viewpoints and philosophies ranging from the relatively conservative to the radical.

More than 100 years later, similar disagreements and tensions split the civil rights movement. Even as

Martin Luther King was delivering his famous "I Have A Dream" speech at the March on Washington in 1963, dissenting voices began to be heard among black leaders.

Some African Americans expressed impatience with King's philosophies, claiming that they were not bringing equality quickly enough. Others rejected the help of sympathetic whites, whom they perceived as hypocritical and conde-

scending. A few African American leaders and organizations rejected the goal of integration entirely, endorsing the idea of black separatism in its place.

Tensions among civil rights leaders and groups sometimes hurt the effectiveness of the movement, just as they did the antislavery movement in the 1840s. *Why do you think tensions and divisions often arise among members of reform movements?*

3. ASSESS

Section 2 Review Answers

1. (a) abolition, see p. 249, (b) emancipation, see p. 249, (c) colonization, see p. 249, (d) underground railroad, see p. 252, (e) gag rule, see p. 253

2. (a) David Walker, see p. 250, (b) William Lloyd Garrison, see p. 250, (c) Frederick Douglass, see p. 251, (d) Harriet Tubman, see p. 252

3. Liberia, see p. 250

4. They wanted to be treated as citizens of the United States, not as misfits to be shipped back to a place they had never known. Colonization was a potential remedy to slavery but it was also coercive, paternalistic, and racist.

Answer to ...

MAKING CONNECTIONS

Participants in the sanctuary movement broke laws to protect a vulnerable group of people from being returned to a place where they would be mistreated, persecuted, and possibly killed. Also, the sanctuary movement comprised a network of individuals who took risks to hide people who were in danger from the authorities.(See Time and Place Activity on page 254.)

In Depth

Biography

Harriet Tubman (1821–1913) was one of eleven children, born into slavery. She ran away to the North alone, later saying, "There was no one to welcome me to the land of freedom. I was a stranger in a strange land." By the beginning of the Civil War in 1861, Tubman had escorted over 300 slaves to freedom, including her brothers, sisters, and parents. Then, as a scout and spy for the Union Army, she helped free more than 750 slaves. In 1896, Tubman founded the National Association of Colored Women.

---

key states as Ohio and New York to throw the 1844 election to Democrat James K. Polk.

Racial tensions further divided the movement. For African Americans, the movement to end slavery had a personal dimension and an urgency that white people could never fully understand. In addition, some black reformers felt patronized by white abolitionists who urged their African American counterparts to keep a low profile and to follow directions. As African American Martin Delany—a frequent critic of white abolitionists—noted:

> We find ourselves occupying the very same position in relation to our Anti-Slavery friends, as we do in relation to the pro-slavery part of the community— a mere secondary, underling position.

Tensions such as these, as well as disagreements over tactics, led Frederick Douglass to break with Garrison in 1847 and found his own antislavery newspaper, *The North Star.*

The Underground Railroad Some members of the antislavery movement insisted that abolitionists use only legal means to advance their cause. Others favored direct action, whether legal or illegal. The best example of direct action in the movement was the **underground railroad**, not a railroad at all, but a network of men and women "conductors" who helped runaway enslaved persons escape to the North and then into Canada. (See "Time and Place: Routes to Freedom," on pages 254–255.)

Although both African American and white abolitionists worked for the underground railroad, African Americans made up the majority of volunteers. The most famous of the railroad's many "conductors" was a courageous former enslaved woman named **Harriet Tubman,** who repeatedly risked her life to lead runaway enslaved persons to freedom. Known as "the Black Moses" among African Americans, Tubman boasted later in life: "I never run my train off the track, and I never lost a passenger." Tubman's work enraged southern slave owners, who offered a $40,000 reward for her capture.

MAKING CONNECTIONS

Individuals and religious groups that participated in the "sanctuary movement" in the 1980s ignored immigration laws in order to prevent Central American political refugees from being returned to countries where they might be tortured, imprisoned, or murdered. Why do you think some people called the sanctuary movement a modern-day underground railroad?

"There's two things I've got a right to . . . death or liberty." So said Harriet Tubman (far left), shown here with a group of formerly enslaved people whom she led to freedom.

RESOURCE DIRECTORY

Teaching Resources

Resistance to Abolitionism

Although the antislavery movement generated a great deal of publicity, it did not enjoy widespread support. In fact, the activities of the abolitionists aroused intense opposition in both the North and the South.

Many northerners reacted negatively to the abolitionist cause. Merchants worried that the antislavery movement would further sour relations between North and South and consequently hurt trade between the two regions. White workers and labor leaders feared competition from free African American workers willing to accept lower wages. Even northerners who opposed slavery did not necessarily want free African Americans, whom they viewed as socially inferior, living in their communities.

Northern opposition to the antislavery movement sometimes became violent. Hostile opponents often booed abolitionists to drown out their messages or used physical threats to prevent them from speaking. William Lloyd Garrison narrowly escaped death in 1835 at the hands of an angry Boston crowd. Abolitionist editor Elijah P. Lovejoy was not so lucky. When he tried to prevent the members of a hostile mob from destroying his printing press in Alton, Illinois, in 1837, they shot and killed him. Many who were not normally sympathetic to the abolitionist cause were angered by Lovejoy's brutal murder.

Not surprisingly, most southerners were outraged by the criticisms the antislavery movement leveled at the institution of slavery. Attacks by northern abolitionists such as Garrison,

together with Nat Turner's 1831 rebellion, made many southerners even more determined to defend the institution of slavery. During the 1830s, it became increasingly rare and dangerous for southerners to speak out in favor of freeing the slaves.

Public officials in the South also joined in the battle against abolitionism. Southern postmasters, for example, refused to deliver abolitionist literature. In 1836, moreover, southern representatives in Congress succeeded in passing the so-called **gag rule,** which for the next eight years automatically tabled all antislavery petitions and thus prevented them from being read in the House. Even Americans who did not have passionate feelings about slavery were angered by this threat to freedom of speech and basic civil liberties.

As the strong resistance to the antislavery movement suggests, abolitionists remained a small minority of the population in the 1830s and 1840s. Only a handful of whites were prepared to fight for the abolition of slavery at this time, and even fewer were interested in racial equality. But the speeches and writings of such abolitionists as Walker, Garrison, Douglass, and others were vitally important in forcing white Americans to recognize the injustice of slavery. At the same time, abolitionism served as an inspiration for American women, who also were interested in winning equal rights.

When abolitionist Jonathan Walker was caught trying to smuggle seven enslaved people from Florida to the Bahamas, authorities branded the letters "SS" onto his hand to mark him as a slave stealer.

5. Walker not only called for an immediate end to slavery, but took great pride in being an African American. The *Appeal* exposed the hypocrisy of white talk about equality and reflected the impatience and anger of African Americans about the continued existence of slavery.

6. Abolitionism gained strength because of the ongoing support of free African Americans, the zealous dedication of leaders such as William Lloyd Garrison, the threats to freedom of speech many Americans saw in the gag rule and attacks on abolitionists, and the growing sense among middle-class northerners that slavery was an evil violation of middle-class morality.

7. Arguments about whether women should be permitted to participate in the movement caused divisions, as did disputes over the value of political action. White racism was a problem even within the abolitionist movement.

8. It suggests that in the mid-1800s few Americans foresaw the day when whites and blacks would have equal rights.

Reteach

Ask students to list the main reasons people supported or opposed the abolition of slavery. Have them identify whether each reason was primarily moral or economic.

Alternative Assessment

Mid-Point Monitoring
Ask students if they have
- Chosen a format for their writing
- Started an outline of major themes or ideas
- Begun any outside research

SECTION 2 REVIEW

Key Terms, People, and Places
1. Define (a) abolition, (b) emancipation, (c) colonization, (d) underground railroad, (e) gag rule.
2. Identify (a) David Walker, (b) William Lloyd Garrison, (c) Frederick Douglass, (d) Harriet Tubman.
3. Identify Liberia.

Key Concepts
4. Why did most free African Americans reject the idea of colonization?

5. Discuss the importance of David Walker's *Appeal*.
6. Why did the abolitionist cause gain strength in the 1830s?
7. What issues created tensions among abolitionists that led to division in the movement?

Critical Thinking
8. **Drawing conclusions** What does the northern response to abolitionism suggest about racial attitudes in American society as a whole during this era?

 Quiz found in the Unit 3 folder, p. 48, covers the main ideas in this section as well as the key terms.

Media and Technology

Transparency
Our Multicultural Heritage, C-5

4. CLOSE

Reinforcing the Big Idea

The antislavery movement caused divisions in United States society. In addition, it inspired another social group—women—to fight for greater freedoms. The next section describes the birth of the women's rights movement in the 1840s.

Routes to Freedom

Focus Ask students if they always travel to and from a location by the shortest possible route. Ask students to think about other factors that affect their choice of route to and from a known location, such as school or the grocery store. Tell students that in this feature they will learn why enslaved Americans took the tortuous route they did as they fled to freedom along the underground railroad.

Instruct After students have read the feature, divide the class into small groups. Ask each group to choose one of the following actual starting points for recorded passengers on the underground railroad: Portsmouth, Virginia; South Florence, Alabama; Martin, Tennessee; Wadesboro, North Carolina; or Eastport, Mississippi. Then, using the map on page 255, additional atlas maps, and the material in the feature, each group should plan a route northward for a group of enslaved people. Groups should prepare a detailed map of their route, including stops of any length.

Extend Ask students to research the escape of one enslaved African American and present the story to the class.

TIME & PLACE
A GEOGRAPHIC PERSPECTIVE

Routes to Freedom

On a map, the routes of the underground railroad look like a confused tangle of lines streaming from the slave states of the South to the freedom of Canada. What logic lies behind that apparent confusion?

The underground railroad was not strictly a railroad, nor was it underground: it was a network of routes, including paths, roads, rivers, and real railways, that led fugitives out of slavery in the South. Geography can help explain the routes marked out by the railroad.

Geographers use themes in their study, much as a workman uses tools. Two of these themes are place—including the physical characteristics of the land—and regions. The routes of the underground railroad depended on certain physical features and regional attitudes in the United States.

Physical Features Lead Out of the South

Several physical features of the South provided relatively protected routes for fugitives traveling to underground railroad connections in the free states. In the West, the valley of the Mississippi River was a natural escape route. Some enslaved people even managed to book riverboat passage northward and reach the underground railroad routes of western Illinois. The Mississippi pathway was dangerous, however, because it constantly brought fugitives into contact with potentially hostile white people.

The east coast, by contrast, boasted a physical feature that offered protection from human pursuers, but posed serious natural dangers. This was the string of low-lying swamps stretching along the Atlantic coast from southern Georgia to southern Virginia. Fugitives who traveled north through the swamps—and survived the hazards of poisonous

snakes and disease-bearing mosquitoes—linked up with one of the eastern underground railroad routes to Canada shown on the map on page 255.

But the physical feature that had the greatest impact on the choice of a southern route was the Appalachian mountain chain. Its narrow, steep-sided valleys, separated by forested ridges, stretch from northern Georgia into Pennsylvania. The Appalachians affected the routes to freedom in two ways. First, their forests and limestone caves sheltered fugitives as they avoided capture on their way north. Second, the Appalachians acted as a barrier that deflected western runaways northward into a region of intense underground railway activity.

> "It is evident that there exist some eighteen or nineteen thoroughly organized thoroughfares through the State of Ohio for the transportation of runaway and stolen slaves."

Regional Attitudes

This busy region was formed by Ohio and parts of the states on either side of it, Indiana and Pennsylvania. As a whole, the region shared a long boundary with two slave states, Virginia and Kentucky.

Once the fugitives crossed into Ohio, they found themselves in a region with an attitude toward

▶ RESOURCE DIRECTORY

Teaching Resources

 Time and Place Activity The Sanctuary Movement in the United States, found in the Unit 3 folder, pp. 55–56, focuses on a modern system of sheltering and transporting refugees that used many of the methods employed by the underground railroad.

Frederick Douglass established a print shop in Rochester that became a depot.

John Brown led fugitives on a midwinter journey from Missouri to Canada via Chicago.

Portuguese fishermen and Native Americans of the Shinnecock group helped transport escaped enslaved persons from Long Island to New England.

Dorchester County was the birthplace of Harriet Tubman. She rescued about 300 enslaved persons on 19 trips to the South.

The home of Presbyterian minister John Rankin in Ripley was one of the most active depots.

Levi Coffin, a Quaker, helped more than 3,000 enslaved persons to escape.

Harriet Beecher Stowe maintained a depot in Walnut Hills.

Slaveholders looked upon the underground railroad as organized theft.

Seminole in Florida offered safe havens for escaped enslaved persons.

Legend:
- The underground railroad
- Slaveholding states
- Swamps
- 1850 boundaries

0   150   300 Miles
0   150   300 Kilometers

ATLANTIC OCEAN

Gulf of Mexico

The photograph on page 254 shows the sort of lengths such people took to aid African Americans.

slavery very different from the one in the region they had left behind. Southern Ohio was home to many Quakers, Covenanters, and others who volunteered their houses as depots, or stations, on religious principles. There, too, lived free African Americans, as well as whites who had moved out of the South because they opposed slavery. In the north and east of the state, many whites had roots in New England and shared its antislavery views. The photograph on page 254 shows the sort of lengths such people took to aid African Americans. This cupboard slid back to reveal a hiding place where several fugitives might conceal themselves if necessary.

The sympathetic attitude of residents throughout much of the Ohio region caused a headache for southern slave owners. "It is evident," an anonymous writer declared indignantly in 1842, "that there exist some eighteen or nineteen thoroughly organized thoroughfares through the State of Ohio for the transportation of runaway and stolen slaves." To the east of Ohio, regional attitudes were similar.

Southern Illinois, however, was a dangerous region for fugitives, because it had been settled by southerners and remained proslavery. Often sympathizers in that area simply ticketed fugitives on a real railroad, the Illinois Central, for swift transit to Chicago. From there they continued on toward Canada, following the North Star as it shone in the night sky and marked their route to freedom.

GEOGRAPHIC CONNECTIONS

1. What physical features in the South offered fugitives protection from pursuers? What dangers also lurked in those areas?
2. Why did so many of the underground railroad routes run through Ohio?

Critical Thinking

3. **Demonstrating Reasoned Judgment** If you had been an enslaved person escaping from the South, which route to freedom would you have taken? Explain your reasoning.

Answers

1. The forested ridges of the Appalachian mountain chain and the limestone caves in the Appalachian Mountains. The string of low-lying swamps stretching along the Atlantic coast from southern Virginia to southern Georgia.

2. Many Ohioans were friendly to the antislavery cause.

3. Answers may be based on any of the three options but should explain the advantages and disadvantages of the choice made.

Connecting to the Big Idea

See page 240B. Women in the early 1800s were expected to dedicate themselves to tending a home and family. Many women, however, were not content with this role and society's expectations. Ask students what caused some people to begin questioning this role.

Objectives

● Describe the traditional view of the role of women in the early 1800s.
● Explain how reform movements of the 1830s and 1840s increased the visibility of women.
● Identify the connection between the abolitionist movement and the early women's movement.

Bellringer

Have students speculate on how a woman of the early 1800s would react if she were somehow transported to the present day. Which aspects of society might she enjoy? Which would she dislike?

Reading Strategy

Finding Evidence Have students identify—and list as they read— ways in which the growth of the women's movement paralleled that of the antislavery movement.

SECTION 3

Women in the Public Sphere: A Turning Point in History

SECTION PREVIEW

Although middle-class women were expected to devote their energies to home, family, and community in the early 1800s, many women were not content with this work. Their participation in the antislavery movement led to the birth of a women's rights movement in the 1840s.

Key Concepts

● According to cultural traditions of the early 1800s, a middle-class woman's place was in the home.
  ● The reform movements of the 1830s and 1840s provided women with new opportunities to speak and act publicly.
  ● Inspired, in part, by the abolitionist movement, some American women started a women's rights movement in the 1840s.

Key Terms, People, and Places

suffrage, cult of domesticity; Catharine Beecher, Lucretia Mott, Elizabeth Cady Stanton, Sojourner Truth; Seneca Falls

Awareness of the plight of women who were enslaved, as shown in this antislavery logo, made many white abolitionist women begin thinking about women's rights.

W omen played a prominent role in almost every reform movement of the first half of the nineteenth century, from temperance to antislavery. In spite of the enormous contribution they made to these movements, their participation was often highly controversial. Although many working-class women in the early 1800s held jobs, the cultural values of the day dictated that a middle-class woman's place was in the domestic sphere, or home. ✪

Cultural attitudes about the proper role of women were deeply ingrained. Middle-class women at this time were expected to raise and educate their children, create a nurturing home, entertain guests, serve their husbands, do community service, and engage in such genteel activities as needlework. Participating in politics or public meetings with men was considered shocking and unladylike. Even a successful public figure like Dorothea Dix found it necessary for a man to present her findings to legislatures.

The cultural attitudes of the period were reinforced by laws. For example, women did not enjoy **suffrage,** or the right to vote, at this time. In most states in the early 1800s, moreover, married women could not own property, make a will, or keep the wages they earned outside the home. Angered by these forms of legal discrimination, as well as by attempts to block their participation in public life, many women reformers in the 1840s began to turn their attention to the struggle for women's rights.

AMERICAN PROFILES

Catharine Beecher

One of the most important advocates of a domestic role for women was **Catharine Beecher** (1800–1878), who tried to win respect for women's contributions as wives, mothers, and teachers. Daughter of the revivalist Lyman Beecher and sister of both the novelist Harriet Beecher Stowe and the prominent Presbyterian minister Henry Ward Beecher, Catharine Beecher grew up in a family devoted to moral improvement and public service.

Born on Long Island in New York, Beecher attended school in Litchfield, Connecticut, and began teaching in 1821. Teaching was considered a proper occupation for a young woman because it was an extension of the role of

---

RESOURCE DIRECTORY

from traditionalists in their views of women's role in society.

Teaching Resources

▢ **Reproducible Lesson Plan** found in the Unit 3 folder, p. 43, provides a summary of the Section 3 lesson plan content.

▢ **Alternate Lesson Plan: Critical Thinking** Identifying Alternatives, found in the Alternate Lesson Plans folder, p. 46, promotes students' understanding of how supporters of the women's rights movement differed

▢ **Guided Reading and Review** found in the Unit 3 folder, p. 49, provides a structure for reading and mastering the key concepts and reviewing the key terms for Section 3. (Guided Practice)

✪▢ **Literature Activity** Advice on Marriage, found in the Unit 3 folder, p. 66, uses an 1831 article from *Godey's Lady's Book* to demonstrate the emphasis placed on money in the consideration of marriage at the time.

mother. In 1823, a year after her fiancé was drowned at sea, Catharine and her sister Mary Beecher established the Hartford Female Seminary. Dedicating herself completely to her career, Catharine never married.

While teaching, Catharine Beecher also started writing about and lobbying for the education of females. She published several books and gained a national reputation as a spokeswoman for what her biographer Kathryn Kish Sklar has termed "a kind of domestic feminism."

Then and now, Beecher's most popular and influential work was *A Treatise on Domestic Economy.* First published in 1841, it was reprinted every year until 1856. In the *Treatise,* Beecher sought to help middle-class women adjust to a new world where they were consumers more than producers and where they were having fewer children. Aside from offering practical advice and household tips, she wrote on a positive note about the contributions that women could make in a democratic and capitalistic society.

Beecher did not believe that women should move beyond the realms of family and education. In her view, being a mother and a wife were important "political" as well as social and economic functions, and she thought these duties should give women their focus in life. Women's work remained as central to the overall economy as it had been in the 1600s, but in different ways. Although middle-class women no longer milked cows or planted vegetables, they were not supposed to become idle or lazy. In fact, it was precisely because they had primary responsibility for the home and the family, Beecher argued, that women were so important.

Everyone knew, wrote Beecher, that "the success of democratic institutions . . . depends upon the intellectual and moral character of the mass of the people." Everyone also agreed that "the formation of the moral

In her *Treatise on Domestic Economy,* Catharine Beecher argued that women should play the central role in managing the household and raising children.

and intellectual character of the young is committed mainly to the female hand." Here, then, was the reason why women were so critically important to the welfare of the United States:

> The mother forms the character of the future man; . . . the wife sways the heart, whose energies may turn for good or for evil the destinies of a nation. . . . Let the women of a country be made virtuous and intelligent, and the men will certainly be the same. The proper education of a man decides the welfare of an individual; but educate a woman, and the interests of a whole family are secured.
>
> Catharine Beecher,
> *A Treatise on Domestic Economy*

Catharine Beecher helped to establish notions about the role of American women that continue to be held by some segments of American society today. Women were important and powerful, but privately, in their duties as mothers and wives. Some historians refer to this as the **cult of domesticity,** or the belief in the importance of women's role in the home.

Beyond the Private Sphere

As influential as Catharine Beecher was, many northern middle-class American women in the first half of the 1800s did not limit themselves to the home and charitable work. Increasingly, women challenged traditional attitudes by becoming involved in political activities. They joined a variety of reform movements, including those advocating temperance and abolitionism; they marched in parades to support their causes and participated in economic boycotts; they gave lectures at public assemblies. Even while Beecher was

2. INSTRUCT

Explain/Discuss

Explain to students that radical reform often comes about through a series of gradual changes in people's lifestyles or attitudes. Also, people at one period in time may achieve breakthroughs that seem huge in their day; as others come along to amplify and improve on their achievements, entrenched attitudes such as discrimination are broken down over time.

Discuss with students how some of Catharine Beecher's peers might have considered her views "radical." Then compare her views to those of reformer Elizabeth Cady Stanton. In what ways do Stanton's views represent a further development of Beecher's ideas about women?

Analyze

The essence of Beecher's philosophy was that the role of women in the home was crucial to the nation's welfare. Some men who opposed feminism argued that women were more pious and virtuous than men (page 258) and that those qualities were needed in the home. Ask students why feminists would argue that these views imprisoned women with flattery.

Media and Technology

 Visions of America: Turning Point Story To enhance students' understanding of the Turning Point topic in this section, play "Speak Out," a story about Harriet Jacobs's escape from slavery and her role in the abolition movement (length: approximately 4 minutes). This selection can be located on side 1 of the videodiscs. This selection can also be located on videotape 2. Lesson plans for Turning Point stories can be found in the Visions of America Guidebook.

 Visions of America: Roundtable Discussion To introduce students to different and differing viewpoints on the Turning Point topic in this section, play all or part of the Roundtable Discussion on "Speak Out," remarks by respected historians and social commentators. This selection can be located on side 1 of the videodiscs. This selection can also be located on videotape 2.

Activity

Teaching Heterogeneous Groups

The public and private spheres were clearly demarcated in the early 1800s. Women in particular were excluded from participating in the public sphere. To help students understand the concept of cultural spheres, ask students of the same gender to sit in circle groupings. Have each "sphere" list five activities in which they participate but the members of the other "sphere" do not. **LEP**

Enrichment

Have students design a logo that might have been used by women and African Americans to illustrate their common bonds in the fight against oppression.

writing her popular books, northern middle-class women were having fewer children and becoming more visible in areas in which they had long been invisible.

Perhaps the most important development for women in this period was a growing sense of what one historian has called "the bonds of womanhood." By participating in reform movements, many northern middle-class women became more conscious of—and consequently more vocal about—their inferior position in American society. At the same time, they formed strong intellectual and emotional ties with other women in similar positions.

Abolitionism was the primary vehicle through which women, both African American and white, emerged from the domestic world of home and family into the public world of politics. By the 1840s, some women were actively protesting their subordinate position within both the antislavery movement and American society in general.

Women who participated in the abolition movement saw obvious parallels between the plight of enslaved African Americans and the status of women. Neither group could vote or hold office, and both were denied the full rights of American citizens. Although white and African American women had been aware of

Elizabeth Cady Stanton (right) issued a manifesto declaring that "all men and women are created equal."

these constraints for decades, the religious revivals and reform movements of the early 1800s heightened their sense of women's potential and power.

In addition to raising their consciousness, abolitionism provided women with a political platform from which they could assert their power. In 1836, for example, South Carolina-born abolitionist Angelina Grimké demanded that the women of the South fight slavery. Although women could not make laws, she said, they could still influence those who do: " If you really suppose *you* can do nothing to overthrow slavery, you are greatly mistaken. . . . You can read. . . . You can pray. . . . You can speak. . . . You can *act*."

The fight for immediate abolition made women prominent public figures. Both black and white women began to attend meetings, gather petitions, give public talks, and write pamphlets and books. Examples of such participation can be seen in the contributions of women such as Lydia Child and Maria Chapman. In addition to serving on the executive committee of the American Anti-Slavery Society, Lydia Child edited that organization's publication, the *National Anti-Slavery Standard,* from 1841 to 1843, and Maria Chapman coedited it from 1844 to 1848.

The involvement of women in the antislavery movement horrified many male abolitionists, who considered it unseemly and an attempt to undermine the existing social order. True, they believed that women were more pious and virtuous than men and that their voices should be heard, but only within families. Although reformers themselves, these men still viewed the spectacle of a women addressing a public meeting as a shocking violation of social norms.

A Movement for Women's Rights

By 1840, when many American abolitionists attended the first World Anti-Slavery Convention in London, England, they were divided by the question of women's participation in the movement. Delegates at the convention immediately fell to squabbling over who should officially participate. The specific

Resolutions

Resolved, That all laws which prevent women from occupying such a station in society as her conscience shall dictate, or which place her in a position inferior to that of man, are contrary to the great precept of nature, and therefore of no force or authority.

Resolved, That woman is man's equal—was intended to be so by the Creator, and the highest good of the race demands that she should be recognized as such...

Resolved, That it is the duty of the women of this country to secure to themselves their sacred right to the elective franchise ......

Resolved, That the speedy success of our cause depends upon the zealous and untiring efforts of both men and women for the overthrow of the monopoly of the pulpit and for the securing to women an equal participation with men in the various trades, professions and commerce.

Resolved, therefore, That, being invested by the Creator with the same capabilities and the same consciousness of responsibility for their exercise, it is demonstrably the right and duty of woman, equally with man, to promote every righteous cause by every righteous means; and especially in regard to the great subjects of morals and religion, it is self-evidently her right to participate with her brother in teaching them, both in private and in public, by writing and by speaking, by any instrumentalities proper to be used, and in any assemblies proper to be held; and this being a self-evident truth growing out of the divinely implanted principles of human nature, any custom or authority adverse to it, whether modern or wearing the hoary sanction of antiquity, is to be regarded as a self-evident falsehood, and at war with mankind.

More than 300 delegates gathered for the first women's rights convention in 1848. The document at left is one of the results of the meeting.

Answer to ...

MAKING CONNECTIONS

In both the 1840s and 1960s, women active in movements for racial justice became aware of the parallels between the plight of African Americans and their own inequality. This awareness inspired them to work for equal rights and full participation in society for women. In both instances, women also gained experience in how to run effective reform movements.

controversy centered on the women delegates from the American Anti-Slavery Society. Although they had legitimate credentials, they were women, and the meeting was a public one. Should they be allowed to participate?

After much debate, the convention voted against female participation. The action angered female abolitionists from the United States and intensified their growing sense that they had a great deal in common with enslaved African Americans. Partly as a result of this experience, two of the humiliated delegates, **Lucretia Mott** and **Elizabeth Cady Stanton,** decided to organize the first convention in history to discuss the question of women's rights. Held at **Seneca Falls,** New York, in 1848, the group issued a *Declaration of Sentiments* signed by sixty-eight women and thirty-two men. Only one African American, Frederick Douglass, was present.

The *Declaration,* written by Stanton, deliberately echoed the form and language of the Declaration of Independence. In addition to protesting women's lack of legal and political rights, it also attacked the double standard that society held for men and women:

The history of mankind is a history of repeated injuries and usurpations [violent seizing of power] on the part of man toward woman, having in direct object the establishment of an absolute tyranny over her. ... [B]ecause women do feel themselves aggrieved [offended], oppressed, and fraudulently deprived of their most sacred moral rights, we insist that they have immediate admission to all the rights and privileges which belong to them as citizens of the United States.
Elizabeth Cady Stanton,
Declaration of Sentiments

Although the vast majority of Americans ignored or dismissed the *Declaration,* the Seneca Falls convention marked the beginning of the organized movement for women's rights in the United States.

MAKING CONNECTIONS

Just as the women's movement of the 1840s was inspired by the abolitionist movement, the women's movement of the 1960s was inspired by the civil rights movement. Why do you think these two movements for racial justice, separated by more than a century, encouraged the rise of movements for women's rights?

Sojourner Truth Speaks Out for Women

African American women also were inspired and empowered by the movement for abolition. Among the most famous of these were three former enslaved women: Harriet Tubman, famous for her activities in the underground railroad; Harriet Brent Jacobs, author of the 1861 book *Incidents in the Life of a Slave Girl;* and **Sojourner Truth.**

Truth, whose original name was Isabella Baumfree, was born in Ulster County, New

In Depth

Then and Now

The struggle for women's rights and the cessation of double standards based on gender is very much an issue in the 1990s. The National Organization for Women, or NOW, (see pages 826–827) is one of the most active organizations for women's rights in the 1990s. "We lead public opinion, we do not follow it," says Patricia Ireland, who has led the organization since 1991. "Taking a leadership position makes people uncomfortable. But my ultimate value isn't comfort. My ultimate value is progress for women."

Section 3 Review Answers

1. (a) suffrage, see p. 256, (b) cult of domesticity, see p. 257

2. (a) Catharine Beecher, see p. 256, (b) Lucretia Mott, see p. 259, (c) Elizabeth Cady Stanton, see p. 259, (d) Sojourner Truth, see p. 259

3. Seneca Falls, see p. 259

4. The latter grew out of the former. Women were prominent members of abolitionist organizations; they spoke out and wrote on the issue of slavery. When they were denied equal treatment within the movement, some abolitionists started a movement to acquire the full rights of American citizenship for women.

5. The home, or domestic sphere, was considered the proper place for women.

6. Along with Harriet Tubman and others, she forcefully and repeatedly reminded white audiences that African American women suffered from both racism and sexism. Her 1851 speech to the Akron convention was a reminder of the strength of African American women and their claim to equal participation in American society.

In Depth

Interdisciplinary

Astronomer Maria Mitchell (1818–1889) was born in the busy whaling port of Nantucket, Massachusetts. As a child, she helped her father record an eclipse of the sun and was encouraged to use his telescope. In 1847, she discovered a comet, which was later named for her. As a teacher, she advised her students to question everything: "We especially need imagination in science. It is not all mathematics, nor all logic, it is somewhat beauty and poetry." (See American Profiles Activity in the Resource Directory.)

TURNING POINTS

Sojourner Truth's commanding presence and powerful speaking style captured people's attention at many antislavery and women's rights meetings.

York, in 1797. Freed in 1827, she initially found work as a domestic servant in New York City but soon became involved in a variety of religious and reform movements of her day. She took the name Sojourner Truth in the early 1840s because she believed her life mission was to travel around the nation telling the truth about slavery and God.

Although she never learned to read or write, Sojourner Truth became a powerful spokesperson in the antislavery cause. She also became one of a small number of African American women in the 1840s and 1850s who were active in the movement for women's rights. No black women attended the Seneca Falls convention, and only a handful came to most other women's rights conventions. For most black women, abolition was the more pressing issue. Truth, however, was often in attendance at these meetings, reminding white women that their African American sisters also had a place in the movement for women's rights.

In 1851, for example, the fifty-four-year-old Truth walked into a convention of white women in Akron, Ohio. Many delegates did not want her to speak, but convention president Frances Dana Gage allowed Truth to come "slowly and solemnly to the front," set aside her bonnet, and address the group:

> I am a woman's rights. I have as much muscle as any man, and can do as much work as any man. . . . I can carry as much as any man, and can eat as much too . . . I have heard the Bible and have learned that Eve caused man to sin. Well if woman upset the world, do give her a chance to set it right side up again.

A Foundation for Change

The activities of such reformers as Elizabeth Cady Stanton and Sojourner Truth did not bring about a sudden, fundamental change in the status of American women. In fact, many Americans continued to agree with Catharine Beecher that women could wield tremendous influence on public affairs through their work in the home. Nevertheless, reformers did succeed in gradually expanding the opportunities available to American women outside the home.

Whereas no seminary or college in the United States admitted women in 1820, by 1890 more than 2,500 women a year were graduating from American colleges and universities. Thanks in part to the benefits of education, women began appearing in professions from which they previously had been excluded. After becoming the first woman to earn a medical diploma, Elizabeth Blackwell began practicing medicine in New York City in 1850 and seven years later founded the first school of nursing in the United States. Astronomer Maria Mitchell was not only a member of the American Academy of Arts and Sciences but also became the first professor of astronomy at newly founded Vassar College for women in 1865. ✪

RESOURCE DIRECTORY

Teaching Resources

✪ **American Profiles Activity** found in the Unit 3 folder, p. 58, profiles Maria Mitchell, who received many academic distinctions as America's first woman astronomer.

In addition to discovering a new comet in 1847, astronomer Maria Mitchell was the first woman elected to the American Academy of Arts and Sciences.

Women also excelled as writers, editors, and publishers. *Uncle Tom's Cabin*, written by Harriet Beecher Stowe and published in 1852, was the most popular and influential antislavery book of the era. Margaret Fuller, the editor of an important philosophical journal, also wrote an 1845 book *Woman in the Nineteenth Century*, in which she criticized cultural traditions that restricted women's roles in society. And as editor of the popular magazine *Godey's Lady's Book*, Sarah Josepha Hale published articles about women's issues for almost fifty years.

Although substantial gains in the struggle for political, economic, and legal equality did not occur until after the Civil War, the emergence of a women's movement in the 1840s marked a point in American history at which a path chosen by many women would change the nation's future. In spite of fierce opposition, the women struggling for equal rights would not be silenced. In the piercing words of Sojourner Truth:

> The women are coming up, blessed be God, and a few of the men are coming up with them. But man is in a tight place, the poor slave is on him, woman is coming on him, and he is surely between a hawk and a buzzard.

SECTION 3 REVIEW

Key Terms, People, and Places
1. Define (a) suffrage, (b) cult of domesticity.
2. Identify (a) Catharine Beecher, (b) Lucretia Mott, (c) Elizabeth Cady Stanton, (d) Sojourner Truth.
3. Identify Seneca Falls.

Key Concepts
4. What was the relationship between abolitionism and the woman's rights movement?

5. During the early 1800s, what was considered the proper place for women?
6. In what sense did Sojourner Truth make a unique contribution to the women's rights movement?

Critical Thinking
7. **Making Comparisons** Compare and contrast the achievements and failures of the antislavery and the women's rights movements.

Quiz found in the Unit 3 folder, p. 50, covers the main ideas in this section as well as the key terms.

7. Both the antislavery and women's rights movements succeeded in making their causes part of the public debate and in winning some important advances. For example, the abolition movement contributed to the start of the Civil War and the emancipation of the slaves; the women's rights movement brought about some important gains in educational opportunities for women. On the other hand, it took more than a century before African Americans and women began to win substantial victories in their struggle for full political and civil rights and full participation in American society.

Reteach
Ask students to list the major steps in the development of the women's movement.

 CLOSE

Reinforcing the Big Idea
Inspired by the antislavery movement, women began fighting for equality. Their demands for reform met with bitter resistance among some cultures and regions in the United States. The next section describes the resentments of working-class people and southerners toward middle-class reform movements.

The Lasting Impact of Women in Public Life

Focus Many women today would feel considerable kinship with the early feminists. They can thank women such as Lucretia Mott and Sojourner Truth for beginning the fight when they did. It was a long struggle, and had the battle not been joined in the 1840s, women today might still be trying to win full voting rights or entrance into law schools.

In this section students will trace the development of the women's rights movement through the Civil War and the triumph of suffrage in 1919.

Instruct After students read the first paragraph of the section, ask them to make a list of "rights and privileges" to which the Seneca Falls delegates might have been referring. As they continue reading, they can check off items on their lists that are mentioned in the section and add to their lists any extra items they find.

Extend Ask students to imagine that they were holding a Seneca Falls convention today. Have them work individually or in small groups to draft a list of demands that women in the 1990s might make.

The Lasting Impact of Women in Public Life

The women delegates who attended the Seneca Falls convention in 1848 adopted a proclamation demanding that women "have immediate admission to all the rights and privileges which belong to them as citizens of the United States." Although it took many long decades to achieve this goal, the women at Seneca Falls set in motion a social movement whose impact is still being felt today. From that point on, women across the United States—either individually or in groups—worked hard for the cause of equal rights and equal opportunity.

The Civil War Opens New Doors

Women's participation in the reform movements of the prewar era had a significant impact on the contribution women were able to make during the war between the North and South. The Civil War offered women many opportunities to experiment with new roles and move into the public sphere. While husbands and fathers were away fighting the war, women took over the management of farms and plantations. Women also filled in for men in schools, factories, mills, munitions plants, banks, shops, and government offices.

In addition, women in the North and South organized some 20,000 relief societies that did everything from collecting medicine and making bandages to helping disabled soldiers find jobs. In the North alone, these relief societies collected about $15 million for the war effort. Whereas nursing had previously been a male-dominated profession, now hundreds of women in both the North

1848 Lucretia Mott was one of the organizers of the Seneca Falls convention, which marked the beginning of the movement for women's rights.

1875 Chief Justice Waite was on the Supreme Court that decided against woman suffrage in the case Minor v. Happersett.

| 1850 | 1865 | 1880 |

1860s As a result of the women's movement, more women began working outside the home in the later 1800s.

RESOURCE DIRECTORY

Teaching Resources

Turning Points Extension Activity
The Lasting Impact of Women in Public Life, found in the Unit 3 folder, pp. 53–54, provides a strategy for students to work cooperatively to address historical issues of the women's movement by creating a twenty-fifth anniversary edition of one of the feminist publications of the 1970s.

and the South volunteered to look after the sick and wounded as army nurses.

By taking advantage of the opportunities the war provided, women were able to win an expanded role in the public and economic life of the nation. As Red Cross founder Clara Barton later put it: "At the war's end, woman was at least fifty years in advance of the normal position which continued peace would have assigned her."

New Educational and Career Opportunities

Following the Civil War, many colleges and universities in the Midwest opened their doors to women. Women also had the chance to pursue a college education at new eastern women's colleges. Many of the women who graduated from these colleges took jobs as teachers, nurses, and social workers. Although women who wished to become lawyers and doctors faced greater obstacles and prejudice, 1,000 women lawyers and 7,500 women doctors had earned degrees in the United States by the turn of the century.

Opportunities for women without college degrees also expanded in the late 1800s. The invention of the typewriter, telephone, and telegraph, together with the growth of department stores, created a large number of new clerical and sales jobs. By 1900, when roughly 500,000 women worked in these kind of positions, women had largely replaced men as office workers.

The Struggle for Suffrage

One of the most important rights the women delegates at the Seneca Falls convention demanded was the right to vote. Although most suffrage activists suspended their activities during the Civil War to contribute to the war effort, they took up the fight for voting rights again as soon as the war had ended.

The struggle for women's suffrage was long and slow, but the seed planted at Seneca Falls eventually began to bear fruit. The continuing impact of a movement that started in the 1840s is illustrated by the suffrage movement, which lasted well into the 1900s.

REVIEWING THE FACTS

1. How was the impact of the women's rights movement apparent during the Civil War?
2. What effect did the increase in educational opportunities for women have on women's place in American society?

Critical Thinking

3. **Expressing Problems Clearly** Why do you think the fight for women's suffrage proved to be so long and difficult?

1884 Belva Lockwood ran a campaign for President, illustrating women's continued push for equal rights.

1895   1910   1925

1920 Suffrage is won at last, marking the end of the struggle on that issue; many battles remain.

SECTION 4

Reform Efforts Highlight Cultural Divisions

Connecting to the Big Idea

See page 240B. Middle-class reformers were deeply resented by people in some segments of society. Ask students why the reformers and their efforts caused such resentment and bitterness.

Objectives

● Explain why working-class people resented the efforts of reformers.
● Analyze how cultural differences between North and South affected reactions to the reform movement.

Bellringer

Ask students how they might feel if their school administration decided to make changes, such as forbidding access to previously open areas or denying open campus privileges, in order to make the school "safer." Describe the kind of reception such "reformers" might get.

Reading Strategy

Structured Overview Have students construct a chart entitled Cultural Differences with the following four column headings: Middle Class, Working Class, Northerners, and Southerners. As students read the section, they should list each group's attitude toward reform in the appropriate column.

SECTION PREVIEW

Not all Americans embraced the crusades of northern middle-class reformers. Working-class people and southerners, in particular, resented interfering reformers who told them how to live their lives.

ATTENTION SOUTHERN MEN! DOWN WITH THE ABOLITION PRESS MEET AT SCHNEIDER'S At 8 o'clock This Night. DECEMBER 26, 1860.

Reformers often met with sentiments such as the one expressed in the poster above.

Key Concepts
• More concerned with economic survival than social reform, working-class people resented reformers' efforts to impose values with which they did not necessarily agree.
• The growing cultural differences between North and South intensified southerners' angry reactions to the criticisms of reformers.

Key Terms, People, and Places
Samuel F. B. Morse

The northern middle-class reformers believed passionately in the causes they supported. Other Americans, however, did not always welcome either the morality they advocated or the kind of reforms they proposed. Many working-class people and southerners viewed reformers as meddlers who had no business interfering in the lives of others. The way these working people and southerners responded to the reform movements of the pre–Civil War era reveals the cultural divisions that existed during this time, particularly the growing division between North and South.

Immigration from Ireland and Germany

The Market Revolution of the early 1800s created a growing population of industrial workers in the United States, many of whom moved from farms to cities to find factory jobs. At the same time, a dramatic increase in immigration between 1830 and 1860 resulted in a more culturally diverse national population. The graph at right shows this huge increase in immigration.

Although some of the new immigrants arrived from Scandinavia and England, most came from Ireland and Germany. Because the system of slave labor in the South limited economic opportunities in that region, the great majority of these immigrants settled in the North. Forced out of their homeland by the disastrous potato famine of the mid-1840s, Irish immigrants tended to settle in northeastern cities and take manual labor jobs in factories or on canals or railroads. German immigrants, on the other hand—many of whom had fled political oppression after the failure of the European revolutions of 1848—bought farmland in the Midwest or settled in northern cities such as New York, Philadelphia, Cincinnati, Chicago, and Milwaukee.

Religious differences immediately created tension between middle-class reformers and working-class immigrants. Nearly all of the Irish immigrants and many of the German immigrants were Roman Catholic. Reformers strongly disapproved of the Catholic religion. They believed that the emphasis Catholicism placed on ritual and the authority of the Pope and bishops made it impossible for individuals to think for themselves and to find their own salvation. Some even suspected that Catholics were part of a conspiracy led by the Pope to rule the world. As inventor and painter **Samuel F. B. Morse** wrote in 1834: "Popery [Catholicism] does not acknowledge *the right of the people to govern;* but claims for itself the supreme right to govern all people and all rulers by divine right."

▶ RESOURCE DIRECTORY

Teaching Resources

Reproducible Lesson Plan found in the Unit 3 folder, p. 44, provides a summary of the Section 4 lesson plan content.

Alternate Lesson Plan: Learning Styles found in the Alternate Lesson Plans folder, p. 47, enhances students' comprehension of the main ideas of the section through the creation of a graphic organizer and is particularly effective for visual learners.

Guided Reading and Review found in the Unit 3 folder, p. 51, provides a structure for reading and mastering the key concepts and reviewing the key terms for Section 4. (Guided Practice)

Immigration to the United States, 1821–1860

Immigration to the United States, 1821–1860

Number of Persons (in thousands) — vertical axis: 0, 100, 200, 300, 400, 500, 600, 700

Legend:
- Great Britain
- Ireland
- Germany
- All Other

Year (horizontal axis): 1821–1825, 1826–1830, 1831–1835, 1836–1840, 1841–1845, 1846–1850, 1851–1855, 1856–1860

Source: *Historical Statistics of the United States*

 Interpreting Graphs
Seeking to escape famine and revolution in Europe, several million immigrants came to the United States in the 1840s and 1850s, changing the character of the United States population in the process. *Which nation sent the largest number of immigrants to the United States in the period from 1846 to 1855?*

For their part, working-class immigrants found that the evangelical Protestant version of character-building and self-improvement were unnecessary luxuries. They were much more concerned with putting food on the table and keeping a roof over their heads than with debating issues of morality. Author Herman Melville summarized this attitude when he wrote in his novel *Moby Dick:*

I n this world, sin that pays its way can travel freely, and without a passport; whereas Virtue, if a pauper, is stopped at all frontiers.

Whether immigrant or native born, working-class people valued different things than most middle-class reformers. Because they had so little power in their working lives, working people wanted to do as they pleased in their leisure time. Alcohol often played an important role in their social lives. Men drank in taverns that were the center of neighborhood society. Women bought beer to enjoy with neighbors on the steps of tenements. The idea that drinking alcohol was an inherently immoral act was a strange one in their view, and they resented temperance activists who preached to them about its evils.

Organized sports played an increasingly important role in working-class lives in the 1840s and 1850s. People who spent much of their lives working in poor-paying, unsatisfying jobs took pleasure in boxing matches, horse races, and newly emerging team sports such as baseball. Gambling and drinking were sometimes part of the fun. Most middle-class reformers were dismayed by these activities. They denounced them as examples of idle behavior and moral weakness and wondered whether working people had the character necessary to become good citizens.

In the end, what many middle-class reformers wanted, particularly evangelical reformers, was for working-class people to become like them. They sought an end to drinking and gambling, a celebration of hard work, and a form of religion that encouraged self-improvement rather than devotion to tradition. Reformers hoped that public schools, together with laws that restricted drinking, gambling, and sporting, would transform working-class men and women into the middle-class idea of model citizens. What working people wanted, on the other hand, was to be left alone to live their lives as they wished.

North Versus South

The tension the reform movements of the 1830s and 1840s sometimes stirred between

Media and Technology

 Transparency
Our Multicultural Heritage, C-13

Explain/Discuss

Explain that during the Market Revolution of the early 1800s, the working-class population increased, in part because many Americans moved from farms to factory jobs in cities and in part because the number of immigrants in the nation's cities also increased. Discuss the many differences between the middle-class reformers and the working-class immigrants and identify differences in religion, leisure activities, personal values, and basic goals.

Ask students how life in the North also became increasingly different from life in the South. Ask students to read and explain Mary Boykin Chesnut's comments on page 266. How might Chesnut's husband have reacted to a northern business associate who suggested that he treat his wife as an equal and free his slaves?

Caption Answer to ...

Interpreting Graphs

Ireland

 In Depth

Multicultural Perspectives

In 1828 a *New York Evening Post* reporter complained about "large groups of men and boys playing ball and filling the air with their shouts and yells." But the noise over baseball was just beginning. In June 1846 the first organized game of baseball was played in New York, and by 1876 a National League was formed. African Americans, however, were largely excluded from playing in the major leagues until 1947—when Jackie Robinson won the pennant for the Brooklyn Dodgers and was named Rookie of the Year. (See pages 760–761 and 764–765.)

Analyze

Ask students to analyze whether reformers had the right to pass laws restricting drinking, gambling, and sporting. Are such laws legitimate if their aims are to improve society?

Activity

Create Needs Pyramids

Ask students to work in groups to create one pyramid reflecting the needs and priorities of the working-class of the early 1800s, and another reflecting the needs and priorities of middle-class reformers at this time. Pyramids should have six to eight layers. Students can first brainstorm ideas and then coordinate responses for each layer.

Enrichment

Ask interested students to research German and Irish immigration in the early and mid-1800s and to report on the character of the neighborhoods and communities these immigrants formed.

3. ASSESS

Section 4 Review Answers

1. Samuel F. B. Morse, see p. 264

2. They clashed mostly as a result of how working-class people spent their leisure time—enjoying sports, drinking in taverns, and gambling. Middle-class evangelicals denounced these activities as idle and self-indulgent. They believed that people should spend their time in more uplifting ways.

3. In the rural world of the South, traditional patriarchal households remained relatively intact. Since southerners were not experiencing the impact of urbanization or industrialization, and since so few middle-class southerners lived in towns, they saw little need for the kind of changes advocated in the North.

Bare-knuckle boxing was a popular American sport in the mid-1800s, as the crowd in this painting illustrates.

middle-class and working-class people was mild compared to the strain these movements created between the North and South.

Southerners bitterly resented the criticisms and activities of the abolitionists. Similarly, southerners did not welcome the advice of northern reformers who told them how to conduct prison reform or prodded them to increase women's rights. Beneath the anger and misunderstanding that often resulted from encounters between northerners and southerners lay the same kind of cultural clash that alienated middle-class and working-class people from one another.

The patriarchal character of plantation life is apparent in this painting, in which the plantation owner's presence overshadows his wife as well as his servants.

⭐ While the North became increasingly industrial and urban in the early 1800s, the South remained primarily agricultural and rural. In fact, the great majority of southern whites in the 1830s and 1840s were farmers who depended on the cash crop of cotton for their living. In most areas of the South, the household remained an important economic unit. Less affected by the Market Revolution that was changing the character of the North, many southern families, both rich and poor, continued to blend work and family activities. They saw little need for restructuring family life or establishing such institutions as public schools.

Social relationships remained quite traditional in the South, especially with regard to matters of gender. Whether small farmers or wealthy planters, southern males viewed themselves as the rulers of their domains. Southern plantations, in particular, were classic examples of patriarchal systems. The master of the plantation exercised power over all of his dependents, including women, children, and enslaved African Americans.

A few southern white women saw parallels between their position in this patriarchal system and that of the enslaved. South Carolina's Mary Boykin Chesnut confided to her diary that her husband was "master of the house. To hear is to obey. . . . All the comforts of my life depend upon his being in a good humor." At times Chesnut was sure that "there is no slave . . . like a wife."

Although southern men idealized their women, these women were less likely to have the moral influence and public role of their northern counterparts. The wives of small farmers often worked with their husbands in the fields, while planters' wives supervised large households and sometimes helped manage the plantation. Many of these women, rich and poor, oversaw their children's education. Because farms and plantations were often miles apart, opportunities to participate in public organizations and community meetings were rare. While in the urban North, women

 RESOURCE DIRECTORY

Teaching Resources

⭐ **Primary Source Activity** Plantation Life, found in the Unit 3 folder, p. 65, presents excerpts from Anne Kemble's *Journal of a Residence on a Georgian Plantation in 1838–39*, in which she comments on differences between paid laborers of the North and slave laborers of the South and the nature of southern chivalry.

such as Elizabeth Cady Stanton and Sojourner Truth attempted to redefine the position of women in American society, in the rural South, women remained locked in traditional roles and activities.

The traditional nature of southern society was also apparent in its inhabitants' highly developed sense of honor. Southern men, in particular, were sensitive about their public reputations. The great emphasis that southern culture put on honor makes it easier to understand the intense anger with which southerners responded to criticism by northern reformers.

MAKING CONNECTIONS

When northerners began to participate in the civil rights movement in the early 1960s, many southerners resented what they viewed as unjustified interference in the southern way of life. Why do you think southerners in both the 1840s and the 1960s were sensitive to criticism by northern whites on racial issues?

Worlds Apart

By the 1840s, the North and South were rapidly moving apart, not only economically, but culturally as well. These growing cultural differences clearly contributed to the rising tension between the two regions, which were quickly becoming like two different worlds.

An armed conflict between North and South would happen, in part, because northern middle-class reformers found southern behavior so unacceptable that they demanded change. And white southerners would eventually decide to leave the union because they would never submit to northern middle-class definitions of morality and social relationships. Although the reform movements of the early 1800s strained relations between North and South, it was ultimately the question of how to develop the vast lands west of the Mississippi River that brought this relationship to the breaking point.

Viewpoints
On Southern and Northern Women

By the mid-1800s, many women in the United States were working for wages outside of the home. *Based on the following viewpoints, how did regional differences affect the type of labor women often performed?*

On Southern Women

"Poor white girls never hired out to do servants' work, but they would come and help another white woman with her sewing or quilting, and take wages for it. . . . That their condition is not as unfortunate by any means as that of Negroes, however, is most obvious, since among them, people may sometimes elevate themselves to positions and habits of usefulness and respectability."

Frederick Law Olmsted, *A Journey in the Seaboard Slave States*, published in 1856

On Northern Women

"Thirteen hours per day of monotonous labor are exacted from these young women. So fatigued are the girls that they go to bed soon after their evening meal. It would be a poor bargain from the industrial point of view to own these workers. . . . The greater number of fortunes accumulated by people in the North in comparison with the South shows that hired labor is more profitable than slave labor."

Report on a visit to the Lowell, Massachusetts, textile mills, published in *The Harbinger*, Lowell, 1846

SECTION 4 REVIEW

Key Terms, People, and Places
1. Identify Samuel F. B. Morse.

Key Concepts
2. How did the working-class and reformers clash?
3. Why did middle-class ideas about reform hold little appeal for southerners?

4. What roles did women play in southern society?

Critical Thinking
5. **Demonstrating Reasoned Judgment** What characteristics of southern society do you think discouraged the rise of reform movements?

Viewpoints Activity On Southern and Northern Women, found in the Unit 3 folder, pp. 59–60, further indicates how women's circumstances differed between the two regions.

Quiz found in the Unit 3 folder, p. 52, covers the main ideas in this section as well as the key terms.

Chapter Test Forms A and B are found in the Unit 3 folder, pp. 71–76.

Answer Keys found in the Unit 3 folder, pp. 116–125, provide answers for all student activities.

Media and Technology

Transparency
Graphic Organizer, G-5

Guided Reading Audiotapes
(English and Spanish)

Computer Test Bank

4. Southern women's roles centered on the home. Farmers' wives helped with farm work. The wives of planters ran large households and helped manage plantations. Southern women were also involved in raising and educating their children.

5. Cultural values that emphasized traditional social relationships; a patriarchal system that stressed obedience to the master/husband/father; the isolated nature of life in the South, where people were often separated by great distances.

Reteach

Have students list three types of conflict during the early 1800s caused by cultural differences and three types caused by regional differences.

Answer to . . .

Viewpoints

Poor women in the South did not accept the lowest forms of labor, which were reserved for slaves, but limited themselves to certain household jobs. In the North, however, poor women performed the most strenuous labor under conditions often worse than slave labor. For a more thorough examination of working women in the mid-1800s, see the Resource Directory below.

Answer to . . .

MAKING CONNECTIONS

Southerners felt betrayed by criticism from members of their own race, who they felt should understand and share their racial attitudes. Southerners also felt that the honor of their region was being attacked by people who behaved as if they were morally superior to southerners.

4. CLOSE

Reinforcing the Big Idea

The reform movement stirred resentment among various segments of United States society and deepened existing cultural divisions.

Understanding Key Terms, People, and Places

Terms
Students should refer to the definitions of the key terms in the chapter to write sentences that show the relation of each word to the reform movements and the growing divisions between North and South from 1815 to 1860.

Matching
1. underground railroad
2. cult of domesticity
3. suffrage
4. gag rule
5. utopian communities

Word Relationships
1. (c) does not belong. Horace Mann, Dorothea Dix, and Henry David Thoreau were dedicated to social reform. Samuel F. B. Morse was an anti-Catholic inventor and painter.

2. (b) does not belong. David Walker, William Lloyd Garrison, and Frederick Douglass were abolitionists. Charles Grandison Finney was a religious revivalist.

3. (d) does not belong. Harriet Tubman, Sojourner Truth, and Harriet Beecher Stowe worked to end slavery. Catharine Beecher advocated respect for women in traditional roles.

Reviewing Main Ideas
1. Many revivalists emphasized individual self-improvement and the possibility of progress, ideas that strongly appealed to reformers.

2. Reforms included prohibiting the use of alcohol, improving conditions for prison inmates and the mentally ill, and making education available for all American children.

3. Utopian communities emphasized sharing property, living in harmony with others, simplicity, and equality among men and women.

4. Abolitionists favored a moderate approach of phasing out slavery; a small minority favored colonization.

5. Some abolitionists, like William Lloyd Garrison, believed that attempts to achieve emancipation through passing laws was pointless. Others disagreed, forming the Liberty party to put pressure on the Whigs and Democrats to get an antislavery candidate elected.

6. Women did not enjoy suffrage; in most states married women could not own property, make a will, or keep earned wages.

Chapter Review

Understanding Key Terms, People, and Places

Key Terms
1. Transcendentalism
2. temperance movement
3. prohibition
4. compulsory education
5. utopian community
6. abolition
7. emancipation
8. colonization
9. underground railroad
10. gag rule
11. suffrage
12. cult of domesticity

People
13. Charles Grandison Finney
14. Lyman Beecher
15. Henry David Thoreau
16. Horace Mann
17. Dorothea Dix
18. David Walker
19. William Lloyd Garrison
20. Frederick Douglass
21. Harriet Tubman
22. Catharine Beecher
23. Lucretia Mott
24. Elizabeth Cady Stanton
25. Sojourner Truth
26. Samuel F. B. Morse

Places
27. Liberia
28. Seneca Falls

Terms For each term above, write a sentence that explains its relation to the reform movements and growing divisions between the North and South from 1815 to 1860.

Matching Review the key terms in the list above. If you are not sure of a term's meaning, review its definition in the chapter. Then choose a term from the list that best matches each description below.

1. the network of men and women who helped runaway enslaved persons escape to the North and into Canada
2. the belief in the importance of women's role at home
3. the right to vote
4. the practice of postponing consideration of antislavery petitions in Congress
5. small societies dedicated to achieving social and political perfection

Word Relationships Three of the people in each of the following sets are related in terms of their accomplishments. Choose the person who does not belong, and explain why he or she does not belong.

1. (a) Horace Mann, (b) Dorothea Dix, (c) Samuel F. B. Morse, (d) Henry David Thoreau
2. (a) David Walker, (b) Charles Grandison Finney, (c) William Lloyd Garrison (d) Frederick Douglass
3. (a) Harriet Tubman, (b) Sojourner Truth, (c) Harriet Beecher Stowe, (d) Catharine Beecher

Reviewing Main Ideas

Section 1 (pp. 242–247)
1. Explain why the evangelical religious revivals of the early 1800s inspired many of the reformers of that era.
2. What were some of the social reforms undertaken by reform-minded citizens?
3. What values did the utopian communities of the period emphasize?

Section 2 (pp. 249–253)
4. What approaches were favored by abolitionists before 1830?
5. Explain the disagreement that arose among abolitionists over the question of political action.

Section 3 (pp. 256–261)
6. Give examples to show that the cultural attitudes toward women in the United States were reinforced by laws in the early 1800s.
7. In what ways did women begin to challenge traditional attitudes?
8. What effect did resistance to their participation in the abolitionist movement have on Lucretia Mott and Elizabeth Cady Stanton?

Section 4 (pp. 264–267)
9. Why did working-class people resent middle-class efforts at reform?
10. Explain why religious differences created tension between the working class and middle-class reformers.
11. Describe three reasons for the growing tensions between the North and the South.

---

7. Women joined reform movements, became involved in political activities, and became more visible members of society.

8. They organized the Seneca Falls convention to discuss women's rights.

9. Working-class people held different moral and cultural values. For example, many working-class people considered drinking a legitimate, simple pleasure rather than an act of moral degradation.

10. Protestant middle-class reformers strongly disapproved of Catholicism's emphasis on ritual and on the power of the Pope rather than the power of the individual. Catholic working-class immigrants judged Protestant notions of self-improvement and character-building to be irrelevant and unnecessary luxuries.

11. Southerners resented not only northern abolitionist views but also northern reformers' advice on prison reform and women's rights. While the North became more industrial, the South remained rural, with the household remaining an important economic unit. While the women's movement was taking hold in the North, social relationships in the South remained quite traditional.

Thinking Critically
1. Answers will vary. Students may point out that some schools have recently begun to include "core values" as part of their curriculum.

1. **Determining Relevance** You have read that during the early 1800s, schools emphasized the teaching of values such as self-discipline, good citizenship, and character-building. Should such values have a place in school curricula today?
2. **Making Comparisons** How did the views of Catharine Beecher differ from those of other women such as Lucretia Mott and Elizabeth Cady Stanton in the women's rights movement? What different voices can you identify in the women's movement today?
3. **Identifying Assumptions** Identify the assumptions that middle-class reformers made about working-class immigrants. How might reformers have avoided alienating the working class?

1. **Evaluating Primary Sources** Review the primary source excerpt on page 259. Explain how the excerpt attacks the double standard that society held for men and women. What other groups in American society have sometimes been treated with a double standard?
2. **Understanding the Visuals** Look at the painting on the bottom of page 266. How does the artist manage to convey through this painting the sense that southern plantations were patriarchal systems?
3. **Writing About the Chapter** Choose a social problem that you feel needs reform, either from the years 1815 to 1860 or from the present. Write a proposal in which you identify the problem and describe possible solutions. First, create a list of reasons why the problem needs to be addressed. Then list the ways in which it might be solved. Note groups or individuals who might help in solving the problem. Next, write a draft of your proposal in which you explain your ideas, offering specific examples when possible. Revise your proposal, making certain that each idea is clearly explained. Proofread your proposal and draft a final copy.
4. **Using the Graphic Organizer** This graphic organizer uses a multiflow map to show the causes and effects of the birth of the women's movement during the 1840s. (a) According to the graphic organizer, what factors contributed to the birth of the women's movement? (b) What were two long-term effects of the birth of the women's movement? (c) On a separate sheet of paper, create your own multiflow map about the antislavery movement, using this graphic organizer as an example.

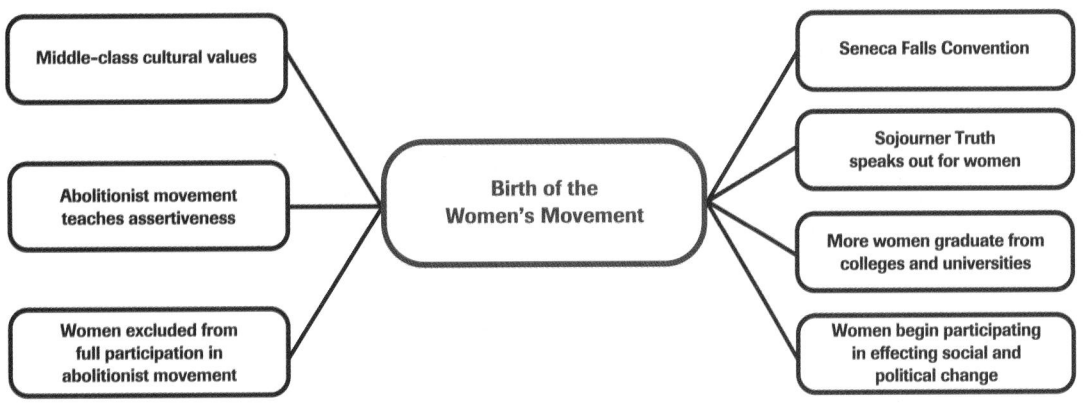

Middle-class cultural values

Abolitionist movement teaches assertiveness

Women excluded from full participation in abolitionist movement

Birth of the Women's Movement

Seneca Falls Convention

Sojourner Truth speaks out for women

More women graduate from colleges and universities

Women begin participating in effecting social and political change

4. (a) Middle-class cultural values, the assertiveness that women learned from their participation in the abolitionist movement, and women's resentment at their exclusion from full participation in the abolitionist movement all contributed to the birth of the women's movement. (b) Long-term effects include higher education for greater numbers of women and the beginnings of women's participation in effecting important social and political changes. (c) Students' graphic organizers should include information about the early abolitionist movement, the growth of more militant abolitionism, and the tensions that developed among abolitionists.

Alternative Assessment

Final Evaluation

Use the following guidelines to evaluate student projects:

● **Evidence of thoughtfulness** Did students include the suggested topics?

● **Evidence of synthesis** Do projects demonstrate an understanding of how topics are related?

● **Communication style** Do the projects convey their purpose to an audience in a clear, appealing way?

● **Evidence of outside research** To what extent did students use outside research materials for their projects?

Allow interested students to present their finished projects to the class.

2. Catharine Beecher believed that although women could make important contributions to the newly emerging capitalist society, their duties as wives and mothers should provide their primary focus in life. Other women were more militant in their demands for equal rights. Students may identify similar trends today.

3. Reformers assumed that working-class immigrants should adhere to middle-class values. Perhaps if the reformers had been more respectful of working-class concerns and values, they could have accomplished reform without arousing resentment.

Making Connections

1. Although the Constitution guarantees citizens of the United States many rights and freedoms, these rights and freedoms had not been extended to women. Other groups with a similar experience are African Americans and Native Americans.

2. By placing the southern planter in a central position in the painting, the artist emphasizes his size and makes him seem to dominate all those around him, not just his servants but his wife and child as well.

3. Issues may include drug or alcohol abuse, poverty, or homelessness.

Chapter 10 Beyond the Mississippi
1800–1860

📁 **Teaching Resources** (See Unit 3 Folder)

	Instruction	Enrichment
Section 1 **The Native Americans of the Plains** (pp. 272–275)	Reproducible Lesson Plan, p. 78 Alternate Lesson Plan, p. 49 Guided Reading and Review, p. 82 Quiz, p. 83	American Profiles Activity, York, p. 90 Literature Activity, Native American Legends: Hiawatha, p. 99
Section 2 **Hispanic North America** (pp. 276–280)	Reproducible Lesson Plan, p. 79 Alternate Lesson Plan, p. 50 Guided Reading and Review, p. 84 Quiz, p. 85	Literature Activity, What Happened in Texas, p. 100
Section 3 **Trails to the West** (pp. 281–284)	Reproducible Lesson Plan, p. 80 Alternate Lesson Plan, p. 51 Guided Reading and Review, p. 86 Quiz, p. 87	Literature Activity, Song of the Pioneers, p. 101 Primary Source Activity, Traveling West, pp. 96–97 Critical Thinking Activity, Determining Relevance, p. 95 Historian's Toolbox Activity, Analyzing Obituaries, p. 94
Section 4 **Conquest of a Continent** (pp. 286–291)	Reproducible Lesson Plan, p. 81 Alternate Lesson Plan, p. 52 Guided Reading and Review, p. 88 Quiz, p. 89 Chapter Test, Forms A & B, pp. 104–109	Visual Learning Activity, The Annexation of Texas, p. 103 Viewpoints Activity, On Expanding into Mexican Territory, pp. 92–93 Visual Learning Activity, Living Dead in Califor-nee, p. 102 Primary Source Activity, Gold! Gold! Gold! p. 98 American Profiles Activity, Kamiakin, p. 91

📁 **Additional Chapter Resources**

Resource Organizer, p. 77
Alternate Lesson Plan, p. 48
Answer Keys, pp. 116–125

Bibliography

For the Teacher

Hill, William E. *The Oregon Trail: Yesterday and Today.* Caxton
Printers, 1990. (Selections from the diaries of travelers going
west.)

Parkman, Francis. *The Oregon Trail.* University of Wisconsin
Press, 1969. (Classic western adventure by a noted writer of
the period.)

de la Peña, José Enrique. *With Santa Anna in Texas.* Translated
and edited by Carmen Perry. Texas A&M University Press,
1975. (A firsthand account by a young officer serving with
Santa Anna in Texas.)

Prentice Hall Literature Excerpts from *The American
Experience,* 1994, including Thoreau, Henry David. *Civil
Disobedience.* Norton, 1966 edition.

Media and Technology

 Fine Art, D-7, D-8, D-13

 Fine Art, D-9; Our Multicultural Heritage, C-10

 The Way It Works, H-9, H-10; Critical Thinking, I-4

 Historical Maps, L-2; Cause and Effect, F-4; Graphic Organizer, G-1

 Guided Reading Audiotapes (English and Spanish)

 Computer Test Bank

For the Student

Jeffrey, J. *Frontier Women: The Trans-Mississippi West, 1840–1880.* Hill & Wang, 1979. (Diaries and letters of ordinary women who crossed the country in the mid-1800s.)

Katz, William Loren. *The Black West.* Open Hand, 1987. (Pictorial history of the African American experience on the frontier.)

The Great West. Charles C. Clark Co. Film/Video. (A dramatized account of the people who went west, told in the words of the pioneers themselves.)

THE BIG IDEA

The Big Idea for the chapter and how the main ideas in each section relate to the Big Idea are graphically displayed below. Comprehension of this chapter's Big Idea is critical to students' understanding of United States history and how we as a nation got where we are today.

CHAPTER 10

Americans pushed westward into Texas, New Mexico, California, and Oregon in search of new opportunities. As their numbers grew, however, tensions developed between the new settlers and the peoples who already claimed these lands as their homes.

SECTION 1

The lives of Native American groups living on the Great Plains had already been greatly affected by European contact by the time white Americans arrived.

SECTION 2

A steady stream of white settlers moving west into Texas, New Mexico, and California created tension with Mexico, which controlled the lands.

SECTION 3

Thousands of settlers traveled west over the perilous Oregon Trail to Oregon and California beginning in the 1830s.

SECTION 4

In the 1840s, white Americans set about fulfilling their dream of an empire that stretched from the Atlantic to the Pacific. Along the way, however, open conflict developed with groups who already lived on the land these new Americans claimed as their own.

270B

Beyond the Mississippi
1800–1860

The Relevance of the Big Idea

In the 1830s and 1840s, white settlers—recent immigrants from Europe—in search of new economic opportunities pushed into lands that Native Americans and Mexicans had lived on for centuries. Conflict and tensions developed as people with different ways of life came into contact with one another. In the 1990s economic opportunity continues to attract immigrants from other nations to the United States; and tension still characterizes the relationship between the newcomers and their more settled neighbors.

Ask students to list some ways in which the culture and traditions of these newcomers differ from American culture. How have these differences sometimes caused problems?

In Depth
Global Connections

In the years that followed the War of 1812, the United States and Britain peacefully settled a number of outstanding issues. After the Oregon Country had been opened to trade, people from both the United States and Britain settled there. In 1846 the two countries finally divided the Oregon Country and agreed on another border—one that reached from the Rockies to the Pacific.

Beyond the Mississippi
1800–1860

*F*ollowing the purchase of Louisiana from France in 1803, a few enterprising American trappers and traders began to explore the vast expanse of territory beyond the Mississippi River. The tales they brought back of a wild and beautiful land encouraged thousands of Americans to begin pushing westward into Texas, New Mexico, California, and Oregon. Although many people found new opportunities in the West, they were invading land that Native Americans and Mexicans had lived on for centuries. The tensions that resulted from these encounters led eventually to conflict with Native Americans and a war with Mexico.

Events in the United States

1800	1804			1821
1800 Forty million buffalo roam the Great Plains.	1804 Lewis and Clark set out to explore the Louisiana Purchase.			1821 Stephen Austin founds a colony of American settlers in Texas.

1800	1806	1812	1818	1824

Events in the World

	1804		1818	1821	1825
	1804 Haiti wins independence from France.		1818 The Zulu empire is founded in Africa.	1821 Mexico wins independence from Spain.	1825 Egyptian forces invade Greece.

RESOURCE DIRECTORY

Teaching Resources

Alternate Lesson Plan: Demonstrating the Big Idea found in the Alternate Lesson Plans folder, p. 48, provides a lesson strategy to instruct students about the Big Idea that tensions and conflict arose from the great westward movements into Texas, New Mexico, California, and Oregon.

Alternative Assessment Handbook provides information, guidance, and strategies for alternative methods of assessment. It includes an essay on new trends in assessment, guidance and strategies for developing performance tasks and portfolios, scoring rubrics, and sample evaluation forms.

Pages 272–275

The Native Americans of the Plains

"Whether the horse was originally a native of this country or not it is out of my power to determine," wrote explorer Meriwether Lewis in 1806 of his encounter with Native Americans and their horses on the Great Plains. In fact, the horse was not native to the plains, and its introduction to Native Americans completely transformed the lives of some.

Pages 276–280

Hispanic North America

When a stream of American traders and settlers began to move into Texas, New Mexico, and California, tensions between Mexico and the United States began to build.

Pages 281–284

Trails to the West

Explorers and fur traders began to bring back reports of the vast, beautiful lands beyond the Rocky Mountains. Hearing them, many Americans packed their bags and headed west in covered wagons along rugged western trails.

Pages 286–291

Conquest of a Continent

The Mexican War extended the nation's boundaries from the Atlantic to the Pacific. The end of the war and the discovery of gold in California transformed a stream of western-moving Americans into a flood, resulting in growing tensions with many Native American groups.

1837 A smallpox epidemic devastates the Native American population of the Missouri River valley.

1848 A gold rush begins in California.
• The Mexican War ends.

1858 Minnesota becomes a state.

1830	1836	1842	1848	1854	1860

1835 Four thousand Boers in South Africa begin the Great Trek to find territory free from British rule.

1842 The Treaty of Nanking ends the Opium War in China.

1854 The United States begins trade with Japan.

1859 Charles Darwin publishes The Origin of the Species.

Alternative Assessment

As an ongoing chapter project, students can illustrate American expansion beyond the Mississippi based on the following scenario: They have been granted a large tract of land in either Texas, Oregon, or California and are responsible for settling it. Encourage students to do outside research to make the project as realistic as possible.

Projects should contain a minimum of three of the following items. Students may also use their own ideas.

● Presentation—in the form of a poster, a local newspaper advertisement, or sales pitch delivered from the town square—to persuade prospective settlers to join them
● Map outlining the route they will follow to get to their destination, with information about the hazards they may encounter along the way
● Plans for the journey west, including a description of how the wagon train will be organized and a list of the supplies needed
● Information about Native American groups living in the area to be settled and attitudes toward them
● Information about the political situation in the region to be settled

Explain that finished projects will be assessed according to the following standards:
● **Unacceptable** Project is not attempted or fails to meet requirements outlined.
● **Limited/Acceptable** Three items are completed, based on material from the textbook.
● **Extensive/Commendable** Three items are completed and reflect some outside research that makes an attempt to give the project authenticity.
● **Extraordinary/Outstanding** More than three items are completed, reflecting extensive research that results in a vivid and realistic project.

For more information and guidance on alternative assessment trends and strategies, see the Alternative Assessment Handbook in the Resource Directory on page 270.

The Native Americans of the Plains

The Native Americans
of the Plains

1. FOCUS

Connecting to the Big Idea

See page 270B. Explain that Native Americans living on the Great Plains had contact with Europeans, principally the Spanish, long before the coming of white Americans. Such contact significantly changed the traditional lives of many Native American groups. Ask how contact with the Spanish altered the lives of Native Americans living on the Great Plains.

Objectives

- Explain how the horse changed the lifestyle of many Native Americans on the Great Plains.
- Explain how nomadic cultures increased the power of Native American men and decreased the influence of women.
- Describe how contact with traders affected Native Americans who lived on the Great Plains.

Bellringer

Ask students to try to recall from films, books, and other sources the names of Native American groups who lived on the Great Plains. Ask them to jot down their names and to consider the cultural images of Native Americans that these sources created.

Reading Strategy

Reading for Evidence Ask students to find evidence as they read the section that European animals and technology affected Native American societies of the Great Plains.

SECTION PREVIEW

"Whether the horse was originally a native of this country or not it is out of my power to determine," wrote explorer Meriwether Lewis in 1806 of his encounter with Native Americans and their horses on the Great Plains. In fact, the horse was not native to the plains, and its introduction to Native Americans completely transformed the lives of some.

The flags and horses on this Sioux beaded vest indicate increasing contact among Native Americans, Europeans, and the United States.

Key Concepts

- The arrival of the horse changed the lifestyle of many Native Americans on the Great Plains.
- Nomadic cultures tended to increase the power of Native American men and weaken the influence that women had exercised in more settled villages.
- Contact with traders brought disease to Native Americans who lived on the Great Plains.

Key Terms, People, and Places

nomad; Meriwether Lewis, William Clark, Sacajawea; Continental Divide, Great Plains

---

E ven before the United States had completed the purchase of Louisiana from France in 1803, a curious President Jefferson was making plans to send an expedition west to explore the nation's new territory. Jefferson hoped this expedition would both establish the political boundaries of Louisiana and gather information about the territory's natural resources that might prove useful for future economic development. In addition, as Jefferson related in an 1806 speech that revealed much about his attitude toward Native Americans,

I ... sent our beloved man, Captain Lewis, ... to go up the Missouri river to get acquainted with all the Indian nations in its neighborhood, to take them by the hand, deliver my talks to them, and to inform us in what way we could be useful to them.

Explorers **Meriwether Lewis** and **William Clark** set out from St. Louis, Missouri, in May 1804 with a small "Corps of Discovery." The roughly fifty men who participated in the expedition journeyed up the Missouri River and over the **Continental Divide,** which is the ridge of the Rocky Mountains that separates rivers that flow west from rivers that flow east. They then journeyed down the Columbia River to the Pacific Ocean before returning east more than two years later. The nation received with much interest the scientific samples, maps of the mountains and rivers of the territory, and information about the Native Americans in the region that the group brought back. ✪

Lewis and Clark's well-organized expedition was a remarkable achievement, but it was not a journey into unsettled territory. Hundreds of thousands of Native Americans lived west of the Mississippi River in the early 1800s. In fact, the expedition owed some of its success to one of these Native Americans—a Shoshone woman named **Sacajawea,** who served as translator and guide for the two explorers.

Lewis and Clark were by no means the first white people that Native Americans west of the Mississippi had encountered. Both animals and technology from Europe had been affecting Native Amer-

German botanist Frederick Pursh drew and classified this evening primrose from a specimen collected by Meriwether Lewis.

 RESOURCE DIRECTORY

Teaching Resources

📄 **Reproducible Lesson Plan** found in the Unit 3 folder, p. 78, provides a summary of the Section 1 lesson plan content.

📄 **Alternate Lesson Plan: Learning Styles** found in the Alternate Lesson Plans folder, p. 49, is especially useful for visual learners and is designed to help students create a graphic organizer explaining how the introduction of the horse changed life for many Native Americans.

📄 **Guided Reading and Review** found in the Unit 3 folder, p. 82, provides a structure for reading and mastering the key concepts and reviewing the key terms for Section 1. (Guided Practice)

✪ 📄 **American Profiles Activity** York, found in the Unit 3 folder, p. 90, profiles William Clark's slave, who proved invaluable on Lewis and Clark's epic journey.

ican societies of the **Great Plains**—the vast grasslands that lie between the Mississippi River and the Rocky Mountains—for almost two centuries.

The Coming of the Horse

One of these European animals, the horse, had a profound impact on the everyday lives of the Native Americans of the plains. The Spanish brought horses to their colonies in New Mexico, and Native Americans acquired them through trading, raids, and the carelessness of the Spanish. By the mid-1700s, horses had spread as far north as the Missouri Valley, the Dakotas, and parts of what are now Oregon and Washington.

Before the arrival of the horse, Native Americans had generally utilized only one domesticated, four-legged animal—the dog, which was useful for hunting and fighting. In contrast, the horse not only improved transportation and communication, but it also changed virtually every aspect of Native American life, from the nature of warfare to the division of labor between men and women.

The Horse Affects Farming and Commerce

Many Native Americans took advantage of the horse without allowing it to transform their cultures. The Pawnee, Mandan, and other Native American nations continued to live primarily as farmers, hunters, and gatherers. As in most Native American societies, the women in these villages did most of the farming, while the men were responsible for the hunting.

The Mandan resided in several villages along the Missouri River in the present-day Dakotas. French men visited them as early as the 1730s, bringing manufactured goods, including blankets, jewelry, tools, and guns. They exchanged these goods for beaver pelts and buffalo hides. By the late 1700s, the Mandan had become part of an international trading system, functioning as both middlemen in the fur trade and discriminating consumers. This trade had a far greater impact on their way of life than did horses.

The Pawnee, on the other hand, became somewhat more mobile than the Mandan following the arrival of the horse. They began to use horses to travel from their homes in the

This Navaho wall painting shows the Spanish bringing horses and other animals into the Southwest. Horses quickly spread north onto the Great Plains.

river valleys onto the plains for semiannual buffalo hunts. Although these hunts became an important part of the year, the Pawnee always returned to their villages afterward, where they continued to farm, hunt, and gather.

The Rise of the Nomads

Other Native Americans rode the horse to an entirely new way of life. They became **nomads**—people who migrate constantly instead of living permanently in a particular place. Carrying their possessions on the backs of horses, they followed the vast herds of buffalo that crisscrossed the Great Plains.

By 1800 the Native Americans of the Great Plains had used horses to hunt the buffalo for more than half a century. During that time they discovered a multitude of purposes for the buffalo. According to James R. Walker, a doctor who lived for a time among the Oglala Sioux, Native Americans used

> their hair for making ropes and pads and for ornamental and ceremonial purposes; the horns and hoofs for making implements and utensils; the bones for making soup and articles to be used in their various occupations and games; the sinews for making their sewing thread and their stronger cords such as bowstrings; the skins for making ropes, tipis, clothing . . . ; the flesh and viscera [intestines] for food.

Most of the nomads who lived on the Great Plains in the early 1800s were recent immigrants to that region. The Crow had long lived on the plains, but the Cheyenne, the Sioux, the Comanche, and the Blackfeet all migrated to that area after horses made it possible for them

Media and Technology

 Transparencies
Fine Art, D-7, D-13

2. INSTRUCT

Explain/Discuss

Discuss the effect of the introduction of the horse. Ask how the horse changed the traditional life of some groups of Native Americans living on the Great Plains.

Discuss how the shift from being settled villagers to living as nomads changed male and female roles. How did the horse affect the relationship between nomadic and village peoples of the Great Plains?

Analyze

Ask students to analyze the horse as a source of power for Native Americans. How did the horse contribute to creating a hierarchy both within and among Native American societies? Compare the influence of the horse on plains society with the influence of the automobile on twentieth century American society.

 Activity

Teaching Heterogeneous Groups
With the introduction of the horse, the lifestyle of many Native Americans on the Great Plains became nomadic rather than agricultural. To help students understand how the introduction of new technology can change people's lives, have them consider how their lives would alter if there were no cars. Have students list five ways in which their lives would change if their community outlawed cars to prevent further pollution. **LEP**

Enrichment

Sign language developed out of the need for a common, easily understood language among the many different Native American groups living on the Great Plains. Ask students to research Native American sign language and to illustrate some of its signals.

New and better machinery and techniques for textile mills and iron foundries spurred the Market Revolution, urbanization, and an increase in the number of industrial workers. The development of the railroad changed the way people traveled, communicated, and did business.

3. ASSESS

Section 1 Review Answers

1. nomad, see p. 273

2. (a) Meriwether Lewis, see p. 272, (b) William Clark, see p. 272, (c) Sacajawea, see p. 272

3. (a) Continental Divide, see p. 272, (b) Great Plains, see p. 273

4. It allowed Native Americans greater mobility; it improved transportation and communication; it allowed some Native Americans to adopt a nomadic lifestyle.

5. One source of women's influence in settled societies was their control over agriculture and the fact that men were often gone on long hunting trips or fighting raids. In nomadic societies, however, buffalo was the primary source of food and wealth. This put a great premium on hunting skills and made agriculture somewhat less important.

6. People lived so close together in Native American village societies that contagious diseases were passed on more easily and did greater damage.

7. By encouraging Native Americans of the plains to focus their entire way of life around a single animal, the introduction of the horse also made them vulnerable to devastating loss in the event that the buffalo was eradicated.

Reteach

Pass a piece of paper around the room and ask each student to list on it one way in which the horse affected Native American societies of the Great Plains. When all students have made an entry, ask a volunteer to read the list aloud.

Alfred Jacob Miller's painting illustrates the nomadic life many Native Americans of the plains adopted after the arrival of the horse. Using the *travois* shown, dogs could pull 40-pound loads five or six miles a day.

to live on the move. Although the seemingly endless herds of buffalo drew them to the plains, these Native Americans also moved westward to avoid the wave of settlers who were pushing toward the Mississippi River and beyond.

MAKING CONNECTIONS

Horses had an enormous impact on the way many Native Americans lived. What technological advances of the early 1800s had a similarly significant impact on East Coast inhabitants of the United States?

Changing Roles for Men and Women

⭐ While there were significant variations from group to group, the nomadic Native Americans of the plains did share some characteristics. Because they depended heavily on skilled riding, hunting, and fighting, which only men learned formally, nomadic societies granted men higher status than women. Men had to be aggressive warriors in dealing with other Native Americans as well as in hunting buffalo. In the early 1800s, Native Americans often conducted raids on one another to obtain horses or to subdue rivals.

Men also benefited because in nomadic life, social and political structures tended to be more fluid than in farming villages. Wealth was determined by the number of horses one had, and power by the skill and daring one showed in battle or during the hunt.

A young Cheyenne named Wilkis remembered when his uncle taught him how to hunt buffalo and gave him the following advice:

> R*ide your horse close up to the buffalo, as close as you can, and then let fly the arrow with all your force. If the buffalo turns to fight, your horse will take you away from it; but, above all things, do not be afraid; you will not kill buffalo if you are afraid to get close to them.*

Eventually Wilkis became exactly what a grown man was supposed to be according to Cheyenne culture: "I was a good hunter; I had a herd of horses, and had been to war, and been well spoken of by the leaders whose war parties I went with."

Women were generally less influential and less well off in nomadic cultures. Because these Native Americans rarely stayed in one place long enough to farm the land, women's responsibilities now involved activities created by a horse-centered culture. For the most part, women spent their time either preparing for the hunt or drying buffalo meat and tanning buffalo hides after it was over.

Female influence in agricultural villages had rested, in part, on the fact that women remained at home and ran the village when the

▶ RESOURCE DIRECTORY

Teaching Resources

 ⭐ **Literature Activity** Native American Legends: Hiawatha, found in the Unit 3 folder, p. 99, uses an excerpt from Henry Wadsworth Longfellow's "Song of Hiawatha" to illustrate his views on the Native American hero.

men left for long periods of hunting and fighting. After Native American nations such as the Sioux and Comanche had adopted a nomadic way of life, however, women followed their husbands and fathers on an endless buffalo hunt. Power that had previously resided in the female-oriented village now rested in the male-dominated hunting parties.

The Decline of Village Societies

Before the arrival of the horse, the nomadic and village people of the Great Plains lived in relative harmony. But as the 1700s wore on, the nomadic Native Americans engaged in a series of destructive raids on more settled Native American groups. To the south, the Comanche drove the Apache and Navaho west into New Mexico. In the North, the Sioux—in alliance with the Arapaho and Cheyenne—emerged as the dominant Native American group by the early 1800s.

Caught between white Americans who were pushing from the east and their nomadic neighbors to the west, agricultural Native Americans suffered greatly. The diseases brought by white settlers added to the tragic effects.

No group was hit harder by European diseases than the Mandan. From a population of close to 10,000 in the mid-1700s, the number of Mandan already had fallen to a total of around 2,000 by June 1837. By October, after the smallpox hit, only 138 were left. American artist George Catlin later claimed that, in addition to disease, another reason the Mandan died in such large numbers was because they were trapped in their villages.

*T*he Mandans were surrounded by several war-parties of their more powerful enemies the Sioux, at that unlucky time, and they could not therefore disperse upon the plains, by which many of them could have been saved.

By the mid-1800s, about 75,000 nomadic Native Americans dominated the Great Plains. In addition, roughly 84,000 Native Americans from the East, forced to relocate by the United States government, lived in what is now Oklahoma. These two groups constituted about 40 percent of the Native American population of North America.

Until the 1840s, their relationship with white Americans had been uneasy but distant, consisting mainly of occasional contacts with fur traders or explorers. But that was about to change. The revolutionary impact of the horse on the people of the Great Plains seems slight when compared with the changes brought by wave after wave of white settlers from the East.

Artist George Catlin lived with and observed the Native Americans of the plains for many years, producing more than 500 sketches and paintings of the Native American way of life. The above painting is entitled *Buffalo Chase—Single Death.*

SECTION 1 REVIEW

Key Terms, People, and Places
1. Define nomad.
2. Identify (a) Meriwether Lewis, (b) William Clark, (c) Sacajawea.
3. Identify (a) Continental Divide, (b) Great Plains.

Key Concepts
4. How did the horse affect Native Americans?
5. Why did Native American women lose power in Native American societies that became nomadic?

6. According to George Catlin, why did European diseases have a worse effect on Native American village societies than on nomadic Native Americans?

Critical Thinking
7. **Predicting Consequences** In making it easier for the Native Americans of the plains to follow and kill buffalo, how did the arrival of the horse also make their way of life more vulnerable?

 Quiz found in the Unit 3 folder, p. 83, covers the main ideas in this section as well as the key terms.

Media and Technology

Transparency
Fine Art, D-8

Reinforcing the Big Idea

By the time white Americans began to explore the territory west of the Mississippi River, contact with the Spanish had already changed traditional Native American life in the Great Plains region. The next section discusses the growing tensions that developed between Mexico and the United States as more and more settlers pushed into areas inhabited by Native Americans and Mexican Americans.

In Depth

Then and Now

Before the arrival of white settlers, about one million Native Americans lived in the continental United States. By the early 1900s, that number had been reduced to a mere 300,000. By 1960, the numbers had climbed back up to about 800,000—half of whom lived on reservations. In the 1990s, nearly two million Native Americans live in the United States; according to the Census Bureau, about four in ten are either Cherokee, Sioux, Navaho, or Chippewa.

SECTION 2

Hispanic North America

1. FOCUS

Connecting to the Big Idea

See page 270B. The westward movement of settlers and traders into Texas, New Mexico, and California caused tension between Mexico and the United States. Ask how Mexico reacted to these new immigrants.

Objectives

- Explain how Spain tried to strengthen its northern colonies in the late 1700s in California, New Mexico, and Texas.
- Explain how the California missions were responsible for the death of thousands of Native Americans.
- Describe the relative power of men and women in New Mexican society.
- Explain how American immigrants who moved into Texas in the 1820s and 1830s established an independent republic.

Bellringer

Provide a map of the United States and ask students to list at least five cities in California, Texas, and New Mexico with names that are Spanish in origin. Ask them if, based on what they know, Mexican and American cultures would be likely to clash.

Reading Strategy

Question Writing Have students read the section's main headings. Then ask students to write a question about each heading and to look for the answers as they read.

SECTION PREVIEW

When a stream of American traders and settlers began to move into Texas, New Mexico, and California, tensions between Mexico and the United States began to build.

Key Concepts

- Spain tried to strengthen its northern colonies in California, New Mexico, and Texas in the late 1700s.
- The California missions led to the death of thousands of Native Americans.
- In New Mexican society, patriarchal authority was weak and the power of women was relatively strong.
- The American immigrants who moved into Texas established an independent republic in 1836.

Key Terms, People, and Places

secularize; Stephen Austin, William Travis, Antonio López de Santa Anna, Sam Houston; Monterey, Santa Fe, the Alamo

These Spanish mission bells were rung at religious services to indicate key points in the Mass.

T he United States government assumed that the Louisiana Purchase would remain part of "Indian Country." But thousands of migrating Americans had other ideas. By the 1830s, many white settlers already were pushing west into Indian Country.

In the North, the stream of migrants was so large and steady that it led to the rapid creation of three new states: Iowa (1846), Wisconsin (1848), and Minnesota (1858). Long before these states came into the Union, however, many Americans in the southern part of the United States were moving west along the coast of the Gulf of Mexico.

The Spanish Attempt to Strengthen Their North American Empire

The Spanish commitment to the conquest of what is now the southwestern United States had always been weak. After the Pueblo revolted against Spanish settlers in present-day New Mexico in the late 1600s, this commitment grew even weaker. In the 1700s, surrounded by increasingly powerful nomadic Native Americans, the Spanish remained confined to a string of small towns along the Rio Grande and in present-day Texas.

Spanish weakness in New Mexico and Texas reflected the larger weakness of the empire as a whole. No longer the most powerful nation in Europe, Spain in the late 1700s faced growing threats to its North American territory from other European nations, including the British, the French, and the Russians from the northern Pacific Coast.

To confront these various threats, the Spanish government attempted to establish better relations with the Comanche and Apache. As a result of these efforts, they were able to achieve a somewhat fitful peace with these Native American groups.

Securing California More dramatic was the Spanish effort to secure the area that is now the state of California, which they feared would fall into the hands of either the British or the Russians. In the late 1700s, Spanish soldiers and priests established a network of missions and presidios, or forts, along the rugged California coastline. Eventually they created a chain of twenty-one missions running north from San Diego to San Francisco.

From the Spanish perspective, the colonizing efforts in California were a great success. While their settlements in New Mexico and Texas remained small, the presidios and missions in California were dynamic, thriving places. Enthusiastic and controversial Franciscan missionaries such as Father Junípero Serra devoted themselves to converting Native Americans to Christianity. In addition to becoming visible symbols of Spanish authority and centers for missionary activity, the California outposts became lively centers of trade.

RESOURCE DIRECTORY

Teaching Resources

Reproducible Lesson Plan found in the Unit 3 folder, p. 79, provides a summary of the Section 2 lesson plan content.

Alternate Lesson Plan: Cooperative Learning found in the Alternate Lesson Plans folder, p. 50, provides a structure for groups of students to make presentations describing and interpreting key events in Texas from various perspectives.

Guided Reading and Review found in the Unit 3 folder, p. 84, provides a structure for reading and mastering the key concepts and reviewing the key terms for Section 2. (Guided Practice)

The missions thrived largely, however, as a result of Native American labor, and the priests who ran these communities were often harsh taskmasters. Because whippings and confinement in irons awaited those who refused to work, some Native Americans chose to leave when opportunities to escape arose. Moreover, the Native Americans who tended the cattle and sheep, farmed the land, built the missions, and wove clothing usually received only food, clothing, and shelter in return for their efforts. Poor living conditions and inadequate medical care contributed to devastating epidemics among the Native Americans on the missions. Between 1769 and 1848, the population of Native Americans in California fell from about 300,000 to about 150,000.

While the number of Native Americans declined, the number of Mexicans grew. Settling along the coast, usually around the missions and presidios, these Mexican colonists re-created the strong extended families that were often found in Spain and Mexico at that time. **Monterey** was the capital of the territory of California, although important settlements also were located at Santa Barbara, San Diego, and Los Angeles.

New Mexico Grows Meanwhile, change also had come to New Mexico. Thanks to long stretches of peace and increased attention from Spain, the Mexican population in the region increased from 3,800 in 1750 to 19,000 by 1800. Unlike eastern North America, however, the powerful nomadic Native Americans and the harsh landscape of New Mexico made it impossible for large numbers of people to spread out over the countryside in small farms. As a result, many people earned a living as craftspeople and traders in large settlements such as Albuquerque.

Population growth and an increase in commercial activity affected social relationships among those living in New Mexico. The authority of parents, particularly fathers, grew weaker. Residents of New Mexico who were not members of the landed aristocracy, or the segment of the wealthy class that owned land, began to choose their own husbands and wives; in the past they had been expected to accept their parents' choice of a partner.

Women in this region enjoyed considerable independence. Wives were able to run businesses, divorce their husbands, own property, and sue in courts of law. In fact, women actually lost rights and influence when New Mexico became part of the United States in 1848.

Oriana Day's painting of the California mission of San Carlos Borromeo depicts Franciscan friars leading a religious procession in the early 1800s. The Native American pictograph shown above captures another view of a Spanish mission.

Media and Technology

Transparency
Fine Art, D-9

2. INSTRUCT

Discuss
Discuss with students the American settlement of Hispanic North America. Encourage discussion with questions such as the following: What was Spain trying to do by establishing missions in California? What role did economics play in the American colonization of Mexico's northern territories? How did Mexico unwittingly encourage the eventual American takeover of Texas?

Analyze
Ask students to analyze the tension caused by the American settlement of Mexico's northern territories. What role might cultural differences have played in the conflict? How do these differences continue to be a source of conflict today in Texas, New Mexico, and California?

Activity
Advertising for Settlers
Ask students to design a poster advertising land opportunities in Texas in the early 1820s.

Enrichment
Tell students that while Native Americans in California allowed Spanish missions to flourish, New Mexico's Native Americans made the establishment of missions there difficult. Ask students to research and compare the cultures of the Native Americans in these two territories and to explain the characteristics that either contributed to or undermined Spanish colonization.

Today's highways link urban settlements, trade routes, and cultural centers—all legacies of yesterday's trails.

3. ASSESS

Section 2 Review Answers

1. secularize, see p. 278

2. (a) Stephen Austin, see p. 279, (b) William Travis, see p. 279, (c) Antonio López de Santa Anna, see p. 279, (d) Sam Houston, see p. 280

3. (a) Monterey, see p. 277, (b) Santa Fe, see p. 278, (c) the Alamo, see p. 279

4. The Spanish, their empire weak and in great danger of being overrun either by other Europeans from the Pacific or by Americans from the east, acted primarily for defensive reasons.

5. From the perspective of the Spanish government, they succeeded because they established a Spanish presence from San Diego to San Francisco; and from the perspective of the priests, they were successful because many Native Americans were baptized; but from the perspective of most Native Americans, the missions in or near which many were forced to live brought only death from diseases and malnutrition.

6. Married Mexican women along the Rio Grande were able to own property, sue in courts of law, and run businesses. In general, authorities upheld female rights. Because women were legally subordinate in American society, females had fewer rights after the American conquest than before.

Yesterday's Trails, Today's Highways

The trails that Native Americans, fur traders, missionaries, and others carved in the landscape (left) became today's superhighways. The photo above shows a group of would-be pioneers who recently reconstructed the journey along the Santa Fe Trail. *Why do you think yesterday's trails have become today's highways?*

Mexican Independence Affects Its Territories

Mexico won its independence from Spain in 1821, after thirteen years of war and economic devastation. Although California, New Mexico, and Texas, then part of Mexico, were far from the fighting, independence still had an effect on their residents. As citizens of Mexico, the men in these territories were now free to elect representatives to the new government in Mexico City.

Because Mexico's new government was hostile to the Roman Catholic church, it **secularized** the missions, meaning it put them under the control of the state rather than the church. By the 1830s, only a handful of priests remained in northern Mexico. In addition, economic reforms designed to bolster the Mexican economy actually widened the gap between rich and poor in Mexico's northern territories. But these reforms also encouraged trade with the United States.

American Economic Influence in New Mexico, California, and Texas

In 1821 William Becknell, a nearly bankrupt American, brought a load of goods from Missouri to the New Mexican capital of **Santa Fe,** where he sold them for mules and silver coins.

Other Americans followed, taking advantage of the commercial opening created by Mexican independence and economic reforms. The high quality and low prices of American goods virtually destroyed New Mexico's trade with the rest of Mexico.

By the early 1830s, caravans of wagons traveled regularly between Independence, Missouri, and New Mexico along the Santa Fe Trail. According to one of the most active American merchants, these caravans shaped the character of Sante Fe: "Instead of the idleness and stagnation which its streets exhibited before, one now sees everywhere the bustle, noise, and activity of a lively market town."

American fur traders and merchants exploited economic openings in other parts of Mexico's northern territories. New Englanders who sailed around South America to reach the West soon dominated the trade with California in fur, cattle hides, and tallow, a waxy substance used to make candles. In return, Californians bought finished goods from the New Englanders. According to one resident of Monterey in the 1840s, "There is not a yard of tape, a pin, or a piece of domestic cotton or even thread that does not come from the United States."

Long before the United States conquered the Mexican provinces of Texas, New Mexico, and

▶ RESOURCE DIRECTORY

Teaching Resources

 Literature Activity What Happened in Texas, found in the Unit 3 folder, p. 100, uses an excerpt from Walt Whitman's "Song of Myself" to demonstrate the popularity of the Alamo in American folklore.

California militarily, it had conquered them economically. By loosening the regulations affecting trade with American merchants, the Mexican government ensured that the commercial ties of its northern provinces would be with the United States, rather than with its own merchants. More important, stronger commercial ties encouraged some Americans to seek new opportunities in Mexico's northern territories.

Texas Wins Independence

Nowhere was the influx of Americans into Mexican territory more apparent in the 1820s than in Texas. **Stephen Austin,** carrying out the plan begun by his father, Moses, received permission from the Mexican government to found a colony of about 300 settlers in east Texas. Austin, twenty-nine years old and a member of the Missouri territorial legislature, led the first organized group of American settlers into Texas in 1822. By 1824, some 2,000 immigrants were living in Austin's colony.

When Americans first started moving into what is now eastern Texas, the new Mexican government adopted a liberal colonization policy. The Mexican Colonization Law of 1824 promised American immigrants cheap land, the protection of the Mexican government, and a four-year tax exemption if they settled in Texas.

Soon other agents were arranging contracts for hundreds of Americans to settle in Texas. By 1830 about 7,000 Americans lived there, more than twice the number of Mexicans in the territory. Worried that they were losing Texas through immigration, Mexico passed a law in 1830 prohibiting any more Americans from settling there. Equally important, they outlawed the importation of enslaved people. Still, Americans continued to flow across the border.

MAKING CONNECTIONS

Many Americans in the 1820s and 1830s migrated to Texas following reports of fertile soil for growing crops. Today, many Mexicans attempt to immigrate to the United States. Do these two groups of people share similar reasons for wanting to settle in a new land?

Tension Erupts Into War By 1835 more than 30,000 Americans and 3,000 enslaved African Americans lived in Texas. As their numbers swelled, these Americans demanded more political freedom. In particular, they wanted slavery to be guaranteed under Mexican law. They were divided between those led by Stephen Austin, who preferred to work within the Mexican system, and those led by a hot-tempered lawyer from Alabama named **William Travis,** who wanted to fight for independence.

Events in Mexico City soon helped Travis's supporters gain the upper hand. When the vain and ambitious General **Antonio López de Santa Anna** declared himself dictator of Mexico, supporters of an independent Texas became even more determined to break away. American settlers united in the cause of independence, and in March 1836, they formally declared the founding of the Republic of Texas. ✪ Santa Anna responded to this defiance of Mexican authority by leading an army of several thousand men north to subdue the rebellion. The Mexican leader won early victories at **the Alamo**, a fortress built on the ruins of a Spanish mission in San Antonio, and at Goliad. At the Alamo, fewer than 200 Texans defended an abandoned Spanish mission for twelve days while inflicting heavy casualties on 4,000 Mexican troops. Before his death, Travis sent this plea for help "to the People of Texas and all the Americans in the World":

Fellow citizens & compatriots, I am besieged by a thousand or more of the Mexicans under Santa Anna. . . . I call on you in the name of Liberty, of patriotism & everything dear to the American character to come to our aid, with all dispatch. . . . If this call is neglected, I am determined to sustain myself as long as possible & die like a soldier who never forgets what is due to his own honor or that of his country.

Bowing to his father's dying wish, Stephen Austin established the first colony of American settlers in Texas in 1822.

Media and Technology

Transparency
Our Multicultural Heritage, C-10

7. Some settlers wanted to be part of the United States. More important, however, was the fact that the Mexican government became more centralized in the 1830s and reneged on some of the promises it had made to settlers in the 1820s. Texans wanted to be left alone, and they wanted to be able to have slaves. When Mexico interfered, they rebelled. The South would take the same course of action against the United States in 1861.

8. Both Spanish missionaries and many white Americans viewed Native Americans as inferior, "uncivilized" human beings whose rights did not need to be considered very seriously.

Reteach

List the following terms on the chalkboard and ask students to use each one in a sentence that relates to the section content: mission, Mexico's northern territories, Santa Fe Trail, Stephen Austin, William Travis, the Alamo, General Antonio López de Santa Anna, and Sam Houston.

Answer to ...

MAKING CONNECTIONS

Americans who moved into Texas in the 1820s were looking for economic opportunities and a new life, the same goals that draw Mexicans into the United States today.

In Depth

Historical Misconceptions

The story that the defense of the Alamo symbolizes brave white settlers' struggle against despotism is under close scrutiny by a new generation of historians. They regard it more as a symbol of United States imperialism and racism over Mexicans and Native Americans. "The Alamo is part of an Anglo-Texan creation myth," says University of Texas history professor Cynthia Orozco. "The Euro-Americans wanted to distinguish themselves from people who were here before them."

Alternative Assessment

Mid-Point Monitoring

Ask students if they have
- Decided what items to include
- Outlined the information to be contained in each item
- Located outside sources

Caption Answer to ...

  Interpreting Maps

The Rio Grande.

  Reinforcing the Big Idea

At first Mexico welcomed American settlers into its northern territories, particularly Texas. But as the settlers' numbers increased, tensions developed. In a war between Mexico and American settlers, the Americans took Texas from Mexico. The next section discusses Americans' push westward over the Oregon Trail.

In Depth

Biography

At fifteen, Sam Houston (1793–1863) ran away to live with the Cherokee, returning home three years later with a Native American name: "The Raven." After studying law, Houston became a member of the United States Congress in 1823, and in 1827 was elected governor of Tennessee. He left public life and returned to the Cherokee until 1832. In 1835 Andrew Jackson made him leader of the Texan forces against Mexico; he reentered public life as Texas's president, then as the state's United States senator, and later as its governor. In 1861, when Texas withdrew from the Union, Houston resigned saying, "I love Texas too well to bring civil strife and bloodshed upon her."

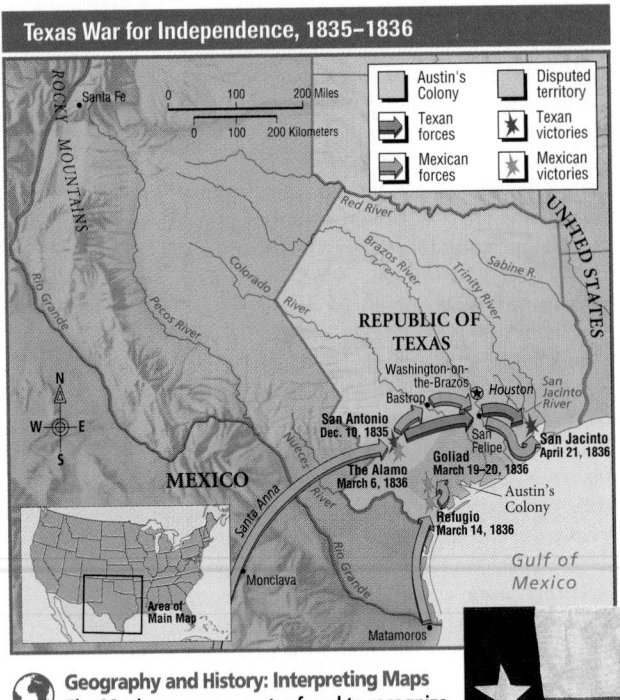

Texas War for Independence, 1835–1836

Legend:
- Austin's Colony
- Texan forces
- Mexican forces
- Disputed territory
- Texan victories
- Mexican victories

Geography and History: Interpreting Maps
The Mexican government refused to recognize the boundaries of the republic Texans established. The Texas flag (right) reflected the new nation's informal name: the Lone Star Republic. *What formed the southernmost edge of the disputed territory?*

Texas Fighters Turn the Tables Still confident of victory, Santa Anna divided his force to finish off the Texan rebels, thousands of whom were fleeing eastward in what became known as the Runaway Scrape. Just when all seemed lost, more than 900 Texans regrouped at the San Jacinto River under **Sam Houston,** a strong-willed former governor of Tennessee. There they surprised the careless and arrogant Santa Anna. Rallying to cries of "Remember the Alamo!" they routed the Mexican troops in a matter of minutes. The map on this page illustrates the war for independence.

In retaliation for the Alamo and Goliad, the Texans killed several hundred of their prisoners and forced Santa Anna to sign a treaty recognizing the Republic of Texas. The Mexican government later denounced that treaty but did not contest it militarily. In the fall of 1836, the citizens of Texas elected Sam Houston as their first president.

By the end of the 1830s, with almost no help from the United States government, American traders and settlers had established a firm presence from Texas to California. They also had succeeded in prying away a large piece of territory from Mexico. As Americans continued to push west during the next decade—and the Mexican government continued to fume over the loss of Texas—tensions between Mexico and the United States grew to the point that war once again became a possibility.

The deaths of the courageous Alamo defenders—including William Travis and the legendary frontiersman Davy Crockett—and the massacre of 371 prisoners captured by the Mexicans at Goliad, enraged and energized Texans to mighty actions for their cause.

SECTION 2 REVIEW

Key Terms, People, and Places
1. Define secularize.
2. Identify (a) Stephen Austin, (b) William Travis, (c) Antonio López de Santa Anna, (d) Sam Houston.
3. Identify (a) Monterey, (b) Sante Fe, (c) the Alamo.

Key Concepts
4. Why did the Spanish try to reform their empire and colonize California in the late 1700s?
5. Were the California missions successful? Explain.

6. In what ways would the American conquest of New Mexico have a negative impact on women there?
7. Why did the Americans in Texas want their independence from Mexico?

Critical Thinking
8. **Making Comparisons** How were the attitudes of Spanish missionaries toward the Native Americans of California similar to the attitudes of many white Americans toward Native Americans at the time?

  RESOURCE DIRECTORY

Teaching Resources

Quiz found in the Unit 3 folder, p. 85, covers the main ideas in this section as well as the key terms.

Trails to the West

SECTION PREVIEW

Explorers and fur traders began to bring back reports of the vast, beautiful lands beyond the Rocky Mountains. Hearing them, many Americans packed their bags and headed west in covered wagons along rugged western trails.

Key Concepts

• Western fur traders in the early 1800s brought back stories of the lands beyond the Rockies.
• Among the earliest American settlers in Oregon were missionaries who hoped to convert the region's Native Americans to Christianity.
• In the 1840s thousands of Americans began to migrate to Oregon and California along a variety of long and difficult western trails.

Key Terms, People, and Places

mountain man; Jason Lee, Narcissa Prentiss Whitman; Oregon Trail, Willamette Valley, Independence, Snake River

---

W hile some Americans were pushing into Texas in the early 1820s, others back east began to hear stories of a beautiful land beyond the Rocky Mountains. This vast territory, known as the Oregon Country, stretched from northern California to the southern border of Alaska. Now called the Pacific Northwest, the area possessed magnificent mountains, seemingly endless forests, and fertile valleys.

Although a variety of Native American groups had lived in Oregon for centuries, by the early 1800s four different nations—the United States, Great Britain, Russia, and Spain—claimed rights to the territory. Ignoring the Native Americans who already lived there, the United States and Britain signed a treaty in 1818 agreeing to joint occupation of the territory. Distracted by other problems, Russia and Spain withdrew their claims to the area in the mid-1820s. By that time, the small but increasing number of enterprising Americans who had

made their way into Oregon were beginning to spread the word of what they had found there.

Fur Traders and Missionaries

Yankee merchants from New England, traveling by ship, first traded for furs with the Native Americans of Oregon in the late 1700s. After Lewis and Clark completed their expedition in 1806, growing numbers of American fur traders such as Jedediah Smith and James Beckwourth began to roam the Rocky Mountains in search of animal pelts. Dubbed **mountain men,** these hardy trappers discovered Native American trails that led through the Rockies to California and Oregon, including the route that came to be known as the **Oregon Trail.**

As news of the Oregon Country filtered back to the East, a few churches decided to send missionaries to the territory to convert Native Americans to Christianity. The first of these missionaries, a Methodist minister named **Jason Lee,** arrived in Oregon in 1834 and promptly built a mission school for Native Americans in the **Willamette Valley.** Encouraged by his example, four Presbyterian missionaries joined Lee in Oregon in 1836. Among them was one of the first white women to cross the Rocky Mountains, **Narcissa Prentiss Whitman.**

This journal recorded the adventures of one pioneer who braved the western trails to find a new home and a new life.

Reproducible Lesson Plan found in the Unit 3 folder, p. 80, provides a summary of the Section 3 lesson plan content.

Alternate Lesson Plan: Learning Styles found in the Alternate Lesson Plans folder, p. 51, is especially effective for auditory and kinesthetic learners, and enhances students' understanding of section content as they prepare and participate in a mock training session for westbound migrants.

Guided Reading and Review found in the Unit 3 folder, p. 86, provides a structure for reading and mastering the key concepts and reviewing the key terms for Section 3. (Guided Practice)

---

1. FOCUS

Connecting to the Big Idea

See page 270B. Attracted by stories of a beautiful and fertile land beyond the Rocky Mountains, settlers began to travel west to the Oregon Country. Ask what the journey west was like for these courageous pioneers.

Objectives

● Explain the role fur traders played in encouraging settlement of the lands beyond the Rocky Mountains.
● Explain why missionaries journeyed to Oregon.
● Describe the journey west made by thousands of settlers to Oregon and California in the late 1840s.

Bellringer

Ask students if they have ever taken a long and difficult trip. If so, ask them to describe how long it took and why it was difficult.

Reading Strategy

Predicting Content Before they read the section, have students predict the challenges American settlers faced as they moved west. Ask students to look for data to support their predictions as they read.

In Depth

Did You Know?

German immigrant John Jacob Astor (1763–1848) led the first effort to establish a permanent settlement in the Oregon Country. Astor made a fortune in the fur trade, and was the richest man in America at the time of his death.

Discuss/Analyze

Discuss the journey across the Oregon Trail and the settlement of the Oregon Country. To encourage discussion, ask students questions such as the following: What kinds of people did the Oregon Country attract? Why was a woman like Narcissa Whitman, who led a comfortable middle-class life, willing to risk the challenges of a trip over the Oregon Trail? What difficulties did settlers encounter?

Analyze

Ask students to analyze the change in relations between Native Americans and American pioneers. What general conclusions about the relations between Native Americans and white settlers might be drawn from the experience of the Whitmans?

Activity

Cooperative Learning

Time: One class period.
Activity: Pioneers moving west over the Oregon Trail faced perilous risks. Have groups develop a skit about one challenge pioneers might have faced while crossing the Oregon Trail.
Grouping: Groups of six students.
Purpose: To help students understand the challenges pioneers might have faced while moving west.
Roles: Skit writers, play director, and actors.
Outcome: Students will empathize with the experience and hardship of the Oregon Trail. **LEP**

Answer to ...

Like the European explorers of the 1500s, the mountain men and missionaries of the early 1800s played the role of pathfinders, blazing trails for thousands of permanent settlers who followed in their footsteps.

AMERICAN PROFILES

Narcissa Prentiss Whitman

Narcissa Prentiss (1808–1847) was born in the small town of Prattsburg, New York, the third of nine children. Her father, Stephen Prentiss, was a successful land and mill owner. Her mother, Clarissa Ward, was a deeply religious woman and the most important influence in her daughter's life.

Living in upstate New York at the height of the Second Great Awakening, Narcissa spent much of her youth immersed in the world of evangelical Protestantism. By the time she was in her late teens, she was determined to become a Christian missionary.

In 1835 Narcissa married Marcus Whitman, a physician. They married primarily to become missionaries rather than for love. Both were committed to spreading the gospel and needed a lifetime partner to assist them.

The following year, the Whitmans were sent to live and work among the Cayuse and Nez Percé in what is now Oregon. Narcissa and another missionary woman became the first two white women to cross the Continental Divide. Narcissa preserved a vivid record of the difficult four-month journey. Two months into their trip, Narcissa wrote to her mother: "We have plenty of dry buffalo meat to eat. I can scarcely eat it, it appears so filthy, but it will keep us alive and we ought to be thankful. Do not think I regret coming. No, far from it. I would not go back for the world." As she arrived at last in the Willamette Valley, she wrote: "Surely my heart is ready to leap for joy, at the thought of being so near the long desired work of teaching the be-nighted ones a knowledge of a Savior."

At first, all went well. The Whitmans established

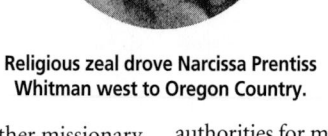

Pioneers often had to discard their possessions along the trail to lighten the load when climbing mountains or crossing rivers. The candle and candle mold below may well have been two of the forsaken items.

Religious zeal drove Narcissa Prentiss Whitman west to Oregon Country.

a small mission and were greeted warmly by the Native Americans. In addition to performing their daily chores, Marcus preached and practiced medicine and Narcissa taught Sunday school.

After their two-year-old daughter was accidentally drowned in 1839, however, the devastated Narcissa lost some of her enthusiasm. From the beginning, she had found it difficult to develop relationships with the Cayuse. She now put less and less energy into working with them.

By the late 1840s, the rapid migration of white settlers into Oregon was beginning to make many of the Cayuse uneasy. This tension gave way to violence in 1847 when Marcus was unable to stop the progress of a serious measles epidemic. On the morning of November 29, several Cayuse mortally wounded Marcus in the Whitmans' kitchen. While trying to tend to her husband's wounds, Narcissa was shot, dragged outside, and beaten to death. The Cayuse killed twelve other white settlers that day and temporarily held another forty-seven hostage. At least five Cayuse were arrested and executed by American authorities for murdering the Whitmans.

Neither Narcissa nor the other missionaries who settled in Oregon had much success in converting the region's Native Americans to Christianity. In fact, their sense of superiority often created more suspicion and hostility than goodwill among local Native Americans. Nevertheless, Narcissa Prentiss Whitman was a brave and persistent woman. Her willingness to undertake the long and dangerous journey across the Great Plains and Rockies captures the pioneering spirit that led many Americans to seek new opportunities in the American West.

MAKING CONNECTIONS

In what sense did the mountain men and missionaries of the early 1800s play a similar role to that of the European explorers of the 1500s?

▶ RESOURCE DIRECTORY

Teaching Resources

✪ **Literature Activity** Song of the Pioneers found in the Unit 3 folder, p. 101, uses the popular wagon song "Sweet Betsy from Pike" to illustrate both the hardships and the spirit of humor along the trail to the West.

The Overland Trails to the West, 1840s

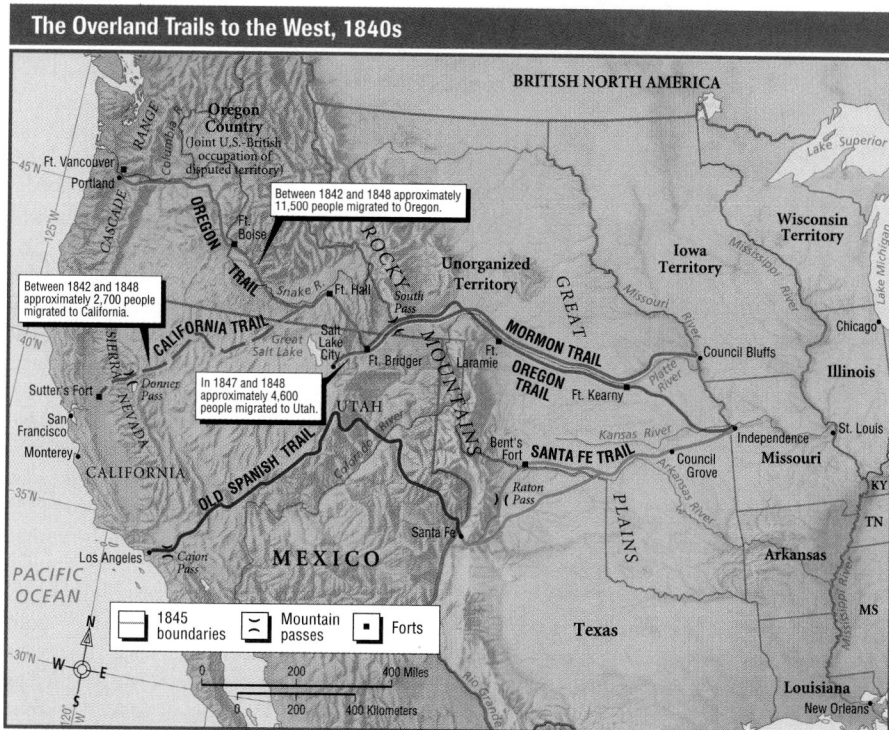

BRITISH NORTH AMERICA

Oregon Country
(Joint U.S.-British occupation of disputed territory)

Ft. Vancouver
Portland

Between 1842 and 1848 approximately 11,500 people migrated to Oregon.

Ft. Boise

Between 1842 and 1848 approximately 2,700 people migrated to California.

Ft. Hall

Snake R.

South Pass

Salt Lake City

Ft. Bridger

Ft. Laramie

In 1847 and 1848 approximately 4,600 people migrated to Utah.

Sutter's Fort

Donner Pass

Great Salt Lake

San Francisco

Monterey

CALIFORNIA

Los Angeles

Cajon Pass

PACIFIC OCEAN

MEXICO

Santa Fe

Raton Pass

Bent's Fort

Council Grove

Independence

Missouri

St. Louis

Chicago

Illinois

Council Bluffs

Platte River

Ft. Kearny

Kansas River

Arkansas River

Wisconsin Territory

Iowa Territory

Unorganized Territory

GREAT PLAINS

Lake Superior

Lake Michigan

Mississippi River

Missouri River

KY

TN

Arkansas

MS

Texas

Louisiana

New Orleans

Rio Grande

| 1845 boundaries | Mountain passes | Forts |

0   200   400 Miles
0   200   400 Kilometers

 Geography and History: Interpreting Maps
Thousands of settlers headed west along various overland trails in the 1840s, facing dry, barren country in some parts of the journey and tall, rugged mountains in others. *Along what important river did the final leg of the Oregon Trail run?*

Traveling the Overland Trail

Starting in 1843, groups met at a small town in western Missouri called **Independence.** From there they began a grueling, 2,000-mile trek across the Great Plains and the Rocky Mountains. Their journey is shown on the map above.

Although the average time of their journeys was 121 days if they were heading for California and 139 days if they were going to Oregon, the trip west sometimes took as long as 6 months. It was an expensive journey as well, costing a typical family between $500 and $1,000.

Normally, the pioneers traveled along the Platte River in present-day Nebraska and through the South Pass in what is now Wyoming. People heading for California would turn southwest at the **Snake River,** follow the Humboldt River across the Sierra Nevada, and descend into the Central Valley of California near Sacramento. Those trying to reach Oregon would continue to the northwest along the Snake River until they reached the settlements along the Columbia and Willamette rivers.

Although some of the pioneers who journeyed west in the 1840s were free African Americans, the majority were white settlers from midwestern states. Often, the trip was the second or third major move in their lives, and most of the migrants went west as part of a family.

⭐ Many pioneers who traveled the Oregon Trail enjoyed the beauty of the plains and the mountains. Still, the trip was a long and difficult one. Getting the heavy covered wagons across rivers, through muddy bogs, and up steep hills was exhausting, backbreaking work. And conditions for travel were often terrible in

Media and Technology

📺 **Transparencies**
The Way It Works, H-9, H-10;
Critical Thinking, I-4

4. They served as trailblazers, bringing back stories of the rich and beautiful lands beyond the Rocky Mountains and showing that it was possible to survive the difficult journey west.

5. Missionaries such as Narcissa Whitman assumed that Native Americans were uncivilized "heathens" who were basically inferior to white people.

6. Disease posed the greatest threat, resulting in far more deaths than occurred from Native American attacks.

7. Many books, films, and television series about the westward expansion of the 1840s have attempted to justify it by portraying Native Americans as hostile, unfriendly people who preyed on brave, innocent pioneers. Most of these fictional accounts have made no attempt to view this period of American history from the point of view of the Native Americans.

Reteach

Ask students to read and correct each of the following statements and to provide evidence from the section to support each correction.
● Immediately after Lewis and Clark completed their expeditions, thousands of settlers flocked to the Oregon Country.
● Narcissa Prentiss Whitman was a poor example of the pioneering spirit that led many Americans west.
● For most pioneers, the trip across the Oregon Trail was a relaxing vacation through beautiful countryside.
● Native Americans posed the greatest threat to the pioneers' safety as they moved across the Oregon Trail.

4. CLOSE

Reinforcing the Big Idea

By 1845 thousands of pioneers had survived the trip west over the Oregon Trail and settled in the Oregon Country, which soon became part of the United States. The next section discusses growing tensions between the American settlers who flooded the west and the Mexicans and Native Americans who already lived there.

Pausing for a photograph in front of their covered wagon, this family was one of many that headed west in the 1840s in search of a better life. ✪

other ways as well, as an anonymous 1852 pioneer makes clear:

> To enjoy such a trip along with such a crowd of emigration, a man must be able to endure heat like a Salamander, mud and water like a muskrat, dust like a toad, and labor like a jackass. He must learn to eat with his unwashed fingers, drink out of the same vessel with his mules, sleep on the ground when it rains, and share his blanket with vermin, and have patience with musketoes. . . . It is a hardship without glory, to be sick without a home, to die and be buried like a dog.

As the months passed and the travelers became more frustrated with the difficulties of the long journey, people's nerves began to fray.

As Oregon Trail traveler Enoch Conyers reported in his diary, "If there is anything in this world that will bring to the surface a man's bad traits, it is a trip across the continent with an ox team." The need to cross over the dangerous Rocky Mountains before the early winter snows arrived only added to the tension.

In fact, the journey via the Oregon Trail was so difficult that some decided to bypass the demanding land trek altogether by sailing from the Atlantic coast of the United States around the tip of South America and up the Pacific coast of North America. The majority of migrants, however, traveled across the overland trails.

Movies and television westerns would have us believe that pioneers and Native Americans were constantly fighting with each other. In fact, they spent more time trading than fighting. White travelers received food and other necessities from Native Americans in return for clothing and tools. It was not until the 1850s that serious conflict developed. Far more deadly than any threats from Native Americans were diseases such as cholera, which killed as many as 10,000 pioneers—or about 4 percent of the total—between 1840 and 1860.

✪ By 1845 more than 5,000 Americans had settled in the Oregon Country. When American settlers in the territory began to outnumber the British in 1843, they drew up a temporary government to be used until Oregon came under the jurisdiction of the United States. Three years later, in the Treaty of 1846, the United States and Great Britain agreed to divide the Oregon Country along the 49th parallel. Because of the growing threat of war with Mexico, this peaceful solution proved to be in the nation's best interest.

SECTION 3 REVIEW

Key Terms, People, and Places
1. Define mountain man.
2. Identify (a) Jason Lee, (b) Narcissa Prentiss Whitman.
3. Identify (a) Oregon Trail, (b) Willamette Valley, (c) Independence, (d) Snake River.

Key Concepts
4. How did fur traders affect the settling of Oregon?
5. What assumptions did missionaries make about the Native Americans they hoped to convert?
6. What posed the biggest threat to those who migrated to California and Oregon on the western trails?

Critical Thinking
7. **Recognizing Bias** Why do you think the media have generally portrayed Native Americans as hostile toward the pioneers when that was not usually their attitude?

 RESOURCE DIRECTORY

Teaching Resources

✪ **Primary Source Activity** Traveling West, found in the Unit 3 folder, pp. 96–97, includes firsthand accounts of westward migration in the mid-1800s from *Women's Diaries of the Westward Journey.*

✪ **Critical Thinking Activity** Determining Relevance, found in the Unit 3 folder, p. 95, encourages students to consider the relationship between the westward migration from 1841 to 1858 and the expansionist policies of the United States.

Quiz found in the Unit 3 folder, p. 87, covers the main ideas in this section as well as the key terms.

Analyzing Tombstones

Have you ever passed an old cemetery and tried to figure out the stories its tombstones and other grave markers tell? They tell you when people lived, how long they lived, and sometimes even how they died and how they were remembered by those they left behind. Whether erected for beloved children who died too soon, brave soldiers who died in battle, or husbands or wives mourned by their spouses, these markers also offer clues about the times in which the people they honor lived.

In a way, the overland trails west were also cemeteries. As one traveler along the Oregon Trail put it, "The road from Independence to Ft. Laramie is a graveyard." Another observer remarked that there was "one dead person every 80 yards along the Oregon Trail." Estimates of the number of people who died on this trek range from 20,000 to 45,000.

Use the following steps to analyze a few of the epitaphs, or inscriptions, on the gravestones that appeared along the Oregon Trail.

1. Identify the time in which the people lived and, if possible, how they met their deaths. (a) What is the time period in which the people remembered here met their deaths? (b) What were the various causes of their deaths?

2. Evaluate what their lives meant to others who knew them. (a) How does the Martess epitaph reflect a deep sense of loss on the part of those who survived her? (b) What tells you that George Winslow was well remembered?

3. Study the grave markers to see what clues they offer about the historical period. (a) According to many of the epitaphs, the Oregon Trail was plagued with an epidemic. What was it? (b) What clues can you find to tell you that the Oregon Trail was hard on small children? (c) What clues can you find to help you identify the dangers of the Oregon Trail?

Died: Of Cholera

(This was the most frequent epitaph found on grave sites along the way.)

Mary Ellis
Died May 7th, 1845
Aged two months

(This epitaph was found on a piece of plank standing up from a grave site, its letters traced by a red-hot piece of iron.)

Marlena Elizabeth Martess
Died Aug. 9th, 1863
Born July 7th, 1862
Friends nor physician could save her from the grave

(This epitaph was followed by a plea to all who might pass to keep the grave in good repair.)

IN MEMORY OF GEORGE WINSLOW
who died on this great highway June 8, 1849
and was buried here by his comrades. . . .
This tablet is affectionately placed by his sons,
George Edward and Orrin Henry Winslow.

Rachel E. Pattison
Aged 18
June 19, '49

(This was a rock, hand-lettered.)

Rebecca Winters,
age 50 years

(This was crudely carved on a wagon wheel, which served as the grave's headstone.)

In Memory
of Charles Hatch HO
Died June 12, 1850

(Scratched on this carved tombstone is "Killed by Indians.")

Pioneer Grave of
John D. Henderson
Died of Thirst
August 9, 1852
Unaware of Nearness of the Malheur River Leaving Independence, Missouri, in May 1852, Mr. Henderson and Companion Name Unknown, Had completed Only Part of the Journey When Their Team Died. They were Compelled to Continue on Foot Carrying Their Few Possessions. The Twenty Miles of Desert Separating the Snake and Maleur Rivers Proved too Great a Struggle for the Weary Travelers

(This marker replaced a stone that gave Henderson's name and date of death.)

Historian's Toolbox Activity Analyzing Obituaries, found in the Unit 3 folder, p. 94, helps students understand what information about a society can be gleaned from death notices.

Conquest of a Continent

Conquest of a Continent

1. FOCUS

Connecting to the Big Idea

See page 270B. As settlers streamed into the West, more and more Americans began to believe it was the destiny of the United States to extend from the Atlantic to the Pacific. Ask how the United States realized its dream of a continental empire.

Objectives

● Explain why President James K. Polk provoked war with Mexico.
● Explain what the United States received in the 1848 Treaty of Guadalupe Hidalgo.
● Explain why tension between the North and the South grew over the issue of slavery.
● Describe how western migration after the Mexican War and the discovery of gold in California increased tensions between Native Americans and white settlers.

Bellringer

Write the word *destiny* on the chalkboard. Ask students to jot down a definition and to think about what the word might have to do with the expanding United States in the mid-1840s.

Reading Strategy

Reading for Evidence Ask students to find evidence as they read the section to support the following statement from page 286: "Increasingly in the 1840s, Americans believed that no other nation should be allowed to keep the United States from fulfilling its destiny."

SECTION PREVIEW

The Mexican War extended the nation's boundaries from the Atlantic to the Pacific. The end of the war and the discovery of gold in California transformed a stream of western-moving Americans into a flood, resulting in growing tensions with many Native American groups.

Key Concepts

• President James K. Polk maneuvered the United States into war with Mexico in the hope of acquiring California and New Mexico.
• In the 1848 Treaty of Guadalupe Hidalgo, the victorious United States received about two fifths of Mexico's territory.
• Tension grew between the North and South over the issue of slavery in the new territories.
• The push of western migration after the Mexican War and the discovery of gold in California increased tensions between Native Americans and white settlers.

Key Terms, People, and Places
manifest destiny, Gadsden Purchase, Wilmot Proviso; John C. Frémont, Joseph Smith, Brigham Young, Kamiakin; Rio Grande

During the Mexican War, American soldiers often wore tall hats called shako caps. The hats showed an eagle spreading its wings as a symbol of manifest destiny.

A s the surge of migrants from the United States into western territories gained momentum in the 1830s and 1840s, some Americans began to dream of a continental empire stretching from the Atlantic to the Pacific. Like the Puritans who envisioned their colony as a "city upon a hill," these Americans believed that the United States had a divine mission to spread liberty across the continent. A New York journalist named John L. O'Sullivan neatly captured this sense of mission when he coined the phrase *manifest destiny.*

Writing in 1845, Sullivan claimed that it was the nation's "manifest destiny to over-

---

spread and to possess the whole of the continent which Providence has given us for the development of the great experiment of liberty and federated self-government entrusted to us." Increasingly in the 1840s, Americans believed that no other nation should be allowed to keep the United States from fulfilling its destiny.

Annexation of Texas

After winning independence from Mexico in 1836, many Texans assumed that the United States would quickly absorb their new republic. Americans were far from united on the question of annexing Texas, however. Southerners and supporters of slavery were eager to carve one or more slave states out of the Texas territory. Northerners feared that the addition of even one slave state would shift the balance of power in Congress and the Electoral College to the South. Many people in both the North and South worried that annexation would lead to war with Mexico. ✪

In the early 1840s, northerners and Whigs held up the annexation of Texas while southerners and Democrats scrambled to find some way to push it through Congress. Although President John Tyler signed a treaty of annexation with Texas in April 1844, the Whig-controlled Senate soundly defeated it. When Democrat James K. Polk, running on an expansionist platform, won the presidency later that year, the tide began to shift. In February 1845, before Polk even took the oath of office, Congress approved annexation. After Texas voters added their approval in December of that year, Texas became the twenty-eighth state in the Union.

War with Mexico

Years before the United States annexed Texas, the steady influx of Americans into Mexico's northern territories had led to growing friction between the two nations. When Congress

---

RESOURCE DIRECTORY

Teaching Resources

Reproducible Lesson Plan found in the Unit 3 folder, p. 81, provides a summary of the Section 4 lesson plan content.

Alternate Lesson Plan: Critical Thinking Determining Relevance, found in the Alternate Lesson Plans folder, p. 52, provides a structure for pairs of students to construct a time line or sequence chain showing the causes and consequences of the Mexican War.

Guided Reading and Review found in the Unit 3 folder, p. 88, provides a structure for reading and mastering the key concepts and reviewing the key terms for Section 4. (Guided Practice)

✪ **Visual Learning Activity** The Annexation of Texas, found in the Unit 3 folder, p. 103, presents a pamphlet opposing the annexation of Texas to demonstrate the controversy surrounding this issue.

approved annexation in early 1845, Mexico immediately broke off diplomatic relations with the United States. Continuing disagreements about the southern border of Texas signaled further trouble ahead.

President Polk and other southern Democrats wanted much more from Mexico than Texas. Polk had dreams of acquiring the entire territory stretching from Texas to the Pacific. In a final attempt to avoid war, he sent Ambassador John Slidell to Mexico City in November 1845 with an offer to buy California and New Mexico for $30 million. But the Mexican government refused even to receive Slidell, let alone consider his offer.

Determined to have his way, the aggressive Polk sent two thousand American troops under General Zachary Taylor into southern Texas to support the American claim that the **Rio Grande** was the official American-Mexican border. Since the Mexican government claimed that the Nueces River, located quite a few miles further north, was the border, it considered Taylor's movements an invasion of Mexican territory. Tensions between the two nations escalated rapidly. Meanwhile, an American expedition under the command of Captain **John C. Frémont** moved into California, probably under orders from the President to stir up trouble.

When Mexican troops engaged in a skirmish with Taylor's forces in early May 1846, Polk had the excuse for which he had long been waiting. Expressing outrage at the loss of "American blood on American soil," the President pushed for an immediate declaration of war. Despite some opposition, Congress gave it to him on May 13, 1846.

The Bear Flag Revolt Before news of the war had reached California, a group of American settlers took matters into their own hands. Led by William B. Ide, these settlers launched a surprise attack on the town of Sonoma on June 14 and proclaimed the California Republic, or Bear Flag Republic—named for their flag, which pictured a grizzly bear and a single star. Frémont quickly assumed control of the rebel forces and drove the Mexican army out of northern California.

Meanwhile, United States troops under the command of General Stephen Kearny crossed into New Mexico. Meeting little or no resistance, American forces occupied Santa Fe by mid-August (see the map below). Kearny then took part of his army and marched west to California to join Frémont. Although the Mexican army won several victories in the fighting that followed, Kearny and Frémont eventually were able to subdue all opposing forces in the territory. By January 1847, the United States had taken control of New Mexico and California.

Fighting in Mexico While Frémont and Kearny were securing Mexico's northern territories for the United States, General Taylor had

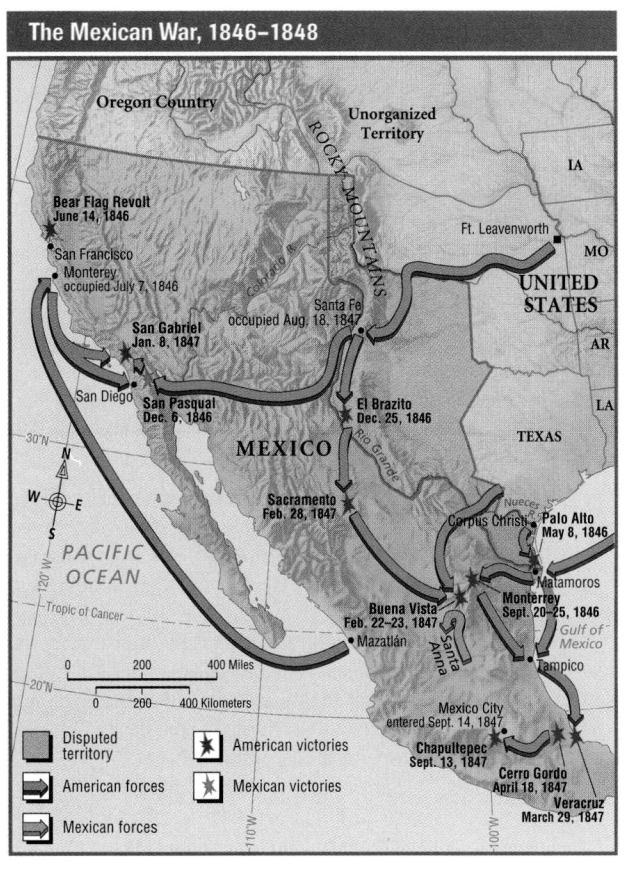

Geography and History: Interpreting Maps
 Many Americans, including President Polk, viewed the Mexican War as an opportunity for the United States to expand its boundaries across the continent. *Looking at this map, what information can you use to make a judgment about who probably won the war?*

Media and Technology

Transparencies
Historical Maps, L-2; Cause and Effect, F-4

2. INSTRUCT

Discuss
Discuss with students the idea of manifest destiny and the American drive to fulfill that destiny. Encourage discussion with questions such as the following: What was meant by the term *manifest destiny*? Why did Americans feel justified in fulfilling their destiny, despite the costs to other nations? What major historical events between 1845 and 1860 illustrate the American drive toward a continental empire? How did westward expansion heighten the tension between North and South over the issue of slavery? How did the westward migration of white Americans affect Native Americans?

Analyze
Have students analyze the attitude of Americans at this time toward other nations. In general, what were their feelings about Native Americans? How did Americans view nations like Mexico, Great Britain, and Spain? Why do you suppose they might have felt morally justified in holding these attitudes toward other peoples?

Caption Answer to ...

🌐 **Interpreting Maps**

Students should infer that the Americans won the war, because the map shows far more American battle victories than Mexican victories.

Viewpoints

O'Sullivan defends expansionism as an American right; Douglass regards the annexation as a shameful example of land grabbing. For a more thorough examination of the expansion into Mexican territory, see the Resource Directory below.

Activity

Designing a Flag

Have students research the societies living in the territories of Utah, Oregon, or New Mexico, or in the new state of Texas. Ask them to design a flag to represent one of these locations.

Enrichment

Probably the best-known writer to describe the California gold rush was Bret Harte. Have students research the work of this writer and read one of his short stories depicting life during the gold rush, for example, "The Luck of Roaring Camp."

In Depth

Biography

Though relatively few of his stories were successful, Bret Harte (1836–1902) played an important role in creating a vivid, lasting portrait of the "Old West." Harte's stories, filled with intriguing characters and expressive dialogue, provided much of post–Civil War America with its first glimpse into western life. (For more on Bret Harte, see Prentice Hall Literature, *The American Experience*, 1994, "The Outcasts of Poker Flat," pp. 452–459.)

Viewpoints
On Expanding into Mexican Territory

Strained relations between North and South intensified when the United States annexed vast Mexican territories in 1848. *How is the spirit of the times reflected in the following viewpoints?*

Pro-Annexation

"The pretense that the annexation has been unrightful and unrighteous is wholly untrue and unjust to ourselves. If Texas became peopled with an American population, it was on the express invitation of Mexico herself. . . . What, then, can be more preposterous than all this clamor by Mexico against annexation as a violation of any rights of hers, any duties of ours?"

John L. O'Sullivan, editorial in *United States Magazine and Democratic Review*, 1845

Anti-Annexation

"They [who favor the Mexican War] have succeeded in robbing Mexico of her territory. And they are rejoicing over their success under the hypocritical pretense of a regard for peace. Had they not succeeded in robbing Mexico of the most important and most valuable part of her territory, many of those now loudest in their cries of favor for peace would be loudest and wildest for war. . . . We are not the people to rejoice. We ought rather blush and hang our heads for shame."

Frederick Douglass, African American leader of the antislavery movement, editorial in *North Star*, March 17, 1848

taken the war into Mexico itself. After crossing the Rio Grande, Taylor won a series of victories, leading finally to the Battle of Buena Vista in February 1847. Here he met Santa Anna, who had brought an army of 20,000 Mexican troops north from Mexico City. Although Taylor won the battle, Santa Anna chose to declare victory and return to Mexico City rather than continue the struggle, which might well have resulted in victory for the Mexicans.

Santa Anna abandoned northeastern Mexico to Taylor, in part because of a more serious threat, this time to his capital. Pressing for complete victory, Polk dispatched forces under General Winfield Scott to take Mexico City. Having captured the port city of Vera Cruz in March 1847, Scott marched his army of 10,000 men toward Mexico City along the route once taken by Spanish conquistador Hernando Cortés. After fierce fighting, Scott defeated Santa Anna's forces and captured the Mexican capital on September 14, bringing the war to an end.

The Treaty of Guadalupe Hidalgo With the defeat of its troops and the fall of their country's capital, the Mexican government was at the mercy of the United States. Although some Americans now had visions of annexing most of all of Mexico, negotiations produced more limited results. Still, by the 1848 Treaty of Guadalupe Hidalgo, Mexico not only recognized the Rio Grande as the border of Texas but also gave up New Mexico and California—more than two fifths of its territory—to the United States. In return, the United States government paid Mexico $15 million and agreed to cover debts owed to United States citizens.

Five years later, in 1853, the Mexican government sold 30,000 square miles of what is now southern New Mexico and Arizona to the United States for $10 million. Known as the **Gadsden Purchase,** this land eventually provided a route for the southern transcontinental railroad. The table on page 291 shows the square miles added to United States territory from 1800 to 1860. The Illustrated Data Bank in the reference section shows the territories that were gradually added to the United States from 1787 to 1899.

Although the Mexican War is often seen as a minor footnote in the history of the United States, the American victory over Mexico had important consequences. The Treaty of Guadalupe Hidalgo, together with the 1846 division of Oregon and the Gadsden Purchase, established the boundaries of the continental United States as we now know them. Referred to by Mexicans as the North American Invasion, the war also left many Mexicans deeply bitter toward the United States and led to decades of poor relations and misunderstandings between the two nations. Finally, the acquisition of a vast expanse of territory in the West opened the doors for a new and even larger wave of western migration.

The Wilmot Proviso Possibly the most important consequence of the Mexican War was the role it played in bringing the question of slavery

RESOURCE DIRECTORY

Teaching Resources

Viewpoints Activity On Expanding into Mexican Territory, found in the Unit 3 folder, pp. 92–93, uses several local contemporary passages to help students understand how regional issues may have influenced arguments for and against mid-1800s expansionism.

to the forefront of American politics. The central issue that confronted Congress was what to do with the vast territory acquired by the United States from Mexico. Northerners did not want the balance of power in the United States to tip to the South and did not want to compete with plantation owners moving west, whose use of slavery drove wages down. As a result, northerners' fear of additional slave states was strong. Partly in response to Whig criticisms of the war, Pennsylvania Democrat David Wilmot attached an amendment to a military appropriations bill in 1846. The **Wilmot Proviso** stated that slavery would not be permitted in any of the territory acquired from Mexico.

Although Congress defeated the proviso, Wilmot laid bare tensions between the North and South. Eventually, the issue of slavery in the western territories would prove to be one of the most important causes of the Civil War. Americans could sidestep the question of slavery within existing states, but they had to confront the issue directly whenever they created new territories and new states.

Mormons Settle Utah

At the time of the Mexican War, the Mormons, one of the largest groups of migrants to head west in the 1840s, were finding a new home in present-day Utah. Mormons, or members of the Church of Jesus Christ of Latter-day Saints, had been looking for a permanent home ever since **Joseph Smith** founded the religion in western New York in 1830. Harrassed by neighbors who were suspicious of their beliefs, the Mormons moved to Ohio, then to Missouri, and finally to Nauvoo, Illinois.

Although the Mormans initially prospered in Illinois, relations with neighbors deteriorated after Smith revealed in 1843 that the Mormons accepted polygyny, the practice of a husband having more than one wife at the same time. After a hostile mob killed Smith and his brother in 1844, the Mormons were forced to move on once again.

The religion's new leader, **Brigham Young,** decided that the Mormons' only hope was to live beyond the borders of the United States of

that time. He and other leaders chose the Great Salt Lake Basin as the Mormons' new home, largely because it was located nearly a thousand miles from other Americans. As Young said in an 1862 sermon:

> We are not going to wait for the angels, . . . to come and build up Zion [the promised land], *but we are going to build it. We will raise our wheat, build our houses, fence our farms, plant our vineyards and orchards, and produce everything that will make our bodies comfortable and happy and in this manner we intend to build up Zion on the earth, and purify and cleanse it from all pollutions.*

Starting in 1847, hundreds of Mormons left their temporary camps in Iowa for new homes near the Great Salt Lake. Within three years, more than 11,000 Mormons had settled in the region. By 1860, about 30,000 Mormons lived in Salt Lake City and more than ninety other towns in present-day Utah.

Despite many difficulties, these settlements were orderly and prosperous. The Mormons skillfully irrigated their desert region and devoted themselves primarily to farming. They also made money from trade with the wagon trains traveling to California and Oregon.

At first the leaders of the Morman church established their own system of government. With the end of the Mexican War, however, Utah became an official territory of the United States and Brigham Young its first governor. Utah eventually entered the Union in 1896 as the forty-fifth state.

MAKING CONNECTIONS

How was the Mormons' decision to establish a settlement in Utah in the 1840s similar to the Puritans' decision to found the Massachusetts Bay Colony in the 1620s?

The Gold Rush in California

No event was more important in attracting settlers to the Far West than the discovery of gold

Answer to ...

MAKING CONNECTIONS

The Puritans wanted to find a home far away from other people where they could practice their religion without fear or interference and establish an ideal society ("city upon a hill") here on earth. Similarly, the Mormons sought out a home in the wilderness where they would be free from persecution and free also to establish the kind of society they wanted.

In Depth

Interdisciplinary

The worst disappointment for gold prospectors was mistaking pyrite, also known as fool's gold, for the real thing. Pyrite, which is not a metal, can be distinguished from gold by pounding it. Real gold will not break when hammered, but pyrite, whose name comes from the Greek word for fire, gives off large sparks when struck hard. In fact it was used by some Native American groups to make fire.

Section 4 Review Answers

1. (a) manifest destiny, see p. 286, (b) Gadsden Purchase, see p. 288, (c) Wilmot Proviso, see p. 289

2. (a) John C. Frémont, see p 287, (b) Joseph Smith, see p. 289, (c) Brigham Young, see p. 289, (d) Kamiakin, see p. 291

3. Rio Grande, see p. 287

4. Mexico ceded about two fifths of its territory for just under $20 million. It had little choice, given the reality of an American occupying army.

5. While President Polk cited boundary disputes and disagreements about trade, the real cause was the American desire to secure its claim to Texas and acquire California and New Mexico.

6. Support for the proviso fell along sectional rather than party lines. Its passage suggested that many northerners (whether Democrats or Whigs) were increasingly unhappy with the South and would oppose the further expansion of slavery into the territories.

7. It brought hundreds of thousands of people to the state, transformed San Francisco into a major commercial center, and destroyed much of what remained of Native American cultures.

8. In both cases, the government's attitude, spurred by a sense of cultural superiority, was that no nation should be allowed to keep the United States from fulfilling its destiny of occupying the entire continent, and that any action toward that end was justifiable.

at Sutter's Mill in California in January 1848. At first, people near the gold strike could not believe it was true. Then, as the lumps of gold were displayed from town to town, they began to realize what the discovery meant. Walter Colton, mayor of Monterey, describes how the news affected his community:

> T*he family who had kept house for me caught the moving fever. Husband and wife were both packing up; the blacksmith dropped his hammer, the carpenter his plane, the mason his trowel, the farmer his sickle, the baker his loaf, and the tapster his bottle. All were off for the mines, some on horses, some on carts, and some on crutches, and one went in a litter.*

Newspapers in the eastern United States were soon full of the news, and people touched by gold fever rushed west by the thousands. California had 14,000 residents in 1848. Within a year, 100,000 people were living in the state, and by 1852 that number had reached 200,000. While some of the hopeful traveled by ship around the tip of South America, or by a combination of ship, rail, and foot via Central America, most went west across the overland trails.

This gold miner was one of many who traveled to California to find his fortune.

A majority of the new immigrants were unmarried men. In fact, only 5 percent of the "forty-niners" who went to California in the 1849 gold rush were women or children. African Americans, both enslaved and free, were also part of the gold rush. Enslaved people worked as servants or searched for gold on their owners' work crews. Some free African Americans, such as the formerly enslaved Moses Ridges, became independent miners.

The gold rush had a tremendous impact on life in California. For Native Americans, the influx of thousands of white immigrants was a disaster. The tens of thousands of miners forced Native Americans to work—the men in the mines, the women in their households. Disease and forced labor reduced the Native American population in California from roughly 150,000 in 1848 to 35,000 by 1860.

While the gold rush devastated Native American societies, it also brought commercial vitality to cities along the Pacific coast. Most impressive was the growth of San Francisco. In 1859 Massachusetts lawyer Richard Henry Dana, who had immortalized a mid-1830s visit to California in his novel *Two Years Before the Mast*, was stunned by the transformation of the sleepy port he knew into

> the great centre of a world-wide commerce. . . . We bore round the point toward the old anchoring-ground of the hide-ships, and there, covering the sand-hills and the valleys, stretching from the water's edge to the base of the great hills, and from the old Presidio to the Mission, flickering all over with the lamps of its streets and houses, lay a city of one hundred thousand inhabitants.

The Mining Frontier

In the wake of the California gold rush came news in the 1850s of gold strikes in Colorado, the Pacific Northwest, Idaho, and Montana. Whenever these reports went out, new towns appeared almost overnight. Men and women came to mine, to open stores, or to run saloons. Although some people have exaggerated the number of fights and murders that

▶ RESOURCE DIRECTORY

Teaching Resources

Visual Learning Activity Living Dead in Califor-nee, found in the Unit 3 folder, p. 102, uses a contemporary cartoon to illustrate the fate of some who sought gold in the California gold rush.

Primary Source Activity Gold! Gold! Gold! found in the Unit 3 folder, p. 98, uses actual accounts from various people in California to show how the populace and the economy there responded and changed after the discovery of gold.

American Profiles Activity found in the Unit 3 folder, p. 91, profiles Kamiakin, an influential Native American and chief of the Yakima during the time the Native American groups of the Northwest were being forced off their land and onto reservations.

took place in these boom towns, it is true that they were often wild and violent places.

Mining towns usually were short lived. During the boom, hundreds of new residents arrived and built scores of houses and businesses with amazing speed. Then, when the mines were spent, the towns went bust and people moved on. Many mining communities slowly decayed and died, turning into abandoned ghost towns. A few of the luckier mining towns were reborn in the late 1900s as tourist and skiing centers.

Western Migration and Native Americans

Until the Mexican War, the United States had proclaimed all land west of the 95th meridian to be "Indian Country." Along the so-called Permanent Indian Frontier, running from Minnesota to Louisiana, the United States Army built a series of forts. As growing numbers of Americans migrated west, however, the United States established military posts further and further west.

Other government groups also dealt with Native Americans. The Bureau of Indian Affairs (1824), or BIA, became part of the newly created Department of the Interior in 1849. The Bureau attempted to "extinguish" Native American land claims through treaties and annuities, or yearly payments. In the 1850s the government increasingly championed the idea of reservations as the ultimate solution to the "Indian problem."

In California, these policies led to the creation of eight reservations by 1858. Native Americans in Oregon and Washington fought back in an 1855 war led by the Yakima chief **Kamiakin.** But there, too, treaties eventually led to the confinement of thousands of people on eight reservations. ⭐

Nomadic Native Americans proved to be the most successful at resisting the government's efforts to control them. Despite treaties of peace signed in the early 1850s, tension increased with every group of white settlers that crossed the Mississippi. By the end of the 1850s, both the United States government and the Plains Indians saw military action as their only option for dealing with each other. Increasing numbers of white Americans wanted to carve farms out of the rugged lands beyond the Mississippi River. Native Americans wanted to follow the buffalo on the wide-open plains as they had for decades. With neither side willing to yield or compromise, violence was the only possible outcome in this conflict of cultures.

Little did the Native Americans of the plains know that another impasse was ahead—one between northerners and southerners of the United States. As the debate over slavery in the western territories grew shriller and political solutions became increasingly less likely, the nation sped toward war. By 1860, decades of tension and debate would erupt in armed conflict between the North and South.

Expansion of the United States, 1800–1860	
Year	Square Miles
1800	888,811
1810	1,716,003
1820	1,788,006
1830	1,788,006
1840	1,788,006
1850	2,992,747
1860	3,022,387

Source: *Historical Statistics of the United States*

Interpreting Tables The United States more than tripled in size between 1800 and 1860. *During what decade did the largest expansion occur?*

SECTION 4 REVIEW

Key Terms, People, and Places
1. Define (a) manifest destiny, (b) Gadsden Purchase, (c) Wilmot Proviso.
2. Identify (a) John C. Frémont, (b) Joseph Smith, (c) Brigham Young, (d) Kamiakin.
3. Identify Rio Grande.

Key Concepts
4. What did Mexico give up in the Treaty of Guadalupe Hidalgo?

5. Why did the United States go to war with Mexico?
6. What was the significance of the Wilmot Proviso?
7. What was the impact of the gold rush on California?

Critical Thinking
8. **Making Comparisons** How was the United States government's attitude about Mexico's northern territories similar to its attitude about the area designated as "Indian Country?"

 Quiz found in the Unit 3 folder, p. 89, covers the main ideas in this section as well as the key terms.

 Chapter Test Forms A and B are found in the Unit 3 folder, pp. 104–109.

 Answer Keys found in the Unit 3 folder, pp. 116–125, provide answers to all student activities.

Media and Technology

📖 **Transparency** Graphic Organizer, G-1

🎧 **Guided Reading Audiotapes** (English and Spanish)

📖 **Computer Test Bank**

Chapter Review

Understanding Key Terms, People, and Places

Terms

Students should refer to the definitions of the key terms in the chapter to write sentences that show the relation of each word to the settlement of lands beyond the Mississippi River.

Matching

1. manifest destiny
2. secularize
3. Wilmot Proviso
4. mountain man

True or False

1. false, Rio Grande
2. false, Kamiakin
3. false, Brigham Young
4. true

Reviewing Main Ideas

1. Men in nomadic societies acquired greater status than women because only they were taught the important skills of riding, hunting, and fighting.

2. Village societies were attacked by nomadic groups and were devastated by European diseases.

3. Nomadic groups such as the Sioux and the Comanche emerged as dominant.

4. They thrived largely as a result of the work of Native Americans, who were treated as a pool of cheap labor.

5. The authority of parents, especially fathers, was weaker than elsewhere; and residents who were not members of the wealthy class could choose their own spouses; women enjoyed considerable independence.

6. Americans in Texas demanded more freedom from the Mexican government and eventually succeeded in breaking away from Mexico.

7. Because many missionaries conveyed an attitude of racial and cultural superiority, Native Americans regarded them and their teachings with suspicion and hostility.

8. Students' descriptions should include evidence demonstrating that the journey was long, difficult, and dangerous.

9. The Treaty of Guadalupe Hidalgo, together with the 1846 division of Oregon and the Gadsden Purchase, established the boundaries of the continental United States as we know them; many Mexicans were left with bitter feelings toward the United States; the acquisition of the vast new territory opened the door for a large westward migration.

Understanding Key Terms, People, and Places

Key Terms
1. nomad
2. secularize
3. mountain man
4. manifest destiny
5. Gadsden Purchase
6. Wilmot Proviso

People
7. Meriwether Lewis
8. William Clark
9. Sacajawea
10. Stephen Austin
11. William Travis
12. Antonio López de Santa Anna
13. Sam Houston
14. Jason Lee
15. Narcissa Prentiss Whitman
16. John C. Frémont
17. Joseph Smith
18. Brigham Young
19. Kamiakin

Places
20. Continental Divide
21. Great Plains
22. Monterey
23. Santa Fe
24. the Alamo
25. Oregon Trail
26. Willamette Valley
27. Independence
28. Snake River
29. Rio Grande

Terms For each term above, write a sentence that explains its relation to the settlement of lands beyond the Mississippi River.

Matching Review the key terms in the list above. If you are not sure of a term's meaning, review its definition in the chapter. Then choose a term from the list that best matches each description below.

1. the belief that the United States had a divine mission to spread liberty across the continent
2. to put under the control of the state rather than the church
3. legislation that forbid slavery in any of the territory acquired from Mexico
4. one of the hardy trappers who discovered Native American trails that led through the Rockies

True or False Determine whether each statement is true or false. If it is true, write "true." If it is false, change the underlined person or place to make the statement true.

1. After the war with the United States, Mexico recognized the <u>Great Plains</u> as the border of Texas.
2. Native Americans in Oregon and Washington fought back in an 1855 war led by <u>Sacajawea.</u>
3. The new leader of the Mormons, <u>William Clark,</u> decided to settle in present-day Utah.
4. <u>Monterey</u> was the capital of the territory of California.

Reviewing Main Ideas

Section 1 (pp. 272–275)
1. How did men acquire greater status than women in nomadic societies?
2. Give two reasons that help explain why Native American village societies declined in the early 1800s.
3. Which Native American groups became dominant on the Great Plains?

Section 2 (pp. 276–280)
4. Why were the California missions able to thrive?
5. Describe the social relationships among people living in New Mexico.
6. What was the ultimate effect of the increasing immigration of Americans into Texas?

Section 3 (pp. 281–284)
7. Why did the missionaries have little success in converting Native Americans to Christianity?
8. Briefly describe a typical overland journey to Oregon during the period of westward expansion.

Section 4 (pp. 286–291)
9. What were three consequences of the Mexican War?
10. How did the Mexican War bring the question of slavery to the forefront of national politics?
11. Explain why the California gold rush led to increased tensions between white settlers and Native Americans.

10. A decision had to be made about whether to allow slavery in the territories acquired by the war.

11. Greater numbers of settlers began to move west into Native American territories.

Thinking Critically

1. The stereotypical Native American is vindictive, bloodthirsty, and usually on horseback. This exaggerated image is based on the behavior of the more warlike nomadic groups, which differed sharply from that of agricultural groups. These seldom appear in popular imagery, however, partly because popular culture favors violence; and partly because whites probably had the most conflict and interaction with the nomadic groups.

2. Utah is a relatively small region with limited resources that eventually would have been surrounded by the United States. It probably would have been difficult and impractical for it to exist as an independent country. Texas is much larger and

Thinking Critically

1. **Distinguishing False from Accurate Images** Briefly describe the popular image of the Native American as portrayed in television westerns and movies. What groups of Native Americans is this image based on? What groups does it ignore?

2. **Identifying Alternatives** Do you think that it would have been possible for Texas or Utah to have remained separate from the United States? Why?

3. **Recognizing Ideologies** While the United States referred to the conflict with Mexico as the Mexican War, Mexicans called the war the North American Invasion. What do these different names suggest about each country's perspective on the war? Was the war in fact an act of aggression on the part of the United States?

Making Connections

1. **Evaluating Primary Sources** Review the primary source excerpt on page 272. Explain what Jefferson's statement reveals about his attitude toward Native Americans. How were future encounters between whites and Native Americans consistent with Jefferson's views? How were they inconsistent?

2. **Understanding the Visuals** Look at the table on page 291. Why might John O'Sullivan see this table as visual evidence that the nation was following his concept of manifest destiny?

3. **Writing About the Chapter** It is 1849. You have just received a letter from your cousin in California urging you to come west. Write a response in which you explain why you will or will not make the journey. First, make a list of the reasons that support your decision. Also note the reasons that support the opposite point of view and why they fail to persuade you. Next, write a draft of your response in which

you explain your intention to travel or to remain at home; use examples from the chapter to support your decision. Revise your response, making sure that you have clearly and persuasively explained your ideas. Proofread your response and draft a final copy.

4. **Using the Graphic Organizer** This graphic organizer uses a web map to organize information about nomadic groups of Native Americans on the Great Plains. In this web, dotted lines are used to show connections between ideas. (a) Why does the graphic organizer show a connection between the two animals central to nomadic culture, the horse and the buffalo? (b) Explain the other connections suggested by this graphic organizer. (c) On a separate sheet of paper, create your own web map about Spanish missions in California, using this graphic organizer as an example.

Centrality of buffalo ---- **Dependence on horses**

Men trained as aggressive hunters — **Nomadic Culture of the Great Plains** — **Women's responsibilities center on activities created by horse-driven culture**

Individual males gain and lose status quickly ---- **Women lack power and influence**

3. Students' letters should weigh the prospects offered by the California gold rush, opportunities in the West, the hardships of the journey, and the spirit of adventure required to undertake such a journey.

4. (a) The horse allowed Native Americans to follow and hunt buffalo. (b) As hunters, men became more aggressive and concerned with status; women consequently lost status. (c) Students' graphic organizers should include information about the purpose of the California missions as well as their negative impact on Native American culture.

Alternative Assessment

Final Evaluation

Use the following guidelines to evaluate student projects:

● **Evidence of outside research** To what extent did students use outside research for their projects?

● **Evidence of synthesis** Do projects demonstrate that students understand how topics are related?

● **Communication style** Do projects convey their information in a clear, appealing way?

---

probably could have prospered independently; but its strong economic ties to the United States and high proportion of United States citizens made its statehood a likely outcome.

3. The United States saw the war as an opportunity to exercise the doctrine of manifest destiny rather than an act of aggression, while Mexico saw it as an act of imperialism. Most students will probably agree that the war was an act of aggression.

Making Connections

1. Jefferson's statement reveals goodwill but is also rather patronizing. Missionaries who tried to convert Native Americans to Christianity were similarly patronizing, as were believers in manifest destiny eager to spread a "superior" culture throughout the continent. In most future encounters, whites did not show goodwill toward Native Americans but stole their lands and treated them with great cruelty.

2. O'Sullivan believed that it was the United States' inevitable fate to occupy the entire continent. This map details the nation's rapid and seemingly unstoppable expansion from a strip of thirteen colonies along the eastern seaboard to a vast nation stretching 3,000 miles from the Atlantic to the Pacific.

Introducing the Unit

Interpreting the Visual During the Civil War, photographers such as Mathew Brady and his assistants followed the armies with their cumbersome equipment, sending image after image of military personnel, battlefields, and bodies back to the nation's cities. Although early photography gave civilians an immediate glimpse into the world of war, its effectiveness was limited. The long exposure time required eliminated any action shots. After a while, the public wanted more.

Sometimes the stillness required by photography became a strength, giving photographers the chance to capture a particular mood or atmosphere. President Lincoln's metaphoric description of the nation as a building is vividly illustrated in the solemn photograph shown on pages 294–295.

Ask students to list suitable adjectives to describe this photograph and then to prepare questions to ask the women in the photograph.

Establishing Chronology Remind students that the previous chapter focused on the growing conflict between the North and the South. This unit covers the years of the Civil War, in which the conflict exploded, and the period of Reconstruction, which brought a different kind of tension between North and South. The war lasted from 1861 until 1865, and Reconstruction was formally ended in 1877.

Division and Uneasy Reunion 1848–1877

"A house divided against itself cannot stand. I believe this government cannot endure permanently, half slave and half free."

—Abraham Lincoln, 1858

*L*ong before the simmering tension between North and South exploded into war in 1861, the United States had come to resemble a "house divided." A series of fragile political compromises in the early 1800s had served only to slow rather than end the growing strain between the two regions. Although the North ultimately prevailed in the Civil War, and Lincoln achieved his dream of preserving the Union, his goal of healing the nation's regional and racial rifts ended with his assassination. The period of Reconstruction that followed the war left a legacy of bitterness, resentment, and broken promises.

 RESOURCE DIRECTORY

Teaching Resources

☐ **Local History Activity** "Rebel Belles in Old New Orleans" and the Local Focus research topic suggestions, found in the Local History Resources folder, pp. 12–14, are designed to help students understand how history affects all lives.

★ **Themes in American History Poster**
Wall-size, illustrated posters, found in the Teaching Resources package, illustrate the four unit themes.

☐ **Unit Test** Forms A and B are found in the Unit 4 folder, pp. 107–112.

This 1865 photograph of Richmond, Virginia, taken by a colleague of photographer Mathew Brady, shows that the Civil War smashed the nation's cities as well as ravaging its battlefields.

Themes in American History

Teachers may wish to discuss specific historical events in the context of historical themes. Here are four suggestions for Unit 4.

Values *A variety of religious, ethical, and moral beliefs have propelled and guided the quest of Americans for a just and ordered society.*

● Northerners began to view slavery as immoral and a threat to families and the nation's character.
● The Civil War saw the emergence of a new type of destructive warfare, directed against civilians.

Economics *Americans have searched for new and better ways to make a living and have struggled to define government's role in this pursuit.*

● The superior economic strength of the North was a deciding factor in the Civil War.
● The federal government's need for arms during the Civil War established a close relationship between business and government that continued long after the war.

Unity and Conflict *Americans have developed unique political systems and laws that affirm a shared commitment to certain goals, such as individual rights and equality. Nevertheless, groups with differing views on how to achieve these goals have often clashed.*

● Debate over slavery reached an impasse and eventually erupted into a full-scale civil war.
● After the war, new forms of enforced labor took the place of slavery in the South.

American Culture *In every period of their history, Americans gave special expression to their views through art, literature, films, music, manners, and morals.*

● The publication of *Uncle Tom's Cabin* rallied northerners against the immorality of slavery.
● The end of the Civil War did not end the regional differences and the mutual distrust between northerners and southerners.

Media and Technology

Visions of America: Scenes of an Era To introduce students to the main idea and events covered in this unit, play "Scenes of an Era: Division and Uneasy Reunion" (length: 2.5 minutes). This selection can be located on side 2 of the videodiscs. This selection can also be located on videotape 2. Lesson plans for "Scenes of an Era" can be found in the Visions of America Guidebook.

Using Multimedia Technology This folder contains instructional tools and strategies for using technology in the classroom.

Transparency Binder Contains full-color transparencies with lesson suggestions. From a large collection divided into twelve categories, specific transparencies are referenced throughout the chapters at appropriate points of use. For this unit, see American Photo, B-4; Cause and Effect, F-5; Links Across Time, J-4; Political Cartoon, K-4; Historical Maps, L-3; and Geographic Setting, M-3 and M-4.

Chapter 11 The Coming of the Civil War
1848–1861

📁 **Teaching Resources** (See Unit 4 Folder)

	Instruction	Enrichment
Section 1 **Two Nations?** (pp. 298–302)	Reproducible Lesson Plan, p. 3 Alternate Lesson Plan, p. 54 Guided Reading and Review, p. 7 Quiz, p. 8	Literature Activity, An Antislavery Best-Seller, pp. 26–27 Literature Activity, A Poem in Defense of Slavery, p. 28
Section 2 **New Political Parties** (pp. 303–309)	Reproducible Lesson Plan, p. 4 Alternate Lesson Plan, p. 55 Guided Reading and Review, p. 9 Quiz, p. 10	Visual Learning Activity, Anthony Burns and the Fugitive Slave Law, p. 29 Historian's Toolbox Activity, Analyzing Political Speeches, p. 21
Section 3 **The System Fails** (pp. 311–315)	Reproducible Lesson Plan, p. 5 Alternate Lesson Plan, p. 56 Guided Reading and Review, p. 11 Quiz, p. 12	Visual Learning Activity, Free Soiler Chokes on Slavery, p. 30 Primary Source Activity, Lincoln–Douglas Senate Campaign, pp. 23–24 Primary Source Activity, An Interview with John Brown, p. 25 American Profiles Activity, John Anthony Copeland, Jr., p. 17 History Might Not . . . Activity, Can Separate Be Equal? pp. 15–16
Section 4 **A Nation Divided Against Itself** (pp. 318–321)	Reproducible Lesson Plan, p. 6 Alternate Lesson Plan, p. 57 Guided Reading and Review, p. 13 Quiz, p. 14 Chapter Test, Forms A & B, pp. 31–36	Viewpoints Activity, On the Southern Secession, pp. 19–20 American Profiles Activity, General P. G. T. Beauregard, p. 18 Critical Thinking Activity, Identifying Assumptions, p. 22

📁 **Additional Chapter Resources**

Resource Organizer, p. 2
Alternate Lesson Plan, p. 53
Answer Keys, pp. 113–122

Bibliography

For the Teacher

Catton, Bruce. *The Coming Fury.* Washington Square Press, 1972. (Traces the split between the North and the South from the election of 1860 through the first Battle of Bull Run.)

Elkins, Stanley M. *Slavery: A Problem in American Institutional and Intellectual Life.* University of Chicago Press, 1976. (A classic study of the issue of slavery.)

Hedrick, Joan D. *Harriet Beecher Stowe, A Life.* Oxford University Press, 1994. (The first biography of Stowe in fifty years, with new material on her life.)

Prentice Hall Literature Excerpts from *The American Experience,* 1994, including "Division, War, and Reconciliation, 1855–1865."

The Big Idea for the chapter and how the main ideas in each section relate to the Big Idea are graphically displayed below. Comprehension of this chapter's Big Idea is critical to students' understanding of United States history and how we as a nation got where we are today.

Media and Technology

 The Way it Works, H-11

 Historical Maps, L-3

 Visions of America: History Might Not Have Happened This Way Game

 Cause and Effect, F-5; Graphic Organizer, G-5

 Guided Reading Audiotapes (English and Spanish)

 Computer Test Bank

For the Student

Holzer, Harold, ed. *Dear Mr. Lincoln: Letters to the President.* Addison-Wesley, 1993. (Letters from ordinary people.)

Neely, Mark E., Jr. *The Last Best Hope of Earth: Abraham Lincoln and the Promise of America.* Harvard University Press, 1993. (Compact study of Lincoln, the politician, by a Pulitzer Prize–winning author.)

Thompson, R. L. *Wiring a Continent: The History of the Telegraph Industry in the United States, 1832–1866.* Ayer Company Publishers, 1972.

CHAPTER 11

The middle of the nineteenth century was a time of deep distrust and escalating hostility between the North and the South. Many Americans no longer believed that the federal government could settle their differences, and the Union, the unified nation, finally shattered.

SECTION 1

In the 1850s the slavery issue and other differences caused increasing numbers of Americans to view the North and the South as two distinct regions. Each side began to view the other as a threat to its way of life.

SECTION 2

When existing political organizations failed to address the question of slavery and other pressing issues of the times, new political parties arose aimed at solving the nation's problems.

SECTION 3

Between 1856 and 1860, a series of violent clashes between antislavery and proslavery forces heightened the tension between the North and the South, and the nation moved closer to war.

SECTION 4

When southern states refused to accept the election of Abraham Lincoln as President, the Union finally failed, and civil war broke out.

The Coming of the Civil War
1848–1861

The Relevance of the Big Idea

In the mid-1800s, the northern and southern regions of the United States were so deeply divided that the democratic process fell apart and Americans embarked on a bloody civil war.

To help students understand the success of the United States as a union in the 1990s, ask them to consider how the United States government works to ensure the balance of regional and national interests. Ask students if there are any current national issues that they think are as divisive as those that caused the Civil War.

In Depth

Global Connections

In 1848 revolutions in many European countries quickly spread, causing many European citizens to move to the United States. German student Carl Schurz was part of this "first migration." He looked to America as "a new world, a free world, a world of great ideas and aims." Upon arrival, Schurz worked for reform movements, including abolition. He distinguished himself as a Civil War general and a senator from Wisconsin.

CHAPTER 11

The Coming of the Civil War
1848–1861

By the 1850s, deep distrust divided northerners and southerners. Worse still, many Americans no longer believed that government could settle their differences. Under the strain of conflict between North and South, the great web of law, compromise, and tradition that had held the United States together for over seventy years snapped. The nation broke apart and began its darkest and most painful trial: the Civil War.

Events in the United States

Events in the World

	1848	1850	1852	1854

Events in the United States:
- 1850 Congress passes the Compromise of 1850. • Senator John Calhoun dies.
- 1852 Harriet Beecher Stowe's Uncle Tom's Cabin becomes an instant best-seller.
- 1854 The American, or Know Nothing, party is formed.

Events in the World:
- 1848 Revolutions sweep Europe. • Franz Josef becomes Emperor of Austria.
- 1850 The Taiping Rebellion begins in China.
- 1851 The Great Exhibition is held at the Crystal Palace in London.
- 1852 The South African Republic is established.
- 1853 The Crimean War begins between Turkey and Russia.

 RESOURCE DIRECTORY

Teaching Resources

Alternate Lesson Plan: Demonstrating the Big Idea found in the Alternate Lesson Plans folder, p. 53, provides a lesson strategy to instruct students about the Big Idea that the middle of the nineteenth century saw an increasing hostility between the North and the South, which ultimately led to the Civil War.

Alternative Assessment Handbook provides information, guidance, and strategies for alternative methods of assessment. It includes an essay on new trends in assessment, guidance and strategies for developing performance tasks and portfolios, scoring rubrics, and sample evaluation forms.

Pages 298–302

Two Nations?

In the 1850s growing numbers of Americans were convinced that the North and South were moving in different directions. Each side saw the other as a threat to the American way of life.

 Pages 303–309

New Political Parties

A compromise during the 1850s failed to end disagreement over slavery in the territories. Meanwhile the second American party system broke down as new political parties arose, aimed at solving the challenging issues of the time.

 Pages 311–315

The System Fails

A series of violent clashes between antislavery and proslavery forces between 1856 and 1860 brought the United States to the boiling point. Americans on each side of the slavery issue became convinced that the other side was acting against law and morality.

 Pages 318–321

A Nation Divided Against Itself

Secession spread like wildfire through the southern states when Abraham Lincoln captured the presidency. While politicians and the people debated how to respond, the first shots were fired, and the broken nation plunged into war.

1856 Debate over slavery erupts into violence in Kansas.

1857 The Supreme Court supports slave owners in the Dred Scott decision.

1859 John Brown, abolitionist, leads a raid against Harpers Ferry, Virginia.

1860 Republican Abraham Lincoln is elected United States President.
• South Carolina secedes from the Union.

1861 The bombardment of Fort Sumter signals the start of the Civil War.

1856	1858	1860	1862	1864

1857 Indian soldiers revolt against the British in the Sepoy Rebellion.

1860 English novelist George Eliot publishes The Mill on the Floss.

1863 The open hearth process for producing steel is developed in France.

Alternative Assessment

As an ongoing chapter project, students can assume the role of historians and explain reasons for the coming of the Civil War. The objective is to chart the growing tension and hostility of the times. Students should conduct research, which may include examining documents and published sources, and visiting a historical museum with an exhibit on the Civil War. Suggestions follow, but students may design the projects in a variety of ways.

• Create and interpret an arrangement of mock artifacts. This may include posters, handbills, newspaper pages, or reproductions of objects associated with pro- and antislavery forces.

• Make an audiotape of simulated interviews with notable figures and common people from the times, and draw conclusions from their comments.

• Develop a historical comic book, that is, a series of sketches accompanied by annotated captions.

Explain that finished projects will be assessed according to the following standards:

• **Unacceptable** Projects are not attempted or fail to meet requirements outlined.

• **Limited/Acceptable** Projects are based on material from the textbook and reflect an effort to show connections among topics.

• **Extensive/Commendable** Projects are based on some outside research and indicate general relationships among topics.

• **Extraordinary/Outstanding** Projects are based on considerable outside research, show specific relationships among topics, and exhibit a high degree of creativity.

For more information and guidance on alternative assessment trends and strategies, see the Alternative Assessment Handbook in the Resource Directory on page 296.

Two Nations?

Connecting to the Big Idea

See page 296B. Explain that in the 1850s, differences between the North and the South increasingly polarized the two regions. Ask what the key differences between the North and the South were.

Objectives

● Describe the different opinions historians hold about the inevitability of the Civil War.

● Explain the effect *Uncle Tom's Cabin* had on northerners.

● Explain how southern thinkers and politicians viewed the relationship between northern capitalists and their workers.

● Describe the deep material differences between the North and the South that contributed to the growing gulf between them.

Bellringer

Ask students to discuss what they know about differences that may exist among regions in the United States today. What effect might these differences have on the nation as a whole?

Reading Strategy

Reading for Evidence Ask students to find and list evidence as they read the section supporting the belief that the differences between the North and the South were so great that these two regions were really distinct nations within the United States.

Two Nations?

SECTION PREVIEW

In the 1850s growing numbers of Americans were convinced that the North and South were moving in different directions. Each side saw the other as a threat to the American way of life.

Key Concepts

• Some historians believe that serious conflict between the North and the South was unavoidable, while others believe better leadership might have prevented it.

• *Uncle Tom's Cabin* helped convince northerners that slavery was immoral and a threat to middle-class families and character.

• Southerners charged that northern capitalists exploited their workers.

• Material differences between the North and South contributed to the growing gulf between these sections.

Key Terms, People, and Places

Civil War, Union; Harriet Beecher Stowe, George Fitzhugh

A spool of thread spun in a mill and a boll of raw cotton symbolize the difference between the industrial power of the North and the agricultural strength of the South in the 1850s.

B etween 1861 and 1865, the southern and northern states clashed with one another in a violent conflict that Americans call the **Civil War.** The result of the war would decide whether the **Union,** as the unified nation was called, would continue unbroken or be shattered forever. This war continually sparks our interest because it is the only time in our history when Americans became so frustrated and disillusioned with their political and legal systems that they saw war as the only way to resolve their differences.

Historians and the Civil War

Some historians have suggested that the Civil War could have been avoided. If the United States had elected better leaders and established stronger political institutions, they believe, wild-eyed extremists on both sides would never have been able to force the nation into war. The reason most of these historians believe that the differences between North and South could have been settled is that they think American society in the middle of the 1800s was relatively similar everywhere. They emphasize that whether in Alabama, Oregon, Indiana, or Massachusetts, Americans were all essentially capitalists who believed strongly in democracy in all areas of life.

Other historians—especially more recent ones—do not accept the idea that American society was similar everywhere. They tend to emphasize differences, including differences between regions, racial groups, and classes in society. These historians do not claim that the actual events of the Civil War could only have happened in one particular way. But because they focus on differences, they believe that the North and South were going in such different directions before 1860 that some kind of major conflict was bound to happen.

This textbook combines both views. While the text has stressed the general commitment of Americans to democratic government, social equality, and capitalism (see Chapters 4, 5, 6, and 7), it has also pointed out growing regional differences in economic and social structures (see Chapters 8, 9, and 10).

Many Americans during the early 1800s noticed the differences between North and South. They said that the two great sections amounted to distinct nations within the United States. And the key difference between North and South—to which all the other differences were connected in some way—was slavery. It was certainly true that nearly all white Americans, including many white abolitionists, were deeply prejudiced against African Americans, believing them to be inferior to white Americans. But prejudiced or not, by the 1850s many

---

 RESOURCE DIRECTORY

Teaching Resources

Reproducible Lesson Plan found in the Unit 4 folder, p. 3, provides a summary of the Section 1 lesson plan content.

Alternate Lesson Plan: Learning Styles found in the Alternate Lesson Plans folder, p. 54, guides students in preparing a graphic organizer to identify differences between North and South before the Civil War, and is especially effective for visual learners.

Guided Reading and Review found in the Unit 4 folder, p. 7, provides a structure for reading and mastering the key concepts and reviewing the key terms for Section 1. (Guided Practice)

Literature Activity An Antislavery Best-Seller, found in the Unit 4 folder, pp. 26–27, uses an excerpt from Harriet Beecher Stowe's novel *Uncle Tom's Cabin* to show how a work of popular literature can influence public opinion.

Christian Americans had become convinced that slavery violated the basic principles not only of the United States but also of the Christian religion. These people were mostly members of the middle class who belonged to the highly democratic Protestant faiths that had been on the rise since the Second Great Awakening. They strongly believed an individual should be able to make choices and develop character. For them, therefore, slavery was simply an evil that could not be tolerated.

The troops that struggled on both sides when the Civil War began were *not* fighting to end slavery or to save it. They were fighting about whether the South would remain part of the United States. Yet the issue of slavery was one of the main differences between North and South that brought on the war.

Uncle Tom's Cabin and the Case Against the South

Without question, the most popular statement about the impact of slavery on white Americans both in this world and the next was a novel by **Harriet Beecher Stowe,** the sister of Catharine Beecher. This book, *Uncle Tom's Cabin,* was published in 1852 and became an instant bestseller. With over 300,000 copies in print in the first year of publication, it sold millions and was translated into twenty languages.

Today, many readers are offended by Stowe's portraits of the enslaved Uncle Tom and his wife, Aunt Chloe. Stowe seems to us to have been condescending and biased in describing them. In fact, "Uncle Tom" has become an insulting nickname for an African American man who passively accepts unequal status. But Stowe intended to portray Uncle Tom as a Christian man: he was simple, passive, and nonthreatening. Her Uncle Tom was

a large, broad-chested, powerfully made man, of a full glossy black, and a face whose truly African features were characterized by an expression of grave and steady good sense, united with much kindliness and benevolence [goodwill]. *There was something about his whole air, self-*

respecting and dignified, yet united with a confiding and humble simplicity.

Because there was no reason to fear such a person, the brutal treatment Uncle Tom received from his master seemed all the more intolerable.

But Stowe did not depend only on the sharp contrast between a kindly enslaved person and his cruel master to make her case against slavery. She also tried to show that slavery was opposed to ideals many northerners cherished: the cult of domesticity, or the importance of women to society, and the ideal of the family. In the novel, the neat, orderly world of Uncle Tom's cabin, formed around his happy family, comes to a tragic end when Uncle Tom's owner has to sell him. Eventually Uncle Tom falls into the hands of another slaveholder, Simon Legree.

By contrast with the saintly Uncle Tom, Simon Legree is everything Stowe's audience in the North feared and despised: an unmarried, anti-Christian, heavy-drinking brute who cares only about satisfying his desires and his greed. Not only does he brutalize the enslaved women of his plantation, but in the end he beats Uncle Tom to death with a whip. It was not a mistake that Stowe made Legree a northerner who lived in the South. She wanted to show how slavery could corrupt even those born outside the system.

To balance these stark images of the

Harriet Beecher Stowe's novel *Uncle Tom's Cabin* offered antislavery forces new encouragement in resisting the slavery system. It inspired songs, plays, a card game, and a children's version (top). An African American family, the Webbs (bottom), toured the North reading the book to audiences.

2. INSTRUCT

Explain/Discuss
Review the economies of the North and the South as discussed in Chapter 8. Ask students to compare the two regions in terms of their economic and material differences. Discuss the way in which slavery divided the North and the South. Ask why so many northerners found slavery morally offensive. Why did southerners accuse northerners of hypocrisy regarding slavery?

Analyze
Have students analyze the roots of the conflict between the North and the South. Why might it be said that slavery was a lightning rod for larger issues between the two regions? Despite their differences, did Americans living in the North and the South share enough basic values, such as the belief in democracy and capitalism, to have been able to avoid the Civil War had the political leadership of the nation been more effective? Explain.

In Depth

Biography

Harriet Beecher Stowe (1811–1896), author of *Uncle Tom's Cabin,* lived in the shadow of two famous men in her family—her father, the Calvinist minister Lyman Beecher, and her brother Henry Ward Beecher, an outspoken and well-known clergyman and orator. Her father wrote to a friend, "Hattie is a genius. I would give a hundred dollars if she was a boy."

Activity

Teaching Heterogeneous Groups

In 1852, the publication of *Uncle Tom's Cabin* ignited the antislavery movement. The author, Harriet Beecher Stowe, created one character who evoked sympathy and a contrasting, despicable character. To assist students in understanding both sides of the Civil War issue, divide the class into small groups. Ask each group to come up with a theme for a book and to create two main characters who would evoke the reader's sympathies toward the South.

Enrichment

Railroads played a central role in widening the economic gap between the North and the South. Later they also played a leading part in the war that erupted between the two regions. Ask students to research the development of railroads in the United States and to draw a map showing the routes of the major railroads in both North and South in the 1850s.

Answer to ...

(See page 301.) Northerners might argue that the Declaration of Independence stated that all men were created equal with certain unalienable rights, which slavery clearly violated; Southerners might point to the statement that people have the right to abolish or alter their government if it does not secure their rights of life, liberty, and the pursuit of happiness, which they might argue included a right to hold slaves.

immoral effects of slavery, Stowe wrote powerful scenes in which northern women influence their husbands to do what is right. Thus she brought the controversy over slavery into the confines of the home, which she saw as the woman's sphere. For instance, in one scene set in a house in Ohio, a wife persuades her husband, a senator, to take no action to prevent some runaway enslaved people from continuing their escape to Canada. When her husband tries to "reason" with her, she replies,

> I don't know anything about politics, but I can read my Bible; and there I see that I must feed the hungry, clothe the naked, and comfort the desolate; and that Bible I mean to follow.

Her husband argues that to help runaway enslaved people would involve breaking the law. But the wife steadily replies:

> Obeying God never brings on public evils. I know it can't. It's always safest, all round, to do as He bids us.

Although it was fiction, Stowe's book had as powerful an effect in her time as Thomas Paine's *Common Sense* had in his. It presented northern readers with a single, vivid picture of both slavery and the South that they could understand and adopt as accurate, even if it was in fact exaggerated. As they sat in the privacy of their parlors reading *Uncle Tom's Cabin*, many northerners became convinced that slavery would be the ruin of the United States. They worried not just about the impact of slavery on African Americans, but about its impact on whites and American society in general. Of this they were sure: they would never allow the United States to become a land full of Simon Legrees.

Cannibals All! and the Case Against the North

While immensely popular in the North, *Uncle Tom's Cabin* was virtually banned in the South. Southern intellectuals and politicians saw it as a book of insulting lies. They admitted that there were some masters who treated enslaved people badly. But the South was hardly home to thousands of Legrees. White southerners had their own exaggerated view of slavery: to them, plantation households were like happy patriarchal families. ✪

But southerners did more than protest what they saw as northern insults. Many began to justify the South and attack the evils they saw in the North. They claimed that most planters took a personal interest in the welfare of the enslaved people who labored for them, providing them with the basic necessities of life. Industrialists, on the other hand, took no personal responsibility for workers and did not care that the meager wages workers were paid could not buy decent food, clothing, and shelter. Most southerners

Southern writers promoted the myth that slavery "raised Africans from savagery" and "civilized" them. These before-and-after pictures are from a pamphlet titled *Bible Defence of Slavery.*

THE NEGRO IN HIS OWN COUNTRY.

THE NEGRO IN AMERICA.

▶ RESOURCE DIRECTORY

Teaching Resources

✪ **Literature Activity** A Poem in Defense of Slavery, found in the Unit 4 folder, p. 28, uses a poem by William J. Grayson of South Carolina to illustrate some of the arguments used in the defense of slavery.

believed that northerners were so intent on making a profit that they had no concern whatever for the human needs of their workers.

Perhaps the most direct statement of this point of view appeared in a book by **George Fitzhugh** published in 1857, titled *Cannibals All!* Attacking northern industrialists, whom he saw as no better than cannibals, Fitzhugh wrote:

Y*ou, with the command over labor which your capital gives you, are a slave owner—a master, without the obligations of a master. They who work for you, who create your income, are slaves, without the rights of slaves. Slaves without a master!*

Outraged by the hypocrisy of antislavery northerners, Fitzhugh exclaimed:

W*hat is falsely called Free Society is a very recent invention. It proposes to make the weak, ignorant, and poor, free, by turning them loose in a world owned exclusively by the few (whom nature and education have made strong and whom property has made stronger) to get a living.*

White southerners argued that they were the true heirs of the American Revolution. They believed that their patriarchal households possessed an order, a grace, a sense of liberty, that Bible-thumping, middle-class reformers and capitalists could not begin to understand. On this point southerners were agreed: they were not about to let northerners, whom they saw as self-righteous, tell them how to live.

MAKING CONNECTIONS

Suggest how the North might use the Declaration of Independence to argue for ending slavery and the South might use it to argue for resisting northern interference.

Material Differences Between North and South

The differences between North and South were not simply a product of exaggerated fiction

Though the North was still largely a land of farms, increasingly its landscape resembled this late-1850s print of Bridgewater, Massachusetts, in which a thundering train passes smoking forges casting metal goods and machinery.

and propaganda. Hard facts also told the story. They showed that the North was becoming still more urban, still more industrial than the South. Its population, two and a half times as large as the population of the South, was becoming even larger and more diverse, as Irish and German immigrants crowded into swelling cities. Of the ten largest cities in the United States in 1860, nine were located in the North.

Like immigration, new technology had a heavier impact on the North than on the South. The biggest technological change was the appearance of railroads. Railroads, developed in Great Britain in the 1820s, were the quickest, most efficient form of transportation the world had ever known. They made canals pointless in a matter of years.

By 1840 about 3,000 miles of track spanned the United States. African American and Irish immigrant workers added another 5,000 miles during the 1840s. It was in the 1850s, however, that the railroads truly came into their own. Over 20,000 miles were laid in that decade.

During this railroad boom, remote places suddenly became the centers of bustling commerce. The small trading village of Chicago grew incredibly. Why? Because railroads made Chicago a central location through which people both to the east and to the west shipped goods such as corn, wheat, and other cereals.

The railroads, however, primarily affected the North. In 1860 the North had 70 percent of the railroad tracks in the United States. The

Media and Technology

 Transparency
The Way It Works, H-11

3. ASSESS

Section 1 Review Answers

1. (a) Civil War, see p. 298, (b) Union, see p. 298

2. Harriet Beecher Stowe, see p. 299

3. Some historians believe that the Civil War could have been avoided if the United States had had better leaders and stronger political institutions. Others, emphasizing the substantial differences between North and South, believe that the conflict was bound to happen.

4. It presented a picture of slavery and the South vivid enough to convince northerners that slavery would be the ruin of the United States.

5. Fitzhugh claimed that northern industrialists took no personal responsibility for their workers and did not care that the meager wages they paid them were not enough to buy decent food, clothing, and shelter. He claimed that northerners were so intent on making a profit that they had no concern whatever for human needs.

6. The North was more urban and industrial. It had a larger population, it had benefited more from new technology, it had more factories and produced more goods.

7. Answers may suggest that as capitalists, both industrialists and slave owners used labor to benefit themselves first, generally supplying the needs of their enslaved people and wage laborers only insofar as it was necessary to keep them working. Conditions among the working poor in the North were terrible, just as were conditions among enslaved people in the South.

Ask students to write two or three sentences in each case explaining how the following topics divided the North and the South: slavery, type of economy, technology.

Answer to ...

The slavery system might have collapsed by itself had southern planters not been dependent on slave labor to produce profits.

Reinforcing the Big Idea

Despite their common political roots, by the 1850s more and more Americans saw the North and the South as two distinct regions with very different values, especially concerning slavery. The next section discusses the new political parties that arose on either side of the issues that divided the nation.

In Depth

Then and Now

The telegraph made it possible for American newspapers to pool their resources into the first wire service, the Associated Press of New York, now known as the Associated Press. During the Civil War (see Chapter 12) telegraph lines were often cut or news transmissions replaced by military bulletins. To get their stories across before interruption, reporters would stack a complete summary of the story in the lead paragraph. This style of news writing, called the *inverted pyramid,* is still in modified use today.

| 1650 | 1700 | 1750 | 1800 | **Links Across Time** | 1850 | 1900 | 1950 | 2000 |

Picking Cotton: Humans vs. Machines

Picking cotton by hand (immediate right, in a photograph from the 1800s) required many workers. Modern mechanical cotton harvesters (far right) need only a few operators. *How might the slavery system have been affected if harvesting machines had been available to pick cotton in the early 1800s?*

South had tracks, and they produced great cities such as Atlanta, Georgia. But southern planters and farmers still tended to rely on transportation by water for their staple crops.

Like the railroad, another invention, the telegraph, also magnified differences between North and South. This early form of electronic communication allowed people to send messages over wire by means of coded pulses of electricity. Because telegraph wires were strung along the ever-growing network of railroad tracks, the communications revolution in the North advanced more quickly than in the South.

Railroads and improved communications nourished the booming industries of the North. In 1860 the North had 110,000 factories, compared to 20,000 in the South; it produced $1.5 billion worth of goods, compared to the South's $155 million. In fact, in terms of numbers, the South outdid the North in only two notable ways: it had more enslaved people and it had more cotton.

Unquestionably, in 1860 the North and the South had much in common. They both had been born in the same revolution and cherished that tradition. They both believed in and practiced capitalism. Even on the issue of the status of African Americans, whites in both North and South displayed tremendous prejudice. But despite these similarities, they differed greatly in their beliefs about what American society should be.

SECTION 1 REVIEW

Key Terms, People, and Places
1. Define (a) Civil War, (b) Union.
2. Identify Harriet Beecher Stowe.

Key Concepts
3. Describe the two main views historians hold about the causes of the Civil War.
4. What effect did *Uncle Tom's Cabin* have on northern views of slavery?

5. Describe George Fitzhugh's criticism of northern capitalists.
6. Describe the material differences that had arisen between the North and the South by 1860.

Critical Thinking
7. **Checking Consistency** Northerners and southerners each accused the other of exploiting labor. Explain how both sides were guilty of this practice.

RESOURCE DIRECTORY

Teaching Resources

Quiz found in the Unit 4 folder, p. 8, covers the main ideas in this section as well as the key terms.

New Political Parties

SECTION PREVIEW

A compromise during the 1850s failed to end disagreement over slavery in the territories. Meanwhile the second American party system broke down as new political parties arose, aimed at solving the challenging issues of the time.

Key Concepts

- Because it failed to deal with the real problem, the Compromise of 1850 was only a temporary solution to the problem of slavery in the territories.
- In the early 1850s, the second American party system came to an end as Americans abandoned the Whig party because it no longer addressed pressing issues.
- In the North, a tremendous increase in immigrants led frightened middle-class and working-class Americans to join new political parties to protect their interests.
- The Kansas-Nebraska Act of 1854 established that the people of those territories could decide for themselves whether they would have slavery.
- The Republicans won voters by campaigning against both immigrants and slavery.

Key Terms, People, and Places

Compromise of 1850, Fugitive Slave Act, states' rights, nativism, naturalization, Kansas-Nebraska Act, the Slave Power; Democratic party, American party, Know Nothings, Stephen Douglas, Republican party

---

S o what if there were differences between North and South? Certainly the differences were bound to cause conflict, but did they have to lead to a four-year war that would kill hundreds of thousands of people? The answer to this question requires an understanding of politics in the 1850s. The war came *when* it did and *how* it did because politicians could not resolve the question of slavery. The rest of this chapter explains that political breakdown.

The Compromise of 1850

Politicians might have been able to keep slavery from tearing the nation apart if Americans had not conquered the trans-Mississippi West. This newly acquired land forced an old question back into politics. That question, first raised by the Missouri Compromise of 1820, was whether or not slavery would be allowed in the territories.

The Slavery Question Grows Heated In theory, the Missouri Compromise had taken care of this problem by establishing 36° 30' N latitude as a permanent boundary between free and slave states. But northerners were unwilling to accept this boundary after the United States acquired a large part of Mexico in the Mexican War. They feared that the new territory would be divided into several slave states, thus giving the South a majority vote in the United States Senate and perhaps in the Electoral College.

Southerners were equally firm in insisting that the national government had no business telling its free citizens they could not take their property to the territories if they wanted to. And property, after all, was what they considered enslaved people to be.

After the Treaty of Guadalupe Hidalgo, the issue of slavery in the territories grew more and more controversial. Though tempers flared and threats flew, Whigs and Jacksonian leaders tried to downplay the issue. Zachary Taylor, a Whig, was elected President in 1848 by avoiding any discussion of slavery in his campaign.

A banner of one of the new political parties of the 1850s—the Republicans—shows John Frémont, candidate for President in 1856, and proclaims the Republicans' refusal to allow slavery in the territories.

Connecting to the Big Idea

See page 296B. Explain to students that existing political organizations in the 1850s failed to deal with the question of slavery. New political parties emerged. Ask what these political parties were. How did they address the issues of the day?

Objectives

- Explain why the Compromise of 1850 was only a temporary solution to the problem of slavery in the territories.
- Describe why the second American party system came to an end in the early 1850s.
- Explain why northerners from the middle and working classes joined new political parties.
- Describe the Kansas-Nebraska Act of 1854.
- Explain how Republicans won voters over to their point of view.

Bellringer

Ask students whether, considering past efforts to compromise on the slavery issue, it was reasonable to expect that the Compromise of 1850 would continue to maintain peace in the United States. Why or why not?

Reading Strategy

Question Writing Have students read the section's main headings and then write a question based on each, filling in the answers as they read.

📄 **Reproducible Lesson Plan** found in the Unit 4 folder, p. 4, provides a summary of the Section 2 lesson plan content.

📄 **Alternate Lesson Plan: Cooperative Learning** found in the Alternate Lesson Plans folder, p. 55, provides a structure for groups of students to prepare oral presentations reflecting the political views of different segments of the American population in 1856.

📄 **Guided Reading and Review** found in the Unit 4 folder, p. 9, provides a structure for reading and mastering the key concepts and reviewing the key terms for Section 2. (Guided Practice)

Explain/Discuss

Discuss with students the inability of politicians to deal with the slavery question. Why were they so ineffective in solving this important issue?

Discuss attempts to end the crisis between the North and the South over slavery. Ask why the Compromise of 1850 provided only a temporary solution to the problem of slavery. What were the reasons Senator John C. Calhoun thought it was impossible for southern interests to be protected by the existing government? How were both northerners and southerners able to justify their stand on slavery in terms of the United States Constitution? Why did the Kansas-Nebraska Act outrage northerners?

Caption Answer to ...

 Interpreting Tables

Slavery was the issue addressed in the Compromise of 1850.

 In Depth

Multicultural Perspectives

The Fugitive Slave Law angered and terrified free African Americans in the North. It permitted the capture not only of newly escaped slaves but of anyone who had ever fled from slavery. Any African American accused of being a fugitive slave had to stand trial before a special commissioner, not a judge. No jury heard the case, and the accused could not testify. Furthermore, the commissioner received a $10 fee for sending the accused back to slavery and only $5 for freeing the person.

But after Taylor died in 1850, President Millard Fillmore found the slavery issue unavoidable. Americans had been thronging into California, especially after the gold rush of 1849, and some decision about slavery there had to be made. In 1850, Fillmore and Congress struggled to put together a deal between the two rival parts of the nation.

A Solution Is Proposed This package of laws, called the **Compromise of 1850,** was designed to balance the interests of the two sections, North and South. The table at right lists the provisions of the compromise. Under the proposal, Congress would admit California as a free state; in return, the people of the territories of New Mexico and Utah were to decide for themselves whether slavery would be legal. Congress also would abolish the sale of enslaved people, but not slavery itself, in Washington, D.C. To win southern approval for this change, the compromise also called for Congress to pass the **Fugitive Slave Act.** This law ordered all citizens of the United States to assist in the return of enslaved people who had escaped from their

owners. It also denied a jury trial to enslaved people who had escaped. ★

Debate over the compromise dragged on for months. On March 4, 1850, the United States Senate gathered to hear the opinion of John C. Calhoun of South Carolina. As it turned out, Calhoun's speech was one of the great summaries of the southern view of the crisis.

The Compromise of 1850

Admitted California as a free state
Allowed citizens in New Mexico and Utah territories to determine for themselves the legal status of slavery
Abolished the sale of enslaved people, but not slavery itself, in Washington, D.C.
Passed the Fugitive Slave Act, which required all citizens to assist in the return of enslaved persons who had escaped from their owners and which denied jury trials to runaways

Interpreting Tables
The Compromise of 1850 was not one but several laws, all of which dealt in various ways with a common issue. *What was that issue?*

During the debate that led to the Compromise of 1850, all the great speakers of Congress had their say. Among them was Henry Clay, shown here in February 1850 as he warned that a failure to compromise would lead to "furious" and "bloody" war.

 RESOURCE DIRECTORY

Teaching Resources

★ **Visual Learning Activity** Anthony Burns and the Fugitive Slave Law, found in the Unit 4 folder, p. 29, features contemporary sketches depicting the escape of Anthony Burns and his subsequent return to slavery as a result of the Fugitive Slave Act of 1850.

AMERICAN PROFILES

John C. Calhoun

Many in the Senate felt great emotion when it was Calhoun's turn to present his views. Everyone knew that the senator was ill and that he probably did not have long to live. So weak was he that he asked James Mason of Virginia to read his speech. But even fading away, Calhoun was still one of the most respected members of the Senate, and people waited in suspense to hear what he had written.

A Champion of the South
Born on March 18 in 1782, the sixty-seven-year-old John Caldwell Calhoun had devoted much of his public life to South Carolina and the United States. For four decades, he had been one of the towering figures in Washington, the equal of Henry Clay and Andrew Jackson. Member of the House of Representatives (1811–1817), secretary of war (1817–1824), Vice President of the United States (1825–1832), secretary of state (1844–1845), and senator (1832–1843, 1845–1850), Calhoun was deeply committed to the Union.

Devoted though he was to the United States, Calhoun was even more devoted to his principles. He had once written:

My politics, I think I may say with perfect truth, has . . . been founded on certain fixed principles; and to carry them into effect has been my highest ambition.

One of Calhoun's principles was a belief in liberty and in fighting anything that threatened it. In the 1820s, it became clear to Calhoun that control of the United States government by the North was a threat to the southern way of life and to liberty as he understood it. Though trained as a lawyer, he was also a gentleman planter and the owner of Fort Hill, a 500-acre plantation in South Carolina and the home of about seventy enslaved people. Therefore Calhoun worked tirelessly throughout the 1830s and 1840s to protect slavery and to keep the North from controlling the federal government. He had great influence among those who believed in **states' rights.** According to this theory, states have the right to nullify acts of the federal government and even to leave the Union if they wish to do so.

"The Greatest and the Gravest Question"
As the speech began, Calhoun—through Senator Mason—stated the problem the nation faced.

I have, Senators, believed from the first that . . . the subject of slavery would, if not prevented by some timely and effective measure, end in disunion [of the United States]. . . . It has reached a point when it can no longer be disguised or denied that the Union is in danger. You have thus had forced upon you the greatest and the gravest question that can ever come under your consideration: How can the Union be preserved?

The "great and primary" cause of the crisis, Calhoun said, was that the North now had

the exclusive power of controlling the Government, which leaves the [South] without any adequate means of protecting itself against . . . encroachment and oppression.

Calhoun was certainly right about this. Over the years, the North had indeed gained power—not only through its greater wealth, but also through its larger population, which gave it more representatives in Congress and more votes in the Electoral College. It also had gained a new understanding of the principle of liberty. Many of its residents no longer would tolerate slavery in any state. Both North and South were now accusing each other of betraying basic American principles, including liberty, unity, and the sharing of power among the states.

The South—Upholder of the Constitution
In his speech, Calhoun made clear that the

Using Historical Evidence John C. Calhoun (left) was once called "the cast iron man." *Find Calhoun in the painting on page 304 by comparing that picture with this portrait.*

Analyze
Have students analyze the end of the second party system and the rise of new political parties. Ask students what Rutherford B. Hayes meant when he said, "Politics is no longer the topic of this country. Its important questions are settled."

Caption Answer to . . .

Using Historical Evidence

Calhoun is to the right of the chair of the president of the Senate.

In Depth

Did You Know?

Photographer Mathew Brady (1826–1896), the son of Irish immigrants, is best known for his "on the spot" studies of the Civil War (see Chapter 12). But by 1844, when he opened a studio in New York City, he was already well known for his portraits of visiting celebrities—including Britain's Prince of Wales and many famous Americans. In 1861, Brady published a portfolio entitled *Gallery of Illustrious Americans,* containing studies of Henry Clay and Daniel Webster and the portrait of John C. Calhoun on this page. Over a fifty-year span, Brady photographed every President from John Quincy Adams to William McKinley, including Abraham Lincoln, his favorite study. More than five thousand of Brady's negatives are now stored in the Library of Congress.

Activity

Writing a Political Slogan for the Know Nothings

Ask students to summarize the political position of the American party (Know Nothings) and to write a campaign slogan for Millard Fillmore, the party's candidate, in the 1856 presidential elections.

Enrichment

The Underground Railroad, a system that helped thousands of enslaved people escape to the North and Canada during the mid-1800s, contributed to the hostility between North and South and encouraged the passage of laws like the Fugitive Slave Law. Have students research how the Underground Railroad operated and share their findings with the class.

South did not want to part ways with the North. But he also stated that the South would not give up its liberty to save the Union:

> The South asks for justice, simple justice, and less she ought not to take. She has no compromise to offer, but the Constitution; and no concession or surrender to make.

Today Americans believe that slavery is morally wrong, because it robs people of their liberty. Calhoun and other white southern planters believed that *stopping* slavery was morally wrong, because it interfered with their liberty to own enslaved people as property. And government, they believed, should protect this basic liberty. Southern planters believed that if the federal government intended to reduce their rights or threaten their property, then it was no longer a government worthy of their respect. From the point of view of Calhoun, it was the northern section of the country, not the southern section, which was twisting the Constitution and the intentions of the Framers. The ringing finale of his speech made this clear:

> I have exerted myself . . . with the intention of saving the Union, if it could be done; and if it could not, [with saving] the section . . . which I sincerely believe has justice and the Constitution on its side.

Although Calhoun warned that the crisis required more drastic measures than mere compromise, his speech did not persuade members from the North. Congress eventually passed the Compromise of 1850.

As Calhoun had foreseen, southerners were not satisfied with the compromise, although the legislation did bring a brief calm to the nation. In reality, it solved nothing beyond determining that California would be a free state. Part of the compromise, the Fugitive Slave Act, actually made the situation worse by infuriating many northerners—including Harriet Beecher Stowe, who expressed her outrage in *Uncle Tom's Cabin.*

Less than a month after Mason read Calhoun's speech on the floor of the Senate, John

Calhoun was dead. His prophetic words and his death proved a fateful beginning for the decade of the 1850s—a time when politics in the United States changed dramatically.

The End of the Second Party System

During the early 1850s, the second American party system broke down. True, the **Democratic party** remained, the descendant of the Jeffersonian Democrat-Republicans and the Jacksonian Democrats. The Democratic party has survived many periods of crisis like the early 1850s because it has always been a collection of diverse groups. But the Whig party was not so diverse, and by the end of the 1850s it had largely disappeared. The slavery issue badly hurt the Whigs, because many of their northern voters were middle-class evangelical Protestants who were disgusted with the politicians' fondness for compromise.

Another reason the Whigs faded away was that the old issues that had divided political parties in the 1830s now seemed largely resolved. Why argue about banks? The United States was prosperous and expanding. The men at the center of the Jacksonian-Whig struggles—Jackson, Clay, Webster, Calhoun—were either dead or dying. Political parties seemed to be lumbering onward only to keep their hold on government jobs and contracts.

Rutherford B. Hayes, a Whig living in Cincinnati, Ohio, and a future President of the United States, argued in the fall of 1852 that the old parties were irrelevant.

> The real grounds of difference upon important political questions no longer correspond with party lines. . . . Politics is no longer the topic of this country. Its important questions are settled. . . . Government no longer has its ancient importance.

In the election of 1852, won by the indecisive Democrat, Franklin Pierce, a few voters seemed very interested in the outcome. The time had come for a new generation of leaders to come forward, and during the 1850s, they did emerge. Whether they would be able to deal with the new issues facing the nation was another question.

The Rise of the Know Nothings

Slavery and disillusionment with politics were not the only issues that brought down the Whigs. The equally powerful issue of **nativism** also played a part in the end of the party. This was a movement to ensure that people born in the United States, who considered themselves "natives," received better treatment than immigrants. Between 1846 and 1854, close to three million Europeans arrived in the United States. Many middle-class evangelical Protestants were particularly disturbed by the Catholic immigrants among them, most of whom had come from Ireland and Germany.

Dislike of Catholics followed a pattern. Many of the same people who objected to slavery in the South also objected to Catholicism. They knew that the Catholic religion was organized into a hierarchy reaching from churchgoers through priests, bishops, and cardinals, up to the Pope, whose word was law. Protestants believed that this hierarchy did not allow for individual free choice. They worried that "Papal Power"—the power of the Pope—would interfere with the rights of citizens in a democracy.

Fear about immigrants led in 1849 to the formation of a secret nativist society called the Order of the Star-Spangled Banner. Within a few years, its membership totaled around a million. The order insisted on complete secrecy from its members, who used passwords and special handshakes. They always replied to questions about the organization with the answer "I know nothing." In 1854 nativists went public by forming a political organization, the **American party.** It pledged to work against Irish Catholic candidates and for laws requiring a longer wait before immigrants could become citizens through the process of **naturalization.** Because it was closely associated with the Order of the Star-Spangled Banner, the American party came to be called the **Know Nothings.**

Know Nothings claimed that they were committed to "the great work of Americanizing Americans." Strongly opposed to Catholicism, they called on

every American and naturalized protestant citizen throughout the Union, to use his

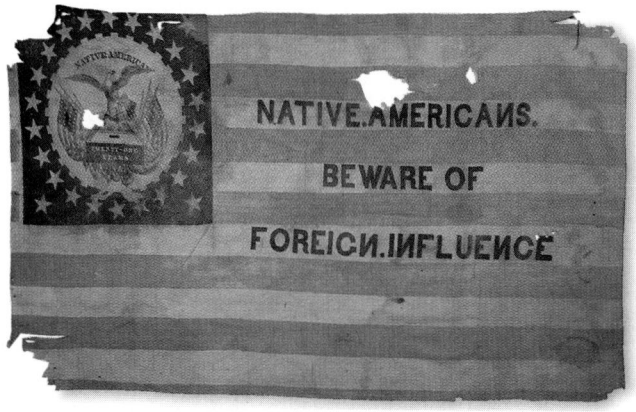

utmost exertions to aid the cause by organizing and freeing the country from that monster [Catholicism] which has long since made its appearance in our midst and is only waiting for the hour to approach to plant its flag of tyranny, persecution, and oppression among us.

The Know Nothings did very well in local elections in northern states. Their main supporters were middle-class Americans worried about the moral impact of immigration, and Protestant working men who were fearful of losing jobs to Irish and German immigrants.

MAKING CONNECTIONS

The term *know-nothingism* also was used later, during the 1900s, to describe a political attitude that included fear of foreigners. What evidence can you offer that this attitude can still be found in the United States today?

The Kansas-Nebraska Act

As if the growing turmoil among the parties was not promising enough trouble for the nation, a Democratic politician again raised the dangerous issue of slavery in the territories. This man, Senator **Stephen Douglas** of Illinois, had two conflicting ambitions. First, he wanted Chicago to benefit from the development of the West. The sooner the territories of Kansas and Nebraska became states, the sooner railroads

The Know Nothings called themselves "Native Americans"—by which they meant Americans born in the United States—and whipped up fears against immigrants.

Answer to ...
MAKING CONNECTIONS

Students may cite occasional violence against immigrants today, government policies that restrict certain types of immigration, or statements by politicians or nativist groups that call for further restrictions on immigration.

In Depth

Did You Know?

The desire to build a railroad all the way across the continent to unite East and West was the American Dream of the 1850s. No American city could hope for a greater prize than to be chosen as the eastern terminus of the nation's transcontinental railway. New Orleans, Memphis, and St. Louis were among many towns competing with Chicago to be selected and so become the bustling headquarters for reaching the wealth and commerce of the West. But Senator Douglas knew that a railroad through the unsettled land of the West could only be built with the aid of government land grants. And these land grants could be made only if the region the railroad passed through was already organized politically and surveyed. With this in mind, Douglas introduced a bill to organize the lands west of Iowa and Missouri—the bill which in its final form provided for a Kansas Territory and a Nebraska Territory.

Section 2 Review Answers

1. (a) Compromise of 1850, see p. 304, (b) Fugitive Slave Act, see p. 304, (c) states' rights, see p. 305, (d) nativism, see p. 307, (e) naturalization, see p. 307, (f) Kansas-Nebraska Act, see p. 308, (g) the Slave Power, see p. 308

2. (a) Democratic party, see p. 306, (b) American party, see p. 307, (c) Know Nothings, see p. 307, (d) Stephen Douglas, see p. 307, (e) Republican party, see p. 308

3. It really addressed only the issue of California, and southerners were not satisfied by it. Stephen Douglas went on to undo the Compromise of 1850 by reopening the issue of slavery in the territories with the Kansas-Nebraska Act.

4. Many Whig voters were disgusted with politicians' fondness for compromise on the slavery issue; the old issues that had divided political parties in the 1830s seemed largely resolved; the politicians of the old system were dead or dying.

5. The issue of nativism.

6. It proposed popular sovereignty.

7. The Republicans adopted the nativist ideas of the American party and drew voters away from that party, making their own party a single powerful force against both slavery and Catholicism.

8. Possible answers: Have one President from the North and one from the South; introduce some kind of veto power for the southern states in Congress; have an equal number of members of Congress from the North and the South.

Reteach

Ask students to write a paragraph summarizing how the failure of politicians to solve the important issues of the day led to the rise of new political parties in the 1850s.

Stephen Douglas champions popular sovereignty in this 1858 cartoon. Douglas believed that slavery in the territories no longer would be a national issue if it were decided by voters in the territories themselves.

could be built across them to link Chicago with the West.

But Douglas also wanted to run for President. To do that, he needed the support of southern Democrats. Pushing statehood for Kansas and Nebraska was not the way to gain supporters in the South, because under the terms of the Missouri Compromise of 1820, Kansas and Nebraska would become free states. The North would then become still more powerful, and southerners would see Douglas as an enemy.

So Douglas tried to score points with both northerners and southerners. His **Kansas-Nebraska Act,** introduced in the United States Senate in January 1854, proclaimed that the people in a territory should decide whether slavery would be allowed there. What Douglas was saying, basically, was that the nation should forget the boundary of 36° 30′ N established by the Missouri Compromise and rely on popular sovereignty. In fact, "popular sovereignty" became a slogan bandied about in the debate over slavery in the territories. As Douglas wrote to a southerner in April 1854:

> The great principle of self-government is at stake, and surely the people of this country are never going to decide that the principle upon which our whole republican system rests is vicious and wrong.

Douglas knew that the Kansas-Nebraska Act would make southerners happy, because it raised the possibility that Kansas and Nebraska might become slave states, which would have been impossible under the Missouri Compromise. But he also figured—incorrectly, as it turned out—that northerners would not object to relying on popular sovereignty to make the decision. He was positive that because agriculture on the Great Plains would not support cotton or slavery, the people of Kansas and Nebraska would peacefully choose to be free states.

Instead of applauding the bill, as Douglas expected, northerners were outraged by it. Northern members of Douglas's own party, the Democrats, denounced Douglas for what they saw as a sellout to **the Slave Power**—the South.

And after Congress passed the Kansas-Nebraska Act, Douglas found out just how wrong he was about a peaceful vote in the territories.

The Rise of the Republican Party

In the uproar over the Kansas-Nebraska Act, the Whig party finally faded from the scene. It had little to offer in the furious debate over slavery. A new organization arose to deal with this very issue. It was the **Republican party,** the direct ancestor of today's party by the same name. While the Know Nothings were against "Papal Power," the Republicans were dedicated to stopping the Slave Power. Yet both believed that Catholics and slaveholders were deliberately working together to destroy American liberty.

The Republicans Gain Support The new Republicans drew their support almost entirely from the North and from Protestant middle-class and working-class voters. The party had several factions. The extremist faction included voters strongly opposed to the Fugitive Slave Act and slavery in the territories. The moderate faction was made up of antislavery voters who wanted to abolish slavery in federal territories but not interfere with the practice where it already existed. Yet another faction was composed of former Whigs still committed to a strong national government that would lead in the development of a national economy. Farmers, professionals, small business owners, craftworkers, hardworking middle-class people—these were the Republicans.

New parties appear frequently in American history. Few last very long. In the mid-1850s, however, the disappearance of the Whigs and the emotional issues of nativism and slavery produced two strong parties, the Know Nothings and the Republicans, competing for the same kinds of voters. The table on page 309 summarizes the views and supporters of these parties, as well as the Democratic party.

In the end, the Republicans survived and the Know Nothings did not. The Republicans succeeded by adopting the nativist ideas of the American party. They drew voters away from the American party, making their own party a single powerful force opposed both to slavery and Catholicism.

 RESOURCE DIRECTORY

Teaching Resources

Political Parties of the 1850s

Party	Views	Supporters
Democrats (North)	Favored deciding issue of slavery in the territories by popular sovereignty	A variety of backgrounds, but particularly northern voters in urban areas and Catholics; some of those born in South who had moved to Old Northwest
Democrats (South)	Favored expanding slavery in territories	Those living in southern areas undergoing growth in economy and population
Republicans	Opposed to slavery, supported nativist movement	People in New England and people born in New England living in the Old Northwest; Protestant English, Scots-Irish immigrants; former American party followers
American Party	Known as "Know Nothings"; anti-Catholic, fearing "Papal Power"; nativist, favoring a longer naturalization period for immigrants; antislavery	Supporters were generally middle-class, northern Protestants born in the United States

 Interpreting Tables
During the 1850s, three major parties jostled for power in the North, but only one major party represented the South. *Why did the Republicans lack support in the South? What views did the Republican party share with the American party that enabled it to win over American party members?*

The Election of 1856 Neither the American party nor the Republican party, however, won the election for President in 1856. The Democratic candidate, James Buchanan, became President, with the backing of southerners. Though an inconsistent politician, Buchanan would do what he could to repay the South for its support. He pledged to stop "the agitation of the slavery issue" in the North.

The American party candidate in the election, former President Millard Fillmore, had little chance of success. He was undistinguished and appealed to few. But the Republican candidate, John C. Frémont, drew a surprising number of votes, particularly in northern states such as Massachusetts, New York, and Ohio. Lack of political experience often helps candidates when voters are disgusted with politics, and Frémont had never been a politician. In addition, he was a hero of the Mexican War and a dynamic figure.

The Republicans had more going for them, however, than a colorful candidate. They received many of their votes from northerners fearful about the slavery issue and about what was now going on in the Kansas Territory. People there were quarreling about whether Kansas would become a free state or a slave state. And all of a sudden they were not just talking about it—they were shooting at each other.

SECTION 2 REVIEW

Key Terms, People, and Places
1. Define (a) Compromise of 1850, (b) Fugitive Slave Act, (c) states' rights, (d) nativism, (e) naturalization, (f) Kansas-Nebraska Act, (g) the Slave Power.
2. Identify (a) Democratic party, (b) American party, (c) Know Nothings, (d) Stephen Douglas, (e) Republican party.

Key Concepts
3. Give two reasons why the Compromise of 1850 failed to solve the issue of slavery in the territories once and for all.

4. Why did many Americans lose faith in the second American party system in the early 1850s?
5. What led to the founding of the American party?
6. How did the Kansas-Nebraska Act propose to settle the issue of slavery in the territories?
7. How did the Republicans gain support in the 1850s?

Critical Thinking
8. **Identifying Alternatives** If you had been Calhoun, what changes to the Constitution would you have proposed to ensure that the South remained as powerful as the North?

 Quiz found in the Unit 4 folder, p. 10, covers the main ideas in this section as well as the key terms.

Media and Technology

Transparency
Historical Maps, L-3

 Alternative Assessment
Mid-Point Monitoring
Ask students if they have
• Chosen a format for their project
• Outlined the main ideas
• Begun outside research and preparation of the bibliography

Caption Answer to ...

 Interpreting Tables

Because they were opposed to slavery. The Republican party was nativist and abolitionist, as was the American party.

4. CLOSE

Reinforcing the Big Idea

New political parties emerged during the 1850s to address the issues of the times. The next section discusses the continuing failure of the political system to solve the biggest issue, slavery, and the growing hostility between proslavery and antislavery forces.

 In Depth

Historical Misconceptions

Because today more than 80 percent of them favor Democratic candidates, African Americans are strongly identified with that party. But until the 1930s, African Americans in the North generally voted Republican. As far back as 1856, a gathering of voters resolved: "That we, the colored citizens of Boston, will support with our voices and our votes, John C. Frémont, of California, as President of the United States. . . . [T]hat while we regard the Republican party as the people's party . . . and while we are willing to unite with them to resist the aggressions of the Slave Power, we do not pledge ourselves to go further with the Republicans than [they] will go with us."

Historical Evidence

Analyzing Political Speeches

Focus Analyze a speech as historical evidence of the politics, issues, and language style of a historical period.

Instruct Explain that political speeches are a particularly useful tool in a government where politicians' success is based on their ability to win popular support for their views. Henry Clay was an extremely successful and popular politician. He was also considered one of the greatest orators of his time and was venerated by Abraham Lincoln for his speeches.

Have a volunteer read the excerpt from Clay's speech aloud, and then ask students to try to identify elements that make it extraordinary. In what special ways does Clay use language to affect the listener?

Extend See Historian's Toolbox Activity in the Resource Directory below.

Answers

1. (a) The main topic is the Compromise of 1850. (b) Clay says specifically that "this measure is the reunion of the Union." (c) Clay believes "our country and our cause" should come before individual and personal concerns.

2. (a) "[A]ll resentments, all passions, all petty jealousies, all personal desires, all love of place, all hungering after . . . power [and] popular fears." (b) He warns that the nation may be torn to pieces and become the victim of military rule or domination by a foreign power. (c) He invokes God, country, conscience, and the Union. (d) Possible answer: Clay's appeal to both emotion and reason is very persuasive.

3. (a) The speech indicates that the people of the time were well aware of the serious danger posed by sectional conflict. (b) The example suggests that speakers were fond of repeating ideas in various ways to achieve poetic effect. (c) Students may point out the high-flown quality of the speech in contrast to modern speeches.

Analyzing Political Speeches

Political speeches are as old as government itself. Their goal has always been to persuade listeners to take a particular view. Such speeches can be about almost anything—what candidate citizens should vote for, what new law they should support, what action the government should take, or what policy it should adopt. They can serve as valuable evidence about people and events in history.

Political speakers use a variety of techniques to win over their listeners. Sometimes they appeal to the self-interest of their audience: "See how doing what I propose will make your life better." Sometimes they appeal to their listeners' social conscience: "See how doing what I propose will benefit the community or the nation as a whole." Often they appeal to patriotism.

Use the following steps to analyze the excerpts from a political speech that Henry Clay made to the Senate at the time it was considering whether to adopt the Compromise of 1850.

1. Identify the main topic of the speech and the speaker's stand on it. Recall what you already know about the speaker and his political philosophy. Skim through the speech to get a general idea of the speaker's topic and aims in making the speech. (a) What is the main topic of the speech? (b) Cite evidence in the speech that Clay believes the compromise will work. (c) What is Clay's stand on the measure?

2. Analyze the techniques the speaker uses to persuade listeners. Of course, political speakers appeal to the minds of their listeners. But because they know that an appeal to the emotions can influence their listeners as well, they also appeal to the feelings of their audience. Evaluate the speaker's persuasiveness and how he or she achieves it. (a) What does Clay tell his listeners to disregard and forget? (b) Give evidence that Clay appeals to reason in his speech. (c) Give evidence that Clay appeals to

his listeners' feelings of patriotism. (d) How would you evaluate Clay's persuasiveness in this speech?

3. Study the speech for clues to what the historical period was like. (a) What does the speech tell you about how serious the tensions between North and South seemed to people at that time? (b) What does it tell you about the style of speeches during that period? (c) Compare and contrast this speech with any modern speeches you may have heard or read.

To the Senate, July 22, 1850

I believe from the bottom of my soul that this measure is the reunion of the Union. And now let us disregard all resentments, all passions, all petty jealousies, all personal desires, all love of place, all hungering after the gilded crumbs which fall from the table of power. Let us forget popular fears, from whatever quarter they may spring. Let us . . . think alone of our God, our country, our conscience, and our glorious Union; that Union without which we shall be torn into hostile fragments, and sooner or later become the victims of military despotism, or foreign domination. . . .

What is an individual man? An atom, almost invisible without a magnifying glass—a mere speck upon the surface of the immense universe—not a second in time, compared to immeasurable, never-beginning, and never-ending eternity; a drop of water in the great deep, which evaporates and is borne off by the winds; a grain of sand, which is soon gathered to the dust from which it sprung. Shall a being so small, so petty, so fleeting, so evanescent [quick to disappear], oppose itself to the onward march of a great nation? . . . Let us look at our country and our cause; elevate ourselves to the dignity of pure and disinterested patriots, wise and enlightened statesmen, and save our country from all impending dangers. . . . What are we—what is any man worth who is not ready and willing to sacrifice himself for the benefit of his country when it is necessary?

—Henry Clay, United States senator from Kentucky

 RESOURCE DIRECTORY

Teaching Resources

Historian's Toolbox Activity Analyzing Political Speeches, found in the Unit 4 folder, p. 21, provides further practice in this skill with an excerpt from President Reagan's 1983 televised speech justifying his proposed increase in the defense budget.

The System Fails

SECTION 3

The System Fails

SECTION PREVIEW

A series of violent clashes between antislavery and proslavery forces between 1856 and 1860 brought the United States to the boiling point. Americans on each side of the slavery issue became convinced that the other side was acting against law and morality.

Key Concepts
- From 1856 to 1858, the Kansas Territory became what amounted to a battlefield for conflict between northern, antislavery forces and southern, proslavery forces.
- In a decision on the *Dred Scott* case, the Supreme Court held that the Constitution protected the rights of slave owners to take enslaved people anywhere in the United States.
- During a senatorial campaign in Illinois in 1858, the North gained a new spokesperson for its antislavery views, Abraham Lincoln.
- An uprising led by abolitionist John Brown deepened the division between the North and South.

Key Terms, People, and Places
Dred Scott v. *Sandford*, Lecompton constitution, Panic of 1857; free soiler, John Brown, Charles Sumner, Chief Justice Roger Taney, Abraham Lincoln; Harpers Ferry

T ension in Kansas began in 1854, when the Kansas-Nebraska bill became law. Antislavery organizations in the Northeast then decided to take action. If the question of slavery in the territories was going to be resolved by voting, they would have to make sure antislavery forces were in the majority there. They set up so-called Emigrant Aid societies and in 1854 and early 1855 sent some 1,200 New Englanders to Kansas to fight against the Slave Power. Like others who were committed to making the territories free, the new settlers were called **free soilers.**

Meanwhile, proslavery settlers in Missouri organized secret societies to oppose the free soilers. Many crossed into Kansas to vote illegally in territorial elections. By 1855 Kansas had—only twenty miles apart—an antislavery capital at Topeka and a proslavery capital at Lecompton.

The First Blood Flows

In 1856 tensions escalated into open violence. The clashes began on May 21 when a group of southerners, with the support of a proslavery federal marshal, looted newspaper offices and homes in Lawrence, Kansas, a center of free-soiler activity.

"Bleeding Kansas" The action of the proslavery looters stirred a swift response from Connecticut-born and Ohio-raised **John Brown,** a stern evangelical who believed that he was a chosen instrument of God. He led several New Englanders by night to a proslavery settlement near Pottawatomie Creek. There, Brown and his men roused five men from their beds, dragged them from their homes, and killed them with swords in front of their families.

The looting in Lawrence and Brown's reaction to it sparked a summer of murderous raids and counterraids throughout Kansas, shown on the map on page 312. The violence won the territory a grim nickname: "Bleeding Kansas." Nor was the bloodshed confined to Kansas; it also spread to the nation's capital.

"Bleeding Sumner" On May 19 and 20, Senator **Charles Sumner** of Massachusetts had given a fiery speech titled "The Crime Against Kansas." Sumner, a leading Republican and one of the most powerful antislavery voices in Congress, bitterly attacked southerners for forcing slavery on the territory. In particular, he charged Senator Andrew Butler of South Carolina, a popular southern politician, with having

During the late 1850s, Americans increasingly turned to violence in an effort to resolve their differences over slavery. Abolitionist John Brown had a blacksmith make a thousand of these pikes to arm enslaved people for a revolt.

1. FOCUS

Connecting to the Big Idea

See page 296B. Explain that between 1856 and 1860, hostilities between antislavery and proslavery forces escalated and moved the nation closer to war. Ask what events took place to increase the tension between the North and the South.

Objectives
- Describe what happened in the Kansas Territory between 1856 and 1858.
- Explain the Supreme Court's *Dred Scott* decision.
- Identify Abraham Lincoln's views on slavery.
- Describe the effect of the uprising led by abolitionist John Brown on relations between the North and the South.

Bellringer

Ask students to make a list of controversial issues in the United States that have incited groups to violence in recent years. Ask when and why people adopt violence to achieve political ends.

Reading Strategy

Structured Overview Ask students to scan the section and to jot down the main headings and subheadings. Have them fill in details from the text under the appropriate heading as they read.

2. INSTRUCT

Discuss

Discuss the breakdown of law and the political process brought about by the government's inability to solve the slavery issue. Ask students why Kansas became a battleground for proslavery and antislavery forces. What was John Brown's role in the escalating violence over the slavery issue? How did Brooks's attack on Sumner illustrate the growing failure of the political process? How did the Supreme Court decision in *Dred Scott* v. *Sandford* and the Lecompton constitution contribute to the breakdown of trust in the law?

Analyze

Ask students to analyze why the beliefs, principles, and government that had held the United States together for seven decades broke down over the issue of slavery. What led some Americans to abandon the democratic process in favor of violence to settle the slavery issue? Is it possible that a similar situation could happen today in the United States?

Caption Answer to . . .

 Interpreting Maps

About 35 miles.

"Bleeding Kansas," 1856

Geography and History: Interpreting Maps
Outsiders from both slave and free states meddled aggressively in Kansas politics. In one election, 5,000 proslavery men from Missouri crossed the border to vote. The final tally totaled four times as many votes as there were registered Kansas voters. *How far is the abolitionist stronghold Lawrence from the Missouri border?*

chosen a mistress to whom he has made his vows, and who, though ugly to others, is always lovely to him; though polluted in the sight of the world, is chaste [pure] in his sight . . . the harlot, Slavery.

Preston Brooks, who was both a member of the House of Representatives and Butler's nephew, was indignant at Sumner's remarks and determined to defend the honor of the South. Normally, he would have challenged Sumner to a duel; but since Brooks did not consider Sumner a gentleman worthy of respect, he planned to punish him as he might have disciplined a misbehaving dog.

Two days after his speech, Sumner was sitting at his desk in the Senate reading mail. Brooks approached him and began beating the senator with his cane. Sumner tried to protect himself, even pulling his desk out of the floor in the process. Southern senators standing nearby made no move to help him. Recalled Brooks:

I . . . gave him about 30 first rate stripes. Toward the last he bellowed like a calf. I wore my cane out completely, but saved the head, which is gold.

Sumner survived the caning, but it took him four years to return to the Senate. In fact, he was never completely healthy again.

Northerners were outraged by Brooks's action. To them it seemed that if a southern member of Congress could beat a United States senator in the middle of the Senate without punishment, then the North was at the mercy of the South. The caning became a symbol of the arrogance and brutality that northerners imagined was typical of southerners.

Southerners, however, saw the caning as a justified response to a terrible insult against their honor. When Brooks resigned his seat in the House to give the voters in his district an opportunity to express their opinion, he was immediately reelected. Furthermore, people across the South voiced their support by sending him canes—including one inscribed "Hit him again."

A Breakdown of the System As bad as the violence in Kansas and the Senate was for the people who experienced it, its larger significance was to reveal the general breakdown of respect for law and the political process. Wrote the New York *Evening Post* shortly after the "Bleeding Sumner" incident:

Violence is the order of the day; the North is to be pushed to the wall by it, and this [southern] plot will succeed if the people of the free states are as apathetic [uninterested] as the slaveholders are insolent [boldly disrespectful].

Confusion Over Law

In March 1857, the Supreme Court added to the breakdown of trust in the law by handing down one of the most controversial decisions in its history, **Dred Scott v. Sandford.** The suit had started when Dred Scott, an enslaved man living in Missouri, had filed suit against his owner. Scott argued that because he and his

▶ RESOURCE DIRECTORY

Teaching Resources

 Visual Learning Activity Free Soiler Chokes on Slavery, found in the Unit 4 folder, p. 30, uses a political cartoon to depict the struggle over the Lecompton constitution in the Kansas territory in 1857.

Using Historical Evidence Preston Brooks raises his cane to strike Senator Charles Sumner in this lithograph by Winslow Homer. *Was this lithograph a piece of northern or southern propaganda? Explain your interpretation.*

wife, Harriet, had once lived in states and territories where slavery was illegal, the couple was in fact free. By a vote of seven to two, the justices ruled against the Scotts.

Dred Scott Supports Slave Owners In his written opinion on the case, **Chief Justice Roger Taney** stated that as an African American, Dred Scott was inferior and without rights. Thus he was not a citizen of the United States and could not sue anyone.

Scott could not be considered free, the Court determined, simply because he had once stood on free soil. As an enslaved person, Scott was property. Taney noted that "the right of property in a slave is distinctly and expressly affirmed in the Constitution." Furthermore, under the Fifth Amendment, Congress had to protect the right of the slave owner, not the enslaved person. Said Taney:

> No word can be found in the Constitution, which gives Congress a greater power over slave property, or which entitles property of that kind to less protection than property of any other description. The only power conferred [granted] is the power coupled with the duty of guarding and protecting the owner in his rights.

This meant that Congress had to protect slavery throughout the Union. It had no power to ban slavery anywhere, including the territories. Taney declared that the Missouri Compromise, which had forbidden slavery in some territories, "is not warranted by the Constitution, and is therefore void."

Today we find the *Dred Scott* decision offensive because of its refusal to recognize the rights of African Americans. But it had the value of being direct and honest. Taney stated that the writers of the Declaration of Independence and the Constitution did not intend those documents to apply to African Americans. The Framers, said Taney, believed African Americans "had no rights which the white man was bound to respect." Therefore no legal basis existed in 1857 for granting any rights to African Americans, even those who were freed. Although Taney's analysis of history was accurate, it was also racist.

Antislavery forces were disgusted with the *Dred Scott* decision. It meant the national government had no power to keep slavery out of the territories. President Buchanan, however, supported the Court's decision for that very reason. He and many other white Americans hoped that now the national government would not be required to deal with the slavery issue.

The Lecompton Constitution Events soon proved, however, that the political fight over slavery had not ended. In Kansas, too, confusion arose over the law. In the fall of 1857, a small proslavery group elected members to a convention to write the constitution required for statehood. Called the **Lecompton constitution,** it was as proslavery as its namesake, the proslavery capital. The majority of people in Kansas were opposed to slavery and refused to even vote on the constitution when it was offered for their approval. President Buchanan, hoping that the problem of slavery in Kansas would go away as soon as the territory became a state, endorsed the Lecompton constitution.

Though Buchanan was a Democrat, his blatant disregard for popular sovereignty and the rule of law was too much for northern Democrats to swallow. Democratic leader Stephen Douglas spoke sharply against the Lecompton

3. ASSESS

Section 3 Review Answers

1. (a) Lecompton constitution, see p. 313, (b) Panic of 1857, see p. 315

2. (a) free soiler, see p. 311, (b) Charles Sumner, see p. 311, (c) Chief Justice Roger Taney, see p. 313

3. Harpers Ferry, see p. 315

4. In 1856 a proslavery group looted offices and homes in Lawrence, Kansas; an antislavery group led by John Brown killed proslavery settlers; and Preston Brooks beat Charles Sumner in the Senate.

5. The rights of white slave owners.

6. Lincoln hoped that if slavery was confined to the states in which it already existed, it would eventually die out.

7. It deepened the division between North and South.

8. Answers should point out that the existing political system, with its party and sectional divisions, was unable to find a compromise that was acceptable in the long term to the majority of Americans. The illegal actions of both proslavery and antislavery forces are proof of this failure.

Answer to ...

MAKING CONNECTIONS

A moral condemnation is more personal than a political criticism. Southern planters could debate slavery as a political issue; but if they were judged guilty of a moral wrong, they could not justify their position.

During his 1858 campaign for the Senate, Abraham Lincoln told one audience that he was driven "by something higher than an anxiety for office," a desire to defend the principle of equality established by the Declaration of Independence.

constitution and criticized Buchanan for accepting it. Congress returned the constitution to Kansas for another vote, and the people now soundly defeated it.

A New Spokesperson Emerges

Senator Douglas denounced the Lecompton constitution in part out of principle and in part because he had to be responsive to public opinion. He faced a difficult reelection campaign in Illinois in 1858, where opinion on slavery was sharply divided.

A short, stout man, Douglas was known popularly as "the Little Giant." Like many whites in the 1850s, he believed that white Americans were superior to African Americans. He went even further, however, and tolerated slavery, because he believed in the absolute right of white citizens to choose the kind of society and government they wanted.

Though Douglas was one of the most influential senators in the nation's history, today people generally remember him only because of the man the Republican party nominated to run against him, **Abraham Lincoln.** The campaign drew nationwide attention when Douglas and Lincoln met in a series of seven debates on the issue of slavery in the territories.

Abraham Lincoln was born in a log cabin in Kentucky in 1809. As a young man, he studied law and worked at various jobs, including postmaster and rail splitter. In 1837 he settled in Springfield, Illinois, where he practiced law. He served one term in Congress in the 1840s. Known for his strength of character, Lincoln won further recognition for his skillful peformance in the Lincoln-Douglas debates.

Lincoln shared many of Douglas's views on African Americans. During the campaign against Douglas, he stated: "I am not nor ever

have been in favor of bringing about in any way the social and political equality of the white and black races." He did not even propose forbidding slavery in the South. He hoped that by confining slavery to the states in which it already existed, it would eventually die out.

Yet Lincoln, like millions of other northerners, knew that slavery was wrong. For him, it was not just a matter of whether the slave states would have equal power in the Senate. He considered slavery a moral issue. During the campaign against Douglas, he quoted both the Bible and the Declaration of Independence to justify his stand.

> The Savior [Jesus Christ] . . . said, "As your Father in Heaven is perfect, be ye also perfect." He set that up as a standard, and [whoever] did most towards reaching that standard attained the highest degree of moral perfection. So I say in relation to the principle that all men are created equal, let it be as nearly reached as we can.

In a now-famous speech in Springfield in June 1858, Lincoln insisted:

> A house divided against itself cannot stand. I believe this government cannot endure, permanently half slave and half free. I do not expect the Union to be dissolved—I do not expect the house to fall—but I do expect it will cease to be divided. It will become all one thing, or all the other.

Though Lincoln gained a large following, Douglas won the election. All the same, the tall, gaunt lawyer from Springfield earned a reputation for eloquence and moral commitment that would serve him and the Republicans well in the presidential election of 1860.

MAKING CONNECTIONS

You have read that Lincoln considered slavery a moral issue. Why would this stand anger and offend southern planters more than if Lincoln had considered slavery only a political issue?

▶ RESOURCE DIRECTORY

Teaching Resources

⭐ **Primary Source Activity** Lincoln–Douglas Senate Campaign, found in the Unit 4 folder, pp. 23–24, presents a passage from Gustave Koerner's impressions of the Lincoln–Douglas debates to demonstrate the differences between the two candidates.

⭐ **Primary Source Activity** An Interview with John Brown, found in the Unit 4 folder, p. 25, presents a transcript of an interview John Brown gave shortly before his execution describing his reasons for attacking the federal arsenal at Harpers Ferry.

⭐ **American Profiles Activity** found in the Unit 4 folder, p. 17, profiles John Anthony Copeland, Jr., one of five African Americans who helped John Brown in his famous raid.

John Brown's Raid

Other factors increased tensions in the late 1850s. One was an economic downturn called the **Panic of 1857.** Another was the continuing growth of the American population. Many people were uneasy; there was a sense that Americans were at sea, that their country was growing and changing so rapidly that it could be controlled no longer.

⭐ John Brown, however, was not one to resign himself to the twists of fate. He would control his own destiny and that of his nation if he could. On October 16, 1859, three years after his nighttime raid along Pottawatomie Creek in Kansas, Brown attacked the federal arsenal at **Harpers Ferry,** Virginia (now West Virginia). With him were twenty-two men, including two African Americans—Shields Green and John Anthony Copeland, a college student. Supported by abolitionists in the North, Brown and his followers hoped to seize the weapons in the arsenal and give them to enslaved people. They had a dream of a massive uprising of enslaved Americans that would end slavery, punish slaveholders, and lead the United States to moral renewal. ⭐

Alerted to the attack, United States troops under the command of Colonel Robert E. Lee bore down on Harpers Ferry and surrounded Brown and his men in the arsenal. The troops killed half of Brown's men—including two of his sons—before the rest surrendered. Convicted of treason against the state of Virginia, John Brown was sentenced to be hanged by the neck until dead.

Just before his execution, Brown wrote a brief note. Although he had failed as a soldier, his final message proved him a prophet:

Behind John Brown's "glittering, gray-blue eyes" lurked a cool willingness to break the law in order to end slavery.

I John Brown am now quite certain *that the crimes of this* guilty land will *never be purged* away; *but with Blood.*

Northerners hailed Brown as a martyr to the cause of justice and freedom. Southerners denounced him as a terrorist and a tool of Republican abolitionists. In short, his raid and his trial only deepened the division between North and South.

As the year 1860 began, it was clear that the majority of northerners would not accept leadership associated with what they called the Slave Power. And southerners now determinedly announced they would not accept leadership by Republicans, who were opposed to the slavery system. The next presidential election was looming. How could the Union possibly survive it?

SECTION 3 REVIEW

Key Terms, People, and Places

1. Define (a) Lecompton constitution, (b) Panic of 1857.
2. Identify (a) free soiler, (b) Charles Sumner, (c) Chief Justice Roger Taney.
3. Identify Harpers Ferry.

Key Concepts

4. Cite examples of disorder in Kansas in 1856.

5. Whose rights were upheld in *Dred Scott* v. *Sandford?*
6. Make a general statement about Abraham Lincoln's position on slavery.
7. What was the greatest impact of John Brown's raid?

Critical Thinking

8. **Testing Conclusions** Explain why the title of this section is "The System Fails."

 Quiz found in the Unit 4 folder, p. 12, covers the main ideas in this section as well as the key terms.

Reteach

Ask students to write front page headlines that sum up newspaper stories on the following events: the attack on Charles Sumner, the decision in *Dred Scott* v. *Sandford* , the defeat of the Lecompton constitution, the presidential campaign of 1858, and John Brown's raid.

4. CLOSE

Reinforcing the Big Idea

After the passage of the Kansas-Nebraska Act, the web of order and government that held the United States together began to unravel. The next section discusses the nation's final descent into war.

In Depth

Interdisciplinary

Less than two months before the Harpers Ferry raid, a technological breakthrough set the stage for a further deepening of the divisions between North and South. On August 29, 1859, Edwin L. Drake drilled the first successful oil well, striking paydirt in Titusville, Pennsylvania. The country's first oil refinery was installed there, and a booming natural gas industry soon formed around it.

The Dred Scott Decision

Focus The Supreme Court had the opportunity to reexamine laws about slavery in the Dred Scott case. Instead, by denying Dred Scott and his wife, Harriet, their freedom in 1857, it chose to support the fragile web of compromise that had so far kept the North and South out of a civil war. Like other efforts on the part of the federal government to avoid direct confrontation over the slavery question, the decision increased tensions between the North and the South. Students are asked to evaluate the ruling and to investigate some of the consequences of other options available to the Court.

Instruct To check students' understanding of the facts of the case, ask them to summarize in a few sentences why Dred Scott felt he and his wife should be freed. Then review the arguments for and against both a narrow and a broad ruling against Scott. Ask students why setting Scott and his wife free was never really an option in the case. Ask students to write their own ruling in this case.

Extend To extend the activity, have students explore how and when African Americans were finally granted United States citizenship, by researching the Fourteenth Amendment.

The Dred Scott Decision

Time Frame:	March 1857
Place:	Washington, D.C.
Key People:	Dred and Harriet Scott, Chief Justice Roger Taney
Situation:	In the 1850s, as controversy raged over slavery, the Supreme Court was faced with a tough question: Did enslaved people become free when they were taken into territories where slavery was against the law?

I n the 1830s, a white man from Missouri named Emerson took Dred Scott, an enslaved African American, into the state of Illinois and the federal territory of Wisconsin. In Wisconsin, Scott met and married his wife, Harriet. Under the Missouri Compromise of 1820, slavery was illegal in both places. In 1838, the Scotts returned to the slave state of Missouri. The husband, Dred Scott—shown in the painting on this page—sued for his family's freedom in 1846. He argued that residence in a free state and then in a free territory had ended his enslavement.

The Court's Options

When the Court finally began considering the case, the justices had to decide between two approaches to the question. They could issue what is called a *narrow ruling*, responding to the legal arguments Dred Scott had made and stating simply whether or not he was free. Or they could issue a *broad ruling*, in which they considered whether the laws involved in the case were constitutional.

Only One Option in a Narrow Ruling The Court could not really use a narrow ruling to declare Scott free. Too many issues would be left unresolved if they did so. After all, the Constitution and federal laws had always upheld the rights of property owners. The Court could not inter-

fere with that right without reexamining the Constitution at length.

The Court could, however, use a narrow ruling to declare that Scott was still enslaved. This decision had already been made by the lower courts that had considered the case. The Supreme Court could simply support their decision.

The Broad Ruling Options The justices did not *have* to make a broad ruling. But throughout its history, the Supreme Court has used certain cases to examine laws and determine if they are constitutional. The justices might well believe it was time to reexamine laws about slavery. Their broad ruling might declare Scott free or declare him enslaved.

Weighing the Options

By setting Scott free, the Court would place human rights above the right of slaveholders to own human property. African Americans and abolitionists would have enthusiastically welcomed this decision. But for

RESOURCE DIRECTORY

Teaching Resources

History Might Not . . . Activity Can Separate Be Equal? found in the Unit 4 folder, pp. 15–16, highlights the case of Homer Adolph Plessy and his attempt to sit in a whites-only railroad car.

GOALS	Determine whether Dred Scott was free; make a decision about the larger issue of slavery		
POSSIBLE ACTIONS	Rule broadly for Scott	Rule narrowly against Scott	Rule broadly against Scott
POSSIBLE RESULTS	• Will place human rights above the right of whites to own enslaved people • Will please African Americans and abolitionists • Will make it easier for enslaved people to escape slavery • Will anger southerners	• Will please southerners and slave holders • Will probably not surprise the majority of northern white people • Will keep the compromises in place, reducing chance of violence	• Will jar compromises over slavery • Might extend slavery into the territories • Would win wide support among white southerners • Might alarm large numbers of white northerners

many whites in the 1850s, the choice was not so clear.

A majority of the Court justices, including Chief Justice Roger Taney, were southerners. Taney himself hated slavery—and proved it by setting free the enslaved people he owned. But he knew that setting Scott free would make it easier for enslaved African Americans everywhere to win their freedom. This would cause a violent backlash from southern slaveholders threatened with the loss of their labor force. And Taney also knew that the Constitution and federal laws had always upheld the right to own property. Setting Scott free would be interfering with that right. So the real question was not whether the Court would rule for Scott. Instead, the question was whether the Court would rule narrowly, or whether it would rule broadly and reconsider federal laws about slavery.

If the Court ruled against Scott narrowly, it would please southerners and slaveholders by making it impossible for slaves to become free simply by entering free territory. And most northern whites would not be surprised by one more court decision that supported slavery. A narrow ruling would not disturb the compromises made over the years between slave states and free states, such as the Missouri Compromise and the Compromise of 1850.

If the Court ruled against Scott broadly, reexamining previous laws, they might jar that fragile web of compromise. They might even use the power of the Court to extend slavery into places where it was not currently legal. Southerners would approve of this, but northerners would be outraged.

When the Court decided the case on March 6, 1857, all nine justices wrote separate statements of their opinions. Taney's was the most influential, however, and the majority of the justices agreed with him. He did not set Scott free. And he combined both a narrow and a broad ruling in his statement on the case.

In the narrow part of his ruling, Taney pointed out that only citizens could sue others. Scott, Taney claimed, could not sue anybody because the Framers of the Constitution had never intended African Americans to be considered citizens.

In the broad part of his ruling, Taney emphasized that the Constitution protected the right to own property, and no federal law could break the Constitution. The Missouri Compromise of 1820 was a federal law that interfered with the right to own property—that is, enslaved people—in certain parts of the United States. Therefore the Missouri Compromise was unconstitutional.

Taney and his colleagues may have hoped that their bold ruling would end the controversy over slavery once and for all. Unfortunately, it only increased tensions.

EVALUATING DECISIONS

1. Why could a narrow ruling not free Scott?
2. Why did Taney decide Dred Scott could not sue?

Critical Thinking
3. **Checking Consistency** If Taney hated slavery, why did he not declare Dred Scott a free man?

Media and Technology

Visions of America: History Might Not Have Happened This Way Game

To encourage students to explore pivotal moments in United States history, have students use the Visions of America software. Refer to the Visions of America Guidebook for viewing objectives, activities, game instructions, and discussion questions.

A Nation Divided Against Itself

SECTION 4

A Nation Divided Against Itself

SECTION PREVIEW

Secession spread like wildfire through the southern states when Abraham Lincoln captured the presidency. While politicians and the people debated how to respond, the first shots were fired, and the broken nation plunged into war.

Key Concepts

- The Republican candidate for President in 1860, Abraham Lincoln, carried no southern states and almost all of the northern states.
- Finding that the North was able to elect an antislavery President despite his complete rejection by the South, southern states left the Union one after another.
- Fort Sumter in South Carolina became a symbol of federal authority. Its bombardment by southern forces was the final challenge that brought on the Civil War.

Key Terms, People, and Places

John C. Breckinridge, William Henry Seward, Constitutional Union party, secessionist, Jefferson Davis; Border States, Lower South, Confederate States of America, Fort Sumter, Upper South

Proudly declaring its independence, South Carolina was the first state to secede from the Union.

A mericans justifiably pride themselves on the peaceful transfer of power from one group of people to another through the electoral process. This process set the new nation apart from others from the early days of the republic. But the success of the American political system depends on the willingness of the losers to accept government by the winners, at least temporarily. Only once—in 1860—has a large group of people refused to accept the outcome of a national election. The result was that the Union failed and the United States broke into two nations.

The Election of 1860

Differences between northern Democrats and southern Democrats finally ripped the Democratic party apart in the summer of 1860. For ten days and 59 ballots, delegates to their national convention sat in Charleston, South Carolina, unable to choose a presidential candidate. When they met again in Baltimore, the Democrats made the division official. Northerners nominated Stephen Douglas of Illinois and southerners chose **John C. Breckinridge,** the current Vice President. He was committed to an aggressive policy of expanding slavery in the territories.

By contrast, Republican **William Henry Seward** of New York was committed to an aggressive policy of ending slavery. Although he was the leading candidate for the Republican nomination when the delegates met in Chicago, they were worried that he was too extreme to attract the voters they needed. They also wanted to ensure victory in Pennyslvania, Indiana, and Illinois, states the Republicans had not won in the presidential election of 1856. But another candidate, Abraham Lincoln, seemed to have more moderate views on slavery than Seward. He could certainly win in his own state, Illinois. They nominated him.

Southerners, however, had heard too much extreme language from the Republicans to trust them. In 1859, for instance, one Republican declared that his party intended

> to check the Slave Power in its aggressive march, to roll back the black and threatening wave of Southern oppression, to teach the Slave Power that it will have absolute need of its utmost efforts to preserve its existence within its present boundaries, without grasping by robbery and bribery the territories of other governments in order to aggrandize and perpetuate [increase and continue] slavery.

---

1. FOCUS

Connecting to the Big Idea

See page 296B. Point out that the election of a Republican President in 1860 was too much for the South to bear. One by one the southern states seceded from the Union. Ask how the nation finally broke apart.

Objectives

- Identify the states that Lincoln carried in the 1860 election for President.
- Explain why the southern states left the Union.
- Explain the significance of Fort Sumter, South Carolina, in relation to the Civil War.

Bellringer

Ask students for names of nations that are currently fighting or have recently fought a civil war, along with the reasons for the conflict. List responses on the chalkboard as a focus for discussion.

Reading Strategy

Predicting Content Ask students to skim the section, list the main headings and subheadings, and write a sentence or phrase under each that predicts the content of that portion. Then have students test their predictions against the actual text.

▶ RESOURCE DIRECTORY

Teaching Resources

📄 **Reproducible Lesson Plan** found in the Unit 4 folder, p. 6, provides a summary of the Section 4 lesson plan content.

📄 **Alternate Lesson Plan: Learning Styles** found in the Alternate Lesson Plans folder, p. 57, is especially suited for visual and auditory learners, and encourages groups of students to create a political commentary with visuals to describe the outcome and identify the consequences of the election of 1860.

📄 **Guided Reading and Review** found in the Unit 4 folder, p. 13, provides a structure for reading and mastering the key concepts and reviewing the key terms for Section 4. (Guided Practice)

Less extreme were those who formed the **Constitutional Union party.** These moderates were mostly southerners who had belonged to the Whig party, along with a few politicians from the **Border States**—Delaware, Maryland, Kentucky, and Missouri. They chose John Bell of Tennessee, a moderate slaveholder, as their presidential nominee.

The November election was essentially two elections, one in the South between Bell and Breckinridge and one in the North between Lincoln and Douglas. The Republicans won a majority in the North, carrying every free state (except New Jersey, which they split with the Douglas Democrats). Breckinridge, meanwhile, won North Carolina, Arkansas, Delaware, Maryland, and the states of the **Lower South**—Texas, Louisiana, Mississippi, Alabama, Florida, Georgia, and South Carolina. Bell carried three border states, Tennessee, Kentucky, and Virginia. Douglas took Missouri.

In the nation as a whole, Lincoln received 180 electoral votes out of 303. These 180 electoral votes were the majority he needed to win the presidency. But he received only 40 percent of the popular vote; Douglas was second with 29 percent, Breckinridge third with 18 percent, and Bell received 13 percent. Contributing to Lincoln's failure to achieve a majority was the fact that he got no votes in the Lower South. His was a decisive victory, but a sectional one.

MAKING CONNECTIONS

Consider the major role southerners had played in the nation's history from its beginnings. Name some southern revolutionaries, Framers, Presidents, and influential members of Congress. Contrast that heritage of government power with the situation after the election of 1860.

The Lower South Secedes

Southerners were outraged that a President could be elected without any southern votes. The government of the nation, it seemed, had passed completely out of their hands. Planters and others who backed slavery called for the South

Viewpoints
On the Southern Secession

Lincoln's election in November 1860 led South Carolina to plan secession. *What issues, according to the following viewpoints, divided the northern and southern states?*

For secession

"In January next we shall take leave of the Union and shall construct with our sister Cotton States a government for ourselves. Whether the other Slave States will join seems very uncertain at least for the present. The condition of affairs at the North since the election of an Abolitionist for President makes it necessary for us to get away as quickly as possible."

E. B. Heyward, South Carolina cotton planter, letter to a friend in Connecticut, dated November 20, 1860

Against secession

"I am for the preservation of the Union; I desire to witness no separation of the States; I have a pecuniary [financial] interest both in the South and in the North. . . . The whole country has just emerged from the exercise of its constitutional and long-established functions, in the choice of a President of the United States. . . . Men of South Carolina, keep to your pledges, and retain your honor and self-respect. No harm will come to you. Mr. Lincoln and his party are your safest and best friends. They will do what is right."

Anonymous northern merchant, letter to the editor, *New York Tribune,* November 22, 1860

to secede. They refused to remain in a Union run by the antislavery Republicans. That party, wrote an Augusta, Georgia, newspaper editor,

stands forth today, hideous, revolting, loathsome, a menace not only to the Union of these states, but to Society, to Liberty, and to Law. It has drawn to it the corrupt, the vile, the licentious [immoral], the profligate [extremely wasteful], the lawless. . . . It is a fiend, the type of lawless Democracy, a law unto itself, its only Lord King Numbers, its decrees but the will of a wild mob.

The **secessionists**—those who wanted the South to secede—argued that since the states had voluntarily joined the United States, they also could choose to leave it. They believed it

Viewpoints Activity On the Southern Secession, found in the Unit 4 folder, pp. 19–20, provides several contemporary opinions on the prospect of southern secession.

2. INSTRUCT

Discuss

Discuss why the southern states seceded from the Union. Ask why southerners felt it was impossible to trust any Republican President. Why were southerners so outraged at the election of Lincoln? Why did the secessionists feel that it was their legitimate right to withdraw from the Union?

Analyze

Analyze Lincoln's choice to stand firm against the seceding states. Would he have done better to allow the southern states to leave the Union in peace? How might that decision have changed the future of the United States?

Answer to . . .

MAKING CONNECTIONS

Students may name Washington, Madison, Jefferson, Jackson, Clay, Calhoun and others. Southerners had always been major shapers of the nation's policy; after the election of 1860, however, they found that their collective electoral power in the presidential election counted for absolutely nothing: the voters of the North alone were able, without regard to southern interests or wishes, to elect a President to govern the entire nation.

Answer to . . .

Viewpoints

Heyward indicates that slavery is the issue leading the South to press for secession; the northern merchant pleads for the preservation of the Union for economic, or business, reasons. For a more thorough examination of the secession issue, see the Resource Directory.

Activity

Cooperative Learning

Time: One class period.
Activity: Create a political campaign.
Grouping: Groups of four to six students.
Purpose: To understand that the primary consideration for presidential candidates in 1860 was how to win in a nation so divided by the question of slavery, have students select a candidate from this election and develop a political campaign for him.
Roles: Candidates and members of the campaign team (campaign manager, secretary, and personal consultants).
Outcome: Students will define and portray the political strategy of one of the candidates in the 1860 presidential campaign.

Caption Answer to ...

 Interpreting Maps

Virginia, North Carolina, Tennessee, and Arkansas.

In Depth

Did You Know?

In December 1860, Congress made some last-ditch efforts to hold the Union together. Kentucky Senator John J. Crittenden proposed a series of "unamendable amendments" to the Constitution, one of which would stretch the Missouri Compromise line (see pages 180–181) to California as the dividing line between slavery and free soil. President Lincoln's Republicans, however, stood firm in refusing to allow slavery to extend into new territories, and the so-called Crittenden Compromise was narrowly defeated in the Senate on March 2, 1861.

---

was an absolute necessity to do so. Typical of the secessionists was Edmund Ruffin of Virginia. He stated that because the Republicans were "a northern sectional party, and majority" in charge of the federal government, they could act constitutionally and legally "to produce the most complete subjection and political bondage, degradation, and ruin of the South."

South Carolina left the Union officially on December 20, 1860. Over the next few weeks, so did six other states of the Lower South. In early February 1861, delegates from the seven states met in Montgomery, Alabama. There they created a new nation, the **Confederate States of America,** also called the Confederacy, shown on the map below. As their president they elected Senator **Jefferson Davis** of Mississippi.

The War Starts

The question on everyone's mind as the winter dragged on was what the national government would do about the secession of seven

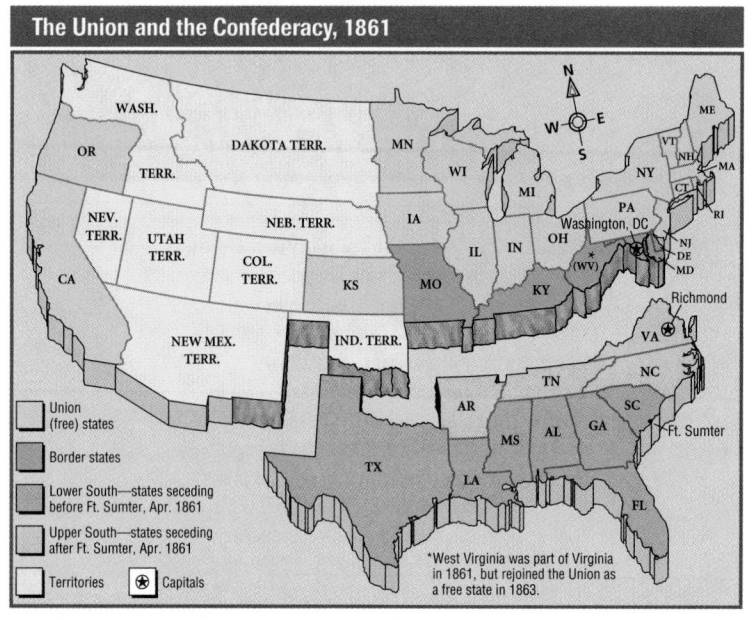

The Union and the Confederacy, 1861

West Virginia was part of Virginia in 1861, but rejoined the Union as a free state in 1863.

Union (free) states
Border states
Lower South—states seceding before Ft. Sumter, Apr. 1861
Upper South—states seceding after Ft. Sumter, Apr. 1861
Territories   ⊛ Capitals

Geography and History: Interpreting Maps
When South Carolina seceded, one Unionist sarcastically observed that the state was "too small for a republic and too big for a lunatic asylum." South Carolina was soon joined by other states, however—making the Confederate republic one of the largest in the world. *Name the states that seceded after the surrender of Fort Sumter.*

of its member states. President Buchanan, as usual, did nothing. Meanwhile, he and the President-elect heard plenty of advice.

Lincoln's Options Some politicians proposed compromises with the South, but few people supported compromises anymore. More serious was a recommendation to allow the seceding states to go in peace. Many opposed this option, including those who believed strongly in the political value of the Union. Northern business people also objected, fearing that profits from their business with the South would be lost.

The third choice was to insist that the southern states return to the Union. After all, how could the United States function as a country if its members could come and go as they pleased? Many northerners, including Stephen Douglas, favored this option, despite the very real chance of war.

The only man in the nation who had the power to make the decision about the government's response left his home in Springfield, Illinois, in early 1861, bound for the White House. Abraham Lincoln believed secession was wrong. He was also strongly committed to stopping the expansion of slavery. But rather than focus on the reasons behind the South's secession, the President-elect emphasized his responsibility to enforce the laws of the United States. On March 4, 1861, Lincoln took the oath of office, swearing, as all Presidents must, to "preserve, protect, and defend the Constitution of the United States."

Fort Sumter, Symbol of the Union As he spoke those words, the attention of the nation was on **Fort Sumter,** a federal fort in the harbor of Charleston, South Carolina. A federal ship sent to supply the fort had been turned back by Confederate forces in January. Now several dozen federal soldiers under the command of Major Robert Anderson were

---

▶ RESOURCE DIRECTORY

Teaching Resources

⊕ **American Profiles Activity** found in the Unit 4 folder, p. 18, profiles General P. G. T. Beauregard, the man who ordered the first shots of the Civil War.

⊕ **Critical Thinking Activity** Identifying Assumptions: War Begins, found in the Unit 4 folder, p. 22, helps students apply this skill by analyzing a contemporary newspaper account of the battle at Fort Sumter.

running out of supplies. If Lincoln did not resupply the fort, it would have to surrender.

Lincoln, along with much of the North and South, saw Fort Sumter as a vital symbol of the Union he had sworn to preserve. Refusing to recognize the Confederate government, on April 6 Lincoln told the governor of South Carolina that he was sending provisions to Fort Sumter. On April 10, before the supplies could arrive, Confederate president Davis ordered General P.G.T. Beauregard to demand that Fort Sumter surrender. If Anderson refused, Beauregard was to take it by force. ⭐

Anderson did refuse, and on April 12, 1861, Beauregard opened fire on the fort. After a twenty-four-hour bombardment, Anderson ordered the Stars and Stripes hauled down and surrendered Fort Sumter to Confederate troops. ⭐ By firing on federal property, the Confederate states had committed an undeniable act of open rebellion. As the defender of the Constitution, Lincoln had no choice but to respond. When he called for volunteers, southerners saw his action as an act of war against them. The **Upper South**—Virginia, North Carolina, Tennessee, and Arkansas—now joined the Lower South in the Confederacy. This left the four border states torn between two hostile nations.

Eighty-four years after the Continental Congress had declared the independence of the United States of America, the nation had come apart. Union with slavery was not possible.

Some in the South called the war the Second War for Independence. Although in the end it did not win independence for the South, the war would indeed prove a second American

As Confederate guns battered Fort Sumter (at the center of the harbor), some onlookers felt excitement and others feared for the future.

Revolution. It would transform the United State as few other events ever have.

But no one in either North or South knew that in 1861. As men marched and women waved good-bye, they expected a short and glorious war. The South was going to teach the North that it could not interfere with the rights of free Americans. The North was going to teach the South that it could not abandon the federal Union the Framers had created. Neither northerners nor southerners imagined the horror that lay ahead of them, or the vastness of the changes they were bringing upon themselves.

SECTION 4 REVIEW

Key Terms, People, and Places
1. Identify (a) John C. Breckinridge, (b) William Henry Seward, (c) Constitutional Union party, (d) secessionist, (e) Jefferson Davis.
2. Identify (a) Border States, (b) Lower South, (c) Confederate States of America, (d) Upper South.

Key Concepts
3. Summarize the results of the election of 1860.
4. How did the Lower South view the election of 1860?

5. Explain the importance of the surrender of Fort Sumter.

Critical Thinking
6. **Recognizing Ideologies** Some thirty different names have been used for the Civil War since 1861. You have read that some southerners called it the Second War for Independence. The North called it the War of the Rebellion. Explain how each name reflects the point of view behind it.

---

3. ASSESS

Section 4 Review Answers

1. (a) John C. Breckinridge, see p. 318, (b) William Henry Seward, see p. 318, (c) Constitutional Union party, see p. 319, (d) secessionist, see p. 319, (e) Jefferson Davis, see p. 320

2. (a) Border States, see p. 319, (b) Lower South, see p. 319, (c) Confederate States of America, see p. 320, (d) Upper South, see p. 321

3. North Carolina and the Lower South generally voted for Breckinridge; three Border States voted for Bell; Missouri voted for Douglas; and most of the North voted for Lincoln.

4. They viewed the result as sufficient cause to secede from the Union.

5. Many saw Fort Sumter as a vital symbol of the Union. By firing on this federal property, the Confederate states had committed an undeniable act of open rebellion.

6. Southerners believed that they were fighting for their right to govern themselves, just as the Patriots had done in the original American Revolution. Northerners took the position that no state had the power to break the Constitution; they branded all who tried to do so rebels.

4. CLOSE

Reinforcing the Big Idea

With the election of Abraham Lincoln in 1860, the southern states no longer felt represented in the Union and decided to secede. After a decade of growing hostility between the North and the South, civil war finally broke out.

Understanding Key Terms, People, and Places

Terms
Students should refer to the definitions of the key terms in the chapter to write sentences that show the relation of each word to the events leading up to the Civil War or the changes in political parties that occurred in the 1850s.

Matching
1. states' rights
2. Kansas-Nebraska Act
3. Panic of 1857
4. nativism

True or False
1. true
2. false, Charles Sumner
3. false, George Fitzhugh
4. false, Fort Sumter

Reviewing Main Ideas

1. By the 1850s, many Americans, especially middle-class Protestants, became convinced that slavery violated the basic principles of the United States. They believed that an individual should be able to make choices and develop character. Thus, slavery was an evil that could not be tolerated.

2. Fitzhugh claimed that northern employers exploited their workers as if their workers were slaves at the same time as they denounced southern slave owners.

3. New technology had a greater impact on the North than on the South. For example, the railroad boom primarily affected the North.

4. The issue of slavery required measures more drastic than compromise.

5. The Whigs no longer addressed the pressing issues of the day, such as slavery.

6. The two main issues were slavery and immigration.

7. Tensions over the issue of slavery escalated into open violence when a group of proslavery southerners looted the newspaper offices and homes of free soilers, leading to a series of raids and counterraids.

8. Douglas argued for the absolute right of white citizens to choose the kind of society and government they wanted; he therefore condoned slavery. Lincoln, although sharing Douglas's views of African Americans as inferior to white Americans, believed that slavery was morally wrong.

Chapter Review

Understanding Key Terms, People, and Places

Key Terms
1. Civil War
2. Union
3. Compromise of 1850
4. Fugitive Slave Act
5. states' rights
6. nativism
7. naturalization
8. Kansas-Nebraska Act
9. Slave Power
10. *Dred Scott* v. *Sandford*
11. Lecompton

constitution
12. Panic of 1857

People
13. Harriet Beecher Stowe
14. George Fitzhugh
15. Democratic party
16. American party
17. Know Nothings
18. Stephen Douglas
19. Republican party

20. free soiler
21. John Brown
22. Charles Sumner
23. Chief Justice Roger Taney
24. Abraham Lincoln
25. John C. Breckinridge
26. William Henry Seward
27. Constitutional Union party

28. secessionist
29. Jefferson Davis

Places
30. Harpers Ferry
31. Border States
32. Confederate States of America
33. Lower South
34. Fort Sumter
35. Upper South

Terms For each term above, write a sentence that explains its relation to the events leading up to the Civil War or the changes in political parties that occurred in the 1850s.

Matching Review the key terms in the list above. If you are not sure of a term's meaning, review its definition in the chapter. Then choose a term from the list that best matches each description below.
1. the theory that states have the right to nullify acts of the federal government
2. legislation proclaiming that the people in a territory should decide whether slavery would be allowed there
3. an economic downturn that increased tensions between North and South before the Civil War

4. the movement to ensure people born in the United States received better treatment than immigrants

True or False Determine whether each statement is true or false. If it is true, write "true." If it is false, change the underlined person or place to make the statement true.
1. Members of the <u>Constitutional Union party</u> were mostly southern moderates who had been Whigs.
2. <u>Stephen Douglas</u> gave a fiery speech entitled "The Crime Against Kansas."
3. <u>Harriet Beecher Stowe</u> attacked northern industrialists in the book *Cannibals All!*
4. After a twenty-four-hour bombardment, <u>Harpers Ferry</u> was surrendered to Confederate troops.

Reviewing Main Ideas

Section 1 (pp. 298–302)
1. Why did slavery seem threatening to northerners?
2. Describe George Fitzhugh's view of the North.
3. Describe technology's effect on North and South.

Section 2 (pp. 303–309)
4. Why was the Compromise of 1850 a failure?
5. Why did the Whig party fade away?
6. What issues helped the Republicans in the 1850s?

Section 3 (pp. 311–315)
7. Why was Kansas called "Bleeding Kansas"?

8. How did Lincoln and Douglas differ in their views?
9. Why did John Brown's raid lead to a greater division between the North and the South?

Section 4 (pp. 318–321)
10. You have read that Lincoln's victory in the election of 1860 was "a decisive victory, but a sectional one." Explain this statement.
11. Why did Lincoln's election prompt secession?
12. Explain why Lincoln was forced to respond to the attack on Fort Sumter.

9. Northerners saw Brown as a martyr to the cause of justice and freedom, while southerners denounced him as a terrorist. The raid was one more reason for the North and South to feel divided.

10. Lincoln received a majority of electoral college votes. However, he received no votes in the Lower South.

11. Lincoln was an antislavery President elected by northerners. The South no longer felt that it had a voice in government.

12. Southerners had fired on federal property, thereby issuing a challenge and committing an act of open rebellion.

Thinking Critically

1. Answers should acknowledge that the South lacked industry and much new technology. It also had a colonial-style economy, which would have limited economic growth.

2. The social contract, nullification, and states' rights.

3. Voters would probably feel that they had lost their voice in government. A President with only regional appeal would encounter great difficulties getting bills through Congress.

Thinking Critically

1. Predicting Consequences What economic difficulties would the South have faced if Lincoln had allowed it to leave the Union peacefully?

2. Determining Relevance The idea that states have the right to secede did not spring out of nowhere. What other beliefs concerning government that you have read about are related to it?

3. Demonstrating Reasoned Judgment Lincoln was elected only by voters from the North. How might voters in other regions of the United States respond today if a President were elected on the basis of winning, for example, only the South and the West? What challenges might a President encounter if he or she had only regional appeal?

Making Connections

1. Expressing Problems Clearly Review the primary source excerpt on page 314. Why did Lincoln believe that the United States could not endure if it was half slave and half free?

2. Understanding the Visuals Examine the before-and-after pictures of the life of enslaved Africans on page 300. How does the artist try to show that slavery "civilized" Africans?

3. Writing About the Chapter You are a newspaper reporter assigned to cover the violence in Kansas in 1856, John Brown's raid on Harpers Ferry, or the surrender of Fort Sumter. First, review the description in the chapter of the event you have chosen. Consider whether you will write your story from the viewpoint of a southern or a northern reporter.

Next, write a draft of your story in which you describe the event. Revise your story, making certain that it is vivid and that it reflects a clear point of view. Proofread your story and draft a final copy.

4. Using the Graphic Organizer This graphic organizer uses a multiflow map to show the sequence of events immediately preceding the outbreak of the Civil War. (a) What examples of a cause-and-effect relationship does the map suggest? (b) What details from the map demonstrate the breakdown of the democratic system of government? (c) On a separate sheet of paper, create your own graphic organizer about the series of clashes between antislavery and proslavery forces between 1856 and 1860, using this graphic organizer as an example.

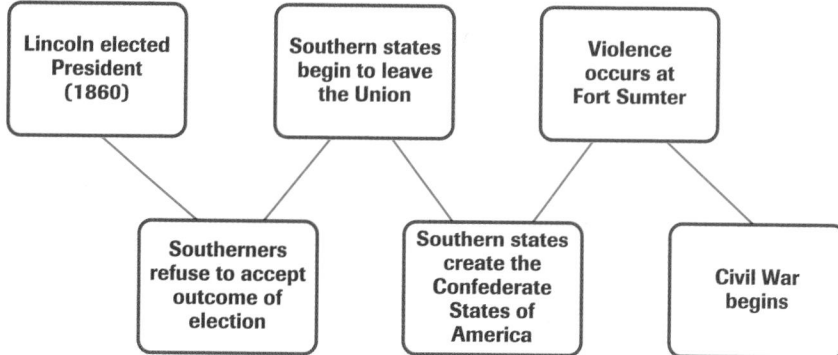

Making Connections

1. Slavery was too explosive and divisive an issue. Compromises had already been tried without success.

2. Answers may suggest that the artist portrayed the African in Africa as a lone killer of other human beings (pointing out the human skeleton and the spear) in a wild setting and the African in America as sitting peacefully with his family in a parlor decorated with paintings and other symbols of the arts.

3. Students' stories should reflect an understanding of the event chosen and an appreciation of how the description of an event is influenced by the point of view of the writer.

4. (a) Examples of cause and effect include the secession of the southern states from the Union as a result of Lincoln's election and the start of the war as a result of the violence at Fort Sumter. (b) The refusal of the South to accept Lincoln as President demonstrated the breakdown of the democratic system of government, in which voters accept the outcome of an election even if their candidate loses. (c) Students' graphic organizers should include information about the Compromise of 1850, the Kansas-Nebraska Act, and the changes that occurred in the political parties of the era.

Chapter 12 The Civil War
1861–1865

📁 **Teaching Resources** (See Unit 4 Folder)

	Instruction	Enrichment
Section 1 **The First Two Years of the Civil War** (pp. 326–332)	Reproducible Lesson Plan, p. 38 Alternate Lesson Plan, p. 59 Guided Reading and Review, p. 42 Quiz, p. 43	Visual Learning Activity, A British View of the Civil War, p. 66 Literature Activity, The Battle of Manassas, p. 63 Viewpoints Activity, On the Purpose of the Civil War, pp. 56–57 Critical Thinking Activity, Recognizing Bias, p. 59 American Profiles Activity, General Robert E. Lee, p. 54
Section 2 **War Brings Change** (pp. 333–339)	Reproducible Lesson Plan, p. 39 Alternate Lesson Plan, p. 60 Guided Reading and Review, p. 44 Quiz, p. 45	Literature Activity, Diary from Dixie, pp. 64–65 American Profiles Activity, Mary Elizabeth Bowser, p. 55 Historian's Toolbox Activity, Using Letters as Primary Sources, p. 58
Section 3 **Turning Point: The Siege of Vicksburg** (pp. 341–345)	Reproducible Lesson Plan, p. 40 Alternate Lesson Plan, p. 61 Guided Reading and Review, p. 46 Quiz, p. 47	Primary Source Activity, A Teenager's Account of War, pp. 61–62 Turning Points Extension Activity, The Lasting Impact of the Siege of Vicksburg, pp. 50–51
Section 4 **A New Birth of Freedom** (pp. 348–351)	Reproducible Lesson Plan, p. 41 Alternate Lesson Plan, p. 62 Guided Reading and Review, p. 48 Quiz, p. 49 Chapter Test, Forms A & B, pp. 68–73	Primary Source Activity, The Gettysburg Address, p. 60 Visual Learning Activity, Defending Atlanta, p. 67 Time and Place Activity, A Cold War Confrontation, pp. 52–53

📁 **Additional Chapter Resources**

Resource Organizer, p. 37
Alternate Lesson Plan, p. 58
Answer Keys, pp. 113–122

Bibliography

For the Teacher
Chesnut, Mary Boykin. *A Diary from Dixie.* Harvard University Press, 1980. (Observations of the war from the southern point of view.)
Quarles, Benjamin. *The Negro in the Civil War.* Little, Brown, 1989. (The role of African Americans in the Civil War.)
Wills, Garry. *Lincoln at Gettysburg: The Words That Remade America.* Simon & Schuster, 1993. (Pulitzer Prize–winning examination of the Gettysburg Address.)

Prentice Hall Literature Excerpts from *The American Experience,* 1994, including "Civil War Voices: A First-Person Narrative of the War."

Media and Technology

 Fine Art, D-10; The Way It Works, H-12

 Geographic Setting, M-3, M-4; The Way It Works, H-13

 Visions of America: Turning Point Story, "Mississippi Siege"

 Visions of America: Roundtable Discussion on "Mississippi Siege"

 Fine Art, D-11; Graphic Organizer, G-4

 Guided Reading Audiotapes (English and Spanish)

 Computer Test Bank

For the Student
Catton, Bruce, ed. *The American Heritage Picture History of the Civil War.* Outlet Book Co., 1985.

Crane, Stephen. *The Red Badge of Courage.* Bantam, 1981. (Classic novel of a Union soldier in the face of enemy fire; originally published in 1895.)

The Civil War. PBS Video. (Acclaimed, multi-part series that combines scholarly analysis and primary sources.)

THE BIG IDEA

The Big Idea for the chapter and how the main ideas in each section relate to the Big Idea are graphically displayed below. Comprehension of this chapter's Big Idea is critical to students' understanding of United States history and how we as a nation got where we are today.

CHAPTER 12

"The Civil War," wrote historian Page Smith, "took place because the southern states felt that they could no longer tolerate their status as members of the Union." After the bloodiest war in the western world in the nineteenth century, enslaved African Americans gained their freedom, while the federal government became a strong force in the lives of citizens.

SECTION 1
During the first two years of the war, the Union put its Anaconda Plan into action by blockading the coasts of the South and taking control of its midwestern part. Union troops failed to take the Confederate capital, however.

SECTION 2
During the Civil War, national government in both the North and the South became more powerful. When the federal government finally permitted African Americans to serve in the armed forces, they earned respect for their courage in battle.

SECTION 3
The successful siege of Vicksburg, Mississippi, which gave the Union control of the entire Mississippi River, was a turning point in the war. In another turning point at Gettysburg, Pennsylvania, the Confederacy suffered a major defeat.

SECTION 4
General Grant and his officers battered the Confederate Army and the South until, finally, Confederate General Lee surrendered at Appomattox Court House.

The Civil War
1861–1865

The Relevance of the Big Idea

Historian Bernard DeVoto posed the question, "Why does the United States consist of just the land area the map now shows; why are there not two or more nations in that area . . . ?" We all know that in the 1860s, we came close to having at least two disunited nations instead of one United States.

Ask students what regions they think exist within the United States today. How different are these regions from one another? Are they as different as separate nations? What conditions might convince one or more of these regions to separate from the rest of the United States?

In Depth

Global Connections

In the 1850s the southern states thought that "King Cotton" could bring them success as a separate nation. More than 80 percent of Britain's cotton came from the South, but by mid-1861 there was a 50 percent oversupply of cotton in the British market. Also, in May 1861 the British government declared its "strict and impartial neutrality" in what was termed the contest between the "Government of the United States of America and certain states styling themselves the Confederate States of America."

The Civil War
1861–1865

*F*or four years, the Civil War raged between the North and the South. Though the South was the main battleground, death and sorrow reached into the North as well. Hundreds of thousands of Americans were killed or maimed, and billions of dollars of property was destroyed. During this great conflict, African Americans won their freedom, and the Union was preserved, despite bad feelings that endured on both sides. The United States also became a completely new kind of nation, in which the federal government proved to be a powerful presence in the lives of the people.

Events in the United States

1861 The Confederacy defeats the Union at the First Battle of Manassas.

1862 Grant leads the Union to victory at the Battle of Shiloh.
• Congress passes the Homestead Act.

1860	1861	1862

Events in the World

1860 Garibaldi wins military victories that lead to the unification of Italy.

1861 Czar Alexander II abolishes serfdom in Russia.

1862 The independence of the African nation of Zanzibar is recognized.

RESOURCE DIRECTORY

Teaching Resources

Alternate Lesson Plan: Demonstrating the Big Idea found in the Alternate Lesson Plans folder, p. 58, provides a lesson strategy to instruct students about the Big Idea that during the four years of the Civil War hundreds of thousands of people lost their lives, African Americans won their freedom, and the federal government emerged as a more powerful presence in the lives of people.

Alternative Assessment Handbook provides information, guidance, and strategies for alternative methods of assessment. It includes an essay on new trends in assessment, guidance and strategies for developing performance tasks and portfolios, scoring rubrics, and sample evaluation forms.

Pages 326–332
The First Two Years of the Civil War
In the first two years of the war, Union armies tried again and again to capture the Confederate capital but were driven back by bolder and more skillful generals. Union forces did succeed, however, in blockading the coasts of the South and seizing control of the great river valleys of its midwestern states.

 Pages 333–339
War Brings Change
During the Civil War, national government in both the North and the South became a powerful presence in the lives of ordinary people. Meanwhile, African Americans in the United States armed forces earned long-overdue respect fighting for the freedom of enslaved people in the South.

 Pages 341–345
Turning Point: The Siege Of Vicksburg, 1863
The tide of war turned in the summer of 1863. Southern forces led by Robert E. Lee invaded Pennsylvania. At the same time, northern forces led by Ulysses S. Grant surrounded Vicksburg, Mississippi, in an attempt to wrest control of the Mississippi River from the Confederacy.

Pages 346–347
The Lasting Impact of the Siege of Vicksburg

 Pages 348–351
A New Birth of Freedom
Northern armies gradually pounded the weakened but persistent South, pushing it toward surrender. As the Civil War came to an end, the conflict became more than a struggle over the Union. It became instead a redefinition of the American nation.

1863 Lincoln proclaims freedom for enslaved people in the Confederacy.	*1864* Sherman leads Union forces in capture of Atlanta and Savannah. • Lincoln wins reelection.	*1865* Lincoln is assassinated. • Lee surrenders to Grant at Appomattox. • The 13th Amendment abolishes slavery.	
1863	**1864**	**1865**	**1866**
1863 The International Red Cross is founded in Switzerland. • Civil war begins in Afghanistan.	*1864* The Taiping Rebellion ends in China. • Prussia defeats Denmark in a brief war.	*1865* Paraguay declares war on Argentina, Brazil, and Uruguay. • Transatlantic telegraph cable is completed.	

Alternative Assessment

As an ongoing chapter project, students can create a short book for elementary school students explaining some of the major events of the Civil War. Students should illustrate their books with maps, drawings, or photocopies of photographs. Books should contain chapters on at least three of the following topics:

• The first two years of the war, including a discussion of the Anaconda Plan and the struggle for the capitals
• The generals and soldiers who fought the war, including information on weapons and supplies
• The effect of the war on African Americans
• Detailed examination of one major battle
• The last two years of the war

Explain that finished projects will be assessed according to the following standards:

• **Unacceptable** Projects are not completed or fail to meet the requirements outlined.
• **Limited/Acceptable** Projects are based on material from the textbook and correctly describe the major events, leaders, and consequences of the war.
• **Extensive/Commendable** Projects incorporate some outside research, correctly describe the major events, leaders, and consequences of the war, and are attractively illustrated.
• **Extraordinary/Outstanding** Projects are based on considerable outside research, summarize and show relationships among events, and are written clearly and vividly. Books are well illustrated with a variety of visual material.

For more information and guidance on alternative assessment trends and strategies, see the Alternative Assessment Handbook in the Resource Directory on page 324.

The First Two Years of the Civil War

1. FOCUS

Connecting to the Big Idea

See page 324B. Explain that during the first two years of the Civil War, each side tried without success to capture the other's capital. Ask why the war looked like a stalemate by 1863.

Objectives

● Explain how new technology and political pressure affected the tactics of the war.
● Describe Union strategy in the western part of the Confederacy.
● Describe the unsuccessful attempts by northern and southern generals to invade each other's territory.

Bellringer

Ask students to think about how new technology has influenced their lives. Which technologies were developed by the military? How has such technology changed the nature of war? How did technology change the nature of warfare during the Civil War?

Reading Strategy

Structured Overview Ask students to write the following column headings on a piece of paper: Union Tactics, Confederate Tactics, Union Victories, Confederate Victories. As they read, they should fill in details from the text in the appropriate column.

SECTION PREVIEW

In the first two years of the war, Union armies tried again and again to capture the Confederate capital but were driven back by bolder and more skillful generals. Union forces did succeed, however, in blockading the coasts of the South and seizing control of the great river valleys of its midwestern states.

Key Concepts

- Both new technology and political pressure greatly affected the tactics of the war.
- In the western part of the Confederacy, northern forces captured most of Kentucky, Tennessee, and the Mississippi Valley.
- Both the North and South resisted attempts to invade their territory in the East.

Key Terms, People, and Places

shell, canister, war of attrition, Anaconda Plan, gunboat; Stonewall Jackson, George McClellan, Ulysses S. Grant, Robert E. Lee; Manassas, Shiloh, Antietam

More than 90 percent of all battle wounds in the Civil War were caused by bullets—many of them by the new, more accurate type shown here.

"Forward to Richmond! Forward to Richmond!" thundered the *New York Tribune* in July 1861. With the secession of the Upper South from the Union, the Confederate states had shifted their capital from Montgomery, Alabama, to Richmond, Virginia. Now northern newspapers demanded immediate action from the volunteers assembled after the surrender of Fort Sumter.

Southerners were just as eager to fight. Wrote the editor of the *Richmond Examiner:*

> The idea of waiting for blows, instead of inflicting them, is altogether unsuited to the genius [nature] of our people. The aggressive policy is the truly defensive one.

Like northern troops, southern soldiers had volunteered for short periods of service. And like their brothers in the North, they were in a hurry to get the war over. ○

The Battle of Manassas

Public pressure for action had its effect in July 1861, when a large Union army tried to march to Richmond and collided with a Confederate army. This first major battle of the war was called both **Manassas**—the name of a nearby town—and the First Battle of Bull Run, after a small river in the area. Many Civil War battles have two names, one given by the South and the other given by the North. The South tended to connect a battle with the nearest town, the North with some physical feature close by the battlefield.

General Irvin McDowell had brought 30,000 Union troops about 30 miles west from Washington, D.C., to attack a southern army under General P.G.T. Beauregard—the officer who had captured Fort Sumter. On the morning of July 21, McDowell sent thousands of poorly trained men on a 10-mile march to strike at the left side of the Confederate army.

Confederate spies, including several women, sighted the Union troops, whose advance was no secret anyway. A huge crowd of civilians had traveled out from Washington behind the army to picnic and watch the battle.

The Confederates were well prepared. Although at first the Union troops nearly broke Beauregard's army, the southerners held their positions. The fighting was fierce: by the time it was over, nearly 5,000 men were killed, wounded, or missing.

In the afternoon, fresh Confederate troops were brought in by railroad—a technology now used in war for the first time—and streamed into the fight. Exhausted, the Union soldiers quit the battle. McDowell ordered a retreat.

But the day was not over. As they turned back, the Union soldiers ran into the crowds of sightseers who had followed them. The result

▶ RESOURCE DIRECTORY

Teaching Resources

Reproducible Lesson Plan found in the Unit 4 folder, p. 38, provides a summary of the Section 1 lesson plan content.

Alternate Lesson Plan: Critical Thinking Identifying Central Issues, found in the Alternate Lesson Plans folder, p. 59, encourages use of this skill to identify and analyze technology, strategy, and key battles in the first two years of the war.

Guided Reading and Review found in the Unit 4 folder, p. 42, provides a structure for reading and mastering the key concepts and reviewing the key terms for Section 1. (Guided Practice)

○ **Visual Learning Activity** A British View of the Civil War, found in the Unit 4 folder, p. 66, depicts European hopes for the war in a political cartoon.

○ **Literature Activity** The Battle of Manassas, found in the Unit 4 folder, p. 63, features poems by Herman Melville describing the famous author's impressions of the battle.

was total confusion. Soldiers and civilians were caught in a tangle of wagons and horses on the narrow road. Terrified that Confederate forces would catch them, troops and picnickers broke into a panic. The army disintegrated; by nightfall it had become a mass of men running headlong for the safety of Washington. ✪

The Tactics of the War

Battles are not always won or lost by dramatic chance events, split-second decisions, or the skill and heroism of one or two individuals. On some occasions, however, such factors do matter. At Manassas, for example, an intensely religious and energetic Confederate officer named Thomas Jonathan Jackson made his troops stand as solidly as a stone wall during a Union attack. He stopped the Union advance and earned the nickname **Stonewall Jackson**.

Though armies need extraordinary soldiers like Stonewall Jackson, more often victory depends on two less colorful factors—organization and training. At Manassas, both armies were poorly organized and trained, and the generals soon realized it. For example, neither McDowell nor Beauregard had a good staff of officers to deliver orders to the battlefield quickly and efficiently. And once the soldiers received their orders, they did not always have the training to know what to do.

Technology Influences Tactics Though both sides quickly learned their lesson about organization and training, they failed to learn that the old ways of fighting a war did not work anymore. Europeans had fought wars for centuries by attacking the enemy's capital city or gathering their forces for one big battle that would decide everything. Cannons and muskets in early times were neither accurate nor capable of repeating fire very quickly. To overwhelm the enemy, generals relied on masses of men moving across open fields.

Almost all the generals of the Civil War had been trained at the United States Military Academy at West Point, New York. They shared a belief in the old-fashioned tactics of gathering their forces in one place, attacking a position with massed troops, and driving the enemy

Viewpoints Activity On the Purpose of the Civil War, found in the Unit 4 folder, pp. 56–57, shows the differing views of North and South on the issue of states' rights.

Viewpoints
On the Purpose of the Civil War

Throughout the years of quarreling between North and South, southerners protested repeatedly that northerners were trampling on their rights, including the right to own slaves as property. *How did the war aims of each side, as described in the viewpoints below, reflect this part of their quarrel?*

The Aims of the South

"We have vainly endeavored to secure tranquility and obtain respect for the rights to which we were entitled. . . . If . . . the integrity of our territory and jurisdiction [legal authority] be assailed [attacked], it will but remain for us with firm resolve to appeal to arms."
President Jefferson Davis, Inaugural Address, February 18, 1861

The Aims of the North

"This war is not waged upon our part in any spirit of oppression, nor for any purpose of conquest or subjugation, nor purpose of overthrowing or interfering with the rights or established institutions of those [seceding] States, but to defend and maintain the supremacy of the Constitution and to preserve the Union, with all the dignity, equality, and rights of the . . . States unimpaired [undamaged]."
House of Representatives, Crittenden Resolution, July 25, 1861

away. The most vital position to attack, they believed, was the enemy's capital. The generals of both North and South had seen such tactics work well in the Mexican War.

In the Civil War, however, American generals gradually had to confront a new technology that had made this strategy suicidal. Gun makers had learned that a long piece of lead with a rounded tip—a bullet—did not drift as it flew, like the older type of ammunition, which was a simple lead ball. They also had discovered that a spiral groove—called rifling—cut on the inside of a gun barrel would make a fired bullet pick up spin and travel in a nearly straight line. These new, more accurate rifles, as they were called, also could be reloaded rapidly. Cannons, too, had been improved. Instead of relying on simple iron cannon balls to smash their targets, gunners had more deadly options. They could fire a cannon **shell** that exploded in the air over the enemy or burst after it hit, or a

Answer to ...

Viewpoints

Davis asserts the independence of the South and its right to bear arms against northern aggression; Crittenden's resolution states that only the preservation of the Union is at stake. For a more thorough examination of the purpose of the Civil War, see the Resource Directory below.

In Depth
Interdisciplinary

Hot air balloons, first employed in warfare by France in 1794, were used by American balloonist Thaddeus Lowe to provide the Union army with information on Confederate troop movements. Lowe conducted the first airborne operation of the recently invented telegraph. He also brought aloft cameras, which were just coming into popular use, to provide panoramic shots of military positions.

2. INSTRUCT

Explain/Discuss

Discuss with students how the expectations of both sides were called into question in the early days of the war. Why did each side wish to capture the other's capital? Ask students to point out the capitals on a map. How far apart were they? (*About 100 miles.*) How did the results of the Battle of Manassas affect those calling for a short war?

Ask students to discuss the tactics of the war. How did tactics lag behind technology? What caused the lag?

Display a wall map and ask students to use it to describe the Anaconda Plan. What sorts of forces did the Anaconda Plan require? Ask students to predict which locations were vital to the success of the Anaconda Plan as they study the map. (*Major ports and river towns such as New Orleans and Vicksburg.*)

Ask students to point out the areas of stalemate in the East and West in 1863, and to predict how these would be broken.

Analyze

Ask students to analyze Grant's victory at Shiloh. Grant himself said that the Battle of Shiloh convinced him that the Confederacy would not collapse after a decisive Union victory but would require "complete conquest." In what ways did Shiloh cause each side to reassess its commitment to the war?

Advantages and Disadvantages of the North and South		
	Northern States*	**Southern States**
Population	21.5 million	9 million
Railroad Mileage	21.7 thousand miles	9 thousand miles
Manufacturing		
Number of Factories	110.1 thousand	20.6 thousand
Number of Workers	1.17 million	111 thousand
Value of Products	$1.62 billion	$155 million
Finance		
Bank Deposits	$207 million	$47 million
Specie	$56 million	$27 million
Agriculture		
Corn (bushels)	446 million	280 million
Wheat (bushels)	132 million	31 million
Oats (bushels)	150 million	20 million
Cotton (bales)	4 thousand	5 million
Tobacco (pounds)	229 million	199 million
Rice (pounds)	50 thousand	187 million
Livestock		
Horses	4.2 million	1.7 million
Donkeys and Mules	300 thousand	800 thousand
Milch Cows	5.7 million	2.7 million
Beef Cattle	6.6 million	7 million
Sheep	16 million	5 million
Swine	16.3 million	15.5 million

* Includes border states

Source: *The American Heritage Picture History of the Civil War*, edited by Richard M. Ketchum

Interpreting Tables
Northerner William T. Sherman warned a southern friend in 1860, "You are bound to fail." *Which advantages would allow the North to raise a larger, better equipped army than the South?*

canister—a special shell filled with lead balls about the size of bullets. Canisters turned cannons into the equivalent of giant shotguns. To cross an open field against such weapons was an act of madness. Some Union and Confederate officers never realized this, though it was clear as early as the first battle at Manassas. Others eventually realized that it was slaughter to send soldiers against bullets, shells, and canister fire, but they continued to do so anyway.

Politics Influences Tactics Why did Civil War generals continue to use the old tactics? The reason is that Americans in both North and South were impatient; they wanted to win

and win today, not tomorrow or next year. The people demanded instant results from their politicians, and the politicians demanded instant results from their generals.

The Confederacy would have had the greatest chance of success if it had worn down the Union in a **war of attrition**. In this kind of war, a weaker army inflicts small but continuous losses of soldiers and material that gradually add up to an unbearable burden for the other side. The table at left shows that the North had tremendous resources. But such an advantage does not always mean victory, as the British had learned during the American Revolution.

Although Confederate president Jefferson Davis apparently recognized the wisdom of waging a war of attrition, his citizens would not let him adopt it. To fight a war of attrition, the army of the weaker side often has to avoid direct confrontations. It has to be able to retreat out of the enemy's way, even if it means giving up territory temporarily. Southerners, however, insisted that their government defend the entire Confederacy. The result was that the South had to stretch its precious soldiers and equipment in a thin line from Virginia to Texas. Its war goal was basically to keep attacking armies out of the Confederacy.

The goal of the North was to conquer the South, but northerners, too, would have been better off avoiding direct confrontations. General Winfield Scott, the hero of the Mexican War and the commander of the United States Army in 1861, knew this well. Scott's recommendation called for Union forces to surround the Confederacy and slowly squeeze it to death. Northern ships could cut the South off from the rest of the world, especially cotton markets in Great Britain and Europe. Union riverboats and armies could cut the Confederacy in two at the Mississippi. This plan would make the best use of the North's advantages—its superiority in population and industry, its more extensive railroads, and its navy.

In the end, the North did make use of Scott's plan. But when word of the strategy was leaked to northern newspapers, they ridiculed it, calling it the **Anaconda Plan**, after a type of snake that coils around its victims and crushes them to death. In 1861 and 1862, most Americans still had dreams of a short war. Much as Manassas

▶ RESOURCE DIRECTORY

Teaching Resources

 Critical Thinking Activity Recognizing Bias: Six Months on the Potomac, found in the Unit 4 folder, p. 59, encourages students to practice identifying point of view and bias with an 1862 cartoon depicting General McClellan and his Confederate counterpart encamped along the Potomac.

horrified soldiers and humbled officers, the political pressure for a quick victory remained strong. This public clamor for results led to more battles like Manassas. They were fought mainly between the two capitals, Richmond and Washington, which lie only 100 miles apart.

The North Begins to Strangle the South

The day after Manassas, President Lincoln appointed **George McClellan** to command the major Union army in the East. This was the Army of the Potomac, named after the river that flows past Washington.

General McClellan was a master organizer. He spent months preparing his men for battle and ensuring that they would have enough food and weapons. McClellan was a favorite with his men because he watched out for their welfare, but he was unpopular with Lincoln and northern politicians, who wanted results.

Though McClellan took no action, other Union officers did. Along the Confederate seacoasts, the United States Navy succeeded in retaking several important federal forts and in setting up a blockade of enemy ports. The great industrial and economic strength of the North came into play as the government built and bought the first of more than six hundred ships it would add to its navy. The anaconda had begun to flex its muscles.

The War on the Rivers In order for the North to squeeze the South, however, Union forces had to gain control of the midwestern part of the Confederacy. Conflict did take place even farther west, in Missouri, Texas, and Oklahoma, which was then called the Indian Territory, but the war in the midwest of the Confederacy is generally referred to as the war in the West. This region, shown on the map on this page, includes Tennessee, Arkansas, Mississippi, and Louisiana. It was a land of waterways, all leading to the Mississippi River. Whoever controlled the rivers would control commerce and military movements throughout the region. Knowing this full well, Confederate forces built Fort Henry on the Tennessee River and Fort Donelson on the Cumberland River, both in the state of Tennessee.

The Civil War in the West, July 1861–May 1863

Geography and History: Interpreting Maps
Union generals in the West such as Grant (shown below) focused their attention on the Mississippi River. "That Mississippi ruins us, if lost," worried southern observer Mary Boykin Chesnut in 1862. *What two key cities on the Mississippi had the Union captured by the summer of 1862?*

But this type of fort was a leftover from an older time. A new and deadly technology, the **gunboat,** made such forts largely useless. The typical gunboat—shown in the illustration on page 330—was basically a small floating fort fitted with rifled cannons. Built to navigate even shallow rivers, driven by steam power, and often protected by iron armor, it brought the destructive power of Union cannon shells deep into the Confederacy.

Under the command of a tough Union general, **Ulysses S. Grant,** gunboats quickly pounded Fort Henry into surrender in February 1862. Not long after, following three days of shelling by gunboats, Fort Donelson surrendered unconditionally—earning U. S. Grant the nickname "Unconditional Surrender" Grant.

The South would be unable to ship large quantities of cotton from its mid-western region; this would drastically affect its ability to earn money to pay for desperately needed supplies.

Gunboats gave Union forces a great advantage in river warfare. One Union naval commander was reported to have preached a Sunday sermon to his sailors in which he said, "Let not your heart be troubled. Ye believe in God; believe also in gunboats."

In Depth

Biography

Mary Boykin Chesnut (1823–1886) is the best known of the Confederate women diarists. A member of a prominent political family, Chesnut's husband, James Chesnut, Jr., was a wealthy senator, and her social circle included President Jefferson Davis. The time in which she lived was one of stress for the entire country, but she limited her observations to what was going on around her. It was her eye for daily life under wartime conditions that makes her diary so valuable. In July 1861 she wrote: "They brought me a Yankee soldier's portfolio from the battlefield. . . . One might shed tears over some of the letters. Women, wives and mothers, are the same everywhere."

The Cumberland and Tennessee rivers now formed Union highways into the heart of the midwestern Confederate states. Nashville soon fell to the Union, and by April General Grant had pushed south nearly to Mississippi and Alabama.

The Slaughter at Shiloh On April 6, however, a southern army unexpectedly struck Grant's forces near Shiloh Church in Tennessee. The Confederates won the first day of this Battle of **Shiloh,** driving the Union troops back nearly into the Tennessee River. But Grant, displaying the determination that would see him through many a crisis in the years ahead, refused to give up. "Retreat?" he scoffed to his doubting officers after the first day. "No. I propose to attack at daylight and whip them."

With the help of reinforcements, Grant was as good as his boast. The North won the battle on April 7. But some 13,000 Union men and 10,000 Confederates had been killed, wounded, or captured. It was the bloodiest single battle that had taken place on the American continent up to that time. Wrote one Tennessee soldier after Shiloh:

I never realized the "pomp and circumstance" of the thing called glorious war until I saw this. Men . . . lying in every conceivable position; the dead . . . with their eyes open, the wounded begging piteously for help.

The Battle of Shiloh showed northern civilians once again that the Confederacy would not collapse overnight. But it also stopped the South from regaining western Tennessee and its river highways.

Action on the Mississippi While Grant was breaking into the Confederacy in Kentucky and Tennessee, Union gunboats and troops were taking many of the Confederate posts on the Mississippi River. In late April 1862, a naval squadron commanded by an iron-willed, sixty-year-old captain named David Farragut forced the surrender of New Orleans, Louisiana. Less than two months later, on June 6, the Union navy also seized Memphis, Tennessee. This city, too, was located in a key position on the Mississippi River.

Slowly, in battle after battle, the Union was putting the Anaconda Plan into operation. In early 1862, Union forces had captured 50,000 square miles, taken control of 1,000 miles of navigable rivers, and seized New Orleans, the largest city in the South. A southern observer, Mary Boykin Chesnut, wrote of her concern about the growing pressure on the Confederacy. Sentences stitched together from her diary over the course of April and May 1862 tell the grim story:

B attle after battle—disaster after disaster. . . . The power they are bringing to bear against our country is tremendous. . . . I have nothing to chronicle [tell] but disasters. . . . The reality is hideous.

Only two major posts on the Mississippi River now remained in Confederate hands—Vicksburg, Mississippi, and Port Hudson, Louisiana. If northern forces could find some way to capture them, the entire Mississippi River valley would be under Union control.

You have read in previous chapters that the South was dependent on its rivers, especially the Mississippi River, to transport cotton for sale abroad. What effect would closing the Mississippi to Confederate boats have on the South's effort to win the war?

RESOURCE DIRECTORY

Teaching Resources

American Profiles Activity General Robert E. Lee, found in the Unit 4 folder, p. 54, profiles the Confederacy's brilliant military commander.

The War for the Capitals

Though Union action on the seas and in the western river valleys was actually far more significant than capturing Richmond, the North was still obsessed with making a quick end of the war by taking the enemy capital. By the spring of 1862, George McClellan had built a huge, well-equipped army. But he was reluctant to move. President Lincoln supposedly became so frustrated with his commander that he quipped: "I will hold McClellan's horse if he will only bring us success."

McClellan's Troops Invade Virginia McClellan thought that going to Richmond through Manassas again would be a mistake. So in the spring of 1862, he moved the Army of the Potomac by ship to the peninsula near Yorktown, Virginia. He inched his troops forward until, by the end of May, he was within a few miles of Richmond (see the map at right).

McClellan had about 100,000 soldiers—twice as many as the Army of Northern Virginia, the Confederate force near Richmond. But the South had two brilliant military leaders.

⭐ The first was General **Robert E. Lee**—the man who had captured John Brown at Harpers Ferry in 1859. Lee took over as the leader of the Confederate forces when General Joseph Johnston was wounded in late May. Lee was an experienced officer, a leader of great courage and intelligence, and a highly dignified and moral man. He had once called slavery "a moral and political evil," but he fought for Virginia because—like many Americans of his day—he felt more loyalty to his state than to the Union. Like all great generals, Lee wanted well-trained men and well-thought-out plans. But he also understood that victory often depends on a willingness to take chances.

The other brilliant leader was General Stonewall Jackson. He drove his men hard and could move his army with a speed that baffled the enemy. While McClellan was creeping close to Richmond, Jackson dashed north of the capital and carried out a series of lightning attacks on Union forces in the Shenandoah Valley in the Blue Ridge Mountains of Virginia. Lincoln was alarmed. Would Jackson attack Washington? To Lincoln and the North, the slippery rebel seemed to be everywhere at once, and his 17,000 men seemed to be three times that number. The Union secretary of war, Edwin M. Stanton, ordered 50,000 Union troops to pursue Jackson instead of joining McClellan. After Jackson had thoroughly confused and alarmed the enemy, he slipped his forces away to help General Lee.

A Union general with the determination of Grant might well have taken the Confederate capital. But McClellan was not Grant. In the Seven Days' Battles, fought from June 25 through July 1, 1862, the outnumbered southerners wore out McClellan's great army and

The Civil War in the East, July 1861–May 1863

 Geography and History: Interpreting Maps
McClellan's extreme caution was his own worst enemy. "No one but McClellan would have hesitated to attack," said Confederate general Joe Johnston during McClellan's slow advance toward Richmond before the Seven Days' Battles. *What action did Lee take after winning the Seven Days' Battles?*

Media and Technology

 Transparency
The Way It Works, H-12

3. ASSESS

Section 1 Review Answers

1. (a) shell, see p. 327, (b) canister, see p. 328, (c) war of attrition, see p. 328, (d) Anaconda Plan, see p. 328, (e) gunboat, see p. 329

2. (a) Stonewall Jackson, see p. 327, (b) George McClellan, see p. 329, (c) Ulysses S. Grant, see p. 329, (d) Robert E. Lee, see p. 331

3. (a) Manassas, see p. 326, (b) Shiloh, see p. 330, (c) Antietam, see p. 332

4. New technology such as bullets, rifle guns, cannons, exploding shells, and canisters turned the tactic of attacking a position with massed troops into an act of madness. Political pressures from both northerners and southerners who wanted instant results from the war drove generals to keep using this tactic, however.

5. Union forces took control of the Cumberland and Tennessee rivers, pushed nearly to Mississippi and Alabama, and captured New Orleans and Memphis.

6. Huge Union armies had failed four times to reach Richmond.

7. Possible answers: Follow the more elastic defense used by George Washington, concentrate on defending a more limited part of the Confederacy, or concentrate forces to break the naval blockade or Union control of the Mississippi River at specific points. Students may also observe that these options probably would not have succeeded.

Caption Answer to ...

🌐 **Interpreting Maps**

He moved northward across Virginia into Maryland.

Ask students to correct each of the following incorrect statements.

- The Battle of Manassas was a Union victory that fed the notion that the war would be won quickly.
- The Confederacy tried to wage a war of attrition against the Union.
- The goal of the Anaconda Plan was to capture Richmond and demand that the Confederates surrender.
- By 1863 the Union was clearly on its way to capturing Richmond and ending the war.

4. CLOSE

Reinforcing the Big Idea

The first two years of the Civil War were terribly bloody and in some ways indecisive. The Union victories in the West, however, were crucial. In the next section, students will see that the war changed the lives of Americans on both sides of the conflict.

In Depth

Then and Now

Before the Civil War, Richmond, Virginia, was a major center for the slave trade. A century later, in 1977, African Americans won five of the nine seats on the Richmond city council, and Henry L. Marsh III was elected Richmond's first African American mayor. In 1982, Marsh was succeeded as mayor by another African American—Roy A. West.

Both Robert E. Lee (left) and Stonewall Jackson (right) believed in a strategy once described by Jackson: "Never fight against heavy odds if . . . you can hurl your own force on only a part . . . of your enemy and crush it."

sent it limping for safety. Again the human cost was nearly unbelievable: some 30,000 Americans were killed or wounded.

The Confederacy Attacks Now that Richmond had been saved, Lee tried to exploit the situation by invading the North. Any show of southern strength could have great benefits, because Great Britain was watching events closely, waiting for a sign that the Confederacy could stand on its own two feet. If Britain could be persuaded to recognize the Confederate States as an independent nation, its assistance in the war would be enormous. Furthermore, a successful invasion of the Northeast might force the United States to end the war.

For a few months, as Lee, Jackson, and other excellent Confederate generals fought their way into Maryland, the Confederacy seemed about to win its independence. But that hope faded on September 17, near Sharpsburg, Maryland, when McClellan's reorganized army met Lee's forces in the Battle of **Antietam.** It was the bloodiest day of the entire war: close to 6,000 soldiers were killed and 17,000 wounded. Neither side won a clear victory. All the same, Lee's heavy losses forced him to turn back to Virginia.

The War Becomes a Stalemate After Antietam, McClellan was replaced. The Union army again tried to take Richmond. In December 1862, General Ambrose Burnside led 110,000 men against Lee's 75,000 men, who were well entrenched along the Rappahannock River near Fredericksburg, Virginia. The Union forces were soundly defeated.

In early May 1863, another Union general, Joseph Hooker, clashed with Lee at Chancellorsville, Virginia. Outnumbered as usual, Lee broke two rules of good generalship: he divided his forces, and he attacked a larger army, rather than waiting to be attacked. He sent Stonewall Jackson and his men on a long, risky march to strike Hooker from behind. The strategy worked brilliantly. Lee thrashed the Union army, though it was twice the size of his own.

Among the many Confederate dead was Stonewall Jackson, who was wounded by his own men in the confusion and died a week later. The North lost about 17,000 men and gave up its lingering hopes for a short war.

In fact, it seemed to northerners that the war had reached a stalemate. In the East, huge Union armies had now failed four times to reach Richmond. In the West, Grant was stuck in the Mississippi Valley, trying to find some way to capture Vicksburg and open up the Mississippi River to Union warships.

But the stalemate would not last long. Ulysses S. Grant was indeed a determined man—as determined as Lee was brilliant.

SECTION 1 REVIEW

Key Terms, People, and Places

1. Define (a) shell, (b) canister, (c) war of attrition, (d) Anaconda Plan, (e) gunboat.
2. Identify (a) Stonewall Jackson, (b) George McClellan, (c) Ulysses S. Grant, (d) Robert E. Lee.
3. Identify (a) Manassas, (b) Shiloh, (c) Antietam.

Key Concepts

4. Give examples of the way in which new technology and political pressure affected the Civil War.

5. What gains did Union forces make in the western part of the Confederacy in the first two years of the Civil War?
6. Why did the war in the East seem like a stalemate by early 1863?

Critical Thinking

7. **Identifying Central Issues** If you had been the president of the Confederacy, how would you have defended your nation against the Anaconda Plan?

RESOURCE DIRECTORY

Teaching Resources

Quiz found in the Unit 4 folder, p. 43, covers the main ideas in this section as well as the key terms.

War Brings Change

SECTION PREVIEW

During the Civil War, national government in both the North and the South became a powerful presence in the lives of ordinary people. Meanwhile, African Americans in the United States armed forces earned long-overdue respect fighting for the freedom of enslaved people in the South.

Key Concepts

• The Confederate government held great power over its citizens, but had difficulty uniting the efforts of its stubbornly independent states.

• President Lincoln limited the rights of the citizens of the North during the war.

• Republicans in Congress passed legislation that later allowed the United States to become a major economic power.

• President Lincoln enlarged the purpose of the war from just saving the Union to abolishing slavery as well.

• During the Civil War, many African Americans set themselves free, and many also fought to free others.

Key Terms, People, and Places

draft, writ of *habeas corpus*, Internal Revenue Act of 1862, greenback, Pacific Railroad Act of 1862, Emancipation Proclamation, contraband; Copperhead, Radical Republican

---

T he Civil War forever changed the relationship between Americans and their government and gave a new meaning to American citizenship. These changes began as both the South and the North responded to the demands of the war.

The Confederacy— Strong and Weak

The branches and powers of the Confederate government were very similar to those of the strong, federal government of the United States. But the men who framed the Confederate constitution also made certain that it explicitly recognized slavery and states' rights. The resulting tension between a strong federal government and strong state governments caused many difficulties for the South during the war.

Strong Federal Power President Jefferson Davis and his government in Richmond faced severe challenges. Unlike their northern counterparts, they had to create a government from scratch and do it while fighting a major war. They lacked money, officials—even furniture for their offices.

Furthermore, like the government in the North, the government of the Confederate States had to persuade an intensely independent and democratic people to sacrifice their personal interests for the common good. But in the South, the problem was even more difficult, because the challenge was to turn rebels into citizens, to forge loyalty to a new government out of disloyalty to an old one. And because the South had fewer people, less money, and less industry than the North, the Confederate war effort required making use of all available human and economic resources.

To meet these needs, the Confederate government passed **draft** laws in April and November of 1862. A draft is a legal means of forcing people to serve in the armed forces. The Confederate draft laws were the first in American history. Under these laws, all white men between eighteen and thirty-five had to fight for the Confederacy, except those who owned a certain number of slaves. Men who were already in the armed forces had to remain there for another three years. Though forcing people to fight for their own independence was a contradiction in terms, the Confederate government had no choice.

Through their own efforts, including outstanding courage in battle, Americans brought dramatic changes to their lives during the Civil War. Medals of Honor like this one were awarded to many, including twenty-one African Americans.

---

1. FOCUS

Connecting to the Big Idea

See page 324B. Explain that the Civil War brought many changes to the lives of both northerners and southerners. Ask students how the national governments of both sides grew in power. How did the war affect the lives of African Americans?

Objectives

● Explain why the Confederate government had difficulty uniting the efforts of its member states.

● Describe how President Lincoln limited the rights of citizens of the North during the war.

● Identify legislation passed during the Civil War that later allowed the United States to become a major economic power.

● Explain how Lincoln issued the Emancipation Proclamation to enlarge the purpose of the war.

● Explain how many African Americans set themselves free during the war and fought to free others.

Bellringer

Ask students to think about how the power of the federal government in the United States changed during its first century as a nation. Then ask them to consider the possible effects of war on the power of government.

Reading Strategy

Reading for Evidence As they read the section, students should look for evidence to support the following statement on page 333: "The Civil War forever changed the relationship between Americans and their government and gave a new meaning to American citizenship."

📋 **Reproducible Lesson Plan** found in the Unit 4 folder, p. 39, provides a summary of the Section 2 lesson plan content.

📋 **Alternate Lesson Plan: Cooperative Learning** found in the Alternate Lesson Plans folder, p. 60, provides a strategy for groups of students to compose letters to the editor representing the views of various segments of Civil War society on their current affairs.

📋 **Guided Reading and Review** found in the Unit 4 folder, p. 44, provides a structure for reading and mastering the key concepts and reviewing the key terms for Section 2. (Guided Practice)

Explain/Discuss

Discuss with students the strengths and weaknesses of the Confederate government. Ask students in what ways it resembled the federal government during the Revolution.

Ask students to list the ways the federal government increased its power during the war. Tell students that Lincoln took on extraordinary power, interfering with freedom of the press and suspending the writ of *habeas corpus* to hold Maryland and the other Border States within the Union. Do students think that Lincoln was justified? What might have happened if he had not acted decisively to hold the Border States?

Ask students to list the permanent increases in federal power described in the section. Ask why the Civil War provided the opportunity for these increases.

Analyze

Have students analyze the following statement by Viscount Palmerston, a contemporary British observer, that in the Emancipation Proclamation, Lincoln attempted "to abolish slavery where he was without power to do so, while protecting it where he had power to destroy it." Ask students to explain and then agree or disagree with the statement. Did Lincoln accomplish his purpose with the Emancipation Proclamation?

"All that has been said by orators and poets since the creation of the world in praise of women . . . would not do them justice for their conduct during the war," said Abraham Lincoln. This woman cared for her children and her soldier husband in a Union camp in 1862.

In addition to directing the use of human resources, the Confederate government also took control of the economy of the South. It determined such matters as the production of wool, cotton, and leather and seized control of southern railroads from private owners. Such actions gave the government of the Confederacy far more power over the lives of its citizens than the government of the Union had ever had.

The South's Weakness: States' Rights

Working against this strong federal control was a fierce southern commitment to states' rights, which harmed the war effort in countless ways. For example, Lee's soldiers often had no boots. The state of North Carolina had boots enough to supply the entire Confederate army—but reserved them for the use of its own troops.

Temporary Increases in Federal Power

Like the central government of the Confederate states, the federal government of the United States also dramatically increased its power during the Civil War. In March 1863 it, too, passed a draft law. The northern draft was weaker than the southern law. Out of 776,000 northern men ordered to report for service in the course of the war, only some 46,000 actually served. About 87,000 paid a fee to avoid the army, and about 74,000 hired substitutes. The rest either moved to Canada or the West, or were exempted from service for some reason such as physical disability.

In response to emergencies created by the war, Lincoln also extended government power into the lives of the people by denying them basic rights. He interfered with freedom of the press by sending the army to shut down newspapers that criticized the policies of his administration. He also suspended the **writ of habeas corpus**, a basic civil liberty protected by the Constitution. This writ is a court order directed to an officer holding a prisoner in jail. It commands the officer to demonstrate to the court that the prisoner is being held for good reason. The Constitution allows suspension of the writ during a rebellion. Lincoln, like President Davis in the South, suspended the writ in various parts of the country. He could then imprison anyone who interfered with the war effort without having to justify his actions. As Secretary of State William Seward told the British ambassador:

> I can touch a bell on my right hand and order the imprisonment of a citizen in New York; and no power on earth except the President can release them.

Lincoln's suspension of the writ of *habeas corpus* was no idle threat. Over 13,000 Americans who objected to federal policies were held in northern prisons without trial during the war.

Permanent Increases in Federal Power

The draft, limits on freedom of the press, and the suspension of the writ of *habeas corpus* were temporary measures in response to the war. Other changes were permanent. Now that southern Democrats had left Congress, Republicans

▶ RESOURCE DIRECTORY

Teaching Resources

✪ **Literature Activity** Diary from Dixie, found in the Unit 4 folder, pp. 64–65, uses excerpts from the diary of Mary Chesnut to describe life in the war-torn South.

had little opposition. They were able to pass several major laws during the Civil War that would have a lasting impact on the United States.

New Tax Laws Many Republicans, including Lincoln, were former Whigs and as such had supported a strong national government that would promote business. Faced with the need to raise money to pay for the war, they passed a tariff that not only would bring in cash, but also would protect American industries from foreign competition.

Other tax measures were aimed mostly at raising money just to wage war. In 1861 the Republican-controlled Congress passed the first federal tax on income in American history. It collected 3 percent of the income of people making more than $800 a year. Then, in the **Internal Revenue Act of 1862**, Congress created taxes on items such as liquor, tobacco, medicine, and newspaper ads. The act even established a stamp tax. While almost all of the taxes ended with the war, the Bureau of Internal Revenue created by Republican legislation became a permanent part of the federal government. It is now known as the Internal Revenue Service (IRS) and is responsible for collecting taxes from individuals and corporations.

Changes in the Nation's Finances In 1863 and 1864, Congress reformed the nation's banking system. Since 1832, when Andrew Jackson vetoed the rechartering of the Second Bank of the United States, Americans had relied on state banks, which issued their own bank notes. Believing that this system was too disorganized, Republicans created a national currency, called **greenbacks** after their color. Though greenbacks were only bank notes, the banks that issued them were chartered not by the states but by the federal government—and the government guaranteed their value.

Promoting American Expansion During the war, President Lincoln also signed several laws that had a powerful impact on the nation's expansion. The **Pacific Railroad Act of 1862** permitted the federal government to offer public land and money to several companies in return for the construction of a railroad from Nebraska to the Pacific Coast. As a result of this act, transcontinental railways would soon link East and West. The Homestead Act of 1862 granted 160 acres of federal land to settlers who lived on the grant and improved it for a period of five years. Under the Morrill Act of 1862, money from the sale of public land was to be used to fund an agricultural college in each state. Many of these colleges later developed into the great universities of the Midwest. The Morrill Act also established the Department of Agriculture to promote farming in the nation.

The Impact of Republican Legislation This Republican legislation as a whole laid the political and economic foundations for the emergence of the United States as the most powerful industrial and agricultural nation in the world. For decades, southern Democrats from Thomas Jefferson to Andrew Jackson had limited the way the federal government could direct the development of the nation's economy. Now, with southerners out of the picture, Republicans made the Civil War Congresses among the most active in American history. They created what amounted to a modified version of the American System promoted by Henry Clay and John Quincy Adams in the 1820s. In the process, they also created a cozy relationship between capitalists and the United States government.

MAKING CONNECTIONS

After the Civil War, people seldom used the term *Union* or used expressions such as "the United States *are*." They were more likely to refer to "the nation" and to say "the United States *is*." Explain how the Republican policy of making government bigger and more powerful helped bring about this change in attitude.

Reaction to Republican Legislation

Because Democrats were in the minority in Congress, they could not stop Republicans from passing such laws. Opponents of the Republicans on the streets of the nation, however, still could raise up their voices in protest. In July 1863, mobs in New York City vented their rage

In Depth

Did You Know?

The Civil War divided the nation in very cruel ways. First Lady Mary Todd Lincoln had four brothers and three brothers-in-law fighting on the Confederate side. Already a controversial figure, accused of willful extravagance and mental instability, Mrs. Lincoln was also alleged to be acting as a rebel spy. The persistence of such rumors led President Lincoln to state: "I, of my own knowledge, know that it is untrue that any of my family hold treasonable communication with the enemy."

Using Historical Evidence

The Union is represented by a woman being attacked by snakes ("Copperheads").

Enrichment

Ask students to research and report on the effect of the Emancipation Proclamation on Great Britain's role in the war.

In Depth

Multicultural Perspectives

Antislavery activities grew in the Border States in anticipation of emancipation. For example, Wisconsin infantryman Stanley Lathrop wrote from northern Arkansas, "We are the first Federal troops who have ever been in this part of the state. Almost all the rich plantation owners have fled as usual, and their negroes are beginning to come to us. . . . Colonel Daniels says he did not persuade them to run away and he will not return them as the Fugitive Slave law privilege of *habeus corpus* etc. are suspended." (See Key Events in the Reference Section.)

at the draft in one of the worst riots in American history. At least 105 people died during four days of looting and destruction. The rioters attacked draft offices, federal property, and the offices of prominent Republican newspapers.

Many members of these mobs were Irish Catholics, who had been targets of Republican nativism for years. But in many ways, the rage of the rioters had more to do with racial prejudice than federal or Republican power. The rioters believed that they were being drafted to fight a war that would benefit only African Americans. A total of eleven African Americans died in the riots, dozens were beaten, and a home for African American orphans was burned to the ground.

Antiwar Democratic politicians—called **Copperheads** after a type of poisonous snake—played on northern racial fears. They wrote editorials and gave speeches warning that Republican policies would bring a tide of African Americans to the North, freed by Union armies. These freed slaves, said Copperheads, would take jobs away from whites. Using such scare tactics, the Copperheads won many congressional and state elections in 1862.

The Emancipation Proclamation

While Copperheads were attacking Lincoln because of his sympathy for African Americans, others were angry with him for not taking a

Using Historical Evidence This cartoon of 1863 echoes Lincoln's warning that "the enemy behind us is more dangerous to the country than the enemy before us." *Explain the symbols in the cartoon.*

strong stand *against* slavery. They included African Americans such as Frederick Douglass and **Radical Republicans** such as Charles Sumner. The Radical Republicans were a wing of the Republican party made up of abolitionists and others hostile to the South.

During the early part of the war, President Lincoln continued to insist that the struggle was about the Union, not about emancipation, or freeing enslaved people. In fact, he promised not to interfere with slavery where it already existed; he did not want to create new enemies in slave states such as Maryland and Kentucky.

Despite Lincoln's focus on restoring the Union, eventually he realized that he could not achieve his purpose without emancipating the enslaved people of the South. In July 1862 he decided to move toward this goal by writing a proclamation to be issued at a time when the Union cause seemed to be winning. Lincoln's **Emancipation Proclamation** stated that as of January 1, 1863, all enslaved people in the areas in open rebellion against the government would "be then, thenceforward, and forever free."

On September 22, five days after Lee and his army abandoned the battlefield at Antietam and retreated south, Lincoln issued his proclamation. It had no immediate effect on enslaved people because they were still under southern control. But it was a promise that they would be free when the North won the war. Just as Lincoln had made slavery in the territories a moral issue during the campaign of 1858, he made slavery in the South a moral issue now. The war was no longer just about the political question of whether the Union would survive. It was about the moral question of whether slavery would fail. As Lincoln told Congress in December 1862:

> Fellow-citizens, we *cannot escape history. . . . The fiery trial through which we pass, will light us down, in honor or dishonor, to the latest* [last] *generation. . . . We hold the power, and bear the responsibility. In giving freedom to the slave, we assure freedom to the free. . . . We shall nobly save, or meanly lose, the last best, hope of earth.*

 RESOURCE DIRECTORY

Teaching Resources

American Profiles Activity found in the Unit 4 folder, p. 55, profiles Mary Elizabeth Bowser, a former slave and important spy for the Union.

African Americans Free Themselves

The Emancipation Proclamation had a practical as well as a moral effect. The Proclamation encouraged enslaved African Americans in the South to set themselves free by moving to territory controlled by Union troops. Actually, they had been doing so since the beginning of the war by means of an unusual feature of the laws of war.

The Contraband Rule During war, the property of the enemy may be seized and declared **contraband.** It then becomes the property of the government. Early in the war, a clever Union general, Benjamin F. Butler, realized that if enslaved African Americans were supposedly the property of the enemy, they too could be considered contraband. The federal government, as their legal owner, could then declare them free. "We," General Butler insisted, "do not need and will not hold such property."

It was a strange irony. Slaveholders had always stubbornly insisted that by law enslaved people were only property. That legal status was now helping enslaved African Americans set themselves free, and they did so by the thousands. After one raid into Mississippi in 1864, a Union general reported: "We bring in some 500 prisoners, a good many refugees, and about ten miles of Negroes." As they left slave plantations, which depended on their labor, African Americans severely weakened the Confederacy.

African Americans Fight for Freedom Once they were free, many African Americans took advantage of another provision of the Proclamation, which allowed them to enlist in the armed forces of the United States. Now they could fight to free others who were still enslaved. The sight of African American soldiers marching across the South was a nightmare come true for white slaveholders. But for African Americans the chance to fight against slavery was a milestone in their history, and 85 percent of the African Americans eligible to fight did so. These African

Americans in the armed forces eventually totalled nearly 180,000 soldiers, almost 10 percent of the Union fighting force.

⭐ Many of the African American soldiers were from free families in the North; some were college educated. But close to 119,000 had once been enslaved. During the war, more than 68,000 were killed or wounded, and 21 won the Medal of Honor, the nation's highest award for courage in combat. One of these was William Harvey Carney, a member of the 54th Massachusetts Regiment.

AMERICAN PROFILES
William Harvey Carney

Occasionally it happens that people who are otherwise unknown achieve a success so remarkable that it flames brightly in the shadows of the past. Such was the case with Sergeant William Harvey Carney.

Carney was born in 1840, but no one is sure where. It was in either New Bedford, Massachusetts, or Norfolk, Virginia. About his family the record is silent. When the Civil War began, he was just another unknown American.

African Americans (top) escape slavery by following the Union army as it retreats across the Rappahannock River in Virginia in 1862. At bottom, a boy named Jackson sheds the rags of slavery to wear the uniform of a drummer.

Section 2 Review Answers

1. (a) draft, see p. 333, (b) writ of *habeas corpus,* see p. 334, (c) Internal Revenue Act of 1862, see p. 335, (d) greenback, see p. 335, (e) Pacific Railroad Act of 1862, see p. 335, (f) Emancipation Proclamation, see p. 336, (g) contraband, see p. 337

2. (a) Copperhead, see p. 336, (b) Radical Republican, see p. 336

3. The South continued the pattern of strong federal government established by the original Constitution, but also tended to weaken federal authority by recognizing states' rights.

4. He limited freedom of the press and suspended the writ of *habeas corpus.*

5. Possible answer: The Pacific Railroad Act provided for the construction of transcontinental railways that linked East and West.

6. It extended them from the political issue of preserving the Union to the moral issue of ending slavery.

7. African Americans abandoned slave plantations, which depended on their labor, severely weakening the South; they also fought in the Union army in huge numbers.

8. Possible answers: The breakdown of law and order in the 1850s, as well as the Civil War itself were connected to the issue of slavery. Northerners were no longer content to let the slave system stand, even in the states in which it had originally been legal under the Missouri Compromise. Lincoln knew that slavery would be an enduring source of friction even if the South could be brought back into the Union with slavery intact in the southern states.

Reteach

Based on what they have learned in the section, ask students to identify the following changes in the federal government as temporary or permanent.

- A draft law supplied troops for the army.
- Congress passed new tax laws, including a federal tax on income.
- Congress created a national currency.
- The President suspended the writ of *habeas corpus*.
- The President shut down newspapers that disagreed with his policies.

In Depth

Then and Now

Students in the 1990s can see the story of the Fifty-fourth Massachusetts Regiment retold in the film *Glory*. The film, which won three Academy Awards in 1989, also won praise for its attention to historical detail. Historian Peter Burchard wrote: "It took great heart . . . to tell the story of the Fifty-fourth as it is told in *Glory*—from the point of view of the regiment's rank and file."

Many years after his heroic actions in the Civil War, William Harvey Carney posed for a photographer. He achieved widespread fame for his refusal to let the American flag touch the ground during battle.

Carney Joins the Regiment In February 1863, a little over a month after the Emancipation Proclamation became official, Carney enlisted in Company C of the 54th Massachusetts Regiment. Hundreds of African American men from all over the northern states signed up with the regiment at the same time.

Carney soon rose to the rank of sergeant. He could not rise higher because, with few exceptions, only whites could be officers. The commander of the 54th Regiment was Colonel Robert Gould Shaw. Despite his youth—he was only twenty-five years old in 1863—Colonel Shaw was an experienced veteran of Antietam. Reserved but kind, he inspired great loyalty in his men.

Even though they wore the blue uniform of the United States, Carney and his fellow soldiers had to endure all kinds of insults. Not only were they paid less than white troops, they were denied adequate supplies and equipment. Overcoming these challenges, the 54th became a disciplined and proud unit.

When the regiment was sent to South Carolina in June, Shaw was eager to get his men into battle. Though as a veteran he knew the horrors of the new kind of warfare, he also knew the 54th had something to prove, something bigger than battlefield courage.

The Charge on Fort Wagner On July 18, 1863, as part of the Union attack on the city of Charleston, the 54th Massachusetts led the assault on Fort Wagner on Morris Island. The regiment was assigned to charge the fort under cover of darkness. The members of the 54th would have to advance along an open beach, easy targets for as many as twenty cannons within the fort and other Confederate artillery elsewhere. In addition to shells and canisters, these guns could fire bursts of grapeshot, or small pellets, and shells filled with shrapnel, a form of larger metal fragment. The 54th would be armed only with rifles and bayonets—a type of long knife fastened onto their gun barrels.

At 7:45 P.M., Carney, Shaw, and the rest of the regiment set out. The advance went well until they approached within about 300 yards of the fort. At that point a savage burst of fire slashed through the ranks of the regiment. Dozens were wounded or killed instantly.

But the rest charged on. They hurled themselves through or over one obstacle after another, including a ditch filled with 4 feet of water. Suddenly they found themselves at the base of the parapet, the main defensive wall of the fort. Not even this could stop them; they climbed it in the darkness and set the flag of their regiment at the top.

As the men of the 54th swarmed over the parapet, the Confederate defenders met them in full force. Shaw was shot dead instantly. Color Sergeant John Wall, whose job it was to carry the flag of the United States, was also hit. But before the symbol of liberty could touch the ground, Sergeant Carney seized it and planted it next to the regimental flag.

Defenders and attackers were now locked together in fierce hand-to-hand combat, which raged along the wall for close to an hour. Carney was wounded in both legs, his right arm, and his chest. But he refused to stop fighting or to let the enemy cut down the flag. When the remaining members of the regiment were

RESOURCE DIRECTORY

Teaching Resources

ordered to pull back from the fort to a position some 700 yards away, Carney carried the flag with him. The 54th held its new position until it was replaced by other troops at 2:00 A.M. on July 19.

The Aftermath of the Assault Of the 600 members of the 54th who had charged Fort Wagner, 259 were dead, wounded, or missing. Sergeant Carney was taken to the field hospital. Other wounded soldiers saw the flag he still carried in his hands and broke into a ragged cheer. "The old flag never touched the ground, boys," he assured them.

Not much is known about Sergeant Carney's life after the charge on Fort Wagner. He reappears in history only once, in 1900. In that year he was awarded the Congressional Medal of Honor for his bravery on the evening of July 18, 1863.

The attack on Fort Wagner was a military failure. But the exploits of the 54th Regiment, widely publicized in the North, had a dramatic impact on white attitudes toward African American soldiers. Wrote a reporter for the *New York Herald*:

I saw them [African Americans] fight at Wagner as none but splendid soldiers, splendidly officered, could fight, dashing through shot and shell, grape, canister and shrapnel, and showers of bullets, and . . . when they did retreat [it was] by command and with choice white troops for company.

The success of the 54th Regiment proved what abolitionist Frederick Douglass had written in August 1863:

Once let a black man get upon his person the brass letters, U.S.; let him get an eagle on his button, and a musket on his shoulder and bullets in his pocket, and there is no power on earth which can deny that he has earned the right to citizenship.

Union troops finally took Fort Wagner seven weeks after the charge of the 54th. One of them, Corporal Henry S. Harmon, wrote soon afterwards:

I am proud to say that I am a member of the 3d United States Colored Troops, and I hope that I am not considered boasting when I say so. Our career has not been unmarked by loss of human life. We have had ten of our number killed and I cannot say exactly how many wounded. . . . When you hear of a white family that has lost father, husband, or brother, you can say of the colored man, we too have borne our share of the burden. We too have suffered and died in defense of that starry banner that floats only over free men.

African Americans wearing the brass letters *U. S.* took a step closer to citizenship as they proved their courage. "Nobody knows anything about these men who has not seen them in battle," boasted one of their officers.

SECTION 2 REVIEW

Key Terms, People, and Places
1. Define (a) draft, (b) writ of *habeas corpus,* (c) Internal Revenue Act of 1862, (d) greenback, (e) Pacific Railroad Act of 1862, (f) Emancipation Proclamation, (g) contraband.
2. Identify (a) Copperhead, (b) Radical Republican.

Key Concepts
3. In what way was the Confederate government both strong and weak?
4. What civil rights did Lincoln suspend during the war?

5. Give an example of Republican legislation and explain how it gave permanent support to economic development.
6. How did the Emancipation Proclamation change the war aims of the Union?
7. How did African Americans bring slavery to an end?

Critical Thinking
8. **Testing Conclusions** Lincoln came to believe that the Union could not survive if slavery was preserved. Give evidence to support this conclusion.

Quiz found in the Unit 4 folder, p. 45, covers the main ideas in this section as well as the key terms.

4. CLOSE

Reinforcing the Big Idea

During the Civil War, the governments of both the North and the South took steps that increased their power. Even before the Emancipation Proclamation, enslaved African Americans acted to free themselves, and many African Americans fought to free others. In the next section, students will learn about the turning point of the war.

In Depth

Multicultural Perspectives

When African American soldiers joined the Union Army they were paid only seven dollars a month compared to the thirteen dollars a month paid other soldiers. James Gooding, an African American soldier, wrote to President Lincoln, "We have done a soldier's duty. Why can't we have a soldier's pay?"

Historical Evidence

Using Letters as Primary Sources

Focus Students analyze letters as a source of historical evidence.

Instruct After students have read the feature, discuss how the information in letters such as those in the feature contributes to our understanding of the Civil War. Discuss how different sorts of letters provide different sorts of historical evidence. Ask students what types of evidence might take the place of letters in the future.

Extend See the Historian's Toolbox Activity in the Resource Directory below.

Answers

1. (a) Letter A refers to a husband and children and to farm matters; clearly it is from a wife and mother living on a farm. Letter B refers to nursing work on the battlefield; clearly the letter is from a woman who is a nurse. (b) Letter A was written to a husband; Letter B was written to a cousin. (c) Letter A was written on June 1, 1862; Letter B was written on July 8, 1863. (d) Letter A: Lowndes County, Alabama (the South); Letter B: Gettysburg, Pennsylvania (the North). (e) Letter A discusses crops, children, farm animals, and the writer's sadness about the absence of her husband. Letter B discusses the conditions of wounded men and the duties of the writer.

2. (a) She mentions that a hired worker has quit and that a horse has gone blind and lame. (b) She gives food and drink to the wounded and writes letters for them.

3. (a) They had difficulties working the crops and caring for livestock without help in addition to their usual task of raising children. (b) They suffered intensely, lying on the ground in rags with only biscuits to eat, and many had to have their limbs amputated. (c) Women contributed both by maintaining business at home and by nursing and working at battle sites.

Using Letters as Primary Sources

When people write letters, they report firsthand about something of interest to them. For this reason, letters are a valuable source of historical evidence. Not only do they present factual information about a subject, but they also give clues to the attitudes of people in a particular historical period.

Use the following steps to analyze the historical evidence in the letters on this page.

1. Lay the groundwork for analyzing the letters by asking who, when, where, and what. (a) What clues do the letters give about the identity of the writers? (b) To whom were the letters written? (c) When were they written? (d) Where were they written? (e) What are the topics of the letters?

2. Analyze the information in each letter. Study the letters to identify their main points. (a) What specific problems does the writer of Letter A describe? (b) What tasks does the writer of Letter B perform?

3. Study each letter to see what it reveals about conditions and attitudes during the period in which it was written. (a) What general difficulties did farm wives face when their husbands were away at war? (b) Summarize what conditions were like for the wounded after Civil War battles. (c) Generalize about the contribution to the war effort made by women during the Civil War.

A *Lowndes County, Alabama, June 1, 1862*
Dear husband, I now take my pen in hand [to] drop you a few lines to let you know that we are all well as common and I am in about the same health that I was when you left. I hopes these lines may find you the same. The boys [her sons] has come home to see me on a furlough [leave from the army] and stayed 10 days. They started back yesterday to the camp. . . . John, my corn is out now and I have not drawed [harvested] any thing yet but I hope I will. My crop is nice but Pane [a hired man] has quit and left my crop in bad fix, but the neighbors says they will help us. You said you wanted me to pray for you. As for prayers, I pray for you all of the time. I pray for you nearly every breath I draw. . . . Your baby is the prettyest thing you ever saw in your life. She can walk by herself and your little grandson is pretty as a pink and grows the fastest in the world. You must come home and see all of your babies and kiss them. I have got the rye cut. . . . Your old mare is gone blind in one eye and something is the matter with one of her feet so she can't hardly walk. Your hogs and cows is coming on very well. I want you to come home for I want to see you so bad I don't know what to do. I must come to a close by saying I remain your loving wife until death. You must write to me as soon as you get this letter. Goodbye to you.
Lucy Lowe to John P. Lowe
Adapted from Katharine M. Jones, *Heroines of Dixie*, 1955

B *Gettysburg, Pennsylvania, July 8th, 1863*
My Dear Cousin, I am very tired tonight; have been on the field all day. . . . There are no words in the English language to express the sufferings I witnessed today. The men lie on the ground; their clothes have been cut off them to dress [bandage] their wounds; they . . . have nothing but hardtack [biscuit] to eat only as Sanitary Commissions, Christian Associations [volunteer workers], and so forth give them. . . . To give you some idea of the extent and numbers of the wounds, four surgeons, none of whom were idle fifteen minutes at a time, were busy all day amputating legs and arms. I gave to every man that had a leg or arm off a gill [measure] of wine, to every wounded in the Third Division, one glass of lemonade, some bread and preserves and tobacco—as much as I am opposed to the latter. . . . I would get on first rate [remain in good spirits] if they would not ask me to write to their wives; that I cannot do without crying, which is not pleasant to either party.
Cornelia
Cornelia Hancock, *South After Gettysburg*, 1956

RESOURCE DIRECTORY

Historian's Toolbox Activity Using Letters as Primary Sources, found in the Unit 4 folder, p. 58, gives further opportunity to examine historical evidence with letters to and from soldiers in Vietnam.

Turning Point: The Siege Of Vicksburg

SECTION PREVIEW

The tide of war turned in the summer of 1863. Southern forces led by Robert E. Lee invaded Pennsylvania. At the same time, northern forces led by Ulysses S. Grant surrounded Vicksburg, Mississippi, in an attempt to wrest control of the Mississippi River from the Confederacy.

Key Concepts

• While Grant spent months trying plan after plan to capture Vicksburg, its residents prepared their defenses.
• In July 1863 Lee was forced to go on the offensive and attack Union general Meade at Gettysburg, Pennsylvania.
• The siege of Vicksburg was a new and extremely destructive kind of warfare directed against civilians as well as soldiers.

Key Terms, People, and Places

Pickett's Charge, siege, total war; William Tecumseh Sherman, George G. Meade; Vicksburg, Gettysburg

---

W hile the armies clashed in the East, a Union army in the West struggled to capture the city of **Vicksburg,** Mississippi. Along with another fortress at Port Hudson, Louisiana, this Confederate stronghold prevented the Union from taking complete control of the Mississippi River.

Vicksburg seemed safe from attack. Not only was the city built on hills high above the Mississippi River, but its defenders had built fortifications along the bank to the north, creating an extended platform from which they could rain cannon shells down on Union ships. A Union officer later described the location as

a long line of high, rugged, irregular bluffs, clearly cut against the sky, crowned with cannon which peered ominously [threateningly] from embrasures [openings] to the right and left as far as the eye could see. . . . The approaches to this position were frightful.

Rail lines to the east linked Vicksburg with the state capital at Jackson 50 miles away. The railroad brought regular supplies and formed a route for quick reinforcement in case of attack.

Vicksburg was not just a military prize. It was the second largest city in Mississippi, with upward of 5,000 people, including about 1,400 enslaved and 31 free African Americans. A major regional commercial center with strong ties to the North, Vicksburg had been against secession. But the city had become defiant in 1862 as Union sailors under David Farragut had swept into the Mississippi Valley, and soldiers under Brigadier General Benjamin Butler had taken control of New Orleans. Vicksburg's military governor, James Autry, had refused to surrender, saying:

M ississippians don't know, and refuse to learn, how to surrender to any enemy. If Commodore Farragut or Brigadier-General Butler can teach them, let them come and try.

Grant Is Determined

The Union general who now faced the task of teaching Vicksburg this lesson was Ulysses S. Grant. This rough-hewn midwesterner was exactly the kind of general the Union needed.

The Anaconda Plan called for the North to capture the Mississippi River in order to "clear out and keep open this great line of communication" for northern armies. This powder flask was issued to a sailor serving on the Mississippi.

---

1. FOCUS

Connecting to the Big Idea

See page 324B. Explain to students that the turning point of the war came in 1863 with the battles of Vicksburg and Gettysburg. Ask why those battles were so important.

Objectives

● Describe the defenses built by the residents of Vicksburg.
● Explain why Lee attacked Union forces at Gettysburg and identify the results of that battle.
● Describe the siege of Vicksburg and explain why it represented a new kind of warfare.

Bellringer

Ask students if they can remember being without electricity for any length of time. If so, ask them to describe how they spent that time. Then ask them to imagine how that experience would compare to living in a cave for several months while an enemy army shelled their city.

Reading Strategy

Reinforcing Key Ideas Ask students to write the headings Gettysburg and Vicksburg on a sheet of paper and to take notes about each battle as they read. When students have finished reading the section, ask them to write two sentences explaining why each battle marked a turning point in the war.

▯ **Reproducible Lesson Plan** found in the Unit 4 folder, p. 40, provides a summary of the Section 3 lesson plan content.

▯ **Alternate Lesson Plan: Learning Styles** found in the Alternate Lesson Plans folder, p. 61, is designed to help students, particularly visual learners, organize information and compare the battles of Vicksburg and Gettysburg.

▯ **Guided Reading and Review** found in the Unit 4 folder, p. 46, provides a structure for reading and mastering the key concepts and reviewing the key terms for Section 3. (Guided Practice)

Explain/Discuss

Remind students that the capture of Vicksburg was part of the Anaconda Plan, by which the Union intended to divide and squeeze the Confederacy. Tell students that Lincoln said, "Vicksburg is the key. The war cannot be brought to a close until the key is in our pocket." Ask students to use a map to explain why Vicksburg was so critical to Union strategy.

Ask students to trace Lee's route to Gettysburg. Tell students that Lee hoped that invading Pennsylvania might encourage foreign countries to recognize and assist the Confederacy and might also dishearten northern civilians.

Analyze

Ask students to speculate about what might have happened if General Meade had pursued Lee's forces after the Battle of Gettysburg. Ask students to create a time line showing events from Gettysburg to the end of the war under those circumstances.

Activity

Mapping the Battle

Ask students to work in groups to make a detailed map of either the siege of Vicksburg or the Battle of Gettysburg. Maps should show major fortifications, troop movements, and assaults. Students may use a Civil War or military atlas for detailed information. Make sure each group plans its map key carefully.

TURNING POINTS

In order to capture Vicksburg, Navy gunboats under Rear Admiral David Porter had to sail past the city at night under heavy fire. "It was as if hell itself were loose," said one observer. Porter himself, with grim humor, remarked: "It was really a jolly scene."

He did not just march armies around, like McClellan. He won battles with them. After the Battle of Shiloh, northern politicians and newspaper editors criticized Grant for his tremendous losses. "I can't spare this man," Lincoln responded bluntly: "He fights."

Like Robert E. Lee, Grant was willing to bend the normal rules of generalship when the time came to do so. But unlike Lee, Grant did not win battles through sheer brilliance—though from time to time he did show flashes of military genius. Instead Grant won mostly through determination. One of his fellow officers once described Grant as the kind of person who

habitually wears an expression as if he had determined to drive his head through a brick wall, and was about to do it.

Banging on a Brick Wall In December of 1862, Grant sent General **William Tecumseh Sherman** and several thousand men to attack Vicksburg. But Grant was unable to link up with Sherman as planned, and the effort failed. Next, Grant tried digging a canal from one part of the Mississippi River to another to bypass Vicksburg altogether, but the canal did not work. Another similar idea called for digging a

connection to the nearby Red River, but this too, proved unworkable. Next Grant tried a scheme to attack Vicksburg from the north by sending gunboats down another river, the Yazoo. Still no success. In yet another plan, Grant sent Sherman and the gunboats on a third roundabout river route. This campaign swiftly became a trap from which Sherman's forces barely escaped alive.

As an early spring came to Vicksburg in 1863, the people of the city took heart from Grant's repeated failures. But they also improved their defenses. One of the biggest businesses in the town was cave building. Twenty dollars would buy protection from bombardments—a one-room hole in the ground. Fifty dollars bought several rooms and timbered supports. In March 1863, one woman described the city as "so honeycombed with caves that the streets look like avenues in a cemetery." ✪

Grant Moves Then, in mid-April, Grant settled on a clever but dangerous plan. He had known all along that the best way to capture Vicksburg was to attack from the land side. But he had not been able to reach that side from his position north of the city, because Vicksburg was protected by the swamps and backwaters of

 RESOURCE DIRECTORY

Teaching Resources

✪ **Primary Source Activity** A Teenager's Account of War, found in the Unit 4 folder, pp. 61–62, uses excerpts from Emma LeConte's diary to show how young southerners viewed and experienced the war.

the Yazoo River. Now Grant decided to send his army south of the city. From that position, he would be able to march inland and attack it on the land side, as shown in the map below.

The plan had many risks. To get south of Vicksburg, the men could march overland on the western bank of the Mississippi River, a safe but difficult route. But the gunboats and transport ships Grant needed would have to make a mad dash by night past the guns of Vicksburg. And once his soldiers were south of the city, they would be cut off from their supplies.

The army marched; the ships fired up their steam engines and raced through the hail of Vicksburg's cannon shells. In late April the navy and army successfully linked up south of the city. The confidence of the white people of Vicksburg gave way to tension and fear. Some packed up and left while they could.

On April 30, Grant headed northeast toward the capital at Jackson. For twenty days, in one of the most ingenious and skillful campaigns of his career, the general and his men raided their way through west-central Mississippi, keeping the enemy in a constant state of confusion. They captured their first objective, the city of Jackson, and burned it to the ground. Vicksburg's supply line was now cut off. Then Grant's forces headed straight for Vicksburg. Confederate defenders

tried to stop them on their way, but the Union army hurled them back on the city. By mid-May, Grant's troops were at Vicksburg's doorstep, chasing the Confederates into the safety of the town.

Grant's determination had brought him to the land side of Vicksburg. But the people of Vicksburg were determined too. They settled down behind their defenses to wait. Grant did not have his victory yet.

The Battle of Gettysburg

Meanwhile, back in the East, another major battle was shaping up. Lee had just defeated Hooker at Chancellorsville. During June 1863, he moved his troops into the North once again. This time he pushed as far as Pennsylvania. His plan was to cut off Washington, D.C., from the rest of the Union and win recognition for Confederate independence.

Once again, the Union army pursued Lee's forces, which were surging toward Harrisburg, Pennsylvania, a key rail center. On July 1, just west of the little village of **Gettysburg**, Union troops clashed with units of the Confederate army as Lee attempted to concentrate his forces. Within hours, tens of thousands of Union and Confederate troops poured into the area. So began the Battle of

Lincoln called capturing Vicksburg "the key" to winning the war; Jefferson Davis said the Confederate stronghold was "the nailhead that holds the South's two halves together." Ulysses S. Grant spent eight months trying to take the city.

Ask students to respond in a short essay to the following statement by Josiah Gorgas, the chief of Confederate ordinance in 1863: "One brief month ago we were apparently at the point of success. Lee was in Pennsylvania. . . . Vicksburg seemed to laugh all Grant's efforts to scorn. . . . Yesterday we rode on the pinnacle of success—today absolute ruin seems to be our portion." In their essays, students should briefly explain why Union victories at Vicksburg and Gettysburg meant "ruin" for the Confederacy.

1 Grant's camp at Millikens Bend Dec. 1862–Apr. 1863

2 Route of Grant's army past Vicksburg Mar. 29–early Apr.

3 Route of Union navy past Vicksburg Apr. 14 & 22

4 Navy ferries army to eastern bank, Apr. 30

5 Vicksburg to Jackson rail line cut, May 13

6 Grant captures and destroys Jackson, Mississippi, May 14

7 Grant defeats Confederate forces at Champions Hill May 16

8 Siege of Vicksburg begins, May 22

Mississippi R.

Raymond

Auburn

Cayuga

Grant's Route

Rocky Springs

Crystal Springs

Pine Bluff

New Orleans & Jackson R.R.

Hard Times Landing

Grant's route

Media and Technology

  Visions of America: Turning Point Story To enhance students' understanding of the Turning Point topic in this section, play "Mississippi Siege," a story about the siege of Vicksburg (length: approximately 4 minutes). This selection can be located on side 2 of the videodiscs. This selection can also be located on videotape 2. Lesson plans for Turning Point stories can be found in the Visions of America Guidebook.

Visions of America: Roundtable Discussion To introduce students to different and differing viewpoints on the Turning Point topic in this section, play all or part of the Roundtable Discussion on "Mississippi Siege," remarks by respected historians and social commentators. This selection can be located on side 2 of the videodiscs. This selection can also be located on the videotape 2.

In Depth

Did You Know?

Cuban-born artist Federico Fernández Cavada served as a captain and engineer in the Union army. Sent aloft in hot-air balloons near the battle lines, Cavada sketched from the air what he could see of Confederate troop movements until he was captured at the Battle of Gettysburg. In 1864 Cavada published *Libby Life*, an account of his cruel treatment in a Confederate prison.

Gettysburg, a struggle that would drag on through three terrible days.

On July 1, the first day of the battle, the Confederates pushed the Union troops through Gettysburg and into defensive positions along a ridge south of the town. The new Union commander, General **George G. Meade,** decided to defend this high ground and force the Confederates to attack.

On July 2, Lee sent repeated shock waves at one part of the Union battle line after another. He tried to capture high ground in two places—Little Round Top and Culp's Hill—so that he could fire down on the enemy. Both of these efforts were pushed back by outnumbered Union troops. Though the Union line stretched for miles along the ridge, Lee could not break it anywhere.

On July 3, Lee ordered a direct attack on the center of the Union line. Known as **Pickett's Charge** after George Pickett, one of the generals who led it, it was a classic confrontation between the old and the new kind of warfare. More than 14,000 Confederates marched the better part of a mile across open ground under withering fire from Union cannons firing shells and canisters. Then they charged up a rise toward the Union guns. Only a few reached the federal lines and fought hand-to-hand with Union troops; most were cut down, and the survivors were captured or forced to retreat.

The next day, July 4, Lee's army, which had suffered 28,000 casualties, left the battlefield and headed south. The exhausted Army of the Potomac, which had 23,000 men dead, wounded, or missing, did not follow the Confederates. Lee and his men escaped, but they would never go on the offensive again.

MAKING CONNECTIONS

Who was usually more successful in the Civil War battles you have read about, the defenders or the attackers? Why was this so?

Vicksburg, Too, Is Determined

Back at Vicksburg, Grant had found he could not take the city by direct attack. A **siege** would be necessary—a form of prolonged attack in which a city is surrounded and starved into surrender. Sieges have been a common form of warfare since ancient times, but at the siege of Vicksburg, the new cannon technology changed them forever.

When Union cannons began to fire on Vicksburg's residents from land and river, it was the first burst in a bombardment that would average about 2,800 shells a day. One civilian, Emma Balfour, described how she barely managed to escape into a shelter:

Confederate troops in George Pickett's charge at Gettysburg temporarily broke the Union line in the action shown here, at a crook in a stone wall called the Angle. After the charge, General Lee told Pickett to re-form his division to repel a possible counterattack. "General Lee," exclaimed Pickett, "I have no division now."

We went into a cave for the first time. . . . Just as we got in several machines [shells] exploded . . . just over our heads, and at the same time two riders were killed in the valley below us by a twenty-four pound shell from the east side, so . . . we were between two fires. As all this rushed over me and the sense of suffocation from being underground, the certainty that there was no way of escape, that we were hemmed in, caged—for one moment my heart seemed to stand still—then my faith and

RESOURCE DIRECTORY

Teaching Resources

courage rose to meet the emergency, and I have felt prepared ever since and cheerful.

The conflict between the North and South had now become **total war**. In this form of war, opponents strike not only against one another's soldiers, but against civilians and the entire economic system of the enemy.

Total War in Vicksburg Hour after hour, day after day for forty-seven days, the people of Vicksburg endured the relentless pounding of three hundred Union guns. As May dragged into hot June, the schedule of the shellings took over everyday life. The people of Vicksburg could not sleep except during pauses in the vast uproar of the guns. They could not always eat when they were hungry or bathe when they were dirty; they had to wait until the shells that rocked their city gave them a few minutes' peace.

But the worst fear of the unfortunate residents of Vicksburg was not the shelling; it was starvation. Food had already been low when Grant surrounded the city, and now no new supplies could reach them. For weeks they had continued to hope that a southern army would come to their rescue. That hope died at the end of June, when they were reduced to eating small portions of rotten meat and moldy rice.

The Turning Point On July 3—as Pickett's men were charging the Union lines at Gettysburg—the Confederate officer in command at Vicksburg, General John C. Pemberton, met with Grant to discuss the terms of a surrender of the city. The next day, the Fourth

of July, 1863, Vicksburg was turned over to the Union.

On the night of July 4, the red glare of rockets lit the sky over the Mississippi River, in celebration of the Union victory in Vicksburg and the eighty-seventh birthday of the United States. A band played festive music. Some of the people of Vicksburg wept; others made the best of the situation, grateful to have food to eat. African Americans greeted the Union troops with rejoicing. For them, the day they had long looked for had come at last.

Five days later, Confederate forces at Port Hudson, Louisiana, surrendered the last Confederate post on the Mississippi River. Though the war would continue for two more years, the Mississippi River would remain under the control of the Union navy. The Confederacy had been cut in two.

Josiah Gorgas, a Confederate officer, wrote in his diary about the tremendous turn of events in early July:

E*vents have succeeded* [followed] *one another with disastrous rapidity. One brief month ago we were apparently at the point of success. Lee was in Pennsylvania, threatening Harrisburg, and even Philadelphia. Vicksburg seemed to laugh all Grant's efforts to scorn. . . . It seems incredible that human power could effect such a change in so brief a space. Yesterday, we rode on the pinnacle of success— today absolute ruin seems to be our portion. The Confederacy totters to its destruction.*

SECTION 3 REVIEW

Key Terms, People, and Places
1. Identify (a) William Tecumseh Sherman, (b) George G. Meade.
2. Identify (a) Vicksburg, (b) Gettysburg.

Key Concepts
3. What quality distinguished Grant as a military leader and allowed him to capture Vicksburg?
4. What were the two most significant events that occurred during the conflicts at Gettysburg and Vicksburg on July 3, 1863?
5. What was new and unusual about the siege of Vicksburg?

Critical Thinking
6. **Identifying Central Issues** Why were the Battle of Gettysburg and the siege of Vicksburg turning points in the Civil War?

Quiz found in the Unit 4 folder, p. 47, covers the main ideas in this section as well as the key terms.

Media and Technology

 Transparencies
The Way It Works, H-13; Geographic Setting, M-3, M-4

---

3. ASSESS

Section 3 Review Answers
1. (a) William Tecumseh Sherman, see p. 342, (b) George G. Meade, see p. 344
2. (a) Vicksburg, see p. 341, (b) Gettysburg, see p. 343
3. Determination.
4. Pickett's Charge and Pemberton's request to talk over terms of surrender.
5. It utilized total warfare.
6. Possible answers: These events were turning points because they defined how each side would be able to operate thereafter. After Gettysburg, Lee never went on the offensive again; he was restricted to operating defensively within the South. After the victory at Vicksburg, however, the Union gained control of the Mississippi River, allowing it access to a huge part of the Confederacy.

Reteach
Ask students which of the following statements apply to the siege of Vicksburg and which to the Battle of Gettysburg.
● Grant's reputation as a successful general was ensured by his victory here.
● This place was important as a transportation and commercial center, as well as a well-positioned fortress above the Mississippi River.
● This city did not surrender until its citizens were starving.
● In this battle, control of the high ground on hills and ridges was crucial.
● This three-day battle was the last time General Lee took the offensive.

4. CLOSE

Reinforcing the Big Idea
The turning point of the Civil War came with bloody Union victories at Vicksburg in the West and Gettysburg in the East. The next section describes the end of the war.

TURNING POINTS

The Lasting Impact of the Siege of Vicksburg

Focus In 1863 Union forces under the command of Ulysses S. Grant broke the months-long siege of Vicksburg. What was the lasting impact of that siege?

Instruct Before students read the material in the feature, ask them to write a definition of the term *war*. Discuss what the combatants in a war wish to accomplish and the means they use to reach their goals. After students have read the feature, ask them to compare their definitions with Grant's view of war.

Ask students to agree or disagree with this statement by Sir Basil Liddell Hart, an English military authority and biographer of Sherman: "Loss of hope is worse than loss of men and land. It was the moral effect, above all, which made Vicksburg the great turning point of the war." Do students think Liddell Hart's statement correctly describes the results of the siege of Vicksburg? Why or why not?

Ask students to list new weapons, technology, and methods of transportation that make total war even more devastating today than during the Civil War. Ask students if there are some weapons and methods of warfare that they believe should not be used. Whose decision is it to use a type of weapon?

Extend Ask students to find out about the shelling of Sarajevo, Bosnia-Herzegovina, in the Bosnian war that began in 1992 and to compare it to the siege of Vicksburg. In what ways were the lives of citizens of Vicksburg and Sarajevo similar? How were they different?

TURNING POINTS

The Lasting Impact of the Siege of Vicksburg

Together with the Union victory at Gettysburg, the fall of Vicksburg ensured the ultimate defeat of the Confederate States of America. But Vicksburg was more than a turning point in the Civil War. It also marked the beginning of a new age in warfare, the age of total war.

Grant's Warfare The tactics that Grant used at Vicksburg were not completely new. In ancient times, armies had burned farmlands and besieged cities, hoping to starve enemies into surrender. But for the most part, wars after the 1600s had been little more than duels between massed armies or fleets. Battles had been limited to one or two days in length. At the end of the battle, whichever side had suffered the worst losses retreated.

Grant refused to limit his fighting in this way. He did not just attack the Confederate army; he attacked anyone and anything that stood between him and victory. That included civilians. He knew well, when he purposefully destroyed Vicksburg's supply line to Jackson, that civilians would soon go hungry as a result. He also knew that the thousands of shells he poured onto Vicksburg would fall among innocent residents of the city.

But Grant's goal was to convince the enemy that defeat meant more than the loss of a distant army. It meant an unacceptable loss of the comfort and security of daily life. Sherman later explained:

War is cruelty, and you cannot refine it. . . . We are not only fighting hostile armies, but a hostile people, and must make old and young, rich and poor, feel the hard hand of war.

For this goal, the new weapons—accurate cannons and explosive shells—were ideal. But simpler

1863 Union cannons at Vicksburg introduce a new age of total warfare.

1940–1945 Nazi warplanes and rockets heavily damage London during World War II.

1900 — **1920** — **1940**

1915 German submarine sinks the Lusitania, a civilian passenger ship, during World War I.

1945 Large parts of Tokyo are destroyed by American fire-bombs.

▶ RESOURCE DIRECTORY

Turning Points Extension Activity
The Lasting Impact of the Siege of Vicksburg, found in the Unit 4 folder, pp. 50–51, describes how technology and tactics became dedicated to a policy of total war following the siege of Vicksburg.

forms of destructive power also worked. In the years after Vicksburg fell, the armies of Grant and Sherman used little more than fire and crowbars to bring large-scale destruction to Georgia, South Carolina, and Virginia.

Such tactics, however, made healing the nation after the war much more difficult. The people of Vicksburg, for example, did not officially celebrate the Fourth of July until 1945, evidence of the enduring anger and bad feelings Grant's total warfare had created.

Americans Wage Total War American troops in the twentieth century would repeatedly find themselves in situations similar to the siege of Vicksburg. In later wars, too, their mission would be to bring the superior numbers and resources of the United States to bear on a well-entrenched enemy. These wars included World War II (1941–1945), the War in Vietnam (1965–1973), and the Persian Gulf War (1991). The United States and other nations would find new technologies for this purpose that would make the horror of Grant's cannons and gunboats seem puny. And more often than not, this warfare would leave in its wake a massive loss of civilian life and destruction of property.

The purpose of this destruction was to persuade the enemy that the struggle was simply not worth the cost. After Vicksburg, civilians were as much a part of war as soldiers; starvation as much of a weapon as the rifle; and victory required not just the surrender of a few troops but the complete demoralization and destruction of vast civilian populations.

The success of Grant at Vicksburg was due to his use of modern warfare—a combination of technology and total war. The people of Vicksburg would not be the last to have to decide whether it was worth losing everything just to hold on to the hope of a later victory.

REVIEWING THE FACTS

1. Why did Grant and Sherman resort to total warfare against the South?
2. In what later wars was the principle of total warfare applied?

Critical Thinking

3. **Distinguishing False from Accurate Images** Americans sometimes think of the Civil War as an old-fashioned war. How is this image false?

1960s–1970s United States planes use napalm (jellied gasoline) to burn Vietnamese villages.

1991 Dictator Saddam Hussein forces Kurds in Iraq to flee to refugee camps.

1960   1980   2000

1991 American bombs and missiles disrupt life in Baghdad during the Persian Gulf War.

Answers

1. They wanted to convince the enemy that continued fighting would mean an unacceptable loss of the comfort and security of daily life.

2. Total warfare was applied in World War II, the Vietnam War, and the Persian Gulf War, among others.

3. Although Civil War technology did not match that of modern warfare, the tactic of total warfare was applied as thoroughly during the Civil War as in any modern war. The willingness of generals such as Grant to attack the civilian population, whether directly or indirectly, puts them in a class with modern military planners.

A New Birth of Freedom

A New Birth of Freedom

Connecting to the Big Idea

See page 324B. Explain that Lee finally surrendered at Appomattox Court House, Virginia, in April 1865. Ask students to consider the costs of the Civil War. What were its major results?

Objectives

● Explain how Lincoln's Gettysburg Address redefined the United States.
● Describe the major conflicts of 1864, including Sherman's march to the sea and Grant's pursuit of Lee's army.
● State the significance of Lincoln's reelection in 1864.
● Describe the terms by which the war ended.

Bellringer

Ask students to think about what it means to surrender. Ask students to describe the feeling of giving up a fight. How does it feel to win a long-fought struggle?

Reading Strategy

Predicting Content Ask students to skim the section, list the main headings and subheadings, and write a sentence or phrase under each one that predicts the content it covers. Students should then test their predictions against the actual text when they have finished reading the section.

"I give thanks to the Almighty," said Lincoln when he was reelected in 1864, "for this evidence of the people's resolution to stand by free government and the rights of humanity."

SECTION PREVIEW

Northern armies gradually pounded the weakened but persistent South, pushing it toward surrender. As the Civil War came to an end, the conflict became more than a struggle over the Union. It became instead a redefinition of the American nation.

Key Concepts

• In the Gettysburg Address, Lincoln redefined the United States, emphasizing that democracy existed to preserve freedom and equality.
• In 1864 Sherman carried total war into Georgia, while Grant threw attack after attack at Lee's army.
• Lincoln won reelection in 1864, demonstrating that he had the nation's approval of his war policy and his stand against slavery.
• Lee, finally hemmed in by Union forces, surrendered to Grant at Appomattox, Virginia.

Key Terms, People, and Places

Gettysburg Address, Thirteenth Amendment; Philip Sheridan, John Wilkes Booth; Atlanta, Savannah, Petersburg, Appomattox Court House

---

After the Battle of Gettysburg, the people of the North decided that all the Americans who had perished there should be honored with burial in a new cemetery. President Lincoln was invited to "make a few appropriate remarks" at the dedication ceremony in Gettysburg on November 19, 1863.

The Gettysburg Address

⭐ The main speaker, Edward Everett of Massachusetts, vividly described the Battle of Gettysburg in a grand, two-hour oration. Then the President spoke for two minutes in his high-pitched voice. Simply, eloquently, Lincoln explained the meaning of the Civil War—and redefined the meaning of the United States.

Lincoln began his speech, now known as the **Gettysburg Address,** by reminding his listeners that in 1776 the American people had

brought forth upon this continent a new nation conceived in liberty and dedicated to the proposition that all men are created equal.

The Civil War, said Lincoln, was a test of whether any nation dedicated to freedom and equality can survive. Freedom and equality, he stressed, were what the Union dead had been fighting for. Americans should now resolve that

these dead shall not have died in vain; this nation, under God, shall have a new birth of freedom; and that government of the people, by the people, for the people, shall not perish from the earth.

Lincoln spoke with a wisdom ahead of his time. Americans in 1863 did not like his speech; they thought it was too short and simple. But in the years since then, people have come to appreciate that Lincoln's words marked a dramatic new definition of the United States. Freedom and equality no longer belonged to a few, as they had in 1776. They were the right of everyone. Democracy and the Union did not exist to serve the interests of white men; they existed to preserve freedom for all. Lincoln's speech marked a great milestone in the gradual expansion of liberty to all people in the United States—an expansion that still continues today.

Sherman Burns and Grant Hammers

Grant's success in 1863 convinced Lincoln that he had found a leader who could win battles. The President called the general to Washington to assume overall command of the northern armies.

▶ **RESOURCE DIRECTORY**

Teaching Resources

📄 **Reproducible Lesson Plan** found in the Unit 4 folder, p. 41, provides a summary of the Section 4 lesson plan content.

📄 **Alternate Lesson Plan: Critical Thinking** Predicting Outcomes, found in the Alternate Lesson Plans folder, p. 62, helps pairs of students analyze the Union victory in the Civil War and how it redefined the United States.

📄 **Guided Reading and Review** found in the Unit 4 folder, p. 48, provides a structure for reading and mastering the key concepts and reviewing the key terms for Section 4. (Guided Practice)

⭐ 📄 **Primary Source Activity** The Gettysburg Address, found in the Unit 4 folder, p. 60, encourages students to appreciate and research Lincoln's famous speech.

Lincoln's Call Is Repeated

In his Gettysburg Address, Lincoln called for Americans to rededicate themselves to the principle that all people are created equal and so should have equal rights. One hundred years later, on August 28, 1963, the African American leader Dr. Martin Luther King, Jr., gave a speech echoing Lincoln's call for "a new birth of freedom." Pointing out that African Americans did not have full political and economic rights even a full century after the Emancipation Proclamation, King said, "We must face the tragic fact that the Negro is still not free." King repeated Lincoln's call for a new dedication to the ideals of the Declaration of Independence, saying, "I have a dream that one day this nation will rise up and live out the true meaning of its creed: 'We hold these truths to be self-evident—that all men are created equal.'"

As a result of the actions of King and others, Congress passed laws to protect the civil rights of African Americans. These laws were a giant step toward the new freedom called for by Lincoln and King. ***Does the United States live up to the ideals of the Declaration of Independence today? Explain your answer.***

Grant brought with him a new plan for winning the war. He would fight Lee's army repeatedly until he exhausted it. And he would send General Sherman into Georgia to do the same to the other major Confederate army there.

Sherman's March to the Sea As it turned out, Sherman could not catch the army he was sent after. Instead he besieged **Atlanta,** Georgia, and captured it in September 1864. Then he proposed a new plan of his own. He would march his troops from Atlanta to the sea, gathering the food he needed from the land and destroying everything he could not take with him. He told Grant:

> If we can march a well-appointed army right through [Jefferson Davis's] territory, it is a demonstration to the world, foreign and domestic, that we have a power which Davis cannot resist.

With Atlanta in flames behind him, Sherman set out for the seacoast city of **Savannah,** Georgia. Cutting a sixty-mile-wide swath across the red earth of the state, he burned the harvest, plundered plantations, uprooted railroad tracks, and smashed bridges, factories, and mills. By December 22, he had reached the coast and captured Savannah. He had succeeded in his purpose—to make the people of Georgia "so sick of war that generations would pass away

before they would again appeal to it." But his march would also make the hatred between North and South still more difficult to heal.

Grant Hammers at Lee Meanwhile, Grant and the Army of the Potomac were pressing toward Richmond, relentlessly hammering at Lee's force, the Army of Northern Virginia. Outnumbered nearly two to one, Lee fought a series of defensive battles that held back the Union advance. But Grant refused to retreat to a distant camp to reorganize, like other Union generals before him. Each time Lee stopped him, Grant simply moved his army to the left and attacked again. "I propose to fight it out on this line if it takes all summer," he told Lincoln. Though northerners were enthusiastic about Grant's determination, they were horrified at its cost: by early June, 65,000 of Grant's men were dead, wounded, or missing.

Unable to reach Richmond or break Lee's army, Grant took his forces south of the Confederate capital in June 1864. There he came to a halt, threatening **Petersburg,** Virginia, the railway center that supplied Richmond. Lee followed, and the armies faced each other once again. The bloody standoff at Petersburg dragged on well into the next year.

The Election of 1864

While Grant and Sherman were fighting their battles on southern soil, Lincoln had a

Media and Technology

Transparency
Fine Art, D-11

Answer to . . .

Links Across Time

Answers may note that while the United States today maintains a theoretical commitment to achieving equality, it has so far failed to achieve full equality in practice.

2. INSTRUCT

Explain/Discuss

Tell students that Lincoln called his speech at Gettysburg a "flat failure." Ask students to summarize in their own words the main points of Lincoln's speech.

Have students trace Sherman's route through Georgia. Ask how Sherman's march and Grant's dogged pursuit of Lee show commitment of both generals to the idea of total war. Discuss how Lincoln's reelection led to the passage by Congress of the Thirteenth Amendment.

In Depth

Then and Now

The New Market Battlefield Historical Park, now maintained by Richmond's Virginia Military Institute (VMI), commemorates one of the lesser battles of the Civil War. In May 1864 about 250 VMI cadets—average age seventeen—stopped some 6,000 Union troops from entering the Shenandoah Valley (see pages 352–353). Needing the cadets to fill out his outnumbered army, Confederate General John C. Breckrinridge is reported to have said: "Put the boys in, and may God forgive me for the order." Before the Union forces were forced into retreat, they had killed or wounded about one in four of the cadets.

They did not outnumber the southern states. Therefore, they did not have the majority needed to ratify such a constitutional amendment. Furthermore, many northerners would have been reluctant to support this kind of amendment, knowing that it might well lead to southern secession.

Analyze

The text states that the Civil War redefined the American nation. Ask small groups to compose an antebellum definition of the nation and a postwar definition.

Activity

Cooperative Learning

Time: One class period.
Activity: Have students plan a research tour through the major battlefields and historic sites of the Civil War.
Grouping: Groups of four students.
Purpose: To identify the significance of specific sites, routes, and battles of the war.
Roles: Members of the research projects' travel department including travel agents, tour planners, guides.
Outcome: Students will identify important battlefields and sites of the Civil War.

Enrichment

Ask students to prepare an oral reading of one of the following: the Gettysburg Address, selections from Stephen Vincent Benet's "John Brown's Body," or Walt Whitman's poem mourning the death of Lincoln, "O Captain! My Captain!"

3. ASSESS

Section 4 Review Answers

1. (a) Gettysburg Address, see p. 348, (b) Thirteenth Amendment, see p. 350
2. (a) Philip Sheridan, see p. 350, (b) John Wilkes Booth, see p. 350

Though Sherman issued orders that civilians were not to be harmed during his march to the sea, one of the soldiers who followed him wrote: "The cruelties practiced on this campaign toward the citizens have been enough to blast a more sacred cause than ours."

political battle of his own to attend to in the North. As the election of 1864 drew near, it seemed very likely that he would lose. The nation was weary of the war, and the Copperheads were calling for peace negotiations.

When Sherman captured Atlanta, however, the mood in the North changed. Lincoln, running against Democratic candidate General George McClellan, won the election with 212 out of 233 electoral votes.

By reelecting Lincoln, voters showed their approval not only of his war policy, but of his stand against slavery. Three months later, in February 1865, members of Congress joined him in that stand and passed the **Thirteenth Amendment** to the Constitution. It was ratified by the states and became law on December 6, 1865. In a few simple words, the amendment ended slavery in the United States forever.

MAKING   CONNECTIONS

Why could the northern states not ban slavery in the Union earlier than the 1860s?

The End of the War

The Confederacy was still holding out. Its leaders tried everything—even signing up enslaved people as soldiers. But the women and men of the South were sick of war. By the end of 1864, more than 50 percent of the soldiers in the Confederate armies had deserted.

The map on page 351 shows the last stages of the war. The standoff at Petersburg continued through March 1865. Then Union general **Philip Sheridan** won a battle that cut off Lee's supplies and put him and his army in danger of being surrounded. Lee's men, already starving, were deserting by the dozen. His only possible hope was to abandon Petersburg and Richmond and try to link up with other Confederate forces to the south.

Again General Sheridan moved, cutting off the retreat of Lee's exhausted men with his swift, horse-mounted troops. Hemmed in by Sheridan and Grant and with no other alternative, Lee sent word that he wanted to discuss surrender.

On Sunday, April 9, 1865, Grant and Lee met in the town of **Appomattox Court House,** Virginia. Lee was as dignified in defeat as he had been courageous and skillful in battle. Grant proved as generous in victory as he had been relentless in war. The two men agreed to the terms of the surrender and were enemies no more.

What Was Lost and What Was Won

Five days later, President and Mrs. Lincoln went to the theater in Washington, D.C. In the middle of the performance, a young actor named **John Wilkes Booth** broke into the presidential box overlooking the stage and shot the President in the head. He then leapt down onto the stage and escaped.

Federal officials immediately began to hunt Booth down. They soon learned he was a member of a group of southern sympathizers who had plotted to murder all the high officials of the federal government. Within days, the army tracked Booth to a barn in Virginia; he died of wounds he received resisting arrest. Several other conspirators were caught and hanged.

RESOURCE DIRECTORY

Teaching Resources

Visual Learning Activity Defending Atlanta, found in the Unit 4 folder, p. 67, promotes understanding of the new weapons technology and strategies of the Civil War through photographs of the fortifications built to counter them.

Lincoln did not die instantly; he lingered until the morning of April 15, though he never regained consciousness. When he perished, the South lost not only its most powerful opponent, but also the man who would probably have become its most powerful friend and protector. Lincoln had already begun to insist that the reunion of the nation after the war should be based on fairness and mercy, not hatred and vengeance. The President, too, now became a victim of the war that had divided the nation.

Like Lincoln, many of the soldiers on both sides did not live to return home. Some 360,000 Union and 258,000 Confederate soldiers died of disease, wounds, or poor medical treatment. Few other wars in history have had so great a human cost.

Lincoln knew well that neither side could truly win such a terrible war. In his Second Inaugural Address he said:

> Both [North and South] read the same Bible, and pray to the same God; and each invokes His aid against the other. . . . The prayers of both could not be answered; that of neither has been answered fully.

The South did not win the independence for which it struggled. The North did not achieve the easy victory that it had hoped for. Instead both sides suffered bitterly.

But if both North and South lost by the war, they both also gained by it. They gained an undivided nation that would go on to become the most powerful country in the world, a

The Final Battles of the Civil War, 1863–1864

Geography and History: Interpreting Maps
After one Civil War battle, a Union general said about the Confederate troops: "I doubt if any soldiers in the world ever needed so much cumulative evidence to convince them they were beaten." The same could be said of the South as a whole. *What were the two main movements of Union forces that brought the war to an end?*

democracy that would continue to seek the equality Lincoln had promised for it. And they gained new fellow citizens—the African Americans who had broken the bonds of slavery and claimed their right to be free and equal, every one.

SECTION 4 REVIEW

Key Terms, People, and Places
1. Define (a) Gettysburg Address, (b) Thirteenth Amendment.
2. Identify (a) Philip Sheridan, (b) John Wilkes Booth.
3. Identify (a) Atlanta, (b) Savannah, (c) Petersburg, (d) Appomattox Court House.

Key Concepts
4. How did Lincoln describe the Civil War in the Gettysburg Address?

5. What plans did Sherman and Grant follow in their campaigns during 1864?
6. What did Lincoln's reelection demonstrate?
7. Why was Lee finally forced to surrender?

Critical Thinking
8. **Making Comparisons** Compare and contrast the condition of the United States at the time of President Lincoln's death with its condition at the time of Washington's first presidency.

 Quiz found in the Unit 4 folder, p. 49, covers the main ideas in this section as well as the key terms.

 Chapter Test Forms A and B are found in the Unit 4 folder, pp. 68–73.

 Answer Keys found in the Unit 4 folder, pp. 113–122, provide answers to all student activities.

Media and Technology

Transparency
Graphic Organizer, G-4

Guided Reading Audiotapes (English and Spanish)

Computer Test Bank

3. (a) Atlanta, see p. 349, (b) Savannah, see p. 349, (c) Petersburg, see p. 349, (d) Appomattox Court House, see p. 350

4. He described it as a test of whether any nation dedicated to freedom and equality can survive.

5. By marching through Georgia, Sherman planned to show that the Union had a power that the Confederacy could not resist. Grant planned to attack Lee's army until he exhausted it.

6. It demonstrated that the majority of northerners approved both of his war policy and his stand against slavery.

7. His supplies were cut off, his men were starving and deserting, and he was in danger of being surrounded.

8. Possible answer: During Washington's first term as President, the political system was just setting out on the road to freedom for all; by the end of Lincoln's presidency, the system was taking steps to include African Americans in the political process. In both cases the Union was intact, although obviously damaged in 1865; sectional differences were not so stark during Washington's presidency.

Reteach

Ask students to identify the significance of the following in relation to the end of the Civil War and the redefinition of the nation: Gettysburg Address, Thirteenth Amendment, Appomattox Court House.

Caption Answer to . . .

 Interpreting Maps

Sherman's march through the South and Grant's movement toward Richmond and Petersburg.

 CLOSE

Reinforcing the Big Idea

The Civil War finally ended in 1865, after Sherman's brutal march through Georgia and Grant's fierce hammering of Lee's exhausted troops. The nation emerged from the war an undivided democracy, with slavery abolished.

Valley of War

Focus Tell students that one skill a military leader needed in the Civil War was the ability to use a piece of land to its best advantage. Both the Confederate and the Union armies used the Shenandoah Valley. However, they used it differently.

Instruct Have the class make a map of the Shenandoah Valley about the same size as the one that belonged to Stonewall Jackson. Then ask students to describe how Jackson used the valley to protect Richmond. Ask students how Sheridan's treatment of the valley differed from Jackson's. Ask students how Sheridan's destruction served the strategy of total war.

Ask students to imagine that they lived on a small farm near Winchester. How would they have responded to Jackson's constant raids? to Sheridan's destruction?

Extend Ask students to research and report on the use of computer technology in modern warfare. How do military strategists use computers to plan their attacks? How do modern weapons render the skill of seeing how to use a piece of land less vital?

Valley of War

One of General Stonewall Jackson's most deadly weapons was a piece of paper eight and a half feet long—a detailed map of the Shenandoah Valley. What made this valley the focus of repeated fighting during the Civil War?

Great generals closely study the geography of the land where they are fighting and use it to their advantage. Like geographers, they pay careful attention to location—the relationship one place has with another. And like geographers, generals are interested in human movement across the land. Finally, military planners also study the characteristics of a place. A look at all three of these themes in geography—location, movement, and place—shows why the Shenandoah Valley played a crucial part in the Civil War.

"The Valley of Humiliation"

The Shenandoah Valley is a corridor about 150 miles long and 25 miles wide between the Blue Ridge Mountains and the Alleghenies. (See the map on page 353.) It stretches from Harpers Ferry in what is now West Virginia to the James River in Virginia. During the Civil War, its location made it mostly useless to northern armies. For them, the valley led nowhere—into rugged hills away from their main target, Richmond. But for southern armies, the valley led close to Washington, D.C. When a Union army pressed toward Richmond, a Confederate army would prowl through the Shenandoah, threatening Washington and drawing troops away from the main Union force.

Hoping to put an end to this threat, northern generals repeatedly tried to take control of the Shenandoah during the early years of the war. Even though they did win parts of it at times, they were soon forced to give up their conquests. One key town in the upper Shenandoah Valley, Winchester, changed hands 72 times between 1861 and 1865. The Shenandoah was soon known to northerners as the Valley of Humiliation.

A Corridor for Travel

Swift and decisive movement was the secret of the Confederate military strategy. Simply because Shenandoah was a valley, it formed an excellent corridor for movement. Its slopes, though forested, were not too steep or rocky for troops on foot or horseback. Furthermore, the Valley Pike, the main road through the Shenandoah, allowed even a large army like that of Robert E. Lee to travel rapidly from the heart of Virginia to the borders of the North. And the many gaps in the Blue Ridge mountain chain allowed southern forces like those of Stonewall Jackson to duck easily in and out of the Shendandoah Valley as it suited their purposes.

"A Barren Waste"

The special characteristics of the valley also made it valuable to the South. For example, the population of the valley was mostly sympathetic to the Confederacy, so Union invaders had to endure constant attacks by armed but unofficial raiders. But a still more beneficial characteristic of the valley—for the South, at least—was its splendid pastures and fields, which supplied the Confederate army in Virginia with meat and grain.

> One key town in the Shenandoah Valley, Winchester, changed hands 72 times between 1861 and 1865.

RESOURCE DIRECTORY

Time and Place Activity A Cold War Confrontation, found in the Unit 4 folder, pp. 52–53, emphasizes the geographic perspective on United States–Cuba hostility and the 1962 Cuban missile crisis.

The commander of Union forces, General Grant, decided in the summer of 1864 that this source of supply had to be shut down once and for all. He determined that the harvest in the valley should be so completely destroyed that "crows flying over it for the balance of the season will have to carry their provender [food] with them." He later gave these specific instructions to General Phil Sheridan: "Do all the damage to railroads and crops you can. Carry off stock of all descriptions, and Negroes so as to prevent further planting. If the war is to last another year we want the Shenandoah Valley to remain a barren waste."

Sheridan carried out these orders to the letter. In the fall of 1864 he wrote Grant:

I have destroyed over 2,000 barns filled with wheat, hay, and farming implements; over 70 mills, filled with flour and wheat; . . . and have killed and issued to the troops not less than 3,000 sheep. . . . The people here are getting sick of the war.

Grant answered: "Keep on, and your good work will cause the fall of Richmond."

In the spring of the next year, Grant's words came true. As one Confederate soldier wrote,

There are a good many of us who believe that this shooting match has been carried on long enough. A government that has run out of rations [food for its army] can't expect to do much more fighting.

Early in April 1865, Lee abandoned Richmond and surrendered. In some respects, the war had been lost months before—in the Shenandoah Valley.

GEOGRAPHIC CONNECTIONS

1. How did the location of the Shenandoah Valley make the valley useful to the South?

2. Why did Grant want to make the Shenandoah Valley "a barren waste"?

Critical Thinking

3. Identifying Central Issues Why do military planners study human movement over the land?

Understanding Key Terms, People, and Places

Terms
Students should refer to the definitions of the key terms in the chapter to write sentences that show the relation of each word to the Civil War.

Matching
1. siege
2. writ of *habeas corpus*
3. gunboat
4. draft
5. greenbacks

Word Relationships
1. (b) does not belong. McClellan, Sherman, and Grant were Union generals; Jackson was a Confederate general.
2. (a) does not belong. Shiloh, Antietam, and Manassas were locations of Civil War battles fought between armies with independent movement; Vicksburg was the location of a siege.
3. (d) does not belong. Atlanta, Savannah, and Petersburg were southern cities. Gettysburg was a northern town.

Reviewing Main Ideas

1. Northerners demanded instant results; southerners did not want to wait for the results of a war of attrition or give up territory even temporarily. The public on both sides demanded direct confrontation.

2. The plan began by capturing key parts of the western region of the Confederacy, including the vital waterways that led to the Mississippi, in an effort to strangle the South.

3. Union troops under Irvin McDowell were repulsed at Manassas in 1861; troops under McClellan were repulsed by Lee in 1862; troops under Burnside were beaten at Fredericksburg in 1862; troops under Hooker were beaten at Chancellorsville in 1863.

4. They had to create a government from scratch while fighting a war. They also had to persuade fiercely independent southerners to sacrifice for the common good.

5. Lincoln suspended the writ so that he could imprison anyone who interfered with the war effort without having to justify his actions.

6. Republicans passed legislation that laid the economic foundations for the United States to become a major world power.

Chapter Review

Understanding Key Terms, People, and Places

Key Terms
1. shell
2. canister
3. war of attrition
4. Anaconda Plan
5. gunboat
6. draft
7. writ of *habeas corpus*
8. Internal Revenue Act of 1862
9. greenback
10. Pacific Railroad Act of 1862
11. Emancipation Proclamation
12. contraband
13. Pickett's Charge
14. siege
15. total war
16. Gettysburg Address
17. Thirteenth Amendment

People
18. Stonewall Jackson
19. George McClellan
20. Ulysses S. Grant
21. Robert E. Lee
22. Copperhead
23. Radical Republican
24. William Tecumseh Sherman
25. George G. Meade
26. Philip Sheridan
27. John Wilkes Booth

Places
28. Manassas
29. Shiloh
30. Antietam
31. Vicksburg
32. Gettysburg
33. Atlanta
34. Savannah
35. Petersburg
36. Appomattox Court House

Terms For each term above, write a sentence that explains its relation to the Civil War.

Matching Review the key terms in the list above. If you are not sure of a term's meaning, review its definition in the chapter. Then choose a term from the list that best matches each description below.
1. a form of prolonged attack in which a city is surrounded and starved into surrender
2. a court order commanding a jail officer to demonstrate that a prisoner is being held for a good reason
3. a small floating fort fitted with cannons
4. a legal means of forcing people to serve in the armed forces
5. national currency created by Republicans

Word Relationships Three of the people and places in each of the following sets are related. Choose the name that does not belong and explain why it does not belong.
1. (a) George McClellan, (b) Stonewall Jackson, (c) William Tecumseh Sherman, (d) Ulysses S. Grant
2. (a) Vicksburg, (b) Shiloh, (c) Antietam, (d) Manassas
3. (a) Atlanta, (b) Savannah, (c) Petersburg, (d) Gettysburg

Reviewing Main Ideas

Section 1 (pp. 326–332)
1. Why did Civil War generals use outmoded tactics?
2. How was the Anaconda Plan put into action?
3. Briefly summarize Union efforts to capture the southern capital of Richmond.

Section 2 (pp. 333–339)
4. What challenges did the new Confederate government face?
5. Why did Lincoln suspend the writ of habeas corpus?
6. What was the permanent effect of the absence of southern Democrats from Congress during the war?
7. What document gave a new moral purpose to the Union's war effort?
8. Who set African Americans free during the Civil War?

Section 3 (pp. 341–345)
9. How did the residents of Vicksburg spend their time while Grant tried unsuccessfully to capture the city?
10. What was the result of the Battle of Gettysburg?
11. In what ways was the siege of Vicksburg total war?

Section 4 (pp. 348–351)
12. Explain how the Gettysburg Address redefined the concept of freedom for Americans.
13. What were the immediate and the long-term effects of Sherman's march to the sea?
14. Briefly describe the events of 1865 that led to Lee's surrender.

---

7. The Emancipation Proclamation.

8. Many enslaved African Americans set themselves free by crossing Union lines; Union troops, including African Americans; and Abraham Lincoln.

9. They improved their defenses—for example, by digging caves.

10. Lee's army was forced to retreat, never to go on the offensive again. Both sides suffered staggering casualties.

11. Union troops struck out against innocent civilians, as well as against opposing soldiers.

12. The speech reflected the idea that freedom and equality no longer belonged to a few white men but were the rights of all.

13. In the short term, Sherman's march brought destruction to the South. In the long term, it made the hatred between North and South more difficult to heal.

14. Sheridan cut off Lee's supplies, forcing him to abandon Petersburg and Richmond. Then, hemmed in by Union forces, Lee surrendered at Appomattox Court House.

Thinking Critically

1. **Distinguishing False from Accurate Images** At the end of the Civil War, General William Tecumseh Sherman was called a traitor to the North because of his generosity to the defeated troops of the South. Yet many people today misjudge Sherman and mistakenly believe he was full of hatred for the South. How did this false image arise?

2. **Formulating Questions** Create three questions to ask William Harvey Carney that could lead to a greater understanding of the role of African Americans during the Civil War.

3. **Identifying Central Issues** How was the charge on Fort Wagner and Pickett's Charge typical of the way in which many Civil War battles were fought?

Making Connections

1. **Evaluating Primary Sources** Review the primary source excerpt on page 336. Explain Lincoln's statement that "in giving freedom to the slave, we assure freedom to the free."

2. **Understanding the Visuals** Examine the painting of Pickett's Charge on page 344. How can you tell that the Confederate forces are about to overrun the enemy lines?

3. **Writing About the Chapter** You are a newspaper reporter filing a story about one of the following events of the Civil War: the Battle of Manassas, the Battle of Vicksburg, the dedication ceremony at Gettysburg, or the surrender at Appomattox Court House. First, make a list of your observations at the event you have chosen. Include your perceptions of the physical setting of the event, the people involved, and the event's significance. Next, write a draft of your story in which you describe the event as you observed it. Revise your story, making sure that details are vividly and clearly described. Proofread your story and draft a final copy.

4. **Using the Graphic Organizer** This graphic organizer uses a flow map to show causes and effects of the Civil War. (a) According to the organizer, what forces clashed in the 1860s? (b) Explain the connection between the Declaration of Independence and the results of the Civil War. (c) On a separate sheet of paper, create your own graphic organizer about events of 1861–1865, using this graphic organizer as an example.

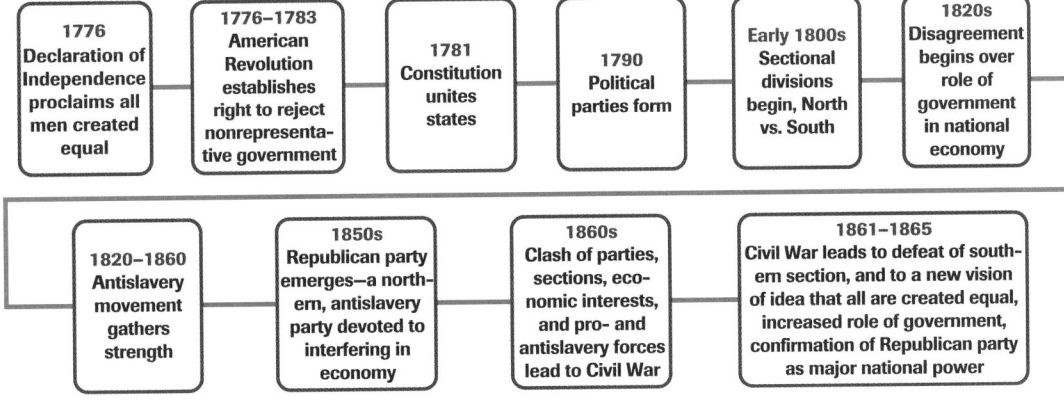

4. (a) Parties, sections, economic interests, and pro- and antislavery forces. (b) The Civil War led to a new vision of the basic principle of the Declaration of Independence that all are created equal. (c) Students' graphic organizers should include information about the basic strategies and events of the Civil War.

 Alternative Assessment

Final Evaluation

Use the following guidelines to evaluate student projects:

- **Evidence of mastery of content** To what extent do projects show knowledge and understanding of the chapter content?
- **Evidence of thoughtfulness** To what extent do projects show an understanding of the importance and significance of events?
- **Evidence of outside research** To what extent do projects use outside research materials?
- **Communication style** To what extent do projects vividly portray the events of the Civil War in a way appropriate for elementary school students?

Thinking Critically

1. Sherman's march to the sea has been interpreted as an expression of hatred for the South rather than as a campaign with deliberate military and political objectives.

2. Possible questions: Why were you willing to fight for the United States despite discrimination? What was your regiment trying to prove besides its courage? What impact did the bravery of your regiment have on white attitudes toward African American soldiers?

3. Despite new technologies that guaranteed heavy casualties, troops advanced upon heavily defended positions. Most troops were easily cut down by enemy fire.

Making Connections

1. Answers should suggest that ending slavery was the only way to end forever the threat to the nation, and thus to American freedom in general, posed by conflict between North and South.

2. They are overrunning a cannon that is pointed directly at them.

3. Students' stories should reveal an understanding of the setting, the people involved, and the importance of the event that they have chosen.

American Album

Explain to students that the Civil War has been endlessly fascinating to Americans, almost from the moment the smoke cleared from the battle-fields. At Gettysburg and other battle sites, souvenir seekers prowled over the fields as soon as the armies had retreated.

Divide the class into small groups. Ask each group to study the feature and answer the following question: What do the objects shown teach us about the Civil War that we would not otherwise know?

Ask students to write a letter from a Union or Confederate soldier in which one of the items displayed is mentioned.

Interested students might do further research on the equipment, medical treatment, and camp life of Civil War soldiers.

Ask students what memorials, monuments, or museum displays exist in their community to commemorate the Civil War. Encourage interested students to visit one or more of these sites and report to the class on the nature of the site, the date it was established, and their opinion of its interest level and appropriateness.

American Album
ARTIFACTS FROM EXHIBITIONS AND COLLECTIONS
AT THE SMITHSONIAN INSTITUTION
NATIONAL MUSEUM OF AMERICAN HISTORY

LIFE AT WAR

When Union and Confederate soldiers set off to war in 1861, both sides expected it to last only a short time. They soon realized that the struggle would not be settled quickly and that they would have to adapt to long months at war. As in most wars, much of what the soldiers did was boring and uncomfortable. Their routine consisted mainly of training for battle, securing food, idling with their fellow soldiers, and traveling. Soldiers far preferred these daily discomforts and boredoms, however, to the deadly horrors they faced from fierce battles, diseases, and infections. More than 600,000 died—the most Americans ever to die in a war. Four of every ten men who went off to the Civil War were killed or wounded. *Why do you think soldiers were willing to pay such a high cost for their side's cause?*

▲ BOWIE KNIFE Many Confederate soldiers carried Bowie knives—named after frontiersman Jim Bowie.

▲ CONFEDERATE UNIFORM John Mosby, a Confederate scout and guerrilla leader, wore this jacket. Mosby and his Partisan Rangers often operated behind enemy lines in Virginia and Maryland.

▲ BULLET IN SHOULDER BELT PLATE
The soldier who wore this shoulder plate was very lucky. The plate saved his life by stopping a musket bullet.

▲ CIVIL WAR MUSKET
Many soldiers during the war used a musket, but the rifle soon replaced it as the standard army weapon. A rifle was easier to load, more accurate over long distances, and misfired less often.

▲ MESS TINS A soldier carried his own eating implements with him. These mess tins took up little space when put away and could be carried easily inside a soldier's pack.

▲ FIELD CUTLERY Soldiers carried utensils like these with their mess tins. Getting food to the soldiers was a problem that slowed down both armies.

◀ HARD TACK Although not very tasty, this chewy bread was very nourishing, lasted a long time without spoiling, and was easy to carry.

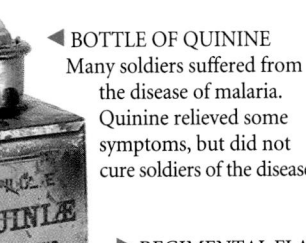

◀ BOTTLE OF QUININE Many soldiers suffered from the disease of malaria. Quinine relieved some symptoms, but did not cure soldiers of the disease.

▶ REGIMENTAL FLAG This flag commemorates some important battles by an African American regiment. About 180,000 of the 2,000,000 Union soldiers were African Americans.

▲ FIELD HOSPITAL More soldiers died from disease and from infections caused by wounds than were killed in battles. Many women served their cause by working in field hospitals.

Chapter 13 Reconstruction
1863–1877

📁 Teaching Resources (See Unit 4 Folder)

	Instruction	Enrichment
Section 1 **The Meaning of Freedom** (pp. 360–365)	Reproducible Lesson Plan, p. 75 Alternate Lesson Plan, p. 64 Guided Reading and Review, p. 79 Quiz, p. 80	Visual Learning Activity, A Symbol of Freedom, p. 99 Literature Activity, The Story of Free Joe, pp. 96–98 American Profiles Activity, Charlotte Forten Grimké, p. 87
Section 2 **Three Plans for Reconstruction** (pp. 366–370)	Reproducible Lesson Plan, p. 76 Alternate Lesson Plan, p. 65 Guided Reading and Review, p. 81 Quiz, p. 82	American Profiles Activity, Thaddeus Stevens, p. 88 Critical Thinking Activity, Identifying Central Issues, p. 92 Primary Source Activity, The Trial of President Johnson, pp. 94–95 Viewpoints Activity, On Voting Rights for African Americans, pp. 89–90
Section 3 **Reconstruction in the South** (pp. 371–375)	Reproducible Lesson Plan, p. 77 Alternate Lesson Plan, p. 66 Guided Reading and Review, p. 83 Quiz, p. 84	Primary Source Activity, A Bleak Future for Freedmen, p. 93 Historian's Toolbox Activity, How Maps Show Change Over Time, p. 91
Section 4 **The Retreat from Reconstruction in the North** (pp. 377–379)	Reproducible Lesson Plan, p. 78 Alternate Lesson Plan, p. 67 Guided Reading and Review, p. 85 Quiz, p. 86 Chapter Test, Forms A & B, pp. 101–106	Visual Learning Activity, America's Birthday Party, p. 100

📁 Additional Chapter Resources

Resource Organizer, p. 74
Alternate Lesson Plan, p. 63
Answer Keys, pp. 113–122

Bibliography

For the Teacher
Carter, Hodding. *The Angry Scar: The Story of Reconstruction.* Greenwood, 1974. (An account of southerners' reactions to Reconstruction.)
Du Bois, W. E. B. *Black Reconstruction.* Kraus-Thomason, 1976. (Classic account by the famous African American scholar.)
Franklin, John Hope. *Reconstruction After the Civil War.* University of Chicago Press, 1970. (Sympathetic treatment of congressional efforts to reconstruct the old Confederacy.)

Prentice Hall Literature Excerpts from *The American Experience,* 1994, including Whitman, Walt. *Complete Poetry and Selected Prose of Walt Whitman.* Houghton Mifflin, 1982 edition.

The Big Idea for the chapter and how the main ideas in each section relate to the Big Idea are graphically displayed below. Comprehension of this chapter's Big Idea is critical to students' understanding of United States history and how we as a nation got where we are today.

Media and Technology

 Critical Thinking, I-2; Geographic Setting, M-4

 Fine Art, D-12; Graphic Organizer, G-3

 Guided Reading Audiotapes (English and Spanish)

 Computer Test Bank

For the Student

Allen, Gay Wilson. *The Solitary Singer: A Critical Biography of Walt Whitman.* University of Chicago Press, 1985. (A life of Walt Whitman.)

Lester, Julius. *This Strange New Feeling.* Scholastic, 1985. (Three short stories about slavery and freedom, based on true accounts.)

Life History of the United States, Vols. 5–7; *The Union Sundered.* 1963; *The Union Restored.* 1977; *The Age of Steel and Steam.* 1974.

CHAPTER 13

Though the outcome of the Civil War cemented the Union, the years that followed plunged the nation headlong into dramatic social and economic changes. While African Americans obtained their liberty and southern society was transformed, Reconstruction involved a redefinition of social, economic, and political relationships between the North and the South as well as between the races.

SECTION 1

In 1865 slavery was finally abolished, making African Americans equal to white people under the law.

SECTION 2

During the years following the Civil War, the federal government undertook to reconstruct the nation through a series of acts and amendments that gave African Americans full United States citizenship and transformed the social order in the South.

SECTION 3

For a while the Republicans were able to bring about significant political and social changes in the South, but eventually their efforts were met by violent resistance that reversed many of the gains.

SECTION 4

As white southerners fought Reconstruction, Republicans in the North began to lose interest in their dream of social equality and justice for African Americans and other powerless groups. Instead, the Republicans began to ally themselves with powerful industrialists.

Reconstruction
1863–1877

The Relevance of the Big Idea

The Reconstruction era, from 1863 to 1877, transformed American society and enabled African Americans to achieve their freedom and move toward social equality and justice. Yet full equality remained elusive. In the 1990s the United States is still struggling to fulfill its promise of justice and equality for all.

To help students understand why the United States could not achieve the goals it envisioned for itself following the Civil War—and still cannot—ask them to consider, given the terms of the surrender, what kind of treatment the South might have expected after the war.

Discuss with students the problems the United States faces in the 1990s that could be regarded in some measure as legacies of the Civil War.

In Depth

Global Connections

With the end of the Civil War, American leaders looked outward. Secretary of State William H. Seward became the champion of expansionism. When the Russians asked whether the United States might want to buy Alaska, he jumped at the chance. In spite of a Civil War debt of $3 billion, the Senate approved the purchase of Alaska for $7.2 million. The purchase turned out to be a bargain—the gold taken from the Yukon Valley since 1897 has paid for Alaska many times over.

Reconstruction
1863–1877

In the years following the Civil War, the people of the United States plunged headlong into accelerating social and economic change. For the formerly enslaved people of the South, freedom opened a new world in which they were at liberty to travel, rebuild relationships, and seek control over their working lives. Yet the fate of African Americans was still intertwined with the will of whites, some of whom respected them and some of whom did not. In the end, most white Americans proved unwilling to commit themselves to full racial equality. Reconstruction transformed the nation, but it failed to fulfill the promise of northern victory in the Civil War.

Events in the United States

1865 The Civil War ends as the last Confederate forces surrender.

1866 The Ku Klux Klan is founded in Tennessee.

1868 Congress impeaches but does not convict President Johnson.

1869 The Wyoming and Utah territories grant women the right to vote.

1863	1865	1867	1869

Events in the World

1865 Englishman Lewis Carroll publishes Alice's Adventures in Wonderland.

1867 The Dominion of Canada is established.

1869 The Suez Canal is completed in Egypt, joining the Mediterranean Sea and the Gulf of Suez.

▶ RESOURCE DIRECTORY

Teaching Resources

Alternate Lesson Plan: Demonstrating the Big Idea found in the Alternate Lesson Plans folder, p. 63, provides a lesson strategy to instruct students about the Big Idea that after the Civil War the United States grappled with large social and economic changes, that African Americans gained new liberties, but the quest for equal rights was often met with bitterness and violence.

Alternative Assessment Handbook provides information, guidance, and strategies for alternative methods of assessment. It includes an essay on new trends in assessment, guidance and strategies for developing performance tasks and portfolios, scoring rubrics, and sample evaluation forms.

Pages 360–365

The Meaning of Freedom

The Civil War was over and slavery was dead. Now liberty swept through the South in the wake of Union armies, and African Americans seized it with enthusiasm, exploring the meaning it held for every aspect of their lives.

Pages 366–370

Three Plans for Reconstruction

The meaning of freedom was clear to the freed people of the South. For Congress, however, the end of the Civil War raised many difficult questions about how to rebuild the nation. The result was a series of acts and amendments that redefined citizenship and attempted to create a new social order in the South.

Pages 371–375

Reconstruction in the South

Republicans stormed the South, bringing ambitious ideas about improving the political and social rights of African Americans. Their policies did lead to significant gains, but they soon found their efforts undermined by a campaign of terror and violence.

Pages 377–379

The Retreat from Reconstruction in the North

The Radical Republican blueprint for Reconstruction was based on a grand dream of social equality and justice. But economic and political changes brought by the war led the Republicans to forsake their commitment to this dream in favor of other, less idealistic, concerns.

1871	1873	1875	1877

1872 President Ulysses S. Grant wins reelection.

1875 Congress passes a Civil Rights Act.

1876 Republican Rutherford B. Hayes wins the presidential election despite losing the popular vote.

1877 The Compromise of 1877 ends military occupation of the South.

1871 The unification of Germany is completed.

1872 Japan introduces universal military service.
• Germany expels the Jesuits.

1873 Slave markets and exports of enslaved people are abolished in Zanzibar in Africa.

1874 The Ashanti War ends in African Ghana.

1876 Korea becomes an independent nation.
• Serbia declares war on Turkey.

1877 First Kaffir War begins in South Africa.
• First tennis championship held at Wimbledon.

Alternative Assessment

As an ongoing chapter project, students can chronicle the history of a southern family, either African American or white, during Reconstruction. The object is to document the changes southerners experienced during Reconstruction and their response to those changes. Encourage students to create a "big picture" of Reconstruction through the story. Students should use primary sources such as diaries and other first-person accounts to help them construct their family's history.

Projects should contain at least three of the following, but may include other items as well:
• Audiotapes of interviews with "relatives" recounting stories handed down over the generations
• Mock letters between relatives and friends describing their living conditions, experiences, and feelings during the Reconstruction era
• Collections of artifacts, such as copies of birth and marriage records, deeds of sale, and labor contracts
• Excerpts from Reconstruction-era diaries and photographs from magazines or books

Explain that finished projects will be assessed according to the following standards:
• **Unacceptable** Projects are not attempted or fail to meet basic requirements.
• **Limited/Acceptable** Projects attempt to give a picture of Reconstruction through the lens of their chosen family.
• **Extensive/Commendable** Projects provide a broad view of Reconstruction through one family's experiences.
• **Extraordinary/Outstanding** Projects successfully provide a detailed view of Reconstruction and one family's experiences in the context of southern society.

For information and guidance on alternative assessment trends and strategies, see the Alternative Assessment Handbook in the Resource Directory on page 358.

SECTION 1

The Meaning of Freedom

1. FOCUS

Connecting to the Big Idea

See page 358B. Explain that the passage of the Thirteenth Amendment in 1865 brought great changes to the southern way of life. African Americans were no longer property at the mercy of their white masters but free human beings who, under the law at least, were equal to white people. Ask how African Americans responded to this new freedom.

Objectives

● Describe how enslaved African Americans took up their freedom and how former owners responded.
● Explain what freedom meant to formerly enslaved African Americans.

Bellringer

Ask students to imagine themselves newly freed citizens after the Civil War. What is the first thing they would want to do to celebrate their free status?

Reading Strategy

Structured Overview Have students write down the main headings and subheadings from the section. Students should then fill in details from the text under the appropriate heading as they read.

SECTION PREVIEW

The Civil War was over and slavery was dead. Now liberty swept through the South in the wake of Union armies, and African Americans seized it with enthusiasm, exploring the meaning it held for every aspect of their lives.

Key Concepts

• Enslaved African Americans took up their freedom with a readiness that surprised white slaveholders.
• To formerly enslaved African Americans, freedom meant the ability to move, to organize, to educate themselves, to participate in politics, to own land, and to decide what to do with their labor.

Key Terms, People, and Places

Reconstruction

Freedom for African Americans meant—among other things—the freedom to worship. After the Civil War, African American churches in the South gained hundreds of thousands of new members. This photograph shows a woman ready to preach.

I n June 1869, A. D. Lewis, an African American citizen of North Carolina, sent a letter to Governor William W. Holden. In it, Lewis describes a dispute he had had with a certain Dr. A. H. Jones.

I was in my field at my own work and this Jones came by me and drove up to a man's gate that live close by . . . and ordered my child to come there and open that gate for him . . . while there was children in the yard at the same time not more than twenty yards from him and just because they were white and mine black he would not call them to open the gate. . . . I spoke gently to him that [the white children] would open the gate. . . . He got out of his buggy . . . and walked nearly hundred yards right into my field where I was at my own work and double his fist and strick me in the face three times and . . .

cursed me as a dumb old Radical. . . . Now governor I wants you to please write me how to bring this man to justice.

It is not known whether Governor Holden ever answered Lewis. But the letter does say a lot about **Reconstruction,** the period of United States history in which the nation tried to adjust to the new conditions created by the Civil War.

In his letter, Lewis mentions himself, his work, and his land in terms that reflect true self-respect. Not only was he outraged by the physical injury Jones did him by striking him in the face, he was offended that Jones had insulted his dignity by giving orders to his child. Clearly, Lewis saw himself as an American citizen with legal rights. He must have believed that the legal system would protect him from assault; otherwise, he would not have written to Governor Holden at all.

Lewis's attitudes and expectations suggest a tremendous change in the American South. No longer were African Americans merely property that could be ordered about at the whim of a white owner. Now they were free citizens whose status—under the law, at least—was equal to that of white people. This change would have a profound impact not just on the southern economy, but on every aspect of the southern way of life.

Breaking Down Slavery

✪ In 1865 the states ratified the Thirteenth Amendment to the Constitution, thereby abolishing slavery. Long before this amendment had been written and proposed, however, African Americans across the South had begun to anticipate its arrival. Whites in the North may have struggled to decide what the Civil War was all about, but African Americans had a clear purpose in mind. They sought nothing less than the abolition of slavery, and they directed their efforts toward that goal.

RESOURCE DIRECTORY

Teaching Resources

Reproducible Lesson Plan found in the Unit 4 folder, p. 75, provides a summary of the Section 1 lesson plan content.

Alternate Lesson Plan: Learning Styles found in the Alternate Lesson Plans folder, p. 64, provides guidance for students working individually and in small groups to create and present journal entries of a former slave to explain the changes brought by freedom.

Guided Reading and Review found in Unit 4 folder, p. 79, provides a structure for reading and mastering the key concepts and reviewing the key terms for Section 1. (Guided Practice)

✪ **Visual Learning Activity** A Symbol of Freedom, found in the Unit 4 folder, p. 99, presents a drawing published in *Leslie's Illustrated Newspaper* on August 5, 1876, showing how a statue called "The Freed Slave" reflected attitudes toward African Americans' new status.

During the war, African Americans in the South often simply ceased paying any attention to the authority of their owners as soon as Union troops were reported to be nearby. They had no doubt they were free. Indeed, the Emancipation Proclamation and the Thirteenth Amendment merely made legal what was already fact throughout the South. As a northern journalist had observed as early as November 1862, slavery was "forever destroyed and worthless, no matter what Mr. Lincoln or anyone else may say on the subject."

The enthusiasm with which African Americans threw off the shackles of slavery actually surprised many whites. Slaveholders often reported feeling deserted or insulted by people they had once considered to be like family members. One nineteen-year-old woman, Susan Bradford, observed with regret the change in the behavior of the enslaved people who had formerly worked for her family: "Never before had I [heard] a word of impudence from any of our black folk," she wrote. Then she added with great understatement, "they are not ours any longer." The bonds that she presumed had linked her to "her people" were gone.

Symbols of the new working relationships between African Americans and white Americans after the Civil War, these two cowhands posed side by side in the 1860s.

R *ight off colored folks started on the move. They seemed to want to get closer to freedom, so they'd know what it was like—like it was a place or a city.*

In the end, many freed people returned to live on or near their old plantations. Yet the excitement of being able to move freely was memorable.

The movement of freed people was not aimless; many traveled with a purpose, for freedom also meant reuniting families. Freed people sometimes walked hundreds of miles looking for relatives separated by the slave trade. Many were successful in their quest. Reconstruction brought together families that had been broken apart by slavery and testified to the deep emotional ties among African Americans. For a time, at least, many African American women worked less time in the fields and devoted more of their attention to home and family.

New African American Organizations Freedom encouraged the formation of new African American organizations. The most visible of these were churches. Across the South, freed people withdrew from congregations with both white and African American members and formed their own churches. They also started

---

MAKING   CONNECTIONS

Recall what you have read about the treatment of enslaved African Americans. How accurate are white slaveholders' claims that they looked upon African Americans as members of their family? Explain your answer.

What Freedom Meant to African Americans

⭐ It was, of course, difficult for white slaveholders such as Susan Bradford to understand the impact of freedom on people who had been enslaved. To the "freed people," as they were called, freedom meant the basic things that whites took for granted. It meant, for example, the freedom to go wherever they wanted. Thus free African Americans often traveled away from the plantations on which they had worked and lived. A formerly enslaved African American from Texas recalled:

⭐ **Literature Activity** The Story of Free Joe, found in the Unit 4 folder, pp. 96–98, was written by Joel Chandler Harris, the creator of Uncle Remus, to describe the life of the free African American in a slave society.

Analyze the reaction of white southerners to the African Americans' new status after the abolition of slavery. Why would the end of slavery intensify white prejudice against African Americans? How did the South's defeat compound the negative feelings of southern whites toward African Americans?

THE ONLY ORIGINAL

University Singers of New Orleans

As freedom opened new possibilities for social participation during Reconstruction, these African Americans in New Orleans formed a choir to raise money for an orphan's home.

thousands of voluntary organizations, including mutual aid societies, temperance clubs, debating clubs, drama societies, and trade associations.

Education Freedom also meant education. Historians estimate that 90 percent of adult freed people were illiterate in 1860. Slave codes had often prohibited teaching enslaved people to read and write. In 1862 a wealthy free African American woman from Philadelphia named Charlotte Forten had gone to Port Royal, South Carolina, to teach African Americans. She later described the enthusiasm she found.

> I never before saw children so eager to learn. . . . Coming to school is a constant delight and recreation to them. . . . Many of the grown people [also] are desirous of learning to read. It is wonderful how a people who have been so long crushed to the earth . . . can have so great a desire for knowledge, and such a capability for attaining it.

After the war, freed people continued eagerly to seek the ability to read and write. Many were taught by white school teachers—often young women—who moved to the South in an effort to help African Americans after the war. Many freed people, however, were self-taught.

African Americans also organized to set up and support schools for higher education.

Between 1865 and 1870, thirty African American colleges were founded. By 1870 those colleges had spent over $1 million in their effort to improve the education of African Americans.

Political Involvement With the end of the Civil War, African Americans throughout the South organized to claim their rights as citizens. They held state conventions and rallies. Although they discussed economic issues, the most common themes were political ones. They wanted the political rights of citizenship: to vote, to hold office, to serve on juries. As Section 3 will show, their participation in politics during Reconstruction was substantial.

Land Ownership Finally, freedom for African Americans meant control of land and labor. It meant the right to own property, the ability to pursue whatever line of work they chose, and the power to determine what they produced.

Freed people throughout the South also sought the redistribution of land. They argued that they were entitled to the land on which they had lived, even though it belonged to white people. After all, freed people argued, enslaved people had cleared the land originally and farmed it for generations.

The most radical experiment in land redistribution occurred in coastal South Carolina and Georgia. With the arrival of General William Tecumseh Sherman and his forces in late 1864, this land came under the military rule of the United States Army. Under pressure from African Americans and Radical Republicans in Congress, General Sherman issued Special Field Order No. 15 on January 16, 1865. Sherman reserved the Sea Islands of Georgia and a 30-mile-wide strip of coastal land south of Charleston for eligible African American families. Each would receive 40 acres.

The Union general saw this order as a war measure; it was intended to punish slaveholders and to help the growing numbers of poor and starving African Americans following his army across South Carolina. By June 1865, roughly 40,000 African Americans were living on 400,000 acres of the land Sherman had set aside for them.

In spite of Sherman's program—and in spite of the dire need of the many freed people

In Depth

Then and Now

A century after the Civil War, African Americans continued to struggle for equal access to education in the South. In 1956, after years of court battles, twenty-seven-year-old Autherine Lucy was admitted to the University of Alabama—only to be expelled a few days later because of violent protests. In 1988, the university revoked its resolution of expulsion and invited Lucy to enroll again. "The University of Alabama is still my alma mater. I just stayed there for three days, but it is still my alma mater," says Lucy. "I did not feel evil toward them because I didn't think they were fighting me. They were fighting tradition and change. It just wasn't my time."

▶ RESOURCE DIRECTORY

Teaching Resources

 American Profiles Activity found in the Unit 4 folder, p. 87, profiles Charlotte Forten Grimké, an African American teacher from a distinguished Philadelphia family who dedicated her life to social reform and the education of formerly enslaved people.

following virtually every Union army—very little land in the South was redistributed. Once the war was over, the United States refused to continue the kind of forced change in land ownership that Sherman had pioneered. In addition, freed people generally lacked the money and could not get the credit they needed to buy land from whites. Those who did buy land, however, were able to take a first step toward economic and psychological independence. A white northerner visiting the South in the fall of 1865 gave this summary of what owning land meant to freed people:

> The sole ambition of the freedman at the present time appears to be to become the owner of a little piece of land, there to erect a humble home, and to dwell in peace and security at his own free will and pleasure. If he wishes to cultivate the ground in cotton on his own account, to be able to do so without anyone to dictate to him hours or system of labor, if he wishes instead to plant corn or sweet potatoes—to be able to do that free from any outside control. . . . That is their idea, their desire and their hope.

These new desires and hopes of African Americans often clashed with the plans of southern whites. The story of the people of White Hall plantation illustrates how both whites and African Americans had to adjust to the realities of life in the South after the Civil War.

AMERICAN PROFILES

The People of White Hall Plantation

The family of Richard and Louisa Arnold was unusual in the mid-1800s. For decades before the Civil War, they had divided their time between a home in Rhode Island and a rice plantation they owned near Savannah, Georgia. Born in the North in 1796, Richard Arnold was both a businessman and a planter. He had purchased his plantation, which he called White Hall, in 1824. He and his wife, Louisa, and their seven children typically spent their summers in the North and their winters on the plantation. They were among the 360,000 white northerners who lived and worked in the South in 1860.

The Arnolds had divided opinions on secession. Louisa favored it, as did most of their children, but Richard opposed it, and the Arnolds spent most of the war in Rhode Island. Richard did, however, sell White Hall to his son Thomas, a Confederate supporter, so that the Confederacy would not seize it. Thomas managed the plantation during the Civil War, but abandoned it as Sherman's army approached in December 1864.

Thanks to Richard Arnold's opposition to secession and his political connections in the North, White Hall was declared exempt from Sherman's Special Field Order No. 15. In November 1865, Thomas went back to the plantation to begin rebuilding it. The Arnolds were lucky. Their money and influence had saved them from losing their plantation, as many southern planters had.

A Postwar Plantation Thomas was shocked by what he found upon his return to White Hall. The war damage to the mansion concerned him, but still more troubling was the new attitude of the African Americans who had long resided at White Hall. These were the formerly enslaved workers whom the Arnolds, like many other white southerners, had called "our people."

Thomas reported to his father that the freed people were unreliable and unfriendly. None of them would even speak to him. In order to get them to work, Thomas brought a Union colonel to "the settlement," the former slave quarters. There the federal official told the thirty or forty assembled African Americans that they would be wise to trust Arnold and agree to work at his plantation for wages. But, Thomas reported,

> Batteast [one of the African Americans] spoke up in behalf of the whole plantation and said they had made up their minds never to work for me again, the Col. told them that they were very foolish and asked Batteast what he intended to do, that they must vacate. [Batteast answered] he did not know, but that God would point out the way.

Activity

Teaching Heterogeneous Groups
To help students reflect on the changed relationships between African Americans and former slaveholders during Reconstruction, have students decide where they would go if they themselves were recently freed from bondage, and how they would provide for their food, shelter, and clothing when they were about to leave home. Students should also list three changes that would occur for their parents. **LEP**

In Depth

Did You Know?

Southern plantations, in spite of their dependence on slavery, were romanticized by southern author Margaret Mitchell in her popular novel *Gone with the Wind*. Published in 1936, the book became the best-selling novel in the United States and sold eight million copies worldwide. *Gone with the Wind* was made into an Academy Award–winning film in 1939, and for over a generation remained the most successful film ever made.

Frederick Douglass was the most famous African American leader in the years following the Civil War. Ask each student to research the achievements of this great man and to write and perform a one-person skit about his accomplishments.

A visitor to White Hall sketched the mansion in 1842 (bottom). Though no picture survives of the slave quarters at White Hall, a traveler drew the children's nursery at Cherry Hill (top), another plantation of Richard Arnold's.

For generations, whites such as the Arnolds had assumed that they shared some sort of a common relationship and affection with their enslaved workers. Thomas Arnold was not the only one who saw that illusion shattered. This has been called "the moment of truth"—the time when white slaveholders finally realized that they did not have the affection and respect of the enslaved people who had worked for them, because slavery and affection could not exist side by side.

Some African Americans did continue to work willingly for their former masters. Forty-five-year-old Amos Morel and his wife Cretia went to Newport, Rhode Island, in 1865 to be with the Arnolds. They came back to White Hall with Thomas in November and went to work rebuilding White Hall into a plantation. Thomas appreciated what he saw as the loyalty of Morel, who he said was "true as steel."

New Working Relationships Richard Arnold purchased White Hall back from his son and resumed the cultivation of rice. In 1869 the place produced a million pounds of the crop; in the early 1870s, it was one of the largest rice plantations in the South. But though rice fields could be rebuilt, plantation life could not. The assertiveness and defiance shown by most of the Arnolds' former enslaved workers did not end. Many freed people had no desire to return to work in swampy fields for the benefit of whites. This was not the meaning of freedom.

The Arnolds had money, however, and spent it freely. They paid $1,700 in wages in May and June of 1867—a generous amount in those days—and spent a total of $60,000 on planting during that year. It was hard to resist good money in hard times. Even so, the Arnolds often had to rely on work gangs of Irish laborers or African Americans who were so deeply impoverished that they had no choice but to work in the rice fields.

The wages paid by the Arnolds gave their African American workers new power. In 1871 Amos Morel took his savings and bought more than 400 acres of land. He then sold pieces of it to other former enslaved workers. Later he bought more than a hundred acres for his daughter. These purchases and sales were a mild form of land redistribution compared to Sherman's famous order. But they were a beginning.

New Living Relationships In many respects, the end of slavery intensified white prejudice against African Americans. Many whites refused to accept freed people who asserted their equality. For instance, Nina Arnold, a relative of Richard Arnold, visited White Hall in 1868. She was shocked when the old nurse of the family, an African American, kissed and hugged her as an equal.

The old prejudices were severely tested in 1870 when the Arnolds gained new neighbors—William and Ellen Craft, who bought the nearby Woodville plantation. The Crafts were African Americans who had escaped slavery in Georgia before the Civil War and gone to England. Now they had returned to their homeland. They made Woodville into a center of education and vocational training for African Americans. Their efforts to empower freed people further widened the gap between the expectations of African Americans in the area around Whitehall, who sought a better life,

In Depth

Did You Know?

In her 1887 book *Memorials of a Southern Planter,* Susan Dabney Smedes tells how her father coped with life after the war: "His chivalrous nature had always revolted from the sight of a woman doing hard work. He determined to spare his daughters all such labor as he could perform. General Sherman had said that he would like to bring every southern woman to the washtub. 'He shall never bring my daughters to the washtub,' Thomas Dabney said. 'I will do the washing myself.' And he did it for two years. He was in his seventieth year when he began to do it."

▶ RESOURCE DIRECTORY

Teaching Resources

Using Historical Evidence A northerner touring the South in 1866 reported, "the whites seem wholly unable to comprehend that freedom for the Negro means the same thing as freedom for them. They . . . believe that they still have the right to exercise over him the old control." *How does this postwar photograph support that observation?*

and former slaveholders, who wanted a return to the old social order.

That return never came about. A Georgia doctor noted: "The revolution of our social fabric is too great, the entire upheaval and overthrow of all the foundations of our society too universal not to affect everybody." Richard Arnold died in 1873. The debts of his estate eventually forced the sale of his land in Georgia. A son-in-law bought White Hall in 1877. The vast rice plantation where white masters had once forced African Americans to work without pay in the fields now became a hunting and fishing preserve for the rich.

Within fifteen years of the end of the Civil War, the ways of the Old South were truly gone from White Hall forever. Most other plantations throughout the South remained working farms, but they too were dramatically changed. Though prejudice remained and white men still held great power over African Americans, the world of slavery had come to an end, destroyed by the combined efforts of the United States armed forces and African Americans eager to assert their independence. In its place was a new order that was still emerging, as will be discussed in the sections ahead.

SECTION 1 REVIEW

Key Terms, People, and Places
1. Define Reconstruction.

Key Concepts
2. How did African Americans react to the prospect of freedom even before the Civil War ended?
3. What did freedom mean to African Americans after the end of the Civil War?

4. Give evidence of the distrust between whites and freed African Americans at White Hall plantation.

Critical Thinking
5. **Demonstrating Reasoned Judgment** What does the exchange between A. D. Lewis and Dr. A. H. Jones, as described in Lewis's letter, suggest about problems facing freed people?

  Quiz found in the Unit 4 folder, p. 80, covers the main ideas in this section as well as the key terms.

Caption Answer to . . .

Using Historical Evidence

It shows a white overseer watching over African Americans working.

3. ASSESS

Section 1 Review Answers

1. Reconstruction, see p. 360

2. They eagerly embraced it. Even before the ratification of the Thirteenth Amendment, African Americans began acting as if they were free.

3. It meant mobility, the opportunity to learn, and the chance to form new institutions and organizations, such as churches, colleges, and self-help groups. In addition, it meant a chance to receive payment for work and to own land.

4. African Americans refused even to speak to Thomas Arnold when he first returned to White Hall; Nina Arnold reacted with disgust to hugs and kisses from an African American woman.

5. Possible answer: The exchange suggests that prejudiced attitudes of whites toward African Americans remained strong, even after emancipation. These attitudes might be expected to hinder efforts to win true equality for African Americans.

Reteach

Have students review the section and formulate ten true/false statements about the section content. Students should then exchange their papers with a partner and indicate whether their partner's statements are true or false.

4. CLOSE

Reinforcing the Big Idea

African Americans took up their new freedom with great enthusiasm. The next section discusses attempts to reconstruct the nation and create a new social order in the South.

SECTION 2

Three Plans for Reconstruction

1. FOCUS

Connecting to the Big Idea

See page 358B. Explain that when the Civil War ended, the federal government struggled with the issue of how to put the nation back together again. Ask students whether they think the South should have been treated harshly or dealt with leniently. What should the government have done to protect the freedom of African Americans?

Objectives

● Explain how the Freedmen's Bureau helped African Americans during the war.

● Explain how Lincoln was able to stop a harsh measure passed by Congress that would have made Reconstruction more difficult.

● Explain how, by refusing to accept moderate changes, white southerners increased northern support for Radical Reconstruction.

● Explain how the Fourteenth Amendment defined American citizenship.

● State the purpose of the Fifteenth Amendment.

Bellringer

Ask students to discuss the meaning of the word *reconstruct*. Ask them to think about how the concept relates to the period after the Civil War.

Reading Strategy

Question Writing

Have students read the section's main headings and then write a question based on each one, filling in the answers as they read.

SECTION PREVIEW

The meaning of freedom was clear to the freed people of the South. For Congress, however, the end of the Civil War raised many difficult questions about how to rebuild the nation. The result was a series of acts and amendments that redefined citizenship and attempted to create a new social order in the South.

The battle between Congress and President Andrew Johnson over Reconstruction reached its lowest point in 1868 when Congress tried to remove Johnson from office. Tickets to the proceedings were in great demand.

Key Concepts

• The Freedmen's Bureau took the first steps to help African Americans freed during the war.

• Lincoln was able to stop a harsh measure passed by Congress that would have made Reconstruction more difficult.

• By refusing to accept moderate changes, white southerners increased northern support for Radical Reconstruction.

• The Fourteenth Amendment clearly defined American citizenship in a manner that included African Americans.

• The Fifteenth Amendment guaranteed all citizens the right to vote.

Key Terms, People, and Places

Freedmen's Bureau, pardon, Fourteenth Amendment, Military Reconstruction Act of 1867, impeach, Fifteenth Amendment; Andrew Johnson

---

F reed people recognized that land, education, and the vote were keys to building a new social order in the South. Meanwhile, politicians in Washington, D.C., were struggling with the many questions raised by the defeat of the Confederacy. What steps should the United States government take to protect the liberties of African Americans? How, and on what terms, should the defeated Confederate states be returned to their former role in the Union? In other words, how should the federal government reconstruct the nation? These issues dominated national politics during the Reconstruction years.

Helping Freed People

One of the more insistent questions confronting the United States government was how to help the former enslaved people. The defeat of the Confederacy brought freedom, but also uncertainty. Without education and jobs, freed people faced continued poverty.

In spite of unrelenting prejudice against African Americans, many whites were committed to helping freed people build new lives. From the time of the Emancipation Proclamation in 1863, the Republican party had defined itself as an organization committed not only to ending slavery, but also to bringing some measure of justice to African Americans.

It was in this spirit that Congress established the **Freedmen's Bureau** in March 1865. The purpose of the bureau was to provide aid to freed people and help them make the adjustment to freedom. Under the leadership of General Oliver O. Howard, the bureau gave out clothing, medical supplies, and millions of meals to refugees of the war, both African American and white. Its most significant work, however, came in the establishment of schools for African Americans. With the help of the bureau, over 250,000 African Americans received their first taste of formal education.

Lincoln's Reconstruction Plan

Another central question facing the United States was how to put the nation back together after the war. In December 1863, while battles were still raging, President Lincoln had proposed a moderate Reconstruction policy. Lincoln offered a **pardon**—an official forgiveness

---

▶ RESOURCE DIRECTORY

Teaching Resources

Reproducible Lesson Plan found in the Unit 4 folder, p. 76, provides a summary of the Section 2 lesson plan content.

Alternate Lesson Plan: Cooperative Learning found in the Alternate Lesson Plans folder, p. 65, organizes groups of students to compare and contrast three plans for Reconstruction and to create their own ideal Reconstruction plan.

Guided Reading and Review found in the Unit 4 folder, p. 81, provides a structure for reading and mastering the key concepts and reviewing the key terms for Section 2. (Guided Practice)

American Profiles Activity found in the Unit 4 folder, p. 88, profiles Thaddeus Stevens, the leader of the Radical Republicans of Congress, who disapproved of President Johnson and pushed for harsher measures against the South.

of a crime—to any Confederate who would swear allegiance to the Union and accept the end of slavery. Confederate military and government officials and those who had killed African American prisoners of war were excluded from Lincoln's offer. When 10 percent of those who had voted in the 1860 election had taken the oath in their state, that state could hold a constitutional convention. After the delegates to the convention had written a constitution endorsing the Thirteenth Amendment, their state could be returned to its proper place in the Union. Lincoln's plan did not require the new constitutions explicitly to ensure African American rights.

Radical Republicans wanted terms that would be much more difficult for southern whites to accept. They wanted to change southern society in order to ensure the rights of African Americans. They also wanted to punish the white South severely for its secession.

With the help of some moderate Republicans, Radical Republicans passed the Wade-Davis Bill in July 1864. Under this legislation, the terms a Confederate state had to meet in order to return to the Union were almost impossible to fulfill. Lincoln refused to sign this legislation. Because Congress had closed for the session after passing the bill, Lincoln's refusal to sign it amounted to a veto of the bill.

Andrew Johnson's Reconstruction Plan

For the next several months, Lincoln and Congress remained at odds over Reconstruction. But in April 1865, John Wilkes Booth's bullet both killed one President and made a new one—former Vice President **Andrew Johnson**.

Johnson Is Moderate Before the war, Johnson had been a Democratic senator from Tennessee. He was the only southerner to remain in Congress after secession. As a gesture of reconciliation toward the South, the Republicans placed him on their ticket with Lincoln in 1864.

Born in Raleigh, North Carolina, Johnson came from a poor family. He became a tailor and learned to read and write with the help of his wife. Johnson then entered politics, where he won success in mountainous eastern Tennessee.

Proud of his humble origins, Johnson had a profound hatred of rich planters and found strong support among poor whites. But to the dismay of Radical Republicans, Johnson was quite forgiving of former Confederates. He made most Confederates eligible for pardons in return for taking an oath of loyalty to the United States. In 1865 Johnson granted 13,000 pardons. He also favored easy terms under which the Confederate

Above left: A teacher and students pose outside a freedmen's school. Above right: To show appreciation for northern aid, Freedmen's Bureau workers sent northern benefactors a photograph of a student wearing his new school clothes and holding a book. They labeled it "*After your boxes came!*"

Discuss/Analyze

Discuss Reconstruction with students. Ask them to summarize and compare the three Reconstruction plans. What was the main intent of the Radical Republican plan for Reconstruction? How did it differ from what Lincoln and Johnson hoped to accomplish with their plans? What did southern states do to undermine Reconstruction? How did the South's refusal to accept Johnson's moderate plan hurt white southerners even more? What important acts and amendments were passed in response to southern resistance to Reconstruction?

In Depth

Then and Now

In the mid-1990s, about 130 years after Robert E. Lee's surrender at Appomattox, the rebel emblem is still saluted across the old Confederacy. In Jackson, Mississippi, for example, in 1994, African American legislators joined the National Association for the Advancement of Colored People (NAACP) in writing bills and filing lawsuits to remove the Confederate emblem from the state flag. Beatrice Branch, president of the Mississippi NAACP, explained: "We want to have the Confederate battle flag taken off the corner of our state flag. We object to it because it signifies to us racism and hatred."

Have students analyze the motives behind the feelings and actions of southerners and northerners regarding Reconstruction. Why were so many northerners eager to punish the South? Why did white southerners feel justified in resisting efforts to reshape southern society?

Answer to . . .

MAKING CONNECTIONS

Possible answer: No. The South traditionally defied northern attempts to outlaw slavery and impose northern values on its way of life.

Caption Answer to . . .

 Interpreting Maps

Tennessee; Virginia, Georgia, Mississippi, and Texas.

Activity

Cooperative Learning

Time: One class period.
Activity: Create a plan for Reconstruction.
Groupings: Groups of four to six students.
Purpose: To decide on what terms to readmit the Confederate states and how to reshape the South's economic, political, and social structure so as to protect the freedom of African Americans.
Roles: Members of the federal government, such as the President and senators and representatives from various states.
Outcome: Students will portray the various political interests, emotions, and lines of reasoning that shaped plans for Reconstruction.

---

states could return to their place in the Union. Under Johnson's plan, states were instructed to hold constitutional conventions. The delegates at each state convention were expected to write a new state constitution that would void secession, abolish slavery, ratify the Thirteenth Amendment, and stop payments of the state's war debts. The convention could then call an election for state offices and members of Congress. 🌐

Southern Defiance Had the South fully accepted Johnson's terms, Reconstruction might have ended earlier. Instead, once southern state governments were established, they acted to weaken Johnson's plan. For example, they quickly enacted black codes, laws that severely restricted the rights of freed people. Some black codes imposed curfews on African Americans and authorized labor contracts that were little better than legalized slavery. Black codes also included vagrancy laws, under which African Americans who were not working—vagrants, under the law—could be arrested and forced to work in order to pay off their fines. The effect of the vagrancy laws, too, was to reestablish slavery by a different name.

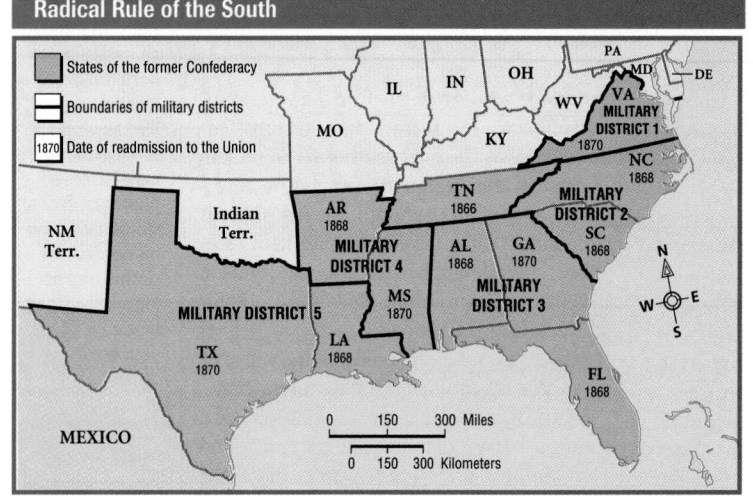

Radical Rule of the South

States of the former Confederacy
Boundaries of military districts
1870 Date of readmission to the Union

PA · MD · DE
IL · IN · OH · WV · VA MILITARY DISTRICT 1 1870
MO · KY · NC 1868
Indian Terr. · AR 1868 · TN 1866 · MILITARY DISTRICT 2 · SC 1868
NM Terr. · MILITARY DISTRICT 4 · AL 1868 · GA 1870
MS 1870 · MILITARY DISTRICT 3
MILITARY DISTRICT 5 · LA 1868
TX 1870 · FL 1868
MEXICO

0 150 300 Miles
0 150 300 Kilometers

🌐 **Geography and History: Interpreting Maps**
In April of 1865, Abraham Lincoln expressed a wish that the nation should put the southern state governments "in successful operation, with order prevailing and the Union reestablished, before . . . December." Under Radical rule, however, many of the former Confederate states did not rejoin the Union for years. *Which state was the first to rejoin the Union? Which states rejoined in 1870?*

Some southern whites also used violence in an effort to regain power over African Americans. In addition to countless individual acts of violence, serious riots erupted in several cities. In May 1866, angry whites killed forty-six African Americans in Memphis, Tennessee. At the end of July of that year, thirty-seven African Americans and three white sympathizers died in a riot by whites in New Orleans.

MAKING CONNECTIONS

Are you surprised by the South's defiant rejection of efforts at Reconstruction? Explain why or why not.

The Radical Plan for Reconstruction

President Johnson and Congress disagreed about how to respond to southern resistance to Reconstruction. In March 1866, Congress passed a Civil Rights Act in order to ensure equal rights for African Americans in spite of the black codes. Johnson vetoed it. Congress overrode his veto. It then switched course and proposed the **Fourteenth Amendment** to the Constitution, which became law two years later.

Protecting Citizen's Rights The Fourteenth Amendment said that everyone born or naturalized in the United States was a citizen and that no state could restrict his or her rights. More specifically, no state could

> *deprive any person of life, liberty, or property, without due process of law, nor deny to any person within its jurisdiction the equal protection of the laws.*

The amendment also provided for the punishment of states that did not permit African Americans to vote. In an effort to limit the President's power to pardon, it gave

---

▶ **RESOURCE DIRECTORY** 🌐

Teaching Resources

⭐ **Critical Thinking Activity** Identifying Central Issues: Granting Amnesty, found in the Unit 4 folder, p. 92, helps students understand why Andrew Johnson granted a general amnesty to former Confederates.

Primary Source Activity The Trial of President Johnson, found in the Unit 4 folder, pp. 94–95, describes President Johnson's trial on the articles of impeachment, in the words of his bodyguard.

Congress alone the power to let former Confederates hold public office. And it forbade any payments of Confederate war debts and any payments to slaveholders to make up for the loss of their slave labor.

Controlling the South White southern defiance contributed to significant Republican gains in the 1866 congressional elections. As a result, Radicals now had enough strength to impose their own conditions—and inflict punishment—on the white South.

The new Congress passed the **Military Reconstruction Act of 1867.** This legislation divided the South into five military districts that were to be governed by northern generals, as shown in the map on page 368. All qualified voters, including African American men, but excluding voters who had supported the Confederacy, had to be allowed to vote for delegates to create new state constitutions. Southern states had to guarantee equal rights to all citizens, permit African Americans to vote, and ratify the Fourteenth Amendment.

Controlling the President At the same time, Congress attempted to limit the power of President Johnson. It passed the Tenure of Office Act, which dealt with the President's power to hire and fire government officials.

Under the Constitution, the Senate has to offer "advice and consent" when the President wants to hire certain government officials. The Constitution does not limit the President's power to dismiss those officials. The Tenure of Office Act, however, said that if a President wanted to fire an official who had earlier been approved by the Senate, the Senate also had to approve of the firing. This act effectively removed the President's power to build an administration to his own liking.

⭐ Johnson and the Congress quickly came into conflict over the Tenure of Office Act. The President tried to fire Secretary of War Edwin Stanton, a Radical Republican. Arguing that the President's action was unconstitutional, the House of Representatives voted to **impeach** him—to charge him formally with wrongdoing in office. Under the Constitution, officials impeached by the House are then tried by the

Viewpoints
On Voting Rights for African Americans

The effort by Radical Republicans to extend voting rights to African Americans in the South was hotly debated in the 1860s. *Summarize the main arguments given in the two viewpoints below.*

In Favor of Voting Rights for African Americans

"If impartial suffrage is excluded in rebel States, then every one of them is sure to send a solid rebel representative delegation to Congress, and cast a solid rebel electoral vote. They . . . would always elect the President and control Congress. . . . I am for negro suffrage in every rebel State. If it be just, it should not be denied; if it be necessary, it should be adopted; if it is a punishment to traitors, they deserve it."
— Thaddeus Stevens, Radical Republican (Pennsylvania), speech in the House of Representatives, January 3, 1867

Against Voting Rights for African Americans

"Most of the whites are disenfranchised [not legally able to vote] and ineligible for office, whilst the Negroes are invested with [granted] the right of voting. The political power is therefore thrown into the hands of a mass of human beings who, having just emerged from a state of servitude [slavery], are ignorant of the forms of government and totally unfit to exercise this, the highest privilege of a free people."
— Henry William Ravenel, South Carolina planter, journal entry for February 24, 1867

Senate, which by a two-thirds majority can convict the official and remove him or her from office. Following this procedure, the Senate tried Johnson in the spring of 1868.

In the end, seven Radicals refused to vote for conviction. As a result, Congress fell one vote short of the two-thirds majority needed to convict. The results of this trial established the precedent that only the most serious offenses could lead to the removal of the President of the United States.

The Last Reconstruction Legislation

The final major piece of Reconstruction legislation was the **Fifteenth Amendment,** proposed in February 1869 and ratified in March 1870. (Congress did pass a Civil Rights Act in

📄 **Viewpoints Activity** On Voting Rights for African Americans, found in the Unit 4 folder, pp. 89–90, demonstrates the pros and cons raised in the debate over the granting of suffrage to African American males during the 1860s.

Media and Technology

Transparencies
Geographic Setting, M-4; Critical Thinking, I-2

Interpreting Tables

The Thirteenth; the Fifteenth.

Reteach

Have students construct a chart showing the major points of the three Reconstruction plans.

 Alternative Assessment

Mid-Point Monitoring

Ask students if they have
- Decided what items to include in their project
- Prepared an outline of information to include in each item
- Visited the library to locate additional sources of information

 4. CLOSE

 Reinforcing the Big Idea

The Radical Republicans finally prevailed and were able to impose their plan for Reconstruction on the South. The next section discusses the Republican efforts to reshape southern society and the eventual backlash against their policies.

Reconstruction Legislation

Legislation	Date	Purpose
13th Amendment	Submitted and ratified 1865	Abolishes slavery in the United States
Freedmen's Bureau	1865 and 1866	Provides services for war refugees and freed people, including food, medical aid, education
Civil Rights Act of 1866	1866	Gives citizenship to African Americans; gives federal government the power to protect African American rights
14th Amendment	Submitted 1866, ratified 1868	Defines citizenship to include African Americans; guarantees due process of law and equal protection under law
Reconstruction Acts	1867	Establish Radical Reconstruction
15th Amendment	Submitted 1869, ratified 1870	Guarantees that voting rights will not be denied on the basis of race
Ku Klux Klan Acts	1871	Seek to outlaw organizations aimed at denying African Americans their rights
Civil Rights Act of 1875	1875	Protects African American rights in public places

Interpreting Tables
During Reconstruction, the federal government struggled to create a new social and political order in the South. *Which amendment ended slavery? Which guaranteed that voting rights would not be denied on the basis of race?*

1875, guaranteeing African American rights in public places, but the act was largely unenforced.) The Fifteenth Amendment stated that no citizen could be denied the right to vote "by the United States or by any State on account of race, color, or previous condition of servitude."

The table on this page shows this amendment as well as other Reconstruction legislation.

The Fifteenth Amendment was inspired in part by the presidential election of 1868. Republican Ulysses S. Grant won a narrow victory that was made possible by the votes of African Americans in the South. The Fifteenth Amendment aimed at ensuring that African Americans would be free to vote in future elections—presumably for Republican candidates. As Chapter 17 reveals, however, southern states eventually found ways to deny African Americans the vote.

Another development linked to Reconstruction legislation was the growing consent of the Supreme Court. In a case known as *Texas* v. *White* in 1869, the Court recognized the right of Congress to reconstruct the governments of the former Confederate states. This decision demonstrated a startling new support for federal power.

Together, African Americans and Congress had redrawn the political and social boundaries of the United States. Many southern whites cooperated with this transformation. Others, however, resisted these changes. If the white South had accepted defeat more gracefully, Radical Republicans likely would not have become as powerful as they did. If the white South had given in to the more moderate plans of Lincoln and Johnson, Reconstruction in the South, as described in the next section, might have been dramatically different.

SECTION 2 REVIEW

Key Terms, People, and Places
1. Define (a) pardon, (b) Fourteenth Amendment, (c) Military Reconstruction Act of 1867, (d) impeach.
2. Identify Andrew Johnson.

Key Concepts
3. What was the Freedmen's Bureau?
4. Why did Lincoln refuse to sign the Wade-Davis Bill?
5. Describe two ways in which southern whites tried to regain the power they had had over African Americans.

6. How was the South to be governed during Reconstruction under the plan of Radical Republicans?
7. What was the purpose of the Fifteenth Amendment?

Critical Thinking
8. **Predicting Consequences** Based on what you have read so far, how effective do you think the federal government will be in creating a new and lasting social order in the South after the Civil War? Explain your answer.

 RESOURCE DIRECTORY

Teaching Resources

Quiz found in the Unit 4 folder, p. 82, covers the main ideas in this section as well as the key terms.

Reconstruction in the South

SECTION PREVIEW

Republicans stormed the South, bringing ambitious ideas about improving the political and social rights of African Americans. Their policies did lead to significant gains, but they soon found their efforts undermined by a campaign of terror and violence.

Key Concepts
- A combination of different groups, including African Americans as well as white northerners and southerners, provided support for the Republican party in the South.
- State governments in the South during Reconstruction took major steps in civil rights, education, and economic development.
- New forms of enforced labor replaced the slave system in the South.
- The initial success of Reconstruction led to a backlash of violence against African Americans and Republicans.

Key Terms, People, and Places
debt peonage; carpetbagger, scalawag, sharecropper, tenant farmer, Ku Klux Klan, Rutherford B. Hayes

I n order for Reconstruction in the South to be effective, two conditions had to be met. First, Republicans had to hold office on the state level. Second, federal officials had to be willing to use their power to support them. For a while, these conditions existed, and Republicans were able to bring about significant change in the South. In the end, however, that success led to a violent resistance that reversed many of the gains of Reconstruction.

Republican Support in the South

Significant problems faced the Republican plan for Reconstruction in the South. After all, the party had had virtually no support in the region before the mid-1860s. And it was unlikely to win large numbers of converts among whites in the post–Civil War years.

White Republicans in the South For these reasons, the Republicans depended for their support in the South on African Americans and on people who are now known as carpetbaggers and scalawags. Both of these terms were originally insulting names given to these groups by southerners.
Carpetbaggers were northern Republicans who moved to the South after the Civil War. Their name referred to a kind of suitcase, and it implied that these northerners had hastily migrated into the region to take advantage of the political situation. Carpetbaggers were mainly former Union army officers and Freedmen's Bureau officials.

Scalawags, a term that means "rascals," were southern whites who became Republicans. They tended to be men who had been Whigs, who were interested in economic development, or who lived in the more isolated areas. Many scalawags were poor.

African Americans in Office African Americans were key, though underrepresented, members of the Republican party in the South. Determined to win their share of political power, they organized to promote the interests of their community. In 1865 the African American state convention addressed these words to the people of South Carolina:

> N ow that we are free men, now that we have been lifted up by the providence of God to manhood, we have resolved to come forward, and, like MEN, speak and act for ourselves.

Many of the northerners who flooded the South hoping to profit from post-war turmoil carried their belongings in cheap suitcases called carpetbags. These bags became a symbol of northern rule of the South.

Reproducible Lesson Plan found in the Unit 4 folder, p. 77, provides a summary of the Section 3 lesson plan content.

Alternate Lesson Plan: Learning Styles found in the Alternate Lesson Plans folder, p. 66, is especially effective for visual learners and helps students understand the new forms of labor that replaced slavery, by creating classified ads for employment in the Reconstruction South.

Guided Reading and Review found in Unit 4 folder, p. 83, provides a structure for reading and mastering the key concepts and reviewing the key terms for Section 3. (Guided Practice)

1. FOCUS

Connecting to the Big Idea

See page 358B. For a time, the Republicans were able to impose their Reconstruction plan on the South and bring radical political and social changes to the region. Ask what gains the Republicans were able to make in the South and how white southerners finally acted to reverse them.

Objectives
- Describe the different groups that supported the Republican party in the South.
- Explain how state governments in the South during Reconstruction took major steps in civil rights, education, and economic development.
- Describe the kinds of labor that replaced the slave system in the South.
- Explain how the initial success of Reconstruction caused a backlash against African Americans and Republicans.

Bellringer

Ask students to think about times in their lives when they experienced change. How did they and others react to the change? Have them speculate why change can spur intense, possibly even violent, behavior on the part of those experiencing it.

Reading Strategy

Predicting Content Ask students to skim the section, list the main headings and subheadings, and write a sentence or phase predicting content under each one. When they have finished reading the section, ask students to test their predictions against the actual text.

Explain/Discuss

Remind students that the southern economy was in ruins at the end of the war. As a result, Reconstruction was a time of great physical and material hardship for southerners. Ask students how they think these conditions influenced white southerners' feelings about the victorious northern Republicans who set about transforming the South.

Discuss with students Republican Reconstruction policies in the South. Ask who provided support for Republican Reconstruction. What changes did Republican policies bring to the South?

Answer to ...

MAKING CONNECTIONS

African Americans do not vote in as high numbers as whites and other groups, and voters commonly elect candidates of their own ethnicity. Furthermore, political machinery, such as the organization of political parties, has been slow to outgrow exclusive practices.

In Depth

Biography

Born enslaved in Virginia, Blanche K. Bruce (1841–1898) fled north to freedom when the Civil War began. After pursuing his education at Oberlin College, he returned to the South. In 1871, while running as a Republican candidate for sheriff in Mississippi, Bruce rebutted the insults of opponents: "It is true that I was a house slave. But I freed myself, educated myself, and raised myself up in the world. If my opponent had started out where I did, he would still be there." Bruce won the election and later served in the Senate from 1875 to 1881.

Sixteen African Americans served with distinction in Congress between 1870 and 1877. One of them, Robert B. Elliot (standing, left), spoke eloquently in response to former Confederate vice president Alexander Stephens in the debate over the Civil Rights Act of 1875. "What you give to one class you must give to all," he said. "What you deny to one class, you shall deny to all."

Between 1867 and 1869, approximately 1,000 men attended state constitutional conventions throughout the South. Some 265 of them were African Americans; at least 107 were former slaves. Many were veterans of the Union army, ministers, artisans, farmers, and teachers.

African Americans held high office in the South during Reconstruction, though the number of such officials was small relative to the African American population. African Americans were, after all, a majority in Louisiana, Mississippi, and South Carolina. One African American, P.B.S. Pinchback, briefly served as governor of Louisiana. Six African Americans were lieutenant governors, and several others held high state office. Meanwhile, sixteen African Americans went to Congress, and Hiram Revels, an educator and minister, became a United States senator from Mississippi in 1870. Mississippi also sent former sheriff Blanche K. Bruce to the Senate in 1874.

In addition, 600 African Americans were members of various state legislatures and hundreds of others held local offices. While some

were illiterate—70 percent of African Americans could not read or write in 1880, compared to under 10 percent of whites—many were educated and virtually all were capable of making informed judgments about major issues.

Many southern whites criticized the presence of African Americans in Reconstruction governments. They accused African American officials of being corrupt or incompetent. In reality, the South's African American officials appeared to have been no worse and no better than their white counterparts. Many served with distinction.

MAKING CONNECTIONS

African Americans are still underrepresented in government. What does this fact suggest?

Republican Policies

State governments controlled by Republicans did bring change to the South. They committed state governments to systems of public education, although these systems were divided along racial lines. They passed civil rights legislation that guaranteed African Americans access to transportation and hotels, though this legislation was largely unenforced. In addition, they repealed black codes and removed restrictions on African American workers.

Economic Development Republicans focused much of their effort on improving economic conditions. Some argued that lasting change could not come to the region without land redistribution. In other words, African Americans would never gain equal rights and economic independence until they owned property. Most white Republicans, however, were unwilling to take such a step, which would have involved taking the land of planters and giving it to people who had been enslaved. This would have violated southerners' constitutional right to security of private property.

Instead, most white Republicans concentrated on economic development. Advocating "the gospel of prosperity," they contended that the key to better times was more railroads,

 RESOURCE DIRECTORY

Teaching Resources

Primary Source Activity A Bleak Future for Freedmen, found in the Unit 4 folder, p. 93, provides an example, through a formerly enslaved man's letter to the editor in Nashville's *Weekly Anglo-African,* of African Americans' difficulties during Reconstruction.

Atlanta Rises from the Ruins

"We have utterly destroyed Atlanta," wrote a Union soldier in 1864. "I don't think any people will want to try and live there now." The ruin of the central train station is shown at left. Yet by 1887 the commercial district (above) was booming. *Basing your answer on the evidence here, what do you think was the key to Atlanta's rebirth?*

banks, and businesses. Southern governments aided in this development with grants, paid for out of higher taxes. But while thousands of miles of railroad track were laid, government aid did little to improve general economic conditions. Most African Americans, and not a few whites, remained mired in poverty.

Voter Anger Republican rule alienated many white voters. Taxes and state debts increased because of expenses such as grants to railroads. As in the North, state officials sometimes accepted bribes, leading to charges of corruption. In addition, the policies seemed to do little to improve economic conditions, though in fact few policies would have made much difference in the war-scarred southern economy. Moreover, worldwide demand for cotton was falling. The 1875 cotton crop equaled that of 1859 in terms of size, but not in profits.

Changes in Southern Agriculture

Devastated by the Civil War, southern planters never recovered the dominance that they had enjoyed before the war. Some sought to re-create the past by finding ways to preserve slavery in a new form. As the economic journal *De Bow's Review* argued in 1868,

We do not mean . . . slavery such as that which has been recently abolished, but some form of subordination of the inferior race that shall compel them to labor, whilst it protects their rights and provides for their wants.

Debt Peonage To achieve this end, planters signed former slaves to labor contracts. Under the terms of these contracts, planters advanced money to laborers in return for signed promises from the workers that they pay all debts before they moved on. Planters then found ways to increase workers' debts while keeping them ignorant of any escape. Year after year, laborers remained bound to work off debts that always got larger. Though slavery was dead, in **debt peonage,** as this system of forced labor came to be called, the South brought some aspects of the slave system back to life.

Answer to . . .

Links Across Time

Atlanta rebuilt its railroad system, which fostered the city's economic rebirth.

Analyze

Ask students to analyze the southern backlash against Reconstruction. If it had been left to white southerners, what kind of society would they have constructed after the Civil War? Why was an organization like the Ku Klux Klan so effective even though the law was on the side of African Americans?

Activity

Writing About Hopes for the Future

Ask each student to imagine living in the year 1865, first as a poor African American sharecropper and then as a white southern planter whose plantation lies in ruins. Students should write two brief essays in which each character tells how they hope their life will be ten years later.

In Depth

Multicultural Perspectives

In her book *The Dispossessed,* historian Jacqueline Jones writes that the sharecropping system had a "superficial simplicity," behind which "lay an intense power struggle between planter and field hand, a struggle that went to the heart of power relations in the rural South." One aspect of that struggle was the practice of fining sharecroppers up to a dollar a day for "time lost" if they refused to devote all their time to field work, as they had been forced to do when they were enslaved.

Ask students to watch the film *Gone with the Wind* and then write an essay comparing Reconstruction as portrayed in the film with its depiction in historical sources. Students may do additional research on Reconstruction to write the essay if they wish.

3. ASSESS

Section 3 Review Answers

1. (a) carpetbagger, see p. 371, (b) scalawag, see p. 371, (c) Ku Klux Klan, see p. 374, (d) Rutherford B. Hayes, see p. 375

2. The groups included carpetbaggers, northern Republicans who came South during Reconstruction; scalawags, southern whites who became Republicans; and African Americans.

3. Republican state governments passed civil rights legislation that guaranteed African Americans access to transportation and hotels, although it was largely unenforced. They repealed black codes and removed restrictions on African American workers. Republicans also committed state governments to public education systems, but the systems were divided along racial lines.

4. Each of these systems is a way of keeping landowners in power while making use of the labor of others. All three systems use debt to keep the laborer in subjugation.

5. Political pressure was combined with a campaign of violent intimidation against African Americans and Republicans to achieve the Compromise of 1877.

6. Possible answer: It suggests that they were more interested in political gain than in actually helping former slaves and other poor people in the South. They were willing to trade political gain for their influence in the region.

An African American couple, possibly sharecroppers or tenant farmers, pose with their children in front of their Florida home—a humble house, but the dwelling of free people.

As part of their campaign of terror, the Ku Klux Klan left miniature coffins like these—containing written death threats—at the doors of African Americans and their white supporters.

Sharecropping Many freed people wanted no part of contract agreements for their labor. In order to make money from their fields, white landowners began to rent their land to African Americans and poor whites. In one common system, farmers called **sharecroppers** grew a crop on land owned by someone else. In return for the use of the land and supplies such as seed and fertilizer, the farmer gave one third to one half of the annual crop to the landowner. Others, called **tenant farmers**, paid cash for the rental of land. They typically agreed to sell their crop to a local merchant, who gave them use of tools and supplies in advance of harvest.

By 1880 one third of the white farmers in the South were sharecroppers or tenant farmers. Where African Americans had grown 90 percent of the cotton before the Civil War, whites now cultivated 30 to 40 percent.

African American sharecroppers and tenant farmers enjoyed more practical freedom than they had possessed as enslaved people. They controlled their own schedules, determined where they lived, and worked without white supervision.

Yet the sharecropping and tenancy systems had serious drawbacks. Low cotton prices that had troubled landowners also made it hard for sharecroppers to earn enough money to survive.

Many had to borrow from local stores for food and supplies, creating debts that grew larger and larger every year. Thus sharecroppers and tenant farmers were trapped in a continuous effort to pay off their debts, just like farmers working under the system of debt peonage.

Whites Attack Reconstruction

From 1868 through 1871, many southern whites launched a counterrevolution against the changes of Reconstruction. The intensity of their violence was a tribute to how far the changes brought by the Republicans had gone. In other words, whites turned to terrorism because Reconstruction was proving successful in transforming the South.

The Ku Klux Klan At the forefront of the campaign was the **Ku Klux Klan,** an organization that began as a social club in Tennessee in 1866. Although Klan members often wore elaborate disguises, including white hoods and robes, members were well known locally. Leaders included planters, merchants, lawyers, and occasionally ministers. Many were former Confederate officers. The oath each member took included a promise to "defend the social and political superiority" of whites, to vote only for white candidates, and to protect whites against what the Klan called the "aggressions of an inferior race."

The goal of the Klan during Reconstruction was to intimidate both African Americans and sympathetic whites so that they became silent and submissive. To keep freed people from voting or asserting themselves, hooded men surrounded the homes of prominent African Americans and harassed and abused them. Whippings were common. So was murder.

In 1871 Thomas Allen, a freed person, told a congressional investigating committee in Atlanta that he had been warned against voting. He and his friends felt safe only in cities, noting that

in a great many places the colored people call the white people master and mistress, just as they ever did; if they do not do it they are whipped.

▶ RESOURCE DIRECTORY

Teaching Resources

As northern anger mounted against southern violence, Congress passed the Enforcement Acts, or the Ku Klux Klan Acts, in 1871. In the next year, the United States used its considerable military and judicial power to break the Klan. But by that time, southern whites had already achieved much of their goal of "redeeming," or winning back, the South from Republican rule by thoroughly intimidating scalawags, African Americans, and carpetbaggers.

Meanwhile, Radical Republicans were beginning to lose their grip on power nationally. In the 1872 presidential race, a group of Republicans known as the Liberals refused to support Grant, whom they viewed as corrupt and incompetent. Although Grant easily trounced Democrat Horace Greeley, the division of the Republicans weakened the party. In the future, Republicans would focus more on winning elections and less on their ideals of justice and equality.

The Compromise of 1877 Final "redemption" for southern whites came in 1877. In the presidential election of 1876, Republican **Rutherford B. Hayes** lost the popular vote to Democrat Samuel Tilden. The electoral vote was in dispute, however. Hayes claimed to have won the presidency based in part on his victories in Florida, Louisiana, and South Carolina, states still under Republican and federal control. Yet another set of returns sent to Washington, D.C., by the Democrats showed Tilden as the victor in those states, and thus in the presidential race.

Congress established a special commission to resolve the crisis. The commission—whose members included more Republicans than

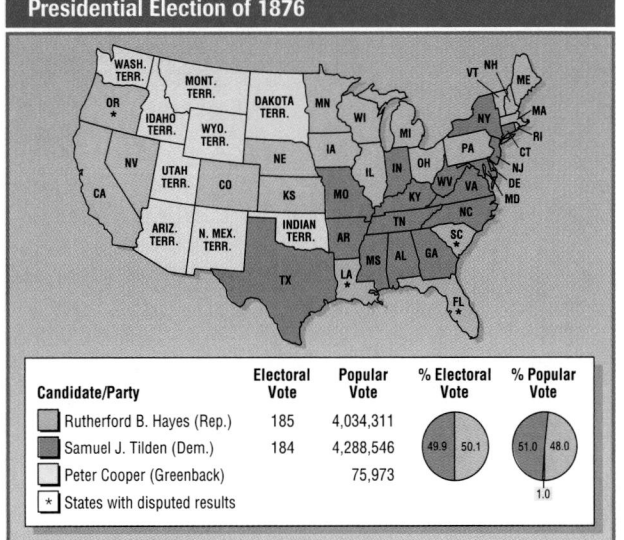

Presidential Election of 1876

Candidate/Party	Electoral Vote	Popular Vote	% Electoral Vote	% Popular Vote
Rutherford B. Hayes (Rep.)	185	4,034,311	49.9	51.0
Samuel J. Tilden (Dem.)	184	4,288,546	50.1	48.0
Peter Cooper (Greenback)		75,973		1.0
* States with disputed results				

Geography and History: Interpreting Maps
In the election of 1876, the electoral votes in three states under federal control were disputed, but eventually went to Hayes when he promised to end Reconstruction. *In which states were results disputed? What would have been the result if even one more state had gone to Tilden? Whom did the majority of Americans favor?*

Democrats—named Hayes the victor, as shown in the election map on this page. Democrats, however, still had enough strength in Congress to reject the commission's decision. But a political deal cleared the way for Hayes's victory. In the Compromise of 1877, Hayes promised that as President, he would remove federal troops from all southern states. Southern Democrats would regain complete control of the region. In return, Democrats would allow Hayes to claim a victory he had not clearly won.

SECTION 3 REVIEW

Key Terms, People, and Places
1. Identify (a) carpetbagger, (b) scalawag, (c) Ku Klux Klan, (d) Rutherford B. Hayes.

Key Concepts
2. What groups formed the basis of support for the Republican party in the South during Reconstruction?
3. What kinds of legislation did Republican state governments in the South pass during Reconstruction?

4. In what ways were debt peonage, sharecropping, and tenant farming alike?
5. How did pressure from southern whites lead to a reversal of Reconstruction?

Critical Thinking
6. **Recognizing Ideologies** What does the Compromise of 1877 suggest about the motives of Republicans in controlling the South?

Quiz found in the Unit 4 folder, p. 84, covers the main ideas in this section as well as the key terms.

Geography

How Maps Show Change Over Time

Focus Compare two historical maps to identify changes in the cultural landscape over time.

Instruct Explain that historical maps provide information about the cultural, or human, traits of a place. Ask students to to use information they already have about the time periods represented by the two maps and supported by visual evidence from the maps to suggest at least one cultural change that may have taken place. Then ask students what a map of this same area might be likely to show today.

Extend See the Historian's Toolbox Activity in the Resource Directory below.

Answers

1. (a) The Barrow Plantation in Oglethorpe County, Georgia. (b) 1860 and 1881 (c) The borders of the plantation, a road crossing it, bodies of water, and buildings.

2. (a) The pre–Civil War slave quarters. (b) The sharecroppers' houses. (c) The church has a cross.

3. (a) The twenty-one years between 1860 and 1881. (b) In 1860 they were concentrated in a single area; by 1881 they had spread out across the entire plantation. (c) A church and a school. (d) Possible answer: By 1881, slavery on the plantation had been replaced by sharecropping. The formerly enslaved people had now spread out and resettled, forming their own community, which replaced the "community" that had been defined and maintained by their owners. Thus the freed people needed their own church and school.

How Maps Show Change Over Time

An important task of historians is to identify change over time. One far-reaching change that took place in American life after the Civil War was the breakup of plantations and the dispersal of freed people. Maps can give important clues to such developments, what changes took place, where they occurred, how extensive they were, and how long they took.

The historical maps below give you an opportunity to identify the changes that occurred over time to 2,000 acres of land in the post–Civil War South. Use the following steps to identify the changes for which the maps provide evidence.

1. Identify the location, time period, and subject matter covered by the maps. To discover what data these maps offer, answer the following questions: (a) What specific area of land do the maps show, and where is it located? (b) What dates are given on the maps? (c) What physical features do the maps show?

2. Analyze the key to determine the type of data that it provides. A map key can help you understand the data in a map. Map keys use symbols and colors to illustrate specific data and to locate the data on a map. (a) What do the colored squares repre-

sent in the map on the left? (b) What do the colored squares represent in the map on the right? (c) How is the symbol for a church distinguishable from the symbol for a school?

3. Analyze the data in the maps. Now compare these maps to draw conclusions about the change over time that they indicate. (a) Over what period of time has the change taken place? (b) How has the location of the dwellings on the plantation changed during this period? (c) What new buildings have been added? (d) How do you explain the changes noted in (b) and (c) above?

The Barrow Plantation, Oglethorpe County, Georgia

Source: Eric Foner, *A Short History of Reconstruction, 1863–1877,* New York: Harper & Row, 1990

RESOURCE DIRECTORY

Teaching Resources

Historian's Toolbox Activity How Maps Show Change Over Time, found in the Unit 4 folder, p. 91, uses maps comparing the numbers of African Americans registered to vote before and after the Voting Rights Act of 1965 to help students evaluate the effect of the legislation.

The Retreat from Reconstruction in the North

SECTION PREVIEW

The Radical Republican blueprint for Reconstruction was based on a grand dream of social equality and justice. But economic and political changes brought by the war led the Republicans to forsake their commitment to this dream in favor of other, less idealistic, concerns.

Key Concepts

• As industry boomed during and after the Civil War, close ties between business leaders and government officials led to widespread corruption.
• Republican governments became increasingly unwilling to serve the needs of African Americans and others among the nation's powerless.

Key Terms, People, and Places

Crédit Mobilier, United States Sanitary Commission

While southern whites were finding new ways to resist Reconstruction, Republicans in the North were also making adjustments to new postwar realities. Increasingly, they chose to ally themselves with leading industrialists rather than African Americans and the poor and powerless in the farms and cities of the North.

Becoming an Industrial Power

The Civil War had an enormous impact on the American economy. The need to arm, clothe, and supply hundreds of thousands of men in the early 1860s stimulated the growth of industries and made the organization of corporations more efficient. Because Republicans were willing to use government to promote economic development, they created a close relationship between corporations and politicians that lasted throughout the century.

As Chapter 14 will discuss, business boomed in the United States in the later part of the 1800s. Fueled by war profits and prodded along by a new generation of business leaders, industrial production in the United States rose by 75 percent between 1865 and 1873. In 1873 the United States reached a new milestone: it now had more industrial workers than farmers. The nation ranked second only to Great Britain as an industrial power.

Railroads set the pace for much of this economic development, in part because railroad companies worked hard to influence state and federal government policies. Governments responded with grants of land and money to pay for costly railroad projects. Politicians at all levels worked closely with influential railroad entrepreneurs; many received favors or illegal payments in return.

The most notorious example of corruption involving railroads was the **Crédit Mobilier** scandal. Crédit Mobilier was a dummy corporation created by the stockholders of the Union Pacific Railroad to oversee construction of that railroad in the 1860s. The shareholders in both corporations were the same. In effect, the owners of the railroad created Crédit Mobilier so they could pay themselves—with federal government grants—to build their own railroad. Crédit Mobilier often billed the Union Pacific for work it never performed. Many members of Congress, too, were involved in the scandal. They received shares in Crédit Mobilier in return for their acceptance of the scheme.

The Union Pacific Railway across the continent was begun with these tools on December 2, 1863. As industries like the railways grew, the nation's politicians abandoned social issues and concentrated on economic growth.

Possible answer: Henry Clay: I am pleased by the rapid expansion of business due to government support. Andrew Jackson: The increased wealth of the privileged has come at great cost to the ordinary citizen.

2. INSTRUCT

Discuss

Discuss the Republicans' retreat from Reconstruction and their growing alliance with business. Ask how the Civil War affected the growth of business. After the Civil War, what role did Republicans play in the country's booming industry?

Analyze

Ask students to analyze the Republicans' changing role in Reconstruction. Why would it be difficult for Republicans to support economic development and social justice at the same time? What connection is there between the Republican party's increasing affiliation with business during Reconstruction and its image today?

Activity

Teaching Heterogeneous Groups

The Radical Republicans' grand dream of social equality and justice for all was abandoned in the interests of business. Ask students to work in small groups to write a slogan in the style of a modern bumper sticker to reflect the feelings of abandonment and betrayal either African Americans, feminists, or working people might have felt toward the Republican party at this time.

During the Civil War, American women threw themselves into public work, only to see their cause ignored by Republicans as Reconstruction ended. This wartime Sanitary Commission worker displays the writing paper, knitted stockings, and other items that cheered Union soldiers.

In general, bribes and other forms of corruption like Crédit Mobilier succeeded in getting corporations what they wanted. Between 1862 and 1872, the United States granted over 100 million acres of federal land and millions of dollars to corporations.

MAKING CONNECTIONS

Imagine that Henry Clay and Andrew Jackson had lived to see the industrial boom after the Civil War. Make a brief comment on the boom from the viewpoint of each of these politicians.

The Republicans Abandon Social Issues

Though government rarely hesitated to aid railroads and other corporations, it was increasingly reluctant to take action for less powerful groups, including African Americans, women, farmers, and factory workers.

African Americans Remain Powerless It is true that in the North, Republicans increased the role of government in civil rights. African Americans won the right to vote and to testify in court. In some places, states passed laws to ensure that African Americans had equal access to hotels and public transportation. In general, however, African Americans in the North—still only 2 percent of the population—remained poor and politically powerless.

The Postponement of Women's Rights Long before the Civil War, women had been prominent as members of the abolitionist movement. During the war, women in both the North and South had further increased their public visibility. For example, 200,000 northern women served in the **United States Sanitary Commission,** formed in 1861. It coordinated local organizations dedicated to providing medical aid and other assistance to soldiers. After the war, many women served in societies to assist freed people, and close to a thousand women went south to teach African Americans. The patriotic work of these women demonstrated the value of women's labor and proved their ability to make vital contributions outside the home.

Feminists such as Elizabeth Cady Stanton and Susan B. Anthony sought far-reaching changes in relationships between men and women. Their primary focus was on the right to vote, however. Lydia Maria Child told Charles Sumner in 1872:

> If I were to give free vent to all my pent-up wrath concerning the subordination of women, I might frighten you. . . . Suffice it, therefore, to say, either the theory of our government is false, or women have a right to vote.

Despite some sympathy from Radical Republicans, the quest for woman suffrage made little progress during Reconstruction. True, Wyoming and Utah territories did grant women the vote in 1869. But they did so for reasons that had little to do with their interest in women's rights. Wyoming wanted to attract female settlers, and Mormons in Utah wanted to increase their power by registering Mormon women as voters.

RESOURCE DIRECTORY

Teaching Resources

Visual Learning Activity America's Birthday Party, found in the Unit 4 folder, p. 100, shows a list published in 1876 in the children's magazine *St. Nicholas* citing major events in the first hundred years of the American Republic.

Unhappy Farmers and Working People Republican failure to satisfy the demands of suffragists paralleled their failures with farmers and working people. As Chapter 15 will show, strong protest movements arose in the late 1800s on the nation's farms. Much of this protest reflected farmers' desire for government regulation of railroads. Most Republicans did not support such regulation.

Working Americans also challenged Republicans to extend more rights to them during this era (see Chapter 14). These workers again focused on the goals of free labor, equality, and independence to which Republicans had been committed in the 1850s. Indeed, directly comparing the labor movement to the antislavery movement, Boston machinist and labor leader Ira Steward pointed out that just as the motive for enslaving someone is to get his or her labor for nothing, similarly,

the motive for employing wage-labor is to secure some of its results for nothing; and, in point of fact, larger fortunes are made out of the profits of wage-labor, than out of the products of slavery.

PUCK.

THE "STRONG" GOVERNMENT 1869–1877.   THE "WEAK" GOVERNMENT 1877–1881.

Using Historical Evidence In the left frame of this Reconstruction cartoon, President Grant, supported by "carpet bag and bayonet rule," rides on an oppressed South. In the right frame, President Hayes plows under the carpet bag. *How did the cartoonist show the effect of each government on the South? What was the bias of the cartoonist?*

The Significance of Reconstruction In 1877 Reconstruction came to an end. In most respects, it had been a tragic failure. Despite the many positive changes that took place, the nation had squandered the opportunity to achieve true equality and social justice. As an African American woman noted, "There is no redress [help] for us from a government that promised to help all under its flag." It would be close to a century before African Americans and whites would truly achieve the legal and political freedoms that were supposedly guaranteed by the legislation of the Reconstruction period. ★

SECTION 4 REVIEW

Key Terms, People, and Places
1. Identify (a) Crédit Mobilier, (b) United States Sanitary Commission.

Key Concepts
2. Explain the impact of the Civil War both on the American economy and on the relationship between federal government officials and business leaders.

3. How did Republicans in the North respond to the concerns of African Americans, women, and working people during Reconstruction?

Critical Thinking
4. **Checking Consistency** The text states that African Americans had many political rights, yet they still lacked power. Explain this apparent inconsistency.

 Quiz found in the Unit 4 folder, p. 86, covers the main ideas in this section as well as the key terms.

 Chapter Test Forms A and B are found in the Unit 4 folder, pp. 101–106.

 Answer Keys found in the Unit 4 folder, pp. 113–122, provide answers to all student activities.

Media and Technology

Transparencies
Fine Art, D-12; Graphic Organizer, G-3

Guided Reading Audiotapes
(English and Spanish)

Computer Test Bank

Chapter Review Answers

Understanding Key Terms, People, and Places

Terms
Students should refer to the definitions of the key terms in the chapter to write sentences that show the relation of each word to Reconstruction and the post–Civil War period.

True or False
1. false, Fifteenth Amendment
2. false, Scalawags
3. false, Ku Klux Klan
4. false, pardon

Matching
1. Rutherford B. Hayes
2. Andrew Johnson

Reviewing Main Ideas

1. Bradford's observations reveal that many white southerners were surprised by the eagerness with which their former slaves embraced freedom; some, who had believed that their slaves considered themselves "part of the family," felt insulted or deserted.

2. Many newly freed African Americans traveled away from the plantation where they had lived, often in order to be reunited with family members. Newly freed people also eagerly sought education, which had been denied them before the Civil War.

3. The Freedmen's Bureau distributed clothing, medical supplies, and meals to refugees of the war. Its most important contribution was the establishment of schools for African Americans.

4. Lincoln proposed a moderate Reconstruction policy under which pardons would be offered to any Confederate who swore allegiance to the Union and accepted the end of slavery. When 10 percent of the number that had voted in a state had taken the oath, the state could hold a constitutional convention. If their new constitution endorsed the Thirteenth Amendment, the state could return to the Union. Radical Republicans wanted to impose much more difficult terms for southern states in order to ensure the rights of African Americans and to punish the South.

5. Although Johnson favored allowing Confederate states to return to the Union on easy terms, white southerners weakened Johnson's plan by enacting black codes and using violence as a means to regain control over African Americans.

Chapter Review

Understanding Key Terms, People, and Places

Key Terms
1. Reconstruction
2. Freedmen's Bureau
3. pardon
4. Fourteenth Amendment
5. Military Reconstruction Act of 1867
6. impeach
7. Fifteenth Amendment
8. debt peonage
9. Crédit Mobilier
10. United States Sanitary Commission

People
11. Andrew Johnson
12. carpetbagger
13. scalawag
14. sharecropper
15. tenant farmer
16. Ku Klux Klan
17. Rutherford B. Hayes

Terms For each term above, write a sentence that explains its relation to Reconstruction and the post–Civil War period.

True or False Determine whether each statement is true or false. If it is true, write "true." If it is false, change the underlined term to make the statement true.
1. The <u>Fourteenth Amendment</u> declared that no citizen could be denied the right to vote.
2. <u>Sharecroppers</u> were southern whites who became Republicans.
3. The <u>Crédit Mobilier</u> supported the use of violence against African Americans and sympathetic whites.
4. Lincoln offered to <u>impeach</u> any Confederate who would swear allegiance to the Union and accept the end of slavery.

Matching Review the key people in the list above. If you are not sure of a person's importance, review his or her significance in the chapter. Then choose a person from the list that best matches each description below.
1. After a disputed presidential election, he promised to remove federal troops from all southern states.
2. The only southerner to remain in Congress after secession, as President he favored easy terms toward Confederates after the war.

Reviewing Main Ideas

Section 1 (pp. 360–365)
1. What do Susan Bradford's observations (page 361) reveal about the response of white southerners to the enthusiasm with which African Americans embraced freedom?
2. How did freedom affect the travel and education of formerly enslaved African Americans?

Section 2 (pp. 366–370)
3. How did the Freedmen's Bureau help African Americans freed during the war?
4. What was Lincoln's Reconstruction plan and how did it differ from that of the Radical Republicans?
5. How did white southerners respond to Andrew Johnson's plan for Reconstruction?
6. Explain how the goals of the Fourteenth and Fifteenth amendments were similar.

Section 3 (pp. 371–375)
7. Give evidence to show that African Americans made significant political contributions in the South after the Civil War.
8. Describe some of the steps taken by Republican state governments in the South in the areas of civil rights, education, and economic development.
9. In what ways did white southerners try to replace the slave system?
10. Why did southern whites launch a violent counterrevolution against Reconstruction?

Section 4 (pp. 377–379)
11. What was the result of the relationship between business and government after the Civil War?
12. Explain how the concerns of the Republican party shifted after the Civil War.

6. Both attempted to create a new social order in the South in which African Americans had equal rights as citizens.

7. Almost one third of the men who attended state constitutional conventions in the South were African Americans. African Americans also held high office and were members of various state legislatures.

8. Republican state governments committed state governments to systems of public education, passed civil rights legislation that guaranteed African Americans access to transportation and hotels, and repealed black codes and removed restrictions on African American workers. They aided in the economic development of railroads, banks, and businesses.

9. They created new forms of enforced labor—including debt peonage, sharecropping, and tenant farming.

10. Reconstruction was proving too successful in changing the South; many southern whites were so intent on returning to the ways of the Old South that they resorted to violence and terrorism.

11. Business and government were closely allied after the Civil War. These close ties often led to corruption, of which the Crédit Mobilier scandal is one example.

12. No longer focusing on the goals of free labor, equality, and independence, Republicans committed themselves to economic development.

1. **Making Comparisons** Evaluate Reconstruction from the point of view of: (a) a former Confederate; (b) a Republican entrepreneur living in the North; (c) an African American living in the inner city at the end of the twentieth century.

2. **Demonstrating Reasoned Judgment** Several wars fought by the United States have been followed by periods of prosperity. Suggest reasons to explain this fact.

3. **Recognizing Ideologies** Imagine that you could interview an enslaved African American and a white slave owner living during the Civil War. Describe how their visions of what the South should be like after the war might differ.

1. **Evaluating Primary Sources** Review the primary source excerpt on page 363. How does the freedman's dream of the kind of life he wants compare with the life goals of many Americans today, as you understand them?

2. **Understanding the Visuals** Examine the cartoon on page 379. Explain the different uses to which weapons are put in each panel of the cartoon.

3. **Writing About the Chapter** Imagine that the Civil War has just ended and you have a brilliant plan for rebuilding the South and reuniting the country. Before sending your plan to the President, first review the three plans for Reconstruction described on pages 364–368 and make a list of their main points. Then make a list of the points of your plan and describe how they are similar to or different from those in the other plans. Note any flaws you see in the three plans and point out how your plan will avoid these flaws. Next, write a draft of your plan in which you explain your ideas. Revise your plan, making certain that each idea is clearly explained. Proofread your plan and draft a final copy.

4. **Using the Graphic Organizer** This graphic organizer uses a tree map to organize main ideas and supporting details about the ways in which formerly enslaved African Americans experienced their new freedom. (a) Which details support the idea that education flourished among African Americans after the Civil War? (b) What conclusions can you draw from the details given under the heading *Land Ownership*? (c) On a separate sheet of paper, create your own graphic organizer about the Republican retreat from Reconstruction, using this graphic organizer as an example.

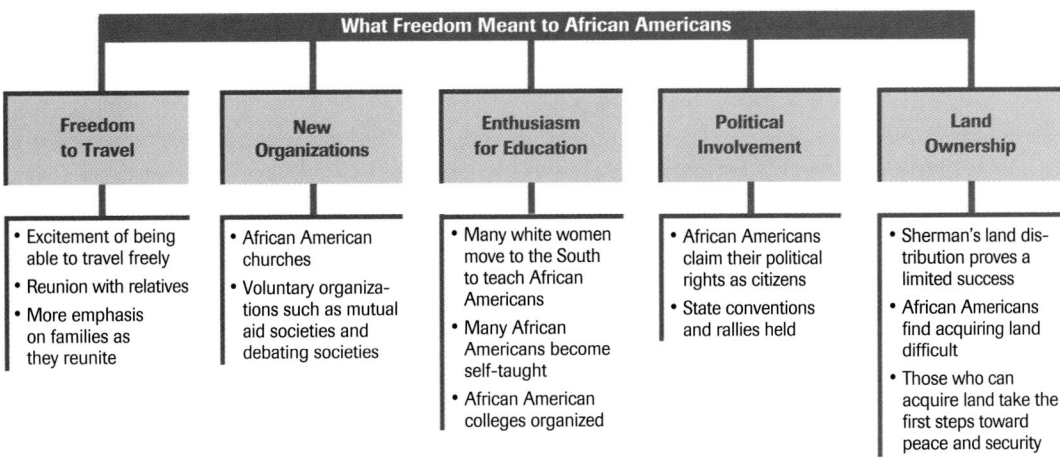

What Freedom Meant to African Americans

Freedom to Travel	New Organizations	Enthusiasm for Education	Political Involvement	Land Ownership
• Excitement of being able to travel freely • Reunion with relatives • More emphasis on families as they reunite	• African American churches • Voluntary organizations such as mutual aid societies and debating societies	• Many white women move to the South to teach African Americans • Many African Americans become self-taught • African American colleges organized	• African Americans claim their political rights as citizens • State conventions and rallies held	• Sherman's land distribution proves a limited success • African Americans find acquiring land difficult • Those who can acquire land take the first steps toward peace and security

Thinking Critically

1. (a) Confederates may have reluctantly accepted Reconstruction or turned to activities such as Klan membership. (b) A Republican entrepreneur would probably have set his sights on the economy rather than on the failures or successes of Reconstruction. (c) An African American today would still be waiting for the equality that Reconstruction failed to deliver.

2. Most wars, including the American Revolution and World Wars I and II, stimulate production and often enforce saving during the conflict, thus releasing money into the system afterward.

3. The enslaved African American would picture a society in which everyone was regarded as equal. The slave owner would picture a society in which he or she still had a superior status.

Making Connections

1. Possible answers: The goals of people today are basically similar, but whereas the freedman was content to have a piece of land and a home, people today might list more possessions and more elaborate forms of financial security when stating their life goals.

2. In the panel on the left, weapons (bayonets) are used to support the oppression of the South. In the panel on the right, weapons (rifles and a sword) form part of the plow that is burying a carpetbag and military rule.

3. Students' plans should consider the ideas of Lincoln, Johnson, and the Radical Republicans, as well as possible ways to avoid the racial tensions and violence that followed the first stages of Reconstruction.

4. (a) Many white women came to the South as teachers, many African Americans were self-taught, and many African American colleges were organized. (b) Although owning land was extremely difficult, in part because of the limited success of land distribution programs, those who did acquire land took the first steps toward peace and security. (c) Students' graphic organizers should contain information about the growing industrialization of the American economy and the Republicans' increasing abandonment of social issues.

Alternative Assessment

Final Evaluation

Use the following guidelines to evaluate students' projects:

● **Evidence of thoughtfulness** To what extent do projects demonstrate an understanding of Reconstruction?

● **Evidence of outside research** To what extent do projects reflect the use of outside research materials?

● **Sensitivity** To what extent do projects reflect an increased awareness of the experiences of different families in the South during Reconstruction?

● **Creativity** To what extent do projects demonstrate creative thought and presentation?

Introducing the Unit

Interpreting the Visual After the Civil War, industry radically changed American life. Poet Walt Whitman's lyricism captures the American spirit of the period as do these words in a St. Louis newspaper: "Rivers run only where nature pleases; railroads run wherever man pleases."

Ask students to study the photograph shown on pages 382–383. Then write two column headings on the chalkboard, Rewards and Costs. Ask students first to list the rewards that the railroad brought to the sightseers shown in the photograph and to their neighbors. Then ask them to identify the environmental costs of the railroad construction visible in the photograph.

Establishing Chronology Remind students that the previous chapter focused on the recovery of the nation after the Civil War. This unit covers the period of zealous American expansion that began just before the Civil War and lasted through World War I. While both the major period of industrial growth and the transformation of the West were largely over by 1900, urban growth and the social change it produced continued through the war years.

Expansion: Rewards and Costs 1860–1920

"Mark the spirit of invention everywhere, thy rapid patents,
Thy continual workshops, foundries, risen or rising,
See, from their chimneys how the tall flame-fires stream."

—Walt Whitman, from "Song of the Exposition," 1872

*T*he explosive growth that Whitman celebrates in these lines sparked a transformation of the United States after the Civil War. The promise of new opportunities attracted thousands of settlers to the West, set off a dramatic wave of immigration, and swelled the populations of cities. Although expansion brought important rewards, such as technological advances, those rewards came with a price. Urban poverty, child labor, and the displacement of Native Americans were some of those costs.

 RESOURCE DIRECTORY

Teaching Resources

Local History Activity "St. Louis, Missouri: 'Meet Me at the Fair'" and the Local Focus research topic suggestions, found in the Local History Resources folder, pp. 15–17, are designed to help students understand how history affects all lives.

★ **Themes in American History Posters** Wall-size, illustrated posters, found in the Teaching Resources package, illustrate the four unit themes.

Unit Test Forms A and B are found in the Unit 5 folder, pp. 143–148.

This photo of an excursion party at Devil's Gate Bridge in Utah captures both rewards and costs of the nation's growth.

Themes in American History

Teachers may wish to discuss specific historical events in the context of historical themes. Here are four suggestions for Unit 5.

Reform Movements *People in the United States have frequently taken action in grass roots movements to right perceived wrongs and to secure improvements in the quality of life.*

● Labor unions, which formed quickly after the Civil War, called major strikes and experienced many violent confrontations with businesses.

● Populists backed the issues of western and southern farmers in the late 1800s.

Technology *Americans' ability to develop new skills and tools and to increase their knowledge of the physical world has greatly affected the way they live and work, and has led to a high standard of living.*

● Electric power transformed life at home and in factories.

● Railroads and the telegraph connected the nation in elaborate transportation and communication networks.

Environment *The geography and available resources of the continent have affected the actions of Americans. Similarly, the actions of Americans have affected the environment and physical landscape.*

● The mechanization of farm machines allowed more western lands to be farmed and thus changed the landscape.

● Rapid urban growth resulted in slums, air and water pollution, and frequent epidemics of disease.

Diversity *Throughout its history America has been made up of a gathering of many peoples from throughout the world. Americans have both benefited from and encountered problems with this diversity.*

● The American West was occupied by Mexican farmers and Native American groups when settlers from the East moved into the area and displaced them.

● Close to 30 million immigrants poured into the United States between 1865 and 1920.

Media and Technology

Visions of America: Scenes of An Era To introduce students to the main idea and events covered in this unit, play "Scenes of an Era: Expansion: Rewards and Costs" (length: 2.5 minutes). This selection can be located on side 2 of the videodiscs. This selection can also be located on videotape 2. Lesson plans for "Scenes of an Era" can be found in the Visions of America Guidebook.

Using Multimedia Technology This folder contains instructional tools and strategies for using technology in the classroom.

Transparency Binder Contains full-color transparencies with lesson suggestions. From a large collection divided into twelve categories, specific transparencies are referenced throughout the chapters at appropriate points of use. For this unit, see American Photo, B-5; Our Multicultural Heritage, C-2 and C-10; Fine Art, D-12 and D-13; Links Across Time, J-5; and Political Cartoon, K-5.

Chapter 14 The Expansion of American Industry
1865–1900

📁 Teaching Resources (See Unit 5 Folder)		
	Instruction	**Enrichment**
Section 1 **A Technological Revolution** (pp. 386–391)	Reproducible Lesson Plan, p. 3 Alternate Lesson Plan, p. 69 Guided Reading and Review, p. 7 Quiz, p. 8	Primary Source Activity, Working on the Railroad, p. 25 American Profiles Activity, Washington A. Roebling, p. 18 Historian's Toolbox Activity, Using Cross-Sectional Maps, p. 21
Section 2 **The Growth of Big Business** (pp. 393–397)	Reproducible Lesson Plan, p. 4 Alternate Lesson Plan, p. 70 Guided Reading and Review, p. 9 Quiz, p. 10	Primary Source Activity, Carnegie's Gospel of Wealth, p. 24 Primary Source Activity, Pestilence in the Cigar, p. 23 Visual Learning Activity, Home of the Trusts, p. 30 Critical Thinking Activity, Making Comparisons, p. 22
Section 3 **Industrialization and Workers** (pp. 398–401)	Reproducible Lesson Plan, p. 5 Alternate Lesson Plan, p. 71 Guided Reading and Review, p. 11 Quiz, p. 12	Visual Learning Activity, The Noble Face of Labor, p. 29 Literature Activity, The Stories of Horatio Alger, p. 26
Section 4 **The Great Strikes: A Turning Point in History** (pp. 402–407)	Reproducible Lesson Plan, p. 6 Alternate Lesson Plan, p. 72 Guided Reading and Review, p. 13 Quiz, p. 14 Chapter Test, Forms A & B, pp. 31–36	Literature Activity, Sister Carrie, pp. 27–28 Viewpoints Activity, On Labor Unions, pp. 19–20 American Profiles Activity, Mary Kenney O'Sullivan, p. 17 Turning Point Extension Activity, The Lasting Impact of the Great Strikes, pp. 15–16

📁 Additional Chapter Resources

Resource Organizer, p. 2
Alternate Lesson Plan, p. 68
Answer Keys, pp. 149–164

Bibliography

For the Teacher

Boorstin, Daniel J. *The Americans: The Democratic Experience.* Random House, 1964.
Wertheimer, Barbara M. *We Were There: The Story of Working Women in America.* Pantheon Books, 1977. (A history of women workers including three chapters on the early nineteenth century.)

Prentice Hall Literature Excerpts from *The American Experience,* 1994, including Wolfe, Thomas. *The Far and the Near.* Macmillan, 1987.

The Big Idea for the chapter and how the main ideas in each section relate to the Big Idea are graphically displayed below. Comprehension of this chapter's Big Idea is critical to students' understanding of United States history and how we as a nation got where we are today.

Media and Technology

 The Way It Works, H-14

 Cause and Effect, F-6

 Visions of America: Turning Point Story, "Company Town" (length: approx. 4 minutes)

 Visions of America: Roundtable Discussion on "Company Town"

 Graphic Organizer, G-5

 Guided Reading Audiotapes (English and Spanish)

 Computer Test Bank

For the Student

Weisberger, Bernard. *Captains of Industry.* American Heritage, Harper & Row, 1966. (A fast-moving, well-illustrated description of industrial leaders.)

Riis, Jacob. *How the Other Half Lives.* Dover, 1971. (The wretchedness of urban slums in 1890 as described by a young New York reporter.)

CHAPTER 14

After the Civil War, rapid industrial progress transformed the United States, but relations between those who managed the industries and those who labored in them were filled with tensions. Conditions for workers grew worse.

SECTION 1

Between 1865 and 1900, new technology revolutionized the way Americans worked, lived, and conducted business.

SECTION 2

Big businesses grew into gigantic enterprises, sometimes through the use of ruthless methods.

SECTION 3

Industrial workers were paid poorly for working long hours in poor conditions. Workers had little opportunity to improve their own or their children's lives.

SECTION 4

Labor unions promised some hope of improving conditions for workers, but fierce opposition from big business slowed the growth of the labor movement.

The Expansion of American Industry
1865–1900

The Relevance of the Big Idea

In the late 1800s, the United States became one of the world's great industrial nations, but tensions between those who managed the industries and those who labored in them intensified. While industrialization and technology improved the quality of life for some, most workers were unable to reap the benefits of their long hours of toil. Labor unions formed to push for improved working conditions, but they faced opposition.

New technology continues to transform everyday life in the United States, and the struggle to achieve fairness in the workplace continues. As advances in communication and transportation capabilities shorten distances and leap borders, the struggle between labor and management takes on the nature of a chase rather than a clash. Instead of dealing with the demands of American labor organizations, business owners often send their jobs overseas to cheaper, less powerfully organized labor markets.

In Depth

Global Connections

Between 1860 and 1910, 23 million people emigrated from Europe and Asia to the United States. Some, like the Irish, left to escape starvation and poverty. Others, like the Russian Jews, fled for their lives. This massive wave of immigration resulted in a population boom for some American cities. Boston and Philadelphia doubled in population while New York and Pittsburgh tripled.

CHAPTER 14

The Expansion of American Industry
1865–1900

After the Civil War, a revolution of new inventions and ideas transformed the United States. Industrial expansion meant new products and conveniences for consumers and business and new sources of wealth for business owners. Industrial growth also put men and women to work, but at the price of a poorer quality of life. As the century came to a close, tensions between workers and employers worsened, finally exploding in a series of violent strikes and confrontations.

Events in the United States

1866 National Labor Union is organized in Baltimore, Maryland.

1869 The transcontinental railroad is completed. • The Knights of Labor are founded.

1877 Edison patents the phonograph. • The railroad strike of 1877 erupts in Pittsburgh.

1880 Andrew Carnegie begins the establishment of Carnegie libraries.

| 1865 | 1870 | 1875 | 1880 |

Events in the World

1867 Austrian Johann Strauss II composes "The Blue Danube" waltz.

1876 Korea becomes an independent nation.

1880 Chile fights the "Pacific War" against Bolivia and Peru.

RESOURCE DIRECTORY

Teaching Resources

Alternate Lesson Plan: Demonstrating the Big Idea found in the Alternate Lesson Plans folder, p. 68, provides a lesson strategy to instruct students about the Big Idea that the Civil War was followed by a revolution of new inventions and ideas that transformed the United States into an industrial nation.

Alternative Assessment Handbook provides information, guidance, and strategies for alternative methods of assessment. It includes an essay on new trends in assessment, guidance and strategies for developing performance tasks and portfolios, scoring rubrics, and sample evaluation forms.

Pages 386–391

A Technological Revolution

A revolution was coming. Not a political revolution—but a technological revolution that would change forever the way people worked, played, traveled, and communicated.

Pages 393–397

The Growth of Big Business

The late 1800s saw the emergence of giant enterprises that controlled vast material and human resources. Big business produced staggering wealth for its owners and for the country. It also prompted controversy and concern over its methods.

Pages 398–401

Industrialization and Workers

For millions of men, women, and children, industrialization was a blessing and a curse. It gave them jobs—but at what cost?

Pages 402–407

The Great Strikes: A Turning Point in History

Many American workers sought relief from their difficult lives through labor unions. What they found in the late 1800s was strong resistance from big business and only fleeting success.

Pages 408–409

The Lasting Impact of the Great Strikes

1883 Railroads adopt standard time zones.
• The Brooklyn Bridge is opened.

1890 Congress passes the Sherman Antitrust Act.

1894 Pullman workers strike.

1900 Western Union sends 63 million telegraph messages.

1885	1890	1895	1900

1885 French scientist Louis Pasteur administers the first successful rabies vaccination.

1891 Building of a railroad across Siberia, in Russia, begins.

1895 Italian physicist Guglielmo Marconi invents a wireless telegraph system.

1899 Boer War begins in South Africa.

Alternative Assessment

As an ongoing chapter project, students can demonstrate their knowledge through an in-depth analysis of the steel industry between 1865 and 1900. Students can demonstrate an understanding of

• The causes for the growth of American industry in the late 1800s
• The effects of industrial developments and new technology on American life
• The changes in the structure of American business
• Conflict between labor and industry

Students may present their study about the growth and development of the steel industry as an essay, oral presentation, or audiotaped presentation in which they summarize and synthesize the above topics.

Explain that projects will be evaluated according to the following guidelines:

• **Unacceptable** Project is not attempted or is incomplete and does not address points for discussion.
• **Limited/Acceptable** Project addresses points for discussion and partially relates them to the growth of American industry.
• **Extensive/Commendable** Project addresses main points thoroughly and is well supported by additional research.
• **Extraordinary/Outstanding** Project addresses main points thoroughly, clearly shows their relationship to the growth of American industry, and reflects extensive outside research on the subject.

For information and guidance on alternative assessment trends and strategies, see the Alternative Assessment Handbook in the Resource Directory on page 384.

SECTION 1

A Technological Revolution

1. FOCUS

Connecting to the Big Idea

See page 384B. Explain to students that the transformation of the United States in the late nineteenth century was due in large part to an outpouring of inventions that changed the way Americans lived and worked. Ask, for example, how the invention of the electric light changed the way people lived.

Objectives

- Identify some of the inventions that transformed American life in the decades following the Civil War.
- Identify how developments in communication and transportation changed American business.
- Describe changes in building and transportation that changed the nation's landscape.

Bellringer

Write the following list of inventions on the chalkboard: typewriter, phonograph, telegraph, telephone. Ask students to decide which they consider the most important and why.

In Depth

Did You Know?

The earliest remaining photographs date from the 1820s. Technological advances in the mid-1800s allowed photographers to produce pictures on paper rather than glass. In the 1880s, George Eastman developed a hand-held camera that could be used by professionals and amateurs alike.

A Technological Revolution

SECTION PREVIEW

A revolution was coming. Not a political revolution—but a technological revolution that would change forever the way people worked, played, traveled, and communicated.

Key Concepts

- Technological change and an explosion of new ideas transformed American life in the post-Civil War years.
- The nature of doing business changed as a result of developments in communications and transportation.
- Changes in transportation and building methods transformed the nation's landscape.

Inventions such as this Singer sewing machine changed daily life for many Americans.

Key Terms, People, and Places

transcontinental railroad; Thomas A. Edison, Alexander Graham Bell; Brooklyn Bridge

---

Americans today flip a switch for light, turn a faucet for water, and communicate in many ways with people they never meet face to face. It is hard to imagine life without these conveniences. In 1865, however, no one had to wonder what such a life was like.

Daily Life in 1865

Indoor electric lighting did not exist in 1865. Instead, the rising and setting of the sun dictated the rhythm of work and play. After dark, people lit candles or oil lamps if they could afford them; if not, they simply went to sleep, to rise at dawn with the first light.

Imagine summers without the benefits of refrigeration. Ice was available in 1865, but only at great cost. Sawn out of frozen ponds during the winter, blocks of ice were packed in sawdust and stored in ice houses for later use.

Communications also were agonizingly slow. In 1860, most mail from the East Coast took ten days to reach the Midwest and three weeks to get to the West. An immigrant living on the frontier would wait months for news from relatives in Europe.

Daily Life Transformed

By 1900, this picture of daily life had changed dramatically for millions of Americans. A combination of factors made this change possible.

The post-Civil War years saw tremendous growth in new ideas and inventions. Between 1790 and 1860, the Patent and Trademark Office of the federal government issued just 36,000 patents. In contrast, in the thirty years between 1860 and 1890, it issued 500,000 for new inventions, such as the typewriter and the phonograph.

While new inventions flooded the patent office, European investors and American business leaders, using profits gained during the Civil War, began to invest heavily in these inventions. This combination of American ingenuity and financial backing created new industries and expanded old ones. By 1900, the industrial productivity and overall standard of living in the United States was in many ways the envy of the world.

The Advent of Electric Power

The blossoming of American ingenuity in the late 1800s had a profound effect on daily life for millions of people. For example, scientists began developing new uses for petroleum, including fuels such as gasoline that would help power new forms of transportation and machinery in the decades ahead.

Electricity, a miracle of light and power, provided another essential energy source. It made possible many significant advances in the nation's industrial development and in people's eating, working, and even sleeping habits.

 RESOURCE DIRECTORY

Teaching Resources

Reproducible Lesson Plan found in the Unit 5 folder, p. 3, provides a summary of the Section 1 lesson plan content.

Alternate Lesson Plan: Learning Styles found in the Alternate Lesson Plans folder, p. 69, provides guidance, especially effective for visual learners, in creating graphic organizers on the technological revolution.

Guided Reading and Review found in the Unit 5 folder, p. 7, provides a structure for reading and mastering the key concepts and reviewing the key terms for Section 1. (Guided Practice)

A Master of Invention The work of **Thomas A. Edison** helped make electricity more widely available. Born in 1847, Edison grew up tinkering with electricity. While working for a New York company, he improved the stock tickers that sent stock and gold prices to other offices. When his boss awarded him a $40,000 bonus, the twenty-three-year-old Edison left his job and set himself up as an inventor.

From his so-called invention factory in New Jersey, Edison and his staff produced "invention to order." Though he had never received any formal science training, the young genius claimed that he could turn out "a minor invention every ten days and a big thing every six months or so." Within a few years, he owned hundreds of patents. Edison's favorite invention, introduced in 1877, was the phonograph, which recorded sounds on metal foil.

Edison also experimented with electric lighting. His goal was to develop affordable, practical, in-home lighting to replace oil lamps. Starting around 1879, Edison and his fellow inventors tried different means of producing light. A key to their search was finding a material that would glow without quickly burning up when charged with an electric current. After experimenting with various threadlike filaments, the team finally found a workable substance. When this filament was placed in a glass bulb, it glowed, Edison said, with "the most beautiful light ever seen."

Edison's ideas were later adapted and improved upon by others. Lewis Latimore, the son of an escaped slave, patented an improved method for producing the filament in bulbs. He worked in Edison's laboratories, where his ingenuity helped develop additional improvements in electricity. He later wrote a landmark book about electric lighting.

Until the early 1880s, anyone using electricity needed their own generator. Hoping to provide affordable lighting to many customers, Edison developed the idea of a central power station. To attract investors, in 1882 Edison built a power plant that lit eighty-five buildings in New York City. Investors were impressed, and Edison's idea spread. By 1890, offices across the country were using electricity to power lamps, fans, printing presses, and other appliances.

Westinghouse and Alternating Current
Edison at first used a form of electricity called direct current to transmit power from his stations. Direct current was expensive to produce, however, and could travel only a mile or two. In the 1880s, George Westinghouse began to experiment with alternating current, which could travel longer distances more cheaply. In addition, Westinghouse used a device called a transformer to produce voltage levels that made home use of electricity practical.

By the early 1890s, financiers built on the Edison and Westinghouse inventions to create the General Electric and Westinghouse Electric companies. These companies' inventions helped spur the growth of electricity. By 1898 nearly three thousand power stations were lighting two million light bulbs across the land.

Electricity's Impact on Daily Life The use of electric current in households revolutionized many aspects of daily life. To take but one example, electricity made possible the refrigeration of foods, reducing food spoilage and the need for ice houses.

Electricity also transformed the world of work and created new job opportunities. For example, foot pedals drove the early sewing machines, which had been introduced in the 1850s. Electrified in 1886, sewing machines enabled the rapid expansion of the ready-made clothing industry. Many of the country's new immigrants, especially women and children, found work making clothing in factories powered by electricity. In addition, many women stopped making their own clothing.

For all its impact, electricity's benefits were not evenly distributed. Rural areas especially went without electricity for many decades. Even where electricity was available, many could not afford its conveniences.

Electricity provided power that made postwar industrial development possible. In turn, electric companies such as General Electric, whose ad appears here, grew into large industrial corporations.

Reading Strategy
Reinforcing Key Ideas Tell students that they will read about daily life in the United States between 1865 and 1900. As they read, have students list the ways in which the United States changed in those thirty-five years.

2. INSTRUCT

Explain

Point out to students that conditions in the United States were ideal for the great surge in industrial activity that occurred. Business leaders had capital to invest, the labor supply was adequate, and abundant forests and mines provided raw materials. Changes in the means of production, including mechanization and electrification, provided the last ingredient needed for the expansion of industry.

In Depth

Biography

African American engineer Elijah McCoy (1843–1929) was born in Canada, to escaped slaves. He studied in Edinburgh, Scotland, before settling in the United States. In 1872, while working for the Michigan Central Railroad, McCoy invented the lubricating cup—a device that continuously oiled the moving parts of a machine. Over the years he adapted his invention to many other machines. It is sometimes said that the expression "the real McCoy," meaning the genuine article, came about because people insisted that the machinery they buy be equipped with McCoy's invention.

Caption Answer to ...

Using Historical Evidence

Women played a significant role in producing the inventions of the era.

Answer to ...

MAKING CONNECTIONS

Answers will vary, but students may identify televisions, stereos, portable telephones, answering machines, and beepers. Benefits might include entertainment and enhanced communications. Drawbacks might include the use of costly and polluting energy. Encourage students to explore how technological developments can affect people's lives both positively and negatively.

In Depth

Did You Know?

Not everyone greeted the improvements in railroad transportation and travel with enthusiasm. The *Boston Courier* printed the following assertion as part of an editorial in 1827: "The project of a railroad from Boston to Albany is impracticable, as every one knows who knows the simplest rule of arithmetic, and the expense would be little less than the market value of the whole of Massachusetts; and which, if practicable, every person of common sense knows would be as useless as a railroad from Boston to the moon."

Using Historical Evidence This drawing appeared in the April 1890 edition of a journal called *The Woman Inventor*. What does it suggest about women's contributions to the industrial growth of the late 1800s?

MAKING CONNECTIONS

Think of a modern convenience that you rely on. What benefits does this item bring to your life? Are there any drawbacks associated with this item?

Improving Transportation Systems

As the Civil War ended, steam-powered ships still provided much of the nation's transportation. During the mid-1800s, however, improvements in railroad travel created interconnecting links on land. Shrewd industrialists seized upon the opportunities offered by these links to make money and stimulate industrial growth.

The Railroads Before the Civil War, most of the nation's thirty thousand miles of track were in short, unconnected lines, almost all of them east of the Mississippi River. Because no system of standard signals existed and brakes were unreliable, train travel was dangerous. Moreover, track width, or gauge, varied among railroad lines. Goods and passengers had to be moved to different cars on different lines, resulting in costly delays and inconvenience.

Matters improved after the Civil War. The most spectacular development came on May 10, 1869. On that day, entrepreneur Leland Stanford drove the golden spike that completed the first **transcontinental railroad.**

The project had begun in 1862, when the absence of southern legislators during the Civil War enabled Congress to agree on a route across the continent. Prior to the war, sectional differences over location of the route had prevented such agreement. Government involvement was vital, for only with federal funding could the massive project be completed. Thus, the government granted huge loans and land grants to two companies. One, the Union Pacific, began work in Omaha, Nebraska, and built toward the West. The other, the Central Pacific, headed east out of Sacramento, California.

Immigrants built the transcontinental line using their bare hands. Irish men on the Union Pacific line hand-dug and -graded rail lines across the Great Plains at the rate of up to six miles a day. Testimony to the backbreaking nature of this work was the railroad saying that there was "an Irishman buried under every tie." Chinese workers shipped in from across the Pacific Ocean by the Central Pacific Railroad chiseled, plowed, and dynamited their way through the rock, ice, and snow of the Sierra Nevada range. Despite deplorable working conditions, they set the one-day record for track laid—an amazing ten miles. ✪

Finally, after seven years of grueling labor, the two crews approached one another in what is now Utah. At a place called Promontory Point, Stanford raised his hammer to drive the final golden spike while a telegraph operator beside the track tapped out a message to crowds throughout the country: "Almost ready now. Hats off. Prayer is being offered. . . . Done!"

Problems and Solutions on the Railroads
Even after such improvements, train travel remained inconvenient for many. Cornelia Adair, an Englishwoman visiting the United States in 1874, recalled the following details about her journey:

> We were obliged to wait all Friday, the afternoon and evening, at Cheyenne [Wyoming]. *The Kansas-Pacific Railway has quarreled with the Union-Pacific, and makes the diabolical arrangement that people must get up at two in the night to go from Cheyenne to Denver [Colorado], and then no sleeping car.*

In addition to their inconvenience and lack of comfort, the railroads aroused the distrust and fear of many. One story of the early railroad days raged against the dangers of train travel, reporting

▶ RESOURCE DIRECTORY

Teaching Resources

 Primary Source Activity Working on the Railroad, found in the Unit 5 folder, p. 25, introduces students to the hard life of an 1880s worker with a folk song by Thomas Casey.

388 **Chapter 14 Section 1**

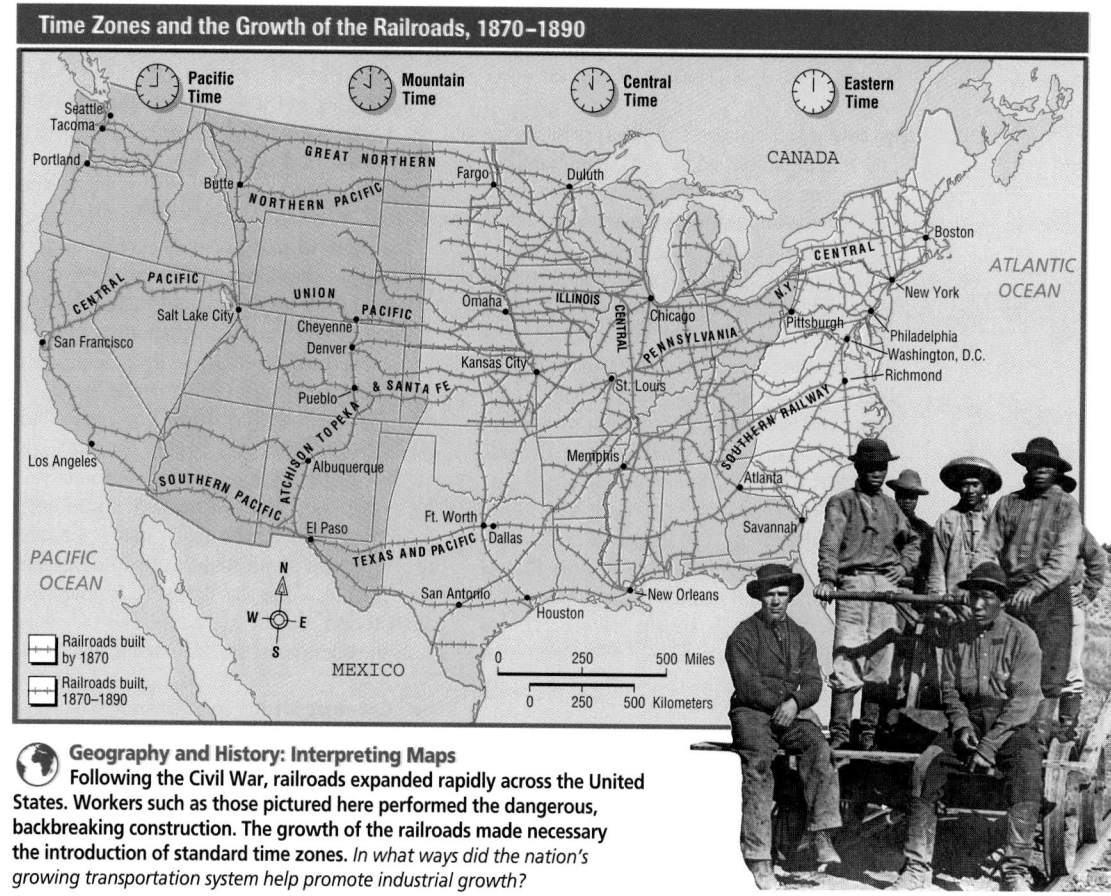

Time Zones and the Growth of the Railroads, 1870–1890

 Geography and History: Interpreting Maps
Following the Civil War, railroads expanded rapidly across the United States. Workers such as those pictured here performed the dangerous, backbreaking construction. The growth of the railroads made necessary the introduction of standard time zones. *In what ways did the nation's growing transportation system help promote industrial growth?*

it is bad enough when the train kills pigs and cows and horses, but if little children get on the track accidental it will run over them too, and even old folks going to church in their buggy. It's enough to make your blood run cold.

From the folk tale
"Railroads Ain't No Good"

In spite of its supposed and real dangers, train travel continued to expand and improve. Steel rails replaced iron rails, track gauges and signals became standardized. In 1883, the railroads helped introduce standardized time zones to improve scheduling nationwide (shown on the map above). Prior to that time, most towns set their clocks independently, creating much confusion.

Railroads also took steps to improve safety. George Westinghouse developed more effective air brakes. Granville Woods invented a telegraph system for communications to and from moving trains, thus reducing collision risks.

Rail improvements made life easier not only for passengers but also for businesses that shipped goods. By the end of the century, shipping costs had dropped: in 1865, shipping a barrel of flour from Chicago to New York cost $3.45; in 1895, it cost 68 cents.

The Power to Communicate

In the late 1800s, thousands of people left their homes in Europe and the eastern United States to seek a new life in the West. Imagine their despair at leaving loved ones. Would they

Discuss

Discuss how the invention of one product often leads to the invention of many others. Have students describe some of the inventions and refinements that resulted from Edison's first light bulb. Ask them to brainstorm as many products and jobs as they can that grew out of the invention of the telephone. Ask what products became available due to the growth of the railroad.

Caption Answer to ...

 Interpreting Maps

Railroads opened vast new regions for American settlement and allowed manufacturers to ship more raw materials and goods to more places.

Activity
Identifying Relationships

Ask students to create a chart that illustrates the relationships among the improvement in railroads, the building of new railroads, the development of new markets for factory goods, the spread of people to new areas, and the demand for more railroads from passengers and businesses.

Enrichment

Many popular American folk songs concern the building of the railroads. Ask students to research the history of railroad songs and to prepare a written report or an oral presentation using an audiotape of the songs they researched. Suggest that students begin their research with books of American folk songs, such as Carl Sandburg's *The American Songbag*.

Section 1 Review Answers

1. transcontinental railroad, see p. 388

2. (a) Thomas Edison, see p. 387,
(b) Alexander Graham Bell, see p. 390,
(c) Brooklyn Bridge, see p. 391

3. Factors include the discovery of new uses for the nation's raw materials and the financial backing of wealthy business leaders.

4. It introduced new means of refrigerating food, lighting and heating homes, and performing work.

5. The nation's physical size required an efficient means of moving goods and sharing ideas. Without these, no one would have been able to sell goods or share important information.

6. Possible answers: by making accessible places not easily reached by ship; by shortening the time required to reach locations via land travel.

Reteach

Have students describe life in the United States before 1865, focusing on transportation, daily schedules, and types of food available. Then ask them to describe how life had changed by the 1900s and to cite the inventions that helped to bring about the changes.

---

ever hear from family and friends again? By 1900, thanks to many advances in communications, such feelings of isolation had diminished.

The Telegraph Samuel F. B. Morse's invention of the telegraph signaled the start of the communications revolution. Using a code of short and long electrical impulses to represent letters of the alphabet, Morse sent his first message in 1844.

After the Civil War, several telegraph companies joined together to form the Western Union Telegraph Company. In 1870, Western Union sent 9 million telegraph messages over 112,000 miles of wire. By 1900, it owned 933,000 miles of wire and was sending 63 million messages a year. Like many companies born in the late 1800s, Western Union still operates today.

The Telephone In 1871, **Alexander Graham Bell** of Scotland immigrated to Boston, Massachusetts, to instruct the hearing impaired. After experimenting with an electric current to transmit sounds, he achieved a "talking telegraph" in 1876. In 1884, Bell and a group of partners set up the American Telephone and Telegraph Company, which still exists today.

Although the first telephone lines could connect only two places, such as a home and a business, soon central switchboards with operators linked homes and businesses in entire cities. President Rutherford B. Hayes had a telephone installed at the White House in 1878. By 1900, 1.5 million telephones were in use.

The Power to Build Things

Throughout the mid-1800s, the nation depended on iron for railroads and for frames for large buildings. But in the 1850s, Henry Bessemer in England and William Kelly in Kentucky independently developed a new process for making steel, a metal that is lighter, stronger, and more flexible than iron. Engineers had long known the benefits of steel, but its high cost had made its widespread use impractical. The Bessemer converter—the name commonly used for the new technology—made possible the production of affordable, plentiful steel. A new age of building was dawning. Perhaps no construction project so exemplified that new age as the building of the Brooklyn Bridge.

The "Greatest Bridge in Existence" As New York City's status as a business center rose, so did its population, many of whom settled in the nearby city of Brooklyn. But the only way to

---

| 1650 | 1700 | 1750 | 1800 | **Links Across Time** | 1850 | 1900 | 1950 | 2000 |

New Ways to Communicate

When Alexander Graham Bell patented the first model of his telephone in 1876, businesses everywhere flocked to buy the new invention. As technology moves into the twenty-first century, a new communications revolution is taking place. The picture telephone technology shown here allows modern businesses to speak with and to see the party whom they have called.

▶ RESOURCE DIRECTORY

Teaching Resources

American Profiles Activity found in the Unit 5 folder, p. 18, profiles Washington A. Roebling, the engineer who supervised the building of the Brooklyn Bridge.

Water Shaft Earth was removed by scoops inside these shafts. Water in the shafts prevented loss of air pressure.

Supply Shaft These shafts allowed workers to get supplies to the work area.

Air Lock These chambers let workers enter and leave the caisson without a loss of air.

Boom Derrick

Granite Blocks

Timber Caisson Each tower was built atop a timber shell, or caisson, under which workers removed earth.

The Brooklyn Bridge included two massive towers, one of which is shown being built here. As workers removed earth beneath the tower and piled granite blocks above it, the tower sank into the ground. When completed, the two towers supported the steel cables that in turn held up the span.

In the dank space under the caisson, workers shoveled earth into the water shafts for removal.

travel between Brooklyn and Manhattan was by ferry across the East River, often impassable in winter due to ice or gales. Could a bridge high enough to clear river traffic be built across such a large distance? Engineer John A. Roebling, a German immigrant, thought it could.

Roebling envisioned a suspension bridge with thick steel cables suspended from high towers to hold up the span. At 1,595 feet long, his **Brooklyn Bridge**—which was completed by his son Washington following his death—would be the longest bridge yet built.

A Symbol of American Ingenuity Sixteen years in the making, the bridge opened on May 24, 1883. President Chester A. Arthur attended the opening ceremony. At nightfall, crowds gasped as a switch was thrown, and electric bulbs strung along the bridge lit up the darkness and shimmered on the river below. Just as suddenly, the lights went out, heralding a magnificent fireworks display. The city celebrated. Indeed, the entire United States celebrated, its ingenuity confirmed for all the world.

Inventions, faster transportation, daring construction—to this list of examples of American ingenuity should be added the new thinking evident in the American business world in the late 1800s. Changes brought about by that business, however, came with a price, as the next section shows.

SECTION 1 REVIEW

Key Terms, People, and Places
1. Identify transcontinental railroad.
2. Identify (a) Thomas A. Edison, (b) Alexander Graham Bell, (c) Brooklyn Bridge.

Key Concepts
3. What were some of the factors that helped spur economic development after the Civil War?
4. How did electricity change daily life?

5. How were effective transportation and communication systems important to economic development?

Critical Thinking
6. **Determining Relevance** Consider the dominant transportation method in the United States before the Civil War. How might railroads have provided a broader, more widespread network than this earlier transportation method?

▯ **Quiz** found in the Unit 5 folder, p. 8, covers the main ideas in this section as well as the key terms.

Media and Technology

▱ **Transparency**
The Way It Works, H-14

---

4. CLOSE

Reinforcing the Big Idea

American life changed dramatically in the decades following the Civil War as a result of inventions and improvements in transportation and communication. The next section describes how American business became "big business" in order to bring those inventions to market.

⬇ **In Depth**

Did You Know?

John Roebling, the engineer who built the Brooklyn Bridge, died six months after construction began, in 1869, of gangrene resulting from a ferry accident. His son Colonel Washington Roebling took over, but he contracted "the bends," or caisson disease, in 1872 and was confined to his bed. His wife, Emily, acted as his messenger, and many consider her to have been in effect the chief engineer during the final phases of construction, which ended in 1883.

Geography

Using Cross-Sectional Maps

Focus Compare the data provided in the cross-sectional map with that of the physical-political map.

Instruct To be sure students understand the information presented in the cross-sectional map, ask them to identify the location on the map at elevation 1,000 feet and 7,000 feet. Have them indicate the elevation at Bitter Creek. Ask students to think about some other useful subjects for cross-sectional maps. (*The ocean floor, rivers and other waterways.*)

Extend See the Historian's Toolbox Activity in the Resource Directory below.

Answers

1. (a) The Rocky Mountains, Salt Lake Valley, Humboldt Valley, and the Sierra Nevada are on the physical-political and cross-sectional maps. (b) No. The cross-sectional maps do not show the land area that lies north or south of the railroads.

2. (a) Union Pacific—the highest elevation was about 7,500 feet above sea level; the lowest about 1,000 feet. Central Pacific—the highest elevation was just over 7,000 feet above sea level, the lowest about 300 feet. (b) The sharpest changes occurred heading east from Sacramento; the most gradual occurred heading west from Omaha.

Using Cross-Sectional Maps

Sometimes it is necessary to use more than one type of map to understand the look of a particular piece of land. Cross-sectional maps show how an area of land would look if viewed from the side. The cross-sectional map below shows the changes in elevation along the route of the first transcontinental railroad, completed in 1869. These changes in elevation appear on the map as sharp spikes and deep depressions. Physical-political maps show the earth's surface as if viewed from above. The physical-political map below gives a bird's-eye view of the vast horizontal distances covered by the railroad.

Steep terrain, snowstorms, floods, and heat all posed great challenges to the workers who built the transcontinental railroad, but the greatest challenges arose from the changes in elevation. Use the following steps to study the cross-sectional map.

1. Study the region shown in the maps. (a) Which landforms on the physical-political map correspond to those on the cross-sectional map? (b) Does the cross-sectional map show all the land area on the political map? Explain.

2. Analyze the information shown in the cross-sectional map. (a) What were the highest and lowest elevations of each railroad route? (b) Where did the sharpest and the most gradual changes occur? (c) Write a paragraph comparing the length and elevation changes of the Central Pacific and Union Pacific routes.

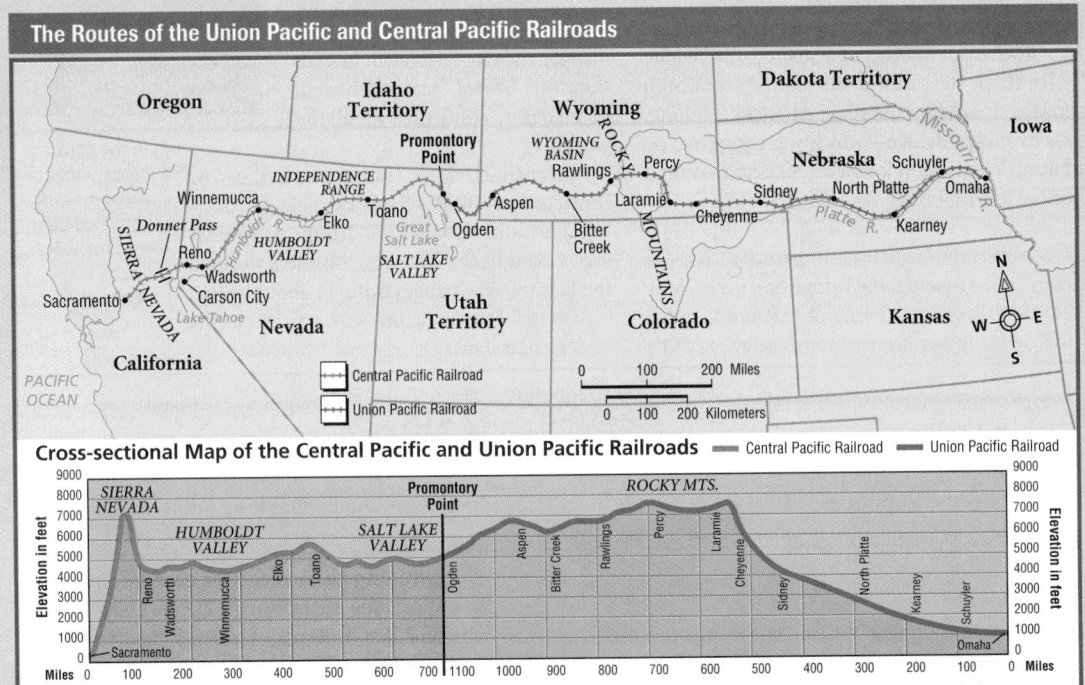

The Routes of the Union Pacific and Central Pacific Railroads

Cross-sectional Map of the Central Pacific and Union Pacific Railroads

RESOURCE DIRECTORY

Teaching Resources

Historian's Toolbox Activity Using Cross-Sectional Maps, found in the Unit 5 folder, p. 21, uses contrasting maps designed to enhance students' application of this skill.

The Growth of Big Business

SECTION PREVIEW

The late 1800s saw the emergence of giant enterprises that controlled vast material and human resources. Big business produced staggering wealth for its owners and for the country. It also prompted controversy and concern over its methods.

Key Concepts

- Only large businesses had the resources needed to exploit new inventions.
- Industrialists were both hated for their ruthlessness and admired for their good works and willingness to take risks.
- Big business sought to control competition through various forms of consolidation.

Key Terms, People, and Places

social Darwinism, monopoly, cartel, trust, horizontal consolidation, vertical consolidation, economy of scale; Andrew Carnegie

---

T he period of invention and discovery following the Civil War set the stage for great industrial growth. But it would take more than ingenuity to bring about the transformation of the United States. Without large outlays of money, inventors could not build great factories, market their new products, or create profitable businesses. To succeed, business leaders had to pool funds and resources into large companies. Thus was born the age of "big business."

Robber Barons or Captains of Industry?

Historians have adopted the terms *robber barons* and *captains of industry* to describe the powerful industrialists who established large businesses in the late 1800s. Each term conjures up strikingly different images, and debate still rages over which is more fitting.

Captains of industry suggests that the business leaders served their nation in a positive way. This view credits them with increasing the availability of goods by building factories, raising productivity, and expanding markets. Furthermore, by creating more jobs, the giant industrialists enabled many Americans to buy their new goods. They also founded and funded many of the nation's great museums, libraries, and universities, many of which still thrive today.

The term *robber barons*, on the other hand, implies that the business leaders built their fortunes by stealing from the public. According to this view, they drained the country of its natural resources and corrupted public officials to interpret laws in their favor. At the same time, these industrialists ruthlessly drove their competitors to ruin and paid meager wages, while forcing their workers to toil under dangerous and unhealthy conditions.

Industrial growth required the contributions of workers and also of business owners, as this illustration suggests.

Andrew Carnegie

Andrew Carnegie (1835–1919) is a fascinating example of an American industrialist of this era. Born in Scotland, Carnegie's father was a skilled weaver. But when industrial growth in Great Britain replaced the need for skilled craft workers, Carnegie's family faced hard times. As a result, they came to the United States in 1848, settling near Pittsburgh, Pennsylvania. Only thirteen years old, Carnegie immediately went out to work.

Carnegie's first job was in a cotton factory at $1.20 a week. Determined to do better, he read avidly to improve himself. When his father's death in 1855 made young Andrew his family's chief earner, his quest for advancement became urgent.

Connecting to the Big Idea

See page 384B. Explain to students that the business organization changes of the late nineteenth century brought both great wealth and great hardship to the country. Ask students what those changes were and how they affected American life.

Objectives

- Explain why only large businesses could exploit new inventions and technologies.
- Present both positive and negative views of the industrialists of the 1800s.
- Show how big business tried to control competition.

Bellringer

Have students describe a "mom and pop" business. Then have them write a definition of "big business" and explain how the two differ.

Reading Strategy

Finding Evidence Ask students to read the section on page 393 titled "Robber Barons or Captains of Industry?" Ask them to look for evidence to support either view of the industrialists of the late 1800s.

Reproducible Lesson Plan found in the Unit 5 folder, p. 4, provides a summary of the Section 2 lesson plan content.

Alternate Lesson Plan: Cooperative Learning found in the Alternate Lesson Plans folder, p. 70, provides guidance for groups of students to produce a news story on a big-business topic of their choice.

Guided Reading and Review found in the Unit 5 folder, p. 9, provides a structure for reading and mastering the key concepts and reviewing the key terms for Section 2. (Guided Practice)

2. INSTRUCT

Explain

Explain to students that the many inventions of the post–Civil War period changed business as well as daily life. To control the large amounts of money needed to produce new inventions and build railroads, bridges, and factories, American businesses grew into giant enterprises, bringing both wealth and hardship to the country. Ask students whether they think the term "big business" has positive or negative associations today. Have them identify some positive and negative associations.

Discuss

Discuss with students the probability that the powerful industrialists of the late 1800s were *both* captains of industry and robber barons. Ask students to explain how that could be.

In Depth

Then and Now

The boom of mergers that took place in the late 1800s was echoed by a massive wave of mergers in the 1980s, when the Reagan administration set out to reverse antitrust laws that had been in place since the early 1900s. The administration's policies resulted in the takeover of about 28 percent of the five hundred largest American corporations. The merging of Time and Warner Communications in 1989 is one example of the many companies affected.

Andrew Carnegie's success in business enabled him to surround himself with comfort. Here he relaxes at his private golf cottage.

After a stint as a telegraph operator, at age eighteen Carnegie won the post of secretary to the superintendent in the Pennsylvania Railroad Company. When Carnegie's boss went off to the War Department during the Civil War, the young Carnegie took over his job.

Forging a Great Enterprise Now well paid, Carnegie began to invest widely. The invention of Henry Bessemer's steel-making process had convinced Carnegie that steel would soon replace iron in many industries. During the early 1870s, Carnegie built two blast furnaces that made pig iron, the material from which steel is made.

Despite a nationwide economic depression in 1873, Carnegie systematically cut his steel prices until he had driven his competitors out of the market. Together with a partner, Henry Clay Frick, Carnegie then took control of the entire steel industry, from the mines that produced iron ore to the ovens and mills that made pig iron and steel. He even took control of the shipping and rail lines necessary for transporting his products to market.

Carnegie as a Public Figure While expanding his business, Carnegie became a major public figure. Through books and speeches, he preached a "gospel of wealth." The essence of his message was simple: People should be free to make as much money as they can. After they make it, however, they should give it away. As he wrote in 1889, "The man who dies . . . rich dies disgraced." Never leave wealth to heirs, he warned, or they will fail to learn how to survive on their own. Never leave it to others to administer, for they will never follow your instruc-

tions. Give it away yourself, he advised, not as charity but as philanthropy, gifts to institutions or to the public that help humankind.

By the turn of the century, Carnegie had built about three thousand free public libraries, supported artistic and research institutions in Pittsburgh, Washington, D.C., and New York City, and set up a fund to study how to abolish war. In these and other ways, Carnegie distributed some $350 million.

Still, not everyone approved of Carnegie's methods. Workers at his steel plants protested vigorously against his company's labor practices. (See Section 4.) Many others questioned the sincerity of his good works. In one satire by humorist Finley Peter Dunne, a fictitious Irish bartender describes what might happen if a beggar asked Carnegie for food:

> Th' pan-handler knocks an' asts f'r a glass iv milk an' a roll. "No sir," says Andhrew Carnaygie. "I will not pauperize this onworthy man. . . . Yet it shall not be said iv me that I give nawthin' to th' poor. Saunders, give him a libry."

⭐ Others admired Carnegie for achieving great things through hard work. He saw himself as "improving the conditions of all" by lowering costs for the masses. In an essay titled "Wealth and Its Uses," he wrote:

> It will be a great mistake for the community to shoot the millionaires, for they are the bees that make the most honey, and contribute most to the hive even after they have gorged themselves full.

Social Darwinism

In statements such as these, Carnegie revealed support for social Darwinism, a popular theory of the late 1800s. This theory applied to society Charles Darwin's theory of evolution, first published in 1859. According to Darwin, all animal life had evolved by a process of "natural selection" through which only the fittest survived to reproduce. ⭐

RESOURCE DIRECTORY

Teaching Resources

⭐ **Primary Source Activity** Carnegie's Gospel of Wealth, found in the Unit 5 folder, p. 24, uses an excerpt from the writing of Andrew Carnegie to explain his philosophy regarding money and philanthropy.

⭐ **Primary Source Activity** Pestilence in the Cigar, found in the Unit 5 folder, p. 23, uses an 1874 newspaper article to enhance students' understanding of the harsh lives of factory workers.

Applying this idea to the struggle between workers and employers, **social Darwinism** held that society should do as little as possible to interfere with the process by which people succeed or fail. If government and other institutions would stay out of the affairs of business, those who were most "fit" would survive—that is, succeed and become rich. Society as a whole would benefit from the success of the fit and the weeding out of the unfit.

Many Americans agreed with the great industrialists that the nation's prosperity depended on a *laissez-faire,* or "hands-off," approach to the economy by the government. As a result, government neither taxed the profits of businesses nor regulated their relations with their workers.

MAKING CONNECTIONS

Based on your understanding of the *laissez-faire* approach of government, what do you predict might happen to those business owners who were less powerful?

Competition in the Age of Big Business

Industrialists used whatever means necessary, fair or foul, to gain a competitive edge over their rivals. They paid as little as they could for raw materials, labor, and shipping. They also sometimes created monopolies and cartels to gain control over competition.

Monopolies and Cartels In order to create a **monopoly,** a business bought out its competitors and all of its patents. The business would thus eliminate all competition for its product, and it could then charge any price it wished.

Toward the end of the 1800s, federal and state governments passed laws to prevent certain monopolistic practices. Those laws did not prevent or destroy all monopolies, however, in part because political leaders were unwilling to attack powerful business leaders.

Cartels are loose associations of businesses making the same product, usually formed in secret. The goal of a cartel is to reduce the harmful effects of competition on the businesses

PUCK.

THE PROTECTORS OF OUR INDUSTRIES.

Using Historical Evidence Some Americans were offended by the argument that business leaders protected jobs. *What does this cartoon suggest about the relationship of workers to business leaders?*

Activity

Understanding Point of View

Ask students to draw, or compile through cutouts, two cartoons, one showing an industrialist of the late 1800s as a captain of industry and one showing the industrialist as a robber baron. Ask them to write a brief explanation of what viewpoint they consider the more accurate.

Enrichment

To illustrate the delicate balance between economic development and fair treatment of workers, ask students to think about how industrialists like Andrew Carnegie, and labor leaders like Samuel Gompers, might have expressed their ideas through mass media in the 1800s. Have students create public service announcements for either industrialists or laborers. Suggest that students brainstorm a list of features that they would want to highlight in their announcement.

Answer to ...

MAKING CONNECTIONS

Students should predict that less powerful businesses would go out of business or be purchased by more powerful enterprises. Assist students as they explore how an abstract concept functions in reality.

Caption Answer to ...

Using Historical Evidence

The cartoon depicts workers struggling to support the business leaders who supposedly protect them.

Caption Answer to ...

Interpreting Charts

Vertical monopoly: Inability to compete on price because of having to pay more for various services. Horizontal monopoly: Lack of competition to help keep prices down and quality up.

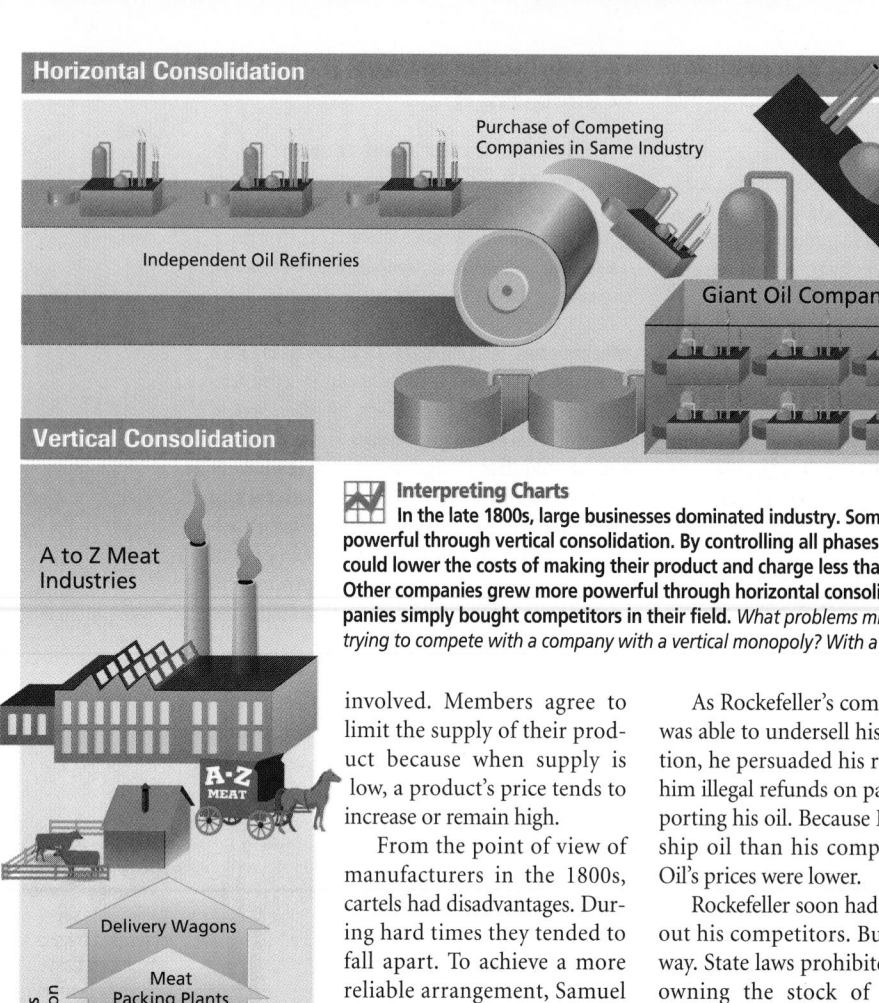

Horizontal Consolidation

Independent Oil Refineries

Purchase of Competing Companies in Same Industry

Giant Oil Company

Vertical Consolidation

A to Z Meat Industries

Purchase of Companies at All Levels of Production

- Delivery Wagons
- Meat Packing Plants
- Cooled Warehouses
- Refrigerated Railroad Cars
- Slaughterhouses
- Cattle

Interpreting Charts

In the late 1800s, large businesses dominated industry. Some companies grew more powerful through vertical consolidation. By controlling all phases of production, they could lower the costs of making their product and charge less than their competitors. Other companies grew more powerful through horizontal consolidation, in which companies simply bought competitors in their field. *What problems might a business face when trying to compete with a company with a vertical monopoly? With a horizontal monopoly?*

involved. Members agree to limit the supply of their product because when supply is low, a product's price tends to increase or remain high.

From the point of view of manufacturers in the 1800s, cartels had disadvantages. During hard times they tended to fall apart. To achieve a more reliable arrangement, Samuel Dodd, a lawyer for oil magnate John D. Rockefeller, invented the trust.

The Standard Oil Trust Born in 1839 in Richford, New York, Rockefeller became rich from a grain and meat partnership during the Civil War. By 1870, he had formed the Standard Oil Company of Ohio. Oil had become a major industry following Edwin L. Drake's 1859 success at Titusville, Pennsylvania. There Drake proved the possibility of extracting oil from under the ground through wells.

As Rockefeller's company sold more oil, he was able to undersell his competitors. In addition, he persuaded his railroad friends to give him illegal refunds on part of the cost of transporting his oil. Because Rockefeller paid less to ship oil than his competitors did, Standard Oil's prices were lower.

Rockefeller soon had enough money to buy out his competitors. But the law stood in his way. State laws prohibited one company from owning the stock of another, since such monopolistic practices reduced competition and therefore "restrained" free trade. ✪

Samuel Dodd's idea of the trust got around this ban. In 1882, the owners of forty companies agreed to turn over their assets to a board of nine trustees. In return, they were promised a share of the profits of the new conglomerate. The board of trustees, which was controlled by Rockefeller, managed the companies as a single unit called a **trust.** Because the companies were not legally merged, no laws were violated. Rockefeller's trust controlled almost all of the nation's oil-refining capacity.

Trusts proved an effective means of limiting industrial competition. As a result, many Americans began to demand that their leaders in government take action to break up the giant

In Depth

Multicultural Perspectives

Many workers came from China to California during the Gold Rush of the mid-1800s. The Chinese workers caught the attention of railroad owners who recruited them when they found it difficult to attract other workers to the hard labor and low wages that were offered. Of the 12,000 men who worked to build the Central Pacific Railroad, 10,000 were Chinese. They were paid about $26 a month—less than the other workers—out of which they paid Central Pacific for their food and lodging. All other workers were paid $35 a month and given free food and lodging.

▶ RESOURCE DIRECTORY

Teaching Resources

✪ **Visual Learning Activity** Home of the Trusts, found in the Unit 5 folder, p. 30, uses an antitrust cartoon by noted political cartoonist Thomas Nast to assist students in analyzing political imagery.

✪ **Critical Thinking Activity** Making Comparisons: Business Consolidations, found in the Unit 5 folder, p. 22, provides an activity for students to apply this skill by using a diagram on consolidating business.

conglomerates. In 1890, the federal government responded by passing the Sherman Antitrust Act. This law aimed to combat restraint of trade or commerce caused by trusts.

The act, however, proved ineffective for nearly fifteen years because the federal government rarely enforced it and its vague wording made it hard to apply in court. When officials did invoke the act, they often used it against labor unions on the grounds that their actions restrained trade.

Vertical and Horizontal Methods of Industrial Control Rockefeller's approach to consolidation—the creation of one giant business from many smaller enterprises—was **horizontal consolidation.** This method involved bringing together many firms in the same business.

Other industrialists practiced **vertical consolidation,** a method by which they gained control of all phases of a product's development. Andrew Carnegie used this method in the steel business. By controlling all phases of steel production, Carnegie could lower his costs and drive competitors out of business. Carnegie could charge less because of a phenomenon called **economy of scale.** As he expanded his enterprises and produced more goods, his cost per item went down.

Public Reaction to Big Business

Few people truly liked trusts and other large business organizations. They knew that such associations did not have consumer or worker interests at heart. In 1873, this anonymous resident of Lynn, Massachusetts, recalled

*I*t is only too evident that the cause now at work in Lynn may render it rich and prosperous as a city, but with a population of overworked, underpaid hirelings, hopelessly dependent upon employers who act upon the good old rule, the simple plan— that they may take who have the power, and they may keep who can.*

But mergers were the wave of the future. By the turn of the century, the mammoth companies that contributed to the United States' enviable levels of wealth and productivity were in place: American Telephone and Telegraph, Swift and Armour, General Electric, Westinghouse, and DuPont are examples.

Rapid industrial growth did lead to strains on the economy. The gigantic markets of big business were subject to sudden fluctuations. When markets became glutted with goods, businesses had to lower prices in order to sell them. They then cut wages and laid off workers.

Other causes of strain included panics, widespread fears that heavily indebted businesses might not be able to pay their debts. When investors rushed to sell stock in affected businesses, stock prices fell and companies went bankrupt. Panics were often followed by depressions, periods of severe shrinking of economic growth. The resulting factory closings and unemployment meant widespread misery.

Unemployment was only one concern of the nation's workers. Indeed, their lives provide a sharp contrast to those of Carnegie, Rockefeller, and their fellow industrialists.

Periods of Economic Depression
1873 to 1879
1882 to 1885
1893 to 1897

The late 1800s were marred by a series of depressions.

SECTION 2 REVIEW

Key Terms, People, and Places
1. Define (a) social Darwinism, (b) monopoly.
2. Identify Andrew Carnegie.

Key Concepts
3. For what reasons were large enterprises necessary for the economic development of the late 1800s?
4. Why did manufacturers form cartels and trusts?

5. What is the difference between vertical and horizontal consolidation?

Critical Thinking
6. **Identifying Assumptions** You have read that government recognized the need to control conglomerates. What does this recognition assume about the nature of businesses?

 Quiz found in the Unit 5 folder, p. 10, covers the main ideas in this section as well as the key terms.

Media and Technology

 Transparency
Cause and Effect, F-6

Industrialization and Workers

1. FOCUS

Connecting to the Big Idea

See page 384B. Review with students that in the late 1800s inventions and technology led to the growth of big business. Explain that in addition to technology and financial backing, workers were needed to make new products for market. Ask students how this increased demand for labor would affect life for most Americans.

Objectives

- Identify labor as an essential ingredient of industrial growth.
- Describe the composition of the American work force in the period of industrialization.
- Describe how harsh working conditions inflicted physical and emotional harm on American workers.

Bellringer

Have students write down the associations that come into their minds as they consider the idea of *work*. Ask them to circle all the positive words and phrases on their list.

Caption Answer to ...

 Interpreting Graphs

The number of agricultural workers as a percentage of the total work force declined.

Children workers such as these labored long hours under hazardous conditions in the late 1800s.

SECTION PREVIEW

For millions of men, women, and children, industrialization was a blessing and a curse. It gave them jobs—but at what cost?

Key Concepts
- Industrial growth depended on the labor of millions of workers.
- Men, women, and children, both native born and immigrant, met the great demand for labor.
- Harsh working conditions inflicted physical and emotional harm.

Key Terms, People, and Places
piecework

Natural resources, inventive minds, risk-taking industrialists—all played central roles in the nation's industrial expansion following the Civil War. This expansion would not have been possible, however, without a growing work force that labored long hours for low wages.

The Growing Work Force

Fourteen million people arrived in the United States from abroad between 1860 and 1900. Most came in the hope of finding work in the booming industrial centers of the United States. The government often encouraged these job-seekers by sending recruiting agents abroad. As described in Chapter 16, however, their reception in the United States and its workplaces was not always warm.

In a population shift almost as dramatic as this immigration, some eight or nine million native-born Americans fled poor economic conditions on the nation's farms to move to its cities during the late 1800s. (See graph at right.) Factory work, in spite of its low pay and long hours, lured most of them.

Until the end of the century, few African Americans took part in this internal migration. Although some moved into cities in the South, the better job opportunities there were closed to them.

A Hard Life for the Factory Laborer

For those who labored in the factories, work was a family affair. Every family member worked in some way. Because wages were low, no one person could earn enough to sustain a household. Children often left school at the age of twelve or thirteen to work. Girls sometimes took factory jobs so that their brothers could stay in school. If a mother could not make some money working at home, she might also take a factory job, leaving babies with older siblings or neighbors. If an adult breadwinner became ill, died, or could not find or keep a job, children as young as six or seven had to bring in cash or go hungry.

Shifts in Nonagricultural and Agricultural Labor Force, 1860–1900

% Nonagricultural workers*

% Agricultural workers

1860 1870 1880 1890 1900
*Mining, construction, manufacturing only
Source: *Historical Statistics of the United States*

 Interpreting Graphs
In the late 1800s, more and more Americans found jobs in industry. *What was the effect of this development on agricultural employment?*

RESOURCE DIRECTORY

Teaching Resources

Reproducible Lesson Plan found in the Unit 5 folder, p. 5, provides a summary of the Section 3 lesson plan content.

Alternate Lesson Plan: Learning Styles found in the Alternate Lesson Plans folder, p. 71, provides an activity, especially effective for visual learners, for students to write captions on topics from the section.

Guided Reading and Review found in the Unit 5 folder, p. 11, provides a structure for reading and mastering the key concepts and reviewing the key terms for Section 3. (Guided Practice)

Using Historical Evidence John Furguson Weir's painting "The Gun Foundry" (1866) presents a vivid image of the nation's industrial might. *What does the painting suggest about the conditions faced by workers?*

Other than private charities, there were no support systems such as today's government welfare programs for families in need. For example, unemployment insurance—payments for workers who are laid off from their jobs—did not exist. In addition, legislators in the late 1800s resisted the idea of creating broad programs of public work to relieve the miseries created by economic crises.

Even charity was of limited help. When an economic crisis hit, charity workers had to spread out their limited resources by making relief more difficult to get. They insisted that applicants prove themselves "worthy," which meant sober and in agreement with the charity's standard of morality.

MAKING CONNECTIONS

Consider the lack of government aid for the poor in the late 1800s. How might the concept of social Darwinism have influenced government policies toward public aid?

The Industrial Laborer at Work

In the 1860s the ordinary work day was about twelve hours, and the work week was six days or longer. By the turn of the century, a ten-hour day prevailed, but in some industries, workers were told "If you don't come in on Sunday, you can forget about Monday." Good jobs were too hard to come by to ignore such a warning.

In many industries, employers paid workers a fixed amount for each finished piece they produced—for example, a few cents for a garment or a number of cigars. This system of **piecework** meant that those who worked fastest and produced the most pieces earned the most money. Piecework favored young and strong workers; older or less able workers suffered.

Increasing Efficiency In the 1880s, management engineer Frederick Winslow Taylor developed time-and-motion studies to get workers to produce more in less time. Taylor's idea was to make the most efficient use of all motion

Reading Strategy

Reinforcing Key Ideas Ask students to recall what they know about the work life of farm families. As they read, ask them to jot down words and phrases that describe the jobs held by millions of American laborers during the late 1800s. When they finish reading, ask students to compare agricultural and industrial work.

2. INSTRUCT

Explain

Help students to visualize the differences between working in a small, owner-operated blacksmith shop in a small town before the Civil War and working as a blacksmith in one of Andrew Carnegie's steel plants. What sort of relationship did worker and employer have in the small smithy? How did industrialization change this relationship? How did the large supply of factory workers affect pay and conditions?

Discuss

Discuss with students why millions of workers migrated from the nation's farms and came from abroad to work in the great industries that developed after the Civil War. Ask why workers, including women and children, tolerated the poor pay and conditions of most industrial jobs.

Answer to ...

MAKING CONNECTIONS

Answers will vary but may include the following: Social Darwinism could have been used to justify the government's unwillingness to supply much public aid, because the theory holds that the "unfit" should be left to fail and that government support for them would interfere with the process in which only the fittest survive.

Cooperative Learning

Time: One class period.

Activity: Create a skit of a piece-work system.

Grouping: Groups of four to six students.

Purpose: Have small groups of students create a skit illustrating how a piecework system favors the employer. Each worker must perform a task, such as create a paper hat or airplane, chosen by the group. Provide the students with the following information to incorporate into their skits: pay per task accomplished, pay scale according to job held, marketability of the product, maintenance of quality control, evaluation of the product.

Roles: Assign workers, foreman or boss, manager, quality control supervisor, and factory owner.

Outcome: Students will portray the frustrations experienced by workers in a piecework system.

Enrichment

In the 1980s and early 1990s, American businesses began to imitate Japanese methods of motivating workers to produce quality products. Ask students to research such business trends as quality circles and worker empowerment and to compare them to management practices of the late 1800s.

3. ASSESS

Section 3 Review Answers

1. piecework, see p. 399

2. Most came for jobs.

3. The government did not have relief or public works programs to help the poor and jobless.

4. They used theories such as Taylor's and speeded up machines.

5. The statements suggest a view of workers as machines.

---

and activity. Workers hated and resisted Taylor's ideas because they imposed an outside control on the way they did their work. They also feared that any increased efficiency caused by Taylor's methods would result in layoffs or a lower rate of pay for each piece of work.

By the early years of the twentieth century, Taylor had used his studies as the basis of an entire system of so-called scientific management in which

> *The work of every workman is fully planned out by the management at least one day in advance, and each man receives in most cases complete written instructions, describing in detail the task which he is to accomplish, as well as the means to be used in doing the work . . . and the exact time allowed for doing it.*
>
> Frederick Winslow Taylor, *The Principles of Scientific Management*, 1911

Industrial growth created jobs for African Americans, though opportunities were limited. For example, these three men were hired for the low-paying job of carrying bricks. White men got the higher-paying jobs as masons.

Taylor's ideas were just one method of improving efficiency. Employers often increased the speed of factory machines or added to workers' loads, especially in hard times. Yet workers' pay did not increase, and their health and safety suffered. When a Fall River, Massachusetts, textile company increased the number of each worker's looms, one woman complained, "They gave us twelve looms, I didn't see that we could make it out alive at all." ✪

Hardships of Factory Work Bosses seldom visited the factory floor where their workers toiled. Workers seldom saw a finished product. Called hands or operatives, they were viewed as cogs in a huge system performing only a small piece of the system's work. One factory manager in 1883 declared,

> *I regard my people as I regard my machinery. So long as they can do my work for what I choose to pay them, I keep them, getting out of them all I can. What they do or how they fare outside my walls I don't know, nor do I consider it my business to know.*

Discipline was strict. A worker could be fined or fired for being late, answering back, refusing to do a task, talking, or other minor offenses. The work was boring, and the noise of the machines was deafening. Lighting and ventilation were poor. Fatigue, faulty equipment, and careless training resulted in frequent fires and accidents. In 1882, the average number of workers killed on the job each week was 675—compared with about 200 today. Worse, there was no system to provide income to workers injured on the job. The courts in the late 1800s held that a worker who sued an employer had to show that the employer was responsible for causing the injury. This was usually impossible.

✪ Despite the harsh conditions, employers suffered no shortage of labor. Thousands of Irish, German, and Italian immigrants, for example, built the Brooklyn Bridge. The nation's factories were likewise jammed with men, women, and children, many desperate for the opportunity to earn even meager wages.

 RESOURCE DIRECTORY ✪

Teaching Resources

✪ **Visual Learning Activity** The Noble Face of Labor, found in the Unit 5 folder, p. 29, features an excerpt from the U.S. Census of 1890 aimed at enhancing students' understanding of the demographics of the time.

Literature Activity The Stories of Horatio Alger, found in the Unit 5 folder, p. 26, uses excerpts from Alger's popular novels to extend students' understanding of the social effects of industrialization.

Industry's Impact on Women and Children

Employers in industry excluded women from the most skilled and highest-paid jobs. Of course, not all men had good jobs, either. But factory owners usually assigned women to the operation of simple machines. More complex machines required machinists and engineers. These were almost always men, for only they had access to training in such fields.

Women enjoyed almost no chances for advancement in factory work. In the garment industry, for example, running the machines that cut out patterns from large stacks of fabric was defined as a man's job. It paid much more than work reserved for women, which usually consisted of performing only one part of the process of sewing a garment.

Children also suffered in the factory system. Today, the use of child labor is strictly regulated by law. In the 1880s, however, children comprised over 5 percent of the industrial labor force. In many households, children's wages meant the difference between going hungry or having food on the table.

Growing children suffered especially from the hazards of the workplace. Working in unhealthful factories or mines, living on inadequate diets, and performing monotonous, dangerous work, many children became stunted in both body and mind. As social commentator Jacob Riis noted, such work left them

grown to manhood and womanhood, just where it found them, knowing no more, and therefore less, than when they began,

Many children went to work in factories and mines. This group of boys were employed in the dangerous, unhealthy work of coal mining. The grime that covers their faces also clogged their lungs, leading to disease.

and with the years that should have prepared them for life's work gone in hopeless and profitless drudgery.
    Jacob Riis, *Children of the Poor*, 1892

The practice of child labor would come under attack in the early 1900s. By 1912, three fourths of the states would have laws limiting the presence of children in the workplace.

SECTION 3 REVIEW

Key Terms, People, and Places
1. Describe piecework.

Key Concepts.
2. What was the reason that prompted most immigrants to come to the United States in the late 1800s?
3. What made life for working people so difficult in times of economic hardship?

4. What efforts did industrialists make to increase efficiency in factories?

Critical Thinking
5. **Identifying Central Issues** Review the quotations by Taylor and the factory manager in this section. What do their statements reveal about their views of working men and women?

Quiz found in the Unit 5 folder, p. 12, covers the main ideas in this section as well as the key terms.

Reteach

Using the graph on page 398 as a guide, ask students to explain how life changed for a worker in the late 1800s. Ask questions such as the following to prompt students: What types of activities were most workers involved in? Who made up the work force?

4. CLOSE

 Reinforcing the Big Idea

Millions of workers, drawn from the nation's farms and from abroad, worked in the great industries that developed after the Civil War. Workers were plentiful, pay was low, and working conditions were poor. The next section highlights the intensity of the strife between labor and management.

 In Depth

Interdisciplinary

Jacob Riis was a New York City police reporter who used his camera to document the squalid conditions of the working poor. Although newspapers lacked the equipment needed to print his photos, in 1888 the *New York Sun* published twelve drawings from his pictures. The photographs in his 1890 book *How the Other Half Lives* proved to be powerful tools in the campaign for social reform.

The Great Strikes: A Turning Point in History

The Great Strikes: A Turning Point in History

1. FOCUS

Connecting to the Big Idea

See page 384B. Explain to students that the late nineteenth century was a period of intense struggle between big business and workers. Workers organized themselves to change working conditions, while management did everything in its power to prevent their success. Explain to students that they will be examining how effective the labor unions formed in the late nineteenth century were in changing working conditions.

Objectives

● Explain why the gap between rich and poor widened in the late 1800s.
● Identify the aims of labor unions to improve workers' wages and working conditions.
● Describe how violent strikes marked relations between labor unions and business owners in the late 1800s.

Bellringer

Have students work in pairs to brainstorm several possible courses of action in the following situation: Workers at a fast-food restaurant are told on Monday that unless they agree to work four additional evening hours each week for no additional pay, they will be fired. As students read the section, have them circle any option that uses the concept of *collective bargaining* as defined on page 404.

Workers in many industries formed unions in the late 1800s.

SECTION PREVIEW

Many American workers sought relief from their difficult lives through labor unions. What they found in the late 1800s was strong resistance from big business and only fleeting success.

Key Concepts
• The gap between rich and poor widened in the late 1800s.
• Labor unions organized to improve the wages and working conditions of workers.
• Violent strikes marked relations between labor unions and business owners in the late 1800s.

Key Terms, People, and Places
socialism, collective bargaining, scab, anarchist; Pinkerton; Haymarket Square, Homestead, Pullman strike

I ndustrialization brought changes and great wealth to the United States. These changes, however, did not bring contentment or prosperity to the nation's working people. Indeed, as the rich grew richer during this era, these workers became increasingly bitter over their own daily struggle for a decent standard of living. During the last quarter of the nineteenth century, working men and women began to take their complaints directly and forcefully to their employers. The resulting turmoil marked a turning point in American history.

The Widening Gulf Between Rich and Poor

The 1890 census revealed that the richest 9 percent of Americans held nearly 75 percent of the national wealth. The nation's workers, however, did not need the census to tell them that they were poor. Able in the best of times to earn only a few hundred dollars a year, workers were well aware of how the elite lived, and they resented it. ❂

Poor families had little hope of relief when hard times hit. Some suffered in silence, trusting that tomorrow would be better; others became politically active in an effort to improve their difficult lives. A few of these individuals were drawn to the idea of socialism then gaining popularity in many European industrialized countries.

Socialism in the Industrial Age

Socialism is an economic and political philosophy that advocates collective or government ownership of factories and property. One goal of socialism is to distribute broadly a society's wealth. In the late 1800s, socialism was strongly influenced by the ideas of Karl Marx, a German philosopher who criticized the capitalist economic system and predicted its eventual overthrow by workers.

Endorsing socialism in the late 1800s was dangerous, however. Most Americans disagreed with socialist theory. They felt that socialism threatened the deeply rooted American ideals of private property and free enterprise—the right of people to compete freely and succeed to whatever extent they can. Most wealthy people also rejected socialism. They would not give up what they owned without a fight. Even though workers had numbers on their side, wealthy Americans knew that if workers tried to bring socialism to the United States by force, the federal government would respond with military action to preserve the nation's economic and political system.

▶ RESOURCE DIRECTORY

Teaching Resources

Reproducible Lesson Plan found in the Unit 5 folder, p. 6, provides a summary of the Section 4 lesson plan content.

Alternate Lesson Plan: Critical Thinking Determining Relevance, found in the Alternate Lesson Plans folder, p. 72, is designed to help students to apply this skill by using a classification system for arranging the section.

Guided Reading and Review found in the Unit 5 folder, p. 13, provides a structure for reading and mastering the key concepts and reviewing the key terms for Section 4. (Guided Practice)

❂ **Literature Activity** *Sister Carrie,* found in the Unit 5 folder, pp. 27–28, introduces students to factory life in the late 1800s with an excerpt from Theodore Dreiser's novel.

Using Historical Evidence Many workers lived in crowded boarding houses, such as the one shown at left. Many wealthy industrialists, on the other hand, enjoyed great personal wealth and luxurious comforts. *How would you expect workers to respond to the contrast between rich and poor?*

The Return of Labor Unions

Socialism itself never achieved a significant following in the United States in the nineteenth century. But the limited appeal of its themes did reflect a growing discontent among the nation's workers. Many of these men and women looked instead to labor unions as a way to improve their standard of living.

Early Labor Unions The early years of industrialization had spawned a few labor unions, organized among workers in certain trades, such as construction and textile manufacturing. But these early unions had not lasted long.

Unions resurfaced after the Civil War. These groups were initially designed to provide help for their members in bad times. Soon they became the means for channeling workers' demands for shorter workdays, higher wages, and better working conditions. The increasing emphasis on protest led to growing opposition to unions among employers.

Unions grew significantly in the 1860s and 1870s. Indeed, labor activists began trying to organize nationally based unions. One, the National Labor Union formed in Baltimore in

1866, nominated a candidate for the presidential election of 1872. This union, however, failed to survive an economic downturn that began the following year. Indeed, unions in general suffered a steep decline in membership as a result of the depression.

The Knights of Labor Another early national union, The Noble Order of the Knights of Labor, was formed in Philadelphia in 1869. The Knights hoped to organize virtually all working men and women into a single union. Membership included farmers, factory workers, and white-collar workers. The union actively recruited African Americans, of whom sixty thousand joined.

Under the dynamic leadership of former machinist Terence Powderly, the Knights pursued broad social reforms. These included equal pay for equal work, the eight-hour day, and an end to child labor.

The leadership of the Knights did not generally advocate the use of strikes, and they did not emphasize higher wages as their primary goal. The majority of members, however, often differed with the leadership. In fact, it was a strike that helped the Knights achieve their

Media and Technology

 Visions of America: Turning Point Story To enhance students' understanding of the Turning Point topic in this section, play "Company Town," a story about the Pullman Strike of 1894 (length: approximately 4 minutes). This selection can be located on side 2 of the videodiscs. This selection can also be located on videotape 3. Lesson plans for Turning Point stories can be found in the Visions of America Guidebook.

Visions of America: Roundtable Discussion To introduce students to different and differing viewpoints on the Turning Point topic in this section, play all or part of the Roundtable Discussion on "Company Town," remarks by respected historians and social commentators. This selection can be located on side 2 of the videodiscs. This selection can also be located on videotape 3.

Side 2, Chapter 17

Side 2, Chapter 18

Viewpoints

The labor leader wants more government protection for workers; the factory manager wants less government involvement with labor. For a more thorough examination of views about labor unions, see the Resource Directory below.

Discuss

Discuss with students how socialism, anarchism, and labor unions were all efforts to solve the problems of workers. Ask them to identify how socialism promised to improve the workers' lives. Then ask what American ideals run counter to the goals of socialism.

Ask students to describe public reaction to the incidents at Haymarket and Homestead. What pattern of events did the Pullman strike set in motion for many years to come?

Activity

Teaching Heterogeneous Groups

To enable all students to understand the different perspectives of the parties involved in labor disputes of the late nineteenth century, assign students the following roles: Pinkerton, scab, anarchist, laborer (skilled and unskilled), recent immigrant, business owner, union leader. Based on their reading, have students write a description of their roles and what they hope to achieve in an industrial dispute.

Enrichment

Ask students to research both socialism and Andrew Carnegie's theories of wealth. Then have them work in pairs to write a dialogue between a socialist and Andrew Carnegie, during which both discuss their beliefs about wealth.

TURNING POINTS

greatest strength. In 1885, when unions affiliated with the Knights forced railroad owner Jay Gould to give up a wage cut, membership quickly soared to 700,000. Yet a series of failed strikes quickly followed, dampening enthusiasm in the Knights. They had largely disappeared as a national force by the 1890s.

The American Federation of Labor A third national union, the American Federation of Labor (AFL) followed the leadership of Samuel Gompers, a London-born cigar maker. Formed in 1886, the AFL differed from the Knights of Labor by seeking to organize only skilled workers in a network of smaller unions, each devoted to a specific craft. Between 1886 and 1892, the AFL gained some 250,000 members. Yet they still represented only a tiny portion of the nation's labor force.

In theory the AFL was open to African Americans. Local unions, however, often found ways to exclude African Americans from their membership. Gompers also opposed women members because he believed that their participation in the work force drove wages down.

> We know to our regret that too often are wives, sisters and children brought into the factories and workshops only to reduce the wages and displace the labor of men—the heads of families.
>
> Samuel Gompers, *Labor and the Employer,* 1887

Gompers and the AFL were primarily interested in issues of wages, hours, and working conditions—so-called bread-and-butter unionism. They sought to force employers to participate in **collective bargaining,** in which workers nego-

---

Viewpoints
On Labor Unions

The Senate Committee on Education and Labor held a series of hearings concerning the relationships between workers and management in 1883. The committee heard these opposing views about the need for labor unions. *What is the major argument presented in each of the two viewpoints below?*

Testimony of a Labor Leader

"*The laws written* [by Congress] *and now in operation to protect the property of the capitalist and the moneyed class generally are almost innumerable, yet nothing has been done to protect the property of the workingmen, the only property that they possess, their working power, their savings bank, their school, and trades union.*"

Samuel Gompers, founder of the American Federation of Labor in 1886

Testimony of a Factory Manager

"*I think that. . .in a free country like this. . .it is perfectly safe for at least the lifetime of this generation to leave the question of how a man shall work, and how long he shall work, and what wages he shall get to himself.*"

Thomas L. Livermore, manager for the Amoskeag Manufacturing Company, Manchester, New Hampshire

---

tiate as a group with employers. The Federation believed that workers acting as a group had more power than a worker acting individually. To strengthen its collective bargaining power, the Federation advocated a "closed shop" that employed only Federation members.

Growing Friction Between Labor and Employers

Not surprisingly, employers disliked and feared unions. They preferred to deal with employees as individuals instead of in powerful groups. Employers took measures to stop unions, such as forbidding union meetings and firing union organizers. They even forced new employees to sign "yellow dog" contracts that exacted a promise never to join a union or to participate in a strike. Some business leaders refused to recognize unions as the workers' legitimate representatives. Wrote one company president:

RESOURCE DIRECTORY

Teaching Resources

Viewpoints Activity On Labor Unions, found in the Unit 5 folder, pp. 19–20, provides additional viewpoints and perspectives on the responsibilities of labor, business, and government in an industrial age.

Rights and interests of the laboring man will be protected and cared for—not by the labor agitators, but by the Christian men to whom God has given control of the property interests of the country.

George F. Baer, mining
company president, 1902

Unions, of course, demanded more than recognition. The competing interests of labor and employers would not be easily reconciled.

MAKING CONNECTIONS

Consider the statement above by George F. Baer. How does it relate to the idea of social Darwinism discussed in Section 2?

The Railroad Strike of 1877

The nation's first major episode of labor unrest occurred in the summer of 1877 in the railroad industry. The strike began when the Baltimore and Ohio Railroad announced a wage cut of 10 percent, the second cut in eight

months. Railroads elsewhere imposed similar cuts, along with orders to run "double headers," trains with two engines, twice as many cars—and an increased risk of accident and worker layoffs. Violent reactions against these moves among railway workers spread rapidly across Pennsylvania and Ohio and on to Chicago, Illinois, and St. Louis, Missouri. When the local militia in Pittsburgh refused to stop the unrest, employers called in troops from Philadelphia, who fired on the demonstrators, killing and wounding many. A crowd of twenty thousand angry men and women reacted to the shootings by setting fire to railroad company property. President Rutherford B. Hayes then sent in federal troops, a move that stopped the riots but caused more deaths.

From the 1877 strike on, employers relied on federal and state troops to repress labor unrest. A new and violent era in labor relations had begun.

Strikes Rock the Nation

The period 1881–1900 was one continuing industrial crisis in the United States. An amazing

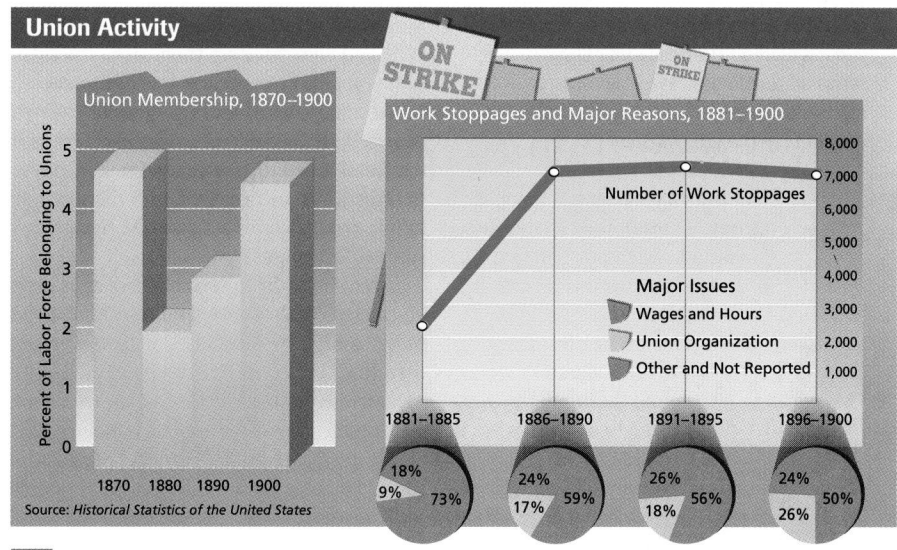

Union Activity

Interpreting Graphs
A severe economic depression helped cause a steep decline in union membership in the 1870s. But the 1880s and 1890s saw growth in the numbers of members and in work stoppages. *What trends can you identify in the causes of work stoppages in the late 1800s?*

 In Depth

Historical Misconceptions

Though the cost of manufactured consumer goods dropped because of industrialization, working-class women had difficulty affording these finished goods. Women's wages and advancement opportunities were far below those of men. African American women were even worse off, being excluded from most factory positions until World War I. Consider the average earnings of a working woman and the price of consumer goods: Factories paid the average woman worker $5 a week; department stores paid $2 a week plus 5 percent commission; and families paid domestic servants $3 a week plus board. A ready-made blouse cost $1, a skirt $2, and a pair of shoes $1.50. Carfare for sales clerks was a nickel each way, and a dormitory bed cost $2.50 a week.

24,000 strikes erupted in the nation's factories, mines, mills, and yards during those two decades alone. Out of this ongoing turmoil, three major incidents of industrial warfare overshadow the rest. ★

Haymarket, 1886 On May 1, 1886, several workers' groups mounted a national demonstration for an eight-hour work day. "Eight hours for work, eight hours for rest, eight hours for what we will," ran the cry. Strikes then broke out in a number of cities. At Chicago's McCormick reaper factory, police broke up a fight between strikers and **scabs,** strikebreakers who replace striking workers and allow a company to continue operating. The police action caused several casualties among the workers.

In protest, **anarchists** called a rally for the evening of May 4 in Chicago's **Haymarket Square.** Anarchists are political radicals who oppose all government on the grounds that it limits individual liberty and acts in the interests of the wealthy, ruling classes. In an effort to whip up the anger of the workers, anarchist newspaper editor August Spies wrote

You have endured the pangs of want and hunger; your children you have sacrificed to the factory-lords. In short, you have been miserable and obedient slaves all these years. Why? To satisfy the insatiable greed, to fill the coffers of your lazy thieving master!

At the May 4 event, someone threw a bomb into a police formation. Seven policemen died, and in the ensuing riot, police and citizen gunfire resulted in dozens of deaths on both sides. Investigators never found the bomb thrower, yet eight anarchists were tried for conspiracy to commit murder. Four were hanged. Another committed suicide in jail. In the belief that the convictions were the result of public hysteria rather than evidence, Governor John P. Altgeld of Illinois later pardoned the remaining three anarchists.

To many unionists, the Haymarket anarchists forever would be heroes. To employers, they remained vicious criminals determined to overthrow law and order. In many people's minds, unions were associated with violence and radical ideas. The Knights of Labor especially suffered from this public reaction.

Homestead, 1892 Continued labor unrest renewed fears of social revolution. It was in this environment that labor strife struck Andrew Carnegie's enterprise.

A union of iron and steel workers associated with the American Federation of Labor had negotiated a labor contract with Andrew Carnegie's steel company. In the summer of 1892, while Carnegie was in Europe, his partner Henry Frick tried to cut wages for company workers. The union at the Carnegie plant in **Homestead,** Pennsylvania, called a strike.

Frick, perhaps with Carnegie's support, was intent on crushing the union. On July 1, Frick called in the **Pinkertons,** a private police force known for its ability to break strikes. Under cover of darkness, three hundred Pinkertons moved up the Monongahela River on barges. When strikers fired on them from the shore, deaths and injuries occurred on both sides.

At first many Americans sympathized with the workers. Then anarchist Alexander Berkman tried and failed to assassinate Frick. Although Berkman was unconnected with the strike, the public associated his act with the rising tide of labor violence.

Eventually, the union acknowledged defeat and called off the strike. Homestead reopened under militia protection. "I will never recognize the Union, never, never!" Frick cried. Meanwhile, Carnegie, who had always claimed to support nonviolent unions, remained silent about the entire affair. Carnegie Steel and its successor (U.S. Steel) remained nonunionized until the mid-1930s.

Pullman, 1894 Like the strike of 1877, the last of the great strikes also involved the railroad industry. This strike also completed a turning

The violence of the Haymarket incident, depicted here, troubled many Americans.

In Depth

Then and Now

In the late 1800s workers injured on the job had no recourse. As the country became more industrialized, worksite accidents became inevitable. Maryland passed the first state compensation law in 1902, but the Supreme Court declared that law, and all compensation laws of that era, unconstitutional. The first state compensation law to be held constitutional, that of Wisconsin, was enacted in 1911. By the end of that year ten states had passed workers' compensation laws. Today, all states have programs, financed by employers, which provide injured workers with both medical and financial benefits.

RESOURCE DIRECTORY

Teaching Resources

★ **American Profiles Activity** found in the Unit 5 folder, p. 17, profiles Mary Kenney O'Sullivan, who campaigned for legislation to regulate and improve working conditions in factories.

point in the federal government's involvement with labor-employer relations.

Sleeping-car maker George Pullman considered himself one of the era's most benevolent industrialists. He built a town for his workers near Chicago that boasted a school, bank, water and gas systems, and comfortable homes.

Conditions in the town, however, took a turn for the worse during a depression in 1893. Pullman laid off workers and cut wages 25 to 40 percent. Meanwhile, he kept rent and food prices in his town at the same levels. In May 1894, a delegation of workers went to him to protest. Pullman's response was to fire three of the workers. When the American Railway Union called a strike, Pullman refused to negotiate and shut down the plant.

The founder of the American Railway Union was Eugene V. Debs, a popular labor organizer from Indiana. By June 1894, Debs had encouraged 120,000 railway workers throughout the region to join in the **Pullman strike.** Though Debs had instructed strikers not to interfere with the nation's mail, the strike led to the complete disruption of western railroad traffic, including the delivery of the mail.

Railroad owners turned to the federal government for help. Arguing that the mail had to get through—and citing the Sherman Antitrust Act—Attorney General Richard Olney won court orders forbidding all union activity that halted railroad traffic. President Grover Cleveland sent in troops to ensure that strikers obeyed the court orders. Twelve deaths and many arrests resulted from ensuing violence.

Debs, who refused to obey the court orders, was jailed for six months. Its leadership in disarray, the American Railway Union and its strike fell apart.

The Pullman strike and its outcome set an important pattern. In the years ahead, factory owners appealed frequently for court orders against unions. The federal government regularly responded to these appeals, denying unions recognition as legally protected organizations. This official government opposition helped limit union gains for over thirty years.

Eugene Debs was a tremendously successful labor organizer in the late 1800s. Later, Debs would combine his energetic style and his belief in socialism to conduct several unsuccessful presidential campaigns as the leader of the Socialist party.

TURNING POINTS

SECTION 4 REVIEW

Key Terms, People, and Places
1. Identify (a) socialism, (b) scab, (c) anarchist, (d) collective bargaining.
2. Identify (a) the Pinkertons, (b) Haymarket Square, (c) Homestead, (d) Pullman strike.

Key Concepts
3. How did industrial growth in the late 1800s affect the distribution of wealth?

4. Explain the purpose and goals of labor unions.
5. How successful were labor unions in the late 1800s?

Critical Thinking
6. **Recognizing Bias** Many labor unions did not include or effectively represent the concerns of women or minorities. What does this fact suggest about their view of worker rights?

 Quiz found in the Unit 5 folder, p. 14, covers the main ideas in this section as well as the key terms.

 Chapter Test Forms A and B are found in the Unit 5 folder, pp. 31–36.

 Answer Keys found in the Unit 5 folder, pp. 149–164, provide answers to all student activities.

Media and Technology

Transparency
Graphic Organizer, G-5

Guided Reading Audiotapes
(English and Spanish)

Computer Test Bank

---

3. ASSESS

Section 4 Review Answers

1. (a) socialism, see p. 402, (b) scab, see p. 406, (c) anarchist, see p. 406, (d) collective bargaining, see p. 404

2. (a) Pinkertons, see p. 406, (b) Haymarket, see p. 406, (c) Homestead, see p. 406, (d) Pullman strike, see p. 407

3. Wealth was heavily concentrated in the hands of a few.

4. Labor unions sought strength in numbers. Their goals included improving workers' wages and working conditions.

5. Labor was generally not successful in the large strikes of the late 1800s.

6. These policies reflect a belief that white men were superior to women and minorities and therefore deserved to have their rights protected first.

Reteach

Ask students to create a two-column chart with the title Labor Movement. Have them label the first column Causes and the second Effects. Under the appropriate column have students list the causes and effects of the development of the labor movement in the 1800s.

4. CLOSE

 Reinforcing the Big Idea

The industrial growth in the late 1800s resulted in a more uneven distribution of wealth, with a widening gap between rich industrialists and poor laborers. Although unions were organized to improve workers' conditions, opposition from employers resulted in violent strikes and enormous suffering.

The Lasting Impact of the Great Strikes

Focus The Great Strikes of the late 1800s caused the federal government to intervene in business-labor disputes, a change from its former "hands off" policy. Since that time, the government has regularly set guidelines and policies for unions and businesses. At the turn of the century, government policy favored business; at other times, government action furthered the cause of labor. Ask students what the lasting impact of government intervention in business-labor disputes has been.

Instruct Divide the class into two groups. Assign one group the year 1890 and the other the year 1990. Ask each group to decide the probable government policy for that date in the following hypothetical situation: The nation's electrical workers go out on strike seeking higher wages and stricter safety regulations. Some other unions, including transportation and communications workers, strike in sympathy with the electrical workers. Soon the nation's communications and transportation will be at a standstill. How does the government act to help resolve the situation?

Review with students the reasons that federal policy began to favor workers during the Great Depression and moved to restrict union activity in the late 1940s.

Ask students to work in small groups to discuss what they consider the ideal government approach to business-labor disputes. Should government policy favor one side or the other? Is a perfectly balanced approach possible or desirable? What do people do if they do not agree with the government's labor policy?

The Lasting Impact of the Great Strikes

The federal government adopted a hands-off approach to business and its relations with its employees throughout much of the 1800s. By the turn of the century, however, government had become a central player in the ongoing struggle between business and labor unions.

The Great Strikes of the late 1800s marked the turning point for this fundamental change in government policy. Since that time, the federal government has regularly involved itself in business-labor relations. The government's position has been either more probusiness or prolabor, depending on the changing circumstances of the day. Over time, while supporting law and order, it has tried more and more often to encourage the two sides to negotiate their grievances.

After the Great Strikes

After the strikes of the late 1800s, many business owners felt little need to deal with unions. They were confident that in the event of labor unrest, government would come to their aid with guns or court orders. Labor, meanwhile, continued its struggle without any government protection. Unions enjoyed no legal right to strike, picket, bargain collectively, or recruit members without interference or threat of losing their jobs.

Some employers did conclude that it was better to work with unions than to fight them. Most, however, remained hostile, while continuing to enjoy the support of the federal government for the first three decades of the twentieth century.

1903 Unions such as the Women's Trade Union of Chicago receive little support from the federal government—or from male-dominated unions.

1932 As the economy crumbles and millions lose their jobs, the government begins to consider offering more support to workers.

| 1900 | 1920 | 1940 |

1935 With President Roosevelt's support, the Wagner Act is passed, guaranteeing workers' rights to join unions and bargain collectively.

 RESOURCE DIRECTORY

Teaching Resources

Turning Point Extension Activity The Lasting Impact of the Great Strikes, found in the Unit 5 folder, pp. 15–16, aims to extend students' understanding of the long-term impact of the Great Strikes by contrasting the views of labor and business, and profiling a case study of a business today.

How the Depression, the New Deal, and World War II Affected Labor

In the 1930s, the federal government again intervened in labor-business relations. Now, however, government took a more prolabor position.

The Great Depression of the 1930s had a deep impact on American attitudes toward business and labor. Sympathy for the cause of labor—and distrust of business—increased among the public and in the federal government. In 1932, Congress passed the Norris-LaGuardia Act, which included provisions that limited the power of the federal courts when acting against unions.

President Franklin Roosevelt's administration also passed several prolabor laws. The most significant was the Wagner Act of 1935, which protected labor's right to organize and to bargain collectively. After more than thirty years of hostility, the federal government was now officially recognizing unions as legitimate organizations.

The federal government again adjusted its position on labor issues following World War II. Postwar prosperity in the United States led labor to seek a greater share of the nation's wealth. The result was a record number of strikes, which aroused national concern. In 1947, the Taft-Hartley Act introduced a number of new restrictions on union activity. For example, the law set guidelines for government response to strikes that involved matters of public health and safety.

Government and Labor in Recent Years

In recent years, the federal government has continued to regulate and monitor the activities of labor unions. In 1981, President Ronald Reagan ordered the firing of striking members of the Professional Air Traffic Controllers Organization, whose walkout violated federal law. And, in the late 1980s, the Justice Department pursued racketeering charges against the Teamsters' Union in response to allegations of widespread corruption and links to organized crime in that union. In settling the charges in 1989, the Teamsters agreed to reform the process by which the union elects its leaders.

REVIEWING THE FACTS

1. For what reason did business choose not to negotiate with unions in the early 1900s?
2. What events helped shape government's approach to labor in the 1900s?

Critical Thinking

3. **Making Comparisons** Summarize the difference between the federal government's approach to labor in 1900 and today.

1947 Unions seek a greater share of the enormous postwar prosperity in a wave of strikes. Congress passes Taft-Hartley Act to curb union power.

1960 **1980** **2000**

1962 President John F. Kennedy issues an executive order that protects federal employees' right to organize and bargain collectively, but not to strike.

1993 The Teamsters union hopes to begin a new era following settlement of its dispute with the federal government over charges of corruption.

Understanding Key Terms, People, and Places

Terms
Students should refer to the definitions of the key terms in the chapter to write sentences that show the relation of each word to technology or to the rise of big business in the late 1800s.

Matching
1. social Darwinism
2. monopoly
3. cartel
4. piecework
5. socialism

True or False
1. true
2. false, Andrew Carnegie
3. false, Homestead
4. true
5. false, Thomas Edison

Reviewing Main Ideas

1. (a) He helped make electricity more widely available, invented the phonograph, perfected the light bulb, and developed the idea of the central power station. (b) He helped make home use of electricity practical and developed more efficient air brakes for trains. (c) He created the first telephone and set up the American Telephone and Telegraph Company.

2. Problems included inconvenient schedules, lack of comfort, and distrust and fear of train travel. Developments included replacement of iron rails with steel, standardization of track gauges and signals, improved safety through more effective air brakes, and a telegraph system for intertrain communication.

3. During the late 1800s, businesses pooled their money and resources, creating giant conglomerates such as American Telephone and Telegraph, General Electric, and Westinghouse.

4. Industrialists increased the availability of goods, provided jobs, and endowed cultural institutions. On the other hand, many were ruthless and corrupt, using any means available to gain control over the competition.

5. Although conglomerates of companies were managed as a single unit, they were not legally merged and thus violated no laws.

6. Workers immigrated from abroad in search of better opportunities. They also migrated from the nation's farms.

Chapter Review

Understanding Key Terms, People, and Places

Key Terms
1. transcontinental railroad
2. Brooklyn Bridge
3. social Darwinism
4. monopoly
5. cartel
6. trust
7. horizontal consolidation
8. vertical consolidation
9. economy of scale
10. piecework
11. socialism
12. collective bargaining
13. scab
14. anarchist

People
15. Thomas A. Edison
16. Alexander Graham Bell
17. Andrew Carnegie
18. Pinkerton

Places
19. Haymarket Square
20. Homestead
21. Pullman strike

Terms For each term above, write a sentence that explains its relation to the technological revolution or the rise of big business in the late 1800s.

Matching Review the key terms in the list above. If you are not sure of a term's meaning, review its definition in the chapter. Then choose a term from the list that best matches each description below.
1. the theory that society should not interfere with the process by which people succeed and fail
2. the result of a business buying out all of its competitors
3. loose associations created by businesses making the same product
4. a system by which employers pay workers a fixed amount for each piece they produce
5. an economic and political philosophy that advocates collective or government ownership of factories

True or False Determine whether each statement is true or false. If it is true, write "true." If it is false, change the underlined person or place to make the statement true.
1. Layoffs and a drop in wages led to the <u>Pullman strike</u> near Chicago.
2. <u>Thomas A. Edison</u> lowered his prices, drove competitors out of business, took control of the steel industry, and then devoted himself to philanthropy.
3. When Henry Frick cut wages at the Carnegie steel plant in <u>Pinkerton</u>, Pennsylvania, the union responded by calling a strike.
4. Violence erupted in Chicago's <u>Haymarket Square</u> when someone threw a bomb during a rally to support striking workers.
5. <u>Alexander Graham Bell</u> set up an "invention" factory in New Jersey.

Reviewing Main Ideas

Section 1 (pp. 386–391)
1. How did each of the following contribute to the technological revolution of the late 1800s: (a) Thomas A. Edison, (b) George Westinghouse, (c) Alexander Graham Bell.
2. Describe the problems that existed on the early railroads and five developments that helped solve them.

Section 2 (pp. 393–397)
3. Explain what is meant by the age of big business.
4. Describe how industrialists could be seen as both captains of industry and robber barons.
5. How did Samuel Dodd's idea of the trust get around laws against monopolies?

Section 3 (pp. 398–401)
6. The growth of industry depended on the movement of millions of people to the nation's industrial centers. Where did most of these workers come from?
7. How did the growth of industry affect women's lives?
8. What were some of the hazards faced by factory workers in the late 1800s?

Section 4 (pp. 402–407)
9. Describe the growth of early labor unions.
10. How did the federal government respond to the Great Strikes of the late 1800s?
11. How did the federal government respond to unions in the years following the Pullman strike?

---

7. It made women's lives harder. In addition to devoting long hours to caring for their families, many women worked in factories, with almost no chance of advancement.

8. Conditions in factories were often unsafe due to inadequate lighting and ventilation, faulty equipment, and improper training. These conditions led to numerous accidents and deaths.

9. The first unions were "brotherhoods" or "orders" designed to help members through bad times. Later unions such as the Knights of Labor helped workers demand better conditions.

10. After the Great Strikes, the government remained opposed to unions for over thirty years.

11. The federal government responded to appeals for court orders by factory owners against labor unions. Unions were denied recognition as legally protected organizations.

Thinking Critically

1. Answers will vary. Students should mention the impact of television, computers, and other electronic inventions. Post–Civil War innovations include the widespread use of electricity, the telegraph, telephones, and typewriters.

Final Evaluation
Use the following guidelines to evaluate students' projects:
● Note how extensively they address the main points of discussion.
● Ask students to rate their own projects in terms of clarity, depth, and presentation.

Students may wish to include finished projects in their portfolios.

Thinking Critically

1. **Making Comparisons** How have the inventions of the past thirty years changed daily life for you? Imagine that it is the year 1900. How have the inventions since the Civil War changed your daily life?

2. **Identifying Assumptions** During the late 1800s, many people began to associate labor unions with violence and radical political ideas. Why did people make this association?

Making Connections

1. **Evaluating Primary Sources** Review the first primary source excerpt on page 394. How does Finley Peter Dunne ridicule Andrew Carnegie's actions as a philanthropist? What underlying concern is being expressed?

2. **Understanding the Visuals** Choose two visuals from the chapter that demonstrate the inequality of labor and business in the late 1800s and explain why you think they demonstrate the point.

3. **Writing About the Chapter** It is 1900. Write a letter to the editor of your local newspaper. Describe the harsh conditions endured by factory workers and recommend changes that factory owners and the government could make that would help improve conditions. First, choose several examples from the chapter that document the difficult life of the factory worker. Then, list some possible improvements. Next, write a draft of your letter, in which you offer

your evidence and your suggestions. Revise your letter, making sure that you have expressed your points clearly and forcefully. Proofread your work and draft a final copy.

4. **Using the Graphic Organizer** This graphic organizer uses a multi-flow map to organize information about the friction between labor and employers in the late 1800s. Multi-flow maps can show the causes and effects of events in history. In this map, the box on the left shows the major cause of unrest, and the boxes on the right show the effects. (a) Based on what you have read in the chapter, why did labor unions grow significantly in the 1860s and 1870s? (b) Based on the multi-flow map, what were the effects of the railroad strike of 1877? (c) On a separate sheet of paper, create your own graphic organizer about the technological revolution using this graphic organizer as an example.

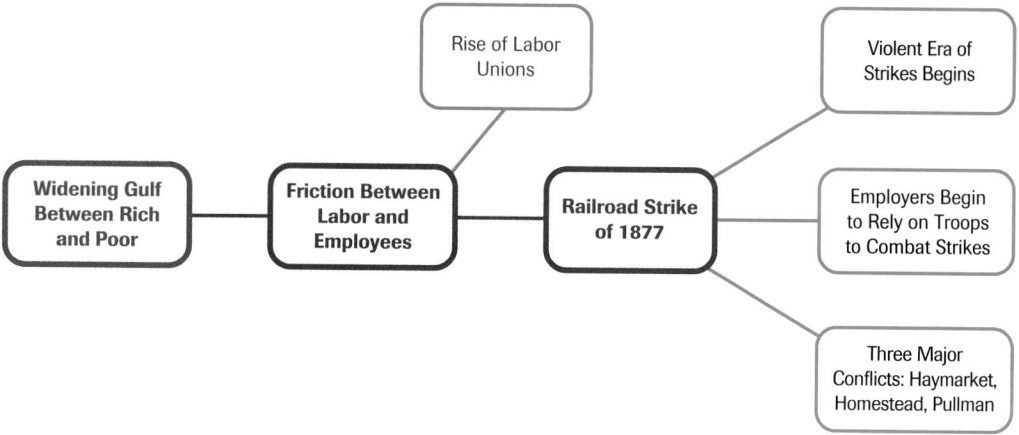

Rise of Labor Unions

Widening Gulf Between Rich and Poor → Friction Between Labor and Employees → Railroad Strike of 1877

Violent Era of Strikes Begins

Employers Begin to Rely on Troops to Combat Strikes

Three Major Conflicts: Haymarket, Homestead, Pullman

2. The public began to equate labor unions in general with the specific actions and violence of anarchists during some labor disputes. Although this violence turned many people against unions, of course not all strikes became violent.

Making Connections

1. Dunne shows Carnegie as appearing to be generous but completely failing to understand the poor man's needs.

2. Students may choose any photographs, drawings, or paintings that demonstrate the harsh conditions under which employees worked and lived in the late 1800s (pages 389, 391, 399, 401, 403) and the comfortable lives of business leaders (pages 394, 403).

Their explanation should show an understanding of the workers' plight and the growing tension of the era.

3. Students' letters should reflect an understanding of factory workers' grievances and possible solutions to their problems. Instruments of change may include: unionization, collective bargaining, and government regulation of wages and working conditions.

4. (a) The increasing disparity of wealth between the rich and poor and the spread of socialist ideals led many workers to organize and join unions. (b) The widening gulf between the rich and poor; friction between labor and management. (c) Students' organizers should include the conditions which made the technological revolution possible.

Chapter 15 Looking to the West
1860–1900

📁 Teaching Resources (See Unit 5 Folder)

	Instruction	Enrichment
Section 1 **Moving West** (pp. 414–417)	Reproducible Lesson Plan, p. 38 Alternate Lesson Plan, p. 74 Guided Reading and Review, p. 43 Quiz, p. 44	Critical Thinking Activity, Formulating Questions, p. 60 Primary Source Activity, African American Settlers, p. 61
Section 2 **The Conquest of the Native Americans** (pp. 418–421)	Reproducible Lesson Plan, p. 39 Alternate Lesson Plan, p. 75 Guided Reading and Review, p. 45 Quiz, p. 46	Visual Learning Activity, Western Expansion into Native American Land, p. 67 Primary Source Activity, Talks with Otoe Chiefs, pp. 62–63 Viewpoints Activity, On Land Use, pp. 57–58
Section 3 **Modernizing, Mining, and Ranching** (pp. 422–425)	Reproducible Lesson Plan, p. 40 Alternate Lesson Plan, p. 76 Guided Reading and Review, p. 47 Quiz, p. 48	Literature Activity, The Californian's Tale, pp. 64–66 Time and Place Activity, The Growth of the Suburbs, pp. 53–54
Section 4 **Populism** (pp. 428–432)	Reproducible Lesson Plan, p. 41 Alternate Lesson Plan, p. 77 Guided Reading and Review, p. 49 Quiz, p. 50	American Profiles Activity, Mary Elizabeth Lease, p. 55 Visual Learning Activity, The Farmers' Complaint, p. 68 Historian's Toolbox Activity, Drawing Conclusions About NAFTA, p. 59
Section 5 **Frontier Myths** (pp. 434–437)	Reproducible Lesson Plan, p. 42 Alternate Lesson Plan, p. 78 Guided Reading and Review, p. 51 Quiz, p. 52 Chapter Test, Forms A & B, pp. 69–74	American Profiles Activity, Nat Love (alias Deadwood Dick), p. 56

📁 Additional Chapter Resources

Resource Organizer, p. 37
Alternate Lesson Plan, p. 73
Answer Keys, pp. 149–164

Bibliography

For the Teacher

Moynihan, Ruth B., Susan Armitage, and Christiane Fischer Dichamp, eds. *So Much to Be Done: Women Settlers on the Mining and Ranching Frontier.* University of Nebraska Press, 1990. (Nineteen narratives by women from diverse environments and backgrounds in the nineteenth-century West.)

Unruh, John D., Jr. *The Overland Emigrants and the Trans-Mississippi West, 1840–60.* University of Illinois Press, 1993. (Reissue of a prizewinning account of the opening of the Oregon Trail.)

Prentice Hall Literature Excerpts from *The American Experience,* 1994, including Twain, Mark. *Life on the Mississippi.* HarperCollins, 1939 edition.

THE BIG IDEA

The Big Idea for the chapter and how the main ideas in each section relate to the Big Idea are graphically displayed below. Comprehension of this chapter's Big Idea is critical to students' understanding of United States history and how we as a nation got where we are today.

Media and Technology

 Critical Thinking, I-5; The Way It Works, H-15

 Cause and Effect, F-4

 Graphic Organizer, G-3

 Guided Reading Audiotapes (English and Spanish)

 Computer Test Bank

For the Student

Time-Life Books Editors. *Time-Life Books: The Old West.* Prentice Hall, 1990. (A richly illustrated companion volume to a ten-hour miniseries, *Faces and Voices of the Wild West.*)

"The Donner Party." KCTS Video, 90 minutes. (Part of the PBS series, *The American Experience;* an ill-fated journey west.)

Dakota Wars and Reservation Life. University of Nebraska. Film. (Depicts the lives of Native Americans of the Plains and their wars, including Custer's last stand.)

CHAPTER 15

After the Civil War, Americans moved west of the Mississippi River, taking over the land for farms, ranches, and mines, and forcing out the original users, the Native Americans. The taming of the West became one of the great American myths.

SECTION 1

American settlers and European immigrants braved the hardships of life on western farms, hoping to build new lives.

SECTION 2

Much of the land in the West claimed by settlers was actually the homeland of Native American groups that had used it for centuries. Native Americans were not only forced off their lands but also lost much of their culture and tradition.

SECTION 3

Mechanized farming made agriculture a "big business" in the West. Mining and ranching were also big businesses, dominated by industrialists who made big investments in their holdings and in modern equipment and tools.

SECTION 4

As farm incomes continued a slow decline, many western farmers protested against tariffs and monopolies and in favor of free silver. The Populist party included many of the farmers' demands in its program.

SECTION 5

Inaccurate as many of the great myths of the Old West were, they exerted a deep influence on the nation in many ways and still affect Americans today.

Looking to the West
1860–1900

The Relevance of the Big Idea

During the trans-Mississippi westward movement (1840s–1880s), popular culture tended to mythologize events and people. The triumph of good over evil was usually the central theme. Reports of cheap land, romance, gold mines and golden sunsets, blaring bugles and blazing guns, courage, and "heathen savages" prompted some people to venture west and see for themselves. Ask students to describe evidence of this theme based on "the West" they've seen on television, in movies, or books.

Have students look for mythical figures or institutions in contemporary society. What is their image of various sports figures, rock stars, and television or movie actors? How accurate do they feel the image is? Where do students find evidence today of the theme of good triumphing over evil?

In Depth

Global Connections

As the American frontier moved to the West, there were similar expansions in Africa whose effects reverberated into the next century. In South Africa, gold was discovered in 1886. By 1900 the gold mines employed 100,000 workers. Johannesburg, which had about a hundred inhabitants in 1885, had over 237,000 by 1910.

Looking to the West
1860–1900

After the Civil War, Americans accelerated their conquest of the lands west of the Mississippi River. The story of that conquest is one of hard-working farm and ranch families and determined miners. It is a tale of the bravery of those who left all behind to try a new life and of the difficulty of working the dry land. Born of these weighty realities, however, is an American myth. This myth focuses on only white Americans and ignores the story of the realized hopes of some African Americans and Asians—and the crushed hopes of others. It also ignores the tragic tale of those from whom the West was taken—the tale of the near destruction of Native American people and their cultures.

Events in the United States

1862 Congress passes the Morrill Land-Grant Act and the Homestead Act to give away public land.

1866 Oliver H. Kelly founds the Grange, an organization for farmers.

1874 Gold lures miners to Dakota's Black Hills.
• J. Glidden invents barbed wire.

1860	1864	1868	1872	1876

Events in the World

1861 Charles Dickens publishes Great Expectations.

1868 Imperial capital of Japan moves to Tokyo.
• Bones of Cro-Magnon are found in France.

 RESOURCE DIRECTORY

Teaching Resources

Alternate Lesson Plan: Demonstrating the Big Idea found in the Alternate Lesson Plans folder, p. 73, provides a strategy designed to instruct students in the Big Idea that settlement of the American West provided opportunity for many, but at the expense of the Native Americans.

Alternative Assessment Handbook provides information, guidance, and strategies for alternative methods of assessment. It includes an essay on new trends in assessment, guidance and strategies for developing performance tasks and portfolios, scoring rubrics, and sample evaluation forms.

Pages 414–417
Moving West

The West promised new opportunities for those who would brave its loneliness and hardships. Though settlers often found more toil than wealth in the West, many found freedoms unavailable to them elsewhere.

Pages 418–421
The Conquest of the Native Americans

Western settlers thought they were building a new life in a new land. But the land was not new at all. Much of it was ancient homeland to a number of Native American groups.

Pages 422–425
Modernization, Mining, and Ranching

The West was home for thousands of years to Native Americans. But modern farming methods, discovery of mineral deposits, and ranching soon made the West attractive to many others, including big business.

Pages 428–432
Populism

By the late 1800s, American farmers were feeding the nation and the world, yet they were increasingly concerned about feeding themselves. Declining incomes created fertile ground for a farmers' protest.

Pages 434–437
Frontier Myths

From modern rodeos to cowboy boots to novels immortalizing the prairie farmer, the wild West captures the imagination. But this image leaves out many other experiences that also helped shape the nation.

1881 Helen Hunt Jackson publishes A Century of Dishonor, protesting Native Americans' treatment.

1885 Annie Oakley joins Buffalo Bill's "Wild West" show.
• Unauthorized fencing of public land is outlawed.

1889 The federal government opens Indian Territory to settlers.

1893 Frederick Jackson Turner delivers the "Turner Thesis."
• Colorado adopts women's suffrage.

1900 Congress passes a gold standard.

| 1880 | 1884 | 1888 | 1892 | 1896 | 1900 |

1880 Rodin's sculpture The Thinker is exhibited.
• Chile begins war with Bolivia and Peru.

1885 Belgian king Leopold II takes possession of the Congo in Africa.

1891 Famine strikes Russia.

1898 Marie and Pierre Curie discover radium and introduce the term radioactivity.

Media and Technology

Transparencies
Time Lines, E-5; Our Multicultural Heritage, C-2

Alternative Assessment

As an ongoing chapter project, students can demonstrate an understanding of the "conquest" of the West and its lingering myths by comparing those myths with reality. Students should identify myths and the stereotypes that exist today, and provide contrasting realistic examples of frontier life. Projects may include material on the homesteaders and farmers, the Native Americans, big business, ranchers, or miners. Projects may be designed in a variety of ways. Suggestions follow, but students may decide on an original format.

● Write an essay responding to the definition of the West by poet Archibald MacLeish as "a state of mind."

● Present a poster talk or oral report illustrated by drawings, charts, or other pictures.

● Prepare and present a videotape or slide show with commentary, contrasting images of myth and reality.

Explain that finished projects will be assessed by the following standards:

● **Unacceptable** Projects are not attempted or fail to meet requirements outlined.

● **Limited/Acceptable** Projects are based on material from the textbook, present some aspects of life in the West, and demonstrate a limited understanding of the differences between the myth of the West and reality.

● **Extensive/Commendable** Projects are based on outside research, present a fairly complete view of aspects of life in the West, and demonstrate an understanding of the reasons for the creation of the myth.

● **Extraordinary/Outstanding** Projects are based on considerable outside research, present an extensive view of aspects of life in the West, and demonstrate a strong understanding of the significance of the frontier myth in American life.

For information and guidance on alternative assessment strategies, see the Alternative Assessment Handbook in the Resource Directory on page 412.

1. FOCUS

Connecting to the Big Idea

See page 412B. Tell students that after the Civil War, large numbers of Americans and Europeans continued to move into "the West," the area between the settled West Coast and the Mississippi River. Ask students what these people hoped to find.

Objectives

- Identify big business as controlling much of the land in the West.
- Explain how settlers obtained land.
- Describe the unique opportunities offered to women and African Americans in the West.
- Describe the difficult work and cooperation demanded of settlers.

Bellringer

Ask students what they would do if they were moving to another part of the country. What difficulties would they face in leaving their old home and in settling into a new one? Why might they want to face these difficulties?

In Depth

Historical Misconceptions

The hard work and rugged individualism of the American frontier were all that many new settlers believed it would take to succeed as a homesteader. This did not take into account, however, the cruel wiles of nature. In the 1890s severe drought gripped Nebraska and the shortage of water caused suffering and loss. One impoverished sod-house dweller said, "We've been here for four years now. We thought we'd have a chance to own a [timber] house . . . but we've never had a single good crop in all that time."

Moving West

SECTION PREVIEW

The West promised new opportunities for those who would brave its loneliness and hardships. Though settlers often found more toil than wealth in the West, many found freedoms unavailable to them elsewhere.

Key Concepts

- Big business controlled much of the land in the West.
- Settlers from the United States acquired land in the West from big business or government grants.
- Women and African Americans found unique opportunities in the West.
- Life in the West meant difficult work and required cooperation among settlers.

Key Terms, People, and Places

Morrill Land-Grant Act, speculators, Homestead Act; Exodusters

Only the settlers' most cherished possessions made the trip west.

A s the nation swelled with new inventions and businesses during the late 1800s, it also expanded across the continent. The story of this expansion is one of rugged frontier families, big businesses, and bold individuals who were willing to take a chance on the unknown.

Seeking Opportunity in the West

By the Civil War, Americans already had settled areas west of the Mississippi and along parts of the West Coast. Following the war, they began filling in the areas in between—the Great Plains, the Pacific Northwest, the Southwest. To most people in the United States, this land was "the West."

Americans and Europeans wanted to settle in the West for many reasons. Most hoped for a new start in life—a chance to own a farm and be their own boss, a goal that seemed increasingly unattainable in the East. Others were fleeing racial prejudice or, for some Europeans, compulsory military service in their homelands. 🟊

Big Business Takes Its Share Much of the western lands to which people were flocking belonged to big businesses—railroad, road and canal, timber, and mining companies. These companies had received huge grants of land from the federal government and made a profit from selling the land to others. When the railroads sold to farmers who worked the land and needed to transport their goods to the cities, the railroads profited even more.

To lure settlers, companies sent agents to Europe who spoke glowingly of immigration to the United States. Businesses also sent out imaginative ads, many of which stretched the truth. One brochure from a western land office falsely described Dakota as a paradise where

mocking birds and gorgeous paroquets [parakeets] and cockatoos warble musical challenges to each other amid the rich foliage of the sweet-bay and mango trees.

Disposing of Government Lands Settlers also bought land as a result of the **Morrill Land-Grant Act** of 1862. This act, plus various other land grants, gave 140 million acres of western lands to state governments. States could then sell the land to fund agricultural colleges. The states sold their land grants at fifty cents an acre to bankers and land **speculators,** people who bought up large areas of land in the hope of later selling it for a profit. Indeed, when settlers began to move westward and demand for land increased, speculators could sell their holdings at five to ten dollars an acre.

The government also gave land directly to settlers through the 1862 **Homestead Act.** This act offered American citizens and immigrants

---

RESOURCE DIRECTORY

Teaching Resources

Reproducible Lesson Plan found in the Unit 5 folder, p. 38, provides a summary of the Section 1 lesson plan content.

Alternate Lesson Plan: Critical Thinking Distinguishing False from Accurate Images, found in the Alternate Lesson Plans folder, p. 74, is designed to help students apply this skill by writing letters from different points of view.

Guided Reading and Review found in the Unit 5 folder, p. 43, provides a structure for reading and mastering the key concepts and reviewing the key terms for Section 1. (Guided Practice)

🟊 **Critical Thinking Activity** Formulating Questions, found in the Unit 5 folder, p. 60, extends students' application of this skill by having them compose questions on immigration from Europe to the United States.

who planned to be citizens 160 acres of public land each for a ten-dollar registration fee. After building a house and living and farming on the land for five consecutive years, the settler could claim ownership.

Thousands of homesteaders benefited from the Homestead Act. Many others, however, could not afford the filing fees, the expense of moving to and setting up a homestead, and the costs of farm machinery. Moreover, most city folk had no farming experience. In the end, experienced farm families migrating from nearby states or from Europe were the most likely homesteaders. Even they had trouble finding good claims near transportation—necessary if they were going to ship their goods to market—for the government gave the railroads much of the land near their tracks. Speculators controlled many other desirable lands.

The Homestead Act also was plagued by fraud. The goal of the act was to give land to people who would then live on it. To prove continuous residence, the government required homesteaders to build permanent shelters on their claims. But speculators simply wheeled portable cabins from plot to plot or built miniature shelters on several plots and then filed phony claims. Land office agents seldom verified them, as distances were too great. Besides, they made their living from the filing fees that those who staked claims were required to pay.

By 1900, individual homesteading families had filed 600,000 claims for 80 million acres. Meanwhile, over six times as much public land had gone to business interests.

Opportunity for African Americans

 Some homesteaders went West to escape violence and exploitation. In the late 1870s, southern African Americans planned a mass "Exodus," similar to the biblical account of the Israelites' flight from Egypt to the promised land. For this reason, these settlers called themselves **Exodusters.** At an 1875 meeting of ministers in New Orleans, one Georgia preacher elaborated on what the African American settlers hoped to find farther north:

Homesteading gave people a chance to become landowners—a dream that had been beyond the reach of most African Americans in the South and East.

Primary Source Activity African American Settlers, found in the Unit 5 folder, p. 61, uses a letter from African Americans wishing to settle in Kansas to extend students' understanding of the status of African Americans in the East.

Media and Technology

Transparency
Critical Thinking, I-5

(Nebraska), or Cheyenne (Wyoming). To make the best decision, the group must study physical, climate, and rainfall maps.

Roles: Have students assume the following responsibilities: physical map and atlas researcher, climate researcher, rainfall researcher, collator, and reporter.

Outcome: Students will learn about the decisions made by homesteaders as they prepared to go West.

Enrichment

Ask students to compare and contrast the following views of the Great Plains in an essay.

Beret, a Norwegian immigrant in O. E. Rolvaag's novel *Giants in the Earth*, reacts to the stillness and bareness of the Great Plains: "How *could* existence go on, she thought desperately. If life is to thrive and endure, it must at least have something to hide behind!"

Chief Ten Bears, a Comanche from Texas, speaks to a group of government commissioners:

"I was born upon the prairie, where the wind blew free and there was nothing to break the light of the sun." [Quoted in *I Have Spoken: American History Through the Voices of the Indians*, compiled by Virginia Irving Armstrong, Ohio U. Press, 1971.]

3. ASSESS

Section 1 Review Answers

1. speculators, see p. 414

2. (a) Morrill Land-Grant Act, see p. 414, (b) Homestead Act, see p. 414, (c) Exodusters, see p. 415

3. Big businesses—railroad, road and canal, timber, and mining companies—controlled most of the land in the West.

Breaking and turning the thick sod was hard work.

Homesteaders burned dried buffalo or cattle dung, corn cobs and stalks, even bundles of grass to keep warm.

Sod also covered the roof, which leaked terribly.

Wind was an abundant energy source. Homesteaders often built windmills to power their water pumps.

All grown members of the household worked the gardens and fields.

Three-foot strips of sod—"Nebraska marble"—were stacked to make the walls.

Soddies were filthy inside. Bugs and mice were frequent visitors.

Wells could be several hundred feet deep.

The geography of the West made homesteading a challenge. Timber was often scarce, so settlers built their first shelters out of the endless expanse of sod. The idea for the "soddy" was borrowed from Native American groups of the region.

We will get what we make, our crops or their value . . . ; and may not have to work on the railroad or levees in chain gangs when we are not guilty of any crime, and not to be whipped as if we were dumb brutes; not hated because we are black.

Life was not easy for the almost fifty thousand Exodusters who migrated to Kansas. Some came with money and property, but many did not. Even after finding work, only a few earned enough for a homestead. For those who did, winters were harsher than in the South, and the resettled farmers lacked experience with the crops, such as wheat and corn, widely grown in Kansas. In addition, the Exodusters could not completely escape racial hatred: Kansas, like other western lands, had an active Ku Klux Klan. In spite of these difficulties, Exodusters with farming skills managed to make a living and in general met with better treatment than they had in the South.

Cooperation in the West

In the West, obtaining even the basic necessities could be a struggle. If settlers were not near water, they had to use buckets or cisterns to collect rainwater for drinking, bathing, and cooking. Such water supplies often carried "prairie fever" or typhoid, so wells were preferable. But until the 1880s, when well-digging machinery became available, settlers had to dig by hand, and groundwater generally lay much deeper in the West than in the East.

Working the tough prairie sod also required backbreaking labor. Even after that work was done, men often had to travel far afield to earn cash for their families' survival while they waited for their crops to come in. Meanwhile,

Teaching Resources

women produced most of the articles that families needed, such as clothing, soap, candles, dairy products, and preserved foods. Wrote homesteader Mary Henderson of Oklahoma of her work on a single day, "I made sausage, rendered lard, molded 4 lbs. butter, halfsoled 3 pairs of shoes, and tonight had to iron [daughter] Agnes a dress."

Settlers relied heavily on each other as they built new communities from the ground up. Families cooperated in raising houses and barns, sewing quilts, husking corn, and providing many other forms of support. "Occasionally a new comer has a 'bee'," noted Howard Ruede about his experience on a Kansas homestead in 1877,

The neighbors for miles around gather at his claim and put up his house in a day. Of course there is no charge for labor in such cases. The women come too, and while the men lay up the sod walls, they prepare dinner for the crowd, and have a very sociable hour at noon.

MAKING CONNECTIONS

You have read about the cooperation among homesteaders in the West. Can you identify and describe similar examples of cooperation in your community today?

A Frontier for Women

Although most homesteaders went West as families, women were able to file claims on their own. Homesteading alone—whether by a man or a woman—was an enormous challenge. Some people, however, such as Wyoming settler Elinore Pruitt Stewart, saw great benefits in the challenge.

It really requires less strength and labor to raise plenty to satisfy a large family than it does to go out to wash, with the added satisfaction of knowing that their job will not be lost to them if they care to keep it. . . . Whatever is raised is the homesteader's own, and there is no house-rent to pay.
Letters of a Woman Homesteader, 1909

Even for those women who were married, the requirements for getting land through homesteading—continuous residence on a claim for five years—often meant long periods of solitude. Such lonely experiences increased western women's eagerness for opportunities outside the home. Some western women campaigned to improve women's professional opportunities, in areas such as business, medicine, and law.

Western women launched successful city and state campaigns for the vote. In 1887 two Kansas towns, Syracuse and Argonia, passed woman suffrage. Syracuse then elected an all-female town council, and Argonia the nation's first female mayor. By 1914, women were voting in eleven states, all but one of which (Illinois) were west of the Mississippi.

For American settlers in the West, hard work was a small price to pay for the opportunity to build a new future. The homesteaders' opportunity, however, represented a threat to Native Americans there.

SECTION 1 REVIEW

Key Terms, People, and Places
1. Describe speculators.
2. Identify (a) Morrill Land-Grant Act, (b) Homestead Act, (c) Exodusters.

Key Concepts
3. What group controlled most of the land in the West?
4. How did Americans acquire lands in the West?

5. Describe some of the hardships homesteaders endured.

Critical Thinking
6. **Distinguishing False from Accurate Images** In your opinion, was the West a land of opportunity? Cite information from the section to support your answer.

 Quiz found in the Unit 5 folder, p. 44, covers the main ideas in this section as well as the key terms.

Media and Technology

 Transparency
The Way It Works, H-15

4. Settlers bought lands from large corporations, who had either bought them from existing state governments or received them as grants from the federal government in return for promises to build on them. Settlers also bought lands directly from the federal government through the Homestead Act.

5. They lived in sod houses and had difficulty finding water; men had to leave home to earn cash, and women had to provide all day-to-day needs. For all settlers, work never stopped.

6. Answers will vary but may include the following: The West gave unique opportunities to people around the world to own farms. It also provided opportunities for African Americans and women that were largely unavailable elsewhere. On the other hand, many of the opportunities of the West were controlled by big business.

Answer to ...

MAKING CONNECTIONS

Answers will vary depending on location and experiences. Encourage students to investigate local organizations for examples of similar occurrences in their own community.

Reteach

Ask students to use the information in the section to answer each of the following questions in one or two sentences:
- *Who* moved to the West?
- *What* was a homestead?
- *Where* did the Exodusters settle?
- *Why* did settlers need to cooperate with one another?
- *How* did women build new opportunities in the West?

4. CLOSE

Reinforcing the Big Idea

Homesteaders and other settlers moved to the West hoping to build new lives. The next section tells about the end of the Native American way of life in the West.

The Conquest of the Native Americans

SECTION 2

The Conquest of the Native Americans

1. FOCUS

Connecting to the Big Idea

See page 412B. Explain that as settlers from both the eastern United States and Europe poured into the West, they took up land that had been home to Native Americans for many generations. Ask students what happened to the Native Americans of the West when the settlers moved in.

Objectives

• Explain how American expansion into the West led to the near destruction of the Native American nations there.

• Explain how reformers seeking to "civilize" surviving Native Americans nearly caused the total loss of their culture and traditions.

Bellringer

Ask students to read Lord Bryce's observation on page 421 under Viewpoints. Ask students to identify what they think might be the effect of such a policy on the land used by the Native Americans.

Reading Strategy

Reinforcing Key Ideas Ask students to write two column headings on a piece of paper: Military Defeats and Cultural Destruction. Have them make notes in the appropriate column as they read the section about the conquest of the Native Americans of the West.

The late 1800s brought the destruction of many vibrant Native American cultures. This war shirt is made of deer hide, cloth, and fur.

SECTION PREVIEW

Western settlers thought they were building a new life in a new land. But the land was not new at all. Much of it was ancient homeland to a number of Native American groups.

Key Concepts

• American expansion into the West led to the near destruction of the Native American nations there.

• When reformers sought to "civilize" surviving Native Americans, their cultures and traditions were all but lost.

Key Terms, People, and Places

squatter, boomer, sooner; George Armstrong Custer, Chief Sitting Bull, Chief Joseph; Wounded Knee

---

For generations, many Americans have envisioned the West as a wild, empty expanse, freely available to those brave enough to tame it. But the West was not empty. Others had laid claim to it centuries before.

The Second Native American Removal

In the 1830s, President Jackson removed Native American groups living in the East to lands west of the Mississippi. By the end of the Civil War, the remaining Native Americans on United States land lived throughout the Great Plains and the West. Others were crowded into Indian Territory in present-day Oklahoma.

Following the Civil War, the railroads began pushing their way deeper into the West. With each rail laid, the Native Americans' chances for survival became bleaker. The Plains soon swarmed with settlers, many of whom felt justified in taking Native American lands because they could produce more food and wealth than did the Native Americans.

Many Native Americans, on the other hand, saw the oncoming settlers as invaders. They wanted to continue to live off their lands as they had for centuries, preserving long-held customs and honoring ancient burial grounds.

A Pattern of Conflict

When settlers from the East began to move westward in the mid-1800s, some Native Americans did not find the newcomers threatening and initiated friendly contacts. Others, however, resisted violently. Many groups, realizing that they were outgunned and outnumbered, signed treaties that sold their lands and accepted federal government demands that they live within reservations set aside for them.

But many of these agreements fell apart, sometimes because not all the members of a group supported them. In addition, Native Americans' and settlers' concepts of owning land differed. When Native Americans signed treaties, they often did not realize that settlers would not let them continue using the land. Isolated acts of violence on both sides set off cycles of revenge and counter-revenge. ✪

The Final Destruction One by one, Native American groups fell. (See the map at right and the Illustrated Data Bank in the reference section.) From the 1860s to the 1880s, the Navaho and the Apache of the Southwest were forced onto reservations, starved, or killed in battle. In the 1860s and 1870s, the Cheyenne were destroyed. The first blow came in 1864, with

---

RESOURCE DIRECTORY

Teaching Resources

Reproducible Lesson Plan found in the Unit 5 folder, p. 39, provides a summary of the Section 2 lesson plan content.

Alternate Lesson Plan: Learning Styles found in the Alternate Lesson Plans folder, p. 75, is especially effective for auditory learners and is designed to help students debate and discuss the conquest of the Native Americans.

Guided Reading and Review found in the Unit 5 folder, p. 45, provides a structure for reading and mastering the key concepts and reviewing the key terms for Section 2. (Guided Practice)

✪ **Visual Learning Activity** Western Expansion into Native American Land, found in the Unit 5 folder, p. 67, uses an 1874 *Harper's Weekly* illustration of a Native American confronting a white settler to enhance students' understanding of the impact of mass media on public opinion.

Colonel John M. Chivington's massacre of men, women, and children in a peaceful village at Sand Creek in present-day Colorado. Some reports put the number of dead as high as 450. After two more wars in 1868 and 1876, the Cheyenne finally surrendered in 1877.

Sitting Bull and the Fall of the Sioux One of the leaders in the destruction of the Cheyenne was Lieutenant Colonel **George Armstrong Custer**. Following that encounter, Custer turned to the Sioux people living in what is now South Dakota. A number of these Sioux had joined **Chief Sitting Bull** and left their Black Hills reservation. In June 1876, Custer moved his cavalry toward the Little Bighorn River in what is now Montana. There he met a larger-than-expected Sioux force. In the clash that followed—the Battle of Little Bighorn—

Custer and the unit he commanded were all killed. Sitting Bull became a fugitive, finally returning to a Sioux reservation five years later.

Following Sitting Bull's death, soldiers of the Seventh Cavalry tried to arrest a group of the chief's followers in 1890. While this was taking place, someone fired a shot. The soldiers then opened fire, killing over two hundred unarmed Sioux in what later became known as the massacre at **Wounded Knee**.

AMERICAN PROFILES
Chief Joseph

The Nez Percé inhabited a large area in what is now Idaho and the eastern sections of Washington and Oregon. In the 1850s and 1860s, some Nez Percé signed treaties agreeing

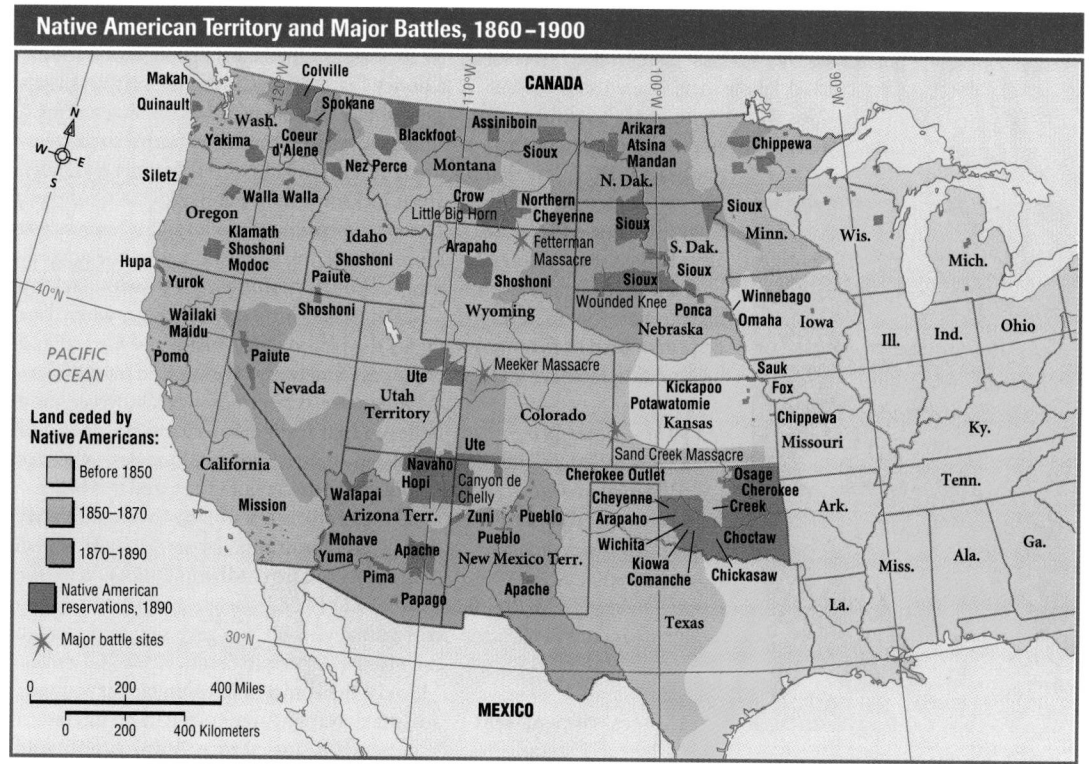

Native American Territory and Major Battles, 1860–1900

Land ceded by Native Americans:
- Before 1850
- 1850–1870
- 1870–1890
- Native American reservations, 1890
- ★ Major battle sites

0   200   400 Miles
0   200   400 Kilometers

Geography and History: Interpreting Maps
Though Native Americans won occasional victories in isolated battles, they were vastly outnumbered and defeat was sure to follow. *What pattern can you see in the location of the remaining Native American reservations in 1890?*

Caption Answer to ...

 Interpreting Maps

Most of the reservation land is located in the central portion of the continent. Much of this was land that American settlers were not interested in.

2. INSTRUCT

Discuss

Discuss with students some of the rationalizations used to justify taking Native American territory and violating agreements made with Native American groups. Ask students to respond to each rationalization.
- White settlers produced more food and wealth for the country.
- White settlers needed to exact revenge for settlers and soldiers killed by Native Americans.
- Native Americans should be concentrated on a few reservations for their own safety.

In Depth
Multicultural Perspectives

The town of Wounded Knee has become a continuing symbol of Native American suffering. In March 1973, more than two hundred members of the American Indian Movement (AIM) seized the trading post at Wounded Knee in an attempt to draw national attention to their platform. AIM leaders wanted reforms in the tribal government and demanded Senate hearings on United States treaties with Native American nations. In response, federal law officers surrounded the area. "You have here," said one government official, "an arguable case of treason." The AIM occupation ended in surrender to the federal authorities, but it mobilized other Native American groups and focused attention on recovering title to their tribal territories. (See page 839.)

Analyze

Ask students to consider the practical results of dividing Native American land into separate plots. What was the effect of the homesteading rush by boomers and sooners in 1889?

Activity

Biographical Sketches

Ask students to write a brief biography of one of the following Native American leaders of the West: Red Cloud, Sitting Bull, Black Kettle, Crazy Horse, Cochise, or Geronimo. Ask students to include the leader's dates and, if possible, a quotation.

Enrichment

Ask students to research to find several illustrations of the Battle of Little Bighorn. Ask them to examine the illustrations and accompanying captions. Have students compare the viewpoints of different illustrators of this historic battle.

3. ASSESS

Section 2 Review Answers

1. (a) George Armstrong Custer, see p. 419, (b) Chief Sitting Bull, see p. 419, (c) Chief Joseph, see p. 420, (d) Wounded Knee, see p. 419

2. (a) squatter, see p. 421, (b) boomer, see p. 421, (c) sooner, see p. 421

3. It brought thousands more white settlers a year to the West.

4. American settlers wanted Native American lands. Broken treaties and acts of violence led to the arrival of federal troops and the extermination of masses of Native Americans.

5. Sooners sneaked in before being officially allowed entry. Settlement by boomers and sooners led to the eventual dominance of the territory (later Oklahoma) by American settlers.

to sell their lands to the government. But the largest group, which lived in the Wallowa Valley at the crossroads of the three states, refused. As the chief of this group lay dying in 1871, he made his son and successor, Joseph, swear never to sell their homeland.

Fulfilling that promise proved impossible. After pressuring **Chief Joseph** (1840–1904) for five years, General Oliver Otis Howard finally ordered him and his people to leave Wallowa Valley for a reservation in Idaho. Faced with the threat of superior force, Chief Joseph felt he must give in. Before he could do so, however, a group of Nez Percé youths attacked some settlers who had been accused of stealing Nez Percé horses. The Nez Percé and the United States government were now at war.

Chief Joseph wanted to stay and fight, but his advisory council thought that they could escape. Pursued by soldiers, the Nez Percé fled. Eventually, Chief Joseph's group reached Montana. Exhausted, they set up camp at Big Hole Basin, but in a surprise 4:30 A.M. raid, United States soldiers attacked, killing men, women, and children.

The Nez Percé who escaped looked to Canada as their last hope for freedom. On September 30, 1877, less than forty miles from Canada, Colonel Nelson Miles's cavalry charged them. Heavily outnumbered, Chief Joseph had no choice but to surrender. "I am tired of fighting," he is reported to have said.

> *T*he old men are dead. The children are freezing to death. Hear me, my chiefs! My heart is sick and sad. From where the sun now stands, I will fight no more forever.
> Chief Joseph, 1877

The government sent Chief Joseph's people to Indian Territory. There, due to heat and malaria, many more Nez Percé died,

Chief Joseph led his Nez Percé on a dramatic flight from United States troops. To his great sadness, he never returned to his homeland.

including all of Joseph's children. In 1885 Chief Joseph and the remaining Nez Percé were allowed to leave the territory for a reservation in present-day Washington state, but the federal government did not allow them to return to their beloved Wallowa Valley.

The Destruction of Native American Cultures

As United States soldiers defeated Native American groups, many aspects of Native American cultures also disappeared. The peoples of the Great Plains, for example, relied on the buffalo for food, clothing, shelter, fuel, and tools. By the 1870s, the great buffalo herds began to disappear, hunted by the railroads to feed their workers and by settlers to clear the range, to satisfy a craze for hides, and for sport. The federal government encouraged the slaughter to wipe out the Plains peoples' food supply, a policy that later destroyed the Native Americans' ability to build new lives on reservations. ✪

Some white Americans found such treatment horrifying. Inspired in part by Helen Hunt Jackson's 1881 publication *A Century of Dishonor*, a national "Indian rights" movement arose. Protesting what she saw as the government's broken promises and treaties, Jackson said, "It makes little difference . . . where one opens the record of the history of the Indians; every page and every year has its dark stain."

As sincere as reformers were, however, most believed that Native Americans needed to be "civilized." Christian missionaries, who ran schools on the reservations, shared this belief.

Other reformers sought to break Native American traditions by requiring Native Americans to farm individual plots. With the Dawes Act of 1887, the government broke up communal villages and gave separate plots to each Native American family headed by a male. Much of the land was not suitable for farming, and many Native Americans had no interest or experience in agriculture. Many simply sold their lands to speculators: between 1887 and 1934, the amount of land owned by Native Americans shrank by 65 percent.

▶ RESOURCE DIRECTORY

Teaching Resources

✪ **Primary Source Activity** Talks with Otoe Chiefs, found in the Unit 5 folder, pp. 62–63, illustrates the United States government's treatment of Native Americans with a transcript of a meeting between Otoe chiefs and the U.S. Commissioner of Indian Affairs.

Does the reformers' desire to "civilize" Native Americans reveal a bias? If so, what is the bias?

The Fate of Indian Territory

Relocation into Indian Territory had been difficult for the nearly seventy groups who were removed there, but worse was to come. Following the Civil War, a flood of whites began to enter the territory. Some worked for Native American landowners as tenants or sharecroppers. Others were **squatters,** people who move onto land that does not belong to them.

Although Native Americans protested and the government tried to stop them, squatters continued to come. Other would-be settlers—so-called **boomers**—pressured Congress to allow legal settlement in the territory. In 1889 Congress responded, opening for homesteading nearly two million acres of lands in Indian Territory that had not yet been assigned to Native Americans. At noon on April 22, soldiers signaled with their pistols and hundreds of homesteaders, called **sooners** if they had sneaked in earlier, rushed across the border to stake claims.

Along the line as far as the eye could reach, with a shout and a yell the swift riders shot out, then followed the light buggies or wagons and last the lumbering prairie schooner and freighters' wagons, with here and there even a man on a bicycle and many too on foot,—above all a

great cloud of dust hovering like smoke over a battlefield.

Newspaper Reporter, 1889

As a result of pressures bearing on Native Americans in the late 1800s, many native populations disappeared. Others survived, slowly increasing their numbers and restoring the memory and practice of their customs.

Viewpoints
On Land Use

As more and more settlers pushed into the West, it became clear that they and the Native Americans held different attitudes toward the land. **Which of the attitudes expressed below do you think is more common today?**

Respecting the Environment

"The ground says, The Great Spirit has placed me here to produce all that grows on me, trees and fruit. The same way the ground says, It was from me man was made. The Great Spirit, in placing men on the earth, desired them to take good care of the ground and to do each other no harm."
— Young Chief of the Cayuse, on opposing selling land in Washington Territory, 1855

Conquering the Environment

"To open the greatest number of mines and extract the greatest quantity of ore, to scatter cattle over a thousand hills, to turn the flower-spangled prairies . . . into wheatfields, . . . to force from nature the most she can be made to yield . . . is preached by Western newspapers as a kind of religion."
— Britain's Lord James Bryce, after visiting the American West in the 1880s

---

Key Terms, People, and Places

1. Identify (a) George Armstrong Custer, (b) Chief Sitting Bull, (c) Chief Joseph, (d) Wounded Knee.
2. Define (a) squatter, (b) boomer, (c) sooner.

Key Concepts

3. How did the extension of the railroad increase the pressure on Native American lands?
4. Why and how did the "second great removal" occur?

5. What was the result of the decision to allow settlement in Indian Territory?

Critical Thinking

6. **Distinguishing False from Accurate Images** Many people in the mid-1800s believed that Native Americans used their land "only" for hunting and subsistence farming. Find information from the text to prove that this belief was untrue.

Viewpoints Activity On Land Use, found in the Unit 5 folder, pp. 57–58, provides additional viewpoints and perspectives on the issue of land use in the nineteenth century.

Quiz found in the Unit 5 folder, p. 46, covers the main ideas in this section as well as the key terms.

---

6. Possible answers: Land represented more than a means of producing food. Native Americans revered their lands as ancestral burial grounds. Communal living on the land was a means of maintaining tribal solidarity and social order for some groups.

Answer to . . .

Viewpoints

Environmentalists and ecological supporters may agree with Young Chief of the Cayuse; developers and businesspeople may support the views of those people quoted by Lord Bryce. For a more thorough examination of the land use issues, see the Resource Directory below.

Answer to . . .

Possible answers: The desire to "civilize" Native Americans is biased, because it is based on the idea that the Native Americans will be better off if they acquire the habits and ways of the reformers.

Reteach

Ask students to rewrite the following incorrect statements:

• In the massacres at Sand Creek and Wounded Knee, Native Americans killed large numbers of United States cavalry.
• Reformers thought that Native Americans should farm individual plots to earn money and become "civilized."

4. CLOSE

Reinforcing the Big Idea

The Native Americans of the West lost access to traditional hunting lands and their traditions, as settlers forced their way onto their lands and reform laws broke up their holdings. The next section describes how technological advances and industry transformed the West yet again.

1. FOCUS

Connecting to the Big Idea

See page 412B. Point out that big business was attracted to the Great Plains by opportunities in mechanized farming, mining, and ranching. Ask students how developments in these areas changed the West.

Objectives

● Explain how modernization, mechanization, and big business methods transformed agriculture in the West.
● Identify opportunities provided by mining and ranching.
● Explain how big business came to dominate the mining and ranching industries.

Bellringer

Write the words *modernization* and *mechanization* on the chalkboard. Ask students to think about the positive and negative effects of these processes.

Reading Strategy

Reinforcing Key Ideas Ask students to write three column headings on a piece of paper: Farming, Mining, and Ranching. Ask students to note in the appropriate column as they read how each of these industries had changed by the late 1800s.

Caption Answer to ...

 Interpreting Tables

Approximately twenty times.

Modernization, Mining, and Ranching

SECTION PREVIEW

The West was home for thousands of years to Native Americans. But modern farming methods, discovery of mineral deposits, and ranching soon made the West attractive to many others, including big business.

Key Concepts
• Modernization, mechanization, and "big business" methods transformed agriculture in the West.
• Mining and ranching in the West and Southwest provided opportunities for some.
• Big business practices came to dominate mining and ranching industries.

American ranchers borrowed techniques and equipment—such as these spurs—from Mexicans of the Southwest.

Key Terms, People, and Places
bonanza farms, cash crops, long drive

The spread of the United States into the West involved many challenges. Two stand out. The first was coming to terms with the native populations already living there, which Americans achieved by conquest. The second challenge lay in making the land fruitful. Inventors and industrialists solved this problem and reaped great riches as a result.

Modernization of Farming on the Great Plains

Despite the misinformation sent out by western land offices and the railroads, the Great Plains was not a farmer's paradise. Rainfall was unpredictable, and never enough. Tough prairie grass, which had thick roots that plunged deep into the earth, plagued farmers who struggled to break its iron grip on the soil. Grasshoppers, locusts, and boll weevils ruined crops and destroyed property. But the same inventiveness that had helped spur industrial expansion in the East helped overcome such difficulties in the West.

Mechanization on the Farm In many of the best farming areas of the East, 80 acres of farmland could provide a farmer with a living. Because the dry climate in parts of the West reduced the land's productivity, a farmer there needed 360 acres—one reason for the Homestead Act's limited success. Because western farms had to be so large, farmers welcomed any mechanical means to reduce the time and effort needed to work the land.

During the 1870s, improvements in farm implements multiplied. Soon farmers were riding behind a plow and plowing several furrows at once. Other inventions included harrows equipped with spring teeth that dislodged debris and automatic drills to spread grain. By 1880, farmers were using automatic grain binders and, later, a "header" drawn by six horses, which cut off the heads of standing grain. Steam-powered threshers arrived on the scene by 1875 and cornhuskers and cornbinders by the 1890s.

Manual vs. Mechanical Harvesting		
Method	Hours Required Per Acre Per Person	Maximum Acreage Harvested
Manual	61	7.5
Mechanical	3	135

 Interpreting Tables
Mechanization meant a dramatic increase in the amount of crop a worker could harvest. *By what factor did mechanization reduce the amount of labor necessary for harvesting?*

▶ RESOURCE DIRECTORY

Teaching Resources

Reproducible Lesson Plan found in the Unit 5 folder, p. 40, provides a summary of the Section 3 lesson plan content.

Alternate Lesson Plan: Critical Thinking Recognizing Cause and Effect, found in the Alternate Lesson Plans folder, p. 76, enhances students' application of this skill by charting causes and consequences of changes in mining, ranching, and farming.

Guided Reading and Review found in the Unit 5 folder, p. 47, provides a structure for reading and mastering the key concepts and reviewing the key terms for Section 3. (Guided Practice)

Irrigation Then and Now

In the late 1800s, some homesteaders in the dry regions of the United States used wind-driven pumps to draw water from the ground. The water was then fed into ditches and out onto their fields. Many farmers in the same regions today use enormous systems that draw water from deep in the earth. The quarter-mile-long arms of these sprinklers rotate like the hands of a clock, creating a large irrigated area. *How have such technologies increased the productivity of the land?*

Agricultural Knowledge Grows Congress established the Department of Agriculture in 1862 as part of the Morrill Land-Grant Act. In the 1880s and 1890s, the department was gathering statistics on markets, crops, and diseases that affected agriculture. It set up divisions to study forestry, the animal and dairy industries, and fruit and vegetable growing.

Working together, government agricultural departments and agricultural colleges funded the work of experiment stations and held institutes that offered entertainment and inspiration to farm families. They also published materials that explained crop rotation, hybridization (the crossing of different plants to produce new varieties), and the preservation of water and topsoil.

The Big Business of "Bonanza" Farms New machines and agricultural knowledge in the late 1800s increased enormously the amount a farm could produce (see chart on page 422). Entrepreneurs who owned large areas of land now hoped to reap a "bonanza" by supplying food to the rising populations of the East. They began applying to farming the same organizational ideas then taking hold in industry. As one observer noted,

> It is no longer left to the small farmer, taking up 160 acres of land, building a log cabin and struggling to secure himself a home. Organized capital is being employed in the work, with all the advantages which organization implies. Companies and partnerships are formed for the cultivation precisely as they are for building railroads, manufactures, etc.
>
> Commercial and Financial
> Chronicle, 1879

Bonanza farms—farms controlled by large businesses and managed by professionals—promised enormous profits to investors. They specialized in single **cash crops** raised for and readily sold at market. But these farms had their down side, as well. When the market became glutted with the enormous quantities of food they produced, prices fell. Small-scale farmers suffered the most, but even corporate giants felt the blow.

By the late 1800s, machines such as those shown in this detail from an advertisement of the time performed many harvesting tasks.

2. INSTRUCT

Explain/Discuss

Explain why a large farm might succeed where a small farm could not. The cost of plowing, planting, and harvesting is not so much greater for a large farm than for a small farm. A farmer has to spend much the same time planning and marketing a crop. Discuss the positive and negative aspects of mechanized farming for farmers.

Explain that during the mining boom, thousands rushed out to claim their fortune. Miners crossed racial barriers and brought enormous energy to their settlements in the West. In the long run, however, the mining frontier existed because of big business. Discuss how only a big business could afford to excavate ore and ship it out.

Analyze

Ask students what allowed the ranching frontier to flourish. What caused its decline?

Activity
Role-Play

Divide the class into groups, assigning two groups each to the farming frontier, the mining frontier, and the ranching frontier. Select one group in each category as a success and the other as a failure. Each group must work out the reasons for its success or failure to present in a skit.

Enrichment

Ask students to research and write an essay about the "romantic" days of the cowboy and the long trail.

3. ASSESS

Section 3 Review Answers

1. (a) cash crops, see p. 423, (b) long drive, see p. 425

2. Mechanized means for cultivation and harvesting were introduced. Also, government and agricultural colleges provided research for new cultivation techniques.

3. They were large-scale farms owned by corporations, run according to systems, and managed by professionals.

4. Machines were costly. Once farmers invested in them, they had to produce the crop for which the machines were designed. When prices for that crop declined, farmers went into debt. Machines also contributed to unemployment for agricultural workers.

5. Only a few became rich. Most riches from America's mines went to large corporations, which alone could afford the costs of deep mining operations.

6. It became a big business in which the average worker did not have much of an opportunity to prosper. The industry declined as a result of falling prices and environmental factors.

7. Possible answers: Mechanization increased productivity. High production also caused price declines that hurt farmers. Mechanization also reduced the need for farm labor, increased start-up costs for farmers, and necessitated crop specialization.

Reteach

Ask students to correct each of the following statements:
- Once they had the proper equipment, small farmers prospered on the Great Plains.
- Big business played a minor role in the mining frontier, where individual prospectors worked to strike it rich.

The Impact of New Farm Machinery Grain binders, threshers, and the like did not always lead to prosperity for farmers. Machines could not protect farmers against insect plagues or bad weather. Moreover, once farmers had invested in machines, they had to produce only the crop for which the machines were designed. If prices for that crop dipped, farmers could not pay off their debts. Such dips in prices were a common problem for many farmers. Wheat, for example, sold at $2.06 a bushel in 1866. By 1895 it had dropped to 51 cents. Even bonanza farmers suffered.

MAKING CONNECTIONS

Can you think of other inventions during the late 1800s that had negative, as well as positive, effects on people?

Boom and Bust Strike the Mining Frontier

⭐ "Gold!" The word alone conjures up the image of a lucky prospector striking it rich. In reality, such individuals were rare and largely a phenomenon of short rushes, such as the California gold rush of 1849. By the late 1850s and early 1860s, most of the precious metals that remained in the West lay deeply buried. Only huge companies could afford the large investments in machinery, mine shafts, and tunnels required to reach these riches.

It is unlikely that this man struck it rich panning for gold. Far more successful were those who "mined the miners," or sold goods to the fortune-seekers.

"Pikes Peak or Bust!" Still, thousands kept coming. In 1859, rumors of gold strikes in the area of Pikes Peak, Colorado, brought on a stampede of wagons with the words "Pikes Peak or Bust!" scrawled on their sides. Also in 1859, Nevada's famed "Comstock Lode," a large silver strike, brought on another rush. Gold and silver strikes throughout the West lured thousands of fortune hunters over the next several years. One of the later strikes in the Black Hills of Dakota in 1874, brought a stampede that led to conflicts with Sioux living there.

Mining communities brought together people of all colors, ethnic backgrounds, and levels of education. Asians, especially men from China who had tired of railway work, often became miners. Clara Brown, who had been enslaved in Virginia, saved enough to buy her freedom and journeyed to Colorado in 1857 to cook and wash clothes for miners. She saved enough to invest in the mines and become one of Colorado's richest citizens.

Miners worked and played hard. Widespread gambling and drunkenness gave mining towns reputations for vice. Actually, most towns settled down quickly. With sufficient population and the arrival of big companies that gave communities stability, territorial government and statehood followed.

The Mining Boom Ends A handful of miners actually struck it rich in the West, but most did not. When prospectors finally realized that all the precious metal was gone, they straggled home, leaving most mining cities deserted ghost towns. Large corporations still brought up copper, tin, and deeply buried gold and silver deposits. Like so many other industries, mining became the realm of big business.

The Cattle Frontier

When American settlers began to arrive in Texas in the early 1800s, they learned the cattle ranching ways of the Mexicans living there. It was not long before Americans had adopted Mexican ranching equipment and dress, and Texas longhorn cattle as their own.

During the 1860s and 1870s, the cattle ranching industry boomed in the West. The destruction of the buffalo and removal of Native Americans to reservations emptied the land for grazing cattle. And the extension of railroads into the West provided a means of shipping cattle to markets across the country.

Entrepreneurs, using techniques borrowed from the industrial East, began to develop profitable large-scale cattle businesses, complete from cattle ranges to stockyards. Individual cattle

▶ RESOURCE DIRECTORY

Teaching Resources

⭐ **Literature Activity** "The Californian's Tale," found in the Unit 5 folder, pp. 64–66, introduces students to the life of a gold prospector in the late 1800s with an excerpt from Mark Twain's short story.

drivers did not do as well. These workers, about a fifth of whom were African American or Mexican, were responsible for the **long drive**—the moving of cattle from distant ranges to busy railroad centers that shipped the cattle to market. Cowboys often led their cattle along well-known cow trails like the Goodnight-Loving and the Chisholm trails.

The long drive was hard, dangerous work and required braving rough, muddy trails, pounding thunderstorms, and attacks by cattle thieves. Stampedes were another danger. Recalled one cowboy of his experience in a stampede, "We found 341 dead cattle, two dead horses, one dead cowboy and two more with broken legs after the herd had passed." Yet cattle drivers and cowboys earned low wages, in the 1870s about thirty dollars a month.

The End of an Era The cattle boom ended in the mid-1880s as a result of several factors. One factor was Joseph Glidden's 1874 invention of barbed wire, which he claimed was "Light as air. . . . Cheaper than dirt. All steel and miles long. The cattle ain't born that can get through it." As a result of this invention, farmers could fence their land and keep out grazing cattle that had caused much conflict between farmers and ranchers. Thus the open range on which ranchers had freely grazed their huge herds began to disappear. The final death knell of the cattle boom sounded when cold winters, dry summers, and cattle fever destroyed many herds and bankrupted thousands of ranchers. Cattle ranching survived, but on a much smaller scale and with new breeds of cattle that largely replaced the Texas longhorn.

Charles Russell's painting "Jerked Down" (1907) illustrates the dangerous work of the cowhand. The open range on which such scenes took place began to disappear with the introduction of barbed wire fencing in the 1870s. The new invention was featured in ads like the one above.

• Ranchers welcomed the invention of barbed wire as a way to keep their cattle within ranch boundaries.

4. CLOSE

Reinforcing the Big Idea

To succeed in the West, farmers, miners, and ranchers needed the capital and methods of big business. The next section examines the way in which farmers began to protest what they claimed was unfair treatment at the hands of government and industry.

Alternative Assessment

Mid-Point Monitoring
Ask students if they have
• Chosen a format for their projects
• Identified one stereotyped image
• Begun their research to provide the contrasting accurate image

In Depth

Did You Know?

More than eight hundred diaries written by women who journeyed west between 1840 and 1870 have been published or cataloged in library archives. The writings offer a glimpse into the pioneer woman's point of view and the particular challenges of being a woman homesteader. Although they seldom mention the fact, about one in five women was pregnant or gave birth during the journey. Taboos against discussions of a personal nature prevented women from writing about childbirth, even in their diaries. A comprehensive collection of pioneer women's diaries is found in Johanna L. Stratton's *Pioneer Women, Voices from the Kansas Frontier*. Simon & Schuster, 1981.

SECTION 3 REVIEW

Key Terms, People, and Places
1. Describe (a) cash crops, (b) long drive.

Key Concepts
2. How were farms modernized in the late nineteenth century?
3. What was bonanza farming? Who used it?
4. What was the impact of mechanization on farming?

5. In the later mining "booms" of the nineteenth century, did many individuals "strike it rich"? Why or why not?
6. Describe the ranching industry in the late 1800s.

Critical Thinking
7. **Identifying Central Issues** Briefly describe the benefits and drawbacks of new farm machinery and knowledge.

Quiz found in the Unit 5 folder, p. 48, covers the main ideas in this section as well as the key terms.

The End of the Open Range

Focus When settlers arrived on the Great Plains and drove off the Native Americans, they changed the land in several ways. Ranchers and farmers had different needs and fought for control of the grasslands until the farmers finally won out.

In this section students will analyze the conflicting needs of ranchers and farmers and the reasons for the eventual decline of the ranching frontier.

Instruct Divide the class into two groups: farmers and ranchers. Ask the farmers to imagine that they are new settlers on an unplowed homestead on the Great Plains. Ask them to list their minimum needs (tools, seeds, etc.) for creating a successful farm on the plains. Ask the ranchers to imagine that they are starting a ranch in northern Texas after the Civil War. What are their minimum needs to create a successful ranch? After students have completed their lists, determine which needs bring the two groups into conflict.

Discuss with students why the farmers eventually won out. Could the farmers have succeeded without the help of the federal government? Could the ranchers have succeeded in the first place without the help of the government? (*The government helped to drive off the Native Americans and allowed ranchers to graze their cattle on government holdings.*)

Extend Ask students to find out about the other group that entered into conflict over the use of the Great Plains: the sheepherders. Why did ranchers oppose sheepherders?

The End of the Open Range

In the last half of the nineteenth century, farmers and ranchers battled over the way that land would be used on the vast western plains. How did this struggle begin, and what was its outcome?

For thousands of years before the first European settlers arrived, Native Americans hunted great bison herds on the vast expanse of grasslands between the Mississippi River and the Rocky Mountains. In the 1800s, however, settlers began to move into the West and drove Native Americans off the land. The new settlers then began to battle with one another over the way this land would be used.

Linking Land Use and Resources

The map on page 427 shows land use in the American West today. Land use is the primary economic activity that takes place in a region. Many categories of economic activity are related to a region's natural resources and climate. Farming, for example, takes place most successfully in a region with good soil, enough water, and a long growing season.

Generally, a single economic activity, or land use, dominates a region. One reason for this is that different economic activities sometimes interfere with one another; for example, if farmers clear trees from land, those trees are not available for forestry. Also, when an economic activity makes intense use of the land and employs many people, it tends to crowd out other land uses.

> *Free-ranging cattle and cattle being driven to market trampled unprotected crops, and the treeless, stoneless prairie supplied no material from which to build fences to keep them out.*

The Growth of Open-Range Ranching

At the beginning of the 1800s, few people looking for land to settle saw a use for the western plains. Until the 1850s, most Americans from east

of the Mississippi River hurried through the plains on their way farther west.

The first Americans to settle on the plains made use of the seemingly limitless grasslands to raise cattle. Cattle ranchers were especially attracted to Texas with its herds of free-roaming longhorns. The ranchers fed their cattle on the available grass and watered them in the open streams and rivers that meandered through the plains. Then the ranchers rounded them up for market.

The ranchers' biggest problem was the great distance that separated their cattle and their customers in the cities of the Northeast. Although the journey could be dangerous, the big demand and the high prices paid for beef convinced cattlemen to take the risk and drive their cattle several hundred miles north to the railroads. The first of these long drives went from Texas to Sedalia, Missouri, in 1866.

As the railroads extended west and south, the distance between grazing land and the railroads decreased. "Cow towns" sprang up on the Great Plains next to the rail lines. Ellsworth, Wichita, and Dodge City in Kansas, Cheyenne and Laramie in Wyoming, and other towns processed millions of head of cattle during the late 1870s and early 1880s.

The Arrival of the Sod Busters

Farmers soon discovered that beneath the grassy surface of the prairies was not sand but as much as six feet of fertile topsoil. The prairie grasses,

RESOURCE DIRECTORY

Teaching Resources

Time and Place Activity The Growth of the Suburbs, found in the Unit 5 folder, pp. 53–54, enriches students' understanding of changing land use patterns by focusing on the cause and effect relationships in the suburbanization of Los Angeles.

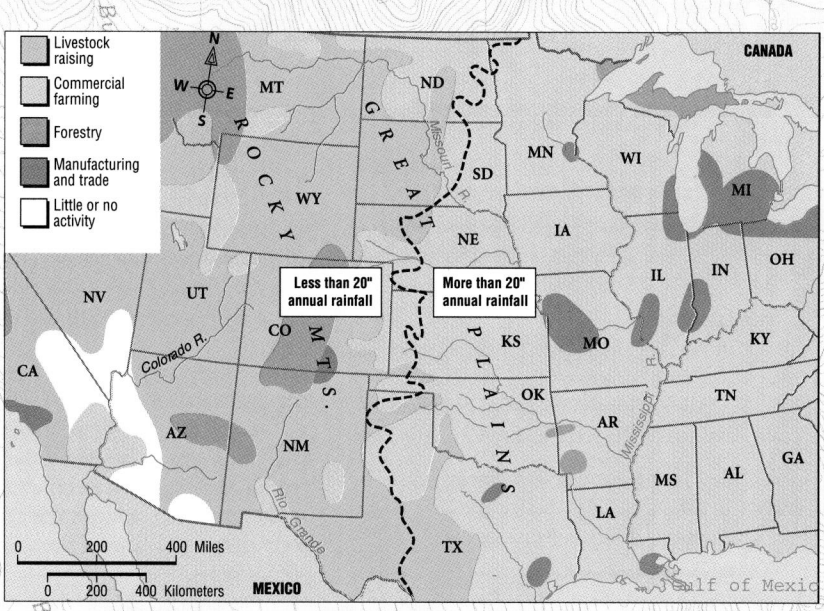

Livestock raising
Commercial farming
Forestry
Manufacturing and trade
Little or no activity

Less than 20" annual rainfall

More than 20" annual rainfall

however, imprisoned this topsoil with a layer of dense roots called sod. Before land could be farmed, the tough, centuries-old sod had to be broken up. Although "sod busting" required the most advanced and expensive plows, farmers arrived by the thousands, encouraged by the federal government and the railroads to make the West their home.

The first homesteaders found that, among other obstacles, open-range ranching threatened their hard-earned farms. Free-ranging cattle and cattle being driven to market trampled unprotected crops, and the treeless, stoneless prairie supplied no material from which to build fences to keep them out. Barbed wire, introduced in 1874, solved this problem but created another.

The Range Wars

Angered by the farmers' attempts to fence off the land, some ranchers started to enclose huge areas. The ranchers' illegal fences sometimes cut farmers off from roads and water supplies. Farmers fought back by cutting the barbed wire and seeking government help. The ranchers mended their fences and protected them with gunfire.

Soon, even cattlemen with fenced ranches were crowded out by the farmers. Farmers could make a living with much less land than cattle ranchers. Because the federal government had a land policy that tried to benefit the largest number of people, it helped the many small farmers more than it helped the few cattle ranchers. Government land-use laws increasingly made open-range ranching impossible. Finally, several years of unusual weather all but destroyed the herds.

GEOGRAPHIC CONNECTIONS

1. In what way were the railroads essential to the success of both ranching and farming on the western plains?
2. Why did the federal government support land-use laws that favored farmers over ranchers?

Critical Thinking

3. **Synthesizing information** The western plains receive less than half the rainfall of those parts closest to the Mississippi River. How does this difference in rainfall help explain the land-use pattern shown on the map?

Media and Technology

Transparency
Cause and Effect, F-4

Populism

Connecting to the Big Idea

See page 412B. Explain that as farmers' incomes declined, they began to join together in protest, and many eventually supported the Populist party. Ask students what the farmers' complaints were. Ask what reforms the Populist party promised to help them institute.

Objectives

● Explain why farmers were in financial difficulty at the close of the century and describe how they began to protest their economic plight.

● Trace the history of the Populist party and describe its reforms.

Bellringer

Ask students why merchants and service industries accept paper money or coins in return for goods and services. What gives these items value?

Reading Strategy

Problem Solving Ask students to imagine that they are farmers in the late 1800s. List some of their problems and identify some of the organizations that promise to help them.

In Depth

Biography

Mary Elizabeth Clyens, better known in history as Mary Lease (1850–1933), one of the most outspoken orators of the populist movement, said in 1890, ". . . the great common people of this country are slaves, and monopoly is the master. The West and South are bound and prostrate before the manufacturing East." (See Teaching Resources on page 430.)

By the late 1800s, American farmers were feeding the nation and the world, yet they were increasingly concerned about feeding themselves. Declining incomes created fertile ground for a farmers' protest.

Key Concepts
• Farmers began to protest their plight at the close of the century.
• A political movement called populism flashed on the scene and quickly faded out.

Key Terms, People, and Places
deflation, currency policy, the Grange; Populists, William Jennings Bryan

Many Americans favored the use of silver to increase the nation's currency supply in the late 1800s.

I n 1869 journalist Henry George arrived in New York City from the West Coast. Side by side with the city's great "palaces of the princely rich," he saw so much poverty that he wondered how such inequality could exist. In his 1879 book, *Progress and Poverty*, he warned that

> So long as all the increased wealth which modern progress brings goes but to build up great fortunes, to increase luxury and make sharper the contrast between the House of Have and the House of Want, progress is not real and cannot be permanent.

Throughout the United States, many other people also began to ask: how could so much progress be surrounded by so much poverty? Farmers were especially vocal in raising this question.

The Farmers' Complaint

Many farmers in the late 1800s were suffering from a long-term decline in crop prices that had begun after the Civil War. New farm machinery and agricultural technologies had increased their yields, but the resulting overproduction had glutted markets, causing prices to fall. Moreover, international competition for markets had increased.

These developments worried the nation's farmers. For solutions, they looked to the federal government's economic policies.

Farmers and Tariffs Tariffs impose duties, or taxes, on imported goods. These taxes discourage people from buying imports by making them more expensive. Thus, the sale of goods produced at home is promoted. In the late 1800s, tariffs also brought money to the federal government, which at the time did not tax people's incomes.

Americans in the late 1800s were divided on the benefit of tariffs. Industrialists claimed that protecting American-made goods protected factory jobs—and their own profits. But because tariffs eliminated foreign competition, they also lead to higher prices on the goods that workers had to buy.

Farmers resented the high prices of manufactured goods, but they did not want foreign farm produce to enter the United States "duty free." On the other hand, tariffs on farm imports prevented foreigners from earning the American currency they needed to buy American crops. Thus, tariffs hurt American farmers in two ways: by raising their living expenses at home and by lowering what they could earn abroad by exporting their crops.

Whenever the government raised tariffs to benefit industry, farmers protested. They felt that government was favoring manufacturers located in the North and Northeast. Yet tariffs were not the chief concern of the agriculture industry in the late 1800s. The dominant issue for many farmers was "free silver."

Goldbugs, Greenbackers, and Silverites In theory, an increase in the supply of money

---

RESOURCE DIRECTORY

Teaching Resources

Reproducible Lesson Plan found in the Unit 5 folder, p. 41, provides a summary of the Section 4 lesson plan content.

Alternate Lesson Plan: Learning Styles found in the Alternate Lesson Plans folder, p. 77, is especially effective for visual learners and is designed to help students create a concept web showing the main ideas of the section.

Guided Reading and Review found in the Unit 5 folder, p. 49, provides a structure for reading and mastering the key concepts and reviewing the key terms for Section 4. (Guided Practice)

should tend to produce inflation, a widespread rise in prices on goods of all kinds. In the years following the Civil War, however, the nation's money supply shrank as the federal government took out of circulation the paper money that had been issued during the war. As a result, the nation experienced a prolonged period of dropping prices called **deflation.**

Deflation hurt farmers, whose income and ability to pay off their debts depended on high prices for their crops. Deflation helped bankers and other lenders, however, because the dollars repaid to them could buy more goods than the dollars they had lent out.

Currency policy, the federal government's plan for the makeup and quantity of the nation's money supply, thus emerged as a major issue in national politics. Supporters of inflation pushed for increasing the amount of money in circulation. Supporters of deflation wanted tight money, or less currency in circulation.

In 1873 the supporters of tight money won a victory. Until that time, United States currency had been on a bimetallic standard; that is, currency consisted of gold or silver coins, or United States treasury notes that could be traded in for gold or silver. In 1873 Congress put the nation's currency on a gold standard in an effort to prevent inflation and secure economic stability. This move reduced the amount of money in circulation.

Conservative "goldbugs" were pleased. Many of them were big lenders, and they liked the idea of being repaid in currency backed by gold. But "silverites," mostly silver-mining interests and western farmers, were furious. They claimed that the end of silver as a monetary standard depressed the prices of farm produce. "Greenbackers" also entered the debate. They argued for more paper money, which was not redeemable in gold or silver, as a means of causing inflation.

Free Silver Economists at the time were vague about the impact on crop prices of currency amounts and standards. Nevertheless, farmer protest in the 1870s revolved increasingly around the call for free silver—the unlimited coining of silver dollars as a means of increasing the money supply.

The dollar of our daddies,
Of silver coinage free,
Will make us rich and happy,
Will bring prosperity,

went a popular rhyme. Silver did make a limited return to the currency supply in the late 1870s—but not as the free silver promoted by many western interests. In the 1890s, most of the farm protest centered on this hope.

Organizing Farmer Protest

Because farmers lived far from one another and tended to be self-reliant, they resisted efforts at organization. In the late nineteenth century, however, improved communication and transportation systems made united action among the nation's farmers more practical. This, coupled with the widespread economic problems facing many farmers, led to the development of several powerful farm protest groups.

The Grange In 1866 the Department of Agriculture sent Oliver H. Kelley on an inspection tour of southern farms. Disturbed by farmers' isolation, the following year he founded the Patrons of Husbandry, or the **Grange,** a term that came from a word meaning "farm."

The Grange soon began helping farmers form cooperatives with the intent of saving money by buying goods in large quantities. The Grange also pressured legislators to regulate the businesses on which farmers depended—for example, grain elevators that stored the farmers' crops and railroads that shipped it. The railroads, which gave better rates to eastern industrialists, received the brunt of farmers' anger.

Although the Grange was popular, by the mid-1870s farmers were turning to other political outlets. A Greenback party, which focused on currency issues, elected fourteen members to Congress in 1878. Its power quickly faded, however, as more and more farmers adopted the free silver position in the currency debate.

Farmers' Alliances Farmers' Alliances followed the Greenback party in the 1880s. The Alliances launched harsh attacks on monopolies, such as those that controlled the railroads.

Using Historical Evidence Farmers' Alliances provided an important channel for farmer protest and political action in the late 1800s. This illustration comes from a book of songs for these organizations. *What do the images on this songbook cover reveal about the ideals of the Farmers' Alliances?*

Mary Elizabeth Lease won fame as a Farmers' Alliance speaker.

Alliance lecturer Napoleon B. Ashby accused the nation's big business millionaires of having made their fortunes by preying upon "the mighty rivers of commerce which the farmers have set flowing."

The Farmers' Alliance in the South, a grassroots organization begun in Texas in the mid-1870s to fight cattle thieving and fraudulent land claims, grew into an especially powerful group. The themes it emphasized found support among many of the nation's farmers: federal regulation of the railroads, a greater circulation of currency, state departments of agriculture, antitrust laws, and farm credit.

Farmer's Alliances held special importance for women, who served as officers and won support for women's political rights. Kansas lawyer Mary Elizabeth Lease, whose voice was said to have "hypnotic qualities," was one of their most popular speakers. ✪

African Americans worked through a separate but parallel "Colored Farmers' Alliance." Formed in 1886 in Lovelady, Texas, the group had a quarter of a million members by 1891.

A series of natural disasters gave special urgency to Farmers' Alliance programs. The Mississippi River flooded in 1882. During 1886 to 1887, twenty-one consecutive months of drought in Texas impoverished 30,000 people. Terrible blizzards, which killed thousands of cattle, struck the West in 1887. The federal government's unwillingness to respond to these disasters alienated sufferers.

The Government Responds
During this era, the Democrats and Republicans produced a series of genial but undistinguished Presidents (see Chapter 16). Some had been influenced by promises of support from the era's powerful business interests. In return, these Presidents protected American industry, whose interests often ran counter to those of western and southern farmers.

At the same time, the country was deeply divided over the issues of the day, including the tariff and currency policy. In every election from 1876 to 1892, no candidate won a majority of the popular vote. Only rarely did a President command a party majority in Congress.

Thus, the federal government seemed incapable of responding to farmers' concerns. It did, however, take some actions. In 1887 Congress passed the Texas Seed bill, which appropriated money for seed grain to aid drought victims. But Democratic President Grover Cleveland vetoed the bill, expressing a then commonly held view that "though the people support the government, the government should not support the people." Cleveland did sign the Interstate Commerce Act of 1887, which regulated the charges paid to move freight, such as farmers' crops, between states. Although the act did not control the monopolistic practices of the railroads that so

Election of 1892

Candidate/Party	Electoral vote	Popular vote
Grover Cleveland (Dem)	277	5,554,414
Benjamin Harrison (Rep.)	145	5,190,802
James Weaver (People's)	22	1,027,329

☐ Territories

Election of 1896

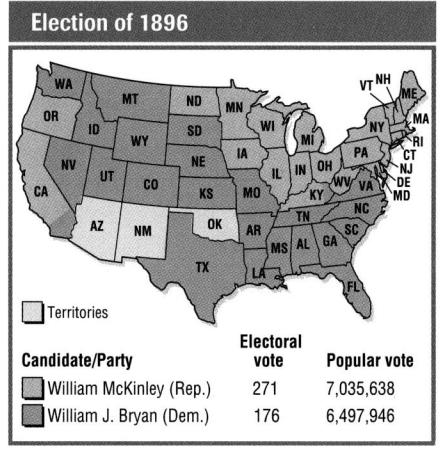

Candidate/Party	Electoral vote	Popular vote
William McKinley (Rep.)	271	7,035,638
William J. Bryan (Dem.)	176	6,497,946

☐ Territories

 Geography and History: Interpreting Maps
In their first presidential election, the People's party ran poorly against both the Democrats and Republicans. In 1896, they shared candidate William Jennings Bryan with the Democrats. *What pattern can you identify in the limited success of the Populists in the presidential elections of 1892 and 1896?*

angered farmers, it did establish the principle that Congress could regulate them. Cleveland's successor, Republican Benjamin Harrison, approved the Sherman Antitrust Act in 1890. As discussed in Chapter 14, this act was meant to curb the power of trusts and monopolies. But during its first decade, enforcement was lax.

MAKING CONNECTIONS

Recall Cleveland's statement that government should not support the people. Is this opinion widely held today? Use examples from current events to support your conclusion.

The Populists Push the Farmers' Program

⭐ In 1890 the various small political parties associated with the Farmers' Alliances began to enjoy success at the ballot box, especially in the South. In 1892 the Alliances founded the People's party, a new national party that demanded radical reform in United States economic and social policies. The **Populists,** as followers of the new party were known, called for an increased circulation of money; a silver standard; and a graduated income tax, which would place a greater tax burden on wealthy industrialists and a lesser one on farmers. The Populist party also called for government ownership of the country's transportation system—which was central to farmers' livelihoods—and communications system. In an effort to attract urban support, they also endorsed an eight-hour work day and opposed the use of Pinkertons as strikebreakers. Finally, they broke through deeply rooted racial prejudice to form a united front of African American and white farmers. As one of the party's most eloquent leaders, Georgian Tom Watson, explained:

> Now, the People's Party says to [whites and African Americans], "You are kept apart that you may be separately fleeced of your earnings. You are made to hate each other because upon that hatred is rested the keystone of the arch of financial despotism [absolute power] which enslaves you both. You are deceived and blinded that you may not see how this race antagonism perpetuates a monetary system which beggars both.

The idea that the poor of different races shared a common cause was unique to populism, but the idea enjoyed only a brief life

Caption Answer to ...

Using Historical Evidence

The cartoon shows Bryan in a negative light. He is trampling upon the Bible and carrying carefully labeled images from his "Cross of Gold" speech.

4. CLOSE

Reinforcing the Big Idea

In the late 1800s, American farmers banded together to protest their economic plight. Many farmers supported the short-lived Populist party. The next section examines the popular vision of the Old West and the realities it ignored.

THE SACRILEGIOUS CANDIDATE.

Using Historical Evidence This cartoon shows William Jennings Bryan wielding the crown of thorns and cross of gold—images that he used in a famous speech. *Is this cartoon presenting Bryan in a positive or a negative light?*

during this period of American politics.

During the 1892 campaign, populism generated great excitement among its followers. But the party's presidential candidate, Iowan James B. Weaver, barely won a million votes. Democratic candidate Grover Cleveland returned to the presidency.

Back in office, Cleveland alienated labor when he put down the Pullman strike. He angered farmers with his support for a gold standard, and manufacturers when he tried to lower the tariff. The 1893 Depression, which had started before he took office, threw millions out of work. When marchers promoting Populist ideas flocked to Washington in 1894, Americans troubled by the great industrial strikes, such as Pullman, added "hayseed socialists" to their list of frightening agitators.

Bryan's "Cross of Gold"

Other Populists looked ahead to the 1896 presidential campaign. In an election that focused mainly on currency issues, the Republicans ran William McKinley on a gold-standard platform. **William Jennings Bryan,** a former silverite congressman from Nebraska and a powerful speaker, captured the Democratic nomination. He overwhelmed his party's convention with a plea for free silver. Using images from the Bible,

he stood with head bowed and arms outstretched and cried out at the climax of his speech,

*Y*ou shall not press down upon the brow *of labor this crown of thorns. You shall not crucify mankind upon a cross of gold!*

Although the Populists were interested in many issues besides free silver, the impact of Bryan's speech was so great that he captured the Populist nomination, too.

Bryan lost the election, carrying the Democratic West and South but not one of the urban and industrial Midwest and northern states. In these states, factory workers feared that free silver might cause inflation, which would eat away the buying power of their wages. Thus, despite populism's broad appeal, it could not bridge the ever-widening gap between America's cities and farms.

Populism's Legacy

By 1897 McKinley's administration had raised the tariff to new heights. In 1900, after gold strikes in South Africa, the Canadian Yukon, and Alaska had added more than $100 million worth of gold to the world's supply, Congress again passed a gold standard. To the surprise of many farmers, crop prices began a slow rise that would last until 1920. The silver movement died, as did populism.

Many of populism's goals, however, did not fade away. In the decades ahead, other political thinkers applied populist ideas to urban and industrial problems. In so doing, they launched new reform programs that shifted the course of United States history.

SECTION 4 REVIEW

Key Terms, People, and Places
1. Describe (a) deflation, (b) currency policy.
2. Identify: (a) Populists, (b) William Jennings Bryan.

Key Concepts
3. What were farmers' objections to tariffs?
4. What was the farmers' position on the currency question?

5. By what means did farmers organize to protest and present their views?

Critical Thinking
6. **Drawing Conclusions** Populism appealed to people in many parts of the country. How can you explain, then, the failure of the Populist party to win the presidential election?

▶ RESOURCE DIRECTORY

Teaching Resources

Quiz found in the Unit 5 folder, p. 50, covers the main ideas in this section as well as the key terms.

Drawing Conclusions

rawing conclusions means finding out an answer or forming an opinion based on information that is suggested but not stated directly. When you read about history or any subject, it is important to be able to draw conclusions. Then you can go beyond what is presented in textbooks and other sources and form new insights about a historical period or event.

Use the following steps and the two passages from the late 1800s that appear on this page to practice drawing conclusions.

1. Study the facts and ideas that the author presents. Read the two passages below, and then answer the following questions about them.
(a) What facts does Washington Gladden present to describe the farmers' problems? (b) What factors does Mary Elizabeth Lease cite to explain the farmers' problems as she perceives them?

2. Make a summary statement as a conclusion about a group of details. A statement that summarizes the major points of an argument is one type of conclusion. Clarify each person's position by summarizing the basic information contained in the two passages. Then answer the following questions.
(a) From passage A, what can you conclude about the farmers' plight? Would farming be more profitable if farmers worked as hard as laborers?

Or, are the farmers' problems beyond their control? (b) From the information in passage B, what can you conclude about the government's response to the problems the farmers are experiencing? Explain your reasoning.

3. Decide whether or not you can draw a conclusion based on what is stated. If an argument does not contain sufficient information, it is possible to jump to a faulty conclusion. Comparing the information in the two passages should raise some questions in your mind. As you answer these questions, you are deciding whether you have enough information to draw conclusions. (a) Given what you read in both passages, what conclusion can you draw about the relationship between farmers and the Populist party? Explain your answer. (b) Based on Lease's ideas in passage B, what conclusion can you draw concerning the ideas of the Populist party and the ideas of the major political parties?

Passage A

"The business of farming has become, for some reasons, extremely unprofitable. With the hardest work and with the sharpest economy, the average farmer is unable to make both ends meet; every year closes with debt, and the mortgage grows till it devours the land. The Labor Bureau of Connecticut has shown, by an investigation of 693 representative farms, that the average annual reward of the farm proprietor of that state for his expenditure of muscle and brain is $181.31, while the average annual wages of the ordinary hired man is $386.36."

—Washington Gladden, Congregational minister, 1890

Passage B

"The parties lie to us and the political speakers mislead us. We were told two years ago to go to work and raise a big crop, that was all we needed. We went to work and plowed and planted; the rains fell, the sun shone, nature smiled, and we raised the big crop that they told us to. . . . Then the politicians said we suffered from over-production. . . . We want money, land, and transportation. We want the abolition of the national banks, and we want the power to make loans direct from the government. We want the accursed foreclosure system wiped out."

—Mary Elizabeth Lease, Populist leader

Historian's Toolbox Activity Drawing Conclusions About NAFTA, found in the Unit 5 folder, p. 59, uses two discourses on the North American Free Trade Agreement to help students apply this skill.

433

Frontier Myths

1. FOCUS

Connecting to the Big Idea

See page 412B. Explain that the history of the American West has been glorified in exciting myths, which have become part of our culture. Ask how the myths compare with the reality of life in the Old West.

Objectives

● Explain why Americans believed that the frontier no longer existed by the turn of the century.

● Describe how myths and misconceptions influenced American understanding of the frontier.

● Give reasons for the continuing presence of myths about the West in the American imagination.

Bellringer

Ask students to identify features of myths. Then ask them to consider familiar American myths, either legends like John Henry and Paul Bunyan, or images like gold rush saloons and shoot-outs at high noon.

Caption Answer to . . .

 Interpreting Tables

Possible answers: The coastal region provided existing sources of transportation that made it an economically viable place to settle. Transportation networks were needed for the interior to become a suitable place to live.

Reading Strategy

Reinforcing Key Ideas Ask students to make a list of myths about the American frontier on the left side of a piece of paper as they read the material in the section. Then ask them to write a sentence about the reality of life on the frontier to the right of each myth.

Frontier Myths

SECTION PREVIEW

From modern rodeos to cowboy boots to novels immortalizing the prairie farmer, the wild West captures the imagination. But this image leaves out many other experiences that also helped shape the nation.

Key Concepts
• By the turn of the century, Americans believed that the American frontier no longer existed.
• Myths and misconceptions influenced American understanding of the frontier.
• Myths about the West still linger in the American imagination.

Key Terms, People, and Places
Frederick Jackson Turner

In the popular imagination, the sheriff's badge is a symbol of justice—wild West style.

T he 1800s were coming to a close, and what had seemed unimaginable a few decades before was happening. The American frontier seemed to be disappearing and an era of special meaning seemed to be ending. But what, exactly, did the era mean? The answer to that question is surrounded by many myths—and is responsible for many of the nation's most cherished images of itself.

The West at the Close of the Nineteenth Century

One by one, areas of the West became territories. Residents then wrote constitutions and applied for statehood. With these developments came the perception that the opportunities of the frontier were fading. As early as 1880, American observers of the West noticed ominous signs of change. The number of tenant farmers—who rented rather than owned land—had risen, along with the number of large farms owned by corporations. Many farmers were deep in debt. "Free" lands were harder to find. In 1890 the superintendent of the census announced the end of the frontier. The country's so-called "unsettled area has been so broken into by isolated bodies of settlement," he declared, "that there can hardly be said to be a frontier line."

This census official exaggerated somewhat. Homesteading continued into the twentieth century. Besides, many western areas that were not suited to agriculture remain sparsely settled still.

Turner's Frontier Thesis Nevertheless, by the 1890s it was clear that an era of special meaning in the history of the United States was closing. In 1893 a young historian named **Frederick Jackson Turner** delivered a speech in which he addressed this issue. He claimed a central role for the frontier in forming the American character.

The West Joins the Union

State	Year of Admission
California	1850
Oregon	1859
Kansas	1861
Nevada	1864
Nebraska	1867
Colorado	1876
North Dakota	1889
South Dakota	1889
Montana	1889
Washington	1889
Wyoming	1890
Idaho	1890
Utah	1896
Oklahoma	1907
New Mexico	1912
Arizona	1912

Interpreting Tables
In the late 1800s and early 1900s, one western territory after another achieved statehood. *Why do you think that the interior of the country was settled later than most of the West Coast?*

 RESOURCE DIRECTORY

Teaching Resources

Reproducible Lesson Plan found in the Unit 5 folder, p. 42, provides a summary of the Section 5 lesson plan content.

Alternate Lesson Plan: Cooperative Learning found in the Alternate Lesson Plans folder, p. 78, provides guidance for groups of students to prepare short tests on Frederick Jackson Turner's thesis.

Guided Reading and Review found in the Unit 5 folder, p. 51, provides a structure for reading and mastering the key concepts and reviewing the key terms for Section 5. (Guided Practice)

The West had forced its Anglo-American and European settlers to shed their old ways and adapt, innovate, and invent, he said. To the frontier, Turner claimed, "American intellect owes its striking characteristics," which he described as

That coarseness and strength combined with acuteness [keen insight] *and inquisitiveness* [curiosity]; *that practical, inventive turn of mind, quick to find expedients* [ways to achieve goals]; *that masterful grasp of material things, lacking the artistic but powerful to effect great ends; that restless, nervous energy; that dominant individualism, working for good and for evil, and withal that buoyancy* [liveliness] *and exuberance which comes with freedom.*

To Turner, it was the frontier that had produced the highly individualistic, restless, and socially mobile American, the person ready for adventure, bent on self-improvement, and committed to democracy.

Turner's Critics The Turner thesis, as his view came to be called, made certain assumptions that historians have since modified. Turner defined settlers as whites of European heritage and saw no difference in the experiences of women and men. He did not consider the importance to the West of African Americans or of the immigrants from Japan and China.

Nor did Turner consider the impact of settlement on Native American and Spanish-speaking inhabitants. Moreover, Turner played down the heavy involvement of government subsidies and of big business in bringing about American achievements in farming, cattle ranching, and mining. And finally, he ignored the extent to which immigrants made use of the many institutions and traditions they brought from their homelands in building farms and contributing to the nation's productivity.

Frontier Realities

A far more complex view of the West now prevails. This view more accurately reflects the reality of the settlement of the West.

The Real Western Settler The West did appeal to the restless, adventurous man, but it also appealed to adventurous women. While many women went west reluctantly and suffered deeply from the pressures of dislocation and deprivation, others not only survived but thrived on the frontier.

Still, the West was hardly a land of unlimited opportunity for either men or women. Boom inevitably led to bust, especially when prices fell for the commodities settlers relied on to make it big. Rare among those who made it big were African Americans, Asians, Mexicans, and single women.

Western settlers were not always eastern whites. Chinese and African American railway workers went into mining and established businesses in western towns. Chinese and Japanese settlers farmed the West Coast; about nine thousand African Americans worked as cowhands on ranches, where they generally suffered less discrimination than in other work. Thousands of Exodusters settled the West. The prosperity that western settlement brought to the United States could not have been achieved without the efforts of many groups.

A Limited View of Democracy The frontier nurtured certain democratic values. These found expression in strong legislatures, short terms for elected officials, and other institutions of popular control over government. Yet many settlers rode roughshod over the rights of the Native American populations they displaced. On the West Coast, white settlers treated Asian immigrants with scorn, segregating them

Frederic Remington's 1902 painting *The Cowboy* reveals that a romanticized image of the American West was well in place in the early twentieth century.

2. INSTRUCT

Discuss

Discuss the association between the close of the nineteenth century and the end of the frontier era. Ask how the myths of that era developed into a lasting American image.

Point out the chart on page 434 and note the number of states admitted to the Union between 1889 and 1912. Ask what advantages statehood provided for residents.

Analyze

Analyze Turner's frontier thesis with students. What was the image this thesis created? In what ways is this image an exclusive one? Ask why proponents of the thesis might emphasize the "new frontiers" of science and exploration.

In Depth

Then and Now

In the 1870s, store owner Levi Strauss and tailor Jacob Davis found a way to answer the need for stronger, heavier, work clothes. They used white tent canvas to make pants with double-stitched seams and small copper rivets pounded into the corners of the front and back pockets. The new clothes were an immediate success and became even more popular when Strauss and Davis switched from canvas to tougher, softer, dyed-blue denim.

In the 1950s and 1960s, blue jeans were seen as the the symbol of restless, idealistic youth. By the 1990s, international designers had turned them into high-fashion clothing. An example of the original "Levi's" now hangs in the Smithsonian Institution in Washington, D.C.

Activity

Teaching Heterogeneous Groups

To encourage settling and governance of the West, the federal government offered statehood to territories that successfully proposed a constitution. Divide students into groups and have each group write a brief proposal for statehood for a fictional state. Each proposal should include the name of the state and its location by longitude and latitude. Each constitution should outline the rights of its citizens and declare to whom these rights are extended.

Enrichment

In 1936, Gertrude Stein wrote: "In the United States there is more space where nobody is than where anybody is. That is what makes America what it is." Ask students to write an essay in response to Stein's statement, analyzing whether or not Stein would support Turner's theory of the frontier.

Caption Answer to . . .

Using Historical Evidence

The poster suggests that white people are in conflict with Native Americans. Both are depicted with weapons.

3. ASSESS

Section 5 Review Answers

1. Frederick Jackson Turner, see p. 434

2. There were few areas into which American settlers had not moved.

3. Developed by historian Frederick Jackson Turner, the thesis argues that the presence of the frontier gave the American character unique traits. Critics point out that Turner saw no difference in the experiences of men and women; he did not take into account the experiences of non-whites or non-Europeans, including Native Americans, in the West; and he played down the heavy role of the government in settling the West.

into neighborhoods and prohibiting them from owning land.

The Impact on the Land Although in the popular mind the settlement of the West meant progress, the costs to the environment were high. Settlers treated the vast natural resources of the West as if they were limitless. Railroad tunnels destroyed mountains. The construction of huge mines scarred the land and depleted forests. Overcultivation eroded fields, and wanton slaughter nearly wiped out the buffalo.

The Influence of Frontier Myths on National Identity

Despite today's deeper understanding of the history of the American West, frontier myths linger on. Through literature, film, and song, they continue to influence how Americans think about themselves.

Creating the Myths The romantic image of the American cowboy began developing as early as the 1870s, popularized in the dime novels of writers like Edward L. Wheeler. In *Deadwood Dick, The Prince of the Road: or, the Black Rider of the Black Hills,* Wheeler painted a hero who was, at various times, outlaw, miner, gang leader, or cowboy and who dealt out righteous justice against evil.

Using Historical Evidence William F. "Buffalo Bill" Cody became famous by playing up the myths of the American West. This 1890 poster promoted his "Wild West" show. *What does the poster tell you about Cody's presentation of the West?*

M ounted upon his midnight steed, and clad in the weird suit of black, he makes an imposing spectacle as he comes fearlessly up. Well may he be bold and fearless, for no one dares to raise a hand against him. . . .
Close up to the side of the coach rides the daring young outlaw, his piercing orbs peering out from the eye-holes in his black mask, one hand clasping the bridle-reins, the other a nickel-plaited seven-shooter.

⭐ Scenes like these kept alive the idea that the West saw little else but stage robberies and killings. And though Wheeler's Deadwood Dick did exist, the real cowboy of that name was no outlaw. He was an African American named Nat Love, who drove cattle north from Texas for twenty years. Entering a rodeo contest in Deadwood, a Dakota Territory mining town, Love won several roping and shooting contests. In his autobiography, Love wrote, "Right there the assembled crowd named me 'Deadwood Dick' and proclaimed me champion roper of the Western cattle country."

In 1883 William F. ("Buffalo Bill") Cody began his Wild West shows, contributing further to frontier myths. These colorful events drew thousands of paying spectators to steer-roping contests, rodeos, and staged battles between "good" cavalry regiments and "bad" Native Americans.

Writers transformed other real figures from the West, such as Wild Bill Hickock and Calamity Jane, into larger than life characters. Here's Wheeler again:

"Who was that chap?" asked Redburn, not a little bewildered.
"That?—why that's Calamity Jane!"
"Calamity Jane? What a name."
"Yes, she's an odd one. Can ride like the wind, shoot like a sharp-shooter, and swear like a trooper. . . . Owns this coop and two or three other lots in Deadwood; a herding ranch at Laramie; an interest in a paying placer claim [mine] near Elizabeth City, and the Lord only knows how much more."
"But it is not a woman?"
"Reckon 'tain't nothin' else."

This sketch helped create the stereotype of the woman who had to act masculine and be "mean with a pistol" in order to survive in the West. Deep down, however, she was always a "real" woman.

▶ RESOURCE DIRECTORY

Teaching Resources

⭐ **American Profiles Activity** found in the Unit 5 folder, p. 56, profiles Nat Love (alias Deadwood Dick), the legendary African American cowboy.

The "Strenuous Life" of the West Most stereotypes from the West were of men. The West was the place where a young man could find freedom and opportunity. He could lead a virtuous life and resist the forces of civilization that were making him soft. Many writers praised the West for having toughened the bodies and souls of young men. In his histories of the West, future President Theodore Roosevelt urged American men to experience the "strenuous life" of the West before they became too weak from the comforts of modern civilization.

Some male themes appealed to women. In 1912 Juliette Low founded the American Girl Scouts in part because she feared that civilization had made girls too soft. Citing as models the ingenuity and hardiness of women homesteaders, she made the scouting techniques of tracking, woodcraft, and wilderness survival the core of her program.

MAKING CONNECTIONS

Consider what you have read about the myths of the West. Have you encountered examples of these myths in television, movies, or other media in your lifetime? Explain.

The Myths of the West Today

Frontier myths have left permanent marks on the nation's character. How many classic American songs arose from the cowboy era? "Home on the Range," where the buffalo roam, "Sweet Betsy from Pike" or "Don't Fence Me In"—all give rise to enduring images of wide open spaces and freedom from the confines of civilization. When Americans hear these songs, they celebrate the richness of their land and the courage of their ancestors. They celebrate the truth that many endured the dangers of a hostile environment and piercing loneliness to "stake a claim" for the future. They set aside for a moment the knowledge that the buffalo are almost gone, that range settlements displaced and nearly destroyed Native American peoples, and that farmers and their barbed-wire fences brought an end to the open range for ranchers and their cattle.

Such were the realities. But who can discount the significance of myths to the spirit of a nation?

The belief that the frontier was disappearing prompted a move to conserve land in the West. Conservationist John Muir and President Theodore Roosevelt, pictured here in 1903, helped lead this conservation effort.

SECTION 5 REVIEW

Key Terms, People, and Places
1. Identify Frederick Jackson Turner.

Key Concepts
2. What did observers mean when they said that the frontier was "closed" in the late 1800s?
3. What is the Turner thesis and what are some criticisms of it?

4. Describe some of the myths of the American West.
5. How have the myths of the American West been perpetuated?

Critical Thinking
6. **Distinguishing False from Accurate Images** Briefly summarize the reality of the American settlement of the West for all groups involved.

 Quiz found in the Unit 5 folder, p. 52, covers the main ideas in this section as well as the key terms.

 Chapter Test Forms A and B are found in the Unit 5 folder, pp. 69–74.

 Answer Keys found in the Unit 5 folder, pp. 149–164, provide answers to all student activities.

Media and Technology

Transparency
Graphic Organizer, G-3

Guided Reading Audiotapes
(English and Spanish)

Computer Test Bank

4. It was full of heroes who were equal parts outlaw and administrators of justice; cowboys were good, Native Americans were bad; women had to be tough and masculine on the outside, "real women" on the inside.

5. In the 1800s, books and "Wild West" shows; today through songs, films, and other forms of popular culture.

6. It provided some opportunities for white Americans, African Americans, and immigrants, though the booms that made some rich led to busts for many others. Native Americans were nearly destroyed, and environmental harm was done. Big business prospered more than individual farmers or miners.

Answer to ...

MAKING CONNECTIONS

Answers will vary according to students' interests and experiences.

Reteach

Ask students to label each statement below as myth or reality.
- The story of the frontier is a story of white, English-speaking males.
- In taming the frontier, settlers destroyed the way of life of Native Americans.
- To succeed in the West, women had to be better at traditionally male skills than most men.
- The environment of the West was deeply scarred by the farming, ranching, and mining frontiers.

4. CLOSE

 Reinforcing the Big Idea

The myth of the American West as a place where strong, restless, white males led lives of daring and adventure while supporting the ideals of democracy still has its appeal today. However, the real story of the West includes immigrants, African Americans, and women, and features the destruction of the Native Americans and the scarring of the environment.

Chapter Review Answers

Understanding Key Terms, People, and Places

Terms
Students should refer to the definitions of the key terms in the chapter to write sentences that show the relation of each word to the settlement of the West, its impact on Native American culture, populism, or myths about the frontier.

Matching
1. speculators
2. currency policy
3. Morrill Land-Grant Act
4. the Grange

True or False
1. false, Exodusters
2. false, Frederick Jackson Turner
3. true
4. false, General George Armstrong Custer

Reviewing Main Ideas

1. Settlers hoped for a chance to own their own farms and be their own boss. African American settlers also hoped to flee racial prejudice, violence, and exploitation.

2. Families cooperated in building houses and barns, making quilts, husking corn, and providing many other forms of support.

3. Western women launched successful city and state campaigns to win the vote. They also campaigned to improve women's professional opportunities in business, medicine, and law.

4. When Native Americans signed treaties handing over their land, they often did not realize that the settlers would not let them continue using it.

5. The government treated Chief Joseph and his people brutally and cruelly, and ignored the fact that the Native Americans had a prior claim to the land.

6. The disappearance of the buffalo eventually destroyed Native Americans' ability to build lives on reservations. Many reformers attempted to "civilize" Native Americans. Also, much of the land given to Native Americans under the Dawes Severalty Act was unsuitable for farming; in addition, many Native Americans had no interest or experience in farming. Many therefore sold their land to speculators.

7. Farmers were challenged by the region's dry climate, tough prairie grass, and plagues of insects.

Chapter Review

Understanding Key Terms, People, and Places

Key Terms
1. Morrill Land-Grant Act
2. speculators
3. Homestead Act
4. squatter
5. boomer
6. sooner
7. bonanza farms
8. cash crops
9. long drive
10. deflation
11. currency policy
12. the Grange

People
13. Exodusters
14. George Armstrong Custer
15. Chief Sitting Bull
16. Chief Joseph
17. Populists
18. William Jennings Bryan
19. Frederick Jackson Turner

Places
20. Wounded Knee

Terms For each term above, write a sentence that explains its relation to the settlement of the West, its impact on Native American culture, populism, or myths about the frontier.

Matching Review the key terms in the list above. If you are not sure of a term's meaning, review its definition in the chapter. Then choose a term from the list that best matches each description below.
1. people who bought up large areas of land to sell later at a profit
2. the federal government's plan for the makeup and quantity of the nation's money supply
3. the act giving western lands to state governments
4. the organization that promoted farmers' interests

True or False Determine whether each statement is true or false. If it is true, write "true." If it is false, change the underlined name to make the statement true.
1. African American homesteaders, who called themselves Populists, traveled West to escape exploitation in the South.
2. Historian William Jennings Bryan wrote about the importance of the frontier in forming the American character.
3. Chief Joseph, leader of the Nez Percé, fled with his people as far as Montana before being attacked by United States soldiers.
4. One of the leaders in the destruction of the Cheyenne was Chief Sitting Bull.

Reviewing Main Ideas

Section 1 (pp. 414–417)
1. Why did settlers want to move west? What additional reasons did African Americans have for moving west?
2. Describe some of the ways settlers relied on each other.
3. What campaigns did women start in the West?

Section 2 (pp. 418–421)
4. Explain how the Native American concept of owning land differed from that of the settlers.
5. Describe the pattern of conflict between the United States government and Native Americans.
6. By what means were Native American cultures destroyed in the late 1800s?

Section 3 (pp. 422–425)
7. What challenges did western land and climate pose for farmers?

8. What ethnic groups might have lived in a western mining town?
9. Describe several factors that led to the cattle ranching boom of the 1860s and 1870s.

Section 4 (pp. 428–432)
10. Why did the nation's farmers suffer from a decline in crop prices in the late 1800s?
11. Describe the currency policy debate of the late 1800s.
12. How did farmers protest their fate in the late 1800s?

Section 5 (pp. 434–437)
13. What was the message of Frederick Jackson Turner's frontier thesis?
14. In what ways was Turner's thesis inaccurate?
15. What has been the impact of frontier myths on the national identity?

---

8. Mining communities brought together people of all ethnic backgrounds, including Asians and African Americans.

9. The cattle ranching boom occurred because the destruction of the buffalo and the removal of Native Americans freed up land for grazing. In addition, the extension of railroads into the West helped ranchers by allowing them to ship cattle to markets throughout the country.

10. By the late 1800s overproduction had glutted markets, causing prices to fall. Also, international competition for markets had increased.

11. Supporters of inflation fought for an increase in the amount of currency, or money, in circulation. Supporters of deflation wanted less currency in cir-

culation. In 1873 Congress put the nation's currency on a gold standard, thus reducing the amount of money in circulation, in an effort to reduce inflation.

12. Several powerful farm protest groups, including the Grange and the Farmers' Alliances, were formed. Improved communication and transportation systems made united action easier and more practical for farmers.

13. Turner claimed that the frontier played a central role in forming the American character. He believed that it produced the essential American—ready for adventure, bent on self-improvement, and committed to democracy.

14. Turner's thesis assumed that settlers were white males of European descent. He did not consider the

---

Thinking Critically

1. **Formulating Questions** Based on what you have read in the chapter, write four questions to ask new homesteaders about their life in the West.
2. **Distinguishing False from Accurate Images** Myths about the frontier led people to believe that the West was a lawless place where everyone could strike it rich. (a) What myths and stereotypes do we have about various regions of the country today? (b) To what extent do you think these stereotypes are accurate?

Making Connections

1. **Evaluating Primary Sources** Review the primary source excerpt on page 423. The excerpt states that farms owned by big business have many advantages. (a) What might be some of these advantages? (b) How might such large farms affect the small farmer?
2. **Understanding the Visuals** Scan the chapter and choose several visuals that illustrate some of the realities and the myths about the West. Write a paragraph that explains what the realities and myths were and how these visuals illustrate them.
3. **Writing About the Chapter** Imagine that the 1892 election is rapidly approaching. Create an informational flyer urging voters to support the Populist party. First decide why voters should support the Populists. Then write a draft of your flyer explaining your point of view. Anticipate and reply to any

potential objections to the Populist platform. Revise your flyer, making certain that your writing is informative and persuasive. Proofread your flyer and draft a final copy.

4. **Using the Graphic Organizer** This graphic organizer uses a tree map to provide information about developing the West. (a) Based on what you have read in the chapter, how did mechanization and new agricultural knowledge lead to the growth of bonanza farms? (b) According to the graphic organizer below, what role did big business play in the development of the West? (c) On a separate sheet of paper, create your own graphic organizer, showing the effects of westward expansion on the Native American groups living in the West.

importance of Native American and ethnic influences, or the significance of big business and government subsidies.

15. Frontier myths have created male and female stereotypes, as well as lasting images of the wide-open spaces, the richness of the land, and the courage of ancestors. The myths deny realities such as the slaughter of the buffalo and the end of the open range.

Thinking Critically

1. Possible questions: Why did you move West? How did you purchase your land? What experience have you had with farming? How do the realities of life in the West fit with your expectations?

2. (a) and (b) Answers will vary. Students may mention stereotypes such as the West Coast as the source of offbeat ideas or the Northeast as industrial and intellectual.

Making Connections

1. (a) Advantages of large commercial farms include the ability to produce more food more efficiently than small family-owned farms. (b) Large farms might force family-owned farms out of business.

2. Students may choose any of the following to represent the reality of the West: pages 415, 416, 419, 424, and 425; and any of the following to represent the myth: pages 425, 435, and 436. Paragraphs should demonstrate an understanding that the reality of western life for homesteaders included hard work and danger as well as the benefits of rural life and freedom from factory or office work. The myth includes romantic images of striking it rich in mining, stage robberies, and killings.

3. Answers will vary. Students' responses should reflect an understanding of populism and the reasons for its rise in popularity.

4. (a) The advances in agricultural techniques and machinery made it possible to farm vastly greater areas of land and increased a farm's output tremendously. Entrepeneurs saw a lucrative new market in the rapidly growing population centers of the East and applied techniques of big business to agriculture in order to meet the demand for food. (b) Big business transformed the formerly small-scale, inefficient occupations of agriculture, mining, and ranching into large, centralized operations that relied on high volume and efficient production. (c) Students' graphic organizers should reflect an understanding of the impact of westward expansion on the various Native American groups living in the West.

 Alternative Assessment

Final Evaluation

Use the following guidelines to evaluate student projects:

● **Evidence of thoughtfulness** To what extent do projects demonstrate an understanding of the role of the myth of the West in American history and life?

● **Evidence of outside research** To what extent do projects reflect outside research?

● **Evidence of sensitivity** To what extent do projects reflect an increased awareness of how myths can create stereotypes?

Chapter 16 Politics, Immigration, and Urban Life
1877–1920

📁 **Teaching Resources** (See Unit 5 Folder)

	Instruction	Enrichment
Section 1 **Politics in the Gilded Age** (pp. 442–447)	Reproducible Lesson Plan, p. 76 Alternate Lesson Plan, p. 80 Guided Reading and Review, p. 80 Quiz, p. 81	Critical Thinking Activity, Distinguishing False from Accurate Images, p. 93
Section 2 **People on the Move** (pp. 448–453)	Reproducible Lesson Plan, p. 77 Alternate Lesson Plan, p. 81 Guided Reading and Review, p. 82 Quiz, p. 83	Visual Learning Activity, Passage to America, p. 100 Literature Activity, The Statue of Liberty, p. 97 Visual Learning Activity, The Chinese Question, p. 101 Viewpoints Activity, On Cultural Ties, pp. 90–91 Literature Activity, Where Is America? pp. 98–99
Section 3 **The Challenge of the Cities** (pp. 454–458)	Reproducible Lesson Plan, p. 78 Alternate Lesson Plan, p. 82 Guided Reading and Review, p. 84 Quiz, p. 85	Primary Source Activity, New York Gangs, p. 94 American Profiles Activity, Thomas Nast, p. 88 Historian's Toolbox Activity, Reading Tables and Analyzing Statistics, p. 92
Section 4 **Ideas for Reform** (pp. 460–463)	Reproducible Lesson Plan, p. 79 Alternate Lesson Plan, p. 83 Guided Reading and Review, p. 86 Quiz, p. 87 Chapter Test, Forms A & B, pp. 102–107	American Profiles Activity, Lillian Wald, p. 89 Primary Source Activity, Hull House, pp. 95–96

📁 **Additional Chapter Resources**

Resource Organizer, p. 75
Alternate Lesson Plan, p. 79
Answer Keys, pp. 149–164

Bibliography

For the Teacher
McKelvey, Blake. *The Urbanization of America, 1860-1915.* Rutgers, 1963. (A detailed book about the growth of American cities in the late 1800s and early 1900s.)
Miller, Kerby A. *Emigrants and Exile: Ireland and the Irish Exodus to North America.* Oxford University Press, 1985.
Takaki, Ronald. *Strangers from a Different Shore: A History of Asian Americans.* Little, Brown, 1989. (A comprehensive account of the Asian American immigrant experience.)

Prentice Hall Literature Excerpts from *The American Experience,* 1994, "Realism and the Frontier, 1865–1915," including Robinson, Edwin Arlington. "Richard Cory," from *The Children of the Night.* Scribner's, 1914.

Media and Technology

 Our Multicultural Heritage, C-2, C-11

 Cause and Effect, F-3

 Graphic Organizer, G-4

 Guided Reading Audiotapes (English and Spanish)

 Computer Test Bank

For the Student

Addams, Jane. *Twenty Years at Hull-House.* University of Illinois, 1989. (The autobiography of a pioneer of the settlement house movement, first published in 1910.)

Martis, Kenneth C. *The Historical Atlas of Political Parties in the United States Congress.* Macmillan, 1989.

Immigration: Growth of a Nation. Random House Media, 1985. Sound filmstrip. (A two-part feature in color.)

THE BIG IDEA

The Big Idea for the chapter and how the main ideas in each section relate to the Big Idea are graphically displayed below. Comprehension of this chapter's Big Idea is critical to students' understanding of United States history and how we as a nation got where we are today.

CHAPTER 16

The years from 1877 to 1920 saw a continuation of the social, economic, and political divisions that had characterized the nation even before the Civil War. This was not a "nation united" as much as it was a collection of political factions and machines, ghettos, neighborhoods, ethnic enclaves, and extremes of rich and poor all competing to realize their view of the "American Dream."

SECTION 1

From 1876 to 1900 alone, the political party occupying the White House changed four times. This was a period when neither of the two major political parties could capture the spirit of the people for very long. The parties themselves were little more than name plates for regional factions and urban machines, often more concerned with their own agendas than a single national one.

SECTION 2

During the late 1800s, millions of immigrants entered the United States, looking for opportunity and freedom. They struggled to find work and acceptance in a nation that welcomed them philosophically yet feared them socially and economically.

SECTION 3

Newcomers from overseas and migrants from the nation's rural areas swelled the populations of America's cities. Cities grew in many exciting ways, but slums and ghettos also grew. Corrupt political machines controlled many of the nation's cities.

SECTION 4

Some reform groups wished to control immigration and behavior; other reformers worked to improve conditions in the nation's cities.

Politics, Immigration, and Urban Life
1877–1920

CHAPTER 16

Politics, Immigration, and Urban Life
1877–1920

 The Relevance of the Big Idea

America seems always to have debated the issue of immigration: clutching the principle and sentiment of being the last best place on earth for the world's "wretched refuse," yet eager to define what is American by a very narrow set of characteristics. During the Gilded Age, for example, some Americans tried to bar the gates against immigration—at least to immigrants they classified as "undesirable." At the same time, the Statue of Liberty was being erected and cheered as a symbol of refuge and hope for the world's oppressed peoples.

Have students quickly brainstorm reasons pro and con continued immigration, directing their discussion to the question of restricted, or limited, versus unlimited immigration.

In the late 1800s and early 1900s, the United States seemed in constant motion. Millions of people were on the move. Immigrants arriving from foreign shores and Americans migrating from rural areas both found new homes in the nation's cities. The urban crowding, poverty, and crime that resulted shocked many people. Reformers suggested various ways to address these problems. But the federal government, troubled with its own corruption and undistinguished leadership, failed to address the challenges faced by its citizens every day.

 In Depth

Global Connections

Through the port of New York City alone, between 1847 and 1860, came over a million people from Ireland. That was nearly half of all Europeans who landed in New York in those years. The Irish came, in large part, because blight destroyed their country's entire potato crop, which was the mainstay of their diet. Eventually over one million died in Ireland from starvation and disease during the potato famine. America seemed a far cry from the disaster. One new arrival wrote, "Every day [in America] is like Christmas Day."

Events in the United States

1875   **1880**   **1885**   **1890**   **1895**

1882 Congress passes the Chinese Exclusion Act.

1886 The Statue of Liberty is erected in New York Harbor.

1892 The federal government opens an immigrant reception center on Ellis Island.

1894 Coxey's army of the unemployed marches on Washington.

Events in the World

1881 Czar Alexander II of Russia is assassinated by revolutionaries.

1889 The Eiffel Tower is constructed for the Paris Exposition.

1896 Ethiopia repels an Italian invasion.

 RESOURCE DIRECTORY

Teaching Resources

Alternate Lesson Plan: Demonstrating the Big Idea found in the Alternate Lesson Plans folder, p. 79, provides a lesson strategy to instruct students about the Big Idea that the rapid influx of people to American cities led to enormous problems, which corrupt government officials had great difficulty solving.

Alternative Assessment Handbook provides information, guidance, and strategies for alternative methods of assessment. It includes an essay on new trends in assessment, guidance and strategies for developing performance tasks and portfolios, scoring rubrics, and sample evaluation forms.

Pages 442–447
Politics in the Gilded Age
In the years after Reconstruction, the United States changed from a nation of farms into one of growing businesses, factories, and cities. Yet despite such changes—and sometimes because of them—many problems festered. Among them were corruption in government and business and a series of Presidents who seemed unable to address the nation's problems.

Pages 448–453
People on the Move
The dreams of the immigrants who came to the United States in the late nineteenth century might have seemed more golden than gilded. Millions left oppression, persecution, and poverty behind to begin new lives as Americans. Most found not streets paved with gold, but unfamiliar roads that they navigated with difficulty.

Pages 454–458
The Challenge of the Cities
As immigrants from Europe and Asia arrived on American shores, most pinned their hopes on the nation's cities. Bustling, noisy, and straining at the seams, the cities were places where the new became neighbors with the old and where progress lived next door to poverty.

Pages 460–463
Ideas for Reform
The flood of newcomers added colorful diversity to the nation's cities in the late 1800s but, at the same time, contributed to a host of problems. Shocked by social, economic, and political conditions in the cities, religious and social groups pushed programs for change.

1901 President William McKinley is assassinated by an anarchist.

1907 Japanese immigration to the United States is limited.

1910s Hundreds of thousands of African Americans migrate from the South to northern cities.

 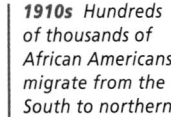

| 1900 | 1905 | 1910 | 1915 | 1920 | 1925 |

1905 Albert Einstein develops his special theory of relativity.

1910 Japan annexes Korea.

1913 The first woman magistrate takes office in England.

1918 A worldwide influenza epidemic kills more than twenty million people.

![Alternative Assessment]

Alternative Assessment

As an ongoing chapter project, students can create a handbook designed to guide and assist would-be immigrants to the United States during the period 1877–1920. Students should analyze and present conditions as they might affect immigrants.

Handbooks should inform immigrants regarding each of the following topics:
- The political scene in the United States; national political parties and their positions
- Current immigration trends and opportunities
- City life and the social scene
- The reform movement

Explain that finished projects will be assessed according to the following standards:
- **Unacceptable** Projects are not attempted, or fail to meet requirements outlined.
- **Limited/Acceptable** Projects are based on material from the textbook, present information about each topic, and provide a limited view of the immigrant perspective.
- **Extensive/Commendable** Projects include some outside research, demonstrate an understanding of the immigrant perspective, and reflect a basic analysis of the topics and trends.
- **Extraordinary/Outstanding** Projects are based on considerable research, demonstrate a thorough understanding of the immigrant perspective, and reflect an in-depth analysis of the topics and trends as they might affect immigrants.

For information and guidance on alternative assessment trends and strategies, see the Alternative Assessment Handbook in the Resource Directory on page 440.

Politics in the Gilded Age

1. FOCUS

Connecting to the Big Idea

See page 440B. Explain that national politics during the Gilded Age were uninspired at best. Reformers tried without much success to end the widespread corruption in politics and business. Ask students what national problems plagued the nation during the Gilded Age and why reformers were unable to end corruption.

Objectives

● Identify business practices that led to new government regulations.
● Describe the respective positions of Democrats and Republicans on issues such as tariffs, currency questions, and political reform.
● Explain why the reforms to end corrupt government practices were largely ineffective.

Bellringer

Ask students to list ideas they associate with the word *reformer*. In what areas of American life are reformers trying to make changes today? What factors work against them?

Reading Strategy

Structured Overview Ask students to write the following headings from Section 1 on a piece of paper: The Political Landscape in the Late 1800s, Presidents and Reforms, Railroad Abuses Lead to New Regulations, Efforts to Regulate Tariffs. Have students scan the section and create subheadings under each of the headings. Have students add details from the text as they read.

Politics in the Gilded Age

SECTION PREVIEW

In the years after Reconstruction, the United States changed from a nation of farms into one of growing businesses, factories, and cities. Yet despite such changes—and sometimes because of them—many problems festered. Among them were corruption in government and business and a series of Presidents who seemed unable to address the nation's problems.

Key Concepts

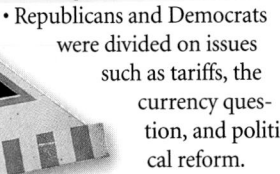

• Unfair business practices led to new government regulations.
• Republicans and Democrats were divided on issues such as tariffs, the currency question, and political reform.
• Political leaders instituted reforms to end corrupt government practices, but these proved largely ineffective.

Political campaigns such as William McKinley's presidential bid aroused wide interest in the late 1800s.

Key Terms, People, and Places

Gilded Age, laissez-faire, blue laws, Pendleton Act, Interstate Commerce Act; Jacob S. Coxey

Many labels have been used to describe the post-Reconstruction era (1877–1900) in the United States. The most famous is the **Gilded Age,** a term coined by writer Mark Twain that implies a thin layer of glitter over a cheap base. Other labels for the period included the Tragic Era and the Dreadful Decades. All of these terms present an unflattering picture of this era. The decades earned their reputation because of widespread corruption in government and business, as well as the failure of the era's Presidents to solve the persistent economic, social, and political problems plaguing the nation.

The Political Landscape in the Late 1800s

The United States faced great challenges as it emerged from Reconstruction. Industrial expansion raised factory and farm productivity, but economic cycles of boom and bust, low wages for workers, and rising farmer debt contributed to feelings of deep discontent among most working people. Others, such as speculators in stocks and land, quickly rose "from rags to riches." Corruption tempted business and political leaders, who also hoped to achieve such dreams of power and wealth. A dissatisfied public demanded reform.

Laissez-Faire Policies In the late 1800s, businesses operated largely without government regulation. This **laissez-faire**, or hands-off, approach to economic matters holds that government should play only a very limited role in business. Supporters of this theory maintain that if government doesn't interfere, the strongest businesses will succeed and bring wealth to the nation as a whole.

In the late nineteenth century, most Americans accepted this philosophy in theory. In practice, however, many supported government involvement when it benefited business. For example, champions of the laissez-faire approach favored high tariffs on imported goods. They argued that raising the prices of imported goods discouraged people from buying them, thus helping American businesses, and eventually the economy, to grow. American businesses also willingly accepted government land grants and subsidies—payments made by the government to encourage the development of certain key industries, such as railroads.

Business giants during the Gilded Age supported friendly politicians with both legal and illegal contributions of money. Between 1875 and 1885, the Central Pacific Railroad (CPR) reportedly budgeted $500,000 annually

---

RESOURCE DIRECTORY

Teaching Resources

Reproducible Lesson Plan found in the Unit 5 folder, p. 76, provides a summary of the Section 1 lesson plan content.

Alternate Lesson Plan: Learning Styles found in the Alternate Lesson Plans folder, p. 80, is especially helpful for kinesthetic learners and is designed to guide students in enacting a Gilded Age time line.

Guided Reading and Review found in the Unit 5 folder, p. 80, provides a structure for reading and mastering the key concepts and reviewing the key terms for Section 1. (Guided Practice)

Critical Thinking Activity Distinguishing False from Accurate Images: Honest Graft, found in the Unit 5 folder, p. 93, is designed to help students apply this skill by examining a politician's attempted justification of "honest graft."

for bribes. CPR cofounder Collis P. Huntington explained, "If you have to pay money to have the right thing done, it is only just and fair to do it."

The Spoils System Another controversial practice in American politics at the time was the spoils system. Under the spoils system, those who were elected to public office were free to appoint friends and supporters to government jobs, regardless of their qualifications—or their honesty. The use of this system became widespread during the presidency of Andrew Jackson, and by the Gilded Age its impact on government had reached a crisis point.

The spoils system appealed to many politicians because it ensured a flock of supporters in future elections. Both Democrats and Republicans handed out jobs to pay off the people who had helped them get elected. But the system led to corruption when dishonest appointees used their jobs for personal profit. ⭐

Political Parties During the Gilded Age, the numbers of Democrats and Republicans in the United States were about equal, but the characteristics of their members were quite different. The two parties also held starkly different positions on the major issues of the day.

Republicans controlled New York state, New England, and the upper Midwest. In general, they favored a tight money supply backed by gold, high tariffs to protect American business, generous pensions for Union soldiers, and government aid to the railroads. They also wanted to restrict immigration and enforce **blue laws**, which prohibited certain personal behaviors, such as drinking alcoholic beverages on Sundays.

As a rule, the Democratic party attracted those in American society who felt—and sometimes were—less privileged. These groups included northern urban immigrants, laborers, and southern planters and western farmers. Democrats claimed to represent the interests of ordinary people and favored free silver as a means of increasing the money supply and raising farm prices. Democrats typically opposed blue laws.

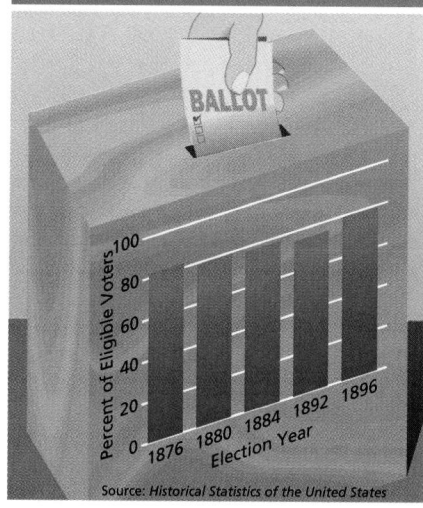

Voter Participation in Presidential Elections, 1876–1896

Percent of Eligible Voters

100 / 80 / 60 / 40 / 20 / 0

1876 1880 1884 1892 1896

Election Year

Source: Historical Statistics of the United States

 Interpreting Graphs
Voter turnout was high in the late 1800s compared to earlier eras. By 1920, it had dropped below 50 percent and never again rose as high as 65 percent. *What factors might help explain the high turnout in the late 1800s?*

Presidents and Reforms

Because the two parties had roughly equal numbers of supporters during the Gilded Age, presidential candidates needed almost total support of the members of their party in order to win an election. Candidates generally avoided taking strong stands on political issues in order not to offend potential supporters. They preferred, instead, to "wave the bloody shirt," which meant they focused on their Civil War records. Once in office, however, each of the era's Presidents did exercise a degree of leadership on the major issues of the day. Indeed, the era witnessed some important reforms of the spoils system, the railroads, and trusts.

Hayes Addresses Currency and Patronage
After his election in 1876, the honest and practical Rutherford B. Hayes faced the money supply debate. Those who favored soft money—the term used to describe an increase in the currency supply—supported the passage of the Bland-Allison Act of 1878. This act favored those

In Depth

Did You Know?

The corruption of this period is illustrated in the story of the Johnstown Flood of 1889. The developer who purchased the South Fork Dam and its reservoir from the commonwealth of Pennsylvania in 1879 had the right friends and political connections. He turned the property into an exclusive fishing and hunting club that counted among its members the entrepreneurs Andrew Mellon and Andrew Carnegie. Officials in the nearby industrial center of Johnstown, about 12 miles east of Stony Creek, persistently warned that the reservoir lake, which could hold approximately five billion gallons of water, was unsafe. They were told by the club's owners: "You and your people are in no danger from our enterprise." However, on May 31, 1889, the South Fork Dam collapsed. One witness described the scene: "In an instant the deserted street became black with people running for their lives. The flood came and licked them up with one eager and ferocious lap." More than two thousand people died in the Johnstown Flood.

Review with students the reasons some Americans demanded reforms after Reconstruction. (*Economic cycles of boom and bust, low wages for workers, rising farm debt, corruption in politics and business.*)

Discuss with students the positions of the two major political parties. Which party was favored by wealthy Americans? (*Republican*) Which party generally attracted the less privileged in society and opposed blue laws? (*Democratic*)

Ask students to list the efforts of Presidents Hayes and Arthur to end patronage. How did President Garfield's assassination contribute to the end of patronage?

Analyze

Ask students to explain why the passage of the Interstate Commerce Act was a hollow victory for those who wished to stop the abuses of the railroads.

Discuss the motives President Harrison might have had for supporting large veterans' pensions.

with high debts, such as farmers and business owners who had borrowed money. It required the federal government to purchase and coin more silver, increasing the currency supply and causing inflation. If prices went up, farmers would make more money for their goods and would more easily pay off debts incurred earlier.

Although Congress passed the act, Hayes vetoed it because he opposed the inflation it would create. Congress overrode Hayes's veto. Nevertheless, Hayes's Treasury Department limited the effectiveness of the act by buying only the minimum silver it required. The Treasury also refused to circulate the silver dollars that the law required it to mint.

Hayes was the first President to turn away from the practice of patronage. He did not have congressional support for his actions, even from members of his own Republican party, but he did what he could through executive orders

President Garfield's assassination by a disappointed office seeker roused the nation to the need for reform of the spoils system.

A GREAT NATION IN GRIEF

PRESIDENT GARFIELD SHOT BY AN ASSASSIN.

THOUGH SERIOUSLY WOUNDED HE STILL SURVIVES.

THE WOULD-BE MURDERER LODGED IN PRISON.

THE PRESIDENT OF THE UNITED STATES ATTACKED AND TERRIBLY WOUNDED BY A FANATICAL OFFICE-SEEKER ON THE EVE OF INDEPENDENCE DAY—THE NATION HORRIFIED AND THE WHOLE CIVILIZED WORLD SHOCKED—THE PRESIDENT STILL ALIVE AND HIS RECOVERY POSSIBLE.

and appointments. Hayes appointed qualified political independents to cabinet posts, outlawed the practice of forcing federal employees to make campaign contributions, and fired those employees who were not needed.

Garfield Assassinated in Office In 1880 the Republican party had three factions. The Stalwarts, followers of New York senator Roscoe Conkling, defended the spoils system. The Half-Breeds followed Maine senator James G. Blaine and tried to balance the need for reform of the spoils system with loyalty to the party. Independents opposed the spoils system altogether. They were sometimes called "googoos," a derisive term that was short for *good government.* In the 1880s, when independents left the party to support a Democrat, they also became known as *Mugwumps.* An Algonquin word for "renegade chief," the term stuck when a newspaper editor joked that it really meant "unreliable Republicans," men whose "mugs" were on one side of the fence and "wumps" on the other.

Hayes had announced at the beginning of his presidency that he would not seek a second term. In 1880, Republicans selected James A. Garfield, a member of Congress from Ohio, as their presidential candidate. Because Garfield was linked to the Half-Breeds, who were only somewhat loyal to old-time Republican policies, the vice-presidential slot went to Chester A. Arthur, a Stalwart.

In the 1880 election, Garfield won a narrow victory against Democratic candidate General Winfield S. Hancock. His term was cut short, however, by an assassin's bullet. On July 2, 1881, a deranged lawyer named Charles Guiteau shot Garfield as the President walked through the Washington, D.C., railroad station. When he fired his fatal shot, Guiteau cried out, "I am a Stalwart and Arthur is President now!" Garfield suffered for nearly three months before dying.

It turned out that Guiteau was a loyal Republican and a disappointed office seeker. He felt that his loyalty had earned him a job under the spoils system, and he became enraged when Garfield passed him over. Guiteau's violent act aroused public outrage at the spoils system.

Arthur Ends Patronage With Garfield's death, Vice President Chester Arthur succeeded to the nation's highest office. During the Hayes administration, Arthur had benefited from the practice of patronage. He had been appointed to a high-paying job in the New York Customs House because of his support of Senator Roscoe Conkling. Once in office, however, he urged Congress to support reform of the spoils system. With Garfield's assassination fresh in the nation's mind, President Arthur was able to garner legislative support for his ideas, and the **Pendleton Act** became law in 1883.

The act empowered three civil service commissioners to classify government jobs and test applicants' fitness for them. It also stated that federal employees could not be required to contribute to campaign funds and could not be fired for political reasons.

Democrats Take Over In the 1884 presidential campaign, the key issues were high tariffs, unfair business practices, and unregulated railroads. The Republicans nominated the eloquent James G. Blaine, a former secretary of state and senator from Maine. The Democratic party chose the genial Grover Cleveland, former mayor of Buffalo and governor of New York. In spite of the serious economic issues of the day, the campaign focused mostly on scandals.

Had James G. Blaine received railroad stock options in return for favorable votes while he was in Congress? No one could prove it. Had Cleveland fathered an illegitimate child when a bachelor in Buffalo? Cleveland admitted it was true. Republicans jeered, "Ma, Ma, where's my Pa?" to which the Democrats responded, "Going to the White House, ha, ha, ha!" In spite of his admission, Cleveland won the election, thereby becoming the first Democrat elected to the presidency since 1856. Cleveland did appoint Democrats to office but avoided giving in to the spoils system. He tried to ensure that his appointments were based on merit.

An advocate of tight money, Cleveland was acceptable to most business interests. Yet he opposed generous pensions and high tariffs, and he took back from the railroads and other interests 81 million acres of land grants on which they had failed to fulfill their obligations. Cleveland also supported regulation of the powerful railroads. He believed that fierce competition among the various railroad lines led to practices, such as secret rebates to high-volume shippers, that hurt small businesses.

Railroad Abuses Lead to New Regulations

Railroad regulation had begun in 1869, when Massachusetts officials investigated rate abuses in that state. By 1880, fourteen states had railroad commissions to look into complaints against railroad practices. Such practices included awarding stock to legislators in return for favors and manipulating the state legal system to win court challenges against rate abuses. In 1877 the Supreme Court decision in *Munn* v. *Illinois* allowed states to regulate certain enterprises within their boundaries. Lawyers for the railroads responded with the argument that, under the Constitution, states could not regulate interstate commerce. Because railroad traffic often crossed state lines, only the federal government could regulate their activities. With this argument the railroads were successful and continued to pursue their disputed practices.

Pressure mounted on Congress to take action to curb railroad company abuses. In 1887 the legislature passed the **Interstate Commerce Act**. The act required that rates be set in proportion to the distance traveled and that rate schedules be made public. The act also outlawed the practice of giving rebates and favors to powerful customers. It set up the nation's first regulatory board, the Interstate Commerce Commission (ICC), to enforce the act.

Unfortunately, the act failed to give the commission the power necessary to set rates, rendering it largely ineffective. To enforce its rulings, the ICC had to take the railroads to court. But of the sixteen cases involving the ICC that came before the Supreme Court between 1887 and 1905, the Court ruled against the ICC fifteen times. Still, the creation of the ICC established the precedent that private enterprise was subject to government control.

3. ASSESS

Section 1 Review Answers

1. (a) Interstate Commerce Act, see p. 445, (b) Jacob S. Coxey, see p. 446

2. (a) laissez-faire, see p. 442, (b) blue laws, see p. 443

3. Superficially, things looked good. There was much wealth and technological progress visible, but beneath that "gilt" appearance, serious problems festered which the era's corrupt politicians and mediocre leaders were unable to solve.

4. Unfair practices by the railroads, such as charging higher rates for shorter hauls and giving secret rebates to high-volume shippers; the Interstate Commerce Act regulated rates, outlawed rebates and other favors, and set up the Interstate Commerce Commission to enforce the act. The Interstate Commerce Act was not very effective because the courts generally ruled in favor of the railroads. The Sherman Antitrust Act attempted to curb the power of corporate trusts. It, too, was not very effective.

5. The people who won elections could appoint their friends to government jobs. Through these acts of patronage, they were guaranteed supporters in future contests. The Pendleton Act empowered civil service commissioners to classify government jobs and test applicants' fitness for them. The act also prevented politicians from requiring federal employees to contribute to their

Using Historical Evidence This cartoon expresses the widespread concern about the harmful effects of monopolies in the late 1800s. *How do the images in this cartoon communicate such a message?*

MAKING CONNECTIONS

How did the passing of the Interstate Commerce Act weaken the policy of laissez-faire?

Efforts to Regulate Tariffs

The White House again found itself with a new tenant when Cleveland lost the 1888 election to Republican Benjamin Harrison. Tariffs provided a focal point for the campaign. Cleveland favored a minor reduction; Harrison campaigned for an increase, a position that won him much business support and, ultimately, the presidency.

Among President Harrison's achievements was the signing of the Sherman Antitrust Act in 1890, described in Chapter 14. Like the Interstate Commerce Act, however, this seemingly bold action failed to curb the power of the largest corporations until well after the turn of the century.

Meanwhile, Harrison also took actions that favored business. In 1890 he approved a huge tariff increase, and he supported legislation on behalf of special business interests. Although he was considered a conservative regarding the public treasury, he was liberal when it came to veterans' pensions. He ate up the last federal surplus in United States history with huge new pensions for the dependents of Civil War soldiers.

In the election of 1892, with many new immigrants swelling Democratic party rolls, and campaigning for lower tariffs, Grover Cleveland was returned to the presidency. By the time his term was over, however, many people were more disillusioned with government than ever before.

Cleveland's Second Term Cleveland's second term started badly. To begin with, he inherited Harrison's treasury deficit. Also, Americans were experiencing the worst depression the country had yet seen. Millions of people lost their jobs or had their wages slashed, yet government offered no help to those out of work. In 1894 **Jacob S. Coxey**, a wealthy Ohio quarry owner turned Populist, demanded that government create jobs for the unemployed. He then called for a march on Washington. "We will send a petition to Washington with boots on," he declared.

Many small "armies" started out on the protest march, but only Coxey's arrived. Police arrested him and a few others for illegally carrying banners on the Capitol grounds and for trampling the grass. Based on the tune of "The Star-Spangled Banner," a song created by Coxey's supporters mocked their government's vigilance in protecting the lawns of the Capitol while ignoring the pleas of the nation's poor.

O h, say, can you see, by the dawn's early light
That grass plot so dear to the hearts of us all?
Is it green yet and fair, in well-nurtured plight,
Unpolluted by the Coxeyites' hated foot-fall?
Midst the yells of police, and swish of clubs through the air,

 RESOURCE DIRECTORY

Teaching Resources

*We could hardly tell if our grass was still
there.
But the green growing grass does in triumph
yet wave,
And the gallant police with their buttons
of brass
Will sure make the Coxeyites keep off the
grass.*

— Anonymous, 1894

In his second term, Cleveland managed to anger not only the unemployed, but almost every group in his party. He angered labor when he sent federal troops to Chicago at the time of the Pullman strike of 1894. He angered farmers by repealing the Silver Purchase Act and returning the country to a gold standard. Having alienated so many fellow Democrats, Cleveland failed to win his party's nomination in 1896.

A Republican Returns to the White House
The Populists had emerged as a political power during the economic hard times of the early 1890s and had made gains in the elections of 1894. But in 1896 William Jennings Bryan, the presidential candidate they shared with the Democrats, lost to Republican William McKinley. Supported by urban workers and the middle class, McKinley won the election with ease.

A new tariff and the gold standard brought Republicans an even more decisive victory against Bryan in 1900. As the economic depression of the 1890s began to loosen its grip, the Republicans claimed credit with their slogan, "A Full Dinner Pail."

McKinley did not live long enough to enjoy the effects of the growing prosperity. On September 6, 1901, a mentally ill, unemployed anarchist named Leon Czolgosz hid a gun in a bandaged hand and shot President McKinley as he greeted the public at the Pan-American Exposition in Buffalo. When McKinley died a few days later, national hysteria followed.

In the public mind, dangerous ideas, many of them associated with foreign people—or those with foreign names such as Czolgosz—were threatening the country. Those blossoming fears would have a profound impact on the nation's huge and growing immigrant population, as the next section describes.

Coxey's Army, shown above, marched through many villages on its way to Washington to demand federal action to resolve the nation's economic problems.

SECTION 1 REVIEW

Key Terms, People, and Places
1. Identify (a) Interstate Commerce Act, (b) Jacob S. Coxey.
2. Define (a) laissez-faire, (b) blue laws.

Key Concepts
3. For what reason(s) is the post-Reconstruction period in national politics referred to as the Gilded Age?
4. Describe the business practices that led to government regulation. What regulations were passed in the Gilded Age, and how effective were they?
5. Describe how the spoils system worked and what action the government took to control it.

Critical Thinking
6. **Determining Relevance** For what reasons do you think political reformers believed that a civil service law could help wipe out corrupt government practices?

Quiz found in the Unit 8 folder, p. 81, covers the main ideas in this section as well as the key terms.

---

campaign funds, and from firing them for political reasons.

6. Possible answer: Officeholders would be appointed on the basis of merit, and appointees would have to prove their fitness for the duties of the job. There would no longer be political favors that had to be repaid.

Reteach
Ask students to correct any of the following statements that are incorrect:
• Government regulations such as the Interstate Commerce Act stopped unfair business practices.
• During the Gilded Age, the positions of the Republicans and Democrats were more or less interchangeable.
• The assassination of President Arthur led to the end of patronage.

4. CLOSE

Reinforcing the Big Idea
During the Gilded Age, a series of ineffective Presidents failed to deal with economic problems and corruption in business and politics. The next section describes the lives of the many immigrants entering the United States during this period.

People on the Move

SECTION 2

People on the Move

Connecting to the Big Idea

See page 440B. Explain to students that during the Gilded Age, millions of immigrants arrived in the United States to begin new lives. Ask students what the lives of these new immigrants were like.

Objectives

• Identify the reasons that caused immigrants to come to the United States in the late 1800s.
• Describe how patterns of immigration changed in the late 1800s.
• Cite some of the difficulties faced by immigrants during their voyage to the United States and their arrival.

Bellringer

Ask students to imagine that they are immigrants entering the United States in 1900. What are their thoughts as they see the Statue of Liberty for the first time? Ask students to explain why the Statue of Liberty remains a potent symbol today, despite the fact that few immigrants now arrive in this country by sailing into New York harbor.

Reading Strategy

Reinforcing Key Ideas Ask students to list the following groups of immigrants on a piece of paper: European, Asian, Hispanic. Ask students to note reasons each group came to the United States, where each group of immigrants was likely to arrive in the United States, and any restrictions on their numbers or activities in this country.

SECTION PREVIEW

The dreams of the immigrants who came to the United States in the late nineteenth century might have seemed more golden than gilded. Millions left oppression, persecution, and poverty behind to begin new lives as Americans. Most found not streets paved with gold, but unfamiliar roads that they navigated with difficulty.

Key Concepts

• Economic hardship and political and religious persecution led immigrants to the United States in the late 1800s.
• Patterns of immigration changed in the late 1800s, and Americans distinguished between "old" and "new" immigrants.
• Immigrants experienced many difficulties during their voyage to the United States and after their arrival.

Millions of immigrants shipped their belongings and their dreams to the United States in the late 1800s.

Key Terms, People, and Places
steerage; Ellis Island, Angel Island

---

s politicians steered their way through the nagging economic and political problems of the late nineteenth century, fascinating human dramas were unfolding far from the spotlight of Washington, D.C. Played out in the nation's gritty ports and grimy back streets, these dramas told tales of triumph and tragedy, with millions of heroes and more than a few villains. These were the stories of the nation's immigrants.

Worldwide Patterns of Movement

In the late 1800s, people in many parts of the world were on the move, from farms to cities and then on to other countries. Immigrants from around the globe were fleeing crop failures, land and job shortages, rising taxes, and famine. Some were also escaping religious or political persecution.

Immigrants to the United States The United States received a huge portion of this migration. In 1860 the resident population of the United States was 31.5 million people. Between 1865 and 1920, close to 30 million additional people entered the country. Some of these newcomers dreamed of making fortunes, or at least of getting free government land through the Homestead Act. Others yearned for more personal freedom. In the United States, they had heard, everyone could go to school, young men were not forced to serve long years in the army, and democratic government meant equality and participation for more people.

In the late 1800s, steam-powered ships could cross the Atlantic Ocean in two to three weeks. By 1900 the crossing took just one week. Even this brief journey, however, could be an ordeal for those who could not afford cabins, and most could not. The majority of immigrants traveled in **steerage**, a large open area beneath the ship's deck with inadequate toilet facilities, no privacy, and poor food, but where tickets cost as little as $15. ★

The Golden Door Immigrants entered the United States through several ports. Those from Europe might come through Boston, Philadelphia, or Baltimore; those from Asia might enter through San Francisco or Seattle. More than 70 percent of all immigrants, however, came through New York City, which came to be called the "Golden Door."

Throughout most of the 1800s, immigrants arriving in New York entered at the Castle Garden depot near the southern tip of Manhattan. Then, in 1892, the federal government opened

---

▶ RESOURCE DIRECTORY

Teaching Resources

Reproducible Lesson Plan found in the Unit 5 folder, p. 77, provides a summary of the Section 2 lesson plan content.

Alternate Lesson Plan: Learning Styles found in the Alternate Lesson Plans folder, p. 81, is particularly effective for tactile learners, and helps students trace the routes of particular immigrants on their way to the United States.

Guided Reading and Review found in the Unit 5 folder, p. 82, provides a structure for reading and mastering the key concepts and reviewing the key terms for Section 2. (Guided Practice)

★ **Visual Learning Activity** Passage to America, found in the Unit 5 folder, p. 100, is designed to enhance students' understanding of the experience of immigrants on their way to America.

a huge reception center for steerage passengers on **Ellis Island** in New York Harbor, near where the Statue of Liberty had been erected in 1886. The statue, a gift of France, celebrated "Liberty Enlightening the World." It became a world symbol of the United States as a place of refuge and hope.

Ellis Island Receives European Immigrants

Information about the number and origins of the nation's immigrants is not exact. For example, officials often misidentified their countries of origin. Also, about a third of all immigrants were "birds of passage"—usually young, single men who worked for a number of months or years and then returned home. Until 1907 Mexican immigrants were not counted. Historians estimate, however, that about 10 million immigrants, mostly northern Europeans from countries such as England and Germany, arrived between 1865 and 1890. In the 1890s, the pattern of immigration shifted dramatically, and most immigrants came from the countries of southern and eastern Europe and the Middle East. Between 1890 and 1920 about 10 million Italians, Greeks, Slavs, Eastern European and Russian Jews, and Armenians arrived.

Arriving in America Before the 1880s, decisions about whom to allow into the country were left to the states. Then, in 1891, the federal government created the Office of the Superintendent of Immigration to determine who was "fit" for life in the United States and who was not. The next year laws required all new immigrants to undergo physical examination, and applicants could be denied admission on medical grounds. Those found to have contagious illnesses such as tuberculosis faced quarantine or even deportation. Those with trachoma, an eye disease that was common among immigrants, were automatically sent back to the country they had just left. Fiorello La Guardia, who later became mayor of New York City, worked as an interpreter at Ellis Island. "It was harrowing to see families separated," he remembered in the book *The Making of an Insurgent.*

*S*ometimes, if it was a young child who suffered from trachoma, one of the parents had to return to the native country with the rejected member of the family. When they learned their fate, they were stunned. They . . . had no homes to return to.

These recent arrivals on Ellis Island contemplate a bewildering yet promising future in their new homeland.

After their physicals, immigrants showed their documents to officials and then collected their baggage. If they had the address of a friend or relative, they took a ferry, boat, or train to find them. Those who were on their own had a harder time. Crooks hung around ports with fake offers of lodgings and jobs, stealing money and baggage from the unwary.

Where the Immigrants Settled Immigrants often settled near their ports of entry. A significant number of immigrants did move inland,

⊗ Literature Activity The Statue of Liberty, found in the Unit 5 folder, p. 97, uses the poem inscribed on the pedestal of the Statue of Liberty to explore a symbolic view of nineteenth-century immigration.

Media and Technology

 Transparency
Our Multicultural Heritage, C-2

Discuss
Ask students why immigrants left their homelands to come to the United States. What might motivate a person, possibly someone with very little money, to go to a country where a different language is spoken?

Ask students what problems immigrants faced in the United States. What special problems did Asian immigrants encounter in the United States?

Analyze
Ask students to analyze the role of fear and racism in discrimination against immigrants from Asia. How did Americans respond to Asian customs and traditions, their willingness to work for low wages, and their success in California agriculture?

In Depth

Historical Misconceptions

Daniel Patrick Moynihan, writing in the *New York Times* in May 1986, confronted a sentimental favorite of American history—the description of immigrants as "the wretched refuse of your teeming shore." Moynihan argues that the majority of the 20 million or so immigrants who arrived in the United States between 1870 and 1910 were neither wretched nor refuse, at least no more than any other immigrant group, including the Pilgrims. These immigrants were energetic and enthusiastic, though most were uneducated and semiskilled. "They were an extraordinary, enterprising, and self-sufficient folk who knew exactly what they were doing, and doing it quite on their own, thank you very much."

Answer to ...

MAKING CONNECTIONS

Answers will vary. Some students may observe that today, as in the late 1800s, certain immigrant groups receive the lowest-paying jobs. Yet certain other immigrant groups, whose members are typically highly trained and educated, often acquire professional, high-paying jobs.

In Depth

Then and Now

The heart of the immigrant experience was vividly recorded by the photographers who provided a lasting, accurate image of Ellis Island. Arrivals were carefully screened for medical problems. For example, a would-be immigrant with trachoma, a highly contagious eye infection that can cause blindness, would not be admitted. Passengers who failed immediate clearance were kept in detention centers, and those with suspected health problems had initials chalked on their clothing to identify the possible problems: *E* for eyes, *L* for lameness, *X* for mental disability. "Their stolid faces hide frightened, throbbing hearts," wrote one observer of arrivals going through the screening process. The steamship companies were responsible for the return of the 2 percent—often as many as one thousand people per month—who were denied immigrant status. Ellis Island officially closed in November 1954, but in September 1990 the Ellis Island Immigration Museum opened as a permanent memorial to the 12 million people who made it their first stop in America.

Chinese immigrants brought distinctive styles and customs to the United States. Traditional dress and shops helped them feel at home—but also set them apart from other Americans, who often had little tolerance for differences.

however, often seeking communities established by previous settlers from their homelands.

In this way, large settlements of Poles and Italians formed in Buffalo, Cleveland, Detroit, and Milwaukee. Chicago—a port, railroad hub, and center for the garment, grain, lumber, and livestock industries—attracted a diverse group of immigrants. Some immigrants continued on to the mining towns of the West. Only 2 percent went to the South, primarily because the area did not offer newcomers enough jobs or land. Louisiana recruited Italian farm laborers, however, and Florida also sought foreign-born agricultural workers.

Once settled, immigrants looked for work. There were never enough jobs, and employers—often immigrants themselves—took advantage of the "greenhorns." They paid them less than other workers and paid women less

than men. Men tailors, for example, working 14 hours a day, 6 days a week, earned $6 to $10 a week. Women seamstresses, doing the same work, earned half that amount. Women domestic servants earned $4 to $10 a month, working 16 hours or more a day and more than 6 days a week.

MAKING CONNECTIONS

How does the treatment of men and women immigrant workers in the nineteenth century compare to the way men and women in the workplace are treated in the United States today?

From Asia to the United States

Most of the immigrants who entered the United States on the West Coast came from Asia. These people, whose cultures differed greatly from those of both Americans and Europeans, faced a unique set of challenges.

In the 1800s, railroad companies recruited about a quarter of a million Chinese workers. Like the indentured servants of the colonial era, the Chinese had to work for their companies until they had paid the cost of their passage and upkeep. Americans called these workers "coolies," a corruption of the Chinese word for "unskilled laborer." Many Chinese paid their debts, settled down, and began to work in other fields, including mining, farming, fishing, factory work, food preparation, and laundering. But the group as a whole had difficulty freeing itself from ethnic stereotypes.

✪ White people ridiculed Chinese dress and their custom of wearing long pony tails, or *queues.* Many Americans condemned them for what they saw as the squalor of crowded Chinese neighborhoods—conveniently disregarding the discrimination and exploitation that helped create such conditions.

Because the Chinese accepted low wages, unions worked to keep them from coming to the United States. Using pseudoscientific evidence, anti-Asian movements fostered racist attitudes. One newspaper's remarks from 1870 were typical:

RESOURCE DIRECTORY

Teaching Resources

✪ **Visual Learning Activity** The Chinese Question, found in the Unit 5 folder, p. 101, encourages students to analyze one common sentiment about immigration and understand the effect of political cartoons.

The Mongoloid [Asian] blood is depraved and debased blood. The Mongoloid type of humanity is an inferior type—inferior in organic structure, in vital force or physical energy, and in the constitutional conditions of development. On this point all anthropologists and ethnologists are agreed.

In reality, some scientists of the time agreed with such incorrect views and many did not. Nevertheless, Congress responded to popular demand by passing the Chinese Exclusion Act in 1882. The act prohibited Chinese laborers from entering the country. It was renewed in 1892 and 1902, and then made permanent. The act was not repealed until 1943.

The act did not prevent entry by those who had previously established residence or who had family already living in the United States. In 1910 the government built a detention center on **Angel Island** in San Francisco Bay, where immigrants' claims of prior residence or relationship to citizens received lengthy examination.

Two hundred thousand Japanese had arrived on the West Coast by 1920, many via Hawaii, which the United States annexed in 1898. Most Japanese settled in the Los Angeles area, and soon they were producing much of southern California's fruits and vegetables.

The success of Japanese immigrants aroused the jealousy of some who gave them the derogatory nickname "The Yellow Peril." In 1905 California's political leaders urged, and two years later won, restrictions on Japanese immigration. This was accomplished when President Theodore Roosevelt made a so-called gentleman's agreement with Japanese officials, who agreed to limit Japanese emigration. In 1913 the California legislature passed an Alien Land Law, which banned noncitizen Asians from owning farmland.

From South to North

In 1902 Congress passed the Newlands National Reclamation Act to stimulate the irrigation of southwestern lands. Over the next decade, irrigation turned millions of acres of desert into fertile farmland in Texas, Arizona, and California.

The new farmland meant new jobs. About 5 percent of Mexico's population, fleeing poverty and debt, entered the United States through El Paso, Texas. The 1909 Mexican Revolution increased the flow. Later, when the Immigration Restriction Act of 1921 limited immigration from Europe and Asia, labor shortages made Mexicans more needed than ever. By 1925 Los Angeles had the largest Spanish-speaking population in any North American city outside of Mexico.

AMERICAN PROFILES
The Immigrant Experience

Facts and figures tell only a part of the story of immigration in the United States. The drama behind the figures is best revealed in the

---

Viewpoints
On Cultural Ties

Many people held opinions on how immigrants could best adjust to their new lives in the United States. Some thought they should give up their own language and customs as quickly as possible; others thought they should hold on to their heritage. ***Do you think that immigrant children or their parents had an easier time adjusting to their new lives? Why?***

On Breaking Cultural Ties

"We wanted to be Americans so quickly that we were embarrassed if our parents couldn't speak English. My father was reading a Polish paper. And somebody was supposed to come to the house. I remember sticking it under something. We were that ashamed of being foreign."

Louise Nagy, a Polish immigrant, 1913

On Preserving Cultural Ties

"We ate the same dishes, spoke the same language, told the same stories, indulged in the same pleasures [as in Syria]. . . . To me the colony [neighborhood] was a habitat so much like the one I had left behind in Syria that its home atmosphere enabled me to maintain a firm hold on life in the face of the many difficulties which confronted me in those days."

Abraham Ribahny, on his neighborhood in New York, 1893

📄 **Viewpoints Activity** On Cultural Ties, found in the Unit 5 folder, pp. 90–91, features additional quotes from immigrants to demonstrate the variety of opinions on settling in America.

Answer to …

Viewpoints

Nagy had a hard time living with immigrant parents while also trying to look and act American. She was ashamed of her parents' ties to the country of their birth. Ribahny's close ties to his immigrant community helped him cope with the new, less comfortable environment. For a more thorough examination of immigrants' adjustment to their new lives, see the Resource Directory below.

Activity
Teaching Heterogeneous Groups

In 1892 the Office of the Superintendent of Immigration was established to determine who was "fit" for immigration into the United States. Divide students into an even number of groups and ask each group to design a test for immigration fitness. Suggest the following tests: physical fitness, intelligence, finances, and knowledge of U.S. history. Have groups administer their tests to each other. Discuss with students their feelings about being tested in this way. `LEP`

Enrichment

Ask students to interview an immigrant to the United States. Before the interview, students should prepare questions about the immigrant's country of origin, the date he or she arrived, reasons for immigrating, impressions of the political system of the United States, and opinions concerning problems currently facing the United States, such as crime and poverty. Students should also ask if the immigrant keeps in touch with friends and relatives in his or her country of origin. Remind students to be sensitive about asking for personal information about finances and visa status. If your school does not have students who have immigrated from another country, students might contact religious, ethnic, or fraternal organizations for help in locating a subject to interview.

Section 2 Review Answers

1. Angel Island, see p. 451

2. The chief reason was economic. Many people were fleeing crop failures, land and job shortages, rising taxes, and famine. Some were escaping religious or political persecution.

3. They hoped to make fortunes, or at least get free government land. Others wanted more personal freedom.

4. They sailed on steam-powered ships in steerage, a large open area with primitive sanitation, no privacy, and poor food. A steerage ticket might cost as little as $15. Eighty percent came through New York City; after 1892 through Ellis Island, near the Statue of Liberty. The rest came through other East Coast ports, Mexico, or West Coast ports such as San Francisco.

5. They came from southern and eastern Europe and the Middle East.

6. Possible answer: Asians' appearance, dress, and customs may have seemed more foreign than those of Europeans; and Americans were less familiar with their culture.

Reteach

Ask students to answer each of the following questions based on information in the chapter section:

• Why did immigrants come to the United States during the Gilded Age?
• From what part of Europe did most European immigrants come before 1890? From what part of Europe did most European immigrants come after 1890?
• How did the United States restrict Asian immigration?

accounts of ordinary people, whose lives and experiences reflect the struggles and triumphs of living day to day in a new land.

Sadie Frowne, Polish Immigrant Young Sadie Frowne lived an unremarkable life in her native Poland. Her mother kept a grocer's shop and worked in the fields with her husband. Sadie, too, worked hard, scrubbing floors and washing dishes, even as a six year old.

When Sadie was ten, however, her father died, shattering the fragile structure of the family's livelihood. Unable to earn enough to buy food, Sadie and her mother looked to the United States, where they hoped to build a new life. Sadie's aunt, who already lived in New York City, encouraged them and took up a collection among her friends to pay for their passage to the United States. Sadie was thirteen years old when she and her mother set out on their immigration journey.

The Frownes' crossing, which took place in 1898, lasted twelve days.

Treasured items from home, such as this stuffed bear and set of spoons, helped provide a link between an immigrant's old and new lives.

There were hundreds of other people packed in with us, men, women and children, and almost all of them were sick. . . . We thought we should die, but at last the voyage was over, and we came up and saw the beautiful bay and the big woman with the spikes on her head and the lamp that is lighted at night in her hand.

Once in the United States, Sadie found a job as a live-in servant. Her mother found employment as a garment worker. Tragedy struck again, however, when Sadie's mother contracted a fatal case of tuberculosis, a disease then raging through the crowded neighborhoods of New York City.

Now orphaned, the need to work was more urgent than ever.

Sadie managed to get a new job as a skirt-maker earning $4 for a six-day week. With this income, she found a room that she shared with another young woman for $1.50 a week.

By keeping her weekly expenses down, Sadie was now able to set aside a dollar a week for "clothing and pleasure" and another dollar for savings. She went to school at night to learn English. She also worked to improve her sewing skills, found a better job, and moved to a nicer place in Brooklyn.

With constant work, sacrifice, and determination, Sadie was living out the dream of millions of immigrants. It was a dream of simple comforts, modest prosperity, and the chance for a better life. ✪

A Japanese Picture Bride Tameji Eto came to the United States from Japan in 1904. After working as a farmhand, he became a foreman for the Pacific Coast Railroad Company and then leased land for his own farm.

Having achieved some security, Tameji began to think of settling down and starting a family. Because few Japanese women had emigrated to the United States, Tameji's thoughts turned to Take, the sister of one of his school friends back in Japan. He wrote her family to ask permission to marry her.

Nineteen-year-old Take had no memory of Tameji, but her parents insisted that she accept his proposal. Because such arranged marriages were typical among the Japanese at that time, Take accepted her fate. Clutching Tameji's photograph, her only means of identifying her future husband, she sailed for the United States.

On board ship, Take met other "picture brides," women whose marriages had been arranged through the exchange of photographs across the Pacific Ocean. Like her companions, Take spent the voyage trying to adapt to strange foods and wondering about her future.

After her arrival and a ten-day quarantine for an eye infection, Take finally met Tameji. Luckily, he looked like his picture, "straight and tall with lots of hair," and he also seemed kind. Together they set out for the frontier town of Grand Arroyo, California.

▶ RESOURCE DIRECTORY

Teaching Resources

✪ **Literature Activity** Where is America? found in the Unit 5 folder, pp. 98–99, uses an excerpt from Anzia Yezierska's *Hungry Hearts* to express some of the hopes of immigrants to the United States.

These Japanese picture brides looked with both hope and apprehension to life in a new land with new husbands they had never met. As part of their traditional dress, many Japanese wore a type of footwear called *geta*, shown below.

Take took up the challenge of daily chores on the frontier and the repeated cultivation necessary to farm their semiarid land. "It was not easy," she later told one of her eight children,

but it was my future as well as [Tameji's], and I wanted to be a part of it. Father never demanded I work so hard. I did it because it was necessary and I wanted to.

The Eto's hard work paid off, and by 1919 they had enough money to buy their own farm. Because of the Alien Land Law, however, they had to buy land under the name of a white friend.

After some difficult years, the farm did well. While caring for her children, Take cooked for a farm crew of forty to fifty men. Finally, after fifteen years of hard work, the Etos felt they could afford a journey back to Japan to see their parents.

The Etos found their success on the American frontier. Opportunities there were greater for many immigrant groups, who faced discrimination in urban areas. Still, most immigrants found homes in one of the nation's large cities. Their impact on urban life in the United States was profound.

SECTION 2 REVIEW

Key Terms, People, and Places
1. Identify Angel Island.

Key Concepts
2. Why were so many people "on the move" in the late nineteenth century?
3. Why did so many people want to come to the United States?

4. How did most immigrants travel to the United States, and where did they enter the country?
5. Where did the "new" immigrants come from?

Critical Thinking
6. **Recognizing Bias** For what reasons do you think Asians were treated more harshly than immigrants from Europe?

 Quiz found in the Unit 5 folder, p. 83, covers the main ideas in this section as well as the key terms.

Media and Technology

Transparency
Our Multicultural Heritage, C-11

 Alternative Assessment

Mid-Point Monitoring
Ask students if they have
● Decided on a format for their projects
● Visited the library to begin their outside research
● Started drafting portions of their handbook

4. CLOSE

Reinforcing the Big Idea

Millions of immigrants sought new lives in the United States after 1865, despite difficulties finding employment and restrictions imposed on certain groups. The next section describes conditions in America's cities, where the majority of immigrants settled.

The Challenge of the Cities

Connecting to the Big Idea

See page 440B. Point out to students that immigrants and migrants flocked to the nation's cities during the Gilded Age. Ask how the nation's cities changed as a result of these dramatic increases in population.

Objectives

- Demonstrate that American cities expanded with the arrival of millions of immigrants.
- Explain the role of migration from within the country in swelling the urban population.
- Describe how the growth of cities contributed to corrupt political practices at the local level.

Bellringer

Ask students to think about the expression "bright lights, big city." Then have them list the advantages and disadvantages of city life.

Reading Strategy

Reading for Evidence Ask students to find evidence to support the statement on page 454, "The arrival of large numbers of newcomers from within and outside the nation radically changed the face of the nation's cities."

The Challenge of the Cities

SECTION PREVIEW

As immigrants from Europe and Asia arrived on American shores, most pinned their hopes on the nation's cities. Bustling, noisy, and straining at the seams, the cities were places where the new became neighbors with the old and where progress lived next door to poverty.

Key Concepts

- American cities expanded upward and outward with the arrival of tremendous numbers of new residents.
- Increased movement of people within the United States added to urban problems caused by immigration.
- The growth of American cities contributed to corrupt political practices at the local level.

Cities such as Chicago, pictured on this postcard, grew upward and outward in the late 1800s.

Key Terms, People, and Places

suburb, ghetto, political machine, political boss, Tammany Hall; William Marcy Tweed

---

While millions of immigrants from around the world were settling into the cities of the United States, growing numbers of Americans were also on the move. Between 1880 and 1920, 11 million Americans left behind the economic hardship of their farms and headed for the opportunities of the cities. This migration within the country, combined with the new immigrants, significantly affected the nation's growing urban centers.

Americans on the Move

Young women were among those who took part in the migration from rural to urban America. As factories produced more of the goods that farm women had once produced, the need for women's labor on farms declined.

Mechanization in agriculture also reduced the need for male farmhands. In 1880 about 72 percent of the population lived on farms. By 1910 that figure was down to 54 percent. Today it is about 3 percent.

Many African Americans also were among the internal migrants. In 1870, fewer than a half million of the nation's 5 million African Americans lived outside the South. By 1890, partly as a result of increased segregationist policies and racial violence in the South, 12 percent of the region's rural-dwelling African Americans had moved into nearby cities, and 150,000 had left the South altogether. Then, in the 1910s, after the boll weevil destroyed cotton crops and floods ruined Alabama and Mississippi farmlands, several hundred thousand more African Americans migrated to northern cities.

How Cities Grew

The arrival of large numbers of newcomers from within and outside the nation radically changed the face of the nation's cities. Between the Civil War and 1900, many features of modern city life first appeared— noise, skyscrapers, traffic jams, slums, air pollution, and sanitation and health problems.

Before the Civil War, cities were small in area—rarely more than 3 or 4 miles across. Most people lived at or near the place where they worked, and they moved about on foot.

Public, horse-drawn streetcars, introduced in the 1850s, changed this pattern somewhat. Those people who could afford the fares moved outside the cities, establishing new communities in the **suburbs**, or areas surrounding the cities. Cable cars and electric trolleys (Richmond, Virginia, had the first in 1888), elevated trains, automobiles (first appeared in 1893), and subways (Boston had the first in 1897), made commuting much easier and speeded suburban growth.

Cities grew upward, too. Before the Civil War, no building stood more than five stories

---

 RESOURCE DIRECTORY

Teaching Resources

Reproducible Lesson Plan found in the Unit 5 folder, p. 78, provides a summary of the Section 3 lesson plan content.

Alternate Lesson Plan: Critical Thinking Testing Conclusions, found in the Alternate Lesson Plans folder, p. 82, is designed to help students test conclusions by identifying sentences that support or refute a given statement.

Guided Reading and Review found in the Unit 5 folder, p. 84, provides a structure for reading and mastering the key concepts and reviewing the key terms for Section 3. (Guided Practice)

Primary Source Activity New York Gangs, found in the Unit 5 folder, p. 94, uses excerpts from journalist Jacob Riis's book *How the Other Half Lives* to help students see some of the repercussions of urbanization.

high. Steam-driven elevators—developed in 1861 by Elisha Graves Otis and electrified by the 1890s—and steel girders permitted the construction of skyscrapers. The first, which was 535 feet high, appeared in Chicago in 1885. Today, the world's tallest building is Chicago's Sears Tower, which is 1,454 feet high.

As a result of expansion, cities developed specialized areas. Banks, financial offices, law firms, and government offices located in one area and retail shops and department stores in another. Industrial, wholesale, and warehouse districts formed a ring around the center.

MAKING CONNECTIONS

Recall the discussion in Chapter 15 about the impact of technology on farms in the late 1800s. How might those same developments have contributed to the growth of cities?

Urban Living Conditions

Some working-class city dwellers moved into housing especially built for them by mill and factory owners. The rest found apartments wherever they could, mostly in buildings converted into multifamily units after being abandoned by middle-class residents who moved to the suburbs. Speculators also built many cheap tenements. These were originally apartment buildings that housed several families, but they

Growing cities lured migrants from within the United States, too. This woman found work as a porter in a subway, itself a product of urban expansion.

came to be identified as dirty, run-down, and overcrowded slums. ✪

Poor Conditions in the Slums Before long, because of poverty, overcrowding, and neglect, the old residential neighborhoods of cities gradually declined. Trees and grass disappeared beneath the new, cheaply built tenements. Soot from coal-fired steam engines and boilers made

Links Across Time

| 1650 | 1700 | 1750 | 1800 | | 1850 | 1900 | 1950 | 2000 |

City Garbage

As cities grew in the late 1800s, so did sanitation problems. More people meant more garbage and more sewage. When the English writer Rudyard Kipling visited New York, he found "a generous scatter of filth and more mixed stinks than the winter wind can carry away."

In crowded tenement houses, people often threw their garbage out of the windows, until the narrow alleys were heaped more than a foot deep. Garbage in other areas was collected and loaded on barges to be dumped in the ocean.

Today, many cities in the United States face serious problems in safely and effectively managing the garbage they generate. Experts estimate that the amount of waste generated in the United States in 1995 will reach 200 million tons, or 4.2 pounds of garbage per person per day. Increasingly, landfills in large cities have reached their capacity and have been closed. *What solutions to the garbage problem are being used by many towns and cities today?*

Answer to ...

MAKING CONNECTIONS

By reducing the need for labor on the nation's farms, technology and mechanization left many farm laborers without work. Many of these people then came to the nation's cities in search of work.

Answer to ...

Links Across Time

Answers will vary but might include the following: supporting programs that call for the recycling of glass, metal, plastic, and paper; arranging for special hazardous waste collection centers in local communities; enforcing illegal dumping laws; designing landfills to prevent pollution.

In Depth

Biography

David Sarnoff (1891–1971) arrived in New York City from Russia in 1900 and exceeded the immigrant promise of America beyond his wildest dreams. Self-educated in Morse code, he got a job as a radio operator for the Marconi Wireless and Telegraph Company. By 1930 Sarnoff was president of the Radio Corporation of America (RCA) and was the brains behind RCA's entry into radio broadcasting. By 1932 Sarnoff had added the National Broadcasting Corporation (NBC) to the ranks of RCA-owned companies. During World War II, Sarnoff postponed plans to expand the then fledgling television industry to serve as General Eisenhower's communications consultant. After the war, Sarnoff aggressively promoted the color television industry for NBC.

Discuss

Point out the statement on page 454, "Between the Civil War and 1900, many features of modern city life first appeared—noise, skyscrapers, traffic jams, slums, air pollution, and sanitation and health problems." Ask how increasing population helped to bring about each of the features of modern city life.

Ask why cities grew outward *and* upward. How could a builder make the most of expensive city property?

Ask what urban problems were caused by overcrowding. Could the development of slums and ghettos have been prevented? How?

Analyze

Ask students to list the positive and negative features of government by political machine. Why might voters support political bosses and political machines?

Activity

Designing a City

Specialized areas such as business districts, retail districts, and industrial districts emerged as a result of city expansion. Ask students to assume the role of city planner for a city of their choice. They should choose one of the specialized areas mentioned and create a drawing of it, trying to arrange it in the best interests of the city. LEP

Enrichment

Frederick Law Olmsted is considered by many to be America's greatest landscape architect. He designed New York City's Central Park, Boston's city park system, and about thirty-eight other major parks. Ask students to find out more about Olmsted's life and to present a report focusing on one of his major projects.

the air seem dark and foul even in daylight. Hundreds of families crammed into spaces meant only for a few. Open sewers and backyard privies attracted rats and other disease-spreading vermin. In 1905 journalist Eleanor McMain quoted a university student who visited a block of tenements in New Orleans' Italian district and described them as "death traps,"

> *closely built, jammed together, with no side openings. Twenty-five per cent of the yard space is damp and gloomy. . . . Where the houses are three or more rooms in depth, the middle ones are dark, without outside ventilator. . . . There is no fire protection whatever.*
> Eleanor McMain, "Behind the Yellow Fever in Little Palermo"

The student went on to describe "the worst features," the toilets. Only 35 of the 144 families in the block he visited had separate toilets. Sometimes, six or seven families shared only one. He found not a single bathtub in the entire block.

Contagious diseases such as cholera, malaria, tuberculosis, diphtheria, and typhoid raged in such conditions. Epidemics, such as the yellow fever that swept through Memphis, Tennessee, in the late 1870s and through New Orleans, Louisiana, in the early 1900s, took thousands of lives. Children were especially vulnerable. In New York City, in one district of tenements, 6 out of 10 babies died before their first birthday.

Fires, such as those that struck Chicago in 1871 and Boston in 1872, were devastating in these crowded neighborhoods. Once a fire started, it leapt from roof to roof, leaving thousands homeless. Crime and vice also flourished, fed by the poverty and hopelessness of the slums.

Ghettos Some urban neighborhoods became **ghettos,** sections of cities in which certain ethnic or racial groups lived. Many immigrants wanted to live near others of their ethnic group because of the comfort of familiar language and traditions. These ethnic neighborhoods strongly reflected the culture of the homeland. Wrote one tenement-house inspector after visiting Philadelphia's "Little Italy,"

> The black-eyed children rolling and tumbling together, the gaily colored dresses of the women and the crowds of street vendors all give the neighborhood a wholly foreign appearance.
> Emily Dinwiddie, "Some Aspects of Italian Housing and Social Conditions in Philadelphia," 1904

In the crowded cities, many immigrants were forced to live in cramped, unsafe apartments. Such conditions troubled many Americans.

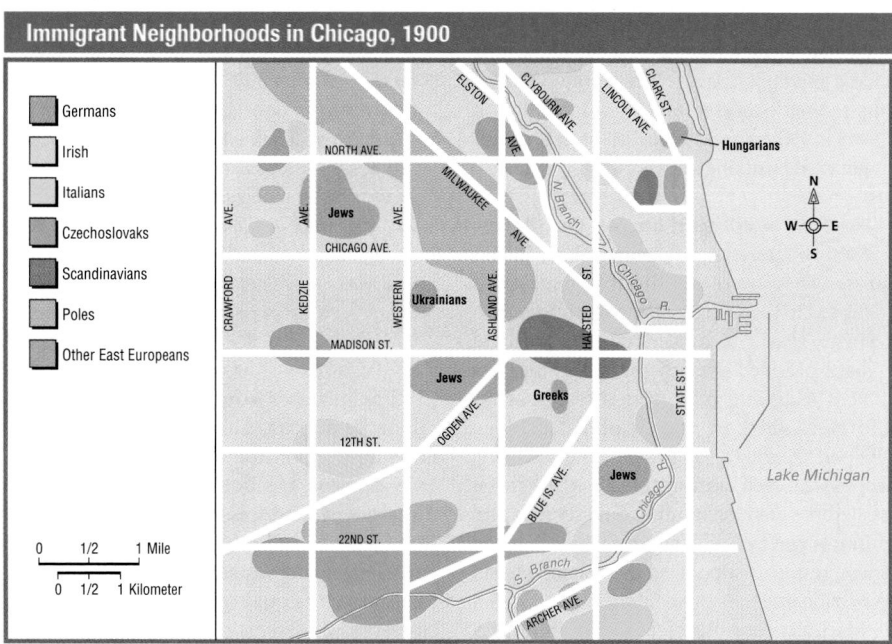

Immigrant Neighborhoods in Chicago, 1900

Germans
Irish
Italians
Czechoslovaks
Scandinavians
Poles
Other East Europeans

0   1/2   1 Mile

0   1/2   1 Kilometer

Hungarians
Jews
Ukrainians
Jews
Greeks
Jews
Lake Michigan

ELSTON AVE.
CLYBOURN AVE.
LINCOLN AVE.
CLARK ST.
NORTH AVE.
MILWAUKEE AVE.
CHICAGO AVE.
CRAWFORD AVE.
KEDZIE AVE.
WESTERN AVE.
ASHLAND AVE.
HALSTED ST.
STATE ST.
MADISON ST.
12TH ST.
OGDEN AVE.
BLUE IS. AVE.
22ND ST.
ARCHER AVE.
S. Branch
N. Branch
Chicago R.

Geography and History: Interpreting Maps
As this map of Chicago shows, immigrants often settled in communities that had been established by others from their homeland. Thus, ethnic neighborhoods developed in many cities. *What advantages and disadvantages might ethnic neighborhoods have offered their residents?*

Dinwiddie's enjoyment of the neighborhood did not lessen her distress at the crowded conditions and poverty that she saw.

Other ghettos were neighborhoods that were segregated by necessity. Usually threats from whites were enough to maintain them. San Francisco's Chinatown had well-known street boundaries: "From Kearny to Powell, and from California to Broadway," recalled one resident. "If you ever passed them and went out there, the white kids would throw stones at you."

Still other ghettos were created by real estate restrictions known as covenants, which prevented the sale or rental of property to certain groups of people. Covenants often prevented African Americans, Mexicans, Asian Americans, and Jews from buying land or houses in the better sections of towns.

The Results of Rapid Urbanization

When the middle and upper classes left the cities for the suburbs beginning in the late 1800s, the gap between the well-to-do and the poor widened. Because many of the poor were foreign-born or people of color, the gap was not just economic, but ethnic and racial as well.

A few cities preserved areas for the most wealthy residents near the city center, such as Boston's Beacon Hill, Chicago's Gold Coast, or San Francisco's Nob Hill. Often, people living in these neighborhoods also owned country estates and were quite isolated from the nearby poverty. As Beacon Hill resident and future Massachusetts senator Henry Cabot Lodge recalled, it was not until the Boston fire of 1872 had rendered thousands of tenement dwellers homeless that he became aware of "how the other half lived."

Political Divisions Urban political divisions stemmed from social divisions. As cities expanded, pressure increased on officials to improve police and fire protection, sewage disposal, electrical and water service, transportation systems, and health care. To deliver these services, cities raised taxes and set up offices.

Caption Answer to ...

Interpreting Maps

Possible advantages: Ethnic neighborhoods helped newcomers by offering support and comfort for those who shared similar experiences. They helped immigrants adjust to life in a new land. Possible disadvantages: Immigrants in ethnic neighborhoods might not learn the ways of the city or nation at large. Also, by sticking together, they maintained their identity as immigrants, thus possibly exposing themselves to anti-immigrant discrimination.

3. ASSESS

Section 3 Review Answers

1. (a) Tammany Hall, see p. 458, (b) William Marcy Tweed, see p. 458

2. suburb, see p. 454

3. With the introduction of streetcars and later cable cars, electric trolleys, automobiles, and subways, people began to move to the outskirts yet continue to work in the city. With the invention of elevators and the use of steel girders, cities grew upward, too.

4. Workers moved into buildings abandoned by middle-class residents and converted into multifamily units, or cheap tenements. With the presence of grime from soot and coal dust, the areas became run-down.

5. Many immigrants chose to live where others of their ethnic group had settled. Forced ghettos were segregated by means of threats from others or by real estate restrictions, known as "covenants."

6. Wide social and political divisions between classes and ethnic and racial groups helped create the rise of political machines and the boss system. In the absence of welfare systems, these machines provided residents with important services in return for loyalty.

7. Possible answer: The immigrants expected that they would be better able to survive among people with whom they shared language and culture.

Reteach

Write the following main ideas from the section on the chalkboard:
- The cities grew rapidly.
- The poor lived in wretched conditions in the cities.
- Political bosses flourished in the period of rapid urban growth.

Ask students to add two supporting facts for each of these main ideas, based on information from the section.

4. CLOSE

Reinforcing the Big Idea

Immigrants and migrants poured into the cities, which changed rapidly as they expanded upward and outward. Living conditions for the poor deteriorated, and political bosses took control in many cities. The next section describes the efforts of reformers to improve American cities and life.

Various groups vied for control of city politics. Some groups represented the remaining middle and upper classes. These groups tended to be well educated and of old immigrant stock. Others were made up of new immigrant and working-class groups.

The Rise of Political Bosses Out of these clashing interests, city **political machines** arose. These were unofficial organizations designed to keep a particular party or group in power. Usually a single, powerful **political boss** presided over them. Sometimes the boss held public office. More often he handpicked others to run for office and then helped them win. An army of ward leaders, people who each administered a city district, assisted the boss by handing out city jobs and contracts and by doing favors for residents. In return, residents supported the machine ticket on election day.

Machines controlled jobs in all administrative offices. They gave their leaders access to graft, or money passed "under the table" in return for favors, such as the granting of a city contract for work.

Many people blamed the success of political machines on the large number of urban immigrants. They thought that the immigrants' lack of education and sophistication made them vulnerable to corrupt political practices. Immigrants did tend to vote for the boss and the followers of his political machine, but this was often because the machine members made up for the lack of a public welfare system. As one Boston ward leader explained,

Is somebody out of a job? We do our best to place him and not necessarily on the public payroll. Does the family run in arrears [in debt] with the landlord or the butcher? Then we lend a helping hand. Do the kids need shoes or clothing, or the mother a doctor? We do what we can, and since as the world is run, such things must be done, we keep old friends and make new ones.

Martin Lomasney, *Boston Globe*, December 2, 1923

Cincinnati's George B. Cox, a former saloon owner, was an unusual example of a fairly honest political boss. A Republican, in 1879 he won election to the city council. Although he used this post to guarantee election victories and business contracts for the party faithful, he worked with local reformers to improve the quality of police officers and city services. He remained in power for almost twenty years.

One of the more notorious bosses of that time period was **William Marcy Tweed.** Tweed was the most powerful politician of **Tammany Hall,** the political club that controlled New York City's Democratic party. He amassed huge amounts of money through various methods, including graft and fraud. But the brilliant political cartoons of German immigrant Thomas Nast helped bring Tweed down by exposing his methods to the public. Convicted of crimes in 1873, Tweed eventually died in jail. Under new leaders, however, Tammany Hall dominated New York politics for another half century.

Using Historical Evidence This bank features a figure who, when coins are placed into his hand, deposits the money into his pocket. *What message is this bank sending about political machines?*

SECTION 3 REVIEW

Key Terms, People, and Places
1. Identify (a) Tammany Hall, (b) William Marcy Tweed.
2. Describe suburb.

Key Concepts
3. What inventions and developments contributed to the growth of cities?
4. How did slums develop?
5. Describe three ways that ghettos developed.

6. How did the growth of cities and urban problems contribute to the rise of political machines and political bosses?

Critical Thinking
7. **Identifying Assumptions** The text states that many immigrants settled among their own people in ethnic ghettos. What does this fact suggest about the immigrants' experience of new life in the United States?

RESOURCE DIRECTORY

Teaching Resources

American Profiles Activity found in the Unit 5 folder, p. 88, profiles cartoonist Thomas Nast, whose powerful political cartoons and caricatures helped bring an end to Boss Tweed's corrupt hold on New York City.

Quiz found in the Unit 5 folder, p. 85, covers the main ideas in this section as well as the key terms.

Media and Technology

Transparency
Cause and Effect, F-3

Reading Tables and Analyzing Statistics

S tatistical tables present large amounts of numerical data clearly and concisely. The patterns suggested by statistics must be carefully analyzed, however, and their sources evaluated for reliability. Statistics should be verified by other historical evidence.

Use the following steps to read and interpret the data below.

1. Determine what type of information is presented, and decide whether the source is reliable. The title of the table and the labels for the rows and columns tell you what information is presented. The source is usually found below the table. (a) What is the table's title? (b) How many decades are covered?

(c) What is the source of the statistics in the table? (d) Can the data be used as historical evidence?

2. Read the information in the table. Note that the table provides the total number of immigrants for each region for a given five-year period. (a) Between 1871 and 1875, how many immigrants came from Asia? (b) Between 1881 and 1885, which region provided the largest number of immigrants? The smallest?

3. Find relationships among the statistics. You can use the data in this table to compare the immigrant populations among different regions or to trace changes in one region's immigration pattern over time.

(a) Which region had the largest total number of immigrants between 1871 and 1920? (b) During which decade did the region called America show the sharpest drop in its number of immigrants? (c) Which region on the table showed the largest increase in its number of immigrants between 1871 and 1920?

4. Use the data in the table to draw conclusions. Between 1891 and 1900, the unemployment rate in the United States averaged 10.5 percent. Between 1901 and 1910, it averaged 4.5 percent. Using the data in the table, what conclusions can you draw about the relationship between the unemployment rate and the immigration rate for those time periods?

Estimated Number of Immigrants to the United States, by Region, 1871–1920								
	North-western Europe	Central Europe	Eastern Europe	Southern Europe	Asia [1]	America [2]	Africa	Oceania
1871–1875	858,325	549,610	15,580	37,070	65,727	193,354	205	6,312
1876–1880	493,866	254,511	24,052	39,248	58,096	210,690	153	4,602
1881–1885	1,193,819	1,128,528	63,443	120,297	60,432	403,977	331	4,406
1886–1890	1,131,844	729,967	157,749	211,399	7,948	22,990	526	8,168
1891–1895	745,433	762,216	251,405	314,625	19,255	14,734	163	2,215
1896–1900	392,907	432,363	270,421	389,608	51,981	24,238	187	1,750
1901–1905	761,527	1,121,234	711,546	1,050,721	115,941	63,774	1,829	6,134
1906–1910	807,020	1,365,530	1,058,024	1,260,424	127,626	298,114	5,539	6,890
1911–1915	652,189	1,027,138	978,931	1,137,539	123,719	528,098	5,847	6,126
1916–1920	201,304	23,276	33,547	322,640	68,840	615,373	2,596	7,301

[1] No record of immigration from Korea prior to 1948 [2] No record of immigration from Mexico for 1886 to 1893
Source: *Historical Statistics of the United States*

Historian's Toolbox Activity Reading Tables and Analyzing Statistics, found in the Unit 5 folder, p. 92, helps students find information and identify relationships in tables of data.

Ideas for Reform

SECTION 4

Ideas for Reform

1. FOCUS

Connecting to the Big Idea

See page 440B. Point out that the rapid growth of the nation's cities led to many urban problems. Reformers worked to improve social, economic, and political conditions in the cities. Ask students what the goals of reformers were. How successful were they in reaching their goals?

Objectives

● Describe the goals of the nativist movement.

● Describe how some reformers sought to control the behavior of the nation's immigrant class and city dwellers.

● Explain how some reformers focused on helping the needy by providing charity and social service.

In Depth

Multicultural Perspectives

By the turn of the century, the largest Chinese community in the United States was in San Francisco; the second largest was in New York City. Racial prejudice drove many Chinese out of small towns and farming and forced them to work for other Chinese in service jobs in laundries and restaurants. Their neighborhoods, called Chinatowns, were tight enclaves built around small businesses such as cigar manufacturing, small grocery stores, barbershops, and Chinese restaurants. Scholar Ronald Takaki described the Chinatowns in American cities as "cultural islands, cut off from the mainland of American society, perceived by whites as strange places to visit as tourists."

SECTION PREVIEW

The flood of newcomers added colorful diversity to the nation's cities in the late 1800s but, at the same time, contributed to a host of problems. Shocked by social, economic, and political conditions in the cities, religious and social groups pushed programs for change.

Key Concepts

• One reform movement sought to limit immigration into the United States.

• Some reformers sought to control the behavior of the nation's immigrant class and city dwellers.

• Other reforms focused on helping the needy by providing charity and social services.

Key Terms, People, and Places

social gospel movement; Jane Addams, Ellen Gates Starr; Hull House

The crusade against alcohol was one example of ideas for reform in the late 1800s.

I n 1890 New York City had as many Italians as Naples, Italy; as many Germans as Hamburg, Germany; twice as many Irish as Dublin, Ireland; and twice as many Jews as Warsaw, Poland. In other cities around the country, immigrant populations were also large. Added to these numbers were many Americans drawn to the cities from the countryside. The steady stream of people to the cities brought serious urban problems that needed solutions.

Controlling Immigration and Behavior

Some reform groups felt that the problems of the cities stemmed from the presence of so many immigrants. Others objected to the habits of certain immigrants. These groups hoped to accomplish change by adopting reforms intended to "control" undesirable social behaviors. They believed that by enacting strict controls, the cities' problems of inadequate housing, pollution, crime, and corruption could be solved.

Reformers who were interested in this approach pursued their goals in two ways: by seeking limits on immigration and by trying to outlaw certain behaviors. In these ways, reformers hoped to return the nation to what they believed was a past of purity and virtue.

Nativism In the 1880s, nativism, the movement to restrict immigration that first began in the 1850s, reappeared. The movement's first success came with the passage in 1882 of the Chinese Exclusion Act. Nativist leanings, however, were not restricted to anti-Asian feelings.

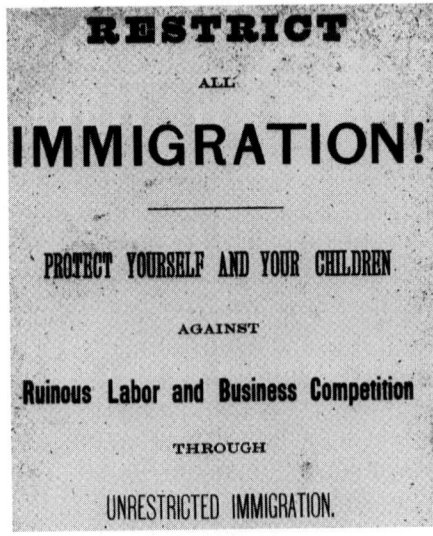

This 1885 brochure reflects the concern that employers would hire immigrants, who would work for lower wages, instead of native-born Americans.

RESOURCE DIRECTORY

Teaching Resources

Reproducible Lesson Plan found in the Unit 5 folder, p. 79, provides a summary of the Section 4 lesson plan content.

Alternate Lesson Plan: Cooperative Learning found in the Alternate Lesson Plans folder, p. 83, is designed to guide students in creating a graphic organizer and discussing social problems and reforms of the late 1800s.

Guided Reading and Review found in the Unit 5 folder, p. 86, provides a structure for reading and mastering the key concepts and reviewing the key terms for Section 4. (Guided Practice)

In the Midwest, the American Protective Association called for the teaching of only American culture and the English language in schools and for tighter rules on citizenship and employment of all "aliens." Nativists across the country fanned public hysteria about the threat that foreigners presented to the country.

Nativists won another victory in 1885 when Congress repealed the contract labor law, which had allowed the recruitment of workers from abroad after the Civil War. Even after the law's repeal, the practice continued illegally. During periods of labor unrest, companies often brought in foreign workers to replace striking employees. These actions served to increase antiforeign feelings among workers.

Upper-class nativism found expression in the Immigration Restriction League, organized in 1894 by some recent graduates of Harvard College. Republican senator Henry Cabot Lodge gave the League a voice in Congress.

The League hoped to exclude "unfit" immigrants by forcing them to pass literacy tests. Its main targets for exclusion were the so-called "new" immigrants from southern and eastern Europe, whose cultures differed significantly from the members of the League.

Prohibition Along with nativism, the temperance movement saw a revival. Three organizations dominated the movement in the late nineteenth century—the Prohibition party (1869), the Woman's Christian Temperance Union (1874), and the Anti-Saloon League (1893). All of these prohibition groups opposed drinking on the grounds that it led to terrible personal tragedies.

Prohibition groups also opposed drinking because of what they saw as the links between saloons, immigrants, and political bosses. Immigrant men often used saloons as "social clubs" where they could pick up information about jobs as well as socialize. To prohibitionists, however, saloons formed the center of a subversive movement to take over the United States. "Foreign control or conquest is rapidly making us un-Christian, with immorality throned in power," wrote Prohibition party supporter A. A. Hopkins in 1908. Had foreigners used "armies and fleets," Hopkins cried,

they could not have achieved greater control. Such views won many followers.

Purity Crusaders As urban populations grew, vice—whether in the form of drugs, gambling, or prostitution—became big business. Vice was not unique to the cities, but large urban populations made vice highly visible and very profitable. Then as now, many residents fought to rid their communities of illegal and immoral activities.

"Purity crusaders" led the way. In 1873 Anthony Comstock founded the New York Society for the Suppression of Vice. The following year he won passage of a law that prohibited sending through the United States mails materials deemed obscene, including those that described methods to prevent unwanted pregnancy. The Comstock Law, as it came to be known, slowed the distribution of information about birth control for decades.

Other purity crusaders attacked political machines on the grounds that machine-controlled police forces actually profited from vice. Police were known to demand payment from gamblers and prostitutes, for example, in return for ignoring illegal activities. Periodically, purity forces joined with other reformers, campaigned on an antivice platform, and threw machine candidates out of office. Usually the machines returned to power in later elections, however, by ridiculing the superior tone of many purists and by arguing that morals were personal issues.

Using Historical Evidence The caption on this *Judge* cartoon reads "Uncle Sam is a man of strong features." *What does the cartoon suggest about the artist's view of immigration?*

Activity

Teaching Heterogeneous Groups

In the late 1800s reform movements took action to alleviate growing problems in urban areas. While their aims were the same, their approaches differed. Divide students into small groups and assign one of the following reformer titles to each: nativist, gospelist, and socialist. Have each reform group design a program to solve an urban problem based on their assigned philosophy. **LEP**

Answer to . . .

MAKING CONNECTIONS

Students might suggest that nativism implies that certain peoples are not as "fit" as others, a notion that lies at the heart of social Darwinism.

Enrichment

Ask students to identify the style of reform favored by Jacob Riis, newspaper reporter and social commentator, based on this quotation from his article "The Battle with the Slum":

"Government by the people must ever rest upon the people's ability to govern themselves, upon their intelligence and public spirit. The slum stands for ignorance, want, unfitness, for mob-rule. . . . Put it this way: you cannot let men live like pigs when you need their votes as freemen."

Ask students to list some of the reforms that they think Riis would have supported. Students may research Riis's life and writings.

3. ASSESS

Section 4 Review Answers

1. (a) Jane Addams, see p. 463, (b) Ellen Gates Starr, see p. 463, (c) Hull House, see p. 463

Some reformers focused their efforts on helping immigrants adjust to life in the United States. This immigrant is learning English—and the American way of life.

MAKING CONNECTIONS

Do you think the idea of nativism relates to the concept of social Darwinism? Explain.

Helping the Needy

Other reformers, moved by social conscience or religious idealism, were developing a "helping" approach to social change. They argued that the middle and upper classes should take responsibility for poverty and try to improve social conditions. Although their methods had limitations—and in fact sometimes attempted to control individual behavior—their primary goal was to help the needy.

The Charity Organization Movement In 1882 Josephine Shaw Lowell founded the New York Charity Organization Society (COS). The COS tried to make charity "scientific" and kept detailed files on those who received help. In part, COS leaders wanted to prevent the duplication of efforts, but they also wanted to help only those they considered the "worthy" poor. This attitude sometimes led to unkind treatment of the needy or to humiliating demands for "proof" of poverty.

Some charity reformers interfered in the lives of immigrants. One clergyman who worked in a southern Italian neighborhood claimed that social workers "burst" into homes of immigrant women and "upset the usual routine of their lives, opening windows, undressing children, giving orders not to eat this and that, not to wrap babies in swaddling clothes." Many COS members wanted immigrants to adopt American, middle-class standards of child-raising, cooking, and cleaning, no matter how strange to residents' cultural backgrounds. While some immigrants found this intrusive, others were grateful for the advice and assistance they received.

The Social Gospel Movement In the 1880s and 1890s, urban churches began to provide social services for the poor who now surrounded them. They also tried to focus prohibition and purity campaigns in new directions. Instead of blaming immigrants for drinking, gambling, and other destructive behaviors, they pointed out the unfortunate circumstances that drove people into such activities.

Soon, a social reform movement developed within religious institutions. Called the **social gospel movement,** it sought to apply the gospel of Jesus directly to society. In 1908, followers of such views formed the Federal Council of the Churches of Christ, an organization that supported improved living conditions and a larger share in the national wealth for all workers. Other religious organizations, such as the Society for Ethical Culture and Jewish synagogues, adapted the social gospel ideal for their own denominations.

The Settlement Movement Thousands of young, educated women and men put the social gospel into practice in an innovative reform program called the social or neighborhood settlement movement. Settlement houses offered social services, believing that charity in the form of money given by well-meaning outsiders never really helped the poor. Idealists decided that in order to find out what would be most helpful, they had to live in poor neighborhoods to witness the effects of poverty firsthand.

 RESOURCE DIRECTORY

Teaching Resources

⭐ **American Profiles Activity** found in the Unit 5 folder, p. 89, describes the life of Lillian Wald, a public-health nurse, activist, fund-raiser, and champion of child welfare and women's rights.

⭐ **Primary Source Activity** Hull House, found in the Unit 5 folder, pp. 95–96, uses excerpts from the writings of Hull House's founder, Jane Addams, to encourage students' investigations of social service organizations.

In 1889, inspired by a settlement movement in London, **Jane Addams** and **Ellen Gates Starr** bought the dilapidated Charles Hull mansion in Chicago, renovated it, and then opened its doors to their immigrant neighbors. At first, Starr and Addams simply wanted to get to know them, offering help when needed. Soon, they began anticipating and responding to the needs of the community as a whole.

 Over the decades that followed, Addams and Starr turned **Hull House** into a center of constructive activities and programs. At Hull House, neighbors could attend cultural events, take classes, or display exhibits of crafts from their home countries. The settlement set up child-care centers, clubs and summer camps for boys and girls, playgrounds and vacation recreation programs, employment and legal aid bureaus, and health-care clinics. It also launched investigations of city economic, political, and social conditions. These actions provided a foundation for many social reforms in the future.

Settlements like Hull House sprang up across the country. Each settlement was unique. The Henry Street Settlement, founded by Lillian Wald on New York's Lower East Side, was originally a nurses' settlement. Wald's plan was to develop a system to offer home care to the poor. Its programs soon expanded to resemble many of those at Hull House.

Other settlements opened up in African American communities. Missionaries founded settlements, in part to gain converts but also to apply social gospel ideas in practical ways. Hundreds of college graduates, especially women excluded from many other professions, became settlement workers.

By 1910, more than four hundred settlements existed. Most were supported by donations and staffed by volunteers or people willing to work for low wages and free room and board. Except for leaders, such as Addams and Wald, most workers spent only a few years in these jobs. Many went on to professional careers in social work, education, or government, but few ever forgot their settlement experience. "I don't know that my attitude changed," wrote one former settlement worker, "but my point of view certainly did, or perhaps it would be more true to say that now I have several points of view." The settlements' ability to widen perspectives on social conditions and close the gap between social divisions may have been their most lasting contribution.

Judith Lathrop (left), Jane Addams (center), and Mary McDowell (right) were a few of the pioneers of the settlement house movement. *Inset:* Reformers offered help to newcomers by watching over their children while they worked.

2. Nativism brought about the exclusion of the Chinese, called for teaching only "American" culture and language, and urged tighter rules on citizenship and the employment of "aliens." Prohibitionism opposed drinking because it led to terrible tragedies, but also because of the links between saloons, immigrants, and political bosses.

3. Purity crusaders attacked vice, sometimes in repressive ways. The 1873 Comstock Law was one example.

4. The charity organization tried to make charity "scientific." It divided the city into districts and kept files on those who received help. Their actions often demeaned or interfered with the poor. The social gospel movement developed in the 1880s and 1890s to get church members to apply the gospel of Jesus Christ directly to contemporary society. The settlements brought young women and men to live in poor neighborhoods to witness the effects of poverty firsthand. By developing centers of activities and programs for communities, settlements tried to bridge the gap between rich and poor.

5. Possible answer: Charity workers tried to tell immigrants how to raise their children, and generally tried to get them to adopt American, middle-class standards for living.

Reteach

Ask students to make a two-column chart showing the goals and successes of the following reform movements: nativism, prohibition, purity crusades, the charity organization movement, the social gospel movement, the settlement movement.

SECTION 4 REVIEW

Key Terms, People, and Places

1. Identify (a) Jane Addams, (b) Ellen Gates Starr, (c) Hull House.

Key Concepts

2. What were the overall goals of the followers of nativism and prohibitionism?
3. Describe some activities of the purity crusaders.

4. Describe the charity organization, social gospel, and settlement movements.

Critical Thinking

5. **Testing Conclusions** The text states that the "helpers" sometimes sought to control people's behavior at the same time they helped them. Can you find examples to support this statement?

---

4. CLOSE

Reinforcing the Big Idea

Shocked by the terrible conditions in the nation's cities, reformers of many types struggled to improve urban conditions. The approaches taken by different reformers varied according to their specific views of the causes of the problems.

Chapter Review Answers

Understanding Key Terms, People, and Places

Terms
Students should refer to the definitions of the key terms in the chapter to write sentences that show an understanding of their relation to politics, immigration issues, urban challenges, or reform movements in the Gilded Age.

Matching
1. laissez-faire
2. nativism
3. steerage
4. ghetto
5. political machines

True or False
1. false, Hull House
2. false, Jacob S. Coxey
3. true
4. false, Angel Island

Reviewing Main Ideas

1. The close relationship between business and government led to bribery. In addition, the spoils system led to abuses associated with patronage.

2. The issues of tariffs, currency questions, and political reform concerned voters during the Gilded Age. The Republican party favored a tight money supply, while the Democrats favored free silver. The Republicans favored high tariffs. Members of both parties favored reform, though certain Republicans resisted. Republicans also favored blue laws, while Democrats generally did not.

3. The Bland-Allison Act required the purchase and coining of silver. The Pendleton Act undermined the spoils system by instituting civil service exams. The Interstate Commerce Act enabled the federal government to regulate railroads. The Sherman Antitrust Act was an attempt to regulate trusts.

4. Immigrants were fleeing crop failures, land and job shortages, rising taxes, famine, and religious or political persecution in their homelands.

5. In the 1890s, the pattern of immigration shifted from northern Europe to southern and eastern Europe and the Middle East.

6. Upon their arrival, immigrants could be deported if they did not pass a physical examination. Once admitted to the United States, they often faced discrimination as well as difficulty finding work.

Chapter Review

Understanding Key Terms, People, and Places

Key Terms
1. Gilded Age
2. laissez-faire
3. blue laws
4. Pendleton Act
5. Interstate

6. steerage
7. suburb
8. ghetto
9. political machine
10. political boss

Commerce Act

11. Tammany Hall
12. social gospel movement

People
13. Jacob S. Coxey
14. William Marcy Tweed

15. Jane Addams
16. Ellen Gates Starr

Places
17. Ellis Island
18. Angel Island
19. Hull House

Terms For each term above, write a sentence that explains its relation to politics, immigration issues, urban challenges, or reform movements in the Gilded Age.

Matching Review the key terms in the list above. If you are not sure of a term's meaning, review its definition in the chapter. Then choose a term from the list that best matches each description below.
1. a hands-off approach to economic issues
2. the movement to restrict immigration
3. the large, open area beneath a ship's deck in which immigrants often traveled
4. a section of a city inhabited mostly by people of one ethnic or racial group
5. unofficial organizations designed to keep a particular party or group in power

True or False Determine whether each statement is true or false. If it is true, write "true." If it is false, change the underlined person or place to make the statement true.
1. At Angel Island, neighbors could attend cultural events or display crafts from their home countries.
2. Populist William Marcy Tweed demanded that the government create jobs for the unemployed.
3. Jane Addams renovated a dilapidated mansion in Chicago and opened its doors to neighborhood immigrants.
4. Most Asian immigrants entered the United States at Ellis Island.

Reviewing Main Ideas

Section 1 (pp. 442–447)
1. What practices bred corruption in American business and politics during the Gilded Age?
2. Describe three economic or political issues that concerned voters during the Gilded Age. What stands did the Republican and Democratic parties take on these issues?
3. What important laws were passed at the national level during the Gilded Age?

Section 2 (pp. 448–453)
4. What conditions in their homelands caused people to immigrate to the United States?
5. How did patterns of immigration change during the late 1800s?
6. What hardships did immigrants face during and after their arrival in the United States?

Section 3 (pp. 454–458)
7. What factors accounted for the tremendous expansion of American cities during the late 1800s?
8. Describe some of the urban problems created by the flood of immigrants and people from within the United States who settled in the nation's cities.
9. What were the advantages and disadvantages of political machines and bosses for urban residents?

Section 4 (pp. 460–463)
10. Describe some of the actions nativists took to restrict immigration.
11. How did purity crusaders attempt to control the behavior of the nation's immigrants and city dwellers?
12. How did the settlement movement seek to help the poor?

7. The late 1800s were a time of massive immigration to the United States. Driven by economic hardship, millions of Americans also moved from the nation's farms to urban areas.

8. Urban problems included severe overcrowding, the absence of fire protection, poor sanitation, epidemics of contagious diseases, and crime.

9. Disadvantages: political machines and bosses were corrupt, surviving on bribery and graft; advantages: they helped people and made up for the lack of a public welfare system.

10. Nativists backed the Chinese Exclusion Act and pressed for the teaching of only American culture and the English language in public schools. They also backed the repeal of the contract labor law which

allowed recruitment of workers from abroad. Upper-class nativists organized the Immigration Restriction League.

11. Purity crusaders fought to rid cities of illegal and so-called immoral activities. To this end, they won passage of the Comstock Law, which prohibited sending materials deemed obscene through the mail. They also attacked political machines, on the grounds that machine-controlled police forces profited from vice.

12. Settlement workers lived in poor neighborhoods in order to witness poverty firsthand. Unlike other charity movements, they offered social services rather than money.

Thinking Critically

1. **Formulating Questions** Imagine that you are interviewing a young adult of the 1890s who is thinking about immigrating to the United States. What five questions would you ask to determine whether he or she is making a well-informed decision?

2. **Making Comparisons** Blue laws that restrict the operation of stores and the sale of liquor on Sundays are still enforced in some parts of the United States. Do you think that the arguments for and against these laws are the same as those used in the late 1800s?

3. **Identifying Assumptions** During the late 1800s, reformers sought to help immigrants by providing charity and social services. Many reformers also wanted immigrants to adopt American standards and customs. Do you consider the Americanization of immigrants a worthwhile objective? Why or why not?

4. **Drawing Conclusions** You have read that before 1890, most immigrants to the United States came from northern Europe. In the 1890s, the pattern shifted so that most immigrants came from southern and eastern Europe and the Middle East. In 1891 the Office of the Superintendent of Immigration was created to determine who was "fit" to live in the United States; all those admitted to the country were required to pass a physical examination. What conclusions can you draw from these facts?

Making Connections

1. **Evaluating Primary Sources** Review the primary source excerpt on page 463. What does the speaker mean by now having several points of view?

2. **Understanding the Visuals** Section 4, page 460, states that "Reformers . . . pursued their goals in two ways: by seeking limits on immigration and by trying to outlaw certain behavior." Find two visuals from Section 4 that illustrate these two methods.

3. **Writing About the Chapter** Reread the profiles of Sadie Frowne and Tameji Eto in Section 2. Then write a fictional profile of a late nineteenth century immigrant. Describe the reasons your character is leaving his or her home country and the experiences he or she might encounter in the United States. Note how your character's experiences are similar to or different from the experiences of other immigrants.

As you write your profile, make sure that you have included enough details to make your account realistic. Proofread your profile and draft a final copy.

4. **Using the Graphic Organizer** This graphic organizer, which shows the results of the rapid expansion of American cities during the late 1800s, uses dotted lines and arrows to show connections between ideas. (a) According to the graphic organizer below, what was the first result of the growth of cities? Based on your reading, why do you think urban problems led to the widening gap between rich and the poor? (b) On a separate piece of paper, fill in the blank boxes with two important examples of urban problems during this era. (c) Create your own graphic organizer about politics during the Gilded Age.

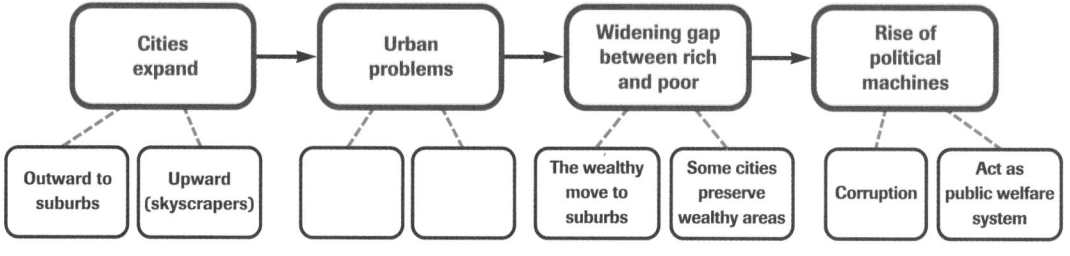

Cities expand → Urban problems → Widening gap between rich and poor → Rise of political machines

- Outward to suburbs
- Upward (skyscrapers)
- The wealthy move to suburbs
- Some cities preserve wealthy areas
- Corruption
- Act as public welfare system

Making Connections

1. The speaker probably began with a sense of compassion and willingness to help that remained unchanged by the settlement experience. However, the speaker is now able to see not only his or her own point of view, but the points of view of people from other parts of the world.

2. The visuals on page 460 illustrate reformers' methods. One shows a crusade against alcohol, the other shows anti-immigrant propaganda.

3. Answers will vary. Students' profiles should reflect an understanding of why immigrants came to the United States and of the difficulties they encountered when they arrived.

4. (a) The first result of the growth of cities was urban problems. Urban problems led to the widening gap between rich and poor because well-to-do residents left the city or insulated themselves in wealthy areas. (b) Examples of urban problems include slums and tenements. (c) Students' graphic organizers should show the connections between politics, poor business practices, and the need for reform in the Gilded Age.

 Alternative Assessment

Final Evaluation
Use the following guidelines to evaluate student projects:
- **Evidence of mastery of content** To what extent do the projects show knowledge and understanding of chapter content?
- **Evidence of thoughtfulness** To what extent do the projects adopt the immigrant perspective on events and trends in the United States?
- **Evidence of outside research** To what extent do the projects use outside research materials?

Thinking Critically

1. Possible questions: How difficult are conditions in your home country compared to the difficulties you might encounter in the United States? What do you expect the voyage to be like? What do you expect life will be like when you reach the United States? Can you pass the physical required to be admitted to the United States? Are you prepared to live with possible discrimination and poverty?

2. Arguments for in 1800s: Sunday is a holy day for Christians; everyone should have a day of rest; drinking should be restricted as much as possible. Arguments against in 1800s: Not everyone is Christian, so not everyone should be forced to rest; people who work all week need to be able to shop on Sundays; retailers need to be able to make a profit seven days a week. Arguments today probably place less emphasis on issues of morality and more emphasis on people's busy schedules than in the past.

3. Possible answers: Americanization is worthwhile because it helps immigrants quickly feel comfortable with American culture. Americanization is not worthwhile; it is patronizing, and American culture loses out by denying the validity of other cultures.

4. Perhaps the tests were designed to limit the number of immigrants from the new areas. Perhaps it was feared that people from the new regions carried more contagious diseases.

Chapter 17 Cultural and Social Transformations
1870–1915

📁 Teaching Resources (See Unit 5 Folder)

	Instruction	Enrichment

Section 1
The Expansion of Education
(pp. 468–471)
	Reproducible Lesson Plan, p. 109
	Alternate Lesson Plan, p. 85
	Guided Reading and Review, p. 113
	Quiz, p. 114
		Literature Activity, The Promised Land,
		    pp. 132–133
		Visual Learning Activity, The Ideal Public
		    School, p. 135
		Primary Source Activity, The Washington–
		    Du Bois Debate, p. 129

Section 2
Recreation for the Masses
(pp. 472–476)
	Reproducible Lesson Plan, p. 110
	Alternate Lesson Plan, p. 86
	Guided Reading and Review, p. 115
	Quiz, p. 116
		Critical Thinking Activity, Recognizing Cause
		    and Effect, p. 128
		American Profiles Activity, George M. Cohan,
		    p. 123
		Literature Activity, Around the World in 72
		    Days, p. 134

Section 3
The World of Jim Crow
(pp. 477–480)
	Reproducible Lesson Plan, p. 111
	Alternate Lesson Plan, p. 87
	Guided Reading and Review, p. 117
	Quiz, p. 118
		Primary Source Activity, Lynchings and Mob
		    Law, pp. 130–131
		Historian's Toolbox Activity, Reading a Political
		    Cartoon, p. 127

Section 4
The Woman Question
(pp. 482–485)
	Reproducible Lesson Plan, p. 112
	Alternate Lesson Plan, p. 88
	Guided Reading and Review, p. 119
	Quiz, p. 120
	Chapter Test, Forms A & B, pp. 137–142
		Visual Learning Activity, The New Woman and
		    the New Man, p. 136
		American Profiles Activity, Lucy Stone, p. 124
		Viewpoints Activity, On the Woman Question,
		    pp. 125–126
		History Might Not . . . Activity, Promoting
		    Women's Rights, pp. 121–122

📁 Additional Chapter Resources

Resource Organizer, p. 108
Alternate Lesson Plan, p. 84
Answer Keys, pp. 149–161

Bibliography

For the Teacher

Abrahams, Roger D. *Singing the Master: The Emergence of African Culture in the Plantation South.* Penguin USA, 1993. (Uses primary sources to trace the impact of plantation traditions and songs on African American performance styles in the nineteenth and twentieth centuries.)

Lewis, David Levering. *W. E. B. Du Bois: 1868–1919, Biography of a Race.* Holt, 1993. (The first fifty–one years of the life of the brilliant African American leader.)

Prentice Hall Literature Excerpts from *The American Experience,* 1994, including Chopin, Kate. "The Story of an Hour," from *The Awakening and Selected Short Stories.* Bantam, 1985 edition.

Media and Technology

 Critical Thinking, I-9

 Fine Art, D-14; Our Multicultural Heritage, C-9

 Visions of America: History Might Not Have Happened This Way Game

 Graphic Organizer, G-3

 Guided Reading Audiotapes (English and Spanish)

 Computer Test Bank

For the Student
Blacks and the Constitution. PBS Video, 1987.
Hymowitz, Carol, and Michaele Weissman. *A History of Women in America.* Bantam, 1978. (A discussion of women's roles from colonial times to the present.)
Washington, Booker T. *Up from Slavery.* Penguin, 1986 edition. (Classic autobiography of the famous civil rights leader.)

THE BIG IDEA

The Big Idea for the chapter and how the main ideas in each section relate to the Big Idea are graphically displayed below. Comprehension of this chapter's Big Idea is critical to students' understanding of United States history and how we as a nation got where we are today.

CHAPTER 17

The growth of industry and urban areas in the late 1800s brought many cultural and social transformations to the United States. At the same time, many Americans feared change and clung to old ideas about social roles, particularly those that affected women and African Americans.

SECTION 1

Educational opportunities expanded. A growing number of Americans, including African Americans, women, and immigrants, took advantage of these opportunities as a way toward economic and social success.

SECTION 2

Urban workers' demand for recreational activities led to new forms of entertainment that collided with traditional codes of behavior.

SECTION 3

Despite widespread discrimination, African Americans worked hard to rise above the hatred to reach high levels of achievement.

SECTION 4

Women's lives changed greatly, and in response they began to demand both an expanded social role and equal political and economic rights, demands that were contested by traditionalists.

Cultural and Social Transformations
1870–1915

CHAPTER 17

Cultural and Social Transformations
1870–1915

The Relevance of the Big Idea

In the period after the Civil War, Americans experienced dramatic cultural and social transformations—in fact, in many of the same areas as in the 1990s. Industrialization and urbanization brought changes in education, the makeup of society, recreational activities, and the role of women. These changes upset long-established patterns and often met with great resistance from certain segments of American society.

Structure a class discussion on the following topic: What social and cultural changes do Americans face in the 1990s? Have students generate a list of areas, such as the family, entertainment, education, the workplace, the roles of men and women, and the ethnic makeup of the United States, and ask students to explain their long-term significance.

In Depth

Global Connections

New methods of transportation, combined with an exploding American interest in travel and leisure, had a profound effect in the early twentieth century. These changes were symbolized by the British luxury liner, *Titanic,* which sank on its maiden voyage. About 1,500 passengers drowned, including many prominent Americans. As a result of the tragedy, the first International Convention for Safety of Life at Sea met in London in 1913 and agreed on stricter maritime laws—including more lifeboat space, more highly skilled crews, and updated communications equipment.

*A*long with the growth of industry and urban areas in the late 1800s came a host of other changes. More children began to attend school, and college became an attainable goal for a growing number of students. A recreation industry, which borrowed heavily from African American culture, emerged to meet the needs of the new urban workers. Yet some segments of society remained mired in the mud of old discriminatory attitudes, refusing to grant such groups as women and African Americans an equal chance at success.

Events in the United States

| 1870 Fewer than half of all American children attend school. | 1873 Boston University opens its doors to women professors. | 1883 Joseph Pulitzer buys the New York World. | 1890 National American Woman Suffrage Association is founded. |

| 1870 | 1875 | 1880 | 1885 | 1890 |

Events in the World

1872 Japan begins universal military service.

RESOURCE DIRECTORY

Teaching Resources

Alternate Lesson Plan: Demonstrating the Big Idea found in the Alternate Lesson Plans folder, p. 84, provides a lesson strategy to instruct students about the Big Idea that in the late 1800s and early 1900s, many social and cultural changes transformed American society, but not all Americans could participate fully in these changes.

Alternative Assessment Handbook provides information, guidance, and strategies for alternative methods of assessment. It includes an essay on new trends in assessment, guidance and strategies for developing performance tasks and portfolios, scoring rubrics, and sample evaluation forms.

Pages 468–471
The Expansion of Education
Education was a lofty goal that was out of reach for most nineteenth-century Americans. As the century came to a close, however, more and more Americans, including women and minorities, gained the opportunity to learn and grow.

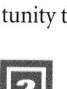
Pages 472–476
Recreation for the Masses
The growing urban working class took its recreation seriously in the late 1800s. Entertainment and sports became new industries that careened onto the American scene and collided with more restrained values.

Pages 477–480
The World of Jim Crow
White society proved quite resourceful at finding ways to repress African Americans in the years after Reconstruction. Yet many African Americans demonstrated an even greater will to rise above the discrimination and hate.

Pages 482–485
The Woman Question
Much had changed for women in the late 1800s—new jobs, new educational opportunities, new roles in the home. Yet much stayed the same, including continued economic and political inequality. This contradiction fueled great debate at the turn of the century.

1896 The Supreme Court legalizes segregation in Plessy v. Ferguson decision.

1903 The movie The Great Train Robbery is a huge popular success.

1910 The National Association for the Advancement of Colored People (NAACP) is founded.

1915 The Supreme Court declares grandfather clauses unconstitutional.

1895	1900	1905	1910	1915

1896 First modern Olympic Games take place in Athens.

1903 Emmeline Pankhurst founds the Women's Social and Political Union in Britain.

1910 The Mexican Revolution begins.

1913 Russian composer Igor Stravinsky revolutionizes music with The Rite of Spring.

The Expansion of Education

Connecting to the Big Idea

See page 466B. Explain that as the United States became more industrialized and urbanized after the Civil War, Americans needed more education. Educational opportunities greatly increased. Ask students in what ways educational opportunities expanded and who benefited.

Objectives

• Describe how opportunities for public education expanded after the Civil War.
• Explain how opportunities for higher education increased in the late 1800s.
• Describe the impact the widening of educational opportunities had on women and African Americans.

Bellringer

Ask students if they think changes need to be made in American education in order to better prepare students for their future roles. Ask them to explain what they think these changes should be.

Reading Strategy

Reinforcing Key Ideas Ask students to list and briefly describe, as they read, the ways in which educational opportunities expanded in the late 1800s.

Answer to ...

(See page 469.) Possible answers: Today's lessons emphasize maintaining individual cultural heritage and valuing the diversity brought to the United States by different immigrant groups, whereas in the late 1800s the emphasis was on Americanization.

SECTION 1

The Expansion of Education

SECTION PREVIEW

Education was a lofty goal that was out of reach for most nineteenth-century Americans. As the century came to a close, however, more and more Americans, including women and minorities, gained the opportunity to learn and grow.

Key Concepts
• Opportunities for public education expanded after the Civil War.
• Opportunities for higher education also expanded in the late 1800s.
  • The wider availability of higher education had a powerful impact on women and African Americans.

Key Terms, People, and Places
Booker T. Washington, W.E.B. Du Bois

Beginning in the late 1800s, a growing number of Americans sought the benefits of education.

Americans had long understood that a democratic society functioned best when its citizens could read and write and communicate effectively. By the late 1800s, however, an education had became more than just a worthy goal. For a growing number of Americans, it was a necessary first step toward economic and social success. In recognition of this fact and in response to public demand, educational opportunities expanded.

Public Schools Gain More Students

By the time of the Civil War, more than half of the nation's white children were receiving some kind of formal education. A high school diploma was still the exception, however: even in 1870, only 2 percent of all seventeen-year-olds graduated from high school. Only a tiny elite went on to college. Because most children had to help their families earn a living, many left school at an early age.

The vast majority of American children had to make do with the basic skills acquired during a few school years, each of which lasted just a few months. As the United States became more industrialized and urbanized in the postwar era, young people began to realize that they needed more than basic skills to advance in life. Parents began pressuring local governments to increase school funding and lengthen the school year. At the same time, reformers pressured state governments to limit child labor. By 1900, thirty-two states had passed compulsory school laws that required children eight to fourteen years old to attend school.

Although unevenly enforced, these laws had a powerful effect. In 1870 overall school enrollment was less than 50 percent of all American children—including fewer than 1 in 10 African Americans. Fewer than 72,000 went to the nation's high schools. By 1910 enrollment was nearly 60 percent, and more than 1,000,000 students were studying in the nation's high schools.

Immigrants and Public Education Immigrants especially treasured American public education. In the mid-1890s, the Russian immigrant father of author Mary Antin was proud to send his children to a Boston public school, convinced "there was no surer way to their advancement and happiness." Adults attended school at night to learn English and civics to qualify for citizenship. ✪

In teaching American standards of cleanliness, thrift, patriotism, and hard work, public schools promoted assimilation of immigrants into the American way of life. In playing games like baseball or basketball or cooking traditional American foods in home economics classes, immigrant children became Americanized and began to forget their native cultures.

Some parents resisted Americanization. Many Greek Orthodox and Eastern European Jewish parents sent their children to religious schools to learn about their cultural heritage in their native languages. Polish parents in Chicago in the early 1900s sent their children to

---

RESOURCE DIRECTORY

Teaching Resources

Reproducible Lesson Plan found in the Unit 5 folder, p. 109, provides a summary of the Section 1 lesson plan content.

Alternate Lesson Plan: Critical Thinking Identifying Assumptions, found in the Alternate Lesson Plans folder, p. 85, encourages students to apply this skill while comparing Booker T. Washington and W.E.B. Du Bois.

Guided Reading and Review found in the Unit 5 folder, p. 113, provides a structure for reading and mastering the key concepts and reviewing the key terms for Section 1. (Guided Practice)

✪ **Literature Activity** The Promised Land, found in the Unit 5 folder, pp. 132–133, an excerpt from the autobiography of Mary Antin, a Jewish immigrant living in Boston, shows the importance of education to immigrant families.

Roman Catholic schools where they learned about Polish history and religion in Polish but studied American history, bookkeeping, and algebra in English.

Immigrants also made their own contributions to American culture. As they shared customs and habits from their homelands, they enriched their new country. Thus, immigrants and Americans each benefited from exposure to one another.

Uneven Support for Schools Though state and local government support for education was expanding, not everyone benefited equally. Compared to white schools, schools for African Americans received less money—sometimes half as much. Writing of her upbringing in Durham, North Carolina, in the 1910s, civil rights activist Pauli Murray remembered vividly the contrast between "what we had and what the white children had."

W e got the greasy, torn, dog-eared books; they got the new ones. They had field day in the city park; we had it on a furrowed stubby hillside. They got wide mention in the newspaper; we got a paragraph at the bottom. . . . We came to know that whatever we had was always inferior.

African Americans were not the only group to receive a separate but unequal education. For example, beginning in the 1890s, Mexican Americans in parts of the Southwest were shuttled off to schools separate from and less well funded than those for white children. Many Asians in California were sent to separate schools. And by 1900, only a small percentage of Native American children were receiving any kind of formal schooling.

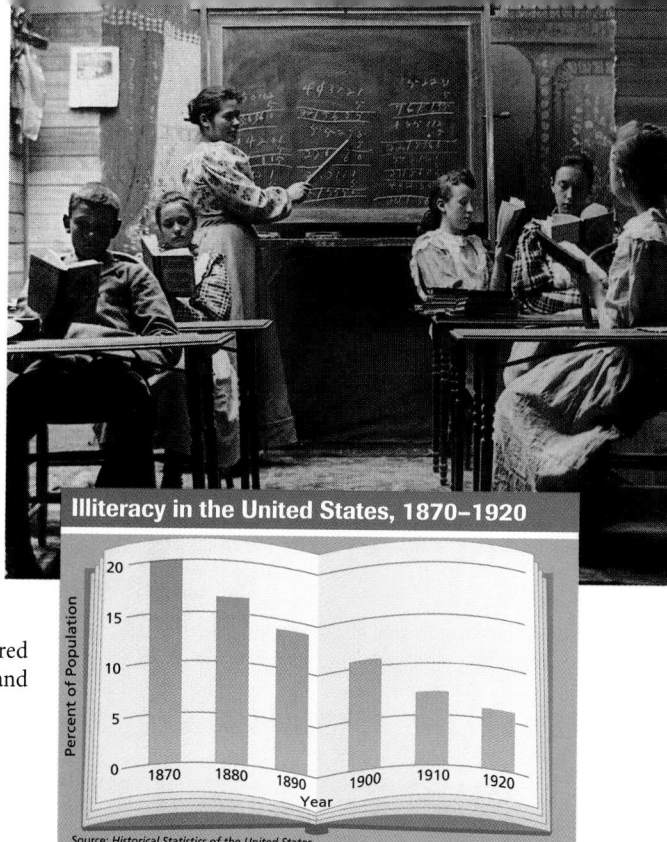

Illiteracy in the United States, 1870–1920

 Interpreting Graphs
The expansion of education meant more students in classrooms, such as this one in Nebraska in 1895. It also meant jobs for women, who filled many teaching posts. *How does the change in the nation's literacy rate reflect the growth of education between 1870 and 1920?*

Higher Education Expands

Between 1880 and 1900, more than 250 new American colleges and universities opened, and college enrollment more than doubled. Wealthy capitalists often endowed institutions of higher learning. For example, in 1885 Leland Stanford, the entrepreneur who had helped build the transcontinental railroad, and his wife, Jane Lathrop Stanford, founded Stanford University. John D. Rockefeller made donations to the University of Chicago that eventually totaled $40 million.

After the Civil War, middle-class women called for greater educational opportunities. In response, educators and philanthropists established private women's colleges with high

---

MAKING CONNECTIONS

What do today's students learn about the role of diverse cultures in American life? How are these lessons different from what students learned in the late 1800s?

 Visual Learning Activity The Ideal Public School, found in the Unit 5 folder, p. 135, uses an 1870 cartoon from *Harper's Weekly* to illustrate contemporary debates over public education.

Media and Technology

Transparency
Critical Thinking, I-9

Caption Answer to ...

 Interpreting Graphs

Not quite. Even though women saw a large increase in college and university attendance, they remained a minority of the overall student population.

Activity

Teaching Heterogeneous Groups

As a growing number of African Americans went on to higher education in the late 1800s, controversy existed regarding the goals of their education. To demonstrate the divergent goals expressed by Booker T. Washington and W. E. B. Du Bois respectively, divide students into two schools: the Washington School and the Du Bois School. Have each group design a day's class schedule to reflect the educational philosophy of their school.

Enrichment

American schools before and after the Civil War reflected the Protestant thinking of the white, male founders of the United States. A series of books by William H. McGuffey, used for teaching students how to read at the time, promoted these values. Locate one of McGuffey's readers and ask students to describe the values it advanced.

3. ASSESS

Section 1 Review Answers

1. (a) Booker T. Washington, see p. 471, (b) W. E. B. Du Bois, see p. 471

2. Most children learned only basic skills and dropped out of school early in order to earn a living. After the Civil War, communities increased funding for schools, lengthened the school year, and required children to stay in school up to age fourteen.

3. It provided the means for success and assimilation, although not all groups welcomed assimilation.

Women Enrolled in Institutions of Higher Learning, 1870–1920

Number of Women Enrolled (in thousands)

Percentage of All Students Enrolled

Year: 1870, 1880, 1890, 1900, 1910, 1920

Source: *A Century of Higher Education for American Women*

 Interpreting Graphs
The women in this 1880 Smith College chemistry class were among the first to benefit from new higher education opportunities. *Did women achieve equality with men in the percentage of enrolled students?*

---

academic standards. The first was New York's Vassar College, which opened in 1865.

Pressure also increased on men's colleges to admit women in the 1880s and 1890s. Rather than do so, some schools founded separate institutions for women that were related to the men's schools. Tulane in Louisiana became the only major southern university to take this step when it established Sophie Newcomb College in 1886. Shortly thereafter, Columbia in New York opened Barnard (1889), Brown in Rhode Island started Pembroke (1891), and Harvard University in Massachusetts established Radcliffe (1894).

Opportunities for men and women to study together—coeducation—also increased. A number of religiously based colleges, including Oberlin, Knox, Antioch, Swarthmore, and Bates, had been coeducational since long before the Civil War. Some colleges also accepted African Americans. In the postwar years, they were joined by institutions such as Cornell and Boston University; the latter announced in 1873 that it welcomed women not only as students but also as professors.

Schools founded for African Americans after the Civil War, such as Fisk and Howard, accepted both women and men. Women's numbers remained small, however, because most of the scholarships that made college study possible went to men. Anna Julia Cooper, an Oberlin graduate who later became an educator, estimated that there were only thirty black college women studying in the United States in 1891.

Women had to fight for full access to most state-funded institutions. For example, in 1863 the coeducational University of Wisconsin required women to stand until all male students had found seats. After 1867 Wisconsin directed women into a "Female College." In 1873, however, when women refused to attend segregated classes, the university was forced to reestablish coeducation.

Who Went to College?

Even with the new opportunities, only a tiny proportion went to college at the turn of the century. Because in the 1890s annual family incomes averaged under a thousand dollars, parents were hard pressed to meet college costs. A few fortunate and gifted students won scholarships or worked their way through college.

Because most scholarships went to men, women had a harder time obtaining a college education. Even those who could afford the cost faced prejudice against educating women. Parents feared that college made daughters too "independent" or unmarriageable or brought them in contact with "unacceptable" friends. When Martha "Minnie" Carey Thomas finally

---

▶ RESOURCE DIRECTORY

Teaching Resources

⭐ **Primary Source Activity** The Washington–Du Bois Debate, found in the Unit 5 folder, p. 129, uses an excerpt from W. E. B. Du Bois's *The Souls of Black Folk* to show how Du Bois took issue with the ideas of Booker T. Washington.

persuaded her Quaker father to allow her to take the Cornell University entrance exams, he said to her, "Well, Minnie, I am proud of thee, but this university is an awful place to swallow thee up."

African Americans and Higher Education
African Americans also had to fight prejudice in institutions of higher learning. In 1890 only 160 African Americans were attending white colleges. Many more were studying at the nation's African American institutions. By 1900, for example, more than 2,000 students had graduated from thirty-four African American colleges.

Foremost among these graduates was **Booker T. Washington.** Born into slavery in 1856, Washington began his studies at Hampton Institute in Virginia in 1872. His education there inspired him to develop a similar institution for African Americans in Tuskegee, Alabama. Washington taught his students skills and attitudes that he thought would help them succeed in an environment of increasing violence and discrimination. He told his students to prepare for productive, profitable work. Washington urged them to bring their intellect "to bear upon the everyday practical things of life, upon something that is needed to be done, and something which they will be permitted to do in the community in which they reside." African Americans could win white acceptance, he predicted, by succeeding in those occupations that whites needed them to fill.

Washington spelled out his approach in a speech he delivered in 1895 at the Atlanta Exposition. In addition to appealing to many African Americans, his ideas relieved those whites who had worried that educated blacks would be difficult to manage. Whites began to consult him on all issues concerning race rela-

tions, and President Theodore Roosevelt invited him to the White House in 1901. Washington's autobiography, *Up From Slavery* (1901), became a classic, and he became a dominant force in the African American community.

W.E.B. Du Bois led the next generation of African Americans in a different direction. Born free in Massachusetts, Du Bois graduated from Tennessee's Fisk University and then in 1895 became the first African American to earn a Ph.D. from Harvard.

⭐ Du Bois rejected Washington's message, which he mockingly called the Atlanta Compromise. Instead, Du Bois argued that the brightest African Americans had to step forward to lead their people. He urged those future leaders to seek an advanced liberal arts education. Only when they had developed "intelligence, broad sympathy, knowledge of the world that was and is, and of the relation of men to it," he wrote, would they be equipped to lead "the Negro race." In writings such as *The Souls of Black Folk,* Du Bois urged blacks not to define themselves as whites saw them, but to take pride in both their African and their American heritages.

Though W.E.B. Du Bois (top) and Booker T. Washington were both influential African Americans, they differed greatly on how blacks might best benefit from education.

Expanding Opportunities While the Washington–Du Bois debate raged, college opportunities continued to grow. By 1915 the college experience was still special but no longer unheard of for most Americans. Families of only middling income began to aspire to a college education for their children. This wide availability of advanced education would distinguish the United States from other industrialized countries.

4. Hundreds of new universities and colleges, some exclusively for women, opened. Coeducational opportunities for women increased. Women's college enrollment increased enormously. Scholarship and work opportunities meant that a college education in the United States would no longer be a privilege only of the elite.

5. Possible answer: Women and blacks would be better able to achieve gains of all sorts. At the same time, such skills would not enable them to overcome the discriminatory attitudes that had served to keep them down in the first place.

Reteach

Ask students to write one sentence describing how each of the following groups benefited from increased educational opportunities: women; African Americans; white, middle-class men; immigrants; and children.

4. CLOSE

Reinforcing the Big Idea

As urbanization and industrialization increased in the late 1800s, a growing number of Americans took advantage of the country's expanding educational opportunities. The next section describes new opportunities for recreation and leisure time.

SECTION 1 REVIEW

Key Terms, People, and Places
1. Identify (a) Booker T. Washington, (b) W.E.B. Du Bois.

Key Concepts
2. What were the educational possibilities before the Civil War? How did this situation change after the war?
3. Why was education so important to many immigrants?

4. What kinds of higher educational opportunities were available after the Civil War, and with what results?

Critical Thinking
5. **Predicting Consequences** How would you expect the increase in educational opportunities to have affected women and African Americans?

Quiz found in the Unit 1 folder, p. 114, covers the main ideas in this section as well as the key terms.

In Depth

Then and Now

Public education brought broad interest in new ideas on the treatment of children. Italian educator Maria Montessori devised her method, based on her belief in the child's right to be treated as an individual, in the early 1900s. Montessori schools were established around the world in countries as different as the United States and India. Today there are more than 450 Montessori schools in the United States.

SECTION 2

Recreation for the Masses

Connecting to the Big Idea

See page 466B. Explain to students that urbanization and industrialization brought in their wake a new commercial entertainment industry. Ask students what the new forms of amusement were in the late 1800s. How did these clash with more traditional codes of behavior?

Objectives

● Describe the new forms of entertainment that emerged in the late nineteenth century.

● Explain the influence of African American musical styles on the new culture.

● Explain why popular amusements caused conflict between the working class and those who wanted to maintain existing codes of behavior.

Bellringer

Ask students how they like to entertain themselves during their free time and if any of their choices cause conflict with the wishes of their parents or other authority figures.

Reading Strategy

Question Writing Have students read the section's main headings. Then ask students to write a question about each heading and to look for answers to their questions as they read.

SECTION PREVIEW

The growing urban working class took its recreation seriously in the late 1800s. Entertainment and sports became new industries that careened onto the American scene and collided with more restrained values.

Key Concepts
• A new mass entertainment and recreation culture emerged in the late nineteenth century.
• The new culture borrowed heavily from African American musical styles.
• Popular amusements stimulated conflict between the working class and those who wanted to maintain existing moral codes.

Key Terms, People, and Places
vaudeville, yellow journalism, minstrel show, ragtime, jazz, Victorianism

Basketball and other sports were popular forms of recreation at the turn of the century.

I n rural America, time spent in play was considered time wasted. Only after the harvest was in or at times of special celebration would rural people allow themselves leisure activities, such as family and community get-togethers. These activities tended to be free—people provided their own food and music.

In contrast, working-class city residents worked by the clock. After long hours on the job, they wanted fun things to do. To meet the need for inexpensive entertainment for the masses, a commercial recreation industry emerged.

Popular Amusements in the Late 1800s

Of all the places where working people gathered in the late 1800s, saloons were the most popular. Denver (population 133,859) had nearly five hundred by 1900; New York City (population 3,437,202) had an estimated ten thousand. Besides providing entertainment, saloons served as places for forging neighborhood and ethnic ties and political alliances. Most of their customers were men. More popular with women were dance halls and cabarets, where patrons watched musical shows and danced the latest dances.

Trolley parks—amusement parks built at the end of trolley lines—were popular with the whole family. Moving pictures also appeared during this era. *The Great Train Robbery,* released in 1903, was a huge success and demonstrated very clearly the commercial possibilities of movies. By 1908 the nation had eight thousand nickelodeons—theaters set up in converted stores or warehouses that charged a nickel admission—showing slapstick comedies and other films to as many as 200,000 people daily.

Sports As leisure time expanded in the late 1800s, sporting events became a favorite pastime. Boxing and horse racing were widely enjoyed spectator sports, but baseball was by far the most popular. ◗

By 1860, groups such as fire fighters, police officers, and teachers had formed baseball clubs in many American cities. When audiences for these games grew, entrepreneurs enclosed fields and charged admission. Teams formed into leagues and began to play championship games. In the 1870s, the sport's best players were paid. The most popular leagues, though open to Native Americans and white immigrants, excluded black players. Even the best African Americans had no alternative but to play in segregated leagues until the late 1940s.

What Americans loved most about baseball was the speed, daring, and split-second timing of the game. Pitcher Christy Mathewson commented, "The American public wants its excitement rolled up in a package and handed out quickly." Baseball fulfilled that desire. Popular writer Mark Twain remarked on the game's need for precision: "In baseball, you've got to do everything just right, or you don't get there."

 RESOURCE DIRECTORY

Teaching Resources

Reproducible Lesson Plan found in the Unit 5 folder, p. 110, provides a summary of the Section 2 lesson plan content.

Alternate Lesson Plan: Cooperative Learning found in the Alternate Lesson Plans folder, p. 86, provides a strategy for students to work together to create a leisure guide or newspaper "Weekend" section describing recreational activities of the period.

Guided Reading and Review found in the Unit 5 folder, p. 115, provides a structure for reading and mastering the key concepts and reviewing the key terms for Section 2. (Guided Practice)

✪ **Critical Thinking Activity** Recognizing Cause and Effect: America's Game, found in the Unit 5 folder, p. 128, focuses on the development of American baseball to help students apply this skill.

Baseball and football, another sport that achieved great popularity in the late 1800s, were exclusively men's games. Women, too, took up sports. Ice-skating had long been a favorite recreation of women. The national bicycling fad of the late 1800s also became popular among women. And because this sport required practical clothing, it helped to liberate women from some of the restrictive clothing styles of the day. "For muscle-play, freedom is the first requisite," a doctor advised in an 1896 article entitled "Bicycling for Women: The Puzzling Question of Costume." Women athletes had to abandon corsets, which wrapped tightly around their torsos and restricted breathing. Thanks to cycling, as well as to sports such as golf and tennis, shirtwaists—or ready-made blouses—that were tucked into shorter or split skirts, became socially acceptable.

Women students also played basketball, an indoor game invented in 1891 to keep athletes fit during winter. On the assumption that stiff competition and hard physical exertion were unhealthy for women, recreation specialists devised less demanding rules for them. Women athletes also learned gymnastics and swam, although social standards required them to wear black cotton stockings under short dresses or bloomers.

*S*uch words as Liar, Slob, Son-of-a-Gun, Devil, Sucker, . . . and all other words unfit for the ears of ladies and children, also any reference to questionable streets, resorts, localities, and bar-rooms, are prohibited under fine of instant discharge.

Like baseball, vaudeville came to be seen as typically American in character. It appealed to men and women of all ages and classes. Like much of what is on television today, vaudeville was entertainment for the masses.

Vaudeville Inexpensive theatrical performances attracted large crowds in this era. **Vaudeville,** a type of variety show that first appeared in the 1870s, was the most popular. Vaudeville performances consisted of comic sketches based on ethnic or racial humor, song-and-dance routines, and ventriloquists, jugglers, and trapeze artists.

Vaudeville was strictly for the family. Theater owners insisted on keeping everything on a "high plane of respectability and moral cleanliness." A "Notice to Performers" posted on the backstage wall of a prominent vaudeville house in 1899 stated that

Newspapers For city residents, newspapers always had been a vital source of information. In the late 1800s, they became a popular form of entertainment. Taking advantage of new production methods, publishers created larger and more interesting publications. They introduced new features, such as comics, sports sections, Sunday editions, women's pages, stories "hot off the wires," and graphic pictures.

Between 1870 and 1899, newspaper circulation soared from 2.8 to 24 million copies a day. Competing heatedly with one another, publishers urged reporters to discover fresh news

Sports were important to both men and women in this era. Baseball was a well-established spectator sport by 1886, when the picture of the team above was taken. Bicycling provided women with exercise, entertainment—and liberation from restrictive clothing.

⊗ 📄 **American Profiles Activity** found in the Unit 5 folder, p. 123, profiles George M. Cohan, the turn-of-the-century entertainer sometimes called "America's greatest showman."

2. **I N S T R U C T**

Discuss
Discuss with students the kinds of popular amusements that emerged in the late 1800s. Ask what part sports played in mass entertainment. What was the role of African American art in popular entertainment?

Analyze
Analyze the conflict aroused by the new forms of entertainment. Contrast the kinds of behavior embraced by forms of entertainment like sports, vaudeville, and dance halls with the code of behavior followed by most middle- and upper-class Americans. In what ways are public amusements still a source of conflict today? You might want to refer to the Bellringer discussion regarding students' choices of entertainment.

⬇ **In Depth**

Biography

The game of basketball was invented in 1891 by Canadian-American James A. Naismith (1861–1939). As head of the physical education department at Springfield College in Massachusetts, Naismith was asked to devise a safe indoor game for play during the cold winter months. Blending aspects of soccer, field hockey, football and other sports, and removing (in theory) physical contact, Naismith invented a basketball game for nine players on each side. He coached the game at the University of Kansas, Lawrence, until 1908.

Activity

Writing an Editorial

Ask students to assume the role of either a factory worker or an upper-class city resident and to write an editorial explaining that citizen's opinion of the new kinds of entertainment sweeping the city.

Enrichment

Many well-known American entertainers got their start in vaudeville. Have students research the early life of W. C. Fields, Charlie Chaplin, Will Rogers, Lillian Russell, or another star who began in vaudeville for a description of the performer's act.

Answer to ...

MAKING CONNECTIONS

(See page 475.) Possible answer: The humor of the minstrel show was based upon the notion that African Americans were not able to understand and function within white society. Such beliefs lay at the heart of white justifications for slavery and other forms of discrimination.

In Depth

Interdisciplinary

By 1905, the phonograph, another Edison invention (see pages 386–388), did for sound what the film projector did for film. Before radio, the phonograph gave the greatest impetus to the spread of popular music, much of it ragtime and jazz, and by 1914 more than half a million phonographs were manufactured each year. Ragtime was, according to African American writer LeRoi Jones (now known as Imamu Amiri Baraka), "a music the Negro came to in imitating white imitations of Negro music."

Newspapers such as the Chicago *Daily News* offered readers information—and entertainment. Magazines also expanded in this era, assisted by a grant of lower postal rates from Congress. ★

sources and lurid details of murders, vice, and scandal—anything to sell more papers. Such "sensational" news coverage came to be called **yellow journalism**, a reference to the yellow ink used in a popular comic strip of the era.

Several publishers became national figures. Hungarian-born Joseph Pulitzer, who owned the St. Louis *Post-Dispatch* and in 1883 bought the New York *World*, hoped to "expose all fraud and sham, fight all public evils and abuses." Californian William Randolph Hearst used his father's gold-mining millions to put out the even more sensational New York *Journal*.

Yellow journalism also troubled many. Critics charged that the "yellow press" intruded into private lives, invented facts, and sensationalized the ordinary with exaggeration.

Absorbing and Transforming African American Culture

As the mass entertainment culture expanded, it absorbed many forms of African American art. In the process, the culture transformed them in order to meet the tastes of white audiences.

The Negro Spiritual In 1871 nine Fisk University students went on a singing tour to raise money for their struggling school. When the Fisk Jubilee Singers began to concentrate solely on spirituals, they excited such interest that triumphal tours of the United States, England, and Europe resulted. Britain's Queen Victoria was so impressed that she had a group portrait of them painted.

In the process of making the spiritual acceptable to white audiences, the Fisk group and others like it transformed the musical form. It acquired characteristics of the European musical tradition with which whites were familiar. This new spiritual became identified as an American art form, as opposed to a purely African American one.

Minstrelsy Other forms of African American culture were also absorbed into the white entertainment world. The **minstrel show** began when white actors discovered they could captivate audiences with exaggerated imitations of African American music, dance, and humor. The shows perpetuated racist stereotypes, generally portraying African Americans as foolish imitators of a white culture they could not understand.

White actors in minstrel shows performed in "blackface"—they blackened their faces and hands and painted on wide grins. African Americans also performed in blackface, as minstrel jobs were often the only stage work they could get.

Minstrelsy peaked between the 1840s and 1870s, but even afterward every major town had a minstrel show. It survived long into the twentieth century, in vaudeville and the movies.

The music of ragtime composer Scott Joplin remains popular today.

Ragtime and Jazz A type of music known as **ragtime** originated among black musicians playing in saloons in the South and Midwest in the 1880s. Consisting of melodies with shifting accents over a steady, marching-band beat, it became a rage in the 1890s. Ragtime composer Scott Joplin, who came from St.

RESOURCE DIRECTORY

Teaching Resources

★ **Literature Activity** *Around the World in 72 Days,* found in the Unit 5 folder, p. 134, features a passage from the writings of Nellie Bly (Elizabeth Cochrane) describing how her record-breaking trip around the world originated.

Louis, Missouri, became famous for his "Maple Leaf Rag" of 1899.

Jazz grew out of the vibrant musical culture of New Orleans, a city with a popular marching-band tradition. After the Civil War, African American bands experimented with new styles of playing, including "raggy" rhythms and call-and-response forms in which singers or instruments respond to a single leader. They also played jazzed-up versions of familiar melodies, such as hymns or the mournful "blues" songs of southern sharecroppers.

New Orleans jazz styles from the 1890s slowly worked their way northward through towns along the Mississippi River. By 1915, thanks in part to the success of the phonograph, jazz—and the dances associated with it—was becoming a national passion.

MAKING CONNECTIONS

How do the attitudes about African Americans as reflected in minstrel shows relate to such issues as slavery and unequal government support for the education of African Americans?

Popular Amusements and Their Critics

Middle- and upper-class city residents had long found much that was offensive in popular amusements. Since well before the Civil War, for example, they had attacked saloons for wasting workers' time and money and helping to cause family abuse. Now, critics charged dance halls and trolley parks with promoting an unsupervised mixing of the sexes. Women especially were at risk of dire consequences associated with unrespectable amusements, critics worried.

Such concerns about the proper behavior of women are examples of **Victorianism,** a term that refers to moral ideas associated with Britain's Queen Victoria, who reigned from 1837 to 1901. Many middle- and upper-class Americans accepted the Victorian morals that dictated proper behavior. They believed that self-control was essential to social progress. Thus, they held personal behavior to a high standard, requiring perfect manners, hard work, sobriety, and, above all, restraint in relations between men and women.

Links Across Time

1650 1700 1750 1800 | 1850 1900 1950 2000

Entertaining a Changing Nation

Films were just emerging as the hottest form of entertainment in the late 1800s. In today's newest form of entertainment, called virtual reality, computers feed images and sounds through a helmet like the one above. *Could virtual reality have the same impact on our culture as films? Explain your thinking.*

Media and Technology

Transparencies
Fine Art, D-14; Our Multicultural Heritage, C-9

Reteach

Ask students to list the key terms and then use them in a paragraph that summarizes the content of the section.

Alternative Assessment

Mid-Point Monitoring

Ask students if they have
- Chosen a format for their project
- Outlined the main ideas
- Begun outside research and preparation of the bibliography

4. CLOSE

Reinforcing the Big Idea

In response to the demand of the urban working class for inexpensive recreational activities, a mass entertainment industry emerged in the late 1800s, challenging the established codes of moral and social behavior. The next section describes how African Americans confronted repression and discrimination.

The 1893 World's Columbian Exposition in Chicago reflected many aspects of American society during this era. The ferris wheel demonstrated a fascination with recreation and amusement. The White City, some of which appears at bottom right, represented an idealistic dream of urban perfection. In another example of social norms for the time, women had a separate building to showcase their accomplishments—it was segregated from the fair's other exhibits.

When critics raised alarms about the moral impact of places of popular amusement, some Victorians proposed extreme action, such as closing down all "evil resorts." Many working-class and immigrant people resisted such attempts. For them, such commercial "resorts" were often their sole sources of amusement. In the end, a compromise evolved.

After the turn of the century, city governments began to license public amusements, requiring them to adhere to health, safety, and liquor codes, and to uphold certain standards of behavior. Kansas City, for example, tried to ban "close dancing." A regulation from 1913 read, "The lady should place her right hand on her partner's arm and not on his shoulder, and partners should keep their bodies free from each other."

Other places tried to encourage moral behavior by providing "wholesome" recreational alternatives in carefully monitored social settings. Settlement houses and voluntary associations sponsored properly chaperoned dances. Educators added activities such as social dancing to their physical education programs. The urban park movement, which had begun in the 1850s, accelerated during this period. By the late 1800s, most cities had gardens for strolling, ponds for boating, baseball diamonds, skating rinks, and even dance pavilions.

By the turn of the century, a balance had emerged between the desires of the masses to amuse themselves and of more elite groups to preserve old codes of behavior. Public amusements, however, would remain a prime area of contention between diverse ethnic, racial, class, and generational groups in the decades ahead.

SECTION 2 REVIEW

Key Terms, People, and Places
1. Describe (a) vaudeville, (b) minstrel show.

Key Concepts
2. Why did mass entertainment and recreation emerge in the late 1800s, and what forms were most popular?
3. What was the role of sports in the entertainment of the masses in the late 1800s?
4. What was yellow journalism?

5. What forms of African American music were absorbed into white culture?
6. What was the basis for the criticism of public amusements, and what was the result of this criticism?

Critical Thinking
7. **Drawing Conclusions** How did the growth of cities help make possible the growth of the entertainment and recreation outlets discussed in this section?

 ## RESOURCE DIRECTORY

Teaching Resources

Quiz found in the Unit 5 folder, p. 116, covers the main ideas in this section as well as the key terms.

The World of Jim Crow

SECTION 3

The World of Jim Crow

SECTION PREVIEW

White society proved quite resourceful at finding ways to repress African Americans in the years after Reconstruction. Yet many African Americans demonstrated an even greater will to rise above the discrimination and hate.

Key Concepts

• White society found a number of ways to discriminate against African Americans after Reconstruction.
• The African American community produced several responses to white discrimination.
• Many African Americans achieved great success in spite of the obstacles placed before them.

Key Terms, People, and Places

poll tax, literacy tests, grandfather clause, Jim Crow, lynching, de facto discrimination, National Association for the Advancement of Colored People (NAACP); Madam C. J. Walker

W ithin a few years after the end of Reconstruction in the 1870s, African Americans began to see many of their newly won freedoms disappear. In the South, they were prevented from exercising their voting rights and were subjected to segregation laws and random violence. Discrimination was also rampant in the North. Despite these developments, African Americans in this era reached high levels of achievement and founded powerful organizations for self-help and protest.

Post-Reconstruction Discrimination

At the same time that white Americans were claiming elements of black culture as their own, racial discrimination and violence were making life harder for African Americans. Booker T. Washington's belief that white Americans would accept hard-working African Americans into equal citizenship was proving too optimistic.

Southern whites, who in the past had always had slavery to repress African Americans, now faced a new situation—free blacks. Whites responded with increasingly vicious methods of oppression.

Voting Restrictions In many southern communities, whites were concerned about the possible impact of African American voters. To deny the vote to blacks—and many lower-class whites with whom African Americans might join forces—southern states employed several tactics during the 1890s. They required voters to own property and to pay a special fee, or **poll tax;** both requirements were beyond the financial reach of most African Americans. Voters also had to demonstrate minimum standards of knowledge by passing **literacy tests.** These tests were rigged to keep African Americans from voting. For example, blacks might be asked questions that were too difficult for most people to answer. White people were given much easier tests.

To ensure that the literacy tests did not keep too many whites from voting, states passed laws that exempted men from certain voting restrictions if they had ancestors who had been allowed to vote before black suffrage. Such laws are examples of **grandfather clauses,** by which groups are exempted from a law if they met certain conditions before that law was passed.

Segregation Also during this period, many states instituted a system of legal segregation that further degraded African Americans. This system was called **Jim Crow,** after a minstrel song-and-dance routine.

Although Jim Crow laws usually are associated with the South, they first appeared in the 1830s, when Massachusetts allowed railroad companies to separate black and white passengers. But it was in the South that Jim Crow became firmly established in many facets of

This hood was part of the costume of the Ku Klux Klan, an organization that began to terrorize African Americans in the late 1800s.

1. FOCUS

Connecting to the Big Idea

See page 466B. Tell students that although African Americans were free, white society found many ways to suppress them. Despite this, many African Americans reached high levels of achievement in the era after Reconstruction. Ask in what ways white society denied African Americans their freedom. How did African Americans rise above these injustices?

Objectives

● Describe the ways in which white society subordinated African Americans after Reconstruction.
● Explain how the African American community responded to discrimination.
● Describe the achievements African Americans made despite the obstacles placed in their way.

Bellringer

Ask students to define the words *discriminate* and *discrimination.* Ask how a discriminating person is different from a discriminatory one.

Reading Strategy

Making Predictions Ask students to skim the section, noting the headings and subheadings. Have them make predictions about the content. Have students verify or correct their predictions as they read.

Reproducible Lesson Plan found in the Unit 5 folder, p. 111, provides a summary of the Section 3 lesson plan content.

Alternate Lesson Plan: Critical Thinking Identifying Alternatives, found in the Alternate Lesson Plans folder, p. 87, provides a strategy for students to apply this skill in examining post-Reconstruction discrimination and the formation of the NAACP and other groups.

Guided Reading and Review found in the Unit 5 folder, p. 117, provides a structure for reading and mastering the key concepts and reviewing the key terms for Section 3. (Guided Practice)

Discuss

Review with students discrimination against African Americans after Reconstruction. Ask what tactics whites used to oppress African Americans. Which tactics legally prohibited African Americans from doing certain things, and which inhibited them from exercising their full rights?

Analyze

Have students analyze the African American response to discrimination. What was the significance of "community" in furthering African American efforts to overcome discrimination?

Caption Answer to ...

 Interpreting Tables

Louisiana, North Carolina, and Alabama adopted voting restrictions in all five categories shown. Virginia also adopted voting restrictions in five categories.

Answer to ...

MAKING CONNECTIONS

Possible answer: White society adapted and sometimes mocked black culture for their own entertainment. Many whites were unable to tolerate free African Americans and introduced repressive means to put them into limited roles.

Adoption of Voting Restrictions in the South, 1889–1908

Year	Poll Tax	Literacy Test	Property Test	Grand-father Clause	Other*
1889	FL				TN, FL
1890	MI, TN	MI			MI
1891					AR
1892	AR				
1893					AL
1894					SC, VA
1895	SC	SC			SC
1896					
1897					LA
1898	LA	LA	LA	LA	
1899					NC
1900	NC	NC	NC	NC	
1901	AL	AL	AL	AI	
1902	VA, TX	VA	VA		VA
1903					TX
1904					
1905					
1906					
1907					
1908		GA	GA	GA	GA

*Registration, multiple-box, secret ballot, understanding clause
Source: *The American Record: Images of the Nation's Past*, Volume Two, edited by William Graebner and Leonard Richards

Interpreting Tables
As shown above, southern states began to adopt voting laws in the late 1800s. Though the laws varied in their techniques, the effect was always the same—African Americans were denied the vote. *Which states had the widest variety of voting restrictions?*

daily life. The laws began to appear in the South a few years after the end of Reconstruction and were solidly in place by 1900.

Jim Crow dominated almost every aspect of daily life by the early 1900s. The laws required the separation of blacks and whites in schools, parks, public buildings, hospitals, and on transportation systems. African Americans and whites could not use the same public toilets or water fountains. They could not sit in the same sections of theaters. Facilities designated for blacks were always inferior.

The Supreme Court legitimized Jim Crow. In 1883 the Court overturned the Civil Rights Act of 1875, ruling that the Fourteenth Amendment did not prevent private organizations from discriminating against others. *Plessy* v. *Ferguson* (1896) legalized separate facilities for African Americans, as long as they were considered to be equal to those provided to whites. The ruling in *Plessy* proved hard to enforce, and schools and other facilities in the South were rarely if ever made truly equal.

Violence The most horrible feature of the post-Reconstruction decline in conditions for African Americans was **lynching.** The term refers to a mob's illegal seizure and execution of a suspected criminal or troublemaker. Sometimes victims were merely individuals who were unlucky enough to be in the wrong place at the wrong time. The seizure sometimes included a mock trial, torture, and even mutilation before the victim—usually a man—was hanged and riddled with bullets. Those who carried out these horrors were rarely pursued or caught, much less punished. ✪

Conditions in the North Decline Many African Americans, though realizing that life in the North was not perfect, moved there in part to escape legal segregation. What they found instead was **de facto discrimination,** or discrimination in fact instead of by law. Through the widespread cooperation of whites, who enforced unwritten agreements to discriminate against African Americans, public areas, schools, housing, and employment were effectively segregated.

African Americans also experienced occasional lynchings in the North. In addition, bloody race riots occurred in 1900 in New York City and in 1908 in Springfield, Illinois—the city where Abraham Lincoln had practiced law in the early 1800s.

MAKING CONNECTIONS

White Americans seemed to be simultaneously repressing African Americans and embracing aspects of their music and culture. Give a possible explanation for how these two developments could have occurred at the same time.

 RESOURCE DIRECTORY

Teaching Resources

✪ **Primary Source Activity** Lynchings and Mob Law, found in the Unit 5 folder, pp. 130–131, provides students with a contemporary account of an Illinois lynching, written by Ida B. Wells.

African Americans Respond to Discrimination

As conditions for African Americans deteriorated, black leaders began to seek new approaches to race problems. For example, Bishop Henry M. Turner of the African Methodist Episcopal church advocated black pride and emigration to Africa. Others criticized Booker T. Washington and his silence on such issues as lynching. Such attacks ignored Washington's quiet support for legal cases against segregation and his financial support for civil rights and African American business activity.

In 1905 a number of outspoken African Americans came together under the leadership of W.E.B. Du Bois to denounce all political, civil, and economic discrimination against African Americans. Meeting in Niagara Falls, Canada, they vowed never to accept "inferiority," bow to "oppression," or apologize "before insult." "We do not hesitate to complain, and to complain loudly and insistently," they warned.

The Niagara Movement, as this group came to be called, gained only about four hundred members and won few concrete victories. But it formed the nucleus of a group that a few years later was joined by concerned whites, who were aroused into action by the 1908 Springfield riot.

Mary White Ovington, a white social worker who had worked in black neighborhoods, was among these concerned individuals. She helped organize a national conference on the "Negro Question" to be held on Lincoln's birthday in 1909. Niagara Movement leaders attended. The following year, this interracial group founded the **National Association for the Advancement of Colored People (NAACP).**

By 1914 the NAACP had fifty branches and six thousand members. Its magazine, the *Crisis,* edited by Du Bois, reached more than thirty thousand readers. The organization worked primarily through the courts. It won its first major victory when the Supreme Court declared grandfather clauses unconstitutional in 1915. In the decades ahead, the NAACP would remain a vital force in the fight for civil rights.

African American Achievement African American mutual aid and benefit societies

also multiplied in this period. Social workers and church groups founded settlement houses in black neighborhoods. The Young Men's and Young Women's Christian Associations developed separate recreational and guidance programs for African American youth. The National Urban League (1911) improved job opportunities and housing for blacks.

Also during this period, African American intellectuals began to publish literature, history, and path-breaking sociological studies. Black-owned businesses appeared everywhere. To help them, Booker T. Washington founded the National Negro Business League in 1900. By 1907 it had 320 branches.

Thanks to the determination and support of many individuals and institutions, African Americans survived the difficult post-Reconstruction era. Some, such as Madam C. J. Walker, actually thrived.

Lynching of African Americans, 1886–1920

Years	Number of Persons Lynched
1886–1890	392
1891–1895	639
1896–1900	493
1901–1905	407
1906–1910	345
1911–1915	279
1916–1920	275

Source: *Historical Statistics of the United States*

Interpreting Tables
Violence against African Americans was an alarmingly frequent phenomenon in the late 1800s. In spite of vocal protests like the one shown below, mobs had killed more than 3,000 African Americans by the 1920s. *In which five-year period did the most lynchings occur?*

Caption Answer to ...

 Interpreting Tables

1891–1895

 Activity

Creating a Slogan

Ask students to create a slogan, together with a logo, for the National Urban League, the National Negro Business Leagues, or another African American self-help organization.

Enrichment

The Supreme Court's decision in *Plessy* v. *Ferguson* introduced the "separate but equal" doctrine that maintained discrimination in the South for the next seventy years. Ask students to research the case and write summaries of the majority decision and the dissenting opinion.

In Depth

Multicultural Perspectives

African American demography has changed rapidly over the past century. In the mid-1870s, more than 90 percent of all African Americans lived in the rural South. In the 1990s, there are three major geographic centers of African American population: the rural South (about 15 percent), the urban South (more than 30 percent), and the urban Northeast, Midwest and West (55 percent).

3. ASSESS

Section 3 Review Answers

1. (a) poll tax, see p. 477, (b) literacy tests, see p. 477, (c) grandfather clause, see p. 477, (d) lynching, see p. 478

2. Madam C. J. Walker, see p. 480

3. Jim Crow laws constituted a system of legal segregation that was legitimized by the Supreme Court in 1883. De facto discrimination resulted in discrimination in practice but was not upheld by written law.

4. African Americans organized to promote black pride and to expose and denounce all forms of discrimination. In 1909, they formed the NAACP, which worked to improve civil rights.

5. African Americans formed their own mutual aid societies and the National Urban League. Intellectuals began to publish, and individuals such as Madam C. J. Walker started their own businesses.

6. Possible answer: African Americans were not truly free because they continued to suffer discrimination that denied them opportunities to improve economically and socially. Whites effectively denied them political rights, thus preventing them from seeking political redress.

Reteach

Ask students to write an agenda for the national conference on the "Negro Question" that Mary White Ovington helped to organize. The agenda should address strategies for surmounting discrimination.

4. CLOSE

Reinforcing the Big Idea

Despite the fact that African Americans were denied their most basic constitutional freedoms in the era following Reconstruction, they were able to reach high levels of achievement and founded powerful organizations. The next section discusses attitudes and changes regarding the status of women.

AMERICAN PROFILES
Madam C. J. Walker

Madam C. J. Walker was an inspiration to many African American women.

In 1912 **Madam C. J. Walker** (1867–1919) asked Booker T. Washington to put her on the program of the annual meeting of the Negro Business League. He refused. But on the last day of the assembly, she spoke to the group anyway, saying:

> I am a woman who came from the cotton fields of the South. I was promoted from there to the washtub. Then I was promoted to the cook kitchen, and from there I promoted myself into the business of manufacturing hair goods and preparations. . . . I have built my own factory on my own ground.

The mostly male audience was so impressed that they invited Walker back the next year as a keynote speaker.

Madam C. J. Walker is a stunning example of African American achievement in the turn-of-the-century era. Born Sarah Breedlove—the name *Walker* would come from a husband—she was the daughter of ex-slaves and sharecroppers. Her first seven years were spent on a Louisiana cotton plantation. Then, after the death of her parents, she moved to Vicksburg, Mississippi, to work as a domestic servant. She later moved to St. Louis, where she worked for seventeen years laundering clothes.

"I got myself a start by giving myself a start," Walker would later say. She did so by deciding in her late thirties to develop her own preparations to style and strengthen the hair of African American women, many of whom suffered hair loss from poor diet, stress, scalp diseases, and damaging hair treatments. After experimenting with different formulas and trying them out on friends, Walker sold her products door to door.

Walker moved to Denver, Colorado, in 1905, where she married C. J. Walker, a newspaper sales agent. There she set up a prosperous mail-order business for her hair products. She also established a string of beauty parlors and training schools for "hair culturists."

Her business a great success, Walker bought property in Harlem, New York, an area that had begun to attract African American residents. Her Harlem town house and later her estate in Irvington-on-Hudson, New York, became gathering places for the country's African American leaders. Walker supported black welfare, education, and civil rights work with large contributions and made many speeches for the antilynching drives of the NAACP and for African American women's organizations.

Walker also created job opportunities for African Americans. In her keynote speech to the National Negro Business League in 1913, Walker summed up her life's work as having "made it possible for many colored women to abandon the washtub for a more pleasant and profitable occupation." By 1916 her company claimed twenty thousand employees.

"The girls and women of our race must not be afraid to take hold of business endeavor," she said in her 1913 speech. "I want to say to every Negro woman present, don't sit down and wait for the opportunities to come. . . . Get up and make them!"

SECTION 3 REVIEW

Key Terms, People, and Places
1. Define (a) poll tax, (b) literacy tests, (c) grandfather clause, (d) lynching.
2. Identify Madam C. J. Walker.

Key Concepts
3. How do Jim Crow laws and de facto discrimination differ?
4. How did African Americans respond to the growing repression following Reconstruction?
5. What are some examples of African American achievement and perseverance during this period?

Critical Thinking
6. **Distinguishing False from Accurate Images** To what extent did the end of slavery and the official granting of political rights bring freedom to African Americans? Explain.

▶ RESOURCE DIRECTORY

Teaching Resources

Quiz found in the Unit 5 folder, p. 118, covers the main ideas in this section as well as the key terms.

Reading a Political Cartoon

Political cartoons can tell you a great deal about the past. For many years, cartoonists have tried to influence public feeling about important issues. To do so, they use visual images to exaggerate or highlight certain details about the facts. This is one reason why cartoons often can make a point more strongly than words alone can.

Study the cartoon below, which was published in 1892. Ask yourself what point about Jim Crow laws the cartoonist was trying to make. Then answer the following questions.

1. Identify the symbols used in the cartoon. Cartoons often use symbols, visual images that stand for some other idea or event. For exam-

ple, a skull and crossbones is a commonly used symbol for death. A dove is a symbol for peace. To understand a cartoon, you must be able to identify the symbols it uses.

Decide what the symbols in this cartoon stand for. (a) What is the figure on the left holding in his right hand? What are the men on the right holding? (b) What is the building at the right meant to be? (c) What is the significance of the cannon and the date printed on it? (d) Based on these symbols, what groups do these people represent?

2. Analyze the meaning of the symbols. Use your reading of this chapter and the cartoon to decide what the symbols refer to. (a) What

do the signs on the building say? (b) What practice is being referred to in this cartoon? (c) Based on your answers to *a* and *b* above, how would you interpret the meaning of the other symbols in the cartoon, which you identified earlier?

3. Interpret the cartoon. Draw conclusions about the cartoonist's point of view. (a) What do you think the cartoonist thought of Jim Crow laws? Give evidence to support your answer. (b) How is the cartoonist trying to influence the public's attitude toward the practice? (c) How does the cartoonist portray the white figures? Is this a sympathetic portrayal?

📓 **Historian's Toolbox Activity** Reading a Political Cartoon, found in the Unit 5 folder, p. 127, focuses on a cartoon about the 1964 Civil Rights Act to enhance students' understanding of the power of cartoons.

| **TOOLBOX** |

Historical Evidence
Reading a Political Cartoon

Focus Analyze a political cartoon as historical evidence of ideas and attitudes about a past event.

Instruct Explain that political cartoons usually take as their theme a topical and highly controversial event. Cartoons are a good primary source of viewpoints that may have been forgotten or reinterpreted over the years.

Ask students to imagine that this cartoon comes from a newspaper published in the South. Does the cartoon reinforce or reject southern sentiment regarding Jim Crow laws? How?

Extend See the Historian's Toolbox Activity in the Resource Directory below.

Answers

1. (a) A ballot marked "Republican vote"; the white men are holding firearms. (b) Both an old Civil War fort and a polling station. (c) The cannon is marked "1861," the year the Civil War began. (d) The African American man represents all African Americans who try to vote; the white men represent those who prevent them from doing so.

2. (a) The signs read as follows: "The Constitution gives the Negro the right to vote but what care we for the Constitution." "Voting done inside by whites only. K. K. K." "Vote Inside / No Negro Votes Taken." (b) The practice is that of preventing African Americans in the late 1800s from exercising their right to vote. (c) Possible answers will include information from the first question.

3. (a) The cartoonist seemed to think that Jim Crow laws were unfair, since those who prevent the African American from entering the polls are portrayed as mean, violent scoundrels. (b) The artist wants the public to applaud the African American for being brave and righteous and condemn the whites for being base and mean. (c) As self-interested protectors of white prerogatives, giving them labels such as "Southern Cracker," "Rebel Brigadier," "Rowdy," "Bulldozer," and dressing some as members of the KKK. It is not a sympathetic portrayal.

The Woman Question

The Woman Question

1. FOCUS

Connecting to the Big Idea

See page 466B. Explain that women's lives were undergoing rapid changes in the late 1880s. Yet many Americans were unwilling to acknowledge these changes and alter their view of women's roles. Ask what women's rights advocates wanted. Why were they opposed by people with more traditional views?

Objectives

● Describe the different attitudes Americans held regarding the role of women in society.
● Explain how women's lives were changing in the late 1800s.
● Identify the economic, political, and social changes women were demanding in the late 1800s.

Bellringer

Ask students if they think women have full equality with men in American society today. Encourage them to explain their answers.

Reading Strategy

Reading for Evidence Write the following statement on the chalkboard: Although much had changed for women in the late 1800s, many Americans were unwilling to acknowledge these changes. Ask students to find evidence to support this statement as they read.

Answer to ...

SECTION PREVIEW

Much had changed for women in the late 1800s—new jobs, new educational opportunities, new roles in the home. Yet much stayed the same, including continued economic and political inequality. This contradiction fueled great debate at the turn of the century.

Key Concepts

• Americans held conflicting attitudes about the status of women in society in the late 1800s.
• Women's lives were changing rapidly as a result of changes in technology, the workplace, and society in general.
• Many women demanded economic and political equality and promoted changes in women's lifestyles.

Many women at the turn of the century began seeking change in their traditional roles—and in their traditional clothing, such as the restrictive corsets advertised above.

Key Terms, People, and Places
woman question

Women hain't no business a votin'," pronounced Josiah Allen, a fictional creation of the popular turn-of-the-century humorist Marietta Holley; "they had better let the laws alone, and tend to their housework. The law loves wimmin and protects 'em." Replied his wife, Samantha, "If the law loves wimmin so well, why don't he give her as much wages as men get for doin' the same work?" ✪

Most Americans around 1900 would have known exactly what Samantha and Josiah were arguing about. They would have called it the **woman question,** a wide-ranging debate about the social role of women that grew out of several major developments of the era. As a result of technological change, industrialization, the expansion of education, and the movement of

people into the cities, women's lives were undergoing rapid change. Yet many Americans were unwilling to acknowledge these changes and expand their view of women's status in society.

What Was the Woman Question?

For women like Samantha Allen, the woman question boiled down to a few key demands: Women should be able to vote. They should be paid the same as men for doing the same work. They should be able to control their own property and income. They should have equal access to higher education and professional jobs. And, they should be free from domestic violence.

Women's rights advocates were countered by traditionalists, who insisted that giving women economic and political power equal to that of men would upset the social order. Some argued that allowing women any public roles would destroy their femininity. As the reality of women's lives changed, however, such arguments against women's rights became increasingly difficult to justify.

MAKING CONNECTIONS

To what extent does the woman question still exist? What aspects of it continue from the past? What are some new features of today's woman question?

Women in the Economy and Society

What was the reality of women's lives at the turn of the century? Women worked in most sectors of the economy and in many areas of public life. Their unpaid work at home continued to be essential. At the same time, because new technologies such as running water and washing machines decreased the time spent doing housework, a growing number of women were earning advanced degrees and entering

▶ RESOURCE DIRECTORY

Teaching Resources

📄 **Reproducible Lesson Plan** found in the Unit 5 folder, p. 112, provides a summary of the Section 4 lesson plan content.

📄 **Alternate Lesson Plan: Learning Styles** found in the Unit 5 folder, p. 88, is especially helpful for kinesthetic and visual learners, and helps all students identify conflicting viewpoints about the roles and status of women in the late 1800s.

📄 **Guided Reading and Review** found in the Unit 5 folder, p. 119, provides a structure for reading and mastering the key concepts and reviewing the key terms for Section 4. (Guided Practice)

✪ 📄 **Visual Learning Activity** The New Woman and the New Man, found in the Unit 5 folder, p. 136, uses a 1909 cartoon to illustrate a satirical point of view about women's suffrage.

professions. Others were building voluntary organizations that took leading roles in reforming education, labor relations, public health, and other areas of society.

Women's Work in the Home As they had for centuries, women continued to perform most of the jobs in the home. Thanks to the era's technological revolution (see Chapter 14), some aspects of this work became less time-consuming. Though technology was not available to all people, it did free many women for wage work, careers, and voluntary activity.

By 1900, fewer women were making their own bread or butchering and preserving their own meat. The number of foods available in tin cans increased fourfold between 1870 and 1880. Almost no one produced clothing from start to finish anymore. Patent medicines replaced remedies previously prepared at home. Even nursing the sick, once a special skill of women, was moving to the hospital and becoming professionalized.

Women still had much to do. In working-class households that could not afford the benefits of technology, housework continued to be strenuous. Many homes were without indoor plumbing. Even as late as 1917, only one quarter of American homes had electricity.

Working Outside the Home In 1870 nearly two million women—one in every eight over the age of ten—worked outside the home. Women worked in each of the 338 occupations listed in the United States census. Most of these women were single. But, in the decades that followed, a rising proportion of married women would go to work.

Most single female workers were between the ages of sixteen and twenty-four. Employers assumed they would leave upon marriage and rarely gave them supervisory jobs or advanced training. They also paid women three to five dollars a week less than men—about 30 to 60 percent less, on average.

Domestic work was an important source of income for many women. In 1900 about one in fifteen American homes employed live-in servants. Most were of foreign or African American origin. Working dawn to bedtime, six-and-a-half

days a week, these women cooked, cleaned, washed and ironed, and cared for children. Many supported their own families who lived elsewhere.

American society accepted the stereotype that women did not have the mental capacity for professional training. In 1873 retired Harvard Medical School professor Edward H. Clarke warned in his famous book *Sex in Education* that young women could not study and learn

and retain uninjured health and a future secure from [sickness], hysteria, and other derangements of the nervous system.

Three years before Clarke made this warning, the United States had 525 physicians, 67 ministers, and 5 lawyers who were women.

New technologies, such as this washing machine, helped lessen women's burdens. But women also had new responsibilities as household consumers as suggested in the ad above.

2. INSTRUCT

Discuss
Discuss with students the ways in which women's lives were different in the late 1890s than in the 1840s. What kinds of changes were women demanding? Why did women want more economic and political rights?

Analyze
Analyze why the demand for equal economic and political rights for women stirred up so much emotional controversy. Why did many men feel threatened by the demands of women's rights advocates? In what ways might some women also feel threatened? Why does the gender question continue to inspire emotional debate today?

In Depth

Historical Misconceptions

The notion that women should not depend on men for survival did not, as some believe, originate with the women's movements of the twentieth century. In her 1898 book, *Women and Economics,* Charlotte Perkins Gilman argued that, "If there should be built and opened. . . [an] apartment house for professional women with families, it would be filled at once. . . . It would be a home where the cleaning was done by [hired] workers. . . and [a] day nursery, and kindergarten, under well-trained professional nurses and teachers, would insure proper care of the children. . . . "

Time: One class period.

Activity: Choose a club focus.

Grouping: Groups of four to six students.

Purpose: For many women in the late 1800s, club membership provided the means to involvement in public life for the first time. Have groups choose a focus for a club and develop an agenda of activities around that focus. Have a recorder from each group report to the class, and discuss common activities.

Roles: Members of a women's club.

Outcome: Students will portray the potential of clubs as a stepping-stone for women's broader participation in American society.

Enrichment

Debate was fierce over the issue of whether or not women should have equal rights with men. Have students research published viewpoints of the time, and write a position paper either for or against equal rights for women in the late 1880s.

3. ASSESS

Section 4 Review Answers

1. the woman question, see p. 482

2. They claimed that women were not capable of learning what they needed to know to play a greater role in society. Furthermore, they argued, women workers were likely to work only until they were married, so they did not deserve the same pay or training as men.

3. Women worked in factories, white-collar jobs, or as domestic servants. They had little chance of advancement and were paid 30 to 60 percent less than men doing the same work. Professional women found jobs primarily in institutions run by and for women.

4. Women joined voluntary associations that became vehicles for improving themselves and society. Women founded libraries, improved education for girls, and worked to achieve temperance, suffrage, and correction of political and social abuses.

During this era, women in growing numbers moved out of the home and into the workplace. Some, such as the telephone operators (top), worked in the new industries that came with industrialization. Domestic work employed many immigrants and minorities such as those in the bottom photograph.

Still, most Americans believed that careers and married life were incompatible. Self-supporting women were allowed to train for professions but discouraged from entering fields that put them in competition with men. Women professionals found opportunities mostly in female-dominated institutions, such as women's colleges, hospitals, and settlement houses.

Volunteering for a Larger Role in Society

Women in both the North and South had performed exemplary voluntary service during the Civil War. Afterward, there was an explosion of interest among middle-class women in voluntary associations.

Women joined these organizations primarily for intellectual stimulation and sociability.

They studied subjects of common interest, gave talks on selected topics, or heard lectures by distinguished guests. Some, such as the New England Woman's Club, founded in 1868, pursued specific causes such as temperance and girls' education. Others founded libraries or playgrounds. African American club women in Atlanta studied a national adult education program. The Chicago Woman's Club read Karl Marx's writings.

Whatever their focus, clubs gave women invaluable experience in speaking, writing, and financial skills. They helped women increase their self-confidence and take their first steps toward public life.

As the number of clubs for women expanded, the idea of forming them into national associations took hold. In 1873 the Association for the Advancement of Women came into being, and in 1890 the General Federation of Women's Clubs was formed. These groups took on increasingly ambitious and far-reaching projects, including suffrage and the correction of political abuses. In doing so, they joined with other groups founded to pursue specific reforms, such as the Woman's Christian Temperance Union, formed in 1874, and the National American Woman Suffrage Association, formed in 1890. This last group would carry the cause of woman suffrage to victory some thirty years later. ✪

▶ RESOURCE DIRECTORY

Teaching Resources

✪ **American Profiles Activity** found in the Unit 5 folder, p. 124, profiles Lucy Stone, a fervent abolitionist and pioneer in the struggle for women's rights.

New Women, New Ideas

During this period of change, women struggled to agree on a proper focus for their activities. By the early 1900s, the woman question had grown to include a number of issues besides economic and political rights.

One issue was the question of lifestyle: How should women dress and behave? As more women entered the work force or went to college, they took this matter into their own hands. In search of more convenient hair styles, they began to "bob" or shorten their hair. They raised hemlines and wore more practical skirts and blouses. The New England Woman's Club even opened a store where women could buy sensible clothing.

Courting and marriage customs also changed. For example, instead of entertaining a man at home, many women now went out on dates without supervision. New women, as they were sometimes called, still hoped to marry. Yet they seemed to have higher expectations of fulfillment in marriage. This expectation was evidenced by the divorce rate, which rose from one in twelve in 1900 to one in nine by 1916. Many married new women began to push for the legalized spread of information about birth control, a campaign led by New York nurse Margaret Sanger. Such developments were shocking to Americans who held on to Victorian morals.

What was the consensus among women on the woman question? At the turn of the century, most women rejected ideas for drastic social change, such as the demand of some that women be freed from all household duties. Though the majority agreed with the principle of greater rights, middle-class women still saw domestic fulfillment as their chief goal. Working-class women seldom had the time to debate the issue.

Voting rights was another matter. The issue of the vote prompted huge numbers of women to campaign or support the movement in some way. Even female workers got caught up in the suffrage movement. Soon the vote would be the one issue on which women from many walks of life would unite.

Viewpoints
On the Woman Question

In the late 1800s and early 1900s, debate over the social, political, and economic roles of women raged in the United States. *Summarize the arguments presented in the viewpoints below.*

For Women's Rights

"These things the women want to do and be and have are not in any sense masculine. They do not belong to men. They never did. They are departments of our social life, hitherto monopolized [until now controlled] by men, but no more made masculine by that use than the wearing of trousers by Turkish women makes trousers feminine. . . ."

Charlotte Perkins Gilman, "Are Women Human Beings?"
Harpers Weekly, May 25, 1912

Against Women's Rights

"So I say deliberately that the so-called woman movement is an attempt to escape the function of woman, a revolt against the fact that woman is not a man, an attempt to enter the field of effort in which man's powers are properly exercised. It is a rising against nature. It is a revolt against God."

Dr. Cyrus Townsend Brady, from a sermon given
October 17, 1915

SECTION 4 REVIEW

Key Terms, People, and Places
1. Define the woman question.

Key Concepts
2. What arguments were used by those Americans who did not want to expand women's roles in the economy and society in the late 1800s?
3. What were the main characteristics of women's work outside the home in this period?

4. Describe women's involvement in volunteer work.
5. What was the general consensus among American women on the woman question?

Critical Thinking
6. **Determining Relevance** How did the growth in women's employment and volunteer activity outside the home support the demands by women for greater political and social roles?

 Viewpoints Activity On the Woman Question, found in the Unit 5 folder, pp. 125–126, provides additional viewpoints and perspectives on the woman question.

 Quiz found in the Unit 5 folder, p. 120, covers the main ideas in this section as well as the key terms.

 Chapter Test Forms A and B are found in the Unit 5 folder, pp. 137–142.

Answer Keys found in the Unit 5 folder, pp. 149–161, provide answers to all student activities.

Media and Technology

 Transparency
Graphic Organizer, G-3

Guided Reading Audiotapes
(English and Spanish)

Computer Test Bank

---

5. Most women rejected radical feminist ideas. Though agreeing generally on the need for more rights for women, most middle-class women held domestic fulfillment as their highest goal, while working women did not have time to debate these ideas. Many women did agree on the need for women's suffrage.

6. Possible answer: Women were assuming greater responsibilities and were proving that they could succeed in the male social and economic world. These achievements refuted the arguments used to deny women better pay, political rights, and so on.

Answer to ...

Viewpoints

Gilman argues that the rights women are seeking belong to them by virtue of their being human beings and have been falsely denied to women on the grounds that these rights belong to men. Brady argues that men and women are different by nature, that society must therefore treat them differently, and that any attempt to do otherwise is sinful. For a more thorough examination of the woman question, see the Resource Directory below.

Reteach

Ask students to create a three-column chart using the section's three main headings and to enter important concepts and supporting details in each column.

 CLOSE

Reinforcing the Big Idea

The changing role of women at the turn of the century spurred women's rights advocates to demand greater economic and political rights for women. These demands were resisted by traditionalists, who were afraid of upsetting the social order.

might not have
History Happened This Way
Key Decisions and Decision Makers

The Decision to Rule Against Women's Suffrage

Focus The Supreme Court's decision to rule against women's suffrage illustrates the unwillingness of many Americans in the late 1800s to acknowledge that women's roles in society had changed and to grant them full economic and political rights. Students are asked to evaluate the Supreme Court decision to uphold the Missouri law that denied women the vote.

Instruct In order to give students more background regarding Virginia and Francis Minor's argument, ask them to read the Fourteenth and Fifteenth amendments. Review with them the definition of citizenship found in Section 1 of the Fourteenth Amendment.

To check student understanding of the arguments for and against women's suffrage, ask students these questions: According to Francis Minor, why did the Constitution give women the right to vote? On what grounds did the Court decide against Virginia Minor and women's suffrage? You might want to have students participate in a role-play of the Supreme Court hearing of the case *Minor v. Happersett.*

Extend To extend the activity, have students explore efforts to get the Equal Rights Amendment passed. Suggest that they research the history of the Amendment, the arguments for and against it, and the Amendment's current status.

The Decision to Rule Against Women's Suffrage

Time Frame:	1869–1875
Places:	St. Louis, Missouri; Washington, D.C.
Key People:	Virginia L. Minor and Francis Minor, Chief Justice Morrison R. Waite, and the Supreme Court
Situation:	Women's rights advocates believed the post-Civil War period to be right for winning the vote. Virginia Minor believed the Fourteenth Amendment made Missouri's ban against woman voters unconstitutional. She asked the Supreme Court to rule for women's suffrage.

In the reform-minded atmosphere immediately after the Civil War, many women became more determined than ever to achieve woman suffrage, for which they had been fighting for decades. After all, new laws and the Fourteenth and Fifteenth amendments to the Constitution were granting rights and privileges, including citizenship and suffrage, to formerly enslaved African Americans. In view of these changes, suffragists reasoned, the nation must be ready to give women the vote.

In 1874, advocates of women's suffrage saw an opportunity to advance their cause. The Supreme Court had agreed to hear the case *Minor v. Happersett.* Depending on its ruling, the Court could make women's suffrage a reality.

Women Make a Move for Suffrage

In the aftermath of the Civil War, Congress passed and the states ratified the Fourteenth and Fifteenth amendments to the Constitution. These amendments were designed to protect the rights of African Americans who had recently been released from slavery. The Fourteenth Amendment extended the rights of citizenship to all Americans, while the Fifteenth guaranteed all races the right to vote.

These amendments split the woman suffrage movement, which had been formed in 1848 at the Seneca Falls Women's Rights Convention in New York. One faction, the National Woman's Suffrage Association (NWSA), refused to endorse the Fifteenth Amendment because it ignored women's voting rights. They continued lobbying for voting and other rights at the federal level. The other faction, known as the American Woman Suffrage Association, supported the Fifteenth Amendment as a step toward winning the vote for women.

Virginia Minor, the president of the Missouri chapter of NWSA, was convinced that women's status in the United States would not be raised until suffrage was won. Her husband, lawyer Francis Minor, enthusiastically supported her endeavors toward this end. In 1869 the couple devised an ingenious argument. They claimed that, of the "rights and privileges" that the Fourteenth Amendment guaranteed to all American citizens, including women, "chief among [them] is the elective franchise"—the right to vote. The NWSA enthusiastically endorsed the Minors' reasoning that embodied in the Constitution itself was the right of woman suffrage.

During the national elections of 1872, NWSA waged a campaign to challenge the ban on women voting. One hundred and fifty of its members tried to vote in ten states. In Missouri, Virginia Minor demanded that the St. Louis registrar, Reese Happersett, register her to vote. When he refused, citing the Missouri constitution, she sued on the basis of the Fourteenth Amendment.

The Logic Behind Minor's Case

Because Missouri state law made it impossible for Minor to bring suit independently of her husband, the Minors jointly took their case to the circuit court at St. Louis and then to the Missouri supreme court. Minor lost her case in the Missouri courts and then appealed to the Supreme Court in 1874. Francis Minor was one of the attorneys who presented the case before the Court. He and the other attorneys asserted that the Constitution gave women the right to vote because women are United States citizens and "there can be no half-way citizenship.

RESOURCE DIRECTORY

History Might Not . . . Activity
Decision Making: Promoting Women's Rights, found in the Unit 5 folder, pp. 121–122, focuses on Belva Lockwood's decision to push for her rights and become the first woman lawyer to practice before the U.S. Supreme Court.

GOAL	Win women's suffrage	
POSSIBLE ACTIONS	The Supreme Court rules that under the Constitution the state of Missouri must allow Virginia Minor to vote	The Supreme Court rules that the state of Missouri has no obligation to allow Virginia Minor to vote
POSSIBLE RESULTS	• Women's suffrage is won under the Constitution.	• Women's suffrage can only be won through constitutional amendment.

Woman, as a citizen of the United States, is entitled to all the benefits of that position, and liable to all its obligations, or to none." Since citizens have the right to vote, and since the Fourteenth Amendment forbade the states from limiting the rights of citizens, then Missouri's ban on women voting was unconstitutional.

Supreme Court Chief Justice Morrison R. Waite, who sat listening to these arguments, was sympathetic to women's rights. Later, his personal physician would be a woman, and he would unsuccessfully argue for admitting women as members of the Supreme Court Bar. It seemed possible that Waite might be willing to embrace a broad reading of the Constitution, one that allowed him to infer women's suffrage from the vague wording of the Fourteenth Amendment.

Yet unfortunately for Minor and the NWSA, the Supreme Court had turned more cautious and respectful of precedent. The Court now tended to opt for more strict readings of the Constitution's language—readings that acknowledged only those rights specifically listed in the document. Realizing that their case had but a slim chance of victory, the Minors and the NWSA nevertheless remained hopeful that the Court would rule for women's suffrage.

The Response of the Supreme Court

The Supreme Court in 1875 decided unanimously that the state of Missouri had no obligation to allow Minor to vote. In the Court's opinion, written by Waite, the justices agreed that women were citizens entitled to the rights and privileges of citizenship, with or without the Fourteenth Amendment. Yet the Constitution and the Fourteenth Amendment never stated specifically that suffrage was one of those rights. Had that been so, they argued, the Fifteenth Amendment guaranteeing African Americans the right to vote would never have been necessary.

The Court further noted that the states always had determined the qualifications for voters. "When the Constitution of the United States was adopted," the justices continued, ". . . in no State were all citizens permitted to vote. Each State determined for itself who should have that power." If the framers of the Constitution meant all citizens to vote, the Court reasoned, they would have stated it explicitly. Waite's opinion concluded by remarking that the justices were not judging the merits of women's suffrage, but only determining the extent of women's constitutional rights.

After the Supreme Court's decision in *Minor* v. *Happersett*, those working for women's suffrage realized what a long road lay ahead. The only way to get a national vote for women would be through the long, difficult process of amending the Constitution. The two women's rights factions reunited in 1890 in the National American Woman Suffrage Association. Under a new generation of leaders, the group worked for thirty more years to achieve passage and ratification of the Nineteenth Amendment in 1920.

EVALUATING DECISIONS

1. (a) According to the Minors, how was women's suffrage implied in the Fourteenth Amendment? (b) Why was this argument attractive to the NWSA?
2. (a) What was the Supreme Court's reasoning in unanimously ruling against the Minors? (b) Why was 1874 an unlikely time to expect the Minors to win?

Critical Thinking

3. **Recognizing Cause and Effect** Waite was said to believe that the people, acting through their elected representatives, knew their own best interest. Explain how such a belief might have led Waite to a make a more strict reading of the Constitution.

Media and Technology

Visions of America: History Might Not Have Happened This Way Game

To encourage students to explore pivotal moments in United States history, have students use the Visions of America software. Refer to the Visions of America Guidebook for viewing objectives, activities, game instructions, and discussion questions.

Chapter Review Answers

Understanding Key Terms, People, and Places

Terms
Students should refer to the definitions of the key terms in the chapter to write sentences that show the relation of each word to the cultural and social transformations of the late 1800s and early 1900s.

Matching
1. Jim Crow
2. vaudeville
3. yellow journalism
4. woman question
5. Victorianism

True or False
1. false, Madam C. J. Walker
2. false, Booker T. Washington
3. true

Reviewing Main Ideas

1. As the United States became more industrialized and urbanized, people realized that they needed more education. To meet this need, school funding was increased, the school year was lengthened, and child labor laws were instituted, thus allowing more students to attend school.

2. Educators and philanthropists established private women's colleges, and pressure increased on men's colleges to admit women. Other opportunities for coeducation increased.

3. Both groups faced prejudice and limited opportunities.

4. Families could visit trolley parks, attend motion pictures and vaudeville shows, and participate in or watch sports such as baseball and football.

5. Ragtime originated among African American musicians playing in saloons in the South and Midwest. Jazz grew out of experiments with new styles of playing among African American musicians in New Orleans.

6. Victorians disapproved of the new forms of entertainment, finding them offensive and immoral.

7. Almost every aspect of the daily lives of African Americans in the South was affected by Jim Crow laws. The laws required the separation of blacks and whites in schools, parks, public buildings, hospitals, and many other facilities. The separate facilities for African Americans were almost always inferior.

8. The NAACP worked primarily through the courts to fight for African American civil rights. The National Urban League worked to improve job opportunities and housing.

9. The profile of Madam C. J. Walker proves that despite repression, some highly motivated and skilled African Americans were able to start their own businesses and achieve success.

10. Some Americans demanded equal economic and political equality for women, while others supported keeping women in traditional roles.

11. Housework for many women became less time-consuming, thus freeing them to work and volunteer outside the home.

12. Many women changed their dress and behavior, cutting their hair, wearing more practical clothing, and going on dates without supervision.

Thinking Critically

1. Students' responses should reflect the fact that in the period immediately following the Civil War, fewer than half of the nation's children were receiving formal education. Only a very small percentage graduated from high school, and even fewer went to college. Opportunities for African Americans and women were even scarcer.

2. Possible answer: Today activities for the family are still important, although theme parks have replaced trolley parks, and movies have replaced vaudeville.

Chapter Review

Understanding Key Terms, People, and Places

Key Terms
1. vaudeville
2. yellow journalism
3. minstrel show
4. ragtime
5. jazz
6. Victorianism
7. poll tax
8. literacy tests
9. grandfather clause
10. Jim Crow
11. lynching
12. de facto discrimination
13. National Association for the Advancement of Colored People (NAACP)
14. woman question

People
15. Booker T. Washington
16. W.E.B. Du Bois
17. Madam C. J. Walker

Terms For each term above, write a sentence that explains its relation to the cultural and social transformations of the late 1800s and early 1900s.

Matching Review the key terms in the list above. If you are not sure of a term's meaning, review its definition in the chapter. Then choose a term from the list that best matches each description below.
1. a system of legal segregation that degraded African Americans
2. a type of family entertainment consisting of comic sketches, song-and-dance routines, ventriloquists, jugglers, and trapeze artists
3. sensationalized news coverage
4. the wide-ranging debate about the social role of women that took place in the late 1800s
5. the beliefs associated with Britain's Queen Victoria, which include commitment to hard work, sobriety, and restraint in relations between men and women

True or False Determine whether each statement is true or false. If it is true, write "true." If it is false, change the underlined name to make the statement true.
1. Booker T. Washington was an African American who persevered through the post-Reconstruction era and established a successful business.
2. Madam C. J. Walker urged African Americans to win white acceptance by succeeding in occupations that whites needed them to fill.
3. W.E.B. Du Bois believed that the brightest African Americans had to step forward to seek advanced educations and lead their people.

Reviewing Main Ideas

Section 1 (pp. 468–471)
1. Why did public schools gain more students in the late 1800s?
2. Give evidence to show that opportunities for higher education increased for women during the late 1800s.
3. In what ways were the experiences of women and African Americans similar with regard to higher education?

Section 2 (pp. 472–476)
4. What kinds of amusements and entertainment were available for families to enjoy during the late 1800s?
5. Where and how did ragtime and jazz originate?
6. What did Victorians think of the new forms of entertainment that evolved during the late 1800s?

Section 3 (pp. 477–480)
7. In what ways did Jim Crow laws affect the daily lives of African Americans in the South?
8. How did the NAACP and the National Urban League help African Americans during the early 1900s?
9. What does the profile of Madam C. J. Walker reveal about the achievements of African Americans?

Section 4 (pp. 482–485)
10. What conflicting attitudes did Americans hold about the proper place of woman in the late 1800s?
11. How did women's lives change as a result of new technologies during this period?
12. Describe how women achieved greater social equality during the early 1900s.

1. **Drawing Conclusions** How might your education have been different if you had lived in the period immediately following the Civil War?
2. **Making Comparisons** As greater numbers of working-class people sought entertainment during the late 1800s, a commercial recreation industry emerged. How are the types of activities available today similar to the types of activities available during the late 1800s?
3. **Expressing Problems Clearly** Jim Crow required the segregation of whites and African Americans. Aside from the fact that facilities for African Americans were inferior, how might segregation have harmed African Americans?

Making Connections

1. **Evaluating Primary Sources** Review the primary source excerpt on page 472. Is Mathewson's assessment of the American public valid today? Give evidence to support your point of view.
2. **Understanding the Visuals** Review the quotations in the "Viewpoints" feature on page 485. Then, scan the chapter to find visuals that could be used to illustrate what each speaker believes is the proper role for women. Write a short paragraph explaining how each photograph supports the quotation.
3. **Writing About the Chapter** Imagine that you are living in the United States around the turn of the century. Write a letter to the editor of the local newspaper in which you take a stand on the woman question. Before you write your letter, draw up an outline of your argument. List several reasons for supporting or opposing expanded rights for women, and identify details or examples to support each of your reasons.

Next, write a draft of your letter. Begin by stating your position, and then present each of your reasons in a separate paragraph. Conclude by encouraging your readers to work for or against expanded women's rights. Read over your draft, carefully refining your arguments and correcting any errors. Then, make a final copy.
4. **Using the Graphic Organizer** This graphic organizer uses a tree map to organize information about the expansion of education in the late 1800s. (a) Based on what you have read in the chapter, how was the experience of higher education different for African Americans and minorities than it was for white males? (b) Describe the experience of higher education for women during the late 1800s. (c) On a separate sheet of paper, create your own graphic organizer about the changes in women's lives during the late 1800s.

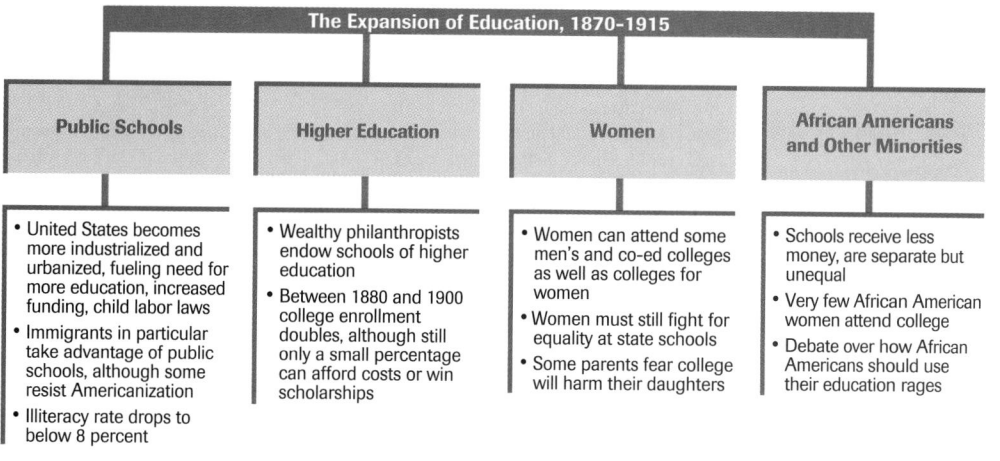

The Expansion of Education, 1870–1915

Public Schools	Higher Education	Women	African Americans and Other Minorities
• United States becomes more industrialized and urbanized, fueling need for more education, increased funding, child labor laws • Immigrants in particular take advantage of public schools, although some resist Americanization • Illiteracy rate drops to below 8 percent	• Wealthy philanthropists endow schools of higher education • Between 1880 and 1900 college enrollment doubles, although still only a small percentage can afford costs or win scholarships	• Women can attend some men's and co-ed colleges as well as colleges for women • Women must still fight for equality at state schools • Some parents fear college will harm their daughters	• Schools receive less money, are separate but unequal • Very few African American women attend college • Debate over how African Americans should use their education rages

3. Students' responses in favor of women's rights might mention the expanding role of women in the workplace and increasing levels of education. Arguments against women's rights might focus on disruption of the existing social order.

4. (a) Although meeting college costs was difficult for all families, including those headed by white males, African Americans faced the added burden of prejudice. (b) Women could attend some male or coeducational colleges or colleges for women, but had to fight for equal status at state-run colleges. Parents often discouraged their daughters from attending college. Very few African American women attended college. (c) Students' graphic organizers should include information about the changes in technology, the workplace, and society in general that affected women's lives in the late 1800s.

Alternative Assessment

Final Evaluation
Use the following guidelines to evaluate student projects:
- **Evidence of thoughtfulness** Did the students include the main topics from the chapter?
- **Evidence of outside research** To what extent did students use outside research materials for their projects?
- **Evidence of synthesis** Do projects demonstrate that students understand how topics are related?
- **Communication style** Do the projects convey their purposes to an audience in a clear, appealing way?

Sports have played an important role in both eras. Many of today's activities, however, such as television viewing and video games, rely on advanced technology. Another difference is that many of these are individual rather than family pursuits.

3. Possible answer: By being forced to use separate public facilities, their self-esteem continued to be undermined. Blacks were effectively told that they were not as good as whites and that whites did not want to be associated with them.

Making Connections

1. Answers will vary. Students may point to the American public's taste for excitement and instant gratification and give examples from sports, movies, and television.

2. For the Charlotte Perkins Gilman quotation, students might choose the photograph of the woman graduate in the chapter opener, or the photograph of women students on page 470. For the Cyrus Townsend Brady quote, students might select the photograph of the woman teacher on page 469, the homemaker on page 483, or the workers on page 484. Explanations should show an understanding of the contrasting ideas each speaker holds on the proper role of women.

Recall with students that the popularity of sports at the turn of the century was a result of the increased availability of leisure time for Americans.

Ask students to study the artifacts and to read the captions on these pages. Using the artifacts and captions as a basis for discussion, ask students what changes in American society were indicated by the growing appeal of sports.

Ask students to examine the effect of technology, communications, and business on sports, and to compare the role of sports in popular culture at the turn of the century to the importance of sports in life today. Ask how technology, communications, and business affected the growth of sports. Is the influence of business on sports good or bad? Is sports of greater of lesser importance to the average American today than it was at the turn of the century? Is there as much criticism of sports today as there was at the turn of the century?

Ask students to make a list of the artifacts they would include in an American Album display about sports of the 1990s. Tell them to choose items that illustrate the wide variety of sports that Americans enjoy.

THE GROWTH OF SPORTS

The great rise in sports at the turn of the century reflected many other changes that were taking part in America at the same time. If not for the country's growing wealth, most adults would not have been free from their constant labor to seek excitement in games. The popularity of sports also signaled a change in the way that Americans viewed health and "idle" entertainments. Before this time, many Americans shunned activities that did not create wealth or improve character. It was now morally acceptable to spend time pursuing interests because they were just plain fun. *How do you think changes taking place in society, technology, communications, and business affected the growth of sports?*

Padded football pants

◀ FOOTBALL AT THE TURN OF THE CENTURY This football card shows that players wore much less protection than modern players. Notice the lack of shoulder pads and helmet. The only protection came from padded pants (also worn by some basketball players of the time), which protected players from leg bruises. A century ago, the game was also less violent.

▼ SKIING Skiing, as we know the sport today, began in Norway in the mid-1800s when the addition of bindings made it possible for skiers to turn and jump. Norwegian immigrants then brought the sport to Minnesota, from where it spread to other snowy areas in the United States. Skiing, however, did not become widely popular until the 1930s with the introduction of the ski tow.

EARLY BASEBALL Baseball achieved its status as the great American pastime in the last third of the 1800s. Many songs celebrated the game's heroes, such as the polka tune shown on this sheet-music cover. Fans of Georgetown University's baseball team dyed the ball (in the mitt on the right) dark blue and painted in the score to honor their team's victory over Yale in 1899.

ICE SKATING A common winter sport before the 1800s, ice skating became even more popular in the late 1800s. One reason for the sport's growth in popularity was the introduction of low-priced "store-bought" skates. ▶

◀ **WOMEN CYCLISTS** Before the late 1800s, outdoor sports activities for women were limited. But women's steady struggle for legal and social rights, as well as improvements in bicycles, contributed to a change. By the 1890s, women had joined the bicycle craze and entered into active, public sport. The athletic demands of riding a bicycle required new, more practical clothing for women, which outraged many people.

◀ On this 1870 bicycle, the pedals connect directly to the front wheels at the axle. The introduction of a chain and foot brakes in the 1890s made pedaling much easier and gave the cyclist more control.

Introducing the Unit

Interpreting the Visual Alfred Thayer Mahan, an American writer on naval affairs quoted on page 492, believed that a nation's greatness lay not in its buildings, factories, or crops but in a strong navy and merchant marine. Mahan's books influenced some of the key figures of his time, including Theodore Roosevelt and Kaiser Wilhelm I of Germany.

By the late 1880s, United States naval power was in decline, partly because investors were more attracted to other ventures, such as railroads and mining. In fact, in 1892 the United States still had more tonnage in sailing ships than in steamships.

Direct students to the photograph on pages 492–493 and point out the Brooklyn Bridge in the background. Ask students to list the kinds of transportation shown in the picture. Then divide the class into discussion groups and ask each group to explain why a vigorously expanding economy continually needs new markets. Ask students to identify the overseas market advertised by the steamship company in the picture.

Establishing Chronology Remind students that the previous chapters focused on the growth of American industry. This unit focuses on the nation's growing role as a world power from 1890 to 1920. From 1898 to 1899, the United States was at war with Spain. From 1917 to 1918, the nation fought in World War I. The progressive movement, which began around 1890, remained strong through the war years.

The United States on the Brink of Change 1890–1920

"Whether they will or not, Americans must now begin to look outward. The growing production of the country demands it."
—Alfred T. Mahan, 1890

The industrial boom at the turn of the century had far-reaching effects. In search of markets for its products, the United States joined the scramble for new territories, leading to international conflict and war. Meanwhile, the serious problems created by the boom inspired a reform movement known as progressivism. Both the ambitions of the imperialists and the ideals of the progressives contributed to the nation's growing role as a world power. This role eventually drew the United States into the horrors of World War I.

CHAPTER 18	Pages 494–519 **Becoming a World Power** 1890–1913
CHAPTER 19	Pages 520–547 **The Era of Progressive Reform** 1890–1920
CHAPTER 20	Pages 548–573 **The World War I Era** 1914–1920

 RESOURCE DIRECTORY

Teaching Resources

Local History Activity "The 'Newsies': A Chicago Street Scene" and the Local Focus research topic suggestions, found in the Local History Resources folder, pp. 18–20, are designed to help students understand how history affects all lives.

★ **Themes in American History Posters** Wall-size, illustrated posters, found in the Teaching Resources package, illustrate the four unit themes.

Unit Test Forms A and B are found in the Unit 6 folder, pp. 110–115.

New York City's docks were teeming with activity in the early 1900s as the United States reached across the Atlantic Ocean in its quest to become an economic and political world power.

Media and Technology

Visions of America: Scenes of an Era To introduce students to the main idea and events covered in this unit, play "Scenes of an Era: The United States on the Brink of Change" (length: 2.5 minutes). This selection can be located on side 2 of the videodiscs. This selection can also be located on videotape 3. Lesson plans for "Scenes of an Era" can be found in the Visions of America Guidebook.

Using Multimedia Technology This folder contains instructional tools and strategies for using technology in the classroom.

Transparency Binder Contains full-color transparencies with lesson suggestions. From a large collection divided into twelve categories, specific transparencies are referenced throughout the chapters at appropriate points of use. For this unit, see American Photo, B-6; Fine Art, D-16; Cause and Effect, F-5; Links Across Time, J-6; Political Cartoon, K-6; and Geographic Setting, M-9.

Themes in American History

Teachers may wish to discuss specific historical events in the context of historical themes. Here are four suggestions for Unit 6.

Reform Movements *People in the United States have frequently taken action in grass roots movements to right perceived wrongs and to secure improvements in the quality of life.*

● The seventy-year quest for women's suffrage ended in 1920 with the adoption of the Nineteenth Amendment.

● Progressivism took root in the late 1800s and led to major changes in urban, state, and federal laws and practices.

Values *A variety of religious, ethical, and moral beliefs have propelled and guided the quest of Americans for a just and ordered society.*

● The argument over American imperialism was shaped by moral, ethical, and religious ideals as well as racial and economic issues.

● The progressives argued that government had a moral responsibility for the welfare of citizens.

Unity and Conflict *Americans have developed unique political systems and laws that affirm a shared commitment to certain goals, such as individual rights and equality. Nevertheless, groups with differing views on how to achieve these goals have often clashed.*

● America's desire to expand its markets clashed with its reluctance to become involved in foreign entanglements and war.

● During World War I, the United States enacted many laws that censored the press and limited personal freedoms.

The United States and the World *America's relationships with other countries have been influenced at different times by a sense of mission, by values, and by self-interest.*

● America's desire to expand its markets led to conflict with Spain and several interventions in Latin America.

● President Wilson took the leading role in defining a vision of global peace after World War I, but Congress and the Allies kept his vision from being realized.

Chapter 18 Becoming a World Power
1890–1913

📁 Teaching Resources (See Unit 6 Folder)

	Instruction	Enrichment
Section 1 **The Pressure to Expand** (pp. 496–499)	Reproducible Lesson Plan, p. 3 Alternate Lesson Plan, p. 90 Guided Reading and Review, p. 7 Quiz, p. 8	Visual Learning Activity, Expansionism, p. 29
Section 2 **Foreign Entanglements, War, and Annexations** (pp. 500–505)	Reproducible Lesson Plan, p. 4 Alternate Lesson Plan, p. 91 Guided Reading and Review, p. 9 Quiz, p. 10	Literature Activity, The Open Boat, pp. 26–27 Critical Thinking Activity, Drawing Conclusions, p. 22 Visual Learning Activity, Wartime Propaganda, p. 30 Primary Source Activity, Teddy Roosevelt: Letters Home, pp. 23–24 American Profiles Activity, Walter Reed, p. 17 Historian's Toolbox Activity, Using a Time Zone Map, p. 21
Section 3 **A Forceful Diplomacy** (pp. 507–511)	Reproducible Lesson Plan, p. 5 Alternate Lesson Plan, p. 92 Guided Reading and Review, p. 11 Quiz, p. 12	Literature Activity, You're All Right, Teddy, p. 28 Primary Source Activity, The Panamanian Revolution, p. 25 Time and Place Activity, Building the Alaska Pipeline, pp. 15–16
Section 4 **The People's Response to Imperialism** (pp. 514–517)	Reproducible Lesson Plan, p. 6 Alternate Lesson Plan, p. 93 Guided Reading and Review, p. 13 Quiz, p. 14 Chapter Test, Forms A & B, pp. 31–36	Viewpoints Activity, On the Race for Empire, pp. 19–20 American Profiles Activity, Juliette Gordon Low, p. 18

📁 Additional Chapter Resources

Resource Organizer, p. 2
Alternate Lesson Plan, p. 89
Answer Keys, pp. 116–128

Bibliography

For the Teacher

Marks, George P., III, ed. *The Black Press Views American Imperialism (1898–1900)*. Arno Press and The New York Times, Inc., 1971. (Includes source material on the annexation of Hawaii, the demand for African American officers, and the Spanish-American War.)

McCullough, David. *The Path Between the Seas: The Creation of the Panama Canal, 1870–1914*. Simon & Schuster, 1977. (Lively and full account contains excerpts from original sources and reads as an epic adventure.)

Prentice Hall Literature Excerpts from *The American Experience*, 1994, including "Realism and the Frontier, 1865–1915."

THE BIG IDEA

The Big Idea for the chapter and how the main ideas in each section relate to the Big Idea are graphically displayed below. Comprehension of this chapter's Big Idea is critical to students' understanding of United States history and how we as a nation got where we are today.

Media and Technology

 Cause and Effect, F-7

 Critical Thinking, I-12; Fine Art, D-15; Geographic Setting, M-9

 Graphic Organizer, G-5

 Guided Reading Audiotapes (English and Spanish)

 Computer Test Bank

For the Student

O'Toole, G. J. A. *The Spanish War: An American Epic–1898.* Norton, 1986. (An anecdotal discussion of the explosion of the *Maine* with recent evidence and an analysis of the McKinley administration's role in the expansion of the conflict.)

St. George, Judith. *Panama Canal: Gateway to the World.* Putnam's, 1989. (Award–winning, illustrated study of the ten-year struggle to build the canal.)

CHAPTER 18

By the 1890s, businesses and political leaders with dreams of empire were pushing into new markets and seizing control of territory abroad. Imperialism on the part of a country founded on freedom from colonialism troubled many United States citizens. The responsibilities of a world power brought conflicting domestic and international agendas of the government to the forefront.

SECTION 1

In the late 1800s, American farms and factories produced more than the nation could consume. The United States thus looked to expand its markets overseas. This drew it into conflicts on foreign soil.

SECTION 2

A swift American victory in the Spanish-American War confirmed the nation's status as a world power and obliged it to wrestle with how to govern newly acquired territories.

SECTION 3

President Theodore Roosevelt conducted an aggressive foreign policy that reflected the nation's new status as a world power. President William Howard Taft continued Roosevelt's policies with a more subtle approach.

SECTION 4

Following the Spanish-American War, anti-imperialists launched moral, political, and practical arguments against the country's foreign ventures. Most citizens, however, supported the interventionist policies of the United States.

Becoming a World Power
1890–1913

CHAPTER 18

Becoming a World Power
1890–1913

The Relevance of the Big Idea

In the 1890s, United States business interests spread throughout the Western Hemisphere and the Pacific. In the 1990s, American multinational corporations operate throughout the world.

In order for students to understand the role of the United States in a global economy, ask them: "How far should the United States go to protect American companies that operate overseas?" Point out that the United States fought the Gulf War in 1991 in large part to protect the oil interests of the United States in Kuwait. Should the United States try to steer countries toward a type of government friendly to American businesses? Should it ever use force to do so?

In Depth

Global Connections

The peace that Teddy Roosevelt arranged between Russia and Japan haunted the United States later in the century. Even though the treaty may have "saved Japan from a beating," Japanese newspapers condemned it as cheating their country out of major territorial gains. Japan defied the terms of the treaty by annexing Korea in 1910. The spread of Japan's influence fueled the country's aspirations for empire in Asia, and its expansionist policies in the 1930s culminated in the bombing of Pearl Harbor and the entry of the United States into World War II.

By the 1890s, farms and factories in the United States were producing more than the nation could consume. Soon, many business and political leaders began to pursue new markets abroad. Inspired by grand dreams of empire, some Americans pushed for new territory as well. As the nation grew into a world power, however, a troubling question arose in some citizens' minds: could a country born in a war for independence from colonial rule become a colonial power itself—without betraying the principles of liberty and equality on which it was founded?

Events in the United States

	1890	1893	1896	1899
	1890 Alfred Mahan publishes The Influence of Sea Power Upon History.	**1893** American planters overthrow Queen Liliuokalani in Hawaii.	**1896** William McKinley defeats William Jennings Bryan in presidential election.	**1898** The Spanish-American War takes place. • The United States annexes Hawaii.

Events in the World

1885 Indian National Congress is founded.	**1895** Japan defeats China in Sino-Japanese War. • Cubans rebel against Spanish rule.	**1900** The Boxer Rebellion breaks out in China.

RESOURCE DIRECTORY

Teaching Resources

Alternate Lesson Plan: Demonstrating the Big Idea found in the Alternate Lesson Plans folder, p. 89, provides a lesson strategy to help students understand the issues that determine the roles the United States plays in the global economy.

Alternative Assessment Handbook provides information, guidance, and strategies for alternative methods of assessment. It includes an essay on new trends in assessment, guidance and strategies for developing performance tasks and portfolios, scoring rubrics, and sample evaluation forms.

Pages 496–499
The Pressure to Expand

In the late 1800s, the United States began bursting at the seams with more goods than the nation could consume. Soon other parts of the world beckoned to government and business leaders eager to sell those extra goods. This economic expansion, however, increasingly led the United States into conflicts on foreign soil.

Pages 500–505
Foreign Entanglements, War, and Annexations

As the United States sought to increase its influence abroad, it frequently found itself feuding with other nations. A swift American victory in the Spanish-American War confirmed the nation's status as a world power, but it left some people arguing over how to govern newly acquired territories.

Pages 507–511
A Forceful Diplomacy

Whether people thought him a hero or a "wild man," most agreed that President Theodore Roosevelt conducted a vigorous foreign policy that suited the new status of the United States as a world power. Although President William Howard Taft continued Roosevelt's policies, he preferred a quieter, more subtle approach to influencing other nations.

Pages 514–517
The People's Response to Imperialism

After the Spanish-American War, the debate intensified over whether it was appropriate for the United States to continue to throw its net around other nations and drag them under American control. Anti-imperialists used a variety of arguments against the acquisition of territories.

1901 President McKinley is assassinated, and Theodore Roosevelt becomes President.

1908 William Howard Taft becomes President.

1910 Boy Scouts and Girl Scouts are introduced to the United States.

1914 Construction of the Panama Canal is completed.

1902	1905	1908	1911	1914	1917

1905 Japan defeats Russia in Russo-Japanese War.

1911 Revolution sweeps China.

1913 Second Balkan War erupts between Bulgaria, Serbia, and Greece.

Alternative Assessment

As an ongoing chapter project, students can write two newspaper editorials that might have appeared in the 1890s. One should take a pro-imperialist stand; the other should be anti-imperialist.

Students might create a scenario involving the possible annexation of a fictional republic; or they might use other real historical examples. Editorials should reflect a firm knowledge of the arguments for or against United States expansionism.

The editorials should attempt to persuade by using reasoned arguments that address moral, economic, social, and political implications. They may be written in a yellow journalism style, employing exaggeration and appeal to jingoism. Students may choose to research and use actual quotations from political and business leaders of the time to help bolster their arguments.

Explain that projects will be evaluated according to the following guidelines:

● **Unacceptable** Editorials are not attempted or fail to meet the basic requirements.

● **Limited/Acceptable** Editorials reflect a basic understanding of the positions of imperialists and anti-imperialists, using information from the chapter.

● **Extensive/Commendable** Editorials reflect an in-depth understanding of the views and motives of imperialists and anti-imperialists, and demonstrate some outside research.

● **Extraordinary/Outstanding** Editorials employ arguments for each viewpoint, demonstrate a clear understanding of yellow journalism, show evidence of considerable outside research, and employ contemporary quotations.

For information and guidance in alternative assessment trends and strategies, see the Alternative Assessment Handbook in the Resource Directory on page 494.

The Pressure to Expand

Connecting to the Big Idea

See page 494B. Explain that in the late 1800s, the United States needed new markets for its goods. Ask students how that economic problem led to political entanglements in foreign countries.

Objectives

● Explain why the United States needed to find new markets for its goods.
● Describe how increased European expansion affected United States foreign policy.
● List the main arguments used by those who favored expansion.
● Analyze why economic expansion led to political entanglements abroad.

Bellringer

Write the following saying on the chalkboard: "The sun never sets on the British Empire." Ask students what they think it means. Explain that in the late 1800s, when this saying was popular and accurate, the United States was beginning to build its own empire. Ask what an empire is.

Reading Strategy

Reinforcing Key Ideas As students read, they should list the pressures and attitudes that led the United States to adopt a policy of political and economic expansion overseas.

SECTION 1
The Pressure to Expand

SECTION PREVIEW

In the late 1800s, the United States began bursting at the seams with more goods than the nation could consume. Soon other parts of the world beckoned to government and business leaders eager to sell those extra goods. This economic expansion, however, increasingly led the United States into conflicts on foreign soil.

Key Concepts
• Overproduction of industrial and agricultural goods threatened the United States economy and created a pressing need for foreign markets.
• The need of the United States for economic expansion occurred at a time when the major European powers were scrambling to seize new territories around the globe.
• Americans who favored expansion used economic, moral, and social Darwinist arguments to justify their position.
• Economic expansion involved the risk of foreign entanglements.

Key Terms, People, and Places
imperialism, annexation, most-favored nation, banana republic; Alfred T. Mahan, Henry Cabot Lodge, Albert J. Beveridge; Hawaii

B y the late 1800s, the industrialists, inventors, and laboring forces of the United States had built a powerful industrial economy. But the nation could not consume food and goods fast enough to prevent harmful cycles of financial panic and depression. Labor and farmers protested their plight, helping to convince business and political leaders that the United States must secure new markets abroad. Some people also began to believe that the United States had a responsibility to carry democratic values and Protestant Christianity to others around the globe.

Business leaders eagerly sought new markets abroad in which to sell goods such as this American-grown fruit.

The Growth of Imperialism Around the World

Meanwhile, Europe had reached new heights in its quest for territories to rule as shown on the map on page 497. Under **imperialism,** stronger nations attempt to create empires by dominating weaker nations—economically, politically, or militarily. This type of policy also has been called expansionism. Although Spain's once-great empire in the Americas and the Pacific had shrunk considerably by 1890, it still held on to a few remaining outposts in Cuba, Puerto Rico, and the Philippines. Meanwhile, developments in transportation and communication made it easier for Great Britain, France, and Russia—nations with long imperialist traditions—to maintain and extend their grip on far-flung lands.

Great Britain, in particular, acquired so much new territory in Africa, Asia, and the Pacific that the saying "The sun never sets on the British Empire" became popular. Competition for new territory grew even more intense when the powerful new German state, unified in 1871, also showed expansionist ambitions in Africa and Asia.

By 1890 the United States was eager to join the international competition for new territories. That year James G. Blaine, secretary of state under President Harrison from 1889 to 1892, summarized the situation as follows:

> W e have developed a volume of manufactures which, in many departments, overruns the demands of the home market. . . . Our great demand is expansion . . . of trade with countries where we can find profitable exchanges.

Blaine denied that the United States was seeking "annexation of territory." But **annexation**—the addition of a new territory to an existing country—did take place.

RESOURCE DIRECTORY

Teaching Resources

Reproducible Lesson Plan found in the Unit 6 folder, p. 3, provides a summary of the Section 1 lesson plan content.

Alternate Lesson Plan: Critical Thinking Recognizing Bias, found in the Alternate Lesson Plans folder, p. 90, provides a structure for students to apply this skill in identifying factors in the drive for U.S. expansion

and how it was justified with economic, moral, and social Darwinist arguments.

Guided Reading and Review found in the Unit 6 folder, p. 7, provides a structure for reading and mastering the key concepts and reviewing the key terms for Section 1. (Guided Practice)

The Tradition of Expansionism in the United States

Despite comments like Blaine's, the United States always had been an expansionist nation. In the 1840s, the concept of "manifest destiny" had captured the popular imagination. The seizure of new territories from Mexico and various Native American nations had followed.

As early as the 1820s, the chief principle of foreign policy in the United States had been the Monroe Doctrine. Under this doctrine, the United States had declared itself interested in anything that happened in the Western Hemisphere and warned European powers to keep out. United States secretaries of state continued to apply the principle after the Civil War. In 1866, for example, William H. Seward sent 50,000 federal troops, still in Texas after the Civil War, into Mexico. The display was meant to convince the French government to withdraw the puppet "emperor" they had placed on the Mexican throne. The following year, Seward bought Alaska from Russia. In addition to gaining more territory, Seward hoped that the presence of the United States on both sides of Canada would force the British out of that region.

Americans also had their eyes on the Pacific. By the 1860s, the United States had won **"most-favored nation"** status in China, which simply meant that it had the same access to trade with China as any other nation. The United States also had established a solid trading relationship with Japan. Now the United States government wanted control of some Pacific islands to use as refueling and repair stations for its naval vessels. To this end, Seward annexed the uninhabited Midway Islands in 1867. Eight years later, the United States government signed a treaty with **Hawaii,** an island nation in the Pacific, that allowed Hawaiians to sell sugar in the United States duty free, as long as they did not sell or lease territory to any foreign power.

Much closer to the United States, and therefore of greater concern, were the Caribbean islands and Latin America. In 1870 President Ulysses S. Grant announced that hereafter the Monroe Doctrine would protect all territories in these two regions from "transfer to a European power."

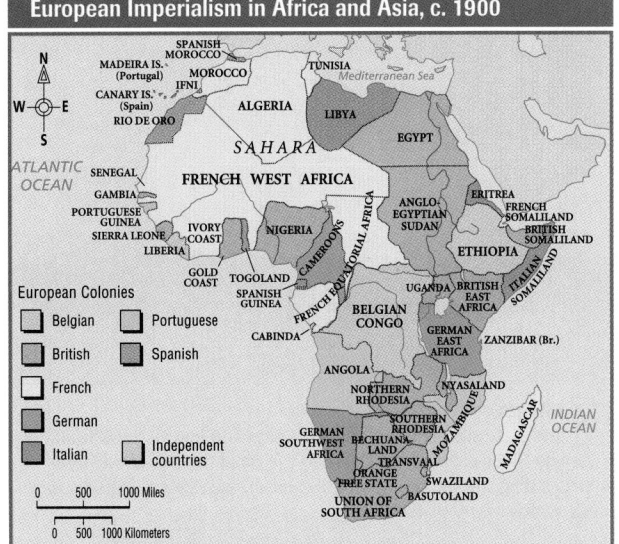

European Imperialism in Africa and Asia, c. 1900

 Geography and History: Interpreting Maps
By 1900, European imperialist nations controlled vast amounts of territory in both Africa and Asia, as the above maps illustrate. *Which African nations retained their independence from imperialist control?*

MAKING CONNECTIONS

In what sense were the expansionist policies of the United States in the late 1800s simply a continuation of the concept of manifest destiny?

Interpreting Graphs

Markets in the United States could not consume the enormous amounts of goods being produced.

Activity

Teaching Heterogeneous Groups

In the late 1800s, overproduction of goods in the United States created a need for American businesses to find foreign markets. Today the United States continues this search, just as other countries seek a place in the American market to sell their goods. For students to understand imports, exports, and the marketplace, have them list the names of the countries where their clothing and accessories originated. Conduct a survey to determine which country has the largest share of the classroom market.

Enrichment

Ask students to research and report on Minor Keith and the activities of his United Fruit Company. Students should find out how United Fruit was able to gain and maintain control of the Central American countries in which it did business.

3. ASSESS

Section 1 Review Answers

1. (a) imperialism, see p. 496 (b) annexation, see p. 496, (c) most-favored nation, see p. 497, (d) banana republic, see p. 498

2. (a) Alfred T. Mahan, see page 498, (b) Henry Cabot Lodge, see p. 499, (c) Albert J. Beveridge, see page 499

3. Hawaii, see p. 497

4. America's industrial and agricultural goods could not be consumed fast enough to prevent recurring cycles of panics and depression; foreign markets were needed to provide a place to sell the nation's surplus products.

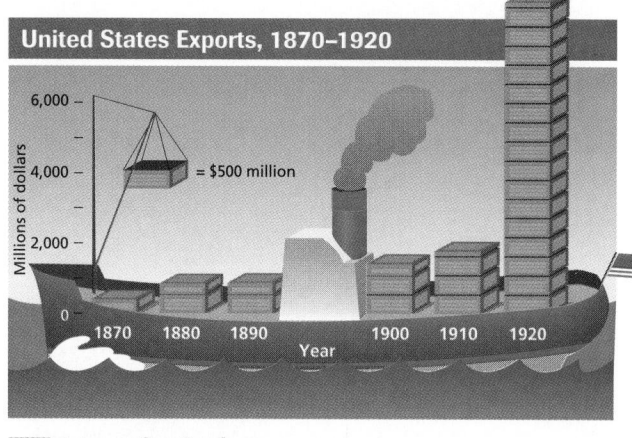

United States Exports, 1870–1920

= $500 million

Interpreting Graphs
The expansion of American businesses into international markets in the late 1800s and early 1900s led to the rapid rise in United States exports during this period. *Why did American businesses wish to sell their goods outside of the United States?*

Americans Debate Expansionism

A debate arose in the 1890s over what foreign policy would best serve the United States in its various interests abroad. Some argued that the country should become even more involved in international economic affairs. Others replied that the country had enough problems of its own without risking foreign entanglements.

Voices Supporting Expansion Many business leaders believed that the economic problems of

As this 1901 political cartoon suggests, the United States relied on the Monroe Doctrine to block European involvement in Latin America.

the nation could be solved by expanding its markets. Some American businesses already dominated international markets. In the 1880s and 1890s, Rockefeller's Standard Oil, Mc-Cormick reapers, American Telegraph and Telephone, Singer Sewing Machine, Kodak Camera, and Sherwin-Williams Paint all became international corporations. Southern cotton farmers and western wheat growers also were involved heavily in overseas trade.

Other business leaders had gone a step farther, by investing directly in the economies of other countries. This step led steadily toward increased political influence in those countries. In Central America, for example, an American named Minor C. Keith won long-term leases for lands and railroad lines by providing financial services to the Costa Rican government. By 1913 Keith's United Fruit Company not only exported 50 million bunches of bananas a year to ports in the United States, but also dominated the political and economic institutions of Costa Rica, Guatemala, and Honduras. As a result, some people began to refer to the Central American nations as **banana republics.**

Lobbyists who favored a strong United States Navy formed a second force pushing for expansion. By the 1880s, United States warships left over from the Civil War were rusting and rotting. Naval officers joined with business interests to convince Congress to build modern steam-powered, steel-hulled ships to protect overseas trade. The most influential of these officers was Captain (later Admiral) **Alfred T. Mahan.** In his 1890 book, *The Influence of Sea Power Upon History, 1660–1783,* Mahan asserted that the economic future of the nation depended on gaining new markets abroad and that a powerful navy would be essential to protect these markets from foreign rivals. Influenced by Mahan's arguments, Congress authorized the building of nine cruisers, including the U.S.S. *Maine,* in the 1890s. Battleships, gunboats, torpedo boats, and more cruisers followed. By 1900, the United States had one of the most powerful navies in the world.

▶ RESOURCE DIRECTORY

Teaching Resources

⭐ **Visual Learning Activity** Expansionism, found in the Unit 6 folder, p. 29, uses a political cartoon from the British magazine *Puck* to present a critical view of United States territorial expansion.

Political and cultural leaders also promoted expansionism. Among them were Massachusetts senator **Henry Cabot Lodge,** historian Frederick Jackson Turner, and a rising young politician from New York named Theodore Roosevelt. Although concerned about the need for new markets abroad, these men saw another purpose in expansionism. Worried about the effects of a closing frontier on the nation's spirit, they feared that the United States was on the brink of losing its vitality. They argued that a quest for empire might restore the country's pioneer spirit.

These and other leaders of the day also drew on the doctrine of social Darwinism to justify the conquest of new territories, just as they had done earlier to defend the treatment of Native Americans. In the opinion of such influential figures as Congregationalist minister Josiah Strong and Indiana senator **Albert J. Beveridge,** the "advanced" civilizations produced by Anglo-Saxon and Teutonic (Germanic) "races" were superior to the "primitive" societies they conquered. Thus, expansionism was not only inevitable but noble, for it introduced Protestant Christianity and modern civilization to those who might otherwise never have encountered such ideas. As Beveridge explained:

> I t is elemental. It is racial. God has not been preparing the English-speaking and Teutonic peoples for a thousand years for nothing but vain and idle self-contemplation and self-admiration. No! . . . He has marked the American people as His chosen Nation finally to lead in the regeneration [rebirth] of the world. . . . American law,

American order, American civilization, and the American flag will plant themselves on shores hitherto bloody and benighted [ignorant], but by those agencies of God henceforth to be made beautiful and bright.
Albert J. Beveridge, *The Meaning of the Times and Other Speeches,* 1908

This postcard of African Zulus with a Singer sewing machine illustrates the spread of American products abroad in the late 1800s.

Public Opinion Leans Toward Expansion
Gradually public opinion warmed to the idea of expansionism. Most Americans did not see themselves as potential rulers of oppressed foreign peoples, but they did want new markets abroad and favorable trade relations. What they soon discovered was that political and military entanglements tended to follow. To maintain a territory's political stability, intervention—and sometimes war—became necessary. When annexation of that territory followed, governing those who resented American interference turned out to be difficult, bloody, and painful.

SECTION 1 REVIEW

Key Terms, People, and Places
1. Define (a) imperialism, (b) annexation, (c) most-favored nation, (d) banana republic.
2. Identify (a) Alfred T. Mahan, (b) Henry Cabot Lodge, (c) Albert J. Beveridge.
3. Identify Hawaii.

Key Concepts
4. Why did United States policy makers feel the need to secure new markets abroad in the late 1800s?

5. In addition to the potential economic benefits of expansion, what were some of the moral arguments that people who favored this policy used?
6. What risks did the United States take in attempting to find new foreign markets?

Critical Thinking
7. **Drawing Conclusions** How did the popular philosophy of social Darwinism make it easier for Americans to embrace imperialist policies in the late 1800s?

Quiz found in the Unit 6 folder, p. 8, covers the main ideas in this section as well as the key terms.

Media and Technology

 Transparency
Cause and Effect, F-7

---

5. They claimed that it would restore the country's pioneer spirit and bring Protestant Christianity and modern civilization to "primitive" peoples.

6. Dangerous rivalries with other powerful countries; costly and disruptive wars; and involvement in the politics of weaker countries.

7. The social Darwinist notions helped many Americans to feel comfortable establishing American rule over colonial peoples.

Reteach
Have students write at least one cause for each of these effects:
• U.S. companies began to dominate the affairs of banana republics.
• Congress authorized an expansion of the United States Navy.
• Public opinion gradually warmed to the idea of expansionism.

 4. CLOSE

Reinforcing the Big Idea
A search for new markets and competition for new territory led the United States to become heavily involved in the affairs of nations in Latin America and the Pacific. The next section describes how U.S. foreign policy would soon become even more aggressive, leading to deeper overseas entanglements—and even war.

In Depth

Multicultural Perspectives
In 1909 a nationwide petition pleaded for an organized attempt to "improve the status of those Americans for whom the Civil War had been fought to set free." The petition helped form the National Association for the Advancement of Colored People (NAACP), one of the best-known organizations in the fight for civil rights. (See Key Events in the Reference Section.)

Connecting to the Big Idea

See page 494B. An aggressive foreign policy brought the United States into conflict with several other nations. Ask what problems the United States faced as a new world power.

Objectives

● Explain how United States foreign policy at the turn of the century reaffirmed the aims of the Monroe Doctrine.
● List the main reasons that the United States went to war with Spain.
● Describe how the United States pursued its expansionist policies in the Pacific.

Bellringer

Write the word *sensationalism* on the chalkboard and ask students to define it. Ask how sensationalism can arouse public energy and response. Discuss types of news coverage that might be considered sensational.

Reading Strategy

Structured Overview Ask students to create a two-column chart entitled "United States Foreign Policy." Students should list countries where the United States pursued expansionist policies in the left-hand column, and the effects of United States policies on each of these countries in the remaining column.

Foreign Entanglements, War, and Annexations

SECTION PREVIEW

As the United States sought to increase its influence abroad, it frequently found itself feuding with other nations. A swift American victory in the Spanish-American War confirmed the nation's status as a world power, but it left some people arguing over how to govern newly acquired territories.

Key Concepts

• The United States took advantage of several incidents in Latin America to reaffirm the validity of the Monroe Doctrine.
• A rebellion in Cuba and the pressure for expansion led the United States into war with Spain.
• While pursuing its interventionist policies, the United States acquired new territories and influence in the Pacific.

Key Terms, People, and Places

guerrilla, jingoism, sphere of influence, Open Door policy; William Randolph Hearst, Joseph Pulitzer, George Dewey; Cuba, Philippine Islands, San Juan Hill

In its drive to become a world power, the United States increasingly became involved in the affairs of Latin American nations.

T hose in the United States who dreamed of expansion looked to three main areas of the world in the late 1800s: Latin America, the islands of the Pacific, and China. In the 1890s, the United States established a pattern of intervention in these three areas that changed its status in world politics. In the process of expanding and becoming a world power, however, the United States increasingly found itself in conflict with other nations.

Stirrings in Latin America

During the 1890s, the United States played an active role in three diplomatic and military conflicts in Latin America. In the first of these incidents, in 1891, the United States government forced Chile to pay $75,000 to the families of United States sailors who were killed or injured by an angry mob during the sailors' shore leave in Valparaíso. Two years later, when a rebellion threatened the friendly republican government of Brazil, President Cleveland ordered naval units to Rio de Janeiro to protect United States shipping. This show of force broke the back of the rebellion.

In the third and most important incident of the era, the United States confronted the nation then considered the most powerful in the world, Great Britain. Since the 1840s, Britain and Venezuela had disputed ownership of a piece of territory located at the border between Venezuela and British Guiana. In the 1880s, the dispute intensified when rumors surfaced of mineral wealth in this border area. When President Cleveland's secretary of state, Richard Olney, warned Britain in July 1895 that the United States would enforce the Monroe Doctrine, the British government replied that the doctrine had no standing in international law. Two years later, however, Britain backed down. Concerned about the rising power of Germany in Africa, the British government realized that it needed to stay on friendly terms with the increasingly powerful United States.

The Spanish-American War

By the mid-1890s, therefore, the United States had not only reaffirmed the Monroe Doctrine but also forced the world's most powerful nation to bow to its will. Encouraged by

---

 RESOURCE DIRECTORY

Teaching Resources

Reproducible Lesson Plan found in the Unit 6 folder, p. 4, provides a summary of the Section 2 lesson plan content.

Alternate Lesson Plan: Learning Styles found in the Alternate Lesson Plans folder, p. 91, enhances students' understanding of the Monroe Doctrine and interventionist policies, and is especially helpful for auditory and visual learners.

Guided Reading and Review found in the Unit 6 folder, p. 9, provides a structure for reading and mastering the key concepts and reviewing the key terms for Section 2. (Guided Practice)

Literature Activity "The Open Boat," found in the Unit 6 folder, pp. 26–27, describes the harrowing experience of author Stephen Crane, who survived the sinking of a munitions supply steamer returning from Cuba in 1897.

Sensational Newspapers

WOMAN TURNS INTO WILD DOG
WW2 BOMBER FOUND ON MOON
REAL AMERICAN MONSTERS AND DRAGONS
WONDERFUL RESULTS FROM MERELY
  HOLDING TUBES OF DRUGS NEAR
  ENTRANCED PATIENTS

Have you ever seen headlines like these while waiting in line at the supermarket? If so, you might be surprised to learn that the first two appeared in 1990, while the last two are from newspapers published in 1896.

Sensational newspapers are not a recent development. In the late 1800s, publishers engaged in fierce competition for the sale of popular daily newspapers. Yellow journalism attempted to attract customers by using sensational, though not necessarily true, photographs, stories, and headlines. If there was no startling news to report, editors would invent some.

One of William Randolph Hearst's editors described the logic behind the so-called "gee whiz" story: "We run our paper so that when the reader opens it, he says, 'Gee Whiz!'" Today's weekly tabloids refer to the same type of story as a "Hey, Martha."

It seems that many subjects are as popular today as they were one hundred years ago: miracle cures, harrowing escapes, gruesome crimes, controversial trials, tragic love stories, and supernatural occurrences. And as anyone can attest who has observed shoppers flipping through newspapers while waiting in today's supermarket lines, these stories still sell newspapers. *Can you think of any issues in the recent past that first surfaced in a tabloid like that described above?*

---

this development, expansionists soon spied an opportunity to make even more spectacular gains in Cuba.

The Cuban Rebellion An island nation off the coast of Florida, **Cuba** first rebelled against Spain in 1868. After ten years of fighting the rebels, Spain finally put in place a few meager reforms to appease the Cuban people. In 1895, after the island's economy had collapsed, Cubans who believed that Spanish rule was oppressive and incompetent rebelled again. This time Spain sent 150,000 troops and its best general, Valeriano Weyler, to put down the rebellion.

Cuban exiles led by journalist José Martí urged the United States to intervene. Even though public support for the rebels was on the rise, both Presidents Cleveland and McKinley refused, unwilling to spend the money that intervention would require and fearing the United States would be saddled with colonial responsibilities it could not handle. Frustrated, Cuban **guerrillas**—soldiers who fight using surprise tactics—turned to the one tactic they knew would attract the United States government's attention: the destruction of American sugar plantations and mills in Cuba. As a result, business owners increased their pressure on the government to act. Newspaper publishers

William Randolph Hearst and **Joseph Pulitzer** vied with one another to publish horrifying stories of "Butcher" Weyler and his barbed-wire concentration camps. Their sensational headlines and stories, known as yellow journalism, whipped up the American public in favor of the rebels. The intense burst of national pride and the desire for an aggressive foreign policy that followed came to be known as **jingoism.** The name came from a line from a British song of the 1870s: "We don't want to fight, yet by Jingo! if we do, We've got the ships, we've got the men, and got the money too." ✪

Pressure for War Builds Early in 1898, riots erupted in Havana, the capital of Cuba. In response, President McKinley moved the U.S.S. *Maine* into the city's harbor to protect American citizens and property. A few months later, in early February 1898, United States newspapers published an intercepted letter from the Spanish ambassador that described McKinley as "weak and a bidder for the admiration of the crowd." War fever mounted.

✪ Then, on February 15, an explosion on the *Maine* killed more than 250 American sailors.

Morning Journal Sales	
1895	30,000
1897	400,000
1898	1,000,000

Source: *American Heritage,* February 1957

Interpreting Tables Sales of William Randolph Hearst's *Morning Journal* soared in 1898 thanks to sensational stories before and during the Spanish-American War.

✪ **Critical Thinking Activity** Drawing Conclusions: The Explosion of the *Maine*, found in the Unit 6 folder, p. 22, presents contemporary reports about the mysterious explosion of the *Maine* to help students apply this skill.

Media and Technology

Transparency
Critical Thinking, I-12

---

2. INSTRUCT

Explain/Discuss

Discuss with students how United States intervention in Latin America, islands in the Pacific, and China resulted in conflict. Ask how conflict in the Caribbean developed into war with Spain. What were the most important causes of the Spanish-American War?

Point out to students that jingoism, as described on page 501, is an "intense burst of national pride and the desire for an aggressive foreign policy." Discuss how these two phenomena could be seen in the events in Chile, Cuba, the Philippines, and Hawaii in the late 1800s. Ask students to note statements and quotations in the text that reflect American jingoism.

DESTRUCTION OF THE WAR SHIP MAINE WAS THE WORK OF AN ENEMY

Headlines and pictures like these stirred the American public's anger following the explosion on the U.S.S. *Maine* in early 1898.

Even though it probably had been caused by a fire that set off ammunition, an enraged American public blamed the Spanish for the disaster and called for war. Still, McKinley hesitated.

On the other side of the world, the people of another of Spain's last remaining possessions, the **Philippine Islands,** also were rebelling. In the view of Theodore Roosevelt, then assistant secretary of the navy, the Philippines could become a key base from which the United States might protect its Asian trade. On February 25, while his boss, the secretary of the navy, was out of the office, Roosevelt cabled naval commanders in the Pacific to prepare for military action against Spain. When President McKinley discovered what Roosevelt had done, he ordered most of the cables withdrawn, but he made an exception in the case of the cable directed to Admiral **George Dewey.** Dewey was told to attack the Spanish fleet in the Philippines if war broke out with Spain.

Late in March, in a final attempt at a peaceful solution, McKinley sent a list of demands to Spain. These included compensation for the *Maine,* an end to the concentration camps, a truce, and Cuban independence. Although Spain accepted most of these demands and agreed to negotiate on the matter of Cuban independence, McKinley decided he could not resist the growing cries for war. On April 11, he sent a war message to Congress. A few days

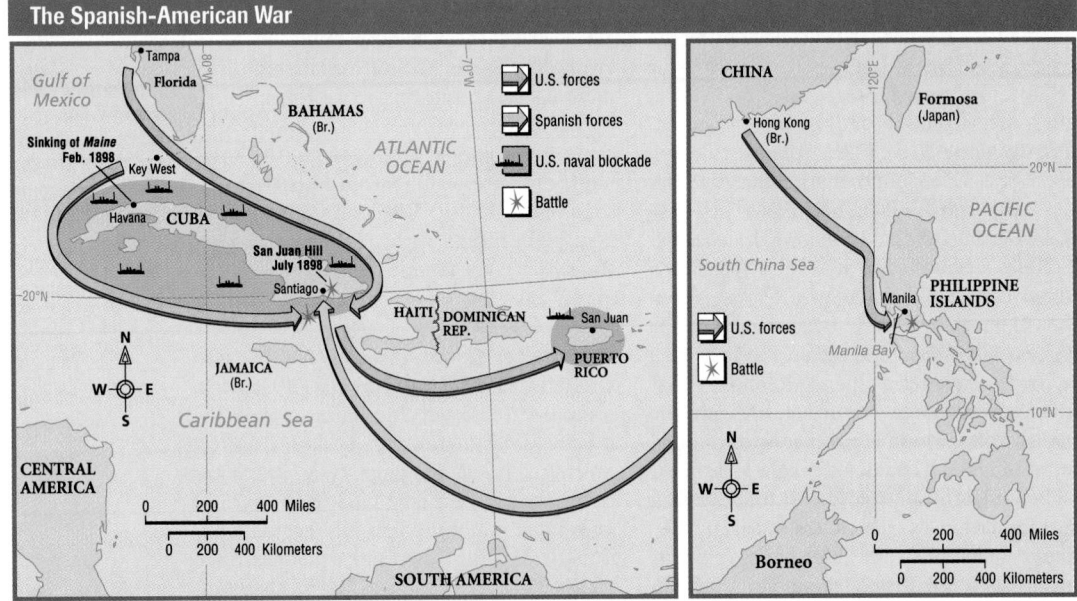

The Spanish-American War

Gulf of Mexico
Tampa
Florida
BAHAMAS (Br.)
ATLANTIC OCEAN
Sinking of *Maine* Feb. 1898
Key West
Havana CUBA
San Juan Hill July 1898
Santiago
HAITI DOMINICAN REP.
San Juan
PUERTO RICO
JAMAICA (Br.)
Caribbean Sea
CENTRAL AMERICA
SOUTH AMERICA

U.S. forces
Spanish forces
U.S. naval blockade
Battle

0 200 400 Miles
0 200 400 Kilometers

CHINA
Hong Kong (Br.)
Formosa (Japan)
PACIFIC OCEAN
South China Sea
Manila PHILIPPINE ISLANDS
Manila Bay
U.S. forces
Battle
Borneo

0 200 400 Miles
0 200 400 Kilometers

 Geography and History: Interpreting Maps
Although the Spanish-American War was fought in two locations on opposite sides of the world, the United States defeated Spain in just three months. *At what specific sites were the major battles of the war fought?*

later, rallying to the cry of "Remember the *Maine!*" Congress recognized Cuban independence and authorized force against Spain.

"A Splendid Little War" The war's first action took place, not in Cuba, but in the Philippines as shown on the map on page 502. On May 1, 1898, Admiral Dewey launched a surprise attack on Spanish ships anchored in Manila Bay, destroying Spain's entire Pacific fleet in just seven hours. In Cuba, meanwhile, United States warships quickly bottled up Spain's Atlantic fleet in the harbor at Santiago. Two months later, Theodore Roosevelt led a group of hastily organized volunteers called the "Rough Riders" in a charge up **San Juan Hill,** which became the most famous incident of the war. Several units of African American troops, known as the "Buffalo Soldiers," also performed superbly in the land war. A white soldier later wrote the Washington Post that "if it had not been for the Negro cavalry, the Rough Riders would have been exterminated."

The Spanish fleet made a desperate attempt to escape the harbor on July 3. In the ensuing battle, the United States Navy sank every Spanish ship, setting off wild Independence Day celebrations back in the United States.

It had all seemed quite simple. Although 2,500 Americans had died in the short war, fewer than 400 died in battle. The remainder died from food poisoning, yellow fever, malaria, and inadequate medical care. Future secretary of state John Hay captured the public mood when he wrote his friend Teddy Roosevelt that it had been "a splendid little war."

Dilemma in the Philippines In the treaty the United States signed with Spain in December 1898, the Spanish government recognized Cuba's independence. In return for a payment of $20 million, Spain also gave up the Philippines, Puerto Rico, and the Pacific island of Guam to the United States. The United States government called these territories "unincorporated," which meant that their residents would not become American citizens.

Although many Americans supported the treaty, others were deeply troubled by it. How could the United States become a colonial power without violating the nation's most basic principle—that all people have the right to liberty? Forced to justify this departure from American ideals, President McKinley explained that rebels in the Philippines were on the edge of war with one another and that the Filipino people were "unfit for self-government." If the United States did not act first, moreover, European powers might seize the islands. After a heated debate, the Senate ratified the treaty in February 1899.

Filipino rebels had fought with American troops in the war against Spain with the expectation that victory would bring independence. But when rebel leader Emilio Aguinaldo issued a proclamation in January 1899 declaring the Philippines a republic, the United States government ignored him. Mounting tensions between the rebel forces and American soldiers finally erupted into war in February. In the bitter three-year war that followed, 4,200 Americans were killed and 2,800 more wounded. Fighting without restraint—and sometimes with great brutality—American forces killed some 16,000 Filipino rebels and hundreds of thousands of Filipino civilians. Occasional fighting continued for years. The Philippines did not gain complete independence until 1946.

The Fate of Cuba and Puerto Rico Although the Teller Amendment, attached to Congress's

African American soldiers in the Tenth United States Cavalry are shown below. Wrote one soldier from this regiment: "If I die on the shores of Cuba my earnest prayer to God is that when death comes to end all, I may meet it calmly and fearlessly."

Media and Technology

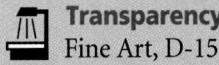
Transparency
Fine Art, D-15

In Depth

Biography

Puerto Rican nationalist Luis Muñoz Rivera (1859–1916) was elected head of a new liberal government in Puerto Rico only months before the United States invasion. In 1910, after sadly accepting the continuing U.S. presence, which he called "unworthy of the United States . . . and of the Puerto Ricans who have to endure it," Muñoz moved to Washington, D.C., as the island's representative in Congress. He died before the passage of the Jones Act of 1917, which granted United States citizenship to all Puerto Ricans who wanted it.

MAKING CONNECTIONS

In both wars the United States swiftly defeated weak and disorganized enemies, and acquired important new territories from the defeated nations in the ensuing peace treaties.

3. ASSESS

Section 2 Review Answers

1. (a) guerrilla, see p. 501, (b) jingoism, see p. 501, (c) sphere of influence, see p. 505, (d) Open Door policy, see p. 505

2. (a) William Randolph Hearst, see p. 501, (b) Joseph Pulitzer, see p. 501, (c) George Dewey, see p. 502.

3. (a) Cuba, see p. 501, (b) the Philippine Islands, see p. 502, (c) San Juan Hill, see p. 503

4. In the 1890s, the American government forced Chile to pay an indemnity for the deaths of American sailors. Also, the United States intervened to prevent the overthrow of a friendly government in Brazil and forced Great Britain to accept its arbitration of a border dispute with Venezuela. Hostilities with Cuba and the explosion of the *Maine* also led to the war.

In Depth

Then and Now

Native Hawaiians waited a hundred years for the United States government to acknowledge its part in the overthrow of the Hawaiian monarchy in 1893. On November 16, 1993, the Congress admitted United States complicity in the 1893 overthrow of the Hawaiian monarchy and called for "reconciliation between the United States and the native Hawaiian people." Three weeks earlier, by a vote of 65–34, the Senate had backed the resolution that offered a formal apology to native Hawaiians.

Filipino civilians suffered the highest casualty rates during the three-year war between the United States and the Philippines.

1898 war resolution against Spain, promised Cubans their independence, United States involvement in Cuba did not end with the victory over Spain. In order to protect American business interests in the chaotic environment that followed the war, President McKinley installed a military government in Cuba that ruled for three years. This government organized a school system and restored economic stability. It also established a commission led by Major Walter Reed of the Army Medical Corps that found a cure for the deadly disease, yellow fever.

When Cubans began to draft a constitution in 1900, however, the United States government insisted that they include a document called the Platt Amendment. According to the provisions of this amendment, the Cuban government could not enter any foreign agreements, must allow the United States to establish two naval bases on the island, and must give the United States the right to intervene whenever necessary. The Platt Amendment remained in force until 1934.

Unlike Cuba, Puerto Rico never gained its independence. In an attempt to stem a growing independence movement, however, the United States government granted Puerto Ricans United States citizenship in 1917.

MAKING CONNECTIONS

In what ways was the Spanish-American War similar to the war between the United States and Mexico in 1846?

Other Gains in the Pacific

The United States government was intervening in other parts of the Pacific at the same time that the Spanish-American War was brewing. This intervention eventually brought about changes in the United States' relationship with Hawaii, Samoa, and China.

Annexation of Hawaii Hawaii had become increasingly important to United States business interests in the late 1800s. When Hawaii and the United States renegotiated their trade treaty in 1887, Hawaii leased Pearl Harbor to the United States as a coaling and repair station for naval vessels. That same year, white Hawaiian-born planters forced the Hawaiian king, Kalakaua, to accept a new constitution that, in effect, gave them control of the government.

When the king died in 1891, his sister Liliuokalani came to the throne. A strong nationalist, Queen Liliuokalani opposed United States control of the islands and sought to reduce the power of foreign merchants. In 1893, with the help of the United States Marines, pineapple planter Sanford B. Dole removed Queen Liliuokalani from power, proclaimed a republic, and requested that Hawaii be annexed by the United States. In 1896, when William McKinley was elected President, he supported the annexation. "We need Hawaii just as much and a good deal more than we did California. It is manifest destiny," McKinley said in early 1898. After briefly considering whether the Hawaiian people wished to be annexed, Congress was swayed by arguments that the United States needed naval stations in Hawaii in order to be a world power. In 1898 Congress approved the annexation of Hawaii.

Samoa The Polynesian islands of Samoa represented another possible stepping-stone to the growing trade with Asia. Back in 1878, the United States had negotiated a treaty with

▶ RESOURCE DIRECTORY

Teaching Resources

⭐ 📄 **American Profiles Activity** found in the Unit 6 folder, p. 17, profiles Walter Reed, the army physician whose scientific method led to the discovery of the cause and prevention of deadly yellow fever.

Samoa offering protection in return for a lease on their fine harbor at Pago Pago. When Britain and Germany began competing for control of these islands in the 1880s, tension between these European powers and the United States almost led to war. Eventually the three nations arranged a three-way protectorate of Samoa in 1889. The withdrawal of Great Britain from Samoa in 1899 left Germany and the United States to divide up the islands. A year after the annexation of Hawaii, the United States had acquired the harbor at Pago Pago as well.

Removed from power by American planters in 1893, Queen Liliuokalani was the last monarch of Hawaii.

An Open Door to China China's population was huge by the late 1800s, and its vast markets were increasingly important to American trade. But the United States was not the only nation interested in China. The Chinese monarchy was weakening, and many other countries—Russia, Germany, Britain, France, and Japan—were seeking **spheres of influence,** or areas of economic control, in China. In 1899 John Hay, now President McKinley's secretary of state, wrote notes to the major European powers trying to persuade them to keep an "open door" to China. He wanted to ensure through his **Open Door policy** that the United States would have equal access to China's millions of consumers.

Meanwhile, many Chinese resented foreign influence of any kind. A secret society called the Righteous and Harmonious Fists (the western press called them Boxers) started a rebellion in the spring of 1900 that led to the massacre of three hundred foreigners and Christian Chinese. Although the European powers eventually defeated the Boxers, Secretary Hay feared that these imperialist nations would use the rebellion as an excuse to seize more Chinese territory. Consequently, he issued a second series of Open Door notes. These notes reaffirmed the principle of open trade in China and made an even stronger statement about the intention of the United States to preserve it.

The Election of 1900

In the election of 1900, populist Democrat William Jennings Bryan and Republican William McKinley faced each other as they had in the election of 1896. McKinley named as his running mate Theodore Roosevelt, a man thoroughly identified with expansionism. American foreign policy had been so successful during McKinley's first term that the anti-imperialist Bryan had to drop the issue from his campaign speeches. Instead, he tried to emphasize the failures of Republican economic policies.

But by 1900, prosperity had returned to the nation. Bryan's complaints were ineffective, and McKinley won even more decisively than in 1896. A year later, however, he was dead—cut down by an assassin's bullet. Theodore Roosevelt, whom McKinley's friend Senator Marcus Hanna had once called a "wild man," was now President.

SECTION 2 REVIEW

Key Terms, People, and Places
1. Define (a) guerrilla, (b) jingoism, (c) sphere of influence, (d) Open Door policy.
2. Identify (a) William Randolph Hearst, (b) Joseph Pulitzer, (c) George Dewey.
3. Identify (a) Cuba, (b) the Philippine Islands, (c) San Juan Hill.

Key Concepts
4. What events led to the Spanish-American War?
5. What was the Open Door policy, and why was it important for the United States?

Critical Thinking
6. **Identifying Central Issues** What argument did anti-imperialists use to convince others that expansionism was wrong?

 Quiz found in the Unit 6 folder, p. 10, covers the main ideas in this section as well as the key terms.

Media and Technology

 Transparency
Geographic Setting, M-9

---

5. The Open Door policy was drafted by John Hay, McKinley's secretary of state, who wanted to preserve access to China's mass markets and opposed the carving up of China by other imperialist nations. The policy ensured American participation in the lucrative China trade.

6. Anti-imperialists questioned the United States' ability to become a colonial power without violating the nation's basic principle of liberty for all.

Reteach
Ask students to list the countries mentioned in the section and to write one sentence for each that summarizes the outcome of United States expansionism in that country.

 Alternative Assessment
Mid-Point Monitoring
Ask students if they have
● Decided on a format for their project and its focus
● Outlined and drafted some ideas
● Begun to identify sources for their project

4. CLOSE

 Reinforcing the Big Idea
In its bid to gain influence in Latin America and the Pacific, the United States seized territory and became enmeshed in complicated efforts to govern other peoples. The next section describes American foreign policy under Presidents Theodore Roosevelt and William Howard Taft.

Geography

Using a Time Zone Map

Focus Students will use a time zone map to calculate times in various locations in the world.

Instruct Ask students if they have seen pictures of the earth from space showing a clear dividing line between day and night. As areas of the earth pass out of the dark side and into the sun's light, people in these areas experience sunrise. We say that sunrise occurs at a specific time in a certain area, but that time is arbitrarily assigned, since sunrise is occurring on a continuous basis as the earth turns. For shuttle astronauts circling the earth many times in 24 hours, no specific time can be assigned for sunrise or sunset; these events cannot be guides for measuring days.

Ask why people on earth need agreed-upon times and time zones. Then guide students to follow steps 1 and 2.

Extend See the Historian's Toolbox Activity in the Resource Directory below.

Answers

1. (a) Moscow: 2:00 P.M.; Denver: 5:00 A.M. (b) 9:00 P.M.; 10:00 A.M. (c) You would have to set your watch back seven hours.

2. Answers will vary depending on students' time zones. Answers are given for the time zones labeled –5 through –10, which include those for the contiguous United States, Alaska, and Hawaii. (a) Zone –5: 11:00 A.M.; Zone –6: 12:00 noon; Zone –7: 1:00 P.M.; Zone –8: 2:00 P.M.; Zone –9: 3:00 P.M.; Zone –10: 4:00 P.M. (b) Zone –5: 10:00 A.M.; Zone –6: 9:00 A.M.; Zone –7: 8:00 A.M.; Zone –8: 7:00 A.M.; Zone –9: 6:00 A.M.; Zone –10: 5:00 A.M. (c) Zone –5: 12:00 noon on Thursday; Zone –6: 1:00 P.M. on Thursday; Zone –7: 2:00 P.M. on Thursday; Zone –8: 3:00 P.M. on Thursday; Zone –9: 4:00 P.M. on Thursday; Zone –10: 5:00 P.M. on Thursday.

Using a Time Zone Map

Until the late 1800s, communities around the world calculated local time by the sun. When railroads began providing rapid long-distance train service between many communities—each with its own version of local time—this method began to cause scheduling nightmares.

In 1884 delegates from twenty-seven nations met in Washington, D.C., to discuss the problem. They eventually agreed on a system of worldwide standard time. Under this system, the world is divided into twenty-four time zones, shown by colored bands on the map below. Time is the same throughout each zone.

The prime meridian, which passes through Greenwich, England at 0° longitude, is the starting point for calculating the time in each zone. The International Date Line—located in the Pacific Ocean at 180° longitude—is where the date changes. The calendar date to the east of this line is one day earlier than that to the west.

Use the following steps to read the time zone map below.

1. Study the information on the map. The numbers at the bottom of the map indicate the number of hours each time zone differs from Greenwich time at the prime meridian. For example, a value of +3 means that the time in that zone is three hours *later* than Greenwich time; –3 means it is three hours *earlier*. The numbers at the top of the map provide examples of how this system works. (a) If it is 12:00 noon, Greenwich time, what time is it in Moscow? In Denver? (b) If it is 2:00 P.M. in Abidjan, Côte d'Ivoire, what time is it in the zone labeled +7? In the zone labeled –4? (c) If you flew west from Cairo, Egypt, to Lima, Peru, how many hours forward or back would you have to set your watch?

2. Compare the time in your zone with others. Find your time zone on the map. (a) If it is 1:00 A.M. in the time zone where you live, what time is it in Karachi, Pakistan? (b) If it is 12:00 noon in São Paolo, Brazil, what time is it where you live? (c) If it is 9:00 P.M. on Wednesday where you live, what time and day is it in Brisbane, Australia?

RESOURCE DIRECTORY

Teaching Resources

Historian's Toolbox Activity Using a Time Zone Map, found in the Unit 6 folder, p. 21, allows students to apply this skill by answering questions about global travel.

A Forceful Diplomacy

SECTION PREVIEW

SECTION PREVIEW

Whether people thought him a hero or a "wild man," most agreed that President Theodore Roosevelt conducted a vigorous foreign policy that suited the new status of the United States as a world power. Although President William Howard Taft continued Roosevelt's policies, he preferred a quieter, more subtle approach to influencing other nations.

Key Concepts

• The forceful and sometimes high-handed manner in which President Theodore Roosevelt conducted foreign policy had the effect of increasing the power of the presidency.
• Under Roosevelt, the United States secured a strip of land in Panama on which it built a canal linking the Atlantic and Pacific oceans.
• President Roosevelt asserted the right of the United States to use military force to preserve stability and order in neighboring countries.
• President William Howard Taft preferred economic pressure to military force in the conduct of American foreign policy.

Key Terms, People, and Places
Roosevelt Corollary, dollar diplomacy;
Theodore Roosevelt, William Howard Taft;
Isthmus of Panama, Colombia

B y 1900 the United States had emerged as a genuine world power, in control of territories overseas. Presidents Theodore Roosevelt and William Howard Taft acknowledged the change by developing a foreign policy to support the nation's new role in the world. Under their leadership, the United States continued to intervene in the domestic affairs of weaker countries of economic and strategic interest to the nation. Roosevelt did so in an independent and sometimes high-handed manner. Taft took a less aggressive approach, preferring economic pressure to military intervention.

AMERICAN PROFILES

Theodore Roosevelt

Was **Theodore Roosevelt** (1858–1919) really a "wild man"? He certainly was energetic. Before becoming President, he was a historian, politician, cowboy, buffalo hunter, crime fighter, reformer, and cavalryman. His active and colorful lifestyle made him famous the world over. The initials of his name were enough to identify him: TR.

The Shaping of a President Born into a wealthy merchant family in New York, TR was raised to be a leader. Although he had asthma as a child, his father insisted that he overcome his illness with rigorous physical exercise. Eventually, he developed a stocky body and fighter's stance.

TR was also studious. In 1876 he entered Harvard College, where he became increasingly interested in history. After graduation, TR married Alice Hathaway Lee and began to study law.

In February 1884, in the course of a single day, TR lost both his wife, who died in childbirth, and his mother, who died of typhoid. To recover from these twin blows, TR went west. Living on a ranch in the Dakota Territory, he hunted, rode, and studied history. There he started work on his most important and popular work, *The Winning of the West*, a glorification of the frontier myth and the "strenuous life." In TR's view, only strong-willed action would save the United States from physical and moral flabbiness.

Like many of his contemporaries, TR also believed in the superiority of the Anglo-Saxon race. He used arguments of racial superiority to justify the destruction of Native Americans. As he explained in his history of the West: "The man who puts the soil to use must of right dispossess the man who does not, or the world will come to a standstill."

This 1904 campaign pin for Teddy Roosevelt consists of a "teddy" bear holding a soldier's hat and sword.

1. FOCUS

Connecting to the Big Idea

See page 494B. The foreign policies of Presidents Theodore Roosevelt and William Howard Taft were both crafted to suit America's new role as a world power. Ask students how their respective approaches differed.

Objectives

● Characterize the effect of President Theodore Roosevelt's foreign policy on the presidency.
● Describe how the Panama Canal came to be built.
● Explain Roosevelt's policy of preserving stability in neighboring countries.
● Analyze President William Howard Taft's approach to foreign policy.

Bellringer

Display a world map for students to observe. Ask students how much time they think it took a ship to travel from New York to San Francisco (a) before and (b) after the building of the Panama Canal. (*About three months and six weeks, respectively.*) Ask the approximate distance between the two cities.

Reading Strategy

Reading for Evidence Ask students to read this statement from the first paragraph of the section: "Under [Roosevelt's and Taft's] leadership, the United States continued to intervene in the domestic affairs of weaker countries of economic and strategic interest to the nation." Have students list specific facts from the section that support this statement.

Reproducible Lesson Plan found in the Unit 6 folder, p. 5, provides a summary of the Section 3 lesson plan content.

Alternate Lesson Plan: Critical Thinking Making Comparisons, found in the Alternate Lesson Plans folder, p. 92, helps students identify similarities and differences in the foreign policies of TR and William Taft by charting their goals, initiatives, and methods.

Guided Reading and Review found in the Unit 6 folder, p. 11, provides a structure for reading and mastering the key concepts and reviewing the key terms for Section 3. (Guided Practice)

Explain/Discuss

Point out to students that the United States did not colonize the territories it seized in the late 1800s and early 1900s. Americans did not move into these new acquisitions in large numbers as the British did in South Africa and other parts of the British Empire.

Why then did Roosevelt and Taft pursue policies that involved direct United States control of other countries? Discuss the motives and values of these two Presidents. Then evaluate their respective methods by comparing the Roosevelt Corollary with Taft's dollar diplomacy. What did each strategy hope to accomplish?

Analyze

Next to Washington, Jefferson, and Lincoln, the fourth stony face on the slopes of Mount Rushmore is that of Theodore Roosevelt. Why might people have wanted Roosevelt to be on this monument? Why might others feel that he did not belong?

In Depth

Did You Know?

In his book *The Path Between the Seas: The Creation of the Panama Canal, 1870–1914,* David McCullough wrote of the construction team: "They were to measure the heights of mountains and the depths of rivers and harbors. They were to gather botanical and geological specimens. They were to take astronomical observations, report on the climate, and observe the character of the Indians encountered." (See pages 512–513 and Key Events in the Reference Section.)

After spending time on the western frontier as a young man (top), Teddy Roosevelt went on to become a war hero and President of the United States (bottom).

Soon after his return to New York City in 1886, TR remarried, this time to a childhood sweetheart, Edith Carow. When President McKinley named him assistant secretary of the navy, he worked hard to build a two-ocean fleet. Like Senators Henry Cabot Lodge and Albert Beveridge, TR was an unapologetic imperialist, who favored war with Spain and the acquisition of new territories abroad. When the Spanish-American War began, he resigned his position in the navy department to organize the First United States Volunteer Cavalry Regiment, made up in part of men he had met out west. The charge of his Rough Riders up San Juan Hill to take a Spanish garrison brought TR lasting fame.

That fall TR narrowly won the New York governorship. Although he ran an impressive administration, he infuriated the conservative bosses of the state Republican party. They were delighted when McKinley asked him to run as his vice-presidential candidate in 1900. The vice presidency was a post of such weakness that they were sure it would bury TR's political career for good. But their celebration proved premature. In September 1901, an assassin's bullet put Theodore Roosevelt in the White House.

Roosevelt as President Roosevelt called the presidency "a bully pulpit," by which he meant that it gave him a wonderful stage from which to win public support for change. Frequently restricted by Congress and other legal checks, Roosevelt still managed to expand the President's powers, especially in foreign affairs.

When Roosevelt was sworn in as President, he was forty-two years old, the youngest man ever to hold the office. As in his own time, many people today consider Roosevelt a hero. He accomplished what most people could only dream of. ✪

The Panama Canal

The Spanish-American War brought home to Americans the need for a quick route between the Pacific and Atlantic oceans. The **Isthmus of Panama** was an ideal location for such a route. At that time Panama was a province of **Colombia,** a country in South America. In 1879 a French company headed by Ferdinand de Lesseps had bought a twenty-five-year concession from Colombia to build a canal across Panama. Defeated by yellow fever and mismanagement, the company abandoned the project ten years later. It offered its remaining rights to the United States for $100 million. When in 1901 the price fell to $40 million, Congress accepted, but a lease on the land still had to be obtained from Colombia.

Colombia, on the other hand, was waiting for the French concession to expire in 1904 so that it could offer the isthmus at a higher price. Roosevelt was enraged by this attempt by Colombian "bandits" to "rob" the United States. As a result, he conspired with an official of the French company to organize a Panamanian "revolution" against Colombia. ✪

The revolt took place in November 1903 with United States warships hovering offshore to provide support for the rebels. The United States immediately recognized an independent Panama and became its protector. In return, it

▶ **RESOURCE DIRECTORY**

Teaching Resources

✪ **Literature Activity** "You're All Right, Teddy," found in the Unit 6 folder, p. 28, uses song lyrics to describe the campaign spirit for President Roosevelt.

✪ **Primary Source Activity** The Panamanian Revolution, found in the Unit 6 folder, p. 25, uses official communications between the Department of State and the U.S. vice consul to appraise United States involvement in the Panamanian Revolution.

Cross-Section of the Panama Canal Zone

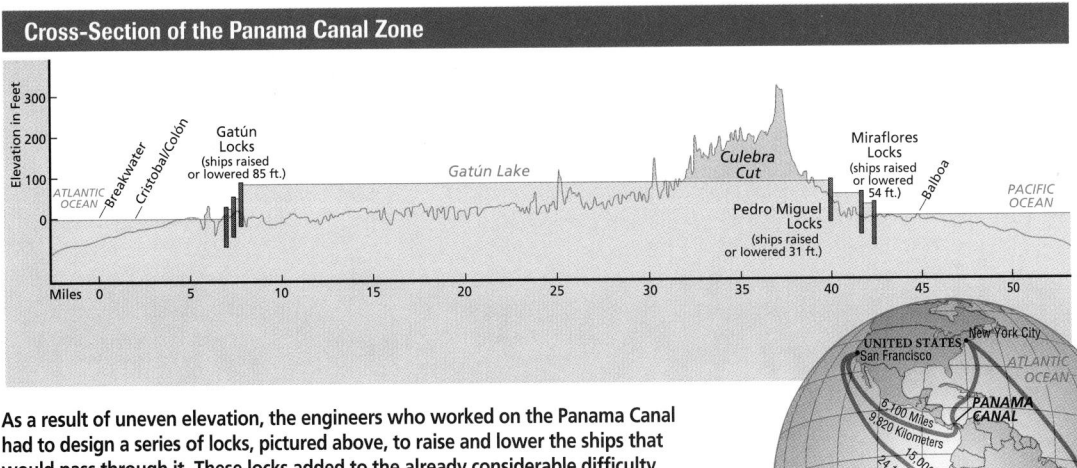

As a result of uneven elevation, the engineers who worked on the Panama Canal had to design a series of locks, pictured above, to raise and lower the ships that would pass through it. These locks added to the already considerable difficulty of constructing the canal. As the map at right shows, the Panama Canal cut thousands of miles off the sea journey from New York to San Francisco.

received a permanent grant of a ten-mile-wide strip of land for a Canal Zone.

Construction of the canal began in 1904. To complete this mammoth task, workers were brought in from several countries. Many of them had no construction experience whatsoever. Yet, after receiving proper training, the workers surpassed all expectations, finishing the canal in 1914, six months ahead of schedule and $23 million under budget.

Roosevelt's opponents did not appreciate the methods he had used to secure the Canal Zone. A newspaper published by William Randolph Hearst commented,

> *B*esides being a rough-riding assault upon another republic over the shattered wreckage of international law . . . it is a quite unexampled instance of foul play in American politics.

Most Americans, however, approved of President Roosevelt's gaining of the Canal Zone in Panama. Two years after leaving office, Theodore Roosevelt gave a speech at the University of California at Berkeley in which he justified his methods in the Canal Zone.

> *I*f I had followed traditional, conservative methods I would have submitted a digni-

fied State paper of probably 200 pages to Congress and the debates on it would have been going on yet; but I took the Canal Zone and let Congress debate; and while the debate goes on the canal does also.

Yet despite its success as a link between the Atlantic and Pacific oceans, the Panama Canal left a long heritage of ill will. In recognition of the illegal means used to acquire the Canal Zone, Congress voted a "guilt" payment of $25 million to Colombia in 1921, after TR had died.

Foreign Policy in the Early 1900s

In 1901 Roosevelt reminded an audience at the Minnesota State Fair of an old saying, "speak softly and carry a big stick; you will go far." In his view, the "big stick" was the American navy. Indeed, the threat of military force allowed Roosevelt to conduct an aggressive foreign policy.

In December 1904, Roosevelt issued a message to Congress that became known as the **Roosevelt Corollary** to the Monroe Doctrine. In this corollary, or extension of a previously accepted idea, Roosevelt denied that the United States was interested in acquiring any more territory. It wanted only "to see neighboring countries stable, orderly, and prosperous," he

Activity
Creating a Political Cartoon

Ask students to create a political cartoon of TR. To help students come up with ideas, have them consider Roosevelt's colorful, aggressive character, his handling of Panama, his receipt of the Nobel Peace Prize, and the criticism of his opponents, such as William Randolph Hearst.

Enrichment

Ask interested students to study Theodore Roosevelt further in order to report on his handling of domestic issues. Encourage students to draw comparisons between TR's foreign and domestic policies, particularly his assault on the nation's big monopolies.

In Depth

Then and Now

Secretary of State John Hay warned Colombia in 1903 that "something unpleasant would happen" if it rejected a treaty giving the United States sovereignty over the land strip desired for canal construction. Rejection led to the clear, though unofficial, United States support of rebels who wrested Panama from Colombian control. In the 1980s the U.S. Central Intelligence Agency covertly trained rebels known as *contras* to fight the Soviet-allied regime in Nicaragua, even though Congress had banned such military aid.

Possessions in the Pacific provided the United States with stepping-stones to the markets of Asia and stations for repair and coaling of their vessels.

3. ASSESS

Section 3 Review Answers

1. (a) Roosevelt Corollary, see p. 509, (b) dollar diplomacy, see p. 511

2. (a) Theodore Roosevelt, see p. 507, (b) William Howard Taft, see p. 511

3. (a) Isthmus of Panama, see p. 508, (b) Colombia, see p. 508

4. He increased the power of the presidency through his aggressive policies and activist, sometimes high-handed, approach.

5. It secretly encouraged a revolution in the Colombian province of Panama, sent military forces to protect it, and in return received a 10-mile strip (the Canal Zone) from Panama through which to build the canal.

6. The message was that the United States would act as an "international policeman" in the Western Hemisphere to maintain order and stability in neighboring countries and to keep powerful European nations out.

7. Both Roosevelt and Taft sought to influence other nations in a way that would advance America's economic, political, and strategic interests. Roosevelt relied on the threat of military force in pursuit of his foreign policy, whereas Taft relied more on economic pressure to influence other nations. On first view, Roosevelt's approach appears to have been more effective, but one could argue that his actions created more resentment toward the United States than did Taft's policy.

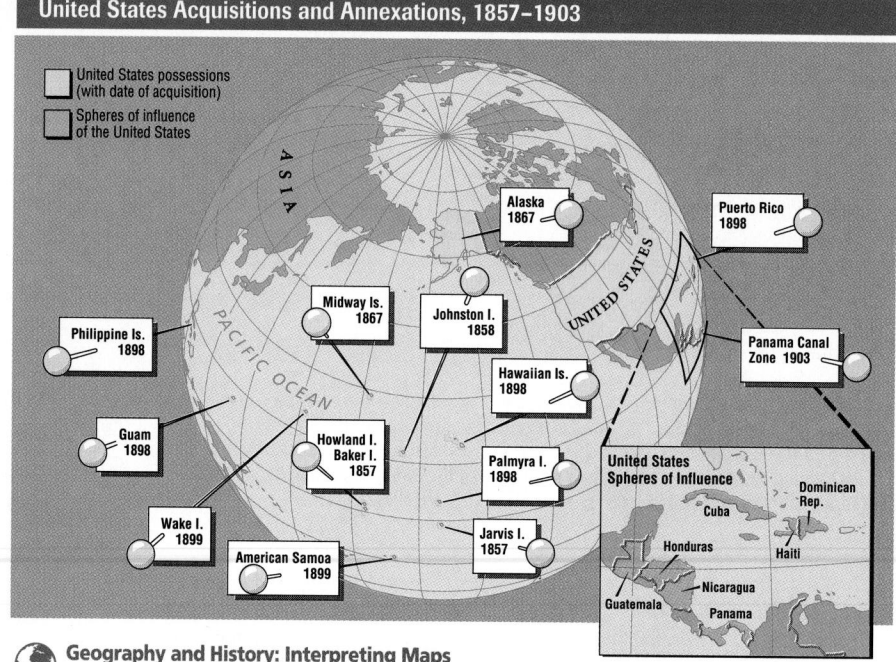

United States Acquisitions and Annexations, 1857–1903

☐ United States possessions (with date of acquisition)
☐ Spheres of influence of the United States

Alaska 1867
Puerto Rico 1898
Midway Is. 1867
Johnston I. 1858
Philippine Is. 1898
Panama Canal Zone 1903
Hawaiian Is. 1898
Guam 1898
Howland I. Baker I. 1857
Palmyra I. 1898
United States Spheres of Influence
Wake I. 1899
Jarvis I. 1857
American Samoa 1899

Cuba, Dominican Rep., Honduras, Haiti, Guatemala, Nicaragua, Panama

🌐 **Geography and History: Interpreting Maps**
Between 1857 and 1903, the United States acquired many new territorial possessions around the globe. *Why do you think so many of these new possessions were islands located in the Pacific Ocean?*

said. But if the countries engaged in activities harmful to the interests of the United States or if their governments collapsed, inviting intervention from stronger nations, then the United States would be forced to exercise "an international police power." In other words, the United States government would intervene to prevent intervention from other powers.

The first test of the Roosevelt Corollary concerned the small Caribbean island republic of Santo Domingo (now the Dominican Republic). When the island went bankrupt, European nations threatened to intervene to collect their money. Quickly Roosevelt made an "executive agreement" with Santo Domingo's president. Bankers in the United States took over the country's finances and paid its European debt.

Under Roosevelt, United States intervention in Latin America became common. This development angered Western Hemisphere countries. Congress also was displeased, for Roosevelt's interventionism meant that presidential powers grew while those of the legislature shrank.

THE WORLD CONSTABLE.

Published after the announcement of the Roosevelt Corollary, this political cartoon depicts Teddy Roosevelt as the world's police officer, using his "big stick" to maintain order and stability in Latin America.

Roosevelt as Peacemaker

Roosevelt's chief concern in Asia was to preserve China's "open door." In order for this to

▶ RESOURCE DIRECTORY

Teaching Resources

happen, Roosevelt believed that both Japan and Russia had to be kept in check. To achieve this, he supported Japan in its war with Russia over supremacy in Asia, but he did not let the war drag on. Roosevelt mediated a peace agreement in 1905 before Japan crushed Russia completely. In this way, he ensured a balance of power in Asia. When Japan accepted the Open Door policy, he invited delegates from the two nations to Portsmouth, New Hampshire, where he persuaded Japan to be satisfied with small grants of land and control over Korea instead of a huge payment of money. He also secured a promise from Russia to vacate Manchuria. Roosevelt's role as mediator won this "war maker" the Nobel Peace Prize.

MAKING CONNECTIONS

How were Teddy Roosevelt and Andrew Jackson similar in the way they used the power of the presidency to achieve their policy goals?

Taft and "Dollar Diplomacy"

William Howard Taft, who succeeded Roosevelt in the White House, was not as aggressive in pursuing foreign policy aims. A distinguished lawyer from Ohio, Taft had served as Roosevelt's secretary of war and headed the commission that governed the Philippines.

Taft's main goals were to maintain the open door to Asia and preserve stability in Latin America. As for the rest, he preferred "substituting dollars for bullets." By this he meant maintaining orderly societies abroad by increasing United States investment in foreign economies. Such an approach, he said, "appeals alike to idealistic humanitarian sentiments, to the dictates of sound policy and strategy, and to legitimate commercial aims." In other words, it pleased public opinion and made money for investors in the United States. Although some of Taft's contemporaries mocked his approach, calling it **"dollar diplomacy,"** Taft himself later used this term with pride.

A Mixed Legacy

Dollar diplomacy did not succeed as well as Taft had hoped. Although it increased the level of United States financial involvement abroad, the results were not always profitable. For example, when Taft's secretary of state, Philander Knox, persuaded bankers to invest in railroad projects in China and Manchuria, Russia and Japan united in an effort to block the influence of the Americans. In addition, many United States investments in China were lost when the country collapsed in revolution in 1911. Dollar diplomacy also created enemies in Latin America, especially in the Caribbean and Central America where local revolutionary movements opposed United States influence. Although the United States reached new heights as an international power under Roosevelt and Taft, anti-colonialism abroad and anti-imperialism at home provided a growing check to further expansion.

Although President William Howard Taft shared Teddy Roosevelt's policy goals, he adopted a less aggressive approach to foreign policy.

SECTION 3 REVIEW

Key Terms, People, and Places
1. Define (a) Roosevelt Corollary, (b) dollar diplomacy.
2. Identify (a) Theodore Roosevelt, (b) William Howard Taft.
3. Identify (a) Isthmus of Panama, (b) Colombia.

Key Concepts
4. What impact did Teddy Roosevelt have on the office of the presidency?

5. How did the United States secure the rights to build a canal through Panama?
6. What was the central message of the Roosevelt Corollary to the Monroe Doctrine?

Critical Thinking
7. **Making Comparisons** How was dollar diplomacy both similar to and different from the approach to foreign policy taken by Theodore Roosevelt?

Quiz found in the Unit 6 folder, p. 12, covers the main ideas in this section as well as the key terms.

Answer to ...

MAKING CONNECTIONS

Both were active Presidents who used aggressive and sometimes high-handed tactics in pursuit of their policy goals. For example, Jackson refused to enforce the Supreme Court's decision stating that the removal of the Cherokee people was illegal; and Roosevelt resorted to "executive agreements" with other nations to avoid the need to win congressional approval for treaties. Both men increased the power of the presidency by such actions.

Reteach

Ask students to make a two-column chart, heading one column Roosevelt and the other column Taft. Have them list major characteristics, attitudes, and accomplishments of each President in the appropriate column. Then ask them to assess which was the more effective President.

4. CLOSE

Reinforcing the Big Idea

Presidents Roosevelt and Taft pursued interventionist foreign policies that many people felt were appropriate to America's status as a world power. Eventually, however, many Americans would come to question United States interference in other countries' internal affairs.

The Building of the Panama Canal: A Geographic Perspective

Focus The building of the Panama Canal is all the more remarkable when one realizes that it was undertaken with the earliest types of earth-moving equipment and without aerial surveillance, computerized geological models, or even thorough knowledge of Panama's rugged jungle environment. In this feature students will identify and categorize some of the key geographic obstacles to building the canal.

Instruct Explain to students that the Panama Canal was the largest engineering accomplishment of its day. The project was far more daunting than the building of Egypt's Suez Canal. In fact, the French company that had built the Suez Canal was overwhelmed with difficulties in Panama. When the company finally ran out of money and abandoned the job, it had already moved enough earth to fill nearly 11,000 of today's Olympic-sized swimming pools.

Explain that the main challenges of the project fell into the categories of location, human-environmental interaction, and the movement of people and goods—three key factors in the study of geography.

Before they read, have students make a chart using these three factors as headings. Ask them to speculate about what specific challenges engineers might have faced and to write down their ideas under the appropriate heading.

Extend After they read, have students add to their chart by filling in factual information under each of the three headings and comparing it with their original, speculative answers.

The Building of the Panama Canal: A Geographic Perspective

On a world map, the Isthmus of Panama seems a mere thread of land. In reality, however, it is dozens of miles wide, formed of violent rivers, dense forests, and towering mountains. How did geographical issues affect the effort to build the canal?

When the United States set out to build the Panama Canal, three geographical factors affected the project. First, engineers had to decide where the canal should be located. Once construction began, the environment of the canal zone presented challenges to workers. Finally, to complete the project, massive amounts of earth had to be moved from one place to another.

Locating the Canal

When the construction team arrived in Panama in 1904, the end points of the canal already had been decided. It would begin at Colón on the Atlantic side and come out close to Panama City on the Pacific side, as the map on page 513 shows. In between lay two major obstacles. One was the Continental Divide, a ridge across Central America that separates rivers that flow west from rivers that flow east. The other obstacle was the wild and unpredictable Chagres River.

The French had never really solved the problem of how to tame the Chagres. The American solution, decided upon in 1906, was to "drown" the river. A vast earthen dam would be laid across the river valley at Gatún (see map opposite). The Chagres would then back up, creating the largest

artificial lake in the world at that time. The Chagres would become the only river in the world to cross a continental divide and flow into two oceans at once.

It was not hard to see where the canal should cross the divide. In the 1880s, a French company had scooped out 19 million cubic yards of dirt and rock from the divide near Culebra. Neither the French nor the Americans guessed that this excavation, the Culebra Cut, would re-quire another 96 million cubic yards of digging before it was finished.

This plan for locating the canal meant that from the entrance at Colón Harbor, ships using the canal would sail 7 miles up a channel and ascend through three locks to a height of 85 feet above sea level. Then they would cross the new and sprawling Gatún Lake for 24 miles, pass through the 9 miles of the Culebra Cut, and descend by one lock to a smaller lake about 1 mile long. Another set of two locks would bring them to sea level and the final 8-mile leg of the canal to the open Pacific.

Against the Environment

While engineers and Congress were wrestling with the location of the canal, army physician

RESOURCE DIRECTORY

Teaching Resources

Time and Place Activity Building the Alaska Pipeline, found in the Unit 6 folder, pp. 15–16, encourages students to explore another, more modern example of humans tackling geographic barriers on a massive scale.

Caribbean Sea

UNITED STATES
Gulf of Mexico
ATLANTIC OCEAN
Caribbean Sea
PACIFIC OCEAN
Area of main map

PANAMA

Colón
Cristóbal
Gatún Locks

PANAMA

Culebra Cut
Culebra
Pedro Miguel Locks
Miraflores Locks
Balboa
Panama City
Fort Amador

9° N
79° 30' W

Canal Zone
Canal
Locks

0   5   10 Miles
0   5   10 Kilometers

PACIFIC OCEAN

William Gorgas was wrestling with an insect. Medical science had learned only a few years before that two of the deadliest tropical diseases, yellow fever and malaria, were transmitted by mosquitoes. The secret of mosquito control, Gorgas found, was to cover, destroy, or drain every place where mosquitoes could lay their eggs—every tank, jar, hollow, and puddle, indoors or out. He divided the cities on the canal route into districts, each with an inspector who entered every house on a daily basis to check for uncovered or standing water. He also gave orders that any pools that could not be drained were to be covered with a film of oil or kerosene to kill the insects.

Gorgas's methods wiped out yellow fever before the end of 1905. Malaria, which was carried by a tougher mosquito, was not eliminated, but was much reduced.

A Problem in Movement

When it came to actually digging the canal, the chief engineer, John F. Stevens, viewed the project as a simple problem of movement: dirt—lots of it—had to be moved. As an experienced builder of railroads, he knew that the cheapest, fastest way to move anything on land was by rail.

Within a week after his arrival, the new chief engineer had ordered double tracks laid. To get the dirt from the ditch to the train cars, Stevens brought in monster steam shovels. President Theodore Roosevelt, on an inspection visit to Panama, wrote, "Now we have taken hold of the job. . . . The huge steam shovels are hard at it, scooping huge masses of rock and gravel and dirt." The shovels were so efficient they filled five hundred trains with debris every day.

The highly efficient railway system could not solve another problem, however. Since Panama could not provide enough supplies to keep tens of thousands of workers fed and busy, ships traveled frequently between Colón and the United States. Ships brought in workers as well, some 45,000 of them, from 97 different nations.

When the canal was completed in 1914, the geographical obstacles of location, interaction with the environment, and movement had been overcome.

GEOGRAPHIC CONNECTIONS

1. What two problems of movement did the building of the canal entail, and how were they solved?
2. How did Dr. Gorgas change the environment of Panama, and what effect did his work have?

Thinking Critically
3. **Making Comparisons** How was building the Panama Canal like building the transcontinental railroad?

Answers

1. The two problems were, first, having enough workers to complete the project and, second, being able to feed those workers and provide other necessary supplies. Both problems were solved by shipping in workers and supplies from other areas.

2. Dr. Gorgas had his workers cover, destroy, or drain every tank, jar, hollow, or puddle indoors and out. Outside the cities, he cut back the jungle that harbored the mosquitoes. He also gave orders that any pools that could not be drained were to be covered with a film of oil or kerosene to kill the insect larva. With methods such as these, Gorgas wiped out the mosquitoes that caused yellow fever and greatly reduced the number of mosquitoes that caused malaria.

3. Both undertakings involved careful study of their location and were essentially problems of moving men and materials, bringing vast supplies over long distances, and managing huge work crews largely composed of foreign labor. In both projects native populations were displaced; both projects had a major impact on the environment and on future movement and settlement patterns; and both united regions that had previously been separated.

The People's Response to Imperialism

The People's Response to Imperialism

1. FOCUS

Connecting to the Big Idea

See page 494B. After the Spanish-American War, anti-imperialists launched heated debates over United States foreign policy. Ask what arguments these anti-imperialists used to support their case. How persuasive were they?

Objectives

● Describe the events that led to debate over United States imperialism.
● Summarize the key arguments of the anti-imperialists.
● Explain why imperialism continued to appeal to Americans at the turn of the century.

Bellringer

Write the following sentence on the chalkboard: The Constitution must follow the flag. Ask students to speculate on what it might mean in relation to the control of other nations by the United States.

Reading Strategy

Structured Overview Have students create a two-column chart with the headings Anti-Imperialists' Arguments and Appeal of Imperialism. Ask them to make entries under the appropriate headings as they read.

SECTION PREVIEW

After the Spanish-American War, the debate intensified over whether it was appropriate for the United States to continue to throw its net around other nations and drag them under American control. Anti-imperialists used a variety of arguments against the acquisition of territories.

Key Concepts

• The annexation of the Philippines led to a spirited debate in the United States over imperialism.
• Anti-imperialists argued that taking over territories betrayed the principles on which the nation was founded.
• Economic benefits, pride in the nation's growing power, and the search for a new frontier made imperialism appealing to many Americans.

Key Terms, People, and Places

paradox of power; Juliette Low

This weathervane from about 1870 reflects national pride in the United States' emerging role as a world power.

B efore the Spanish-American War, United States citizens already were debating the consequences of an expanded role in world affairs. Walter Gresham, President Cleveland's secretary of state in 1894, was one government official who worried about the issue. He cautioned against "the evils of interference in affairs that do not specially concern us." Until the annexation of the Philippines in 1898, however, most citizens supported the idea of overseas involvement.

The Anti-Imperialists

After the annexation, opposition to imperialism grew. In November 1898, opponents of

United States policy in the Philippines established the Anti-Imperialist League. Most of its organizers were upper-middle-class professionals, such as the prominent Republican and former senator Carl Schurz, editor E. L. Godkin, Democratic politician William Jennings Bryan, settlement house leader Jane Addams, charity reformer Josephine Shaw Lowell, novelist Mark Twain, and Harvard philosopher William James. Steel industrialist Andrew Carnegie contributed thousands of dollars to the cause.

Moral and Political Arguments The anti-imperialists used a variety of arguments to support their position. The strongest of these were moral and political in nature. "Any nation," wrote Boston pacifist Lucia Mead in 1900,

> whether it be monarchy or republic, which buys or takes by conquest another people, and dominates them without promise of granting them independence or . . . guaranteeing future Statehood, has adopted an imperialist policy.

Such behavior, the anti-imperialists asserted, was a rejection of the nation's foundation of "liberty for all."

As Carl Schurz explained in 1899:

> We regret that it has become necessary in the land of Washington and Lincoln to reaffirm that all men, of whatever race or color, are entitled to life, liberty, and the pursuit of happiness.

Others said it more concisely: "The Constitution must follow the flag," by which they meant that the United States flag and United States laws went together, and that people in territories controlled by the United States should be entitled to the guarantees in the United States Constitution.

RESOURCE DIRECTORY

Teaching Resources

Reproducible Lesson Plan found in the Unit 6 folder, p. 6, provides a summary of the Section 4 lesson plan content.

Alternate Lesson Plan: Learning Styles found in the Alternate Lesson Plans folder, p. 93, is particularly useful for auditory learners and directs students working in teams to identify conflicting viewpoints on imperialistic policies in the early 1900s.

Guided Reading and Review found in the Unit 6 folder, p. 13, provides a structure for reading and mastering the key concepts and reviewing the key terms for Section 4. (Guided Practice)

United States Interventions, 1890–1920

U.S. expeditionary force, 1916–1917

UNITED STATES

ATLANTIC OCEAN

Parral

U.S. occupation, 1915–1934

U.S. possession, 1898

MEXICO

U.S. occupation, 1898–1902, 1906–1909, 1912, 1917–1922

U.S. occupation, 1916–1924

Purchased from Denmark, 1917

Tampico

U.S. seizure, 1914

Bahamas (Br.)

Havana

Antigua (Br.)

CUBA

Guantanamo

Puerto Rico

Virgin Is.

Mexico City

Veracruz

U.S. leased naval base, 1903

HAITI

Guadeloupe (Fr.)

Dominica (Br.)

Martinique (Fr.)

St. Lucia (Br.)

Barbados (Br.)

Grenada (Br.)

BR. HONDURAS

Jamaica (Br.)

DOMINICAN REP.

Caribbean Sea

GUATEMALA

HONDURAS

U.S. occupation, 1924–1925

United Fruit Co. organized for banana trade, 1899

EL SALVADOR

NICARAGUA

U.S. leased Corn Is., 1914

Trinidad (Br.)

U.S. occupation, 1909–1910 1912–1925, 1926–1933 Canal proposed, 1916

COSTA RICA

VENEZUELA

PANAMA

PACIFIC OCEAN

U.S. acquired Canal Zone, 1903 Canal completed, 1914

COLOMBIA

0   250   500 Miles

0   250   500 Kilometers

 Geography and History: Interpreting Maps
The above map illustrates how frequently the United States intervened in the affairs of Latin American countries in the early 1900s. The United States government defended these interventions as necessary for the protection of the nation's economic and political interests. *What economic interests were served by having influence in these nations?*

President of the American Federation of Labor Samuel Gompers objected to taking over countries in which United States labor laws did not apply. He pointed out that in Hawaii, half of the population consisted of "contract laborers, practically slaves," who did not benefit from the laws that protected American workers.

Expansionists replied that the people of the Caribbean and the Pacific were not ready for democracy and that the United States was preparing them for liberty. For example, Major General Arthur McArthur, military governor of the Philippines in 1900, said, "We are planting in those islands . . . the best traditions, the best characteristics of Americanism." The anti-imperialists responded that no people should be forced to wait to enjoy liberty.

Finally, anti-imperialists noted that imperialism endangered the nation's democratic institutions. Imperialist wars required large standing armies that could be used to crush dissent at home just as easily as to bring other nations under United States control.

A Race War? Other anti-imperialists saw racism at work in imperialism. Like Theodore Roosevelt, many Americans of this period believed that people of Anglo-Saxon heritage were superior to other races. The public officials who developed the country's imperialist policies shared these sentiments.

African Americans were at first torn about imperialistic issues. As United States citizens, they wanted to support their country in a time of war. But they recognized the racism that underlay imperialism. Bishop Alexander Walters of the A.M.E. Zion Church said in 1899,

Had the Filipinos been white and fought as bravely as they have, the war would have been ended and their independence granted a long time ago.

Caption Answer to ...

 Interpreting Maps

The United States was able to gain new markets for its goods.

2. INSTRUCT

Discuss

Discuss with students why upper-middle-class professionals, southern Democrats, labor leaders, and African Americans opposed imperialism.

Ask students in what way racism entered into the arguments of both imperialists and anti-imperialists. Have them use examples from the text to support their explanations.

Analyze

Explain that a paradox is a statement that seems contradictory but may actually be true. How does the term "paradox of power" apply to the United States during the era of imperialism?

In Depth

Historical Misconceptions

The Filipino people were not blind to the irony of facing African American soldiers serving in the war against the Philippines (1898–1902). Joining the military was a way for African Americans to prove their patriotism, but as one African American soldier wrote from the Philippines, "I was struck by a question a little Filipino boy asked me, which ran this way: 'Why does the American Negro come . . . to fight us. . . ? Why don't you fight those people in America who burn Negroes?' "

Answer to ...
Viewpoints

Sumner's point is that other people's customs and beliefs should be respected and that they should have the freedom to practice them; therefore, his statement is more in keeping with America's founding principles of equality and liberty. For a more thorough examination of imperialism, see the Resource Directory below.

Activity
Cooperative Learning

Time: One class period.
Activity: Role-play interviews on imperialism.
Grouping: Four to six students.
Purpose: One student conducts interviews with others playing various types of citizens to elicit their views on the subject of United States imperialism. Interviewees assume imperialist or anti-imperialist positions.
Roles: Reporter; interview subjects such as a Filipino immigrant, a social worker, a U.S. general, a coal miner, a cowboy, and a pineapple grower.
Outcome: Students will come to understand different perspectives regarding United States imperialism.

Enrichment

Students can read and evaluate excerpts from Theodore Roosevelt's *The Rough Riders*. They should state whether the book changed their opinion of Roosevelt or of United States imperialism, and if so, how.

3. ASSESS

Section 4 Review Answers

1. paradox of power, see p. 517

2. Juliette Low, see p. 517

3. Anti-imperialists objected to extending a protectorate over another country without also extending the protection and rights available to U.S. citizens under the Constitution. They believed that people in U.S. protectorates should not have to wait to enjoy the universal right of liberty. Imperialism was racist

---

Viewpoints
On the Race for Empire

The Spanish-American War heightened the debate between imperialist and anti-imperialist factions at home. *Which of the following viewpoints do you think best represents the political ideals of liberty and equality on which the United States was founded?*

Anti-Imperialist
"We assume that what we like and practice, and what we think better, must come as a welcome blessing to Spanish-Americans and Filipinos. This is grossly and obviously untrue. They hate our ways. They are hostile to our ideas. Our religion, language, institutions, and manners offend them.
William G. Sumner, Yale University professor, in an 1898 speech

Pro-Imperialist
"Think of the thousands of Americans who will pour into Hawaii and Puerto Rico when the republic's laws cover those islands with justice and safety! Think of the tens of thousands of Americans who will invade mine and field and forest in the Philippines when a liberal government, protected and controlled by this republic, if not the government of the republic itself, shall establish order and equity there!"
Albert J. Beveridge, leading imperialist and later United States senator, in an 1898 speech

---

Although most southern Democrats also opposed imperialism, they did so for different reasons. Many southern politicians feared the effects of having to absorb more people of different races into the United States. Consequently, southern Democrats led the movement in the Senate against ratifying the treaty with Spain.

A number of anti-imperialists outside the South, including William Jennings Bryan and Samuel Gompers, also opposed imperialist policies because of the fear that they would encourage people of different racial backgrounds to move to the United States. Reformer Carl Schurz wrote about these concerns:

> The prospects of the consequences which would follow the admission of the Spanish creoles and . . . the negroes . . . to participation in the conduct of our

government is so alarming that you instinctively pause before taking the step.

Practical Objections Finally, anti-imperialists raised practical objections to expansionist policies. In the view of these thinkers, it was not a good time for the United States to expand. First, expansion involved too many costs. Maintaining the necessary armed forces required more taxation, debt, and possibly even compulsory military service. Second, as African American leader Booker T. Washington said, the United States already had enough difficulties at home. "Until our nation has settled the Negro and Indian problems I do not believe that we have a right to assume more social problems," he argued.

Samuel Gompers raised a third point. He argued that laborers coming to the United States from annexed territories would compete with American workers for jobs. Since these immigrants would work for lower wages, their presence would drive all wages down. Industrialists also pointed out that goods produced cheaply in annexed countries could be imported to the United States without customs duties, which would hurt many American industries in the process.

Imperialism's Appeal to the American Imagination

Despite the strength of many anti-imperialist arguments, imperialism maintained a powerful hold on the American imagination. The director of the census had declared the frontier "closed" in the 1890 census. The America of explorers and pioneers, who bravely charted unknown territories, overcame great obstacles, and accomplished great deeds, was fast disappearing into the shadows of memory. What would keep Americans from growing too soft, from losing their competitive edge? Some looked to a new frontier abroad to answer this question.

The growth and popularity of youth scouting programs during this period shows that many middle-class Americans shared a "frontier mentality." Sir Robert Baden-Powell, an army officer of the British Empire, had used scouting techniques (tracking, woodcraft, and

---

RESOURCE DIRECTORY

Teaching Resources

Viewpoints Activity On the Race for Empire, found in the Unit 6 folder, pp. 19–20, provides several contemporary speeches on the pros and cons of American imperialism.

American Profiles Activity found in the Unit 6 folder, p. 18, profiles Juliette Gordon Low, who founded the American Girl Scouts in 1912.

wilderness survival) to great success in a battle in South Africa. A few years after he returned to Britain as a war hero, Baden-Powell founded the Boy Scout movement. Scouting appeared in the United States in 1910 and soon became immensely popular. Two years later, **Juliette Low,** a close friend and admirer of Baden-Powell, founded the American Girl Scouts. Low hoped to use the program both to build moral character in girls and to teach them skills that would make them "hardy" and "handy."

In addition, the popular media glorified the accomplishments of imperialist frontier heroes. Theodore Roosevelt's book on his heroic charge, *The Rough Riders,* drew much praise. However, satirist Finley Peter Dunne's character, "Mr. Dooley," suggested the book should be called *Alone in Cuba* to emphasize Roosevelt's boastfulness. Another book of this era, *Conquest of the Tropics* (1914), describes the history of the United Fruit Company, portraying railroad entrepreneur Minor Keith as one of "the hardy American type which listens and responds eagerly to the call of the wild."

THE·GIRL·SCOUT·PROMISE
On my honor, I will try:
To do my duty to God
· · · · · and my country,
To help other people at all times,
To obey the Girl Scout Laws.

MAKING CONNECTIONS

How was the popular media's glorification of imperialist heroes such as Minor Keith similar to the often romantic portrayal of the men and women settlers of the American West?

The Paradox of Power

Having begun a pattern of international involvements, shown on the map on page 515,

the United States discovered that these actions frequently took on a life of their own. Unforeseen difficulties arose. In the Caribbean and Central America, for example, the United States often had to defend governments that were friendly to its economic and political interests but unpopular with local inhabitants. In Latin America, the cry "Yankee, Go Home!" began to be heard.

On the other hand, because the United States was quickly becoming so powerful, other countries—even those fearful about maintaining their independence—increasingly were turning to the United States government for help. This state of affairs illustrated the **paradox of power.** Both admired and hated, welcomed and rejected, the United States would spend the rest of the century trying to decide the best way to reconcile its growing power and national interests with its relationships with other nations and peoples.

As "The Girl Scout's Promise" suggests, founder Juliette Low (bottom) saw scouting as a way of teaching moral character as well as frontier skills. ⭐

and would result in the necessity of absorbing other races into an already complex and difficult racial system.

4. Now that the western frontier had been declared closed, an imperialist foreign policy gave Americans other opportunities to act in a forceful, heroic fashion in demanding circumstances. Imperialism also brought the United States economic rewards.

5. Imperialism led the United States into diplomatic conflicts and costly military engagements with other nations. By failing to extend the guarantees of the Constitution to peoples living in United States territories, the policy betrayed the democratic principles upon which the United States had been founded.

6. One can infer from the arguments of the anti-imperialists that they believed the United States should promote democratic principles and institutions around the world and that all peoples of the world deserved access to these rights, principles, and institutions.

Answer to …

MAKING CONNECTIONS

Both emphasized brave, rugged individuals who had amazing adventures and overcame great obstacles while taming wild new frontiers.

Reteach

Ask students to create a newspaper advertisement that attempts to persuade Americans to support the anti-imperialists' arguments. Students should focus on these issues for their ad: anti-imperialist arguments; effective ways to counter the appeal of imperialism; and the effect of imperialism on the image of the United States in Latin America and the Pacific.

SECTION 4 REVIEW

Key Terms, People, and Places
1. Define paradox of power.
2. Identify Juliette Low.

Key Concepts
3. Name some of the major arguments of the anti-imperialists.
4. Explain why imperialism was so appealing to many United States citizens.

5. What were some of the disadvantages of imperialism for the United States?

Critical Thinking
6. **Identifying Assumptions** Based on the arguments they used against imperialism, what kind of role do you think the anti-imperialists believed the United States should play in world affairs?

 Quiz found in the Unit 6 folder, p. 14, covers the main ideas in this section as well as the key terms.

 Chapter Test Forms A and B are found in the Unit 6 folder, pp. 31–36.

 Answer Keys found in the Unit 6 folder, pp. 116–128, provide answers to all student activities.

Media and Technology

Transparency Graphic Organizer, G-5

Guided Reading Audiotapes (English and Spanish)

Computer Test Bank

4. CLOSE

 Reinforcing the Big Idea

After the Spanish-American War, the debate over United States imperialism intensified. Strong arguments by anti-imperialists, however, failed to dampen the appeal of imperialism to the American imagination.

Chapter Review Answers

Understanding Key Terms, People, and Places

Terms
Students should refer to the definitions of the key terms in the chapter to write sentences that show the relation of each word to the growth of the United States as a world power.

Matching
1. guerrillas
2. imperialism
3. annexation
4. dollar diplomacy
5. jingoism

Word Relationships
1. George Dewey was an admiral in the Spanish-American War, which was fought in the Philippine Islands and Cuba. William Howard Taft, President Roosevelt's successor, discouraged the use of military force.
2. William Randolph Hearst and Joseph Pulitzer published sensational stories that whipped up public sentiment in favor of the war against Spain, of which the charge up San Juan Hill was the most famous incident. The Isthmus of Panama was the site of the Panama Canal.
3. Alfred T. Mahan, Henry Cabot Lodge, and Theodore Roosevelt supported American expansionism. Juliette Low founded the American Girl Scouts in order to make American girls more hardy.

Reviewing Main Ideas
1. The economy was producing more than the nation could consume.
2. New developments in communication and transportation fueled intensified competition among nations with long traditions of imperialism, now joined by the newly unified Germany.
3. Mahan argued that the economic future of the United States depended on new markets abroad and a navy to protect these markets. Lodge worried about the effects of a disappearing frontier. Beveridge believed that expansionism was necessary because it introduced the ideas and customs of "superior" races to "primitive" societies.
4. The British government eventually backed down when warned that the United States would enforce the Monroe Doctrine.
5. Yellow journalism, which played on the human rights abuses taking place in Cuba and fanned public outrage over the destruction of American property in Cuba, was partly responsible for an

518

CHAPTER 18

Chapter Review

Understanding Key Terms, People, and Places

Key Terms
1. imperialism
2. annexation
3. most-favored nation
4. banana republic
5. guerrilla
6. jingoism
7. sphere of influence
8. Open Door policy
9. Roosevelt Corollary
10. dollar diplomacy
11. paradox of power

People
12. Alfred T. Mahan
13. Henry Cabot Lodge
14. Albert J. Beveridge
15. William Randolph Hearst
16. Joseph Pulitzer
17. George Dewey
18. Theodore Roosevelt
19. William Howard Taft
20. Juliette Low

Place
21. Hawaii
22. Cuba
23. Philippine Islands
24. San Juan Hill
25. Isthmus of Panama
26. Colombia

Terms For each term above, write a sentence that explains its relation to the growth of the United States as a world power.

Matching Review the key terms in the list above. If you are not sure of a term's meaning, review its definition in the chapter. Then choose a term from the list that best matches each description below.
1. soldiers who fight using surprise tactics
2. the policy under which stronger nations attempt to create empires by dominating dominance over weaker nations
3. the addition of a new territory to an existing country
4. W. H. Taft's policy of "substituting dollars for bullets"
5. an intense burst of national pride and the desire for an aggressive foreign policy

Word Relationships Three of the terms in each of the following sets are related. Choose the term that does not belong and explain why it does not belong.
1. William Howard Taft, George Dewey, Philippine Islands, Cuba
2. William Randolph Hearst, Isthmus of Panama, Joseph Pulitzer, San Juan Hill
3. Alfred T. Mahan, Juliette Low, Henry Cabot Lodge, Theodore Roosevelt

Reviewing Main Ideas

Section 1 (pp. 496–499)
1. Describe the status of the United States economy in the late 1800s.
2. Why were the major European powers scrambling to seize new territory?
3. Briefly explain the arguments of Alfred T. Mahan, Henry Cabot Lodge, and Albert J. Beveridge regarding expansionism.

Section 2 (pp. 500–505)
4. Describe how the 1880 dispute between the United States and Great Britain reaffirmed the validity of the Monroe Doctrine.
5. Why did the American public favor war with Spain?
6. What new territories and influence did the United

States gain in the Pacific as a result of its interventionist policies?

Section 3 (pp. 507–511)
7. Describe Theodore Roosevelt's approach to foreign policy.
8. How did the Roosevelt Corollary affect United States policy in Latin America?
9. What were President Taft's main foreign policy goals and how did he plan to accomplish them?

Section 4 (pp. 514–517)
10. Explain why anti-imperialists believed that imperialism betrayed basic American principles.
11. What was the connection between imperialism and the closing of the American frontier?

---

intense burst of national pride in favor of war. In addition, the public blamed the Spanish for the explosion aboard the *Maine*.

6. The United States gained the Philippines, Puerto Rico, Guam, the harbor at Pago Pago, and Hawaii. It also gained influence in China.

7. Roosevelt conducted an aggressive and vigorous foreign policy. He often dealt with other countries in a high-handed manner, assuming that what he wanted for each country was necessarily in its best interests. He used his position as President to win public support for change, especially in foreign affairs.

8. The Roosevelt Corollary caused United States military intervention to become standard policy in Latin America.

9. Taft wanted to maintain the Open Door policy in Asia and to preserve stability in Latin America. He planned to accomplish these goals through economic rather than military pressure (dollar diplomacy).

10. Anti-imperialists believed that imperialism rejected the basic tenet of liberty for all peoples.

11. Many Americans saw expansion abroad as a way to continue the spirit and excitement of the frontier.

Thinking Critically

1. **Distinguishing Fact from Opinion** Future secretary of state John Hay referred to the Spanish-American War as "a splendid little war." Can you think of any Americans, in addition to anti-imperialists, who might disagree with Hay?
2. **Demonstrating Reasoned Judgment** You have read that although some people today question Teddy Roosevelt's militaristic and racial beliefs, in his own time many people considered him a hero. How can you account for this change in public perception?
3. **Drawing Conclusions** During the late 1800s, the press fanned the flames of the Spanish-American War by publishing sensational stories about Spanish cruelties in Cuba. On what current issues do you think the press has played a major role in influencing public opinion? Has sensationalism played a part in influencing the public?

Making Connections

1. **Evaluating Primary Sources** Review the primary source excerpt on page 507. What does Roosevelt assume about Native American land use? Do you think that his assumption is accurate?
2. **Understanding the Visuals** Choose one visual from the chapter that provides an argument in favor of expansionism and one that provides an argument against expansionism. Explain how each visual argues its position.
3. **Writing About the Chapter** Imagine that you are living during the early 1900s. Write a letter to the editor of your local newspaper in which you argue either for or against an interventionist foreign policy. First, create a list of arguments that support your position. Note any opposing arguments to which you wish to reply. Next, write a draft of your letter in which you offer your ideas. Revise your letter, making sure that your opinions are well supported. Proofread your letter and draft a final copy.
4. **Using the Graphic Organizer** This graphic organizer uses a multi-flow map to show the causes and effects of American expansion during the late 1800s and early 1900s. (a) Based on the graphic organizer, what was the major negative effect of American expansion for Americans? (b) On a separate sheet of paper, create your own graphic organizer about the causes and effects of the Spanish-American War, using this graphic organizer as an example.

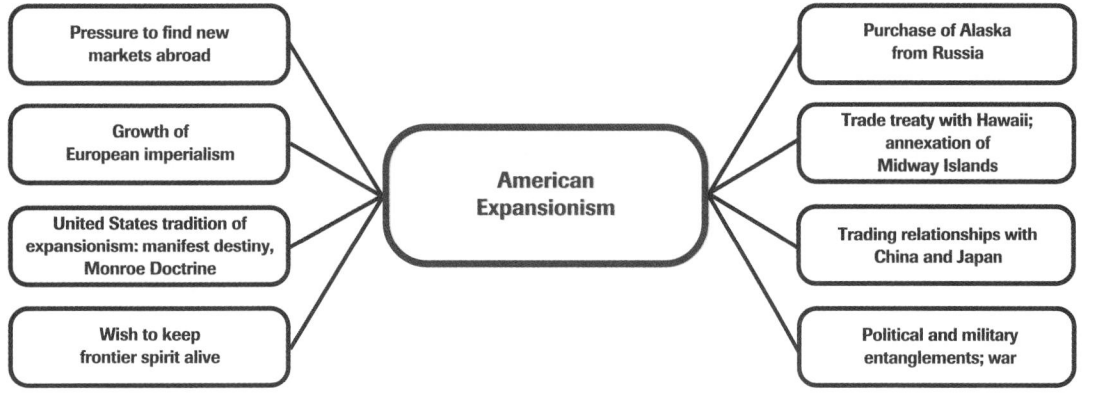

Pressure to find new markets abroad

Growth of European imperialism

United States tradition of expansionism: manifest destiny, Monroe Doctrine

Wish to keep frontier spirit alive

American Expansionism

Purchase of Alaska from Russia

Trade treaty with Hawaii; annexation of Midway Islands

Trading relationships with China and Japan

Political and military entanglements; war

2. Pro-expansionism—students may choose any of the following visuals: the photograph on page 499, which shows that involvement in other countries would result in new markets for U.S. goods; the Panama Canal illustrations on page 509, which show that expansionism could have positive results such as this new route from the East to West coasts. Anti-expansionism—students may choose any of the following visuals: the painting and headline on page 502 or the photograph on page 504, which both show that involvement in the affairs of other nations can result in violence and bloodshed for Americans.

3. Students' letters should take into account the imperialist and anti-imperialist arguments advanced in Sections 1 and 4.

4. (a) The primary negative effect of expansion was foreign entanglement. (b) Students' graphic organizers should show the main causes (including rebellion in Cuba and the pressure for expansion) and effects (acquisition of new territories and influence) of the Spanish-American War.

 Alternative Assessment

Final Evaluation

Use the following criteria to evaluate student projects:
- **Evidence of thoughtfulness** Are editorials well reasoned, making a strong claim and supporting it with appropriate facts and reasons?
- **Evidence of synthesis** Do editorials effectively use a combination of moral, economic, social, and political arguments?
- **Communication style** Are editorials logical, forceful, and persuasive?
- **Evidence of outside research** Do editorials use actual quotations from outside sources to support their claims?

Thinking Critically

1. The families of people who were injured or killed in the war would probably disagree with Hay, as would anyone who suffered as a result of the war.
2. Partly as a result of the civil rights movement, people today are more sensitive to the values of other races and cultures than was the case in the early part of the century. Also, expansionism is now viewed with disfavor, in part because Americans have experienced so much bloodshed as a result of foreign entanglements.
3. Answers will vary. Students might cite press coverage of any issue currently in the news. Students may point out that the degree of sensationalism usually depends on the source that is covering the story.

Making Connections

1. Roosevelt assumes that Native Americans made poor use of the land and that white Americans used the land to better advantage. Many students will disagree with Roosevelt's assumption, noting that Native Americans and white Americans simply used the land differently, but that this difference did not entitle white Americans to seize Native Americans lands.

Chapter 19 The Era of Progressive Reform
1890–1920

📁 Teaching Resources (See Unit 6 Folder)

	Instruction	Enrichment
Section 1 **The Origins of Progressivism** (pp. 522–526)	Reproducible Lesson Plan, p. 38 Alternate Lesson Plan, p. 95 Guided Reading and Review, p. 42 Quiz, p. 43	Visual Learning Activity, A Different Kind of Wild West Show, p. 66 American Profiles Activity, Ida Tarbell, p. 54 Literature Activity, Horrors of the Meat-Packing Industry, pp. 63–64
Section 2 **Progressivism: Its Legislative Impact** (pp. 527–531)	Reproducible Lesson Plan, p. 39 Alternate Lesson Plan, p. 96 Guided Reading and Review, p. 44 Quiz, p. 45	Primary Source Activity, The Shame of the People, p. 60 Primary Source Activity, Giving the Child a Chance, pp. 61–62 History Might Not . . . Activity, Marching for Child Labor Laws, pp. 52–53
Section 3 **Progressivism: Its Impact on National Politics** (pp. 534–537)	Reproducible Lesson Plan, p. 40 Alternate Lesson Plan, p. 97 Guided Reading and Review, p. 46 Quiz, p. 47	Critical Thinking Activity, Distinguishing False from Accurate Images, p. 59 American Profiles Activity, Louis D. Brandeis, p. 55 Historian's Toolbox Activity, Testing Conclusions, p. 58
Section 4 **Suffrage at Last: A Turning Point in History** (pp. 539–543)	Reproducible Lesson Plan, p. 41 Alternate Lesson Plan, p. 98 Guided Reading and Review, p. 48 Quiz, p. 49 Chapter Test, Forms A & B, pp. 68–73	Literature Activity, The New Woman, p. 65 Viewpoints Activity, On the Nineteenth Amendment, pp. 56–57 Visual Learning Activity, When Women Have Rights, p. 67 Turning Points Extension Activity, The Lasting Impact of the Nineteenth Amendment, pp. 50–51

📁 Additional Chapter Resources

Resource Organizer, p. 37
Alternate Lesson Plan, p. 94
Answer Keys, pp. 116–126

Bibliography

For the Teacher
Cott, Nancy F. *Root of Bitterness: Documents of the Social History of American Women.* Dutton, 1972. (Examines the range and depth of women's experience through historical sources such as diaries, letters, and petitions.)

Prentice Hall Literature Excerpts from *The American Experience,* 1994, "Realism and the Frontier, 1865–1915."

The Big Idea for the chapter and how the main ideas in each section relate to the Big Idea are graphically displayed below. Comprehension of this chapter's Big Idea is critical to students' understanding of United States history and how we as a nation got where we are today.

Media and Technology

 Cause and Effect, F-3;
Our Multicultural Heritage, C-13

 Visions of America: History Might Not Have Happened This Way Game

 Critical Thinking, I-8

 Visions of America: Turning Point Story, "Sister Suffragette" (length: approx. 4 minutes)

  Visions of America: Roundtable Discussion on "Sister Suffragette"

 Graphic Organizer, G-3

 Guided Reading Audiotapes (English and Spanish)

 Computer Test Bank

For the Student

Life History of the United States, Vols. 8–10. *The Progressive Era*. 1964. (Richly illustrated series by editors of *Life* magazine.)

The Progressives. McGraw Hill Films. (A brief history of the period.)

The Women Get the Vote. McGraw Hill Films. (Traces the history of the suffrage movement through the passage of the Nineteenth Amendment.)

CHAPTER 19

At the turn of the century, many Americans hoped to change American society for the better. These reform-minded citizens, who were called progressives, worked for many different causes at the national, state, and local levels. Many of their reforms had lasting effects on American society.

SECTION 1

At the turn of the century, many educated, middle-class Americans began to think that the reforms needed in the nation were too great for private efforts. Progressives wanted the government to bring about reform.

SECTION 2

Progressives working at the federal, state, and local levels enacted many reform programs.

SECTION 3

In 1912, some progressives formed a political party. Although the Progressive party did not win the election, progressives continued to implement their reform programs until World War I focused the nation's attention on events in Europe.

SECTION 4

The Nineteenth Amendment was ratified in 1920, ending the long struggle of American women for enfranchisement.

The Era of Progressive Reform
1890–1920

The Relevance of the Big Idea

During the heady days of the progressive movement, muckraking journalists exposed corruption and scandal, stirring public opinion and supporting calls for reform.

One hundred years later, almost every major newspaper and television network employs an "investigative" team of reporters assigned to search out and report on scandals and corruption in government and industry. Some people think that investigative journalism has gone too far and that the media should exercise greater restraint.

Discuss with students the pros and cons of investigative journalism and how it does or does not help in reforming social and political ills.

In Depth

Global Connections

In 1905, as progressivism caught fire in the United States, Einstein's theory of relativity—the idea that space and time are connected and that nothing is absolute, that even the passage of time is not uniform but varies in relation to an object's velocity—set the stage for a major rethinking of scientific truth. Publication of the more sweeping theory of general relativity in 1916 brought with it a questioning of the status quo and justified, some felt, revolutionary calls for change.

CHAPTER 19

The Era of Progressive Reform
1890–1920

GIVE YOUR CHILDREN EQUAL RIGHTS
VOTE YES Nov. 2
On the AMENDMENT ENABLING WOMAN TO VOTE

At the turn of the century, a spirit of reform known as progressivism took hold of many American people. Less a united movement than a loose collection of informal and unlikely alliances, progressivism targeted the massive problems of an urban, industrialized nation. In spite of opposition, progressives were able to redefine government's role in American life, make a serious run for the White House, and enact such lasting reforms as woman suffrage.

NO ONE CARES FOR ME
WORDS AND MUSIC BY TELL TAYLOR

Events in the United States

1890 National American Woman Suffrage Association formed.
• Yosemite declared a national park.

1893 Illinois passes law prohibiting child labor.
• A depression rocks the nation.

1899 National Consumers League forms to investigate conditions under which goods are made.

1903 Teddy Roosevelt proposes arbitration to end the United Mine Workers' strike.

| 1890 | 1893 | 1896 | 1899 | 1902 |

Events in the World

1890 Japan holds its first general elections.
• Swiss government introduces social insurance.

1894 Japan and Korea declare war on China.
• British obtain control of Uganda.

 RESOURCE DIRECTORY

Teaching Resources

Alternate Lesson Plan: Demonstrating the Big Idea found in the Alternate Lesson Plans folder, p. 94, provides a lesson strategy to instruct students about the Big Idea that many of the reforms made during the progressive era had lasting effects on American society.

Alternative Assessment Handbook provides information, guidance, and strategies for alternative methods of assessment. It includes an essay on new trends in assessment, guidance and strategies for developing performance tasks and portfolios, scoring rubrics, and sample evaluation forms.

1906 Upton Sinclair publishes The Jungle, *an exposé of the meat-packing industry.*

1908 *The Supreme Court upholds an Oregon law limiting hours for women laundry workers.*

1912 *Massachusetts becomes the first state to adopt a minimum wage.*
• *Woodrow Wilson is elected President.*

1919 *State legislatures ratify the 18th Amendment, enacting prohibition.*

1920 *Women win the vote with the ratification of the 19th Amendment.*

1905	1908	1911	1914	1917	1920

1904 *Ten-hour work day established in France.*

1907 *Universal direct suffrage instituted in Austria.*

1911 *Turkish-Italian war begins.*
• *Mexican Civil War ends.*

Alternative Assessment

As an ongoing chapter project, students can write an essay responding to the following analysis: The progressives had three basic goals: to end corruption and abuses of power in government and business; to reform social institutions so as to provide opportunity for every citizen; and to apply scientific principles to political and social institutions. Student essays should include information that either supports or challenges each of the three parts of the quotation and backs up their point of view with specific examples of progressive actions. Students may research the progressive movement and include in their essays information they discover.

Explain that finished projects will be assessed according to the following standards:

• **Unacceptable** Essays are not completed or fail to meet requirements outlined.

• **Limited/Acceptable** Essays are based on material from the textbook and provide a response to each of the three parts of the quotation.

• **Extensive/Commendable** Essays respond to each part of the quotation with a thoughtful stance of agreement or challenge, provide examples of progressive actions that support the students' opinions, and show evidence of some outside research.

• **Extraordinary/Outstanding** Essays respond to each part of the quotation, provide a variety of examples of progressive actions that support the students' opinions, and show evidence of extensive outside research.

For information and guidance on alternative assessment trends and strategies, see the Alternative Assessment Handbook in the Resource Directory on page 520.

SECTION 1

The Origins of Progressivism

Connecting to the Big Idea

See page 520B. In the 1880s and 1890s, many concerned citizens worked to reform American society. Their efforts became known as progressivism. Ask what the characteristics of the progressive movement were. How did it affect American life?

Objectives

● Describe the new reform ideas popular at the turn of the century.
● Define progressivism as a movement made up of many reform activities.
● Explain that progressives did not all share the same ideas and beliefs but often used similar methods.

Bellringer

Ask students what cues they look for to determine whether they are making progress, possibly in a course or with a project. How does a society or a nation measure its progress? How would students define progress in a national context? In what areas would students like to see the United States make progress today?

Reading Strategy

Structured Overview Ask students to write the term *progressivism* in the center of a piece of paper. As they read, students should write six phrases summarizing important characteristics of progressivism or the progressive movement around the central concept.

SECTION PREVIEW

In the twilight of the 1800s, many citizens could see that existing efforts to solve the massive problems of industrialization were failing. Could government heal the nation's ills?

Key Concepts

• The turn of the century brought a variety of new reform ideas.
• The many plans for reform fed into a stream of ideas that came to be called progressivism.
• Though progressives did not all share the same ideas and beliefs, they often used similar methods.

Key Terms, People, and Places

home rule, progressivism, social welfare program, muckraker; Henry George, Edward Bellamy, Florence Kelley

One popular cause in the early 1900s was the campaign for pure food and medicine, referred to in the magazine cover above.

By the end of the 1800s, many citizens were aware of the massive problems resulting from rapid industrialization. Unemployment, unsafe working conditions, and political corruption were just a few of these concerns, which have been discussed in earlier chapters. Citizens also realized that private efforts to address these issues, such as charity or settlement-house work, were inadequate. These concerned citizens—most of them educated middle- and upper-class men and women— began to argue that government had to become more actively involved in addressing the nation's ills. Their ideas soon redefined the United States government's role in society.

A Spirit of Reform in the late 1800s

The 1880s and 1890s were filled with lively debates about how to reform society. The ideas of journalists Henry George and Edward Bellamy were among the most popular. Socialists, unionists, and city government reformers also had many followers.

Two Visionaries In 1879 **Henry George** had written the book *Progress and Poverty* in an effort to explain why an advanced civilization seemed to increase rather than eliminate poverty. He concluded that poverty arose because private interests—speculators—bought and held land until its price went up. This practice prevented others from using land productively.

George proposed to solve this problem by ending taxes on improvements on land, such as houses and cultivation. State and local governments raised much of their income from these taxes. Instead, George proposed only a single tax—on the value of land itself. Such a tax would make speculation in land less attractive by increasing the cost of holding land without using it.

George's ideas had a powerful effect. "Single-tax" clubs sprang up everywhere. In 1894, club members from Iowa, Ohio, Minnesota, and Pennsylvania migrated to Fairhope, Alabama, to establish a single-tax colony.

In 1888 newspaper editor **Edward Bellamy** published a novel called *Looking Backward*. In it, a man undergoes hypnosis in 1887 and wakes up in the year 2000. He finds the United States transformed. The harsh working conditions, gaps between social classes, and political corruption of the late 1800s have disappeared. The reason for the change was that government had nationalized the great trusts and organized industrial management to meet human needs rather than to make profits. Writes Bellamy,

*I*n a word, the people of the United States concluded to assume the conduct of their own business, just as one hundred odd years before they had assumed the conduct of their own government.

▶ **RESOURCE DIRECTORY**

Teaching Resources

Reproducible Lesson Plan found in the Unit 6 folder, p. 38, provides a summary of the Section 1 lesson plan content.

Alternate Lesson Plan: Learning Styles found in the Alternate Lesson Plans folder, p. 95, especially helpful for tactile learners, encourages students to identify the era's reform ideas by compiling a scrapbook of newspaper headlines representative of the views of progressives.

Guided Reading and Review found in the Unit 6 folder, p. 42, provides a structure for reading and mastering the key concepts and reviewing the key terms for Section 1. (Guided Practice)

Bellamy's novel was a phenomenal best seller. In response to its vision, hundreds of "Nationalist" clubs formed.

Socialists Bellamy's views were related to the widely discussed ideas of socialism, an economic and political system featuring collective or government ownership of a nation's wealth. (See Chapter 14.) Many American socialists in this era wanted to end the capitalist system, distribute wealth more equally, and nationalize American industries—but through the ballot box, not through revolution. In 1901 they formed a Socialist Party of America, which by 1912 had won more than one thousand municipal offices. Although the party never became a political force on the national level, many reform-minded Americans gave consideration to its ideas at some time.

The Labor Movement Like members of the Socialist party, union members also hoped for economic change for the masses. Unions, however, concentrated on hours, wages, and conditions in the workplace. Reformers around the turn of the century supported many union goals.

The union movement grew in the 1890s, but slowly. Union membership was risky. Big business easily got the courts to prohibit strikes with court orders called injunctions.

Municipal Reform The spirit of social reform was also felt at the municipal, or city government, level. Municipal reformers opposed the influence that political bosses wielded and sought honest, cost-efficient government through a professional, nonpolitical civil service. They also worked for **home rule,** under which cities exercise a limited degree of self-rule. At that time, home rule helped cities escape domination by state governments, which often were controlled by political machines or rural interests.

Municipal reformers sometimes appeared naive in their belief that they could abolish corruption. Some of them also held negative views of immigrants, whom they felt were responsible for many city problems. Still, their ideas formed an important element of the era's spirit of reform.

Progressivism Takes Hold

Aspects of all the reform visions and programs discussed above influenced citizens at the end of the century. Other movements were also influential at this time—including nativism, prohibitionism, the purity crusade, charity reform, social gospel, and the settlement house movement, all discussed in Chapter 16. Together these fed into the stream of ideas that became known as **progressivism.** The Populist movement formed another, though less central, current in the progressive movement.

Progressives did not agree on all points. The movement was made up of a series of temporary alliances among diverse interests pursuing different but related goals. Yet many reformers identified themselves as progressives, and for a number of years, many progressives organized themselves into a formal political party.

The Views of Progressives As mentioned before, many progressives were well-to-do Americans. They recognized that the nation's free enterprise system often could be unfair, but they did not want to lose the high standard of living and personal liberty it had given them, and they deeply feared the violence of revolution. Thus, progressives were faced with the question of how to preserve what was good about the United States while reforming the bad.

In spite of the obstacles facing unions, the International Ladies Garment Workers Union (ILGWU) formed in 1900. After the 1909 strike shown below, which included 20,000 New York City women garment workers, the ILGWU won the right to bargain collectively.

Media and Technology

Transparencies
Cause and Effect, F-3; Our Multicultural Heritage, C-13

2. INSTRUCT

Explain/Discuss

Discuss the theme of reform. In what ways does the progressive movement resemble the populist movement?

Ask students to compare the ideas of Henry George and Edward Bellamy. How did George want the government to act to eliminate poverty? What actions did Bellamy think the government should take to transform American society?

Discuss how the motives of progressive reformers were often mixed. How much self-interest was involved in the progressives' desire to maintain order and stability and the nation's high standard of living? Does self-interest on the part of reformers affect the value of their reforms?

Analyze

Discuss why American reformers were often wealthy or financially comfortable. Then ask students why women progressives tended to work for reforms that affected the lives of women and children.

In Depth

Then and Now

In the early 1920s, less than 10 percent of the nation's wage earners were organized into labor unions. By the 1940s and 1950s, over 30 percent of all working Americans were union members, and as recently as 1975 union membership still accounted for fully 25 percent of the labor force. In the 1990s, however, only about seventeen million Americans, less than 14 percent of the nation's labor force, belong to unions.

Teaching Heterogeneous Groups

While they did not have voting power, women often created ways to push progressive reform when legislators were slow to cooperate. Businesses that supported progressive social reform, for example, were placed on a list of places where women should do their shopping. In order to be named on this "White List," businesses needed to meet certain criteria in harmony with reform. Divide students into groups to create at least five criteria suitable for a White List of today. Then have the groups compare their lists and justify their choices. **LEP**

Enrichment

Ask students to research and report on the reforms suggested and implemented by progressive educator John Dewey. Ask students to identify progressive elements in their own education, such as "hands-on" math and science activities.

In Depth

Did You Know?

Progressive ideas were slow to gain acceptance in the world of literature. Theodore Dreiser's first novel, *Sister Carrie* (1900), with its gritty depiction of urban life and a heroine who goes unpunished for her sins, was apparently too shocking for its time. The book failed miserably at first, selling fewer than 700 copies. In 1981, the unedited original version was published by the University of Pennsylvania Press.

Progressives argued that government must play a larger role in regulating economic activity. This regulation would prevent businesses from treating workers and competing enterprises unfairly. Progressives opposed government control of businesses, except of those companies that supplied essential services such as water, electricity, and transportation. They wanted to allow other businesses the freedom to operate independently—as long as society's needs came first. ✪

Progressives also believed that government ought to increase its responsibility for human welfare. Capitalism, progressives argued, often forced workers into poverty through no fault of their own. Workers had no protection against substandard wages, unemployment, or workplace hazards. Progressives proposed that government protect workers from such miseries. They also wanted government to develop more **social welfare programs,** which would help ensure a basic standard of living for all Americans. These programs might include unemployment and accident and health insurance, as well as a social security system to cover disability and old age. Progressives expected that government would rely on trained experts and scientists to plan efficient

LAD FELL TO DEATH IN BIG COAL CHUTE

Workers of all ages enjoyed little protection against workplace hazards—and few benefits when an accident befell them on the job. The fate of injured or killed workers aroused public sympathy and demands for reform.

programs, which professionals, not politicians, would manage.

Suffrage and Progressivism The cause of votes for women was important to many progressives. As social worker Jane Addams explained in a 1910 *Ladies Home Journal* article, women had a special interest in the reform of American society.

> W omen who live in the country sweep their own dooryards and may either feed the refuse [trash] of the table to a flock of chickens or allow it innocently to decay in the open air and sunshine. In a crowded city quarter, however, if the street is not cleaned by the city authorities no amount of private sweeping will keep the tenement free from grime; if the garbage is not properly collected and destroyed a tenement house mother may see her children sicken and die of diseases.

In short, Addams argued, women in cities could not care for their families without government help—so government had to allow women to make known their needs through voting.

Women activists did not all agree on how to change society. Many focused on outlawing alcohol, others on reforming conditions in the workplace. But whatever their focus, it was widely agreed that women were powerless without political rights.

Progressive Regulation and Control In order to protect vulnerable citizens, progressives accepted an increased level of government control over areas once considered private, such as housing, health care, and the content of the movies people watched or the dancing styles they enjoyed. This aspect of progressivism aroused resistance, often among the very people progressives hoped most to help. For example, progressives saw child labor laws as critical to social progress. Naturally, employers who relied on cheap child labor opposed the laws. But poor people who could not survive without sending their children out to work also objected. Such disputes added to the perception that typically well-to-do progressives were insensitive to the plight of the poor.

▶ RESOURCE DIRECTORY

Teaching Resources

✪ **Visual Learning Activity** A Different Kind of "Wild West" Show, found in the Unit 6 folder, p. 66, depicts the goal of most progressives as the control of businesses, such as railroads, that affected the public interest.

✪ **American Profiles Activity** found in the Unit 6 folder, p. 54, profiles Ida Tarbell, a muckraker for *McClure's* magazine, who exposed the coercion and ruthless business practices of John D. Rockefeller and Standard Oil.

✪ **Literature Activity** Horrors of the Meat-Packing Industry, found in the Unit 6 folder, pp. 63–64, uses excerpts from Upton Sinclair's *The Jungle* to provide insight into the plight of immigrant workers in Chicago.

MAKING CONNECTIONS

At what other points in American history have reformers helped bring about social or political change?

Progressive Methods

Progressives worked for reforms in a systematic manner. First, relying heavily on scientific data and expert testimony, they investigated issues of concern, such as slum or sweatshop conditions. Next, they publicized the results of their investigations and put pressure on legislators to get laws passed and enforced. Women's organizations, such as clubs and charitable groups, were a key means of increasing grass roots support and pressuring officials to take some action.

Using the new mass-circulation publications, journalists also alerted the public to wrongdoing on the part of political bosses or big business. Theodore Roosevelt called such writers **muckrakers,** an allusion to a character in John Bunyan's 1678 book *Pilgrim's Progress* who was too busy raking filth to look to heaven. While TR disapproved of those who whitewashed wrongdoing, he condemned those who "earn their livelihood by telling . . . scandalous falsehoods about honest men."

⭐ Despite Roosevelt's criticism, the muckrakers included respected writers who identified and exposed real abuses. Lincoln Steffens, for example, exposed political corruption in St. Louis and other cities. Ida Tarbell revealed the abuses committed by the huge Standard Oil trust. *The Jungle* (1906), a novel by Upton Sinclair, laid bare the horrors of the meat-packing industry. Wrote Sinclair of the nation's corrupt and filthy canneries,

I t seemed they must have agencies all over the country, to hunt out old and crippled and diseased cattle to be canned. . . . It was stuff such as this that made the "embalmed beef" that had killed several times as many United States soldiers as all the bullets of the Spaniards [in the Spanish-American War].

Although it was meant to promote socialism, Sinclair's book did little for workers. Its revelations, however, turned people's stomachs and thus led to a federal meat inspection program. ⭐

This cartoon shows that TR himself was willing to wield the muckrake to attack difficult problems. Here, TR tries to clean up the nation's meatpacking industry.

AMERICAN PROFILES
Florence Kelley

When you shop for clothing, do you ever wonder under what conditions it was made? When you buy medicines or a package of meat, do you worry about possible harmful effects to your health? At the turn of the century, issues such as these bothered many consumers. Because women tended to be the shoppers for their families, they were often the most vocal in asking such questions.

Florence Kelley (1859–1932) became a leader in the search for answers. She came from a prominent Pennsylvania family. Her father, William Darrah Kelley, was a fifteen-term member of Congress. Her great-aunt, Sarah Pugh, had a strong influence on her. An abolitionist and suffragist, Pugh had once refused to use cotton and sugar because slave labor produced them.

After completing her education at Cornell and at the University of Zurich in Switzerland, Kelley became a resident in Jane Addams's Hull House in Chicago. When federal officials asked Addams to investigate labor conditions in the neighborhood, Addams recommended Kelley for the job.

Answer to . . .

MAKING CONNECTIONS

Possible answers: Abolitionists in the early to mid-1800s brought the issue of slavery to the forefront. In the later 1800s, political reformers sought to reform the spoils system that pervaded national politics.

3. ASSESS

Section 1 Review Answers

1. (a) home rule, see p. 523, (b) social welfare program, see p. 524, (c) muckraker, see p. 525

2. (a) Henry George, see p. 522, (b) Edward Bellamy, see p. 522, (c) Florence Kelley, see p. 525

3. Single-tax ideas, Bellamyite "nationalism," socialism, unionism, and municipal reform. Single-taxers wanted to tax only the value of land; "nationalists" wanted to nationalize industry; socialists wanted to end capitalism and distribute wealth equally; unionists wanted to improve workplace conditions; and municipal reformers wanted to professionalize government and make it more honest.

4. Progressives were a coalition of primarily urban social reformers, professionals, and businesspeople who wanted to keep the free enterprise system basically intact but also give more regulatory power to government. They also believed that government should take up a greater part of the burden of securing human welfare.

5. Because women were generally the primary consumers, they led the way in questioning the process by which consumer goods were produced. Also, suffrage was a key issue of the progressive movement; for women reformers the vote would clearly enhance their ability to exert pressure for government reforms.

6. Reformers investigated issues of concern, then publicized their findings in an effort to win grassroots support. Muckrakers—journalists who specialized in exposés of corruption or abuses —led the way.

7. Possible answer: Government, and not private interests and agencies, is the best authority to provide relief for massive, society-wide problems.

Reteach

Ask students to identify with the letter *P* all of the following statements that identify a belief or goal of progressive reformers at the turn of the century.

- Progressive reformers did not agree on all points.
- The progressive movement was part of the general world socialist movement.
- Progressives accepted an increased level of government control in the lives of citizens.
- Progressives used scientific methods and data and worked systematically for reform.

4. CLOSE

Reinforcing the Big Idea

At the turn of the century, a spirit of reform known as progressivism swept through the country, especially in the cities. In the next section, students will learn about the progressive bills passed by local, state, and federal legislatures.

Florence Kelley led the way in several areas of progressive reform, including workplace and municipal reform.

Kelley's Early Career "Hull-House was . . . surrounded in every direction by home work carried on under the sweating system," Kelley wrote later, referring to a system of labor featuring poor conditions and pay. "From the age of eighteen months few children able to sit in high chairs at tables were safe from being required to pull basting threads." Once, Kelley reported, a public official who was supposed to visit a sweatshop refused to enter, fearing contamination from one of the many diseases, such as tuberculosis, that raged through the tenements at that time.

Largely through her efforts, in 1893 Illinois passed a law prohibiting child labor, limiting working hours for women, and regulating sweatshop conditions. The governor put Kelley in charge of enforcing it. She became so frustrated by the district attorney's refusal to prosecute cases that she earned a law degree in order to take legal action herself.

In 1897 a new governor replaced Kelley as factory inspector with a political friend who did nothing to enforce the 1893 law. It was this experience that drew Kelley into municipal reform. Only a civil service based on merit instead of favors, she realized, would keep unqualified political appointees out of important regulatory jobs.

Leading Consumer Action In 1899 a National Consumers' League (NCL) was organized to unite local consumers' leagues that had formed in the 1890s across the country. The NCL's board invited Florence Kelley to become general secretary, a post she held until her death. Through the consumers' leagues, women around the country investigated the conditions under which goods were made and sold. Local leagues urged women to patronize only those shops on a "White List"—that is, shops that did not employ children or require overtime. Leagues also insisted that factories obey state factory inspection laws and, later, pay a minimum wage.

Under Kelley's leadership, the NCL spearheaded national movements to outlaw child labor and protect workers, especially women. When criticized over this issue, Kelley would ask why "seals, bears, reindeer, fish, wild game in the national parks, buffalo" and numerous other creatures were worthy of government protection, "but not the children of our race and their mothers."

Kelley's legacy lasted long after her death. In 1954 Supreme Court justice Felix Frankfurter said that Florence Kelley "had probably the largest single share in shaping the social history of the United States during the first thirty years of this century."

SECTION 1 REVIEW

Key Terms, People, and Places

1. Define (a) home rule, (b) social welfare program, (c) muckraker.
2. Identify (a) Henry George, (b) Edward Bellamy, (c) Florence Kelley.

Key Concepts

3. What were some of the reform ideas at the turn of the century?

4. Who were the progressives and what did they want?
5. Describe the special role of women in the progressive movement.
6. Describe the methods of progressives.

Critical Thinking

7. **Recognizing Ideologies** What beliefs about the proper role of government lie at the heart of the progressive movement?

 RESOURCE DIRECTORY

Teaching Resources

Quiz found in the Unit 6 folder, p. 43, covers the main ideas in this section as well as the key terms.

Progressivism: Its Legislative Impact

SECTION PREVIEW

Driven by the rising tide of public demand, a torrent of progressive reform programs flowed through local, state, and federal legislatures. Targets for the proposed reforms included politics, society, and the economy.

Key Concepts

• The progressive era produced several different kinds of reforms.
• Reform took place at the urban, state, and federal levels.
• Reformers found unlikely allies in political machines.

Key Terms, People, and Places

direct primary, arbitration, holding company

T he unleashing of the progressive impulse led to a tremendous amount of legislation in the early 1900s. Reform took place at all levels of government—city, state, and federal.

Urban Reform

Much of the progressive reform began in the cities as opposed to the state or federal levels. In part this was because the less extensive the government, the easier it is to change that government. Also, cities were home to most of the settlement workers, club members, professionals, and business leaders who were pushing many of the reforms. Thus, they were on hand to maintain the pressure for change.

Attacking the Bosses Political machines and bosses sustained heavy criticism in the progressive period, but always seemed able to withstand such attacks. New York City provides a good example. In 1896 Columbia University president Seth Low ran for mayor, supported by municipal reformers and settlement work-

ers. To help his campaign against Tammany Hall's ward bosses, settlement houses sent out children with handbills to post in their neighborhoods. Low lost, but he tried again in 1901 and won, only to see the Tammany Hall machine return to power in the next election. Over the following decades, New York seesawed between turning to reform or sticking with the old political bosses.

In some cities, voter support for reforms prompted machine politicians to work with reformers. Together they registered voters, improved city services, established public health programs, and enforced tenement codes. Such alliances could bring about astonishing improvements in urban life.

Cities Take Over Utilities Reformers made efforts to regulate or dislodge the monopolies that provided city utilities such as water, gas, and electricity. Reform mayors Hazen S. Pingree of Detroit (1889–1897), Samuel M. "Golden Rule" Jones of Toledo (1897–1904), and Tom Johnson of Cleveland (1901–1909) pioneered city control or ownership of utilities, thus providing residents with more affordable services. By 1915, nearly two out of three cities had some form of city-owned utilities.

Providing Welfare Services Some reform mayors led movements for city-supported welfare services. Hazen Pingree provided public baths, parks, and, to combat the 1893 depression, a work-relief program. "Golden Rule" Jones opened playgrounds and free kindergartens and built lodging houses for the homeless. "Nobody has a right to rule anybody else," he once said. In his view, all people would be good if social conditions were good.

Progressive-era legislation resulted in the regulation of the meatpacking industry. This stamp was used by federal officials who inspected meat for freshness.

1. FOCUS

Connecting to the Big Idea

See page 520B. Progressives succeeded in passing many reform bills in local, state, and federal legislatures. Ask students what these laws were. What did they accomplish?

Objectives

● Describe the different kinds of reforms introduced during the progressive era.
● Give examples of progressive reform at the urban, state, and federal levels.
● Explain how progressives found unlikely allies in political machines.

Bellringer

Ask students to consider this statement by former Speaker of the House Thomas P. (Tip) O'Neill, Jr., "All politics are local [politics]." Do students agree or disagree with this view?

Reading Strategy

Structured Overview Ask students to write the following headings on a piece of paper: Urban Reforms; Reforms at the State Level; Reforms at the Federal Level. Have students then scan the section for subheadings and write them under the appropriate heading. Have students fill in details from the text as they read.

📄 **Reproducible Lesson Plan** found in the Unit 6 folder, p. 39, provides a summary of the Section 2 lesson plan content.

📄 **Alternate Lesson Plan: Critical Thinking** Determining Relevance, found in the Alternate Lesson Plans folder, p. 96, provides a strategy for applying this skill that helps students determine how reformers, ideas, and results of reforms are related, and understand the effects of progressivism at the local, state, and national levels.

📄 **Guided Reading and Review** found in the Unit 6 folder, p. 44, provides a structure for reading and mastering the key concepts and reviewing the key terms for Section 2. (Guided Practice)

2. INSTRUCT

Explain/Discuss

Discuss the accommodations made by machine politicians and progressive reformers in order for the two groups to work together. Do students think that reformers compromised their own ethics by working with the political machines?

Do students agree with "Golden Rule" Jones that people would be good if social conditions were good? How can that theory be proved or disproved?

Ask students whether progressives were justified in resorting to arguments about safeguarding mothers and prospective mothers in order to pass legislation protecting women workers. Why were such arguments successful? What harm did they do?

Explain that when the antitrust action against Northern Securities began, the head of Northern Securities, J. P. Morgan, said to President Roosevelt, "If we have done anything wrong, send your man to my man and they can fix it up." What attitude toward government does Morgan's statement reveal?

Gains Made by Voters During the Progressive Era

Referendum
Legislature refers measure to voters for approval or rejection

Initiative
Voters force placement of measure on the ballot

Sign Petitions

Voters

Sign Petitions

Recall
Voters force elected officials to stand for reelection

Interpreting Charts
Voters sought and won greater control over their state governments during the progressive era. By 1912, a dozen states had the initiative and referendum. Seven had recall. *Explain how these measures would help voters exert greater control over government.*

MAKING CONNECTIONS

Given what you read in Chapter 16 about political machines and immigrants, are you surprised to read about machines cooperating with progressive reformers? Explain.

Reforms at the State Level

⭐ Progressive governors and state legislators also were active. Governors Robert "Battling Bob" La Follette in Wisconsin and Hiram Johnson in California, among others, introduced reforms to make government more efficient and responsive to voters. They also championed state labor and factory legislation, motivated in part by the Triangle Shirtwaist Factory fire in New York City, in which inadequate and unenforced safety regulations contributed to 146 deaths (see "History Might Not Have Happened This Way," pages 532–533).

La Follette became a reformer out of disgust, after a Republican party boss offered him a bribe. In 1900 he won the Wisconsin governorship. By 1904 he had brought about a **direct primary,** an election in which voters cast ballots to select nominees for upcoming elections. Direct primaries replaced the handpicking of candidates by party leaders. By 1916 all but three states had direct primaries.

Reforms of the Workplace Activists also targeted the workplace. Applying the principle that employers and employees had to negotiate over differences, individual states established labor departments to provide information and dispute-resolution services to both sides.

States also worked toward ending exploitative and unsafe working conditions. They developed a workers' accident insurance and compensation system, and by 1920 all but five states had taken steps to make it easier for workers to collect payment for workplace accidents.

Government efforts to control working conditions met legal opposition at every turn. In a case known as *Lochner* v. *New York* (1905), for example, the Supreme Court struck down a law setting maximum hours for bakers on the ground that it "was an illegal interference with the rights of individuals . . . to make contracts."

Frustrated, reformers took another approach: they tried to convince the courts that government had to control conditions to protect women. This approach achieved a breakthrough in 1908, when in *Muller* v. *Oregon* the United States Supreme Court upheld an Oregon law that limited hours for women laundry workers to ten hours a day.

Labor reformers were successful on some other fronts as well. By 1907 the National Child Labor Committee had convinced some thirty states to abolish child labor—often defined as

▶ RESOURCE DIRECTORY

Teaching Resources

⭐ **Primary Source Activity** The Shame of the People, found in the Unit 6 folder, p. 60, uses Lincoln Steffens's introduction to *The Shame of the Cities* to show the scope of graft and corruption found in the United States at the turn of the century.

Protecting Workers from Their Workplace

During the progressive era (left), reformers sought to eliminate the dangerous conditions of factories. Today (above), workers are protected by strict guidelines established by the Occupational Safety and Health Administration (OSHA). These guidelines require the use of protective clothing and equipment in the workplace. *What other reforms might progressives try to implement in today's workplaces?*

employment of children under age fourteen. Minimum wage legislation for women and children also made headway. Florence Kelley led the national campaign, and after Massachusetts adopted a minimum wage in 1912, eight other states followed.

The Paradox of Protective Legislation Laws that singled out particular groups for protection had both positive and negative results. Maximum hour and minimum wage legislation for women led some employers to replace women with men, who were willing to work longer hours for lower wages. Special protection for women also fostered beliefs about female weakness, hurting women's case for voting and work rights equal to those of men. In the *Muller* decision, for example, Justice David J. Brewer had said that

> *continuance for a long time on her feet at work, repeating this from day to day, tends to injurious effects upon the body, and, as healthy mothers are essential to vigorous offspring, the physical well-being of woman becomes an object of public interest.*

Many progressives believed that laws protecting women would eventually break down the opposition to protection for all workers. This prediction came true: over the following decades, most protective legislation came to apply to both sexes.

Reforms at the Federal Level

Progressivism appeared at the federal level in labor and industrial relations, in the regulation of business and commerce, in the preservation of the environment, and in social legislation.

Theodore Roosevelt's "Square Deal" As President, Theodore Roosevelt was determined to use his powers vigorously. He got his chance in May 1902, when the United Mine Workers called a strike because of their low wages. As winter approached and mine owners continued to refuse to talk to the union, TR decided to intervene. Without coal, he realized, the nation would be without a key source of heating fuel.

TR insisted that both sides submit to **arbitration,** a process in which an impartial third party decides on a legally binding solution.

Most of these lands are in the western portion of the United States, a part of the country that has traditionally been sparsely populated.

Enrichment

Tell students that in 1905, after eighteen college players were killed playing football, President Roosevelt called a White House conference on the game. Ask students to research the results of this event and to present their findings in a report that examines the conference as a part of the progressive movement.

3. ASSESS

Section 2 Review Answers

1. (a) direct primary, see p. 528, (b) arbitration, see p. 529, (c) holding company, see p. 530

2. Examples include city control of or operation of utilities and provision of welfare services. When the machine politicians discovered that the reforms were popular with voters, in some cases they joined forces with reformers.

3. There were structural reforms, such as the direct primary and the initiative, referendum, and recall; workplace reforms such as child labor laws; and protective legislation for women.

4. Legislation designed to protect women and children interfered with private family life and stigmatized women as weak and unable to work outside the home. Yet without such legislation inhumane conditions would have persisted, and reformers might never have won protective laws for all workers.

5. TR was an aggressive regulator of trusts and of the nation's transportation system. He strengthened regulation of food and drugs. He also introduced a number of environmental reforms, though some conservationists disagreed with his willingness to use public land for mining, water projects, and logging. His "square deal" represented a compromise between business and labor interests.

National Forests, Parks, and Monuments, c. 1908

National parks and monuments created prior to Theodore Roosevelt's administration

National parks and monuments created during the Roosevelt administration

National forests and other federal land created during the Roosevelt administration

(43 million acres of national forest were created prior to Roosevelt; 151 million additional acres were created during his administration)

Geography and History: Interpreting Maps
TR was convinced that "vigorous action must be taken" to save the nation's natural environment. Among the millions of acres of public land he set aside are sixteen national monuments and fifty-one wildlife refuges. *What do you notice about the location of the nation's parks, forests, and preserves?*

To encourage mine owners to accept this step, he threatened to use the army to seize and operate the mines. In 1903 arbitrators granted the miners a 10 percent raise and reduced their hours from ten to nine—but did not grant official recognition of their union. When TR called this a "square deal" for both sides, the phrase became a slogan of his presidency.

Reelected easily in 1904, TR focused on regulating railroads and food and drugs. In 1906 the Hepburn Act authorized the Interstate Commerce Commission to limit rates if shippers complained of unfair treatment. Also in 1906 the Pure Food and Drug Act and the Meat Inspection Act required accurate labeling of ingredients, strict sanitary conditions, and a rating system for meats.

Antitrust Activism Although the Sherman Antitrust Act (1890) was in place as a check on big business, it had never been vigorously enforced. Calling for an end to special privileges for capitalists, TR had his attorney general use the act to sue a huge holding company, the Northern Securities Company, which controlled railroads in the Northwest. **Holding companies** are corporations that hold the stocks and bonds of—and thus exert control over—numerous companies, thus achieving a monopoly. In 1904 the government won its case against Northern Securities in the Supreme Court.

By the time TR had completed his second term in 1909, the government had filed forty-two antitrust actions. The beef trust, Standard Oil, and the American Tobacco Company were either broken up or forced to reorganize. TR was not antibusiness. He did not wish to destroy trusts that he deemed "good," or not harmful to the public. But he believed that they should be supervised and controlled.

RESOURCE DIRECTORY

Teaching Resources

Primary Source Activity Giving the Child a Chance, found in the Unit 6 folder, pp. 61–62, illustrates attempts made to stimulate interest in the crusade for children's rights using an article published in *Harper's Weekly.*

The Environment As settlement expanded into the West, people began to realize that the land, water, and forests there needed to be protected. At the urging of explorers and nature writers such as John Wesley Powell and John Muir, in 1872 Congress established Yellowstone in Wyoming as the nation's first national park and in 1890 made Yosemite in California a national park. Presidents Harrison and Cleveland preserved some 35 million acres of forest land.

In the early 1900s, reflecting the era's reliance on scientific data, the federal government called in experts to develop a workable policy for land and water use. In 1905 Roosevelt named Gifford Pinchot, a scientific forester, to head a new United States Forest Service. At his recommendation, TR set aside more than 200 million acres of land for national forests, mineral reserves, and water projects, shown on the map on page 530. A National Reclamation Act (1902) aimed at planning and developing irrigation projects aroused controversy between farmers and city residents in the Southwest over the use of scarce water resources that persist to this day.

Social Legislation Although most social legislation took place in the states, the federal government was active too. In response to pressure from women's clubs and labor organizations, in 1912 the government established a Children's Bureau within the Department of Labor, itself a new cabinet department. A Women's Bureau was formed in 1920. These two bureaus supported advocates of legislation that would benefit women and children. Both were headed by women, Julia Lathrop and Mary Anderson, the first female bureau heads at the federal level.

Progressive Era Amendments

Amendment	Result
16th Amendment Gives Congress power to levy an income tax	Allowed government to raise more revenue from wealthy people's incomes and less from tariffs that hurt the working poor
17th Amendment Provides for direct election of senators	By taking the election of senators out of the hands of the legislature, voters were able to play a more direct role in government

 Interpreting Tables
By 1913, the progressive era had produced the Sixteenth and Seventeenth amendments. *How did the Seventeenth Amendment relate to the initiative, referendum, and recall that had passed in many states?*

National Prohibition Although not all progressives favored prohibition, many thought it would protect society from the poverty and violence associated with drinking. Women's support for it prompted brewery and liquor interests to oppose woman suffrage.

A number of states had passed prohibition laws in the 1800s, though most soon repealed them. The expansion of prohibition increased in the early 1900s, however. The states of the South and West (except for California) had outlawed the sale and manufacture of liquor by the time national prohibition arrived with the ratification of the Eighteenth Amendment in 1919. Until its repeal in 1933, Americans could not legally make, sell, or import liquor. They could still drink, however, and they proved very resourceful at obtaining alcohol illegally.

Prohibition is but one of the many distinct interests that came under the banner of progressivism in the early 1900s. Eventually supporters of many of those interests joined forces in a national political party.

SECTION 2 REVIEW

Key Terms, People, and Places
1. Define (a) direct primary, (b) arbitration, (c) holding company.

Key Concepts
2. What kinds of reforms took place at the city level and how did political machines become involved?
3. Briefly describe state-level reforms.

4. What is the "paradox of protective legislation"?
5. Briefly describe TR's progressive record.

Critical Thinking
6. **Testing Conclusions** Progressivism was not a single, unified movement, but a collection of distinct causes and concerns. Find evidence in this section to support this conclusion.

Quiz found in the Unit 6 folder, p. 45, covers the main ideas in this section as well as the key terms.

The Decision to Lock the Doors at the Triangle Shirtwaist Company

Focus Before students read about the event, ask them to imagine that their community has few regulations for fire safety in public buildings such as schools, and existing regulations are not enforced. Ask them to further imagine that there is a terrible fire in a school located in a busy area, and 146 children are killed, many because they jumped from the burning building. The fire receives a great deal of publicity. What do students think would be the results of the fire?

Instruct Ask students to read the feature and to explain why the Triangle fire had such significant results.

Ask students to think of possible ways the Triangle owners might have met the fire regulations and continued to make money. Then divide the class into groups and ask the groups to consider some similar issues confronting business owners today. Many small business owners complain that if they comply with antipollution regulations they cannot make a profit and stay in business.

Ask each group to imagine that they are the owners of a small, barely profitable paper company. In order to meet new antipollution regulations, they must completely refit their main factory, requiring loans at high interest. Ask students to brainstorm choices they could make as factory owners in this situation. Then ask each group to select three possible choices and list the likely results of each course of action. Ask each group to try to arrive at a consensus.

Extend Tell students that Frances Perkins witnessed the Triangle fire. In 1933, President Franklin Roosevelt chose Perkins as his secretary of labor. Ask students to write a short biography of this interesting reformer.

The Decision to Lock the Doors at the Triangle Shirtwaist Company

Time Frame:	1909–1911
Place:	The Asch Building in New York City's Greenwich Village
Key People:	Max Blanck and Isaac Harris, owners of the Triangle Shirtwaist Company; Triangle workers
Situation:	In New York's highly competitive garment manufacturing industry, the owners of the Triangle Shirtwaist Company had to decide how to cut spending in order to save money.

I n the early 1900s, the Triangle Shirtwaist Company was one of the numerous garment manufacturing companies operating sweatshops in New York City. Seeking to boost profits, such manufacturers often tried to cut the costs involved in obeying the few existing fire safety laws. The Triangle Shirtwaist Company and others were able to take this approach in part because public officials failed to enforce safety and labor regulations adequately. The Triangle owners also tried to save money by preventing employees from leaving the workplace with materials supplied by the company—lace trims and fabric scraps, for example.

Sweatshop Conditions at Triangle

One of the largest garment manufacturers in New York, the Triangle company was also known as one of the hardest on its workers. Owners Max Blanck and Isaac Harris hired mostly immigrant women, who worked for less than men. Blanck and Harris also charged their workers for needles, the use of lockers and chairs, and any clothing that did not turn out right.

Avoiding the Costs of Meeting Fire Regulations

Aware that factories were hardly ever inspected for safety violations, the Triangle company routinely ignored local fire laws in an effort to save money. Like many of the sweatshops in downtown Manhattan, the ten-story Asch Building—and especially the top three floors that housed the Triangle Shirtwaist Company—was riddled with fire hazards. Blanck and Harris crammed as much equipment as possible into the factory, blocking access to fire hoses and stairways. They gave their employees no instruction in fire safety, nor did they hold fire drills.

Blanck and Harris were not alone in their willingness to avoid costs by ignoring fire safety standards. When the New York fire department tried to strengthen regulations and enforcement early in 1911, numerous local manufacturers blocked them at an emergency meeting on Wall Street. Claiming that the financial burden of the new regulations would be unreasonable, manufacturers convinced public officials that stricter fire laws should wait.

Locking Doors to Prevent Employee Theft Avoiding the costs of meeting fire regulations was not the only way Triangle's owners tried to save money. They also saved money by taking measures to prevent employee theft. According to

a newspaper report, the owners of the company ordered two hall doors and a single fire escape door on each floor to be locked "to safeguard employers from the loss of goods by the departure of workers through fire exits." Workers

RESOURCE DIRECTORY

Teaching Resources

History Might Not . . . Activity
Marching for Child Labor Laws, found in the Unit 6 folder, pp. 52–53, focuses on the decisions made by the reformer "Mother Jones" and others in an effort to establish child labor laws in the early 1900s.

GOALS	Reduce business expenses and operating costs to save money and remain competitive in New York City's garment industry	
ACTIONS	Ignore fire safety standards or avoid the cost of meeting them.	Prevent employee theft of company goods.
OUTCOMES	• Block fire hoses and stairways with equipment. • Provide no fire drills or fire safety instruction. • Triangle employees are exposed to hazardous working conditions.	• Lock fire exits. • Have workers leave through one door. • Post a guard to check employees leaving work. • Triangle saves money.

left the company through one door, where a guard searched for stolen materials.

A Horrifying Disaster

Late in the afternoon on Saturday, March 25, 1911, tragedy struck. As about five hundred Triangle workers prepared to leave work, a carelessly tossed match or cigarette butt ignited some fabric cuttings on the eighth floor. Within seconds, a fire engulfed all three floors of the Triangle factory. A mere ten minutes later, more than 140 people lay dead.

The fire exposed the terrible potential of the Triangle company's violation of safety standards. As the flames spread, workers ran for the exits—and found most of them locked. A few dozen people made it to the elevator and reached the street before fire knocked the elevator out. There was one fire escape on the building, but those who were able to reach it found that the small, rusted structure could not support them. The fire escape collapsed to the ground, carrying people to their deaths. By the time firefighters could break down the factory's locked fire exits, scores of workers had burned to death, while many others had jumped to their deaths down the elevator shafts or out the windows. When it was all over, 146 workers were dead, and New York City had witnessed one of the most horrifying and tragic disasters in its history.

Response and Reform

The decision to lock the doors at Triangle was made without regard to the Triangle workers. The decisions that followed the blaze, however, helped to safeguard the lives, health, and welfare of workers throughout the state. The horror of the Triangle fire roused the public to immediate action. The day after the tragedy, the Women's Trade Union League and the Red Cross formed a committee to improve fire safety standards. It called on the city to appoint fire inspectors, to make fire drills compulsory, and to unlock and fireproof exits. The city building department declared the Asch Building unsafe, and fire officials began to improve the city's fire codes.

Labor unions demonstrated, calling on New York state to investigate factory conditions and enact stricter safety laws. In response, the state legislature formed a Factory Investigating Commission to look into working conditions. Its findings eventually prompted the state to redraft its entire labor code, making it the most ambitious in the nation.

EVALUATING DECISIONS

1. What actions did the Triangle Shirtwaist Company take that endangered its employees?
2. Why did the owners of the Triangle Shirtwaist Company decide to take those actions?

Critical Thinking

3. **Determining Relevance** The owners of the Triangle Shirtwaist Company were not alone in disregarding safety laws. How might this fact have affected their decisions?

Media and Technology

Visions of America: History Might Not Have Happened This Way Game

To encourage students to explore pivotal moments in United States history, have students use the Visions of America software. Refer to the Visions of America Guidebook for viewing objectives, activities, game instructions, and discussion questions.

Progressivism: Its Impact on National Politics

Progressivism: Its Impact on National Politics

1. FOCUS

Connecting to the Big Idea

See page 520B. In 1912, many groups associated with the progressive movement established a formal political party. Although the Progressive party candidate did not win the presidential election, the new President, Woodrow Wilson, continued to institute progressive reforms. Ask what led the progressives to form a political party. What was the legacy of progressive reform?

Objectives

● Describe the progressive legislation enacted during Taft's administration.
● Explain why Roosevelt abandoned Taft and led the "Bull Moose" movement.
● Describe how Wilson continued progressivism until the approach of World War I.

Bellringer

Ask students to imagine an election for class president with four students running for office. What would happen if all the girls agreed to vote for one nominee and the boys voted for several? Who would win? Explain how the election of 1912 was determined by the Taft-Roosevelt split in a similar fashion.

Reading Strategy

Reinforcing Key Ideas Ask students to list the names of the presidential candidates in 1912—Debs, Taft, Roosevelt, and Wilson—at the top of a piece of paper. Ask students to make notes under each name as they read, identifying each candidate, his political party in 1912, and his claim to be called a progressive, even if he was not a member of the Progressive party.

SECTION PREVIEW

In 1912 several of the loosely allied interests that made up progressivism joined forces in a new political party. Hitching their campaign wagon to a bull moose named TR, they set a course for the White House. Though they lost, the victors promoted many progressive ideas—until a distant war cast a shadow across the country.

Many progressives joined forces in a new political party in 1912, taking as their symbol the mighty Bull Moose.

Key Concepts

• Taft's presidency was marked by progressive legislation—and a rebel movement within his own party.
• Roosevelt abandoned Taft and led the "Bull Moose" movement.
• Wilson continued progressivism—until the movement came to an end with the approach of World War I.

Key Terms, People, and Places

New Nationalism, Bull Moose party, New Freedom

The progressive movement had always been little more than a series of informal alliances. In 1912, however, a number of interests and groups associated with this movement came together into a formal political party. Though this party did not win the presidential election that year, its ideas continued to hold the attention of American voters and politicians—for a few more years, at least.

The Presidency After Roosevelt

The day after his election in 1904, TR announced he would not seek another presidential term. As the campaign of 1908 neared, he handpicked the next Republican presidential nominee—his secretary of war, William Howard Taft. On the Democratic side, William Jennings Bryan tried for a third (and last) time to win the office. Taft won easily.

President Taft had pledged to carry on TR's progressive program. He fulfilled that promise, pursuing some ninety antitrust cases and supporting numerous other reforms. Taft, however, had neither Roosevelt's energy nor strength of personality. He gave in to the Republican "old guard" that resisted many progressive programs. One such issue was tariff reduction, a favorite cause of progressives because tariffs favored business and hurt consumers. Taft's failure to reduce the tariff angered progressives in his own party, and an insurgent, or rebel, movement arose.

The Ballinger-Pinchot Affair A party crisis over conservation worsened matters for Taft. Ignoring the protests of conservationists, Taft's secretary of the interior, Richard A. Ballinger, allowed a private group to obtain several million acres of Alaskan public lands that contained rich coal deposits. Gifford Pinchot, TR's appointee to head the Forest Service, felt that Ballinger had shown special preference to the purchasing group and protested to a congressional committee. Taft fired Pinchot.

Upset over Taft's handling of the affair, insurgent House Republicans rebelled against their party leader. They joined with Democrats in a vote to investigate Ballinger. Although never found guilty of wrongdoing, Ballinger eventually resigned.

Insurgents also took action against the Republican old guard, who, by controlling the vital House Rules Committee, had blocked much reform legislation. The insurgents managed to change the committee's membership by making it elective and excluding powerful House Speaker, Joseph G. Cannon, a Republican reform opponent.

RESOURCE DIRECTORY

Teaching Resources

Reproducible Lesson Plan found in the Unit 6 folder, p. 40, provides a summary of the Section 3 lesson plan content.

Alternate Lesson Plan: Cooperative Learning found in the Alternate Lesson Plans folder, p. 97, organizes groups of students to write campaign speeches for each of the four presidential candidates in 1912.

Guided Reading and Review found in the Unit 6 folder, p. 46, provides a structure for reading and mastering the key concepts and reviewing the key terms for Section 3. (Guided Practice)

Critical Thinking Activity Distinguishing False from Accurate Images, found in the Unit 6 folder, p. 59, encourages students to apply this skill by analyzing a political cartoon.

The Midterm Elections of 1910 TR returned from a hunting trip in Africa to find a storm of protest rising against Taft. At first he kept clear of it, but soon he began speaking out in support of insurgent Republican candidates in the 1910 midterm elections. He called for more federal regulation of business, welfare legislation, and progressive reforms such as stronger workplace protections for women and children, income and inheritance taxes, direct primaries, and the initiative, referendum, and recall. TR called this program the **New Nationalism.**

In the election, the Republicans lost seats as the Democrats captured the House of Representatives. A progressive group of Democratic and Republican insurgents dominated the Senate. Roosevelt, back in the political picture, announced by early 1912 that he would oppose Taft for the Republican presidential nomination.

Taft's Record Taft did not have a bad record on progressive causes. He had reserved more public lands and brought more antitrust suits in four years than TR had in seven. He also had supported the Children's Bureau, the Sixteenth and Seventeenth amendments, and the Mann-Elkins Act (1910), which placed telephone and telegraph rates under the control of the Interstate Commerce Commission rather than big businesses. In the end, however, Taft never recovered from the Ballinger-Pinchot affair.

MAKING CONNECTIONS

How influential are the opinions of former Presidents who are alive today? Do Americans listen to them or seek their views? Give examples.

The Election of 1912

⭐ As TR and Taft vied for the nomination in the primaries of 1912, TR's challenge began to succeed. Still, Taft controlled the central party machinery. When the Republican national convention met in Chicago in June, the Taft group disqualified the delegates TR had won in the primaries. Charging Taft's group with fraud, TR's supporters marched out, vowing to form their own party. In August they held their own convention and formed the Progressive party. When TR was asked about his physical readiness for a campaign, he said, "I feel fit as a bull moose!" The **Bull Moose party** became the nickname of the Progressive party.

The Bull Moose platform included tariff reduction, woman suffrage, more regulation of business, an end to child labor, an eight-hour work day, a federal workers' compensation system, and the popular election of senators. Many women joined the party, campaigned for Progressive candidates, and in those states that already had won woman suffrage, ran for state and local offices. California's progressive crusader, Hiram Johnson, was TR's running mate.

TR ran a vigorous campaign that became legendary. For example, despite bleeding from a chest wound he suffered in an assassination attempt in Milwaukee, TR spoke for an hour and a half before seeking medical aid. "It takes more than this to kill a bull moose," he said as he showed the crowd his bloodstained shirt. Many Americans began to think of him as the people's champion and a hero.

A Four-Way Election Four men sought the presidency in 1912. Labor leader Eugene V. Debs ran on the Socialist ticket. Taft was the Republican candidate, and Roosevelt represented his Bull Moose progressives. Woodrow Wilson, a political newcomer and governor of New Jersey, headed the Democratic ticket. Wilson ran on a reform platform, too, but, unlike Roosevelt, he criticized both big business and big government.

Using Historical Evidence
In spite of his respectable record on progressive issues, Taft's presidency became entangled in controversy and conflict with Congress. *What does this cartoon suggest about TR's reaction to Taft's difficulties?*

Media and Technology

 Transparency
Critical Thinking, I-8

2. INSTRUCT

Explain/Discuss
Explain that while Roosevelt said, "I believe in a strong executive. I believe in power," Taft felt that the President should use power with restraint.

Discuss why Taft's unwillingness or inability to influence Congress angered progressives. Discuss the expectations Roosevelt and his followers had for Taft. In what ways did Taft disappoint them? Ask students to explain in their own words why Roosevelt threw his hat into the ring in 1912. How did Wilson increase the powers of the federal government?

Caption Answer to ...

Using Historical Evidence

TR disapproves of Taft. He observes that Taft cannot be effective because he has become entangled.

Answer to ...

MAKING CONNECTIONS

Possible answer: Since former Presidents are out of the public eye, it is hard for most Americans to know what their opinions are, or how influential they might be privately.

In Depth

Historical Misconceptions

Death and taxes are said to be the only certainties in life. But the progressives had to wage a long fight to institute the income tax—now the largest single source of revenue in the United States. In 1894, an income tax amendment to the Wilson-Gorman (Tariff) Bill was ruled unconstitutional by the Supreme Court, on the grounds that the income tax was a direct tax and must be levied equally among the states. A national income tax was not levied in the United States until 1913, when the Sixteenth Amendment made the federal income tax constitutional.

Interpreting Tables

Taft would have won with over 50 percent of the vote.

Analyze

Ask students to analyze the election of 1912 in terms of the personalities of Taft, Roosevelt, and Wilson. How did the candidates' personalities affect the outcome of the election?

Activity

Name That Candidate

Ask each student to write two statements about each of the six candidates in the presidential election of 1912, following this format: "This candidate _____." Then invite pairs of students to exchange papers and identify the candidates described in each statement.

Enrichment

Ask students to research the background of Woodrow Wilson and explain how his education, experience, and religion influenced his political career.

In Depth

Multicultural Perspectives

Although they were mainly ignored by progressives, there were a few serious attempts to publicize the exclusion of African Americans from American society. The first movie extravaganza that became a box-office smash in 1915—D.W. Griffith's *The Birth of a Nation*—illustrated the depth of the exclusion. "It started people to thinking," one reviewer wrote. "The people of Chicago saw. . . the reason the South wants the Negro to 'keep in his place.' They saw in it a new conception of southern problems." (See page 537.)

Presidential Election of 1912

Candidate and Party	Popular vote	Percent	Electoral vote
Woodrow Wilson/Democrat	6,296,547	41.8	435
Theodore Roosevelt/Progressive	4,118,571	27.4	88
William H. Taft/Republican	3,486,720	23.2	8
Eugene V. Debs/Socialist	900,672	6.0	–
Eugene Chafin/Prohibition	206,275	1.4	–
Arthur E. Reimer/Socialist Labor	28,750	0.8	–

Source: *Historical Statistics of the United States*

Interpreting Tables
In the 1912 election, progressive ideas played a part in the platforms of the Democrats, Progressives, Republicans, and Socialists. The button below shows Woodrow Wilson, the winner of the election. *What would have happened if TR had not run and Taft had received TR's votes?*

Calling his policy a **New Freedom,** he promised to enforce antitrust laws without threatening free economic competition.

Roosevelt trounced Taft, as the table above shows. But Wilson outdistanced them all, and the Democratic party took both houses of Congress.

Impact of the Wilson Victory An eloquent speaker and talented politician, Wilson could compromise when necessary—but also could hold unbendingly to his principles. As the governor of New Jersey, he had acquired a reputation as a reformer (see Section 2).

Wilson was not opposed to federal regulation, but he wanted to preserve as much free economic competition as possible. As he explained during the 1912 campaign, the world had become too interdependent for government to remain distant. "We used to think in the old-fashioned days," he said, "that all that government had to do was to put on a policeman's uniform, and say, 'Now don't anybody hurt anybody else.'" But life in the early 1900s had become so complex that Wilson believed government had "to step in and create new conditions."

Thus, following up on measures taken under TR, Wilson in 1914 created a Federal Trade Commission to be sure business complied with federal trade regulations. Also in 1914, the Clayton Antitrust Act spelled out specific activities big businesses could not do in restraint of trade, thus strengthening the nation's antitrust laws. Of great importance to labor unions, this act also exempted union activities from antitrust lawsuits, unless those activities led to "irreparable injury to property."

Wilson also lowered many tariffs and instituted major financial reforms. In 1913 he helped establish the Federal Reserve System. This system let banks borrow money to meet short-term demands, thus helping to prevent bank failures that occurred when large numbers of depositors withdrew funds during an economic panic. Such bank failures could cause widespread job loss and misery. Another Wilson financial reform was the establishment of the Federal Farm Loan Board in 1916, which made low-interest loans available to farmers.

Wilson was less active in social justice legislation. He allowed his cabinet officers to extend the Jim Crow practice of separating the races in federal offices—a practice that had begun under Taft. He also opposed a constitutional amendment on woman suffrage because his party platform had not endorsed it.

A Controversial Appointment Early in 1916 Wilson nominated progressive lawyer Louis D. Brandeis to the Supreme Court. Born in 1856 in Louisville, Kentucky, Brandeis was known for his brilliance and for fighting many public causes, often without fee. His work earned him the name "the people's lawyer." ⭐

Brandeis supported Wilson in 1912 and advised him during the campaign. When Wilson nominated him to the Supreme Court, the action drew a storm of protest. Opponents, who included former President Taft, accused Brandeis of being too radical. Anti-Semitism also played a part in opposition to Brandeis, as he was the first Jewish Supreme Court nominee. Nevertheless, Brandeis won his seat on the Court and served with distinction until 1939. His appointment marked the peak of progressive reform at the federal level.

 RESOURCE DIRECTORY

Teaching Resources

⭐ **American Profiles Activity** found in the Unit 6 folder, p. 55, profiles the progressive Supreme Court justice, Louis D. Brandeis.

Wilson Wins a Second Term Wilson ran for reelection in 1916. By then, the ties binding the Progressive party were weakening. TR did not want to run again. Instead, he endorsed Wilson's Republican opponent, Charles Evans Hughes, a former governor of New York and Supreme Court justice. Promising to keep the country out of war, Wilson won a narrow victory.

The Legacy of Progressive Reform

By the mid-1910s, progressives could take pride in the many changes they had helped bring about, such as redefining the role of government in business and politics.

A Limited View of Progress Progressives so identified themselves because they believed they were working toward progress. Usually this term has a positive meaning. But what seems progressive to one class, race, or region might seem regressive, even repressive, to another.

For example, many African Americans felt ignored by progressives. Only a tiny group of progressives, those who helped found the NAACP, concerned themselves with the worsening race relations of the era. At the 1912 Progressive party convention, Roosevelt declined to seat southern African American delegates for fear of alienating white southern supporters. In addition, some white southern progressives who favored the women's vote did so with the racist argument that the white vote would double if suffrage passed. African Americans, on the other hand, would fall further behind because of their lower population and the effectiveness of voting restrictions in the South.

EQUALITY

This lithograph trumpets one of the few bright spots in relations between African Americans and whites during this era: Booker T. Washington's visit to Teddy Roosevelt's White House in 1901.

Progressives also focused narrowly on the problems of cities, ignoring the plight of tenant and migrant farmers and of nonunionized workers in general. Some supported immigration restriction and literacy tests.

Finally, many progressives uncritically supported the imperialistic adventures of the day. Just as they believed in the uplift of the slums and ghettos of American cities, they favored the "civilizing" of undeveloped nations, no matter what the residents of those countries wanted.

The End of the Progressive Coalition In August 1914, war began in Europe, and many nations began to assemble troops and supplies. Americans worried about how long they could remain uninvolved in the conflict. Soon, calls to prepare for war drowned out calls for reform in the United States. By the end of 1916 the reform spirit had sputtered out—with the exception of the drive for woman suffrage.

SECTION 3 REVIEW

Key Terms, People, and Places
1. Identify (a) New Nationalism, (b) Bull Moose party, (c) New Freedom.

Key Concepts
2. In what ways did President Taft support the progressive agenda?
3. Why did an insurgent movement arise during Taft's presidency?
4. Who ran for President in 1912?

5. In what ways did Wilson support progressivism?
6. Did the progressives deserve the name *progressive*? Explain.

Critical Thinking
7. **Recognizing Cause and Effect** Consider what you have read about the nature of the progressive movement in the early 1900s. How does this help explain the failure of the Bull Moose challenge in 1912?

Quiz found in the Unit 6 folder, p. 47, covers the main ideas in this section as well as the key terms.

3. ASSESS

Section 3 Review Answers

1. (a) New Nationalism, see p. 535, (b) Bull Moose party, see p. 535, (c) New Freedom, see p. 536

2. He pursued some ninety antitrust cases; supported the Sixteenth and Seventeenth amendments, the Children's Bureau, and the Mann-Elkins Act; and reserved many forest lands for public use.

3. Progressive Republicans were unhappy over the Ballinger-Pinchot affair.

4. Socialist Eugene V. Debs, Bull Moose Roosevelt, Republican Taft, and Democrat Woodrow Wilson.

5. He created the Federal Trade Commission, supported the Clayton Antitrust Act, lowered tariffs, and appointed reformist lawyer Louis Brandeis to the Supreme Court.

6. Answers will vary. Some students may agree that they deserved the name; others may argue that progressives did not believe in progress for all people.

7. Possible answer: The progressive movement was not a single-minded entity, but comprised diverse groups. No single political party, therefore, could hope to capture the loyalty of all progressives.

Reteach

Ask students to identify the leader described in the statements below.
● Although he chose not to run for President in 1908, he ran as a third-party candidate in 1912.
● This Democrat won the election of 1912.
● He began the practice of separating the races in federal offices.

4. CLOSE

Reinforcing the Big Idea

Although some progressives formed their own political party, Republican President Taft and Democratic President Wilson continued the flow of progressive reforms. The next section discusses a turning point in American life: women's suffrage.

TOOLBOX

Critical Thinking

Testing Conclusions

Focus Students test the validity of conclusions by checking to see if they are supported by known data.

Instruct Divide students into groups and ask each group to decide what kind of data they would need to test the validity of the following conclusions, each made by a prominent historian:

"The United States has had the bloodiest and most violent labor history of any industrial nation in the world." (Philip Taft and Philip Ross)

"The railroads. . . gave an enormous stimulus to industrial growth." (Page Smith)

"A good index of the industrial development of the Middle West is the rise of ship tonnage passing through the 'Soo' [Sault Ste. Marie] Canal between Lakes Superior and Huron." (Samuel Eliot Morison)

Compare responses from different groups.

Extend See the Historian's Toolbox Activity in the Resource Directory below.

Answers

1. (a) The work force, labor union membership, and earnings between 1900 and 1920. (b) Yes, the conclusions appear to be based on the data provided.

2. (a) Conclusion 1 requires data over a period of time because it is based on a trend. (b) no

3. (a) contradict (b) It is not valid—more information is needed. While students can conclude that builders had more union members than the other industries shown, they cannot conclude that builders had more union members than any other industry. (c) No. No data is given that indicates the earnings that were lost due to work stoppages. Therefore, conclusion 4 is not a valid conclusion.

Testing Conclusions

Testing conclusions means checking statements or opinions to see whether or not they are supported by known data. Data that is known to be valid can be used as criteria for testing a conclusion. If the data supports the conclusion, then you have reason to believe that the conclusion is sound. Use the following steps to test the validity of conclusions.

1. Study the conclusions to recognize the type of data that is necessary to verify them. If supporting data is provided, decide if it is useful for testing the conclusions. Read the conclusions at right, examine the data in the tables, and answer the following questions: (a) Upon what information are the conclusions based? (b) Is there a relationship between the conclusions and the evidence provided?

2. Decide on the criteria by which the conclusions could be tested most effectively. Some conclusions are based upon trends and must be tested against data that covers a period of time. Other conclusions are more specific and may need exact data for verification. (a) Does conclusion 1 deal with a trend or with a specific point in time? (b) Would data covering a period of time be needed to support conclusion 2?

3. Test the conclusions by comparing them with the data. Decide if the data supports or contradicts the conclusions and whether additional information is needed to determine the validity of some conclusions. (a) Do the facts support or contradict conclusion 3? (b) According to the data, is conclusion 5 valid or not? Why? (c) Do you agree with conclusion 4? Explain.

Conclusions:

1. The twenty-year period between 1900 and 1920 saw a steady and significant growth in union membership.
2. By 1920, union workers earned more money than nonunion workers while working fewer hours.
3. In terms of a percent of the work force, more workers were union members in 1910 than in 1920.
4. The reason why the vast majority of workers did not join labor unions in the early 1900s was that work stoppages led to pay stoppages and decreased earnings.
5. In 1900 builders claimed more union members than any other industry.

Work Force and Labor Union Membership			
Year	Total Workers	Total Union Membership	Percentage of Work Force in Unions
1900	29,073,000	868,000	3.0
1910	37,371,000	2,140,000	5.7
1920	42,434,000	5,048,000	11.9

Union Membership by Industry			
Year	Building	Textiles	Public Service
1900	153,000	8,000	15,000
1910	459,000	21,000	58,000
1920	888,000	149,000	161,000

Average Union and Nonunion Hours and Earnings in Manufacturing Industries				
	Union		Nonunion	
Year	Weekly Hours	Hourly Earnings	Weekly Hours	Hourly Earnings
1900	53.0	$0.341	62.1	$0.152
1910	50.1	$0.403	59.8	$0.188
1920	45.7	$0.884	53.5	$0.561

Source: *Historical Statistics of the United States*

 ## RESOURCE DIRECTORY

Teaching Resources

Historian's Toolbox Activity Testing Conclusions, found in the Unit 6 folder, p. 58, provides further practice in interpreting quantitative data to examine conclusions.

Suffrage at Last:
A Turning Point in History

SECTION PREVIEW

With a long, bitter campaign, women finally won the right to vote—and at the same time they demonstrated their skills as organizers and activists.

Key Concepts
- The quest for woman suffrage took more than seventy years and required great effort.
- The earliest victories for suffrage took place at the state level, and mostly in the western states.
- The campaign experienced internal division before finally achieving victory.

Key Terms, People, and Places
Carrie Chapman Catt, Alice Paul

I n August 1920, Tennessee's state legislature faced a tough issue. Thirty-five states had voted to ratify the Nineteenth Amendment, which established national woman suffrage. By the terms of the Constitution, the measure needed the approval of one more state in order to win ratification. Would Tennessee be the "perfect thirty-sixth"?

Gathered in the state capitol, the all-male Tennessee legislature made a rowdy spectacle. Despite prohibition, liquor flowed freely. Rumors of vote-buying circulated. Those on the suffrage side, the "suffs," wore yellow roses in their lapels. The "antis," or antisuffragists, wore red.

Both sides had supporters in hotels across the street. Suffrage leader Carrie Chapman Catt directed the lobbying effort for the suffs. "I've been here a month," she wrote a friend on August 15. "It is hot, muggy, nasty, and this last battle is desperate. . . . Even if we win, we who have been here will never remember it with anything but a shudder."

The Tennessee senate passed the amendment easily, voting 25 to 4. But the state house of representatives was bitterly divided. For day after sweltering day, the women and men who had fought for or against this moment anxiously followed every debate, every strategic move. Before learning the outcome, a review of the events preceding it will put the moment in perspective.

Suffrage at the Turn of the Century

Seventy-two years had passed since the 1848 meeting in Seneca Falls, New York, when activists formally demanded the vote for women. The struggle had cost a great deal of personal energy and money. People had grown old and died in the movement.

Divisions had plagued suffrage activists throughout. The movement had split in 1869 over different approaches to the goal. In 1890 a younger generation of leaders reconciled competing groups to form a united organization, the National American Woman Suffrage Association (NAWSA). ⭐

Women's Rights By the time of NAWSA's founding, women had won many rights. For example, married women could now buy, sell, and will property. Yet many challenges remained. Legal attempts to win suffrage had failed (see "History Might Not Have Happened This Way," a feature on *Minor* v. *Happersett*, pages 486–487). Perhaps more troubling to suffrage workers were the widely held attitudes about women and their proper

This deck of playing cards promotes the battle for woman suffrage—a battle that finally ended in 1920.

1. FOCUS

Connecting to the Big Idea

See page 520B. Women won the right to vote in 1920 after a long, bitter fight. Ask students how the suffrage campaign achieved success.

Objectives
- Describe the long campaign and great effort required to achieve women's suffrage.
- Identify the earliest victories for suffrage as occurring at the state level, mostly in western states.
- Describe the internal division in the campaign before victory was achieved.

Bellringer

Ask students if they intend to vote at every opportunity after they reach the age of eighteen. How would they feel if a constitutional amendment raised the minimum voting age to twenty-five?

Reading Strategy

Reinforcing Key Ideas Ask students to note these sentences on page 543: "Woman suffrage was not granted to women. They fought for it, long and hard." As they read, students should list and briefly describe the ways women fought for the right to vote.

📄 **Reproducible Lesson Plan** found in the Unit 6 folder, p. 41, provides a summary of the Section 4 lesson plan content.

📄 **Alternate Lesson Plan: Learning Styles** found in the Alternate Lesson Plans folder, p. 98, is especially suited for visual learners, encouraging students to think about the campaign for women's suffrage by creating slogans and posters for a demonstration.

📄 **Guided Reading and Review** found in the Unit 6 folder, p. 48, provides a structure for reading and mastering the key concepts and reviewing the key terms for Section 4. (Guided Practice)

⭐ 📄 **Literature Activity** The "New" Woman, found in the Unit 6 folder, p. 65, provides insight into the psychological and social oppression of women at the turn of the century with excerpts from Kate Chopin's novel, *The Awakening*.

Answer to ...

MAKING   CONNECTIONS

Possible answer: In spite of the fact that they did not enjoy suffrage, women were able to wield considerable political power through their involvement in various groups and causes.

2. INSTRUCT

Explain/Discuss

Explain to students that many progressives wanted women to vote because they thought that women would support reform measures. Ask students how the passage of prohibition affected the cause of women's suffrage?

Ask students to compare the tactics favored by Catt and the NAWSA with those adopted by Paul and the CU. How did the actions of both groups help the cause? Read students the following comment from a 1974 interview with Alice Paul, then eighty-nine years old: "I always feel . . . the movement is a sort of mosaic. Each of us puts in one little stone, and then you get a great mosaic at the end." (Quoted in Garraty, John A., ed. *Historical Viewpoints,* Vol. II. Harper & Row, 1983, p. 195.)

Analyze

Ask students to list arguments used against women's suffrage. Then ask for volunteers to refute each of the arguments.

Activity

Make a Time Line
Ask students to make a time line that shows the major events in the campaign for women's suffrage. Time lines should start in 1848 and end in 1920.

Caption Answer to ...

Using Historical Evidence

That the vote would cause women to misplace their attention and would undermine their childrearing role.

social roles. When lawyer Myra Bradwell of Chicago was denied a state license to practice law in 1869, she took her case to the Supreme Court. In *Bradwell* v. *Illinois* (1873), the Court upheld the denial, reaffirming the "wide difference in the respective spheres and destinies of man and woman." Although Illinois had given Bradwell her license by 1890, for most Americans, woman's proper sphere remained the home, not the workplace.

By 1900, however, even larger numbers of traditional women were feeling justified in demanding the vote. Many women were participating in voluntary organizations that were investigating social conditions, publicizing their findings, suggesting reforms, lobbying officials, and monitoring enforcement of new laws. Working women were becoming more active in unions, picketing, and getting arrested. To

Using Historical Evidence Antisuffragists argued that suffragists were fooling themselves by expecting the vote to lead to fulfillment. *What does this cartoon suggest about how the vote would affect women?*

many of these women, it seemed ridiculous to deny women the vote with arguments about "woman's proper sphere."

The Opposition Mobilizes As the suffrage movement became more energetic, an antisuffrage movement mobilized. Antis made two basic arguments. The first was that women were powerful enough without the vote. The second was the old notion that giving women the vote would blur the distinctions between the sexes and make women more masculine. Suffrage opponents also included liquor interests, who assumed that women voters would quickly establish prohibition.

MAKING   CONNECTIONS

Consider what you read in Section 2 about the role of women in the progressive era. How does this information relate to the antisuffrage argument that women had enough power without the vote?

Suffragist Strategies

Suffragists followed two paths toward their goal. One path was to press for a constitutional amendment. The most commonly used method of amending the Constitution required two thirds of each house of Congress to pass a measure, which then had to be ratified by three fourths of the state legislatures.

The other path pursued by suffragists was to get individual states to permit women to vote. At first this approach was more successful (see the map on page 543), especially in the western states. There, survival on the frontier depended on the combined efforts of men and women—and thus encouraged a greater sense of equality.

Pushing for a federal amendment proved the more difficult approach. First introduced in Congress in 1868, a proposed amendment stalled. In 1878 it adopted the wording of suffrage leader Susan B. Anthony: "The right of citizens of the United States to vote shall not be denied or abridged by the United States or by any state on account of sex." With this language, the

▶ RESOURCE DIRECTORY

Teaching Resources

Viewpoints Activity On the Nineteenth Amendment, found in the Unit 6 folder, pp. 56–57, offers several contemporary arguments for and against women's suffrage.

proposed amendment received its first committee hearing. Elizabeth Cady Stanton described the experience:

*I*n the whole course of our struggle for equal rights, I never felt more exasperated than on this occasion, standing before a committee of men many years my junior, all comfortably seated in armchairs.

The chair of the committee, Senator Wadleigh of New Hampshire, was a picture of "inattention and contempt." "He stretched, yawned, gazed at the ceiling, cut his nails, sharpened his pencil, changing his occupation and position every two minutes."

Stalled again, the bill was not debated until 1887. It was then defeated in the Senate by a vote of 16 for, 34 against, and 26 absent. Supporters reintroduced the "Anthony Amendment," as the bill came to be called, every year until 1896. Then it disappeared, and did not resurface again until 1913.

The Movement Heats Up in the 1910s At the turn of the century, the idea of votes for women had become more acceptable to a wider proportion of the population. Prominent and working women supported it. Increasing numbers of men supported it. But the suffrage movement itself was in the doldrums. New leadership and new techniques were desperately needed to give it added momentum.

One of these new leaders was **Carrie Chapman Catt,** a former high school principal and superintendent of schools in Mason City, Iowa. A talented speaker and organizer, she headed NAWSA from 1900 to 1904, and then again after 1915. Catt systematized NAWSA techniques, insisting on close, precinct-by-precinct political work.

Alice Paul also came on the scene. She had experienced the aggressive English suffrage movement while she was a student in England. In January 1913, she and a friend, Lucy Burns, took over the NAWSA committee that was supposed to work on congressional passage of the federal amendment.

Two months later, the two women had organized a parade of five thousand women in Washington, D.C. Taking place on the day before Woodrow Wilson's inauguration, it drew so much attention that, when Wilson arrived at the train station, no crowd was there to greet him. Flushed with success, Paul transformed her committee into a new organization, the Congressional Union (CU).

A Collision over Strategy At this point, division tore the movement in two. Paul's CU called for an all-out national campaign for the constitutional amendment. She planned to enter different states, bypass the suffrage organizations there, and set up new ones.

The leadership of NAWSA felt that Paul's actions were premature, and in February 1914 expelled her group from the organization. When Paul adopted aggressive, militant protests—demonstrating in front of the White House, burning copies of President Wilson's speeches and even a life-size dummy made to look like Wilson—all attempts at smoothing

Viewpoints
On the Nineteenth Amendment

Woman suffrage had been a subject of debate in the United States since the mid-1800s. In the early 1900s, that debate heated up. *Summarize the arguments presented in the viewpoints below.*

Pro-Woman Suffrage
"The great doctrine of the American Republic that 'all governments derive their just powers from the consent of the governed' justifies the plea of one-half of the people, the women, to exercise the suffrage. The doctrine of the American Revolutionary War that taxation without representation is unendurable justifies women in exercising the suffrage."
Robert L. Owen, senator from Oklahoma, 1910

Anti-Suffrage
"In political warfare, it is perfectly fitting that actual strife and battle should be apportioned [given out] to man, and that the influence of woman, radiating from the homes of our land, should inspire to lofty aims and purposes those who struggle for the right. I am thoroughly convinced that woman can in no better way than this usefully serve the cause of political betterment."
Grover Cleveland, "Would Woman Suffrage Be Unwise?"
Ladies' Home Journal, October 1905

In Depth
Biography

Born into slavery, Ida Bell Wells-Barnett (1862–1931) founded what was probably the first African American women's suffrage group, Chicago's Alpha Suffrage Club. As a journalist she was a strident crusader against the lynching of African Americans in the South, and in 1909 she helped organize the National Association for the Advancement of Colored People (NAACP). Her memoirs, *Crusade for Justice,* were published posthumously in 1970.

Media and Technology

Visions of America: Turning Point Story To enhance students' understanding of the Turning Point topic in this section, play "Sister Suffragette," a story about the beginnings of the women's rights movement (length: approx. 4 minutes). This selection can be located on side 2 of the videodiscs. This selection can also be located on videotape 3. Lesson plans for Turning Point stories can be found in the Visions of America Guidebook.

Visions of America: Roundtable Discussion To introduce students to different and differing viewpoints on the Turning Point topic in this section, play all or part of the Roundtable Discussion on "Sister Suffragette," remarks by respected historians and social commentators. This selection can be located on side 2 of the videodiscs. This selection can also be located on videotape 3.

Section 4 Review Answers

1. (a) Carrie Chapman Catt, see p. 541, (b) Alice Paul, see p. 541

2. Tennessee was the thirty-sixth state to ratify women's suffrage. Under the Constitution, three fourths of the states (forty-eight at that time) had to approve suffrage in order for the Nineteenth Amendment to be ratified.

3. One strategy was to win suffrage for women in individual states. Another was to work for a constitutional amendment.

4. They felt that women had enough political power without the vote, and they worried that the vote would blur distinctions between men and women.

5. A number of states had enacted women's suffrage, increasing the political pressure; World War I demonstrated women's many contributions; and the fact that prohibition had already been passed meant that liquor interests no longer opposed votes for women.

6. They fought long and hard for it. Since announcing it as a goal in 1848, women waged hundreds of campaigns and spent countless hours lobbying legislators for state constitutional amendments and the federal amendment. They were not successful until 1920.

7. In both cases, women won the vote for making contributions to society that were similar in nature to those made by men.

A journalist covering a suffrage march in New York City in 1912 described "women striding five abreast" up Fifth Avenue. Such colorful parades became a favorite technique of suffragists in the 1910s.

"The question of woman suffrage is a very simple one," said Carrie Chapman Catt (left) in 1901. "The plea is dignified, calm, and logical."

over their differences failed. When CU members ended up in jail for their demonstrations, went on hunger strikes over prison conditions, and then were force-fed, NAWSA condemned them, not their treatment.

NAWSA's state campaigns continued. Hopes had centered on four eastern states, New York, Pennsylvania, Massachusetts, and New Jersey. In 1915 the suffrage campaigns failed in all four. At that point, Catt was put back at NAWSA's helm and was given free rein to bring about victory. Out of this challenge came her "Winning Plan."

This plan consisted of developing a large troop of totally committed, full-time leaders to work in "red-hot" campaigns for six years. The days of amateur dabbling were over. In addition, NAWSA decided to focus on getting Congress to propose the federal amendment.

By 1917, NAWSA had two million members. It was the largest voluntary organization in the country. In the fall, New York state finally voted in woman suffrage, raising to 172 the number of electoral votes from states with woman suffrage.

Impact of the War The United States entered World War I in April 1917. As women hastened to do their patriotic duty—volunteering for ambulance corps and medical work and taking up jobs left by men— their accomplishments came into the public eye. Talk about separate spheres for women and men seemed even more ridiculous. Moreover, in the spirit of national sacrifice inspired by the war, Congress adopted the prohibition amendment (the Eighteenth Amendment). Liquor interests no longer had reason to fight suffrage.

The Final Victory for Suffrage

In 1918 Congress formally proposed the suffrage amendment. Its members finally succumbed to the political forces of states that had passed suffrage and to the unrelenting work of NAWSA. They also had been keenly embarrassed and disturbed by the treatment the women of Paul's CU had received in jail.

Following the proposal of the amendment in Congress came the ratification battle. It would end in Tennessee.

Ratification Harry Burn, the Tennessee legislature's youngest member, had originally lined up with the antis. At the last moment he received a letter from his widowed mother. "Don't forget to be a good boy and help Mrs. Catt put the 'rat' in ratification," she wrote.

In deciding to vote "yes" for his mother, Burn broke a tie in the House. Realizing this, the speaker (an anti) voted *for* suffrage, and then called to reconsider the entire vote. (According to the legislature's rules, only by voting for a bill could a member move to

RESOURCE DIRECTORY

Teaching Resources

Visual Learning Activity When Women Have Rights found in the Unit 6 folder, p. 67, uses a 1913 cartoon to illustrate the antisuffrage argument that granting women the vote would make them more masculine.

reconsider it.) With this tactical move, the speaker hoped to gain time to rally the opposition.

The antis then took a daring step. They reasoned that if they left the capitol, the legislature would no longer have a quorum—the minimum number of members legally necessary to hold a vote. A large group of antis took a train to Alabama. The strategy backfired, however. When the house next met, the speaker claimed there was no quorum. But prosuffrage legislators held that the speaker was in violation of the rules and sent the suffrage bill to the governor.

On August 24, Tennessee's governor signed the suffrage bill. The news was rushed to Washington, D.C., and on August 26, the Nineteenth Amendment was declared ratified.

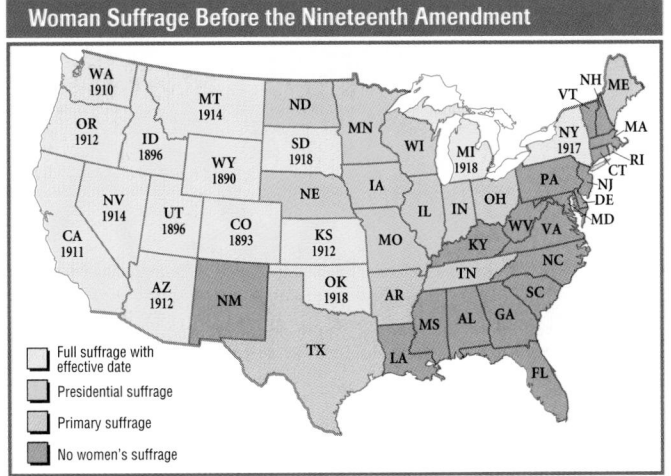

Woman Suffrage Before the Nineteenth Amendment

Full suffrage with effective date
Presidential suffrage
Primary suffrage
No women's suffrage

 Geography and History: Interpreting Maps
Suffrage was already a reality in many states by the time of the Nineteenth Amendment's ratification. *What pattern do you notice in the locations of states that did and did not pass suffrage at the state level?*

A Hard-Won Victory Woman suffrage was not granted to women. They fought for it, long and hard. When it was all over, Catt tried to calculate the effort. She counted

fifty-six campaigns of referenda to male voters; 480 campaigns to get Legislatures to submit suffrage amendments to voters; 47 campaigns to get State constitutional conventions to write woman suffrage into state constitutions; 277 campaigns to get State party conventions to include woman suffrage planks; 30 campaigns to get presidential party conventions to adopt woman suffrage planks in party platforms, and 19 campaigns with 19 successive Congresses.

Imagine the triumphant feelings after such an effort! Imagine, also, the bitterness at how long it had taken and the exhaustion of many women at its end. As Carrie Chapman Catt commented when the fight was all over, "It is doubtful that any man . . . ever realized what the suffrage struggle came to mean to women, . . . It leaves its mark on one, such a struggle."

The ratification of the Nineteenth Amendment marked the last major reform of the progressive era and was a turning point in American history. With suffrage finally won, women activists looked forward to a host of new battles in the long and difficult struggle to achieve true equality for women.

SECTION 4 REVIEW

Key Terms, People, and Places
1. Identify (a) Carrie Chapman Catt, (b) Alice Paul.

Key Concepts
2. What is the significance of the phrase "the perfect thirty-sixth"?
3. What were the two main strategies of the suffrage movement during the late 1800s and early 1900s?
4. On what grounds did people resist suffrage?

5. What factors finally turned the tide for suffrage?
6. Why is it incorrect to say that the vote was granted to women?

Critical Thinking
7. **Recognizing Ideologies** Recall what you have read about the reasons for the passage of suffrage in the West and at the national level. In the end, what seemed to "prove" women's fitness to vote?

 Quiz found in the Unit 6 folder, p. 49, covers the main ideas in this section as well as the key terms.

 Chapter Test Forms A and B are found in the Unit 6 folder, pp. 68–73.

 Answer Keys found in the Unit 6 folder, pp. 116–126, provide answers to all student activities.

Media and Technology

Transparency
Graphic Organizer, G-3

Guided Reading Audiotapes
(English and Spanish)

Computer Test Bank

Caption Answer to . . .

Interpreting Maps

Suffrage had been passed throughout nearly all of the West. The South and southeast, however, did not support it.

Reteach
Ask students to read and correct the following statements and to cite evidence from the text to support their correction.
• The campaign for suffrage began in 1920.
• Alice Paul founded the National American Woman Suffrage Association.
• Supporters of prohibition tended to oppose suffrage.
• The first states in which women won the right to vote were large eastern states.
• Predictions of a coming world war helped the passage of the suffrage amendment.

4. CLOSE

 Reinforcing the Big Idea
The campaign for women's suffrage in the United States was a long, hard struggle. The passage of the Nineteenth Amendment marks a turning point in American history.

The Lasting Impact of the Nineteenth Amendment

Focus In 1920 women won the vote. What has been the lasting impact of women's suffrage?

Instruct After students have read the feature, ask them to state the immediate results of the Nineteenth Amendment. Then ask them to list some of the long-term results of women's suffrage.

Discuss with students the great advantage the vote gave women in working for equality in other arenas such as careers, unions, and academic institutions.

Ask students to discuss why there is no consistent women's bloc among voters. Why do women vote along party lines rather than uniting as a political force?

Present students with the following quotations about the movement for women's rights. Ask students to guess the year each statement was made:

"NOW is a new national organization and has been formed 'To take action to bring women into full participation in the mainstream of American society NOW, exercising all the privileges and responsibilities thereof in equal partnership with men.'" (1966— National Organization for Women.)

"There are many discriminations in the laws against women. The discriminations show the need for the proposed equal rights amendment.

"The woman, even in the home— that place so often designated as her 'appropriate sphere'—does not share equally in the husband's authority." (1931—Testimony before the Senate of Burnita Matthews, chairwoman of the National Woman's Party Lawyer's Council.)

"The world will talk to you about the duties of wives & mothers & housekeepers, but all these incidental relations should ever be subordinated to the greater fact of womanhood. You may never be wives, or mothers, or housekeepers, but you will be women, therefore labor for the grander, more universal fact of your

The Lasting Impact of the Nineteenth Amendment

The passage of woman suffrage was a turning point not just for American women but for men as well. Women's admittance into full citizenship (or almost full—some important rights remained to be won) changed everyone's lives, forever. After suffrage, women did not bring about dramatic improvements in American political and social life, and they made few inroads into political office until many decades later. But at least women now had the dignity of individual citizenship. Thus, suffrage is a central part of the larger story of the nation's gradual achievement of its democratic promise.

Concrete Impact Of course, the women's vote did have more than a symbolic impact. Although many doors remained closed to women for years to come,

the vote opened political and occupational opportunities previously unavailable to them. Women became eligible for posts within national party organizations, and public recognition and acceptance of women as professionals grew.

In addition, those who had been involved in the struggle were changed forever. Through participating in social reform movements, they had learned how to influence the making of social and public policy. The suffrage battle further honed their skills and made many of them even more aggressive in working for change. This experience helped women secure passage and state-by-state implementation of the Sheppard-Towner Act (1921), which allocated federal money for prenatal and infant health care. Later, women activists helped lead the fight for the repeal of prohibition.

1920 Suffragists celebrate ratification of the Nineteenth Amendment by painting in Tennessee on their suffrage map.

1933 Frances Perkins becomes the first woman to hold a cabinet post when Franklin Delano Roosevelt appoints her secretary of labor.

| 1900 | 1920 | 1940 |

1942 Women workers fill the nation's factories, making the planes, tanks, and other goods that help the United States win World War II.

SOLDIERS *without guns*

 RESOURCE DIRECTORY

Turning Points Extension Activity
The Lasting Impact of the Nineteenth Amendment found in the Unit 6 folder, pp. 50–51, provides a strategy for groups of students to explore gender equality issues that have been prominent in the public sphere since passage of the Nineteenth Amendment.

Continuing Divisions Another legacy of the suffrage movement was conflict. Almost immediately following the passage of the Nineteenth Amendment, the divisions over tactics that had marked the final years of the suffrage battle surfaced again. Alice Paul was less interested in pursuing the reforms of the progressive era than in achieving complete legal equality with men. In 1923 her National Woman's party launched a new constitutional amendment campaign, this time for an Equal Rights Amendment (ERA) that would make women and men equal before the law.

Because of the potential of ERA to make illegal all the protective legislation for working women that progressive reformers had struggled for since the 1890s, many former suffragists opposed it. The League of Women Voters, the successor organization to NAWSA, led the opposition of many women's groups, including the Women's Trade Union League and Florence Kelley's Consumers' League.

The struggle over ERA tore apart what remained of the suffrage movement in the 1920s. Although the two sides cooperated on some legislation, such as winning the right to jury service for women, for the most part they stood on opposite sides for several decades. It was only with the renewed women's movement of the 1960s and 1970s that the issue was resolved among those who worked for feminist causes. Even then, however, the rest of the nation was opposed to an ERA and refused to ratify it.

REVIEWING THE FACTS

1. In what sense was the Nineteenth Amendment a *symbolic* victory for the American people?
2. In what sense was the Nineteenth Amendment a *concrete* victory?

Critical Thinking

3. **Making Comparisons** Compare the divisions of the women's movement before and after suffrage.

1972 Congress passes the Equal Rights Amendment, touching off an unsuccessful ratification battle across the United States.

1992 Carol Mosely Braun becomes the first African American woman elected to the United States Senate. She is one of five women elected to the Senate that November.

| 1960 | 1980 | 2000 |

The famous bestseller that ignited women's liberation

BETTY FRIEDAN

THE FEMININE MYSTIQUE

1963 Feminist Betty Friedan's groundbreaking book The Feminine Mystique *helps inspire a new generation of women activists in the 1960s and beyond.*

existence." (*1870s*—Elizabeth Cady Stanton, lecture.)

(All quoted in Papachristou, Judith, ed. *Women Together: A History in Documents of the Women's Movement in the United States.* A Ms. Book, 1976.)

After students have heard all three quotes, ask them what generalizations they can make about the campaign for women's rights and the achievement of suffrage.

Extend Tell students that in 1902, Carrie Chapman Catt defined prejudice in her presidential address to the NAWSA:

"What is prejudice? An opinion, which is not based upon reason; a judgment, without having heard the argument; a feeling, without being able to trace from whence it came." (Quoted in Ravitch, Diane, ed. *The American Reader.* HarperCollins, 1990, p. 214.) Ask students in what way women defeated prejudice in 1920. What prejudices remain against women in American society?

Answers

1. Its passage did not have an immediate effect on the nature of American political and social life, or on the condition of women in the country.

2. The struggle to gain suffrage showed reformers, especially women, how they could influence social and public policy; suffrage opened the door a little further for women in politics and professions.

3. Before ratification of the amendment, the movement was divided over what kind of tactics to use to reach the common goal; after suffrage, the movement was divided over the goals themselves.

Chapter Review Answers

Understanding Key Terms, People, and Places

Terms

Students should refer to the definitions of the key terms in the chapter to write sentences that show the relation of each word to the era of progressive reform.

Matching

1. New Freedom
2. home rule
3. holding company
4. direct primary
5. arbitration

True or False

1. false, Florence Kelley
2. false, Edward Bellamy's
3. true

Reviewing Main Ideas

1. Bellamy proposed that government nationalize the nation's trusts and organize industry to meet human needs rather than to make a profit. Socialists similarly wanted to end capitalism, distribute wealth more equally, and nationalize industry.

2. Progressives valued the high standard of living and personal liberty of the free enterprise system. However, they wanted to change the unfair aspects of the system.

3. Progressives typically studied a social problem using scientific methods. Then they publicized their results to put pressure on lawmakers. Muckraking journalists helped publicize many progressive causes.

4. State reformers aimed at making government more responsive and efficient, for example, through direct primaries. They also championed labor and factory legislation. Urban reformers attacked political machines, took over utilities, and expanded welfare services.

5. The alliance accomplished many improvements in urban life, such as public health programs and enforcement of tenement codes.

6. TR went after certain "bad" trusts and sought to conserve the nation's natural resources. The federal government also established the Women's Bureau and the Children's Bureau.

Chapter Review

Understanding Key Terms, People, and Places

Key Terms
1. home rule
2. progressivism
3. social welfare program
4. muckraker
5. direct primary

6. arbitration
7. holding company
8. New Nationalism
9. Bull Moose party
10. New Freedom

People
11. Henry George
12. Edward Bellamy
13. Florence Kelley
14. Carrie Chapman Catt
15. Alice Paul

Terms For each term above, write a sentence that explains its relation to the era of progressive reform.

Matching Review the key terms in the list above. If you are not sure of a term's meaning, review its definition in the chapter. Then choose a term from the list that best matches each description below.

1. Woodrow Wilson's policy in which he promised to enforce antitrust laws without threatening free economic competition
2. the system under which cities exercise a limited degree of self-government
3. a corporation that owns the stocks and bonds of numerous companies
4. an election in which voters cast ballots to select nominees for upcoming elections
5. a process in which an impartial third party decides on a legally binding solution to a dispute

True or False Determine whether each statement is true or false. If it is true, write "true." If it is false, change the underlined name to make the statement true.

1. Under the leadership of <u>Edward Bellamy,</u> the National Consumers' League spearheaded national movements to outlaw child labor and protect workers.
2. In <u>Henry George's</u> novel, a man undergoes hypnosis and wakes up in the year 2000 to find the United States transformed.
3. The National American Woman Suffrage Association believed that the tactics of <u>Alice Paul</u> in trying to win the vote for women were too extreme.

Reviewing Main Ideas

Section 1 (pp. 522–526)
1. What reform programs did Edward Bellamy envision and how were they similar to the widely discussed ideas of socialism?
2. What did progressives see as good about the United States? What did they want to reform?
3. What were the typical methods of progressive reformers?

Section 2 (pp. 527–531)
4. Briefly describe progressive reforms at the state and municipal levels.
5. What did the alliance of progressive reformers and political machines accomplish?
6. Briefly describe progressive reforms at the national level.

Section 3 (pp. 534–537)
7. Briefly describe the successes and failures of the Taft presidency.
8. Why did progressivism—with the exception of the suffrage movement—come to an end?

Section 4 (pp. 539–543)
9. After the victory for woman suffrage, Carrie Chapman Catt made a count of the campaigns that achieved passage of the Nineteenth Amendment. What does her tally reveal?
10. Where did campaigns to achieve suffrage first meet with success?
11. How did the Congressional Union (CU) and the National American Woman Suffrage Association (NAWSA) differ in their strategies?

7. Taft achieved many progressive goals, such as increased prosecution of antitrust cases. Yet he lost progressive support because of events such as the Ballinger-Pinchot affair and his failure to lower the tariff.

8. Preparations for war began to occupy the nation.

9. Her tally reveals the enormous hard work that it took to achieve suffrage.

10. Early campaigns met with the greatest success on the state level, mostly in the West, since survival there depended on the efforts of both men and women.

11. The CU's strategy, calling for an all-out campaign for a constitutional amendment, was more militant than that of NAWSA, which planned long-term (six-year) campaigns focused on getting Congress to propose the amendment.

Making Connections

1. The behavior of Senator Wadleigh and his committee suggests that they feel smug, bored, and sure that the amendment before them is unworthy of their attention. They have no interest in its passage.

Thinking Critically

1. **Drawing Conclusions** What does the profile of Florence Kelley reveal about progressive concerns and methods?

2. **Identifying Central Issues** What does the fate of Taft's presidency suggest about the nature of the presidency and presidential leadership?

3. **Demonstrating Reasoned Judgment** Progressives were sometimes criticized for being insensitive to the needs of the poor. Do you think that this criticism was justified?

Making Connections

1. **Evaluating Primary Sources** Review the primary source excerpts quoting Elizabeth Cady Stanton on page 541. What bias is revealed by the behavior of Senator Wadleigh and the other committee members?

2. **Understanding the Visuals** What visual evidence can you find in the chapter to indicate that the efforts of the progressive era have had a positive impact on the nation today?

3. **Writing About the Chapter** You are running for student council on the progressive ticket. Write a progressive campaign statement for your school. Before you begin, create a list of the goals of the progressive era. Decide which of them you can apply or adapt to your school. Consider any areas in which you feel progressivism failed, and suggest changes

you think are necessary. Next, write a draft of your statement in which you explain your ideas. Revise your statement, making certain that each idea is clearly explained. Proofread your statement and draft a final copy.

4. **Using the Graphic Organizer** This graphic organizer uses a tree map to organize information about progressivism's legislative impact at the city, state, and federal levels. (a) What do the three levels of government have in common in terms of the types of reforms undertaken? (b) What were the four general areas of reform on the federal level? (c) On a separate sheet of paper, create your own tree map about the national political impact of progressivism (section 3), using this graphic organizer as an example.

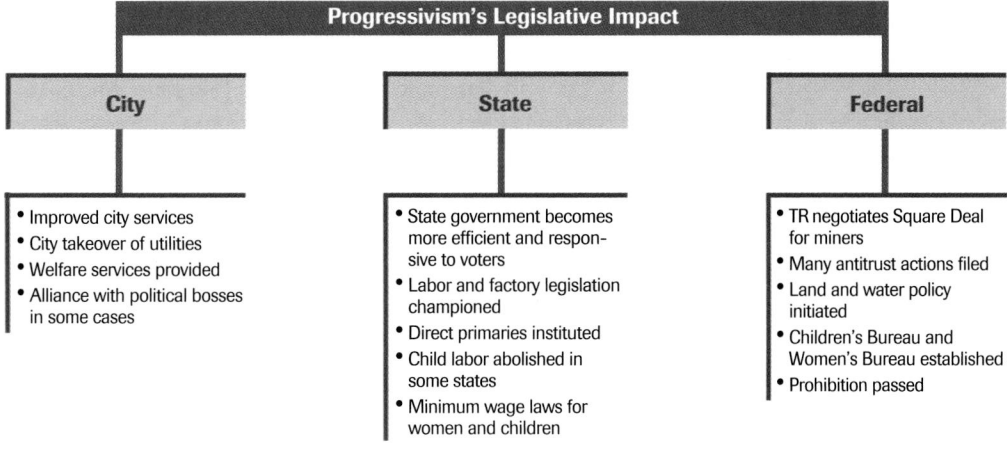

Progressivism's Legislative Impact

City	State	Federal
• Improved city services • City takeover of utilities • Welfare services provided • Alliance with political bosses in some cases	• State government becomes more efficient and responsive to voters • Labor and factory legislation championed • Direct primaries instituted • Child labor abolished in some states • Minimum wage laws for women and children	• TR negotiates Square Deal for miners • Many antitrust actions filed • Land and water policy initiated • Children's Bureau and Women's Bureau established • Prohibition passed

2. Possible answers: The chart on page 528 illustrates the initiative, referendum, and recall system, which gave voters greater power; Links Across Time on page 529 indicates improvements in worker protection; the table on page 531 summarizes the Sixteenth and Seventeenth amendments; the lithograph on page 537 depicts African American Booker T. Washington and white President Teddy Roosevelt sitting at a table called equality.

3. Statements should focus on reforms that guarantee greater equality and social welfare for students, show an awareness that progressivism failed to address the needs of some groups, such as African Americans, and include a strategy for avoiding these flaws.

4. (a) Each level focused on social welfare. (b) The four general areas of reform were labor and industrial relations, the regulation of business and commerce, the preservation of the environment, and social legislation. (c) Graphic organizers should contain information about the Taft presidency, the Bull Moose movement, and Wilson's attempts to continue progressivism.

 Alternative Assessment

Final Evaluation
Use the following guidelines to evaluate student projects:

• **Evidence of mastery of content** To what extent do essays show knowledge and understanding of chapter content?

• **Evidence of thoughtfulness** To what extent do essays show that students have formed an opinion about the goals of the progressives based on progressive actions?

• **Evidence of outside research** To what extent do projects use materials and information from outside research sources?

• **Communication style** Are the arguments clear and easy to follow?

Thinking Critically

1. The profile reveals Kelley's concerns about the general welfare of Americans, including child labor, consumers' rights, and workers' protection, especially for women. Kelley worked for reforms in a systematic manner, earning a law degree so that she could take legal action herself, and headed the consumers' leagues that investigated conditions under which goods were bought and sold.

2. Possible answer: Taft's fate suggests that a President must be able not only to achieve stated goals but to be perceived as an effective leader. Once a President loses political support, he is ineffective.

3. Possible answer: Some students might say that progressives worked to improve conditions for all people, and that they thus were not insensitive. Others might argue that progressive programs often hurt those they were designed to help, because progressives put their own goals ahead of the interests of the disadvantaged.

Chapter 20 The World War I Era
1914–1920

📁 Teaching Resources (See Unit 6 Folder)

	Instruction	Enrichment

Section 1
The Road to War
(pp. 550–553)
	Reproducible Lesson Plan, p. 75
	Alternate Lesson Plan, p. 100
	Guided Reading and Review, p. 80
	Quiz, p. 81
		Primary Source Activity, Thoughts on the War,
		  p. 96
		Historian's Toolbox Activity, Identifying
		  Alternatives, p. 94

Section 2
The United States Declares War
(pp. 555–558)
	Reproducible Lesson Plan, p. 76
	Alternate Lesson Plan, p. 101
	Guided Reading and Review, p. 82
	Quiz, p. 83
		Critical Thinking Activity, Identifying Central
		  Issues, p. 95
		Visual Learning Activity, Uncle Sam's Pledge,
		  p. 102
		American Profiles Activity, Jeannette Rankin,
		  p. 90

Section 3
Americans on the European Front
(pp. 559–563)
	Reproducible Lesson Plan, p. 77
	Alternate Lesson Plan, p. 102
	Guided Reading and Review, p. 84
	Quiz, p. 85
		Primary Source Activity, Women on the War
		  Front, p. 97
		Literature Activity, A War Song, p. 99
		American Profiles Activity, Henry Johnson,
		  p. 91
		Literature Activity, A Poet Describes War, p. 101

Section 4 **On the Home Front** (pp. 564–567)	Reproducible Lesson Plan, p. 78 Alternate Lesson Plan, p. 103 Guided Reading and Review, p. 86 Quiz, p. 87	Literature Activity, Selling the War, p. 100 Visual Learning Activity, Women's Roles in World War I, p. 103

Section 5
Global Peacemaker
(pp. 568–571)
	Reproducible Lesson Plan, p. 79
	Alternate Lesson Plan, p. 104
	Guided Reading and Review, p. 88
	Quiz, p. 89
	Chapter Test, Forms A & B, pp. 104–109
		Viewpoints Activity, On the League of Nations,
		  pp. 92–93
		Primary Source Activity, Mrs. Wilson's Role,
		  p. 98

📁 Additional Chapter Resources

Resource Organizer, p. 74
Alternate Lesson Plan, p. 99
Answer Keys, pp. 116–126

Bibliography

For the Teacher

American Heritage editors. *American Heritage History of World War I.* American Heritage, 1964. (Richly illustrated coverage of the war.)

Rickards, Maurice. *Posters of the First World War.* Evelyn, Adams & Mackay, 1968. (Recruitment and propaganda posters, organized by their country of origin.)

Tuchman, Barbara W. *Guns of August.* Macmillan, 1962. (Chronicle of the events that resulted in World War I.)

Prentice Hall Literature *The American Experience,* 1994, including Hemingway, Ernest. "In Another Country" from *Men Without Women.* Charles Scribner's Sons, 1927.

The Big Idea for the chapter and how the main ideas in each section relate to the Big Idea are graphically displayed below. Comprehension of this chapter's Big Idea is critical to students' understanding of United States history and how we as a nation got where we are today.

Media and Technology

 Cause and Effect, F-8

 The Way It Works, H-17

Critical Thinking, I-13

 Graphic Organizer, G-4

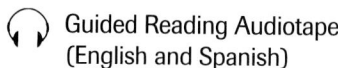 Guided Reading Audiotapes (English and Spanish)

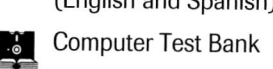 Computer Test Bank

For the Student

Remarque, Erich Maria. *All Quiet on the Western Front.* Fawcett, 1987. (Classic novel of the war from the German viewpoint; first published in 1929.)

Stallings, Laurence. *The Doughboys.* Harper & Row, 1963. (A first-person account of serving on the western front.)

Time-Life Books editors. *Time-Life Books: This Fabulous Century, Vol. 2. 1910-1920.* Time-Life, 1969. (Richly illustrated, comprehensive study of the era.)

CHAPTER 20

In the second decade of the twentieth century, a terrible war began in Europe, with the death toll eventually totaling an estimated eight million combatants—and many times more civilians. At first the United States vowed to maintain its neutrality. However, the nation finally declared war in order to support its allies and defend its commercial interests.

SECTION 1

When war broke out in Europe in 1914, the United States tried to maintain neutrality but also began to prepare for the possibility of war.

SECTION 2

Because of growing conflict between the two countries, the United States declared war on Germany and its allies to "make the world safe for democracy."

SECTION 3

Americans, serving in Europe in many capacities, helped the Allies to win the war.

SECTION 4

In its efforts to maintain order and preparedness during the war, the government took new responsibility for regulating the economy and controlling news and information. The government also repressed certain civil liberties for the sake of the war effort.

SECTION 5

The years immediately following the war were disillusioning for many Americans. Europeans rejected many of President Wilson's idealistic peace proposals, and he failed to secure Senate approval of the final treaty ending the war.

The World War I Era
1914-1920

The World War I Era
1914-1920

The conflict began with a few shots fired by a single assassin. Within months, much of Europe was at war. Most Americans were reluctant to get involved, but powerful forces—including German submarines and American commercial interests—pulled the nation into the battle. By 1917 United States soldiers had joined Europeans in the trenches and terrors of the war. When the guns finally quieted, President Wilson launched a campaign for a treaty and a new international organization that would prevent such a tragedy from ever happening again. Meanwhile, the American people struggled to make peace in their own minds with the horrors of the war.

OVER ★ THERE

The Relevance of the Big Idea

The United States had been reluctant to enter World War I at first but later became involved, along with other nations, in a war that began in the Balkan Peninsula. In the 1990s, war in the Balkans once more captured the attention of the world, and the role of the United States was again questioned.

Ask students to locate the Balkans on a map of the world. If they were advisers to the President of the United States, what role would they recommend for the United States? Discuss the pros and cons of United States policy in Bosnia-Herzegovina.

Events in the United States

| 1914 The United States declares itself officially neutral in World War I. | 1915 Jane Addams and Carrie Chapman Catt organize the Woman's Peace party. | 1916 Woodrow Wilson is reelected United States President on a peace platform. |

| 1913 | 1914 | 1915 | 1916 |

Events in the World

| 1914 The assassination of Archduke Francis Ferdinand sets off World War I. | 1915 German submarines sink the British Lusitania. |

In Depth

Global Connections

In 1918, a devastating, worldwide epidemic of influenza—the worst outbreak of disease since the Black Death more than five hundred years earlier—left some 20 million people dead, including more than 500,000 in the United States. All in all, the epidemic killed twice as many people in one year as did all four years of World War I.

RESOURCE DIRECTORY

Teaching Resources

Alternate Lesson Plan: Demonstrating the Big Idea found in the Alternate Lesson Plans folder, p. 99, provides a strategy to instruct students about the Big Idea that although initially neutral, the United States was drawn by various factors into World War I, affecting life at home in spite of America's distance from the battle front.

Alternative Assessment Handbook provides information, guidance, and strategies for alternative methods of assessment. It includes an essay on new trends in assessment, guidance and strategies for developing performance tasks and portfolios, scoring rubrics, and sample evaluation forms.

Pages 550–553
The Road to War
With the outbreak of war in Europe, Americans responded with claims of neutrality. Yet as the war dragged on, the need to defend American commercial and political interests drew the United States toward active involvement in the struggle.

 Pages 555–558
The United States Declares War
The United States struggled to avoid the horrors of World War I. But the nation could not prevent its slow slide into the conflict.

 Pages 559–563
Americans on the European Front
On entering the war, the United States saw itself merely as "associate" to the Allies. The Americans were quickly promoted to a leading role, however. Yankee soldiers and volunteers poured onto foreign battlefields and served nobly in many capacities.

 Pages 564–567
On the Home Front
World War I was fought at home, too. To win that war, the government took control of the economy—and of people's minds—to an extent never before attempted.

 Pages 568–571
Global Peacemaker
President Wilson's lofty vision for peace was brought back to earth by contentious allies and Congress. Meanwhile, many Americans experienced keen disappointment over postwar conditions at home.

1917 The United States enters World War I. • Congress passes the Selective Service Act.	1918 Congress passes the last of the Sedition and Espionage Acts. • President Wilson announces his peace plan.	1919 The states ratify the Eighteenth Amendment, prohibiting the manufacture and sale of alcohol.	1920 Warren G. Harding is elected United States President.
1917	**1918**	**1919**	**1920** **1921**
1917 The Russian Revolution ends the reign of the czars.	1918 Germany surrenders to the Allies. • Women over 30 win the right to vote in Britain.	1919 The Versailles Treaty marks the official end of World War I. • The Allies establish the League of Nations.	1920 Adolf Hitler helps organize the Nazi party in Germany.

Media and Technology
 Transparency
Time Lines, E-6

 Alternative Assessment

As an ongoing chapter project, students can prepare an in-depth essay or oral report describing a particular diplomatic, political, or military event of World War I and explain how the event affected life in the United States during that time.

Explain that finished projects will be assessed according to the following standards:

- **Unacceptable** Projects are not attempted, or fail to meet requirements outlined.
- **Limited/Acceptable** Projects are based on material from the textbook and attempt to explain the importance of the events to the United States.
- **Extensive/Commendable** Projects are based on some outside research and provide clear explanation of the importance of the event to the United States.
- **Extraordinary/Outstanding** Projects are based on considerable outside research and thoroughly explain the importance of the event to the United States.

For more information and guidance on alternative assessment trends and strategies, see the Alternative Assessment Handbook in the Resource Directory on page 548.

1. FOCUS

Connecting to the Big Idea

See page 548B. Explain that when war first broke out in Europe, most Americans wished to maintain strict neutrality. However, as the war continued, the United States moved toward more active involvement. Ask what prompted this change in direction.

Objectives

● Identify World War I as a conflict of global origins and dimensions.
● Describe the new weapons and military techniques used in the war.
● Explain how the United States responded to the war with calls for neutrality and for war preparedness.

Bellringer

Ask students to define the word *neutral*. Ask them to think of situations in which they chose to remain neutral and others in which they took a stand. What conditions encouraged them to take a stand rather than remain neutral?

Reading Strategy

Reading for Evidence Ask students to find evidence as they read the section that Americans responded to the war with "calls for neutrality and for war preparedness," as stated in the key concepts on page 550.

The Road to War

SECTION PREVIEW

With the outbreak of war in Europe, Americans responded with claims of neutrality. Yet as the war dragged on, the need to defend American commercial and political interests drew the United States toward active involvement in the struggle.

Key Concepts
• World War I was a conflict of global origins and dimensions.
• The war saw the introduction of destructive new weapons and techniques.
• Americans responded with calls for neutrality and for war preparedness.

Key Terms, People, and Places
Central Powers, Allies; Kaiser Wilhelm, autocrat

Soldiers in World War I wore gas masks such as this to protect themselves from poison gas, a horrible new weapon introduced in the war.

B y the early 1900s, war in Europe was hardly a new phenomenon. The Germans had fought often with France over Alsace-Lorraine, the coal- and iron-rich region near the border between the two countries. Austria-Hungary had fought to hold onto the many ethnic groups subject to its control. Russia's ancient quest for a warm-water port had led to frequent clashes on its frontiers. The French and British had warred repeatedly over territorial claims in Europe and in their colonies.

In 1914 all five of Europe's major powers went to war. The conflict—eventually known as World War I—divided them into two sides: Germany and Austria-Hungary made up the **Central Powers;** Russia, France, and Great Britain were called the **Allies.**

Archduke Francis Ferdinand: his assassination sparked the fighting.

Each side felt confident of swift victory. Six weeks, experts said, and it would all be over. The experts were wrong. Relatively equal in force and ability, the two sides quickly reached a bloody stalemate that would last more than four years and cost millions of lives.

What Caused World War I?

A complicated system of secret treaties had developed among the nations of Europe during the late nineteenth century. Designed to bolster each nation's security, the treaties bound the great powers to come to each other's aid in the event of attack. For many decades this system created a fragile balance of power that no nation dared disrupt. In 1914 the very system that had kept the peace led its creators into war.

The spark that ignited World War I was the June 28, 1914, assassination of the heir to the Austrian-Hungarian throne, Archduke Francis Ferdinand, and his wife, Sophie. They were gunned down during a visit to Sarajevo, the capital of Bosnia, a province within the Austrian-Hungarian Empire.

At the time of the assassinations, Bosnia was the focal point of a dispute between Austria-Hungary and the neighboring nation of Serbia. This dispute involved Serbia's efforts to achieve union with ethnic Serbs living in Bosnia by promoting Bosnian resistance to Austrian-Hungarian rule.

The Austrian-Hungarian government was convinced that Serbia was behind the assassinations, and used the event as an excuse to crush its small enemy. In late July Austria-Hungary insisted that Serbia apologize and made a number of other demands that interfered with Serbia's sovereignty. When Serbia refused to meet every one of the demands, Austria-Hungary declared war.

RESOURCE DIRECTORY

Teaching Resources

Reproducible Lesson Plan found in the Unit 6 folder, p. 75, provides a summary of the Section 1 lesson plan content.

Alternate Lesson Plan: Learning Styles found in the Alternate Lesson Plans folder, p. 100, helps students create a graphic organizer showing the steps leading to World War I and is particularly effective for visual learners.

Guided Reading and Review found in the Unit 6 folder, p. 80, provides a structure for reading and mastering the key concepts and reviewing the key terms for Section 1. (Guided Practice)

Primary Source Activity Thoughts on the War, found in the Unit 6 folder, p. 96, presents a passage written by Walter Hines Page, the United States ambassador to Great Britain, to show predictions about the consequences of World War I.

The Conflict Expands

The Austrian-Hungarian declaration of war set off a chain reaction that worked its way through Europe's complex web of alliances. Nation after nation became entangled. Serbia had the promise of protection from Russia, so Russia started amassing its troops. Two days later, Germany, Austria-Hungary's chief ally, demanded that Russia stop its mobilization. Russia refused. At that point, Russia's ally, France, began to ready its troops. Germany realized that soon it would be trapped between France attacking from the west and Russia from the east. So Germany too mobilized and, on August 1, declared war on Russia. Convinced that the French were ready to invade, Germany's military leaders decided to strike first. To reach France as fast as possible, however, they had to pass through Luxembourg and Belgium. This invasion brought Great Britain, Belgium's protector, into the conflict. A large proportion of the European continent was now at war.

Stalemate In earlier wars, a forceful offense led by a heroic cavalry often was enough to secure victory. Now, defensive forces could use modern firepower to stop such advances. In September 1914, German forces had advanced to within 30 miles of Paris. There, at the river Marne, a combined French and British force stopped their progress. Both sides then dug in. Holed up in a line of muddy, lice- and rat-infested trenches, the two sides faced each other across an empty "no man's land" (see the illustration on page 552). For months each side tried to reach the other's lines to destroy or at least push back the enemy. But neither side was able to gain more than a few miles, and that only at appalling human cost.

Meanwhile, an Austrian army was taking Belgrade, the Serbian capital. Combined German and Austrian-Hungarian forces were pushing the Russian lines back. At the end of 1914, the Ottoman Empire, centered in what is now Turkey, entered the war on the side of the Central Powers; and in the spring of 1915, Italy joined the Allies. Many more costly battles took place, but without significant gain for either side.

European Alliances in World War I

Geography and History: Interpreting Maps
Before the war, Europe was a land of empires and alliances. Thus when Austria-Hungary declared war on Serbia, much of the continent was drawn into the conflict. *Based on this map, which side, if any, had a geographical advantage in the war? Explain.*

Modern Warfare The number of soldiers killed or wounded was horrifying. Industrialization had produced new killing machines of terrible efficiency. In 1914 the youth of Europe had marched off to fight, eager for a chance at heroism. Ripped apart by machine guns, hand grenades, or artillery shells, and asphyxiated or disabled by poison gases, soldiers found that heroism came at a ghastly price.

"It was the machine gun that froze the front," one historian has written. If soldiers charging across no-man's land toward the enemy survived the shelling that rained down upon them, the enemy's machine guns, firing 450 rounds a minute, mowed them down. The generals, unaccustomed to the new weaponry, were confused. Again and again they gave the order to attack. But such tactics produced only a mounting pile of infantry dead. In one 1916 battle, for example, the British suffered 60,000 casualties in a single day of combat.

Morale sank. Desperate, troops began using any tactic available. They slaughtered prisoners of war. Erasing the distinction between soldier

Caption Answer to ...

 Interpreting Maps

Possible answer: The Allies had a geographical advantage because the Central Powers were nearly enveloped by enemy nations.

2. INSTRUCT

Explain/Discuss

Discuss the reasons why Serbia, Russia, Germany, France, Great Britain, and Austria-Hungary each became involved in the early days of the war. Then ask why the system of secret alliances that bound the nations of Europe to one another failed to maintain the peace. Ask in what way the system of alliances itself contributed to the war.

Discuss the possibility of being both neutral and prepared. Did building up arms and troops ensure that the United States would enter the war? Why or why not?

Analyze

Ask students to analyze why the United States was at first so removed from the conflict in Europe. Have students list the forces that beckoned the United States toward war and then to rank them in order of strength.

In Depth

Historical Misconceptions

Allied newspapers published graphic accounts of German atrocities in order to muster support. One common story was that German troops chopped off the hands of Belgian babies. After the war, when censorship was lifted, people learned that wartime propaganda had been efficient. Journalist William Shepherd reported: "I couldn't find atrocities. . . [or even] photographs of children whose hands had been cut off or who had been wounded or injured in other ways."

Activity

Cooperative Learning

Time: One class period.
Activity: Prepare a briefing book on the countries of Europe for President Wilson.
Grouping: Groups of four to six students with each group being the expert on one nation.
Purpose: To prepare a document describing the major nations of Europe in June 1914, including sections on the head of state and form of government; major geographical features; economy, including major projects and trade partners; military leaders; and ethnic and religious composition of the population. Each student should assume responsibility for one section of the document for the group's assigned nation.
Roles: Researchers, writers.
Outcome: Students will identify and outline significant information on each of the major powers of Europe at the onset of World War I.

Enrichment

Britain's Queen Victoria, who reigned from 1837 to 1901, has been called "Europe's grandmother" because so many monarchs were descended from her five children. Ask students to make a family tree tracing Victoria's descendants up to 1920. Ask them to highlight the names of the cousins who reigned during World War I.

Front-line Trench Warfare

No man's land	Support trench
XX Barbed wire	Reserve trench
Firing trench	Communications trench
Cover trench	

 Interpreting Charts
Trench networks allowed armies to fire on the enemy, get supplies and reinforcements, and find cover from enemy fire. But soldiers leaving the trench to press the battle faced deadly machine gun fire. *How did trench warfare contribute to a stalemate in World War I?*

and civilian, they burned fields and poisoned wells. On the seas, German submarines struck any ship they believed to be carrying arms to the Allies. A British naval blockade slowly starved the German people. Soon the war was one of attrition—meaning that each side tried to wear down the enemy gradually by inflicting enormous losses.

MAKING CONNECTIONS

The United States today has many security alliances that are similar to those that drew so many countries into World War I. Do you think the United States should be willing to fight to protect the interests of its allies?

The American Response

July 29: AUSTRIA DECLARES WAR, RUSHES VAST ARMY INTO SERBIA; RUSSIA MASSES 80,000 MEN ON BORDER

August 2: GERMANY DECLARES WAR ON RUSSIA; FRANCE PREPARES TO JOIN HER ALLY

Americans read these 1914 headlines with mounting alarm. How could all these great countries of beauty, taste, and culture be at war with one another?

Some Americans felt personally involved. More than a third of the nation's 92 million people were first- or second-generation immi-grants who still felt close ties to their old countries. About a quarter of these were German American, and another eighth were Irish American. Both groups harbored hostile feelings toward Great Britain due to past conflicts and the current war in Europe.

Most Americans favored the Allies, however. Germany, one of the Central Powers, was ruled by **Kaiser Wilhelm.** The Kaiser, or emperor, was an **autocrat**—a ruler with unlimited power. Americans saw the Germans as a people of frightening militarism and cold-blooded efficiency. Reporters who had rushed to Belgium in August 1914 to witness the German advance toward France fueled this view. Richard Harding Davis described the event for New York *Tribune* readers as "not men marching, but a force of nature like a tidal wave, an avalanche, or a river flooding its banks."

At the sight of the first few regiments of the enemy we were thrilled. After, for three hours, they had passed in one unbroken steel-gray column, we were bored. But when hour after hour passed and there was no halt, no breathing time, no open spaces in the ranks, the thing became uncanny, unhuman.

Other Americans held a more neutral but cynical attitude. They looked at the European war as a great financial boon to the United States. One newspaper said that the war was "a supreme opportunity for American manufacturers to gain world-wide markets."

The United States Declares Neutrality In the end, the nation's business interests had a stronger impact on United States policy than the feelings of the American people. The war imperiled United States commercial investments overseas, which between 1897 and 1914 had increased fivefold, from $700 million to $3.5 billion. Now, German submarines and a British naval blockade of the North Sea were putting those investments at risk. To protect those investments, the United States declared itself officially neutral, protested the actions of both sides, and tried to act as peacemaker.

The Preparedness Movement At the same time that they pushed for neutrality, American business leaders who had strong commercial ties to Great Britain urged that the United States get ready for war. Their watchword was preparedness, and they wanted their country to be ready to aid Great Britain, if necessary. In December 1914, preparedness advocates organized a National Security League to "promote patriotic education and national sentiment and service among people of the United States."

By the late summer of 1915, the movement had won over President Wilson. The government set up camps to train American men for combat. By the summer of 1916, President Wilson and Congress had worked out an agreement for large increases in the armed forces.

The Peace Movement When world war broke out, a peace movement also swung into gear. In the early 1900s, peace advocates consisted primarily of former populists, midwest progressives, and social reformers.

Women were particularly active in the movement. On August 29, suffragists, dressed in black and carrying a banner of a dove, marched down New York City's Fifth Avenue to the slow beat of a muffled drum. In November 1915, a group of women and men social reformers founded the American Union Against Militarism.

Congress also had some peace advocates. Aiming to remind Americans of the costs of war, they insisted on paying for preparedness through a tax on the makers of arms and through higher income taxes. Claude Kitchin, member of Congress from North Carolina, predicted that when people discovered "that the income tax will have to pay for the increase in the army and navy, . . . preparedness will not be so popular with them as it now is."

Congress did increase taxes, but the preparedness movement remained strong. As you will read, the United States could not resist the forces pushing it toward entry into the conflict.

Jane Addams, second from the left in the front row, joined the delegation on this "peace ship," which journeyed to Europe in 1915 with hopes of ending the war.

SECTION 1 REVIEW

Key Terms, People, and Places
1. Define (a) Central Powers, (b) Allies,
2. Identify (a) Kaiser Wilhelm, (b) autocrat.

Key Concepts
3. Why did the dispute between Austria-Hungary and Serbia escalate?
4. For what reasons was this war so destructive?

5. What were the reactions in the United States to the outbreak of World War I?

Critical Thinking
6. **Checking Consistency** The alliance system in Europe in 1914 was designed to maintain peace. Yet it seemed to make the conflict worse once the fighting began. Explain this apparent inconsistency.

Quiz found in the Unit 6 folder, p. 81, covers the main ideas in this section as well as the key terms.

Section 1 Review Answers

1. (a) Central Powers, see p. 550, (b) Allies, see p. 550

2. (a) Kaiser Wilhelm, see p. 552, (b) autocrat, see p. 552

3. A system of mutual defense alliances brought Russia to Serbia's defense. This led Germany, Austria's ally, to mobilize for war against Russia and Russia's ally, France. The Germans' invasion of neutral Belgium on their way to invade France drew Great Britain, Belgium's ally, into the war.

4. Industrialization had produced more destructive weapons, namely machine guns. Thus, deaths rose and desperate troops began to use any tactics available including killing civilians.

5. Most Americans were pro-British. President Wilson decided on a position of neutrality. Both the preparedness movement, which urged the United States to get ready for war, and the peace movement were very active.

6. Possible answer: Once a war starts, alliances tend to widen the conflict by involving nations with no real interest in or concern with the issues that caused the war.

Reteach

Ask students to correct each of the following incorrect statements:
● World War I began with the assassination of a German archduke in Bosnia.
● Great Britain and Germany fought together against Russia and Austria-Hungary.

Reinforcing the Big Idea

When war began in Europe in 1914, the United States resolved to preserve its neutrality. Given the nation's commercial and personal interests abroad, this policy would be difficult to maintain. The next section describes how the nation finally joined the war.

Critical Thinking

Identifying Alternatives

Focus Students will identify and analyze alternatives, or possible solutions to a problem.

Instruct As a class, work through the question in steps 1 to 3. You might want to divide students into small groups for consideration of step 4. Ask each group to submit a sentence stating the goal of the United States regarding the war in Europe and at least three steps likely to achieve that goal. Have each group describe which of these steps the nation actually took.

Extend See Historian's Toolbox Activity in the Resource Directory below.

Answers

1. (a) World War I and the United States' response to it. (b) No, they differ in their approach.

2. (a) Passage A proposes that the United States react without judgment and without acting for or against any power. (b) Passage B suggests that the United States act forcefully and swiftly for the side that it determines to be "right." (c) Passage A proposes caution and restraint; Passage B proposes swift action.

3. Possible answers: (a) It is difficult to expect people not to judge or feel strong sympathy with one side or another. (b) If the United States does not act in its own best interests, its interests may be injured. (c) Roosevelt does not clarify what he means by "[doing] ill." (d) Roosevelt does not give an answer to this question. It is presumed that this standard is clearly understood by all.

4. Possible answer: (a) A desirable goal is staying out of the war or joining the war on behalf of the side America feels is most worthy of its help. (b) Make sure students explain their answers.

Identifying Alternatives

Identifying alternatives means finding one or more possible solutions to a problem. In the previous section, you read about the conflict in the United States over how to react to the war raging in Europe. The passages on this page make the case for two responses the United States might have made. Passage A presents the views of then President Woodrow Wilson, as stated in August 1914. Passage B, which was published in January 1915, presents the thoughts of former President Theodore Roosevelt.

Use the following steps to identify and analyze the alternatives presented in the passages.

1. Identify the nature of the problem under discussion. Before you can identify alternative solutions to a problem, you must understand what the problem is. (a) What is the issue that both passages address? (b) Does each passage present the same approach to the problem?

2. Identify the solutions proposed in the two passages. (a) What does Passage A suggest is the proper response of the United States to the war raging in Europe? (b) How does Passage B propose that the United States respond to the war? (c) In what ways are these two viewpoints similar or different?

3. Evaluate the potential effectiveness of each view. Consider the strengths and weaknesses of each proposal. For example, you might ask the following questions about Passages A and B: (a) What difficulties do you see in Wilson's suggestion that the United States not judge the actions of other nations? (b) What might happen if the United States acts in a "disinterested" way, as Wilson suggests? (c) Does Roosevelt make clear what he means when he refers to a nation that "does ill"? (d) Does Roosevelt explain the basis by which nations should be judged "highly civilized" or "well behaved"?

4. Consider other alternatives. Recall the nature of the problem under discussion. Then, using insights you gained above, think of other possible solutions. Ask: (a) What should be the goal of the United States in responding to the war in Europe? (b) What steps are most likely to achieve that goal?

Passage A

"My thought is of America. . . . [T]his great country of ours . . . should show herself in this time of peculiar trial a Nation fit beyond others to exhibit the fine poise of undisturbed judgment, the dignity of self-control, the efficiency of dispassionate [unemotional] action; a Nation that neither sits in judgment upon others nor is disturbed in her own counsels and which keeps herself fit and free to do what is honest and disinterested and truly serviceable for the peace of the world."

Woodrow Wilson, *Appeal for Neutrality*, August 19, 1914

Passage B

"Our true course should be to judge each nation on its conduct, unhesitatingly to antagonize every nation that does ill [at the point] it does ill, and equally without hesitation to act. . . .

One of the greatest of international duties ought to be the protection of small, highly civilized, well-behaved and self-respecting states from oppression and conquest by their powerful military neighbors. . . .

I feel in the strongest way that we should have interfered, at least to the extent of the most emphatic diplomatic protest and at the very outset—and then by whatever further action was necessary—[when Germany invaded Belgium]."

Theodore Roosevelt, *America and the World War*, 1915

 RESOURCE DIRECTORY

Teaching Resources

Historian's Toolbox Activity Identifying Alternatives, found in the Unit 6 folder, p. 94, extends students' opportunity to practice this skill by analyzing three 1993 policy proposals for United States response to the war in Bosnia-Herzegovina.

The United States Declares War

SECTION PREVIEW

The United States struggled to avoid the horrors of World War I. But the nation could not prevent its slow slide into the conflict.

Key Concepts

• Germany's unrestricted submarine warfare had a powerful impact on American attitudes toward the war.

• Wilson won reelection in 1916 based on his success at keeping the United States out of the war.

• A series of events finally pushed Congress to declare war on the Central Powers—an act that was met with mixed reactions by the American people.

Key Terms, People, and Places

U-boat, *Lusitania,* Zimmerman note

From 1915 to 1917, growing conflict between the United States and Germany increased the popularity of the preparedness position and intensified the pressure for war. Ultimately, both Congress and the President were pushed toward entering World War I on the side of the Allies.

German Submarine Warfare

One factor pushing the United States toward war was the German use of submarine warfare. This tactic was effective militarily, but it cost the Germans dearly in terms of American public opinion.

The German **U-boat,** short for *Unterseeboot,* or submarine, was a terrifying new weapon that changed the rules of naval warfare. Submarine attacks depended on the element of surprise, so unlike other naval ships, U-boats issued no warning to their targets. This situation troubled many Americans. Though the British blockade threatened freedom of the seas

and led to the slow starvation of the German people, the American public felt that such action was reasonable during wartime. In contrast, German attempts to break the blockade with submarines seemed unfair, even uncivilized.

The British encouraged such anti-German feeling. Shortly after the war began, the British cut the transatlantic cable connecting Germany and the United States. All news of the European front henceforth flowed through London. Its pro-Allied bias helped shape the opinion of the people in the United States in favor of punishing Germany for its alleged atrocities.

American public opinion of the Germans sank even lower on May 7, 1915, when a U-boat sighted the **Lusitania,** a British passenger liner, in the Irish Sea. Suspecting correctly that the ship carried weapons for the Allies, the U-boat fired on the liner. Eighteen minutes later the *Lusitania* disappeared beneath the waves along with its 1,198 passengers. Included among the dead were 128 Americans, who had boarded the *Lusitania* in spite of German warnings to stay off British ships. Nevertheless, the American press went wild over this German act of "barbarism."

Wilson counseled patience. He directed his secretary of state, William Jennings Bryan, to demand that Germany renounce unrestricted submarine warfare and make payments to the victims' survivors. Germany's reply that the ship carried small arms and ammunition did not quiet American anger.

Wilson ordered a second, stronger note. This time, however, Bryan refused to sign it, fearing it would lead to war. Bryan also insisted that Wilson send an equally strong note to

This German poster urges its U-boats on in their mission. The translation is, "Submarines: [come] out!"

📄 **Reproducible Lesson Plan** found in the Unit 6 folder, p. 76, provides a summary of the Section 2 lesson plan content.

📄 **Alternate Lesson Plan: Cooperative Learning** found in the Alternate Lesson Plans folder, p. 101, helps groups of students prepare and present interviews exploring different American opinions about the conflict in Europe.

📄 **Guided Reading and Review** found in the Unit 6 folder, p. 82, provides a structure for reading and mastering the key concepts and reviewing the key terms for Section 2. (Guided Practice)

Media and Technology

 Transparency
Cause and Effect, F-8

SECTION 2

The United States Declares War

1. FOCUS

Connecting to the Big Idea

See page 548B. Explain that from 1915 to 1917, relations between the United States and Germany deteriorated, and pressure for war increased. Ask why the United States finally declared war on the Central Powers.

Objectives

● Describe the impact of Germany's unrestricted submarine warfare on American attitudes toward the war.
● Identify President Wilson's avoidance of war as the key factor that helped him win the election of 1916.
● Explain why the United States Congress finally declared war on the Central Powers and describe the mixed reaction of the American people to the declaration.

Bellringer

Ask students what makes a country one of the great nations of the world. What domestic conditions and foreign alliances characterize a great nation? What countries are great nations today? Why?

Reading Strategy

Solving Problems Have students imagine that they are members of Congress in 1917. They must decide whether the United States should go to war with Germany and the other Central Powers. As they read the section, students should list the events that influence their decision.

Explain/Discuss

Discuss the reasons Germany said that submarines could not follow the traditions of international law. Ask students to respond to the German argument that the submarines should not be denied their weapon of surprise.

Ask students to list the options open to President Wilson in April 1917 in dealing with the war and to consider the consequences of each option.

Ask students to discuss whether President Wilson acted in good faith in the 1916 election when he campaigned on his success in maintaining the nation's neutrality. What evidence is there either to back up Wilson's assertion of neutrality or to show that he supported Great Britain?

Answer to ...

MAKING CONNECTIONS

The public perceived the Germans as militaristic and coldly efficient. Thus they judged German actions more cruel than those of the British, even though British actions had similarly harmful effects on noncombatants.

In Depth

Biography

In 1916, Jeannette Rankin of Montana (1880–1973) became the first woman elected to Congress. A staunch pacifist, she was in the minority in the House of Representatives in voting against the war resolution. "Little woman, you cannot afford not to vote," a veteran House member whispered to her prior to the vote. "You represent the womanhood of the country." When the roll call came, however, Rankin announced: "I want to stand by my country, but I cannot vote for war. I vote no."

NOTICE!

TRAVELLERS intending to embark on the Atlantic voyage are reminded that a state of war exists between Germany and her allies and GreatBritian and her allies; that the zone of war includes the waters adjacent to the British Isles; that, in accordance with formal notice given by the Imperial German Government, vessels flying the flag of Great Britian, or of any of her allies, are liable to destruction in those waters and that travellers sailing in the war zone on ships of Great Britian or her allies do so at their own risk.

IMPERIAL GERMAN EMBASSY,
WASHINGTON, D. C., APRIL 22, 1915.

CUNARD

EUROPE VIA LIVERPOOL

LUSITANIA

Fastest and Largest Steamer now in Atlantic Service Sails
SATURDAY, MAY 1, 10 A. M.
Transylvania - Fri., May 7, 5 P.M.
Orduna, - - - Tues., May 18, 10 A.M.
Tuscania, - - - Fri., May 21, 5 P.M.
LUSITANIA, - Sat., May 29, 10 A.M.
Transylvania, - - - - - - 5 P.M.

American public opinion was extremely critical of Germany and its use of U-boats. The cartoon above right suggests that Germany felt no remorse for the loss of American lives. However, Germany did warn travelers—including passengers of the *Lusitania*—to stay out of the war zone (left).

Great Britain protesting its blockade. Wilson refused and Bryan resigned. His successor, Robert Lansing, signed the note to Germany. In response, Germany promised to stop sinking passenger ships without warning, as long as the ship's crew offered no resistance to German search or seizure.

Still, U-boats continued to sink British and French liners. The loss of American lives was small but infuriating. Wilson protested and, in response, Germany pledged restraint. Because Wilson could not threaten force without entering the war, however, he felt fairly powerless. But during this time, Wilson did embrace the concept of preparedness. He also authorized New York bankers to make a huge loan to the Allies. American neutrality was beginning to lose its meaning. ✪

MAKING CONNECTIONS

Consider public feelings about Germany discussed in Section 1. How might these feelings explain public condemnation of U-boat warfare—and public acceptance of the British blockade?

Moving Toward the Brink of War

On February 1, 1917, Germany once again began unrestricted submarine warfare. Wilson had been reelected in November of 1916 with the slogan "He kept us out of war." Now his hope of maintaining freedom of the seas—and American neutrality—was dashed. Two days later, the United States broke off diplomatic relations with Germany, and Wilson asked Congress for permission to arm American merchant ships.

The Zimmerman Telegram In the Senate, a group of antiwar senators tried to prevent action on Wilson's request by using a filibuster. A filibuster is a tactic in which senators take the floor, begin talking, and refuse to stop talking to permit a vote on a measure. While this was taking place, the British revealed the contents of an intercepted German telegram to Mexico. In it, Arthur Zimmerman, Germany's foreign secretary, wrote:

> We shall endeavor to keep the United States neutral. In the event of this not succeeding, we make Mexico a proposal of alliance. . . : Make war together, make peace together, . . . and . . . Mexico is to

RESOURCE DIRECTORY

Teaching Resources

✪ **Critical Thinking Activity** Identifying Central Issues: Provocations of War, found in the Unit 6 folder, p. 95, encourages students to apply this skill in examining a 1917 political cartoon.

✪ **Visual Learning Activity** Uncle Sam's Pledge, found in the Unit 6 folder, p. 102, uses a Library of Congress drawing to show how symbols were used to promote public support for World War I.

reconquer the lost territory in Texas, New Mexico, and Arizona.

Neither Wilson nor Mexico took this telegram—the so-called **Zimmerman note**—seriously. Its release, however, scored another propaganda victory for Great Britain. War fever mounted.

Revolution in Russia By early 1917, Russia already had suffered enormous casualties in the war: 1.8 million killed, 2.4 million taken prisoner, and 2.8 million sick or wounded. Austrian and German forces had advanced deep into Russian territory. Ill-shod, ill-fed, and miserably equipped, the Russians fell back farther and farther into their interior.

Then, in March 1917, revolutionaries overthrew Czar Nicholas II, Russia's autocratic monarch, replacing him with a republican government. This event elated the prowar faction in the United States. Concern over being allied with the czar had helped slow the nation's move toward entry into the war. By overthrowing the czar, the Russian revolution removed a last stumbling block to a full American commitment to the Allies.

The War Resolution Meanwhile, between March 16 and March 18, Germany sank the United States ships *City of Memphis, Illinois,* and *Vigilancia.* On March 20 Wilson's cabinet voted unanimously for war. Casting the issue in idealistic terms, on April 2 Wilson told Congress that "The world must be made safe for democracy." ✪

> I t is a fearful thing to lead this great peaceful people into war, the most terrible and disastrous of all wars, civilization itself seeming to be in the balance. But the right is more precious than peace.

Antiwar forces were devastated. Social worker Jane Addams used her considerable prestige to appeal directly to the President, but to no avail. An Emergency Peace Federation was formed to pressure Congress not to say yes to war. But a war resolution passed 82 to 6 in the Senate and 373 to 50 in the House. On April 6, the President signed it.

The United States entry into World War I broke some long-standing alliances among progressives.

President Woodrow Wilson reluctantly led the nation into World War I.

1650   1700   1750   1800   Links Across Time   1850   1900

Making the World Safe for Democracy

According to President Wilson, the United States entered World War I to make the world safe for democracy. By fighting its enemies, Wilson said, the United States would "bring peace and safety to all nations and make the world at last free." On a number of occasions since that time, the United States has followed a similar policy—using military action as well as diplomatic means in an attempt to achieve peace, security, and democracy.

After World War II, the United States, acting under this policy, committed itself to strong resistance to

communism. This policy contributed to American involvement in several wars and military actions. In July 1950, for example, the United Nations Security Council backed the use of military action to combat the communists in North Korea who were trying to conquer South Korea. Led by the United States, the South Koreans received "assistance to repel armed attack and restore international peace and security in the area."

In the Vietnam War, the United States gave military and economic aid to the southeast Asian country of South Vietnam in an attempt to stop

a takeover by communist North Vietnam. Despite the efforts of thousands of American troops, South Vietnam fell to communist forces in 1975.

More recently, President Bush echoed Wilson's policy in 1991 when he obtained Congress's approval to send American troops to liberate the Persian Gulf nation of Kuwait from an invasion by its neighbor Iraq. The action came after about six months of diplomatic pressures and economic sanctions against Iraq. *How successful do you think the United States has been in its policy of making "the world safe for democracy"?*

Analyze
Ask students to analyze the reasons for declaring war against Germany and then to decide which was the most compelling. Have students explain their reasoning.

Activity
Writing Editorials
Ask students to assume the role of editor of a United States newspaper in early March 1917. Students should write an editorial either urging the United States into the war or cautioning the nation against further involvement in the conflict.

Enrichment
Ask students to research and report on either the Russian Revolution of 1917 or the Irish uprising of 1916. Reports should briefly describe the rebellion's goals, its leaders, the main events, and its effect on the United States.

Answer to ...
Links Across Time

Possible answers: Successful, because the United States' involvement in the Persian Gulf War let other countries know that the United States would not tolerate conflicts that threaten world peace; not successful, because as the century draws to a close, people in many countries are still struggling to achieve democracy.

3. ASSESS

Section 2 Review Answers
1. (a) U-boat, see p. 555, (b) *Lusitania*, see p. 555, (c) Zimmerman note, see p. 557

2. The United States broke off diplomatic relations with Germany, and President Wilson asked Congress for permission to prepare American merchant ships for war.

3. He ran on a combined peace and social reform platform. The party of his opponent, Charles Evans Hughes, did not present a unified platform. It was divided among advocates of preparedness, war, and social reform.

4. Russia was one of the Allies but a dictatorship. It had been difficult for Americans to think of joining the war on the Allied side as long as the Russian czar remained in power. When he was overthrown, Americans became much more sympathetic to Russia.

5. Feelings were divided. Fifty-six members of Congress, including Jeannette Rankin, voted against the war resolution. Most former progressives went along with the resolution, but some split off and continued to work in the peace movements. Many saw the war as an opportunity for the United States to enter a new age of peace and democracy.

6. Possible answer: The United States could have avoided the confrontations with Germany by keeping its commercial vessels out of waters patrolled by U-boats. This may have been politically impossible given that many commercial interests in the United States were at stake. It also may have been more costly to lose the commercial ties than to engage in war.

Reteach

Ask students to write the following events in chronological order:
- Germany begins unrestricted submarine warfare.
- A German U-boat sinks the *Lusitania.*
- Congress declares war.
- Bryan resigns as secretary of state.
- Wilson reveals the contents of the Zimmerman note.

4. CLOSE

Reinforcing the Big Idea

Although the United States tried to maintain its neutrality, events pushed Congress into a declaration of war. The next section describes the role of Americans overseas in the war.

Jeannette Rankin of Montana, the first woman member of the House of Representatives, cast one of the few votes against the United States war resolution. She remained opposed to the war and lost her congressional seat in 1919.

Teddy Roosevelt pushed for war. La Follette favored peace. Settlement worker Lillian Wald resigned from the American Union Against Militarism, but Jane Addams stayed a member. Carrie Chapman Catt dedicated her suffrage association to serve the war effort, an act that prompted President Wilson to tell the Senate in 1918 that the passage of woman suffrage was "vital to the winning of the war."

Why Did the United States Go to War?

After years of reluctance, the United States was finally at war. Why? In the United States people believed that Germany's refusal to respect American claims to neutrality had forced the United States to retaliate. From Germany's perspective, however, its refusal was understandable. "Neutral noncombatant" hardly described the United States between 1914 and 1917. United States money and munitions had been flowing to the Allies long before its troops left for Europe.

⭐ The decision also can be seen as the result of long-standing commercial interests. As Jeannette Rankin, the first woman member of Congress, said in defense of her vote against the war, "I knew we were asked to vote for a commercial war." Indeed, in 1912, Wilson had announced, "Our industries have expanded to such a point that they will burst their jackets if they cannot find a free outlet to the markets of the world." In addition, British propaganda had helped promote anti-German feeling. Finally, many believed that the world *could* be made safe for democracy. If the United States hoped to benefit from a new world of peace and freedom, then the nation would have to be a player in the drama.

Political commentator Walter Lippmann saw the war as an opportunity for the United States to tap "new sources of energy" in its people that would make "the impossible . . . possible." "We can dare to hope for things which we never dared to hope for in the past," he wrote. Lippmann was convinced that democracy would be realized not just abroad but at home as well. "We shall turn with fresh interest to our own tyrannies—to our Colorado mines, our autocratic steel industries, our sweatshops and our slums."

In short, many Americans felt that the United States was on the brink of greatness. Its participation in World War I would hasten progress toward that goal.

SECTION 2 REVIEW

Key Terms, People, and Places
1. Define (a) U-boat, (b) *Lusitania,* (c) Zimmerman note.

Key Concepts
2. What was the impact in the United States of Germany's unrestricted submarine warfare?
3. State the reason for Wilson's reelection in 1916.
4. Why did the March 1917 revolution in Russia push the United States toward war?

5. How did the American people respond to the declaration of war?

Critical Thinking
6. Identifying Alternatives Consider the causes that brought the United States into World War I. What would the United States have had to do to avoid the conflict altogether? For what reasons did the United States not take such steps?

RESOURCE DIRECTORY

Teaching Resources

⭐ **American Profiles Activity** found in the Unit 6 folder, p. 90, profiles Jeannette Rankin, the first woman elected to Congress and one of the fifty-six members to vote against United States entry into World War I.

Quiz found in the Unit 6 folder, p. 83, covers the main ideas in this section as well as the key terms.

Americans on the European Front

SECTION PREVIEW

On entering the war, the United States saw itself merely as "associate" to the Allies. The Americans were quickly promoted to a leading role, however. Yankee soldiers and volunteers poured onto foreign battlefields and served nobly in many capacities.

Key Concepts
- At first, Americans envisioned a limited role for themselves in World War I.
- The role of the United States quickly expanded, and millions of draftees and volunteers, both women and men, became part of the effort.
- American military involvement helped turn the tide of the war.

Key Terms, People, and Places
American Expeditionary Force, armistice; doughboy

The United States was now at war. Would Americans achieve greatness in the mighty conflict? Pacifists looked to the future and saw European battlefields strewn with American corpses. Enthusiastic patriots, anxious for an unrestrained American commitment to the war, saw glory for the nation. United States officials, however, focused on the present and took a more cautious approach.

The United States Slowly Gets Involved

At first, President Wilson envisioned Americans as "associates" in the war, rather than equal partners with the Allies. Congress therefore authorized $3 billion in loans, naval support, supplies, and arms—but did not send troops.

For the Allies, this contribution was not enough. They insisted on an armed force, even a token one, to boost morale. Thus, in June 1917 the United States War Department, which had no formal plans for a European military operation, sent over General John J. "Black Jack" Pershing, a cold, tough veteran of the Spanish-American War, and a contingent of 14,500 men. Pershing quickly realized that he needed more troops.

Draftees and Volunteers At the time of Pershing's request, American troop strength fell far short of needs. When the United States entered World War I, the armed forces numbered only 120,000 enlisted men and 80,000 National Guardsmen. Thus, in May 1917 Congress passed a Selective Service Act, authorizing a draft of young men for military service.

During the Civil War, the draft had sparked riots. Now, however, the general feeling that this would be the "war to end all wars" resulted in wide acceptance for the program. By November 1918, over 24 million men had registered for the draft. From those, a lottery picked three million draftees. Volunteers and National Guardsmen made up the remainder of what was called the **American Expeditionary Force** (AEF). ✪

Included in this American force was a new group of people—women. Eleven thousand women volunteered to serve in uniform as nurses, drivers, clerks, and telephone operators. Another 14,000 women served abroad as civilians working for the government or in private agencies. As Addie Hunton and Kathryn Johnson, two of the few African American women who made it to the front, later wrote: "We had the greatest opportunity for service that we have ever known."

The Convoy System In addition to building a fighting force, the War Department also had to worry about getting troops and supplies

In 1917 American soldiers began marching off to war, carrying items such as this trench shaving kit.

1. FOCUS

Connecting to the Big Idea

See page 548B. Point out that the United States quickly became fully involved in the war. Ask what roles Americans played abroad. What were the results of American efforts in the war?

Objectives
- Describe the limited role Americans at first envisioned for themselves in World War I.
- Describe how the role of the United States in the war quickly expanded.
- Explain how American military involvement helped to turn the tide of the war.

Bellringer

Are allies automatically equals? Can allies exist without a common enemy? Ask students what relationship allies share.

Reading Strategy

Predicting Content Ask students to skim Section 3, list the main headings and subheadings, and write a sentence or phrase under each heading that predicts the content that follows. When they have finished reading the section, ask students to test their predictions against the actual text.

📄 **Reproducible Lesson Plan** found in the Unit 6 folder, p. 77, provides a summary of the Section 3 lesson plan content.

📄 **Alternate Lesson Plan: Learning Styles** found in the Alternate Lesson Plans folder, p. 102, helps students use maps and other information to describe United States participation in the war in Europe and is especially useful for visual learners.

📄 **Guided Reading and Review** found in the Unit 6 folder, p. 84, provides a structure for reading and mastering the key concepts and reviewing the key terms for Section 3. (Guided Practice)

✪ 📄 **Primary Source Activity** Women on the War Front, found in the Unit 6 folder, p. 97, shows how African American women came to contribute to the war effort through an excerpt from Addie Hunton and Kathryn Johnson's *Two Colored Women with the American Expeditionary Forces.*

Explain/Discuss

Ask students to estimate the original number of U.S. troops sent to Europe with General Pershing (*14,500*) and the total number who eventually served overseas (*two million*). Write the actual numbers on the chalkboard. Ask students to account for the huge disparity between the two numbers. Work with students to list the steps required to create an army large enough to fight a war on that scale.

Ask students to locate on a map the major battles of the war involving American troops.

Analyze

Ask students to analyze Pershing's insistence on keeping the American troops separate from the Allied forces. Why did Pershing want to keep the Americans under American command? Why did some American troops wish to be transferred to French command?

Answer to ...

MAKING CONNECTIONS

Possible answer: The treatment of African Americans was inconsistent with the claim to be making the world safe for democracy, since that rationale seemed to imply that full democracy existed in the United States.

In Depth

Multicultural Perspectives

In 1919, when the 369th United States Infantry marched triumphantly through New York, its sixty-piece band, led by Lieutenant James Europe, switched to jazz when it reached Harlem. The band had played the same music to wildly enthusiastic crowds in Britain, France, Belgium, and Germany.

---

overseas. Toward this end, officials developed a system that protected merchant and troop ships from German U-boats by surrounding American ships with a convoy of small destroyers. The speed of the destroyers enabled them to mount counterattacks against U-boats or scare them off altogether. Between April and December 1917, merchant marine losses dropped by half.

American Soldiers in Europe "I don't know what the war's about, But I guess, by heck, I'll soon find out!" So went a popular World War I song that expressed the thoughts of the 2 million soldiers who eventually crossed the Atlantic Ocean. Infantrymen were called **doughboys**, a term that originated during the Civil War in reference to the dumpling-shaped buttons on Union infantry uniforms. ⭐

Once the American soldiers had arrived on foreign shores, Pershing did not integrate them with Allied troops, who in Pershing's view had become too accustomed to defensive action. He wanted to save his men's strength for offensive moves.

Segregation occurred not only between the American and Allied troops, but also within the American ranks. The more than 300,000 African Americans who volunteered or were drafted into service were kept separate from white troops. Though many African Americans fought with distinction and 3,925 died or were wounded, most never saw combat. The marines refused to accept African Americans

altogether, and the navy used them for menial tasks only. The army, too, used African Americans mostly for manual labor.

These assignments distressed many African Americans. The 369th Infantry Regiment, who came to be known as the Harlem Hell Fighters, was especially eager to fight. Its members convinced their white officers to loan them to the French, who did not practice segregation. Because of their distinguished service, the French awarded the entire regiment their highest combat medal, the *Croix de Guerre.*

Consider Wilson's justification for entering the war, which was discussed in Section 2. Is the military's treatment of African Americans consistent with this justification? Explain.

AMERICAN PROFILES
Mary E. Gladwin

Many women did not wait for American entry into the war to find ways to serve. As early as the fall of 1914, women traveled to Europe as volunteers for the Red Cross, YWCA, or other service organizations. One such volunteer was Mary E. Gladwin.

Gladwin had become a nurse in her thirties after a career in teaching. She served as an American Red Cross volunteer in Georgia,

African American soldiers endured segregation overseas. But that did not keep the 369th Infantry, pictured here, from fighting valiantly and winning recognition for their bravery. ⭐

▶ RESOURCE DIRECTORY

Teaching Resources

⭐ **Literature Activity** A War Song, found in the Unit 6 folder, p. 99, highlights "Hinky Dinky Parlay-Voo," a song popular with the American Expeditionary Force, to demonstrate the soldiers' outlook during that time.

⭐ **American Profiles Activity** found in the Unit 6 folder, p. 91, profiles Henry Johnson, the most famous African American soldier of World War I.

Puerto Rico, and the Philippines during the Spanish-American War, and in Hiroshima, Japan, during the Russo-Japanese War of 1905. After a major flood in Dayton, Ohio, in 1913, she supervised a staff of 110 nurses there.

Gladwin was fifty-three years old when she responded to a call to assist in Europe. As chief nurse in a unit of three doctors and twelve nurses, she set sail on a freighter on September 13, 1914. Her ultimate destination was Belgrade, the capital of Serbia. Awaiting an Austrian occupation, the city was almost deserted.

Gladwin's unit set itself up in a walled hospital complex that stood on a bluff overlooking the Danube and Sava rivers. Aside from the picturesque setting, the situation at the hospital was desperate. Every window had been blown out by the fighting. The volunteers arrived to find no food or equipment and 250 patients waiting for help. Gladwin threw herself into her rounds. With an interpreter, she worked her way through the confusing mixture of German, French, Serbian, and Russian tongues spoken by those at the hospital. Wrote Gladwin,

> I used to tumble into bed at two or three o'clock in the morning, and hear those men. They begged and prayed . . . for help. They swore, they tore their bandages and the nights when I got up (it took all my strength of mind to stay in bed), I knew exactly what I would find . . . the men in their agony tearing off the dressings, the dark streams of blood on the floor.

The hospital lacked blankets and coal for heat. Fleas and lice were everywhere. Pneumonia, pleurisy, scarlet fever, typhoid, and tetanus raged among patients and staff. In March 1915, three nurses and two physicians had to return home. Chief surgeon Dr. Edward Ryan contracted typhus.

The American Red Cross set a date for the recall of all its overseas medical units—October 1, 1915. As the date approached, however, Gladwin's unit was pinned down by fighting in the area and could not move. Although she finally left in November, a year later she was back on the eastern front. For the remainder of the war, she served with the Serbian Red Cross,

now from a station in Salonika, Greece. In 1920 the Red Cross awarded her the Florence Nightingale Medal.

Red Cross units had their critics. Before the United States entered the war, some asked what business American volunteers such as Gladwin had in a European war. By helping to heal soldiers and returning them to the front, were they not prolonging the conflict? But when the United States finally entered the war, the experience of people such as Gladwin would greatly assist the work of the Army Medical Corps in saving American lives.

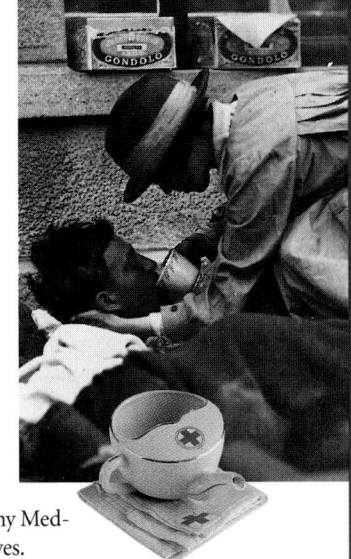

New Factors in the War

As the United States was expanding its involvement in the war, a major development occurred within the alliance. In November 1917, Vladimir Lenin led a new government to power in Russia.

Prior to his takeover, Lenin had been living in Switzerland and had promised to make peace with Germany if he ever gained control in Russia. Thus, Germany had helped arrange his return to Russia in April 1917. By November, Lenin had taken over the country.

Lenin's new regime immediately faced opposition from within the country. When civil war broke out, Lenin made peace with Germany on March 3, 1918.

Russia's exit from the war freed the Germans from the two-front war they had been forced to fight. From March through May 1918, German forces turned all their energies toward pounding at the French and British lines. They finally broke through, and by June 3, they were a mere 56 miles from Paris.

American forces came to the rescue. Marching out from Paris, the men received this word from their leader, Brigadier General James G. Harbord: "We dig no trenches to fall back on. The Marines will hold where they stand." And

The efforts of American women like Mary Gladwin and the nurse shown above saved lives and contributed to the Allies' success. According to the Women's Overseas Service League, 348 women died during the war from bombardments or disease.

Activity

Question and Answer

Ask students in small groups to write *who, what, where, when,* and *why* questions for the section content. After groups exchange question sheets, they should continue to work together to answer the questions.

Enrichment

Ask students to locate the lyrics for some of the songs popular with troops and civilians alike during the war. Possibilities include "Over There," "Tipperary," and "Pack Up Your Troubles."

In Depth

Then and Now

When the war broke out, Wilson asked Americans to be "impartial in thought as well as in action." Even after declaring war against Germany, Wilson saw America as a mere "associate" on the allied side. In the 1990s, the United States assumes much more of a leadership role in global conflict resolution. In January 1991, the United States under President Bush led a coalition including French, British, and Middle Eastern forces against Iraq's Saddam Hussein, who had invaded Kuwait. Of 700,000 troops assembled by the allies, 540,000 were Americans.

Interpreting Maps

The Central Powers had made the greatest territorial gains in the east.

3. ASSESS

Section 3 Review Answers

1. (a) American Expeditionary Force, see p. 559, (b) armistice, see p. 563

2. doughboy, see p. 560

3. The convoy system, in which destroyers protected merchant and troop ships from submarine attack; the use of tanks and airplane bombers in the last months of the war.

4. About eleven thousand wore the uniform of the AEF, working primarily as nurses, telephone operators, drivers, and clerks. Another fourteen thousand volunteered for service organizations throughout the war, even before the United States entered the conflict.

In Depth

Interdisciplinary

One of the inventions that revolutionized twentieth-century warfare was the tank. By mounting the body of an armored car onto a tractor, the British improvised the first armored, tracked vehicle in July 1915. The prototype tank, called "Little Willie," was quickly succeeded by "Big Willie." The new weapon proved itself at the Battle of Cambrai in late 1917, where 474 British tanks breached German lines. But the tanks were too slow to exploit the victory, necessitating the development of faster armored vehicles.

they did. At a loss of over half of their forces, they saved Paris, blunted the edge of the German advance, and began to turn the tide of the war.

Allied Counterattack The German command was astounded. "Nerves of the Americans are still unshaken," a general wrote to his headquarters. After turning back Germany at Paris, the Allied counteroffensive began in earnest in July. Using British tanks, a new machine that gave troops protection as well as mobility, the Allies began to break the German lines. On August 8, the battle of Amiens stopped the German advance once and for all. On August 11, German general Erich von Ludendorff sensed that the end was near. He advised Kaiser Wilhelm to seek terms for ending the war with the Allies.

The Allies, however, were not interested in any agreement in which Germany could win concessions from the Allies in return for peace.

They wanted total surrender. In September some 500,000 American troops, assisted by 100,000 French, began to hit the final German strongholds. Soon after the Germans were in full retreat.

The Allies also began to use airplanes to drop bombs. Aerial dogfights already had taken place. Each side had its "aces," such as the American captain Eddie Rickenbacker, who took down twenty-six enemy fighters. Now, Colonel Billy Mitchell organized a fleet of over 1,400 bomb-carrying planes. Although not very effective in this first attempt, aerial bombing raids would be devastating in future warfare.

Armistice The final Allied assault came on September 26. Over a million AEF troops began the drive to expel the Germans from France and cut their supply lines. Many individual acts of heroism shone during these final

World War I, 1917

Geography and History: Interpreting Maps
At the point of the United States entry into the war, the Central Powers had made gains in both the east and the west. Americans went immediately to work fighting against the Germans in France. *On which front had the Central Powers made the greatest gains?*

▶ RESOURCE DIRECTORY

Teaching Resources

⭐ **Literature Activity** A Poet Describes War, found in the Unit 6 folder, p. 101, uses e. e. cummings's short poem, "look at this)," to express the tragedy of war.

105-horsepower, six-cylinder engine

Driver

Commander

One of four Lewis machine guns

One of two 57-mm pedestal-mounted guns

Armor plating

Pressed steel track plate

months. Sergeant Alvin York of Tennessee, for example, saved an entire platoon by picking off machine gunners with his rifle and then, armed only with a pistol, captured 132 prisoners.

The Allies pressed on against their enemy. The German commanders begged for peace, but still hoped to dictate some terms. The Allies refused. Revenge was too sweet. By the time **armistice,** or a cease-fire, came, the Kaiser had fled. On November 11, the guns finally fell silent.

The War's Toll More than 50,000 American soldiers died in battle, and many more died of disease. The physical scars—and the mental scars—ran deep. Twenty-one-year-old Corporal Elmer Sherwood of Indiana wrote after one bloody battle in August 1918:

H*undreds of bodies of our brave boys lie on Hill 212, captured with such a great loss of blood. We will never be able to* explain war to our loved ones back home even if we are permitted to live and return. It is too gigantic and awesome for expression through words.*

American losses were minute in comparison to those suffered by the Europeans. The total death toll of 8 million soldiers and sailors is only an estimate. The French alone suffered over 1 million war dead and 4,000 towns destroyed. Great Britain lost 900,000 troops and suffered 2 million wounded. As mentioned earlier, Russian deaths also were high. Across Europe, the war killed 20 million civilians during and immediately after the fighting, from starvation, disease, or related injuries.

This terrible slaughter took place on the battlefields of Europe. But the war also was "fought" on other fronts, as well. The next section discusses the impact of World War I on the American home front.

The tank was another new weapon introduced in World War I. The British and the Americans collaborated on designing and building tanks like the one shown above.

SECTION 3 REVIEW

Key Terms, People, and Places
1. Define (a) American Expeditionary Force, (b) armistice.
2. Identify doughboy.

Key Concepts
3. What were some of the military innovations introduced during World War I?
4. In what ways did American women serve in World War I?

5. How did American troops help turn the tide of the war on the battlefield?
6. How many people were killed and wounded as a result of World War I?

Critical Thinking
7. **Demonstrating Reasoned Judgment** The United States failed in its original plan to be a mere "associate" in the war. Do you think it is possible to be anything less than a "full partner" in a war? Explain.

Quiz found in the Unit 6 folder, p. 85, covers the main ideas in this section as well as the key terms.

Media and Technology

Transparency
The Way It Works, H-17

---

5. They stopped the German attack toward Paris, then led a counterattack that helped bring about the end of the war.

6. Estimates of the war dead are about eight million. Another 20 million civilians died during and immediately after the war.

7. Answers will vary. Some students might observe that a country entering a war is committed to doing whatever is necessary to win it.

Reteach

Ask small groups to work together to write ten sentences, some true and some false, based on Section 3. Sentences should cover the following topics: the draft system, the selective service system, the convoy system, segregation in the army, the American Red Cross, the armistice, and the casualty toll. After a spokesperson from each group reads the completed sentences aloud, ask for volunteers to identify the incorrect statements and provide corrections.

 Alternative Assessment

Mid-Point Monitoring
Ask students if they have
● Chosen an event upon which to base their projects
● Decided on a format for their projects
● Begun their outside research

4. CLOSE

Reinforcing the Big Idea
American troops reached Europe in time to turn the course of the war and bring about an armistice. The cost of the war in lives and devastation was enormous. In the next section, students will read about how the war affected life at home.

SECTION 4

On the Home Front

SECTION PREVIEW

World War I was fought at home, too. To win that war, the government took control of the economy—and of people's minds—to an extent never before attempted.

1. FOCUS

Connecting to the Big Idea

See page 548B. Point out that World War I brought many changes at home, including unprecedented government control of the economy and of news and information. Ask how the government's actions changed American life.

Objectives

● Describe the financial and managerial efforts required on the home front to support the war effort.

● Explain how an atmosphere of war hysteria enabled the United States government to control and manipulate information and to repress free speech.

● Identify the significant cultural and social changes caused by the war.

Bellringer

Ask students what the term *home front* implies about the nature of life in the United States during the war. Why could life not continue normally while the nation was involved in a "total" war?

Reading Strategy

Reading for Evidence Ask students to find evidence as they read to support the following statement on page 564: "Waging war required many sacrifices at home." Ask students to list as many kinds of sacrifices made by Americans as they can.

SECTION PREVIEW

World War I was fought at home, too. To win that war, the government took control of the economy—and of people's minds—to an extent never before attempted.

Key Concepts

• Waging World War I involved tremendous financial and managerial efforts on the home front.

• The atmosphere of war hysteria enabled the United States government to control and manipulate information and to repress free speech.

• The war spurred significant cultural and social changes.

Key Terms, People, and Places

Liberty Bond, Industrial Workers of the World

The United States government whipped up sentiment against the "Huns"—the Germans—with posters such as this.

Waging war required many sacrifices at home. Despite the efforts of the preparedness movement, the economy was not ready to meet the demands of modern warfare. In this era, war required huge amounts of money and personnel. As President Wilson explained, now "there are no armies . . . ; there are entire nations armed."

Financing the War

As those in Congress who had argued for peace had made clear, preparedness was costly. Taxes went up. Most of the money for the war, however, came from patriotic private citizens. The government launched a vigorous campaign to raise money from the American people, a plan created by Secretary of the Treasury William Gibbs McAdoo. By selling **Liberty Bonds** to enthusiastic Americans, McAdoo raised millions of dollars, which he then loaned to the Allies at low interest rates. People who purchased the bonds could later redeem them, collecting what they paid for the bonds plus interest.

Teams of salespeople across the country sold the bonds to the "patriotic people." Responding to the slogan "Every Scout to Save a Soldier," Boy Scouts and Girl Scouts set up booths on street corners and sold bonds. The government hired popular commercial artists to draw colorful posters and recruited famous screen actors to host bond rallies. An army of 75,000 "four-minute men" gave brief (four-minute) speeches before films, plays, and school or union meetings to persuade audiences to buy bonds.

Managing the Economy

The government also needed industry to convert to the production of war goods. In 1918 Wilson won authority to set up a huge bureaucracy to manage this process. Business leaders—so-called "dollar-a-year" men and women—gave their service for a token salary and flocked to Washington to take up posts in thousands of new agencies.

New Government Agencies A War Industries Board, headed by financier Bernard Baruch, oversaw the whole war effort. The board's control was almost dictatorial. It doled out raw materials, told manufacturers what and how much to produce, and even fixed prices. A Fuel Administration introduced gasless days and daylight saving time, which increased the number of daylight hours and thus lowered fuel consumption. A War Trade Board licensed foreign trade and punished firms suspected of dealing with the enemy.

A National War Labor Board, set up in April 1918 under former President Taft, mediated those labor disputes that might hinder the war effort. Labor leader Samuel Gompers promised to limit labor strife in war production industries. A separate War Labor Policies Board, headed by Harvard law professor Felix

▶ RESOURCE DIRECTORY

Teaching Resources

📄 **Reproducible Lesson Plan** found in the Unit 6 folder, p. 78, provides a summary of the Section 4 lesson plan content.

📄 **Alternate Lesson Plan: Critical Thinking** Recognizing Cause and Effect, found in the Alternate Lesson Plans folder, p. 103, helps students practice this skill through examining the changes World War I brought to the American home front.

📄 **Guided Reading and Review** found in the Unit 6 folder, p. 86, provides a structure for reading and mastering the key concepts and reviewing the key terms for Section 4. (Guided Practice)

⭐📄 **Literature Activity** Selling the War, found in the Unit 6 folder, p. 100, uses an excerpt from the propaganda booklet *Why America Fights Germany* to show how the government galvanized public sentiment against Germany.

Frankfurter, standardized wages, hours, and working conditions in the war industries. Labor unions won limited rights to organize and bargain collectively.

Regulating Food Consumption Using the slogan "food will win the war," the government began regulating food consumption. Under the leadership of engineer and future President Herbert Hoover, a Food Administration (1917) worked to increase agricultural output and reduce waste. Opposed to price controls and rationing, Hoover hoped that voluntary restraint and increased efficiency would accomplish these goals.

Women, assumed to be in charge of America's kitchens, were a key part of his program. Writing to women in August 1917, Hoover preached a "Gospel of the Clean Plate."

Stop, before throwing any food away, and ask "Can it be used?" . . . Stop catering to different appetites. No second helpings. Stop all eating between meals. . . . Stop all refreshments at parties, dances, etc. . . . One meatless day a week. One wheatless meal a day. . . . No butter in cooking: use substitutes.

"The American woman and the American home," he concluded, "can bring to a successful end the greatest national task that has ever been accepted by the American people." Eager for a chance to play a purposeful part in the war, women across the country responded to this patriotic challenge.

A Progressive Victory? Thanks to the war, some aspects of progressive-era visions had come to pass. Government now regulated American economic life to an extent most progressives had never dreamed possible. When regulation spilled over into more private areas of life, however, some progressives wondered if the growth in public power had become excessive. In addition, regulation had not lessened the power of the corporate world. Indeed, during the war, the government relaxed its pursuit of antitrust suits, the influence of business leaders grew, and corporate profits tripled.

FOOD WILL WIN THE WAR
You came here seeking Freedom
You must now help to preserve it
WHEAT is needed for the allies
Waste nothing
UNITED STATES FOOD ADMINISTRATION

Using Historical Evidence This poster served a dual purpose. It encouraged Americans to save food and also promoted patriotism among immigrants. *What symbols and ideas in this poster are aimed at immigrants?*

MAKING CONNECTIONS

How does the involvement of the federal government in the regulation of business during World War I differ from government policies toward business in the late 1800s? What factors account for this change?

Controlling Hearts and Minds

News and information also came under federal control during World War I. George Creel, a Denver journalist and former muckraker, headed a Committee on Public Information, the country's first propaganda machine. Creel's office coordinated the production of short propaganda films, pamphlets explaining war aims, and posters selling recruitment and Liberty Bonds. Study plans distributed to teachers from Creel's office put the entire blame for the war on Germany. ✪

Enforcing Loyalty As in all wars, fear of spies and sabotage was widespread. A few months after the sinking of the *Lusitania,* a staff

Media and Technology

 Transparency
Critical Thinking, I-13

---

2. INSTRUCT

Explain/Discuss

Have the students first brainstorm a list of changes in American life caused by the war and then put the changes into categories.

Ask students how the War Industries Board controlled industry. Have students compare the operations of a small manufacturing company before the war with its operations during the war. Students should consider such activities as obtaining raw materials, negotiating with workers, and deciding how much of a given product to produce at what price. Ask in what ways the War Labor Policies Board controlled workers. Why did business and labor cooperate with these boards? Would business and labor have cooperated with them in peacetime? Why?

Caption Answer to ...

Using Historical Evidence

The words on the base of the Statue of Liberty refer to the United States as a land that welcomes all people. The words on the poster remind immigrants that the United States has welcomed them and that they thus owe their allegiance in return.

Answer to ...

MAKING CONNECTIONS

Government's heavy involvement in the regulation of business differs sharply with the laissez-faire policies of the late 1800s and early 1900s. Explanations for this change include the changing attitudes brought by the progressive era and the wartime need for more drastic government intervention.

Analyze

Analyze the way in which war hysteria led to the suppression of civil liberties. Tell students that in 1929, Herbert Hoover said, "Absolute freedom of the press to discuss public questions is a foundation stone of American liberty." How would Woodrow Wilson have responded if Hoover had made that statement in 1917? Do students agree with Hoover or with Wilson?

Activity

Teaching Heterogeneous Groups

As President Wilson exclaimed, "there are no armies. . . , there are entire nations armed," Americans mobilized their talents and efforts to support the war. To help students understand the consequences of this mobilization, divide the class into small groups. Have groups list as many jobs on the home front as possible that were essential to the war effort. Then have students list who would fill those jobs. **LEP**

Enrichment

For decades after the war, American schoolchildren memorized the poem "In Flanders Field," written by John McCrae, a Canadian physician killed in action. After helping students find the poem in an anthology, ask them to read it and then write a short report on its message.

3. ASSESS

Section 4 Review Answers

1. Industrial Workers of the World, see p. 566

2. Through higher taxes and the sale of Liberty Bonds.

3. They set up numerous agencies to regulate and control many aspects of the economy, including production, fuel usage, trade, labor relations, and food consumption. Boards included the War Industries Board, the War Trade Board, the Fuel Administration, the National War Labor Board, and the Food Administration.

member of the German embassy left his briefcase on a train. In it were plans for undermining pro-Allied sentiment and disrupting the American economy. Henceforth, the government was on the alert for sabotage.

Once the United States declared war, this alertness approached hysteria. Nativism revived, this time more vigorously than before. Having won its battle for preparedness, the National Security League began to preach "100 Percent Americanism." In 1917 the League finally got Congress to pass, over Wilson's veto, a literacy test for immigrants. This test excluded those who could not read or write a language—relatively few immigrants, as it turned out. Limits on immigration would become more severe after the war.

"Hate the Hun!" The war also spurred hostility toward Germans, who were called Huns in reference to an Asiatic people who brutally invaded Europe in the fourth and fifth centuries. German composers and musicians were banned from symphony concerts. German measles became "liberty measles," a hamburger

"I am afraid we are going to have a good many instances of people roughly treated on very slight evidence of disloyalty," wrote Secretary of War Newton Baker. Indeed, as this 1917 photograph shows, anti-German feeling in the United States led to the arrest of many citizens of German descent.

a "liberty sandwich." The California Board of Education condemned German as a language that spread "the ideals of autocracy, brutality and hatred." Yet it was a brutal mob of Americans that, in April 1918, lynched German-born citizen Robert Prager near St. Louis, in spite of the fact that Prager had tried to enlist in the navy. This act was but one of numerous wartime attacks on people of German descent.

Repression of Civil Liberties Wilson had claimed that the United States was now fighting for liberty and democracy. Many Americans, including women still denied the vote, found the claim ironic. It was particularly galling to those who suffered from wartime restrictions on their civil liberties.

When Wilson addressed Congress on the war resolution, he had warned that disloyalty would be "dealt with with a firm hand of repression." Accordingly, Congress passed the Espionage Act (1917), which made it illegal to interfere with the draft. This was followed by the Sedition Act (1918), which made it illegal to obstruct the sale of Liberty Bonds or to discuss anything "disloyal, profane, scurrilous, or abusive" about the American form of government, the Constitution, or the army and navy.

The government imposed censorship on the press and banned some publications from the mails. It pursued more than 1,500 prosecutions and won over 1,000 convictions. Socialist and former presidential candidate Eugene Debs drew a ten-year jail sentence for criticizing the American government and business leaders and urging people to "resist militarism." From prison he ran again for President in 1920 and won nearly a million votes. The victor in that race, Warren G. Harding, pardoned him in 1921.

Controlling Political Radicals Socialists such as Debs argued that the war was merely a quarrel among imperialist capitalists. This view became a rallying point for antiwar sentiment. In the elections of 1917 in New York, Ohio, and Pennsylvania, socialists made impressive gains. The **Industrial Workers of the World,** a radical labor organization seeking the overthrow of capitalism, also gained new supporters. The IWW (also known as the "Wobblies") was

RESOURCE DIRECTORY

Teaching Resources

⭐ **Visual Learning Activity** Women's Roles in World War I, found in the Unit 6 folder, p. 103, uses recruitment posters from the United States to illustrate the roles promoted for women during World War I.

founded in 1905. Unlike the labor movement Samuel Gompers led, the IWW focused on unskilled workers. It consisted mostly of western miners, lumbermen, migrant farm workers, and some eastern textile workers.

The views of socialists and the IWW distressed moderate labor leaders like Gompers, who had pledged union cooperation with the war effort. The police hounded the IWW. Raids in September 1917 led to the conviction of nearly two hundred members in trials held in Illinois, California, and Oklahoma. Vigilante groups, citizens who take the law into their own hands, lynched and horsewhipped others.

Cultural and Social Changes

Despite American criticism of Germany for its militarism, American patriotism and war fever made military styles and activities acceptable at home. Scouting programs, which for both boys and girls involved military-style uniforms, marching, and patriotic exercises, grew in popularity. Military drill became part of many school programs. By the summer of 1918, all able-bodied males in colleges and universities became army privates, subject to military discipline.

Social Mobility for Women and Minorities
Americans turned against militarism after the war. But other social changes had more lasting implications. ✪

The war propelled certain people into higher paid work. As the war cut off the flow of immigrants from Europe, factories that used to discriminate against African Americans and Mexican Americans now actively recruited them. The Women's Land Army put women to work on farms. White women moved into jobs previously closed to them, such as telegraph messenger, elevator operator, and letter carrier. Middle-class white women moved into management positions.

As a result of the war, about 400,000 women joined the industrial work force for the first time. In 1917 a speaker for the Women's Trade Union League exulted, "At last, after centuries of disabilities and discrimination, women are coming into the labor and festival of life on equal terms with men." In 1919 a study appeared with the optimistic title, "A New Day for the Colored Woman Worker." These pronouncements, while premature, celebrated what seemed to be major change.

Prohibition Finally Passes In 1917 the temperance movement was almost a century old. In that year, Congress proposed prohibition. The Eighteenth Amendment was passed less out of concern for the health of alcoholics and their families than to show patriotism. Because of the war, the grain that used to make alcohol would now make bread to meet needs at home and overseas. The states ratified the amendment in 1919.

The IWW gained strength during World War I. They also became the target of government crackdowns, part of a wider effort to control political radicals.

4. The government convinced Americans to support the war with both carrot and stick: The Committee on Public Information disseminated propaganda urging support; restriction of civil liberties, such as outlawing criticism of the army and navy, made not supporting the war difficult or dangerous.

5. So-called hyphenated Americans, such as German Americans; anyone who spoke up against the draft; radicals, such as the IWW; and the radical press.

6. Militarism gained popularity, as evidenced in scouting programs and military drill in schools; women and minorities made gains in social mobility; and after almost a century of struggle, the temperance movement finally won prohibition.

7. Possible answer: The American people's support was viewed as crucial to the success of the war effort.

Reteach
Ask students to read and correct each of the following statements:
● Most of the money to pay for the war came from taxes.
● The purpose of the War Industries Board was to run the nation's businesses so that their profits could help pay for the war.
● The Food Administration used price controls and rationing to make Americans conserve food supplies.
● The Committee on Public Information encouraged Congress to introduce a literacy test for immigrants.
● The Sedition and Espionage acts limited the rights of workers to bargain collectively.

SECTION 4 REVIEW

Key Terms, People, and Places
1. Identify Industrial Workers of the World.

Key Concepts
2. How did the United States finance its involvement in World War I?
3. In what ways did the government try to control the economy?
4. By what means did the government try to convince Americans to support the war?

5. Whose civil liberties were sacrificed in this effort to win the war?
6. What were some social and cultural changes that took place as a result of the war?

Critical Thinking
7. **Recognizing Ideologies** The federal government went to great lengths to control public opinion. What do these actions suggest about government's view of public opinion and its role in the war effort?

4. CLOSE

Reinforcing the Big Idea

To support the war effort, the government took unprecedented control of the economy and of news and information. The next section describes the difficult task of shaping the peace that ended the war.

Quiz found in the Unit 6 folder, p. 87, covers the main ideas in this section as well as the key terms.

Global Peacemaker

President Wilson's lofty vision for peace was brought back to earth by contentious allies and Congress. Meanwhile, many Americans experienced keen disappointment over postwar conditions at home.

Key Concepts

- At the postwar peace talks, Wilson's grand vision for peace was welcomed—but not wholeheartedly embraced.
- In the United States, reaction to the Versailles Treaty and to Wilson's proposal for a League of Nations was cool.
- The immediate postwar years in the United States were marred by disillusionment and economic disorder.

Key Terms, People, and Places

Fourteen Points, self-determination, League of Nations, reparations, Versailles Treaty

Enthusiasm for the war effort, demonstrated by this game board cover, gave way to despair in the postwar years.

1. FOCUS

Connecting to the Big Idea

See page 548B. Explain that President Wilson's vision of postwar peace, summarized in his Fourteen Points, was not shared by the Allies. Nor did the United States Congress accept the final treaty ending the war. Ask what Wilson's Fourteen Points were. What were the provisions of the Versailles Treaty?

Objectives

- Describe the reception President Wilson's peace plan received from the Allies.
- Describe the reaction at home to Wilson's peace plan and to the Versailles Treaty.
- Identify the immediate postwar years as marred by disillusionment, and economic disorder.

Bellringer

Ask students to consider and explain the expression "At what cost peace?" How could this expression be applied to other wars the United States had fought?

Reading Strategy

Reinforcing Key Ideas Ask students to take notes as they read the section listing the steps involved in the creation of the Versailles Treaty and the decision of the United States Senate to withhold ratification of the treaty.

W ith the fighting in Europe over, the nations involved in the conflict began the difficult task of shaping the peace. President Wilson, who feared that the failure to craft a treaty acceptable to all parties would lead to future wars, was determined to play a large role in this effort. But the postwar world—in Europe and at home—seemed almost as divided as before the war.

Wilson's Vision for Postwar Peace

On January 8, 1918, President Wilson delivered a peace program to Congress, which came to be called the **Fourteen Points** for the number of provisions it included. Among the program's key points were a call for an end to secret alliances, the restoration of freedom of the seas, and a reduction in armaments. The plan called for European colonial powers to handle all claims to each other's colonies with respect for the native populations. Wilson also demanded that Austria-Hungary allow its several ethnic groups to determine their own futures, a principle called **self-determination.** Finally, he called for an association of nations to join together in a single organization to secure world peace.

Wilson hoped that these points would form the basis of peace negotiations. At first, the Allies appeared to cooperate. After a while, as new political realities intervened, the fourteen points began to unravel.

The Paris Peace Conference In January 1919 an international peace conference met in Paris. Wilson decided to head the United States delegation himself. He also chose not to name any Republicans or senators to the group, a snub that would not be forgotten.

When Wilson arrived in Paris, Parisians threw flowers in his path and greeted the American President as a conquering hero. Wilson claimed he was not interested in gaining rewards for the United States, but sought only the establishment of a permanent agency to guarantee international stability. As he had said two years earlier, "There must be not a balance of power, but a community of power; not organized rivalries, but an organized common peace."

Wilson Is Forced to Compromise All would not go Wilson's way. First, the Allies *were* interested in reward. In particular, they wanted to divide up Germany's colonies. The French, determined never to be invaded again, wanted the total humiliation if not destruction of Germany. Russia, although absent from the conference, was on everyone's mind. In March, civil war had erupted there. British, French, and American forces had become involved in the fray on the side of Lenin's opponents. Would

---

▶ RESOURCE DIRECTORY

Teaching Resources

Reproducible Lesson Plan found in the Unit 6 folder, p. 79, provides a summary of the Section 5 lesson plan content.

Alternate Lesson Plan: Learning Styles found in the Alternate Lesson Plans folder, p. 104, extends students' understanding of the armistice through role-playing a press conference at the Treaty of Versailles and is especially effective for kinesthetic learners.

Guided Reading and Review found in the Unit 6 folder, p. 88, provides a structure for reading and mastering the key concepts and reviewing the key terms for Section 5. (Guided Practice)

Lenin's government collapse or prevail? Would it press for war claims?

From the start of the conference, Wilson was forced to compromise on his plans. He had to give up, for example, on the idea of self-determination for Germany's colonies, agreeing that the Allied powers could take them over.

Wilson did, however, get the other powers to postpone further discussion of Germany's fate and to move directly to his ideas for collective security. After ten days of hard work, he produced a plan for the **League of Nations,** an organization in which the nations of the world would join together to ensure security and peace for all members. Wilson then left for home, hoping to persuade Congress and the nation to accept his ideas.

Article 10 For Wilson, the heart of his proposal for the League of Nations was "Article 10." This provision pledged members to regard an attack on one as an attack on all. Since the League would not have any military power, the force of the article was moral only. Nevertheless, thirty-nine Republican senators or senators-elect signed a statement rejecting it, fearing the loss of American diplomatic independence.

MAKING CONNECTIONS

Were Wilson's goals for the peace process, as outlined in his Fourteen Points, consistent with his stated reasons for entering the war? Explain.

The Peace Treaty

In March, Wilson returned to the peace conference. The Big Four—Britain, France, Italy, and the United States—dominated the proceedings. Though the Allies accepted Wilson's plan for the League of Nations, French premier Georges Clemenceau used Wilson's embarrassment over American opposition to the League to exact harsh conditions against Germany. These included a fifteen-year French control of the mineral resources in Alsace-Lorraine. Wilson feared that this decision would lead to future wars, but he could not get Clemenceau to budge.

Viewpoints
On the League of Nations

Joining the League of Nations would involve a major commitment for the United States. The wisdom of making such a commitment was discussed from every angle. *On what basis does each speaker below support or oppose American entry into the League?*

For Joining the League of Nations
"The United States will, indeed, undertake . . . to 'respect and preserve as against external aggression the territorial integrity and existing political independence of all members of the League,' and that engagement constitutes a very grave and solemn moral obligation. But it is a moral, not a legal, obligation, and leaves our Congress absolutely free to put its own interpretation upon it."

President Woodrow Wilson, testifying before the Foreign Relations Committee, August 19, 1919

Against Joining the League of Nations
"Shall we go there, Mr. President, to sit in judgment, and in case that judgment works for peace join with our allies, but in case it works for war withdraw our cooperation? How long would we stand as we now stand, a great Republic commanding the respect and holding the leadership of the world, if we should adopt any such course?"

Senator William Borah (Idaho), testifying in the Senate, November 19, 1919

Wilson had to compromise elsewhere. Self-determination for the peoples of Austria-Hungary proved hard to apply. Central Europe was (and still is) an ethnic mixture of monumental complexity. As the map on page 570 shows, the conference created the new nations of Czechoslovakia and Yugoslavia, more nearly following ethnic lines than before the war. But these arrangements failed to resolve all ethnic tensions, which in the early 1990s contributed to the breakup of these nations.

War Guilt and Reparations Wilson met his greatest defeat when he gave in to French insistence on German war guilt and financial responsibility. The French wanted to cripple Germany. The British wanted **reparations**—payment from its enemy for the economic injury suffered in the war. In 1921 a Reparations

Viewpoints Activity On the League of Nations, found in the Unit 6 folder, pp. 92–93, expands on opinions both favoring and opposing the establishment of the League.

Answer to . . .

Viewpoints

Wilson supports joining the League to attain collective security; Borah views League membership as an excuse for drawing the United States into foreign quarrels and, therefore, foreign wars. For a more thorough examination of the League of Nations issue, see the Resource Directory below.

Answer to . . .

MAKING CONNECTIONS

Possible answer: Yes. Wilson entered the war with the goal of making the world safe for democracy. His Fourteen Points expressed his desire to have all nations respect one another's integrity.

2. INSTRUCT

Explain/Discuss

Explain that Wilson made several political mistakes that cost him support for his peace plan. Ask why the loss of Republican support hurt Wilson's efforts to negotiate and fulfill his promise to "make the world safe for democracy."

Discuss why such harsh conditions were imposed on Germany. How do students think the German people reacted to the treaty? Ask students whether they agree that the seeds of World War II were sown in the Versailles Treaty. Why or why not?

Discuss the problems caused by the sudden return of the troops from overseas. What did the returning veterans need? How did their return affect women workers?

Analyze

Ask students to explain why Americans were disillusioned at the start of the 1920s. What ideals had been shattered by the war? In what ways did the nation's successes during the war—in battle, in building support for the war, and in reorganizing the economy—contribute to the disillusionment that followed the war?

Caption Answer to ...

Interpreting Maps

The new map includes several new nations, for example, Poland, Czechoslovakia, and Yugoslavia. These nations resulted in part from Wilson's demand for self-determination.

Activity

Debate

Ask students to prepare arguments for or against United States membership in the League of Nations. Ask for pairs of volunteers to present their arguments at three-minute intervals. Ask one or two students to summarize the arguments on the chalkboard.

Enrichment

Ask students to research and report on the history of the League of Nations. How effective was it? What actions did it take? When was it dissolved? What organization eventually replaced it?

In Depth

Did You Know?

Many historians have shared German criticism of the terms of the Versailles Treaty on the grounds that it was unusually punitive and led to the growth of totalitarianism. Yet in March 1918 (see page 561), the Germans themselves had imposed just as harsh terms on the Russian Bolsheviks. Under the Treaty of Brest-Litovsk, the Bolsheviks yielded all of Poland, Lithuania, the Ukraine, Finland, the Baltic provinces, and neighboring territories. All told, they gave up the source of 90 percent of Russia's coal and 80 percent of its iron.

Europe After World War I

New nations

Allied-occupied zones

Geography and History: Interpreting Maps
The peace process helped lead to the transformation of the map of Europe.
In what ways does this map of Europe differ from the map on page 551?

Committee ruled that Germany owed the Allies $33 billion, an amount far beyond its ability to pay. As Wilson had feared, Germany never forgot or forgave this humiliation.

Signing the Treaty The Allies presented the treaty to the Germans on May 7, 1919. Insisting that the treaty violated the Fourteen Points, the Germans at first refused to sign. They soon gave in, however, when threatened with a French invasion. On June 28 the powers signed the treaty at Versailles, the former home of the French kings outside of Paris. Thus, the treaty is known as the **Versailles Treaty.**

Seeking Approval at Home

On July 8, treaty in hand, Wilson returned home to great acclaim. But many legislators had doubts. Some senators, called the "irreconcilables," opposed the treaty because it included American commitment to the League of Nations. Irreconcilables argued that joining the League would weaken American independence.

Senator Henry Cabot Lodge, chair of the Foreign Relations Committee, led another group called the "reservationists." This group wanted to impose reservations on American participation in the League. In particular they wanted a guarantee that the Monroe Doctrine would remain in force. Wilson's point that compliance with League decisions was "binding in conscience only, not in law," failed to persuade them.

Wilson Barnstorms the Country

Determined to win grass roots support for the League, Wilson took to the road. In twenty-three days he delivered three dozen speeches. In the midst of this tremendous effort, he suffered a stroke that paralyzed one side of his body. He would remain an invalid, isolated from his cabinet and visitors, for the rest of his term.

In his illness, Wilson grew increasingly inflexible. Congress would accept the treaty and the League as he envisioned it, or not at all. In November the Senate voted on the treaty with Lodge's reservations included. The vote was 39 for, 55 against. When the treaty came up without the reservations, it went down again, 38 to 53. In the face of popular dismay at this outcome, the Senate reconsidered the treaty in March, but once again the treaty failed to win approval. ✪

A Formal End to Hostilities On May 20, 1920, Congress voted to declare the war officially over. Steadfast to his principles, Wilson vetoed it. Finally, on July 2, 1921, another joint resolution to end the war passed. By that time a new President, Warren Harding, was in office and signed it. Congress ratified separate peace treaties with Germany, Austria, and Hungary that October.

Difficult Postwar Adjustments

The biggest winners from the war were American business and financial interests. The United States was now the world's richest creditor. In 1922 a Senate debt commission calculated that Europe owed the United States $11.5 billion.

RESOURCE DIRECTORY

Teaching Resources

✪ **Primary Source Activity** Mrs. Wilson's Role, found in the Unit 6 folder, p. 98, illustrates how First Lady Edith Wilson became the "voice" of President Wilson after her husband suffered a stroke.

The return to peace caused problems for the general population, however. There was no plan for reintegrating returning troops into society. The federal agencies that had controlled the economy during the war abruptly cancelled war contracts. By April 1919, about 4,000 servicemen a day were being mustered out of the armed forces. But jobs proved scarce. The women who had taken men's places in factories and offices also faced readjustment. Late in 1918, Mary Van Kleeck, head of the Women in Industry Service, reported that "the question heard most frequently was whether women would now retire from industry." Many women did, either voluntarily or because they were fired.

Postwar Despair Many artists and intellectuals in the United States faced the postwar years with disillusionment. Some progressives had been encouraged by the government-business collaboration during the war. But for most other reformers, the war years marked the end of an era of optimism.

This disillusionment was not unique to artists and intellectuals. Wrote Alice Lord O'Brian, a military post exchange director from Buffalo who was twice decorated,

> We all started out with high ideals . . . after being right up here almost at the front line . . . I cannot understand what it is all about or what has been accomplished by all this waste of youth.

African American Troops at Home Like white troops, African American soldiers

came home heroes. When the soldiers went to find jobs, however, the reception was quite different.

W.E.B. Du Bois, editor of the NAACP's magazine, the *Crisis*, had supported the war. In July 1918 he had written, "Let us, while this war lasts, forget our special grievances and close our ranks . . . with our white citizens and the allied nations that are fighting for democracy." A year later, after more lynchings of African Americans, including some still in uniform, his message became defiant. "This country of ours, despite all its better souls have done and dreamed, is yet a shameful land," he wrote in May 1919. "It **lynches**. . . . It steals from us. . . . It insults us. . . . We **return**. We **return from fighting**. We **return fighting**."

Du Bois's views, shared by many, heralded a new era in the struggle for equality. Indeed, the entire United States was on the threshold of a stormy era—the 1920s.

Weariness and fear line the face of Corporal Johnson of the 58th Regiment as he rests during a pause in battle. The experience of war left deep scars in the bodies and minds of many Americans.

SECTION 5 REVIEW

Key Terms, People, and Places
1. Describe (a) self-determination, (b) League of Nations, (c) reparations, (d) Versailles Treaty.

Key Concepts
2. What were Wilson's Fourteen Points, and what were its key elements?
3. What factors forced Wilson to compromise on his plans at the Paris peace conference?

4. What was the American reaction to the Treaty of Versailles and the League of Nations?
5. What factors contributed to the difficult postwar adjustment in the United States?

Critical Thinking
6. **Expressing Problems Clearly** It is often said that Wilson won the war but "lost the peace." Explain your understanding of this statement.

 Quiz found in the Unit 6 folder, p. 89, covers the main ideas in this section as well as the key terms.

 Chapter Test Forms A and B are found in the Unit 6 folder, pp. 104–109.

 Answer Keys found in the Unit 6 folder, pp. 116–126, provide answers to all student activities.

Media and Technology

Transparency
Graphic Organizer, G-4

Guided Reading Audiotapes
(English and Spanish)

Computer Test Bank

3. ASSESS

Section 5 Review Answers

1. (a) self-determination, see p. 568, (b) League of Nations, see p. 569, (c) reparations, see p. 569, (d) Versailles Treaty, see p. 570

2. The Fourteen Points were Wilson's peace program for the postwar era. They included a call for an end to secret alliances, restoration of freedom of the seas, arms reduction, self-determination for subject nationalities, and an association of nations to secure the peace.

3. The Allies demanded that Germany accept war guilt and financial responsibility, and they wanted pieces of Germany's colonies. Wilson wasn't interested in reward and wanted self-determination for the colonies.

4. There was widespread popular support for the Treaty, but many congressional representatives were against membership in the League.

5. Unemployment was a problem for many Americans who felt despair because the abstract ideals for which they had fought now seemed to be illusions. African Americans who had served overseas did not feel rewarded for their loyal service.

6. Possible answer: Wilson had directed the United States' victorious effort in the war. Yet at the peace conference, where Wilson hoped to parlay his influence into the shaping of a "noble peace," he was forced to give in to the bitterness of his allies.

Reteach

Ask students to write two headings on a piece of paper: Fourteen Points and Versailles Treaty. Have them list the key points of each in the appropriate column.

4. CLOSE

 Reinforcing the Big Idea

President Wilson's idealistic hopes for the provisions of the peace settlement were dashed by the Allies and by the United States Congress. The mood of the country as it entered the 1920s was stormy and disillusioned.

Chapter Review Answers

Understanding Key Terms, People, and Places

Terms
Students should refer to the definitions of the key terms in the chapter to write sentences that show the relation of each word to the outbreak of World War I, United States involvement in the war, or events that followed the conflict.

True or False
1. false, Allies
2. false, Industrial Workers of the World
3. false, reparations
4. true
5. false, Fourteen Points

Reviewing Main Ideas

1. Before 1914, the treaty system created a fragile balance of power. In 1914, however, the complex system of treaties and alliances brought most of Europe into a war that began as a dispute between Serbia and Austria-Hungary.

2. Because military leaders were not experienced in fighting with modern weaponry, no one was able to achieve victory. The mounting death toll that resulted led to loss of morale and acts of desperation.

3. Some American business leaders saw the war as an opportunity for economic expansion. Others pushed for neutrality, and some also urged preparedness, so that the United States would be ready to protect its commercial interests.

4. Americans developed an anti-German attitude because of German submarine warfare, British propaganda, and the revelation of the Zimmerman note.

5. Germany resumed its unrestricted submarine warfare.

6. Reasons included pressure from commercial interests and wide popular support, shaped in part by British propaganda.

7. At first, Americans envisioned themselves as playing only a supporting role in the war, but the Allies demanded that the United States send troops to help boost morale. The Allies' military needs also led to greater American involvement.

8. General Pershing at first sought to keep his troops separate from other Allied troops. Within American ranks, African Americans were segregated from white troops.

9. Holding firmly to their positions, American troops were able to save Paris and blunt the edge of the German advance.

Chapter Review

Understanding Key Terms, People, and Places

Key Terms
1. Central Powers
2. Allies
3. U-boat
4. *Lusitania*
5. Zimmerman note
6. American Expeditionary Force
7. armistice
8. Liberty Bond
9. Industrial Workers of the World
10. Fourteen Points
11. self-determination
12. League of Nations
13. reparations
14. Versailles Treaty

People
15. Kaiser Wilhelm
16. autocrat
17. doughboy

Terms For each term above, write a sentence that explains its relation to the outbreak of World War I, United States involvement in the war, or events that followed the conflict.

True or False Determine whether each statement is true or false. If it is true, write "true." If it is false, change the underlined term to make the statement true.
1. At the outbreak of World War I, the <u>Central Powers</u> consisted of Russia, France, and Great Britain.
2. The <u>American Expeditionary Force,</u> a radical labor organization, sought the overthrow of capitalism.
3. After the war, the European Allies demanded harsh <u>self-determination</u> from Germany.
4. Americans bought <u>Liberty Bonds</u> to help finance the war.
5. Wilson's peace program came to be called the <u>Zimmerman note</u>.

Reviewing Main Ideas

Section 1 (pp. 550–553)
1. How did the role of secret European treaties shift in 1914?
2. Why did troops fighting in the war resort to acts of desperation?
3. What position did businesses in the United States take regarding the war?

Section 2 (pp. 555–558)
4. For what reasons did many Americans develop an anti-German attitude?
5. Why was Wilson unable to keep his campaign promise to maintain neutrality?
6. In addition to Germany's refusal to respect American claims to neutrality, name two other reasons why the United States entered the war.

Section 3 (pp. 559–563)
7. Describe how Americans envisioned their role when they first entered the war. What led to the expansion of the American role in World War I?

8. What types of segregation occurred during the war?
9. Explain how the Allies were able to turn the tide of the war.

Section 4 (pp. 564–567)
10. Describe the changes in American life brought about by the War Industries Board, the National War Labor Board, and other new government agencies.
11. What was the result of news and media coming under government control during the war?
12. In what ways were people's civil liberties limited during the war?
13. Name some positive effects of the war.

Section 5 (pp. 568–571)
14. What was the response of the French and British to Wilson's peace plan?
15. Briefly describe congressional opposition to the League of Nations.
16. Describe the postwar adjustment for African Americans.

10. Answers include gasless days, daylight savings time, punishment for firms suspected of dealing with the enemy, and the mediation of labor disputes that might hinder the war effort.

11. The government was able to control the public's response to the war through propaganda.

12. The federal government actively attacked dissent with strict, harsh laws. Also, nativist sentiment was unleashed against German Americans, leading to much abuse.

13. The war propelled certain people into higher paid work and temporarily diminished discrimination against African Americans, Mexican Americans, and women.

14. They wanted harsher treatment for Germany.

15. The Reservationists wanted a guarantee that the Monroe Doctrine would remain in force.

16. Despite a triumphant return, African Americans again faced unemployment, discrimination, and even lynchings on their return home.

Alternative Assessment

Final Evaluation
Use the following guidelines to evaluate student projects:
● **Evidence of mastery of content** To what extent do projects demonstrate knowledge and understanding of chapter content?
● **Evidence of thoughtfulness** To what extent do projects demonstrate an understanding of the importance and significance of events?
● **Evidence of outside research** To what extent do projects use outside research materials?

Thinking Critically

1. **Recognizing Ideologies** When the United States entered World War I, it hoped to play a supporting role as an "associate." What does this assumption suggest about the country's view of itself at the time?
2. **Identifying Central Issues** In what ways did World War I differ from previous wars involving the United States?
3. **Checking Consistency** Many members of Congress worried that the League of Nations would limit the independence of the United States. Based on what you have read about World War I, how independent was the United States from the affairs of Europe?

Making Connections

1. **Evaluating Primary Sources** Review the primary source excerpt on page 563. How would you expect such attitudes to affect soldiers returning from World War I?
2. **Understanding the Visuals** Examine the cartoon and the newspaper clippings on page 556. Do the cartoon and the clipping on the left support or refute each other? Explain your answer.
3. **Writing About the Chapter** Imagine that World War I has recently ended. Write a statement to Congress in which you express your opinion of President Wilson's proposal for the League of Nations. First, create a list of what you see as the positive aspects of Wilson's plan. Then, list the negative features. Note any suggestions you have for improvements. Next, write a draft of your statement in which you offer your ideas. Revise your statement, making certain that each idea is clearly explained. Proofread your statement and draft a final copy.
4. **Using the Graphic Organizer** This graphic organizer uses a modified flow map to organize information about the events leading to World War I and about early responses to the war on the part of Americans. Flow maps can show both a sequence of events or what happened as the result of an event. (a) Based on the chart, what was the cause of Americans becoming increasingly alarmed about the war? (b) What was the effect of American alarm? (c) On a separate sheet of paper, create your own flow map about American involvement in World War I in Europe and on the home front, using this graphic organizer as an example.

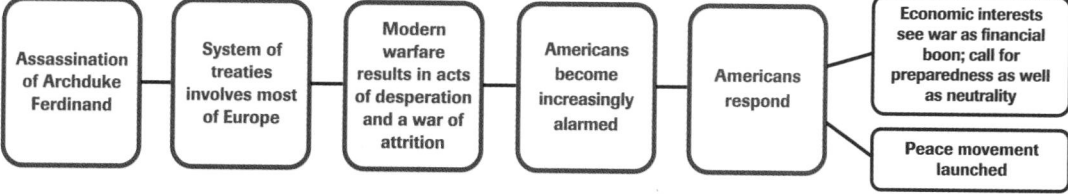

Thinking Critically

1. The United States considered itself independent of the affairs of Europe.

2. It differed in the number of countries and regions involved, the fact that the war was fought entirely outside North America, and the effect of new weapons of mass destruction.

3. Possible answer: The fact that the United States was drawn into World War I indicates that the United States could never keep itself completely independent of European affairs.

Making Connections

1. Possible answer: Returning soldiers might face difficulty finding meaning in their war experience and readjusting to life during peacetime.

2. The visuals refute each other. Although the cartoon illustrates an uncaring and unconcerned Germany, the newspaper clipping shows that Germany did take some measures to warn the public not to board the *Lusitania*.

3. Statements should contain students' opinions of both positive and negative aspects of the League, as well as specific ideas for improvements.

Tell students that contemporary African American poet Margaret Walker calls the South the "sorrow home." Ask students why thousands of African Americans left their homes and communities to move to the cities of the North.

Ask students to scan the images in the American Album feature and to classify them into two categories. First have students identify those items that represent conditions in the South that pushed African Americans toward migration. (*doll, record book, home school, plow*) Then ask them to identify those that represent the attraction pulling African Americans to the North. (*job poster, soldiers*) Discuss the significance of the suitcase and the Bibles in terms of the community the migrants had to leave.

Explain to students that in 1940 and 1941, African American artist Jacob Lawrence painted a series of sixty panels, called "The Migration of the Negro," that tell the story of the extraordinary movement of people from South to North. (See the Transparency Binder in the Resource Directory on page 547.) Ask students to work in groups to plan a mural depicting items or conditions—such as those displayed in the American Album—that reflect an African American family's decision to leave their home in the rural South. Students should prepare a brief description of each panel in the mural.

FROM FIELD TO FACTORY

Beginning in 1915, hundreds of thousands of African Americans moved from the rural South to the cities of the North. Most African Americans made this "Great Migration" to take advantage of job opportunities in the North. Others, however, moved to escape the poverty and discrimination they faced in the Jim Crow South. This migration changed the lives of the African Americans who made the journey, and it changed the nature of race relations in the North. *How did the lives of African Americans change when they moved from the fields of the South to the factories of northern cities?*

▲ HANDMADE DOLL
Cash-poor African Americans made or grew much of what they used in the South. This doll had its own handmade cradle and blankets.

▲ STORE OWNER'S RECORD BOOK The southern store owner kept track of sharecroppers' debts and payments in a ledger like this. Few African American sharecroppers ever made enough money to pay what they owed the store owner.

▲ PLOW More than two thirds of the African Americans living in the South were sharecropping farmers. Farming was back-breaking work for the whole family and seldom yielded more than survival. Farmers walked behind a mule-drawn plow like this one to break the land.

▼ SUITCASE AND BIBLES African Americans in the South had strong community ties, which centered around the local church. Leaving this community, even to escape hardships, was difficult.

LABORERS WANTED
AT
HOG ISLAND
GOVERNMENT SHIPBUILDING
35¢ AN HOUR
$3.85 A DAY
A CHANCE TO LEARN A GOOD TRADE AND GET
HIGHER WAGES
Apply 150 3rd Ave.—15-St.

▲ JOB OPPORTUNITIES Because of World War I, industries could not get new laborers from Europe. Also, many native-born workers were drawn into the armed forces. African Americans streamed north to fill these open jobs.

◄ HOME SCHOOLING There were few schools for African Americans in the rural South, and the ones that existed were poor. Parents frequently were forced to be their children's teachers.

WORLD WAR I SOLDIERS ► Many African Americans learned about the opportunities in the North when they served as soldiers during World War I. For most soldiers, this was the first time they traveled more than a few miles from home.

Boom Times to Hard Times
1919–1938

Introducing the Unit

Interpreting the Visual In March 1936, Dorothea Lange (1895–1965) made the photograph on pages 576–577 for the Farm Security Administration (FSA), a New Deal agency for which she took photographs from 1935 to 1939. "I saw and approached the hungry and desperate mother as if drawn by a magnet." Lange's evocative images of migrant farm families suffering terrible hardships during the Depression had great political impact, inspiring support for government relief programs. The FSA compiled the largest archive of Depression photographs, some 216,000 in all.

Herbert Hoover's words on page 576 provide an ironic contrast to Lange's photograph. Read the quote from Hoover to the class and ask students to determine which occurred first, the scene in the photograph or the quote.

Divide the class into two groups. Ask one group to write questions that they would like to ask the woman in the photograph. Ask the other half to pretend that they are the woman and to write questions for President Hoover about the country's economy.

Ask students to compare Lange's photograph to images of victims of poverty, war, and natural disasters appearing today in newspapers and newsmagazines. What gave Lange's work such impact?

Establishing Chronology Remind students that the previous chapter focused on the period of World War I, which ended in 1918. Explain that Unit 7 covers the two decades between the world wars. During the 1920s, the nation's economy soared, only to collapse in 1929. The 1930s were the bleak years of the Great Depression and the attempts of FDR's New Deal to restore the nation's vitality.

Boom Times to Hard Times
1919–1938

"We in America today are nearer to the final triumph over poverty than ever before."

—Herbert Hoover, 1928

When President Herbert Hoover spoke these words, he expressed the optimism and faith in business and technology that characterized the United States in the 1920s. Following the stock market crash of October 1929, however, the fragile prosperity of the decade gave way to a period of severe economic distress known as the Great Depression. In the election of 1932, voters chose Franklin Delano Roosevelt for President, a choice that marked a turning point in the way Americans would view their Presidents.

CHAPTER 21
Pages 578–605
A Stormy Era 1919–1929

CHAPTER 22
Pages 608–637
Crash and Depression 1929–1933

CHAPTER 23
Pages 638–659
The New Deal 1933–1938

▶ RESOURCE DIRECTORY

Teaching Resources

 Local History Activity "Down and Out in Newark" and the Local Focus research topic suggestions, found in the Local History Resources folder, pp. 21–23, are designed to help students understand how history affects all lives.

★ **Themes in American History Posters** Wall-size, illustrated posters, found in the Teaching Resources package, illustrate the four unit themes.

Unit Test Forms A and B are found in the Unit 7 folder, pp. 110–115.

During the Great Depression, poverty and suffering were constant traveling companions to families like the one above, forced to move from town to town to look for work.

Media and Technology

Visions of America: Scenes of an Era To introduce students to the main idea and events covered in this unit, play "Scenes of an Era: Boom Times to Hard Times" (length: 2.5 minutes). This selection can be located on side 3 of the videodiscs. This selection can also be located on videotape 4. Lesson plans for "Scenes of an Era" can be found in the Visions of America Guidebook.

Using Multimedia Technology This folder contains instructional tools and strategies for using technology in the classroom.

Transparency Binder Contains full-color transparencies with lesson suggestions. From a large collection divided into twelve categories, specific transparencies are referenced throughout the chapter at appropriate points of use. For this unit, see American Photo, B-7; Fine Art, D-8; Cause and Effect, F-9; The Way It Works, H-18; Links Across Time, J-7; and Political Cartoon, K-7.

Themes in American History

Teachers may wish to discuss specific historical events in the context of historical themes. Here are four suggestions for Unit 7.

Diversity *Throughout its history America has been made up of a gathering of many peoples from throughout the world. Americans have both benefited from and encountered problems with this diversity.*

● Immigration from southern and eastern European countries, which had been increasing since the late 1800s, was abruptly halted in the 1920s because of restrictive quotas.
● Many African Americans moved from the South to northern cities. They found opportunities, but also faced discrimination and violence.

American Culture *In every period of their history, Americans gave special expression to their views through art, literature, films, music, manners, and morals.*

● The 1920s experienced a rapid shift in fashions, music, manners, and morality that marked a dramatic break with the past. African Americans experienced a "black renaissance."
● A revolution in communications led to a period of bigger-than-life heroes and a growth in consumer products.

Economics *Americans have searched for new and better ways to make a living and have struggled to define government's role in this pursuit.*

● Americans demanded that their government take an active role to relieve the despair and suffering of the Depression. New Deal programs provided relief.

Environment *The geography and available resources of the continent have affected the actions of Americans. Similarly, the actions of Americans have affected the environment and physical landscape.*

● Unwise farming practices in the Great Plains and an extended drought caused the area to become a dust bowl.
● Massive public projects built dams to harness hydroelectric power and to control flooding.

Chapter 21 A Stormy Era
1919–1929

📁 **Teaching Resources** (See Unit 7 Folder)

	Instruction	Enrichment
Section 1 **Postwar Adjustments** (pp. 580–583)	Reproducible Lesson Plan, p. 3 Alternate Lesson Plan, p. 106 Guided Reading and Review, p. 8 Quiz, p. 9	History Might Not . . . Activity, Lobbying for Indian Immigration, pp. 18–19
Section 2 **Social and Political Developments** (pp. 586–590)	Reproducible Lesson Plan, p. 4 Alternate Lesson Plan, p. 107 Guided Reading and Review, p. 10 Quiz, p. 11	Primary Source Activity, Growing Up Black, pp. 26–27 Literature Activity, The Weary Blues, p. 31 American Profiles Activity, Bessie Smith, p. 20

Section 3
New Manners, New Morals
(pp. 591–594)
	Reproducible Lesson Plan, p. 5
	Alternate Lesson Plan, p. 108
	Guided Reading and Review, p. 12
	Quiz, p. 13
		Critical Thinking Activity, Testing Conclusions,
		  p. 25
		American Profiles Activity, Lillian Moller
		  Gilbreth, p. 21
		Historian's Toolbox Activity, Analyzing Adver-
		  tisements, p. 24

Section 4
Creating a Shared Culture
(pp. 596–599)
	Reproducible Lesson Plan, p. 6
	Alternate Lesson Plan, p. 109
	Guided Reading and Review, p. 14
	Quiz, p. 15
		Visual Learning Activity, Advertising Tech-
		  niques of the 1920s, p. 33
		Primary Source Activity, Teens and Cigarette
		  Smoking, p. 28

Section 5
Stemming the Tide of Change
(pp. 600–603)
	Reproducible Lesson Plan, p. 7
	Alternate Lesson Plan, p. 110
	Guided Reading and Review, p. 16
	Quiz, p. 17
	Chapter Test, Forms A & B, pp. 34–39
		Viewpoints Activity, On the Eighteenth
		  Amendment, pp. 22–23
		Visual Learning Activity, The Ku Klux Klan,
		  p. 32
		Literature Activity, Tales of the Jazz Age,
		  pp. 29–30

📁 **Additional Chapter Resources**

Resource Organizer, p. 2
Alternate Lesson Plan, p. 105
Answer Keys, pp. 116–128

Bibliography

For the Teacher

Delany, Sarah Louise and Annie Elizabeth. *Having Our Say: The Delany Sisters' First 100 Years.* Kodansha,1993. (History as lived by the Delany sisters—from Jim Crow, through Harlem migration and Depression, to the present day.)

Lemann, Nicholas. *The Promised Land, The Great Black Migration and How It Changed America.* Alfred A. Knopf, Inc., 1991. (A recent study of African American migration.)

Prentice Hall Literature Excerpts from *The American Experience,* 1994, including Hurston, Zora Neale. *Dust Tracks on a Road.* HarperCollins,1970 edition.

The Big Idea for the chapter and how the main ideas in each section relate to the Big Idea are graphically displayed below. Comprehension of this chapter's Big Idea is critical to students' understanding of United States history and how we as a nation got where we are today.

Media and Technology

Visions of America: History Might Not Have Happened This Way Game

Fine Art, D-16, D-17; Our Multicultural Heritage, C-12

The Way It Works, H-18

Graphic Organizer, G-3

Guided Reading Audiotapes (English and Spanish)

Computer Test Bank

For the Student

Bogart, Max, ed. *The Jazz Age.* Macmillan, 1969. (An anthology of literature of the 1920s.)

Willis-Braithwaite, Deborah. *Van Der Zee.* Harry N. Abrams, 1993. (Harlem in its heyday as seen by its most famous photographer.)

CHAPTER 21

American society changed in many ways following World War I. Conflict existed between those Americans ready to adopt new manners and new ways and those Americans who tried to resist the forces of change.

SECTION 1

After World War I, fear of radicals and communism turned many Americans against progressive ideas of reform.

SECTION 2

After the war, important social and political developments included women's suffrage and the Great Migration north by African Americans. During this time Republicans gained national support.

SECTION 3

The Jazz Age introduced a variety of new styles, tastes, and manners; and popular media spread the new image.

SECTION 4

Population movement and developments in communication and transportation helped to create a national culture as Americans throughout the country began to share the same information and experiences.

SECTION 5

Some Americans tried to slow the pace of change that followed the war. Whether through prohibition or through the terrorism of the Ku Klux Klan, such attempts were generally unsuccessful.

A Stormy Era
1919–1929

CHAPTER 21

A Stormy Era
1919–1929

The Relevance of the Big Idea

Tell students that in the 1920s, Americans were divided over issues such as the ones discussed in this chapter. Manners and styles changed quickly after World War I. Young urban Americans in particular adopted the new styles and manners, while some other Americans tried to stop what they saw as the nation's moral decay.

Structure a class discussion on the following topic: What are the issues about which Americans of different generations disagree? Have students generate a list of issues, such as fashions, hairstyles, movies, television programming, and music, and explain why these issues have become subjects of generational controversy.

"*My candle burns at both ends . . . *" wrote poet Edna St. Vincent Millay in 1920, a phrase that can be used to symbolize a divided nation during the entire decade. Some people wanted to put aside the horrible memories of war and so embraced anything new, be it product, attitude, or behavior. Others wanted to shield their eyes from the responsibility that came with being a new global power and tried to pull the nation back to attitudes and behaviors that were known and "safe."

In Depth

Global Connections

After the devastation of the war in Europe and the deaths of more than 100,000 Americans out of two million who had been shipped "over there," Americans worked to withdraw from world affairs and focus on improving their lives at home. Material dreams, not the idealistic dreams that sent Americans to fight in Europe, were the important ones. Coolidge defined business as "one of the great contributing forces to the moral and spiritual advancement of the race."

Events in the United States

Events in the World

1919 Attorney General Palmer begins raids on suspected radicals. • Chicago race riot occurs.	**1920** Warren Harding elected President. • The first commercial radio broadcast is made.		**1922** T. S. Eliot publishes "The Wasteland."	**1923** Harding dies; Calvin Coolidge takes office. • Bessie Smith records her first jazz album.	
1919	**1920**	**1921**	**1922**	**1923**	
	1920 The Treaty of Versailles ends World War I. • The League of Nations is formed.	**1921** Takashi Hara, Premier of Japan, is assassinated.		**1923** Adolf Hitler fails in an attempted coup in Germany.	

RESOURCE DIRECTORY

Teaching Resources

Alternate Lesson Plan: Demonstrating the Big Idea found in the Alternate Lesson Plans folder, p. 105, provides a lesson strategy to instruct students about the Big Idea that the 1920s were years of change as well as resistance to change.

Alternative Assessment Handbook provides information, guidance, and strategies for alternative methods of assessment. It includes an essay on new trends in assessment, guidance and strategies for developing performance tasks and portfolios, scoring rubrics, and sample evaluation forms.

Pages 580–583
Postwar Adjustments

With the shadow of World War I finally lifting, some Americans hoped the way toward progressive-style reform would be relighted. Others, however, began to view such ideas for change with suspicion and fear.

 Pages 586–590
Social and Political Developments

After the war, women and African Americans faced a world of new opportunities and old disappointments. In the political realm, Republicans won Americans' support—and votes.

 Pages 591–594
New Manners, New Morals

From rising hemlines to the energetic sounds of jazz, the 1920s daringly broke with tradition. New social freedoms created opportunity—and dilemmas—for women. But beneath it all lay a nagging question: How much had really changed?

 Pages 596–599
Creating a Shared Culture

People in city apartments, country farmhouses, and everywhere in between were connected in new ways in the 1920s. Such links allowed sweeping changes to envelop the entire nation.

 Pages 600–603
Stemming the Tide of Change

Jazz music, moving pictures, fast cars—American life moved at a dizzying pace in the 1920s. All the motion left some people feeling queasy, and they sought to slow the pace of change.

	1925 The Charleston becomes a dance craze. • John Scopes is tried for teaching evolution.		**1927** Charles Lindbergh flies solo across the Atlantic Ocean. • Ford begins production of the Model A.	**1928** Republican Herbert Hoover is elected President.	**1929** Ten million families own radios.
1924	**1925**	**1926**	**1927**	**1928**	**1929**
1924 V. I. Lenin, founder of the Soviet Union, dies. • France hosts the first Winter Olympics.		**1926** Ibn Saud becomes king of Saudi Arabia. • French painter Claude Monet dies.		**1928** Chiang Kai-shek becomes president of China.	**1929** The term apartheid is introduced in South Africa.

Media and Technology

 Transparencies
Time Lines, E-6; Historical Maps, L-5

 ## Alternative Assessment

As an ongoing chapter project, students can create a decade-in-review project for the 1920s entitled "The 1920s: Change and Opposition." The objective is to illustrate the concept of change and opposition to change. Students need to use information from the chapter as well as conduct additional research. Research may include examination of documents and published sources, or interviews. Students might design the projects in a variety of ways. Suggestions follow, but students may come up with an original format.

• Develop a point of view to be published in a newsmagazine.
• Create a newspaper page, including photographs and illustrations with captions as well as short news pieces.
• Make an audiotape of a simulated radio program and include interviews with notable figures from the decade or the person on the street.

Explain that finished projects will be assessed according to the following standards:

• **Unacceptable** Activity not attempted; projects fail to meet requirements outlined.
• **Limited/Acceptable** Projects are based on material from the textbook and reflect some effort to show connections among topics.
• **Extensive/Commendable** Projects are based on some outside research, indicate general relationships among topics, and reflect the student's own position.
• **Extraordinary/Outstanding** Projects are based on considerable outside research, highlight specific as well as general relationships among topics, and reflect an in-depth position by the student.

Students may choose to include finished projects in their portfolio.

For information and guidance on alternative assessment trends and strategies, see Alternative Assessment Handbook in the Resource Directory on page 578.

SECTION 1

Postwar Adjustments

Connecting to the Big Idea

See page 578B. Tell students that after the war Americans tried to return to their normal lives. While progressives hoped to continue the prewar era of reform, many Americans viewed proposals for change with fear and suspicion. Ask students what events caused Americans to grow anxious about change.

Objectives

● Describe the postwar economic adjustments and labor unrest that troubled the nation after World War I.
● Describe the causes and results of the "red scare."
● Show how the United States limited immigration and foreign entanglements in the 1920s.

Bellringer

Write the word *optimism* on the board. Ask students to jot down a definition and to think about what the word might have to do with the climate in the United States during the early postwar years.

Reading Strategy

Reading for Evidence As they read the section, ask students to find evidence that some Americans looked on proposals for changing and improving society with "suspicion and fear" as stated on page 580.

Explain/Discuss

Review with students the progressives' belief that solutions could be found for the problems of the nation and of its citizens. Why did progressives think that the problems of the nation could be solved?

SECTION PREVIEW

With the shadow of World War I finally lifting, some Americans hoped the way toward progressive-style reform would be relighted. Others, however, began to view such ideas for change with suspicion and fear.

Key Concepts
• Postwar economic adjustments and labor unrest troubled the nation.
  • Fears that the ideas of the Russian Revolution would spread led to a "red scare" in the United States.
  • Efforts to limit immigration and foreign entanglements won wide support in the 1920s.

Key Terms, People, and Places
communist, red scare, general strike; Vladimir I. Lenin, Nicola Sacco, Bartolomeo Vanzetti

After the Russian Revolution, many Americans saw the Communist hammer and sickle as a symbol of a threat to the United States.

World War I was over. Now was the time, progressive reformers thought, to relaunch plans for economic and social change, such as unemployment insurance and housing initiatives, put on hold during the war.

The times, however, were less ripe for change than reformers hoped. The unprecedented brutality of the war had wounded the nation's spirit. Europe, once the model of enlightened civilization, was now viewed with disgust. Fear about the worldwide effects of revolution in Russia swept the country. And as the United States endured a bumpy transition back to peacetime, many Americans began to view proposals for changing society with suspicion and fear.

Postwar Economic Adjustments

During the war, American factories geared up to meet the demand for ships, guns, food, and other goods. When this demand dropped after the war, the economy entered a difficult period of adjustment. Returning veterans faced unemployment. When they got their jobs back, they did so by taking those that had been filled by women and minorities. In addition, food prices and rents shot up in the spring of 1919, and by 1920 the cost of living was more than double what it had been before the war. Farmers suffered as wartime orders declined and European farmers began producing crops again. Prices for wheat, corn, and hay dropped by half.

Labor unrest became increasingly common. From 1916 through 1920, the United States experienced between 3,350 and 4,450 strikes a year, most caused by disputes over wages and hours. When factory owners discovered that the absence of unions in the South helped make southern labor costs much lower than those in the North, many moved their businesses south, leaving northern mill towns to die. Union members responded with outrage.

The Russian Revolution Causes a Red Scare

The end of World War I did not bring an end to the turmoil overseas. As the fighting in Europe entered its final months, Russia erupted in revolution. Few foreign events would have as long-lasting an impact on the United States.

In March 1917, revolutionary forces overthrew the Russian monarchy headed by Czar Nicholas II and set up a representative form of government. Under the leadership of Aleksandr Kerensky, a lawyer who had defended opponents of the czarist regime, the new government pledged to continue in the European war. This pledge hurt Kerensky's standing with Russia's hungry workers and peasants, to whom the war seemed remote and unrelated.

Revolutionary leader **Vladimir I. Lenin** soon undermined Kerensky's power with

---

RESOURCE DIRECTORY

Teaching Resources

Reproducible Lesson Plan found in the Unit 7 folder, p. 3, provides a summary of the Section 1 lesson plan content.

Alternate Lesson Plan: Critical Thinking Recognizing Cause and Effect, found in the Alternate Lesson Plans folder, p. 106, is an alternate lesson plan that helps students clearly recognize cause and effect through construction of a graphic organizer.

Guided Reading and Review found in the Unit 7 folder, p. 8, provides a structure for reading and mastering the key concepts and reviewing the key terms for Section 1. (Guided Practice)

promises of "peace, land, and bread." This message offered hope to Russia's weary people.

Although in the minority, Lenin and his followers believed that they represented all of Russia's workers. They therefore took the name *Bolsheviks*, the Russian word for *the majority*. They also adopted the red flag as their emblem.

In November 1917, the Bolsheviks overthrew Kerensky. Their new state, which eventually became the Union of Soviet Socialist Republics, made peace with Germany. It adopted socialism, a political and economic system in which all of society—represented by the government—jointly owns all property. Lenin also referred to his new regime as **communist**, a term that comes from the writings of German philosopher Karl Marx. It describes the revolutionary system that exists when workers have taken over a society and proclaimed an end to all differences between social and economic classes.

Lenin's ideas appealed to many poor Russians. But others resisted violently, and in early 1918, Russia erupted in civil war. Soldiers from Britain, France, Japan, and the United States intervened militarily on the side of Lenin's opponents to protect their countries' investments in the former Russia.

Lenin's "Reds" eventually won the civil war in 1920, and they resolved to fulfill Marx's ideology by spreading communism to other nations. From then on, the United States regarded the Bolshevik Reds as the world's villain.

National Unrest Is Blamed on the Reds In the United States, a rash of labor strikes and terrorist acts convinced many that the Reds were about to take over. A **red scare**—the fear of communism, socialism, or other so-called extreme ideas—gripped the nation.

One major strike took place in Seattle in January 1919. Shipworkers walked off their jobs and later were joined by workers in other industries. This action, one in which many unions participate as a show of worker unity, is known as a **general strike**. The Seattle strike paralyzed industry, trade, and the delivery of essential services in the area for five days. It also convinced many Americans that the United States was on the brink of revolution.

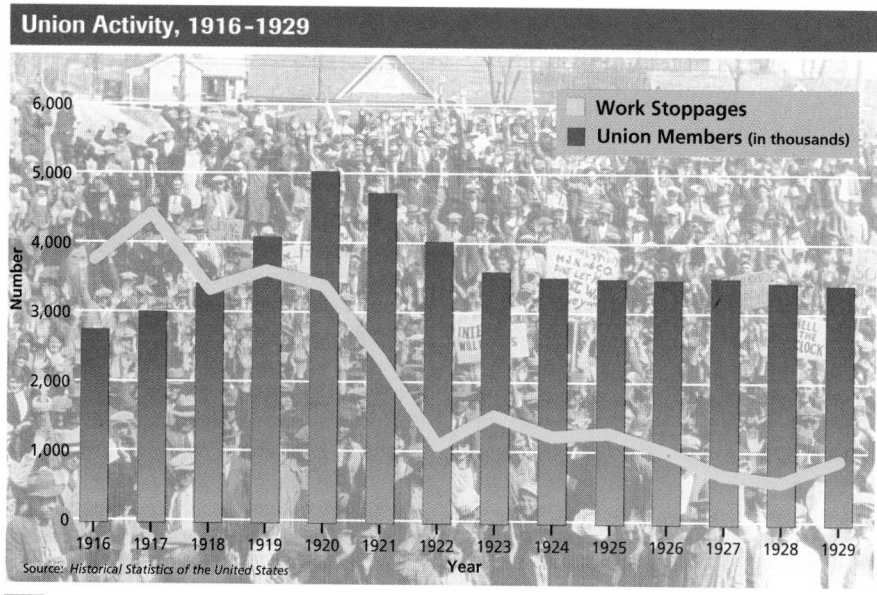

Union Activity, 1916–1929

Work Stoppages
Union Members (in thousands)

Source: *Historical Statistics of the United States*

 Interpreting Graphs
The post–World War I years were stormy ones for labor and business. The number of annual strikes was high and union membership also rose slightly. *Based on this information, how would you summarize the condition of organized labor in the 1920s?*

Discuss with students how a long, brutal war might have changed people's view of the world. Encourage discussion with questions such as: How did postwar economic adjustments make Americans anxious? Why did demand lessen for the products of American factories and farms? Why did labor disputes increase? Why did many factory owners move their operations to the South?

Analyze

Have students analyze Americans' fear of communism. In what ways did the communist government established in Russia by Lenin differ from the government of the United States? Why did Lenin encourage communist revolutions in other countries?

Have students define the red scare and tell how it affected reform proposals. How did events such as the Palmer raids and the Sacco and Vanzetti trial affect legislation regarding immigration?

Caption Answer to ...

Interpreting Graphs

Union membership declined slightly and reached a more or less stable level. The remaining union workers struck far less often than they had in the postwar years.

 In Depth

Did You Know?

Radio became a popular medium for evangelists in the 1920s. The best known of these was Billy Sunday, a one-time professional baseball player. His nativist views were heard by thousands throughout the country. When 249 aliens were deported to Russia on December 21, 1919, Sunday preached, "If I had my way with these ornery wild-eyed Socialists and I.W.W.'s, I would stand them up before a firing squad and save space on our ships."

The case of Sacco and Vanzetti, who are pictured below, inspired much protest, including this piece of folk art.

Such fears set the stage for violent attacks on unions. In September, steelworkers in Gary, Indiana, and several other cities struck over hours, wages, shop conditions, and company recognition of their union. Claiming that the strike was the work of communists, the United States Steel Corporation used force to break it, killing eighteen and beating hundreds more.

Also that fall, Boston's police force tried to win their first pay raise since the start of World War I. When the police commissioner fired nineteen officers for union activity, the whole force voted to strike.

Many Bostonians were frightened and outraged by the police strike. But Massachusetts governor Calvin Coolidge responded quickly, proclaiming, "There is no right to strike against the public safety by anybody, anywhere, anytime." He received national attention for his firm response to the police walkout.

The Palmer Raids Convinced by the events of 1919 that the country was about to fall to radicals, many Americans grew anxious. Attorney General A. Mitchell Palmer, a man with political ambitions combined with a genuine fear of the communist threat, responded with enthusiasm. He set up an antiradical division to raid organizations suspected of so-called radical activity. These included communist and anarchist groups.

Thousands of individuals, mostly foreign-born and many innocent of any crime, were jailed as a result of the raids. Eventually, over five hundred people were deported without being formally charged with or convicted of any crimes. The army's chief of staff recommended that they be sent away on "ships of stone with sails of lead," and preacher Billy Sunday recommended a firing squad to save money on the ships.

The antiradical campaign then sputtered out, in part because some of its followers went too far. For example, in January 1920 the New York State Assembly voted to expel five socialist members, even though they had been legally elected and had violated no rules or laws. The assembly's defiance of the democratic process aroused wide protests.

Although the red scare faded, fear of revolution lingered. Indeed, these fears put a halt to reformers' postwar plans. Skillful use of terms such as *un-American* or *Bolshevik* by reform opponents was enough to denounce any proposal. Plans for state-supported housing initiatives, health and unemployment insurance, and a social-security system received little support.

MAKING CONNECTIONS

The United States Constitution is designed to protect expression of most ideas—even those that are unpopular. Did the Palmer raids violate this design? At what point is it acceptable to limit political speech?

The Sacco and Vanzetti Case

The red scare played a part in one of the most controversial events in United States history. The story began on April 15, 1920, when gunmen robbed and killed the guard and paymaster of a South Braintree, Massachusetts, shoe factory. A few weeks later, police arrested two Italian immigrants, shoemaker **Nicola Sacco** and fish peddler **Bartolomeo Vanzetti**, in connection with the crimes. Both were carrying guns at the time of their arrest, and Sacco's was the same model used in the crime. They were convicted and sentenced to die.

At the time, many Americans felt that the trial of Sacco and Vanzetti was unfair. The two admitted to being anarchists, and it seemed clear that their political views—as well as their

Italian heritage—had played a bigger role in their conviction than had any evidence against them. Appeals went on for years, but the original decision stood. In 1927, the two men were electrocuted.

The Sacco and Vanzetti case divided the country and provoked an international outcry. Some thought they were innocent. Others felt that, regardless of the pair's guilt or innocence, they had not been fairly tried. The two men, dignified to the end, went to their deaths comforted only by the thought that their fate would spark wider discussion of important issues. A writer who visited Vanzetti two days before his execution reported him as saying,

> This is our career and our triumph. Never in our full life could we hope to do such work for tolerance, for justice, for man's understanding of man as we now do by accident.

Renewed Isolationism and Nativism

Hostility to foreign people and ideas in the 1920s found expression in a renewed isolationism. The League of Nations was, as President Warren G. Harding said, "as dead as slavery." As for concerns about the security and safety of European countries, many Americans decided Europe would have to deal with them alone.

Nativism, a movement to limit immigration, first appeared in the 1800s. Not surprisingly, it revived after the war. Nativists now claimed that people from foreign countries could never be fully loyal to the United States.

When immigration swelled after the war, Congress reacted. In 1921, it limited annual immigration to 350,000 and set up quotas for certain nationalities. In 1924 it passed a law slashing immigration to 164,000. In addition to excluding Asians entirely, the law set quotas for each country at 2 percent of the total number of that country's immigrants living in the United States in 1890. The goal was to reduce immigration from southern and eastern Europe, for few immigrants from those countries had arrived in the United States before 1890. Nativists had long regarded these immigrants as undesirable, in part because of such cultural characteristics as their Catholic religion. (See Chapter 16.) As Washington congressman Albert Johnson declared in 1927,

This song, written in the 1920s, expressed the anti-immigration sentiment of the era.

> The United States is our land. . . . We intend to maintain it so. The day of unalloyed [pure] welcome to all peoples, the day of indiscriminate acceptance of all races, has definitely ended.

Distrust of people and things "un-American," like the concerns over strikes and the spread of communism, contributed to a political climate that was hostile to reformers in the postwar years. But while the nation held firm against the invasion of ideas and people from abroad, individuals within the country were transforming the nation's political and social landscape.

SECTION 1 REVIEW

Key Terms, People, and Places
1. Define (a) communist, (b) general strike.

Key Concepts
2. How did the difficult postwar economic adjustments in the United States affect workers?
3. Who were the Bolsheviks?
4. What was the red scare?

5. Who were Sacco and Vanzetti, and why are they remembered?
6. Why did Congress restrict immigration in the 1920s?

Critical Thinking
7. **Expressing Problems Clearly** Summarize the obstacles facing those who wished to reintroduce reforms in the postwar United States.

Quiz found in the Unit 7 folder, p. 9, covers the main ideas in this section as well as the key terms.

The Decision to Restrict Immigration

Focus Congress's passage of laws restricting immigration provides a vivid illustration of the postwar desire to curb the forces of change, to protect the United States from alien ideas, and to restore the United States to the kind of "normalcy" it enjoyed before the war. Students are asked to evaluate the congressional decisions to restrict immigration in the 1920s and to predict some of the consequences.

Instruct In order to give students a chronological framework for the material, ask them to make entries on a time line showing the changes in immigration law that are discussed in the text.

To check student understanding of the facts of immigration restriction, provide the following dates: 1913, 1926, 1967. Ask students which year or years each of the following would-be immigrants would most likely *not* have been admitted to the country.
- A Russian Jew, literate in two languages, but not in English, skilled at clock making and clock repair (*1926*)
- A Japanese teacher, literate in English (*1913, 1926*)
- An Italian chef (*1926*)
- An agricultural specialist from Nigeria (*1913, 1926*)

Review the arguments for and against immigration restriction. Ask volunteers to participate in a role-play of the congressional debate in 1924.

Extend To extend the activity, have students explore current trends in immigration, researching the latest census figures on the national origins of immigrants, their settlement patterns, and current discussions about immigration restriction.

The Decision to Restrict Immigration

Time Frame:	1917–1924
Place:	Washington, D.C.
Key People:	Members of United States Congress
Situation:	When some citizens strongly expressed their fear that new immigrants were threatening American character and institutions, Congress debated whether or not to control who would be allowed to enter the United States.

Congress has debated immigration policy every year since its first meeting in 1790. During World War I and in the years immediately after, the debate heated up. Congress faced strong pressure from the public to create an immigration policy that would severely restrict the numbers of newcomers from abroad.

Background to the Decision

Until the mid 1800s, most immigrants coming to the United States quickly blended in with old, established residents. Most of these immigrants to the United States came from western and northern Europe. They were culturally similar in many ways to the native-born descendants of America's first white settlers.

The "New" Immigrants Between 1880 and 1920 more than 23 million people left Europe to come to the United States. These "new" immigrants, as they were called, came from southern and eastern European countries such as Italy, Poland, and Russia. Their unfamiliar clothing, customs, and languages seemed "foreign" to many. Their religions were Catholicism, Orthodox Christianity, or Judaism—not Protestantism like most of the old immigrants. Many did not read or write any language, and few spoke English.

The new immigrants crowded into the cities. Some people blamed the growth of urban slums, the political corruption of cities, and other problems on the new immigrants. Others feared that they would take jobs away from "Americans."

The new immigrants, argued some, came from the most unstable parts of Europe—the places where the war had started and communism had been born. If newcomers did not already carry dangerous political ideas, many believed they were certainly vulnerable to these ideas. Furthermore, a number of respected scholars spread false notions that southern and eastern Europeans were inferior to other white people.

In Favor of Immigration Not everyone opposed immigration. To many, the United States was a "golden door" that all who wished to better themselves could enter.

THE ONLY WAY TO HANDLE IT.

 RESOURCE DIRECTORY

Teaching Resources

History Might Not . . . Activity Lobbying for Indian Immigration, found in the Unit 7 folder, pp. 18–19, shows how J. J. Singh, an Indian immigrant himself, successfully lobbied Congress to revoke laws that obstructed Indian immigration to the United States.

Others believed that the poverty and illiteracy of the new immigrants showed a lack of opportunity, not a lack of ability. They pointed to the thousands of immigrants in the past who had contributed greatly to the growth of the country.

DECISION	Should immigration to the United States be restricted?				
ARGUMENTS OF PEOPLE FAVORING RESTRICTIONS	Immigrants are too "different."	Immigrants are creating slums.	Immigrants corrupt democracy.	Immigrants bring radical ideas.	Immigrants are inferior.
ARGUMENTS OF PEOPLE OPPOSED TO RESTRICTIONS	The U.S. represents hope to people all over the world.	Open immigration is an American tradition.	Immigrants bring needed talent to U.S.	Restriction would be discriminatory.	With opportunity, immigrants would contribute to America.

Congress Chooses Immigration Restriction

In 1924 the debate in Congress was not about open immigration, but about restricting immigration from some parts of Europe. Non-European immigration was already restricted. In 1882 Congress had banned Chinese immigration. A 1908 agreement with the Japanese government had halted Japanese immigration.

The crisis created by World War I gave immigration restriction a push forward. The fear of foreigners increased because of the communist revolution in Russia. A wave of terrorism also made many citizens nervous. In 1917 Congress passed a series of laws restricting immigration. The new laws barred political radicals and "undesirables," including those who could not read.

After the war, immigration from war-torn Europe began to rise again. Fears rose that the cities would fill with jobless, desperate, foreign radicals. In response, Congress passed new immigration laws in both 1921 and 1924. These immigration acts established a quota system based on national origins. The cartoon at left comments on the 1921 law, which set quotas at 3 percent of each country's white immigrants living in the United States in 1910.

Immigration Laws Since 1924

The decision to enact restrictive immigration laws in 1921 and 1924 reflected an American fear of diversity in the 1920s. Since then, Congress has continued to debate immigration. In the 1950s and 1960s, Americans closely examined their views on immigration and diversity, in large part because of the African American struggle for civil rights. Congress recognized that the immigration

laws written in the 1920s discriminated against immigrants from most parts of the world. It passed new legislation in 1952, which greatly changed the quotas for each country. For the first time, individuals from any country in the world could enter the United States. In 1965 a new immigration act eliminated quotas altogether.

Immigration policy continues to be debated in Congress. The debate focuses on jobs, the country's ability to absorb new immigrants, and to what extent the United States should be a refuge for people seeking freedom. After twenty-five years, the Immigration Act of 1990 was passed. This law favors immigrants who are close relatives of American citizens and those who have skills that are in short supply. The new law also excludes some individuals: for example, criminals and drug abusers. No provisions of the current law, however, limit the entry of immigrants based on national origin.

EVALUATING DECISIONS

1. What caused many Americans to change their attitudes about immigration after 1880?
2. How did World War I and its aftermath create a mood favorable to immigration restriction?

Critical Thinking

3. **Predicting Consequences** How do you think the immigration acts of 1921 and 1924 affected the way that people from eastern and southern Europe viewed the United States?

Media and Technology

Visions of America: History Might Not Have Happened This Way Game

To encourage students to explore pivotal moments in United States history, have students use the Visions of America software. Refer to the Visions of America Guidebook for viewing objectives, activities, game instructions, and discussion questions.

SECTION 2

Social and Political Developments

Connecting to the Big Idea

See page 578B. Point out that important political and social developments changed the United States during the 1920s. Ask students how women's suffrage and the northward migration of African Americans affected the country.

Objectives

● Describe the impact of women's suffrage on American politics in the 1920s.
● Explain why many African Americans migrated to the North during the 1920s.
● Describe the Harlem Renaissance.
● Describe the candidates and issues of the presidential election of 1928.

Bellringer

Ask students if they have ever moved, and if so, for what reasons their family moved. Then ask students to decide which state or region of the country they think currently provides the best opportunity for good jobs and advancement. Have students consider why their family might have to move to this or another area.

Reading Strategy

Reinforcing Key Ideas Ask students to note this sentence on page 586: "Out of the postwar climate of fear of things foreign or new came several important political and social developments." As they read, ask students to list and briefly describe the political and social developments discussed in this section.

SECTION PREVIEW

After the war, women and African Americans faced a world of new opportunities and old disappointments. In the political realm, Republicans won Americans' support—and votes.

Key Concepts

• The newly won women's vote did not lead to widespread change in American politics.
• Many African Americans moved to the North; some experienced repression and others, a renaissance.
• The Republican party controlled national politics.

Key Terms, People, and Places

Harlem Renaissance, Teapot Dome; Marcus Garvey, Warren G. Harding, Calvin Coolidge, Herbert Hoover

Performers such as Louis Armstrong helped jazz find a home in northern cities.

O ut of the postwar climate of fear of things foreign or new came several important political and social developments. Women looked to flex their political muscles after securing the right to vote. Southern African Americans sought greater opportunity in the North. Meanwhile, the nation's ailing economy began to show signs of improvement in the early 1920s, and voters gave the credit to the Republican party.

The Women's Movement Fades

Having won the right to vote in 1920, women voters now faced the daunting challenge of fulfilling their promises to themselves and the nation. Would women vote in significant numbers? Would men give women equality in political parties? These questions worried those who had fought for women's rights.

The Impact of Suffrage In fact, women did not flock to the polls in huge numbers. This was partly because the percentage of voter turnout continued a decline that had begun more than twenty years before. Because women's suffrage was new, however, observers focused more attention on how few women voted than on how many did.

In addition, women's votes did not seem to change politics as much as suffragists had hoped. In national elections especially, women voted in patterns similar to men. Only in local contests did women seem to have a noticeable impact.

After gaining the right to vote, many women joined the Republican and Democratic parties and sought central roles in them. But men who ran these parties gave women only minor posts and rarely nominated women for office. Women therefore continued working largely from behind the scenes or in groups such as the League of Women Voters that were not connected to any political party. A few women became active in the newly formed National Woman's party, which was founded by militant

To celebrate the passage of the Nineteenth Amendment in 1920, Alice Paul adds the "ratification star" to the flag of the National Woman's Party.

 RESOURCE DIRECTORY

Teaching Resources

Reproducible Lesson Plan found in the Unit 7 folder, p. 4, provides a summary of the Section 2 lesson plan content.

Alternate Lesson Plan: Cooperative Learning found in the Alternate Lesson Plans folder, p. 107, is an alternate lesson plan that provides guidance for having students collectively produce a newspaper on the major issues of the 1920s.

Guided Reading and Review found in the Unit 7 folder, p. 10, provides a structure for reading and mastering the key concepts and reviewing the key terms for Section 2. (Guided Practice)

Primary Source Activity Growing Up Black, found in the Unit 7 folder, pp. 26–27, profiles Daisy Bates—a child of the South of the 1920s. The effects of segregation on seven-year-old Daisy and her neighbors—both African American and white—are described in Daisy's autobiography.

suffragist Alice Paul. Among the party's causes was an unsuccessful campaign for an Equal Rights Amendment (ERA) to the Constitution.

The Successes of Suffrage Suffrage did lead to some immediate gains for women. Polling places moved out of saloons and into more neutral public spaces, and women in twenty-one states began to serve on juries. National victories included the Sheppard-Towner Act (1921), which allocated federal money for pre-natal and infant health care. Also, the Cable Act (1922) allowed women who married foreigners to keep their United States citizenship. But perhaps more important than any concrete legislative or political success, suffrage marked an important first step for women on which they would base future gains in jobs, civil rights, and politics.

African Americans and the Great Migration

Throughout the early 1900s, jobs for African Americans, most of whom lived in the South, were scarce and low paying. Many factory jobs simply were closed to them. Opportunities for education were inadequate. In addition, lynchings and other forms of racial violence claimed the lives of dozens of innocent African Americans each year and terrorized countless others.

During World War I, factories in the North expanded production to meet the demands of the war, and many white factory workers left their jobs to join the battle overseas. These two developments created many new employment opportunities for African Americans in the North.

As a result of conditions in the South and new job opportunities in the North, half a million African Americans made the move to northern states by 1920, as the map below shows. Hundreds of thousands more followed later in the decade.

The trip from the South to the North was no small undertaking. The *Chicago Defender*, an African American newspaper, received thousands of letters like this one from a New Orleans man in 1917:

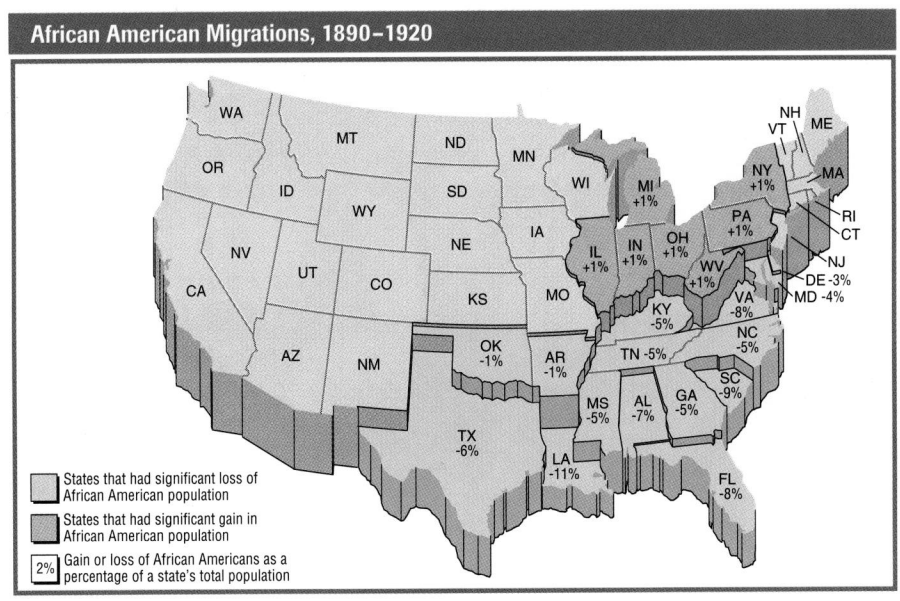

African American Migrations, 1890–1920

- States that had significant loss of African American population
- States that had significant gain in African American population
- 2% Gain or loss of African Americans as a percentage of a state's total population

Geography and History: Interpreting Maps
The migration of African Americans from the South to the North helped alter the populations of both regions. *Which states lost the most population?*

Media and Technology

Transparency
Fine Art, D-16

Role Play—Voting Preference

Ask students to summarize the issues in the 1928 election. Play the part of a roving reporter, while students role-play the following voters: heir to a large furniture manufacturing company, Irish immigrant chauffeur, African American teacher, midwestern farmer and Roman Catholic head of a temperance movement in a small midwestern city. Ask the "voters" to explain their preference in the upcoming election.

In Depth

Multicultural Perspectives

The Harlem Renaissance inspired many artists to create masterpieces of language and tone. Claude McKay's "The Tropics in New York," Jean Toomer's "Cane," and Georgia Douglas Johnson's "Common Dust" are among the many works that express the feelings of both urban and rural African Americans. Langston Hughes's poem "I, Too" epitomizes the sense of possibility and the deep frustrations that African Americans felt at the time. Carl Van Doren, the editor of *Century* Magazine and a Pulitzer winner for biography, observed: "What American literature decidedly needs at this moment is color, music, gusto, the free expression of gay or desperate moods. If the Negroes are not in a position to contribute to these items, I don't know what Americans are."

I f there is any way that you could get a pass please try and do that much for us as we are a party of four good working men the southern white are trying very hard to keep us from the north but still they wont give us no work to do.

The Reality of the North The North did offer more opportunities, but it was not a promised land, free of discrimination or hardship. Many African American women, for instance, found work as maids in white-owned homes. These jobs paid higher wages than most jobs in the South—but not enough to lift the women out of poverty. As one woman remarked in 1917, "They give you big money for what you do but they charge you big things for what you get." In addition, African American factory workers often met hostility from whites, who felt that the migrants threatened their jobs and wages.

African Americans also found that moving to the north did not ensure freedom from racial violence. Serious race riots occurred in 1917 in East St. Louis, Illinois, and in 1919 in Washington, D.C., and many other northern cities. ✪

Perhaps the worst racial disturbance took place in Chicago. On Sunday, July 27, 1919, an African American youth went for a swim. New to town, he knew nothing of the invisible racial divisions that segregated the beach. When he drifted onto the "white" side, a white man threw a stone at him. The rock injured the youth, and he drowned. In retaliation, blacks began attacking whites. The riot left almost forty people dead, hundreds injured, and thousands homeless.

Racial tension clearly lay at the heart of the riots. But the fighting further unnerved a nation already troubled by the specter of radical violence and labor unrest. Attorney General Palmer even suggested that the rioting was the work of communists.

The Harlem Renaissance With the migration to northern cities, the number of African Americans living in New York's Harlem grew from 14,000 in 1914 to about 200,000 in 1930. At that time—prior to the economic devastation of the Depression in the 1930s—Harlem was a fashionable and exciting place to live. ✪

People flocked to Harlem nightspots to hear jazz, a musical form with roots deep in the African American South. With the Great

Writers Langston Hughes (left) and Zora Neale Hurston (right) helped make Harlem a leading artistic center. Harlem was also a vital social hub in the 1920s.

Jazz singer Bessie Smith helped fill jazz nightspots in the North.

▶ RESOURCE DIRECTORY ✪

Teaching Resources

✪ **Literature Activity** *The Weary Blues,* found in the Unit 7 folder, p. 31, expresses the pain and frustration of Langston Hughes, a leading figure of the Harlem Renaissance, and serves as a pointed comparison to the indulgences of the flapper culture.

American Profiles Activity found in the Unit 7 folder, p. 20, profiles singer Bessie Smith whose life—from poverty, through migration, to success as a great interpreter of the blues—is a microcosm of the African American experience of the times.

Migration, jazz enjoyed a golden age. Singers Bessie Smith and Ma Rainey, pianist Duke Ellington, and trumpeter Louis "Satchmo" Armstrong became widely known performers.

Literary life among African Americans also flowered, part of a movement that came to be called the **Harlem Renaissance**. Publishers began printing novels and other writings by African American writers such as Countee Cullen, Zora Neale Hurston, Claude McKay, and Langston Hughes. Alain Locke's 1925 book titled *The New Negro* celebrated this development. Locke argued that being of both African and American heritage need not be a cause of conflict but rather of mutual enrichment.

The Garvey Movement New York City was home to another notable African American named **Marcus Garvey**. Garvey came to New York from his native Jamaica in 1916 to establish a new headquarters for his Universal Negro Improvement Association (UNIA). The UNIA sought to build up African Americans' self-respect. Its message of racial pride attracted masses of followers.

Garvey urged followers to return to "Motherland Africa." He also invested his followers' money in the Black Star steamship line. When Garvey oversold stock in this enterprise, he was jailed on fraud charges in 1925. The UNIA collapsed, but Garvey's ideas remained an inspiration to later "black pride" movements.

MAKING   CONNECTIONS

Consider what you have read about postwar economic conditions in the United States. How might these conditions have contributed to the problems facing African Americans following their migration to the North?

A Decade of Republican Dominance

During the 1920s, the Republican party took a firm hold on the White House. One reason was that in the early 1920s, the economy began to rebound from the hard times that followed World War I. Industrial productivity soared, unemployment went down, and the number of strikes dropped. Voters gave the Republicans credit for the nation's recovery.

For the presidential election of 1920, Republican conservatives nominated **Warren G. Harding**, an Ohio senator. **Calvin Coolidge**, of the Boston police strike fame, was his running mate. The handsome, silver-haired Harding seemed the very picture of an American President, and many voters were attracted to his promise of a "return to normalcy." The Republicans overwhelmed the Democratic ticket of James Cox and Franklin D. Roosevelt.

A Scandal-Ridden Administration Harding, considered by many observers to be an "amiable second-rater," did make some good cabinet appointments, such as the highly regarded Herbert Hoover for secretary of commerce. Yet Harding also selected a number of unqualified friends for key posts. Some of these pals brought scandal down upon Harding's administration.

Harding himself did not have to deal with these troubles. He died on August 2, 1923, two-and-a-half years into his first term. By 1924, however, the full extent of the corruption in his administration was exposed. One Harding appointee had stolen government funds, others had taken payments in return for influence. Several other officials also were accused of wrongdoing, and two committed suicide.

The worst Harding scandal came to be known as **Teapot Dome**. It involved Harding's secretary of the interior, Albert B. Fall, who leased critical government oil reserves in Elk Hill, California, and Teapot Dome, Wyoming, to two private oil companies. In return, Fall received illegal payments and so-called loans that totaled over $300,000. Fall later went to jail for his role in the scandal.

The Democrats in 1924 tried to use public anger over the Teapot Dome affair to defeat the Republicans. The object below carried the Democratic message.

The Election of 1924 Voters apparently did not hold Vice President Calvin Coolidge responsible for these scandals. Following Harding's death, Coolidge completed the term. He then easily won his own election in 1924 over the Democratic ticket of John W. Davis and Charles Bryan and the Progressive candidate Bob La Follette.

6. Students might formulate questions about whether or not employment or overall earning rates increased in the North as compared to the South. They might also question whether African Americans experienced increases or decreases in poverty rates and incidents of racial violence.

Reteach

Tell students that the following statements are incorrect. Ask them to read and correct each of the statements and provide evidence from the section to support each correction.

● The women's vote had a major impact on American politics, since women voted in large numbers for Democrats.
● African Americans moving to the North found freedom from racial violence.
● *Harlem Renaissance* refers to the popularity of jazz in that part of New York City during the 1920s.
● In 1928 the Republicans appealed to those Americans who supported the repeal of prohibition.
● Democrat Al Smith was elected President in 1928.

Caption Answer to ...

Using Historical Evidence

The cartoon suggests that big business is quite happy with Coolidge. Big business is depicted as an energetic flapper who is enjoying dancing to Coolidge's music.

4. CLOSE

Reinforcing the Big Idea

The social and political changes examined in this section, women's suffrage, the northward migration of many African Americans, and the scandals of the Harding administration each changed the nation in different ways. The next section describes some of the changes in the social life, manners, and styles during the "roaring twenties."

Using Historical Evidence Calvin Coolidge, depicted here with a saxophone, was known for his support of big business. *What does this cartoon suggest about big business's reaction to Coolidge's policies?*

"Silent Cal" Coolidge, as he was nicknamed, was a shy man known for using few words. His other memorable trait was an uncritical support for the interests of American business, as the cartoon at left illustrates. "The chief business of the American people is business," he told a group of newspaper editors in 1925. Coolidge demonstrated his beliefs by raising tariffs. This helped American manufacturers by making foreign goods more expensive and American goods more attractive to buyers.

Coolidge was less willing to use the federal government to aid ordinary citizens. For example, he rejected aid for victims of a Mississippi River flood, saying that government had no duty to protect citizens "against the hazards of the elements."

The Election of 1928 As Coolidge neared the end of his first full term, he announced that he would not seek reelection in 1928. In his place, the Republicans nominated the well-respected **Herbert Hoover**. During and after World War I, Hoover achieved spectacular success running relief programs in Europe and the Food Administration in the United States. Later, he held cabinet posts in both the Harding and Coolidge administrations. Voters seemed to trust that he would provide sound leadership for the nation. Indeed, Hoover easily won election over the Democratic candidate, New York governor Al Smith.

In fact, the 1928 election returns did reveal some signs of weakness in the Republican armor, as you will read in Section 5. These political shifts, however, were subtle and hard to detect. Far more obvious were the dramatic changes in morals, manners, and fashion being flaunted by the energetic youth of the nation's growing urban centers.

SECTION 2 REVIEW

Key Terms, People, and Places
1. Define (a) Harlem Renaissance, (b) Teapot Dome.
2. Identify (a) Marcus Garvey, (b) Warren G. Harding, (c) Calvin Coolidge, (d) Herbert Hoover.

Key Concepts
3. What were some of the disappointments and successes of suffrage?
4. For what reasons did African Americans move north, and what was the result?
5. What factors helped lead to Republican success in the 1920s?

Critical Thinking
6. **Formulating Questions** What questions might you examine to determine whether or not African American migration in the early 1900s improved the lives of migrants generally?

 RESOURCE DIRECTORY

Teaching Resources

Quiz found in the Unit 7 folder, p. 11, covers the main ideas in this section as well as the key terms.

New Manners, New Morals

SECTION 3

New Manners, New Morals

From rising hemlines to the energetic sounds of jazz, the 1920s daringly broke with tradition. New social freedoms created opportunity—and dilemmas—for women. But beneath it all lay a nagging question: How much had really changed?

Key Concepts
- Many American youth were eager for social changes after the war.
- The Jazz Age introduced many new tastes and manners, especially for women.
- The changes were not as widespread as presented in popular media.

Key Terms, People, and Places
Jazz Age, flapper

For many Americans, World War I was a watershed event. By bringing to a crashing close most of the monarchies of Europe, the war made the code of values and morals that they represented seem dreadfully old-fashioned. Many Americans longed to shed these old ideas and, with them, the horrors and disillusionment of World War I.

Young people were especially eager for change. They experimented with new social freedoms that took root first in the cities and then spread across the country. Yet, though the brash new ways of the urban youth became a symbol of the 1920s, many changes of the era turned out to be superficial.

Jazz Age Manners

Several factors contributed to the cultural changes taking place following World War I. As more youth finished high school and went on to college, they looked to each other rather than to their parents for standards of behavior. Soldiers returning home from the war brought new styles and habits to their hometowns.

Advances in communications rapidly spread the emerging culture. (See Section 4.)

Along with the great postwar African American migration from the South to the North came jazz, blues, and Dixieland music, which quickly found a home in northern urban nightspots. The wide availability of phonograph records and record players meant that people could play the music wherever they gathered. Jazz had such a strong influence on the tastes and manners of the age that the 1920s became known as the **Jazz Age.**

The exciting rhythms of jazz captivated young people and blossomed on dance floors. Dance marathons—in which couples competed to see who could stay on the dance floor longest—became a popular fad. Young Americans let off steam in other zany ways as well: Flagpole sitting and goldfish eating became crazes during the 1920s.

Like jazz itself, most American dance rages of the early 1900s came from African American culture. As Carl Van Vechten, an admirer of black culture in the twenties, explained, the dances would start on street corners in African American communities, move into saloons and nightclubs, and from there onto the music-hall stage and into the larger culture. "This has been the history of the Cake-Walk, the Bunny Hug, the Turkey Trot, the Charleston, and the Black Bottom," he wrote, referring to several dances of the early 1900s.

Older generations mocked the new dances. A writer in 1920 sneered about how the youth of his day "trot like foxes, limp like lame ducks, . . . all to the barbaric yawp of strange instruments. . . ." But by mid-decade, critics celebrated

Jazz music, played on records and phonographs like these, lay at the heart of a dramatic change in fashion, manners, and morals.

---

1. FOCUS

Connecting to the Big Idea

See page 578B. Explain to students that the 1920s were the years of the flapper, the Jazz Age, new manners and new styles. Ask if changes in the social life, manners, and styles of urban youth marked a significant change in American life.

Objectives
- Explain why American youth were eager for social change after the war.
- Describe the new tastes and manners introduced during the Jazz Age.
- Show evidence that changes in the 1920s were not as widespread as presented by the media.

Bellringer

Ask students to list current fashions, music, fads, or pastimes that appeal to young people. Ask how these styles or activities are perceived by others of their generation or of their parents' generation.

In Depth

Biography

Margaret Sanger (1883–1966) established the first birth control clinic in the United States in Brooklyn, New York, in 1916. Within weeks, the police closed the clinic, arrested Sanger, and jailed her for thirty days. However, in 1921 she organized the first American Birth Control Conference and in 1923 the Clinical Research Bureau of New York. The merger of these two organizations in 1938 eventually became the modern-day Planned Parenthood Federation of America.

Reproducible Lesson Plan found in the Unit 7 folder, p. 5, provides a summary of the Section 3 lesson plan content.

Alternate Lesson Plan: Critical Thinking Making Comparisons, found in the Alternate Lesson Plans folder, p. 108, is an alternate lesson plan that provides a chart activity that helps students compare the social changes of the 1920s to those of the 1990s.

Guided Reading and Review found in the Unit 7 folder, p. 12, provides a structure for reading and mastering the key concepts and reviewing the key terms for Section 3. (Guided Practice)

Reading Strategy

Finding Evidence Write the following statement on the board: In spite of new manners and trends, life continued much as usual. Ask students to find evidence of superficial changes in the 1920s.

 INSTRUCT

Discuss

Tell students that the image of the 1920s as the "roaring twenties," the era of the flapper and the rake, is still prevalent. Why are these images popular with Americans? Do the gilded youth of the 1920s represent characteristics that Americans value? Why would young people want to embrace behaviors that were so different from those of their parents' generation?

Ask why the prevalence of the automobile brought about changes in manners and, perhaps, in morals.

Analyze

Discuss the fact that women went to work in large numbers in the 1920s. Ask students to decide if and how they think women's lives improved in the 1920s.

 Activity

Teaching Heterogeneous Groups

The desire for change and progress by youth during the Jazz Age was embodied in the flapper and the rake. Styles and manners today also illustrate the feelings and desires of youth. In small groups, have students name and describe three or four symbols to illustrate the styles and manners of today's youth culture. Have students compare these symbols to the symbols of the 1920s.

LEP

Enrichment

Ask students to research the life and writings of F. Scott Fitzgerald in order to determine if he invented the flapper.

During dance marathons in the 1920s, people frequently fainted from exhaustion. This 1928 marathon consisted of an 8-mile dance down the highway to a ballroom, where the marathon continued.

jazz as a positive force. Leopold Stokowski, a well-known symphony conductor, observed that jazz had "come to stay because it is an expression of the times, of the breathless, energetic, superactive times in which we are living."

Breaking Social Conventions in the Jazz Age

During the twenties, young men and women displayed growing freedom in their relations with one another. They dated without chaperones, talked slang, danced with their bodies touching, and in general defied the social conventions of the time. Poet Edna St. Vincent Millay voiced this youthful, some would say reckless, new spirit when she wrote:

My candle burns at both ends;
It will not last the night;
But ah, my foes, and, oh my friends—
It gives a lovely light.

"First Fig," 1920

Changes in fashion reflected the new morals and manners. Women's clothing became more revealing, exposing arms and knees. Makeup, once associated only with the stage and prostitutes, appeared on the faces of ordinary women for the first time.

The wider availability of cars in the 1920s shaped some aspects of youth behavior. Instead of meeting at a young woman's home, young men increasingly took their partners out on dates. In an automobile, they could escape all supervision. This development had far-reaching implications: Fearing a rise in sexually transmitted diseases and unwanted pregnancies, some teachers and social workers urged a more open discussion of sex.

The new freedoms, however, created a dilemma for many young women. In the twenties, women's behavior was still judged by stricter standards than men's. As a result, women were torn by conflicting social pressures that encouraged them both to adopt new standards of behavior and to adhere to old ones.

The Flapper The ultimate symbol of Jazz Age behavior was the youthful woman known as the **flapper**. The term came from a popular drawing of a dancing woman with her boots open and flapping. As author Preston Slosson

▶ RESOURCE DIRECTORY

Teaching Resources

Critical Thinking Activity Testing Conclusions: The Jazz Age, found in the Unit 7 folder, p. 25, provides a partial glossary of Jazz Age terms and expressions to help students test their conclusions on the values and mores of the era.

observed in his 1930 work *The Great Crusade and After,* the flapper was

breezy, slangy, and informal in manner; slim and boyish in form; covered in silk and fur that clung to her as close as onion skin; with carmined [vivid red] cheeks and lips, plucked eyebrows and close-fitting helmet of hair; gay, plucky and confident.

Jazz Age men had their symbol, too—the "rake," with his careening automobile, reckless drinking, and irresponsible flirting. But the flapper became the more widely used symbol of the rebellious youth culture. Perhaps this was because standards of behavior for women had always been more constrained than for men. Thus, the new styles and manners seemed more startling when women adopted them. ⭐

MAKING CONNECTIONS

Compare the flapper to women from the suffrage or the abolition movements of the past or the feminist movement of recent years. In what ways are they similar and different?

How Widespread Was the New Youth Culture?

In reality, the urban youth culture represented by the flapper was not as widespread as the popular media suggested. Although the economy appeared healthy, deeply rooted problems, especially on the nation's farms, had many Americans worrying more about their economic survival than how to do the hottest new dance. Large numbers of young people did not rebel against traditional social and religious standards. Women everywhere experimented with cropped hair and short skirts, but many did so out of convenience rather than out of identification with flappers.

Reality for Women For women, especially, many of the new social freedoms turned out to be limited. Single women in large numbers moved into office, sales, and service jobs during the 1920s. Yet employers continued to assume that women were in the labor force only until they were married, and thus did not train them for advancement or pay them as well as men. Many hospitals and law firms refused to hire women physicians and lawyers.

Flappers defined a whole new style of dress and behavior.

Links Across Time

1650   1700   1750   1800   1850   1900   1950   2000

Women's Fashions

The flappers of the 1920s broke the mold of traditional dress for women. Over the course of history, women's clothing has undergone many such changes. In the late 1800s, for example, many women took pains to present an "hourglass" figure. Because few women possessed the desirable tiny waist naturally, they often wore restrictive corsets that were reinforced with whalebone for added stiffness. Usually, a helper was needed to pull the laces of the corset tight enough to reduce the waist as much as possible. These corsets restricted the abdomen so much that they were blamed by physicians for contributing to many kinds of internal health problems.

Within a few years, young women wanted to achieve just the opposite look—a boyish, straight silhouette. Fashion changes in the 1920s reflected new morals and manners among the nation's youth. Ankle-length dresses and cotton stockings gave way to short, tight dresses worn with silk stockings rolled down to the knees. Young women bobbed their long hair into short, boyish styles, often to the horror of their more traditional mothers.

Following World War II, the desire for stability in the 1950s home contributed to another fashion shift toward longer skirts and a return to the hourglass figure ideal. But then the social revolution of 1960s youth led again to a fashion revolution. For the first time, slacks were considered acceptable garb for women and hemlines rose again—this time to the previously unseen heights of the miniskirt. *What effects might accepted standards of beauty and fashion have on women?*

Answer to …

Links Across Time

The *New York Times Magazine* of October 1993 described fifty years of women's fashion in the following way: "The salon trussed her. Advertising seduced her. Rock released her. Then the market indulged her, until just getting dressed became a complex but liberating challenge to her identity."

Answer to …

MAKING CONNECTIONS

A possible response might be that unlike abolitionists and suffrage workers, flappers had no specific political agenda. Like feminists of recent years, flappers sought to redefine the social perception of women.

3. ASSESS

Section 3 Review Answers

1. flapper, see p. 592

2. Many Americans were anxious to shed old values and morals. A growing number of Americans were going to college and finding their own standards of behavior. Soldiers returning from the war brought new styles and habits that influenced young Americans.

3. Women's behavior was judged by stricter standards than that of men. Rebellion for them was thus more startling.

4. It was mainly an urban rebellion. Economic survival prevailed and though more women moved into the work force, the wage structure and other forms of discrimination held them back.

5. The developments of the decade seemed to offer new freedoms. At the same time, double standards still led to harsh judgments of many women's behavior, and technological improvements that were supposed to make women's work easier in fact created a new set of higher expectations.

Reteach

Write the following phrases on the chalkboard: flappers and rakes; students and workers. Ask each student to write at least two generalizations about each phrase.

Alternative Assessment

Mid-Point Monitoring

You may want to confer with students to see if they have
- Chosen a format for their project
- Outlined the main ideas
- Begun outside research and preparation of the bibliography

4. CLOSE

Reinforcing the Big Idea

Many young Americans, eager for change after World War I, adopted the manners, styles, and customs of the Jazz Age and challenged the culture of their parents' generation. The next section describes how sweeping technological changes affected the entire nation.

Using Historical Evidence Thanks to new electrical appliances, the nature of housework changed, but the demands on women remained. *What does this ad suggest about the responsibilities of women?*

The number of married women combining work, careers, and family life also rose slowly during the 1920s. But married women's working lives remained restricted. Employers often fired white women when they became pregnant. African American women had different experiences. White employers expected—and their own economic need often required—that they work even after they became pregnant.

In spite of workplace inequalities, many women enjoyed the independence that came with a job. Yet many also felt the pull of traditional roles of wife and mother. Former suffragist Sue Shelton White expressed the dilemma as a choice "between the frying pan and the fire—both very uncomfortable." ⬛

The Impact of Technological Change For the majority of women, it was technological change more than flapperism or jazz that seemed to promise real liberation. Thanks to cars, women could more easily shop for food. As manufacturers lowered prices for electrical products and as merchants introduced installment-plan buying, more women bought sewing machines, vacuum cleaners, and other labor-saving devices.

These developments eased life, but by no means freed women from drudgery. In fact, they raised expectations of household work. Kitchens and clothes now could be—and thus had to be—spotless. "By Their Floors Ye Shall Judge Them," warned a floor-polisher ad. "It is written that floors are like unto a mirror, reflecting the character of the housewife."

Of course, technological change in the 1920s changed more than the ways women did housework. Enormous changes in communications technology helped to create a whole new culture.

SECTION 3 REVIEW

Key Terms, People, and Places
1. Define flapper.

Key Concepts
2. What factors led many Americans to challenge existing social norms following World War I?
3. Why did the Jazz Age changes in manners appear to have a greater impact on women than on men?

4. How far-reaching were Jazz Age changes? Explain.

Critical Thinking
5. **Demonstrating Reasoned Judgment** "The developments of the 1920s, including the changing manners and the technological developments of the era, were a mixed blessing for women." Explain the meaning of this statement.

Analyzing Advertisements

Print advertisements—ads that appear as posters or in newspapers and magazines—offer important visual evidence about the consumer goods and services that were promoted during a historical period. Advertisements also can offer useful clues to the widely held ideas, attitudes, and values of the past. When using advertisements as historical evidence, however, it is important to bear in mind that advertisers rely on many different types of techniques in order to influence people's buying decisions. Ads may reflect certain lifestyles to which advertisers want consumers to aspire, rather than lifestyles that reflect reality for the majority of people during a certain historical period.

By the 1920s, the previously straightforward "what-it-is and what-it-does" mode of advertising was giving way to "situational" ads. These ads depicted not only the products, but also the ways in which those products might increase personal satisfaction or enhance the lives of typical consumers. One such advertisement from the 1920s appears at right.

Use the following steps to analyze the ad.

1. Identify the subject of the ad.
(a) What product or service is being promoted? (b) What facts about the product does the ad provide? (c) What issue does this advertisement use to appeal particularly to men? To women?

2. Analyze the ad's reliability as historical evidence. (a) Do you think that the people depicted in the ad portray typical consumers of the 1920s? Explain. (b) What is the unstated message that the advertiser is using in this case to persuade people to buy the product?

3. Study the ad to learn more about the historical period. (a) What social or cultural values are being promoted in the advertisement? (b) In general, do you think that advertisements reflect consumers' desires for products or create the desire for such products? Explain.

—and he wonders why she said "NO!"

 Could he have read her thoughts he would not have lost her. A picture of neatness herself, she detested slovenliness. And not once, but many times, she had noticed his ungartered socks crumpling down around his shoe tops. To have to apologize to her friends for a husband's careless habits was too much to ask. So she had to say "NO"—and in spite of his pleading couldn't tell him WHY.

No SOX Appeal Without

 PARIS GARTERS
SINGLE GRIP   DOUBLE GRIP
NO METAL CAN TOUCH YOU
25c to $2
Dress Well and Succeed

Historian's Toolbox Activity Analyzing Advertisements, found in the Unit 7 folder, p. 24, uses an advertisement of the 1990s to assist students in analyzing visual evidence as a tool to research history; and as a guide to the social and cultural values of today.

Creating a Shared Culture

Connecting to the Big Idea

See page 578B. In the 1920s, the nation began to develop a truly national culture. Ask what changes helped to create this new culture.

Objectives

● Show how population movements and developments in communications and transportation helped create a common culture.

● Describe how developments in radio, movies, advertising, and the automobile industry furthered the process of creating a national culture.

Bellringer

Ask students to imagine that a new student joins your class from another part of the country. In what ways would they expect this new student to be different from other students? What might account for the new student's familiarity with the same slang, clothing, food, music, movies, and books?

Reading Strategy

Predicting Content Ask students to skim Section 4, list the main and subheadings, and write a sentence or phrase under each heading that predicts the content of each section. When they have finished reading the section, ask students to test their predictions against the actual text.

Caption Answer to ...

 Interpreting Tables

Possible answers: There was also growth in broadcasting, as well as in all entertaining media that were carried on the radio, such as music and sports. Advertising also found a huge new market.

Creating a Shared Culture

SECTION PREVIEW

People in city apartments, country farmhouses, and everywhere in between were connected in new ways in the 1920s. Such links allowed sweeping changes to envelop the entire nation.

Key Concepts
• Population movements and new developments in communications and transportation helped create a culture common to many Americans.
• Developments in radio, movies, advertising, and the automobile industry furthered the process of creating a national culture.

Key Terms, People, and Places
Charles A. Lindbergh, Henry Ford

Caps like this were worn by aviators in the 1920s. Heroes of aviation, as well as sports and movies, were products of the new entertainment media.

C hange—resisted by some and welcomed by others—remained a constant force during the 1920s. During this decade, 14.6 million Americans moved from rural to urban areas and from one state to another. This included the migration of African Americans described in Section 2.

As people moved, they interacted with people in other regions to an extent never before possible. In addition, expanding mass media and advances in transportation led to a wider sharing of tastes, values, and experiences among people all across the country.

Americans at Leisure

Partly as the result of decades of union campaigns for shorter hours, the average factory workweek in the mid-1920s was just over fifty hours, down from nearly sixty hours in 1900. Men and women began exploring new ways to spend their growing leisure time. Industry and commerce stood ready to meet this need.

The Radio In 1920, only about twenty thousand people using homemade sets were receiving wireless radio messages. As an experiment, Frank Conrad of the Westinghouse Company in East Pittsburgh began to broadcast recorded music and baseball scores over the radio. The response was so great that the company began broadcasting new programs on a regular basis. By the fall of 1920, the country had its first radio station operated as a commercial enterprise, Pittsburgh's KDKA.

By 1922, over five hundred stations had formed, with newspapers controlling about a quarter of them. Listeners could now hear music, news, sports events, and religious services over the air. To reach more people, networks such as the National Broadcasting Company (NBC) brought together many individual stations, and each station in the network played the same programming. Soon much of the country was sharing the same jokes, commercials, and music.

The Movies By 1917, the movies had become big business. Luxury movie theaters began to replace storefront nickelodeons. As with radio, corporate giants took control. The studios of

Households with Radios, 1920–1930

Year	Number of Households with Radio Sets
1920	20,000
1922	60,000
1924	1,250,000
1926	4,500,000
1928	8,000,000
1930	13,750,000

Source: *Historical Statistics of the United States*

Interpreting Tables
Radio—once the hobby of a few dedicated enthusiasts—soon became a household fixture. *What industries probably benefited from the growth in the number of household radios?*

RESOURCE DIRECTORY

Teaching Resources

Reproducible Lesson Plan found in the Unit 7 folder, p. 6, provides a summary of the Section 4 lesson plan content.

Alternate Lesson Plan: Learning Styles found in the Alternate Lesson Plans folder, p. 109, is an alternate lesson plan that provides a group activity, especially effective for visual and auditory learners, around the theme of shared cultures.

Guided Reading and Review found in the Unit 7 folder, p. 14, provides a structure for reading and mastering the key concepts and reviewing the key terms for Section 4. (Guided Practice)

Visual Learning Activity Advertising Techniques of the 1920s, found in the Unit 7 folder, p. 33, helps students understand how advertisers market their brands to specific groups of consumers; and how companies shape images to their own products.

Metro-Goldwyn-Mayer, Warner Brothers, and Columbia dominated the field. Talkies—movies with sound—arrived in 1927 with *The Jazz Singer,* starring stage performer Al Jolson. By 1930, patrons were buying 100 million movie tickets a week.

MAKING CONNECTIONS

What leisure activities are important to young people today? In what ways are these activities similar to or different from the leisure activities of the 1920s?

The Worship of National Idols

The new entertainment media helped create national idols. The American people, eager for someone to look up to after the trauma of World War I, embraced them. From the movies, the ever-innocent Mary Pickford became America's Sweetheart; Clara Bow, the It Girl—a "good girl" who had "it," or sexual allure. Charlie Chaplin was the Little Tramp, and Rudolph Valentino, the Sheik.

Sports Heroes After the movie stars came sports figures. Among the most famous were Babe Ruth, the New York Yankee hitter of sixty home runs in 1927; prizefighters Jack Dempsey and Gene Tunney; and Gertrude Ederle, the first woman to swim the English Channel.

Lindbergh's Historic Flight The decade's ultimate hero, **Charles A. Lindbergh,** was from Minnesota. Lindbergh was a stunt flyer and air-mail pilot. In May 1927, the twenty-five-year-old competed for a $25,000 prize offered to the first aviator to fly nonstop across the Atlantic Ocean from New York to Paris. Except for a team of two flyers who landed in a sleepy Irish bog in 1919, everyone else attempting the crossing had crashed or disappeared.

Flying his *Spirit of St. Louis* with a dangerous overload of fuel, struggling through ice storms and fatigue, Lindbergh managed to cross the great ocean and land safely on May 21 at Le Bourget airfield near Paris. He became an instant hero. A poem in the *New York*

Sun ignored the industrial know-how that had made his flight possible and celebrated Lindbergh as the ultimate lone conqueror:

> No kingly plane for him;
> No endless data, com-
>   rades, moneyed chums;
> No boards, no councils,
>   no directors grim—
> He plans ALONE and
>   takes luck as it comes."

To many Americans, the tall, handsome, independent Lindbergh came to symbolize their national spirit. *The New Republic* declared, he is "ours. . . . He is no longer permitted to be himself. He is US personified. He is the United States."

Daring Charles Lindbergh, who was the first aviator to fly nonstop across the Atlantic Ocean, embodied the American ideal of the lone conqueror.

Selling New Products and Ideas

While many Americans were adoring the same heroes, other aspects of their daily lives also became increasingly similar. Chain supermarkets spread, along with products known mostly by brand names. The A&P grocery chain, which had 5,000 stores in 1922, had 15,500 by 1929. The nation's first shopping center (in Kansas City) and first fast-food chain (A & W Root Beer) appeared in the twenties. Soon people across the country were shopping in the same stores for the same goods.

The advertising industry boomed, rising to the challenge of selling the country's many new products. Agents and salesmen grew from 11,000 in 1910 to 25,000 in 1920. Through advertising, products became synonymous with brand names. Paper hankies became "Kleenex," record players became "Victrolas."

In aggressive campaigns, advertisers convinced people that they needed to buy new products. When the Lambert Company discovered it could sell more Listerine as a cure for bad breath than as a general antiseptic, its advertising agents introduced the term *halitosis*—a new

Cars were assembled by dozens of workers as they passed by on a conveyor.

Even the detailed and skillful work of upholstering seats was performed on an assembly line.

Each worker on the line performed the same step over and over.

Model T bodies moved down a slide to be fitted on the chassis.

Henry Ford's ingenious production methods were based on two key ideas: the assembly line and uniformity of product. The assembly line, shown above, broke down car production into precise steps. Uniformity of product held that each car should be identical—an idea never before applied to such complicated machinery.

"scientific" word for an age-old problem. "What secret is your mirror holding back?" ads asked. "Even your best friend won't tell you."

Manufacturers put huge amounts of money into advertising. In 1922 Lambert's advertising budget came to $100,000. By 1928, it was spending $5 million and still raking in huge profits.

An Affordable Automobile

The automobile, invented in the 1890s, came of age in the 1920s. Over the decade, the number of registered automobiles rose from 8 million to over 23 million.

By freeing individuals to set their own schedules, automobiles individualized travel. People who were not wealthy traveled more often and over greater distances. To accommodate them, the government built new road systems, parks, and beaches for everyone, not just the rich. These developments had a powerful impact on the economy, stimulating the construction, rubber, gasoline and petroleum, advertising, and tourist industries. ✪

The United States owed much of the boom in the auto industry to one man. His genius helped revolutionize industry at the same time that it changed the face of the nation itself.

AMERICAN PROFILES

Henry Ford

Henry Ford was born on a Michigan farm in 1863. Early in life he showed an aptitude for things mechanical, and he seemed destined for a career working with machines.

In the late 1880s, while an engineer at the Detroit Illuminating Company, Ford began working on a horseless carriage powered by an engine. In 1896 he produced a "quadricycle," the lightest of the current gasoline-driven models. Ford started his own company in 1903 to manufacture automobiles. By 1910, he was selling over thirty thousand of his Model T's.

Pioneering Production Methods Ford had even higher ambitions. He wanted to "democratize the automobile," producing more cars at prices ordinary people could afford. Toward this end, he developed the revolutionary assembly line illustrated above.

Ford's system worked. By making large numbers of identical automobiles in an identical way, Ford could take advantage of the economy of scale to lower his costs for producing each car. In 1914, the first year his assembly line was fully operational, his company sold 248,000 cars at $490 each, almost half of what a car had cost in 1910. The following year he dropped the price to $390. By the early 1920s he was producing 60 percent of the nation's automobiles. He led the world market as well.

Others improved upon Ford's success. In the mid-twenties, General Motors surpassed Ford by introducing the Chevrolet in colors. Ford had failed to grasp the growing impor-

Even small items such as wheels assembled separately

tance of style and color to the American people. He joked that his customers could get their "Tin Lizzies" in any color they liked, as long as it was black. But in 1927, Ford began producing a new car, the Model A, in colors.

Running the Business In 1914, Ford had won praise by introducing the five-dollar-a-day pay rate for many of his workers, double what other factories paid. Yet Ford was not always well regarded by his workers. He was notorious for authorizing the use of spies and violence in an effort to combat unions in his plants.

Ford ruled his business like a dictator. "We expect the men to do what they are told," he explained in his 1922 book, *My Life and Work.*

The organization is so highly specialized and one part is so dependent upon another that we could not for a moment consider allowing men to have their own way. . . . Anyone who does not like to work in our way may always leave.

Ford's reputation also suffered when, in 1920, he allowed his newspaper, the *Dearborn Independent,* to engage in an anti-Semitic campaign. The attacks on Jews upset many people.

Ford's outbursts were a symptom of the age. Upset by social and moral changes of which he disapproved, Ford found a scapegoat in the Jews. As the next section discusses, he was not the only person to reach out for such simplistic solutions.

Henry Ford (above) began his career when horseless carriages like this were state of the art.

SECTION 4 REVIEW

Key Terms, People, and Places
1. Identify (a) Charles A. Lindbergh, (b) Henry Ford.

Key Concepts
2. How did commerce and industry respond to the increase in leisure time in the twenties?
3. How did the expanded advertising industry affect the American consumer?

4. What was the impact of easily available automobiles on American society?
5. What were the key features of Ford's assembly line?

Critical Thinking
6. **Recognizing Cause and Effect** How did the growth of mass media, such as radio and movies, lead to the creation of national heroes?

 Quiz found in the Unit 7 folder, p. 15, covers the main ideas in this section as well as the key terms.

Media and Technology

▭ **Transparency**
The Way It Works, H-18

3. ASSESS

Section 4 Review Answers
1. (a) Charles A. Lindbergh, see p. 597, (b) Henry Ford, see p. 598

2. They increased radio broadcasting nationwide; created the movie industry and national idols; and speeded up the building of a national culture.

3. It created an identity between brand names and products and a new set of needs for the American public.

4. It liberated travel and thus speeded up the homogenization of American culture.

5. Making large numbers of automobiles in an identical way, and selling cars at affordable prices.

6. A possible answer is because the mass media can reach millions of people with the exact same message, and large numbers of people can share in events and information that help create heroes.

Reteach

Ask students to tell how each of the following helped create a national culture: migration from one state to another, the radio, the movies, the advertising industry, and the affordable automobile.

---

4. CLOSE

Reinforcing the Big Idea

Changes such as the population movement and developments in communication, transportation, industry, and the media worked to create a new national culture in America. The next section will describe how some Americans tried to slow down the fast pace of change.

SECTION 5

Stemming the Tide of Change

1. FOCUS

Connecting to the Big Idea

See page 578B. Explain to students that some Americans were alarmed by the ways in which American life and culture changed after World War I. They tried to slow down the pace of change. Ask how those Americans tried to halt what they considered the nation's moral and intellectual decay.

Objectives

● Evaluate the results of prohibition.
● Show how developments such as censorship and the growth of the Ku Klux Klan reflected a desire to slow changes in morals and manners in the 1920s.
● Describe how some artists responded to the changes in the nation with despair and self-exile.
● Describe how the election of 1928 revealed the social and political divisions in the United States.

Bellringer

Ask students to consider what might happen if the making, selling, transporting, importing, and exporting of soft drinks were made illegal. Do students think all Americans would stop drinking sodas? What undesirable effects might such a law have?

Reading Strategy

Structured Overview Ask students to write on their papers the following headings: Moral Controls, Controls on Beliefs, A Campaign of Political Action and Terror, and A Different Form of Social Protest. Have students scan the section and create subheadings under each of the headings. As students read, have them fill in details from the text.

SECTION PREVIEW

Jazz music, moving pictures, fast cars—American life moved at a dizzying pace in the 1920s. All the motion left some people feeling queasy, and they sought to slow the pace of change.

Prohibition forced many beer companies to find new beverages to brew. Above are labels from such products.

Key Concepts

• Prohibition, censorship, the growth of the Ku Klux Klan, and other developments reflected a desire to slow the changes in morals and manners in the 1920s.
• Some artists responded to the changes in the nation with despair and self-exile.
• The 1928 election dramatically demonstrated the social and political divisions in the United States.

Key Terms, People, and Places

speakeasies, bootlegging, fundamentalism, Scopes trial; T. S. Eliot, F. Scott Fitzgerald

T he social and cultural changes taking place in the United States in the 1920s were exhilarating to many people. Other Americans, however, were quite alarmed at what they saw as the nation's moral and intellectual decay.

Moral Controls

Throughout United States history, various groups had worked for the prohibition of alcoholic beverages. In 1919, prohibitionists finally achieved their goal with the ratification of the Eighteenth Amendment to the Constitution. The amendment outlawed the making, selling, transporting, importing, or exporting of any intoxicating beverages.

Prohibition's supporters believed that the Eighteenth Amendment would stop people from drinking alcohol. They thought some of the most undesirable features of modern urban life might thus be curbed. As preacher Billy Sunday declared,

> T he reign of tears is over. The slums will soon be only a memory. We will turn our prisons into factories and our jails into storehouses and corncribs. Men will walk upright now. Women will smile and children will laugh. Hell will be forever for rent.

Prohibition in Practice The use of alcohol did decrease for a few years after 1919, especially among the poor. Prohibition, however, proved impossible to enforce. Congressman Thomas Spencer Crago of Pennsylvania had predicted that the attempt to enforce prohibition would breed "a discontent and disrespect for law in this country beyond anything we have ever witnessed before." He was right. For many, openly defying prohibition was almost fun. Others only pretended to comply, sneaking liquor into their homes or slinking off to **speakeasies,** bars where liquor was served illegally.

During prohibition, many crooks made fortunes **bootlegging**—smuggling liquor across the border from Canada, shipping it from the West Indies or Mexico, or distilling their own moonshine. Organized gangs, the most famous of which was Al Capone's in Chicago, fought to gain control over the illegal but highly profitable traffic in liquor. Designed to wipe out crime, prohibition created new ones. By decade's end, many people began to call for reform.

Morality at the Movies In an effort to draw bigger audiences, filmmakers in the early 1920s began to include more sexually explicit content. This development prompted a movement to control the industry. To avoid censorship from outside the movies, filmmakers decided to censor themselves. In 1922, they set up their own organization, which devised a production code

---

RESOURCE DIRECTORY

Teaching Resources

Reproducible Lesson Plan found in the Unit 7 folder, p. 7, provides a summary of the Section 5 lesson plan content.

Alternate Lesson Plan: Learning Styles found in the Alternate Lesson Plans folder, p. 110, is an alternate lesson plan especially effective for auditory learners that provides a team activity centered on a radio interview of a 1928 congressional candidate.

Guided Reading and Review found in the Unit 7 folder, p. 16, provides a structure for reading and mastering the key concepts and reviewing the key terms for Section 5. (Guided Practice)

for movies that limited the amount of love-making, bare skin, and crime a film could show.

Laws for the Dance Floor Considered a sign of the decay of modern morals, dancing to that "Unspeakable Jazz" aroused widespread criticism in the early 1920s. "Anyone who says that 'youths of both sexes can mingle in close embrace'—with limbs intertwined and torso in contact—without suffering harm lies," accused a writer in the *Ladies Home Journal* in 1921.

To discourage close dancing, respectable dance halls required couples to remain six inches apart and ceased moonlight dances—those with the lights turned low. By 1929, cities and states across the country passed over three hundred laws to control dancing and dance halls. Most were easily evaded.

MAKING CONNECTIONS

Consider some of the laws that regulate behavior today. Do you think these laws will still be enforced in one hundred years? Explain.

Controls on Beliefs

During the early twentieth century, the rising prestige of science, changing social roles for women, and social gospel reform movements challenged many traditional religious beliefs. In reaction, religious traditionalists published a series of pamphlets called *The Fundamentals.* These tracts, which appeared between 1909 and 1914, insisted that every word in the Bible was inspired by God, and that every biblical story was literally true. The pamphlets gave birth to a religious movement called **fundamentalism.**

The Scopes Trial In 1923 and 1924, fundamentalist legislators in at least twelve states introduced laws to ban the teaching of evolution in the public schools. *Evolution* is the name for Charles Darwin's theory, put forward in 1859, that holds that humans and all other species developed over time from lower to more complex forms. Fundamentalists argued that the theory of evolution contradicted biblical accounts of the creation of the world.

Viewpoints
On the Eighteenth Amendment

Flagrant violations of prohibition led to loud cries for reform, or repeal of the Eighteenth Amendment. The speakers below are addressing a Senate committee investigating violations of the law. *What basic value underlies each argument?*

For Reform or Repeal of the National Prohibition Act
"It is impossible to tell whether prohibition is a good thing or a bad thing. It has never been enforced in this country. . . . I will concede that the saloon was odious [offensive], but now we have delicatessen stores, pool rooms, drug stores, millinery shops, private parlors, and 57 other varieties of speakeasies selling liquor and flourishing."
New York congressman Fiorello La Guardia, 1926

Against Reform or Repeal of the National Prohibition Act
"Permit me to show another side of the picture, and propose that instead of lowering our standards, we urge that the law be strengthened. . . . The closing of the open saloon . . . has resulted in better national health, children are born under better conditions, homes are better, and the mother is delivered from the fear of a drunken husband."
Ella A. Boole, president of the
National Woman's Christian Temperance Union, 1926

Several states passed an antievolution law. The American Civil Liberties Union (ACLU), however, felt that the laws violated the Constitution. In 1925, the ACLU announced that it would defend any teacher willing to challenge the statutes. John T. Scopes, a young high school biology teacher from Dayton, Tennessee, accepted. He read to his class a description of Darwin's theory. His arrest followed.

Thanks to radio, the **Scopes trial** became a national sensation. Famed lawyer Clarence Darrow headed the ACLU defense team. Former presidential candidate William Jennings Bryan defended the antievolution law. The climax came when Bryan insisted that everything in the Bible was literally true. Darrow got Bryan to admit that even he interpreted figuratively some biblical stories and ideas. Bryan, widely ridiculed, died soon after the trial.

Because Scopes had violated the law, the trial jury convicted him and imposed a one-hundred

Viewpoints Activity On the Eighteenth Amendment, found in the Unit 7 folder, pp. 22–23, provides additional viewpoints and perspectives on the Eighteenth Amendment.

Answer to . . .

Viewpoints

La Guardia emphasizes the unenforce-ability of the law; Boole argues that prohibition leads to a better economic and moral climate in the country. For a thorough understanding of the Eighteenth Amendment, see Resource Directory below.

Answer to . . .

MAKING CONNECTIONS

Answers will vary. Students may cite generally accepted laws such as those regulating school attendance, or they may mention more controversial laws such as those concerning drug use. Encourage students to consider 1920s efforts at moral control in light of similar efforts today.

2. INSTRUCT

Explain/Discuss

Explain that many of the Americans who favored prohibition lived in small towns and on farms. Discuss the ways that the passing of a prohibition amendment and its failure to control the use of alcohol pointed up divisions in American society.

In Depth

Then and Now

In the 1920s, the Klan gained a foothold in the industrial Northeast as well as in the South, Midwest, and West. In a court battle pitting the Empire Knights of the Ku Klux Klan against the Southern Poverty Law Center, the Klan group agreed to surrender its name, its mailing list, and all its assets. The settlement followed a guilty verdict in a case involving a Klan-led attack on a group of African Americans in Georgia.

Ask students what other sorts of behavior those concerned about moral decay tried to regulate. Do students think censorship or related activities are desirable? Who should develop the standards for movies, rock concerts, or books available in the library?

Analyze

Ask students why John Scopes went to jail after the famous Scopes trial and what the lasting importance of the Scopes trial was.

How did the Ku Klux Klan try to halt what it saw as the nation's moral decline? Discuss why the actions of the Klan were illegal and immoral.

Caption Answer to ...

 Interpreting Maps

Strongest in the North Central and Southwest regions; weakest in the North Atlantic and Far West regions.

Activity

Teaching Heterogeneous Groups

For all students to understand censorship as a tool to regulate behavior, have them work in small groups and choose an industry, such as music, to censor. Have them select one criterion on which to censor that industry. Criteria for censorship might include language, behavior, or styles.

Enrichment

Tell students that in 1925 the first issue of *The New Yorker* magazine appeared, with a famous editorial statement vowing that the slick, expensive magazine of fiction, essays, cartoons, and reviews was not designed for "the old lady from Dubuque." Ask students to write a brief essay about the divisions in American society pointed up by that statement. What did the editors of *The New Yorker* see as the difference between the urbane elite they hoped would read their magazine and the middle class of rural America?

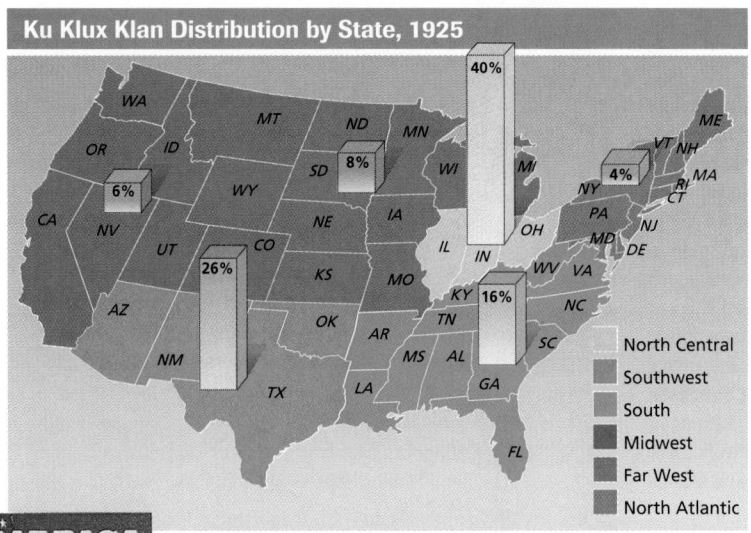
Ku Klux Klan Distribution by State, 1925

- North Central
- Southwest
- South
- Midwest
- Far West
- North Atlantic

Geography and History: Interpreting Maps
The resurgence of the Ku Klux Klan in the 1920s occurred in all corners of the country. *In which regions was the Klan the strongest? The weakest?*

dollar fine. The Tennessee Supreme Court threw out the fine—and a chance to test the law's constitutionality—on a technicality. The United States Supreme Court has since ruled, however, that similar laws violate the Constitution by promoting certain religious views. Nevertheless, debate over the proper place of evolution theory in American education continues today.

A Campaign of Political Action and Terror
In June 1920, the Ku Klux Klan (KKK), which had revived in 1915, launched a recruitment campaign using mass-marketing techniques of the advertising age. By October 1921, it had 85,000 new recruits. At its high point in the 1920s, the Klan boasted membership of between three and five million.

The Klan's political power extended across the country. In Oklahoma, Klan votes removed an anti-Klan governor. In Oregon, they dealt a blow to Catholic schools by getting a law passed requiring all children to attend public schools. In the South, they terrorized African Americans, and in the Southwest, pursued violators of prohibition. In the Northeast and West, they targeted Jews. They also went after Catholics, then 36 percent of the population and pre-

sumed by the Klan to be more loyal to their Pope than to the United States.

The Klan's goal was to restore white Protestants to a dominant place in American society and to halt the nation's so-called moral decline. According to the KKK's Imperial Wizard Hiram Wesley Evans, the Klan by 1926 was well on its way toward success. "When the Klan first appeared," he wrote, "the invasion of aliens and alien ideas" had brought about the destruction of cherished moral values. "After ten years of the Klan [the nation] is in arms for defense," Evans boasted.

The Klan movement of the 1920s collapsed suddenly under the weight of its violent nature. In 1928 the Grand Dragon of Indiana, David Stephenson, was jailed on second-degree murder charges. Stephenson took revenge on the politicians who failed to get him released by revealing the extent of Klan influence and political corruption in the state. Stephenson's revelations caused a scandal that broke the movement, at least for a time.

A Different Form of Social Protest

Efforts at moral, intellectual, and political control were not the only responses to the changes taking place in the United States in the 1920s. Some rebellious spirits were critical of their times for completely different reasons.

Before World War I, in urban artistic colonies such as New York City's Greenwich Village, artists and intellectuals had created hotbeds for discussion of new ideas in politics, theater, art, literature, and music. These thinkers felt themselves to be on the brink of artistic and intellectual triumph over nineteenth-century values and ideals. Then came World War I, a conflict of such brutality that belief in human progress seemed impossible to these artists. Following that came a period in which unconventional ideas were denounced as radical. Disillusioned, a whole group of artists turned

 RESOURCE DIRECTORY

Teaching Resources

Visual Learning Activity The Ku Klux Klan, found in the Unit 7 folder, p. 32, uses a 1923 drawing from *Life* magazine to enhance students' understanding of how symbols are used by artists to convey political viewpoints.

Literature Activity *Tales of the Jazz Age*, found in the Unit 7 folder, pp. 29–30, highlights the shallow, carefree rebellion of the flapper culture, and can be compared to the strong, poignant voices of *The Weary Blues*.

against their culture, depicting it in biting satires or choosing, instead, to flee from it altogether.

Poet Ezra Pound wrote of "a botched civilization." **T. S. Eliot's** "The Waste Land" became the symbolic poem of the generation. Novelist **F. Scott Fitzgerald** wrote of the youth of his times as "the beautiful and the damned." His 1925 masterpiece, *The Great Gatsby,* exposed what he saw as the shallow self-involvement and illusions of the Jazz Age rich. ✪

To these disillusioned artists, old ideals no longer inspired faith. Progressivism and related reform ideas now seemed dull. "If I am convinced of anything," journalist H. L. Mencken wrote, "It is that Doing Good is in bad taste."

Rejecting the American mass culture and ethic of success, some artists went into self-exile, many to Paris. Soon, they found it just as hard to live there. Ironically, when they came back, some got jobs in advertising or the book trade, the very businesses they had earlier despised.

The Election of 1928 Reflects the Conflicts of the Era

No single event more dramatically reflected the divisions of the era than the presidential election of 1928. On the Democratic side was New York governor Al Smith, a Roman Catholic from a family of recent immigrants, and a "wet," or opponent of prohibition. Smith's formal education had ended at the eighth grade. But after New York's Democratic political machine, Tammany Hall, got him a seat in the New York State Assembly, Smith educated himself and became a champion of workers' rights. Because of his record in New York, Smith in 1928 had the support of many progressives—even though he was a product of Tammany Hall, which progressives despised.

The Republicans ran Herbert Hoover, a Protestant Quaker from West Branch, Iowa; a Stanford-educated friend of big business; and a "dry," or supporter of prohibition. In contrast to Smith, who was a fiery campaigner, Hoover was dull but polished. He was especially popular among women voters.

For the first time, radio played an extensive role in an election. Over the airwaves, Hoover came across as moderate, sensible, and trustworthy. In contrast, Smith's thick New York City accent made him sound uneducated and brash to many audiences. Smith also suffered the effects of an anti-Catholic propaganda campaign that sought to raise fears among voters about Smith's loyalty to the United States.

These factors—combined with the widespread though not entirely accurate belief that the economy was strong—gave Hoover a landslide victory. Yet Hoover's win did hide some dark clouds on the Republican horizon. Smith carried the nation's twelve largest cities, an important development in the increasingly urban United States. He also broke into the midwestern belt of unhappy, indebted farmers, who were experiencing economic hard times in spite of the nation's apparent prosperity.

From the vantage point of 1928, however, Hoover's victory seemed decisive. Indeed, with the election over, the roar of the 1920s seemed to quiet down. Yet it would not be long before it would rise again—this time driven by panic.

SECTION 5 REVIEW

Key Terms, People, and Places
1. Define (a) speakeasy, (b) bootlegging, (c) fundamentalism.

Key Concepts
2. For what reasons did Prohibition fail?
3. What attempts were made in the 1920s to control morals, and how successful were they?
4. Explain the facts and significance of the Scopes trial.

5. What were some of the goals of the Ku Klux Klan in the 1920s?
6. What group do T. S. Eliot and F. Scott Fitzgerald represent?

Critical Thinking
7. **Demonstrating Reasoned Judgment** In what ways did the 1928 election reflect the social and political divisions of the era?

 Quiz found in the Unit 7 folder, p. 17, covers the main ideas in this section as well as the key terms.

 Chapter Test Forms A and B are found in the Unit 7 folder, pp. 34–39.

 Answer Keys found in the Unit 7 folder, pp. 116–128, provide answers to all student activities.

Media and Technology

Transparency
Graphic Organizer, G-3

Guided Reading Audiotapes (English and Spanish)

Computer Test Bank

Chapter Review

Understanding Key Terms, People, and Places

Key Terms
1. communist
2. red scare
3. general strike
4. Harlem Renaissance
5. Teapot Dome
6. Jazz Age
7. flapper
8. speakeasies
9. bootlegging
10. fundamentalism
11. Scopes trial

People
12. Vladimir I. Lenin
13. Nicola Sacco
14. Bartolomeo Vanzetti
15. Marcus Garvey
16. Warren G. Harding
17. Calvin Coolidge
18. Herbert Hoover
19. Charles A. Lindbergh
20. Henry Ford
21. T. S. Eliot
22. F. Scott Fitzgerald

Terms For each term above, write a sentence that explains its relation to the social and technological changes that took place in the 1920s.

Matching Review the key terms in the list above. If you are not sure of a term's meaning, review its definition in the chapter. Then choose a term from the list that best matches each description below.
1. bars where liquor was served illegally
2. youthful woman symbolizing the spirit of the 1920s
3. smuggling or distilling liquor illegally
4. period when artistic life flowered among African Americans

True or False Determine whether each statement is true or false. If it is true, write "true." If it is false. change the underlined person or place to make the statement true.
1. Warren G. Harding sought to build up African Americans' self-respect and racial pride.
2. Many people believed that shoemaker Nicola Sacco had been unfairly tried because of his Italian heritage and political views.
3. T. S. Eliot's novel *The Great Gatsby* exposed what he saw as the self-involvement of the Jazz Age.
4. Bartolomeo Vanzetti became a national hero after his solo flight across the Atlantic Ocean.

Reviewing Main Ideas

Section 1 (pp. 580–583)
1. Briefly describe conditions in the American economy in the first few years following World War I.
2. What events of 1919 led many Americans to fear that the Russian Revolution would spread to the United States? How did politicians respond?
3. How did Congress limit immigration in the 1920s?

Section 2 (pp. 586–590)
4. Why did women's votes fail to change politics as much as suffragists had hoped?
5. Describe the general experience of African American migrants to the North in the postwar years.
6. In what sense was the 1920s a "Republican decade"?

Section 3 (pp. 591–594)
7. In what ways did young people defy social conventions after World War I?

8. How did changes in fashion for women reflect the new morals and manners of the Jazz Age?
9. How were new social possibilities still limited for women during the Jazz Age?

Section 4 (pp. 596–599)
10. How did the growth of leisure time help lead to the creation of a national culture?
11. What role did chain supermarkets, advertisers, and fast-food chains play in creating a common culture?
12. How did Henry Ford "democratize the automobile"?

Section 5 (pp. 600–603)
13. Briefly describe some of the efforts to control Americans' morals and beliefs in the 1920s.
14. Why were many writers disillusioned in the 1920s?
15. In what ways did the election of 1928 reflect the divisions of the era?

Chapter Review Answers

Understanding Key Terms, People, and Places

Terms Students should refer to the definitions of the key terms in the chapter to write sentences that show understanding of their relationship to the social and technological changes that took place in the 1920s.

Matching
1. speakeasies
2. flapper
3. bootlegging
4. Harlem Renaissance

True or False
1. false, Marcus Garvey
2. true
3. false, F. Scott Fitzgerald
4. false, Charles A. Lindbergh

Reviewing Main Ideas

1. Veterans faced unemployment; farmers suffered as prices for crops dropped; inflation was high; labor unrest increased.

2. Labor strikes and terrorist acts caused many people to believe that the fabric of society was tearing apart. Politicians' responses included the Palmer raids and the defeat of many progressive reforms.

3. Congress set quotas for each country at 2 percent of the total number of immigrants from that country living in the United States in 1890. The law reduced immigration from southern and eastern Europe.

4. Women did not vote in large numbers. Especially in national elections, women voted in patterns similar to men.

5. African Americans left the South to find work, but they were unable to substantially improve their standard of living. Also, discrimination and racial violence continued to plague them in the North. But many African Americans helped build vital new communities, such as Harlem in New York City.

6. Republicans capitalized on improvements in the economy to win each presidential election in the 1920s.

7. Fads such as dance marathons became popular. The young also displayed growing freedom in their social relations.

8. Women's clothing exposed arms and knees for the first time; ordinary women began to wear makeup.

9. Large numbers of women entered the work force, at lower pay than men. White women were often fired when they became pregnant; most African American women were forced by economic circumstances to keep working.

10. Commerce and industry produced and sold new products such as the radio and automobile. Also the expanding communications industry led to a wide sharing of experiences among people throughout the country.

11. People across the country could shop in the same stores for the same products. Advertisers helped make brand names synonymous with certain types of products.

12. By applying the ideas of uniformity of product and the assembly line, Ford produced cars at prices that working people could afford.

13. Prohibition tried to outlaw the consumption of alcohol. The Ku Klux Klan tried to return white Protestants to a place of superiority. Fundamentalists helped push the passage of anti-evolution laws.

14. After the brutality of World War I, belief in human progress seemed impossible to many writers.

15. Smith, a Catholic of immigrant roots and an opponent of prohibition, represented one side of a number of the divisive issues of the decade. Hoover represented the opposite side of those issues.

Thinking Critically

1. **Recognizing Ideologies** During the 1920s, terms such as "un-American" and "Bolshevik" were used to ignite people's fears and obscure complex issues. Describe terms that play a similar role today.
2. **Demonstrating Reasoned Judgment** "For many African Americans, the migration to the North was a mixed success." Explain the meaning of this statement.

3. **Distinguishing False from Accurate Images** The flapper was a popular image of the 1920s that, in fact, represented only a small number of American women. Are there symbols that represent the present era? If so, what are they? What role does the media play in promoting this image? Who does the image truly represent?

Making Connections

1. **Evaluating Primary Sources** Review the primary source excerpt on page 599. If you were a business manager, what would be your opinion of this method of running a business? If you were a worker? If you were running a business, would you emphasize creativity or efficiency? What are the benefits and drawbacks of each approach?
2. **Understanding the Visuals** Write a short paragraph explaining how the information in the graph on page 581 and the photo of sheet music on page 583 are related.
3. **Writing About the Chapter** You are a newspaper editor in the early 1920s. Write an editorial in which you offer your opinion about the outcome of the Sacco and Vanzetti case. Before you begin, review the chapter for details about the red scare and the treatment of immigrants, and consider how these factors might have influenced the trial. As you write a draft of your editorial, consider the following questions: Is

there any valid reason to consider Sacco and Vanzetti's political beliefs in their trial? What if Sacco and Vanzetti are in fact guilty—does it matter whether they received a fair trial? Proofread your work and draft a final copy.
4. **Using the Graphic Organizer** This graphic organizer uses a web to organize information about the changes in technology and culture that took place in the 1920s. Webs often can show connections between seemingly unconnected ideas. In this web, dotted lines are used to show these connections. (a) Based on what you have read in the chapter, what is the connection between increased leisure time and the rise in popularity of the radio and movies? (b) According to the graphic organizer below, what did chain stores and the auto industry have in common in the 1920s? (c) On a separate sheet of paper, create your own graphic organizer about the new manners and social freedoms that arose during the Jazz Age.

Alternative Assessment

Final Evaluation
Use the following guidelines to evaluate student projects:
● **Evidence of thoughtfulness** Did the student include the main topics from the chapter?
● **Evidence of outside research** To what extent did students use outside research materials for their projects?
● **Evidence of synthesis** Do projects demonstrate that students understand how topics are related?
● **Communication style** Does the project convey its purpose to an audience in a clear, appealing way?

Thinking Critically

1. Answers will vary. Students might respond that such terms as *communist, liberal, welfare state,* and *gay* are sometimes used today as negative labels.
2. African Americans who migrated North found some improvement in their lives, but not what many hoped for. But the Great Migration led to the flowering of African American culture in Harlem.
3. Answers will vary. Students may point to symbols of youth culture today, such as pencil-thin models and rock stars. Such images are promoted by the media and bear little resemblance to real lives.

Making Connections

1. From a business viewpoint, Ford's way is highly efficient. From the viewpoint of a worker, however, it might be dehumanizing. Students may offer ways of combining efficiency and creativity, perhaps by offering workers incentives for creative ideas.
2. When strikes and labor unrest broke out in the 1920s, many people blamed this on communism and feared an uprising in the United States. Such sentiments led to a fear of foreigners and renewed isolationism, which became so widespread that songs were written about it, such as this one, "O! Close the Gates."
3. Students' editorials should reflect serious thought about the purpose and meaning of the right to a fair trial.

Recall with students that the 1920s were referred to as the "Jazz Age," and whether Americans enjoyed or disapproved of jazz, the music and the idea were in the air.

Ask students to study the artifacts and to read the captions. Using the artifacts and captions as a basis for discussion, ask students why radio was important in making jazz familiar to the American public. Discuss how radio brought jazz to white audiences who were less likely to attend clubs where African American jazz musicians performed.

Ask students to compare the importance of jazz in the 1920s to the importance of rock music in all its many styles and varieties in the 1990s. Prompt discussion with questions such as: Is rock as prevalent as jazz was? Do people have more or less opportunity to hear rock as people did to hear jazz? Is rock as shocking to the older generation in the 1990s as jazz was in the 1920s?

Ask students to make a list of the artifacts they would include in an American Album display about the music of the 1990s. Tell them to choose items that illustrate the many aspects of life that rock touches.

If possible, play some jazz from the 1920s in the classroom. One good compilation is the *Smithsonian Collection of Classic Jazz*.

THE JAZZ AGE

No music was more important to an era than jazz was to the 1920s. This unique American music grew from the culture of southern African Americans and traveled north with them. Jazz was more than mere music, however. Much of the country's youth—African American and white—saw jazz as the symbol of their new generation. *Compare the importance of jazz in the 1920s with the importance of "rock and roll" to later generations.*

▲1930s RADIO Radio, more than any other medium, made jazz familiar to the American public. The jazz heard on the radio was adapted by all-white bands to appeal to largely white audiences.

▲ DUKE ELLINGTON The jazz clubs of Harlem and Chicago were one of the few places where African American musicians could perform their music for white audiences. Duke Ellington, pictured on the sheet music of one of his famous compositions, became a Harlem headliner in 1923.

DIZZIE GILLESPIE'S ▶ TRUMPET Jazz musicians developed their own playing styles and unique signatures. Dizzy Gillespie, whose bent horn distinguished him from other trumpet players, pioneered the modern jazz and bebop styles. His career, which began in the 1930s, spanned seven decades.

◄ HYMIE SHERTZER
The well-known sax-
ophonist worked
with many bands
as well as in
recording
studios and
in radio.

FLAPPER'S DRESS ►
AND BEADS The symbol of
the Jazz Age was the flapper
with her "jazz style" clothes. The
flapper's short skirts, silk stockings, and fake jewelry were new
and daring, shocking many in the
older generation. Flapper clothes
were a must for doing the newest
dances to jazz music.

◄
SHERTZER'S
SAXOPHONE
The saxophone
was invented in
Europe in 1840
but never became
a popular orchestral
instrument. Musicians
like Shertzer, however, made the sax's
smooth, easily blended sound one of the
major voices of the jazz band.

◄ BENNY GOODMAN'S
CLARINET Known as the "King of
Swing," Goodman began his jazz career in
1926. His "big band" helped make jazz
popular with white audiences, but he preferred small groups. Goodman's 1936
trio with African American musicians
Lionel Hampton and Teddy Wilson
was the first popular racially
mixed jazz group. Goodman
was also a classical performer
who made recordings with
leading symphony
orchestras.

◄ 1920s JAZZ BAND
Most jazz artists strug-
gled to earn a living and
remained anonymous.
This band, which was
photographed in St. Louis
in the 1920s, is unidentified. The band played the
New Orleans style jazz.

Chapter 22 Crash and Depression
1929–1933

📁 **Teaching Resources** (See Unit 7 Folder)

	Instruction	Enrichment
Section 1 **The Economy in the Late 1920s** (pp. 610–613)	Reproducible Lesson Plan, p. 41 Alternate Lesson Plan, p. 112 Guided Reading and Review, p. 46 Quiz, p. 47	Critical Thinking Activity, Identifying Central Issues, p. 65 Visual Learning Activity, Hard Times for Farmers, p. 73
Section 2 **The Stock Market Crash** (pp. 614–617)	Reproducible Lesson Plan, p. 42 Alternate Lesson Plan, p. 113 Guided Reading and Review, p. 48 Quiz, p. 49	Literature Activity, The Stock Market Crash, p. 69 American Profiles Activity, Woody Guthrie, p. 60 Time and Place Activity, The Great Flood of 1993, pp. 58–59
Section 3 **Social Effects of the Depression** (pp. 620–624)	Reproducible Lesson Plan, p. 43 Alternate Lesson Plan, p. 114 Guided Reading and Review, p. 50 Quiz, p. 51	Literature Activity, The Psychological Effects of the Depression, pp. 70–71 Primary Source Activity, Hard Times in Oklahoma, p. 66 Historian's Toolbox Activity, Distinguishing False from Accurate Images, p. 64
Section 4 **Surviving the Great Depression** (pp. 626–628)	Reproducible Lesson Plan, p. 44 Alternate Lesson Plan, p. 115 Guided Reading and Review, p. 52 Quiz, p. 53	American Profiles Activity, Babe Didrikson Zaharias, p. 61 Primary Source Activity, The Forgotten Man, pp. 67–68
Section 5 **The Election of 1932: A Turning Point in History** (pp. 629–633)	Reproducible Lesson Plan, p. 45 Alternate Lesson Plan, p. 116 Guided Reading and Review, p. 54 Quiz, p. 55 Chapter Test, Forms A & B, pp. 74–79	Visual Learning Activity, Veterans March on Washington, p. 72 Viewpoints Activity, On Ending the Depression, pp. 62–63 Turning Point Extension Activity, The Lasting Impact of the Election of 1932, pp. 56–57

📁 **Additional Chapter Resources**

Resource Organizer, p. 40
Alternate Lesson Plan, p. 111
Answer Keys, pp. 116–128

Bibliography

For the Teacher
Watkins, T. H. *The Great Depression: America in the 1930s.*
Little, Brown, 1993. (Companion volume to the PBS video.)

Prentice Hall Literature Excerpts from *The American
Experience*, 1994, including Wright, Richard. *Black Boy: A
Record of Childhood and Youth.* HarperCollins, 1993 edition.

THE BIG IDEA

The Big Idea for the chapter and how the main ideas in each section relate to the Big Idea are graphically displayed below. Comprehension of this chapter's Big Idea is critical to students' understanding of United States history and how we as a nation got where we are today.

Media and Technology

 Time Lines, E-6

  Visions of America: Turning Point Story, "Regulating Riches" (length: approx. 4 minutes)

  Visions of America: Roundtable Discussion on "Regulating Riches"

 Fine Art, D-18; Cause and Effect, F-9; Graphic Organizer, G-3

🎧 Guided Reading Audiotapes (English and Spanish)

 Computer Test Bank

For the Student

The Great Depression. 420 minutes. PBS Video, 1993. Color. (Seven one-hour segments produced by Public Broadcasting Service.)
The Grapes of Wrath. 129 minutes. Zenger. Black and white film. (Dramatization of John Steinbeck's novel on the Depression.)

CHAPTER 22

When the high-flying 1920s crashed in 1929, the bleak years of the Great Depression began. Behind the headlines and photos of stock-buying frenzy and destitution grew a debate that cut to the very political, social, and economic fiber of the country and changed forever how Americans look at government.

SECTION 1

During the 1920s most Americans had great confidence in the country's economy. However, the seemingly booming economy was actually not healthy and there were signs of troubled times ahead.

SECTION 2

The stock market crashed in October 1929, bringing about a depression more severe than any the country had ever experienced.

SECTION 3

At first the Depression affected only certain Americans, but gradually it came to change the lives, and affect the physical and mental health, of almost all citizens.

SECTION 4

Life during the Great Depression was an unforgettable experience. In spite of the hard times, many Americans faced the future with courage.

SECTION 5

Republican President Hoover failed to control the Depression, and in 1932, for the first time in twelve years, voters elected a Democratic President who changed the concept of American government.

Crash and Depression
1929–1933

The Relevance of the Big Idea

Despite President Hoover's insistence that the economy was "fundamentally sound," and that "prosperity was just around the corner," business confidence failed in the late 1920s and unemployment became the norm. The Great Depression that followed brought a misery and fear that was unprecedented for most Americans. After taking office, President Roosevelt acted quickly to enact relief, recovery, and reform programs.

The stark policy differences between Hoover and FDR exemplified the political debate that has engaged all modern American Presidents: How best do we serve—with direct aid and intervention to the people or by encouraging business? Ask how policies of recent Presidents Bush (for an investment tax credit) and Clinton (for national health care) fit into this debate.

In Depth

Global Connections

The breadlines symbolic of the Great Depression were common in most major industrial countries. Germany was racked by inflation, crippled industrially, and buried under war reparations debt. Newsreel cameras filmed consumers using carts to carry deutsche marks to market—inflation had made them so worthless that millions were needed just to buy a loaf of bread. As a leader rose in America promising "relief, recovery, and reform," a different kind of leader came to power in Germany. Within days of FDR taking office in 1933, Adolf Hitler became Germany's dictator.

Crash and Depression
1929–1933

*T*he surface prosperity of the late 1920s hid deep faults in the American economy. When stock prices began to fall in October 1929, panic brought the economy crashing down. The United States sank into a long-lasting depression that brought widespread suffering. President Hoover's policies proved ineffective in turning the economy around, so Americans were eager to hear presidential candidate Franklin D. Roosevelt's proposals. In the 1932 election, voters chose Roosevelt, marking a major turning point in American history.

Events in the United States

1928 The automobile, steel, rubber, glass, and housing industries are in recession.	1929 Stock market hits record high in September, then crashes in October.	1931 Empire State Building opens in New York, becoming the world's tallest skyscraper.

1928	**1929**	**1930**	**1931**

Events in the World

1928 Fifteen nations sign the Kellogg-Briand Pact renouncing war.	1930 U.S., Britain, Japan, France, and Italy sign naval disarmament treaty.	1931 Japanese troops occupy Manchuria. • Spain is declared a republic.

▶ RESOURCE DIRECTORY

Teaching Resources

Alternate Lesson Plan: Demonstrating the Big Idea found in the Alternate Lesson Plans folder, p. 111, provides a lesson strategy to instruct students about the Big Idea that the difficult years of the Great Depression led to dramatic changes in the American way of life.

Alternative Assessment Handbook provides information, guidance, and strategies for alternative methods of assessment. It includes an essay on new trends in assessment, guidance and strategies on developing performance tasks and portfolios, scoring rubrics, and sample evaluation forms.

Pages 610–613

The Economy in the Late 1920s

Optimism and faith in business continued throughout the 1920s. But while many were buying goods on credit and investing in the booming stock market, millions more had no share in the country's prosperity.

Pages 614–617

The Stock Market Crash

In 1929 the foundation of the seemingly prosperous economy was so unstable that the stock market crash in October led to a severe depression whose effects spread worldwide.

Pages 620–624

Social Effects of the Depression

Most people were not immediately affected by the 1929 stock market crash, but by the early 1930s, wage cuts and growing unemployment brought widespread suffering.

Pages 626–628

Surviving the Great Depression

Living through the Great Depression was an unforgettable experience. Despite the hard times, many Americans learned to face troubles together with courage and humor.

Pages 629–633

The 1932 Election: A Turning Point in History

As the Depression worsened, people came to blame Hoover and the Republicans for their misery. The 1932 presidential election brought a sweeping victory for Democrat Franklin D. Roosevelt, and a new direction for American government.

Pages 634–635

The Lasting Impact of the 1932 Election

	1933 Prohibition is repealed. • Franklin D. Roosevelt is inaugurated as President.	1934 Farm families leave drought-stricken Great Plains and move west to California.	
1932 Veterans in the Bonus Army protest in Washington, D.C.			
1932	**1933**	**1934**	**1935**
1932 Amelia Earhart is the first woman to fly solo across the Atlantic.		1934 Nationalists force communists under Mao Zedong into "Long March" across China.	

Media and Technology

Transparency
Historical Maps, L-5

The Economy in the Late 1920s

SECTION 1

The Economy in the Late 1920s

1. FOCUS

Connecting to the Big Idea

See page 608B. Explain to students that all three Presidents of the decade took a hands-off approach to government and the economy. As a result, stock market practices were largely unregulated. The stock market boomed in this climate, and many Americans thought prosperity was here to stay. Millions of other Americans, however, did not share in the good times, and that in fact was one of the signs of trouble to come. Ask what other signs pointed to serious flaws in the economy.

Objectives

● Relate Hoover's election in 1928 to voters' expectations of continuing prosperity.
● Explain why the government and many Americans believed that business prosperity was in the national interest.
● Analyze the increase of personal debt in the 1920s as an economic indicator.
● Identify farmers and industrial workers as groups not sharing in the prosperity of the 1920s.

Bellringer

Have students describe what happens when a consumer makes a purchase on credit. Suggest that they consider factors such as how a consumer gets credit, how buying on credit can add to the cost of the purchase, and consequences for those who are unable to pay for purchases made on credit.

Reading Strategy

Reading for Evidence As they read, ask students to look for reasons for optimism about the economy in the 1920s and also for reasons for concern about the economy.

SECTION PREVIEW

Optimism and faith in business continued throughout the 1920s. But while many were buying goods on credit and investing in the booming stock market, millions more had no share in the country's prosperity.

Key Concepts
- Voters believed Herbert Hoover's administration would continue the good times.
- The government and many people believed that business prosperity served national interests.
- People went into debt to buy products and to invest in the stock market.
- Farmers and many industrial workers did not share in the general prosperity of the 1920s.

During the 1920s catalogs brimming with new goods tempted consumers to buy on credit.

Key Terms, People, and Places
real wages, welfare capitalism, installment buying, speculation, buy on margin

---

T he mood of most Americans in the late 1920s was optimistic, and for good reason. Medical advances had greatly reduced deaths from whooping cough, diphtheria, and other serious diseases. Since 1900, the number of infant deaths had declined, and life expectancy had lengthened more than 10 years, to 59 years for men and 63 years for women.

The brightest hopes seemed to come from the economy. In his final message to Congress, President Calvin Coolidge said that the country could "regard the present with satisfaction and anticipate the future with optimism." His successor, Herbert Hoover, predicted that "poverty will be banished from this nation."

The Economy Inspires Trust

Coolidge chose not to run in 1928, but years of prosperity under the Republicans made victory easy for Hoover. A self-made millionaire, Hoover was widely admired for the way he had organized food relief in Europe during and after World War I. He had also been an effective secretary of commerce for Presidents Harding and Coolidge. People expected that the good times would get even better under Hoover.

"Wonderful Prosperity" The United States economy seemed to be in fine shape. In 1925, the market value of all stocks was $27 billion. Over the next few years, it soared: in 1928 alone, stock values rose by almost $11.4 billion. Because the stock market was widely regarded as the nation's economic weathervane, the *New York Times* could describe the year as one "of unprecedented advance, of wonderful prosperity." By early October 1929, stock values hit $87 billion.

Working people also seemed better off. Since 1914, **real wages**—what money could actually buy—had increased more than 40 percent. Although some industries were troubled, and some workers lost jobs to assembly-line machinery, unemployment in general averaged below 4 percent.

Even critics of capitalism made optimistic predictions. In 1928, former muckraker Lincoln Steffens wrote:

B ig business in America is producing what the Socialists held up as their goal: food, shelter and clothing for all. You will see it during the Hoover administration.

"Everybody Ought to Be Rich" People had unusually high confidence in the business world during the 1920s. For some, business success became almost a religion. One of the

---

▶ RESOURCE DIRECTORY

Teaching Resources

📄 **Reproducible Lesson Plan** found in the Unit 7 folder, p. 41, provides a summary of the Section 1 lesson plan content.

📄 **Alternate Lesson Plan: Cooperative Learning** found in the Alternate Lesson Plans folder, p. 112, is an alternate lesson plan that provides guidance for groups of students to prepare oral presentations on economic conditions of the 1920s.

📄 **Guided Reading and Review** found in the Unit 7 folder, p. 46, provides a structure for reading and mastering the key concepts and reviewing the key terms for Section 1. (Guided Practice)

Higher Compression with *any* Gas!

*Plus Willys-Knight Silence, Velvet
Smoothness, Graceful Lines, Rich Colors*

BEAUTIFUL NEW COLORS

WILLYS·KNIGHT

$1295

This car advertisement from 1927 reflects the apparent prosperity and optimism of those years.

decade's best-selling books was *The Man Nobody Knows* (1925). Written by Bruce Barton, an advertising executive, it told Jesus' life story in business terms. Barton portrayed Jesus as a managerial genius who "picked up twelve men from the bottom ranks of business and forged them into an organization that conquered the world."

Similarly, Americans trusted the advice of corporate leaders such as John J. Raskob. In a 1929 article, "Everybody Ought to Be Rich," he stated that savings of only $15 a week over twenty years could bring a $400-a-month income from investments. "And because income can do that," Raskob said, "I am firm in my belief that anyone not only can be rich, but ought to be rich."

The three Republican Presidents of the 1920s equated the interests of the nation with the interests of the business world. They, too, expressed great confidence in business. Although people in the late 1920s were wildly buying stocks with borrowed money, the Hoover administration did nothing to discourage such borrowing.

Welfare Capitalism Partly because workers' standard of living seemed to be improving, organized labor lost members during the 1920s. To counter moves by outside union organizers and keep workers contented, companies met some of their workers' needs without prompting by unions. This new approach to labor relations was known as **welfare capitalism**. Employers raised wages and provided benefits such as paid vacations, health plans, and even English classes for recent immigrants.

MAKING CONNECTIONS

Although vacations and health plans were unusual benefits in the 1920s, more and more working people today expect them. What does this change show about the relative status of workers in the 1920s and 1990s?

Signs of Trouble

Despite the apparent prosperity, all was not well. Only later, however, did many people recognize the warning signs of an unsound economy.

Uneven Riches In reality, the economy of the 1920s was seriously out of balance. Despite some stock market success stories, it was mainly the rich who got richer. Huge corporations, rather than small businesses, dominated American industry. In 1929, 200 large companies controlled 49 percent of American industry.

Activity

Teaching Heterogeneous Groups

In the 1920s, farms and factories borrowed money to take advantage of new technology to increase production. Soon however, production exceeded demand. In order for students to understand how supply exceeded demand due to overproduction, divide the class into small groups representing farms and factories. Have students in each group list items required for production. For example, the auto industry would list rubber and steel. Then have students identify the other industries that might be affected should their industry overproduce and not be able to sell its goods, setting in motion a domino effect throughout the economy. **LEP**

Enrichment

Ask students to create a campaign poster or song for Herbert Hoover in the election of 1928, based on the Republican promise that Hoover would safeguard the nation's prosperity. Students might research some of the actual slogans used in the campaign.

 In Depth

Historical Misconceptions

The crash is usually seen as the result of bad business practices in the stock market and, therefore, avoidable. But the crash was, in the words of historian George Soule, "no easily preventable accident. While it is now possible to identify certain major infections that were developing, there seems to be no simple inoculation, the injection of which into the economic body would have maintained its health."

Income Distribution and Depression Era Prices

- $10,000 and over
- $5,000 – $9,999
- $2,000 – $4,999
- $1,999 and under

1%
5%
65%   29%

Income Distribution, 1929

Source: *Historical Statistics of the United States*

Depression Era Prices	
Item	Price
1 Dozen Eggs	$0.29
Quart of Milk	$0.10
Loaf of Bread	$0.05
Gasoline (per gallon)	$0.18
Vacuum Cleaner	$18.75
Gas Stove	$23.95
Wool Dress	$1.95
Men's Trousers	$2.00
New Car (Chrysler sedan)	$995.00
Double Bed and Spring Mattress	$14.95
Catcher's Mitt	$1.19
Two-Wheeled Bike	$10.95
Modern 6-Room House With 2-Car Garage	$2,800.00

Source: *This Fabulous Century*, Vol. IV, by Time-Life Books

This political cartoon, symbolic of the stock market frenzy, shows greedy brokers "fishing" for new clients from the top of the New York Stock Exchange building.

 Interpreting Graphs
The pie graph shows how unevenly the country's wealth was distributed in the 1920s. *What percentage of Americans earned less than $2,000 a year? Looking at the list of prices and assuming that you didn't buy on credit, find what you could have bought with that income—a monthly income of $165 or less.*

Similarly, personal wealth was concentrated in a tiny percentage of American families. (See the graph above.) In 1929, the richest Americans—24,000 families, or just 0.1 percent of the population—had incomes of more than $100,000. They also held 34 percent of the country's total savings. Of those families, 513 were millionaires.

By contrast, 71 percent of American individuals and families earned less than $2,500 a year. About 21.5 million households—nearly 80 percent of all families—had no savings. Many people earned so little that almost everyone in a family, including children, had to work just to get by.

Buying on Credit Another sign of trouble was an increase in personal debt. Traditionally, Americans feared debt and resisted buying goods unless they had the cash to pay for them. In the 1920s, however, assembly-line production lowered the cost of many consumer items, making them affordable for more people. People also were eager to forget World War I. They flocked to buy radios, vacuum cleaners, refrigerators, and other exciting new products, whether or not they could afford them.

Advertising made new goods irresistible. Store owners also had enough confidence in the economy to let people buy goods "on time." **Installment buying** let people purchase expensive items such as automobiles and furniture and pay for them (with interest) over many months.

"Get Rich Quick" A "get-rich-quick" attitude prevailed during the 1920s. Stock prices were on a dizzy climb, and the press quickly reported success stories of ordinary people who had made fortunes.

Before World War I, only the wealthy played the stock market. Now, with stock prices rising, **speculation**—taking chances in the stock market—became widespread. Small investors entered the market, often with their life savings. If they could not afford to buy stocks at face value, stockbrokers let them **buy on margin**.

RESOURCE DIRECTORY

Teaching Resources

⭐ **Critical Thinking Activity** Identifying Central Issues: Signs of Trouble, found in the Unit 7 folder, p. 65, helps students to identify central issues by analyzing a graph on income distribution in the United States in 1929.

⭐ **Visual Learning Activity** Hard Times for Farmers, found in the Unit 7 folder, p. 73, uses photographs and oral accounts to extend students' understanding of government attempts to draw attention to the plight of farmers during the Depression.

They paid a fraction of the price (10 to 50 percent) and borrowed the rest.

Brokers charged high interest and could demand payment of the loan at any time. But if the price of the stocks went up, the borrower could sell at a price high enough to pay off the loan and interest charges and still make money.

Too Many Goods, Too Little Demand By the late 1920s, the country's warehouses held piles of unbought consumer goods. Wages had risen, but not as fast as production. People could not afford to buy goods as fast as they were made.

Although the stock market kept rising, overproduction caused some industries to slow in the late 1920s. The automobile industry, which had helped create American prosperity, slumped after 1925. Industries that depended on it—steel, rubber, and glass—also were in recession. Housing construction fell by 25 percent between 1928 and 1929.

Hard Times Most farmers never shared in the 1920s prosperity. New machinery enabled them to grow more crops, but the huge postwar demand for food ended as European farmers recovered. As a result, crop prices in the United States fell so low that farmers could not pay what they owed for land and machinery. Rural banks suffered when loans were not repaid, and about 6,000 failed. "We were in the Depression before 1929, we just didn't call it that," recalled a rural Tennessean.

Outside agriculture, factory workers faced low wages and long hours. Conditions were especially bad in coal mines and southern

Farm families faced hard times in the 1920s. Many had to watch while their homes, land, and animals were sold at auction.

textile mills. In the rayon mills of Elizabethton, Tennessee, for instance, women worked 56-hour weeks, earning 16 to 18 cents an hour—about $10 a week.

To some observers, these factors—uneven wealth, rising debt, speculation in the stock market, overproduction, and hard times for many workers—clearly signaled trouble in the economy. In 1928, Belle Moskowitz, who had managed Al Smith's losing presidential campaign that year, predicted that "growing unemployment, business depression or some false step" would soon trigger a reaction against Hoover and his policies. Although the collapse did not come till the next year, she soon was proved right.

SECTION 1 REVIEW

Key Terms, People, and Places
1. Define (a) real wages, (b) welfare capitalism, (c) installment buying, (d) speculation, (e) buy on margin.

Key Concepts
2. Why was there so much optimism in the United States in the late 1920s?
3. How did most Americans regard the business world in the 1920s?

4. In what ways had many Americans gone deeply into debt? Why?
5. Which groups were experiencing hard times in the 1920s despite the general prosperity in the United States?

Critical Thinking
6. **Identifying Central Issues** Why did most people not realize that the economy in the 1920s was not as healthy as it seemed?

Quiz found in the Unit 7 folder, p. 47, covers the main ideas in this section as well as the key terms.

3. ASSESS

Section 1 Review Answers

1. (a) real wages, see p. 610, (b) welfare capitalism, see p. 611, (c) installment buying, see p. 612, (d) speculation, see p. 612, (e) buy on margin, see p. 612

2. Medical advances had increased human life expectancy by about ten years for both sexes. The booming stock market made it seem that the economy was very prosperous.

3. People had confidence in business prosperity and in business leaders; they believed people could achieve success.

4. They bought consumer goods on installment plans; they bought stocks on margin, borrowing from the broker. The mood was one of confidence and trust in business.

5. Farmers, industrial workers.

6. The economy appeared deceptively healthy because the stock market was rising, real wages had improved, and employers were giving more benefits. People also had confidence in business leaders and in Presidents Coolidge and Hoover; moreover, they wanted to forget problems and look to a bright future after World War I.

Reteach

Ask students to make two columns on a piece of paper. Ask them to list the 1920s economy's positive signs in the right-hand column and the negative signs in the left-hand column. Then ask them to write one or two sentences explaining the seriousness of the negative indications.

4. CLOSE

Reinforcing the Big Idea

Most Americans were optimistic about the continued growth of the economy in 1928 and early 1929. Certain key signs, however, showed that the economy was in trouble. The next section deals with the stock market crash in October 1929.

SECTION 2

The Stock Market Crash

SECTION 2

1. FOCUS

Connecting to the Big Idea

See page 608B. Explain to students that the stock market crash in October 1929 brought on a depression more severe than any the nation had ever experienced. Ask what the lasting effects of the Depression were on government, politics, and American thought.

Objectives

● Describe how a sudden fall in stock prices in late October 1929 brought on a stock market crash.

● Explain how the stock market crash led to a general decline in the United States economy.

● Account for the worldwide effects of the stock market crash.

Bellringer

Ask students to imagine themselves as a bank customer who wants to withdraw savings and is told by the bank teller that there is no money. What might be the cause of such a situation? What options would be available to the customer?

Reading Strategy

Predicting Content Ask students to skim Section 2, list the main headings and subheadings and write a sentence or phrase to predict the content of each section. When they have finished reading Section 2, ask them to review their predictions and test them against the actual text.

2. INSTRUCT

Explain/Discuss

Explain to students that the sense of prosperity described in the previous section came to a sudden halt as stock prices fell, investors began to sell, and prices fell even more. Ask students to explain how Richard

---

SECTION PREVIEW

The Long and the Short of it

Ticker-tape machines, which report stock market activity, brought both good news and bad to investors, as this drawing from a 1930 *Life* **cover shows.**

In 1929 the foundation of the seemingly prosperous economy was so unstable that the stock market crash in October led to a severe depression whose effects spread worldwide.

Key Concepts

• A sudden fall in stock prices in late October 1929 brought a wave of panic selling.

• The crash contributed to a severe decline in the overall United States economy.

• The results of the stock market crash were felt worldwide.

Key Terms, People, and Places
Dow Jones industrial average, Gross National Product (GNP), collateral

---

After Herbert Hoover's 1928 election, stock prices continued to climb. Early that year, the **Dow Jones industrial average**, an average of stock prices of leading industries, was 191. By inauguration day, March 4, 1929, it had risen another 122 points. Prices faltered in April, but brokers said, "Buy!" On September 3, the Dow Jones reached an all-time high of 381.

The Market Crashes

The rising stock market dominated the news. Keeping track of prices was almost as popular as counting Babe Ruth's home runs. Eager, nervous investors filled brokerage houses around the country to catch the latest news coming in on the ticker tape or posted on blackboards. Prices for many stocks soared far above their real value, in terms of the company's earnings and assets.

Black Thursday, Black Tuesday After the peak in September, stock prices fell slowly. Some brokers began to call in loans, but others loaned even more. Business leaders such as Charles E. Mitchell, head of the National City Bank of New York, assured the nervous public: "Although in some cases speculation has gone too far, . . . the markets generally are now in a healthy condition."

As the stock market closed on October 23, the Dow Jones average dropped 21 points in an hour. The next day, Thursday, October 24, worried investors began to sell, and stock prices fell. Falling prices panicked others, who also sold quickly—at any price. Investors who had bought General Electric stock at $400 a share sold it for $283 a share. U.S. Steel stock fell from 261 3/4 to 193 1/2.

Again, business and political leaders told the country not to worry. Colonel Leonard P. Ayres, a banking executive, said that only a nation as rich as the United States could "withstand the shock of a $3 billion paper loss on the Stock Exchange in a single day without serious effects to the average citizen." President Hoover announced: "The fundamental business of the country . . . is on a sound and prosperous basis."

To stop the panic, a group of bankers pooled their money to buy stock. Banker Richard Whitney, a Stock Exchange official, went to the floor and, in a few minutes, made offers for $20 to $30 million worth of stock. This action stabilized prices, but only for a few days. By Monday prices were falling again. Investors all over the country raced to get out of the stock market. On October 29, known as Black Tuesday, a record 16.4 million shares were sold, compared with 4 to 8 million shares a day, earlier in the year. ✪

The collapse continued. By November 13, the Dow Jones had fallen from its September high of 381 to 198.7. Overall losses amounted to $30 billion.

RESOURCE DIRECTORY

Teaching Resources

Reproducible Lesson Plan found in the Unit 7 folder, p. 42, provides a summary of the Section 2 lesson plan content.

Alternate Lesson Plan: Critical Thinking Predicting Consequences, found in the Alternate Lesson Plans folder, p. 113, is an alternate lesson plan that provides students with the skills to predict consequences by analyzing a newspaper stock market page.

Guided Reading and Review found in the Unit 7 folder, p. 48, provides a structure for reading and mastering the key concepts and reviewing the key terms for Section 2. (Guided Practice)

✪ **Literature Activity** The Stock Market Crash, found in the Unit 7 folder, p. 69, describes the mood on the floor of the New York Stock Exchange on Black Tuesday, October 29, 1929.

Coming to Terms It took time for people to recognize the extent of the disaster caused by the crash. Arthur Crew Inman, a wealthy Boston resident, lost heavily in the market. He wrote in his diary, "The profit in my little book melted yesterday to seven thousand. It is probably nil today. . . . My dreams of a million—where are they?" Inman, however, had a secure income of $12,000 a year. Although upset, he viewed the situation with wry humor, adding this mock prayer:

> O *Stock Market, God of American gamblers, be merciful to me, a petty and insignificant worshipper at your shrine! If I have been greedy, forgive me! Leave me my remnants, O Stock Market!*

For people like Inman, whose entire wealth did not depend on the stock market, life went on much as before, with perhaps a few cutbacks. Others, even wealthy families, lost everything. Brokers and banks called in their loans, but people did not have cash to pay them.

When the stock market crashed, many investors—large and small—stockbrokers, bankers, and manufacturers fell too. As the economic slide got steeper, it took more and more ordinary people down with it. The graph below shows the fluctuations in the stock market from 1925 to 1933.

MAKING CONNECTIONS

Many people today use credit cards and charge accounts to buy on credit. Is it as dangerous now as it was in 1929? Why or why not?

The Crash Affects Millions

⭐ By 1929, about 4 million people, out of a population of 120 million, had invested in the stock market. They were the first to suffer from the crash, but it soon affected millions who had

As stock market prices fell, the ticker tape could not report market activity fast enough. Nervous investors crowded into Wall Street, hoping to hear the latest news.

Stock Prices,* 1925–1933

Price Index — values from 0 to 30, Years 1925–1933

*Standard and Poor's index of common stocks
Source: *Historical Statistics of the United States*

Interpreting Graphs
With only a few pauses, stock market prices climbed steadily during the 1920s. *According to this graph, when did market prices reach their lowest point before starting to rise again?*

The New York Times
NEW YORK, TUESDAY, OCTOBER 29, 1929.

STOCK PRICES SLUMP $14,000,000,000 IN NATION-WIDE STAMPEDE TO UNLOAD; BANKERS TO SUPPORT MARKET TODAY

⭐ **American Profiles Activity** found in the Unit 7 folder, p. 60, profiles folk song writer and singer Woody Guthrie, who used his considerable talent to chronicle the woes of ordinary Americans during the Depression.

Whitney and other bankers attempted to stop the panic, and what the outcome was.

Ask students to think about conditions in the United States on October 30, 1929, the day after the great stock market crash. Explain that much had changed, although few people really understood what had happened on the stock market. It took time for the effects of the crash to reach businesses and services. Ask students how a general economic failure would likely affect such employers as a zipper manufacturer, a restaurant in a small town, and a college.

Analyze

Have students examine the reasons for bank failures. Ask them to compare the plight of an investor who lost on the stock market and a worker who lost life savings.

Ask students to list and explain the underlying causes of the Great Depression. Ask why the government did not regulate the stock market.

Caption Answer to . . .

📈 **Interpreting Graphs**

1932

Answer to . . .

MAKING CONNECTIONS

Answers may vary but are likely to reflect students' own experience or family background. Some students may know that nearly all credit cards place credit limits on buying but that people can still get into trouble with credit buying.

Activity

Cooperative Learning

Time: One class period.
Activity: Create a sequential chart that illustrates the effects of the stock market crash on different segments of the American economy.
Grouping: Groups of four to six students.
Purpose: In each group, let one student represent a given segment of the American economy. Each student should create an appropriate symbol for his or her segment. The group should create a flow chart showing the effects of the stock market on each segment and how each segment in turn affected all the others on the chart.
Roles: Assign the following roles: large manufacturing corporation, small manufacturing company, farm, American family, store owner, restaurant owner, etc.
Outcome: Students will demonstrate how the stock market crash affected different segments of the economy.

Enrichment

Suggest that students learn how to read the stock market reports in the daily newspaper. Ask them to pick one or two stocks that are traded on the New York Stock Exchange and chart the progress of their stocks for at least one week. Students might also be interested in writing to the corporations for annual reports. Addresses can be found in a business directory such as the one published by Standard & Poor's.

never owned a single share of stock. Eventually, like ripples from a stone thrown into a pond, its effects spread beyond the United States. The Great Depression had begun.

Workers and Farmers Lose Out As income and profits fell, American factories began to close. Week after week, thousands of workers lost their jobs or had their pay cut. In August 1931, Henry Ford shut down his Detroit automobile factories, putting at least 75,000 people out of work.

In several European countries, workers had government unemployment insurance, but the United States had no such program. By 1932, nearly 13 million were unemployed, about a quarter of the labor force (see graph on page 617). Others worked only part time or had their wages cut. The **Gross National Product (GNP)**—the total annual value of goods and services a country produces— was $103 billion in 1929. By 1933 it was only $56 billion.

The effects of the crash spread. Restaurants and other small businesses closed because customers could no longer afford to patronize them. Once-wealthy families dismissed household workers. Farm prices, already low, fell

even more, bringing final disaster to many families (see graph below). In 1929, a bushel of wheat had sold at the low price of $1.04; in 1932 it brought 38 cents. Cotton dropped from 17 to 6.5 cents a pound. In 1930 a severe drought parched farmlands in the Great Plains, a foretaste of the weather that would turn the area into a dust bowl. (See "Time and Place: The Black Blizzards," pages 618–619.)

Banks Close Unpaid farm loans already had ruined many rural banks. Now city banks were in trouble. Banks exist on the interest they earn from lending out their deposits. They assume that not everyone will claim their deposits at once. After the stock market crash, people with loans to repay as well as nervous depositors rushed to withdraw their money.

Thousands of banks closed their doors when they could not return their depositors' money or sell foreclosed properties. In just a few years, more than 5,500 banks failed. By 1933, the money from nine million savings accounts had vanished.

Worldwide Repercussions The crash would have been serious even if it had hurt only the United States. But by the 1930s, international banking, manufacturing, and trade had made nations interdependent. When the world's leading economy fell, the global economic system began to crumble.

After World War I, the United States had insisted that France and England, its wartime allies, repay their war debts. At the same time, Congress kept import taxes high, making it hard for European nations to sell goods in the United States. With economies weakened by the war and little chance of selling goods in the United States, the Allies had to rely on Germany's reparations payments for income.

As long as United States companies invested in Germany, reparations payments continued. But with the Depression, investments fell off. German banks failed, Germany suspended reparations, and the Allies in turn stopped

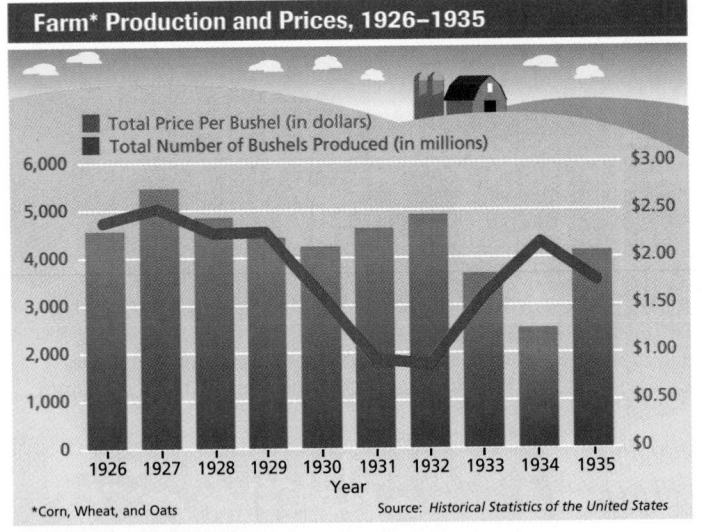

Farm* Production and Prices, 1926–1935

- Total Price Per Bushel (in dollars)
- Total Number of Bushels Produced (in millions)

*Corn, Wheat, and Oats

Source: *Historical Statistics of the United States*

Interpreting Graphs
American farmers invested heavily to meet the postwar need for food, but demand suddenly fell—and crop prices dropped as a result. *In what year did farm prices drop the most?*

▶ **RESOURCE DIRECTORY**

Teaching Resources

Unemployment, 1926–1933

Number Unemployed (in thousands)

12,000
8,000
4,000
0

1926 1927 1928 1929 1930 1931 1932 1933
Year

Source: *Historical Statistics of the United States*

Interpreting Graphs
The number of people without jobs increased each year after the crash. *What caused unemployment to rise sharply after 1929?*

paying their debts. Europeans no longer could afford to buy American-made goods. Thus the American stock market crash started a downward cycle in the global economy.

What Caused the Great Depression?

The stock market crash of 1929, though devastating to investors, was only the final push that toppled the fragile structure of the American economy. Deeper problems were the real underlying causes of the Great Depression.

Overspeculation During the 1920s, speculators bought stocks with borrowed money, then pledged those stocks as **collateral,** or security, for loans to buy more stocks. Brokers' loans went from under $5 million in mid-1928 to

1929. Based on borrowed money and optimism instead of real value, the stock market boom was as unsteady as a house of cards. When investors lost confidence, it collapsed, taking them with it.

Government Policies Mistakes in monetary policy were also to blame. During the 1920s the Federal Reserve system, which regulates the amount of money in circulation, cut interest rates to spur economic growth. Then in 1929, worried about overspeculation, it introduced a tight-money policy, seeking to dry up credit. After the Crash, however, this meant that there was so little money in circulation that the economy was unable to recover.

An Unstable Economy Overall, the seemingly prosperous economy lacked a firm base. National wealth was unevenly distributed, with the most money in the hands of a few families, who tended to save or invest rather than buying goods. Industry produced more goods than most consumers wanted or could afford. While some people profited, most felt that their incomes had not kept up with prices. Farmers and many workers had not shared in the economic boom. The unevenness of the 1920s prosperity made rapid recovery impossible.

SECTION 2 REVIEW

Key Terms, People, and Places
1. Define (a) Dow-Jones industrial average, (b) Gross National Product, (c) collateral.

Key Concepts
2. What were the main events leading up to Black Tuesday in 1929?
3. Who were the first to feel the effects of the crash?
4. Why did banks fail?

5. What effect did the United States stock market crash have on the world economy?

Critical Thinking
6. **Identifying Assumptions** In the 1930s, the United States did not provide any type of unemployment insurance. What beliefs support the idea that government should provide workers with unemployment insurance?

Quiz found in the Unit 7 folder, p. 49, covers the main ideas in this section as well as the key terms.

Media and Technology

Transparency
Time Lines, E-6

Section 2 Review Answers

1. (a) Dow Jones industrial average, see p. 614, (b) Gross National Product, see p. 616, (c) collateral, see p. 617

2. Stock prices reached an all-time high in September 1929, then began to slide. After a sudden drop on October 23, investors panicked and began to sell the next day. After a brief stabilization, prices fell drastically on Black Tuesday, October 29.

3. Investors who had speculated heavily, bought on margin, and risked all their assets and income.

4. Banks rely for profits on lending all but a portion of their deposits. When depositors tried to withdraw their savings all at once, the banks had no cash to pay them and had to close.

5. It stopped investment in Germany, which stopped paying reparations to the Allies, who in turn stopped paying war debts. European economies grew weaker, and international trade also slowed.

6. Answers may vary, but should touch on the question of whether government does or does not have some responsibility for citizens' well-being.

Reteach

Ask students to draw three concentric circles on a sheet of paper. Have them label the circles Causes of the Stock Market Crash, Immediate Effects of the Crash, and Later Effects of the Crash. Ask students to review the major sections of the chapter and to list three causes, one immediate effect, and three later effects of the crash.

4. CLOSE

Reinforcing the Big Idea

The crash of the stock market in October 1929 brought on a depression more severe than any other in the nation's history. The Depression had repercussions around the world. The next section deals with some of the suffering endured by Americans in that bleak time.

The Black Blizzards

Focus Some of the most vivid images of the Great Depression are those of farms on the Great Plains, dust covered and abandoned, and those of Great Plains farm families on the road, headed for a new life. Their plight, vividly described in John Steinbeck's American classic *The Grapes of Wrath*, symbolized the misery of the Depression. The loss of their lands and the lessons of the Dust Bowl changed American farming.

In this section students will identify the natural and human causes of the Dust Bowl.

Instruct Explain to students that in the 1930s a great natural disaster—a series of terrible dust storms—destroyed many farms in the Great Plains. Point out that natural causes, as well as human actions, contributed to the disaster.

Before students read the feature, ask them to locate the Great Plains on a map of the United States.

Trace the history of farming on the Great Plains by creating a time line for the period between 1800 and 1950. Ask students to place the following events on the time line:
• Great Plains identified as desert.
• Richness of the Great Plains discovered.
• Hard winter wheat introduced.
• World War I causes rise in wheat prices.
• Four million acres under plow.
• Prices for wheat fall.
• First dust storms.
• Rain relieves drought.

Ask students to explain if it was a bitter coincidence that the dust storms came at the same time as the Depression or if the Depression helped to cause them. (*An early sign of the Depression was a drop in farm income, and farmers plowed up more land for wheat in an effort to survive.*)

Extend Ask students to explain how each of the following factors contributed to the Dust Bowl: extensive wheat farming on the Great Plains,

TIME & PLACE
A GEOGRAPHIC PERSPECTIVE

The Black Blizzards

Between 1933 and 1940, so much earth blew out of the central and southern Great Plains that the area became known as the Dust Bowl. What factors contributed to this environmental disaster?

The Great Plains is famous the world over as "America's breadbasket." Deep, fertile soils, a growing season long enough for most crops, and flat land give the region its farming advantage. But because the region is dry, farming on the plains is a risky undertaking.

The Plow that Broke the Plains

It was the dryness of the region that early settlers noticed first. For this reason, maps in the early 1800s referred to the Great Plains as the Great American Desert. By the late 1800s, however, farmers discovered the truth of the Great American Desert—when there was water, the Great Plains was one of the world's best farming regions.

Early farmers faced a major obstacle. The soils of the Great Plains were protected by a thick layer of native grasses with roots that were difficult to cut. To break the roots required expensive steel plows and months of hard labor. Yet, from the time that hard winter wheat was first introduced in central Kansas in the mid 1870s, farmers in the plains sank their plow blades into the sod and turned it over to make wheat fields.

In the early years of the twentieth century, wheat brought good prices, and farmers continually increased the acres of plowed land at the expense of the native grasses. In 1917 prices went even higher, spurred upward by the great demand caused by World War I. The price increases stimulated an even

Violent winds picked up the dark, nutrient-rich topsoil and carried it eastward, sometimes for hundreds of miles, leaving behind barren, shifting dunes of grit and sand.

greater fervor to plow more land to grow wheat: "Plant more wheat! Wheat will win the war!" was the slogan. By 1919 farmers plowed under nearly 4 million acres of grassland. Even after the war ended, the big plow-up continued.

It was new technology that allowed so much land to be plowed. Plowing with tractors allowed farmers to turn over far more acres in a day than they ever could have without those machines. When prices for wheat began to fall in the early 1920s, farmers responded by growing even more wheat. In the five years between 1925 and 1930 alone, more than 5 million additional acres of grassland disappeared, converted to wheat fields by the relentless plow blades.

Interaction: Drought and Human Activity Led to Dust Storms

At the time the first dust storms occurred in the early 1930s, farmers blamed them on the severe and lengthy drought that began and lasted until the end of the decade. While drought was a major factor in creating the Dust Bowl, it was not the only factor. Farming practices contributed as much as the weather to the disaster.

The plains region experiences great variations. Hot and humid tropical air masses move into the region from the Gulf of Mexico and cold polar air masses push southward from above the Arctic Circle. When these two air masses collide, powerful storms with fierce updrafts are created.

RESOURCE DIRECTORY

Teaching Resources

Time and Place Activity The Great Flood of 1993, found in the Unit 7 folder, pp. 58–59, explains the impact of human interaction with the environment by analyzing the great flood of the Mississippi River in 1993.

Severe wind erosion

Slight wind erosion

Dust Bowl

Great Plains

Area of main map

invention and use of tractors, drought, high winds. Students might want to learn about current farming practices in the Great Plains to see if topsoil loss is still a problem and how current techniques help prevent erosion.

Answers

1. The black blizzards were caused by drought and heavy winds that blew topsoil exposed by poor farming practices.
2. (a) Rich soil, ample growing season, and flat land. (b) Frequent droughts and strong wind storms.
3. Answers may vary, but should include strategies for protecting the topsoil from drought and high winds.

Severe weather could not harm the environment as long as the thick layer of prairie grasses protected the topsoil. But when farmers stripped the soil of its natural protection by plowing the land, they opened the door to a major disaster.

Not Enough Rain

The most severe storms of the dry years were dubbed "black blizzards." Violent winds picked up the dark, nutrient-rich topsoil and carried it eastward, sometimes for hundreds of miles, leaving behind barren, shifting dunes of grit and sand. The map above shows the extent of soil erosion across the plains.

Time after time, dirt was sucked up off the parched plains and dropped by the ton over states and cities to the east. The dirt darkened the sky in New York City and Washington, D.C. It stained the snows of New England red and dropped on ships hundreds of miles off the Atlantic coast. The drought and winds persisted for more than seven years, bringing ruin to farmers.

The combination of terrible weather and very low prices for farm products caused 60 percent of the people in the Dust Bowl to lose their farms. Relief did not come until the early 1940s when the rains finally arrived and World War II drove farm prices up. By that time the damage was done. Driven by their need to grow more wheat to pay their growing debts, Dust Bowl farmers were the agents of their own destruction in the "Dirty Thirties."

GEOGRAPHIC CONNECTIONS

1. What caused the black blizzards of the 1930s?
2. (a) What features of land and climate make the Great Plains a good farming region? (b) What features make it a poor farming region?

Critical Thinking

3. Identifying Alternatives What might the farmers of the Great Plains do to prevent another Dust Bowl?

Social Effects of the Depression

SECTION 3

Social Effects of the Depression

SECTION PREVIEW

Most people were not immediately affected by the 1929 stock market crash, but by the early 1930s, wage cuts and growing unemployment brought widespread suffering.

Key Concepts
• Wage cuts and unemployment affected all levels of society, making many people homeless.
• Those groups already experiencing economic difficulty, such as farmers, faced harder times.
• The Depression affected people's mental and physical health.
• Conditions for African Americans worsened during the Depression.

Key Terms, People, and Places
Hooverville; Father Divine, Scottsboro Boys

"Apples 5 cents" became a familiar sign in many cities in the 1930s, as out-of-work people struggled to make a living.

Not everyone felt the impact of the crash immediately. Many thought the depression that followed would not last. For them, reality hit in 1931 or 1932. As hard times spread to all levels of society, a song from a 1932 Broadway revue became a theme song of the times:

Once I built a railroad, made it run,
Made it race against time.
Once I built a railroad, now it's done.
Brother, can you spare a dime?

Brother, Can You Spare A Dime?

Imagine that the bank where you had a savings account suddenly closed. Your money was gone. Or your parents lost their jobs and could not pay the rent. One day you came home to find your furniture on the sidewalk—you had been evicted. ✪

People at all levels of society faced these situations. Professionals and white-collar workers, who had felt more secure than laborers, were laid off suddenly with no prospects of finding another job. Those whose savings disappeared found it hard to understand why banks no longer had the money they had deposited for safekeeping.

"Hoovervilles" The hardest hit were those at the bottom of the economic ladder. Some unemployed laborers, unable to pay their rent, moved in with relatives. Others drifted. In 1931, census takers estimated the homeless in New York City alone at 15,000.

Homeless people sometimes built shanty towns, with shacks of tar paper, cardboard, or scrap material. These homes for the homeless came to be called **Hoovervilles,** mocking the President whom people blamed for the crisis. A woman living in Oklahoma visited one Hooverville:

Here were all these people living in old, rusted-out car bodies. . . . There were people living in shacks made of orange crates. One family with a whole lot of kids were living in a piano box.

Farm Distress Farm families suffered as low food prices cut their income. When they could not pay their mortgages, they lost their farms to the banks, which sold them at auction. In the South, landowners expelled tenant farmers and sharecroppers. In protest against low farm prices, farmers dumped thousands of gallons of milk and destroyed other crops. These desperate actions shocked a hungry nation.

Migration from the Dust Bowl For thousands of farm families in the Dust Bowl, the harsh conditions of the Depression were made even worse by the drought and dust storms that took place in the Great Plains for much of the 1930s. (See "Time and Place: The Black Blizzards," pages 618–619.) In the face of low farm prices and terrible weather, many families lost or gave up their farms. More than 440,000 people left Oklahoma during the 1930s. Nearly 300,000 people left Kansas. Thousands of families in Oklahoma, Texas, Kansas, and other southwestern Plains states migrated to California. Many found work on California's farms as laborers. About 100,000 of the Dust Bowl migrants headed to cities, such as Los Angeles, San Francisco, and San Diego.

Hardships Create New Problems

As it wore on, the Depression had a serious physical and psychological impact on the entire nation. Unemployment and fear of losing a job caused great anxiety. People became depressed; many considered suicide, and some took their own lives.

Impact on Health "No one has starved," President Hoover declared, but some did, and thousands more went hungry. Those who could not afford food or shelter got sick more easily. Children suffered most from the long-term effects of poor diet and inadequate medical care. One boy tramp recalled:

All last winter we never had a fire except about once a day when Mother used to cook some mush or something. When the kids were cold they went to bed. I quit high school of course.

In the country, people grew food and ate berries and other wild plants. In cities, they sold apples and pencils, begged for money to buy food, and fought over the contents of restaurant garbage cans. Families who had land planted "relief gardens" to feed themselves or to barter food for other items.

Family Problems Living conditions declined as families moved in together, crowding into small houses or apartments. The divorce rate dropped because people could not afford separate households. Other couples postponed wedding plans. People gave up even small pleasures like an ice cream cone or a movie ticket.

Men who had lost jobs or investments often felt like failures because they could no longer provide for their families. If their wives or children were working, men thought their own status had fallen. It embarrassed them to be seen at home during normal work hours. They were ashamed to apply for relief or ask friends for help.

Women faced other problems. Those who worked at home and were used to depending

Makeshift huts were homes for homeless and the unemployed in this Hooverville in downtown New York.

⭐ **Primary Source Activity** Hard Times in Oklahoma, found in the Unit 7 folder, p. 66, focuses on Peggy Terry, a resident of Oklahoma City during the Depression, who describes in her own words how good times often accompanied the hard times.

2. INSTRUCT

Explain/Discuss

Explain to students that the effects of the 1929 crash took a while to reach all Americans, but the repercussions were powerful and long lasting. Point out that the crash immediately affected those with the least money.

Have students describe how the Depression affected each of the following segments of the population: farm families, men, women, African Americans in the North, African Americans in the South. Discuss with students how rural poverty differed from urban poverty. Ask students if they think they could have survived the Depression more easily in the country or in a large city. You might want to refer back to the Bellringer discussion about dealing with limited cash funds.

In Depth

Biography

Gordon Parks, the first African American photographer on staff at *Life* magazine, joined the Civilian Conservation Corps (CCC)—one of the agencies set up during the New Deal to counteract the hopelessness of the breadlines. By 1936, Parks was working as a Pullman porter and during breaks looked through discarded magazines on the trains. Some had collections of photographs of the Farm Security Administration (FSA), an agency established to help starving farmers. The power of the FSA photographs of hungry migrants, both black and white, made Parks realize the power of the camera. He went on to take photographs for the FSA and then for *Life* and many other prestigious periodicals.

Analyze

Ask students to use the profile of Wilson Ledford on pages 623–624 to analyze the personality traits that helped people to survive in the Depression.

Answer to ...

Answer to ...

Links Across Time

Answers will vary, but are likely to include social security, unemployment insurance, minimum wage laws, federal housing projects, and drug rehabilitation programs.

In Depth

Did You Know?

Although there are many familiar images of Wall Street brokers leaping to their deaths from skyscraper windows, most Depression-era suicides were ordinary people. In 1930, a Pennsylvania man caught stealing a loaf of bread for his children was so overcome by shame that he hanged himself. San Diego, California, had the highest suicide rate of any city in the country during these years.

on a husband's paycheck worried about feeding their hungry children. Working women were accused of taking jobs away from men. Even in the better times of the 1920s, Henry Ford had fired 82 married women. "We do not employ married women whose husbands have jobs," he explained. In the Depression, this practice became common. In 1931, the American Federation of Labor endorsed it. Most school districts would not hire married women teachers, and many fired those who got married.

Many women continued to find work, however, because poor-paying jobs such as domestic service, typing, and nursing were considered "women's work." The greatest job losses of the Depression were in industry and other areas that seldom hired women. Even on the same job, however, women usually were paid less than men.

MAKING CONNECTIONS

Depression attitudes and policies discriminated against working women. Have attitudes toward working women today changed? If so, how?

Discrimination Increases

African Americans continued to leave the South, though not as many as in the 1920s. They worked as janitors or porters in northern cities but soon lost even those jobs to whites. Black unemployment soared—56 percent of black Americans were out of work in 1932. Photographer Gordon Parks, who rode the rails to Harlem, later wrote:

> To most blacks who had flocked in from all over the land, the struggle to survive was savage. Poverty coiled around them and me with merciless fingers.

Because relief programs discriminated against African Americans, black churches and organizations like the National Urban League gave private help. The followers of M. J. Divine, a Harlem evangelist known as **Father Divine,** opened soup kitchens that fed hungry thousands every day.

Discrimination increased for African Americans in the South. Some white Americans declared openly that African Americans had no right to a job if whites were out of work. African Americans were denied civil rights such as access to education, voting, and health care. Lynchings increased.

The justice system often ignored black rights. In March 1931, near Scottsboro, Alabama, nine African American youths who had been riding the rails were arrested and accused of raping two white women on the train. Without being given the chance to hire a defense lawyer, eight of the nine were quickly convicted by an all-white jury and sentenced to die.

| 1650 | 1700 | 1750 | 1800 | **Links Across Time** | 1850 | 1900 | 1950 | 2000 |

Homelessness

So many homeless young men and women were riding freight trains and searching for work in 1933, that railroad officials often hired people to search the cars and remove the homeless they found there—by force, if necessary. Homelessness has become a growing problem in the 1990s as it was during the 1930s.

The economic conditions that brought about widespread unemployment during the Depression were a clear cause of homelessness. People point to a variety of reasons for the rapid increase in the number of homeless in the 1990s—unemployment, a decline in low-rent housing for the poor, changes in qualifications for government disability payments, and the premature release of many patients from mental-health facilities. Experts estimate that about 20 percent of homeless people have jobs, 33 percent are families with children, and 10 percent are single women. *What assistance for the homeless is available in the 1990s that was not available in the 1930s?*

Poverty was especially hard on sharecroppers in the South, who had to live in improvised camps after being evicted from their farms by landowners.

Like the Sacco and Vanzetti case a few years earlier, saving the so-called **Scottsboro Boys** became a national cause. Eventually the Supreme Court decided the youths had not had a fair trial and ordered new trials.

AMERICAN PROFILES
Wilson Ledford

Americans survived the Depression in many ways. Here, Wilson Ledford, who was then a teenager in rural Tennessee, remembers the early years.

Wilson first felt the effects of the Depression in March 1930 when he was fifteen, living in Chattanooga with his mother and younger sister. Wilson had worked part time and after school in a grocery store since he was eleven. By 1930, his family could no longer afford Chattanooga. They moved back to Cleveland, Tennessee, a nearby small town where one of Wilson's brothers had left a house when he moved West. Like many farmhouses then, it had no running water or electricity.

Wilson's mother owned another house and 15 acres of land, which brought in $6 a month rent—except when the tenants were out of work. After taxes and insurance, the family had about a dollar a week to live on.

Wilson "swapped work with neighbors." He looked after the family horse and cow, chopped wood for the fireplace, tended the garden that provided family food, and raised corn to feed the animals:

> We had to raise most of what we ate since money was so scarce. . . . Sometimes I plowed for other people when I could get the work. . . . I got 15 cents an hour for plowing and I furnished the horse and plow.

Nothing was wasted. His mother kept chickens and traded eggs at the store for things they could not raise. Overalls cost 98 cents; shoes were $2. She bought a pig for $3 and raised it for meat, and made jelly from wild blackberries. Despite the family's own poverty, Wilson's mother gave extra milk and butter to

Activity
Teaching Heterogeneous Groups

During the Depression, people found ways to acquire, without money, the basic necessities to survive. For students to appreciate the cooperation and creativity necessary to survive during the Depression, have them list skills and resources they could have exchanged if they had lived during that time. In small groups, have students barter with each other. **LEP**

Enrichment

Ask students to choose a section from Studs Terkel's book *Hard Times,* Jeane Westin's *Making Do: How Women Survived the '30s,* or other collections of personal reminiscences from the Depression years. Students should present their selection to the class as either an oral reading or on audiotape.

3. ASSESS

Section 3 Review Answers

1. Hoovervilles, see p. 620

2. (a) Father Divine, see p. 622, (b) Scottsboro Boys, see p. 623

3. When banks failed, people lost their savings; when they lost their jobs, they couldn't pay mortgages or rent. Many became homeless.

4. Crop prices went even lower than they already had been in the late twenties. Many lost their land to bank foreclosures.

5. Men were depressed by losing their status as providers and were ashamed to ask for relief; women worried about their children and often lost their jobs. Families had to combine households; marriages and divorces both declined.

6. Conditions became worse; African Americans lost their jobs to white workers; they were discriminated against by relief agencies; in the South, civil rights violations increased.

7. Answers may vary but are likely to include how rural people worked and got by during the Depression; how they cooperated with one another and found ways to entertain themselves; and how hard it was to find work.

Have students work individually or in small groups to create a poster showing the effects of the Depression, including its impact on health and family problems, and its effect on women and African Americans.

Alternative Assessment

Mid-Point Monitoring
Ask students if they have
● Decided which materials they intend to include
● Located a subject and prepared questions for the interview
● Visited the local library and/or historical society to locate sources of information

4. CLOSE

Reinforcing the Big Idea

The Depression eventually touched the lives of nearly all Americans with wage cuts and unemployment. Those on the lowest end of the economic scale were most severely affected. The next section explains how some Americans made it through those difficult years.

In Depth

Did You Know?

Evictions were commonplace during the 1930s. In Chicago, an angry crowd in the street protested the eviction of an African American family. "All we want is to see that these people, our people, get back into their home," said one protestor. Those already marginalized before the Depression suffered heavily. Writer Langston Hughes observed, "[T]he Depression had brought everyone down a peg or two. And the Negroes had but a few pegs to fall."

"If they come to take my farm, I'm going to fight. I'd rather be killed outright than die by starvation." Although farm families were hard hit by the Depression, the fighting spirit represented by this quote was seen across the country.

"some poor people, a woman with three small children who lived in a one-room shack with a dirt floor."

Wilson never got to high school, "as survival was more important then than getting an education was, and I had to work to survive." The Ledfords had no radio, but he and his neighbors made their own entertainment. Wilson and some other boys cleaned the rocks off a field, graded it, and made a baseball diamond. Baseballs were precious. "You could buy a pretty good baseball for a quarter and a real good one for 50 cents. . . . If we lost a ball during the game, everyone had to go hunt for it."

In the summer of 1932, when he was seventeen, Wilson got a job in Chattanooga with another brother, delivering ice. At the end of the summer, the brother bought him a 1924 Model T Ford for $25. The next summer, too, Wilson hauled ice: "I worked twelve hours a day, six days a week and made $3.00 a week."

When the icehouse closed in the fall, Wilson hitchhiked throughout the Southeast looking for work, but never had any success. "I pumped up so many tires for people I rode with, I had blisters all in my hands. Finally I got back home."

In the next few years, Wilson bought a truck to haul coal, cotton, and oranges, then worked nights in a woolen mill while carrying ice during the day. Finally, "I got a call from Chickamauga Dam and I went to work there. That was a good job working on the dam, I made 60 cents an hour. Times were better by then, but did not start booming until World War II started."

SECTION 3 REVIEW

Key Terms, People, and Places
1. Define Hoovervilles.
2. Identify (a) Father Divine, (b) Scottsboro Boys.

Key Concepts
3. What were the earliest social effects of the Depression?
4. How did the Depression affect farmers?

5. How did the Depression affect family life?
6. How did conditions for African Americans change during the Depression?

Critical Thinking
7. **Determining Relevance** What can you learn about the Depression from Wilson Ledford's experiences?

RESOURCE DIRECTORY

Teaching Resources

Quiz found in the Unit 7 folder, p. 51, covers the main ideas in this section as well as the key terms.

Distinguishing False from Accurate Images

Distinguishing false from accurate images means examining widely held beliefs about a person, a thing, or an event to determine whether or not those beliefs are based in fact. When studying history, you may uncover source materials such as newspaper and magazine articles that use stereotypes or that put forth misleading ideas. Learning to recognize the differences between false and accurate images will help you to reach your own conclusions about a statement.

The letter excerpted below was written to President Herbert Hoover during the early years of the Depression. Practice distinguishing between false and accurate images by using the following steps.

1. Summarize the main message of the passage. The first step in evaluating a piece of information is to understand what its central message is. Read the excerpt below and answer the following question: What is the main point of the letter?

2. Look for generalizations and overstatements in the passage. Generalizations are broad and over-simplified statements about people, events, or issues that are presented as being accurate in all cases. Overstatements exaggerate or stretch the truth. These techniques often signal claims that are unsupported by facts and, therefore, may indicate the use of false images. (a) What generalizations

can you find in the letter? (b) What overstatements or unsupported claims do you find?

3. Look for supporting facts or evidence. Accurate statements are usually backed up by statistics, quotations, or other verifiable evidence.

Facts can be fabricated and used in misleading ways, however, so always check them for accuracy. (a) What verifiable facts, if any, are given in the letter below? (b) Based on the use of facts in the letter, what can you conclude about the accuracy of its message?

Annapolis, Maryland
September 10, 1931

My dear Mr. Hoover,

In these days of unrest and general dissatisfaction it is absolutely impossible for a man in your position to get a clear and impartial view of the general conditions of things in America today. But, of this fact I am very positive, that there is not five per cent of the poverty, distress, and general unemployment that many of your enemies would have us believe. It is true, that there is much unrest, but this unrest is largely caused . . . by the excessive prosperity and general debauchery through which the country has traveled since the period of the war. The result being that in three cases out of four, the unemployed [person] is looking for a very light job at a very heavy pay, and with the privilege of being provided with an automobile if he is required to walk more than four or five blocks a day.

National Relief Director, Walter S. Gifford, and his committee are entirely unnecessary at this time, as it has a tendency to cause communities to neglect any temporary relief to any of their people, with the thought of passing the burden on to the National Committee. . . .

. . . Believe me to be one of your well wishers in this ocean of conflict.

Yours sincerely,
W. H. H.

📄 **Historian's Toolbox Activity** Distinguishing False from Accurate Images, found in the Unit 7 folder, p. 64, uses President Clinton's presentation before Congress of his health-care plan to enhance students' application of this skill.

TOOLBOX

Critical Thinking
Distinguishing False from Accurate Images

Focus Students will distinguish true from false images by identifying generalizations and overstatements and by citing the presence or lack of evidence to support statements.

Instruct Ask students to generate examples of generalizations and overstatements on a given topic, such as "Television plays a harmful role in the development of American children."

You might want to display W.H.H.'s letter on an overhead projector, and invite students as a group to underline generalizations and overstatements and circle verifiable evidence.

Extend See the Historian's Toolbox Activity in the Resource Directory below.

Answers

1. The main point of the letter is that the overwhelming majority of Americans in 1931 were not suffering economically.
2. (a) Generalizations include that most unemployed persons are looking for light work at high pay; that people would refuse a job that required them to walk four or five blocks; that local communities would, given the opportunity, neglect their responsibilities and freeload on the national government. (b) Overstatements and unsupported claims include "absolutely impossible," "of this fact I am very positive," "there is not five per cent of the poverty, distress, and general unemployment," "unrest is largely caused . . . by the excessive prosperity and general debauchery," "in three cases out of four, the unemployed [person] is . . .," and "entirely unnecessary."
3. (a) No verifiable facts are given. Although the letter includes statements such as "not five per cent" and "three cases out of four," no sources for these figures are cited and verification is not possible. (b) Because the letter contains no verifiable evidence and because it contains so many generalizations and overstatements, the accuracy of its contents is suspect.

1. FOCUS

Connecting to the Big Idea

See page 608B. Explain to students that Americans who lived through the Great Depression never forgot the pain of that time, and their feelings about banks, business, government, and money changed forever. Ask what characteristics helped Americans to survive those troubled times.

Objectives

- Give examples of the lasting effects of the Great Depression on those who lived through it.
- Describe some of the positive experiences of life in the Depression.
- Explain why the Depression ended an era.

Bellringer

Ask students to recall a time in their lives when friends, neighbors, or strangers worked together to solve a problem or helped one another through an unpleasant situation.

Reading Strategy

Relating to Topic Ask students to think about the meaning of the two main subheadings of the section: Working Together for Change and Looking Ahead. Ask them to take note of the ways in which Americans worked together during the Depression and of the signs of change that gave them hope as they looked ahead.

Surviving the Great Depression

SECTION PREVIEW

Living through the Great Depression was an unforgettable experience. Despite the hard times, many Americans learned to face troubles together with courage and humor.

For the homeless of the Depression, this "kind-hearted woman" symbol on a sidewalk or fence in front of a house meant that the family inside would help provide food or clothing.

Key Concepts

- The Great Depression left a lasting impression on those who lived through it.
- People had good memories of working together and helping each other.
- The Depression ended the era of the 1920s.

Key Terms, People, and Places

Socialists, Twenty-first Amendment; Norman Thomas; Empire State Building

---

N o one who lived through the Great Depression ever forgot it. It changed people's feelings about banks, business, government—and money. Even after the economy recovered, the "Depression generation" would continue to pinch and save before buying anything.

Working Together for Change

Not all the memories of the Depression were bad or despairing. Writing in 1932, reporter Gerald W. Johnson noted:

The great majority of Americans may be depressed. They may not be well pleased with the way business and government have been carried on, and they may not be at all sure that they know exactly how to remedy the trouble. They may be feeling dispirited. But there is one thing they are not, and that is—beaten.

People pulled together to help each other. Tenant groups formed to protest rent increases and evictions. Religious, political, and charitable groups set up soup kitchens and breadlines to feed the hungry. In some farm communities, people agreed to keep bids low when foreclosed farms were auctioned. Buyers then returned the farms to their original owners.

Many individual acts of kindness shone as people helped those they saw as worse off than themselves. One woman, Kitty McCulloch, remembered:

There were many beggars, who would come to your back door, and they would say they were hungry. I wouldn't give them money because I didn't have it. But I did take them in and put them in my kitchen and give them something to eat.

She also gave one beggar a pinstripe suit belonging to her husband, who, she explained, already had three others.

Moves to the Political Left As bad as conditions were, only a few called for radical political change. In Europe, economic problems had brought riots and political upheaval, but in the United States most citizens trusted in the democratic process to solve them. As writer William Saroyan observed in 1936:

Ten million unemployed continue law-abiding. No riots, no trouble, no multi-millionaires cooked and served with cranberry sauce, alas.

For some Americans, however, radical and reform movements offered new solutions to the country's problems, promising a fairer distribution of wealth. Membership in the Communist party, consisting mainly of intellectuals and labor organizers, was 14,000, and in the 1932 election, the Communist candidate polled just

---

 RESOURCE DIRECTORY

Teaching Resources

Reproducible Lesson Plan found in the Unit 7 folder, p. 44, provides a summary of the Section 4 lesson plan content.

Alternate Lesson Plan: Critical Thinking Formulating Questions, found in the Alternate Lesson Plans folder, p. 115, is an alternate lesson plan that provides an opportunity for students to learn to formulate questions by interviewing people who survived the Depression.

Guided Reading and Review found in the Unit 7 folder, p. 52, provides a structure for reading and mastering the key concepts and reviewing the key terms for Section 4. (Guided Practice)

American Profiles Activity found in the Unit 7 folder, p. 61, profiles Babe Didrikson Zaharias—an outstanding athlete whose gold-medal performances at the 1932 Olympic Games helped raise the spirits of a Depression-weary country.

over 100,000 votes. More people than the numbers suggest, however, also believed that the new Communist government in the Soviet Union might have the right answers.

Socialists, who called for gradual social and economic changes rather than revolution, did better politically. Their presidential candidate, **Norman Thomas,** won 881,951 votes in 1932, about 2.2 percent of the total vote. Others who might have supported Thomas voted for Franklin D. Roosevelt simply to defeat Hoover.

Voting figures and party membership do not reflect the widespread interest in radical and reform movements in the 1930s. Those who were part of those movements remember the decade as a high point of cooperation among different groups of Americans—students, workers, writers, artists, and professionals of all races. They worked together for social justice in cases such as that of the Scottsboro Boys.

MAKING CONNECTIONS

Third-party candidates, such as the Socialists, have almost no chance of winning presidential elections. Why, then, do they present candidates? What influence do minor parties have?

Looking Ahead

For the most part, Americans gritted their teeth and waited out the hard times. They looked for change and signs of hope. ✪

Depression Humor Wry jokes and cartoons kept people laughing through their troubles. The term "Hooverville" was at first a joke. People who slept on park benches huddled under "Hoover blankets"—old newspapers. Empty pockets turned inside out were termed "Hoover flags." When Babe Ruth was criticized for requesting a salary of $80,000—higher than President Hoover's—he joked, "I had a better year than he did." ✪

People fought despair by laughing at it. In 1929 humorist Will Rogers quipped, "When Wall Street took that tail spin, you had to stand in line to get a window to jump out of." A cartoon that showed two men jumping out of a

Above: To get a warm meal, many people—even those who had once been relatively prosperous—had to stand in breadlines or outside soup kitchens run by churches and community groups. *Below:* Showing the darker side of Depression humor, an end-of-the-year cartoon in *Life* magazine summed up the hopes and disasters of 1929.

window arm-in-arm was captioned "The speculators who had a joint account."

Prohibition Is Repealed In February 1933, Congress voted to repeal the ban on alcoholic beverages. The **Twenty-first Amendment** was ratified by the end of the year. Some people, including President Hoover, regretted the end of this social experiment limiting the sale of alcohol, but most welcomed repeal as an end to national hypocrisy and as a curb on gangsters who prospered from bootlegging.

✪ **Primary Source Activity** The "Forgotten Man," found in the Unit 7 folder, pp. 67–68, uses two letters written to President Hoover during the Depression to show the way many American workers viewed their President and the economic breakdown of the country.

Answer to ...
MAKING CONNECTIONS
Students should understand that many issues raised by third or minor parties have later been adopted by one of the two major parties. Third-party candidates often represent deeply felt ideologies or social policies that later enter the mainstream.

2. INSTRUCT

Discuss

Discuss with students how living through the Great Depression brought out characteristics of courage, kindness, charity, and humor in many Americans. Ask why they think crises bring out these characteristics. You might want to have students share their recollections from the Bellringer activity.

Discuss the signs of changing times that gave Americans hope. Ask students to explain the impact of the repeal of prohibition restrictions.

Analyze

Discuss the characteristics that defined the era of the 1920s. Ask students to explain why the Depression ended that era. Ask them to consider how Depression survivors might view savings banks, the stock market, or installment buying.

Activity

Creating Editorials

Ask students to draw an editorial cartoon about one of the following:
● Norman Thomas runs for President in 1932 (a brave crusade or a foolish gesture).
● Poor people call their shanty towns "Hoovervilles" (justified or unjustified slam at the President).
● Completion of the Empire State Building (marvelous accomplishment or questionable use of money).

The Empire State Building, the Chrysler Building, and Rockefeller Center were designed in the Art Deco style. Ask students to bring to class copies of photographs of some section of one of these buildings that illustrates the Art Deco style, and describe its prominent features.

3. ASSESS

Section 4 Review Answers

1. (a) Socialists, see p. 627, (b) Twenty-first Amendment, see p. 627

2. (a) Norman Thomas, see p. 627, (b) Empire State Building, see p. 628

3. The Socialist and Communist parties offered new answers to social problems.

4. People pulled together and helped each other through the hard times; Americans continued to believe in the democratic process; prohibition was repealed; "Depression humor" kept people's spirits up; the Empire State Building became a symbol of progress.

5. Sports heroes retired; Henry Ford lost popularity; the Lindbergh baby was killed; Coolidge died.

6. Answers will vary but may focus on daily life, search for jobs, bank closings, and similar topics.

Reteach

Have one student write on a piece of paper a sentence about how the Depression affected Americans or about signs that the Depression might end. Have another student add a sentence to the first. When the paper has circulated to all students, have a spokesperson read the resulting document aloud.

4. CLOSE

Reinforcing the Big Idea

The Depression changed the Americans who lived through it. Above all, an era ended. The next section shows the nation taking a new direction—through the exciting election of 1932.

Despite the economic hardships of the 1930s, American architects and developers raced to build the world's tallest building. Workers like the man shown above looked out over the rest of New York City as they labored to complete the Empire State Building.

The end of prohibition and return of legalized alcohol stimulated parts of the economy—grain growing, breweries and distilleries, even the pretzel industry. Control of alcohol returned to the states, eight of which chose to continue the ban on liquor sales.

The Empire State Building For many, a dramatic symbol of hope was the new **Empire State Building**, begun in 1930. John J. Raskob, the developer of the gleaming new skyscraper, won the race to build the world's tallest building.

One hundred and two stories high, the Empire State Building soared 1,250 feet into the sky and was topped with a mooring mast for blimps. Sixty-seven elevators, traveling 1,000 feet per minute, brought visitors to its observation deck. On the first Sunday after it opened, over 4,000 people paid a dollar each to make the trip.

The End of An Era By 1933, it was clear that an era was ending. One by one, symbols of the 1920s faded away. Gangster Al Capone went to prison for tax evasion. Boxer Jack Dempsey was defeated. Babe Ruth retired. The Depression-era labor policies of car-maker Henry Ford, once admired for his efficiency, made him labor's prime enemy.

In 1932 the nation was shocked when the infant son of aviation hero Charles Lindbergh and Anne Morrow Lindbergh was kidnapped and murdered. Somehow this tragedy seemed to echo the nation's woeful condition and its fall from the energy and heroism of the 1920s. Finally, eight weeks before Roosevelt's inauguration in 1933, former President Calvin Coolidge, a symbol of the age of prosperity, died.

SECTION 4 REVIEW

Key Terms, People and Places
1. Define (a) Socialists, (b) Twenty-first Amendment.
2. Identify (a) Norman Thomas, (b) Empire State Building.

Key Concepts
3. Why did radical political groups gain support in the early 1930s?

4. What Depression memories might some people remember as good?
5. What were signs that the 1920s era had ended?

Critical Thinking
6. **Formulating Questions** What questions could you ask people who lived in the Depression era in order to understand its effects on both their lives and their attitudes?

▶ RESOURCE DIRECTORY

Teaching Resources

Quiz found in the Unit 7 folder, p. 53, covers the main ideas in this section as well as the key terms.

The Election of 1932: A Turning Point in History

SECTION PREVIEW

As the Depression worsened, people came to blame Hoover and the Republicans for their misery. The 1932 presidential election brought a sweeping victory for Democrat Franklin D. Roosevelt, and a new direction for American government.

Key Concepts

• President Hoover hoped to use voluntary action to end the Depression.
• Federal government action and funds for relief were inadequate under Hoover.
• Promising a "new deal," the Democratic candidate, Franklin D. Roosevelt, won an overwhelming victory in the presidential election of 1932.

Key Terms, People, Places

Hawley-Smoot tariff, Reconstruction Finance Corporation; John Maynard Keynes, Bonus Army, Franklin Delano Roosevelt, Eleanor Roosevelt

F or a few months after the stock market crash, President Hoover, along with business leaders, insisted that the key to recovery was confidence. Hoover blamed the Depression on "world-wide economic conditions beyond our control"—not on problems in the United States economy.

Hoover Tries to End the Crisis

Taking Hoover's advice, business and government leaders tried to maintain public confidence in the economy. Even as factories closed and breadlines formed, Hoover administration officials insisted that things would get better soon.

Voluntary Action Fails Hoover believed deeply that voluntary controls in the business world were the best way to end the economic crisis. He quickly organized a White House conference of business leaders and got their promise to maintain wage rates. At first, many firms kept wages up. By the end of 1931, however, many quietly cut workers' pay.

Hoover meant well, but he held rigidly to this principle of voluntary action. A shy man, successful in business but inexperienced in politics, he could not make his plan attractive to the American people. After a year of misery, they began to blame him and the Republicans for the crisis.

The Government Acts Hoover then took more action. To create jobs, the government spent more on new public buildings, roads, parks, and dams. Boulder Dam (later renamed Hoover Dam) was begun in 1930. A President's Emergency Committee on Employment advised local relief programs.

Trying to protect domestic industries from foreign imports, in 1930 Congress passed the **Hawley-Smoot tariff,** the highest import tax in history. The tariff backfired. European countries raised their own tariffs, bringing a sudden slowdown in international trade. Hoover suspended the Allies' payments of their war debts, but Europe's economies grew weaker.

In 1932, Hoover set up the **Reconstruction Finance Corporation** (RFC), which gave government credit to banks so that they could extend loans. The RFC reflected the theory that prosperity at the top would help the economy as a whole. To many people, however, it seemed that the government was helping bankers while ordinary people went hungry.

The Democrats in 1932 based their campaign on the promise that Franklin Roosevelt would end the Depression.

---

1. FOCUS

 Connecting to the Big Idea

See page 608B. Recall with students that by 1932, President Hoover was unable to curb the ravages of the Depression. The 1932 presidential election presented an opportunity for change. Ask what the outcome of this election was. How did this administration change the direction of American government?

Objectives

• Explain how President Hoover hoped voluntary action would end the Depression.
• Describe the amount of governmental action and funds for relief provided under Hoover.
• Identify Franklin D. Roosevelt as the successful candidate for President who defeated Hoover in 1932.

Bellringer

Ask students to consider why elections are important and provide specific examples showing how elections are an avenue of change.

 In Depth

Interdisciplinary

Edward Hopper's (1882–1967) paintings reflected the character of the people and the land realistically and objectively. Hopper saw America as a lonely place, often silhouetted in harsh but true shades of light, as depicted in his paintings "Early Sunday Morning" (1930) or "Room in Brooklyn" (1932). In the midst of the Depression, Hopper's works achieved national recognition when New York's Museum of Modern Art mounted a one-man retrospective show in 1933.

Reproducible Lesson Plan found in the Unit 7 folder, p. 45, provides a summary of the Section 5 lesson plan content.

Alternate Lesson Plan: Learning Styles found in the Alternate Lesson Plans folder, p. 116, is an alternate lesson plan, especially effective for auditory learners, that provides a structure for a radio debate on the differences between Hoover and FDR.

Guided Reading and Review found in the Unit 7 folder, p. 54, provides a structure for reading and mastering the key concepts and reviewing the key terms for Section 5. (Guided Practice)

Media and Technology

 Transparency Fine Art, D-18

Answer to . . .

MAKING CONNECTIONS

Answers may vary but should suggest that, since the Depression and the New Deal, the government has been more receptive to hearing "ordinary" people's opinions, and that there is more recognition and public appreciation of the rights of different groups.

In Depth

Multicultural Perspectives

Hardships for rural African Americans mounted during the Depression, often spurred by policies of the New Deal that were of benefit to the nation as a whole. Historian Jacqueline Jones writes in her book *The Dispossessed* that NRA (National Recovery Act) minimum-wage legislation spurred mechanization of the tobacco industry and put many African American men and women out of work. The crop-reduction programs of the AAA (Agricultural Adjustment Administration) severely cut demand for farm labor and provided ready cash for planters to invest in labor-saving machinery. The long-term effects of major development programs such as the TVA (Tennessee Valley Authority) are well known, but the fates of 841 Santee-Cooper (South Carolina) families living along the floodplain of a proposed dam are all but forgotten.

TURNING POINTS

President Hoover's apparent inaction made people everywhere eager to blame him for their troubles, as this cartoon from 1931 shows.

Some government efforts helped, but not enough. Hoover wanted state and local governments to handle relief, but their programs never had enough money. Despite the RFC, banks continued to fail.

Hoover's Unpopularity Grows Many people blamed Hoover—not always fairly—for all their problems. "The 1932nd Psalm" was a popular take-off on Psalm 23:

> Hoover is my Shepherd, I am in want,
> He maketh me to lie down on
>   park benches,
> He leadeth me by still factories,
> He restoreth my doubt in the
>   Republican Party.

Hoover argued that direct federal relief would destroy people's self-respect and create a large bureaucracy. His refusal to help brought bitter public reaction and negative publicity.

Although his World War I relief work had made him the "Great Humanitarian," Hoover's attitude toward Depression relief made him seem cold and hard-hearted. While people went hungry, newspapers showed a photograph of him feeding his dog on the White House lawn. People booed when he said such things as "Our people have been protected from hunger and cold."

Private charities and local officials could not meet the demands for relief, as Hoover wanted. Finally in 1932, Hoover broke with tradition and let the RFC lend the states money for unemployment relief. But it was too little and too late.

As the Depression deepened, some economists backed the ideas of British economist **John Maynard Keynes.** He said that massive government spending could help a collapsing economy and encourage more private spending. This economic theory was not yet widely accepted, however.

Veterans March on Washington A low point for Hoover came in the summer of 1932, when 20,000 jobless World War I veterans and their families encamped in Washington, D.C. They wanted immediate payment of a pension bonus that had been promised for 1945. The House of Representatives agreed, but the Senate said no. Most of the **Bonus Army** then went home, but a few thousand stayed, living in shacks. ✪

Although the bonus marchers were generally peaceful, a few violent incidents prompted Hoover to call in the army. General Douglas MacArthur decided to use force to drive the marchers out of Washington. Armed with bricks and stones, the Bonus Army faced guns, tanks, and tear gas. Many were injured. Hoover was horrified but took responsibility for MacArthur's actions. In the next election, the lingering image of this ugly scene would help defeat him.

MAKING CONNECTIONS

In recent decades, the government has actually helped protesters to hold marches in Washington. What reasons can you give for this difference in treatment?

 RESOURCE DIRECTORY

Teaching Resources

✪ **Visual Learning Activity** Veterans March on Washington, found in the Unit 7 folder, p. 72, especially effective for visual learners, enriches the section content by using a political cartoon.

World War I veterans from all parts of the country demonstrated on the steps of the Capitol in Washington, D.C., in 1932, hoping that their promised bonus would help them survive unemployment and homelessness.

A "New Deal" for America

"I pledge myself to a new deal for the American people," announced presidential candidate **Franklin Delano Roosevelt** as he accepted the Democratic party's nomination at its Chicago convention in July 1932. Delegates cheered, and an organ thundered out the song "Happy Days Are Here Again."

The Republicans, in June, had again named Hoover. As the presidential campaign took shape, the differences between the two candidates became very clear.

The Roosevelts In Franklin and **Eleanor Roosevelt,** the Democrats had a remarkable political couple to bring them victory. Franklin, nicknamed "FDR" by the press, was born in 1882. He graduated from Harvard University and took a job in a law firm, although his main interest was politics. He was elected twice to the New York State Senate, then became assistant secretary of the navy in President Woodrow Wilson's cabinet.

In 1920, FDR ran for Vice President but lost. The following summer, he came down with polio and he never walked without help again. He spent much of the 1920s recovering at Warm Springs, Georgia, but kept up his political interests.

Franklin and Eleanor Roosevelt (at right)—seen here a few years after their marriage—followed a family tradition of political and social activism.

Explain

Explain to students that Hoover believed that a positive outlook and the voluntary cooperation of business leaders would result in an end to the economic crisis. His administration did, however, take more direct action than government had taken in the past. Ask students to state the purpose and the results of the Hawley-Smoot tariff and the Reconstruction Finance Corporation.

Discuss/Analyze

Discuss students' reactions to Hoover's image problems. Analyze with students the problems of image in a presidential campaign. Prompt discussion with questions such as: In what ways is image unavoidable? In what ways can image mask the truth? Did Hoover's image mask his real strengths? What was FDR's image? What about his image appealed to many Americans?

Activity

Teaching Heterogeneous Groups

The 1932 presidential election was, in President Hoover's words, "a contest between two philosophies of government." To help students remember how this election would change the way people viewed the role of government, have groups of students design campaign posters for either of the 1932 candidates, Hoover or Roosevelt. Help students focus on their candidate's ideas for bringing the United States out of the Depression. **LEP**

Media and Technology

Visions of America: Turning Point Story To enhance students' understanding of the Turning Point topic, play "Regulating Riches," a story about the stock market speculation and depression that culminated in the election of 1932 (length: approximately 4 minutes). This selection can be located on side 3 of the videodiscs. This selection can also be located on videotape 4. Lesson plans for Turning Point stories can be found in the Visions of America Guidebook.

Side 3, Chapter 25

Visions of America: Roundtable Discussion To introduce students to different and differing viewpoints on the Turning Point topic, play all or part of the Roundtable Discussion on "Regulating Riches," remarks by respected historians and social commentators. This selection can be found on side 3 of the videodiscs. This selection can also be located on videotape 4.

Side 3, Chapter 26

Viewpoints

Hoover wanted to preserve the limited role of national government; Roosevelt proposed change through greater government involvement. For a more thorough examination of 1932 campaign issues, see the Resource Directory below.

Enrichment

Ask students to decide which of the following Presidents would have agreed with FDR and which would have supported Hoover on the issue of controls on business growth and power: Washington, McKinley, Theodore Roosevelt, Coolidge, Wilson. Ask students to explain their decisions based on evidence from the words and actions of the former Presidents.

3. ASSESS

Section 5 Review Answers

1. (a) Hawley-Smoot tariff, see p. 629, (b) Reconstruction Finance Corporation, see p. 629

2. (a) John Maynard Keynes, see p. 630, (b) Bonus Army , see p. 630, (c) Franklin Delano Roosevelt, see p. 631, (d) Eleanor Roosevelt, see p. 631

3. He hoped to wait it out, urged everyone to have confidence, and believed that voluntary actions would be enough.

4. It was intended to protect American industries, but actually caused higher European tariffs and a drop in trade.

5. Urban workers, coal miners, and recent immigrants of Catholic and Jewish descent; people voting against Hoover's policies.

6. Answers will vary but may point out that one person's policies and personality probably could not have compensated for the deep flaws in the economy. On the other hand, Hoover appeared cold and hardhearted, unwilling to provide enough government money either for relief or to stimulate industrial recovery.

TURNING POINTS

Eleanor Roosevelt, a niece of Theodore Roosevelt, was born in 1884 into a wealthy family. Educated in an English boarding school, she later worked at a social settlement house in New York City. She married her distant cousin Franklin in 1905 and they had six children.

By the 1920s, the marriage was shaky, but the couple stayed together. In New York state, Eleanor worked for legislation about public housing, state government reform, birth control, and better conditions for working women. By 1928, when FDR was persuaded to run for governor of New York, she was an experienced political worker and social reformer.

After FDR's success as governor of New York (1929–1932), his supporters believed him ready to try for the presidency. With his broad smile and genial manner, he represented a spirit of optimism that the country badly needed.

Unlike Hoover, FDR was ready to experiment with governmental roles. Though from a wealthy background, he had genuine compassion for ordinary people, in part because of his own struggle with illness. He was also moved by the great gap between the nation's wealthy and the poor.

As governor of New York, he had worked vigorously for Depression relief. In 1931, he set up an unemployment commission and a relief administration, the first state agencies to aid the poor in the Depression era. When, as a presidential candidate, FDR promised the country a "new deal," he had similar programs in mind.

Roosevelt and Hoover The two candidates and their proposed programs contrasted sharply. In October 1932, Hoover said:

Viewpoints
On Ending the Depression

Sharp philosophical differences characterized the presidential campaign of 1932. *How do both viewpoints below support what you know about the approach of Hoover and Roosevelt to ending the Depression?*

Against Drastic Measures
We are told by the opposition that we must have a change, that we must have a new deal. It is not the change . . . to which I object but the proposal to alter the whole foundations of our national life which have been built through generations of testing and struggle.

Herbert Hoover, speech at Madison Square Garden, October 31, 1932

For Drastic Measures
I have recounted to you in other speeches, and it is a matter of general information, that for at least two years after the crash, the only efforts made by the [Hoover administration] to cope with the distress of unemployment were to deny its existence.

Franklin D. Roosevelt, campaign address, October 13, 1932

This campaign is more than a contest between two men. . . . It is a contest between two philosophies of government.

Still arguing for voluntary aid, Hoover attacked the Democratic platform. If its ideas were adopted, he said, "this will not be the America which we have known in the past." He sternly resisted the idea of giving the national government more power.

Roosevelt, by contrast, called for "a reappraisal of values" and controls on business:

I feel that we are coming to a view through the drift of our legislation and our public thinking in the past quarter century that private economic power is . . . a public trust as well.

While statements like this showed FDR's new approach, probably any Democratic candidate could have beaten Hoover in 1932. Even long-time Republicans deserted him. Reserved by nature, Hoover became grumpy and isolated.

RESOURCE DIRECTORY

Teaching Resources

Viewpoints Activity On Ending the Depression, found in the Unit 7 folder, pp. 62–63, provides additional opinions and perspectives to extend students' understanding of the presidential campaign of 1932.

THE NEW YORKER

Mar. 4. 1933   Price 15 cents

This *New Yorker* cover drawn for the inauguration clearly shows how people saw Roosevelt, the new President, in contrast with Hoover.

He gave few campaign speeches. Crowds jeered his motorcade.

FDR won the presidency by a huge margin—seven million popular votes. (See the map above.) Much of his support came from groups that had begun to turn to the Democrats in 1928: urban workers, coal miners, and immigrants of Catholic and Jewish descent. Some people did not really vote for Roosevelt, they

Election of 1932

Candidate/Party	Electoral Vote	Popular Vote
Franklin D. Roosevelt (Dem.)	472	22,821,857
Herbert Hoover (Rep.)	59	15,761,841
Minor parties		1,160,615

 Geography and History: Interpreting Maps
Franklin D. Roosevelt and the Democratic party won the popular vote in 1932 as well as a huge margin of electoral votes. *Which states' electoral votes did Hoover win?*

simply voted *against* Hoover and the Republican policies. Still, the words of FDR's inaugural address gave most of the country renewed hope:

> So first of all let me assert my firm belief that the only thing we have to fear is fear itself.

With these words, Roosevelt reassured a frightened nation and began a journey into a new era of government involvement and presidential activism.

Caption Answer to ...

 Interpreting Maps

Maine, New Hampshire, Vermont, Connecticut, Pennsylvania, Delaware

Reteach

Ask students to write an editorial for a 1932 newspaper. The editorial should summarize Hoover's major efforts to end the Depression, and either urge voters to reelect him or urge them to vote for Franklin D. Roosevelt.

4. CLOSE

Reinforcing the Big Idea

At first President Hoover tried to curb the Depression through voluntary controls. Hoover's later attempts at direct federal action and relief were inadequate. In 1932 voters swept in the Democratic candidate Franklin Delano Roosevelt and waited to see if he could indeed deliver a "New Deal."

SECTION 5 REVIEW

Key Terms, People, and Places
1. Define (a) Hawley-Smoot tariff, (b) Reconstruction Finance Corporation.
2. Identify (a) John Maynard Keynes, (b) Bonus Army (c) Franklin Delano Roosevelt, (d) Eleanor Roosevelt.

Key Concepts
3. How did President Hoover hope to end the Depression and its hardships?

4. What was the intent of the Hawley-Smoot tariff?
5. In the 1932 election, what groups supported Roosevelt?

Critical Thinking
6. **Distinguishing False from Accurate Images** Was Hoover's great unpopularity justified, or would the economic crisis have defeated anyone?

 Quiz found in the Unit 7 folder, p. 55, covers the main ideas in this section as well as the key terms.

 Chapter Test Forms A and B are found in the Unit 7 folder, pp. 74–79

 Answer Keys found in the Unit 7 folder, pp. 116–128, provide answers to all student activities.

Media and Technology

Transparencies Cause and Effect, F-9; Graphic Organizer, G-3

Guided Reading Audiotapes (English and Spanish)

Computer Test Bank

TURNING POINTS

The Lasting Impact of the Election of 1932

Focus During FDR's administration, the federal government took on broad powers and responsibilities for regulating business and for promoting the welfare of all citizens. What has been the lasting impact of those powers and responsibilities?

Instruct Tell students that before FDR's administration, many familiar government programs such as social security, unemployment insurance, federal housing projects, and minimum wage laws did not exist. The federal government had never before taken the direct responsibility to see that each American enjoyed a minimum standard of living. Government was much smaller and much less expensive.

Review with students the reasons that Americans turned to the federal government in 1932 for relief from the Depression. What other sources of relief had failed? What government programs had been ineffective? Did citizens have any reason to expect that the federal government could end the Depression?

Ask students to discuss in small groups one critical current human problem such as homelessness or the spread of AIDS. Ask them to consider the following questions: Whose problems are these? What other institutions, groups, or segments of society are involved in attempts to solve these problems? Should the federal government take full responsibility for finding solutions and administering the programs that might correct these situations? What might be the harmful effects of such governmental action? Do students think that the federal government should take charge of solving such problems?

The Lasting Impact of the Election of 1932

On a rainy day in 1933, FDR stood before a Depression-weary crowd and took the oath of office of President of the United States. As reporter Thomas Stokes observed, a stirring of hope moved through the crowd when Roosevelt began, "This nation asks for action and action now."

Phrases like this foreshadowed a sweeping change in the style of presidential leadership and government response to its citizens' needs. Ultimately, such changes altered the way many Americans viewed their government and its responsibilities.

A Revolutionary Change

In the depths of the Great Depression, many Americans had to give up cherished traditional beliefs in "making it on their own." They turned to the government as their only hope. Thus, the Roosevelt years saw the beginning of many programs that changed the role of the government in American society.

Presidential Activism In general, the Presidents since FDR—whatever their politics and personality—have carried on the tradition begun by Roosevelt and responded actively to people's needs. Harry Truman inherited the presidency when Roosevelt died in 1945. His domestic program extended the social welfare commitments that Roosevelt had made, such as social security and unemployment insurance. He also argued that government should provide medical care programs to its citizens.

Even supposedly nonactivist Presidents such as Dwight Eisenhower have acted when necessary. For example, in 1957 Eisenhower sent army troops to Little Rock, Arkansas, to protect black students entering a formerly all-white high school.

Government Involvement Continues In the 1960s, President Lyndon Johnson was even more successful at working with Congress than FDR had been. Johnson's proposal of programs like Medicare

1933 Roosevelt's inauguration begins a new age of activist Presidents.

1957 President Dwight Eisenhower sends troops to integrate Arkansas high school.

1930	1940	1950

1948 President Truman bans racial segregation in the military.

RESOURCE DIRECTORY

Teaching Resources

Turning Point Extension Activity
The Lasting Impact of the Election of 1932, found in the Unit 7 folder, pp. 56–57, extends students' understanding of the Depression era by discussing the long-term impact of social programs that grew out of New Deal legislation.

and Medicaid, which offered health care benefits to the elderly and the poor, extended the ideas of social welfare.

Attempts at a More Limited Role Fail

During the 1970s and 1980s, several Presidents attempted to take a more limited role in social welfare. President Richard Nixon sought to scale back involvement in social issues, but because the American public had come to expect this commitment, he failed. At the same time, people began to complain about the "imperial presidency" as Nixon acted aggressively to maintain law and order at home.

Presidents Ford and Carter, too, fashioned a more modest role for themselves and the government during their presidencies, but found that without strong leadership, the American government could not operate effectively.

When Ronald Reagan took office in 1981, he waged a campaign against "entitlements"—those programs that provide basic support for elderly, unemployed, or impoverished people. Because these programs were taking the largest share of the federal budget, Reagan argued that they should be cut back, maintaining that the government should not be so involved in the social welfare of its citizens. But he still acknowledged the need for a basic safety net that would catch those who were unable to help themselves.

The People Choose Social Intervention

After such attempts to reduce government's role in people's lives, voters elected a President in 1992 who argued that the government has a responsibility to help citizens. President Bill Clinton acted on this belief often during his first year in office. When rain-swollen rivers flooded the Midwest in 1993, he authorized federal disaster funds and—as people expected—personally visited flooded towns and farmlands. He also presented a plan to Congress for a national health care program.

REVIEWING THE FACTS

1. How did Roosevelt's election affect people's expectations of the role of the President?
2. What actions has President Clinton taken that follow in President Roosevelt's footsteps?

Critical Thinking

3. **Expressing Problems Clearly** What are possible consequences of both a large government role in social welfare and a limited government role?

1971 President Richard Nixon imposes a freeze on wages and prices.

1965 President Lyndon Johnson signs bills on Medicare and aid to education into law.

1984 President Reagan introduces programs to aid farmers.

1993 President Bill Clinton visits flood-damaged areas in the Midwest.

1960　　1970　　1980　　1990

TURNING POINTS

Extend Ask students to review the presidential campaigns of 1992, 1988, 1984, and 1980. Which candidates proposed new governmental welfare programs? Which candidates vowed to cut back federal welfare programs? Did any candidates promise to do both?

Answers

1. After Roosevelt's election, people began to expect the President to take a more active role in the social welfare of the nation.
2. President Clinton approved relief for the Midwest after floods, personally visited towns there, and proposed to Congress a national health-care plan.
3. Answers will vary, but should indicate an understanding of the consequences of greater or lesser government involvement in social welfare issues. Greater government involvement might result in the creation and extension of programs such as health-care benefits. Lesser government involvement might be accompanied by an emphasis on areas such as foreign policy.

Understanding Key Terms, People, and Places

Terms
Students should refer to the definitions of the key terms in the chapter to write sentences that show understanding of the economy of the 1920s and the causes and effects of the Great Depression.

Matching
1. real wages
2. Gross National Product (GNP)
3. speculation
4. Reconstruction Finance Corporation

True or False
1. false, Father Divine
2. false, Bonus Army
3. true
4. false, Norman Thomas
5. false, John Maynard Keynes

Reviewing Main Ideas

1. People assumed that prosperity would continue under the Republicans, and the stock market seemed to be doing remarkably well.

2. A few people made fortunes, but generally, wealth remained concentrated in a small percentage of the population.

3. As European farmers recovered from World War I, crop prices in the United States fell. Farmers could not meet their payments on loans for land and machinery.

4. Worried investors began to sell, causing stock prices to fall. Falling prices caused a wave of panic selling.

5. The United States stopped investing in Germany; Germany could no longer meet its reparations payments to the Allies who in turn could no longer pay their debts or afford to buy American goods.

6. Some people moved in with relatives or lived in shanty towns; many became drifters.

7. When low crop prices resulting from the Depression cut their incomes, many farmers lost their farms to the banks.

8. African Americans lost jobs to whites; relief programs discriminated against them; civil rights violations grew worse in the South.

9. Examples include tenant groups forming to protest rent increases and evictions, groups setting up soup kitchens and breadlines, and people agreeing to keep bids low when foreclosed farms were sold.

Chapter Review

Understanding Key Terms, People, and Places

Key Terms
1. real wages
2. welfare capitalism
3. installment buying
4. speculation
5. buy on margin
6. Dow Jones industrial average
7. Gross National Product (GNP)
8. collateral
9. Hooverville
10. Socialists
11. Twenty-first Amendment
12. Hawley-Smoot tariff
13. Reconstruction Finance Corporation

People
14. Father Divine
15. Scottsboro Boys
16. Norman Thomas
17. John Maynard Keynes
18. Bonus Army
19. Franklin Delano Roosevelt
20. Eleanor Roosevelt

Places
21. Empire State Building

Terms For each term above, write a sentence that explains its relation to the economy of the late 1920s and the Great Depression.

Matching Review the key terms in the list above. If you are not sure of a term's meaning, review its definition in the chapter. Then choose a term from the list that best matches each description below.
1. what money can actually buy
2. the total annual value of goods and services a country produces
3. taking chances in the stock market
4. agency that gave government credit to banks so that they could extend loans

True or False Determine whether each statement is true or false. If it is true, write "true." If it is false, change the underlined name to make the statement true.
1. Herbert Hoover opened soup kitchens in Harlem during the Depression.
2. The Scottsboro Boys marched on Washington in the summer of 1932 to demand immediate payment of their pension bonuses.
3. Franklin Delano Roosevelt won the 1932 election by a huge margin.
4. In 1932 John Maynard Keynes ran for President on the Socialist ticket.
5. Eleanor Roosevelt supported massive government spending to revive the economy.

Reviewing Main Ideas

Section 1 (pp. 610–613)
1. Why did the economy of the 1920s inspire trust?
2. How did the rising stock market affect the way wealth was distributed in the United States?
3. Why did farmers fail to share in the 1920s prosperity?

Section 2 (pp. 614–617)
4. What were the results for investors when the Dow Jones average dropped suddenly?
5. Explain how the stock market crash started a downward cycle in the global economy.

Section 3 (pp. 620–624)
6. How did the Depression affect those at the bottom of the economic scale?

7. Why were farm families hit particularly hard by the Depression?
8. In what ways did the Depression affect African Americans more severely than white Americans?

Section 4 (pp. 626–628)
9. What were some ways in which people pulled together to help each other during the Depression?
10. In what ways did the end of Prohibition mark the end of an era?

Section 5 (pp. 629–633)
11. What government actions did Hoover finally take to try to end the Depression? Why did his program fail?
12. What programs had Roosevelt set up as governor of New York that foreshadowed his "new deal"?

---

10. The end of prohibition marked an end to a social experiment; it also ended a period of national hypocrisy, since many people drank anyway, thus encouraging gangsters and bootleggers.

11. Hoover set up the Emergency Committee on Employment to advise local relief programs, and tried to protect domestic industries with the Hawley-Smoot tariff. He also set up the Reconstruction Finance Corporation to give government credit to banks. These actions proved inadequate.

12. Roosevelt had set up an unemployment commission and a relief administration to provide Depression relief.

Thinking Critically

1. Answers will vary. Some students will point out that overspeculation, short-sighted government economic policies, and an unstable economy would have made it obvious that a depression was looming. Others will note that these warning signs were probably not as clear to people at the time as they are in retrospect.

2. Answers will vary. Some students will be aware that today the government spends much more money on social programs than it did before the Depression.

3. Answers will vary, but students should relate the general mood of the 1920s (Chapter 21) to these actions.

Final Evaluation
Allow students to present their portfolios during individual conferences. You might also want to display finished projects for students to observe and discuss.

Use the following guidelines to evaluate students' projects:
● Type and variety of material included
● Evidence of synthesis
● Creativity of thought and presentation

Thinking Critically

1. **Predicting Consequences** If you had lived during the 1920s, what evidence would you have had of the coming Depression?
2. **Determining Relevance** During the Depression, some economists turned to the ideas of British economist John Maynard Keynes, who argued that massive government spending could help a collapsing economy. Do you agree with Keynes's approach? To what extent are Keynes's views still at work in the United States economy today?
3. **Recognizing Cause and Effect** Looking back, the stock market speculation and installment buying of the late 1920s may seem irresponsible. What reasons can you find for the way people were behaving at that time?

Making Connections

1. **Evaluating Primary Sources** Review the primary source quotation on page 632. Do you agree with Hoover's assessment that the election of 1932 was a contest between two different philosophies of government? Explain your answer.
2. **Understanding the Visuals** Much of the "humor" of Depression jokes and cartoons is bitter rather than funny, like the cartoon on page 627. Look at the cartoons on pages 612 and 630 and answer the following questions: (a) What issues do they address? (b) What is the tone of the humor in each case?
3. **Writing About the Chapter** It is 1932. You want to preserve this period in history in a letter that your grandchildren can read in the 1990s. First list the main points you wish to make about events leading up to the Depression, daily life in difficult economic times, and the upcoming election. Note how your life has been permanently changed by the Depression. Then write a draft of a letter in which you explain your experiences and those of the people around you. Revise your letter, making sure that you have used enough detail to bring your experiences to life. Proofread your letter and draft a final copy.
4. **Using the Graphic Organizer** This graphic organizer uses a tree map to organize information about the social effects of the Depression. (a) Based on the graphic organizer below, what were the five social effects of the Depression? (b) According to the graphic organizer, which groups suffered increased discrimination due to the Depression? (c) On a separate sheet of paper, create your own graphic organizer about signs of trouble in the 1920s economy, using this graphic organizer as an example.

Social Effects of the Depression

Homelessness	Farmers suffer	Poor diet and inadequate medical care	Family problems	Increased discrimination against African Americans
• Hoovervilles	• Many lose farms	• Children especially hard hit	• Families move in together • Men feel sense of failure • Women face job discrimination • Divorces and marriages both decline	• Civil rights violations worsen • Unemployment soars to 56 percent for African Americans

Making Connections

1. Hoover believed that voluntary aid could solve the country's economic problems; he resisted the idea of a powerful central government. Roosevelt believed that government must play an active role in turning the economy around.

2. The cartoon on page 612 examines speculation on the stock market. Its tone is critical. The cartoon on page 630 examines public opinion about President Hoover. Its tone is accusatory.

3. Answers will vary. Students' letters should reflect a grasp of the causes and effects of the Depression. They should also mention some of the issues involved in the 1932 election.

4. (a) The five social effects were: homelessness, farmers suffer, poor diet and inadequate medical care, family problems, and increased discrimination against African Americans. (b) Women and African Americans. (c) Students' graphic organizers should include the increase in personal debt, overspeculation, overproduction, uneven distribution of wealth, and economic hard times for many workers.

Chapter 23 The New Deal
1933–1938

📁 Teaching Resources (See Unit 7 Folder)		
	Instruction	**Enrichment**
Section 1 **Forging a New Deal** (pp. 640–646)	Reproducible Lesson Plan, p. 81 Alternate Lesson Plan, p. 118 Guided Reading and Review, p. 84 Quiz, p. 85	Primary Source Activity, A Fireside Chat: The NIRA, p. 98 Primary Source Activity, Providing Emergency Relief, pp. 96–97 Visual Learning Activity, Promoting the WPA, p. 102 Critical Thinking Activity, Recognizing Ideologies, p. 95
Section 2 **The New Deal's Critics** (pp. 647–651)	Reproducible Lesson Plan, p. 82 Alternate Lesson Plan, p. 119 Guided Reading and Review, p. 86 Quiz, p. 87	Literature Activity, In Search of Work: African Americans, p. 101 Visual Learning Activity, FDR Tries to Pack the Court, p. 103 Viewpoints Activity, On the New Deal, pp. 92–93 Historian's Toolbox Activity, Distinguishing Fact from Opinion, p. 94
Section 3 **Enduring Legacies of the New Deal** (pp. 653–657)	Reproducible Lesson Plan, p. 83 Alternate Lesson Plan, p. 120 Guided Reading and Review, p. 88 Quiz, p. 89 Chapter Test, Forms A & B, pp. 104–109	American Profiles Activity, Emma Tenayuca, p. 90 Literature Activity, In Search of Work: Migrant Farmers, pp. 99–100 American Profiles Activity, Jacob Lawrence, p. 91

📁 Additional Chapter Resources	**Bibliography**
Resource Organizer, p. 80 Alternate Lesson Plan, p. 117 Answer Keys, pp. 116–125	**For the Teacher** Brinkley, A. *Voices of Protest: Huey Long, Father Coughlin, and the Great Depression.* Knopf, 1982. Bunche, Ralph. *The Political Status of the Negro in the Age of F.D.R.* University of Chicago Press, 1975. (The view of an African American who served as ambassador to the United Nations.) Lash, Joseph P. *Eleanor and Franklin: The Story of Their Relationship, Based on Eleanor Roosevelt's Personal Papers.* Norton, 1971. Schraff, Anne E. *The Great Depression and the New Deal: America's Economic Collapse and Recovery.* Watts, 1990. (Includes an analysis of the impact of FDR's New Deal on American society.) ***Prentice Hall Literature*** Excerpts from *The American Experience,* 1994, including Porter, Katherine Anne. "The Jilting of Granny Weatherall," from *Flowering Judas and Other Stories.* Harcourt Brace, 1958 edition.

The Big Idea for the chapter and how the main ideas in each section relate to the Big Idea are graphically displayed below. Comprehension of this chapter's Big Idea is critical to students' understanding of United States history and how we as a nation got where we are today.

Media and Technology

 Cause and Effect, F-9; Critical Thinking, I-11

 Critical Thinking, I-17

 Graphic Organizer, G-3

 Guided Reading Audiotapes (English and Spanish)

 Computer Test Bank

For the Student

Life History of the United States. Vol. 2. *New Deal and Global War.* 1964. (Illustrated account by the editors of *Life* magazine.)

Leuchtenburg, William E. *Franklin D. Roosevelt and the New Deal, 1932–1940.* Harper & Row, 1963. (An introduction to the New Deal.)

Warren, Robert Penn. *All the King's Men.* Random House, 1960. (A fictionalized account of the life of Huey Long.)

CHAPTER 23

President Roosevelt's New Deal—the name given to the vast collection of programs and policies formulated to combat the Depression—proved only a partial success at ending the nation's misery. Though critics were quick to point to the many failures, it was hard to argue against its resounding success in bringing hope to a weary nation. Moreover, the New Deal influenced the social, political, and cultural life and attitudes of Americans in ways that are still apparent six decades later.

SECTION 1

Roosevelt delivered on his promise of vigorous action. New Deal programs aided and uplifted millions and attacked root causes of the Depression. After the Supreme Court struck down key parts of the New Deal, the President pushed through a second set of programs.

SECTION 2

Not everyone was pleased with Roosevelt and the New Deal. Critics from all points on the political spectrum noted the President's failures or attacked his methods.

SECTION 3

The New Deal did not bring an end to the Depression. Yet the federal government's programs and policies helped transform the nation in lasting ways. Many physical, political, and cultural transformations are still evident today.

CHAPTER 23

The New Deal
1933–1938

The Relevance of the Big Idea

The Depression was a crisis that threatened the lives and security of millions of Americans. In response, President Roosevelt's New Deal instituted sweeping programs that changed the basic relationship between government and those it represented and governed.

Ask students what some of the major national issues are in the 1990s. Discuss issues such as health care, job retraining, AIDS research, the rights of minorities such as homosexuals, the breakup of the family, the inner-city underclass, foreign aid, drug abuse and rehabilitation, and education. What should the government's role be in any or all of these areas?

In Depth

Global Connections

The Great Depression had a catastrophic impact on the United States. But it was equally damaging to economies of other nations, whose fortunes were becoming ever more tightly interconnected. Japan's burden of a rapidly growing population and a lack of territorial resources was exacerbated by the economic depression. In response, militarist Japanese leaders promoted aggressive expansion into areas rich in natural resources, such as the northern Chinese province of Manchuria. The stage was thus being set for World War II, President Roosevelt's greatest challenge.

The New Deal
1933–1938

*F*ranklin Roosevelt breezed into the White House, raising people's hopes with a promise to change the relationship between government and the economy. When the dust from FDR's first flurry of programs settled, critics were quick to point out the President's failures. Indeed, though the New Deal did help millions of Americans, it left many people out and failed to end the Depression. Still, the New Deal left permanent marks on American political, social, and cultural life—and on citizens' attitudes about their government.

Events in the United States				
	1932 Franklin Delano Roosevelt is elected President of the United States.	**1933** Frances Perkins becomes the first woman cabinet member.	**1934** Congress passes the Indian Reorganization Act.	**1935** Congress passes the Social Security Act.
1932	**1933**	**1934**	**1935**	

Events in the World				
	1932 Bolivia and Paraguay begin a three-year territorial war in which more than 100,000 people die.	**1933** Hitler and the Nazis take over Germany. • The Philippines gain independence from the United States.	**1934** Stalin launches the Great Purge in the Soviet Union.	**1935** Italy invades Ethiopia. • German Jews lose citizenship under Nuremburg Laws.

RESOURCE DIRECTORY

Teaching Resources

Alternate Lesson Plan: Demonstrating the Big Idea found in the Alternate Lesson Plans folder, p. 117, provides a lesson strategy to instruct students about the Big Idea that Roosevelt's New Deal, although it had many failures, influenced social, political, and cultural life for the next fifty years.

Alternative Assessment Handbook provides information, guidance, and strategies for alternative methods of assessment. It includes an essay on new trends in assessment, guidance and strategies for developing performance tasks and portfolios, scoring rubrics, and sample evaluation forms.

Pages 640–646

Forging a New Deal

FDR came to office with a breezy confidence—and no detailed plan of action. But act he did, pushing program after program to spur recovery and reduce misery. Not all of his ideas worked as planned, but they did manage to give the nation hope.

Pages 647–651

The New Deal's Critics

For millions of Americans, the New Deal meant survival, security, and even opportunity. Others, including many women and minorities, noted its failures with bitterness. As the New Deal continued to disappoint, its critics accumulated large followings across the political spectrum.

Pages 653–657

Enduring Legacies of the New Deal

The New Deal attacked the Great Depression with a barrage of programs and agencies. The Depression withstood this onslaught and refused to loosen its grip on the economy. Yet the New Deal was not without effect; it left a legacy that endures to this day.

1936 President Roosevelt wins reelection in a landslide.
• Auto workers strike in Michigan.

1937 Roosevelt's attempt to pack the Supreme Court fails.

1938 The Fair Labor Standards Act bans child labor.
• Orson Welles's radio production of H. G. Wells's War of the Worlds causes national panic.

1939 Author John Steinbeck publishes The Grapes of Wrath.
• Hollywood releases The Wizard of Oz.

1936	1937	1938	1939	1940

1936 The Spanish Civil War begins.
• Olympic Games held in Berlin.

1937 Japan launches a full-scale war against China.

1938 Mexico nationalizes its oil fields.

1939 Germany and the Soviet Union sign the Nazi-Soviet Pact.
• World War II begins.

Media and Technology

Transparency
Time Lines, E-7

Alternative Assessment

As an ongoing chapter project, have students write three personal letters to President Franklin D. Roosevelt. Students should write the letters from the points of view of the following people:

• A beneficiary of a New Deal program living in the 1930s
• A critic of the New Deal living in the 1930s
• A recipient of social security benefits living in the 1990s

Students are free to choose which programs and aspects of the New Deal they want to write about. In all cases, however, the letters should be as specific and rich in detail as possible. In addition to the information provided in the textbook, students should seek information from newspapers, periodicals, biographies, and other sources. Students may also want to use primary sources such as interviews with relatives or neighbors who lived during the Depression. Students should submit a bibliography for their project.

Explain that projects will be assessed according to the following standards:

• **Unacceptable** Projects are not completed or fail to meet the requirements outlined.
• **Limited/Acceptable** Projects are based primarily on material from the textbook and present a limited view of the New Deal.
• **Extensive/Commendable** Projects are based on some outside resources as well as material from the textbook and present an in-depth picture of the period and its legacy.
• **Extraordinary/Outstanding** Projects are based on considerable outside research and present a detailed picture of the events, programs, and people of the time in the context of their relevance today.

For more information and guidance on alternative assessment trends and strategies, see the Alternative Assessment Handbook in the Resource Directory on page 638.

639

Forging a New Deal

Connecting to the Big Idea

See page 638B. Explain that President Roosevelt promised action to combat the Depression and that he fulfilled that promise. Though the New Deal suffered setbacks, Roosevelt's attitude and programs uplifted the nation. Ask students to consider the ways in which the New Deal sought to overcome the Depression.

Objectives

● Explain how the Roosevelt administration restored the American people's optimism.

● Explain the results of the New Deal and determine why Roosevelt launched the Second New Deal.

In Depth

Did You Know?

With FDR's enactment of the New Deal, a horde of young, idealistic lawyers came to Washington eager to reform American society. These students and protégés of Harvard University's Felix Frankfurter (see page 526 and pages 564–565)—who were accordingly nicknamed "hot dogs"—incurred the disapproval of conservatives. One bureaucratic spokesperson complained of the "plague of young lawyers settled upon Washington."

Forging a New Deal

FDR came to office with a breezy confidence—and no detailed plan of action. But act he did, pushing program after program to spur recovery and reduce misery. Not all of his ideas worked as planned, but they did manage to give the nation hope.

Key Concepts

• The Roosevelt administration restored the optimism of the American people.

• After achieving mixed results with his New Deal, Roosevelt launched the Second New Deal.

Key Terms, People, and Places

New Deal, hundred days, public works program, Wagner Act, Social Security Act; Frances Perkins, Mary McLeod Bethune

Many victims of the Depression found work and relief through such government programs as the Civilian Conservation Corps—the CCC.

W hen Franklin Roosevelt took office in 1933, he had big plans for the country—the so-called **New Deal.** Even Roosevelt himself, however, was not sure exactly how the New Deal would work. Nevertheless, the new President's personality and willingness to experiment won him the support of the American people. As humorist Will Rogers said, "The whole country is with him, just so he does something. If he burned down the capital we would cheer and say, 'Well, we at least got a fire started anyhow.'"

Restoring the Nation's Hope

Shortly after FDR took office, World War I veterans staged a second Bonus March on Washington. This time, the new administration provided campsites for the veterans. Even more astounding, Eleanor Roosevelt paid them a visit.

When she drove up, "They looked at me curiously and one of them asked my name and what I wanted," she recalled. By the time she left an hour later, the veterans were waving and calling out, "Good-by and good luck to you!" The First Lady later told reporters how polite the marchers had been. By this act she both soothed popular fears about renewed radical agitation and demonstrated the new administration's approach to unrest.

FDR also soothed the public. In his inaugural address of March 4, 1933, he tried to restore confidence: "Let me assert my firm belief that the only thing we have to fear is fear itself." The first Sunday after taking office, Roosevelt spoke to the nation over the radio in what became regular "fireside chats." His easy manner and confidence calmed his listeners. His words contained little of substance, but they made people feel better.

The First Hundred Days In campaigning for the White House, FDR had promised "bold, persistent experimentation." No one knew exactly what that experimentation would entail, only that someone was going to do something. As reporter Arthur Krock expressed it, Washington "welcomes the 'new deal,' even though it is not sure what the new deal is going to be."

Americans soon found out. From March to June 1933, during a period known as the **hundred days,** FDR feverishly pushed program after program through Congress to provide relief, create jobs, and stimulate economic recovery. Some of these programs were based on federal agencies that had controlled the economy during World War I, or on programs started under Hoover or by state governors. Former progressives figured prominently, inspiring New Deal legislation or administering programs.

Closing the Banks FDR's first step was to restore public confidence in the nation's banks. On March 6 he ordered all banks to close. He then pushed Congress to pass the Emergency

---

RESOURCE DIRECTORY

Teaching Resources

Reproducible Lesson Plan found in the Unit 7 folder, p. 81, provides a summary of the Section 1 lesson plan content.

Alternate Lesson Plan: Learning Styles found in the Alternate Lesson Plans folder, p. 118 is designed to help students create a graphic organizer identifying New Deal programs and agencies, as well as their goals and effects, and is particularly effective for visual learners.

Guided Reading and Review found in the Unit 7 folder, p. 84, provides a structure for reading and mastering the key concepts and reviewing the key terms for Section 1. (Guided Practice)

Banking Act, which authorized the government to inspect the financial health of all banks. Congress also established a Federal Deposit Insurance Corporation (FDIC) to insure deposits up to $5,000.

These acts reassured the American people, many of whom had been terrified by the prospect of losing all their savings in a bank failure. Government inspectors found that most banks were healthy, and two thirds had reopened by March 15. After the brief "bank holiday," deposits at last exceeded withdrawals.

Providing Relief and Creating Jobs FDR's next step was to replenish badly depleted local relief agencies. Harry Hopkins, a former social worker, directed a Federal Emergency Relief Administration (FERA) that sent funds to these agencies. He was in office barely two hours before he had given out $5 million. At the same time, Hopkins professed a strong belief in helping people find work. He said,

> G ive a man a dole [handout], *and you save his body and destroy his spirit. Give him a job and pay him an assured wage and you save both the body and the spirit.*

The government also put federal money behind **public works programs**—government-funded projects to build public facilities. Its

President Roosevelt's manner both radiated and inspired confidence. At Hilltop Cottage in Hyde Park, New York, FDR chats with the caretaker's granddaughter in 1941.

first such effort along these lines was the Civil Works Administration (CWA), which gave the unemployed jobs building or improving roads, parks, airports, and other facilities. The CWA was a tremendous morale booster to its 4 million employees. As a former insurance salesman from Alabama remarked, "When I got that [CWA identification] card it was the biggest day in my whole life. At last I could say, 'I've got a job.'"

FDR believed fervently in conservation of the environment. For this reason, the Civilian Conservation Corps (CCC), which put 2.5 million unmarried male workers into forest, beach, and

1650 | 1700 | 1750 | 1800

Links Across Time

1850 | 1900 | 1950 | 2000

Putting People to Work

When President Roosevelt took office in 1933, at least one of every four American workers was unemployed. Among FDR's first initiatives were programs to provide work—programs similar to ones Bill Clinton proposed during his presidential campaign in 1992.

New Deal programs created a variety of work agencies, such as the Civilian Conservation Corps (CCC), the Public Works Administration (PWA),

and the National Youth Administration (NYA). These organizations provided work to people who would otherwise have had none.

In 1993 Bill Clinton responded to high unemployment figures by proposing to invest $100 billion dollars in building and repairing roads, bridges, sewers, airports, and communication systems. He also proposed spending federal money on a job-training program that would

include classes and apprenticeships. Clinton hoped that his spending programs would provide work for unemployed Americans.

Roosevelt was able to put his plans into action. President Clinton hoped to use similar programs to help people learn skills and earn a living. *Based on what you know about reactions to the New Deal, what do you think were the reactions to President Clinton's plan?*

Bellringer
Ask students to imagine that all members of their household—and many people in the country—were out of work, had no hope of finding a job, and had no government benefits. Ask them to consider how they would want their government leaders to respond to such a crisis.

Reading Strategy
Structured Overview Have students write two column headings on a piece of paper: The New Deal and The Second New Deal. Then ask them to list details from the section in the appropriate column and note the significance of each detail.

Answer to ...

Links Across Time

Possible answer: Clinton's plan was likely to be approved by Congress, which had a Democratic majority; however, Clinton's plans would be as subject to criticism as were those of Roosevelt's New Deal.

In Depth

Did You Know?

Eleanor Roosevelt was personally responsible for persuading Harry Hopkins to create a women's division within the Federal Emergency Relief Administration (FERA). And in late 1933, Mrs. Roosevelt sponsored a White House Conference on the Emergency Needs of Women. By spring 1934, more than 300,000 women—more than 50 percent of those who qualified for relief—were employed on various public works projects. At the same time, these women were usually paid less than men.

Explain/Discuss

Explain that the Depression had deeply demoralized the nation by the time Roosevelt became President. Ask students to consider how prolonged joblessness with little prospect for relief might affect people. Ask how people might respond in such circumstances to the government programs that put people back to work and tried to address the root causes of such widespread unemployment and misery.

Explain that Roosevelt's New Deal was in many ways a revolutionary program; no President had ever attempted such far-reaching changes in the structure of the economy. Indeed, the Supreme Court found some New Deal programs unconstitutional. Ask students to identify the ways in which the Second New Deal addressed the shortcomings of the first New Deal.

Analyze

Ask students to analyze how the New Deal affected the relationship between the people and their government. As a result of the New Deal, would people expect more or less from government in future crises? Why?

The CCC gave young people jobs and preserved the nation's natural resources. This worker is planting seedlings in Montana.

NRA participants displayed the blue eagle label shown below.

NRA MEMBER
U.S.
WE DO OUR PART

park maintenance and restoration projects, was his favorite program. CCC workers earned only $1 a day but were boarded in camps and received job training. One participant commented that CCC work "gives a fellow self-confidence and teaches them how to get along by themselves." Thanks to Eleanor Roosevelt's intervention, from 1934 to 1937 the CCC funded similar programs for young women, though only 8,500 women benefited.

Public works programs also helped Native Americans. John Collier, FDR's commissioner of Indian affairs, used New Deal funds and Native American workers to build schools, hospitals, and irrigation systems. Native Americans also benefited from the Indian Reorganization Act of 1934, which ended the sale of tribal lands begun under the Dawes Act (1887) and restored ownership of unallocated lands to Native American groups.

A Helping Hand to Business The sharp decline of industrial prices in the early 1930s had caused many business failures—and also much unemployment. The National Industrial Recovery Act (NIRA) of June 1933 sought to bolster those prices and thus help businesses and individuals.

The NIRA allowed trade associations in many industries to draw up codes to regulate wages, working conditions, production, and even prices. The act also set a minimum wage and gave organized labor collective bargaining rights.

For a brief time, the codes stopped the tailspin of industrial prices. But by the fall of 1933, when higher wages went into effect, prices rose, too. Consumers stopped buying. The cycle of overproduction and underconsumption returned, and many businesses failed. Businesses soon complained that the codes were too complicated and that control by the National Recovery Administration (NRA) was too rigid. Critics joked that NRA really stood for "National Run Around" or "No Recovery Allowed."

The best part of the NIRA may have been its Public Works Administration (PWA). Directed by Secretary of the Interior Harold Ickes, the PWA launched projects ranging from the Grand Coulee Dam on the Columbia River in the state of Washington, to the causeway connecting Key West to the Florida mainland, to New York's Triborough Bridge.

Another New Deal act was less pleasing to business. A Federal Securities Act (May 1933) required full disclosure of information about stock offered for sale. The next year, Congress set up the Securities and Exchange Commission (SEC) to regulate the stock market. Congress also gave the Federal Reserve Board power to regulate the purchase of stock on margin—a practice that had contributed heavily to the crash.

Saving Homes and Farms The New Deal helped people keep their homes and farms. The Home Owners' Loan Corporation (HOLC) refinanced mortgages of middle-income home owners. An Agricultural Adjustment Administration (AAA) tried to raise farm prices. The AAA used proceeds from a new tax to pay farmers not to raise certain crops and animals. Lower production, it was hoped, would raise prices.

Under this program, some farmers also destroyed animals and plowed under growing crops. Many Americans, however, could not understand how the federal government could encourage the destruction of food while so many Americans were hungry.

Improving the Quality of Life One public works project proved especially popular. The Tennessee Valley Authority (TVA), created in May 1933, helped farmers and created jobs in one of the country's least modernized regions. By

---

▶ RESOURCE DIRECTORY

Teaching Resources

Primary Source Activity A Fireside Chat: The NIRA, found in the Unit 7 folder, p. 98, provides an example of Roosevelt's use of radio to introduce and build support for his programs.

Primary Source Activity Providing Emergency Relief, found in the Unit 7 folder, pp. 96–97, uses excerpts from Frances Perkins's *The Roosevelt I Knew* to demonstrate her impressions of the New Deal President.

The Tennessee Valley Authority

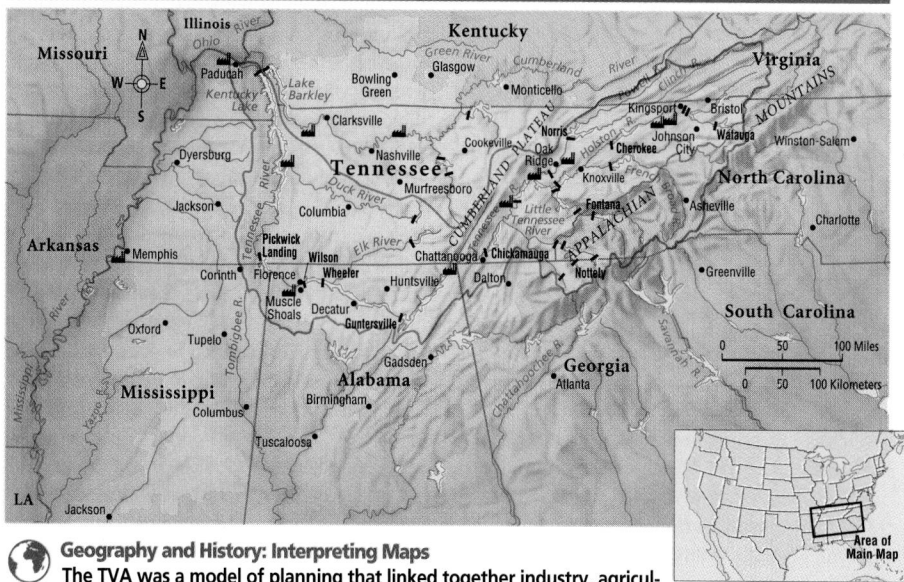

Geography and History: Interpreting Maps
The TVA was a model of planning that linked together industry, agriculture, forestry science, and flood prevention. To many critics, however, the TVA was also the emblem of big government. *In how many states did the TVA provide service and benefits?*

reactivating a hydroelectric power facility started during World War I, the TVA provided cheap electric power, flood control, and recreational opportunities to the entire Tennessee River valley, as shown on the map above.

MAKING CONNECTIONS

What are the major differences between FDR's approach to the Depression and Hoover's?

New Deal Personnel

FDR surrounded himself with eager and hardworking advisers. Some, like Hopkins and Ickes, went directly into his cabinet or headed one of the new agencies. Others, such as Raymond Moley, Adolf A. Berle, and Rexford G. Tugwell, were part of a so-called brain trust, an informal group of intellectuals who helped Roosevelt devise policies. For the first time, a woman held a cabinet post. **Frances Perkins** became secretary of labor, a job she held until 1945. Perkins was one of almost thirty women who held key New Deal positions.

Eleanor Roosevelt Among FDR's most important colleagues was his wife, Eleanor Roosevelt. She threw herself into supporting New Deal programs and traveled widely for her husband, visiting coal mines, sewing rooms, and housing projects. She held her own press conferences, and in 1935 started her own newspaper column, "My Day," in which she drummed up support for the New Deal.

At times, ER took stands that embarrassed her husband. For example, in 1938 at a Birmingham, Alabama, meeting of the Southern Conference for Human Welfare, an interracial group, she knew she had to obey local Jim Crow laws that required African Americans and whites to sit in separate parts of the auditorium. In protest, she sat in the center aisle between the divided races. Her act

Eleanor Roosevelt surprised many Americans with her activism. In 1933 alone, she traveled 40,000 miles. Here, the First Lady emerges from an inspection of an Ohio coal mine.

Enrichment

Ask students to research a particular New Deal public works program, such as the CWA, CCC, or PWA. Students should focus on the attitudes and experiences of the individuals whose lives were affected by these programs. Students can present their findings in a written or oral report.

In Depth

Interdisciplinary

In 1933, FDR established the Tennessee Valley Authority (TVA) to oversee "a land use experiment on a regional scale, one embracing many states." In spite of considerable opposition, the TVA revitalized the economic life of the Tennessee Valley. Building projects brought $500 million into the region and employed 200,000 men and women. Fertilizers produced from local minerals in river-powered factories nourished the thin soil. Exhausted corn, cotton, and tobacco fields soon became rich pastures for livestock. One resident of Decatur, Alabama, in the 1940s described the change: "Fifteen years ago we were dozing in the sunshine waiting for that once-a-year payroll brought by cotton and wearing out our second finest resource, the land. Today the cash income from all farm products in the area surrounding Decatur is $43 million." (See pages 642–643.)

received wide publicity, and no one missed its symbolism.

Many Americans were confused by ER's activities. In their view, a First Lady should take care of her husband and serve graciously at state dinners. Gradually, the public got used to ER, and many came to admire her for her idealism and humanity.

AMERICAN PROFILES

Mary McLeod Bethune

FDR's administration broke new ground by hiring African Americans to more than one hundred policy-making posts. One of Roosevelt's key appointments was **Mary McLeod Bethune** (1875–1955), who held the highest position of any black woman in the New Deal.

The President was not the first to recognize Bethune's talents. From the mid-1920s on, she had been one of the country's most influential spokespersons for African American concerns. Bethune achieved this status through her efforts in three areas: education, women's voluntary associations, and government.

Improving African American Education Born near Mayesville, South Carolina, Bethune was the fifteenth of seventeen children born to for-

"Your road may be somewhat less rugged because of the struggles we have made." So stated Mary McLeod Bethune of efforts in the New Deal era to further the interests of women and African Americans.

merly enslaved parents. With the help of a scholarship and money she earned by ironing, cooking, and cleaning, she received an education at the Scotia Seminary in Concord, North Carolina. Bethune's opportunity did not come without sacrifice. For example, during one period at Scotia, Bethune owned only one dress, which she washed out each night and wore again the next day.

In 1895 Bethune began training for missionary work in Africa, only to discover a year later that her church sent out only white missionaries. Undaunted, she turned her missionary spirit toward teaching, and in 1904 moved to Daytona Beach, Florida, determined to open a school for African American girls. Describing how she started this enterprise, Bethune later wrote:

On October 3, 1904, I opened the doors of my school, with an enrollment of five little girls, aged from eight to twelve, whose parents paid me fifty cents weekly tuition. . . . Though I hadn't a penny left, I considered cash money as the smallest part of my resources. I had faith in a living God, faith in myself, and a desire to serve.

Later, Bethune moved her school to the site of an old dumping ground. She purchased the land with a five-dollar down payment, which she raised by selling ice cream and sweet-potato pies to local laborers.

That was how the Daytona Normal and Industrial Institute got started. Despite its humble beginnings, the school prospered. By 1918 Bethune had added a four-year high school. In 1923 it merged with Cookman Institute, a coeducational school in Jacksonville. This institution was renamed Bethune-Cookman College in 1929, and Bethune became its president.

Volunteerism Bethune was also active in voluntary groups, including the NAACP, National Urban League, and National Association of Colored Women. Assuming the presidency of this last group in 1924, Bethune developed international contacts to forge "a significant link between the peoples of color throughout the world." In 1935 she founded the National Council of Negro Women, which represented thirty African American women's organizations.

RESOURCE DIRECTORY

Teaching Resources

⭐ **Visual Learning Activity** Promoting the WPA, found in Unit 7 folder, p 102, uses a poster created under the Works Project Administration to show how the agency simultaneously employed artists, historians, and others, and promoted public interest issues.

Serving in Government Also in 1935, the New Deal's National Youth Administration made her a consultant to its advisory council. This work eventually earned her an appointment to the post of director of the Division of Negro Affairs.

In her government posts, Bethune encouraged programs that aided African Americans. She also sought a share of New Deal posts for African Americans. "The White man has been thinking for us too long," she said, expressing her belief that African American officeholders would be more sensitive to African American concerns. She forged a united stand among black officeholders by organizing a Federal Council on Negro Affairs in August 1936. This unofficial group, known as the black cabinet, met weekly to hammer out priorities and to increase African American support for the New Deal.

At a time when no governmental commitment to the improvement of the lives of African Americans existed, Bethune helped create one. Recipient in 1935 of the NAACP's most prestigious award, the Spingarn Medal, and twelve honorary degrees, Bethune reached an extraordinary level of influence for women and for African Americans. Speaking about Bethune, Roosevelt once remarked, "I believe in her because she has her feet on the ground; not only on the ground but deep down in the plowed soil."

The End of the Honeymoon

The zeal and energy with which New Dealers attacked the Depression pleased most observers. But when the new programs failed to bring about significant economic improvement, criticism began to mount. Many worried about the increasing power that New Deal agencies were giving to the federal government. Former President Hoover warned against "a state-controlled or state-directed social or economic system. . . . That is not liberalism; it is tyranny," he said. Other criticisms of the New Deal are discussed in Section 2.

In 1935 the Supreme Court declared the NRA unconstitutional because it gave the President law-making powers and regulated local, rather than interstate, commerce. The following year, the Court ruled that the tax that funded AAA subsidies to farmers was also unconstitutional. The New Deal's most important programs had crumbled. It was time to reassess.

A Second New Deal

Meanwhile, most of the public remained behind Roosevelt. The midterm elections of 1934 showed stunning nationwide support for FDR's administration. In 1935 he launched a new, even bolder burst of legislative activity. Some have called this period the Second New Deal. In part, it was a response to his various critics. The Second New Deal included more social welfare benefits, stricter controls over business, stronger support for unions, and higher taxes on the rich.

New and Expanded Agencies New agencies attacked joblessness even more aggressively than before. The Works Progress Administration (WPA), an agency set up in 1935 and lasting eight years, provided work for more than eight million citizens. The WPA constructed or improved more than 20,000 playgrounds, schools, hospitals, and airfields, and supported the creative work of many artists and writers (see Section 3). ✪

The Second New Deal responded to the worsening plight of agricultural workers. The original AAA had ignored many of the farm workers who did not own land. In the Southwest, for example, Mexican American farm workers struggled to survive. Many were forced to return to Mexico; others tried to form unions, inspiring fierce resistance from farmer associations. In the South, landlords had pocketed AAA subsidies, taken land out of production, and left tenants and sharecroppers to shift for themselves.

In May 1935 Rexford Tugwell set up a Resettlement Administration that loaned money to owners of small farms and helped resettle tenants and sharecroppers on productive land. In 1937 a Farm Security Administration (FSA) replaced Tugwell's agency. It loaned more than $1 billion to farmers and set up camps for migrant workers.

New Labor Legislation Labor unions had liked the NIRA provision—known as 7a—that

Media and Technology

 Transparencies
Cause and Effect, F-9; Critical Thinking, I-11

3. ASSESS

Section 1 Review Answers

1. (a) New Deal, see p. 640, (b) hundred days, see p. 640, (c) Wagner Act, see p. 646, (d) Social Security Act, see p. 646

2. Frances Perkins, see p. 643

3. FDR gave a stirring inaugural address and began proposing legislation to Congress at a feverish pace. Instead of driving the bonus marchers out of Washington, the government provided camp sites for them and Eleanor Roosevelt visited them.

4. After declaring a four-day bank holiday, FDR increased relief and created public works programs. He then launched a National Industrial Recovery Act, which did not work very well and was eventually declared unconstitutional. Farmers were somewhat helped by an Agricultural Adjustment Act, and agencies were created to help people refinance their mortgages. The Tennessee Valley Authority brought cheap electric power and flood control to one of the nation's poorest and least modernized areas. The CCC provided jobs and engaged in conservation projects.

5. She promoted African American education by founding a school, which later became a college. She worked on behalf of several African American volunteer associations. She also held a post in the New Deal administration, which she used to promote African American interests.

6. A Works Progress Administration, a National Youth Administration, the Wagner Act (which legalized unions), and the Social Security Act.

7. Possible answer: FDR gave the appearance of confidence. He also appeared willing to take whatever steps necessary to get results.

Write the following questions on the chalkboard: Why was there a New Deal? Why was there a Second New Deal? Then ask students to formulate answers to these questions, and to give examples of how Roosevelt's goals were met.

Alternative Assessment

Mid-Point Monitoring

Ask students if they have
● Identified the programs and points of view on which their letters will be based
● Begun outside research on the New Deal
● Started drafts of their letters

 Reinforcing the Big Idea

The New Deal uplifted millions by its vigorous response to the Depression. The next section explores some of the many criticisms that President Roosevelt and the New Deal provoked.

A major Second New Deal program was the Social Security Act, which provided a variety of benefits to many retired, disabled, and unemployed workers. The original social security program did not cover agricultural or domestic workers.

granted them the right to organize and bargain collectively. When the NIRA was declared unconstitutional, however, workers began to demand new legislation to protect their rights.

In July 1935, Congress responded. It passed a National Labor Relations Act, called the **Wagner Act** after its leading advocate, New York senator Robert Wagner. The Wagner Act legalized practices allowed only unevenly in the past, such as closed shops—in which only union members can work—and collective bargaining. It also outlawed spying on union activities and blacklisting—a practice in which employers agreed not to hire union leaders. The act also set up a National Labor Relations Board (NLRB) to enforce its provisions.

In 1938 a Fair Labor Standards Act banned child labor and established a minimum wage for all workers covered under the act. This law was a long-awaited triumph for progressive-era social reformers.

Social Legislation Congress also passed the **Social Security Act,** establishing a system that provided old-age pensions for workers; survivors' benefits for victims of industrial accidents; unemployment insurance; and aid for dependent mothers and children, the blind, and the physically disabled. The act was based in part on models from European welfare states, and it was funded through contributions from employers and workers, which were then later paid out to people covered by the system who were not earning a wage.

Though the original Social Security Act did not cover many farm and domestic workers, it did help millions of beneficiaries feel more secure. Its importance to the American people has continued to grow, and its success has helped inspire numerous other social welfare programs.

The 1936 Election

No one expected the Republican presidential candidate of 1936, Kansas governor Alfred M. Landon, to beat FDR. But few predicted the extent of FDR's landslide. FDR carried every state except Maine and Vermont. Although Depression conditions had increased support for radical movements, no effective third party emerged to challenge the capitalist system. FDR buried Socialist Norman Thomas, who received fewer than 200,000 votes, and Communist candidate Earl Browder, who won only 80,000 votes.

Indeed, a broad cross section of the country's population supported the New Deal. Forming a new Democratic majority were farmers, recent immigrants, skilled and unskilled workers, northern African Americans, and women. Democrats also received support from the unions. Yet the New Deal was not without its critics, as the next section discusses.

SECTION 1 REVIEW

Key Terms, People, and Places
1. Describe (a) New Deal, (b) hundred days, (c) Wagner Act, (d) Social Security Act.
2. Identify Frances Perkins.

Key Concepts
3. What were some of the ways in which the Roosevelt administration restored hope to the nation?
4. What were some of the first New Deal programs?

5. In what ways did Mary McLeod Bethune seek to help African Americans?
6. What were the most important features of the Second New Deal?

Critical Thinking
7. **Drawing Conclusions** How do you explain the popularity of FDR with American voters?

 RESOURCE DIRECTORY

Teaching Resources

Critical Thinking Activity Recognizing Ideologies: The Role of Government, found in the Unit 7 folder, p. 95, helps students understand the ideology behind the implementation of the Social Security Act in 1935.

Quiz found in the Unit 7 folder, p. 85, covers the main ideas in this section as well as the key terms.

The New Deal's Critics

SECTION 2

The New Deal's Critics

For millions of Americans, the New Deal meant survival, security, and even opportunity. Others, including many women and minorities, noted its failures with bitterness. As the New Deal continued to disappoint, its critics accumulated large followings across the political spectrum.

Key Concepts
• New Deal programs often treated women and minorities unfairly.
• The New Deal was criticized both for what it did and for what it did not do.

Key Terms, People, and Places
political right, political left, demagogue; Father Charles E. Coughlin, Huey Long

---

F ranklin Roosevelt's success at the polls in 1936 suggests overwhelming approval of his New Deal. Indeed, vast numbers of Americans benefited from the relief and employment programs of the New Deal. Letters thanking the President poured into the White House. One example read:

I 'm proud of our United States and every time I hear the "Star-Spangled Banner" I feel a lump in my throat. There ain't no other nation in the world that would have sense enough to think of WPA and all the other A's.

Yet the New Deal had its failures—and inspired its share of critics. Another letter to Roosevelt read:

I f you could get around the country as I have and seen the distress forced upon the American people, you would throw your darn NRA and AAA, and every other . . . A into the sea.

The Limits of the New Deal

For all its success, the New Deal fell short of expectations. The Fair Labor Standards Act, for example, covered fewer than one quarter of all gainfully employed workers and set the minimum wage at twenty-five cents an hour—well below what most covered workers already made. New Deal agencies also were generally less helpful to women and minority groups than they were to white men.

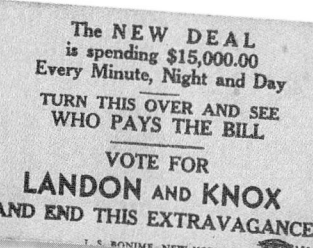

The NEW DEAL is spending $15,000.00 Every Minute, Night and Day
TURN THIS OVER AND SEE WHO PAYS THE BILL
VOTE FOR
LANDON AND KNOX
AND END THIS EXTRAVAGANCE
J. S. BONIME. NEW YORK

Women Many aspects of New Deal legislation put women at a disadvantage. The NRA codes, for example, permitted lower wages for women's work in almost a fourth of all cases. In relief and jobs programs, men and boys received strong preference. Jobs went to male "heads of families," unless the men were unable to work. No New Deal provision protected domestic service, the largest female occupation. In 1942 an African American domestic worker in St. Louis pleaded with the President to ask the "rich people" to "give us some hours to rest in and some Sundays off and pay us more wages." Working fourteen-hour days, she earned only $6.50 per week. An official matter-of-factly wrote back,

S tate and Federal labor laws, which offer protection to workers in so many occupations, have so far not set up standards for working conditions in domestic situations. There is nothing that can be done . . . to help you and others in this kind of employment.

African Americans In the South, federal relief programs reinforced racial segregation. No person of color received a job at a professional level. Segregation prevailed on public works

Millions of Americans benefited from the New Deal. But critics, including FDR's 1936 opponent Alf Landon, were quick to point out the program's problems and shortcomings.

Caption Answer to ...

Using Historical Evidence

All the people in the relief line are African American. The billboard, which trumpets the nation's high standard of living, features only white people.

2. INSTRUCT

Explain/Discuss

Explain that for all its successes, the New Deal did not solve the problems of many people. Ask students in what way the New Deal failed to address the problems of many women and African Americans.

Explain that other people objected to the New Deal because of what it did or did not do. Ask students to describe the opposition from the right and the left, respectively. Discuss the role of anti–New Dealers such as Huey Long and Father Coughlin, and ask students to consider why such demagogues are often effective critics. Then explore the Court-packing scheme. Ask how that episode provoked widespread public disapproval of Roosevelt and damaged his standing in Congress.

WORLD'S HIGHEST STANDARD OF LIVING

There's no way like the American Way

Using Historical Evidence This picture, taken at a relief center in Louisville, Kentucky, highlights the struggle of African Americans to overcome both the Depression and the effects of prejudice. *What elements of this picture contribute to its ironic effect?*

projects, and African Americans received lower pay than whites and were kept from skilled jobs on dam and electric power projects. Because the Social Security Act excluded both farmers and domestic workers, it failed to cover nearly two thirds of working African Americans. ⭐

African Americans in the North had not supported FDR in 1932. By 1936 they had joined his camp. Often the last hired and first fired, they had experienced the highest unemployment rates of any group during the Depression. They therefore appreciated many New Deal programs.

Yet the New Deal did nothing to end distressing discriminatory practices in the North. Especially troubling was the employment of only whites in white-owned businesses in black neighborhoods. In the absence of help from the federal government, African Americans took matters into their own hands. Protesters picketed and boycotted such businesses with the slogan "Don't shop where you can't work."

The early Depression also had seen an alarming rise in the number of lynchings. The federal government again offered no relief. In 1935 and 1938, bills to make lynching a federal crime went down to narrow defeat. NAACP head Walter White recalled in 1948 that FDR had given this explanation for his refusal to support these measures:

S outherners, by reason of seniority rule in Congress, are chairmen or occupy strategic places on most of the Senate and House committees. If I come out for the anti-lynching bill now, they will block every bill I ask Congress to pass to keep America from collapsing. I just can't take that risk.

Of course, FDR's record with African Americans was not all bad. FDR appointed more than a hundred African Americans to policy-making posts. The Roosevelts also conveyed an apparently genuine concern for the fate of African Americans. These factors help to explain FDR's wide support among black voters.

Criticism of the New Deal

African Americans may have supported FDR. But many others, at each end of the political spectrum, criticized the New Deal.

Criticism from the Right The **political right**—typically made up of those who want to preserve a current system or power structure—opposed Roosevelt. These critics included many wealthy people, who regarded FDR as their enemy. Early in the New Deal, they had disapproved of programs such as the TVA,

▶ RESOURCE DIRECTORY

Teaching Resources

 Literature Activity In Search of Work: African Americans, found in the Unit 7 folder, p. 101, uses the characters found in Zora Neale Hurston's novel *Their Eyes Were Watching God* to depict the lives of African American migrant workers.

which they considered to be socialistic. The Second New Deal gave them even more to hate, as FDR pushed through a series of higher taxes aimed at the rich.

The Social Security Act also aroused opposition from the right. Some people felt that it penalized successful, hardworking people. Other critics saw the assignment of social security numbers as the first step toward a militaristic, regimented society. They predicted that soon people would have to wear metal dog tags engraved with their social security numbers.

A group called the American Liberty League (1934) spearheaded much right-wing opposition to the New Deal. It was led by former Democratic presidential candidate Alfred E. Smith, the National Association of Manufacturers, and business figures such as John J. Raskob and the Du Pont family.

The league charged the New Deal with limiting individual freedom in an unconstitutional, "un-American" manner. To them, programs such as compulsory unemployment insurance smacked of "Bolshevism." They advised instead that people take responsibility for themselves and practice "thrift and self-denial."

Socialists and Progressives Others attacked the New Deal from the left. The **political left** generally seeks governmental change—sometimes radical change—as a means of helping the common people. These critics accused the New Deal of not going far enough in addressing the nation's ills.

In 1934 muckraking novelist and socialist Upton Sinclair ran for governor of California on the Democratic ticket. His platform, "End Poverty in California" (EPIC), called for a new economic system in which the state would take over factories and farms. EPIC clubs formed throughout the state, and Sinclair won the primary. Terrified, opponents used dirty tricks to discredit Sinclair. They produced fake newsreels showing people speaking in a Russian accent and endorsing Sinclair. Associated unfairly with Soviet communism, Sinclair lost the election.

The limited success of the New Deal in eliminating poverty helped lead to a revival of progressivism in Minnesota and Wisconsin. Running for the United States Senate, Wisconsin progressive Robert La Follette, Jr., argued that "devices which seek to preserve the unequal distribution of wealth . . . will halt the progress of mankind and, in the end, will retard or prevent recovery." His brother, Philip, also took a radical stand, calling for the redistribution of income. Philip's ideas persuaded the state Socialist party to join his progressives after he won the Wisconsin governorship in 1934.

MAKING CONNECTIONS

Consider what you have read about the poverty caused by the Depression. Do you agree with the criticisms of the political left or the political right? Explain why.

Using Historical Evidence The artist who created this cartoon had little faith that FDR's New Deal programs were in the country's best interest. *What is it that has put the "patient" to sleep? What does the cartoon imply will happen when the "patient" wakes up?*

UNCLE "GUINEA PIG"

NEW DEAL CLINIC

TRY OUT YOUR EXPERIMENT BEFORE THE PATIENT WAKES UP.

IT'S MY TURN AFTER YOU!

I HOPE THEY DON'T WEAR HIM OUT BEFORE I HAVE A CHANCE TO TRY MY EXPERIMENT.

NEW DEALER

U.S.A.

ETHER PROPAGANDA

Copyright, 1934, by The Chicago Tribune.

Caption Answer to ...

Using Historical Evidence

The patient (the country) has been put to sleep by government propaganda. The cartoon implies that when the country "wakes up," it will no longer tolerate the New Deal's experimental programs.

Answer to ...

MAKING CONNECTIONS

Answers will vary. Encourage students to compare the political rhetoric of an era with the known facts.

Analyze

Ask students to analyze the difficulties of forging government programs that provide equal benefit and satisfaction to all citizens. Have students consider what limits the democratic process places on the ability of a government to implement broad new programs, such as universal health care.

In Depth

Multicultural Perspectives

Many African Americans felt left out by the New Deal and turned to the Communist party. Hosea Hudson, for example, an African American farmer from rural Georgia, joined the party. Angered by the 1931 case of the Scottsboro Boys (see page 623), Hudson organized unemployed African Americans in Birmingham, Alabama, to meet weekly and discuss social issues. The Communist party's legal arm, the International Labor Defense (ILD) defended the Scottsboro Boys.

Other New Deal Critics

Some New Deal critics were **demagogues**—charismatic leaders who manipulate people with half-truths, deceptive promises, and scare tactics. One such demagogue was **Father Charles E. Coughlin,** who used the radio to broadcast his message. In the early 1930s, the so-called Radio Priest was holding national audiences spellbound.

Coughlin achieved popularity in spite of the fact that his ideas were not consistent. Sometimes he advocated nationalizing the banks and redistributing wealth. At others, he defended the sanctity of private property. After first endorsing the New Deal, in 1934 he formed a "National Union for Social Justice," which denounced it. His increasing attacks on FDR grew reckless. In 1936 he called Franklin "Double-crossing" Roosevelt a "great betrayer and liar."

By the end of the 1930s, Coughlin was issuing openly anti-Semitic statements and showering praise on Adolf Hitler and Benito Mussolini, two menacing leaders who were then rising to power in Europe. Coughlin's actions alarmed many, and he lost some of his support. In the early 1940s, Roman Catholic officials ordered him to cease his broadcasts.

Huey Long—also known as the Kingfish—was a different type of demagogue. A country lawyer, he won the governorship of Louisiana in 1928 and became a United States senator in 1932. Unlike many other southern Democrats, Long never used racial attacks as the basis of his power. Instead, he worked to help the underprivileged, improving education, medical care, and public services. He also built an extraordinarily powerful and ruthless political machine.

Huey Long (below) achieved great popularity in the 1930s with his motto, "Every man a king." He had his eye on the presidency before his assassination.

Originally a supporter of FDR, he broke with him early in the New Deal. "Unless we provide for redistribution of wealth in this country, the country is doomed," he said. Calling his program "Share Our Wealth" (SOW) and using the motto "Every man a king," Long in 1934 proposed high taxes on large fortunes and inheritances, and grants of $5,000 to each American family.

Long's overly simplistic plan for helping all Americans achieve wealth attracted many followers. His success helped push FDR to propose new taxes on wealthy Americans in the Second New Deal. Meanwhile, Long began to eye the presidency. But in September 1935, the son-in-law of one of his political enemies shot and killed him.

Long and Coughlin never seriously threatened FDR or the New Deal. But their popularity warned Roosevelt that if he failed to spread the country's wealth more widely, he risked losing popular support.

The Court-Packing Scheme

⭐ Roosevelt received criticism not only for his programs, but also for his actions. No act aroused more opposition than his attempt to pack the Supreme Court.

Throughout the early New Deal, the Supreme Court had caused FDR his greatest frustration. The Court, which included four conservative justices, had invalidated the NRA, the AAA, and many state laws from the progressive era. In February 1937, FDR proposed a major court reform bill.

The Constitution had not specified the number of Supreme Court justices. Congress had last changed the number in 1869. But by Roosevelt's time, the number nine had become well established. Arguing dishonestly that he wanted to lighten the burden of the aging justices, FDR asked Congress to pass his reform, enabling him to appoint as many as six additional justices, one for each justice over seventy years of age. Most people understood Roosevelt's real intention. He wanted to "pack" the Court with judges favorable to the New Deal.

Negative reaction came swiftly from all sides. The President, critics raged, was trying to inject politics into the judiciary and was attacking the constitutional principle of separation of powers. With Hitler, Mussolini, and Stalin ruling as dictators in Germany, Italy, and the Soviet Union, the world seemed already to be tilting toward tyranny. If Congress let FDR reshape the Supreme Court, critics worried, the United States might follow. Sam E. Roberts of Kansas wrote his representative in Congress:

Our liberty is much more important than any whim of the President's. He might be a kind dictator himself, but after the stage is set the next President might be a Hitler or Mussolini.

California's aging senator Hiram W. Johnson expressed the views of many legislators when he said:

Shall the Congress make the Supreme Court subservient to [subject to] the presidency? The implications of this are so grave and far-reaching, I can do but one thing, and that is, . . . oppose this extraordinary legislation.

FDR was forced to withdraw his reform. He also suffered much political damage. Southern Democrats and conservative Republicans united against further New Deal legislation. This alliance remained a force for years to come.

FDR did wind up with a liberal majority on the Court. Some older justices retired, allowing FDR to appoint his own justices. Even earlier, the Court had begun to uphold measures from the Second New Deal, including the Wagner Act—perhaps because the laws had been better thought out and drafted.

Viewpoints
On The New Deal

FDR's promise to improve life for all Americans with a New Deal did not win approval from all quarters. *Why, according to the viewpoints below, were some people pleased and some displeased with the New Deal?*

For the New Deal

"Roosevelt is the only President we ever had that thought the Constitution belonged to the pore [poor] man too. . . . Yessir, it took Roosevelt to read in the Constitution and find out them folks way back yonder that made it was talkin' about the pore man right along with the rich one. I am a Roosevelt man."

Testimony by mill worker George Dobbin, 1939. Collected in *These Are Our Lives,* Federal Writers Project of the Works Progress Administration (1939).

Against the New Deal

"All the prosperity he had brought to the country has been legislated and is not real. Nothing he has ever started has been finished. My common way of expressing it is that we are in the middle of the ocean like a ship without an anchor. No good times can come to the country as long as there is so much discrimination practiced. . . . I don't see much chance for our people to get anywhere when the color line instead of ability determines the opportunities to get ahead economically."

Testimony by Sam T. Mayhew, 1939. Collected in *Such As Us* (1978).

SECTION 2 REVIEW

Key Terms, People, and Places
1. Define (a) political right, (b) political left, (c) demagogue.
2. Identify (a) Father Charles E. Coughlin, (b) Huey Long.

Key Concepts
3. How did New Deal programs discriminate against or neglect women and minorities?
4. Why did people criticize FDR and the New Deal?

5. What was Franklin Roosevelt's attitude toward African American concerns about lynching?

Critical Thinking
6. **Checking Consistency** The text says that Roosevelt had critics at both ends of the political spectrum during the New Deal. Yet Roosevelt was easily reelected in 1936. How do you explain these two apparently conflicting facts?

Viewpoints Activity On the New Deal, found in the Unit 7 folder, pp. 92–93, expands the discussion with extended quotations for and against the New Deal.

Quiz found in the Unit 7 folder, p. 87, covers the main ideas in this section as well as the key terms.

5. He told the head of the NAACP that he could not support federal antilynching bills for fear of losing the support of southern Democrats for New Deal programs.

6. Possible answer: Roosevelt had many critics, but the vast majority of people supported his ideas. In other words, Roosevelt's critics did not attract significant mainstream support.

Answer to ...

Viewpoints

Dobbin supports the New Deal because it addresses the problems of working people like himself; Mayhew thinks the New Deal legislation falls short of inclusion of African Americans. For a more thorough examination of New Deal legislation, see the Resource Directory below.

Reteach

Ask students to construct a two-column chart that identifies conservative critics of the New Deal in one column and the reasons behind their criticisms in the other; then have them create a similar chart identifying the liberals who criticized FDR and their reasons for doing so.

4. CLOSE

Reinforcing the Big Idea

President Roosevelt and the New Deal faced many criticisms, from all points along the political spectrum. The next section examines how the New Deal left a permanent mark on the United States in spite of its inability to end the Depression.

Critical Thinking

Distinguishing Fact from Opinion

Focus Analyze a speaker's use of facts and opinions in a political speech.

Instruct Divide students into small groups to examine the speech and identify the various facts and opinions used by the speaker. Ask each group to report its findings. If groups draw different conclusions about which statements are facts and which are opinions, have the whole class discuss the examples. Then ask students whether or not they think the speaker in this case has made an effective argument. What facts might he have used to strengthen his points? Which statements of opinion were effective? Why?

Extend See the Historian's Toolbox Activity in the Resource Directory below.

Answers

1. (a) The decisions of the Supreme Court are matters of public record and can thus be easily verified. (b) Possible answer: The statements about the growth of the national debt and the growth in the number of public officials are facts, which can be checked in public records.

2. (a) It winds up a sweeping accusation of the executive and the Congress. (b) Possible answer: The charge that the Congress has abandoned its responsibility and that New Deal developments have polluted the fountain of liberty are both opinions.

3. (a) He states that they were overthrown by the Supreme Court, the guardian of constitutional rights. (b) No, he gives no specific examples—just makes a sweeping accusation. (c) Students may be divided on how well or badly he has done, according to their own views of what government should and should not do.

Distinguishing Fact from Opinion

When you read historical materials—such as speeches, letters, and diaries—you will find that their authors express both facts and opinions. A fact is something that can be proved to be true by checking other sources. An opinion is a judgment that reflects beliefs or feelings—it may or may not be true.

To determine the soundness of an author's ideas, you need to be able to distinguish between fact and opinion. The ability to do so will help you evaluate what you read and reach your own conclusions about historical events.

Use the following steps to distinguish between fact and opinion in Herbert Hoover's criticism of the New Deal, excerpted from his speech to the Republican National Convention in 1936.

1. Determine which statements are facts. Remember that facts can be checked and confirmed by other sources. (a) For what reason is Hoover's first statement, about the Supreme Court, easily recognizable as a fact? (b) Choose two other statements of fact in the excerpt. Explain how you might prove that each statement is a fact.

2. Determine which statements are opinions. Sometimes authors signal opinions with phrases such as "I believe" or "I think," but often they do not. Other clues that indicate opinions are sweeping generalizations and emotion-packed words. (a) What indicates that the final sentence of the

first paragraph is an opinion rather than a fact? (b) Choose two other statements of opinion, and explain what tells you that they are opinions.

3. Separate facts from opinions as you read. Generally, an opinion is more reliable when an author gives facts to support it. (a) How does Hoover support his opinion that many New Deal acts "were a violation of the rights of men and of self-government"? (b) Does he present any facts to support his statement that the Congress has "abandoned its responsibility"? (c) In your opinion, how good a job has Hoover done in supporting his opinions? Explain your answer.

"The Supreme Court has reversed some ten or twelve of the New Deal major enactments. Many of these acts were a violation of the rights of men and of self-government. Despite the sworn duty of the Executive and Congress to defend these rights, they have sought to take them into their own hands. That is an attack on the foundations of freedom.

More than this, the independence of the Congress, the Supreme Court, and the Executive are pillars at the door of liberty. For three years the word "must" has invaded the independence of Congress. And the Congress has abandoned its responsibility to check even the expenditures [spending] of money. . . .

We have seen these gigantic expenditures and this torrent of waste pile up a national debt which two generations cannot repay. One time I told a Democratic Congress that "You cannot spend your way into prosperity." You recall that advice did not take then. It hasn't taken yet.

Billions have been spent to prime the economic pump. It did employ a horde of paid officials upon the pump handle. We have seen the frantic attempts to find new taxes on the rich. Yet three-quarters of the bill will be sent to the average man and the poor. He and his wife and his grandchildren will be giving a quarter of all their working days to pay taxes. Freedom to work for himself is changed into a slavery of work for the follies of government. . . .

We have seen the building up of a horde of political officials. We have seen the pressures upon the helpless and destitute to trade political support for relief. Both are a pollution of the very fountains of liberty."

—Herbert Hoover, excerpted from
American Ideals Versus the New Deal

 RESOURCE DIRECTORY

Teaching Resources

Historian's Toolbox Activity Distinguishing Fact from Opinion, found in the Unit 7 folder, p. 94, gives students further opportunity to apply this skill by evaluating President Bush's address to Congress after Iraq's 1990 invasion of Kuwait.

Enduring Legacies of the New Deal

SECTION PREVIEW

The New Deal attacked the Great Depression with a barrage of programs and agencies. The Depression withstood this onslaught and refused to loosen its grip on the economy. Yet the New Deal was not without effect; it left a legacy that endures to this day.

Key Concepts
• The New Deal did not resolve the economic problems of the Depression.
• The New Deal did leave a significant legacy that has affected the presidency, labor unions, and American cultural life.

Key Terms, People, and Places
national debt, Congress of Industrial Organizations, sit-down strike

---

The New Deal did not attempt truly radical solutions to the problems of the American economy in the 1930s. Neither did it end the nation's suffering. It did, however, lead to some profound and lasting changes in American politics and social life.

FDR and the New Deal increased the public's expectations of the presidency. Voters began to expect a President to formulate programs and solve problems. Government now was authorized to intervene in major ways, and business could no longer resist regulation—or unionization—with claims about the sanctity of private property.

In addition to its effects on the economy, the New Deal also helped enhance American cultural life. Americans of the 1930s—and of future generations—were entertained and enriched due to programs aimed at helping artists.

The Recession of 1937

The New Deal did not put an end to the Great Depression. As predicted by economist John Maynard Keynes (see Chapter 22), the New Deal's massive government spending did lead to some economic improvement. But the economy collapsed again in August 1937, as you can see on the graph on page 654.

Reductions in consumer income from social security payroll deductions were partly to blame. Americans had less money in their pockets, and so bought fewer goods. Consumers also had less money because FDR had cut back on programs such as the WPA. The President—who campaigned in 1932 with a promise to balance the budget—had become distressed at the rising **national debt.** This is the total amount of money the federal government has borrowed and has yet to pay back. Because the government spent more than it took in, the debt rose from $21 billion in 1933 to $43 billion by 1940.

After 1937, Harry Hopkins and others convinced FDR to start up the suspended programs in 1938. Joblessness and misery slowly decreased. Still, hard times lasted well into the 1940s, until the nation's entry into World War II.

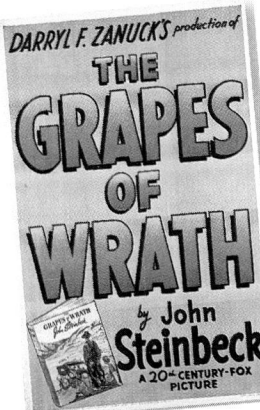

The Depression era produced many lasting works of art, including the novel *The Grapes of Wrath* and the movie that was based on it.

The Triumph of the Labor Unions

By legalizing unions, the New Deal permanently changed the relations between workers and employers in America. Union membership rose from 3 million in 1933 to 10.5 million by 1941, a figure representing 28 percent of the nonagricultural work force. By 1945, 36 percent were unionized, the high-water mark for unions in the United States.

A New Labor Organization Activism by powerful union leaders helped to increase membership. The cautious and craft-based American Federation of Labor (AFL) had done

1. FOCUS

Connecting to the Big Idea

See page 638B. Point out that the New Deal did not succeed in ending the Depression but that it did have a great impact on the nation's political, social, and cultural life. Ask students how that impact is felt today.

Objectives
● Explain that the New Deal did not resolve the economic problems of the Depression.
● Identify the ways in which the New Deal had a lasting effect on the presidency, labor unions, and American cultural life.

Bellringer
Write the words *federal government* on the chalkboard. Ask students to brainstorm a list of words they associate with the term. Explain that many modern attitudes and beliefs concerning the government stem from the New Deal era.

Reading Strategy
Structured Outline Have students take notes on the following topics as they read the section:
● The New Deal's impact on the Depression
● The New Deal and labor
● Cultural life in the 1930s
● Lasting monuments of the New Deal

Reproducible Lesson Plan found in the Unit 7 folder, p. 83, provides a summary of the Section 3 lesson plan content.

Alternate Lesson Plan: Cooperative Learning found in the Alternate Lesson Plans folder, p. 120, provides a strategy for groups of students to prepare presentations explaining the enduring legacy of the New Deal on different aspects of American life.

Guided Reading and Review found in the Unit 7 folder, p. 88, provides a structure for reading and mastering the key concepts and reviewing the key terms for Section 3. (Guided Practice)

2. INSTRUCT

Explain/Discuss

Explain that the New Deal did not by itself resolve the problems that were causing the Depression. Ask students what the Recession of 1937 revealed about the New Deal and the economy.

Discuss the real changes that the New Deal did introduce to the nation. Ask students to describe changes affecting labor unions. Ask them to consider the role of government in helping to make union gains possible.

Discuss government support for the arts as an important part of the New Deal. Ask students to discuss the benefits and drawbacks of government funding of art.

In Depth

Interdisciplinary

Technological developments changed the culture of this period. Specifically, the integration of sound with moving pictures revitalized the motion picture industry (see page 597). Adding sound was first accomplished by using a sound-on-film synchronization system, Phonofilm, patented by Lee DeForest in 1919. By 1933, when techniques had been developed to eliminate camera noise from recordings, improve microphones (so that actors could move while they spoke), and edit a soundtrack, all of the major studios had converted to sound, increasing their profits by 600 percent.

Federal Public Debt, 1933–1940

Source: *Historical Statistics of the United States*

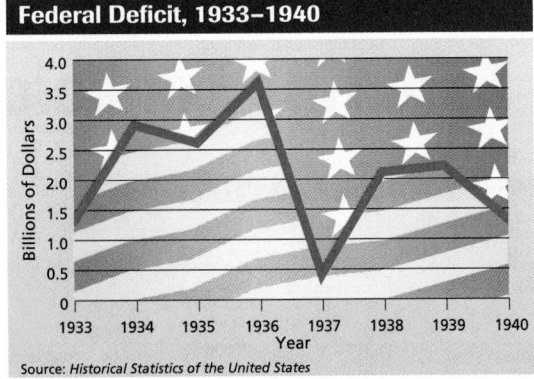

Federal Deficit, 1933–1940

Source: *Historical Statistics of the United States*

Interpreting Graphs
The New Deal was paid for by huge increases in government spending. Because of yearly deficits, the national debt expanded greatly during the Depression. *In which year was the deficit the greatest? The lowest?*

little to attract unskilled industrial workers during its half-century of existence. In 1935 United Mine Workers president John L. Lewis, whose bushy eyebrows made him a familiar front-page figure, joined with other AFL unions to create a Committee for Industrial Organizations (CIO) within the AFL. Though the AFL did not support its efforts, the CIO sought to organize the nation's unskilled workers. It sent organizers into steel mills, auto plants, and southern textile mills and welcomed all workers regardless of sex, color, or skill. The AFL suspended the CIO unions in 1936. Nevertheless, by 1938 the CIO had two million members. The group then changed its name to the **Congress of Industrial Organizations** and in November of that year it formed a new union.

Thanks in part to the Wagner Act and the efforts of the CIO, union membership soared in the 1930s. By 1939, nearly 30 percent of nonagricultural workers belonged to unions.

An Era of Strikes The Wagner Act legalized collective bargaining and told management it had to bargain in good faith with certified union representatives. But the act could not force a company to accept union demands. Although the Wagner Act was designed to bring about industrial peace, in the short run it led to a wave of some of the country's most spectacular strikes.

Many of these work stoppages were known as **sit-down strikes,** in which workers stopped work and refused to leave the premises. Supporters outside then organized picket lines. Together the strikers and the picket line prevented the company from bringing in scabs, or substitute workers, and the business was paralyzed.

Sit-down strikes began in the rubber tire plants in Akron, Ohio. The most famous took place in the winter of 1936 to 1937 in Flint, Michigan. In this strike, workers associated with the United Auto Workers (UAW) occupied General Motors' Fisher body plants. GM executives turned off the heat and blocked entry to the plants so that the workers could not receive food. They also sent in police against picketers outside. Violence erupted. The wife of a striker then grabbed a bullhorn and urged other wives to join the picketers. The group became so large that the police could not control them. Women later organized food deliveries to supply the strikers, set up a speakers' bureau to present the union's position to the public, and formed a Women's Emergency Brigade to take up picket duty. Governor Frank Murphy of Michigan and President Roosevelt refused to use the militia against the strike. By

▶ RESOURCE DIRECTORY

Teaching Resources

⭐ **American Profiles Activity** found in the Unit 7 folder, p. 90, profiles Emma Tenayuca, a prominent labor organizer and community activist of the 1930s.

✪ **Literature Activity** In Search of Work: Migrant Farmers, found in the Unit 7 folder, pp. 99–100, uses an excerpt from John Steinbeck's *The Grapes of Wrath* to illustrate the plight of tenant farmers in the Depression and the harsh realities of a nation divided into economic classes.

early February, General Motors had given in.

Not all strikes were as successful. Henry Ford continued to resist unionism. In 1937 at a Ford plant near Detroit, his men viciously beat UAW officials when the unionists tried to distribute leaflets. Walter Reuther, a beating victim and future president of the UAW later testified,

> They picked me up about eight different times and threw me down on my back on the concrete. While I was on the ground they kicked me in the face, head, and other parts of my body. . . . I never raised a hand.

Like the Ford Company, Republic Steel Company refused to sign with steelworkers' unions until war loomed in 1941. At one bloody strike at Republic Steel on Memorial Day 1937, Chicago police killed ten picketers. Southern textile workers and clerical workers, both made up primarily of women, also remained unorganized in spite of New Deal efforts.

Cultural Life in the Thirties

Hard times stimulated a great release of creative energy in the United States during the Depression. In addition, Congress allocated federal funds to support the popular and fine arts. As a result, despite general unemployment among professionals, the arts not only thrived but created some enduring cultural legacies for the nation.

Literature Works of literature destined to become classics emerged during this period. Three examples are Pearl Buck's *The Good Earth* (1931), a saga of peasant struggle in China; John Steinbeck's *The Grapes of Wrath* (1939), a powerful tale about dust-bowl victims who travel to California; and Margaret Mitchell's fictional re-creation of the Old South, *Gone With the Wind* (1936). In 1936 Tennessee writer James Agee and photographer Walker Evans lived for a few

weeks with sharecropper families in Alabama and produced a masterpiece of nonfiction literature, *Let Us Now Praise Famous Men* (1941). Folklorist Zora Neale Hurston wrote the classic *Their Eyes Are Watching God* (1937), a novel about an African American woman in Florida.

Radio and Movies Radio became the major medium of entertainment for most American families. In particular, comedy shows peaked in the thirties, producing stars such as Jack Benny, Fred Allen, George Burns, and Gracie Allen. The first soap operas—so called because they often were sponsored by soap companies—emerged in this period. These fifteen-minute stories designed to promote strong emotional responses were aimed at women who remained at home during the day. Symphony music and opera also thrived over the radio. By 1939 the country boasted 270 symphony orchestras.

By 1933 the movies had recovered from the initial setback caused by the early Depression. For a quarter, customers could see a double feature (introduced in 1931) or take the whole family to a drive-in (1933). Federal agencies used motion pictures to publicize their work. The Farm Security Administration, for example, produced classic documentaries of American agricultural life.

Some Hollywood studios concentrated on optimistic films about common people who

The successful sit-down strike at the Fisher body plant in the winter of 1936–37 demonstrated the effectiveness of the new technique. Here, workers guard a window during the strike.

Analyze

Ask students to analyze the ways in which the New Deal's impact can still be felt. Based on these considerations, ask students to carry out a critical evaluation of the success and/or failure of the New Deal. What parts of the New Deal legacy do they value?

Activity
Cooperative Learning

Time: One or two class periods.
Activity: Create a newspaper special edition about the New Deal.
Grouping: Groups of four to six students.
Purpose: To have students create a newspaper that highlights the major people and events of the New Deal. The newspaper could include such features as news stories about New Deal programs or developments, profiles of key personnel, political cartoons about people or events, and an editorial.
Roles: Cartoonist, editorial writer, reporters, layout and production designers.
Outcome: Students will understand the importance of prominent people and events of the New Deal.

In Depth

Then and Now

Labor unions in the 1930s exhibited formidable strength and identified clearly the issues that brought them political influence. In the 1990s, labor's power and reach have diminished considerably, as demonstrated in November, 1993, when Congress passed the North American Free Trade Agreement (NAFTA). This measure was enacted over the protestations of organized labor, which feared American jobs would move to Mexico as a result.

Answers will vary. Encourage students to defend their positions.

Enrichment

Ask students to investigate the social security system of the United States today. Students might gather information about benefits, numbers of people receiving benefits, and budget. Students should contact a local social security office and consult government documents at a library.

3. ASSESS

Section 3 Review Answers

1. (a) national debt, see p. 653, (b) Congress of Industrial Organizations, see p. 654, (c) sit-down strike, see p. 654

2. It did not fundamentally change the structure of the economy, nor did it end the Depression. Some of its programs, such as social security, offered limited benefits. But it brought more security to ordinary citizens and introduced more government regulation into the economy.

3. The social security program took money out of circulation. Also, FDR scaled back many spending programs out of concern over the rising deficit.

4. The Wagner Act legalized collective bargaining and outlawed unfair labor practices. This strengthened union membership. The CIO was formed, and a series of sit-down strikes succeeded in bringing industry management to the bargaining table.

5. Federal programs supported the arts, the collection of historical materials, and literature, heralding a period of intense creativity in American cultural life.

6. Possible answers: Though the New Deal did not solve all the nation's problems, it did help people feel better about their lives and the future; the major positive effect of the New Deal—the uplifting of American morale—could have been accomplished without significant government spending.

triumphed over evil, such as Warner Brothers' *Mr. Smith Goes to Washington* (1939). In this era, the zany Marx Brothers produced such comic classics as *Monkey Business* (1931) and *Duck Soup* (1933). The greatest box-office hits were escapist, such as the gangster films that memorialized the prohibition era and the musicals featuring large orchestras and exquisitely choreographed dancers in luxurious costumes. No one understood the needs of Depression-era audiences better than Walt Disney, whose Mickey Mouse cartoons delighted moviegoers everywhere. Classics such as *Snow White and the Seven Dwarfs* (1937) and *The Wizard of Oz* (1939) came out in this period, as well as Charlie Chaplin's satire of capitalist society and its efficiency, *Modern Times* (1936).

In spite of the poverty of the Depression, cultural life bloomed in the 1930s. Charlie Chaplin's classic *Modern Times*, a satire about work in a modern factory, was released in 1936.

The WPA and the Arts FDR believed that the arts were not luxuries that people should give up in hard times. He thus earmarked WPA funds to support unemployed artists, musicians, historians, theater people, and writers. The Federal Writers' Project assisted more than six thousand writers, such as Richard Wright, Saul Bellow, Margaret Walker, and Ralph Ellison. Historians surveyed the nation's local government records, wrote state guidebooks, and collected life stories from about two thousand former slaves. Without this project, their stories would have been lost.

Other projects supported music and the visual arts. The Federal Music Project started community symphonies, organized free music lessons, and sent musicologists to lumber camps, prisons, and small towns to record a fast-disappearing folk heritage. The Federal Art Project hired artists to paint murals in the nation's public buildings. ✪

The Federal Theatre Project (FTP), directed by Vassar College professor Hallie Flanagan, was the most controversial. Flanagan used drama to create awareness of social problems. Her project launched the careers of many actors, play-

wrights, and directors who later became famous including Burt Lancaster, Arthur Miller, John Houseman, and Orson Welles.

Accusing the FTP of being a propaganda machine for international communism, the House of Representatives' Un-American Activities Committee (HUAC) investigated the project in 1938 and 1939. In July 1939 Congress killed the FTP appropriation.

Americans still debate the role of government in funding the arts. In your opinion, should government pay to support art that criticizes it or offends certain taxpayers? Explain.

Lasting New Deal Monuments

The great public works of the Depression era—the bridges, dams, tunnels, public buildings, sewage systems, port facilities, and hospitals—remind us of this extraordinary period of government support for the national welfare. Constructed with great efficiency and durability, they stand to this day. In national and state parks and on mountain trails and oceanfront walks, Americans still reap advantages from the restoration and conservation work of the Civilian Conservation Corps.

Some of the federal agencies from the New Deal era have endured. The Tennessee Valley Authority remains a model of government planning. The Federal Deposit Insurance Corporation still guarantees bank deposits. The Securities and Exchange Commission continues to monitor the workings of the stock exchange. And in rural America, farmers still plant according to federal crop allotment strategies, which were put in place to conserve soil and reduce acreage after the Supreme Court struck down AAA crop reduction plans.

Social Security Almost everyone in the United States has come to depend on the social security system. Few people today seriously question its place in American society.

Over the years, however, social security has had many critics. You read about some of these

RESOURCE DIRECTORY

Teaching Resources

✪ **American Profiles Activity** found in the Unit 7 folder, p. 91, profiles Jacob Lawrence, one of the finest artists in the WPA Federal Arts Project, and long considered the foremost African American painter of his time.

critics in Section 2. Others attacked social security because, at first, payments were very low, and the program excluded millions of farmers, domestic workers, and the self-employed. For a long time the system discriminated against women. It assumed, for example, that the male-headed household was typical. A mother could lose benefits for her children if a man, whether providing support for her or not, lived in her house. Women who went to work when their children started school rarely stayed in the work force long enough or earned high enough wages to receive the maximum benefits from the system.

In addition, unlike every other industrialized country in the world except South Africa, the American social security system did not guarantee health insurance for all citizens. For decades this omission prompted calls for further legislation. Only recently has the executive branch of the government begun to tackle this problem.

A Legacy of Hope

In August 1939, Mrs. Renee Lohrback of San Antonio, Texas, wrote a sad letter to Eleanor Roosevelt. Lohrback was a typist who could not find work. Four children depended on her. The WPA had rejected her work application because she had a three-month-old baby to care for. The entire family lived in one damp basement room. Wrote Lohrback:

M rs. Roosevelt, I'm begging you with all my heart to please help me if you can. I love my babies dearly and won't sub-

Government support for the arts led to many lasting works, including this mural painted by Thomas Hart Benton in 1930 for the New School of Social Research in New York City. Audrey McMahon, New York director of the WPA, said: "We did the best we could, and that best was very good."

mit to them being put in a home away from me. I would simply die apart from them.

This letter was typical of thousands both Eleanor and Franklin Roosevelt received daily in the late Depression era. As the letter indicates, personal suffering continued in the late 1930s, and people still despaired. But as the above letter also suggests, in their desperation people were now looking to their government for support. Indeed, government programs did mean the difference between survival and starvation for millions of Americans.

Shortly after Mrs. Lohrback wrote her letter, the event that would ultimately bring a lasting recovery to the United States was set in motion on the battlefields of Europe. Several years would pass before that recovery would reach the United States. When it did arrive, it came in the form of another tremendous test of the character of the United States: world war.

SECTION 3 REVIEW

Key Terms, People, and Places
1. Define (a) national debt, (b) Congress of Industrial Organizations, (c) sit-down strike.

Key Concepts
2. What effect did the New Deal have on the American economy?
3. What factors contributed to the economic collapse of 1937?

4. In what sense did labor unions triumph in the thirties?
5. What was the impact of the New Deal on American cultural life?

Critical Thinking
6. **Identifying Central Issues** In your opinion, was the New Deal a success or a failure? Explain, citing information from the chapter.

 Quiz found in the Unit 7 folder, p. 89, covers the main ideas in this section as well as the key terms.

 Chapter Test Forms A and B are found in the Unit 7 folder, pp. 104–109.

 Answer Key found in the Unit 7 folder, pp. 116–125.

Media and Technology

Transparency
Graphic Organizer, G-3

Guided Reading Audiotapes
(English and Spanish)

Computer Test Bank

Reteach
Ask students to identify and correct the errors in the sentences below:
- The New Deal brought an end to the Depression by the late 1930s.
- In spite of government support, unions failed to grow in the 1930s because of a lack of strong leadership.
- The New Deal helped Depression victims, but otherwise it had little impact on the nation.

  4. CLOSE

Reinforcing the Big Idea

The New Deal failed to bring an end to the Depression. Yet it helped bring about many important developments, whose impact can still be felt.

In Depth

Historical Misconceptions

It would be a mistake to assume that public confidence in FDR was unqualified. Many Americans considered FDR a power-hungry dictator who set a dangerous precedent by serving four terms, thus violating the unwritten rule against more than two terms. In 1947 the Eightieth Congress, which according to historian Daniel Boorstin "was really attacking the New Deal and the four-term President, FDR," passed the Twenty-second Amendment to limit any President to two terms in office.

Chapter Review Answers

Understanding Key Terms, People, and Places

Terms
Students should refer to the definitions of the key terms in the chapter to write sentences that show the relation of each word to the New Deal or the legacies of the New Deal.

True or False
1. false, political left
2. false, public works programs
3. true
4. false, Wagner Act
5. true

Matching
1. Huey Long
2. Frances Perkins
3. Mary McLeod Bethune
4. Father Charles E. Coughlin

Reviewing Main Ideas

1. FDR was confident, optimistic, energetic, and willing to experiment.

2. Public works programs such as the CWA, CCC, and TVA put the unemployed to work building, repairing, or improving public facilities. They raised morale and provided incomes for many hitherto jobless people. The facilities that were built also benefited the nation.

3. The Second New Deal attacked joblessness more aggressively, turned attention toward the worsening plight of agricultural workers, and included more social welfare benefits, stricter controls over business, stronger support for unions, and higher taxes on the rich.

4. The New Deal was a limited success for women and minorities.

5. Those on the right saw some New Deal programs as socialistic and "un-American." They also believed that the Social Security Act penalized people for success and hard work.

6. The Supreme Court had struck down some New Deal programs, such as the NRA. Roosevelt's plan aroused great opposition, forcing him to withdraw his proposed reform. In the end, however, he was able to appoint some new justices when older justices retired; in addition, the Court had begun to uphold measures of the Second New Deal.

7. It indicated that although the New Deal had helped alleviate suffering, it had not solved the nation's economic problems.

8. People began to expect the President to intervene in major ways, formulate programs, and solve problems.

Chapter Review

Understanding Key Terms, People, and Places

Key Terms
1. New Deal
2. hundred days
3. public works program
4. Wagner Act
5. Social Security Act
6. political right
7. political left
8. demagogue
9. national debt
10. Congress of Industrial Organizations
11. sit-down strike

People
12. Frances Perkins
13. Mary McLeod Bethune
14. Father Charles E. Coughlin
15. Huey Long

Terms For each term above, write a sentence that explains its relation to the New Deal or the legacies of the New Deal.

True or False Determine whether each statement is true or false. If it is true, write "true." If it is false, change the underlined term to make the statement true.
1. People on the <u>political right</u> accused Roosevelt's social programs of not going far enough in addressing the nation's problems.
2. The first <u>Congress of Industrial Organizations</u> employed the jobless to build or improve roads, parks, airports, and other public facilities.
3. Some critics of Roosevelt's programs were <u>demagogues</u> who manipulated people's emotions.
4. The <u>Social Security Act</u> legalized closed shops and collective bargaining.
5. President Roosevelt's <u>New Deal</u> programs provided jobs and improved the quality of life for some Americans.

Matching Review the key people in the list above. If you are not sure of a person's importance, review his or her significance in the chapter. Then choose a person from the list who best matches each description below.
1. a southern Democrat, known as the Kingfish, who called for the redistribution of wealth
2. the first woman to hold a cabinet post
3. the person who held the highest position of any African American woman in the New Deal
4. the radio broadcaster who first supported and then opposed the New Deal

Reviewing Main Ideas

Section 1 (pp. 640–646)
1. What characteristics of FDR's personality helped inspire hope in the American people?
2. Briefly describe the New Deal's public works programs and their purpose.
3. Explain how the Second New Deal differed from the original New Deal.

Section 2 (pp. 647–651)
4. For which groups in particular was the New Deal of limited success?
5. What was the basis of the political right's opposition to the New Deal?

6. Why did FDR want to pack the Supreme Court? Describe the consequences of his plan, citing details to support your statements.

Section 3 (pp. 653–657)
7. What did the Recession of 1937 indicate about the success of the New Deal?
8. What was the impact of the New Deal on the public's expectations of the presidency?
9. What permanent changes occurred for labor unions as a result of the New Deal?
10. Briefly describe the cultural impact of the New Deal, citing examples to support your description.

---

9. Because the New Deal legalized unions, relations between workers and employers were permanently changed, and unions became more powerful.

10. The New Deal gave financial support to the arts, facilitating the creation of many lasting artistic works. The era also produced many classics in literature and film.

Thinking Critically

1. Possible answer: People now expect government to be able to provide a basic standard of living for almost all citizens, regardless of the reasons for their inability to provide for themselves.

2. The fact that voters were willing to follow "bold, consistent experimentation" suggests that people were desperate for any possible relief from the Depression. Although some people vote solely for change in every election, the national readiness to accept such radical measures indicates that the mood of the country must have been desperate. Answers to the second question will vary.

3. ER perceived herself as taking an active role in alleviating suffering and promoting programs. Several contemporary First Ladies, such as Rosalyn Carter and Hillary Rodham Clinton, have also taken assertive roles in public life.

Final Evaluation
Use the following guidelines to evaluate student projects:
● **Evidence of thoughtfulness** To
what extent do projects demonstrate
an understanding of the New Deal,
its limitations, and its legacy?
● **Evidence of outside research** To
what extent do projects reflect use of
outside research materials?
● **Evidence of sensitivity** To what
extent do projects reflect an increased
awareness of government's power to
affect people, now and in the future?
● **Communication style** To what
extent do projects convey information in a clear, appealing way?

Thinking Critically

1. **Recognizing Ideology** What does the endurance and success of the Social Security Act suggest about the current attitudes of Americans toward government's role in their lives?

2. **Demonstrating Reasoned Judgment** You have read that voters were willing to follow the "bold, consistent experimentation" of the New Deal. What does this willingness suggest about the mood of the country when FDR was elected? Do you think that people would vote for bold experimentation today?

3. **Making Comparisons** Describe how Eleanor Roosevelt perceived her role as First Lady. How have the roles of more recent first ladies been similar to or different from that of Eleanor Roosevelt?

Making Connections

1. **Evaluating Primary Sources** Review the second primary source excerpt on page 651. Explain how the balance of power among the branches of government would be affected if Congress made the Supreme Court subject to the presidency.

2. **Understanding the Visuals** Skim through the chapter and find photographs, artwork, or other illustrations that both support and oppose the New Deal. Explain how each visual conveys its message of approval or disapproval.

3. **Writing About the Chapter** The New Deal tried to solve the nation's economic and social problems during the Depression. Write a proposal for a New Deal kind of program that would help end a social or economic problem today. First, choose a contemporary issue that you would like to see addressed. Then, jot down ideas for a government program that could help solve the problem. Include your ideas about how the program is to be financed. Next, write a draft of your proposal in which you explain your ideas. Revise your proposal, making certain that your solution is clearly explained, with as many details as possible about its implementation. Proof-read your proposal and draft a final copy.

4. **Using the Graphic Organizer** This graphic orga-nizer uses a tree map to organize main ideas and supporting details about the effects of the New Deal. (a) What were three main sources of enter-tainment during the 1930s, and what role did the government play in funding the arts? (b) If you were to travel throughout the United States today, what evidence of New Deal programs listed on the graphic organizer might you encounter? (c) On a separate sheet of paper, create your own tree map about the New Deal's critics, using this graphic organizer as an example.

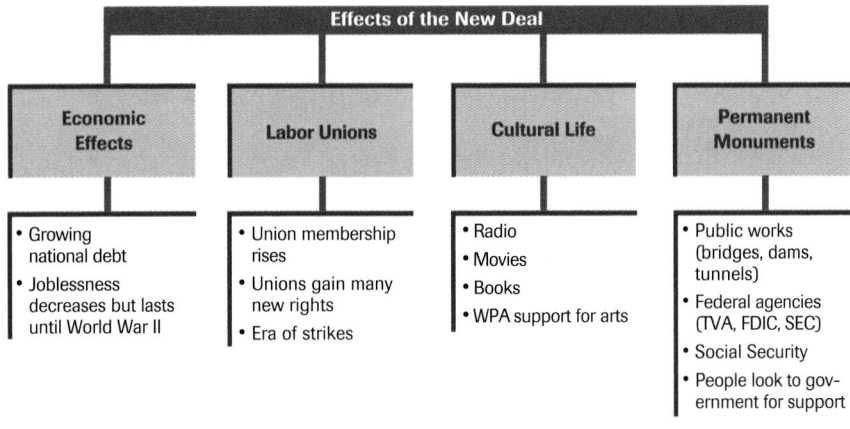

Effects of the New Deal

Economic Effects	Labor Unions	Cultural Life	Permanent Monuments
• Growing national debt	• Union membership rises	• Radio	• Public works (bridges, dams, tunnels)
• Joblessness decreases but lasts until World War II	• Unions gain many new rights	• Movies	• Federal agencies (TVA, FDIC, SEC)
	• Era of strikes	• Books	• Social Security
		• WPA support for arts	• People look to gov-ernment for support

Making Connections

1. There would no longer be a true balance of power, because the three branches of government would not be separate. The executive branch (the President) could simply alter the judicial branch if the courts did not support the President's program. There would be no judicial check on the executive's power.

2. Visuals that support the New Deal appear on the following pages: 638 (needle book and sheet music), 640, and 646. Visuals that disapprove of the New Deal appear on these pages: 638 (button), 647, and 649.

3. Students' proposals may deal with such challenges as homelessness, street violence, or environmental degradation. Government programs might, for example, provide housing, offer incentives for con-tinuing education, or provide jobs in environmental protection. Programs could be financed by higher taxes, a special assessment to finance a particular program, cutbacks elsewhere, or by allowing a greater federal deficit.

4. (a) Sources of entertainment included radio, movies, and literature; many arts activities were sup-ported with WPA funds. (b) You might encounter bridges, dams, and tunnels, as well as evidence of CCC restoration and conservation projects. (c) Stu-dents' graphic organizers should include information about the limits of the New Deal and the criticisms of women and minorities.

Introducing the Unit

Interpreting the Visual In contrast to today, when television brings wars and battlefronts instantly into American living rooms, in World War II only press photographers, newspaper reporters, and radio journalists reported to the folks back home. Dwight Eisenhower, the supreme Allied commander, describes the natural conflict between the press and the military in his book *Crusade in Europe*: "Complete wartime . . . co-operation can never be achieved between the press and military authorities. For the commander, secrecy is a defensive weapon; to the press it is anathema."

Ask students to study the picture on pages 660–661. What can they learn from the picture and the caption alone about the course of the war at that moment? For example, how closely can they identify the region where the picture was taken?

Ask students to imagine being one of the soldiers in the picture and to write a letter home describing conditions during the last few months of the war.

Establishing Chronology Remind students that the previous chapter focused on the New Deal and the ending of the Great Depression. This unit focuses on World War II and the cold war years that followed. The war began in Europe in 1939, but the United States did not declare war until the Japanese bombed Pearl Harbor in December 1941. After the war ended in 1945 came fifteen "hot" cold war years, during which a nuclear war seemed all too possible.

UNIT 8

Hot and Cold War
1939–1960

"We have to face the fact that either all of us are going to die together or we are going to learn to live together, and if we are to live together we have to talk."

—Eleanor Roosevelt, 1960

M*any Americans were determined to stay out of another European conflict, but Japan's attack on Pearl Harbor finally shattered their resolve and American isolationism ended forever. After the war, the nation barely had time to enjoy its hard-won peace before a "cold war" developed between the United States and the Soviet Union. That conflict and the threat of nuclear destruction cast a long shadow across the postwar era.*

▶ RESOURCE DIRECTORY

Teaching Resources

 Local History Activity "Seattle at War" and the Local Focus research topic suggestions, found in the Local History Resources folder, pp. 24–26, are designed to help students understand how history affects all lives.

★ **Themes in American History Posters** Wall-size, illustrated posters, found in the Teaching Resources package, illustrate the four unit themes.

Unit Test Forms A and B are found in the Unit 8 folder, pp. 140–145.

Weary American infantrymen line up in the cold for a meal. Despite the fatigue of the soldiers and the world, World War II would rage in Europe for another four months after this January 1945 photograph was taken.

Teachers may wish to discuss specific historical events in the context of historical themes. Here are four suggestions for Unit 8.

Technology *Americans' ability to develop new skills and tools and to increase their knowledge of the physical world has greatly affected the way they live and work, and has led to a high standard of living.*

● The Manhattan Project to build the atomic bomb was the largest scientific project ever undertaken.
● American factories made a dramatic conversion to the production of war goods during World War II.

American Democracy *The concepts of democratic representation, equality under the law, and freedom from discrimination have been gradually broadened to include previously excluded groups.*

● Events on the home front stimulated a movement for equal rights for African Americans.
● The United States, believing that Japanese Americans posed a military threat on the West Coast, forcibly removed them to internment camps.

Unity and Conflict *Americans have developed unique political systems and laws that affirm a shared commitment to certain goals, such as individual rights and equality. Nevertheless, groups with differing views on how to achieve these goals have often clashed.*

● After more than a decade of economic depression, America's mood during the war turned to cooperation, unity, and resolve.
● Fear of communist subversives after the war led to attacks on the patriotism of many Americans.

The United States and the World *America's relationships with other countries have been influenced at different times by a sense of mission, by values, and by self-interest.*

● The Japanese attack on Pearl Harbor finally brought the United States into World War II.
● Relations between the United States and the Soviet Union broke down after the war, leading to a prolonged cold war.

Media and Technology

Visions of America: Scenes of an Era To introduce students to the main idea and events covered in this unit, play "Scenes of an Era: Hot and Cold War" (length: 2.5 minutes). This selection can be located on side 3 of the videodiscs. This selection can also be located on videotape 4. Lesson plans for "Scenes of an Era" can be found in the Visions of America Guidebook.

Using Multimedia Technology This folder contains instructional tools and strategies for using technology in the classroom.

Transparency Binder Contains full-color transparencies with lesson suggestions. From a large collection divided into twelve categories, specific transparencies are referenced throughout the chapters at appropriate points of use. For this unit, see American Photo, B-8; Time Lines, E-7 and E-8; Cause and Effect, F-10; The Way It Works, H-19 and H-20; Links Across Time, J-8; and Political Cartoon, K-8.

Chapter 24 World War II
1939–1945

📁 Teaching Resources (See Unit 8 Folder)

	Instruction	Enrichment
Section 1 **Prelude to War** (pp. 664–669)	Reproducible Lesson Plan, p. 3 Alternate Lesson Plan, p. 122 Guided Reading and Review, p. 7 Quiz, p. 8	Visual Learning Activity, Books Are Weapons, p. 29
Section 2 **The Military Struggle** (pp. 670–676)	Reproducible Lesson Plan, p. 4 Alternate Lesson Plan, p. 123 Guided Reading and Review, p. 9 Quiz, p. 10	Visual Learning Activity, The North African Front, p. 30 Primary Source Activity, Guadalcanal, p. 23 American Profiles Activity, Navaho Code Talkers, p. 18 Literature Activity, Dispatches from the Battle Front, pp. 26–27
Section 3 **Americans on the Battle Fronts** (pp. 677–680)	Reproducible Lesson Plan, p. 5 Alternate Lesson Plan, p. 124 Guided Reading and Review, p. 11 Quiz, p. 12	American Profiles Activity, Jacqueline Cochran, p. 17 Critical Thinking Activity, Predicting Consequences, p. 22 Primary Source Activity, Experiences of an African American Soldier, pp. 24–25 Viewpoints Activity, On the Integration of the Military, pp. 19–20 Historian's Toolbox Activity, Examining Photographs, p. 21
Section 4 **Dropping the Atomic Bomb:** **A Turning Point in History** (pp. 682–685)	Reproducible Lesson Plan, p. 6 Alternate Lesson Plan, p. 125 Guided Reading and Review, p. 13 Quiz, p. 14 Chapter Test, Forms A & B, pp. 31–36	Literature Activity, Hiroshima, p. 28 Turning Point Extension Activity, The Lasting Impact of the Atomic Bomb, pp. 15–16

📁 Additional Chapter Resources

Resource Organizer, p. 2
Alternate Lesson Plan, p. 121
Answer Keys, pp. 146–160

Bibliography

For the Teacher
Roeder, George. *The Censored War: American Visual Experience During World War II.* Yale University Press, 1993. (A collection of wartime photographs, many used for propaganda, and many from the National Archives.)

Prentice Hall Literature Excerpts from *The American Experience,* 1994, including "The Modern Age, 1915–1916."

The Big Idea for the chapter and how the main ideas in each section relate to the Big Idea are graphically displayed below. Comprehension of this chapter's Big Idea is critical to students' understanding of United States history and how we as a nation got where we are today.

Media and Technology

 Time Lines, E-7

 The Way It Works, H-19

 Critical Thinking, I-2

 Visions of America: Turning Point Story, "Atomic Cloud," (length: approx. 4 minutes)

 Visions of America: Roundtable Discussion on "Atomic Cloud"

 Graphic Organizer, G-5

 Guided Reading Audiotapes (English and Spanish)

 Computer Test Bank

For the Student

Hersey, John. *Into the Valley: A Skirmish of the Marines.* Knopf, 1942. (Eyewitness account of the battle for Guadalcanal.)

Selden, Kyoko and Mark Selden, eds. *The Atomic Bomb: Voices from Hiroshima and Nagasaki.* Sharpe, 1989.

CHAPTER 24

"The peace, freedom, and security of 90 percent of the population of the world is being jeopardized by the remaining 10 percent…" is the way President Roosevelt viewed the war raging in Europe. But many Americans did not want to intervene. After Pearl Harbor and the American entry into World War II, there was no question about the role of the United States in world affairs.

SECTION 1

After World War I, the aggression of the fascist allies—Italy, Germany, and Japan—led to conflict around the world, and eventually caused a second world war. After attempting to remain neutral, the United States entered the war when Japan bombed Pearl Harbor in Hawaii.

SECTION 2

World War II was a global war, fought on fronts in Europe, North Africa, and the Pacific. Success for the Allies required tremendous organization of people and resources.

SECTION 3

The 12 million Americans who fought in World War II endured terrible hardships. Women, African Americans, and members of other minority groups in the armed services helped to win the war, although discrimination reduced their effectiveness.

SECTION 4

In an attempt to hasten the end of the war, the United States dropped a devastating new weapon, the atomic bomb, on two Japanese cities in August 1945. Japan surrendered on August 14, 1945.

CHAPTER 24

World War II
1939–1945

The Relevance of the Big Idea

As the war clouds massed over Europe and Asia, Americans debated their nation's role in the growing conflict. President Roosevelt helped the Allies in many ways short of engaging in combat until the bombing of Pearl Harbor propelled the nation into war.

Tell students that in the decade of the 1990s, the United States must balance requests and demands for military help in conflicts throughout the world—in such diverse places as Haiti, Somalia, and the former Yugoslavia—with its own political and economic needs.

In Depth

Global Connections

Between 1936 and 1939, Spain was consumed by civil war. Italian and German leaders aided Spanish General Francisco Franco's Nationalists in their effort to install a fascist state. Soviet leaders sent weapons and advisers to Spain's Republican government. Britain, France, and the United States did not officially take sides, but fear of fascism ran high, and many people from these countries volunteered to fight with "international brigades" on the Republican side. In December 1936 the first of 3,300 American volunteers sailed for Spain; sixteen hundred died. The Spanish Civil War was a battleground for European conflicts of the 1930s, and is often described as a prelude to World War II.

World War II
1939–1945

In the 1930s a frightening series of events overseas showed that the world war Americans had fought from 1917 to 1918 had not succeeded in making the world "safe for democracy." As ruthless dictators devoured whole nations in Europe, northern Africa, and Asia, many Americans fervently hoped that the United States could remain uninvolved. This proved impossible, and in December 1941 the nation fully committed its material and human resources to a second global conflict that would end United States isolationism forever.

Events in the United States

1935 To keep the United States out of war in Europe, Congress passes Neutrality Acts.

1938 Severe recession hits the United States economy.

1935	1936	1937	1938	1939

Events in the World

1936 Spanish Civil War begins.

1939 German invasion of Poland sets off World War II.

▶ RESOURCE DIRECTORY

Teaching Resources

Alternate Lesson Plan: Demonstrating the Big Idea found in the Alternate Lesson Plans folder, p. 121, provides a lesson strategy designed to instruct students in the Big Idea that the United States' involvement in World War II changed the country's status from an isolated nation to a world power.

Alternative Assessment Handbook provides information, guidance, and strategies for alternative methods of assessment. It includes an essay on new trends in assessment, guidance and strategies for developing performance tasks and portfolios, scoring rubrics, and sample evaluation forms.

Pages 664–669
Prelude to War

World War I had left deep scars in Europe. Wounded national pride and devastated economies laid the foundation for the rise of fascist dictators and a second global conflict.

Pages 670–676
The Military Struggle

By December 1941, only an exhausted Britain stood between the Nazis and their dream of dominating the European continent. The United States finally cast its lot with the British—but was it already too late?

Pages 677–680
Americans on the Battle Fronts

The grim reality of combat far from home was tough on all soldiers. Discrimination in the armed forces made the experience even more painful for many Americans.

Pages 682–685
Dropping the Atomic Bomb: A Turning Point in History

A collaboration of the top scientists in the world put a devastating secret weapon in American hands. Desperate to end the war as quickly as possible, the United States decided to unleash the terrible force of the atomic bomb on two unsuspecting Japanese cities.

Pages 686–687
The Lasting Impact of the Atomic Bomb

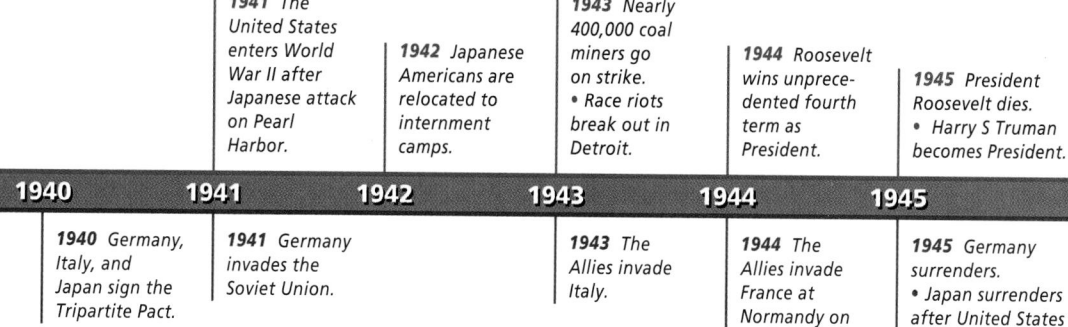

1941 The United States enters World War II after Japanese attack on Pearl Harbor.

1942 Japanese Americans are relocated to internment camps.

1943 Nearly 400,000 coal miners go on strike.
• Race riots break out in Detroit.

1944 Roosevelt wins unprecedented fourth term as President.

1945 President Roosevelt dies.
• Harry S Truman becomes President.

1940	1941	1942	1943	1944	1945

1940 Germany, Italy, and Japan sign the Tripartite Pact.

1941 Germany invades the Soviet Union.

1943 The Allies invade Italy.

1944 The Allies invade France at Normandy on D-Day.

1945 Germany surrenders.
• Japan surrenders after United States drops atomic bombs.

Prelude to War

Connecting to the Big Idea

See page 662B. Fascist dictators seized control in several nations scarred by World War I, while military leaders in Japan insisted on a policy of expansion. Ask students how the United States responded to the growing worldwide conflict and what finally propelled the United States into the war.

Objectives

● Identify the aggressive nations of Europe and Asia and their leaders.
● Explain how the United States struggled to remain neutral while supporting the Allies with economic aid.
● Identify Japan's attack on Pearl Harbor as the aggressive action that propelled the United States into war.

Bellringer

Ask students to choose a current "hot spot," or place in the world where there is armed conflict, and to describe the United States' involvement in that area, if any. Ask them to consider under what conditions the United States should intervene in a conflict within another nation or between nations.

Reading Strategy

Graphic Organizer Ask students to make a concept map of this section by drawing three large circles on a piece of paper, labeled Fascism and Nazism in Europe, Japan Builds an Empire, and The American Response to Axis Aggression. Have students add supporting information in smaller circles, and draw lines connecting them to the appropriate large circles.

Prelude to War

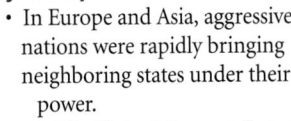

SECTION PREVIEW

World War I had left deep scars in Europe. Wounded national pride and devastated economies laid the foundation for the rise of fascist dictators and a second global conflict.

Key Concepts

• In Europe and Asia, aggressive nations were rapidly bringing neighboring states under their power.
• The United States at first struggled to stay out of the fighting abroad, while supporting the Allies with economic aid.
• The Japanese attack on Pearl Harbor finally dragged the United States into the war.

Nazis singled out Jews for persecution by forcing them to wear yellow Stars of David like this one.

Key Terms, People, and Places

fascism, Nazi party, anti-Semitism, appeasement, Lend-Lease Act; Benito Mussolini, Adolf Hitler, Winston Churchill; Rhineland, Manchuria, Pearl Harbor

---

Throughout the 1930s, Americans watched warily as dictators in Germany, Italy, and Japan sought to extend their power around the globe. Even so, most Americans wanted to stay out of the conflict. World War I had not made the world a better place; why, then, should they be eager to enter another foreign war? Besides, the American people had enough trouble at home, as the Depression stubbornly kept a grip on the economy. Yet as the struggle unfolded, it became clear that democracy everywhere was threatened by the dictators.

Fascism and Nazism in Europe

By the mid-1930s, Italian and German dictators had ruthlessly established their authority on the European continent. They took advantage of the humiliation felt by many Italians and Germans after World War I by promising to restore their nations to a position of glory.

Benito Mussolini was an Italian schoolteacher, journalist, and political activist who had been wounded in World War I. Along with many Italians, Mussolini felt that his country had been shortchanged in the peace settlement after the war. The few small territories Italy received from the former German and Turkish empires paled in comparison to those claimed by its fellow Allies, Britain and France. In 1919 Mussolini banded together with a group of war veterans, who also were dissatisfied, to found the revolutionary Fascist party.

The term *fascism* refers to a political philosophy that values the nation or the race above the individual. During World War II, Italy, Germany, and Japan all were ruled by fascist governments that wielded absolute power. The fascist powers each looked back in history to their nation's great and glorious past—a crucial difference between them and the communists, who looked forward to a transformation of society for a glorious new future.

Mussolini Becomes "the Leader" In 1922 Mussolini threatened a march on Rome unless his authority was recognized. King Victor Emmanuel III, who feared the disruption that could occur, asked him to become prime minister. Three years later, calling himself *Il Duce* ("the leader"), Mussolini declared a dictatorship that extended throughout the country.

Mussolini and the Fascists attempted to promote Italian power, in spite of the serious political and economic instability following World War I. Claiming that efficiency and order were necessary to make Italy as great as they felt it had been in the past, Mussolini and his party suspended elections, centralized the economy under state control, and began modernizing the armed forces. In order to supply

---

RESOURCE DIRECTORY

Teaching Resources

Reproducible Lesson Plan found in the Unit 8 folder, p. 3, provides a summary of the Section 1 lesson plan content.

Alternate Lesson Plan: Learning Styles found in the Alternate Lesson Plans folder, p. 122, is particularly effective for auditory learners and is designed to guide students thorough a mock interview with world leaders of the World War II years.

Guided Reading and Review found in the Unit 8 folder, p. 7, provides a structure for reading and mastering the key concepts and reviewing the key terms for Section 1. (Guided Practice)

colonies for his modern-day Roman Empire, he pursued an aggressive foreign policy. Under his direction, Italy invaded Ethiopia in 1935, and by the next year, it dominated that East African nation.

Hitler's Rise to Power At the same time, **Adolf Hitler,** a poorly educated Austrian who supported himself as a painter, rose to power in Germany. Hitler had been wounded and temporarily blinded in World War I. The war left him feeling enraged by Germany's defeat and by the degrading terms of the Treaty of Versailles.

In 1919 Hitler joined the forty-member German Workers' party. With his powerful public speaking, he soon became a leader in the growing party. In 1920 the group changed its name to the National Socialist German Workers' party, or **Nazi party**. In November 1923, by which time the party's membership had swelled to 55,000, Hitler and the Nazis attempted to seize power in the city of Munich.

Although many citizens of Munich supported Hitler, the rebellion was put down quickly. Hitler was found guilty of high treason and spent nine months in jail. During this time he began writing an autobiography titled *Mein Kampf* ("My Struggle"), in which he described his diagnosis of Germany's problems and how he planned to cure them.

Hitler and the Nazis continued their crusade throughout the 1920s and 1930s. They appealed to Germans ravaged by the Great Depression. Saddled with insurmountable war debts from World War I, Germany also faced terrible unemployment and massive inflation. Hitler promised to stabilize the country, rebuild the economy, and revive the German empire that had been shattered in the war.

As a result of such promises, Hitler won a large following. In addition, his tremendous personal magnetism swayed many to his views. One witness who observed Hitler speaking later recalled:

> I cannot remember in my entire life such a change in the attitude of a crowd in a few minutes, almost a few seconds. There were certainly many who were not converted yet. But the mood of the majority

Adolf Hitler was once described as looking rather ordinary, "like a waiter in a railway station restaurant" (right). When he spoke, however, his passion and charisma electrified audiences.

> abruptly changed. Hitler had turned them inside out, as one turns a glove inside out, with a few sentences. It had almost something of hocus-pocus, or magic about it.
>
> Karl Alexander von Müller,
> German historian

Hitler Becomes *Der Führer* In January 1933, the Nazi party was the largest group in the Reichstag (the German parliament), and Hitler was named chancellor. The next month he squelched his opposition in the Reichstag and suspended civil liberties. An act of parliament gave him dictatorial powers in the new government, known as the Third Reich. He was now *Der Führer* ("the leader").

Hitler appealed to a form of prejudice with a long and deep-rooted history in Western civilization: **anti-Semitism**, or the hatred of Jews. Hitler blamed Jews for Germany's problems and preached that so-called Aryans—blond, blue-eyed Germans—belonged to a dominant "master race." Anti-Semitism became a cornerstone of Hitler's program. He soon ordered the boycott of Jewish shops, the burning of books written by Jewish authors, and the imprisonment of Jews in concentration camps.

Explain/Discuss

Recall with students that the world-wide effects of the Great Depression were widespread and pervasive. Economic instability, inflation, and unemployment raged. Point out that the climate was ripe for the rise of dictators. Explain that dictators such as Mussolini and Hitler promised to restore economic strength.

Examine the similarities and differences between the two dominant dictatorships of this period: Communist Russia and Nazi Germany. Explore Hitler and the Nazi party's rise to power. Ask how and why the Jews became Hitler's scapegoat.

Analyze

Point out that it is believed that the United States became involved in World War II to support our allies against Nazi and fascist aggression and to respond to Japanese aggression in the Pacific.

In Depth

Biography

Jesse Owens (1913–1980), the tenth child of African American sharecroppers in the South, gave an outstanding performance at the 1936 Olympic Games in Berlin, Germany. The Nazi dictator, Adolf Hitler, expected the Games to showcase German athletes' superiority since he believed that they were destined to rule "non-Aryan" or "inferior peoples." Before the eyes of the world, Owens proved Hitler wrong by winning four gold medals in track and field events. After the Games, Owens said, "I learned that the false leaders and sick movements of this earth must be stopped in the beginning, for they turn humanity against itself."

Regions of Axis and Allied Control, 1941

Axis powers
Areas under Axis control, 1941
Allies and areas under Allied control, 1941
Neutral nations

Geography and History: Interpreting Maps
Millions of people like this Czechoslovakian woman, shown reluctantly saluting the Nazis in 1938, saw their homelands conquered by the Axis powers. *How does this map illustrate the dire situation of the Allies in 1941?*

Like Mussolini, Hitler saw foreign policy as a way to bolster national pride. He, too, was determined to return Germany to a dominant position in the world. In 1936 he marched troops into the **Rhineland**—a section of western Germany from which the Treaty of Versailles had excluded German forces since the end of World War I. (See the map above.) In that same year, Hitler formed an alliance with Mussolini, and Italy and Germany became known as the Axis Powers.

The German Empire Grows German aggression continued as the decade of the 1930s drew to a close. Early in 1938 Hitler annexed Austria. Later that year, he demanded possession of the Sudetenland, a section of Czechoslovakia inhabited by an ethnic German population.

The League of Nations, which had been organized after World War I to try to maintain international peace, proved powerless to resist German aggression. England and France, reluctant to become involved in another conflict after the devastation of World War I, adopted a policy known as **appeasement**. To *appease* means to "keep the peace by giving in to someone's demands." Over and over England and France allowed Hitler to seize control of European territories, on the assumption that he finally would be satisfied.

Their assumption was wrong. Hitler's appetite proved insatiable, and he moved relentlessly to take over all of Czechoslovakia. Then, in September 1939, after signing a non-aggression pact with the Soviet Union so he would not have to fear a Soviet assault, Germany invaded Poland. Two days after this attack, leaders in England and France decided they would appease Hitler no longer. Angry and frustrated over his steady encroachment on the European continent, they finally declared war on Germany.

Japan Builds an Empire

In Asia in the 1930s, Japan was every bit as eager as Germany and Italy to establish itself as a world power. Japan consisted of a chain of small islands in the Pacific and lacked the raw materials needed for a booming industrial economy. Military leaders who dominated the government resented their dependence on the United States and other nations for such necessary resources as iron, coal, and petroleum. High tariffs prevented Japan from enjoying a profitable export trade with the United States and led to a prolonged economic depression in Japan. To make Japan self-sufficient, its leaders were determined to incorporate part of the Asian mainland into what they called the Greater East Asia Co-Prosperity Sphere.

In 1931 Japan attacked **Manchuria**, a region in northern China rich in minerals. By the next year, Japan controlled Manchuria. It quickly established a puppet government and renamed the area Manchukuo. Despite condemnation by the League of Nations, Japan continued its aggression in China. In 1937 Japanese troops launched an attack and seized Shanghai, Nanjing, Beijng, and other Chinese cities.

Japanese aggression continued over the next few years. Ever hungry for more resources, raw materials, and markets, Japan also sought control of Southeast Asia, as the map below shows. In 1940 the island nation signed an alliance with Germany and Italy, known as the Tripartite Pact. Now all three of the world's major fascist powers were partners. Secure in that alliance, the Japanese invaded southern Indochina—then ruled by France—in the middle of 1941.

MAKING CONNECTIONS

How do you think different groups of Americans reacted to German and Japanese aggression? How might their memories of World War I have affected their responses? Compare your answers to the information that follows.

The American Response to Axis Aggression

The United States watched the storm clouds rising in Europe and Asia but hoped to remain uninvolved. Most Americans remained

Regions of Japanese Control, 1941

 Geography and History: Interpreting Maps
The terrified baby at right somehow escaped harm during the 1937 bombing of a Shanghai train station by the Japanese. *Judging from this map, what regions in 1941 appear to have been in the greatest danger of being attacked next by Japan?*

Answer to ...
MAKING CONNECTIONS

Some Americans may have felt that the events in Europe and Asia were a threat to American national security and that the United States should join the military effort to defeat the Axis. Others, remembering the limited results of U.S. involvement in World War I, may have wanted to stay out of the conflict.

Caption Answer to ...
 Interpreting Maps

The areas on the fringes of Japanese control, such as the Philippines, the Dutch East Indies, and the rest of China, would logically be the next targets of Japanese aggression.

In Depth
Did You Know?

On May 13, 1939, the Hamburg-American liner *St. Louis* left Germany bound for Cuba, carrying 930 Jewish refugees, 734 of whom were carrying United States immigration papers. When the *St. Louis* docked in Havana on May 27, however, the refugees were told that Cuban authorities would not allow them ashore. United States officials refused to waive quota restrictions then in effect, and the doomed vessel sailed back to Europe. Frantic workers from Jewish relief agencies finally persuaded four European countries to take in the refugees—but only those who settled in Britain remained free of Nazi persecution.

Section 1 Review Answers

1. (a) fascism, see p. 664, (b) Nazi party, see p. 665, (c) anti-Semitism, see p. 665, (d) appeasement, see p. 666, (e) Lend-Lease Act, see p. 668

2. (a) Benito Mussolini, see p. 664, (b) Adolf Hitler, see p. 665, (c) Winston Churchill, see p. 668

3. (a) Rhineland, see p. 666, (b) Manchuria, see p. 667, (c) Pearl Harbor, see p. 668

4. Hitler and Mussolini exploited the humiliation many people in Germany and Italy felt after defeat in World War I. Hitler also used anti-Semitic prejudices to his advantage. Japan invaded Manchuria and several other major population centers of China in order to gain influence and access to raw materials.

5. Most Americans wanted to stay out of the conflict. In the 1930s, Congress passed a series of Neutrality Acts to distance the United States from direct involvement in Europe and Asia.

In Depth

Historical Misconceptions

American isolationism in the late 1930s was quite significant. The America First Committee was not only vocal but also influential in gathering support from a cross-section of Americans *against* intervening in the war in Europe. Among the public figures who supported the America First Committee were former President Herbert Hoover, labor leader John L. Lewis, historian Charles Beard, architect Frank Lloyd Wright, chairman of Sears, Roebuck Robert Wood, and the most famous American of his generation—Charles Lindbergh.

People opposed to the United States entering World War II voiced their opinions on bumper stickers such as the one above, or wore pins that read "America First" (below). Those who favored United States involvement in the war urged "Bundles [of supplies] for Britain" (below).

disillusioned by World War I; they had fought to make the world safe for democracy, but questioned later whether their actions had made any difference at all. Many Americans wanted to follow a policy of isolationism, believing that American interests could best be served by staying out of the quarrels of other nations entirely. Isolationists formed the America First Committee to denounce any move by the government toward involvement in the war.

Congress responded to isolationist sentiment in the 1930s by passing a series of three neutrality acts. Taken together, these laws declared that the United States would withhold weapons and loans from all nations at war and would sell other goods to warring powers only if they paid cash and picked up the goods themselves, a policy known as "cash and carry." The third and last of these acts was passed in 1937, thus completing American neutrality policy. In early 1941 a Gallup poll revealed that 88 percent of the American people still opposed entering the war.

Challenges to Neutrality Despite most Americans' desire for noninvolvement, the ominous events of the war convinced other Americans that the United States should help the Allies. Between September 1939 and June 1940, the Axis Powers in Europe defeated Poland, Norway, Denmark, Belgium, Luxembourg, and France. In Asia, Japan was swallowing up French and Dutch colonies. Unless something was done quickly, England—which was single-handedly resisting the Axis in Europe—might not survive. In May 1940, journalist William Allen White organized the Committee to Defend America by Aiding the Allies,

which worked vigorously to enlist the support of the American people. ✪

The Arsenal of Democracy That same year, while seeking and winning a third presidential term, Roosevelt moved to help Great Britain directly. When British prime minister **Winston Churchill** asked for American destroyers to convoy supplies across the Atlantic, Roosevelt agreed to trade fifty old American ships in return for sites on which to build eight naval and air bases on British territory in the Western Hemisphere.

The next year, Roosevelt helped push the **Lend-Lease Act** through Congress. Britain desperately needed economic help to continue its struggle against the Axis. Under Lend-Lease, the United States would provide war supplies to Britain and worry about payment later. It was like lending a garden hose to a neighbor whose house was burning, Roosevelt said. You loaned it to him, and he returned it when the fire was out. With that commitment, the United States became, in FDR's words, "the great arsenal of democracy."

The Attack on Pearl Harbor

As the war in Europe unfolded, tensions between the United States and Japan increased. In 1940 the United States stopped selling airplanes to Japan, then moved to terminate a long-standing trade agreement. By mid-1940, the United States had ceased selling other crucial items, such as scrap metal and oil, to Japan. After Japan's attack on Indochina, it froze all Japanese financial assets in the United States. Desperate for oil in particular, Japan was determined to do whatever was necessary to attain its militaristic aims. The United States naval fleet based in Hawaii stood directly in the way of Japan's plans to dominate eastern Asia and the Pacific.

The Japanese took matters into their own hands. Hoping to knock out the United States Pacific Fleet before an all-out military conflict could begin, Japan launched a surprise attack on the American naval base at **Pearl Harbor**, Hawaii, on December 7, 1941. The attack destroyed five battleships, three cruisers, and

▶ RESOURCE DIRECTORY

Teaching Resources

✪ **Visual Learning Activity** Books Are Weapons, found in the Unit 8 folder, p. 29, enhances students' understanding of wartime propaganda and the power of the written word through a poster issued by the U.S. Office of War Information, depicting a Nazi book burning.

several smaller vessels, while wiping out almost 200 airplanes. Nearly 2,400 people died. Fortunately, the Pacific Fleet's aircraft carriers were on a mission elsewhere in the Pacific and so were spared destruction.

The attack stunned the American people. Then, in the wake of the initial shock, came a feeling of determination. A college student recalled hearing the news:

*I*n an incredibly short time—
it seemed to be almost a matter of moments—a wave of patriotism swept the country. As we drove home we felt, This is our country, and we're going to fight to defend it. When we got home that evening we were glued to the radio. "The Star-Spangled Banner" was played, and everyone in the room automatically rose. And we were disillusioned college students— the 1940s version of the 1960s kids.*

Dellie Hahne, a student at Santa Barbara State College, California

In recent years Roosevelt had come to believe that the United States could not avoid involvement in World War II. The attack on Pearl Harbor meant that the nation could hesitate no longer. The day after the raid, in one of his most stirring speeches, the President told the Congress and the American people that December 7, 1941, was "a date which will live in infamy." He called on Congress to declare war against Japan. Congress quickly

Anti-Japanese propaganda (right) kept the Pearl Harbor attack (above) fresh in Americans' minds.

complied. Three days later, Japan's allies, Germany and Italy, declared war on the United States. The American people now were committed to this war. Their contributions would make the difference between victory and defeat for the Allies.

SECTION 1 REVIEW

Key Terms, People, and Places
1. Define (a) fascism, (b) Nazi party, (c) anti-Semitism, (d) appeasement, (e) Lend-Lease Act.
2. Identify (a) Benito Mussolini, (b) Adolf Hitler, (c) Winston Churchill.
3. Identify (a) Rhineland, (b) Manchuria, (c) Pearl Harbor.

Key Concepts
4. What steps did Italy, Germany, and Japan take early in 1935 to extend their power?

5. How did the United States respond to international upheaval in the 1930s?

Critical Thinking
6. **Testing Conclusions** "In the years leading up to the attack on Pearl Harbor, the United States was gradually becoming more and more involved in the war. Even if the attack had never happened, the United States would eventually have become involved in the fighting." Explain why you agree or disagree with this conclusion.

 Quiz found in the Unit 8 folder, p. 8, covers the main ideas in this section as well as the key terms.

Media and Technology

Transparency
Time Lines, E-7

---

6. Possible answers: Students may point out that it took the attack on Pearl Harbor to unite Americans behind the decision to enter World War II. On the other hand, some Americans had argued for joining the war long before Pearl Harbor.

Reteach
Ask students to identify the nation described in each statement below as Italy, Germany, Japan, or the United States.
- Benito Mussolini promised to restore this country's efficiency and order.
- This country's dictator blamed its problems on the Jews.
- Military leaders dominated the emperor of this country.
- This country bombed an American naval base on December 7, 1941.
- Britain and France declared war when this country invaded Poland.

4. CLOSE

Reinforcing the Big Idea

The United States overtly tried to remain neutral when the fascist powers began a second world war. However, the United States did give increasing amounts of aid to the Allies. When Japan bombed Pearl Harbor in 1941, the United States entered World War II. The next section describes the course of the war from that point.

The Military Struggle

SECTION 2

The Military Struggle

Connecting to the Big Idea

See page 662B. When the United States entered the war, the Allies were on the defensive. Ask students to consider how the Allies planned to win the war and shape the world during the postwar peace.

Objectives

● Identify American military strength as the ingredient that helped the Allies defeat their Axis foes.

● Explain why the Allies chose to concentrate on Europe and North Africa and then to focus on the Pacific.

● Define the Nazi holocaust and describe its terrors.

Bellringer

Ask students to decide what they consider the most basic human freedoms. Then have them compare their lists to President Roosevelt's: freedom of speech, freedom of worship, freedom from want, and freedom from fear.

In Depth

Multicultural Perspectives

The United States' "Good Neighbor policy" paid dividends during the war. The Latin American nations provided vital war materials—rubber, quinine, tin—along with naval and air bases. Brazil sent troops to Europe, and Mexico had an air squadron in the Pacific. The Mexican and Cuban navies patrolled the Caribbean for German submarines. In return, the United States provided military equipment and loans to these nations.

SECTION PREVIEW

By December 1941, only an exhausted Britain stood between the Nazis and their dream of dominating the European continent. The United States finally cast its lot with the British—but was it already too late?

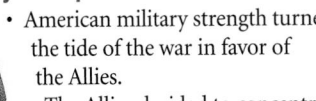

Key Concepts

• American military strength turned the tide of the war in favor of the Allies.

• The Allies decided to concentrate first on winning the war in Europe and North Africa and then focus on the Pacific.

• At the end of the war in Europe, the American public discovered the horrors of the holocaust.

Key Terms, People, and Places

blitzkrieg, Battle of the Bulge, holocaust; Douglas MacArthur, Dwight D. Eisenhower, Chester Nimitz, Joseph Stalin; Midway Island, Guadalcanal, Normandy

This helmet was worn by General George Patton, whose brilliant use of tanks helped sweep the Germans out of France in 1944.

W orld War II was a global war in an even greater sense than World War I. With campaigns occurring on many fronts at the same time, the war required enormous coordination of people and resources. If they hoped to defeat their Axis foes, Allied military strategists had to look at the "big picture" formed by a mosaic of smaller objectives.

Allied War Aims

While the immediate objective was to win the war, the United States was from the start planning to shape the postwar peace. Months before the United States entered the war, Roosevelt had shared his vision of what the world should be like. In a speech to Congress in early 1941, the President spoke of the "four

essential human freedoms"—freedom of speech, freedom of worship, freedom from want, and freedom from fear. That summer, he met with British prime minister Winston Churchill off the coast of Newfoundland, and the two leaders issued the Atlantic Charter. This document described their notion of a free and democratic postwar world. It demanded self-determination for all nations, so that people everywhere could decide what kind of government they wanted; equal trading rights for all, so that every country could share in the world's riches; and a system of general security to help keep peace.

While the four freedoms and the Atlantic Charter defined the United States' formal aims in the war, most Americans fought for more personal reasons. As soldiers huddled in filthy foxholes overseas, they dreamed of home and a cherished way of life. War correspondent John Hersey once asked a young marine on the Pacific front what he was fighting for. After reflecting for a moment, the soldier just sighed, "What I'd give for a piece of blueberry pie."

Early Danger

The Allies were in deep trouble by the time the United States entered the war. With fighting occurring around the globe, they found themselves on the defensive on virtually every front. To have any chance of victory, they had to determine military priorities. Soon after Pearl Harbor, Roosevelt and Churchill decided that they would concentrate on defeating Germany and its European supporters first, while waging a defensive war against Japan in the Pacific. Only after the Nazis had been defeated would they devote full attention to the Asian front.

The European and North African Fronts The situation was desperate in Europe and North Africa. The German **blitzkrieg** ("lightning war")—a series of sudden military attacks

---

RESOURCE DIRECTORY

Teaching Resources

Reproducible Lesson Plan found in the Unit 8 folder, p. 4, provides a summary of the Section 2 lesson plan content.

Alternate Lesson Plan: Learning Styles found in the Alternate Lesson Plans folder, p. 123, is especially effective for tactile learners and is designed to help students understand the military struggle of World War II.

Guided Reading and Review found in the Unit 8 folder, p. 9, provides a structure for reading and mastering the key concepts and reviewing the key terms for Section 2. (Guided Practice)

by land and air—had extended Germany's control across Europe. England had survived the Battle of Britain, a relentless air attack that lasted from July 1940 to June 1941, but the German bombings of cities like London had taken a heavy toll. Suspicious of Soviet intentions in eastern Europe, Hitler broke his nonaggression pact with the Soviet Union in early 1942. German troops drove deep into the Soviet Union, gaining substantial territory. In North Africa, a German army led by Field Marshal Erwin Rommel, known as the "Desert Fox" for his shrewd tactics, was equally successful.

The Pacific Front Conditions for the Allies were not much better in the Pacific. The attack on Pearl Harbor had destroyed much of the American fleet, although not its aircraft carriers. Japan already controlled a large part of eastern and southern Asia. After years of fighting, China had been ground down. India, a British colony, was threatened from east and west, and Australia, part of the British Commonwealth, was expecting a Japanese invasion soon.

After Pearl Harbor, Japan moved successfully against the Pacific islands of Guam and Wake and against the British colony of Hong Kong in China and the British naval base at Singapore, just south of the Malay Peninsula. (See the map below.) In the spring of 1942, Japanese forces defeated Filipino and American troops in the Philippines and drove General **Douglas MacArthur** from the islands. After the defeat on March 10, 1942, MacArthur promised the Filipinos and American soldiers: "I shall return."

Turnaround The situation began to improve toward the end of 1942. Despite initial German

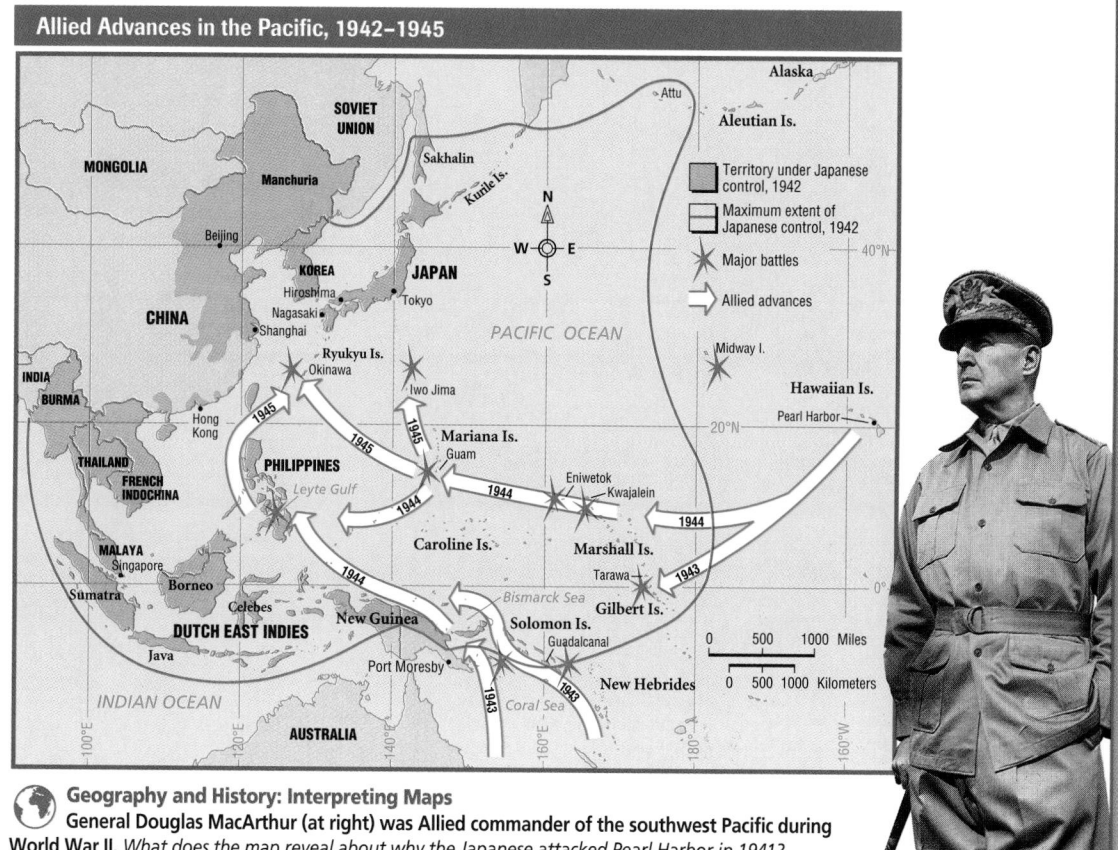

Allied Advances in the Pacific, 1942–1945

Territory under Japanese control, 1942
Maximum extent of Japanese control, 1942
★ Major battles
⟹ Allied advances

🌍 **Geography and History: Interpreting Maps**
General Douglas MacArthur (at right) was Allied commander of the southwest Pacific during World War II. *What does the map reveal about why the Japanese attacked Pearl Harbor in 1941?*

Reading Strategy

Structured Overview Have students create four columns on a sheet of paper and label them 1941, 1942, 1943, and 1944. In each column have them list the major battles and events in the European, North African, and Asian theaters of war for that year.

2. INSTRUCT

Explain/Discuss

Explain to students that the vision of a free and democratic postwar world posited by FDR and Churchill included the right of all nations to determine their own kind of government, to enjoy equal trading rights, and to live in peace. Discuss how the goals of the major wartime conferences support the conclusion that one of Roosevelt's main goals for entering the war was to ensure his role in the postwar peace talks.

Review the military strategy agreed upon by Churchill and Roosevelt. Ask students to describe the significance of Midway, Guadalcanal, Normandy, and the Battle of the Bulge. Have students describe how the use of radar and sonar equipment aided the Allies.

Ask students why the Soviet Union continually pressured the Allies to open a front in western Europe. Why did Churchill insist on attacking Germany through North Africa and Italy? What were the repercussions of this decision on future United States—Soviet relations?

Caption Answer to ...

🌍 **Interpreting Maps**

The arrows leading from the Hawaiian islands show that Pearl Harbor was the base from which Allied initiatives were launched in the Pacific.

Ask why the holocaust was referred to as Hitler's "final solution." What was the impact of the discovery of the atrocities committed against millions of Jews and others whom the Nazis considered to be undesirable?

 Activity

Creating Maps

Ask students to work in groups to make a detailed map of one theater of the war, including lines of battle and the dates of important events.

LEP

Enrichment

Ask students to prepare a detailed report about one battle of World War II or about one military leader. Suggest that students locate old issues of *Yank* magazine in the library and read eyewitness accounts written by soldiers who actually participated in the battles.

Caption Answer to ...

 Interpreting Maps

The arrow labeled "1944" that crosses the English Channel into France represents the D-Day invasion; the arrows that cross North Africa and move through Sicily into Italy represent the "soft underbelly" strategy.

---

triumphs in the Soviet Union, the Soviets were helped by the fact that Hitler repeated the same mistake made by the French emperor Napoleon more than a hundred years earlier. German troops advanced into the Soviet Union far beyond their country's ability to support them, and they were not equipped to deal with harsh Russian winters. The Soviets managed to withstand a long and costly attack on the city of Stalingrad. In September 1942, the Germans began bombing the city, while 300,000 German soldiers waited to attack. The Soviets took up positions in the rubble left by the bombing. When the Germans advanced, the Soviets engaged them in bitter house-to-house fighting for the next four months. At the end of that time, the Germans had been repulsed. In the process of defending Stalingrad, however, the

Soviet Union suffered more casualties than the United States experienced in the entire war.

In the Atlantic, the Allies used radar (which had been crucial in the Battle of Britain) and sonar to find and destroy German submarines. Without that ability, troops would have been left without weapons or food, for the Germans had sunk 125 Allied ships in May 1942 alone.

⭐ Meanwhile, the Allies took the offensive in North Africa (see the map below). In early 1943, Roosevelt and Churchill met at Casablanca, in the North African nation of Morocco, to decide where to strike back. The Soviet Union, which was fighting alone on the eastern front, desperately wanted the other Allies to open up a second front in western Europe. Churchill, however, was determined not to launch a frontal invasion until he felt Germany was likely to fall.

Allied Advances in Europe and Northern Africa, 1942–1945

Axis powers
Areas under Axis control, 1942
Allies and areas under Allied control, 1942
Neutral nations
Allied advances

 Geography and History: Interpreting Maps
General Dwight Eisenhower (at right) commanded many Allied initiatives in Europe, including the D-Day landing at Normandy in 1944. *Which arrow on the map represents this landing? Which arrows show the strategy of attacking the "soft underbelly" of the Axis?*

▶ **RESOURCE DIRECTORY**

Teaching Resources

⭐ **Visual Learning Activity** The North African Front, found in the Unit 8 folder, p. 30, uses information from the chapter and a photograph of American soldiers in Tunisia to challenge students' perception of detail.

⭐ **Primary Source Activity** Guadalcanal, found in the Unit 8 folder, p. 23, uses a passage written by Eleanor Roosevelt on the aftermath of the battle for Guadalcanal to express the sorrows of war and the ideals for which American soldiers died.

Instead, he persuaded Roosevelt to attack what he called the "soft underbelly" of the enemy, moving from North Africa to Sicily and Italy. The Soviets felt that by postponing the attack in western Europe, Britain and the United States "sacrificed" the Soviets in order to pursue their own war aims. Many thousands of Soviet soldiers died—and the German army was weakened—in the following months. Bitterness over this strategic decision would affect United States-Soviet relations in the postwar years.

Operation Torch, as the North African campaign was called, began in November 1942. It was a combined Anglo-American operation under the command of General **Dwight D. Eisenhower**. The Allied forces landed first in Morocco and Algeria, controlled by German puppet governments. The Allies easily triumphed, then moved east to Tunisia, where they encountered Rommel's Afrika Corps. In May 1943, the Axis forces in that region surrendered.

After their victory in North Africa, the Allies turned toward Italy. In July 1943, paratroopers of the 82nd Airborne Division jumped into Sicily, the island just off the "toe" of Italy; the invasion was a success. Next, Allied forces assaulted the Italian mainland and pushed toward Rome. The Italians overthrew Mussolini after the Sicily invasion and surrendered in September. German soldiers stationed in Italy dug in, though, and contested every mile of territory as the Allies moved up the Italian peninsula. In early 1944, the Allies landed, via sea, on the beaches of Anzio, and six months later they liberated the nearby city of Rome. The war was hardly over, but in the Italian campaign, the Allies had taken a major step forward. (See the map on page 672.)

MAKING CONNECTIONS

What are some of the differences between fighting a war on your own soil and going somewhere else to fight?

Midway and Guadalcanal At about the same time, battles over two small but highly strategic islands in the Pacific shifted the balance of power between the Allies and Japan. Japanese

admiral Isoroku Yamamoto wanted to engage the United States Navy at **Midway Island**, near Hawaii, in an attempt to destroy the aircraft carriers that the Pearl Harbor bombing had missed. When, in April 1942, Colonel James Doolittle launched a successful air raid on Tokyo from the carrier USS *Hornet*, which had departed from Midway, Japanese officials approved Yamamoto's plan.

Before the attack on Midway, the Japanese intended to secure their position around Australia by landing troops at Port Moresby in New Guinea. (See the map on page 671.) The United States had broken the Japanese military code, so American officials were aware of this strategy. In May 1942, in the Battle of the Coral Sea, planes launched from the American carriers *Lexington* and *Yorktown* fought a Japanese fleet for four days, finally forcing the enemy to turn back. This Allied victory slowed the Japanese drive toward Australia.

Americans again intercepted Japanese code messages and were prepared for the attack on Midway on June 4, 1942. Even so, the battle did not go well for the American forces at first. Most of the planes that Admiral **Chester Nimitz** sent from the island to attack the Japanese fleet were quickly shot down, as were those launched from American carriers. It was a bit of sheer luck that finally favored the Americans. At about 10:25 A.M., when the Japanese believed they had seen the last of the American fighter planes and were refueling for a final attack on the island, a group of dive-bombers that had gotten lost suddenly found their target. Three of the four Japanese carriers were swiftly demolished as fuel hoses and bombs on the Japanese ships exploded. The fourth was later destroyed while trying to escape. As a result of this tremendous blow to Japan's naval power, Midway would be the last Japanese offensive operation in the war.

⭐ At this point, the Allies took the offensive in the Pacific. Their first goal would be to secure the island of **Guadalcanal**, in the Solomon Islands. (See the map on page 671.) United States marines landed on the island beginning on August 7, 1942. Japanese leaders deemed Guadalcanal "the fork in the road which leads

Americans wore pins like this one of General Eisenhower to show their support of the Allied military effort.

Answer to . . .

MAKING CONNECTIONS

Fighting on home territory means familiarity with the terrain and a very personal connection to the struggle. Soldiers fighting on foreign soil may not know the geography, feel no personal connection to the area, and may wonder if the conflict is worth dying for.

In Depth

Then and Now

The United Service Organizations (USO), founded in 1941, assembled volunteer touring companies of actors, comedians, bandleaders, singers, and dancers to entertain the armed forces overseas. USO camp shows performed wherever American troops were stationed—in the North African desert, in bombed-out opera houses in Italy, or in the steamy rain forests of New Guinea. The USO has toured in every American war zone since then. In the early 1990s, about forty thousand volunteers around the world keep USO active.

Periscopes

Showers & toilets · Radio tower · Escape hatch · Anchor

Bunks · Galley · Conning tower

Engineers' room

Electric engines

Diesel engines · Radio room · Batteries · Torpedoes

Ammunition · Control room · Officers' quarters

In the early years of the war, submarines—especially German U-boats—were able to terrorize surface ships with sneak attacks. They could approach other ships undetected, with their sailors viewing targets through the periscope (left). Later in the war, however, Allied aircraft equipped with radar were able to detect a submarine replenishing its supply of fresh air at the surface and alert destroyer ships to the submarine's location.

In Depth

Interdisciplinary

Photography played a vital role in bringing the war to the American people at home. One acclaimed photograph, which became emblematic of the American effort in World War II, was Joe Rosenthal's study of six victorious marines hoisting the American flag on the captured isle of Iwo Jima. Rosenthal said of the shot: "I want[ed] to get at least *one* picture of an American flag on top of this hill." One writer later suggested that more people learned about the fight for Iwo Jima because of Rosenthal's photograph than because of any books or articles they have read on the subject. (For more on the role of photography in war see Historian's Toolbox on page 681.)

to victory for them or for us," so they made an all-out effort to recapture it.

Months of heavy fighting followed. In mid-November, the naval Battle of Guadalcanal ended with American control of the waters around the island, cutting off Japanese supply lines. In February 1943, American marines finally secured the island. From Guadalcanal, American forces would begin their strategy of "island-hopping," moving north through the Pacific by selectively attacking a few Japanese-held islands, their final objective being the Japanese homeland. The last two major battles in the Pacific war were fought on the small islands of Iwo Jima and Okinawa. The Japanese defended them fiercely, and both sides suffered heavy casualties before the Allies prevailed. ✪

The Road to Victory in Europe The Allies were ready to tighten the noose. In Europe they now looked to liberate Germany itself from the Nazis. Toward the end of 1943, Churchill, Roosevelt, and Soviet leader **Joseph Stalin** met together for the first time in Tehran, Iran. They

agreed that an invasion across the English channel should come next.

Air attacks throughout 1943 and 1944 softened German resistance. Yet even though the Allies destroyed military, industrial, and transportation facilities, the Nazis fought on.

Then came Operation Overlord, which aimed to drive the Germans out of France and defeat the Third Reich itself. D-Day began before dawn on June 6, 1944. It was the largest amphibious invasion—a landing by sea—in history. More than 150,000 Allied soldiers in 600 warships and 4,000 other vessels crossed the English channel and came ashore along 60 miles of the **Normandy** coast in northern France. (See the map on page 672.) The Germans knew an attack was coming, but they expected it near Calais, where the English channel was narrowest. Despite the advice of his generals to counterattack, Hitler hesitated, for he still feared a larger invasion at Calais. The Allies, under the command of General Dwight Eisenhower, were thus able to land safely on the beach. In the course of the first week, they placed 326,000 soldiers, 50,000 vehicles, and

▶ RESOURCE DIRECTORY ✪

Teaching Resources

 American Profiles Activity Navaho Code Talkers, found in the Unit 8 folder, p. 18, profiles a corps of 420 radio operators who transmitted secret codes in the Navaho language during World War II.

Literature Activity Dispatches from the Battle Front, found in the Unit 8 folder, pp. 26–27, features war correspondent Ernie Pyle's descriptions of the front lines of the European theater and the lives of the U.S. servicemen who fought there.

100,000 tons of supplies on the French coast. By the time the invasion of Normandy was over in July, the Allied forces had landed more than a million men.

⭐ Bitter fighting followed as the Allies pushed toward Paris. At the end of August, they liberated the French capital, then freed Brussels and Antwerp in Belgium a few days later.

The Germans launched a counterattack in Belgium and Luxembourg in December 1944, called the **Battle of the Bulge** because it caused a large bulge in the Allied line. When it sputtered out after one month, the way into Germany was clear. As Allied bombers continued to hammer major German cities, the Soviets pushed into Germany from the east, while American forces crossed the Rhine River and drove in from the west.

The Holocaust

As the Allies moved toward final victory, they discovered the horrors of what Hitler called the "Final Solution"—his effort to exterminate all Jews and other people he considered enemies of the Aryan state. For the duration of the war, the Nazis had engaged in a systematic campaign to liquidate the entire Jewish population of Europe. The extermination camps of Auschwitz, Maidanek, and Treblinka were located in Poland; Buchenwald and Dachau were in Germany. In these and other camps, the Nazis killed 6 million Jews in what we now call the **holocaust**, from the Greek term for "total destruction by fire." They also murdered another 5 million Slavs, Gypsies, and other people they considered undesirable—political enemies (especially communists), homosexuals, and the physically and mentally disabled.

Nazi doctors performed cruel experiments on their victims, often as an excuse to torture them as much as for any scientific purpose. Many victims were told to remove all their clothing and report to a bath house, which was actually a lethal gas chamber. Their bodies were then stripped of gold teeth, rings, and other valuables and burned in large ovens.

In liberating the concentration camps, American troops found the gaunt survivors who had somehow escaped death in the gas chambers and crematoriums. Second Lieutenant Dick Winters from Pennsylvania recorded the following impressions when he first saw Dachau:

Links Across Time

1650 1700 1750 1800 — 1850 1900 1950 2000

The "Final Solution" and "Ethnic Cleansing"

As Hitler and the Nazi party rose to power in Germany in the 1930s, they blamed Germany's recent economic and social troubles on the Jewish people and other minority groups.

Eventually, the Nazis decided on the "Final Solution" to what they termed the "Jewish problem." Their solution amounted to genocide, or systematic extermination of an entire ethnic group. When the realities of the "final solution" came to light, a horrified world community promised, "Never again."

In 1992 long-standing conflicts between Serb, Croat, and Muslim ethnic groups intensified in the former country of Yugoslavia. The Serbs wanted the areas they controlled to be the home of Serbians only, although Muslims had lived there for centuries. To bring about their aims, the Serbs followed a policy of "ethnic cleansing," including camps for the torture, rape, starvation, and execution of thousands of Slavic Muslim and ethnic Croat civilians. The United States State Department asserted that the Serbian abuse "dwarfs anything seen in Europe since the Nazis."

In 1993 the International Court of Justice in The Hague (in the Netherlands) implied that Serb aggression in Bosnia was "tantamount to genocide." The United Nations Security Council voted unanimously to establish a war crimes tribunal to bring to justice anyone found guilty of atrocities. **What do you think are the responsibilities of the United States when faced with strong evidence of genocide in another country?**

Media and Technology

 Transparency
The Way It Works, H-19

Answer to ...

Links Across Time

Possible answers: The United States should publicly protest genocide in another country, use its influence to protest in the United Nations, impose economic sanctions, and support a United Nations peacekeeping force.

3. ASSESS

Section 2 Review Answers

1. (a) blitzkrieg, see p. 670, (b) Battle of the Bulge, see p. 675

2. (a) Douglas MacArthur, see p. 671, (b) Dwight D. Eisenhower, see p. 673, (c) Chester Nimitz, see p. 673, (d) Joseph Stalin, see p. 674

3. (a) Midway Island, see p. 673, (b) Guadalcanal, see p. 673, (c) Normandy, see p. 674

4. The holocaust refers to the Nazi program of murdering Jews in concentration camps.

5. The United States' entry into the war allowed the Allies to keep the Japanese at bay in the Pacific while concentrating on dividing and conquering German forces in Europe and North Africa. The allies were then able to concentrate on defeating Japanese forces.

6. Possible questions: What are the strengths and weaknesses of both the Allies and the Axis powers? What are some possible strategies? How many Allied soldiers would be required to execute each strategy? What actions would most hurt enemy morale?

Ask students to use information in the section to correct the following incorrect statements.

- The Atlantic Charter declared the right of the United States to decide what kind of government nations would have after the war.
- The Allies decided to concentrate on defeating Japan while waging a defensive war in Europe.
- The Allied victory in the Philippines marked the last Japanese offensive operation in the war.
- The horrors of the holocaust were directed primarily at Muslims.
- The war in the Pacific ended before the war in Europe.

Alternative Assessment

Mid-Point Monitoring

Ask students if they have
- Divided responsibilities within the group
- Decided on an oral or written format for their album
- Obtained outside resources and found persons to interview

4. CLOSE

Reinforcing the Big Idea

In early 1941, the United States decided to join forces with the Allies, then on the defensive. Aided by American military strength, the Allies eventually gained control of Europe and North Africa. Germany at last surrendered, but the war in the Pacific continued. The next section describes life in the United States military during the war.

The memory of starved, dazed men, who dropped their eyes and heads when we looked at them through the chain-link fence, in the same manner that a beaten, mistreated dog would cringe, leaves feelings that cannot be described and will never be forgotten. The impact of seeing those people behind that fence left me saying, only to myself, "Now I know why I am here!"

Survivors of the Nazi holocaust were a chilling sight. Their bodies were emaciated from lack of food, and their eyes appeared haunted by memories of horrible torture.

The End of the War in Europe

In early 1945, Roosevelt, Churchill, and Stalin met again, this time at Yalta, a city in the Soviet Union near the Black Sea. After the "Big Three" Allied leaders had decided to split Germany into peacekeeping zones and to reorganize the government of Poland, the Soviets agreed to enter the war in the Pacific three months after the defeat of Germany.

The end of the European war was not far off. The Third Reich was in shambles. Hitler fulfilled a vow he had made in 1939: "I shall stand or fall in this struggle. I shall never survive the defeat of my people." On April 30, 1945, he committed suicide in a Berlin bunker. On May 8, Germany's unconditional surrender took effect, and the European war came to a close. American soldiers rejoiced, and civilians celebrated at home. But Japan still had to be defeated.

In the Pacific, the United States was embarking on a relentless drive toward the Japanese home islands. (See the map on page 671.) Pushing north from Australia and west through the islands of the central Pacific, American troops slowly gained control. Marines, with help from naval forces, took the islands of Tarawa, Kwajalein, and Guam. Meanwhile, MacArthur returned to the Philippines, as he had promised, with a dramatic landing on the island of Leyte. By the end of 1944, American bombers were close enough to attack the Japanese islands themselves and dropped hundred of tons of explosives on Japanese cities.

In one final meeting of the Big Three, Allied leaders met at Potsdam, Germany, in mid-1945. By this time Roosevelt was dead, and his successor, Harry S Truman, had to oversee the end of the war. The three heads of state warned the Japanese to surrender or face "prompt and utter destruction."

Around the same time, a meeting of delegates from fifty nations met in San Francisco to plan for an international organization to keep the peace. That conference created and approved the charter of the United Nations. While the conference was going on, however, there was still work to be done on the battlefields, carried out by the men and women who actually fought and won the war.

SECTION 2 REVIEW

Key Terms, People, and Places
1. Define (a) blitzkrieg, (b) Battle of the Bulge.
2. Identify (a) Douglas MacArthur, (b) Dwight D. Eisenhower, (c) Chester Nimitz, (d) Joseph Stalin.
3. Identify (a) Midway Island, (b) Guadalcanal, (c) Normandy.

Key Concepts
4. What was the holocaust?

5. How did the United States entry into the war affect the Allied position?

Critical Thinking
6. **Formulating Questions** Imagine that you are responsible for deciding Allied military strategy at the point when the United States entered World War II. Develop a list of questions that you would ask your military advisers before firming up your strategy.

RESOURCE DIRECTORY

Teaching Resources

Quiz found in the Unit 8 folder, p. 10, covers the main ideas in this section as well as the key terms.

Americans on the Battle Fronts

SECTION PREVIEW

The grim reality of combat far from home was tough on all soldiers. Discrimination in the armed forces made the experience even more painful for many Americans.

Key Concepts
- Life for American soldiers on the war fronts was brutal and frightening.
- Several groups—including women, African Americans, Latino Americans, and Native Americans—served in the armed forces despite discrimination.
- While their families were interned at home, Japanese Americans bravely defended their country overseas.

Key Terms, People, and Places
GI, WAC

World War II changed the lives of the men and women who were uprooted from home and sent far away from loved ones to provide the military muscle that won the war. The 15 million Americans who served as soldiers, sailors, and aviators made their way through distant deserts, jungles, swamps, turbulent seas, and forbidding skies. Anxious to engage the enemy, fearful of what would happen when they did, for them the war was often a desperate struggle just to stay alive.

The GI War

American soldiers called themselves **GIs**, after the "Government Issue" stamp on all shoes, clothes, guns, and other equipment provided by the military. Thousands entered the service when they received their official draft notices: "Greetings. You are hereby ordered for induction into the Armed Forces of the United States. . . ." Even more rushed to volunteer after the attack on Pearl Harbor.

In the field, the war was hardly the romantic struggle portrayed in some books and films. The miserable conditions were described in the newspaper columns of Ernie Pyle, the popular war correspondent who lived with the enlisted men on the battle fronts and wrote about the war from their perspective. Pyle sent reports back to the United States six times a week until he died from a sniper's bullet in the Pacific campaign in 1945. He characterized the life of a typical soldier as follows:

The front-line soldier has lived like an animal for months and is a veteran of the cruel fierce world of death. Everything has been abnormal and unstable in his life for months. He has been filthy dirty, has eaten if and when, has slept on the hard ground without cover. His clothes have been greasy, he has lived in a constant haze of dust, pestered by flies and the heat, moving constantly, deprived of all the things that once meant stability. Things such as walls, chairs, floors, windows, faucets, shelves, Coca-Colas and the greatly important little matter of knowing you'll go to bed tonight in the same place you got up in this morning.
Written aboard a navy ship in the Allied invasion fleet headed for Sicily, July 16, 1943

The army Medal of Honor (above) paid tribute to gallantry in action above and beyond the call of duty. Fatigues (below) were standard wear for American soldiers.

AMERICAN PROFILES
Charles Rigaud, Marine

Ernie Pyle's description of combat life would have been all too familiar to Charles Alfred Rigaud. Marine Captain Rigaud was

Reproducible Lesson Plan found in the Unit 8 folder, p. 5, provides a summary of the Section 3 lesson plan content.

Alternate Lesson Plan: Critical Thinking Identifying Central Issues, found in the Alternate Lesson Plans folder, p. 124, is designed to help students apply this skill by writing letters focusing on life at the battle fronts.

Guided Reading and Review found in the Unit 8 folder, p. 11, provides a structure for reading and mastering the key concepts and reviewing the key terms for Section 3. (Guided Practice)

1. FOCUS

Connecting to the Big Idea

See page 662B. Service in the armed forces was difficult. Ask students how overt discrimination and racial segregation affected some groups of Americans in the military.

Objectives
- Describe conditions for American soldiers on the war fronts.
- Identify groups of Americans who served in the armed forces despite discrimination.
- Describe the contribution of Japanese Americans in the armed services.

Bellringer

Ask students to describe how Hollywood would portray the typical World War II soldier, seaman, or airman. Have students compare their descriptions to see if stereotypes emerge.

Reading Strategy

Structured Outline Ask students to take notes on the following topics:
- Conditions on the battlefield
- Role played by women in the military
- Effects of discrimination on African American soldiers
- Military contributions of Mexican Americans, Native Americans, and Japanese Americans

2. INSTRUCT

Explain/Discuss

Explain to students that Americans on the battle front confronted perilous situations, miserable conditions, and loneliness. Discuss with students the characteristics, exemplified by Charles Rigaud, that made the American armed forces so efficient. (*Courage, fraternity, obedience, modesty, willingness to assume responsibility.*)

Ask students to tell how what they have read in the section supports or refutes the stereotype or typical Hollywood soldier described in the Bellringer activity.

Analyze

Some scholars trace the beginning of the civil rights movement to the experience of African Americans in the military during World War II. Which facet of this experience do students think was most important in beginning the movement for equality? Discuss the importance of leadership, the importance of experience in a large institution such as the military, and the significance of the contrast between the nation's stated goals and its discriminatory actions.

Activity

A Letter to Roosevelt

Explain that the average age of the typical soldier in World War II ranged from late teens to early twenties. Ask students to assume the role of a voting-age citizen during World War II. Have them write a letter to President Roosevelt explaining their views on one of the following topics: the role of women in the military; segregation in the armed forces; or the policy of separating army blood plasma by the race of the donor. Letters should respectfully suggest to Roosevelt a change the students feel is acceptable. Ask why they think the government did not change its policies at the time.

responsible for leading his men into battle against the Japanese on the island of Guadalcanal. John Hersey, another well-known war correspondent, was with Rigaud and his unit during the Third Battle of the Mataniko River. While this battle was not among the most famous of the war, Hersey's vivid account reveals that it was fraught with terror, death, heartache—and remarkable courage.

Rigaud's mission in the Third Battle was to push the Japanese, who were advancing toward the American camp, back across the Mataniko River. To reach the river, Rigaud's unit would have to pass through a jungle valley filled with Japanese snipers. Once there, they would face machine gun and mortar fire from established Japanese battle positions. Rigaud, the veteran marine in charge of this operation, looked to Hersey "like anything except a killer who took no prisoners. He had a boy's face. . . . His mustache was not quite convincing."

Marine Captain Charles Rigaud was recommended for decoration after his brave fighting on the island of Tulagi in the Pacific.

Charles Rigaud had grown up in Oriskany Falls, New York, almost ten thousand miles from the jungles of Guadalcanal. Back home he played the violin, both in orchestras and at square dances. Rigaud also loved the outdoors and he often went on hunting and trapping trips with a close friend.

Rigaud attended Syracuse University, where he joined ROTC (Reserve Officers' Training Corps) and graduated with a commission as a second lieutenant. He joined the marines just as the war began. In command in the field, he was responsible for his company. He had led them through other battles on Guadalcanal and on the nearby island of Tulagi. Success had come at no small cost—twenty-two of his men were dead.

Now, on October 8, 1942, Rigaud and his unit were slowly making their way through the jungle into another perilous situation. They walked single file down a narrow path, keeping five paces between them so that any snipers in the area would not have a big target. Before they reached the river, one marine lay dead in the path, killed by a Japanese sharpshooter.

After hours of difficult marching, the trees began to thin and the river was in sight. Then a single "high flat snap [that] was easily recognizable as a Japanese sound" broke the silence. Within seconds the air was filled with sniper fire, followed quickly by machine gun and mortar fire from across the river. Rigaud's company had walked right into a Japanese trap.

Marines carrying machine gun parts came together in bunches to set them up. Under heavy fire from the Japanese, however, no more than two guns were ever assembled. As his men took cover and tried to fight back, Rigaud rushed about checking on all of them. The Japanese fire was terrifying, and before long, a desperate rumor began to circulate that the order to withdraw had been given. As his men headed back toward the jungle, Rigaud stood up and shouted, "Who . . . gave that order? . . . Where do you guys think you're going? . . . Get back in there." Soon, however, he did give the order for withdrawal. He knew they could not hold their position.

Rigaud and most of his men survived to fight another day. The Third Battle of the Mataniko River was won by other companies of marines who forced a Japanese retreat on October 9. John Hersey, when preparing to leave Guadalcanal, asked if he could do anything for Rigaud when he got back to the United States. Rigaud answered, "Well, if you go through a place called Oriskany Falls, wish you'd tell my folks you saw me."

Women in the Armed Forces

Not all soldiers were men. By the war's end, over 300,000 American women had served in the military. Faced with serious personnel needs, officials were willing to use women's help in virtually all areas except combat.

Oveta Culp Hobby, director of the Women's Army Auxiliary Corps (WAAC—later shortened to **WAC**, Women's Army Corps), told potential recruits, "This is *your* war." Women

RESOURCE DIRECTORY

Teaching Resources

American Profiles Activity found in the Unit 8 folder, p. 17, profiles Jacqueline Cochran, veteran of the World War II Women's Air Force Service Pilots.

Critical Thinking Activity Predicting Consequences: After the Army—What? found in the Unit 8 folder, p. 22, helps students to apply this skill by having them explore possible postwar lifestyle changes for returning servicewomen.

Primary Source Activity Experiences of an African American Soldier, found in the Unit 8 folder, pp. 24–25, uses narrative by World War II veteran Timuel Black to illustrate some of the hardships and injustices faced by African American soldiers.

worked as typists and clerks, but also as control tower operators, radio operators, parachute riggers, and mechanics. The navy had a similar organization, the WAVES (Women Accepted for Volunteer Emergency Service). One quarter of all WAVES served in naval aviation. Women Air Force Service Pilots (WASPs) ferried planes around the country, and they towed targets for antiaircraft gunnery practice missions as well. ✪

How has the role of women in the United States military changed since World War II?

Equality in the Armed Forces

✪ Although the military discriminated against African Americans, their participation as soldiers helped win the war. The all-African American 92nd Infantry Division, known as the Buffaloes, fought in the bloody Italian campaign of 1943 and 1944. The 333rd Field Artillery Battalion served with distinction with General George Patton's Third Army in France. These are only a few examples.

According to official policy, African Americans were not allowed to join either the air force or the marines. In the navy, they could only enlist in the messman's branch, which provided food services for the troops. The army, like the Red Cross, separated the blood plasma donated by African Americans.

Near the end of the war, however, shortages of soldiers led military officials to bend the

Using Historical Evidence How does this 1943 magazine cover demonstrate the new opportunities women had during World War II?

To defeat the Japanese in the Pacific, United States marines had to keep their strategies from the enemy. Navaho code talkers, using their native language for secret military communications, allowed the Allies to stay one step ahead of the Japanese.

Media and Technology

 Transparency
Critical Thinking, I-2

Caption Answer to ...

Using Historical Evidence

The woman pictured on the cover is an air force pilot, operating in a field newly opened to women during the war. Her clothing (pantsuit) also suggests a wartime acceptance of new roles for women.

Answer to ...

In the years since World War II, the military has extended many more opportunities to women. They may now become officers and participate in most fields of duty. In 1993 women pilots were finally allowed to compete for assignments in combat missions.

Enrichment

Ask students to find out about, visit, and describe World War II memorials in your community. Students might interview a veteran of the war (possibly through contacting the local VFW post), and ask questions about his or her branch of service, locations of service, assignments, rank, and conditions experienced.

3. ASSESS

Section 3 Review Answers

1. (a) GI, see p. 677, (b) WAC, see p. 678

2. Rigaud's profile reveals that many American soldiers were ordinary men who became extraordinary leaders when faced with life-and-death situations.

3. Women served in all capacities except combat. They worked as typists, clerks, control tower operators, radio operators, parachute riggers, and mechanics.

4. African American participation helped win the war. For example, the "all-Negro" (as it was then called) 92nd Infantry Division fought in the Italian campaign of 1943 and 1944; the 333rd Field Artillery Battalion served with Patton's Third Army in France.

5. Possible answers: The United States was fighting for the liberties of those overseas, while the liberties of women and minorities were being curtailed at home.

Answer to ...

Viewpoints

Poage argues that keeping up the morale of the southern white volunteers is more important to winning the war than serving the interests of African Americans. A. Philip Randolph argues that the military is fighting for democracy—if it remains segregated, then the African American volunteers have won nothing. For a more thorough examination of the integration of the military, see the Resource Directory below.

Reteach

Write the following statements on the chalkboard and ask students to find details in the section to support each one:
- Americans serving on the war fronts suffered many hardships.
- Women served in the military in all areas except combat.
- The armed services segregated African American and Japanese troops.
- Minority groups helped to win the war despite discrimination.

4. CLOSE

Reinforcing the Big Idea

The stated goals the United States fought for during World War II were essentially inconsistent with its treatment of women and minorities. They suffered not only the hardships of war but also the added burden of discrimination. The next section describes the decision to use the atomic bomb to end the war.

Viewpoints
On the Integration of the Military

Discussion about desegregating the armed forces during World War II aroused strong feelings on both sides. Below are two opposing viewpoints. *What arguments does each side use to support its viewpoint?*

Against Integration

"In this hour of national crisis, it is much more important that we have the full-hearted co-operation of the thirty million white southern Americans than that we satisfy the National Association for the Advancement of Colored People. . . . If they be forced to serve with Negroes, they will cease to volunteer; and when drafted, they will not serve with that enthusiasm and high morale that has always characterized the soldiers and sailors of the southern states."

W. R. Poage, Texas state representative, 1941

For Integration

"Though I have found no Negroes who want to see the United Nations lose this war, I have found many who, before the war ends, want to see the stuffing knocked out of white supremacy. . . . If freedom and equality are not vouchsafed [granted] the peoples of color, the war for democracy will not be won. . . . We demand the abolition of segregation and discrimination in . . . [all] branches of national defense."

A. Philip Randolph, "Why Should We March?" November 1942

---

rules. An army program begun in January 1945 allowed 20,000 volunteers—including over 4,500 African Americans—to train for infantry duty. From March until the end of the war in Europe, African Americans fought alongside whites in these volunteer combat units. In 1944 the navy organized twenty-five supply ships with integrated crews. The marines finally invited African Americans to enlist in the corps in 1945.

Nearly 350,000 Mexican Americans served in the military during World War II, most enlisting in the army. Mexican American soldiers made up a quarter of the combat troops defending Bataan in the Philippines shortly after Pearl Harbor. They faced Erwin Rommel in North Africa and played a major role in the D-Day invasion of 1944. Guy Gabaldón, who had been raised by a Japanese American family in Los Angeles, earned the Silver Star for his actions in the Battle of Saipan, an island in the Marianas in the western Pacific. Using his language skills, he persuaded more than a thousand Japanese soldiers to surrender to the Allies. By the end of the war, seventeen Mexican Americans had earned the Congressional Medal of Honor.

Though Native Americans were denied the right to vote in three states, they were still eligible for the draft, and eventually 25,000 served in the army and other branches of the military. Ira Hayes, a Pima from Arizona, was one of three survivors at Mount Suribachi on Iwo Jima. Some Navahos worked as code talkers in the marines, using their unique language as a means of transmitting messages by radio and phone.

While tens of thousands of Japanese Americans were interned in camps in the United States (see Chapter 25, Section 4), others seized the opportunity offered them to fight. The 442nd Regimental Combat Team eventually fought in Italy under General Mark Clark and then moved into France. There, they took almost ten thousand casualties and became the most decorated unit in the war.

SECTION 3 REVIEW

Key Terms, People, and Places
1. Define (a) GI, (b) WAC.

Key Concepts
2. What does the profile of Charles Rigaud reveal about the soldiers who fought in the war?
3. Describe the roles that women played during World War II.

4. What contributions did African Americans make in the military during World War II?

Critical Thinking
5. **Checking Consistency** Were the goals the United States was fighting for in World War II consistent with its treatment of women and minorities? Explain why you answered yes or no.

▶ RESOURCE DIRECTORY

Teaching Resources

Viewpoints Activity On the Integration of the Military, found in the Unit 8 folder, pp. 19–20, provides additional viewpoints and perspectives on the arguments for and against the integration of the military.

Quiz found in the Unit 8 folder, p. 12, covers the main ideas in this section as well as the key terms.

Examining Photographs

Photographs are a form of visual evidence that can provide valuable information about an event or historical period. They can show what people or places in recent history looked like and can document momentous occasions. Photographers, however, like other observers of events, have their own points of view. Therefore, you must analyze their photographs carefully.

By their choice of subject, lighting, and camera angle, photographers can influence what is seen and how it is perceived. They may choose to photograph a scene that strikes them as particularly interesting, dramatic, or revealing but that, in reality, is not typical or representative. Photographers may also distort the appearance of objects in their pictures to create an illusion or convey a particular mood. By making these choices, photographers affect what is learned from their pictures.

The photograph at right was taken during World War II on a Pacific island southeast of the Philippines that was the scene of bitter fighting during the fall of 1944. Use the following steps to analyze the photograph.

1. Study the photograph to identify the subject. Look at the photograph as a whole, then study the details. (a) What do you see in the picture? (b) What broad subject or issue does the photograph address? (c) Was the photograph likely taken before, during, or after a tough battle? Explain.

2. Analyze the reliability of the photograph as a source of information. (a) What mood or emotion is captured in this photograph? (b) What aspects of the photograph capture this mood? (c) Does the photograph look as if it has been altered in any way by the photographer? Explain. (d) Does it seem as if the soldier posed or was unaware that he was being photographed?

3. Study the photograph to learn more about the historical period. Refer to the photograph and what you have read about World War II to answer the following questions. (a) What could you learn about the Pacific front if this photograph was your only source of information? (b) What can photographs such as this one contribute to a person's knowledge about an event that written sources cannot? (c) From what you have read in this chapter about the fighting on the Pacific islands during World War II, do you think this photograph presents a realistic picture of the war? Explain.

Historian's Toolbox Activity Examining Photographs, found in the Unit 8 folder, p. 21, provides further opportunity for students to determine a photographer's intent and other information from a photograph.

Historical Evidence
Examining Photographs

Focus Analyze a photograph as historical evidence, taking into account the point of view of the photographer.

Instruct If possible, display collections of World War II photographs, such as the Time-Life Series on World War II or the work of Robert Capa or Margaret Bourke-White, for students to observe. Ask students to note the subjects, background, and qualities of light and mood in the photographs. Encourage them to try to determine the style, or point of view, of the photographer. Discuss the importance of being able to analyze a photographer's point of view when using photographs to learn about a particular period in history.

Extend See the Historian's Toolbox Activity in the Resource Directory below.

Answers

1. (a) The picture shows a soldier sitting alone in a desolate area with his head bowed, surrounded by debris. (b) It addresses the aftermath of war. (c) It was taken after; the devastation of battle is evident, but all lies quiet.

2. (a) The photograph conveys exhaustion and sorrow. (b) The soldier's despairing posture, seen up close; the wide swath of destruction all around him. (c) The photo does not appear to have been altered. Even the object in the foreground has not been moved. (d) The soldier appears unposed. He probably did not know he was being photographed, as his face is in his hands.

3. (a) One could gather what type of terrain was being fought over, the level of destruction that followed, and the feelings of at least some of the soldiers. (b) Photographs can sometimes present a powerful, emotionally graphic portrayal of an event that cannot be described in words. (c) It is realistic but incomplete. The photograph conveys more of a mood than it does a detailed account of the death and destruction that took place. Ideally, one would have access to both text and pictures for a full, historical account.

Dropping the Atomic Bomb: A Turning Point in History

SECTION 4

Dropping the Atomic Bomb: A Turning Point in History

1. FOCUS

Connecting to the Big Idea

See page 662B. To bring the war to an end as quickly as possible, the United States used a new weapon, the atomic bomb, against Japan. Ask students what was special or unique about the bomb and what were the results of its use.

Objectives

• Identify the Manhattan Project and the atomic bomb.
• Explain why President Truman chose to use the atomic bomb on Japan.
• Describe the results of the bombing of Hiroshima and Nagasaki.

Bellringer

Ask students to write one sentence describing what they think is the most important way the use of nuclear power has changed the world.

In Depth

Interdisciplinary

A number of factors helped win the war for the Allies; among them were the inventions of scientific tools. One of these was radar, an electronic tracking system. By 1943, airplanes using radar could locate submarines or direct ships to attack. In addition, navy ships using sonar, an apparatus that transmits high frequency sound waves through water, could detect distant propeller noises from objects such as submarines.

SECTION PREVIEW

A collaboration of the top scientists in the world put a devastating secret weapon in American hands. Desperate to end the war as quickly as possible, the United States decided to unleash the terrible force of the atomic bomb on two unsuspecting Japanese cities.

Key Concepts

• The top secret Manhattan Project, which began before the United States entered the war, took years to develop the atomic bomb.
  • Alternatives to using the bomb on Japan were considered, but President Truman believed that the bomb would actually save many lives.
  • Two atomic bombs demolished Hiroshima and Nagasaki; the long-term effects on survivors were unpredictable.

This watch was stopped and partially melted when an atomic bomb exploded over Hiroshima, Japan, in 1945.

Key Terms, People, and Places

Manhattan Project, Interim Committee; Albert Einstein, J. Robert Oppenheimer, Harry S Truman; Hiroshima, Nagasaki

---

World War II was a technological war. Aircraft were now more maneuverable and could fly longer distances without refueling. The aircraft carrier introduced a new type of naval battle at Midway: one in which the opposing vessels were never in sight of one another. Specialized landing craft and dive-bombers made amphibious landings such as the Normandy invasion possible. But the world could scarcely imagine the destructive capacity of the new bomb being secretly developed in the United States.

The Manhattan Project

A letter written by physicist **Albert Einstein** in August 1939 helped set in motion the process of developing this new kind of bomb in the United States. Einstein was known worldwide for developing the theory of relativity, which describes how time and space function in the universe. He speculated that enormous energy might be released if atoms could be split in a particular way. In his letter to President Roosevelt, he wrote, "It is conceivable . . . that extremely powerful bombs of a new type may . . . be constructed," and he hinted that the Germans were already trying to build such a weapon. Einstein's letter reached Roosevelt just as World War II was starting in Europe.

Intrigued with the possibility of a new weapon and concerned that Germany might develop it first, Roosevelt established an Advisory Committee on Uranium to look into the matter. After the United States entered the war, the venture was reorganized and became known as the **Manhattan Project**.

The Manhattan Project developed into one of the greatest engineering enterprises of all time. During the final three years of the war, this top secret undertaking involved the building of thirty-seven installations in the United States and Canada. It employed 120,000 people and cost $2 billion—an unimaginable sum at the time. Scientists already had succeeded in splitting the nucleus of the uranium atom. Now they needed to produce a self-sustaining atomic chain reaction, in which particles released from the splitting of one atom would cause another atom to break apart, and so on. In December 1942, a physicist working with Italian scientist Enrico Fermi at the University of Chicago placed a phone call including a coded message to be relayed to President Roosevelt:

RESOURCE DIRECTORY

Teaching Resources

Reproducible Lesson Plan found in the Unit 8 folder, p. 6, provides a summary of the Section 4 lesson plan content.

Alternate Lesson Plan: Critical Thinking Identifying Alternatives, found in the Alternate Lesson Plans folder, p. 125, is designed to help students apply this skill by charting and discussing President Truman's decision to drop the atomic bomb.

Guided Reading and Review found in the Unit 8 folder, p. 13, provides a structure for reading and mastering the key concepts and reviewing the key terms for Section 4. (Guided Practice)

"You'll be interested to know," the physicist said, "that the Italian navigator [Fermi] has just landed in the New World. The earth was not as large as he had estimated, and he arrived in the New World sooner than he had expected."

"Is that so?" he was asked. "Were the natives friendly?"

"Everyone landed safe and happy." The message meant that the chain reaction had been accomplished without blowing up the laboratory in the process. Next, scientists had to find ways to gather enough of a special kind of uranium—or produce a new element, plutonium—to mold into a bomb.

On July 16, 1945, they tested their effort. In the desert at Alamogordo, New Mexico, scientists detonated the world's first atomic device. It left a huge crater in the earth's floor and shattered windows 125 miles away. As he watched the first blast, physicist **J. Robert Oppenheimer**, who had spearheaded the entire project, remembered the words of the *Bhagavad Gita*, the Hindu holy book: "Now I am become Death, the destroyer of worlds."

The Decision to Drop the Bomb

Once the bomb was ready, American policymakers had to decide if and when to use it. The war in Europe was over, but the Pacific struggle still ground on. There were other courses of action besides dropping the bomb that might end the war. Allied planners had already worked out the details of a massive invasion of the Japanese islands. But this was a frightening prospect. Art Rittenberg, who joined the marines after he graduated from high school in 1942, describes the prospect of invading Japan from the point of view of an enlisted soldier:

M*ake no mistake about it, the Japanese were great fighters and everyone respected . . . them and feared them. They fought like [crazy] for Iwo [Jima] . . . , a two-and-a-half-mile long piece of volcanic sand and rock. What are they going to fight like in the home islands?*

The estimated cost of the invasion in American lives was as high as one million.

Using Historical Evidence This painting by Jacob Lawrence depicts a Hiroshima family after the atomic blast. *Why has the artist made the people's faces and the furniture look as they do?*

A naval blockade or continued bombing might also help defeat Japan. A demonstration on a deserted island might show the Japanese the bomb's awesome power. Some diplomats believed that Japan might surrender more quickly if the United States simply softened its insistence on "unconditional surrender" and guaranteed that the emperor could keep his throne.

American officials debated these possibilities in the **Interim Committee**, a group that included both government leaders and scientists. In the end, they were unwilling to choose any of the alternatives to dropping the bomb. They did not want to incur further casualties or let the long war drag on still longer. They did not want to suffer the embarrassment of a failed demonstration. Besides bringing Japan to its knees, some historians have speculated that the new bomb offered a dramatic display of

TURNING POINTS

Reading Strategy

Relating to Topic Ask students to write two column headings on a piece of paper: Alternatives to Using the Bomb and Reasons to Use the Bomb. Ask students to write notes in the appropriate column as they read.

2. INSTRUCT

Explain/Discuss

Explain to students that the Manhattan Project was conducted in complete secrecy. Discuss the necessity and morality of such secret undertakings. What might have happened if the Manhattan Project had been public knowledge? Is a government justified in keeping secrets from its citizens in wartime, or at any time?

Analyze

Remind students how new atomic power was to the world: the bomb was tested for the first time in July and deployed in August. Do students think that Truman would have made a different decision if he had understood the delayed effects of the bomb? (*Truman himself emphatically defended his decision throughout his life, saying that his goal was to end the war with the loss of as few American lives as possible.*)

Caption Answer to . . .

Using Historical Evidence

Students may suggest that the people's faces look like skulls, as if they are dead or almost dead. A part of them—their innocence, perhaps—has surely died. The broken furniture suggests the physical devastation wrought by the blast; it may also symbolize the people's broken lives.

CHAPTER 24 SECTION 4 **683**

On August 6, 1945, the United States dropped a uranium bomb on Hiroshima, Japan, killing thousands of people. Survivors later told stories about their terrifying experiences. Have students take the point of view of a survivor, possibly a child, mother or father, student, factory worker, or business owner, and write a fictional journal entry reflecting how the bombing affected that character on that day. Encourage students to describe what happened before, during, and after the explosion. **LEP**

Enrichment

Simulate a meeting of the Interim Committee by having students argue in favor of one of the following positions: a naval blockade or A-bomb demonstration; the invasion of Japan; immediate use of the atomic bomb; relaxation of the position on unconditional surrender. Students might research the opinions of a top policymaker—such as Henry L. Stimson, Ralph A. Bard, or James Frank—regarding the use of the atomic bomb.

Answer to ...
MAKING CONNECTIONS

Students may argue that a subtle racism contributed to the decision. Prejudice against Japanese Americans was clear, given the internment policy instituted earlier in the war. On the other hand, students may argue, since Allied forces had mercilessly bombed German cities just before Germany surrendered, the United States might well have used the atomic bomb there had it been ready in time.

Allied might and served as an example of American power to the Russians. Although they were allies during the war, the United States and the Soviet Union had very different ideas about the shape of the postwar world. The deployment of a new atomic weapon allowed the United States to flex its muscles before the eyes of its communist rival.

The Interim Committee therefore recommended dropping the new bomb. **Harry S Truman**, President for barely four months after Franklin Roosevelt's death in April 1945, would have had a difficult time arguing against using the weapon that had consumed so many resources over the past five years. Truman, however, had no intention of arguing. He recorded in his memoirs that he "regarded the bomb as a military weapon and never had any doubt that it should be used." Winston Churchill agreed. Speaking for the military and political leaders of the day, he explained, "The decision whether or not to use the atomic bomb to compel the surrender of Japan was never even an issue. There was unanimous, automatic, unquestioned agreement around our table."

Truman's decision came down to two main reasons. One was the fact that invading Japan would result in high casualty figures. Second was the bitterness Americans felt toward the Japanese in the first place. "You should do your weeping at Pearl Harbor," said Truman in 1963, "where thousands of American boys are underneath the waves caused by a Japanese sneak attack."

MAKING CONNECTIONS

Do you think Truman would have been more reluctant to use the atomic bomb on Germany or Italy, if they had not yet surrendered in August 1945, than he was to use it on Japan? Why or why not?

The Bombs in Japan

On August 6, 1945, an American plane dropped "Little Boy," a uranium bomb, on the Japanese city of **Hiroshima**. It killed 70,000

---

people immediately or soon thereafter and injured 70,000 more. Three days later, another plane dropped "Fat Man," a plutonium bomb, on the city of **Nagasaki**, killing 40,000 people and injuring a like number.

The bombs were a terrifying experience for those people who managed to escape instant death. Novelist Masuji Ibuse recalled the Hiroshima blast: "I saw a ball of blindingly intense light, and simultaneously I was plunged into total, unseeing darkness." Then followed the screams of pain as the city descended into chaos. The black cloud of dust that had instantly turned day into night soon formed a mushroom cloud over the region. People wandered around in confusion looking for friends and family or simply in shock. ●

Hiroshima was ablaze after the explosion. The bomb ignited fires near where it had detonated, and more fires began as hot wires were exposed in crumbling buildings. People suffering from terrible burns—many of whom would die within a few days—rushed to plunge themselves into one of Hiroshima's seven rivers. The white-hot blast had burned people's clothes off their bodies; some people had designs from their kimonos scorched into their flesh. Author Tatsue Urata pictured a victim in Nagasaki:

> The skin was peeling off his face and chest and hands. He was black all over—I suppose it was dirt that had stuck to him where the skin had peeled off; his whole body was coated with it and the blood trickling from his wounds made red streaks in the black.

People who survived the fires still had much to endure. Schoolchildren who had been outside when the bombs hit were so badly disfigured that they became social outcasts. Radiation poisoning—an effect that few people had even considered before the bomb was actually dropped—continued to produce unpredictable symptoms and to claim more victims in the years that followed.

Bombs in both cities demolished buildings, too. Hiroshima and Nagasaki were little more than mounds of rubble near where the bombs had hit. Similar damage had been done in

---

RESOURCE DIRECTORY

Teaching Resources

● **Literature Activity** *Hiroshima,* an excerpt from the writings of war correspondent John Hersey, found in the Unit 8 folder, p. 28, helps students understand the experiences of six Japanese who survived the atomic blast over Hiroshima in 1945.

A moment before "Little Boy" leveled Hiroshima, the American GI above would have been standing in the midst of a thriving city. The photo at left shows the mushroom cloud that formed over Nagasaki when "Fat Man" exploded.

Tokyo and other cities by hundreds of conventional weapons, but this destruction had been caused by just one bomb.

The Japanese were dazed by the blasts. They were already considering surrender when the Soviet Union entered the war on the Chinese front two days after Hiroshima. Following the Nagasaki explosion, they sought to end the conflict any way they could. On August 14, 1945, Japanese leaders accepted American terms. The island nation formally surrendered on September 2, bringing the long and destructive war to a final end.

SECTION 4 REVIEW

Key Terms, People, and Places

1. Define Interim Committee.
2. Identify (a) Albert Einstein, (b) J. Robert Oppenheimer, (c) Harry S Truman.
3. Identify (a) Hiroshima, (b) Nagasaki.

Key Concepts

4. What was the purpose of the Manhattan Project, and what resources were required to accomplish this purpose?
5. What were some alternatives to dropping the atomic bomb on Japan?

Critical Thinking

6. **Demonstrating Reasoned Judgment** World War II veteran Art Rittenberg recalls that war propaganda "heavily influenced the way we viewed the Japanese. I never thought of them as people like myself who had gone to high school, who had gone to a dance, who had friends, who had parents. They were 'the Japs.'" List three reasons that such attitudes may have affected the decision to drop two atomic bombs on Japan and three reasons they may not have.

Quiz found in the Unit 8 folder, p. 14, covers the main ideas in this section as well as the key terms.

Chapter Test Forms A and B are found in the Unit 8 folder, pp. 31–36.

Answer Keys found in the Unit 8 folder, pp. 146–160, provide answers to all student activities.

Media and Technology

Transparency
Graphic Organizer, G-5

Guided Reading Audiotapes
(English and Spanish)

Computer Test Bank

Section 4 Review Answers

1. Interim Committee, see p. 683

2. (a) Albert Einstein, see p. 682, (b) J. Robert Oppenheimer, see p. 683, (c) Harry S Truman, see p. 684

3. (a) Hiroshima, see, p. 684, (b) Nagasaki, see p. 684

4. The Manhattan Project was established to research and develop a weapon that used a sustained nuclear reaction. The project involved thirty-seven sites in the United States and Canada, employed 120,000 people, and cost $2 billion.

5. Alternatives included an invasion, a blockade, a demonstration, or relaxation of the unconditional surrender formula.

6. Answers will vary, but students should support their answers with well-reasoned arguments.

Reteach

Ask students to complete each of the following statements, using information from the chapter section.

- The Manhattan Project was a top-secret plan to develop _____.
- The decision to drop the bomb was made by _____.
- The bomb was dropped on _____.
- The war in the Pacific ended eight days after _____.

Reinforcing the Big Idea

The United States ended the war with Japan by using a terrible new weapon, the atomic bomb. The war was finally over, but the world would never be the same again.

The Lasting Impact of the Atomic Bomb

Focus During World War II, the United States developed a secret weapon, the atomic bomb. In the summer of 1945, the United States made the momentous decision to use this new weapon against Japan in order to bring an end to the war. What has been the lasting impact of the development of atomic power?

Instruct Tell students that in the 1950s, schools regularly scheduled air raid drills and students practiced hiding under their desks and shielding their eyes in case of a nuclear attack. Many Americans built and stocked air raid shelters for their families. Families without shelters planned where to go along the evacuation routes out of major cities. As tension between the United States and the Soviet Union tightened or relaxed, people around the world lived above all with the threat that the world might suffer nuclear destruction.

Discuss the arms race with students. Why did Americans think that the way to prevent a nuclear war was to make more and better nuclear weapons? In what way can history prove them correct? What are some of the unforeseen problems of nuclear power that continue to await solutions?

Ask students to work in pairs to find out more about nuclear power and the arms race. Ask pairs to summarize their findings about the arms race and nuclear power plants and their impact on the environment.

Extend Ask students to bring in articles from newspapers, magazines, and other sources about new uses for nuclear power or about problems and proposed solutions concerning nuclear waste. You may want to display these pieces on a bulletin board.

The Lasting Impact of the Atomic Bomb

The atomic bomb did more than simply end the war. The nuclear technology developed by the Manhattan Project launched a wide range of political and economic changes in the postwar world. The Soviet Union tested its first atomic weapon in 1949, and the specter of nuclear war between the superpowers cast a dark shadow over international affairs.

The Arms Race

The arms race was on. The United States tested a new and even more destructive nuclear weapon, the hydrogen bomb, in 1952. The Soviets soon had their own hydrogen bomb. Besides increasing tension and fear between the superpowers, tests in the 1950s and 1960s produced large quantities of fallout, radioactive dust in the atmosphere that drifted down to earth and contaminated every-thing it touched. Water, milk, and all kinds of foods could become toxic. In response, the United States, the Soviet Union, and Great Britain—now also a member of the "nuclear club"—signed a treaty in 1963 banning above-ground testing of nuclear devices.

Both the United States and the Soviet Union continued to produce many thousands of nuclear devices. By 1983 the United States possessed about 26,000 nuclear warheads, a number closely matched by the Soviet stockpile. Despite the proliferation of weapons, however, leaders were in no hurry to spark a nuclear conflict. The possibility of "mutu-ally assured destruction" acted as a strong deterrent. This situation meant that a country could not win a nuclear war because it would be destroyed by its opponent's defensive weapons.

The Soviet Union and the United States, as well as other countries, continued to devote much of

1945 Physicist J. Robert Oppenheimer and General Leslie R. Groves oversee first atomic bomb test in New Mexico desert.

| 1900 | 1920 | 1940 |

1939 Albert Einstein informs President Roosevelt that atomic weapons are possible.

RESOURCE DIRECTORY

Turning Point Extension Activity The Lasting Impact of the Atomic Bomb, found in the Unit 8 folder, pp. 15–16, extends students' understanding of the postwar era by discussing the long-term impact of the arms race.

their defense budgets to the development of conventional (nonnuclear) weapons. Atomic weapons were a deterrent against atomic weapons, but "limited" wars employing conventional weapons still played a central role in the postwar world. The war between the United States and Iraq in 1991, called the Persian Gulf War, is a good example. This brief conflict introduced the sophisticated new Patriot missile, which is capable of seeking out and destroying incoming missiles in midair.

Peaceful Applications

Nuclear technology has other applications besides the machinery of war. In 1953 Britain harnessed the power of the atom to produce electricity, completing the first nuclear power plant. By 1957 the United States had an operating nuclear plant in Shippingport, Pennsylvania. Many more were to follow. But in the late 1960s and early 1970s, some citizens began to question the safety of nuclear power. The possibility of radiation leaks and the risks involved in storing atomic waste, which remains dangerously radioactive for tens of thousands of years, frightened many people. By 1978 orders for new nuclear power plants

had dropped to zero, and many plants under construction in the 1980s were abandoned before they were finished.

New technologies that have grown out of nuclear research have been useful in the medical field. For example, methods of isotope separation developed by the Manhattan Project have given birth to nuclear medicine, in which small amounts of radioactive chemicals can be injected into and traced throughout the body to diagnose certain diseases. The atom contains an awesome and terrifying force, but it can also be tamed for human benefit.

REVIEWING THE FACTS

1. Did nuclear weapons make conventional war obsolete? Explain your answer.
2. What are some of the peaceful applications of nuclear technology?

Critical Thinking
3. **Formulating Questions** If your local utility company were planning to build a nuclear power plant in your community, what questions would you want to ask a nuclear scientist about the plant?

1952 United States tests first megaton-class hydrogen bomb on Pacific island of Eniwetok.

1982 Nearly one million people join an antinuclear demonstration in New York City.

1990s A bone scan using radioisotope tracers can determine whether cancer in one part of the body has spread to the bones.

| 1960 | 1980 | 2000 |

1950s American companies market backyard fallout shelters to families fearful of nuclear war.

1957 First American light-water nuclear power plant begins generating electricity in Shippingport, Pennsylvania.

Answers

1. The killing of vast numbers of people over the course of many years using conventional weapons would no longer be practical, since one atomic bomb could cause enormous destruction instantaneously.

2. These include nuclear power—a new source of energy—and nuclear medicine.

3. Answers should demonstrate students' understanding of the potential hazards of nuclear power. Possible questions: What provisions do you have in place in the event of a radiation leak? What safeguards do you have against a nuclear meltdown? How do you plan to dispose of nuclear waste?

..
Chapter Review Answers

Understanding Key Terms, People, and Places

Terms
Students should refer to the definitions of the key terms in the chapter to write sentences that show the relation of each word to World War II.

Matching
1. appeasement
2. blitzkrieg
3. Battle of the Bulge
4. GI
5. Interim Committee

Word Relationships
1. Mussolini, dictator of Italy during World War II, does not belong. Einstein and Oppenheimer were associated with the development of the atomic bomb and Truman with its deployment.

2. Churchill, the British prime minister, does not belong. Generals MacArthur and Eisenhower and Admiral Nimitz were American military leaders.

3. The Rhineland, one of the first areas occupied by Hitler in 1936, does not belong. Pearl Harbor, Guadalcanal, and Midway Island were all scenes of important battles in the Pacific.

Reviewing Main Ideas

1. Japan, a resource-poor chain of islands, hoped to gain access to raw materials and new markets.

2. In order to help the Allies, President Roosevelt traded American ships to convoy supplies across the Atlantic. The next year, in 1941, he supported the Lend-Lease Act to provide war supplies to Britain.

3. Japan hoped to knock out the U.S. Pacific Fleet so that nothing would stand in the way of Japanese control of the Pacific.

4. In Europe, the failed German invasion of the Soviet Union and the successful Allied offensives in North Africa and Italy helped turn the tide in favor of the Allies. In the Pacific, the Allies won key strategic victories on the islands of Midway and Guadalcanal.

5. The Nazis' "final solution" was to get rid of all Jews and other "undesirables" by gathering them in concentration camps and killing them.

6. Their families were interned in camps in the United States and not allowed to leave.

7. Official policy forced African Americans to fight in segregated units in the

army. For most of the war, they were not allowed to join the air corps or the marine corps, and in the navy they could enlist only in the messman's branch.

8. The Navaho used their language to transmit secret messages by radio and telephone.

9. Because the Japanese were fierce fighters who would be defending their homeland, many people thought that the potential casualties of an invasion of Japan would be intolerable.

10. Buildings were demolished; seventy thousand people in Hiroshima and forty thousand in Nagasaki were killed; thousands more suffered terrible burns and radiation sickness; Japan finally agreed to surrender to the Allies.

Chapter Review

Understanding Key Terms, People, and Places

Key Terms
1. fascism
2. Nazi party
3. anti-Semitism
4. appeasement
5. Lend-Lease Act
6. blitzkrieg
7. Battle of the Bulge
8. holocaust
9. GI
10. WAC
11. Manhattan Project
12. Interim Committee

People
13. Benito Mussolini
14. Adolf Hitler
15. Winston Churchill
16. Douglas MacArthur
17. Dwight D. Eisenhower
18. Chester Nimitz
19. Joseph Stalin
20. Albert Einstein
21. J. Robert Oppenheimer
22. Harry S Truman

Places
23. Rhineland
24. Manchuria
25. Pearl Harbor
26. Midway Island
27. Guadalcanal
28. Normandy
29. Hiroshima
30. Nagasaki

Terms For each term above, write a sentence that explains its relation to World War II.

Matching Review the key terms in the list above. If you are not sure of a term's meaning, review its definition in the chapter. Then choose a term from the list that best matches each description below.
1. a policy of keeping the peace by giving in to someone's demands
2. a series of sudden military attacks by land and air
3. the German counterattack in Belgium and Luxembourg in December 1944
4. the nickname for an American soldier
5. the group of American officials who studied alternative methods of ending the war in the Pacific

Word Relationships Three of the terms in each of the following sets of terms are related. Choose the term that does not belong, and explain why it does not belong.
1. (a) Albert Einstein, (b) Benito Mussolini, (c) J. Robert Oppenheimer, (d) Harry S Truman
2. (a) Chester Nimitz, (b) Douglas MacArthur, (c) Winston Churchill, (d) Dwight D. Eisenhower
3. (a) Pearl Harbor, (b) Rhineland, (c) Guadalcanal, (d) Midway Island

Reviewing Main Ideas

Section 1 (pp. 664–669)
1. What did Japan hope to gain by invading Manchuria and other parts of the Asian mainland?
2. How did the United States support the Allies with economic aid while staying out of the fighting?
3. Why did Japan attack Pearl Harbor?

Section 2 (pp. 670–676)
4. What events helped turn the tide of war in favor of the Allies?
5. What was Hitler's "Final Solution"?

Section 3 (pp. 677–680)
6. While some Japanese Americans were fighting the

enemy overseas, what was happening to many of their families in the United States?
7. In what ways did the United States government discriminate against African Americans during World War II?
8. What unique contribution were Native Americans able to make to the American military effort?

Section 4 (pp. 682–685)
9. Why did the United States government reject the idea of invading Japan in order to end the war?
10. What were the immediate effects of using the atomic bomb on Hiroshima and Nagasaki?

Thinking Critically

1. Serious personnel shortages led military officials to bend the rules against women and African Americans in the military.

2. The United States and the Soviet Union had different ideas about what the postwar world should look like. The fact that the Soviet Union was excluded from the Manhattan Project showed a lack of trust and led to Soviet resentment. The United States deployed the atomic bomb in part to demonstrate America's strength to the Soviet Union.

3. Video games make war seem exciting and death seem unreal and impersonal. The actual experience of combat is numbingly terrifying; daily life is miserable and unstable.

- **Evidence of thoughtfulness** Did students include the major events presented in the chapter?
- **Evidence of outside research** To what extent did students use outside research materials?
- **Evidence of synthesis** Do the students' classification systems show how events are related? How complex are the relationships?
- **Communication style** Is the time line clear and easy to follow?

Thinking Critically

1. **Expressing Problems Clearly** What situation often motivated the armed forces to relax their discrimination against women and African Americans?
2. **Expressing Problems Clearly** The Soviet Union fought alongside the Allies during World War II, yet soon after became a bitter enemy of the United States. Give evidence to show that the seeds of conflict between the United States and the Soviet Union were already present during World War II.
3. **Distinguishing False from Accurate Images** Many popular video games deal with war. Do you think that the images of war presented in such games accurately portray the real experience of fighting in a war? Why or why not?

Making Connections

1. **Evaluating Primary Sources** Review the first primary source excerpt on page 684. Dwight Eisenhower disagreed with President Truman's decision to end the war by using the atomic bomb. Are Eisenhower's reasons convincing? Explain why or why not.
2. **Understanding the Visuals** Look through the chapter to find visuals that reveal the attitude of the United States toward the war before and after Pearl Harbor. Write a paragraph to accompany your choice of visuals, explaining what the attitude was and what change, if any, it underwent.
3. **Writing About the Chapter** Imagine that you are living in London during the Battle of Britain, the devastating German air attack that was most intense during the summer and fall of 1940. Write a letter to a relative in the United States, explaining your fears and uncertainties. First, review the chapter for details about the war. Next, write a draft of your letter, adding details from your imagination as you picture yourself living with the relentless bombing and the knowledge that much of Europe is under Nazi control. Revise your letter, making sure that it is written from the point of view of someone who does not know how the conflict will end. Proofread your letter and draft a final copy.
4. **Using the Graphic Organizer** This graphic organizer uses a multi-flow chart to organize information about the causes and effects of Britain and France's declaration of war on Germany in September 1939. Causes of that event appear in the boxes at left. Effects of the event are listed to the right. (a) According to the graphic organizer, what were two major causes of this event? (b) On a separate sheet of paper, create your own multi-flow chart. In the center box, write "Japanese bombing of Pearl Harbor draws U.S. into war." Add three causes and three effects of this event to the appropriate boxes.

Treaty of Versailles harshly punishes Germany after World War I

Depression destroys German economy in the 1930s

Adolf Hitler and his Nazi party rise to power

Germany takes over Rhineland and Czechoslovakia and attacks Poland

Britain and France declare war on Germany in September 1939

France falls to Germany in 1940

United States aids Britain through Lend-Lease Act

Japan signs treaty with Germany and Italy

Japanese bombing of Pearl Harbor draws United States into war

---

Making Connections

1. Answers will vary. Some students may argue that it was necessary to use the atomic bomb to ensure a quick end to the war; others may say that the United States should have tried other alternatives before using such a horrible weapon.

2. Students should use the visual "America First" on page 668 to demonstrate American isolationism before the war. To show the shift in the American attitude, they might use any of the photos or maps on pages 671, 672, 679, and 685. Students' paragraphs should demonstrate an understanding of the shift that the United States underwent from isolationism to interventionism.

3. Students' letters should be written from the viewpoint of someone living during the bombings and should reflect the uncertainty and fear of not knowing who will ultimately win the war.

4. (a) Answers should include two of the following: the Treaty of Versailles, depression in Germany, Hitler's rise to power, German aggression in Europe. (b) Causes may include American trade sanctions on Japan, Japanese desire for control over East Asia, and the threat of the Pacific Fleet to Japanese plans. Effects may include battles over tiny Pacific islands, anti-Japanese feelings in the United States, and the use of the atomic bomb.

Chapter 25 World War II at Home
1941–1945

📁 Teaching Resources (See Unit 8 Folder)

	Instruction	Enrichment
Section 1 **The Shift to Wartime Production** (pp. 692–695)	Reproducible Lesson Plan, p. 38 Alternate Lesson Plan, p. 127 Guided Reading and Review, p. 42 Quiz, p. 43	Visual Learning Activity, Campaign on the Home Front, p. 63 Critical Thinking Activity, Identifying Alternatives, p. 55
Section 2 **Daily Life on the Home Front** (pp. 696–699)	Reproducible Lesson Plan, p. 39 Alternate Lesson Plan, p. 128 Guided Reading and Review, p. 44 Quiz, p. 45	Literature Activity, How to Win Friends and Influence People, p. 59 Visual Learning Activity, The Nature of the Enemy, p. 62
Section 3 **Women and the War** (pp. 700–704)	Reproducible Lesson Plan, p. 40 Alternate Lesson Plan, p. 129 Guided Reading and Review, p. 46 Quiz, p. 47	Primary Source Activity, Working Conditions for Women of Color, pp. 57–58 Historian's Toolbox Activity, Identifying Assumptions, p. 54
Section 4 **The Struggle for Justice at Home** (pp. 706–711)	Reproducible Lesson Plan, p. 41 Alternate Lesson Plan, p. 130 Guided Reading and Review, p. 48 Quiz, p. 49 Chapter Test, Forms A & B, pp. 64–69	Literature Activity, Black Boy, pp. 60–61 American Profiles Activity, James Farmer, p. 50 American Profiles Activity, Daniel K. Inouye, p. 51 Viewpoints Activity, On Japanese American Internment, pp. 52–53 Primary Source Activity, Anti-Japanese Sentiment, p. 56

📁 Additional Chapter Resources

Resource Organizer, p. 37
Alternate Lesson Plan, p. 126
Answer Keys, pp. 146–158

Bibliography

For the Teacher
O'Neill, William L. *A Democracy at War: America's Fight at Home and Abroad in World War II.* Free Press, 1993.
Winkler, Allan M. *Home Front, U.S.A.: America During World War II.* Harlan Davidson, 1986. (A concise volume with a chapter devoted to ethnic minorities and women.)
Motley, Mary Penick, ed. *The Invisible Soldier: The Experience of the Black Soldier, World War II.* Wayne State University Press, 1975. (Personal accounts of African American soldiers during the war; illustrated with photographs and maps.)

Prentice Hall Literature Excerpts from *The American Experience,* 1994, "The Modern Age, 1915–1946."

Media and Technology

 Fine Art, D-18; Critical Thinking, I-10

 Graphic Organizer, G-3

 Guided Reading Audiotapes (English and Spanish)

 Computer Test Bank

For the Student

Frank, Miriam, et al. *The Life and Times of Rosie the Riveter.* Clarity, 1982. (Photographs and interviews provide a lively account of women and African American workers on the home front.)

Armour, John, and Peter Wright. *Manzanar.* Random House, 1988. (Uses text and photographs by Ansel Adams to tell the story of one Japanese internment camp.)

Harris, Mark Jonathan, et al. *The Home Front: America During World War II.* G.P. Putnam's Sons, 1984. (An informal anthology of interviews with ordinary citizens, including women and minorities, describing life during the war.)

THE BIG IDEA

The Big Idea for the chapter and how the main ideas in each section relate to the Big Idea are graphically displayed below. Comprehension of this chapter's Big Idea is critical to students' understanding of United States history and how we as a nation got where we are today.

CHAPTER 25

World War II affected every aspect of American life, from jobs and wages to the kind of food that appeared on the nation's dinner tables. Americans were asked to examine the ideals they were fighting for overseas and compare them with practices at home.

SECTION 1

World War II brought an end to the Great Depression as American factories and workers began to produce goods needed to win the war.

SECTION 2

Americans on the home front supported the war effort by conserving resources and coping with rationing.

SECTION 3

Thousands of American women took jobs in defense plants during the war.

SECTION 4

The need for workers during the war temporarily broke down some racial barriers in the job market. Japanese Americans, however, were treated with bitter prejudice and many were forced into internment camps.

World War II at Home
1941–1945

The Relevance of the Big Idea

World War II required large numbers of American men to fight in Europe and Asia. At the same time, workers were needed in industries at home. As a result, a major change in the American workplace took place: Women and minorities entered the work force in unprecedented numbers—and in fields previously off-limits to them. Executive orders barred racial discrimination in government war production jobs, but African Americans continued to suffer from widespread discrimination. In the midst of the cheerfully portrayed flurry of the war effort at home, Japanese Americans were interned in remote camps and their civil rights suspended.

Discuss the contrast of these conditions with the ideals put forth as the reasons Americans were fighting the war. Tell students that the civil rights movement of the sixties and some aspects of the women's movement of the seventies have their roots during this period.

In Depth

Global Connections

The Great Depression ended with the start of World War II. By 1943, there was virtually no unemployment in the United States. The war fueled economic growth not only in the United States but also in the other countries involved in the war. Germany and Japan both entered the war hoping that their economies would get a much-needed boost. In Japan, 3.2 million people became employed during the war years. In Great Britain, the labor force grew by 2.9 million.

World War II at Home
1941–1945

As war clouds gathered over Europe and Asia in the late 1930s, the United States government faced an enormous challenge. How would it convert a depressed peacetime economy and a public that still remembered the horrors of World War I into an efficient war production machine? This massive organizational project required not only mobilizing American businesses but also "selling" the American public on the war. Families who had known terrible hardship during the Depression and who were sending their loved ones into combat would have to be convinced to sacrifice still more. With slogans such as "Remember Pearl Harbor" and "Don't You Know There's A War On?" the government launched a massive campaign that reminded people at every turn to conserve, participate, and sacrifice.

Events in the United States

1939 Robert de Graff starts the Pocket Books company.

1940 Roosevelt asks Congress to approve the production of 50,000 airplanes per year.

1941 A. Philip Randolph suggests a march on Washington to end discrimination.

1938	1939	1940	1941

Events in the World

1939 First evacuation of women and children from London.

1940 Rationing begins in Britain.

RESOURCE DIRECTORY

Teaching Resources

 Alternate Lesson Plan: Demonstrating the Big Idea found in the Alternate Lesson Plans folder, p. 126, provides a lesson strategy to instruct students about the Big Idea that the wartime economy involved unprecedented public effort in financing and participating in the massive war effort.

 Alternative Assessment Handbook provides information, guidance, and strategies for alternative methods of assessment. It includes an essay on new trends in assessment, guidance and strategies for developing performance tasks and portfolios, scoring rubrics, and sample evaluation forms.

Pages 692–695
The Shift to Wartime Production

Despite its horrors, World War II did bring an end to the Depression in America. Millions of workers streamed back into the factories to produce airplanes, tanks, and guns—and to receive a welcome paycheck.

Pages 696–699
Daily Life on the Home Front

While American soldiers crouched in foxholes overseas, friends and families supported their struggle on the home front. Rationing and conserving resources like gasoline, scrap metal, and rubber drew most of the country into the war effort.

Pages 700–704
Women and the War

During World War II, thousands of American women rolled up their sleeves and went to work in defense plants and shipyards. Adapting quickly to work usually done by men and overcoming a sometimes cold welcome from fellow male employees, they helped satisfy the Allies' urgent need for military goods.

Pages 706–711
The Struggle for Justice at Home

For many Americans, the war broke down racial barriers in the job market. Japanese Americans, however, fell victim to bitter prejudice at home as the United States battled Japan abroad.

1942 Popular movies such as Casablanca glorify the war effort and inspire troops.

1943 Race riots in Los Angeles.
• Congress passes Smith-Connally Act limiting strikes.

1944 The number of working women rises to over 19 million, up from 14.6 million in 1941.

1945 Japanese Americans are released from internment camps.

1942	1943	1944	1945	1946

1942 Great Britain produces 23,671 aircraft, 8,611 tanks, and 173 major vessels.

1943 Germans give up after 900-day siege of Stalingrad.

1944 Anne Frank and her family arrested by Nazis in Amsterdam.

1945 Hitler commits suicide in an underground bunker in Germany.

Alternative Assessment

As an ongoing chapter project, students can demonstrate their understanding of the changes in American life during World War II by preparing a "Guide to Life on the Home Front" for returning veterans. Point out that many of the veterans have had little contact with home for several years. The guides should address all of the following topics:

• The economy and the shift to wartime production
• Daily life at home
• Women and the war
• The struggle for justice at home

Students may prepare a booklet, an audiotape, or an oral presentation. Guides should be interesting, easy to follow, and appropriately humorous. Explain that projects will be evaluated according to the following guidelines:

• **Unacceptable** Activity not attempted; guide does not describe topics as outlined above.
• **Limited/Acceptable** Guide provides a limited description of changes in each area and states causes.
• **Extensive/Commendable** Guide provides an extensive description of changes in each area with analysis of causes.
• **Extraordinary/Outstanding** Guide contains a lively, in-depth description of changes in each area with thoughtful analysis of causes and includes information from sources other than the textbook.

For information and guidance on alternative assessment trends and strategies, see the Alternative Assessment Handbook in the Resource Directory on page 690.

The Shift to Wartime Production

1. FOCUS

Connecting to the Big Idea

See page 690B. Explain to students that World War II changed American life by helping to end the Depression—putting Americans back to work. As factories shifted into wartime production, there were new opportunities for workers, businesses, and entrepreneurs. Ask students what these new opportunities were and how they changed life in America.

Objectives

● Describe the changes in the American economy as it converted to wartime production.
● Explain how World War II ended the Depression in the United States.
● Explain how the United States paid for the cost of the war.

In Depth

Did You Know?

When Coca-Cola was developed in 1885, it was sold as a cure for headaches. Concocted by John Pemberton, an Atlanta pharmacist, the original drink was a syrup made with wine, cocaine, and a few other ingredients. A year later, Pemberton took out the wine and cocaine, adding caffeine and kola nut extract for flavor. By 1889, drugstores sold drinks made of Coca-Cola syrup and carbonated water. By 1919, Coca-Cola was so popular that the company was sold for $25 million.

SECTION PREVIEW

Despite its horrors, World War II did bring an end to the Depression in America. Millions of workers streamed back into the factories to produce airplanes, tanks, and guns—and to receive a welcome paycheck.

Key Concepts

Many advertisements linked their products to wartime patriotism.

• During World War II, the American economy converted to producing materials for the war.
• World War II ended the Great Depression as millions joined the wartime labor force and, after the United States joined the war, the military.
• The war was paid for with taxes and by government borrowing.

Key Terms, People, and Places

cost-plus system, wildcat strike, deficit spending; John L. Lewis

A t the start of World War II, supplying goods to the Allied forces helped boost the American economy. With the cloud of the Depression finally beginning to lift, companies were eager to start making cars, refrigerators, and washing machines again, and consumers were eager to buy them. The government would have to campaign vigorously to convince Americans to continue to sacrifice such items for the sake of the war effort.

Mobilizing the War Economy

President Roosevelt understood that the outcome of the war would ultimately depend on America's ability to produce war materials such as bombers, tanks, and uniforms. He knew that the government would have to take a firm hand in coordinating the production efforts of hundreds of American businesses used to pursuing their own interests. In May 1943 FDR organized the Office of War Mobilization under the direction of James F. Byrnes. A former Supreme Court justice, Byrnes was a skillful negotiator whose guidance made wartime production run smoothly. ⊗

Conversion of the Auto Industry After the bombing of Pearl Harbor, the nation was convinced of the need to produce large amounts of war materials. The automobile industry responded to this need by converting its factories to produce bombers. On February 10, 1942, as the last cars rolled off the assembly lines, workers began taking apart automobile machinery and packing it for storage.

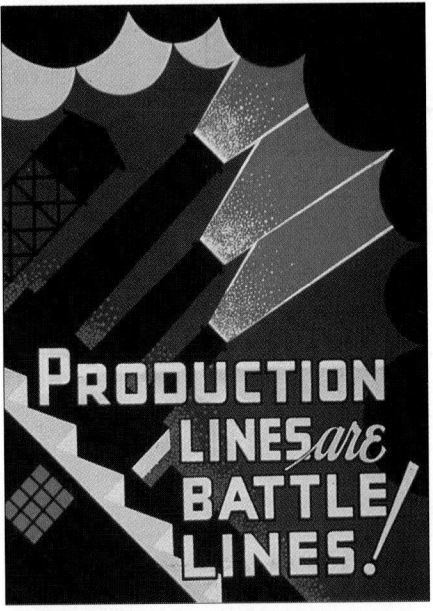

The government used posters such as this one, designed by Ches Cobb, to remind people on the home front of their responsibility to the war effort.

RESOURCE DIRECTORY

Teaching Resources

📄 **Reproducible Lesson Plan** found in the Unit 8 folder, p. 38, provides a summary of the Section 1 lesson plan content.

📄 **Alternate Lesson Plan: Learning Styles** found in the Alternate Lesson Plans folder, p. 127, is especially effective for visual learners and uses unnumbered graphs designed to extend students' understanding of how the war was financed.

📄 **Guided Reading and Review** found in the Unit 8 folder, p. 42, provides a structure for reading and mastering the key concepts and reviewing the key terms for Section 1. (Guided Practice)

⊗ 📄 **Visual Learning Activity** Campaigns on the Home Front, found in the Unit 8 folder, p. 63, uses government posters to help students understand the techniques used to "sell" Americans on making sacrifices for the war.

Passenger Car and Military Aircraft Production, 1939–1946

Passenger Car Production
(in millions)

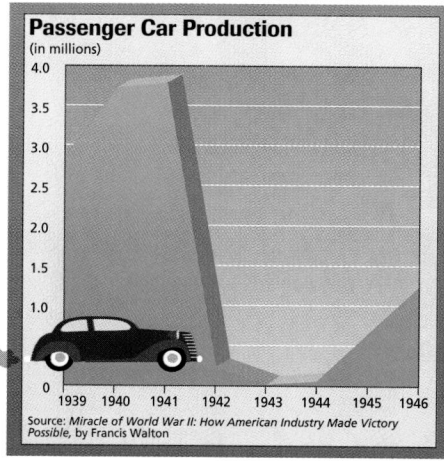

Source: *Miracle of World War II: How American Industry Made Victory Possible*, by Francis Walton

Military Aircraft Production
(in thousands)

Source: *Historical Statistics of the United States*

Interpreting Graphs
What overall trends in auto production and military aircraft production do these graphs show? Do you think the effect of assembly-line production on the aircraft industry can be judged from the information in the graph on the right? Explain your answer.

While many existing plants were being converted, Henry Ford was planning to build an immense new factory to produce B-24 Liberator bombers. Ford wanted to use assembly-line techniques, which had never before been applied in the aircraft industry, to produce planes faster and more efficiently. To achieve his goal, Ford conceived the huge Willow Run bomber plant near Ann Arbor, Michigan. Willow Run covered 975 acres with an assembly line that stretched a full mile across a flat meadowland. When operating at full capacity, the plant employed more than 42,000 people.

MAKING CONNECTIONS

How do you suppose the government encouraged businesses to undertake the expensive process of wartime conversion? Compare your response to the information that follows.

New Opportunities for Profit Secretary of War Henry L. Stimson understood that "if you are going to try to go to war, or to prepare for war, in a capitalist country, you have to let business make money out of the process or business won't work." To that end, the government established the **cost-plus system,** in which the government paid all development and production costs plus a percentage of those costs as profit on anything a company made for the war.

Thousands of business executives went to Washington to work in war agencies responsible for coordinating production. Many accepted token salaries of one dollar from the government while remaining on their own companies' payrolls. From inside war agencies, these "dollar-a-year men" helped to decide which firms would receive profitable contracts.

New Markets and Methods Entrepreneurs prospered during World War II. Some succeeded in creating profitable new markets for their products. Robert Woodruff, head of Coca-Cola, declared in December 1941: "We will see that every man in uniform gets a bottle of Coca-Cola for five cents wherever he is and whatever it costs [the company]." By the time the war was over, American troops had drunk five billion bottles of Coca-Cola. At the same time, Woodruff's company had established a new "army" of civilian consumers who had enjoyed the drink while in uniform.

Caption Answer to ...

Interpreting Graphs

A steep decline in auto production and a sharp increase in military aircraft. Assembly-line production may be one factor affecting the graph on the right, but the increased demand for military planes and the conversion of many more factories to their production are other factors.

Bellringer

Ask students to imagine themselves in President Roosevelt's shoes on December 8, 1941. Now that the United States is at war, what are the three most important things that must be done at once to help the country fight it?

Reading Strategy

Predicting Content Ask students to skim the section, looking at the illustrations and reading the headings. Ask them to predict the content of the section by completing the following sentences: During the war, American factories and businesses concentrated on making goods for _____. Union membership _____ during the war. The government paid for the war through taxes and _____.

Answer to ...

MAKING CONNECTIONS

Students may predict that the government provided financial incentives for businesses to convert to wartime production. In fact, as the text goes on to explain, the government started the cost-plus system and allowed business executives to influence the distribution of government contracts.

Interpreting Graphs

More workers had jobs, and they earned higher wages.

2. INSTRUCT

Discuss

Point out the slogan on the poster on page 692: "Production lines are battle lines." Ask students to restate the slogan in their own words. Have students list the types of goods that were needed, and describe the incentives used by the government to mobilize industries to produce them.

Ask students to explain the reduction in unemployment after the country entered the war.

Analyze

Ask students to explain why putting money into the economy by deficit spending would get the economy moving.

Activity

Teaching Heterogeneous Groups

War can bring new opportunities for business expansion. To illustrate this concept for all students, have them work in groups to design an ad campaign for a product to be sold during wartime. This product might be one that both soldiers and those on the home front can use, such as Coca-Cola or chewing gum. Suggest that students identify which of their product's features the ad should promote, as well as the audience that it is designed to reach.

Enrichment

Ask students to research some of the new products developed by the petrochemical industry during the war, such as artificial rubber, nylon, and plastics. Suggest that they find out why these new products were needed.

Percent of Labor Force Unemployed, 1935–1945

Rise in Wages, 1935-1945

*Manufacturing industries

Source: *Historical Statistics of the United States, Colonial Times to 1970*, U.S. Department of Commerce

 Interpreting Graphs
The conversion of the United States economy during the war brought businesses huge profits from government contracts. According to these graphs, in what two ways did workers benefit during the war?

Other entrepreneurs pioneered modern production methods. Henry J. Kaiser, for example, introduced mass production techniques to shipbuilding. The vessels that made him famous were called Liberty ships. In 1941 it took 355 days to build one Liberty ship. By the end of the war, Kaiser's shipyard located in Portland, Oregon, could assemble a ship in just 14 days.

Workers, the War, and Unions

Business owners were not the only group to benefit from war production. War production brought an end to the devastating unemployment of the 1930s. As the graph shows, by 1943 unemployment had fallen dramatically. Average weekly wages in

Welder Benny Chan gives the "V for Victory" sign.

manufacturing, adjusted for inflation, rose 27 percent in a little over three years.

With more people working, union membership rose. Between 1940 and 1941, the number of workers belonging to unions increased by 1.5 million. Union membership continued to rise sharply once the United States entered the war, from 10.5 million in 1941 to 14.8 million in 1945. ✪

Two weeks after the attack on Pearl Harbor, labor and business representatives agreed to refrain from strikes and lockouts—a tactic in which an employer "locks" employees out of their jobs to avoid meeting their demands. The no-strike agreement became hard to honor, however, as the cost of living rose during the war and Pearl Harbor faded from memory. The government had to remind citizens continually of the importance of the agreement. Leonard Williamson, a superintendent for a large construction company, recalled the government's involvement in the building of a military base in New Jersey:

▶ RESOURCE DIRECTORY

Teaching Resources

✪ **Critical Thinking Activity** Identifying Alternatives: Mobilizing a Wartime Labor Force, found in the Unit 8 folder, p. 55, uses one of Roosevelt's fireside chats to help students apply this skill.

They started at one time to develop a strike there, and some big guy from the Pentagon came down, and he just laid the cards on the table: "There'll be no strikes." Everybody kind of buckled down, and we finished the thing in record time.

Still, the number of strikers doubled between 1942 and 1943, and it continued to rise in the last two years of the war. Some of the strikes were **wildcat strikes**—that is, they were organized by the workers themselves and not endorsed by the unions.

The most serious confrontations organized by unions occurred in the coalfields, where **John L. Lewis,** head of the United Mine Workers union, called strikes on four different occasions in 1943. Lewis and the miners, seeing industry profits soar while their wages stayed the same, demanded a pay raise to compensate for the rising cost of living. Secretary of the Interior Harold J. Ickes finally negotiated an agreement with Lewis. Meanwhile, Congress passed the Smith-Connally Act in June 1943 to place limits on future strike activity.

Financing the War

In World War II, the United States government was willing to spend whatever it cost to energize war production and maintain a "fighting" mentality at home. Federal spending increased from $9.4 billion in 1939 to $95.2 billion in 1945, and the gross national product more than doubled in that time.

A raise in taxes paid for approximately 41 percent of the cost of the war. The Revenue Act of 1942 increased the number of Americans who paid income taxes, levying a flat 5 percent tax on all incomes over $624 a year. The rest of the money was borrowed from banks, private investors, and the public. The United States Treasury launched a series of bond drives to borrow money from individual Americans, raising a total of $135 billion.

Massive wartime spending ended the Great Depression. In the 1930s most economists believed that the economy would fix itself if the government did not interfere. English economist John Maynard Keynes, on the other hand, argued that **deficit spending**—government spending of borrowed money—should be used to get a depressed economy moving again. Deficit spending during World War II turned the economy around overnight. Unfortunately, it also catapulted the nation into a habit of deficit spending, causing economic problems that continue to this day.

The results of wartime spending were stupendous. Each year the United States raised its production goals for military materials, and each year it met them. By the middle of 1945, the nation had produced 80,000 landing craft, 100,000 tanks and armored cars, 300,000 airplanes, 15 million guns, and 41 billion rounds of ammunition. The country had indeed become, in Franklin Roosevelt's words, the "arsenal of democracy."

Don't Let That Shadow Touch Them *Buy* **WAR BONDS**

This poster, designed to appeal to people's emotions, encouraged Americans to sacrifice and helped raise money for the war.

SECTION 1 REVIEW

Key Terms, People, and Places
1. Define (a) cost-plus system, (b) wildcat strike.
2. Identify John L. Lewis.

Key Concepts
3. What were the major problems involved in mobilizing the American economy in World War II?
4. How did World War II end the Great Depression?

5. How did deficit spending help the war effort?

Critical Thinking
6. **Formulating Questions** Imagine that you are a business owner in 1942, and that the government has asked you to produce materials for the war. Develop a list of questions that you would want to ask before you agreed to cooperate.

 Quiz found in the Unit 8 folder, p. 43, covers the main ideas in this section as well as the key terms.

Media and Technology

 Transparencies
Fine Art, D-18; Critical Thinking, I-10

3. ASSESS

Section 1 Review Answers

1. (a) cost-plus system, see p. 693, (b) wildcat strike, see p. 695

2. John L. Lewis, see p. 695

3. Businesses were reluctant to turn away customers now that the demand for consumer goods was on the rise; plants had to be retooled in order to make war materials.

4. The urgent need for war products created jobs for many Americans, and the new policy of deficit spending helped get the economy moving again.

5. Deficit spending—government spending of borrowed money—helped end the Depression and boost the economy.

6. Possible questions: How will production be financed? How will the product(s) be marketed? Who will supply the raw materials and machinery needed for production?

Reteach

Ask students to correct any of the following statements that are false:
• The coming of the war made the Depression worse because many workers lost their jobs.
• The government paid for goods and services needed to fight the war by borrowing money.
• During the war, factories switched from producing consumer goods to producing war materials.

4. CLOSE

Reinforcing the Big Idea

Involvement in the war stimulated the domestic economy and ended the Depression. The geared-up factories and industries needed workers. In the next section, students will learn who kept the assembly lines moving during the war.

Daily Life on the Home Front

Daily Life on the Home Front

1. FOCUS

Connecting to the Big Idea

See page 690B. Explain to students that Americans at home were continually reminded of the war. Almost every American had a relative, friend, or neighbor overseas. Constant effort was required to support the war. Ask students how daily life in America changed as a result of these efforts.

Objectives

- Describe the mood on the American home front during the war.
- Explain the change in Americans' spending habits.
- Describe the shortages that plagued American consumers during the war.
- Explain how the government used public relations to maintain morale at home.

Bellringer

Ask students to think about how their lives would change if their family could buy only three gallons of gasoline a week—the amount that Americans were allowed under rationing during World War II.

Reading Strategy

Question Writing Ask students to read the section's three main headings and rewrite each as a question. Have them jot down answers to their questions as they read the chapter.

SECTION PREVIEW

While American soldiers crouched in foxholes overseas, friends and families supported their struggle on the home front. Rationing and conserving resources like gasoline, scrap metal, and rubber drew most of the country into the war effort.

Key Concepts

- The mood on the American home front was one of cooperation and determined optimism.
  - American consumers had money in their pockets for the first time in years, and they looked for ways to spend it.
    - Shortages of many basic items, such as sugar, meat, and gasoline, plagued the wartime economy.
  - The government sought to maintain morale at home through various public relations campaigns.

Key Terms, People, and Places

rationing

Rationing coupons set limits on the amount of scarce items each family could buy during the war.

The daily life of most Americans during World War II was filled with constant reminders of the war. To escape, many used the first extra cash they had earned since the Depression to purchase paperback books and go to the movies or baseball games, among other popular diversions. Rubber and aluminum drives, encouraged by the government, were designed to make most Americans feel part of the war effort.

Prosperity and Popular Culture

In the middle of the war, seven out of ten Americans felt that they had not had to make any "real sacrifices" because of the war. Morale was quite high as the Depression subsided. In 1941, 34 percent of all American families had incomes of less than $1000 a year, but new jobs created by the war brought that figure down below 20 percent by 1945. One measure of people's optimism was an increase in the birthrate. The population grew by 7.5 million between 1940 and 1945, nearly double the rate of growth for the 1930s. The so-called postwar baby boom that extended through the 1950s really began during the war.

Money to Burn As the wartime economy gathered speed, many Americans who had gone without steady paychecks for years suddenly found themselves earning more money than they needed just for basic necessities. They were hungry for ways to spend this extra income—they wanted new cars and trucks and appliances. Unfortunately, wartime conversion meant that most of these goods were unavailable, so they had to look for other ways to spend their money.

Among the items that people did buy were books. The new Pocket Books company, founded by Robert de Graff in 1939, developed a market for paperback books. De Graff believed that more Americans would read if books were more widely available and at lower prices. His instinct proved correct when he sold 34,000 copies of the first Pocket Book, titled *How to Win Friends and Influence People,* in two months. Soldiers carried Pocket Books with them into combat, and when the war was over, these men joined a sizeable new market for paperbacks. ✪

Approximately 85 million Americans, or 62 percent of the population, went to the movies each week during the war. Many of these films were in the "escapist" category: love stories, adventure tales, or light comedies that took audiences' minds off the serious business of war. Others dealt with the war directly and promoted themes of patriotism and American victory. Hollywood, too, was "doing its part" to contribute to the war effort.

▶ RESOURCE DIRECTORY

Teaching Resources

Reproducible Lesson Plan found in the Unit 8 folder, p. 39, provides a summary of the Section 2 lesson plan content.

Alternate Lesson Plan: Critical Thinking Determining Reasoned Judgment, found in the Alternate Lesson Plans folder, p. 128, extends students' application of this skill by completing a chart on the section content.

Guided Reading and Review found in the Unit 8 folder, p. 44, provides a structure for reading and mastering the key concepts and reviewing the key terms for Section 2. (Guided Practice)

✪ **Literature Activity** *How To Win Friends and Influence People,* found in the Unit 8 folder, p. 59, introduces students to the spirit of the times with excerpts from Dale Carnegie's best-seller.

Baseball and Popular Music Though more than 4,000 of the 5,700 major and minor league players were in the military services, Americans still flocked to baseball games during the war. Ball clubs had to scramble to make up for the losses in their ranks. To fill their rosters, many had to place want ads in newspapers:

> *If you are a free agent and have previous professional experience, we may be able to place you to your advantage on one of our clubs. We have positions open on our AA, B, and D classification clubs. If you believe you can qualify for one of these good baseball jobs, tell us about yourself.*
> Sporting News, February 25, 1943

Women ball players also took to the fields to lift the spirits of war-weary Americans. In 1943 Philip Wrigley founded the All-American Girls' Softball League, which became the All-American Girls' Baseball League in 1945. Women who played for teams such as the Rockford (Illinois) Peaches and the South Bend (Indiana) Blue Sox had to attend charm school and wear impractical skirted uniforms. But they endured such inconveniences for the chance to play professional ball, and they attracted scores of devoted fans.

As in World War I, many popular songs during World War II were written to inspire hope and patriotism. Frank Loesser's "Praise the Lord and Pass the Ammunition"—based on a true story—told of a navy chaplain who took over an anti-aircraft gun at Pearl Harbor after several of his fellow sailors had been killed. "There's a Star-Spangled Banner Waving Somewhere" was one of the best-selling records of 1942 and 1943. "White Christmas," from the 1942 film *Holiday Inn,* was the sentimental favorite, both for soldiers overseas and for civilians at home.

Shortages and Controls

The war brought its share of problems along with increased prosperity and a high-spirited popular culture. Although they had money to spend, Americans had to live with shortages and disruptions throughout the war.

Pete Gray, a one-armed outfielder, did his part for the war effort by playing for the St. Louis Browns and giving the "troops" at home a lift.

Some consumer items were simply unavailable. Metal to make zippers was used for guns; rubber for girdles went into tanks and trucks; fabric for dresses became military uniforms instead. In an effort to save cloth, government regulations required the elimination of vests, patch pockets, and cuffs in men's suits. They also limited the length and width of women's skirts, which grew shorter and narrower during the war period. Two-piece bathing suits for women—considered somewhat shocking in the 1920s and 1930s—could now be justified on the basis of military need because they required less fabric.

Some foods were also in limited supply during the war. Sugar became scarce when the major source of American imports, the Philippines, fell to the Japanese and shipping lanes from other countries were closed. Coffee could not be transported easily from Brazil. Meat and countless other items were likewise scarce.

Worried that shortages would lead to price increases, the government used tough measures to head off inflation.

VICTORY SPEED 35 MILES

2. INSTRUCT

Explain

Explain that during the war, jobs were plentiful and workers made good wages. Point out the subheading Money to Burn on page 696 and ask students to describe the forms of entertainment that Americans supported and enjoyed with their extra money. Also note that many basic necessities were not available. Have students explain why rationing was instituted and how, in essence, this policy was an example of home-front support.

Discuss

Discuss the many reasons the government wanted to maintain high morale among its citizens. Ask students to brainstorm reasons and then to rank them in order of importance.

In Depth

Interdisciplinary

The economics of supporting a war was brought home in 1942, after the attack on Pearl Harbor. President Roosevelt created the War Production Board to oversee the changeover from a peacetime to a wartime economy. The board regulated all home-based industries that were engaged in war work and had the power to confiscate materials considered essential to the war effort. The board could also order industries to convert to war production. After 1942, in response to the need, all manufacturers of civilian automobiles switched over to full-time production of tanks, trucks, armored personnel carriers, and aircraft parts. Shirt factories redesigned assembly lines to make mosquito netting; model-train producers made bomb fuses; and kitchen sink factories were converted to produce cartridge casings.

Activity

Teaching Heterogeneous Groups

To help students understand the shortages and rationing during World War II, have them make a list of what they are wearing or what they might eat in the course of a day. Then have them identify the raw materials that make up the listed items. Finally, ask students to list what materials or food they would have had to sacrifice to support the war effort in the 1940s. **LEP**

Enrichment

Ask students to choose one year during the war and find the following information: the movie that won the Academy Award for best picture; a popular song and the artist who recorded it; the team that won a popular sports event; a best-selling book; the nation's GNP for the year. Encourage students to review their answers to see if they reflect common aspects of the wartime mood.

Answer to ...

MAKING CONNECTIONS

The Pearl Harbor attack had united most Americans behind the war effort. Since rationing was necessary for the war and since everyone had to sacrifice together, rationing probably contributed to a spirit of patriotism.

3. ASSESS

Section 2 Review Answers

1. (a) rationing, see p. 698

2. There were shortages of sugar, coffee, meat, butter, shoes, and gasoline. The OPA established a rationing system to conserve these resources, and government campaigns encouraged people to collect scrap metal, rubber, and other recyclable items.

3. Styles that used less cloth came into fashion, such as suits without vests for men and two-piece bathing suits for women.

4. Government campaigns were designed to foster a sense of home-front participation in the war as well as to use human and other resources wisely.

Children, too, did their part for the war effort. These boys in New York City used their powers of persuasion—and noisemaking—to urge their neighbors to contribute to an aluminum drive.

began **rationing,** or distributing goods in a fixed amount by using coupons. It assigned point values to scarce items such as sugar, coffee, meat, butter, shoes, and gasoline. Consumers were issued coupons worth a certain number of points. Once they had used up their points, they were not allowed to buy any more of the rationed items until additional coupons were issued.

MAKING CONNECTIONS

What effect do you think wartime shortages and rationing had on people's morale? Do you suppose it made people feel angry at the government or more patriotic?

Campaigns at Home

The government understood the need to maintain morale. While making rationing seem fun was not an easy task, the government had to create a sense of patriotism and participation in the war effort while convincing citizens to conserve precious resources. ★

President Roosevelt created the Office of Price Administration (OPA) in mid-1941, and the following year he gave the agency the authority to freeze prices. In the middle of 1942, OPA

| 1650 | 1700 | 1750 | 1800 | Links Across Time | 1850 | 1900 | 1950 | 2000 |

Taking Care of the Troops

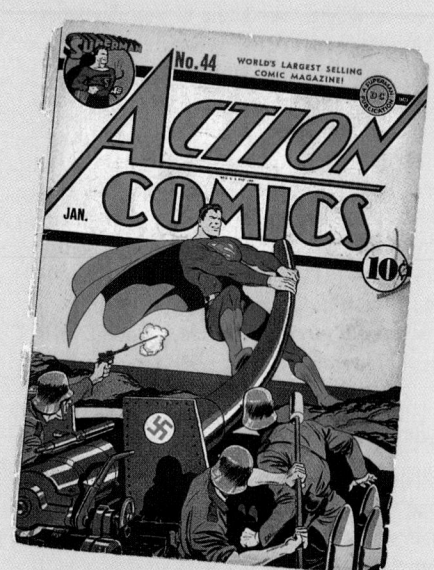

During wartime, America's businesses have always played their part by producing items designed specifically to boost the morale of those on the front lines. During World War II, special editions of certain comic books, such as Action Comics, were printed and sent to cheer up the soldiers overseas. Similarly, Hershey Foods developed a nonmelting chocolate bar for the troops in the Persian Gulf War of 1991 that was specially formulated "for desert or tropical conditions."

▶ RESOURCE DIRECTORY

Teaching Resources

★ **Visual Learning Activity** "The Nature of the Enemy," found in the Unit 8 folder, p. 62, presents a Nazi photo from an OWI exhibit in order to extend students' understanding of wartime propaganda.

In one campaign, Americans were asked to save scrap metal and other materials that could be used for war machinery. Huge drives collected tin cans, pots and pans, razor blades, old shovels, and even old lipstick tubes. In Virginia, collectors raised sunken ships from the James River; in Wyoming they took apart an old steam engine to use the parts. When rubber was in short supply, people collected rubber hoses, raincoats, and bathing caps. Americans were asked to save kitchen fats because the glycerin could be used to make powder for bullets or shells. Some historians have questioned whether the items collected were ever really used for their intended purpose. Whether they were or not, the collection process served another important purpose: it was another way the government kept the American public's attention focused on the war effort.

Another campaign encouraged Americans to buy savings bonds to finance the war. In the spring of 1941, Secretary of the Treasury Henry Morgenthau, Jr., decided "to use *bonds* to sell the *war,* rather than *vice versa.*" Morgenthau realized that selling war bonds would give people "a financial stake in American democracy—an opportunity to contribute toward the defense of that democracy."

"Play your part." "Conserve and collect." "Use it up, wear it out, make it do or do without"—these refrains echoed throughout the United States, constantly reminding Americans of their patriotic duty in the wartime campaign.

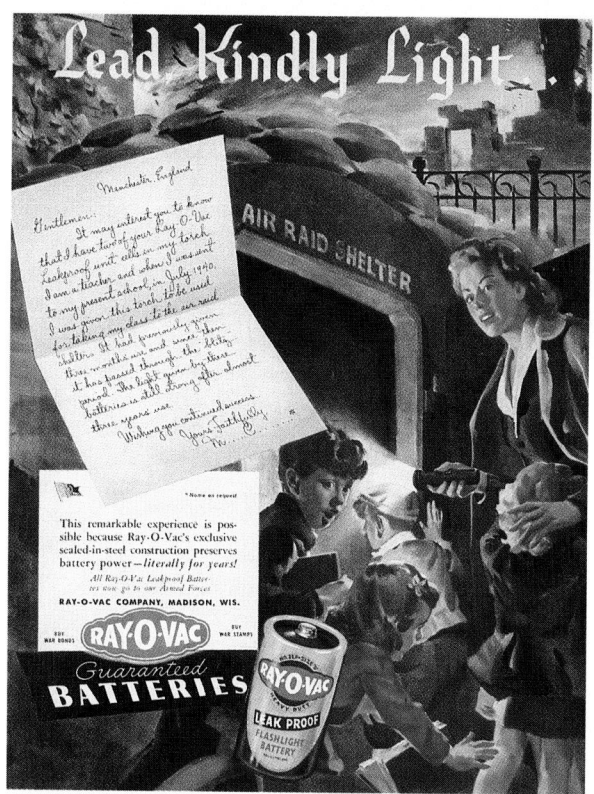

Using Historical Evidence Besides emphasizing quality and value, advertisers used a war-related setting and emotion to sell their products during the war. *How are all of those used in this ad?*

SECTION 2 REVIEW

Key Terms, People, and Places
1. Define rationing.

Key Concepts
2. What items were in short supply during the war, and how did the government respond to these shortages?
3. How did the scarcity of cloth during World War II affect clothing fashions?

4. What was the purpose of government campaigns such as the war bond campaign?

Critical Thinking
5. **Identifying Assumptions** What underlying beliefs was the United States government acting upon when it waged its massive effort to "sell" the war to Americans at home?

Quiz found in the Unit 8 folder, p. 45, covers the main ideas in this section as well as the key terms.

---

5. Answers will vary but some underlying beliefs might be that the American people needed to be "sold" on the war if they were not convinced the goals of fighting for freedom and democracy were enough; the belief that the cause of the war was a good enough one to launch the huge propaganda campaign; the belief that it is acceptable for a government to use propaganda on its own citizens in certain cases.

Reteach
Ask students to read and complete the following sentences with a short phrase.
● During the war, many Americans used their extra income to buy

_____.
● In order to cope with shortages of items such as sugar and gasoline, the government began a policy of

_____.
● Americans collected scrap metal because _____.

 Alternative Assessment

Mid-Point Monitoring
Ask students if they have
● Chosen a format for their guide
● Completed notes for each section

Caption Answer to ...

Using Historical Evidence

The poster shows a dramatic scene of an air raid in Britain during the war and tells the story of a schoolteacher who used a flashlight with Ray-O-Vac batteries to lead her young students to a shelter. The text of the poster claims that the batteries last a long time because of their "sealed-in-steel construction" and appeals to the parental concerns for safety.

---

 4. CLOSE

Reinforcing the Big Idea
The war touched Americans at home in many ways. The next section describes the dramatic ways in which the war changed the lives of many American women.

Women and the War

SECTION 3

Women and the War

1. FOCUS

Connecting to the Big Idea

See page 690B. Explain that during the war, women responded to the urgent demand for workers in factories and shipyards. They quickly adapted to their new status and responsibilities. Just as quickly, most gave up their jobs when the war ended. Ask students what impact the war actually had on the lives of women.

Objectives

● Understand that American women of all ages went to work during World War II.
● Describe how women overcame hardships and discrimination to become successful at their new jobs.
● Explain why women were strongly encouraged to leave their jobs at the end of the war.

Bellringer

Have students list their hobbies, after-school activities, and responsibilities at home. Then ask them to imagine that they were of the opposite sex. How might their lists change? How might expectations of parents and others be different?

Reading Strategy

Predicting Content Ask students to look at the illustrations and skim the headings of this section. Ask them to predict as many ways as they can in which the lives of American women changed during World War II.

SECTION PREVIEW

During World War II, thousands of American women rolled up their sleeves and went to work in defense plants and shipyards. Adapting quickly to work usually done by men and overcoming a sometimes cold welcome from fellow male employees, they helped satisfy the Allies' urgent need for military goods.

Key Concepts

• During World War II, American women of all ages went to work.
• Women were successful in their new jobs despite the hardships and discrimination they faced.
• At the end of the war, women were strongly encouraged to leave their jobs, whether they wanted to or not.

Key Terms, People, and Places
Rosie the Riveter

The motto of the women's Auxiliary Reserve Pool (ARP) during World War II was "Prepared and Faithful."

A popular song during World War II paid tribute to a fictional young woman named **Rosie the Riveter,** who worked in a defense plant while her boyfriend Charlie served in the marines. The government used images of Rosie the Riveter in posters and propaganda films of the 1940s to attract women to the work force. In general, the Rosie created by the government was young, white, and middle class. Patriotism was her main motive for taking a war job—she wanted to do her part on the home front while her brother, husband, or boyfriend fought on the military front. In reality, the wartime economy made it essential for American women of all ages and ethnic and economic backgrounds to work. And, despite the ideals that the government set before them, they worked for a variety of reasons beyond patriotism.

Shifting Patterns of Employment

Before the war, most women who worked for wages were single and young. Even during the hard times of the Depression, most people disapproved of a married woman working outside the home to earn money. This social opposition was reinforced by the fear that working women took jobs away from unemployed men. According to a poll taken in 1936, 82 percent of Americans believed that a married woman should not work if her husband had a job. Nevertheless, by 1940 about 15.5 percent of all married women were working.

Women often worked as sales clerks and household servants because many other fields were closed to them. Men dominated the machinery, steel, and automobile industries, while women more commonly worked in industries that produced clothing, textiles, and shoes. In the jobs they did hold, women usually earned much less than men.

Like World War I, World War II brought many women into the work force. As men were drafted into the armed forces, a large number of factory jobs fell vacant. News of these well-paying job openings brought women who were already working in traditional women's jobs to take over these positions. But these women were not enough. So the Office of War Information launched a propaganda campaign to fill the rest of the positions with women who normally would not have considered working outside the home: older, married women.

Posters and advertisements told women that it was their patriotic duty to work for their country. "An American homemaker with the strength and ability to run a house and raise a family . . . has the strength and ability to take her place in a vital War industry," declared one government advertisement. As a result of this campaign, the number of working women rose from 14.6 million in 1941 to about 19.4 million in 1944. (See the graph on page 702.)

 RESOURCE DIRECTORY

Teaching Resources

Reproducible Lesson Plan found in the Unit 8 folder, p. 40, provides a summary of the Section 3 lesson plan content.

Alternate Lesson Plan: Cooperative Learning found in the Alternate Lesson Plans folder, p. 129, gives students, in groups of six, guidance in creating a question-and-answer activity to summarize information on the effects of women workers on the labor force.

Guided Reading and Review found in the Unit 8 folder, p. 46, provides a structure for reading and mastering the key concepts and reviewing the key terms for Section 3. (Guided Practice)

More than half of all American women were employed at some point during the war; at its peak, women made up 36 percent of the total civilian labor force.

Along with growing numbers of women in the work force, the type of women who worked changed significantly during the war. Married women accounted for almost three quarters of the increase; for the first time in American history, they outnumbered single working women. More than two million women over the age of thirty-five found jobs, and by the end of the war, half of all women workers were over age thirty-five.

An even more striking change occurred in the kind of work women did. Increasingly they moved out of domestic service and into manufacturing, particularly the defense industries. Now women worked in airplane plants and shipyards as steelworkers, riveters, and welders. Rosie the Riveter—strong, determined, and capable—became the ideal to which American women were supposed to aspire.

MAKING CONNECTIONS

Rosie the Riveter was the image of the working woman promoted by the government. Why did the government have to create a character such as Rosie the Riveter?

The Wartime Working Experience

Despite resistance in the past, employers were usually pleased to have women workers—although often for reasons many Americans find misguided today. Employers believed, for instance, that women could do certain welding tasks better than men, for they could squeeze into smaller places. They also made assumptions about women's mental abilities that led them to think that women could do simple, repetitive tasks more effectively than men.

Working Conditions for Women of Color

African American women had long worked in greater proportion than married white women, but they had been largely restricted to domestic work. In addition to gender stereotyping,

This war worker is assembling one part of an aircraft in a California factory.

African American women often faced racial discrimination when they applied for defense jobs. Wanita Allen, who wanted to work at Murray Auto Body in Detroit, Michigan, described her experience this way:

I didn't have any problem getting in the training program. They said you have to have 300 hours to get a job in the plant, and I got my 300, 400, going on 500 hours, and was learning blueprint and everything else, but still no job. They would come in from the plant proper to pick women who'd maybe been there just a couple of days on the training program, and they would put them to work. But they were white women.

Allen later helped gather evidence for a lawsuit against the plant, and she and many other African American women were eventually hired at Murray Auto. Through lawsuits and other forms of protest, African American women changed their profile in the work force. Between 1940 and 1944, the proportion of African American women in industrial jobs

2. INSTRUCT

Discuss

Ask students to explain why women went to work during the war. Then have them provide examples of how women felt about their work experience, especially regarding working conditions, attitudes, employment benefits, stresses of family life, salaries, and discrimination against African American women. Ask students if attitudes regarding these issues have changed and, if so, how.

Answer to ...

MAKING CONNECTIONS

The government needed to convince women to take the factory jobs that were falling vacant as men were drafted into the armed forces. Rosie the Riveter introduced a new model for women's behavior, showing that during the war it was "right" for women to take jobs normally reserved for men.

In Depth

Then and Now

Almost 2,000 women flew non-combat air missions during World War II. The Women's Airforce Service Pilots, known as WASP, flew every airplane in the U.S. air arsenal, including the B-29 Superfortress and the super-quick P-51 Mustang fighter. Although they were highly skilled, the women had to fight for advanced training and more challenging assignments. Even today there is still debate over the role of women in combat.

Analyze

Just as women were urged to join the work force during the war, they were urged to return home after the war. While some women were quite agreeable to these conditions, others were ambivalent about giving up what they had earned during the war. Ask students to identify the reasons for this ambivalence felt by many women.

Activity

Cooperative Learning

Time: One class period.
Activity: Produce a script for a newsreel for a particular event during World War II.
Grouping: Groups of four to six students.
Purpose: Have students work to research a topic related to the war front or the home front during World War II and to write a brief newsreel-style story about it. Possible subjects include a war hero, entertainment, movies, or clothes.
Roles: Have students assign the following roles: researchers, editors, broadcasters.
Outcome: Students will learn how newsreel stories were used as part of the government's propaganda campaign during World War II.

Enrichment

Ask students to read interviews with women in Studs Terkel's book *The Good War: An Oral History of World War II* or pertinent chapters in Richard R. Lingeman's *Don't You Know There's a War On? The American Home Front, 1940–1945.* Have them summarize what they read.

Caption Answer to ...

 Interpreting Graphs

The number of women employed rose during the war, but since the number of men in the labor force increased as well, the ratio of women to men stayed about the same.

These women welders at the Kaiser shipyard in Richmond, California, are working on the Liberty ship S.S. *George Washington Carver.*

increased from 6.8 percent to 18 percent, while the number working in domestic service dropped from 59.9 percent to 44.6 percent.

Benefits of Employment On the whole, women were delighted to be employed. To many, the money they earned made a difference in their lives. Josephine McKee, a Seattle mother of nine who worked at the Boeing Aircraft Company, was able to pay off debts from the Depression. Leola Houghland, also from Seattle, used her earnings at Associated

Shipyards to pay for her family's home. Other women simply found the work more exciting than what they had done before. Evelyn Knight described why she left a position as a cook to work in a navy yard: "After all, I've got to keep body and soul together, and I'd rather earn a living this way than to cook over a hot stove." Still other women took jobs for patriotic reasons. One rubber plant worker declared, "Every time I test a batch of rubber, I know it's going to help bring my three sons home quicker."

Many women also were eager to prove that they could do whatever their jobs required. Adele Erenberg left a position as a Los Angeles cosmetics clerk to work in a machine shop when the war began. The noisy atmosphere was intimidating at first, and it was two weeks before fellow employees spoke to her. Her response was: "Okay, . . . I'm going to prove to you I can do anything you can do, and maybe better than some of you."

AMERICAN PROFILES

Beatrice Morales Clifton

Beatrice Morales Clifton never imagined herself as Rosie the Riveter. In 1942 she was living in Pasadena, California, with her husband Julio and four children. Her teenage niece wanted to get a job, so Clifton took her to apply for work in the aircraft industry.

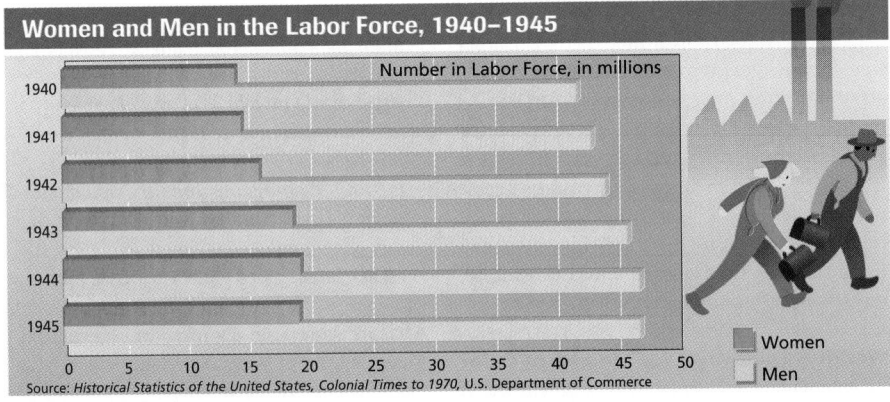

Women and Men in the Labor Force, 1940–1945

Number in Labor Force, in millions

Source: *Historical Statistics of the United States, Colonial Times to 1970,* U.S. Department of Commerce

 Interpreting Graphs
What was the overall trend in women's employment during World War II, according to this graph? Why did the ratio of women to men in the labor force remain about constant during the war?

▶ RESOURCE DIRECTORY

Teaching Resources

⭐ 📄 **Primary Source Activity** Working Conditions for Women of Color, found in the Unit 8 folder, pp. 57–58, profiles Sybil Lewis, an African American worker who tells of discrimination in the wartime work place.

Clifton was surprised when the man in the employment office suggested that she herself fill out an application; she had been married at age fifteen and had never considered looking for work outside the home. "But," she later explained, "the more I kept thinking about it, the more I said, 'That's a good idea.'" Her husband was initially opposed to her plan, but Clifton was determined. She told him, "I've made up my mind. I'm going to go to work."

⭐ Clifton was hired by Lockheed Aircraft in Los Angeles. When she arrived for her first day of work, she found the factory "exciting and scary at the same time." The male worker assigned to teach Clifton her job resented working women. When she made a slight slip with the rivet gun, he told her, "You're not worth the money Lockheed pays you."

With the support of her female co-workers, however, Clifton soon learned to enjoy her work. Her confidence grew as she mastered one skill after another. She later explained:

I felt proud of myself and felt good [because] I had never done anything like that. I felt good that I could do something, and being that it was war, I felt that I was doing my part.
   I went from 65 cents to $1.05 [an hour]. That was top pay. It felt good and, besides, it was my own money. I could do whatever I wanted with it.

After leaving her wartime job for several years, Clifton returned to Lockheed in 1951. By the time she retired in 1978, she was a supervisor for about fifty other workers, half of them men. Asked how her work experiences affected her life, Clifton said,

My life, it was changed from day to night. . . . The changes started when I first started working. They started a little bit, and from then on it kept on going. Because after I quit . . . at Lockheed, I wasn't satisfied. I started looking for ways of getting out and going to work. See, and before, I had never had that thought of going out.

Problems for Working Women

For all the positive aspects of employment, working women experienced a number of problems. Some faced hostile reactions from other workers, particularly in jobs previously held only by men. Restrictions imposed by managers who worried about mixing the sexes in their plants irritated other women. General Motors, for example, fired male supervisors and female employees found "fraternizing," or socializing with one another.

Many working women worried about leaving their children. More than half a million women with children under ten worked during the war, and day-care centers were scarce. Even when the government provided such facilities, most women preferred to have their children cared for by family members or friends, and this often required making complicated arrangements. Women were encouraged to work, but at the same time they continued to bear complete responsibility for both their children and for many of the chores in the home.

Women also earned significantly less than men doing the same jobs. Although the National War Labor Board declared in the fall of 1942 that women who performed "work of the same quality and quantity" as men should receive equal pay, the policy often was ignored. Women began at the bottom, with the lowest-paying jobs. Because they had less seniority, they frequently advanced more slowly. Their wages reflected these patterns. At the Willow Run plant in 1945, women earned a yearly average of $2,928, compared with $3,363 for men. Conditions improved toward the end of the war, but the gap never closed.

Beatrice Morales Clifton worked at Lockheed Aircraft during World War II.

MAKING CONNECTIONS

Women were encouraged to enter the work force and provided essential labor for the war effort, but they were never paid the same as men. What do you predict happened to these workers when the war ended?

Answer to . . .

MAKING CONNECTIONS

Students may predict that since women remained second-class citizens in the wartime economy, they were expected to give up their jobs when servicemen returned from overseas.

3. ASSESS

Section 3 Review Answers

1. Rosie the Riveter, see p. 700

2. Women over thirty-five and married women entered the work force, taking jobs previously reserved for men.

3. Propaganda featuring Rosie the Riveter made defense jobs seem glamorous as well as patriotic. The government initially used Rosie to fill the jobs it needed to produce the materials to win the war, and later to remind women of their "proper" role as homemakers once the war was over.

4. Women encountered hostile reactions from men in the factories, received lower wages than men doing the same work, and had to juggle child care and domestic responsibilities with their factory work schedules.

In Depth

Did You Know?

"There was a passion for marriage in wartime America," observed historian William Tuttle in Daddy's Gone to War, that was almost absent in the 1930s. Two reasons help explain why.

Hope—As people went back to work, they felt better about themselves. That and rising wages made the proposal easier to consider.

Fear—War made young draftees and enlisted men face the question of survival: "As a soldier, will I even live through the war?" Young women faced a similar dilemma: "If I don't get married now, will I have a second chance?" Not wanting to hear "I won't," both rushed to the altar in record numbers to say "I do."

5. Women were pressured to leave their defense jobs. Some returned to their jobs as full-time homemakers. Others continued to work part-time or full-time despite the pressure to return home.

6. Some possible underlying beliefs are that women really belonged in the home and that it was more important for men to have jobs than for women.

Reteach

Have students construct a concept map of the section, with a central circle labeled Women Go to Work During WW II. Ask them to write statements in outer circles about changing patterns of employment, working conditions for women of color, advantages of employment, and problems for working women.

4. CLOSE

Reinforcing the Big Idea

World War II changed the lives of millions of American women who went to work outside their homes for the first time or moved into jobs previously held by men. The next section describes how African Americans, Mexican Americans, Native Americans, and Japanese Americans were involved in World War II.

Sisters under the apron—Yesterday's war worker becomes today's housewife.

What's Become of Rosie the Riveter?

Government propaganda aimed at women did an about-face once the war was over. Posters such as this one now urged women to give up their factory jobs and return to full-time homemaking.

The Postwar Push to "Demobilize" Women

The government propaganda campaign that urged women to report to the defense plants also assumed that when the war was over, women would leave their jobs and return to their homes. The following script excerpt from the recruitment film *Women of Steel*, produced by the Office of War Information, demonstrates this assumption.

> NARRATOR: *Women make good drivers, too. American girls raised to drive the family car have no trouble at all handling trucks and tractors. Edith Stoner's husband is in Alaska. She took this job for the duration. . . . How do you like your job, Mrs. Stoner?*

EDITH STONER: *I love it.*
NARRATOR: *How about after the war? Are you going to keep on working?*
EDITH STONER: *I should say not. When my husband comes back, I'm going to be busy at home.*
NARRATOR: *Good for you!*

At the war's end, many women in fact wanted to continue working, but the pressures to return home were intense. Servicemen wanted "their" jobs back, and they longed to return to the familiar family arrangements they had known before the war. A new campaign by industrialists and government officials now encouraged women to leave their jobs. Articles in women's magazines changed their tune after the war, too. Ammunitions worker Margaret Wright recalled:

> Y ou know, during the war they [were] telling you to cook dishes that you could cook quick and get on to work. Now, they were telling you how to cook dishes that took a full day. There were more articles in there about raising your child. . . .

During demobilization, twice as many women as men lost factory jobs.

Some women were tired of their defense jobs—which in many cases were not very fulfilling once the war's sense of urgency had ended—and looked forward to their work at home. Others, like Beatrice Clifton, would never again feel satisfied being full-time homemakers. After the war, many women continued to work part-time to supplement their families' incomes.

SECTION 3 REVIEW

Key Terms, People, and Places
1. Identify Rosie the Riveter.

Key Concepts
2. How did the profile of women in the work force change during World War II?
3. How did the government use Rosie the Riveter to accomplish its wartime goals?
4. What problems did women encounter as they worked?

5. What options did women defense workers have at the war's end?

Critical Thinking
6. Recognizing Bias At the end of the war, government and business responded to the need to provide jobs for returning soldiers by pressuring women to leave their jobs. What underlying beliefs does this response suggest?

RESOURCE DIRECTORY

Teaching Resources

Quiz found in the Unit 8 folder, p. 47, covers the main ideas in this section as well as the key terms.

Identifying Assumptions

Identifying assumptions means recognizing the unstated beliefs that may underlie a statement or action. An assumption is an idea that a person takes for granted as true. In fact, it may prove either true or false, but in order to determine the accuracy of an assumption, you must first be able to recognize it as such.

Editorials, opinion pieces, and illustrations frequently contain many assumptions. Magazine covers, such as the one shown here, are often excellent sources of information about public attitudes toward historical events. At the same time, illustrations may be drawn in such a way that they also reveal assumptions of the artist.

By the time artist Norman Rockwell's portrayal of "Rosie the Riveter" appeared on the cover of *The Saturday Evening Post* in 1943, American women by the thousands were already making history. They were working in nontraditional factory jobs, assembling ships and airplanes for the country's war effort.

To examine the accuracy of the image portrayed in this painting, use the following steps to identify and evaluate the assumptions on which it may be based.

1. Determine the subject of the cover illustration. Study the illustration carefully and answer the following questions. (a) What is the woman in the illustration doing? (b) Who is "Rosie the Riveter" supposed to represent? (c) What general subject or issue does the illustration address? (d) What is the overall message of the illustration?

2. Define the artist's point of view. To help determine if the artist is presenting a particular viewpoint,

answer the following questions. (a) What seems to be the artist's purpose in creating this illustration? (b) How would you describe the artist's attitude toward the subject? (c) What aspects of the illustration clearly express this point of view? (d) Are there any elements in the illustration that contrast with each other? If so, what might the artist be trying to convey through these contrasts?

3. Identify the assumptions on which the artist's viewpoint is based and decide whether they are valid. To help decide if the artist's assumptions can be supported by facts, answer the following questions. (a) What assumptions, if any, does the artist make about the nature of the work performed by the woman in the illustration? Does the artist make any assumptions about why she holds this job? (b) What assumptions, if any, does the artist make about the women who work in nontraditional jobs? (c) Can any aspects of a person's physical appearance, such as clothes or posture, be reliably linked to his or her occupation? Explain. (d) How can you find out if the artist's apparent assumptions are valid?

Historian's Toolbox Activity Identifying Assumptions, found in the Unit 8 folder, p. 54, uses a recruitment brochure for the United States Air Force to help students apply this skill.

Critical Thinking
Identifying Assumptions

Focus Identify and evaluate assumptions in historical sources such as editorials, speeches, or works of art.

Instruct Ask students to brainstorm a list of adjectives that describe "Rosie the Riveter," the symbol of women workers during World War II. Have them work in small groups to identify the assumptions that underlie the lists they have generated. Compare their assumptions to those of Norman Rockwell's magazine cover. Ask why some of their assumptions might be different from Rockwell's.

Extend See the Historian's Toolbox Activity in the Resource Directory below.

Answers

1. (a) Taking a break from work to eat lunch. (b) American women during World War II. (c) Women in the workplace. (d) Women are capable of doing work that was traditionally done by men.

2. (a) To show support for women in the workplace. (b) He seems to admire women workers supporting the home front. (c) The woman looks strong, capable, and confident. (d) The woman's muscular body contrasts with her childish face, and her rough work clothes contrast with the dainty mirror in her pocket. The artist may be suggesting an inherent contradiction in a young woman doing a traditional "man's" job.

3. (a) The artist seems to assume that the work is physically demanding and "men's" work. The American flag background suggests that the woman has taken a factory job for patriotic reasons. (b) The artist seems to assume that women have had to give up their femininity and are somewhat masculine in appearance and/or attitude. (c) Answers will vary. Some students may think that a muscular appearance may mean that a person performs physically demanding work or that a person who wears a dress or suit must work in an office. Others may say that appearances are often wrongly interpreted as stereotypes and are in fact not reliable indicators. (d) Read biographies of women, or interview women, who lived during World War II.

The Struggle for Justice at Home

1. FOCUS

Connecting to the Big Idea

See page 690B. Point out to students that just as women were mobilized to support the war effort, Americans of different races and ethnic groups were also heavily recruited. Explain that in spite of this, discrimination continued at many levels. Ask students what impact the involvement in the war had on these Americans.

Objectives

● Explain how events on the home front stimulated the movement for equal rights for African Americans.
● Cite the effect of the war on the employment of Mexican Americans and Native Americans.
● Describe how many Japanese Americans were forced into internment camps during the war.

Bellringer

Write the words *injustice* and *inequality* on the chalkboard. Have students describe an incident that they associate with these words. Encourage students to explain why the incident serves as an example of injustice or inequality.

Reading Strategy

Reinforcing Key Concepts As they read, ask students to see how our policies at home toward women and minorities compared to our goals for fighting abroad.

The Struggle for Justice at Home

For many Americans, the war broke down racial barriers in the job market. Japanese Americans, however, fell victim to bitter prejudice at home as the United States battled Japan abroad.

Key Concepts

• Events on the home front helped stimulate the movement for equal rights for African Americans.

• Mexican Americans and Native Americans battled discrimination at home and entered the work force in greater numbers during the war.

• A large number of Japanese Americans were forced into internment camps by the United States government during the war, while others served courageously in the military.

Key Terms, People, and Places

"Double V" campaign, bracero, internment camp; A. Philip Randolph

Clinging to her most precious belongings, this little girl waits to be moved to an internment camp.

P resident Roosevelt, in his 1942 Columbus Day speech, expressed the need to set aside bigotry for the sake of the wartime effort:

I n some communities employers dislike to hire women. In others they are reluctant to hire Negroes. We can no longer afford to indulge such prejudice.

In fact, the war did bring greater opportunities for a number of groups in America. But racial prejudice did not disappear during the war years. On the contrary, the war fanned the flames of many conflicts that had been smoldering for decades.

The Wartime Struggle Against Jim Crow

Although the effort to end discrimination toward African Americans had long been under way by the time the United States entered World War II, the Jim Crow system—which provided for the rigid separation of the races—remained firmly in place in the South. In the North, fewer laws enforcing segregation were on the books, but African Americans still were discriminated against in employment, education, and housing patterns. During the 1940s, over two million African Americans migrated from the South to northern and western cities (see map on page 707). There they found new opportunities, but they also found themselves concentrated in urban ghettos, or sections of a city in which many members of a particular minority group live due to economic pressure or discrimination. A survey taken in 1941 showed that 50 percent of all African American homes were substandard, versus only 14 percent of white homes.

When the war began, African American unemployment remained high—one out of five potential workers was unemployed. The United States Employment Service, a government agency created during the Depression to provide unemployed Americans with job counseling and placement, continued to honor employers' requests for "whites only," thereby continuing existing patterns of discrimination.

⭐ The war turned a spotlight on the injustice of racism in the United States. Alexander J. Allen, who worked for the Baltimore Urban League during the war, remarked, "It made a mockery of wartime goals to fight overseas against fascism only to come back to the same kind of discrimination and racism here in this country." One poignant example of this "mockery" occurred when a group of African American GIs was refused service by the owner of a lunch counter:

RESOURCE DIRECTORY

Teaching Resources

Reproducible Lesson Plan found in the Unit 8 folder, p. 41, provides a summary of the Section 4 lesson plan content.

Alternate Lesson Plan: Learning Styles found in the Alternate Lesson Plans folder, p. 130, is especially effective for auditory learners, and gives students guidance in creating a television report on prejudice.

Guided Reading and Review found in Unit 8 folder, p. 48, provides a structure for reading and mastering the key concepts and reviewing the key terms for Section 4. (Guided Practice)

⭐ **Literature Activity** *Black Boy,* found in the Unit 8 folder, pp. 60–61, focuses on Richard Wright's novel about the struggle to survive in the segregated United States.

African American Migration, 1940–1950

States that had significant loss of African American population

States that had significant gain in African American population

2% Gain or loss of African Americans as a percentage of a state's total population

WA, MT, ND, MN, WI, MI +3%, NY +3%, VT, ME, NH, MA, RI
OR, ID, SD, IA, IL +3%, IN +1%, OH +2%, PA +2%, CT, NJ +1%, DE, MD
WY, NE, MO +3%, KY -2%, WV, VA -5%
NV, UT, CO, KS, TN -2%, NC -3%
CA, AZ, NM, OK -1%, AR -4%, MS -5%, AL -4%, GA -6%, SC -7%
TX -2%, LA -4%, FL -7%

Geography and History: Interpreting Maps

All of their possessions loaded into the family car, these young people are moving north. *According to this map, what states lost the greatest percentage of their African American populations in the 1940s? How do you think the wartime economy affected African American migration?*

"You know we don't serve coloreds here," the man repeated. . . .

We ignored him, and just stood there inside the door, staring at what we had come to see—the German prisoners of war who were having lunch at the counter. . . .

We continued to stare. This was really happening. It was no jive talk. The people of Salina would serve these enemy soldiers and turn away black American GIs.

Lloyd Brown, an American soldier stationed in Salina, Kansas

African Americans and others experienced discrimination not only at lunch counters. In the United States military, where men were risking their lives to defend their country, white and African American troops were strictly segregated.

Many white Americans, however, saw no problems in these racial practices. A 1942 poll revealed that six out of ten whites felt that African Americans were satisfied with existing conditions and needed no additional opportunities. Mirroring the lack of concern felt by much of white America, the government did not seem eager to improve the situations of African Americans. Franklin Roosevelt, preoccupied with military matters, was not willing to disrupt the war effort to promote social equality. "I don't think, quite frankly," he said in late 1943, "that we can bring about the millennium [a period of human perfection] at this time."

African Americans disagreed with the President and began organizing for change on their own. The Pittsburgh *Courier,* an African American newspaper, launched a **"Double V" campaign:** *V* for victory in the war against the Axis powers, *V* for victory in the struggle for equality at home. **A. Philip Randolph**—head of the Brotherhood

Discuss

Although the war provided opportunities for African Americans, it did not put an end to discrimination at home. Have students list examples of continued discrimination, and describe efforts to promote racial equality. Then ask them to consider whether the advances outweighed the setbacks.

Caption Answer to ...

Interpreting Maps

VA, SC, FL, GA, MS; the concentration of wartime industries—and jobs—in the North attracted people to the region.

In Depth

Then and Now

The 99th Fighter Squadron, formed in 1942, were the first African Americans to fly in the Army Air Corps. They were known as the "Black Eagles" because of their success in escorting all-white bomber crews over Europe. The 99th was commanded by Benjamin O. Davis, Jr., the son of the man who became the first African American general. In 1991, Davis wrote about the exploits of the Black Eagles in his autobiography. By the early 1990s, 5,527 African American officers made up 5.6 percent of the officers in the United States Air Force.

In Depth

Biography

Adam Clayton Powell, Jr. (1908–1972), charismatic minister from Harlem, used the pulpit and his oratorical skills to mobilize frustrated African Americans into positive political action. He echoed the sentiments of many fellow African Americans of his time when he said: "If the Negro is good enough to drive tanks on the battlefronts of Europe and Asia, he's good enough to work on the assembly lines of America." In 1944, Powell became one of only two African Americans in Congress and gained admiration for his "Powell Amendments"—attachments to bills that called for the cut-off of federal funds to any organization that practiced racial discrimination.

Using Historical Evidence This man is protesting outside a Chicago milk company in 1941. *How does the injustice the man is protesting conflict with the issues being fought for abroad during World War II?*

of Sleeping Car Porters, a labor union with a largely African American membership—proposed a massive march on Washington in early 1941 to demand an end to discrimination in all areas of American society. Worried about the possibility of violence in the nation's capital, Roosevelt tried to talk Randolph out of the march. Randolph agreed only when, on June 25, 1941, the President signed Executive Order 8802, which opened jobs and job training programs in defense plants to all Americans regardless of race.

The order also created the Fair Employment Practices Committee (FEPC) to hear complaints about job discrimination in defense industries as well as in the government. While the FEPC was only moderately successful, it did highlight the issue of discrimination, and it opened the way for employers to fill their job openings by hiring African Americans.

Meanwhile, African Americans were beginning to take direct action to promote equality. The Congress of Racial Equality (CORE), committed to using nonviolent techniques to end racism, was founded in Chicago in 1942. In May 1943 CORE organized its first sit-in at a restaurant called the Jack Spratt Coffee House. Groups of CORE members, each including at least one African American, filled the restaurant's counter and booths and refused to leave until everyone was served. They succeeded in ending Jack Spratt's discriminatory policies, and the sit-in technique quickly spread to CORE groups in other cities. These efforts paved the way for later civil rights activity but could not head off major race riots during the summer of 1943. Thirty-four people died in Detroit on June 16, and New York City was the scene of another riot on August 1 and 2. ✪

MAKING CONNECTIONS

In what ways did the war speed up, and in what ways did it retard, the movement toward equal rights for African Americans?

Mexican Americans and Braceros During World War II

Like African Americans, Mexicans working in the United States and Mexican American citizens faced discrimination during the war. At the same time, the war did bring new employment opportunities for Mexican Americans. Planning for future needs, the Labor Department's Office of Education established vocational schools in a number of southwestern cities and provided training for rural Americans—including Mexican Americans—that eased the transition to war work.

Mexican Americans made major gains on the industrial front during World War II. By 1944, 17,000 were employed in the Los Angeles shipyards, where none had worked three years before. Mexican Americans also found jobs in shipyards and aircraft factories elsewhere in California and in Washington, Texas, and New Mexico. Some headed for other war production centers in places such as Detroit, Chicago, Kansas City, and New York.

The Bracero Program On the agricultural front, a shortage of farm laborers led the United States to seek help from Mexico. In 1942 an agreement between the two nations provided for transportation, food, shelter, and medical care for thousands of **braceros** (Spanish for "workers"), Mexican farm laborers brought to work in the United States. Between 1942 and 1947, more than 200,000 braceros participated in the program. When their contracts expired, however, they were quickly transported back to Mexico.

Despite their vital contributions to the war effort, Mexicans and Mexican Americans continued to suffer discrimination. Braceros endured miserable working conditions, and employers sometimes withheld their wages. Industrial workers occasionally received lower wages for the same work done by people of other ethnic backgrounds. Crowded cities often bred racial tensions. In Los Angeles, where many Mexican Americans lived, those tensions erupted in a bloody race riot in mid-1943.

Zoot Suit Riots Los Angeles was a popular city for sailors on leave from nearby military bases. In April and May 1943, street fighting broke out between sailors and residents of Mexican descent. Many Mexican American men wore a popular style of clothing known as the "zoot suit," which had baggy pants and a long jacket. Gangs of sailors roamed the streets looking for men wearing such suits, whom they attacked and humiliated. Although one Spanish newspaper, *La Opinión*, encouraged the victims not to respond with more violence, some Mexican American youths took revenge on the sailors when they had the chance.

The fighting turned into a full-scale riot during the first weeks of June 1943. Local newspapers usually blamed Mexican Americans for the violence. Police often arrested the victims rather than the sailors who had initiated the attacks. Finally, army and navy officials intervened by restricting soldiers' off-duty access to Los Angeles. By mid-June the riots had subsided.

Native Americans and the War at Home

Despite their history of oppression by the United States government, Native Americans behaved patriotically during World War II. Thousands enlisted in the armed forces or migrated to urban centers to work in defense plants. Government propaganda held up these Native Americans as models of loyal service.

Nearly fifty thousand Native Americans worked in war industries around the country. Over two thousand Navaho helped build a large supply depot in New Mexico. Iroquois worked in aluminum plants and mining operations in New York state. Other Native Americans constructed airplanes on the West Coast and made tanks and ships in other war production centers.

Thousands of Native Americans who left reservations to take military or industrial jobs

had to adapt quickly to white culture. At the end of the war, Native Americans who had served abroad or worked in industrial centers in the United States were less likely to return home. For some Native Americans, the cultural transition brought a sense of alienation and rootlessness that left lasting scars.

The Japanese American Internment

Japanese Americans suffered the worst discrimination during the war. In late 1941, they comprised a tiny minority in the United States. Numbering but 127,000—or one tenth of one percent of the entire population—they were concentrated on the West Coast, where prejudice against them had been festering for decades. About two thirds of the Japanese Americans had been born in the United States and were therefore American citizens, but their citizenship mattered little in the heat of war.

Anti-Japanese sentiment grew stronger after Japan attacked Pearl Harbor. Rumors of sabotage on the West Coast spread quickly. One report that reached President Roosevelt's desk, while noting that the Japanese Americans there were almost all loyal citizens, went on to say that "there are still Japanese in the United States who will tie dynamite around their waist and make a human bomb out of themselves." The report also suggested that "dams could be blown and half of California could actually die of thirst."

Mexican American "zoot suiters" were the target of attacks in 1943, but they themselves were often blamed by police for the violence.

Analyze

Ask students to consider in what ways service in the armed forces broke down prejudices against Mexican Americans and Native Americans, as well as increasing the desire of these Americans to achieve their full civil rights. Then have students decide what civil rights of Japanese Americans were violated by their internment. What factors may have played a part in the internment of Japanese Americans?

Activity
Writing an Editorial

Ask students to imagine that they are writing for a magazine distributed to the armed services during World War II. Ask them to write an editorial about the Zoot Suit riots, expressing an opinion about the actions of sailors before and during the riot.

Enrichment

Ask students to research the life of A. Philip Randolph and to write a short biography of this prominent African American.

In Depth

Multicultural Perspectives

In 1942, the U.S. government forced thousands of Italian and German immigrants to leave their homes in California. (Among those evacuated were the parents of baseball star Joe DiMaggio.) These people, perceived as a threat to American security, were taken to guarded army camps in the interior of the country. Four months later, the government realized its mistake and allowed the Italian and German aliens to return home. Japanese Americans, nevertheless, remained in internment camps for the entire war.

3. ASSESS

Section 4 Review Answers

1. (a) "Double V" campaign, see p. 707, (b) bracero, see p. 708, (c) internment camp, see p. 710

2. A. Philip Randolph , see p. 707

3. African Americans used the "Double V" campaign, the March on Washington movement, and peaceful demonstrations to demand equal rights during the war.

4. The war brought new employment opportunities for Mexican Americans, but it also saw racial tensions erupt into race riots in Los Angeles in 1943.

5. Thousands of Native Americans worked in war industries; for some the war also sped the process of their assimilation into white culture.

6. The belief that some Japanese Americans were cooperating with Japan and that Japanese people were fanatical and would even sacrifice their lives to sabotage the West Coast laid the groundwork for the policy of internment.

7. Answers will vary. Students may suggest that since Japanese Americans were such a small minority and looked physically different from the Caucasian population, it was easier for white Americans to believe the wild rumors about them and to make them scapegoats.

Reteach

Ask students to make four columns on a piece of paper, with the headings African Americans, Mexican Americans, Native Americans, and Japanese Americans. Ask them to summarize under each heading the major effects of the war on members of that group.

Viewpoints
On the Internment of Japanese Americans

The forced internment of Japanese Americans produced strong feelings on both sides of the issue. Two views are given below. *How does each of these viewpoints address the issue of constitutional rights?*

For Internment

"It is a fact that the Japanese navy has been reconnoitering [investigating] the Pacific Coast. . . . It is [a] fact that communication takes place between the enemy at sea and enemy agents on land. The Pacific Coast is officially a combat zone: some part of it may at any moment be a battlefield. Nobody's constitutional rights include the right to reside and do business on a battlefield."

Walter Lippmann, American columnist,
February 12, 1942

Against Internment

"Racial discrimination in any form and in any degree has no justifiable part whatever in our democratic way of life. . . . All residents of this nation are kin in some way by blood or culture to a foreign land. Yet they are primarily and necessarily a part of . . . the United States [and are] . . . entitled to all rights and freedoms guaranteed by the Constitution."

Supreme Court Justice Frank Murphy's dissenting opinion,
Korematsu v. United States, 1944

The press capitalized on people's fears. Headlines such as "Jap Boat Flashes Message Ashore" and "Japanese Here Sent Vital Data to Tokyo" gave newspaper readers the feeling that Japanese spies were everywhere. *Time* and *Life* magazines told readers how to tell the Chinese, who were allies, from the Japanese, who were enemies: "The Chinese expression is likely to be more placid, kindly, open; the Japanese more positive, dogmatic, arrogant." ✪

As a result of these fears and prejudices, the government decided to remove all Japanese from the West Coast. On February 19, 1942, President Roosevelt signed Executive Order 9066 authorizing the secretary of war to establish military zones and to remove "any or all persons" from such zones. The War Relocation Authority (WRA) was created to move 110,000 Japanese Americans—citizens and noncitizens alike—to ten **internment camps** in remote areas across the country.

The relocation process took place hastily, and Japanese Americans had little time to secure their property before they left for the camps. Many lost their businesses, homes, and other property. Henry Murakami, a resident of California, remembers losing the $55,000 worth of fishing nets that had been his livelihood:

*W*hen we were sent to Fort Lincoln [in Bismarck, North Dakota] *I asked the FBI men about my nets. They said, "Don't worry. Everything is going to be taken care of." But I never saw the nets again, nor my brand-new 1941 Plymouth, nor our furniture. It all just disappeared. I lost everything.*

Japanese Americans had no idea where they were going when they boarded the buses for the internment camps. Monica Sone, who lived in Seattle before the war, imagined her camp would be "out somewhere deep in a snow-bound forest, an American Siberia. I saw myself plunging chest deep in the snow, hunting for small game to keep us alive." She and her family packed winter clothes, only to end up in Camp Minidoka, on the sun-baked prairie of central Idaho. Normal July temperature there is about 90 degrees Fahrenheit.

All of the internment camps were located in desolate areas. They consisted of wooden barracks covered with tar paper and were protected by barbed wire and armed guards. Rooms inside the barracks had only cots, blankets, and a light bulb. Toilet, bathing, and dining facilities were communal.

Despite these injustices, more than 17,000 Japanese Americans served in the armed forces. About 1,200 of the Japanese Americans who volunteered for service did so from relocation centers. Many more volunteers came from Hawaii, where no internment had taken place. The 442nd Regimental Combat Team, composed entirely of Japanese Americans, won more medals for bravery than any other unit in United States history.

 RESOURCE DIRECTORY ✪

Teaching Resources

📄 **Viewpoints Activity** On Japanese American Internment, found in the Unit 8 folder, pp. 52–53, provides additional viewpoints and perspectives on the internment of Japanese Americans during the war.

📄 **Primary Source Activity** Anti-Japanese Sentiment, found in the Unit 8 folder, p. 56, profiles Mary Tsukamoto, who experienced anti-Japanese sentiment in the United States firsthand.

Although the vast majority of Japanese Americans abided by the policy of internment, a few did challenge it in the courts. Four cases eventually reached the Supreme Court, which in each case upheld the constitutionality of the wartime relocation. In one case, California resident Fred Toyosaburo Korematsu was convicted of violating Executive Order 9066 because he failed to report to an assembly center for relocation. The Supreme Court ruled in *Korematsu* v. *United States* (1944) that "Korematsu was not excluded from the Military Area because of hostility to him or his race," but that "the military urgency of the situation demanded that all citizens of Japanese ancestry be segregated from the West Coast temporarily." The dissenting opinion, however, labeled the policy "an obvious racial discrimination."

Finally, early in 1945, all Japanese Americans were allowed to leave the camps. Some were able to return to their homes and resume their lives. Others, finding that their property had been seized, had no place to go. It was not until 1988 that the United States government took responsibility for this gross violation of civil liberties. At that time Congress passed and President Ronald Reagan signed a law awarding each surviving Japanese American internee a tax-free payment of $20,000. These monetary reparations could not undo the damage that had been done decades earlier, but the law at least acknowledged the injustice.

Using Historical Evidence Tags with family identification numbers were attached to each piece of luggage and each family member at assembly centers for Japanese Americans. Permitted to take only a few possessions with them, many tried to sell their belongings but were forced to abandon what they could not carry or sell. *How do you think each person in this photo is feeling about the situation?*

Reinforcing the Big Idea

World War II hastened the demand for and the rate of social change on the home front. Although minority groups broke through some racial barriers during the war, discrimination and injustice continued to affect many Americans.

Caption Answer to ...

Using Historical Evidence

Answers will vary but may include the following: The elderly man is proud, attempting to maintain his dignity; the children are innocent and uncertain.

SECTION 4 REVIEW

Key Terms, People, and Places
1. Define (a) "Double V" campaign, (b) bracero, (c) internment camp.
2. Identify A. Philip Randolph.

Key Concepts
3. What strategies did African Americans use in their struggle for equal rights during World War II?
4. What were the major effects of World War II on the lives of Mexican Americans?
5. What impact did World War II have on the lives of Native Americans?

6. What fears and prejudices led to the internment of Japanese Americans during World War II?

Critical Thinking
7. **Recognizing Cause and Effect** Although some German Americans and Italian Americans were relocated from the West Coast during the war, this action was on a much smaller scale than the internment of Japanese Americans. What do you think caused the harsher treatment of Japanese Americans?

 Quiz found in the Unit 8 folder, p. 49, covers the main ideas in this section as well as the key terms.

 Chapter Test Forms A and B are found in the Unit 8 folder, pp. 64–69.

 Answer Keys found in the Unit 8 folder, pp. 146–160, provide answers to all student activities.

Media and Technology

Transparency
Graphic Organizer, G-3

Guided Reading Audiotape
(English and Spanish)

Computer Test Bank

 In Depth

Historical Misconceptions

There is debate about how much of a surprise the attack on Pearl Harbor really was. Some historians suggest that Roosevelt deliberately exposed the Pacific Fleet in Hawaii to provoke a Japanese attack. Fleet commanders *had* been put on war alert, but never anticipated the bombing of Pearl Harbor. Most felt that before attacking American bases, the Japanese would strike closer to home. Planes approaching Pearl Harbor were seen on radar but were thought to be American, although the radar indicated a flight path from the north, not the east—the likely direction for an American approach. Eleven months before the attack, the American ambassador to Japan heard a rumor that the Japanese were planning a surprise attack on Pearl Harbor. No action was taken.

Understanding Key Terms, People, and Places

Terms
Students should refer to the definitions of the key terms in the chapter to write sentences that show the relation of each word to America during World War II.

True or False
1. true
2. false, wildcat strikes
3. true
4. false, braceros
5. false, "Double V" campaign

True or False
1. true
2. false, John L. Lewis
3. false, A. Philip Randolph

Reviewing Main Ideas

1. President Roosevelt established the Office of War Mobilization and appointed James F. Byrnes its director. The government also established the cost-plus system so that businesses could make money on what they produced for the war.

2. Robert Woodruff of Coca-Cola and Philip K. Wrigley created new markets for their products. Other entrepreneurs, including Henry Ford and Henry J. Kaiser, introduced new methods such as mass production to their companies.

3. More workers in the work force resulted in more union members. The rise in the cost of living during the war, coupled with increased union membership, led to more frequent strikes despite agreements to refrain from striking.

4. Deficit spending turned the economy around and helped finance the war. Unfortunately it also created huge debts, causing economic problems that continue to this day.

5. With the Depression over, people were able to find new jobs and had money in their pockets for the first time in many years. In addition, the government waged a massive propaganda war to encourage a sense of cooperation. Participation in the war effort also contributed to the mood of optimism.

6. People spent their free time and newly earned money buying and reading the new paperback books created by the Pocket Book company, going to movies, watching professional baseball (both women's and men's leagues), and listening to popular music.

7. The government froze prices and began a rationing program. It tried to

---

Chapter Review

Understanding Key Terms, People, and Places

Key Terms
1. cost-plus system
2. wildcat strike
3. deficit spending
4. rationing
5. "Double V" campaign
6. bracero
7. internment camp

People
8. John L. Lewis
9. Rosie the Riveter
10. A. Philip Randolph

Terms For each term above, write a sentence that explains its relation to World War II in the United States, from 1941 to 1945.

True or False Determine whether each statement is true or false. If it is true, write "true." If it is false, change the underlined term to make the statement true.
1. During World War II, Japanese citizens and noncitizens alike were sent to <u>internment camps</u> in remote areas of the country.
2. <u>Braceros</u> are organized by workers themselves and not endorsed by the union.
3. A government program called <u>rationing</u> distributed scarce goods among consumers by using a point value system and issuing coupons.
4. In 1942 a shortage of farm labor led the United States to seek help from Mexican <u>wildcat strikes.</u>
5. African Americans launched the <u>cost-plus system</u>, with the goals of victory against the Axis powers and victory in the struggle for equality.

True or False Determine whether each statement is true or false. If it is true, write "true." If it is false, change the underlined name to make the statement true.
1. <u>Rosie the Riveter</u> was a fictional defense plant worker in World War II.
2. <u>A. Philip Randolph</u> called strikes in 1943 to demand pay raises.
3. <u>John L. Lewis</u> proposed a massive march on Washington in 1941 to demand an end to discrimination.

Reviewing Main Ideas

Section 1 (pp. 692–695)
1. How did the United States government help businesses convert to wartime production?
2. Give examples to show how entrepreneurs were able to profit during the war.
3. What effect did the increased work force during the war have on union membership?
4. Describe the positive and negative effects of deficit spending during World War II.

Section 2 (pp. 696–699)
5. What factors account for the mood of optimism on the home front?
6. Name several new ways in which people spent their free time and newly earned money during the war.
7. How did the government deal with wartime shortages?
8. What campaigns did the government undertake to encourage Americans to participate in the war effort?

Section 3 (pp. 700–704)
9. What changes took place in the kinds of jobs women held before and during World War II?
10. How did their new jobs benefit women?
11. Why did government campaigns strongly encourage women to return home after the war?

Section 4 (pp. 706–711)
12. Explain how the war turned a spotlight on the injustice of racism in American society.
13. Describe some of the opportunities and some of the problems encountered by Mexican Americans during the war.
14. How did the war speed the process of assimilation for Native Americans?
15. What factors influenced the government's decision to intern Japanese Americans on the West Coast during World War II?

---

maintain morale by encouraging patriotism and a sense of participation in the war effort.

8. One campaign asked Americans to conserve resources by saving items such as scrap metal and rubber. Another encouraged Americans to buy savings bonds.

9. Before the war women often worked as sales clerks or household servants. During the war many women took jobs in manufacturing, especially in the defense industry.

10. Women were able to make their own money. Many felt that their lives became more exciting and enjoyed a new sense of accomplishment.

11. The government assumed that women's proper role was in the home. In addition, men wanted

"their" jobs back and wanted to return to home life as it had been before the war.

12. During the war many people realized the incongruity of fighting fascism overseas while ignoring racism and discrimination at home.

13. During the war Mexican Americans were able to find jobs in defense industries that had been closed to them before. As they moved to cities like Los Angeles to take advantage of these opportunities, however, they often encountered racial prejudice that sometimes led to violence and rioting.

14. Native Americans who left reservations to take military or industrial jobs had to adjust quickly to white culture. This transition brought with it a sense of alienation for some Native Americans.

Making Connections (right column)

1. Although many women had to leave their jobs after the war, the numbers of women who joined the work force during the war sowed the seeds for women to work outside the home in the future. The movement of women into jobs traditionally reserved for men also encouraged women to seek better, more challenging jobs than they had in the past.

2. The poster on page 692 seems to convey that "we're all in this together" and reminds citizens that their work in the factories is needed to help win the war. The photographs on pages 708 and 711 demonstrate the inequalities that still existed in American society at the time. Students' explanations should show an understanding of the contradiction between what the government was asking its citizens to do and how it treated some segments of society. Primary source excerpts that support this idea can be found on pages 706 and 707 (Alexander J. Allen and Lloyd Brown).

3. Possible answers: reading paperback books; attending movies; playing and attending baseball games; saving aluminum and rubber; shortages of foods such as sugar and meat; clothing styles that conserve cloth; wartime songs, slogans, and posters; women in the work force; minorities in the work force; their struggle for justice.

4. (a) The tree map cites the end of the Depression and the introduction of defense jobs and participation in wartime campaigns as factors that contributed to the mood of the home front. (b) Possible answers: Robert Woodruff's sending Coca-Cola to troops overseas, Robert de Graff's establishing a market for paperback books, and Henry Kaiser's applying mass production techniques to shipbuilding. (c) Answers will vary. Students' graphic organizers should show an awareness of the main ideas and supporting details that explain these struggles.

Alternative Assessment

Final Evaluation

Display written guides and allow students to present their taped or spoken guides.

Use the following criteria to evaluate students' projects:
- Extensiveness of their description of changes
- Effectiveness of their analysis of the causes for change

Thinking Critically

1. **Making Comparisons** Many entrepreneurs prospered during the war. What did Robert de Graff's Pocket Books company have in common with Robert Woodruff's Coca-Cola company?
2. **Predicting Consequences** At the end of the war, government propaganda urged women to resume their traditional roles as homemakers. How do you think this campaign influenced family patterns and women's self-perception in the postwar years?
3. **Identifying Assumptions** Explain the assumptions underlying the 1942 poll that revealed that six out of ten whites felt that African Americans were satisfied with existing conditions and opportunities (page 707).

Making Connections

1. **Evaluating Primary Sources** Review the primary source excerpts on page 703. What long-term effects did joining the work force during the war have for some women?
2. **Understanding the Visuals** Write a short paragraph explaining the contradiction demonstrated by the poster on page 692 and the photos on page 708 and 711. Find a primary source excerpt in Section 4 that supports your explanation.
3. **Writing About the Chapter** Write a letter from the viewpoint of an American teenager in the early 1940s to a soldier who is serving in World War II. In your letter explain how your life and the lives of people around you have changed because of the war, including the lives of women, minorities, and local entrepreneurs. First, make a list of the changes that are affecting your life such as shortages and rationing. Note new ways in which you spend your leisure time. Write a draft of your letter, in which you describe your present life. Revise your letter, making sure that you have presented a detailed and interesting picture of life on the home front. Proofread your letter and draft a final copy.
4. **Using the Graphic Organizer** This graphic organizer uses a tree map to organize information about daily life on the home front during the war. Tree maps can help classify main ideas and supporting details. (a) According to the tree map, what are two factors that contributed to the mood of optimism and cooperation on the home front? (b) What supporting details could be included under a new main idea on the tree map: "Entrepreneurs profited from the war"? (c) On a separate sheet of paper, create your own graphic organizer about the struggle for justice among minorities during the war, using this graphic organizer as an example.

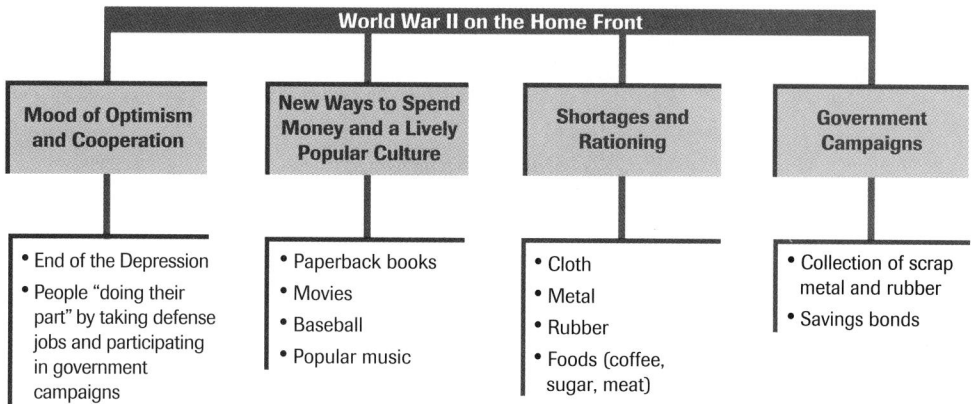

15. Some of the factors included prejudice against Japanese Americans that had existed for many years on the West Coast; wild rumors, supported by the press, that suggested Japanese Americans were assisting Japan in the war; the attack on Pearl Harbor that shocked and infuriated Americans; and a report to President Roosevelt that outlined the possibilities for sabotage in the United States.

Thinking Critically

1. Both entrepreneurs created new markets for their products among American GIs. Woodruff sent Coca-Cola overseas and de Graff lowered the price of books and made them more widely available so that soldiers could carry them into combat.

2. Answers will vary. Students may predict that the homemaker image promoted for women led to an idealization of the nuclear family consisting of a wife who stayed at home while her husband worked, and that women—even those who attended college—did not see themselves as destined for lifelong careers outside the home.

3. The attitude expressed in the poll assumes that African Americans did not want or were unable to take advantage of the same opportunities available to white Americans. It also suggests that some white Americans believed that the hierarchy of race that existed in the United States was somehow "natural" or inevitable.

Review with students the ways in which the United States government attempted to bolster morale and enlist support for the war effort. Recall the ways in which the government appealed to the conscience of every American.

Using the images and captions highlighted in the American Album as a basis for discussion, ask why the propaganda campaigns were important and necessary for American victory in World War II. Point out that campaigns, rationing, slogans, posters, songs, and movies delivered a powerful message during the war. Have students identify the different segments of the population targeted by the various campaigns through a study of the various artifacts.

Ask students how messages are delivered to Americans today. Discuss the role of television in advertising. Ask how "infomercials" help create images for political candidates. Have students identify other forms of advertising. Ask how billboards, posters, and magazine photographs are used by clothing, tobacco, and other manufacturers to appeal to specific groups. Discuss the ways in which radio programming and videos appeal to Americans of different generations.

You might want to have students bring to class examples of advertising artifacts of the 1990s.

American Album

BRINGING THE WAR HOME

Americans living and working "stateside" seldom forgot about the war overseas. Almost everyone had relatives and close friends who faced constant danger from the fighting. Besides, the government wouldn't let Americans forget about the war. Rationing, pleas for conservation, a steady stream of patriotic messages, even requests to donate the family dog to the army— all this and more reminded Americans that their country was in a life-and-death struggle against totalitarian dictatorships. *What effect do you think these reminders had on the morale of soldiers and on Americans living in the United States?*

▲ LABEL ON MILK BOTTLE This label conveyed the message that conserving resources was every American's patriotic duty. The recycling effort included hundreds of products, especially those made with metal or rubber.

◄ "E" BUTTON The army and navy awarded these "E" (for excellence) pins to civilian workers who met production quotas or did outstanding work.

◄ RATION CARDS AND STAMPS Shoppers during the war needed their ration books to purchase many items that were either in short supply or needed by the armed forces. Notice the initials OPA, which stood for the Office of Price Administration. This agency distributed the ration books and also had the authority to set prices for items in short supply.

▲ HITLER AND UNCLE SAM This button used gallows humor to ask everyone to "pull" together to win the war. The need to put aside disagreements among Americans was a common government message.

◀ WAR RELIEF EFFORT While the American economy boomed during the war, Europe and Asia were devastated. Americans proudly wore pins like this one to indicate that they had contributed money to help people in other countries.

VICTORY ▶ BUTTON The letter *V*, for victory, was the most common symbol of the war effort. Many businesses used the *V* and the American flag to send a patriotic and a promotional message.

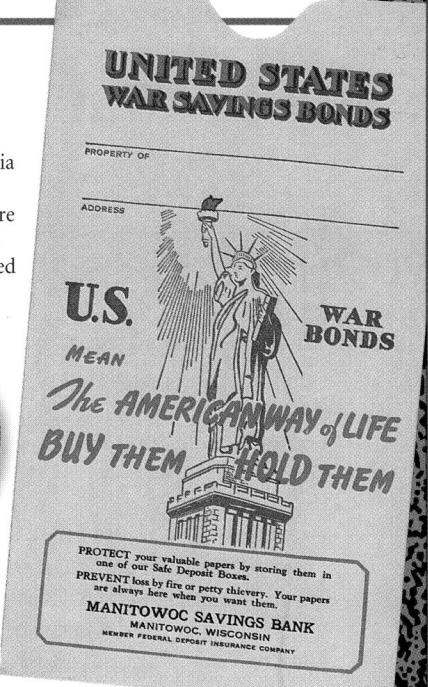

SLEEVE FOR U.S. WAR BONDS ▲ The government borrowed an incredible 135 billion dollars from individual Americans to finance the war effort. These War Savings Bonds not only helped finance the war, but they gave thousands of Americans a personal and financial stake in the outcome of the war and preserving "the American way of life."

◀ DOGS FOR DEFENSE The armed forces needed dogs for sentry duty, to sniff out explosives, and for many other tasks. Citizens who donated dogs to the military could proudly wear this button.

PROPAGANDA POSTERS No matter where they went—at work, on the street, at the movies—Americans saw wonderfully creative posters reminding them that their way of life depended on the outcome of the war. The posters shown at right encouraged people to work hard at their jobs to win the war. The posters used images of happy families to stir up even more support for the war effort. ▶

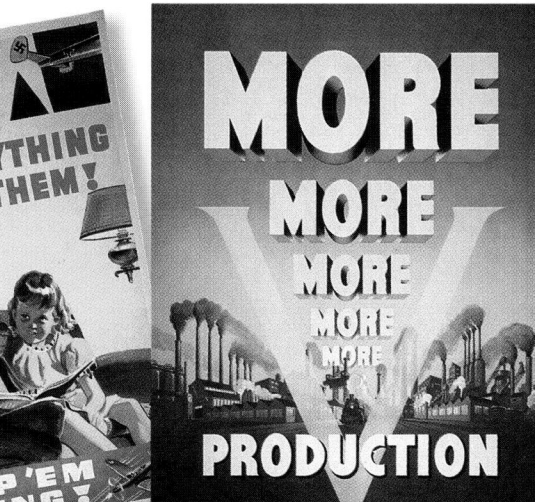

Chapter 26 The Cold War and American Society
1945–1960

📁 **Teaching Resources** (See Unit 8 Folder)

	Instruction	Enrichment
Section 1 **Origins of the Cold War** (pp. 718–721)	Reproducible Lesson Plan, p. 71 Alternate Lesson Plan, p. 132 Guided Reading and Review, p. 75 Quiz, p. 76	Primary Source Activity, Uncle Joe, p. 89 Visual Learning Activity, What They Fear Most, p. 95 Historian's Toolbox Activity, Recognizing Cause and Effect, p. 87
Section 2 **Containment** (pp. 723–727)	Reproducible Lesson Plan, p. 72 Alternate Lesson Plan, p. 133 Guided Reading and Review, p. 77 Quiz, p. 78	American Profiles Activity, George F. Kennan, p. 83 Viewpoints Activity, On Joining NATO, pp. 85–86 Critical Thinking Activity, Identifying Central Issues, p. 88
Section 3 **The Cold War in Asia, the Middle East, and Latin America** (pp. 728–732)	Reproducible Lesson Plan, p. 73 Alternate Lesson Plan, p. 134 Guided Reading and Review, p. 79 Quiz, p. 80	American Profiles Activity, Marguerite Higgins, p. 84 Visual Learning Activity, Civilian Control of the Military, p. 96 Literature Activity, The Ugly American, p. 92
Section 4 **The Cold War in the United States** (pp. 733–737)	Reproducible Lesson Plan, p. 74 Alternate Lesson Plan, p. 135 Guided Reading and Review, p. 81 Quiz, p. 82 Chapter Test, Forms A & B, pp. 97–102	Primary Source Activity, The Rise of Joseph McCarthy, pp. 90–91 Literature Activity, The Hunt for Witches and Communists, pp. 93–94

📁 **Additional Chapter Resources**

Resource Organizer, p. 70
Alternate Lesson Plan p. 131
Answer Keys pp. 146–158

Bibliography

For the Teacher
Gimbel, John. *The Origins of the Marshall Plan.* Stanford University, 1976.
Kennan, George F. *Memoirs: 1925–1959.* Pantheon, 1983. (A personal view of the era by the definitive statesman of the policy of "containment.")
McCullough, David. *Truman.* Simon & Schuster, 1992. (A comprehensive biography of the cold war President.)

Prentice Hall Literature Excerpts from *The American Experience,* 1994, including Momaday, N. Scott. "A Vision Beyond Time and Place." *Life,* 1971.

The Big Idea for the chapter and how the main ideas in each section relate to the Big Idea are graphically displayed below. Comprehension of this chapter's Big Idea is critical to students' understanding of United States history and how we as a nation got where we are today.

Media and Technology

 Cause and Effect, F-10

 Critical Thinking, I-2

 Graphic Organizer, G-5

 Guided Reading Audiotapes (English and Spanish)

 Computer Test Bank

For the Student
Macridis, Roy C., and Steven L. Burg. *Introduction to Comparative Politics: Political Regimes and Political Change.* HarperCollins, 1991.

Orwell, George. *Nineteen Eighty-Four.* Buccaneer, 1982. (A haunting, futuristic indictment of the totalitarian state.)

Solzhenitsyn, Aleksandr I. *One Day in the Life of Ivan Denisovich.* Bantam, 1984. (A famous Russian dissident's moving account of life in a Soviet prison camp.)

White, Theodore H. *In Search of History: A Personal Adventure.* Harper and Row, 1978. (A well-known writer's personal look at the unfolding of United States history.)

CHAPTER 26

American foreign policy after World War II remained consistent with the nation's wartime activities: force would be used to oppose authoritarian regimes that the United States considered a threat to the free world. At home the federal government would use strong, and sometimes questionable, measures to counter what it perceived to be threats to the nation's internal security.

SECTION 1

World War II forced communist and capitalist nations into a temporary alliance. In the postwar era, however, they began to compete for power and territory.

SECTION 2

To counter possible communist influence in Europe, the United States embarked on a foreign policy strategy known as containment.

SECTION 3

As communist movements arose outside Europe, the United States extended its policy of containment to Asia, the Middle East, and Latin America.

SECTION 4

The United States launched a cold war at home, embarking on an ugly crusade to root out suspected communists among its own citizens.

The Relevance of the Big Idea

War costs money—even a cold war. The cold war between the superpowers lasted for more than forty years. It affected the political systems and economies of nearly every nation on earth. We are still paying the costs of that war.

With the end of the cold war in the late 1980s, Americans began a long debate over how to spend the "peace dividend," the money saved from cuts in the defense budget that could be used in other programs.

Ask students to list ways in which the government could spend the peace dividend. List their responses on the chalkboard. Have students work in small groups to rank the items listed in order of importance. Compare the groups' lists, noting similarities and differences. Ask students what the results reveal about American values.

 In Depth

Global Connections

At the end of World War II, Europe was in political disarray and economic ruin. In war-torn France and Italy, Soviet-backed Communist parties began to gain strength. Civil war broke out in Greece, where the right-wing government came under fire from communist rebels. The growing tension between the United States and the Soviet Union added to the political uncertainty and in turn impeded economic recovery. It also made maintenance of Europe's security in the face of Soviet domination the central focus of the cold war.

The Cold War and American Society
1945–1960

*T*he United States and the Soviet Union temporarily ignored their differences during World War II. After the war, however, these differences began to pull the two nations apart again. Soon the world was divided into two camps, formed around communist and capitalist beliefs. The bitterness of the conflict affected both international relations and relations among Americans at home. In its effort to counteract communism around the world, the United States government contributed to a frenzied mood of suspicion within its own borders.

Events in the United States

1945 Fifty nations adopt the United Nations charter in San Francisco.	1946 Winston Churchill gives his famous "iron curtain" speech in Fulton, Missouri.	1948 George Orwell's frightening novel 1984 is published.	1949 North Atlantic Treaty Organization (NATO) is established.	1952 Dwight D. Eisenhower is elected President.

1945	1947	1949	1951

 Events in the World

	1948 The Berlin airlift begins. • Israel is founded.	1949 Communists seize control of China. • Soviet Union tests its first atomic bomb.	1950 The Korean War begins.

▶ **RESOURCE DIRECTORY**

Teaching Resources

📄 **Alternate Lesson Plan: Demonstrating the Big Idea** found in the Alternate Lesson Plans folder, p. 131, provides a lesson strategy to instruct students about the big idea that the wartime alliance of the capitalist United States and the communist Soviet Union crumbled into an increasingly hostile ideological struggle affecting both international and domestic affairs.

📄 **Alternative Assessment Handbook** provides information, guidance, and strategies for alternative methods of assessment. It includes an essay on new trends in assessment, guidance and strategies for developing performance tasks and portfolios, scoring rubrics, and sample evaluation forms.

1953 The Rosenbergs are executed for espionage.

1954 Nationally televised McCarthy hearings lead to Joseph McCarthy's downfall.

1957 President Eisenhower formulates a plan to protect the Middle East from communism.

1959 The United States cuts diplomatic ties with Cuba after Fidel Castro seizes power.

1953	1955	1957	1959	1961

1954 The Vietnamese defeat the French at Dien Bien Phu.

1956 The Soviet Union crushes a popular uprising in Hungary.

1957 The African nation of Ghana wins independence.

1959 Revolutionary leader Fidel Castro overthrows dictatorship in Cuba.

1960 The Soviet Union shoots down a United States spy plane.

Media and Technology

Transparency
Time Lines, E-8

SECTION 1

Origins of the Cold War

Connecting to the Big Idea

See page 716B. Having defeated a common enemy in World War II, the United States and the Soviet Union then became enemies. Ask students what both sides sought to gain after the war.

Objectives

● Summarize the relationship between the United States and the Soviet Union during World War II.
● Explain why relations between the United States and the Soviet Union broke down after World War II.
● Identify the main goals of the superpowers in the postwar period and explain why those goals were in conflict.

Bellringer

Write the following questions on the chalkboard and ask students to jot down an answer: What do you think a "cold war" is? Why was this war considered "cold" and not "hot"? What made it a war?

Reading Strategy

Reading for Evidence Explain that the United States and the Soviet Union went from being allies to being enemies in a very short period of time. Ask students to identify turning points in this process as they read, and find reasons for the rapid political shift.

SECTION PREVIEW

During World War II, a common enemy forced communist and democratic nations together in a shaky alliance. Once the shooting stopped, however, political and economic differences divided the globe along new lines.

Key Concepts
• The Soviet Union and the United States suppressed their disagreements during World War II.
• Diplomatic relations between the United States and the Soviet Union quickly broke down after the war.
• The beliefs of communism and capitalism created different goals for the two superpowers in the postwar period.

Key Terms, People, and Places
cold war, proletariat, totalitarian, iron curtain

The mass media helped spread tension during the cold war years. This 1947 comic book described how the Soviets might be planning to conquer and enslave the people of the United States.

T he **cold war** was the bitter state of indirect conflict that existed between the United States and the Soviet Union for more than four decades after the end of World War II. This conflict developed out of long-standing disagreements between the two nations. After the Russian Revolution of 1917, the United States had refused to extend formal diplomatic recognition to the new communist nation until 1933. Americans were angered when the Soviet Union signed a nonaggression pact with Germany in 1939, but found themselves on the same side as the Soviets when Hitler broke the agreement and attacked the Soviet Union in 1941. The Allies pulled together to defeat the Axis powers, but by the end of the war, relations between the United States and Britain on the one hand and the Soviet Union on the other became increasingly tense.

Wartime Problems

At Tehran in 1943 and at Yalta in 1945, President Franklin Roosevelt had met with British prime minister Winston Churchill and Soviet leader Joseph Stalin to work out disagreements about the future of Germany and Poland. The three leaders had finally agreed to partition Germany into four zones—one American, one British, one French, and one Soviet. They also had agreed that in Poland a government sympathetic to the Soviet Union should control postwar policy. This new Polish government should, however, include representatives sympathetic to the West, and democratic elections should be held in the future. In diplomatic fashion, these agreements were left vague so that everyone could agree to them. Their imprecise terms, however, left room for disputes in the future.

Adding to this tension over Germany and Poland, the Soviet Union blamed the United States for delaying the opening of a western front in Europe during the war. While the Allies attacked the "soft underbelly" of the Axis Powers in southern Europe, the Soviets sustained heavy losses fighting the Germans alone on the eastern front. The Soviets were on their own for two years before Operation Overlord finally took some of the pressure off in June 1944.

Tension also arose during the development of the atomic bomb. The United States had relied on British help in the Manhattan Project while consciously excluding the Soviet Union. President Truman, Stalin, and Churchill had met at the Berlin suburb of Potsdam in 1945 to discuss ending the war in Japan and postwar plans for Europe. At that time, Truman hinted to Stalin that the United States had a new weapon of extraordinary force, but he said nothing more about it. Stalin, who knew about the bomb from Soviet spies in New Mexico, simply nodded and said that he hoped it would be put to good use. Stalin's casual manner hid, for

---

 RESOURCE DIRECTORY

Teaching Resources

Reproducible Lesson Plan found in the Unit 8 folder, p. 71, provides a summary of the Section 1 lesson plan content.

Alternate Lesson Plan: Critical Thinking Recognizing Ideologies, found in the Alternate Lesson Plans folder, p. 132, is designed to provide students with the skills to identify ideologies by focusing on ideologies in conflict during the cold war.

Guided Reading and Review found in the Unit 8 folder, p. 75, provides a structure for reading and mastering the key concepts and reviewing the key terms for Section 1. (Guided Practice)

★ **Primary Source Activity** "Uncle Joe," found in the Unit 8 folder, p. 89, presents excerpts from Svetlana Stalin's memoirs to afford students a personal glimpse of her father, Joseph Stalin.

the moment, the Soviets' resentment over being left out of the atom bomb project.

The Allies Follow Separate Postwar Paths

Americans became increasingly disillusioned with the Soviet Union as the war drew to a close. During the struggle, they had viewed the Soviets sympathetically. Newspapers and magazines encouraged support for the Americans' long-suffering ally. Journalist Joseph Goulden, who grew up in Texas during the war, recalled how he and his friends had played war games and pretended to be Soviet soldiers:

> We assembled new sabotage devices with fingers stiffened by the subzero temperatures of Mother Russia—old soup cans hand-packed with dirt and cinders—and climbed back up the embankment. . . . Another successful sabotage by Russian guerrillas. Under cross-examination none of the band could have distinguished a Communist from a logarithm. But we did know from movies that the Russians were brave and skilled partisans; in our minds their heroic stand at Stalingrad was equal to the defense of the Alamo.

Franklin Roosevelt affectionately referred to Stalin as "Uncle Joe." *Time* magazine even chose the Soviet leader as "Man of the Year" in 1940. But near the end of the war, the gaping divide between the two nations' postwar goals could be ignored no longer. ⭐

American Aims The United States fought in World War II to protect its vision of the American dream. The nation hoped to share with the world the essential elements of a democratic life—liberty, equality, and representative government. The United States also sought to create a world in which its own economic interests would be served by worldwide markets for its products. As a major contributor to victory in the war, the United States was determined to see its vision survive in the postwar world.

HOLLYWOOD'S FIRST DRAMA OF RUSSIA'S YOUNG HERO

THE BOY FROM STALINGRAD

with BOBBY SAMARZICH · CONRAD BINYON · MARY LOU HARRINGTON
SCOTTY BECKETT · STEVEN MULLER · Screen Play by Ferdinand Reyher
Produced by COLBERT CLARK · Directed by SIDNEY SALKOW
A COLUMBIA PICTURE

MAKING CONNECTIONS

How would communism, a system in which private property does not exist and resources are shared by everyone, present a threat to American capitalism?

The 1943 film advertised in this poster promoted a heroic image of our Soviet allies. When World War II was over, however, Hollywood portrayed the "Commies" as sly and dangerous enemies.

The Soviet Stance The Soviets approached the postwar world very differently from the United States. Communism predicted that through a process of class struggle, the workers of the world would eventually triumph. The first step toward that triumph involved removing the resources necessary for production from the hands of private business owners. If this happened, then members of the **proletariat**—working-class men and women—would join together for the common good, sharing resources equally among themselves.

Until the proletariat established a true communist state, however, a strong central government would control the society's resources. In practice, the Soviet state under Stalin was vastly different from the ideal state under communism. He created a **totalitarian** dictatorship in which the central government ruled by terror and held absolute control over its citizens' lives.

The map shows how the Soviet Union secured compliant nations along its European borders.

Enrichment

Have students write an essay in response to this question: Had the United States and the Soviet Union been able to avoid the deep split that made them enemies and instead remain allies, what benefits might have resulted?

3. ASSESS

Section 1 Review Answers

1. (a) cold war, see p. 718, (b) proletariat, see p. 719, (c) totalitarian, see p. 719, (d) iron curtain, see p. 721

2. There were disagreements over the fate of Germany and Poland. The Soviet Union was also irritated at having been left out of the effort to develop the atomic bomb.

3. The United States wanted to keep foreign markets open for the benefit of its own capitalist economy. Thus, it supported governments sympathetic to capitalism around the world. The Soviet Union demanded communist regimes along its western borders for its own security.

4. Americans went from considering the Russians brave allies to thinking of the Soviet Union as a harsh dictatorship that repressed its people and could not be trusted to cooperate with the United States.

5. Capitalism rests on a free market system in which private owners of resources make their own decisions on how to use the resources. Communism is predicated on a future proletarian state in which people will forgo their selfish goals to promote the common good; in the meantime, a powerful central government controls economic resources and makes decisions for everyone.

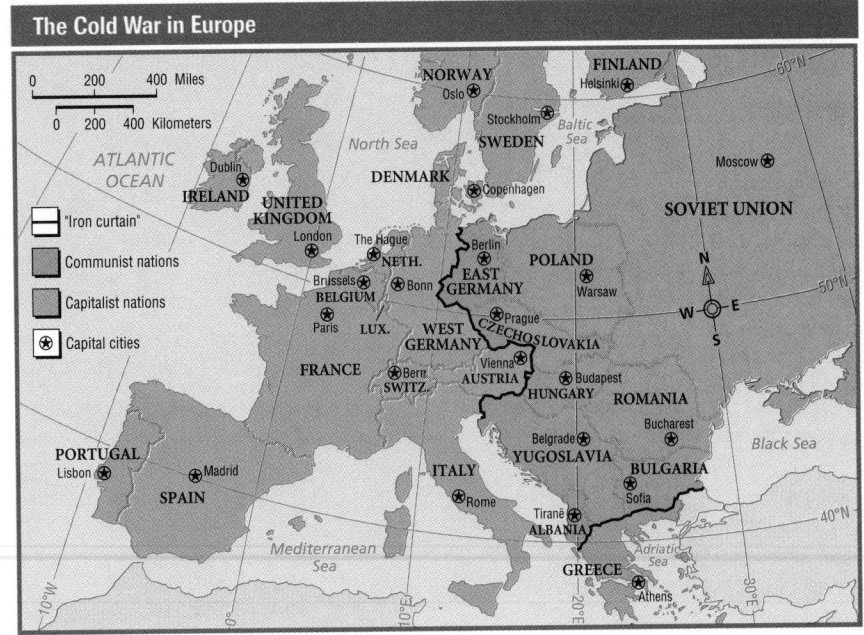

The Cold War in Europe

	"Iron curtain"
	Communist nations
	Capitalist nations
✴	Capital cities

Geography and History: Interpreting Maps
This map shows the territories controlled by communist and capitalist countries. After World War II, the Soviet Union was every bit as concerned about protecting its national security as was the United States. *How does this map illustrate the policy pursued by the Soviet Union to protect itself from its capitalist rivals in Europe?*

After losing twenty million people—about as many as live in New York state today—and suffering the destruction of cities such as Stalingrad in the war, the Soviet Union was determined to rebuild on its own terms. One part of that rebuilding required having friendly nations along the western borders of the Soviet Union. Several times in the past century and a half, the Soviet Union had faced attack from the west. Having repelled first Napoleon and then Hitler, the Soviets wanted regimes in Eastern Europe sympathetic to their own aims.

Postwar Clashes The United States and the Soviet Union clashed first over Poland. The loosely worded Yalta agreement called for a new Polish government influenced strongly by the Soviet Union but including a few representatives sympathetic to the West. President Truman met with Soviet foreign minister Vyacheslav Molotov on April 23, 1945, and told him that "the United States Government . . . could not agree to be a party to the formation of a Polish government which was not representative of all Polish democratic elements." Truman insisted that the Soviets were not keeping their part of the Yalta agreement, and he demanded bluntly that the Soviets do exactly as they were told. Molotov protested, "I have never been talked to like that in my life." "Carry out your agreements and you won't get talked to like that," Truman retorted.

The next evening President Truman received an answer from Molotov's boss. Stalin sent a message in which he emphasized that because Poland bordered the Soviet Union, the Soviets must be allowed to have a strong influence there. He said that securing friendly neighbors along Soviet borders was "demanded by the blood of the Soviet people abundantly shed on the fields of Poland," and he concluded:

> I am ready to fulfill your request and do everything possible to reach a harmonious solution. But you demand too much of me. In other words, you demand that I renounce the interests of security of the Soviet Union, but I cannot turn against my country.

It was clear from the determined tone of Stalin's message that there was to be no such "harmonious solution" to the Poland problem.

American and British officials were not the only ones grappling with the alarming actions of their former ally. Polls reflected the American public's shifting views of the Soviet Union. A poll in September 1945 found that 54 percent

RESOURCE DIRECTORY

Teaching Resources

 Visual Learning Activity What They Fear Most, found in the Unit 8 folder, p. 95, uses a 1952 cartoon to illustrate fears on both sides of the cold war.

of the respondents trusted the Soviets to cooperate with Americans in the postwar period. Two months later, the number fell to 44 percent, and by February 1946, it had dropped still further to 35 percent.

As they soured on the Soviet Union, Americans began to transfer their wartime hatred of Nazi Germany to the communist Soviet Union. Both nations, according to authors, journalists, and government officials, were totalitarian regimes whose leaders had absolute control and the ability to eliminate any opposition. George Orwell's haunting novel *1984,* published in the United States in 1949, described a frightening future world in which a totalitarian state, represented by the ever-present face of "Big Brother," monitors and controls every aspect of people's lives. *Life* magazine called Big Brother a mating of Hitler and Stalin. Truman himself declared the next year that "there isn't any difference between the totalitarian Russian government and the Hitler government."

Declaration of the Cold War While there was no formal declaration of war, two speeches marked the onset of the struggle. In 1946 Stalin declared his confidence in the ultimate triumph of the Soviet system. The Soviet Union would strengthen its military forces and do whatever was necessary to ensure its survival in a struggle with the West.

Winston Churchill, now out of office, responded that same year. Speaking in Fulton, Missouri, Churchill said that "from Stettin in the Baltic to Trieste in the Adriatic, an iron curtain has descended across the [European] Continent." This so-called **iron curtain**, the new battlefront of the cold war, sharply divided the capitalist West from the communist East. The map on page 720 shows these divisions. In his speech, Churchill stressed that the English-speaking peoples had to work together to stop the Soviet Union from closing the iron curtain around any more nations.

Using Historical Evidence Winston Churchill (right) is shown making the 1946 speech in which he introduced the idea of the iron curtain. *In the cartoon (left), why is United States secretary of state James Byrnes portrayed as a determined suitor? Whom is he courting? How does the cartoonist rate his chances of success?*

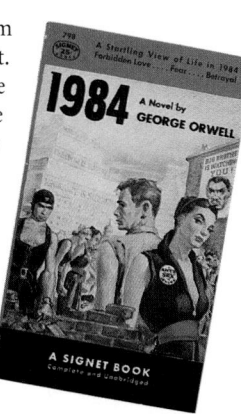

Orwell's *1984*—a story of "forbidden love and terror in a world many of us may live to see"—painted a dismal picture of life under a communist dictatorship.

SECTION 1 REVIEW

Key Terms, People, and Places
1. Define (a) cold war, (b) proletariat, (c) totalitarian, (d) iron curtain.

Key Concepts
2. What wartime issues paved the way for the cold war?
3. How did American aims and Soviet aims for the postwar period differ?

4. How did American public opinion about the Soviet Union change after World War II?

Critical Thinking
5. **Identifying Central Issues** What are the main points that separate the capitalist from the communist vision of society?

Quiz found in the Unit 8 folder, p. 76, covers the main ideas in this section as well as the key terms.

Media and Technology

Transparency
Cause and Effect, F-10

Caption Answer to ...

Using Historical Evidence

Byrnes represents the United States trying to pursue friendly relations with the nations of Eastern Europe. The cartoonist seems to believe that the effort is futile: the iron curtain dwarfs Byrnes and his bouquet of roses, and Stalin looks over the top and just smiles.

Reteach

Ask students to explain what the iron curtain was. Have students list facts about life on both sides of the iron curtain.

4. CLOSE

Reinforcing the Big Idea

Deep and bitter divisions emerged between the United States and the Soviet Union after World War II. The next section describes how the Soviets' dream of spreading communism soon fueled a massive American effort to stop it.

TOOLBOX

Critical Thinking

Recognizing Cause and Effect

Focus Distinguish between causes and effects; recognize multiple causes and effects.

Instruct Present this quotation from Harry Truman: "There is nothing new in the world except the history you do not know." Why, then, is it important to study the causes and effects of historical events?

Ask students to cite causes of the cold war. Discuss events in the world today that are similar to those that caused the cold war, such as the tensions caused by the spread of nuclear technology to developing countries.

Extend See the Historian's Toolbox Activity in the Resource Directory.

Answers

1. (a) Statements A and B. (b) Statement A cause: President Roosevelt believed that postwar cooperation with the Soviet Union was possible. Effect: He viewed Stalin as a partner—if not an ally—in formulating a Great Powers peace. Statement B cause: President Truman was persuaded by advisers that the Soviet Union would become a "world bully" after the war. Effect: He adopted a "get tough" policy whose aim was to block any possibility of Soviet expansion. (c) *Because* signals cause. *As a result* signals effect.

2. (a) Cause: mounting distrust between the United States and the Soviet Union. Effects: Peace negotiations were viewed as opportunities to test each other's global objectives. Negotiations on Poland, the former German satellite states, and the occupation of Germany were used as tests. (b) Effect: the cold war. Causes: mounting distrust; negotiations viewed as opportunities to test global objectives; negotiations used as tests; defensive positions seen as aggressive stances.

3. Distrust between the United States and the Soviet Union mounted. ➔ Peace negotiations were viewed as an opportunity to test the other's global objectives. ➔ Negotiations on Poland, the former German satellite states, and the occupation of Germany were used as tests. ➔ Defensive positions of each power were viewed as aggressive stances by the other. ➔ The cold war began.

722

Recognizing Cause and Effect

History is more than a list of events; it is a study of the relationships among events. Recognizing cause and effect means examining how one event or action brings about others. If you can understand how events or ideas relate to and affect each other, you can begin to formulate workable solutions to problems.

Follow the steps below to practice recognizing cause and effect.

1. Identify the two parts of a cause-effect relationship. A cause is an event or action that brings about an effect. As you read, look for key words that signal a cause-effect relationship. Words such as *because, due to,* and *on account of* signal causes. Words such as *so, thus, therefore,* and *as a result* signal effects. Read statements A through C at right, and answer the following questions. (a) Which statements contain both a cause and an effect? (b) Which is the cause and which is the effect in each statement? (c) What words, if any, signal the cause-effect relationship?

2. Remember that an event can have more than one cause and more than one effect. Several causes can lead to one event. So, too, can a single cause have several effects. Read statement D at right, and respond to the following. (a) Find an example of a cause that has more than one effect. (b) Find an example of an effect that has more than one cause.

3. Understand that an event can be both a cause and an effect. A cause can lead to an effect, which in turn can be the cause of another event. In this way, causes and effects can form a chain of related events. You can diagram the following statements to show such a chain: The United States feared Soviet expansion in Europe. ➔ The United States began a military buildup. ➔ The Soviet Union began a military buildup. ➔ An arms race between the two countries began. Now read statement D below, and using arrows, draw a diagram of the causes and effects that shows the chain of related events.

Statements

A Because President Roosevelt believed that postwar cooperation with the Soviet Union was necessary, he viewed Stalin as a partner—if not an ally—in formulating a peace.

B Unlike Roosevelt, President Truman was persuaded by advisers that the Soviet Union would become a "world bully" after the war. As a result, he adopted a "get tough" policy whose aim was to block any possibility of Soviet expansion.

C The Soviets, for their part, believed that the United States was intent on global domination and meant to encircle the Soviet Union with anticommunist states.

D Due to mounting distrust between the United States and the Soviet Union, each power came to view the postwar peace negotiations as an opportunity to test the other's global objectives. Thus, negotiating the status of Poland became the first such test. Other tests included the plans for former German satellite states and the policies for the occupation of Germany. Each power regarded its own positions in these negotiations as essentially defensive, but each viewed the other's stances as aggressive and expansionist. Together these tests and stances produced the cold war, an armed and dangerous truce that lasted for forty-five years.

RESOURCE DIRECTORY

Historian's Toolbox Activity Recognizing Cause and Effect, found in the Unit 8 folder, p. 87, helps students apply this skill by focusing on the end of the cold war.

Containment

SECTION PREVIEW

The United States government viewed Soviet communist influence as a disease that was rapidly spreading around the globe. Foreign policy in the postwar years focused on preventing any more capitalist nations from becoming "infected."

Key Concepts
- American foreign policy in the postwar years was summed up by the term *containment,* which meant preventing nations around the world from adopting communism.
- Containment was spelled out in a series of speeches, plans, and documents.
- Despite talk of liberating the nations dominated by the Soviet Union during the 1950s, containment continued to shape American foreign policy under President Eisenhower.

Key Terms, People, and Places
United Nations, containment, Truman Doctrine, Marshall Plan, Berlin airlift, NATO, NSC-68, satellite nation; George C. Marshall, Mao Zedong

T he founding of the United Nations in 1945 ignited new hope for international peace and understanding. Deep differences between Western democracy and communism, however, made it difficult for the UN to fulfill its great promise. Afraid of Soviet communist expansion, American leaders developed programs aimed at preventing the Soviets from extending their influence any further.

The United Nations

Near the end of World War II, diplomats hoped to create a new international peace-keeping organization. The League of Nations, founded at the end of World War I, had failed, largely because the United States had refused to join. This time, American policymakers succeeded in securing the support of the United States Congress for the **United Nations.**

In April 1945, delegates from fifty nations met in San Francisco to adopt a charter, or document setting down official rules, for the new organization. The United Nations charter pledged that member countries would seek to settle their disagreements peacefully. It also committed them to try to stop wars from occurring and to end those that did break out. All member nations belonged to the General Assembly. Eleven countries sat on the Security Council. Five of those—the United States, the Soviet Union, Great Britain, France, and China—had permanent seats and a chance to veto any policies under consideration. This veto power, exercised by both communist and capitalist powers, limited the UN's ability to take action in the early postwar years and led the United States to explore other approaches to controlling the Soviet Union.

On June 26, 1945, after the UN charter had been signed by representatives from all fifty nations, Harry Truman delivered a speech to the assembly. He said,

> T he Charter of the United Nations which you have just signed is a solid structure upon which we can build a better world. History will honor you for it. Between the victory in Europe and the final victory in Japan, in this most destructive of all wars, you have won a victory against war itself.

The Policy of Containment

Despite the hopeful sentiments expressed in Truman's speech to the UN and the fact that the Soviet economy was in ruins following World War II, American leaders still perceived a serious threat to United States interests from the Soviet Union. To address their concerns, officials developed a policy known as **containment.**

After World War II, the Marshall Plan provided United States aid to European nations. Some of this aid went to purchase food, such as this load of sugar.

Explain/Discuss

Explain to students that during the course of the cold war, there were several flashpoints in hostilities between the United States and the Soviet Union. One took place in Berlin, Germany, in 1948–49. The news that the Soviets had blockaded West Berlin, a Western-controlled area surrounded by East Germany, raised world tensions.

Discuss with students why they think the blockade of one city caused so much anxiety to people around the world. Why did the West see the action as provocation? What might the Soviets have hoped to gain by such a move? Why is the incident a good example of the cold war and of the policy of containment?

Analyze

Ask students to identify the major United States foreign policy efforts discussed in this section. Then have them analyze those actions and decide whether each was aimed more at confrontation or at peacemaking. Students should support their analysis with specific facts from the text.

Answer to ...

Vandenberg advised Truman to scare Americans into supporting the Truman Doctrine, which Truman did by describing the Soviet Union as a threat to the rights of "free peoples." Similarly, Reagan used his "evil empire" rhetoric to rally public support for increasing the military budget.

At its birth, the United Nations was hailed by President Harry Truman as "a victory against war itself." In this photograph, Truman and representatives from other member nations look on as Secretary of State Edward Stettinius signs the UN charter in June 1945.

The definition of containment came from George Kennan, a top-ranking American diplomat stationed in Moscow. In early 1946, he sent an eight-thousand-word telegram back to the State Department analyzing Soviet policy. The Soviet Union was not going to yield, he believed, and the United States needed to remove any opportunities for its enemy to establish communist governments in other countries. ✪

The Truman Doctrine Truman was an unassuming man, with a straightforward approach to the job he inherited from Franklin Roosevelt. He had a chance to apply the policy of containment in early 1947. When Great Britain informed the United States that it could no longer continue to provide Greece and Turkey with economic and military aid, Truman was afraid that those two nations might embrace communist strategies to ease their economic troubles. The State Department therefore developed a program for American assistance and then had to sell the plan to Congress. Undersecretary of State Dean Acheson told congressional leaders that "like apples in a barrel infected by one rotten one, the corruption of Greece would infect Iran and all to the east."

Meanwhile, Truman followed the advice of Senator Arthur Vandenberg of Michigan. The President, a

This sign, which sat on Truman's desk, expressed his belief that the President of the United States cannot "pass the buck"—or shirk responsibility for tough decisions.

Democrat, was determined to enlist Republicans in his foreign policy initiatives, and Vandenberg was the ranking Republican in this area. Vandenberg told Truman that if he wanted his program passed to assist Greece and Turkey, he had to generate public support—and that meant he had to "scare the hell out of the country." In his speeches, Truman warned the American people about the serious threat to national security posed by Soviet influence abroad. In a statement to Congress that came to be called the **Truman Doctrine,** he said, "I believe that it must be the policy of the United States to support free peoples who are resisting attempted subjugation [conquering] by armed minorities or by outside pressures." Responding to his plea, Congress appropriated $400 million for Turkey and Greece.

In the 1980s, President Ronald Reagan referred to the Soviet Union as "the evil empire." How does this compare to Arthur Vandenberg's advice to President Truman?

The Marshall Plan By 1947, Communist parties were growing stronger in a number of countries, and American policymakers were afraid that the Soviet Union might intervene to support local communist movements. At the same time, they were eager to open new markets for American goods. That year, Secretary of State **George C. Marshall** carried containment a step further with a plan to address both concerns.

Marshall unveiled his plan in a speech at Harvard University in June 1947. The **Marshall Plan** called for the nations of Europe—including the Soviet Union and other communist countries—to draw up a program for economic recovery from the war. The United States would then support the program with financial aid.

The Soviet Union and its Eastern European neighbors (under Soviet pressure) did not participate. Soviet foreign minister Molotov called the plan "nothing but a vicious American scheme for using dollars to buy its way" into European affairs. Sixteen Western European

▶ **RESOURCE DIRECTORY**

Teaching Resources

✪ **American Profiles Activity** found in the Unit 8 folder, p. 83, profiles George F. Kennan, the diplomat and scholar who developed the containment doctrine on which the United States based its postwar foreign policy.

nations, however, hammered out a plan requesting $17 billion over a four-year period. In 1948 Congress approved the Marshall Plan, also called the European Recovery Program. The United States sent over $13 billion in aid to Europe over the next four years. The Western European economy was quickly restored to health, and the United States was rewarded with strong trading partners in that region of the world.

One of the nations to benefit from the Marshall Plan was West Germany. At the end of World War II, Germany had been split into four zones occupied by the Soviet Union, France, Britain, and the United States. The city of Berlin, located in the Soviet zone, was likewise divided among the four Allies. When the Western powers united the French, British, and American zones to form West Germany and introduced a West German currency in the western part of Berlin, the Soviets reacted by blockading all ground and water routes to West Berlin in June 1948.

Truman did not want to risk starting a war with the Soviet Union by forcing open the transportation routes; nor did he want to give up West Berlin to the Soviets. Instead he began the **Berlin airlift,** moving supplies into West Berlin by plane. Food, coal, and other vital supplies were flown into the city every day for over a year. The Soviets finally ended the blockade in May 1949, and the airlift ended the following September. By this time the Marshall Plan had resulted in progress toward economic stability in the capitalist nations of Western Europe, including West Germany. Nevertheless, the tension that resulted from the airlift helped convince the Western powers that they needed to form a peacetime alliance for security against the Soviet threat.

NATO In 1949 the United States helped to establish the North Atlantic Treaty Organization—**NATO**—shown on the map on page 726. The twelve nations in the alliance—Belgium, Britain, Canada, Denmark, France, Iceland, Italy, Luxembourg, the Netherlands, Norway, Portugal, and the United States—vowed that an attack against one would be viewed as an attack against all. Dropping its opposition to military treaties with Europe for the first time since the American Revolution, the United States was now actively involved in European affairs.

Two disturbing events in 1949 prompted more drastic action from the United States. In April of that year, Chinese nationalists led by General Chiang Kai-shek lost control of their country to **Mao Zedong** and his communist followers. Civil war between these two factions had torn China since the early part of the century, and not even the need to fight off a common enemy—Japan—during World War II could unite the nation.

Despite support from the United States in the postwar years, Chiang was unable to stop Mao from steadily taking over control of China. Now, in mid-1949, Roosevelt's intended "anchor" of democracy in East Asia had turned into a communist dictatorship. Chiang was forced to retreat to the island of Taiwan off the southeast coast of China. The United States continued to

Viewpoints
On Joining NATO

Debates over whether or not the United States should join the North Atlantic Treaty Organization (NATO) were held in Congress and in the press. *What fears underlie the following arguments for and against the United States joining this peacetime alliance?*

For Joining NATO
"From now on, no one will misread our motives or underestimate our determination to stand in defense of our freedom. . . . The greatest obstacle that stands in the way of complete recovery [from World War II] is the pervading and paralyzing sense of insecurity. The treaty is a powerful antidote to this poison. . . . With this protection afforded by the Atlantic Pact, western Europe can breathe easier again."
Senator Tom Connally (Texas), Chairman, Committee on Foreign Relations, address before the United States Senate, 1949

Against Joining NATO
"This whole program in my opinion is not a peace program; it is a war program. . . . We are committing ourselves to a policy of war, not a policy of peace. We are building up armaments. We are undertaking to arm half the world against the other half. We are inevitably starting an armament race. . . . The general history of armament races in the world is that they have led to war, not to peace."
Senator Robert A. Taft (Ohio), address before the United States Senate, 1949

Viewpoints Activity On Joining NATO, found in the Unit 8 folder, pp. 85–86, encourages discussion of the North Atlantic Treaty Organization and helps students evaluate predictions.

Activity
Teaching Heterogeneous Groups
Fearing the threat of communism, the United States government established a containment policy to provide financial and military support to countries potentially subject to communist influence. Have students on their own describe an example of a threat their parents fear might influence them. Ask them to list three ways their parents try to "contain" this threatening influence. Then, as a group, make a list of parental containment policies and compare them with the postwar containment policies of the United States government.
LEP

Enrichment
Have students in a group enact a meeting of the United Nations General Assembly. Ask them to choose a current or historical world event to discuss in the meeting. Students can assume the roles of the secretary general and delegates from member nations. Students should debate the situation and vote on a proposed solution.

Answer to . . .

Viewpoints

The argument in favor of joining NATO is based on the fear that Western Europe and North America are vulnerable to attack; underlying the argument against joining NATO is the fear that an arms buildup will inevitably lead to another war. For a more thorough examination of the debate over joining NATO, see the Resource Directory below.

Section 2 Review Answers

1. (a) containment, see p. 723,
(b) Truman Doctrine, see p. 724,
(c) Marshall Plan, see p. 724, (d) Berlin airlift, see p. 725, (e) NATO, see p. 725,
(f) satellite nation, see p. 727

2. (a) George C. Marshall, see p. 724,
(b) Mao Zedong, p. 725

3. (a) The UN sought to settle disagreements between nations peacefully and to put an end to wars. (b) The veto power exercised by both capitalist and communist nations in the UN Security Council made it difficult for the body to reach any agreements.

4. The Truman Doctrine and the Marshall Plan, both of which provided aid to foreign countries thought to be vulnerable to communist takeover, expressed the determination of the United States to prevent communism from spreading.

5. NSC-68 recommended that the United States triple its defense budget.

6. Eisenhower exercised caution because he did not want to involve the United States in a full-scale shooting war with the Soviet Union.

7. Over the course of its history, Russia had suffered terrible losses in successive attacks by hostile European neighbors. After World War II, the Soviet Union hoped to insulate itself from possible future invasion by controlling the neighbors along its borders.

Caption Answer to ...

 Interpreting Maps

After almost two hundred years of isolationism, the United States finally formed peacetime ties with European nations. The United States recognized that its interests now extended around the world.

The NATO Alliance, 1949

- NATO member nations
- Soviet Union and its satellite nations

 Geography and History: Interpreting Maps
This map shows the nations that sided with the United States during the cold war and those that aligned with the Soviet Union. *How does the map illustrate the new global perspective gained by American leaders after World War II?*

recognize Chiang's government (now located on Taiwan) as the official government of all China, but Chiang would never regain control from the communists. The "loss of China" would become, in the minds of many Americans, a stain on the record of the Truman administration. The desire to prevent other nations in Asia from following the same path would be used to justify many future cold war policies, including involvement in the Korean and Vietnam wars.

More bad news surfaced later in 1949. On September 23, Truman made a brief but terrifying announcement to the nation: "We have evidence that within recent weeks an atomic explosion occurred in the USSR." Years sooner than some officials expected, the Soviet Union had broken the West's monopoly on nuclear weapons.

NSC-68 In response to these events, the National Security Council spelled out American policy in a document known as **NSC-68.** The National Security Council had been created in 1947 to develop broad policy concepts on which the President could build specific strategies.

NSC-68 outlined several policies that the United States might adopt in light of the current state of international affairs. The paper said, however, that only one of these policies could be seriously considered. It stated that the United States should triple its defense budget—and some leaders suggested quadrupling it from about $13 billion to $50 billion annually. This unprecedented level of peacetime defense spending was justified by NSC-68 and its supporters on the basis of the new demands of global security. According to this policy, only a vigorous

▶ RESOURCE DIRECTORY

Teaching Resources

✪ 📄 **Critical Thinking Activity** Identifying Central Issues: Cold War Policy, found in the Unit 8 folder, p. 88, uses a speech by Christian A. Herter, undersecretary of state in 1957, to help students apply this skill in examining the nation's cold war policy.

defense effort could keep communism in check and ensure the survival of the free world.

Containment in the 1950s

 When Dwight Eisenhower succeeded Harry Truman in 1953, the Republican party redefined American foreign policy. Secretary of State John Foster Dulles was a deeply religious person who hated communism because it denied the existence of God. Containment, he believed, was too cautious an approach to the communist threat. Instead, he proposed a policy of liberation, to roll back communism where it had already taken hold.

This approach proved impossible to put into practice. Eisenhower, who had helped keep the Allies together during World War II, understood the need for caution in dealing with the Soviet Union. Less rigid than his secretary of state, he recognized that the United States could not change the governments of Soviet **satellite nations**—countries controlled politically and economically by the Soviet Union—in Eastern Europe. When East Germans demonstrated against the Soviet Union in 1953, the United States merely stood back and watched. Three years later, when freedom fighters in Hungary rose up against Soviet domination, the United States again kept its distance as Soviet soldiers crushed the uprising. President Eisenhower recognized that any other response by the United States might have led to a larger war, and he wanted to avoid that at all costs.

On November 4, 1956, newspaper headlines announced that Soviet tanks had attacked Budapest and other cities in Hungary to squash the resistance of anticommunist rebels. Hungarian premier Imre Nagy was taken prisoner; Joseph Cardinal Mindszenty, the Roman Catholic bishop of Hungary, took refuge with the American diplomatic staff in Budapest.

Throughout the 1950s, despite talk of liberating Soviet satellite nations, the policy of containment remained in effect. Containment itself proved difficult enough. Before long the United States would be putting to use some of the weapons NSC-68 had recommended it build.

SECTION 2 REVIEW

Key Terms, People, and Places
1. Define (a) containment, (b) Truman Doctrine, (c) Marshall Plan, (d) Berlin airlift, (e) NATO, (f) satellite nation.
2. Identify (a) George C. Marshall, (b) Mao Zedong.

Key Concepts
3. (a) What were the goals of the United Nations in 1945? (b) What prevented the UN from achieving these goals?
4. How were the Truman Doctrine and the Marshall Plan expressions of the containment policy?

5. What did NSC-68 recommend that the United States do to defend against the communist threat?
6. Why did President Eisenhower not follow the advice of John Foster Dulles and attempt to "roll back communism" in Germany and Hungary?

Critical Thinking
7. **Recognizing Cause and Effect** In 1946 George Kennan described "the traditional and instinctive Russian sense of insecurity" on which the Soviet view of world affairs was based. What events in Russian history may have caused such insecurity?

 Quiz found in the Unit 8 folder, p. 78, covers the main ideas in this section as well as the key terms.

Media and Technology

Transparency
Critical Thinking, I-2

SECTION 3

The Cold War in Asia, the Middle East, and Latin America

Connecting to the Big Idea

See page 716B. In the postwar era, countries in Asia, the Middle East, and Latin America began to lean toward the communist model of government. Ask what the United States did in response.

Objectives

● Explain why the United States became involved in the affairs of Korea and Vietnam.
● Identify the factors that complicated United States containment policy in the Middle East.
● Describe the superpowers' struggle for control in Latin America.

Bellringer

Set up a row of dominos in the front of the classroom. Knock over the first domino so that it causes the whole line to fall. Ask students to explain what this "domino effect" has to do with containing communism in the 1950s.

Reading Strategy

Reinforcing Key Ideas Read the following sentence on page 728: "As communist movements developed in Asia, the Middle East, and Latin America, however, the United States extended the policy to meet challenges around the world." As students read the section, they should list the incidents that drew the United States into other countries' affairs.

SECTION PREVIEW

The policy of containment had been created with the aim of maintaining European stability. As communist movements developed in Asia, the Middle East, and Latin America, however, the United States extended the policy to meet challenges around the world.

Key Concepts

• Both the Korean War and early American involvement in Vietnam stemmed from cold war tension.
• The United States juggled oil interests and political sympathies in the Middle East while trying to control communist influence there.
• In Latin America, the United States and the Soviet Union struggled for control in unstable countries.

This cover illustration from a 1959 *Newsweek* magazine shows that the fate of the world hung on the uneasy balance of power between Khrushchev and Eisenhower, each of whom commanded many nuclear warheads.

Key Terms, People, and Places

38th parallel, domino theory, 17th parallel; Ho Chi Minh, Fidel Castro; Indochina

---

The policy of containment soon was broadened to apply not only to Europe but also to Asia, the Middle East, Latin America—in short, anywhere United States government and military officials perceived a communist threat. Political struggles in countries that had seemed to have little impact on the United States before 1945, such as Korea, Vietnam, Iran, and Cuba, became vital issues of national security when viewed through the lens of the cold war. Each "minor" war in which the United States took part reflected the delicate balance between its two major foreign policy objectives: avoiding another world war and keeping a tight lid on communism.

The Korean War

The policy followed by the Allies at the very end of World War II created the context for the Korean War. Korea, which had been occupied by Japan for decades, hoped for its independence once the Japanese finally were defeated. The war ended, however, before careful plans could be worked out, and the Allies resorted to a short-term solution. Soviet soldiers accepted the surrender of Japanese troops north of the **38th parallel,** the latitude line that runs through Korea at 38°N; American forces did the same south of the parallel. While the dividing line was never intended to be permanent, the Soviet Union set up and supported a government in the north, and the United States did the same in the south. The major powers left Korea but continued to support the regimes they had created.

Both North and South Korea hoped to unify the country, but each wanted to do so on its own terms. In June 1950, the North Korean army moved across the 38th parallel intending to bring about this unification. The United States felt certain—wrongly, it turned out—that the maneuver had been directed by the Soviets. Faced with what he viewed as a clear case of aggression, Truman was determined to respond. He recalled in his memoirs:

I n my generation, this was not the first occasion when the strong had attacked the weak. I recalled some earlier instances: Manchuria, Ethiopia, Austria. I remembered how each time that the democracies failed to act it had encouraged the aggressors to keep going ahead. . . . If this was allowed to go unchallenged, it would mean a third world war, just as similar incidents brought on the second world war.

RESOURCE DIRECTORY

Teaching Resources

Reproducible Lesson Plan found in the Unit 8 folder, p. 73, provides a summary of the Section 3 lesson plan content.

Alternate Lesson Plan: Cooperative Learning Activity found in the Alternate Lesson Plans folder, p. 134, helps students work together to understand U.S. foreign policy in Asia, the Middle East, and Latin America during the cold war.

Guided Reading and Review found in the Unit 8 folder, p. 79, provides a structure for reading and mastering the key concepts and reviewing the key terms for Section 3. (Guided Practice)

American Profiles Activity found in the Unit 8 folder, p. 84, profiles Marguerite Higgins, a journalist who became a frontline war correspondent in Korea, despite the opposition she faced as a woman.

Rather than respond alone, the United States went to the UN Security Council. With the new People's Republic of China excluded and the Soviet delegation absent in protest of that exclusion, the United States gained unanimous approval for resolutions branding North Korea the aggressor and calling on UN member states to assist in restoring peace.

⭐ General Douglas MacArthur planned a bold strategy to drive the North Koreans out of South Korea. In September 1950, while most North Korean troops were fighting near Pusan in the southeast, marines landed at the western port city of Inchon. The landing allowed UN forces to cut off North Korean supply lines through Inchon and to sandwich enemy troops between MacArthur at Inchon and the other UN troops at Pusan.

MacArthur's strategy was an overwhelming success. UN troops pushed the North Koreans back across the 38th parallel and continued into the north. With these early victories behind them, they hoped to unify the country on South Korea's terms. As they approached China's border, however, the Chinese warned them against going any farther. MacArthur ignored the warning, and in October 1950 Chinese troops entered the war. In fierce fighting, the Chinese and North Koreans pushed the UN forces back into the south (see the map at right).

As the war bogged down, Truman found himself in conflict with his most colorful general. MacArthur wanted to teach the Chinese a lesson, and proposed using atomic weapons or blockading the Chinese mainland. Truman wanted to do everything he could to keep the conflict limited and refused to expand the war.

⭐ MacArthur would not back down, however. In March 1951 he sent a letter to Joseph W. Martin, the minority leader of the House of Representatives, that contained a thinly veiled attack on the Truman administration's failure to see the gravity of the situation in Asia. After Martin read the letter in the House on April 5, Truman fired MacArthur for insubordination.

MacArthur returned home to a hero's welcome. When he addressed a joint session of Congress on April 19, his speech was often interrupted by bursts of applause. Finally, he said an emotional farewell:

S ince I took the oath at West Point, the hopes and dreams [of youth] have all vanished. But I still remember the refrain of one of the most popular barracks ballads of that day, which proclaimed most proudly that old soldiers never die, they just fade away.

And like the old soldier of that ballad, I now close my military career and just fade away, an old soldier who tried to do his duty as God gave him the light to see that duty.

Good-bye.

Once tempers had cooled, MacArthur did, in fact, fade from view, and Truman was able to proceed with his plan to keep the war limited. The struggle dragged on for two more years. Finally, a truce was signed in 1953, leaving the

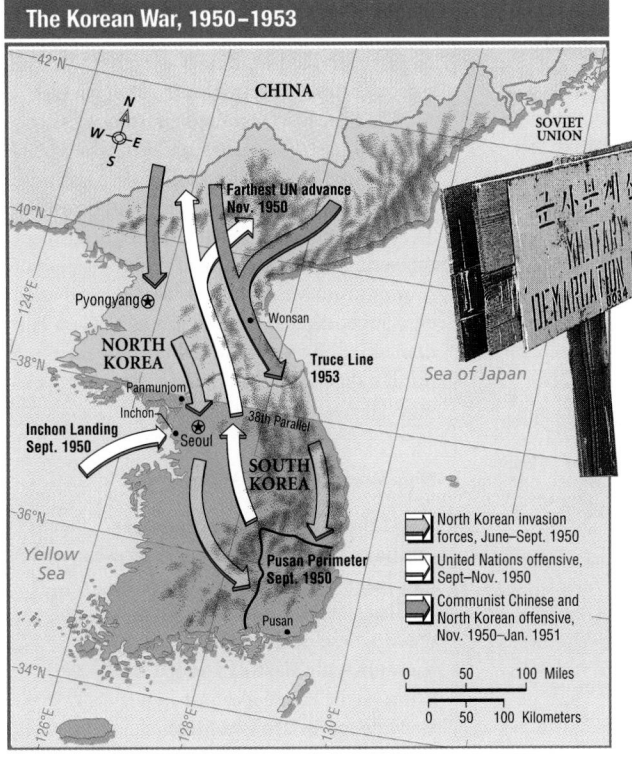

The Korean War, 1950–1953

CHINA

SOVIET UNION

Farthest UN advance Nov. 1950

Pyongyang

Wonsan

NORTH KOREA

Truce Line 1953

Sea of Japan

Panmunjom

Inchon

Inchon Landing Sept. 1950

38th Parallel

Seoul

SOUTH KOREA

Yellow Sea

Pusan Perimeter Sept. 1950

Pusan

North Korean invasion forces, June–Sept. 1950

United Nations offensive, Sept.–Nov. 1950

Communist Chinese and North Korean offensive, Nov. 1950–Jan. 1951

0   50   100 Miles
0   50   100 Kilometers

🌐 **Geography and History: Interpreting Maps**
This map shows the major battles of the Korean War. The sign shown above marked the final truce line in Korea, near the 38th parallel. *How does the map illustrate the back-and-forth nature of the war? What did MacArthur accomplish by landing his troops at Inchon rather than Pusan?*

⭐ 📋 **Visual Learning Activity** Civilian Control of the Military, found in the Unit 8 folder, p. 96, uses a cartoon to present one view of Truman's controversial firing of General MacArthur during the Korean War.

Explain/Discuss
Explain that in its efforts to fight communist aggression, the United States engaged in its own aggressive policies. Ask students to identify United States actions that other countries saw as aggressive. Discuss whether those actions were justified in order to contain communism. Encourage students to support their opinions with facts and reasoning.

Caption Answer to …

🌐 **Interpreting Maps**

The arrows on the map show the first North Korean offensive, which pushed the South Koreans to the Pusan perimeter; the counterattack of UN forces, which extended almost to the Chinese border; and the final push of the Chinese and North Koreans back to the 38th parallel. MacArthur was able to open up another front by landing at Inchon, thus sandwiching the North Koreans between Inchon and Pusan.

In Depth

Multicultural Perspectives

Following President Truman's 1948 order to desegregate the military, the Korean War was the first in which African American and white soldiers fought side by side. A 1951 NAACP investigation, however, unearthed a striking disparity in military justice. It found that of thirty-four soldiers convicted of misconduct in combat, two were white and received minimal sentences. The thirty-two convicted African Americans received extremely harsh sentences including one death sentence and fifteen life sentences.

Have students compare and contrast the leadership of Vietnam's Ho Chi Minh and Cuba's Fidel Castro. What was each leader trying to achieve? What made both turn to the Soviet Union for help?

Activity

Analyzing the Leaders

Have students work in small groups to analyze the conflict between President Truman and General MacArthur. Have them list two or three beliefs held by each. What goals did they have in common? Why did they come into conflict? Whose views do students favor more?

Enrichment

Have students evaluate the following questions in regard to the CIA: Could there be any situation in which it would be right for the CIA to topple governments and assassinate leaders? Was there justification for such actions in Guatemala and Cuba? How far should the United States go to protect American companies in foreign lands?

In this oft-repeated scene from the war, South Korean civilians flee from North Korean invaders while United States troops advance to meet the enemy.

country divided at almost exactly the same place as before the war, near the 38th parallel.

The Korean War caused enormous frustration at home. Americans wondered why 54,000 of their soldiers had been killed, and far more had been wounded, for such limited results. They also wondered whether their government was serious about wanting to stop the spread of communism. Meanwhile, the war also led to an ever-larger defense budget, just as NSC-68 had demanded. By 1950 the military took up one third of the total federal budget. Ten years later, it consumed one half.

The Early War in Vietnam

At the same time, another war was unfolding in **Indochina.** France had long controlled this part of Southeast Asia, which had fallen to the Japanese during World War II. Vietnam, one part of Indochina, now sought independence in a struggle led by **Ho Chi Minh,** the leader of the Indochina Communist party. Although Ho was sympathetic to the principles of communism, he was really more of a Vietnamese nationalist than a Soviet sympathizer. In his battle for Vietnamese independence, he used the American Revolutionary War as his model for independence. Ho and his political organization, the Viet Minh, established the Democratic Republic of Vietnam in 1945. He then had to fight France, which was determined to reclaim its empire.

An ugly war unfolded and attracted the attention of American officials. The United States needed the assistance of France for its policy of containment in Europe. American leaders doubted that France could survive a long colonial war in Asia without help. While Ho Chi Minh did not have close ties with the Soviet Union, he was still dedicated to the ideas of Karl Marx, and Americans were persuaded that communism was the same everywhere and had to be resisted wherever it surfaced. The United States therefore provided France with large amounts of economic aid for reconstruction at home, and that assistance allowed France to use its own resources in Vietnam. By 1954 the United States was giving France aid amounting to more than three fourths the cost of the war. ✪

Even so, the war was not going well. France's position deteriorated at about the time Eisenhower took over the presidency, and in 1954 the Vietnamese defeated France in a major battle at Dien Bien Phu, an outpost in northern Vietnam. This worried Eisenhower, who believed in the **domino theory.** This theory

ON BEHALF OF VIETNAM GOVERNMENT AND PEOPLE I BEG TO INFORM YOU THAT IN COURSE OF CONVERSATIONS BETWEEN VIETNAM GOVERNMENT AND FRENCH REPRESENTATIVES THE LATTER REQUIRE THE SECESSION OF COCHINCHINA AND THE RETURN OF FRENCH TROOPS IN HANOI STOP MEANWHILE FRENCH POPULATION AND TROOPS ARE MAKING ACTIVE PREPARATIONS FOR A COUP DE MAIN IN HANOI AND FOR MILITARY AGGRESSION STOP I THEREFORE MOST EARNESTLY APPEAL TO YOU PERSONALLY AND TO THE AMERICAN PEOPLE TO INTERFERE URGENTLY IN SUPPORT OF OUR INDEPENDENCE AND HELP MAKING THE NEGOTIATIONS MORE IN KEEPING WITH THE PRINCIPLES OF THE ATLANTIC AND SAN FRANCISCO CHARTERS RESPECTFULLY

HOCHIMINH

Ho Chi Minh (left) sent this urgent telegram to President Truman in October 1945 asking for United States support of Vietnamese independence. Not wanting to jeopardize relations with France, Truman ignored Ho's plea.

▶ RESOURCE DIRECTORY

Teaching Resources

✪ **Literature Activity** *The Ugly American,* found in the Unit 8 folder, p. 92, presents excerpts from the 1953 book that brought into focus the negative impressions made by Americans—especially officials—while abroad.

French Indochina, 1954

BURMA
CHINA
Tonkin
Dien Bien Phu
Haiphong
Hanoi
Luang Prabang
Gulf of Tonkin
LAOS
Vientiane
VIETNAM
17th Parallel
Hue
Annam
South China Sea
THAILAND
CAMBODIA
Cochin-China
Phnom Penh
Saigon
Gulf of Siam

ASIA

Areas of French control
Areas of Viet Minh control

0 100 200 Miles
0 100 200 Kilometers

Geography and History: Interpreting Maps
Reread Ho Chi Minh's telegram on page 730. *What did the French demand in 1945? According to this map, how many of their objectives had the French achieved by 1954?*

compared countries to dominos and held that "you have a row of dominos set up, you knock over the first one, and what will happen to the last one is the certainty that it will go over very quickly." Thus, if one country in Indochina fell to communism, other countries in the area would soon follow. Still, Eisenhower did not want the United States to become further involved.

Instead, an international conference in Geneva decided to draw a dividing line, similar to the ones drawn in Germany and Korea following World War II. Vietnam would be divided along the **17th parallel,** with Ho Chi Minh holding power in the north and an anti-communist government in charge in the south.

For the time being, the United States provided military aid to the South Vietnamese government but resisted greater involvement. That course would change in the next decade.

The Middle East

The cold war was also played out in the Middle East. This area had strategic importance because of its large supplies of oil. During World War II, the Allies had occupied Iran, a large nation just south of the Soviet Union. After the war, the United States and Britain departed; the Soviet Union did not. The United States became increasingly concerned as Soviet tanks rumbled toward the Iranian border, and threatened vigorous American action unless the Soviets pulled back. In the face of that determined stance, the Soviets withdrew.

Two years later, in 1948, the UN divided Palestine into an Arab state and a Jewish state. Zionist Jews had for years hoped to establish a Jewish nation in Palestine, but it was not until World War II, when thousands of European Jews immigrated to the region, that the Jewish population was large enough to form a new state. Tensions between Palestinian Jews and Arabs erupted with the UN announcement of the new Jewish state, called Israel, on May 14, 1948. The United States and the Soviet Union immediately recognized Israel, but Israel was soon invaded by surrounding Arab states. Israel defeated those states and annexed most of the Palestinian territory, as shown on the map on page 732. While sympathetic to Israel, the United States tried to maintain ties with the oil-rich Arab nations of the region and to prevent them from falling into the Soviet orbit.

MAKING CONNECTIONS

What conflicts over oil-rich Middle East nations has the United States been drawn into in recent years?

The Cold War in Latin America

The cold war likewise affected United States policy in Latin America. For decades the United States had dominated economic affairs in this part of the world. By the mid-1920s, the United States had gained control over the economies of ten Latin American countries.

Reteach

Ask students to write the column headings Problem and Solution on a piece of paper. In the first column have them list the problems faced by the United States in Asia, the Middle East, and Latin America, and in the second have them write the solutions the United States attempted to carry out.

Caption Answer to ...

 Interpreting Maps

The fact that the Soviet Union lies next to Iran and very close to the rest of the Middle Eastern nations may have fueled U.S. concerns that it could easily gain control over the oil in this region.

---

4. CLOSE

 Reinforcing the Big Idea

In an expansion of its containment policy, the United States battled communism in smaller countries throughout the world. The next section describes how America's fear of communism would eventually lead it to suspect its own citizens.

 In Depth

Biography

The bloody fighting between Arabs and Jews that erupted after Israel's declaration of independence in 1948 ended with a truce in 1949. The chief mediator of that truce was UN diplomat Ralph J. Bunche (1904–1971). Formerly a U.S. State Department official, Bunche joined the United Nations at its inception and later oversaw UN peacekeeping operations in the Suez, the Congo, and Cyprus. For his mediation of the Arab-Israeli war, Bunche became the first African American to be awarded the Nobel Peace Prize.

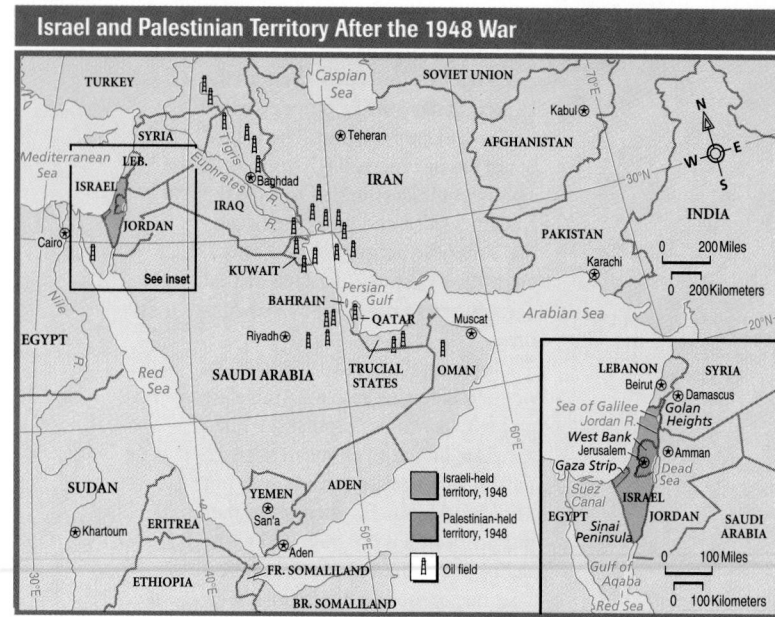

Israel and Palestinian Territory After the 1948 War

Israeli-held territory, 1948

Palestinian-held territory, 1948

Oil field

Geography and History: Interpreting Maps
After the 1948 war, Palestinian-held territory was annexed by Egypt and Jordan. *How might the location of the Soviet Union in relation to that of Middle Eastern countries have fueled concerns in the United States?*

American troops also had invaded Honduras and Nicaragua to prop up leaders who supported United States interests. After World War II, the fear of Soviet communist influence led the United States government to protect Latin American nations where United States corporations had large financial investments.

In 1954 the United States feared possible communist activity in Guatemala. As a result, the Central Intelligence Agency (CIA) helped to overthrow Jacobo Arbenz Guzmán, a reform-minded leader, on the grounds that he was sympathetic to radical causes. The CIA takeover restored the property of an American corporation called the United Fruit Company, which had been seized by the government in Guatemala. This action also demonstrated that where it sensed a communist threat, the United States would do almost anything to restore stability and to install leadership it found more sympathetic. Such actions also fueled the Soviet perception that the United States was escalating the cold war.

In 1959 another crisis occurred as revolutionary leader **Fidel Castro** overthrew a long-standing dictatorial regime in Cuba. When Castro seized American property in Cuba, the United States responded by severing diplomatic ties and cutting off exports. In response, Cuba turned to the Soviet Union for economic and military support, which continued for several decades.

SECTION 3 REVIEW

Key Terms, People, and Places
1. Define (a) 38th parallel, (b) 17th parallel.
2. Identify (a) Ho Chi Minh, (b) Fidel Castro.
3. Identify Indochina.

Key Concepts
4. How were the seeds of the Korean War planted at the end of World War II?
5. What was the connection between the war in Vietnam and the cold war in Europe?

6. Why was the United States especially concerned about the possibility of communist control in the Middle East?
7. What economic factors led the United States to intervene in Guatemala and Cuba?

Critical Thinking
8. **Determining Relevance** Explain how Eisenhower's "domino theory" expressed the basic assumptions of American cold war policy.

RESOURCE DIRECTORY

Teaching Resources

 Quiz found in the Unit 8 folder, p. 80, covers the main ideas in this section as well as the key terms.

The Cold War in the United States

SECTION PREVIEW

The effort to contain communism abroad made Americans fear subversion at home. The nation became swept up in an ugly campaign to expose suspected communists among its own citizens.

Key Concepts

- The fear of subversion by communist sympathizers in the United States led President Truman to create the Federal Employee Loyalty Program.
- A congressional committee investigated "un-American activity" in the late 1940s and 1950s.
- Senator Joseph McCarthy led a vicious crusade against American radicals that destroyed the careers and lives of many citizens.

Key Terms, People, and Places

House Un-American Activities Committee (HUAC); Alger Hiss, Julius and Ethel Rosenberg, Joseph R. McCarthy

---

D uring the Great Depression, tens of thousands of Americans had joined the Communist party, which was a legal organization. They were looking for answers to the question of why the American economic system no longer seemed to work. After World War II, some of these citizens were still Communist party members, although most had withdrawn. Now, in an atmosphere of cold war fears, their past came back to haunt them.

In the administrations of both Harry Truman and Dwight Eisenhower, concern over the growing appeal of communism around the world led to wholesale violations of civil liberties at home. The fear of subversion, or conspiracy to overthrow the government, launched a crusade that persecuted not only people who had ties to the Communist party but also anyone whose views leaned toward the left. The political left is made up of people who generally want to see the existing political system changed—sometimes radically—to benefit the common person. The political right is composed of people who generally wish to preserve the current system. During the late 1940s and 1950s, people were afraid to make statements that could in any way identify them with the political left. The government's loyalty program removed the left from power while effectively silencing any real political debate in the United States.

Truman's Loyalty Program and HUAC

As the Truman administration pursued support for its containment program, it pictured the cold war struggle in life-or-death terms. In his speeches, the President declared that the issue facing the world was whether "tyranny or freedom" would win out. Godless communism was a "threat to our liberties and to our faith," Truman said. It had to be stopped at all costs.

Administration officials feared that communism was infiltrating the United States. Exposure of a number of wartime spy rings in 1946 increased American anxiety. When the Republican party made significant gains in the midterm congressional elections that year, Truman became concerned that his political opponents would use the loyalty issue for their own ends. He therefore began his own investigation. He established a Federal Employee Loyalty Program in early 1947.

Under the terms of this program, the FBI was to check its files for individuals who might be engaged in suspicious activity. Cases would then move to a new Loyalty Review Board. While civil rights were supposed to be safeguarded, in fact those accused of disloyalty to

Anticommunist films like *The Red Menace* (1949) played on Americans' fear of communist activity in the United States. Such films also gave Hollywood studios a chance to prove their loyalty and patriotism.

1. FOCUS

Connecting to the Big Idea

See page 716B. In its effort to uncover communist spies and revolutionaries at home, the United States government embarked on an anticommunist purge. Ask students what dangers resulted from this red scare.

Objectives

- Describe President Truman's Federal Employee Loyalty Program.
- List the outcomes of congressional investigations of "un-American activity" in the 1940s and 1950s.
- Explain Senator Joseph McCarthy's role in the anticommunist crusade.

Bellringer

Ask students to list three elements that define loyalty. Does criticism of one's country constitute disloyalty?

Reading Strategy

Predicting Content Ask students to read the first paragraph of Section 4 and skim the headings and subheadings in the section. Have them predict the main idea and possible conclusion of the section. When they have finished reading the section, ask students to test their predictions against the actual text.

Explain/Discuss

Explain to students that in the name of patriotism, the United States in the early 1950s embarked on a crusade that deprived citizens of their constitutional rights. Why, in the end, did this witch hunt threaten democracy more than any communist plots? Why is it important for the United States to allow dissent?

Analyze

Many people knew that Senator McCarthy's claims were exaggerated at best. Why, then, was he able to gain so much power and ruin the lives of so many people?

Activity

Teaching Heterogeneous Groups

In the late 1940s and early 1950s, the film and television industries were often a target of investigation by the House Un-American Activities Committee (HUAC). Have students work in small groups to list three activities by the film and television industry today that might be considered un-American, and three activities that would be considered "good" for Americans.

In Depth

Then and Now

The Alger Hiss controversy was refueled in 1992 when the chairman of the Russian Military Intelligence Archives announced that, based on his review of Soviet archives, the espionage charges against Hiss were groundless. The official subsequently admitted that he could not fully clear Hiss; given the size and complexity of Soviet archives, perhaps no one could. The debate thus remains very much alive.

I'M NO COMMUNIST

Actor Humphrey Bogart (top) flew to Washington, D.C., in 1947 to protest the congressional committee's actions against other actors. He then had to launch a public relations campaign to clear his own name. *Red Channels* **(bottom), an index of blacklisted actors, was published in 1950.**

their country often found themselves under attack with little chance to defend themselves. Rather than being innocent until proven guilty, they found that the accusation alone made it difficult for them to clear their names.

Although the Truman loyalty program examined several million employees, it only dismissed several hundred. Still, it helped create a dangerous climate of suspicion throughout the country.

Meanwhile, Congress began its own loyalty program. The **House Un-American Activities Committee (HUAC),** which had been established a decade earlier to investigate disloyalty on the eve of war, now began a probe of the motion picture industry. It argued that films had tremendous power to corrupt the American public and suggested that numerous Hollywood figures had left-wing inclinations that compromised their work.

Many stars protested the procedures. Singer Judy Garland urged Americans to "write your Congressman a letter" denouncing the campaign. Actor Frederic March asked Americans to consider the question: "Who's next? . . . Is it you, who will have to look around nervously before you can say what's on your mind? . . . This reaches into every American city and town!" But HUAC pressed on. ✪

AMERICAN PROFILES

The Hollywood Ten

In October 1947, HUAC called nineteen Hollywood figures to testify. According to rumors, all were either members of, or had close associations with, the Communist party. These Hollywood personalities—writers, directors, producers, actors—were a distinguished lot. Ring Lardner, Jr., had shared an Academy Award for writing *Woman of the Year* in 1942; Howard Koch had coauthored *Casablanca* that same year. Others too were responsible for some of the best films of the previous ten years.

Facing the committee, the celebrities who stood accused had no chance to defend themselves. Chairman J. Parnell Thomas first called friendly witnesses (those whose views were in line with the committee's), allowing them to make accusations and to slander whomever they chose. Then he turned his attention to the Hollywood activists themselves. Over and over the committee asked, "Are you now or have you ever been a member of the Communist party?" When some of the writers attempted to make their own statements, Thomas denied them the floor. Ten of the accused refused to answer his question by invoking rights guaranteed by the First Amendment. This amendment protects individuals, as the Supreme Court recently had ruled in *West Virginia Board of Education* v. *Barnette* (1942), against government officials who try to "prescribe what shall be orthodox in politics, nationalism, religion, or other matters of opinion." The committee responded by threatening prison terms if the Hollywood Ten failed to testify, but they held their ground. When the committee likewise stood firm, the Ten went to jail for contempt of Congress and served sentences ranging from six months to a year.

Worse still, Hollywood gave in totally to the committee. The day Congress voted the contempt citations, fifty motion picture executives held a meeting at the Waldorf-Astoria Hotel in New York. They announced that the Hollywood Ten had "been a disservice to their employers" and had "impaired their usefulness to the industry." They were discharged without compensation until they had "purged" themselves, or demonstrated their loyalty in some undefined way. So began the blacklist—a list of persons who would not be allowed to work. The blacklist included not only the Hollywood Ten but also many others who seemed in some way "subversive."

The hearings had a powerful impact on American films. In the immediate postwar years, the industry had been willing to make movies dealing with controversial subjects such as racism and anti-Semitism. Now studios resisted all films dealing with social problems and emphasized "pure entertainment" instead.

RESOURCE DIRECTORY

Teaching Resources

✪ **Primary Source Activity** The Rise of Joseph McCarthy, found in the Unit 8 folder, pp. 90–91, provides students with an insider's description of how the stage was set for the McCarthy hearings with a chapter from Senator Charles E. Potter's book, *Days of Shame.*

Spy Cases Inflame the Nation

Several spy cases at the start of the cold war helped fuel suspicion of a communist conspiracy in the United States. In 1948, HUAC investigated **Alger Hiss,** who had been a high-ranking State Department official before he left government service. Whittaker Chambers, a former Communist who had become a successful *Time* magazine editor, accused Hiss of having been a Communist in the 1930s. Hiss denied the charge and sued Chambers for libel. Chambers then went one step further and declared that Hiss had been a Soviet spy.

After two trials, Hiss was convicted of perjury—too much time had passed for the espionage charge to be pressed—and in 1950 he went to prison for four years. Not all Americans were convinced he was guilty—indeed, even today Americans still debate the Hiss case—but for most people at the time the case seemed to prove that there was a real communist threat in the United States.

Several months after Hiss's conviction, **Julius and Ethel Rosenberg,** a husband and wife who held radical views, were accused of passing atomic secrets to the Soviets during the war. While opinion about the Rosenbergs' guilt was split, they were nonetheless convicted of espionage and executed in the electric chair in 1953. Like the Hiss case, the Rosenberg trial focused attention on a possible internal threat and inflamed anticommunist passions.

The McCarthy Era

Joseph R. McCarthy, a Republican senator from Wisconsin, took the anticommunist crusade even further. Through his skillful use of the media and his willingness to make wild accusations about almost anyone, he quickly landed himself on center stage.

McCarthy's Rise to Power McCarthy attracted attention in early 1950 with a speech in Wheeling, West Virginia. He would be up for reelection in two years, and he figured that he could gain support by identifying himself as a leader in the fight against communism in the United States government. So he claimed he

held in his hand a list with the names of 205 known Communists in the State Department. In fact he had no such list, simply names of people accused of disloyalty under the Federal Employee Loyalty Program and still in their jobs. But such minor complications never stopped McCarthy. When pressed for details, he declared that he would show his list to the President; then he reduced the number from 205 to 57.

McCarthy soon took on other targets. He lashed out at Dean Acheson, the current secretary of state, calling him a "pompous diplomat in striped pants," and at George Marshall, a former secretary of state, referring to him as "a man steeped in falsehood" for his inability to prevent the fall of China to the communists. Marshall was a national hero and a man of unquestioned integrity, but McCarthy made the incredible claim that he was involved in "a conspiracy so immense and an infamy so black as to dwarf any such previous venture in the history of man."

McCarthy gained support through these tactics because Truman's loyalty program had planted fears in the minds of many Americans about the supposed communist threat at home. But McCarthy also succeeded because he knew how to give journalists what they needed for newspaper stories. He knew when their deadlines

Ethel and Julius Rosenberg, shown above just after her conviction in 1951, were the first U.S. civilians to be executed for espionage. They were accused of passing top-secret data on nuclear weapons to the Soviets.

Welch looks dazed and frustrated, probably unable to comprehend McCarthy's relentless attack on his associate, Fred Fisher.

Answer to ...

MAKING CONNECTIONS

Students may suggest that certain segments of the media, such as tabloid newspapers, are able to make unsupported claims about people and thus shape public opinion about their subjects.

Answer to ...

Links Across Time

Possible answers: Fear verging on hysteria is an emotion commonly associated with both the witch trials and McCarthy's hunt for communists.

In Depth

Interdisciplinary

The ritualism and quasireligious fervor of McCarthy's anticommunist crusade were mirrored in *The Crucible,* Arthur Miller's allegorical dramatization of the Salem witch trials. Miller, who later became the target of a HUAC hearing, created a parable of American society under McCarthyism in his play. It was poorly received when it opened on Broadway in 1953 but went on to become Miller's most frequently produced play. (See Literature Activity in the Resource Directory.)

Using Historical Evidence Army counsel Joseph Welch (seated at table) listens to Senator McCarthy discuss communist infiltration with the aid of a giant map. *How does this photo show Welch's reaction to McCarthy's tactics?*

occurred and recognized that they needed stories for their editors. He provided material at just the right time. When he had nothing to report, he would call a press conference to announce that new disclosures would be coming soon.

Some Republican politicians, who hoped McCarthy's campaign would damage the reputation of the Democratic administration in the eyes of voters, encouraged McCarthy. Robert Taft, a senator from Ohio, told his colleague, "If one case doesn't work, try another." McCarthy did.

The public responded favorably to McCarthy's attacks. By the end of 1953, 50 percent of the sample in one Gallup poll had a positive opinion of McCarthy, with only 29 percent holding an unfavorable view.

MAKING CONNECTIONS

McCarthy had the power to ruin a person's reputation with a mere accusation. What people or institutions today have a similar power?

McCarthy's Fall McCarthy finally overreached himself when he took on the United States Army. In 1953 the army drafted McCarthy's assistant G. David Schine. When the military refused the request of Roy Cohn, another influential McCarthy assistant, to give Schine special treatment, McCarthy decided to investigate army security. Congress then began to examine the complaint.

⊗ The Army-McCarthy hearings began in April 1954, were televised nationally, and lasted for thirty-six days. They reached a climax when McCarthy charged that Fred Fisher, an assistant to army counsel Joseph Welch, had been a member of an organization sympathetic to the

| 1650 | 1700 | 1750 | 1800 | **Links Across Time** | 1850 | 1900 | 1950 | 2000 |

The Hunt for Witches and Communists

Between June and September of 1692, fourteen women and five men were hanged in Salem, Massachusetts, as witches. Those who "confessed" to witchcraft were spared; many who maintained their innocence were hanged. Historians today compare Salem in 1692 to the United States in the 1950s. The Puritans had recently resisted hostile Native Americans in King Philip's War and outlasted all challenges to their religious beliefs. Instead of feeling secure, however, the Puritans suddenly saw the devil in the very heart

of their community. Similarly, the United States in the 1950s had just defeated its enemies in World War II and recovered from the Depression. Yet, many Americans feared that evil forces within their community posed a grave threat. Senator Joseph R. McCarthy seized upon this fear to start a "witch-hunt" of his own.

The stress of the cold war with the Soviet Union frightened Americans. On very little evidence, they began to suspect a strong communist conspiracy to take over the United States. In what has been called "the

McCarthy terror," thousands of innocent people were accused of being communists or communist sympathizers. At numerous public hearings, those who refused to answer questions were treated as guilty.

In 1954, after being condemned by the Senate for his activities, McCarthy's reign of terror ended. As in Salem more than two centuries earlier, the witch-hunt was over. *What emotion seems to have allowed both the Salem witch trials and the McCarthy hunt for communists to happen?*

 RESOURCE DIRECTORY

Teaching Resources

⊗ 📄 **Literature Activity** The Hunt for Witches and Communists, found in the Unit 8 folder, pp. 93–94, focuses on *The Crucible*, Arthur Miller's play about the Salem witch trials of 1692, which he wrote in response to the McCarthy hearings.

Communist party. Welch, an eloquent Boston lawyer, was furious:

> *U*ntil this moment, Senator, I think I never really gauged your cruelty or your recklessness. . . . If it were in my power to forgive you for your reckless cruelty, I would do so. I like to think I am a gentleman, but your forgiveness will have to come from someone other than me. . . . Let us not assassinate this lad [Fisher] further, Senator. You have done enough. Have you no sense of decency, sir, at long last? Have you left no sense of decency?*

The Senate, once frightened by McCarthy's power, now condemned him for his reckless attacks. Although he remained in office, his strength was gone. He died three years later, a broken man.

McCarthy's Impact In his peak years in power, though, McCarthy had a powerful impact on American society. He, and the others who participated in the anticommunist crusade, generated a sense of fear and suspicion that filtered down to all levels. In the late 1940s and early 1950s, it seemed impossible to dissent in the United States. Civil servants, government workers, teachers, and writers all came under attack and found their right to defend themselves restricted. Often an accusation alone was enough to end a person's career.

Examples of abuse extended throughout American life. Subway workers in New York were fired for refusing to answer questions about their political beliefs and actions. A fire department officer in Seattle was dismissed just forty days before reaching twenty-five years of service (and gaining retirement benefits) because, although he denied that he was a current member of the Communist party, he declined to speak about his past involvement. Investigations of university faculties in 1952 and 1953 led to dismissals of professors who refused to cooperate with hostile congressional committees. Navaho in Arizona and New Mexico were denied all government assistance during one brutal winter on the grounds that their communal way of life was un-American. Latino workers sometimes faced deportation for belonging to unions that seemed radical.

Eventually, this second red scare, like the first one following World War I, subsided. But for a time it created widespread fear and confusion in the United States. Some of the victims were fortunate enough to reclaim their careers. Others suffered for years to come. The entire nation suffered from the era's suppression of free speech and honest debate.

These demonstrators show the depth of anticommunist feeling among many Americans in the postwar period.

SECTION 4 REVIEW

Key Terms, People, and Places
1. Identify (a) Alger Hiss, (b) Julius and Ethel Rosenberg, (c) Joseph R. McCarthy.

Key Concepts
2. Why did Harry Truman launch his Federal Employee Loyalty Program?
3. What was the HUAC and why did it make Hollywood a specific target of its investigations?

4. How did Senator McCarthy create an atmosphere of suspicion and paranoia in the United States?

Critical Thinking
5. **Identifying Assumptions** HUAC forced Americans to answer the question "Are you now or have you ever been a member of the Communist party?" What assumptions was this question based on?

 Quiz found in the Unit 8 folder, p. 82, covers the main ideas in this section as well as the key terms.

 Chapter Test Forms A and B are found in the Unit 8 folder, pp. 97–102

 Answer Keys found in the Unit 8 folder, pp. 146–158, provide answers to all student activities.

Media and Technology

 Transparency
Graphic Organizer, G-5

 Guided Reading Audiotapes
(English and Spanish)

Computer Test Bank

Understanding Key Terms, People, and Places

Terms
Students should refer to the definitions of key terms in the chapter to create sentences that show an understanding of their relation to the post–World War II period.

Matching
1. 38th parallel
2. domino theory
3. cold war
4. iron curtain

True or False
1. false, Alger Hiss
2. false, Joseph R. McCarthy
3. false, Ho Chi Minh
4. true

Reviewing Main Ideas

1. The United States and the Soviet Union suppressed their disagreements and worked together in a shaky alliance against their common enemy.

2. The Soviet Union wanted to create a Polish government sympathetic to Soviet interests. The United States demanded a democratic government in Poland—one that would be friendly to American interests. This conflict over the loyalty of foreign governments would become a pattern in United States–Soviet relations during the cold war.

3. The two countries' goals differed in part because of their different economic and political systems. The Soviet Union looked forward to the collapse of capitalism worldwide and wanted to establish friendly foreign governments along its borders. The United States wanted to open as many foreign markets as possible.

4. Containment meant that the United States would take action to prevent the Soviet Union from extending its influence beyond the satellite nations it controlled in 1946.

5. The Truman Doctrine declared the United States responsible for helping "free peoples" resist communist influence. The Marshall Plan provided American money to rebuild Western European economies, thus preventing the Soviets from exerting their influence there. NSC-68 proposed tripling the peacetime defense budget to allow the United States to fight communism worldwide.

Chapter Review

Understanding Key Terms, People, and Places

Key Terms
1. cold war
2. proletariat
3. totalitarian
4. iron curtain
5. United Nations
6. containment
7. Truman Doctrine
8. Marshall Plan
9. Berlin airlift
10. NATO
11. NSC-68
12. satellite nation
13. 38th parallel
14. domino theory
15. 17th parallel
16. HUAC

People
17. George C. Marshall
18. Mao Zedong
19. Ho Chi Minh
20. Fidel Castro
21. Alger Hiss
22. Julius and Ethel Rosenberg
23. Joseph R. McCarthy

Places
24. Indochina

Terms For each term above, write a sentence that explains its relation to the post–World War II period.

Matching Review the key terms in the list above. If you are not sure of a term's meaning, review its definition in the chapter. Then choose a term from the list that best matches each description below.

1. division line between North and South Korea
2. belief that if one country falls to communism, neighboring countries will fall as well
3. state of indirect conflict between the United States and the Soviet Union after World War II
4. division between the capitalist West and the communist East in Europe

True or False Determine whether each statement is true or false. If it is true, write "true." If it is false, change the underlined name to make the statement true.

1. After two trials, <u>Joseph R. McCarthy</u> went to prison for four years on perjury charges.
2. <u>George C. Marshall</u> rose to power by accusing people of disloyalty to the United States.
3. <u>Fidel Castro</u> led the struggle for independence in Vietnam.
4. After their conviction on charges of espionage, <u>Julius and Ethel Rosenberg</u> were executed in 1953.

Reviewing Main Ideas

Section 1 (pp. 718–721)
1. Describe the relationship between the United States and the Soviet Union during World War II.
2. How did the issue of Poland's government cause diplomacy between the United States and the Soviet Union to break down after World War II?
3. Why did the United States and the Soviet Union have different goals for the postwar period?

Section 2 (pp. 723–727)
4. Summarize the policy of containment pursued by the United States during the cold war.
5. How were the Truman Doctrine, the Marshall Plan, and NSC-68 expressions of containment policy?
6. How did President Eisenhower and Secretary of State Dulles differ in their views of foreign policy?

Section 3 (pp. 728–732)
7. What two foreign policy objectives did Presidents Truman and Eisenhower have to balance in their handling of the Korean War and the early Vietnam War?
8. What conflicts did the United States face in shaping foreign policy in the Middle East?
9. How did the cold war affect United States policy in Latin America?

Section 4 (pp. 733–737)
10. What were the purpose and effects of Truman's Federal Employee Loyalty Program?
11. What accusations did HUAC make against the nineteen Hollywood figures that it called in to testify?
12. What impact did Senator McCarthy's anticommunist crusade have on American society?

---

6. Dulles wanted to liberate other nations from communism. Eisenhower followed a more cautious approach, favoring containment instead.

7. Truman and Eisenhower had to balance the foreign policy objectives of containing the spread of communism while avoiding another world war.

8. While sympathetic to the new Jewish state of Israel, the United States also wanted to remain friendly with the oil-rich nations of the Middle East in order to prevent them from falling under Soviet influence.

9. Fear of communist activity led the United States to take decisive action to protect its economic interests in Latin America. For example, the United States helped overthrow Jacobo Arbenz Guzmán of

Guatemala on the grounds that he was sympathetic to communism.

10. The Federal Employee Loyalty Program was established to investigate government workers for possible ties to the Communist party. The program created an atmosphere of fear and suspicion throughout the country.

11. HUAC accused the Hollywood figures of membership in or association with the Communist party.

12. The anticommunist crusade generated fear and suspicion on all levels of society. People found that dissent was nearly impossible, that their rights to defend themselves were curtailed, and that accusations alone could end their careers.

Possible questions: Will the Truman Doctrine be modified if support for capitalist governments is leading to world war? Where will the money come from to finance this support? Will the United States support repressive governments that resist communism? Will support be financial, humanitarian, or military?

2. Students' paragraphs should observe that the United States was reluctant to provoke the Soviet Union into a conflict that might involve nuclear weapons.

3. Students' statements should reflect an understanding of McCarthyism and the atmosphere of suspicion that it created.

4. (a) The Marshall Plan restored the European economy and created new markets for American goods in Europe in order to head off communist involvement. In doing so, it took action on a much larger scale than Truman had taken in Greece and Turkey. (b) The communist takeover of China and the Soviet explosion of an atomic bomb led to the recommendation in NSC-68 to increase defense spending. (c) Students' graphic organizers should demonstrate an understanding of the origins of the cold war, including the reasons diplomatic relations between the United States and the Soviet Union broke down after World War II and how communism and capitalism represented a mutual threat.

 Alternative Assessment

Final Evaluation
Use the following guidelines to evaluate student projects:

● **Evidence of mastery of content** Do students' reports reflect at least one main idea from each of the sections in the chapter?

● **Evidence of outside research** To what extent did students use outside research materials for their reports?

● **Evidence of synthesis** Do students' reports demonstrate that they understand the overall significance of the topics they chose?

● **Communication style** Do the reports convey their purpose to an audience in a clear, appealing way?

Allow interested students to present their "broadcasts" to the class.

Thinking Critically

1. **Making Comparisons** You have read about the different political and economic ideas that motivated the United States and the Soviet Union during the cold war. How were the foreign policy aims of the two countries similar?

2. **Drawing Conclusions** During the cold war, fear and hostility toward communism were the driving forces behind many of the social and foreign policies in the United States. How much of this fear actually was grounded in reality?

3. **Identifying Alternatives** Imagine that you are an adviser to President Eisenhower. The President has asked you to draw up a list of alternatives to help him decide on his policy about the emerging conflict in Vietnam. What alternatives can you propose? Which alternative will you advise the President to use?

Making Connections

1. **Evaluating Primary Sources** Review the statement of the Truman Doctrine on page 724. Create four questions that, if answered, would help explore what Truman's statement meant for foreign policy in the future.

2. **Understanding the Visuals** Look at the image in the section preview showing Khrushchev and Eisenhower on page 728, and then at the photograph on page 727. Write a short paragraph explaining how the illustration of the two cold war leaders explains one reason why the United States was reluctant to become involved in the event shown in the photograph on page 727.

3. **Writing About the Chapter** You have been accused by HUAC of participating in a communist conspiracy. Write a statement in which you defend yourself against these charges. First create a list of the reasons why the accusation is false. Note ways in which the anticommunist hysteria of the times has contributed to your false accusation. Then write a draft of your statement in which you respectfully but firmly defend yourself. Revise your statement, making certain that each point is clearly explained. Proofread your statement and draft a final copy.

4. **Using the Graphic Organizer** This graphic organizer uses a modified flow map to outline developments on the policy of containment during the 1940s and 1950s. Large boxes show main developments; smaller boxes add details. (a) Based on your reading of the chapter and this graphic organizer, explain how the Marshall Plan implemented the Truman Doctrine and took it a step further. (b) According to the flow map, what events led to the NSC-68 recommendation for a massive increase in defense spending? (c) On a separate sheet of paper, create your own graphic organizer about the origins of the cold war, using this graphic organizer as an example.

Thinking Critically

1. Both the Soviet Union and the United States were trying to create a global context in which their respective political and economic systems could flourish.

2. On the one hand, the Soviet Union had refused to relinquish control in countries such as Poland, where the Allies had agreed on a temporary presence. Also, the Soviets believed that communism would one day spread throughout the world. Thus some fear was justified. On the other hand, Senator McCarthy's anticommunist campaign led to a hysteria that was quite out of proportion to the actual threat.

3. Alternatives include a "get tough" policy against Ho Chi Minh and an attempt to negotiate a settlement between France and the Viet Minh. Students' advice should take into account what was believed about Soviet aggression at the time, rather than what is known in hindsight.

Chapter 27 The Postwar Years at Home
1945–1960

📁 Teaching Resources (See Unit 8 Folder)

	Instruction	Enrichment
Section 1 **The Postwar Economy** (pp. 742–746)	Reproducible Lesson Plan, p. 104 Alternate Lesson Plan, p. 137 Guided Reading and Review, p. 108 Quiz, p. 109	American Profiles Activity, Ray A. Kroc, p. 120 Visual Learning Activity, The Miracle of Television, p. 133 Historian's Toolbox Activity, Evaluating Magazine Advertisements, p. 124
Section 2 **The Mood of the 1950s** (pp. 748–751)	Reproducible Lesson Plan, p. 105 Alternate Lesson Plan, p. 138 Guided Reading and Review, p. 110 Quiz, p. 111	Literature Activity, Conformity in the 1950s, pp. 129–130 Critical Thinking Activity, Determining Relevance, p. 125 Literature Activity, Nonconformity in the 1950s, p. 131 Viewpoints Activity, On Rock and Roll, pp. 122–123 Time and Place Activity, Edge Cities, pp. 118–119
Section 3 **Domestic Politics and Policy** (pp. 754–759)	Reproducible Lesson Plan, p. 106 Alternate Lesson Plan, p. 139 Guided Reading and Review, p. 112 Quiz, p. 113	Visual Learning Activity, Auto Strike, 1950, p. 132 Primary Source Activity, Harry Truman: Off the Record, pp. 126–127
Section 4 **The Continuing Struggle for Equality** (pp. 760–763)	Reproducible Lesson Plan, p. 107 Alternate Lesson Plan, p. 140 Guided Reading and Review, p. 114 Quiz, p. 115 Chapter Test, Forms A & B, pp. 134–139	Primary Source Activity, Enforcing Brown v. Board of Education, p. 128 American Profiles Activity, Maria Latigo Hernandez and Pedro Hernandez, p. 121 History Might Not . . . Activity, Integrating the University of Georgia, pp. 116–117

📁 Additional Chapter Resources

Resource Organizer, p. 103
Alternate Lesson Plan, p. 136
Answer Keys, pp. 146–158

Bibliography

For the Teacher
Halberstam, David. *The Fifties.* Villard Books, 1993. (A comprehensive look at the social, political, economic, and cultural history of the 1950s.)
Handlin, Oscar. *Fire-Bell in the Night: Crisis in Civil Rights.* Little, Brown, 1964. (A study of the racial crises of the 1950s.)

Prentice Hall Literature Excerpts from *The American Experience,* 1994, including Ellison, Ralph. "Hidden Name and Complex Fate," from *Shadow and Act.* Random House, 1953.

The Big Idea for the chapter and how the main ideas in each section relate to the Big Idea are graphically displayed below. Comprehension of this chapter's Big Idea is critical to students' understanding of United States history and how we as a nation got where we are today.

Media and Technology

 Historical Maps, L-5

 Critical Thinking, I-4

 The Way It Works, H-20

 Visions of America: History Might Not Have Happened This Way Game

 Graphic Organizer, G-2

 Guided Reading Audiotapes (English and Spanish)

 Computer Test Bank

For the Student

Ellison, Ralph. *Invisible Man.* Random House, 1989. (Awarded the 1952 National Book Award for fiction, uses the experiences of an idealistic young African American to depict the alienation of American society.)

Time-Life Books editors. *This Fabulous Century. Vol. 6, 1950–1960.* Time-Life Books, 1969. (Richly illustrated and comprehensive study of the 1950s.)

CHAPTER 27

Emerging from World War II, the nation momentarily reveled in its triumph of good over evil. The American Dream of having a secure job, owning a house, and using labor-saving appliances came within reach of many after the war. The economy, fueled by the postwar baby boom, rocketed in the late 1940s and 1950s. The dividends of the triumph of democracy eluded many, however. The civil rights movement gained momentum as it brought into focus the democratic principles that the United States had fought for in World War II.

SECTION 1

During the postwar years, the economy of the United States had one of its greatest periods of expansion, as Americans began families, purchased brand-new homes, and spent their wartime savings.

SECTION 2

The American Dream—a life of wealth, success, and leisure time—seemed more accessible than ever before during the 1950s; but critics claimed that the dream encouraged conformity and was sterile.

SECTION 3

President Truman concentrated on helping the nation adjust to peacetime and tried to continue the New Deal spirit of reform. The next President, Dwight D. Eisenhower, believed in more limited presidential power and attempted to reduce the size and authority of government.

SECTION 4

The civil rights movement gained fresh momentum and new victories in the courts and through boycotts and protests.

The Postwar Years at Home
1945–1960

The Relevance of the Big Idea

Much of the way of life familiar to Americans in the 1990s took shape in the 1950s. Mass media, especially television, created a national culture; radio offered teenagers their own music; advertising defined the American Dream; franchise businesses sprouted in shopping centers in the suburbs, "bedroom communities" near large cities and towns. People who had previously lived in either crowded cities or on isolated farms now moved to these new towns. More and more people wore white rather than blue collars to work, similar to the 1990s, and began to grapple with many of the social issues—urban flight to suburbs, the changing roles of women, continuing discrimination in various forms, and lasting pockets of poverty—that exist within an affluent society.

Discuss aspects of these social issues that remain in the forefront of life in America in the 1990s.

In Depth

Global Connections

After World War II, as demands for independence increased, European countries—most notably Britain—gradually began to quit colonial possessions in Asia and Africa. In 1947, the former British colony of India was partitioned into two independent countries, India and Pakistan, signaling the dissolution of the British Empire, the largest in history. As two centuries of British world dominance ended, the United States rose to superpower status in the West.

The Postwar Years at Home
1945–1960

Americans had dreamed of peace and prosperity through sixteen grueling years of economic depression and world war. After the war, they expected to enjoy the benefits of their new standing as a military and economic superpower. People embraced a wide array of technological developments that promised to make their lives easier, and they relished the chance to live more comfortably than their parents had. While not all groups shared in the prosperity, most Americans now were able to buy the homes, cars, and other items that they had once only imagined owning.

Events in the United States

	1945	1947	1949	1951
		1947 Jackie Robinson becomes the first African American to play major league baseball.	**1948** Scientists invent the transistor. • President Truman desegregates the armed forces.	**1951** J. D. Salinger publishes his novel The Catcher in the Rye.

Events in the World

	1945	1947	1949	1951
	1945 The British Labour party nationalizes major industries after winning power.	**1947** India is divided into India and Pakistan. • Japan adopts a new constitution.	**1948** South African Alan Paton's Cry the Beloved Country examines racial segregation in his country.	**1951** United States occupation of Japan ends.

RESOURCE DIRECTORY

Teaching Resources

Alternate Lesson Plan: Demonstrating the Big Idea found in the Alternate Lesson Plans folder, p. 136, provides a lesson strategy to instruct students about the Big Idea that many Americans benefited from postwar prosperity, but not all could enjoy these middle-class advantages, and the civil rights movement thus gained momentum.

Alternative Assessment Handbook provides information, guidance, and strategies for alternative methods of assessment. It includes an essay on new trends in assessment, guidance and strategies for developing performance tasks and portfolios, scoring rubrics, and sample evaluation forms.

Pages 742–746
The Postwar Economy

The American Dream—a home in the suburbs, a car in the garage—materialized for many people in the postwar years.

Pages 748–751
The Mood of the 1950s

After World War II, many Americans were blessed with wealth, success, and leisure. Conformity seemed the order of the day, although some groups made it their business to avoid the popularly accepted lifestyles of the 1950s.

Pages 754–759
Domestic Politics and Policy

The postwar period created many challenges for American leaders—including the conversion back to a peacetime economy and the debate over the proper role of government in the nation's economic and social affairs. Presidents Harry Truman and Dwight Eisenhower used two very different styles of leadership to meet these challenges.

Pages 760–763
The Continuing Struggle for Equality

The events of World War II—including the fight against fascism abroad and the African American migration at home—breathed new life into the civil rights movement. The actions of many courageous Americans brought significant results in the postwar years.

1953 Two thirds of all families in the United States own televisions.

1954 Supreme Court issues *Brown v. Board of Education* ruling desegregating schools.

1955 Ray Kroc opens his first McDonald's fast-food restaurant.
• Montgomery bus boycott begins.

1957 First commercial nuclear power plant opens in Shippingport, Pennsylvania.

1960 Gross National Product reaches $504 billion, more than double that of 1945.

1953	1955	1957	1959	1961

1953 Soviet leader Joseph Stalin dies.

1955 Juan Perón is deposed as dictator of Argentina.
• Soviet Union forms Warsaw Pact.

1957 The Soviet Union launches Sputnik satellite.

1960 Organization of Petroleum Exporting Countries (OPEC) is formed.

Media and Technology

Transparency
Time Lines, E-8

Alternative Assessment

As an ongoing chapter project, students can explore the "Affluent Society," the United States at home in the postwar years.

Students may design their projects in one of the following ways to analyze issues, events and trends as they affected the American family.
● Create a photo-essay of the lifestyle of the 1950s or prepare a position paper on the Affluent Society.
● Produce a documentary-style videotape or audiotape of a simulated news program, using interviews with notable figures and ordinary families to assess the period.

Projects should present information and viewpoints on each of the following topics:
● Postwar economic growth and the growth of suburbs
● The respective roles of religion in society, of women in the family, and of television in creating a society of consumers
● The domestic policies of Presidents Truman and Eisenhower
● The campaign for civil rights

Finished projects will be assessed according to the following standards:
● **Unacceptable** Projects are not attempted, or fail to meet requirements outlined.
● **Limited/Acceptable** Projects are based on material from the textbook, include information about each of the topics listed, and present personal assessments of the period.
● **Extensive/Commendable** Projects are based on some outside research and present material about each of the topics listed in a manner that helps to support personal assessments of the period.
● **Extraordinary/Outstanding** Projects are based on considerable outside research, present material about each of the topics listed, and develop strong support for personal assessments of the period.

For information and guidance on alternative assessment trends and strategies, see the Alternative Assessment Handbook in the Resource Directory on page 740.

The Postwar Economy

SECTION 1

The Postwar Economy

Connecting to the Big Idea

See page 740B. The nation's economy boomed during the postwar years. Ask students how economic growth changed the jobs available to Americans and the communities they lived in.

Objectives

● Describe how the nation's economy grew after World War II.
● Give examples of technological advances, such as atomic energy and computers, that spurred economic growth and altered American life.
● Explain why the economy was increasingly driven by the needs and wants of affluent consumers prepared to buy on credit.

Bellringer

Have students think of inventions that would be totally new to a person from the 1930s who was suddenly transported to the 1990s.

Reading Strategy

Reading for Evidence Have students note the statement on page 742 that after the war, the United States "embarked on one of the greatest periods of economic expansion in its history." Ask students to find evidence to support this statement as they read the section, including information on each of the following topics: corporations, technology, changes in the work force, farm work and life, suburbs, and consumer credit.

SECTION PREVIEW

The American Dream—a home in the suburbs, a car in the garage—materialized for many people in the postwar years.

Even some children's games in the 1950s reflected the ideal middle-class life. These game pieces are from "Merry Milkman," in which players delivered milk, eggs, and butter to suburban homes.

Key Concepts
• After World War II, the American economy grew rapidly. People could buy more with their money and created new ways of organizing businesses.
• Technological advances such as atomic energy and computers altered American life.
• The economy was increasingly driven by the needs and wants of affluent consumers.

Key Terms, People, and Places
per capita income, real purchasing power, diversified conglomerate, franchise, agribusiness, baby boom, GI Bill; William J. Levitt

---

W hen American soldiers returned from the battlefields, they wanted nothing more than to put the horrors of the war behind them and enjoy the comforts of home and family. As large numbers of young people married and started families, they wanted homes, furniture, and other household items. During the war, when most items were rationed or not produced at all, many people had simply put their money into savings. Now most Americans were eager to acquire everything the war—and before that, the Depression—had denied them.

Thus the United States embarked on one of the greatest periods of economic expansion in its history. The Gross National Product (GNP) more than doubled, jumping from $212 billion in 1945 to $504 billion in 1960. During the same period, **per capita income**—the average income per person—increased from $1,526 to

$2,788. **Real purchasing power**—what people actually could buy with their money—grew by about 22 percent. The United States was now the richest nation in the world.

Corporations Create New Jobs

Major corporate expansion accompanied economic growth. In the 1950s, a few huge firms dominated many industries. General Motors, Ford, and Chrysler overshadowed all competitors in the automobile industry; General Electric and Westinghouse enjoyed similar positions in the electrical business. Giant corporations, fearful after the Depression of investing all their resources in one business, became **diversified conglomerates.** They acquired companies that produced entirely different goods and services, so that if one area of the economy failed, their investments in another area would be safe. International Telephone and Telegraph, for example, purchased Avis Rent-a-Car, Sheraton Hotels, Hartford Fire Insurance, and Continental Baking.

At the same time, another kind of expansion took place. In 1954 Ray Kroc, who sold milk-shake machines called Multimixers, was amazed when two brothers who owned a restaurant in San Bernardino, California, ordered their tenth Multimixer. With ten machines, the restaurant could make fifty milk shakes at once. Because of the restaurant's fast, efficient service and its prime location along a busy highway, it was enjoying great success. Intrigued by the possibilities, Kroc purchased the two brothers' idea of assembly-line food production. He also acquired the name of the brothers' restaurant: McDonald's. Kroc took his fast food nationwide by selling **franchises**—the right to open McDonald's restaurants using the same system—to other eager entrepreneurs. Hundreds of other restaurant franchises, such as Burger King and Kentucky Fried Chicken, followed. ✪

The franchise system flourished in the 1950s. It worked so well that it was applied to

---

▶ RESOURCE DIRECTORY

Teaching Resources

📄 **Reproducible Lesson Plan** found in the Unit 8 folder, p. 104, provides a summary of the Section 1 lesson plan content.

📄 **Alternate Lesson Plan: Learning Styles** found in the Alternate Lesson Plans folder, p. 137, is especially effective for visual learners and helps students understand the effects of economic and social change in the

postwar period through the creation of a graphic organizer.

📄 **Guided Reading and Review** found in the Unit 8 folder, p. 108, provides a structure for reading and mastering the key concepts and reviewing the key terms for Section 1. (Guided Practice)

✪📄 **American Profiles Activity** found in the Unit 8 folder, p. 120, profiles Ray A. Kroc, founder of the McDonald's fast-food restaurant chain.

other kinds of businesses, such as clothing stores and automobile muffler shops. The system's advantage lay in the fact that an individual with only a few thousand dollars could own a small business that enjoyed the support—especially in terms of national advertising—of a multimillion-dollar parent company. The system also created countless low-paying jobs across the nation. But with the growth of the franchise system, many small, unique stores with ties to the local community were replaced by nationwide chains that were the same everywhere in the country.

Technology Transforms Life

New developments in technology also spurred industrial growth. An entirely new industry—the generation of electrical power through the use of atomic energy—resulted from the research that had produced the atomic bomb. In 1956 film producer Walt Disney voiced Americans' hopes and fears about atomic power in his book and film *Our Friend the Atom*. Disney began with a story about a fisherman who found a sealed bottle. When the fisherman opened the bottle, a genie escaped and threatened to kill him. The fisherman got the genie back into the bottle and would only open it again when the genie promised to grant him three wishes. "The story of the atom is like that tale," Disney explained:

> The fable . . . has a happy ending; perhaps our story can, too. Like the Fisherman we must bestir our wits [think carefully before we act]. *We have the scientific knowledge to turn the Genie's might into peaceful and useful channels.*

The next year, Navy captain Hyman G. Rickover oversaw the development of the first commercial nuclear power plant in Shippingport, Pennsylvania. The new plant promised the peaceful use of atomic energy that Walt Disney had imagined.

The Computer Industry At the same time that Americans were looking forward to inexpensive energy from nuclear reactors, they reached out to embrace the computer industry. Wartime research led to the development of ever more powerful calculators. Grace Hopper, a research fellow at Harvard University's computation laboratory, led the way in the creation of the software that runs computers. She also introduced the term *debugging*, which was born when she removed a moth caught in a relay switch that had caused a large computer to shut down. Today the term means "ridding a computer program of errors."

In 1947 scientists at Bell Laboratories invented the transistor, a tiny circuit that did the work of a much larger vacuum tube. Because of the transistor, giant machines that once filled whole rooms could now fit on a desk. Calculations that had taken hours could now be computed in fractions of a second. The Census Bureau purchased one of the first computer systems to tally the 1950 census. Soon hotels, airlines, and countless other industries used computers to keep track of their customers.

This sign at the original fast-food restaurant in San Bernardino, California, advertised the McDonald brothers' mass-produced hamburgers.

MAKING CONNECTIONS

Today the government and many businesses use computers to create files with information on every American. How might this use of computers threaten people's right to privacy?

Television Americans fell in love with another invention in the 1950s: television. Developed in the 1930s, television became enormously popular after World War II. By 1953 two thirds of all American families owned TVs.

In 1955 the average American family watched television four to five hours a day. Children grew up on such programs as "Howdy Doody Time" and "The Mickey Mouse Club." Teenagers danced to the rock-and-roll music played on "American Bandstand," a predecessor of today's MTV. Other viewers followed situation comedies like "I Love Lucy" and "Father Knows Best."

Television networks raised the money to broadcast these shows by selling advertising

 Visual Learning Activity The Miracle of Television, found in the Unit 8 folder, p. 133, uses a 1949 advertisement to enhance students' understanding of the impact the introduction of television had on American life.

Media and Technology

Transparency
Historical Maps, L-5

Explain/Discuss

Discuss how the end of the war also marked the end of the Great Depression. However, fear of another depression governed many economic decisions of the time.

Discuss how a technological advance such as the development of commercial nuclear power or of the computer industry creates jobs.

Ask students why a credit-driven economy moves faster than a cash-only economy. What industries profit from credit use?

Analyze

The baby boom was both a result of increased economic growth and the cause of more growth. Ask how babies created what syndicated economics writer Sylvia Porter called "the biggest, boomiest boom ever known in history."

Answer to . . .

MAKING CONNECTIONS

Computers make it easy both to collect and store information and to transfer it from one place to another. Thus, confidential information may be available to anyone with a modem or other means of accessing computer data.

 In Depth

Interdisciplinary

The new nuclear technology had few detractors and fewer restrictions. From the 1940s to the early 1970s, the federal government exposed as many as 1,800 people to radiation in experiments that provided little or no medical benefit. In early 1994, Congressman Ed Markey (D–Massachusetts) said that "the appalling truth is that in some cases American citizens were used as nuclear calibration instruments."

Possible answers: People can do more work much faster; they can take their work with them as they travel; simple tasks such as writing letters or more complicated ones such as preparing tax returns can be performed quickly on a computer; volumes of information are now instantly accessible—whether at the grocery store, the post office, the airport, or the bank's automated teller machine—thanks to computer processing.

Activity

Teaching Heterogeneous Groups

Today we take business franchises for granted, but after World War II the franchise was a new concept, designed to address the growing consumer demand in the United States. Divide students into small groups and have them list as many franchises as possible in five minutes. Discuss with students how the increasing number of franchises contributed to the growing economy after World War II. Then have the groups list two positive and two negative effects of franchises. **LEP**

Enrichment

Invite students to watch episodes from some children's television series of the 1950s, such as "Kukla, Fran, and Ollie," "Howdy Doody," "The Lone Ranger," "Hopalong Cassidy," or "The Mickey Mouse Club." Some of these programs are broadcast on cable networks, and some are available on video. Students may compare the subject matter, format, types of people and groups represented, and level of sophistication of these programs with current children's television programs.

The Incredible Shrinking Computer

In their early days, computers filled entire rooms and performed calculations at a snail's pace (left). Over the years, improvements in technology have reduced the size of computers—such as the laptop model above—to fit almost anywhere. Computers now have the power to do many complex operations at lightning speed. *How has the computer revolution increased the pace of life for all Americans?*

Situation comedies like "Leave It to Beaver" (TV inset) entertained audiences while promoting the family values of the 1950s. Frozen foods allowed TV viewers to cook dinner during commercial breaks.

time. Television commercials gave Americans constant exposure to products they supposedly needed to live a comfortable life. Children grew up singing lyrics to commercials, which they sometimes knew even better than popular songs. Companies got their money's worth from advertising dollars: millions of viewers were persuaded to buy the items they saw on television commercials.

Changes in the Work Force

Using the nearly miraculous technology of the post–World War II years, Americans invented their way out of their manufacturing jobs and into new ones. In earlier years, most Americans made a living as blue-collar workers, or those who produce goods. After the war, however, new machines performed many of the jobs previously done by people. By 1956 a majority of all American workers held white-collar jobs, in which they no longer produced goods but instead performed services for others, working at counters or in offices.

The new white-collar workers felt encouraged by the working conditions they found: clean, bright offices rather than the dark, often dangerous factories of the recent past. But they soon realized that office jobs had drawbacks as well. Work in large corporations was often impersonal. White-collar workers sometimes never saw the products that their companies made. Employers might pressure employees to dress, think, and act alike. Some workers felt they sacrificed individuality for the sake of the corporation. Sociologist C. Wright Mills had this scathing comment: "When white-collar people get jobs, they sell not only their time and energy but their personalities as well."

For those who kept their blue-collar jobs, working conditions and wages improved during the 1940s and 1950s. Labor unions continued to work for change, and their strength reached an all-time high as the war ended. In 1955 the two largest unions, the American Federation of Labor (AFL) and the Congress of Industrial Organizations (CIO) merged. The AFL-CIO, a new and more powerful organization, remains a major force today. Workers won gains that we now take for granted, such as guaranteed cost-of-living increases.

Changes in Farm Work and Life

The world of American agriculture was also transformed in the postwar period. Technological improvements made planting and harvesting easier. Fertilizers, fungicides, and pesticides promoted and protected plant growth. As farming became more profitable, it underwent the same kind of consolidation experienced by industry.

Once again, Americans had invented themselves out of their old jobs. Hundreds of thousands of small farmers who could no longer compete with farms using high-tech machinery abandoned rural America in search of new lives in the cities and suburbs. They left their farms behind to be bought up by big businesses. Americans called this new industry **agribusiness.**

Americans Move to the Suburbs

With so many people working and making a better living than ever before, the **baby boom** that had begun during World War II continued. The birthrate, which had fallen to 19 births per one thousand people during the Depression, soared to more than 25 births per thousand in its peak year of 1947. (See the graph at right.)

Large families seeking new houses and wanting to enjoy the benefits of a booming economy retreated from the aging cities to suburbs that ringed the urban areas. World War II veterans enjoyed the benefits of the Servicemen's Readjustment Act of 1944, commonly known as the **GI Bill,** which gave them low-interest mortgages to purchase their new homes.

Developers like **William J. Levitt** built new communities in the suburbs. He pioneered mass-production techniques in home building by buying precut and preassembled materials and building houses in weeks instead of

months. Proud of his creations, Levitt gave his name to the new towns. Soon there was a Levittown in New York, another in Pennsylvania, and a third in New Jersey. Others quickly adopted Levitt's techniques, and new communities sprang up all over the United States.

The houses were affordable, but they all bore a monotonous resemblance to one another. Folk singer Malvina Reynolds expressed her revulsion for the new communities with these words from "Little Boxes," a popular song of the era:

Little boxes on the hillside
Little boxes made of ticky-tacky
Little boxes on the hillside
Little boxes all the same.
There's a green one and a pink one
And a blue one and a yellow one
And they're all made out of ticky-tacky
And they all look just the same.

Suburban growth depended on automobiles and roads. To meet the demand, auto makers produced up to 8 million new cars each year in the 1950s. The 1956 Interstate Highway Act provided $26 billion to build an interstate highway

As reported in a 1953 article in *Life* magazine, "Every day, including Saturdays and Sundays, is moving day in Los Angeles." Four hundred people a day moved into the suburbs around that city in the 1950s.

Birth Rate, 1930–1960

Live Births (per 1,000 people) — Year axis 1930 to 1960, values 16 to 28

Source: *Historical Statistics of the United States*

Interpreting Graphs
What was the overall trend in the birth rate after World War II? How might the lack of consumer goods during the war have contributed to this trend?

3. ASSESS

Section 1 Review Answers

1. (a) per capita income, see p. 742, (b) real purchasing power, see p. 742, (c) baby boom, see p. 745, (d) GI Bill, see p. 745

2. William J. Levitt, see p. 745

3. The diversified conglomerate led to the formation of giant corporations that owned businesses in many different areas of the economy. The franchise system meant that unique local businesses were sometimes pushed out of business by chains that were uniform throughout the country. Agribusiness shifted much control of the nation's farms from individual farmers to large corporations.

4. Atomic generation of electrical energy, computer technology, and television-related industries had a powerful impact on Americans after World War II.

5. Suburbs developed because of urban decay; an increase in population due to the postwar baby boom; cheap, plentiful housing; improved roads; and availability of automobiles and fuel.

6. Americans were eager to buy everything they were denied during the Depression and the war.

Caption Answer to ...

Interpreting Graphs

The overall trend was that the birth rate increased dramatically. The unavailability of consumer goods during World War II meant that families saved more money, which made the expense of raising a family after the war more manageable. Thus, people began to have more children.

Caption Answer to . . .

Interpreting Graphs

Consumer credit increased by a factor of six—about $2.5 billion to about $15 billion—between 1945 and 1950. It increased by about $20 billion between 1950 and 1958.

Reteach

Ask students to write one or two sentences showing how each of the following developments changed American life during the postwar period: corporate expansion, technological advances, changes in the work force, changes in farm work and life, the move to the suburbs, and consumer credit.

4. CLOSE

Reinforcing the Big Idea

After World War II, the nation's economy boomed. Many Americans enjoyed a comfortable lifestyle, with a new house in the suburbs and a car to drive to work. In the next section, students will learn why some critics claimed that conformity was the cost of comfort.

In Depth

Then and Now

Between 1947 and 1951 William Levitt built more than 17,000 nearly identical 800-square-foot houses in Levittown, New York, which sold for as little as $6,990 —with no down payments for veterans. "I'm not here just to build houses," Levitt said in 1952. "To be perfectly frank, I'm looking for a little glory, too." By the 1990s, these houses were selling for more than $150,000.

Estimated Outstanding Consumer Credit, 1945–1958

Source: *Historical Statistics of the United States*

Interpreting Graphs
The consumer credit shown in this graph includes automobile and home loans as well as credit card debts. *By approximately what factor did consumer credit increase between 1945 and 1950? How many more dollars worth of consumer credit was accumulated between 1950 and 1958?*

Consumer Credit Finances Growth

The postwar American economy required enormous consumption of goods to remain healthy. The increase in real purchasing power helped pay for some consumer goods but not all. After years of depression and war, Americans willingly went into debt to make up the difference, as the graph at left shows. Lending agencies created new ways to make borrowing easy, such as the credit card. The Diner's Club credit card appeared in 1950, followed at the end of the decade by the American Express card, and then by the BankAmericard (later called Visa).

system more than 40,000 miles long. The project provided a national web of new roads and allowed the evacuation of major cities in the event of nuclear attack. As President Eisenhower noted,

> The total pavement of the system would make a parking lot big enough to hold two thirds of all the automobiles in the United States. The amount of concrete poured to form these roadways would build . . . six sidewalks to the moon.

Advertisers persuaded consumers that only by buying new products could they attain status and success. Americans responded by using their credit to purchase washing machines, vacuum cleaners, and television sets. The United States had become, in the words of economist John Kenneth Galbraith, "the affluent society."

A decade before, the nation had faced the problems of scarcity and want. Now it would have to deal with the consequences of abundance.

SECTION 1 REVIEW

Key Terms, People, and Places
1. Define (a) per capita income, (b) real purchasing power, (c) baby boom, (d) GI Bill.
2. Identify William J. Levitt.

Key Concepts
3. How did the diversified conglomerate, the franchise system, and agribusiness each change the American economy after World War II?

4. What technological advances had an important impact on Americans in the decade after World War II?
5. What factors contributed to suburban development from 1945 to 1960?

Critical Thinking
6. **Recognizing Cause and Effect** In what ways did the Depression and World War II contribute to the postwar economic boom of the 1950s?

 RESOURCE DIRECTORY

Teaching Resources

Quiz found in the Unit 8 folder, p. 109, covers the main ideas in this section as well as the key terms.

Evaluating Magazine Advertisements

Magazine advertisements can be a rich and colorful source of evidence about the past. Because popular weekly or monthly magazines are aimed at a broad audience, advertisements frequently reflect a society's prevailing attitudes and values. Remember, though, that every ad also reflects the purpose of the company whose products are being advertised—namely, to sell their products. Therefore, an ad may present a slanted view of the desirable American life, designed to make people want to buy certain products.

Use the following steps to evaluate the advertisement at right, which appeared in the *Saturday Evening Post* in April 1958.

1. Identify the nature of the advertisement. (a) What is the point of this advertisement? What does it encourage readers to do? (b) What company created this ad? What product does the company make? (c) What other products are shown in the ad? (d) Who is the intended audience for the advertisement?

2. Study the advertisement to evaluate the underlying messages it contains. (a) What things seem to make the people shown in the advertisement happy? (b) Does this ad suggest a preference for suburban life or city life? Explain why you think so. (c) What does this ad suggest is the "good life" toward which Americans should strive?

3. Study the advertisement to learn more about the historical period. Use the information in the ad to help you answer the following questions. (a) Based on what you see in this ad, how closely linked were happiness and material wealth in the minds of many Americans in the 1950s?

(b) Would everyone in the 1950s have been able to afford to buy the items shown in the ad? What reasons does the ad suggest for why credit cards became so popular during this period? (c) Are your conclusions consistent with what you already know about the United States in the 1950s? Explain.

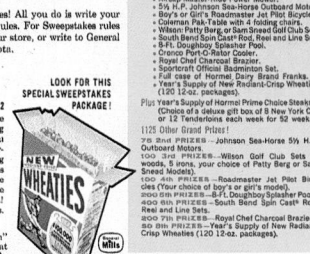

Historian's Toolbox Activity Evaluating Magazine Advertisements, found in the Unit 8 folder, p. 124, encourages students to apply this skill in a modern setting, using a 1993 magazine ad for the sporting goods retailer L.L. Bean.

SECTION 2

The Mood of the 1950s

1. FOCUS

Connecting to the Big Idea

See page 740B. In the 1950s, many Americans enjoyed unprecedented prosperity and security. Ask students if this comfort was worth the price of conformity and frustration.

Objectives

● Describe the value assigned to comfort and security by middle-class Americans in the 1950s.

● Explain how the media and society fostered expectations about the proper roles for men and women.

Bellringer

Ask students to decide what they consider the "proper" roles for men and women in today's society. Have them consider how their views of gender-based roles might differ from those of their parents or grandparents.

Reading Strategy

Reinforcing Key Ideas Ask students to write two headings on a piece of paper: Conformity and Nonconformity. As they read the section, students should note relevant information in the appropriate column. When they have finished, ask students to write one sentence explaining whether conformity or nonconformity was more prevalent in the 1950s than in their present life.

2. INSTRUCT

Explain/Discuss

Ask students how people behave when they want to fit into a group. Ask why Americans wanted to fit in after the war. How did the Great Depression and World War II affect Americans' need for comfort and security?

SECTION PREVIEW

After World War II, many Americans were blessed with wealth, success, and leisure. Conformity seemed the order of the day, although some groups made it their business to avoid the popularly accepted lifestyles of the 1950s.

Key Concepts
• Middle-class Americans valued comfort and security during the 1950s.
• Expectations about the proper roles for men and women were fostered by the media and society.

Key Terms, People, and Places
beatniks; Benjamin Spock, Betty Friedan, J. D. Salinger

In the 1950s, the "happy house-wife" portrayed in the media used state-of-the-art appliances to cook and clean, and she looked glamorous while doing so. Poodle skirts (below) were part of the uniform for teenage girls.

Middle-class Americans were comfortable during the 1950s. Most did not question whether the images of prosperous, suburban white families frequently seen on television represented "typical" American experiences. They valued the apparent harmony that minimized differences between individuals and groups in the United States. Compromise, rather than conflict, was the way disagreements could be settled. After the deprivations of depression and war, people wanted to enjoy their newly won prosperity and provide even better opportunities for their children.

Americans Value Conformity

The 1950s were years of conformity in the United States. Throughout the country, members of middle-class society seemed to want to imitate those around them rather than search out unique experiences. Even the descendants of the immigrants of the early 1900s seemed to value American middle-class culture above their own diverse cultural heritages.

In the past, sociologist David Riesman observed, Americans had valued individuality. Now they strained to conform. Riesman cited *Tootle the Engine,* a children's story in the popular Little Golden Book series. Tootle, a young train engine, found it was more fun to play in the fields than it was to stay on the tracks. His fellow citizens in "Engineville" worked hard to break him of the habit. Tootle finally absorbed the lesson of his peers: "Always stay on the track no matter what." The story, Riesman believed, was a powerful parable for the young people of the 1950s.

Some called the middle-class youth of the 1950s the "silent generation." The silent generation seemed to have little interest in the problems and crises of the larger world; its members were content to let other people worry about such issues. Instead, many middle-class young people appeared to devote their energies to joining fraternities and sororities, organizing parties and pranks, and generally pursuing entertainment and fun.

Movies generally portrayed the girls of the silent generation in poodle skirts and bobby socks and the boys in letter sweaters. The image of 1950s youth as cheerleaders and football heroes was not entirely accurate, however. Many young people rejected the values of their parents and felt misunderstood and alone. A few films, such as *Rebel Without a Cause* in 1955, captured these feelings of alienation.

Religion Revives in the United States In the 1950s Americans who had drifted away from religion in earlier years flocked back to their churches or synagogues. Evangelists like Billy Graham used radio and television to spread

---

▶ RESOURCE DIRECTORY

Teaching Resources

▢ **Reproducible Lesson Plan** found in the Unit 8 folder, p. 105, provides a summary of the Section 2 lesson plan content.

▢ **Alternate Lesson Plan: Critical Thinking** Making Comparisons, found in the Alternate Lesson Plans folder, p. 138, helps students use this skill to identify the values of middle-class Americans in the 1950s and compare and contrast them to those of the 1990s.

▢ **Guided Reading and Review** found in the Unit 8 folder, p. 110, provides a structure for reading and mastering the key concepts and reviewing the key terms for Section 2. (Guided Practice)

✪ ▢ **Literature Activity** Conformity in the 1950s, found in the Unit 8 folder, pp. 129–130, uses an excerpt from Sloan Wilson's novel *The Man in the Gray Flannel Suit* to provide students with a perspective on the shortcomings of unquestioned conformity.

Thousands gathered to hear evangelist Billy Graham preach. He conducted large-scale crusades in major American cities, including this one in New York in 1957.

their messages to more people than ever before. The new interest in religion stemmed in part from the cold war struggle against "godless communism," in part from an effort to find hope in the face of the threat of nuclear war, and in part from a desire to do what everyone else seemed to be doing.

Evidence of the newfound commitment to religion was everywhere. In 1954 Congress added the words "under God" to the Pledge of Allegiance, and the next year it required the phrase "In God We Trust" to appear on all American currency. Religion also became commercial. Those in need could Dial-a-Prayer for the first time, and new slogans such as "The family that prays together stays together" became commonplace. By the end of the 1950s, 95 percent of all Americans felt linked to some formal religious group, even if they never attended services.

Women's and Men's Roles Americans in the post-World War II years were keenly aware of the roles that they were expected to play as men and women. Men were supposed to go to school and then find jobs to support wives and children. Theirs was the public sphere, the world away from home where they earned money and made important political, economic, and social decisions. Men of this time often judged themselves and others by what they could buy with the money they earned.

Women in the 1950s were expected to play a supporting role for their husbands' lives in the public sphere. They kept house, cooked meals, and raised children. Many women had enjoyed working outside the home during World War II and were reluctant to give up good jobs. But propaganda from both employers and the government made it clear that women were expected to give their jobs to returning soldiers. In 1947 *Life* magazine recorded women's frustration in a photo essay titled "The American Woman's Dilemma."

By the 1950s the dilemma seemed solved. Most middle-class women settled into the demands of raising children and decorating their suburban homes. In 1956 *Life* produced a special edition on women that carried a very different message from the issue of nine years before. In a story entitled "Busy Wife's Achievements," *Life* profiled Marjorie Sutton, a happy housewife who had married at the age of sixteen, had four children, and now kept busy with the PTA, Campfire

These Chicago-area commuters may have identified with the characters in *The Man in the Gray Flannel Suit.* The 1955 novel told the story of a couple who seemed to be living the American dream but who felt strangely discontented with their lives.

Discuss other factors in American life that led to increased conformity. Recall that corporations expected their employees to accept and follow the company code. Explain that the postwar fear of communism and the related fear of being branded a communist or communist sympathizer also contributed to the desire to conform and blend in.

Analyze

Ask students to consider this statement by Annie Dillard about her young life in *An American Childhood:* "Every woman stayed alone in her house in those days, like a coin in a safe. Amy [Dillard's sister] and I lived alone with our mother most of the day." What is the mood of Dillard's statement? What image does she create of a woman's life in the 1950s?

In Depth

Did You Know?

Embracing the postwar view that "a woman's place is in the home," Future Homemakers of America was founded in 1945. Its aim was to teach girls how to cook, sew, decorate a home, and raise children. In the last two decades, Future Homemakers has broadened its focus to appeal to both sexes, stressing communications and family management skills as much as cooking and cleaning. As a result, boys now make up 16 percent of the group's membership; and the president of Future Homemakers of America in 1993 was a boy.

Activity

Cooperative Learning

Time: One class period.

Activity: Prepare questions and select potential subjects for interviews about life in the 1950s.

Grouping: Four to six students.

Purpose: Have students work in groups to brainstorm topics concerning life in the 1950s, write questions for potential interviews, and select possible subjects to interview. Students may focus their interview questions on a specific population, for example, women.

Roles: Topic specialists, writers, editors, interviewers, spokesperson.

Outcome: Students will identify significant aspects of life in the 1950s and learn about them through first-person accounts.

Enrichment

Have students work in groups to prepare a dramatic presentation based on an excerpt of their choice from J. D. Salinger's *The Catcher in the Rye.*

Caption Answer to ...

 Interpreting Graphs

More women were joining the work force; approximately 5 million between 1950 and 1960.

3. ASSESS

Section 2 Review Answers

1. beatniks, see p. 751

2. (a) Benjamin Spock, see p. 750,
(b) Betty Friedan, see p. 750,
(c) J. D. Salinger, see p. 751

3. Conformity was in evidence in the bureaucratic workplace, schools, churches, and in the acceptance of traditional gender roles.

Girls, and charity causes. She served as "home manager, mother, hostess, and useful civic worker," and even found time to exercise twice a week "to help preserve her size 12 figure."

Pediatrician **Benjamin Spock** assured American families that mothers should stay home with their young children. In his *Common Sense Book of Baby and Child Care,* published in 1946 and still selling today (though in revised form), he advised a mother to remain with her children if she wanted them to grow up stable and secure. Adlai Stevenson, Democratic candidate for President in 1952 and 1956, reinforced this message when he told a group of female college students that "the assignment for you, as wives and mothers, you can do in the living room with a baby in your lap or in the kitchen with a can opener in your hand."

Despite such expectations, more women than ever before—many of them married with children—held paying jobs in the 1950s. Besides the satisfaction of earning their own money, women wanted to be able to buy the items that were part of the media image of "the good life"—automobiles, electric appliances, and so on.

In 1950, 22 percent of all married American women had jobs; by 1960 the figure had risen to 31 percent. Married women with jobs had first begun to outnumber unmarried women with jobs near the end of World War II; in the postwar years, the gap grew even larger. The graph below shows these trends. 🅒

In 1963 **Betty Friedan** published an explosive critique of the 1950s ideal of womanhood. Friedan had graduated with top honors from Smith College in 1942 but had given up her career as a journalist to become a full-time homemaker and mother. In her book *The Feminine Mystique,* Friedan lashed out at the culture that denied creative roles to women:

> It was unquestioned gospel [in the 1950s] that women could identify with nothing beyond the home—not politics, not art, not science, not events large or small, war or peace, in the United States or the world,

Female Labor Force, 1950–1960

Number of Women (in millions)

Single* / Married / Total (single and married)

25 / 20 / 15 / 10 / 5 / 0

1950 1952 1954 1956 1958 1960

* Includes widowed and divorced.
Source: *Historical Statistics of the United States*

Interpreting Graphs
As the *Post* cover (above right) suggests, women in the 1950s were encouraged to link their self-esteem to their success in the kitchen and home. *According to the graph, what was actually happening to American women during this period? How many women joined the work force between 1950 and 1960?*

▶ RESOURCE DIRECTORY 🅒

Teaching Resources

🅒 **Critical Thinking Activity** Determining Relevance: Wages, Hours, and Unions, found in the Unit 8 folder, p. 125, uses graphs of wages, working hours, and union membership in the United States between 1900 and 1960 to help students apply this skill.

🅒 **Literature Activity** Nonconformity in the 1950s, found in the Unit 8 folder, p. 131, features a passage from the novel *On the Road* by Jack Kerouac, the author whose work and life are often considered synonymous with the "Beat Generation" counterculture.

unless it could be approached through female experience as a wife or mother or translated into domestic detail!

Millions of women, Friedan charged, were frustrated with their roles in the 1950s.

MAKING CONNECTIONS

In what ways are women and men today pressured to conform to social standards?

Pockets of Nonconformity Appear

Occasional challenges to the rigid expectations of 1950s society did erupt. Holden Caulfield, the main figure in **J. D. Salinger's** 1951 novel *The Catcher in the Rye,* was troubled by the hypocrisy of the "phonies" he saw at boarding school and in the world at large. His effort to preserve his own integrity despite the fierce pressure to conform was an experience to which many readers could relate. ★

Members of the "Beat Generation," called **beatniks** by middle-class observers, launched a different kind of challenge. Beatniks, some of them writers, some artists, some simply participants in the movement, stressed spontaneity and spirituality instead of apathy and conformity. They challenged traditional patterns of respectability and shocked other Americans with their more open sexuality and their use of illegal drugs.

Author Jack Kerouac, the spiritual leader of the beatniks, gathered with others in coffee houses in San Francisco, California, where they shared ideas and experiences. The unconventional Kerouac typed his best-selling novel *On the Road,* published in 1957, on a 250-foot roll of paper. The novel's lack of standard punctuation and paragraph structure was meant to reflect an open approach to life.

Such challenges to conformity were not the norm. Most Americans were willing to seize the comfort offered by the postwar economy and preferred to live their lives in the relative safety of the suburbs. Many people pleased with this lifestyle eventually began to expect the government to ensure that the "good life" continued.

Viewpoints
On Rock-and-Roll Music

When the defiant beat of rock and roll burst onto the American scene in the mid-1950s, few people remained impartial about its sound or its impact. *What does each viewpoint below say about the relationship between rock music and delinquency?*

Against Rock and Roll

"Rock 'n' roll . . . is sung, played and written for the most part by [mentally deficient] goons and by means of its almost imbecilic repetition and sly, lewd, in plain fact, dirty lyrics . . . it manages to be the [warlike] music of every sideburned delinquent on the face of the earth."

Singer Frank Sinatra, The *New York Times,* January 12, 1958

For Rock and Roll

"If my kids are home at night listening to my radio program, and get interested enough to go out and buy records and have a collection to listen to and dance to, I think I'm fighting delinquency."

Radio disc jockey Alan Freed, The *New York Times,* January 12, 1958

SECTION 2 REVIEW

Key Terms, People, and Places
1. Define beatniks.
2. Identify (a) Benjamin Spock, (b) Betty Friedan, (c) J. D. Salinger.

Key Concepts
3. In what aspects of American life was conformity most visible during the period between 1945 and 1960?

4. What social and economic roles were men and women expected to play in the 1950s?

Critical Thinking
5. **Making Comparisons** In what ways was the "Beat Generation" of the 1950s similar to or different from the rebellious youth of the 1920s?

 Viewpoints Activity On Rock and Roll, found in the Unit 8 folder, pp. 122–123, provides a basis for discussion of censorship of free speech and artistic expression.

Quiz found in the Unit 8 folder, p. 111, covers the main ideas in this section as well as the key terms.

Media and Technology

Transparency
Critical Thinking, I-4

The Suburban Explosion

Focus Before the postwar building boom, only the wealthy could afford to live in the suburbs, although many Americans longed to escape life in dingy city apartments and crowded houses. After the war, prosperity and government programs to finance mortgages started a suburban building spree that changed the way many Americans lived.

Instruct Using an overhead projector, show students a fairly detailed map of the nearest large city and its surrounding suburbs. Ask students to point out the core city, beltways, and "edge cities" near suburban shopping malls.

Ask students to list ways in which the development of suburban housing changed American life. Ask them to consider each of the following aspects:
- The family: How did suburban housing encourage nuclear, as opposed to extended, families?
- The environment: What impact did the growth of suburbs have on wildlife, quality of air and water, amount of farmland, and so on?
- Integration: Did the growth of suburbs encourage or discourage integration of housing and schools?

Extend Many observers thought that the suburban shopping mall would become the "community center" of the suburbs, filling the roles of Main Street, the town common, the city square, and the neighborhood playground. Ask students how successful they think shopping malls have been in creating a sense of community. What activities other than shopping, such as eating meals or snacks, taking an exercise class, or going to a movie, are available in shopping malls?

TIME & PLACE
A GEOGRAPHIC PERSPECTIVE

The Suburban Explosion

After World War II, American cities rapidly expanded outward as people moved into suburbs that first housed them and then became major centers for shopping, working, and recreation. What factors contributed to this suburban explosion?

Both nature and people can change a place. Changes in the landscape, such as those caused by a hurricane or drought, often are dramatic. The changes that people make in the environment can be just as striking. At no time in United States history were these changes more evident than in the decades following World War II.

Movement: Railroads and Streetcars Lead to Suburban Growth

The largest cities in the United States in the 1700s were commercial centers situated at key waterfront locations. This was because goods and people could move much more rapidly and easily on water than over land. Workplaces in these cities were clustered near the waterfront, while residences crowded nearby, so working people could walk between their homes and jobs.

These compact, circular-shaped cities began to expand when railroads first cut paths outward from the centers. In the decades before and after the Civil War, small residential communities sprouted around railroad stations that were situated six or more miles from the central cities, as the map of Newport in 1775 shows. These small communities provided quiet, pastoral settings for those with sufficient money to afford daily rail trips to and from their jobs in the city.

Even more urban residents could consider moving away from the city centers after the late 1880s, when electric-powered streetcar lines reached into the surrounding countryside. Many of the newer dwellings accessible by streetcar were larger than city homes and sat in the middle of pleasant yards. By World War I, some of the larger cities extended out as far as ten miles from their centers, where most people still worked and shopped. Because streetcar lines did not extend as far in some directions as in others, the overall shape of the cities were star-like, shown in the map of Detroit in 1920.

Population Growth, Automobiles, and Highways Continue the Trend

The Great Depression and World War II required most Americans to defer their desire for new, larger houses in pleasant settings. Once the war ended, however, millions of people returned to the nation's cities, where they married, produced children in record numbers, and searched for bigger homes. Available housing within cities filled quickly, but the automobiles that many veterans purchased permitted them to consider locations outside cities. The GI Bill made money readily available for housing. The result was construction at a rate unprecedented in the nation's history. Between 1947 and 1965, at least 1.25 million new houses were built each year, with more than one half of those units in the expanding suburbs.

After the nation's first enclosed, climate-controlled shopping center opened in 1956, the suburban mall became the new mecca for American consumers.

In the first decade after the war ended, the number of automobiles owned by city dwellers increased dramatically. In 1956 the federal government established an interstate highway system to connect

RESOURCE DIRECTORY

Teaching Resources

Time and Place Activity Edge Cities, found in the Unit 8 folder, pp. 118–119, focuses on the "third wave" of the suburban explosion, when job opportunities followed retail businesses and residential developments out of the center cities, creating altogether new—and different—cities.

Newport, 1775

N W E S

Narragansett Bay

■ Buildings

0   50   100 Feet
0   100 Meters

Detroit, 1920

···· Detroit city limits

▦ Developed areas

☐ Streetcar and bus lines

0   1   3 Miles
0   1   3 Kilometers

Detroit R.

N W E S

major cities. In addition to highways radiating out from city centers, engineers constructed "beltways" that circled cities at distances ranging from six to twenty miles from the core. The result was a dramatic reshaping of metropolitan areas.

Stores and Jobs Follow

As suburban neighborhoods grew, traveling to stores in the city center was no longer convenient. Store owners soon recognized this and built new establishments in suburban locations. Starting in the early 1950s, groups of stores began to cluster together in shopping centers surrounded by large parking lots. After the nation's first enclosed, climate-controlled shopping center opened in 1956, the suburban mall became the new mecca for American consumers.

A major reason for the success of suburban shopping malls was their easy access from freeways. Such locations also were recognized as ideal sites for offices, factories, service providers, and many other forms of economic activity. These businesses grouped themselves in dozens of low buildings straddling heavily traveled freeways and streets and formed what journalist Joel Garreau has called "edge cities."

The growth of edge cities was not without its difficulties. As suburbs became more densely settled, they began to experience the same pollution, crime, and other problems formerly associated with central cities. Of greatest concern to the people who worked, shopped, and lived in edge cities was the increasing traffic congestion. The easy access that attracted so many people to the suburbs was becoming a distant memory. Urban observers today wonder what new forms of transportation will evolve to move people and goods more quickly and easily—and how those new forms once again will transform the geography of American cities.

GEOGRAPHIC CONNECTIONS

1. Why did the earliest large cities develop in waterfront locations?
2. What factors contributed to the boom in suburban housing construction after World War II?

Critical Thinking

3. **Predicting Consequences** Many cities have considered banning cars from downtown streets. How would this affect both cities and suburbs?

Answers

1. Major cities were located on waterways because people and goods could be moved more quickly and easily over water than they could over land.

2. After the war millions of military personnel returned to the nation's cities, married, had families, and looked for housing. The shortage of urban housing, the availability of government-guaranteed bank loans, and the increased availability of automobiles allowed people to buy new, larger homes farther from the cities where they worked.

3. A ban on automobile transportation would force many more suburban commuters to use public transportation such as buses and trains and would probably mean that fewer people would be willing to commute into the city to work. More businesses might relocate to the suburbs as a result, thus contributing to the further growth and problems of "edge cities." The decreased congestion and pollution in the city cores, however, might make them more attractive for shoppers, city residents, and tourists.

SECTION 3

Domestic Politics and Policy

1. FOCUS

Connecting to the Big Idea

See page 740B. Presidents Truman and Eisenhower presented Americans with different approaches to government and to the challenges facing the postwar nation. Ask students in what ways Eisenhower and Truman disagreed about the proper role of government and the way to solve the nation's social problems.

Objectives

● Identify Truman's main task as President as converting the nation to a peacetime economy.
● Describe Truman's Fair Deal as a continuation of the principles of the New Deal.
● Describe Eisenhower's modern Republicanism.

Bellringer

Ask students to think of someone in a leadership position whom they admire, for example, a teacher, school administrator, coach, or member of the clergy. Ask students to describe that person's leadership style and explain why they think it is effective.

Reading Strategy

Problem Solving Ask students to imagine that they must evaluate Presidents Truman and Eisenhower for their administrations' handling of domestic affairs. As they read, students should note positive and negative points about the administration of each President. Have students write a brief analysis of both Presidents and use it to give each a grade. Students should give specific reasons for the grades.

SECTION PREVIEW

The postwar period created many challenges for American leaders—including the conversion back to a peacetime economy and the debate over the proper role of government in the nation's economic and social affairs. Presidents Harry Truman and Dwight Eisenhower used two very different styles of leadership to meet these challenges.

Key Concepts

- Truman's main task as President was converting a powerful wartime economy to peacetime production.
- Truman wanted to advance the principles of the New Deal through his own Fair Deal.
- In 1952 Americans favored Dwight Eisenhower's modern republicanism, which encouraged expansion without destroying the economic and social programs of the 1930s.

Key Terms, People, and Places

Taft-Hartley Act, modern republicanism, *Sputnik*; Adlai Stevenson, Richard M. Nixon

Enthusiastic Eisenhower supporters during the 1952 election campaign could add this colorful scarf to their wardrobe.

I n the postwar years, political events reflected the economic and social patterns of the country. Middle-class Americans, who grew more numerous all the time, pressured the government to help maintain the nation's newly won prosperity. Democrat Harry S Truman first struggled with the problems of reconversion to a peacetime economy, then fought for a reform program blocked repeatedly by Congress. Republican Dwight D. Eisenhower took a more low-key approach to the presidency. His genial, reassuring manner made him one of the most popular Presidents in the years following World War II.

Reconversion and the Fair Deal

Harry Truman wanted to follow in Franklin Roosevelt's footsteps, but he often appeared ill-prepared for the presidency. He seemed to have a scattershot approach to governing, offering a different batch of new proposals in every speech. People wondered where his focus lay.

Truman's first priority was reconversion—the social and economic transition from wartime to peacetime. Soldiers wanted to return home, and politicians were flooded with messages that warned, "No boats, no votes." Truman responded quickly and got most soldiers home by 1946.

Lifting the economic controls that had kept wartime inflation in check proved a more difficult challenge. Americans had done without thousands of consumer goods during World War II. Now they wanted those goods, and they wanted them right away. The government eased the controls, and prices soared, in the words of one political cartoonist, "over the moon!" Since wages failed to keep up with prices, many people still could not enjoy the fruits of their years of sacrifice.

Meanwhile, angry workers demanded wage increases that they had forgone for the sake of the war effort. In 1946, 4.6 million workers went on strike, more than ever before in the United States. Strikes hit the automobile, steel, electrical, coal, and railroad industries and affected nearly everyone in the country. ◎

Though Truman agreed that workers deserved high wages, he thought that their demands were inflationary—that is, he believed that such increases would push the prices of goods still higher. In his view, workers failed to understand that big wage increases might destroy the health of the economy.

Angry at the disruptions, Truman threatened to draft some striking workers and order them as soldiers to stay on the job. Truman's White House took other steps as well. When

---

RESOURCE DIRECTORY

Teaching Resources

Reproducible Lesson Plan found in the Unit 8 folder, p. 106, provides a summary of the Section 3 lesson plan content.

Alternate Lesson Plan: Critical Thinking Drawing Conclusions, found in the Alternate Lesson Plans folder, p. 139, provides a structure for students to analyze the Truman and Eisenhower administrations.

Guided Reading and Review found in Unit 8 folder, p. 112, provides a structure for reading and mastering the key concepts and reviewing the key terms for Section 3. (Guided Practice)

◎ **Visual Learning Activity** Auto Strike, 1950, found in the Unit 8 folder, p. 132, uses a photograph of United Auto Workers members preparing for a strike to illustrate the continuing rift between workers and management.

John L. Lewis and his United Mine Workers defied a court order against a strike, the Truman administration asked a judge to serve Lewis with a contempt of court citation. The court fined Lewis $10,000 and his union $3.5 million.

Congress went even further than Truman. In 1947 it passed the **Taft-Hartley Act.** This act allowed the President to declare an eighty-day cooling-off period, during which strikers in industries that affected the national interest had to return to work while the government conducted a study of the situation. Reflecting the widespread anticommunist paranoia gripping the United States at the time, the measure also required union officials to sign noncommunist oaths. Furious union leaders complained bitterly about the measure, and Truman vetoed it. Congress passed the act over Truman's veto.

MAKING CONNECTIONS

Why might Congress have been especially concerned about possible communist ties among union officials?

Truman's Fair Deal Truman had supported Roosevelt's New Deal, and now, playing on the well-known name, he devised a program he called the Fair Deal. The Fair Deal extended the New Deal's goals.

Truman agreed with FDR that government needed to play an active role in securing economic justice for all American citizens. As the war ended, he introduced a twenty-one point program that included legislation designed to promote full employment, a higher minimum wage, greater unemployment compensation for workers without jobs, housing assistance, and a variety of other items. Over the next ten weeks, Truman added more proposals. By early 1946 he had asked for a national health insurance program and legislation to control atomic energy.

In attempting to promote his program, Truman ran into tremendous political opposition. A coalition of conservative Democrats and Republicans opposed him at every turn.

As the 1946 midterm elections approached, Truman seemed little more than another bungling bureaucrat. Some people commented,

"You just sort of forget about Harry until he makes another mistake." Others adapted a well-known saying: "To err is Truman." Truman's support in one poll dropped from 87 percent just after he assumed the presidency to 32 percent in November 1946. In the 1946 elections, Republicans won majorities of both houses of Congress.

The 80th Congress battered the President for the next two years. Under the leadership of conservative Republican senator Robert A. Taft of Ohio, commonly known as "Mr. Republican," the Republican party did whatever it could to reduce the size and the power of the federal government, to decrease taxes, and to stymie Truman's liberal goals.

The Election of 1948 Truman decided to seek another term as President in 1948. He had no reason to expect victory, however, because even in his own party, his support was disintegrating. The southern wing of the Democratic party, protesting a moderate civil rights plank in the party platform, split off from the main party. These segregationists formed the States' Rights, or Dixiecrat, party and nominated

Some supporters of the Truman-Barkley ticket in 1948 attached this sign to their cars' license plates.

In 1948 Truman became the first President ever to campaign in Harlem. The button at left announced his commitment to the civil rights cause.

2. INSTRUCT

Explain/Discuss

Almost as quickly as the nation had mobilized for war, it needed to demobilize once the war was over. Discuss with students the tasks that needed to be accomplished to return the nation to a peacetime footing, including bringing the troops home; lifting wartime economic controls, such as price restrictions and rationing; controlling inflation; and finding jobs for returning troops whose jobs had been taken by women during the war. Ask students to assess how well Truman carried out each of these tasks and show how Truman was a New Dealer in his view of the appropriate role of government in American life. In which of his policies did Truman follow in the footsteps of Franklin Roosevelt?

Ask students to compare Eisenhower's view of government with Truman's. What other Presidents would have agreed with Eisenhower's policy of "modern republicanism"? Ask students to explain the significance of Eisenhower's willingness to accept the welfare programs of the New Deal.

Analyze

Ask students to compare the personalities of Truman and Eisenhower. Ask how Eisenhower's personality helped him win the election of 1952. Encourage students to use what they know about the 1950s to explain how Eisenhower's style fit the mood of the country at the time.

Answer to ...

MAKING CONNECTIONS

The demands and tactics of union leaders often went against the interests of big business. Their activities pointed out the failure of capitalism to meet the needs of workers, which may have been interpreted as a "communist" point of view.

Ask students to prepare for the role of either Stevenson or Eisenhower in a press conference during the election of 1952. Students should prepare to answer questions about their candidate's experience, record, goals, style, and view of government as part of the role-play.

Ask each student to write one question for the press conference and put it in a bowl or box. Choose random pairs of students to role-play the two candidates, and ask for volunteers to select and read the questions to them. Any student may object to an answer presented by one of the "candidates" and present an alternative answer; he or she then must take over as the "candidate" and continue answering new questions. Ask students to evaluate both answers in that event.

In Depth

Historical Misconceptions

Far from being a passive President, as was the common perception at the time, historians today argue that Dwight Eisenhower was an astute behind-the-scenes policymaker who only gave the appearance of not being involved. He kept Secretary of State John Foster Dulles in check and refused to intervene on the side of the French when they faced defeat in Vietnam. He once joked, when asked how he would answer questions about a delicate issue at a press conference, that he would simply confuse the audience if that issue arose. Ike's public style reflected later generations' perception of the 1950s—there was a lot more underneath than met the eye.

Governor J. Strom Thurmond of South Carolina for President.

Meanwhile, the left wing of the Democratic party deserted Truman to follow Henry Wallace, who had been Roosevelt's third Vice President. Many Democrats believed that Wallace was the right person to carry on the ideas begun by Franklin Roosevelt. Most recently Wallace had served as Truman's secretary of commerce. Wallace had resigned, however, because he did not support Truman's cold war policies.

Running against Republican Thomas E. Dewey, governor of New York, Truman crisscrossed the country by train, campaigning not so much against Dewey as against the Republican Congress, which the President repeatedly mocked as the "do-nothing" 80th Congress. Truman's campaign style was electrifying. In off-the-cuff speeches, he challenged all Americans: "If you send another Republican Congress to Washington, you're a bigger bunch of suckers than I think you are." "Give 'em hell, Harry," the people yelled as Truman got going. And he did. ✪

Among other things, Truman vehemently attacked Congress's farm policy. In the past, a federal price-support program permitted farmers to borrow money to store surplus crops until someone bought the produce. Recently, however, Congress had failed to provide additional storage bins, just as a good harvest loomed on the horizon. Truman told the farmers:

The Chicago Tribune was so certain of Truman's defeat that it printed this edition before the final election results were tallied. Truman was delighted to see the headline proved wrong.

The Republican Congress has already stuck a pitchfork in the farmers' backs. . . . When you have to sell your grain below the support price because you have no place to store it, you can thank this same Republican Congress.

On election day, although virtually all experts and polls picked Dewey to win, Truman scored an astounding upset. He now stepped out of FDR's shadow to claim the presidency in his own right, with a chance to push further for his liberal legislative goals. But over the next four years, the Fair Deal scored only occasional successes, and on balance was disappointing compared to the New Deal the decade before. Truman decided not to run for reelection in 1952. Instead, the Democrats chose **Adlai Stevenson,** governor of Illinois, as their presidential candidate.

Dwight Eisenhower and the Republican Approach

Running against Stevenson for the Republicans was Dwight Eisenhower. As a public figure, Eisenhower's approach to politics differed from Harry Truman's. Whereas Truman was a scrappy fighter, Ike—as the people affectionately called Eisenhower—had always been a talented diplomat. During World War II, Eisenhower forged agreements among Allied military commanders; now his easy-going charm gave Americans a sense of security.

By 1952, Americans across the land chanted, "I Like Ike." The Republicans used a "K_1C_2" formula for victory, which focused on the three problems of Korea, communism, and corruption. Eisenhower promised to end the Korean War, and the Republican party guaranteed a tough approach to the communist challenge. Eisenhower's vice-presidential running mate, Californian **Richard M. Nixon,** hammered on the topic of corruption in government.

The Checkers Speech In spite of his overwhelming popularity, Eisenhower's candidacy hit a snag in September 1952. Newspapers accused Richard Nixon of having a special fund, set up by rich Republican supporters.

RESOURCE DIRECTORY

Teaching Resources

✪ **Primary Source Activity** Harry Truman: Off the Record, found in the Unit 8 folder, pp. 126–127, uses excerpts from the private papers of the former President to provide students with an additional perspective on the issues of that era.

"Secret Nixon Fund!" and "Secret Rich Man's Trust Fund Keeps Nixon in Style Beyond His Salary," screamed typical headlines. In fact, Nixon had done nothing wrong, but the accusation that he had received illegal gifts from political friends was hard to shake.

Soon, cries arose for Eisenhower to dump Nixon from the ticket. Eisenhower decided to allow Nixon to save himself, if he could. On September 23, Nixon went on television to explain the situation in his own words. With Ike joining a national audience, Nixon delivered one of the most memorable speeches in recent political history. He emotionally denied wrongful use of campaign funds. He gave a detailed account of his personal finances, including his $4,000 life insurance policy and the $38,500 debt on his house and other items. In response to the charge that he was living above his means, he described his wife, Pat, as wearing a "good old Republican cloth coat."

The emotional climax of the speech came when Nixon admitted that he had, in fact, received one gift from a political supporter:

> *It was a little cocker spaniel dog. . . . Black and white spotted. And our little girl— Tricia, the six-year-old—named it Checkers. And you know the kids love that dog and I just want to say this right now, that regardless of what they say about it, we're going to keep it.*

At the end of his speech, Nixon requested that the American people contact the Eisenhower campaign headquarters to register their opinions as to whether or not he should stay on the Republican ticket. The response was overwhelming. People from all across the nation called, wired, and wrote to Eisenhower, demanding that Nixon continue as his running mate. Nixon had turned a political disaster into a public relations bonanza.

In the election, Democratic candidate Adlai Stevenson never had a chance. Ike got 55 percent of the popular vote and swept into office with a Republican Congress as well.

Four years later, despite a number of serious illnesses during his first term in office, the American people wanted Ike back. Eisenhower won reelection—again over Stevenson—with almost 58 percent of the vote. After 1952, however, the Democrats regained control of Congress.

Modern Republicanism
In domestic matters, the President was determined to slow the growth of the federal government. He also wanted to limit the President's power and raise the legislature's and the courts' authority.

Ike's priorities included cutting spending, reducing taxes, and balancing the budget. He called this approach to government "dynamic conservatism" or **"modern republicanism."** He intended to be "conservative when it comes to money, liberal when it comes to human beings."

Ike's natural inclination was to work behind the scenes. One writer has described his style as the "hidden hand." "I am not one of those desk-pounding types that likes to stick out his jaw and look like he is bossing the show," Eisenhower said. Critics misinterpreted his apparent lack of leadership, joking about an Eisenhower doll— you wound it up and it did nothing for eight years. But the American people approved of Ike's style. Eisenhower defended his approach, declaring,

> *Now, look, I happen to know a little about leadership. I've had to work with a lot of nations, for that matter, at odds with each other. And I tell you this: you do not lead by hitting people over the head. . . . I'll tell you what leadership is. It's persuasion—and conciliation—and education—and patience. It's long, slow tough work. That's the only kind of leadership I know or believe in—or will practice.*

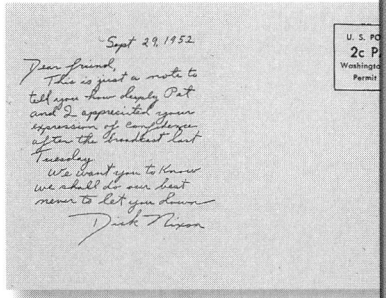

Using Historical Evidence Richard Nixon thanked the voters who had shown their support after his "Checkers" speech with this postcard. *What image of Nixon does the photograph promote?*

The "I Like Ike" message was seen everywhere in 1952, even on women's compacts.

In Depth

Biography

The period of history that this chapter covers has many truly heroic figures, but none more memorable than Thurgood Marshall. The great-grandson of a freed slave, Thoroughgood (he later changed the name to Thurgood) Marshall (1908–1993) spent more than twenty years challenging institutional racism as the NAACP's chief legal counsel. In 1967, President Johnson appointed Marshall the Supreme Court's first African American associate justice. Marshall maintained a staunchly liberal presence on what soon became an increasingly conservative Court. He opposed the death penalty and favored affirmative action and other remedies for discrimination. By the time he retired in 1991 he had become, in the words of one Harvard Law School professor, "the great dissenter . . . part of the conscience of the Court." (See Section 4.)

Section 3 Review Answers

1. (a) Taft-Hartley Act, see p. 755, (b) modern republicanism, see p. 757

2. (a) Adlai Stevenson, see p. 756, (b) Richard M. Nixon, see p. 756

3. Truman's main problem was releasing the American economy from wartime price controls, which created postwar inflation.

4. The Fair Deal included legislation designed to promote full employment, a higher minimum wage, greater unemployment compensation for workers without jobs, housing assistance, and a variety of other items. Truman later added other proposals: a national health insurance program and legislation to control atomic energy.

5. *Sputnik* was the first artificial satellite to orbit the earth. When the Soviet Union launched it in 1957, the United States awoke from its dream of scientific superiority with a rude shock and began taking steps to catch up with the Soviets in that area. Legislation provided incentives for people to become teachers and funds for schools to build science and foreign language facilities.

In Depth

Then and Now

Eisenhower's Atoms for Peace program was an attempt to ease cold war tensions by promoting the commercial uses of nuclear power. By the time Eisenhower left office in 1960, three nuclear power plants were operating in the United States with a total generating capacity of 350 megawatts. (A megawatt equals one million watts or 10,000 100-watt light bulbs.) In the 1990s, nuclear power is America's second-largest provider of electricity (after coal). Over ninety nuclear power plants, representing a total capacity of over 85,000 megawatts, supply 13 percent of the nation's electricity.

Sputnik sparked real fears of nuclear attack. Many Americans hoped they could survive a nuclear war in a basement fallout shelter. After an atomic explosion, radioactive particles attach themselves to dust in the atmosphere, which continues to rain down upon the earth for as long as two weeks. In the shelter shown above, an air filter protects people from breathing radioactive dust, and a Geiger counter tells them when the radioactivity outside has returned to a safe level.

In the tradition of past Republican Presidents such as Coolidge and Hoover, Eisenhower favored big business. His cabinet was composed mostly of successful businessmen, plus one union leader, which prompted critics to charge that the cabinet consisted of "eight millionaires and a plumber." For secretary of defense he chose Charles E. Wilson, former president of General Motors, who believed that "what was good for our country was good for General Motors, and vice versa."

Modern republicanism did everything possible to aid corporate America. It transferred control of about $40 billion worth of offshore oil lands from the federal government to the states so that the states could lease oil rights to corporations. The administration also tried to end government competition with big business. For example, Eisenhower sought to eliminate the Tennessee Valley Authority, the New Deal enterprise that provided electrical energy to the public at low cost. Though he failed, in this effort Ike revealed his preference for private power companies.

Ike's attempt to balance the budget backfired. His cuts in government spending caused the economy to slump. When that happened, tax revenues dropped, and the deficit grew larger instead of smaller. Economic growth, which had averaged 4.3 percent between 1947 and 1952, fell to 2.5 percent between 1953 and 1960. The country suffered three economic recessions during Eisenhower's presidency, from 1953 to 1954, from 1957 to 1958, and again from 1960 to 1961.

RESOURCE DIRECTORY

Teaching Resources

Eisenhower's Achievements Despite economic troubles, Eisenhower helped maintain a mood of stability in America. He also underscored the basic commitment the government had made during the New Deal to ensure the economic security of all Americans. For example, in 1954 and 1956 Social Security was extended to make eligible 10 million additional workers. In 1955 minimum wage was raised from 75 cents to one dollar an hour.

Sputnik Shocks Americans In 1957 the Soviet Union launched *Sputnik,* the first artificial satellite to orbit the earth. *Sputnik* sped around the world every 96 minutes at a rate of 18,000 miles per hour. The United States, which had viewed itself as the world's foremost scientific power, was mortified. Worse yet, the United States' own rocket, rushed to the launching pad before it was ready, rose only a foot before crashing to the ground.

Critics charged that the apparent stability and security of the United States was, in fact, only smugness and self-satisfaction. Perhaps the institutions most vulnerable to critics' attacks were the nation's schools. Americans questioned whether their children were learning to read, write, and calculate well enough to succeed in an increasingly competitive world.

Another fear prompted by *Sputnik* was the possibility of nuclear attack. The Soviet rocket that launched the satellite might also be used to send a hydrogen bomb to American shores. In one response to anxiety about a nuclear attack, millions of Americans constructed bomb shelters in their basements. The art on page 758 shows a typical bomb shelter of the 1950s.

Less than a year after the launching of *Sputnik* shredded Americans' confidence, Congress passed and President Eisenhower signed into law the National Defense Education Act of 1958. The act provided millions of dollars in low-cost loans to college students and significant reductions in repayments if they ultimately became teachers. The federal government also granted millions to state schools for building science and foreign language facilities.

Besides the jolt to their confidence caused by *Sputnik,* Americans had other reasons to doubt the health of the nation in the postwar years. Some people began to wonder whether the inequalities in American society might be just as dangerous to the United States as threats from foreign nations. The people still liked Ike, but deep troubles were becoming more and more visible.

The blow that *Sputnik* delivered to American self-assurance is reflected in this "Space Race" card game from the 1950s, in which those dealt the *Sputnik* card would lose two turns.

SECTION 3 REVIEW

Key Terms, People, and Places
1. Define (a) Taft-Hartley Act, (b) modern republicanism.
2. Identify (a) Adlai Stevenson, (b) Richard M. Nixon.

Key Concepts
3. What problem did Harry Truman face in reconverting the nation to a peacetime economy after World War II?

4. What were some of the goals of Harry Truman's Fair Deal program?
5. What was *Sputnik,* and what impact did it have in the United States?

Critical Thinking
6. **Recognizing Ideologies** How did Truman's and Eisenhower's approaches to the role of the federal government in solving domestic problems differ?

Quiz found in the Unit 8 folder, p. 113, covers the main ideas in this section as well as the key terms.

Media and Technology

Transparency
The Way It Works, H-20

---

6. Truman believed in an active, positive role for the federal government in social and economic matters; Eisenhower wanted to curb the role of the federal government in these matters.

Reteach
Write the following sentences on the chalkboard and ask students to decide which of them apply to President Truman and which to President Eisenhower.
- He stood by his running mate in 1952 despite accusations that the vice-presidential candidate had accepted illegal gifts.
- His victory in 1948 was a surprise to experts and pollsters.
- He failed to get his social program through Congress.
- He thought government should aid business.
- Although he wanted to reduce the size of government, he accepted FDR's welfare state.

Alternative Assessment

Mid-Point Monitoring
Ask students if they have
- Decided on a format for their projects
- Begun their outside research
- Started drafting portions of their projects

4. CLOSE

Reinforcing the Big Idea
The Presidents of the 1950s, Truman and Eisenhower, differed greatly in style and political philosophy. The next section presents material on the growth of a great social movement that grew during both of their administrations—the civil rights movement.

The Continuing Struggle for Equality

SECTION 4

The Continuing Struggle for Equality

1. FOCUS

Connecting to the Big Idea

See page 740B. The civil rights movement took on a new momentum in the years following World War II. Ask what methods Americans used in the struggle to attain racial justice.

Objectives

● Describe the changes in American society that led African Americans to demand more equality between the races.
● Identify the methods used by African Americans to wage their battle for racial justice.
● Explain how other minority groups began to follow the example of the African American movement for equality.

Bellringer

Ask students to consider the role of sports in American life. Ask if sports stars should be considered heroes. Is there a difference between a "star" and a "hero"? What qualities does a "hero" possess? Ask students who their heroes are. Why?

Reading Strategy

Reading for Evidence Note with students the opening sentence on page 760: "The events of World War II . . . breathed new life into the civil rights movement." Ask students to look for evidence to support that statement and to describe the change as they read the section.

SECTION PREVIEW

The events of World War II—including the fight against fascism abroad and the African American migration at home—breathed new life into the civil rights movement. The actions of many courageous Americans brought significant results in the postwar years.

The NAACP was one organization devoted to fighting racial injustice in the United States. In the South, African Americans had to use separate facilities at all public places.

Key Concepts
• World War II caused changes in American society that led African Americans to demand more equality between the races.
• African Americans used the courts and a protest movement to wage their battle for racial justice.
• Other minorities began to follow the example set by the African American movement.

Key Terms, People, and Places
termination policy; Jackie Robinson, Thurgood Marshall, Martin Luther King, Jr.

B efore and during World War II, African Americans were not treated as equals by a large portion of American society. After the war, however, the campaign for civil rights began to accelerate. Thousands of African Americans had served their country during the war and felt this service was a mockery if they were not allowed equal rights in their own country. Hundreds of thousands had moved to northern cities during the war and experienced a new sense of freedom there, in spite of poor living conditions. Millions more simply believed that the time had come to demand that the nation live up to its creed that all are equal before the law.

President Truman, while holding in private many of the racial prejudices he had learned growing up in the South, recognized that as President he had to take action. In 1948 he wrote in a letter to a friend,

I am not asking for social equality, because no such things exist, but I am asking for equality of opportunity for all human beings, and, as long as I stay [in the White House], I am going to continue that fight.

In July 1948 Truman banned discrimination in the hiring of federal employees. He also ordered an end to segregation and discrimination in the armed forces. Real change came slowly, however. Only with the onset of the Korean War in 1950 did the armed forces make significant progress in ending segregation.

AMERICAN PROFILES

Jackie Robinson

The battle against racial segregation was taken up not only in the military but on the professional baseball diamond as well. For years, major league baseball had banned African Americans, forcing them to play in the separate Negro Leagues. In 1946 Branch Rickey, general manager of the Brooklyn Dodgers, decided to challenge the ban. (See "History Might Not Have Happened This Way," page 764.)

Rickey selected **Jackie Robinson** (1919–1972) to be the first African American to break the color line. Robinson had grown up in Pasadena, California, and attended the University of California in Los Angeles. In college Robinson earned letters in football, basketball, baseball, and track and was also a superb golfer, swimmer, and tennis player.

Robinson had a record of standing up against racial injustice. While he was in the army during World War II, a bus driver had snarled at him, "Get in the back where you belong or there'll be trouble." Robinson knew that buses on the army post were not segregated, so he stood his ground. Although he had not broken any rules, Robinson had to undergo a court-martial before clearing his name.

▶ RESOURCE DIRECTORY

Teaching Resources

Reproducible Lesson Plan found in the Unit 8 folder, p. 107, provides a summary of the Section 4 lesson plan content.

Alternate Lesson Plan: Cooperative Learning found in the Alternate Lesson Plans folder, p. 140, provides a strategy for groups of students to identify contributions of African Americans to the postwar struggle for racial equality.

Guided Reading and Review found in the Unit 8 folder, p. 114, provides a structure for reading and mastering the key concepts and reviewing the key terms for Section 4. (Guided Practice)

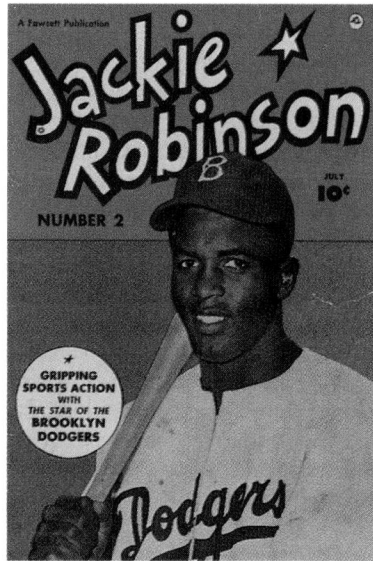

After his brilliant first season with the Brooklyn Dodgers, Jackie Robinson was featured on baseball cards such as the one above, issued in 1951.

The mental toughness that Robinson acquired from such experiences and his ability to rise above the injustices he encountered served him well during his baseball career. He faced prejudice from fans, opponents on the field, and even his own teammates. Robinson later recalled his first interview with Branch Rickey:

> I am a normal man with the feelings of any normal man. If anything, my competitive instincts are so sharp that I will eagerly challenge any man who challenges me. But Mr. Rickey made entirely clear to me that day that I could not behave normally. . . . On my ability to measure up to the challenge would depend not only my future but the future of my race in baseball.

Despite many instances of prejudice, Robinson behaved with dignity and had a sparkling first season. He was Rookie of the Year in 1947 and kept improving with time. Just as important, Robinson fostered pride in African Americans around the country and opened the way for other African Americans to follow him into professional sports.

MAKING CONNECTIONS

In the 1990s Charles Barkley, an African American professional basketball player, insisted, "I am not a role model!" How might the American public have reacted if Jackie Robinson had made that statement in 1947?

Brown v. Board of Education

Beginning in the 1930s, the National Association for the Advancement of Colored People, NAACP, launched a series of court cases aimed at overturning the 1896 *Plessy* v. *Ferguson* Supreme Court decision. *Plessy* v. *Ferguson* held that segregation of the races in public institutions and accommodations was constitutional as long as facilities were "separate but equal."

In 1951 Oliver Brown sued the Topeka, Kansas, Board of Education to allow his eight-year-old daughter Linda to attend a school that only white children were allowed to attend. She passed the school on her way to the bus that took her to a distant school for African Americans. After appeals, the case reached the Supreme

Linda Brown (inset) was at the center of the landmark *Brown* v. *Board of Education* case. African American students like Elizabeth Echford of Little Rock, Arkansas, (below) still had to endure the insults of white students who disagreed with the Court's decision.

Teaching Heterogeneous Groups

Beginning in the 1930s the NAACP took action by bringing a series of court cases aimed at overturning the 1896 Supreme Court decision that segregation in public institutions was constitutional as long as facilities were "separate but equal." To illustrate the inherent unfairness of this decision, divide students into small groups. Have each group design, justify, and implement a "separate but equal" seating chart for the classroom. For example, students might segregate the classroom according to clothing color. Have students who were segregated tell how they felt in that role. **LEP**

Enrichment

Martin Luther King, Jr., was one of the nation's great orators and writers. Ask students to assemble a collection of quotations from King's speeches and writings. Students should arrange their quotes by date or theme, preparing their collections in pamphlet form.

Caption Answer to ...

Using Historical Evidence

It showed that groups could peacefully force change by straining an institution's pocketbook.

3. ASSESS

Section 4 Review Answers

1. termination policy, see p. 763

2. (a) Jackie Robinson, see p. 760, (b) Thurgood Marshall, see p. 762, (c) Martin Luther King, Jr., see p. 762

3. (a) Thousands of African Americans had served their country during World War II and felt they had earned the right to equality. Hundreds of thousands now living in northern cities experienced a new sense of freedom. (b) Marches and boycotts.

Court. There a brilliant African American lawyer named **Thurgood Marshall** argued on behalf of Brown and against segregation in America's schools.

On May 17, 1954, in *Brown* v. *Board of Education of Topeka, Kansas,* the Supreme Court issued its ruling. It declared unanimously that "separate facilities are inherently unequal." The "separate but equal" doctrine was no longer permissible in public education. President Eisenhower, who privately disagreed with the *Brown* ruling, refused to take a stand, saying only that "the Supreme Court has spoken and I am sworn to uphold the constitutional processes in this country; I will obey." A year later, the Court ruled that local school boards should move to desegregate "with all deliberate speed."

The ruling in *Brown* v. *Board of Education* caused fear and angry resistance in many southern whites. The worst confrontation came at Central High School in Little Rock, Arkansas. Just before the start of the 1957 school year, Governor Orval Faubus declared that he could not keep order if integration occurred. He posted the Arkansas National Guard at the school, and guardsmen turned away nine African American students who tried to enter.

Eisenhower could no longer avoid the issue of segregation. Faubus's actions were a direct challenge to the Constitution and to his own authority as President. Eisenhower therefore placed the National Guard under federal command. With paratroopers and other soldiers on guard in Arkansas to protect the nine African American children, the long, slow process of school integration began. ✪

The Montgomery Bus Boycott

In December 1955, in Montgomery, Alabama, Rosa Parks, a seamstress who had been secretary of the Montgomery NAACP for twelve years, took a seat in the middle section of a bus, where both African Americans and whites usually were allowed to sit. When a white man got on at the next stop and had no seat, however, the bus driver ordered Parks to give up hers. She refused. Even when threatened with arrest, she held her ground. At the next stop, police seized her and ordered her to stand trial for violating the segregation laws.

African American civil rights officials in Montgomery made the most of the incident. Fifty African American leaders met and, after Jo Ann Robinson of the Women's Political Council (WPC) suggested the idea, decided to organize a boycott of the entire bus system. Robinson and other members of the WPC wrote and distributed leaflets announcing the boycott. **Martin Luther King, Jr.,** the twenty-six-year-old minister of the Baptist church where the original boycott meeting took place, eventually became the spokesperson for the protest movement. He proclaimed:

> There comes a time when people get tired . . . tired of being segregated and humiliated, tired of being kicked about by the brutal feet of oppression. We have no alternative but to protest.

Using Historical Evidence These participants in the Montgomery bus boycott seemed not to mind getting a little wet as they walked to work. *How did the boycott demonstrate the effectiveness of applying economic pressure to promote social change?*

▶ RESOURCE DIRECTORY ✪

Teaching Resources

✪ **Primary Source Activity** Enforcing *Brown* v. *Board of Education,* found in the Unit 8 folder, p. 128, uses excerpts from an Eisenhower press conference in 1957 to illustrate the federal government's role in enforcing the integration of public schools in the South.

American Profiles Activity Maria Latigo Hernandez and Pedro Hernandez, found in the Unit 8 folder, p. 121, profiles two Mexican immigrants who sought relief in the United States from Mexico's famine and chaos in the early twentieth century.

The morning of the first day of the boycott, King prowled the streets of Montgomery anxiously to see how many African Americans would participate. Here are excerpts from his account of that morning:

During the rush hours the sidewalks were crowded with laborers and domestic workers, many of them well past middle age, trudging patiently to their jobs and home again, sometimes as much as twelve miles. They knew why they walked, and the knowledge was evident in the way they carried themselves. And as I watched them I knew that there is nothing more majestic than the determined courage of individuals willing to suffer and sacrifice for their freedom and dignity.

Over the next year, fifty thousand African Americans in Montgomery walked, rode bicycles, or joined car pools to avoid the city buses. Despite losing money, the bus company refused to change its policies. Finally, the Supreme Court ruled that bus segregation, like school segregation, was unconstitutional.

The Montgomery bus boycott produced a new generation of leaders in the African American community, particularly Martin Luther King, Jr. In addition, it introduced nonviolent protest as a means of achieving equality for minority groups in the United States.

Other Voices of Protest

⭐ Mexican Americans also demanded equal rights after World War II. A court case in Texas involving a funeral home that refused to bury a Mexican American war casualty led to the soldier's burial in Arlington National Cemetery in Washington, D.C. Groups like the Community Service Organization and the Asociación Nacional México-Americana found that peaceful protest could slowly bring about some of the results Mexican Americans desired.

Native Americans faced discrimination unique to their situation. The federal government managed the reservations where most Native Americans lived. In 1953, however, the government adopted a new approach, known as "termination," which sought to eliminate Native American reservations altogether. The administration used its **termination policy** to promote assimilation of Native Americans into the mainstream of American life.

Such assimilation did more harm than good. A 1954 Seminole petition to President Eisenhower eloquently stated the Native Americans' pride in their heritage:

We are not White Men but Indians, do not wish to become White Men but wish to remain Indians, and have an outlook on all things different from the outlook of the White Man.

In time the federal government discarded the termination policy. Yet the problems of the Native Americans remained: poverty, discrimination, and little real political representation. For Native Americans, the civil rights advances of the 1950s were mere tokens of the real gains that were needed.

This young protester was part of a 1958 Tuscarora picket in New York. The Native Americans were attempting to block a state power project on their reservation.

SECTION 4 REVIEW

Key Terms, People, and Places
1. Define termination policy.
2. Identify (a) Jackie Robinson, (b) Thurgood Marshall, (c) Martin Luther King, Jr.

Key Concepts
3. (a) For what reasons did the civil rights movement accelerate after World War II? (b) What avenues of protest did civil rights activists use in their struggle?

4. What was the principle behind the Supreme Court's ruling in *Brown* v. *Board of Education?*
5. How did Mexican Americans and Native Americans assert their rights in the 1950s?

Critical Thinking
6. **Determining Relevance** Why did Eisenhower feel bound to respond to the use of the National Guard to prevent school integration in Little Rock?

 Quiz found in the Unit 8 folder, p. 115, covers the main ideas in this section as well as the key terms.

 Chapter Test Forms A and B are found in the Unit 8 folder, pp. 134–139.

 Answer Keys found in the Unit 8 folder, pp. 146–158, provide answers to all student activities.

Media and Technology

Transparency
Graphic Organizer, G-2

Guided Reading Audiotapes
(English and Spanish)

Computer Test Bank

---

4. The main principle underlying the decision was that there can be no such thing as "separate but equal"; segregated facilities are by definition not equal.

5. Mexican American groups used peaceful protest to demand equal rights. Native Americans protested the federal government's termination policy, which threatened to destroy their culture, and eventually the policy was abandoned.

6. Eisenhower believed it was his duty as President to uphold constitutional processes, including enforcement of Supreme Court decisions. The Court had ordered integration of public schools, but Faubus used his state's resources to block the Court's ruling. Eisenhower was therefore forced to respond to Faubus's challenge.

Reteach

Ask students to use the information in the section to correct each of these following incorrect statements.
● The civil rights movement slowed after World War II.
● In *Brown* v. *Board of Education* the Supreme Court ruled that separate schools for African Americans were constitutional.
● The Montgomery bus boycott introduced Jackie Robinson as a new leader of the civil rights movement.
● The purpose of the termination policy of the federal government was to end the demands of Native Americans for advances in civil rights.

4. CLOSE

Reinforcing the Big Idea

The civil rights movement accelerated quickly following World War II. African Americans worked for their rights through the courts and on the streets in nonviolent protests, and other minority groups also began to demand equal rights.

The Decision to Integrate Major League Baseball

Focus Branch Rickey's decision to hire Jackie Robinson for the Brooklyn Dodgers, integrating major league baseball, preceded the great civil rights struggles of the 1950s and 1960s. However, as the English believed that "The battle of Waterloo was won on the playing fields of Eton," so some part of the civil rights struggle was won on the ball diamonds, courts, and fields of this nation.

Robinson signed with the Dodgers in 1945. In 1946 he played with the Montreal Royals, a Dodgers' farm team, against the New York Giants. It was the Giants' first game since the end of the war. Robinson grounded out his first time at bat. His second time up, he hit a home run over the left-field fence.

Instruct Ask students to review Rickey's options, to integrate or not, and to speculate about the results of each option in both the long and short term.

Ask students to list the circumstances that came together to make Rickey's decision possible, starting with Rickey himself. (*Rickey's motivation to integrate big league baseball, his ability to hire Robinson, Robinson's spectacular ability, willingness to sign on, and ability to withstand abuse.*)

Extend Ask students to find out when other sports were integrated, including professional football, basketball, and the United States Davis Cup tennis team. Have students examine issues of racial barriers today, including the lack of African American football coaches, sport executives, and team owners.

The Decision to Integrate Major League Baseball

Time Frame	1945
Place	New York City
Key People	Branch Rickey, general manager of the Brooklyn Dodgers baseball team, and Jackie Robinson, an African American athlete
Situation	Branch Rickey wanted to hire the first African American baseball player in the major leagues and prove that integration was possible. His decision could further African American civil rights in sports and other areas.

Unbelievable as it may seem today, in 1945 African American baseball players were not allowed to play in the major leagues. Many people at the time were beginning to fight for African American civil rights, and the situation in professional baseball attracted their attention. African Americans pointed with pride to athletes like Joe Louis, who was the world heavyweight boxing champion, and Jesse Owens, who won an unprecedented four gold medals in track and field in the 1936 Olympic games. Civil rights activists wanted to see the integration of baseball as well. Branch Rickey, the general manager of the Brooklyn Dodgers, recognized the possibilities integration offered to baseball. Jackie Robinson, a spectacular African American athlete from California, was the man Rickey identified as he considered his options. Rickey began to wonder whether the time had come to end segregation in baseball. As he considered the sensitive issue of integration, Rickey could have chosen any one of several possible avenues.

To Integrate or Not, and If So, How?

One possible avenue Rickey could have chosen was to drop the idea of integrating the major leagues altogether. Although baseball commissioner Kenesaw Mountain Landis declared in 1942 that "There is no rule, formal or informal, or any understanding—unwritten, subterranean, or sub-anything—against the hiring of Negro players by the teams of organized ball," baseball remained rigidly segregated. Most owners and other leaders of the game wanted to keep it that way. Many white Americans agreed.

Another option was to try to enlist the support of other teams before attempting to hire an African American player. Rather than working alone, Rickey knew that persuading other important baseball figures of the merits of opening the major leagues to African Americans would make it more likely that integration would succeed.

A third option was to find a superb African American athlete, such as Robinson, who could endure the taunts and jeers he was certain to receive when he took the field, and to work with him to show other teams—and American society as a whole—that integrated baseball could work.

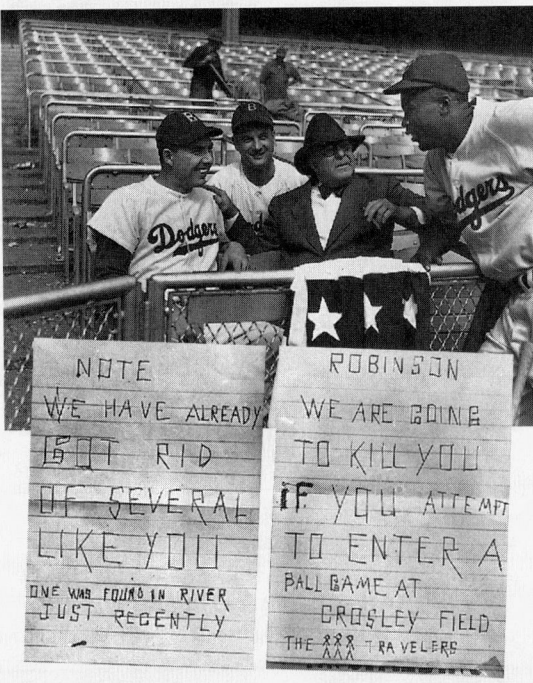

NOTE
WE HAVE ALREADY
GOT RID
OF SEVERAL
LIKE YOU
ONE WAS FOUND IN RIVER
JUST RECENTLY

ROBINSON
WE ARE GOING
TO KILL YOU
IF YOU ATTEMPT
TO ENTER A
BALL GAME AT
CROSLEY FIELD
THE XXX TRAVELERS

▶ RESOURCE DIRECTORY

Teaching Resources

 History Might Not . . . Activity
Decision Making: Integrating the University of Georgia, found in the Unit 8 folder, pp. 116–117, provides students an opportunity to role-play decision makers and those who influenced them in the decision of Charlayne Hunter and Hamilton Holmes to push for admittance to, and thus integration of, the University of Georgia.

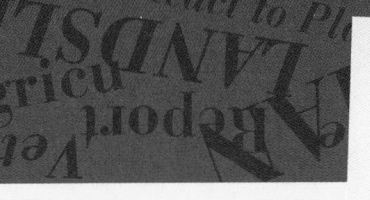

Possible Repercussions

Rickey knew that the safest course was to leave the situation alone and abandon the idea of integration. Major league baseball was prospering, and many people were reluctant to rock the boat. African American players had their own Negro Leagues, such people reasoned, so they had a chance to play. Taking no action was the best way to ensure stability on the field.

Seeking support from other teams, Rickey believed, would backfire. Baseball commissioner Landis and other top officials already had derailed the efforts of Bill Veeck, Jr., the bold young son of the former president of the Chicago Cubs, to buy the Philadelphia Phillies and hire black players. The more people who were involved, the more likely any integration plan was to fail.

Rickey also realized that the final option, simply hiring Jackie Robinson, might well erupt in violence both on and off the field. White ballplayers might refuse to play with Robinson. Fans might stay away from the game. Robinson himself might be hurt.

Rickey's Decision

Rickey decided that he would take what was in some ways the riskiest option: he would hire Jackie Robinson to play for the Brooklyn Dodgers.

Rickey called Robinson into his office on August 28, 1945 and told the ballplayer of his plan. Then, in a calculated move to test how Robinson would respond to the pressure he was likely to face, Rickey acted the part of those who might try to discourage him. He roared insults at Robinson, abused him, and threatened him with violence. "Mr. Rickey," Robinson finally said, "do you want a ballplayer who's afraid to fight back?" Rickey answered, "I want a player with guts enough not to fight back."

Rickey's decision paid off. Robinson played first for the Montreal Royals, a minor league team, then joined the Brooklyn Dodgers to become the first African Ameri-

Goal	To integrate major league baseball		
Possible Actions	Do nothing and hope integration would eventually take place	Enlist the support of other baseball teams	Hire an African American player
Possible Results	• Continue the tradition of segregated baseball, as integration was not likely to occur without some major impetus	• Unlikely to succeed in integrating the major leagues, because strong resistance to integration existed in the baseball community	• Might convince baseball leaders and society in general that integration could work, but might lead to violence both on and off the field

can to play in the major leagues. The photograph at left shows Rickey, seated and wearing a suit, and Robinson (far right). At first, he did have to endure much abuse, including threatening letters like the one on page 764. Robinson's wife, Rachel, worried about him:

> *At the end of his first season in baseball, I became extremely worried about Jack. I knew nobody could go along day after day, week after week, month after month bottling up his emotion. . . . He couldn't eat, and at night he'd toss constantly in his sleep. . . . But Jack wouldn't give it up.*

Robinson's bravery and Branch Rickey's willingness to take a chance paved the way for future African American baseball players.

EVALUATING DECISIONS

1. Why did Branch Rickey choose not to work with other teams in bringing African Americans into major league baseball?
2. What did Rickey want Jackie Robinson to do when taunted by other players and fans?

Critical Thinking

3. **Predicting Consequences** What do you think Rickey hoped would happen if Jackie Robinson proved to be a success? What might have happened if he had failed?

Media and Technology

Visions of America: History Might Not Have Happened This Way Game

To encourage students to explore pivotal moments in United States history, have students use the Visions of America software. Refer to the Visions of America Guidebook for viewing objectives, activities, game instructions, and discussion questions.

Chapter Review

Chapter Review Answers

Understanding Key Terms, People, and Places

Terms

Students should refer to the definitions of key terms in the chapter to create sentences which show an understanding of their relation to the postwar years in the United States.

True or False

1. false, termination policy
2. false, franchises
3. true
4. false, real purchasing power
5. false, modern republicanism

Matching

1. Thurgood Marshall
2. Adlai Stevenson
3. Richard M. Nixon
4. William J. Levitt
5. Betty Friedan

Reviewing Main Ideas

1. After the war, people who had put their money into savings were eager to buy everything that the war and the Depression had denied them. In addition, new technological advances spurred the economy.

2. After the war, giant corporations organized themselves into diversified conglomerates. In addition, franchises began to flourish.

3. The work force shifted from a blue-collar to a white-collar majority. This change occurred because machines now did the work once done by people; thus fewer people were needed to produce goods and instead performed services.

4. The middle class generally valued comfort, security, and conformity.

5. *Life* magazine produced a special edition featuring a happy housewife. Benjamin Spock advised mothers to remain home with their children. Adlai Stevenson told female college students that their "assignment" was to care for children and to cook.

6. Beatniks challenged traditional patterns of respectability. Authors J. D. Salinger and Jack Kerouac wrote novels whose themes challenged 1950s conformity.

7. Truman's first priority was to accomplish the transition from wartime to peacetime by bringing soldiers home from abroad and lifting controls on the economy.

8. Truman was concerned about controlling inflation, and he believed that wage increases demanded by workers would inflate the prices of consumer goods.

766

Understanding Key Terms, People, and Places

Key Terms
1. per capita income
2. real purchasing power
3. diversified conglomerate
4. franchise
5. agribusiness
6. baby boom
7. GI Bill
8. beatniks
9. Taft-Hartley Act
10. modern republicanism
11. *Sputnik*
12. termination policy

People
13. William J. Levitt
14. Benjamin Spock
15. Betty Friedan
16. J. D. Salinger
17. Adlai Stevenson
18. Richard M. Nixon
19. Jackie Robinson
20. Thurgood Marshall
21. Martin Luther King, Jr.

Terms For each term above, write a sentence that explains its relation to the postwar years in the United States.

True or False Determine whether each statement is true or false. If it is true, write "true." If it is false, change the underlined term to make the statement true.
1. The <u>Taft-Hartley Act</u> sought to eliminate Native American reservations.
2. Ray Kroc started the first <u>diversified conglomerate</u>.
3. The launching of <u>Sputnik</u> embarrassed the United States, which viewed itself as the world's greatest scientific power.
4. <u>Per capita income</u>, what people actually could buy with their money, grew by about 22 percent in the postwar period.
5. President Eisenhower called his approach to government <u>agribusiness</u>.

Matching Review the key people listed above. If you are not sure of a person's significance, review his or her importance in the chapter. Then choose a name from the list that best matches each description below.
1. African American lawyer who argued on the side of Oliver Brown in *Brown* v. *Board of Education*
2. Democratic candidate for President in 1952 and 1956
3. accused of receiving illegal gifts from political friends
4. pioneered mass-production techniques in home building
5. author of a book that criticized society for limiting the roles of women

Reviewing Main Ideas

Section 1 (pp. 742–746)
1. Why did the United States economy grow so rapidly after World War II?
2. What changes occurred in American business after the war?
3. What changes took place in the work force after World War II? What accounts for this change?

Section 2 (pp. 748–751)
4. What values did middle-class Americans cherish most during the 1950s?
5. Give examples showing how the media fostered expectations about the proper role of women.
6. What challenges to the rigid expectations of the period arose during the 1950s?

Section 3 (pp. 754–759)
7. What was President Truman's first priority after World War II?
8. Why did Truman oppose the demand of labor for higher wages?
9. What were Eisenhower's goals for the presidency? How successful was he in achieving these goals?

Section 4 (pp. 760–763)
10. What steps did President Truman take that helped African Americans achieve racial justice?
11. How did African Americans use the courts and nonviolent protest in their battle for equality?
12. Why did Native Americans protest against the federal government's termination policy in the 1950s?

9. Eisenhower wanted to cut spending, reduce taxes, and balance the budget. He was largely unsuccessful in achieving these goals, because his cuts in government spending caused the economy to slump.

10. Truman banned discrimination in the hiring of federal employees and ordered an end to segregation and discrimination in the military.

11. The NAACP launched a series of court cases that culminated in the Supreme Court's *Brown* v. *Board of Education* decision overturning the "separate but equal" doctrine. African Americans also successfully used nonviolent protest in the Montgomery bus boycott.

12. The federal government's termination policy promoted the assimilation of Native Americans and in the process undermined their tribal society.

Thinking Critically

1. Answers will vary. Students may point out that television has been blamed for such problems as obesity, violence, and consumerism; computers have become ordinary elements of daily life, changing the nature of work and recreation; and atomic weapons have altered whole generations' outlooks on the future.

2. Positive effects include a higher standard of living for more people. Negative effects include materialism and preoccupation with wealth.

1. Demonstrating Reasoned Judgment Which technological advance of the 1950s—atomic energy, computers, or television—do you think has had the most far-reaching impact on the way Americans live? Explain why you think so.

2. Drawing Conclusions During the 1950s the United States became, in the words of economist John Kenneth Galbraith, "the affluent society." What might be some of the consequences, both positive and negative, of this abundance?

3. Making Comparisons During the 1990s many politicians, religious leaders, and ordinary citizens have called for a return to "family values." What do these family values have in common with the values of the 1950s?

4. Predicting Consequences In 1957, the launch of the Soviet satellite *Sputnik* jolted Americans' sense of stability and security. Do you think that a major scientific breakthrough by another nation would have the same effect today?

1. Evaluating Primary Sources Review the primary source excerpt on page 763. What assumptions did the federal government make when it created the termination policy to promote Native American assimilation into mainstream American culture?

2. Understanding the Visuals Examine the visuals on pages 742, 745, and 746 and describe how the issues represented may have contributed to the dilemma faced by women in the 1950s.

3. Writing About the Chapter You have read that in 1956, *Life* magazine published a photo essay titled "Busy Wife's Achievements" about a happy full-time mother of four. Write the text for a *Life* magazine photo essay about a working mother's life in the 1990s. First make a list describing some of the activities in a typical working mother's day, noting her job, number of chil-

dren, and responsibilities. Next, write a draft of your essay in which you describe the typical working mother today, including her achievements and the challenges she faces. Revise your essay, making certain that each idea is clearly explained. Proofread your essay and draft a final copy. If you wish, you may include ideas for photos and captions to accompany the text.

4. Using the Graphic Organizer This graphic organizer uses a double web to compare and contrast the presidencies of Harry Truman and Dwight Eisenhower. (a) Based on the information in the web, how were Truman and Eisenhower similar as Presidents? (b) How does the web contrast Truman's personality with Eisenhower's? (c) Create your own graphic organizer comparing and contrasting the concerns of men and women in the 1950s.

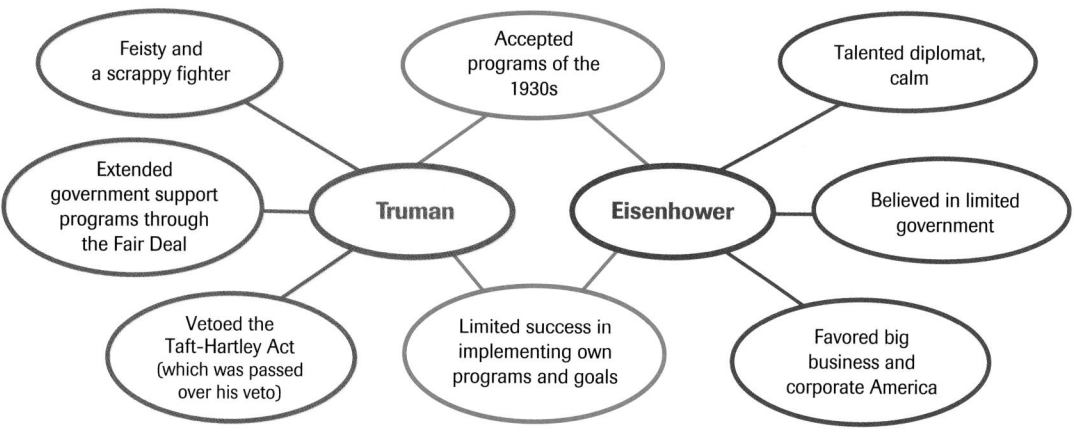

Truman
- Feisty and a scrappy fighter
- Extended government support programs through the Fair Deal
- Vetoed the Taft-Hartley Act (which was passed over his veto)
- Accepted programs of the 1930s
- Limited success in implementing own programs and goals

Eisenhower
- Talented diplomat, calm
- Believed in limited government
- Favored big business and corporate America

---

3. "Family values" share with some 1950s values the notion that women should stay at home as full-time mothers, emphasizing the well-being of children and the importance of religion.

4. Answers will vary. Students may point out that since the end of the cold war has opened the global marketplace for ideas and technology, a major scientific breakthrough by another country today would not only be less devastating than *Sputnik*, it would probably be a positive development.

Making Connections

1. The federal government assumed that Native Americans wanted to give up their culture and be like "white men."

2. The images depict suburban houses and an increasing birth rate, representing home and family, which women were supposed to consider their sole domain, even though many had held jobs during the war; increased consumer spending also presented women with a dilemma, since without a job they could not make money of their own.

3. Students' essays should show an awareness of the complexity and stresses of the lives of many women today as they struggle to balance work and family responsibilities.

4. (a) Both embraced the programs of the 1930s but had some difficulty implementing their own programs. (b) Whereas Truman was a scrappy fighter in the political arena, Eisenhower was diplomatic and affable. (c) Students' graphic organizers should indicate that men and women shared the values of home and family and the acquisition of material goods, although their roles were very different.

 Alternative Assessment

Final Evaluation
Use the following guidelines to evaluate student projects:

● **Evidence of mastery of content** To what extent do the projects demonstrate knowledge and understanding of chapter content?

● **Evidence of thoughtfulness** To what extent do the projects present a personal assessment of the period with evidence to support it?

● **Evidence of outside research** To what extent are the projects based on materials and information from outside research materials?

● **Communication style** Do the projects convey a purpose in a clear appealing way?

Introducing the Unit

Interpreting the Visual The 1960s and early 1970s were years of unrest and change. John F. Kennedy's inauguration as President marked the political shift of a new generation. His words on page 768 form a concise summary of the nation's mood over the next two decades. Many Americans, determined to reform the nation, worked to bring change quickly; other Americans resisted their efforts. The energy and confidence of the marchers in the photograph reprinted on pages 768–769 constitute an apt image for the spirit and determination of the civil rights movement, the first of the social struggles of the sixties.

John Lewis, one of the marchers at Selma, recalls his feelings in these words: "You didn't get tired, you really didn't get weary, you had to go. It was more than an ordinary march. . . . It was the sense of community moving there."

Ask students to think of a title for this photograph that appropriately conveys its mood and feeling.

Establishing Chronology Remind students that the previous chapter focused on the postwar years at home. This unit covers the tumultuous years from 1960 to 1975. From 1960 to 1968, a strong civil rights movement worked for equality at home, equality which the previous generation of African Americans had hoped to gain after their valiant participation in World War II. From 1960 to 1975, other movements for social change emerged. The Vietnam War defined these years by challenging the nation's military ability and by leading antiwar activists to challenge the nation's values.

UNIT 9

The Upheaval of the Sixties
1960–1975

"Today our concern must be with the future. For the world is changing. The old era is ending. The old ways will not do."
—John F. Kennedy, 1960

When John F. Kennedy became President in 1961, Americans sensed a new era was dawning. Buoyed by the promise of change, African Americans pushed hard to end a century of inequality. Inspired by the civil rights movement, women, Latinos, Native Americans, and others also pressed for equality. Although much progress was achieved in the sixties, the promise that began this turbulent decade was shattered by a series of assassinations, a wave of urban riots, and a controversial war in Southeast Asia.

RESOURCE DIRECTORY

Teaching Resources

 Local History Activity "The Second Battle of Atlanta" and the Local Focus research topic suggestions, found in the Local History Resources folder, pp. 27–29, are designed to help students understand how history affects all lives.

★ **Themes in American History Posters** Wall-size, illustrated posters, found in the Teaching Resources package, illustrate the four unit themes.

Unit Test Forms A and B are found in the Unit 9 folder, pp. 140–145.

Inspired by the righteousness of their cause, civil rights workers march toward a better future in this 1965 voter registration drive in Selma, Alabama.

Media and Technology

Visions of America: Scenes of an Era To introduce students to the main idea and events covered in this unit, play "Scenes of an Era: The Upheaval of the Sixties" (length: 2.5 minutes). This selection can be located on side 4 of the videodiscs. This selection can also be located on videotape 5. Lesson plans for "Scenes of an Era" can be found in the Visions of America Guidebook.

Using Multimedia Technology This folder contains instructional tools and strategies for using technology in the classroom.

Transparency Binder Contains full-color transparencies with lesson suggestions. From a large collection divided into twelve categories, specific transparencies are referenced throughout the chapters at appropriate points of use. For this unit, see American Photo, B-9; Our Multicultural Heritage, C-15; Fine Art, D-20; Links Across Time, J-9; and Political Cartoon, K-9.

Themes in American History

Teachers may wish to discuss specific historical events in the context of historical themes. Here are four suggestions for Unit 9.

Reform Movements *People in the United States have frequently taken action in grass roots movements to right perceived wrongs and to secure improvements in the quality of life.*

- African Americans used the courts and nonviolent protests to win reforms.
- The women's movement urged the end of all discrimination based on gender.

Environment *The geography and available resources of the continent have affected the actions of Americans. Similarly, the actions of Americans have affected the environment and physical landscape.*

- Rachel Carson's book *Silent Spring* spurred the modern environmental movement.
- The Environmental Protection Agency (EPA) was established by Congress to be the nation's watchdog against polluters.

American Culture *In every period of their history, Americans gave special expression to their views through art, literature, films, music, manners, and morals.*

- The 1950s saw the growth of suburbs and consumerism—the purchase of consumer goods to achieve success and status.
- The counterculture in the 1960s and early 1970s advanced new attitudes about personal relationships, drugs, and music.

The United States and the World *America's relationships with other countries have been influenced at different times by a sense of mission, by values, and by self-interest.*

- During the Cuban missile crisis, the world came closer than ever before to nuclear war.
- The United States became involved in Vietnam in an effort to contain communism, but soon became bogged down in a war that American citizens did not understand.

Chapter 28 The Kennedy and Johnson Years
1960–1968

📁 Teaching Resources (See Unit 9 Folder)

	Instruction	Enrichment
Section 1 **The New Frontier** (pp. 772–775)	Reproducible Lesson Plan, p. 3 Alternate Lesson Plan, p. 142 Guided Reading and Review, p. 6 Quiz, p. 7	Visual Learning Activity, Creating Images of the Candidates, p. 26 American Profiles Activity, Dr. Frances Kelsey, p. 14 Literature Activity, A Grieving Nation, pp. 23–24 Historian's Toolbox Activity, Exploring Oral History, p. 18
Section 2 **The Great Society** (pp. 777–781)	Reproducible Lesson Plan, p. 4 Alternate Lesson Plan, p. 143 Guided Reading and Review, p. 8 Quiz, p. 9	Primary Source Activity, President Johnson's Thanksgiving Address, p. 20 Critical Thinking Activity, Recognizing Cause and Effect, p. 19 Visual Learning Activity, The Job Corps, p. 27 Literature Activity, The Invisible Poor, p. 25 History Might Not . . . Activity, Building an International Manned Space Station, pp. 12–13
Section 3 **Foreign Policy in the 1960s** (pp. 784–791)	Reproducible Lesson Plan, p. 5 Alternate Lesson Plan, p. 144 Guided Reading and Review, p. 10 Quiz, p. 11 Chapter Test, Forms A & B, pp. 28–33	Primary Source Activity, Cuban Missile Crisis, pp. 21–22 American Profiles Activity, Robert F. Kennedy, p. 15 Viewpoints Activity, On the Cold War, pp. 16–17

📁 Additional Chapter Resources

Resource Organizer, p. 2
Alternate Lesson Plan, p. 141
Answer Keys, pp. 146–160

Bibliography

For the Teacher

Hodgson, Godfrey. *America in Our Time: From World War II to Nixon, What Happened and Why.* Vintage Books, 1976. (Includes the New Frontier, civil rights movement, and Vietnam.)

Miller, Merle. *Lyndon: An Oral Biography.* Ballantine, 1987. (Lyndon Johnson's presidency by people who knew him.)

Reeves, Richard. *President Kennedy: Profile of Power.* Simon & Schuster, 1993. (A study of Kennedy written thirty years after his death.)

White, Theodore H. *The Making of the President, 1960: A Narrative History of American Politics in Action.* Macmillan, 1988. (Comprehensive coverage of the 1960 presidential campaign of John F. Kennedy.)

Prentice Hall Literature Excerpts from *The American Experience*, 1994, "Contemporary Writers, 1946–Present."

The Big Idea for the chapter and how the main ideas in each section relate to the Big Idea are graphically displayed below. Comprehension of this chapter's Big Idea is critical to students' understanding of United States history and how we as a nation got where we are today.

Media and Technology

 Our Multicultural Heritage, C-3

 Critical Thinking, I-13

 Visions of America: History Might Not Have Happened This Way Game

 Graphic Organizer, G-4

 Guided Reading Audiotapes (English and Spanish)

 Computer Test Bank

For the Student

Brown, Claude. *Manchild in the Promised Land.* Macmillan, 1965. (Autobiography of an African American youth from poverty in Harlem to a law degree from Howard University.)

Kennedy, Robert F. *Thirteen Days.* Norton, 1971. (Gripping account of the Cuban missile crisis by the President's brother and closest adviser, who served as attorney general of the United States.)

Schlesinger, A. M., Jr. *A Thousand Days.* Houghton Mifflin, 1965. (The Kennedy presidency as viewed by members of the White House staff.)

CHAPTER 28

The contrast between the presidencies of John Kennedy and Lyndon Johnson is striking. While Kennedy articulated plans for domestic reform, few of his programs actually advanced through Congress, perhaps because he was preoccupied with foreign affairs. When Johnson took office after Kennedy's death, he used his legislative skills to push through Congress some of the most significant social programs in the nation's history.

SECTION 1

Young, energetic, and popular, President Kennedy proposed a New Frontier for the United States but was unable to move his program through Congress before his assassination.

SECTION 2

President Johnson hoped to create a "Great Society," and pushed an extraordinary number of social reform bills through Congress.

SECTION 3

Both Presidents Kennedy and Johnson continued to wage the cold war. Both Presidents reacted boldly to communist challenges, bringing the nation into serious confrontations and threatening world peace.

The Kennedy and Johnson Years
1960-1968

The Relevance of the Big Idea

For the baby-boom generation born right after World War II, the Kennedy style was full of youth, humor, and vigor. "For those who lived during his times," wrote journalist Richard Reeves, "Kennedy seemed to be the beginning of the new."

The promise of the new was actually fulfilled by Lyndon Johnson, who lacked Kennedy's appeal but had a style very much his own. A master builder of coalitions, he used these skills to pass some of the most lasting social legislation of this century—Medicare, the Voting Rights Act, the Civil Rights Act, Head Start, and many others.

Discuss with students the extent to which the Great Society legislation affects their lives.

In Depth

Global Connections

"From Korea to Berlin to Cuba to Vietnam, the Truman Doctrine governed America's response to the Communist world," was how Senator Fulbright explained the United States' foreign policy in the 1960s. By then, however, the economic position of the United States relative to the rest of the world was slowly declining. And the war-shattered Soviet Union had rebuilt its military strength, thus making it possible for the Soviets to challenge the United States in Cuba.

The Kennedy and Johnson Years
1960-1968

Our 35th PRESIDENT John F. KENNEDY

*B*old phrases such as "the New Frontier" and "the Great Society" captured the spirit of optimism that energized the United States in the early 1960s. John F. Kennedy, the youngest President ever elected, promised vigorous leadership. His focus on cold war politics and problems with an uncompromising Congress, however, left little room for domestic reform. Kennedy's successor, Lyndon Johnson, did more to help Americans at home. He rallied Congress and the country behind the most ambitious social program since the New Deal of the 1930s. Johnson's foreign policy, based on the assumption that communists were determined to take over the world, led the nation into conflicts with other countries.

Events in the United States

1960	1961	1962	1963
1960 John F. Kennedy and Richard Nixon appear in the first televised presidential debates.	1961 President Kennedy establishes the Peace Corps. • Bay of Pigs invasion in Cuba fails.	1962 The Cuban missile crisis occurs.	1963 President Kennedy is assassinated. • Lyndon Johnson becomes President.

Events in the World

1960 The Soviets shoot down U.S. spy plane. • The Congo gains independence from Belgium.	1961 The Soviets build the Berlin Wall. • Soviet cosmonaut is first to orbit the earth.		

▶ RESOURCE DIRECTORY

Teaching Resources

Alternate Lesson Plan: Demonstrating the Big Idea found in the Alternate Lesson Plans folder, p. 141, provides a lesson strategy to instruct students about the Big Idea that Kennedy focused primarily on dealing with the cold war abroad while Johnson pushed a broad domestic agenda through Congress.

Alternative Assessment Handbook provides information, guidance, and strategies for alternative methods of assessment. It includes an essay on new trends in assessment, guidance and strategies for developing performance tasks and portfolios, scoring rubrics, and sample evaluation forms.

Pages 772–775
The New Frontier

President John F. Kennedy's first years in office did not bear the legislative fruit he promised in his inspiring campaign speeches. More interested in foreign affairs than in affairs at home, Kennedy did not shepherd his proposals along the legislative path. Congress, which fought him at every step, contributed to the lack of progress.

 Pages 777–781
The Great Society

Lyndon Johnson picked up the domestic agenda after John Kennedy's death. In the greatest triumph of social legislation since Franklin Roosevelt's New Deal, he launched a remarkable reform program that offered something for everyone and for a time promised to ease the inequalities in American life.

 Pages 784–791
Foreign Policy in the 1960s

The drama and seriousness of events on the world stage beckoned Kennedy more than did the problems at home. He performed boldly on several foreign policy issues, with decisions grounded in familiar cold war assumptions about the intentions of the Soviet Union. When Johnson took office, he saw foreign affairs as something of a nuisance, but continued Kennedy's policies.

Timeline:

1964 Congress passes the Civil Rights Act.

1965 Congress passes the Voting Rights Act and establishes Medicare and Medicaid.

1966 Miranda v. Arizona ruling establishes that suspects must be informed of their rights before questioning.

1964	1965	1966	1967	1968

1964 Khrushchev is removed from power in the Soviet Union.
• The military leads coup in Brazil.

1965 Ferdinand Marcos becomes president of the Philippines.

1966 Chinese Cultural Revolution begins.
• Indira Gandhi becomes Indian prime minister.

1967 Israel defeats Arab states in Six-Day War.
• Civil war breaks out in Nigeria.

1968 Student uprising shakes France.
• The Soviet Union invades Czechoslovakia.

◆ Alternative Assessment

As an ongoing chapter project, students can compare the goals and achievements of the New Frontier with the goals and achievements of the Great Society, and express their own opinions on their findings. Students may wish to focus on comparisons of the cabinet and team of presidential advisers, or on the style and images of the two Presidents and their families. Students may design their projects in the formats suggested or create an original one.

• Make an audiotape of a simulated radio program consisting of interviews with historians and commentators.

• Create an article for a newsmagazine, entitled "Presidents of the 1960s in Review."

Explain that finished projects will be assessed according to the following standards:

• **Unacceptable** Projects are not attempted or fail to meet requirements outlined.

• **Limited/Acceptable** Projects are based on material from the textbook and reflect some effort to make and support comparisons and distinctions concerning the strengths and weaknesses of both Presidents.

• **Extensive/Commendable** Projects are based on some outside research, make and support broad comparisons and distinctions concerning the strengths and weaknesses of both Presidents, and reflect the student's own position.

• **Extraordinary/Outstanding** Projects are based on considerable outside research, make and support broad comparisons and distinctions concerning the strengths and weaknesses of both Presidents, and reflect a strong personal position.

For information and guidance on alternative assessment trends and strategies, see the Alternative Assessment Handbook in the Resource Directory on page 770.

The New Frontier

Connecting to the Big Idea

See page 770B. During the close-fought election of 1960, John F. Kennedy promised new programs of reform. Ask what those programs were. Why did few of them make it through Congress?

Objectives

- Identify John F. Kennedy and describe his popular image.
- Describe Kennedy's proposed domestic program, including a tax cut, the space program, and direct aid to the poor.
- Explain why Kennedy's legislative proposals on domestic policy suffered defeat in Congress.

Bellringer

Ask students to imagine a political campaign for President waged without television appearances, interviews, or campaign commercials. How would voters learn about the candidates? What do voters learn about candidates from television? How valuable is this information?

Reading Strategy

Structured Overview Ask students to write two column headings on a piece of paper: Kennedy's Image and Kennedy's Actual Domestic Accomplishments. Ask students to take notes in the appropriate column as they read the section.

The New Frontier

SECTION PREVIEW

President John F. Kennedy's first years in office did not bear the legislative fruit he promised in his inspiring campaign speeches. More interested in foreign affairs than in affairs at home, Kennedy did not shepherd his proposals along the legislative path. Congress, which fought him at every step, contributed to the lack of progress.

Key Concepts

- The youthful President Kennedy created a popular image that appealed to Americans eager for change.
- Kennedy's program included the space program, a tax cut to restore prosperity, and, near the end of his presidency, direct aid to the poor.
- Kennedy's legislative proposals on domestic policy suffered defeat in Congress.

Key Terms, People, and Places

liberal consensus, mandate, New Frontier, Warren Commission; John F. Kennedy, Earl Warren

Images of the new President and his family flooded popular culture in the early 1960s, appearing even in board games such as the one shown above.

President Eisenhower had steered the nation along a moderate course through the 1950s. In an era of conformity, the popular Eisenhower had presided over a consensus, or general agreement, within the government that the United States was in good shape.

When **John F. Kennedy** took office, he adopted this **liberal consensus** view. According to this view, held by many in government and the public, capitalism was the best economic system and the United States was threatened more by communism abroad than by domestic problems such as poverty and racial injustice. Only at the end of his time in office, when he could no longer ignore the signs that the fabric of American society was being torn apart, did Kennedy earnestly move toward addressing these domestic problems.

The Election of 1960

Kennedy, a Massachusetts Democrat who had served in the United States House of Representatives and Senate, faced serious obstacles in his quest for the presidency. He was only forty-three years old, and many questioned whether he had the experience needed for the nation's highest office. His Roman Catholic religion also seemed a potential problem to some. No Catholic had ever been elected President, and some feared he would be controlled by the Catholic church in Rome. Kennedy defused the religion issue in the primary campaign, when he won in the largely Protestant state of West Virginia. With that hurdle behind him, he campaigned hard, with promises to spur the sluggish economy. During the Eisenhower administration, the Gross National Product (GNP) had grown very slowly, and the economy had suffered several recessions. Kennedy proclaimed that it was time to "get America moving again."

⭐ Television played a key role in the election. Kennedy and Republican candidate Richard Nixon, who was Eisenhower's Vice President, squared off in the first televised debates ever held. Television sets now glowed in a majority of American households, and the debates made a major difference in the outcome of the election. Both candidates expressed their views well, but Kennedy, who had hired professional television consultants to help him with makeup and clothes, looked more polished and relaxed. While Nixon looked out at the studio audience, Kennedy looked directly at the camera and thus into the eyes of every television viewer. At the end of the first debate, momentum had shifted Kennedy's way. A CBS poll estimated that 57 percent of the people voting in November felt that the debates had affected their choice.

RESOURCE DIRECTORY

Teaching Resources

📄 **Reproducible Lesson Plan** found in the Unit 9 folder, p. 3, provides a summary of the Section 1 lesson plan content.

📄 **Alternate Lesson Plan: Learning Styles** found in the Alternate Lesson Plans folder, p. 142, is especially useful for visual or tactile learners and is designed to help students identify reasons for Kennedy's popularity and explain the New Frontier program.

📄 **Guided Reading and Review** found in the Unit 9 folder, p. 6, provides a structure for reading and mastering the key concepts and reviewing the key terms for Section 1. (Guided Practice)

⭐ 📄 **Visual Learning Activity** Creating Images of the Candidates, found in the Unit 9 folder, p. 26, shows how the candidates in the 1960 presidential campaign tried to manipulate their images with buttons, T-shirts, and other items.

In the election, Kennedy won by an extraordinarily close margin. Though the electoral vote was 303 to 219, Kennedy won by only 120,000 popular votes out of more than 34 million cast. If but a few thousand voters in Illinois or Texas had cast ballots for Nixon, the Republicans would have won. The razor-thin victory would affect policy decisions when Kennedy took office. With only borderline support, he did not have a **mandate,** or the backing of voters, to push his more controversial measures through Congress.

The Promise of Camelot

No matter how slim his margin of victory, Kennedy was now President. In ringing phrases he declared in his inaugural address that "the torch has been passed to a new generation of Americans." He pledged the United States to defend the interests of western democracies at any cost:

> Let every nation know, whether it wishes us well or ill, that we shall pay any price, bear any burden, meet any hardship, support any friend, oppose any foe to assure the survival and the success of liberty.
> Inaugural Address, January 20, 1961

The new administration was buoyant and energetic. Jacqueline Kennedy, the President's attractive young wife, charmed the country with her grace. Nobel Prize winners visited the White House. The Kennedys and their friends loved to play touch football on the lawn or take long hikes. The administration, which seemed full of idealism and youth, earned the nickname Camelot after a 1960 Broadway musical that portrayed the legendary kingdom of the British king Arthur. Arthur dreamed of transforming medieval Britain from a country in which "might makes right"—or the strong always get their way—into one where might, or power, would be used to achieve right. The sentimental idealism of Broadway's *Camelot* seemed the perfect image for President Kennedy.

Jacqueline and John Kennedy dazzled the nation with their beauty, glamour, and youth.

MAKING CONNECTIONS

In what ways might an image of youthful energy help—and hurt—a new President?

Kennedy's Economic Program

In a speech early in his administration, Kennedy said that the nation was poised at the edge of a **New Frontier,** and the name stuck to the reform programs he proposed. The proposals focused on the economy, aid to the poor, and the space program.

Concerned about the continuing recession, Kennedy hoped to work with the business community to restore prosperity to the nation. Often, however, he faced resistance from executives who were suspicious of his plans. The worst fears of business leaders were realized in the spring of 1962. When the U.S. Steel Company announced that it was raising the price of steel by $6 a ton, other firms did the same. Worried about inflation, Kennedy called the price increase unjustifiable and charged that it showed "utter contempt for the public interest." He ordered a federal investigation into the possibility of price-fixing. Under that pressure, U.S. Steel and the other companies backed down. But business

Media and Technology

 Transparency
Our Multicultural Heritage, C-3

Explain/Discuss

Discuss the importance of a "mandate for change" for a reform-minded President. Ask how lack of such a mandate hampered Kennedy. Who were his opponents in Congress?

Ask which of the powers of the presidency Kennedy used to "encourage" U.S. Steel and other companies to comply with his voluntary limits on price hikes. What did this action reveal about Kennedy's view of the presidency? Students might compare JFK's handling of business interests such as U.S. Steel with Teddy Roosevelt's handling of the trusts.

Analyze

One way to analyze JFK's presidency is to evaluate his performance in each of these roles: chief of state; chief administrator; chief diplomat; commander in chief of the armed forces; chief legislator; leader of his political party; and representative of all the people. Ask students to find references to as many of the roles as they can in the section.

Answer to ...

MAKING CONNECTIONS

Such an image might give people a feeling of hope for progressive change, thus increasing the President's chances of public support for new programs. On the other hand, a young President might appear inexperienced or naive and thus lose public confidence.

Caption Answer to ...

 Interpreting Charts

Eighteen percent. The graph shows that most Americans were not wealthy; Harrington said that one fifth of the population could be classified as poor.

Activity

Cooperative Learning

Time: Two class periods.
Grouping: Groups of four to six students.
Activity: Create an oral history of the Kennedy assassination.

First day: preparation for interviews. Students should create a list of open-ended questions about people's memories of and reactions to Kennedy's assassination.

Outside class: interviews and preparation of finished project. Each group member should use the questions to interview one or two adults over the age of forty.

Second day: presentations. Students may present the results of their interviews in a magazine-type collage, or in the form of a television newsmagazine segment.
Purpose: To study the impact of the Kennedy assassination on the American public.
Roles: Interviewers, designers, writers, editor, broadcasters, director.
Outcome: Students will compile an oral history of the Kennedy assassination and understand its impact at the time.

Enrichment

Ask students to research and report on the folk revival in popular music in the early 1960s (focusing on artists such as Joan Baez and Bob Dylan) and its relation to increasing demands for social reform in the nation.

Caption Answer to ...

 Interpreting Graphs

About $800 million. After *Sputnik*, NASA funding increased significantly, because the United States wanted to remain competitive with the Soviets.

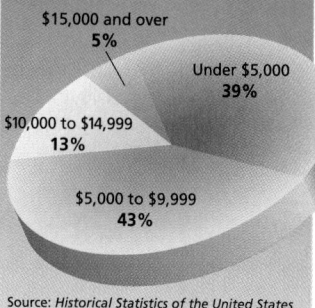

Distribution of Families, by Annual Income, 1962

- $15,000 and over **5%**
- $10,000 to $14,999 **13%**
- Under $5,000 **39%**
- $5,000 to $9,999 **43%**

Source: *Historical Statistics of the United States*

Interpreting Charts
What percentage of American families in 1962 had an annual income of $10,000 or more? How does the pie chart support what Michael Harrington wrote in The Other America?

---

leaders remained angry, and the stock market fell in the steepest drop since the Great Crash of 1929.

On the larger issue of ending the economic slump, Kennedy proposed cutting taxes. In 1963 the President called for a $13.5 billion cut in taxes over three years. The measure would reduce government income and create a budget deficit at first, but Kennedy believed that the extra cash in taxpayers' wallets would stimulate the economy and bring added tax revenues in the end. Many people, both conservative and liberal, vigorously opposed the policy. Economist John Kenneth Galbraith claimed that the deficit would cause frivolous spending without addressing serious national problems:

> I am not sure what the advantage is in having a few more dollars if the air is too dirty to breathe, the water too polluted to drink, the commuters are losing out on the struggle to get in and out of the cities, the streets are filthy, and the schools are so bad that the young, perhaps wisely, stay away, and hoodlums roll citizens for some of the dollars that they save in taxes.

The tax-cut proposal, like many others Kennedy made, was soon bottled up in a congressional committee and stood little chance of passage.

Kennedy also was eager to take action against poverty. In his first two years in office, Kennedy hoped that he could help the poor simply by stimulating the economy. With his privileged background, Kennedy was out of touch with the brutal realities of poverty. In 1962 author Michael Harrington publicized this problem in a book he called *The Other America*. Harrington revealed that while middle-class Americans were enjoying the prosperity of the 1950s, a shocking one fifth of the population was living below the poverty line. The chart at left shows income distribution in the United States in 1962. Kennedy, who had seen poverty firsthand during the 1960 campaign, read Harrington's book and realized that the situation demanded direct aid to the poor. Despite his concern, however, Kennedy acted to address the poverty problem too late in his presidency, and he never succeeded in pushing legislation through Congress.

Kennedy was more successful in his effort to breathe life into the space program. As astronaut Alan Shepard was launched 115 miles into space in 1961, Kennedy committed the United States to landing a man on the moon before the end of the decade. As the graph at left shows, Congress increased National Aeronautics and Space Administration (NASA) funding for this project.

Camelot in Perspective

⭐ Kennedy energized the country with his eloquent call for action, but his legislative record was mixed at best. Foreign policy, covered in Section 3, really concerned Kennedy the most, and his domestic vision was not as focused. He also wanted to avoid making enemies in Congress by pushing unpopular programs; such enemies might refuse to give him the votes he

---

Federal Funding of NASA* Research and Development, 1950–1965

Millions of Dollars (y-axis: 0, 1,000, 2,000, 3,000, 4,000, 5,000, 6,000)
Year (x-axis: 1950, 1953, 1956, 1959, 1962, 1965)

Launching of *Sputnik*, 1957

*National Aeronautics and Space Administration
Source: *Historical Statistics of the United States*

Interpreting Graphs
Approximately how much federal funding did NASA receive in 1961, the year Alan Shepard flew in space? How does the graph illustrate the influence of the Soviet Union's Sputnik on United States policy?

▶ RESOURCE DIRECTORY

Teaching Resources

⭐ **American Profiles Activity** found in the Unit 9 folder, p. 14, focuses on Dr. Frances Kelsey, whose struggle to prevent FDA approval of thalidomide, a drug later linked to severe birth defects, won her the Distinguished Civilian Service Medal from President Kennedy.

⭐ **Literature Activity** A Grieving Nation, found in the Unit 9 folder, pp. 23–24, features a detailed account of JFK's funeral from William Manchester's *Death of a President* to help students understand the impact of Kennedy's assassination throughout the nation and the world.

needed to progress on foreign policy. Kennedy's lack of experience as a legislative leader further eroded his effectiveness. Finally, the Congress, though Democratic, was determined to follow its own agenda and seemed to thwart Kennedy at every turn. For all these reasons, most of Kennedy's proposals died in Congress. Measures that did finally work their way into law, like a modest increase in the minimum wage, barely made a dent in the nation's problems.

The Nation Mourns Still, Kennedy pressed on. On November 22, 1963, as he looked ahead to reelection the following year, he went to Texas to mobilize support. As he rode through Dallas in an open car, shots rang out. Fatally wounded, President Kennedy was pronounced dead soon after his arrival at a nearby hospital.

The country was shattered. Jimmy Carter, a Georgia farmer who later became President, had just gotten down from his tractor when he heard the news: "I wept openly for the first time in ten years, for the first time since my own father died." Millions of Americans remained glued to their television sets for the next four days as the impact of the tragedy sank in. Just as members of an earlier generation remembered where they had been when the Japanese attacked Pearl Harbor, Americans would always recall vividly what they were doing in 1963 when they learned that their President had been shot. ✪

The Assassination Debate Shortly after Kennedy's death, a commission headed by Chief Justice **Earl Warren** was formed to investigate the crime. Despite the fact that the prime

suspect, Lee Harvey Oswald, was himself gunned down two days after Kennedy was killed, the **Warren Commission** declared that Oswald had worked alone in shooting the President. Since then, however, some people have argued that Oswald was involved in a larger conspiracy, and that he was killed in order to protect others who had helped plan Kennedy's murder.

For a time the assassination embellished the Kennedy myth. The myth began to fade with time, but Lyndon Johnson, who succeeded Kennedy as President, made good use of the spirit of hope and the desire for change that Kennedy had inspired. He saw enacted much of the legislation that his predecessor had failed to push through Congress.

Millions of Americans watched President Kennedy's funeral on television. *Inset: A Life* magazine cover shows Jacqueline Kennedy and her children during the funeral.

SECTION 1 REVIEW

Key Terms, People, and Places
1. Define (a) liberal consensus, (b) mandate, (c) New Frontier, (d) Warren Commission.
2. Identify (a) John F. Kennedy, (b) Earl Warren.

Key Concepts
3. How did President Kennedy hope to stimulate the economy?
4. Why was the Kennedy administration nicknamed Camelot?

5. (a) What did Kennedy try to accomplish in his domestic program? (b) How successful was he?

Critical Thinking
6. **Drawing Conclusions** Kennedy remarked that in the 1960 election, "it was TV more than anything else that turned the tide." Do you think that television may have given Kennedy an unfair advantage over Nixon, or did it provide voters with information they needed to make an intelligent decision?

Quiz found in the Unit 9 folder, p. 7, covers the main ideas in this section as well as the key terms.

3. ASSESS

Section 1 Review Answers

1. (a) liberal consensus, see p. 772, (b) mandate, see p. 773, (c) New Frontier, see p. 773, (d) Warren Commission, see p. 775

2. (a) John F. Kennedy, see p. 772, (b) Earl Warren, see p. 775

3. In 1963 Kennedy proposed cutting taxes by $13.5 billion over three years.

4. The youth, vigor, and idealism that the Kennedy administration exuded was compared with the idealistic and energetic reign of the legendary King Arthur, portrayed in the 1960 Broadway musical hit *Camelot*.

5. (a) Kennedy's domestic proposals focused on the economy, aid to the poor, and the space program. (b) With the exception of the space program, his record was not very successful at all. Most legislative proposals were stymied by Congress.

6. Possible answers: Kennedy did gain an unfair advantage because his skill in presenting himself to a television audience said little about his ability to govern; voters were able to see the candidates in an impromptu speaking situation and could evaluate how each performed under pressure.

Reteach

Ask students to correct the following incorrect statements.
- Kennedy defeated Nixon by a wide margin in 1960.
- Kennedy was able to move most of his New Frontier legislation through Congress.
- Kennedy was killed at the end of his fourth year as President.

4. CLOSE

Reinforcing the Big Idea

John F. Kennedy inspired and invigorated the nation, but he was unable to get many of his reform bills through Congress. The next section describes how Lyndon Johnson pushed much new legislation through Congress.

Historical Evidence

Exploring Oral History

Focus Students will analyze the content of oral history excerpts.

Instruct Ask students to work in groups to consider the following: Twenty Americans have been selected to answer questions about the presidency of John Kennedy. Ask each group to write questions about the characteristics of the twenty citizens that might provide useful information when historians try to evaluate their testimony. (Questions might include age, level of political activity, level of education.) Ask why such information is critical.

Extend See the Historian's Toolbox Activity in the Resource Directory below.

Answers

1. (a) John Lewis, Atlanta city council member and civil rights leader. (b) 1983 (c) He loved and admired President Kennedy and was saddened by his assassination. (d) No. Lewis's admiration has not lessened over time.

2. (a) Answers will vary, but Lewis worked closely with Kennedy on difficult issues. It is likely that his views are accurate, not sentimentalized. (b) Lewis likely sees Kennedy as instrumental in the passage of civil rights legislation that occurred after his death. If successful legislation had not been passed, he may have viewed Kennedy in a different light. (c) They reveal that he favored government intervention on domestic issues such as civil rights, and that he believed government should be accessible to the people.

3. (a) Lewis believes that Kennedy was a sincere and caring President and that he gave people, especially African Americans, feelings of hope that his administration cared about the American people and would work on domestic issues such as civil rights. (b) Lewis's account indicates that Kennedy may not have been universally admired as a President, but that many people felt for the first time that there was a friend in the White House.

Exploring Oral History

Oral history is made up of people's verbal accounts and recollections of former times and events. As historical evidence, it is one of the oldest and most universal methods by which people have acquired information about the past.

Historians preserve oral history by interviewing people and recording their words on audio- or videotape or in written transcripts. Historians may gather oral history at the time an event takes place or at some later date, perhaps years or even decades later.

Historians often seek out oral histories because they give a unique perspective on the past. Oral histories are a type of primary source and therefore are more valuable to historians than secondary sources. Oral histories record not only facts about the past, but also people's opinions, feelings, and impressions—all important to a historian in putting together a picture of the past.

The excerpt at right is taken from a 1983 interview with John Lewis, an Atlanta city council member, on the twentieth anniversary of President Kennedy's death. In 1963 Lewis was chairperson of the Student Nonviolent Coordinating Committee and one of the leaders of the civil rights March on Washington.

Read the oral account at right and then use the following steps to analyze its content.

1. Identify the nature of the oral account. (a) Who was interviewed?

(b) When did the interview take place? (c) What was Lewis's attitude toward Kennedy at the time of his death? (d) Did that attitude change in any way over time?

2. Determine the reliability of the evidence. (a) How might Lewis's role in the events being recollected affect his interpretation of those events? (b) How might events after Kennedy's

death have affected the account? (c) What do Lewis's views reveal about his political perspective?

3. Study the evidence to learn more about the historical event. (a) What impact does Lewis think Kennedy's presidency had on government policy and the nation? (b) What can you learn about Kennedy's presidency from Lewis's account?

An Interview with John Lewis:
Remembering President Kennedy's Assassination

"I was living in Atlanta then, but I had gone back to Nashville for a trial. I was getting into a car to go to the Nashville airport when I heard it on the radio. And to me, it was the saddest moment in my life. I had grown up to love and to admire President Kennedy. I remember crying on the plane.

I saw him as a sort of guy that listened. Sincere. Caring. People argue and say that he didn't really do anything. But he did listen, and during that period from 1961 to 1963, I'll tell you, I think probably for the first time in modern American history, we felt, "Well, we have a friend in the White House." On some things we disagreed. We'd call them up and argue and debate with them on some issue, and we said a lot of different things, and sometimes it was harsh. But we saw the Kennedy administration during that period as a sympathetic referee in the whole struggle for civil rights.

His campaign had created a sense of hope, a sense of optimism for many of us. When someone asked him about the civil rights sit-ins that year, he said, 'By sitting down, these young people are standing up for the very best in American tradition.' "

—*Newsweek,* November 28, 1983

RESOURCE DIRECTORY

Teaching Resources

Historian's Toolbox Activity Exploring Oral History, found in the Unit 9 folder, p. 18, provides a further example of what oral history can reveal about public affairs in a *U.S. News & World Report* interview with President Clinton using readers' questions on health care.

The Great Society

SECTION PREVIEW

Lyndon Johnson picked up the domestic agenda after John Kennedy's death. In the greatest triumph of social legislation since Franklin Roosevelt's New Deal, he launched a remarkable reform program that offered something for everyone and for a time promised to ease the inequalities in American life.

Key Concepts

- Lyndon Johnson was a skillful politician who used his forceful personality to get measures passed in Congress.
- Johnson's Great Society included a tax cut, a "war on poverty," health-care legislation, aid to education, and other proposals.
- Supreme Court decisions in the 1960s supported the Great Society, but the program also had many critics.

Key Terms, People, and Places

Great Society, Volunteers in Service to America (VISTA), Medicare, Immigration Act of 1965; Lyndon B. Johnson

L yndon B. Johnson succeeded where Kennedy had failed. Vice President under JFK, Johnson found himself elevated to the presidency when Kennedy was assassinated. Once in office, he used all the talents he had developed as Senate majority leader to push through Congress an extraordinary program of reforms on domestic issues.

LBJ's Path to the White House

Lyndon B. Johnson arrived in Congress in 1937 as a New Deal Democrat from Texas. Johnson took a conservative stance in order to appeal to more Texas voters during his quest for a Senate seat. He won the seat in 1948 by a tiny margin of only eighty-seven votes and was promptly dubbed "Landslide Lyndon"—a

nickname that stuck for the rest of his career. In the Senate, Johnson demonstrated both his talent and his ambition by winning leadership posts. In the six years from 1954 to 1960, he became famous for his ability to manipulate the political system to accomplish his goals.

Johnson was a forceful, energetic man. He was "not a very likable man," as former Secretary of State Dean Acheson once told him, but Johnson was more concerned with accomplishment than popularity, and his single-minded intensity enabled him to get his way. Other senators marveled at the "Johnson treatment," in which he carefully researched a bill, then approached in a hallway or office the legislator whose vote he needed. If he thought it was the best way to persuade the legislator, he would attack, "his face a scant millimeter from his target, his eyes widening and narrowing, his eyebrows rising and falling," according to columnists Rowland Evans, Jr., and Robert Novak. He might grab his victim by the lapels or by the shoulders, flattering, cajoling, shouting in turn. And without fail he got the vote.

Johnson was a master of behind-the-scenes dealing in the Senate, but John Kennedy knew more about how to win a presidential nomination. When Johnson's bid for the Democratic nomination failed in 1960, he accepted Kennedy's invitation to run for the vice presidency. Once in office, however, Johnson suffered miserably. He was uncomfortable with the Kennedy crowd, whose Ivy League educations made him feel intellectually inferior. He also was frustrated with the powerlessness of the vice presidency and upset at being away from Congress, where he had been so effective. Then came the assassination, and suddenly he was President.

Johnson sensed the profound shock gripping the nation. He knew that millions of Americans viewed him as the wrongful heir to the Kennedy tradition. He also was aware that he had less than a year to convince the American

The fiberglass sculpture above, which was a gift to President Johnson, portrays him as a rough-and-ready Texan.

Connecting to the Big Idea

See page 770B. Lyndon Johnson, taking office after Kennedy's assassination, moved many reform bills through Congress as part of his goal of achieving a "Great Society." Ask what Johnson's most important reform bills were. Why did some Americans criticize Johnson's program?

Objectives

- Describe the qualities that allowed Lyndon Johnson to move his programs through Congress.
- Identify some of the major proposals that made up the Great Society legislation.
- Explain why criticism of the Great Society came from many different segments of American society.

Bellringer

Ask students what they think is great about American society. Was it as great or less so in Johnson's time? What differences are evident?

Reading Strategy

Reading for Evidence As they read students should look for evidence that "Lyndon B. Johnson succeeded where Kennedy had failed," as stated on page 777.

📄 **Reproducible Lesson Plan** found in the Unit 9 folder, p. 4, provides a summary of the Section 2 lesson plan content.

📄 **Alternate Lesson Plan: Critical Thinking** Determining Relevance, found in the Alternate Lesson Plans folder, p. 143, helps students identify the impact of various aspects of the Great Society programs and the role of Supreme Court decisions during this time.

📄 **Guided Reading and Review** found in the Unit 9 folder, p. 8, provides a structure for reading and mastering the key concepts and reviewing the key terms for Section 2. (Guided Practice)

Explain/Discuss

Discuss with students why LBJ was able to succeed where Kennedy had failed. Remind students that Congress, as well as LBJ, wanted to pass legislation proposed by the slain President as a memorial and as a way of reassuring the country. Ask students to what extent LBJ's political experience helped him move legislation through Congress.

Ask students to list the programs instituted by LBJ. What areas of American life did they touch? Ask students to consider what sort of bureaucracy was required to keep such programs going. Do students see any potential for overlapping programs in the list of legislation? Read students the following comment by Sargent Shriver, head of the Office of Economic Opportunity and chief administrator of the War on Poverty, concerning the multitude of programs: "It's like we went down to Cape Kennedy and launched a half dozen rockets at once."

In Depth

Multicultural Perspectives

The war on poverty is continuing into the late twentieth century. The focal point of poverty, however, is not predominantly among African Americans in the North and in urban areas, as popular perception might have it. The 1990 census data shows that poor whites (21 million) outnumber poor African Americans (9 million) by more than two to one. However, African Americans do bear a disproportionate burden of poverty—28 percent compared to 8.8 percent of the white population.

When Lyndon Johnson was elected President in 1964, he renewed his pledge to follow through on Kennedy's programs.

Despite strong publicity efforts, including advertising on bars of soap, Republican candidate Barry Goldwater's run for the presidency in 1964 was unsuccessful. It did signal the beginnings of a conservative movement in the United States, however.

people of his competence before running for the presidency in 1964.

Speaking to the nation for the first time after Kennedy's death, Johnson expressed his grief at the loss. "All I have," he declared in this address, "I would have given gladly not to be standing here today." He went on to convey his determination to carry on where the slain President had left off. Johnson's theme was "Let us continue," and he asked Congress to pass the measures that Kennedy had sought.

The Great Society

Congress, also aware that the American people needed some action that would heal the wound caused by the loss of their President, responded to Johnson's appeal. Swift passage of Kennedy's civil rights and tax-cut bills followed. Soon Johnson branched out and sought laws to aid public education, provide medical care for the elderly, and eliminate poverty. By the spring of 1964, he had begun to use the phrase **"Great Society"** to describe his goals. In a speech at the University of Michigan in May 1964, he told students:

> Your imagination, your initiative, and your indignation will determine whether we build a society where progress is the servant of our needs, or a society where old values and new visions are buried under unbridled [unrestrained] growth. For in your time we have the opportunity to move not only toward the rich society and the powerful society, but upward toward the Great Society.

Johnson's early successes paved the way to a true landslide victory over Republican Barry Goldwater in the election of 1964. Goldwater, a senator from Arizona, held views that seemed frighteningly radical to many Americans. For example, he

opposed civil rights legislation, and he believed that military commanders should be allowed to use nuclear bombs as they saw fit on the battlefield. The Johnson campaign capitalized on voters' fears of nuclear war and aired a television commercial in which a little girl's innocent counting game turned into the countdown for a nuclear explosion. Johnson received 61 percent of the popular vote and an overwhelming 486 to 52 tally in the Electoral College. Democratic majorities were established in both houses of Congress: 295 to 140 in the House of Representatives and 68 to 32 in the Senate. Landslide Lyndon now had the mandate to move ahead even more aggressively.

The Tax Cut Johnson accepted the idea that had been supported by Kennedy that carefully controlled budget deficits could bring about prosperity. To gain conservative support for Kennedy's tax-cut bill, he agreed to cut spending. Once that was done, the measure passed, and it worked just as planned. As the tax cut went into effect, the Gross National Product (GNP) rose 7.1 percent in 1964, 8.1 percent in 1965, and 9.5 percent in 1966. The deficit, which many people feared would grow, shrank, while the revival of prosperity generated new tax revenues. Unemployment fell, and inflation remained in check.

The War on Poverty Next, LBJ pressed for the poverty program that Kennedy had begun to consider. In his 1964 State of the Union message he vowed, "This administration today, here and now, declares unconditional war on poverty in America." The Economic Opportunity Act, passed in the summer of 1964, created **Volunteers in Service to America (VISTA)**, which sent volunteers to help people in poor communities. The act also set up "community action programs" to give the poor a voice in defining housing, health, and education policies in their own neighborhoods. Poor people were to participate in decisions about the distribution of government money and resources.

Medicare Johnson also focused attention on the increasing cost of medical care. Twenty years before, Harry Truman had proposed a

RESOURCE DIRECTORY

Teaching Resources

Primary Source Activity President Johnson's Thanksgiving Address, found in the Unit 9 folder, p. 20, includes portions of the first national speech LBJ made as President— after only seven days in office.

Critical Thinking Activity Recognizing Cause and Effect, found in the Unit 9 folder, p. 19, helps students apply this skill with a graph showing trends in poverty and the economy from 1948 to 1987.

Federal Dollars to Public Schools,* 1959–1971

Millions of Dollars

School Year
1959–60
1961–62
1963–64
1965–66
1967–68
1969–70
1970–71

* Elementary and secondary
Source: *Digest of Education Statistics*

 Interpreting Graphs
Congress passed President Johnson's Elementary and Secondary Education Act in 1965. *How does the graph illustrate the overall effect of this legislation? By how much did the federal education budget increase between the 1963–1964 and 1965–1966 school years?*

medical assistance plan as part of his Fair Deal program, but it had never been passed into law. Johnson provided the necessary leadership by tying **Medicare**—which would provide health care for the elderly—to social security and confining the new approach to people over the age of sixty-five. "No longer will older Americans be denied the healing miracle of modern medicine," Johnson declared. "No longer will illness crush and destroy the savings that they have so carefully put away." Another program, called Medicaid, met the needs of poor Americans of any age who could not afford their own private health insurance. This broad-based health care program was the most important piece of social welfare legislation since the passage of the Social Security Act in 1935. It demonstrated the government's commitment to provide help to those Americans who needed it.

Aid to Education Johnson was equally successful in his effort to provide funds for elementary and secondary education. Kennedy had fought for a bill to aid public education but

was defeated when Catholics insisted on equal support for parochial, or private Catholic, schools. Bending over backwards to prove that his own Catholicism was not influencing policy decisions, Kennedy had opposed the Catholics, saying that such a provision would be a violation of the separation of church and state. In the process he had lost the entire bill. Johnson endorsed a measure to provide aid to states based on the number of children from low-income homes. That money could then be distributed to public as well as private schools, including parochial schools. The bill passed, and Johnson signed it into law in the small Texas school he had attended as a child. The graph above shows federal aid to schools from 1959 to 1971.

Other Measures As a result of White House prodding, Congress passed a measure to give rent supplements to the poor. It created a new Department of Housing and Urban Development, thus elevating the importance of housing issues. It provided substantial aid to colleges

Media and Technology

 Transparency
Critical Thinking, I-13

Caption Answer to ...

 Interpreting Graphs

The overall effect of the law was to increase federal spending for public schools. The budget increased by approximately $1.1 billion between the 1963–64 and 1965–66 school years.

Analyze
Ask students to analyze the criticisms leveled against Great Society legislation. Ask which, if any, of the criticisms seem justified.

Activity
Drawing a Political Cartoon
Ask students to draw a political cartoon illustrating either a criticism of Johnson's Great Society legislation or a response to LBJ's critics.

Enrichment
Three Supreme Court cases, *Gideon* v. *Wainwright, Escobedo* v. *Illinois,* and *Miranda* v. *Arizona,* dealt with the rights of individuals accused of crimes. Ask students to work in groups to write dialogue for a drama in which police officers, suspects, and lawyers refer to these cases and discuss instances in which the rights of the accused may have been violated.

 In Depth

Then and Now

An enduring legacy of LBJ's aid to education is Head Start—a program begun in 1965 to prepare economically disadvantaged preschoolers for school. Now administered by the Department of Health and Human Services, Head Start works through local communities to provide nutritious lunches, medical and family services, and educational preparation. Head Start receives bipartisan support in Congress, and serves over 11 million children, mostly under age five.

Caption Answer to …

Interpreting Graphs

An increase in immigration from Asia and from southern and eastern Europe and a decrease in immigration from northwestern Europe. It eliminated some of the restrictions on immigration from areas outside northwestern Europe.

3. ASSESS

Section 2 Review Answers

1. (a) VISTA, see p. 778, (b) Medicare, see p. 779, (c) Immigration Act of 1965, see p. 780

2. Lyndon B. Johnson, see p. 777

3. Johnson invoked Kennedy's memory and asked legislators to pass the bills Kennedy had supported.

4. The Great Society included bills guaranteeing civil rights, providing medical care for the aged (and poor), and mandating a tax cut. It also organized an antipoverty program, offered aid to education, and gave federal support to artists and scholars.

5. Middle-class Americans felt the burden of aiding the poor. Conservatives argued that Great Society programs went too far. Radicals argued that they didn't go far enough.

In Depth

Biography

In 1965, lawyer Marian Wright Edelman (b. 1939) became the first African American woman admitted to the Mississippi bar. Edelman is the founder and president of the Children's Defense Fund, an advocacy group that promotes the health and welfare of children. Edelman summarizes the Fund's philosophy as follows: "Children cannot eat rhetoric and they cannot be sheltered by commissions. I don't want to see another commission that studies the needs of kids. We need to help them."

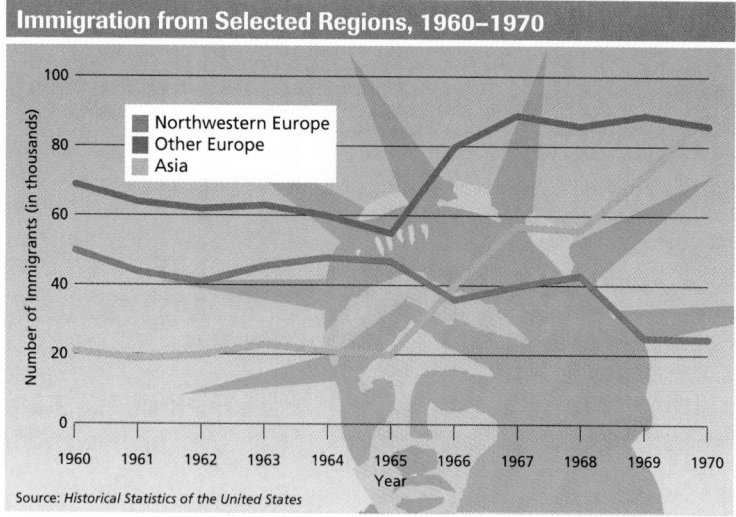

Immigration from Selected Regions, 1960–1970

Number of Immigrants (in thousands)

Legend:
- Northwestern Europe
- Other Europe
- Asia

Source: *Historical Statistics of the United States*

Interpreting Graphs
What general trends in immigration during the 1960s are shown by the graph? How did the Immigration Act of 1965 contribute to these trends?

and universities. It offered grants to artists through a new National Endowment for the Arts and to scholars through a similar National Endowment for the Humanities. This was the first assistance for such groups since the Works Progress Administration of the New Deal.

The Great Society also reformed the restrictive immigration policy that had been in place since 1924. The **Immigration Act of 1965** eliminated the quotas that had discriminated against all immigrants from areas outside northern and western Europe. It now had a much more flexible limit of 170,000 people from the Eastern Hemisphere and 120,000 from the Western Hemisphere. Family members of United States citizens were exempted from the quotas, as were political refugees. In the 1960s approximately 350,000 immigrants entered the United States each year; in the 1970s the number rose to more than 400,000 a year. ✪

Supreme Court Support

The Supreme Court under Chief Justice Earl Warren supported the actions of Johnson's Great Society in the 1960s. The 1954 *Brown* v. *Board of Education* decision outlawing school segregation signaled that the Warren Court was prepared to play an active role in politics. As the Johnson administration made good on its promise to promote civil rights, the Court backed up this program. It upheld all measures aimed at guaranteeing African American rights and demonstrated that discrimination would no longer be tolerated.

The Supreme Court handed down several decisions protecting the rights of persons accused of crimes. In the *Gideon* v. *Wainwright* case in 1963, the Court ruled that suspects in criminal cases who could not afford a lawyer had the right to free legal aid. In *Escobedo* v. *Illinois,* 1964, the justices said that accused individuals had to be given access to an attorney while being questioned. In 1966 the Court ruled, in *Miranda* v. *Arizona,* that a suspect must be warned of his or her rights before being questioned. Police must now read all suspects a Miranda warning, which informs accused persons that they have the right to remain silent and that anything they do say may be used against them in court.

In 1965 the Court struck down a Connecticut law that prohibited the use of birth control devices and prevented doctors from sharing information about contraceptives, even with married couples. *Griswold* v. *Connecticut* held that such a law violated a couple's right to privacy. Although the Constitution does not explicitly mention a right to privacy, the Court ruled that such a right was implied because without it, the rights that are specifically guaranteed would be meaningless.

In *Baker* v. *Carr,* 1962, the Court declared that congressional districts had to be apportioned on the basis of "one person, one vote." This prevented the party in power from gerrymandering electoral districts—drawing the lines that established the districts in unfair ways to give themselves more votes. In another area, the Court ruled that religious prayer in public schools was unconstitutional

RESOURCE DIRECTORY

Teaching Resources

Visual Learning Activity The Job Corps, found in the Unit 9 folder, p. 27, uses a photograph from a Job Corps training course to illustrate how job training was considered a major weapon in Johnson's war on poverty.

Literature Activity The Invisible Poor, found in the Unit 9 folder, p. 25, features an excerpt from Michael Harrington's bestseller, *The Other America,* which inspired Kennedy and shocked middle-class Americans into supporting action against poverty.

according to the First Amendment principle of separation of church and state. In yet another significant decision, the Court decreed that obscenity laws could not restrict material that might have some "redeeming social value."

The Supreme Court's decisions in the 1960s were controversial. Some conservatives argued that the justices had gone too far and began a long struggle to turn back the new decisions.

MAKING CONNECTIONS

Is the Supreme Court any less political—any less affected by its members' liberal or conservative views—than Congress? Should it be?

Challenges to the Great Society

At first the Great Society seemed enormously successful. Opinion polls taken after Johnson's speech of May 22, 1964, in which he introduced his vision of the Great Society, showed Johnson more popular than Kennedy had been at a comparable point in his presidency. Pressed by Johnson, Congress had passed Kennedy's tax-cut bill early in 1964, and, as detailed on page 778, the state of the economy improved significantly.

Soon, however, criticisms began to surface. New programs raised expectations, and disillusionment followed when not all demands could be met. Middle-class Americans complained that too many of their tax dollars were being spent on poor people. Other critics argued that Great Society programs put too much author-

ity in the hands of the federal government, which could not possibly respond well to the particular needs of local communities across the nation.

At the same time, others complained that the Great Society did not fundamentally alter the distribution of wealth and power in a capitalist economy. Some critics charged that the program sought simply to maintain the middle class and to provide the poor with middle-class values, but not middle-class incomes. Antipoverty measures were criticized for not allotting enough money to carry out their stated goals. Michael Harrington, who had helped focus attention on poverty with his book *The Other America*, argued that the amount of money the government spent was not nearly enough: "What was supposed to be a social war turned out to be a skirmish and, in any case, poverty won."

Before his death, John Kennedy had been more concerned about foreign affairs than domestic; when Johnson took office, he placed the emphasis on the latter. The next section describes Kennedy's actions on the world stage and, after his death, the beginnings of a conflict in Southeast Asia that began to consume the resources that Johnson had hoped to spend on his programs at home. His inability to keep that conflict under control undermined and finally ended the Great Society.

Johnson was both criticized and praised for his Great Society but to him, the programs were all good—"major accomplishments without equal or close parallel in the present era."

SECTION 2 REVIEW

Key Terms, People, and Places
1. Define (a) VISTA, (b) Medicare, (c) Immigration Act of 1965.
2. Identify Lyndon B. Johnson.

Key Concepts
3. How did Lyndon Johnson mobilize support for his domestic programs when he became President?
4. What were the key elements of the Great Society?

5. What were some criticisms of the Great Society?

Critical Thinking
6. **Determining Relevance** What role did the principle of judicial interpretation—the power of the courts to interpret the law—play in the 1965 Supreme Court case *Griswold* v. *Connecticut*? Would the case have been decided differently if the Court did not have this power?

Quiz found in the Unit 9 folder, p. 9, covers the main ideas in this section as well as the key terms.

6. Judicial interpretation allowed the court to extrapolate the right of privacy (not expressly written in the Bill of Rights) from the existence of other guaranteed rights. It may have been harder for the court to rule as it did in *Griswold* without this interpretation, and the effects of the ruling would not have been as far-reaching.

Reteach

Have students locate the key concepts on page 777. Ask each student to write one question based on each of the key concepts. Have students exchange papers with a classmate and answer the questions. Pairs of students can work together to correct their answers.

Alternative Assessment

Mid-Point Monitoring
Ask students if they have
• Decided on a format for their finished project
• Started taking notes about the topic
• Begun their outside research

Answer to ...
MAKING CONNECTIONS

The Court's decisions are certainly affected by the political views of its members. Since the justices are not elected but are appointed for life, they probably feel less political pressure than members of Congress do. Most people would argue that the Supreme Court should be as apolitical as possible.

4. CLOSE

Reinforcing the Big Idea

Lyndon Johnson moved an astonishingly comprehensive reform program through Congress in an attempt to build a "Great Society" and wage a war on poverty. The next section discusses foreign affairs during the Kennedy and Johnson administrations.

Kennedy's Decision to Send an American to the Moon

Focus Ask students which of the following programs they would recommend cutting from the nation's budget in order to reduce government spending:

- Preschool programs and food supplements for children at risk
- Repairs to highways, bridges, harbors, and other parts of the transportation system
- Research on AIDS
- Space programs, including a program to land astronauts on the surface of Mars
- Hazardous waste cleanup programs at government installations

Tally student responses. Allow students to debate their decisions briefly and to explain their reasons for choosing a particular program to cut. Point out that the debate over the value of space exploration began decades ago and continues today.

Instruct Explain that in 1969, when American astronauts actually landed on the moon, many Americans were not convinced that the tremendous outlay of money and talent devoted to the space program was worthwhile.

In the July 7, 1969, issue of *Newsweek,* several Americans voiced negative opinions regarding the upcoming moon walk. Ralph Abernathy, then president of the Southern Christian Leadership Conference, said that United States society had "failed to use its ability to rid itself of the scourges of racism, poverty and war, all of which were brutally scarring the nation even as it mobilized for the assault on the solar system." (*Newsweek*, July 7, 1969, p. 60.)

The tribal secretary of the Laguna Pueblos in Paguate, New Mexico, said: "What we could do with that money!" Others favored the project, such as the physicist who hoped, "This seemingly lifeless moon may tell us about the origins of life on the earth . . .a feeling of intense excitement grips the scientific community."

Kennedy's Decision to Send an American to the Moon

Time Frame:	November 1960–May 1961
Place:	Washington, D.C.
Key People:	President John F. Kennedy, physicist Jerome Wiesner, NASA head James Webb
Situation:	When John F. Kennedy was elected President, the Soviet Union was rapidly widening its lead in space exploration. The United States needed to find a way to catch up and, if possible, surpass the Soviets in space.

When the Soviet Union launched *Sputnik*, the first artificial satellite, in 1957, a shocked American public worried that the Soviets were gaining a dramatic lead in space. Senator Henry Jackson captured the dismay of many Americans when he declared that *Sputnik* represented "a devastating blow to the prestige of the United States as the leader of the scientific and technical world."

When Kennedy took office in 1960, he assigned a task force, headed by MIT physicist Jerome Wiesner, to evaluate the future direction of the space program. Wiesner's team concluded that the potential scientific payoffs of sending astronauts into space were not worth the enormous costs. They recommended that NASA concentrate on exploratory missions without human crews.

In April 1961, however, Soviet Yuri Gagarin became the first person to complete an orbital flight around the earth. Gagarin's flight rekindled Americans' fears that the United States was falling behind the Soviet Union. Under fire for neglecting his campaign promise to revitalize the space program, the President began to press his advisers for ways to beat the Soviets in space.

Lunar Politics

In the early 1960s, many experts remained skeptical about the scientific merits of sending human beings into space. Sending a person to the moon seemed particularly foolish, both because the moon held little scientific interest and because robots and other instruments could explore it without risking human life.

Financial considerations made the goal of landing a person on the moon even more problematic. Estimates placed the cost of a 10-year project to send an American to the moon at $30 billion to $40 billion. Opponents of the plan questioned the wisdom of diverting so much money and energy to a high-stakes project of questionable scientific value. They pointed to the nation's need for greater spending on public education and social welfare programs. As President Eisenhower bluntly put it, "Anybody who would spend $40 billion in a race to the moon for national prestige is nuts."

Yet a growing number of politicians and scientists—including Vice President Lyndon Johnson and NASA head James Webb—supported sending a person to the

▶ RESOURCE DIRECTORY

Teaching Resources

History Might Not . . . Activity Decision Making: Building an International Manned Space Station, found in the Unit 9 folder, pp. 12–13, provides a structure for groups of students to understand the interests involved, weigh the pros and cons, and debate the issues while simulating a congressional subcommittee hearing on the decision to fund a manned space station.

GOALS	Prevent the Soviets from taking control of space; protect American prestige and security		
POSSIBLE ACTIONS	Continue current uncrewed program of space exploration	Begin crewed space program to land an American on the moon within 10 years	Begin crewed program to land on the moon when space technology makes it safe to do so
POSSIBLE RESULTS	• Enable NASA to emphasize scientific discovery at a much lower cost • United States will have more money to spend on domestic problems • Soviet Union may increase lead in space, thus winning greater international prestige	• Project will fail, causing great embarrassment and, possibly, loss of life • Project will succeed, keeping Soviets from dominating space • Project will prove more costly and less scientifically valuable than an uncrewed space program	• Domestic problems will worsen as funds go to space program • Project will lose momentum and never be completed • Project will succeed, putting American space program ahead and advancing scientific knowledge

moon. They believed that the risks could be addressed by careful engineering and that a human could gather much more information than a robot.

The supporters of a crewed space program believed that the race to the moon represented an important battle in the cold war. If the Soviets won in space, the rest of the world might see it as a victory of communism over capitalism. The United States would have to resign itself, as the Vice President put it, "to going to bed each night by the light of a Communist moon."

People who favored a crewed flight to the moon also believed that there were economic benefits to this approach. The race to the moon meant huge contracts and thousands of new jobs for the aerospace industry. In the view of those who supported such a race, science, industry, and education also would profit from technological advances made by a crewed space program.

Some scientists who supported sending people into space favored a third approach. They believed that NASA should wait until space technology was further advanced before attempting to send a person to the moon. They recognized that this emphasis on safety meant it might take several decades to land an American on the moon rather than the relatively short space of ten years.

Kennedy's Decision

Despite the objections, President Kennedy came to believe that a highly visible space program would distract attention from problems at home and abroad. "I am tired of the headlines," he told an aide. "All they describe is crisis, and they give the impression that we have our backs against the wall everywhere in the world." A successful lunar program could erase that impression.

On May 5, 1961, as part of Project Mercury, Alan Shepard became the first American to travel in space. The public's enthusiastic response convinced Kennedy that it was time to submit the moon launch proposal.

In his May 25 special message to the Congress, the President issued a bold challenge to the nation. Rather than continuing an uncrewed space program or taking a go-slow approach in the moon race, he said, the United States "should commit itself to achieving the goal, before this decade is out, of landing a man on the moon." Kennedy's decision finally yielded results on July 20, 1969, when astronaut Neil Armstrong became the first person to set foot on the moon.

EVALUATING DECISIONS

1. What were some reasons in favor of starting a project to put an American on the moon?
2. Why did some people oppose the moon program?

Critical Thinking

3. **Determining Relevance** Lyndon Johnson said that "control of space means control of the world." To what extent was this idea behind Kennedy's decision to send an astronaut to the moon? What other factors contributed to his decision?

Media and Technology

Visions of America: History Might Not Have Happened This Way Game

To encourage students to explore pivotal moments in United States history, have students use the Visions of America software. Refer to the Visions of America Guidebook for viewing objectives, activities, game instructions, and discussion questions.

Foreign Policy in the 1960s

1. FOCUS

Connecting to the Big Idea

See page 770B. The foreign policies of Presidents Kennedy and Johnson were grounded in the cold war. Ask how Kennedy reacted to communist challenges. How did Johnson intervene in South American countries?

Objectives

- Identify the Peace Corps and describe its purpose.
- Explain how Kennedy's commitment to the cold war and inexperience in foreign affairs affected his handling of foreign policy.
- Describe the events of the Cuban missile crisis of 1962.
- Describe President Johnson's attitude toward foreign affairs.

Bellringer

Ask students to think about foreign policy—the way the United States pursues relationships with other countries. Ask them to list what they think should be the goals of our foreign policy.

Reading Strategy

Structured Overview Before students begin reading the section, ask them to write two column headings on a piece of paper: Kennedy's Trouble Spots and Johnson's Trouble Spots. As they read the section, students should list each of the foreign affairs crises discussed in the section in the appropriate column and briefly describe the crisis and its resolution.

Foreign Policy in the 1960s

SECTION PREVIEW

The drama and seriousness of events on the world stage beckoned Kennedy more than did the problems at home. He performed boldly on several foreign policy issues, with decisions grounded in familiar cold war assumptions about the intentions of the Soviet Union. When Johnson took office, he saw foreign affairs as something of a nuisance, but
- continued Kennedy's policies.

Key Concepts
- Kennedy promoted a new program called the Peace Corps.
- Kennedy's commitment to the cold war and his inexperience in foreign affairs showed in his handling of an invasion of Cuba and in his dealings with the Soviet Union.
- The Cuban missile crisis brought the United States and the Soviet Union perilously close to nuclear war.
- President Johnson continued the cold war against communism abroad.

Key Terms, People, and Places
Peace Corps, Berlin Wall, Cuban missile crisis, Limited Test Ban Treaty; Nikita Khrushchev; Bay of Pigs

Long-range missiles capable of carrying nuclear explosives heightened cold war tension. The Soviet Union and the United States could launch nuclear attacks against each other with the push of a button.

W hile Presidents Kennedy and Johnson promised to seek a "new frontier" and a "great society" in domestic affairs, their foreign policy stayed strictly within the limits of the cold war. Communist challenges and the Presidents' reactions to them led to confrontations that seriously threatened world peace.

Kennedy's Approach to Foreign Policy

The rhetoric of Kennedy's inaugural address proclaimed that the United States would do anything to uphold its version of freedom throughout the world. By this, the new President was referring to defending United States interests against the Soviet Union and its allies.

The Alliance for Progress One focus of Kennedy's foreign policy was the promotion of "peaceful revolution" in developing countries around the world. In other words, he wanted to promote changes in foreign countries that would serve the capitalist interests of the United States in order to prevent those countries from aligning with the Soviet Union. To counter procommunist revolutionary movements, the United States wanted to help countries in Latin America, Asia, and Africa. To do so, Kennedy believed that modern transportation and communication systems and stable governments sympathetic to the United States were necessary. Two months after taking office, Kennedy called on

all the people of the hemisphere to join in a new Alliance for Progress—Alianza para Progreso—a vast cooperative effort, unparalleled in magnitude and nobility of purpose, to satisfy the basic needs of the American people for homes, work and land, health and schools.
Address to Latin American diplomats,
March 13, 1961

The administration devoted $100 billion to public and private funding to promote economic development and social reform and to sidetrack revolution before it occurred. All citizens in the Western Hemisphere, Kennedy declared, had "a right to social justice," and that included "land for the landless, and education for those who are denied education." Soon, however, Latin Americans began to question whether what was good for the United States was necessarily good for their countries. Because of such doubts, the Alliance for Progress never lived up to Kennedy's expectations.

RESOURCE DIRECTORY

Teaching Resources

Reproducible Lesson Plan found in the Unit 9 folder, p. 5, provides a summary of the Section 3 lesson plan content.

Alternate Lesson Plan: Learning Styles found in the Alternate Lesson Plans folder, p. 144, helps students identify Kennedy's cold war policies around the world by locating "hot spots" on a world map—especially helpful for tactile and auditory learners.

Guided Reading and Review found in the Unit 9 folder, p. 10, provides a structure for reading and mastering the key concepts and reviewing the key terms for Section 3. (Guided Practice)

One answer to such charges that the United States was more interested in its own agenda than it was in helping other countries was the **Peace Corps.** This new program of JFK's would send volunteers abroad to help developing nations around the world. It would, aide Arthur M. Schlesinger, Jr., declared,

replace protocol-minded, striped-pants officials [with] reform-minded missionaries of democracy who mixed with the people, spoke the native dialects, ate the food, and involved themselves in local struggles against ignorance and want.

AMERICAN PROFILES

Paul Cowan

Paul Cowan was one such "reform-minded missionary." After college in 1963 he worked in the civil rights movement tutoring African American children in Maryland. In 1965 Cowan and his wife, Rachel, joined the Peace Corps and prepared to work in Ecuador in South America. After a training program at the University of New Mexico, they went to the city of Guayaquil to do community development work. Their task would be to raise the standard of living in poor areas by pressuring local governments to provide services such as garbage disposal and clean water.

The job turned out to be far more complicated and frustrating than the Cowans had anticipated. An inefficient bureaucracy constantly hampered their work. The local government was almost as poor as the people it served, and its lack of funds made it essentially powerless. "From the day we moved into the *barrio* [neighborhood]," Paul Cowan later recalled, "the question we were most frequently asked by the people we were supposed to be organizing was whether we would leave them our clothes when we returned to the States."

The Peace Corps bureaucracy, which was too often insensitive to the local culture in which the volunteers were

Paul Cowan volunteered for the Peace Corps in Ecuador.

immersed, also frustrated the couple. Cowan returned home upset, like so many students of his generation, with the slow pace and the twisted path toward progress. Yet, as he looked back on his experience, he wrote:

After all the tragedies and frustrations of this past decade, I still believe that someday we will create an America which realizes, with the great Cuban revolutionary José Martí, that "los niños son la esperanza del futuro del mundo" [the children are the hope of the future of the world] and create a society based on that homily.

The executive order that created the Peace Corps stated, "They will live at the same level as the citizens of the countries which they are sent to, doing the same work, eating the same food, speaking the same language." The Peace Corps volunteer above is teaching sewing skills to women in Sri Lanka.

A Series of Global Crises

The Peace Corps program was one for which Kennedy was, in general, praised. Other actions of his on the foreign scene were viewed less positively. Kennedy's first serious problem arose in Cuba, an island approximately 90 miles off the Florida coast.

The Bay of Pigs The United States had worried about Cuba ever since Fidel Castro, a former lawyer, had seized power there in 1959.

2. INSTRUCT

Explain/Discuss

Explain to students that in the first three years of the Peace Corps, ten thousand Americans volunteered for duty. During the program's first twenty years, some eighty thousand volunteers served in eighty-eight countries. The Peace Corps, like the Alliance for Progress, had an underlying political goal: to build goodwill in developing nations and to prevent them from forming ties with the Soviet Union. Ask students why Kennedy was so concerned with winning the favor of developing nations. How successful do students think he was in South America and in other parts of the world?

Discuss the Bay of Pigs fiasco. Why was the United States concerned about Castro? Why did Kennedy agree to support the invasion?

Have students make a time line of the Cuban missile crisis events on the chalkboard. Ask them to identify the most critical time period of the crisis. Ask students to explain the following statement by Secretary of State Dean Rusk at the moment the first Soviet ships began to turn back: "We're eyeball to eyeball, and I think the other fellow just blinked."

Ask students to compare the actions taken by Presidents Kennedy and Johnson in South America with Kennedy's stated goals for the Alliance for Progress. How do students think the gap between the actions and the rhetoric could be bridged?

Possible answers: In Panama, the United States took action because of Noriega's involvement in drug trafficking and because he had refused to heed his country's democratic election by stepping down. All of the previous United States invasions were prompted by fears of the spread of communism in the Western Hemisphere.

Analyze

Ask students to think of other ways in which Kennedy's goals for the Alliance for Progress might have been reached.

Activity

Teaching Heterogeneous Groups

Foreign policy during the Kennedy and Johnson administrations consisted of maintaining safety from nuclear threat by blocking the establishment of communist governments in other—particularly neighboring—countries. To help students relate to this concept, have them describe their neighborhoods. Then ask them to list characteristics of their neighborhoods that make them feel safe and those that make them feel threatened. **LEP**

Many Cubans had supported Castro because he promised to improve the lives of poor people who were being exploited by wealthy Cubans and by United States companies operating in Cuba. Castro had taken over private property, including that of the United States corporations that had dominated the Cuban economy for decades. He also developed ties to the Soviet Union, particularly after the United States broke diplomatic relations and refused to accept him as the legitimate leader of Cuba. United States officials feared that he could become a model for revolutionary upheaval throughout Latin America.

When Kennedy became President, he learned that President Eisenhower had approved a plan in 1960, in which the Central Intelligence Agency (CIA) was providing military training for Cuban opponents of Castro in Guatemala, a nearby Central American country. When training was complete, an invasion of Cuba at a place called the **Bay of Pigs** was planned. With the expectation that when the invasion began, the Cuban people would use the opportunity to overthrow Castro, Kennedy gave the CIA the go-ahead.

Resistance to the plan soon surfaced, however. When Senator J. William Fulbright, Democratic chairman of the Foreign Relations Committee, learned of the scheme, he called it an "endless can of worms" and declared:

> To give this activity even covert [secretive] *support is of a piece with the hypocrisy and cynicism for which the United States is constantly denouncing [condemning] the Soviet Union in the United Nations and elsewhere. This point will not be lost on the rest of the world—nor on our own consciences. . . . The Castro regime is a thorn in the flesh; but it is not a dagger in the heart.*
>
> Memorandum to President Kennedy,
> March 29, 1961

Despite such reservations and those of some military leaders, Kennedy accepted the advice of the Joint Chiefs of Staff to push ahead.

| 1650 | 1700 | 1750 | 1800 | **Links·Across·Time** | 1850 | 1900 | 1950 | 2000 |

Intervention in Latin America

When the United States invaded Cuba at the Bay of Pigs in 1961, it was neither the first time nor the last that the United States invaded a Latin American country. The United States has often intervened militarily in Latin America to protect its own interests.

Plans for the invasion of Cuba were, in fact, modeled on an invasion of Guatemala, in Central America, that took place in 1954 during the Eisenhower administration. The CIA had backed a group of guerrillas who opposed the elected, procommunist president, Jacobo Arbenz Guzmán. Concerned that Guatemala would become a communist foothold in Latin America, the United States funded a military coup that overthrew the government. Only later did people learn of the CIA's role in the coup.

More recently, the United States invaded both Grenada, an island nation off the coast of Venezuela, and Panama, in Central America. After Grenada's leader, Maurice Bishop, was killed by procommunist members of his own party in October 1983, President Ronald Reagan sent a force of 6,000 United States troops and 300 from several Caribbean countries to Grenada. They removed the leaders of the coup and returned power to the country's original anticommunist government.

Six years later, in 1989, the United States launched an invasion of Panama to oust Manuel Noriega, the head of the Panamanian military. Noriega was indicted in the United States in 1988 on charges of drug trafficking. Although Noriega lost an election in 1989, he disregarded election results and declared himself "maximum leader." At first the United States supported Panamanians who wanted to overthrow Noriega. When their attempt failed, President George Bush ordered an invasion. Noriega surrendered to United States authorities early in 1990, after 24,000 United States troops invaded Panama to ensure his arrest. *How did the reasons for the invasion of Panama differ from those in Cuba, Guatemala, and Grenada?*

The Bay of Pigs Invasion, 1961

B26 Bomber

420

3 CIA training camp for Cuban exile recruits

Florida
Homestead   Miami

Large Cuban exile population from which Cuban Brigade recruited most of its invasion force

Cuban Brigade lands on two beaches, Apr. 17

Bay of Pigs

Havana

4 Cuban forces led by Fidel Castro sink two ships and capture 1,200 men of the invasion force, Apr. 17

CUBA

ATLANTIC OCEAN

BAHAMAS

CIA advanced training base for more than 1,400 Cuban exiles

1

Six B26 bombers, flown by Cuban exiles, attack Cuban airfields and assist invasion force on beaches, Apr. 15

JAMAICA

HAITI   DOMINICAN REP.

Puerto Rico

MEXICO

BR. HONDURAS

GUATEMALA

2 Seven U.S. Navy ships and planes assist landing of Cuban Brigade but take no part in the fighting, Apr. 17

Caribbean Sea

HONDURAS

Puerto Cabezas

EL SALVADOR

CIA-constructed air base used to train Cuban exile pilots

NICARAGUA

Staging area for invasion force

PACIFIC   OCEAN

⟹ U.S. naval forces
⟹ Transport ships with Cuban invasion troops
⟹ Flight path of B26 bombers
⟹ Cuban airfields bombed
✳ Battle

0   200   400 Miles
0   200   400 Kilometers

UNITED STATES
CUBA
Area of main map

Geography and History: Interpreting Maps
This map outlines the ill-fated Bay of Pigs invasion authorized by President Kennedy in 1961. *How were Guatemala and Nicaragua involved in the plan? How does the map show why the United States would want to maintain friendly governments in Latin American nations?*

The invasion, depicted in the map above, took place on April 17, 1961, and was a total disaster. An air strike failed to destroy Cuba's air power. Castro was therefore able to stop the United States–supported troops from coming ashore. When advisers urged Kennedy to use United States planes to provide air cover for the soldiers, he refused. Rather than continue a hopeless effort, he chose simply to cut his losses and accept defeat.

The United States lost a great deal of prestige in the disastrous attack. The nation's illegal effort to overthrow a legitimate government was exposed to the world. The United States faced anger from other countries in Latin America for violating agreements not to interfere in the rest of the Western Hemisphere. And the invasion itself was clumsy and incompetent. European leaders, who initially had high hopes for the new President, were concerned about the kind of leadership he planned to provide.

The Berlin Crisis Upset by the experience at the Bay of Pigs, Kennedy was now even more determined to respond firmly to what he perceived as a growing communist threat. Unfortunately, his first meeting with Soviet leader **Nikita Khrushchev** was another disaster.

This time the issue was Germany. After World War II, the Allies had divided Germany into zones, with the United States, Great Britain, the Soviet Union, and France each controlling one sector of the country. While the original intention was that the zones would be temporary, the lines had hardened as cold war tensions pitted the former Allies against each other. In time the western regions had been combined into one, creating the nation of West Germany, while the sector controlled by the Soviet Union became East Germany. The city of Berlin, lying inside East Germany, had been likewise divided. The Soviet effort to cut off access to Berlin in 1948 had failed as a result of President Truman's

Friendly governments in nations such as Guatemala and Nicaragua allowed the CIA to establish bases from which to prepare for the invasion. Such sympathetic governments were thus essential to United States foreign policy in the region.

Enrichment
The threat of a nuclear holocaust was very real in the 1960s. Ask students to use the *Reader's Guide to Periodical Literature* to locate and report on contemporary magazine articles about building, stocking, and maintaining fallout shelters.

 In Depth

Then and Now

When the Berlin Wall that divided East and West Germany for thirty years was torn down on November 9, 1989, a witness said that protesters "seemed to be drawn by the sense that . . . the barrier of concrete and steel that had figured so prominently in the history of this city and the world, might soon be relegated to history." And the reunification of Germany one year later proved to be just part of the collapse of the monolithic "iron curtain."

Using Historical Evidence A West Berlin resident walks along his side of the Berlin Wall. *Why was the wall an appropriate symbol of the cold war?*

to be prepared if the confrontation over Berlin led to a nuclear war. Kennedy appeared on television to tell the American people that West Berlin was "the great testing place of Western courage and will, a focal point where our solemn commitments . . . and Soviet ambitions now meet in basic confrontation." The United States, he said, would not be pushed around: "We do not want to fight—but we have fought before." This address, strategic analyst Michael Mandelbaum later declared, was "one of the most alarming speeches by an American President in the whole, nerve-wracking course of the cold war."

The Soviets responded by building a wall in Berlin. It effectively sealed East Berliners in their region of the city (and in East Germany) and so ended the immediate crisis. The **Berlin Wall** became an enduring symbol of East-West conflict for the next three decades.

The Cuban Missile Crisis Kennedy had a chance to regain his prestige in another confrontation in Cuba. The Soviet Union, disturbed by the attempted invasion at the Bay of Pigs, had pledged to support Cuba. In October 1962, photographs taken from a United States spy plane revealed that the Soviets were placing offensive missiles on Cuban soil. Khrushchev may have been trying to bolster Soviet standing in the international community by positioning missiles so close to the United States. He may have been trying to show that the Soviets would not allow their Cuban allies to be shoved around. In any event, the missiles did not alter the overall strategic balance, for the Soviets could already inflict serious damage on the United States from missile bases within their own country. But Kennedy was convinced that the missiles in Cuba presented a direct challenge to which he must respond. ❖

The President quickly convened his top advisers in a series of secret meetings. His brother Robert, serving as the nation's attorney general and his most influential adviser, argued against an air strike to knock out the missiles. It seemed, he said, too much like the Japanese attack on Pearl Harbor that had started World War II. Nonetheless, President Kennedy ordered United States forces on full alert. Bombers and missiles were armed with nuclear weapons. The

successful Berlin airlift. Now the Soviets made another effort to resolve problems in Berlin on their own terms. They demanded a peace treaty that would make the division of the city permanent and cut off the flow of East Germans into West Germany, particularly through Berlin.

Kennedy feared that the Soviet effort in Germany was part of a larger plan to take over the rest of Europe. Despite his need to establish himself as a leader in the international community, Kennedy's first conversation with Khrushchev in Vienna, Austria, in June 1961 went poorly. Kennedy felt bullied by the Soviet leader, and he knew he came off second best.

Upon returning home, Kennedy decided to show the Soviets that the United States would not be intimidated. He asked Congress for a huge increase of more than $3 billion for defense. He requested more men for the army, navy, and air force. He doubled the number of young men being drafted into the armed services, and he called up reserve forces for active duty. At the same time, he sought over $200 million for a program to build fallout shelters across the country, with the argument that the United States had fleet was ready to move. Soldiers were prepared to invade Cuba at a moment's notice.

Kennedy's advisers in the National Security Council realized the dangerousness of the situation in this **Cuban missile crisis,** especially with nuclear warheads poised ready for use. At one point former Secretary of State Dean Acheson joined the deliberations and declared that the United States had to knock out the Soviet missiles. He was then asked what would happen next. The following conversation records his response.

> ACHESON: *I know the Soviet Union well. I know what they are required to do in the light of their history and their posture around the world. I think they will knock out our missiles in Turkey.*
> AN NSC ADVISER: *Well, then what do we do?*
> ACHESON: *I believe under our NATO treaty . . . we would be required to respond by knocking out a missile base inside the Soviet Union.*
> ANOTHER ADVISER: *Then what do they do?*
> ACHESON: *That's when we hope that cooler heads will prevail, and they'll stop and talk.*

After preparing his forces, Kennedy went on television to tell the public about the missiles and to demand that the Soviets remove them. The United States, he said, would not shrink from the risk of nuclear war. He then announced a naval "quarantine" around Cuba to prevent the Soviets from bringing in more missiles. He was careful not to call the action a "blockade," because a blockade is an act of war.

For two days the two most powerful nations in the world stood teetering on the brink of disaster. Soviet ships steamed toward the quarantine line. United States forces were ready to respond as soon as the line was crossed. Then Khrushchev called the ships back, though work on the missile sites inside Cuba continued. A few days later Khrushchev sent Kennedy a long letter in which he pledged to remove the missiles if Kennedy promised that the United States would end the quarantine and stay out of Cuba. A second letter demanded that the United States remove its missiles from Turkey

Viewpoints
On the Cold War

The United States and its allies continued to battle against communist expansion in the 1960s. *What strategy did each of the following speakers want to pursue during the cold war?*

For Civility in the Cold War
"The issues called the cold war . . . will not be scolded away by invective [abusive language] nor frightened away by bluster. They must be met with determination, confidence, and sophistication. Unnecessary or pointless irritations should be removed; channels of communication should be kept open. . . . Our discussion, public or private, should be marked by civility; our manners should conform to our own dignity and power and to our good repute throughout the world."
Secretary of State Dean Rusk in a speech at the University of California, Berkeley, California, March 20, 1961

For Aggression in the Cold War
"It is our purpose to win the cold war, not merely wage it in the hope of attaining a standoff. . . . [I]t is really astounding that our government has never stated its purpose to be that of complete victory over the tyrannical forces of international communism. . . . We need a declaration that our intention is victory. . . . And we need an official act, such as the resumption of nuclear testing, to show our own peoples and the other freedom-loving peoples of the world that we mean business."
Senator Barry Goldwater of Arizona in an address to the United States Senate, July 14, 1961

in exchange for the withdrawal of Soviet missiles in Cuba. The United States accepted the terms of the first note and ignored the second. With that, the crisis was over. As Secretary of State Dean Rusk observed to President Kennedy, "We have won a considerable victory. You and I are still alive."

In the Cuban missile crisis, the world was closer than ever before to nuclear war. Far more powerful hydrogen bombs had replaced the first atomic weapons, and this was the closest the superpowers had come to using them. For a time, Kennedy emerged from the confrontation as a hero. He had stood up to the Soviets and shown that the United States would not be pushed around. His reputation, and that of the Democratic party, improved, and popular support

Viewpoints Activity On the Cold War, found in the Unit 9 folder, pp. 16–17, presents an expanded discussion of different views of the cold war and the policies proposed for battling communism.

Answer to . . .

Viewpoints

Rusk favors encouraging civil dialogue among nations throughout the world; Goldwater seeks a stated policy of armed aggression to crush communism. For a more thorough examination of the cold war, see the Resource Directory below.

In Depth
Historical Misconceptions

Although the outcome of the Cuban missile crisis seemed to limit the Soviet role there, the removal of Soviet missiles from Cuba in 1962 did not in fact lessen Soviet influence nor rid Cuba of dictatorship. "There is a good deal of unfinished business in Cuba," said Kennedy. "[Castro] still remains a major danger to the United States." Castro was still in power more than thirty years later when the breakup of the Soviet Union led to the departure of Russian troops in 1993.

3. ASSESS

Section 3 Review Answers

1. (a) Peace Corps, see p. 785, (b) Berlin Wall, see p. 788, (c) Limited Test Ban Treaty, see p. 790

2. Nikita Khrushchev, see p. 787

3. Bay of Pigs, see p. 786

4. The confrontation over Berlin showed Kennedy's willingness to do anything to avoid being pushed around. When Kennedy felt bullied by Khrushchev at their first meeting in Vienna, he responded by calling for more troops and for civil defense measures to show he was ready for war.

5. Satellite photography revealed that the Soviet Union was developing a missile base in Cuba, which the United States interpreted as a threatening gesture. Both sides talked of aggressive action. Khrushchev backed down. Faced with the American quarantine, he called Soviet ships back and agreed to remove offensive missiles from Cuba if the United States ended the blockade and promised not to invade Cuba.

6. Johnson's approach to foreign affairs differed from Kennedy's. Kennedy had been most interested in foreign affairs; Johnson considered them something of a nuisance. Both leaders agreed, however, in the view that the Soviet Union was trying to spread communism and in responding aggressively to any perceived threat.

DON'T WORRY.
THEY'RE STILL 90 MILES AWAY!

The tongue-in-cheek slogan on this bumper sticker refers to the Soviet missiles in Cuba, which marked the presence of the enemy only 90 miles off the Florida coast.

helped with mid-term congressional elections just weeks away. In time, however, critics came to suggest that what Kennedy felt was his finest hour was actually a rash and extreme response to a situation that could have been handled more rationally. Kennedy had not used traditional diplomatic channels to try to defuse the crisis, but rather had proclaimed his willingness to move to the brink of nuclear war and even beyond. He avoided disaster, Dean Acheson later observed, by "plain dumb luck."

The Cuban missile crisis did lead to a number of efforts to reduce the risk of nuclear war. Once the confrontation was over, Kennedy and Khrushchev established a "hot line" between their two nations to allow for immediate discussion in the event of a future crisis. In the summer of 1963, they also signed the first nuclear treaty since the development of the atomic bomb. The **Limited Test Ban Treaty** banned nuclear testing above the ground, and so eliminated the radioactive fallout that was threatening to contaminate human, animal, and plant life. It still permitted underground testing, and scientists proved

After coming close to war with the Soviets early in his presidency, Kennedy signed the Limited Test Ban Treaty in 1963. In a nation-wide television address following the signing, Kennedy said, "Let us, if we can, step back from the shadows of war and seek out the way of peace."

resourceful in creating bigger and better bombs that way, but it was nonetheless, as Kennedy noted, "an important first step toward peace, a step toward reason, a step away from war."

Yet despite such steps, turmoil still afflicted the relationship between the United States and the Soviet Union. In Southeast Asia, conflict between communist North Vietnam and United States–backed South Vietnam was escalating. In the years ahead, it would lead the United States into war.

MAKING CONNECTIONS

Do you agree with Robert Kennedy that for the United States to strike Soviet missile sites in Cuba would have been similar to the Japanese attack on Pearl Harbor? Explain your answer.

LBJ and Foreign Affairs

Whereas Kennedy had been passionately concerned with the world abroad, President Johnson was preoccupied with domestic policy. Johnson was convinced that he could cajole foreign leaders with the same ease with which he controlled policymakers at home. His dismissive attitude toward smaller countries led the United States into some large and costly conflicts.

Trouble in Panama Johnson was frustrated by what he called those "piddly little" countries in Latin America. Soon after he had assumed the presidency, Panama asked for a renegotiation of the treaty Theodore Roosevelt had signed in 1903 guaranteeing the United States access to the Canal Zone. The symbolic issue of which flag—the United States or the Panamanian—should fly in the zone led to a riot and loss of life. Johnson phoned the Panamanian leader and helped cool the situation, then authorized discussions that eventually led to a new treaty.

Invasion of the Dominican Republic In the Dominican Republic, Johnson acted more aggressively. In 1965 he heard that the military rulers in this Caribbean nation close to Cuba had been attacked by rebels, and that the

▶ **RESOURCE DIRECTORY**

Teaching Resources

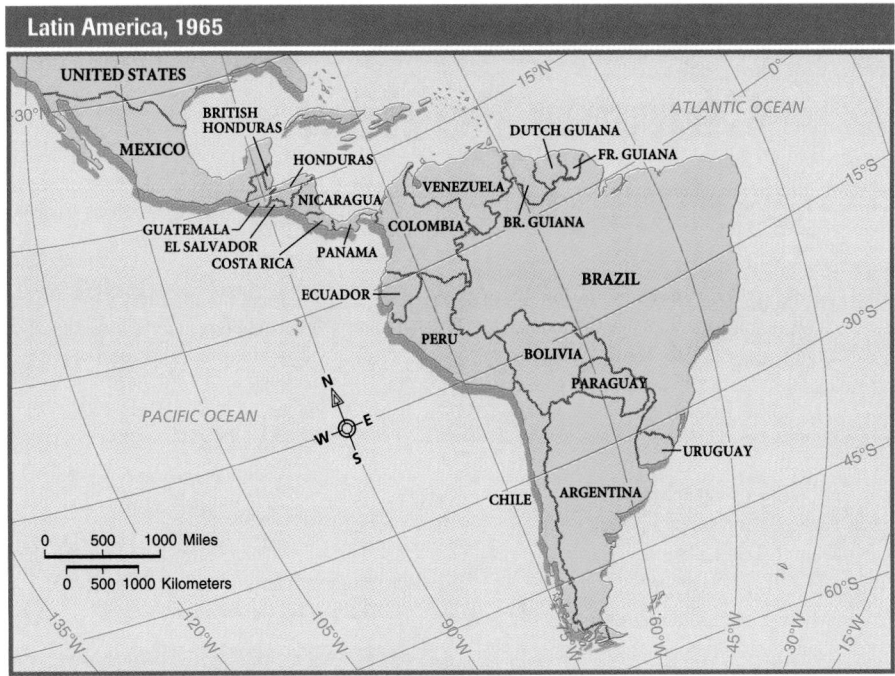

Latin America, 1965

UNITED STATES
MEXICO
BRITISH HONDURAS
HONDURAS
GUATEMALA
EL SALVADOR
COSTA RICA
NICARAGUA
PANAMA
ECUADOR
PERU
BOLIVIA
CHILE
ATLANTIC OCEAN
DUTCH GUIANA
FR. GUIANA
VENEZUELA
COLOMBIA
BR. GUIANA
BRAZIL
PARAGUAY
URUGUAY
ARGENTINA
PACIFIC OCEAN

0   500   1000 Miles
0   500 1000 Kilometers

Geography and History: Interpreting Maps
President Johnson often felt annoyed when faced with problems in Latin America that took his attention away from domestic policy. *In the context of the cold war, why did United States leaders consider it important to maintain a strong presence in this part of the world?*

disruption might endanger United States citizens living there. LBJ was livid. Arguing (wrongly, it turned out) that communist elements were causing the disruption, he sent 22,000 marines to the Dominican Republic. The presence of the United States forces tipped the balance away from the rebels. Johnson's action promoted stability in the Dominican

Republic, but only at the cost of supporting a repressive military government.

Meanwhile, the Vietnam War began and soon consumed more and more resources. Johnson tried to take the same approach in Vietnam as he had in the Dominican Republic. As will be discussed in Chapter 31, his policy there had much more disastrous results.

SECTION 3 REVIEW

Key Terms, People, and Places
1. Define (a) Peace Corps, (b) Berlin Wall, (c) Limited Test Ban Treaty.
2. Identify Nikita Khrushchev.
3. Identify Bay of Pigs.

Key Concepts
4. What was the significance of Kennedy's confrontation with Khrushchev over Berlin?
5. What was the Cuban missile crisis, and how did it end?

6. Was President Johnson's approach to foreign affairs similar to or different from Kennedy's? Explain your answer.

Critical Thinking
7. **Demonstrating Reasoned Judgment** Dean Acheson called Kennedy's success in the Cuban missile crisis a result of "plain dumb luck." Do you agree or disagree with this opinion? Give reasons to support your answer.

 Quiz found in the Unit 9 folder, p. 11, covers the main ideas in this section as well as the key terms.

 Chapter Test Forms A and B are found in the Unit 9 folder, pp. 28–33.

 Answer Keys found in the Unit 9 folder, pp. 146–159, provides answers to all student activities.

Media and Technology

Transparency
Graphic Organizer, G-4

Guided Reading Audiotapes
(English and Spanish)

Computer Test Bank

---

7. Answers will vary. Students may cite Kennedy's lack of experience and his failure to use normal diplomatic channels to deal with the crisis as evidence to support Acheson's claim. Others may suggest that Kennedy instinctively sensed that the only way to deal with Khrushchev was to bully him, as Khrushchev had bullied Kennedy in Vienna.

Caption Answer to ...

 Interpreting Maps

During the cold war, United States leaders sought to contain communist influence all over the world. Communist governments in Latin America seemed especially threatening because this region was so close to the United States.

Reteach

Ask students to identify the following cold war crises by writing the name of the country in which each occurred.

• The United States and the Soviet Union came close to war over a buildup of Soviet missiles here.
• When the Soviets demanded a peace treaty that permanently divided this city, Kennedy responded forcefully.
• The bungled invasion here by opponents of Fidel Castro was organized by the United States.
• President Johnson sent troops to this country in 1965 to put down a rebellion.

4. CLOSE

 Reinforcing the Big Idea

President Kennedy acted boldly to maintain United States strength in the cold war, at times bringing the nation perilously close to war. President Johnson, though little interested in foreign affairs, sent United States troops to quell a rebellion in the Dominican Republic.

Chapter Review Answers

Understanding Key Terms, People, and Places

Terms
Students should refer to the definitions of the key terms in the chapter to write sentences that show the relation of each word to domestic and foreign policy during the presidencies of John F. Kennedy and Lyndon B. Johnson.

True or False
1. false, Great Society
2. false, Peace Corps
3. false, Limited Test Ban Treaty
4. false, Medicare
5. false, Immigration Act of 1965

Matching
1. Earl Warren
2. John F. Kennedy
3. Lyndon B. Johnson

Reviewing Main Ideas

1. In the legendary kingdom of Camelot, King Arthur wanted to transform Britain into a country where strength was used to achieve right. Americans saw the Kennedy administration as symbolizing a similar idealism.

2. Kennedy wanted to stimulate the economy with a large tax cut, which he thought would help the poor indirectly. Later he proposed direct aid to the poor. He also expanded the space program.

3. Kennedy lacked a mandate from the electorate and was unable to push his programs through Congress. In addition, he addressed the problem of poverty too late in his presidency.

4. (a) The nation was shattered. Millions of Americans mourned as they watched the tragedy unfold on television. (b) The Warren Commission was formed to investigate the crime.

5. Johnson was forceful, energetic, and ambitious. His ability to win people over to his point of view helped him to get the votes he needed to pass the legislation he supported.

6. The Great Society was Johnson's program to increase the social well-being of all Americans. This program aimed to create a truly humane society that was more than simply rich and powerful.

7. In *Gideon* v. *Wainwright* (1963), the Supreme Court upheld the rights of persons accused of crimes by defending the right to free legal aid. *Escobedo* v. *Illinois* (1964) guaranteed defendants access to an attorney during questioning, and *Miranda* v. *Arizona* (1966) held that a

---

Chapter Review

Understanding Key Terms, People, and Places

Key Terms
1. liberal consensus
2. mandate
3. New Frontier
4. Warren Commission
5. Great Society
6. Volunteers in Service to America
7. Medicare
8. Immigration Act of 1965
9. Peace Corps
10. Berlin Wall
11. Cuban missile crisis
12. Limited Test Ban Treaty

People
13. John F. Kennedy
14. Earl Warren
15. Lyndon B. Johnson
16. Nikita Khrushchev

Places
17. Bay of Pigs

Terms For each term above, write a sentence that explains how it relates to domestic and foreign policy during the presidencies of John F. Kennedy and Lyndon B. Johnson.

True or False Determine whether each statement is true or false. If it is true, write "true." If it is false, change the underlined term to make the statement true.
1. Lyndon Johnson's <u>New Frontier</u> focused on domestic policy.
2. President Kennedy's <u>Medicare</u> program sent American volunteers abroad to help people in developing countries.
3. The <u>Warren Commission</u> prohibited above-ground nuclear testing.
4. <u>VISTA</u> was designed to provide medical care for older Americans.
5. The <u>Limited Test Ban Treaty</u> eliminated quotas that had discriminated against immigrants from areas outside northern and western Europe.

Matching Review the key people in the list above. If you are not sure of a person's significance, review that person in the chapter. Then choose a name from the list that best matches each description below.
1. the head of the group that investigated the Kennedy assassination
2. the leader who ordered United States forces on full alert during the Cuban missile crisis
3. the creator of the Great Society

Reviewing Main Ideas

Section 1 (pp. 772–775)
1. Explain why the Kennedy administration was compared to the Broadway musical *Camelot*.
2. What domestic programs did Kennedy propose?
3. Why was Kennedy's domestic policy largely unsuccessful?
4. (a) How did the nation react to Kennedy's assassination in 1963? (b) What later actions were taken to investigate his death?

Section 2 (pp. 777–781)
5. How did Lyndon Johnson's personality help him advance his political career?
6. Explain Johnson's statement to University of Michigan students that they had the opportunity to move "upward toward the Great Society."

7. Describe three Supreme Court decisions of the 1960s that supported the ideals of the Great Society.
8. What criticisms of the Great Society surfaced?

Section 3 (pp. 784–791)
9. For what reasons did President Kennedy initiate the Peace Corps?
10. What did the invasion at the Bay of Pigs and the Berlin crisis reveal about President Kennedy's foreign policy?
11. How did President Kennedy interpret the presence of Soviet missiles in Cuba?
12. What was Johnson's approach to foreign policy?
13. How did foreign affairs affect Johnson's Great Society programs?

---

suspect must be informed of his or her rights before questioning. In *Griswold* v. *Connecticut* (1965) the Court upheld a couple's right to privacy.

8. Middle-class Americans felt that too many of their tax dollars were being spent on the poor; critics argued that the federal government could not respond appropriately to the needs of local communities; radicals argued that programs did not go far enough; conservatives argued that they went too far.

9. Kennedy initiated the Peace Corps to help people in developing nations.

10. These incidents revealed that Kennedy was firmly anticommunist, inexperienced in foreign affairs, and willing to take great risks.

11. He saw the missiles as a direct threat to national security requiring an immediate response.

12. Johnson was more interested in domestic than foreign policy. However, he was militantly anticommunist, as he demonstrated when he sent United States forces to fight rebels in the Dominican Republic who he thought were backed by communists.

13. Johnson's contemptuous attitude toward smaller foreign nations resulted in costly conflicts for the United States. Foreign affairs diverted Johnson's attention from Great Society programs, as well as the money to support them.

1. **Making Comparisons** Describe the programs you would implement if you were to create a Great Society today. In what ways would they be similar to the programs of Johnson's Great Society?

2. **Predicting Consequences** How did the beliefs of Kennedy and Johnson about the spread of communism abroad lead to United States involvement in the Vietnam War?

1. **Evaluating Primary Sources** Review the first primary source excerpt on page 789. What does this conversation reveal about the way in which ideologies—fundamental political beliefs—determined the actions of the United States and Soviet governments during the cold war?

2. **Understanding the Visuals** Look at the tables on page 774. How might the facts illustrated in the table on income distribution have affected President Kennedy's ability to influence Congress to change NASA spending, as shown in the second table?

3. **Writing About the Chapter** You are a top adviser to President Kennedy when photos from a United States spy plane reveal the presence of Soviet missiles in Cuba. Write a memo advising the President on how to handle the situation. First, make a list of the various actions that the President might take. Note both the positive and negative aspects of each. Next,

write a draft of your memo in which you offer each possibility, describe its pros and cons, and finish with your recommendation for the best course of action. Revise your memo, making certain that each possible course of action is clearly explained. Proofread your memo and draft a final copy.

4. **Using the Graphic Organizer** This graphic organizer uses a flow map to organize information about foreign policy in the 1960s. (a) Based on the information in the flow map, what earlier event may have caused President Kennedy to need to regain the respect of the international community during the Cuban missile crisis? (b) What was the Soviet response to Kennedy's declaration that West Berlin was a testing ground for Western resolve? (c) On a separate sheet of paper, create your own flow map about the Great Society, using this flow map as an example.

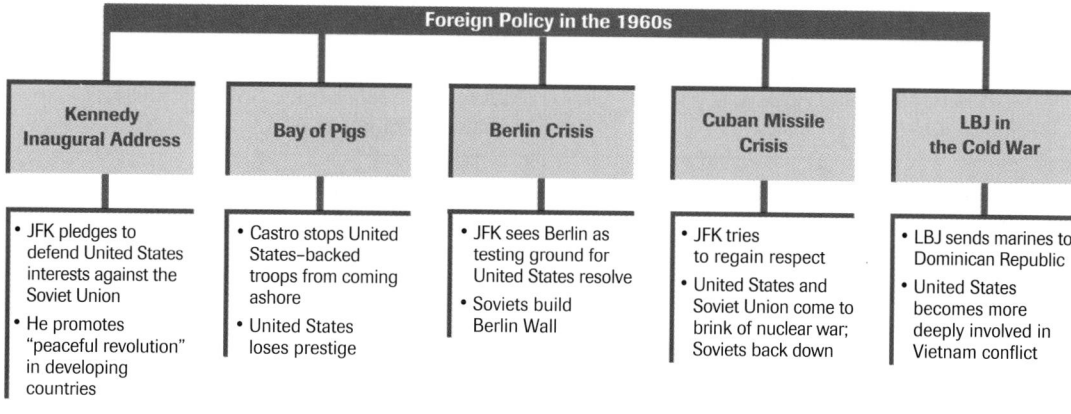

Foreign Policy in the 1960s

Kennedy Inaugural Address	Bay of Pigs	Berlin Crisis	Cuban Missile Crisis	LBJ in the Cold War
• JFK pledges to defend United States interests against the Soviet Union • He promotes "peaceful revolution" in developing countries	• Castro stops United States–backed troops from coming ashore • United States loses prestige	• JFK sees Berlin as testing ground for United States resolve • Soviets build Berlin Wall	• JFK tries to regain respect • United States and Soviet Union come to brink of nuclear war; Soviets back down	• LBJ sends marines to Dominican Republic • United States becomes more deeply involved in Vietnam conflict

3. Students' memos should mention alternative solutions to the crisis such as ignoring the Soviet missiles, negotiation, and economic or political pressure. They should also mention the pros and cons of each and conclude with a recommendation for a course of action.

4. (a) The flow map indicates that the United States lost prestige during the Bay of Pigs affair. (b) The Soviets' response was to build the Berlin Wall. (c) Students' graphic organizers should include information about Johnson's tax cut, his war on poverty, health care legislation, aid to education, and other proposals.

 Alternative Assessment

Final Evaluation
Use the following guidelines to evaluate student projects:
● **Evidence of mastery of content** To what extent do projects show knowledge and understanding of chapter content?
● **Evidence of thoughtfulness** To what extent do projects reflect a personal position?
● **Evidence of outside research** To what extent do projects reflect outside research?

Thinking Critically

1. Students may propose a variety of social welfare programs to combat such contemporary problems as homelessness and unemployment. Students may mention that while the focus has shifted somewhat, many of the issues of the 1960s, such as civil rights and affordable medical care, are still unresolved.

2. Both Kennedy and Johnson were convinced that communism needed to be fought wherever it turned up, or else the Soviet Union and its allies would take control of the world. Thus they were willing to send United States troops to fight the forces of Ho Chi Minh in Vietnam.

Making Connections

1. Both superpowers had an almost blind, irrational fear of the threat each nation posed to the other. Thus, a United States strike in Cuba would "require" the Soviet Union to hit missile sites in Turkey, and so on. The cold war made honest diplomatic talks seem a last resort rather than an obvious first step toward solving disputes.

2. Because of the huge expense of the space program—especially compared with Americans' salaries—members of Congress were probably under pressure from constituents not to increase spending on such programs. Thus, Congress was likely to make it difficult for Kennedy to pass legislation increasing spending on NASA.

Chapter 29 The Civil Rights Movement
1960–1968

📁 Teaching Resources (See Unit 9 Folder)

	Instruction	Enrichment
Section 1 **Leaders and Strategies** (pp. 796–801)	Reproducible Lesson Plan, p. 35 Alternate Lesson Plan, p. 146 Guided Reading and Review, p. 39 Quiz, p. 40	American Profiles Activity, Thurgood Marshall, p. 50 Viewpoints Activity, On School Integration, pp. 51–52 Visual Learning Activity, Passive Resistance, p. 61 Literature Activity, SNCC Workers, pp. 58–59 Historian's Toolbox Activity, Using Autobiography and Biography, p. 53
Section 2 **Nonviolent Confrontation: A Turning Point in History** (pp. 803–807)	Reproducible Lesson Plan, p. 36 Alternate Lesson Plan, p. 147 Guided Reading and Review, p. 41 Quiz, p. 42	American Profiles Activity, Sidney Poitier, p. 49 Primary Source Activity, Protecting the Freedom Riders, p. 55 Turning Points Extension Activity, The Lasting Impact of Nonviolent Confrontation, pp. 47–48
Section 3 **The Political Response** (pp. 810–814)	Reproducible Lesson Plan, p. 37 Alternate Lesson Plan, p. 148 Guided Reading and Review, p. 43 Quiz, p. 44	Primary Source Activity, Registering to Vote in Mississippi, pp. 56–57 Visual Learning Activity, A White House Demonstration, p. 62
Section 4 **The Challenge of Black Power** (pp. 815–819)	Reproducible Lesson Plan, p. 38 Alternate Lesson Plan, p. 149 Guided Reading and Review, p. 45 Quiz, p. 46 Chapter Test, Forms A & B, pp. 63–68	Literature Activity, Sins of the Fathers, p. 60 Critical Thinking Activity, Demonstrating Reasoned Judgment, p. 54

📁 Additional Chapter Resources

Resource Organizer, p. 34
Alternate Lesson Plan, p. 145
Answer Keys, pp. 149–159

Bibliography

For the Teacher

Branch, Taylor. *Parting the Waters: America in the King Years, 1954–1963.* Simon & Schuster, 1988. (Chronicles the times from Eisenhower to Kennedy.)

Davis, Flora. *Moving the Mountain: The Women's Movement in America Since 1960.* Simon & Schuster, 1991. (Blends archival material with interviews to trace the movement from the 1960s to the early 1990s.)

Prentice Hall Literature Excerpts from *The American Experience,* 1994, including Walker, Alice. "Everyday Use," from *In Love and Trouble: Stories of Black Women.* Harcourt Brace, 1967.

THE BIG IDEA

The Big Idea for the chapter and how the main ideas in each section relate to the Big Idea are graphically displayed below. Comprehension of this chapter's Big Idea is critical to students' understanding of United States history and how we as a nation got where we are today.

Media and Technology

  Visions of America: Turning Point Story, "Nonviolent Solutions" (length: approx. 4 minutes)

  Visions of America: Roundtable Discussion of "Nonviolent Solutions"

 Critical Thinking, I-17; Graphic Organizer, G-3

 Guided Reading Audiotapes (English and Spanish)

 Computer Test Bank

For the Student

"Eyes on the Prize." PBS Video. (Comprehensive six-part series on the history of the civil rights movement from 1954.)

Raines, Howell. *My Soul Is Rested: Movement Days in the Deep South Remembered.* Penguin, 1983 edition. (First-person accounts of participants in major civil rights events.)

CHAPTER 29

The 1960s were a time of great progress and great frustration for African Americans. Through nonviolent protests and an extremely focused civil rights struggle, African Americans ended institutional segregation and secured voting rights in the South. Lack of progress in economic issues, especially in urban areas, however, drove some to vent their anger through bitter violence.

SECTION 1

The civil rights movement was diverse in its tactics but united in its goal of halting segregation.

SECTION 2

Nonviolent protests—on segregated buses and at whites-only lunch counters—brought both violence and victories and revealed the courage of ordinary Americans in standing up for their convictions.

SECTION 3

As the voices of protest grew, politicians could no longer ignore the issue of civil rights.

SECTION 4

Not content with limited progress and continuing discrimination, African American frustration turned to violence—and the civil rights movement split on its response to discrimination.

The Civil Rights Movement
1960–1968

 The Relevance of the Big Idea

The civil rights movement of the 1990s is similar to the 1960s movement in some significant ways—progress and frustration are still its major characteristics. African Americans are no longer fighting for the right to vote; they are steadily increasing their representation in legislative bodies across the country. Yet they still face problems of housing and job discrimination, as well as high poverty and mortality rates. The impoverished ghettos of urban America and starkly poor rural communities still simmer—and sometimes boil over, as witnessed in the Los Angeles riots of 1992.

Ask students to list ways in which African Americans today are trying to call attention to the inequities that they suffer. Discuss the goals of each method.

 In Depth

Global Connections

While the civil rights movement of the 1960s forced the American people to turn inward, the nation was also experiencing a revolution in international communications. In 1965, the first operational communications satellite, *Early Bird,* was launched; and by the late 1960s, satellite telecasts could be seen by 500 million viewers in thirty nations. The war in Vietnam, civil rights marches, and riots in the street all appeared on the nation's TV screens at home. This leap forward in communications has been compared to the 1866 opening of the first transatlantic telegraph link.

The Civil Rights Movement
1960–1968

After scoring major legal victories through the 1950s, the civil rights movement enjoyed a groundswell of popular support in the 1960s. African Americans and others focused their attention on ending segregation and securing voting rights in the South. The battle against inequality was a bitter and often violent one, but it yielded significant results by the middle of the decade. Once desegregation was under way, the movement began to address the more subtle issues of economic injustice that plagued the nation's urban centers.

Events in the United States

1960	1961	1962	1963
	1961 Freedom Riders challenge segregation on interstate buses.	**1962** James Meredith becomes the first African American student to attend the University of Mississippi.	**1963** Martin Luther King writes his "Letter from a Birmingham Jail." • The March on Washington takes place.

Events in the World

1960	1961	1962	1963
1960 Congo and Nigeria win independence. • South Africa bans the African National Congress.	**1961** Mao Zedong's economic plan, the Great Leap Forward, ends in China.	**1962** Algeria and Uganda win independence. • The Soviet Union removes missiles from Cuba.	**1963** The Organization of African Unity is founded.

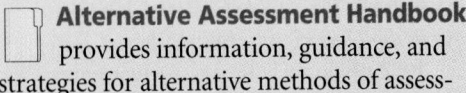 **RESOURCE DIRECTORY**

Teaching Resources

Alternate Lesson Plan Demonstrating the Big Idea, found in the Alternate Lesson Plans folder, p. 145, provides a strategy to instruct students about the Big Idea that a highly focused civil rights movement in the 1960s resulted in some progress, but frustration and disagreement eventually split the movement.

Alternative Assessment Handbook provides information, guidance, and strategies for alternative methods of assessment. It includes an essay on new trends in assessment, guidance and strategies for developing performance tasks and portfolios, scoring rubrics, and sample evaluation forms.

Pages 796–801

Leaders and Strategies

Civil rights groups in the 1960s were as diverse as the people in the movement. Each group had its own priorities, but all spoke up against violence and unfair treatment of African Americans with a clear, strong voice that said, "No more."

Pages 803–807

Nonviolent Confrontation: A Turning Point in History

"We Shall Overcome," sang civil rights protesters, revealing both their spirit of nonviolence and their steadfast commitment to the cause. Acts such as sitting at "whites only" lunch counters brought vicious responses, but also showed the courage and determination of the protesters.

Pages 808–809

The Lasting Impact of Nonviolent Confrontation

Pages 810–814

The Political Response

For politicians in the early 1960s, taking a firm stand in favor of civil rights was a risky business. As the decade wore on, however, the rising voice of protest no longer could be ignored in Washington.

Pages 815–819

The Challenge of Black Power

During the civil rights movement, change happened slowly and at times appeared to have ground to a halt. The response from some African Americans was a call for self-defense—even if it meant using violence.

1964 Congress passes the Civil Rights Act. • Three young civil rights activists are killed in Mississippi.	1965 Congress passes Voting Rights Act. • Malcolm X is assassinated. • Watts riot occurs.	1966 The militant Black Panther party is founded. • Splits develop in civil rights movement.		1968 The Kerner Commission publishes its report on civil disobedience.
1964	**1965**	**1966**	**1967**	**1968**
1964 The Beatles achieve international fame as rock musicians. • Palestine Liberation Organization is founded.		1966 The Cultural Revolution begins in China.	1967 First successful human heart transplant takes place in South Africa. • Israel defeats Arabs in Six-Day War.	1968 Japanese novelist Kawabata Yasunari wins Nobel Prize in literature.

Media and Technology

Transparency
Fine Art, D-19

1. FOCUS

Connecting to the Big Idea

See page 794B. Explain to students that the civil rights movement was not a monolithic organization under the sway of one leader. The groups were as diverse as the people in the movement. Ask students to note in what ways it was diverse and in what ways it was united.

Objectives

● Describe the variety of opinions and goals within the civil rights movement.

● Identify Martin Luther King, Jr., and explain his role in the civil rights movement.

Bellringer

Ask students to think of ways in which people can protest without resorting to violence. What advantages do these tactics have?

Reading Strategy

Question Writing Ask students to read the section headings and subheadings and formulate a question pertaining to each. Then have them answer the questions they have written as they read.

Leaders and Strategies

SECTION PREVIEW

Civil rights groups in the 1960s were as diverse as the people in the movement. Each group had its own priorities, but all spoke up against violence and unfair treatment of African Americans with a clear, strong voice that said, "No more."

The Congress of Racial Equality was one of many civil rights groups committed to improving the status of African Americans. This hat was designed to be worn at the 1963 March on Washington.

Key Concepts

● The civil rights movement consisted of many separate groups, each with a slightly different aim within the larger goal of social equality.

● Martin Luther King, Jr., was a Southern Baptist minister who became a leader in the civil rights movement through his powerful speaking and commitment to nonviolent resistance.

Key Terms, People, and Places

interracial, Congress of Racial Equality (CORE), Southern Christian Leadership Conference (SCLC), Student Nonviolent Coordinating Committee (SNCC)

T he civil rights movement was composed of ordinary citizens whose courage and determination to end racial injustice in the United States brought remarkable changes to the nation. As in all grassroots movements, the motivation for change came from the experiences and beliefs of a large number of people at the local level, not from a central organization directing activities. Several groups did form, however, out of the need to share information and coordinate activities within the movement. Each of the groups described in this section had its own goals and concerns, but all of them helped to focus the energies of thousands of Americans committed to securing civil rights for all citizens.

The NAACP Focuses on Legal Issues

By the time the civil rights movement began to make its impact felt in the 1960s, the National Association for the Advancement of Colored People (NAACP) was one of the oldest civil rights organizations in the United States. It had been founded in 1910 to promote equality, remove obstacles to voting for all Americans, and secure full legal equality. W.E.B. Du Bois, a prominent African American scholar who had been one of the founding members, summarized the NAACP's goals in a memo to its board of directors:

> T he main object of this association is to secure for colored people, and particularly for Americans of Negro descent, free and equal participation in the democracy of modern culture. This means the clearing away of obstructions to such participation, effort toward fitting these people for this participation, and it means also the making of a world democracy in which all men may participate.

The NAACP was **interracial**—it consisted of both African Americans and white Americans working together for the common goal of equality. Du Bois, who was the first African American to receive a doctoral degree from Harvard University, served as director of publicity and research. He also edited the NAACP magazine, the *Crisis*.

One major focus of NAACP activity was to put an end to lynching. The organization's efforts succeeded in getting two antilynching bills passed by the House of Representatives in the 1930s. Southern leaders in the Senate prevented these bills from becoming law, but the NAACP kept the issue of lynching in the public eye.

The NAACP was more successful in its court battles. In the 1920s and 1930s, it had won a number of legal battles in the areas of

---

▶ RESOURCE DIRECTORY

Teaching Resources

Reproducible Lesson Plan found in the Unit 9 folder, p. 35, provides a summary of the Section 1 lesson plan content.

Alternate Lesson Plan: Cooperative Learning found in the Alternate Lesson Plans folder, p. 146, helps groups of students focus on the goals and strategies of civil rights activists through writing speeches for civil rights leaders.

Guided Reading and Review found in the Unit 9 folder, p. 39, provides a structure for reading and mastering the key concepts and reviewing the key terms for Section 1. (Guided Practice)

✪ **American Profiles Activity** found in the Unit 9 folder, p. 50, profiles Thurgood Marshall, the first African American justice on the U.S. Supreme Court, whose remarkable legal career was devoted to championing civil rights.

In its efforts to desegregate public schools, the NAACP leadership frequently met with civil rights leaders in the South, where school segregation was especially entrenched. In a 1955 meeting in Atlanta, Georgia, NAACP leaders met with African American leaders from southern states to discuss the latest Supreme Court ruling that public school desegregation begin "with all deliberate speed." Seated at the table second from the left is Thurgood Marshall, NAACP chief counsel.

housing and education and scored a major victory in the 1954 *Brown* v. *Board of Education* decision. (See Chapter 27, Section 4.) ✪

Although the NAACP appealed primarily to middle- and upper-class African Americans, it also welcomed the support of whites in the effort to end social and political discrimination. Sometimes, in its emphasis on achieving legal equality for all races, the organization appeared out of touch with the more basic issues of economic survival faced by many African American citizens.

Other organizations emerged to fill that gap. The National Urban League, founded in 1911, sought to assist people moving to major American cities. It helped African Americans moving out of the South find homes and jobs and made sure that they received fair treatment at work. Urban League workers looked for migrant families on ship docks and at train stations. They placed them in apartments they had inspected, and they insisted factory owners and union leaders teach African American workers the skills that could lead to better jobs. Urban League activities complemented those of the NAACP.

CORE Continues Its Fight

The **Congress of Racial Equality (CORE)** took another approach. It had been founded in 1942 by pacifists dedicated to bringing about change through peaceful confrontation. It too was interracial, including both African American and white members. During World War II, CORE had organized demonstrations against segregation in cities including Baltimore, Chicago, Denver, and Detroit.

In the years after World War II, CORE director James Farmer worked without pay in order to keep the organization alive. The growing interest in civil rights in the 1950s gave him a new base of support and allowed him to turn CORE into a national organization. It would soon play a major role in the confrontations that lay ahead.

SCLC: A Southern Group Emerges

Another key organization in the civil rights movement was the **Southern Christian Leadership Conference (SCLC).** It was founded in 1957 by Martin Luther King, Jr.,

Discuss

Ask students to read the quotation by Martin Luther King, Jr., at the top of page 799. Then discuss these questions: Do you agree with King's view that the failure to fight oppression made African Americans guilty of cooperating with evil? What values and beliefs did King hold that caused him to view the struggle this way?

Analyze

Ask students to respond to this question: Why did the civil rights movement splinter into many factions instead of uniting as one?

In Depth

Biography

Baptist minister Jesse Jackson (b. 1941) was a close aide to Martin Luther King, Jr. Jackson headed Operation Breadbasket, a Southern Christian Leadership Conference (SCLC) program to expand educational and job opportunities for African Americans, until 1971. He then founded People United to Save Humanity (PUSH), which grew to a membership of 80,000. PUSH brought Jackson into the national spotlight. In 1984, he unsuccessfully ran for the Democratic presidential nomination, but his candidacy spurred African American voter registration. "Hands that picked cotton in 1884," said Jackson, "will pick the President in 1984."

Answer to ...

Viewpoints

Kennedy expresses frustration at the slow course of change in the civil rights area of school integration; Wallace symbolizes the intransigence of the South. For a more thorough examination of the school integration issue, see the Resource Directory below.

In Depth

Historical Misconceptions

Dorothy Cotton, a leader of the Southern Christian Leadership Conference (SCLC), found that internally the group fell short of its egalitarian goals and was instead more of a microcosm of society at large. "I'm conscious of the fact that I did have a decision-making role," she states. "But I'm also very conscious of the male chauvinism that existed within the Movement. I was on the executive staff, and that's where a lot of the decisions got made, but I'm also aware that like any other place . . . historically, where there was a female sitting, she was always asked to go get the coffee and take notes."

Viewpoints
On School Integration

In parts of the Deep South, the battle for equal rights continued to be fought at the nation's schoolhouse doors each September, even after the Supreme Court ordered schools to desegregate in 1954. *How do the viewpoints below reflect the course of the civil rights movement of the 1960s?*

For School Integration

"Nearly nine years have elapsed since the Supreme Court ruled that state laws requiring or permitting segregated schools violate the Constitution. That decision represented both good law and good judgment—it was both legally and morally right. Since that time it has become increasingly clear that neither violence nor legalistic measures will be tolerated as a means of thwarting court-ordered desegregation."

President John F. Kennedy,
message to Congress, February 28, 1963

Against School Integration

"I draw the line in the dust and toss the gauntlet before the feet of tyranny and I say segregation today, segregation tomorrow, segregation forever."

Governor George Wallace (Alabama),
inaugural address, January 14, 1963

and other African American clergymen after their success in the Montgomery bus boycott (see Chapter 27). Initially, sixty African Americans from ten states convened in Atlanta, Georgia, and agreed that they needed to coordinate their efforts. They urged African Americans "to assert their human dignity" and to refuse "further cooperation with evil." A month later, one hundred African American ministers took the next step they had agreed on and met in New Orleans, Louisiana. Later they elected King president of what came to be called the Southern Christian Leadership Conference. In its first official statement, SCLC called on African Americans

to understand that nonviolence is not a symbol of weakness or cowardice, but as Jesus demonstrated, nonviolent resistance transforms weakness into strength and breeds courage in the face of danger.

It was SCLC that shifted the focus of the civil rights movement to the South. Other civil rights organizations had been dominated by northerners. Now southern African American church leaders moved into the forefront of the struggle for equal rights.

Martin Luther King Leads a Movement
King used his post at SCLC to become a leader in the national civil rights movement. He had been born in Atlanta and raised in a prominent Baptist family. Both his father and his grandfather were ministers, and he followed in their footsteps. King grew up memorizing biblical passages and watching members of his family fight for African American rights. He went to Morehouse College in Atlanta, then received a divinity degree from the Crozer Theological Seminary in Pennsylvania. He later earned his Ph.D. from Boston University. He preached to his first congregation in Montgomery, Alabama. Before he was thirty years old, King was playing a central role in the civil rights movement as a result of his articulate leadership of the bus boycott.

King was influenced by the beliefs of Mohandas Gandhi. Gandhi was a great Indian leader who had won a fierce struggle to gain his country's independence from Great Britain in 1947. Gandhi preached that nonviolence was the only way to achieve victory against much stronger foes. It would not help to fight violence with violence. Rather, those who fought for justice must peacefully refuse to obey unjust laws and must remain nonviolent—regardless of the violent reaction such peaceful resistance might provoke. ✪

Nonviolence Training As the Montgomery boycott came to a successful conclusion, King began training followers for what they might expect in the months ahead. Films describing Gandhi's activities were shown regularly in African American congregations. Songs and theatrical skits served to underscore the success of passive resistance in India. A leaflet urged bus boycotters to follow seventeen rules for maintaining a nonviolent approach as they prepared to ride newly desegregated vehicles. Among those rules were:

RESOURCE DIRECTORY

Teaching Resources

Viewpoints Activity On School Integration, found in the Unit 9 folder, pp. 51–52, presents extended quotations from the debate on school desegregation, reflecting the course of the civil rights movement of the 1960s.

Visual Learning Activity Passive Resistance, found in the Unit 9 folder, p. 61, uses a poster to spur discussion on nonviolence and passive resistance, ideals shared by Martin Luther King, Jr., and Mohandas Gandhi.

*P*ray for guidance and commit yourself to complete nonviolence in word and action as you enter the bus. . . . Be loving enough to absorb evil and understanding enough to turn an enemy into a friend. . . . If cursed, do not curse back. If pushed, do not push back. If struck, do not strike back, but evidence love and goodwill at all times. . . . If another person is being molested, do not arise to go to his defense, but pray for the oppressor and use moral and spiritual force to carry on the struggle for justice. . . . Do not be afraid to experiment with new and creative techniques for achieving reconciliation and social change. . . . If you feel you cannot take it, walk for another week or two [rather than ride the bus].

Nonviolent protest was a practical strategy in the civil rights struggle, but it also represented a moral philosophy. "To accept passively an unjust system is to cooperate with that system; thereby the oppressed become as evil as the oppressor," King said. "Noncooperation with evil is as much a moral obligation as is cooperation with good." King's message, eloquently delivered, told African Americans that they would be victorious in the end. At the same time, it forced whites to confront the difficulties African Americans faced and persuaded many of them to offer their support to the movement for change.

MAKING CONNECTIONS

What do you think are some of the strengths and weaknesses of nonviolent protest as a means to bring about social change? Do you think this approach would be effective in the 1990s?

SNCC Breaks Away

The **Student Nonviolent Coordinating Committee (SNCC,** pronounced "snick") was originally part of SCLC. In the spring of 1960, as the movement was heating up, SCLC executive director Ella Baker organized a conference

for students active in the struggle. Baker believed that the NAACP and SCLC had not kept up with the demands of young African Americans, and she wanted to provide a way for them to play an even greater role in the movement. More than two hundred students showed up for her meeting in North Carolina. Most came from southern communities, but some northerners attended as well.

Baker delivered the opening address. "The younger generation is challenging you and me," she told the adults present. "They are asking us to forget our laziness and doubt and fear, and follow our dedication to the truth to the bitter end." Martin Luther King spoke next and called the civil rights movement

a revolt against the apathy and complacency of adults in the Negro community; against Negroes in the middle class who indulge in buying cars and homes instead of taking on the great cause that will really solve their problems; against those who have become so afraid they have yielded to the system.

At the end of the meeting, the participants organized a temporary coordinating committee. A month later, fifteen student leaders met with Baker and other SCLC and CORE leaders and

On the night of April 26, 1960, burning crosses—the symbol of the Ku Klux Klan—appeared in the front yards of many African American residents of Atlanta. Above, Martin Luther King, Jr., removes a cross from his lawn as his young son looks on.

Section 1 Review Answers

1. (a) interracial, see p. 796, (b) CORE, see p. 797, (c) SCLC, see p. 797, (d) SNCC, see p. 799

2. The National Urban League addressed the concerns of poor African Americans living in urban areas, unlike the NAACP, which was geared mostly to upper- and middle-class people.

3. King was committed to the notion of nonviolence and counseled nonviolent direct action to attain the movement's goals. In this kind of passive resistance, people were asked to turn the other cheek in response to violence.

4. SNCC gave the movement a younger focus and energized it. Its members were idealistic activists who pushed for social change and forced others to confront their demands.

5. Possible answers: The oppressed are not as evil as the oppressors because their role is passive rather than active and because they live under the constant threat of brutal retaliation from a stronger force if they resist their own oppression. The oppressed are just as evil, because the lack of self-respect that allows a person to put up with injustice is just as evil as the lack of respect for others that allows another person to act unjustly.

Reteach

Have students list the key organizations and people mentioned in this section and describe the contributions of each to the civil rights movement.

Robert Moses helped train SNCC volunteers in Ohio in 1964. His low-key style was well suited to SNCC, which strove for democracy rather than rigid leadership. SNCC member Jane Stembridge summed up the philosophy: "Finally it all boils down to human relationships. . . . Love alone is radical. Political statements are not."

One focus of SNCC activities was African American voter registration in the South. Those involved were jailed, beaten, and even killed for their efforts.

voted to maintain their independence from other civil rights groups. By the end of the year, the Student Nonviolent Coordinating Committee was a permanent and separate organization.

SNCC filled its own niche in the civil rights movement. It gave young African Americans a chance to make decisions about priorities and tactics, and it shifted the focus away from church leaders alone. SNCC was also more militant, or willing to resort to more extreme measures to achieve immediate change, than were most of the older organizations committed to gradual change.

Robert Moses was one of the most influential leaders of SNCC. He had been a mathematics teacher in Harlem, a largely African American section of New York City, as the civil rights movement developed. Like many others, he wanted to be involved. He first went to work for SNCC in Atlanta, and later headed for Mississippi to encourage other African

American students to come to SNCC meetings. While Martin Luther King spoke with eloquence and passion, Moses was much more soft spoken. He took time to gather his thoughts, and then he spoke slowly. Todd Gitlin, a white student activist leader, later noted that Moses was loved and trusted *"precisely because* he seemed humble, ordinary, accessible." Gitlin went on to describe Moses's style:

> He liked to make his points with his hand, starting with palm down-turned, then opening his hand outward toward his audience, as if delivering the point for inspection, nothing up his sleeve. The words seemed to be extruded [thrust forth], with difficulty, out of his depths. What he said seemed earned. . . . To teach his unimportance, he was wont [accustomed] to crouch in the corner or speak from the back of the room, hoping to hear the popular voice reveal itself.

AMERICAN PROFILES
Anne Moody

⭐ Anne Moody was one of the many young Americans who became involved in the civil rights movement in the 1960s. As a child in the rural Mississippi town of Centreville, Moody grew up wondering what "the white folks' secret" was. "Their homes were large and beautiful with indoor toilets and every other convenience that I knew of at the time," she observed. "Every house I had ever lived in was a one- or two-room shack with an outdoor toilet." When fourteen-year-old Emmett Till, visiting from Chicago, was killed in Mississippi, supposedly because he had whistled at a white woman, Moody was horrified. She became increasingly disturbed as she noticed how the African Americans she knew passively accepted constant humiliation by white southerners. "I began to look upon Negro men as cowards," she said. "I could not respect them for smiling in a white man's face, addressing him as Mr. So-and-So, saying yessuh and nossuh when after they were

▶ RESOURCE DIRECTORY

Teaching Resources

⭐ 📄 **Literature Activity** SNCC Workers, found in the Unit 9 folder, pp. 58–59, features an excerpt from *Coming of Age in Mississippi*, in which Anne Moody describes what it was like to be an African American in Mississippi in the 1960s.

home behind closed doors" they would curse that same man.

Because she was bright and did well in school, Moody became the first member of her family to go to college. She completed her sophomore year at a small school called Natchez Junior College, then spent her last two years at Tougaloo College near Jackson, Mississippi. At Tougaloo she became involved in the civil rights movement. She joined the NAACP and also worked with CORE and SNCC. The professor who coordinated NAACP activities at Tougaloo asked Moody to take part in the first sit-ins in Jackson in 1963. She agreed to lead groups of students in still more sit-ins to desegregate local businesses, and she gave self-defense workshops for demonstrators.

Moody was amazed at the violent reaction she and other demonstrators—both African American and white—provoked when they sat down at a Woolworth's lunch counter in Jackson. (See photo on page 804.) After three hours of being humiliated—screamed at, beaten, and smeared with ketchup and mustard—Moody went back to the NAACP office. She sat there and reflected on her experience:

> All I could think of was how sick Mississippi whites were. They believed so much in the segregated Southern way of life, they would kill to preserve it. . . . Before the sit-in, I had always hated the whites in Mississippi. Now I knew it was impossible for me to hate sickness. The whites had a disease, an incurable disease in its final stages.

Like so many other students in the 1960s, Moody was jailed for taking part in civil rights demonstrations. The jail cells in Jackson were segregated, and she and her African American friends were separated from their white colleagues. Facilities for the African Americans were crude, with no curtain around the shower.

Worse was the reaction from her family at home. Her mother, afraid for the lives of her relatives, begged Moody to end her involvement with the civil rights movement. The local sheriff had warned that Moody should never return to her hometown. Her brother had been beaten up and almost lynched by a group of white boys. Moody's sister angrily told her that her activism was threatening the life of every African American in Centreville.

Against all that resistance, Moody persevered. She participated in demonstrations, helped force the desegregation of facilities, and remained determined to do everything she could to make the South a better place for African Americans. But it was never easy, and the gains came at tremendous personal cost. Like many other Americans committed to changing their society through nonviolent means, Moody learned that challenging white supremacy often provoked an ugly and violent reaction.

Anne Moody joined a SNCC voter registration drive during her first year at Tougaloo College. She said of her fellow SNCC workers, "I had never known people so willing and determined to help others."

4. CLOSE

Reinforcing the Big Idea

The civil rights movement was made up of many groups that differed on tactics but agreed on the urgent need to halt segregation. As the next section describes, the first battle lines were drawn on the whites-only buses and lunch counters of the South.

SECTION 1 REVIEW

Key Terms, People, and Places
1. Define (a) interracial, (b) CORE, (c) SCLC, (d) SNCC.

Key Concepts
2. What function did the National Urban League perform for African Americans?
3. What was Martin Luther King, Jr.'s, contribution to the civil rights movement?
4. What role did SNCC play in the movement?

Critical Thinking
5. **Demonstrating Reasoned Judgment** Martin Luther King, Jr., said, "To accept passively an unjust system is to cooperate with that system; thereby the oppressed become as evil as the oppressor." Drawing on your knowledge of the section, give a concrete example of what this statement means, and explain why you do or do not agree with it.

 Quiz found in the Unit 9 folder, p. 40, covers the main ideas in this section as well as the key terms.

In Depth

Multicultural Perspectives

After the death of Martin Luther King, Jr., in 1968, his widow Coretta Scott King (b. 1927) remained active in various civil rights issues. In the 1993 edition of her book, *My Life with Martin Luther King, Jr.,* she wrote: "One reason so many young people became involved in the Movement was television. The Movement began in Montgomery just when the electronic era was beginning. Students were educated about social issues through the nightly news."

Historical Evidence

Using Autobiography and Biography

Focus Use autobiography and biography as sources of clues about society at a given time.

Instruct Ask students to read the feature and work through the questions. Discuss their responses. Then divide students into groups and ask each group to use the library to choose an important figure in American history for whom they can locate both a biography and an autobiography. Suggest that students focus on one important event in the person's life. Ask students to use the questions in the feature as a guide to compare the sources and decide which is more reliable.

Extend See the Historian's Toolbox Activity in the Resource Directory below.

Answers

1. (a) An autobiography, as evidenced by the use of the first person. (b) He is describing the events surrounding the nonviolent struggle for civil rights in the 1960s. This can be determined by his references to nonviolence, arrests, and Martin [Luther King].

2. (a) He was right on the scene, training the protesters in nonviolent tactics. (b) He operates from a firm belief in the justice of the civil rights cause and is a partisan of it. (c) Students will probably find his account quite accurate; he was an eyewitness, his tone is matter-of-fact, and his presentation does not seem exaggerated.

3. (a) Whites who resist the civil rights movements and African Americans who support it. (b) Physical attacks with billy clubs, fists, rocks, and bottles attest to a high degree of violence. (c) They are willing to act violently in the midst of it. (d) They are willing to withstand the physical abuse to further their cause.

Using Autobiography and Biography

Autobiography and biography are two major sources of evidence about a historical period. An autobiography is an account of a person's life as written by that person. A biography is an account of a person's life written by someone else. Both sources offer clues—revealed in the narrative—of what society was like at the time the person lived. As well as describing the person's life, an autobiography or biography also describes the kind of conditions under which people lived, how they reacted to those conditions, and the attitudes and values prevailing at that time.

An autobiography can be especially helpful in capturing a moment in time because it is a firsthand account. But both autobiography and biography must be judged on their reliability. How objective is the writer about the facts presented? Do the facts seem colored by the writer's desire to cast the person profiled in a good or bad light? Or do the facts seem straightforward and believable?

Use the following steps to analyze an excerpt from *And the Walls Came Tumbling Down*, by Ralph Abernathy. Abernathy was a civil rights leader who worked with Martin Luther King, Jr., in organizing the Montgomery bus boycott and who later founded the SCLC with King.

1. Identify the kind of account and the subject of the profile. (a) Is the excerpt from an autobiography or a biography? How can you tell? (b) What events is Abernathy describing? How can you tell?

2. Analyze the source's reliability as historical evidence. (a) How well acquainted is the writer with the facts he describes? (b) What is his point of view toward them? (c) How accurate do you judge his report to be? Explain why.

3. Search for clues that tell what the historical period was like. (a) What groups are in conflict and why? (b) What can you learn about the level of violence that exists in some parts of society? (c) What is the attitude of certain whites to the struggle? (d) What is the attitude of the African Americans involved?

> Though we knew that our people could follow the path of nonviolence while in control of themselves, we also knew that in moments of sudden anger almost anybody could be tempted to strike back—and one injured policeman could nullify the work of weeks. So we took particular care to teach our people to count to ten before they responded in any way to verbal or physical abuse.
>
> We also showed them how to march along bent over, elbows guarding their stomachs and hands covering their ears and temples. We devised this technique for use in the event that we were bombarded with rocks and bottles while demonstrating. We also taught a modified version of the same maneuver for use while being beaten with fists or billy clubs.
>
> Then, too, we told everyone to go limp when anyone laid hands on them during an arrest. In the first place, it signaled to the arresting officer that he would encounter no active resistance; hence there was no need for excessive force. But equally important, a limp body was harder to handle, took more time to haul into a paddy wagon, and therefore limited the efficiency of the police. . . .
>
> It is surprising how many of the situations we would later face were actually anticipated and discussed in these Saturday workshops. By the time we reached the end of our years together, Martin and I had seen people assaulted with fists, clubs, bottles, and rocks and were moved by the manner in which they endured such abuse. Almost without exception they behaved exactly as we taught them to behave. They protected themselves from the full force of blows, but they didn't strike back, even when their lives were endangered; and for the most part they replied with courtesy and charity.
>
> —From *And the Walls Came Tumbling Down*, by Rev. Ralph David Abernathy, 1989

 RESOURCE DIRECTORY

Historian's Toolbox Activity Using Autobiography and Biography, found in the Unit 9 folder, p. 53, provides students further practice in this skill with a passage written by Elizabeth Dole in 1988.

Nonviolent Confrontation: A Turning Point in History

TURNING POINTS

SECTION PREVIEW

"We Shall Overcome," sang civil rights protesters, revealing both their spirit of nonviolence and their steadfast commitment to the cause. Acts such as sitting at "whites only" lunch counters brought vicious responses, but also showed the courage and determination of the protesters.

Key Concepts

• The sit-in technique, pioneered by CORE in the 1940s, became a popular and effective tool among civil rights activists in the 1960s.
• Nonviolent protest took the form of Freedom Rides in 1961, when activists bravely desegregated the interstate bus system.
• The violence that erupted during peaceful marches in Birmingham, Alabama, shocked the nation and created sympathy for the civil rights movement.

Key Terms, People, and Places

sit-in, Freedom Rides, Albany Movement

B uilding on the success of the Montgomery bus boycott, African American students took the next step in the campaign for equal rights. With quiet dignity, they insisted on fair treatment in facilities that had been segregated for decades. When their peaceful protests caused angry whites to strike back violently, they refused to respond with violence. Throughout the early 1960s, they maintained their commitment to passive resistance and in the process generated nationwide support for their goals. ✪

Sit-Ins Test the Limits of Inequality

The Congress of Racial Equality (CORE) created the **sit-in** in 1943 when it desegregated the

Jack Spratt Coffee House in Chicago. (See Chapter 25, Section 4.) The sit-in technique meant that African American CORE members, often accompanied by white members, simply sat down in a segregated establishment and refused to leave until they were served or accommodated. By testing the limits of segregation policies and putting business owners' profits at risk by causing a disruption, CORE brought an end to segregation in the facilities it targeted. Sit-ins became common practice for many groups participating in the civil rights movement.

On January 31, 1960, Ezell Blair, Jr., an African American freshman at the Agricultural and Technical College in Greensboro, North Carolina, asked his parents if they would be troubled if he caused a disturbance in the community. They were puzzled by the strange question and wanted to know why. "Because," he said, "tomorrow we're going to do something that will shake up this town."

The next day, Blair and three other African American students from the college walked into a Woolworth's store in Greensboro and purchased a few items. Then they sat down at a lunch counter reserved for "whites only." When a surprised waitress wanted to know what they were doing, one of them answered, "We believe since we buy books and papers in the other part of the store, we should get served in this part."

The manager refused to allow them to be served. Rather than leave, Blair and his friends simply remained where they were until the store closed. The next day, twenty students returned to participate in a sit-in at the store. Members of the press poured into Greensboro, and the publicity led to other sit-ins across the state.

John Lewis, an African American activist who participated in sit-ins in Nashville, Tennessee, reflected on his experience in a similar store:

This student picketed a restaurant in Georgia that refused to serve African Americans unless they stood up at the lunch counter.

1. FOCUS

Connecting to the Big Idea

See page 794B. Explain that as civil rights activists put the philosophy of nonviolence into action, protests began to sweep the South. Ask students to describe what happened as a result of these protests.

Objectives

● Describe the sit-in technique and explain why it was an effective form of protest.
● Explain the significance of the Freedom Rides.
● Analyze how white violence against nonviolent protesters affected public opinion.

Bellringer

Read aloud the quotation by John Lewis on page 804. Then ask students to weigh carefully this question: Could you have endured what the lunch-counter protesters did without either fleeing or defending yourself? Ask what motivated Lewis and the other protesters to suffer the abuse of the white segregationists.

Reading Strategy

Problem Solving Explain to students that the "weapons" of civil rights protesters differed greatly from those of their opponents. Ask students to list as they read the nonviolent "weapons" (that is, tactics) of the freedom fighters and the methods that were used to try to stop them.

📋 **Reproducible Lesson Plan** found in the Unit 9 folder, p. 36, provides a summary of the Section 2 lesson plan content.

📋 **Alternate Lesson Plan: Learning Styles** found in the Alternate Lesson Plans folder, p. 147, guides pairs of students to create a simulated radio broadcast about an event from this section and is especially helpful for auditory or kinesthetic learners.

📋 **Guided Reading and Review** found in the Unit 9 folder, p. 41, provides a structure for reading and mastering the key concepts and reviewing the key terms for Section 2. (Guided Practice)

✪ 📋 **American Profiles Activity** found in the Unit 9 folder, p. 49, profiles Sidney Poitier, whose movies in the 1950s and 1960s dramatically portrayed the evils of racism in United States society.

Discuss

Discuss with students what issues made the civil rights movement so unstoppable. Ask students to consider the following factors in their examination of the movement: the particular people involved; the tactics; the moral philosophy of the movement; the reactions of whites; television and newspaper images of the violence.

Analyze

After students have read the statement by Assistant Attorney General Burke Marshall on page 805, ask them to analyze why, indeed, whites reacted as they did to the Freedom Rides. What was at stake from the point of view of white segregationists? Why did African Americans riding a bus alongside whites seem so threatening to them?

Answer to ...

MAKING CONNECTIONS

Possible answers: Anti-abortion groups have used sit-ins to try to block the entrances to clinics. In some cases these protesters have temporarily succeeded, but their actions have also been treated as criminal violations, as well as generating anger among their opponents. In addition, some anti-abortion activists have not adhered to the principle of nonviolence.

TURNING POINTS

John Salter, Jr., Joan Trumpauer, and Anne Moody (left to right) held a sit-in at a Jackson, Mississippi, lunch counter in May 1963. A hostile crowd registered their response by mocking and pouring food on the three activists.

I t was a Woolworth in the heart of the downtown area, and we occupied every seat at the lunch counter, every seat in the restaurant. . . . A group of young white men came in and they started pulling and beating primarily the young women. They put lighted cigarettes down their backs, in their hair, and they were really beating people. In a short time police officials came in and placed all of us under arrest, and not a single member of the white group, the people that were opposing our sit-in, was arrested.

But the students persisted, and soon thousands were involved in the campaign. The sit-ins gained the support of SCLC. Martin Luther King told students that arrest was a "badge of honor." In the next year, some 70,000 students participated in the sit-ins, and 3,600 served time in jail. The protests failed to change southern customs immediately, but they began a process of change that could be contained no longer.

MAKING CONNECTIONS

What groups in recent times have used nonviolent protests such as sit-ins to affect public policy? Have their tactics been effective?

Freedom Rides

In the spring of 1961, CORE led an effort to test a recent Supreme Court decision. In *Boynton* v. *Virginia*, 1960, the Court had expanded on an earlier ruling that prohibited segregation on buses traveling across state lines. As a result of the *Boynton* decision, waiting rooms and dining facilities that served interstate travelers now could not be segregated, either. The **Freedom Rides,** organized by CORE with aid from SNCC, placed groups of African American and white activists on interstate buses heading south and stopping at terminals on the way, as the map on page 805 shows.

At first the Freedom Riders encountered little trouble. When they reached the Deep South, however, they faced a ferocious response. In Anniston, Alabama, a bus was met by a mob of white men at the terminal. They carried weapons—guns, knives, blackjacks, chains—all clearly visible and meant to intimidate. The Freedom Riders decided not to test the facilities there and prepared to move on. James Farmer described what happened next:

B efore the bus pulled out, however, members of the mob took their sharp instruments and slashed tires. The bus

RESOURCE DIRECTORY

Teaching Resources

Primary Source Activity Protecting the Freedom Riders, found in the Unit 9 folder, p. 55, uses excerpts from interviews with Robert Kennedy and his assistant attorney general for civil rights to reveal the complications of the Freedom Rides.

got to the outskirts of Anniston and the tires blew out and the bus ground to a halt. Members of the mob had boarded cars and followed the bus, and now with the disabled bus standing there, the members of the mob surrounded it, held the door closed, and a member of the mob threw a firebomb into the bus, breaking a window to do so. Incidentally, there were some local policemen mingling with the mob, fraternizing with them while this was going on.

The riders escaped before the bus burst into flames, but many were beaten by the mob as they stumbled, choking on the smoke, out of the vehicle. They had anticipated trouble, and indeed, their strategy was meant to provoke a confrontation. But the level of violence took them by surprise.

As a result of the savage response, CORE director James Farmer contemplated calling the project off. But SNCC leaders begged to be allowed to continue. When Farmer warned,

"You know that may be suicide," student activist Diane Nash answered, "If we let them stop us with violence, the movement is dead! . . . Your troops have been badly battered. Let us pick up the baton and run with it."

Photographs of the charred and battered bus in Anniston, with flames and black smoke rising from its smashed windows, horrified the country. Burke Marshall, Assistant Attorney General, expressed astonishment "that people—presumably otherwise sane, sensible, rational—would have this kind of reaction simply to where people were sitting on a bus." His boss, Attorney General Robert Kennedy, who initially had been reluctant to lend federal support to the protest, finally assigned federal marshals to protect the Freedom Riders. Kennedy and the Justice Department also pressured the Interstate Commerce Commission to issue a ruling prohibiting segregation in interstate transportation, and the federal government forced local communities to follow the new regulations. ✪

Freedom Rides, 1961

Geography and History: Interpreting Maps
According to the map, where did the Freedom Rides begin? What was the originally planned end point for the Freedom Rides? How far did the Riders actually get? On what date was the bus shown in the photo at right firebombed in Anniston, Alabama?

Activity

Cooperative Learning
Time: One class period.
Activity: Make a collage depicting the civil rights movement.
Grouping: Groups of three students.
Purpose: Have each student in the group find or make three images relating to the civil rights movement to include in the collage. The group should decide on a title for the artwork, perhaps borrowing a film or television series title (*Mississippi Burning* or "Eyes on the Prize"), using a line from a speech ("I Have a Dream"), or making up a title. One student from each group should present the finished collage to the class.
Roles: Art designers, caption writers, presenters.
Outcome: Students will identify images that express the goals, attitudes, controversies, and sentiments surrounding the civil rights movement in the 1960s.

Caption Answer to . . .

Interpreting Maps

The route was supposed to begin in Washington, D.C., and end in New Orleans, Louisiana. The riders made it as far as Jackson, Mississippi, where they were arrested. The firebombing took place on May 14, 1961.

Media and Technology

Visions of America: Turning Point Story To enhance students' understanding of the Turning Point topic in this section, play "Nonviolent Solutions," a story about the role of nonviolent action in the civil rights movement (length: approximately 4 minutes). This selection can be located on side 4 of the videodiscs. This selection can also be located on videotape 5. Lesson plans for Turning Point stories can be found in the Visions of America Guidebook.

Visions of America: Roundtable Discussion To introduce students to different and differing viewpoints on the Turning Point topic in this section, play all or part of the Roundtable Discussion on "Nonviolent Solutions," remarks by respected historians and social commentators. This selection can be located on side 4 of the videodiscs. This selection can also be located on videotape 5.

Side 4, Chapter 33

Side 4, Chapter 34

Enrichment

Ask students to compare the civil rights movement in the United States with the African independence movements of the late 1950s and early 1960s. Suggest that students present their findings in either narrative or chart form. Encourage them to research the leaders, goals, and respective challenges of the movements, as well as any inspirational symbols, slogans, or songs. Ask them to conclude with a paragraph addressing this question: How did events in Africa challenge America's image as the protector of democracy?

Police in Birmingham, Alabama, used high-powered hoses to break up civil rights marches in 1963. Television coverage of this brutal treatment of peaceful demonstrators prompted widespread sympathy for the movement.

The Albany Movement

The Freedom Rides exacted a heavy toll from civil rights workers, but the campaign did lead to significant gains in the desegregation of interstate bus travel. A campaign that began soon after the Freedom Rides did not fare so well.

In October 1961, African Americans in Albany, Georgia, who had joined together and called themselves the **Albany Movement,** began a year-long campaign of protest marches. They demanded the desegregation of bus terminals, and they wanted to open talks with white community leaders to address racial injustices. In December, Martin Luther King arrived in Albany, hoping to lead the movement toward its goals.

While King's presence did inspire many African Americans to join the demonstrations, it also irritated some local civil rights leaders, who resented the way King seemed to swoop in and take charge of the movement. The Albany police chief, Laurie Pritchett, also did not help the movement. He shrewdly kept the national press from seeing and reporting on the worst violations of civil rights committed by his forces. Once he even joined a group of demonstrators in prayer before they were carted off to jail. His tactic of "nonviolent" opposition to the civil rights protests kept the Albany Movement from stirring up the same nationwide sympathy that the Freedom Rides had created.

King was jailed at one point but promptly released when Albany authorities learned that volunteers were mobilizing to protest the arrest. As the campaign seemed to be failing, King began to turn his attention elsewhere. The Albany Movement had largely fizzled out by the end of 1962, with few real accomplishments to show for a difficult year.

The Integration of Ole Miss

In September of 1962, James Meredith had better success in his personal quest for civil rights. The African American air force veteran was a student at Jackson State College but wanted to transfer to the all-white University of Mississippi (known as Ole Miss). When he was denied entrance on racial grounds, he sued and carried his case to the Supreme Court, which upheld his claim. Mississippi governor Ross Barnett had other ideas. He declared that Meredith would not be allowed to enroll, whatever the Court declared, and at one point personally blocked the way to the admissions office.

With the lines of confrontation drawn, a major riot began. One angry resident tried to drive a bulldozer into the administration building. Agitated whites destroyed vehicles bringing marshals to campus. Tear gas covered the grounds. Two men died and hundreds were hurt. Army troops sent by President Kennedy finally restored order, and Meredith entered the university with troops to guarantee his safety. He remained until he graduated in 1963.

The Birmingham Confrontation

In late 1962 Fred Shuttlesworth, head of the Alabama Christian Movement for Human Rights in Birmingham, Alabama, decided that his city would be the perfect site for another nonviolent campaign. Birmingham, which was 40 percent African American, was rigidly segregated. Victory there could serve as a model for future resistance elsewhere. Shuttlesworth therefore invited Martin Luther King to visit the city in April 1963.

RESOURCE DIRECTORY

Teaching Resources

In Depth

Interdisciplinary

Most Americans in the early 1960s were more focused on President-elect Kennedy's New Frontier and its faith in a future based on science and technology than on civil rights activism. In January 1961, *Time* magazine chose fifteen scientists as its "Men of the Year" with the following glowing testimonial: "Statesmen and savants, builders and even priests are their servants . . . . Science is at the apogee of its power."

Local business leaders, afraid of the money they would lose if King's visit touched off demonstrations throughout the city, tried to negotiate with Shuttlesworth to call off the plan. These negotiations did not go very far, however, and King arrived on schedule.

Civil rights activists faced Eugene "Bull" Connor, the Birmingham police commissioner who was committed to crushing the protest. When reporters wanted to know how long King planned to stay, King drew on a biblical story and told them he would remain until "Pharaoh let his people go." Bull Connor replied, "I got plenty of room in the jail."

Activists, still committed to their peaceful approach, challenged discriminatory hiring practices and segregated public facilities. City officials declared that protest marches violated a regulation prohibiting parades without a permit and arrested King. When a group of white clergy criticized the campaign as an ill-timed threat to law and order, King responded from his cell. In his "Letter from a Birmingham Jail," he defended his tactics and his timing:

F or years now I have heard the word "Wait!" It rings in the ear of every Negro with a piercing familiarity. . . . But when you have seen vicious mobs lynch your mothers and fathers at will and drown your sisters and brothers at whim; when you have seen hate filled policemen curse, kick, brutalize and even kill your black brothers and sisters with impunity; . . . when you have to concoct an answer for a five-year-old son who is asking in agonizing pathos: "Daddy, why do white people treat colored people so mean?" . . . then you will understand why we find it difficult to wait.

After more than a week, King posted bail and emerged from jail. Soon after, he decided to allow children to participate in the campaign to test the conscience of the Birmingham authorities and the nation. As they marched with the adults, Bull Connor arrested more than 900 of the children. Police turned high-pressure fire hoses, able to tear the bark from trees, on the demonstrators. They also brought out trained police dogs that attacked the arms and legs of marchers. When protesters fell to the ground, policemen beat them with clubs and took them off to jail.

Television cameras recorded the scenes of appalling violence for people around the country. Even those unsympathetic to the civil rights movement were revolted. As reporter Eric Sevareid observed, "A newspaper or television picture of a snarling police dog set upon a human being is recorded in the permanent photo-electric file of every human brain."

In the end, the protesters won. A compromise arranged by Assistant Attorney General Burke Marshall led to desegregation of city facilities, fairer hiring practices, and organization of a biracial committee to keep channels of communication open. The success of the Birmingham marches was just one example that proved the effectiveness of nonviolent protest. While the technique did not always work—or worked only slowly—nonviolent confrontation as a means to social change had earned itself a place of honor in the history of civil rights in the United States.

SECTION 2 REVIEW

Key Terms, People, and Places
1. Define (a) sit-in, (b) Freedom Rides, (c) Albany Movement.

Key Concepts
2. What was the significance of the sit-in movement?
3. What was the point of the Freedom Rides?
4. What was the aim of the Birmingham campaign?

Critical Thinking
5. **Drawing Conclusions** In May 1961, an article in *The New York Times* encouraged the Freedom Riders to call off their program, arguing, "Non-violence that deliberately provokes violence is a logical contradiction." Explain why you agree or disagree with this statement as it applies to the Freedom Rides.

Quiz found in the Unit 9 folder, p. 42, covers the main ideas in this section as well as the key terms.

---

3. ASSESS

Section 2 Review Answers
1. (a) sit-in, see p. 803, (b) Freedom Rides, see p. 804, (c) Albany Movement, see p. 806

2. The sit-ins mobilized students in the civil rights movement. They also generated tremendous publicity around the country, which helped the larger movement gain momentum.

3. The Freedom Riders hoped to test a recent Supreme Court decision calling for an end to segregation in interstate transportation.

4. Martin Luther King, Jr., wanted to bring about the integration of public facilities and to end discrimination in hiring practices. He also wanted to use Birmingham as a model for the desegregation of other southern cities.

5. Answers will vary. Encourage students to support their responses with examples.

Reteach
Ask students to create a three-column chart listing the locations of major civil rights protests, immediate purposes, and the outcomes of each.

 Alternative Assessment

Mid-Point Monitoring
Ask students if they have
● Chosen the subjects for their biographical entries
● Begun to collect information
● Decided what visuals to include

 4. CLOSE

 Reinforcing the Big Idea
Nonviolent protests sparked violent responses but caught the attention and sympathy of the nation. In the next section students will read about how politicians, slow to acknowledge the civil rights issue, finally were forced to take action.

The Lasting Impact of Nonviolent Confrontation

Focus It is difficult for young people today to imagine living in a world in which segregation was the law and a person could be arrested for sitting in the wrong seat. It is equally difficult for them to comprehend how baffling southerners found the rapid changes in civil rights legislation.

In this section students will learn how nonviolent protests brought about the transformation of the South. They will also see how both the gains and the continuing battles today are rooted in the struggles of the 1960s.

Instruct On the chalkboard, make a flow chart consisting of these terms: *colored, Negro, black, Afro-American, African American.* Explain that the preferred term for Americans of African descent has changed over the years. Ask students what these name changes indicate. Then ask them to read this feature and discuss the questions at the end.

Extend Ask students to list and/or draw examples of how African American pride is expressed today. Have volunteers share their examples.

TURNING POINTS

The Lasting Impact of Nonviolent Confrontation

The nonviolent, direct-action campaigns of the early 1960s marked the beginning of a new chapter in the African American struggle for equal rights. The sit-ins, the Freedom Rides, and the marches forced a shift in American attitudes and created a climate within which reform could take place.

Prior to the movement, most Americans had taken white supremacy for granted. Most white southerners were not significantly different from Melton McLaurin, who grew up in the rural town of Wade, North Carolina, in the 1950s. "Like many such families in small southern towns," he later recalled, "we assumed that the blacks of the village were in residence primarily to serve us, and we used their labor to support our comfortable lifestyle." The civil rights movement of the 1960s, however, brought a shift in perspective that made McLaurin

different from his parents. Returning home for a visit in 1984, he watched his father deliver a gift to an African American family at Christmas. It was a gracious gesture from a 65-year-year-old man who accepted changes without fully understanding them. At the same time, McLaurin observed, his father "remained, spiritually, emotionally, a resident of the Wade I had left and to which I could never return."

African Americans themselves experienced even more dramatic changes. In the late 1960s, Henry Louis Gates, a high school student from West Virginia, applied for admission to Yale University in Connecticut. In his application, which earned him a spot at the school, he described how the civil rights movement had brought changes in his own life: "My grandfather was colored; my father was Negro; and I am black." In other words, the movement

1960s African American students around the nation demand that their colleges create Black Studies programs.

| 1965 | 1970 | 1975 |

1960s African Americans' pride in their heritage is shown in the popularity of traditional African clothing.

▶ **RESOURCE DIRECTORY**

Teaching Resources

📄 **Turning Points Extension Activity**
The Lasting Impact of Nonviolent Confrontation, found in the Unit 9 folder, pp. 47–48, provides background and structure for groups of students to work on task forces promoting nonviolence today.

brought a shift in African Americans' sense of identity and in the way they wanted to be viewed by the larger culture. African Americans looked back toward their African roots, and with that rediscovery came a powerful pride in their ethnic identity. Some African American students began wearing *dashikis*—brightly colored African shirts—while others stopped straightening their hair and wore it longer in a style called the Afro.

Those were surface changes, to be sure, but they reflected larger cultural shifts. In the course of the next several decades, as you will read in the following chapters, the civil rights movement itself shifted course. African Americans refused to accept the second-class citizenship that had been forced upon them for the past one hundred years. They discovered that beyond segregation lay more subtle forms of discrimination, and they continued the fight to secure their full rights.

In time, however, their efforts sparked an opposing reaction on the part of previously sympathetic whites, who felt that change was coming too quickly and often at their expense. For example, Americans were divided on the issue of affirmative action programs, which sought to make up for past discrimination by requiring employers to make a special effort to hire African Americans. The civil rights movement, so passionate in the 1960s, has today lost some of its steam. But the results remain visible. And the struggle to attain equality continues, especially in the economic sphere.

REVIEWING THE FACTS

1. How did the civil rights movement change the way some African Americans perceived their own identity?
2. What obstacles did the movement toward full equality for African Americans face after the 1960s?

Critical Thinking
3. **Formulating Questions** Imagine that you are conducting a study on how far the civil rights movement has come as of the 1990s. Create a list of questions that your study would seek to answer. Some of the questions may involve statistics, while others may deal with how African Americans and others perceive the situation today.

1970s The women's rights movement employs nonviolent protests like those of the civil rights movement.

1992 Spike Lee's film Malcolm X *marks a renewed interest in the slain civil rights leader.*

1980　　　**1985**　　　**1990**

1980s Multicultural curriculums reflect the growing diversity in American classrooms.

809

The Political Response

The Political Response

The Political Response

1. FOCUS

Connecting to the Big Idea

See page 794B. Explain to students that few politicians of the early 1960s were willing to risk taking a strong stand for civil rights. Ask students to note what forced them to change their minds.

Objectives

- Characterize John F. Kennedy's response to civil rights at the beginning of his presidency.
- Summarize Kennedy's efforts on the civil rights issue.
- Identify the key civil rights accomplishments of Lyndon B. Johnson.

Bellringer

Ask students if they plan to vote when they are of age. Why or why not? How many students would vote if it meant facing possible harassment or violence? Explain that protection of voters' rights was an important aspect of the civil rights movement.

Reading Strategy

Finding Evidence Ask students to look for evidence as they read the section to support this statement: As nonviolent protests continued, civil rights became not only a moral issue but also a political one.

AMHERST COLLEGE
We ask the
PRESIDENT
To
STAND UP
For
CIVIL RIGHTS

When President Kennedy avoided committing himself to the politically charged civil rights struggle, students demanded leadership from the White House.

SECTION PREVIEW

For politicians in the early 1960s, taking a firm stand in favor of civil rights was a risky business. As the decade wore on, however, the rising voice of protest no longer could be ignored in Washington.

Key Concepts
- At the start of his presidency, John F. Kennedy was hesitant to embrace the civil rights cause.
- Kennedy finally took a moral stand for civil rights but was unable to secure passage of his bill.
- Lyndon Johnson succeeded in gaining passage of the Civil Rights Act of 1964 and the Voting Rights Act of 1965.

Key Terms, People, and Places
March on Washington, Civil Rights Act of 1964, Voting Rights Act of 1965

T he protest activities of the early 1960s forced a political response. At first President John F. Kennedy, worried about his narrow electoral victory, hoped to avoid getting involved in the struggle. Finally, when the violence became extreme, he provided the moral leadership that President Eisenhower had not and committed himself to full support for a civil rights bill. The bill remained bottled up in a congressional committee when he died late in 1963, however. Kennedy's successor, Lyndon B. Johnson, harnessed a wave of popular sympathy after Kennedy's assassination and made the cause his own. Through LBJ's efforts, the civil rights movement reached its high point in the middle of the decade.

John Kennedy's Reaction

Kennedy had sought to straddle the fence at the start of his presidency. As a member of Congress, he had voted for civil rights measures but never embraced the cause wholeheartedly. In his presidential campaign, he had sought and won many African American votes with bold rhetoric. In 1960 he proclaimed, "If the President does not himself wage the struggle for equal rights—if he stands above the battle—then the battle will inevitably be lost." He also declared that a "stroke of the pen" could eliminate racial discrimination in federal housing.

In October 1960, just weeks before the election, Kennedy had an opportunity to make a powerful gesture of goodwill toward African Americans. Martin Luther King had been arrested in Alabama and sentenced to four months of hard labor. His family feared for his life in the prison camp. Kennedy called Coretta Scott King, Dr. King's wife, and said, "If there is anything I can do to help, please feel free to call on me." Then Robert Kennedy called the Alabama judge who had sentenced King and persuaded the judge to release him on bail. Word of the Kennedys' actions spread quickly through the African American community, and many switched their votes from Nixon to Kennedy. These votes were crucial in Kennedy's slim margin of victory in the election.

Once in office, though, Kennedy moved slowly. He did not want to alienate southern senators, whose votes he would need to achieve his foreign policy goals, by taking a strong stand on civil rights. He appointed a number of African Americans to prominent positions. Thurgood Marshall, for example, joined the United States Circuit Court and later became the first African American Supreme Court justice. But at the same time, Kennedy named a number of segregationists to federal courts. He also conveniently forgot about his pledge to end housing discrimination.

But Kennedy was deeply disturbed by the scenes of violence in the South that were flooding the media. The race riots surrounding the Freedom Rides in 1961 had been an embarrassment

▶ RESOURCE DIRECTORY

Teaching Resources

Reproducible Lesson Plan found in the Unit 9 folder, p. 37, provides a summary of the Section 3 lesson plan content.

Alternate Lesson Plan: Learning Styles found in the Alternate Lesson Plans folder, p. 148, highlights the responses of Kennedy and Johnson to the civil rights movement and is particularly effective for visual learners.

Guided Reading and Review found in the Unit 9 folder, p. 43, provides a structure for reading and mastering the key concepts and reviewing the key terms for Section 3. (Guided Practice)

to Kennedy when he met with Nikita Khrushchev in Vienna. To observers around the world, the upheaval in Birmingham looked even more like the beginning of a revolution. Aware that he had to do something, Kennedy spoke to the American people on nationwide television. He called the quest for equality "a moral issue" and underscored the need for action:

> We preach freedom around the world, and we mean it, and we cherish our freedom, here at home, but are we to say to the world, and much more importantly, to each other that this is a land of the free except for the Negroes? . . . The time has come for this nation to fulfill its promise.

Several months earlier, Kennedy had proposed a modest civil rights bill to help support African American voting rights and to aid schools beginning to desegregate. The Birmingham crisis pushed him further. He introduced a far stronger bill that would prohibit segregation in public places, ban discrimination wherever federal funding was involved, and advance the effort to desegregate schools. It was the most comprehensive civil rights measure ever endorsed by a United States President. The public stood behind Kennedy; a Gallup poll soon after his televised speech showed that 61 percent of the nation approved of the way he was doing his job. But Congress, still dominated by white southerners, proved resistant and kept the bill from coming up for a vote.

The March on Washington

Civil rights leaders proposed a march on Washington to lobby for passage of Kennedy's civil rights bill. Like Franklin Roosevelt when he was faced with a similar march in 1941, Kennedy tried to sidetrack the proposal. He feared it would simply alienate Congress and might result in serious racial violence in the United States capital. But his efforts to get organizers to call off the demonstration failed. Vice President Johnson warned civil rights leaders that the march might

backfire, and that it was time instead for political deal making in Congress. But Martin Luther King noted, "I have never engaged in any direct action movement which did not seem ill-timed." In the end, Kennedy bowed to the inevitable and supported the march.

The **March on Washington** took place in August 1963. More than 200,000 people came from all over the country to call for jobs and freedom. Prominent African American celebrities were present: government official Ralph Bunche, author James Baldwin, entertainer Sammy Davis, Jr., singer Harry Belafonte, baseball player Jackie Robinson. Many of the leading folk singers of the early 1960s were also there. Peter, Paul, and Mary; Joan Baez; and Bob Dylan all sang songs like "Blowin' in the Wind" and "We Shall Overcome," which had become the unofficial anthem of the struggle. The leaders of the major civil rights organizations all addressed the crowd.

At the march, Martin Luther King delivered what was to become his best-known address. With power, eloquence, and passion, he spoke to the demonstrators and to the nation at large:

> I have a dream that one day this nation will rise up and live out the true meaning

"Jobs and Freedom" was the official slogan for the March on Washington in 1963. Thousands like the young woman in the inset turned out to show their support for the civil rights movement.

2. INSTRUCT

Discuss

Explain to students that John Kennedy was from Massachusetts and Lyndon Johnson was from Texas. Discuss Kennedy's and Johnson's reactions to the civil rights crisis. Was one of them more genuinely concerned about the issue than the other? How might each man's origins have played a role in his handling of civil rights issues?

Analyze

Ask students to reread the passage from the famous speech by Martin Luther King, Jr., on pages 811 and 812. Have them identify the moral, political, and religious ideas his words reflect and consider why the speech is regarded as one of the most powerful in American history. Encourage students to consider both substance and style.

In Depth

Then and Now

In August 1993, 75,000 people—far fewer than the 250,000 who came in 1963—gathered in Washington, D.C., for the 30th anniversary of the March on Washington. The theme of the 1993 march, "Jobs, Justice and Peace," was chosen by African American leaders to focus on the gap between the promise of 1963 and the reality thirty years later. "When we were segregated, we said, if we could sit all over the bus, things would be all right," said one civil rights leader. "We have since discovered the bus has flat tires and burned out pistons. We have got to rebuild the bus."

Activity

Creating a Symbol

Symbols of unity were an important inspiration to the civil rights movement. Ask students to create a logo, song, poem, or slogan that represents the moral tone of the struggle and the bravery of its participants.

Answer to . . .

MAKING CONNECTIONS

As students will recall from Chapter 28, Johnson was a master of political deal making in Congress, and so it was natural for him to use that method—rather than the unpredictable and uncontrollable March on Washington—to get civil rights legislation passed.

Caption Answer to . . .

 Interpreting Graphs

Approximately two million new voters registered between 1960 and 1970.

 In Depth

Then and Now

The struggle for equal rights is an ongoing one. Assistant Attorney General for Civil Rights Deval L. Patrick, appointed by President Clinton in 1994, defined the issue of race in a 1993 commencement address at Milton Academy in Massachusetts. "As a nation, we are still not free. For it is undoubtedly true that legions of African Americans feel less of a sense of opportunity, less assured of our equality, and less confident of fair treatment today than we have in many, many years. . . . We lack a national consensus on civil rights today. More ominously, in my view, we lack the national interest to build one."

of its creed, "We hold these truths to be self-evident, that all men are created equal." I have a dream that one day on the red hills of Georgia, sons of former slaves and the sons of former slave owners will be able to sit down together at the table of brotherhood. . . . I have a dream that my four little children will one day live in a nation where they will not be judged by the color of their skin, but by the content of their character. . . . When we allow freedom to ring, when we let it ring from every village and every hamlet, from every state and every city, we will be able to speed up that day when all of God's children, black men and white men, Jews and Gentiles, Protestants and Catholics, will be able to join hands and sing in the words of the old Negro spiritual: "Free at last. Free at last. Thank God Almighty, we are free at last."*

King's words echoed around the country. President Kennedy, watching the speech on television, was impressed with King's skill. But still the civil rights bill remained stalled in Congress.

MAKING CONNECTIONS

Why do you think Vice President Johnson preferred to use politics to get the civil rights bill passed rather than relying on demonstrations?

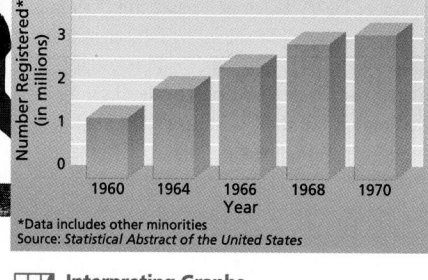

African American Voter Registration in the South, 1960–1970

*Data includes other minorities
Source: Statistical Abstract of the United States

 Interpreting Graphs
Civil rights workers like the woman at left had already begun registering African Americans years before the Voting Rights Act of 1965. *How many new African American voters registered between 1960 and 1970?*

Lyndon Johnson's Role

Three months after the March on Washington, President Kennedy was dead and his civil rights bill was not much closer to passage. Lyndon Johnson was finally able to move the legislation along. Although he had voted against civil rights measures early in his congressional career, as Senate majority leader Johnson had worked to get a civil rights bill passed in 1957. Upon becoming President, he was eager to use his political skills to build support for Kennedy's bill. In his first public address, he told Congress and the country that nothing "could more eloquently honor President Kennedy's memory than the earliest possible passage of the civil rights bill." Johnson promised African American leaders that he would push for the measure "with every energy [he] possessed," and he made good on that commitment.

Johnson let Congress know that he would accept no compromise on civil rights. After the House of Representatives passed the bill, the Senate became caught in a lengthy filibuster, in which southern members exercised their privilege of unlimited debate. Johnson finally enlisted his old colleague, Republican minority leader Everett Dirksen, to support cloture—a two-thirds vote to cut off debate. Never before had such a procedure been used for a civil rights measure. In June 1964 the Senate voted for cloture. Soon after, it passed the bill.

The **Civil Rights Act of 1964** banned discrimination in all public accommodations and gave the Justice Department authority to act more vigorously in school segregation and voting rights cases. It also included an equal-opportunity provision that prohibited discriminatory hiring on the basis of race, sex, religion, or national origin in companies with more than twenty-five employees, as shown in the chart on page 813.

Johnson was satisfied, but the struggle moved on with a momentum of its own. In 1964 leaders of the major civil rights groups organized a voter registration drive in Mississippi. About a thousand African American and white volunteers, most of them college students, went to Mississippi to participate in what came to be called Freedom Summer. The

▶ RESOURCE DIRECTORY

Teaching Resources

✪ 📄 **Primary Source Activity** Registering to Vote in Mississippi, found in the Unit 9 folder, pp. 56–57, uses the testimony of Fannie Lou Hamer to show why hundreds of civil rights workers volunteered to spend the summer of 1964 with the Mississippi Summer Project.

Civil Rights Act of 1964

Title I	Prohibits different registration standards for white and African American voting applicants
Title II	Prohibits discrimination in the use of public accommodations
Title III	Guarantees equal access to and treatment in all public-owned and -operated facilities
Title IV	Authorizes the federal government to provide technical and financial aid to all school districts in the process of desegregation
Title V	Extends tenure of Civil Rights Commission until January 31, 1968
Title VI	Guarantees that no individual will be subjected to racial discrimination in any program that is receiving federal financial aid
Title VII	Prohibits discrimination by employers or unions with more than 100 employees or members during the first four years the Act is in effect, and thereafter for more than 25 employees or members Establishes a commission to investigate and to mediate charges of discrimination
Title VIII	Directs the Census Bureau to compile voting statistics by race in regions designated by the Civil Rights Commission
Title IX	Allows higher federal courts to prevent lower federal courts from remanding a civil rights case to a state or local court
Title X	Establishes a Community Relations Service in the Department of Commerce to mediate racial disputes at the local level
Title XI	Guarantees the right of jury trial in criminal contempt cases that grow out of any part of the Act, except for Title I Provides that the Civil Rights Act cannot be invalidated as a whole even if a single portion of it is invalidated

Source: *The Negro Almanac: A Reference Work on the Afro American*

Interpreting Tables
One of the landmark achievements of the Johnson administration was the passage of the Civil Rights Act of 1964. *Which provision of the act allows the federal government to assist in school desegregation with money or other forms of aid?*

Ku Klux Klan held rallies to intimidate the volunteers. In August FBI agents found the bodies of three civil rights workers—James Chaney, Andrew Goodman, and Michael Schwerner—who had been murdered by opponents. This violence was only part of the turbulence seen that summer. Civil rights leaders reported three deaths, thirty-five shootings, thirty firebombings, and eighty mob attacks. A thousand volunteers were arrested.

In order to claim their full political rights, newly registered Mississippi voters, along with members of SNCC, organized the Mississippi Freedom Democratic party. The MFDP sent delegates to the Democratic National Convention in the summer of 1964. These delegates argued that they, rather than segregationist politicians, were the rightful representatives of the state.

Fannie Lou Hamer, a timekeeper on a cotton plantation who had lost her job when she tried to register to vote, addressed the convention in a speech carried on national television. She related the treatment she had received in one voter drive:

> I began to scream, and one white man got up and began to beat me on my head and tell me to "hush." . . . All of this on account we want to register, to become first class citizens. [If] the Freedom Democratic Party is not seated now, I question America.

Lyndon Johnson offered a compromise to the Freedom party: he would seat two MFDP delegates of his own choosing, and he promised that the rules of the convention would be

Enrichment

Encourage interested students to examine the book or video version of "Eyes on the Prize" or another source of firsthand information on the civil rights movement. Then ask them to write a short essay addressing these questions: Was it right for "outsiders" (northern African Americans and whites) to come to southern towns to spark confrontations over civil rights? Were some southern whites and African Americans justified in accusing these activists of "meddling" by inflaming hatred and igniting violence with their nonviolent actions?

Caption Answer to . . .

Interpreting Tables

Title IV

In Depth

Did You Know?

Southerners were caught off guard when Representative Charles Weltner (D–Georgia) voted in favor of the Civil Rights Act of 1964, arguing, "We can offer resistance and defiance, with their harvest of strife and tumult. We can suffer continued demonstrations, with their wake of violence and disorder. Or, we can acknowledge this measure as the law of the land. We can accept the verdict of the Nation. . . . I would urge that we at home now move on to the unfinished task of building a new South. We must not remain forever bound to another lost cause."

Section 3 Review Answers

1. (a) March on Washington, see p. 811, (b) Civil Rights Act of 1964, see p. 812, (c) Voting Rights Act of 1965, see p. 814

2. Having won the presidency by a very narrow margin, JFK was afraid of alienating white southerners, whose votes he needed to support other measures. He soon decided to back stronger civil rights legislation.

3. After making passage of Kennedy's civil rights bill his first priority upon assuming the presidency, Lyndon Johnson threw his support behind another measure aimed at securing voting rights.

4. The United States was probably not ready for the Civil Rights Act and the Voting Rights Act in the 1940s. The nation was fighting a world war and had little energy left to focus on civil rights. The march might have had some impact, but most likely Randolph decided to settle for Roosevelt's promise to form the FEPC because he knew it was about the best possible outcome at the time.

Reteach

Have students review the section by listing ways in which politicians responded to the civil rights conflict. Next to each item, have students grade each type of response as *strong* or *weak*.

4. CLOSE

Reinforcing the Big Idea

Politicians belatedly joined the issue of civil rights. Yet their efforts left many wrongs unrighted, and some African Americans became disillusioned with nonviolence as a solution to continuing discrimination. The next section describes the reactions of those African Americans.

When Fannie Lou Hamer registered to vote in her home state of Mississippi, the owner of the plantation where she lived promptly evicted her. She told her story at the 1968 Democratic National Convention (right), reaching a television audience of millions.

changed in 1968 so there would be no more discrimination in the Mississippi delegation. The MFDP rejected the compromise. Johnson went on to win reelection in a landslide, but he knew he had to do something about the issue of voting rights for African Americans.

⚫ In early 1965 Johnson addressed a joint session of Congress and a national television audience. He was at his most eloquent as he spoke about the right to vote: "The command of the Constitution is plain. There is no moral issue. It is wrong—deadly wrong—to deny any of your fellow Americans the right to vote in this country."

At one point in his speech, Johnson paused, raised his arms, and repeated the words that had become the marching song of the civil rights movement: "And . . . we . . . shall . . . overcome." Johnson got the response he wanted. After turning back another filibuster, Congress passed the **Voting Rights Act of 1965.**

The Voting Rights Act authorized the attorney general to appoint federal examiners to register voters where local officials prevented African Americans from exercising their constitutional right. The act singled out the South, for six states and part of another did not pass the test of having 50 percent of the voting-age population registered in 1964. In the year following passage, over 400,000 African Americans registered to vote in the Deep South, as shown by the chart on page 812. By 1968 the number reached 1 million. This act changed the nature of southern politics. It created an entirely new voting population, and it led to African American representation at local, state, and national levels.

The Civil Rights Act and the Voting Rights Act were landmarks in the history of civil rights in the United States, and they had a real impact. For some African Americans, however, these legislative accomplishments were not nearly enough. Impatient with the slow pace of progress, many African Americans turned a receptive ear to radical leaders who voiced the fury born of centuries of oppression. Pride and power, rather than peaceful resistance, were the watchwords for this new outgrowth of the civil rights movement.

SECTION 3 REVIEW

Key Terms, People, and Places

1. Define (a) March on Washington, (b) Civil Rights Act of 1964, (c) Voting Rights Act of 1965.

Key Concepts

2. Why was Kennedy initially reluctant to support civil rights wholeheartedly? How did his position change?

3. What role did Lyndon Johnson play in the passage of civil rights legislation?

Critical Thinking

4. Demonstrating Reasoned Judgment Reflect on the struggle for civil rights up to 1965. Then explain why you agree or disagree with the following statement: "If A. Philip Randolph had gone ahead with his plans for the 1941 March on Washington, legislation such as the Civil Rights Act and the Voting Rights Act would have been passed twenty years earlier."

RESOURCE DIRECTORY

Teaching Resources

⚫ **Visual Learning Activity** A White House Demonstration, found in the Unit 9 folder, p. 62, enriches students' understanding of the pressure on Washington to pass the Voting Rights Act with a 1965 photo of a civil rights demonstration.

Quiz found in the Unit 9 folder, p. 44, covers the main ideas in this section as well as the key terms.

The Challenge of Black Power

SECTION PREVIEW

During the civil rights movement, change happened slowly and at times appeared to have ground to a halt. The response from some African Americans was a call for self-defense—even if it meant using violence.

Key Concepts
• The anger felt by many African Americans was expressed in the words of writer James Baldwin, activist Malcolm X, and others.
• Malcolm X preached that African Americans could expect nothing from white society in the United States and therefore needed to create a separate society.
• Street riots erupted in some cities in the late 1960s.

Key Terms, People, and Places
de jure segregation, de facto segregation, Nation of Islam, Black Power; James Baldwin, Malcolm X

Son, a collection of essays published in 1955, he told of the damaging effects of segregation in the United States. He attacked not simply **de jure segregation**—the rigid pattern of separation dictated by law in the South—but also **de facto segregation**—the separation that resulted from the ghetto conditions in many northern cities. This pattern is shown on the map below. In 1963, in his best seller *The Fire Next Time*, Baldwin argued that these conditions could not continue. African American anger was ready to erupt. In one essay he described the horrors of the recent past—

this past, the Negro's past, of rope, fire, torture, castration, infanticide, rape; death and humiliation; fear by day and night; fear as deep as the marrow of the bone; doubt that he was worthy of life, since everyone around

A raised fist became the symbol of the Black Power movement, a militant outgrowth of the earlier civil rights movement. ✪

A
fter passage of the two civil rights acts in 1964 and 1965, the movement shifted course. Racial discrimination continued, both in the North and in the South. African Americans became frustrated at the slow and sometimes halting pace of change. Their growing anger found expression in the speeches and essays of a number of critics, who challenged the nonviolent approach that had guided the movement in the early 1960s. More militant calls for reform changed the nature of the struggle and led to increasing division in the movement and in the United States as a whole.

African American Anger

James Baldwin was a gifted writer who described the African American experience in his works and became a spokesperson for the civil rights movement. In his *Notes of a Native*

De Facto Segregation in the North, c. 1965

Cleveland, c.1965

■ Area of city more than 70% African American

⌐-⌐ Cleveland city limits

0 2.5 5 Miles
0 2.5 5 Kilometers

Lake Erie

SUPERIOR AVE.
EUCLID AVE.
CARNEGIE AVE.
LORAIN AVE.
BROADWAY
KINSMAN BLVD.
MILES AVE.
PEARL RD.

🌍 **Geography and History: Interpreting Maps**
This map shows the areas of Cleveland, Ohio, with the highest concentrations of African Americans in the 1960s. *What social and economic factors may have contributed to this pattern of settlement?*

☐ **Reproducible Lesson Plan** found in the Unit 9 folder, p. 38, provides a summary of the Section 4 lesson plan content.

☐ **Alternate Lesson Plan: Critical Thinking** Making Comparisons, found in the Alternate Lesson Plans folder, p. 149, encourages students to apply this skill by examining the evolution of various civil rights groups.

☐ **Guided Reading and Review** found in the Unit 9 folder, p. 45, provides a structure for reading and mastering the key concepts and reviewing the key terms for Section 4. (Guided Practice)

✪ ☐ **Literature Activity** Sins of the Fathers, found in the Unit 9 folder, p. 60, uses an essay from Eldridge Cleaver's *Soul on Ice* to show Cleaver's view that there could be mutual respect between the races if "white youth" could repudiate the evils of the past.

1. FOCUS

Connecting to the Big Idea

See page 794B. Explain to students that nonviolent protests earned early gains, but that progress subsequently seemed to stall. Ask students how African Americans reacted to continuing discrimination.

Objectives
● Identify the figures who expressed the rage that many African Americans felt during the 1960s.
● Summarize the main ideas preached by Malcolm X.
● Describe how nonviolence gave way to violent protests in the late 1960s.

Bellringer

Ask students what kinds of activities go on in school that are officially against the rules. Then explain the difference between the terms *de jure* and *de facto*.

Reading Strategy

Structured Overview Have students make a two-column chart headed Problems and Solutions. As they read, they should write in the appropriate columns the problems African American leaders identified and the solutions that they advocated.

Caption Answer to ...

🌍 Interpreting Maps

The fact that African Americans were discriminated against in the work force meant that many had to accept low-paying jobs and could not afford to live in affluent neighborhoods. African Americans also may not have been able to buy homes in white neighborhoods because of prejudice on the part of realtors and white residents.

Answers will vary but students can be encouraged to research and report on the extent of equal access for disabled students in their school cafeterias, classrooms, and libraries, for example.

2. INSTRUCT

Discuss

Point out President Johnson's comment on page 819. Then discuss with students the answers to his and the following questions: Why, after so much progress on civil rights, did so much anger and violence erupt? Why did African Americans become cynical about the goal of nonviolent integration pursued by Martin Luther King, Jr.?

Analyze

Have students analyze why de facto segregation was so much harder to identify and extinguish than de jure segregation. How did the Black Power movement seek to solve the problem of de facto segregation?

Equal Rights Movements

The civil rights movement of the 1960s resulted in federal laws that forbade discrimination against African Americans. The success of the civil rights movement has inspired other minority groups to fight for equal rights. Latinos, Asian Americans, women, children, the elderly, and people with disabilities are among those groups who have also used demonstrations and sit-ins, court challenges, and legislative pressure to demand their constitutional guarantee of equal rights.

Victory was gained by one group when President Bush, in his 1990 State of the Union message, spoke of the need for a "better America" where "for the first time, the American mainstream includes all our disabled citizens." In July 1990 the Americans with Disabilities Act was finally approved by both houses of Congress. This law was the result of a long struggle by physically or mentally disabled people to ensure equal access to employment, transportation, telecommunications, and public accommodations.

Businesses that employ twenty-five or more workers are now forbidden to refuse to hire or promote a qualified disabled job applicant. In addition, nearly all businesses are required to provide access for people with disabilities. For example, aisles in stores must be wide enough for a wheelchair.

Railroads, bus lines, mass transit systems, and public school bus companies are required to ensure that all new vehicles are accessible to disabled persons. Telephone companies must provide services so that hearing- or voice-impaired people can use their systems. *What facilities and programs in your school ensure equal access for disabled students?*

---

him denied it; sorrow for his women, for his kinfolk, for his children, who needed his protection, and whom he could not protect; rage, hatred, and murder, hatred for white men so deep that it often turned against him and his own, and made all love, all trust, all joy impossible.

In this essay and others published in the popular press, Baldwin warned Americans that unless change occurred soon, the nation could expect uncontrollable violence.

Malcolm X

Another leader who expressed the deeply felt anger of many African Americans was **Malcolm X.** He was born Malcolm Little in Omaha, Nebraska, in 1925. His father, a Baptist minister, spread the "back-to-Africa" message of Marcus Garvey but died when Little was a child. Little was raised in ghettos in Detroit, Boston, and New York, where he spent his youth involved in various criminal activities. At age twenty, he was arrested for an attempted burglary and served seven years in prison. While in jail he read widely and became interested in a group called the **Nation of Islam.**

The Nation of Islam was founded in 1933 in Chicago by Elijah Muhammad. He taught that Allah, the God of Islam, would bring about a "Black Nation" composed of all the nonwhite peoples of the world. According to Elijah Muhammad, one of the keys to self-knowledge was knowing one's enemy, and the enemy of the Nation of Islam was the white man and white supremacy. Members of the Nation of Islam did not seek change through political means but waited for Allah to create the Black Nation. In the meantime, they led a righteous life and worked hard to become economically self-sufficient.

Released from prison in 1952, Malcolm Little converted to the Nation of Islam, changed his name to Malcolm X, and became a disciple of Elijah Muhammad. He spent the next twelve years spreading the gospel of his new faith.

Malcolm X disagreed with both the tactics and the goals of the early civil rights movement. He called the March on Washington the "Farce on Washington" and voiced his irritation at "all of this non-violent, begging-the-white-man kind of dying . . . all of this sitting-in, sliding-in, wading-in, eating-in, diving-in, and all the rest." He preached that integration would not work and that African Americans had to take their destiny into their own hands:

No sane black man really wants integration! No sane white man really wants integration! No sane black man really believes that the white man ever will give the black man anything more than token integration. No! The Honorable Elijah Muhammad teaches that for the black man in America the only solution is complete separation from the white man . . . . The American black man should be focusing his effort toward building his own businesses, and decent homes for himself. As other ethnic groups have done, let the black people, wherever possible, however possible, patronize their own kind, hire their own kind, and start in those ways to build up the black race's ability to do for itself. That's the only way the American black man is ever going to get respect.

Before long Malcolm X had attracted a wide following. By 1963 Elijah Muhammad had become increasingly jealous of the attention that Malcolm X was receiving. When Elijah Muhammad objected to a remark Malcolm X had made about the Kennedy assassination, Malcolm X left the Nation of Islam and formed his own religious organization, called Muslim Mosque, Inc. He then made a pilgrimage to Mecca, the holy city of Islam in Saudi Arabia. When he returned, he proclaimed that he had been wrong to preach the hatred of white people. Malcolm X was assassinated in February 1965; three members of the Nation of Islam were charged with the murder. But his message lived on, and it attracted the attention of many of the young workers in SNCC.

Elijah Muhammad (above left) called African Americans "the lost-found Nation of Islam in the wilderness of North America." Malcolm X (above right) was a leading minister of the Nation of Islam until 1963.

MAKING CONNECTIONS

The Nation of Islam had its historical roots in the ideas of Marcus Garvey's "back-to-Africa" movement. How were the ideas behind each movement related to each other?

Black Power Rages

One of the SNCC leaders influenced by Malcolm X was Stokely Carmichael. He had been born in Trinidad, in the West Indies, and came to the United States at the age of eleven. He grew up interested in political affairs and involved in African American protest. At Howard University in Washington, D.C., he and other students took over the Washington chapter of SNCC. He was beaten and jailed for his participation in demonstrations and finally got tired of civil disobedience. Carmichael called on SNCC workers to carry guns for self-defense. He also argued that African Americans should cease deferring to whites and make SNCC into an exclusively African American organization. His election as head of the organization in 1966 was a reflection of SNCC's growing radicalism.

A turning point in the civil rights movement came in June 1966, at a march that took place in Greenwood, Mississippi. As Martin Luther King's followers sang "We Shall Overcome," Carmichael's supporters drowned them out by singing "We Shall Overrun." Then Carmichael, just out of jail, jumped into the back of an open truck to address the group:

This is the twenty-seventh time I have been arrested, and I ain't going to jail no more! . . . The only way we gonna stop them white men from whuppin' us is to take over. We been saying freedom for six years—and we ain't got nothin.' What we gonna start saying now is "Black Power!"

Activity

A Panel Debate

Stage a mock panel debate between supporters of nonviolent protest, such as Martin Luther King, Jr., and Black Power advocates, such as Malcom X or Stokely Carmichael, in 1966. Panel members on both sides should become familiar with the moral, social, and political arguments of their positions and try to refute the arguments of the opposition.

Enrichment

Ask students to locate protest poems, prose, songs, and art from the 1960s and to include several in a notebook. Suggest that they begin by examining the writings of James Baldwin and Malcolm X.

Answer to . . .

MAKING CONNECTIONS

Both Marcus Garvey and Elijah Muhammad preached that African Americans could succeed only by separating themselves from white society.

In Depth

Multicultural Perspectives

In 1975, congressional committees in the House and Senate began inquiries into the infiltration activities of the Federal Bureau of Investigation (FBI) into certain civil rights groups. The government found, according to scholar Howard Zinn, that "[t]he FBI had sent forged letters, engaged in burglaries (it admitted to ninety-two between 1960 and 1966), opened mail illegally, and, in the case of Black Panther leader Fred Hampton, seems to have conspired in murder."

Section 4 Review Answers

1. (a) de jure segregation, see p. 815,
(b) de facto segregation, see p. 815,
(c) Nation of Islam, see p. 816,
(d) Black Power, see p. 818

2. James Baldwin was a writer whose essays described the experience of African Americans growing up in a white-dominated culture. He predicted that the anger engendered by centuries of unjust treatment of African Americans would soon explode into violence if it were not addressed seriously.

3. Malcolm X argued that integration was not sufficient and insisted that African Americans had to develop a sense of racial pride and a willingness to help themselves. He also declared that the moderate civil rights movement would not help them achieve their ends, so African Americans would have to create their own separate society within the United States.

4. African Americans remained frustrated, despite gains made. Small gains only whetted their appetite for more progress, but some whites felt that too much had already been done. These bitterly opposed viewpoints eventually erupted into violence in areas where African Americans and whites lived close together.

5. Possible answers: Separate communities would reject King's dream of "sitting down together at the table of brotherhood," and would probably be difficult to maintain on a practical level. Separate communities might decrease African American frustration, in line with Malcolm X's warning that African Americans ought not to expect anything more than "token integration" from the white establishment.

As he repeated "We . . . want . . . Black . . . Power!" the audience responded with the same words in a thunderous echo. Carmichael's idea of **Black Power** called on African Americans "to unite, to recognize their heritage, to build a sense of community . . . to begin to define their own goals, to lead their own organizations and support those organizations."

In the fall of 1966, a number of African American militants founded a new political party—the Black Panthers. The Panthers wanted African Americans to lead their own communities and demanded that the federal government rebuild the nation's ghettos in repayment for years of discrimination. Huey Newton, one of the founders of the group, repeated the words of Chinese leader Mao Zedong: "Power flows from the barrel of a gun." At the same time, the organization had a gentler side and developed day-care centers, health-care facilities, and free breakfast programs in communities where it took hold.

Black Power gave rise to the "Black Is Beautiful" slogan that helped foster a sense of racial pride. It also led to a serious split in the civil rights movement, as radical groups like SNCC and

Members of the Black Panther party marched through the streets of New York City in 1968 to protest the trial of one of their leaders, Huey P. Newton.

the Black Panthers moved away from the NAACP and other more conservative organizations. ✪

Riots in the Streets

Riots in a number of American cities were symptoms of the continuing poor conditions under which many African Americans were forced to live in the mid-1960s. There were no "whites only" signs above water fountains in northern cities, but more subtle forms of discrimination kept African Americans living in poverty. African Americans were kept out of well-paying jobs, job training programs, and suburban housing. Police officers assigned to ghetto neighborhoods were viewed by African American residents as dangerous oppressors rather than upholders of justice. James Baldwin remarked that a white police officer in one of these neighborhoods was "like an occupying soldier in a bitterly hostile country."

Riots ravaged Rochester, New York; New York City; and several cities in New Jersey in 1964. One of the most violent riots began in the Watts neighborhood of Los Angeles on August 11, 1965. On that steamy summer day, police pulled over a twenty-one-year-old African American man for drunk driving. At first the interaction was friendly between the police, the suspect, and the crowd of Watts residents that had gathered around. When the suspect resisted arrest, however, one police officer panicked and began swinging his riot baton. The crowd was outraged, and the scene touched off six days of rioting. Thousands of people filled the streets, burning cars and stores, stealing merchandise, and sniping at fire fighters. When the national guard and local police finally gained control, thirty-four people were dead and more than a thousand were injured.

Violence spread to other cities in 1966 and 1967. Cries of "Get Whitey" and "Burn, Baby, Burn" replaced the gentler slogans of the earlier civil rights movement. The

RESOURCE DIRECTORY

Teaching Resources

✪ **Critical Thinking Activity** Demonstrating Reasoned Judgment: How to Respond, found in the Unit 9 folder, p. 54, presents passages from four of America's most powerful civil rights leaders to help students apply this skill.

National Advisory Commission on Civil Disorders, known as the Kerner Commission, noted in a report in 1968: "The nation is rapidly moving toward two increasingly separate Americas."

The Legacy of the Movement

African Americans and whites both wondered at times whether progress in civil rights was possible. Anne Moody felt frustrated when the movement failed to bring the quick change activists sought. As she listened to others sing civil rights songs during one demonstration, she found herself unable to forget the suffering that continued. "We Shall Overcome" echoed around her, but all she could think was, "I wonder. I really wonder."

Lyndon Johnson was devastated by the violence that exploded near the end of his presidency. "How is it possible," he asked, "after all we've accomplished? How could it be? Is the world topsy turvy?" While the measures passed by his administration had brought good results, they were not nearly enough.

Despite the need for further progress, the movement had brought tremendous change. Segregation was now illegal. African Americans were assured the right to vote, and the power they wielded changed the nature of American political life. Between 1970 and 1975, the number of African American elected officials rose by 88 percent. African Americans served as mayors in large cities like Atlanta, Detroit, Los Angeles, and Newark and served in Congress in larger numbers as well. Black studies courses

began to appear in high schools and colleges. African Americans had a new sense of identity and pride in their ethnic heritage.

African American congresswoman Barbara Jordan noted the impact of the movement:

> The civil rights movement called America to look at itself in a giant mirror. . . . Do the black people who were born on this soil, who are American citizens, do they really feel that this is the land of opportunity, the land of the free. . . . America had to say no.

The response to that question was the first step toward making the United States a fairer society for all.

The rallying cry "Burn, Baby, Burn" became a nightmarish reality in the streets of Los Angeles in 1965. After fire fighters quenched the flames in buildings all over Watts, crowds of looters moved in to carry off the spoils.

SECTION 4 REVIEW

Key Terms, People, and Places
1. Define (a) de jure segregation, (b) de facto segregation, (c) Nation of Islam, (d) Black Power.

Key Concepts
2. How did James Baldwin give voice to African American anger?

3. When Malcolm X belonged to the Nation of Islam, what did he preach about the future of race relations in the United States?

4. Why was there rioting in many cities across the United States in the late 1960s?

Critical Thinking
5. Drawing Conclusions The Nation of Islam and the Black Power movement both taught that African Americans should seek to establish their own communities separate from white Americans. Explain why you do or do not believe that such a goal is possible.

Quiz found in the Unit 9 folder, p. 46, covers the main ideas in this section as well as the key terms.

Chapter Test Forms A and B are found in the Unit 9 folder, pp. 63–68.

Answer Keys found in the Unit 9 folder, pp. 146–159, provide answers to all student activities.

Media and Technology

 Transparencies Critical Thinking, I-17; Graphic Organizer, G-3

Guided Reading Audiotapes (English and Spanish)

Computer Test Bank

Reteach
Have students make a chart illustrating the key occurrences in the chain of events that led from nonviolent protests to the ghetto riots.

4. CLOSE

Reinforcing the Big Idea
Delays in achieving full equality caused increasing frustration among some African Americans, whose anger boiled over into violence.

In Depth

Then and Now

In January 1994, activist Tom Hayden, then a state senator and gubernatorial candidate in California, looked back on the 1960s. "We made long strides in a short time: ending segregation, reforming presidential primaries, the eighteen-year-old vote, the birth of the environmental and women's movements. It may have caused the Nixon reaction, but it also made Clinton-Gore possible."

Chapter Review

Chapter Review Answers

Understanding Key Terms, People, and Places

Terms
Students should refer to the definitions of the key terms in the chapter to write sentences that show the relation of each word to the civil rights movement.

Matching
1. Freedom Rides
2. SNCC
3. Civil Rights Act of 1964
4. Nation of Islam
5. Albany Movement

Matching
1. James Baldwin
2. Malcolm X

Reviewing Main Ideas

1. The NAACP emphasized legal equality, while CORE was dedicated to effecting change through peaceful confrontation.

2. King favored nonviolent resistance; he was influenced by the ideas implemented by Mohandas Gandhi during India's struggle for independence from Britain.

3. SNCC was made up of young people and was more radical than the SCLC.

4. Sit-ins were effective because they demonstrated the unfairness of segregationist policies and put business owners' profits at risk.

5. Activists placed groups of African Americans and whites on Freedom Rides to the South. After the Freedom Riders were attacked at many bus terminals, the federal government finally stepped in and forced local authorities to uphold desegregation policies for interstate travelers.

6. The violence shocked people throughout the country and created sympathy for the civil rights movement.

7. On the one hand, Kennedy talked boldly about the need for civil rights; on the other hand, he was careful not to alienate white southern leaders in Congress by taking effective action.

8. Besides being an organizer of the march, King, always an eloquent and inspiring speaker, delivered his best-known and most inspiring address on this occasion.

9. Johnson used his skills as a political consensus builder and played on the nation's sorrow over Kennedy's death to ensure passage of the Civil Rights Act of 1964 and the Voting Rights Act of 1965.

10. Baldwin warned that violence would erupt if change did not come soon.

Understanding Key Terms, People, and Places

Key Terms
1. interracial
2. Congress of Racial Equality
3. Southern Christian Leadership Conference (SCLC)
4. Student Nonviolent Coordinating Committee (SNCC)
5. sit-in
6. Freedom Rides
7. Albany Movement
8. March on Washington
9. Civil Rights Act of 1964
10. Voting Rights Act of 1965
11. de jure segregation
12. de facto segregation
13. Nation of Islam
14. Black Power

People
15. James Baldwin
16. Malcolm X

Terms For each term above, write a sentence that explains its relation to the civil rights movement.

Matching Review the key terms in the list above. If you are not sure of a term's meaning, review its definition in the chapter. Then choose a term from the list that best matches each description below.
1. bus trips on which groups of African American and white activists traveled south to protest segregation on interstate transportation facilities
2. an organization that grew out of a conference for students active in the civil rights struggle
3. the legislation that banned discrimination in all public accommodations
4. a religious group whose members believed that Allah would create a Black Nation
5. a group of African Americans who joined together in Georgia for a year-long campaign of protest marches

Matching Review the key people in the list above. Then choose a name from the list that best matches each description below.
1. an author who wrote about the damaging effects of segregation in his book *Notes of a Native Son*
2. a member of the Nation of Islam who preached that neither African Americans nor whites wanted integration

Reviewing Main Ideas

Section 1 (pp. 796–801)
1. How did CORE differ from the NAACP in its approach?
2. What methods did Martin Luther King, Jr., favor to achieve equality, and where did these methods originate?
3. How did SNCC differ from SCLC?

Section 2 (pp. 803–807)
4. Why was the sit-in strategy effective in ending segregation policies?
5. How did activists desegregate the interstate bus system?
6. Describe the effect of the violence that erupted during the 1963 Birmingham marches, explaining both its local and national impact.

Section 3 (pp. 810–814)
7. In what ways did President Kennedy straddle the fence in his civil rights policies?
8. What role did Martin Luther King, Jr., play in the March on Washington?
9. How did Lyndon Johnson secure passage of major civil rights legislation during his presidency?

Section 4 (pp. 815–819)
10. What did author James Baldwin warn might happen if change in the area of civil rights did not occur quickly?
11. What message for African Americans did Malcolm X preach as a member of the Nation of Islam?
12. What were the underlying causes of the riots that occurred in many cities in the mid- to late 1960s?

11. Malcolm X preached that African Americans must create a separate society.

12. Continuing discrimination against African Americans that kept many from gaining access to economic opportunities fueled the anger that erupted in street riots across the nation.

Thinking Critically

1. Possible questions: Why did you join the civil rights movement? What was your family's response to your participation in the civil rights movement? How did your opinions of race relations change as a result of your participation? Do you agree that the use of nonviolent confrontation is the most effective way of achieving equality?

2. Answers will vary, but students may suggest issues related to racial or other forms of injustice or to the environment and land development. Alternatives to nonviolent protest include working through established political channels, voting for candidates sympathetic to one's position, and letter-writing campaigns.

1. **Formulating Questions** Create four questions to ask civil rights activist Anne Moody that would, if answered, lead to a deeper understanding of what participating in the civil rights movement of the early 1960s was like.

2. **Identifying Alternatives** What issues could provoke a sit-in or other nonviolent protest in your community? What other options for effecting change are available to members of your community?

3. **Distinguishing Fact from Opinion** Malcolm X once said that for African Americans, "The only solution is complete separation from the white man." Explain why you think this statement is a fact or an opinion.

1. **Evaluating Primary Sources** Review the primary source excerpt on pages 811–812. In what ways has Martin Luther King's dream come closer to being a reality? In what ways is it still a dream for the future? Use as many specific examples as possible, from both your personal experience and your knowledge of current events, to support your conclusions.

2. **Understanding the Visuals** In the primary source excerpt on page 807, Martin Luther King says, "For years now I have heard the word 'Wait!'" Find visuals in the chapter that illustrate why the people who fought for civil rights found it impossible to "wait" any longer to be treated fairly.

3. **Writing About the Chapter** It is the spring of 1960. SCLC executive director Ella Baker has asked you, a young African American, to attend a meeting of a new organization, the Student Nonviolent Coordinating Committee (SNCC). Write a letter in which you reply to Baker's invitation, explaining why you will or will not attend this meeting. First, create a list of what you see as the potential benefits of SNCC. Then list its possible negative features. Note any suggestions you have for the new organization. Next, write a draft of your reply to Baker's invitation in which you offer your ideas. Revise your letter, making sure that each idea is clearly expressed. Proofread your letter and draft a final copy.

4. **Using the Graphic Organizer** This graphic organizer uses a tree map to organize information about nonviolent confrontation during the civil rights movement. A tree map shows how details support a main idea. On this tree map, blue entries show the results of various events. (a) What was the result of each of the protests mentioned on the chart? (b) Which method of protest listed was the most effective as a nonviolent protest? (c) On a separate sheet of paper, create your own tree map about the challenge of Black Power, using this graphic organizer as an example.

Nonviolent Confrontation During the Early Civil Rights Movement

Sit-ins	Freedom Rides	Albany Movement	Integration of Ole Miss	Birmingham Confrontation
• Test limits of segregation policies • Put business profits at risk • Become an effective way to integrate restaurants and stores	• Activists travel on interstate buses • Violence erupts in Deep South • Segregation prohibited on interstate transportation	• Activists plan a year of protests • Local leaders angered when Martin Luther King, Jr., takes charge • Movement fizzles	• Lines of confrontation drawn when James Meredith tries to gain admission to Ole Miss • Violence erupts • Ole Miss becomes integrated	• Activists challenging discriminatory hiring practices and segregated city facilities met with violence • Protesters win desegregated city facilities, fairer hiring practices, biracial committee

4. (a) Successes include the integration of many stores and restaurants, the prohibition of segregation on interstate transportation, the integration of Ole Miss, and the desegregation of city facilities and fairer hiring practices in Birmingham. (b) The sit-ins seem to have been the most effective nonviolent means of protest, as most of the other nonviolent tactics degenerated into violence. (c) Students' graphic organizers should include details that illustrate the influence of Black Power during the mid- and late l960s.

Alternative Assessment

Final Evaluation

Use the following guidelines to evaluate student projects:

● **Evidence of thoughtfulness** Did students include significant leaders of the civil rights movement?

● **Evidence of outside research** To what extent did students use outside research materials for their projects?

● **Evidence of synthesis** Do projects demonstrate that students understand the relationships among the subjects and their spheres of influence?

● **Communication style** Do projects convey their purpose to an audience in a clear, appealing way?

Allow interested students to present their finished projects to the class.

3. The statement is an opinion; it expresses Malcolm X's conclusion about the complex problem of race relations in the United States, but other conclusions are possible.

Making Connections

1. Answers will vary but should demonstrate an awareness that although progress has been made toward achieving equality, much still remains to be done.

2. Students may cite any of the following visuals to illustrate the injustices faced by African Americans: lynching on page 797, burnt cross in King's yard on page 799, sit-in on page 804, violence of Freedom Rides indicated on map on page 805, firemen directing hoses at people on page 806, de facto segregation shown on map on page 815.

3. Answers will vary, but letters should demonstrate an awareness of the goals of SNCC.

Chapter 30 Continuing Social Revolution
1960–1975

📁 Teaching Resources (See Unit 9 Folder)		
	Instruction	**Enrichment**
Section 1 **The Women's Movement** (pp. 824–829)	Reproducible Lesson Plan, p. 70 Alternate Lesson Plan, p. 151 Guided Reading and Review, p. 74 Quiz, p. 75	Literature Activity, A Changing Sense of Self, p. 93 Primary Source Activity, The Equal Rights Amendment, p. 90 Viewpoints Activity, On Working Mothers, pp. 86–87 Historian's Toolbox Activity, Recognizing Bias, p. 88
Section 2 **Ethnic Minorities Seek Equality** (pp. 831–835)	Reproducible Lesson Plan, p. 71 Alternate Lesson Plan, p. 152 Guided Reading and Review, p. 76 Quiz, p. 77	Literature Activity, Perspectives by Women of Color, p. 95 American Profiles Activity, Delores Huerta, p. 84
Section 3 **Native American Struggles** (pp. 836–840)	Reproducible Lesson Plan, p. 72 Alternate Lesson Plan, p. 153 Guided Reading and Review, p. 78 Quiz, p. 79	Visual Learning Activity, Changing Attitudes Toward Native Americans, p. 96 American Profiles Activity, Vine Deloria, Jr., p. 85 Critical Thinking Activity, Identifying Assumptions, p. 89 Literature Activity, Native American Voices, p. 94
Section 4 **Environmental and Consumer Movements** (pp. 841–843)	Reproducible Lesson Plan, p. 73 Alternate Lesson Plan, p. 154 Guided Reading and Review, p. 80 Quiz, p. 81 Chapter Test, Forms A & B, pp. 98–103	Primary Source Activity, The Desecration of America, pp. 91–92 Visual Learning Activity, Preserving the Environment, p. 97 Time and Place Activity, The Costs of Environmental Protection, pp. 82–83

📁 Additional Chapter Resources	Bibliography
Resource Organizer, p. 69 Alternate Lesson Plan, p. 150 Answer Keys, pp. 146–159	**For the Teacher** Carson, Rachel. *Silent Spring.* Houghton Mifflin, 1962. (Classic, ground-breaking book on environmental awareness.) Friedan, Betty. *The Feminine Mystique.* Dell, 1984 edition. (A critique of postwar inequities and discrimination against women.) *Voices from Wounded Knee.* Akwesasne Notes, 1973. (Anthology of critically praised expressions of Native American militancy during the late 1960s and early 1970s.) ***Prentice Hall Literature*** Excerpts from *The American Experience,* 1994, including Lopez, Barry H. *Arctic Dreams: Imagination and Desire in a Western Landscape.* Charles Scribner's Sons, 1986.

Media and Technology

 Fine Art, D-20

 Our Multicultural Heritage, C-15

 Critical Thinking, I-9

 Graphic Organizer, G-3

 Guided Reading Audiotapes (English and Spanish)

 Computer Test Bank

For the Student

Darling, Frank Fraser. *Wilderness and Plenty.* Houghton Mifflin, 1970. (On shrinking natural resources, the effects of accelerated technology, and conservation.)

Momaday, N. Scott. *House Made of Dawn.* New American Library, 1969. (The Pulitzer Prize–winning novel of a young Native American caught between the white world and the ways of his people; written by an Oklahoma Kiowa.)

Time-Life Books editors. *This Fabulous Century, Vol. 7, 1960–1970.* Time-Life Books, 1970. (Illustrated and comprehensive study.)

THE BIG IDEA

The Big Idea for the chapter and how the main ideas in each section relate to the Big Idea are graphically displayed below. Comprehension of this chapter's Big Idea is critical to students' understanding of United States history and how we as a nation got where we are today.

CHAPTER 30

Inspired by the civil rights movement, women, Latino Americans, Asian Americans, and Native Americans struggled to achieve equality in the 1960s and early 1970s through protests. The movement for social change affected almost every aspect of American society—from the environment to consumer awareness.

SECTION 1

The civil rights movement encouraged many American women to face their own inequality in society. These women worked to end discrimination based on gender and experienced considerable success.

SECTION 2

The civil rights movement also inspired Latino Americans and Asian Americans to work for equality.

SECTION 3

In the 1960s and early 1970s, Native Americans worked to gain equality and control over their own lives and land.

SECTION 4

Activists in the environmental and consumer movements used tactics introduced by the civil rights movement to bring about changes in public awareness, attitudes, and public policy.

The Relevance of the Big Idea

In the 1990s advertising agencies, school administrators, movie producers, book publishers, and politicians strive to attain "political correctness" (p.c.), or calculated inoffensiveness. Those who maintain a high level of p.c. try to avoid offending groups working against discrimination. Support for the environment is also considered politically correct. Concerned observers note that p.c. can be superficial and hypocritical. Real gains, which cannot be lost when the next political or advertising fashion comes along, must come from the courts, the legislatures, and through significant social change.

Have students discuss briefly what they think are real gains and changes for the better in American society over the last twenty years.

In Depth

Global Connections

The youth revolution was just as powerfully expressed in Europe as in the United States. In 1963, the irreverent, working-class Beatles, heavily influenced by American pop and rock music, were the first of a number of British groups to find wide appeal in the youth-dominated popular music markets in both Europe and America. From clothes to politics, the youth cultures across the Atlantic were similar. In 1968, as the Democratic National Convention in Chicago was besieged by protesters, university sit-ins in France played a major role in the demise of the French government.

Continuing Social Revolution
1960–1975

*C*hange. Upheaval. Action. These words describe the social revolution of the 1960s and early 1970s. Far from occurring in a vacuum, the 1960s civil rights movement breathed new life into other issues. Women, Latinos, Asian Americans, and Native Americans adapted civil rights tactics to achieve their own goals of equality. Similar tactics helped launch movements to protect the environment and improve the quality and safety of certain consumer goods.

Events in the United States

1960 Asian Americans represent Hawaii in Congress.	1962 Biologist Rachel Carson publishes Silent Spring.	1963 Feminist Betty Friedan publishes The Feminine Mystique.	1965 César Chávez organizes farm workers. • Ralph Nader publishes Unsafe at Any Speed.	1966 The National Organization for Women is founded.

| 1960 | 1962 | 1964 | 1966 |

Events in the World

	1961 The Berlin Wall is built to divide East and West Berlin.		1964 Jomo Kenyatta becomes president of independent Kenya.	1966 Indira Gandhi becomes prime minister of India.

RESOURCE DIRECTORY

Teaching Resources

Alternate Lesson Plan: Demonstrating the Big Idea found in the Alternate Lesson Plans folder, p. 150, provides a lesson strategy to instruct students about the Big Idea that the movement for social change affected almost every aspect of American life.

Alternative Assessment Handbook provides information, guidance, and strategies for alternative methods of assessment. It includes an essay on new trends in assessment, guidance and strategies for developing performance tasks and portfolios, scoring rubrics, and sample evaluation forms.

Pages 824–829
The Women's Movement

For generations, many American women had realized they were being treated as second-class citizens. Encouraged by the gains of the civil rights movement, women united behind the goal of ending discrimination based on gender.

 Pages 831–835
Ethnic Minorities Seek Equality

Inspired by the civil rights movement, Latinos and Asian Americans launched their own movements to overcome racial discrimination. Each group faced different obstacles in its struggles for equal treatment.

 Pages 836–840
Native American Struggles

Most Native Americans in the 1960s were living under conditions that were the result of centuries of discrimination and constantly changing government policies. They too took their cue from the civil rights movement to work for self-determination.

 Pages 841–843
Environmental and Consumer Movements

The mood of protest in the 1960s energized movements to preserve the environment and challenge the safety of certain consumer products.

1968 *Activists found American Indian Movement (AIM).*	**1970** *The federal government sets up the Environmental Protection Agency.*	**1972** *Ms. magazine is founded.*	**1973** *Native Americans stage a protest at Wounded Knee, South Dakota.*	**1975** *Congress passes the Indian Self-Determination and Education Assistance Acts.*
1968	**1970**	**1972**	**1974**	**1976**
1969 *Golda Meir becomes prime minister of Israel.*	**1970** *Salvador Allende is elected president of Chile.*	**1972** *Bangladesh becomes an independent nation.*	**1974** *Haile Selassie is deposed as ruler of Ethiopia.*	**1975** *Margaret Thatcher becomes head of Britain's Conservative party.*

Media and Technology

 Transparency
Time Lines, E-9

 Alternative Assessment

As an ongoing chapter project, students can select one of the major movements discussed in the chapter—the women's movement, Latino American movement, Asian American movement, Native American movement, environmental movement, or consumer movement—and present a report about its major activities in their community between 1960 and 1975. Student reports may be written or tape-recorded.

Explain that finished projects will be assessed according to the following standards:

● **Unacceptable** Projects are not attempted or fail to meet requirements outlined.

● **Limited/Acceptable** Projects present some information about the activities of one movement in the community based on limited outside research.

● **Extensive/Commendable** Projects present information about the activities of one movement in the community based on some outside research. Reports attempt to relate local activities to the national movement's goals and activities.

● **Extraordinary/Outstanding** Projects present detailed information about one movement in your community based on extensive outside research. Reports effectively relate local activities to the national movement's goals and activities.

For information and guidance on alternative assessment trends and strategies, see the Alternative Assessment Handbook in the Resource Organizer on page 822.

The Women's Movement

1. FOCUS

Connecting to the Big Idea

See page 822B. Women were among the first groups to note the successes of the civil rights movement and to apply them to the inequalities of their own lives. Ask students how the women's movement affected American society.

Objectives

● Describe ways in which American society discriminated against women economically and socially in the 1950s.
● Explain how women learned legal and political techniques to fight discrimination from the civil rights movement.
● Describe how feminist leaders organized groups to advocate women's rights.
● Describe the backlash the feminist movement provoked among those who wanted to preserve traditional roles.

Bellringer

Write the terms *feminist* and *women's libber* on the chalkboard. Ask students to list five words that help describe each. Have them rank the words in order from most positive to most negative.

Reading Strategy

Structured Overview Ask students to write the following three column headings on a piece of paper: Social Conditions for Women in the 1950s, Steps Taken by Feminists to Change Conditions, and Backlash Against the Feminist Movement. As students read the section, ask them to note relevant information in the appropriate column.

The Women's Movement

The new women's movement chose symbols for its cause that represented power.

SECTION PREVIEW

For generations, many American women had realized they were being treated as second-class citizens. Encouraged by the gains of the civil rights movement, women united behind the goal of ending discrimination based on gender.

Key Concepts
- American society in the 1950s discriminated against women economically and socially.
- From the civil rights movement, women learned legal and political techniques to fight discrimination.
  - Feminist leaders organized groups to advocate women's rights.
  - The feminist movement produced a backlash among some who wanted to preserve traditional roles.

Key Terms, People, and Places
feminism, feminist, National Organization for Women (NOW), Equal Rights Amendment (ERA); Gloria Steinem, Phyllis Schlafly

T he African American struggle for civil rights made other citizens keenly aware of inequalities in American life. Women, though not a minority in numbers, recognized certain disadvantages they had accepted for years and were determined to do something about them. From working in civil rights and other movements, many women had learned techniques that would help them gain a more equal role in American life.

The women's movement of the 1960s, although influenced by the civil rights movement, was not a new development in the nation's history. In the 1800s, particularly, women had worked for the right to vote and for equality in education and in jobs. The term **feminism** first came into recorded use in 1895 as a word to describe the theory of political, economic, and social equality of men and women. **Feminists** were those who believed in or acted on behalf of this theory.

Social Conditions Set the Stage for the Feminist Movement

The women's movement of the 1960s sought to change the style of American life that had been accepted for decades. Society expected women always to put home and family first.

During and after World War II, however, more and more women entered the labor force. As described in Chapter 27, the popular image of the 1950s put women at home, married, and raising children, but in fact more and more married women were employed. By the beginning of the 1960s, about half of all women held jobs.

Working women, however, earned less than working men doing similar or even the same jobs. In 1963, for example, women, on average, were paid only 63 cents for each dollar that men earned. By 1973 this figure had dropped to 57 cents. This financial inequality created a growing sense of frustration among women and led to demands for change.

In those same years, more and more women were going to college. In 1950 only 25 percent of all Bachelor of Arts degrees had gone to women. Twenty years later, in 1970, it was 41 percent. Better-educated women had high hopes for the future but often were discouraged by the discrimination they faced when they looked for jobs or tried to advance in their professions. Many employers, for example, acting under the belief that home and family should be a woman's only responsibility, denied women job opportunities for which they were qualified. Women who did enter the work force often found themselves underemployed, performing jobs and earning salaries far below their abilities. The graph on page 825 shows median incomes of men and women from 1950 to 1975. Now this generation of women was ready to act to change these conditions.

▶ RESOURCE DIRECTORY

Teaching Resources

📄 **Reproducible Lesson Plan** found in the Unit 9 folder, p. 70, provides a summary of the Section 1 lesson plan content.

📁 **Alternate Lesson Plan: Critical Thinking** Identifying Central Issues and Demonstrating Reasoned Judgment, found in the Alternate Lesson Plans folder, p. 151, helps students practice these skills in examining the growth of and reaction to the feminist movement.

📁 **Guided Reading and Review** found in the Unit 9 folder, p. 74, provides a structure for reading and mastering the key concepts and reviewing the key terms for Section 1. (Guided Practice)

The Impact of the Civil Rights Movement

While social conditions set the scene for the women's movement, the civil rights movement provided a model for techniques and an inspiration for action. Black and white women joined in the struggle for civil rights, but they often found that they were expected to make coffee and do clerical work while men made most of the policy decisions.

At the same time, women gained valuable skills from their work in the movement. They learned the value of direct action and the usefulness of political pressure in making society respond. They saw the importance of strong publicity in making others understand the conditions they were trying to change.

The civil rights movement also provided women with legal tools to fight discrimination. One important piece of legislation was the 1964 Civil Rights Act (see Chapter 29).

Originally, the section of the act called Title VII prohibited discrimination based on race, religion, or national origin. When Congress debated the bill, however, some opponents of civil rights added an amendment to outlaw discrimination on the basis of gender. This action was a strategy to make the entire bill look ridiculous, so that it would fail in the final vote. To the dismay of its opponents, both the amendment and the bill passed. The new Civil Rights Act now had a provision that gave women a legal framework to use to fight discrimination.

Even with the added boost of the new legislation, progress took time. Women soon discovered that the Equal Employment Opportunity Commission (EEOC) set up by the bill took women's claims less seriously than those of African Americans. Nevertheless, Title VII would be tremendously important as the women's movement gained steam.

Women's Groups Raise "Consciousness"

As the 1960s unfolded, women began to meet together to compare experiences. Civil rights workers met to look for ways in which they could play a larger role in the struggle.

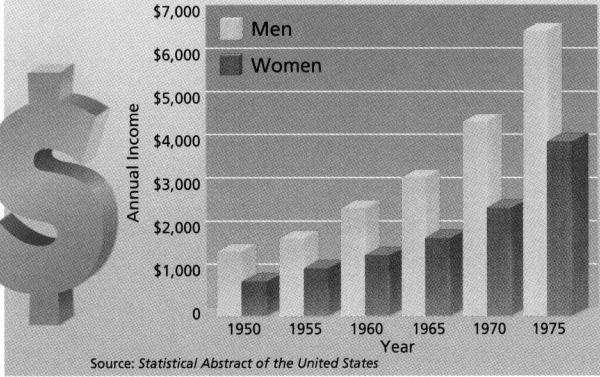

Median Incomes of Men and Women, 1950–1975

Source: *Statistical Abstract of the United States*

 Interpreting Graphs
Women's incomes continued to lag behind men's earnings, partly because many low-paying fields were traditionally considered "women's work." *Did the gap increase or decrease between 1950 and 1975?*

Soon they went beyond politics, exploring other aspects of their lives. The growing movement drew women who were active in other forms of protest and reform—student radicals, opponents of the draft, and workers for welfare rights and other social issues.

Another important influence was Betty Friedan's 1963 book *The Feminine Mystique* (see Chapter 27). Friedan described the cultural patterns that prevented women from achieving their full potential. Many readers recognized what she called "the problem that has no name"—the despair that came from trying to be the perfect wife and mother, the only roles society granted women.

Meeting in kitchens and living rooms, women in "consciousness-raising" groups began to talk about their lives in new ways. One participant, Nancy Hawley, a community activist in Boston, Massachusetts, was troubled by patterns she saw in her work for other social issues. "Though many of us were working harder than the men," she noted, "we realized we were not listened to and often ignored."

Betty Friedan voiced many women's feelings in her influential book *The Feminine Mystique.*

2. INSTRUCT

Explain/Discuss

Discuss with students the conditions in American society that feminists wanted to change. Ask students to list the ways in which employers discriminated—and in some cases continue to discriminate—against women.

Ask students to list the kinds of action taken by feminists to improve conditions for women. Which actions do students think were most successful? How strong do students consider the subsequent backlash against the women's movement to be?

In Depth

Did You Know?

In the late 1960s and early 1970s, women created a vast network of health clinics, legal centers, newspapers, counseling centers, and professional caucuses for their needs. But since "men and institutions resisted radical challenges," according to one historian, women found it difficult to break through the "glass ceiling" in business. Women with college degrees were earning half as much as men with similar education, and one third of all working women held clerical jobs. Even by the late 1970s, very few women were executives or upper-level managers.

MAKING CONNECTIONS

Students are likely to agree that people today expect women to have a job or career, whereas people in the 1950s expected that women would stay home, raise children, and keep house. You might want to contrast media images such as popular television programs from the two periods.

Analyze

Tell students that the following states did not ratify the Equal Rights Amendment: Alabama, Arkansas, Arizona, Florida, Georgia, Illinois, Louisiana, Missouri, Mississippi, Nevada, Oklahoma, North Carolina, South Carolina, Utah, Virginia. Have them locate these states on a map and then ask what generalizations students can make about them.

In Depth

Biography

In 1970 Betty Friedan (b. 1921) helped create the National Women's Political Caucus, and led a national Women's Strike for Equality. Friedan continually stirred women "to march, to picket, and to speak up for equal rights." A frequent target of her attacks was the advertising industry, which she claimed promoted an image of women as the "weaker sex." In her 1981 book *The Second Stage,* Friedan assumed a more moderate stance, and criticized earlier feminists for trying to emulate the male realm rather than "affirm the differences between men and women." (See Key Events in Reference Section.)

Women from different backgrounds shared their stories in informal meetings and found they had common experiences.

Throughout the country, more and more women recognized the negative attitudes directed toward them. In New Orleans, Louisiana, civil rights activist Cathy Cade mentioned that her boyfriend had made fun of her for going to a "women's meeting." Others in her group began to tell stories of being teased or ridiculed for coming to a women's group. Such lack of support outside the group made their bond stronger within the group. As Cade put it:

> One thing became clear: that in the black movement I had been fighting for someone else's oppression and now there was a way that I could fight for my own freedom, and I was going to be much stronger than I ever was.

In San Francisco, Mimi Feingold, also a veteran of the civil rights and draft resistance movements, felt the same sense of exhilaration at her group's first meeting:

> It was something that we had all been waiting for, for a long time. It was a really liberating experience for all of us. . . . This was finally permission to look at our own lives and talk about how unhappy we were.

MAKING CONNECTIONS

What is the popular image of women today, and how does it differ from the image of women in the 1950s?

Women Organize NOW

In 1966 a small group of women decided to form an organization to pursue their goal of achieving equality. These women were frustrated that existing women's groups were unwilling to pressure the Equal Employment Opportunity Commission to take women's grievances more seriously. Twenty-eight professional women, including Betty Friedan, established the **National Organization for Women (NOW)** "to take action to bring American women into full participation in the mainstream of American society *now.*"

NOW sought fair pay and equal job opportunities. It attacked the "false image of women" in the media, such as advertising that used sexist slogans or photographs. In one such ad in the 1960s, for example, an oven manufacturer asked, "Can a woman ever feel right cooking on a dirty range?" thus reinforcing the popular notion that a woman's sole contribution was to be a homemaker. NOW also called for more balance in marriages, with men and women sharing parenting and household responsibilities. A year after NOW was founded, it had 1,000 members.

On August 26, 1970, the anniversary of the passage of the constitutional amendment on women's suffrage, thousands of women left jobs and household chores to observe "Women's Equality Day."

 RESOURCE DIRECTORY

Teaching Resources

⭐ **Literature Activity** A Changing Sense of Self, found in the Unit 9 folder, p. 93, describes the early steps taken in the women's movement, in an excerpt from *Our Bodies, Ourselves.*

Four years later there were 15,000. Today, about 280,000 women belong to NOW.

For some women, NOW seemed too extreme; for others it was not extreme enough. Some saw NOW—and the women's movement in general—as mainly for the benefit of white, middle-class women. Nonetheless, NOW served as a rallying point in the movement to end sex discrimination and promote greater equality for all women.

The Impact of Feminism

The women's movement came of age in the early 1970s. Songs were one expression of the energy of the struggle. In 1971 pop singer Helen Reddy recorded a song that was soon broadcast on radio stations around the country. Delivered in the ringing, forceful style of an anthem, Reddy's hit song proclaimed:

> I am woman, hear me roar
> In numbers too big to ignore,
> And I know too much to go back
>   and pretend. . . .
>
> Yes, I've paid the price
> But look how much I gained.
> If I have to, I can do anything.
> I am strong, I am invincible,
> I am woman.

Reddy's lyrics reflected a new sense of women's self-confidence and a strength that drove the movement on.

⭐ Books and magazines likewise promoted the cause. *Our Bodies, Ourselves,* a handbook published by a women's health collective in Boston, encouraged women to understand their own health issues. It sold 200,000 copies in the first several years after its publication and three million by 1990. In 1972 journalist **Gloria Steinem** and several other women founded *Ms.* magazine, which was devoted to feminist issues and provided women with viewpoints that were decid-

edly different from those in *Good House-keeping, Ladies' Home Journal,* and other women's magazines of the day. The preview issue of 300,000 copies sold out in eight days, and by 1973 *Ms.* had nearly 200,000 subscribers. While not all readers considered themselves feminists, they became familiar with the arguments of the movement from the magazine.

Slowly the women's movement brought a shift in attitudes. For example, a survey of first-year college students revealed a significant change in career goals. In 1970, men interested in fields such as business, law, engineering, and medicine outnumbered women by eight to one. Five years later, the margin had dropped to three to one. More women entered law school and medical school. They were finally admitted to military academies and trained as officers. The graph on page 828 clearly illustrates this trend in women's career paths.

Feminist Issues on the National Stage

Despite many shared concerns, the women's movement continued to be divided on its goals. In 1972 *Time* magazine observed, "The aims of the movement range from the modest, sensible amelioration [betterment] of the female condition to extreme and revolutionary visions." The more radical feminists emphasized the need to end male domination, sometimes rejecting men, marriage, and child-bearing.

The cover at left from the first edition of *Ms.* magazine, begun by Gloria Steinem (above), shows the many roles women had to fill.

The graph on page 828

Activity
Teaching Heterogeneous Groups

During the civil rights movement, women learned protest tactics that they then used to fight their own battle against discrimination. To enable students to apply protest tactics, divide them into small groups to design a campaign for youth rights. Each group must create an identifying acronym, give one example of a discriminatory practice against youth, and describe a nonviolent tactic that could be used to change it.

Enrichment

Ask students to review issues of *Ms.* magazine from 1972 through the 1980s and to report on how the focus, appearance, and editorial policy of the magazine changed during this time.

In Depth

Then and Now

Some of the lasting effects of the social movements of the 1960s and 1970s were in the areas of environmental awareness and health education. When DDT manufacturers fought back against Rachel Carson, it was just one of many occasions in American history when businesses gave profits a higher priority than safety. Until well into the 1990s, tobacco companies refused to accept evidence showing that cigarette smoking can cause cancer. Sometimes companies cover up facts they have discovered; in the early 1990s, Dow Corning was cited for ignoring evidence that their silicone breast implants might be harmful to women.

Interpreting Graphs

The smallest increase was in doctoral degrees.

3. ASSESS

Section 1 Review Answers

1. (a) feminism, see p. 824, (b) feminist, see p. 824, (c) National Organization for Women (NOW), see p. 826, (d) Equal Rights Amendment (ERA), see p. 828

2. (a) Gloria Steinem, see p. 827, (b) Phyllis Schlafly, see p. 829

3. The civil rights movement made women realize that they too could fight back against long-standing discrimination; it trained them in techniques of resistance and political action. Title VII of the 1964 Civil Rights Act prohibited sex discrimination.

4. NOW fought for equal pay, equal job opportunities, the end of false media images, more equality in marriages, and a woman's right to abortion.

5. She was describing the frustration of trying to live up to traditional mother/wife roles and the limitations they placed on women.

6. Some men rejected the idea; some women defended traditional roles, while others opposed what they claimed would be the effects of the ERA.

7. Possible answers: the realization that many attitudes and practices were unfair, that women were underpaid, and that society's expectations prevented them from realizing their ambitions.

Reteach

Ask students to correct the following incorrect statements.
- In the 1960s, women workers were paid the same wages as male workers.
- The civil rights movement learned techniques and tactics from the women's movement.
- The 1964 Civil Rights Act was passed in response to demands from NOW and other women's groups.
- The ERA was ratified in 1973.
- American women welcomed the advances brought by the women's movement.

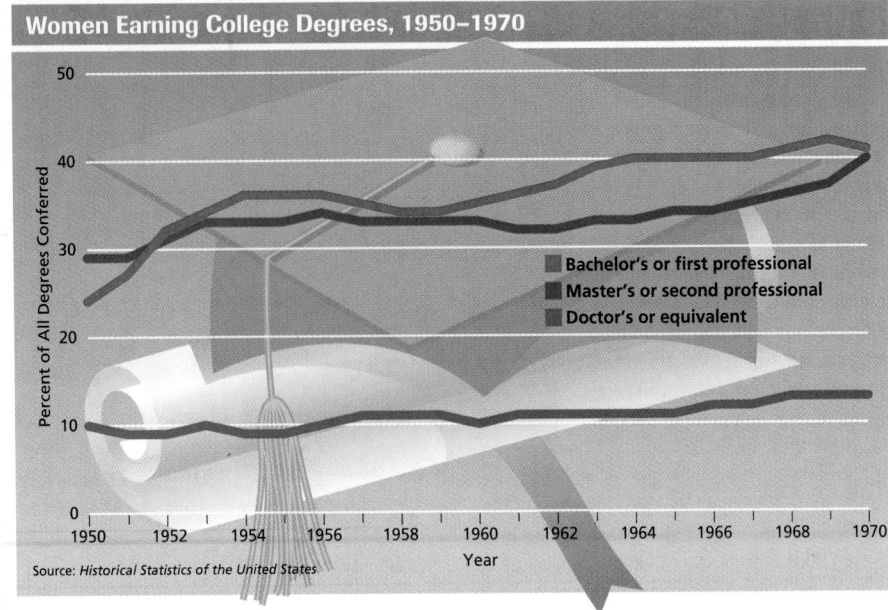

Women Earning College Degrees, 1950–1970

Percent of All Degrees Conferred vs. Year

Legend:
- Bachelor's or first professional
- Master's or second professional
- Doctor's or equivalent

Source: *Historical Statistics of the United States*

 Interpreting Graphs
As women's educational levels rose, so did their expectations of good jobs and fair salaries. *At which degree level—bachelor's, master's, or doctoral—did women gain the least?*

The Equal Rights Amendment NOW and other groups pressed for equal employment opportunities and facilities like day-care centers to make life more manageable for working parents. An even wider group took part in the campaign for constitutional change. In 1972 Congress passed the **Equal Rights Amendment (ERA)** to the Constitution:

> Equality of rights under the law shall not be denied or abridged by the United States or by any State on account of sex.

To become law, the amendment had to be ratified by thirty-eight states. Thirty states complied quickly, then a few others, and approval at first seemed certain. Strong opposition surfaced, however, and the struggle for ratification went on until 1982 and then died. ✪

Roe v. Wade NOW also worked to reform the laws governing a woman's right to choose an abortion instead of continuing an unwanted pregnancy. Many states outlawed or severely restricted access to abortion. Women who could afford to travel to another state could usually find legal medical services, but poorer women turned to abortion methods that were not only illegal but frighteningly unsafe. A landmark social change came in 1973, when the Supreme Court legalized abortion in the controversial *Roe* v. *Wade* decision. The justices based their decision on a constitutional right to personal privacy, but they still allowed states to restrict abortions.

Backlash Against the Women's Movement

Many men at first were hostile to the feminist movement, which became known as "women's liberation" or "Women's Lib." Nor were all women sympathetic. Some responded by stressing their desire to remain at home and raise children and their satisfaction with traditional roles.

Marabel Morgan, a housewife from Florida, was one of those who argued that a woman's highest purpose in life should be to stay home

▶ RESOURCE DIRECTORY

Teaching Resources

✪ **Primary Source Activity** The Equal Rights Amendment, found in the Unit 9 folder, p. 90, uses Congresswoman Shirley Chisholm's 1969 speech proposing the ERA to Congress as an example of the arguments in its favor.

and help her husband. In her book *The Total Woman*, published in 1973, she said:

> It is only when a woman surrenders her life to her husband, reveres and worships him, and is willing to serve him, that she becomes really beautiful to him. She becomes a priceless jewel, the glory of femininity, his queen!

Morgan suggested the "4A" approach: accept, admire, adapt, appreciate. She advised women readers how to make their marriages move from "fizzle to sizzle." Her tactic of defining a woman's self-worth in terms of beauty won her an approving audience. Two years after publication, her book had sold 500,000 copies.

Conservative political activist **Phyllis Schlafly** led a national campaign to block ratification of the ERA, saying:

> It won't do anything to help women, and it will take away from women the rights they already have, such as the right of a wife to be supported by her husband, the right of a woman to be exempted from military combat, and the right . . . to go to a single-sex college.

Schlafly also helped spread false ideas about the supposed effects of the ERA, such as coed bathrooms and the end of alimony. Women already had legal backing for their rights, she argued. Eventually, such arguments would prevent the ERA from being ratified within the time limit.

Viewpoints
On Working Mothers

The paragraphs below are from two of the books most widely read by women in the years from 1950 to 1975. **What argument does each author use to support his or her opinion?**

Against Working Mothers

"To work or not to work? *Some* mothers *have* to work to make a living. Usually their children turn out all right, because some reasonably good arrangement is made for their care. But others grow up neglected and maladjusted. . . . It doesn't make sense to let mothers go to work making dresses in a factory or tapping typewriters in an office, and have them pay other people to do a poorer job of bringing up their children."

Benjamin Spock, M.D., *Baby and Childcare*, 1957 edition, first published in 1945

For Working Mothers

"At the present time, one can say anything—good or bad—about children of employed mothers and support the statement by some research finding. But there is no definitive evidence that children are less happy, healthy, adjusted, because their mothers work. The studies that show working women to be happier, better, more mature mothers do not get much publicity. Since juvenile delinquency is increasing, and more women work or 'are educated for some kind of intellectual work,' there is surely a direct cause-and-effect relationship, one says. Except that evidence indicates there is not."

Betty Friedan, *The Feminine Mystique*, 1963

Answer to ...

Viewpoints

According to Benjamin Spock, some children are harmed because their mothers work; therefore, it would be better if they did not work. According to Betty Friedan, there is no proven cause-and-effect relationship between working mothers and maladjusted children. For a more thorough examination of the subject of working mothers, see the Resource Directory below.

4. CLOSE

Reinforcing the Big Idea

American women were encouraged by the successes of the civil rights movement to work for greater equality for their sex. The women's rights movement made some significant gains but produced a backlash among those who wished to preserve traditional roles. As students will read in the next section, other groups also learned from the civil rights movement.

SECTION 1 REVIEW

Key Terms, People, and Places

1. Define (a) feminism, (b) feminist, (c) National Organization for Women (NOW), (d) Equal Rights Amendment (ERA).
2. Identify (a) Gloria Steinem, (b) Phyllis Schlafly.

Key Concepts

3. How did the civil rights movement influence the women's movement?
4. What were some goals of NOW?

5. What did Betty Friedan identify as "the problem that has no name"?
6. What opposition did the women's movement encounter?

Critical Thinking

7. **Identifying Assumptions** What beliefs prompted many women to join the women's movement and groups such as NOW in the 1960s?

 Viewpoints Activity On Working Mothers, found in the Unit 9 folder, pp. 86–87, presents several facets of the debate about the effect of working mothers on children.

Quiz found in the Unit 9 folder, p. 75, covers the main ideas in this section as well as the key terms.

Media and Technology

Transparency
Fine Art, D-20

Critical Thinking

Recognizing Bias

Focus Students will practice recognizing bias in two written selections.

Instruct After students have read the selections, ask them to analyze this quote using the questions presented in the feature.

"As radical feminists we recognize that we are engaged in a power struggle with men, and that the agent of our oppression is man insofar as he identifies with and carries out the supremacy privileges of the male role. For while we realize that the liberation of women will ultimately mean the liberation of men from their destructive role as oppressor, we have no illusion that men will welcome this liberation without a struggle."

Answers

1. (a) Excerpt A: Black women distrust Women's Lib because it is white, and see white women as a racist enemy. Excerpt B: Passing the Equal Rights Amendment will solve the problem of legal discrimination against women at both the state and national levels. (b) Both excerpts A and B.

2. (a) Excerpt A: The phrase "faces of those white women hovering behind that black girl at the Little Rock school in 1957." Excerpt B: The text of the Fourteenth and Fifteenth amendments; Susan B. Anthony's arrest, trial, and conviction for voting in 1872; the number of legal discriminations against women contained in state statutes in 1969; and the text of the Equal Rights Amendment. (b) Yes. In excerpt A, the writer presents as facts what are actually her own opinions of black women's attitudes toward Women's Lib, white feminist organizations, and white women.

3. Excerpt A: All black women have the same distrustful view of Women's Lib, white feminist organizations, and white women; all white women share the racism apparent in the expressions of a few white women in Little Rock in 1957. Excerpt B: Women are not now protected by the Constitution.

4. Excerpt B is the less biased, although it favors both legal equality for women and passage of the ERA.

Recognizing Bias

Recognizing bias means being aware of information and ideas that are one-sided or that present only a partial view of a subject. Knowing how to recognize bias is important because this skill helps you to better understand not only historical events, but also current issues. Campaign speeches, debates on controversial topics, and opinions expressed in the media all contain elements of bias. The ability to spot bias will help you analyze information about the present and the past.

Bias often is attached to issues that have an impact on people's emotions. One such issue is the women's movement, which questions the role of women in American life. Both of the excerpts on this page were taken from articles written during the reappearance of the women's movement in the 1960s and early 1970s. Use the following questions to help you determine whether either of these writings is biased.

1. Decide whether the excerpt presents only one side of an issue, while suggesting it covers all sides. Writing from a single viewpoint signals imbalance—and bias. (a) What is the overall message of each excerpt? (b) Which presents only one side of the issue while suggesting that it is a complete picture?

2. Determine whether the issue as described is supported by opinions or verifiable facts. Sometimes what appear to be facts are actually opinions disguised as facts. (a) Which details presented in the excerpts can be checked for accuracy? (b) Are any opinions presented as though they were facts? Give an example from the excerpts.

3. Examine the excerpts for hidden assumptions or generalizations that are not supported by facts. What hidden assumptions or generalizations does excerpt A contain? Excerpt B?

4. Analyze the excerpts for bias. Which excerpt is the least biased? Explain your answer.

A "What do black women feel about Women's Lib? Distrust. It is white, therefore suspect. They don't want to be used again to help somebody gain power—a power that is carefully kept out of their hands. They look at white women and see them as the enemy—for they know that racism is not confined to white men. . . . The faces of those white women hovering behind that black girl at the Little Rock school in 1957 do not soon leave the retina of the mind."
—Toni Morrison, "What the Black Woman Thinks About Women's Lib," *The New York Times Magazine,* August 22, 1971

B "The 14th and 15th amendments, written in 1868 and 1870, said: "ALL PERSONS BORN OR NATURALIZED IN THE U.S. ARE CITIZENS AND HAVE THE RIGHT TO VOTE."
Susan B. Anthony, considering herself to be a person, registered and voted in 1872. She was arrested, brought to trial, convicted of the crime of voting—because she was a woman, and the word PERSONS mentioned in our Constitution *DID NOT MEAN WOMEN*. . . . If she were alive today, Susan B. Anthony might vote, but she would still see 1000 legal discriminations against women upon various state statute books. . . .
The solution of the problem of giving women 100 per cent protection of the Constitution . . . is the adoption of the Equal Rights for Women Amendment which reads: "EQUALITY OF RIGHTS UNDER LAW SHALL NOT BE DENIED OR ABRIDGED BY THE UNITED STATES OR BY ANY STATE ON ACCOUNT OF SEX."
—Marjorie Longwell, "The American Woman—Then and Now," *Delta Kappa Gamma Magazine,* Fall 1969

 RESOURCE DIRECTORY

Teaching Resources

Historian's Toolbox Activity Recognizing Bias, found in the Unit 9 folder, p. 88, uses both statements and questions about the women's movement to help students identify bias.

Ethnic Minorities Seek Equality

SECTION PREVIEW

Inspired by the civil rights movement, Latinos and Asian Americans launched their own movements to overcome racial discrimination. Each group faced different obstacles in its struggles for equal treatment.

Key Concepts

• Latinos used tactics from the civil rights movement to overcome discrimination.
• Education and cultural pride were the major goals of the Latino movement.
• The United Farm Workers, led by César Chávez, sought better conditions for Mexican American farm workers.
• Asian Americans faced racial discrimination, particularly during World War II and the cold war.
• Asian Americans made economic and political gains in the 1960s and 1970s.

Key Terms, People, and Places

Latino, Anglo, *barrio,* migratory farm workers, United Farm Workers, Japanese American Citizens League; César Chávez

T he United States is home to many ethnic and racial groups. Throughout the country's history, each group has faced different kinds of prejudice and discrimination. Latinos and Asian Americans have lived in the United States for many years. Yet both have had to fight for equality in mainstream American society.

The Latino Population

Spanish-speaking Americans, or **Latinos,** come from many places, although they share the same language and some elements of culture. But whether they come from Puerto Rico, Cuba, Mexico, or other parts of the Americas, Latinos often have been seen as outsiders and denied equal opportunities in many aspects of life, including employment, education, and housing.

In the 1960s and early 1970s, more and more people arrived from Central America and South America. Between 1970 and 1980, census figures for people "of Spanish origin" rose from 9 million to 14.6 million. Different groups tended to settle in certain areas. Americans of Cuban descent concentrated in Florida, Puerto Rican in the Northeast, and Mexican in the West and Southwest. As their population grew, Latinos throughout the country found and expressed a new pride in their heritage. ✪

Mexican American Protests

Mexican Americans, often known as Chicanos, always have been the most numerous Latinos in the United States. In the 1960s, they began to organize against discrimination in education, jobs, and the legal system, leading to *el Movimiento Chicano*—the Chicano movement.

Cultural Identity Activists began encouraging pride in Mexican American culture and its dual heritage from Spain and the ancient cultures of Mexico. In 1967 Rodolfo "Corky" Gonzales, a Denver activist, wrote a long poem that raised Mexican Americans' self-awareness nationwide. *Yo Soy Joaquin* ("I am Joaquin") expresses the importance of cultural identity in Mexican history and the modern world. It begins:

> I am Joaquin
> lost in a world of confusion
> caught up in the whirl of a gringo [white]
>   society,
> confused by the rules,
> scorned by attitudes,
> suppressed by manipulation
> and destroyed by modern society.

Nationwide boycotts made the United Farm Workers' symbol, the eagle, well known.

1. FOCUS

Connecting to the Big Idea

See page 822B. Inspired by the civil rights movement, other ethnic minorities such as Latino Americans and Asian Americans began to struggle for greater equality. Ask how their struggles were different.

Objectives

● Describe how Latino Americans used tactics from the civil rights movement to overcome discrimination.
● Identify César Chávez and describe his efforts to obtain better conditions for Mexican American farm workers.
● Describe the types of discrimination faced by Asian Americans during World War II and the cold war.
● Identify the political and economic gains made by Asian Americans in the 1960s and 1970s.

Bellringer

Ask students to consider the dilemma faced by all ethnic Americans from the early days of mass immigration: whether to assimilate or to try to retain their native culture and language. Ask students to note what is gained and what is lost by assimilation.

Reading Strategy

Structured Overview Ask students to make a chart on a piece of paper comprising two vertical columns, headed Latino Americans and Asian Americans, and two horizontal rows, headed Reasons for Protest and Results of Protest. Ask students to fill in the chart as they read the section.

Reproducible Lesson Plan found in the Unit 9 folder, p. 71, provides a summary of the Section 2 lesson plan content.

Alternate Lesson Plan: Learning Styles found in the Alternate Lesson Plans folder, p. 152, helps students identify and compare discrimination faced by Latinos and Asian Americans, and is especially helpful for visual learners.

Guided Reading and Review found in the Unit 9 folder, p. 76, provides a structure for reading and mastering the key concepts and reviewing the key terms for Section 2. (Guided Practice)

✪ **Literature Activity** Perspectives by Women of Color, found in the Unit 9 folder, p. 95, personalizes the hopes of women of color with a poem by Puerto Rican–born poet Judith Ortiz Cofer.

Explain/Discuss

Discuss how cultural differences among different groups of Latinos have led to many Latino movements rather than a single unified effort for equality in American society. Read this comment by Daniel Villanueva, a TV executive: "We need a Spanish Bobby Kennedy or Martin Luther King. Right now he's just not there." Discuss what a "Spanish Martin Luther King" might have been able to do that César Chávez did not do.

Ask how differences in language and culture affect any unified Asian American movement. Discuss why the admission of Hawaii to the Union was a step forward for Asian Americans throughout the United States.

Analyze

Ask students to analyze the success of the grape boycott and compare it with the Montgomery bus boycott. What made them different? Have students compare the work and tactics of César Chávez with those of Martin Luther King, Jr.

In Depth

Historical Misconceptions

The 1989 movie *Stand and Deliver* chronicled a true story belying the common assumption that young Americans from low-income areas plagued by drugs and gang violence have nowhere to go but down. A high school math teacher, Jaime Escalante, inspired his class of unprepared, predominantly Latino students from Garfield High School in East Los Angeles to become a team of motivated mathematicians. In 1982, eighteen of Escalante's students passed the Advanced Placement calculus exam, and Garfield High attained high national ranking in math. One student said of Escalante, "He made us feel powerful, that we could do anything."

Gonzales emphasized that **Anglos**—English-speaking, non-Latinos—had undermined Mexican Americans' control over their lives. Gonzales said that Anglos had done this through economic pressure and through institutions such as the schools, the Roman Catholic church, and the media.

Education Many Chicanos wanted changes in education. Schools in the *barrios,* or Latino neighborhoods, were crowded and run-down, with high dropout rates. In March 1968, ten thousand Mexican American students walked out of five such Los Angeles high schools to protest their unequal treatment. Students in Colorado, Texas, and other parts of California followed their example. Students demanded better courses and facilities and Latino teachers and counselors.

As leader of the United Farm Workers, César Chávez once said the "truest act of courage . . . is to sacrifice ourselves for others in a totally nonviolent struggle for justice."

AMERICAN PROFILES
César Chávez

César Chávez (1927–1993), founder of the United Farm Workers, became a hero to millions of Americans, both Latino and Anglo. He was born in Yuma, Arizona, where his family had farmed for three generations. During the Great Depression, they lost their adobe farmhouse because they could not afford the taxes. Moving to California, they became **migratory farm workers,** who make a living moving from farm to farm to provide the labor needed to plant, cultivate, and harvest crops.

Chávez later remembered how his family fostered a powerful sense of independence:

> I don't want to suggest we were that radical, but I know we were probably one of the strikingest families in California, the first ones to leave the fields if anyone shouted "Huelga!" — which is Spanish for "Strike!"

As he grew up among farm workers, Chávez gradually came to believe that unions were a way to resist employers' economic power. Migratory farm workers were some of the most exploited workers in the country, spending long hours doing backbreaking work for little pay. In the 1960s Chávez began to organize Mexican field hands into what became the **United Farm Workers** (UFW). He and a group of loyal followers went from door to door and field to field. By 1965 the union had 1,700 members. ✪

The UFW's first target was the grape growers of California. Chávez, like Martin Luther King, Jr., believed in nonviolent action. In 1967, when growers refused to grant more pay, better working conditions, and union recognition, Chávez organized a successful nationwide consumer boycott of grapes picked on nonunion farms. Later boycotts of lettuce and other crops also won consumer support.

Chávez's efforts created many angry enemies and even brought him death threats. He responded by saying:

> It's not me who counts, it's the Movement. And I think that in terms of stopping the Movement—this one or other movements by poor people around the country—the possibility is very remote. . . . The tide for change now has gone too far.

In 1975 California passed a measure that required collective bargaining between growers and union representatives. Workers now had a legal basis to ask for better working conditions. Chávez's efforts not only made him a national hero but also brought migratory farm workers into the broader movement for civil rights.

Other Latino Protests

Mexican Americans had other heroes too. Some formed organizations that took a militant approach, while others used political action.

Brown Berets In East Los Angeles, David Sanchez and other young Mexican Americans formed a community action group that took

---

▶ RESOURCE DIRECTORY

Teaching Resources

✪ **American Profiles Activity** found in the Unit 9 folder, p. 84, profiles Delores Huerta, who cofounded the United Farm Workers and worked for social justice.

A mural in Los Angeles illustrates Mexican American pride.

on a semi-military style. Known as the Brown Berets, they later started branches in other cities. The group regarded itself as "defensive," protecting Mexican Americans against police and other authorities and sometimes acting outside the law. Sanchez said:

> We're not a violent or a nonviolent organization . . . we are an emergency organization. . . . If we see a cop beating up a Chicano, we move in and stop the cop, we try to be ready for every emergency.

Political Action Some Latinos worked within mainstream politics. In 1961 voters in San Antonio, Texas, elected Henry B. González to Congress. Another Texan, Elizo "Kika" de la Garza, went to the House of Representatives in 1964, while Joseph Montoya of New Mexico was elected to the Senate.

New political groups formed to support Latino interests. For example, José Angel Gutiérrez brought together Mexican American groups in Crystal City, Texas, leading to the formation of the political party *La Raza Unida* in 1970. The new party worked for better housing and jobs and backed Mexican American political candidates.

Another leader, Reies López Tijerina, argued that the Anglo culture had stolen the Chicanos' land and heritage. To call attention to broken treaties, in 1966 his *Alianza Federal de Mercedes* (Federal Alliance of Land Grants) marched on the New Mexico state capital. At about the same time, the Mexican American Legal Defense and Educational Fund (MALDEF), was founded. It has provided legal aid to help Mexican Americans gain civil rights and encouraged Mexican American students to become lawyers.

MAKING CONNECTIONS

Different regions of the United States are home to larger numbers of certain ethnic groups. What ethnic groups are prominent in your area and what discrimination do they face, if any?

Media and Technology

 Transparency
Our Multicultural Heritage, C-15

Activity
Making a Map

Divide students into groups and assign each group a region of the United States. Distribute outline maps of the United States, or ask students to sketch or trace such maps. Students can use almanacs or Census Bureau documents to find statistics about the number of Latino Americans in each state. Have students find or calculate the percentage of Latino Americans in their state and display that information on their maps.

Then ask students to compare this information with the percentage of African Americans in their state's population.

Answer to ...
MAKING CONNECTIONS

Answers will vary depending on the ethnic composition of the area, but should indicate an awareness of their own and other groups' status and position in the community. In many places, large numbers of students may themselves be members of minority groups.

In Depth
Biography

Writer Amy Tan was born in Oakland, California, in 1952. Her childhood typifies the difficulties inherent in cultural assimilation in the United States during the 1950s and 1960s. Her mother always spoke to her in Mandarin, but Amy would always answer in English. As Tan explains, "With assimilation you have a dominant culture and the underlying message is you have to reject your other culture." Drawing from her experiences, Tan has written successful novels, including *The Joy Luck Club* and *The Kitchen God's Wife*, about Asian American life in the United States.

Ask students to research the Congressional Hispanic Caucus. Who are its members? What are its goals? How successful has the caucus been in reaching its goals?

 3. ASSESS

Section 2 Review Answers

1. (a) Latino, see p. 831, (b) Anglo, see p. 832, (c) *barrio*, see p. 832, (d) migratory farm workers, see p. 832, (e) United Farm Workers, see p. 832, (f) Japanese American Citizens League, see p. 834

2. César Chávez, see p. 832

3. It emphasized Mexican American self-identity in history and the modern world.

4. He formed the United Farm Workers in order to win better conditions for migratory workers. By winning in California, he drew national attention to the cause.

5. Chicano high school students walked out of schools; organizations like the Brown Berets engaged in defensive patrol actions; others joined mainstream politics or used the court system.

6. World War II and the communist takeover in China increased prejudices.

7. It gave them political influence in Congress.

8. Answers should point out that Asian Americans are physically distinguishable from those of European ancestry and that they are often perceived as having closer ties to the countries from which their ancestors came.

Reteach

Ask students to list the goals, tactics, and gains of Latinos and Asian Americans, based on information from the section.

Caption Answer to ...

 Interpreting Maps

Japan and China sent the most immigrants in the 1950s, Korea and the Philippines in the 1970s.

Asian Americans Fight Discrimination

Ever since their arrival in the United States, Americans of Chinese and Japanese ancestry have faced racial discrimination. Prejudice against Japanese Americans reached a peak during World War II, and the communist takeover of China in 1949 influenced attitudes toward Chinese Americans. In general, the years after the war brought many hopeful and positive changes for Asian Americans.

Japanese Americans After the War A major issue for Japanese Americans was compensation for the losses they had suffered during their wartime internment in the 1940s. As discussed in Chapter 26, Japanese American citizens living along the West Coast were forced to relocate to internment camps after the government decided they were a risk to American security once the nation declared war on Japan. Not only had their lives been disrupted, but they had lost hundreds of millions of dollars in homes, farms, and businesses. The main voice for Japanese Americans, the **Japanese American Citizens League** (JACL), in 1948 won passage of the Japanese American Claims Act, under which Congress eventually paid relatively small amounts for property losses. JACL also worked for changes in anti-Asian immigration laws.

About two thirds of Japanese Americans who had been relocated returned to the Pacific Coast, but others moved to cities east of the Rockies. Their new communities were more a part of mainstream society than the prewar *nihonmachis*—"Japantown"—had been.

Economic Changes Although Asian Americans as a group were well educated, in 1960 they earned less than white Americans. In California, for example, for each $51 a white male was paid, a Chinese man would earn $38 and a Japanese man, $43. College graduates faced prejudice in attempting to move into management jobs.

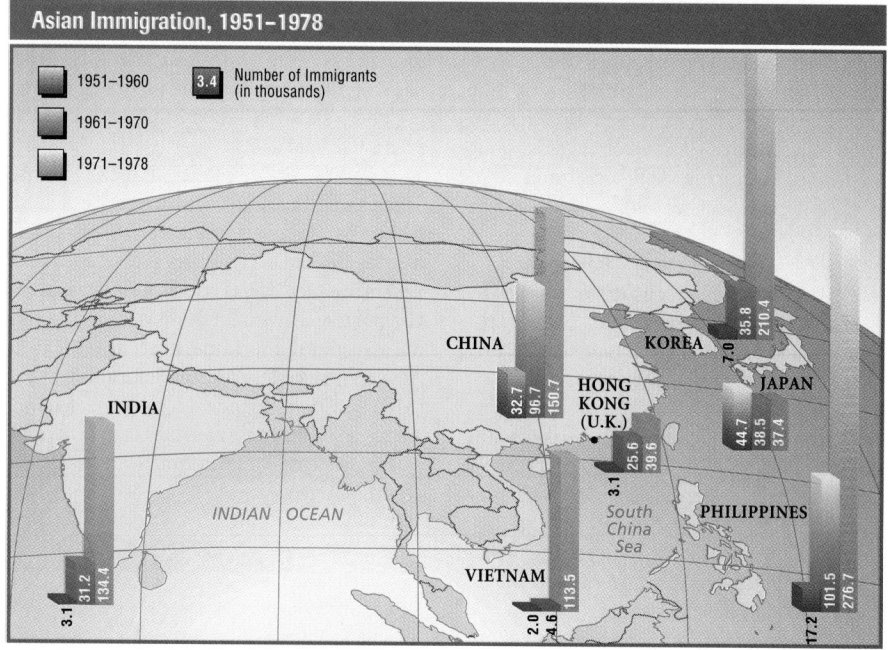

Asian Immigration, 1951–1978

- 1951–1960
- 1961–1970
- 1971–1978

3.4 Number of Immigrants (in thousands)

CHINA 32.7 / 96.7 / 150.7

KOREA 7.0 / 35.8 / 210.4

HONG KONG (U.K.) 3.1 / 25.6 / 39.6

JAPAN 44.7 / 38.5 / 37.4

INDIA 3.1 / 31.2 / 134.4

VIETNAM 2.0 / 4.6 / 113.5

PHILIPPINES 17.2 / 101.5 / 276.7

INDIAN OCEAN

South China Sea

Geography and History: Interpreting Maps
Patterns of immigration from Asia changed dramatically in the 1950s, 1960s, and 1970s. *Which two countries sent the greatest number of people in the 1950s? In the 1970s?*

▶ RESOURCE DIRECTORY

Teaching Resources

Statehood for Hawaii created, for the first time, a state in which most voters were of Asian or part-Asian ancestry. Members of Congress from the new state, such as Daniel Inouye (above), reflected the islands' cultural diversity.

As a group, Asian Americans in the 1960s and 1970s were making economic gains faster than other minorities. Nonetheless, they still faced discrimination and relied on the example of the civil rights movement to push for gains. Some Chinese American community activists in the 1970s asked for federal help in overcoming problems of unemployment, health, and language barriers. Another development in the 1970s was an increase in immigration from other Asian countries, especially Korea, India, and Vietnam, as illustrated by the map on page 834.

Political Representation A major step forward for Asian Americans' self-image was the granting of statehood to Hawaii in 1959. The new state sent Hiram Leong Fong, a Chinese American, to the Senate, and Daniel K. Inouye, a Japanese American, to the House of Representatives. Other Asian American lawmakers have since been elected from Hawaii and California.

SECTION 2 REVIEW

Key Terms, People, and Places
1. Define (a) Latino, (b) Anglo, (c) *barrio*, (d) migratory farm workers, (e) United Farm Workers, (f) Japanese American Citizens League.
2. Identify César Chávez.

Key Concepts
3. What was the importance of the poem *Yo Soy Joaquin*?
4. What role did César Chávez play in the Chicano struggle for equal rights?

5. What were other forms of Chicano protest?
6. What world events influenced prejudice against Asian Americans?
7. Why was Hawaiian statehood significant for Asian Americans?

Critical Thinking
8. **Recognizing Bias** What factors might have made prejudice against Asian Americans last longer than discrimination against people of European ancestry?

 Quiz found in the Unit 9 folder, p. 77, covers the main ideas in this section as well as the key terms.

 Alternative Assessment

Mid-Point Monitoring
Ask students if they have
● Selected a movement for their report
● Begun to research the activities of your community
● Begun to do outside research about the national movements

 4. CLOSE

 Reinforcing the Big Idea

Latino Americans and Asian Americans, diverse groups with different problems, used the techniques of the civil rights movement to overcome racial discrimination. The next section describes the struggle of Native Americans for self-determination.

In Depth

Interdisciplinary

The 1983 Nobel prize in physics was won by an Indian American, Subrahmayan Chandrasekhar. As a student at Cambridge University in England, he questioned the existing theory that stars become "white dwarfs," very old stars that no longer make much light, because they lack hydrogen gas. Chandrasekhar, who moved to the United States in 1937, agreed that the theory applied to small stars, but not to big ones. Gravity, he argued, would make big stars shrink until they were much smaller than white dwarfs, until they turned into what would later be called "black holes."

Native American Struggles

1. FOCUS

Connecting to the Big Idea

See page 822B. As a result of discrimination and shifting governmental policies, most Native Americans lived in poverty in the 1960s. Ask how Native Americans tried to change government policy and win more self-determination.

Objectives

- Explain why Native Americans faced unique problems of poverty and discrimination.
- Describe how many Native American activists worked to maintain their traditional culture and identity as a people.
- Identify the focus of the American Indian Movement as urban problems and protests.
- Cite gains in self-determination achieved by Native Americans through protests and legal challenges.

Bellringer

Ask students to write a definition for *self-determination*. Ask them to what extent they think that they themselves are now self-determining. In what areas do they not make decisions for themselves? When do students think they might become completely self-determining?

Reading Strategy

Predicting Content Before students begin reading the section, write the main headings from the section on the chalkboard: Native Americans Face Unique Problems, Roots of Native American Activism, Confronting the Government. Ask students to formulate at least two questions for each heading and to look for answers to their questions as they read.

SECTION PREVIEW

Most Native Americans in the 1960s were living under conditions that were the result of centuries of discrimination and constantly changing government policies. They too took their cue from the civil rights movement to work for self-determination.

A Sioux woman joins a protest against federal policies for Native Americans.

Key Concepts

- Native Americans faced unique problems in terms of poverty and discrimination.
- Many Native American activists worked to maintain their traditional culture and identity as a people.
- The American Indian Movement focused on urban problems and spearheaded protests.
- Protests and legal challenges won Native Americans more self-determination.

Key Terms, People, and Places
American Indian Movement (AIM); Dennis Banks, Russell Means; Alcatraz

---

Native Americans were another minority who were inspired by the civil rights movement to seek equality and control over their own lives. Overall, Native Americans were perhaps the country's most troubled nonwhite group, in part because of government policies. Activists used legal challenges and direct action to reach their goals.

Native Americans Face Unique Problems

As the original inhabitants of North America, Native Americans have occupied a unique social and legal position. Although their cultures and languages are varied, white society has seen "Indians" as one group. The Constitution excluded them from citizenship, and Congress assumed the right to supervise them.

From the 1800s on, government agencies limited self-government for Native Americans and often worked to erase their traditional lifestyles. Until 1924, many Native Americans did not have full citizenship rights. Today they are citizens of both the United States and their own nations or tribal groups.

As a whole, Native Americans have routinely been denied equal opportunities. They have had higher rates of unemployment, alcoholism, and suicide, as well as a shorter life expectancy, than white Americans. Poverty and poor living conditions were once common in their communities. Like other nonwhite groups, Native Americans were the victims of centuries-old stereotypes, reinforced by the way movies and other media depicted them. ✪

Native Americans also had some grievances that were unique. **Dennis Banks,** a Chippewa, explained why he became an activist:

> *I t was a question of this government being responsible to me, and not seeing to it that I had an opportunity to lead a decent life, or to own a piece of land, or to find a good job, like they had promised my ancestors in all these treaties. They broke all of those promises. They stole everything from them and wrecked their way of life—which was a good way.*

Roots of Native American Activism

An important part of the Native Americans' way of life was their tie to the land and what it stood for. "Everything is tied to our homeland," declared D'Arcy McNickle, a Native American anthropologist, in 1961. Yet, many years after pioneers first moved onto Indian territory, state and federal governments continued to take over traditional tribal lands. Protecting what was left became a major goal of Native Americans.

▶ RESOURCE DIRECTORY

Teaching Resources

Reproducible Lesson Plan found in the Unit 9 folder, p. 72, provides a summary of the Section 3 lesson plan content.

Alternate Lesson Plan: Cooperative Learning found in the Alternate Lesson Plans folder, p. 153, helps groups of students focus on the goals of Native American activists by writing headlines and brief articles.

Guided Reading and Review found in the Unit 9 folder, p. 78, provides a structure for reading and mastering the key concepts and reviewing the key terms for Section 3. (Guided Practice)

✪ **Visual Learning Activity** Changing Attitudes Toward Native Americans, found in the Unit 9 folder, p. 96, portrays attempts made in the 1960s and 1970s to challenge stereotypes about Native Americans.

Native American Pride and Sports Team Names

The Native American movement of the 1960s and early 1970s influenced changes in more areas than one might expect. One example of the effects of the reawakening of Native American pride can be found in the sports world, where Native American names and images often have been used as team names and mascots. Arguing that using Native American names in such a way is degrading and racially offensive and that other races are not used for the same purpose, Native Americans began to request that some teams change their names. In response,

in 1969 Dartmouth College, in New Hampshire, changed its team name from the Indians to the Big Green to avoid racial insensitivity. In 1972, Stanford University, in California, whose team name was also the Indians, likewise changed its name. Stanford chose the Cardinal to replace its previous name. Syracuse University followed suit not much later, abandoning its original mascot, the Saltine Warrior, for an orange with arms and legs.

The attitudes that prompted these changes have affected professional sports teams as well. In 1991

the Atlanta Braves sparked considerable debate over both their name and their rallying cry, the "Tomahawk Chop." The same year, controversy over the Washington Redskins reached fever pitch with the introduction of a bill before Congress. Senator Ben Nighthorse Campbell of Colorado proposed that no federal land be allotted for the Redskins' new stadium until the team changed its name. Thus far, the name change has not taken place. *What other popular names or symbols might some groups find offensive?*

Land Claims A government project in New York state triggered one early protest. According to a 1794 treaty, the Seneca Nation held the land on its Allegany reservation. The federal government, however, had long planned to build a dam there as part of a flood control project. The Kinzua Dam would affect 10,000 acres of hunting and fishing land, as well as homes and sacred sites.

In 1956 Congress held hearings, which did not include the Seneca, and appropriated funds for the dam. After legal appeals failed, the Seneca in 1961 went to President John Kennedy, but he supported the government claim. Once the dam was built, Congress agreed to pay $15 million in damages, but this did not restore the land.

Other Native Americans responded to this decision by bringing lawsuits for violations of treaty rights and failure to make promised payments. Court rulings supported many claims. For example, in 1967 the Court of Claims ruled that the federal government had forced the Seminole to give up Florida lands in 1823 for an unreasonably low price. The court directed the government to pay more to the Seminole community.

The American Indian Movement One of the leading activist movements began in Minneapolis in 1968, led by Dennis Banks and George Mitchell, both Chippewa. At a meeting of 250 people representing twenty Native American organizations, Banks set forth the goals: "Let's get a new organized effort going, a new coalition that will fight for Indian treaty rights and better conditions and opportunities for our people."

The new organization came to be called the **American Indian Movement (AIM).** It originally focused on the special problems of Native Americans living in cities. Following the example of militant black groups, AIM set up Indian patrols to monitor street activity. It also began survival schools to encourage racial and cultural pride in young people.

Many people, both white and Native American, criticized AIM's militant approach. On the group's second anniversary, however, Banks repeated its goals:

We must commit ourselves to changing the social pattern in which we have been forced to live. . . . The government and churches have demoralized, dehumanized, massacred, robbed, raped,

2. INSTRUCT

Explain/Discuss

Discuss with students how the federal government came to make special treaties with Native Americans. Recall that for years, Native Americans were considered members of tribal nations with whom the United States negotiated as with a foreign country.

Ask students to discuss the problems of contemporary Americans who think they own land that by treaty belongs to a group of Native Americans. If the government returns the land to the Native Americans, how should the "owners" be compensated?

Discuss what Native Americans accomplished at Alcatraz and Wounded Knee. Then ask what they accomplished through legal battles. Which route do students think was more effective?

In Depth

Biography

During the turbulent decade of the sixties, Northern Cheyenne Ben Nighthorse Campbell (b. 1933) channeled an angry adolescence into the study of martial arts. It eventually earned him the captaincy of the 1964 United States Olympic Judo Team at the Tokyo games. In 1982, Campbell became the first Native American to serve in Congress since the 1930s. In 1992, he was elected to represent Colorado in the United States Senate.

promised, made treaty after treaty, and lied to us. . . . We must now destroy this political machine that man has built to prevent us from self-determination.

MAKING CONNECTIONS

One goal of Native American activists has been to force the federal government to honor treaties made in the 1800s. Why were so many treaties made—and then broken?

Echoes of past history surrounded the Sioux village of Wounded Knee, where AIM members, led by Russell Means (left) and others, protested past and present federal government actions against Native Americans.

Confronting the Government

Trying to call attention to issues long ignored, Native Americans staged several standoffs with the federal government. In 1972, demonstrators formed the Broken Treaties Caravan, traveled to Washington, D.C., and occupied the federal government's Bureau of Indian Affairs' offices for six days. Other protests were even more dramatic.

The Occupation of Alcatraz In November 1969, seventy-eight protesters from several Native American groups landed on

Alcatraz, an island in San Francisco Bay on which stood an abandoned federal prison. They claimed the 13-acre rock under the terms of the Fort Laramie Treaty of 1868, which allowed male Native Americans to file homestead claims on federal lands. The occupation also was a protest against the policies and methods of the Bureau of Indian Affairs.

✪ Others joined the original group, planning to turn the deserted island into an educational and cultural center. In March 1970, author Vine Deloria, Jr., a Standing Rock Sioux, wrote hopefully about the project in the *New York Times:*

B y making Alcatraz an experimental Indian center operated and planned by Indian people, we would be given a chance to see what we could do toward developing answers to modern social problems. Ancient tribalism can be incorporated with modern technology in an urban setting. Perhaps we would not succeed in the effort. . . . It just seems to a lot of Indians that this continent was a lot better off when we were running it.

The occupation failed to achieve the desired results. Federal marshals eventually removed

Activity

Teaching Heterogeneous Groups

Cultural pride and education were very important tools for gaining self-determination. For students to understand the importance of cultural heritage and the ways in which it is taught, have them list as many aspects as possible of their cultural heritage and recall briefly how they learned about them. **LEP**

Enrichment

A number of Native American groups have opened gambling casinos on their reservations. Ask students to prepare a report explaining the casino openings, their financial success, and why some Native American leaders oppose them.

3. ASSESS

Section 3 Review Answers

1. American Indian Movement, see p. 837

2. (a) Dennis Banks, see p. 836, (b) Russell Means, see p. 839, (c) Alcatraz, see p. 838

3. They faced poverty, high unemployment, alcoholism, suicide, and low life expectancy.

4. Native Americans followed African American groups' example of direct action and militant tactics; they worked to instill racial and cultural pride.

5. It focused on Native Americans in cities.

---

the last protesters after a year and a half. But the episode dramatized Native American grievances and gained important national exposure.

Confrontation at Wounded Knee An even more dramatic confrontation came in 1973 at the Oglala Sioux village of Wounded Knee, South Dakota. There, in 1890, the army's Seventh Cavalry had massacred more than two hundred Sioux men, women, and children.

The Pine Ridge reservation around the village was one of the country's poorest, with half its families living on welfare. In February 1973, AIM leaders **Russell Means** and Dennis Banks and some two hundred AIM members took over the village. AIM sought to draw attention to conditions on the reservation and to the 371 treaties it said the government had broken over the years.

Other Native American leaders came out in support of the occupation. Onondaga Chief Oren Lyons, speaking for the Iroquois, said:

W e support the Oglala Sioux Nation or any Indian Nation that will fight for its sovereignty. . . . The issue

here at Wounded Knee is the recognition of the treaties between the United States Government and the sovereign nations that were here before.

Federal marshals and FBI agents then surrounded the village, allowing only occasional shipments of supplies. From time to time, gunfire broke out. As the siege went on, agents arrested some three hundred people, including news reporters and outside supporters.

By the time the standoff finally ended in May, two AIM members had been killed and about a dozen people hurt, including two federal marshals. The government agreed to re-examine treaty rights. ✪

The Government Responds Native American activism brought some responses from the government. The Kennedy and Johnson administrations in the 1960s tried to bring jobs and income to some reservations by encouraging industries to locate there and leasing reservation lands to energy and development corporations. But many Native Americans worried about the effects

AIM leader Dennis Banks leads a protest march at Mount Rushmore, South Dakota.

Media and Technology

 Transparency
Critical Thinking, I-9

6. They wanted to assert their claims to lands that were important to them, to gain redress for treaties the government had broken in past years, and have more control over their own communities.

7. Possible answer: Native Americans struggled to claim certain sovereign rights granted to them through treaty with the United States government; African Americans for the most part fought to gain rights granted to U.S. citizens by the Constitution.

Reteach

Ask students to work in pairs or groups of three to develop a set of five questions about the section content. Each group should have a question beginning with *who, what, why, when,* and *how.* Have groups exchange question sheets and decide on consensus answers.

4. CLOSE

Reinforcing the Big Idea

Native Americans in the 1960s continued to suffer poverty and discrimination, largely the result of long standing government policies. Native Americans worked for self-determination through protests and court cases. The next section describes the efforts of the environmental and consumer movements.

Many Native American groups went to court to win back land and other rights. Wearing traditional ceremonial dress, George Crows Fly High and Martha Grass, along with civil rights leader Ralph Abernathy, seek a meeting with Supreme Court justices.

these projects would have on the land. In the 1970s, the Navaho, Crow, Northern Cheyenne, and others sought to renegotiate or cancel many of the leases.

Pressure by Native Americans also led to their inclusion in "Great Society" programs dealing with housing, health, and education. Government agencies made resources available and let Native Americans plan and run their own programs and, in some places, their own schools. ★

A number of laws passed in the 1970s favored Native American rights. The Indian Education Act of 1972 gave parents and tribal councils more control over schools and school programs. The Indian Self-Determination and Education Assistance Acts of 1975 upheld Native American autonomy and let local leaders administer federally supported social programs for housing and education.

Native Americans also continued to win legal battles to regain land, mineral, and water rights. For example, in 1971 the Alaska Federation of Natives was given $1 billion and 40 million acres of land. In 1970, after rejecting a cash settlement, the Taos in New Mexico won back Blue Lake, a religious shrine, as well as 48,000 acres of land. A Taos representative said:

> We don't have gold temples in this lake, but we have a sign of a living God to whom we pray—the living trees, the evergreen and spruce . . . and the lake itself. . . . We are taking that water to give us strength so we can gain in knowledge and wisdom.

SECTION 3 REVIEW

Key Terms, People, and Places
1. Define American Indian Movement.
2. Identify (a) Dennis Banks, (b) Russell Means, (c) Alcatraz.

Key Concepts
3. What problems were typical of Native American communities in the 1960s?
4. How did the African American civil rights movement influence the tactics of Native American groups?

5. What group was the original focus of the American Indian Movement?
6. What did Native Americans hope to accomplish by lawsuits?

Critical Thinking
7. **Making Comparisons** How was the social and political situation of Native Americans different from that of African Americans?

▶ RESOURCE DIRECTORY

Teaching Resources

 Literature Activity Native American Voices, found in the Unit 9 folder, p. 94, presents a poem that expresses the hope of Native Americans in the 1970s.

Quiz found in the Unit 9 folder, p. 79, covers the main ideas in this section as well as the key terms.

Environmental and Consumer Movements

SECTION PREVIEW

The mood of protest in the 1960s energized movements to preserve the environment and to challenge the safety of certain consumer products.

Key Concepts
- The activism of minorities in the 1960s spurred environmentalists and consumers to take action.
- The modern environmental movement was triggered by Rachel Carson's *Silent Spring*.
- Ralph Nader was a major figure in beginning the movement for consumers' rights.

Key Terms, People, and Places
Environmental Protection Agency (EPA); Rachel Carson, Ralph Nader

I n the 1960s and early 1970s, the mood of protest surrounding the civil rights movement inspired a number of other movements. Environmentalists demanded actions that would preserve and restore the earth's environment and resources. Similarly, consumers and vigilant consumer advocates used proven protest techniques to ensure that American industries would be accountable to their customers and workers. Their efforts brought changes in public attitudes and public policy—changes that affect the lives of Americans to this day.

The Environmental Movement

Like the women's movement, the environmental movement did not spring up in the 1960s but had roots in the American past. In the late 1890s and early 1900s, progressives had worked to make public lands and parks available for the people. New Deal programs of the 1930s included tree-planting projects in an effort to put people back to work—as well as to conserve forests and farmlands.

Rachel Carson The modern environmental movement stemmed even more directly, however, from the work of marine biologist **Rachel Carson.** She had once hoped to become a writer but initially followed her interest in zoology. In the 1930s and 1940s, however, she combined her talents and began to write about scientific subjects for general audiences. In 1951 Carson published *The Sea Around Us*, which was an immediate best seller. Her major—and most influential—book was *Silent Spring*, published in 1962.

In *Silent Spring*, Carson attacked the use of chemical pesticides, particularly DDT, which had increased agricultural productivity but killed various plants and animals other than the insect pests that were its target:

> T *he most alarming of all man's assaults upon the environment is the contamination of air, earth, rivers, and sea with dangerous and even lethal materials. This pollution is for the most part irrecoverable. . . . In this now universal contamination of the environment, chemicals are the sinister and little-recognized partners of radiation in changing the very nature of the world.*

As Carson explained, chemicals sprayed on crops entered into living organisms and moved from one to another in a chain of poisoning and death. Specifically, the lingering effects of DDT threatened to destroy many species of birds and fish, including the national symbol, the bald eagle.

Environmental activists battled for a variety of issues in the 1960s.

Connecting to the Big Idea

See page 822B. Inspired by other protest movements, environmentalists and consumer advocates demanded action to preserve the environment and protect the buyers and users of products in America. Ask students what triggered the environmental and consumer movements. How successful were they?

Objectives

- Explain how the activism of minorities in the 1960s spurred environmentalists and consumers to take action.
- Identify Rachel Carson's *Silent Spring* as the trigger for the modern environmental movement.
- Identify Ralph Nader as the major figure in the early movement for consumer rights.

Bellringer

Ask students to recall how many purchases they made on each day of the past week and how long they spent shopping. Have them use the information to estimate how much money and how much time a year they spend as consumers. Discuss the importance of consumers in our economy.

Reading Strategy

Reading for Evidence Note the statement on page 841 that the efforts of environmentalists and consumerists " . . . brought changes in public attitudes and public policy—changes that affect the lives of Americans to this day." Ask students to look for evidence to support this statement as they read.

Reproducible Lesson Plan found in the Unit 9 folder, p. 73, provides a summary of the Section 4 lesson plan content.

Alternate Lesson Plan: Learning Styles found in the Alternate Lesson Plans folder, p. 154, is useful for many types of learners and helps students identify and describe issues and concerns raised by environmental and consumer groups.

Guided Reading and Review found in the Unit 9 folder, p. 80, provides a structure for reading and mastering the key concepts and reviewing the key terms for Section 4. (Guided Practice)

Explain/Discuss

Explain that many environmental problems grew out of the rapid development of technology, industry, and transportation after World War II.

Have students list some voluntary measures that people undertake to preserve the environment. Next ask how big a role they think the federal government should play in regulating our care of the environment. Should government determine how communities dispose of trash and regulate speed limits, or how manufacturers package items?

Analyze

Ask students why *Silent Spring* and *Unsafe at Any Speed* had such immediate impact and produced such far-reaching effects. Ask what conditions came together for Carson's and Nader's books to attract the immediate attention of the nation.

Answer to ...

MAKING CONNECTIONS

Answers will vary depending on local events and activism, as well as on students' own families' interest in the environment and conservation.

Activity

Cooperative Learning

Time: One class period.
Activity: Create an Earth Day celebration.
Grouping: Four to six students.
Purpose: The first Earth Day was celebrated in 1970. Have groups decide on a focus, theme, or goal for an Earth Day celebration and plan a day's schedule, including entertainment, speakers, and other events coordinated with the focus.
Roles: Community committee members, each responsible for one aspect of the celebration.
Outcome: Students will identify ways in which the community can celebrate the preservation of the environment.

Disturbed by the changes she saw in her environment, biologist Rachel Carson sounded a trumpet call to action in her book *Silent Spring,* inspiring others to join a strong environmental movement.

Silent Spring was a bombshell. The chemical industry fought back vigorously, arguing that Carson confused the issues and left readers "unable to sort fact from fancy." The public was not persuaded by this attack. So great was national concern that a special presidential advisory committee was appointed. It called for continued research and warned against the widespread use of pesticides. Eventually DDT was banned in the United States, and other chemicals were controlled more strictly. For more information about the impact of *Silent Spring,* see the feature "Time and Place: A Geographic Perspective" on page 844.

It was not only DDT that worried people. They became more conscious of poisonous fumes in the air, oil spills on beaches, and toxic wastes buried in the ground. In the mid-1960s, President Lyndon Johnson's administration addressed environmental concerns as part of the "Great Society." Johnson hoped for "an environment that is pleasing to the senses and healthy to live in." Environmental legislation was part of his broader reform program.

Nuclear Power Another issue arose toward the end of the 1960s, as environmentalists focused on the problems of nuclear power plants built to generate electricity. While nuclear plants caused less air pollution than coal-burning plants, they produced steam that was then discharged into local waterways. The steam raised water temperatures, killing fish and plant life. People also worried about the possibility of nuclear plant accidents.

Public Response Grassroots environmental movements sprang up in many places, supporting conservation efforts and opposing actions such as the building of new nuclear plants. In 1970 Americans celebrated the first Earth Day, which would become a yearly observance aimed at heightening awareness of environmental issues and marked by day-long activities to clean up pollution and litter. Besides Rachel Carson, other scientists were alarmed by environmental problems. For example, in his 1971 book *The Closing Circle,* biologist Barry Commoner warned about rapid increases in pollution.

The efforts of the environmentalists helped spur the federal government to create new policies. Responding to public concerns about air and water pollution, in 1970 Congress passed the Water Quality Improvement Act and the Clean Air Act. Also in 1970, President Richard Nixon's administration established the **Environmental Protection Agency (EPA).** The EPA combined existing federal agencies concerned with air and water pollution. As the nation's watchdog against polluters, the EPA today monitors and reduces air and water pollution and regulates the disposal of solid waste and the use of pesticides and toxic substances.

MAKING CONNECTIONS

Do you think that concern for the environment has increased or decreased since the 1970s? What evidence have you seen?

The Consumer Movement

The consumer movement was yet another outgrowth of the 1960s protests. It too had roots

---

RESOURCE DIRECTORY

Teaching Resources

Primary Source Activity The Desecration of America, found in the Unit 9 folder, pp. 91–92, features excerpts from a 1961 *Atlantic Monthly* article by Vance Packard in which he examines the state of the countryside with dismay.

Visual Learning Activity Preserving the Environment, found in the Unit 9 folder, p. 97, helps students understand and visually express specific environmental issues.

in earlier years. The Pure Food and Drug Act of 1906, for example, was one early effort to maintain standards and protect the public. In the 1960s and early 1970s, however, the movement grew far stronger and involved more people.

Attorney **Ralph Nader** spearheaded the new consumer effort. Nader had been a serious activist all his life. While a student at Princeton University in the early 1950s, Nader protested the spraying of campus trees with DDT. His interest in automobile safety began at Harvard Law School and continued into his law practice in Hartford, Connecticut. In 1964 Daniel Patrick Moynihan, then assistant secretary of labor, hired Nader as a consultant on the issue of automobile safety regulations.

The government report Nader wrote soon became a book, *Unsafe at Any Speed: The Designed-in Dangers of the American Automobile*. It began:

> For over half a century the automobile has brought death, injury, and the most inestimable sorrow and deprivation to millions of people. With Medea-like intensity, this mass trauma began rising sharply four years ago reflecting new and unexpected ravages by the motor vehicle. A 1959 Department of Commerce report projected that 51,000 persons would be killed by automobiles in 1975. That figure will probably be reached in 1965, a decade ahead of schedule.

Like the muckrakers of the Progressive era, Nader used facts to support his passionate argument that car manufacturers would be responsible for many of these deaths. He called many cars "coffins on wheels," pointing to dangers such as a tendency to flip over. The industry, he charged,

knowingly continued to build over one million cars before confronting the safety problems.

Nader's book was a sensation, and in 1966 he testified before Congress about automobile hazards. That year, Congress passed the National Traffic and Motor Vehicle Safety Act. The *Washington Post* noted that, "Most of the credit for making possible this important legislation belongs to one man—Ralph Nader. . . . A one-man lobby for the public prevailed over the nation's most powerful industry."

Nader broadened his efforts and investigated the meatpacking business, helping to secure support for the Wholesome Meat Act of 1967. He next looked into consumer problems in other industries. Scores of volunteers, called "Nader's Raiders," signed on to help. They turned out report after report and inspired consumer activism. As ordinary Americans began to stand up for their rights, consumer protection offices had to respond to a flood of complaints.

Concern for the earth and its health prompted Earth Day rallies and clean-ups, including such events as a roadway "lie-down" by 5,000 people to protest car fumes in Italy and a Cheyenne ceremony at dawn outside Bozeman, Montana.

SECTION 4 REVIEW

Key Terms, People, and Places
1. Define Environmental Protection Agency.
2. Identify (a) Rachel Carson, (b) Ralph Nader.

Key Concepts
3. What was the target of Rachel Carson's book *Silent Spring*?

4. What role did Ralph Nader play in the consumer movement?

Critical Thinking
5. **Recognizing Cause and Effect** What were some of the results of Rachel Carson's book *Silent Spring*?

Quiz found in the Unit 9 folder, p. 81, covers the main ideas in this section as well as the key terms.

Chapter Test Forms A and B are found in the Unit 9 folder, pp. 98–103.

Answer Keys found in the Unit 9 folder, pp. 146–159, provide answers to all student activities.

Media and Technology

Transparency Graphic Organizer, G-3

Guided Reading Audiotape (English and Spanish)

Computer Test Bank

TIME & PLACE
A GEOGRAPHIC PERSPECTIVE

After *Silent Spring*

Focus Tell students that when *Silent Spring* appeared in 1962, *ecology* was not a familiar word in the vocabularies of most Americans. There was virtually no way for Americans to recycle glass, paper, metal, or plastic. The Environmental Protection Agency did not exist. Few Americans considered the environment when they went shopping; fewer still would refuse to purchase an item because of its excessive packaging. Most Americans did not know about the ozone layer, much less worry about it when buying hair spray or air conditioners; and store clerks would have cast strange looks at a shopper who wanted to reuse grocery bags. When did Americans start learning about the environment? When did "environmentally conscious" become a compliment? When did *green* start to mean a lifestyle as well as a color? A trend such as the environmental movement seldom begins at one specific time, but the publication of *Silent Spring* marks the moment when the American public began to learn about the choices required to safeguard the earth.

Instruct Divide the class into small groups. Ask students to discuss the information on DDT presented in the feature and to brainstorm as many groups as possible who were hurt in any way by restrictions on the use of DDT. *(Farmers who lost crops, manufacturers, suppliers, stockholders, employees, etc.)* Then make a list of these groups with the whole class and ask students to decide if the benefit to the world as a whole from the banning of DDT outweighed the cost to the groups on the list. Ask who makes such cost-benefit decisions. *(Individuals; federal, state, and local governments; the courts.)*

After *Silent Spring*

Although many of her concerns were shared by other scientists, Rachel Carson's book Silent Spring *was a landmark in the environmental movement. Why did Carson's book have such an impact?*

The publication of Rachel Carson's book *Silent Spring* in 1962 is usually described as a landmark event in the history of the environmental movement. Carson, concerned about the disappearance of songbirds from America's towns and cities, blamed the immensely successful and widely used pesticide DDT. Scientists already were beginning to weigh the environmental costs of DDT against its proven benefits in controlling insects. Their voices, however, tended to be overridden by the chemical companies and the agricultural lobby, both of which favored continued DDT use.

What Carson did was to plant in the mind of the general public an important concept: that humans are a part of a living ecological system, not outside of it or dominant over it. Geographers and other scientists had long been interested in the concept that people, plants, and animals are all part of the same ecosystem. After *Silent Spring*, however, a growing awareness of the theme of interaction between humans and the environment led to a national movement that continues to this day.

> *What Carson did was to plant in the mind of the general public an important concept: that humans are a part of a living ecological system, not outside of it or dominant over it.*

some time, at first in Europe, and much later in the United States. This was the concern that "progress" in science and technology was a two-edged sword. Such progress, people worried, might bring about negative as well as positive outcomes, and unintended as well as intended consequences. One such worry focused on the massive increase in the number of automobiles. While cars made it possible for many Americans to live outside of the cities where they worked, their use also brought increased air pollution. By the end of the 1960s, cars and trucks were identified as being the sources of more than half the air pollution in the United States.

It was into this troubled decade that Rachel Carson brought the environmental movement in 1962. During the 1960s, the environmental movement grew to a mass movement, partly because of court cases against the use of DDT brought late in the decade by the Environmental Defense Fund, one of many activist groups. At the close of the decade, the movement won official government recognition with the founding of the Environmental Protection Agency in 1970.

Human and Environmental Interaction: Background to a Movement

By pointing out that DDT not only poisoned insects, but also killed birds that ate the poisoned insects, Carson questioned humankind's relationship with the natural world. Her views were part of a much larger concern that had been building for

DDT: A Case Study of a Shift in Ideology

Until the 1960s, most Americans generally accepted the idea that humans should use the natural world for their own ends. Science and technology were the tools that let them do so. A case in point was the use of DDT by large-scale commercial farmers. Many important and profitable American

RESOURCE DIRECTORY

Teaching Resources

Time and Place Activity
The Costs of Environmental Protection, found in the Unit 9 folder, pp. 82–83, discusses more recent concerns about the environment and encourages understanding of the link between economics and conservation.

A Shift in Public Opinion: The Environment

"Which of these problems would you like to see government devote most of its attention to in the next two years? — Gallup Poll question

	Percent of Public Mentioning Item		
Issue	1965	1970	Five-Year Change
Reducing amount of crime	41	56	15%
Reducing pollution of air and water	17	53	36%
Improving public education	45	31	-14%
Helping people in poor areas	32	30	-2%
Conquering "killer" diseases	37	29	-14%
Improving housing, clearing slums	21	27	6%
Reducing racial discrimination	29	25	-4%
Reducing unemployment	35	25	-10%
Improving highway safety	18	13	-5%
Beautifying America	3	5	2%

Source: *The Politics of Environmental Concern*, by Walter A. Rosenbaum

farm crops came originally from Europe and Asia, bringing their own insect pests with them. By the early 1900s, farmers were ready to use any easy-to-use, inexpensive method to kill insects that gobbled up corn, wheat, and other crops.

Farmers turned enthusiastically to chemical insecticides, but many of these poisons contained metals such as lead or arsenic that were deadly to humans. Against this background, DDT—which was apparently not toxic to humans even in massive doses—seemed like a wonderful solution.

By the 1960s, however, new research findings caused some people to question the assumption that humans should freely exploit nature. Rachel Carson brought some of that new research to light. She based her book on observations of the negative effect of DDT caused by massive spraying in American urban areas in an attempt to protect Dutch Elm trees from insect pests. As it turned out, DDT was a poison that remained in the ecosystem long after it had destroyed insect pests. It built up in the fatty tissues of birds and fish that ate the poisoned insects, and its long-term effects could be fatal. In birds, for example, DDT weakened shell formation so that young birds did not hatch. Predator birds

high in the food chain, such as hawks and eagles, reached the crisis stage first because they ate smaller birds, fish, and rodents.

Silent Spring sparked a debate that in 1972 resulted in the banning of almost all uses of DDT in the United States. Even more significantly, by questioning the popular ideology that nature exists for the benefit of humanity, Carson and other scientists and historians helped introduce a new ideology. Within a decade, environmentalism grew from something that interested only a small number of geographers and scientists to a nationwide movement embraced by a majority of citizens.

GEOGRAPHIC CONNECTIONS

1. Why were American crops such as wheat and corn susceptible to insect pests?
2. How did farmers' use of DDT affect other parts of the environment?

Critical Thinking

3. **Recognizing Ideologies** How did people's beliefs about their relationship with the natural environment change during the 1960s?

Answers

1. The crops came from Europe and Asia and brought insect pests from those countries with them. The pests' natural predators, however, usually did not come along.

2. DDT was consumed by birds and fish that ate the poisoned insects from the crops. The chemical buildup in their fatty tissues could be fatal.

3. At first, people believed that the environment existed for humans to use as they wished, with no regard to the effects such use might have on the environment. Later, people began to realize that perhaps the environment must be treated with more care in order to preserve it for all of its inhabitants.

Chapter Review

Understanding Key Terms, People, and Places

Understanding Key Terms, People, and Places (left column answers)

Terms
Students should refer to the definitions of the key terms in the chapter to write sentences that show the relation of each word to consumer activism and the social revolution of the 1960s and early 1970s.

Matching
1. feminism
2. *barrio*
3. Environmental Protection Agency
4. Anglos
5. migratory farm workers

True or False
1. false, Rachel Carson
2. false, Ralph Nader
3. false, Betty Friedan
4. true

Reviewing Main Ideas

1. The only long-term role considered acceptable for women was that of wife and mother. Women who did work outside the home earned less than men, even when they held similar or identical jobs. They also often faced discrimination by employers who denied them job opportunities for which they were qualified.

2. Women learned the value of direct action, political pressure, and the importance of publicity in making others understand their positions.

3. Women organized local feminist groups as well as the national organization for women's rights, NOW. They also promoted the cause through publications like *The Feminine Mystique, Our Bodies, Ourselves,* and *Ms.* magazine. They supported the Equal Rights Amendment and worked to reform the laws that governed abortion.

4. Beliefs that women would lose existing rights, such as the right to be supported by a husband, and fears about coed bathrooms and the end of alimony eventually prevented ratification.

5. The goals of the Chicano movement were to instill cultural pride, improve education for Chicanos, and fight discrimination.

6. The profile of César Chávez reveals that Latino Americans used nonviolent tactics, such as boycotts, borrowed from the civil rights movement.

7. Japanese Americans were eventually paid some compensation for property losses incurred because of forced relocation during World War II. In addition,

---

Understanding Key Terms, People, and Places

Key Terms
1. feminism
2. feminist
3. National Organization for Women (NOW)
4. Equal Rights Amendment (ERA)
5. Latino
6. Anglo
7. *barrio*
8. migratory farm workers
9. United Farm Workers (UFW)
10. Japanese American Citizens League
11. American Indian Movement (AIM)
12. Environmental Protection Agency (EPA)

People
13. Gloria Steinem
14. Phyllis Schlafly
15. César Chávez
16. Dennis Banks
17. Russell Means
18. Rachel Carson
19. Ralph Nader

Places
20. Alcatraz

Terms For each term above, write a sentence that explains its relation to citizen activism and the social revolution of the l960s and early 1970s.

Matching Review the key terms in the list above. If you are not sure of a term's meaning, review its definition in the chapter. Then choose a term from the list that best matches each description below.
1. the theory of the political, economic, and social equality of men and women
2. a Latino neighborhood
3. the nation's watchdog against polluters
4. English-speaking, non-Latino Americans
5. people who make a living moving from place to place to plant, cultivate, and harvest crops

True or False Determine whether each statement is true or false. If it is true, write "true." If it is false, change the underlined name to make the statement true.
1. Gloria Steinem began the environmental movement by writing *Silent Spring*.
2. César Chávez spearheaded the consumer effort by attacking automobile safety.
3. In *The Feminine Mystique*, Dennis Banks described the cultural patterns that prevented women from reaching their full potential.
4. The American Indian Movement leader Russell Means helped take over the village of Wounded Knee as a protest against the American government.

Reviewing Main Ideas

Section 1 (pp. 824–829)
1. Describe how society in the 1950s discriminated against women.
2. What political skills did women learn from their work in the civil rights movement?
3. Name at least three of the ways in which women tried to fight discrimination during the l960s and early 1970s.
4. Describe the beliefs and fears that eventually prevented ratification of the ERA.

Section 2 (pp. 831–835)
5. Describe the goals of the Chicano movement.
6. What does the profile of César Chávez reveal about the tactics used by Latinos to overcome discrimination?
7. What positive changes did the years after World War II bring for Asian Americans?

Section 3 (pp. 836–840)
8. How did the United States government contribute to the discrimination faced by Native Americans?
9. What was the major issue over which Native American activists confronted the federal government?
10. Describe some of the tactics used by the American Indian Movement.
11. How successful was Native American activism in achieving its goals?

Section 4 (pp. 841–843)
12. What were the goals of the consumer movement?
13. Describe how Rachel Carson's *Silent Spring* initiated the environmental movement.
14. What were two of the targets of Ralph Nader's consumer movement?

Asian Americans as a group made faster gains than other minorities. Politically, Asian American pride was boosted by Hawaiian statehood.

8. Native Americans were excluded from citizenship by the Constitution and did not have full citizenship rights until 1924. Government agencies limited self-government and often worked to erase Native American traditions.

9. Activists wanted to protect what was left of traditional tribal lands, such as the Senecan lands on which the Kinzua Dam was built, and protested the government's many broken treaties.

10. AIM set up patrols to monitor street activity and began survival schools to encourage racial and cultural pride.

11. Activism was somewhat successful. In the l960s the federal government tried to bring jobs to reservations. Native Americans were also included in President Johnson's Great Society programs; and a number of laws passed in the 1970s favored Native American rights.

12. The consumer movement wanted to hold American industries accountable to their customers and workers and to ensure the safety of consumer products.

13. *Silent Spring* initiated the environmental movement by calling attention to the dangers of pesticides in the environment.

14. Nader targeted automobile safety and the meat-packing industry.

Thinking Critically

1. **Drawing Conclusions** During the l960 and l970s, César Chávez's United Farm Workers organized boycotts of grapes, lettuce, and other crops. Explain the purpose of these boycotts. What issues might lead you to join in a boycott?

2. **Demonstrating Reasoned Judgment** Think of a local concern that affects your community, such as a new housing development that threatens to destroy your favorite patch of trees or the need for increased recycling in your neighborhood. Following the examples of any of the activists you have read about in the chapter—such as Gloria Steinem, César Chávez, Rachel Carson, or Ralph Nader—what could you do to champion your cause?

Making Connections

1. **Evaluating Primary Sources** Review the second primary source excerpt on page 829. What assumptions is Phyllis Schlafly making when she explains her arguments against the ERA?

2. **Understanding the Visuals** Look at the graph of median incomes for men and women on page 825. What does this graph tell you about the legitimacy of the drive for passage of the Equal Rights Amendment?

3. **Writing About the Chapter** Choose one of the following characters: a woman, a Chicano, a Native American, or an Asian American during the 1960s. As your chosen character, you are to testify to a congressional subcommittee regarding the discrimination faced by you and your group. First, create a list of examples illustrating the discrimination you face. Note any historical explanations for this discrimination and any suggestions you have for improving the

situation. Next, write a draft of your testimony in which you explain your experiences and those of your group. Revise your testimony, making sure that each example, explanation, and suggestion is clearly explained. Proofread your testimony and draft a final copy.

4. **Using the Graphic Organizer** This graphic organizer uses a tree map to organize information about the women's movement. (a) According to the graphic organizer, how did the women's movement benefit from legal action? (b) What was the connection between consciousness-raising and women's groups? (c) On a separate sheet of paper, create your own graphic organizer about Native American struggles against discrimination, using this graphic organizer as an example.

The Women's Movement, 1960–1975

Forms of Discrimination	Goals	Strategies	Results
• Society defines women's roles as wives and mothers • Women earn less than men for the same or a similar job • Women denied jobs for which they are qualified; are often underemployed	• To raise women's "consciousness" • To achieve equality	• Direct action • Political pressure • Strong publicity • Legal action	• Title VII of the Civil Rights Act prohibits gender discrimination • Women's groups; NOW • Feminist issues become part of the national agenda • Antifeminist backlash

Thinking Critically

1. Boycotts were organized to show support for the United Farm Workers union. Students might join in boycotts related to a variety of social, political, and environmental concerns.

2. Possible answers: speak and write to inform people about the issue, organize boycotts, propose legal challenges, and carry out more militant actions such as sit-ins.

Making Connections

1. She is assuming that other women will see the conditions she mentions—wives supported by husbands, women exempted from combat, and female students attending all-female colleges—as rights.

2. The graph shows that women consistently make less money than men, justifying the need for the Equal Rights Amendment.

3. Students' responses should demonstrate an understanding of the origins and nature of discrimination against their chosen group, and suggest ways to end such discrimination.

Chapter 31 The Vietnam War and American Society 1960–1975

Teaching Resources (See Unit 9 Folder)

	Instruction	Enrichment
Section 1 **The War in the 1960s** (pp. 850–853)	Reproducible Lesson Plan, p. 105 Alternate Lesson Plan, p. 156 Guided Reading and Review, p. 110 Quiz, p. 111	American Profiles Activity, Colin Powell, p. 120

Section 2
The Brutality of the War
(pp. 854–857)
	Reproducible Lesson Plan, p. 106
	Alternate Lesson Plan, p. 157
	Guided Reading and Review, p. 112
	Quiz, p. 113
		Literature Activity, Experiences of a Young
		  Soldier in Vietnam, pp. 129–130
		Primary Source Activity, An Army Nurse
		  Remembers, p. 126

Section 3
Student Protest
(pp. 858–861)
	Reproducible Lesson Plan, p. 107
	Alternate Lesson Plan, p. 158
	Guided Reading and Review, p. 114
	Quiz, p. 115
		American Profiles Activity, Joan Baez, p. 121
		Visual Learning Activity, Antiwar
		  Demonstrations, p. 132
		Historian's Toolbox Activity, Checking
		  Consistency, p. 124

Section 4 **The Counterculture** (pp. 863–866)	Reproducible Lesson Plan, p. 108 Alternate Lesson Plan, p. 159 Guided Reading and Review, p. 116 Quiz, p. 117	Visual Learning Activity, Reflections of the Counterculture, p. 133 Literature Activity, The Flower Children, p. 131

Section 5
The End of the War
(pp. 867–871)
	Reproducible Lesson Plan, p. 109
	Alternate Lesson Plan, p. 160
	Guided Reading and Review, p. 118
	Quiz, p. 119
	Chapter Test, Forms A & B, pp. 134–139
		Primary Source Activity, LBJ Withdraws from
		  the Race, pp. 127–128
		Viewpoints Activity, On the Tragedy of Kent
		  State, pp. 122–123
		Critical Thinking Activity, Drawing
		  Conclusions, p. 125

Additional Chapter Resources

Resource Organizer, p. 104
Alternate Lesson Plan, p. 155
Answer Keys, pp. 146–159

Bibliography

For the Teacher

Fitzgerald, Frances. *Fire in the Lake: The Vietnamese and the Americans in Vietnam.* Random House, 1989 edition. (Considered the classic history of the war.)

Severo, Richard, and Lewis Milford. *The Wages of War: When America's Soldiers Came Home—From Valley Forge to Vietnam.* Simon & Schuster, 1989. (A social history of America's returning soldiers.)

Sheehan, Neil. *A Bright Shining Lie: John Paul Vann and America in Vietnam.* Random House, 1989. (The war seen through the story of one American officer.)

Prentice Hall Literature Excerpts from *The American Experience,* 1994, including Jarrell, Randall. "The Death of the Ball Turret Gunner," and "Losses," from *The Complete Poems.* Farrar, Straus and Giroux, 1969 edition.

The Big Idea for the chapter and how the main ideas in each section relate to the Big Idea are graphically displayed below. Comprehension of this chapter's Big Idea is critical to students' understanding of United States history and how we as a nation got where we are today.

Media and Technology

 Critical Thinking, I-13

 Critical Thinking, I-12; Graphic Organizer, G-4

 Guided Reading Audiotapes (English and Spanish)

 Computer Test Bank

For the Student

Kovic, Ron. *Born on the Fourth of July.* McGraw-Hill, 1976. (A personal account by a disillusioned Vietnam veteran; later made into an Academy Award–winning film.)

O'Brien, Tim. *The Things They Carried.* Viking Penguin, 1991. (A blending of fact and fiction on coming to terms with Vietnam.)

Rottmann, Larry, Jan Barry, and Basil T. Paquet, eds. *Winning Hearts and Minds: War Poems by Vietnam Veterans.* 1st Casualty Press, 1972.

Vietnam: A Television History. PBS Video. (Award-winning thirteen-hour history of the war.)

CHAPTER 31

The 1960s and 1970s were decades of deep division and turmoil in the United States. Under Presidents Kennedy and Johnson, the country became increasingly involved in stopping a communist takeover in Vietnam. As the war continued to cost more and more in lives and money while achieving little apparent success, many Americans began to question their government's role there. At the same time, a youthful counterculture arose, criticizing the traditional values of many Americans.

SECTION 1

When communists threatened to take over South Vietnam in the 1960s, Presidents Kennedy and Johnson sent thousands of American troops to fight them, supporting repressive but anti-communist governments in Indochina.

SECTION 2

Americans at home learned from televised broadcasts, and American soldiers learned while trying to fight a hidden enemy, that the war was a brutal guerrilla struggle lacking clear objectives.

SECTION 3

Students, already primed by activists on behalf of civil rights and the free speech movement, were among the first to protest against the Vietnam War.

SECTION 4

In the 1960s, many young Americans rejected the traditional norms of American life in favor of the counterculture, experimenting with alternative lifestyles.

SECTION 5

The antiwar movement finally grew strong enough to persuade the government to find a way out of Vietnam, and in 1973, a cease-fire was proclaimed.

The Vietnam War and American Society
1960–1975

The Relevance of the Big Idea

For most Americans, the name *Vietnam* connotes tragedy, failure, doubt, and confusion. By the 1970s, the Vietnam War had become the longest, most expensive war in American history—and the least successful. The war split the nation into "hawks" and "doves," and returning GIs bore much of the bitterness of the nation's failure.

To help students understand the relevance of this conflict, point out that failure in Vietnam dimmed the nation's view of its own power. However, it also led to demands for more openness and accountability in government, and Congress limited the powers of the President to commit United States troops abroad.

In Depth

Global Connections

President Eisenhower claimed Vietnam was like the first in a row of "standing dominoes." If communists toppled it over, the other dominoes, the neighboring countries, would also fall to communism. The Central Intelligence Agency supplied anticommunist guerrillas with arms in Laos as early as 1962 to ensure that Laos would not fall into communist hands. By 1975, however, Laos had been taken over by communists. In 1970, American and South Vietnamese forces crossed the Cambodian border to destroy North Vietnamese supply bases there. Soon after, Cambodia too was plunged into civil war, and in 1975 its government fell to the communist Khmer Rouge.

The Vietnam War and American Society
1960–1975

*T*he Vietnam War was one of the most tragic events of the cold war. United States Presidents from Eisenhower to Nixon spent billions of dollars and sent half a million soldiers to Vietnam. Over time, as the war consumed more and more resources, many Americans questioned whether the United States should remain involved in this faraway conflict. The Vietnam War was only one of many issues that divided American society in the 1960s, but it cut deep and left lasting scars.

Events in the United States

1960 Student activists establish Students for a Democratic Society (SDS).

1963 President Kennedy is assassinated.
• The Bob Dylan song "The Times They Are A-Changin' " is a hit.

1964 Lyndon Johnson wins reelection to the presidency.

1965 President Johnson rapidly increases the number of American troops in Vietnam.

1967 Antiwar protesters march on the Pentagon.

| 1960 | 1962 | 1964 | 1966 |

Events in the World

1963 South Vietnamese leader Diem is assassinated.
• Kenya wins independence.

1964 Civil war escalates in Vietnam.
• United Nations troops restore order in the Congo.

1965 European Common Market nations eliminate industrial tariffs.

1967 Israel defeats the Arabs in the Six-Day War.
• Civil war begins in Nigeria.

▶ RESOURCE DIRECTORY

Teaching Resources

Alternate Lesson Plan: Demonstrating the Big Idea found in the Alternate Lesson Plans folder, p. 155, provides a lesson strategy to instruct students about the Big Idea that the Vietnam War not only consumed many lives and billions of dollars but also deeply wounded the American psyche.

Alternative Assessment Handbook provides information, guidance, and strategies for alternative methods of assessment. It includes an essay on new trends in assessment, guidance and strategies for developing performance tasks and portfolios, scoring rubrics, and sample evaluation forms.

Pages 850–853
The War in the 1960s
Determined to defeat Ho Chi Minh's communist forces, Presidents Kennedy and Johnson supported dictatorships and sent thousands of American soldiers to fight and die in Vietnam.

Pages 854–857
The Brutality of the War
Vietnam was the first war that Americans witnessed on their television screens. They were not prepared for the awful violence they saw, but neither were those who experienced the war firsthand.

Pages 858–861
Student Protest
"The times they are a-changin'," folksinger Bob Dylan sang in the 1960s. Student activists demanded many changes during this period, but the Vietnam War took center stage in the protest movement.

Pages 863–866
The Counterculture
In the 1960s, a youth culture that stressed freedom and individuality created for some people a promising new "space" in which to explore themselves. At the same time, it filled others with fear and disgust.

Pages 867–871
The End of the War
The antiwar movement finally convinced politicians in Washington that it was time to pull out of Vietnam, but American troops withdrew very slowly, and the fighting was far from over.

1968 Richard Nixon is elected United States President.

1970 Rock stars Janis Joplin and Jimi Hendrix die of drug overdoses.
• Four students are shot at Kent State.

1972 Nixon is reelected.

1973 The United States withdraws final troops from Vietnam.

1968	1970	1972	1974	1976

1969 Golda Meir becomes prime minister of Israel.

1970 The Aswan Dam is completed in Egypt.

1971 East Pakistan becomes the independent nation of Bangladesh.

1972 Ferdinand Marcos declares martial law in the Philippines.

1974 Argentinian dictator Juan Perón dies.

1975 The South Vietnamese government surrenders to North Vietnam.

SECTION 1

The War in the 1960s

1. FOCUS

Connecting to the Big Idea

See page 848B. Explain that in the 1960s, Presidents Kennedy and Johnson were determined to maintain South Vietnam under an anticommunist government. Ask why the United States became involved in Vietnam. How did the American presence in Vietnam escalate?

Objectives

● Explain why the United States supported the repressive regime of Ngo Dinh Diem.
● Describe how President Kennedy increased American involvement in Vietnam in the early 1960s.
● Describe how President Johnson used the Gulf of Tonkin incident to intensify the war.

Bellringer

Ask students to brainstorm words, phrases, and images that come to mind when they hear the word *Vietnam*.

Reading Strategy

Structured Overview Ask students to write the following column headings on a piece of paper: Background of the War, John Kennedy's Policy in Vietnam, and Lyndon Johnson's War. Ask students to take notes in the appropriate column as they read the section.

SECTION PREVIEW

Determined to defeat Ho Chi Minh's communist forces, Presidents Kennedy and Johnson supported dictatorships and sent thousands of American soldiers to fight and die in Vietnam.

Key Concepts
• Fearing that communist forces would take over Vietnam, the United States supported the repressive government of Ngo Dinh Diem in southern Vietnam.
   • President Kennedy increased American involvement in the early 1960s by sending military advisers to South Vietnam.
   • President Johnson used the Gulf of Tonkin incident as an excuse to begin bombing North Vietnam and sending thousands more American troops to the country.

Key Terms, People, and Places
Viet Cong, Gulf of Tonkin Resolution, escalation, Tet Offensive; Ngo Dinh Diem; Saigon

The fates of three nations—Vietnam, the United States, and France—became interwoven in the struggle for control over Vietnam.

By the mid-twentieth century, Vietnam had a history of nationalism that extended back nearly 2,000 years. Two Vietnamese sisters, Trung Trac and Trung Nhi, organized the first major revolt against Chinese oppressors in A.D. 39. The Vietnamese continued to resist Chinese domination for centuries afterward. In the 1800s, France established itself as a new colonial power in Vietnam. Ho Chi Minh, the leader of the Vietnamese independence movement after World War II, continued his country's tradition of nationalism in his resistance to Chinese and French control. Policy makers in the United States, however, saw Ho merely as a communist and therefore an enemy in the cold war. As the independence movement in Vietnam turned into a civil war

in the 1960s, the United States was determined to support the anticommunist government it had helped create in the south.

Background of the War

The United States became involved in Vietnam because of the demands of the cold war. As discussed in Chapter 26, American policy makers supported the French effort to crush Ho Chi Minh's independence movement because they needed French support to make the policy of containment work in Europe. The French attempt to reestablish control over its former colony failed in 1954. After the French were defeated at Dien Bien Phu, a conference was held in Geneva, Switzerland, to discuss the situation in Indochina. The conference included representatives of Ho Chi Minh, Vietnamese emperor Bao Dai, Cambodia, Laos, France, the United States, the Soviet Union, China, and Britain.

As a result of the Geneva Conference, Vietnam was divided into two separate nations. Ho Chi Minh, a nationalist leader sympathetic to communist ideas, controlled North Vietnam. **Ngo Dinh Diem,** a former official in Bao Dai's government who had been living in exile in the United States and Europe, became the new prime minister of South Vietnam, with the support of the United States. France and North Vietnam agreed that elections would be held in 1956 to unify the country. Diem and his United States supporters, however, did not commit to the elections, which they feared would remove Diem from power. The elections never took place.

John Kennedy's Policy in Vietnam

President Eisenhower gave his firm support to Diem's South Vietnamese government, providing some 675 United States military advisers to assist in the continuing struggle against the north. When President Kennedy took office, he decided to do even more.

▶ RESOURCE DIRECTORY

Teaching Resources

Reproducible Lesson Plan found in the Unit 9 folder, p. 105, provides a summary of the Section 1 lesson plan content.

Alternate Lesson Plan: Critical Thinking Recognizing Cause and Effect, found in the Alternate Lesson Plans folder, p. 156, helps students identify the sequence of events leading to the military escalation in Vietnam and analyze the United States' role in terms of cold war policy.

Guided Reading and Review found in the Unit 9 folder, p. 110, provides a structure for reading and mastering the key concepts and reviewing the key terms for Section 1. (Guided Practice)

Kennedy was a cold warrior, like most other United States leaders after World War II. He was determined to prevent the spread of communism at all costs. Early in his term, Kennedy sent Vice President Lyndon Johnson to Vietnam to assess the situation. Referring to the great British leader of World War II, Johnson called Diem "the Winston Churchill of Southeast Asia." He argued that if South Vietnam was to survive, it needed even more aid. In response, Kennedy increased the number of American military advisers to Vietnam. By the end of 1963, that number had grown to more than 16,000.

But military aid by itself could not ensure success. The problem was that Diem lacked support in his own country. He imprisoned people who criticized his government in "re-education centers." He filled many powerful government positions with members of his own family. United States aid earmarked for economic reforms went instead to the military and into the pockets of corrupt officials. Diem launched an enormously unpopular program to move peasants from their ancestral lands to "strategic hamlets"—government-run farming communities that isolated the peasants from communist influences seeping into South Vietnam. On top of everything else, Diem was a Catholic in a largely Buddhist country, and he often dismissed the religious concerns of others.

When Diem insisted that Buddhists obey Catholic religious laws, serious opposition developed. In June 1963, a Buddhist monk doused himself with gasoline and burned himself to death. Photographs showing his silent, grisly protest appeared on the front pages of newspapers around the world. Other monks followed the example, but their martyrdom did not budge Diem. Kennedy finally realized that Diem would never reform and acknowledged that the struggle against communism in Vietnam could not be won under Diem's rule.

United States officials told South Vietnamese military leaders that the United States would not object to Diem's overthrow. With that encouragement, Vietnamese troops struck in early November 1963, assassinated Diem, and seized control of the government.

Lyndon Johnson's War

Three weeks after Diem's assassination, Kennedy himself was dead, and the new military government in South Vietnam was already in trouble. While the ruling generals bickered among themselves and failed to direct the South Vietnamese army effectively, communist guerrillas in the south, known as **Viet Cong,** gained control over more territory and earned the loyalty of an increasing number of South Vietnamese. Throughout the struggle, the Viet Cong received assistance from Ho Chi Minh and the North Vietnamese.

Lyndon Johnson, the new United States President, was as much of a cold warrior as Kennedy, and he was equally suspicious of the communist

3. ASSESS

Section 1 Review Answers

1. (a) Viet Cong, see p. 851, (b) Gulf of Tonkin Resolution, see p. 852, (c) escalation, see p. 852, (d) Tet Offensive, see p. 853

2. Ngo Dinh Diem, see p. 850

3. Saigon, see p. 853

4. United States leaders wanted to make sure that Ho Chi Minh, the communist North Vietnamese leader, did not take control of the entire country, so they supported Ngo Dinh Diem in the south.

In Depth

Biography

By the early 1990s, Brigadier General Sherian Grace Cadoria, born in Marksville, Louisiana, in 1940, was the highest-ranking African American woman in the United States armed forces. She served in Vietnam from January 1967 to October 1969. She remembers her arrival: "I interviewed for a protocol job. When I got there, the colonel told me I couldn't do the job. He said, 'You can't travel, you can't carry luggage, it's too heavy. Women can't do this.' And I said, 'Nobody said I couldn't carry those hundred-pound bags of cotton when I was just a child.'"

sympathies of Ho Chi Minh. He commented about the continuing need for containment:

> *The Communists' desire to dominate the world is just like the lawyer's desire to be the ultimate judge on the Supreme Court or the politician's desire to be President. You see, the Communists want to rule the world, and if we don't stand up to them, they will do it. And we'll be slaves. Now I'm not one of those folks seeing Communists under every bed. But I do know about the principles of power, and when one side is weak, the other steps in.*

Just after he assumed office, Johnson met with Henry Cabot Lodge, United States ambassador to South Vietnam. Lodge told the new President that if he wanted to save Vietnam, he faced some tough choices. Johnson was determined to do whatever necessary to win the war. "I am not going to lose Vietnam," he said. Referring to the communist takeover of China in 1949, he went on: "I am not going to be the President who saw Southeast Asia go the way China went."

In his campaign for reelection as President in 1964, Johnson posed as a man of peace. "We are not about to send American boys nine or ten thousand miles away from home to do what Asian boys ought to be doing for themselves," he declared. He called Barry Goldwater, his Republican opponent in the election, a

General William Westmoreland (below) believed he could win the war with enough American troop strength, but he and President Johnson vastly underestimated the determination of the communist forces operating throughout Vietnam.

 RESOURCE DIRECTORY

Teaching Resources

⭐ **American Profiles Activity** found in the Unit 9 folder, p. 120, profiles Bob Kerrey, Vietnam veteran and Senator from Nebraska.

warmonger. He attacked critics who suggested using American bombs in Vietnam.

MAKING CONNECTIONS

President Johnson vowed not to let Vietnam "go the way China went." What do you think Johnson believed the Truman administration should have done in 1949?

Intensifying the War Meanwhile, however, war planning was under way. During the election campaign, LBJ cleverly secured congressional authorization for deepening American involvement in Vietnam. He did so in August 1964 by announcing that North Vietnamese torpedo boats had attacked United States destroyers in the international waters of the Gulf of Tonkin, thirty miles from North Vietnam. He did not mention that the United States ships appeared to the North Vietnamese to be participating in combat raids against North Vietnam, nor that the commander of one United States ship was not sure that an attack really had taken place. Despite the confusion over these details, Johnson asked for and obtained a resolution giving him authority to "take all necessary measures to repel any armed attack against the forces of the United States and to prevent further aggression."

Congress passed this **Gulf of Tonkin Resolution** by a vote of 416 to 0 in the House of Representatives and 88 to 2 in the Senate. Johnson had been waiting for some time for an opportunity to propose the resolution, which, he noted, "covered everything." The President now had nearly complete control over what the United States did in Vietnam—without Congress ever officially declaring war.

After his reelection, Johnson began a drastic military **escalation,** or expansion, of the war by devoting more and more American money and personnel to the conflict. In February 1965, after a Viet Cong attack at Pleiku in South Vietnam killed eight Americans and wounded 126, Johnson authorized retaliatory bombing of North Vietnam. Two weeks after the Pleiku attack, General William Westmoreland, the commander of United States forces in Vietnam, asked Johnson to send two battalions of marines to protect the American airfield at Danang. Johnson heeded the request, beginning a rapid buildup of American troops. At the start of 1965, nearly 25,000 American soldiers were stationed in Vietnam; by the end of the year, the number rose to 184,000. That number had climbed to 385,000 by 1966, to 485,000 by 1967, and to 543,000 by 1968. ★

Initially, United States soldiers had gone to Vietnam to advise the South Vietnamese. Now they took responsibility for trying to prop up the South Vietnamese government. Led by military men Nguyen Van Thieu and Nguyen Cao Ky, the new government was more effective than Diem's but remained dictatorial. Despite the large United States presence in Vietnam, the communist forces only intensified their efforts.

The Tet Offensive On January 30, 1968, the North Vietnamese mounted a major offensive during Tet, the Vietnamese new year. The **Tet Offensive,** shown in the map at right, included strikes on numerous provincial and district capitals and other towns in South Vietnam. In **Saigon,** the South Vietnamese capital, the Viet Cong attacked the American embassy, Tan Son Nhut air base, and the presidential palace. Even though they were turned back, the Viet Cong won a psychological victory. In contrast to official reports that claimed the North Vietnamese were on the verge of surrender, the Tet Offensive dramatically demonstrated that the Viet Cong could launch a massive attack on targets throughout South Vietnam. Furthermore, as images of

Vietnam, 1964–1968

Vietnamese defeat of the French, 1954.

CHINA

NORTH VIETNAM

BURMA

Dien Bien Phu

Hanoi • Haiphong

Gulf of Tonkin August 1964
Gulf of Tonkin

LAOS

Vientiane

Khe Sanh Jan.–June 1964
Hue
Danang

The marines (first U.S. ground troops) arrive, March 1965.

THAILAND

Bangkok

Pleiku Nov. 1965

South China Sea

CAMBODIA

SOUTH VIETNAM

Phnom Penh

Saigon

Tet Offensive begins, Jan. 30, 1968. North Vietnamese army and Viet Cong attack many major cities.

Gulf of Thailand

Mekong Delta

★ Major battles

⚝ Tet Offensive, 1968

0   150   300 Miles
0   150   300 Kilometers

 Geography and History: Interpreting Maps
The Ho Chi Minh Trail, shown in the map above, was a supply route from North Vietnam through Laos and Cambodia into South Vietnam. *How might the Ho Chi Minh Trail have contributed to the execution of the Tet Offensive?*

the fighting flooded American television, many people at home began to express reservations about United States involvement in Vietnam.

SECTION 1 REVIEW

Key Terms, People, and Places
1. Define (a) Viet Cong, (b) Gulf of Tonkin Resolution, (c) escalation, (d) Tet Offensive.
2. Identify Ngo Dinh Diem.
3. Identify Saigon.

Key Concepts
4. Why did the United States support the government of Ngo Dinh Diem in South Vietnam?
5. How did President Kennedy increase United States involvement in Vietnam's civil war in the early 1960s?

6. How did President Johnson use the Gulf of Tonkin incident to further his goals in the Vietnam conflict?

Critical Thinking
7. **Checking Consistency** Based on what you have read about Ngo Dinh Diem's government in South Vietnam, do you think that supporting this government was consistent with the stated aim of United States foreign policy: to defend freedom around the world? Explain why or why not.

Quiz found in the Unit 9 folder, p. 111, covers the main ideas in this section as well as the key terms.

---

5. Kennedy sent Vice President Lyndon Johnson to South Vietnam, then dramatically increased the number of United States military advisers there.

6. Just after North Vietnamese torpedo boats supposedly attacked American ships in the Gulf of Tonkin, Johnson convinced Congress to give him broad powers to control United States actions in the war.

7. Since Diem's government oppressed the South Vietnamese people, supporting it seems to have contradicted America's foreign policy aim of defending freedom. United States leaders at the time, however, believed that by preventing the spread of communism they were defending freedom in a fundamental sense.

Reteach

Ask students to write one or two sentences describing the level of United States involvement in the Vietnam War under Presidents Eisenhower, Kennedy, and Johnson, respectively.

Caption Answer to ...

 Interpreting Maps

The Ho Chi Minh Trail allowed the North Vietnamese government to provide the Viet Cong with ammunition and other supplies for use in the Tet Offensive.

4. CLOSE

Reinforcing the Big Idea

Attempting to keep communism out of Vietnam, Presidents Kennedy and Johnson supported dictatorships and sent thousands of American troops to Southeast Asia. The next section describes the brutality of the war.

The Brutality of the War

1. FOCUS

Connecting to the Big Idea

See page 848B. American soldiers were not prepared for the brutality of the fighting in Vietnam, and Americans at home were not prepared for the violence they were to witness on their television screens. Ask why American forces had little success in Vietnam. How did the war affect Vietnamese civilians?

Objectives

• Describe the effect of the war on the morale of American troops.
• Describe how the war affected Vietnamese civilians.
• Explain the effects of the My Lai massacre on Americans.

Bellringer

Ask students to consider how they would define a "just" war. Is any war just? Does the way the war is waged, including the type of weapons and damage inflicted, determine whether or not it can be considered just?

Reading Strategy

Reading for Evidence Have students read the first paragraph of the section, which states that American soldiers and Vietnamese civilians suffered during the war. Then ask students to list as they read, the different ways in which the soldiers and the civilians suffered.

The Brutality of the War

SECTION PREVIEW

Vietnam was the first war that Americans witnessed on their television screens. They were not prepared for the awful violence they saw, but neither were those who experienced the war firsthand.

Images of brutality and bloodshed, such as this one of a Vietnamese child wounded in the war, made American television viewers question United States involvement in Vietnam.

Key Concepts

• Many American soldiers went to Vietnam eager to do their patriotic duty, but they quickly learned that fighting the Viet Cong was a cruel and nerve-wracking ordeal.
• Vietnamese civilians were under constant attack from the air and the ground by United States troops, who could not distinguish them from Viet Cong or North Vietnamese soldiers.
• The massacre at My Lai brought the horrifying reality of the war home to many Americans.

Key Terms, People, and Places

My Lai massacre

T he Vietnam War was a long, brutal struggle. American soldiers were fighting a guerrilla war against a hidden enemy, and so they were often unable to tell friendly South Vietnamese peasants from Viet Cong soldiers waiting for an opportunity to attack them. As buddies fell before sniper bullets, land mines, and booby traps, GIs grew increasingly frustrated by the demands of a war that seemed to be accomplishing few clear objectives. Meanwhile, Vietnamese civilians in both the north and the south suffered heavy casualties in the ferocious destruction of their land and way of life.

The American Soldiers' War

Many American soldiers went to war enthusiastic about the job they were being asked to do. Many, like Ron Kovic of Long Island, had dreamed of being heroes when they grew up. Television characters such as the Lone Ranger and the Cisco Kid—rugged heroes of the American West—shaped their ideas about what it meant to be an American. They learned patriotism by watching actor John Wayne perform daring deeds in his movie roles.

Kovic, like many Americans, worried about the communist threat and was afraid that communists "were infiltrating our schools, trying to take over our classes and control our minds." After high school, he joined the marines to do his part to defend his country. He proudly served a tour in Vietnam and signed up for a second tour. This second tour of duty would take a terrible toll on Kovic's body and mind.

He and other soldiers were finding the war confusing and disturbing. They were trying to defend the freedom of the South Vietnamese, but the population, reared in an altogether different political tradition, seemed indifferent to their effort. "We are the unwilling working for the unqualified to do the unnecessary for the ungrateful," Kit Bowen of the First Infantry Division wrote to his father in Oregon.

⚙ Fighting conditions were also different from those they had seen in films. Carrying sixty-pound packs, they had to walk through jungles of ten-foot-tall elephant grass and across flooded rice paddies. Much of the time they fought leeches, fever, and jungle rot—a tropical fungus that infected the skin. Racial tensions within the American ranks destroyed morale. Death always lurked around the corner. American troops never knew what to expect next, and they never could be sure who was a friend and who was an enemy. The Vietnamese woman selling soft drinks by the roadside might be a Viet Cong ally, counting enemy soldiers as they

---

RESOURCE DIRECTORY

Teaching Resources

📄 **Reproducible Lesson Plan** found in the Unit 9 folder, p. 106, provides a summary of the Section 2 lesson plan content.

📄 **Alternate Lesson Plan: Cooperative Learning** found in the Alternate Lesson Plans folder, p. 157, guides groups of students in preparing and presenting scripts for a mock radio or TV broadcast describing the war from the perspective of various people in Vietnam.

📄 **Guided Reading and Review** found in the Unit 9 folder, p. 112, provides a structure for reading and mastering the key concepts and reviewing the key terms for Section 2. (Guided Practice)

⭐ 📄 **Literature Activity** Experiences of a Young Soldier in Vietnam, found in the Unit 9 folder, pp. 129–130, relates the Vietnam experiences of Charles Coe in an excerpt from his book *Young Man in Vietnam*.

passed. A child peddling candy might be concealing a live grenade.

The Viet Cong lacked the sophisticated equipment of the United States troops, so they avoided head-on clashes. Instead they used guerrilla warfare tactics, working in small groups to launch sneak attacks and practice sabotage. They were skilled in setting clever traps. For example, they might bury a land mine in a path that they expected a platoon of marines to take. When a soldier stepped on the mine, platoon leaders and others would gather around the wounded man, and Viet Cong snipers would have their guns aimed at the spot, ready to kill them.

Angel Quintana, an American soldier, described life in Vietnam:

An infantryman almost never sleeps. Even if you have time to sleep, you can't because you have all these memories in your head. If you're near a fire-support base, then you sleep even less with the noise of the cannons—the 155s, the 105s, the 4.2s, all firing at the same time. It's like an earthquake. And when you're in the jungle, you're afraid. As macho as you may be, you feel it. You know that death is behind you. You don't know whose turn it is. There are times when you lose the fear because something happens, like they kill a friend of yours. For five or six days it goes away because you're so shook up from losing your friend that life means nothing to you. Then it passes, and you start to be interested in life again.

Ron Kovic confronted his fears by making an aggressive effort to be a good soldier. But the horrors of war came to haunt him after he accidentally killed a United States corporal. Later, he shot at shadowy figures in a village hut, only to learn that his unit had killed and wounded innocent children. The final blow came when a sniper's bullet entered his spine. As his spinal column was severed and he lost all sensation in his legs, all he could feel was "the worthlessness of dying right here in this place at this moment for nothing." He was paralyzed from the chest down, after which he felt, in his words, "like a big clumsy puppet with all his strings cut."

MAKING CONNECTIONS

In what ways were the experiences of American soldiers who served in Vietnam and in the Pacific theater during World War II similar? How were they different?

Vietnamese Civilians and the War

The war was even more devastating for Vietnamese civilians in both the north and the south. Because American soldiers were never sure who might be sympathetic to the Viet Cong, civilians suffered as much as soldiers. As the struggle intensified, the destruction worsened. Saturation bombing—air raids that dropped thousands of tons of explosives over large areas—tore North Vietnam apart. The fragmentation bombs used in these raids, which threw pieces of their thick metal casings in all directions when they exploded, were not confined to the north alone; they were also used in the south, where they killed and maimed countless civilians.

United States forces also used chemical weapons against the Vietnamese. In order to expose Viet Cong hiding places, an herbicide known as Agent Orange was dropped on jungle landscapes, causing the leaves to fall off trees. Agent Orange also killed crops, and later it was discovered to cause health problems in humans and livestock. (See "History Might Not Have Happened This Way," pages 928–929.) Another destructive chemical used in Vietnam was called napalm. This jellylike substance, dropped from planes, burned uncontrollably as it stuck to people's bodies and seared off their flesh.

The war touched everyone in Vietnam. As Le Thanh, a North Vietnamese child in the 1960s, recalled,

Nobody could get away from the war. It didn't matter if you were in the countryside or the city. While I was living in the country I saw terrible things. . . . I saw children who had been killed, pagodas and churches that had been destroyed, monks and priests dead in the ruins, schoolboys who were killed when schools were bombed.

2. INSTRUCT

Explain/Discuss

Ask students to explain how a guerrilla war differs from a conventional war. Discuss why the superior firepower and technology of the American forces was not more successful against the Viet Cong guerrillas.

Ask students whether the Vietnam War meets the definition of "total war," one in which destruction of property and civilian life is carried out to persuade the enemy that continuing the conflict is not worth the cost. (See pages 346–347.) Ask students to describe American attempts at total warfare and to explain why these efforts were not successful.

Answer to . . .

MAKING CONNECTIONS

The jungle fighting conditions were similar, but in Vietnam, American soldiers never knew whom they were fighting—it was often impossible for them to tell friendly South Vietnamese from the Viet Cong.

In Depth

Interdisciplinary

As American herbicides destroyed crops in the South Vietnamese countryside, in the United States the Environmental Protection Agency (EPA) ordered a near-total ban on the pesticide dichlorodiphenyltrichloroethane (DDT). Although the use of DDT had resulted in dramatically increased crop yields, it was suspected to be a carcinogen and a possible cause of birth defects in humans and animals. DDT was banned in the United States and most other industrialized countries in the early 1970s.

Analyze

Explain that thousands of Vietnamese civilians were killed in the war. Ask students what made the My Lai massacre stand out. Why was it so shocking to Americans at home?

Activity

Researching War Images

Ask students to find illustrated books and magazines about the Vietnam War and to select one image that they think best represents the entire war. Students may present their chosen image to the class with a description and explanation of why they chose it.

Enrichment

Present to the class the following quotation by an American army officer after the total destruction of the village of Ben Tre in January 1968: "It became necessary to destroy the town in order to save it." Then ask students to explain why those opposed to the war frequently quoted this statement.

3. ASSESS

Section 2 Review Answers

1. My Lai massacre, see p. 857

2. American soldiers never knew who among the Vietnamese were enemies and who were friends. The fighting conditions in the jungle climate were also difficult.

3. Vietnamese civilians suffered heavy casualties as they watched their land and traditional way of life destroyed.

4. Over a hundred Vietnamese villagers were massacred by United States troops at My Lai. Reports of the massacre horrified Americans at home and made them wonder what kind of war their government was waging in Vietnam.

5. Many GIs probably felt that bringing Western culture to other people meant enlightenment and a better life for those people. The Vietnamese, however, were happy with their own way of life and did not want to see it overshadowed by Western culture with all of its "bewildering machines."

Although death was a constant presence in the war, few could harden their hearts against it. From the medic trying in vain to save a dying comrade, to the marine finally giving in to anguished tears in a lonely barracks, the war left few untouched. ★

The situation was similar in the south. Near the village of My Thuy Phuong, one peasant remembered this incident:

One day I was walking back home from the ricefield, carrying tools on my shoulder. Then behind me I heard a large, loud noise. A very bad noise. I looked back and saw an American helicopter following me, shooting down the path toward me. I was very scared, so [I] jumped into the water by the side. Just one moment later, the bullets went right by. So scary.

AMERICAN PROFILES

Le Ly Hayslip

Born in a tiny village in the northern part of South Vietnam, Le Ly Hayslip now lives in the United States and is an American citizen. Like other Vietnamese, as a child she learned "to love God, my family, our traditions, and the people we could not see: our ancestors." Then, when she was twelve years old, American helicopters came to Ky La, and the war intruded on her life.

For the next three years Le Ly fought for the Viet Cong. She and others were taught to follow Uncle Ho—Ho Chi Minh—in the struggle against the South Vietnamese government. For them, " 'Western culture' meant bars, brothels, black markets, and *xa hoi van minh*—bewildering machines—most of them destructive."

Life for Le Ly was never safe. Because she had ties to the Viet Cong, she always had to be alert to the moves of South Vietnamese soldiers. They often "took out their frustration on us: arresting nearby farmers and beating or shooting them on the spot, or carting anyone who looked suspicious off to jail." Captured by the South Vietnamese, she was questioned and then released. Later she was detained again, and this time tortured. Though she was fortunate enough to be freed once again, she now found herself suspected by the Viet Cong, since they could not understand why she had been released twice. She was caught in the middle. "If the [South

▶ RESOURCE DIRECTORY

Teaching Resources

★ **Primary Source Activity** An Army Nurse Remembers, found in the Unit 9 folder, p. 126, provides insight into the lives of women who served in Vietnam through the remembrances of army nurse Grace Barolet O'Brien.

Le Ly Hayslip endured both physical and emotional pain during the Vietnam War.

Vietnamese] were like elephants trampling our village," she observed, "the Viet Cong were like snakes who came at us in the night."

After the Viet Cong sentenced her to death, Le Ly's life was filled with the terror of being discovered. She realized she could not stay in Ky La. She also realized that her life had changed forever: "From now on, I promised myself, I would only flow with the strongest current and drift with the steadiest wind—and not resist."

Determined to leave Vietnam, Le Ly began to spend time with American soldiers and civilians. Eventually she met Ed Hayslip, a civilian contractor, who wanted to marry her and take her and her son back to the United States.

Le Ly accepted his proposal and became an immigrant to the United States. Still a young woman, she had seen more than most people see in a lifetime. For her, the war would never go away, and she devoted her life to trying to break down the barriers between the old world where she had been raised and the new world where she now lived.

The My Lai Massacre

In March 1968, the brutality of the war came into sharp focus in a massacre at My Lai, a small village in South Vietnam. In response to word that the community was sheltering 250 members of the Viet Cong, a United States infantry company moved in to clear out the village. Rather than enemy soldiers, the company found women, children, and old men. The American troops already had suffered heavy combat losses. They were worn down by the uncertainties and terrors of fighting a guerrilla war. Some lost control.

Lieutenant William L. Calley, Jr., was in charge. He first ordered, "Round everybody up," and then gave the order for the prisoners to be killed. One soldier, Private Paul Meadlo, later described what happened:

We huddled them up. We made them squat down. . . . I poured about four clips [about 68 shots] into the group. . . . The mothers kept hugging their children. . . . Well, we kept right on firing. . . . I still dream about it. About the women and children in my sleep. . . . Some nights, I can't even sleep. I just lay there thinking about it.

Stories of the horrible **My Lai massacre,** in which more than a hundred Vietnamese were slaughtered, shocked Americans at home. This was more than the nation had bargained for when it went to war.

Reteach

Ask students to write two or three sentences about the hardships and dangers confronting American soldiers in Vietnam and two or three sentences about the hardships and dangers that the war brought to Vietnamese civilians.

 Alternative Assessment

Mid-Point Monitoring
Ask students if they have
● Decided which materials to include
● Begun to locate sources of information

 Reinforcing the Big Idea

The Vietnam War took an enormous toll both on the American soldiers who tried to fight it and on the Vietnamese civilians who tried to survive it. The televised images of the war shocked Americans at home. The next section describes how the student protest movements of the time developed into the antiwar movement.

SECTION 2 REVIEW

Key Terms, People, and Places
1. Define My Lai massacre.

Key Concepts
2. Why was the war so hard on American troops?
3. How did the war affect Vietnamese civilians?
4. What happened at My Lai, and how did it affect Americans' perception of the war?

Critical Thinking
5. **Making Comparisons** Le Ly Hayslip and her fellow Viet Cong were willing to fight and die to keep "Western culture" out of Vietnam. How did their perception of American values differ from that of the GIs who grew up watching the Lone Ranger on television?

Quiz found in the Unit 9 folder, p. 113, covers the main ideas in this section as well as the key terms.

Student Protest

Student Protest

Connecting to the Big Idea

See page 848B. Explain that during the 1960s, college campuses erupted in student protest. The most dramatic, and perhaps the most effective, student protests were against the war in Vietnam. Ask why college students became activists during the 1960s.

Objectives

• Explain why the United States was ripe for change in the early 1960s and describe how college students at that time challenged the foundations of American life.

• Identify the Vietnam War as the focus of the protest movement in the 1960s.

• Describe the methods used by student protesters to voice their opinions.

Bellringer

Ask students whether the decade in which they are living seems to have a particular theme or identity. Ask them to suggest adjectives that might describe its general tone and spirit. What was the tone and spirit of the 1960s and early 1970s?

Reading Strategy

Structured Overview Ask students to write the main headings Student Activism and Changing Times and Resistance to War in the center of a piece of paper. Ask them to add important details from the relevant part of the section to support each main idea.

SECTION PREVIEW

"The times they are a-changin'," folksinger Bob Dylan sang in the 1960s. Student activists demanded many changes during this period, but the Vietnam War took center stage in the protest movement.

This 1969 poster advertised one of many antiwar demonstrations that shook the nation during the Vietnam War era.

Key Concepts

• The United States was ripe for change in the early 1960s, and students began to challenge the foundations of American life.

• The Vietnam War became the focus of the protest movement in the 1960s.

• Student protesters used peaceful demonstrations, teach-ins, educational campaigns, and sometimes violence to voice their opinions.

Key Terms, People, and Places

Students for a Democratic Society (SDS), New Left, teach-in, conscientious objector

---

I n June 1971, the *New York Times* published the first in a series of articles based on a classified government study of United States involvement in the Vietnam War. The Pentagon Papers, as the study came to be called, revealed that government officials, including President Johnson, had lied to Congress and the American public about the war. Although many were shocked by these revelations, others had long suspected that there were ugly truths hiding behind the optimistic statements of politicians and military leaders. In fact, opposition to the war had been growing steadily since the early 1960s.

Students were in the forefront of the antiwar movement, and their activism undermined support for the war in the population at large. Still, many Americans remained patriotically devoted to their country's involvement in Vietnam, and the issue created deep rifts within the United States.

Student Activism and Changing Times

Student activism began in the early 1960s. When members of the baby boom generation graduated from high school, college and university enrollments swelled with more students than ever before. Unlike previous generations of students, who needed to work after high school, members of this generation had time to experiment before they went out into the world.

Change was in the air. Even in the conformist years of the 1950s, popular culture—including rock-and-roll music and rebellious youths on the movie screen—had indicated that many young Americans were not satisfied with the values of their parents. The early 1960s saw a widening of this generation gap. In 1963 folksinger Bob Dylan captured the new mood in a song entitled "The Times They Are A-Changin'":

> *C ome mothers and fathers*
> *Throughout the land*
> *And don't criticize*
> *What you can't understand*
> *Your sons and your daughters*
> *Are beyond your command*
> *There's a battle*
> *Outside and it's ragin'*
> *It'll soon shake your windows*
> *And rattle your walls . . .*
> *For the times they are a-changin'.*

The civil rights movement, discussed in Chapter 29, was a stepping-stone to other movements for change. Civil rights activists were among those who organized **Students for a Democratic Society (SDS)** in 1960. Its manifesto, the Port Huron Statement, appeared

---

▶ RESOURCE DIRECTORY

Teaching Resources

Reproducible Lesson Plan found in the Unit 9 folder, p. 107, provides a summary of the Section 3 lesson plan content.

Alternate Lesson Plan: Learning Styles found in the Alternate Lesson Plans folder, p. 158, is particularly effective for auditory learners, and focuses on lyrics of protest songs and other methods of activism in reaction to the Vietnam War.

Guided Reading and Review found in the Unit 9 folder, p. 114, provides a structure for reading and mastering the key concepts and reviewing the key terms for Section 3. (Guided Practice)

⭐ **American Profiles Activity** found in the Unit 9 folder, p. 121, profiles Joan Baez, considered by many to be the "queen of the folk singers," who used her considerable talents to further the antiwar movement.

in 1962. It was written largely by Tom Hayden, a student at the University of Michigan. The statement declared:

> We are people of this generation, bred in at least modest comfort, housed now in universities, looking uncomfortably at the world we inherit.
>
> When we were kids the United States was the wealthiest and strongest country in the world. . . . As we grew, however, our comfort was penetrated by events too troubling to dismiss. . . . We would replace power rooted in possession, privilege, or circumstance by power and uniqueness rooted in love, reflectiveness, reason, and creativity. As a social system we seek the establishment of a democracy of individual participation.

Although it was but a tiny organization at the start, SDS was a major force in the development of a new political movement that came to be called the **New Left**. Members of the New Left believed that radical changes were the only way to solve problems such as poverty and racism in the United States.

MAKING CONNECTIONS

The Port Huron Statement rejected a system of "power rooted in possession, privilege, or circumstance." What other social movements have you read about that criticized similar aspects of American society?

The Free Speech Movement The first blow of the student revolution came at the University of California at Berkeley in September 1964. Civil rights workers became angry when the university refused to allow them to distribute leaflets outside the main gate of the campus. The students, who had fought for equal rights in the South, argued that their right to free speech was being challenged, and they resisted the university's effort to restrict their political activity. When police came to arrest one of their leaders, students surrounded the police car and kept it from moving. The free speech movement was under way.

Eventually the administration tried to find a compromise. Then, however, the governing board that had the final word over university policy decided to hold student leaders responsible for their actions and filed charges against some. Irate students took over Sproul Hall, the main administration building. Student leader Mario Savio declared that the university was no more than a vast, impersonal bureaucracy:

In October 1964, Berkeley student Mario Savio stood atop a police car to address a crowd of protesters demanding free speech (above). The building in the background is Sproul Hall.

> There comes a time when the operation of the machine becomes so odious [hateful], makes you so sick at heart, that you can't take part, you can't even tacitly [silently] take part. And you've got to put your bodies upon the gears and upon the wheels, upon the levers, upon all the apparatus, and you've got to make it stop.

✪ Students wore buttons echoing the instructions on their university registration cards and protesting the impersonal treatment they received from the school. "I am a U.C. Student," the buttons read. "Do not Fold, Bend, or Mutilate." Folksinger Joan Baez came to the school and sang "We Shall Overcome," the marching song of the civil rights movement. When police arrested students in Sproul Hall, other students, supported by the faculty, went on strike and stopped attending classes to show their support for the free speech demonstrators.

Berkeley remained the most radical campus, but the agitation there spread to other campuses across the United States. In the spring of 1965, activists challenged regulations they felt unfairly curbed their freedom, such as restrictions on the hours when women and men could visit each others' dorms. Students also sought greater involvement in college

Activity

Cooperative Learning

Time: Two class periods.

Activity: Students should create and administer a questionnaire about the 1960s to people who were of college age during that time.

Grouping: Four to six students.

Purpose: The questionnaire should ask open-ended but focused questions about college attendance, work, attitudes toward SDS and other protest movements, feelings about the Vietnam War, and participation in or opposition to the antiwar movement.

Roles: Researchers, question writers, analysts.

Outcome: Students will understand the primary concerns of Americans of college age during the 1960s.

Enrichment

Dr. Benjamin Spock, author of the perennial best-selling child care manual, *Baby and Child Care*, joined the antiwar movement when LBJ ordered the bombing of North Vietnam. Ask students to research the activities of Spock, Daniel Berrigan, Philip Berrigan, Jane Fonda, or William Sloane Coffin in the antiwar movement.

Caption Answer to ...

 Interpreting Graphs

There were approximately 185,000 American troops in Vietnam in 1965 and 485,000 in 1967. As the 1960s progressed, the increasing number of both draftees and casualties fueled antiwar protest. The Tet Offensive took place in 1968—the peak year for American troops in Vietnam. The fact that the offensive could happen despite the presence of so many troops there pointed to the hopelessness of the American war effort; after 1968, the number of troops began to decline.

 Interpreting Graphs
How many United States soldiers were in Vietnam in 1965? In 1967? How do the graphs show some reasons for antiwar protest, especially among students? Explain how the top graph might relate to the Tet Offensive (January 1968) and its effect on public opinion in the United States.

affairs. SDS recruited some of these discontented students to work in campaigns to improve conditions in the cities of the United States.

The Teach-in Movement Then the Vietnam War intervened. As escalation began, students were among the first to protest American involvement in the war. Some opposed what they regarded as American imperialism. Others questioned American interests in a civil war. All called for withdrawal. The Tet Offensive in early 1968 finally turned a majority of Americans against the war, but the student protest movement had been registering many young people's disapproval for years. The graphs above give some indication of the statistics students found disturbing.

The first **teach-in** took place at the University of Michigan in March 1965. When a small group of faculty members planned a strike to protest the war, the Michigan legislature threatened to fire them. Instead, an even larger group decided to make a public statement. Fifty or sixty professors decided to teach a special night session in which issues concerning the war could be aired. To their surprise, several thousand people showed up and made the evening a monumental success. Soon other teach-ins followed at colleges around the country. Both supporters and opponents of the war appeared at the early teach-ins, but soon antiwar voices dominated the proceedings.

Resistance to War

At about the same time that the first teach-ins were taking place, resistance to the military draft was beginning to sweep the country. A selective service act allowing the government to draft men between the ages of eighteen and twenty-six had been in place since 1951. As more and more young men were being called into service and sent to fight in Vietnam, Americans began to question the morality and fairness of the draft. College students could receive deferments, which meant they did not have to go to war, but those who could not afford college did not have this avenue open to them. Many other young men tried to avoid the draft by leaving the country or by claiming that they were **conscientious objectors**—they opposed fighting in the war on moral grounds.

SDS grew by leaps and bounds as it embarked on a campaign against the draft. Leaders encouraged men to refuse to report for duty. The organization also launched attacks on campus units of the Reserve Officers' Training Corps (ROTC), on CIA recruiters, and on companies producing napalm and other tools of destruction. "Hey, hey, LBJ. How many kids did you kill today?" marchers chanted during demonstrations around the country. In 1967 some 300,000 opponents of the war marched in New York City, while 100,000 tried to close down the Pentagon, home of the Defense Department, near Washington, D.C. In 1969 the National Chicano Moratorium Committee staged its own antiwar

 RESOURCE DIRECTORY

Teaching Resources

✪ 📄 **Visual Learning Activity** Antiwar Demonstrations, found in the Unit 9 folder, p. 132, shows two pictures of protesters to illustrate the way the antiwar movement won broad support in late 1969.

demonstrations. These protesters argued that Vietnam was a racial war, with black and brown Americans being used against their brothers and sisters in developing nations.

Protest became a way of life. In the first six months of 1968, more than 200 major demonstrations erupted at colleges and universities around the country. The most dramatic confrontation came at Columbia University in New York. There the issues of civil rights and the war were closely related. An SDS chapter sought to get the university to cut its ties with a research institute that did work for the military. At the same time, an African American students' organization tried to halt construction of a gymnasium that would encroach upon an adjacent neighborhood. Together, these two groups took over the president's office. Finally the president called the police, and hundreds of students were arrested. A student sympathy strike followed, and the university closed early that spring.

Sometimes the radical movement turned violent. Activists in one SDS faction called themselves the Weathermen, after a line in a Bob Dylan song—"You don't need a weatherman to know which way the wind blows." They were determined to bring about a revolution immediately. In October 1969, the group converged on Chicago. Members dressed in hard hats, boots, and work gloves rampaged through the streets wielding pipes, clubs, rocks, and chains. They tangled with police (as they had planned), regrouped, and came back for still another confrontation.

Bo Burlingham, a participant from Ohio, explained why he had joined in the attack:

This antiwar protest took place in San Francisco in 1967. ⭐

W hy did we do it? The status quo meant to us war, poverty, inequality, ignorance, famine and disease in most of the world. To accept it was to condone and help perpetuate it. We felt like miners trapped in a terrible poisonous shaft with no light to guide us out. We resolved to destroy the tunnel even if we risked destroying ourselves in the process.

The violent measures of groups like the Weathermen represented the extreme expression of youthful discontent in the 1960s. The spirit of change led most members of the counterculture to work for reforms in peaceful ways, but that same spirit led others simply to "drop out" of the traditional culture they were rejecting.

SECTION 3 REVIEW

Key Terms, People, and Places
1. Define (a) SDS, (b) New Left, (c) teach-in, (d) conscientious objector.

Key Concepts
2. What were the roots of student activism in the 1960s?
3. What was the role of SDS in the growing protest movement?
4. How did the Vietnam War affect the student protest movement?

5. What did activists hope to accomplish, and what methods did they use?

Critical Thinking
6. **Distinguishing False from Accurate Images** Mario Savio described the university as a huge machine with gears and wheels. Explain why you think that this image does or does not accurately reflect the nature of any large institution.

📄 **Quiz** found in the Unit 9 folder, p. 115, covers the main ideas in this section as well as the key terms.

Section 3 Review Answers

1. (a) SDS, see p. 858, (b) New Left, see p. 859, (c) teach-in, see p. 860, (d) conscientious objector, see p. 860

2. Baby boomers in college had time to experiment before getting jobs, and they were dissatisfied with the traditional values of their parents. The model of the civil rights movement helped spark other movements for change.

3. SDS formed the core of the New Left, and it led the protest against the draft as the Vietnam War progressed. Some radical SDS members formed the Weathermen, who used violent methods of protest.

4. The Vietnam War took center stage in the student protest movement as more and more young men were drafted.

5. Activists hoped to challenge the corporate values that had defined the 1950s and, more specifically, to change unfair university policies and to stop the Vietnam War. Their methods included draft resistance, protest marches, and strikes.

6. Possible answers: The machine image works well because each person plays a small part in achieving a larger purpose, even though they may not be happy as tiny parts of huge machines that are out of their direct control. The machine image is inaccurate because the human element in institutions will always keep them more dynamic and changeable than mere machines.

Reteach

Ask students to describe the goals and methods of the free speech movement, draft resistance, and antiwar protest.

Reinforcing the Big Idea

Student protesters demanded many changes during the 1960s, but the primary focus of their protest became the Vietnam War. The next section describes the development of the counterculture.

Critical Thinking

Checking Consistency

Focus Students check for consistency between what they have read about the Vietnam era and the passages provided.

Instruct Divide the class into pairs and ask students to work with their partners to answer the questions in the feature. Ask for a show of hands to indicate how many find the passages in Item A inconsistent. Do the same for Item B. Then ask for volunteers to explain the inconsistency they find. Ask those who find the items consistent to explain their reasoning.

Extend See the Historian's Toolbox Activity in the Resource Directory below.

Answers

1. (a) The First Amendment of the Constitution, which guarantees freedom of the press. (b) Johnson's highly sympathetic depiction of the North Vietnamese in 1965 suggested policy objectives geared toward peaceful settlement rather than military victory in Vietnam. (c) Johnson's language and imagery, used in support of a policy of peace, can serve as the basis of comparison with his language, imagery, and policy objectives on the same subject at a later date.

2. (a) The U.S. Supreme Court turned down the government's request to keep two newspapers from publishing "The Pentagon Papers." (b) The ruling meant that the newspapers were free to publish the material, which they probably did. (c) In 1966 Johnson's depiction of the North Vietnamese in harsh, flatly threatening terms suggested policy objectives geared toward a military victory rather than a peaceful settlement in Vietnam. He now painted a menacing, inhuman picture of the North Vietnamese.

3. (a) The Supreme Court's ruling against the government agreed with the constitutional requirement of the First Amendment that no law interfere with the freedom of the press. (b) No, it was not consistent. In 1965 Johnson's policy objective was portrayed as a peaceful settlement with the North Vietnamese. In 1966 it was portrayed as a military victory over the North Vietnamese.

Checking Consistency

Checking consistency means determining whether ideas that should agree—or follow logically one from the other—actually do. Government actions, for example, should always agree with the Constitution. Where no such overriding rules apply—in the creation of foreign policy, for instance—policy objectives are expected to be consistent with past decisions on similar issues. Checking for consistency will help reveal whether the government is in fact operating as it should.

Use the following steps and what you have read about the Vietnam era to check for consistency in the examples at right.

1. Identify the principle or other factor to be used as the baseline for checking consistency. You should expect certain facts, ideas, or actions to agree—either with one another or with an overriding principle. Read the information in Items A and B at right. (a) What rule or principle serves as the baseline for checking consistency in Item A? (b) In Item B, what did Johnson's description of the North Vietnamese in 1965 suggest about the goals of his policy in Vietnam at the time? (c) How can Johnson's statement serve as the baseline for checking his consistency in other statements about Vietnam?

2. Note the corresponding action or idea to be checked for consistency. (a) In Item A, what action did the Supreme Court take? (b) What probably happened as a result of this action? (c) In Item B, what did Johnson's description of the North Vietnamese (the "Communists") in 1966 suggest about the goals of his policy in Vietnam at the time?

3. Check for consistency between the principle or baseline factor and the corresponding action or idea. In the examples below, compare the second action or idea against the baseline you have identified to see if the two ideas are consistent with or contradict each other. (a) In Item A, did the action taken by the Supreme Court agree or conflict with the constitutional requirement of the First Amendment? Explain your answer. (b) In Item B, was Johnson's statement of his policy objective in 1966 consistent with the statement he had made in 1965? Explain your answer.

A "Congress shall make no law . . . abridging the freedom of speech, or of the press. . . ."

—First Amendment, United States Constitution

In 1971 the United States Supreme Court denied the government's request to prohibit two newspapers from publishing "The Pentagon Papers," a highly classified documentary history of United States involvement in Vietnam through May 1968.

B "This war, like most wars, is filled with terrible irony. For what do the people of North Vietnam want? They want what their neighbors also desire: food for their hunger, health for their bodies, . . . an end to the bondage of material misery. . . . Neither independence nor human dignity will ever be won by arms alone. It also requires the works of peace."

—President Lyndon B. Johnson, address at Johns Hopkins University (April 7, 1965)

"Aggression is on the march and the enslavement of free men is its goal. . . . If we allow the Communists to win in Vietnam, it will become easier and more appetizing for them to take over other countries in other parts of the world. . . . That is why it is vitally important to every American family that we stop the Communists in South Vietnam."

—President Lyndon B. Johnson, Honolulu Conference (February 6, 1966)

RESOURCE DIRECTORY

Teaching Resources

Historian's Toolbox Activity Checking Consistency, found in the Unit 9 folder, p. 124, provides passages in which students can practice this skill by determining whether words and actions follow a given principle.

The Counterculture

SECTION PREVIEW

In the 1960s, a youth culture that stressed freedom and individuality created for some people a promising new "space" in which to explore themselves. At the same time, it filled others with fear and disgust.

Key Concepts
- Rejecting the conventional lifestyles of older Americans, many young people in the 1960s became part of a counterculture that sought to promote freedom and creativity.
- The counterculture advanced new attitudes about personal relationships, drugs, and music.
- Many Americans were shocked by the new values of the counterculture.

Key Terms, People, and Places
counterculture, hippie, psychedelic drug, Woodstock

I n the 1960s, many Americans began to look for alternatives to traditional patterns of living. Young people in particular were involved in what became known as the **counterculture.** Drawing on the example of the Beat Generation of the 1950s, members of the counterculture rejected conventional customs. They experimented with new forms of dress, different attitudes toward sexual relationships, and the use of drugs. Some members of the counterculture were politically involved; most were not. But their challenge to traditional norms was visible both in the political protests of the 1960s and in the changing social patterns of American life.

Reflections of the Counterculture

People's appearances reflected the changes that were taking place. The **hippies** of the 1960s—men and women who self-consciously rejected conventional norms—tried to look different. Women chose freer fashions, such as miniskirts and loose-fitting dresses. Men let their hair grow long and wore beards. Many hippies adopted the dress of working people, which seemed somehow more "authentic" than the school clothes of middle-class youth. Therefore, men and women wore jeans, muslin (plain-woven cotton) shirts, and other simple garments that were intended to look handmade.

The Sexual Revolution The new views about sexual behavior advanced by the counterculture were labeled "the sexual revolution." The young people who led this revolution demanded more freedom to make personal choices. Some argued that sex should be separated from its traditional ties to family life. Lynn Ferrin, who moved to San Francisco to become part of the counterculture in California, remembered her feelings at the time:

I was among the women in that whole vanguard of sexual freedom who were very excited by being free women. . . . In my circles, you wouldn't think of getting married, settling down with one person. The suburbs and the station wagon full of Cub Scouts became something you didn't want anything to do with.

The sexual revolution in the counterculture led to more open discussion of sexual subjects. Newspapers, magazines, and books published articles that might not have been printed, even in the recent past. The 1962 book by Helen Gurley Brown, *Sex and the Single Girl,* became a best-seller. In 1966 William H. Masters and Virginia E. Johnson shocked many people when they published *Human Sexual Response,* a report on their scientific studies of sexuality.

One way in which 1960s youth expressed themselves was by turning everyday objects into works of art. Country Joe McDonald of the popular rock group Country Joe and the Fish decorated his guitar (above) with antiwar symbols. Others decorated their clothing with colorful embroidery. ✪

1. FOCUS

Connecting to the Big Idea

See page 848B. Explain that in the 1960s, a youth culture rejected conventional norms and values. Ask what norms and values were embraced by the counterculture. How did the counterculture affect American life?

Objectives
- Explain the ways in which many young people in the 1960s sought to promote freedom and creativity in a counterculture that rejected the conventional lifestyles of older Americans.
- Describe the attitudes of the counterculture toward personal relationships, drugs, and music.
- Describe the shocked reaction of many older Americans to the new values of the counterculture.

Bellringer

Ask students to think about the meaning of the compound word *counterculture.* Ask them to consider how far the values, attitudes, and activities of young people in the 1960s ran "counter" to traditional American culture.

Reading Strategy

Reinforcing Key Ideas Ask students to note examples from the section to support this sentence on page 863: "In the 1960s, many Americans began to look for alternatives to traditional patterns of living."

📘 **Reproducible Lesson Plan** found in the Unit 9 folder, p. 108, provides a summary of the Section 4 lesson plan content.

📘 **Alternate Lesson Plan: Learning Styles** found in the Alternate Lesson Plans folder, p. 159, encourages students to identify values and styles of the counterculture, and is especially effective for visual learners.

📘 **Guided Reading and Review** found in the Unit 9 folder, p. 116, provides a structure for reading and mastering the key concepts and reviewing the key terms for Section 4. (Guided Practice)

✪ 📘 **Visual Learning Activity** Reflections of the Counterculture, found in the Unit 9 folder, p. 133, displays many of the popular buttons that were worn in the 1960s to express views on current subjects.

Explain/Discuss

Discuss the aspects of American life that hippies rejected. What sort of life did hippies want to build for themselves?

Discuss the reactions of other Americans to hippies and would-be hippies. Why did hippies attract so much attention? Why did some more conservative Americans feel threatened by the hippie lifestyle? Ask students what aspects of the counterculture were dangerous.

Answer to ...

MAKING CONNECTIONS

Young people in the 1960s may have been trying to escape the lives of conformity and materialism their parents were living—as well as all of the normal problems that accompany growing up. Today, many young people also seek to escape problems through experimentation and rebellion.

In Depth

Historical Misconceptions

The common belief concerning antiwar sentiments during this period was that they were held exclusively by the young and the highly educated. But a May 1971 Gallup Poll found that 75 percent of those with only a grade school education opposed the war, against 66 percent of college graduates. "A careful review of public opinion data over the last seven years [1965–72]," stated a 1972 University of Michigan Survey Research Center study, "shows that on most war-related issues, the greatest opposition to continued American involvement has come from the least educated parts of the population."

This group of hippies lived together in the New Buffalo Commune. They turned out for the 1968 Fourth of July parade in El Rito, New Mexico, in their outrageously painted bus.

Novels like D. H. Lawrence's *Lady Chatterly's Lover,* which had been banned in the United States since 1928 for being too explicit, now became available.

Many men and women also experimented with new living patterns. Some hippies rejected traditional relationships and lived together in communal groups. More and more people simply lived together as couples, without getting married.

The Drug Scene Also part of the 1960s counterculture were **psychedelic drugs,** which are drugs that cause the brain to behave abnormally. As a result, the brain produces hallucinations and other altered perceptions of reality. The beatniks had experimented with drugs a decade before, but they had been in the minority. Now drug use became more widespread among the nation's youth.

One early proponent of psychedelic drug use was researcher Timothy Leary, who worked at Harvard University with Richard Alpert on the chemical compound lysergic acid diethyl amide, commonly known as LSD. The two men were fired from their research posts for using undergraduates in experiments with the drug. Leary then began to preach that drugs could help free the mind. He advised listeners, "Tune in, turn on, drop out."

Soldiers who had used drugs in Vietnam brought them home when their tours of duty were completed. Marijuana became common among middle-class college students. Todd Gitlin, a radical activist who became president of SDS, explained that "the point was to open up a new space, an *inner* space, so that we could *space out,* live for the sheer exultant point of living."

On the other side of the drug issue, however, was serious danger. Overdoses and deaths from accidents that occurred while under the influence of drugs caused concern in many quarters. Three leading musicians—Janis Joplin, Jim Morrison, and Jimi Hendrix—died of complications from drug overdoses. They were not the only ones. Their deaths represented the tragic excesses to which some people were driven by their reliance on drugs as an escape.

MAKING CONNECTIONS

What might some young people in the 1960s have been trying to escape by seeking a spiritual "inner space"? In what ways do young people today seek similar escapes?

▶ RESOURCE DIRECTORY

Teaching Resources

 Literature Activity The Flower Children, found in the Unit 9 folder, p. 131, uses lyrics from the song "San Francisco (Be Sure to Wear Flowers in Your Hair)" to describe the group of young people who called themselves "flower children."

The Music World

⭐ Music likewise reflected and contributed to the cultural changes. The rock and roll of the 1950s and the folk music of the early 1960s gave way to a new kind of rock. The Beatles, a group of performers from England, heavily influenced the music of this period, taking first England and then the United States by storm. Mick Jagger of the Rolling Stones was an aggressive, sometimes violent showman on stage. Janis Joplin was a hard-driving, hard-drinking singer whose powerful interpretations of classic blues songs catapulted her to superstardom before her death in 1970.

Woodstock The diverse strands of the counterculture all came together at the Woodstock Music and Art Fair in upstate New York in August 1969. About 300,000 people gathered for several days in a large pasture in Bethel, New York, to listen to the major bands of the rock world. Despite brutal heat and bursts of rain, those who attended **Woodstock** recalled the festival with something of a sense of awe for the fellowship they experienced there. Tom Law, one participant at Woodstock, commented on the mood:

> The music had very little to do with it. The music was great and it was there and kept everybody focused on that. But the event was so much bigger than the music. It was a phenomenon. It was absolutely a phenomenon. And it was also the most peaceful, civilized gathering that was probably happening on the planet at the time.

The weekend was trouble-free. Police avoided confrontations with those attending by choosing not to enforce drug laws. The crowd remained under control. After the festival, many supporters spoke about the "Woodstock Nation" as a model for the new and better world to come.

Other Americans, however, viewed both the festival and the mood it reflected with distaste. Even as older people began growing their hair

Links Across Time

| 1650 | 1700 | 1750 | 1800 | | 1850 | 1900 | 1950 | 2000 |

Music: The Sound of Rebellion

The 1960s were not the first time that Americans were shocked by the music their children were listening to. In the 1920s, the jazz sound of Louis Armstrong and the Hot Five (left) was too hot for many older listeners—but the young flappers and rakes loved it. The performances of rock bands in the 1960s (above) were similarly lost to the older generation. **Does any of the music you listen to today leave the older people you know baffled?**

Analyze

Ask students to analyze what ultimately happened to the 1960s counterculture. Why did most hippies melt back into the middle class, and why had many who protested against capitalistic values in the 1960s become business executives by the 1980s? What aspects of American life were permanently changed by the counterculture?

Activity

Teaching Heterogeneous Groups

In protest against conventional lifestyles, many young people in the 1960s adopted alternative ways of dressing and behaving. To understand the purpose of this form of expression, divide students into small groups to define today's counterculture in terms of dress and behavior. In order to do this, each group must first describe the conventional customs that this counterculture rejects. Students should then state what change today's counterculture seeks to realize. **LEP**

Enrichment

Ask students to research the various kinds of communes that were formed in the 1960s. Ask students to present a brief report on their findings to the class.

Answer to ...

Links Across Time

Answers will vary but should reflect an understanding that trends in music often evolve along generational lines.

Section 4 Review Answers

1. (a) hippie, see p. 863, (b) psychedelic drug, see p. 864, (c) Woodstock, see p. 865

2. The counterculture rejected the conformity and traditional values that had marked the 1950s. Instead, it emphasized freedom and individuality.

3. The counterculture valued individual freedom and experimentation; its members tried new types of sexual relationships, experimented with mind-altering drugs, and enjoyed new forms of rock music.

4. Many outside the counterculture viewed it with distaste because it seemed childish and vulgar and rejected time-honored values.

5. The assumption is that marriage is boring and restricting. Students may agree with this view, or they may point out that marriage allows for a kind of personal growth that living without commitment does not.

Reteach

Ask students to read and correct each of the following statements and to provide evidence from the section to support their correction.

● The counterculture began as an attempt by older Americans to halt the spreading student protest movement.

● The term *sexual revolution* refers to women's demands for equality with men in the workplace.

● LSD is a kind of music that was popular in the 1960s.

● The rock festival at Woodstock was marred by violence.

 CLOSE

 Reinforcing the Big Idea

In the 1960s, many young Americans traded traditional patterns of living for a counterculture that stressed freedom and individuality. The next section describes the success of the antiwar movement in bringing an end to the Vietnam War.

The young people who attended the Woodstock Music and Art Fair in 1969 reflected the new fashions and social values of their times.

longer and wearing more colorful clothes, they were not interested in the more fundamental changes they saw occurring around them. Some young people also disliked these changes. In particular, opponents deplored the drugs, sex, and nudity they saw at the Woodstock festival and around the country. To them, the counterculture represented a rejection of morals and honored values and seemed a childish reaction to the problems of the era.

Altamont The fears of those who criticized Woodstock came true at another rock festival that took place at the Altamont Speedway in California in December 1969. There, 300,000 people gathered for a concert concluding an American tour by the Rolling Stones. When promoters of the concert failed to provide adequate security, the Stones hired a band of Hell's Angels, the infamous and lawless motorcycle gang, to keep order. The cyclists battered any people who annoyed them and ended up beating one man to death when he ventured on stage.

The violence at the Altamont concert was not the only sign of contradictions within the counterculture. Despite their celebration of simple lifestyles, most hippies were children of the comfortable middle class, and they melted right back into it when the counterculture fell apart. American corporations seized on the opportunity to market items such as blue jeans and stereo equipment to members of the counterculture, who eagerly bought the products. By the 1980s, many baby boomers who had protested the capitalistic values of the 1950s and 1960s would be holding executive positions in the same corporations they had once denounced.

SECTION 4 REVIEW

Key Terms, People, and Places

1. Define (a) hippie, (b) psychedelic drug, (c) Woodstock.

Key Concepts

2. Describe the values that were rejected and those that were embraced by the counterculture of the 1960s.

3. How was the counterculture reflected in the sexual values, drug use, and music of its members?

4. How did Americans outside the counterculture view the movement?

Critical Thinking

5. Identifying Assumptions Lynn Ferrin recalled being part of a group of women in the 1960s "who were very excited by being free women" and "wouldn't think of getting married, settling down with one person." What assumptions about marriage are revealed in this statement? Explain why you think these assumptions are or are not valid.

▶ **RESOURCE DIRECTORY**

Teaching Resources

Quiz found in the Unit 9 folder, p. 117, covers the main ideas in this section as well as the key terms.

The End of the War

SECTION 5

The End of the War

SECTION PREVIEW

The antiwar movement finally convinced politicians in Washington that it was time to pull out of Vietnam, but American troops withdrew very slowly, and the fighting was far from over.

Key Concepts

- Growing opposition to the war convinced Lyndon Johnson not to run for reelection and helped Richard Nixon to become President in 1968.
- Nixon gradually replaced American troops with South Vietnamese, but at the same time he began a new bombing assault on Cambodia that enraged antiwar protesters.
- A cease-fire was finally signed in 1973, but by 1975 North Vietnamese leaders had taken control of the entire country.
- The war left permanent scars in the Vietnamese countryside as well as in the hearts of Vietnamese and Americans.

Key Terms, People, and Places

Vietnamization; Kent State University

T he antiwar movement created serious opposition to American involvement in Vietnam. It also polarized the United States. Deep rifts in the Democratic party and in the country as a whole forced Lyndon Johnson to leave the presidency at the end of his term and paved the way for the election of Republican Richard Nixon in 1968. Nixon made good on a pledge to withdraw the United States from the Southeast Asian struggle, but only after expanding the war outside Vietnam and creating even more violent protest at home.

Mounting Opposition

By 1968 the antiwar movement was in full swing. Political activists drew on all of their resources to mount the most extensive resistance campaign in American history. Marchers took to the streets, while artists, authors, and musicians contributed their talents to the antiwar crusade.

Years of protest and a growing list of American casualties had steadily increased public opposition to the war. In a 1965 Gallup poll, 62 percent of those interviewed felt that the United States was handling the war in Vietnam "as well as could be expected." In 1966 only 41 percent approved of Johnson's Vietnam policy; that figure dropped to 35 percent in 1968. At the same time, disapproval of Johnson's actions increased from 37 percent in 1966 to 50 percent in 1968. In 1968, 49 percent of those polled felt that the United States had made a mistake in sending troops into the war. Details on these statistics can be found in the table on page 868.

Johnson finally succumbed to the opposition. As resistance to the war mounted, his own popularity fell accordingly. After the Tet Offensive, when the North Vietnamese demonstrated that they still had the resources to carry out a broad-based attack in South Vietnam, Johnson recognized that American public opinion had shifted in such a way that he could not win another election.

The Vietnam Women's Memorial in Washington, D.C., shows two nurses helping a wounded soldier. The memorial sculpture was erected in 1993 to honor the thousands of women who had served in the war.

1. FOCUS

Connecting to the Big Idea

See page 848B. Explain that antiwar protests grew in strength and frequency until finally President Nixon managed to bring the war to a close. Ask how opposition to the war affected the election of 1968. How did the war finally end?

Objectives

- Explain how growing opposition to the war persuaded Lyndon Johnson not to run for reelection and helped Richard Nixon become President in 1968.
- Explain how Nixon gradually replaced American troops with South Vietnamese forces but also initiated a bombing assault on Cambodia in 1970.
- Explain how American involvement in Vietnam finally ended in 1973 and describe the takeover of South Vietnam by North Vietnamese leaders.
- Describe the permanent scars left by the war in Vietnam.

Bellringer

Ask students whether it is possible for a United States President to continue a course of action strongly opposed by most of the American people. In what ways can the people make their opinions known to the President?

Reading Strategy

Predicting Content Ask students to skim the section, list the main headings and subheadings, and write a sentence or phrase predicting the content under each one. When they have finished reading the section, ask students to test their predictions against the actual text.

Reproducible Lesson Plan found in the Unit 9 folder, p. 109, provides a summary of the Section 5 lesson plan content.

Alternate Lesson Plan: Critical Thinking Testing Conclusions, found in the Alternate Lesson Plans folder, p. 160, is designed to help students apply this skill by citing evidence to support or refute a set of statements.

Guided Reading and Review found in the Unit 9 folder, p. 118, provides a structure for reading and mastering the key concepts and reviewing the key terms for Section 5. (Guided Practice)

Explain/Discuss

Ask students to list the reasons for growing opposition to the war. Ask why Lyndon Johnson could not end the war. What steps finally led to the cease-fire and withdrawal of American forces? Why did Nixon's escalation of the bombing and the invasion of Cambodia cause such outrage? Tell students that Nixon's adviser Henry Kissinger hoped that "jugular diplomacy" would force the North Vietnamese into making some concessions at the negotiating table.

Analyze

Explain that once President Nixon had determined that the United States should no longer seek victory in Vietnam, he tried to find a way to gain "peace with honor." Ask students how the Vietnamization policy seemed to placate both antiwar protesters and conservatives who did not think the United States should abandon Vietnam to its fate. Then ask students to determine how successful the policy was as a military strategy.

Caption Answer to ...

  Interpreting Tables

In December 1965, 56 percent of those polled approved of Johnson's handling of the war; by February 1968, that number had dropped to 35 percent. Between May 1966 and February 1968, the percentage of people who thought the United States had made a mistake in sending troops to Vietnam increased from 36 percent to 49 percent.

Answer to ...

MAKING CONNECTIONS

Answers will vary, but students should note that the American public obtains information from a variety of sources, including print, radio, television, online computer services, and others. The topic choices these media sources make, their analysis of issues, and their heavy use of poll-takers all influence public opinion.

Public Opinion of United States Involvement in Vietnam

"Do you approve or disapprove of the way President Johnson is handling the situation in Vietnam?"

	Approve	Disapprove	No opinion
December 1965	56%	26%	18%
May 1966	41%	37%	22%
April 1967	43%	42%	15%
July 1967	33%	52%	15%
December 1967	39%	49%	12%
February 1968*	35%	50%	15%

* During Tet Offensive

"In view of the developments since we entered the fighting in Vietnam, do you think the United States made a mistake sending troops to fight in Vietnam?"

	Yes, made mistake	No, did not	No opinion
May 1966	36%	49%	15%
April 1967	37%	50%	13%
July 1967	41%	48%	11%
February 1968†	49%	41%	10%

† After Tet Offensive

Source: *The Gallup Poll: Public Opinion 1935–1971*, by George H. Gallup

Interpreting Tables
What percentage of those polled in 1965 approved of Lyndon Johnson's handling of the war? What percentage approved in 1968? Between 1966 and 1968, what happened to the percentage of people who thought the United States should never have entered the war?

Johnson rarely left the White House near the end of his presidency for fear of being assaulted by angry, shouting crowds of protesters. He felt like "a jackrabbit in a hailstorm, hunkering up and taking it."

After watching the campaign of antiwar candidate Eugene McCarthy gain momentum in the Democratic primaries, President Johnson declared dramatically in a nationally televised speech that he would not run for another term as President. He knew that he had lost his base of support. He hoped that by ordering a pause in the relentless bombing of Vietnam he could encourage peace talks to end the war and so restore unity in the United States as he left public life. ✪

RESOURCE DIRECTORY

Teaching Resources

✪ **Primary Source Activity** LBJ Withdraws from the Race, found in the Unit 9 folder, pp. 127–128, describes the reasons behind President Johnson's decision to withdraw from the 1968 presidential race, in a passage from his memoirs.

The media—especially television—strongly influenced public opinion during the Vietnam War. What are the major issues facing the people of the United States today, and how are people's opinions on these issues affected by the media?

Richard Nixon's Approach

Eugene McCarthy's campaign faltered, and Robert Kennedy, who likewise challenged Johnson, was assassinated (see Chapter 32). Another candidate, Hubert Humphrey, eventually was nominated by the Democrats. For the Republicans, Richard Nixon ran for the presidency with the claim that he had a secret plan to end the war in Vietnam. He never divulged the details, and critics doubted that a plan really existed, but his pledge still helped secure his election over Humphrey. Once in the White House, Nixon dedicated himself to a policy of **Vietnamization,** which involved removing American forces and replacing them with South Vietnamese soldiers. Between 1968 and 1972, American troop strength dropped from 543,000 to 39,000, and opposition to the war among people in the United States declined.

Even as he moved to bring American soldiers home, Nixon himself became caught up in the war. As much as he wanted to defuse antiwar sentiment at home, he was determined not to lose the war, either. And so, as he withdrew American troops, he resumed bombing raids, keeping his actions secret from his critics. The map on page 869 shows the major targets of those bombing raids.

President Nixon also widened the war beyond the borders of Vietnam. In April 1970, he announced that United States and South Vietnamese forces were moving into neighboring Cambodia to clear out communist camps there, from which the enemy was mounting attacks on South Vietnam. The United States, he asserted, would not stand by like "a pitiful helpless giant" while the Viet Cong attacks from Cambodia went on:

We take this action not for the purpose of expanding the war into Cambodia but for the purpose of ending the war in Vietnam and winning the just peace we all desire. We have made and we will continue to make every possible effort to end this war through negotiation at the conference table rather than through more fighting on the battlefield.

His actions belied his words, however, and the move brought chaos and civil war in Cambodia and a fresh wave of protests at home.

Renewed Protests

Nixon's invasion of Cambodia in 1970 reignited the protest movement on college campuses in the United States. At **Kent State University** in Ohio, students reacted angrily to the President's action. On the weekend following his speech, they broke windows in the business district downtown and burned the army ROTC building on campus, which had become a hated symbol of the war.

In response, the governor of Ohio ordered the National Guard to Kent State. Tension mounted. When students threw rocks and empty tear gas canisters at them, the soldiers loaded their guns and donned gas masks. They knelt down and aimed their rifles at the students, as if warning them to stop. Then the guardsmen retreated to another position. At the top of a hill, they suddenly turned and began firing on the students below.

Tom Grace was a sophomore crossing campus just before the outburst. He was more than 150 feet away and thought he was keeping a safe distance from the disturbance. He was wrong:

When the National Guardsmen got to the top of the hill, all of a sudden there was just a quick movement, a flurry of activity, and then a crack, or two cracks of rifle fire, and I thought, Oh my God! I turned and started running as fast as I could. I don't think I got more than a step or two, and all of a sudden I was on the ground. It was just like somebody had come over and given me a body blow and knocked me right down. The bullet had entered my left heel and had

literally knocked me off my feet. I tried to raise myself, and I heard someone yelling, "Stay down, stay down! It's buckshot!" . . . The bullet blew the shoe right off my foot, and there was a bone sticking through my green sock. It looked like somebody had put my foot through a meat grinder.

Grace was relatively lucky. After just thirteen seconds of firing, four students lay dead, with nine others wounded. Two of the dead had been demonstrators more than 250 feet away from the soldiers. The other two were bystanders, almost 400 feet away.

A similar attack occurred at Jackson State University in Mississippi. Policemen and highway patrolmen fired into a women's dormitory there without warning. Two people were killed, and more were wounded.

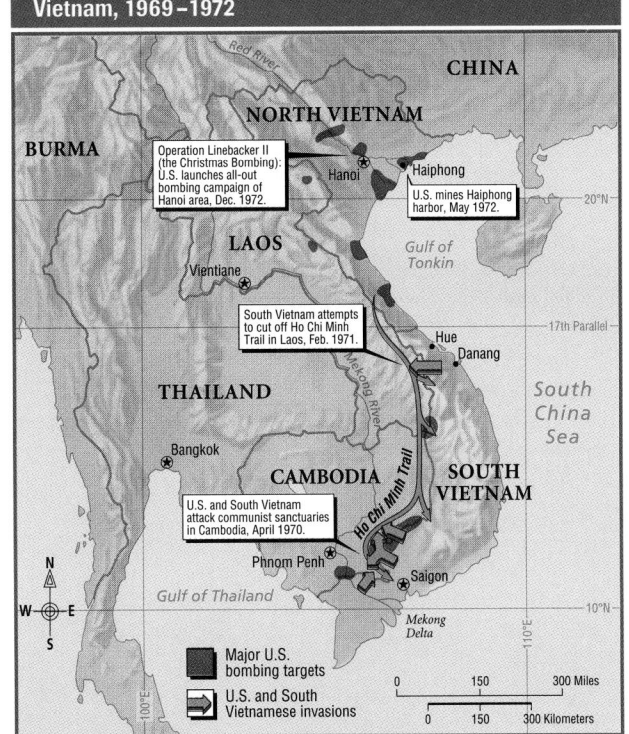

Vietnam, 1969–1972

Operation Linebacker II (the Christmas Bombing): U.S. launches all-out bombing campaign of Hanoi area, Dec. 1972.

U.S. mines Haiphong harbor, May 1972.

South Vietnam attempts to cut off Ho Chi Minh Trail in Laos, Feb. 1971.

U.S. and South Vietnam attack communist sanctuaries in Cambodia, April 1970.

Major U.S. bombing targets

U.S. and South Vietnamese invasions

 Geography and History: Interpreting Maps
According to this map, in what areas were United States bombing raids concentrated during the later years of the war? What do you think these bombing raids were supposed to accomplish?

 Activity

Making a Time Line

Ask students to make time lines identifying the major dates in the Vietnam War, starting their time lines in 1960.

Enrichment

The fate of the Americans taken prisoner during the war in Vietnam (POWs), and those missing in action (MIAs), was of great concern for years after the hostilities ended. Ask students to find out how many POWs were held in Vietnam, how many were released, and how many remained unaccounted for in the 1990s. Ask students also to find out how many MIAs are still unaccounted for.

Caption Answer to . . .

 Interpreting Maps

The later bombing raids were concentrated on the Vietnam-Cambodia border and in the Hanoi area. One goal of these raids was to cut off supplies being carried along the Ho Chi Minh Trail to the Viet Cong.

In Depth

Multicultural Perspectives

Of Americans who served in Vietnam, including professional military personnel and volunteers, the greatest percentage were draftees from minority and low-income families. In Lawrence Baskir and William Strauss's *Chance and Circumstance: The Draft, the War and the Vietnam Generation*, S. L. A. Marshall, a military historian, is quoted as saying that "in the average rifle company, the strength was 50 percent composed of Negroes, Southwestern Mexicans, Puerto Ricans, Guamians, Nisei, and so on. But a real cross-section of American youth? Almost never."

Viewpoints

The mother accuses the government of initiating the violence; the wife accuses the students of threatening the National Guard and making the violence inevitable. For a more thorough examination of the Kent State tragedy, see the Resource Directory below.

3. ASSESS

Section 5 Review Answers

1. Vietnamization, see p. 868

2. Kent State University, see p. 869

3. President Johnson decided not to run for reelection in 1968.

4. Nixon planned to gradually replace United States troops with Vietnamese troops. At the same time, he was determined not to lose the war.

5. The United States withdrew from the war in 1973. The South Vietnamese army could not hold back the North Vietnamese on their own, and the communists took control of the country in 1975.

In Depth

Then and Now

"I felt like Lady Macbeth. I couldn't get the blood of Vietnam off my hands," remembers Jean Fury, who served as a nurse in the war. "Part of me had held on, hoping that I'd be proven right, that all those sacrifices were worth something." On Veterans' Day, 1993, Fury was one of the 11,500 women who had served in Vietnam to be honored with a permanent tribute in the form of a bronze statue of two service-women in action. "I didn't realize how much your sacrifice equaled and even exceeded that of the men," said General Colin Powell at the groundbreaking ceremony for the memorial in July 1993. (See page 867.)

Viewpoints
On the Tragedy of Kent State

In May 1970, four students were killed at Kent State University when the National Guard opened fire on a crowd of antiwar protesters. *How do the following viewpoints reflect the issues that tore apart American society at that time?*

From the mother of a student
"President Nixon wants people to believe Jeff turned to violence. That is not true. What kind of sympathy is this? When four kids are dead he gave no comfort. Nixon acts as if the kids had it coming. But shooting into a crowd of students, that is violence. They say it could happen again if the Guard is threatened. They consider stones threat enough to kill children. I think the violence comes from the government."
Mother of Jeffrey Glenn Miller, one of four students killed at Kent State, quoted in *Life* magazine, May 15, 1970

From the wife of a Guardsman
"They didn't go to Kent State to kill anyone. I know he'd rather have stayed home and mowed the lawn. He told me so. He told me they didn't fire those shots to scare the students off. He told me they fired those shots because they knew the students were coming after them, coming for their guns. People are calling my husband a murderer; my husband is not a murderer. He was afraid."
Wife of a member of the National Guard, quoted in *Newsweek* magazine, May 18, 1970

Americans were horrified by these attacks. They had hoped that the rifts of the past few years between the youth of the United States and those in positions of power were starting to heal. Now the wounds were opened even wider than before.

The United States Withdraws

The war dragged on as Nixon ran for a second term as President in 1972, and South Vietnam refused to accept a proposed settlement. To reassure the South Vietnamese of continuing American concern, Nixon ordered the most intense bombing campaign of the war in the spring of 1972. The United States bombed Hanoi, the North Vietnamese capital, and mined North Vietnamese harbors. Just days before the election, National Security adviser

Henry Kissinger announced, "Peace is at hand." In January 1973, after Nixon was reelected, a cease-fire was finally signed, and United States involvement in the war came to an end.

But the civil war continued for another two years in Vietnam. After the withdrawal of United States forces, South Vietnamese soldiers steadily lost ground to their North Vietnamese enemies. In the spring of 1975, the North Vietnamese launched a campaign of strikes against strategic cities throughout South Vietnam, the final objective being the seat of government in Saigon. South Vietnamese forces crumpled in the face of this campaign. On April 29, with communist forces surrounding Saigon, the United States carried out a dramatic last-minute evacuation. More than 1,000 Americans and nearly 6,000 Vietnamese were taken from the city by helicopter to aircraft carriers waiting offshore. On April 30, the Saigon government officially surrendered to the North Vietnamese.

Legacy of the War

The Vietnam War was the longest and least successful war in which the United States had ever participated. It resulted in 58,000 Americans dead and about 300,000 wounded. It cost more than $150 billion and disrupted the American economy in the process. The costs of the war were even higher in Vietnam itself. The Vietnamese were bombarded by more bombs than had fallen on all Axis powers during World War II. The number of dead and wounded Vietnamese soldiers ran into the millions, with countless civilian casualties. The landscape itself would long reveal the scars of war. ✪

In the United States, the war also fractured the liberal consensus that had guided the nation during and after World War II. Americans had believed that they could defend the world from communism anywhere, at any time. American technology and money, they assumed, could always bring victory. That assumption was proved false in Vietnam, and the United States now had to reassess its global mission.

RESOURCE DIRECTORY

Teaching Resources

Viewpoints Activity On the Tragedy of Kent State, found in the Unit 9 folder, pp. 122–123, provides extended comments on the 1970 shooting of student protesters.

Critical Thinking Activity Drawing Conclusions: Military Spending, found in the Unit 9 folder, p. 125, charts the increase in military spending that many people thought was prolonging the Vietnam War.

The legacy of the war lingered on long after the last bomb had been dropped. Soldiers came home to a different reception than their fathers and grandfathers had in World War II. The war had been so unpopular that some of the outrage felt by antiwar Americans was transferred to the GIs who had fought in Vietnam. It was often hard for returning soldiers to rationalize their participation in Vietnam, and it was harder still to integrate themselves back into American life. Ron Kovic, who was paralyzed in the war, summed up his feelings about his smashed dreams and body in a haunting poem. He had been born on the fourth of July, a date that had once underscored his patriotism. Now it seemed a bitter joke.

*I am the living death
the memorial day on wheels
I am your yankee doodle dandy
your john wayne come home
your fourth of july firecracker
exploding in the grave*

The Vietnam Veterans Memorial in Washington, D.C., was created to recognize the courage of American GIs during the Vietnam ordeal and to help heal the wounds the war had caused. An open competition, announced in 1980, specified that the memorial should be a quiet, contemplative structure that included a list of the war dead. It was won by Maya Ying Lin, a twenty-two-year-old Chinese American architecture student.

The memorial is a starkly beautiful structure, elegant in its simplicity. It consists of two long black marble slabs, intersecting in a V shape, with all the names of the known dead inscribed chronologically according to date of death. In 1993 a Vietnam Women's Memorial was unveiled near the wall to honor the more than 11,000 women who served in Vietnam.

In 1975 Nha Trang in South Vietnam was evacuated just before communist troops took over. The man above was punched by an American official as he tried to board the last plane out, which was already overcrowded with fleeing refugees.

SECTION 5 REVIEW

Key Terms, People, and Places
1. Define Vietnamization.
2. Identify Kent State University.

Key Concepts
3. What were the political effects of growing public disapproval of the war in 1968?
4. What was Richard Nixon's approach to the war in Vietnam?
5. How did the war in Vietnam finally end?

6. What was the lasting impact of the war in Vietnam and in the United States?

Critical Thinking
7. **Determining Relevance** The counterculture of the 1960s was despised by many Americans who saw it as a senseless rejection of time-honored values. Explain how such feelings might have played a part in the violence that erupted at Kent State University in 1970.

 Quiz found in the Unit 9 folder, p. 119, covers the main ideas in this section as well as the key terms.

 Chapter Test Forms A and B are found in the Unit 9 folder, pp. 134–139.

 Answer Keys found in the Unit 9 folder, pp. 146–159, provide answers to all student activities.

Media and Technology

Transparencies
Critical Thinking, I-12; Graphic Organizer, G-4

Guided Reading Audiotapes (English and Spanish)

Computer Test Bank

In Depth

Then and Now

In February 1994 President Bill Clinton lifted the nineteen-year trade embargo on Vietnam. Senator John McCain (R–Arizona), a former prisoner of war in Vietnam, and Senator John Kerry (D–Massachusetts), a thrice-wounded, decorated Vietnam veteran, were chief sponsors of the Senate resolution to lift the trade ban. "I have made the judgment," said Clinton to critics of the action, "that the best way to ensure cooperation from Vietnam, and to continue getting the information Americans want on POWs and MIAs, is to end the trade embargo."

Chapter Review

Chapter Review Answers

Understanding Key Terms, People, and Places

Terms
Students should refer to the definitions of the key terms in the chapter to write sentences that show the relation of each word to the Vietnam War or to American society during the 1960s.

True or False
1. true
2. false, escalation
3. false, New Left
4. false, Tet Offensive
5. true

Matching
1. Saigon
2. Kent State University
3. Ngo Dinh Diem

Reviewing Main Ideas

1. Diem's government was repressive, corrupt, and did not enjoy popular support.

2. A committed cold warrior, Kennedy increased American involvement in the war by sending military aid.

3. Johnson used the Gulf of Tonkin incident as an excuse to devote increasing amounts of American money and personnel to the war and to bomb North Vietnam.

4. Many American soldiers were worried about the communist threat and wanted to do their patriotic duty. They thought that the war would be as exciting as the battles they had seen in the movies. In reality, the war was dangerous, disturbing, confusing, and frustrating.

5. Americans used saturation bombing and chemical weapons, such as Agent Orange and napalm, which had a destructive effect on civilian life in both North and South Vietnam.

6. The My Lai massacre shocked Americans at home into the realization that the course of the war was out of control.

7. Many young Americans rejected the conservative values of their parents.

8. Students demanded free speech and an end to poverty and racism. Their primary demand, however, was an end to the Vietnam War.

9. Women rejected confining clothing in favor of freer fashions; men let their hair grow long and wore beards. People wore jeans, "working people's" clothes, and colorful garments intended to convey their sense of individuality.

10. They saw the counterculture as a rejection of traditional morals and values.

11. Johnson had become so unpopular because of continuing American involvement in the Vietnam War that he could not possibly win an election.

12. Nixon bombed Cambodia in order to destroy North Vietnamese bases there.

13. North Vietnam took over South Vietnam.

14. The purpose of the memorial is to honor the American GIs who died in the war, to recognize the courage of those who returned only to become scapegoats for public anger toward government policies during the war, and to help heal the wounds that the war caused.

Understanding Key Terms, People, and Places

Key Terms
1. Viet Cong
2. Gulf of Tonkin Resolution
3. escalation
4. Tet Offensive
5. My Lai massacre
6. Students for a Democratic Society (SDS)
7. New Left
8. teach-in
9. conscientious objector
10. counterculture
11. hippie
12. psychedelic drug
13. Woodstock
14. Vietnamization

People
15. Ngo Dinh Diem

Places
16. Saigon
17. Kent State University

Terms For each term above, write a sentence that explains its relation to the Vietnam War or to American society during the 1960s.

True or False Determine whether each statement is true or false. If it is true, write "true." If it is false, change the underlined term to make the statement true.
1. People who attended Woodstock remembered the sense of fellowship they experienced there.
2. After his reelection, Johnson began the Vietnamization of the war.
3. Members of a new political movement called the Viet Cong believed that radical change was the only way to solve poverty and racism in the United States.
4. The Gulf of Tonkin Resolution included strikes on provincial and district capitals and other towns in South Vietnam.
5. The use of psychedelic drugs, which alter perceptions of reality, was part of the 1960s counterculture.

Matching Review the key people and places in the list above. If you are not sure of their significance, review the information given in the chapter. Then choose a person or place from the list that best matches each description below.
1. the site of major strikes during the Tet Offensive
2. the site of violent protests against the American invasion of Cambodia
3. the repressive prime minister of South Vietnam

Reviewing Main Ideas

Section 1 (pp. 850–853)
1. Describe the government of Ngo Dinh Diem.
2. What was President Kennedy's policy toward Vietnam in the early 1960s?
3. Describe how the Vietnam War escalated under President Johnson.

Section 2 (pp. 854–857)
4. Explain why many American soldiers were eager to go to Vietnam. Why did many feel different once they actually began to fight?
5. Why was the war so devastating for Vietnamese civilians?
6. Explain how the My Lai massacre affected the attitudes of Americans at home toward the Vietnam War.

Section 3 (pp. 858–861)
7. What was the source of the 1960s "generation gap"?

8. What were some of the changes that student activists demanded during the 1960s?

Section 4 (pp. 863–866)
9. How did the styles of dress in the 1960s reflect counterculture values of freedom and individuality?
10. Why did many Americans view the counterculture with shock and dismay?

Section 5 (pp. 867–871)
11. Why did Lyndon Johnson decide not to run for reelection in 1968?
12. Why did Richard Nixon authorize the invasion of Cambodia in 1970?
13. What happened in Vietnam after the United States withdrew?
14. What is the purpose of the Vietnam Veterans Memorial in Washington, D.C.?

Thinking Critically

1. Students' answers should demonstrate an understanding that many people's views changed from acceptance to strong disapproval over the course of the war. Factors that influenced this shift in opinion included television coverage of the brutality of war and student protests.

2. The warning cautions against becoming involved in distant conflicts that are difficult to pull out of, that consume great amounts of money and numbers of lives, and that are probably doomed to failure.

3. Possible questions: Was the reality of the war what you expected? Did you feel that you were fighting for a worthwhile cause? How were you received when you returned home?

Thinking Critically

1. **Demonstrating Reasoned Judgment** If you had been a student during the Vietnam War, do you think that your views of the conflict would have changed or remained the same throughout the course of the war? What factors might have influenced your views?

2. **Expressing Problems Clearly** Since the end of the Vietnam War, government officials have advised caution in global affairs so that the United States does not get involved in "another Vietnam." Explain what is meant by this warning.

3. **Formulating Questions** Create three questions that you might ask a soldier who fought in Vietnam that, if answered, would give some idea of what participating in the war was like.

Making Connections

1. **Evaluating Primary Sources** Review the primary source excerpt on page 852. What underlying beliefs are revealed in Johnson's statement? Did history prove his beliefs to be correct?

2. **Understanding the Visuals** A protest sign carried in a 1967 antiwar demonstration in San Francisco read, "No war on children." Find an image in the chapter that might have inspired such a slogan. In general, how do the visuals in the chapter support the idea that the 1960s were a turbulent and confusing era?

3. **Writing About the Chapter** It is 1968. Write a letter to the editor of your school newspaper explaining why you will or will not participate in the upcoming student demonstration against the Vietnam War. First, create a list of the reasons why you do or do not support the war. Note your opinion about peaceful demonstrations as a way to effect change. Next, write a draft of your letter in which you explain your point of view. Revise your letter, making certain that each idea is clearly explained. Proofread your letter and draft a final copy.

4. **Using the Graphic Organizer** This graphic organizer uses a flow map to show the sequence of events leading to the end of the Vietnam War. (a) According to the map, what was one result of Nixon's bombing of Cambodia? (b) What contradiction in Nixon's policy toward Vietnam is shown by the flow map? (c) On a separate sheet of paper, create your own flow map about the beginnings of the Vietnam War, using this graphic organizer as an example.

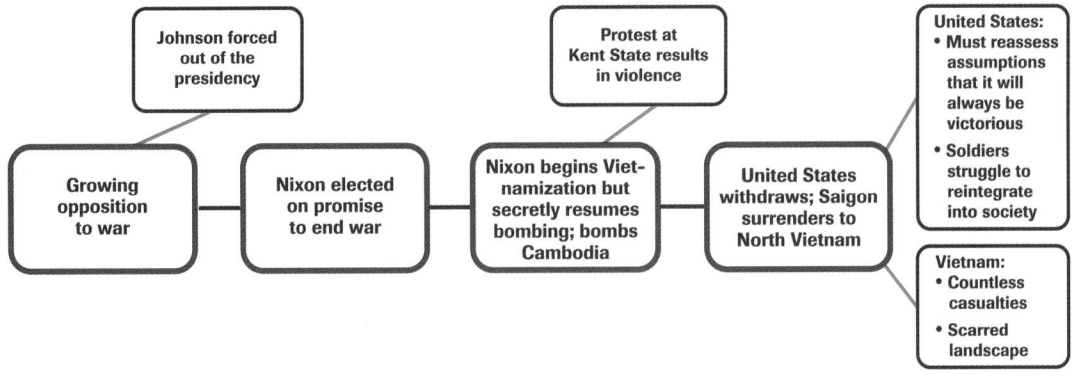

Making Connections

1. Johnson believed that communists would take over the world if the United States did not stand up to them. The collapse of communism in the Soviet Union and Eastern bloc in the early 1990s proved Johnson's assumptions wrong.

2. Possible answer: The image of the wounded Vietnamese child on page 854. The visuals in the chapter—photographs and posters of antiwar protest, a memorial sculpture, a medic trying in vain to save a dying soldier, an anguished marine, the counterculture on display at Woodstock—support the idea that the 1960s were a turbulent and confusing era.

3. Students' responses should consider reasons for supporting the war, such as stopping the threat of communism, or reasons for opposing the war, such as loss of American lives and brutality toward Vietnamese civilians.

4. (a) The bombing of Cambodia sparked protest at Kent State, which resulted in violence. (b) Nixon seemed to be pulling the United States out of the war with his policy of Vietnamization while at the same time he secretly resumed bombing raids and expanded the war beyond the borders of Vietnam by bombing Cambodia. (c) Students' graphic organizers should contain information about United States support of Ngo Dinh Diem and about the policies of Kennedy and Johnson toward Vietnam.

The United States' involvement in the Vietnam War divided the country into two angry camps: those who opposed the war and those who supported it. When the war ended and Saigon fell to the North Vietnamese, many Americans felt strongly that the years of agony and the loss of life had been in vain. Vietnam veterans returned to face anger and confusion, not the honor and gratitude of their country. Some vets were asked about the children they had killed or about their lack of success in the war. Many veterans suffered physically and mentally from the effects of the violence they had witnessed during the war. The indifference of the nation to their sacrifices only increased their stress and difficulty in becoming rehabilitated.

A change in attitude was evident when the Vietnam Veterans Memorial was unveiled in 1982 in Washington, D.C. Ask students to read the feature and to look at the personal memorials left at the "Wall." Ask students to focus on various images and discuss the significance of each to a combat soldier or to a member of a soldier's family.

Ask students to compare the items belonging to soldiers who fought in Vietnam with the artifacts from the Civil War shown on pages 356–357. Then ask students to list similar experiences common to veterans of both conflicts.

PERSONAL LEGACY

The V-shaped Vietnam Veterans Memorial, unlike most other monuments in Washington, D.C., is built on a small, human scale. Visitors find themselves drawn to its two polished black-granite walls, on which are inscribed more than 58,000 names of Americans killed and missing in the war. When this memorial opened in 1982, something unusual and unexpected began to occur: visitors left personal tokens at the base of the walls to honor and remember the soldiers who fought the war. This practice continues today. The usual gifts of flowers, wreaths, and small American flags mix with the most common items of a soldier in Vietnam—helmets, combat boots, and dog tags. Some mourners leave the items that gave soldiers comfort, such as favorite magazines, beverages, and items of clothing. A few visitors leave things, such as notes, jewelry, and stuffed animals, that carry memories of the bond between soldier and mourner. This practice continues today, and the National Park Service collects and preserves the artifacts. *What do the objects shown here tell you about the life of a combat soldier in Vietnam?*

▲ The photo above shows one of the thousands of personal memorials left beside the Vietnam Veterans Memorial in Washington, D.C.

Continuity and Change
1968–Present

Introducing the Unit

Interpreting the Visual Continuity and change are key features of American government and politics. At regular intervals, Americans have the opportunity to choose another President, to elect new legislators, and thus to change the party in power. Despite these changes, however, the government continues to function in an orderly manner, and the new President and legislators must abide by the Constitution and the traditions of government.

In 1993, when Bill Clinton, a Democrat opposed to the policies of his two Republican predecessors, Reagan and Bush, took the oath of office, the ritual of orderly transfer of power was repeated and the strength of the Republic once again reaffirmed.

Ask students to imagine that they must explain the significance of the photograph reproduced on pages 876–877 to a citizen of a nondemocratic nation. In their explanations, students should answer the following questions:
• Why is the inauguration a time for festivity and celebration?
• Why does the outgoing President attend the inauguration?
• Who can become President?

Establishing Chronology Remind students that the previous chapter focused on the politically divisive years of the Vietnam War. This unit covers four distinct political periods since 1968, beginning with the election of Richard Nixon, who resigned amid the disgrace of Watergate in 1974. From 1974 to 1980, the nation tried to recover from the damage of Watergate. Conservative Republicans again held the White House from 1980 until 1992, when Democrat Bill Clinton was elected. In the 1994 midterm election, the Republican party gained control of Congress for the first time in over 40 years.

Continuity and Change 1968–Present

"In this present crisis, government is not the solution to our problem; government is the problem."
—Ronald Reagan, 1981

By 1968 many Americans were tired of the turmoil of the sixties. The election of Richard Nixon as President that year marked the emergence of a Republican majority that lasted, with one brief exception, for more than twenty years. A long recession following the election of George Bush in 1988, however, created growing dissatisfaction with Republican policies. When Democrat Bill Clinton defeated Bush in the 1992 presidential election, Americans seemed ready to head in a new direction.

RESOURCE DIRECTORY

Teaching Resources

Local History Activity "'Boom and Bust' in Houston" and the Local Focus research topic suggestions, found in the Local History Resources folder, pp. 30–32, are designed to help students understand how history affects all lives.

Themes in American History Wall-size, illustrated posters, fou_ Teaching Resources package, illustrate unit themes.

Unit Test Forms A and B are fo_ Unit 10 folder, pp. 137–142.

With a handshake and a smile, presidential power passed from Republican George Bush to Democrat Bill Clinton on a sunny day in January 1993.

Themes in American History

Teachers may wish to discuss specific historical events in the context of historical themes. Here are four suggestions for Unit 10.

Values *A variety of religious, ethical, and moral beliefs have propelled and guided the quest of Americans for a just and ordered society.*

● President Carter introduced a foreign policy based on a moral commitment to human rights, freedom, and democracy.
● The issue of abortion stirred a debate over morality, religious beliefs, and freedom of choice.

Economics *Americans have searched for new and better ways to make a living and have struggled to define government's role in this pursuit.*

● The energy crisis of the 1970s and high rates of inflation created an unstable economy.
● Presidents Carter, Reagan, and Bush all moved toward deregulation, reducing or removing controls on industry.

Diversity *Throughout its history America has been made up of a gathering of many peoples from throughout the world. Americans have both benefited from and encountered problems with this diversity.*

● New immigrants from Asia and Latin America added to America's cultural diversity.
● The debate over multiculturalism heightened Americans' awareness of the country's diversity.

American Democracy *The concepts of democratic representation, equality under the law, and freedom from discrimination have been gradually broadened to include previously excluded groups.*

● Shock at the unethical actions represented by Watergate forced President Nixon's resignation and some reform of the presidential election process.
● The civil rights movement grew to include Latinos, Native Americans, and gays.

Media and Technology

Visions of America: Scenes of an Era To introduce students to the main idea and events covered in this unit, play "Scenes of an Era: Republican Revival and Decline" (length: 2.5 minutes). This selection can be located on side 4 of the videodiscs. This selection can also be located on videotape 5. Lesson plans for "Scenes of an Era" can be found in the Visions of America Guidebook.

Using Multimedia Technology This folder contains instructional tools and strategies for using technology in the classroom.

Transparency Binder Contains full-color transparencies with lesson suggestions. From a large collection divided into twelve categories, specific transparencies are referenced throughout the chapters at appropriate points of use. For this unit, see American Photo, B-10; Our Multicultural Heritage, C-3; Links Across Time, J-10; Political Cartoon, K-10; and Historical Maps, L-5.

Chapter 32 The Nixon Years
1968–1974

📁 **Teaching Resources** (See Unit 10 Folder)		
	Instruction	**Enrichment**
Section 1 **1968: A Turning Point in History** (pp. 880–883)	Reproducible Lesson Plan, p. 3 Alternate Lesson Plan, p. 162 Guided Reading and Review, p. 7 Quiz, p. 8	Primary Source Activity, Selling Candidate Nixon, pp. 23–24 Turning Points Extension Activity, The Lasting Impact of the Year 1968, pp. 15–16
Section 2 **The Nixon Administration** (pp. 886–891)	Reproducible Lesson Plan, p. 4 Alternate Lesson Plan, p. 163 Guided Reading and Review, p. 9 Quiz, p. 10	Visual Learning Activity, The Imperial President, p. 29 Critical Thinking Activity, Predicting Consequences, p. 22 American Profiles Activity, Maggie Kuhn, p. 17
Section 3 **Nixon's Foreign Policy** (pp. 892–896)	Reproducible Lesson Plan, p. 5 Alternate Lesson Plan, p. 164 Guided Reading and Review, p. 11 Quiz, p. 12	Primary Source Activity, The Trip to China: Diplomacy and Publicity, p. 25
Section 4 **The Watergate Scandal** (pp. 897–902)	Reproducible Lesson Plan, p. 6 Alternate Lesson Plan, p. 165 Guided Reading and Review, p. 13 Quiz, p. 14 Chapter Test, Forms A & B, pp. 31–36	Visual Learning Activity, Wanted, p. 30 American Profiles Activity, John J. Sirica, p. 18 Literature Activity, Unraveling the Story of Watergate, pp. 26–28 Viewpoints Activity, On Nixon's Impeachment, pp. 19–20 Historian's Toolbox Activity, Analyzing Presidential Records, p. 21

📁 **Additional Chapter Resources**	**Bibliography**
Resource Organizer, p. 2 Alternate Lesson Plan, p. 161 Answer Keys, pp. 143–156	**For the Teacher** Hersh, S. M. *The Price of Power: Kissinger in the Nixon White House.* Summit Books, 1983. (A critical study of Nixon's secretary of state.) Lukas, J. Anthony. *Common Ground: A Turbulent Decade in the Lives of Three American Families.* Random House, 1986. (A study of the impact of school busing on three economically diverse families.) Wills, Garry. *Nixon Agonistes: The Crisis of the Self-Made Man.* Houghton Mifflin, 1970. (A critical and probing analysis of Richard Nixon and his most famous crisis.) ***Prentice Hall Literature*** Excerpts from *The American Experience,* 1994, including Oates, Joyce Carol. "Journey," from *The Poisoned Kiss and Other Stories from the Portuguese.* Vanguard, 1975.

THE BIG IDEA

The Big Idea for the chapter and how the main ideas in each section relate to the Big Idea are graphically displayed below. Comprehension of this chapter's Big Idea is critical to students' understanding of United States history and how we as a nation got where we are today.

Media and Technology

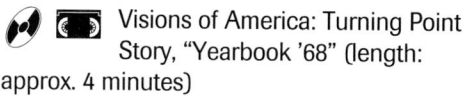 Visions of America: Turning Point Story, "Yearbook '68" (length: approx. 4 minutes)

 Visions of America: Roundtable Discussion on "Yearbook '68"

 Time Lines, E-9

 Critical Thinking, I-14

 Graphic Organizer, G-4

 Guided Reading Audiotapes (English and Spanish)

 Computer Test Bank

For the Student

The Right Stuff. Warner Communications, 1983. Film/Video. (Award–winning look at astronauts, based on Tom Wolfe's best-seller.)

All the President's Men. Warner Home Video, 1976. Video. (Fast-paced depiction of *Washington Post* reporters Bob Woodward and Carl Bernstein and the story they uncovered about the Watergate break-in.)

CHAPTER 32

A series of tumultuous events in 1968 helped pave the way for the presidency of Richard Nixon and a twenty-year era of almost uninterrupted Republican control of the White House. The new President's domestic and foreign policies marked a shift in national politics. But Nixon's leadership style led to scandal and his own shattering downfall.

SECTION 1

In 1968, events in Vietnam and assassinations at home ripped the nation and the Democrats apart. Nixon and the Republicans took advantage of the chaos to win the White House.

SECTION 2

Nixon adopted a conservative approach to domestic policies. From the economy, to crime, to race relations, Nixon tried to take the nation in a new direction.

SECTION 3

Nixon used his credentials as a tough anticommunist to forge new, positive relationships with China and the Soviet Union. The President relied heavily on adviser Henry Kissinger.

SECTION 4

The President's willingness to exploit presidential power for personal political aims led to scandal. Nixon himself was tainted and forced to resign.

878B

The Nixon Years
1968–1974

The Relevance of the Big Idea

In 1968, voters in the United States elected Richard Nixon, ushering in an era of Republican dominance in national politics. Nixon's policies at home and abroad marked a shift from the Democratic policies that began with the New Deal and continued through most of the 1960s. Though Nixon himself was undone by his personal failings, his Republican successors generally followed a similar political line.

In the 1990s, the nation appears to be considering another shift in political direction. In 1992, voters put Democrat Bill Clinton in the White House; it remained to be seen whether this election marks a lasting shift similar to the one the nation experienced in 1968. Ask students if they can identify a significant change in the direction of the country in the 1990s compared with the 1980s.

In Depth
Global Connections

Richard Nixon forged an active and bold foreign policy. Besides rebuilding relations with China and making peace in Vietnam, he turned his attention to the explosive Middle East. During the Arab-Israeli war of 1973, Secretary of State Henry Kissinger helped engineer a cease-fire, then traveled back and forth between countries trying to work out a peace treaty. The success of this "shuttle diplomacy" was limited but it did result in Egypt and Israel's agreement to pull back their troops and establish a buffer zone between them. By the 1990s, shuttle diplomacy had become an established way of negotiating disputes between nations.

The Nixon Years
1968–1974

*A*merican politics shifted dramatically in 1968, as violence and confrontation divided the country. Republican Richard Nixon capitalized on the disruption to gain the presidency. In office, Nixon was mainly interested in foreign affairs, and he took bold steps in changing relations with China and the Soviet Union. The Watergate scandal, involving Nixon's 1972 reelection campaign, angered Americans and forced Nixon to an action never before taken by a United States President.

Events in the United States

1968	1969	1970	1971
1968 Martin Luther King, Jr., and Robert Kennedy are assassinated. • Violence disrupts the Democratic National Convention.	**1969** Richard Nixon is sworn in as President. • United States astronauts land on the moon.	**1970** Four Kent State University students are killed by the Ohio National Guard at an antiwar protest.	**1971** The Supreme Court allows school busing for desegregation.

Events in the World

1968	1969	1970	1971
1968 Pierre Trudeau is elected prime minister of Canada.	**1969** Civil war continues in Nigeria.		**1971** China is admitted to the United Nations. • Idi Amin seizes power in Uganda and begins a reign of terror.

RESOURCE DIRECTORY

Teaching Resources

Alternate Lesson Plan: Demonstrating the Big Idea found in the Alternate Lesson Plans folder, p. 161, provides a lesson strategy to instruct students about the Big Idea that Republican President Richard Nixon's policies signaled a shift in national politics, but Nixon's leadership style ultimately led to scandal and personal ruin.

Alternative Assessment Handbook provides information, guidance, and strategies for alternative methods of assessment. It includes an essay on new trends in assessment, guidance and strategies for developing performance tasks and portfolios, scoring rubrics, and sample evaluation forms.

Pages 880–883
1968: A Turning Point in History
A crisis-filled year of assassinations, antiwar protest, and violence polarized the country in 1968. The turmoil paved the way for the election of Richard Nixon and the emergence of a Republican majority in national politics.

Pages 884–885
The Lasting Impact of the Year 1968

Pages 886–891
The Nixon Administration
Having gained the presidency, Richard Nixon was determined to maintain his power at all costs. He kept tight control of his administration and took a conservative direction on the national front.

Pages 892–896
Nixon's Foreign Policy
Nixon's main interest was in foreign affairs, where he made significant changes. Working closely with Henry Kissinger, he took dramatic steps toward new relationships with both China and the Soviet Union.

Pages 897–902
The Watergate Scandal
Richard Nixon was willing to use presidential power to do whatever was necessary to remain in the White House. Eventually this approach compromised the presidency itself. The resulting Watergate scandal angered the nation and moved Nixon to take drastic steps.

MR. PRESIDENT:
RELEASE the TAPES!

1972	1973	1974	1975	1976
1972 Nixon visits China. • Break-in at Democratic headquarters sets off the Watergate scandal.	*1973 The Senate begins investigating the Watergate affair.* • Spiro Agnew resigns as Vice President.	*1974 Nixon resigns the presidency.* • Vice President Gerald Ford becomes President.	*1975 White House aides go to jail for Watergate crimes.*	
1972 SALT I treaty between the United States and the Soviet Union limits nuclear weapons.	*1973 The fourth Arab-Israeli war begins on Yom Kippur.* • OPEC places embargo on oil shipments.	*1974 Writer Alexander Solzhenitsyn is exiled from the Soviet Union.*	*1975 Civil war begins in Lebanon.* • Mozambique wins independence from Portugal.	

SECTION 1

1968: A Turning Point in History

See page 878B.

1. FOCUS

1968: A Turning Point in History

Connecting to the Big Idea

See page 878B. Explain to students that in 1968 the American people endured a series of traumatic shocks, shaking the nation's faith in itself. Americans seemed interested in changing direction politically. Ask students how the Republicans and Richard Nixon took advantage of these changing attitudes.

Objectives

● Identify the Tet Offensive and its impact on American attitudes toward the Vietnam War.
● Explain the impact of the assassinations of Dr. Martin Luther King, Jr., and Robert Kennedy.
● Describe the events at the Democratic National Convention in Chicago and their effect on Democrats.
● Explain how public reaction against violence helped Republican Richard Nixon win the presidency.

Bellringer

Ask students to imagine the following situation: The United States is losing a war and violence is breaking out in cities across the country. How might the nation react under such circumstances? Who would be held responsible for the state of affairs?

Reading Strategy

Finding Evidence Ask students to jot down facts as they read the section supporting the idea stated on page 880 that 1968 was "the most shattering year" of the 1960s.

1968: A Turning Point in History

LBJ's political career is crushed in "The Time Machine," shown in this 1967 British cartoon.

SECTION PREVIEW

A crisis-filled year of assassinations, antiwar protest, and violence polarized the country in 1968. The turmoil paved the way for the election of Richard Nixon and the emergence of a Republican majority in national politics.

Key Concepts
• The Tet Offensive increased protests over American involvement in Vietnam.
• The assassinations of Dr. Martin Luther King, Jr., and Robert Kennedy increased divisions in the country.
• Violence at the Democratic presidential convention polarized people politically and caused disunity in the party.
• Reaction against violence helped Republican Richard Nixon win the presidency.

Key Terms, People, and Places
Poor People's Campaign; Robert F. Kennedy, Eugene McCarthy, Hubert Humphrey, George C. Wallace, Richard M. Nixon, Spiro Agnew

I n the troubled decade of the 1960s, perhaps the most shattering year was 1968. A series of tragic events hit with such force that, month by month, the nation seemed to be coming apart. In the midst of the turmoil—and, in part, as a result of it—the way was paved for the election of Richard Nixon and the emergence of a Republican majority in national politics that would last for the next twenty years. The nation experienced an emotional shift as well as a political one. Against a backdrop of domestic violence, chaos, and confrontation, many Americans saw as hopeless the chance of achieving peaceful social change through political activism.

The Tet Offensive Increases Antiwar Sentiment at Home

The Vietnam War continued to rage in 1968. One encounter during the war had a profound effect on the American people and made 1968 a turning point in the conflict.

Beginning on January 30, the Viet Cong launched a massive three-week surprise attack against South Vietnam. While the Tet Offensive, as this attack was called, ended in military defeat for North Vietnam, it caused more and more Americans to question whether winning the Vietnam War was possible. After three years of escalation under the Johnson administration, many Americans wondered what had been achieved if the enemy could mount such a blistering offensive. Television news coverage of Tet increased the impact the attack had on the American public. Millions watched as news anchor Walter Cronkite, known for his objective viewpoint, said in February, "It now seems more certain than ever that the bloody experience in Vietnam is to end in stalemate."

After Tet, public opinion polls showed that a majority of Americans opposed the war. From a military perspective, Tet was a major defeat for the Viet Cong. But from a political perspective, it was a major defeat for the United States—and for the Johnson administration.

Popular Leaders Fall to Violence

For many Americans, the memory of President John F. Kennedy's assassination in 1963 was still vivid and haunting five years later. They looked to other leaders to carry on the spirit and idealism of the Kennedy years. But in 1968, people's hopes were again shattered by the burst of bullets from assassins' guns.

Tragedy Strikes The major spokesperson for African Americans in the decade after 1955 was Martin Luther King, Jr. By the mid-1960s,

RESOURCE DIRECTORY

Teaching Resources

Reproducible Lesson Plan found in the Unit 10 folder, p. 3, provides a summary of the Section 1 lesson plan content.

Alternate Lesson Plan: Cooperative Learning found in the Alternate Lesson Plans folder, p. 162, guides groups of students in identifying the events that made 1968 a turning point in history, by creating photo captions for a TV documentary on that year.

Guided Reading and Review found in the Unit 10 folder, p. 7, provides a structure for reading and mastering the key concepts and reviewing the key terms for Section 1. (Guided Practice)

King, convinced that poverty bred violence, broadened his crusade to attack all economic injustice.

In 1968 King began the **Poor People's Campaign,** planning a march on Washington like that in 1963. Traveling around the United States to mobilize support, he went to Memphis, Tennessee, in early April to support striking garbage workers seeking better working conditions. On April 3, King spoke eloquently, referring to threats made against his life:

Seconds after shots ring out, Martin Luther King lies mortally wounded, while companions point frantically to the direction from which the shots were fired.

W*e've got some difficult days ahead. But it doesn't matter with me now, because I've been to the mountain top. And I don't mind. Like anybody, I would like to live a long life. . . . But I'm not concerned about that now. I just want to do God's will. And He's allowed me to go up to the mountain. And I've looked over. And I've seen the promised land.*

The next day, as King stood on the balcony of his motel, a shot from a high-powered rifle ripped through his jaw. An hour later, King was dead.

King's assassination sparked violent reactions across the nation. In an outburst of rage and frustration, some African Americans rioted, setting fires and looting stores in 124 cities. Riots and police responses left forty-five people dead. President Johnson ordered flags on federal buildings to be flown at half-mast to honor King, but it took more than 5,500 troops to quell the violence. For many Americans of all races, the death of King eroded faith in the idea of nonviolent change.

Another Leader Falls Robert F. Kennedy, who had served his brother John as attorney general, was now running for President himself. Earlier in the year, in March, Senator **Eugene McCarthy** of Minnesota had come out against the war and challenged Lyndon Johnson in the New Hampshire Democratic primary. When McCarthy did well—42 percent to the President's 49 percent—Kennedy saw that

Johnson was vulnerable and entered the campaign himself. Kennedy's bid received a critical boost later that month when, on March 31, LBJ addressed the American people on television. After announcing that he had ordered a reduction in the bombing of North Vietnam as a step toward furthering peace negotiations, Johnson stunned the nation by saying he would not run for a second term as President.

In the years since his brother's death, Bobby Kennedy had reached out to many Americans—Chicanos in the California fields, Native Americans in the Southwest, African Americans in the Mississippi delta, poor white families in New York tenements. Morally and politically opposed to the Vietnam War, he condemned the killing of both Americans and Vietnamese. And he criticized the Johnson administration for financing a war instead of the programs needed to help the poor and disadvantaged at home.

Kennedy spent the spring of 1968 battling McCarthy in the Democratic primary elections. In June he won a key victory in California's primary. But on the evening of the primary, after giving his victory speech, Robert Kennedy was shot by an assassin and died a day later.

When the shooting was reported, several campaign workers who had watched the speech

2. INSTRUCT

Explain/Discuss

Explain that the 1960s was a time of great political and social upheaval. Discuss the impact of the Tet Offensive. Encourage discussion by asking students why Tet made many Americans feel that they had been misled about the struggle in Vietnam.

Ask students to explain why the deaths of Robert Kennedy and Martin Luther King, Jr., led many to feel that their hopes for the future were disappearing. Why were these acts of violence a signal to many of a major social development?

Analyze

Ask students to examine the election of 1968 and explain how the Republicans benefited from the events taking place in the United States and in the Democratic party. Ask students if they think people generally hold a political party responsible for events in the country.

📐 Activity

Writing a Letter to the Editor

Ask each student to assume the role of a Republican party official in 1968 and to write a letter to a newspaper editor encouraging voters to support Republican candidates in the 1968 elections.

TURNING POINTS

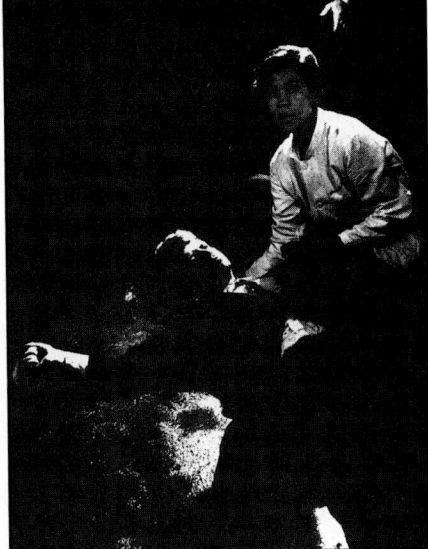

Busboy Juan Romero was the first to reach Robert Kennedy after he was shot in a hotel kitchen just after winning the California primary.

on TV were waiting for Kennedy in his Los Angeles hotel room. One of them, civil rights leader John Lewis, later said, "We all just fell to the floor and started crying. To me that was like the darkest, saddest moment." In a 1987 statement, Lewis also described the funeral journey to Arlington National Cemetery and reflected on the killings that had shattered the country:

> *All along the way, you saw people coming up to the train crying and these hand-made signs saying, "We love you, Bobby," "Goodbye, Bobby," "God bless you, Bobby," and so forth. . . . Something was taken from us. The type of leadership that we had in a sense invested in, that we had helped to make and to nourish, was taken from us.*

Kennedy's death ended many people's hopes for reform or reconciliation.

MAKING CONNECTIONS

Many people who lived through the 1960s would agree with John Lewis that the country lost its sense of hope after the assassinations. Do you think that people in the United States today have regained a sense of hope?

The 1968 Democratic Convention

By the time the Democrats convened in Chicago that summer, the party was in shreds. Eugene McCarthy was still a prominent antiwar candidate, but party regulars thought he was too far from the mainstream. They supported Vice President **Hubert Humphrey,** who had long been a strong advocate of social justice and civil rights.

Humphrey, however, was hurt by his support of administration policies on Vietnam. In the face of growing antiwar protest, he hardly seemed the one to bring the party together. Robert Kennedy, the one candidate who might have succeeded, was dead.

"The Whole World Is Watching" The prospect of thousands of demonstrators at the Democratic convention—radicals, peace marchers, hippies—enraged Chicago mayor Richard J. Daley. He had the convention hall protected by barbed wire and chain-link fencing. He also ordered police to clear out protesters gathered in Lincoln Park along the lake shore. As the police went in with tear gas and clubs, several violent confrontations took place.

The climax came as the delegates voted down a peace resolution and seemed ready to nominate Humphrey. As thousands of protesters gathered for a rally near the convention hotel, the police moved in, using their nightsticks to club anyone on the street, including passersby, hotel guests, and reporters.

Historian Theodore H. White, the even-handed chronicler of presidential elections, recorded the scene this way:

> *Slam! Like a fist jolting, like a piston exploding from its chamber, comes a hurtling column of police . . . into the intersection, and all things happen too fast: first the charge as the police wedge cleaves through the mob; then screams, whistles, confusion . . . And as the scene clears, there are little knots in the open clearing—police clubbing youngsters, police dragging youngsters, police rushing them by the elbows, their heels dragging, to patrol wagons . . .*

 RESOURCE DIRECTORY

Teaching Resources

Primary Source Activity "Selling" Candidate Nixon, found in the Unit 10 folder, pp. 23–24, uses transcripts of commercials from Richard Nixon's presidential campaign to show how Nixon appealed to the voters' feelings through television.

Much of the violence took place in front of television cameras, while crowds chanted "The whole world is watching." As convention delegates voted, Senator Abraham Ribicoff of Connecticut denounced the "Gestapo tactics on the streets of Chicago," provoking an angry scene with Daley. Humphrey was nominated, but the party had been torn apart.

Wallace Woos Voters Adding to the Democrats' problems was a third-party candidate in the race. Alabama governor **George C. Wallace** had gained national fame for playing on racial tensions among southerners. Now he turned to blue-collar voters in the North who resented campus radicals and liberal antiwar forces. Wallace won support by attacking "left-wing theoreticians, briefcase-totin' bureaucrats, ivory-tower guideline writers, bearded anarchists, smart-aleck editorial writers and pointy-headed professors."

The Election of 1968

The Republicans chose **Richard M. Nixon,** who had narrowly lost to John Kennedy in 1960. In his campaign, Nixon backed law and order and claimed to have a secret plan to end the war in Vietnam. Earlier, Nixon had often seemed harsh and angry, but this time he let his running mate, Governor **Spiro Agnew** of Maryland,

Determined to stop protests at the 1968 Democratic Convention, Chicago police and National Guardsmen used nightsticks, tear gas, and rifles against demonstrators and others who were caught up in the violence.

deliver nasty rhetoric, such as calling Humphrey "squishy soft" on communism.

Nixon's campaign was well run and well financed. Late in the campaign, Humphrey began to catch up. But even though President Johnson stopped the bombing of North Vietnam on October 31, it was too late. Many disillusioned Democrats stayed home on election day, voting for no one.

In the popular vote, Nixon squeaked by with only 43.4 percent—less than one percentage point ahead of Humphrey's 42.7 percent. Wallace won the rest. Although Democrats kept control of both houses of Congress, the Republicans were back in the White House.

SECTION 1 REVIEW

Key Terms, People, and Places
1. Define Poor People's Campaign.
2. Identify (a) Robert F. Kennedy, (b) Eugene McCarthy, (c) Hubert Humphrey, (d) George C. Wallace, (e) Richard M. Nixon, (f) Spiro Agnew.

Key Concepts
3. How did the Tet Offensive contribute to the turbulence of 1968?

4. What were some aftereffects of the assassination of Martin Luther King, Jr.?
5. From what groups did Wallace try to attract support?
6. What issues did Nixon emphasize in his campaign?

Critical Thinking
7. **Recognizing Cause and Effect** How did the assassination of Robert Kennedy affect the chances of the Democrats in the 1968 presidential election?

Quiz found in the Unit 10 folder, p. 8, covers the main ideas in this section as well as the key terms.

Media and Technology

Transparency
Time Lines, E-9

3. ASSESS

Section 1 Review Answers
1. Poor People's Campaign, see p. 881
2. (a) Robert F. Kennedy, see p. 881,
(b) Eugene McCarthy, see p. 881,
(c) Hubert Humphrey, see p. 882,
(d) George C. Wallace, see p. 883,
(e) Richard M. Nixon, see p. 883,
(f) Spiro Agnew, see p. 883

3. Since the enemy was able to mount such a successful attack in spite of escalation during the Johnson administration, many Americans began to question the possibility of winning the war. Also, television news coverage of Tet increased the awareness of the American public.

4. It destroyed people's confidence in the possibility of peaceful reform, convinced many African Americans that nonviolence did not work, and caused angry riots in many American cities.

5. White conservative southerners, northern blue-collar Democrats.

6. He tried to appeal to conservatives and blue-collar workers, emphasizing law and order and an end to unrest; he promised a plan to end the war in Vietnam.

7. It hurt Democratic chances; antiwar supporters found it hard to support Humphrey; Kennedy was probably the only candidate who could have united the party.

Reteach

Have students create a time line of the events of 1968. Students should be able to explain the significance of each event they include.

4. CLOSE

Reinforcing the Big Idea
The traumatic events of 1968 revealed the deep divisions in the nation and helped clear the way for a Republican victory. The next section examines the domestic policies introduced by President Richard Nixon as he sought to lead the country in a more conservative direction.

The Lasting Impact of the Year 1968

Focus Events of the year 1968 helped lead to a shift in the direction of the nation's domestic and foreign policies. Attitudes toward the nation's use of military power changed dramatically, and the government sharply reduced its commitment to social programs. Ask students to describe how the events of 1968 helped to shape the political world in which they live today.

Instruct Remind students that the war in Vietnam had resulted from an aggressive policy, which many Americans supported, of resisting communist expansion around the world. The failure of the United States in Vietnam gave the nation reason to question that policy. The failure also caused people to question the authority of the President alone to commit the nation to armed conflict. Ask students to review Article I, Section 8, Clause 11, and Article II, Section 2, Clause 1, of the Constitution. In what ways do these two clauses leave open the question of whether or not a President alone can commit the nation to war?

Review also with students massive government programs such as the New Deal and the Great Society, which greatly expanded government's role in people's lives. Following the election of 1968, the federal government slowly retreated from some of those programs. After Ronald Reagan was elected President in 1980, many social programs were drastically cut. Ask students to discuss current attitudes toward government support for programs such as welfare, social security, or health care.

Extend Have students work in pairs to research and prepare a report on the War Powers Act. Students should research the congressional debate on this act, and examine the ongoing debate over the constitutionality of the War Powers Act, particularly in the Reagan and Bush administrations. Students can present their findings in an oral or written report.

The Lasting Impact of the Year 1968

The year 1968 was a turning point in American political life, bringing a shift in the direction of both foreign and domestic policies. The turmoil of the year also had a psychological impact on many people.

Foreign Policy Attitudes

The turbulence sparked by Vietnam, which reached a peak in 1968, destroyed the nation's consensus on foreign policy. Now many Americans wondered whether they could—or should—support the aims of the United States around the world. Questions about Vietnam would haunt the country for decades.

Presidential War Powers Opposition to the war also brought a challenge to the President's powers as commander in chief. Many Americans were disturbed by the way Lyndon Johnson had maneuvered the United States into Vietnam and by Nixon's order to bomb Cambodia, thereby escalating the war. The War Powers Act, passed over Nixon's veto in 1973, required the President to notify Congress quickly if troops were sent overseas. The act then required congressional approval of such troop movements.

The war powers issue continued to cause controversy. In the Reagan administration, for example, members of Congress filed lawsuits to stop military actions in Central America and on the island of Grenada. The question arose again in 1990 when President George Bush sent American troops to Kuwait after the Iraqi invasion. Bush finally asked for—and got—Congress's approval of the Persian Gulf War.

1977 When Jimmy Carter won the presidency, he served as a lone Democrat in the midst of over twenty years of Republicans in the White House.

1980	1982	1984

1984 Despite protests from members of Congress, President Reagan orders military action in Grenada.

 RESOURCE DIRECTORY

Teaching Resources

Turning Points Extension Activity
The Lasting Impact of the Year 1968, found in the Unit 10 folder, pp. 15–16, focuses on the election of President Nixon as a turning point in U.S. relations with communist powers.

Changes at Home

In domestic affairs, the events of 1968 brought significant change, both political and social. As the war eroded many "Great Society" programs, conservative Americans challenged the entire liberal approach toward government assistance for those in need. Since Franklin Roosevelt's New Deal in the 1930s, the range of social programs had grown. Few people wanted to eliminate programs like social security or Medicare, but Republicans were committed to cutting back the role of government. Winning the White House in 1968 gave them the chance to do so. Their successors went even further—in particular, the Reagan administration in the 1980s drastically cut funds for social programs.

The 1968 election also brought an end to the Democratic domination of national politics that had lasted for more than thirty years. Joined together by President Roosevelt in 1936, the party included working-class Americans, first- and second-generation immigrants, and African Americans. The events of 1968 split that group. What followed was seen by some analysts as an emerging Republican majority. Although a Democrat won the White House in 1976, Republicans won the presidency in every other election from 1980 to 1988. In congressional politics, Republicans encouraged the growth of a new conservative movement, reflected in legislation and in several significant decisions by the Supreme Court.

Emotionally, the violence of 1968 also left its mark on the nation, ending what for many had been an era of idealism. After Bobby Kennedy's death, civil rights worker John Lewis said:

> There are people today who are afraid, in a sense, to hope or to have hope again, because of what happened in 1963, and particularly what happened in 1968.

REVIEWING THE FACTS

1. What groups were included in the old Democratic party?
2. What was the significance of Richard Nixon's victory in 1968?

Critical Thinking

3. **Identifying Assumptions** Why did Congress believe it was necessary to pass the War Powers Act in 1973?

1980s Republicans continued their push for a new conservative movement with Supreme Court nominations that moved the Court to the right.

1991 The question of presidential war powers arose again when President George Bush sent troops to the Persian Gulf.

1986 **1988** **1990**

1989 As social programs were cut back during the years of Republican government, homelessness and other local problems increased.

SECTION 2

The Nixon Administration

See page 878B.

1. FOCUS

Connecting to the Big Idea

See page 878B. Explain that as President, Nixon employed a closed, secretive style in his effort to steer the nation in a more conservative direction than had his Democratic predecessors. Ask how Nixon's style influenced his presidency.

Objectives

● Describe Nixon's reserved, secretive style and how it influenced his administration.
● Explain how Nixon sought to take a more conservative stance with regard to economic policies and crime.
● Explain how Nixon tried to slow the pace of civil rights advances as part of an effort to win white support in the South.

Bellringer

Write the word *leadership* on the chalkboard. Ask students to brainstorm a list of words and ideas they associate with this term. Explain that Nixon, upon taking office, exercised a new type of leadership.

Reading Strategy

Reinforcing Key Ideas Have students write two column headings on a piece of paper: Nixon's Personality and Nixon's Domestic Policies. As they read the section, students should write words and details describing Nixon's personal traits and his policies in the appropriate column.

SECTION PREVIEW

Having gained the presidency, Richard Nixon was determined to maintain his power at all costs. He kept tight control of his administration and took a conservative direction on the national front.

Key Concepts

• Nixon's reserved, secretive personality influenced his staff and his style of governing.
• Nixon tried to take a more conservative stance in dealing with the economy and with issues such as law and order.
• Nixon slowed the advancement of civil rights with his policies, aimed in part at winning support in the South.

Key Terms, People, and Places

imperial presidency, Organization of Petroleum Exporting Countries (OPEC), embargo, busing; Henry A. Kissinger, H. R. Haldeman, John Ehrlichman, John Mitchell

This crocheted replica of the presidential seal was sent to President Nixon by a well-wisher early in his presidency.

R ichard Nixon had struggled hard during a twenty-year political career mixed with setbacks and successes. He suffered a number of bitter defeats but came back to national politics each time. Having worked hard to gain the presidency, he was determined to maintain strict control over his administration.

Nixon in Person

Richard Nixon was a shy and remote man. Although uncomfortable with people, he put up a front when he campaigned, and he used new techniques such as television to good advantage. He often seemed stiff and lacking in humor and charm, however. Many Americans respected Nixon for his abilities and his skillful handling of the vice presidency under Eisenhower, but many others neither trusted nor liked him.

Nixon's family was poor, and he never got over his sense of being an outsider. In 1963 he described how that feeling drove him to achieve:

W*hat starts the process really are laughs and slights and snubs when you are a kid. Sometimes it's because you're poor or Irish or Jewish or Catholic or ugly or simply that you are skinny. But if you are reasonably intelligent and if your anger is deep enough and strong enough, you learn that you can change those attitudes by excellence, personal gut performance.*

According to Pat Buchanan, then a Nixon speech writer, there was "a mean side to his nature." He was willing to say or do anything to defeat his enemies. Adlai Stevenson, who ran

Despite his shy personality, Nixon knew how to play a crowd and often put on an "imperial" aspect when appearing in public.

RESOURCE DIRECTORY

Teaching Resources

Reproducible Lesson Plan found in the Unit 10 folder, p. 4, provides a summary of the Section 2 lesson plan content.

Alternate Lesson Plan: Critical Thinking Identifying Assumptions, found in the Alternate Lesson Plans folder, p. 163, is designed to promote understanding of how political considerations and concerns for reelection can influence policy.

Guided Reading and Review found in the Unit 10 folder, p. 9, provides a structure for reading and mastering the key concepts and reviewing the key terms for Section 2. (Guided Practice)

Visual Learning Activity The Imperial President, found in the Unit 10 folder, p. 29, depicts what some people termed Nixon's "imperial presidency" in two humorous posters from the early 1970s.

unsuccessfully for the presidency twice in the 1950s, spoke of a place called "Nixonland—a land of slander and scare, of sly innuendo, of a poison pen, the anonymous phone call, and hustling, pushing, shoving—the land of smash and grab and anything to win."

Nixon had few close friends, insulating himself from people and the press. He took support and security from his family—his wife, Pat, and their two daughters. Away from the White House, he secluded himself at his estates in Florida and California, both lavishly redone at government expense. He dreamed of what historian Arthur Schlesinger, Jr., has called an **imperial presidency,** meaning an executive branch that dominates the branches of government to an extreme degree. By his own choice, his administration reflected a closed, secretive style. ✪

The Oval Office in the White House saw many meetings of Nixon and his inner circle of close advisers—here, left to right, are Kissinger, Ehrlichman, the President, and Haldeman.

Nixon's Top Staff People

Nixon's staff gave him support and loyalty. His cabinet members were all wealthy, white, male Republicans, sympathetic to his views. Yet Nixon generally worked around his cabinet and more often relied on a few other key appointees for advice.

One was **Henry A. Kissinger,** a Harvard government professor, who joined the Nixon administration as head of the National Security Council and in 1973 became Nixon's secretary of state. He played a major role in shaping foreign policy, both as an adviser to the President and in behind-the-scenes diplomacy.

Two influential staff members shielded Nixon from the outside world and carried out his orders. **H. R. Haldeman,** an advertising executive who had campaigned tirelessly for Nixon, became chief of staff. He once observed, "I get done what he wants done and I take the heat instead of him."

Lawyer **John Ehrlichman** served first as legal counselor, then rose to the post of chief domestic adviser. He and Haldeman framed issues and narrowed options for the President. Together they became known as the "Berlin Wall" for the way they protected Nixon's privacy.

Finally, there was **John Mitchell,** a lawyer who had worked with Nixon in New York and then managed his campaign. He was named attorney general and wielded great influence, speaking with Nixon several times a day. White House staff members called Mitchell "El Supremo" for his stature as a top aide.

MAKING CONNECTIONS

A President's personality can greatly affect the style and actions of an administration. What kind of personalities have recent Presidents such as Reagan, Bush, and Clinton had?

Domestic Policy Issues: A Different Direction

The Vietnam War and domestic issues had both been important in the 1968 political campaigns. Domestically, Nixon took a different course than his Democratic predecessors.

2. INSTRUCT

Explain/Discuss

Explain that in the domestic area, Nixon pursued a conservative direction—one that favored the existing power structure. This proved most difficult in the realm of economics, where inflation caused by war spending forced Nixon to act contrary to his stated goals. Explain that the oil crisis further aggravated the nation's economic problems. Discuss how many aspects of the nation's economy depend on petroleum. Ask students what might happen if fuel prices rose suddenly today.

Explain that Nixon was more successful in instituting conservative policies in the area of social programs and law and order. Discuss Nixon's campaign position that programs such as welfare and aid to the poor discouraged welfare recipients from working. Do students agree or disagree? Review also Nixon's position on law and order. Ask students if government should actively oppose people who protest against the government.

Answer to ...

MAKING CONNECTIONS

Students are likely to characterize all three recent Presidents as outgoing; current events and media coverage will influence other ideas.

Ask students to read Nixon's words quoted on page 886. Ask how Nixon's personal characteristics and the qualities he valued in his aides are exemplified in this quote. Ask how these qualities may have both helped and hurt his presidency.

Activity

Understanding Points of View

Have students reread Nixon's views and statements on student protests quoted on pages 889–890. Then ask students to respond in a brief essay explaining whether or not they share Nixon's views. Students' essays should explore their understanding of the proper role of protest in a democratic society.

Caption Answer to ...

 Interpreting Graphs

Early in 1974; the peak was very brief and prices quickly and steadily declined until 1975.

Economic Problems The economy was shaky when Nixon took office. Largely because of spending for the Vietnam War, inflation had doubled between 1965 and 1968. At the same time, unemployment continued to grow. Nixon's first priority was to halt inflation. He felt that federal spending had gotten out of control and wanted to cut back, even if it led to further unemployment.

At the same time, he was determined to avoid economic controls. He had seen such controls in action while working for the Office of Price Administration during World War II. "I will not take the nation down the road of wage and price controls, however politically expedient they may seem," he said in 1970.

During his first few years in office, however, controlling spending proved difficult. Both unemployment and inflation continued to rise. Lawrence O'Brien, head of the Democratic National Committee, called the new situation "Nixonomics":

> All the things that should go up—the stock market, corporate profits, real spendable income, productivity—go down, and all the things that should go down—unemployment, prices, interest rates—go up.

Although Republicans traditionally aimed for a balanced budget, Nixon began to consider deficit spending—spending beyond the budget in order to stimulate the economy. This was the approach that

English economist John Maynard Keynes had called for during the Depression and that many Democrats had supported. "I am now a Keynesian in economics," Nixon announced in 1971, to the surprise of many.

To slow the high rate of inflation, shown in the graph below, he imposed a ninety-day freeze on wages, prices, and rents, but then pressure from business and labor led him to lift controls. Inflation soared again.

Unrest in the Middle East brought more disruptions to the troubled economy. Americans depended on cheap, imported oil for about a third of their energy needs. But in 1973, Israel and the Arab nations of Egypt and Syria went to war. When the United States backed its ally Israel, the Arab members of the **Organization of Petroleum Exporting Countries (OPEC)** angrily responded by imposing an **embargo,** or restriction, on oil shipped to the United States. OPEC, a group of nations that sets oil prices and production, also quadrupled its prices. Oil prices soared, even after the embargo ended in 1974. The map on page 889 shows the nations that belong to OPEC.

The oil crisis affected everyone. A loaf of bread that had cost twenty-eight cents earlier in the 1970s now was eighty-nine cents. Americans

Because Americans depended so heavily on oil from the Middle East for gasoline and heating fuel, Arab oil producers had an effective weapon in the threat of raising prices.

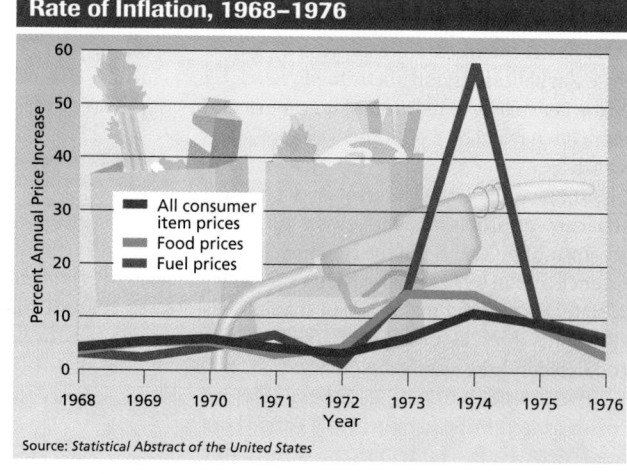

Rate of Inflation, 1968–1976

(graph legend: All consumer item prices; Food prices; Fuel prices)

Source: *Statistical Abstract of the United States*

Interpreting Graphs
Rising oil prices in the 1970s had a strong impact on all parts of the American economy. *When did oil prices reach their peak? How long did high prices last?*

▶ **RESOURCE DIRECTORY**

Teaching Resources

⭐ **Critical Thinking Activity** Predicting Consequences: Wage-Price Freeze, found in the Unit 10 folder, p. 22, presents an excerpt from President Nixon's televised national address announcing a ninety-day wage and price freeze.

⭐ **American Profiles Activity** Maggie Kuhn, found in the Unit 10 folder, p. 17, profiles the founder of the Gray Panthers, a new protest group to emerge in the early 1970s.

Organization of Petroleum Exporting Countries (OPEC), c. 1970

Geography and History: Interpreting Maps
OPEC brought together the world's major oil producers. *In what region of the world are many of these nations concentrated? What political effects did this have? What oil-producing nations are located in the Americas?*

Enrichment

To help students gain a better insight into the racial climate during the Nixon administration, ask them to research the history of busing as a means of integrating schools. Students should prepare a brief report demonstrating the successes and failures of busing. Reports may take the form of a photo or video montage.

Caption Answer to ...

 Interpreting Maps

Africa and the Middle East; strained relations between the United States and these countries; Venezuela and Ecuador.

who were used to paying twenty-five cents a gallon for gas now paid sixty-five cents. Higher energy prices fueled inflation, which in turn led consumers to cut back on spending. The result was another recession. Unemployment reached 9 percent, the highest rate since the 1930s.

Social Programs Meanwhile, Nixon was trying to stop the growth of government spending on social programs that were part of Lyndon Johnson's Great Society. Critics claimed that the programs were wasteful, encouraged "welfare cheaters," and discouraged people from seeking work.

Nixon had exploited that frustration in his campaign, but he now faced a dilemma. On the one hand, he wanted to please conservative voters in the South who demanded cutbacks. On the other hand, he hoped to appeal to traditionally Democratic blue-collar voters, who wanted to keep the programs that benefited them.

The administration suggested a work-incentive program that would give families a basic minimum income, while requiring them to register for job training and accept a job when one was found. The Family Assistance

Plan failed to pass the Senate but did gain Nixon political points with some voters.

Law and Order Another important campaign issue had been the need to restore "law and order" in the country. President Nixon recognized that a strong backlash had developed against student radicals, antiwar protesters, and the youth counterculture in general. Many older working-class and middle-class Americans held those groups responsible not only for demonstrations in the streets but also for rising crime, growing drug use, and permissive attitudes toward sex.

To strengthen his position on law and order, Nixon's strategy was to discourage any kind of protest. In speeches, he lashed out at all demonstrators, once calling students "bums." After National Guardsmen shot and killed student protesters at Kent State University, Nixon implied that the students themselves had caused the tragedy. Speaking at Kansas State University later in 1970, he said:

The time has come for us to recognize that violence and terror have no place in a free society. Whatever the purported

Media and Technology

 Transparency
Critical Thinking, I-14

In Depth

Interdisciplinary

In July, 1969, after nine years of preparation, Americans set out to land on the moon. Manned by astronauts Collins, Armstrong, and Aldrin, *Apollo 11* (see pages 782–783) successfully completed its mission. It was not only an unprecedented scientific and technical achievement, but it also diverted attention from the social unrest rocking the United States at the time. Part of the lunar module remains on the moon with a plaque that, rather than boasting of an American achievement, proclaims the hope of the world: "Here men from the planet earth first set foot upon the moon, July 1969, A.D. We came in peace for all mankind."

Section 2 Review Answers

1. (a) imperial presidency, see p. 887, (b) OPEC, see p. 888, (c) embargo, see p. 888, (d) busing, see p. 890

2. (a) Henry A. Kissinger, see p. 887, (b) H. R. Haldeman, see p. 887, (c) John Ehrlichman, see p. 887, (d) John Mitchell, see p. 887

3. Though Nixon wanted to avoid wage and price controls, he eventually imposed controls and turned to budget deficits to stimulate the economy.

4. He hoped to appeal to older and middle-class Americans who were disturbed by the radical protest movements of the 1960s.

5. Nixon decided not to strive for the African American vote, but to try instead to win white southerners over to the Republican party. He slowed civil rights reforms and opposed busing.

6. Possible answer: Nixon felt himself an outsider, was reserved and secretive, and ran his administration in a private, closed way. He also resented what he saw as other people's good luck and easy successes, which may have accounted for his hostility to student protesters.

Answer to ...

Links Across Time

Possible answer: One common way for political terms to become part of the American language is through the media. Newspaper reporters, headline writers, news commentators, and television reporters all take up and publicize these until a term with political origins becomes part of everyday usage.

[supposed] *cause of the perpetrators may be . . . no cause justifies violence.*

Other members of the administration backed him up. Attorney General Mitchell stepped up the Justice Department's campaign against crime. Using his gift for colorful rhetoric, Vice President Spiro Agnew called student protesters and professors an "effete corps of impudent snobs," *effete* meaning they were weak and *impudent* meaning they were rude and disrespectful. Unhappy with press coverage of the White House, Agnew also accused television reporters and producers of distorting administration actions.

The "Southern Strategy" Nixon felt that he had little to gain by supporting advances in civil rights. Few African Americans had voted for him in the 1960 race against John Kennedy, and in 1968 he had gotten just 12 percent of the black vote. Besides, he reasoned, any attempt to court the black electorate could threaten the white southern vote in a reelection bid. Thus, while there were some civil rights gains in the Nixon years, the record was generally weak.

Explaining his position, Nixon once observed that "there are those who want instant integration and those who want segregation forever. I believe that we need to have a middle course between those two extremes." Given the strong resistance to change that persisted in many places, this meant a slowdown in desegregation.

Nixon's aim was to find the proper "southern strategy" to win over the Democratic white South. Senator Strom Thurmond of South Carolina, who had left the Democratic party in 1948, was now a Republican and became Nixon's strongest southern supporter. To keep him and his colleagues happy, Nixon sought to reduce the appropriation needed for enforcing fair housing, and he eased guidelines for desegregation.

The Justice Department, headed by John Mitchell, tried to prevent the extension of the Voting Rights Act of 1965, which had greatly increased the number of African Americans who could vote in the South. Congress went ahead with the extension, but Nixon had made his point to white southern voters.

Another controversial issue was the use of **busing** to end school segregation. In several cities, federal courts ordered school systems to

---

| 1650 | 1700 | 1750 | 1800 | **Links Across Time** | 1850 | 1900 | 1950 | 2000 |

To Coin a Phrase

The language of American politics gained a new entry when Spiro Agnew uttered the phrase "effete corps of impudent snobs" in a speech he made in 1969. American political language has had a long and colorful past. Since the early republic, American politicians have invented their own words and phrases or borrowed them from other people, such as journalists or members of the military. Some of the terms and phrases coined by politicians from the past to the present include:

silk stocking A wealthy person; dates back to colonial times when only the rich could afford to wear silk stockings.

cookie pusher A diplomat who spends time attending social teas rather than doing any real work; dates from the 1940s.

fishing expedition An investigation with no specific goal, usually made by one political party into the business of another; popularized in the 1940s.

pooh-bah A self-important high official; a popular term in American politics since the 1950s.

nervous Nellies People who become easily disturbed or upset; popularized by President Johnson, who used the term to describe some critics of his policy in Vietnam.

waxworks The honored guests at a political dinner who sit on a raised platform, so named because of the frozen, or waxen, smiles they keep on their faces; dates from the late 1960s.

break all the china To obey an order regardless of the obstacles; a favorite Nixon phrase.

FOB Friend of Bill's; a phrase meant to describe a personal friend of President Clinton, popularized in the press since Clinton's inauguration.

How might a term or a phrase coined by a politician become commonly used by Americans?

RESOURCE DIRECTORY

Teaching Resources

bus students to other schools to end the pattern of all-black or all-white schools. Particularly in northern cities, such as Detroit and Boston, some white students and their parents met incoming black students with boycotts or violent protests.

In 1971 guidelines for busing were laid down by a Supreme Court decision that went against Nixon's views. A federal judge in North Carolina had ruled that voluntary integration efforts were not working. In *Swann* v. *Charlotte-Mecklenburg Board of Education,* the Court agreed, saying that busing was one possible option for ending school desegregation.

Nixon had long been opposed to busing. He now went on national television to say that he would ask Congress to halt it. He also allowed the Department of Health, Education, and Welfare to restore federal funding to school districts where segregation persisted. Although busing continued in some places, Nixon's position was clear to voters in the South.

Nixon and the Supreme Court

During the campaign, Nixon had criticized the Supreme Court as too liberal and soft on criminals. In his first term, four justices died, resigned, or retired, giving him the extraordinary opportunity to name four new justices and thus reshape the Court. He first named Warren Burger as Chief Justice, replacing Earl Warren. Burger was a moderate who was easily confirmed by the Senate.

Later nominations reflected Nixon's southern strategy and conservative views. The Senate rejected his first nominees from the South: Clement Haynsworth of South Carolina and G. Harrold Carswell of Florida. Opponents

These demonstrators expressed their unhappiness with busing by burying a school bus and erecting the following epitaph nearby: "Here lies a school bus/No mourning from us./No more fuming/No more fussing/May this be the end of busing."

charged that both choices showed racial bias. Haynsworth was also suspected of conflict of interest in some court rulings, while Carswell was seen as intellectually mediocre. Bitterly, Nixon told the press, "I cannot successfully nominate to the Supreme Court any federal appellate judge from the South who believes as I do in the strict construction of the Constitution." Eventually Nixon appointed Harry A. Blackmun, Lewis F. Powell, Jr., and William H. Rehnquist, all qualified jurists, who generally tilted the Court in a more conservative direction.

While Nixon developed domestic policies to "bring Americans together again," as he said in his inaugural speech, he took a greater interest in what he could do to shape foreign policy. The outcome of his plans to play an important role in world affairs is discussed in the next section.

SECTION 2 REVIEW

Key Terms, People, and Places
1. Define (a) imperial presidency, (b) OPEC, (c) embargo, (d) busing.
2. Identify (a) Henry A. Kissinger, (b) H. R. Haldeman, (c) John Ehrlichman, (d) John Mitchell.

Key Concepts
3. What steps did Nixon take to fix the economy?

4. Why did Nixon strongly advocate law and order?
5. What was Nixon's "southern strategy"?

Critical Thinking
6. **Determining Relevance** How did Nixon's background and philosophy influence his style of governing?

Quiz found in the Unit 10 folder, p. 10, covers the main ideas in this section as well as the key terms.

Reteach

Ask students to review the lists and notes they created during the Reading Strategy exercise for this section. Have students use the information they gathered to describe briefly the key features of Nixon's staff and the administration's domestic policy.

Alternative Assessment

Mid-Point Monitoring
Ask students if they have
• Created an outline for their profile
• Identified materials to incorporate into their profile
• Begun research on Nixon's presidency

4. CLOSE

Reinforcing the Big Idea

In the domestic sphere, Nixon tried to take the nation in a new, more conservative direction than Johnson and Kennedy before him. The next section examines Nixon's efforts in the foreign policy field.

Nixon's Foreign Policy

1. FOCUS

Connecting to the Big Idea

See Page 878B. Tell students that Nixon hoped to have an especially powerful impact as President in the field of foreign policy. Ask students how Nixon's efforts might be said to have benefited the American people.

Objectives

● Explain Henry Kissinger's key role in shaping foreign policy in the Nixon administration.
● Identify the bold steps taken by Nixon to relax international tensions.
● Describe how Nixon reversed existing American policy toward the People's Republic of China.
● Explain the initial steps toward arms control between the United States and the Soviet Union.

Bellringer

Ask students to imagine the following situation: The United States has been for several years locked in a costly competition with powerful enemies for influence around the world. Neither side seems to be winning. What should the United States do to break the stalemate? Explain to students that Nixon faced a similar dilemma during his presidency.

Reading Strategy

Structured Outline Have students take notes on the following topics as they read the section:
● Henry Kissinger and American foreign policy
● United States relations with China during Nixon's administration
● United States relations with the Soviet Union during Nixon's administration

Nixon's Foreign Policy

SECTION PREVIEW

Nixon's main interest was in foreign affairs, where he made significant changes. Working closely with Henry Kissinger, he took dramatic steps toward new relationships with both China and the Soviet Union.

Key Concepts
• Henry Kissinger played an important role in shaping the foreign policy of the Nixon administration.
• Nixon took bold steps in relaxing international tensions.
• Nixon reversed American policy in relations with the People's Republic of China.
• The United States and the Soviet Union moved toward arms control.

Key Terms, People, and Places
realpolitik, détente, Strategic Arms Limitation Talks (SALT)

This panda bear was one of two given to the people of the United States from the People's Republic of China on the occasion of President Nixon's visit there in 1972.

A s President, Nixon's greatest achievements were in the field of foreign policy. "I've always thought this country could run itself domestically without a President," he once observed. He understood the implications of strategic planning and diplomacy in foreign affairs, and took a creative approach that helped ease the tensions of the cold war. Aided by the skillful diplomacy of Henry Kissinger, Nixon opened the way to establishing relations with China and crafted a better relationship with the Soviet Union.

AMERICAN PROFILES

Henry Kissinger

While Nixon had an astute grasp of foreign policy, he still relied heavily on Henry Kissinger in charting his course. The German-born Kissinger quickly gained the President's confidence and became a dominant figure in the administration.

Henry (originally Heinz) Kissinger came from a Jewish family that fled Nazi Germany in 1938 when he was fifteen. The Kissingers settled in New York City that same year. In New York, Kissinger worked during the day at a shaving brush company, finished high school at night, and then attended City College. He was drafted in 1943, and an army teacher and historian encouraged him to go to Harvard University at the end of the war. There he completed both undergraduate and graduate degrees and wrote his doctoral dissertation on Klemens von Metternich, a nineteenth-century Austrian statesman and diplomat who helped maintain stability in Europe in the face of liberal change. Kissinger's studies gave him an admiration for *realpolitik,* a German term for "practical politics" based on achieving power.

On the faculty at Harvard, Kissinger rose quickly through university positions, gaining a reputation for being brilliant but arrogant and abrasive. By 1962 he was a full professor of government.

Outside the university, Kissinger soon became a recognized expert on foreign relations. His first book, *Nuclear Weapons and Foreign Policy,* published in 1957, argued that President Eisenhower's doctrine of massive retaliation was a mistake, and that a limited nuclear war could be fought successfully. He also worked with Nelson Rockefeller, governor of New York, who recommended him to Nixon.

Kissinger understood how to deal with the insecure President. Nixon needed to be flattered, and he liked people who could talk tough. Kissinger was willing to accommodate him and soon became the man Nixon talked to most. "Henry, of course, was not a personal friend," Nixon later said, but the two spoke five

▶ RESOURCE DIRECTORY

Teaching Resources

Reproducible Lesson Plan found in the Unit 10 folder, p. 5, provides a summary of the Section 3 lesson plan content.

Alternate Lesson Plan: Learning Styles found in the Alternate Lesson Plans folder, p. 164, guides students in the creation of a time line tracing the evolution of relations between the superpowers, and is particularly helpful for visual or tactile learners.

Guided Reading and Review found in the Unit 10 folder, p. 11, provides a structure for reading and mastering the key concepts and reviewing the key terms for Section 3. (Guided Practice)

Henry Kissinger was a major architect of American foreign policy in the 1970s.

or six times a day, sometimes in person, sometimes by phone, and often for hours at a time.

Kissinger's actual influence in shaping American foreign policy was broader than his official roles—first as national security adviser and then as secretary of state. He knew how to frame questions in ways the President wanted. He could distill foreign policy issues into briefing papers that gave Nixon options for making decisions. In his memoirs, Kissinger wrote:

N ixon could be very decisive. Almost invariably during his Presidency his decisions were courageous and strong and often taken in loneliness against all expert advice. But wherever possible Nixon made these decisions in solitude on the basis of memoranda or with a few very intimate aides.

Kissinger saw to it that he was with the President when such decisions were made.

Both men were suspicious and secretive. Together, they took an almost conspiratorial approach to foreign policy. "They tried not to let anyone else have a full picture, even if it meant deceiving them," Lawrence Eagleburger, a State Department official, observed.

Kissinger also had a remarkable ability to manipulate the press. Journalists depended on him for stories and were wary of antagonizing him. A *Time* magazine reporter noted how Kissinger worked: "You know you are being played like a violin, but it's still extremely seductive."

His efforts in ending the Vietnam War and easing cold war tensions made Kissinger a celebrity. He shared the 1973 Nobel Peace Prize with North Vietnam's Le Duc Tho (who refused it), appeared on twenty-one *Time* covers, and in 1973 was first in a Gallup Poll listing the most-admired Americans. He left a lasting mark on American foreign policy.

Superpower Tensions Relax

Nixon's greatest accomplishment was in bringing about **détente,** a relaxation in the tensions between the superpowers. This role was ironic, for in the 1950s Richard Nixon had been one of the most bitter and active anti-communists in government. He had made his reputation as someone willing to demand extraordinary action in response to the communist threat. As President, however, Nixon dealt imaginatively with both China and the Soviet Union. Bypassing Congress, and often bypassing his own advisers, he and Kissinger reversed the direction of postwar American foreign policy.

Nixon drew on Kissinger's understanding that foreign affairs were more complex than a simple standoff between the United States and the threat of communism. Kissinger pointed out that there were deep rifts in the communist world itself, noting, "The deepest international conflict in the world today is not between us and the Soviet Union but between the Soviet Union and Communist China."

A New Approach to China

The most surprising policy shift was toward China. When the communist revolution ended in 1949, establishing the People's Republic of China, Americans saw all communists in Asia

2. INSTRUCT

Explain/Discuss

Discuss the role of Henry Kissinger in shaping Nixon's foreign policy. What skills made Kissinger such a valued aide? What did he offer Nixon that other advisers could not?

Tell students that United States–China relations were tense during Nixon's presidency. Ask how Nixon's reputation as a strong anti-communist enabled him to approach China. Ask what might have happened had a President with weaker anticommunist credentials attempted a similar maneuver.

Analyze

Analyze Nixon's effort to play one communist country off against the other. Ask how such efforts would improve the position of the United States. Help students see that Nixon believed that if the United States became friendly with China, the Soviet Union would grow insecure and more willing to get closer to the United States.

In Depth

Then and Now

By the 1990s détente no longer defined United States foreign policy. But traditional alliances have prolonged the civil war in Bosnia-Herzegovina (see Chapter 35, pages 967–968) and increased the dangers of prolonged conflict. Russia has sided with its old allies and fellow Slavs, the Serbs, while the United States and its Western allies have sided with the Serbs' Muslim and Croat enemies.

During the Nixon administration, United States relations with the Soviet Union and communist China changed dramatically. Going against the anticommunist sentiment of the 1950s, Nixon negotiated with these countries for strategic aims. Ask students to think of the different ways in which conflicts are resolved. Have students work in small groups to choose a conflict experienced by a member of the group. Then have groups list three ways in which the conflict might be resolved, and evaluate the benefits and drawbacks of each method.

Enrichment

The SALT I treaty negotiated between the Soviet Union and the United States marked a major step forward in relations between the two countries. Have students create an illustrated time line of the history of arms control negotiations between the Soviet Union (and the independent republics) and the United States. The time line should highlight the important successes and failures of these negotiations.

The President and First Lady Pat Nixon head a group touring the Great Wall of China on this historic first visit to the People's Republic of China.

as part of a united plot to dominate the world. Ignoring reality, the United States did not extend formal diplomatic recognition to the new Chinese government—in effect, officially pretending instead that it did not exist. Even when a Chinese-Soviet alliance crumbled, the United States clung to its rigid position. It insisted that the government of Chiang Kai-shek, set up on the island of Taiwan when the Nationalists fled the Chinese mainland, was the rightful government of all China.

Quietly, Nixon began to prepare the way for change. In his inaugural address in 1969, he referred indirectly to China when he declared, "We seek an open world . . . a world in which no people, great or small, will live in angry isolation." His first foreign policy report to Congress in 1970 began:

> The Chinese are a great and vital people who should not remain isolated from the international community. . . . United States policy is not likely soon to have much impact on China's behavior, let alone its

ideological outlook. But it is certainly in our interest, and in the interest of peace and stability in Asia and the world, that we take what steps we can toward improved practical relations with Peking [Beijing].

The next year, the administration relaxed some regulations toward China. Then the Chinese invited an American table-tennis team to visit the mainland, and the United States began to ease some trading restrictions. In July 1971, after extensive secret diplomacy by Kissinger, Nixon made the dramatic announcement that he planned to visit China the following year. He would be the first United States President to travel to that country.

Nixon understood that the People's Republic was an established government and would not simply disappear. Other nations had recognized the new government, and it was time for the United States to do the same. Similarly, other countries wanted to give China's seat in the United Nations to the People's Republic, and the United States could no longer muster international opinion against this change.

Nixon had other motives as well. He recognized that he could use Chinese friendship as a bargaining chip in his negotiations with the Soviet Union. Press coverage of the trip would give him a boost at home. Also, he believed that he could take the action without political damage, because of his past reputation as a strong anticommunist.

✪ Nixon traveled to China in February 1972. He met with Mao Zedong, the Chinese leader who had spearheaded the revolution in 1949. He spoke with Premier Zhou Enlai about international problems and ways of dealing with them. He and his wife, Pat, toured the Great Wall and other Chinese sights, all in front of television cameras that sent historic pictures home. When he returned to the United States, he waited in his plane until prime time so his return would be seen by as many television viewers as possible. Formal relations were not yet restored—that

RESOURCE DIRECTORY

Teaching Resources

✪ 📘 **Primary Source Activity** The Trip to China: Diplomacy and Publicity, found in the Unit 10 folder, p. 25, demonstrates the importance Nixon placed on the China trip as well as his intense distrust of the media through a 1972 memo from the President to Bob Haldeman.

would take a few more years—but the basis for diplomatic ties had been established.

Strengthening Ties with the Soviet Union

At the same time that he was dealing with China, Nixon turned his attention to the Soviet Union. He and Kissinger hoped to play off one communist state against the other. In 1971 he outlined his aim for East-West relations in Europe:

E ast-West conflict in Europe springs from historical and objective causes, not transient [changing] moods or personal misunderstandings. For 25 years Europe has been divided by opposing national interests and contrary philosophies. . . . To relax tensions means a patient and persistent effort to deal with specific sources and not only with their manifestations [obvious appearances]. . . . We in the West are convinced by the history of the postwar period that a détente that does not apply equally to Eastern and Western Europe will be inherently [basically] unstable.

Several months after his China trip, Nixon visited the Soviet Union. He was welcomed as warmly in Moscow as he had been in Beijing. In a series of cordial meetings with Premier Leonid Brezhnev, the two nations negotiated a weapons pact, agreed to work together to explore space, and eased long-standing trade limits.

As reporters catch the event for the world, Chinese premier Zhou Enlai and President Richard Nixon congratulate each other on the new ties between their nations.

MAKING CONNECTIONS

What are the relations between the United States and Russia today? How have they changed since the 1970s?

The Superpowers Agree to Limit Weapons

Nixon saw arms control as part of the process in tying the various strands of his foreign policy program together. Like many Americans, he was worried about the widespread proliferation of nuclear weapons. The Limited Test Ban Treaty of 1963 had ended atmospheric testing of new bombs, but underground testing continued. Bigger and better bombs were being made all the time, and some people feared that the world might be destroyed unless these weapons were brought under control.

Nixon was determined to address the nuclear threat and to deal creatively with the Soviet Union at the same time. He had entered office intent on achieving superiority over the Soviet Union, but came to recognize that superiority made little sense in an era in which each nation had more than enough weapons to

In Depth

Interdisciplinary

In the 1970s, the Soviet Union's rise as a nuclear superpower intensified the cold war. In 1971, for the first time, the Soviet Union passed the United States in total number of land- and submarine-based nuclear missiles. A confident Foreign Minister Andrei Gromyko boasted that in world affairs, "No question of any significance . . . can now be decided without the Soviet Union or in opposition to it."

The Cold War warmed slightly as Soviet premier Leonid Brezhnev and President Nixon met and SALT I was signed.

destroy their enemies many times over. This ability is known as overkill. Balance between the superpowers was what the nuclear age demanded. The United States and the Soviet Union therefore began **Strategic Arms Limitation Talks,** known as SALT. Once again,

Kissinger kept tight control of the negotiating process. In 1971 Nixon noted:

> *Perhaps for the first time, the evolving strategic balance allows a Soviet-American agreement which yields no unilateral [one-sided] advantages. The fact [that] we have begun to discuss strategic arms with the USSR is in itself important. Agreement in such a vital area could create a new commitment to stability, and influence attitudes toward other issues.*

Thirty months of talks culminated in an important pact to limit offensive nuclear weapons, ready to be signed when Nixon went to Moscow.

The SALT I treaty included a five-year interim agreement that held the number of intercontinental ballistic missiles (ICBMs) and submarine-launched ballistic missiles at 1972 levels. The treaty also included an agreement restricting the development and deployment of defensive antiballistic missile systems.

SALT I was a diplomatic triumph and an important step forward. But it did little to limit the number of warheads the two nations possessed or to stop them from improving nuclear weapons systems in other ways. The practical Kissinger called for respecting the limits imposed while improving defenses. "The way for us to use this freeze is for us to catch up," he said soon after the summit. "If we don't do this we don't deserve to be in office." Still, SALT I showed that arms control agreements were possible, paving the way for more progress in the future.

SECTION 3 REVIEW

Key Terms, People, and Places
1. Define (a) *realpolitik*, (b) détente, (c) Strategic Arms Limitation Talks (SALT).

Key Concepts
2. What were Henry Kissinger's official and actual roles in the Nixon administration?
3. What was Kissinger's relationship with the press?
4. How did Nixon alter American relations with the People's Republic of China? Why did he believe it was important to effect such changes?
5. What actions did President Nixon take toward the Soviet Union?

Critical Thinking
6. **Demonstrating Reasoned Judgment** Considering its weaknesses, how important was the SALT I treaty?

 RESOURCE DIRECTORY

The Watergate Scandal

SECTION PREVIEW

Richard Nixon was willing to use presidential power to do whatever was necessary to remain in the White House. Eventually this approach compromised the presidency itself. The resulting Watergate scandal angered the nation and moved Nixon to take drastic steps.

Key Concepts
• The Nixon White House operated in an atmosphere of suspicion.
• Nixon and his supporters were willing to take extreme measures to win the 1972 election.
• When the Watergate break-in was traced to the White House, the President himself became involved in trying to cover it up.
• Nixon's involvement in Watergate made his impeachment likely, causing him to resign.

Key Terms, People, and Places
Watergate, Pentagon Papers, perjury; Plumbers, Daniel Ellsberg, John J. Sirica

L ooking toward the 1972 election, Nixon was determined to win an overwhelming mandate for a second term. Fiercely loyal aides were prepared to do anything for him, even if it meant breaking the law. When Nixon tried to hide their actions, he implicated himself in what became known as **Watergate,** a scandalous series of events that ended his presidency and threatened the foundations of American government.

Suspicion and Deceit at the White House

Reflecting Nixon's suspicious mind, the White House operated as if it was in a state of siege, surrounded by enemies. Nixon's staff responded to the President's attitude by trying to protect him at all costs from anything that might weaken his position.

One result of this mind-set was what became known as the "enemies list." Special counsel Charles W. Colson helped develop a list of prominent people unsympathetic to the administration. It included politicians such as Senator Edward Kennedy, members of the media such as reporter Daniel Schorr, and a number of outspoken performers including comedian Dick Gregory and actors Jane Fonda and Steve McQueen. Aides then considered how to harass these White House "enemies." One idea, for example, was to arrange income tax investigations of people on the list.

Despite his dedication to a domestic policy of law and order, Nixon was sometimes willing to take illegal actions more serious than the activities they were meant to control. For example, when he suspected that news stories were being leaked by the National Security Council, he ordered Kissinger to wiretap the phones of his own staff. When stories began to circulate about the secret bombing of Cambodia, Nixon had reporters' phones tapped, too.

At the same time, he sought tighter coordination of American intelligence activities. Both the FBI and the CIA were already illegally monitoring radical activists by tapping their phones and opening mail. In mid-1970 Nixon's staff proposed a plan for wiretaps and other investigations that was so far outside the law that even FBI director J. Edgar Hoover rejected the plan.

The White House then organized its own unit—nicknamed the **Plumbers**—to stop government security leaks. The group included E. Howard Hunt, a spy novelist and former CIA agent, and G. Gordon Liddy, once an FBI agent. In the spring of 1971, **Daniel Ellsberg,** a

MR. PRESIDENT:
RELEASE the TAPES!

After persistent public demands for the release of the tapes containing information about Watergate, President Nixon finally complied—then resigned three days later. His resignation letter is shown above.

Reproducible Lesson Plan found in the Unit 10 folder, p. 6, provides a summary of the Section 4 lesson plan content.

Alternate Lesson Plan: Critical Thinking Drawing Conclusions, found in the Alternate Lesson Plans folder, p. 165, encourages students to use this skill in identifying the abuses of power that led to the Watergate scandal, and the effect that had on the Nixon presidency.

Guided Reading and Review found in the Unit 10 folder, p. 13, provides a structure for reading and mastering the key concepts and reviewing the key terms for Section 4. (Guided Practice)

1. FOCUS

Connecting to the Big Idea
See page 878B. Tell students that Nixon's suspicious nature and his willingness to use his presidential power for partisan political ends set in motion a series of events that compromised the presidency itself. Ask students how the people of the United States reacted to presidential wrongdoing.

Objectives
● Describe the atmosphere of suspicion that existed in the Nixon White House.
● Explain that Nixon and his team went to extreme lengths to secure his reelection.
● Describe Nixon's efforts to cover up his involvement in the Watergate break-in.
● Explain that Nixon's involvement led to the likelihood of his impeachment, and thus his resignation.

Bellringer
Ask students how they would feel if they discovered that the President might have broken the law. Ask them to discuss the impact of such a piece of news, and the symbolic role of the President.

Reading Strategy
Graphic Organizer Tell students that the Watergate scandal involved several causes and effects. Have students make a cause-and-effect chart of this section comprising three columns on a piece of paper. They should head the first column Causes of the Break-In, the second The Break-In, and the third Effects of the Break-In. Have students write notes in the appropriate column as they read.

Discuss

Discuss the atmosphere in the White House as described in the section. What does the existence of the "enemies list" reveal about Nixon's view of the world? Ask students to react to the fact that Nixon harassed those he perceived as hostile by arranging income tax investigations of them. Do they view such actions as an abuse of power? Why or why not?

Discuss the activities of the Plumbers and the "dirty tricks" conducted by CREEP. Ask students how they felt as they read about these activities.

Discuss Nixon's responses as the scandal grew larger and closer to him. Ask students to speculate on why the President was so damaged by his attempts to fire the special prosecutor.

Answer to ...

MAKING CONNECTIONS

Answers will vary but should serve as the basis for a discussion about ethics and about the proper roles of Congress, the President, and agencies such as the FBI.

---

former Defense Department official, had given the *New York Times* the **"Pentagon Papers"**—a huge, secret Pentagon study of the Vietnam War. The *New York Times* began to publish the Pentagon Papers in June 1971. The documents showed that the executive branch often had deceived the Congress and American people about the real situation in Vietnam and had deliberately escalated the conflict. Intent on stopping further leaks, Nixon approved the plan to create the Plumbers. With approval from White House chief domestic adviser John Ehrlichman, the undercover unit broke into the office of Ellsberg's psychiatrist in an effort to discover damaging information about Ellsberg's private life.

MAKING CONNECTIONS

Other than its illegality, what problem can you see with a President assuming as much power as did Nixon?

Nixon's Campaign for Reelection

Determined to ensure Nixon's victory in 1972, the Committee to Reelect the President—known as CREEP—used other questionable tactics. Headed by John Mitchell, CREEP launched a fund-raising campaign to collect as much money as possible before a new law made it necessary to report such contributions. The money would fund both routine campaign activities and "dirty tricks" kept hidden from the public.

CREEP funded a variety of questionable actions. For example, people on its payroll leaked a fabricated letter to a conservative New Hampshire newspaper to discredit presidential contender Edmund Muskie, a Democratic senator from Maine. Charging Muskie with making insulting remarks about French Canadians living in the state, the letter was timed to arrive two weeks before the New Hampshire primary. The normally calm and composed Muskie responded by breaking down in tears in front of television cameras, which seriously damaged his reputation. Other "dirty tricks" carried out by CREEP included sending hecklers to disrupt Democratic campaign meetings and assigning

The Watergate scandal began when security guard Frank Willis (above) discovered a door left ajar by CREEP "burglars" trying to break in and install wiretaps in the Democratic party headquarters.

undercover "spies" to join the campaigns of major candidates.

"Dirty Tricks" at the Watergate Complex An intelligence branch within CREEP, which included "Plumbers" Liddy and Hunt, masterminded outlandish plans. One elaborate scheme called for the wiretapping of top Democrats to try to compromise them at their convention. Twice Mitchell refused to go along, not because the plan was illegal, but because it was too risky and expensive. Finally in 1972 he approved another idea: tapping the phones at Democratic National Committee headquarters in the Watergate apartment complex in Washington, D.C.
★ The first break-in to install illegal listening devices failed. A second attempt, on the night of June 16, 1972, ended with the arrest of the five men involved. One suspect was James McCord, a former CIA officer working for CREEP as a security officer. The Watergate "burglars" carried money that could be traced to CREEP and thus implicated Nixon's reelection campaign.

Top officials, including Nixon himself, had to decide what to do to conceal the incident. When

---

▶ RESOURCE DIRECTORY

Teaching Resources

★ **Visual Learning Activity** Wanted, found in the Unit 10 folder, p. 30, illustrates in a poster the number of Nixon's staff and campaign personnel who were arrested as a result of the Watergate scandal.

★ **American Profiles Activity** found in the Unit 10 folder, p. 18, profiles John J. Sirica, whose tough sentences as the judge in the Watergate scandal helped break the case.

★ **Literature Activity** Unraveling the Story of Watergate, found in the Unit 10 folder, pp. 26–28, presents excerpts from Woodward and Bernstein's book *All the President's Men*, describing the actions of Nixon and his supporters.

the FBI traced the money carried by the Watergate burglars to CREEP, Nixon authorized the CIA to call off the FBI on the grounds that the matter involved "national security." Though he had not been involved in planning the break-in, the President was now part of the illegal cover-up.

As the Watergate case went on, the White House became more deeply involved. Nixon authorized the payment of hush money to keep Hunt and others quiet. Top officials, including Mitchell, committed **perjury**—lying under oath—in court to shield the President and others.

The 1972 Presidential Election Still, Watergate had barely reached the public's notice. In the 1972 presidential election, the Democrats ran George McGovern, a liberal senator from South Dakota, who lost to Nixon by a landslide. Nixon won a popular majority of 47 million to 29 million votes and swamped the Electoral College by a tally of 520 to 17. He had the mandate he wanted, though he did not get a Republican majority in either house of Congress.

The Watergate Story Continues

Despite Nixon's victory, the Watergate case refused to disappear. Nixon himself had proclaimed publicly that "no one in the White House staff, no one in this administration, presently employed, was involved in this very bizarre incident." At the trial in early 1973, the Watergate burglars either pleaded guilty or were found guilty. At sentencing time, however, Judge **John J. Sirica** was not convinced that he had gotten to the bottom of the matter. Criticizing the prosecution, he said:

> I have not been satisfied, and I am still not satisfied that all the pertinent facts that might be available—I say might be available—have been produced before an American jury. . . . I would hope that the Senate committee is granted the power by Congress . . . to try to get to the bottom of what happened in this case.

To prompt the burglars to talk, Sirica sentenced them to long prison terms.

Meanwhile, *Washington Post* reporters Bob Woodward and Carl Bernstein were following a trail of leads. Even before the election, they had learned about the secret funds at CREEP and had begun to write about the political intelligence effort and the sabotage campaign. As they began to realize who was involved, they called Mitchell and asked him to verify their story. He denied it angrily.

Investigative reporters Bob Woodward (left) and Carl Bernstein (right) persisted in tracking down information to uncover the Watergate story. ⭐

Analyze

Tell students that the televised investigation of the President was a first in American history. Not since Andrew Johnson in the 1860s had a President come under such heavy suspicion. Ask students to consider the American state of mind during Nixon's final days.

In Depth

Historical Misconceptions

The 1972 Republican campaign was not devoid of support from young people, as might be assumed from Nixon's and Agnew's assaults on youth in general (see pages 889–890) and the still-fresh memories of Kent State (see pages 868–870). Young Republicans, according to *Life* magazine in September 1972, comprised "the nation's largest bloc of first-time voters, 2.5 million of them, mostly 18–24-year-olds." By early fall 1972, "Young Voters for the President" claimed 10,000 college volunteers on more than ninety campuses—many established far ahead of McGovern's youth workers. On election day Nixon got 52 percent of the votes cast by those under thirty.

Activity

Cooperative Learning

Time: Two class periods.

Activity: Have students debate whether or not Richard Nixon should be impeached for his involvement in the Watergate scandal.

Grouping: Groups of four students.

Purpose: To explore the Constitution's guidelines for impeachment, as well as the charges and evidence against Nixon and the question of whether Nixon's removal from office serves the best interests of the country.

Roles: Proponents and opponents of impeachment.

Outcome: Students will learn about the questions and issues surrounding the decision to impeach a high official.

Enrichment

Suggest that students research and prepare a biographical file of the major figures in Watergate, their roles, and what happened to them in the aftermath of the scandal. The file could include figures in the Nixon administration, in the press, and in Congress.

In Depth

Biography

Senator Samuel Ervin, Jr., (1896–1985) of North Carolina headed the seven-member Senate committee on Watergate. He won praise not only for his easy southern manner but for his doggedness in pursuing evidence against Nixon and resisting the President's claims to "executive privilege." Ervin, who called the United States Constitution "the finest thing to come out of the mind of man," served in the United States Senate for more than twenty years until he retired in 1974. He wrote two books, *The Whole Truth: The Watergate Conspiracy* (1980) and *Humor of a Country Lawyer* (1983).

A Watergate Chronology

1972

June Five members of CREEP are arrested for breaking into Democratic National Committee headquarters in the Watergate Office Building. Two former Nixon aides are also arrested.

1973

January All seven men arrested plead or are found guilty.

April Nixon denies knowledge of the break-in.

May Nixon appoints special prosecutor Archibald Cox. The Senate establishes a Select Committee on Presidential Campaign Activities, which begins Watergate hearings.

June John Dean tells the Select Committee that Nixon authorized a cover-up.

July The Select Committee learns that Nixon had been secretly recording presidential conversations since 1971 and asks Nixon to release certain tapes. Nixon refuses.

Dean testifies before the Select Committee.

The tapes become the center of the controversy.

August Cox sues Nixon for the tapes. Judge John J. Sirica orders Nixon to release the tapes. Nixon appeals, but the appeals court supports Sirica.

October Nixon offers summaries of the tapes, which Cox rejects. Nixon has Cox fired, setting off a series of firings and resignations known as the "Saturday Night Massacre." The House of Representatives begins steps to impeach Nixon. Nixon finally releases the tapes, but investigators find two are missing.

November An eighteen-and-a-half minute gap is found on one of the tapes. The White House blames accidental erasure, but later investigation proves that the tape was deliberately erased.

1974

January Nixon claims "executive privilege."

April Attorney Leon Jaworski, the new special prosecutor, and the House Judiciary Committee subpoena Nixon to surrender tapes and related documents. Nixon supplies 1,254 pages of edited transcripts. Jaworski sues Nixon for the originals.

July The Supreme Court orders Nixon to give Jaworski the tapes and documents. The House Judiciary Committee recommends three articles of impeachment.

August Nixon releases additional transcripts, which show that he learned of the break-in as early as June 23, 1972 and ordered the cover-up. Nixon resigns August 9.

Nixon leaves Washington, D.C.

The Senate Investigates At the same time, a Senate Select Committee on Presidential Campaign Activities began to investigate the Watergate affair. James McCord, one of the convicted Watergate burglars, responded to his lengthy prison sentence by testifying before the committee, giving members a sense of what had gone on. The newspaper stories by Woodward and Bernstein helped the investigation, while leads from the Senate committee in turn aided the reporters.

As rumors grew that the White House was involved, Nixon tried to protect himself. In April 1973 he fired Haldeman and Ehrlichman, his two closest aides. On national television, he proclaimed that he would take final responsibility for the mistakes of others, for "there can be no whitewash at the White House."

Still the investigation ground on. In May 1973 the Senate committee, chaired by Senator Sam Ervin of North Carolina, began televised public hearings on Watergate. Millions of Americans watched, fascinated, as the story unfolded like a mystery thriller. John Dean, seeking to save himself, testified that Nixon knew about the cover-up. Other staffers described the various illegal activities undertaken in the White House.

The most dramatic moment came when one aide revealed the existence of a secret taping system in the President's office that recorded all meetings and telephone conversations—supposedly to provide a historical record of Nixon's presidency. Now those tapes could show whether or not Nixon had actually been involved in the cover-up.

The "Saturday Night Massacre" In an effort to prove his honesty, Nixon agreed to the appointment of a special Watergate prosecutor in the Justice Department. Archibald Cox, a Harvard law professor, took the post and immediately asked for the tapes. Nixon refused to release them. When Cox persisted, Nixon ordered him fired during the weekend of October 20, 1973, triggering a series of resignations and firings that became known as the "Saturday Night Massacre."

An Administration in Jeopardy By this time, Nixon was in serious trouble. His public

RESOURCE DIRECTORY

approval rating plummeted. After Cox's firing, *Time* magazine declared "The President Should Resign."

Nixon appointed another special prosecutor, Leon Jaworski of Texas, who also asked for the tapes. Nixon then tried to show his innocence by releasing edited transcripts of some of his White House conversations. He carefully excised the most damaging evidence, but many people were angry and disillusioned when they read the actual words of some of the conversations in the Oval Office.

There was a subplot in the troubled White House. Vice President Spiro Agnew, accused of evading income taxes and taking bribes, resigned in disgrace early in October 1973, just ten days before the "Saturday Night Massacre." To succeed him, Nixon named Gerald R. Ford, the House minority leader. For nearly two months, until the Senate confirmed Ford, the nation had a President in trouble—and no Vice President.

Impeachment Ahead? Nixon had to do something. After the "Saturday Night Massacre," Congress had begun the process that could lead to impeachment—bringing charges and holding a trial to determine whether he should remain in office. In July 1974, the House Judiciary Committee, which included twenty-one Democrats and seventeen Republicans, began to hold hearings to determine if there were adequate grounds for impeachment.

This debate, like the earlier hearings, was televised nationally. The country watched anxiously as even Republicans deserted the President. Representative M. Caldwell Butler of Virginia spoke for many of them when he said:

> For years we Republicans have campaigned against corruption and misconduct. . . . But Watergate is our shame. Those things have happened in our house and it is our responsibility to do what we can to clear it up. . . . It is a sad chapter in American history, but I cannot condone what I have heard; I cannot excuse it; and I cannot and will not stand for it.

By sizable tallies, the House Judiciary Committee voted to impeach the President on

📁 **Viewpoints Activity** On Nixon's Impeachment, found in the Unit 10 folder, pp. 19–20, presents several excerpts from impeachment hearings to further the discussion on presidential conduct.

Viewpoints
On Nixon's Impeachment

In July 1974, the House Judiciary Committee conducted its televised debate on the possible impeachment of President Richard Nixon. *What attitudes about Nixon's impeachment are expressed in the two statements below?*

For Impeachment

"My faith in the Constitution is whole, it is complete, it is total. I am not going to sit here and be an idle spectator to the diminution [lessening], the subversion [overthrow], the destruction of the Constitution. . . . The Framers confided in the Congress the power if need be to remove . . . a President swollen with power and grown tyrannical."

Representative Barbara Jordan, Democrat (Texas)

Against Impeachment

"As the trust is placed in Congress to safeguard the liberties of the people through the awesome and extraordinary powers to remove a President, so must Congress's vigilance be fierce in seeing that the trust is not abused. . . . Not only do I not believe that any crimes by the President have been proved beyond a reasonable doubt, but I do not think the proof even approaches the lesser standards of proof which some of my colleagues, I believe, have injudiciously [with poor judgment] suggested we apply."

Representative Edward Hutchinson, Republican (Michigan)

Americans were fascinated but dismayed by the conversations taped in the Oval Office. This cartoonist saw Nixon as a man trapped by his own plots.

Answer to . . .

Viewpoints

Jordan points to the constitutional basis for impeachment; Hutchinson argues that legislative grounds for impeachment have not yet been fulfilled. For a thorough examination of the impeachment issue, see the Resource Directory below.

In Depth
Then and Now

When Richard Milhous Nixon died on April 22, 1994, at age eighty-one, biographer Garry Wills wrote of him: "In some areas of politics, he seemed to know almost everything about anything—except about himself. His strengths and weaknesses fed upon each other. He was a small bitter man and a very grand diplomat. Who can read that riddle? Some of us have spent much of our lives trying to read it, with little better success than his own."

Section 3 Review Answers

1. (a) Watergate, see p. 897, (b) Pentagon Papers, see p. 897, (c) perjury, see p. 899

2. (a) Plumbers, see p. 897, (b) Daniel Ellsberg, see p. 897, (c) John J. Sirica, see p. 899

3. To monitor Democratic party headquarters activities.

4. Money carried by the burglars was traced back to CREEP (the Committee to Reelect the President), involving campaign manager John Mitchell, the former attorney general.

5. Nixon became involved in the cover-up when he authorized the CIA to call off the FBI investigation on the grounds that national security was involved and when he approved the payment of hush money to keep the burglars quiet.

6. It was clear that he would be impeached if he did not resign.

7. While the upheaval in leadership was unusual for the United States and had many repercussions, the transition was legal and peaceful, and the basic structure of government and law remained intact.

Reteach

Have students use information from this section to answer the following questions in one or two sentences:

● Who were Nixon's "enemies"?

● What methods did Nixon use to win reelection?

● Where were the Watergate burglars captured and arrested?

● Why did Nixon fire special prosecutor Archibald Cox?

● How did Nixon respond to the threat of impeachment?

Reinforcing the Big Idea

Nixon's White House was one of suspicion and abuse of power. His efforts to use the presidency for his own political gain led to scandal—and to the end of his presidency.

In the midst of the Watergate hearings, a worn Nixon finds the energy to shake hands with some sightseers at the White House.

charges of obstruction of justice, abuse of power, and refusal to obey a congressional order to turn over his tapes. To remove him from office, the full House of Representatives would have to vote for impeachment, and the Senate would have to hold a trial. The outcome seemed obvious in this case.

Nixon Resigns from Office On August 5, after a brief delay, Nixon finally obeyed a Supreme Court ruling and released the tapes. Despite a disturbing gap of eighteen and a half minutes where the conversation had been mysteriously erased, the tapes gave clear evidence of Nixon's involvement in the cover-up. Three days later, Nixon appeared on national television and painfully announced that he would resign the office of the President the next day. On August 9, Nixon resigned, the first President ever to do so. In a smooth constitutional transition, Vice President Gerald Ford was sworn in, telling the country "our long national nightmare is over."

Why Watergate?

Watergate raised many questions about the use and abuse of power. Richard Nixon was committed to winning in 1972 at any cost. He had gone further than his predecessors in creating an "imperial presidency," surrounding himself with subordinates who believed he could do no wrong. Though many of them were lawyers, they did not let the law stand in their way. They paid a high price, for most of them spent time in prison because of the Watergate cover-up. Nixon himself was never indicted and remained free by virtue of a presidential pardon granted by Gerald Ford.

SECTION 4 REVIEW

Key Terms, People, and Places

1. Define (a) Watergate, (b) Pentagon Papers, (c) perjury.
2. Identify (a) Plumbers, (b) Daniel Ellsberg, (c) John J. Sirica.

Key Concepts

3. Why did the White House undertake illegal wiretaps?
4. How was the Watergate break-in linked to the White House?

5. How did Richard Nixon become involved in the Watergate cover-up?
6. What was the ultimate reason for Nixon's resignation?

Critical Thinking

7. **Determining Relevance** In what way did the ending of the Watergate affair demonstrate the strength of the Constitution?

RESOURCE DIRECTORY

Teaching Resources

 Quiz found in the Unit 10 folder, p. 14, covers the main ideas in this section as well as the key terms.

 Chapter Test Forms A and B are found in the Unit 10 folder, pp. 31–36.

 Answer Keys found in the Unit 10 folder, p. 143–156, provides answers to all student activities.

Media and Technology

Transparency Graphic Organizer, G-4

Guided Reading Audiotapes (English and Spanish)

Computer Test Bank

Analyzing Presidential Records

Presidential papers record a President's time in office. Letters, memorandums, notes on meetings, speeches, transcripts of press conferences—nearly every word the President utters seems to find its way into these papers. Thus, they provide a good source of information when trying to piece together historical evidence about the past.

In more recent times, technology has added new forms of "papers" as historical evidence—audio- and video-tapes. President Nixon's audiotapes, recorded in the Oval Office, loomed large in the Watergate affair. In fact, it was a tape that finally ended the affair—a recording of a conversation that took place just a few days after the Watergate break-in on June 16, 1972. Not released until August 5, 1974, it proved that Nixon knew of the cover-up all along.

Use the following steps to analyze excerpts from this tape.

1. Identify the source by asking *who*, *when*, *where*, and *what*.
(a) Who are the speakers on the tape? (b) Who else is mentioned in it? (c) When did the conversation take place? (d) Where? (e) What is the major topic?

2. Identify the main points of information in the excerpts.
(a) Why is Haldeman concerned about the FBI? (b) What recommendation does he put forward about using the CIA to end the investigation? (c) How does President Nixon respond to the recommendation?

3. Study the tape to find clues to the historical period. (a) What can you infer about the extent of the powers that Nixon believed he had over FBI and CIA operations? (b) What can you infer about Nixon's sense of priorities at the time the recording was made? (c) What can you infer about the extent of Haldeman's influence?

CAST OF CHARACTERS
PRESIDENT NIXON
H. R. HALDEMAN, *Chief of Staff*
PAT GRAY, *Acting FBI Director*
JOHN MITCHELL, *Chairman of CREEP*
VERNON WALTERS, *Deputy CIA Director*

June 23, 1972

HALDEMAN Now, on to the investigation, you know the Democratic break-in thing. We're back in the problem area because the FBI is not under control, because Gray doesn't exactly know how to control it and . .. their investigation is now leading into some productive areas—because they've been able to trace the money. . . . Mitchell's recommendation [is] that the way to handle this now is for us to have Walters call Pat Gray and just say, "Stay . . . out of this—this is ah, business here we don't want you to go any further on it." That's not an unusual development, and ah, that would take care of it.

NIXON What about Pat Gray—you mean Pat Gray doesn't want to?

HALDEMAN Pat does want to. He doesn't know how to, and he doesn't have any basis for doing it. Given [Walters' call], he will then have the basis.

NIXON Yeah.

HALDEMAN [Gray will] say, "We've got this signal from across the river [the CIA] to put a hold on this." And that will fit rather well because the FBI agents who are working the case, at this point, feel that's what it is.

NIXON They've traced the money [the money that was found on the Watergate burglars]? Who'd they trace it to?

[Haldeman describes various people who contributed to CREEP and Nixon wonders if these people will say that the burglars, not CREEP, asked for the money.]

HALDEMAN Well, if they will. But then we're relying on more and more people all the time. That's the problem and they'll stop if we could take this other route.

NIXON All right.

HALDEMAN And you seem to think the thing to do is get [the FBI] to stop?

NIXON Right, fine.

Excerpted from *The New York Times,* Tuesday, August 6, 1974

Historian's Toolbox Activity Analyzing Presidential Records, found in the Unit 10 folder, p. 21, focuses on the inaugural address of President Clinton for further examination of presidential documents as historical evidence.

TOOLBOX

Historical Evidence
Analyzing Presidential Records

Focus Examine the transcript of an actual presidential conversation to analyze its value as historical evidence.

Instruct Ask for student volunteers to read and act out the transcript. After the performance, ask students to discuss what strikes them as interesting or important about the conversation. Was it what they expected of a "presidential" conversation? Why or why not? What does the conversation reveal about Nixon and his leadership style? Ask students how they think American citizens might benefit by reading such presidential records.

Extend See Historian's Toolbox Activity in the Resource Directory below.

Answers

1. (a) Chief of Staff H. R. Haldeman and President Richard Nixon. (b) Pat Gray of the FBI, John Mitchell of CREEP, and Vernon Walters of the CIA. (c) June 23, 1972 (d) The Oval Office. (e) How to stop the investigation of the Watergate break-in.

2. (a) They have traced the money the burglars were carrying to people who contributed to CREEP. (b) He describes Mitchell's recommendation that the CIA tell the FBI to stop the investigation because it involves the CIA. (c) He agrees to it.

3. (a) Nixon obviously believes that he can order one government agency to lie to another if it is expedient for his needs. (b) He must believe that protecting his administration and getting himself reelected take precedence over honesty and proper use of government agencies. (c) Haldeman seems to know what is happening at every phase of the operation; his suggestions are readily accepted by the President.

Chapter Review Answers

Understanding Key Terms, People, and Places

Terms
Students should refer to the definitions of the key terms in the chapter to write sentences that show the relation of each word to the events of 1968 or the Nixon years.

True or False
1. true
2. false, *realpolitik*
3. false, Poor People's Campaign
4. false, embargo
5. true

Word Relationships
1. (b) does not belong. Humphrey, Wallace, and Nixon all ran for President in 1968. Kissinger was Nixon's national security adviser and secretary of state.

2. (a) does not belong. Haldeman, Ehrlichman, and Mitchell were members of Nixon's staff; McCarthy, an antiwar candidate, ran for the Democratic nomination in the 1968 election.

3. (c) does not belong. The Plumbers were men organized by the White House to stop security leaks. They broke into the office of Ellsberg's psychiatrist after Ellsberg released the "Pentagon Papers"; and Sirica investigated their burglary of the Democratic party headquarters at the Watergate complex. Kennedy was assassinated while running for President in 1968.

Reviewing Main Ideas

1. Americans' beliefs in nonviolent change were threatened; and many people felt disillusioned. Some African Americans showed their frustration and rage by rioting; 124 cities experienced riots after King's death.

2. The party was in disarray because of differing attitudes toward the Vietnam War, the lack of a candidate who could draw the party together, and the propensity of counterculture groups to annoy the establishment.

3. Voters were reacting against the recent assassinations of King and Kennedy and the violence at the Democratic convention.

4. Nixon's staff was fiercely loyal and willing to go to any lengths to protect him or to help him achieve his goals.

5. Nixon took a more conservative stance, although he eventually resorted to deficit spending and ninety-day freezes. He also tried to stop increased government spending on social programs.

Chapter Review

Understanding Key Terms, People, and Places

Key Terms
1. Poor People's Campaign
2. imperial presidency
3. Organization of Petroleum Exporting Countries (OPEC)
4. embargo
5. busing
6. *realpolitik*
7. détente
8. Strategic Arms Limitation Talks (SALT)
9. Watergate
10. Pentagon Papers
11. perjury

People
12. Robert F. Kennedy
13. Eugene McCarthy
14. Hubert Humphrey
15. George C. Wallace
16. Richard M. Nixon
17. Spiro Agnew
18. Henry A. Kissinger
19. H. R. Haldeman
20. John Ehrlichman
21. John Mitchell
22. Plumbers
23. Daniel Ellsberg
24. John J. Sirica

Terms For each term above, write a sentence that explains its relation to the events of 1968 or to the Nixon years.

True or False Determine whether each statement is true or false. If it is true, write "true." If it is false, change the underlined term to make the statement true.
1. In the spring of 1971, newspapers published the Pentagon Papers, a huge, secret government study of the Vietnam War.
2. Henry Kissinger was an admirer of détente, or politics based on achieving power.
3. In 1968 Martin Luther King, Jr., began the Strategic Arms Limitation Talks.
4. Because the United States supported Israel in the war in the Middle East, Saudi Arabia imposed a perjury on oil shipments.
5. Oil prices soared when members of OPEC quadrupled their prices.

Word Relationships Three of the people in each of the following sets are related in terms of their activities and accomplishments. Choose the person who does not belong and explain why he does not belong.
1. (a) Hubert Humphrey, (b) Henry A. Kissinger, (c) Richard M. Nixon, (d) George C. Wallace
2. (a) Eugene McCarthy, (b) John Ehrlichman, (c) John Mitchell, (d) H. R. Haldeman
3. (a) Plumbers, (b) Daniel Ellsberg, (c) Robert F. Kennedy, (d) John J. Sirica

Reviewing Main Ideas

Section 1 (pp. 880–883)
1. How did the assassinations of Martin Luther King, Jr., and Robert Kennedy affect Americans?
2. Why was the Democratic party in such a state of disunity and disarray at the 1968 convention?
3. How did Nixon's law and order stance help him win the presidency?

Section 2 (pp. 886–891)
4. Describe Nixon's relationship to the key members of his staff.
5. How did Nixon differ from his predecessors on issues of the economy and social programs?
6. Describe Nixon's civil rights policies and their effect on the civil rights movement.

Section 3 (pp. 892–896)
7. Explain why Henry Kissinger left a lasting mark on American foreign policy.
8. Describe how Nixon reversed United States policy toward China.
9. What was the result of Nixon's negotiations with the Soviet Union on arms control?

Section 4 (pp. 897–902)
10. What measures did the Committee to Reelect the President take to win the 1972 election?
11. Describe Nixon's involvement in the Watergate cover-up.
12. What were the impeachment charges brought against Nixon? Why was he not impeached?

6. Nixon opposed busing and did not support reform to advance the status of minorities; his policies slowed the civil rights movement.

7. Kissinger worked to ease cold war tensions and to end the Vietnam War.

8. Nixon reversed the policy of refusing to give diplomatic recognition to the communist government of China by relaxing some regulations and finally becoming the first American President to visit the country.

9. The result was the SALT I treaty, which was an important first step in limiting nuclear weapons.

10. The Committee to Reelect the President (CREEP) lied to discredit opposition candidates. For example, it falsely charged presidential contender Edmund Muskie with making insulting remarks about French Canadian residents of New Hampshire just two weeks before the New Hampshire primary. CREEP also sent hecklers to disturb Democratic campaign meetings. And a special unit within CREEP, the Plumbers, tried to wiretap the Democratic party headquarters at the Watergate complex in Washington, D.C.

11. Nixon tried to protect himself by firing his closest aides; he at first refused to release tapes from his secret taping system, then released edited transcripts of the tapes with the most damaging evidence excised; he fired special prosecutor Archibald Cox when Cox demanded the release of the tapes.

1. **Testing Conclusions** Some commentators have observed that only a Republican veteran of the cold war like Richard Nixon would have been able to reestablish relations with China. Do you agree, or do you feel that a Democratic President might have been equally successful?

2. **Demonstrating Reasoned Judgment** Should Nixon have been pardoned? Explain your reasoning.

3. **Predicting Consequences** What kind of President do you think Americans were looking for after Watergate and the Nixon resignation?

4. **Distinguishing False from Accurate Images** Adlai Stevenson described "Nixonland" as a place where the President would do "anything to win." Do you agree or disagree with Stevenson's observation? Explain your answer.

1. **Evaluating Primary Sources** Review the primary source excerpt on page 886. What does this statement reveal about Nixon's motivations? What other possible responses might someone have to being an outsider? Can you think of anyone with whom you are familiar in your personal life or from your reading whose ambition stems from anger?

2. **Understanding the Visuals** On page 886, Nixon is described as a shy and remote man who put up a front when he campaigned for office. The picture on page 886 shows Nixon on the campaign trail. Based on this picture, what conclusions can you make about the public side of Nixon's personality?

3. **Writing About the Chapter** You have been asked to write a preface to a new biography of Richard Nixon, in which you evaluate his presidency. First,

make a list of the positive accomplishments of the Nixon administration. Then, make a list of the negative aspects of Nixon's presidency. Note which events you think have had the most lasting impact. Next, write a draft of your preface in which you summarize your conclusions. Revise your preface, making sure that each idea is clearly explained. Proofread your preface and draft a final copy.

4. **Using the Graphic Organizer** This graphic organizer uses a flow map to show the sequence of events in 1968. (a) What was the result of the 1968 Democratic convention? (b) List three factors that contributed to Nixon's victory in the 1968 election. (c) On a separate sheet of paper, create your own flow map about the Watergate scandal, using this graphic organizer as an example.

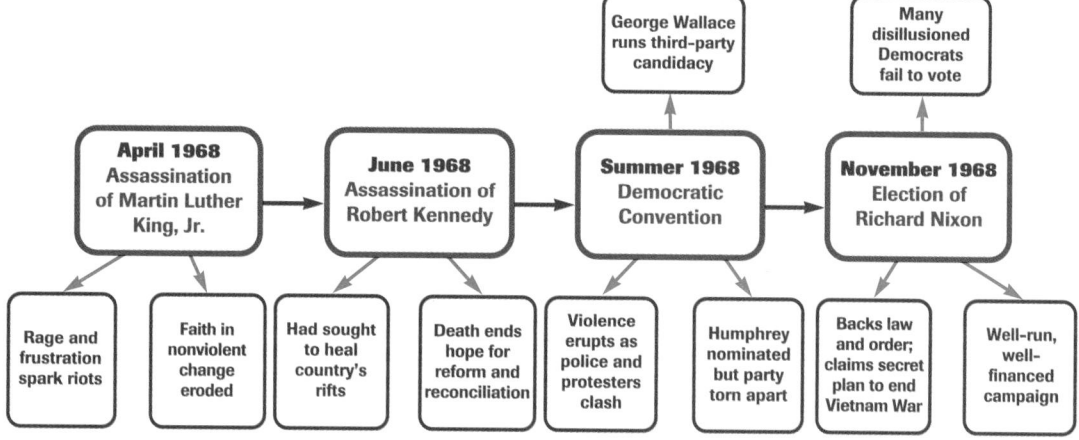

12. Nixon was charged with obstruction of justice, abuse of power, and refusal to obey a congressional order to turn over his tapes. He resigned before he could be impeached.

Thinking Critically

1. Students' responses should demonstrate an awareness that a hard-liner like Nixon was less likely to encounter conservative opposition than a Democrat.

2. Some students may believe that Nixon should have been imprisoned, as were many of his subordinates. Others may feel that the healing gesture suggested by the pardon was more important than censure.

3. Americans were probably looking for a President who could instill trust in the government.

4. Students should find ample evidence to support Stevenson's statement. Besides Watergate, Nixon's domestic policies on law and order and his "southern strategy" were both designed to win votes; in foreign policy, his trip to China was partly arranged to give him a boost at home.

Making Connections

1. Nixon was motivated by anger at being an outsider. Being an outsider could, for example, make someone more compassionate toward other outsiders or wish to educate others about acceptance of differences. The ambition of many dictators is thought to stem from anger.

2. The picture shows Nixon standing on the hood of a car with his arms stretched out high over his head in an effusive, triumphant gesture. Students should conclude that, based on this image, the public side of Nixon's personality was outgoing and exuberant.

3. Positive accomplishments include Nixon's foreign policy achievements; negative aspects include Watergate and Nixon's civil rights policies. Watergate had a lasting impact on the issue of trust in government, and Nixon's policy of détente had a lasting effect on foreign relations.

4. (a) Hubert Humphrey was nominated, but the party was torn apart. (b) Nixon backed law and order and claimed a secret plan to end the Vietnam War; his campaign was well run and well financed; the Democrats were not united behind Humphrey. (c) Students' graphic organizers should include events leading to the Watergate break-in, Nixon's involvement in the cover-up, and Nixon's resignation.

 ## Alternative Assessment

Final Evaluation
Use the following guidelines to evaluate student projects:

● **Evidence of thoughtfulness** To what extent do projects demonstrate an understanding of Nixon's policies and his successes and failures?

● **Evidence of outside research** To what extent do projects reflect use of outside research materials?

● **Sensitivity** To what extent do projects reflect an increased awareness of the role of Nixon's personality and personal style in his successes and failures as President?

Chapter 33 The Post-Watergate Period
1974–1980

📁 Teaching Resources (See Unit 10 Folder)

	Instruction	Enrichment

Section 1
The Ford Administration
(pp. 908–912)
	Reproducible Lesson Plan, p. 38
	Alternate Lesson Plan, p. 167
	Guided Reading and Review, p. 42
	Quiz, p. 43
		Literature Activity, A Search for Roots,
		  pp. 61–63
		Primary Source Activity, 1976: The
		  Bicentennial Year, p. 58

Section 2
The Carter Transition
(pp. 913–916)
	Reproducible Lesson Plan, p. 39
	Alternate Lesson Plan, p. 168
	Guided Reading and Review, p. 44
	Quiz, p. 45
		American Profiles Activity, Patricia Roberts
		  Harris, p. 52
		Primary Source Activity, A Crisis of
		  Confidence, pp. 59–60

Section 3
Carter's Foreign Policy
(pp. 917–921)
	Reproducible Lesson Plan, p. 40
	Alternate Lesson Plan, p. 169
	Guided Reading and Review, p. 46
	Quiz, p. 47
		American Profiles Activity, Andrew Young,
		  p. 53
		Visual Learning Activity, The Hostage Crisis as
		  a Media Event, p. 64
		Historian's Toolbox Activity, Recognizing
		  Ideologies, p. 56

Section 4
Carter's Domestic Problems
(pp. 923–927)
	Reproducible Lesson Plan, p. 41
	Alternate Lesson Plan, p. 170
	Guided Reading and Review, p. 48
	Quiz, p. 49
	Chapter Test, Forms A & B, pp. 66–71
		Critical Thinking Activity, Formulating
		  Questions, p. 57
		Visual Learning Activity, Responding to the
		  Energy Crisis, p. 65
		Viewpoints Activity, On Nuclear Energy,
		  pp. 54–55
		History Might Not . . . Activity, Helping to Heal
		  a War-Torn Nation, pp. 50–51

📁 Additional Chapter Resources

Resource Organizer, p. 37
Alternate Lesson Plan, p. 166
Answer Keys, pp. 143–156

Bibliography

For the Teacher

Lasch, C. *The Culture of Narcissism: American Life in an Age of Diminishing Expectations.* Warner Books, 1979.

Lasky, Victor. *Jimmy Carter: The Man and the Myth.* Marek, 1979. (An analysis of the Carter presidency.)

Sheehan, Neil. *After the War Was Over: Hanoi and Saigon.* Vintage, 1993. (A look at Vietnam's recovery in the 1990s.)

Terkel, S. *Working: People Talk About What They Do All Day and How They Feel About What They Do.* Pantheon, 1974, and *American Dreams: Lost and Found.* Pantheon, 1980. (Oral histories on the American Dream in the seventies and eighties.)

Prentice Hall Literature Excerpts from *The American Experience,* 1994, including Walker, Alice. "Everyday Use," from *In Love and Trouble: Stories of Black Women.* Harcourt Brace Jovanovich, 1973 edition.

THE BIG IDEA

The Big Idea for the chapter and how the main ideas in each section relate to the Big Idea are graphically displayed below. Comprehension of this chapter's Big Idea is critical to students' understanding of United States history and how we as a nation got where we are today.

Media and Technology

 Visions of America: History Might Not Have Happened This Way Game

 The Way It Works, H-21; Critical Thinking, I-5; Graphic Organizer, G-3

 Guided Reading Audiotapes (English and Spanish)

 Computer Test Bank

For the Student

Colby, Anne, and William Damon. *Some Do Care: Contemporary Lives of Moral Commitment.* The Free Press, 1993. (Profiles individuals who have made lifetime commitments to social change.)

Kidder, Tracy. *The Soul of a New Machine.* Little, Brown, 1981. (A study of the growth of the computer industry in the 1970s.)

Nader, Ralph. *Civics for Democracy: A Journey for Teachers and Students.* Essential Books, 1993. (Teaches citizenship by profiling students across the country working to improve their communities, and covers a history of the civil rights and women's rights movements.)

CHAPTER 33

The political scandal dubbed *Watergate* profoundly shook the people's faith in their leaders. Coming on the heels of the turbulence of the 1960s, the scandal's reach into the highest, most trusted offices of the government seemed to confirm the country's worst fears about the abuse of power. It was no surprise, then, when an outsider to Washington politics, Jimmy Carter, was elected President.

SECTION 1

When Nixon resigned, Vice President Gerald Ford, a modest and popular politician, became President. Ford's presidency was lackluster in addition to being plagued by economic stagnation and an undefined foreign policy. Ford's pardon of Nixon for any Watergate crimes was extremely unpopular.

SECTION 2

In 1976 Jimmy Carter, former governor of Georgia, was elected President. Carter, who had campaigned as an outsider to the world of Washington politics, discovered that his inexperience in and unfamiliarity with the federal government made it difficult for him to get his programs enacted.

SECTION 3

Carter had some great successes in foreign affairs by emphasizing negotiations, peacemaking, and human rights; however, his approach also brought about some serious crises, one of which played a central role in his failure to win reelection.

SECTION 4

Carter was generally unsuccessful in creating domestic programs and working with Congress to see them enacted.

The Post-Watergate Period
1974–1980

The Relevance of the Big Idea

After the Watergate scandal, the American people and the press began to scrutinize the nation's leaders and political candidates more closely than ever. Any hint of potential scandal became headline news. Almost all presidential candidates since Watergate have had to explain (some with more success than others) an embarrassing skeleton dug out of their closet. Tell students that in 1994, President Clinton and First Lady Hillary Rodham Clinton were challenged on their investment in the Whitewater real estate venture, which formed part of a confusing series of financial dealings carried out when Clinton held office in his home state of Arkansas.

Ask students to list minimum standards of conduct that should apply to all public officials.

In Depth

Global Connections

Early in his presidency Jimmy Carter made human rights a cornerstone of American foreign policy. He condemned the Soviet Union's treatment of dissidents and South Africa's policy of apartheid; and he also chastised South Korea, Ethiopia, and several Latin American nations for repressive policies. But Carter found it necessary to reconcile his convictions about human rights with pledges of support for repressive anticommunist regimes. He praised Iran under the dictatorship of the shah, for example, as an "island of stability."

906

CHAPTER 33

The Post-Watergate Period
1974–1980

*T*he upheaval from the Watergate scandal continued to disrupt American society even after Richard Nixon resigned. People wondered whether any President could heal the rifts that tore the country apart. Gerald Ford, the man who took Nixon's place, tried to revive the confidence that had sustained the United States through past troubles. But after two years in office, he lost the presidency to a little-known Democrat, Jimmy Carter, who promised the country honesty and morality.

Events in the United States

1973 Henry Kissinger wins the Nobel Peace Prize.
• Congress enacts the War Powers Act.

1974 Gerald Ford becomes President after Nixon resigns.

1976 Americans celebrate their bicentennial.
• Jimmy Carter is elected President.

| 1973 | 1974 | 1975 | 1976 |

Events in the World

1973 President Allende of Chile is killed in a military coup.

1974 Giscard d'Estaing becomes president of France.

1975 The Khmer Rouge takes power in Cambodia.

1976 Chinese leader Mao Zedong dies.

▶ RESOURCE DIRECTORY

Teaching Resources

Alternate Lesson Plan: Demonstrating the Big Idea found in the Alternate Lesson Plans folder, p. 166, provides a lesson strategy to instruct students about the Big Idea that the Watergate scandal had far-reaching consequences in American politics, hampering Ford's attempts to lead after Nixon and enabling Carter, with his promises of honest government, to be elected.

Alternative Assessment Handbook provides information, guidance, and strategies for alternative methods of assessment. It includes an essay on new trends in assessment, guidance and strategies for developing performance tasks and portfolios, scoring rubrics, and sample evaluation forms.

Pages 908–912
The Ford Administration

Gerald Ford faced difficulties with the presidency he inherited. Although he wanted to help the nation recover from the Watergate affair, he never managed to step forward as a strong leader or deal effectively with problems that dogged the economy.

Pages 913–916
The Carter Transition

The Watergate scandal continued to influence the nation's political decisions as the people chose a Democrat, Jimmy Carter, for President in 1976. Carter tried to bring a new spirit of trust and honesty to Washington.

Pages 917–921
Carter's Foreign Policy

Carter's religious beliefs led him to emphasize peacemaking and human rights in foreign affairs, resulting in some outstanding successes. Those same beliefs also played a part in preventing his reelection.

Pages 923–927
Carter's Domestic Problems

In addition to crises overseas, domestic issues brought more trouble for the Carter presidency. The administration could not effectively create and pass legislation, dooming Carter's energy program and efforts to stabilize the economy.

The New York Times
LATE CITY EDITION
VOL. CXXIII...No. 42,591
NEW YORK, MONDAY, SEPTEMBER 9, 1974
15 CENTS
All the News That's Fit to Print

FORD GIVES PARDON TO NIXON, WHO REGRETS 'MY MISTAKES'

Jimmy Carter '76

SORRY NO GAS

1977 President Carter establishes the Department of Energy. • The Panama Canal treaties are signed.	1978 President Carter visits Nigeria and Liberia. • Egyptian and Israeli leaders meet at Camp David.	1979 Americans are taken hostage in Iran. • A nuclear accident occurs at Three Mile Island in Pennsylvania.	1980 Jimmy Carter loses the presidency to Ronald Reagan.
1977	**1978**	**1979**	**1980** **1981**
1977 South Africa declares the black homeland of Bophuthatswana independent.	1978 Civil war begins in Nicaragua.	1979 Egypt and Israel sign a peace treaty. • Margaret Thatcher becomes British	1980 War begins between Iran and Iraq.

The Ford Administration

SECTION 1

The Ford Administration

1. FOCUS

Connecting to the Big Idea

See page 906B. Explain that when Vice President Ford stepped up to the presidency after Nixon resigned in 1974, Americans were cheered by his honesty and simplicity. However, his administration proved mediocre. Ask what problems plagued the Ford administration.

Objectives

● Describe Gerald Ford's congressional experience and explain why some critics questioned his qualifications for President.
● Describe the economic troubles of the mid-1970s.
● Describe Ford's foreign policy.

Bellringer

Ask students to think of a time when they excused, or forgave, a friend, classmate, or family member. What does offering a pardon imply about the guilt or innocence of the person pardoned?

Reading Strategy

Relating to Topic Ask students to think about the meaning of the subheading on page 908, "A Ford, not a Lincoln." Then ask them to note the various failings of the Ford presidency described in the section.

SECTION PREVIEW

Gerald Ford faced difficulties with the presidency he inherited. Although he wanted to help the nation recover from the Watergate affair, he never managed to step forward as a strong leader or deal effectively with problems that dogged the economy.

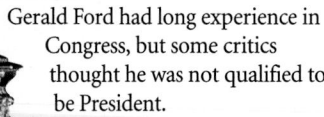

Key Concepts

• Gerald Ford had long experience in Congress, but some critics thought he was not qualified to be President.

• Neglected during Watergate, the economy was in trouble by the mid-1970s.

• Ford continued the foreign policies initiated under Nixon.

This ornate soup tureen was a gift from Queen Elizabeth II of Great Britain to President Ford to commemorate the American bicentennial.

Key Terms, People, and Places
stagflation, Helsinki Accords; Gerald R. Ford, Nelson Rockefeller

---

T he new President, **Gerald R. Ford,** was a decent man who faced a difficult job. He had to help the United States emerge from its worst political scandal at a time when the economy was in trouble and the war in Vietnam was ending in defeat. Ford began on the wrong foot, with a well-meant pardon for Richard Nixon that outraged many. In the months that followed, he never managed to provide the leadership the country needed.

"A Ford, not a Lincoln"

Gerald Ford was one of the most popular politicians in Washington when he was appointed Vice President in October 1973, after Spiro Agnew resigned in disgrace for accepting bribes. In a long career in Congress, Ford had risen to become minority leader of the House of Representatives, where he was well-liked by members of both parties. He was an unassuming, midwestern Republican from Michigan, who believed in traditional American virtues such as hard work and self-reliance. His stands on the issues of the day reflected these beliefs. Over the years, he had opposed federal aid to education, the antipoverty program, and government funds for mass transit. He supported measures for law and order and defense spending.

Nixon chose Ford as a noncontroversial figure who might bolster his own support from Congress. When Ford was confirmed, Congress and the public were interested mainly in his honesty and stability, not his qualifications for the presidency. In fact, during his years in Washington, Ford had often been the target of jokes. One was attributed to President Lyndon Johnson, who could be cruel when fighting political opponents. Knowing that Ford had played football on the University of Michigan championship team in the 1930s, Johnson remarked that perhaps he had played too long without a helmet.

While the choice of Ford as Vice President was generally well received, it brought new criticism of the man from those concerned about his qualifications for taking over the presidency should the need arise. Journalist Richard Rovere wrote in *The New Yorker*:

> *That he is thoroughly equipped to serve as Vice President seems unarguable; the office requires only a warm body and occasionally a nimble tongue. However . . . neither Richard Nixon nor anyone else has come forward to explain Gerald Ford's qualifications to serve as Chief Executive. He altogether lacks administrative experience. If his knowledge of foreign affairs*

 RESOURCE DIRECTORY

Teaching Resources

Reproducible Lesson Plan found in the Unit 10 folder, p. 38, provides a summary of the Section 1 lesson plan content.

Alternate Lesson Plan: Critical Thinking Determining Relevance, found in the Alternate Lesson Plans folder, p. 167, identifies the issues Ford confronted and analyzes his approach to problem solving.

Guided Reading and Review found in the Unit 10 folder, p. 42, provides a structure for reading and mastering the key concepts and reviewing the key terms for Section 1. (Guided Practice)

exceeds that of the average literate citizen, the fact has yet to be demonstrated.

Ford acknowledged his own limitations when he was sworn in, saying, "I am a Ford, not a Lincoln."

When Nixon resigned eight months later, Ford became the first nonelected President. Other Vice Presidents who had moved into the White House had at least been elected to the vice presidency as part of the national ticket. To fill the vice-presidential vacancy, Ford named former New York governor **Nelson Rockefeller**—creating the unique situation of having both a President and a Vice President who had been appointed, but not elected.

MAKING CONNECTIONS

The Twenty-fifth Amendment to the Constitution, which allows the President to appoint a replacement when the vice presidency is vacant, was passed in 1967, only a few years before Watergate. Is this the best way to fill such a high office? What other method would you suggest?

The Nixon Pardon

Ford became President in the midst of what he called "our long national nightmare." The nation was embittered by Watergate and did not look forward to the prospect of an impeachment trial—which would be only the second in United States history. Many Americans wondered whether the Constitution would survive such seeming disrespect from the nation's leaders. When Ford assumed the presidency, the nation needed a leader who could take it beyond the ugliness of Watergate.

In response to this public mood, President Ford declared that it was a time for "communication, conciliation, compromise and cooperation." Americans were on his side. *Time* magazine noted "a mood of good feeling and even exhilaration in Washington that the city had not experienced for many years."

All too quickly, however, Ford lost that popular support. Barely a month after Nixon had

resigned, Ford pardoned the former President for "all offenses" he might have committed, preventing further prosecution. On national television, Ford explained that he had looked to God and his own conscience in deciding "the right thing" to do about Nixon and "his loyal wife and family":

> T heirs is an American tragedy in which we have all played a part. It could go on and on and on, or someone must write the end to it. I have concluded that only I can do that, and if I can I must. . . . My conscience tells me that only I, as President, have the constitutional power to firmly shut and seal this book. My conscience tells me that it is my duty not merely to proclaim domestic tranquillity but to use every means that I have to ensure it.

Ford knew critics would surface, but he thought, "Most Americans will understand." He was wrong. While many of Nixon's loyalists

Betty Ford described her husband as "an accidental Vice President, and an accidental President, and in both jobs he replaced disgraced leaders." One of Ford's first presidential acts—pardoning Richard Nixon—stirred up a storm of controversy.

2. INSTRUCT

Explain/Discuss

Review the constitutional requirements for the office of President and discuss Ford's qualifications. What about Ford made him suitable as Nixon's Vice President, but less suitable as President?

Discuss Ford's reasons for pardoning Nixon. Then review the public reaction to Ford's well-intentioned action.

Discuss the efforts of the Ford administration to control inflation and increase productivity. Ask students to consider the results of these efforts. Why was the WIN program such a disaster for Ford?

Answer to . . .

MAKING CONNECTIONS

Students may suggest that Congress should have the right to appoint a new Vice President, that there be a special election, or that some other person in the executive branch be automatically next in line.

In Depth

Historical Misconceptions

The popular image of Gerald Ford as a bumbling, guy-next-door, caretaker politician is far from the truth. Social critic Michael Medved writes: "The guy next door doesn't spend sixteen hours a day and twenty-five years of his life in a nonstop quest for votes, power, and admiration. Like most politicians, Ford is a driven man."

Analyze

Ask students to analyze the concept of presidential leadership. Everett Carl Ladd, executive director of the Roper Center for Public Opinion Research, observes in his book *American Polity*: "At its best, presidential leadership moves the nation as far as possible in the directions the public favors, by means that are acceptable given prevailing values and institutional requirements." When did Ford act according to Ladd's definition of presidential leadership? Which of the methods Ford tried to use to solve problems were in opposition to prevailing values?

In Depth

Did You Know?

In the mid-1970s, Ford's case-by-case clemency offer to thousands of Vietnam-era draft resisters and military deserters was as controversial as his presidential pardon of Nixon. The Clemency Board found that though thousands had been either prosecuted and punished, or officially forgiven, the question remained "whether the American people will continue to condemn them."

faced prison for their role in Watergate, the former President walked away without a penalty. Ford's generous gesture backfired, making people wonder what kind of bargain had been made when Nixon resigned. They questioned the new President's judgment and ability as he tried to move ahead. Ford found himself booed when he made public speeches, just as Johnson and Nixon had been. He, too, had to leave speaking engagements from back doors to avoid angry demonstrators.

Ford Tries to Move Ahead

Recovery from Watergate was not the only difficult issue Ford had to face. While focused on the scandal, the nation seemed to have stood still, but some conditions had grown worse. Now, at a time when the country needed direction, the new administration seemed unclear about what course to take.

Problems with inflation and unemployment prompted one cartoonist to send President Ford this comment on the issue.

The Economy Stagnates Preoccupation with Watergate had hurt Nixon's ability to deal with the economy, and it was still in sorry shape. Inflation hovered around 11 percent a year, significantly higher than it had been in the past, while unemployment climbed to 5.3 percent, as the graph on page 911 shows. Home building, usually a sign of a healthy economy, stalled as interest rates rose. The fears of worried investors brought a drop in stock prices.

In the past, economists had believed that a moderate rise in inflation could help control the rate of unemployment. Conversely, rising unemployment would counterbalance an increase in inflation. Federal policy makers had sought to strike a satisfactory balance between the two. Now, however, inflation and unemployment both rose, while the economy remained stalled and stagnant. Economists named this new situation **stagflation,** but giving it a name did not make it go away. Nixon's preoccupation with Watergate had compromised his effort to deal with economic difficulties. By the time Ford assumed the presidency, the situation had reached crisis levels. Not since Franklin Roosevelt took office during the Great Depression had a new President faced such harsh economic troubles.

Ford's approach—like Herbert Hoover's in the early 1930s—was to try to restore public confidence. The centerpiece of his economic program was the "Whip Inflation Now," or "WIN," campaign. The President asked Americans to wear red and white "WIN" buttons, to save a portion of their incomes, and to plant vegetable gardens to challenge rising prices in the stores. This effort to manage the economy by coordinating the everyday actions of millions of people was doomed from the start. The plan had no real incentives and soon faded away.

Eventually, Ford's administration recognized that the government must act, but its initial attempts backfired. A policy to curb inflation by controlling the money supply led to the worst recession since the 1930s, with widespread job layoffs. Unemployment soared to 9 percent in 1975. Congress then backed an antirecession spending program, and Ford, reversing his previous course, backed an increase in unemployment benefits and a multibillion dollar tax cut. The economy recovered slightly, but inflation and unemployment remained high and the deficit increased.

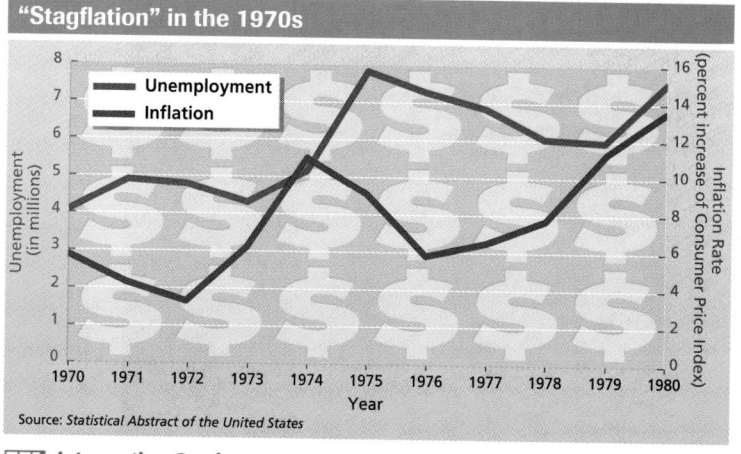

"Stagflation" in the 1970s

Source: Statistical Abstract of the United States

Interpreting Graphs
Upon assuming office, President Ford declared war on inflation, calling it "Public Enemy No. 1." Ford's administration, however, saw the worst economic slump in the United States since the Great Depression. *In what year did the highest consumer prices coincide with the second highest level of unemployment in the decade?*

Conflicts with Congress In spite of having served many years in the House of Representatives, President Ford was often locked in combat with the Democratic Congress. His basic dilemma was that he believed in limited government at a time when strong executive leadership was needed to get the nation on its feet. Jerold F. terHorst, his first press secretary, once noted how Ford's own sense of decency came into conflict with his view of presidential power:

If he saw a schoolkid in front of the White House who needed clothing, he'd give him the shirt off his back, literally. Then he'd go right in the White House and veto a school-lunch bill.

Ford vetoed bills to create a consumer protection agency and to fund programs for education, housing, and health care. Congress responded by overriding a higher percentage of presidential vetoes than it had since the presidency of Franklin Pierce in the 1850s.

Foreign Policy Actions In foreign policy, Ford followed the basic outlines of Nixon's approach, keeping Henry Kissinger on as secretary of state. During the Ford years, the United States continued forging ties with China, freeing the country from its involvement in Vietnam, and refocusing its attention on Europe.

Congress asserted itself on foreign policy as it did on domestic policy. Irritated at the growth of the "imperial presidency," it had passed the War Powers Act in 1973 over Nixon's veto. This law let Congress either approve or disapprove the President's sending troops overseas and bringing forces home. Congress now used its power to stop new United States military action in Southeast Asia as the North Vietnamese strengthened control over all Vietnam in 1975. It also refused to become involved in political unrest in Turkey and Angola.

Despite Congress's effort to play a greater role in foreign affairs, the Ford administration did initiate some foreign policy actions. In mid-1975, soldiers from communist Cambodia captured the *Mayaguez*, an American merchant ship cruising in Cambodian waters. When protests went unanswered, Ford sent 250 marines to rescue the ship's crew. The rescue succeeded, but 41 Americans were killed—probably needlessly, as later investigations showed that the Cambodian government apparently was preparing to return both ship and crew. For Ford and Kissinger, however, the incident was a chance to counteract the impression that Vietnam had weakened the United States internationally.

Activity

Cooperative Learning

Time: One class period.
Activity: Create a public relations campaign for a presidential program.
Grouping: Groups of four students.
Purpose: To create a program designed to increase public acceptance of Ford's WIN campaign and then rate the campaign's potential effectiveness.
Roles: Planners, writers, editors, media and marketing specialists.
Outcome: Students will identify key aspects of Ford's WIN program and analyze its potential.

Enrichment

Ask interested students to research and report on the celebration of the bicentennial in your community. Reports should include descriptions of special projects and festivities.

 In Depth

Did You Know?

Beginning on July 4, 1976, in Washington, D.C., the Declaration of Independence, the Constitution, and the Bill of Rights were on display for seventy-six consecutive hours to accommodate the thousands of tourists visiting the capital. In 1976 the nation had still not recovered from the divisive war in Vietnam. However, celebration of the nation's 200th birthday was a time for drawing together and for renewing the spirit of independence.

Section 1 Review Answers

1. (a) stagflation, see p. 910,
(b) Helsinki Accords, see p. 912

2. (a) Gerald R. Ford, see p. 908,
(b) Nelson Rockefeller, see p. 909

3. He had long experience in Congress and was well liked but had no experience as an executive or leader; he lacked foreign policy experience and knowledge.

4. Unemployment and inflation were both high; Ford's WIN program was ineffective. Efforts to control money brought a recession and higher unemployment.

5. Ford retained Kissinger as secretary of state; they continued the initiatives begun in the Nixon years.

6. Ford's good relationship with Congress deteriorated after he became President.

7. Whether or not they agree with Ford's decision to grant the pardon, students should demonstrate an understanding both of Ford's wish to bring Watergate to an end and of the widespread negative public reaction to his decision.

Reteach

Ask students to assess President Ford's effectiveness in healing the wounds of Watergate, restoring the health of the economy, and maintaining peace and good relationships with other nations.

 Reinforcing the Big Idea

Since President Ford's administration failed to develop and carry out coherent policies, Ford was not perceived as a strong leader. The next section describes the presidential campaign of 1976 and Carter's approach to the presidency.

"Uncle Sam" leads a joyful parade in honor of the 200th anniversary of the Declaration of Independence. All across the country, bicentennial celebrations drew people together and stirred up feelings of national pride. ✪

signed the **Helsinki Accords**, a series of agreements made at a summit meeting in Finland. There, thirty-five nations, including the Soviet Union, pledged to cooperate economically and to promote human rights. As revolutions in Africa and elsewhere around the world toppled colonial governments, the administration took steps toward developing relationships with the new regimes.

Foreign policy in the Ford years was mainly a reaction to outside events. Still, the United States remained at peace, avoided major confrontations, and continued the difficult process of redefining its role abroad.

The Country Celebrates a Birthday

Amidst lingering recession and the memory of Watergate, Americans seized the chance to forget their problems at a nationwide birthday party. July 4, 1976, marked the bicentennial, or two hundredth anniversary, of the Declaration of Independence. Across the country, people in small towns and great cities celebrated with parades, concerts, air shows, political speeches, and fireworks. ✪

The climax of the national party was the Fourth of July itself. In New York City, more than two hundred sailing ships, including majestic "tall ships," sailed into the harbor while millions watched from the shore. Other cities competed to have the most spectacular fireworks display or the longest parade. Many observers saw the bicentennial mood as an optimistic revival after years of gloom.

On other foreign policy fronts, Ford's record was stronger. Ford continued Strategic Arms Limitation Talks (SALT) and held out hope for further nuclear disarmament. He also

---

SECTION 1 REVIEW

Key Terms, People, and Places

1. Define (a) stagflation, (b) Helsinki Accords.
2. Identify (a) Gerald R. Ford, (b) Nelson Rockefeller.

Key Concepts

3. What were Ford's strengths and weaknesses as President?
4. What problems did the economy face during the Ford administration? How did President Ford attempt to address those problems?

5. What was the direction of Ford's foreign policy?
6. What was the relationship like between President Ford and Congress?

Critical Thinking

7. **Demonstrating Reasoned Judgment** Should Gerald Ford have pardoned Richard Nixon? Why or why not? Consider both the explanations that Ford gave and your own assessment of what the pardon did and did not accomplish.

 RESOURCE DIRECTORY ✪

Teaching Resources

✪ **Literature Activity** A Search for Roots, found in the Unit 10 folder, pp. 61–63, describes Alex Haley's search for his ancestral identity, in an excerpt from his book *Roots*, published in 1976.

Primary Source Activity 1976: The Bicentennial Year, found in the Unit 10 folder, p. 58, presents quotations from various demographic groups commenting on issues important in contemporary American society.

Quiz found in the Unit 10 folder, p. 43, covers the main ideas in this section as well as the key terms.

The Carter Transition

SECTION PREVIEW

The Watergate scandal continued to influence the nation's political decisions as the people chose a Democrat, Jimmy Carter, for President in 1976. Carter tried to bring a new spirit of trust and honesty to Washington.

Key Concepts

• Gerald Ford did not appear "presidential" to many voters in the 1976 election.

• Jimmy Carter's campaign emphasized his trustworthiness and his status as a Washington outsider.

• Carter's small-town background and deep religious beliefs influenced his style and policies as President.

Key Terms, People, and Places

James Earl Carter, Jr.

In a reaction against the Watergate scandal and economic woes, voters elected a Democrat, Jimmy Carter, as President in 1976. **James Earl Carter, Jr.,** a businessman and former naval officer who had been governor of Georgia, promised to bring a fresh approach to the White House. At first Carter enjoyed his status as a "Washington outsider," but in time that position lessened his ability to lead effectively.

The Election of 1976

Although Gerald Ford initially said that he would not seek election to the office he had inherited, by 1976 he had changed his mind. But as he campaigned to win the nation's approval, a number of personal liabilities continued to hurt his chances for success.

In the public's perception, Ford did not appear "presidential," and while people liked him, he never completely captured their confidence. He was a wooden speaker, and, as

described by the English journalist Alistair Cooke, "always seemed to be battling gamely with a language he had only recently acquired." At the Republican convention, Ford narrowly won the nomination against a strong challenge from Ronald Reagan, a former actor and governor of California, who represented the conservative wing of the party.

Ford faced Jimmy Carter, who, as governor of Georgia, had worked against racial discrimination in his state. Nationally, Carter began as a virtual unknown, with a broad smile and soft southern accent. In addition to his political activities, he also owned a successful peanut farm in Georgia. In a skillful primary campaign, he appealed to a wide audience and easily won the Democratic nomination. His running mate was Walter Mondale, a progressive senator from Minnesota.

Carter played on the backlash that followed Watergate. Over and over, he stressed that he was not part of the Washington establishment and so would bring a different perspective to the nation's capital. He distanced himself from many involved in the scandal by pointing out that he was not a lawyer but just "a peanut farmer."

Carter presented himself as honest and straightforward. In *Why Not the Best?*—an autobiography published in 1975—he said, "There is no need for lying. Our best national defense is the truth." In a later memoir, he recalled his campaign approach:

> I ran as though I would have to govern—always careful about what I promised, and determined not to betray those who gave me their support. Sometimes I irritated my opponents and the news reporters by firmly refusing to respond to questions to which I did not know the answers. And

Jimmy Carter's smile was famous. One writer described it as "the biggest grin of any President since TR."

---

1. FOCUS

  Connecting to the Big Idea

See page 906B. Explain that in 1976, Jimmy Carter, former governor of Georgia, was elected President. Ask what promises Carter made to the American people.

Objectives

● Describe how Ford's inability to project a presidential image affected his showing in the 1976 election.

● Describe how Jimmy Carter's campaign emphasized his trustworthiness and his status as a Washington outsider.

● Explain how Carter's small-town background and deep religious beliefs influenced his style and policies as President.

 In Depth

Biography

Barbara Jordan (b. 1933) represented the "New South" that the Carter presidency brought to national prominence. Elected to the Texas Senate in 1966, she was the first African American to sit in that body since 1883 and became one of its most articulate members. Jordan was elected to the United States House of Representatives in 1972, where she served for three terms. She delivered the keynote address at the Democratic convention in 1976, warning: "This is the great danger America faces. That we will cease to be one nation and become instead a collection of interest groups: city against suburb, region against region, individual against individual. Each seeking to satisfy private wants."

Ask students how they would rate the honesty of the current President and administration. Ask if they can envision any situation in which a President should be less than completely open and honest with the public.

Reading Strategy

Structured Overview Ask students to write the name *Jimmy Carter* in the center of a piece of paper and to note important details about Carter around his name as they read the section.

2. INSTRUCT

Explain/Discuss

Discuss how Ford's failure to convey a "presidential" image on television affected the election of 1976. Ask students which recent President they think had the strongest "presidential" image, and whether that President was also a good leader.

Ask students whether they think a campaign such as that waged by Carter tells voters what they really need to know about a candidate.

Discuss how Carter's outsider status, and his choice of other outsiders as his key advisers, hampered his ability to work with Congress.

Answer to ...

MAKING CONNECTIONS

Students should note that a vein of public distrust of officials and politicians runs through American political history, and that being an "outsider" separates a candidate from people's current discontent.

Caption Answer to ...

 Interpreting Maps

Ford was from the Midwest himself. His belief in traditional American values would appeal to many voters in this traditionally conservative area of the country.

---

repeatedly I told supporters, *"If I ever lie to you, if I ever make a misleading statement, don't vote for me. I would not deserve to be your President."*

Carter's appeal succeeded. The basic issue in 1976 was trust, and he used it superbly. Patrick Caddell, a public opinion pollster, noted:

> Without the trust thing, he couldn't have made it.... Most people would really rather trust other people than distrust them, except in politics; most people have a reason to distrust most candidates. Jimmy was a stranger in town. They had no reason to distrust him and he didn't give them one.

Carter began the campaign with a lead, then nearly lost it as voters wondered whether he could really govern. Ford hurt his own cause with a number of embarrassing mistakes, such as declaring in a television debate that the Soviets did not dominate Eastern Europe. One observer commented that the campaign was like the Indianapolis 500, the nation's largest auto race, with people watching to see who would crash next.

In the end, Carter gained the support of most elements of the old Democratic coalition. He was successful with blue collar, African American, and some Catholic voters. He also won most of the South. Though Democrats in races for Congress and local contests generally swept the election, Carter's own margin was narrow: he won 50 percent of the popular vote to Ford's 48 percent. The electoral vote, 297 to 240, was also close. The map below left shows these election results.

MAKING CONNECTIONS

Like Jimmy Carter, candidates for Congress and the presidency often point out that they are "Washington outsiders," not part of the establishment. Why do you think this argument appeals to some voters?

The President from Plains, Georgia

Jimmy Carter—a southerner with a short career in politics—*was* different from his recent predecessors in the White House. His family had lived for generations in the rural South; the population of his hometown of Plains was six hundred. After graduating in 1946 from the United States Naval Academy, where he was trained as an engineer, he served on nuclear submarines. Later he took over management of his family's prosperous peanut farm and warehouse. He did not enter Georgia state politics until 1962.

Carter's deeply felt religious faith dominated his view of the world and led to considerable curiosity and questioning from reporters. He was a born-again Baptist, who noted that his life had been "shaped in the church." He relied on the Bible and read it daily—often in Spanish to improve his skill with the language. His faith, he believed, would keep him from taking on "the same frame of mind that Nixon or Johnson did—lying, cheating and distorting the truth."

On the other hand, Carter believed strongly in personal freedom. In Georgia, for instance, he had rejected calls for prayer in the public

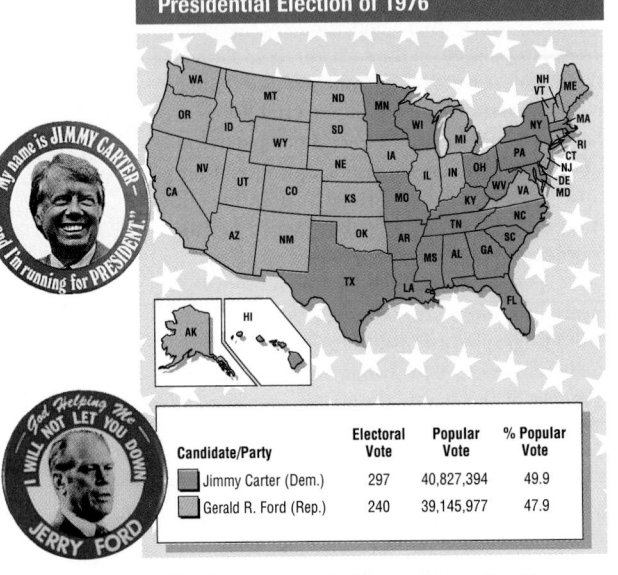

Presidential Election of 1976

Candidate/Party	Electoral Vote	Popular Vote	% Popular Vote
Jimmy Carter (Dem.)	297	40,827,394	49.9
Gerald R. Ford (Rep.)	240	39,145,977	47.9

Geography and History: Interpreting Maps
This map shows that Ford captured the vote of most of the Midwest. *What do you know about Ford's background that might help to explain this?*

RESOURCE DIRECTORY

Teaching Resources

American Profiles Activity Patricia Roberts Harris, found in the Unit 10 folder, p. 52, profiles the woman who, in addition to being the head of Carter's Department of Housing and Urban Development, was also the first African American woman to head a law school and the first to serve as an American ambassador.

Refusing the traditional limousine ride, President Jimmy Carter takes an inaugural stroll with his wife, Rosalynn, and daughter, Amy.

schools. Despite his strong religious beliefs, he would not use the presidency as a "pulpit" to promote them.

Personal Abilities Carter was thoughtful, able, and precise. Alistair Cooke called him the "most intelligent" and "best-informed" President the nation had known in years. Yet, Cooke said, Carter

> unfortunately used his intelligence to identify, and articulate, 12 sides to every question. . . . He wound up bearing a distressing resemblance to a stalled centipede. All the feelers were wiggling, but the body itself was immobile.

Approach to the Presidency In the first months of Carter's presidency, he appeared to be a reform Democrat. When he accepted his party's nomination, he demanded "an end to discrimination because of race or sex," challenged the established "political and economic elite," and suggested new welfare and health-care programs.

 He began by appointing significantly more women and minorities to his staff than previous administrations had done. Of 1,195 full-time appointees, 12 percent were women, 12 percent were African American, and another 4 percent were Hispanic. In nominating federal

judges, he chose four times as many women as had all previous Presidents combined.

In other areas, however, Carter began to look more conservative. As a result, his support from his own party gradually began to dwindle. He had won in 1976 by a narrower margin than other Democratic candidates, who consequently felt that they owed him less than if he had won a sweeping victory that carried them into office as well. The press, too, became more critical as the Carter presidency seemed to lose its momentum.

Staff Problems The "outsider" role became a disadvantage in the White House, too. Carter surrounded himself with southern, mostly Georgian, advisers, who had little sense of how crucial it was for the President to work with Congress. Carter himself was uneasy with congressional expectations and demands, and found it difficult to bargain effectively to pass legislation. Without any congressional experience, he lacked the kind of ability that Lyndon Johnson had to wheel and deal and win over reluctant politicians.

Carter also suffered from hints of scandal in an administration that took pride in being pure. Banker Bert Lance, the director of the Office of Management and Budget, was an old friend from Georgia on whom the President relied. When Lance was accused of allowing large bank overdrafts and other irregularities in

Analyze

Explain that Carter won nearly 90 percent of the African American and Mexican American vote in the 1976 election. President Ford did best among middle- and upper-middle class voters. Ask students to analyze these results in terms of each political candidate's party, and in terms of the problems of the economy under President Ford.

Activity

Preparing a Press Release

In order to have students understand the central issues of the 1976 presidential campaign, ask students to prepare a brief press release. Present to the class one of the broad themes of either the Carter or Ford campaign. Members of the class, acting as the press, may address questions to each "press official."

Enrichment

Ask students to research and report on the controversial role of Rosalynn Carter as her husband's most trusted adviser and on the major activities of the presidential spouses since Carter.

In Depth

Then and Now

A legacy of the Carter era is the link between human rights and diplomacy. As Winston Lord, assistant secretary of state for East Asian and Pacific affairs, described the post–cold war 1990s: "There are still security considerations but increasingly the thrust of the debate in foreign policy today is economics versus human rights. . . . I find myself going from a meeting with Amnesty International or Asia Watch in the morning to one with the Chamber of Commerce in the afternoon."

Section 2 Review Answers

1. James Earl Carter, Jr., see p. 913

2. Ford failed to convince people that he was "presidential" or a strong leader; also, many Americans were still reacting against the Republicans because of Watergate.

3. Carter chose advisers who were also outsiders; both he and they lacked skills and experience in establishing relations with Congress and passing legislation.

4. He tried at first to move away from the imperial presidency to a more casual, simple style. People liked it at first, but some critics charged that he was not being presidential enough.

5. Voters may have concluded that a sincerely religious person would bring honesty and integrity to act as an "antidote" to Watergate.

Reteach

Ask students to write either a newspaper editorial endorsing Carter for President in 1976 or an editorial column analyzing why Ford lost.

Alternative Assessment

Mid-Point Monitoring
Ask students if they have
• Selected a presidential subject
• Decided which materials to include
• Begun to locate sources of information

Reinforcing the Big Idea

In 1976 American voters selected Jimmy Carter, a Washington outsider and former governor of Georgia, as the nation's new President. Carter, who had a small-town background and strong religious beliefs, vowed to bring honesty to government. The next section focuses on Carter's foreign policy.

The Carters brought a folksy style to the presidency, a style some people criticized as undignified. In spite of the President's low-key image, he was known among friends as a "super-achiever." One friend called Carter "the most disciplined person I've ever seen."

his bank in the past, Carter came strongly to his defense but finally had to conclude that Lance must resign.

Carter's brother Billy posed other problems. He was a flamboyant, irreverent character who relished the attention he received as part of the presidential family. His careless, sometimes anti-Semitic, comments were embarrassing, and his acceptance of $200,000 in "loans" from friends in Libya made it look as if family business was entwined with foreign affairs.

A Question of Style Finally, Carter's image suffered from his attempt to discard the aloof, ceremonial style of the presidency for one of greater simplicity. At first, people responded warmly to his informal, "down home" approach. They loved it when he and his wife, Rosalynn, dismissed the limousine and strolled down Pennsylvania Avenue after the inauguration. Carter wore jeans in the White House and spoke to the nation on television wearing a cardigan sweater instead of a business suit. Critics, however, soon complained about the lack of dignity and ceremony. ✪

Carter finally discarded his low-key approach. After a few months, he let the band play "Hail to the Chief" on "special occasions," noting, "I found it to be impressive and enjoyed it." The honesty that prompted the President to make this comment also influenced his decisions in foreign policy, as the next section shows.

SECTION 2 REVIEW

Key Terms, People, and Places
1. Identify James Earl Carter, Jr.

Key Concepts
2. What problems during Ford's first term plagued him in the 1976 election?
3. How did Carter's "outsider" image hurt his effectiveness in office?

4. What was Carter's presidential style? How did the American people react to this style?

Critical Thinking
5. **Determining Relevance** How might Carter's outspokenness about his religious beliefs have affected the 1976 election?

▶ RESOURCE DIRECTORY

Teaching Resources

✪ **Primary Source Activity** A Crisis of Confidence, found in the Unit 10 folder, pp. 59–60, presents an excerpt from a televised address in which President Carter talked about what he saw as "threatening to destroy the social and the political fabric of America."

Quiz found in the Unit 10 folder, p. 45, covers the main ideas in this section as well as the key terms.

Carter's Foreign Policy

SECTION PREVIEW

Carter's religious beliefs led him to emphasize peacemaking and human rights in foreign affairs, resulting in some outstanding successes. Those same beliefs also played a part in preventing his reelection.

Key Concepts
- Carter's peacemaking efforts helped bring some stability to the Middle East.
- Carter's beliefs also guided his actions in Latin America and Africa.
- Relations with the Soviet Union worsened because of Carter's stand on certain issues.
- A hostage crisis in Iran gravely damaged the Carter presidency.

Key Terms, People, and Places
shuttle diplomacy, Camp David Accords, dissident; Anwar el-Sadat, Menachem Begin, Cyrus Vance, Shah Mohammad Reza Pahlavi, Ayatollah Ruholla Khomeini

P resident Carter achieved his greatest successes in foreign policy. Although he had little diplomatic experience when he took office, he brought the standards that governed his personal life into foreign affairs. While that approach brought notable achievements, it also complicated the relationship of the United States with some nations and ultimately hurt his chance for reelection.

Human Rights Diplomacy

Carter was unwilling to compromise his powerful sense of morality. This trait guided his approach to foreign policy. In his inaugural speech, he declared, "Our commitment to human rights must be absolute. . . . We can never be indifferent to the fate of freedom elsewhere." Support for human rights became the cornerstone of his foreign policy.

Carter later wrote, "Our country has been strongest and most effective when morality and a commitment to freedom and democracy have been most clearly emphasized in our foreign policy." But since the Truman era, he went on, the country had not kept to that standard:

> I nstead of promoting freedom and democratic principles, our government seemed to believe that in any struggle with evil, we could not compete effectively unless we played by the same rules or lack of rules as the evildoers. . . . When I announced my candidacy in December 1974, I expressed a dream: "That this country set a standard within the community of nations of courage, compassion, integrity, and dedication to basic human rights and freedoms."

MAKING CONNECTIONS

Jimmy Carter set certain standards for foreign policy. Do you think foreign policy today is based on some or all of those principles? Should it be? Why or why not?

A Step Toward Middle East Peace

Carter's commitment to finding ethical solutions to prickly problems was most visible in the Middle East question, and there he had the greatest success. In that unstable region, conflicts between Israel and the Arab nations had existed for nearly thirty years, most recently in 1967 and 1973. After the last Arab-Israeli war, Henry Kissinger had undertaken **shuttle diplomacy**, moving back and forth between nations in an attempt to arrange peace in the region, but conflicts continued.

At first, Carter hoped to call an international conference on the Middle East. Then leader

444 DAYS in CAPTIVITY
WELCOME BACK TO FREEDOM
GOD BLESS AMERICA

WELCOME HOME TO FREEDOM

Yellow ribbons became the symbol of hope for the safe return of the Americans held hostage in Iran. The ribbons seemed to decorate every available space when the hostages finally were freed.

1. FOCUS

Connecting to the Big Idea

See page 906B. Point out that President Carter's greatest successes were in the area of foreign policy. Ask what those successes were. How did Carter's stand on certain issues create problems with other nations?

Objectives
- Describe how Carter's peacemaking efforts brought some stability to the Middle East.
- Identify Carter's major actions in Latin America and Africa and show how they related to his emphasis on human rights and peacemaking.
- Explain how Carter's stance on human rights and the Soviet invasion of Afghanistan led to a worsening of relations with the Soviet Union.
- Describe the Iran hostage crisis and explain how it damaged the Carter presidency.

Bellringer

Ask students to list the rights that they would include in a definition of the term *human rights*.

Reading Strategy

Structured Overview Ask students to write the names of the following countries on a piece of paper: Israel, Egypt, Panama, China, Africa, Soviet Union, Iran. Ask students to take notes on Carter's major dealings with each country as they read the section.

Answer to . . .

MAKING CONNECTIONS

Answers will vary, but this is a good starting point for discussion of the role of human rights in United States foreign policy.

Explain/Discuss

Ask students to create a definition of *human rights*, using their thoughts from the Bellringer activity above. Ask them to compare their definitions with that of the Carter administration.

Ask why boycotting the Olympic Games was a serious demonstration of dissatisfaction with the Soviet invasion of Afghanistan. Tell students that, in addition, Carter imposed a grain embargo preventing the Soviet Union from importing grain from the United States. Ask how such an embargo hurt the Soviet Union. How would it hurt the United States?

Review the events leading up to the Iran hostage crisis. Ask what other measures Carter might have taken to free the hostages. Why was the situation so frustrating for Americans?

In Depth

Interdisciplinary

While at Harvard, An Wang (1920–1990) started his own business, Wang Laboratories, in 1951. During the 1970s and early 1980s, the company became a $3 billion operation. He also helped fund a student exchange program between the United States and China and was awarded the Medal of Liberty at the relighting of the Statue of Liberty in 1986. (See the Resource Directory on page 936.)

A jubilant President Carter congratulates Egypt's President Sadat (left) and Israeli prime minister Begin (right) on the signing of the Camp David Accords, a historic step toward peace in the Middle East.

Anwar el-Sadat of Egypt made a historic visit to Israel, beginning negotiations with Prime Minister **Menachem Begin.** The two men had such different personalities, however, that they had trouble compromising. Carter intervened, sending Secretary of State **Cyrus Vance** to invite them to Camp David, the rustic presidential retreat in the Maryland hills. In such a setting, he hoped that he could smooth their differences and move the peace process forward.

Carter knew it was a bold step. In his diary entry for July 31, 1978, he wrote, "We understand the political pitfalls involved, but the situation is getting into an extreme state." He and the two Middle Eastern leaders maintained tight secrecy about the coming conference.

At Camp David in September 1978, Carter assumed the role of peacemaker and practiced highly effective personal diplomacy to bridge the gap between Sadat and Begin. They finally agreed on a framework for peace that became known as the **Camp David Accords.** Under the resulting peace treaty, Israel would withdraw from the Sinai peninsula, which it had occupied in 1967. Egypt, in return, became the first Arab country to recognize Israel's existence as a nation.

The Camp David Accords, of course, did not solve all the problems of the Middle East. Foremost was the question of what to do about the Palestinians, many of whom had fled their homes when Arab nations declared war on Israel immediately after that country was established in 1948. Still, as Secretary of State Vance noted:

> The Camp David Accords rank as one of the most important achievements of the Carter administration. First, they opened the way to peace between Egypt

and Israel, which transformed the entire political, military, and strategic character of the Middle East dispute. Genuine peace between Egypt and Israel meant there would be no major Arab-Israeli war, whatever the positions of [other Arab groups].

Moreover, Vance pointed out, the agreement also let negotiators focus on the Palestinian question and established a process for future talks.

Foreign Policy Takes New Directions

Carter's foreign policy team took new steps in other parts of the world as well. Often these reflected the President's own philosophy.

The Panama Canal Another diplomatic milestone was Carter's successful fight to have the Senate ratify treaties returning the Panama Canal to Panama by the year 2000. Once again, his morality guided his approach to foreign policy.

In the early 1900s, President Theodore Roosevelt was proud of the way he had gained control of Panamanian land for the canal. Now Panama and other Latin American countries were increasingly unhappy with the continuing United States presence. It was time to give up some control over that region.

Returning the canal caused bitter debate in Congress, but the Senate finally accepted the pacts by a close margin of one vote. While agreeing to return the canal, the United States reserved the right to intervene militarily, if necessary, to keep it open. The pacts gave the United States security while improving relations with Latin America.

Recognition of China Building on Nixon's initiative in Asia, Carter took the next step and established diplomatic relations with the People's Republic of China as of January 1979. The Chinese wanted American technology and expertise in modernizing their country, while the United States hoped that closer ties with China would keep the Soviet Union on guard. Businesses in the United States also were eager to open the Chinese market of nearly a billion people.

RESOURCE DIRECTORY

Teaching Resources

 American Profiles Activity found in the Unit 10 folder, p. 53, profiles Andrew Young, President Carter's ambassador to the United Nations.

New African Nations Great changes were taking place in Africa, as countries that had been dominated by colonial powers revolted and became independent nations. Under Carter, relations with many nations in Africa improved, guided by Andrew Young, United States ambassador to the United Nations.

⭐ Young, a minister and civil rights leader who had served in Congress, shared many of Carter's views. He convinced the President that the United States should not interfere with African leaders as they shaped new governments. When Carter visited Nigeria and Liberia in March 1978, the popularity of this approach was shown as thousands cheered him in the streets.

Soviet-American Relations

Several issues complicated the relationship between the United States and the Soviet Union. Détente—a relaxation of the tensions between the superpowers—was at a high point when Carter took office. In his first year, he declared optimistically that the United States would forge even closer ties with the Soviet Union.

Then Carter's commitment to human rights alienated Soviet leaders, undermining efforts to work together. The Soviets were annoyed when the President verbally supported **dissidents,** Soviet writers and other activists who opposed the actions of their government.

SALT II In particular, this situation slowed efforts to reach further agreement on arms control. Negotiations were already underway for a second Strategic Arms Limitation Treaty (SALT II). Misjudging the Soviets, Carter offered new weapons reduction proposals that went further than earlier agreements. The Soviets, already suspicious of Carter because the United States had recognized China and was vocally supporting human rights, balked at the proposals.

Finally, Carter and Soviet president Leonid Brezhnev signed the new treaty in Vienna in June 1979. More complicated than SALT I, it limited the number of nuclear warheads and missiles each power retained. SALT II still had to be ratified by the Senate, however.

Andrew Young (left) believed strongly in black majority rule in Africa. In 1981 he would be elected mayor of Atlanta, Georgia.

Afghanistan SALT II seemed to have little chance of passage when the Soviet Union invaded Afghanistan, a country on its southern border. To end agitation against the Soviet-supported government there, Soviet troops invaded in December 1979.

Carter reacted by calling Brezhnev on the "hot line," the open telephone line between Washington and Moscow, and telling him that the invasion was "a clear threat to the peace." He also added, "Unless you draw back from your present course of action, this will inevitably jeopardize the course of United States–Soviet relations throughout the world."

Carter took other steps to emphasize United States disapproval of Soviet aggression. Realizing that SALT II surely would be turned down, he postponed sending it to the Senate. He also imposed a boycott on the summer Olympic Games scheduled to be held in Moscow in 1980. Eventually, some sixty other nations joined the boycott. Détente was effectively dead.

Iran Holds Americans Hostage

The worst foreign policy crisis that Carter faced occurred in Iran, on the Persian Gulf. For years the United States had supported the rule of **Shah Mohammad Reza Pahlavi,** who had taken many steps to modernize Iran.

Analyze

Have students analyze to what extent a President's personal beliefs should affect administration policy and presidential actions. Ask whether or not Carter's insertion of his own morality into his foreign policy was appropriate.

Activity
Teaching Heterogeneous Groups

To emphasize the importance of the Carter administration in bringing stability to the Middle East, divide students into groups of three to form peace negotiation teams. Each group should assign one student to play Anwar el-Sadat of Egypt, another to be Menachem Begin of Israel, and the third to play President Carter. Have each group then role-play the Camp David peace negotiations.

Enrichment

Ask students to respond to the following statement by President Carter in a 1977 speech on humane purposes in foreign policy: "The great democracies are not free because we are strong and prosperous. I believe we are strong and influential because we are free." (Speech at Notre Dame commencement, 1977.) Students should explain the relationship between freedom and strength.

Section 3 Review Answers

1. (a) shuttle diplomacy, see p. 917, (b) Camp David Accords, see p. 918, (c) dissident, see p. 919

2. (a) Anwar el-Sadat, see p. 918, (b) Menachem Begin, see p. 918, (c) Cyrus Vance, see p. 918, (d) Shah Mohammad Reza Pahlavi, see p. 919, (e) Ayatollah Ruholla Khomeini, see p. 920

3. Egypt was the first Arab nation to recognize Israel's existence and make peace with it; the agreement would discourage other Arab countries or groups from going to war; it was an important first step.

4. Carter believed that morality had to govern foreign policy, and that concern for human rights everywhere must be integral to foreign policy. He respected the rights of developing nations to make their own policies.

In Depth

Then and Now

In 1976 women won an important equal rights victory when Congress passed a bill authorizing the admission of women to military academies. Eight years later, in 1984, Kristine Holderied became the first woman to graduate, at the top of her class, from the United States Naval Academy in Annapolis, Maryland. As late as 1994, however, legal action was required to compel the Citadel, a South Carolina military college, to allow its first female student, Shannon Faulkner, to attend classes.

Americans overlooked the corruption and harsh repression of the shah's government because he was a reliable supplier of oil and a pro-Western force. Carter himself praised the shah in a visit to Tehran, Iran's capital, in late 1977.

In January 1979, revolution broke out in Iran, led by Muslim fundamentalists who wanted to bring back old ways, and liberal critics who wanted political and economic reform. The shah fled the country and was replaced by an elderly Islamic leader, the **Ayatollah Ruholla Khomeini,** who had been in exile. Khomeini and his followers were aggressively anti-Western, determined to make Iran a strict Islamic state.

In October, in what was intended as a humanitarian gesture, Carter let the exiled shah enter the United States for medical treatment. Many Iranians were outraged. On November 4, angry students seized the American embassy in Tehran and took sixty-six Americans hostage. Though a few were soon released, more than fifty were held for over a year, creating bitter animosity between the United States and Iran.

President Carter and Soviet president Leonid Brezhnev sign SALT II in Vienna, Austria. Carter believed that the arms limitation agreement would "make the world a safer place for both sides."

AMERICAN PROFILES

Kathryn Koob

One of the American hostages was Kathryn Koob, a diplomat. The eldest of six daughters

who grew up on an Iowa farm, she loved to travel. After graduating from Wartburg College in Iowa and earning a master's degree at the University of Denver, she joined the Foreign Service. She became a diplomat, working to promote American aims abroad.

Kate Koob arrived in Iran in July 1979, when the revolution was in full swing. She was director of the Iran-American Society, which promoted cultural exchange. On November 4, her staff heard that students had occupied the American embassy. The next day, she herself was taken hostage.

It was a brutal experience. During the day, zealous young women revolutionaries were her guards, while the "brothers" came at night with threats and questions. "The next day passed, and the next, and the next," she later wrote, "with more interrogations, more comings and goings. And always, the ever-present chanting of the mob outside the gates."

Sometimes imprisoned alone, sometimes with other women, she never knew whether any of them would survive:

The biggest fear was not knowing what the future held and not knowing what was happening to my colleagues. And then there was the undercurrent: threats of trials and executions.

Usually she could maintain her resolve:

A they're-not-going-to-get-us attitude began to set in. . . . Each day we survived was to our benefit. I decided the challenge each morning was to get through the day.

Sometimes, though, fear broke through, intensified by thoughts of her worried family and by constant stress:

And the sounds outside the embassy were nerve-wracking. . . . There seemed to be a continuous crowd of people shouting anti-American slogans, listening to the exhortations [cries] of the students and mullahs [clergymen] who were always on hand. In addition to the crowd noises,

RESOURCE DIRECTORY

Teaching Resources

Visual Learning Activity The Hostage Crisis as a Media Event, found in the Unit 10 folder, p. 64, demonstrates, in a political cartoon by Mark Alan Stamaty of the *Village Voice,* the perception that the media sometimes overshadow the story they are trying to cover.

*there were three or four loud-
speakers blaring newscasts. . . .
As I sat confined in my chair I
thought,* I can't take this, I just
can't take this.

The Hostage Crisis Ends

The ordeal of Kate Koob and the
other hostages continued for 444
days. They were blindfolded and
moved from place to place. Some
were tied up and beaten. Others
spent time in solitary confinement
and faced mock executions in-
tended to keep them constantly afraid. Meanwhile, the American public became increasingly frustrated and impatient for the
hostages' release. Nightly newscasts made the
crisis a national issue. ★

People expected the President to secure the
hostages' freedom. When his efforts failed, his
hopes for reelection were doomed. Carter broke
diplomatic relations with Iran and froze all
Iranian assets in the United States. Khomeini
held out, insisting that the shah be sent back.
Under pressure, Carter finally authorized a daring commando rescue mission, but it ended in
disaster when several helicopters broke down in
the desert sands and eight American soldiers
were killed. The government was humiliated,
and Carter's popularity dropped even further.

Carter was torn apart by the crisis. At one
point, just weeks after the Americans had been
taken prisoner, he confided his feelings to
Hamilton Jordan, one of his closest aides:

Y*ou know, I've been wor-
ried all week about the
hostages as a problem for the
country and as a political
problem for me. But it wasn't
until I saw the grief and hope on the
faces of their wives and mothers and
fathers that I felt the personal responsibility for their lives. It's an awesome
burden.*

After months of secret talks, in early 1981
the Iranians agreed to release the 52 hostages.
Not until the day Carter left office, however,
were they allowed to come home. Buses carried
them, blindfolded, to the airport where—
almost in disbelief—they saw the airplanes that
would take them out of Iran. Because Carter
was not reelected, however, it was his successor,
Ronald Reagan, who greeted them as they
arrived on American soil.

**In spite of the
sentiments of
anti-American
Iranians (left),
personnel from
the United States
embassy in
Tehran, Iran,
reach freedom
after being held
as hostages for
more than a year
(above). Among
them is Kathryn
Koob (second
from bottom).**

SECTION 3 REVIEW

Key Terms, People, and Places
1. Define (a) shuttle diplomacy, (b) Camp David
   Accords, (c) dissident.
2. Identify (a) Anwar el-Sadat, (b) Menachem Begin,
   (c) Cyrus Vance, (d) Shah Mohammad Reza Pahlavi,
   (e) Ayatollah Ruholla Khomeini.

Key Concepts
3. What was the significance of the Egypt-Israel agreements made at Camp David?

4. How did Carter's personal beliefs affect his actions in
   Latin America and Africa?
5. What factors led to the worsening of relations with
   the Soviet Union?
6. How did Carter respond to the Iran hostage crisis?

Critical Thinking
7. **Making Comparisons** How did Carter's commitment to acting on moral principles compare with
   Nixon and Kissinger's emphasis on *realpolitik*?

---

5. Carter's support for Russian dissidents angered Soviet leaders; he
strongly criticized the Soviet invasion of
Afghanistan; SALT II was not ratified.

6. He broke diplomatic relations, seized
Iranian assets in the United States, and
later authorized a rescue raid that failed.
Secret talks finally won the hostages'
release.

7. Students should note the increasing
emphasis on human rights and self-
determination under Carter, in contrast
to the maneuvering for power that
characterizes *realpolitik*.

Reteach

Ask students to describe the major
events of Carter's administration
affecting each of the following countries: Israel, Egypt, Panama, China,
Soviet Union, Iran.

4. CLOSE

**Reinforcing
the Big Idea**

Carter tried to emphasize human
rights and peacemaking in his foreign policy, but his actions complicated United States relationships
with the Soviet Union and Iran. The
hostage crisis in Iran cost Carter
much support in the United States.
The next section describes Carter's
domestic problems.

Critical Thinking

Recognizing Ideologies

Focus Students will learn the importance of recognizing the ideology of a speaker or writer.

Instruct After students have read and discussed the feature, ask if they think that President Theodore Roosevelt, who said, "Speak softly and carry a big stick," shared the ideology of Senator Thurmond or of President Carter.

Ask students to work in small groups to identify several current issues and to draft a list of questions about those issues designed to reveal a presidential candidate's ideologies.

Extend See the Historian's Toolbox Activity in the Resource Directory below.

Answers

1. (a) Whether or not treaties should be ratified that would turn control and operation of the Panama Canal over to the Panamanians. (b) Passage A: Senator Strom Thurmond in opposition; Passage B: President Jimmy Carter in support. (c) Thurmond: legislative branch; Carter: executive branch. (d) Thurmond: Republican; Carter: Democratic.

2. (a) The Panama Canal belongs to the United States, not to Panama, so it is our right to retain it. It would show weakness to give it up. (b) It is in our national interest, and it is the right and fair thing to do.

3. (a) They take precedence over everything else. We bought and paid for the canal, and therefore it is ours. (b) Strength, with never a sign of weakness. (c) It should take precedence—Panama is a sovereign country and we should respect that sovereignty. (d) Fairness and honor toward smaller countries; generosity, as well as strength.

Recognizing Ideologies

An ideology might be defined as the beliefs that underlie the actions or statements of a person, a group, or a culture. An important critical thinking skill is being able to identify such beliefs. If you can recognize ideologies, you can better understand why certain actions are taken or statements are made.

Use the following steps to help you recognize the ideologies that underlie two opposing statements made during the debate over the Panama Canal treaties.

1. Identify the main topic of the statements and the people who made them. (a) What is the subject under debate in these statements? (b) Who made each statement? (c) In which branch of government does each speaker serve? (d) To what party does each belong?

2. Locate the major points that each speaker makes. (a) What reasons does Speaker A give for rejecting the proposed change? (b) What reasons does Speaker B give for accepting it?

3. Identify the beliefs that underlie the reasons given. (a) What does Speaker A believe about the rights of property with regard to the Panama Canal? (b) What attribute of the national character does he believe should guide United States foreign policy on this issue? (c) What does Speaker B believe about the role of fairness with regard to the canal? (d) What attributes of national character does he think should guide United States foreign policy?

Passage A

The case for rejecting the proposed treat[ies] . . . begins with one crucial point: The Panama Canal is United States property, and the Canal Zone is United States territory. According to the terms of the 1903 treaty with Panama, we acquired sovereign rights over the Canal Zone "in perpetuity" [forever]. The Supreme Court upheld our exercise of sovereignty in 1907. . . . Moreover, the maps of the world show the Canal Zone as part of the United States.

Thus, it is clear that the burden of proof rests on those who favor the treaties; those who oppose them are merely standing up for American rights. Proponents must show that it is in the national interest to dispose of American property which, in addition to its strategic and economic value, represents a cumulative investment of roughly $7 billion.

. . . Would we give up Alaska to the Russians if they were suddenly to demand it? Such weakness is entirely contrary to our national character and heritage.

—Strom Thurmond, Republican (South Carolina),
"Why the U.S. Should Keep the Panama Canal,"
The Christian Science Monitor, September 13, 1977

Passage B

The most important reason, the only reason, to ratify the treaties is that they are in the highest national interest of the United States and will strengthen our position in the world. Our security interest will be stronger; our trade opportunities will be improved. We will demonstrate that as a large and powerful country we are able to deal fairly and honorably with a proud but smaller sovereign nation.

. . . We Americans want a more humane and stable world. We believe in goodwill and fairness as well as strength. This agreement with Panama is something we want because we know it is right.

. . . If Theodore Roosevelt were to endorse the treaties, as I'm quite sure he would, it would be mainly because he could see the decision as one by which we are demonstrating the kind of great power we wish to be. . . . In this historic decision, he would join us in our pride for being a great and generous people with a national strength and wisdom to do what is right for us and what is fair to others.

—President Jimmy Carter,
televised speech, February 1, 1978

 RESOURCE DIRECTORY

Teaching Resources

Historian's Toolbox Activity Recognizing Ideologies, found in the Unit 10 folder, p. 56, helps students apply the skill by analyzing two opposing viewpoints on the topic of taxing America's richer people to alleviate the federal deficit.

Carter's Domestic Problems

SECTION PREVIEW

In addition to crises overseas, domestic issues brought more trouble for the Carter presidency. The administration could not effectively create and pass legislation, dooming Carter's energy program and efforts to stabilize the economy.

Key Concepts
- The Carter administration had trouble getting its domestic programs through Congress.
- Economic policy under Carter was inconsistent and ineffective.
- Congress blocked Carter's ambitious energy conservation goals.
- Carter gave stronger support to civil rights than Nixon or Ford had done.

Key Terms, People, and Places
Nuclear Regulatory Commission, deregulation, amnesty; Allan Bakke; Three Mile Island

W hile Jimmy Carter had several triumphs in foreign affairs, he had little success in programs at home. He could not find a way to work effectively with Congress and its leaders, which stalled his plans in many areas, especially energy and the economy. Looking back, he wrote, "I quickly learned that it is a lot easier to hold a meeting, reach a tentative agreement, or make a speech than to get a controversial program through Congress."

That was not the only problem. As *New York Times* columnist Tom Wicker observed, Carter "never established a politically coherent administration." His strategies were not clearly defined. Public support, which had been with him at first, faded as his programs floundered.

The Economy Wobbles

Carter inherited an unstable economy and had trouble finding a way to balance inflation and growth. Inflation also had been a problem

for Ford, but had seemed under control after the recession that lasted from 1974 to 1976. To prevent another recession, Carter tried to stimulate growth with government deficit spending. As deficits grew, the Federal Reserve Board increased the money supply, but inflation then rose to about 10 percent.

To stop inflation, Carter tried to slow the economy and reduce the deficit by cutting spending. Cuts fell mostly on social programs, angering reform-minded Democrats. At the same time, the slowdown in the economy increased unemployment and the number of business failures.

Things got worse in 1980, when the new federal budget showed continued high spending. In reaction, bond prices fell and interest rates soared. Borrowers were angry at having to pay high interest rates—sometimes over 20 percent, which is about 3 times higher than they are today—for mortgages and other loans.

People lost confidence in Carter and his economic advisers. The administration's vacillating efforts—trying first one approach, then another—gave the impression that it had no idea what was happening or how to fix it. When Carter left the White House, economist Robert J. Samuelson commented:

W hat was most consistent about the Carter administration was its inability to make a proposal in January that could survive until June. . . . The Carter administration never projected a clear economic program or philosophy because it never had one.

A Carter Crusade: Saving Energy

Carter made energy conservation a major goal, but he had trouble winning support from Congress and the public. Despite earlier

When a revolution in Iran caused oil shortages at home, American drivers faced long lines at the gas pumps—when gas was available at all.

1. FOCUS

Connecting to the Big Idea

See page 906B. Explain that President Carter was not successful in creating and passing legislation on domestic issues. Ask how historians have so far assessed Carter's presidency.

Objectives
- Explain why the Carter presidency had trouble getting its domestic programs through Congress.
- Describe Carter's attempts to regulate the economy.
- Identify the successes and failures of Carter's energy conservation program.
- Compare Carter's support for civil rights with the policies of Nixon and Ford.

Bellringer

Ask students to think of four or five reasons why saving energy is important. Discuss whether arguments are convincing.

Reading Strategy

Reading for Evidence Ask students to find evidence as they read to support the statement on page 923 that President Carter "had little success in programs at home."

Reproducible Lesson Plan found in the Unit 10 folder, p. 41, provides a summary of the Section 4 lesson plan content.

Alternate Lesson Plan: Learning Styles found in the Alternate Lesson Plans folder, p. 170, helps students identify the causes and results of Carter's domestic policies, describe the effects of the Three Mile Island accident, and explain the significance of the *Bakke* decision; especially effective for auditory and visual learners.

Guided Reading and Review found in the Unit 10 folder, p. 48, provides a structure for reading and mastering the key concepts and reviewing the key terms for Section 4. (Guided Practice)

Explain/Discuss

Discuss Carter's various attempts to regulate the economy and the results of each attempt. Ask students to test Samuelson's comment on page 923 by trying to find a clear relationship among the attempts they have listed.

Ask why energy conservation became especially important during the Carter presidency. Discuss Carter's various energy proposals and ask students to identify those that became law. Ask students to classify the complaints about nuclear power plants into two categories: environmental concerns and financial concerns.

Discuss the *Bakke* case and ask students to define *reverse discrimination* in their own words. Ask them if the Supreme Court decision in the *Bakke* case is consistent with their own ideas of fairness.

Analyze

Ask students to state the connection between the high cost of imported oil and the high inflation rate during Carter's presidency.

Answer to ...

Links Across Time

Answers will vary according to students' perceptions of former Presidents' visibility.

In Depth

Did You Know?

Jimmy Carter reflected thus on his presidency: "I have found it much more difficult to be a leader in a time of calm than in a time of crisis. Leaders are very popular in a time of crisis because it is easy to arouse support for the interest of those who are concerned with the crisis itself. But to take action to prevent a future crisis that can't be easily detected nor proved is a very difficult task indeed."

embargoes and shortages, Americans still depended heavily on imported oil. In the late 1970s, more than 40 percent of the oil used in the United States was imported. Some thought the country should be energy self-sufficient instead of depending on supplies from other countries.

OPEC, the Organization of Petroleum Exporting Countries, had been raising oil prices steadily since 1973. People grumbled about rising prices, shortages, and long lines at the gas station. Although Carter was not responsible for oil prices or shortages, he often was the focus of people's complaints. ✪

In April 1977, Carter presented his comprehensive energy program to Congress and the people. He asked people to save fuel by driving less and keeping homes and offices cooler. He also created a new cabinet department, the Department of Energy, to bring together a variety of federal programs promoting conservation and looking for new energy sources. But when he called the need for conservation the "moral equivalent of war," critics seized on the acronym MEOW (from the first letter of each word) to make fun of it.

The energy proposals bogged down in Congress for months, opposed fiercely by representatives from states that produced oil and gas. Eventually, however, the National Energy Act taxed "gas-guzzling" cars, required utilities to use coal rather than oil, removed price controls on domestic oil and natural gas, and allowed tax credits and research funds for alternative energy sources such as solar energy and synthetic fuels. ✪

Three Mile Island Nuclear power seemed one exciting alternative energy source, but serious questions persisted about its costs and safety. Since the 1960s, grassroots activists and some scientists had been criticizing the nuclear power industry. In March 1979, people's doubts and fears seemed to be confirmed by an accident at the nuclear power plant at **Three Mile Island,** near Harrisburg, Pennsylvania.

A small leak through a faulty seal in the cooling system stopped the pumps that circulated the coolant. Temperatures in the reactor core rose, but plant operators misread the symptoms and shut down an emergency cooling system. A partial meltdown of the core occurred, releasing some radiation.

Links Across Time

| 1650 | 1700 | 1750 | 1800 | 1850 | 1900 | 1950 | 2000 |

Carter's Commitment to Public Service

Jimmy Carter had entered public service years before he became President in 1976 (near right). After he lost the presidency to Ronald Reagan in 1980, Carter remained committed to public service. Among other activities, Carter is a leading member of Habitat for Humanity (far right), which volunteers its members' time and energy to build houses for the homeless. *Can you think of any Presidents since Carter who have continued their involvement in public life?*

RESOURCE DIRECTORY

Teaching Resources

✪ **Critical Thinking Activity** Formulating Questions: Prices at the Pump, found in the Unit 10 folder, p. 57, helps students practice this skill by analyzing the 1970s oil shortage.

✪ **Visual Learning Activity** Responding to the Energy Crisis, found in the Unit 10 folder, p. 65, illustrates one solution to the problem of dwindling natural resources in a poster issued by the Hawaii Department of Planning and Natural Resources.

Containment building

Turbogenerators

Steam generators

Reactor

Control room

Unused fuel storage

Water pumps

Steam lines

Condenser

Used fuel storage

Nuclear energy generates enormous amounts of heat, which then is used to make steam. The steam then produces electricity. To make heat, the reactor splits the nuclei of uranium or plutonium in half. Despite the strides made in understanding such reactions, scientists have not yet been able to make use of the full potential of nuclear energy, which could supply the world's electricity for millions of years.

People near the plant were terrified by the idea of a radioactive leak, and 140,000 people fled their homes. Panic increased when the film *The China Syndrome*—in which the plot centers on a fictional reactor meltdown—opened in town. As reporters flocked to Three Mile Island, the story made headlines around the world.

The Future of Nuclear Power Carter named a commission to investigate the accident at Three Mile Island. Its report identified operator errors that had made the initial problem worse. In his response to the report, Carter noted "very serious shortcomings in the way that both the Government and the utility industry regulate and manage nuclear power." He proposed reorganizing the **Nuclear Regulatory Commission,** the agency in charge of nuclear power, and called on utility companies to improve standards:

> The steps that I am taking today will help to assure that nuclear power plants are operated safely. Safety, as it always has been and will remain, is my top priority. . . . I challenge our utility companies to bend every effort to improve the safety of nuclear power.

In spite of Carter's efforts, the nuclear industry fell on hard times. People were angry at cost overruns in building new plants, often reflected in their electric bills. Protesters blocked building sites. Orders for new plants were canceled, and some construction was halted.

 Activity

Responding to a Poll

Ask students the following question, used in a 1988 Harris poll: "I'd like to ask you about the last nine Presidents of the United States. Please keep in mind Roosevelt, Truman, Eisenhower, Kennedy, Johnson, Nixon, Ford, Carter, and Reagan. If you had to choose one, which President do you think was best on domestic affairs? best on foreign affairs? was least able to get things done? most inspired confidence? set the lowest moral standards? was the most likely to be viewed by history as the best over all?" Compile and display the class responses. Tell the class that 46 percent of those polled at the time chose Carter as the least able to get things done, and that Ford came in second, with 15 percent. Only 1 percent of those polled chose either Carter or Ford as the President "most likely to be viewed by history as the best over all."

Enrichment

In 1976, writer Tom Wolfe proclaimed the 1970s as the "me decade," a comment on the high level of interest in self-improvement. Ask students to research and report on both the human-potential movement and the fascination with health and physical fitness of the 1970s.

Answer to ...

Viewpoints

McClure argues that nuclear energy is tied to the economic growth, or future well-being, of the United States; Caldicott pleads for restraint, on the grounds that a nuclear meltdown would have disastrous effects on people in every way. For a more thorough examination of the nuclear energy issue, see the Resource Directory below.

Answer to ...

MAKING CONNECTIONS

Answers will vary. Examples of concern might include recycling, the marketing of "green" products, efforts to promote mass transport, production of fuel-efficient cars, and so on.

In Depth

Multicultural Perspectives

The Voting Rights Act of 1965 (see page 814), a landmark in civil rights history, has been extended through amendments four times —in 1970, 1975, 1982, and 1992. In 1975 literacy requirements were abolished for any state or county where more than 5 percent of the population of voting age included persons of Spanish heritage, Native Americans, Asian Americans, and Alaskan Natives. In such areas, all ballots and official election materials must be printed both in English and in the language of the minority or minorities involved. In 1992 minority provisions were amended: they now apply to any community that has a minority-language population of 10,000 or more.

Viewpoints
On Nuclear Energy

The need to reduce the dependence of the United States on foreign oil prompted viewpoints strongly for and against nuclear power. *What concerns do the following viewpoints address?*

For Nuclear Energy

"When you debate the issue of nuclear energy, you are actually debating the issue of growth. Growth will be the key issue for the remainder of this century, and it is the resolution of that issue which will determine the lifestyles of most Americans for generations to come. . . . Economic growth has been inextricably linked to the growth of the supply of energy throughout history."
Senator James A. McClure (Idaho), address before the National Conference on Energy Advocacy, February 2, 1979

Against Nuclear Energy

"If this country . . . continues to rely more and more on nuclear power a meltdown disaster is almost predictable, and when it does occur, disaster and chaos from the medical and psychological effects as well as the shutdown of electricity from all nuclear power plants will be the result. For years now, the utilities and nuclear power industry have refused to listen to scientific logic and reasoning concerning the dangers of this technology. . . . Perhaps it is time for emotion and for passion and for commitment to stir our souls and our hearts and our minds once again into action."
Dr. Helen Caldicott, in *Nuclear Madness, What You Can Do!* 1980

MAKING CONNECTIONS

Carter tried to emphasize the importance of using energy wisely and conserving oil. Are many Americans today concerned about this issue? What examples can you give?

Steps Toward Deregulation

Carter also moved toward **deregulation,** or reducing or removing government controls, in several industries. In the late 1800s and early 1900s, agencies such as the Interstate Commerce Commission had been established to regulate rates and business practices in certain industries. Over the years, regulations had multiplied, and now Carter argued that they hurt competition and increased consumer costs.

RESOURCE DIRECTORY

Teaching Resources

Viewpoints Activity On Nuclear Energy, found in the unit 10 folder, pp. 54–55, provides different opinions on the issue of nuclear power.

Carter's energy plan included proposals to take controls off oil and natural gas prices. He also took steps to deregulate railroads, trucking, and airlines.

Many liberal Democrats and consumer groups were upset. They argued that regulation was a way of assuring that businesses would be accountable to the public. Critics also worried that companies would not maintain safety standards and that airlines and railroads, for example, would cut service to less profitable areas of the country. Deregulation continued during the next two administrations, both Republican, though not always with the promised benefits to consumers.

Other Domestic Issues

Concern for moral values influenced the President's approach to domestic questions as well as foreign policy. Some of his actions were controversial. Once in office, for example, Carter carried out his promise to grant **amnesty**—a general pardon—to those who had evaded the draft during the Vietnam War. Because the war still divided Americans, reactions were mixed.

Civil Rights Carter was more sympathetic to the goal of equal rights than either Ford or Nixon had been. During the 1976 campaign, he had won African American support with what columnist David Broder called "an eloquence, a simplicity, a directness that moved listeners of both races."

Carter also tried to move beyond the civil rights battles of the 1950s and 1960s. As a white southerner himself, he understood the South's need to overcome the negative images of the past decades:

> The most important [message] was that we in the South were ready for reconciliation, to be accepted as equals, to rejoin the mainstream of American political life. This yearning for what might be called political redemption was a significant factor in my successful campaign.

Carter won the approval of African Americans with his staff appointments, particularly to visible, prestigious posts such as the United Nations ambassadorship for Andrew Young. On the other hand, African Americans were disappointed by his weak support of social programs and his concentration on economic problems and foreign affairs instead of on civil rights.

The Bakke Case In 1978 the Supreme Court ruled on a case that had important implications for civil rights and affirmative action policies. **Allan Bakke,** who was white, applied to the medical school at the University of California at Davis in 1973 and 1974. After being turned down twice, he sued the school for "reverse discrimination." Bakke charged that the policy of reserving sixteen of one hundred class spaces for minority group applicants violated both the Civil Rights Act of 1964 and the Constitution.

In a complex ruling in *Regents of the University of California* v. *Bakke,* the justices wrote six separate opinions. While the Court ordered Bakke's admission to the California medical school, it also upheld the consideration of race as one factor in admission decisions, though it did not allow actual quotas. The decision supported the concept of affirmative action, but the case signaled the start of a white backlash against the policy.

It Bakke WINS
We All LOSE
in:
Employment,
Education,
Housing

Allan Bakke took his case against affirmative action all the way to the Supreme Court when he claimed to be a victim of reverse discrimination. People argued both sides of the issue and some marched to voice their views.

Evaluating the Carter Presidency

Historians continue to assess Jimmy Carter's presidency. Some explain it as mainly a reaction to Watergate, a brief period of Democratic rule in a long period of Republican dominance. They also find serious flaws in the administration itself, mainly in its inability to create and stick with a consistent policy or to display strong leadership. After Carter's defeat in 1980, economist Robert J. Samuelson observed that Charles Schultze, retiring head of the Council of Economic Advisers, was typical of the entire team:

*I*n many ways, Schultze symbolizes the puzzle of the departing Carter administration: that a lot of good people went into government four years ago, and a government of good people didn't produce a good government.

SECTION 4 REVIEW

Key Terms, People, and Places
1. Define (a) Nuclear Regulatory Commission, (b) deregulation, (c) amnesty.
2. Identify Allan Bakke.
3. Identify Three Mile Island.

Key Concepts
4. What were the problems with Carter's economic policy?

5. What were Carter's energy goals?
6. What developments in civil rights took place during the Carter administration?

Critical Thinking
7. **Recognizing Cause and Effect** Carter won the presidency on the strength of being a Washington "outsider." How did this ultimately hurt his administration?

 Quiz found in the Unit 10 folder, p. 49, covers the main ideas in this section as well as the key terms.

 Chapter Tests Forms A and B are found in the Unit 10 folder, pp. 66–71.

 Answer Keys found in the Unit 10 folder, pp. 143–156, provide answers to all student activities.

Media and Technology

Transparency
Graphic Organizer, G-3

Guided Reading Audiotapes
(English and Spanish)

Computer Test Bank

3. ASSESS

Section 4 Review Answers
1. (a) Nuclear Regulatory Commission, see p. 925, (b) deregulation, see p. 926, (c) amnesty, see p. 926

2. Allan Bakke, see p. 927

3. Three Mile Island, see p. 924

4. Policy was not consistent and lacked direction. Efforts to avoid recession increased inflation; cutbacks brought unemployment and high interest rates as well as hurting social programs.

5. He wanted to encourage energy conservation, reduce fuel use, lessen dependency on foreign oil, and find new energy sources at home, such as solar and nuclear energy and synthetic fuels.

6. Carter appointed many African Americans and other minorities to important positions but failed to extend social programs that benefited the poor. The *Bakke* case upheld the idea of affirmative action but signaled the beginning of a backlash.

7. As an outsider, Carter lacked skills in dealing with Congress and getting his programs through; since he chose advisers who were also not part of the political establishment, he could not overcome this problem.

Reteach
Have students work individually or in small groups to create a poster showing Carter's successes and failures in controlling the economy, passing energy conservation legislation, and promoting civil rights.

4. CLOSE

 Reinforcing the Big Idea
President Carter was not successful at proposing and carrying out a clear economic program. Neither was he successful at creating or passing other domestic legislation.

The Decision to Reveal the Effects of Agent Orange

Focus Before students read the feature, ask them to consider to what extent they think one average citizen can change policy. Encourage them to evaluate Maude de Victor's decision to expose the effects of Agent Orange, and the future impact of her decision, as they read.

Instruct Ask students to read the feature. Play the part of the roving reporter, interviewing students role-playing the following citizens: Vietnam veteran with no visible effects of Agent Orange, Vietnam veteran with disease attributable to Agent Orange exposure, taxpayer, VA official. Ask the "citizens" to explain how Maude de Victor's decision to reveal the effects of Agent Orange will affect each of their lives.

Discuss with students the role of the media in American society. How were the media instrumental in getting compensation for veterans damaged by Agent Orange?

Ask students to consider how Jimmy Carter would respond to Maude de Victor's decision. What do students think Carter would have advised de Victor to do? Why?

might not have
History Happened This Way
Key Decisions and Decision Makers

The Decision to Reveal the Effects of Agent Orange

Time Frame:	1977–1978
Place:	Chicago, Illinois
Key People:	Maude de Victor, Ethel Owens, Bill Kurtis
Situation:	Veterans Administration counselor Maude de Victor found evidence that mysterious illnesses among Vietnam veterans were due to exposure to the chemical Agent Orange, but had to decide what to do about her discovery.

During and after the Vietnam War, the federal Veterans Administration (the VA) was faced with helping a new generation of veterans who were troubled by the physical and psychological aftereffects of a confusing and unpopular war. Many Vietnam veterans could not find work or resume a normal life, for they had come home emotionally shattered, alcoholic, or addicted to drugs. In addition, many developed mysterious ailments. Some blamed these health problems on exposure to Agent Orange, a chemical used by the American military to destroy vegetation in Vietnam. The photograph at right shows a before-and-after shot of one area in Vietnam that was treated with the chemical. The VA rejected the claims against Agent Orange, but one dedicated VA employee became convinced that it had harmed many soldiers.

Looking for the Truth

Maude de Victor was a benefits counselor at the VA in Chicago. She had been a corpsman at a naval hospital from 1959 to 1961, then joined the VA. Perhaps because of her work on an experimental program in radiation therapy while in the navy, she contracted breast cancer in 1976. She was still recovering from treatment when she began to hear complaints about Agent Orange from Vietnam veterans.

In 1977 Ethel Owens called de Victor to say that her husband Charlie, a thirty-year air force veteran, was dying of cancer. Charlie, Ethel said, had once told her that if he died of cancer, "it was because of the chemicals used in Vietnam." De Victor sent Owens's file to Washington but was told the illness had nothing to do with Vietnam. When Owens died, the VA did not pay full benefits, saying his death was not service related.

De Victor began to track down military and chemical company records. She learned about Operation Ranch Hand, the program to defoliate Vietnamese forests and crops by spraying chemical herbicides from the air. One chemical, Agent Orange, contained a type of dioxin considered highly toxic. Between 1965 and 1970, nearly 12 million gallons of Agent

▶ RESOURCE DIRECTORY

Teaching Resources

History Might Not ... Activity Decision Making: Helping to Heal a War-Torn Nation, found in the Unit 10 folder, pp. 50–51, helps students apply this skill through the story of Jan Scruggs, the initiator of the Vietnam Memorial in Washington.

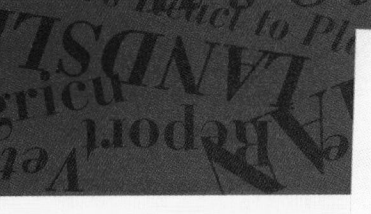

Orange were sprayed on Vietnam. Soldiers in helicopters flew through clouds of the defoliant, while chemical fog drifted down onto troops and Vietnamese civilians on the ground.

De Victor talked to veterans who had a variety of bizarre illnesses—rashes, headaches, strange lumps and sores, mood swings, or cancers. Others told her of their children's birth defects or their wives' miscarriages. Mapping the use of Agent Orange in Vietnam, she found that these ailing veterans had served in the areas sprayed with the chemical.

By early 1978, she had more than fifty case histories showing a link between Agent Orange and medical problems. She also had evidence that the government knew the dangers of Agent Orange. She showed her data to her superiors at the VA, but the they dismissed her findings and ordered her to stop her investigation.

Disobeying Orders

At that point, Maude de Victor could have dropped the investigation as she had been told to do. She understood why the VA would not admit the dangers of Agent Orange—the government feared a flood of disability claims and lawsuits from sick veterans and Vietnamese survivors, as well as condemnation from the world community. But she decided that getting help for sick veterans and their families was important.

Again, there were choices. She could go on applying pressure within the VA. Or she could risk her job and go to officials elsewhere in government. Both courses could be slow—and possibly useless. She wanted the world to know the story—so she turned to the news media.

Bill Kurtis, a Chicago news anchor, put on an hour-long documentary about her findings. "Agent Orange: The Deadly Fog" aired on March 23, 1978, and drew a torrent of calls from journalists, politicians, and Vietnam vets. The VA did not let de Victor take the calls and transferred her to another department, but she continued to discuss the issue. Claims related to Agent Orange began to pour into the VA, which still denied its harmful effects.

De Victor lost her job at the VA in 1984, but she had started a movement. Veterans formed lobbying organizations and filed a class action suit against chemical companies. They turned up evidence that the government and manufacturers had known the risks of using Agent Orange. In 1984 Vietnam veterans injured by Agent Orange were awarded millions of dollars in compensation.

EVALUATING DECISIONS

1. Why did Maude de Victor go to the media with her findings?
2. What was the impact of de Victor's decision to publicize the harmful effects of Agent Orange?

Critical Thinking

3. **Determining Relevance** What element of de Victor's personal life may have contributed to her commitment to the Agent Orange cause?

GOALS	Get medical and financial help for Vietnam veterans suffering from the results of exposure to Agent Orange			
POSSIBLE ACTIONS	Drop the investigation as ordered by superiors	Apply pressure for action within the VA	Take the information outside the VA	Publicize the situation through the news media
POSSIBLE RESULTS	• Victims of Agent Orange will be ignored, and VA policy will not change. • The VA will eventually recognize the claims of Agent Orange victims and help them.	• The VA will not change its position, and veterans will not receive help. • The VA will, in time, take responsibility for helping Agent Orange victims.	• Officials will protect the military's image. • Some politicians may take up the cause of Agent Orange victims but fail to change VA policy. • Sympathetic politicians will act to change the VA policy.	• The media will not pursue the story. • The media will publicize, but the public will not respond. • Publicity will prompt public outrage, but no results. • Publicity and outrage will bring help for victims.

Visions of America: History Might Not Have Happened This Way Game

To encourage students to explore pivotal moments in United States history, have students use the Visions of America software. Refer to the Visions of America Guidebook for viewing objectives, activities, game instructions, and discussion questions.

Answers

1. The VA refused to take any action in response to what she had learned, and her other options for gaining a response seemed slow and uncertain.

2. Many veterans learned why they were sick; organizations formed to fight for Agent Orange victims' rights; veterans took their cases to court and gained recognition of and compensation for their suffering.

3. The fact that her own cancer may have been caused by the work she did while in the navy may have made her particularly sympathetic to other veterans in similar circumstances.

Chapter Review Answers

Understanding Key Terms, People, and Places

Terms
Students should refer to the definitions of the key terms in the chapter to write sentences that show the relation of each word to the events of the Ford or Carter administrations.

Matching
1. amnesty
2. dissident
3. stagflation
4. Helsinki Accords
5. deregulation

True or False
1. false, Alan Bakke
2. false, Shah Mohammad Reza Pahlavi
3. true

Reviewing Main Ideas

1. A midwestern Republican, Ford believed in traditional values such as hard work and self-reliance. In Congress he had opposed federal funds for education and mass transit, and the antipoverty program. He supported law and order and defense spending. Critics cited his lack of administrative and foreign policy experience.

2. Ford inherited the problems of healing the country after the Watergate scandal and nagging problems in the economy, including inflation and unemployment (stagflation).

3. Ford's rescue of the *Mayaguez* succeeded in sending a message of American strength, although probably with needless loss of life. He continued the SALT talks, signed the Helsinki Accords, and took steps toward new relationships with African nations. The nation remained at peace, although Ford's foreign policy was mainly a reaction to outside events.

4. Carter presented himself as trustworthy and honest; he also emphasized his status as a Washington outsider.

5. Carter was deeply religious but also believed strongly in personal freedom of conscience. His personal style was low-key and unassuming. He was intelligent, well informed, and precise. Sometimes, however, his focus on all sides of a question made him unable to make decisions.

6. Carter sent Cyrus Vance to invite Sadat and Begin to Camp David in order to move the peace process forward. While at Camp David, Carter assumed the role of peacemaker and practiced personal diplomacy to bridge the gap between the two leaders.

7. Persuaded by Andrew Young, U.S. ambassador to the United Nations, Carter did not interfere with the newly emerging nations of Africa.

8. Ties between the United States and the Soviet Union actually worsened under Carter because of Carter's insistence on human rights and the sanctions he adopted following the Soviet invasion of Afghanistan.

9. People expected Carter to secure the hostages' release. In addition, the country was humiliated when a rescue mission failed, killing eight Americans.

10. Carter did not find a way to work effectively with Congress, which stalled his plans for energy conservation and the economy.

Chapter Review

Understanding Key Terms, People, and Places

Key Terms
1. stagflation
2. Helsinki Accords
3. shuttle diplomacy
4. Camp David Accords
5. dissident
6. Nuclear Regulatory Commision
7. deregulation
8. amnesty

People
9. Gerald R. Ford
10. Nelson Rockefeller
11. James Earl Carter, Jr.
12. Anwar el-Sadat
13. Menachem Begin
14. Cyrus Vance
15. Shah Mohammad Reza Pahlavi
16. Ayatollah Ruholla Khomeini
17. Allan Bakke

Places
18. Three Mile Island

Terms For each term above, write a sentence that explains its relation to the events of the Ford or Carter administrations.

Matching Review the key terms in the list above. If you are not sure of a term's meaning, review its definition in the chapter. Then choose a term from the list that best matches each description below.
1. a general pardon
2. a writer or other activist who opposes the actions of his or her government
3. a condition in which the economy remains stalled during a period of high inflation and rising unemployment
4. a series of agreements in which thirty-five nations pledged to cooperate economically and to promote human rights
5. the process of reducing or removing government controls

True or False Determine whether each statement is true or false. If it is true, write "true." If it is false, change the underlined name to make the statement true.
1. In 1978 <u>Nelson Rockefeller</u> sued the University of California at Davis for "reverse discrimination."
2. <u>Menachem Begin</u> took many steps to modernize Iran, but his government was corrupt and repressive.
3. Egyptian leader <u>Anwar el-Sadat</u> made a historic visit to Israel to try to establish peace between the two countries.

Reviewing Main Ideas

Section 1 (pp. 908–912)
1. Briefly describe Gerald Ford's beliefs and his voting record in Congress. Why did some critics feel that he was not qualified to be President?
2. Describe two major challenges that Ford inherited when he took office.
3. Briefly describe the successes and failures of Ford's foreign policy.

Section 2 (pp. 913–916)
4. Why did Jimmy Carter's candidacy appeal to voters eager to recover from the Watergate scandal?
5. Describe Carter's personal beliefs, his personal style, and his special abilities.

Section 3 (pp. 917–921)
6. What was President Carter's role in establishing the Camp David Accords?

7. Describe President Carter's policy toward Africa.
8. In Carter's first year, he said that the United States would forge closer ties with the Soviet Union. Why did his statement prove to be premature?
9. Why did the Iran hostage crisis damage Carter's presidency?

Section 4 (pp. 923–927)
10. What problems did Carter experience in his dealings with Congress?
11. You have read columnist Tom Wicker's observation that Carter "never established a politically coherent administration." How can this observation be applied to Carter's economic policies?
12. Explain why Americans faced oil shortages and high prices in the late 1970s. Why was Carter unable to reach his energy conservation goals?

---

11. The Carter administration continually shifted its economic policies as new problems arose, thus appearing to have no coherent economic program. For example, Carter tried to stimulate growth with deficit spending. When an increase in the money supply resulted in inflation, he then tried to reduce the deficit through cuts in government spending, including social programs.

12. OPEC had been raising prices since 1973. Carter was unable to reach his energy goals because he had trouble winning support from Congress and from the public.

1. **Testing Conclusions** Both Ford and Carter were branded as ineffective leaders by their critics. Yet both inherited serious economic and social problems from previous administrations. To what extent do you think the ineffectiveness of these Presidents was due to inherited problems and to what extent was it due to inadequate leadership?

2. **Demonstrating Reasoned Judgment** Do you think that Jimmy Carter would have been a more effective or a less effective President if he had been less concerned with moral values? Give evidence from the chapter to support your point of view.

3. **Checking Consistency** Although people complained about gas lines and fuel shortages during the 1970s, many did not back Carter's energy policies. How do you account for this discrepancy?

4. **Identifying Central Issues** You have read that in the election of 1976 the most important issue was trust. What do think is the most important issue for voters today when electing a President?

1. **Evaluating Primary Sources** Review the primary source excerpt on page 917. Based on your reading of the chapter, to what extent was Carter able to live up to his ideals in his foreign and domestic policies?

2. **Understanding the Visuals** Look at the map on page 914. How did your state vote in the 1976 election? Is this consistent with its voting pattern today?

3. **Writing About the Chapter** You are running as a third-party candidate in the presidential election of 1976. You want to combine the best aspects of both Carter and Ford while avoiding their weaknesses. Write a speech in which you announce your candidacy and the reasons why you should be elected. First, create a list detailing Ford's and Carter's positions on important issues. Note how your positions will improve upon theirs. Next, write a draft of your speech in which you explain your positions. Revise your speech, making sure that your ideas are clearly explained, then proofread and draft a final copy.

4. **Using the Graphic Organizer** This graphic organizer uses a tree map to organize main ideas and supporting details about Carter's foreign policy. (a) One reason for the breakdown of détente in the Carter years was due to Carter's commitment to human rights. According to the map, what was a second reason? (b) According to the map, what events led to the capture of American hostages in Iran? (c) Create your own tree map about Carter's domestic policy, using this graphic organizer as an example.

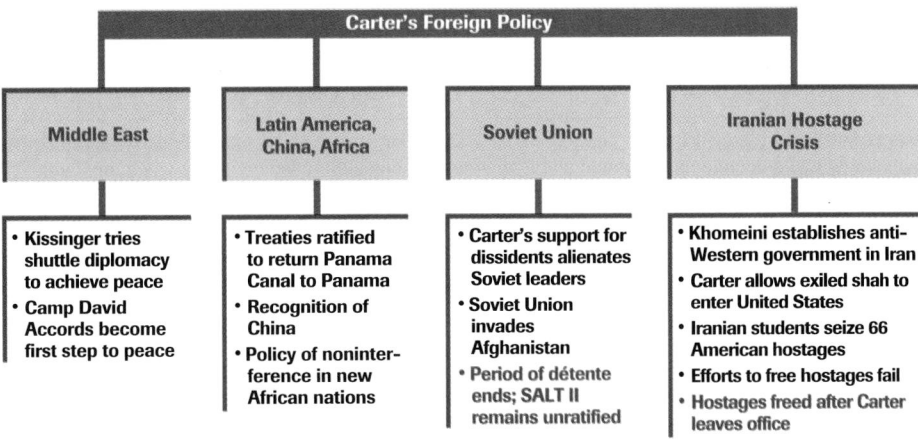

Carter's Foreign Policy

Middle East	Latin America, China, Africa	Soviet Union	Iranian Hostage Crisis
• Kissinger tries shuttle diplomacy to achieve peace • Camp David Accords become first step to peace	• Treaties ratified to return Panama Canal to Panama • Recognition of China • Policy of noninterference in new African nations	• Carter's support for dissidents alienates Soviet leaders • Soviet Union invades Afghanistan • Period of détente ends; SALT II remains unratified	• Khomeini establishes anti-Western government in Iran • Carter allows exiled shah to enter United States • Iranian students seize 66 American hostages • Efforts to free hostages fail • Hostages freed after Carter leaves office

Thinking Critically

1. Responses should consider the economic and social effects of Watergate inherited by Ford and the continuing economic problems inherited by Carter.

2. Responses should consider, for example, the worsening relations with the Soviet Union caused by Carter's stand on human rights.

3. Possible answers: Carter did not effectively promote his energy policies; Americans might have been unwilling to make sacrifices under any circumstances, despite inconvenience and high prices.

4. Possible answer: The ability to solve economic and social problems.

Making Connections

1. Responses should consider the areas of foreign policy in which Carter successfully carried out his ideals of promoting peace and compassion, such as the Camp David Accords. They should also consider the compromises the President was forced to make in cutting social programs in order to lower the deficit.

2. Answers will vary.

3. Students' speeches should consider Ford's and Carter's respective positions on and goals for the economy and foreign affairs as well as their qualifications for the presidency.

4. (a) The Soviet invasion of Afghanistan. (b) Carter allowed the exiled shah of Iran into the United States for medical treatment after a radical, anti-Western government gained control of his country. (c) Students' graphic organizers should indicate Carter's efforts to stabilize the economy, his energy program, steps toward deregulation, and his civil rights record.

Alternative Assessment

Final Evaluation
Use the following guidelines to evaluate student projects:

● **Evidence of thoughtfulness** To what extent do projects demonstrate an understanding of the presidency?

● **Evidence of outside research** To what extent do projects use outside research materials?

● **Evidence of synthesis** To what extent do projects demonstrate an understanding of relationships among topics?

● **Communication style** Do projects convey their purpose to an audience in a clear, appealing way?

Chapter 34 The Conservative Revolution
1980–1992

📁 Teaching Resources (See Unit 10 Folder)

	Instruction	Enrichment
Section 1 **Roots of the New Conservatism** (pp. 934–937)	Reproducible Lesson Plan, p. 73 Alternate Lesson Plan, p. 172 Guided Reading and Review, p. 77 Quiz, p. 78	Primary Source Activity, Speaking for the President, p. 93
Section 2 **The Reagan Revolution** (pp. 938–942)	Reproducible Lesson Plan, p. 74 Alternate Lesson Plan, p. 173 Guided Reading and Review, p. 79 Quiz, p. 80	Visual Learning Activity, Passing the Economy Buck, p. 100
Section 3 **Reagan's Second Term** (pp. 943–948)	Reproducible Lesson Plan, p. 75 Alternate Lesson Plan, p. 174 Guided Reading and Review, p. 81 Quiz, p. 82	Literature Activity, Masters of the Universe, p. 96 Viewpoints Activity, On the Legacy of the Civil Rights Movement, pp. 89–90 Visual Learning Activity, Wages for Housework, p. 99 Critical Thinking Activity, Recognizing Ideologies, p. 92 American Profiles Activity, Sandra Day O'Connor, p. 88 Primary Source Activity, An Explanation of Iran-Contra, pp. 94–95
Section 4 **The Bush Presidency** (pp. 949–952)	Reproducible Lesson Plan, p. 76 Alternate Lesson Plan, p. 175 Guided Reading and Review, p. 83 Quiz, p. 84 Chapter Test, Forms A & B, pp. 101–106	American Profiles Activity, Melissa Rathbun-Nealy, p. 87 Literature Activity, Operation Desert Storm, pp. 97–98 Historian's Toolbox Activity, Demonstrating Reasoned Judgment, p. 91 Time and Place Activity, The Baby Boomers Grow Up, pp. 85–86

📁 Additional Chapter Resources

Resource Organizer, p. 72
Alternate Lesson Plan, p. 171
Answer Keys, pp. 143–156

Bibliography

For the Teacher

Atkinson, Rick. *Crusade: The Untold Story of the Persian Gulf War.* Houghton Mifflin, 1993. (A *Washington Post* reporter looks at the war three years later.)

Evans, Rowland, and Robert Novak. *The Reagan Revolution.* Dutton, 1981. (Account of Ronald Reagan's political and economic ideas.)

Hunter-Gault, Charlayne. *In My Place.* Vintage, 1993. (A successful journalist remembers her youth as one of the first two African American students at the University of Georgia.)

Prentice Hall Literature Excerpts from *The American Experience,* 1994, including Beattie, Ann. "Imagined Scenes," from *Distortions.* International Creative Management, 1976.

THE BIG IDEA

The Big Idea for the chapter and how the main ideas in each section relate to the Big Idea are graphically displayed below. Comprehension of this chapter's Big Idea is critical to students' understanding of United States history and how we as a nation got where we are today.

Media and Technology

 Critical Thinking, I-3

 Critical Thinking, I-11

 Graphic Organizer, G-1

 Guided Reading Audiotapes (English and Spanish)

 Computer Test Bank

For the Student

Ashe, Arthur, and Arnold Rampersad. *Days of Grace: A Memoir.* Random House, 1993. (Reflections by the African American tennis champion and activist who died of AIDS.)

Erdrich, Louise. *Love Medicine: New and Expanded Version.* HarperCollins, 1993. (Updated version of the author's first novel of Native American life.)

Salzman, Marian, and Ann O'Reilly. *War and Peace in the Persian Gulf: What Teenagers Want to Know.* Peterson's Guides, 1991.

CHAPTER 34

After the political, social, and cultural upheavals of the 1960s and 1970s, many Americans felt change had gone too far and wanted to return to smaller government and more conservative ideas. The policies of Ronald Reagan and his successor, George Bush, carried out the social and economic goals of "New Right" conservatives.

SECTION 1

After five decades of social change and growth of government programs, conservatives banded together in 1980 to elect Ronald Reagan and begin a reversal in policies.

SECTION 2

Reagan's goals as President were to encourage business and drastically reduce government programs and spending, except in defense.

SECTION 3

Reagan's personal popularity and conservative policies continued throughout his second term, despite issues involving the domestic economy and foreign affairs.

SECTION 4

Continuing Reagan's policies, President Bush took strong actions in foreign policy as the cold war came to an end, but he could not match Reagan's successes or popularity at home.

The Conservative Revolution
1980–1992

The Relevance of the Big Idea

The conservative movement of the "New Right" in the 1980s tapped into the feelings of many Americans who felt liberalism and social change had gone too far. Like Ronald Reagan, the New Right's articulate, charismatic spokesman, many Americans looked back to an older, more traditional time and the values they associated with it.

The fall of the Soviet Union and the end of the cold war removed one old enemy—Soviet communism—for the New Right, but their intent to bring about economic and social change at home remained strong. Discuss with students what some of these traditional ideas are and how they have affected national policies.

In Depth

Global Connections

President Reagan found a conservative colleague in British Prime Minister Margaret Thatcher (b. 1925). In 1979, as leader of the Conservative party, Thatcher became Britain's first woman prime minister. Former Secretary of State Henry Kissinger described her influence: "During the Reagan administration, she achieved an influence over American decisions . . . not seen since Churchill's day." Not as personally well-liked as Reagan, the authoritarian Thatcher was known as the Iron Lady. In November 1990 she lost her party's support and resigned. She was later named a life peer; as Lady Thatcher, she would be in the House of Lords.

The Conservative Revolution
1980–1992

In the 1980s the Republican party—now controlled by conservatives—scored major electoral victories. Under the leadership of Ronald Reagan and then George Bush, the Republicans rolled back the liberal agenda that had shaped national policy ever since the New Deal of Franklin D. Roosevelt. The Republicans' main thrust was an attempt to revive the moral values of the nation, which conservatives felt had eroded in an increasingly permissive society.

Building on America's Strength
GEORGE BUSH
PRESIDENT

Events in the United States

1979 Religious conservatives found the Moral Majority.	**1980** Republican Ronald Reagan defeats Democrat Jimmy Carter for the presidency.	**1982** The Equal Rights Amendment fails to win ratification.	**1984** Democrat Geraldine Ferraro becomes the first woman to run for the vice presidency on a major party ticket.

1978	1980	1982	1984

Events in the World

1979 The Soviet Union invades Afghanistan.	**1980** Rhodesia, in Africa, is renamed Zimbabwe.	**1982** Britain and Argentina engage in the Falklands War.	**1984** South African archbishop Desmond Tutu receives the Nobel Peace Prize.

932

RESOURCE DIRECTORY

Teaching Resources

Alternate Lesson Plan: Demonstrating the Big Idea found in the Alternate Lesson Plans folder, p. 171, provides a lesson strategy to instruct students about the Big Idea that with Ronald Reagan's victory in 1980, the Republican party began to roll back the liberal agenda that had shaped national policy since the New Deal, attempting to institutionalize conservative social values as well as economic ones.

Alternative Assessment Handbook provides information, guidance, and strategies for alternative methods of assessment. It includes an essay on new trends in assessment, guidance and strategies for developing performance tasks and portfolios, scoring rubrics, and sample evaluation forms.

1 Pages 934–937
Roots of the New Conservatism

Since the expansion of the federal government in the 1930s, conservatives had argued for a smaller government. Conservatives also objected to many of the social and cultural changes of the 1960s and 1970s. By 1980 the conservative message had gained enough appeal to elect Ronald Reagan as President.

2 Pages 938–942
The Reagan Revolution

Ronald Reagan came into office determined to cut taxes, shrink the size of the federal government, and increase defense spending. In this way, he hoped to bolster American prosperity and pride.

3 Pages 943–948
Reagan's Second Term

After a decisive reelection victory in 1984, Reagan continued his conservative policies on economic and social issues. In domestic and foreign affairs, the administration had key successes but also serious missteps.

4 Pages 949–952
The Bush Presidency

George Bush's foreign policy successes, including a successful end to the cold war, had their roots in Reagan's initiatives. Likewise, his failures on the domestic front, where the economy battled slow growth and rising debt, were rooted in the policies of the Reagan years.

1986 The Iran-contra affair becomes public.

1987 The Senate rejects Robert Bork's nomination to the Supreme Court.

1988 Vice President George Bush wins the presidential election.

1990 A severe economic recession deepens.

1991 The United States and United Nations troops defeat Iraq in the Persian Gulf War.

1986	1988	1990	1992

1986 Corazon Aquino is elected president of the Philippines.

1987 Syrian troops invade Lebanon.
• Riots break out in Israel's West Bank territory.

1988 Civil wars sweep Ethiopia and the Sudan.
• Pakistan elects Benazir Bhutto

1989 The Berlin Wall is torn down.
• Japanese emperor Hirohito dies.

1990 Violetta Chamorro is elected president of Nicaragua.
• Namibia becomes an independent country.

1992 Somalia is torn by war and famine.

933

SECTION 1

Roots of the New Conservatism

SECTION PREVIEW

Since the expansion of the federal government in the 1930s, conservatives had argued for a smaller government. Many Americans also objected to many of the social and cultural changes of the 1960s and 1970s. By 1980 their message had gained enough appeal to elect Ronald Reagan as President.

Key Concepts
- The New Deal's expansion of government created many vocal opponents.
- Government continued to grow in the decades after the New Deal.
- As more Americans came to oppose big government and changes in traditional lifestyles, conservatism gained popularity.

Key Terms, People, and Places
coalition, affirmative action, New Right, televangelism; Ronald Reagan

With this 1980 campaign poster, Ronald Reagan appealed to the patriotism of those voters who felt that President Carter had not provided strong guidance in managing the economy or foreign affairs.

The inauguration of **Ronald Reagan** in early 1981 marked a major shift in American politics. The new President voiced the growing frustrations of voters around the country who believed that government had grown too large and had lost touch with the needs of the people. Reagan's own political journey reflected the growing conservatism of millions of Americans.

Reagan began as a Democrat and voted for Franklin D. Roosevelt, architect of the New Deal, in 1933. After Reagan moved to Hollywood and began a career as a movie actor, he was actively involved in the affairs of the actors' union.

After World War II, however, Reagan found himself less comfortable with the Democratic approach and joined the Republican party. In the 1950s he served as a spokesman for General Electric, making speeches praising capitalism and corporate values and attacking government regulation. He also spoke out strongly against communists in the United States. Ronald Reagan was now clearly in the conservative camp.

Reagan gained national attention in 1966, when he was elected governor of California. Likeable, photogenic, genial—and committed to conservative values—he gained support for cutbacks in social programs in his state. He also called for the same approach on the national stage. Reagan's emergence as a national figure showed that conservatives, who had complained for decades about the growth of government, were gaining strength.

New Deal Opponents

Americans have debated the proper size and scope of government since this nation's founding. That debate greatly intensified in the 1930s, however. The New Deal—Franklin Roosevelt's effort to cope with the Great Depression through relief, recovery, and reform—brought about a tremendous expansion in the size of the federal government.

New Deal agencies, which furnished banking regulation, assistance to farmers, aid for the unemployed, and a great deal more, changed the role of the President and the government as a whole. Federal spending increased dramatically to pay for new programs. Critics argued that in a capitalist country, government should not undertake these tasks, and that the nation could not afford the high government spending that resulted.

Some of these critics joined together in the American Liberty League. Established in 1934, this organization included both industrialists and disgruntled politicians. The Liberty League sought to teach respect for the rights of individuals and property and to underscore the importance of individual enterprise. All of these values, members claimed, were being undermined by FDR's oversized government programs.

In 1937 Roosevelt attempted to "pack" the Supreme Court by adding new justices when older ones, whom he called "nine old men," failed to retire. Opponents of FDR's plan joined forces to create a **coalition**—a union of several groups that work together to achieve a common goal. This coalition, made up of both Democrats and Republicans and forming a strong voting bloc, opposed any further New Deal legislation. It also resisted measures of liberal reform during World War II.

From Eisenhower to Goldwater

The election of Dwight D. Eisenhower as President in 1952 began eight years of Republican rule. Ike, the popular hero of World War II, called his approach to government "modern Republicanism." He accepted the basic outlines of the New Deal and made no effort to roll it back. He never attempted to dismantle the federal bureaucracy. It provided essential services, such as Social Security payments, to millions of Americans. There was even occasional bureaucratic expansion, as when the government established a new Department of Health, Education, and Welfare, headed by Oveta Culp Hobby.

In 1964 the Republican candidate for President, Senator Barry Goldwater of Arizona, preached a brand of conservatism quite unlike that of Eisenhower. Running against Democrat Lyndon B. Johnson, Goldwater opposed government activism, including civil rights laws and antipoverty programs. He also demanded a military buildup against an expected Soviet attack.

Johnson portrayed Goldwater as a dangerous extremist and crushed him in the 1964 election. Some analysts concluded that Goldwater's conservatism would never gain wide support. But others—including Ronald Reagan, who had won national attention with a stirring speech endorsing Goldwater—saw that Goldwater's messages of less government and strict anticommunism could have real power.

Johnson's Great Society

Conservatives found themselves silenced for a time following Goldwater's decisive defeat in 1964. Liberals seemed to have the upper hand in the mid-1960s, as President Johnson pushed ahead with his Great Society program, an extension of the New Deal. "Is a new world coming?" he asked. "We welcome it, and we will bend it to the hopes of man."

The Great Society had something for everyone. The Office of Economic Opportunity helped the poor and gave them a voice in handling their own affairs. Medicare provided for medical care for the elderly, while Medicaid gave similar assistance to the poor. Aid to education, in the most far-reaching school support program in American history, offered funds at the elementary, secondary, and college levels. A new Department of Housing and Urban Development gave Cabinet-level visibility to the effort to revive the cities of the United States.

Nixon and the Welfare State

In 1968 Richard Nixon won the presidency, bringing Republicans back into power. Much like Eisenhower, whom he had served as Vice President, Nixon hoped to restrain the growth of the federal government. He wanted to trim social welfare programs, which he claimed encouraged people not to work. He wanted to bring the budget under control. And he wanted "to reverse the flow of power and resources" toward the federal government by moving responsibility back to state and local authorities. Yet, like Eisenhower, Nixon did not attempt to dismantle the basic framework of the welfare state.

In fact, the federal government continued to grow during Nixon's presidency. The Occupational Safety and Health Act of 1970 provided for employee rights in the workplace and demanded that safety standards be maintained, with federal regulation to ensure enforcement. Also in 1970 the Environmental Protection Agency was created to oversee federal antipollution regulations.

Opponents of government growth bridled at these efforts. These initiatives, they claimed, were going too far. It was time to roll these programs back.

Senator Barry Goldwater's conservative message failed to win him the presidency in 1964. Sixteen years later, however, Ronald Reagan would use a similar message to propel himself into the White House.

2. INSTRUCT

Explain/Discuss

Explain that the conservative movement of the 1980s was not new, but was part of an ongoing opposition to the growth of government after the 1930s. Review with students the major shift in the role of government brought by the New Deal.

Discuss with students the aims of the various government programs that were instituted over the years. Did critics argue with those aims, with the methods, or with both?

Have students also discuss the social issues that helped bring the New Right together. Are such questions a different kind of issue?

Analyze

Have students analyze the approaches to government growth taken by different Republican leaders: Eisenhower, Goldwater, Nixon, Reagan. How did each one's philosophy reflect the times? What factors made Reagan's viewpoint "an idea whose time had come"?

In Depth

Biography

The title "Father of the New Right" may belong to former Senator Barry M. Goldwater (b. 1909) of Arizona. He was a transport pilot in World War II, then ran for the Senate in 1952. There he became a critic of the Eisenhower administration and led conservative Republicans. Goldwater lost the presidential race in 1964 by 16 million votes, partly because his tough pro-military rhetoric frightened many people. So did his famous quote: "Extremism in the defense of liberty is no vice." He was reelected to the Senate in 1968 and served until his retirement in 1987.

Activity

Role-Play a Reporter

Ask students to take on the role of a journalist covering a political campaign. Each student should prepare six questions to ask as he or she interviews one candidate from the New Right and one with liberal views. Other students can take on the candidate's role and answer the questions.

Enrichment

Ask students to research the strategies, slogans, and advertisements used by the three candidates in their 1980 presidential campaigns. Have them demonstrate or read samples from each campaign in class.

Caption Answer to ...

Using Historical Evidence

The sign one person is holding argues that "Choice is the American Way." Other people are holding signs arguing that their point of view is the one that best supports the rights of women. Still others have signs arguing that their point of view is the more "caring" one.

3. ASSESS

Section 1 Review Answers

1. (a) coalition, see p. 935, (b) affirmative action, see p. 936, (c) New Right, see p. 936, (d) televangelism, see p. 936.

2. Ronald Reagan, see p. 934.

3. Conservatives believed that the nation could not afford increased government spending for New Deal programs, which they did not think were the job of government; and that business should not be regulated by government.

4. Possible examples: Eisenhower kept much of the New Deal bureaucracy; the Department of Health, Education, and Welfare was added. Johnson expanded the welfare state, adding social programs such as aid to education, Medicare, and Medicaid; created the Office of Economic Opportunity and the Department of Housing and Urban

Social Issues

Other critics were equally unhappy, but for cultural rather than economic reasons. For example, the sometimes abrasive lyrics of rock music troubled them, as did performers who lost all inhibitions on stage. The spread in the use of drugs horrified many Americans. First marijuana, then other drugs, became common features of campus life. Some Americans feared the emerging "drug culture" was both a sign and a cause of increased immorality in American life.

The sexual revolution was another source of controversy. The use of the birth control pill encouraged a more flexible—and, to critics, less responsible—attitude toward sexual relationships. Also, after the 1973 Supreme Court ruling in *Roe* v. *Wade* legalized abortion, "pro-life" forces launched a campaign to overturn that ruling. The movement for gay and lesbian rights further infuriated many Americans, who deplored the shifting moral codes that threatened traditional values.

The women's movement caused still another rift. As women worked for equal rights and began to gain new opportunities, some Americans reacted vigorously. A woman's place was at home, they argued. Phyllis Schlafly, who campaigned against ratification of the Equal Rights Amendment, echoed their desire to retain women's traditional roles.

Another workplace controversy revolved around **affirmative action**. This is a policy whereby employers try to make up for past discrimination by giving special consideration to the hiring of women and people from minority groups. When the government and various private institutions adopted affirmative action, some critics called this policy "reverse discrimination." This issue attracted some traditionally Democratic blue-collar workers to the ranks of the Republican party.

The New Right Coalition

By 1980, Americans who were disgruntled about all of these things had formed a movement known as the **New Right**. The New Right was a coalition of a wide range of conservative groups. The groups did not always agree on specific ends, but they all contributed to the overall strength of the movement.

Some in the New Right coalition were most concerned with the role of government in the economy. They argued that the nation was faced with enormous inefficiency and waste. It was time, they said, to reduce the size of government, cut taxes, and get rid of government regulations that limited economic competition. One way they proposed to reduce government was to make cuts in government-supported social programs, such as those that provided assistance to the poor.

Some groups in the New Right movement wanted to restore what they considered Christian values to society. Members of the Moral Majority, led by the Reverend Jerry Falwell of Virginia, wanted to follow the dictates of the Bible and revive the traditional values they believed had strengthened the country in the past.

Falwell and other evangelists used the power of television brilliantly to reach millions of people. In a format that became known as **televangelism**, they appealed to viewers to contribute money to their campaign. They delivered fervent sermons on specific political issues and used the money they raised to back conservative politicians.

The debate over abortion continues to be one of the most divisive issues in American politics. Both "pro-life" and "pro-choice" forces gathered at this rally. **Using Historical Evidence** *What arguments are people in the photo using to support their point of view on this issue?*

 RESOURCE DIRECTORY

Teaching Resources

⭐ **Primary Source Activity** Speaking for the President, found in the Unit 10 folder, p. 93, highlights the writings of Peggy Noonan, who worked as a speech writer for Ronald Reagan and George Bush.

New Right strategists made a number of innovations in campaign tactics. They used brief, powerful television images that conveyed their message visually. They crafted "sound bites"—short, memorable statements that would be repeated on the evening news. Strategists pioneered in "spinning" the news, or giving events the best possible interpretation from their candidate's point of view. They used mass mailings to raise huge sums of money and mobilize supporters.

MAKING CONNECTIONS

In what ways did the New Right resemble the progressive movement of the early 1900s? In what ways was it different?

The Election of 1980

In 1976, Ronald Reagan had challenged President Gerald Ford for the Republican nomination. He lost by a narrow margin. In 1980 Reagan again sought the nomination. Though Republican moderates claimed that he, like Goldwater in 1964, was too conservative to defeat the Democratic President, the growing strength of conservatives in the party gave Reagan the nomination.

⭐ During the 1980 campaign, Reagan seized on growing discontent. His attacks on incumbent Jimmy Carter's handling of the economy were particularly effective. Criticizing Carter's economic record, he poked fun at the President's use of technical language:

I'm talking in human terms and he is hiding behind a dictionary. If he wants a definition, I'll give him one. A recession is when your neighbor loses his job. A depression is when you lose yours. A recovery is when Jimmy Carter loses his.

The continuing hostage crisis in Iran, as well as other issues, worked against Carter, and Reagan won a landslide victory. He gained 51 percent of the popular vote to Carter's 41 percent. (John Anderson, a member of Congress from Illinois, ran as a third-party candidate.) Carried along by Reagan's popularity, the Republicans gained control of the Senate for the first time in 25 years. Conservatism now controlled the nation's agenda.

Jerry Falwell and other televangelists helped change the way political candidates portrayed themselves and their opponents in the media.

Development. The Environmental Protection Agency began under Nixon.

5. Cultural issues that bothered conservatives included the lyrics of much rock music, the increase in drug use, the birth control pill, legalized abortion, the movement for gay and lesbian rights, the women's movement, and affirmative action programs.

6. Reagan used television effectively, speaking to voters in everyday language, using humor and acting techniques to promote a pleasing image of himself as a trusted friend and a person with deep convictions.

Reteach

Ask students to write the heading "Roots of the New Conservatism" and then list at least six issues that helped to unite conservatives in forming the New Right.

Answer to ...
MAKING CONNECTIONS

Both the progressives and the New Right were coalitions of groups with related goals, which worked together to achieve common political ends. The two groups, however, held opposite views of government's role. Progressives urged reforms that often involved government programs and regulation, while the New Right wanted to shrink the federal government.

4. CLOSE

 Reinforcing the Big Idea

For decades, federal government programs had expanded, despite the objections of many Americans. By the late 1970s, this discontent had combined with unhappiness about social changes to bring together a powerful coalition that elected a conservative President, Ronald Reagan, in 1980.

SECTION 1 REVIEW

Key Terms, People, and Places
1. Define (a) coalition, (b) affirmative action, (c) New Right, (d) televangelism.
2. Identify Ronald Reagan.

Key Concepts
3. For what reasons did conservatives oppose FDR's expansion of the federal government?

4. Give several examples of how government continued to grow after the New Deal.
5. Which social and cultural changes in the United States angered conservatives?

Critical Thinking
6. **Recognizing Cause and Effect** How did Reagan use modern technology and new political techniques to increase his popularity?

Quiz found in the Unit 10 folder, p. 78, covers the main ideas in this section as well as the key terms.

SECTION 2

The Reagan Revolution

1. FOCUS

Connecting to the Big Idea

See page 932B. Explain that Reagan's actions and policies in his first term as President were intended to carry out the conservative ideas and principles on which he had campaigned. Ask students to name those principles.

Objectives

● Describe Reagan's economic policies and the steps he took to put them into action.

● Explain why and in what ways Reagan increased defense spending and what effects this had on the American economy.

● Trace the pattern of the U.S. economy during Reagan's first term.

Bellringer

Ask students to suggest their own ideas for a fair method of taxing people to pay for government services. What kinds of income or purchases would they tax? How would they make sure the tax was fair?

Reading Strategy

Asking Questions Ask students to look at the main headings and subheads in the section, then turn each of them into a *how*, *why*, or *what* question. As they read, students should look for the answers to those questions.

Answer to ...

MAKING CONNECTIONS

Reagan and his Republican predecessors in the 1920s—Coolidge and Harding—all believed that helping the wealthiest segment of the economy would improve the overall economy, creating prosperity that would eventually trickle down to the poor.

SECTION PREVIEW

Ronald Reagan came into office determined to cut taxes, shrink the size of the federal government, and increase defense spending. In this way, he hoped to bolster American prosperity and pride.

Key Concepts

• Reagan cut taxes and government regulation to expand economic and personal freedom.

• Under Reagan, the United States launched a huge military buildup and was actively involved in events around the globe.

• After a severe recession in 1981–1982, the economy began to improve, but the nation's debt soared.

Key Terms, People, and Places

supply-side economics, New Federalism, Strategic Defense Initiative, federal deficit

Critics of supply-side economics warned that Reagan's policies would cause Americans to "lose their shirts." Supporters answered that the President's policies would bring widespread prosperity.

During the 1980 campaign, Ronald Reagan stressed three broad policies that he would pursue if elected President: slashing taxes, eliminating unnecessary government programs, and bolstering the defense capability of the United States. In his first term, he moved aggressively to implement those policies.

Supply-Side Economics

Reagan's main goal was to spur business growth. His economic program, known as "Reaganomics," rested on the theory of **supply-side economics**. This theory reversed earlier policies based on the ideas of English economist John Maynard Keynes.

In the 1920s and 1930s, Keynes had argued that the government could best improve the economy by increasing consumers' demand for goods. This meant giving people more money—either directly, through government aid, or indirectly, by creating jobs. Once people had more money to spend, Keynes argued, they would purchase more goods and services, which would cause the economy to grow.

Keynesian theory had helped explain the Great Depression, and the recovery that took place as the United States began a massive military spending program during World War II. In the postwar years, most economists accepted Keynesian arguments.

In contrast to Keynesians, "supply-siders" focused not on the demand for goods but on the supply of goods. Supply-siders argued that cutting taxes would put more money into the hands of businesses and investors—those who supplied the goods for consumers to buy. The theory assumed that businesses would then hire more people and produce more goods and services, making the economy grow faster. The real key, therefore, was encouraging business leaders to invest. Their individual actions would promote greater national economic abundance. Prosperity would eventually "trickle down" from the top to those at the lower levels of the economy.

George Bush, a rival candidate for the Republican presidential nomination, called Reagan's economic plan "voodoo economics." Only later, when he became Reagan's running mate, did Bush change his mind.

MAKING CONNECTIONS

How was Reaganomics similar to the economic policies of Presidents Harding and Coolidge in the 1920s?

RESOURCE DIRECTORY

Teaching Resources

Reproducible Lesson Plan found in the Unit 10 folder, p. 74, provides a summary of the Section 2 lesson plan content.

Alternate Lesson Plan: Critical Thinking Making Comparisons, found in the Alternate Lesson Plans folder, p. 173, guides students in practicing this skill by making a chart comparing the policies of the Republican Presidents from the 1920s and 1980s.

Guided Reading and Review found in the Unit 10 folder, p. 79, provides a structure for reading and mastering the key concepts and reviewing the key terms for Section 2. (Guided Practice)

Cutting Taxes

Reagan's first priority was a tax cut. In October 1981, a 5 percent cut went into effect, followed by 10 percent cuts in 1982 and 1983. In 1986, during Reagan's second term, Congress passed the most sweeping tax reform measure in American history. The new law closed loopholes that had allowed some people to avoid their fair share of taxes. It also simplified the tax system by reducing the number of brackets that determined what percentage of income a person paid. While all taxpaying Americans benefited from these measures, wealthy Americans benefited most of all. The maximum tax rate—the rate on the highest incomes—dropped from 50 percent to 38 percent.

Cutting Regulations

Meanwhile, Reagan embarked on a major program of deregulation. Like President Carter before him, Reagan wanted to eliminate those government regulations that, in his opinion, stifled competition in the free market economy.

By the time of Reagan's presidency, regulation had been expanding for nearly a century. The Interstate Commerce Commission, established in 1887, was the first step. Government regulations grew during the Progressive era of the early 1900s and in the New Deal years of the 1930s. Regulation was intended to protect companies from unfair competition, workers from unsafe working conditions, and consumers from ineffective or unsafe products.

While Carter's deregulation efforts had focused on the oil and transportation indus-

tries, Reagan sought to reduce government controls in virtually all areas of the economy. Reagan argued that regulations made life difficult for producers, which in turn meant fewer jobs for workers and higher prices for consumers. The more that businesses spent to comply with government rules, he charged, the less they could spend to invest in new factories and equipment.

Slowing the Growth of Government

Meanwhile, Reagan embarked upon an effort to cut back the size of the federal government. The President began with a passionate belief that anyone in the United States could succeed through individual effort. This faith in individual initiative ran counter to the argument on which the welfare state was based: that the government should help people who could not help themselves.

Reagan charged that the government had become too intrusive in people's lives. In his first Inaugural Address in 1981, he declared:

This Washington, D.C., building is a looming symbol for the United States' massive federal government. The building once housed both the Defense and State departments, but today it is too small even to contain all the President's aides.

2. INSTRUCT

Explain/Discuss

Explain the two competing theories of economics that modern U.S. governments have followed. Explore with students the rather complex subject of how tax policies and other actions, such as deregulation, are outgrowths of the economic policy that an administration is following.

Discuss with students how the military buildup, increased spending on weapons, and overseas military expeditions such as the invasion of Grenada fit in with Reagan's agenda.

Analyze

Have students analyze the continuing Republican effort in the 1990s toward the "New Federalism," shifting responsibility for programs from the federal government to states and cities. Ask students to find local examples of such changes. What effects have they had?

Activity

Drawing a Political Cartoon

Have students choose one of the major topics or issues of Reagan's first term—for instance, supply-side economics, Grenada, or "Star Wars"—and draw a political cartoon that expresses an opinion or point of view about that issue. Display finished cartoons in class.

Caption Answer to . . .

Interpreting Graphs

The defense budget under Reagan more than doubled, from approximately $130 billion to $290 billion. Under Bush it increased slightly, although it dropped between 1989 and 1991.

It is . . . my intention . . . to make [government] work—work with us, not over us; to stand by our side, not ride on our back. Government can and must provide opportunity, not smother it; foster productivity, not stifle it.

Drawing support from opponents of the programs created by Lyndon Johnson's Great Society, Reagan attacked these programs head-on. The administration eliminated public service jobs that were part of an employment training program. It reduced unemployment compensation. It lowered welfare benefits and reduced allocations for food stamps. It raised fees for Medicare patients. Altogether, federal spending for human assistance fell by $101 billion between 1980 and 1982.

While he cut back the role of the federal government, Reagan sought to give more responsibility to state and local governments. Borrowing a term from the Nixon administration, he called his plan the **New Federalism**. Under this plan, the federal government would no longer tell states exactly how federal aid had to be used, but rather would let states create and pay for programs as they saw fit. This effort

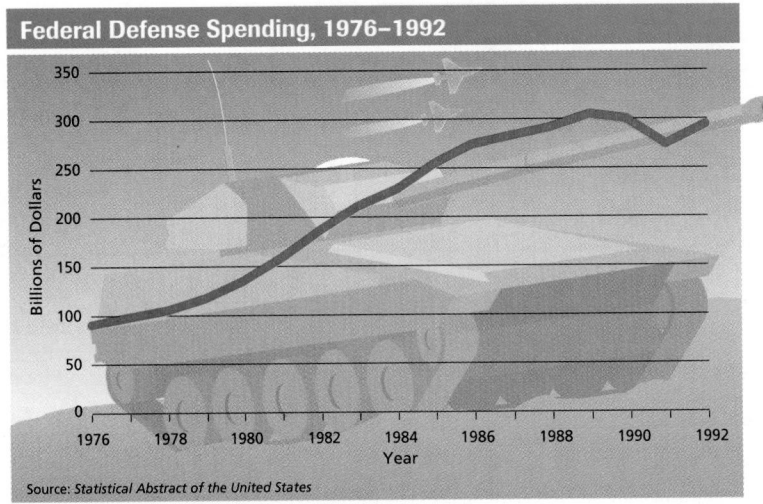

Federal Defense Spending, 1976–1992

Source: *Statistical Abstract of the United States*

Interpreting Graphs
Notice the change in defense spending in the early 1980s. *By how much did the defense budget increase during President Reagan's two terms in office? What happened to defense spending when President Bush took office in 1989?*

never worked as planned. A recession early in Reagan's presidency left a number of cities and states nearly bankrupt, for they now had responsibility but not enough money for programs formerly funded by Washington.

A Tough Line Toward Communism

While taking decisive measures to change the direction of domestic policy, Reagan was equally determined to defend American interests in the cold war. He believed in a tough approach toward the Soviet Union, which he called an "evil empire," and favored large defense budgets to strengthen both conventional military forces and the supply of nuclear weapons.

Military Buildup The costs of the buildup were enormous. Over a five-year period, the United States spent $1.5 trillion on defense, an amount far higher than ever before. By 1985, the United States was spending half a million dollars every minute on defense. These expenditures contributed to the growing budget deficits at home.

Much of this money went into new weapons. The United States continued to develop new missiles, such as the intercontinental MX, as well as new bombers and submarines that could carry nuclear weapons. At the same time, Reagan explored ways to protect Americans against nuclear attack. In 1983 Reagan announced the **Strategic Defense Initiative** (SDI), popularly known as "Star Wars" after a 1977 film. SDI proposed the creation of a massive satellite shield in outer space to intercept and destroy incoming Soviet missiles.

Reagan's Foreign Policy Relations with the Soviet Union remained frosty during Reagan's first term. The Soviets criticized the

---

▶ RESOURCE DIRECTORY

Teaching Resources

Visual Learning Activity "Passing the Economy Buck," found in the Unit 10 folder, p. 100, reveals two cartoonists' suggestions of why successive administrations were unable to control government waste and inefficiency.

American defense buildup. They also complained when the United States stationed new intermediate-range nuclear missiles in Western Europe.

The United States was active outside Europe as well. In the Middle East, Lebanon had become a battleground in the hostilities between Israel and the Palestine Liberation Organization (PLO). In 1982, Reagan sent several thousand marines to Beirut, the Lebanese capital, as part of a peacekeeping force. In October 1983 a terrorist truck loaded with explosives crashed through the gates of a marine barracks, killing 241 Americans. Many Americans demanded an immediate withdrawal from Lebanon, and by the following February, all the troops left.

Latin America was equally troubled. Reagan feared that communist forces there would gain power and threaten American interests. In El Salvador, the United States aided a repressive military regime in resisting guerrillas, some of whom were Marxists. Reagan increased military assistance to El Salvador to the level of about $1 million a day. In Nicaragua, as you will read in the next section, the United States helped guerrillas who were fighting to overthrow that nation's leftist government.

Reagan claimed a victory on the tiny Caribbean island of Grenada. He ordered United States military forces to Grenada in October 1983, after a military coup installed a government sympathetic to communist Cuba. The official aim of the invasion was to safeguard several hundred American medical students. However, United States forces also overthrew the new Grenadian government and remained in Grenada to oversee free elections.

Recession and Recovery

⭐ During Reagan's first two years in office, the United States experienced the worst recession it

American troops won a swift victory on the Caribbean island of Grenada. **Using Historical Evidence** *How might photos like this one have boosted President Reagan's popularity during his first term?*

5. Possible answers: Positive—The economy began to recover from recession; tax cuts led to increased consumer spending; business leaders increased investments; the stock market moved up. Negative—Tax cuts benefited wealthy Americans most; cities and the poor suffered from spending cuts; the federal deficit and the national debt both ballooned because of tax cuts and defense spending.

6. Environmental Protection Agency: pollution and health problems might increase. Consumer Product Safety Commission: consumers might be hurt by unsafe consumer goods. Occupational Safety and Health Administration: people working in unsafe workplaces could be hurt or killed in accidents.

Reteach

Ask students to make a cause-and-effect chart that shows, first, Reagan's policy priorities in his first term; second, the moves taken to implement them; and third, the results.

Caption Answer to ...

 Interpreting Graphs

During Reagan's administration, the federal deficit rose from nearly $80 billion to a peak of $221 billion. Reagan's policy of high defense spending contributed to that trend

 Alternative Assessment

Mid-Point Monitoring

Ask students if they have:
● Chosen the format they will use for their project.
● Outlined the main ideas.
● Begun outside research and collection of materials.

 CLOSE

 Reinforcing the Big Idea

In his first term, Ronald Reagan worked steadfastly to carry out conservative policies. His successes—and the many voters who approved of them—would carry him into a second term.

Federal Budget Deficit, 1980–1992

Billions of Dollars (y-axis: 0, 20, 40, 60, 80, 100, 120, 140, 160, 180, 200, 220, 240, 260, 280, 300, 320)

Year (x-axis: 1980, 1982, 1984, 1986, 1988, 1990, 1992)

Source: Statistical Abstract of the United States

Interpreting Graphs
Examine the graph above showing the federal deficit from 1980 to 1992. *What happened to the federal deficit during Reagan's years in office? How did Reagan's policies contribute to that trend?*

---

had seen since the Great Depression. High interest rates discouraged Americans from borrowing to purchase goods or invest in new equipment. Foreign competition cost thousands of American jobs. By 1982 several hundred American businesses were going bankrupt each week.

The 1981–1982 recession did, however, pave the way for an economic recovery. The high interest rates cooled down inflation, and as Reagan's tax cuts took effect, consumer spending began to rise. By 1983, both inflation and unemployment had dropped below 10 percent. Business leaders gained new confidence and increased their investments. The stock market pushed upward. Republicans claimed that the recovery demonstrated the wisdom of supply-side economics.

Yet an important prediction of the supply-side theorists had not come true. Cuts in tax rates were supposed to generate so much economic growth that the government's tax revenues would actually increase. As a result, the **federal deficit**, or the amount by which the government's spending exceeds its income in a given year, was supposed to decrease. During the 1980 campaign, Reagan had complained about the federal deficit and had vowed to balance the federal budget if elected. And yet under Reagan, the combination of the tax cuts and the huge defense spending increases pushed the deficit up, not down. The deficit ballooned from nearly $80 billion in 1980 to a peak of $221 billion in 1986.

Even worse, each year's deficit drove the nation as a whole deeper and deeper into debt. The national debt—the total amount of money owed by the government—rose from $914 billion in 1980 to $3.1 trillion in 1990. Future generations would have to bear the burden of interest payments on this monumental debt.

Yet in spite of these problems, most Americans supported Reagan. They shared his values and principles. In 1981, Reagan was wounded in an assassination attempt. The courage and humor with which he faced the situation ("Please tell me you're all Republicans," he quipped to the doctors treating him) only reinforced Americans' respect for their President.

SECTION 2 REVIEW

Key Terms, People, and Places
1. Define (a) supply-side economics, (b) New Federalism, (c) Strategic Defense Initiative, (d) federal deficit.

Key Concepts
2. How, according to Reaganomics, would a cut in taxes help the economy?
3. Why did Reagan want to cut government spending?
4. How did the Reagan administration respond to the threat of communism as represented by the Soviet Union? by left-wing forces in Latin America?
5. Give one positive and one negative effect of Reagan's economic policies.

Critical Thinking
6. **Predicting Consequences** What problems could result from cutting regulations enforced by the Environmental Protection Agency, the Consumer Product Safety Commission, and the Occupational Safety and Health Administration?

▶ RESOURCE DIRECTORY

Teaching Resources

Quiz found in the Unit 10 folder, p. 80, covers the main ideas in this section as well as the key terms.

Reagan's Second Term

SECTION PREVIEW

SECTION PREVIEW

After a decisive reelection victory in 1984, Reagan continued his conservative policies on economic and social issues. In domestic and foreign affairs, the administration had key successes but also serious missteps.

Key Concepts

- Reagan encouraged a rebirth of American patriotic pride.
- Growing economic inequality and disagreements over social issues divided Americans.
- Reagan remained a popular President despite several missteps.

Key Terms, People, and Places

AIDS, S & L, Sandinista, contra, Iran-contra affair, INF Treaty, entitlement; Sandra Day O'Connor

C ampaigning for reelection in 1984, Ronald Reagan asked voters if they were better off than they had been four years before. As they roared their approval, he told them, "You ain't seen nothing yet." His campaign advertisements, such as one depicting "Morning in America," heralded a new day of optimism.

To oppose Reagan, the Democrats nominated Senator Walter Mondale, who had been Carter's Vice President. Mondale chose as his running mate Geraldine Ferraro, a member of Congress from New York. Ferraro was the first woman ever to be nominated on a major party's presidential ticket.

The relative strength of the economy and Reagan's personal popularity combined to give Reagan a landslide victory over Mondale. Reagan took 59 percent of the popular vote and all of the electoral votes except those of the District of Columbia and Mondale's home state of Minnesota. It was a resounding triumph, the largest electoral-vote margin in history.

Patriotic Renewal

What accounted for Reagan's sweeping popularity? For one thing he represented an America in which men and women were independent and strong. He recognized the public's hunger for heroes and used his own personal charisma to respond to that need. Ever optimistic, he conveyed, as President Bill Clinton later wrote (page 1083, Unit 10 Source Readings), "a sense that the possibilities of America go on forever."

Reagan wanted to recreate the sense of community he had known and loved in his youth, and to help people revive the virtues that had made America strong. The nation had endured continued turbulence in the years following the war in Vietnam. It had doubted its aims after that ill-fated struggle. Now was the time for patriotic renewal, and the 1980s offered several opportunities to celebrate that renewal.

1984 Olympic Games In the summer of 1984 the Olympic Games were held in Los Angeles. This was the first time the Summer Games had been held in the United States in half a century, and the nation made the most of it. The opening and closing ceremonies, televised worldwide to hundreds of millions of viewers, were festive, patriotic affairs.

Statue of Liberty Centennial Two years later, in 1986, the nation celebrated the centennial of the Statue of Liberty in New York harbor. This monument, the first structure many immigrants had seen as they entered the United States, was a symbol of freedom around the

Ronald Reagan was one of the most popular American presidents. During the 1980s, he helped Americans feel a sense of pride in their country that many felt had been missing in the previous decade.

Explain/Discuss

Discuss with students the economic, social, and judicial issues that developed during the Reagan era, such as the growing gap between rich and poor, the arrival of recession, the defeat of the Equal Rights Amendment, the appointment of conservatives to the Supreme Court, and the extension of the Voting Rights Act of 1965. Do they think that these events strengthened or weakened the conservative cause?

Explain the rapid changes going on in the Soviet Union in this period. Discuss with students the effects of Reagan's relationship with Mikhail Gorbachev on these changes.

Analyze

Have students analyze the characteristics that made Reagan so popular both during his terms as President and afterward. How important are charisma and personal appeal for a President?

Fireworks lit up New York harbor in 1986 to celebrate the 100th anniversary of the Statue of Liberty.

world. Unfortunately, it had deteriorated over the course of 100 years. Now, after a massive campaign to refurbish the statue, the nation held a monumental celebration to mark its anniversary. Hundreds of boats, including a large number of tall ships with sails and masts, converged on the harbor. Fireworks, more elaborate than those in any celebration before, illuminated the event.

Bicentennial of the Constitution The following year the United States celebrated the 200th anniversary of the Constitution, drafted in 1787. This celebration, less dramatic than that of the Statue of Liberty but equally important, commemorated one of the fundamental documents in American history. Throughout the year, Americans attended lectures, workshops, and meetings focusing on the features of the Constitution that had made the nation strong. This observance helped renew public appreciation of such ideas as balanced government and separation of powers, which had helped enable the American system of government to endure for two centuries.

The Unequal Divide

⭐ While the American people as a whole celebrated their nation's heritage, not all Americans had reason to celebrate the economic changes of the Reagan years. The gap between rich and poor grew larger.

Economic Hardships A small group of people prospered most in the 1980s. The net worth of the *Forbes* magazine 400 richest Americans nearly tripled in the Reagan years. Political analyst Kevin Phillips described this new class of "upper America."

> I t was the truly wealthy, more than anyone else, who flourished under Reagan. . . . The truth is that the critical concentration of wealth in the United States was developing at higher levels—decamillionaires, centimillionaires, half-billionaires and billionaires. Garden variety millionaires had become so common that there were about 1.5 million of them by 1989.

By the end of the 1980s, wealth was more unevenly shared than at any time since the end

---

 RESOURCE DIRECTORY

Teaching Resources

⭐ **Literature Activity** Masters of the Universe, found in the Unit 10 folder, p. 96, presents an excerpt from a popular novel by author Tom Wolfe that pokes fun at the attitudes of some investment brokers during the 1980s.

⭐ **Visual Learning Activity** Wages for Housework, found in the Unit 10 folder, p. 99, illustrates in a poster by Betsy Warrior the backlash from women who felt that their traditional role in the home was being unfairly devalued by the women's movement.

of World War II. Many families were able to increase their total income by having both husband and wife work outside the home. Individual salaries, however, declined. And for the poorest one fifth of the population, even total family income dropped. The gap between the rich and poor, first publicized widely during the Reagan years has, in fact, grown even more pronounced in recent years. It remains one of our nation's greatest challenges.

Continuing Social Debates

As you have read, in the years leading to Reagan's election, conservatives gained public support with their stands on social issues as well as economic ones. In the 1980s, conservative policies on social issues made these "hot" issues even hotter. None of the issues have been resolved in the late 1990s. They all continue to be debated by Americans.

Viewpoints
On the Legacy of the Civil Rights Movement

Decades after the civil rights movement demanded racial justice in the United States, Americans disagreed on how much progress had been made. **What does each of the viewpoints below say about the impact of the movement on race relations in the early 1990s?**

Substantial Progress

"Before the civil rights movement, there was a very wide separation between blacks and whites. I don't think the separation is as great today. There has been more speaking out. Blacks now let themselves open up and say how they feel in no uncertain terms. I think there are friendships between blacks and whites that didn't exist before. In spite of everything, I think the racial situation is healthier than it was before. Blacks are no longer invisible."

Eileen Barth, retired social worker and child care professional, quoted in Studs Terkel, *Race,* 1992

Little or No Progress

"The country is more segregated today than it was when [Martin Luther] King and [Robert] Kennedy were alive. What Dr. King and Bobby were fighting was segregation and discrimination imposed by law, by the state. . . . All of that has changed. . . . But in the North, everybody knows what's happened in the cities. At universities, there's much more black withdrawal into separate communities. I grew up thinking we were going to have an integrated society, not just an end to official racism."

Anthony Lewis, columnist for the *New York Times,* quoted in *Life,* April 1993

Civil Rights The federal commitment to extend voting rights had given the vote to millions of African Americans who had been denied it for decades. These new voters elected an increasing number of African American candidates to local, state, and national offices.

Resistance to civil rights initiatives was growing, however, as critics complained that many of these policies trampled on the rights of state and local governments. Reagan tried to prevent the extension of the Voting Rights Act of 1965, backing off only after intense criticism. He appointed judges to the federal courts who were less sympathetic to civil rights goals, including school desegregation. The adminis-

tration also worked to end some affirmative action programs.

The Women's Movement As women gained increasing access to jobs and other opportunities previously denied to them, the women's movement met with a backlash. One sign of this backlash was the defeat of the proposed Equal Rights Amendment to the Constitution, which failed to gain the approval of enough state legislatures. ✪

Pro-life groups also took aim at the right to abortion, granted in the 1973 *Roe* v. *Wade* Supreme Court decision. Opponents lobbied to cut off federal funds that paid for abortions for

📄 **Viewpoints Activity** On the Legacy of the Civil Rights Movement, found in the Unit 10 folder, pp. 89–90, provides differing perspectives on the topic of race relations in the 1990s.

Answer to ...

Viewpoints

Barth thinks that African Americans are more hopeful and more visible in society in the 1990s; Lewis sees less promise of integration than when Dr. King was alive. For a more thorough examination of the civil rights movement, see the Resource Directory below.

Activity
Teaching Heterogeneous Groups

The 1984 presidential election was historic in several ways: it included the first woman candidate for a major party and the greatest electoral-vote margin for the victor. Have students discuss and "replay" the election in light of what they now know about the events of Reagan's second term. Have one group represent the Reagan–Bush campaign team; the other Mondale–Ferraro. Each group should decide what issues they will emphasize and why.

Enrichment

A President's ability to choose Supreme Court Justices can have long-term effects. Have students research the biographies and judicial histories of the Justices named by Reagan, tracing their votes and influence from their appointment to today.

Answer to ...

MAKING CONNECTIONS

Seeing the problems that persisted into the 1990s, some African Americans might feel that the song's promise remained unfulfilled.

In Depth

Then and Now

Randy Shilts, a reporter for the *San Francisco Chronicle*, was one of the first writers to recognize AIDS as an epidemic. His 1987 book *And the Band Played On: Politics, People, and the AIDS Epidemic* was a national best-seller. "Our society didn't grapple with AIDS in the '80s, because it was the disease of gay men," said Shilts. "But in the '90s . . . our society is being split into two worlds. For people who have AIDS it is a factor in your life that dwarfs any other concerns. For people who don't have it, the disease is a trivial concern, unless you actually know someone who is dying from it." Randy Shilts died of AIDS in 1994 at the age of 42.

Sandra Day O'Connor became the first woman on the United States Supreme Court in 1981. President Reagan took her conservative views into account when selecting her as a nominee.

the poor. They also pressed successfully for the appointment of judges who would restrict abortion rights.

Sexual Orientation The campaign for gay and lesbian rights caused similar polarization. The discovery of **acquired immuno-deficiency syndrome (AIDS)** in 1981 contributed to the backlash. At first, most of its victims were intravenous drug users and gay men. Some Americans therefore viewed AIDS as a curse that punished certain people for their habits and lifestyles. Even as AIDS spread into the larger community, the resistance to gay rights grew more pronounced.

MAKING CONNECTIONS

Why might the song "We Shall Overcome," which had inspired civil rights activists in the 1960s and 1970s, cause a feeling of disappointment for some African Americans in the 1990s?

Conservatives in the Courts

Many of these controversial social issues wound up in the courts, and Reagan used his eight years in office to appoint conservatives as federal judges. In 1981 he made his first Supreme Court appointment by selecting Arizona judge

Sandra Day O'Connor, who became the first woman Supreme Court justice. In 1986 Reagan chose another conservative, Antonin Scalia, for the Supreme Court. ✪

While O'Connor and Scalia won Senate confirmation, Reagan's next Supreme Court appointment, judge and former law professor Robert Bork, did not. Liberal groups joined together in 1987 to convince the Senate to reject Bork's nomination. The nominee whom the Senate finally approved, Anthony Kennedy, was known as a moderate conservative. ✪

Reagan's Hands-off Approach

Ronald Reagan favored less government regulation of the economy. A decade later, neither party—the Republicans or the Democrats—would argue with that.

Reagan also followed a hands-off approach in running the government. He delegated authority to those who worked for him rather than be involved in every decision. Several times this approach led to notable problems.

The S & L Scandal "Thrift institutions" or savings and loan banks, often called **S & L**s, made home mortgage loans to individuals. The Reagan administration, with the help of Democrats in Congress, pressed for the deregulation of

RESOURCE DIRECTORY

Teaching Resources

✪ **American Profiles Activity** found in the Unit 10 folder, p. 88, profiles Sandra Day O'Connor, the first woman appointed to serve on the United States Supreme Court.

✪ **Critical Thinking Activity** Recognizing Ideologies: The Bork Nomination, found in the Unit 10 folder, p. 92, helps students apply this skill by analyzing the Senate debate about one of Reagan's nominees to the Supreme Court, Robert H. Bork.

✪ **Primary Source Activity** An Explanation of Iran-Contra, found in the Unit 10 folder, pp. 94–95, presents an excerpt from President Reagan's televised address on March 4, 1987, to demonstrate how he defended his involvement in the scandal.

S & Ls to permit them to make riskier but more profitable investments.

Officials at a number of unregulated S & Ls took advantage of the new laws to make huge fortunes for themselves while driving their banks into failure. Because bank accounts are insured by the federal government, taxpayers had to make up the millions of dollars squandered in bad investments. A number of banking officials were prosecuted for their dishonest actions, but the money itself could not be recovered. Critics charged that the congressional rescue plan of almost $250 billion was another example of Reaganomics at work.

The Iran-contra Affair In Nicaragua, the Reagan administration sought to undermine the Marxist **Sandinista** government—named after a Nicaraguan freedom fighter from the 1920s—which had seized power in 1979. Reagan feared the spread of revolution to other Latin American countries. Working through the Central Intelligence Agency, the United States trained and armed Nicaraguan guerrilla fighters known as **contras** (from the Spanish word for "counterrevolutionaries"). This policy, however, violated United States neutrality laws.

Congress discovered these secret missions and in 1984 cut off military aid to the contras. Some members of the Reagan administration still believed, however, that aid to the contras was justified. These officials took the profits from secret arms sales to Iran and then sent those profits to the contras. (The arms sales were meant to encourage the release of American hostages held in Lebanon by pro-Iranian terrorists.)

 When the secret actions became public in the fall of 1986, Oliver North, the marine colonel who had made the arrangements, took the blame. The **Iran-contra affair**, as this scandal came to be called, caused the most serious criticism that the Reagan administration ever faced.

The Reagan Legacy

The Iran-contra affair did not damage Ronald Reagan's personal approval ratings. When he left office in 1989, polls showed that

Relations between the United States and the Soviet Union warmed considerably during Reagan's second term. Here, Reagan and Soviet President Mikhail Gorbachev meet outside St. Basil's Cathedral in Moscow.

over 60 percent of the American people gave him high marks for his overall performance.

Foreign Policy Success One reason was the tremendous improvement in U.S.-Soviet relations during Reagan's second term. Despite his long-standing anticommunism, Reagan developed a close relationship with Mikhail Gorbachev, who became the new Soviet leader in 1985. To reform the ailing Soviet system, Gorbachev proposed a program of *glasnost*—political openness—and *perestroika*—economic restructuring. These moves paved the way toward better relations with the United States. In 1987, Reagan and Gorbachev signed the **Intermediate-Range Nuclear Forces (INF) Treaty** that provided for the destruction of 2,500 Soviet and American missiles in Europe.

3. ASSESS

Section 3 Review Answers

1. (a) AIDS, see p. 946, (b) S & L, see p. 946, (c) Sandinista, see p. 947, (d) contra, see p. 947, (e) Iran-contra affair, see p. 947, (f) INF Treaty, see p. 947, (g) entitlement, see p. 948.

2. (a) Sandra Day O'Connor, see p. 946.

3. The 1984 summer Olympic Games, the first Summer Games held in the United States since 1932; the celebration of the centennial of the Statue of Liberty; and the 200th anniversary of the U.S. Constitution.

4. Reagan's economic policies, such as certain tax cuts, benefited the rich and concentrated wealth; recession, economic insecurity, and cuts in federal programs hurt the middle class and left the poor without resources or sources of help.

5. Civil rights initiatives: For—programs such as affirmative action and school desegregation help provide equal opportunity for minorities. Against—these programs interfere with the rights of state and local governments. The

In Depth

Global Connections

Nicaragua had been controlled by the wealthy Somoza family for 40 years when the Sandinista National Liberation Front led the overthrow of the government in 1979. The Sandinistas nationalized industry and took land from the rich to give to the peasants. Nicaraguans who were unhappy with some reforms then joined with Somoza supporters to fight the Sandinista government. These guerrillas—known as *contras*, which means "against"—attacked from bases across the border in Honduras and Costa Rica. Thousands in Nicaragua and neighboring countries died as fighting raged through the 1980s. A negotiated cease-fire in 1990 let Nicaraguans choose their first democratically elected government.

women's movement: For—women should be guaranteed equal rights by law, and should have the right to have an abortion. Against—the Equal Rights Amendment should not become law, and abortion should be illegal. The gay and lesbian movement: For—Gays and lesbians should not be discriminated against. Against—AIDS is a curse that punishes gays and lesbians for their lifestyles.

6. Because deregulation allowed S & Ls to make riskier but more profitable investments, some S & L officials took undue risks and sent their banks into failure, while making fortunes for themselves.

7. Answers will vary. Students should consider not only the positive and negative effects of Reagan's policies but also the long-term impact of the "Reagan revolution" in changing the country's direction.

Caption Answer to . . .

 Interpreting Graphs

During Reagan's first term in office, unemployment first rose dramatically, then began to fall during 1983. It continued to fall throughout his second term. The 1983 drop in unemployment may have helped to convince voters that Reagan's economic policies were good for the nation, which may have helped him get reelected.

Reteach

Ask students to write two or three sentences describing positive and successful events in Reagan's second term (1984–1988). Then have them write two or three sentences about the problems that arose in the same period.

 CLOSE

 Reinforcing the Big Idea

Reagan's continuing popularity helped maintain support for conservative policies throughout his two terms and enabled George Bush to "inherit" the presidency. However, Reagan's shoes would prove hard to fill.

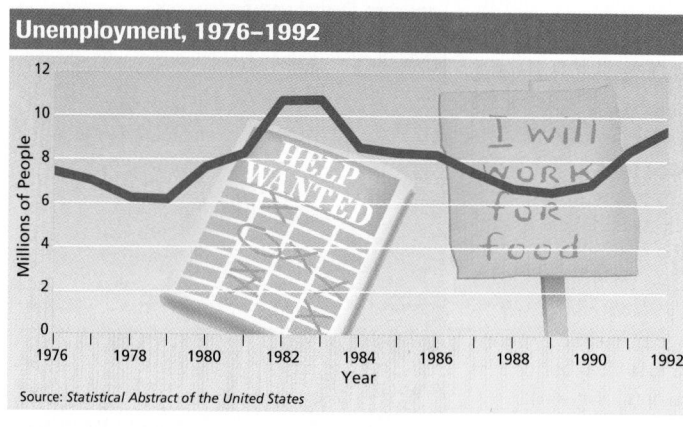

Unemployment, 1976–1992

Source: *Statistical Abstract of the United States*

 Interpreting Graphs
Examine the graph above showing unemployment statistics from 1976 to 1992. *What happened to unemployment during Reagan's years in office? How do you think those statistics might have contributed to Reagan's reelection in 1984?*

Domestic Policy Initiatives Another reason for Reagan's continued popularity was his stated commitment to reducing government. Reagan's policies, however, did not succeed in dramatically reducing Washington bloat. **Entitlements**—programs like Social Security, Medicare, and Medicaid, for which spending rises automatically each year—grew faster than policymakers expected. Social Security expenditures, for example, skyrocketed as the nation's elderly population continued to rise. Reagan failed to restrain the growth of these programs.

Economic difficulties surfaced dramatically near the end of Reagan's presidency. Investor fears about the huge budget deficits and rising national debt prompted a stock market crash in 1987. Following six weeks of falling prices, the market suffered a huge 22.6 percent drop on Monday, October 19. The speculative bubble of the 1980s had burst. While the stock market did recover, George Bush inherited some of the same problems. By the end of the decade the nation found itself in the midst of another recession, as more and more Americans lost their jobs.

For most Americans, Ronald Reagan's two-term presidency was marked by his vigorous emphasis on national pride and the force of his own optimistic personality. Reagan's presidency made Americans feel confident for the first time since the Kennedy years (see Chapter 19, page 770). President Clinton later summed it up when he wrote (page 1083, Unit 10 Source Readings), " . . . Ronald Reagan's greatest gift as President [was] the way his unwavering hopefulness reminded us that optimism is one of our most fundamental virtues."

SECTION 3 REVIEW

Key Terms, People, and Places
1. Define (a) AIDS, (b) S & L, (c) Sandinista, (d) contra, (e) Iran-contra affair, (f) INF Treaty, (g) entitlement.
2. Identify Sandra Day O'Connor.

Key Concepts
3. What events and celebrations during Reagan's presidency contributed to a rebirth in American patriotism?
4. How did Reagan's economic policies affect the gap between the rich and the poor?

5. List the controversies over social issues during the 1980s and, for each issue, explain the opposing arguments.

Critical Thinking
6. Making Comparisons Some historians consider the presidency of Franklin Roosevelt to be the most significant in this century. Do you think later historians will view the Reagan presidency as equally significant? Explain your answer.

 RESOURCE DIRECTORY

Teaching Resources

Quiz found in the Unit 10 folder, p. 82, covers the main ideas in this section as well as the key terms.

Media and Technology

Transparency
Critical Thinking, I-11

The Bush Presidency

SECTION PREVIEW

George Bush's foreign policy successes, including a successful end to the cold war, had their roots in Reagan's initiatives. Likewise, his failures on the domestic front, where the economy battled slow growth and rising debt, were rooted in the policies of the Reagan years.

Key Concepts
- Though not fully accepted by conservative Republicans, George Bush used a hard-hitting campaign to win the presidency in 1988.
- Bush enjoyed major foreign policy triumphs as the Soviet Union collapsed and Iraq was expelled from Kuwait.
- Economic recession and rising national debt cut into Bush's popularity.

Key Terms, People, and Places
START, Persian Gulf War, downsizing; George Bush, Clarence Thomas

I t's tough to follow a legendary President. **George Bush** had the same problem as William Howard Taft, who succeeded Theodore Roosevelt in 1909, and Harry S Truman, who inherited the presidency upon the death of Franklin D. Roosevelt in 1945. Ronald Reagan remained enormously popular as he left office in 1989, and Bush sought to continue the revolution his predecessor had begun. But he lacked Reagan's charismatic appeal and found that it was not always easy to measure up.

Bush's Background

The son of a well-to-do Connecticut senator, Bush began his career in the Texas oil industry, then served in government as a member of Congress, as an envoy to China, and as head of the CIA. In the Nixon years, he led the Republican National Committee. He was well-connected, with a reputation as a moderate and a loyal Republican.

Despite these impressive credentials, Bush lacked the support of conservatives in the GOP. Some Republicans whose hero was Ronald Reagan questioned Bush's commitment to their cause. They were concerned about his apparent early sympathy for abortion rights. They never truly forgave him for his characterization of Reagan's economic plans as "voodoo economics" during the 1980 campaign. Bush's loyal service as Reagan's Vice President for eight years failed to ease their fears.

Despite long years of public service and loyalty to the Republican party, George Bush was never as popular with conservatives—or with the American public as a whole—as his predecessor, Ronald Reagan.

The 1988 Campaign

Bush began the 1988 campaign far behind his Democratic opponent, Governor Michael Dukakis of Massachusetts. Dukakis had revived his state after years of economic distress and promised to do the same thing at the national level. Four months before the election, he enjoyed a 17 percentage point lead.

Bush took the offensive in what became a nasty contest. He vowed to continue Reagan's transformation of the United States. One part of his campaign was a pledge that there would be "no new taxes." Reagan's tax cuts, though enormously popular, had contributed to the huge budget deficit and growing national debt. Whoever succeeded Reagan would be under great pressure to raise taxes in order to reduce the deficit. Yet Bush publicly committed himself to holding the line on taxes.

Bush also attacked Dukakis as soft on crime. One particularly devastating television

Possible answer: As long as the people of a city wanted to be united—or, as in the case of Berliners, remember a united past—a wall would not last.

2. INSTRUCT

Explain/Discuss

Explain that, as President, Bush inherited a "mixed bag" of policies from his popular predecessor. Bush concentrated on foreign policy—where his own background and strengths lay—but also had to deal with domestic economic problems inherited from the Reagan administration.

Analyze

Ask students to look at the Bush administration and several previous administrations and analyze what makes a President choose to emphasize foreign or domestic policies. Is the main reason the course of world events? Or are some leaders naturally more interested in either foreign policy or domestic affairs?

Activity

Cooperative Learning

Time: One class period.
Activity: Research some of the nations that underwent major changes in the period 1988–1992.
Grouping: Groups of four students. Three are to do research as "experts"; the fourth acts as the recorder/spokesperson.
Purpose: Have each group research one of the countries that underwent major upheavals between 1988 and 1992. One student in a group should research each of these aspects: political system and leaders, economy, culture. The fourth person in the group will collect data, summarize it in chart form, and present it in class.
Outcome: Students will gain an understanding of world events in the 1980s. Have them save their research for a follow-up activity in Chapter 35.

| 1650 | 1700 | 1750 | 1800 | **Links Across Time** | 1850 | 1900 | 1950 | 2000 |

The Wall: Its Rise and Fall

Begun in 1961, the Berlin Wall was still being reinforced by East German workers—under the watchful eyes of armed border patrols—in 1967 (left). When the border finally opened in 1989, Berliners celebrated with a joyous all-night party (above). *Do you think it would be possible for a barrier such as the Berlin Wall to keep a city permanently divided?*

commercial featured an African American convict named Willie Horton. While on a furlough from prison through a Massachusetts weekend release program, Horton committed another brutal crime. The advertisement never mentioned race directly. Still, Democrats charged that it was intended to increase racial tensions and draw white voters toward the Republican ticket.

By election day, many Americans were complaining that neither candidate had addressed the major issues facing the country. Nearly half of all eligible voters stayed home in frustration. Among those who did vote, Bush won 54 percent of the popular vote and carried 40 states in a 426-111 electoral vote win. But he failed to gain the mandate Reagan had enjoyed, as Democrats now controlled both houses of Congress.

Foreign Policy Successes

Bush's major triumphs as President came in the field of foreign policy. Even more than Reagan, Bush benefited from the historic changes in the communist world unleashed by Mikhail Gorbachev. Some of the most dramatic changes occurred in Eastern Europe.

Eastern Europe While past Soviet leaders had stifled reform movements in Eastern Europe—using force when necessary—Gorbachev made it clear that he favored reform in Eastern Europe as well as the Soviet Union. The people of Eastern Europe needed no further encouragement. In 1989 Poland held its first free elections in half a century, leading to the election of Lech Walesa as president. Also in 1989, a writer once persecuted by the Communists, Vaclav Havel, was elected president of Czechoslovakia. Eventually, new regimes took charge in Bulgaria, Hungary, Romania, and Albania as well.

Probably the most dramatic event of 1989 took place in East Germany. In November 1989, that country's communist leader suddenly declared that East Germans could travel freely to West Germany. As border guards stepped aside, East Germans flooded across the hated Berlin Wall. The wall, the most potent symbol of the cold war, had been breached. A year later East and West Germany reunified, helping heal a once-divided Europe.

The Soviet Union By the end of 1991 the Soviet Union no longer existed, replaced by a loose Commonwealth of Independent States.

▶ RESOURCE DIRECTORY

Teaching Resources

American Profiles Activity Melissa Rathbun-Nealy, found in the Unit 10 folder, p. 87, profiles the first American woman soldier taken prisoner by the Iraqis during the Persian Gulf War.

Literature Activity Operation Desert Storm, found in the Unit 10 folder, pp. 97–98, dramatically illustrates the events surrounding the Allied action in Kuwait. The excerpt is from General Norman Schwarzkopf's autobiography, *It Doesn't Take a Hero.*

Post–Cold War Europe, 1994

 Geography and History: Interpreting Maps
In the late 1980s the Eastern bloc shattered into a jigsaw puzzle of diverse republics. *What kinds of problems do you think might follow the break-up of such a large nation as the Soviet Union?*

Boris Yeltsin, head of Russia, emerged as dominant leader in this fragmented land.

As the Soviet Union disintegrated, Bush continued arms-control talks with Soviet leader Gorbachev and later with Russian leader Yeltsin. The Soviets and Americans signed a number of pacts that signaled the end of the cold war. Agreements in 1989 and 1990 limited the buildup of both nuclear and chemical weapons. Then the **Strategic Arms Reduction Treaty (START)**, signed in 1991, called for dramatic reductions in the two nations' supply of long-range nuclear weapons. "The cold war is now behind us," Gorbachev proclaimed. "Let us not wrangle over who won it." But the victor was clear. The United States was now the world's lone remaining superpower.

⭐ **The Gulf War** In August 1990, Saddam Hussein, the dictator of Iraq, invaded Kuwait, a small nation rich in oil. Worried about the flow of oil to the West, Bush responded strongly:

> There is much in the modern world that is subject to doubts or questions— washed in shades of gray. But not the brutal aggression of Saddam Hussein against a peaceful, sovereign nation and its people. It's black and white. The facts are clear. The choice is unambiguous—right versus wrong.

 Working through the United Nations, the United States mobilized an alliance of 28 nations and struck at Iraq in January 1991 in "Operation Desert Storm." The **Persian Gulf War** lasted just 42 days. UN forces liberated Kuwait at the cost of just 240 soldiers, while tens of thousands of Iraqi troops died. Yet Hussein remained in power in Iraq.

MAKING CONNECTIONS

Reread the excerpt from President Bush. How does his description of Saddam Hussein echo the cold war speeches of earlier Presidents?

Enrichment

Have students do further research on aspects of the Gulf War that interest them. Possible topics: media coverage, health questions for veterans, women's participation in military actions, environmental issues, political and cultural characteristics of Iran, Kuwait or Saudi Arabia, lasting effects of the war.

Caption Answer to ...

🌐 **Interpreting Maps**

Possible answer: Ethnic conflicts might arise between groups vying for power in the new governments; groups might fight over economic resources.

Answer to ...

MAKING CONNECTIONS

By painting the situation in Kuwait in terms of "black and white" and "right versus wrong," Bush echoes the cold-war Presidents before him who had in the same way perceived anything or anyone connected with communism as automatically evil.

In Depth

Interdisciplinary

As the Persian Gulf War was ending, Iraqi troops set some 600 oil well fires and deliberately spilled more than 6 million barrels of oil into the Persian Gulf. The fires spread pollution through the air; marine life in the Gulf still shows acute toxicity from the oil spills. In late 1993 the Geological Society of America found that the Persian Gulf War "caused severe and lasting damage to Kuwait's desert, economic resources, and ecosystems." A 1991 EPA report called the environmental damage "tragic." Wetlands, wildlife, and vegetation around the Persian Gulf will suffer the effects of the war for decades.

Section 4 Review Answers

1. (a) START, see p. 951, (b) Persian Gulf War, see p. 951, (c) downsizing, see p. 952.

2. (a) George Bush, see p. 949, (b) Clarence Thomas, see p. 952.

3. Bush promised to continue Reagan's policies and not raise taxes; he attacked Dukakis as soft on crime and played on racial fears.

4. As Soviet control relaxed in Eastern Europe, several countries rejected communism and held free elections. The Berlin Wall fell, and East and West Germany reunited. Finally, the Soviet Union itself disintegrated as its republics became independent nations.

5. Victorious UN forces, led by the United States, liberated Kuwait and devastated the Iraqi army; Saddam Hussein remained in power.

6. There was a general economic downturn, as a recession began in the early 1990s. Unemployment increased, companies "downsized," and budget deficits continued.

7. Answers will vary. Some students may take a firm moral stance against breaking a promise. Others may argue that breaking a pledge for the good of the country is an acceptable action. Still others may recognize that campaign promises are frequently broken.

Reteach

Ask students to write two headings: "World" and "United States." Under each heading they should list the major events that took place in each region during the Bush administration.

Reinforcing the Big Idea

While George Bush never rivaled Reagan in popularity, history was made during his administration. With the end of the cold war, the United States and other world leaders had to rethink their policies.

AMERICAN PROFILES
Colin Powell

When war broke out in the Persian Gulf, President Bush turned to General Colin Powell to organize the military operations against Iraq. The general's battle plan was simple—use airpower to destroy Iraq's ability to wage war and then smash the Iraqi forces occupying Kuwait. UN forces, directed by General Powell, did just that. By war's end, Powell was a hero.

Colin Powell was born in 1937 in the Harlem section of New York City. During his military career, he rose quickly through the ranks. In 1979, at age 42, he became the Army's youngest brigadier general. In 1987, he became the first African American to serve as the President's National Security Advisor. In 1989, he was named the nation's top military officer—Chairman of the Joint Chiefs of Staff—and its youngest one ever.

Powell retired from government service in 1993. As a respected military hero in the mold of Dwight Eisenhower, Powell seemed destined for political office. Yet in 1996, Powell declared that he would not seek any political position. He did not, however, rule out a future run for office. "If I ever do decide to enter politics . . .,"

General Colin Powell

he stated in his autobiography, "I would enter only because I had a vision for this country."

Domestic Problems

Bush pleased conservatives—but angered many moderates and liberals—with his nomination of **Clarence Thomas** to the Supreme Court in 1991. A year earlier, Bush's nomination of David Souter of New Hampshire to fill an opening on the Court had won easy Senate confirmation. Thomas, in contrast, faced grilling about his views on civil rights and about episodes of possible sexual harassment in his past. An African American, Thomas also faced criticism from some black organizations for his conservative views. Thomas won confirmation, but only after televised Senate hearings had caused a storm of public debate on the issue of sexual harassment.

Bush's strong leadership during the Persian Gulf War drove his approval rate up to an astounding 91 percent. However, a recession, with roots in the Reagan years, began in the early 1990s. Unemployment climbed once again. A new word—downsizing—described the process by which companies laid off workers in order to cut costs. By 1991 the unemployment rate reached 7 percent, the highest level in nearly 5 years.

Bush countered by slowing spending for social programs. Finally, he agreed to a deficit reduction plan that included new taxes. This agreement, which violated Bush's promise of the 1988 campaign, angered the public.

SECTION 4 REVIEW

Key Terms, People, and Places
1. Define (a) START, (b) Persian Gulf War, (c) downsizing.
2. Identify (a) George Bush, (b) Clarence Thomas.

Key Concepts
3. Describe the main elements of Bush's strategy in the 1988 presidential campaign.
4. What historic changes in Eastern Europe and the Soviet Union took place during Bush's presidency?

5. Summarize the results of the Persian Gulf War.
6. What economic problems did the United States experience under Bush?

Critical Thinking
7. **Demonstrating Reasoned Judgment** Bush was widely criticized for breaking his "no new taxes" pledge. In your opinion, should a President break a promise if he believes that changed circumstances require him to do so? Explain your answer.

RESOURCE DIRECTORY

Teaching Resources

Quiz found in the Unit 10 folder, p. 84, covers the main ideas in this section as well as the key terms.

Chapter Test Forms A and B are found in the Unit 10 folder, pp. 101–106.

Answer Keys found in the Unit 10 folder pp. 143–156, provide answers to all student activities.

Media and Technology

Transparencies Graphic Organizer, G-1

Guided Reading Audiotapes (English and Spanish)

Computer Test Bank

Demonstrating Reasoned Judgment

Making connections between ideas is the basis for reasoned judgment. This critical thinking skill enables you to analyze the merits of a statement or opinion and thus reach your own conclusions about its validity.

Iraq invaded Kuwait in early August 1990 in what seemed to be an unprovoked attempt to grab Kuwait's oil resources. President Bush reacted quickly. Within a few days, the United States had sent troops and planes to nearby Saudi Arabia, assembled a naval force in the Persian Gulf, and backed a UN trade embargo against Iraq. By early September, U.S. combat aircraft had begun to arrive in the region. Clearly, Bush was sending a message to Saddam Hussein—if you do not leave Kuwait, the United States will force you to leave. The passage at right presents one person's response to the saber rattling (or intense military buildup) in the Persian Gulf.

Read the passage. Then use the following steps to analyze the response and to test the reasonableness of both the speaker's judgment and your own.

1. Examine the source and nature of the evidence by asking who, when, where, and what.
(a) Who offered the response? (b) When? (c) Where was the speech presented? (d) What are the speaker's qualifications for addressing this subject? (e) Might the speaker have any biases that affected his view of Bush's actions in the Persian Gulf?

2. Identify the major points in the response. (a) Why does the speaker remind his audience of World War II and the Vietnam War? (b) What false premises—propositions used as the basis for an argument—does he point out, and what does he think they are being used to do? (c) What does the speaker believe is missing in this conflict?

3. Evaluate the evidence offered and the speaker's reasoning. (a) What does the speaker seem to be arguing for? (b) How convincing do you find his arguments? Explain why. (c) What grade—from A down to F (failing)—would you give the speaker on how well he demonstrates reasoned judgment? Why did you choose that grade?

The war that formed George Bush began because of Adolf Hitler. The Allied effort was successful because the evil of Hitler and his plan became clear to Americans as the war progressed. We were convinced of the need for the sacrifice required to wage it. . . .

The war that formed me began because of a need to contain communism. We failed in that war because in the end our leaders did not adequately convince the American people that Ho Chi Minh was a threat requiring our prolonged sacrifice.

I had hoped that we in this nation could act differently in the Persian Gulf than we did in Vietnam. Now I am not so sure. I am profoundly uneasy about the instant deployment of more than 100,000 American troops that was sold to the American people on the false premises that Saddam Hussein is Adolf Hitler, that our way of life is at clear and present danger, that we have as much at stake as we did in World War II. . . .

What is missing in this conflict is the grim-faced attitude of a people who really believe that the United States, or at least a strategic asset of unquestionable importance, is at risk. Missing is the conviction that we must fight with our lives because we are fighting for our lives. Although the President says that this is the first post-Cold War test of our mettle, it simply, honestly, does not feel like it. . . .

What is needed in this crisis, above all, is honesty. Our actions in the Gulf should not exceed the scope of informed public consent and informed public support.

—Senator Bob Kerrey, Democrat from Nebraska and a veteran of the Vietnam War, from a speech to the Senate, September 19, 1990

953

📄 **Historian's Toolbox Activity** Demonstrating Reasoned Judgment, found in the Unit 10 folder, p. 91, helps students apply this skill by analyzing Reagan's criticism of big government.

TOOLBOX

Critical Thinking
Demonstrating Reasoned Judgment

Focus Analyze a passage on the Gulf War to judge its validity.

Instruct After students have read the passage, have them identify the main idea of the statement. Then have them list key pieces of evidence that support the main message. Ask students if the writer includes any information that does not necessarily support an argument. Point out that it is important to be able to recognize this when making reasoned judgments.

Extend See the Historian's Toolbox Activity in the Resource Directory below.

Answers

1. (a) Senator Bob Kerrey of Nebraska (b) September 19, 1990 (c) In the U.S. Senate (d) As a senator and a veteran of the Vietnam War, presumably he would know about military matters and about foreign policy. (e) As a Democrat, he might be inclined to oppose a Republican policy or at least offer a viewpoint to balance it.

2. (a) He is measuring the Persian Gulf conflict against two wars: one that had a clear enemy and ended in American victory; and one in which the threat was less clear and the outcome was American failure. (b) The premises that "Saddam Hussein is Adolf Hitler, that our way of life is at clear and present danger, that we have as much at stake as we did in World War II" are being used to persuade the American people to send more than 100,000 troops to the Gulf. (c) The certainty that this is a conflict worth fighting and dying for is missing.

3. (a) He argues for honesty from administration officials and for keeping the American people informed so that they can use facts, not false comparisons, to decide what policies to support. (b) and (c) Answers will vary.

The Rise of the Sunbelt

Focus Point out to students that there have always been distinctive differences between regions of the United States. Until the mid-twentieth century, most of the states in the South were mainly agricultural. They lagged behind the rest of the country in industries, wages, racial attitudes, spending on health and education, and other measures. The cities of the Northeast and North Central regions dominated business, banking, and manufacturing, and so had political power as well.

In this feature, students will learn how the balance between regions has changed in the recent past, giving new influence to the Sunbelt.

Instruct Ask students to describe, in general terms, economic and political changes they have observed in their own communities within their own lifetimes. What earlier changes do they know about? How do those changes compare with those described for the Sunbelt states? If your community is part of the Sunbelt, how have the trends affected it?

To guide the discussion, have them focus on specific aspects:

- **Population** Has the population of the community grown or declined since the 1970s? What factors have caused the change? What effects have population changes had on community services such as schools and medical care?
- **Business and industry** Have new firms and factories located in the area? Or have businesses closed or downsized? Has the number of available jobs increased? What about service businesses such as supermarkets or video rentals?
- **Politics** Is the community traditionally Democratic or Republican? Liberal or conservative? What political issues are important in the community?
- **Environment** Have air and water quality improved or declined? Do growing populations put pressure on water supplies and other resources? (For instance, are there seasonal limits on water use? Are wetlands threatened by development?)

TIME & PLACE
A GEOGRAPHIC PERSPECTIVE

The Rise of the Sunbelt

By the 1990s, one region of the United States—the Sunbelt— had gained new influence. What caused this change? And how did it affect politics and the economy?

In the years after World War II, the southern states—mainly agricultural, often poor—suddenly exploded into growth and prosperity. Writers in the 1970s used the term "Sunbelt" in describing this change. Generally, the Sunbelt included the warm-weather states south of the 37th parallel, from North Carolina to Arizona. Neighboring states such as California and Colorado also shared in the boom.

New manufacturing industries were started in the South or moved there from other areas. People from places where times were harder and weather colder flocked to the warmer Sunbelt. They left behind decaying industries and cities in northern states, which soon acquired a number of unflattering nicknames—Frost Belt, Rust Belt.

Sunbelt cities such as Houston, Dallas, and Atlanta grew quickly, with more room to spread out than crowded metropolitan areas in the North. Of the 20 cities expected to grow the most between 1995 and 2005, 15 were in Sunbelt states (including Colorado). Eleven were in just three states: Texas, Florida, and California. Eighteen of the 20 cities with the fastest projected job growth for the same period were also in the South and West.

Drawing Business and Industry

The key reason for Sunbelt growth was jobs, both new and transplanted. Other factors made the South attractive to business. Hydroelectric power was inexpensive and widely available. Warmer weather reduced the expense of heating fuels. And lower taxes and costs of living attracted both workers and industry. Southern economic expansion coincided with the expansion of defense industries and allied companies such as aerospace and electronics.

As manufacturing jobs increased, other types of businesses grew too. Newcomers built homes and offices, bringing a boom in construction and building supplies. Service businesses opened to serve people moving in—from realtors to supermarkets to video rentals. Southern cities won franchises for expansion teams—even for that most wintry sport, ice hockey.

> The key reason for Sunbelt growth was jobs, both new and transplanted.

Attracting People

Many people who moved to the Sunbelt were either following or looking for jobs. Good weather and mild winters also drew retired people and families. For younger families, one big reason was "quality of life"—things such as a slower-paced way of life, clean air, a friendlier, safer atmosphere, and more chances for outdoor recreation.

For the first time in decades, many new southerners were African Americans. Earlier in the century, thousands had flocked north to escape racial prejudice and find jobs in industry. Now, many black Americans decided that racial attitudes and quality of life were better in the South than in many northern cities.

▶ RESOURCE DIRECTORY

Teaching Resources

Time and Place Activity The Baby Boomers Grow Up, found in the Unit 10 folder, pp. 85–86, focuses on another feature of American demographics—the impact of the large Baby Boomer population group as it has moved from school age to family life and on into middle age.

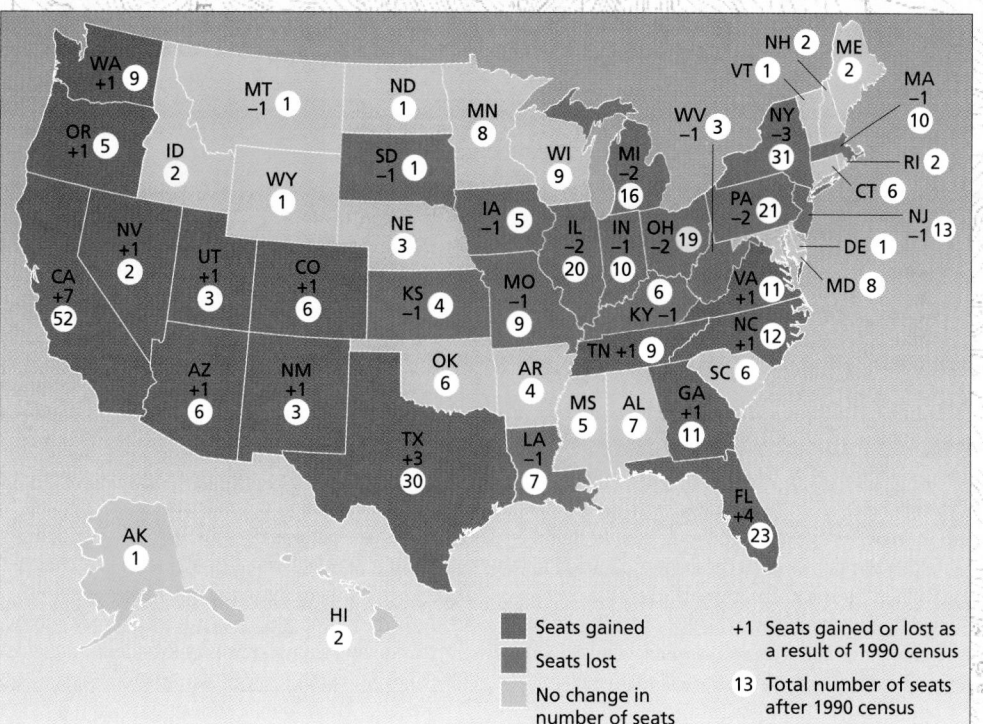

Map Legend:
- Seats gained
- Seats lost
- No change in number of seats
- +1 Seats gained or lost as a result of 1990 census
- 13 Total number of seats after 1990 census

State data (from map):
WA +1 (9), OR +1 (5), ID (2), MT −1 (1), ND (1), MN (8), WI (9), MI −2 (16), NH (2), VT (1), ME (2), MA −1 (10), NY −3 (31), WV −1 (3), RI (2), CT (6), NJ −1 (13), PA −2 (21), DE (1), MD (8), NV +1 (2), CA +7 (52), UT +1 (3), WY (1), CO +1 (6), SD −1 (1), NE (3), IA −1 (5), IL −2 (20), IN −1 (10), OH −2 (19), VA +1 (11), KS −1 (4), MO −1 (9), KY −1 (6), NC +1 (12), TN +1 (9), SC (6), AZ +1 (6), NM +1 (3), OK (6), AR (4), MS (5), AL (7), GA +1 (11), TX +3 (30), LA −1 (7), FL +4 (23), AK (1), HI (2)

A New National Voice

The shift of people to the South has brought a dramatic shift in national political power too. Every ten years, after the census, the 435 seats in the U.S. House of Representatives are reapportioned among the states on the basis of population changes. As the map shows, after both the 1980 and 1990 censuses, many southern and western states added congressional seats, while the Northeast lost representatives. These shifts have given the South and West greater influence on both politics and social issues.

The voting strength of the Sunbelt is strongly reflected in presidential politics. Since the mid-1960s, all Presidents except one—Gerald Ford, from Michigan—have been from Sunbelt states. They are: Democrats Lyndon Johnson of Texas, Jimmy Carter of Georgia, and Bill Clinton of Arkansas; Republicans Richard Nixon and Ronald Reagan from California, and George Bush, elected from Texas. In 1996, for the first time, southern Republicans led both houses of Congress: Speaker of the House Newt Gingrich of Georgia and Senate Majority Leader Trent Lott of Mississippi.

Southern voting patterns also changed. Once a stronghold for Democrats, the South became more strongly Republican and conservative. According to a recent poll, the South's approach to national problems favored a smaller government role in the economy but more government oversight in issues of culture and morality.

GEOGRAPHIC CONNECTIONS

1. What were some factors that attracted people and businesses to the Sunbelt?
2. What political changes took place as a result of the growth of the Sunbelt?

Critical Thinking

3. **Identifying Alternatives** What could northern states and communities do to keep businesses and people from moving to the Sunbelt?

Chapter Review Answers

Understanding Key Terms, People, and Places

Terms
Students should refer to the definitions of the key terms in the chapter to write sentences that show the relation of each word to the social, political, and economic changes that took place during the rise of the conservative movement.

Matching
1. supply-side economics
2. federal deficit
3. S & L
4. Strategic Defense Initiative
5. downsizing

True or False
1. false, Ronald Reagan
2. false, Clarence Thomas's
3. true

Reviewing Main Ideas

1. The New Deal expanded the size and role of government, greatly increased federal spending, imposed business regulations, and, according to conservatives, undermined American values such as self-reliance.

2. Eisenhower accepted the basic idea of the New Deal but tried to slow government growth. During Nixon's administration, the federal government continued to grow, as several new regulatory agencies were added.

3. Many people in the country felt that government had grown too large; others disapproved of various social changes. Groups with different conservative agendas came together in the coalition known as the New Right. The coalition used innovative tactics in Reagan's successful campaign for the presidency.

4. Reagan pushed for tax cuts in 1981, 1982, and 1983. In 1986, Congress passed a sweeping tax reform measure that benefited the wealthy most. In theory, this benefit should have "trickled down" to help the economy.

5. He argued for ending many government regulations that he claimed discouraged business growth. The Reagan administration also eliminated some public service jobs, slashed aid to cities, and sharply reduced federal spending for human assistance, shifting responsibility to state and local governments.

6. No, he favored large defense budgets and a military buildup, in order to take a tough stance against the Soviet Union.

7. Yes and no. The economy recovered from the recession of 1981–1982, and

---

Chapter Review

Understanding Key Terms, People, and Places

Key Terms
1. coalition
2. affirmative action
3. New Right
4. televangelism
5. supply-side economics
6. New Federalism
7. Strategic Defense Initiative
8. federal deficit
9. AIDS
10. S & L
11. Sandinista
12. contra
13. Iran-contra affair
14. INF Treaty
15. entitlement
16. START
17. Persian Gulf War
18. downsizing

People
19. Ronald Reagan
20. Sandra Day O'Connor
21. George Bush
22. Clarence Thomas

Terms For each term above, write a sentence that explains its relation to the social, political, and economic changes that took place during the rise of the conservative movement.

Matching Review the key terms in the list above. If you are not sure of a term's meaning, review its definition in the chapter. Then choose a term from the list that best matches each description below.
1. the theory that lower taxes will stimulate the economy by encouraging business leaders to invest
2. the amount by which the government's spending exceeds its income in a given year
3. one of the generally small, stable banks that were deregulated during the Reagan administration
4. the proposal to create a satellite shield intended to intercept incoming missiles
5. a process by which companies laid off workers in order to cut costs

True or False Determine whether each statement is true or false. If it is true, write "true." If it is false, change the underlined name to make the statement true.
1. A former actor, <u>George Bush</u> was tremendously popular during his two terms as President.
2. <u>Sandra Day O'Connor's</u> nomination hearings generated a storm of public controversy when the nominee was accused of sexual harassment.
3. Some members of the Reagan administration secretly arranged for money to be sent to the <u>contras</u>.

Reviewing Main Ideas

Section 1 (pp. 934–937)
1. Why was the New Deal so difficult for conservatives to accept?
2. What did Republican Presidents Eisenhower and Nixon do about the growth of government?
3. How did the conservative movement finally gain success in the 1980s?

Section 2 (pp. 938–942)
4. How did Ronald Reagan apply the theory of supply-side economics as President?
5. How else did Reagan try to apply conservative principles to the federal government?
6. Did Reagan cut the defense budget? Why or why not?
7. Was "Reaganomics" a successful economic program?

Section 3 (pp. 943–948)
8. How did the national celebrations that took place in the 1980s fit Reagan's view of what America should be?
9. How did Reagan's economic policies affect the distribution of wealth in the United States?
10. Describe the two major scandals that erupted during Reagan's presidency.

Section 4 (pp. 949–952)
11. Why did some conservatives hesitate to support George Bush during the 1988 presidential campaign?
12. How did Bush win the presidential race in 1988?
13. Give evidence to show that President Bush was more successful at foreign policy than domestic policy.

---

inflation and unemployment dropped, but the federal deficit skyrocketed; tax cuts did not generate the economic growth that supply-side economic theory predicted.

8. The Olympic Games, the centennial of the Statue of Liberty, and the 200th anniversary of the Constitution all fit Reagan's romantic vision of a strong, patriotic, virtuous America.

9. The gap between rich and poor widened; wealth became more concentrated in the hands of a few. The middle class faced economic insecurity as high-paying industrial jobs disappeared.

10. S & Ls: After deregulation, a number of small banks (S & Ls) failed because of risky investments, while some bank officials grew rich. Iran-contra affair: Some members of the Reagan administration acted illegally by selling weapons to Iran and using the profits to illegally aid contras in Nicaragua.

11. Conservatives did not trust Bush as a genuine conservative, because he had once seemed to accept abortion rights and had called Reagan's plan "voodoo economics."

12. He pledged "no new taxes" and attacked the Democratic candidate as soft on crime.

13. The United States and its allies won the Persian Gulf War, forcing Saddam Hussein's troops to retreat from Kuwait. Meanwhile, Bush's policies were unable to stop unemployment in the United States from rising.

Thinking Critically

1. Demonstrating Reasoned Judgment You have read that Ronald Reagan enjoyed a high approval rating when he left office, despite the scandals that marred his presidency. How do you account for Reagan's popularity?

2. Determining Relevance If Reagan had attended the Constitutional Convention in 1787, how might he have advised the Framers as to the proper role of the federal government?

3. Formulating Questions Write three questions that you might ask former President Bush concerning actions he took during his political career. The goal of your questions should be to gain insight into the decision-making process or to determine whether Bush regrets any of his past actions.

4. Predicting Consequences In what specific ways might your adult life be different because the cold war ended?

Making Connections

1. Evaluating Primary Sources Review the primary source excerpt on page 944. According to Phillips, who was most financially successful during Reagan's administration? Based on what Phillips says, do you think Reagan's economic policies were successful?

2. Understanding the Visuals Look at the photos on pages 932, 933, 934, and 943. How do they help explain Ronald Reagan's enduring popularity with the American people?

3. Writing About the Chapter A newsmagazine has asked you to write an essay that looks back at the 1980s. You are to focus on either the social, political, or economic changes that occurred in the United States during that decade. First, review the chapter and make a list of the points you plan to cover. Next,

write a draft of your essay. Revise your essay, making certain that each idea is clearly explained. Proofread your essay and draft a final copy.

4. Using the Graphic Organizer This graphic organizer uses a web to organize information about Republican policies during the 1980s and early 1990s. The dashed lines show connections between seemingly unconnected elements. (a) What is the connection between tax reform, increased spending for defense, and cuts in social programs? (b) How do deregulation and the New Federalism demonstrate a similar view of the role of government? (c) On a separate sheet of paper, create your own web to organize information about the conservative movement. Use this graphic organizer as an example.

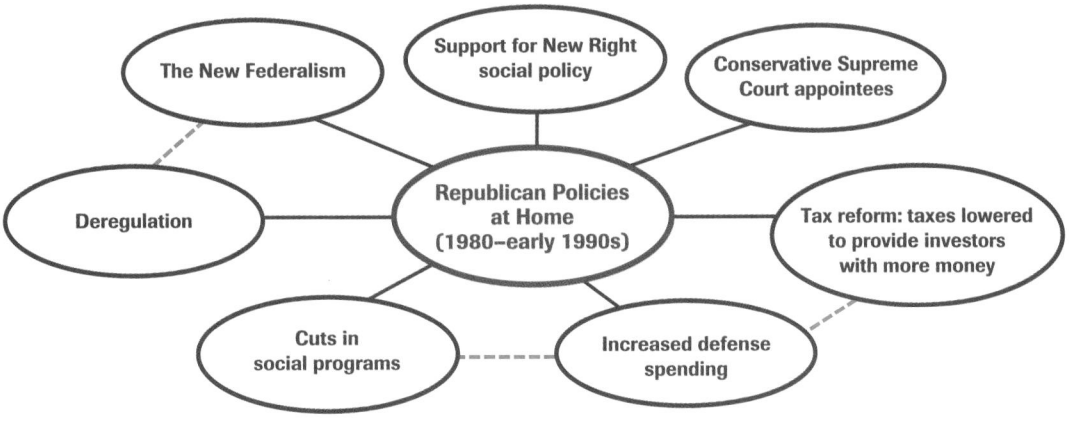

3. Students' essays should demonstrate an understanding of the social, political, and economic changes that took place in the 1980s as a result of the influence of the conservative movement.

4. (a) Because of increase in defense spending and a decrease in revenues due to tax cuts, the government had less money and chose to cut social programs. (b) Both policies aim to limit the federal government's role in business and the economy. (c) Students' graphic organizers should include information about groups that formed the New Right coalition, the policies and issues they supported and opposed, and the role of television and other techniques in promoting the conservative agenda.

 Alternative Assessment

Final Evaluation
Use the following guidelines to evaluate student projects:

● **Evidence of thoughtfulness** Did students include the main topics from the chapter?

● **Evidence of outside research** To what extent did students use outside research materials for their project?

● **Evidence of synthesis** Do projects demonstrate an understanding of how topics are related?

● **Communication style** Do projects convey their purpose to an audience in a clear, appealing way?

Encourage students to present their finished projects to the class.

Thinking Critically

1. Responses should mention Reagan's great personal charm and communication skills, as well as the appeal of his conservative policies to many Americans.

2. Possible answer: Reagan probably would have advocated a very limited role for the federal government in economic and social matters but an aggressive role in foreign affairs.

3. Possible question topics: campaign ads against Dukakis; the "no new taxes" pledge or why it was broken; signing the START treaty; going to war in the Persian Gulf War; nominating Clarence Thomas to the Supreme Court.

4. Answers will vary but should recognize the tensions formerly created by the cold war, including the threat of nuclear war.

Making Connections

1. According to Phillips, the truly wealthy were the most successful during Reagan's administration. Based on what Phillips says, Reagan's policies were successful for the rich, but less successful for other sections of the population.

2. The photos shows that Reagan was an appealing, charismatic person with strong, patriotic ideals about America. He kept up a tough stance against the Soviet Union until Mikhail Gorbachev indicated that the Soviets were ready to back down; then he was gracious in victory.

Chapter 35 Entering a New Era
1992–Present

📁 **Teaching Resources** (See Unit 10 Folder)

	Instruction	Enrichment

Section 1
The Clinton Presidency
(pp. 960–965)
	Reproducible Lesson Plan, p. 108
	Alternate Lesson Plan, p. 177
	Guided Reading and Review, p. 111
	Quiz, p. 112
		American Profiles Activity, Ron Brown,
		  p. 117
		Primary Source Activity, Defining Economic
		  Goals, pp. 123–124
		Critical Thinking Activity, Drawing
		  Conclusions, p. 122
		Visual Learning Activity, Campaign
		  Strategies '96, p. 130

Section 2 **The United States in a New World** (pp. 966–971)	Reproducible Lesson Plan, p. 109 Alternate Lesson Plan, p. 178 Guided Reading and Review, p. 113 Quiz, p. 114	Visual Learning Activity, Clinton's Foreign Policy, p. 129

Section 3
Twenty-First Century Americans
(pp. 972–976)
	Reproducible Lesson Plan, p. 110
	Alternate Lesson Plan, p. 179
	Guided Reading and Review, p. 115
	Quiz, p. 116
	Chapter Test, Forms A & B, pp. 131–136
		American Profiles Activity, Amy Tan, p. 118
		Primary Source Activity, Trying to Break the
		  Cycle of Crime, p. 125
		Literature Activity, Living in a New World,
		  pp. 126–128
		Viewpoints Activity, On Immigration Policy,
		  pp. 119–120
		Historian's Toolbox Activity, Predicting
		  Consequences, p. 121

📁 **Additional Chapter Resources**

Resource Organizer, p. 107
Alternate Lesson Plan, p. 176
Answer Keys, pp. 143–156

Bibliography

For the Teacher

Bell, Derrick. *Faces at the Bottom of the Well: The Permanence of Racism.* Basic, 1993. (Attitudes toward race revealed through dialogues and myths.)

Glickman, Rose L. *Daughters of Feminists.* St. Martin's Press, 1993. (Reports on fifty women raised by feminist mothers.)

Takaki, Ronald. *A Different Mirror: A History of Multicultural America.* Little, Brown, 1993. (An attempt to view all of American history from a multicultural perspective.)

Prentice Hall Literature Excerpts from *The American Experience,* 1994, including McElroy, Colleen J. "For My Children," from *What Madness Brought Me Here: New and Selected Poems, 1968–1988.* University Press of New England, 1990.

The Big Idea for the chapter and how the main ideas in each section relate to the Big Idea are graphically displayed below. Comprehension of this chapter's Big Idea is critical to students' understanding of United States history and how we as a nation got where we are today.

Media and Technology

 Historical Maps, L-5; Our Multicultural Heritage, C-3, C-14; Graphic Organizer, G-1

 Guided Reading Audiotapes (English and Spanish)

Computer Test Bank

For the Student

Ashabranner, Brent. *An Ancient Heritage: The Arab American Minority.* HarperCollins, 1993. (Personal reflections on the experience of being Arab American.)

Cisneros, Sandra. *The House on Mango Street.* Arte Publico, 1989. (A short story collection by a Mexican American writer.)

Santiago, Esmeralda. *When I Was Puerto Rican.* Addison-Wesley, 1993.

Smith, Jessie Carney. *Black Firsts: 2,000 Years of Extraordinary Achievement.* Visible Ink Press, 1994. (Chronicles the "firsts" among people of color.)

CHAPTER 35

Sweeping changes in world affairs in the early 1990s changed the face of world politics. While the cold war was over, these developments offered new challenges to the United States, now the only superpower, and to its President, Bill Clinton. The United States also faced new issues at home, as immigration and an aging population changed the demographics of American society.

SECTION 1

Economic issues, plus the appeal of youth and fresh ideas, brought Democrat Bill Clinton to the presidency in 1992. Then, in 1994, Republican victory in Congress seemed to herald a new conservative movement. However, congressional opposition ultimately helped Clinton's popularity, winning him reelection in 1996.

SECTION 2

The end of the cold war changed not only the United States' relationship with Russia but its entire approach to foreign affairs. The Clinton administration had to find new ways to meet change and tensions in various parts of the world.

SECTION 3

As the 21st century approached, the United States itself was changing. The population, on average, was growing older, while immigration increased the country's ethnic and cultural diversity and sometimes challenged its unity.

Entering a New Era
1992–Present

The Relevance of the Big Idea

The beginning of a new century is always a milestone, but the coming of the 21st century seemed to pose a startling array of challenges for the United States, its citizens, and its leaders.

After spending half the century engaged in a cold war, the United States was now the only superpower, trying to help its old enemy Russia make the transition to democracy. Around the world, many other nations were undergoing painful transitions, which sometimes involved the United States as peacekeeper or police officer.

Closer to home, the United States itself was becoming a different society—older and more diverse. Ask students to list some situations or issues that they think will be important in the new century.

In Depth

Global Connections

The 1996 summer Olympic Games, celebrating the centennial of the modern Olympics (revived in 1896 in Athens, Greece), were the first games of the post-cold war period. For the first time, every country invited sent a team to the games in Atlanta, Georgia—197 delegations with some 10,000 athletes competing. The world TV audience was estimated at 3.5 billion. This global community reflected the "new world": post-apartheid South Africa returned to world sports, while the countries of the former Soviet Union—from Belarus to Kazakhstan—competed as independent national teams.

Entering a New Era
1992–Present

In 1992 Democrat Bill Clinton ended twelve years of Republican rule in the White House when he became the forty-second president of the United States. In 1996, he became the first Democratic President since Franklin D. Roosevelt to win a second term. In the 1990s, with the end of the cold war abroad and a rapidly changing cultural climate at home, President Clinton and the American people would need to find creative solutions to many complex problems.

Events in the United States

1990 Congress passes the Immigration Act of 1990.

1992 Democrat Bill Clinton defeats Republican George Bush in the presidential election.

1989	1990	1991	1992

Events in the World

1991 Yugoslavian republics of Slovenia and Croatia declare their independence.
• The Haitian president is overthrown.

1992 The European Community drops many trade barriers between members.
• Boris Yeltsin is elected president of Russia.

RESOURCE DIRECTORY

Teaching Resources

Alternate Lesson Plan: Demonstrating the Big Idea found in the Alternate Lesson Plans folder, p. 176, provides a lesson strategy to instruct students about the Big Idea that as the twentieth century drew to a close, the United States faced new challenges in technology, foreign affairs, and culture.

Alternative Assessment Handbook provides information, guidance, and strategies for alternative methods of assessment. It includes an essay on new trends in assessment, guidance and strategies for developing performance tasks and portfolios, scoring rubrics, and sample evaluation forms.

Pages 960–965
The Clinton Presidency

American voters, concerned with an ailing economy, elected Democrat Bill Clinton to the presidency in 1992. Congress approved Clinton's first budget, but rejected his plan to reform the health-care system. A Republican sweep of the House and Senate in the 1994 mid-term elections spelled trouble for Clinton, but battling a hostile Congress actually boosted the President's popularity. Clinton rode that popularity to victory in the 1996 presidential election.

THE CHOICE
BOB WOODWARD

Pages 966–971
The United States in a New World

The end of the cold war in the 1990s left the Clinton administration struggling to find its way through uncharted waters in international relations. The collapse of communism and the increase in ethnic tensions in various parts of the world created new problems for the nation.

Pages 972–976
Twenty-First Century Americans

By the 1990s, immigration and an aging population had changed the makeup of the United States. Minority groups comprised a much larger percentage of the population than ever before, and older Americans made up the fastest-growing age group in the country. The United States sought to find new ways to create unity out of its ethnic and cultural diversity and deal with the consequences of an "aging revolution."

CAUTION

PROHIBIDO

1993 President Clinton appoints Ruth Bader Ginsburg to the Supreme Court.
• Congress passes the North American Free Trade Agreement.

1994 President Clinton pushes for reform of the health-care and welfare systems.

1995 A Republican majority enters Congress on the promise of the "Contract with America."

1996 President Clinton signs the Welfare Reform bill.
• Bill Clinton is reelected president of the United States.

1997 Bill Clinton begins second term as president of the United States.

1993   1994   1995   1996   1997

1993 Israel and the Palestine Liberation Organization sign a peace treaty.

1994 War continues between Serbia and Bosnia-Herzegovina.
• The Winter Olympics are held in Lillehammer, Norway.

1995 Yitzhak Rabin, Prime Minister of Israel, is assassinated.

1996 Boris Yeltsin is reelected president of Russia.

Alternative Assessment

As an ongoing project, students can organize "Project 2000," in which small groups look at important trends and issues of the coming century. Students should choose five to seven topics (one per group) that they believe will be important to the country and to themselves personally. Possibilities include demographic changes (future cities, changes in lifestyle); or political and economic issues (poverty, jobs).

Possible formats for presenting topic reports include the following:
• Audiotaped or videotaped interviews with experts on the particular issue.
• Interviews with "trendsetters" or forecasters.
• Oral presentations exploring potential policies, with charts or maps.
• Scrapbooks of newspaper or magazine articles on the topic.
• Oral presentations including statistics or other factual evidence supporting a trend.

Explain that projects will be evaluated according to the following guidelines.
• **Unacceptable** Projects are not attempted or do not address a relevant issue.
• **Limited/Acceptable** Projects use material from the textbook and show a limited exploration of the issue.
• **Extensive/Commendable** Projects are based on outside research and present information in a well-organized and interesting way.
• **Extraordinary/Outstanding** Projects are based on extensive research and display thoughtful interpretation as well as original thought and creativity.

This project can serve as an interesting prologue to Unit 11.

For more information and guidance on alternative assessment trends and strategies, see the Alternative Assessment Handbook in the Resource Directory on page 958.

The Clinton Presidency

1. FOCUS

Connecting to the Big Idea

See page 958B. Explain to students that American voters chose Bill Clinton, a Democrat, after 12 years of Republican presidents. Two years later, however, they chose a record number of Republicans to represent them in Congress. Ask students to describe the two parties' differences on issues, where they have moved closer together, and where they still strongly differ.

Objectives

• Describe Clinton's plans for the economy and health-care reform.
• Identify the pledges made by Republican lawmakers in the "Contract with America."
• Describe the course and outcome of the 1996 presidential campaign.

Bellringer

Ask students to imagine that they are making a decision about how to vote in the 1996 presidential election. What factors and issues would influence their decision? How would they have voted?

Reading Strategy

Question Writing Have students read through the section headings and write a *what*, *why*, or *how* question for each. As they read, they should look for the answers to each question.

The Clinton Presidency

SECTION PREVIEW

American voters, concerned with an ailing economy, elected Democrat Bill Clinton to the presidency in 1992. Congress approved Clinton's first budget, but rejected his plan to reform the health-care system. A Republican sweep of the House and Senate in the 1994 mid-term elections spelled trouble for Clinton, but battling a hostile Congress actually boosted the President's popularity. Clinton rode that popularity to victory in the 1996 presidential election.

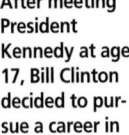

After meeting President Kennedy at age 17, Bill Clinton decided to pursue a career in politics.

Key Concepts

• In his first year as President, Bill Clinton proposed ways to stimulate the economy and reform the health-care system.
• The Republicans, whose victory in the 1994 elections gave them control of Congress, set out to honor the promises made in their "Contract with America."
• Clinton won a second term by defeating Republican Bob Dole in the 1996 presidential election.

Key Terms, People, and Places

Bill Clinton, Al Gore, Ross Perot, Newt Gingrich, Bob Dole

A t the age of 17, **Bill Clinton** shook hands with the President. A hard-working student from the small town of Hope, Arkansas, Clinton was chosen to participate in Boys Nation, a summer program in which high school students learn about politics. The group traveled to Washington, D.C.,

and met President John F. Kennedy at the White House. This experience helped persuade Clinton to pursue a career in politics. In 1993, some three decades after meeting President Kennedy, Clinton once again went to the White House. This time he brought his luggage and moved right in, for he was now the forty-second President of the United States.

Clinton's Path to the Presidency

Clinton's political career got off to a fast start. In 1976, three years after earning his law degree, Clinton was elected Arkansas attorney general. In 1978, at age 32, he won election as Arkansas governor. Defeated for reelection in 1980, he made a comeback in the 1982 election and held the office of governor through the 1980s.

One of Clinton's closest advisors was his wife, Hillary Rodham Clinton, whom he had met at law school. In the 1980s Mrs. Clinton chaired the Arkansas Education Standards Committee, which proposed educational reforms. She was praised by some for her intelligence and energy but criticized by others, who argued that a governor's wife should confine herself to ceremonial duties.

As the 1992 presidential election approached, several prominent Democrats, discouraged by President Bush's high approval ratings, chose not to try for the Democratic nomination. That created an opening for Bill Clinton. Known as an articulate reformist governor and a superb campaigner, Clinton won the nomination.

The 1992 Campaign for President

The 1992 election was a three-way race. Like the 1912 campaign, which also involved three candidates—Wilson, Taft, and Theodore Roosevelt—the presence of a third major candidate played a major role in the contest.

RESOURCE DIRECTORY

Teaching Resources

Reproducible Lesson Plan found in the Unit 10 folder, p. 108, provides a summary of the Section 1 lesson plan content.

Alternate Lesson Plan: Cooperative Learning found in the Alternate Lesson Plans folder, p. 177, helps groups of students identify the early goals of President Clinton, explain the ups and downs of Clinton's first years in office, and identify the main political characters of the period.

Guided Reading and Review found in the Unit 10 folder, p. 111, provides a structure for reading and mastering the key concepts and reviewing the key terms for Section 1. (Guided Practice)

On the Republican side, President George Bush was seeking a second term. Bush survived a challenge for the Republican nomination from right-wing journalist Patrick Buchanan. The confrontation, which showed once again that conservative Republicans did not fully accept Bush, persuaded Bush to take a more conservative stance.

On the Democratic side, Clinton was the surprise nominee. During the campaign, Clinton's critics charged that he would say whatever he needed to say—regardless of the complete truth—to get what he wanted. Clinton's statements about how and why he had avoided the draft during the Vietnam War, for example, seemed evasive. In reply, Clinton's supporters pointed to his refusal to quit in the face of criticism and called him the "comeback kid." That nickname also reminded voters that Clinton, at 46, was a full generation younger than the 68-year-old Bush. Clinton's running mate, former senator **Al Gore** of Tennessee, was likewise in his forties. Both Clinton and Gore hoped to reach out to their peers—the large population of voters who had been born during the post-World War II baby boom.

The third candidate was **H. Ross Perot,** a billionaire businessman from Texas who had made a fortune in computer data processing. Perot entered the race out of frustration at the federal government's policies on the budget and the economy. With no party base, he organized a large network of volunteers who collected the necessary signatures to get his name on the ballot in all 50 states.

Economic Issues

Economic issues dominated the campaign. The recession of the early 1990s continued, and the government seemed unable to control the budget deficit. Something needed to be done to get the country out of this mess. Though Bush had won wide praise for his role in ending the cold war and winning the Gulf War, voters in the fall of 1992 were more concerned with conditions at home. A sign taped to the wall of Clinton's campaign headquarters best captured the public's mood: "It's the economy, stupid!"

Even before he ran for president of the United States, Bill Clinton had a reputation as a brilliant campaigner. Here he greets a crowd of supporters during his successful 1992 presidential campaign. **Using Historical Evidence** *How does this photo illustrate some of the challenges of campaigning for President?*

Bush claimed that Republican policies of the preceding 12 years had turned the nation around. The economy had begun to revive, he argued, and would continue to improve with reliance on individual initiative. Further cutbacks in the federal bureaucracy were necessary, Bush claimed, for "government is too big and spends too much."

Clinton, in contrast, promised to use government to end the recession, reduce the deficit, and help improve the nation's ailing health-care system. Like his hero, John F. Kennedy, he believed that government was necessary "to make America work again." At the same time, however, Clinton called himself a "New Democrat"—someone who would make government more efficient and responsive. This message appealed to voters increasingly frustrated at "gridlock" in Congress and eager for change.

Like the other candidates, Perot focused on the economy. As a successful businessman, he argued, he had the necessary skills to cut costs, balance the budget, and restore prosperity. As a non-politician, Perot continued, he had no ties to special interest groups and thus would consider the needs of the country as a whole.

Television played a crucial role in the campaign. In addition to formal debates, all three

Hillary Rodham Clinton's strong and visible role in the Clinton administration helped to make her a controversial figure. Ask students what they, and what the American public in general, expect of a First Lady. How willing are people to accept changes or a new style in that role?

Activity

Run a Presidential Campaign
To better understand the issues that decided the 1992 and 1996 presidential campaigns, have students act as spokespersons for the candidates in each of the campaigns. They should create a short "capsule campaign" for each candidate: devise a campaign slogan, list five to eight "planks" in a platform, and write a press release detailing the candidate's position. Each "campaign manager" should present the campaign in class.

Answer to ...

MAKING CONNECTIONS

Answers will vary, but may include mention of Kennedy as a strong role model for Clinton.

---

candidates made informal appearances on talk shows and interview programs in an effort to shape public opinion. Perot was a frequent guest on "Larry King Live," while Clinton played his saxophone on the "Arsenio Hall Show" and appeared on MTV.

Clinton Elected President

On election day, Clinton received only 43 percent of the popular vote, but Perot's strong showing (19 percent) meant that 43 percent was enough to win the presidency. Bush gained 38 percent of the vote. In the electoral college, Clinton won 357 votes versus 160 for Bush and none for Perot. Clinton entered the White House with Democratic majorities in both houses of Congress as well.

MAKING CONNECTIONS

As a young man, Bill Clinton met President Kennedy. How do you think that meeting affected Clinton's rise to the presidency?

Clinton's First Year in Office

In 1993, Clinton tried to follow a middle course. He wanted to end the lingering reces-sion by raising spending or cutting taxes. At the same time, he knew he needed to reduce the budget deficit, which meant cutting spending or raising taxes. Trying to stimulate the economy and reduce the deficit involved contradictory initiatives—like a driver putting one foot on the gas pedal and the other on the brake, some said.

Over and over, Clinton spoke of the need to "grow the economy." He wanted new spending to provide the economic boost. Even with Democratic majorities in Congress, however, he lacked the necessary support. Legislators recognized the conservative mood in the country and refused to pass Clinton's spending package. The middle way was going to be more difficult than Clinton had thought.

Congress did approve Clinton's first budget, but just barely. In the House of Representatives, the budget passed by a 218-216 margin. In the Senate, Vice President Gore had to break a 50–50 tie to pass the measure. To reduce the deficit, the budget included both spending cuts and tax increases. Neither was popular with the public. The gas tax that was finally approved— 4.3 cents per gallon—caused complaints. Higher income taxes and taxes on Social Security benefits were equally unpopular. The tax increases fell most heavily on the wealthiest Americans but still irritated people in other income brackets.

First Lady Hillary Clinton led the Clinton administration's task force on health care. In this speech, she addressed the issue of the thousands of people who lost health care under the system that was in place in the early 1990s.

▶ **RESOURCE DIRECTORY**

Teaching Resources

Primary Source Activity Defining Economic Goals, found in the Unit 10 folder, pp. 123–124, presents a speech by Bill Clinton to an economic conference shortly after his election outlining national economic goals.

Critical Thinking Activity Drawing Conclusions: Comparing Budget Categories, found in the Unit 10 folder, p. 122, helps students apply this skill by analyzing brief descriptions of parts of the 1995–1996 budget submitted to Congress by President Clinton.

American Profiles Activity Ron Brown, found in the Unit 10 folder, p. 117, profiles President Clinton's first Secretary of Commerce, who died in a plane crash in 1996 while on an official tour of Bosnia.

Clinton succeeded with another economic initiative, though this too was controversial. In September 1993, after a bitter battle, he won Senate ratification of the North American Free Trade Agreement (NAFTA), which aimed at promoting free trade among Canada, Mexico, and the United States. (You will read more about NAFTA in the next section.) ⭐

The Battle over Health Care

Also in September 1993, Clinton appeared on national television and declared to Congress and the country:

> *T his health-care system of ours is badly broken, and it is time to fix it. Despite the dedication of literally millions of talented health-care professionals, our health care is too uncertain and too expensive, too bureaucratic and too wasteful. It has too much fraud and too much greed. At long last, after decades of false starts, we must make this our most urgent priority.*

An estimated 37 million Americans lacked health insurance, and the number was rising. Early in 1993 Clinton had appointed his wife Hillary to direct the task force that would analyze the problem and propose a solution. In November 1993 the President presented the new plan to Congress. Under Clinton's plan, each state would create health alliances to pay health care claims. Networks of doctors, hospitals, and insurers would work with the alliances to provide health care. The plan, in the President's words, "guarantees every single American a comprehensive package of health benefits . . . that can never be taken away." The health-care bill met with strong opposition in Congress, and was eventually rejected. Clinton was unable to make his plan a reality.

The 1994 Republican Sweep

The defeat of his health-care plan was a sign of coming political trouble for Clinton. In the 1994 mid-term elections, Republicans scored a historic victory. During the campaign **Newt Gingrich,** a representative from Georgia, called on Republican candidates to endorse a

"Contract with America" to scale back the role of the federal government, eliminate bothersome regulations, reduce taxes, and balance the budget. Many voters, feeling that the Democratic-controlled Congress had lost touch with their concerns, responded enthusiastically.

Republicans took control of both the House of Representatives and the Senate for the first time in four decades. In the House, they scored their largest gains since 1946. They defeated some of the strongest and most senior Democrats, including House Speaker Thomas Foley.

First-term Republicans were now a potent force in the House, and for leadership they looked to Gingrich, who was elected Speaker of the House. Gingrich pushed through changes in the House rules that gave him far greater power than his predecessor. Conservatives now had the tools to fulfill what they considered their mandate to cut government. There was talk of a new era in American politics in which Congress, not the President, set the nation's course.

Congress Versus the President

Republicans in the new 104th Congress moved quickly to keep the promises they had made during the campaign. Under Gingrich's

Newt Gingrich led a group of enthusiastic Republican representatives who worked to fulfill the promises they made in the "Contract with America." In an outdoor press conference, Gingrich described how he and his fellow Republicans had accomplished many of the goals set forth in the Contract.

In Depth

Then and Now

President Clinton's first chance to appoint a Supreme Court Justice came late in 1993 with the retirement of Byron White. Clinton's choice was Ruth Bader Ginsburg (b. 1933), a Brooklyn-born law professor and expert on constitutional law, who had been a judge on the U.S. Court of Appeals. Judge Ginsburg became the second woman to serve on the Court, joining Sandra Day O'Connor. At her confirmation hearings, Ginsburg pointed out: "What a distance we have traveled from the day President Thomas Jefferson told his Secretary of State the appointment of women to public office is an innovation for which the public is not prepared. 'Nor,' Jefferson added, 'am I.'"

Section 1 Review Answers

1. (a) Bill Clinton, see p. 960, (b) Al Gore, see p. 961, (c) H. Ross Perot, see p. 961, (d) Newt Gingrich, see p. 963, (e) Bob Dole, see p. 964.

2. Clinton promised to use government to end the recession, reduce the deficit, and improve the health-care system, while at the same time making government more efficient and responsive.

3. The plan died in Congress because of strong opposition.

4. The Republican "Contract with America" promised to reduce the role of the federal government, eliminate many federal regulations, reduce taxes, and balance the budget. In Congress, they demanded that the budget be balanced in seven years and proposed cuts in most social services and the elimination of three Cabinet departments.

5. Clinton maneuvered several popular bills through Congress; he appealed to conservative voters by supporting welfare reform and a balanced budget; he benefited from a strong economy and from a Dole campaign that failed to impress most voters.

6. Answers will vary. Students should recognize that the long fight over the budget ended with an agreement between Congress and the President that was worked out through compromise; such agreements are rarely clear victories for either side. Also, the budget fight apparently raised Clinton's standing in the polls and hurt Republicans.

leadership, they demanded that the budget be balanced within seven years. They proposed cuts in virtually all social services and the elimination of three Cabinet departments. Referring back to FDR's remarkable achievements in the first hundred days of the New Deal in 1933, Gingrich demanded action on all these items within the first hundred days of the session, and in most cases he succeeded.

Yet many of the bills passed by the House never became law. Some were rejected by the Senate, while others passed the Senate but were vetoed by Clinton. Even so, Gingrich could say with some satisfaction that he had "changed the whole debate in American politics." That is, Americans were no longer debating whether to cut government and balance the budget, but rather *how* to do so.

The budget remained a point of contention. At the end of 1995, Clinton and Gingrich clashed over the size of budget cuts and the timetable for balancing the budget. When they proved unable to compromise, the government shut down and 800,000 federal employees found themselves temporarily out of work. Not until the spring of 1996 did Congress and the President come to a permanent agreement.

The fight over the budget signaled the start of a Clinton comeback. Voters increasingly regarded congressional Republicans as too extreme, while Clinton scored points for standing up for groups dependent upon government help. Presenting himself as someone who would make needed reforms but not mean-spirited cuts, Clinton rose in the polls.

Bill Clinton (left) and Bob Dole (right) had a solid working relationship when Dole was Senate Majority Leader. In his book *The Choice*, reporter Bob Woodward takes a behind-the-scenes look at each candidate's campaign.

The Election of 1996

After the Republicans took control of Congress in 1994, Clinton's chances for a second term seemed slim. His opponents' message had great appeal to voters. To win, Clinton would have to counter that message while showing that he was not a "tax-and-spend liberal." He would also have to turn back a vigorous challenge from the Republicans and from a new third party.

The Challengers Several Republicans sought their party's nomination for President. The eventual winner was Bob Dole, a respected member of Congress for 35 years who rose to the position of Senate Majority Leader.

Other Republican contenders included Lamar Alexander, a former governor of Tennessee, and Steve Forbes, a wealthy magazine publisher. The main test for Dole, however, came from Patrick Buchanan, a journalist and former speechwriter for Richard Nixon. Buchanan's calls to put "America first" struck a chord with many Americans, but his provocative statements did not please mainstream Republicans.

As he had in 1992, billionaire H. Ross Perot entered the presidential race, this time as the nominee of the newly created Reform Party. He once again demanded a balanced budget, an end to NAFTA, and campaign reforms.

⬤ With the election approaching, Clinton successfully maneuvered several popular bills through Congress, including a higher minimum wage. He also appealed to conservative voters by supporting welfare reform and a balanced budget. Clinton began asking the question that had worked so well for Ronald Reagan in 1980: "Are you better off now than you were four years ago?" Back then, the answer was "No." In 1996, thanks to a strong economy, most Americans answered "Yes."

The Choice

By the summer of 1996, polls showed Clinton far ahead of Dole. Dole hoped to cut into that lead by introducing the centerpiece of his campaign—a 15 percent tax cut. He backed up

▶ RESOURCE DIRECTORY

Teaching Resources

✪ 📄 **Visual Learning Activity** "Campaign Strategies '96", found in the Unit 10 folder, p. 130, uses a cartoon to illustrate Clinton as quick to change his mind on campaign issues and to illustrate Dole as having a slim chance for victory in the race for the presidency.

that proposal by choosing a champion of tax reduction, former congressman and Cabinet officer Jack Kemp, as his running mate. Clinton criticized Dole's plan as a return to supply-side economics. "I am unalterably opposed to going back to the mistake we made before and having big tax cuts that are not paid for," he said.

Dole's tax plan did not impress the voters, either. With the election just three weeks away, he was forced to try a new, more aggressive strategy. Despite Americans' distaste for negative campaigning, he began attacking Clinton on "the character issue." Dole accused Clinton of "ethical failure" and "endless violations of the public trust." He was referring to the several potential scandals that beset the Clinton administration. One incident, called "Filegate," involved a White House staffer's gathering of confidential FBI background files, many on former Republican officials.

Clinton countered Dole's accusations with a plea to address the issues. "No attack ever created a job or educated a child or helped a family make ends meet," he said. "No insult ever cleaned up a toxic waste dump or helped an elderly person."

In the end, voters ignored the character issue. Clinton won the election with 49 percent of the popular vote, compared with 41 percent for Dole and 8 percent for Perot. In the Electoral College, Clinton gained 379 votes, versus 159 for Dole. Republicans retained control of both houses of Congress.

First Lady Hillary Clinton (left), daughter Chelsea (center), and President Bill Clinton (right) at the closing ceremonies of the 1996 Democratic National Convention in Chicago.

Clinton's Second Term

Bill Clinton became the first Democratic President to win a second term since FDR. His momentous victory allowed him to pursue his agenda for the next four years. That agenda included balancing the budget, helping workers cope with the shift to a global economy, expanding free trade, and pushing for reforms in education, taxation, and health care. These and other issues, at home and abroad, would not be resolved easily. But the American people, working together on the solutions, could look forward to a new century with hope.

Reteach

Have students write two headings: "Clinton" and "Congress." Under each heading, students should list the major goals and issues that concerned each side during Clinton's first term. They should then write an outcome for each issue, noting whether a compromise was reached or one side "won."

4. CLOSE

Reinforcing the Big Idea

The 1994 mid-term elections seemed to spell disaster for the Clinton administration, but the sweeping plans of House Republicans were slowed by a more moderate Senate and several presidential vetoes. Many of the strongest Republican demands, in fact, helped Clinton's popularity.

SECTION 1 REVIEW

Key Terms, People, and Places

1. Identify (a) Bill Clinton, (b) Al Gore, (c) H. Ross Perot, (d) Newt Gingrich, (e) Bob Dole.

Key Concepts

2. Describe Clinton's message to voters in the 1992 presidential election.
3. Why did the Clinton health-care plan fail?
4. What goals did Republicans in the 104th Congress set for themselves?

5. How did Clinton win a second term as President in 1996?

Critical Thinking

6. **Distinguishing Fact from Opinion** After much wrangling, Congress finally approved the annual budget in the spring of 1996. Republican John Kasich called the vote to approve the budget "a clear victory for Republicans." Do you agree with his evaluation? Explain your answer.

Quiz found in the Unit 10 folder, p. 112, covers the main ideas in this section as well as the key terms.

The United States in a New World

Connecting to the Big Idea

See page 958B. Explain to students that for fifty years American foreign policy had been based on the attitudes and needs of the cold war. Now, the administration not only had to find new ways of dealing with a former enemy superpower, it also faced challenges in other trouble spots around the world. Ask students to suggest how this "new world" offered both hopes and challenges.

Objectives

- Understand the relationship between the United States and the new government in Russia.
- Describe the United States policies aimed at keeping peace in world trouble spots.
- Identify the American policies that helped expand the global economy.

Bellringer

Ask students what countries they have heard about on radio or TV news in the last few weeks. What kinds of problems are going on there? Do they involve the United States or not? What is the United States' responsibility to those countries?

Reading Strategy

Reading for Evidence Ask students, as they read, to find evidence for the statement in the Section Preview, "The collapse of communism and the increase in ethnic tensions in various parts of the world created new problems for the nation."

The United States in a New World

SECTION PREVIEW

The end of the cold war in the 1990s left the Clinton administration struggling to find its way through uncharted waters in international relations. The collapse of communism and the increase in ethnic tensions in various parts of the world created new problems for the nation.

Key Concepts

- The Clinton administration backed Boris Yeltsin in his efforts to promote democratic and economic reforms in Russia.
- The United States supported attempts in South Africa, the Middle East, and Bosnia to bring a peaceful end to long-standing conflicts.

F.W. de Klerk and Nelson Mandela shared the 1993 Nobel Peace Prize for their work in ending apartheid.

- The European Union and the North American Free Trade Agreement marked the expansion of the global economy in the 1990s.

Key Terms, People, and Places

apartheid, economic sanction, North American Free Trade Agreement (NAFTA); Boris Yeltsin; Bosnia

W itnessing the collapse of communism in the Soviet Union and Eastern Europe, President Bush had spoken hopefully of the dawn of a "New World Order." By this, he meant a more stable and peaceful world, in which "the strong respect the rights of the weak." But President Clinton found that the world was in some ways becoming less stable. While some nations had thrown off repres-

sive governments and become more free, others were being torn apart by racial, cultural, or religious tensions. A few observers joked grimly of a "New World Disorder." Meanwhile, economic ties between nations continued to grow.

The Search for Peace and Freedom

Communism in the Soviet Union, racial oppression in South Africa, conflict in the Middle East—for decades, American foreign policy had dealt with these seemingly permanent problems. But by the mid-1990s, historic events had radically changed life in these areas.

Russia and Eastern Europe As the old Soviet empire crumbled, the United States tried to promote the move toward Western-style democracy in the former Soviet republics. It applauded the election of **Boris Yeltsin** as president of Russia. The United States, Clinton declared, "supports the historic movement toward democratic political reform in Russia. President Yeltsin is the leader of that process."

To help Russia create a free enterprise economy, the United States offered a $2.5 billion aid package. Yet even that was not enough. Goods remained in short supply, and the economy remained unstable. In the fall of 1993, the Russian parliament resisted reforms that Yeltsin argued were necessary. Yeltsin dissolved the parliament and later ordered troops to storm the parliament building. He also tightened censorship in a bid to silence his political opponents.

Russian reformers, angry at these curbs on freedom, grew angrier in 1994. That year, Yeltsin ordered Russian troops into the Russian republic of Chechnya, which was seeking independence. The war in Chechnya cost thousands of lives and cost Yeltsin much of his public support.

RESOURCE DIRECTORY

Teaching Resources

Reproducible Lesson Plan found in the Unit 10 folder, p. 109, provides a summary of the Section 2 lesson plan content.

Alternate Lesson Plan: Critical Thinking Predicting Consequences, found in the Alternate Lesson Plans folder, p. 178, helps pairs or groups of students analyze a world hot spot of the early 1990s and apply this skill to the resolution of conflicts there.

Guided Reading and Review found in the Unit 10 folder, p. 113, provides a structure for reading and mastering the key concepts and reviewing the key terms for Section 2. (Guided Practice)

As Russian voters lost confidence in Yeltsin, many considered supporting right-wing nationalists or Communists, who spoke of reviving the Soviet Union. In the 1996 presidential election, however, Yeltsin defeated his nearest rival, a Communist, and won another term. American officials pointed to the election as proof that democracy was taking root in Russia.

Communists made a more successful comeback in parts of Eastern Europe. In the early 1990s Poland, led by Solidarity hero Lech Walesa, had undertaken bold economic reforms to create a free market. But these reforms required enormous investment and caused much short-term suffering, such as unemployment and inflation. In 1995, Polish voters showed their discontent by electing a former Communist, Aleksander Kwasniewski, as president.

South Africa The United States and nations around the world hailed South Africa's effort to overturn **apartheid**—the systematic separation of the black and white races. South Africa's white minority, which made up only 15 percent of the population, had long denied equal rights to the black majority. The United States and other nations had used **economic sanctions**—trade restrictions—to encourage reform. Finally, in 1990, Prime Minister F. W. de Klerk released anti-apartheid leader Nelson Mandela

Israel, 1994

Final status of West Bank and Gaza Strip to be negotiated within three years of 1993 agreement

1993 agreement between Israel and the Palestine Liberation Organization calls for Israeli military withdrawal from the Gaza Strip and gradual takeover of administration by Palestinians

1993 agreement between Israel and the Palestine Liberation Organization turns Jericho over to Palestinian administration

0   30   60 Miles
0   30   60 Kilometers

Land occupied by Israel following the 1967 war

Major Israeli settlements in the West Bank

Geography and History: Interpreting Maps
President Clinton presided over the signing of the 1993 peace accord between Israel's Yitzhak Rabin (above left) and the PLO's Yasir Arafat (above right). *How did the accord affect the West Bank and Gaza Strip?*

from jail. Mandela had been held prisoner for 27 years.

Together, former rivals Mandela and de Klerk worked to end apartheid. In 1994 South Africa held its first free elections, in which blacks as well as whites voted. These elections produced a new government, led by the African National Congress (ANC), Mandela's anti-apartheid organization. Mandela himself became South Africa's new president. While South Africa still faced serious troubles, such as economic development and ethnic tension, South Africans were justly proud of their recent accomplishments.

The Middle East In September 1993, in a dramatic ceremony on the White House lawn, Palestine Liberation Organization (PLO) leader Yasir Arafat and Israeli prime minister Yitzhak

Ask students to analyze the problems faced by people in a newly free nation—such as Russia or Haiti—that has little or no tradition of democracy. What steps can its leaders take to build democracy? Is a transition stage necessary? Ask students to think of reasons why people in such a country might be nostalgic for the "bad old days."

 Activity

Deliver a News Report

Ask students to imagine they are foreign correspondents for radio or television news. Divide students into groups and assign (or let students choose) one of the regions mentioned in the section or one of those they surveyed in Chapter 34 (Activity: Cooperative Learning). Each group should research recent newspaper and magazine articles about events in their region, then prepare a report to broadcast back to the United States, explaining the situation there.

Caption Answer to ...

 Interpreting Maps

The map shows that, after the dissolution of a strong central government, many groups formerly within that nation often compete for political power and control over land. The former Yugoslavia is just one example of an Eastern bloc country that experienced such problems at the end of the cold war.

The Former Yugoslavia, 1994

Boundary of the former Yugoslavia

Portion of Bosnia Herzegovina under Muslim control

Portion of Bosnia Herzegovina under Serbian control

Portion of Bosnia Herzegovina under Croatian control

0   50   100 Miles
0   50   100 Kilometers

Geography and History: Interpreting Maps
This map shows the regions of Bosnia-Herzegovina controlled by various groups in 1994. *How does it demonstrate the problems in many former communist nations after their governments collapsed in the late 1980s and early 1990s?*

Rabin shook hands and signed a historic peace agreement. It was a difficult step for both sides, but as Rabin noted, "Peace is not made with friends. Peace is made with enemies." The pact provided for Palestinian self-rule in the Gaza Strip (between Israel and the Sinai Peninsula) and in the town of Jericho, on the West Bank of the Jordan River. Israel had seized these areas in the Six-Day War of 1967. In return, the PLO recognized Israel's right to exist.

The Middle Eastern peace process had other successes. In 1994 Israel and Jordan signed a treaty ending the state of war that had existed between them. Israel and Syria began talks as well. Extremists on both sides tried to destroy prospects for peace through terrorist attacks, most tragically in 1995, when a Jewish extremist assassinated Rabin. In 1996, Benjamin

Netanyahu won a slim majority of the popular vote, defeating Shimon Peres, who had taken over as Prime Minister after Rabin's death. Netanyahu formed a coalition government headed by the Likud party. Though many parts of the peace accords were now in question, the United States continued to press the governments in the region to work toward peace.

Other nations Several other nations likewise took steps toward democracy and stability. In Haiti, military leaders had overthrown the first freely elected president, Jean-Bertrand Aristide, in 1991. Three years later the threat of a United States invasion led the military to give up power. U.S. troops went to Haiti to help restore democracy. In Northern Ireland, the United States encouraged renewed efforts to end the violence between Protestants and Catholics.

Nations Torn by Conflict

For the United States, encouraging peace and the spread of democracy in places like the former Soviet Union was a satisfying foreign policy challenge. Far less satisfying was the task of trying to stop the terrifying violence that erupted within several disintegrating countries. Clinton had to balance Americans' desire to help other nations against Americans' fear of costly commitments, a fear magnified by memories of the Vietnam War.

Bosnia The Balkan region of southern Europe had long been a powder keg. In 1914, a political spark there ignited World War I. In 1918 the nation of Yugoslavia was created in an effort to unite the region's different ethnic and religious groups. Following World War II, Yugoslavia became a communist nation, with a strict dictator—Josip Tito—who maintained order. Yet beneath the surface, ethnic and religious tensions remained.

As the cold war came to an end, the situation in Yugoslavia became more volatile. The different Yugoslav republics had different priorities. Serbia and its leader, Slobodan Milosevic, wanted to preserve a unified Yugoslavia, which Serbia had dominated. When two other republics—Slovenia and

 RESOURCE DIRECTORY

Teaching Resources

Visual Learning Activity Clinton's Foreign Policy, found in the Unit 10 folder, p. 129, uses a cartoon to illustrate the problems that can result from a policy of supporting one candidate exclusively in foreign elections.

Croatia—declared their independence in 1991, many ethnic Serbs living there feared repression by the new governments.

Fighting soon broke out among Serbs, Croats, and Muslims. The powder keg had once again been ignited and the violence quickly spread, this time to the nearby republic of Bosnia-Herzegovina. When the Muslim and Croatian majority in **Bosnia** declared their independence, Bosnian Serbs, backed by Milosevic and Serbia, attacked. They began a siege of the city of Sarajevo and an even more ferocious "ethnic cleansing" campaign to force non-Serbs out of Bosnia. Brutal killing became commonplace, and defenseless civilians suffered most of all.

Other nations searched for ways to end the conflict. The United Nations sent humanitarian aid and peacekeeping troops, but the fighting continued. Various peace plans were discussed and then abandoned. Campaigning for President in 1992, Clinton promised strong action in Bosnia, but once in office he hesitated. Finally, in mid-1995, a NATO bombing campaign forced the Bosnian Serbs into peace talks. Hosted by the United States in Dayton, Ohio, these talks produced a cease-fire and the commitment of foreign peace-keeping troops, including thousands from the United States. Yet despite this success, tensions in the region remained extremely high.

Somalia In the early 1990s the East African nation of Somalia suffered from a devastating famine, made worse by a civil war. In 1992 President Bush sent American troops to assist a United Nations relief effort. The food crisis eased, but Somalia's government remained unable to control the armed groups that ruled the countryside. The fol-

Links Across Time

Sarajevo Then and Now

Before the breakup of Yugoslavia, Sarajevo was a bustling modern city (above). With the outbreak of civil war in 1991, however, Sarajevo found itself under siege by Serbian forces. Much of the city was reduced to rubble, including the Bosnian National Library—where an undaunted Sarajevo Orchestra rehearsed in 1993 (left). *What might such destruction mean for the people of a city?*

MAKING CONNECTIONS

Both conflicts began because of a dispute concerning ethnic Serbs living in Bosnia and other parts of former Yugoslavia. Serb nationalism played a major role in triggering both conflicts.

3. ASSESS

Section 2 Review Answers

1. (a) apartheid, see p. 967, (b) economic sanction, see p. 967, (c) North American Free Trade Agreement (NAFTA), see p. 971.

2. Boris Yeltsin, see p. 966.

3. Bosnia, see p. 969.

4. The United States supported the election and reelection of Boris Yeltsin, who promised reforms; it offered Russia $2.5 billion in aid.

5. In South Africa the white minority had long denied equal rights to the black majority. In Israel the Palestinians sought self-rule in territories seized by the Israelis in the Six-Day War in 1967. In Bosnia, Muslims and Croats wanted

Caption Answer to . . .

Using Historical Evidence

The workers' signs indicate that some of them do not believe that NAFTA "puts people first," or "respects workers' rights." Their signs also indicate that they believe NAFTA would take good jobs out of the United States.

In Depth

Global Connections

NAFTA is not the only trade bloc in the Western Hemisphere. The Caribbean region has the Association of Caribbean States (ACS), while Argentina's Carlos Menem has worked to create Mercosur, the Southern Common Market, with Argentina's neighbors Brazil, Paraguay, and Uruguay. In the Pacific, ASEAN (Association of Southeast Asian Nations) is emerging as an economic bloc.

lowing year, when several U.S. soldiers were killed in a battle with Somali rebels, some Americans demanded immediate withdrawal. Clinton recalled the troops later in 1993 without having restored order.

Rwanda The United States was equally baffled by a crisis in Rwanda, in Central Africa. In 1994, the death of Rwanda's president in a suspicious plane crash wrecked an uneasy peace that had existed between the nation's two main ethnic groups, the Tutsis and the Hutus. Hutus blamed Tutsis for the crash and embarked on a massive genocidal campaign, slaughtering hundreds of thousands of Tutsis and moderate Hutus. Later in 1994, Tutsi rebels overthrew the Hutu government. An estimated one million Hutus then fled the country out of fear that they would be killed in revenge. Other nations looked on, horrified by the senseless violence yet unwilling to risk the lives of their soldiers to try to stop it.

MAKING CONNECTIONS

How was the dispute that led to conflict in Bosnia similar to the dispute that started World War I?

Members of many workers' unions protested the ratification of NAFTA.
Using Historical Evidence *What does this photo tell you about workers' concerns regarding NAFTA?*

The Expanding Global Economy

Despite these dramatic events within countries, the most important world development of the mid-1990s may have been one that took place between countries: the continuing growth of global trade. The United States was active in promoting closer economic ties with other countries. As European nations joined together in the European Union, American policymakers sought to define a new relationship with this huge trading bloc. Meanwhile, they worked to create their own regional economic community through the North American Free Trade Agreement.

The European Union Beginning with the formation of the European Coal and Steel Community in 1951, Western European nations made several agreements to increase economic cooperation. In 1957 six European nations set up the European Economic Community (also called the Common Market), which sought to coordinate economic and trade policies. Over time new

 RESOURCE DIRECTORY

Teaching Resources

nations joined the Common Market, and in 1986, member nations agreed to dismantle all tariffs on each other's exports, thereby creating a single market. In 1993 they formed the European Union (EU) to provide political and monetary coordination as well. The EU, now with more than a dozen members, has a parliament and a council representing member governments and is moving toward establishment of a common currency.

The United States has supported the progress toward European economic cooperation. As a Clinton administration official stated, "Close partnership between the United States and the European Union is essential to our common agenda of democratic renewal." This partnership has real benefits for Americans, for the European Union is the largest trading partner of the United States today, accounting for more than $200 billion each year. Close to 20 percent of all American trade is with the European Union.

NAFTA Meanwhile, the United States also sought to encourage greater economic cooperation in its own back yard. The **North American Free Trade Agreement (NAFTA)**, a landmark agreement that took effect in 1994, called for the removal of trade restrictions among the United States, Mexico, and Canada. The resulting free trade zone would create a single market, similar to—but much larger than—the market of the European

Union. NAFTA was the first free trade agreement between a developing country and a developed country.

NAFTA aroused tremendous controversy in the United States. Ross Perot made opposition to NAFTA a large part of his 1992 presidential campaign, while Bush and Clinton supported the agreement. Perot and other NAFTA opponents worried that manufacturers would move factories—and jobs—from the United States to Mexico, where wages were lower and government regulations (like environmental controls) were less stringent. Supporters of NAFTA claimed that it would create new American jobs by raising exports to Canada and Mexico. In the end, the United States Senate ratified the treaty, but only after a bruising battle. Free trade in the Western Hemisphere moved forward another step.

The North American Free Trade Agreement (NAFTA), 1994		
The Agreement	**The Result**	**The Controversies**
The United States, Canada, and Mexico will remove tariffs and most other mutual trade restrictions over the next 15 years.	The resulting free-trade zone will form a single market similar to, but much larger than, the European Community.	Despite NAFTA's "side agreements" and other provisions, concern remains over its potential effects on the environment and on the United States job market.

 Interpreting Tables
President Clinton called NAFTA "more than a trading bloc—it's a building block in our efforts to assert America's global leadership on behalf of American jobs and opportunity." *According to the table, what new trading opportunities does NAFTA provide?*

SECTION 2 REVIEW

Key Terms, People, and Places
1. Define (a) apartheid, (b) economic sanction, (c) North American Free Trade Agreement (NAFTA).
2. Identify Boris Yeltsin.
3. Identify Bosnia.

Key Concepts
4. How did the United States support Russian efforts to reform its political system and its economy?

5. Identify the opposing groups and describe the conflicts in South Africa, in Israel, and in Bosnia.
6. How did NAFTA give the United States, Canada, and Mexico greater influence in the global economy?

Critical Thinking
7. **Drawing Conclusions** Why do you think President Clinton hesitated to take strong action to end the fighting in Bosnia?

Quiz found in the Unit 10 folder, p. 114, covers the main ideas in this section as well as the key terms.

---

to be independent of Serbia (former Yugoslavia) but were attacked by Bosnian Serbs.

6. By joining in NAFTA, the three nations made trading easier among themselves and created a much larger, unified North American market that would increase their influence in the world economy.

7. Answers will vary, but students should recognize the American reluctance to send troops overseas unless a situation threatens the United States, as well as the volatile history of the Balkans and the brutality of the fighting.

Caption Answer to ...

 Interpreting Tables

NAFTA would remove trade barriers between the United States, Canada, and Mexico, allowing each country's products to compete unimpeded in neighboring markets.

Reteach

Ask students to write the names of the following countries: Canada, Mexico, Russia, Bosnia, Haiti, Israel, South Africa. After each one, they should write one sentence describing how that country related to American foreign policy in the mid-1990s.

Alternative Assessment

Mid-Point Monitoring
Ask students if they have:
● Chosen a topic to research.
● Begun their research.
● Chosen a format to present their findings.

 4. CLOSE

Reinforcing the Big Idea

Changes around the world in the 1990s challenged American foreign policymakers to find new directions and new approaches. At the same time, as the next section discusses, the United States was facing major changes in its own society.

Twenty-First Century Americans

Connecting to the Big Idea

See page 958B. The face of America was changing in the late 1990s. More Americans immigrated from places outside Europe, especially from Asia and Latin America. Americans, as a group, were also growing older. Ask what challenges these changes posed for the United States in the early years of the 21st century.

Objectives

- Understand how patterns of immigration shifted to bring more new Americans from Asia and Latin America.
- Describe the divided attitudes of Americans toward diversity.
- Explain why Americans as a population are growing older and what effects this trend is likely to have.

Bellringer

Ask students to take a multicultural poll of their classroom or their neighborhood. What ethnic and national groups are represented? Do they belong to the "old" immigrants, who came in the 1800s and early 1900s (or earlier)? Or are they part of the newer immigration? How do the results of the student poll compare with the pie chart on page 973?

Reading Strategy

Predicting Content Ask students to skim the section, list the main headings and subheadings, and write a sentence predicting the content under each one. When they have read the section, ask them to test the accuracy of their predictions.

SECTION PREVIEW

By the 1990s, immigration and an aging population had changed the makeup of the United States. Minority groups comprised a much larger percentage of the population than ever before, and older Americans made up the fastest growing age group in the country. The United States sought to find new ways to create unity out of its ethnic and cultural diversity and deal with the consequences of an "aging revolution."

Key Concepts
- Near the end of the twentieth century, most immigrants came to the United States from Asia and Latin America.
- Many Americans supported attempts to make diversity work, but others worried that this effort could damage the unity of American society.
- The aging of America's population had important political and economic effects.

Key Terms, People, and Places
multiculturalism, Internet

Hundreds of thousands of legal immigrants arrive in the United States each year. Scores of others seek to enter the country illegally. This California road sign warns drivers to be on the lookout for undocumented aliens who might have crossed the border from Mexico.

T he motto of the United States, found on American coins, is "E pluribus unum"—a Latin phrase that means "From many, one." This brief phrase reflects the patterns of this nation's past and the possibilities for its future. The United States was created when 13 separate colonies agreed to join in a single union. Since then, immigrants from an astonishing variety of lands have come to the United States, contributing their cultural heritage and their individual effort to enrich the culture of their adopted nation. The process continued in the 1990s. New immigrants con-

tinued to come to American shores, and new priorities emerged as the nation matured. But creating unity in the midst of diversity remained the United States' biggest challenge—and its greatest asset.

A Nation of Immigrants

In the 1990s, as a result of the latest in a series of waves of immigration, the United States was more diverse than ever before. Throughout history, each wave of immigrants has been dominated by settlers from a different part of the world: England in the 1600s, Germany and Ireland in the mid-1800s, and southern and eastern Europe in the late 1800s and early 1900s. Near the end of the 1900s, close to 90 percent of all legal immigrants came from Asia and Latin America. As the point of origin shifted away from Europe, Los Angeles became the major port of entry, just as the New York City had been a century before.

These new immigrants changed the face of America. According to the 1990 census, an all-time high of 23 percent of the population were African American, Latino, Asian American, or Native American. While the total percentage of minority groups had reached an all-time high, the percentage of African Americans was not as great as it had been in the nation's early history, when the slave trade was at its peak. Nor was the percentage of foreign born as great as it had been in the heyday of American immigration—the early 1900s. Still, the expanding diversity of the American people meant that the United States was becoming, in the words of writer Ben J. Wattenberg, "the first universal nation."

American immigration policy contributed to the nation's growing diversity. Laws passed in the 1920s had strictly limited immigration and had given preference to immigrants from northern and western Europe. Beginning in 1965, new laws made immigration easier and

---

RESOURCE DIRECTORY

Teaching Resources

Reproducible Lesson Plan found in the Unit 10 folder, p. 110, provides a summary of the Section 3 lesson plan content.

Alternate Lesson Plan: Learning Styles found in the Alternate Lesson Plans folder, p. 179, guides class debate on differing viewpoints of multiculturalism in education, and is especially effective for auditory learners.

Guided Reading and Review found in the Unit 10 folder, p. 115, provides a structure for reading and mastering the key concepts and reviewing the key terms for Section 3. (Guided Practice)

American Profiles Activity found in the Unit 10 folder, p. 118, profiles Amy Tan, author of the best-selling novel *The Joy Luck Club*, which depicts life in America from the perspective of Chinese American women.

fairer. The Immigration Act of 1965 eliminated the bias in favor of European immigration. The Immigration Reform and Control Act of 1986 sought to curb illegal immigration while permitting aliens who had lived in the United States since 1982 to register to become citizens. The Immigration Act of 1990 increased immigration quotas by 40 percent and eased restrictions that had denied entrance to many people in the past.

⭐ Changes in immigration caused changes in demographics. While earlier immigrants had settled mostly on the east coast, many of the new arrivals chose the so-called Sunbelt, which stretched from Florida to California. The new arrivals congregated in urban areas. In 15 of the nation's 28 largest cities in 1990, "minorities" made up at least half of the population. African Americans predominated in Detroit, Washington, D.C., New Orleans, and Chicago. Latinos were more heavily concentrated in Phoenix, El Paso, and San Antonio. Asian Americans settled heavily in San Francisco. Los Angeles contained the most dramatic variety of all—newcomers like Koreans, Vietnamese, Cambodians, Samoans, and Taiwanese, as well as more established groups, such as Mexican Americans, African Americans, and European Americans. Like the many nationalities that had crowded into New York City a century earlier, these groups competed with one another for jobs and housing.

As minority groups grew in size, they became more politically active. In 1992 Carol Moseley Braun, a Democrat, became the first African American woman to serve in the United States Senate. After the 1994 election, 38 African American representatives, including Republican J.C. Watts, the first African American representative elected from Oklahoma, were serving in the House. Eighteen Latino representatives, including Democrat Nydia M. Velázquez from New York, were also serving in the House after 1994. These representatives were committed to bringing fresh ideas to

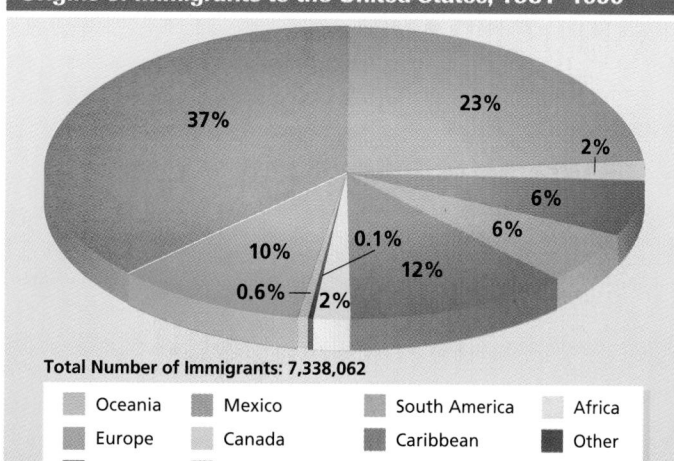

Origins of Immigrants to the United States, 1981–1990

37%
23%
2%
6%
6%
0.1%
12%
10%
0.6%
2%

Total Number of Immigrants: 7,338,062

Oceania | Mexico | South America | Africa
Europe | Canada | Caribbean | Other
Asia | Central America

Source: *New York Times*, May 31, 1992

 Interpreting Charts
Which group comprised the largest percentage of immigrants to the United States in the 1980s? What was the second largest group? How would you expect these statistics to affect the overall ethnic composition of the United States over several decades?

Congress. As Congresswoman Velázquez said, "Many of the new members were elected on [the promise of] changing business as usual."

Making Diversity Work

In the United States, governments at all levels—as well as private organizations and individual citizens—undertook efforts to make diversity work. Some of these efforts, however, created bitter controversy.

Affirmative Action One of the most heated debates concerned affirmative action. Supporters of affirmative action argued that it had given educational and professional opportunities to tens of thousands of women and minorities. Opponents argued that giving preferential treatment to some groups was unfair to everyone else. As California Governor Pete Wilson argued, Americans should not "trample individual rights" in this way. Among the increasingly vocal critics of affirmative action were some well-known African Americans, including Supreme Court justice Clarence Thomas.

Media and Technology

Transparencies
Historical Maps, L-5; Our Multicultural Heritage, C-14

2. INSTRUCT

Explain/Discuss

Explain that, while nearly all Americans (excepting only Native Americans) are immigrants or the descendants of immigrants, it has often been difficult for the newest group of newcomers to be accepted. Ask students to discuss the kinds of problems and prejudice that newer immigrants face. What kinds of factors or events contribute to increased prejudice?

Discuss the various ways in which Americans have tried to make diversity work. Which approaches are effective? Which do little good?

Have students discuss their views of the coming decade. For example, how might the "aging of America" affect relationships in their families?

Analyze

Ask students to analyze the statement by Jaime S. Wurzel on page 974 and compare it with Arthur Schlesinger's comment about "ethnic cheerleading." What are the benefits of multiculturalism? Can it be carried too far? Is "ethnic cheerleading" necessarily either good or bad? Ask students to suggest an "ideal" way to teach the history of the United States that would include basic ideas as well as minority contributions.

Caption Answer to ...

Interpreting Charts

Mexicans were the largest group, with Asians in second place. Students may predict an increase in the percentage of Asian Americans and Mexican Americans in the population.

Answer to ...

Viewpoints

Both writers look at immigration as an economic issue, and both agree that immigrants take jobs that might otherwise go to American citizens. Lehigh focuses narrowly on the question of how immigration hurts unskilled American laborers. Legomsky presents a broader view, noting the net effects of job loss and job creation as well as other positive aspects of immigration. For a more thorough examination of the issue of immigration, see the Resource Directory below.

Answer to ...

MAKING CONNECTIONS

Recent legislation, both state and federal, has already targeted immigrants and immigration, citing concerns about jobs and social welfare. Students might suggest that if a significant number of Americans believe that immigrants from Asia or Latin America are a threat to their jobs, some specific kind of exclusion might be enacted again.

Activity

Cooperative Learning
Time: One class period.
Activity: Create a poster for use in American schools and travel offices abroad, illustrating and reflecting the diversity of the United States.
Grouping: Groups of four to six students, who share ideas and cooperate in making the poster, using colored markers, poster paint, or collage materials.
Purpose: To present the United States in a global context as a diverse society.
Outcome: Students will explore their own ideas about diversity as they work to interpret it graphically.

Viewpoints
On Immigration Policy

In the 1990s, the influx of immigrants from less developed nations led to disagreements about U.S. immigration policy. **Compare and contrast the following statements on the issue.**

For Restricting Immigration
"The dynamic is as simple as supply and demand. With America experiencing only moderate economic growth, the nation's immigration policies have contributed to an excess of labor. Loose labor markets, which see workers vying for jobs rather than employers competing for wages, always spells lower relative wages."
  Scot Lehigh, staff writer, in an essay in *The Boston Globe*, June 23, 1996

Against Restricting Immigration
"Yes, immigrants take jobs. But they also create jobs by consuming goods and services, lending their expertise to newly vibrant American export companies, starting businesses, and revitalizing cities. Yes, some immigrants receive welfare. But immigrants also pay taxes—income, sales, property, gasoline, and Social Security. . . . Of course, immigration does far more than this. It reunites husbands with wives and parents with children. It enriches us culturally. It is, ultimately, the quintessential American value."
  Stephen H. Legomsky, law professor, quoted in *The Wall Street Journal*, November 27, 1995

The Supreme Court and other courts considered a variety of affirmative action cases, but the complexity of the issue made it difficult to decide. Can race be the deciding factor in a decision such as hiring, or just one of many factors? Is it proper for an organization to set numerical targets for hiring minorities or women? Should a less-qualified applicant ever be hired or promoted over a more-qualified one? These questions show that while affirmative action's supporters and opponents alike support the idea of fairness, fairness is not always easy to define.

Multiculturalism Another effort to help make diversity work was **multiculturalism**, a movement that called for greater attention to non-European cultures in such areas as education. As professor of education Jaime S. Wurzel writes,

The multicultural person questions the arbitrary nature of his or her own culture and accepts the proposition that others who are culturally different can enrich their experience.

Advocates of multicultural education argued, among other things, that school textbooks should encourage tolerance by celebrating the contributions of people from all groups.

Others disapproved of this approach. Historian Arthur M. Schlesinger, Jr., criticized what he called "ethnic cheerleading"—using history to make people feel good about themselves rather than to discover the truth about the past. Critics worried that extreme versions of multiculturalism could damage the unity of American society by emphasizing the differences between groups rather than the shared values and experiences of all Americans.

The Future of Immigration Not just debates over diversity, but also concerns over the economic effects of increased immigration led in the 1990s to calls for a tougher immigration policy. Proposals included lowering the number of legal immigrants allowed to enter the country each year and limiting the rights of illegal immigrants.

In 1994, for example, California voters approved Proposition 187, which required teachers and clinic doctors to deny assistance to illegal aliens and to report them to the police. Supporters of the measure argued that high-immigration states like California were being unfairly burdened by high social welfare costs. The debate over immigration was but a new wrinkle in the uniquely American effort to create a unified nation from diverse peoples. (See Chapter 36, pp. 984–991.)

MAKING CONNECTIONS

The Chinese Exclusion Act of 1882 prohibited Chinese laborers from entering the United States. Do you think that the same kind of exclusion might someday be applied to all Asians or to Latin Americans? Explain your answer.

RESOURCE DIRECTORY

Teaching Resources

Viewpoints Activity On Immigration Policy, found in the Unit 10 folder, pp. 119–120, presents different opinions on the issue of immigration into the United States.

Primary Source Activity Trying to Break the Cycle of Crime, found in the Unit 10 folder, p. 125, gives the text of a pledge introduced by Jesse L. Jackson to high school students in the Washington, D.C., area.

Literature Activity Living in a New World, found in the Unit 10 folder, pp. 126–128, describes the life of a new immigrant in New York through an excerpt from *When I Was Puerto Rican*, by Esmeralda Santiago.

America's Aging Population

As the United States approached the turn of the century, its population was older than ever before. Elderly people made up the fastest growing age group in the country. In the years between 1900 and 1980, the number of people over the age of 65 increased eightfold, while the total population of the country only tripled. Advances in medical care increased average life expectancy from 47 to 74 years. During the 1980s alone, the number of people over 75 grew by more than 27 percent. An "aging revolution" was underway.

The "graying of America" had important political and economic effects. Many older Americans, wanting to continue working, pushed successfully for legislation that prohibited forced retirement at a given age. But because many other older Americans were retiring, entitlement payments increased astronomically. The Social Security system, for example, faced serious difficulties because the number of retired citizens receiving benefits was rising faster than the number of working citizens paying taxes. In 1983 the federal government tried to deal with the crisis by raising taxes for those still working and setting a later age for benefits to begin. Experts warned that more radical steps would have to be taken before the baby boom generation began retiring in the next century.

There was similar pressure on the medical care system. Medicare, established during the Great Society of the 1960s, provided substantial support for the medical expenses of the elderly. But as the number of recipients and the cost of health care per recipient rose, Medicare costs exploded—from $7.5 billion in 1970 to $178 billion in 1995. President Clinton and the Republican-controlled Congress agreed that reform was needed but could not agree how to do it.

Rethinking Entitlements

In August 1996, Congress and President Clinton did, however, agree on a historic piece of legislation that affected 12.8 million people receiving Aid to Families with Dependent Children (AFDC), commonly referred to as welfare.

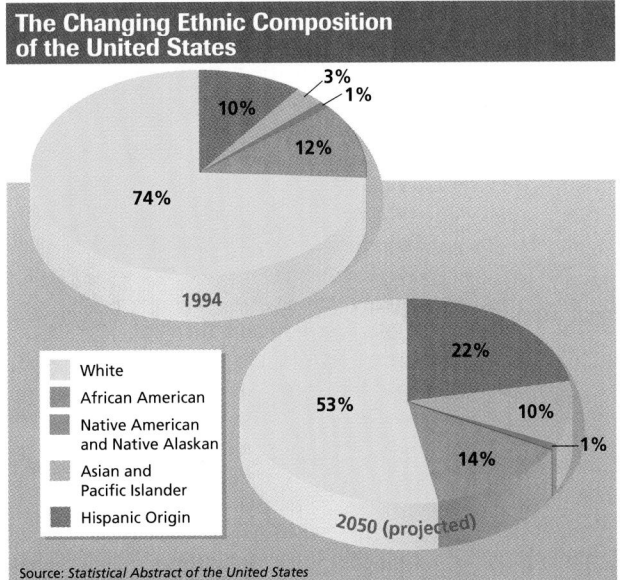

The Changing Ethnic Composition of the United States

1994: White 74%, 10%, 3%, 1%, 12%

Legend:
- White
- African American
- Native American and Native Alaskan
- Asian and Pacific Islander
- Hispanic Origin

2050 (projected): White 53%, 22%, 10%, 1%, 14%

Source: *Statistical Abstract of the United States*

Interpreting Charts

According to the charts, which group in the United States will experience the most dramatic rate of growth between 1994 and 2050? What will happen to the white population as a percent of the total population?

The bill also affected 25.6 million people who receive food stamps. In a bill that was endorsed by President Clinton, the House approved by a vote of 329 to 101 sweeping social welfare reform that reversed six decades of legislation dating back to the New Deal Social Security Act of 1935.

The bill would eliminate the Federal guarantee of cash assistance. It would give states authority to run their own welfare and workfare programs with block grants of Federal money. It would establish a lifetime limit of five years for any family receiving aid. It would also require most adults to work within two years of receiving aid. (See Chapter 39, pp. 1006–1014.)

Education for the Next Century

The pace of change today is increasing, and the computer is perhaps the best symbol of this change. Between 1983 and 1995, the percentage of American households with a computer jumped from 7 percent to 37 percent. Computers navigate spacecraft, route telephone calls,

Section 3 Review Answers

1. (a) multiculturalism, see p. 974, (b) Internet, see p. 976.

2. Asia and Latin America

3. New laws after the 1960s made immigration easier and fairer: the Immigration Act of 1965 eliminated the bias in favor of Europeans; the Immigration Reform and Control Act of 1986 permitted many resident aliens to register to become citizens; the Immigration Act of 1990 increased immigration quotas and eased restrictions.

4. Supporters argued that education should pay attention to non-European cultures; textbooks should celebrate the contributions of people from all groups. Opponents argued that textbooks should use history to discover the truth about the past, not to make people feel good about themselves; some feared that extreme multiculturalism would emphasize differences and damage the unity of American society.

5. The number of people reaching retirement age and collecting Social Security benefits is increasing faster than the number of working people paying into the system.

6. Possible answer: Diversity can be divisive. Students may suggest that opposing groups could develop hostility toward one another, resulting in political battles or other forms of conflict.

Reteach

Ask students to write a paragraph in which they describe four ways in which the United States was changing in the closing years of the 1990s.

4. **CLOSE**

Reinforcing the Big Idea

The United States, part of a changing world, was itself changing as the 21st century approached. Immigration, an aging population, and technological change were some of the future challenges foreseen at the time.

---

and assist in all kinds of scientific research. The **Internet**, the computer network that currently links tens of millions of people around the world, may well revolutionize American education and industry.

How will these changes affect employment? In many cases, computers—like other modern machines—are taking the place of humans, thereby decreasing jobs. On the other hand, the growth of "high-tech" industries has created thousands of new jobs as well. These jobs, however, demand skills, and an important feature of the emerging economy is the lack of stable, well-paying jobs for unskilled workers. Education, therefore, has become more important than ever before. (See Chapter 42, pp. 1034–1045.)

Bill Gates

AMERICAN PROFILES

Bill Gates

In 1975, Bill Gates envisioned the future of computers and set to work turning that vision into reality. That year, Gates remembers, he and his friend Paul Allen first read about a kit computer in *Popular Electronics* magazine: "Paul and I didn't know exactly how it would be used, but we were sure it would change us and the world of computing."

At first, people couldn't make the kit computer do much. Gates and Allen changed that by writing a program, or software, to run on the computer. Programming transformed the simple computer from a machine with limited uses into a general-purpose computer similar to those we use today—though much less powerful. That same year, the two friends decided to start their own company to market their software. Their company, later named Microsoft, grew to become a giant in the computer industry.

Today, Bill Gates believes that the most valuable use for personal computers might be in the classroom. Some people may think his ideas are farfetched, but not Bill Gates. He has learned to trust his vision of the future.

For all Americans, especially the young, the future is of immense importance. In the future lie our hopes and dreams as well as the struggles that bind us together as a nation. The next seven chapters focus on the issues of our common future. By tackling these issues, we will make our own future together.

Near the end of his life, Thomas Jefferson, who envisioned a magnificent future over two hundred years ago, wrote in a letter, "If a nation expects to be ignorant and free, in a state of civilization, it expects what never was and never will be." True as this statement was for America in the age of quill pens and horse-drawn carriages, it is all the more true as we enter a century whose advances we can scarcely imagine.

SECTION 3 REVIEW

Key Terms, People, and Places
1. Define (a) multiculturalism, (b) Internet.

Key Concepts
2. What two parts of the world provided the most immigrants to the United States toward the end of the 1900s?
3. How did federal immigration policy add to the diversity of the United States?

4. Describe the views of supporters and opponents of multicultural education.
5. How has the increase in older Americans caused difficulties for the Social Security system?

Critical Thinking
6. **Predicting Consequences** If Americans fail to make diversity work in the United States, what might happen in the future?

RESOURCE DIRECTORY

Media and Technology

Teaching Resources

Quiz found in the Unit 10 folder, p. 116, covers the main ideas in this section as well as the key terms.

Chapter Test Forms A and B are found in the Unit 10 folder, pp. 131–136.

Answer Keys found in the Unit 10 folder pp. 143–156, provide answers to all student activities.

Transparencies
Our Multicultural Heritage, C-3; Graphic Organizer, G-1

 Guided Reading Audiotapes (English and Spanish)

 Computer Test Bank

Predicting Consequences

Many social scientists, especially those who work for the government, try to look into the future. They study what has happened in the past, and on the basis of that, they try to predict what might happen next.

Every ten years the government takes a census of the national population. Social scientists study the evidence from the census to see what they can predict from it. For example, what has been the rate of population growth over the past decades? What does this suggest about the rate of population growth we might expect in the next few years? Which groups are likely to grow faster and which slower?

The table at right focuses on census information on the changing number of families in three ethnic groups in the United States and family income in those groups over a fifteen-year period. Use the following steps to analyze the information in the table and draw on your understanding of history to predict possible trends into the twenty-first century.

1. Identify the kinds of information in the table. (a) What does this table tell you about the number of families in various ethnic groups in the United States? (b) By what percentage did the number of Latino families increase between 1980 and 1985? (c) The median income for a given group represents the center of the income distribution—in each group, exactly half of the families earn more

and half earn less than the median income. What does it mean if one group has a lower median income than another group?

2. Analyze the rate of change. (a) Which group of families is growing at the fastest rate? (b) Which group's median income has grown at the fastest rate? (c) Which group seems the most economically vulnerable—that is, which has the least stable median income?

3. Use your knowledge of history to predict the consequences that your findings might have in the future. You have read in the chapter that the Immigration Act of

1965 allowed more people from places other than Europe to immigrate to the United States, and that the Immigration Act of 1990 further increased immigration quotas by 40 percent. (a) How might the table illustrate the consequences of the 1965 law? (b) What consequences might the 1990 law have by the year 2005? (c) If an economic recession began in the first years of the twenty-first century, which group's median income would you expect to drop the most? (d) What changes in the trends shown on the table would have to take place in order to alter your predictions?

Change in Number of Families and Median Income,* by Selected Ethnic Groups, 1980–1994

	Year	Number of Families (in thousands)	Percent Change (from preceding figure)	Median Income (dollars)	Percent Change (from preceding figure)
White Families	1980	52,710	—	39,443	—
	1985	54,991	+4.3	40,152	+1.8
	1990	56,803	+3.3	41,858	+4.2
	1994	58,444	+2.9	40,884	−2.3
African American Families	1980	6,317	—	22,822	—
	1985	6,921	+9.6	23,120	+1.3
	1990	7,471	+7.9	24,291	+5.1
	1994	8,093	+8.3	24,698	+1.7
Latino Families	1980	3,235	—	26,500	—
	1985	4,206	+30.0	26,206	−1.1
	1990	4,981	+18.4	26,568	+1.4
	1994	6,202	+24.5	24,318	−8.5

* In 1994 dollars
Source: *Bureau of the Census*

977

Historian's Toolbox Activity Predicting Consequences, found in the Unit 10 folder p. 121, helps students apply the skill by identifying trends and possible consequences of those trends as revealed by an age distribution graph of the United States for the years 1992–2050.

TOOLBOX

Critical Thinking
Predicting Consequences

Focus Students will use the statistics in a table to predict patterns of population growth and median income for three ethnic groups.

Instruct Have students examine the title and headings in the table. Make sure that they understand, in particular, what the numbers in the Percent Change columns mean. If necessary, explain that a "+" means an increase and a "−" means a decrease, and that the percentage in the 1994 row covers the period from 1990 to 1994. Ask them to compare the percentages for the three ethnic groups and to note any outstanding differences among them.

Extend See the Historian's Toolbox Activity in the Resource Directory below.

Answers

1. (a) In the period from 1980 to 1994, the number of white families in the United States greatly outnumbered African American and Latino families. (b) 30 percent (c) More than half of the families in the group with a lower median income earn less than the median income for the other group.

2. (a) Latinos, nearly doubling between 1980 and 1994 (b) African Americans (c) Latinos

3. (a) The rapid increase in the number of Latino families between 1980 and 1994 reflects the continuing rise in the number of immigrants coming from Latin America after 1965. (b) Possible answer: The number of Latino families in the United States will continue to grow at a much faster rate than the number of white or African American families. (c) Possible answer: An economic recession would be more likely to cause a decrease in the median income of Latino families. (d) Predictions might not be so easy if the trend for the number of Latino families dropped to single digits and the Latino median income stabilized.

Chapter Review Answers

Understanding Key Terms, People, and Places

Terms
Students should refer to the definitions of the key terms in the chapter to write sentences that show the relation of each word to the Clinton presidency, to United States foreign policy in the mid-1990s, or to American society in the late 1990s.

Matching
1. North American Free Trade Agreement (NAFTA)
2. apartheid
3. Internet
4. multiculturalism

True or False
1. false, Newt Gingrich
2. true
3. false, Boris Yeltsin
4. false, Bill Clinton

Reviewing Main Ideas

1. Voters wanted the candidates to address the recession, the budget deficit, and other economic problems.

2. The budget included both spending cuts and tax increases such as a gas tax.

3. It faced strong opposition in Congress, especially from Republicans.

4. Republicans won a majority in both houses of Congress in the 1994 mid-term elections for the first time in 40 years; many backed the "Contract for America," a plan for cutting government that was laid out by conservative Newt Gingrich, who was chosen Speaker of the House.

5. Although both sides agreed that the budget should be balanced, they disagreed about the size of budget cuts, the programs to be cut, and the timetable for a balanced budget.

6. Russia's problems included an unstable economy; disagreements among Yeltsin, reformers, and a parliament resisting reform; war in the republic of Chechnya.

7. Besides taking part in the NATO bombing campaign that forced the Bosnian Serbs to seek peace, the United States hosted peace talks in Dayton, Ohio, that produced a cease-fire.

8. Supporters said that NAFTA would create new American jobs by increasing exports to Canada and Mexico. Opponents claimed that manufacturers would move factories and jobs to Mexico, where wages were lower and environmental controls were less strict.

Chapter Review

Understanding Key Terms, People, and Places

Key Terms
1. apartheid
2. economic sanction
3. North American Free Trade Agreement (NAFTA)
4. multiculturalism

People
5. Internet

6. Bill Clinton
7. Al Gore
8. H. Ross Perot
9. Bob Dole

10. Newt Gingrich
11. Boris Yeltsin

Places
12. Bosnia

Terms For each term above, write a sentence that explains its relation to the Clinton presidency, United States foreign policy in the 1990s, or American society in the 1990s.

Matching Review the key terms in the list above. If you are not sure of a term's meaning, review its definition in the chapter. Then choose a term from the list that best matches each description below.
1. the treaty promoting free trade between Canada, Mexico, and the United States
2. a systematic separation of the races
3. the computer network linking people around the world
4. a movement calling for greater respect for non-European cultures

True or False Determine whether each statement is true or false. If it is true, write "true." If it is false, change the underlined name to make the statement true.
1. Georgia's <u>Ross Perot</u> was elected Speaker of the House after the Republicans swept Congress in 1994.
2. <u>Bob Dole</u> challenged Bill Clinton for the presidency of the United States in 1996.
3. In 1996, <u>Newt Gingrich</u> won another term as president of Russia by defeating his Communist rival.
4. In November 1993, <u>Al Gore</u> presented his new health-care plan to Congress.

Reviewing Main Ideas

Section 1 (pp. 960–965)
1. What issues did American voters want the presidential candidates to address in 1992?
2. How did Clinton's first budget aim to reduce the budget deficit?
3. Why did Clinton's health-care plan fail to become law?
4. After 1994, why did conservatives in Congress believe that they had a mandate to reduce the size of the federal government?
5. Explain how Clinton and congressional Republicans differed on the issue of balancing the budget.

Section 2 (pp. 966–971)
6. What problems slowed Russia's pursuit of political and economic freedom?

7. What role did the United States play in producing a cease-fire in Bosnia?
8. Give reasons why some people supported NAFTA and others opposed it.

Section 3 (pp. 972–976)
9. How did the Immigration Act of 1965 contribute to the diversity of the United States?
10. What arguments were made against multiculturalism?
11. What were the political and economic effects of the increase in older Americans?
12. Why will education be so important to workers of the twenty-first century?

---

9. The Immigration Act of 1965 eliminated the bias in favor of European immigration, increasing the number of immigrants from Asia, Africa, and Latin America.

10. Some critics of multicultural education argued that it made people feel good about themselves rather than showing the truth about the past. Others said that extreme multiculturalism could damage American unity by emphasizing differences.

11. Older Americans succeeded in getting legislation passed that prohibited forced retirement at a given age; the number of people entitled to Social Security was increasing faster than payments, threatening a crisis in the system. Medicare costs increased.

12. Education will provide the skills needed for employment in the "high-tech" industries that are expected to dominate in the twenty-first century.

Making Connections

1. The image of a "badly broken" system is easy to understand. The words describing health care as "too uncertain, . . . expensive, too bureaucratic and too wasteful," are simple statements addressing a variety of Americans' concerns. The last sentence offers hope that the problem can be solved.

2. Answers will vary, but may include news conferences and meeting voters face-to-face.

3. Students' scripts should mention Clinton's budget battles, his health-care plan, NAFTA, and events in Russia, South Africa, the Middle East, Bosnia, and Haiti.

4. (a) Peace treaty between the PLO and Israel, quest for racial equality in South Africa, NAFTA (b) Russia, Bosnia, Somalia, Rwanda (c) Students' graphic organizers should contain information about immigration, affirmative action, multiculturalism, and the aging of the population.

Thinking Critically

1. Identifying Alternatives Republicans in the 104th Congress demanded cuts in social services as part of their plan to balance the federal budget. If you wanted to find other ways to balance the budget, how would you begin to research this issue?

2. Demonstrating Reasoned Judgment In the 1990s, the United States intervened in conflicts in Bosnia, Somalia, and Haiti, and it became involved to a lesser degree in crises in Russia, South Africa, and the Middle East. What should be the role of the United States in future conflicts throughout the world?

3. Identifying Assumptions Affirmative action has helped many African Americans by giving them educational and professional opportunities. Why would some African Americans, such as Supreme Court justice Clarence Thomas, oppose affirmative action?

Making Connections

1. Evaluating Primary Sources Review the primary source excerpt on page 963. The complexity of the health-care issue bewildered many Americans. Does Clinton's description clarify the issue? Is it persuasive? Does it offer a solution? Explain your answers.

2. Understanding the Visuals Look at the images in Section 1 of this chapter. How do they illustrate some of the methods that public figures use to get their messages across to the public?

3. Writing About the Chapter Write a television script entitled "Clinton's First Term in Review." First, create a list of what you see as the accomplishments of Clinton's presidency. Then make a list of the problems that still exist and the ways in which they might be solved. Next write a draft of your script in which you present your ideas and note what kind of image—such as television news footage or a photograph—could be used to illustrate each point. Revise your script, making certain that each idea is clearly explained. Proofread your script and draft a final copy.

4. Using the Graphic Organizer This graphic organizer uses a web to organize international events during the early years of the Clinton administration. (a) Which events show a trend toward peace and global unity? (b) Which regions present ongoing challenges? (c) On a separate sheet of paper, create your own web about American society in the 1990s, using this graphic organizer as an example.

United States supports South Africa's quest for racial equality

Slaughter in Rwanda reflects deeply rooted ethnic hatred

NAFTA promotes free trade between Canada, Mexico, and the United States

Disorder continues in Somalia after United States troops are withdrawn

International Events During the Clinton Years

NATO and UN intervention leads to an uneasy cease-fire in Bosnia

Treaty between Israel and the PLO holds out hope for peace

Russia endures unstable economy, resistance to reforms, and curbs on freedoms

Thinking Critically

1. The first step might be to list all the federal government's sources of revenue and expenses; the next steps might be to determine how much must be cut to balance the budget; and then to consider different ways to achieve that goal, either by increasing revenue or reducing expenses other than social services.

2. Students may suggest that the United States, as the world's lone superpower, has an obligation to take on the role of "world police officer." Others might decide that becoming involved in dangerous situations such as Bosnia or Somalia may be too costly in money or lives.

3. Possible answers: Some African Americans might believe that affirmative action is a crutch—that preferential treatment robs people of their dignity or self-worth.

American Album

ARTIFACTS FROM EXHIBITIONS AND COLLECTIONS
AT THE SMITHSONIAN INSTITUTION
NATIONAL MUSEUM OF AMERICAN HISTORY

THE INFORMATION AGE

Ever since people began recording and exchanging information, they've asked four practical questions: What is the best way to store the information? How much information can be put in a space of a certain size? How can later users of the information retrieve it? How can the information be sent to people in other places? You hold one of the best and earliest answers to these questions in your hands—a book. Starting in the last century, people began to develop new forms of communication—the telegraph, the telephone, and the radio. In the last few decades, many more ways to store, retrieve, and transmit information have created an information explosion. *How does each object shown here help send or process information?*

▲ WATERGATE BUGS The burglars who broke into the Democratic National Committee headquarters carried these "bugs." The ability to listen in on private conversations and invade privacy is an unwelcome by-product of the information age.

▼ COMMUNICATIONS SATELLITE Telstar was the world's first communications satellite, relaying signals from one part of earth to another. On the day it was launched, July 10, 1962, it transmitted the first live television pictures from the United States to Europe.

◄ FIBER–OPTIC CABLE Hair-thin glass fibers can carry sound and data long distances using coded light pulses. Cables made of these optical fibers are lighter, cost less to use, and can carry much more information than metal cables.

▲ LASER HEAD Theodore Maiman developed this early laser in 1960. Laser light can carry more information than radio waves. Laser light is used to decode information stored on CD-ROM and compact audio disks.

▶ COMPUTER PIONEER
Grace Murray Hopper stands next to the UNIVAC, one of the earliest computers. Hopper pioneered the compiler—the link between a computer's circuits and the computer program. Her work also served as a foundation for COBOL, the most widely used computer language for business applications.

◀ HAND-HELD COMPUTER
The ability of a single silicon chip to store and process information has shrunk the size of the computer. A person can carry this computer anywhere and operate it at any time with a small stylus.

▶ SILICON CHIP
The miracle of the information age is this chip of impure silicon—a microprocessor. Computers with silicon chips are more complex, faster, and can handle many times more information than the original room-size computers that used vacuum tubes and transistors.

▶ EARLY COMPUTER
The very first computers had no keyboards to enter information, no screens to view what was entered, and no storage devices. The Osborne, shown here, was a personal computer that offered the user all these improvements.

▲ BAR CODES Mad Magazine makes fun of bar codes—lines of varying thickness carrying information that can be read by laser light.

Unit 11 Pathways to the Future

📁 Teaching Resources (See Unit 11 Folder)

	Instruction	Enrichment
Chapter 36 **Immigration and the Golden Door** (pp. 984–991)	Reproducible Lesson Plan, p. 3 Alternate Lesson Plan, p. 181 Guided Reading and Review, p. 4 Chapter Test, Forms A & B, pp. 9–10	Literature Activity, Immigrant Dreams, pp. 7–8 Debating the Future Activity, The Debate on Immigration, pp. 5–6
Chapter 37 **Gun Control and Crime** (pp. 992–998)	Reproducible Lesson Plan, p. 12 Alternate Lesson Plan, p. 182 Guided Reading and Review, p. 13 Chapter Test, Forms A & B, pp. 18–19	Literature Activity, Roots of the Brady Law, pp. 16–17 Debating the Future Activity, The Debate on Gun Control and Violence, pp. 14–15
Chapter 38 **Minimum Wage and the Role of Government** (pp. 999–1005)	Reproducible Lesson Plan, p. 21 Alternate Lesson Plan, p. 183 Guided Reading and Review, p. 22 Chapter Test, Forms A & B, pp. 27–28	Literature Activity, No Work 'Till Spring, pp. 25–26 Debating the Future Activity, The Debate on Minimum Wage, pp. 23–24
Chapter 39 **Entitlements: Rethinking Government Guarantees** (pp. 1006–1014)	Reproducible Lesson Plan, p. 30 Alternate Lesson Plan, p. 184 Guided Reading and Review, p. 31 Chapter Test, Forms A & B, pp. 36–37	Literature Activity, Responsibility, Not Entitlement, pp. 34–35 Debating the Future Activity, The Debate on Entitlements, pp. 32–33
Chapter 40 **The United States in the Western Hemisphere** (pp. 1015–1023)	Reproducible Lesson Plan, p. 39 Alternate Lesson Plan, p. 185 Guided Reading and Review, p. 40 Chapter Test, Forms A & B, pp. 45–46	Literature Activity, The Banana Republics, pp. 43–44 Debating the Future Activity, The Debate over NAFTA, pp. 41–42
Chapter 41 **Foreign Policy After the Cold War** (pp. 1024–1031)	Reproducible Lesson Plan, p. 48 Alternate Lesson Plan, p. 186 Guided Reading and Review, p. 49 Chapter Test, Forms A & B, pp. 54–55	Literature Activity, Toward a New Century, pp. 52–53 Debating the Future Activity, The Debate over Foreign Policy After the Cold War, pp. 50–51
Chapter 42 **Technology and You in the Next Century** (pp. 1032–1043)	Reproducible Lesson Plan, p. 57 Alternate Lesson Plan, p. 187 Guided Reading and Review, p. 58 Chapter Test, Forms A & B, pp. 63–64	Literature Activity, The Information Revolution, pp. 61–62 Debating the Future Activity, Should Funding Technology Be a Priority? pp. 59–60

📁 Additional Chapter Resources

Resource Organizers, pp. 2, 11, 20, 29, 38, 47, 56
Alternate Lesson Plan, p. 180
Answer Keys, pp. 65-72

Bibliography

For the Teacher
Johnson, Haynes. *Divided We Fall.* W. W. Norton, 1994 (A portrait of a country framed by the problems confronting it and the personal narratives of the many citizens exploring the challenges of change.)

The Big Idea for the unit and how the main ideas in each chapter relate to the Big Idea are graphically displayed below. Comprehension of this unit's Big Idea is critical to students' understanding of United States history and how we as a nation got where we are today.

Media and Technology

Our Times Multimedia Encyclopedia of the 20th Century
Decision America: Visual Explorations of America's Enduring Issues

Our Times Multimedia Encyclopedia of the 20th Century
Decision America: Visual Explorations of America's Enduring Issues

Our Times Multimedia Encyclopedia of the 20th Century
Decision America: Visual Explorations of America's Enduring Issues

Our Times Multimedia Encyclopedia of the 20th Century
Decision America: Visual Explorations of America's Enduring Issues

Our Times Multimedia Encyclopedia of the 20th Century
Decision America: Visual Explorations of America's Enduring Issues

Our Times Multimedia Encyclopedia of the 20th Century
Decision America: Visual Explorations of America's Enduring Issues

Our Times Multimedia Encyclopedia of the 20th Century
Decision America: Visual Explorations of America's Enduring Issues

For the Student
Our Times Multimedia Encyclopedia of the 20th Century CD-ROM. Vicarious, 1996. (Available through Prentice Hall, this CD-ROM offers interactive timelines, video stories, and authoritative reference articles.)

UNIT 11

As the twenty-first century approached, the United States faced a number of critical issues. Some were new challenges, posed by social and technological change. Others were reappraisals of ongoing questions, such as the role of government. Despite differences, Americans continued to work together to seek solutions.

CHAPTER 36
Increasing numbers of immigrants from different cultures have had widespread effects on American society, raising questions about the nation's historic policy of welcoming newcomers.

CHAPTER 37
An increase in violent crime caused many people to demand limits on private gun ownership, while others defended it as a fundamental right of American citizens.

CHAPTER 38
As the gap between the rich and the poor increased, debate continued over the proper role of government in assuring workers a minimum wage.

CHAPTER 39
The role of government in providing for the general welfare came into conflict with budgetary constraints.

CHAPTER 40
As relationships within the Western Hemisphere shifted, the United States had to rethink its policies on trade and cooperation.

CHAPTER 41
The end of the cold war did not, as hoped, guarantee world peace. The United States had to define its new global role.

CHAPTER 42
Computerization of many everyday tasks has brought changes to almost every aspect of life. This trend has raised questions about the use of computers in classrooms.

UNIT 11

Pathways to the Future:
Themes for the
Twenty-First Century

Introducing the Unit

Interpreting the Visual Have students look at the photo on pp. 982–983 and suggest reasons for this tickertape parade—perhaps a hero's welcome, or a new year. Point out that the year 2000 will bring not only a new year but also a new century.

The twentieth century has been marked by American achievement and success. It is not an exaggeration to call it "the American century." The late 1990s, however, found many Americans uncertain about the coming century. This thematic unit explores some of the issues.

Establishing Chronology The chapters focus on national issues. Some are part of an ongoing national debate about the role of government. Others reflect changes in society and technology.

Teachers may want to set these specific issues in the context of broader historical themes:

Economics
- Budgetary constraints raised questions about entitlements such as AFDC and Medicare.
- NAFTA brought debate over free trade in the Western Hemisphere.

Unity and Conflict
- Some Americans charged that immigration hurt national unity.
- Americans disagreed sharply about controls on gun ownership.

Diversity
- Immigration from different cultures increased diversity in American society.

The United States and the World
- The end of the cold war meant a reshaping of American foreign policy.
- Trade changed the United States' relationships with Latin America.

Technology
- The spread of computer networks raised questions about their use in education.

Pathways to the Future

Themes for the
Twenty-First Century

How will Americans apply the lessons from their rich history to meet the challenges of the next century?

CHAPTER 36   *Pages 984-991*

Immigration and the Golden Door

In the 1990s, immigrants had a profound impact on the nation. Both the sheer numbers of immigrants and their cultural diversity have had an effect on everything from foods and phone books to schools and politics.

CHAPTER 37   *Pages 992-998*

Gun Control and Crime

In recent years, America has experienced a wave of violent crime, with a significant percentage of these crimes involving the use of guns. The Second Amendment to the Constitution protects the right to "keep and bear arms." Does it refer only to states' need for security or does it include individuals' as well?

CHAPTER 38   *Pages 999-1005*

Minimum Wage and the Role of Government

In the 1990s the gap between the rich and the poor continued to widen. To narrow this gap, President Clinton proposed an increase in the minimum wage. While economists and politicians debated the effect of such a raise on the economy, others questioned whether the federal government should be setting a minimum wage at all.

 RESOURCE DIRECTORY

Teaching Resources

📄 **Alternate Lesson Plan: Demonstrating the Big Idea** found in the Alternate Lesson Plans folder, p. 180, provides a lesson strategy to instruct students about the Big Idea that the United States has successfully met difficult challenges in the past, and it will continue to meet and overcome challenges in the future.

📄 **Alternative Assessment Handbook** provides information, guidance, and strategies for alternative methods of assessment. It includes an essay on new trends in assessment, guidance, and strategies for developing performance tasks and portfolios, scoring rubrics, and sample evaluation forms.

⭐ **Themes in American History Posters** Wall-size, illustrated posters, found in the Teaching Resources package, illustrate the unit themes.

Tickertape parade,
New York City

Using Multimedia Technology This folder contains strategies for using technology in the classroom and the latest offerings from Prentice Hall.

Using the Internet This folder contains lesson plans and strategies for student use of the World Wide Web resources.

Spanish Resources This folder provides key terms, key concepts, and quizzes for all chapters in Unit 11 in Spanish.

Nystrom *Our Country* Atlas Historical atlas with illustrated timeline helps students make connections between geography and history.

American History Block Scheduling Support Contains 40 interdisciplinary folders on major topics in American history. Includes introductory folder on block scheduling options, lesson strategies, and sample unit lessons.

Transparency Binder Contains full-color transparencies with lesson suggestions. From a large collection divided into twelve categories, specific transparencies are referenced throughout the chapters at appropriate points of use.

Technology Corner

Listed below are the technology tools that *America: Pathways to the Present* offers.

Our Times Multimedia Encyclopedia of the 20th Century CD-ROM

A flexible and authoritative reference tool, this CD-ROM contains *The Columbia Encyclopedia*, which is cross-referenced and linked to interactive timelines. A Teacher's Guidebook with lesson plans is included. Especially appropriate for independent student research and review.

Decision America: Visual Explorations of America's Enduring Issues Videodiscs/Videotapes

A collection of videodiscs and videotapes that helps students understand and analyze some of the critical issues that face the nation. Teacher's Guidebook is included.

Visions of America Videodiscs/Videotapes

This award-winning integrated multimedia package was developed for *America: Pathways to the Present.* The program includes a Teacher's Guidebook that familiarizes you with the program, provides sample lessons, and provides extension activities. Especially appropriate for student use in Reviewing the Past in this unit.

RESOURCE PRO

America: Pathways to the Present Teaching Resources on CD-ROM offers lesson planning flexibility and resource manageability.

▶▶▶ USING THE INTERNET
Prentice Hall's Home Page offers student-appropriate Internet activities and links as well as resources for teachers.

Visit **http://www.phschool.com**

Immigration and the Golden Door

1. FOCUS

Connecting to the Big Idea

See page 982B. Remind students of the waves of immigration that have contributed to building the United States. Why do immigration patterns today appear different to many people? How has this influenced attitudes toward new immigrants?

Objectives

- Explain the challenges presented by the increasing numbers and diversity of immigrants to the United States.
- Understand historic patterns of immigration.
- Identify the arguments offered by those for and against tighter controls on immigration.

Bellringer

Ask students why they think people want to come to the United States. What do they think is the most common reason?

Reading Strategy

Reading for Evidence Ask students, as they read, to look for evidence supporting both sides of the question posed in "Introducing the Theme:" "Should we continue to welcome so many from other lands, or do we need to restrict immigration in some ways?"

Immigration and the Golden Door

INTRODUCING THE THEME

Give me your tired, your poor,
Your huddled masses yearning to breathe free,
The wretched refuse of your teeming shore.
Send these, the homeless, tempest tossed to me:
I lift my lamp beside the golden door!

Emma Lazarus wrote these words in the poem "The New Colossus" in 1883, when a new wave of immigration was beginning to arrive in the United States. More than a hundred years later, we find ourselves in the midst of another huge wave of immigrants. Both the sheer numbers of immigrants and their cultural diversity have had a profound impact on American society—everything from foods and phone books to schools and politics.

Debate Should we continue to welcome people from other lands, or do we need to restrict immigration?

Key Terms, People, Places
undocumented immigrants, political asylum, green cards, nativists, bilingual education; William Penn, Pete Wilson

VIEWING THE PRESENT

Ovidiu Colea spent five years in a Romanian labor camp as punishment for trying to escape to the United States. He finally emigrated in 1978 and settled in New York. In 1985 he won the only contract to make replicas of the Statue of Liberty for the centennial celebration the next year. Today he's still making the statues, with the help of about two dozen other immigrants in his factory in Blissville, Queens. Colea and his business are very successful, manufacturing the very symbol of the American dream.

Not all immigrant stories end so happily. In El Monte, California, 72 immigrants from Thailand lived and worked locked inside an apartment complex surrounded by razor wire. They sewed garments for up to 115 hours a week in cramped sweatshops, receiving only meager wages, from which was deducted the nearly $5,000 cost of transportation to the United States. "Living in there was like death, never able to see the world outside," said one woman. Eventually a worker escaped and notified authorities, who freed the others.

Ovidiu Colea with one of his replicas of the Statue of Liberty.

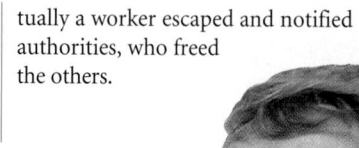

▶ RESOURCE DIRECTORY

Teaching Resources

📁 **Reproducible Lesson Plan** found in the Unit 11 folder, p. 3, provides a summary of the Chapter 36 lesson plan content.

📁 **Alternate Lesson Plan: Learning Styles** found in the Alternate Lesson Plans folder, p. 181, is especially effective for tactile and visual learners, and is designed to help students understand the immigration issue by mapping historical immigration patterns.

📁 **Guided Reading and Review** found in the Unit 11 folder, p. 4, provides a structure for reading and mastering the key concepts and reviewing the key terms for Chapter 36. (Guided Practice)

📁 **Spanish Resources** provides key terms and key concepts for Chapter 36 in Spanish.

How Many Recent Immigrants Are There?

Between the extremes of these two experiences lie the stories of millions of newcomers to the United States in recent years. In the 1980s, immigration skyrocketed. During that decade, the number of newcomers soared to about 7.3 million, more than one and a half times what it had been in the previous decade. This surge continued into the 1990s. In just one year—1991—1,827,200 people entered the United States officially. The figures began to drop in succeeding years, with 720,461 arriving in 1995. To appreciate the full impact of recent immigration, however, you need to add to these figures the number of **undocumented immigrants**. (These are immigrants who have entered the United States illegally.) The Census Bureau estimated that in 1994 between 3.5 million and 4 million people were living in this country illegally.

Why Do They Come?

Immigrants can legally enter the United States for the following reasons:

1. They have relatives who are American citizens.
2. They possess needed job skills.
3. They are refugees from war or are seeking **political asylum** to escape persecution.

The principal reason for coming is family ties. In 1993, about 53 percent of legal immigrants were family members of U.S. citizens. Another 16 percent were granted entry because they had specialized work skills. About 14 percent were refugees and asylum seekers. The

rest fell into special categories of the immigration law.

Where Have They Come From?

The largest number of immigrants in 1993—about 40 percent—came from Asia, with China in the lead, followed by the Philippines, Vietnam, and India. Approximately one-third of all immigrants in that year came from North and Central

Which of the foods in this photo can you find in your local grocery store? Do those foods reflect the backgrounds of people who live in your area? How do they reflect the diversity of America as a whole?

America and the Caribbean, with the largest contingent from Mexico. About 18 percent came from Europe, 6 percent from South America, and 3 percent from Africa. All in all, more people are coming to America from more countries than ever before.

Endless Challenges

Once they arrive, newcomers face seemingly endless challenges, the first of which is finding a place to live. Immigrants move to every state of the Union, with the greatest concentrations in California, Texas,

Florida, and New York. Most settle in cities with ethnic neighborhoods where they can find familiar food, language, and customs, as well as a network of people to help them learn the new ways of America. Nur Emirgil, a Turkish immigrant to Queens, New York, describes how her neighborhood works: "Somebody calls or knocks on the door and asks, 'Can this person stay on your couch for a few days?' 'Do you know any job they

can get, someplace that doesn't care about **green cards** [work permits for foreigners]?' 'Can you go with them to the doctor to translate?'"

The Changes

Striking the balance between old ways and new can be tricky. Many immigrants discover they have to give up their old line of work and take the lowest-paying unskilled jobs just to be employed at all. While they want their children to learn English, they also want them to maintain their heritage.

Discuss

Discuss how people's point of view about immigration may be influenced by personal factors such as having/not having a job, affluence/poverty, and the like. Ask students to suggest what some of those factors might be and how they would influence attitudes.

Analyze

Ask students to analyze the types of problems that confront new immigrants to the United States today. How are they similar to or different from those encountered by earlier immigrants? Why?

In Depth

Interdisciplinary

Several artists contributed to the making of "Liberty Enlightening the World," the formal name of the Statue of Liberty. It was created by French sculptor Frédéric-Auguste Bartholdi (1834–1904), whose other masterpiece is the "Lion of Belfort," a war monument. The colossal Statue of Liberty, a gift from the people of France, was made of copper sheets hammered into shape by hand. Gustave Eiffel, designer of Paris's Eiffel Tower, made the steel framework that supports the statue. Once completed, the statue was disassembled, shipped to New York, and mounted on its pedestal on an island in New York harbor. It was dedicated in 1886. Poet and playwright Emma Lazarus (1849-1887) wrote her now-famous sonnet in 1883. Only its last lines are on the statue.

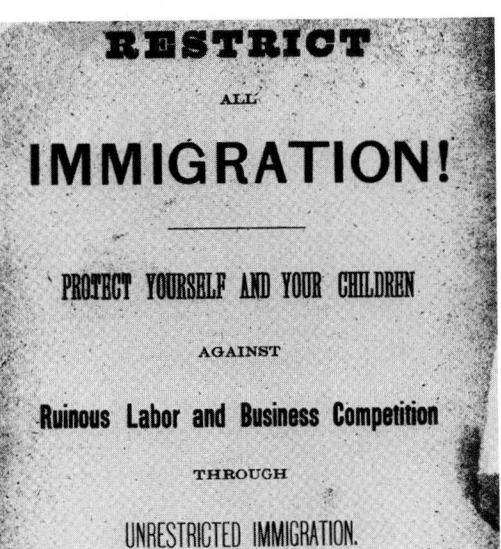

This 1885 brochure reflects the concern that employers would hire immigrants, who would work for lower wages, instead of native-born Americans.

⭐ Just as immigrants change to adjust to America, so does America change to adjust to the immigrants. With almost 9 percent of the population foreign-born, new products and services have appeared to meet immigrant needs. Television and radio now broadcast in dozens of languages. Yellow pages appear for different ethnic groups. Foods imported from places as different as Southeast Asia and Mexico line the shelves of grocery stores in small towns like Garden City, Kansas.

The Costs

The most difficult challenge to America is how to provide social services for so many immigrants of such diverse origins. Areas with large foreign-born populations must provide ballots in one or more languages besides English. Big-city school systems like Chicago and Los Angeles must teach children who speak more than 100 different languages. Public hospitals must take care of poor immigrants who cannot pay, and the government must provide public assistance for the poorest. All of these services cost money at a time when federal, state, and local governments have less to spend.

REVIEWING THE PAST

We are, as President Kennedy put it, a "nation of immigrants." With the exception of Africans, who were brought to the Americas against their will, all other immigrants have come here in search of a better life. They see America as a land of opportunity. But opportunity has always involved risk, loss, and change. Coming to America has meant wrenching changes for immigrants leaving behind their homelands and adapting to new circumstances. It has also meant the growth of a unique culture in America. Some call it a melting pot. Others describe it as a salad bowl or a mosaic. But whatever the metaphor, American society is indeed the product of many people from many nations.

Colonial America

Archaeologists say that perhaps as long as 40,000 years ago, people began migrating to the Americas across a land bridge from Asia. Their descendants, today's Native Americans, dispute that their ancestors were immigrants, saying their people have lived in the Americas since the creation of the earth. Whether they were the first immigrants or not, Native Americans had formed about 500 nations by the time Europeans began colonization in the 16th and 17th centuries.

Differences in purpose led to differences in immigration patterns in the various European colonies of North America. The Spanish set up colonies to extract wealth from the land and to convert Native Americans, but not

This Russian family came to the United States in the early 1900s. In those years, thousands of new arrivals passed through the Ellis Island immigration center each day.

▶ RESOURCE DIRECTORY

Teaching Resources

⭐ 📄 **Literature Activity** Immigrant Dreams, found in the Unit 11 folder, p. 7, is an interview with Miguel Cortez, who immigrated to the United States from Cuba.

SOURCE READINGS

The Source Readings for Unit 11, found on pp. 1084–1087, provide students with links to America's future through literature.

Nystrom *Our Country* Atlas Historical atlas with illustrated timeline helps students make connections between geography and history. See pp. 24–25, 30–31, and 36–37.

primarily to relocate Spaniards. The French, similarly, did not emphasize settlement. They too wanted the riches of the land, and in the 17th and 18th centuries, that meant trapping and trading with Native Americans for furs. The English and Dutch, on the other hand, did want to settle. New Amsterdam had to advertise to recruit people. They were so successful in drawing people from many places that as early as 1644, 18 languages were spoken there. **William Penn** also advertised throughout Europe for people to come to Pennsylvania. By 1750, the population of the English colonies was slightly less than half English. Almost 20 percent were African, and the rest were Scots-Irish, German, Irish, Scottish, Welsh, Dutch, French, and Swedish.

The New Nation

In his 1782 *Letters from an American Farmer,* J. Hector St. John de Crèvecoeur wrote, "I could point out to you a family whose grandfather was an Englishman, whose wife was Dutch, whose son married a French woman, and whose present four sons have now four wives of different nations." As the new nation, founded on principles of equality, grew, so did its immigration from many nations. Until 1846, those nations were mostly in western and northern Europe, and almost all their emigrants were Protestant. In America there were land and jobs enough for all.

Starting in 1846, the immigrant population changed rapidly as the potato famine in Ireland sent hundreds of thousands of Irish Catholics to America. Joining them in the early 1850s were hundreds of thousands of German immigrants fleeing political oppression. This new wave of immigrants settled largely in the cities of

THE ONLY WAY TO HANDLE IT.

Americans have long debated immigration policy. This cartoon refers to a 1921 law that restricted immigration from European countries. That law set quotas based on national origin: immigration from a particular country could not exceed 3 percent of the number of people living in the United States in 1910 whose background was from that very country.

Using Historical Evidence *How do you think the cartoonist felt about the 1921 immigration law? How does the cartoon portray immigrants?*

the Northeast and Midwest. The Irish and many of the Germans were Catholic. Some native-born Americans, fearing control by the Pope and loss of jobs to newcomers, responded with hostility toward the foreign-born. Many of these **nativists** formed the Know-Nothing Party, which became an important political force in 1854. The Know-Nothings wanted to keep all Catholics and foreigners out of public office and to require a 21-year

residence period for immigrants to qualify for citizenship.

Although the Know-Nothing Party fell apart, such nativist sentiment grew as Chinese immigrants arrived in the mid-1800s. Fearing competition for jobs, nativists succeeded in passing the Chinese Exclusion Act of 1882. This federal law cut off all immigration from China. Anti-Asian sentiment would also curtail Japanese immigration with the so-called "gentleman's agreement" of 1907.

Media and Technology

 Transparencies Our Multicultural Heritage, C-2 and C-3

 Decision America Will help motivate students to analyze and understand contemporary issues in American society. See Issue 1, "Can One Voice Make a Difference? The School Prayer Case" (disc 1, side 1; tape 1; approx. 8 min.).

 Activity

Interdisciplinary

Divide students into groups to compile a "Who's Who" list of immigrants to the United States who have made notable contributions. Each group will focus on a specific discipline such as Science, Technology, Business, Arts, or Entertainment. They will provide brief biographies and, if possible, pictures for a display. To help students begin, suggest historical figures such as Enrico Fermi, Alexander Graham Bell, Nikola Tesla, Andrew Carnegie, Baron von Steuben, and Irving Berlin.

Enrichment

Suggest to students that they use the library computer or reading lists to find and read one of the first-person accounts, autobiographies, or novels based on the immigrant experience.

Caption Answer to ...

Using Historical Evidence

The cartoonist approved of the 1921 law. The cartoon portrays immigrants as part of a huge mob trying to pour into the United States.

 In Depth

Then and Now

The 1990s is not the first decade in which people have worried about the primacy of English as the language of the United States. In the early 1700s, William Penn's colony of Pennsylvania drew thousands of immigrants from Germany. By 1776 they numbered 100,000. The Pennsylvania Germans tended to keep to themselves, forming a cultural island with German-language schools, churches, and printing presses. Even tolerant Benjamin Franklin wanted to divert German immigrants to other colonies or, he said, English speakers might be outnumbered and "be not able to preserve our language."

Alternative Assessment

Monitoring Progress

Check with students to see whether they have

- Chosen a list of films and TV shows to analyze.
- Begun their analysis and research.
- Decided on a format.

Explain that projects will be evaluated according to the following guidelines.

- **Unacceptable** Projects are not attempted or do not address the topic.
- **Limited/Acceptable** Projects show some research and a limited exploration of the issue.
- **Extensive/Commendable** Projects are based on outside research and present information in a well-organized and interesting way.
- **Extraordinary/Outstanding** Projects are based on extensive research and display thoughtful interpretation as well as original thought and creativity.

Caption Answer to ...

Interpreting Charts

In previous eras, most immigrants came from Europe. In the late 1980s, most came from Latin America and Asia.

In Depth

Global Connections

The definition of "citizenship" varies from country to country but depends generally on one of two criteria: being born in a country or being born to a citizen or to someone with citizen's rights. Although changes have been proposed, the Constitution gives American citizenship to anyone born on U.S. territory, regardless of the citizenship of his or her parents. Only a few other countries grant such birthright citizenship, including Canada, India, New Zealand, and Spain.

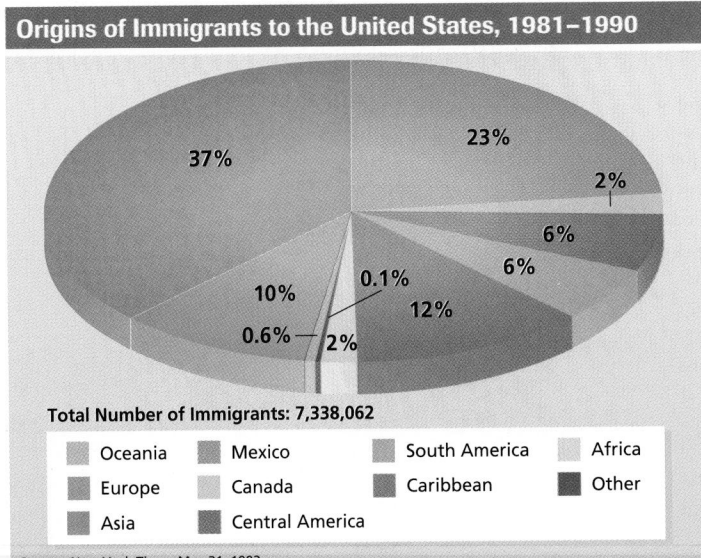

Origins of Immigrants to the United States, 1981–1990

Total Number of Immigrants: 7,338,062

23% · 2% · 6% · 6% · 12% · 2% · 0.6% · 10% · 0.1% · 37%

Legend:
- Oceania
- Europe
- Asia
- Mexico
- Canada
- Central America
- South America
- Caribbean
- Africa
- Other

Source: *New York Times*, May 31, 1992

Interpreting Charts
As the 1900s drew to a close, immigration was helping to create an increasingly diverse American population. Look at the graphs on pages 265 and 780. *How did immigration in those eras compare with immigration in the late1980s?*

The New Immigration

Beginning in the 1880s, immigration to the United States increased rapidly. Between 1870 and the end of the 1880s, immigration doubled. This new wave of immigrants was different from the ones before. Instead of coming from western and northern Europe, as they had done previously, they came from southern and eastern Europe. Instead of being Protestant, they were Catholic and Jewish. Instead of spreading out over the farmlands of the Midwest and Great Plains, they settled in cities, where they found work in factories and mills.

Even as these newcomers were becoming part of the country's mainstream, opposition to immigrants continued to flourish. During World War I, government propaganda fanned nativist sentiment.

Immigration Laws

After the war, America went through a period of intense fear of foreigners. Believing political radicals were spreading communism and revolution, the Justice

Many Americans today believe that immigration to the United States should be restricted or even stopped completely.

Department jailed or deported hundreds of innocent people between 1919 and 1921. Wanting no part of European politics, American foreign policy became isolationist. In this spirit, Congress passed the Immigration Law of 1921, which limited immigration to 350,000 people per year and set up quotas for nationalities. The Immigration Law of 1924 went even further. It capped immigration at 164,000, banned all Asians, and limited each nationality's immigration to 2 percent of that country's emigrants to the United States in 1890. This last provision aimed to halt immigration from southern and eastern Europe.

With these laws in place, immigration slowed to a trickle. During the next 30 years, only about 100,000 people came to the United States each year. Then in 1965 Congress passed a new law lifting all immigration quotas, thus opening the Golden Door to more non-Europeans. As a result, the number of immigrants has greatly increased, and their countries of origin have changed. Between 1930 and 1960,

RESOURCE DIRECTORY

Teaching Resources

Debating the Future The Debate on Immigration, in the Unit 11 folder, pp. 5–6, allows students to debate the immigration issue using the 1996 platforms of the Republican and Democratic parties as background.

Using the Internet Provides additional lesson activities using the resources of the World Wide Web and the Internet.

about 80 percent of all immigrants came from Europe or Canada. Since 1960, about 80 percent are from Asia, Latin America, and the Caribbean.

As the number of legal immigrants has grown, so has the number of illegal, or undocumented, immigrants. To combat this problem, Congress passed the Immigration Reform and Control Act of 1986. This law punished employers who knowingly hired illegals. It also granted amnesty to illegals who had lived in the United States since 1982, to enable them to register to become citizens. The Immigration Act of 1990 raised immigration totals and removed certain restrictions on people who had been denied entry in the past. The impact of these laws is reflected in the change of composition of American society. By the mid-1990s, nearly 10 percent of the population was foreign-born, the highest level since 1940. This greater diversity has, in turn, sparked intense debate about the continuation of this immigration policy. ✪

DEBATING THE FUTURE

Massive immigration will destroy America, says author Lawrence Auster. "As whites lose their numerical, political, and cultural dominance, American civilization with all its constituent virtues will also come to an end." Not so, counters Julian L. Simon, a professor at the University of Maryland. He believes that "Talented young immigrants help us achieve every one of our national goals. They make us richer and not poorer, stronger and not weaker." Arguments such as these are representative of much of the national debate about immigration policy.

In Favor of Tighter Controls on Immigration

Opponents of current policy argue that high levels of immigration hurt the American economy. "How

Time magazine created this computer-generated portrait by combining the characteristics of all the groups present in the United States in 1993.

can we keep bringing people into this country when our own people don't have jobs?" asks Clark Yates, an auto mechanic in Chicago.

Economic Arguments Because immigrants are willing to work for low wages, many fear they will take jobs away from Americans. Illegal immigrants, in particular, will work for less than minimum wage, which drives down other workers' pay. "Undocumented immigrants tend to compete unfairly for low-skilled jobs, and they can sometimes bring down the level of wages and working conditions," according to Charles Wheeler, executive director of the National Immigration Law Center.

Political Arguments The federal government sets immigration policy, but by and large it is state and local governments that must pay for services—welfare, health care, and education—for immigrants and their children, who are citizens if born in the United States. Many Californians oppose immigration because their state receives the largest number of immigrants, both legal and illegal, and must pay for their social services. In 1994 Governor **Pete Wilson** asked the President to declare an emergency in California and repay the state the $2.4 billion it spends each year on undocumented aliens. Said a California state assembly aide in 1993,

> The state is broke. We've had a multibillion-dollar deficit three years in a row, and yet we continue to pay medical benefits for these illegal immigrants. We take better care of them than of our own people.

Cultural Arguments Immigration opponents see the new immigrant groups as fragmenting American society, dividing it into ethnic enclaves rather than adapting to American culture. Language has become a rallying point, with campaigns for "English only" as the official language. In 1975, Congress amended the voting rights act to require bilingual ballots. English-only advocates point out that naturalized citizens are supposed to know the language, but many have cheated to pass the exam. "Citizens who are

Using the Internet
Prentice Hall has reviewed the Internet site listed in this activity. However, due to the changing nature of the Internet, all sites should be previewed before students explore on their own.

Immigration Today

Objective Use the Internet to research and graph data on United States immigration and emigration.

Have students follow these instructions:

1. Enter the following URL: **http://www.usdoj.gov/ins/public/index.html**

2. Click the link "Immigration Fact Sheet."

3. Use the data to create a bar graph showing immigration to and emigration from the United States, by decade, since 1900.

4. Create a bar graph to compare the foreign-born population with the total United States population since 1900.

5. Use the graphs to answer these questions: (a) In which decade did immigration to the United States increase most? (b) In which year was the percentage of the foreign-born population the highest?

In Depth

Biography

The first foreign-born officer to become chairman of the Joint Chiefs of Staff—the main military adviser to the President—is General John Shalikashvili (b. 1937), who suceeded Colin Powell in 1993. Shalikashvili grew up in Warsaw, Poland. His family came to the United States in 1952. Shalikashvili was drafted into the army in 1958. He gained combat, command, and diplomatic experience in Vietnam, South Korea, and Germany. In 1991, he led the relief effort to the Kurdish refugees, Operation Provide Comfort. That mission, he said, made him realize the good that such military relief operations could do. He became a four-star general in 1992 as NATO commander.

Media and Technology

Our Times Multimedia Encyclopedia of the 20th Century CD-ROM Will help students of all abilities to link the past to the present. Students can access the timeline, listen to and read about immigration in the early part of the century, review the interactive essays in the *Encyclopedia,* and watch the Decade Video, 1900–1909.

 Decision America Will help motivate students to analyze and understand contemporary issues in American society. See Issue 3, "Why Vote? Encouraging Political Participation" (disc 1, side 1; tape 1; approx. 11 min.).

Chapter 36 Review
Answers (page 991)

1. undocumented immigrants, see p. 985

2. political asylum, see p. 985

3. green cards, see p. 985

4. nativists, see p. 987

5. bilingual education, see p. 990

6. William Penn, see p. 987

7. Pete Wilson, see p. 989

8. Students' timelines should include events such as the Irish potato famine and World War I, as well as major pieces of legislation.

9. Answers will vary, but should reflect an understanding of broad immigration trends in American history. Answers may include:

[boxes across the top]: German/Irish wave of immigration; New era of open immigration

[boxes across the bottom]: Prehistoric Native American immigration; Fears of job competition; Religious prejudice; Immigration Act of 1965; New immigration debates (e.g., bilingual education)

10. Student presentations should show both creativity and a thoughtful approach to the issue.

11. Student presentations should be clear and to the point, as required in the assignment.

For more guidance on scoring, see the Alternative Assessment Handbook in the Resource Directory on page 982.

---

not proficient in English cannot, in most cases, follow a political campaign, talk with candidates, or petition their representatives. They are citizens in name only and are unable to exercise their rights. Providing them with bilingual ballots does not enable them to exercise those rights in any meaningful way," argues John Silber, chairman of the Massachusetts State Board of Education.

Bilingual education is another source of frustration for those who want to limit immigration. In bilingual programs, students are taught subject matter like science and math in their native language, while they learn English in other classes. Opponents of bilingual education argue that these programs only perpetuate separateness rather than promote assimilation into the American mainstream. Without a common language, they believe our common culture is in danger.

Opposed to Tighter Controls on Immigration

Immigrants help, not hurt, the economy, claim immigration supporters. They come highly motivated to work, with strong family units that promote discipline and high standards.

Economic Arguments Immigrants contribute to the economy as consumers, small-business owners, and taxpayers. They also take jobs few native-born Americans want. "My brother . . . has a business, and the Mexicans work hard for him 12 hours a day and they don't complain," reports Eddy Jerena, a Chicago carpenter. "You get these American-born guys, they don't work like that. This country was built by immigrants. The Mexicans deserve to be here."

The Statue of Liberty was what many immigrants first saw when they arrived in the United States. For some of those people, trunks like the one shown here carried all the possessions they were able to bring from their native lands.

Political Arguments Immigration supporters point out that, contrary to popular belief, most immigrants do not receive public assistance. Most legal immigrants have to wait three years to be eligible for welfare,

and illegal immigrants are not eligible for any social services except emergency Medicaid. A recent study showed that 6.6 percent of immigrants get help, in contrast to 4.9 percent of the native-born population. But a significant portion of those immigrants are refugees or the elderly, who do not qualify for Social Security as older Americans do. Looking only at working-age immigrants who are not refugees, only 5.1 percent get welfare, compared to 5.3 percent of native-born.

Cultural Arguments Supporters say immigration is an investment that will pay off in a trained workforce and future taxpayers. To those who would deny education to the children of illegal immigrants, Indianapolis, Indiana Superintendent of Schools Esperanza Zendejas replies,

These kids are going to be here for a long time. So the question is whether we want to educate these kids now or pay for increased social welfare costs later down the line. I think it's an easy choice.

The Debate Continues

While both supporters and opponents of immigration believe it is necessary to exert greater control over illegal immigrants, they disagree over how to do it. They also disagree over the level of legal immigration and whether legal immigrants should be eligible for social services. Voters will need to weigh the Statue of Liberty's promise against their perception of America's ability to keep it.

RESOURCE DIRECTORY

Spanish Resources provides Key Terms Quiz with Answer Key in Spanish.

Teaching Resources

Chapter Test Forms A and B are found in the Unit 11 folder, pp. 9-10.

Answer Keys found in the Unit 11 folder, pp. 65-72, provide answers to all student activities.

Chapter Review

DEFINE AND IDENTIFY

Key Terms
1. undocumented immigrants
2. political asylum
3. green cards
4. nativists
5. bilingual education

People
6. William Penn
7. Pete Wilson

MAKING CONNECTIONS

Create a Timeline
8. To set the events of this chapter in context, construct a timeline that includes eight to ten significant milestones in the modern history (since colonial times) of immigration to the United States. Include both events and legislation. You can refer to previous chapters of this textbook for information.

Use a Graphic Organizer
9. Review the arguments in the Debating the Future section of the chapter. Then fill in the blanks in the graphic organizer below that shows political movements and legislation affecting immigration between the mid-1800s and the 1990s. Large boxes show the major developments or laws. Specific details or effects appear in the smaller boxes. You can copy the web on another sheet of paper.

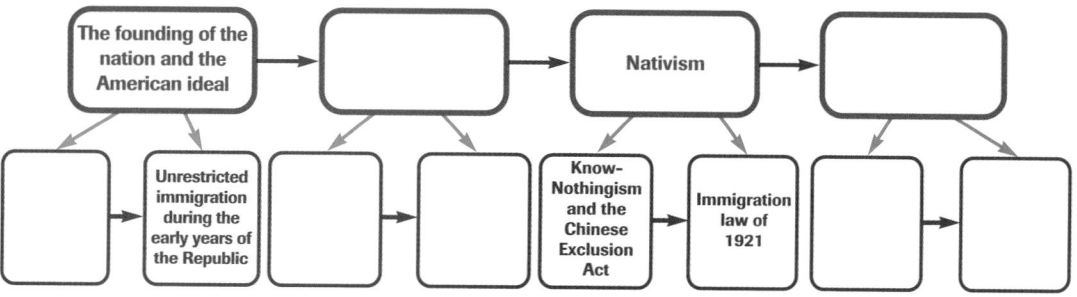

- The founding of the nation and the American ideal
- Nativism
- Unrestricted immigration during the early years of the Republic
- Know-Nothingism and the Chinese Exclusion Act
- Immigration law of 1921

ACTIVITIES

For Your Portfolio
10. Think about your own attitudes toward immigration and the services to which immigrants are entitled. Then consider how you can best express this opinion: for instance, a newspaper editorial, a pictorial essay, a series of interviews, a poem, a cartoon or drawing, a poster. When you have chosen a presentation that is acceptable to your teacher, put it in an appropriate format.

▶▶▶ **USING THE INTERNET**
Access Prentice Hall's site at: **http://www.phschool.com** for related links on United States history.

11. Go to Congress's Web site for legislative information at http://thomas.loc.gov/ and find a bill pending in Congress. Summarize the bill and explain two arguments for and against passing it. Present your summary to the class for discussion.

Media and Technology

 Computer Test Bank

 RESOURCE ⊙ PRO

Teaching Resources on CD-ROM contains all instructional and enrichment material for Chapter 36. Includes all quizzes and tests. You can print directly from the CD-ROM.

Reteach
Have students write the heading "More Controls on Immigration" and make two columns, "For" and "Against." In each column, they should list at least four reasons presented in the chapter.

Alternative Assessment

Final Evaluation
Use the following guidelines to evaluate student projects:
- **Evidence of thoughtfulness** Did students show an understanding of the issue and its impact on the community?
- **Evidence of outside research** To what extent did students use outside research and interviews for their projects?
- **Communication style** Do projects convey their purpose in a clear, appealing way?

4. CLOSE

 Reinforcing the Big Idea

New patterns of immigration were just one of the issues that challenged people in the United States as the twentieth century drew to a close. Immigrants came from new parts of the world, increasing cultural diversity but challenging some elements of society.

Connecting to the Big Idea

See page 982B. Explain to students that violent crime was one of the issues that Americans worried about most in the 1990s. They disagreed, however, on ways to combat it. The focus of the debate was the question of gun control. Why is this issue so "hot," or charged with emotion, for many Americans?

Objectives

● Understand the changing patterns of violent crime in the United States.
● Trace the growth of American attitudes toward gun ownership since frontier days.
● Identify the arguments offered by opponents and supporters of gun control.

Bellringer

Ask students how crime or the fear of crime affects them in their daily lives. Do they, like many Americans, rank violent crime as one of the things that frighten and worry them the most?

Reading Strategy

Predicting Content Have students read the introductory paragraph and the boldface section and subsection headings in the section. Ask them to predict the content of the chapter and then read to confirm or change this prediction.

Gun Control and Crime

As this 1779 woodcut shows, guns have been part of American life since colonial times.

INTRODUCING THE THEME

Violent crime has too often been part of life in America, with many crimes involving the use of guns. At the same time, more private citizens are arming themselves in self-defense. Since the earliest days of this nation, Americans have debated the right to private ownership of guns. The Second Amendment to the Constitution protects the right to "keep and bear arms." But does it refer only to states' needs for security or does it include individuals' as well?

Debate Given the rising tide of violent crime, is stiffer gun control an effective way to restore tranquillity?

Key Terms, People, and Places

homicide, militias, Second Amendment, National Rifle Association (NRA); James Brady

VIEWING THE PRESENT

Under a Chicago railroad bridge the police found "Yummy" in a mud puddle, his face torn apart by bullets fired through the back of his head. Eleven-year-old Robert "Yummy" Sandifer had been gunned down by members of his own gang. He was supposed to shoot members of a rival gang, but killed an innocent 14-year-old girl instead. When police went after him, Yummy became too big a risk and fell victim to gang violence himself.

In Collingswood, New Jersey, Amy Fleming practices loading her handgun in the dark in five seconds flat. She lives with her son Justy, her dog, and her fear of her ex-husband, Ed. A drug user who has been convicted of two violent assaults and theft of a firearm, Ed has repeatedly threatened to kill Amy. No help is available from the police, who can only recommend that she run away and hide. Since Ed has no trouble finding out where she lives, Amy feels that her gun is the only protection she has.

Signs of the Times

How typical are these two stories? While they don't give the full picture, they do put human faces on some startling statistics. Every two minutes someone is shot in this country. The

Many people today say that the high rate of crime in the United States makes them feel unsafe. Some, like this woman, find that owning a handgun makes them feel more secure.

▶ RESOURCE DIRECTORY

Teaching Resources

Reproducible Lesson Plan found in the Unit 11 folder, p. 12, provides a summary of the Chapter 37 lesson plan content.

Alternate Lesson Plan: Critical Thinking Formulating Questions, found in the Alternate Lesson Plans folder, p. 182, is designed to help students clarify arguments put forward by supporters and opponents of gun control by preparing questions and answers.

Guided Reading and Review found in the Unit 11 folder, p. 13, provides a structure for reading and mastering the key concepts and reviewing the key terms for Chapter 37. (Guided Practice)

Spanish Resources provides key terms and key concepts for Chapter 37 in Spanish.

Federal Bureau of Investigation reports that Americans are now more likely to be the victim of violent crime—murder, rape, robbery, and aggravated assault—than to be hurt in a traffic accident. Between 1983 and 1992, violent crime increased 54 percent in the United States. Not surprisingly, crime soared to first place among national concerns in a Gallup poll in 1993.

Three years later, crime still topped the list in a poll conducted by the *San Jose Mercury News* and Knight-Ridder Publications. What is surprising is that serious crimes actually decreased overall in 1995 for the fourth year in a row. (Serious crimes include violent crimes and crimes against property—burglary, larceny, motor vehicle theft, and arson.) Yet people continue to think of crime as a more serious problem than other urgent concerns like unemployment or taxes. Why?

Reasons for Increase

Criminologists, social scientists who study crime, cannot say for certain what makes crime rates increase or decrease. Still, they can identify historical trends. During the 1940s and 1950s, the United States enjoyed relatively low crime rates. Things began to change in the mid-1960s, as a look at the rate of **homicide**, or murder, reveals. In 1965 the murder rate was about 5 per 100,000 people; by 1974 it had doubled. Falling in the mid-1970s, it rose to 10 per 100,000 people in 1980, then dropped again until the late 1980s. According to the FBI the murder rate in 1994 was 9 per 100,000 people.

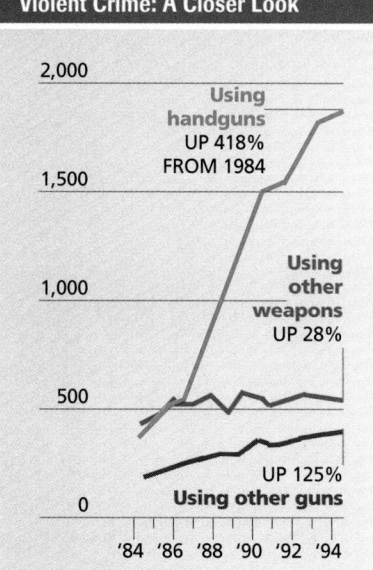

Violent Crime: A Closer Look

Using handguns UP 418% FROM 1984

Using other weapons UP 28%

UP 125% Using other guns

'84 '86 '88 '90 '92 '94

Source: Trends in Juvenile Justice: Report to the U.S. Attorney General, James Alan Fox, Northeastern University

Interpreting Graphs
Homicides, particularly with handguns, have risen sharply since 1984. *What reasons would you give for this enormous rise?*

There are no clear-cut explanations of these ups and downs. Still, Professor Lawrence M. Friedman of Stanford University suggests that fluctuations in crime may be connected with larger social, economic, and cultural trends. For example, the rise in murder rates in the late 1960s took place during a period of great social and political turmoil. The increase in murder rates in the late 1980s coincides with high inner-city unemployment and poverty and the get-rich-quick appeal of the crack cocaine trade.

Why Is Crime the Number One Problem?

There is a direct link between drugs and violent crime. Drug deal-ers use weapons to defend their profitable but illegal trade. Crime increases as addicts steal and kill to support their habits. In many places, the drug trade is controlled by gun-toting youth gangs. Los Angeles is one such city, with murder rates that reveal the depth of the problem. Gang-related murders numbered 158 in 1982, but jumped to 618 in 1992. Of these, the number of drive-by shootings skyrocketed from 57 in 1987 to 211 in 1992.

Los Angeles is just one city. Still, its statistics help to explain why crime is people's Number One fear.

Guns and Crime: A Deadly Combination

Crime, especially murder, is reported widely in newspapers and on television and radio. Major television networks tripled their news coverage of murder stories in 1993. These broadcasts draw attention to the fact that crime increasingly involves young people. Between 1983 and 1992, the rate of juvenile arrests for violent crime doubled. In 1995 alone, the number of murders committed by 14- to 17-year-olds rose 22 percent. And an overwhelming proportion of violent crimes,

In the popular imagination, the sheriff's badge is a symbol of frontier justice, Wild West–style.

Discuss

Discuss with students the national debate about gun control and why those who resist controls feel so strongly. What issues—besides actual gun ownership—are involved in the resistance by the National Rifle Association and those who agree with it? How do they relate to attitudes toward government regulation in general?

Analyze

Point out that the American people hold a wide range of attitudes about gun control. Using the chalkboard, have students analyze the varying points of view and arrange them along the continuum, from an outright ban on private gun ownership to no controls at all. Where do they think most Americans stand on the issue?

In Depth

Global Connections

World crime statistics vary wildly, depending on who collects them and what is counted. Among industrialized nations, the United States has often been in the position of leading in both gun ownership and rate of homicides. (The #2 gun-owning nation is Norway.) But according to a 1995 story in *U.S. News and World Report*, a soaring crime rate in South Africa gave it the world's highest homicide rate: 53.5 per 100,000 people. South Africa had a murder every 29 minutes, with carjacking and armed robbery as other frequent violent crimes.

During the War for Independence, volunteers such as these organized themselves into militias, or small defense forces, known as the minutemen. They got their name because they were ready to respond at a minute's notice to fight British troops.

whether juvenile or adult, are committed with a gun. In 1993, 70 percent of all homicides involved firearms, and four out of five of these were handguns. Of the other violent crimes, a majority, 86 percent, involved handguns.

⭐ So is stiffer gun control an effective way to reduce crime?

REVIEWING THE PAST

Foreign visitors are often surprised by the number of guns—some 200 million—owned by civilians in the United States. In many other countries, guns are banned or tightly controlled. For example, Britain now limits gun ownership mostly to members of gun clubs, who must store their weapons at the club. Since the assassinations of President Kennedy, Martin Luther King, Jr., and Robert F. Kennedy, there have been a number of attempts to pass gun-control laws. Each bill has met with heated debate because of the history of gun ownership in this country.

The English Tradition on American Shores

Guns have been part of the American way of life since the first Europeans came to North America. There were as many guns as colonists in early Jamestown. In a new setting, people needed guns to hunt and to protect themselves.

The colonists also had English tradition to support their ownership of weapons—the right to defend oneself and one's home and the duty to have weapons to protect the public peace. Dating back to the Middle Ages, the English chose to arm themselves for defense rather than have an army under the direction of a monarch. They felt that the monarch could become a tyrant and use the army against them.

Keeping Guns for Common Defense

Over time, tensions increased as the English kings sought more power. After the Glorious Revolution of 1688 overthrew James II, Parliament placed limits on the monarchy through the Bill of Rights. For one thing, it established the right to keep arms for the common defense. Thus English people, both before and after the Glorious Revolution, brought to the American colonies their strongly held belief in their rights to own guns and to protect themselves from absolute government power.

The Colonists Fight for Their Rights

When colonists felt that the British were trying to limit their rights, they fought back. The colonists had enjoyed a fair amount of self-government until Britain

---

RESOURCE DIRECTORY

Teaching Resources

⭐ **Literature Activity** Roots of the Brady Law, found in the Unit 11 folder, pp. 16–17, describes how Sarah Brady began to work towards passage of the Brady Law.

SOURCE READINGS

The Source Readings for Unit 11, found on pp. 1084–1087, provide students with links to America's future through literature.

Nystrom *Our Country* Atlas Historical atlas with illustrated timeline helps students make connections between geography and history. See pp. 14–15 and 20–23.

began to tighten its control after the French and Indian War. Maintaining its vast new North American empire, the British kept a standing army in the colonies and expected the colonists to help pay for it. Resistance to the British grew after passage of the Stamp Act, and **militias**—bands of citizens armed to defend themselves—began to form in 1774 and 1775. One such group, known as minutemen, fought the British to protect supplies of ammunition at Lexington and Concord in Massachusetts. This "shot heard round the world" touched off the American War for Independence.

The Constitution and the Second Amendment

After the War for Independence, the new nation had to form a stable, unified government. The result was the Constitution. That document, however, met with stiff resistance from those who feared it would not protect individuals' and states' rights. In order to get the Constitution ratified, its sponsors agreed to add a Bill of Rights, which was made up of the first ten amendments.

Americans had fought the War for Independence to preserve their rights to self-defense and self-taxation. They had been able to resist the British because they had had their own militias. Following the war, Americans were not about to give up that protection. After all, who knew how the new government would turn out? During the debate on ratifying the Constitution, there was great demand to include bearing arms in a Bill of Rights. As a result, James Madison drafted the **Second Amendment**. In its final form it states, "A well-regulated militia being necessary to the security of a free state, the right

of the people to keep and bear arms shall not be infringed."

American Ideal: Rugged Individualism

 Thus guns were present at the creation of this country and became part of the law of the land. Firearms have also become the stuff of American legend. Think of the mountain man, the pioneer woman, and that popular American symbol, the cowhand—strong, independent, free, a rugged individual. What happens to that symbol when you think of cowhands without their guns? But given the facts that the United States is now far more urban than rural and that gun violence is so high, should the right to

have a gun continue to be part of the American way of life? Americans have wrestled with that question and have put some restrictions on the books.

Existing Gun Regulations

There are about 20,000 laws regulating firearms in the United States in the 1990s. Most of these are local laws that license gun dealers, set up purchase requirements, and mandate background checks. On the federal level, the amended 1968 Gun Control Act prohibits criminals, minors, the mentally ill, and illegal aliens from owning guns. The 1994 Brady law requires a five-day waiting period for a background check before the purchase of a gun. (This

Prentice Hall has reviewed the Internet site listed in this activity. However, due to the changing nature of the Internet, all sites should be previewed before students explore on their own.

Party Platforms and Gun Control

Objective Use the Internet to research political party platforms.

Have students follow these instructions:

1. Go to the Web sites for the Democratic and Republican parties at the following URLs: Democratic Party: **http://www.democrats.org/** Republican Party: **http://www.rnc.org/**

2. Use links at each site to learn about each party's position on gun control.

3. Write an essay describing each party's position on gun control. Cite information from the parties' current platforms.

4. Do you agree with the position taken by either party? Write a paragraph outlining your position on gun control and how it is similar to or different from the positions of the major political parties.

Alternative Assessment

Monitoring Progress

Ask students if they have:

● Located sources of information.

● Chosen a format.

● Begun their research and interviews.

Explain that projects will be evaluated according to the following guidelines.

● **Unacceptable** Projects are not attempted or do not address the topic.

● **Limited/Acceptable** Projects show a lack of research and limited understanding of the issue.

● **Extensive/Commendable** Projects are based on outside research and present information in a well-organized and interesting way.

● **Extraordinary/Outstanding** Projects are based on extensive research and display thoughtful interpretation as well as original thought and creativity.

law was named for **James Brady**, who was paralyzed by a gunshot intended for President Reagan.) Another federal law passed in 1994, the Assault Weapons Act, bans certain types of semiautomatic firearms. If there are regulations on firearms, what more is necessary?

DEBATING THE FUTURE

Natisha Campbell, whose friend Hank Lloyd was shot and killed in Washington, D.C., asks, "Why should you be able to have a gun laying under your pillow so that a baby can pick it up and shoot themselves?"

"I say all guns are good guns," counters Joe Foss, former president of the **National Rifle Association (NRA),** the leading organization against gun control. "There are no bad guns. I say the whole nation should be an armed nation. Period."

Against Gun Control

The National Rifle Association's members cite the Second Amendment phrase, "the right of the people to keep and bear arms shall not be infringed" as the basis for their belief that individuals have the right to own guns.

Gun prohibition, besides being unconstitutional, would endanger society, says the NRA. Members believe people must have guns to protect themselves against criminals. They point out that most gun owners are law-abiding citizens. Says Mary Sue Faulkner of the NRA, "We know criminals fear armed citizens

more than they do the police." Statistics support this statement: handguns are used more often in repelling crimes (about 645,000 annually) than in committing them (about 580,000 annually). As one Florida rifle association member put it, "If I want to mug someone, I'll avoid a person who may have a handgun."

Moreover, NRA members say

Using Historical Evidence Some Americans believe that the right to keep and bear arms, without federal or state regulations, is part of their constitutional rights as stated in the Second Amendment. *Do you agree or disagree with the sentiments expressed in this photo? Explain.*

that gun control is not the answer to the crime problem. "Gun control is a cop-out," said NRA lobbyist James Jay Baker, "an easy solution to a complex problem. And it doesn't work." People bent on committing crime will find a way. So will people intent on getting a gun. "There is absolutely no way the legislation is going to

stop the bad guys from getting guns," says a veteran Maryland police officer. A 1991 Justice department study showed that only 27 percent of state-prison inmates had bought their guns legally. The others got them from family or friends, stole them, or purchased them on the black market. Commented one gun shop customer, "It's easier to get a firearm delivered in the Washington area than it is to get a pizza."

Many members of the NRA feel that any attempt to regulate firearms will lead to total gun prohibition. Before the 1994 federal laws were passed, former NRA president Jim Reinke said,

If we give in on the gun waiting period and assault rifles, we'd lose half our membership, and six months later the antigunners will want our long guns.

⊙ If gun control is not the answer to violent crime, what is? The NRA's J. Warren Cassidy, an executive vice president, said in 1990:

Tough laws designed to incarcerate violent offenders offer something gun control cannot: swift, sure justice meted out with no accompanying erosion of individual liberty.

For Gun Control

Supporters of gun control focus on the first phrase of the Second Amendment, "A well-regulated militia being necessary to the security of

---

 RESOURCE DIRECTORY

Teaching Resources

⊙ **Debating the Future: Simulation** The Debate on Gun Control and Violence, found in the Unit 11 folder, pp. 14–15, allows students to hold a simulated town meeting to discuss this question: "Should we outlaw guns within 200 yards of the high school?"

Using the Internet Provides additional lesson activities using the resources of the World Wide Web and the Internet.

a free state." They emphasize that the purpose of the amendment is to provide for protection for the entire community.

Restricting criminals' access to guns is absolutely essential to reduce violent crime, argues Dewey Stokes, national president of the Fraternal Order of Police. "The police are definitely outgunned in this country." Criminals are carrying more dangerous weapons, and are more willing to use them. Al Baker of the Houston Police Department says,

> *Just about everybody committing a crime has a gun. Not cheap Saturday-night specials, but guns they can count on. And they're willing to shoot it out rather than go to jail.*

Gun-control advocates point out that in 1939 the Supreme Court upheld a law against short-barreled shotguns because their use could not "contribute to the common defense." In 1983, the Court refused to hear a case challenging the first ban on handguns in the nation.

Far from making society safer, gun-control advocates say guns kept for defense against criminals make life more dangerous. Police estimates show that if a gun in a house is ever used, it is six times more likely to shoot a family member or friend than an intruder.

For these reasons, many law-enforcement organizations back gun-control legislation.

James Brady, White House press secretary during President Reagan's first term, is shown here in front of the Capitol. After he was paralyzed by a gunshot wound during an assassination attempt on President Reagan in 1981, Brady and his wife, Sarah, became strong advocates of gun control. Their efforts brought about the 1994 passage of the Brady law.

The Debate Continues

A *TIME*/CNN poll in December 1993 showed that 70 percent of Americans favor gun control, and 78 percent support mandatory registration of all guns. Even so, 74 percent oppose a ban on handguns. Moreover, less than half think that stronger gun control would have any effect on violent crime. Given these mixed feelings, Americans will need to look beyond the bumper-sticker slogans of both sides on the gun-control issue to develop effective public policy in combating crime.

Media and Technology

 Our Times Multimedia Encyclopedia of the 20th Century CD-ROM Will help students of all abilities to link the past to the present. Students can access the timeline, listen to and read about the assassination attempt on President Reagan in 1981.

Decision America Will help motivate students to analyze and understand contemporary issues in American society. See Issue 2, "Should Privacy Be Protected? Drug Testing and the Fourth Amendment" (disc 1, side 1; tape 1; approx. 12 min.), and Issue 13, "What Is a Fair Trial? The Use of Trial Consultants" (disc 2, side 2; tape 4; approx. 6 min.).

3. ASSESS

Chapter 37 Review Answers (page 998)

1. homicide, see p. 993.
2. militias, see p. 995
3. Second Amendment, see p. 995
4. National Rifle Association (NRA), see p. 996
5. James Brady, see p. 996.
6. Student timelines should trace the historic tensions between people and government that English settlers brought to the colonies and reinforced on the frontier.

Caption Answer to ...

Using Historical Evidence

(See p. 996.) Answers will vary.

In Depth

Biography

Personal tragedy helped lead Sarah Brady to become an advocate for gun control. In 1981, her husband, White House press secretary James Brady, was gravely wounded in an assassination attempt on President Ronald Reagan. Brady, a witty and articulate man known to his friends as "the Bear," was shot in the head. He suffered brain damage, which affected his speech and memory, and was partly paralyzed. After months of therapy, Brady could use a cane but often was in a wheelchair. In 1984, after a gun incident also endangered their son, Sarah Brady became a volunteer for Handgun Control, a gun-control lobby. Her efforts helped bring passage of the "Brady Bill," which imposes a waiting period for gun purchases.

7. Answers will vary, but should reflect an understanding of the debate. Possible answers may include: (left side blank web)—Sees link between guns and violent crime; (bottom blank web)—In favor of civil liberties; (right side blank web)—Focuses on long traditions of free gun ownership.

8. Student presentations should show both creativity and a thoughtful approach to the issue.

9. Student presentations should be clear and to the point, as required in the assignment.

For more guidance on scoring, see the Alternative Assessment Handbook in the Resource Directory on page 982.

Reteach

Have students create a chart with two columns: "For More Gun Control" and "Against Gun Control." In each column have them list people who hold that point of view and at least two reasons why.

 ## Alternative Assessment

Final Evaluation
Use the following guidelines to evaluate student projects:
- **Evidence of thoughtfulness**
Did students show an understanding of the issue? Have they effectively analyzed the films and TV programs they chose?
- **Evidence of outside research** To what extent did students use outside research and interviews for their projects? Did they survey films and TV from the appropriate period?
- **Communication style** Do projects convey their purpose in a clear, appealing way?

 4. CLOSE

Reinforcing the Big Idea

Crime remains a major issue for Americans, although they are divided on the question of increasing controls on private gun ownership.

Chapter Review

DEFINE AND IDENTIFY

Key Terms
1. homicide
2. militias

3. Second Amendment
4. National Rifle Association (NRA)

People
5. James Brady

MAKING CONNECTIONS

Create a Timeline
6. To place the issue of gun control in context, construct a timeline that traces the English and American traditions toward gun ownership from the Middle Ages to the inclusion of the Second Amendment in the Constitution (from the Reviewing the Past section). Use your textbook as a reference.

Use a Graphic Organizer
7. Review the arguments in the Debating the Future section of the chapter. Then fill in the blank webs in the graphic organizer below that compares and contrasts views on gun control. You can copy the web on a separate sheet of paper.

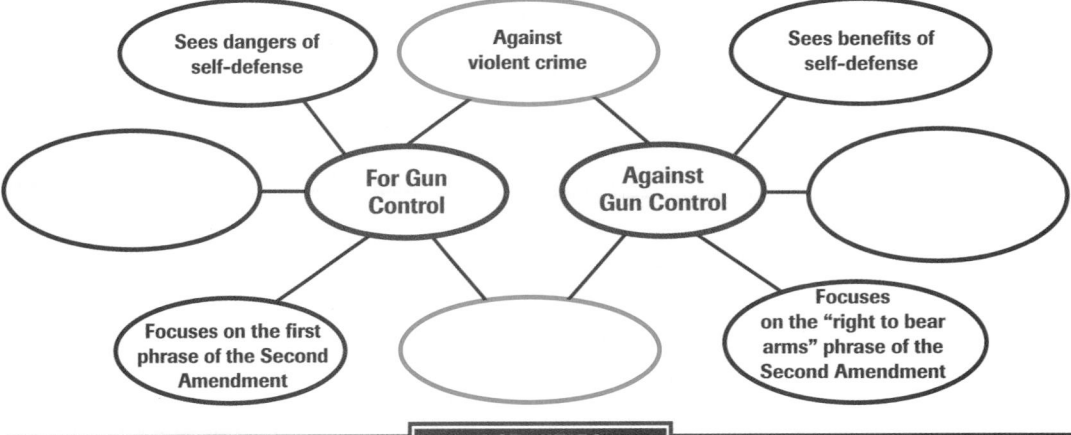

ACTIVITIES

For Your Portfolio
8. Think about your own opinions about crime and the role of gun control in reducing violent crime. Express the opinions in your own way. Consider the following: a poster or drawing, a letter to the editor, a poem or personal essay, a photo essay. When you have chosen a presentation that is acceptable to your teacher, put it in an appropriate format.

▶▶▶ **USING THE INTERNET**
Access Prentice Hall's site at: **http://www.phschool.com** for related links on United States history.

9. Go to the Wiretap Gopher site at gopher://wiretap.spies.com/11/Gov/World and review two constitutions from nations other than the United States for information on firearms. How do they compare to the Second Amendment to the Constitution?

▶ RESOURCE DIRECTORY

Teaching Resources

📁 **Chapter Test** Forms A and B are found in the Unit 11 folder, pp. 18–19.

📁 **Answer Keys** found in the Unit 11 folder, pp. 65-72, provide answers to all student activities.

📁 **Spanish Resources** provides Key Terms Quiz with Answer Key in Spanish.

Media and Technology

 Computer Test Bank

RESOURCE⊙PRO

Teaching Resources on CD-ROM contains all instructional and enrichment material for Chapter 37. Includes all quizzes and tests. You can print directly from the CD-ROM.

Minimum Wage and the Role of Government

INTRODUCING THE THEME

For the last century, the role of the federal government in the economic life of its citizens has been hotly debated. Should government regulate industries in a free enterprise system? Regulations for various industries, product safety issues, and worker's safety and compensation are among the concerns that Americans continue to debate. Setting a minimum wage is one widely argued topic.

 Debate What should be the proper role of the federal government in protecting workers' incomes?

Key Terms, People, Places

progressives, New Deal, work ethic; Frances Perkins, Franklin D. Roosevelt; Triangle Shirtwaist Factory

VIEWING THE PRESENT

Jacqueline Barnes wants to be a doctor. To pay her way through medical school, she works eight-hour shifts at a sandwich shop in Washington, D.C., between semesters. In 1996 the minimum-wage raise would increase her earnings by 15 cents an hour. Does she turn her nose up at such a small raise? Not at all. "Fifteen cents might not sound like much, but you know what? Even after taxes that's enough to buy me at least one extra textbook at college."

Barnes works for a large chain of sandwich shops, but across town Karen Audia Shannon runs her own restaurant. She worries that an increase in the minimum wage would have a ripple effect, forcing her to increase wages to her lowest-paid employees, even though they earn slightly more than the minimum now. Said Shannon, "It would put my business in serious jeopardy, so much so that I almost feel I'd be forced to close. I would be put in a position where operating as a profitable restaurant would no longer be a possibility." If the restaurant closed, she and her 26 employees would be out of a job.

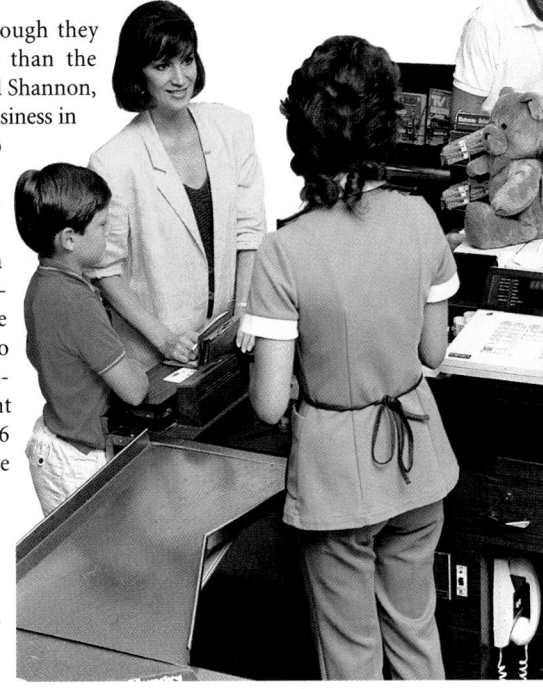

The majority of minimum-wage workers are adults. Half of all people making a minimum wage are also women.

Teaching Resources

Reproducible Lesson Plan found in the Unit 11 folder, p. 21, provides a summary of the Chapter 38 lesson plan content.

Alternate Lesson Plan: Learning Styles found in the Alternate Lesson Plans folder, p. 183, is designed to help students, especially auditory and visual learners, understand the history of government involvement in labor issues and explain the debate over the minimum wage by having students teach parts of the chapter.

Guided Reading and Review found in the Unit 11 folder, p. 22, provides a structure for reading and mastering the key concepts and reviewing the key terms for Chapter 38. (Guided Practice)

Spanish Resources provides key terms and key concepts for Chapter 38 in Spanish.

1. FOCUS

Connecting to the Big Idea

See page 982B. Explain to students that many people in the 1990s were questioning the proper role of government in the economy. One part of that debate was the minimum wage, which Congress sets by law. Advocates succeeded in raising the minimum wage in the summer of 1996, but questions remained. What factors make changes in the minimum wage necessary?

Objectives

- Understand the current situation for minimum-wage workers.
- Trace the historic development of government regulations and standards protecting workers.
- Identify the arguments offered by those for and against a higher minimum-wage standard.

Bellringer

Ask students what kinds of jobs are available to them and others their age. What do they think is a fair hourly wage?

Reading Strategy

Problem Solving Ask students, "What would you do if you worked full time but still did not earn enough to live on? Is it strictly your problem, or should the government help?" Then ask them to look for answers to those questions as they read.

During the progressive era, reformers tried to make factories less dangerous and working conditions in them better. The photograph shown here is of a factory from that period.

How Many Americans Work for Minimum Wage?

In 1991 Congress set the minimum wage at $4.25 per hour for most jobs. (Those whose jobs are not covered by the law earn even less.) Out of 107 million workers in the United States, about 2.1 million earn minimum wage. Another 9.6 million earn between $4.25 and $5.15, the proposed target for a two-year minimum-wage increase. Who are these workers? What kinds of jobs do they have? Where do they live?

Minimum-Wage Worker: A Profile

When you think of someone making minimum wage, you probably picture a teenager flipping hamburgers at a fast-food restaurant. But as with most stereotypes, the reality is much more complex.

1. The majority of minimum-wage earners—63 percent—are adults, while the minority are teenagers.

2. Most workers at this level—62 percent—share a home with someone else who works, so the minimum wage is not the only paycheck.

3. The remaining 38 percent are the only source of income for their household.

4. Of these, 11 percent are the sole breadwinners in families with children.

5. Department of Labor statistics show that half of all minimum-wage earners are women.

Jobs paying minimum wage include retail sales in shops and malls, restaurant work, gardening, farm work, motel cleaning, dry cleaning, child care, and garment work. These jobs can be found all over the country. Some, however, are more concentrated in particular areas. They include farm work in California, garment work in the Northeast, San Francisco, and Los Angeles, and textile jobs in the Southeast. Overall, the South has the highest concentration of minimum-wage workers.

The idea of government legislation to protect workers began with the **progressives** in the late 1800s and early 1900s. The progressives, largely well-educated middle-class people, were appalled by the effects of rapid industrial growth. They saw corrupt politicians lining their own pockets, captains of industry amassing great wealth, and workers laboring long hours in unsafe conditions for low wages. To improve society, various progressive groups worked to end corruption in government. They also tried to limit the abuses of power by giant corporations. And they worked to improve the living and working conditions of the poor.

Progressives and State Government

Instead of counting on public opinion or private charity to bring about social reform, the progressives looked to government to solve problems. They believed government had to increase its responsibility for the well-being of its citizens. To protect workers, progressives pushed for state laws regulating workplace conditions, maximum hours, and minimum wages. They met with stiff resistance, however. At that time, such laws were considered restrictions on personal liberties. In 1905, for example, the Supreme Court overturned a New York law setting a maximum ten-hour workday for bakers. Wrote Supreme Court Justice Peckham, "[Statutes] limiting the hours in which grown and intelligent men may labor to earn their living, are mere meddlesome interferences with the rights of the individual."

It took a terrible tragedy to galvanize public demand for more legislation to protect workers. On March 25, 1911, fire swept through the **Triangle Shirtwaist Factory** in New York City. Locked doors and an inadequate fire escape system trapped many young women workers. More than 140 were killed. Some plunged to their death from the eighth, ninth, and tenth floors. As a result, the New York state legislature formed the Factory Inspection Commission. The Commission recommended legislation on factory safety, workman's compensation, protection for women and children in industry, and minimum wages. The commission's work led to the adoption of a new Industrial Code in New York. This code became a model for legislation in other states.

Shall There Be Another ?

FIRE PROOF BUILDING HORROR! 141 LIVES SACRIFICED.

BROOKLYN EAGLE

EXIT

CLEVELAND PLAIN DEALER

The fire at the Triangle Shirtwaist Factory in New York City brought national attention to the issue of workplace safety and workers' rights.

First Minimum-Wage Law

Progressives like **Frances Perkins,** who had worked to set up the Factory Inspection Commission, believed the minimum wage was essential. In 1912 Massachusetts became the first state to pass a minimum-wage law. That year Theodore Roosevelt made the minimum wage a part of his Progressive Party platform, and in 1913 eight additional states passed minimum-wage laws.

When the United States entered World War I, the federal government took on a larger role. It regulated wages, hours, and working conditions under the War Labor Policies Board to ensure defense production. After the war, however, the military need for regulation ended, and public interest in workers' conditions dropped off.

Depression and New Deal

⭐ When the glamour of the Roaring Twenties gave way to the grim realities of the Great Depression, there was renewed interest in protection for workers. As more and more people lost their jobs, those still employed often saw their wages drop. Between 1928 and 1932, for example, the average weekly earnings for factory workers dropped from $27.80 to $17.05.

When he took office in 1933, President **Franklin D. Roosevelt** made good on his campaign promise of a **New Deal** for Americans. He offered programs to provide relief, create jobs, and stimulate the economy. He also appointed Frances Perkins to be secretary of labor, the first woman to hold a cabinet post. Perkins, who had fought tirelessly for worker protection in New York, continued her crusade in Washington.

The New Deal's first attempt to set minimum wages and shorter

Enrichment

Ask students to use the library's periodicals indexes to find stories about people hurt by trends in today's economy. They should choose one example and write a short summary report about the human impact on people's economic lives.

Caption Answer to ...

Using Historical Evidence

Laws and guarantees include the five-day week, shorter hours, the right to organize, the prohibition of child labor, the right to bargain collectively, and Social Security.

Alternative Assessment

Monitoring Progress

Check with students to see whether they have
- Assigned roles within the team for the panel discussion.
- Begun their research.

Explain that projects will be evaluated according to the following guidelines.
- **Unacceptable** Projects are not attempted or do not address the topic.
- **Limited/Acceptable** Projects show a limited exploration of the issue.
- **Extensive/Commendable** Projects use outside research and present information in a well-organized and interesting way.
- **Extraordinary/Outstanding** Projects are based on extensive research and display thoughtful interpretation as well as original thought and creativity.

Using Historical Evidence Many of the labor laws that we have become accustomed to in the late 1990s were either enacted or proposed during FDR's New Deal. *How many familiar workplace laws and guarantees can you identify in this painting?*

The Works Progress Administration (WPA) was a New Deal agency set up in 1935. It lasted for eight years and provided work for more than eight million Americans.

hours was part of the National Industrial Recovery Act of 1933. When the Supreme Court declared it unconstitutional, workers renewed their demands for protection. With Perkins's help, FDR sent the Fair Labor Standards bill to Congress in 1937. He said, "A self-supporting and self-respecting democracy can plead no justification for the existence of child labor, no economic reason for chiseling workers' wages or stretching workers' hours."

Congress passed the Fair Labor Standards Act the next year. It banned child labor and set the minimum wage at 25¢ per hour, increasing to 40¢ per hour over seven years. The maximum work week was set at 44 hours, to drop to 40 hours in the next three years. When the law took effect in 1938, it immediately helped about 300,000 workers earning less than 25¢ an hour and 1,384,000 others working more than 44 hours a week. The next year, when the minimum wage went up to 30¢ and maximum hours went down to 42, three million more workers benefited. ✪

Recent Developments

Since 1938 the minimum wage has become part of American working life. Following the New Deal came Harry Truman's Fair Deal, during which Congress raised the minimum wage to 75¢ an hour. Six years later it rose to $1 an hour, and another six years took it to $1.25. It has inched upward since then until it reached $4.25 in 1991. Congress debated raising the minimum wage in the election year of 1996 and finally passed it in the Senate, voting 74-24.

▶ RESOURCE DIRECTORY

Using the Internet Provides additional lesson activities using the resources of the World Wide Web and the Internet.

Teaching Resources

✪ **Debating the Future** The Debate on Minimum Wage, found in the Unit 11 folder, pp. 23–24, allows students to use two opposing viewpoints to begin a debate on the issues involved in the minimum-wage controversy.

J ill Mattioli could no longer afford an apartment in Telluride, Colorado. She had to move to the woods outside of town. "If I wait [tables] and serve these people," she says, "I should be able to live here and have a decent standard of living." But to do so would involve raising the minimum wage. That is something Atlanta radio talk show host Sean Hannity opposes. "How much more can you pay someone who flips burgers for a living? Are you willing to pay more for a hamburger?" he argues.

A national poll taken by the *Los Angeles Times* in 1996 showed that more than three-fourths of Americans favored increasing the minimum wage. Moreover, more than half of the people surveyed in every Gallup poll taken on this topic since 1945 supported it. Yet despite public opinion and Congressional action, debate continues to swirl around the minimum-wage issue.

In Favor of Raising the Minimum Wage

In 1965, chief executive officers of 30 big corporations earned 44 times as much as the average worker. By 1995, they were earning 212 times more. Proponents of increasing the minimum wage point to the vast gap between the rich and poor in America to argue their case. "It's a moral issue," says Representative John Lewis of Georgia. "Raising the minimum wage is the right thing to do."

It is the right thing, argue those in favor, because in 1996 a minimum-wage earner working full time earned $8,500. If that worker had three dependents, his or her earnings fell far below the federal poverty

line of $15,600. Said Philadelphian John Trendler of the $4.25 minimum wage,

I don't know of anyone trying to support a family who can get by on that.

Getting by at that level requires food stamps and even welfare. Inflation is one reason it's so hard to support a family on a minimum wage.

Reduced buying power means minimum-wage earners must skimp on everything. That skimping, in turn, has far-reaching consequences for society as a whole. For example, an uninsured driver who gets into an accident forces someone else to pay and drives up everyone else's premiums. Pregnant women who do not get adequate medical care are more at risk for having babies with birth defects. Caring for these children drives up medical costs.

Those who support a rise in the minimum wage say that most families cannot support themselves on a low minimum wage. The burden would fall on public assistance programs and the consequences would be far-reaching.

Opposed to Raising the Minimum Wage

Restaurant owner Robert Bobbitt, Sr., of Canton, Ohio, argues that wages are not a matter of "employer whim." Mr. Bobbitt worked a second job at night to get enough training to qualify for ownership of a McDonald's franchise. Now he owns four McDonald's. He opposes a wage increase. "Before, I would have thought of the minimum wage as a social issue. Then you start working for yourself, and all the risk and responsibilities are on you. Raising the minimum wage will take money out of the entrepreneur's [business owner's] pocket," Bobbitt claims. In other words, the level of wages can make or break a small business.

Opponents of an increase say holding the minimum wage steady is also important to consumers. Typically, a producer of goods or services passes along any increase in costs to

In Depth

Biography

One of the most influential creators of the New Deal's protections for workers was Secretary of Labor Frances Perkins (1882–1965), the first woman to hold a Cabinet post. An eyewitness to the Triangle Shirtwaist Factory tragedy, she began to work for legislation that would bring safer workplaces, shorter hours, and higher wages. She was a member of President Franklin D. Roosevelt's Cabinet from 1933 to 1945. Perkins was one of the writers of the original Social Security Act.

Chapter 38 Review
Answers (page 1005)

1. progressives, see p. 1000.

2. New Deal, see p. 1001.

3. work ethic, see p. 1004.

4. Frances Perkins, see p. 1001.

5. Franklin D. Roosevelt, see p. 1001.

6. Triangle Shirtwaist Factory, see p. 1001.

7. Timelines should include New Deal legislation and later adjustments to the minimum wage.

8. Answers will vary, but should show an understanding of minimum-wage issues. Possible answers may include: (top left blank web)—Minimum wage leaves workers below poverty level; (middle left blank web)—At minimum wage, workers need federal support; (bottom blank web)—Three out of four Americans support raising the minimum wage; (right side blank web): Raising the minimum wage may stifle entrepreneurs

---

In Depth

Interdisciplinary

Many writers helped raise the public's perceptions of the poverty and unsafe conditions endured by many workers. Upton Sinclair, a leading progressive, exposed the horrors of the meat-packing industry in his novel *The Jungle* (1906), while "muckraking" investigative journalists such as Ida M. Tarbell and Lincoln Steffens urged government action. During the Depression, books like *The Grapes of Wrath* (1939) by John Steinbeck and *Let Us Now Praise Famous Men* by James Agee with photographer Walker Evans, made people's hardships vividly real.

Robert Bobbitt, Sr., of Canton, Ohio, is a restaurant owner. He, like many small-business owners, fears that a rise in the minimum wage cannot be absorbed by a small business like his. He thinks the rise will result in worker layoffs.

customers. "Businesses simply don't absorb increased wage costs," according to presidential adviser Rob Shapiro. "They pass them on in the form of higher prices, which are regressive [hardest on the poor] because they're borne equally by all." Higher prices hurt those least able to pay. They can also trigger inflation.

Consumers aren't the only ones who will suffer from raising the minimum wage, opponents say. Workers on the lowest rungs of the economic ladder will be hurt, too. When employers must raise the minimum wage, they often have to cut employee hours or drop employees from the payroll. Like Robert Bobbitt of Ohio, Maryland restaurant owner Chris Gallant says,

These people need their jobs. Congress would only be hurting us, and our employees, if they raised the minimum wage.

So what is the value of the minimum wage? The laws of supply and demand in the marketplace should determine wages, not the government, according to these opponents of the minimum wage.

The Debate Continues

The majority of the American people favor increasing the minimum wage. Yet the debate among politicians over the minimum wage is intense because it pits two deeply held American values against each other. Americans hold fast to their belief in the **work ethic**—the idea that hard work will produce a decent life. The American dream, after all, is based on the notion that anyone who tries hard enough can achieve a comfortable standard of living.

On the other hand, Americans also believe in free enterprise. Government regulation that restricts free enterprise interferes with the workings of the marketplace and will ultimately hurt the economy. The challenge to Americans, then, is to find a way to reconcile these two beliefs in an era when government regulation is mistrusted but poverty is increasing.

▶ **RESOURCE DIRECTORY**

Teaching Resources

📄 **Chapter Test** Forms A and B are found in the Unit 11 folder, pp. 27–28.

📄 **Answer Keys** found in the Unit 11 folder, pp. 65-72, provide answers to all student activities.

📄 **Spanish Resources** provides Key Terms Quiz with Answer Key in Spanish.

Chapter Review

DEFINE AND IDENTIFY

Key Terms
1. progressives
2. New Deal
3. work ethic

People
4. Frances Perkins
5. Franklin D. Roosevelt

Places
6. Triangle Shirtwaist Factory

MAKING CONNECTIONS

Create a Timeline

7. To set the issues of this chapter in context, construct a timeline that includes major events and legislation in twentieth-century United States history related to worker protection and the minimum wage, beginning with the Triangle Shirtwaist Factory fire. You can use your textbook as a reference.

Use a Graphic Organizer

8. Review the arguments in the Debating the Future section of the chapter. Fill in the blank webs in the graphic organizer below that shows the connections among employers, wage earners, and the government. You can copy the web on a separate sheet of paper.

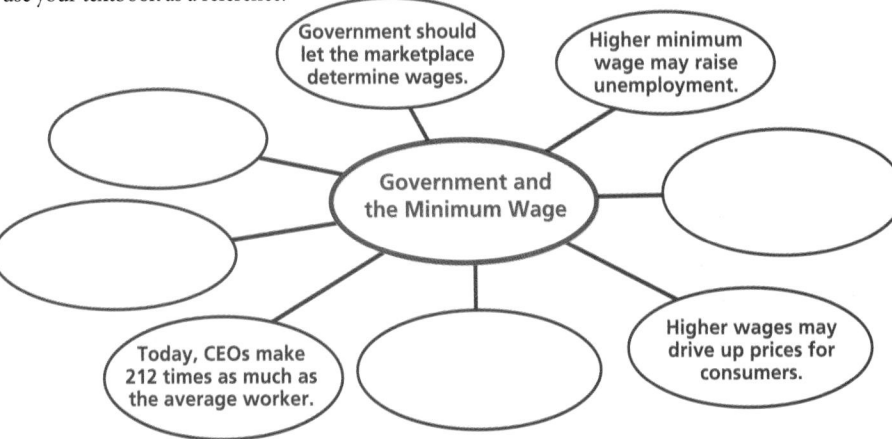

Government should let the marketplace determine wages.

Higher minimum wage may raise unemployment.

Government and the Minimum Wage

Today, CEOs make 212 times as much as the average worker.

Higher wages may drive up prices for consumers.

ACTIVITIES

For Your Portfolio

9. Review the issues of the debate about the minimum wage in the Debating the Future section of the chapter. How do they affect you personally and the country as a whole? Choose a way to express your opinion. Draw a cartoon, write a letter to a member of Congress, or construct a poster. When you have chosen a presentation that is acceptable to your teacher, put it in an appropriate format.

 ►►► **USING THE INTERNET**

Access Prentice Hall's site at: **http://www.phschool.com** for related links on United States history.

10. Go to the Economic Policy Institute's web site at http://epinet.org/ and access links to find information on the workplace in the United States today. Write a report on the connections between wages, corporate responsibility, and living standards.

Media and Technology

Our Times Multimedia Encyclopedia of the 20th Century CD-ROM Will help students of all abilities to link the past to the present. Students can access the timeline to learn about the first hundred days of President Franklin D. Roosevelt's first administration in 1933, which set in motion many of the entitlement programs now being scrutinized.

 Decision America Will help motivate students to analyze and understand contemporary issues in American society. See Issue 12, "Is Politics for Professionals Only? The Life of a State Representative" (disc 2, side 2; tape 4; approx. 8 min.).

 Computer Test Bank

RESOURCE PRO

Teaching Resources on CD-ROM contains all instructional and enrichment material for Chapter 38. Includes all quizzes and tests. You can print directly from the CD-ROM.

---

9. Student presentations should show creativity and a thoughtful approach to the issue.

10. Student presentations should be clear and to the point, as required in the assignment.

For more guidance on scoring, see the Alternative Assessment Handbook in the Resource Directory on page 982.

Reteach

Ask students to write one or two sentences on each of these topics: who earns the minimum wage; problems with trying to live on the minimum wage; problems involved in raising the minimum wage.

Alternative Assessment

Final Evaluation

Use the following guidelines to evaluate student projects:

● **Evidence of thoughtfulness** Did students show an understanding of the issue and its impact on different people?

● **Evidence of outside research** To what extent did students use outside research and interviews?

● **Communication style** Do projects convey their purpose in a clear, appealing way? Have students brought insight to their roles?

4. CLOSE

Reinforcing the Big Idea

The economy is an ongoing concern among Americans. Raising the minimum wage is part of that concern, but it still remains controversial.

Entitlements: Rethinking
Government Guarantees

1. FOCUS

Connecting to the Big Idea

See page 982B. Explain to students that some social welfare programs have been in effect since the New Deal of the 1930s, while others were started as part of the Great Society in the 1960s. What factors forced a reappraisal of those programs in the 1990s? What criticisms were due to changes in the programs themselves?

Objectives

● Define the major social welfare programs known as "entitlements."
● Understand the growth of social welfare programs beginning with the New Deal.
● Identify the different plans offered for changing or eliminating welfare programs.

Bellringer

Ask students for their own suggestions about ways to help people who live in poverty. What government or private programs do they know about? What does "promote the general welfare" mean to them?

Reading Strategy

Question Writing Ask students to read the chapter section headings and subheadings and write *how*, *what*, *when*, and *why* questions about each one. As they read, they should look for answers to those questions.

Entitlements: Rethinking Government Guarantees

INTRODUCING THE THEME

Increasing numbers of people in the 1990s are receiving assistance in the form of cash benefits, food stamps, and medical care. This puts a strain on the federal budget and increases the national debt.

Debate How do we balance the needs of the poor and the elderly against the needs of the budget, both for the present and the future?

Key Terms, People, Places
entitlements, AFDC, Medicare, federal deficit, national debt, block grants; Michael Harrington

VIEWING THE PRESENT

When she was in the tenth grade in Milwaukee, Keyola Lackey dropped out of school because she was pregnant. Only a year after her baby was born, she had another child. Without a husband and without job skills, Keyola got by on welfare, or public assistance. She fit the welfare stereotype almost exactly: an unwed teenage mother with several kids and no way to support them.

When 75-year-old J. S. Russell learned that he needed heart surgery, his family worried a lot about how to pay for it. The costs of a pacemaker, the operation itself, and a week of care at Stanford University Hospital seemed enormous. As it turned out, the family had to pay much less than they feared. Medicare, the federal health insurance program for elderly and disabled Americans, paid for almost everything except Mr. Russell's medications.

What Are Entitlements?

Welfare and Medicare are two examples of federal programs called **entitlements**. Entitlements are social welfare programs that people are "entitled to" by being at a certain income level or age. The federal government guarantees assistance for all those who qualify. As the number of people who qualify increases, so do

Aid to Families with Dependent Children (AFDC) costs the federal and state governments about $50 billion a year. This includes the cost of food stamps, Medicaid, social services, and housing.

▶ RESOURCE DIRECTORY

Teaching Resources

Reproducible Lesson Plan found in the Unit 11 folder, p. 30, covers the main ideas in this section as well as the key terms.

Alternate Lesson Plan: Cooperative Learning found in the Alternate Lesson Plans folder, p 184, helps groups of students summarize important aspects of the entitlements issue by writing headlines and brief articles.

Guided Reading and Review found in the Unit 11 folder, p. 31, provides a structure for reading and mastering the key concepts and reviewing the key terms for Chapter 39. (Guided Practice)

Spanish Resources provides key terms and key concepts for Chapter 39 in Spanish.

Almost all Americans aged sixty-five and over are insured by Medicare.

the costs. As a result, managing costs has become a major concern.

In the 1990s, politicians were quick to attack the idea of welfare but reluctant to question the need for Medicare. A 1995 *TIME*/CNN poll reflects this split. Some 65 percent of those surveyed favored cutting welfare benefits, while 81 percent opposed cuts in Medicare. Yet despite these differences in public opinion, most Americans agree that both programs need to be reformed. There is little agreement, however, on how to do it.

What Is AFDC?

Welfare is a broad term that covers many forms of public assistance. Yet when most people hear "welfare," they think of Aid to Families with Dependent Children (**AFDC**), the largest and best-known program. Federal outlays to AFDC families make up roughly 4 percent of the national budget. Medicaid, which provides health care for those on AFDC and others receiving public assistance, accounts for about 6 percent of the budget.

The federal government sets the guidelines for who can receive AFDC and Medicaid and how money is distributed. Slightly more than half of the costs of AFDC are paid for by the federal government. The rest is paid by the states. The federal government also pays at least half of each state's Medicaid expenses.

Who Gets AFDC?

In 1996, roughly 12.8 million people received AFDC, about two-thirds of them children. Approximately one in seven American children is on AFDC, and of these AFDC children, nearly 60 percent are African American or Hispanic. While some people are able to leave welfare after a short time, many others become dependent on it. According to Ladonna Pavetti of the Urban Institute, about 63 percent of those receiving welfare at any given time will eventually spend nine years or more on public assistance.

What Is Medicare?

Medicare provides health insurance for Americans over 65—about 33 million people in 1995. Medicare pays for both hospital care and doctors' visits, but it does so in different ways. Money for Part A of Medicare, which covers hospital expenses, comes from a payroll tax paid for by workers and employers. About one fourth of the money for Part B, which covers doctors' visits, comes from premiums paid by Medicare recipients themselves. The other three-fourths comes from Congressional outlays. In 1995, government Medicare payments accounted for 11 percent of the federal budget.

Discuss

Discuss with students the two main entitlement programs—AFDC and Medicare—and the different missions and aims of each program. What problems does each face? Discuss why these programs have become such major budget issues.

Have students list some of the proposals made for changing welfare and Medicare. Discuss what arguments can be made for and against the various proposals.

Caption Answer to ...

 Interpreting Charts

Since the number of people on AFDC rose sharply in the 1970s and remained high throughout the 1980s and early 1990s, the public may have begun to assume that once people begin to receive AFDC, they will not want to stop on their own.

In Depth

Global Connections

The United States has been a latecomer in providing government social welfare programs, particularly medical care. In Europe, a large, well-unionized urban working class won benefits in the late 1800s and early 1900s. Germany under Bismarck gave workers health insurance in 1883 and old age benefits and workmen's compensation a few years later. France, Britain, and Sweden enacted old-age pensions in the early 1900s. In 1946, Britain's postwar Labour government began the National Health Service, providing universal medical care regardless of ability to pay.

Millions of People on AFDC, 1940–1995

Average number of people receiving Aid to Families with Dependent Children, in millions, for selected years.

Source: Department of Health and Human Services, Administration for Children and Families/Social Security Administration

Interpreting Charts
The number of people receiving AFDC has grown rapidly in recent years. *What connection is there between these figures and the public's view of welfare?*

Medicare faces several problems. The hospital insurance fund, which had a surplus in the mid-1990s, is expected to run out of money by 2001 because of soaring costs. The main reason for the rising costs of medical care is the expense of new technology.

Who Gets Medicare?

The number of people eligible for Medicare is growing steadily. By 2010, when baby boomers start to retire, the number of Americans over 65 will be about 40 million. Adding to the problem is the fact that the fastest-growing population group is also the group needing the most medical care. This is the group over age 85.

Unlike welfare, eligibility for Medicare does not depend on income but on age. In 1995, the ratio of employed people paying Medicare taxes to Medicare recipients was four to one. By the middle of next century that ratio is predicted to be two to one.

Why Rethink Entitlements?

Each year since 1970 the United States has spent more money than it has taken in through taxes, thus creating a **federal deficit**. Each year's deficit gets added to the **national debt**—all the money that the federal government owes. By mid-1996, the national debt had reached around $5 trillion.

Like anyone who borrows money, the federal government must pay interest on this debt. For the fiscal year ending in September 1995, that interest totaled more than $332 billion—about 15 percent of the federal budget.

Another way to understand these numbers would be to consider that a family might spend 15 percent of its annual income on interest for a mortgage. However, the family would get a home in return. The American taxpayer, on the other hand, receives nothing substantial for the approximately $800 that he or she paid just for interest on the 1995 debt. Taxpayer frustration,

therefore, is high, making tax hikes unacceptable. Shrinking the deficit would slow down our mounting debt, but to do so requires bringing federal spending in line with federal revenues. Entitlements have, therefore, become a logical target for budget cuts.

REVIEWING THE PAST

T o most people the "American Dream" is the belief that through hard work and perseverance, anyone can become successful in America. For most of America's history, people did not believe it was the government's responsibility to help the poor or the needy.

However, by the end of the 19th century, some said it had become much more difficult for people to make it on their own. As working and living conditions in the growing cities became harsh, progressives worked for government regulation of some aspects of private industry. Passage of

---

 RESOURCE DIRECTORY

Teaching Resources

Nystrom *Our Country* Atlas Historical atlas with illustrated timeline helps students make connections between geography and history. See p. 34.

---

these laws signaled a shift in public opinion. It paved the way for greater government involvement in solving social problems.

FDR's New Deal

The economic crisis of the Great Depression motivated President Franklin D. Roosevelt to set up a number of social welfare programs in the United States. Under his New Deal, work-relief projects like the Works Progress Administration provided billions of dollars for jobs for the poor and kept many families from starving. The Social Security Act provided retirement pensions for workers over 65 and unemployment benefits for those who lost their jobs. Social Security would be funded by deductions from workers' paychecks and contributions from employers. Added to the original Social Security Act was a section to provide Aid to Dependent Children (ADC)—direct payments to children whose fathers had died or deserted the family. Money for ADC was to come from both the federal government and the

The Social Security Act of 1935 provided direct payments to children whose fathers had died or deserted the family. The photograph on the left of a family during the Depression was taken by Dorothea Lange in 1936. A social security card from the period is shown above.

Media and Technology

Transparencies Cause-and-Effect Charts, F-9, and Political Cartoons, K-7

Analyze

On the chalkboard, list the major entitlement programs—AFDC, Medicare, Social Security—and the populations each one serves. Have students analyze the political impact and influence of each. Students should notice that a program often affects people other than the direct recipients—for example, the families of elderly people who might be bankrupted by high medical costs.

Activity

Interdisciplinary

Divide the class into two groups. Each group will plan a 30-minute roundtable discussion on one of the two major programs discussed in the chapter: Medicare and AFDC. To prepare for the panel, students should prepare to represent different points of view: advocates for the elderly or the poor, people affected by the programs, economists, supporters of moderate reform, those who want to abolish the programs altogether. Allow class time on successive days for each group to present its discussion. **LEP**

In Depth

Then and Now

Before the Civil War, the local "poorhouse" was the only recourse for America's poor. In the late 1800s and early 1900s, reformers and private charities tried to help the urban poor with day nurseries, milk stations, libraries, and classes to teach English and other skills. Neighbors helped, too. One woman remembered: ". . . it's the women that got together, collected food. When they saw a woman in the butcher shop or the grocery not buying enough and they knew how many children she had, my mother would go to a few neighbors, collect money and bring food, and put it under the door and walk away."

Alternative Assessment

Mid-Point Monitoring

Check with students to see whether they have

● Decided which program to study.

● Chosen a format.

● Made appointments for interviews or photographs.

● Started to collect information.

Explain that projects will be evaluated according to the following guidelines.

● **Unacceptable** Projects are not attempted or do not address the issue.

● **Limited/Acceptable** Projects show evidence of some research and a limited exploration of the issue.

● **Extensive/Commendable** Projects are based on outside research and present information in a well-organized and interesting way.

● **Extraordinary/Outstanding** Projects are based on extensive research and display thoughtful interpretation as well as original thought and creativity.

states, with the federal government handling a larger share.

ADC became Aid to Families with Dependent Children (AFDC) in 1950. In that year, Congress broadened its coverage to include mothers in its benefits. During the prosperous 1950s AFDC received little attention. But unknown to most Americans, pockets of poverty existed in the midst of national prosperity—in Appalachia, in the Deep South, and in the big cities of the Northeast and Midwest. **Michael Harrington** brought these problems to light in his widely read 1962 book, *The Other America*. In response, President Kennedy asked Congress for laws to eliminate poverty. One direct result was the food stamp program to help feed the poor. ✪

Johnson's Great Society

After Kennedy's death, President Lyndon Johnson enlarged JFK's ideas into his own vision of "The Great Society." To create it, he declared "an unconditional war on poverty in America." In 1964 and 1965 Congress passed laws that raised AFDC payments and broadened eligibility, increased Social Security benefits, set up Medicare and Medicaid, and established job training and education programs

This comic book cover shows the energy with which President Johnson rallied Congress and the country behind his ambitious social programs.

The food stamp program in the United States came about in part because of the publication of *The Other America*. Shown here is the original cover of the 1962 book.

like Head Start. Johnson, who had begun his political career as an ardent New Dealer, believed that the federal government could and should solve the problems of poverty in America.

During the Johnson administration, federal welfare spending increased each year. It continued to grow during the Nixon, Ford, and Carter administrations as well. One reason for the increase was the growing number of people on welfare. Yet spending more money on more people did not create a Great Society. It did, however, generate a major backlash against federal anti-poverty programs.

Reagan's Revolution

Ronald Reagan was elected President in 1980, declaring that "government is not the solution to our problem. Government is the problem." Reagan wanted to reduce the size of government in most areas. Social welfare programs were a prime target. Welfare payments

▶ RESOURCE DIRECTORY

Teaching Resources

 Literature Activity Responsibility, Not Entitlement, found in the Unit 11 folder, pp. 34–35, is an excerpt from Robert J. Samuelson's book, *The Good Life and Its Discontents*. In the excerpt, Samuelson suggests that more responsibility, not more entitlement, will help Americans create a better society.

SOURCE READINGS

The Source Readings for Unit 11, found on pp. 1084–1087, provide students with links to America's future through literature.

Using the Internet Provides additional lesson activities using the resources of the World Wide Web and the Internet.

robbed people of their dignity and of their drive to work, Reagan believed. Promising to maintain a "safety net" for the neediest, he made dramatic cuts in social welfare budgets. For example, during the Reagan years, funding for food stamps dropped 18.8 percent, and funding for AFDC decreased 17.7 percent. About 600,000 people found themselves excluded from Medicaid.

After Ronald Reagan

George Bush, elected President in 1988, carried on Reagan's legacy and continued to cut spending for social programs. Although Bush was defeated in 1992, the conservative desire to spend less on social programs gained momentum. Democrat Bill Clinton promised to "end welfare as we have known it" in his campaign for the Presidency in 1992. When conservative Republicans won control of Congress in 1994, their "Contract With America" agenda called for sweeping welfare reforms.

The Clinton Initiative

In 1996, President Clinton signed the Welfare Reform bill, which made the most sweeping changes to the original AFDC guarantees made in 1935. Passage of the bill placed the issue of entitlements squarely in front of all Americans. 🔲

DEBATING THE FUTURE

Andrew Cuomo, assistant secretary of housing and urban development in the Clinton administration, says that "Nobody likes welfare. Nobody thinks it works." There is similar agreement on the need to revamp Medicare. According to Frank Luntz, a Republican pollster, "When the public realizes and personalizes the financial situation of Medicare,

they end up backing significant reform." Yet that is about as far as agreement goes. Opinions differ widely on what shape the needed reforms should take.

In Favor of Deep Cuts

Although welfare makes up a small part of the federal budget, it provokes sharp attacks. Many people see welfare as a threat to the American belief in individual effort. They believe welfare recipients would rather take a handout than work. They see people getting something for nothing while the rest of America works hard and pays high taxes.

The debate over Medicare has been heated. President Clinton's popularity increased when he insisted on not touching Medicare as a way of balancing the federal budget.

HEALTH CARE
THAT'S ALWAYS THERE.
THE NATIONAL HEALTH CARE CAMPAIGN

Congress and Entitlements

Objective Use the Internet to track Congressional votes and debates on entitlements.

Have students follow these instructions:
1. Enter the following URL: **http://www.epolitics.com/**

2. Click the link "the Library of Congress" under Member Voting Records.

3. Choose one of your Senators or your Representative. Then choose an entitlement program to research. Follow the instructions to enter your search.

4. Use links to research the voting record and positions of your Senator or Representative on the entitlement program you chose.

5. Write a brief summary of your Senator or Representative's position on the issue.

6. Draft a letter to your Senator or Representative about whether you agree or disagree with specific votes cast and debates held in Congress.

Media and Technology

🎞 📼 *Decision America* Will help motivate students to analyze and understand contemporary issues in American society. See Issue 5, "How Are We Represented? A Typical Day for Two Members of Congress" (disc 1 side 2; tape 2; approx. 11 min.).

Tom Delay, Republican whip in the House of Representatives, sums up the argument:

*T*he current welfare system *undermines incentives to work, encourages expansion of the underclass, breaks up families, and promotes welfare as a way of life.*

Delay and others argue that sharply limiting the time people can receive assistance will get them out into the workforce. For teenage mothers, programs such as Wisconsin's Learnfare require young people to stay in school or lose their benefits. Keyola Lackey supports Learnfare because it made her return to school to prepare for a job. "The people who criticize it want the money free and do nothing for it. But nothing comes free," she says.

Welfare critics also suggest that Congress allocate a fixed amount of money for welfare each year, instead of funding open-ended entitlements. To promote efficiency, reformers of welfare want the states, not the federal government, to administer welfare programs. In 1996 Congress passed a bill changing welfare funding to lump sum amounts called **block grants**, to be administered by the states as they see fit.

⭐ Those who want to make stiff cuts in Medicare believe that it too suffers from inefficiency and overgenerosity. They point out that Medicare covers everyone, even those who could afford to pay for their own health care. Clyle Dwyer, retired truck driver in Fargo, North Dakota, reports that "Medicare is too generous. I know guys who have stuff done that they shouldn't because Medicare will pay for it."

To rein in the growth of Medicare, cost cutters like Speaker of the House Newt Gingrich advocate several measures. One is raising Part B premiums (see page 1007) for those with higher incomes. Others involve turning health care for senior citizens over to private insurers, either by encouraging them to use Health Maintenance Organizations (HMOs) or by establishing a voucher program to set up medical savings accounts. Gingrich believes the private sector can do a better job than the government. He predicts that the Health Care Financing Administration, which handles Medicare, "will wither on the vine

States pay part of the public-assistance bills. Now, as the political cartoon shows, the federal government is making the management of public-assistance programs a state responsibility as well.

In Depth

Biography

One advocate for strengthening Medicare was Donna Shalala (b. 1941), Secretary of Health and Human Services in the Clinton administration. In 1995, she wrote, "What we need is a powerful combination of government, science, public health, medicine, and personal responsibility." Before joining the Cabinet, Shalala was the first woman to head a Big Ten university: the University of Wisconsin. She had also worked for HUD in the Carter administration, with an emphasis on policies toward women. She held several high academic posts before returning to government in 1993.

 RESOURCE DIRECTORY

Teaching Resources

⭐ **Debating the Future: Simulation** The Debate on Entitlements, found in the Unit 11 folder, pp. 32–33, uses a simulated demonstration outside a welfare office to help students identify different points of view on the issue of government entitlements.

because we think people are voluntarily going to leave it."

In Favor of Moderate Cuts

Increasing poverty accounts for the growth in the welfare population far more than individual laziness. So say those who favor moderate welfare cuts. Rebecca Blank, a leading poverty economist, explains:

The welfare rolls are not increasing because of generous benefits or because single mothers are working less. They're working more.

They have to, because inflation decreased the value of food stamps and AFDC 26 percent between 1972 and 1992.

Those who favor moderate cuts also point out that most people who receive benefits want to work but cannot find jobs that pay a decent wage. Many lack job skills. According to Christopher Jencks, a professor at Northwestern University:

For a very large proportion of single mothers, it's impossible to find a job that pays as well as being on welfare.

Removing these women from the welfare rolls will send them into minimum-wage jobs, observers point out. There they will earn less. They will also lose Medicaid coverage for themselves and their children.

Deep welfare cuts would harm children the most, say the moderates, and block grants would remove the federal guarantee of protection for all. Since each state can administer its money as it chooses, there may be areas where people completely lose their safety net. Reverend Sam Myskens of Wichita, Kansas, gives this illustration: "If the wheat crop is bad one year or Boeing lays off 5,000 people, there will be more hungry children but no more money available to feed them."

Moreover, cutting back welfare will not amount to great savings, say the moderates. A better long-term solution would include child care and job training. While these programs would cost money, they would be investments in a better-educated workforce and healthier children.

Reform Challenges

Privatizing Medicare will not produce the desired savings in Medicare, argue some specialists. Studies have shown that private insurers are no more cost-effective than Medicare. Furthermore, shifting additional responsibilities for financing Medicare Part B (see page 1007) to senior citizens does nothing to stop pressures driving health-care inflation. Among those pressures is the soaring cost of new medical technology. Moreover, this scheme does not rescue Part A, the hospital insurance fund.

The Debate Continues

The need to reduce the federal deficit is very real. Clearly, entitlements are one area of spending that can be cut to help balance the budget. Like a household budget, the federal budget is more than a list of numbers—it is also a statement of priorities. The statement would have to consider what is most important to the household at the present time and how it will affect the household in the future. How America's leaders ultimately rethink and revise entitlements will reflect the nation's priorities for the future.

One of the challenges welfare reformers face is providing education and training for people on public assistance. Parents of young children require child care while they learn job skills that will pay enough to support the entire family.

Media and Technology

 ***Our Times Multimedia Encyclopedia of the 20th Century* CD-ROM** Will help students of all abilities to link the past to the present. Students can access the timeline, listen to and read about the history of entitlement programs in the United States.

In Depth

Interdisciplinary

A study of health care costs in Canada and Germany showed that operating costs there were 25 percent to 33 percent less than in the United States, mainly because fewer hospitals had expensive high-tech equipment or did certain highly specialized procedures. For every one million people, at least twice as many U.S. hospitals have units for open-heart surgery, organ transplants, and MRI's as do Canadian hospitals. Of Canada's 68 teaching hospitals, only 37 have open-heart surgery units.

10. Presentations should show creativity and a thoughtful approach to the issue.

11. Student presentations should be clear and to the point, as required in the assignment.

For more guidance on scoring, see the Alternative Assessment Handbook in the Resource Directory on page 982.

Reteach

Have students write down the terms "AFDC" and "Medicare." Ask them to write, first, a sentence explaining what each program does; and next, one or two sentences giving some of the criticisms made of each program.

Alternative Assessment

Final Evaluation

Use the following guidelines to evaluate student projects:

● **Evidence of thoughtfulness** Did students show an understanding of the issue and how to portray it?

● **Evidence of outside research** To what extent did students use appropriate outside research and interviews for their projects?

● **Communication style** Do projects convey their purpose in a clear, appealing way? Are different media used effectively?

4. CLOSE

Reinforcing the Big Idea

Questions about entitlement programs pose major dilemmas for the American public, as the costs of such programs soar and government budgets are tight, but the needs continue.

Chapter Review

DEFINE AND IDENTIFY

Key Terms
1. entitlements
2. AFDC

3. Medicare
4. federal deficit

5. national debt
6. block grants

People
7. Michael Harrington

MAKING CONNECTIONS

Create a Timeline
8. To set a background for the entitlements debate, construct a timeline that includes six to ten significant events and legislation related to social welfare programs from the New Deal to the present.

Use a Graphic Organizer
9. Review the arguments in the Debating the Future section of the chapter. The graphic organizer below shows arguments for making moderate cuts in entitlement spending. Use a separate sheet of paper to create a web that shows arguments for making deep cuts.

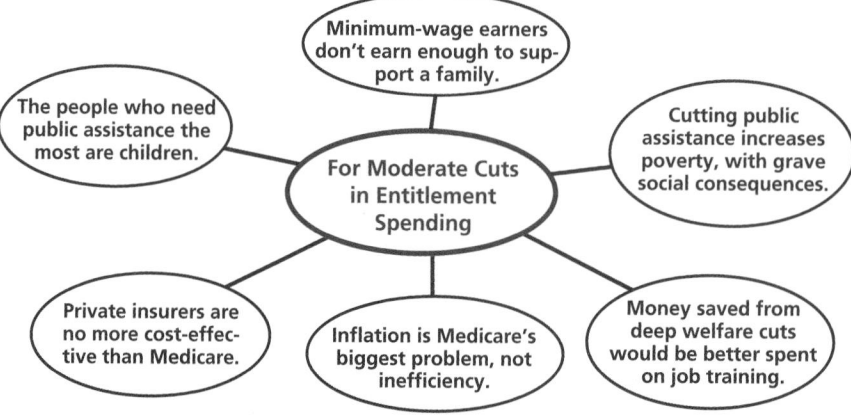

ACTIVITIES

For Your Portfolio
10. Think about the history of social welfare programs in the United States. What events or legislation do you think were the most important in creating the system of entitlements that exists today? Choose one or two of these landmarks and describe them in your own way. You may make a poster, an album of magazine or newspaper photographs, or choose another format acceptable to your teacher.

 ▶ ▶ ▶ USING THE INTERNET
Access Prentice Hall's site at: **http://www.phschool.com** for related links on United States history.

11. Go to Policy.com at http: // www.policy.com and click the hypertext link "Issues Forum." Using the information there, write a report explaining the debate over Social Security. Include references to at least three experts on Social Security.

 RESOURCE DIRECTORY

Teaching Resources

Chapter Test Forms A and B are found in the Unit 11 folder, pp. 36–37.

Answer Keys found in the Unit 11 folder, pp. 65–72, provide answers to all student activities.

Spanish Resources provides Key Terms Quiz with Answer Key in Spanish.

Media and Technology

Computer Test Bank

RESOURCE ⊙ PRO

Teaching Resources on CD-ROM contains all instructional and enrichment material for Chapter 39. Includes all quizzes and tests. You can print directly from the CD-ROM.

The United States in the Western Hemisphere

INTRODUCING THE THEME

When the North American Free Trade Agreement (NAFTA) took effect on January 1, 1994, the economy of the United States became more closely linked with the economies of Canada and Mexico. Since then, NAFTA has been a lightning rod for debate over free trade. For one thing, it may well be the model for a trade agreement proposed for 2005 that would include all of North and South America.

Debate How well has NAFTA worked? How good a model is it for our dealings with the other countries of the Americas?

Key Terms, People, Places

NAFTA, tariffs, trade deficit, trade surplus, Helms-Burton Act, Monroe Doctrine, Roosevelt Corollary, Good Neighbor Policy, maquiladoras; H. Ross Perot, Theodore Roosevelt, Franklin D. Roosevelt, Fidel Castro

Tall hats called shako caps were worn by American soldiers during the Mexican War.

VIEWING THE PRESENT

Nelson Silva used to operate a fork lift at a TV-assembly plant in Elmwood Park, New Jersey. When the factory shut down and moved to Tijuana, Mexico, in 1995, he lost his job. "I'm bitter that we lost these people, lost these jobs, not just at JVC but all over America," he says. "We invented the television in the United States, and they're going to take it completely out of the country."

Key Tronic Corporation used to manufacture computer keyboards in Spokane, Washington. It too moved to Mexico. Although Key Tronic had to lay off workers, chief financial officer Ronald F. Klawitter points out that the move turned out to be good for Spokane. Lower labor costs for his company meant lower prices for the keyboards. Lower prices, in turn, meant more sales, which increased the demand for keyboard components made in Spokane. A greater number of people in Washington ended up with jobs making parts that are then assembled in Mexico.

Workers in an assembly factory based in Mexico. Products that are assembled at plants such as these are made almost exclusively for markets in the United States.

Ross Perot, the independent candidate in the 1992 and 1996 presidential elections, opposed the North American Free Trade Agreement.

What Is NAFTA?

NAFTA (the North American Free Trade Agreement) was the reason for the relocation of both these factories. Their stories illustrate both sides of the argument for or against NAFTA.

The main purpose of NAFTA is to stimulate economic growth in Canada, the United States, and Mexico. To this end NAFTA removed **tariffs**—import taxes—and other barriers to trade, thereby creating a continent-wide free-trade zone. Without tariffs, companies can sell their goods more cheaply to a larger market. Since lower prices will bring higher sales, companies like JVC and Key Tronic moved their plants to Mexico, where labor costs less. They no longer have to pay tariffs if they want to sell such foreign-made goods in the United States.

Before 1994, when NAFTA took effect, opponents argued that it would mean an enormous loss of American jobs to Mexico. In 1992, **H. Ross Perot** described the potential disaster as a "giant sucking sound" of jobs heading south of the border. Supporters of NAFTA like Presidents Bush and Clinton countered that the increased demand for American goods would create more higher-skilled, higher-paying jobs in the United States, as well as more investment opportunities.

NAFTA and Canada

The United States' trade with Canada has been strong for a long time. President Kennedy summed up this relationship: "Geography made us neighbors. History made us friends. And economics made us partners." Even before NAFTA, Canada and the United States were each other's largest trading partner. In 1988, the two countries signed the Free Trade Agreement. Six years before NAFTA, this pact eliminated tariffs over a ten-year period. Since NAFTA took effect, both countries have greatly increased exports to each other. The United States, however, buys more than it sells to Canada, producing a **trade deficit**.

NAFTA and Mexico

The effect of trade with Mexico since NAFTA is more complicated. On the one hand, fewer jobs disappeared than had been predicted. Instead of the 6 million jobs that Perot claimed would be lost, the Labor Department reported in 1996

The North American Free Trade Agreement (NAFTA), 1994		
The Agreement	**The Result**	**The Controversies**
The United States, Canada, and Mexico will remove tariffs and most other mutual trade restrictions over the next 15 years.	The resulting free-trade zone will form a single market similar to, but much larger than, the European Community.	Despite NAFTA's "side agreements" and other provisions, concern remains over its potential effects on the environment and on the United States job market.

Interpreting Tables
This table provides an overview of the NAFTA agreement and its consequences. *As you read this chapter, look for examples of the controversies mentioned in the table. Did NAFTA create other controversies? If so, what were they?*

Opponents of NAFTA argued that many of the new jobs created in Mexico would pay low wages. They also argued that Mexican workers would take work that otherwise would be performed by Americans.

2. INSTRUCT

Discuss

Discuss with students the basic differences and disagreements between people who favor free trade and those who favor protective tariffs and other kinds of limits. Can they point to any common thread that links people who are pro-NAFTA or anti-NAFTA?

that 66,600 job losses were NAFTA-related. On the other hand, not as many new jobs were created as had been anticipated. Supporters of NAFTA had predicted that it would bring about 200,000 new jobs in its first year. That did not happen. While the number of people employed in the United States has risen steadily since NAFTA, it is impossible to say how many of the new jobs are directly a result of the free-trade agreement.

Mexican Debt Crisis

Overall, the two-way trade between the United States and Mexico rose about 30 percent between 1993 and 1995. Still, the balance of trade was not always in favor of the United States. During NAFTA's first year, 1994, exports from the United States to Mexico rose from $41.6 billion to $50.8 billion and also produced a **trade surplus**. This meant that the United States sold more than

it bought. During 1995, however, the United States' exports dropped to $46.3 billion, but imports soared, leaving a trade deficit.

This shift in balance of payments resulted from a drop in the value of the Mexican peso in December 1994. With that drop, a severe recession hit Mexico. Foreign investors became nervous. It did not help to have a financial crisis, an uprising for land reform, and a scandal involving Mexico's president, all at the same time.

The NAFTA Puzzle

These interlocking puzzle pieces illustrate the relationship between the three economies of the United States, Canada, and Mexico.

In Depth

Then and Now

Free trade was a controversial issue even in the first American government. George Washington's Secretary of the Treasury, Alexander Hamilton, favored tariffs on imports as a way both to encourage young American industries and to provide revenue for the government. In the early 1800s, protective tariffs as high as 40 percent were placed on products such as cotton, wool, and iron. Tariffs then became a heated issue between northern manufacturers and southern planters. Before the income tax was enacted in 1913, customs duties were the federal government's greatest source of income.

Analyze

Using the chalkboard, list some of the major milestones in the United States' diplomatic attitudes toward Latin America, from the Monroe Doctrine through "gunboat diplomacy" to today. Have students analyze how each step represented a changing or continuing policy.

Activity

Interdisciplinary

To deepen their understanding of the United States' partners in NAFTA, divide students into two groups to learn more about the cultures of Canada and Mexico. Within each group, some students should investigate these fields: the people (ethnic groups and background), landscape and geography, famous artists and writers, sports and popular entertainment, food, science and technology, holidays. They should prepare short oral reports on each of those aspects, including examples or illustrations. Allow class time for each group to deliver the report on its country.

Teddy Roosevelt called the 1898 Spanish-American War "a splendid little war." It marked the beginning of United States involvement in Latin America for the next century. Shown here are the African American soldiers of the Tenth United States Cavalry, who fought in Cuba.

United States Loan to Mexico

To promote stability, the United States loaned Mexico $12.5 billion. With this help, Mexico was able to start recovery. By mid-1996, it had paid back more than half of the bailout. This was ahead of schedule and much to the surprise of many Americans. Mexico also began making political reforms in 1996. Even so, the Mexican recession left many Americans wondering whether it was wise to be so closely tied economically to an unstable neighbor.

Balance Between Economics and Politics

NAFTA raises political as well as economic questions. While the agreement sets up a special economic relationship with the United States and its immediate neighbors, what impact does it have on political

relations with them? What happens, for example, when neighbors trade with a country to which the United States has restricted trade? In 1996 Congress passed the **Helms-Burton Act.** That act penalizes foreign companies that do business with Cuba. Canada, Mexico, and other nations of Latin America loudly objected to it. They claimed that it violated NAFTA and international law. They saw the Helms-Burton Act as an abuse of United States power and the

latest example of Uncle Sam's muscle-flexing in the Western Hemisphere.

REVIEWING THE PAST

The history of the United States' relations with Latin America shows how hard it is to separate economics and politics. In 1995 Deputy Secretary of State Strobe Talbott stated the gov-

This 1901 political cartoon suggests how the United States applied the Monroe Doctrine.

 RESOURCE DIRECTORY

Teaching Resources

⭐ 📄 **Literature Activity** The Banana Republics, found in the Unit 11 folder, pp. 43–44, describes the enormous political power of the United Fruit Company in Honduras.

📖 **Nystrom *Our Country* Atlas** Historical atlas with illustrated timeline helps students make connections between geography and history. See pp. 32–33.

ernment's two main goals in the Americas. He said, ". . . one is to support the growth of democratic institutions; the other is to advance prosperity through open markets and free trade." These objectives, democracy and trade, have shaped American foreign policy in the Western Hemisphere from the nation's earliest days. However, the ways the United States has chosen to pursue these goals have often made its neighbors wary of American power.

The Monroe Doctrine

In the early 1820s, independence movements rocked the American colonies of Spain and Portugal. When it looked as if several European monarchies were going to help these countries regain their former colonies, the United States issued the **Monroe Doctrine**. Remembering its own recent colonial status, the United States warned that "The American continents, by the free and independent condition which they have assumed and maintain, are henceforth not to be considered as subject for future colonization by any European powers."

Behind this hands-off message was the desire to promote trade. One enterprising American was Minor C. Keith, who built a railroad and banana plantations in Costa Rica in the late 1800s. Keith and his partners made their business, the United Fruit Company, the largest employer in Central America. With its vast economic power, United Fruit also had enormous political power. Its influence was especially strong in Costa Rica, Guatemala, and Honduras—the so-called "banana republics." ✪

In most of these countries a small number of families controlled the wealth, leaving the rest of the population in poverty. Although able to win their independence, the ruling class of the new nations had little experience in running their own governments. Dictators filled this power vacuum, often replacing each other in rapid succession. Yet political stability was essential to maintain the profitability of American investments in the region.

Gunboats and Dollars

Extending the Monroe Doctrine, President **Theodore Roosevelt** announced in 1904 that the United States would exercise "international police power" to promote stability in Latin America. He called this policy the **Roosevelt Corollary**. It aimed to prevent European interference in the weak and unstable governments of the region. In practice, it meant that the United States sent troops to the Dominican Republic, Cuba, Nicaragua, and Haiti to keep the peace and protect American property.

In contrast to this style of "gunboat diplomacy," Roosevelt's successor, William Howard Taft, favored "dollar diplomacy." This term was used to describe building regional stability through American investments in Latin America. Mexico, for example, attracted American investors. In time, Americans owned a large share of that nation's oil, railroads, mines, and rubber plantations. Yet dollar diplomacy just masked gunboat diplomacy. The

Teddy Roosevelt's vigorous policies set the course for the United States as a world power. The campaign pin (right) consists of a "teddy" bear with a soldier's hat and rifle.

Using Historical Evidence Teddy Roosevelt was seen as the world's policeman with a "big stick," in this 1904 cartoon. *How does this explain the Roosevelt Corollary?*

Ask students if they have
• Determined what country each group or individual will represent.
• Made notes of questions in preparation for writing their "trade position paper."
• Begun their outside research into trade and economy.

Explain that projects will be evaluated according to the following guidelines.

• **Unacceptable** Projects are not attempted or do not address the topic.
• **Limited/Acceptable** Projects use accurate research and show a limited exploration of the issue.
• **Extensive/Commendable** Projects are based on thorough research and present information in a well-organized and interesting way.
• **Extraordinary/Outstanding** Projects are based on extensive research and display thoughtful interpretation as well as original thought and creativity.

United States still wielded military power in Latin America to protect its interests, and many Latin Americans resented it bitterly.

Good Neighbors

After World War I, the United States no longer needed to warn European nations away, and during the Depression it could no longer afford military occupation in Latin America. Instead of direct intervention, President **Franklin D. Roosevelt** promoted the **Good Neighbor Policy**. Stability would come from a higher standard of living, Roosevelt believed, and so he encouraged trade by lowering tariffs. The United States also loaned money to Latin American governments to build public works such as bridges, roads, schools, hospitals, and water systems.

Economic development was sorely needed. A number of corrupt

By the 1990s, the United States was the most important world power.

dictators still controlled countries where the majority of people lived in poverty.

After World War II

Protecting American interests after World War II meant opposing communism. Americans worried that the impoverished masses of Latin America might be attracted by communism's philosophy. When **Fidel Castro** nationalized American property in Cuba and allied his country with the Soviet Union, Americans feared that he would export communism to the rest of Latin America. To gain support in blocking the spread of communism, the United States backed a number of governments headed by military strongmen.

While these leaders tightly controlled their countries, they mismanaged the finances. Many had

This bumper sticker refers to Soviet missiles in Cuba in 1961. At the height of the cold war, the United States was determined to block the spread of communism in Latin America.

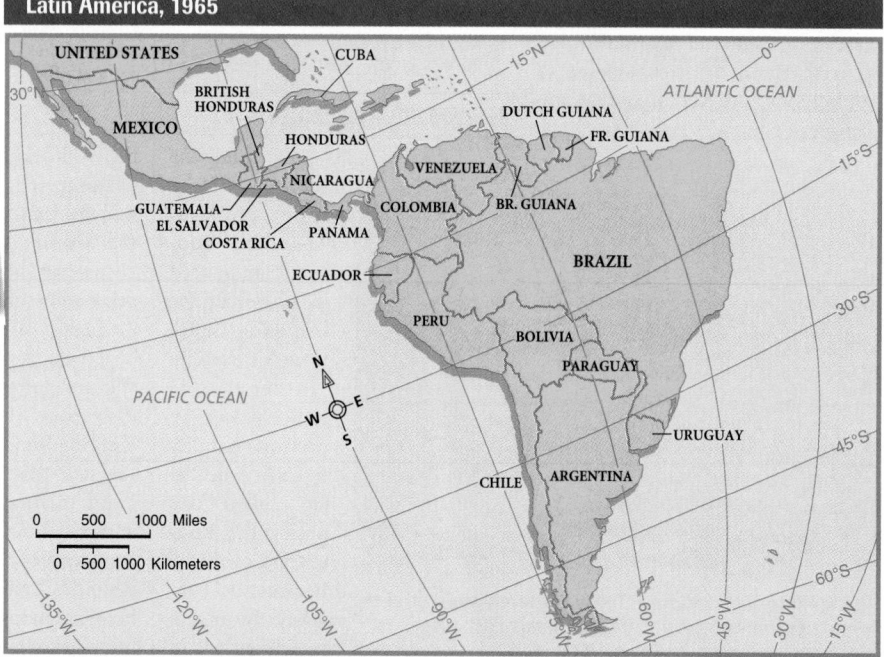

Latin America, 1965

UNITED STATES
CUBA
ATLANTIC OCEAN
BRITISH HONDURAS
MEXICO
HONDURAS
DUTCH GUIANA
FR. GUIANA
NICARAGUA
VENEZUELA
GUATEMALA
EL SALVADOR
COSTA RICA
PANAMA
COLOMBIA
BR. GUIANA
ECUADOR
BRAZIL
PERU
BOLIVIA
PARAGUAY
PACIFIC OCEAN
URUGUAY
CHILE
ARGENTINA

0 500 1000 Miles
0 500 1000 Kilometers

▶ RESOURCE DIRECTORY

Teaching Resources

⭐ **Debating the Future** The Debate over NAFTA, found in the Unit 11 folder, pp. 41–42, allows students to hold a classroom debate in which they discuss the issues involved in expanding a free trade zone to include other nations in the Americas.

Using the Internet Provides additional lesson activities using the resources of the World Wide Web and the Internet.

borrowed huge sums from foreign banks. By the early 1980s, the loans could not be paid off and Latin America plunged into a debt crisis. To get out of it, governments had to agree to plans that led to the restructuring of their economies. In time, better economic management brought new foreign investment.

In the course of these economic changes, governments were changing, too. Democracy was spreading throughout Latin America, given an added boost by the collapse of the Soviet Union. By 1995, all of the governments of the Western Hemisphere except Cuba had democratic institutions. As economies improved, political stability grew. So too did the potential for increased trade among the nations of the region.

DEBATING THE FUTURE

Opponents of NAFTA argue that the agreement is not fair to the United States. Politician Pat Buchanan believes the American people were sold a bill of goods with NAFTA because none of the promises made about it have been kept. He says, "NAFTA should be canceled. A contract negotiated in deceit is no contract at all." President Clinton, on the other hand, says "NAFTA . . . is working superbly." What does our experience with NAFTA teach us about free trade and international relations? ✪

In Favor of NAFTA

"The premise of NAFTA is that trade is not a zero-sum game," says Labor Secretary Robert B. Reich. In other words, both players win. Benefits for the United States include a net increase in jobs and a 25 percent growth in exports to Mexico and Canada in NAFTA's first two years.

How the Maquiladoras Work

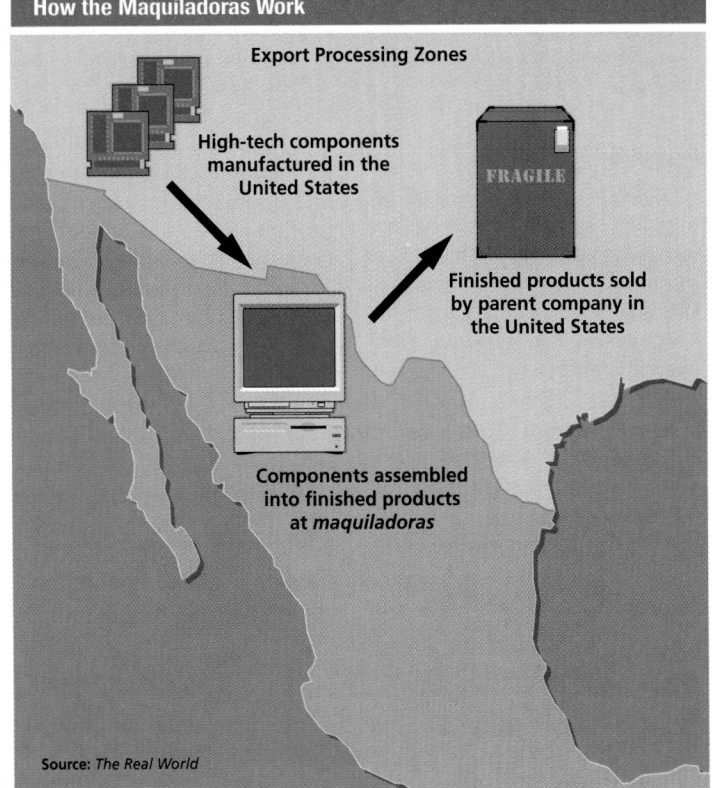

Export Processing Zones

High-tech components manufactured in the United States

FRAGILE

Finished products sold by parent company in the United States

Components assembled into finished products at *maquiladoras*

Source: *The Real World*

This illustration shows how both the United States and Mexico benefit from free trade.

Both Canada and Mexico have enjoyed an increase in exports, too. NAFTA has also created jobs, particularly in the **maquiladoras**, Mexican border factories that assemble imported parts.

Some might say that these short-term gains are small. But those who support free trade point to the importance of the long-term confidence in the economy that NAFTA builds. Explains Professor Edward Leamers of Yale and UCLA:

NAFTA *guarantees that tariffs won't suddenly be raised. It is a major risk reduction document for investors. If your time clock is year by year, then*

NAFTA was definitely oversold. If your clock runs decade by decade, this is a more important event.

Advocates believe that free trade will improve the Mexican economy over time. This, they say, is the best way to build political stability in Mexico. A more stable and successful Mexico will also mean fewer illegal immigrants to the United States.

Based on NAFTA, supporters believe free trade is the wave of the future. Free trade "is simply going to happen, and no President or Congress can stand in the way of it or they will be eaten alive," predicts former Congressman Bill Frenzel. A free-trade agreement is essential,

💻 Using the Internet

Prentice Hall has reviewed the Internet site listed in this activity. However, due to the changing nature of the Internet, all sites should be previewed before students explore on their own.

The United States and International Trade

Objective Use the Internet to locate and graph statistics on the United States' international trade.

Have students follow these instructions:

1. Enter the following URL: **http://www.census.gov/foreign-trade/www/**

2. Click the link "Top 10 International Trading Partners."

3. Create a bar graph comparing the value of United States trade for one month with the value of trade for each of the United States' top ten trading partners for that month. Then add bars to show the year-to-date total for each country.

4. Create bar graphs to show the following data: the ten countries with which the United States has its highest trade surplus; the ten countries with which the United States has its highest trade deficit.

5. Use your graphs to analyze United States trade with its NAFTA partners. Write a paragraph explaining the statistics you find.

3. ASSESS

Chapter 40 Review
Answers (page 1023)

1. NAFTA, see p. 1016.

2. tariff, see p. 1016.

3. trade deficit, see p. 1016.

4. trade surplus, see p. 1017.

5. Helms-Burton Act, see p. 1018.

6. Monroe Doctrine, see p. 1019.

7. Roosevelt Corollary, see p. 1019.

8. Good Neighbor Policy, see p. 1020.

9. maquiladoras, see p. 1021.

10. H. Ross Perot, see p. 1016.

11. Theodore Roosevelt, see p. 1019.

12. Franklin D. Roosevelt, see p. 1020.

13. Fidel Castro, see p. 1020.

14. Timelines should include such major items as the Monroe Doctrine, the Spanish-American War, and the Roosevelt Corollary.

In Depth

Interdisciplinary

Free trade among Spanish-speaking Mexico, English- and French-speaking Canada, and the English-speaking United States posed new language problems. Directions for cooking, washing, or assembling a product made in one country now had to be written in three languages so that the others could understand them. Alternatively, manufacturers would have to stock three separate inventories of goods for each market. One solution proposed by clothing manufacturers was a nonverbal label for washing instructions. It used icons and symbols for information such as "wash cold" and "do not bleach."

says G. Philip Hughes, former ambassador to Barbados, because "We simply cannot afford to be left behind."

Against NAFTA

NAFTA has been a bad deal, say opponents of free trade. It has not increased trade to the levels that were promised. It has mostly benefited large multinational corporations but hurt workers. Public Citizen, a lobbying group, says,

> *N*AFTA is causing the loss of existing jobs, while the new jobs that were promised aren't being created.

To make matters worse, NAFTA is pushing down wages for some existing jobs. For these reasons, labor unions have vigorously opposed NAFTA.

NAFTA has not been uniformly good for Mexico either, opponents say. Mexican workers are still paid too little and work in unsafe conditions. Factory growth is strong only in the north, but investment in the rest of the country has dried up. Small businesses find it very hard to compete. Mexican farmers suffer when American crops like corn undersell theirs. With these economic woes, NAFTA has not made good on its promise to stem the tide of illegal immigration into the United States.

Opponents like Ross Perot claim the United States makes a great mistake by tying its economy to that of an unstable country. A crisis in that country could cost thousands of jobs in the United States. It could also wipe out billions of dollars in investments.

Other critics say that free trade is not unavoidable. Nor should it be the driving force in government policy. Says Lori Wallach of Public Citizen,

> *T*he notion that free trade is inevitable is just not right; trade is a conscious choice. The problem is, recently, trade has become an end in itself. . . . Public policy should not be determined solely by the global marketplace.

The Debate Continues

In December 1994, the leaders of 34 nations in the Western Hemisphere met at the Summit of the Americas in Florida and agreed to work for the creation of a Free Trade Area of the Americas by 2005. Since that meeting, government committees have begun work on shaping the new agreement.

Clearly, economic isolationism is no longer possible in the age of multinational corporations. But just what form the new trade pact will take remains to be seen. Like NAFTA, it will need to be ratified by Congress. As in the case of NAFTA, the debate is sure to be lively.

Most labor unions have strongly opposed NAFTA.

 RESOURCE DIRECTORY

Teaching Resources

Chapter Test Forms A and B are found in the Unit 11 folder, pp. 45–46.

Answer Keys found in the Unit 11 folder, pp. 65–72, provide answers to all student activities.

Spanish Resources provides Key Terms Quiz with Answer Key in Spanish.

Chapter Review

DEFINE AND IDENTIFY

Key Terms
1. NAFTA
2. tariffs
3. trade deficit
4. trade surplus
5. Helms-Burton Act
6. Monroe Doctrine
7. Roosevelt Corollary
8. Good Neighbor Policy
9. maquiladoras

People
10. H. Ross Perot
11. Theodore Roosevelt
12. Franklin D. Roosevelt
13. Fidel Castro

MAKING CONNECTIONS

Create a Timeline
14. To see the pattern of United States relations with Latin America, construct a timeline tracing major events and developments from the Monroe Doctrine to NAFTA. Include at least six items and be sure you can explain the significance of each event on the timeline.

Use a Graphic Organizer
15. Review the arguments in the Debating the Future section of the chapter. Then fill in the blank portion in the graphic organizer below that shows the different major stages in the policies of the United States toward its neighbors. There should be at least three supporting details. You can copy the organizer on another sheet of paper.

U.S. Foreign Policy in the Western Hemisphere

Monroe Doctrine
- Anti-colonialism
- Pro-democracy
- Trade encouraged

Dollar Diplomacy
- Regional stability promoted
- United States corporate investment
- Military enforcement of stability

Good Neighbor Policy
- Low tariffs
- Stability in Latin America through better standard of living
- United States loans for building schools, roads, bridges, parks

NAFTA

ACTIVITIES

For Your Portfolio
16. Decide whether you agree with those who favor NAFTA or those who oppose it, and why. Then choose a way to express these opinions, such as an editorial, a cartoon, a photo essay, a letter to the President or your representatives in Congress, or another format that is acceptable to your teacher.

 ▶ ▶ ▶ USING THE INTERNET
Access Prentice Hall's site at: **http://www.phschool.com** for related links on United States history.

17. Go to the U.S.-Mexico Chamber of Commerce web site at http://www.cais.net/usmcoc/ and access the link "NAFTA." Create an economic report on U.S.-Mexico trade, including descriptions of goods traded and graphs of their value.

Media and Technology

 Computer Test Bank

RESOURCE ⊙ PRO

Teaching Resources on CD-ROM contains all instructional and enrichment material for Chapter 40. Includes all quizzes and tests. You can print directly from the CD-ROM.

---

15. Answers will vary, but should include at least three details concerning United States policy on NAFTA. Possible answers may include: removal of all tariffs and trade obstructions in 15 years; pro-growth, pro-investment for the region's economy; support Mexican stability through economic growth; fears of regulatory leveling.

16. Presentations should show creativity, careful reasoning, and a thoughtful approach to the issue.

17. Student presentations should be clear and to the point, as required in the assignment.

For more guidance on scoring, see the Alternative Assessment Handbook in the Resource Directory on page 982.

Reteach
Ask students to write six sentences about NAFTA. The first two should explain what it is and what it was intended to do. The next two sentences should present positive aspects or arguments in favor of the agreement. The final two will offer criticisms or negative points of view.

 Alternative Assessment

Final Evaluation
Use the following guidelines to evaluate student projects:
● **Evidence of thoughtfulness** Did students show an understanding of the country and its economy?
● **Evidence of outside research** To what extent did students use appropriate outside research for their projects?
● **Communication style** Do projects convey their purpose in a clear, appealing way?

4. CLOSE

Reinforcing the Big Idea
Trade relationships between the United States and the world continue to change. Whatever the debate about NAFTA, the country must reconsider its trade policies in the hemisphere as a whole.

CHAPTER 41

Foreign Policy After the Cold War

See page 982B.

Foreign Policy After the Cold War

INTRODUCING THE THEME

From Theodore Roosevelt's "big stick diplomacy" to Ronald Reagan's talk of the Soviet Union as an "evil empire," the question has remained the same: What role should America play in the world?

Debate What should be the American role in world affairs now that the cold war is over?

Key Terms, People, and Places

cold war, Truman Doctrine, NATO, Warsaw Pact; Woodrow Wilson, Mikhail Gorbachev; Korea, Vietnam

1. FOCUS

Connecting to the Big Idea

Remind students that for about fifty years, the United States dealt with the rest of the world mainly in terms of whether they were "with us" or "with them"—the Soviet Union. With the end of the cold war, what did people expect and hope for? What are the realities of the post-cold war world?

Objectives

• Describe the new challenges brought by the end of the cold war.
• Understand the philosophies and events that have guided American foreign policy since the 1790s.
• Identify the arguments for and against maintaining defense commitments to other nations.

Bellringer

Ask students to name some countries in the news. Where are those countries? What events are taking place there? How, if at all, do those events involve the United States?

Reading Strategy

Predicting Content Ask students to skim the chapter, list the main headings and subheadings, and write a sentence or phrase that predicts the content under each one. After they have read the chapter, have them test their predictions against the actual content.

VIEWING THE PRESENT

In Woodside, California, Stephen Shapiro slices up vegetables for a Malaysian gourmet dinner he's preparing. Formerly an equipment operator in the Missile and Space Division of Lockheed Corporation—one of the nation's leading weapons manufacturers—Shapiro was laid off after Lockheed's government contracts began drying up. Now he works as a cook in an artists' colony.

Three thousand miles away, in Valley Forge, Pennsylvania, Sally Kain looks out her office window at a crab apple tree she planted in a company ceremony in 1971. Employed for the past twenty-eight years by Martin Marietta Corporation, another major weapons producer, Kain is losing her job as well. Her layoff is one part of a company-wide reorganization announced after Lockheed and Martin Marietta merged in 1995, creating a new company called Lockheed Martin.

The Defense Boom Busts

Shapiro and Kain are two unlikely victims of the end of the cold war. From the 1950s through the 1980s the United States required an enormous military force to protect itself and its allies against the Soviet Union. Billions were spent each year on defense—as much as $300 billion a year by the late 1980s. Companies that made weapons thrived.

As cold war tensions began to ease, defense spending fell. Defense contractors reacted in three ways. First, they laid off workers. Employment in airplane manufacturing, for example, fell from around 905,000 to around 585,000 between 1989 and 1994. Lockheed cut more than 10,000 jobs in its San Francisco–area plants alone.

Defense contractors also negotiated mergers and takeovers with their competitors. Stronger companies swallowed weaker ones, and troubled companies sought stability

The cold war required an enormous military force to defend the United States against the Soviet Union.

One of the roles of the United States in the 1990s is that of a peacekeeper. United States troops were sent to Somalia in 1993 to distribute much-needed food supplies. They also restrained feuding clans from stealing and hoarding food and medical supplies while the population was starving.

by growing larger. Combining companies made more job cuts necessary to eliminate duplication of services. The merger of Lockheed and Martin Marietta resulted in the closing of 12 plants and the layoffs of 12,000 workers, some 7 percent of the companies' combined workforce.

The defense contractors' third response to the budget cuts was to move into non-defense areas of production. They believed that companies less dependent on the size of the government's military budget would be more stable over the long run. Lockheed's Missiles and Space Division—Stephen Shapiro's former employer—worked on the Hubble space telescope. It also signed a large contract with Motorola to build a string of communications satellites. Still, more than half of Lockheed Martin's sales come from defense

contracts, which have declined by about 70 percent since their peak in the late 1980s.

Which New World Order?

Just as the health of the defense industry reflects changes in the military budget, the size of the military budget reflects the threats to American security. Cuts in the military budget have taken place because the collapse of the Soviet Union and the end of the

Operation Restore Hope helped distribute truckloads of food and other vital supplies in famine-stricken Somalia.

cold war eliminated the United States' most dangerous rival.

Now the world—like the American defense industry—is in a state of transition. Will the next century be more dangerous, less dangerous, or

Discuss

Discuss with students the changes that have occurred in the world since the collapse of the Soviet Union in late 1991. What changes and events do students think had the most troubling effects on the United States? Ask students to consider whether military superiority is the only way the United States can maintain its position as a superpower.

Analyze

Point out to students that Americans have a long-standing tendency toward isolationism. Using the chalkboard, ask them to analyze this tendency and list some reasons for it. Then ask them to list factors that weigh against isolationism as a current policy.

Caption Answer to ...

Using Historical Evidence

The masks protected them from poison gases such as mustard gas.

In Depth

Then and Now

American isolationism reached a peak in the 1930s, when the mood of Congress supported "Fortress America." One congressman, for example, predicted that a state visit by the king and queen of England would return America to colonial status. When President Franklin D. Roosevelt suggested a global "quarantine" of aggressors (meaning Hitler and Japan), people protested heatedly. In 1938 an Indiana congressman even introduced a bill requiring Congress to get majority approval in a nationwide referendum before declaring war. Though a poll suggested that 73 percent of Americans supported this idea, it never passed the House of Representatives.

simply dangerous in a different way from the cold war era? And how will the United States deal with this new world? These questions lie at the heart of the present debate over the future of American foreign policy. ★

REVIEWING THE PAST

George Washington advised in his Farewell Address in 1796, "The great rule of conduct for us in regard to foreign nations is, in extending our commercial relations, to have with them as little political connection as possible." In other words, trade with other nations should benefit Americans. Entanglements in foreign conflicts—and the large military forces that they required—could only threaten American democracy.

Most American leaders of the 1800s followed Washington's advice.

The pin with the title of the song that George M. Cohan wrote, and the gas mask are two easily recognizable items from World War I.

Events during the first half of the twentieth century, however, led the United States into foreign wars, permanent alliances, and involvement around the globe.

World War I

Millions of Americans had ties to the nations involved in World War I. Yet when the war started in 1914, most Americans wanted to stay out of it, just as they had stayed out of earlier European conflicts.

For three years the United States remained neutral. Still, the government and a majority of the people sympathized more with Britain and France than with Germany. German submarine attacks on American ships inflamed American anger at Germany and, in 1917, led the United States to enter the war on the side of Britain and France.

American soldiers helped turn back the last great German offensive in 1918. By November 1918, Germany was ready to sign an armistice.

Having played a key role in the war, the United States was in a position to help shape Europe's future. President **Woodrow Wilson** looked forward to a strong American presence in the League of Nations, the newly created international peacekeeping body. Still, the war had not converted Americans to the cause of global

involvement. Americans worried that the League might dictate American foreign policy and even drag the United States into future European wars.

In 1919 the United States Senate rejected American participation in the League of Nations. For the next two decades, the United States would

Using Historical Evidence About 2 million American soldiers fought in World War I. The stereoscope photos above and the statue below show some of the equipment the soldiers used. *Why did the soldiers wear masks such as these?*

 RESOURCE DIRECTORY

Teaching Resources

★ **Literature Activity** Toward a New Century, found in the Unit 11 folder, pp. 52–53, is an excerpt from a speech by Anthony Lake, national security advisor under President Clinton. In the excerpt, Lake reminds students that though the cold war has ended, Americans still have many responsibilities to the nations of the world.

SOURCE READINGS

The Source Readings for Unit 11, found on pp. 1084–1087, provide students with links to America's future through literature.

Nystrom *Our Country* Atlas Historical atlas with illustrated timeline helps students make connections between geography and history. See pp. 36–37.

revert to its long-standing policy of seeking trading partners around the world while avoiding political entanglements.

World War II

The American people opposed involvement in World War II at first, just as they had in World War I. In fact, since the United States had entered World War I with the goal of creating lasting peace in Europe, many Americans saw the outbreak of World War II in 1939 as proof that no good could come of American participation in European wars. Nor did Americans favor war against Japan, despite Japanese aggression in East Asia. In August 1941, for example, a proposal to extend the service of Army draftees passed the House of Representatives by only one vote.

That attitude changed in a single day. On December 7, 1941, Japanese war planes attacked Pearl Harbor, Hawaii. Shocked and angered, Americans of all backgrounds rallied in defense of their nation. When the other Axis powers—Germany and Italy—declared war on the United States three days later, Americans realized they were now part of a global war.

To a far greater degree than World War I, World War II was a global war. Involvement in that war helped make the United States a truly global power. American troops fought battles from the Philippines to Morocco to France. American ships confronted both German U-boats in the North Atlantic and Japanese aircraft carriers in the South Pacific. Ameri-

A World War II poster

can bombers and supply planes crossed tens of thousands of miles of land and sea.

When the war ended with an Allied victory in 1945, the United States had the power to shape events nearly everywhere on the globe. It had done more than any other nation to defeat the Axis powers, and its economy was bigger than that of all other nations combined. Finally, only the United States possessed the awesome destructive power of the atomic bomb.

All these factors meant that the United States would not return to isolation, as it had after World War I. Like Woodrow Wilson, President Franklin Roosevelt wanted to create an international peacekeeping body—the United Nations—and he wanted the United States to be a strong member. This time, most Americans agreed.

Photographer Joe Rosenthal's study of victorious marines hoisting the American flag on the Pacific island of Iwo Jima is one of the most famous photographs of World War II.

Media and Technology

🖥 **Transparencies** Cause-and-Effect Charts, F-7, F-8, F-10

💿 📼 ***Decision America*** Will help motivate students to analyze and understand contemporary issues in American society. See Issue 6, "A New Role for the Military? An Interview with Colin Powell" (disc 1 side 2; tape 2; approx. 8 min.).

Activity

Interdisciplinary
Divide students into groups and have each one prepare a short illustrated report on one of the recent missions in which U.S. military forces have carried out military, humanitarian, or peacekeeping efforts, including (but not limited to) the Persian Gulf War, Operation Provide Comfort (Kurdish refugees), Haiti, Somalia, Zaire, and Bosnia. Have them locate the country or countries on a map of the world. **LEP**

Enrichment

The role of the United Nations is a controversial aspect of U.S. foreign policy. Have students do research to find out more about the United Nations and the work of its various agencies.

In Depth

Global Connections

"Neutrality," in international law, is not an isolationist policy but the official position of not taking sides in a conflict. A few nations, notably Sweden and Switzerland, have remained resolutely neutral throughout the twentieth century, thus avoiding large defense budgets. They do, however, take part in international organizations. A nation can declare its neutrality at the beginning of a specific conflict, with the option of changing its mind later. In World War II, Ireland, Spain, and Portugal were nominally neutral, although fascist Spain sympathized with Nazi Germany, as did some anti-British groups in Ireland. Neutral Sweden served as a haven for many Jews fleeing Europe.

Mid-Point Monitoring

Ask students if they have
- Chosen a region to study and noted important points about it.
- Decided on a format.
- Begun their research on their chosen region.

Explain that projects will be evaluated according to the following guidelines:

- **Unacceptable** Projects are not attempted or do not follow the assignment.
- **Limited/Acceptable** Projects use material from the textbook and show a limited exploration of the issue.
- **Extensive/Commendable** Projects are based on outside research and present information in a well-organized and interesting way.
- **Extraordinary/Outstanding** Projects are based on extensive research and display thoughtful interpretation as well as original thought and creativity.

In Depth

Interdisciplinary

Changes in communications technology have dramatically altered how Americans think about military missions. Television has brought bloodshed, bombings, and the horrors of war into American living rooms. The Vietnam War was the first televised war, shocking people at home with images of napalm and wounded children. During the Persian Gulf War, viewers could see CNN reporters broadcasting live from their Baghdad hotel, watching tracer fire cross the sky. Once they could see where their soldiers were, and what they were encountering, many Americans had a new view of military involvement.

The Cold War

Between 1945 and 1950, as the United States and Soviet Union changed from wartime allies to bitter rivals, a new American foreign policy took shape. The Soviet Union aimed at world conquest, American leaders said, and only the United States had the strength to lead the free world against it. From roughly 1947 to 1991, the cold war was the centerpiece of American foreign policy.

In the **Truman Doctrine** in 1947, President Truman committed the United States to defend "free peoples who are resisting attempted subjugation by armed minorities or by outside pressures." The United States, in other words, would intervene wherever communism threatened to expand. Under this commitment, the United States helped create **NATO** (the North Atlantic Treaty Organization), promising to defend Western Europe against attack. The United States also signed agreements with other allies, such as Japan, and made large commitments to small and distant countries that faced a communist threat.

Wars in Korea and Vietnam

Twice in Asia, the United States joined wars within divided nations to stop the spread of communism. In **Korea**, American forces rushed to defend South Korea after an invasion by communist North Korea in 1950. Three years of bloody fighting brought stalemate on the battlefield and frustration within the United States. Still, American intervention had saved South Korea.

The United States would not manage to save South **Vietnam**.

Soviet and American leaders Khrushchev and Eisenhower balanced on a 1959 *Newsweek* cover.

Despite American military involvement from 1961 to 1973, communist North Vietnam overran South Vietnam and reunified the country in 1975. The war cost the United States some 58,000 lives and more than $150 billion. It also convinced most Americans that the United States

The Vietnam Women's Memorial in Washington, D.C.

should reduce its foreign commitments. The United States, more and more Americans argued, could not afford to be what some called "the world's policeman."

Reagan and the Collapse of Communism

Whether and when to intervene in foreign countries remained controversial issues throughout the 1970s and 1980s. Americans still feared communist expansion. But they did not think that they alone could, or should, fight it. American defense spending declined after the Vietnam War, but then rose sharply in the 1980s under President Reagan, who won election in 1980 on a promise of a stronger anti-Soviet policy. Americans supported the

RESOURCE DIRECTORY

Teaching Resources

⭐ **Debating the Future** The Debate over Foreign Policy After the Cold War, found in the Unit 11 folder, pp. 50–51, provides students with selections that offer three different points of view on the issue of U.S. foreign policy after the cold war. Students can use those selections and others in the Student Edition to help debate the topic.

Using the Internet Provides additional lesson activities using the resources of the World Wide Web and the Internet.

defense increases but remained wary of military intervention abroad.

While Americans were questioning their commitment to the cold war, the cold war enemy—the Soviet Union and its Eastern European allies—was beginning to collapse. One by one the nations of Eastern Europe, fed up with the brutalities and inefficiencies of communism, rejected their communist leaders. Soviet leader **Mikhail Gorbachev**, who took power in 1985, tried to reform the Soviet system but only quickened the pace of its decline. On December 31, 1991, the Soviet Union officially ceased to exist. The cold war was over.

DEBATING THE FUTURE

E -mailing American troops stationed in Bosnia in 1996, a student in the "horrible terrifying 6th grade" in Melbourne, Florida, wrote, "I would like to thank you for putting your life on the line for our country." From Jackson, Mississippi, came this message: "Being a Vietnam vet, I know how hard it is being away from family and friends." Another American wrote, "It seems that having U.S. troops abroad has become a traditional part of the holiday season. Please know that we miss you guys and are proud of the commitment that you have made to serve your country. . . . Hurry Home!"

While these letters use the new technology of the Internet, they contain a message that is as old as American commitments abroad. Americans are proud of their country's global role. Yet they also hope that Americans serving abroad will soon be able to return home.
⭐ As you have read, during the cold war the United States took on many

One of the most prominent symbols of the cold war was the barbed wire and concrete of the Berlin Wall. Shown here is the celebration of its destruction in 1989.

foreign commitments, promising to protect other nations in case of attack. To meet these commitments, the United States spent hundreds of billions of dollars each year on defense. As the United States approaches the next century, it must confront two basic foreign policy questions:

1. Now that the Soviet Union has collapsed, should the United States maintain its foreign commitments?
2. Now that the national debt has skyrocketed and other nations have become stiff trading competitors, can the United States afford to maintain its foreign commitments?

1. Should the United States Maintain Its Foreign Commitments?

Some foreign-policy analysts argue that the United States should cancel cold war–era alliances like NATO and defense treaties with other nations, like Japan and South Korea. "It is time to recognize that with the disintegration of the Soviet Union, the mission of America's cold war alliances has been accomplished," writes Ted Galen Carpenter, a foreign-policy analyst at a research organization called the Cato Institute.

NATO, for example, was created to defend Western Europe against attack by Soviet and **Warsaw Pact** forces. Carpenter and others point out that Russia and the Eastern European nations that once made up the Warsaw Pact are now more interested in joining NATO than attacking it. There is no reason, they argue, to defend Western Europe against an enemy that no longer exists.

Other analysts disagree. One, former President Richard Nixon, wrote in his book *Seize the Moment: America's Challenge in a One-Superpower World:*

F *or many on the American left and right, the knee-jerk response to the decline of the Soviet Union . . . is to withdraw into a new isolationism. But in*

Using the Internet
Prentice Hall has reviewed the Internet site listed in this activity. However, due to the changing nature of the Internet, all sites should be previewed before students explore on their own.

Conflict in Bosnia

Objective Use the Internet to research the United States' and United Nations' roles in the war in the former Yugoslavia.

Have students follow these instructions:
1. Go to CNN's Mission: Peace Web page at **http//www.cnn.com/ WORLD/Bosnia/index.html**

2. Use links to explore the history of the conflict in the former Yugoslavia.

3. Take notes on United States and United Nations involvement in the Bosnian crisis.

4. Create a timeline of significant events in the crisis. Highlight events in which the United States and United Nations played a role.

5. Write an essay explaining the roots of the conflict and the goal of the United States and the United Nations in the former Yugoslavia. Include your opinion on whether the United States and the UN should be involved in the peace process. Be sure to support your argument.

Media and Technology

💿 📼 *Decision America* Will help motivate students to analyze and understand contemporary issues in American society. See Issue 7, "Is America Still the Free-World Leader? The View from Overseas" (disc 2 side 1; tape 3; approx. 10 min.).

💿 *Our Times Multimedia Encyclopedia of the 20th Century* **CD-ROM** Will help students of all abilities to link the past to the present. Students can access the timeline, and listen to and read about the major stories for 1989, including the destruction of the Berlin Wall. Articles in the *Encyclopedia* are interactive.

Chapter 41 Review
Answers (page 1031)

1. cold war, see p. 1024.

2. Truman Doctrine, see p. 1028.

3. NATO, see p. 1028.

4. Warsaw Pact, see p. 1029.

5. Woodrow Wilson, see p. 1026.

6. Mikhail Gorbachev, see p. 1029.

7. Korea, see p. 1028.

8. Vietnam, see p. 1028.

9. Timelines should include such major items as World Wars I and II, Pearl Harbor, and the Korean War.

10. Answers will vary, but should reflect an understanding of the United States' role in world affairs. Possible answers may include: (bottom left web)—The cold war threat has ended; (top web)—Defense cuts cause economic difficulties; (bottom right web)—New threats may emerge in formerly communist areas of the world.

11. Presentations should show creativity and a thoughtful approach to the issue.

12. Student presentations should be clear and to the point, as required in the assignment.

For more guidance on scoring, see the Alternative Assessment Handbook in the Resource Directory on page 982.

Reteach

Ask students to write short answers to these questions, based on information in the chapter:

● What was the cold war, and what brought it to an end?

● What was American foreign policy during the Reagan and Bush administrations?

● Why do some people think the United States should end its defense commitments to other nations?

---

fact American world leadership will be indispensable in the coming decades. . . .

The real world revolves not around wishful thinking about "peace breaking out all over" but around the enduring realities of geopolitics. . . . In a world of competing states, clashing interests and national conflicts are inevitable. . .

AMERICAN PEACE SIGN   BALKAN PEACE SIGN

STAHLER @THE CINCINNATI POST 1995

This political cartoon points out the uncertainty of the outcome of American involvement in Bosnia in the mid-1990s.

Put most simply, Nixon's point is that nations will always need friends because they will always have enemies. Although the collapse of the Soviet Union removed the United States' chief rival, Nixon argued, other rivals will surely emerge. The United States will need the help of allies against those new rivals. As Caspar Weinberger, who was secretary of defense under President Reagan, wrote:

Clearly, no nation is strong enough alone to keep its own freedom. Every nation requires alliances, friendships or associations of one kind or another with other countries who share its goals and ideals.

2. Can the United States Afford Foreign Commitments?

"Today there is not, as some argue, a single superpower, the United States," columnist William Pfaff wrote in the quarterly *Foreign Affairs*. "There are none." Pfaff and others claim that the United States, with a national debt of around $5 trillion, is simply not wealthy enough to try to control events all over the world.

The Cato Institute's Ted Galen Carpenter agrees, writing, "We cannot afford to maintain alliances for the sake of having alliances." He continues:

The NATO commitment alone cost American taxpayers more than $120 billion a year during the latter stages of the cold war. . . . Washington's obligation to defend Japan, South Korea, and other East Asian allies costs another $40 billion. . . .

The United States currently spends nearly seven times as much on the military as does any other member of the [major] industrial powers. Indeed, it spends some 60 percent more than all of the other [major industrial] countries combined.

"A nation that faces [serious] domestic problems . . . can ill afford" this burden, Carpenter concludes. High American defense spending not only takes money away from domestic programs like education, Carpenter and others argue. It also enables the United States' trading competitors like Germany and Japan to spend less on

---

defense, because those countries can rely on American military protection.

A number of other analysts believe that the United States can indeed afford the cost of remaining a superpower. Caspar Weinberger, for example, writes that "The United States could obviously afford larger defense budgets, provided that sacrifices were made elsewhere." Former President Nixon argued that in the long run, reducing foreign commitments would cost the United States even more money than maintaining them:

The security of our home in this . . . interdependent world is affected by changes everywhere. Walking away from global challenges will carry a dangerous price. History may once again produce nations aspiring to regional or global dominance. . . . With imports and exports comprising over 20 percent of our economy, our prosperity depends on international stability.

The Debate Continues

The two questions outlined here have no simple or permanent answers. The United States' need for foreign commitments is influenced by events around the world. These can create or remove threats to American security almost overnight. The United States' ability to afford foreign commitments depends on the constantly changing health of the American economy. Each generation of Americans, therefore, must decide for itself the role its nation will play in the world.

 RESOURCE DIRECTORY

Spanish Resources provides Key Terms Quiz with Answer Key in Spanish.

Teaching Resources

Chapter Test Forms A and B are found in the Unit 11 folder, pp. 54–55.

Answer Keys found in the Unit 11 folder, pp. 65–72, provide answers to all student activities.

Chapter Review

DEFINE AND IDENTIFY

Key Terms
1. cold war
2. Truman Doctrine

3. NATO
4. Warsaw Pact

People
5. Woodrow Wilson
6. Mikhail Gorbachev

Places
7. Korea
8. Vietnam

MAKING CONNECTIONS

Create a Timeline

9. To see this chapter in context, construct a timeline showing six to twelve major events of the twentieth century that had an important impact on American foreign policy.

Use a Graphic Organizer

10. Review the arguments in the Debating the Future section of the chapter. Then fill in the blank webs in the graphic organizer below that shows the connection between various issues and arguments that have affected United States foreign policy in the years after the cold war. You can copy the web on a separate sheet of paper.

Growing debt constrains foreign policy.

Foreign Policy After the Cold War

Alliances with other nations are essential.

A legacy of commitments: NATO and Warsaw Pact

ACTIVITIES

For Your Portfolio

11. Decide which point of view on foreign policy you generally agree with and choose a way to express it: a selection of magazine or newspaper articles; a poster or cartoon; a letter to your representatives in government; an editorial; or some other format acceptable to your teacher.

▶▶▶ **USING THE INTERNET**

Access Prentice Hall's site at: **http://www.phschool.com** for related links on United States history.

12. Go to the U.S. Department of State web site at http:// www.state.gov/index.html and access hypertext links to explore current foreign-policy topics. Make a list of three or more foreign-policy issues you see there and explain them to your class.

Media and Technology

 Computer Test Bank

RESOURCE◉PRO

Teaching Resources on CD-ROM contains all instructional and enrichment material for Chapter 41. Includes all quizzes and tests. You can print directly from the CD-ROM.

 Alternative Assessment

Final Evaluation

Use the following guidelines to evaluate student projects:

● **Evidence of thoughtfulness**
Did students show an understanding of the region and what information was important for this project?

● **Evidence of outside research** To what extent did students use appropriate outside research materials for their projects?

● **Communication style** Do projects convey their purpose in a clear, appealing way?

4. CLOSE

 Reinforcing the Big Idea

The end of the cold war removed the issue that had been the focus of American foreign policy and began a debate about the country's future role in the world.

Technology and You in the Next Century

Technology and You in the Next Century

1. FOCUS

Connecting to the Big Idea

See page 982B. Point out to students that rapidly changing technology is influencing almost everyone, every day, everywhere. While some of these changes are desirable, there is debate about whether all of them are necessary. Ask why the Internet has become a controversial issue.

Objectives

● Understand the interlocking trends of globalization, transition from manufacturing to service jobs, and computer networking.
● Describe the development of automation and the computer age.
● Identify the arguments offered by those who are for and against more emphasis on computer use in schools.

Bellringer

Ask students to describe when they most recently used a computer or came into contact with computer technology. Remind them of such not-so-obvious uses of new technology as supermarket scanners or automated phone messages. How often during a single day do they use computer technology?

Reading Strategy

Structured Overview Ask students to skim the chapter for key terms and concepts. Then have them create an outline using the main headings and subheadings, and including important terms. Have them revise the outline and terms as they read.

INTRODUCING THE THEME

Technological advances have changed the face of America many times. The cotton gin made possible the rise of King Cotton. Following the Bessemer steelmaking process came the expansion of the railroads and the rise of modern industry. The automobile revolutionized not only how people traveled, but also where they lived and how they spent their time. However, nothing before it can be compared to the computer.

Debate How can schools best prepare students to use and take advantage of the technology of the next century?

Key Terms, People, Places

globalization, e-mail, modem, telecommunications, software, productivity, automation, World Wide Web; Henry Ford, Herman Hollerith

VIEWING THE PRESENT

"**B**uy American," the principal told the school librarian, so she ordered a computer from a California company. Yet when she opened the boxes, she was surprised. She found a monitor made in Japan, a mouse made in China, a keyboard manufactured in Mexico from American parts, and a computer assembled in Taiwan. The memory chips were from Malaysia, the floppy disk drive from Korea, and the hard disk drive, central processing unit, and power supply from the United States.

It took not only many countries but also many computers to deliver the finished product. To order this computer, the librarian had sent a fax to a dealer, whose computerized inventory system noted the sale and kept track of how many more computers to buy. Each month the dealer places orders by electronic mail with the computer's California manufacturer. From the company's computerized order department, the information goes electronically to the billing department, the shipping department, and also the manufacturing department. There, computers auto-

Computers have made many tasks easier. Students often use computers in classrooms for research projects. They also use computers at home for both school projects and for their own entertainment.

▶ RESOURCE DIRECTORY

Teaching Resources

Reproducible Lesson Plan found in the Unit 11 folder, p. 57, provides a summary of the Chapter 42 lesson plan content.

Alternate Lesson Plan: Cooperative Learning found in the Alternate Lesson Plans folder, p. 187, helps groups of students investigate the real-world applications of classroom learning, with a focus on computer technology.

Guided Reading and Review found in the Unit 11 folder, p. 58, provides a structure for reading and mastering the key concepts and reviewing the key terms for Chapter 42. (Guided Practice)

Spanish Resources provides key terms and key concepts for Chapter 42 in Spanish.

"I KNEW WE WERE GETTING TELEPHONE SERVICE THROUGH OUR CABLE TV, AND TRANSMITTING DOCUMENTS THROUGH OUR COPIER, BUT WHEN DID WE START GETTING FAXES THROUGH OUR TOASTER OVEN?"

Many people find computer technology confusing and frustrating, as this cartoon humorously points out.

matically tally the demand and send orders to each of the suppliers in Asia. With computers talking to computers, this information can travel within the company and halfway around the globe in seconds.

Alexander Graham Bell's patent of the first model of the telephone (above) is contrasted with today's picture telephone technology (left).

The Global Economy

How typical is this computer use for the average American product? More typical than you might think. It illustrates an economic trend called **globalization**. This refers to a system of producing and selling goods that involves many countries. It also highlights the increasing importance of computer networks.

Reflecting this trend, Boeing, an American aerospace company, advertised, "It takes the entire world to pay our bills. . . . 70% of all our airplanes are sold outside the U.S." Foreign trade, like exporting planes and importing televisions, occupies a

Discuss

Discuss with students the interlocking of three trends in American society and industry: globalization, the change from a manufacturing base to an information base, and finally, the importance of computer networks. If you think it useful, use the chalkboard to show these links. Ask students to suggest ways in which these trends affect them.

In order to help students understand the debate over how best to use computer technology in schools, have students discuss their school's computer resources and how they use them.

Ask them to discuss ideas and suggestions about improving school computer systems or using them in better ways.

larger and larger position in the economy.

As the computer example shows, the Asian countries of the Pacific Rim have become important trading partners of the United States. The computer also illustrates another side of globalization, the blurring of national boundaries in making products. Says Jeffrey Garten, dean of the Yale School of Management, "An increasing number of the goods we make are composed of both foreign and American components, and multinational companies, with plants all over the world, are responsible for an increased portion of international trade." American companies not only buy foreign parts but also own factories in other countries. For example, Ford makes cars on every continent except Antarctica. Likewise, foreign companies like Honda build their cars in the United States. In some places, like the NUMMI plant in Fremont, California, foreign and domestic companies team up to manufacture cars.

In the 1990s, computers have become one of the most important tools in the global marketplace. They are needed for communication, information storage, and information delivery.

Shift from Manufacturing Jobs to Service Jobs

⭐ Why are American companies buying foreign parts and building factories overseas? One reason is lower labor costs. Since the 1970s, foreign countries like Japan and Korea have been able to sell their products in the United States at lower prices than American products. To be competitive, American companies

So Many Changes in So Little Time

1775 ◆ James Watt perfects his invention of the steam engine.

1793 ◆ Eli Whitney invents the cotton gin.

1793 ◆ Samuel Slater builds first mill to spin cotton.

1876 ◆ Alexander Graham Bell invents the telephone.

INDUSTRIAL REVOLUTION
mid-1700s–1876

▶ RESOURCE DIRECTORY

Teaching Resources

⭐ **Literature Activity** The Information Revolution, found in the Unit 11 folder, pp. 61–62, argues that American schools and businesses must help students prepare for the information-based work of the twenty-first century.

SOURCE READINGS

The Source Readings for Unit 11, found on pp. 1084–1087, provide students with links to America's future through literature.

have had to reduce their costs, the biggest of which is labor. The result has been more and more traditional manufacturing jobs leaving the United States for other countries.

Meanwhile, service industries have grown strong in the American economy. Gaining importance within the service sector are jobs that involve managing information. Think of what happened when the librarian ordered the computer. Workers in California handled the flow of information that generated the bill, directed shipping, regulated the supply of parts, and determined levels of production. Most of the manufacturing was done abroad. Still, it was American engineers who had designed these complex computer systems.

As the economies of the world grow more interconnected, countries are starting to specialize in what they do well. Countries with low labor costs are specializing in manufacturing, while the United States is specializing in managing information. For example, large American corporations with plants around the world still centralize their accounting in the United States.

Importance of Computer Networks

What makes these two trends possible is the widespread use of computer networks. A network enables one computer to send information to another through a central computer called a server. While a single computer can store massive amounts of data, it is much more valuable when it can share data at lightning speed with other computers. Some businesses and schools have local area networks that link all of their computers together. As a result, they can send data and **e-mail**—electronic messages—back and forth.

Now picture a network so large that it would link computers around the world. This is the Internet. The Internet is a global network that connects computers by sending electronic information over telephone lines. Each computer needs a device called a **modem** to transmit its data to a phone line.

1974 ◆ The first fax machine transmits one page in six minutes.

1983 ◆ The Federal Communications Commission issues a license for the first cellular phone system.

1984 ◆ Philips and Sony develop the compact disc read-only memory (CD-ROM).

1992 ◆ The World Wide Web is released by the European Laboratory for Particle Physics.

Analyze
To emphasize the concept of globalization, ask students to analyze a computer system (mouse, keyboard, monitor, printer, CD-ROM drive, speakers) and identify where each component was made or assembled. Then have them analyze other items in the classroom or school. Where was each one made?

1877 ◆ Thomas Edison invents the phonograph.

1893 ◆ Henry Ford builds his first car.

1969 ◆ Neil Armstrong walks on the surface of the moon.

ELECTRIC AGE
1877–1946

ELECTRONIC AGE
1947–1972

INFORMATION AGE
1973–present

Media and Technology

Decision America Will help motivate students to analyze and understand contemporary issues in American society. See Issue 4, "Who Tells Us What to Think? Television and Political Image-Making" (disc 1, side 2; tape 2; approx. 6 min.).

In Depth

Global Connections

The Internet makes so much information easily available that some governments fear it as a subversive tool that could aid dissidents or tell people news that the government would like to censor. China is worried about Internet links between pro-democracy students at home and overseas. One government firm is building a closed, China-specific version of the Internet that, its CEO says, will carry no "smut, politics, or decadent Western culture." Chinese officials have considered creating a network that would link China's 1,000-plus universities but would screen overseas connections. Experts, however, point out that such screening software would be easy to bypass—with other software.

Activity

Interdisciplinary
Ask students to draw cartoons or short (four- to five-panel) comic strips that comment on computer technology and how it is affecting them, their school, or people's everyday lives.

As an alternate activity, ask students to construct an illustrated timeline of the revolution in the production process. They can go through their textbook's earlier chapters and select illustrations that would signify the major changes from the late eighteenth century. **LEP**

Not only do computers have the power to do many complex operations at lightning speed, they can also share the information with other computers almost instantly. This telecommunications network map of the United States illustrates the idea.

The Internet makes it possible for students to use a computer to conduct research all over the world. It also makes it possible for anyone to send and receive information almost instantaneously.

Using this global computer network is a prime example of **telecommunications**—sending information over long distances. Says one California executive, "A modern company operating globally can't do anything without telecommunications." For example, his company has computer programmers in India, writing **software**—instructions telling the computer what to do—for a new product. At the end of the day, the programmers can send their work via the Internet to California to be tested. While the programmers are sleeping, workers twelve hours away go to work, test the program, and send it back over the Internet, in time for the next work day in India.

Computers and Education

In this increasingly high-tech world, schools face the question of

Electricity changed people's eating, working, and sleeping habits. Electric companies such as General Electric grew into large industrial corporations.

how best to prepare students for the next century. How much should they use computers to teach? How much should they teach students about using computers? Or should schools concentrate on traditional writing, computation, and thinking skills, since computers are, after all, only as smart as the people using them?

Some people argue that computers are the answer to preparing America's students for the future. But are they really?

REVIEWING THE PAST

The computer has brought American society to the turning point of a new age. Yet it is only the latest in a series of inventions that have changed the way Americans live, work, and learn. The automobile, electric power, and the telephone are probably the only other technologies that have had such a profound effect on American life.

Before the Industrial Revolution, America was a land of farmers and

RESOURCE DIRECTORY

Teaching Resources

 Nystrom *Our Country* Atlas Historical atlas with illustrated timeline helps students make connections between geography and history. See pp. 26–27.

independent artisans. In today's terms, they would be considered "small-business people," owning their own tools and working for themselves. A craftsman like Paul Revere would make his products in his own workshop, fashioning each piece of silver by hand from start to finish. Learning these skills took many years.

The Production Revolution

Making goods by machine began in the United States in 1793 when Samuel Slater built the first mill to spin cotton in Rhode Island. Soon, New England had a number of factories to spin and weave cotton, each built beside a river. Water powered the machines, and workers kept them running smoothly. Many of these workers were young women who had left subsistence farms and moved near the factories. Unlike their mothers, who had to know all the steps of carding, spinning, and weaving wool to make cloth, these workers had to learn only one job—how to run the machines.

Manufacturing grew rapidly in the early 1800s, especially in the Northeast. In addition to textiles, factories turned out guns, shoes, and other goods. However, most American goods in this era were still made by skilled craftsmen.

In the early 1800s, the textile mills of the Northeast had plenty of rivers and streams suitable for mill sites, busy ports for shipping, and plenty of people in search of work.

Not until the Civil War did industrialization really take off. After the war, cities grew rapidly as new factories attracted workers, both native-born and immigrant. In the 1870s and 1880s, factories replaced workshops in the production of goods.

In this industrial transformation, workers no longer made all parts of a product. Instead, they performed only one step in the production process. Craftsmen's skills learned through long years of apprenticeship were no longer needed. Industrial workers typically had to know only one task, learned on the job.

The automobile profoundly changed the way Americans lived. Ordinary Americans used the car to travel regularly, not as a necessity, but for pleasure. The government began building roads and public spaces such as parks and beaches to which people could drive.

Technology and Education

Objective Use the Internet to research current technology initiatives of the United States Department of Education.

Have students follow these instructions:

1. Go to the U. S. Department of Education Technology Initiatives Web site at: **http://www.ed.gov/Technology/**

2. Access the link "Getting America's Students Ready for the 21st Century: Meeting the Technology Challenge," for background on the Department's goals.

3. Research at least three government initiatives to promote technology literacy. Take notes.

In Depth

Biography

During the 1980s and 1990s, young "techno-wizards" revolutionized information technology. While attending college at the University of Illinois, a programmer named Marc Andreessen decided to create a way to make it simple and fun to travel the Internet. He worked with a group to produce the "browser" program Mosaic.

After moving to California, Andreessen got advice and funding from an earlier computer pioneer, Jim Clark, founder of Silicon Graphics. With Clark's help, Andreessen co-founded a company called Netscape in 1994, when he was just 23 years old. Today, Netscape makes software that millions use to cruise the Internet's World Wide Web.

When he introduced the assembly line in 1913, **Henry Ford** ushered in the age of mass production. Now workers stood behind a moving conveyor belt to assemble a product. Each worker added one part, performing the same step over and over at a steady pace. This innovation greatly increased **productivity**, the amount each worker produces in a given period of time.

Automation Productivity grew even faster after World War II with the advent of **automation**—the use of sophisticated machines instead of human labor in farming, mining, and manufacturing. In some cases, one worker could now produce as much in a day as 100 people had in the past.

While automation reduced the number of workers needed in manufacturing, more and more Americans found jobs in sales and service. The service sector included not only jobs like auto repair and dry cleaning, but also work done in offices. These jobs involved reading, writing, and calculating—skills learned in school rather than on the job. The typewriter and telephone were tools that increased productivity among office workers, but these improvements pale beside the achievements of the computer.

The telephone brought mass communication within the reach of many. New industries and jobs opened up as well. Women found work as telephone switchboard operators.

Using Historical Evidence Advances and inventions in technology, such as Edison's moving images, often have great popular appeal. *Can you name some inventions that have made possible the entertainment that you and your friends enjoy?*

The Computer Age

The workplace of the 1990s has changed profoundly because of the computer. The American inspiration for it came not from a car factory or law office, but from the United States census. **Herman Hollerith,** an 1890 census agent, devised a time-saving machine that used punch cards to tabulate data. By 1946 scientists had developed the Electronic Numerical Integrator and Computer—ENIAC for short. ENIAC could do 5,000 addition problems per second. But its tremendous size and weight made it impractical for most uses.

Since ENIAC, transistors have replaced vacuum tubes, and computers have become smaller, faster, and more sophisticated. In the 1960s and 1970s, computers in universities, businesses, and government offices were still large calculating machines operated by a few workers. A handful of offices had a central computer, with connections to terminals beside a few workers' desks. Computer skills were limited to specially trained employees.

RESOURCE DIRECTORY

Teaching Resources

Using the Internet Provides additional lesson activities using the resources of the World Wide Web and the Internet.

During the 1980s, several breakthroughs in computer technology revolutionized the workplace. When the personal computer appeared early in the decade, millions of workers gained a computer on their desk. Once they had learned how to use it to write, calculate, and sort data, workers found that their productivity increased. Another time-saver of the 1980s was the facsimile (fax) machine, which used computer technology to scan a page, turn its contents into electronic signals, and transmit them over telephone lines, to be decoded at the other end. An even faster way to send information was through computer networks, which were operating in many businesses by the end of the decade.

The Internet became the world's hottest communications tool in the 1990s. Begun in the 1960s as a government project to link university science departments, the Internet grew to include millions of business, governmental, educational, and individual computers. To help users find what they're looking for, the Internet has a system called the **World Wide Web**. Using software called a Web browser, users can retrieve electronic files to get information and use links to jump to related files. Access to the Internet has spread to schools, businesses, libraries, homes, and even cafes, where "Net-surfing" replaced video games to attract customers. With a global audience of millions, businesses scrambled to find ways to use the Internet.

DEBATING THE FUTURE

A high school junior in a tiny town in Alaska is writing a term paper on the migration of gray whales. The nearest public library is more than a hundred miles away, but she is able to do research at school. Using a computer and modem, she browses the World Wide Web and within a few hours finds the most up-to-date information. Her teacher is very pleased with her paper because her research far exceeded what the library has to offer.

At a high school in California, two seniors create a multimedia presentation on the stegosaurus for a geology assignment. They scan pictures into the computer, color them, and add sound clips downloaded from the Internet. While their presentation amuses their classmates, the teacher is not impressed. He says it's too little information dressed up in a flashy package.

How much do computers really add to a student's educational expe-

In 1946, University of Pennsylvania's Electronic Numerical Integrator and Computer (ENIAC) took up a huge room, weighed 30 tons, and had 17,000 vacuum tubes.

4. Create a report that outlines the initiatives you chose. Include information on the status of the programs. Use specific examples of the programs in action wherever possible.

5. Write an analysis of the initiatives in your report, describing whether you think the programs are or will be effective. Include one idea of your own that would promote technology literacy. Present your report to your class.

Caption Answer to ...

Using Historical Evidence

(See p. 1038.) Answers will vary, but may include the moving picture camera, the video camera, the computer, the microphone, the cassette tape recorder, and the CD player.

In Depth

Then and Now

Technology has changed political campaigning. Political conventions were first televised in the 1950s, with news reporters covering the speeches and roll-call votes. The presence of TV, combined with changes in voting practices, gradually turned the conventions into entertainment, with real news happening off-screen. TV also made new demands on candidates. After the first televised presidential debates, between Nixon and Kennedy in 1960, candidates learned to use the media. Today they know how to speak following the text on a Teleprompter, and to tailor remarks to contain "sound bites" that can be excerpted on evening TV news broadcasts. By the 1996 elections, politicians were at home at Web sites on the Internet.

Media and Technology

Transparencies Cause-and-Effect Charts, F-9, and Political Cartoons, K-7

Mid-Point Monitoring

Check with students to see whether they have

● Chosen the format they will use for their project.

● Set up interviews.

● Made arrangements for computer/Internet time.

● Begun outside research and collection of materials.

Explain that projects will be evaluated according to the following guidelines:

● **Unacceptable** Projects are not attempted or do not address the topic.

● **Limited/Acceptable** Projects are based on material from the textbook but demonstrate some effort to show the impact of technology.

● **Extensive/Commendable** Projects are based on thorough outside research, show an understanding of the subject, and reflect the student's own interpretation.

● **Extraordinary/Outstanding** Projects are based on extensive research, show the impact of technology in an effective way, and display original thought.

---

rience? Stories such as these fuel the debate over what place computer technology should have in school. ⊗

High-Tech Is the Way to Go

One of the most important jobs of the schools is to prepare students for work. Computer skills have become absolutely essential in the workplace, say advocates of educational technology. To support this position, they point to "What Work Requires of Schools," a 1991 report from the Department of Labor. The report states that understanding and applying technology and using computers to process information are essential requirements for workers. Colleges have already recognized the importance of computer skills. Some even require freshmen to bring their own computer to college.

Like today's mechanic who analyzes a car's problems electronically instead of poking around under the hood, more and more jobs of the future will rely on computers. Labor economist Audrey Freedman says:

> The jobs that are being created are computer-using jobs. They're service, white-collar types of work.

Moreover, computer users earn more money than workers without computers in similar jobs—about 15 percent more in 1995. To prevent widening the gap between haves and have-nots in this country, high-tech boosters warn that all students must learn how to use computers.

Adaptability is the key to the future in America's constantly changing workplace, and computer skills

provide that adaptability, supporters claim. They cite examples like Lizanne Gottung, a manager in a Connecticut factory, who says, "When we hire now, we're thinking about how easily a person can be trained to do different jobs." Mike Thomas, one of her employees, knows how adaptable workers need to be. "I'm an old dog who's adjusted to three product changes in the last year," he reports. He monitors computers that control production. Without his computer skills, he would have been out of a job.

Advantages of Technology Use

Using computers in schools not only prepares students for the future, advocates say, but also improves the quality of education. Computer-assisted learning gives students a

---

An Introduction to the Internet

What is the Internet?

The Internet is a global network of computers that are all linked together. It was set up as a government project to link university science departments in the 1960s. Today, the Internet is used by individuals, businesses, schools, and by other groups as well.

What is the World Wide Web?

The Web is a group of electronic documents (called Web pages) and links that lead from one document to another. Documents can contain text, pictures, audio clips, and video clips.

Who uses the Web?

Millions of people use the Web every day. More than 100,000 companies and individuals have Web sites, called home pages.

How do you get on the Web?

To get on the Web, you need a computer, a modem, and a computer application called a browser. The modem provides the link between your computer and the other computers on the Web. The browser lets you find and read Web pages.

What does the future hold?

Today, people can do everything from grocery shopping to medical research over the Internet. Over time, it will have even more uses. Almost any use you can think of for the Internet may someday become a reality. You could even be the one to make your ideas come true.

▶ RESOURCE DIRECTORY

Teaching Resources

⊗ **Debating the Future: Simulation** Should Funding Technology Be a Priority? found in the Unit 11 folder, pp. 59–60, will introduce students to differing points of view and help them draw conclusions using a simulation activity. Student handouts are provided.

In less than fifty years, technological advances have quickened the pace of change. Early computers (left) filled an entire room. Now computers weigh only a few pounds (above) and can be carried in a briefcase.

chance to advance at their own pace, giving them immediate feedback and repeating a lesson as many times as necessary. Computer programs like word processing, spreadsheets, and databases let students write, calculate, and do research more efficiently than ever before. In addition, computers enable handicapped students to complete many educational tasks they could not perform in the past.

Computers with access to the Internet can connect students to a huge global pool of information. Says Jim Dunnigan, a high school teacher in Seattle, Washington:

W*e have students in my school district who know no bounds to the classroom walls. They use electronic mail to talk with archaeologists in South America; they publish Civil War history research projects on the Internet; and they maintain e-mail correspondence with other students in the Czech Republic.*

Using computers has enriched these students' education in ways previously unimaginable. When they enter the increasingly global workplace, they will know how to find information and communicate internationally.

High-Tech Is Not the Answer

Good teaching is far more important than electronic gadgets, say critics of computers in education. Clifford Stoll, an astrophysicist and one of the best-known critics of educational technology, describes the most important thing in a classroom:

A*good teacher interacting with motivated students. Anything else that separates them—filmstrips, instructional videos, multimedia displays, e-mail, TV sets, interactive computers—is of questionable educational value.*

Stoll and others would rather have school districts spend their limited funds on more teachers instead of on computers.

Computer-assisted instruction sugarcoats the learning process, opponents argue. Learning takes hard work, concentration, and self-discipline—far more sustained effort than zapping an alien on a computer

Media and Technology

Our Times Multimedia Encyclopedia of the 20th Century CD-ROM Will help students of all abilities to link the past to the present. Students can access the timeline, listen to and read about the major stories for 1946 in the United States and in other parts of the world. They can also choose to read a detailed, interactive essay on the ENIAC.

In Depth

Interdisciplinary

Computer-generated imaging has brought new magic to movies and video, giving film animators a powerful new tool. To create the images of T-rex, velociraptors, and the other scary inhabitants of *Jurassic Park*, animators used dinosaur models to draw wire mesh skeletal outlines that were recorded on a computer screen. The computer added color, shadow, texture, and other elements, and the dinosaur images were then processed into live action scenes. Another software program created the dinosaurs' realistic movements. Filmmakers also have produced films entirely with computer animation. A feature-length one, *Toy Story*, won a Special Achievement Award from the Academy of Motion Picture Arts and Sciences.

Chapter 42 Review Answers (page 1043)

1. globalization, see p. 1033.

2. e-mail, see p. 1035.

3. modem, see p. 1035.

4. telecommunications, see p. 1036.

5. software, see p. 1036.

6. productivity, see p. 1038.

7. automation, see p. 1038.

8. World Wide Web, see p. 1039.

9. Henry Ford, see p. 1038.

10. Herman Hollerith, see p. 1038.

11. Timelines should include an appropriate span of events from Slater's mill to the Internet.

12. Students' multi-flow charts will vary considerably, but should reflect an understanding of how information travels in the era of telecommunications. Information in the multi-flow chart might include:

(top left box: source of information)—Library at State U. has valuable information; (bottom left box: source of information)—Regional School System Headquarters has proposed plan for bringing computers to the schools; (middle left box: route for information)—via fax, modem, internet; (middle right box: route for information)—student's e-mail address or fax number; (top right box: how paper is presented)—paper turned in to teacher in classroom; (middle right box: how paper is presented)—paper published in local newspaper; (bottom right box: how paper is presented)—paper sent to Regional School System Headquarters.

13. Presentations should show creativity and a thoughtful approach to the issue.

14. Student presentations should be clear and to the point, as required in the assignment.

For more guidance on scoring, see the Alternative Assessment Handbook in the Resource Directory on page 982.

---

screen to get a right answer. This type of instruction promotes a short attention span, not dedicated study or critical thinking. Moreover, computer simulations are no substitute for real life. Students need to know how to conduct experiments and perform calculations in the real world, not just on the computer.

Disadvantages of Technology Use

By focusing on technology, computer lovers have missed the main point of the "What Work Requires of Schools" report, say those who favor a more traditional approach to education. The Labor Department report pays far more attention to other requirements, which are based on fundamental academic skills, think-

ing skills, and personal qualities. Critics of educational technology believe that emphasizing computer skills is not the best way to prepare students for the workplace. Even more than computer literacy, jobs of the future will require educated workers who can reason well, express themselves clearly, and work well with others.

Indeed, computer skills are easy to acquire and can be learned outside of school. Critics point out that, with computers in many public libraries and in almost 40 percent of American households, free time is better than school time for developing computer expertise. Moreover, school assignments that require high-tech delivery distract students from the subject matter they should be studying. Students end up spending more time using the software than they do on researching and thinking.

Turning students loose on the Internet to do research makes a lot of data available to them but gives them no organization or context for it, say

opponents. It is also easy for students to download a file from the Internet, then cut and paste parts of it into their own work. Missing is any critical thought about the value of the source or any understanding of the true purpose of doing research.

Debating the Future

While computers have become an essential part of American society, their use in schools is still being determined. The challenge will be to find the right balance between teaching new skills and finding new ways of adapting the technology to reinforce traditional skills. To find the money for schools to fund all that will be the biggest challenge.

Technology by itself, after all, has never been the answer to any nation's problems. The answer might be in the balance between developing new technology, understanding it, using it for personal improvement, and adapting it to improve society.

The computer has been called "the children's machine," because of the ease with which most children approach this marvel of technology. Using computers is a requirement in many colleges today. It is even more common in the workplace.

RESOURCE DIRECTORY

Teaching Resources

📁 **Chapter Test** Forms A and B are found in the Unit 11 folder, p. 63-64.

📁 **Answer Keys** found in the Unit 11 folder, pp. 65-72, provide answers to all student activities.

📁 **Spanish Resources** provides Key Terms Quiz with Answer Key in Spanish.

Chapter Review

DEFINE AND IDENTIFY

Key Terms
1. globalization
2. e-mail

3. modem
4. telecommunications
5. software

6. productivity
7. automation
8. World Wide Web

People
9. Henry Ford
10. Herman Hollerith

MAKING CONNECTIONS

Create a Timeline

11. Using information in the Reviewing the Past section, construct a timeline that shows the progress and changes in American technology. Include six to eight major developments, and be ready to explain why each step was important.

Use a Graphic Organizer

12. The multi-flow chart below gives an example of the ways that information could travel in the 1990s. On a separate piece of paper, construct a similar chart to show how you would gather information from different sources to present a paper on why and how schools would use computers.

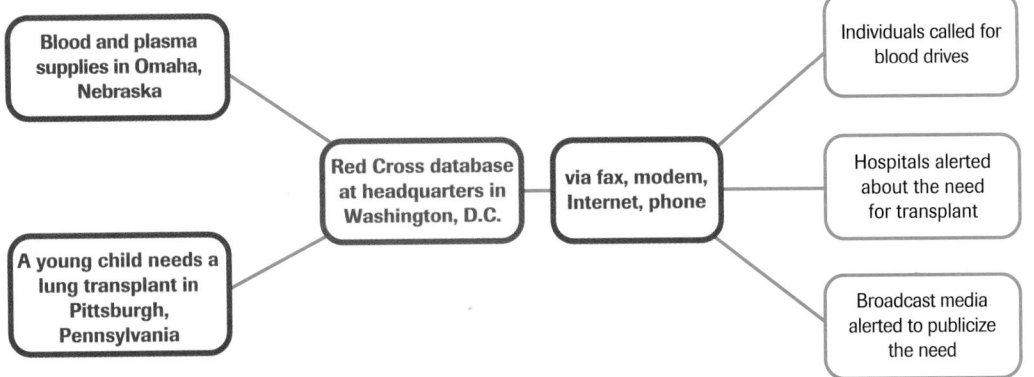

- Blood and plasma supplies in Omaha, Nebraska
- A young child needs a lung transplant in Pittsburgh, Pennsylvania
→ Red Cross database at headquarters in Washington, D.C. → via fax, modem, Internet, phone →
- Individuals called for blood drives
- Hospitals alerted about the need for transplant
- Broadcast media alerted to publicize the need

ACTIVITIES

For Your Portfolio

13. From your experience and from the information in this chapter, decide what you think about how useful computers are and could be in schools. Then choose a way to express your point of view: a selection of magazine or newspaper articles, a poster or cartoon, a letter to the editor, or another format acceptable to your teacher. If possible, use a computer to prepare or present your project.

▶▶▶ **USING THE INTERNET**

Access Prentice Hall's site at: **http://www.phschool.com** for related links on United States history.

14. Go to EdWeb at http://k12.cnidr.org:90/resource.cntnts.html and use links to explore the issues of technology and education today. Write a report that outlines both sides of the debate on the role of technology in the classroom.

Media and Technology

 Computer Test Bank

RESOURCE◉PRO

Teaching Resources on CD-ROM contains all instructional and enrichment material for Chapter 42. Includes all quizzes and tests. You can print directly from the CD-ROM.

Reteach

Have students write these three terms: globalization, automation, computer network. Then ask them to write one sentence about each of the three terms, plus a final sentence or two that explains how the terms are related.

 Alternative Assessment

Final Evaluation

Use the following guidelines to evaluate student projects:

- **Evidence of thoughtfulness** Did students show an understanding of the issue and how to portray it?
- **Evidence of outside research** To what extent did students use appropriate outside research and interviews for their projects?
- **Communication style** Do projects convey their purpose in a clear, appealing way? Are different media used effectively?

4. CLOSE

 Reinforcing the Big Idea

Computer technology has brought profound changes in all aspects of American life, including education. Its role in schools still is a question for debate.

A Nation Looks Ahead

As the 1990s come to a close, Americans look forward to the new century with a sense of hope. In spite of the many challenges they foresee, the people of our country have tremendous resources to use as they face the future. Together, Americans must take advantage of those strengths in order to meet those challenges.

Foremost of those strengths is the nation's unique system of government, which allows Americans to face the future with confidence. Our representative democracy strikes a balance between the rights of the people and the responsibilities that are assigned to the government. The tone of our various national debates might sometimes be shrill, but the discussion itself is a testament to the power of democracy as a means of settling disputes.

Americans have always tried their best to work together. Separated by race, religion, and culture, all have played a part in building a strong nation. Now, as we face the challenges of the future we look, as always, to the lessons of the past.

More than half a century ago, President Franklin D. Roosevelt could not possibily have imagined the world in which future generations of Americans would live. Nevertheless, in a famous speech that he delivered before both houses of Congress on January 6, 1941, President Roosevelt outlined what he hoped would be goals for all Americans. Those goals are worth remembering today.

There is nothing mysterious about the foundations of a healthy and strong democracy. The basic things expected by our people of their political and economic systems are simple. They are:

◆ *Equality of opportunity for youth and for others.*

◆ *Jobs for those who can work.*

◆ *Security for those who need it.*

◆ *The ending of special privilege for a few.*

◆ *The preservation of civil liberties for all.*

◆ *The enjoyment of the fruits of scientific progress in a wider and constantly rising standard of living.*

These are simple and basic things that must never be lost sight of in the turmoil and unbelievable complexity of the modern world. The inner and abiding strength of our economic and political systems is dependent upon the degree to which they fulfill these expectations. . . .

Americans have built a nation that is unique. It is unique in its diversity, its exciting opportunities, and the ability of its citizens to meet new challenges.

In the future days, which we seek to make secure, we look forward to a world founded upon four essential human freedoms.

THE FIRST IS FREEDOM OF SPEECH and expression everywhere in the world.

THE SECOND IS THE FREEDOM OF EVERY PERSON TO WORSHIP GOD in his own way everywhere in the world.

THE THIRD IS FREEDOM FROM WANT which, translated into world terms, means economic understandings which will secure to every nation a healthy peacetime life for its inhabitants everywhere in the world.

THE FOURTH IS FREEDOM FROM FEAR which, translated into world terms, means a worldwide reduction of armaments to such a point and in such a thorough fashion that no nation will be in a position to commit an act of physical aggression against any neighbor— anywhere in the world. . . . Since the beginning of our American history we have engaged in change—in perpetual peaceful revolution—a revolution which goes on steadily, quietly adjusting itself to changing conditions. . . .

Freedom means the supremacy of human rights everywhere. Our support goes to those who struggle to gain those rights or keep them. Our strength is in our unity of purpose.

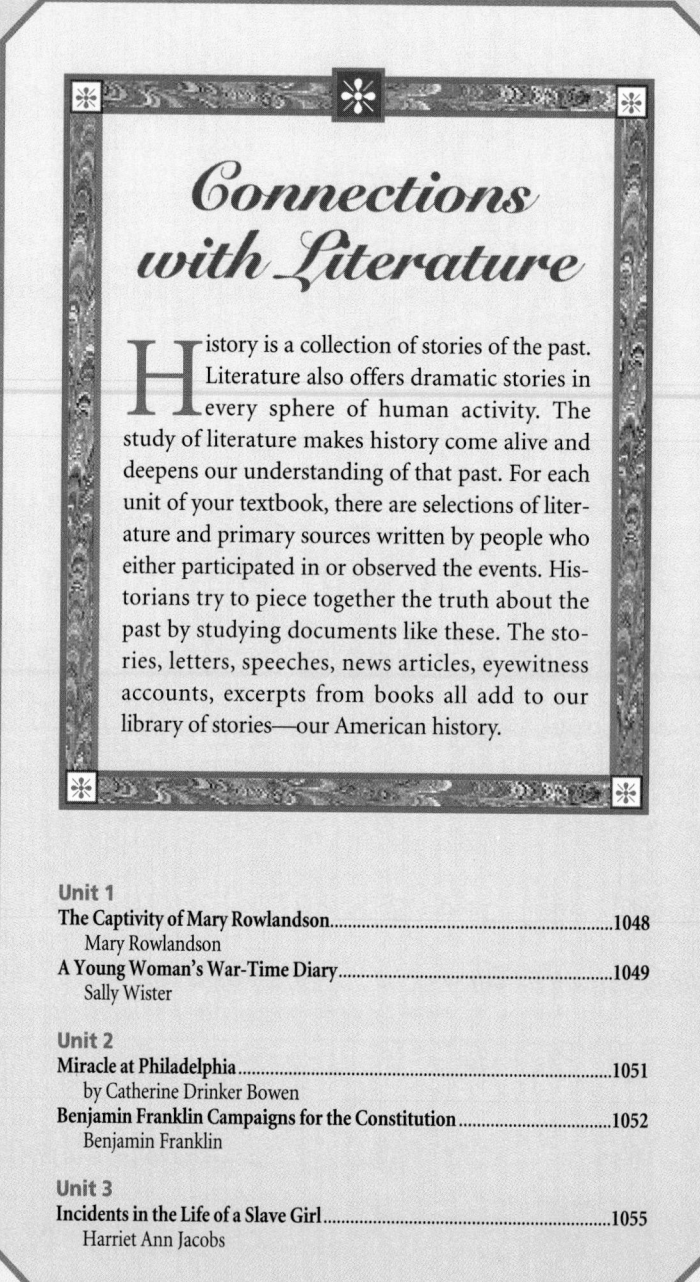

Connections with Literature

History is a collection of stories of the past. Literature also offers dramatic stories in every sphere of human activity. The study of literature makes history come alive and deepens our understanding of that past. For each unit of your textbook, there are selections of literature and primary sources written by people who either participated in or observed the events. Historians try to piece together the truth about the past by studying documents like these. The stories, letters, speeches, news articles, eyewitness accounts, excerpts from books all add to our library of stories—our American history.

FOCUS

Connecting Literature and History

In the 1400s, the area that is now the United States was peopled with varied and distinct Native American groups. In the late 1400s, when Europeans began arriving, conflicts arose between settlers and Native Americans. Tell students that this source reading chronicles one of these conflicts, King Philip's War.

INSTRUCT

Point out that events such as that experienced by Mary Rowlandson were often the result of misunderstanding and lack of toleration. Tell students that it has only been in recent years that more balanced and comprehensive information about the role of Native Americans in United States history has been included in textbooks. Ask students why it might be that such information had been so sparse. Point out that the Native American tradition of oral history led to a lack of written accounts, which made it difficult for historians to trace the events and lives of Native Americans. Finally, ask students to consider what role prejudice against Native Americans, begun in part by such accounts as Mary Rowlandson's, might have played in keeping Native Americans out of history textbooks.

EXTEND

Ask students to research your local area to learn about the Native Americans who inhabited it. Students can begin their search at local libraries, historical societies, and town halls. Students should try to determine what Native American group lived in the area, what their relationship was to settlers there, and what happened to them. Have students write their findings in a report that they present to the class.

The Captivity of Mary Rowlandson

Primary Source

INTRODUCTION One of the most famous victims of King Philip's War was Mary Rowlandson, the wife of the minister of the town of Lancaster, which was attacked in February 1675. Mrs. Rowlandson spent eleven weeks as a captive of the Narragansett. After her release, she returned to Lancaster where she recorded her experiences. Her narrative, *A True History of the Captivity and Restoration of Mrs.* *Mary Rowlandson*, published in 1682, may have been the first American best-seller.

VOCABULARY Before you read the selection, find the meaning of these words in a dictionary: doleful, ravenous, barbarous, vexation.

On the tenth of February, 1675, came the *Indians* with great number upon Lancaster. . . . I had often before this said, that if the Indians should come, I would chuse rather to be killed by them than taken alive; but when it came to the trial my mind changed; their glittering Weapons so daunted my spirit, that I chose rather to go along with those (as I may say) ravenous Bears, than that moment to end my daies. . . .

The first Remove.—Now away we must go with those Barbarous Creatures, with our bodies wounded and bleeding, and our hearts no less than our bodies. About a mile we went that night; up upon a hill, within sight of the Town, where they intended to lodge. . . . This was the dolefullest night that ever my eyes saw: oh the roaring, and singing, and dancing, and yelling. . . . And as miserable was the waste that was there made of Horses, Cattle, Sheep, Swine, Calves, Lambs, Roasting Pigs, and Fowls, (which they had plundered in the Town,) . . . to feed our merciless Enemies. . . .

The twelfth Remove.—It was upon a Sabbath-day morning that they prepared for their Travel. . . . My Mistress. . . snatched [my bible] hastily out of my hand, and threw it out of doors; I ran out and catcht it up, and put it into my pocket, and never let her see it afterward.

The twentieth Remove.—I was with the Enemy eleven weeks and five days; and not one Week passed without the fury of the Enemy, and some desolation by fire and sword upon one place or other. . . . They would boast much of their Victories; saying, that in two hours time, they had destroyed such a Captain and his Company in such a place . . . and boast how many Towns they had destroyed, and then scoff, and say, they had done them a good turn to send them to Heaven so soon. . . .

I have seen the extreme vanity of this World; one hour I have been in health and wealth, wanting nothing; but the next hour in sickness, and wounds, and death, having nothing but sorrow and affliction. . . . The Lord hath shewed me the vanity of these outward things, that they are . . . but a shadow, . . . that we must rely on God himself, and our whole dependence must be upon him.

THINKING ABOUT THE SELECTION

1. What were some of Mrs. Rowlandson's experiences during captivity?
2. How did her eleven weeks in captivity change Rowlandson?

Critical Thinking

3. **Predicting Consequences** Mrs. Rowlandson's narrative became one of the popular books of the seventeenth century, both in the colonies and in Britain. What effect do you think the book might have had on relations between British settlers and Native Americans?

ANSWERS TO

Thinking About the Selection

1. Rowlandson describes injuries from the fighting in Lancaster, the celebrations of the Native Americans when they did well in battle, and the boasts of the Native Americans after they destroyed settlers' towns.

2. During her captivity, Rowlandson realized that small misfortunes or discomforts are nothing compared with how difficult and painful life can become. She learned to trust in God and appreciate small things.

3. The book paints an unfavorable picture of Native Americans, referring to them as "ravenous," "barbarous," and boastful. Thus, the book most likely inflamed anti–Native American sentiments and contributed to the British settlers' negative perception of Native Americans.

A Young Woman's War-Time Diary

Primary Source

Sally Wister

INTRODUCTION In 1777, in the midst of the War for Independence, fifteen-year-old Sally Wister and her family left Philadelphia and went to a relative's country house. They hoped to avoid the British army, who they believed were about to occupy the city. The following excerpts are from a diary Wister kept during the time. She wrote the entries as though she were addressing letters to her friend Deborah Norris.

VOCABULARY Before you read the selection, find the meaning of these words in a dictionary: dispel, chintz, kenton.

September, 1777.

Yesterday, which was the 24th of September, two Virginia officers called at our home, and informed us that the British army had crossed the Schuylkill[1]. Presently after, another person stopped, and confirmed what they had said, and that General Washington and army were near Pottsgrove. Well, thee may be sure we were sufficiently scared; however, the road was very still till evening. About seven o'clock we heard a great noise. To the door we all went. A large number of waggons, with about three hundred of the Philadelphia militia. They begged for drink, and several pushed into the house. One of those that entered was a little tipsy, and had a mind to be [rude]. I then thought it time for me to retreat; so figure me (mightily scared, as not having presence of mind enough to face so many of the military) running in at one door, and out at another, all in a shake with fear; but after a little, seeing the officers appear gentlemanly and the soldiers civil, I called reason to my aid. My fears were in some measure dispelled, tho' my teeth rattled, and my hand shook like an aspen leaf. They did not offer to take their quarters with us; so, with many blessings, and as many adieus, they marched off.

Fifth Day, September 26th.

About 12 o'clock cousin Jesse heard that General Howe's army had moved down towards Philadelphia. Then, my dear, our hopes and fears were engaged for you. However, my advice is, summon up all your resolution, call Fortitude to your aid, don't suffer your spirits to sink, my dear; there's nothing like courage; 'tis what I stand in need of myself, but unfortunately have but little of it in my composition.

I was standing in the kitchen about 12, when somebody came to me in a hurry, screaming, "Sally, Sally, here are the light horse!"[2] This was by far the greatest fright I had endured. . . . I ran immediately to the western door, where the family were assembled, anxiously waiting for the event. They rode up to the door and halted, and enquired if we had horses to sell; he answered negatively. "Have not you, sir," to my father, "two black horses?"— "Yes, but have no mind to dispose of them." My terror had by this time nearly subsided. The officer and men behaved perfectly civil; the first drank two glasses of wine, rode away, bidding his men to follow, which, after adieus in number, they did. The officer was Lieutenant Lindsay, of Bland's's regiment, Lee's troop. The men, to our great joy, were Americans, and but 4 in all. What made us imagine them British, they wore blue and red, which with us is not common.

December 5th, Sixth Day.

Oh, gracious Debby, I am all alive with fear. The English have come out to attack (as we imagine) our army, three miles this side. What will become of us,

---
[1] a tributary of the Delaware River

[2] cavalry

FOCUS

Connecting Literature and History

When learning the important dates and names of the War for Independence, it is easy for students to overlook the drama and tension of those days. This excerpt from the diary that a young girl kept during the war will bring home to students the fact that the war affected individual lives in a very personal way.

INSTRUCT

Ask students to imagine that they are Sally Wister, the young diarist in the selection. Have students write another day's entry in Wister's diary.

Students should explore in their diary entries whether or not the Wister family ever encounters the British army, how long the British army remains in Philadelphia, and what course the war takes following the British occupation of that city. Students should draw on the information presented in the chapter to write their diary entries. After students finish their writing, have several of them read their work aloud to the class.

Point out to students that the American Revolution could never have happened without individuals who were independent thinkers and who had strong personalities. Ask students to find a person who contributed to the revolution in some way. The person can be either a famous figure, such as Samuel Adams, Benjamin Franklin, or Patrick Henry, or a little-known figure, such as Sally Wister, who nonetheless contributed to the American effort in some way. Then have students collect information and write a one-page biography about the person's life and involvement in the American Revolution. To choose a subject, students could use their textbooks or sources such as *The Ethnic Contribution to the American Revolution*, edited by Frederick Harling and Martin Kaufman, or *Patriots: The Men who Started the American Revolution*, by A. J. Languth. To write their biographies, students should look for other biographies on the person they have chosen, or read materials written by that person. Students should be sure their biographies answer the following questions: Who is the person? How was he/she involved in the American Revolution? What thoughts and beliefs did this person have about the revolution? What happened to the person after the war was won?

only six miles distant? We are in hourly expectation of an engagement. I fear we shall be in the midst of it. Heaven defend us from so dreadful a sight. The battle of Germantown, and the horrors of that day, are recent in my mind. It will be sufficiently dreadful, if we are only in hearing of the firing, to think how many of our fellow creatures are plung'd into the boundless ocean of eternity, few of them prepar'd to meet their fate. But they are summon'd before an all-merciful judge, from whom they have a great deal to hope.

Sixth Day, June 5th, Morn, 11 o'clock.

Last night we were a little alarm'd. I was awaken'd about 12, with somebody's opening the chamber door. I observ'd cousin Prissa talking to mamma. I asked what was the matter. "Only a party of light horse." "Are they Americans?" I quickly said. She answer'd in the affirmative, (which dispell'd my fears), and told me Major Jameson commanded, and that Captains Call and Nixon were with him. With that intelligence she left us. . . . This morning I rose by, or near seven, dress'd in my light chintz, which is made gown-fashion, kenton handkerchief, and linen apron. . . .

Dress'd as above, down I came, and went down to our kitchen, which is a small distance from the house. As I came back, I saw Jameson at the window. He met me in the entry, bow'd: — "How do you do, Miss Sally?" . . . I invited him into our parlour. He

Woodcut, 1779

followed me in. We chatted very sociably. . . .

I ask'd him whether Dandridge was on this side the Delaware [river]. He said, "Yes." I wanted sadly to hear his opinion, but he said not a word. The conversation turn'd upon the British leaving Philadelphia. He firmly believ'd they were going. I sincerely wish'd it might be true, but was afraid to flatter myself. I had heard it so often that I was quite faithless. . . . He smiled and assur'd me they were going away.

He was summon'd to breakfast. I ask'd him to stay with us. He declin'd the invitation with politeness, adding that he was in a hurry,—oblig'd to go to camp as soon as he could. He bow'd, "Your servant, ladies," and withdrew immediately. After breakfast they set off for Valley Forge, where Gen'l Washington's army still are.

THINKING ABOUT THE SELECTION

1. What is Wister afraid will happen near the house where she is staying?
2. Based on this excerpt and on the information in the chapter, who won the battle when the British finally did attack Philadelphia?

Critical Thinking

3. **Drawing Conclusions** What events in Wister's recent experience might help explain her fear of encountering the British army?

ANSWERS TO

Thinking About the Selection

1. She is afraid to see more destruction and suffering from a nearby battle.
2. Based on Wister's discussion with Jameson ("The conversation turn'd upon the British leaving Philadelphia. He firmly believ'd they were going. I sincerely wish'd it might be true, but was afraid to flatter myself. I had heard it so often that I was quite faithless. . . . He smiled and assur'd me they were going away.") and the information in the text, students should know that the British won the battle.

3. Wister refers to the "the battle of Germantown, and the horrors of that day" and wishes to be spared such a sight again. Thus, her own negative experience has led her to fear the British and the war.

Miracle at Philadelphia

 Literature

Catherine Drinker Bowen

INTRODUCTION Despite the stifling heat of Philadelphia in the summer of 1787, delegates to the Constitutional Convention often sat with the windows of the east chamber of the State House tightly closed. They did so in order that passers-by on the street or eavesdroppers from local newspapers could not hear the debates raging inside. The excerpt below, from the book *Miracle at Philadelphia*, describes the delegates' struggle to avoid discussing the Convention with outsiders and the seriousness with which they took their promise of secrecy and their task of developing a new plan of government.

VOCABULARY Before you read the selection, find the meaning of these words in a dictionary: convivial, entreat, repose, dissipate.

It must have been difficult to maintain the rule of secrecy. Delegates were questioned on all sides; one meets it in their letters. [Delegate] Pierce of Georgia was apt to be talkative, especially when he went over to the meetings of Congress in New York. As for old Dr. Franklin, it seemed impossible to keep him quiet; it is said a discreet member attended the Doctor's convivial dinners, heading off the conversation when Franklin in one of his anecdotes threatened to reveal secrets of the Convention.

There was criticism of the secrecy rule; Jefferson did not like it when he heard. Yet it is difficult to see how a Constitution could have evolved had the Convention been open to abuse and suggestion from the public. Sentries were placed at the State House doors; members could not copy the daily journal without permission. . . .

One anecdote, . . . from [delegate] Pierce, shows the seriousness with which the secrecy rule was regarded, shows also the awe in which delegates held their chairman,

¹ George Washington

the President of the Convention.¹ As the meeting rose one afternoon, a member dropped a paper on the floor. It was picked up and handed to Washington. Pierce tells how, next day, when debate was over and the question for adjournment called for, the General rose from his seat. "Gentlemen!" he said. "I am sorry to find that some one member of this body has been so neglectful of the secrets of the Convention as to drop in the State House a copy of their proceedings,

"Independence Hall," by William Birch, 1790.

---

which by accident was picked up and delivered to me this morning. I must entreat gentlemen to be more careful, lest our transactions get into the newspapers and disturb the public repose by premature speculations. I know not whose paper it is, but there it is [throwing it down on the table], let him who owns it take it."

"At the same time he bowed," Pierce's notes continue, "picked up his hat and quitted the room with a dignity so severe that every person seemed alarmed; for my part I was extremely so, for putting my hand in my pocket I missed my copy of the same paper, but advancing up to the table my fears soon dissipated; I found it to be in the handwriting of another person. When I went to my lodgings at the Indian Queen, I found my copy in a coat pocket which I had pulled off

that morning. It is something remarkable that no person ever owned the paper."

THINKING ABOUT THE SELECTION

1. Based on what you know about the compromises that were hammered out at the Convention, why do you think the delegates decided to keep the proceedings secret until a final document was crafted?
2. Why was Pierce especially alarmed when Washington reprimanded the group for finding some notes of the proceedings on the floor?

Critical Thinking
3. **Identifying Alternatives** What other courses of action might the delegates have agreed upon, other than secrecy, for keeping public speculation and opinions from influencing their work?

Benjamin Franklin Campaigns for the Constitution

Primary Source

INTRODUCTION "It is much easier to pull down a government . . . than to build up, at such a season as the present," wrote John Adams early in 1787. Considering the chaos that seemed to have descended on the United States in those days and the differences in background and intent of the delegates to the Constitutional Convention, many would have agreed with Adams. Yet on September 17, 1787, the completed Constitution of the United States was put before the delegates for their signatures. It was fitting

that Benjamin Franklin, who for so long had been part of the revolutionary changes sweeping the nation, should rise at that point and urge the delegates to approve the document, despite all its faults and imperfections.

VOCABULARY Before you read the selection, find the meaning of these words in a dictionary: sect, infallible, despotism, constituents, partisan, salutary, manifest, vicissitude.

Monday, September 17, 1787: In Convention:

The engrossed[1] Constitution being read, Doctor FRANKLIN rose with a speech in his hand, which he had reduced to writing for his own conveniency, and which Mr. Wilson read in the words following.

Mr. President

I confess that there are several parts of this constitution which I do not at present approve, but I am not sure I shall never approve them: For having

lived long, I have experienced many instances of being obliged by better information, or fuller consideration, to change opinions even on important subjects, which I once thought right, but found to be otherwise. It is therefore that the older I grow, the more apt I am to doubt my own judgment, and to pay more respect to the judgment of others. Most men indeed as well as most sects in Religion, think themselves in possession of all truth, and that wherever others differ from them it is so far error. Steele, a Protestant, in a Dedication tells the Pope that the only difference between our

[1]formally written out, on parchment

ANSWERS TO

Thinking About the Selection

1. So many possible forms of government were considered during the convention that if the public had been aware of the specific debates they might have become alarmed at something that was only considered briefly by the convention and then discarded. In addition, the delegates might have been overly influenced by the opinions of those who were not part of the proceedings or been subject to the harsh criticism of those who did not agree with their decisions.

2. Pierce could not find his own notes and thought that those given to Washington might have belonged to him.

3. The delegates might have agreed to release daily reports to the press which included only those details they deemed appropriate. They might also have sequestered the delegates completely, allowing them no contact with the public at all.

Churches in their opinions of the certainty of their doctrines is, the Church of Rome is infallible and the Church of England is never in the wrong. But though many private persons think almost as highly of their own infallibility as of that of their sect, few express it so naturally as a certain french lady, who in a dispute with her sister, said "I don't know how it happens, Sister but I meet with no body but myself, that's always in the right—Il n'y a que moi qui a toujours raison."

In these sentiments, Sir, I agree to this Constitution with all its faults, if they are such; because I think a general Government necessary for us, and there is no form of Government but what may be a blessing to the people if well administered, and believe farther that this is likely to be well administered for a course of

Benjamin Franklin

years, and can only end in Despotism, as other forms have done before it, when the people shall became so corrupted as to need despotic Government, being incapable of any other. I doubt too whether any other Convention we can obtain, may be able to make a better Constitution. For when you assemble a number of men to have the advantage of their joint wisdom, you inevitably assemble with those men, all their prejudices, their passions, their errors of opinion, their local interests, and their selfish views. From such an assembly can a perfect production be expected? It therefore astonishes me, Sir, to find this system approaching so near to perfection as it does; and I think it will astonish our enemies, who are waiting with confidence to hear that our councils are confounded like those of the

In this painting by Howard Chandler Christy, delegates to the Constitutional Convention sign the Constitution of the United States.

Using newspaper accounts and books on the subject, have students compare the inauguration of President Washington in 1789 to that of President Clinton in 1993. The comparisons should examine the role of the federal government in relation to those of the states at the time of the two inaugurations, public opinion about the two men, the backgrounds of the two men, and public attitudes toward the presidency in general.

As another part of this exercise, students could interview family members, neighbors, and other teachers about their views on the presidency. Students could draft a list of questions that they wish to ask interviewees, such as: Do you think the President of the United States has too much power? Too little power? Why do you think so? Do you think the President is in touch with the needs and desires of ordinary people of the United States? What one thing would you want to tell the President if you could meet with him today?

After having their questions reviewed and approved, students can conduct their interviews, tape recording or videotaping them if possible. The interviews can then be played back to the classroom or read aloud from a transcript. Discuss with students the differing views on the presidency and the issues that people are concerned about today. Ask them what issues the people of the United States might have been concerned about in Washington's day.

Builders of Babel; and that our States are on the point of separation, only to meet hereafter for the purpose of cutting one another's throats. Thus I consent, Sir, to this Constitution because I expect no better, and because I am not sure, that it is not the best. The opinions I have had of its errors, I sacrifice to the public good. I have never whispered a syllable of them abroad. Within these walls they were born, and here they shall die. If every one of us in returning to our Constituents were to report the objections he has had to it, and endeavor to gain partizans [partisans] in support of them, we might prevent its being generally received, and thereby lose all the salutary effects & great advantages resulting naturally in our favor among foreign Nations as well as among ourselves, from our real or apparent unanimity. Much of the strength & efficiency of any Government in procuring and securing happiness to the people, depends, on opinion, on the general opinion of the goodness of the Government, as well as of the wisdom and integrity of its Governors. I hope therefore that for our own sakes as a part of the people, and for the sake of posterity, we shall act heartily and unanimously in recommending this Constitution (if approved by Congress & confirmed by the Conventions) wherever our influence may extend, and turn

A detail of the sun decoration from the chair in which George Washington sat during the Constitutional Convention.

our future thoughts & endeavors to the means of having it well administered.

On the whole, Sir, I can not help expressing a wish that every member of the Convention who may still have objections to it, would with me, on this occasion doubt a little of his own infallibility, and to make manifest our unanimity, put his name to this instrument. . . .

Whilst the last members were signing it Doctor FRANKLIN looking towards the President's Chair, at the back of which a rising sun happened to be painted, observed to a few members near him, that Painters had found it difficult to distinguish in their art a rising from a setting sun. I have, said he, . . . often in the course of the Session, and the vicissitudes [vicissitudes] of my hopes and fears as to its issue, looked at that behind the President without being able to tell whether it was rising or setting: But now at length I have the happiness to know that it is a rising and not a setting Sun.

The Constitution being signed by all the members except Mr. [Edmund] Randolph [of Virginia], Mr. Mason, and Mr. Gerry who declined giving it the sanction of their names, the Convention dissolved itself by an Adjournment sine die—

THINKING ABOUT THE SELECTION

1. Why does Franklin believe the Constitution should be approved?

2. What does Franklin mean when he urges the delegates to "doubt a little of [their] own infallibility"?

Critical Thinking

3. **Identifying Assumptions** What assumption was Franklin making about the delegates when he wrote this speech?

ANSWERS TO

Thinking About the Selection

1. Franklin believes that government is necessary for the new nation to succeed and that no other group is likely to write a document is that is any more satisfactory than that of the Convention.

2. He refers to each person's belief that they are right and the others wrong, and he asks them to consider that perhaps other viewpoints are also valid.

3. Franklin was assuming that some delegates were undecided about whether or not they would sign the Constitution.

Incidents in the Life of a Slave Girl

Primary Source

Harriet Ann Jacobs

INTRODUCTION Harriet Ann Jacobs was born into slavery in Edenton, North Carolina, in 1813 and achieved freedom in 1852. Her long and remarkable road to freedom began in 1835, when she and her two young children went into hiding in her hometown. In 1842, Jacobs escaped to New York with her son and daughter. There, she made a home for her children and was eventually purchased by the Colonization Society and freed in 1852. Shortly afterward she wrote her autobiography, which provides a personal account of what it was like to be enslaved in the 1800s. These excerpts describe parts of her early childhood and the circumstances that were forced upon her and her family.

VOCABULARY Before you read the selection, find the meaning of these words in a dictionary: toilsome, bequeath, chattel, defrauded.

I was born a slave; but I never knew it till six years of happy childhood had passed away. My father was a carpenter, and considered so intelligent and skillful in his trade, that, when buildings out of the common line were to be erected, he was sent for from long distances, to be head workman. On condition of paying his mistress two hundred dollars a year, and supporting himself, he was allowed to work at his trade, and manage his own affairs. His strongest wish was to purchase his children; but, though he several times offered his hard earnings for that purpose, he never succeeded.

I was so fondly shielded that I never dreamed I was a piece of merchandise, trusted to them for safe keeping, and liable to be demanded of them at any moment. . . .

Such were the unusually fortunate circumstances of my early childhood. When I was six years old, my mother died; and then, for the first time, I learned, by the talk around me, that I was a slave. My mother's mistress was the daughter of my grandmother's mistress. She was the foster sister of my mother; they were both nourished at my grandmother's breast. In fact, my mother had been weaned at three months old, that the babe of the mistress might obtain sufficient food. They played together as children; and, when they became women, my mother was a most faithful servant to her white foster sister. On her death-bed her mistress promised that her children should never suffer for any thing; and during her lifetime she kept her word. They all spoke kindly of my dead mother, who had been a slave merely in name, but in nature was noble and womanly. I grieved for her, and my young mind was troubled with the thought who would now take of me and my little brother. I was told that my home was now to be with her mistress; and I found it a happy one. No toilsome or disagreeable duties were imposed upon me. My mistress was so kind to me that I was always glad to

Antislavery logo symbolizing the link between the women's rights movement and the abolitionist movement.

Have students research the daily life of an enslaved person on a southern plantation or some other figure from Unit 3. Students might use such sources as *Six Women's Slave Narratives* by William Andrews. Students should each then prepare a ten-minute, one-person skit that will demonstrate what the daily life of their chosen person was like. Afterwards, discuss with the class what the skit revealed about the person and the history of the time. If possible, videotape the skits for viewing by other classes.

do her bidding, and proud to labor for her as much as my young years would permit. . . .

When I was nearly twelve years old, my kind mistress sickened and died. As I saw the cheek grow paler, and the eye more glassy, how earnestly I prayed in my heart that she might live! I loved her; for she had been almost like a mother to me. My prayers were not answered. She died, and they buried her in the little churchyard, where, day after day, my tears fell upon her grave.

I was sent to spend a week with my grandmother. I was now old enough to begin to think of the future; and again and again I asked myself what they would do with me. I felt sure I should never find another mistress so kind as the one who was gone. She had promised my dying mother that her children would never suffer for any thing; and when I remembered that, and recalled her many proofs of attachment to me, I could not help having some hopes that she had left me free. . . .

After a brief period of suspense . . . we learned that she had bequeathed me to her sister's daughter, a child of five years old. So vanished our hopes. My mistress had taught me the precepts of God's Word: "Thou shalt love thy neighbor as thyself." "Whatsoever ye would that men should do unto you, do ye even so unto them." But I was her slave, and I suppose she did not recognize me as her neighbor. I would give much to blot out from my memory that one great wrong. As a child, I loved my mistress; and, looking back on the happy days I spent with her, I try to think with less bitterness of this act of injustice. While I was with her, she taught me to read and spell; and for this privilege, which so rarely falls to the lot of a slave, I bless her memory. . . .

My grandmother's mistress had always promised her that, at her death, she should be free; and it was said that in her will she made good the promise. But when the estate was settled, Dr. Flint told the faithful old servant that, under existing circumstances, it was necessary she should be sold.

On the appointed day, the customary advertisement was posted up, proclaiming that there would be a "public sale of negroes, horses, &c." Dr. Flint called to tell my grandmother that he was unwilling to wound her feelings by putting her up at auction, and that he would prefer to dispose of her at private sale. My grandmother saw through his hypocrisy; she understood very well that he was ashamed of the job. She was a very spirited woman, and if he was base enough to sell her, when her mistress intended she should be free, she was determined the public should know it. She had for a long time supplied many families with crackers and preserves; consequently, "Aunt Marthy," as she was called, was generally known, and every body who knew her respected her intelligence and good character. Her long and faithful service in the family was also well known, and the intention of her mistress to leave her free. When the day of sale came, she took her place among the chattels, and at the first call she sprang upon the auction-block. Many voices called out, "Shame! Shame! Who is going to sell you, Aunt Marthy? Don't stand there! That is no place for you." Without saying a word, she quietly awaited her fate. No one bid for her. At last, a feeble voice said, "Fifty dollars." It came from a maiden lady, seventy years old, the sister of my grandmother's deceased mistress. She had lived forty years under the same roof with my grandmother; she knew how faithfully she had served her owners, and how cruelly she had been defrauded of her rights; and she resolved to protect her.

THINKING ABOUT THE SELECTION

1. What skill did Jacobs' former mistress teach her? How important was this skill to Jacobs?
2. Why did Dr. Flint want to sell Jacobs' grandmother at a private auction?

Critical Thinking
3. **Formulating Questions** What questions might you ask of Jacobs to learn more about her life?

ANSWERS TO

Thinking About the Selection
1. Jacobs's mistress taught her how to read and write. The skill proved to be quite important both to Jacobs and to history because she used it to write of her life as an enslaved person.
2. Because he knew that the community would be enraged at the idea of selling her at all and wanted to do it secretly.
3. Questions might include: What sort of work did you do as an enslaved person? How did white children treat you? What books did you read and what did you learn from them? How did you escape from slavery?

To a Locomotive in Winter

Walt Whitman

INTRODUCTION Walt Whitman gave Americans poetry that was uniquely theirs. He departed from the traditional European style of writing in favor of a freer form that would give voice to the vastness and energy of the new United States. At first, his work was not popular, but by the time the poem below was written, in 1881, he was revered as one of the foremost literary figures in the world. "To a Locomotive in Winter" celebrates the railroads, which, with their expansion in the later part of the 1800s, gave a new excitement and urgency to the movement of the people of the United States.

VOCABULARY Before you read the selection, find the meaning of these words in a dictionary: recitative, panoply, ponderous, metrical, Muse, debonair, glib, unpent.

> Thee for my recitative,
> Thee in the driving storm even as now, the snow, the winter-day declining,
> Thee in thy panoply, thy measur'd dual throbbing and thy beat convulsive,
> Thy black cylindric body, golden brass and silvery steel,
> Thy ponderous side-bars, parallel and connecting rods, gyrating, shuttling at thy sides,
> Thy metrical, now swelling pant and roar, now tapering in the distance,
> Thy great protruding head-light fix'd in front,
> Thy long, pale, floating vapor-pennants, tinged with delicate purple,
> The dense and murky clouds out-belching from thy smoke-stack,
> Thy knitted frame, thy springs and valves, the tremulous twinkle of thy wheels,
> Thy train of cars behind, obedient, merrily following,
> Through gale or calm, now swift, now slack, yet steadily careering;
> Type of the modern—emblem of motion and power—pulse of the
>   continent,
> For once come serve the Muse and merge in verse, even as here I
>   see thee,
> With storm and buffeting gusts of wind and falling snow,
> By day thy warning ringing bell to sound its notes,
> By night thy silent signal lamps to swing.

Walt Whitman

FOCUS

Connecting Literature and History

In Walt Whitman's poem, students will find a passionate expression of the invigorating growth of the United States during the 1800s that is unparalleled by any mere recounting of facts and figures.

INSTRUCT

Tell students to analyze the poem. Have them begin by carefully reading the poem several times. Then ask them to discuss the language used in the piece. Is it angry? Thoughtful? Excited? Then have students make a list of the words that contribute to the overall feel of the piece. Finally, ask students to turn to Unit 3 in their textbooks and to find passages that are supported by this source reading.

After students have finished, have them share their lists with the rest of the class. Discuss the fact that primary sources such as speeches and letters are used as evidence by historians when they are piecing together the events of the past. Pieces of literature such as Walt Whitman's poem often provide further evidence of the mood of the nation and the events that unfolded at a particular time.

Have students write a poem or short story that relates to other events or themes that appear in Unit 3, such as the issuing of the Monroe Doctrine in 1823 or President Jackson's goal to move all Native Americans west of the Mississippi. Encourage students to research those events further in such sources as *Hunted Like a Wolf: The Story of the Seminole War* by Milton Meltzer or *The Making of the Monroe Doctrine* by E. R. May. Read some of the students' work to the class.

"Lazell, Perkins and Co., Bridge-water, Ma." painted in 1858 by J.P. Newell.

Fierce-throated beauty!
Roll through my chant with all thy lawless music, thy swinging lamps at night,
Thy madly-whistled laughter, echoing, rumbling like an earthquake, rousing all,
Law of thyself complete, thine own track firmly holding,
(No sweetness debonair of tearful harp or glib piano thine,)
Thy trills of shrieks by rocks and hills return'd,
Launch'd o'er the prairies wide, across the lakes,
To the free skies unpent and glad and strong.

THINKING ABOUT THE SELECTION

1. What image of the railroad does Whitman's poem evoke? Give examples of words or phrases from the poem that help to convey this image.
2. How might a Native American writer of the late 1800s have described the railroad? Would the description likely be similar to Whitman's or different? Explain your answer.

Critical Thinking

3. **Demonstrating Reasoned Judgment** This poem was written in 1881, at the time when the railroads were relatively new in the United States. How does this poem describe the railroad and other aspects of the United States at the time?

ANSWERS TO

Thinking About the Selection

1. Whitman's poem evokes an image of the railroad as powerful and full of energy. Words and phrases used include: "throbbing," "ponderous," "pant and roar," "protruding," "dense," "emblem of motion and power," "pulse of the continent," "fierce-throated beauty," "earthquake," "strong."

2. One possible answer is that a Native American writer might see the railroad as an unwelcome intruder that brings noise and dirt into the natural world. The description and tone would likely differ from Whitman's.

3. The poem conveys the sense of newness, energy, and motion that was characteristic of the United States at the time.

Diary of a Southern Woman *Primary Source*

Mary Boykin Chesnut

INTRODUCTION Mary Boykin Chesnut of South Carolina was a well-to-do southerner who kept a diary of the days before the start of the Civil War. Because her husband, James Chesnut, Jr., served as an aide to Jefferson Davis, president of the Confederacy, Mary Boykin Chesnut knew members of the Confederate cabinet and many of the Confederacy's most important generals, including Robert E. Lee.

VOCABULARY Before you read the selection, find the meaning of these words in a dictionary: forestall, stagnant, clandestine, prowess, sanguine.

June 10, 1861

The war is making us all tenderly sentimental. No casualties yet, no real mourning, nobody hurt; so it is all parade, fuss and fine feathers. There is no imagination here to forestall woe, and only the excitement and wild awakening from everyday stagnant life is felt; that is, when one gets away from the two or three sensible men who are still left in the world. . . .

In Charleston, a butcher has been clandestinely supplying the Yankee fleet outside of the Bar with beef. They say he gave the information which led to the capture of the *Savannah*. They will hang him. . . .

June 28, 1861

In Mrs. Davis's drawing-room last night, the President[1] took a seat by me on the sofa where I sat. He talked for nearly an hour. He laughed at our faith in our own prowess. We are like the British; we think every Southerner equal to three Yankees at least, but we will have to be equivalent to a dozen now. After his experience of the fighting qualities of Southerners in Mexico, Mr. Davis believes that we will do all that can be done by pluck and muscle, endurance and dogged courage, dash and red-hot patriotism, and yet his tone was not sanguine. There was a sad refrain running through it all. For one thing, either way, he thinks it will be a long war. That floored me at once. It has been too long for me already. . . .

October 13, 1861

I was shocked to hear that dear friends of mine refused to take work for the soldiers because their seamstresses had their winter clothes to make. I told them true patriotesses would be willing to wear the same clothes until our siege was raised. They did not seem to care. They have seen no ragged, dirty, sick and miserable soldiers lying in the hospital, no lack of woman's nursing, no lack of woman's tears, but an awful lack of a proper change in clean clothes. They know nothing of the horrors of war. One has to see to believe. They take it easy, and are not yet willing to make personal sacrifices. The time is coming when they will not be given a choice in the matter.

THINKING ABOUT THE SELECTION

1. What is Jefferson Davis's opinion of the fighting abilities of the northerners?
2. Why is Chesnut's attitude about clothing different from that of her friends?

Critical Thinking

3. **Drawing Conclusions** What can you determine about the mood of some southerners from Chesnut's diary? Give examples to support your answer.

---

[1] Jefferson Davis, President of the Confederate States.

ANSWERS TO

Thinking About the Selection
1. He thinks that they are able and courageous fighters.
2. She has seen soldiers in the hospital who are "ragged, dirty, sick and miserable." Her friends have not seen the soldiers and "know nothing of the horrors of war."

3. Their mood is "tenderly sentimental," "all parade, fuss and fine feathers." They feel "excitement and wild awakening." According to Davis, the southerners think highly of their own fighting abilities and are of a low opinion of the northerners' abilities. Finally, Chesnut reveals that some southerners are not yet aware of the sacrifices and hardship that the war will entail.

The Gettysburg Address

Primary Source

Abraham Lincoln

INTRODUCTION Edward Everett, a former United States senator from Massachusetts and known as one of the greatest orators of his day, spoke for two hours at the ceremony dedicating the cemetery at Gettysburg. When President Lincoln rose after Everett to give his dedication, the crowd fell silent in anticipation. At just 267 words, the speech was short, so short that a photographer who meant to take a picture of Lincoln delivering the speech did not have time to focus his camera. Later Everett wrote to Lincoln, "I should be glad if I could flatter myself that I came as near to the central idea of the occasion in two hours as you did in two minutes." Indeed, Lincoln's address, criticized at the time for its brevity, encapsulated an ideal that citizens continue to cherish today.

VOCABULARY Before you read the selection, find the meaning of this word in a dictionary: consecrate.

Four score and seven years ago our fathers brought forth on this continent, a new nation, conceived in Liberty, and dedicated to the proposition that all men are created equal.

Now we are engaged in a great civil war, testing whether that nation, or any nation so conceived and so dedicated, can long endure. We are met on a great battlefield of that war. We have come to dedicate a portion of that field, as a final resting place for those who here gave their lives that that nation might live. It is altogether fitting and proper that we should do this.

But, in a larger sense, we can not dedicate—we cannot consecrate—we can not hallow—this ground. The brave men, living and dead, who struggled here, have consecrated it, far above our poor power to add or detract. The world will little note nor long remember what we say here, but it can never forget what they did here. It is for us the living, rather, to be dedicated here to the unfinished work which they who fought here have thus far so nobly advanced. It is rather for us to be here dedicated to the great task remaining before us—that from these honored dead we take increased devotion to that cause for which they gave the last full measure of devotion—that we here highly resolve that these dead shall not have died in vain—that this nation, under God, shall have a new birth of freedom—and that government of the people, by the people, for the people, shall not perish from the earth.

President Abraham Lincoln

THINKING ABOUT THE SELECTION

1. How does Lincoln describe the soldiers who died at Gettysburg?
2. Why does Lincoln say that the people attending this ceremony cannot really dedicate the cemetery?

Critical Thinking
3. **Determining Relevance** What are some of the ideals expressed in the Gettysburg Address that we still find relevant today?

ANSWERS TO

Thinking About the Selection
1. He describes them as "brave," noble, and "honored."
2. He says that the deaths of the men who fought in the battle have dedicated it more than can those who gather to honor them.
3. The ideal that all are created equal, that those who fight for their country should be honored, and that a government of the people, by the people, and for the people is worth fighting for.

Where Is America?

Literature

Anzia Yezierska

INTRODUCTION Like many other immigrants who flooded into the nation's cities during the late 1800s, Anzia Yezierska and her family came to New York to escape ethnic persecution in their homeland. In her autobiography, *Hungry Hearts,* Yezierska describes what it was like to leave her Russian village and begin a new life in the United States.

VOCABULARY Before you read the selection, find the meaning of these words in a dictionary: Cossack, dilapidated, maw, galling.

Steerage—dirty bundles—foul odors—seasick humanity—but I saw and heard nothing of the foulness and ugliness around me. I floated in showers of sunshine. Vision upon vision of the new world opened before me. From everyone's lips flowed the golden legend of the golden country:

"In America you can say what you feel—you can join your friends in the open streets without fear of Cossack."

"In America is a home for everyone. The land is your land. Not like in Russia where you feel yourself a stranger in the village where you were born and lived—the village in which your father and grandfather lie buried." . . .

"Everybody can do what he wants with his life in America."

"There are no high or low in America. Even the President holds hands with Gedalyeh Mindel."

"Plenty for all. Learning flows free like milk and honey."

"Learning flows free."

The words painted pictures in my mind. I saw before me free schools, free colleges, free libraries, where I could learn and learn and keep on learning. . . .

"Land! Land!" came the joyous shout.

"America! We're in America!" cried my mother, almost smothering us in her rapture.

All crowded and pushed on deck. They strained and stretched to get the first glimpse of the "golden country," lifting their children on their shoulders that they might see beyond them.

Men fell on their knees to pray. Women hugged their babies and wept. Children danced. Strangers embraced and kissed like old friends. Old men and women had in their eyes a look of young people in love.

Age-old visions sang themselves in me—songs of freedom of an oppressed people.

America! America! . . .

Between buildings that loomed like mountains, we struggled with our bundles, spreading around us the smell of the steerage. Up Broadway, under the bridge, and through the swarming streets of the ghetto, we followed Gedalyeh Mindel.

I looked about the narrow streets of squeezed-in stores and houses, ragged clothes, dirty bedding oozing out of the windows, ash cans and garbage cans cluttering the sidewalk. A vague sadness pressed down my heart—the first doubt of America.

"Where are the green fields and open spaces in America?" cried my heart. "Where is the golden country of my dreams?"

A loneliness for the fragrant silence of the woods that lay beyond our mud hut welled up in my heart, a longing for the soft, responsive earth of our village streets. All about me was the hardness of brick and stone, the stinking smells of crowded poverty.

America, the destination of millions of immigrants in the late 1800s, is stamped in gold letters on the side of this steamer trunk.

Have students ask their parents or other relatives whether their ancestors immigrated to the United States from Europe during the late 1800s. If so, have students interview any living relative who remembers some details about the immigrant. Students should ask questions such as: Why did [relative] decide to leave his or her native country? How much did it cost to make the trip? What was the journey across the ocean like? Where did [relative] live on arriving in the United States? What did [relative] do for a living? Students can tape record their interviews and play them back to the class. Have them write a one-page paper describing the contents of the tape and what they learned about European immigrants in doing the interview. If a student does not have a relative who emigrated from Europe, have them check with neighbors or other people in the community to find someone who does. Students can then interview that person for memories about the immigrant.

"Here's your house with separate rooms like in a palace." Gedalyeh Mindel flung open the door of a dingy, airless flat.

"Oi weh!" my mother cried in dismay. "Where's the sunshine in America?"

She went to the window and looked out at the blank wall of the next house. "Gottuniu! Like in a grave so dark."

"It ain't so dark, it's only a little shady." Gedalyeh Mindel lighted the gas. "Look only." He pointed with pride to the dim gaslight. "No candles, no kerosene lamps in America, you turn on a screw and put to it a match and you got it light like with sunshine."

Again the shadow fell over me, again the doubt of America!

In America were rooms without sunlight, rooms to sleep in, to eat in, to cook in, but without sunshine. And Gedalyeh Mindel was happy. Could I be satisfied with just a place to sleep and eat in, and a door to shut people out—to take the place of sunlight? Or would I always need the sunlight to be happy?

And where was there a place in America for me to play? I looked out into the alley below and saw pale-faced children scrambling in the gutter. "Where is America?" cried my heart. . . .

"Heart of mine!" my mother's voice moaned above me. "Father is already gone an hour. You know how they'll squeeze from you a nickel for every minute you're late. Quick only!"

I seized my bread and herring and tumbled down the stairs and out into the street. I ate running, blindly pressing through the hurrying throngs of workers—my haste and fear choking each mouthful.

I felt a strangling in my throat as I neared the sweatshop prison[1]; all my nerves screwed together into iron hardness to endure the day's torture.

For an instant I hesitated as I faced the grated window of the old dilapidated building—dirt and decay cried out from every crumbling brick.

In the maw of the shop, raging around me the roar and the clatter, the clatter and the roar, the merciless grind of the pounding machines. Half maddened, half deadened, I struggled to think, to feel, to remember—what am I—who am I—why was I here?

[1] Factory where Yezierska worked

I struggled in vain—bewildered and lost in a whirlpool of noise.

"America—America—where was America?"

It cried in my heart.

The factory whistle—the slowing-down of the machines—the shout of release hailing the noon hour.

I woke as from a tense nightmare—a weary waking to pain.

In the dark chaos of my brain reason began to dawn. In my stifled heart feelings began to pulse. The wound of my wasted life began to throb and ache. My childhood choked with drudgery—must my youth too die—unlived?

The odor of herring and garlic—the ravenous munching of food—laughing and loud, vulgar jokes. Was it only I who was so wretched? I looked at those around me. Were they happy or only insensible to their slavery? How could they laugh and joke? Why were they not torn with rebellion against this galling grind—the crushing, deadening movements of the body, where only hands live and hearts and brains must die?

A touch on my shoulder. I looked up. It was Yetta Solomon from the machine next to mine.

"Here's your tea."

I stared at her, half hearing.

"Ain't you going to eat nothing?"

"Oi weh! Yetta! I can't stand it!" The cry broke from me. "I didn't come to America to turn into a machine. I came to America to make from myself a person. Does America want only my hands—only the strength of my body—not my heart—not my feelings—my thoughts?"

THINKING ABOUT THE SELECTION

1. What were Anzia Yezierska's expectations of life in the United States?
2. What did the author first miss about her village, once she had been shown the family's new residence?

Critical Thinking

3. **Identifying Central Issues** What was the author's biggest disillusionment with the United States?

ANSWERS TO

1. She expected to find freedom, choices, equality, and the opportunity to attend school and learn as much as she could.
2. She longed for the "fragrant silence of the woods" and the "soft, responsive earth of our village streets."
3. She was disillusioned when it seemed that the United States wanted only the labor of her hands, and was not interested in her thoughts or feelings.

Separate but Equal

Primary Source

INTRODUCTION The Fourteenth and Fifteenth amendments to the Constitution were passed after the Civil War to extend citizenship to formerly enslaved people and to protect African Americans' right to vote. A series of Supreme Court decisions in the late 1800s weakened the force of those amendments, however. One such case, *Plessy* v. *Ferguson* (1896), involved a Louisiana law that allowed separate accommodations for white and African American passengers on railroads in the state. Homer Plessy was arrested after refusing to sit in the car designated for African Americans. After being convicted in the state courts, he appealed to the Supreme Court. The Court's ruling in the case undercut the Fourteenth Amendment by upholding the idea that separate facilities for African Americans were acceptable, as long as those facilities were equal to those provided for white Americans. The Court's decision, delivered by Justice Henry Brown, denied the claim that separate facilities were, by nature, inferior and unequal. The excerpt below from the Court's decision details its reasoning on this matter and also includes a portion of the dissenting opinion.

VOCABULARY Before you read the selection, find the meaning of these words in a dictionary: commingle, competency, usage, conveyance, fallacy, plaintiff, relegate, acquiesce, affinity, beneficent, abridge, indissolubly, sanction, servitude.

MR. JUSTICE BROWN DELIVERED THE OPINION OF THE COURT:

The object of the [14th] amendment was undoubtedly to enforce the absolute equality of the two races before the law, but in the nature of things it could not have been intended to abolish distinctions based upon color, or to enforce social, as distinguished from political, equality, or a commingling of the two races upon terms unsatisfactory to either. Laws permitting, and even requiring their separation in places where they are liable to be brought into contact do not necessarily imply the inferiority of either race to the other, and have been generally, if not universally, recognized as within the competency of the state legislatures in the exercise of their police power. The most common instance of this is connected with the establishment of separate schools for white and colored children, which have been held to be a valid exercise of the legislative power even by courts of states where the political rights of the colored race have been longest and most earnestly enforced. . . .

So far, then, as a conflict with the 14th Amendment is concerned, the case reduces itself to the question whether the statute of Louisiana is a reasonable regulation, and with respect to this there must necessarily be a large discretion on the part of the legislature. In determining the question of reasonableness it is at liberty to act with reference to the established usages, customs, and traditions of the people, and with a view to the promotion of their comfort, and the preservation of the public peace and good order. Gauged by this standard, we cannot say that a law which authorizes or even requires the separation of the two races in public conveyances is unreasonable or more obnoxious to the 14th Amendment than the acts of Congress requiring separate schools for colored children in the District of Columbia, the constitutionality of which does not seem to have been questioned, or the corresponding acts of state legislatures.

We consider the underlying fallacy of the plaintiff's argument to consist in the assumption that the enforced separation of the two races stamps the colored

Finally, ask students to comment on the text of the decision. Do they think this ruling was consistent with the attitudes of the period? Ask students to consider what the Court would have risked if it had ruled in Plessy's favor.

EXTEND

Ask students to think about how they would go about proving in a court of law that separate facilities are inherently unequal. Ask them to consider what evidence they would gather, whom they would call as witnesses, and how they would word their final argument. Then have students write a report explaining their approach.

Review students' reports and offer suggestions where needed. Then have students work in groups of five or six. One student should be the lawyer, one the judge, and the rest should be witnesses called to the stand by the lawyer. The students should then role-play for the class the trial of the separate but equal doctrine, acting out only the side of the prosecution (those attacking the doctrine).

race with a badge of inferiority. If this be so, it is not by reason of anything found in the act, but solely because the colored race chooses to put that construction upon it. The argument necessarily assumes that if, as has been more than once the case, and is not unlikely to be so again, the colored race should become the dominant power in the state legislature, and should enact a law in precisely similar terms, it would thereby relegate the white race to an inferior position. We imagine that the white race, at least, would not acquiesce in this assumption. The argument also assumes that social prejudices may be overcome by legislation, and that equal rights can not be secured to the negro except by an enforced commingling of the two races. We cannot accept this proposition. If the two races are to meet on terms of social equality, it must be the result of natural affinities, a mutual appreciation of each other's merits and a voluntary consent of individuals. . . .

Despite Supreme Court rulings that legitimized segregation, African Americans protested against the many forms of discrimination in the post-Reconstruction era, including lynching.

MR. JUSTICE HARLAN DISSENTING . . .
The present decision, it may well be apprehended, will not only stimulate aggressions, more or less brutal and irritating, upon the admitted rights of colored citizens, but will encourage the belief that it is possible, by means of state enactments, to defeat the beneficent purposes which the people of the United States had in view when they adopted the recent amendments of the Constitution, by one of which the blacks of this country were made citizens of the United States and of the states in which they respectively reside and whose privileges and immunities, as citizens, the states are forbidden to abridge. Sixty millions of whites are in no danger from the presence here of eight millions of blacks. The destinies of the two races in this country are indissolubly linked together, and the interests of both require that the common government of all shall

not permit the seeds of race hate to be planted under the sanction of law. What can more certainly arouse race hate, what more certainly create and perpetuate a feeling of distrust between these races, than state enactments which in fact proceed on the ground that colored citizens are so inferior and degraded that they cannot be allowed to sit in public coaches occupied by white citizens? That, as all will admit, is the real meaning of such legislation as was enacted in Louisana. . . .

If evils will result from the commingling of the two races upon public highways established for the benefit of all, they will be infinitely less than those that will surely come from state legislation regulating the enjoyment of civil rights upon the basis of race. We boast of the freedom enjoyed by our people above all other peoples. But it is difficult to reconcile that boast with a state of the law which, practically, puts the brand of servitude and degradation upon a large class of our fellow citizens, our equals before the law. The thin disguise of "equal" accommodations for passengers in railroad coaches will not mislead anyone, or atone for the wrong this day done.

THINKING ABOUT THE SELECTION

1. What does the decision state that the Fourteenth Amendment was meant to do? What does it say the Amendment was not meant to do?
2. According to this decision, how does the Supreme Court determine the reasonableness of a particular law?

Critical Thinking

3. **Expressing Problems Clearly** What does the Court believe is wrong with the argument that separate facilities are unequal?

ANSWERS TO

Thinking About the Selection
1. The Court's decision states that the Fourteenth Amendment was meant to "enforce the absolute equality of the two races before the law." The decision states that the amendment was not meant to "abolish distinctions based upon color, or to enforce social, as distinguished from political, equality, or a commingling of the two races upon terms unsatisfactory to either."

2. The Court uses established usage, customs, and traditions, keeping in mind the people's comfort and the preservation of the public peace and order.
3. The Court believes that separate does not necessarily mean unequal because if this were so, then a state legislature controlled by African Americans, acting under a similar law, would place white Americans in an unequal position. In addition, the Court does not believe that social prejudices can be overcome by legislation or that equal rights can be secured by forced commingling.

The United States Looking Outward

Alfred T. Mahan

Primary Source

INTRODUCTION Naval historian and admiral Alfred T. Mahan believed that the United States should follow the example of Great Britain in order to gain dominance in world affairs. The most important act the country could undertake, according to Mahan, was to enlarge and strengthen its naval fleet so that no other nation could challenge it when trading overseas. In the excerpt below from "The United States Looking Outward," published in the

Atlantic Monthly in 1890, Mahan explains his reasoning for such a policy. Mahan's writings led to the United States Navy becoming one of the most powerful in the world. For many years his books were standard reading for all naval officers.

VOCABULARY Before you read the selection, find the meaning of these words in a dictionary: temperament, ominous, prudent, inanition.

For nearly the lifetime of a generation, American industries have been protected[1] until the practice has assumed the force of a tradition. At bottom, however, the temperament of the American people is essentially alien to such a sluggish attitude. Independently of all bias for or against protection, it is safe to predict that, when the opportunities for gain abroad are understood, American enterprise will try to reach them. The importance of distant markets and their relation to our own production imply the recognition of the link that joins the products and the markets—that is, the carrying trade.[2] We need not follow far this line of thought before America's unique position becomes clear. Facing the older worlds of the East and West, America's shores are lapped by the oceans which touch the one or the other but which are common to her alone.

Together with these signs of change in our own policy there is a restlessness in the world at large which is deeply significant, if not ominous. There is no sound reason for believing that the world has passed into a period of peace outside the limits of Europe. Unsettled political conditions exist in Haiti,

Central America, and many of the Pacific islands, especially the Hawaiian group. When combined with great military or commercial importance, these conditions contain dangerous germs of quarrel, against which it is at least prudent to be prepared.

Despite a superior geographical location, the United States is woefully unready to assert its influence in the Caribbean and Central America. We have not the navy. And, what is worse, we are not willing to have the navy that will weigh seriously in any disputes with those nations whose interests conflict with our own. We have not, and we are not anxious to provide, the defense of the Atlantic seaboard which will leave the navy free for its work at sea.

Whether they will or not, Americans must now begin to look outward. The growing production of the country demands it. An increasing volume of public sentiment demands it. The position of the United States, between the two Old Worlds and the two great oceans, makes the same claim, which will soon be strengthened by the creation of the new link joining the Atlantic and Pacific. The tendency will be increased by the growth of the European colonies in the Pacific, by the advancing civilization of Japan, and by the rapid peopling of our Pacific states.

The military needs of the Pacific states, as well as their supreme importance to the whole country, are yet a matter of the future. But this future is so near that

---

[1] Mahan is referring to protective tariffs that increase the price of imported goods so that American-made goods will be less expensive.

[2] The carrying trade refers to the fleets of merchant ships that carry products to markets overseas.

describing whether Mahan would agree or disagree with Bryan. Students should use examples from the excerpt to support their arguments.

EXTEND

Ask students to write a poem that expresses the imperialist sentiments voiced by Alfred Mahan and Albert Beveridge. If they prefer, students can draw a political cartoon or other picture that illustrates in some way either the imperialist or the anti-imperialist side. Display students' work around the room and allow the class time to review the poems and drawings.

Mahan believed that a powerful navy was needed to protect the nation's "carrying trade," symbolized by this busy New York dock in the early 1900s.

provision should immediately begin to weigh their importance. To provide this, three things are needed: First, protection of the chief harbors by fortifications and coast-defense ships. Second, naval force, the arm of offensive power, which alone enables a country to extend its influence outward. Third, it should be an unshakeable resolution of our national policy that no European state should henceforth acquire a coaling position within 3,000 miles of San Francisco—a distance which includes the Sandwich and Galapagos islands and the coast of Central America. For fuel is the life of modern naval war. It is the food of the ship. Without it the modern monsters of the deep die of inanition. Around it, therefore, cluster some of the most important considerations of naval strategy.

THINKING ABOUT THE SELECTION

1. For what geographical reasons does Mahan believe that the United States is in a unique position to become a powerful international trading force?
2. For what economic reasons does Mahan believe the United States must begin looking to distant markets for trading opportunities?

Critical Thinking

3. **Formulating Questions** What questions would you ask Mahan in order to understand how qualified he is to draw the conclusions stated in this excerpt?

ANSWERS TO

Thinking About the Selection
1. The United States is positioned geographically between Europe and Asia and has coasts on both the Pacific and the Atlantic oceans, whereas Europe and Asia each have shores on only one of these oceans. In addition, the building of the Panama Canal ("the new link joining the Atlantic and Pacific") will further strengthen the United States' position for engaging in international trade.

2. Mahan states that the "growing production of the country demands" that Americans begin to look outward. He refers to the surplus of goods that modern technology has allowed the United States to produce.

3. Questions might include: Describe your career in the navy. What studies have you made of the American economy? From where does your knowledge of foreign affairs come? Why do you believe that the United States should imitate British policy with regard to its navy?

All Quiet on the Western Front

Erich Maria Remarque

Literature

INTRODUCTION In 1929 Erich Maria Remarque wrote *All Quiet on the Western Front,* an autobiographical account of the war which became the most celebrated novel of its time. Remarque emigrated to the United States in 1939 after his books were banned by the Nazis and his citizenship revoked. In the excerpt below, the book's main character, a soldier in whose voice the novel is told, describes a visit home on a leave.

VOCABULARY Before you read the selection, find the meaning of these words in a dictionary: garrison, apoplexy, parapet.

For a moment I am shy and lower my head, then I take off my helmet and look up. Yes, it is my eldest sister.

"Paul," she cries, "Paul—"

I nod, my pack bumps against the banisters; my rifle is so heavy.

She pulls a door open and calls: "Mother, Mother, Paul is here."

I can go no further—Mother, Mother, Paul is here.

I lean against the wall and grip my helmet and rifle. I hold them as tight as I can, but I cannot take another step, the staircase fades before my eyes, I support myself with the butt of my rifle against my feet and clench my teeth fiercely, but I cannot speak a word, my sister's call has made me powerless, I can do nothing, I struggle to make myself laugh, to speak, but no word comes, and so I stand on the steps, miserable, helpless, paralysed, and against my will the tears run down my cheeks.

My sister comes back and says: "Why, what is the matter?"

Then I pull myself together and stagger on to the landing. I lean my rifle in a corner, I set my pack against the wall, place my helmet on it, and fling down my equipment and baggage. Then I say fiercely: "Bring me a handkerchief."

She gives me one from the cupboard and I dry my face. Above me on the wall hangs the glass case with the coloured butterflies that once I collected.

Now I hear my mother's voice. It comes from the bedroom.

"Is she in bed?" I ask my sister.

"She is ill—" she replies.

I go in to her, give her my hand and say as calmly as I can: "Here I am, Mother."

She lies still in the dim light. Then she asks anxiously:

"Are you wounded?" and I feel her searching glance.

"No, I have got leave."

My mother is very pale. I am afraid to make a light.

"Here I lie now," says she, "and cry instead of being glad."

"Are you sick, Mother?" I ask.

"I am going to get up a little to-day," she says and turns to my sister, who is continually running to the kitchen to watch that the food does not burn: "And put out the jar of preserved whortleberries—you like that, don't you?" she asks me.

"Yes, Mother, I haven't had any for a long time."

"We might almost have known you were coming," laughs my sister, "there is just your favourite dish, potato-cakes, and even whortleberries to go with them, too."

"And it is Saturday," I add.

"Sit here beside me," says my mother.

FOCUS
Connecting Literature and History

Tell students that the death toll in World War I is estimated at 8 million soldiers, which is roughly equal to the population of the entire state of Ohio. In addition, 20 million civilians were killed or died during or immediately following the war; this figure is slightly more than the population of the entire state of New York. Remind students that new weapons used in combination with old fighting tactics resulted in these huge figures. Tell students that soldiers fighting on the battlefronts are the best source of information on what it was like to endure such a war, day after day. Explain to students that the source readings will help them develop an understanding of soldiers' war experiences.

INSTRUCT

Ask students to review the excerpt from the viewpoint of a World War I historian. Ask: What information about World War I can you gain from the excerpt? What information can you discern from it about the emotions and morale of troops? What questions would a historian need to answer before using the excerpt to learn about World War I?

Have students read Remarque's book *All Quiet on the Western Front*. Ask students to write a critique of the book in which they compare the description of the war in the book to that found in Unit 6 of their texts. In their critiques students should also comment on the effectiveness of Remarque's writing and how it differs from a first-person account written by a soldier who was in the war, such as that found on page 563. What are the pros and cons of each type of writing?

She looks at me. Her hands are white and sickly and frail compared with mine. We say very little, and I am thankful that she asks me nothing. What ought I to say? Everything I could have wished for has happened. I have come out of it safely and sit here beside her. And in the kitchen stands my sister making the evening bread and singing.

"Dear boy," says my mother softly.

We were never very demonstrative in our family; poor folk who toil and are full of cares are not so. It is not their way to protest what they already know. When my mother says to me "dear boy," it means much more than when another uses it. I know well enough that the jar of whortleberries is the only one they have had for months, and that she has kept it for me; and the somewhat stale cakes that she gives me too. She has taken a favourable opportunity of getting a few and has put them all by for me.

I sit by her bed, and through the window the chestnut trees in the beer garden opposite glow in brown and gold. I breathe deeply and say over to myself:— "You are at home, you are at home." But a sense of strangeness will not leave me, I can find nothing of myself in all these things. There is my mother, there is my sister, there my case of butterflies, and there the mahogany piano—but I am not myself there. There is a distance, a veil between us.

I go and fetch my pack to the bedside and turn out the things I have brought—a whole Edam cheese, that Kat provided me with, two loaves of army bread, three-quarters of a pound of butter, two tins of liversausage, a pound of dripping and a little bag of rice.

"I suppose you can make some use of that—" They nod.

"Is it pretty bad for food here?" I enquire.

Two soldiers fire at the enemy from a trench. They wear masks to protect themselves against poison gas.

"Yes, there's not much. Do you get enough out there?"

I smile and point to the things I have brought. "Not always quite so much as that, of course, but we fare reasonably well."

Erna goes out to bring in the food. Suddenly my mother seizes hold of my hand and asks falteringly: "Was it very bad out there, Paul?"

Mother, what should I answer to that! You would not understand, and never realize it. And you never should realize it. Was it bad, you ask.—You, Mother,—I shake my head and say: "No, Mother, not so very. There are always a lot of us together so it isn't so bad."

"Yes, but Heinrich Bredemeyer was here just lately and he said it was terrible out there now, with the gas and all the rest of it."

It is my mother who says that. She says: "With the gas and all the rest of it." She does not know what she is saying, she is merely anxious for me. Should I tell her how we once found three enemy trenches with their garrison all stiff as though stricken with apoplexy? Against the parapet, in the dug-outs, just where they were, the men stood and lay about, with blue faces, dead.

"No, Mother, that's only talk," I answer, "there's not very much in what Bredemeyer says."

1. Why does the author begin to cry when his sister calls to his mother that he is there?
2. Why does the author stress the strangeness of having his mother ask him about the horrors of the war?

Critical Thinking

3. **Identifying Central Issues** Why does the author feel "a distance" from his family and home?

Thinking About the Selection

1. He begins to cry because the familiarity of home, with its smells, sights, and sounds, is so powerful to him, and he has dreamed of it so often. His sister's calling to his mother that "Paul is here" must seem like a dream that he never thought would come true.

2. The horrors of the war seem so separate from his home and his mother that he cannot seem to conceive of her even asking about the war. It is impossible for her to ever understand what he has experienced.

3. He has dreamed so often and so longingly of being allowed to return home, and of living to return home, that he is almost unable to comprehend that it has actually happened. The familiarity of his surroundings is enveloping him. Yet he himself has changed so drastically while at war that he cannot fit himself back into the old picture.

The Rich Boy

F. Scott Fitzgerald

INTRODUCTION The fiction of F. Scott Fitzgerald helped to define the wealthy people of the Jazz Age, at the same time exposing the shallowness and disillusionment that lurked on the fringes of their lives. Fitzgerald begins "The Rich Boy," a short story which was the first serious work he produced after *The Great Gatsby*, with this famous pronouncement: "Let me tell you about the very rich. They are different from you and me." Thus saying, Fitzgerald introduces the theme of the story and, in some sense, invites readers to share his own curiosity and fascination with the 1920s world of the very wealthy.

VOCABULARY Before you read the selection, find the meaning of these words in a dictionary: deference, feudal, brusque, débutante, dissipation, convivial, bawdy, avid, sardonic.

Anson was the eldest of six children who would some day divide a fortune of fifteen million dollars, and he reached the age of reason—is it seven?—at the beginning of the century when daring young women were already gliding along Fifth Avenue in electric "mobiles." In those days he and his brother had an English governess who spoke the language very clearly and crisply and well, so that the two boys grew to speak as she did—their words and sentences were all crisp and clear and not run together as ours are. They didn't talk exactly like English children but acquired an accent that is peculiar to fashionable people in the city of New York.

In the summer the six children were moved from the house on 71st Street to a big estate in northern Connecticut. It was not a fashionable locality—Anson's father wanted to delay as long as possible his children's knowledge of that side of life. He was a man somewhat superior to his class, which composed New York society, and to his period, which was the snobbish and formalized vulgarity of the Gilded Age, and he wanted his sons to learn habits of concentration and have sound constitutions and grow up into right-living and successful men. He and his wife kept an eye on them as well as they were able until the two older boys went away to school, but in huge establishments this is difficult—it was much simpler in the series of small and medium-sized houses in which my own youth was spent—I was never far out of the reach of my mother's voice, of the sense of her presence, her approval or disapproval.

Anson's first sense of his superiority came to him when he realized the half-grudging American deference that was paid to him in the Connecticut village. The parents of the boys he played with always inquired after his father and mother, and were vaguely excited when their own children were asked to the Hunters' house. He accepted this as the natural state of things, and a sort of impatience with all groups of which he was not the centre—in money, in position, in authority—remained with him for the rest of his life. He disdained to struggle with other boys for precedence—he expected it to be given him freely, and when it wasn't he withdrew into his family. His family was sufficient, for in the East money is still a somewhat feudal thing, a clan-forming thing. In the snobbish West, money separates families to form "sets."

At eighteen, when he went to New Haven, Anson was tall and thick-set, with a clear complexion and a healthy color from the ordered life he had led in school. His hair was yellow and grew in a funny way on his head, his nose was beaked—these two things kept him from being handsome—but he

F. Scott Fitzgerald

Have students think about a type of lifestyle in the United States today that is very different from their own and learn more about it. Examples might include the lives of those struggling with poverty, an urban lifestyle (if students live in a rural area), a rural lifestyle (if students live in an urban area), or life in a state like Alaska. Have students write a one-page essay about what they imagine life in the "unknown" area to be like. Then have them do research to compile a factual picture. Students should write a report on their findings and compare the facts with their earlier recorded perceptions.

had a confident charm and a certain brusque style, and the upper-class men who passed him on the street knew without being told that he was a rich boy and had gone to one of the best schools. Nevertheless, his very superiority kept him from being a success in college—the independence was mistaken for egotism, and the refusal to accept Yale standards with the proper awe seemed to belittle all those who had. So, long before he graduated, he began to shift the centre of his life to New York.

He was at home in New York—there was his own house with "the kind of servants you can't get any more"—and his own family, of which, because of his good humor and a certain ability to make things go, he was rapidly becoming the centre, and the débutante parties, and the correct manly world of the men's clubs, and the occasional wild spree with the gallant girls whom New Haven only knew from the fifth row. His aspirations were conventional enough—they included even the irreproachable shadow he would some day marry, but they differed from the aspirations of the majority of young men in that there was no mist over them, none of that quality which is variously known as "idealism" or "illusion." Anson accepted without reservation the world of high finance and high extravagance, of divorce and dissipation, of snobbery and of privilege. Most of our lives end as a compromise—it was as a compromise that his life began.

He and I first met in the late summer of 1917 when he was just out of Yale, and, like the rest of us, was swept up into the systematized hysteria of the war. In the blue-green uniform of the naval aviation he came down to Pensacola, where the hotel orchestras played "I'm sorry, dear," and we young officers danced with the girls. Every one liked him, and though he ran with the drinkers and wasn't an especially good pilot, even the instructors treated him with a certain respect. He was always having long talks with them in his confident, logical voice—talks which ended by his getting himself, or, more frequently, another officer, out of some impending trouble. He was convivial, bawdy, robustly avid for

pleasure, and we were all surprised when he fell in love with a conservative and rather proper girl.

Her name was Paula Legendre, a dark, serious beauty from somewhere in California. Her family kept a winter residence just outside of town, and in spite of her primness she was enormously popular; there is a large class of men whose egotism can't endure humor in a woman. But Anson wasn't that sort, and I couldn't understand the attraction of her "sincerity"—that was the thing to say about her—for his keen and somewhat sardonic mind.

Nevertheless, they fell in love. . . . One evening after a dance they agreed to marry, and he wrote a long letter about her to his mother. The next day Paula told him that she was rich, that she had a personal fortune of nearly a million dollars.

Jazz was originally played on phonographs like this one.

THINKING ABOUT THE SELECTION

1. When did Anson first realize that his situation was different from that of many others?
2. Why was Anson uncomfortable at Yale?

Critical Thinking
3. **Recognizing Ideologies** Why does Anson's father not want to live in a fashionable area? What ideology does this reveal?

ANSWERS TO

Thinking About the Selection

1. He first realized that his situation was different during his summers in Connecticut; the other boys treated him differently and their parents were excited when their children were invited to his house.

2. People mistook his independence for egotism and did not like his refusal to be awed by Yale; in addition, he was unhappy when he was not the center of attention, which was probably the case at Yale.

3. Anson's father does not want to live in a fashionable area because he wants to keep this "side of life" from his children. In other words, he does not wish them to know too early that they are rich, so that they will develop the ability to think for themselves and to be successful in their own right. His thinking reflects a belief that each person should make his or her own way in the world and not rely on the moneyed world of privilege and power.

Letters from the Forgotten Man

Primary Source

INTRODUCTION The introduction to *Down and Out in the Great Depression: Letters from the Forgotten Man* begins with this quotation from an unemployed man in 1935: "We're about down and out and the only good thing about it that I see is that there's not much further down we can go." The letters that fill the book echo this sentiment, many written by citizens who are in despair; having exhausted all means they know to support themselves, they now turn to the government to ask for help, to voice their anger, and to merely inform the President of how things are going "out here." The President, with his conversational fireside chats and comforting manner, seemed like someone they could confide in; the First Lady was something of a mother figure. And so the letters poured in. Here are a few from that collection.

Troy, New York
January 2, 1935

Dear Mrs. Roosevelt,

About a month ago I wrote you asking if you would buy some baby clothes for me with the understanding that I was to repay you as soon as my husband got enough work. Several weeks later I received a reply to apply to a Welfare Association so I might receive the aid I needed. Do you remember?

Please Mrs. Roosevelt, I do not want charity, only a chance from someone who will trust me until we can get enough money to repay the amount spent for the things I need. As a proof that I really am sincere, I am sending you two of my dearest possessions to keep as security, a ring my husband gave me before we were married, and a ring my mother used to wear. Perhaps the actual value of them is not high, but they are worth a lot to me. If you will consider buying the baby clothes, please keep them (rings) until I send you the money you spent. It is very hard to face bearing a baby we cannot afford to have, and the fact that it is due to arrive soon, and still there is no money for the hospital or clothing, does not make it any easier. I have decided to stay home, keeping my 7-year-old daughter from school to help with the smaller children when my husband has work. The oldest little girl is sick now, and has never been strong, so I would not depend on her. The 7-year-old is a good willing little worker and somehow we must manage—but without charity.

If you still feel you cannot trust me, it is allright and I can only say I donot blame you, but if you decide my word is worth anything with so small a security, here is a list of what I will need—but I will need it very soon.

2 shirts, silk and wool. size 2
3 pr. stockings, silk and wool, 4 1/2 or 4
3 straight flannel bands
2 slips—outing flannel
2 muslin dresses
1 sweater
1 wool bonnet
2 pr. wool booties
2 doz. diapers 30 x 30—or 27 x 27
1 large blanket (baby) about 45" or 50"
3 outing flannel nightgowns

If you will get these for me I would rather no one knew about it. I promise to repay the cost of the layette as soon as possible. We will all be very grateful to you, and I will be more than happy.

Sincerely yours,
Mrs. H.E.C.

Have students prepare a "Report on the Great Depression in Pictures" by finding in books photographs and paintings that illustrate the experiences of the nation during the Great Depression. Students should compile the photographs along with captions that explain them. Tell students to be sure their reports show the range of experiences during the time period, from the farmer, to the stock market broker, to the politician, and so on.

December 11, 1934
President Roosevelt,
Washington, D.C.

Dear President:
I am in debt needing help the worst in the world. I own my own little home and a few live stock. Nine (9) head of red white face cattle and a span of mules. I have them all mortgaged to a man and he is fixing to foreclose me.

I have done all I could to pay the note and have failed on everything I've tried. I fell short on my crop this time and he didn't allow me even one nickel out of it to feed myself while I was gathering it and now winter is here and I have a wife and three (3) little children, haven't got clothes enough to hardly keep them from freezing. My house got burned up three years ago and I'm living in just a hole of a house and we are in a suffering condition. My little children talking about Santa Claus and I hate to see Xmas come this time because I know it will be one of the dullest Xmas they ever witnessed.

I have tried to compromise with the man I am in debt to and he wont except nothing but the money or my stock and I can't borrow the money and I need my stock so I am asking you for help of some kind please.

So I remain,

Your humble servant,
N.S.
Sulphur Springs, Texas

P.S. That man won't even agree for me to have my stock fed.

Forest
February 24, 1936

Dear President Roosevelt,
You speak about the good neighbor idea and Mr. Farley speaks about the humane treatment the poor are receiving. Do you think it is humane to load a lot of old infirm men in steel bottom trucks—no protection from the storms or cold—send them 25 miles into the county and place them in the charge of tyrants and slave driver bosses, with no place to hang their coat or leave their dinner pails, only a snow bank and serve them dinner in a frozen state, also in a snow bank. Then if some have the misfortune to get sick and are sick 5 days cut them off from W.P.A. and relief for a month just because they happen to get sick. Is that humane? Is it right to give has-been Republicans all of the jobs as timekeepers and bosses whose cellars are full and who have farms, cows, pigs, chickens, and full and plenty to live on, leave us Democrats out in the cold. You pay them $65.00, $75.00, $90.00 and on up. You give us a starvation $48.00 and use us like dogs. You would be arrested if you treated a dog or any other dumb animal that way. Then Mr. Farley has the nerve to stand up and tell how humane we are being treated. You can remedy this by cutting the bosses' pay and giving us a little more so we can live as well as them. There is no reason they should be paid over $10.00 a month more than we are. Don't consider them skilled workmen because they are not. Out of every 1000 white collar jobs, how many Democrats will you find? No more than 10. Do you think us poor fools cannot see and understand what is going on? Oh yes, we can and don't blame us if we have to prove it when the time comes.

Yes, we realize you are trying to do your best and how you are being kept from doing it but we don't think you know what the men in charge of this W.P.A. and relief are doing. Will you try to change the program a little so there will not be so much dissatisfaction and starvation and unequalization?

A Poor Icicle

WORK-IS-WHAT-I
WANT-AND-NOT-CHARITY
WHO-WILL-HELP-ME-
GET-A-JOB-7YEARS-
IN-DETROIT. NO MONEY
SENT AWAY. FURNISH
BEST-OF-REFERENCES
PHONE RANDOLPH 8381. Room 439.

THINKING ABOUT THE SELECTION

1. What evidence can you find in the letters that shows these people have suffered much before finally appealing to the government for help?
2. What concerns does the author of the letter from Sulphur Springs, Texas, have?

Critical Thinking

3. **Expressing Problems Clearly** What complaint does "A Poor Icicle" have about the Republicans?

ANSWERS TO

Thinking About the Selection

1. The letter writers have suffered hardships other than those they mention in their letters. The first writer has no money to pay for the hospital bill when she delivers her baby, and her oldest daughter is sick. The second writer's house was destroyed by fire.

2. The letter writer from Sulphur Springs, Texas, is worried that he will be foreclosed on and lose his stock. He despairs at how such a foreclosure will affect his impoverished family.

3. He complains that the Republicans take all the higher-paying, white-collar jobs and leave the manual labor, lower-paying jobs for the Democrats.

Survivors of the Holocaust Remember

Primary Source

Claude Landzmann

INTRODUCTION The excerpts below are from the text of the 1985 film *Shoah, An Oral History of the Holocaust*. In the excerpts, two survivors describe their first hours at Treblinka, one of the concentration camps in which millions of Jewish people and others were murdered by the Nazis. At these camps, those prisoners who had skills that the Nazis found useful were spared. The rest were herded into vans or "showers" and killed with gas. By the end of World War II, 800,000 Jewish men, women, and children had been murdered at Treblinka.

VOCABULARY Before you read the selection, find the meaning of these words in a dictionary: barracks, uncoupled.

Richard Glazar: We were taken to a barracks. The whole place stank. Piled about five feet high in a jumbled mass, were all the things people could conceivably have brought. Clothes, suitcases, everything stacked in a solid mass. On top of it, jumping around like demons, people were making bundles and carrying them outside. It was turned over to one of these men. His armband said "Squad Leader." He shouted, and I understood that I was also to pick up clothing, bundle it, and take it somewhere. As I worked, I asked him: "What's going on? Where are the ones who stripped?" And he replied: "Dead! All dead!". . .

Abraham Bomba: At that time we started working in that place they called Treblinka. Still I couldn't believe what had happened over there on the other side of the gate, where the people went in, everything disappeared, and everything got quiet. But in a minute we find out, when we start to ask the people who worked here before us what had happened to the others, they said: "What do you mean, what happened? Don't you know that? They're all gassed, all killed." It was impossible to say anything—we were just like stones. We couldn't ask what had happened to the wife, to the kid. "What do you mean—wife, kid? Nobody is anymore!" How could they kill, how could they gas so many people at once? But they had a way to do it.

Richard Glazar: All I could think of then was my friend Carel Unger. He'd been at the rear of the train, in a section that had been uncoupled and left outside. I needed someone. Near me. With me. Then I saw him. He was in the second group. He'd been spared too. On the way, somehow, he had learned, he already knew. He looked at me. All he said was: "Richard, my father, mother, brother . . ." He had learned on the way there. . . . I left the barracks and had my first look at the vast space that I soon learned was called "the sorting place." It was buried under mountains of objects of all kinds. Mountains of shoes, of clothes, thirty feet high. I thought about it and said to Carel: "It's a hurricane, a raging sea. We're shipwrecked. And we're still alive. We must do nothing . . . but watch for every new wave, float on it, get ready for the next wave, and ride the wave at all costs. And nothing else."

THINKING ABOUT THE SELECTION

1. What were the belongings piled in the "sorting place"? To whom did they belong?

Critical Thinking

2. **Identifying Central Issues** Why does Glazer say that "We must do nothing . . . but watch for every new wave, float on it, get ready for the next wave, and ride the wave at all costs. And nothing else"?

ANSWERS TO

Thinking About the Selection
1. They were shoes, clothing, and other articles that had belonged to the prisoners who were killed in the gas chambers.
2. He says this because in order to survive they could not resist, could not even think about the horrors they were witnessing and experiencing.

A Londoner Describes Life During the Blitz

Primary Source

INTRODUCTION The excerpt below is from an oral account by Jean Wood, a Londoner who had four children during World War II. Wood's narrative appeared in *"The Good War": An Oral History of World War II*, by historian Studs Terkel. Here she describes the bombing of London and how people adapted to living with the constant fear and uncertainty of life in a city under siege.

VOCABULARY Before you read the selection, find the meaning of this word in a dictionary: staccato.

I never thought I could sit and read to children, say, about Cinderella, while you could hear the German planes coming. Sometimes a thousand a night came over, in waves. We had a saying, (says it staccato) I'm gonna getcha, I'm gonna getcha. That's how the planes sounded. You'd hear the bomb drop so many hundred yards that way. And you'd think, Oh, that missed us. You'd think, My God, the next one's going to be a direct hit. But you'd continue to read: "And the ugly sister said"—and you'd say "Don't fidget, dear." And you'd think, My God, I can't stand it. But you bore up. And I wasn't the bravest of people, believe me.

You had hunches. About half past three you'd say, "I won't sleep over there tonight. I'll put them all over here 'cause I have a hunch that that part of the wall will come down." Or what few neighbors were left would say, "Why don't you bring all the kids over to me tonight and let's all sing and play cards. We won't bother with Jerry[1] tonight." Now would it be safer that side of the road or this side? We'll go over there.

I did fire-watch. And that's frightening. You got up on the roof with a steel helmet on. You're supposed to have a protective jacket. The fire bombs were round balls. They'd come onto roofs and start fires. So the government gave you a bucket of sand and a shovel. Charming. (Laughs.) You stood there till the bomb fell. And you'd shovel it up quick and throw it into the bucket of sand. . . .

I had an aunt who was bombed out three times. My grandmother, who was eighty-odd, was bombed out and left clinging to the stairs, with her hair alight. The air-raid wardens got her out. She said, "I must go back for my hat." They took her in a truck with a lot of other elderly people to a safety zone.

I had to stay with my mother-in-law once. Sometimes the raids came before the siren went off, so you weren't down in the shelter. Land mines came down by parachute and laid whole streets low. It was like a bombed-out piece of land. This airplane was very low dropping the fire bombs, dropping them everywhere she was going. She did this terrific zigzag all across this field, hopping and leaping, hopping and leaping. Afterwards, people ran to get the parachute, 'cause with this parachute, we could make ourselves clothes. Clothes rationing was terribly strict. My husband got me a piece, and I made the children little dresses out of this nylon.

A lot of flowers grew on these bombed spaces, especially one in particular. It was a stalk with a lot of little red spots. It was like a weed, really. It was called London pride.

There was the blitz, when all London caught fire, except Saint Paul's Cathedral, thank God. That's why every time I go to Saint Paul's, I say, Oh, you're still there, thank God. Everything was in flames that night. It was like daylight, the flames.

[1] "Jerry" was a name used for the Germans during the war.

THINKING ABOUT THE SELECTION

1. Why did the Londoners gather up the parachutes from the bombs after they exploded?
2. Why might the flowers that grew on the bombed spaces have been called "London pride"?

Critical Thinking

3. **Drawing Conclusions** What does the excerpt show about Wood's personality that might have helped her cope with the bombings?

1984

 Literature

George Orwell

INTRODUCTION From the first sentence of George Orwell's novel, *1984*, the reader knows they have entered another world. The clock is just striking thirteen and the city is readying itself for Hate Week. Yet, although this world is much different from that of 1949, when it was written, or from today, it is not far from the imaginings of the people of the United States at the start of the cold war. British author George Orwell successfully captured the fears and concerns of much of the Western world when he wrote of a government that monitored all actions, taught people to hate, and dealt out death sentences for any thoughts or beliefs that were not specifically authorized. To the minds of many, the communist government in the Soviet Union was headed in precisely that direction. The timing of Orwell's novel was such that it contributed to the anti-communist feeling in the United States by painting a vivid picture of what life under communist rule might be like.

VOCABULARY Before you read the selection, find the meaning of these words in a dictionary: sanguine, scrutinize.

It was a bright cold day in April, and the clocks were striking thirteen. Winston Smith, his chin nuzzled into his breast in an effort to escape the vile wind, slipped quickly through the glass doors of Victory Mansions, though not quickly enough to prevent a swirl of gritty dust from entering along with him.

The hallway smelt of boiled cabbage and old rag mats. At one end of it a colored poster, too large for indoor display, had been tacked to the wall. It depicted simply an enormous face, more than a meter wide: the face of a man of about forty-five, with a heavy black mustache and ruggedly handsome features. Winston made for the stairs. It was no use trying the lift. Even at the best of times it was seldom working, and at present the electric current was cut off during daylight hours. It was part of the economy drive in preparation for Hate Week. The flat was seven flights up, and Winston, who was

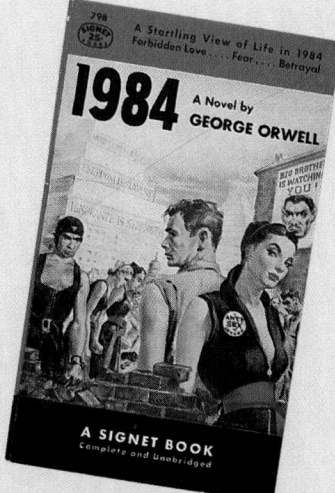

Shown above is a copy of *1984*. Visible on the front cover —posted on the wall at the right—is one of the book's most famous slogans, "Big Brother Is Watching You."

thirty-nine and had a varicose ulcer above his right ankle, went slowly, resting several times on the way. On each landing, opposite the lift shaft, the poster with the enormous face gazed from the wall. It was one of those pictures which are so contrived that the eyes follow you about when you move. BIG BROTHER IS WATCHING YOU, the caption beneath it ran.

Inside the flat a fruity voice was reading out a list of figures which had something to do with the production of pig iron. The voice came from an oblong metal plaque like a dulled mirror which formed part of the surface of the right-hand wall. Winston turned a switch and the voice sank somewhat, though the words were still distinguishable. The instrument (the telescreen, it was called) could be dimmed, but there was no way of shutting it off completely. He moved over to the window: a smallish, frail figure, the meagerness of his body

Have students take another issue from Unit 8 and explore the most far-reaching consequences that could have evolved from that issue, as Orwell did with his novel. Students can write a short play, a poem, or draw a poster depicting a future world in which something that began in the 1950s went out of control. For example, students might examine the policy of containment gone awry or the House Un-American Activities Committee with too much power.

merely emphasized by the blue overalls which were the uniform of the Party. His hair was very fair, his face naturally sanguine, his skin roughened by coarse soap and blunt razor blades and the cold of the winter that had just ended.

Outside, even through the shut window pane, the world looked cold. Down in the street little eddies of wind were whirling dust and torn paper into spirals, and though the sun was shining and the sky a harsh blue, there seemed to be no color in anything except the posters that were plastered everywhere. The black-mustachio'd face gazed down from every commanding corner. There was one on the house front immediately opposite. BIG BROTHER IS WATCHING YOU, the caption said, while the dark eyes looked deep into Winston's own. Down at street level another poster, torn at one corner, flapped fitfully in the wind, alternately covering and uncovering the single word ING-SOC.[1] In the far distance a helicopter skimmed down between the roofs, hovered for an instant like a blue-bottle, and darted away again with a curving flight. It was the Police Patrol, snooping into people's windows. The patrols did not matter, however. Only the Thought Police mattered.

Behind Winston's back the voice from the tele-screen was still babbling away about pig iron and the overfulfillment of the Ninth Three-Year Plan. The telescreen received and transmitted simultaneously. Any sound that Winston made, above the level of a very low whisper, would be picked up by it; moreover, so long as he remained within the field of vision which the metal plaque commanded, he could be seen as well as heard. There was of course no way of knowing whether you were being watched at any given moment. How often, or on what system, the Thought Police plugged in on any individual wire was guesswork. It was even conceivable that they watched everybody all the time. But at any rate they could plug in your wire whenever they wanted to. You had to live—did live, from habit that became instinct—in the assumption that every sound you made was overheard, and, except in darkness, every movement scrutinized.

[1] Orwell defines this as English Socialism.

Winston kept his back turned to the telescreen. It was safer; though, as he well knew, even a back can be revealing. A kilometer away the Ministry of Truth, his place of work, towered vast and white above the grimy landscape. . . .

The Ministry of Truth—Minitrue, in Newspeak[2]—was startlingly different from any other object in sight. It was an enormous pyramidal structure of glittering white concrete, soaring up, terrace after terrace, three hundred meters into the air. From where Winston stood it was just possible to read, picked out on its white face in elegant lettering, the three slogans of the Party:

WAR IS PEACE

FREEDOM IS SLAVERY

IGNORANCE IS STRENGTH.

[2] Newspeak was the offical language of Oceania. Orwell describes its purpose in the Appendix to *1984* as "not only to provide a medium of expression for the world-view and mental habits proper to the devotees of Ingsoc, but to make all other modes of thought impossible." In other words, freedom of expression and even thought would be ended by making it impossible to find the word to describe concepts such as democracy or liberty.

THINKING ABOUT THE SELECTION

1. What was the telescreen, and how was it used by the government?
2. What was the government trying to accomplish by hanging Big Brother posters everywhere? What did the slogan on the posters mean?

Critical Thinking
3. **Distinguishing False from Accurate Images**
   Reread the three slogans of the Ministry of Truth. How do these slogans contradict the name of the ministry? How might such contradictions affect a society?

ANSWERS TO

Thinking About the Selection

1. The telescreen was like a television screen, except that it both transmitted and received a signal. One was put in every citizen's home in order to feed government propaganda into the home and to monitor the people's actions.

2. The posters were meant to remind people of the ever-watchful eye of the government. Their presence kept people from acting in ways that were against government rules by reminding them that their actions were being watched at all times. The slogan on the poster was meant to have a double meaning. It reminded the people that they were being watched and it also was meant to comfort them, to make them believe that Big Brother, or the government, was looking out for their best interests.

3. Although the ministry is called the Ministry of Truth, the slogans are lies, or distortions of the truth. The constant bombardment of a society by such contradictions or lies would no doubt produce a psychologically damaged society, capable of doing anything the government demands, because there would no longer be any truth against which to measure what they were being told.

President Kennedy's Inaugural Address

Primary Source

INTRODUCTION John F. Kennedy's bold inaugural address seemed to many Americans to signal a fresh new start for the country. In the address, Kennedy spoke to the American people, to the friends of the United States, and to the nation's most threatening foe—the Soviet Union.

VOCABULARY Before you read the selection, find the meaning of these words in a dictionary: forebears, belabor, eradicate.

We observe today not a victory of party but a celebration of freedom—symbolizing an end as well as a beginning—signifying renewal as well as change. For I have sworn before you and Almighty God the same solemn oath our forebears prescribed nearly a century and three-quarters ago.

The world is very different now. For man holds in his mortal hands the power to abolish all forms of human poverty and all forms of human life. And yet the same revolutionary beliefs for which our forebears fought are still at issue around the globe—the belief that the rights of man come not from the generosity of the state but from the hand of God.

We dare not forget today that we are the heirs of that first revolution. Let the word go forth from this time and place, to friend and foe alike, that the torch has been passed to a new generation of Americans—born in this century, tempered by war, disciplined by a hard and bitter peace, proud of our ancient heritage—and unwilling to witness or permit the slow undoing of those human rights to which this nation has

President Kennedy delivers his Inaugural Address.

always been committed, and to which we are committed today at home and around the world.

Let every nation know, whether it wishes us well or ill, that we shall pay any price, bear any burden, meet any hardship, support any friend, oppose any foe to assure the survival and the success of liberty. . . .

So let us begin anew—remembering on both sides that civility is not a sign of weakness, and sincerity is always subject to proof. Let us never negotiate out of fear. But let us never fear to negotiate.

Let both sides explore what problems unite us instead of belaboring those problems which divide us.

Let both sides, for the first time, formulate serious and precise proposals for the inspection and control of arms—and bring the absolute power to destroy other nations under the absolute control of all nations.

Let both sides seek to invoke the wonders of science instead of its terrors. Together let us explore the stars, conquer the deserts, eradicate disease, tap the ocean depths, and encourage the arts and commerce.

Let both sides unite to heed in all corners of the earth the command

Using a source such as the Department of State Bulletins, have students locate and read the full text of Kennedy's 1961 inaugural address. Then have them locate and read the full text of President Clinton's inaugural address, given in 1993. Students should then write a paper that compares the tone, content, and style of the two addresses. It should also use the text of the addresses to explain the different world and domestic situations facing the nation in 1961 and 1993.

FOCUS

Connecting Literature and History

Throughout history leaders have used the spoken word to gain followers, to reason with opponents, and to inform the ignorant. Until we read their words, we often do not have a real understanding of what made a particular person great, or loved, or influential. Tell students that this source reading sheds some light on the personality and the crusade of a great man.

---

of Isaiah—to "undo the heavy burdens . . .[and] let the oppressed go free."

And if a beachhead of co-operation may push back the jungle of suspicion, let both sides join in creating a new endeavor, not a new balance of power, but a new world of law, where the strong are just and the weak secure and the peace preserved.

All this will not be finished in the first one hundred days. Nor will it be finished in the first one thousand days, nor in the life of this administration, nor even perhaps in our lifetime on this planet. But let us begin. . . .

And so, my fellow Americans: ask not what your country can do for you—ask what you can do for your country.

My fellow citizens of the world: ask not what America will do for you, but what together we can do for the freedom of man.

Finally, whether you are citizens of America or citizens of the world, ask of us here the same high standards of strength and sacrifice which we ask of you. With a good conscience our only sure reward, with history the final judge of our deeds, let us go forth to lead the land we love, asking His blessing and His help, but knowing that here on earth God's work must truly be our own.

THINKING ABOUT THE SELECTION

1. What are the "terrors" of science to which Kennedy refers in his speech?
2. What five proposals does Kennedy make to both sides in the cold war?

Critical Thinking

3. **Testing Conclusions** "The United States was in the midst of the cold war when Kennedy took office in 1961." Find evidence from the excerpt to support or refute this statement.

Letter from Birmingham Jail

Primary Source

Martin Luther King, Jr.

INTRODUCTION In 1963 the Reverend Martin Luther King, Jr., and the Southern Christian Leadership Conference staged a mass protest in Birmingham, Alabama. King was arrested for his participation in the protest, and he wrote a letter which is excerpted below, from his jail cell. The letter was his answer to eight Birmingham clergymen who had condemned the demonstration and claimed King was in their city as an "outside agitator."

VOCABULARY Before you read the selection, find the meaning of these words in a dictionary: deplore, unduly, ominous, complacency, incorrigible, solace, manifest.

My Dear Fellow Clergymen:

You deplore the demonstrations taking place in Birmingham. But your statement, I am sorry to say, fails to express a similar concern for the conditions that brought about the demonstrations. . . .

We know through painful experience that freedom is never voluntarily given by the oppressor; it must be demanded by the oppressed. Frankly, I have yet to engage in a direct-action campaign that was "well timed" in the view of those who have not suffered unduly from the disease of segregation. For years now I have heard the word "Wait!" It rings in the ear of every Negro with piercing familiarity. This "Wait!" has almost always meant "Never." We must come to see, with one of our distinguished jurists, that "justice too long delayed is justice denied." . . .

Perhaps it is easy for those who have never felt the stinging darts of segregation to say, "Wait." But when you have seen vicious mobs lynch your mothers and fathers at will and drown your sisters and brothers at

---

ANSWERS TO

Thinking About the Selection

1. Kennedy is referring to the atomic bomb.
2. He proposes: (1) that both sides explore the problems that they can solve together; (2) that both sides formulate a plan for arms control and inspection; (3) that both sides work to develop positive scientific advances, rather than destructive ones; (4) that both sides work to help the oppressed of the world; and (5) that both sides help to create a world of justice.

3. The evidence supports this statement. Specific examples include Kennedy's statement of strength and warning, meant for the Soviet Union, that we will fight to preserve democracy in the world; his reference to the atomic bomb and the need to prevent a nuclear war; his use of the traditional cold war term "balance of power."

whim; when you have seen hate-filled policemen curse, kick, and even kill your black brothers and sisters; when you see the vast majority of your twenty million Negro brothers smothering in an airtight cage of poverty in the midst of an affluent society; when you suddenly find your tongue twisted and your speech stammering as you seek to explain to your six-year-old daughter why she can't go to the public amusement park that has just been advertised on television, and see tears welling up in her eyes when she is told that Funtown is closed to colored children, and see ominous clouds of inferiority beginning to form in her little mental sky, and see her beginning to distort her personality by developing an unconscious bitterness toward white people. . . then you will understand why we find it difficult to wait. . . .

You speak of our activity in Birmingham as extreme. At first I was rather disappointed that fellow clergymen would see my nonviolent efforts as those of an extremist. I began thinking about the fact that I stand in the middle of two opposing forces in the Negro community. One is a force of complacency, made up in part of Negroes who, as a result of long years of oppression, are so drained of self-respect and a sense of "somebodiness" that they have adjusted to segregation; and in part of a few middle-class Negroes who, because of a degree of academic and economic security and because in some ways they profit by segregation, have become insensitive to the problems of the masses. The other force is one of bitterness and hatred, and it comes perilously close to advocating

As shown in this picture, Martin Luther King, Jr., experienced racial hatred firsthand. As his son looks on, King removes a cross set on fire—a symbol of the Ku Klux Klan—in front of his home in Atlanta, Georgia, in 1960.

violence. It is expressed in the various black nationalist groups that are springing up across the nation, the largest and best-known being Elijah Muhammad's Muslim movement. . . .

I have tried to stand between these two forces, saying that we need emulate neither the "do-nothingism" of the complacent nor the hatred and despair of the black nationalist. For there is the more excellent way of love and nonviolent protest. I am grateful to God that, through the influence of the Negro church, the way of nonviolence became an integral part of our struggle. . . .

Oppressed people cannot remain oppressed forever. The yearning for freedom eventually manifests itself, and that is what has happened to the American Negro. Something within has reminded him of his birthright of freedom, and something without has reminded him that it can be gained.

THINKING ABOUT THE SELECTION

1. According to King, why can African Americans no longer wait for their freedom?
2. Why does King find fault with the criticism leveled against him by the Birmingham clergy?

Critical Thinking

3. **Recognizing Ideologies** What two ideologies does King describe in the African American community? Where does he place himself in relation to these two ideologies?

ANSWERS TO

Thinking About the Selection

1. They can no longer wait because they have suffered for 340 years. King poignantly describes this suffering and says "Oppressed people cannot remain oppressed forever. The yearning for freedom eventually manifests itself."

2. He disagrees with the criticism because he thinks the clergy should be more concerned about the conditions in Birmingham that brought about the protest than about the protests themselves.

3. King describes the "complacent," those who are willing to let segregation continue, and the "black nationalists," who are willing to use violence to overcome segregation. He places himself between these two groups as a force that is trying to find an approach between the "do-nothing" and the violent.

INSTRUCT

Ask students whether they believe it is important to have the right to vote. After reaching general agreement that it is important, lead students in a discussion as to the reasons why. Students should understand that being able to vote means being able to elect the representatives to government who most closely agree with one's own political beliefs. Thus, by voting we are exercising our right to have a voice in government. In order to illustrate why this is important, ask students to consider this scenario: A representative in Congress has just proposed a new amendment to the Constitution that would ban any person below the age of twenty-one from purchasing any music on compact disc without the written consent of an adult. Because voter turnout in the age group 18 to 21 has historically been low, that group is underrepresented in Congress. Thus, the bill stands a better chance of being passed than it would if this age group had elected a sizable proportion of the Congress with its votes. Explain to students that without the ability to elect representatives to local, state, and national posts, African Americans were essentially powerless to effect change in American politics.

EXTEND

Have students draw a picture or a political cartoon, or write a ten-minute play that relates to the struggle for civil rights in the 1960s. Alternatively, students can research whether any polls were taken during the 1960s that gauge public opinion on civil rights for African Americans. Gallup polls would likely be a good source for students to begin their search; students should be able to find *The Gallup Poll: Public Opinion 1935–1971* in their public libraries. Newspapers and newsmagazines such as *Newsweek* or *Time* would also be likely sources for such information. Students should compile the statistics they find to report to the class.

1079

Tell students that invisible lines linked Vietnam soldiers and their families and friends during the war. These invisible lines were the international and United States mail routes, on which most people depended to keep in contact with each other.

Read the following statement to students: "Soldiers in the Vietnam War reacted to the dangers constantly surrounding them by becoming more and more suspicious of anyone they encountered, including the friends with whom they fought. The war resulted in a soldier who cared for no one and who fought for nothing but his own survival." Ask students to use the letter in the source reading to find evidence that either supports or refutes this statement.

Have students conduct a poll to determine the general feeling today about United States involvement in the Vietnam War. Students should ask parents, neighbors, or teachers the following question: Do you think the United States should or should not have been involved in the Vietnam War? To gauge the person's basis for answering the question as well as to learn how many people were directly influenced by the war, students should also ask: Do you know anyone who fought in the Vietnam War? Students should each poll at least five people. Then, as a class, compile the results and form a conclusion as to current public opinion about the war and how many people in your community were directly affected by the conflict.

Letter Home from Vietnam

Primary Source

INTRODUCTION Letters from home provided the American soldier in Vietnam with a link to reality, something that often seemed to recede during the long days of war. Writing home provided many soldiers with a way to voice the feelings they were experiencing. In their letters, they released the powerful emotions of fear, despair, pride, and bravery that brought them through their tours of duty and home to the people they loved.

Lance Corporal Perron Shinneman returns home from Vietnam to Sioux Falls, South Dakota, in 1966.

Dearest Bev,

Last night we had the VC all around us. [We] had some trapped near the water hole, but I guess they got away. Bev, don't ever tell Mother this, but at times I feel I will never come home. The VC are getting much stronger, so I think this war is going to get worse before it gets better...

The days are fairly peaceful, but the nights are pure hell! I look up at the stars, and it's so hard to believe that the same stars shine over you and such a different world as you live in. I look at this war in the sense that it is an experience that can never be equaled and that someday I can make something [out of it]. I guess if I had it to do over, I would do it again!

I try and take great pride in my unit and the men I work with. A lot of the men have been in a lot of trouble and have no education or money. But I feel honored to have them call me a friend. In my heart I know these are the men that build America, not the rich or the well educated. I hope to spend my life in their behalf and try to help them all I can. I have been so very lucky to have had the chances I have had, so I hope I can put these chances to work in a good cause! ... If something does happen, my family can always say that I died for a good cause and that I did accomplish just a little in my lifetime....

All my love,
Al

THINKING ABOUT THE SELECTION

1. What does Al say in his letter that shows his respect for the men in his unit?

Critical Thinking

2. **Recognizing Cause and Effect** Based on his letter, how do you think fighting in Vietnam changed Al?

ANSWERS TO

Thinking About the Selection
1. He says that he feels "honored to have them call me a friend. . . . these are the men that build America."

2. It gave him great respect for the men with whom he fought, and made him realize how lucky he was to have had good opportunities in his life. Knowing this, he now wants to "put those chances to work for a good cause."

"These Are the Boys of Point du Hoc"

Primary Source

Ronald Reagan

Introduction On June 6, 1984, President Reagan gave a speech at Point du Hoc, France, on the occasion of the fortieth anniversary of D-Day—the day the Allies launched an invasion of German-occupied France along Normandy, France's northern coast. Elegant and powerful, Reagan's Point du Hoc speech reminded Americans of the nation's effort to stop totalitarianism and promote democracy. It also showcases his ability as a communicator. His presidential style—unassuming, personable, candid, and fervently optimistic—is remembered by many Americans, among them President Bill Clinton.

VOCABULARY Before you read the selection, find the meaning of these words in a dictionary: desolate, deter, valor.

We're here to mark that day in history when the Allied armies joined in battle to reclaim this continent to liberty. . . .

We stand on a lonely, windswept point on the northern shore of France. The air is soft, but forty years ago at this moment, the air was dense with smoke and the cries of men, and the air was filled with the crack of rifle fire and the roar of cannon. At dawn, on the morning of the 6th of June, 1944, 225 Rangers jumped off the British landing craft and ran to the bottom of these cliffs. Their mission was one of the most difficult and daring of the invasion: to climb these sheer and desolate cliffs and take out the enemy guns. The Allies had been told that some of the mightiest of these guns were here and they would be trained on the beaches to stop the Allied advance.

The Rangers looked up and saw the enemy soldiers—at the edge of the cliffs shooting down at them with machine guns and throwing grenades. And the American Rangers began to climb. They shot rope ladders over the face of these cliffs and began to pull themselves up. When one rope was cut, a Ranger would grab another and begin his climb again. They climbed, shot back, and held their footing. Soon, one by one, the Rangers pulled themselves over the top, and in seizing the firm land at the top of these cliffs, they began to seize back the continent of Europe. Two hundred and twenty-five came here. After two days of fighting, only ninety could still bear arms.

President Reagan and Nancy Reagan laying flowers at the graves of American soldiers killed in the 1944 Normandy invasion.

Behind me is a memorial that symbolizes the Ranger daggers that were thrust into the top of these cliffs. And before me are the men who put them there.

These are the boys of Point du Hoc. These are the men who took the cliffs. These are the champions who helped free a continent. These are the heroes who helped end a war. . . .

Forty summers have passed since the battle that you fought here. You were young the day you took these cliffs; some of you were hardly more than boys, with the deepest joys of life before you. Yet, you risked everything here. Why? Why did you do it? What impelled you to put aside the instinct for self-preservation and risk your lives to take these cliffs? What inspired all the men of the armies that met here? We look at you, and somehow we know the answer. It was faith and belief; it was loyalty and love.

The men of Normandy had faith that what they were doing was right, faith that they fought for all humanity, faith that a just God would grant them

Have students research the early life and times of Ronald Reagan. Ask them to look for influences and events in his early life that may have helped shape his conservative viewpoint.

As an alternative assignment, students should look through *Time*, *Newsweek*, and other magazines from the early 1980s and try to find evidence of the resurgence of conservative ideals in society in general. Tell students to pay particular attention to advertisements. Do the advertisements in these magazines attempt to win sales by promoting conservatism in some manner? Students should bring photocopies of the advertisements they find to class and explain how they do or do not reflect the nation's shift to conservatism.

cmercy on this beachhead or on the next. It was the deep knowledge—and pray God we have not lost it—that there is a profound moral difference between the use of force for liberation and the use of force for conquest. You were here to liberate, not to conquer, and so you and those others did not doubt your cause. And you were right not to doubt.

You all knew that some things are worth dying for. One's country is worth dying for, and democracy is worth dying for, because it's the most deeply honorable form of government ever devised by man. All of you loved liberty. All of you were willing to fight tyranny, and you knew the people of your countries were behind you. . . .

When the war was over, there were lives to be rebuilt and governments to be returned to the people. There were nations to be reborn. Above all, there was a new peace to be assured. These were huge and daunting tasks. But the Allies summoned strength from the faith, belief, loyalty, and love of those who fell here. They built a new Europe together. . . .

In spite of our great efforts and successes, not all that followed the end of the war was happy or planned. Some liberated countries were lost. The great sadness of this loss echoes down to our own time in the streets of Warsaw, Prague, and East Berlin. Soviet troops that came to the center of this continent did not leave when peace came. They're still there, uninvited, unwanted, unyielding, almost forty years after the war. Because of this, allied forces still stand on this continent. Today, as forty years ago, our armies are here for only one purpose—to protect and defend democracy. The only territories we hold are memorials like this one and graveyards where our heroes rest. . . .

It's fitting to remember here the great losses also suffered by the Russian people during World War II: 20 million perished, a terrible price that testifies to all the world the necessity of ending war. I tell you from my heart that we in the United States do not want war. We want to wipe from the face of the earth the terrible weapons that man now has in his hands. And I tell you, we are ready to seize that beachhead. We look for some sign from the Soviet Union that they are willing to move forward, that they share our desire and love for peace, and that they will give up the ways of conquest. There must be a changing there that will allow us to turn our hope into action. . . .

Here, in this place where the West held together, let us make a vow to our dead. Let us show them by our actions that we understand what they died for. . . . Strengthened by their courage, heartened by their valor, and borne by their memory, let us continue to stand for the ideals for which they lived and died.

Thank you very much, and God bless you all.

An Oval Room with a View

Primary Source

Bill Clinton

There is a room on the second floor of the White House called the Yellow Oval Room, and I gather that this remains President Reagan's favorite place in the great house that we have both been privileged to inhabit. I bring this up because the Yellow Oval Room, more than any other place in this magnificent old building, best sums up Ronald Reagan's greatest gift to us as President—the way his own unwavering hopefulness reminded us that optimism is one of our most fundamental virtues.

No one room could better represent what Americans love about President Reagan. We remember the sunniness of his temperament during eight years in office: the room's color gives it a steady glow during clear days and stormy ones alike. Its view is expansive. From it, you can see the Jefferson Memorial, the Washington Monument, the broad Potomac, even the foothills of Virginia. The landscape conveys a sense

Thinking About the Selection

1. President Reagan refers to the fact that some countries were taken over by the Communist Soviet Union after World War II and thus were "lost" to communism.

2. In 1987 the United States and the Soviet Union signed the Intermediate-Range Nuclear Forces (INF) Treaty, which provided for the destruction of 2,500 Soviet and American nuclear missiles in Europe. In 1991 President George Bush and Soviet leader Mikhail Gorbachev signed the Strategic Arms Reduction Treaty (START). This treaty dramatically decreased the number of long-range weapons that both superpowers had stockpiled.

3. Responses should include three of the following: "unwavering hopefulness," "optimism," "sunniness," "hopeful exuberance," "he genuinely liked Americans."

4. His speech praises the military for its bravery during World War II and condemns the Soviet Union for refusing to leave Europe following the war. In addition, Reagan talks of the lessons learned by the United States during two

The Reagans and the Thatchers in the Yellow Oval Room.

that the possibilities of America go on forever. President Reagan had that gift, too.

As President, Ronald Reagan made us feel that he genuinely liked Americans. I imagine that what he enjoyed most about this room is that the view is not limited to the monuments.

From its window, you can also see families walking along the Mall, people driving to work along Constitution Avenue, children playing softball on the Ellipse. And they can look up from what they are doing and almost see inside a bit, too. The Yellow Oval Room, located in the center of the building, and ringed by the Truman Balcony, is where your gaze falls naturally if you're looking at the White House from the south. In that way, this room represents something unique about the American sense of democracy. It is situated in such a way that we—voters and Presidents—can keep one another always in mind.

As he turns 85, President Reagan is still very much in our minds. And though he's been back in California for a few years now, I think a little of his hopeful exuberance stayed behind in the Yellow Oval Room to cheer his fellow citizens—indoors and out.

THINKING ABOUT THE SELECTION

1. What did President Reagan mean when he said that some European countries were "lost" after World War II?

2. Based on your reading of the chapter, what step did the United States and the Soviet Union take to "wipe from the face of the earth the terrible weapons that man now has in his hands"?

3. What are three phrases that President Clinton uses to describe President Reagan's appeal to Americans? Write a sentence for each to explain your choices.

Critical Thinking

4. **Checking Consistency** President Reagan believed in a strong military to protect the nation's interests. He also strongly opposed communism. How does the Point du Hoc speech reflect these beliefs?

5. **Drawing Conclusions** In reading President Clinton's essay, what do you think is an important presidential role?

world wars: "It is better to be here ready to protect the peace, than to take blind shelter across the sea, rushing to respond only after freedom is lost." This is an argument for preparedness and a strong military.

5. Answers should include mention of how the President should help the American people feel good about their future and about their country.

My American Journey

 Literature

Colin Powell

Introduction As our nation heads toward the twenty-first century, many citizens are seeking to recover a sense of community that has sustained the United States at key points in the past. They hope that the fundamental values Americans hold in common will bring the nation together to work for a better future. In spite of the many challenges it faces, the United States has tremendous advantages to use in confronting the modern world. First among them are the American people themselves, who have proven themselves capable not only of economic miracles but also of acts of inspiring generosity. Both abilities will be needed as the world enters the twenty-first century.

The challenges that face our country in the 1990s seem both familiar and brand-new as we head into the future from our vantage point of knowing the past. Like the immigrants of the late 1800s and early 1900s, like the ordinary citizens who struggled through the Great Depression, and like the Americans who are debating the issues that are discussed in this final unit of your textbook, our paths will be full of decisions and unexpected turns. As we choose our way among the paths of the present, we, too, are shaping the nation's future.

The selections that follow are both testimonials to the American spirit, written by two keen observers of the American landscape. Colin Powell is probably the most famous person on the American political scene in the 1990s who is not a politician (see page 952). Haynes Johnson is a Pulitzer Prize-winning journalist, author, and political commentator.

Vocabulary Before you read the selections, find the meaning of these words in a dictionary: hyphenated, fractious, resilience, hybrid, affix, insular, introspection.

As I travel around the country, I invite questions from my audiences, which range from trade associations to motivational seminars, from prison inmates to the youngsters at my pride and joy, the Colin L. Powell Elementary School in Woodlands, Texas. What people ask gives me a good idea of what is on America's mind. . . .

American voters [are] looking, in my judgment. . . for a different spirit in the land, something better. How do we find our way again? How do we reestablish moral standards? How do we end the ethnic fragmentation that is making us an increasingly hyphenated people? How do we restore a sense of family to our national life? On the speech circuit, I tell a story that goes to the heart of America's longing. The ABC correspondent Sam Donaldson was interviewing a young African-American soldier in a tank platoon on the eve of battle in Desert Storm. Donaldson asked, "How do you think the battle will go? Are you afraid?"

"We'll do okay. We're well trained. And I'm not afraid," the GI answered, gesturing toward his buddies around him. "I'm not afraid because I'm with my family."

According to Colin Powell, American voters in the 1990s were looking for "a different spirit in the land, something better."

The other soldiers shouted, "Tell him again. He didn't hear you."

The soldier re-peated, "This is my family and we'll take care of each other."

That story never fails to touch me or the audience. It is a metaphor for what we have to do as a nation. We have to start thinking of America as a family. We have to stop screeching at each other, stop hurting each other, and instead start caring for, sacrificing for, and sharing with each other. We have to stop constantly criticizing, which is the way of the malcontent, and instead get back to the can-do attitude that made America. We have to keep trying, and risk failing, in order to solve this country's problems. We cannot move forward if cynics and critics swoop down and pick apart anything that goes wrong to a point where we lose sight of what is right, decent, and uniquely good about America. . . .

We are a fractious nation, always searching, always dissatisfied, yet always hopeful. We have an infinite capacity to rejuvenate ourselves. We are self-correcting. And we are capable of caring about each other. . . .

We will prevail over our present trials. We will come through because our founders bequeathed us a political system of genius, a system flexible enough for all ages and inspiring noble aspirations for all time. We will continue to flourish because our diverse American society has the strength, hardiness, and resilience of the hybrid plant we are. . . . Jefferson once wrote, "There is a debt of service due from every man to his country, proportioned to the bounties which nature and fortune have measured to him." . . . My responsibility, our responsibility as lucky Americans, is to try to give back to this country as much as it has given to us, as we continue our American journey together.

"Reclaiming the Dream"

Haynes Johnson

Literature

Twice before, Americans have gone through periods like the present when they knew, deep in the bone, that their world was changing forever. The first was in the years between 1846 and 1861. As the Civil War drew closer and closer, new forces collided, forcing decisions about old questions: whether America would be an agrarian or industrial nation; whether it would be one nation or a loose confederation of independent states; whether it would sanction slavery or uphold the principles of freedom and equality explicit in its founding charters.

Americans understand that by working together, we can achieve our goals in the twenty-first century.

Point out to students that, as Haynes Johnson says, Americans have faced other difficult periods, notably after the Civil War and during the Great Depression. Discuss what events and issues today—political, economic, social—may be contributing to people's unease and insecurity. Have students recall some of the solutions that Powell suggests as remedies for the national mood.

Have students read the list of chapter titles for this final unit and discuss how each of those issues relates to the observations made by Powell and Johnson.

The second period came after the financial crash of 1929 ushered in the Great Depression and subsequently World War II. Americans emerged from those challenges aware that they and their country were forever changed. Never again would they be as insular, never again could they cling to the isolationism of their past, never again could they brush aside the pressures for racial and social change within their own society. With the signing of the World War II peace accords aboard the battleship *USS Missouri* in Tokyo Bay on September 2, 1945, the United States stepped fully onto the world stage, enjoying a time of unbounded confidence in the American future, a time that gradually gave way to the present doubts over America's prospects, not only for competing abroad but for binding itself together at home.

Against this awareness, the new introspection flourishes. In another change from the past, I found Americans no longer assigning as much blame to the usual suspects: to Japanese ... to welfare "cheats" ... to "shiftless" members of this or that minority ... to liberals or to conservatives. More and more, Americans are affixing responsibility for the nation's troubles on the country and its leaders—and on themselves. They do not need to be told that their country no longer enjoys the unsurpassed position it held for a generation after World War II. Everyone knows this. Yet they also know America still possesses enormous resources, backed

From Sea to Shining Sea by Jacqueline Paton, Merrimack, New Hampshire

ANSWERS TO

Thinking About the Selection
1. Answers will vary, but should include a combination of the following: the can-do attitude; valuing family and community; being self-correcting, caring, hardy, and resilient.
2. The first was the period just before the Civil War. At that time, the United States faced the questions of whether it should be an agrarian or industrial nation; whether it should sanction slavery; whether it would be one nation or a loose federation of independent states. The second was the period between 1929 and the end of World War II in 1945. During that period, the Depression and the war helped Americans cast aside isolationism, bring the nation together to fight a war, and, in the war's aftermath, create confidence in the future.
3. Powell quotes Thomas Jefferson and suggests that citizens have the responsibility of giving back to the country as much as it has given them.

by an energetic, resourceful people. As the historian D. W. Brogan noted long ago, the hardest task for a people forced to change is to acquire new attitudes and unlearn old lessons. Americans I met understand this; they say it, in private conversation, over and over again. I am convinced they are eager to respond to a strong challenge for unified action—and, yes, willing to sacrifice to achieve clearly defined national goals.

In all, I traveled to fifteen states—Maine, Massachusetts, Connecticut, New York, North Carolina, South Carolina, Alabama, Florida, Iowa, Illinois, Michigan, Oklahoma, Texas, New Mexico, Califorrnia—and spoke with people in cities as large as New York and Los Angeles and as small as the rural communities of Selma, Alabama, and Waverly, Iowa. After listening to these people, and especially after hearing some of them again nearly two years later, I do not feel that I have been writing the obituary of the American Dream. I believe I have been writing about an interlude in the reclaiming of that Dream.

THINKING ABOUT THE SELECTION

1. What does Powell see as the most important American traits?
2. What were the two similar periods in America's past according to Johnson?

Critical Thinking

3. **Drawing Conclusions** According to Powell, what is the responsibility for every American?
4. **Identifying Assumptions** What is Johnson's central unstated belief?

4. Johnson assumes that the United States is going through a period of enormous change and that we have to be prepared to seek new approaches to solve the problems that confront us.

A Correlation to Prentice Hall Literature
The American Experience

LITERATURE CORRELATION

A Correlation to Prentice Hall Literature *The American Experience* (continued)

Chapter	Author	Title	Genre
UNIT SEVEN Boom Times to Hard Times, 1919–1938			
21 **A Stormy Era, 1919–1929**	John Dos Passos	*Tin Lizzie* Page 670	biography
22 **Crash and Depression, 1929–1938**	F. Scott Fitzgerald	*Winter Dreams* Page 588	short story
23 **The New Deal, 1933–1938**	Carl Sandburg	From "The People, Yes" Page 740	poem
UNIT EIGHT Hot and Cold War, 1939–1960			
24 **World War II, 1939–1945**	Randall Jarrell	"The Death of the Ball Turret Gunner" Page 979	poem
25 **World War II at Home, 1941–1945**	W. H. Auden	"The Unknown Citizen" Page 783	poem
26 **The Cold War and American Society, 1945–1960**	Ezra Pound	"In a Station of the Metro" "The River Merchant's Wife: A Letter" Pages 700–701	poems
27 **The Postwar Years at Home, 1945–1960**	Joan Didion	*On the Mall* Page 916	essay
UNIT NINE The Upheaval of the Sixties, 1960–1975			
28 **The Kennedy and Johnson Years, 1960–1968**	Robert Hayden	"Frederick Douglass" Page 1004	poem
29 **The Civil Rights Movement, 1960–1968**	Colleen McElroy	"For My Children" Page 1010	poem
30 **Continuing Social Revolution, 1960–1975**	N. Scott Momaday	*A Vision Beyond Time and Place* Page 924	essay
31 **The Vietnam War and American Society, 1960–1975**	Carson McCullers	*The Mortgaged Heart* Page 902	essay
UNIT TEN Continuity and Change, 1968–Present			
32 **The Nixon Years, 1968–1974**	John Updike	*The Slump* Page 854	short story
33 **The Post-Watergate Period, 1974–1980**	Simon Ortiz	"Hunger in New York City" Page 1020	poem
34 **The Conservative Revolution 1980–1992**	Sandra Cisneros	*Straw Into Gold: The Metamorphosis of the Everyday* Page 930	essay
35 **Entering a New Era 1992– Present**	Amy Tan	*Mother Tongue* Page 946	essay
UNIT ELEVEN Pathways to the Future			
36 **Immigration and the Golden Door**	Claude McKay	"The Tropics in New York" Page 790	poem
37 **Gun Control and Crime**	Henry Wadsworth Longfellow	"The Arsenal at Springfield" Page 304	poem
38 **Minimum Wage and the Role of Government**	Robert Frost	"The Death of the Hired Man" Page 770	poem
39 **Entitlements: Rethinking Government Guarantees**	Katherine Anne Porter	*The Jilting of Granny Weatherall* Page 606	short story
40 **The United States in the Western Hemisphere**	Lorna Dee Cervantes	"Freeway 280" Page 1029	poem
41 **Foreign Policy After the Cold War**	Robert Frost	"Mending Wall" Page 768	poem
42 **Technology and You in the Next Century**	William Faulkner	"Nobel Prize Acceptance Speech" Page 658	speech

Reference Section

The Declaration of Independence

In Congress, July 4, 1776

THE UNANIMOUS DECLARATION OF THE THIRTEEN UNITED STATES OF AMERICA,

When in the Course of human events, it becomes necessary for one people to dissolve the political bands which have connected them with another, and to assume among the Powers of the earth, the separate and equal station to which the Laws of Nature and of Nature's God entitle them, a decent respect to the opinions of mankind requires that they should declare the causes which impel them to the separation.

We hold these truths to be self-evident, that all men are created equal, that they are endowed by their Creator with certain unalienable Rights, that among these are Life, Liberty and the pursuit of Happiness. That to secure these rights, Governments are instituted among Men, deriving their just powers from the consent of the governed, That whenever any Form of Government becomes destructive of these ends, it is the Right of the People to alter or to abolish it, and to institute new Government, laying its foundation on such principles and organizing its powers in such form, as to them shall seem most likely to effect their Safety and Happiness. Prudence, indeed, will dictate that Governments long established should not be changed for light and transient causes; and accordingly all experience hath shown, that mankind are more disposed to suffer, while evils are sufferable, than to right themselves by abolishing the forms to which they are accustomed. But when a long train of abuses and usurpations, pursuing invariably the same Object evinces a design to reduce them under absolute Despotism, it is their right, it is their duty, to throw off such Government, and to provide new Guards for their future security.—Such has been the patient sufferance of these Colonies; and such is now the necessity which constrains them to alter their former Systems of Government. The history of the present King of Great Britain is a history of repeated injuries and usurpations, all having in direct object the establishment of an absolute Tyranny over these States. To prove this, let Facts be submitted to a candid world.

He has refused his Assent to Laws, the most wholesome and necessary for the public good.

He has forbidden his Governors to pass Laws of immediate and pressing importance, unless suspended in their operation till his Assent should be obtained; and when so suspended, he has utterly neglected to attend to them.

He has refused to pass other Laws for the accommodation of large districts of people, unless those people would relinquish the right of Representation in the Legislature, a right inestimable to them and formidable to tyrants only.

He has called together legislative bodies at places unusual, uncomfortable, and distant from the depository of their Public Records, for the sole purpose of fatiguing them into compliance with his measures.

He has dissolved Representative Houses repeatedly, for opposing with manly firmness his invasions on the rights of the people.

He has refused for a long time, after such dissolutions, to cause others to be elected; whereby the Legislative powers, incapable of Annihilation, have returned to the People at large for their exercise; the State remaining in the mean time exposed to all the dangers of invasions from without, and convulsions within.

He has endeavored to prevent the population of these States; for that purpose obstructing the Laws for Naturalization of Foreigners; refusing to pass others to encourage their migration hither, and raising the conditions of new Appropriations of Lands.

He has obstructed the Administration of Justice, by refusing his Assent to Laws for establishing Judiciary powers.

He has made Judges dependent on his Will alone for the tenure of their offices, and the amount and payment of their salaries.

He has erected a multitude of New Offices, and sent hither swarms of Officers to harass our people and eat out their substance.

He has kept among us in time of peace, Standing Armies, without the Consent of our legislature.

He has affected to render the Military independent of and superior to the Civil power.

He has combined with others to subject us to a jurisdiction foreign to our constitutions, and unacknowledged by our laws; giving his Assent to their Acts of pretended Legislation:

For Quartering large bodies of armed troops among us:

For protecting them, by a mock Trial, from Punishment for any Murders which they should commit on the Inhabitants of these States:

For cutting off our Trade with all parts of the world:

For imposing taxes on us without our Consent:

For depriving us in many cases, of the benefits of Trial by Jury:

For transporting us beyond Seas to be tried for pretended offenses:

For abolishing the free System of English Laws in a neighbouring Province, establishing therein an Arbitrary government, and enlarging its Boundaries so as to render it at once an example and fit instrument for introducing the same absolute rule into these Colonies:

For taking away our Charters, abolishing our most valuable Laws, and altering fundamentally the Forms of our Governments;

For suspending our own Legislature, and declaring themselves invested with Power to legislate for us in all cases whatsoever.

He has abdicated Government here, by declaring us out of his Protection, and waging War against us.

He has plundered our seas, ravaged our Coasts, burned our towns, and destroyed the lives of our people.

He is at this time transporting large armies of foreign mercenaries to compleat the works of death, desolation and tyranny, already begun with circumstances of Cruelty and perfidy scarcely paralleled in the most barbarous ages, and totally unworthy the Head of a civilized nation.

He has constrained our fellow Citizens taken Captive on the high Seas to bear Arms against their Country, to become the executioners of their friends and Brethren, or to fall themselves by their Hands.

He has excited domestic insurrections amongst us, and has endeavored to bring on the inhabitants of our frontiers the merciless Indian Savages, whose known rule of warfare, is an undistinguished destruction of all ages, sexes, and conditions.

In every stage of these Oppressions We have Petitioned for Redress in the most humble terms. Our repeated Petitions have been answered only by repeated injury. A Prince, whose character is thus marked by every act which may define a Tyrant, is unfit to be the ruler of a free People.

Nor have We been wanting in attentions to our British brethren. We have warned them from time to time of attempts by their legislature to extend an unwarrantable jurisdiction over us. We have reminded them of the circumstances of our emigration and settlement here. We have appealed to their native justice and magnanimity, and we have conjured them by the ties of our common kindred to disavow these usurpations, which, would inevitably interrupt our connections and correspondence. They too have been deaf to the voice of justice and of consanguinity. We must, therefore, acquiesce in the necessity, which denounces our Separation, and hold them, as we hold the rest of mankind, Enemies in War, in Peace Friends.

We, therefore, the Representatives of the united States of America, in General Congress, Assembled, appealing to the Supreme Judge of the world for the rectitude of our intentions, do, in the Name, and by the Authority of the good People of these Colonies, solemnly publish and declare, That these United Colonies are, and of Right ought to be Free and Independent States; that they are Absolved from all Allegiance to the British Crown, and that all political connection between them and the State of Great Britain, is and ought to be totally dissolved, and that as Free and Independent States, they have full Power to levy War, conclude Peace, contract Alliances, establish Commerce, and to do all other Acts and Things which Independent States may of right do. And for the support of this Declaration, with a firm reliance on the protection of Divine Providence, we mutually pledge to each other our Lives, our Fortunes and our sacred Honor.

JOHN HANCOCK
President of the Continental Congress 1775–1777

NEW HAMPSHIRE
Josiah Bartlett
William Whipple
Matthew Thornton
MASSACHUSETTS BAY
Samuel Adams
John Adams
Robert Treat Paine
Elbridge Gerry
RHODE ISLAND
Stephan Hopkins
William Ellery
CONNECTICUT
Roger Sherman
Samuel Huntington
William Williams
Oliver Wolcott
NEW YORK
William Floyd
Philip Livingston
Francis Lewis
Lewis Morris

NEW JERSEY
Richard Stockton
John Witherspoon
Francis Hopkinson
John Hart
Abraham Clark
DELAWARE
Caesar Rodney
George Read
Thomas McKean
MARYLAND
Samuel Chase
William Paca
Thomas Stone
Charles Carroll
of Carrollton

VIRGINIA
George Wythe
Richard Henry Lee
Thomas Jefferson
Benjamin Harrison
Thomas Nelson, Jr.
Francis Lightfoot Lee
Carter Braxton
PENNSYLVANIA
Robert Morris
Benjamin Rush
Benjamin Franklin
John Morton
George Clymer
James Smith
George Taylor
James Wilson
George Ross

NORTH CAROLINA
William Hooper
Joseph Hewes
John Penn
SOUTH CAROLINA
Edward Rutledge
Thomas Heyward, Jr.
Thomas Lynch, Jr.
Arthur Middleton
GEORGIA
Button Gwinnett
Lyman Hall
George Walton

Source: Documents of American History, Volume I

The Constitution of the United States of America

PREAMBLE

We the people of the United States, in order to form a more perfect union, establish justice, insure domestic tranquility, provide for the common defense, promote the general welfare, and secure the blessings of liberty to ourselves and our posterity, do ordain and establish this Constitution for the United States of America.

The Preamble, or opening paragraph of the Constitution, establishes the fundamental assumption of American government: that government derives its power from the people. "We the people" are the most important words in the Constitution, as President Abraham Lincoln emphasized in 1863 when he called the United States a "government of the people, by the people, and for the people" in his Gettysburg Address. Presidents and other politicians today regularly invoke "the people" as the source of their power when making important speeches.

The Preamble also states, however, that the purpose of the Constitution is to create an orderly, stable, and just society. The authors of the Constitution were worried about the impact of too much democracy in the new American nation, fearing that what "We the people" wanted would not always lead to "a more perfect union" or insure "domestic tranquility." In fact, the tension between the desire for democracy and the wish for a stable social order is one of the most important and enduring themes in American history.

Article I
LEGISLATIVE BRANCH
Section 1 *Legislative Powers; The Congress*

All legislative powers herein granted shall be vested in a Congress of the United States, which shall consist of a Senate and House of Representatives.

SECTION 1 The Constitution outlines the legislative branch first, for this part of the federal government is the closest and most directly responsible to the people. The men who wrote the Constitution deliberately established a bicameral, or two-part, legislative branch, whose two houses would not only balance each other but also modify the impact of "the people." All legislation requires the approval of both the House of Representatives and the Senate.

Section 2 *House of Representatives*

1. Election of Members The House of Representatives shall be composed of members chosen every second year by the people of the several states, and the electors in each state shall have the qualifications requisite for electors of the most numerous branch of the state legislature.

CLAUSE 1 The Founding Fathers wanted the House of Representatives to be the part of the federal government most responsive to the will of the people. They made sure that voters could change the membership of the House frequently by requiring every member to run for office every two years. Today, the House is the only part of the federal government the people could change in one election; if the people wished, they could replace all 435 members of the House every two years.

2. Qualifications No person shall be a representative who shall not have attained to the age of twenty-five years, and been seven years a citizen of the United States, and who shall not, when elected, be an inhabitant of that state in which he shall be chosen.

CLAUSE 2 The purpose of these requirements was to make certain that representatives actually live among the people whom they represent. The authors of the Constitution wanted to avoid absentee legislators—representatives who did not actually live in their districts—something that happened frequently in the British Parliament. They wanted to ensure direct contact between the people and their representatives.

3. Apportionment Representatives and direct taxes* shall be apportioned among the several states which may be included within this Union, according to their respective numbers, which shall be determined by adding to the whole number of free persons, including those bound to service for a term of years and excluding Indians not taxed, three fifths of all other persons. The actual enumeration shall be made within three years after the first meeting of the Congress of the United States, and within every subsequent term of ten years, in such manner as they shall by law direct. The number of representatives shall not exceed one for every thirty thousand, but each state shall have at least one representative; and until such enumeration shall be made, the state of New Hampshire shall be entitled to choose three, Massachusetts eight, Rhode Island and Providence Plantations one, Connecticut five, New York six, New Jersey four, Pennsylvania eight,

---

* The black lines indicate portions of the Constitution altered by subsequent amendments to the document or that no longer apply.

Note: Spelling and capitalization have been modernized.

Source: Documents of American History, Volume I

Delaware one, Maryland six, Virginia ten, North Carolina five, South Carolina five, and Georgia three.

CLAUSE 3 As a result of this provision, the United States government must conduct a census of the population every ten years. The primary purpose of the census is to determine how many members of Congress each state will have. The decision to count only three fifths of the total number of enslaved persons was a compromise between southerners, who wanted the total number to be counted in order to have more members in Congress, and northerners, who wanted southerners to have fewer representatives and consequently less influence in the legislature. This clause became controversial in the 1800s when abolitionists and slaveholders began to argue about whether the Constitution sanctioned slavery. Notice that the language is very vague. The word *slaves* does not appear, just "other persons." The Thirteenth Amendment effectively repealed this clause when it made slavery illegal in 1865 following the Civil War.

4. Filling Vacancies When vacancies happen in the representation from any state, the executive authority thereof shall issue writs of election to fill such vacancies.

CLAUSE 4 This clause allows the governor of each state to call special elections to replace members of Congress who die or resign in the middle of their terms.

5. Officers; Impeachment The House of Representatives shall choose their speaker and other officers; and shall have the sole power of impeachment.

CLAUSE 5 Both the British Parliament and the colonial legislatures had fought long and hard to obtain the right to control their own affairs, meaning that the members rather than a king or president would choose their officers. Imagine how much more power the President of the United States would have in Congress if he or she could simply appoint the Speaker of the House and other officials. Another cherished right was the power to impeach, or accuse, government officials of committing crimes or abusing their offices. Impeachment proceedings against a federal official or judge must always begin in the House.

Section 3 *Senate*

1. Composition; Term The Senate of the United States shall be composed of two senators from each state chosen by the legislature thereof, for six years; and each senator shall have one vote.

CLAUSE 1 By giving each state two senators, the authors of the Constitution sought to prevent large states with bigger populations from dominating smaller states. To make the Senate less directly responsive to the people's wishes, senators were to have six-year terms and be chosen by state legislators. The people did not directly elect senators until the Seventeenth Amendment was ratified in 1913.

2. Classification; Filling Vacancies Immediately after they shall be assembled in consequence of the first election, they shall be divided as equally as may be into three classes. The seats of the senators of the first class shall be vacated at the expiration of the second year, of the second class at the expiration of the fourth

year, and of the third class at the expiration of the sixth year, so that one third may be chosen every second year; and if vacancies happen by resignation, or otherwise, during the recess of the legislature of any State, the executive thereof may make temporary appointments until the next meeting of the legislature, which shall then fill such vacancies.

CLAUSE 2 This clause ensures that the membership of the Senate, unlike that of the House, cannot be changed in one election. In the Senate, terms are staggered, so it would take three elections and six years to replace all 100 senators. Longer terms tend to make the Senate a more independent body than the House; its members are a little more likely to vote the way they wish rather than the way they think people might want them to vote.

3. Qualifications No person shall be a senator who shall not have attained to the age of thirty years, and been nine years a citizen of the United States, and who shall not, when elected, be an inhabitant of that state for which he shall be chosen.

CLAUSE 3 This clause is meant to ensure that senators will not be absentees, that they will represent the people and places they know. When politicians who have grown up in one state run for the Senate in another state, they are often accused of being outsiders. Massachusetts native Robert F. Kennedy overcame this charge when he was elected senator from New York in 1964, but Connecticut-born George Bush could not do so when he ran for the Senate from Texas and lost in 1970.

4. President of the Senate The Vice President of the United States shall be president of the Senate, but shall have no vote, unless they be equally divided.

CLAUSE 4 During the first few decades of the republic, the Vice President generally attended the meetings of the Senate. Now he usually attends only on ceremonial occasions or when the Senate is equally divided over a bill.

5. Other Officers The Senate shall choose their other officers, and also a president pro tempore, in the absence of the Vice President, or when he shall exercise the office of the President of the United States.

CLAUSE 5 This sentence ensures that no other officials, such as the President, can exercise undue influence in the Senate by controlling the selection of its officers.

6. Impeachment Trials The Senate shall have the sole power to try all impeachments. When sitting for that purpose, they shall be on oath or affirmation. When the President of the United States is tried, the Chief Justice shall preside: and no person shall be convicted without the concurrence of two thirds of the members present.

CLAUSE 6 If the House votes to impeach, or indict, a federal official, the Senate becomes a court to try that person. The senators are like members of a jury. They listen to lawyers present evidence for and against the accused and then vote to convict or acquit. To make sure that an official is not impeached for frivolous or partisan reasons, the Constitution requires a two thirds vote in the Senate in order to convict someone. In 1974 President

Richard Nixon resigned the presidency when he realized that more than 67 senators would vote to convict him.

7. Penalty on Conviction Judgment in cases of impeachment shall not extend further than to removal from office, and disqualification to hold and enjoy any office of honor, trust or profit under the United States: but the party convicted shall nevertheless be liable and subject to indictment, trial, judgment and punishment, according to law.

CLAUSE 7 Under the Constitution, the only punishment for officials who are impeached and convicted is that they can no longer be part of the United States government. The regular criminal court system must determine all jail terms, fines, and other punishments. In 1974 President Gerald Ford pardoned Richard Nixon for all illegal acts he may have committed as President, even though Nixon was never actually convicted of any specific crime.

Section 4 *Elections and Meetings*

1. Election of Congress The times, places and manner of holding elections for senators and representatives, shall be prescribed in each state by the legislature thereof; but the Congress may at any time by law make or alter such regulations, except as to the places of choosing senators.

CLAUSE 1 The states decide how and when to choose members of Congress, although Congress reserves the right to change the ways in which they do it. In 1842 Congress required that elections be held on the first Tuesday after the first Monday in November in even-numbered years.

2. Sessions The Congress shall assemble at least once in every year, and such meeting shall be on the first Monday in December, unless they shall by law appoint a different day.

CLAUSE 2 This clause guarantees that Congress will meet on a regular basis. A few decades before the American Revolution, kings and royal governors had called legislatures into session and dismissed them at their pleasure. In the 1630s, King Charles I refused to call Parliament and tried to govern England without a legislature. The Constitution makes certain that this cannot happen in the United States. Congress, not the President, decides when it will meet. In 1933 the Twentieth Amendment set the annual opening date as January 3, rather than the first Monday in December.

Section 5 *Legislative Proceedings*

1. Organization Each house shall be the judge of the elections, returns and qualifications of its own members, and a majority of each shall constitute a quorum to do business; but a smaller number may adjourn from day to day, and may be authorized to compel the attendance of absent members, in such manner, and under such penalties, as each house may provide.

2. Rules Each house may determine the rules of its proceedings, punish its members for disorderly behavior, and, with the concurrence of two thirds, expel a member.

CLAUSES 1 AND 2 These clauses were also designed to ensure that Congress would maintain control of its activities. They protect the integrity of the people's representatives from interference by the President or judges.

3. Record Each house shall keep a journal of its proceedings, and from time to time publish the same, excepting such parts as may in their judgment require secrecy; and the yeas and nays of the members of either house on any question, shall, at the desire of one fifth of those present, be entered on the journal.

CLAUSE 3 The Founders recognized that the people needed some sort of record of what their representatives said and how they voted in order to hold them accountable for their actions. Although the Constitution requires Congress to maintain a journal—today published as the *Congressional Record*—it also gives Congress the power to keep some matters secret. For example, representatives might not want to publish their debates on an issue involving national security.

4. Adjournment Neither house, during the session of Congress, shall, without the consent of the other, adjourn for more than three days, nor to any other place than that in which the two houses shall be sitting.

CLAUSE 4 Some of the Constitution's clauses may seem strange today. Why, for example, would the men who wrote the Constitution care about adjournments? The answer lies in colonial and British history. Sometimes one house of Parliament or a colonial legislature would leave or adjourn in order to prevent some legislation from passing or to hold up proceedings. This clause guarantees that, while they may not always agree with each other, the two houses of Congress must deal with each other. One house cannot adjourn unless the other agrees to an adjournment.

Section 6 *Compensation, Immunities, and Disabilities of Members*

1. Salaries; Immunities The senators and representatives shall receive a compensation for their services, to be ascertained by law, and paid out of the treasury of the United States. They shall, in all cases, except treason, felony and breach of the peace, be privileged from arrest during their attendance at the session of their respective houses, and in going to and returning from the same; and for any speech or debate in either house, they shall not be questioned in any other place.

CLAUSE 1 Imagine what would happen if members of Congress could be arrested for what they say. This idea may seem ridiculous now, but it actually happened in the 1600s and 1700s. If Presidents or judges could arrest members of Congress, they could directly interfere with their proceedings. This clause essentially guaranteed that members of Congress did not have to worry about arbitrary interference by the executive and judicial branches.

2. Restrictions on Other Employment No senator or representative shall, during the time for which he was elected, be appointed to any civil office under the authority of the United States, which shall have been created, or the emoluments whereof shall have been increased during such time; and no person holding any office under the United States shall be a member of either house during his continuance in office.

CLAUSE 2 In Great Britain and in some of the American colonies, government officials had also held seats in Parliament or in legislatures. The authors of the Constitution feared that this practice encouraged corruption and discouraged independent decisions. If cabinet officers or presidential appointees were members of Congress, they would probably vote the way the President wanted them to. They might be more beholden to the President than to their constituents. Today, no federal officer may also be a member of Congress. In Great Britain, on the other hand, the prime minister and other cabinet officers are all members of Parliament.

Section 7 *Revenue Bills, President's Veto*

1. Revenue Bills **All bills for raising revenue shall originate in the House of Representatives; but the Senate may propose or concur with amendments as on other bills.**

CLAUSE 1 Because the House of Representatives is the body closest to the people, the Constitution requires that all legislation regarding taxes must begin there. The idea is that the people's representatives are the most appropriate guardians of the people's pocketbooks. Even today, if the President of the United States wants to raise taxes, the bill must begin in the House, not the Senate.

2. How a Bill Becomes a Law; the Veto **Every bill which shall have passed the House of Representatives and the Senate, shall, before it become a law, be presented to the President of the United States; if he approve he shall sign it, but if not he shall return it, with his objections to that house in which it shall have originated, who shall enter the objections at large on their journal, and proceed to reconsider it. If after such reconsideration two thirds of that house shall agree to pass the bill, it shall be sent, together with the objections, to the other house, by which it shall likewise be reconsidered, and if approved by two thirds of that house, it shall become a law. But in all such cases the votes of both houses shall be determined by yeas and nays, and the names of the persons voting for and against the bill shall be entered on the journal of each house respectively. If any bill shall not be returned by the President within ten days (Sundays excepted) after it shall have been presented to him, the same shall be a law, in like manner as if he had signed it, unless the Congress by their adjournment prevent its return, in which case it shall not be a law.**

3. Resolutions Passed by Congress **Every order, resolution, or vote to which the concurrence of the Senate and House of Representatives may be necessary (except on a question of adjournment) shall be presented to the President of the United States; and before the same shall take effect, shall be approved by him, or being disapproved by him, shall be repassed by two thirds of the Senate and House of Representatives, according to the rules and limitations prescribed in the case of a bill.**

CLAUSES 2 AND 3 These two clauses carefully regulate the balance of power between the legislative and executive branches while trying to maintain the independence of both. Thus, the President has the right to reject any bill the Congress passes, but only if one third of the members agree with him after further deliberation. A presidential veto—when a President refuses to sign a bill into law—

makes the President equally powerful with Congress but not completely independent of it. The President cannot veto a bill without some congressional support. These clauses prevent either the Congress or the President from acting arbitrarily or impulsively.

Section 8 *Powers of Congress*
The Congress shall have power

1. To lay and collect taxes, duties, imposts and excises, to pay the debts and provide for the common defense and general welfare of the United States; but all duties, imposts and excises shall be uniform throughout the United States;

CLAUSE 1 This clause gives the federal government power it did not have under the Articles of Confederation, specifically, the right to tax. It is one of the most important provisions of the Constitution, for without the power to raise revenues, the government would not have the money to operate itself or fund programs. This clause also ensures that the government must tax every part of the country equally. For example, federal taxes must be the same in Arizona as in Maine.

The phrase "provide for the common defense and general welfare of the United States" is one of the vague phrases in the Constitution that Presidents, Congress, and judges have often interpreted very broadly in order to take actions not specifically mentioned in the Constitution. Because Congress theoretically has the power to act for the "general welfare," it can take any steps it deems necessary to guarantee the defense and welfare of the nation as a whole.

2. To borrow money on the credit of the United States;

CLAUSE 2 The power to borrow money allows Congress to spend money beyond the amount it is able to tax. Secretary of the Treasury Alexander Hamilton's financial program in the 1790s, most wartime spending, and many of the social programs of the 1900s would have been impossible without this clause.

3. To regulate commerce with foreign nations, and among the several states, and with the Indian tribes;

CLAUSE 3 As a result of this clause, Congress possesses the power to supervise all commerce, both among the various states and between the United States and foreign nations. Without this provision, the states might have established tariffs on imports and exports, and trade in the United States would have become a complex patchwork of regulations and taxes. Imagine, for example, if states in the middle of the country taxed or regulated trade between the eastern and western halves of the United States. Congress did not have the power to regulate commerce under the Articles of Confederation. This clause was designed to create a clear, uncomplicated system of trade that would advance the economic interests of the nation.

4. To establish an uniform rule of naturalization, and uniform laws on the subject of bankruptcies throughout the United States;

CLAUSE 4 Only Congress, not the states, can regulate the way in which immigrants become citizens of the United States. In addition, only Congress can regulate the handling of bankruptcies, another attempt to create uniform economic regulations throughout the United States.

5. To coin money, regulate the value thereof, and of foreign coin, and fix the standard of weights and measures;

6. To provide for the punishment of counterfeiting the securities and current coin of the United States;

CLAUSES 5 AND 6 These two clauses ensure that there is only one kind of money in the United States. Without such regulation, the states or private institutions could issue their own money. The members of the Constitutional Convention included these clauses to create a stable and predictable medium of exchange throughout the United States.

7. To establish post offices and post roads;

CLAUSE 7 Just as Congress has the power to regulate commerce—the exchange of goods—so, too, it has the power to regulate the exchange of information and news through the mails. Without this power, Americans might have to contend with fifty different postal services in the United States.

8. To promote the progress of science and useful arts, by securing for limited times to authors and inventors the exclusive right to their respective writings and discoveries;

CLAUSE 8 This clause gives Congress the power to regulate the exchange of knowledge in the United States. Congress, not the states, issues patents and copyright protection to people who come up with new ideas or technology.

9. To constitute tribunals inferior to the Supreme Court;

CLAUSE 9 This brief clause grants Congress an important power—the right to create the federal court system below the level of the Supreme Court. Because the Constitution itself does not explain the judicial system in great detail, Congress has had enormous leeway in the creation of this system.

10. To define and punish piracies and felonies committed on the high seas and offenses against the law of nations;

11. To declare war, grant letters of marque and reprisal, and make rules concerning captures on land and water;

CLAUSES 10 AND 11 Congress also has the power to regulate international relations, particularly any matters concerning war.

12. To raise and support armies, but no appropriation of money to that use shall be for a longer term than two years;

CLAUSE 12 Although Congress can form armies to defend American interests, it can only pay for them for two years at a time. This clause reflects the deep fear the Founders and other former colonists had about standing, or professional, armies. They worried that government officials might use permanent armies to stifle opposition and take away liberties, as kings had done in the past.

13. To provide and maintain a navy;

CLAUSE 13 Following a British constitutional tradition, the delegates at the Constitutional Convention felt no need to restrict naval expenditures to two years. They viewed the navy as far less of a threat to civil authority than the army.

14. To make rules for the government and regulation of the land and naval forces;

CLAUSE 14 These rules are spelled out in the Uniform Code of Military Justice, passed by Congress in 1950.

15. To provide for calling forth the militia to execute the laws of the Union, suppress insurrections and repel invasions;

16. To provide for organizing, arming, and disciplining, the militia, and for governing such part of them as may be employed in the service of the United States, reserving to the states respectively, the appointment of the officers, and the authority of training the militia according to the discipline prescribed by Congress;

CLAUSES 15 AND 16 The National Defense Act of 1916 made each state's militia part of the National Guard. Under normal circumstances, each state's governor is in charge of that state's National Guard; however, the President has the power to call into federal service any or all National Guard units when necessary, as President George Bush did during the 1991 Persian Gulf War.

17. To exercise exclusive legislation in all cases whatsoever, over such district (not exceeding ten miles square) as may, by cession of particular states, and the acceptance of Congress, become the seat of the government of the United States, and to exercise like authority over all places purchased by the consent of the legislature of the state in which the same shall be, for the erection of forts, magazines, arsenals, dockyards, and other needful buildings; and

CLAUSE 17 This clause provides for what would become the nation's capital, Washington, D.C., and for federal establishments in the states. Without this provision, Philadelphia or some other large city might have become the nation's permanent capital.

18. To make all laws which shall be necessary and proper for carrying into execution the foregoing powers, and all other powers vested by this Constitution in the government of the United States, or in any department or officer thereof.

CLAUSE 18 No other clause in the Constitution has been used more often by judges and federal officials to increase the power of the federal government. Read loosely, the "necessary and proper," or "elastic," clause says that Congress may take any steps not otherwise prohibited by the Constitution to guarantee that the other provisions of the Constitution are carried out.

Section 9 *Powers Denied to Congress*

1. The Slave Trade ~~The migration or importation of such persons as any of the states now existing shall think proper to admit, shall not be prohibited by the Congress prior to the year one thousand eight hundred and eight, but a tax or duty may be imposed on such importation, not exceeding ten dollars for each person.~~

CLAUSE 1 Although the Constitution outlawed the importation of enslaved persons into the United States, this provision did not take effect until two decades after the ratification of the document. Notice again how careful the language is. The word "slave" does not appear, only "such persons as any of the States now existing shall think proper."

2. Writ of Habeas Corpus The privilege of the writ of habeas corpus shall not be suspended, unless when in cases of rebellion or invasion the public safety may require it.

CLAUSE 2 The writ of habeas corpus directs a sheriff, public official, or other person who is holding citizens against their will to produce them so that the legality of their detention can be determined. This clause protects American citizens from being held in prison without being formally charged with a crime. Without the writ, the government could simply put people it did not like in jail and hold them there without explanation. President Abraham Lincoln, who called the Civil War a rebellion, did suspend the writ of habeas corpus and imprison people without showing cause.

3. Bills of Attainder; *Ex Post Facto* Laws No bill of attainder or ex post facto law shall be passed.

CLAUSE 3 A bill of attainder is a legislative act that punishes a person without a trial in court. An ex post facto law is a retroactive one; it declares that an action is a crime after it has been committed. These important provisions prevent the government from arresting and punishing people without due process of law.

4. Apportionment of Direct Taxes No capitation, ~~or other direct,~~ tax shall be laid, unless in proportion to the census or enumeration herein before directed to be taken.

CLAUSE 4 This provision outlawed all direct taxes on individuals until the Sixteenth Amendment (1913) gave Congress the power to tax personal incomes.

5. Taxes on Exports No tax or duty shall be laid on articles exported from any state.

CLAUSE 5 Congress cannot tax anything sent out of a state, although it does have the power to tax imported goods.

6. Special Preference for Trade No preference shall be given by any regulation of commerce or revenue to the ports of one state over those of another: nor shall vessels bound to, or from, one state, be obliged to enter, clear, or pay duties in another.

CLAUSE 6 These specific restrictions on the states keep them from trying to regulate trade outside their own boundaries. Interstate trade is solely the business of the national government.

7. Spending No money shall be drawn from the treasury, but in consequence of appropriations made by law; and a regular statement and account of the receipts and expenditures of all public money shall be published from time to time.

CLAUSE 7 Like many other parts of the Constitution, this paragraph reflects eighteenth-century fears about corruption and power. The purpose of the clause was to prevent Presidents or other officials from thwarting the will of Congress and the people by spending money in secret on projects prohibited by Congress. It is a significant check on presidential power. The Iran-contra scandal involved government officials who attempted to raise and spend money in support of the contras in Nicaragua, an activity that Congress had made illegal.

8. Titles of Nobility No title of nobility shall be granted by the United States: and no person holding any office of profit or trust under them, shall, without the consent of the Congress, accept of any present, emolument, office, or title, of any kind whatever, from any king, prince or foreign state.

CLAUSE 8 The Founders included this provision to prevent the establishment of an aristocracy in the United States. The clause was also designed to discourage foreign nations from attempting to bribe or otherwise corrupt government officials. Today, exceptions are made, usually in the case of retired officials. Presidents Ronald Reagan and George Bush, for example, received formal recognition from the government of Great Britain after their public careers were over.

Section 10 *Powers Denied to the States*

1. Unconditional Prohibitions No state shall enter into any treaty, alliance, or confederation; grant letters of marque and reprisal; coin money; emit bills of credit; make any thing but gold and silver coin a tender in payment of debts; pass any bill of attainder, ex post facto law, or law impairing the obligation of contracts, or grant any title of nobility.

2. Powers Conditionally Denied No state shall, without the consent of the Congress, lay any imposts or duties on imports or exports, except what may be absolutely necessary for executing its inspection laws: and the net produce of all duties and imposts, laid by any state on imports or exports, shall be for the use of the treasury of the United States; and all such laws shall be subject to the revision and control of the Congress.

3. Other Denied Powers No state shall, without the consent of Congress, lay any duty of tonnage, keep troops, or ships of war in time of peace, enter into any agreement or compact with another state, or with a foreign power, or engage in war, unless actually invaded, or in such imminent danger as will not admit of delay.

CLAUSES 1, 2, AND 3 These three clauses specifically prohibit the states from getting involved in foreign affairs or interstate commerce. Their purpose is to limit the power of the states to internal affairs. Anything that affects more than one state, economically or militarily, is properly the business of the national government.

Article II
EXECUTIVE BRANCH
Section 1 *President and Vice President*

1. Chief Executive; Term The executive power shall be vested in a President of the United States of America. He shall hold his office during the term of four years, and, together with the Vice President, chosen for the same term, be elected, as follows:

CLAUSE 1 The Founders deliberately left the duties of the President vague. During the past century, Presidents have assumed great power, in part because the Constitution does not put many specific restrictions on the office. Although the presidential term is four years, many members of the Constitutional Convention expected incumbents to be reelected more than once. In fact, they thought most Presidents would serve for a long time. But after Franklin Roosevelt was elected to four terms between 1932 and

1944, the Twenty-second Amendment (1951) restricted Presidents to two terms. There is no such limit on Vice Presidents.

2. Electoral College Each state shall appoint, in such manner as the legislature thereof may direct, a number of electors, equal to the whole number of senators and representatives to which the state may be entitled in the Congress: but no senator or representative, or person holding an office of trust or profit under the United States, shall be appointed an elector.

CLAUSE 2 This clause establishes what we call the Electoral College, the group of people who elect the President. State legislatures decide how electors for that state will be chosen. The number of electoral votes each state has is equal to the number of its senators and representatives added together.

3. Former Electoral Method The electors shall meet in their respective states, and vote by ballot for two persons, of whom one at least shall not be an inhabitant of the same state with themselves. And they shall make a list of all the persons voted for, and of the number of votes for each; which list they shall sign and certify, and transmit sealed to the seat of the government of the United States, directed to the president of the Senate. The president of the Senate shall, in the presence of the Senate and House of Representatives, open all the certificates, and the votes shall then be counted. The person having the greatest number of votes shall be the President, if such number be a majority of the whole number of Electors appointed; and if there be more than one who have such majority, and have an equal number of votes, then the House of Representatives shall immediately choose by ballot one of them for President; and if no person have a majority, then from the five highest on the list the said House shall in like manner choose the President. But in choosing the President, the votes shall be taken by states, the representation from each state having one vote; a quorum for this purpose shall consist of a member or members from two thirds of the states, and a majority of all the states shall be necessary to a choice. In every case, after the choice of the President, the person having the greatest number of votes of the electors shall be the Vice President. But if there should remain two or more who have equal votes, the Senate shall choose from them by ballot the Vice President.

CLAUSE 3 The Twelfth Amendment (1804) replaced this paragraph, which is no longer in force.

4. Time of Elections The Congress may determine the time of choosing the electors, and the day on which they shall give their votes; which day shall be the same throughout the United States.

CLAUSE 4 Congress has established the Tuesday after the first Monday in November every fourth year as the time to choose electors. By law, the electors cast their ballots on the Monday after the second Wednesday in December.

5. Qualifications for President No person except a natural-born citizen, or a citizen of the United States at the time of the adoption of this Constitution, shall be eligible to the office of President; neither shall any person be eligible to that office who shall not have attained to the age of thirty-five years, and been fourteen years a resident within the United States.

CLAUSE 5 This provision ensures that the President of the United States will be a mature person, who is not only a natural-born citizen of the United States but has also lived in the nation for at least fourteen years.

6. Presidential Succession In case of the removal of the President from office, or of his death, resignation, or inability to discharge the powers and duties of the said office, the same shall devolve on the Vice President, and the Congress may by law provide for the case of removal, death, resignation or inability, both of the President and Vice President, declaring what officer shall then act as President, and such officer shall act accordingly, until the disability be removed, or a President shall be elected.

CLAUSE 6 The Twenty-fifth Amendment (1967) supersedes the first half of this provision, more clearly explaining when and how a Vice President becomes President.

7. Salary The President shall, at stated times, receive for his services, a compensation, which shall neither be increased nor diminished during the period for which he shall have been elected, and he shall not receive within that period any other emolument from the United States, or any of them.

CLAUSE 7 This clause prohibits Congress from changing a President's salary while he or she is in office. The authors of the Constitution were afraid that Congress might use its power to corrupt or punish a President. Without this clause, for example, Congress could threaten to lower a President's salary to prevent him or her from vetoing a bill. Today, the President of the United States is paid $200,000 a year, plus $50,000 in a taxable expense account. Additional benefits include residence in the White House, Secret Service protection, and means of transportation. Congress cannot give a President a valuable gift ("an emolument") while he or she is in office.

8. Oath of Office Before he enter on the execution of his office, he shall take the following oath or affirmation:—"I do solemnly swear (or affirm) that I will faithfully execute the office of the President of the United States, and will to the best of my ability, preserve, protect and defend the Constitution of the United States."

CLAUSE 8 Note that the President swears to uphold the Constitution, not the United States. When Presidents take the oath of office, they commit themselves to the form of government outlined in this document. Remember that people in the 1780s and 1790s did not assume that the Constitution would be permanent; after all, the Articles of Confederation had lasted only a decade. The oath commits the President to this Constitution and no others.

Section 2 Powers of the President

1. Military Powers The President shall be commander in chief of the army and navy of the United States, and of the militia of the several states, when called into the actual service of the United States; he may require the opinion, in writing, of the

principal officer in each of the executive departments, upon any subject relating to the duties of their respective offices, and he shall have power to grant reprieves and pardons for offenses against the United States, except in cases of impeachment.

CLAUSE 1 Even though the President is a civilian, he or she is the supreme commander of the military. The phrase "require the opinion, in writing" is one of the few places in which the Constitution refers to what is called the cabinet, the heads of the executive departments. The President's power to grant pardons is limited to federal crimes.

2. Treaties; Appointments He shall have power, by and with the advice and consent of the Senate, to make treaties, provided two thirds of the senators present concur; and he shall nominate, and by and with the advice and consent of the Senate, shall appoint ambassadors, other public ministers and consuls, judges of the Supreme Court, and all other officers of the United States, whose appointments are not herein otherwise provided for, and which shall be established by law: but the Congress may by law vest the appointment of such inferior officers, as they think proper, in the President alone, in the courts of law, or in the heads of departments.

CLAUSE 2 To make major agreements with foreign countries or to appoint major public officials, the President has to seek the advice and consent of the Senate. The aim of this provision is to prevent the President from conducting personal diplomacy, committing the United States to something only he or she wants, and from appointing only his or her friends to judgeships and federal offices.

3. Temporary Appointments The President shall have power to fill up all vacancies that may happen during the recess of the Senate, by granting commissions which shall expire at the end of their next session.

CLAUSE 3 This clause simply allows the President to make temporary appointments when Congress is not in session.

Section 3 *Duties of the President*
He shall from time to time give to the Congress information of the state of the Union, and recommend to their consideration such measures as he shall judge necessary and expedient; he may, on extraordinary occasions, convene both houses, or either of them, and in case of disagreement between them, with respect to the time of adjournment, he may adjourn them to such time as he shall think proper; he shall receive ambassadors and other public ministers; he shall take care that the laws be faithfully executed, and shall commission all the officers of the United States.

SECTION 3 This paragraph lists the specific duties and responsibilities of the President. He must give a State of the Union address occasionally (usually once a year). In addition, he may call special sessions of Congress, adjourn Congress if the two houses are divided about it, receive ambassadors, and commission officers. Finally, he must see "that the laws [of the United States] be faithfully executed." These are important duties. But notice how general they are and how few in number. Compare them with the lengthy list of specific things the Congress can and

cannot do. The members of the Constitutional Convention were not as sure of what the office of the presidency would be as they were of Congress. Much of the job has been defined by the men who have held the office.

Section 4 *Impeachment*
The President, Vice President and all civil officers of the United States, shall be removed from office on impeachment for, and conviction of, treason, bribery, or other high crimes and misdemeanors.

SECTION 4 If the President goes too far in assuming powers and breaks the law in the opinion of a majority of the members of the House of Representatives, he can be impeached and tried by the Senate. This event has happened once in American history. President Andrew Johnson was impeached by the House of Representatives in 1867. Although a majority of senators voted that he was guilty, more than a third had doubts, so Johnson remained in office. In 1974 the House Judiciary Committee voted to recommend the impeachment of President Richard Nixon, but he resigned before the full House was able to vote on the recommendation.

Article III
JUDICIAL BRANCH
Section 1 *Courts, Terms of Office*
The judicial power of the United States, shall be vested in one Supreme Court, and in such inferior courts as the Congress may from time to time ordain and establish. The judges, both of the Supreme and inferior courts, shall hold their offices during good behavior, and shall, at stated times, receive for their services, a compensation which shall not be diminished during their continuance in office.

SECTION 1 Although the Constitution makes provisions for a federal court system to hear and decide cases, it only specifically creates the Supreme Court. Acts of Congress have created all other federal courts, as well as established the number of Supreme Court justices. In order to preserve the integrity and independence of judges from both the executive and legislative branches, federal judges serve "during good behavior," which basically means as long as they live, and cannot have their salaries reduced.

Section 2 *Jurisdiction*
1. Scope of Judicial Power The judicial power shall extend to all cases, in law and equity, arising under this Constitution, the laws of the United States, and treaties made, or which shall be made, under their authority;—to all cases affecting ambassadors, other public ministers and consuls;—to all cases of admiralty and maritime jurisdiction;—to controversies to which the United States shall be a party;—to controversies between two or more states; between a state and citizens of another state; between citizens of different states;—between citizens of the same state claiming lands under grants of different states, and between a state, or the citizens thereof, and foreign states, citizens or subjects.

CLAUSE 1 This paragraph lists the kinds of cases federal courts can hear and decide on. They have jurisdiction over cases relating to the Constitution, federal laws, treaties, and diplomatic offi-cials. They also have jurisdiction over cases involving disputes between the United States and someone else, between two states, or between citizens of different states. The Eleventh Amendment (1795) substantially restricted the jurisdiction of federal courts in cases involving states.

2. Supreme Court In all cases affecting ambassadors, other public ministers and consuls, and those in which a state shall be a party, the Supreme Court shall have original jurisdiction. In all the other cases before mentioned, the Supreme Court shall have appellate jurisdiction, both as to law and fact, with such excep-tions, and under such regulations as the Congress shall make.

CLAUSE 2 Under this clause, the Supreme Court has both original and appellate jurisdiction. That is, the Court is first to hear and decide cases involving foreign ambassadors and individual states. But it also has appellate jurisdiction, meaning people can appeal the decisions of lower courts to the Supreme Court.

3. Trial by Jury The trial of all crimes, except in cases of impeachment, shall be by jury; and such trial shall be held in the state where the said crimes shall have been committed; but when not committed within any state, the trial shall be at such place or places as the Congress may by law have directed.

CLAUSE 3 In reaction to cases in English constitutional history, the members of the Constitutional Convention guaranteed American citizens the right to trial by jury in federal cases and the right to have the trial in the place where the crime supposedly occurred. The Founders feared the power of government to take defendants to distant places to try them quickly and without a jury.

Section 3 *Treason*

1. Definition Treason against the United States shall consist only in levying war against them, or in adhering to their enemies, giving them aid and comfort. No person shall be convicted of treason unless on the testimony of two witnesses to the same overt act, or on confession in open court.

CLAUSE 1 The definition of treason is very specific because the authors of the Constitution wanted to make certain that people were not imprisoned or punished simply for criticizing the gov-ernment. The crime of treason can apply only to citizens or resi-dent aliens, and even then only in time of war.

2. Punishment The Congress shall have power to declare the punishment of treason, but no attainder of treason shall work corruption of blood, or forfeiture except during the life of the person attained.

CLAUSE 2 Although the United States has never executed anyone for treason, death remains the maximum punishment for some-one convicted of this charge. The minimum punishment, by act of Congress, is five years in prison and/or a $10,000 fine. The phrase "corruption of blood, or forfeiture" means that punish-ment for treason affects only the person convicted of it; neither the traitor's family nor descendants can be punished.

Article IV
RELATIONS AMONG THE STATES
Section 1 *Full Faith and Credit*

Full faith and credit shall be given in each state to the public acts, records, and judicial proceedings of every other state. And the Congress may by general laws prescribe the manner in which such acts, records and proceedings shall be proved, and the effect thereof.

SECTION 1 In this clause, the authors of the Constitution were again asserting the supremacy of the federal government. Con-gress would have responsibility for making sure that each state respected the legal actions of the others.

Section 2 *Privileges and Immunities of Citizens*

1. Privileges The citizens of each state shall be entitled to all privileges and immunities of citizens in the several states.

CLAUSE 1 The Constitution ensures that states cannot discrimi-nate against people from other states. The federal government will make certain that citizens of the United States enjoy their full rights in every part of the nation.

2. Extradition A person charged in any state with treason, felony, or other crime, who shall flee from justice, and be found in another state, shall on demand of the executive authority of the state from which he fled, be delivered up, to be removed to the state having jurisdiction of the crime.

CLAUSE 2 The legal term for this process is *extradition*. If some-one commits a crime in Minnesota, for example, and then flees to Montana, the governor of Montana must arrange to transport the alleged criminal back to Minnesota for trial if the governor of Minnesota requests this action. Although governors sometimes delay complying with such requests for political reasons, the fed-eral government has the power to force governors to comply.

3. Fugitive Slaves ~~No person held to service or labor in one state, under the laws thereof, escaping into another, shall, in con-sequence of any law or regulation therein, be discharged from such service or labor, but shall be delivered up on claim of the party to whom such service or labor may be due.~~

CLAUSE 3 This clause was nullified by the Thirteenth Amend-ment in 1865, which made slavery illegal throughout the United States.

Section 3 *New States and Territories*

1. New States New states may be admitted by the Congress into this Union; but no new states shall be formed or erected within the jurisdiction of any other state, nor any state be formed by the junction of two or more states, or parts of states, without the consent of the legislatures of the states concerned as well as of the Congress.

CLAUSE 1 Only the federal government can create new states. Congress decides on the rules and procedures for admitting new states to the Union. It cannot, however, make new states out of old ones unless the legislature of a particular state agrees to this course of action. Since 1789 Congress has created thirty-seven states. Five of these—Vermont, Kentucky, Tennessee, Maine, and West Virginia—were originally parts of other states. One—Texas—was an independent republic. One—California—was part of Mexico before it became a state. The other thirty states have become parts of the United States after first being territories. The Northwest Ordinance of 1787 outlines the process by which a territory becomes a state.

2. Federal Lands The Congress shall have power to dispose of and make all needful rules and regulations respecting the territory or other property belonging to the United States; and nothing in this Constitution shall be so construed as to prejudice any claims of the United States, or of any particular state.

CLAUSE 2 Simply put, this clause gives Congress the power to govern all federal territory and other property as it sees fit. In theory, state governments have no say when it comes to the regulation or disposal of federal lands. This clause led to controversy in the 1800s because Congress had the power to abolish slavery on federal property if it wished. Controversy has continued in the 1900s because of the question of how to handle the vast acreage in national parks and other preserves owned and operated by the federal government, particularly in western states.

Section 4 *Protection Afforded to States by the Nation*
The United States shall guarantee to every state in this Union a republican form of government, and shall protect each of them against invasion; and on application of the legislature, or of the executive (when the legislature cannot be convened) against domestic violence.

SECTION 4 The federal government is the most powerful government in the United States. Not only will it protect the states from all enemies, foreign and domestic, it will ensure that each state has a "republican form of government." Officials and judges today assume that "republican" means a representative government. But the Constitution leaves it up to Congress to decide what is "republican" and what is not.

Article V
PROVISIONS FOR AMENDMENT
The Congress, whenever two thirds of both houses shall deem it necessary, shall propose amendments to this Constitution, or, on the application of the legislatures of two thirds of the several states, shall call a convention for proposing amendments, which, in either case, shall be valid to all intents and purposes, as part of this Constitution, when ratified by the legislatures of three fourths of the several states, or by conventions in three fourths thereof, as the one or the other mode of ratification may be proposed by the Congress; provided ~~that no amendment which may be made prior to the year one thousand eight hundred and eight shall in any manner affect the first and fourth clauses in the ninth section of the first Article; and~~ that no state, without its consent, shall be deprived of its equal suffrage in the Senate.

ARTICLE V One of the most democratic features of the Constitution is its ability to be changed. Amendments to the Constitution are essentially revisions of the original document.

While the authors of the Constitution wanted the people to be able to change this document, they did not want it changed for frivolous reasons. Consequently, they made sure that the process of amending the Constitution would take a great deal of consensus as well as time. Proposing an amendment to the Constitution requires either a two thirds vote in each house of Congress or the approval of a national convention called by two thirds of the state legislatures. After an amendment has been proposed, either the legislatures or special conventions of three fourths of the states must approve the amendment before it can become law. All twenty-seven amendments to the Constitution have originated in Congress.

Article VI
NATIONAL DEBTS, SUPREMACY OF NATIONAL LAW, OATH
Section 1 *Validity of Debts*
All debts contracted and engagements entered into, before the adoption of this Constitution, shall be as valid against the United States under this Constitution, as under the Confederation.

SECTION 1 One of the major reasons some Americans supported the Constitution was because this document would enable the new nation to pay off the huge debts contracted during the American Revolution. Under the Articles of Confederation, Congress had lacked the power to tax; to pay for the war effort, it had been forced to borrow millions of dollars. Once the Constitution went into effect, this clause promised creditors of the United States that the new government would pay all bills contracted under the Articles of Confederation.

Section 2 *Supremacy of National Law*
This Constitution, and the laws of the United States which shall be made in pursuance thereof; and all treaties made, or which shall be made, under the authority of the United States, shall be the supreme law of the land; and the judges in every state shall be bound thereby, anything in the constitution or laws of any state to the contrary notwithstanding.

SECTION 2 This is the "supremacy clause." In very general terms, it says that federal laws rank above state or local laws. No other government in the United States can make or enforce any law that is in conflict with the Constitution, acts of Congress, diplomatic treaties, or orders issued by the executive branch. In other words, the federal government is supreme in the United States.

Section 3 *Oaths of Office*
The senators and representatives before mentioned, and the members of the several state legislatures, and all executive and judicial officers, both of the United States and of the several states, shall be bound by oath or affirmation, to support this Constitution; but no religious test shall ever be required as a qualification to any office or public trust under the United States.

SECTION 3 This clause simply reinforces the supremacy clause. It requires that everyone holding office within the borders of the United States swear to uphold the Constitution.

The Framers of the Constitution specifically forbid the exclusion of anyone from government office for religious reasons. Americans take this right for granted today, but in the 1700s it was a relatively novel idea. In Great Britain, people who were not members of the Church of England could not hold office until the 1800s; Catholics, Jews, and Protestant Dissenters were effectively barred from government service.

Article VII
RATIFICATION OF CONSTITUTION
The ratification of the conventions of nine states shall be sufficient for the establishment of this Constitution between the states so ratifying the same.

ARTICLE VII The Framers required only nine of thirteen states to approve the Constitution, in large part because they knew it would be extremely difficult to win unanimous approval. Because they also had doubts about whether state legislatures would approve their new government, they provided for specially elected conventions to make the decision.

Done in convention by the unanimous consent of the states present the seventeenth day of September in the year of our Lord one thousand seven hundred and eighty-seven, and of the independence of the United States of America the twelfth. *In Witness* whereof we have hereunto subscribed our names.

ATTEST:
William Jackson, SECRETARY
George Washington, PRESIDENT
and deputy from Virginia

NEW HAMPSHIRE
John Langdon
Nicholas Gilman

MASSACHUSETTS
Nathaniel Gorham
Rufus King

CONNECTICUT
William Samuel Johnson
Roger Sherman

NEW YORK
Alexander Hamilton

NEW JERSEY
William Livingston
David Brearley
William Paterson
Jonathan Dayton

PENNSYLVANIA
Benjamin Franklin
Thomas Mifflin
Robert Morris
George Clymer
Thomas Fitzsimons
Jared Ingersoll
James Wilson
Gouverneur Morris

DELAWARE
George Read
Gunning Bedford, Jr.
John Dickinson
Richard Bassett
Jacob Broom

MARYLAND
James McHenry
Dan of St. Thomas Jennifer
Daniel Carroll

VIRGINIA
John Blair
James Madison, Jr.

NORTH CAROLINA
William Blount
Richard Dobbs Spaight
Hugh Williamson

SOUTH CAROLINA
John Rutledge
Charles Cotesworth Pinckney
Charles Pinckney
Pierce Butler

GEORGIA
William Few
Abraham Baldwin

THE CONSTITUTION

AMENDMENTS

The supporters of the Constitution had to agree to several changes in order to win the approval of the required nine states. The first ten amendments to the Constitution—or the Bill of Rights—incorporate most of the revisions called for by critics of the Constitution. Basically, the Bill of Rights protects the hard-won rights of citizens from a powerful national government. These amendments were originally meant to restrict only the federal government; however, the Supreme Court on occasion has held that most of them also apply to the states. The justices have based this extension on the due process clause of the Fourteenth Amendment. The amendments in the Bill of Rights were proposed by Congress on September 25, 1789, and ratified by December 15, 1791.

FIRST AMENDMENT (1791) *Freedom of Religion, Speech, Press, Assembly, and Petition*

Congress shall make no law respecting an establishment of religion, or prohibiting the free exercise thereof; or abridging the freedom of speech, or of the press; or the right of the people peaceably to assemble, and to petition the government for a redress of grievances.

FIRST AMENDMENT The First Amendment prohibits Congress from restricting five basic liberties—the right of the people to practice their religion as they wish; the right of the people to speak, publish, and express their views; and the right of the people to join together publicly with others to discuss issues and to petition, or ask, their government to change laws they think are unfair. Although most Americans now take these basic rights for granted, they are a vital part of the democratic system of government established by the Founders.

SECOND AMENDMENT (1791) *Bearing Arms*

A well-regulated militia being necessary to the security of a free state, the right of the people to keep and bear arms shall not be infringed.

SECOND AMENDMENT Although Congress must allow each state to maintain a militia, or national guard, for its protection, all state governments regulate the possession and use of firearms by private citizens. In the eighteenth century, when people were very distrustful of powerful governments, the right to bear arms was a cherished liberty. After all, the American Revolution began in April 1775 when men grabbed muskets and rifles to resist a British army marching from Boston to Concord, Massachusetts. Today, however, this amendment is more controversial. Some Americans continue to think of the right to bear arms as an essential right; others argue that because our times are so different from the late 1700s, the amendment is outdated.

THIRD AMENDMENT (1791) *Quartering of Troops*

No soldier shall, in time of peace be quartered in any house, without the consent of the owner, nor in time of war, but in a manner to be prescribed by law.

THIRD AMENDMENT It was a common practice for governments in the 1700s to house troops in private homes in order to save money on food and shelter. Before the American Revolution, the British government frequently quartered, or housed, troops in the homes of Americans. The colonists resented the practice, and it was one of the major grievances with Great Britain listed in the Declaration of Independence. Determined to prevent the practice in the United States, many Americans demanded and won this amendment to the Constitution. As a result, the United States government cannot quarter troops in private homes.

FOURTH AMENDMENT (1791) *Searches and Seizures*

The right of the people to be secure in their persons, houses, papers, and effects, against unreasonable searches and seizures, shall not be violated, and no warrants shall issue, but upon probable cause, supported by oath or affirmation, and particularly describing the place to be searched, and the persons or things to be seized.

FOURTH AMENDMENT This amendment protects another "right of the people" from a potentially intrusive government. No one can search for or seize evidence in an American citizen's house or arrest a citizen without a court order issued for "probable cause." The Supreme Court has reinforced this right with the "exclusionary rule," which holds that illegally obtained evidence cannot be used against a person in a court of law.

FIFTH AMENDMENT (1791) *Criminal Proceedings; Due Process; Eminent Domain*

No person shall be held to answer for a capital, or otherwise infamous crime, unless on a presentment or indictment of a grand jury, except in cases arising in the land or naval forces, or in the militia, when in actual service in time of war or public danger; nor shall any person be subject for the same offense to be twice put in jeopardy of life or limb; nor shall be compelled in any criminal case to be a witness against himself, nor be deprived of life, liberty, or property, without due process of law; nor shall private property be taken for public use, without just compensation.

FIFTH AMENDMENT This amendment, like the others in the Bill of Rights, provides people with protection from a powerful government. It outlines the ways in which the United States government must treat its citizens, even when it suspects them of criminal activity. For example, people cannot be tried unless they have been formally indicted, or accused, by a grand jury. They cannot be tried twice for the same crime. They cannot be required to give evidence against themselves. And they are entitled to "due process of law." If the government takes their property, it must pay them for what it took. In other words, government officials cannot behave in an unfair or arbitrary manner. By respecting due process in dealing with alleged criminals, the Constitution respects and protects the rights of all Americans.

SIXTH AMENDMENT (1791) *Criminal Proceedings*

In all criminal prosecutions, the accused shall enjoy the right to a speedy and public trial, by an impartial jury of the state and district wherein the crime shall have been committed, which district shall have been previously ascertained by law, and to be informed of the nature and cause of the accusation; to be confronted with the witnesses against him; to have compulsory process for obtaining witnesses in his favor, and to have the assistance of counsel for his defense.

SIXTH AMENDMENT This amendment guarantees that even citizens who stand accused of a crime have rights when dealing with their government. They have the right to a relatively quick and open trial before a jury of their peers. They also have the right to be represented by an attorney, to know the charges against them, to examine witnesses, and to present evidence in their own defense.

SEVENTH AMENDMENT (1791) *Civil Trials*
In suits at common law, where the value in controversy shall exceed twenty dollars, the right of trial by jury shall be preserved, and no fact tried by a jury shall be otherwise re-examined in any court of the United States, than according to the rules of the common law.

SEVENTH AMENDMENT This amendment applies only to civil cases—that is, cases heard in federal courts that involve the rights of private individuals and involve no criminal behavior. People have a right to a jury trial in cases involving more than twenty dollars, a fairly large amount of money in the 1700s, unless both parties agree to waive, or give up, that right.

EIGHTH AMENDMENT (1791) *Punishment for Crimes*
Excessive bail shall not be required, nor excessive fines imposed, nor cruel and unusual punishments inflicted.

EIGHTH AMENDMENT Bail is the sum of money that a person accused of a crime may be required to post, or deposit with the court, in order to guarantee his or her appearance before the court at the proper time. Governments in the United States may require bail. They may also punish people convicted of crimes. The purpose of this amendment is to make certain that both bail and punishments are reasonable and fair. For example, executing someone for stealing a small amount of money would be unreasonable; however, the question of what constitutes a fair and reasonable punishment is not always easy to determine. Today, for example, many Americans disagree about whether capital punishment, or the execution of a convicted criminal, is by definition a "cruel and unusual" punishment.

NINTH AMENDMENT (1791) *Unenumerated Rights*
The enumeration in the Constitution, of certain rights, shall not be construed to deny or disparage others retained by the people.

NINTH AMENDMENT The Constitution lists many, but not all, of the rights enjoyed by the people. In other words, because a right is not spelled out in the Constitution does not necessarily mean that the people do not have this right. The point of this amendment was to prevent governments from denying people a right simply because it was not specifically listed in the Constitution.

TENTH AMENDMENT (1791) *Powers Reserved to the States*
The powers not delegated to the United States by the Constitution, nor prohibited by it to the States, are reserved to the states respectively, or to the people.

TENTH AMENDMENT The states are free to exercise whatever powers are not specifically given to the federal government or denied the states by the Constitution. In other words, states can do whatever they wish, as long as the Constitution does not prohibit the activity or reserve it solely for the federal government.

ELEVENTH AMENDMENT (1798) *Suits Against States*
The judicial power of the United States shall not be construed to extend to any suit in law or equity, commenced or prosecuted against one of the United States by citizens of another state, or by citizens or subjects of any foreign state.

ELEVENTH AMENDMENT People from other states or from foreign countries may not sue a state in federal court. For example, a resident of Pennsylvania, a citizen of France, or the government of France may not sue the state of Ohio in federal court.

Proposed by Congress March 4, 1794; ratified February 7, 1795; officially announced January 8, 1798.

TWELFTH AMENDMENT (1804) *Election of President and Vice President*
The electors shall meet in their respective states, and vote by ballot for President and Vice President, one of whom, at least, shall not be an inhabitant of the same state with themselves; they shall name in their ballots the person voted for as President, and in distinct ballots the person voted for as Vice President, and they shall make distinct lists of all persons voted for as President, and of all persons voted for as Vice President, and of the number of votes for each, which lists they shall sign and certify, and transmit sealed to the seat of the government of the United States, directed to the president of the Senate; the president of the Senate shall, in the presence of the Senate and the House of Representatives, open all the certificates and the votes shall then be counted;—the person having the greatest number of votes for President shall be the President, if such number be a majority of the whole number of electors appointed; and if no person have such a majority, then from the persons having the highest numbers not exceeding three on the list of those voted for as President, the House of Representatives shall choose immediately, by ballot, the President. But in choosing the President, the votes shall be taken by states, the representation from each state having one vote; a quorum for this purpose shall consist of a member or members from two thirds of the states, and a majority of all the states shall be necessary to a choice. And if the House of Representatives shall not choose a President whenever the right of choice shall devolve upon them, ~~before the fourth day of March next following,~~ then the Vice President, shall act as President, as in the case of the death or other constitutional disability of the President.—The person having the greatest number of votes as Vice President, shall be the Vice President, if such number be a majority of the whole number of electors appointed, and if no person have a majority, then from the two highest numbers on the list, the Senate shall choose the Vice President; a quorum for the purpose shall consist of two thirds of the whole number of senators, and a majority of the whole number shall be necessary to a choice. But

no person constitutionally ineligible to the office of President shall be eligible to that of Vice President of the United States.

TWELFTH AMENDMENT This amendment was a response to the election of 1800. Article II, Section 1, Clause 3 stated that each member of the Electoral College should vote for two people for President of the United States; the one with the most votes would win, and the person who finished second would become Vice President. In 1800, however, Thomas Jefferson and Aaron Burr ended up with the same number of electoral votes. To prevent another tie, the Twelfth Amendment separates the voting for the two offices. Each elector now casts one vote for President and another for Vice President.

The Twentieth Amendment (1933) changed inauguration day from March 4 to January 20, mainly because of the sense of national emergency during the Depression and the problems created by Franklin Roosevelt having to wait from November to March to become President.

Proposed by Congress December 9, 1803; ratified June 15, 1804.

THIRTEENTH AMENDMENT (1865) *Slavery and Involuntary Servitude*
Section 1 *Outlawing Slavery*
Neither slavery nor involuntary servitude, except as a punishment for crime whereof the party shall have been duly convicted, shall exist within the United States, or any place subject to their jurisdiction.

Section 2 *Enforcement*
Congress shall have power to enforce this article by appropriate legislation.

THIRTEENTH AMENDMENT With the addition of this amendment following the North's victory in the Civil War, the Constitution forbade the practice of slavery anywhere in the United States. American citizens may not be held against their will unless they have been convicted of a crime. Section 2 simply gave Congress the power to enforce the abolition of slavery.

Proposed by Congress January 31, 1865; ratified December 6, 1865.

FOURTEENTH AMENDMENT (1868) *Rights of Citizens*
Section 1 *Citizenship*
All persons born or naturalized in the United States, and subject to the jurisdiction thereof, are citizens of the United States and of the state wherein they reside. No state shall make or enforce any law which shall abridge the privileges or immunities of citizens of the United States; nor shall any state deprive any person of life, liberty, or property, without due process of law; nor deny to any person within its jurisdiction the equal protection of the laws.

SECTION 1 Until the Civil War, constitutional amendments had been directed primarily at restricting the power of the national government. The Fourteenth Amendment, on the other hand, protects citizens against the states. Congress passed this amendment during the Reconstruction era, when some northerners were angry about the attempts by southern states to evade or ignore legislation dealing with the rights of African Americans.

This section of the amendment defines citizenship. People are citizens of the United States if they are born within its territorial borders or if they have been naturalized through the legal process. States can neither deprive American citizens of any of their rights and privileges without "due process of law," nor discriminate against them. They are entitled to "equal protection of the laws" simply because they are citizens of the United States. The purpose of this amendment was to protect former enslaved persons from state governments, many of which were trying to restrict their rights. Here the federal government is no longer viewed as the potential enemy of the people, as it had been in most of the first thirteen amendments. Now it is an ally of the people against potentially oppressive state governments.

It would be difficult to overestimate the importance of this section of the Fourteenth Amendment in the history of the United States. Through the "due process" provision, the Supreme Court has extended to the state governments the restrictions on government action listed in the first eight amendments.

Section 2 *Apportionment of Representatives*
Representatives shall be apportioned among the several states according to their respective numbers, counting the whole number of persons in each state, excluding Indians not taxed. But when the right to vote at any election for the choice of electors for President and Vice President of the United States, representatives in Congress, the executive and judicial officers of a state, or the members of the legislature thereof, is denied to any of the male inhabitants of such state, being twenty-one years of age, and citizens of the United States, or in any way abridged, except for participation in rebellion, or other crime, the basis of representation therein shall be reduced in the proportion which the number of such male citizens shall bear to the whole number of male citizens twenty-one years of age in such state.

SECTION 2 The first sentence replaces Article I, Section 2, Clause 3. From this point forward, all people were to be counted equally in the census.

Section 3 *Former Confederate Officials*
No person shall be a senator or representative in Congress, or elector of President and Vice President, or hold any office, civil or military, under the United States, or under any state, who, having previously taken an oath, as a member of Congress, or as an officer of the United States, or as a member of any state legislature, or as an executive or judicial officer of any state, to support the Constitution of the United States, shall have engaged in insurrection or rebellion against the same, or given aid or comfort to the enemies thereof. But Congress may, by a vote of two thirds of each house, remove such disability.

SECTION 3 This paragraph concerns the pardoning of the men who led the Confederate States of America during the Civil War. Many members of Congress were upset with President Andrew Johnson's liberal pardon policy. This provision essentially gave

Congress the power to pardon former Confederates. Congress repealed this section in 1898.

Section 4 *Public Debt*
The validity of the public debt of the United States, authorized by law, including debts incurred for payment of pensions and bounties for services in suppressing insurrection or rebellion, shall not be questioned. But neither the United States nor any state shall assume or pay any debt or obligation incurred in aid of insurrection or rebellion against the United States, or any claim for the loss or emancipation of any slave; but all such debts, obligations and claims shall be held illegal and void.

SECTION 4 According to this section, the public debt of the United States, including that incurred in fighting the Civil War, was legal and would be paid. The public debt of the Confederate States of America, however, was illegal and would not be paid. No one could recover any money they loaned the Confederacy or any expense they had incurred in supporting the South during the Civil War. Nor could they receive compensation for the loss of enslaved persons. This section was simply a punishment designed to hurt those who had engaged in, or supported, rebellion against the Union.

Section 5 *Enforcement*
The Congress shall have power to enforce, by appropriate legislation, the provisions of this article.

SECTION 5 Congress may do what is necessary to make sure Americans obey the provisions of the Fourteenth Amendment.

Proposed by Congress June 13, 1866; ratified July 9, 1868.

FIFTEENTH AMENDMENT (1870) *Right to Vote—Race, Color, Servitude*
Section 1 *Extending the Right to Vote*
The right of citizens of the United States to vote shall not be denied or abridged by the United States or by any state on account of race, color, or previous condition of servitude.

Section 2 *Enforcement*
The Congress shall have power to enforce this article by appropriate legislation.

FIFTEENTH AMENDMENT Like the Fourteenth Amendment, the purpose of the Fifteenth Amendment was to protect African Americans from the attempts of southern states to restrict their rights. As a result of this amendment, no state could deny persons the right to vote on the basis of race or color or because they had once been enslaved.

Proposed by Congress February 26, 1869; ratified February 3, 1870.

SIXTEENTH AMENDMENT (1913) *Income Tax*
The Congress shall have power to lay and collect taxes on incomes, from whatever source derived, without apportionment among the several states, and without regard to any census or enumeration.

SIXTEENTH AMENDMENT This amendment gives Congress the right to collect an income tax. Both the United States and its gov-

ernment had grown larger and more expensive to run, and the purpose of the income tax was to ensure a fair and regular source of income. The amendment modified Article I, Section, 2, Clause 3 and Section 9, Clause 4.

Proposed by Congress July 12, 1909; ratified February 3, 1913.

SEVENTEENTH AMENDMENT (1913) *Popular Election of Senators*
Section 1 *Method of Election*
The senate of the United State shall be composed of two senators from each state, elected by the people thereof, for six years; and each senator shall have one vote. The electors in each state shall have the qualifications requisite for electors of the most numerous branch of the state legislatures.

SECTION 1 Repealing parts of Article I, Section 3, Clauses 1 and 2, this amendment provides for the direct election of United States senators. As a result, voters, rather than state legislatures, choose their senators. Any person who is qualified to vote for state representatives can vote for United States senators.

Section 2 *Vacancies*
When vacancies happen in the representation of any state in the Senate, the executive authority of such state shall issue writs of election to fill such vacancies: provided, that the legislature of any state may empower the executive thereof to make temporary appointments until the people fill the vacancies by election as the legislature may direct.

SECTION 2 If a senator dies or resigns while in office, the governor of that state may appoint someone to serve until an election can be held, if the legislature of his or her state grants the governor such power.

Section 3 *Those Elected Under Previous Procedure*
~~This amendment shall not be so construed as to affect the election or term of any senator chosen before it becomes valid as part of the Constitution.~~

SECTION 3 Anyone who was serving in the Senate when this amendment was passed by Congress could complete his or her term.

Proposed by Congress May 13, 1912; ratified April 8, 1913.

EIGHTEENTH AMENDMENT (1919) *Prohibition of Intoxicating Liquors*
Section 1 *Ban on Alcohol*
~~After one year from the ratification of this article, the manufacture, sale, or transportation of intoxicating liquors within, the importation thereof into, or the exportation thereof from the United States and all territory subject to the jurisdiction thereof for beverage purposes is hereby prohibited.~~

Section 2 *Enforcement*
~~The Congress and the several states shall have concurrent power to enforce this article by appropriate legislation.~~

Section 3 *Method of Ratification*
~~This article shall be inoperative unless it shall have been ratified as an amendment to the Constitution by the legislatures of the~~

several states, as provided in the Constitution, within seven years from the date of the submission hereof to the states by Congress.

EIGHTEENTH AMENDMENT Climaxing a long campaign against alcohol that had begun in the early 1800s, this amendment forbid the making, selling, transporting, importing, and exporting of alcoholic beverages in the United States. Called prohibition, it was later repealed by the Twenty-first Amendment.

Proposed by Congress December 18, 1917; ratified January 16, 1919.

NINETEENTH AMENDMENT (1920) *Women's Suffrage*

The right of citizens of the United States to vote shall not be denied or abridged by the United states or by any state on account of sex.

Congress shall have power to enforce this article by appropriate legislation.

NINETEENTH AMENDMENT Like the Thirteenth Amendment, which made slavery illegal, this amendment testifies to the Constitution's reputation as a "living document," one that can be revised to reflect major social changes. The authors of the Constitution could scarcely have imagined a world in which women could vote. By the early 1900s, however, many Americans believed women were entitled to a voice in their own government. This amendment gives them the right to vote. Notice how the language restricts both the federal and the state governments from denying someone the vote on the basis of their sex.

Proposed by Congress June 4, 1919; ratified August 18, 1920.

TWENTIETH AMENDMENT (1933) *Commencement of Terms; Sessions of Congress; Death or Disqualification of President-Elect*

Section 1 *Beginning of Terms*

The terms of the President and Vice President shall end at noon on the 20th day of January, and the terms of senators and representatives at noon on the 3d day of January, of the years in which such terms would have ended if this article had not been ratified; and the terms of their successors shall then begin.

Section 2 *Congressional Sessions*

The Congress shall assemble at least once in every year, and such meeting shall begin at noon on the 3d day of January, unless they shall by law appoint a different day.

TWENTIETH AMENDMENT Largely a housekeeping amendment, its purpose was to speed up the transfer of power from one President to another and to limit the time that a defeated or retiring member of Congress—"a lame duck"—could serve. This amendment was a response to the long delay between Franklin Roosevelt's election in 1932 and his assumption of the presidency in 1933 at a time when the nation was in crisis. The amendment changed inauguration day from March 4 to January 20.

Section 3 *Presidential Succession*

If, at the time fixed for the beginning of the term of the President, the President-elect shall have died, the Vice President-elect shall become President. If a President shall not have been chosen before the time fixed for the beginning of his term, or if the President-elect shall have failed to qualify, then the Vice President-elect shall act as President until a President shall have qualified; and the Congress may by law provide for the case wherein neither a President-elect nor a Vice President-elect shall have qualified, declaring who shall then act as President, or the manner in which one who is to act shall be selected, and such person shall act accordingly until a President or Vice President shall have qualified.

SECTION 3 These provisions deal with hypothetical cases. No situation like the ones described in this paragraph has ever occurred.

Section 4 *Elections Decided by Congress*

The Congress may by law provide for the case of the death of any of the persons from whom the House of Representatives may choose a President whenever the right of choice shall have devolved upon them, and for the case of the death of any of the persons from whom the Senate may choose a Vice President whenever the right of choice shall have devolved upon them.

SECTION 4 Congress has never passed such a law, largely because the situation described in the section is an extremely unlikely one. Essentially, this section provides a procedure for replacing presidential candidates who die before a final choice of President can be made, assuming no one received a majority of Electoral College votes in the first place.

Section 5 *Date of Implementation*

Sections 1 and 2 shall take effect on the 15th day of October following the ratification of this article.

Section 6 *Ratification Period*

This article shall be inoperative unless it shall have been ratified as an amendment to the Constitution by the legislatures of three fourths of the several states within seven years from the date of its submission.

SECTIONS 5 AND 6 Beginning with the Eighteenth Amendment, Congress set a limit of seven years for the ratification process.

Proposed by Congress March 2, 1932; ratified January 23, 1933.

TWENTY-FIRST AMENDMENT (1933) *Repeal of Prohibition*

Section 1 *Repeal*

The eighteenth article of amendment to the Constitution of the United States is hereby repealed.

Section 2 *State Laws*

The transportation or importation into any state, territory, or possession of the United States for delivery or use therein of intoxicating liquors, in violation of the laws thereof, is hereby prohibited.

Section 3 *Ratification Period*

This article shall be inoperative unless it shall have been ratified as an amendment to the Constitution by conventions in the several states, as provided in the Constitution, within seven years from the date of the submission hereof to the states by the Congress.

TWENTY-FIRST AMENDMENT This amendment, the only one submitted to state conventions rather than to legislatures, repealed the Eighteenth Amendment and marked the failure of prohibition. Section 2 does give states power to regulate the distribution and use of intoxicating beverages in ways that would be unconstitutional with any other commodity.

Proposed by Congress February 20, 1933; ratified December 5, 1933.

TWENTY-SECOND AMENDMENT (1951) *Presidential Tenure*
Section 1 *Two-Term Limit*
No person shall be elected to the office of the President more than twice, and no person who has held the office of President, or acted as President for more than two years of a term to which some other person was elected President shall be elected to the office of the President more than once. ~~But this article shall not apply to any person holding the office of President when this article was proposed by the Congress, and shall not prevent any person who may be holding the office of President, or acting as President, during the term within which this article becomes operative from holding the office of President or acting as President during the remainder of such term.~~

Section 2 *Ratification Period*
~~This article shall be inoperative unless it shall have been ratified as an amendment to the Constitution by the legislatures of three fourths of the several states within seven years from the date of its submission to the States by the Congress.~~

TWENTY-SECOND AMENDMENT Written in reaction to Franklin Roosevelt's four terms as President, this amendment limited future Presidents (after President Harry Truman, who was in office at the time) to two terms. If a Vice President succeeded a President when the latter was more than halfway through his term, then that Vice President could run for two more terms. For example, Lyndon Johnson became President during President Kennedy's third year in office; Johnson ran for President in 1964 and won. He could have run again in 1968, if he had chosen to do so. But no President can serve more than ten years. In the nation's history, only Franklin Roosevelt has been President for more than eight years; he served a little more than twelve.

Proposed by Congress March 24, 1947; ratified February 27, 1951.

TWENTY-THIRD AMENDMENT (1961) *Presidential Electors for the District of Columbia*
Section 1 *Determining Number of Electors*
The district constituting the seat of government of the United States shall appoint in such manner as the Congress may direct:

A number of electors of President and Vice President equal to the whole number of senators and representatives in Congress to which the district would be entitled if it were a state, but in no event more than the least populous state; they shall be in addition to those appointed by the states, but they shall be considered, for the purposes of the election of President and Vice President, to be electors appointed by a state; and they shall meet in the district

and perform such duties as provided by the twelfth article of amendment.

Section 2 *Enforcement*
The Congress shall have power to enforce this article by appropriate legislation.

TWENTY-THIRD AMENDMENT Until this amendment became law in 1961, residents of Washington, D.C., could not vote for President of the United States. The Twenty-third Amendment gives them that right. The District has three electoral votes; it cannot have more than any state. Residents of Washington still do not have voting representatives in the United States Senate or in the House of Representatives. In fact, Congress governed the capital city until 1968, when it granted residents the right to elect their own mayor and city council.

Proposed by Congress June 16, 1960; ratified March 29, 1961.

TWENTY-FOURTH AMENDMENT (1964) *Right to Vote in Federal Elections—Tax Payment*
Section 1 *Poll Tax Banned*
The right of citizens of the United States to vote in any primary or other election for President or Vice President, for electors for President or Vice President, or for senator or representative in Congress, shall not be denied or abridged by the United States or any state by reason of failure to pay any poll tax or other tax.

Section 2 *Enforcement*
The Congress shall have the power to enforce this article by appropriate legislation.

TWENTY-FOURTH AMENDMENT Some states used poll taxes in order to keep African Americans and poor Americans from voting in elections. This amendment made it illegal to require people to pay a tax in order to vote for a federal officeholder. Like the Reconstruction amendments (Thirteenth to Fifteenth), its purpose is to keep states from infringing on the rights of any of their citizens.

Proposed by Congress September 14, 1962; ratified January 23, 1964.

TWENTY-FIFTH AMENDMENT (1967) *Presidential Succession, Vice Presidential Vacancy, Presidential Inability*
Section 1 *President's Death or Resignation*
In case of the removal of the President from office or of his death or resignation, the Vice President shall become President.

SECTION 1 Written shortly after the assassination of President John F. Kennedy, this section simply clarified Article II, Section 1, Clause 6. It followed the precedent established by Vice President John Tyler when he became President upon the death of President William Henry Harrison in 1841.

Section 2 *Vacancies in Vice Presidency*
Whenever there is a vacancy in the office of the Vice President, the President shall nominate a Vice President who shall take office upon confirmation by a majority vote of both houses of Congress.

SECTION 2 The purpose of this paragraph was to outline a procedure for filling a vacancy in the office of Vice President. After the assassination of President Kennedy in November 1963, the United States did not have a Vice President until January 1965. The vacancy marked the sixteenth time in American history that such a situation had occurred. This section provided a procedure for choosing a new Vice President; it has been used only twice. The first time occurred in 1973, when Spiro T. Agnew resigned the vice presidency. President Richard Nixon nominated and Congress confirmed Gerald R. Ford as Vice President. In 1974, when President Nixon resigned, Ford became President and chose Nelson Rockefeller to be the Vice President.

Section 3 *Disability of the President*

Whenever the President transmits to the president pro tempore of the Senate and the Speaker of the House of Representatives his written declaration that he is unable to discharge the powers and duties of his office, and until he transmits to them a written declaration to the contrary, such powers and duties shall be discharged by the Vice President as acting President.

SECTION 3 This section provides for a situation in which a President is too sick, too mentally incapacitated, or too gravely wounded to carry out the duties of his office.

Section 4
Vice President as Acting President

Whenever the Vice President and a majority of either the principal officers of the executive departments or of such other body as Congress may by law provide, transmit to the president pro tempore of the Senate and the Speaker of the House of Representatives their written declaration that the President is unable to discharge the powers and duties of his office, the Vice President shall immediately assume the powers and duties of the office as acting President.

Thereafter, when the President transmits to the president pro tempore of the Senate and the Speaker of the House of Representatives his written declaration that no inability exists, he shall resume the powers and duties of his office unless the Vice President and a majority of either the principal officers of the executive department or of such other body as Congress may by law provide, transmit within four days to the president pro tempore of the Senate and the Speaker of the House of Representatives their written declaration that the President is unable to discharge the powers and duties of his office. Thereupon Congress shall decide the issue, assembling within forty-eight hours for that purpose if not in session. If the Congress, within twenty-one days after receipt of the latter written declaration, or, if Congress in not in session, within twenty-one days after Congress is required to assemble, determines by two thirds vote of both Houses that the President is unable to discharge the powers and duties of his office, the Vice President shall continue to discharge the same as acting President; otherwise, the President shall resume the powers and duties of his office.

SECTION 4 This section creates the procedure whereby somebody other than the President determines whether he or she is inca-

pable of performing his or her duties. Initiating such an action requires the agreement of the Vice President and a majority of the cabinet. This procedure has never been used.

Proposed by Congress July 6, 1965; ratified February 10, 1967.

TWENTY-SIXTH AMENDMENT (1971) *Right to Vote—Age*
Section 1 *Lowering of Voting Age*

The right of citizens of the United States, who are eighteen years of age or older, shall not be denied or abridged by the United States or by any state on account of age.

Section 2 *Enforcement*

The Congress shall have the power to enforce this article by appropriate legislation.

TWENTY-SIXTH AMENDMENT In response to the size and influence of the "baby boom" generation, Congress lowered the minimum age to eighteen for voting in elections in the United States. A state could, if it wished, make the minimum age even lower.

Proposed by Congress March 23, 1971; ratified July 1, 1971.

TWENTY-SEVENTH AMENDMENT (1992) *Congressional Pay*

No law, varying the compensation for the services of the senators and representatives, shall take effect until an election of representatives shall have intervened.

TWENTY-SEVENTH AMENDMENT Congress can vote an increase in the pay of its members, but that increase may not take effect until after the next election. In other words, it gives "the people" a chance to express their opinion on the subject before it becomes law.

Proposed by Congress September 25, 1989; ratified May 18, 1992.

Illustrated Data Bank

T he maps, tables, and graphs that make up this Illustrated Data Bank are designed as reference materials to help you in your study of United States history. The first six pages present data that is organized chronologically. This page and the facing page show a demographic picture of the nation in 1790. Pages 1114 and 1115 show three maps that describe the United States population in 1890 and territorial growth. Page 1116 compares birth rate and median age over time and page 1117 presents a demographic picture of the United States in 1990 and 1995. Pages 1118 to 1122 contain a physical-political map of the United States, a world political map, and a table of information about the fifty states. The last five pages of the Illustrated Data Bank hold a comprehensive list of the presidents of the United States that includes each president's portrait, years in office, political party, home state, and vice president(s).

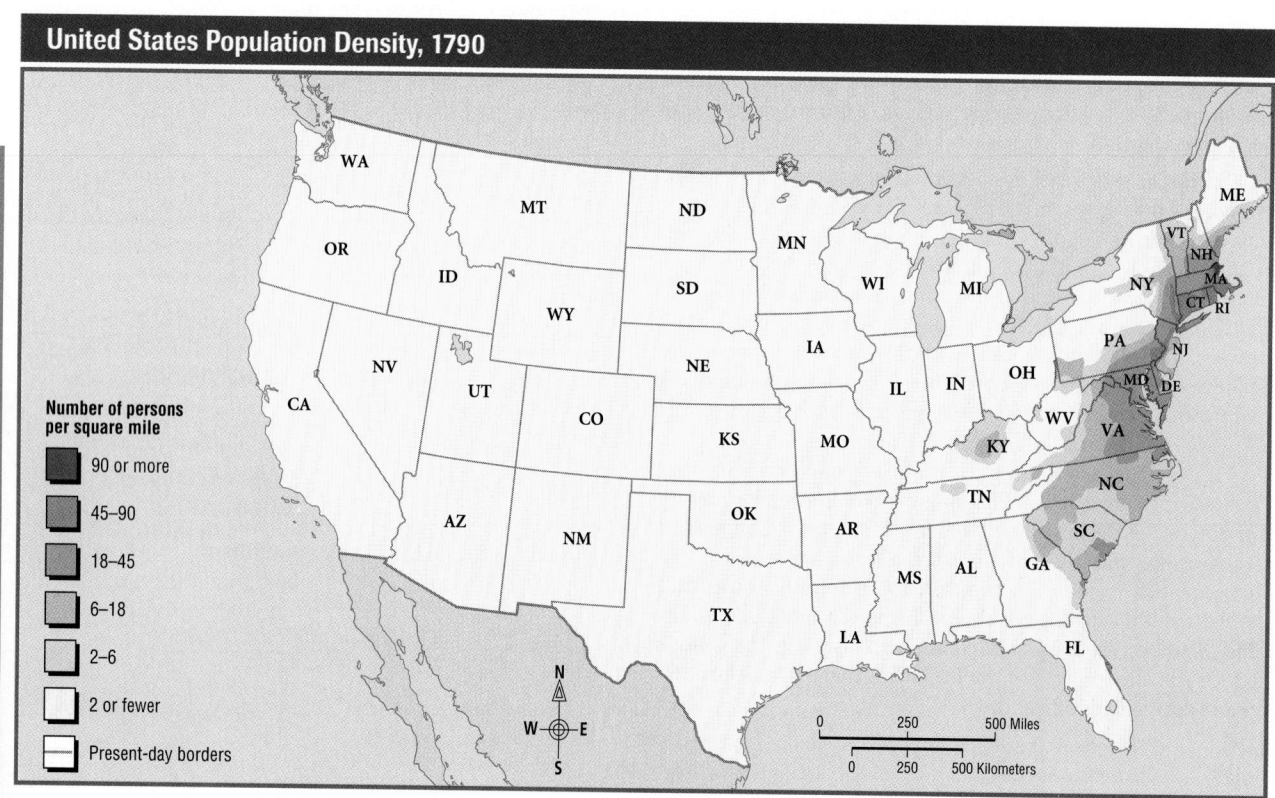

United States Population Density, 1790

Number of persons per square mile
- 90 or more
- 45–90
- 18–45
- 6–18
- 2–6
- 2 or fewer
- Present-day borders

United States Ethnic Groups, 1790

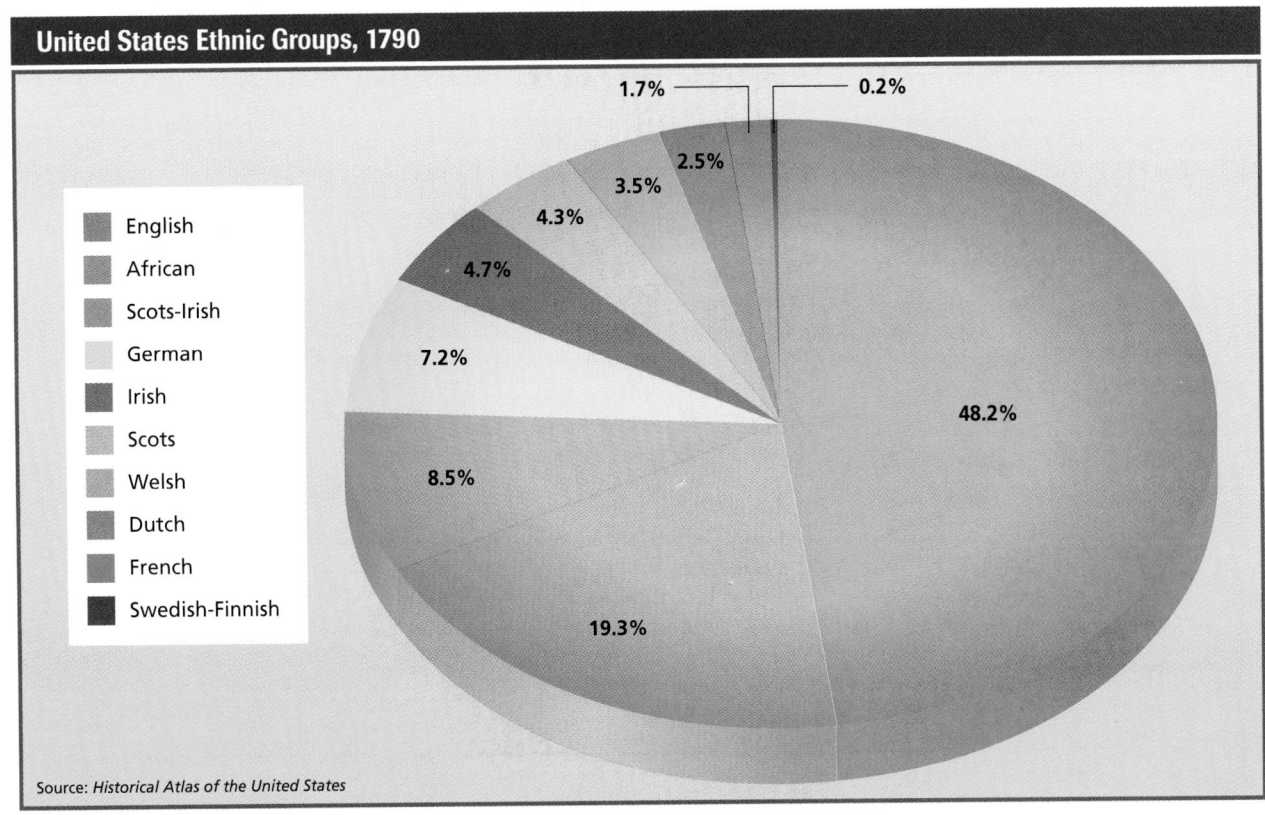

Legend:
- English
- African
- Scots-Irish
- German
- Irish
- Scots
- Welsh
- Dutch
- French
- Swedish-Finnish

Pie chart values: 48.2%, 19.3%, 8.5%, 7.2%, 4.7%, 4.3%, 3.5%, 2.5%, 1.7%, 0.2%

Source: *Historical Atlas of the United States*

Enslaved Population of the United States, 1790

State	Total Population	Enslaved Population	Percent Enslaved
Connecticut	237,946	2,648	1.11
Delaware	59,096	8,837	14.95
Georgia	82,548	29,624	35.89
Maryland	319,728	103,036	32.33
Massachusetts	475,307	0	0.00
New Hampshire	141,885	157	0.11
New Jersey	184,139	11,423	6.20
New York	340,120	21,193	6.23
North Carolina	393,751	100,783	25.60
Pennsylvania	434,373	3,707	0.85
Rhode Island	68,825	958	1.39
South Carolina	249,073	107,094	43.00
Virginia	747,600	292,627	39.14

Source: *Historical Statistics of the United States*

United States Population Density, 1890

Number of persons per square mile

- 90 or more
- 45–90
- 18–45
- 6–18
- 2–6
- 2 or fewer
- No data available
- Present-day borders

0   250   500 Miles

0   250   500 Kilometers

United States Foreign-Born Population, 1890

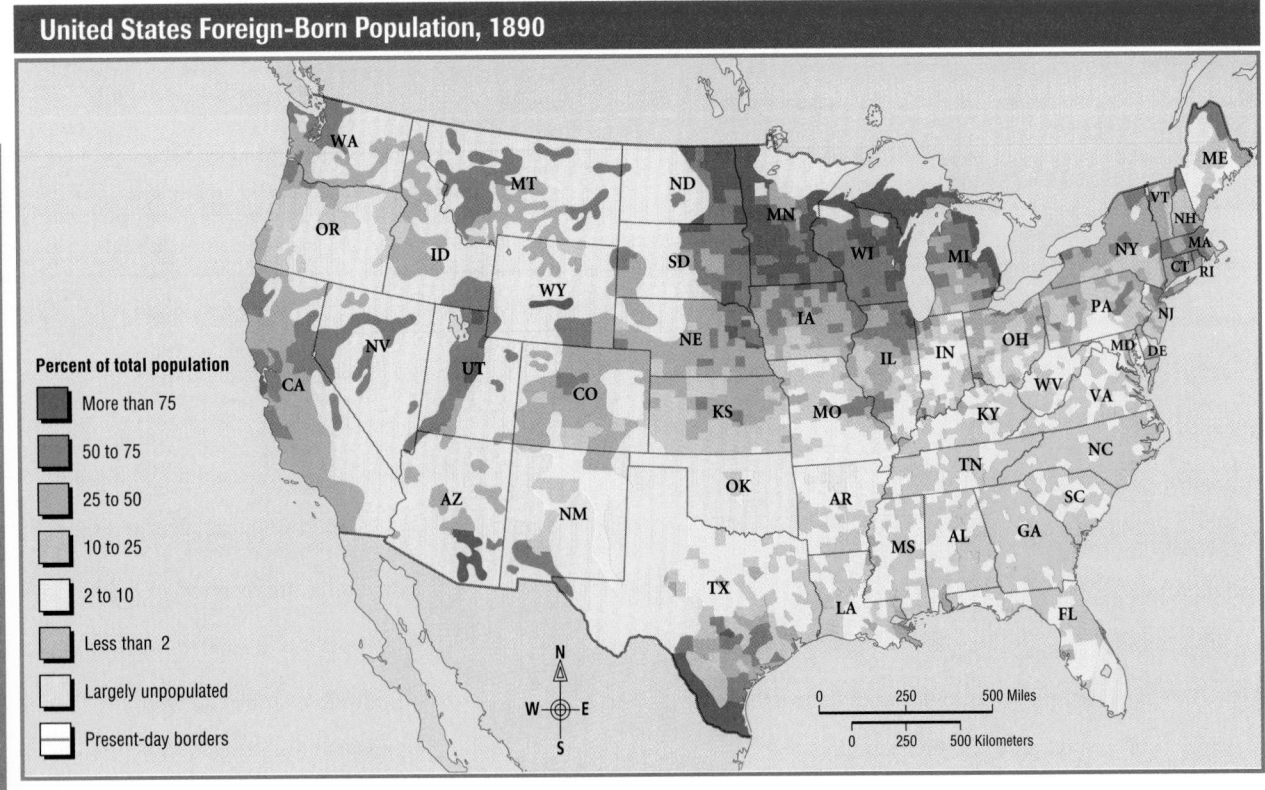

Percent of total population

- More than 75
- 50 to 75
- 25 to 50
- 10 to 25
- 2 to 10
- Less than 2
- Largely unpopulated
- Present-day borders

0   250   500 Miles

0   250   500 Kilometers

United States Territorial Growth

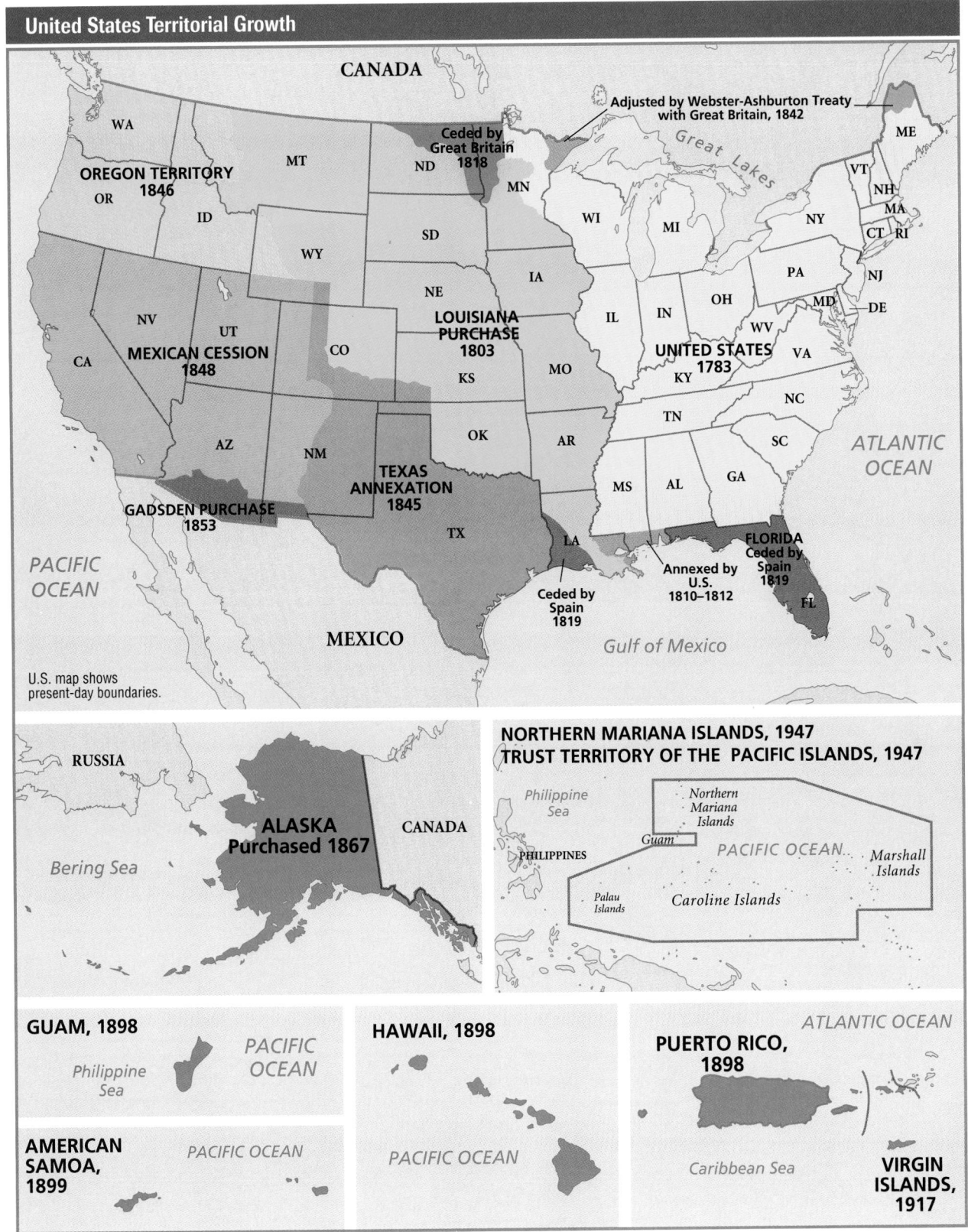

CANADA

WA

OREGON TERRITORY
1846

OR

ID

MT

ND

Ceded by
Great Britain
1818

MN

Adjusted by Webster-Ashburton Treaty
with Great Britain, 1842

ME

Great Lakes

VT

NH

SD

WY

WI

MI

NY

MA
CT RI

NV

UT

MEXICAN CESSION
1848

CA

CO

NE

LOUISIANA
PURCHASE
1803

KS

IA

IL

IN

OH

PA

NJ

MD
DE

WV

UNITED STATES
1783

VA

KY

MO

NC

AZ

NM

TEXAS
ANNEXATION
1845

OK

AR

TN

SC

GADSDEN PURCHASE
1853

TX

LA

MS

AL

GA

ATLANTIC
OCEAN

PACIFIC
OCEAN

Ceded by
Spain
1819

Annexed by
U.S.
1810–1812

FLORIDA
Ceded by
Spain
1819

FL

MEXICO

Gulf of Mexico

U.S. map shows
present-day boundaries.

RUSSIA

ALASKA
Purchased 1867

CANADA

Bering Sea

NORTHERN MARIANA ISLANDS, 1947
TRUST TERRITORY OF THE PACIFIC ISLANDS, 1947

Philippine
Sea

Northern
Mariana
Islands

PHILIPPINES

Guam

PACIFIC OCEAN

Marshall
Islands

Palau
Islands

Caroline Islands

GUAM, 1898

PACIFIC
OCEAN

Philippine
Sea

HAWAII, 1898

PACIFIC OCEAN

ATLANTIC OCEAN

PUERTO RICO,
1898

AMERICAN
SAMOA,
1899

PACIFIC OCEAN

Caribbean Sea

VIRGIN
ISLANDS,
1917

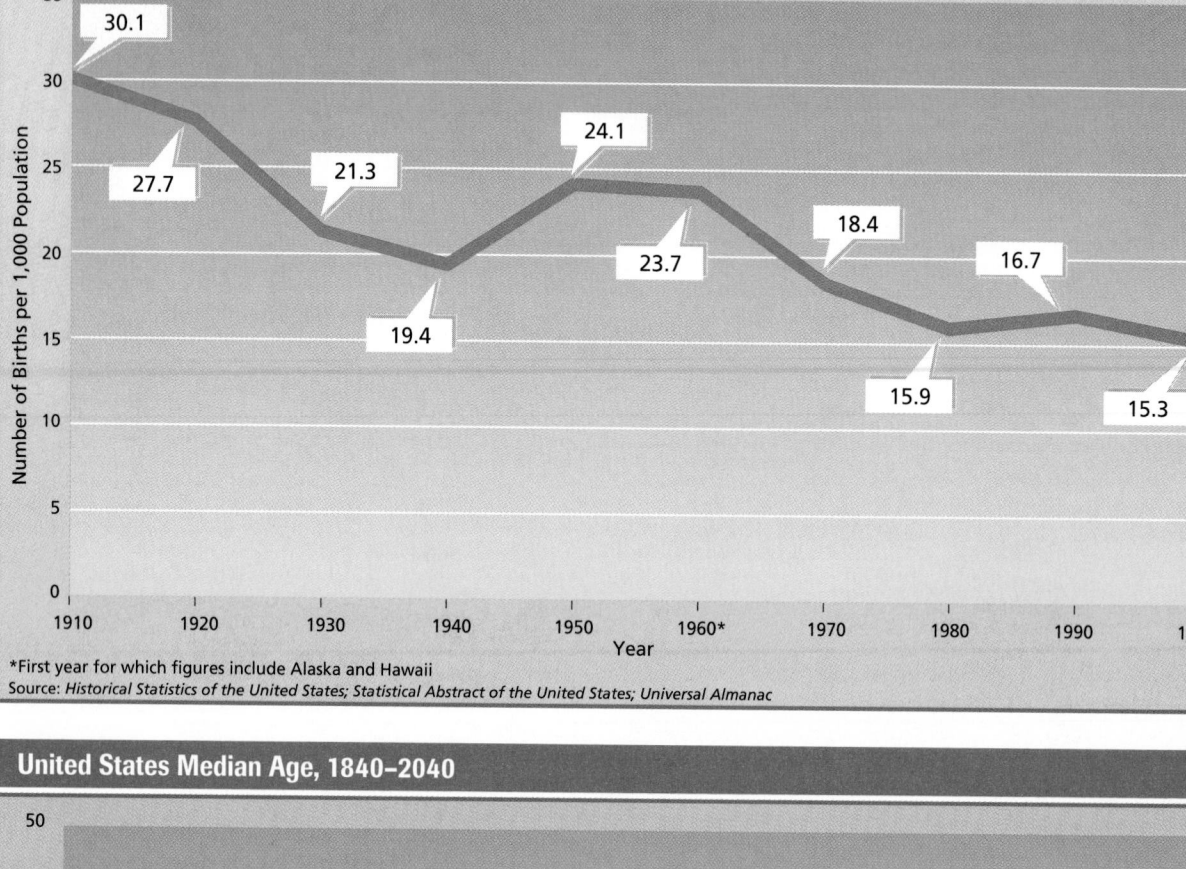

United States Birth Rate, 1910–1994

Number of Births per 1,000 Population

- 30.1
- 27.7
- 21.3
- 19.4
- 24.1
- 23.7
- 18.4
- 16.7
- 15.9
- 15.3

Year: 1910, 1920, 1930, 1940, 1950, 1960*, 1970, 1980, 1990, 1994

*First year for which figures include Alaska and Hawaii
Source: *Historical Statistics of the United States; Statistical Abstract of the United States; Universal Almanac*

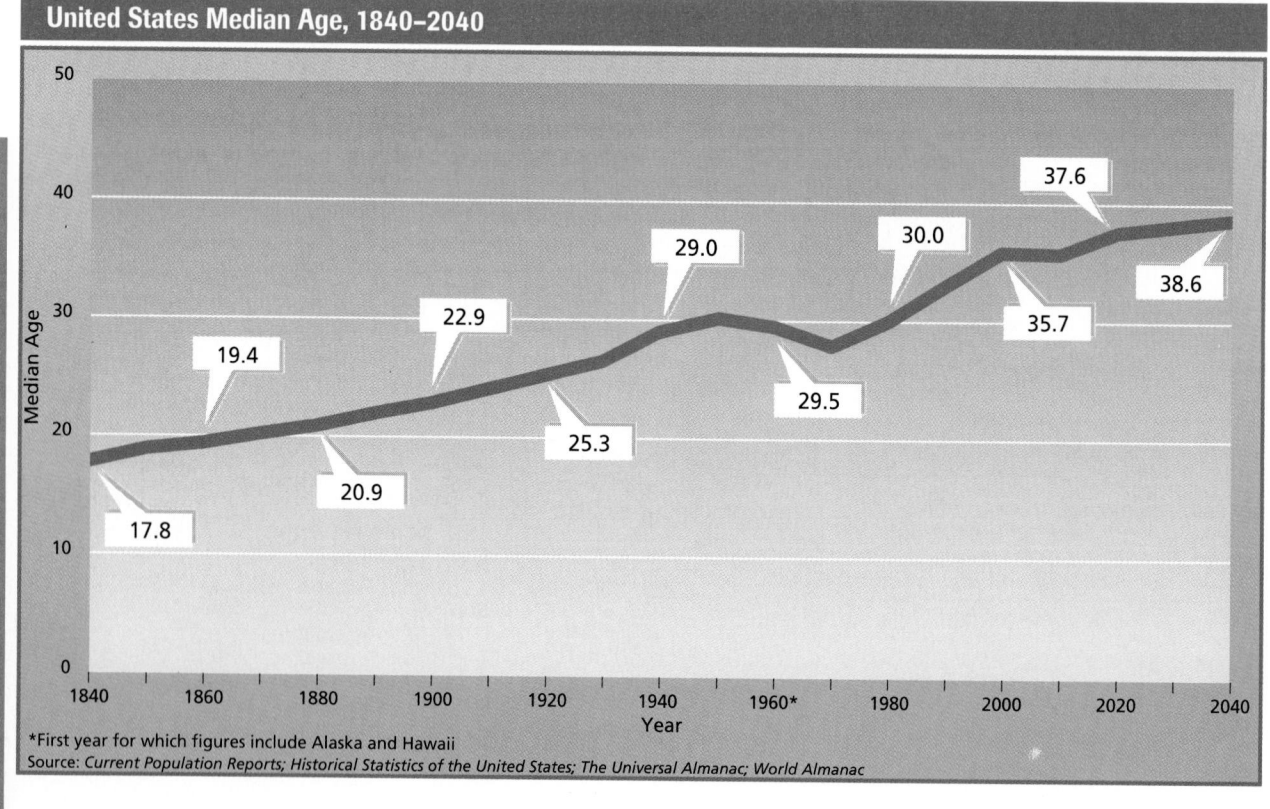

United States Median Age, 1840–2040

Median Age

- 17.8
- 19.4
- 20.9
- 22.9
- 25.3
- 29.0
- 29.5
- 30.0
- 35.7
- 37.6
- 38.6

Year: 1840, 1860, 1880, 1900, 1920, 1940, 1960*, 1980, 2000, 2020, 2040

*First year for which figures include Alaska and Hawaii
Source: *Current Population Reports; Historical Statistics of the United States; The Universal Almanac; World Almanac*

United States Population by Race, 1990

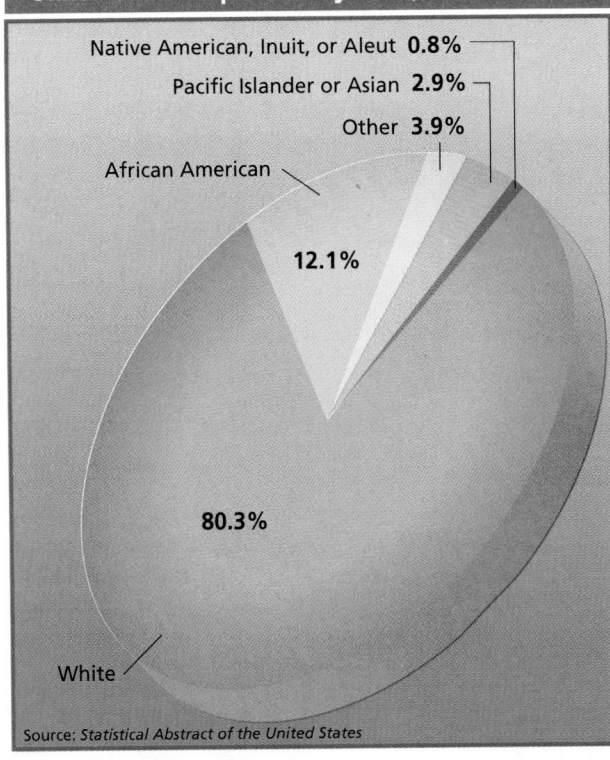

- Native American, Inuit, or Aleut **0.8%**
- Pacific Islander or Asian **2.9%**
- Other **3.9%**
- African American **12.1%**
- White **80.3%**

Source: *Statistical Abstract of the United States*

United States Latino Population, 1990

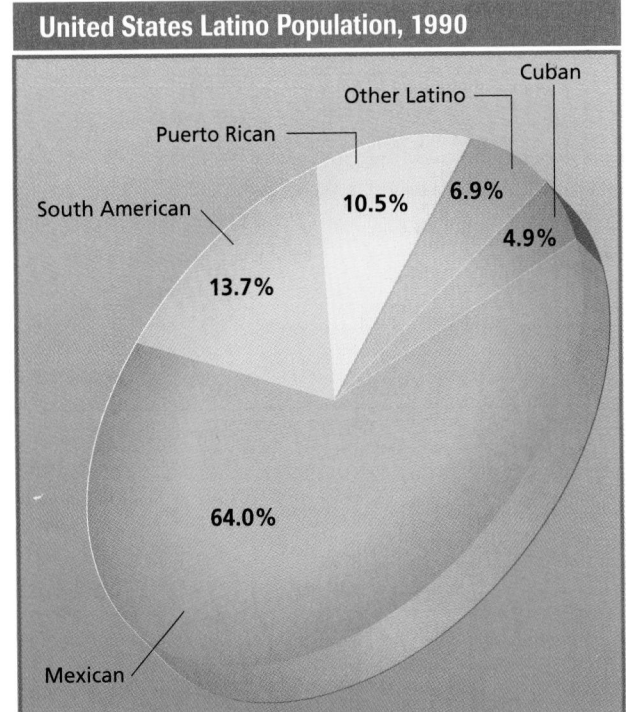

- Cuban
- Other Latino **6.9%**
- Puerto Rican **10.5%**
- **4.9%**
- South American **13.7%**
- Mexican **64.0%**

Source: *The Universal Almanac*, 1993

United States Population Density, 1995

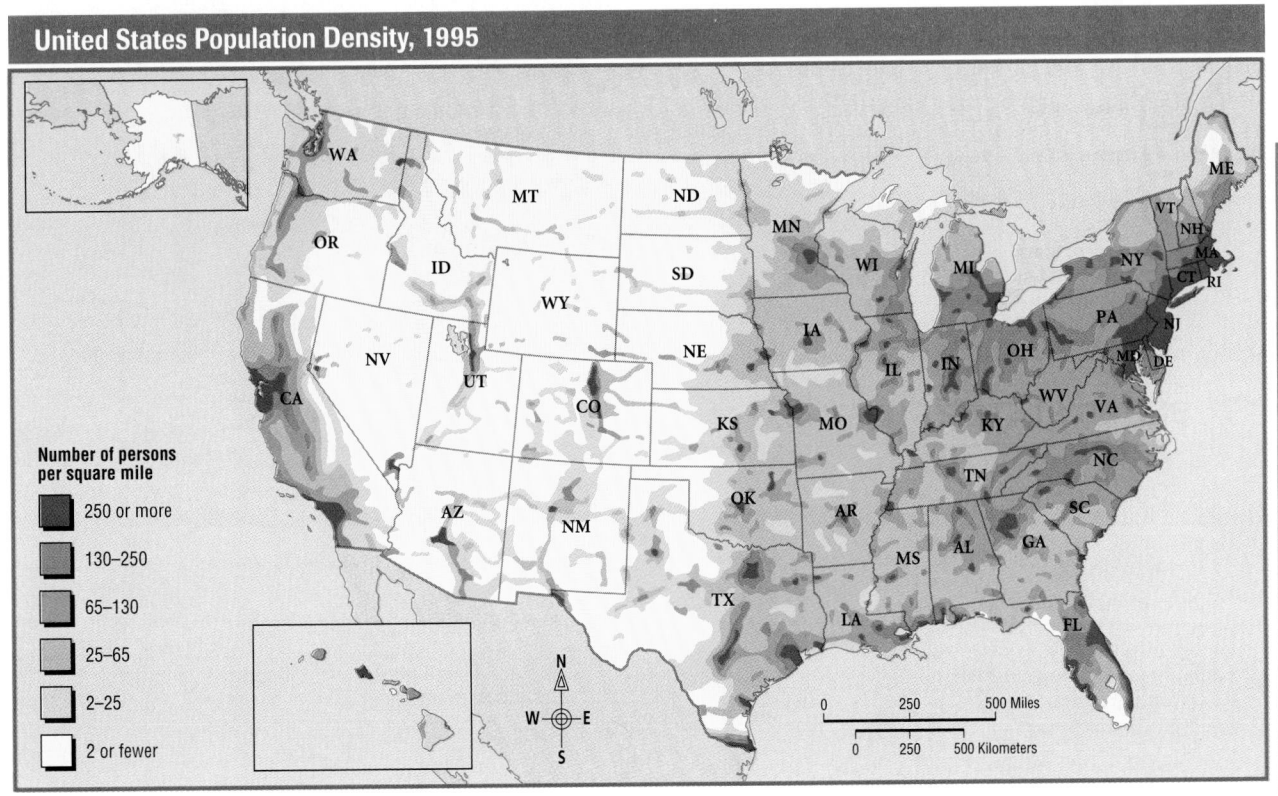

Number of persons per square mile

- 250 or more
- 130–250
- 65–130
- 25–65
- 2–25
- 2 or fewer

WA, OR, ID, MT, ND, MN, WI, MI, NY, VT, NH, ME, MA, CT, RI, PA, NJ, OH, IN, IL, IA, SD, WY, NE, NV, UT, CO, KS, MO, KY, WV, VA, MD, DE, NC, TN, OK, AR, SC, CA, AZ, NM, TX, LA, MS, AL, GA, FL

N
W—E
S

0 250 500 Miles
0 250 500 Kilometers

UNITED STATES: PHYSICAL-POLITICAL

Elevations

Feet		Meters
13,120		4,000
6,560		2,000
1,640		500
656		200
0		0
Below sea level		Below sea level

★ National capital
★ State capitals
• Other cities
▲ Mountain peaks

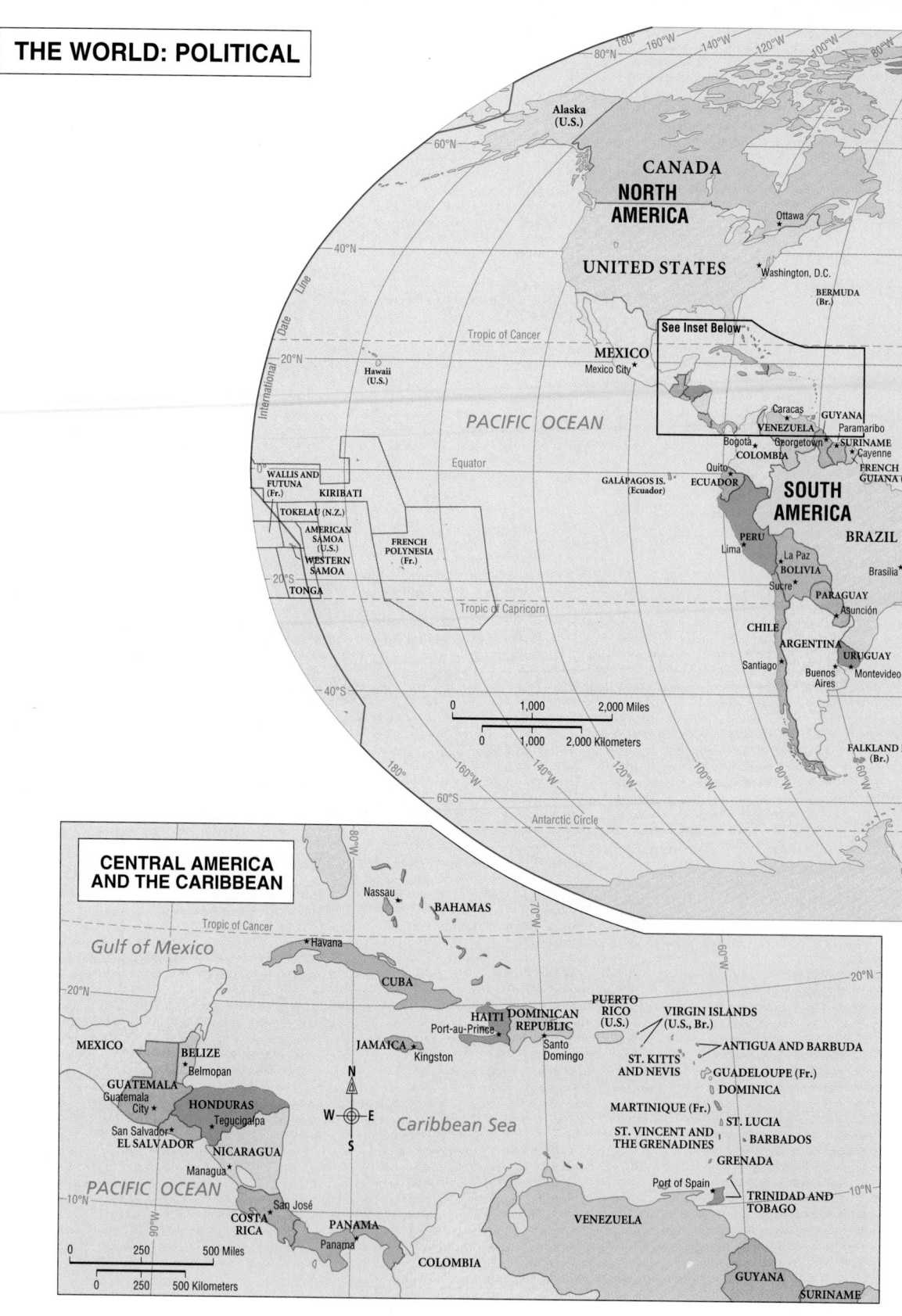

THE WORLD: POLITICAL

CANADA
NORTH AMERICA
Ottawa ★

Alaska (U.S.)

UNITED STATES
★ Washington, D.C.

BERMUDA (Br.)

See Inset Below

Tropic of Cancer

MEXICO
Mexico City ★

Hawaii (U.S.)

PACIFIC OCEAN

Caracas ★ GUYANA
VENEZUELA Paramaribo ★
Georgetown ★ SURINAME ★
Bogotá ★ Cayenne ★
COLOMBIA FRENCH GUIANA (Fr.)

Equator

GALÁPAGOS IS. (Ecuador) Quito ★
ECUADOR

SOUTH AMERICA

WALLIS AND FUTUNA (Fr.)

KIRIBATI

TOKELAU (N.Z.)

AMERICAN SAMOA (U.S.)
WESTERN SAMOA

FRENCH POLYNESIA (Fr.)

PERU
Lima ★
La Paz ★
BOLIVIA
Sucre ★

BRAZIL

Brasília ★

PARAGUAY
Asunción ★

TONGA

International Date Line

Tropic of Capricorn

CHILE
ARGENTINA URUGUAY
Santiago ★ Buenos Aires ★ Montevideo ★

0	1,000	2,000 Miles

0	1,000	2,000 Kilometers

FALKLAND IS. (Br.)

Antarctic Circle

CENTRAL AMERICA AND THE CARIBBEAN

Nassau ★
BAHAMAS

Tropic of Cancer

Gulf of Mexico
★ Havana
CUBA

MEXICO

BELIZE
★ Belmopan

GUATEMALA
Guatemala City ★
HONDURAS
Tegucigalpa ★
San Salvador ★
EL SALVADOR
NICARAGUA
Managua ★

JAMAICA
Kingston ★

HAITI
Port-au-Prince ★

DOMINICAN REPUBLIC
Santo Domingo ★

PUERTO RICO (U.S.)

VIRGIN ISLANDS (U.S., Br.)

ANTIGUA AND BARBUDA

ST. KITTS AND NEVIS
GUADELOUPE (Fr.)
DOMINICA
MARTINIQUE (Fr.)
ST. LUCIA
ST. VINCENT AND THE GRENADINES
BARBADOS
GRENADA

Caribbean Sea

N
W E
S

PACIFIC OCEAN

COSTA RICA
San José ★
PANAMA
Panama ★

VENEZUELA

Port of Spain ★
TRINIDAD AND TOBAGO

COLOMBIA

GUYANA
SURINAME

0	250	500 Miles

0	250	500 Kilometers

ILLUSTRATED DATA BANK

ILLUSTRATED DATA BANK

State	Capital	Entered Union	Population (1994)	Population Rank	Land Area (Square Miles)	Land Area Rank
Alabama	Montgomery	1819	4,218,792	22nd	51,705	29th
Alaska	Juneau	1959	606,276	48th	591,004	1st
Arizona	Phoenix	1912	4,075,052	23rd	114,000	6th
Arkansas	Little Rock	1836	2,452,671	33rd	53,187	27th
California	Sacramento	1850	31,430,697	1st	158,706	3rd
Colorado	Denver	1876	3,655,647	26th	104,091	8th
Connecticut	Hartford	1788	3,275,251	27th	5,018	48th
Delaware	Dover	1787	706,351	46th	2,044	49th
Florida	Tallahassee	1845	13,952,714	4th	58,664	22nd
Georgia	Atlanta	1788	7,055,336	11th	58,910	21st
Hawaii	Honolulu	1959	1,178,564	40th	6,470	47th
Idaho	Boise	1890	1,133,034	42nd	83,564	13th
Illinois	Springfield	1818	11,751,774	6th	56,345	24th
Indiana	Indianapolis	1816	5,752,073	14th	36,185	38th
Iowa	Des Moines	1846	2,829,252	30th	56,275	25th
Kansas	Topeka	1861	2,554,047	32nd	82,277	14th
Kentucky	Frankfort	1792	3,826,794	24th	40,409	37th
Louisiana	Baton Rouge	1812	4,315,085	21st	47,751	31st
Maine	Augusta	1820	1,240,209	39th	33,265	39th
Maryland	Annapolis	1788	5,006,265	19th	10,460	42nd
Massachusetts	Boston	1788	6,041,123	13th	8,284	45th
Michigan	Lansing	1837	9,496,147	8th	58,527	23rd
Minnesota	St. Paul	1858	4,567,267	20th	84,402	12th
Mississippi	Jackson	1817	2,669,111	31st	47,689	32nd
Missouri	Jefferson City	1821	5,277,640	16th	69,697	19th
Montana	Helena	1889	856,047	44th	147,046	4th
Nebraska	Lincoln	1867	1,622,858	37th	77,355	15th
Nevada	Carson City	1864	1,457,028	38th	110,561	7th
New Hampshire	Concord	1788	1,136,820	41st	9,279	44th
New Jersey	Trenton	1787	7,903,925	9th	7,787	46th
New Mexico	Santa Fe	1912	1,653,521	36th	121,593	5th
New York	Albany	1788	18,169,051	3rd	49,108	30th
North Carolina	Raleigh	1789	7,069,836	10th	52,669	28th
North Dakota	Bismarck	1889	637,988	47th	70,703	17th
Ohio	Columbus	1803	11,102,198	7th	41,330	35th
Oklahoma	Oklahoma City	1907	3,258,069	28th	69,956	18th
Oregon	Salem	1859	3,086,188	29th	97,073	10th
Pennsylvania	Harrisburg	1787	12,052,367	5th	45,308	33rd
Rhode Island	Providence	1790	996,757	43rd	1,212	50th
South Carolina	Columbia	1788	3,663,984	25th	31,113	40th
South Dakota	Pierre	1889	721,164	45th	77,116	16th
Tennessee	Nashville	1796	5,175,240	17th	42,144	34th
Texas	Austin	1845	18,378,185	2nd	266,807	2nd
Utah	Salt Lake City	1896	1,907,936	34th	84,899	11th
Vermont	Montpelier	1791	580,209	49th	9,614	43rd
Virginia	Richmond	1788	6,551,522	12th	40,767	36th
Washington	Olympia	1889	5,343,090	15th	68,138	20th
West Virginia	Charleston	1863	1,822,021	35th	24,231	41st
Wisconsin	Madison	1848	5,081,658	18th	56,153	26th
Wyoming	Cheyenne	1890	475,981	50th	97,809	9th

Source: *World Almanac,* 1996

ILLUSTRATED DATA BANK

1

2

1. **George Washington** (1732–1799)
   Years in office: 1789–1797
   No political party
   Elected from: Virginia
   Vice Pres.: John Adams

2. **John Adams** (1735–1826)
   Years in office: 1797–1801
   Federalist party
   Elected from: Massachusetts
   Vice Pres.: Thomas Jefferson

3. **Thomas Jefferson** (1743–1826)
   Years in office: 1801–1809
   Democratic Republican party
   Elected from: Virginia
   Vice Pres.: Aaron Burr, George Clinton

4. **James Madison** (1751–1836)
   Years in office: 1809–1817
   Democratic Republican party
   Elected from: Virginia
   Vice Pres.: George Clinton,
                     Elbridge Gerry

5. **James Monroe** (1758–1831)
   Years in office: 1817–1825
   Democratic Republican party
   Elected from: Virginia
   Vice Pres.: Daniel Tompkins

6. **John Quincy Adams** (1767–1848)
   Years in office: 1825–1829
   National Republican party
   Elected from: Massachusetts
   Vice Pres.: John Calhoun

7. **Andrew Jackson** (1767–1845)
   Years in office: 1829–1837
   Democratic party
   Elected from: Tennessee
   Vice Pres.: John Calhoun,
                     Martin Van Buren

8. **Martin Van Buren** (1782–1862)
   Years in office: 1837–1841
   Democratic party
   Elected from: New York
   Vice Pres.: Richard Johnson

3

4

5

6

7

8

ILLUSTRATED DATA BANK

9

9. **William Henry Harrison*** (1773–1841)
   Years in office: 1841
   Whig party
   Elected from: Ohio
   Vice Pres.: John Tyler

10

10. **John Tyler** (1790–1862)
    Years in office: 1841–1845
    Whig party
    Elected from: Virginia
    Vice Pres.: none

11. **James K. Polk** (1795–1849)
    Years in office: 1845–1849
    Democratic party
    Elected from: Tennessee
    Vice Pres.: George Dallas

11

12. **Zachary Taylor*** (1784–1850)
    Years in office: 1849–1850
    Whig party
    Elected from: Louisiana
    Vice Pres.: Millard Fillmore

12

13. **Millard Fillmore** (1800–1874)
    Years in office: 1850–1853
    Whig party
    Elected from: New York
    Vice Pres.: none

14. **Franklin Pierce** (1804–1869)
    Years in office: 1853–1857
    Democratic party
    Elected from: New Hampshire
    Vice Pres.: William King

13

14

15. **James Buchanan** (1791–1868)
    Years in office: 1857–1861
    Democratic party
    Elected from: Pennsylvania
    Vice Pres.: John Breckinridge

16. **Abraham Lincoln**** (1809–1865)
    Years in office: 1861–1865
    Republican party
    Elected from: Illinois
    Vice Pres.: Hannibal Hamlin,
                Andrew Johnson

16

15

*Died in office   **Assassinated

17

19

21

23

25

17. **Andrew Johnson** (1808–1875)
    Years in office: 1865–1869
    Republican party
    Elected from: Tennessee
    Vice Pres.: none

18. **Ulysses S. Grant** (1822–1885)
    Years in office: 1869–1877
    Republican party
    Elected from: Illinois
    Vice Pres.: Schuyler Colfax,
       Henry Wilson

19. **Rutherford B. Hayes** (1822–1893)
    Years in office: 1877–1881
    Republican party
    Elected from: Ohio
    Vice Pres.: William Wheeler

20. **James A. Garfield**** (1831–1881)
    Years in office: 1881
    Republican party
    Elected from: Ohio
    Vice Pres.: Chester A. Arthur

21. **Chester A. Arthur** (1830–1886)
    Years in office: 1881–1885
    Republican party
    Elected from: New York
    Vice Pres.: none

22. **Grover Cleveland** (1837–1908)
    Years in office: 1885–1889
    Democratic party
    Elected from: New York
    Vice Pres.: Thomas Hendricks

23. **Benjamin Harrison** (1833–1901)
    Years in office: 1889–1893
    Republican party
    Elected from: Indiana
    Vice Pres.: Levi Morton

24. **Grover Cleveland** (1837–1908)
    Years in office: 1893–1897
    Democratic party
    Elected from: New York
    Vice Pres.: Adlai Stevenson

25. **William McKinley**** (1843–1901)
    Years in office: 1897–1901
    Republican party
    Elected from: Ohio
    Vice Pres.: Garret Hobart,
       Theodore Roosevelt

26. **Theodore Roosevelt** (1858–1919)
    Years in office: 1901–1909
    Republican party
    Elected from: New York
    Vice Pres.: Charles Fairbanks

18

20

22

24

26

27

28

29

30

31

32

33

34

35

36

27. **William Howard Taft** (1857–1930)
Years in office: 1909–1913
Republican party
Elected from: Ohio
Vice Pres.: James Sherman

28. **Woodrow Wilson** (1856–1924)
Years in office: 1913–1921
Democratic party
Elected from: New Jersey
Vice Pres.: Thomas Marshall

29. **Warren G. Harding*** (1865–1923)
Years in office: 1921–1923
Republican party
Elected from: Ohio
Vice Pres.: Calvin Coolidge

30. **Calvin Coolidge** (1872–1933)
Years in office: 1923–1929
Republican party
Elected from: Massachusetts
Vice Pres.: Charles Dawes

31. **Herbert C. Hoover** (1874–1964)
Years in office: 1929–1933
Republican party
Elected from: California
Vice Pres.: Charles Curtis

32. **Franklin D. Roosevelt*** (1882–1945)
Years in office: 1933–1945
Democratic party
Elected from: New York
Vice Pres.: John Garner, Henry
Wallace, Harry S. Truman

33. **Harry S. Truman** (1884–1972)
Years in office: 1945–1953
Democratic party
Elected from: Missouri
Vice Pres.: Alben Barkley

34. **Dwight D. Eisenhower** (1890–1969)
Years in office: 1953–1961
Republican party
Elected from: New York
Vice Pres.: Richard M. Nixon

35. **John F. Kennedy**** (1917–1963)
Years in office: 1961–1963
Democratic party
Elected from: Massachusetts
Vice Pres.: Lyndon B. Johnson

36. **Lyndon B. Johnson** (1908–1973)
Years in office: 1963–1969
Democratic party
Elected from: Texas
Vice Pres.: Hubert Humphrey

37. **Richard M. Nixon***** (1913–1994)
    Years in office: 1969–1974
    Republican party
    Elected from: New York
    Vice Pres.: Spiro Agnew,
                Gerald Ford

38. **Gerald R. Ford** (1913–)
    Years in office: 1974–1977
    Republican party
    Elected from: Michigan
    Vice Pres.: Nelson Rockefeller

39. **Jimmy Carter** (1924–)
    Years in office: 1977–1981
    Democratic party
    Elected from: Georgia
    Vice Pres.: Walter Mondale

40. **Ronald W. Reagan** (1911–)
    Years in office: 1981–1989
    Republican party
    Elected from: California
    Vice Pres.: George H.W. Bush

41. **George H.W. Bush** (1924–)
    Years in office: 1989–1993
    Republican party
    Elected from: Texas
    Vice Pres.: J. Danforth Quayle

42. **William J. Clinton** (1946–)
    Years in office: 1993–2000
    Democratic party
    Elected from: Arkansas
    Vice Pres.: Albert Gore, Jr.

***Resigned

⭑ All pictures in Presidents of the United States are official portraits.

Key Events That Shaped the Nation

In addition to the ten "Turning Point" events discussed in detail in this book, the list that follows describes key events (arranged in chronological order) that have shaped the United States. Like all such lists, this one is biased—representing the personal opinions of this textbook's authors. The list is not intended to include every event of lasting importance. If it were, the result would be a list many times longer. You are invited to think about the events on this list, debate their significance with your classmates, and add events of your own.

1607 Jamestown and Tobacco

Jamestown, the first permanent English settlement in the Americas, teetered on the edge of ruin for the first decade of its existence. The colony was saved, however, when John Rolfe recognized that tobacco, which was highly prized in Europe, thrived in the climate and soil of Virginia. The lure of wealth from tobacco farming ensured the colony a steady stream of colonists. At the same time, Jamestown provided England with a foothold in North America and helped inspire further attempts at colonization.

1619 The Arrival of Enslaved Africans in North America

In 1619, Dutch traders sold twenty Africans to the English colonists in Jamestown. Unfamiliar with the concept of slavery, the colonists treated the Africans the same way they treated English indentured servants, who were freed after working off debts incurred in their passage to North America. It was not until the 1680s that the use of enslaved Africans became widespread. By 1760 about 325,000 enslaved Africans labored in England's North American colonies.

1651 The Navigation Acts

In the 1600s, England and the Netherlands clashed over which nation would control trade in Europe and the Americas. This economic competition caused the English government to enact a series of Navigation Acts beginning in 1651. These acts sought to cut the Dutch out of the profitable colonial trade by forcing the English colonies to limit their trade in certain goods to England alone. As the result of a series of wars between the two European powers, the English captured and retained the prosperous Dutch colony of New Amsterdam in 1664, renaming it New York. New York City became one of the most profitable commercial centers in the English colonies.

1720s–1760s The Great Awakening

A series of religious revivals swept through the colonies between 1720 and 1760, igniting religious fervor with an emphasis on achieving salvation. The so-called Great Awakening reached its peak in 1739, thanks to the preaching of George Whitefield. The twenty-four-year-old Whitefield, an Anglican priest, won converts by the thousands with his dramatic sermons. The Great Awakening helped shape the colonists' commitment to religious pluralism and equality, which later would help to shape their commitment to revolution against the British Empire.

1759 The Fall of Quebec

After five long years of defeat in the French and Indian War, the British finally turned the tides in 1759. Brigadier General James Wolfe decided to attempt the capture of Quebec, the capital of New France. Wolfe surrounded the fortress, eventually drawing out the French commander, Montcalm, into open battle. When the conflict was over, Wolfe and Montcalm lay dead, and the British controlled Quebec. This victory foreshadowed an overall French defeat in the war and the loss of all the French holdings in North America.

1765 The Stamp Act

In an attempt to raise money and pay the cost of an army to protect the colonies, Parliament passed the Stamp Act in 1765. This law required colonists to buy official stamps—in effect, pay a tax—for items such as legal documents. The British had had such a tax for 100 years, and Parliament felt justified requiring it in the colonies. But Parliament underestimated colonial reaction to the act. The direct taxation of the Stamp Act outraged and united the colonies. Colonial assemblies passed resolutions claiming the sole right to pass taxes, and riots broke out in numerous port cities. Colonial sentiment against Great Britain deepened.

1775 Lexington and Concord

As relations between colonists and the British worsened, colonists began collecting weapons in preparation for war. On April 19, 1775, General Thomas Gage, the British military commander in Boston, sent about 700 British soldiers on a raid to seize weapons in nearby Concord. Warned in advance, colonial militiamen assembled on the village green in Lexington, a town through which the British would pass on their way to Concord. Upon arriving in Lexington, the British ordered the colonials to disperse. An unknown person then fired a shot, and both sides began shooting. When the smoke cleared, eight colonials lay dead. Marching on to Concord, the British found a much larger force of armed colonists waiting. After a battle in Concord, the British retreated toward Boston. Along the way, colonists fired on the British from the roadside, inflicting 273 casualties. The Revolutionary War had begun.

1776 The Declaration of Independence

The Second Continental Congress established a committee of five men to write a declaration of American independence. The committee insisted that Thomas Jefferson, a young Virginian, write the original draft. The Continental Congress approved the document, with some revisions, and on July 4, the thirteen colonies declared their independence from Great Britain.

1787 The Northwest Ordinance

The United States faced a serious problem after the Revolutionary War: sorting out land claims in its huge territory west of the Appalachian Mountains. States with large land claims in this territory insisted they be given the land; states with no claims argued for congressional control of the territory. Congress passed the Northwest Ordinance to solve these problems. This act reduced tensions over land claims, granted settlers the right to form their own territorial governments, and provided for an orderly admission of the new territories into statehood. This act guaranteed Americans in the new states equal representation in government, which set the stage for the rapid expansion of the United States.

1787 The Constitutional Convention

The weak American government created under the Articles of Confederation had become a serious concern to a powerful group of American leaders. The very survival of the republic seemed at stake. So when Congress called a convention to reform the Articles, the delegates quickly decided to go beyond their assigned task and form an entirely new government. The result of their efforts was the Constitution. In 1788 the Constitution was ratified, creating a new, powerful central government that would alter the nature of American democracy.

1793 The Invention of the Cotton Gin

Although it is a matter of some debate who invented the cotton gin, Eli Whitney gained credit for the machine. The simple box contraption separated seeds from cotton fifty times faster than could be done by hand. The gin helped make possible a great expansion in cotton production. Increasing cotton production led to an increase in the practice of slavery in the South. Cotton and cotton products were the most important American exports until 1839, helping to fuel the expanding American economy.

1803 Marbury v. Madison

In the final hours of his presidency, John Adams appointed William Marbury to a judicial post. When President Jefferson took office, however, he declared that Marbury's appointment would not be honored. Marbury sued, taking the case to the Supreme Court. Chief Justice John Marshall denied Marbury's argument on a technicality. In the process, Marshall held that the courts have the power to declare acts of Congress unconstitutional. This landmark decision established the principle of judicial review, which gave great authority to the Supreme Court.

1803 The Louisiana Purchase

President Jefferson and the Senate nearly doubled the size of the nation by purchasing the Louisiana territory from France. The Louisiana territory was an enormous area of land that extended from the Mississippi River to the Rocky Mountains and from the Louisiana coast to Canada. The United States paid about $15 million for more than 800 million acres of land, a cost of about 1.8 cents per acre. Territory from the Louisiana Purchase created all or part of thirteen states.

1820 The Missouri Compromise

In 1819 the United States consisted of eleven free states and eleven slave states. "Free" Maine and "slave" Missouri were seeking statehood. At this point, Representative James Tallmadge introduced an amendment providing for gradual emancipation in Missouri. This sparked off a round of bitter debate. Henry Clay offered a compromise. Missouri would be slave and Maine free. And, in cases of territories seeking statehood in the future, land north of latitude 36° 30' would be free, and land south of the line would be open to slavery. The compromise temporarily quieted congressional debate over slavery and preserved the balance between the opposing sides in Congress.

1825 The Opening of the Erie Canal

The Erie Canal opened in 1825 after seven years of construction. The canal was a marvel of engineering: 40 feet wide and 364 miles long. Its closest competitor was only 28 miles long. The canal greatly improved shipping between the Great Lakes region and New York City. The Erie Canal encouraged commerce and economic growth all along its route, and it also made New York City a vital center for western trade. The Erie Canal's success represented the transportation revolution in the United States that accelerated the growth of the economy.

1830 The Indian Removal Act

President Andrew Jackson supported the Indian Removal Act, which made provisions for the relocation of Native Americans living in the Southeast to what is today Oklahoma. In spite of the act, however, most of the Cherokee people living within the borders of Georgia and other states remained in their homes. But in 1837 and 1838, the United States Army forcibly moved the Cherokee west. The event came to be known as the "Trail of Tears," because as many as one quarter of the 15,000 Cherokee who made the trek died. The removal opened up vast tracts of land in the Southeast for white settlement, but Native Americans paid a terrible price.

1832 The Nullification Crisis

South Carolina grew increasingly fearful of the federal government's power in the wake of spreading abolitionist views. Vice President John C. Calhoun, a South Carolinian, developed the doctrine of nullification, which held that a state had the right to nullify any law harmful to its interests. This doctrine struck at the heart of the dispute over the rights of the states versus the power of the federal government. President Andrew Jackson threatened to use force if South Carolina defied federal law. Meanwhile, Congress worked out a compromise that temporarily ended the standoff. The debate over states' rights, however, remained unresolved and would be decided only by the Civil War.

1834 – early 1850s The Settlement of the Oregon Country

The Oregon Country, home to numerous Native American groups for centuries, extended from northern California to the southern border of Alaska. Ignoring the Native Americans who already lived there, the United States and Britain signed a treaty in 1818 agreeing to joint occupation. Starting off from Independence, Missouri, settlers traveled along the Oregon Trail, a 2,000-mile trek across the Great Plains and the Rocky Mountains. Between 1842 and 1848, approximately 11,500 pioneers migrated to Oregon. In 1846, the United States and Britain agreed to divide the Oregon Country along the 49th parallel.

1836 The Founding of the Texas Republic

In 1822 Stephen Austin founded a colony of about 300 settlers in Texas, which then belonged to Mexico. By 1835 more than 30,000 Americans and 3,000 enslaved African Americans lived in Texas. In March 1836, supporters of a Texas independence movement formally declared the founding of the Republic of Texas. Mexico's leader, General Santa Anna, led an army of several thousand men to subdue the rebellion. At the Alamo, a former mission in San Antonio, fewer than 200 Texans held off 4,000 Mexican troops but ultimately were defeated. At the Battle of San Jacinto in April 1836

KEY EVENTS

the Texas rebels routed Mexican troops and later forced Santa Anna to sign a treaty recognizing the republic. With almost no help from the United States government, Texas settlers had succeeded in gaining a large piece of territory from Mexico.

1848 The Discovery of Gold at Sutter's Mill, California

No event was more important in attracting settlers to the West than the discovery of gold at Sutter's Mill near the city of Sacramento in California in 1848. Lured by the promise of gold, people rushed west by the thousands. California had 14,000 residents in 1848; within a year its population was 100,000, and by 1852 the number had reached 200,000. The gold rush had a tremendous impact on life in California. Native Americans were forced to work in the mines, and disease and forced labor greatly reduced their population. While the gold rush devastated the Native Americans, it also brought growth to Pacific coast cities.

1848 The Treaty of Guadalupe Hidalgo

The Treaty of Guadalupe Hidalgo ended the Mexican War, which took place between 1846 and 1848 over a dispute between the United States and Mexico about the southern border of Texas. Under the terms of the Treaty of Guadalupe Hidalgo, Mexico ceded the United States one third of its territory, including present-day California, New Mexico, Nevada, Utah, and Arizona. The territorial acquisition, however, once again sparked bitter controversy over the extension of slavery and the balance of slave and free states in Congress.

1857 Dred Scott v. Sandford

Dred Scott, an enslaved African American living in Missouri, filed suit against his owner. He argued that because he and his wife, Harriet, had once lived in states and territories where slavery was illegal, the couple was in fact free. The case reached the Supreme Court, and, in one of its most controversial rulings, the justices ruled against the Scotts. The Court held that as an African American, Scott was not a citizen and could not sue anyone. The Court also held that, because enslaved persons were property, Congress had to protect the rights of the slave owner. This decision stayed in force until the passage of the Fourteenth Amendment, which in 1868 guaranteed citizenship to African Americans.

1861 The Secession of the South

The election of Republican Abraham Lincoln to the presidency in the 1860 election demonstrated to the white South that northerners had the ability to elect a purely regional—and antislavery—candidate. Within a matter of months, seven southern states seceded and formed the Confederate States of America. Calmer heads on both sides sought to avoid the crisis, but events had proceeded beyond their control. The decisive incident came on April 12, 1861, when Confederate forces bombarded and captured the federal garrison of Fort Sumter in South Carolina, starting the Civil War. The United States had run out of peaceful compromises, and as a result over 600,000 Americans would die.

1863 The Emancipation Proclamation

President Lincoln issued the Emancipation Proclamation on New Year's Day, 1863. Lincoln had long said that the purpose of the Civil War was to save the Union. But he now realized that the war must also be a crusade against slavery. Critics noted that the declaration did not physically free a single enslaved person. The proclamation changed the nature of the war for the Union, however, adding to the war's purpose the freeing of enslaved people. The pronouncement also helped the Union politically by reducing the likelihood that Great Britain, which hated slavery, would support the South.

1863 The Battle of Gettysburg

In the summer of 1863, General Robert E. Lee led a Confederate army into the North. Lee thought he could end the Civil War by defeating a Union army on its own soil, which would compel the war-weary Union to recognize Confederate independence. Lee's army met the Union forces under General George Meade at Gettysburg, a small Pennsylvania town. The bloody fighting ended with Lee withdrawing his mauled army. The three days of battle cost nearly 50,000 casualties on both sides. Lee's shattered Confederate army never recovered and Union victories mounted. America's most costly war ended in 1865, with the Confederacy's surrender.

1865 African American Higher Education

Reconstruction offered African Americans an era of new promise. The African American community saw a great need for a core of educated leaders. Responding to this need, the American Missionary Association, the African Methodist Episcopal Church, and numerous other religious groups and philanthropists founded educational institutions throughout the country. Out of these efforts emerged the nation's leading black institutions of higher education, including Howard, Fisk, Atlanta, Dillard, Tougaloo, Morehouse, and Spelman. These colleges and universities were invaluable to African Americans, nurturing future political and social leaders.

1865–1870 The Reconstruction Amendments

The Thirteenth, Fourteenth, and Fifteenth amendments to the Constitution represented the central efforts of the Radical Republicans to benefit African Americans in the post–Civil War era. The Thirteenth Amendment abolished forever the institution of slavery. The Fourteenth and Fifteenth amendments guaranteed African Americans full citizenship and stated that the right to vote could not be denied on the basis of color or creed. After 1877, however, northern apathy for the issue of African American rights enabled southern states to deny African Americans many protections of the Fourteenth and Fifteenth amendments. Not until the 1960s were these injustices remedied.

1869 The Transcontinental Railroad

During the Civil War, the Union government promoted the building of railroads by offering generous land grants. One such project was a railroad that would link the West Coast with the East. The line was to be built by two different companies: the Central Pacific and the Union Pacific. In 1869, the two lines linked up in Utah, completing the first transcontinental railroad. The railroads promoted settlement of the West and helped create a nationwide transportation system that sparked tremendous growth in the American economy.

1869 Women's Suffrage in the Wyoming Territory

Western territories, with their rugged life styles and small populations, depended on women to take roles in social and political life that were unavailable to them in the eastern United States. In 1869 the Wyoming Territory passed into law a bill that granted women the right to vote and fully participate in national politics. This set a trend followed by many of Wyoming's neighbors. By 1914 every state in the western third of the nation, except New Mexico, had passed women's suffrage bills. The trailblazing of these western states helped pave the way for the ratification of the Nineteenth Amendment, which guaranteed all women the right to vote, in 1920.

1876 The Invention of the Telephone

On March 10, 1876, Alexander Graham Bell uttered the words, "Mr. Watson, come here. I want you." These few words, transmitted over a Bell invention called the telephone, altered communications technology forever. In the years ahead, Bell's American Telephone and Telegraph Company (AT&T) organized telephone line service and made widespread use of the telephone practical. By 1899 about one million telephones were operating in the United States. That number had grown to ten million by 1915. The telephone created a reliable, nationwide communication system that would play a vital part in American economic expansion.

1886 AF of L Formed

As the Noble Order of the Knights of Labor foundered in the 1890s, a new organization emerged to replace it as the leading national labor union. In 1886 Samuel Gompers organized the American Federation of Labor (AF of L). Gompers and the AF of L focused on such issues as a shorter workday, better wages, and safer working conditions. By 1900 the AF of L had one million members, and was the most important national union.

1887 The Dawes Severalty Act

Native American people in the West suffered greatly as settlers moved onto their lands. Reformers concerned with the fate of the Native Americans believed strongly that only by adopting the customs and values of white civilization could Native Americans be saved. Toward this end, Congress passed the Dawes Severalty Act. The law broke up tribal lands and allotted land parcels to individuals. Government officials hoped that individual land ownership would encourage Native Americans to farm like white Americans. In reality, relatively few Native Americans were able or willing to farm on their individual plots. Many sold their land to whites. As a result, Native American land holdings dwindled.

1890 The Formation of the National American Woman Suffrage Association

As the drive for women's suffrage heated up in the late 1800s, two leading woman suffrage groups joined forces to form the National American Woman Suffrage Association (NAWSA). NAWSA coordinated the efforts of state suffrage groups and utilized pressure tactics to convince legislators to vote for suffrage bills. The group's efforts finally paid off in 1920, when the Nineteenth Amendment was ratified.

1893 The First Automobiles

Inventors first developed prototypes of automobiles in 1893. This mode of transportation did not become common, however, until the 1910s and 1920s. It was then that Henry Ford's car company began to mass-produce cars at a cost low enough for working people to afford. By 1929 there were almost 27 million registered cars in the United States. The automobile industry became a dominant force in the American economy. Cars, trucks, and buses revolutionized American transportation and helped to spur the continued growth of the suburbs.

1896 Plessy v. Ferguson

By the 1880s, the United States government clearly had retreated from its commitment to African American equality. Southern state and local governments passed laws that segregated public facilities. The Supreme Court ruled on the constitutionality of these laws in the landmark case *Plessy* v. *Ferguson*. In its ruling, the Court held that "separate but equal" facilities did not violate the Fourteenth Amendment. Until the 1950s, southern states continued their systematic segregation of southern society and denial of African American voting and civil rights.

1898 The Spanish-American War and the Annexation of Hawaii

A powerful group of Americans sought to expand United States' influence beyond its own shores in the late 1890s. The Cuban revolt from Spain provided an opportunity, as public sentiment turned against the Spanish. In addition to its alleged mistreatment of the Cuban people, Spain was blamed for the mysterious sinking of the American battleship *Maine* in Havana harbor. The Spanish-American War lasted for three months, and victory gave the United States control of Puerto Rico and Guam. The United States also annexed the Philippines. Meanwhile, in Hawaii, an 1893 coup by American planters led to the overthrow of the Hawaiian government, and the islands were annexed by the United States government in 1898.

1909 The Founding of the NAACP

A prominent group of white and African American reformers joined together in 1909 to form the National Association for the Advancement of Colored People (NAACP). This organization fought important battles for voting rights and against segregation and lynching. In 1915 the NAACP scored its first major victory when the Supreme Court declared so-called grandfather clauses unconstitutional. These laws had been used throughout the South as part of an effort to deny African Americans their voting rights. The NAACP continued to fight discrimination and white violence and remains a leading civil rights organization today.

1914 The Opening of the Panama Canal

The Isthmus of Panama was an ideal location for a quick route between the Atlantic and Pacific oceans. After supporting a Panamanian revolt against Colombia in 1903, the United States received a permanent grant of a 10-mile-wide Canal Zone across the isthmus. Construction began in 1904 and ended ten years later. At a cost of $400 million, the United States now had easy access between two oceans and a greater ability to extend its power to other parts of the world.

1917 The United States Entry into World War I

After several years of claiming neutrality in World War I, the United States finally entered the war on the side of the Allies in 1917. American forces delivered an Allied victory, but after the war, revenge-minded Allied leaders frustrated Wilson's visions for postwar peace and security, opting instead to humiliate the defeated Germans. The Germans never forgot nor forgave their treatment at the hands of the Allies. The treaty contained the seeds of future conflict between the powers of Europe.

1929 The Stock Market Crash

In October 1929, stock prices plummeted. The stock market crash helped push the American economy into a deep downward cycle that would come to be known as the Great Depression. Unregulated speculation on the stock market, overvalued stocks, bad government policy, and a decline in purchasing power all contributed to the downturn. The Depression caused thousands of banks to close. By 1932 median income had been cut in half. Unemployment remained high throughout the 1930s, ranging from 20 to 38 percent. More than merely an economic crisis, the Depression shattered many Americans' faith in government and business.

1935 The Social Security Act

During the Depression, President Franklin Roosevelt initiated reforms to ensure that no future depression would have such a devastating effect on the nation. The Social Security Act grew out of these efforts. This act provided income for retired workers, compensation to the unemployed, and assistance for dependent children. The program was funded by joint employee-employer contributions. The Social Security Act was a landmark piece of legislation that helped to create the foundation for the modern welfare state. The first bill to revise significant sections of government welfare was signed by President Clinton in 1996.

1935 The Wagner Act

Prior to 1935, President Roosevelt had not been interested in extending labor protections through new legislation. But when the Supreme Court struck down existing legislation that included key protections for labor, Roosevelt gave his support to the National Labor Relations Act, commonly known as the Wagner Act. This act outlawed blacklisting—by which employers conspired not to hire certain workers—and guaranteed labor the right to organize and bargain collectively. After decades of outright hostility toward unions, the United States government now officially recognized the right of labor unions to exist and represent workers in their relations with employers.

1941 The Attack on Pearl Harbor

On December 7, 1941, a Japanese force launched a surprise attack upon the American naval base at Pearl Harbor, Hawaii. Japanese leaders believed that the United States was blocking Japanese

expansion in the Pacific, and they decided a lightning thrust would disable the American navy. The attack killed over 2,335 American soldiers and 68 civilians and destroyed 19 ships and 150 planes. On December 8, Congress voted in favor of a declaration of war against Japan, and the United States entered World War II.

1942–1945 The Battles of Guadalcanal and Iwo Jima

Allied victories on the small islands of Guadalcanal and Iwo Jima were turning points of the war in the Pacific. On August 7, 1942, some 20,000 marines landed on Guadalcanal and the neighboring island of Tulagi in an effort to reclaim them from Japan. After months of hand-to-hand combat, the Japanese evacuated Guadalcanal—and ended their advance across the Pacific—on February 9, 1943. After Guadalcanal, a two-year struggle began to regain the other islands of the Pacific. On Iwo Jima, desperate fighting from February to March 1945 brought victory to the Allies, but at the cost of 5,000 American dead. With the capture of Iwo Jima, the Allies were within striking distance of the Japanese homeland.

1944 The Normandy Invasion

The Normandy invasion was the beginning of the end of World War II. With a force of 175,000 soldiers, 600 warships, and 11,000 planes, combined American and British forces landed on the northern coast of German-controlled France in June 1944. Within one month, over a million Allied troops had moved into France, and the defeat of Germany took less than a year. The Soviet Union, the United States wartime ally, never forgave the late date of the invasion, because the Soviets had been suffering terribly at the hands of the Germans since 1942. This contributed to postwar American-Soviet hostility.

1944 The Serviceman's Readjustment Act

In gratitude for the service of World War II veterans, Congress passed the Serviceman's Readjustment Act, commonly known as the GI Bill, in 1944. The act granted returning veterans job guidance, priority for jobs, loans, mortgage assistance, technical training, and educational benefits. This bill contributed to the peacetime success of World War II veterans, who as a group earned 40 percent more than nonveterans. Few women and minorities, however, received full benefits under the act.

1945 The Formation of the United Nations

Near the end of World War II, diplomats hoped to create a new international peacekeeping organization. In April 1945, delegates from fifty nations met in San Francisco to adopt a charter for the new organization, called the United Nations (UN). Members pledged to settle their disagreements peacefully and to try to prevent wars from occurring and stop those that did break out. The formation of the UN provided new hope for an era of international peace and understanding.

1947 The Desegregation of Major League Baseball

After World War II, African Americans began to make louder demands for equality. Mild-mannered Jackie Robinson proved to be one of the trailblazers. In 1947 Robinson took the field for the Brooklyn Dodgers, thus ending the exclusion of African Americans from major league baseball. Within a few years, more African American players entered professional baseball, football, and basketball. In coming years, athletes such as Hank Aaron, Lawrence Taylor, and Michael Jordan would rise to the top of their respective sports.

1947 The Truman Doctrine

The years after World War II witnessed increasing hostility between the United States and the Soviet Union. Postwar American policy came to be dominated by the goal of resisting communist expansion. This policy was first expressed officially in the Truman Doctrine. In 1947, Truman announced that it was the duty of the United States to protect the "free peoples" of the world from "subjugation by armed minorities or outside pressures." If America failed in this duty, Truman warned, communism could take over the world. The Truman Doctrine helped shape a United States foreign policy that contributed to the tensions of the cold war.

1949 The Formation of the North Atlantic Treaty Organization

The United States committed its economic resources to rebuild war-torn Western Europe, partially in an effort to prevent communist gains there. To provide military protection for Western Europe, the United States created a military alliance known as the North Atlantic Treaty Organization (NATO) in 1949. Twelve nations joined NATO, pledging mutual military protection. The United Sates provided military aid to all the members. NATO ensured that Western Europe would be protected from Soviet invasion and provided the United States with a cold war weapon that could be used to contain any threat of communist aggression.

1954 The Army-McCarthy Hearings

The tense cold war atmosphere of the 1950s in the United States produced a fear of Soviet infiltration. In this atmosphere, Wisconsin senator Joseph McCarthy won fame with his accusations of communist infiltration of American government. His attacks continued for four years, while producing little evidence of communist activity in the government. McCarthy's accusations against the army led to televised hearings, in which Americans for the first time recognized the reckless and ruthless nature of his tactics. Defeated and censured by his colleagues in Congress, McCarthy lost his influence. His anticommunist crusade, however, contributed to the cold war fears in the United States.

1954 Brown v. Board of Education of Topeka

Civil rights leaders in the 1950s determined that they had to overturn the "separate but equal" doctrine established by *Plessy* v. *Ferguson* in 1896. The NAACP's Legal Defense Fund fought segregation in the courts, and in 1951 it helped Oliver Brown sue the Topeka, Kansas, school board for not allowing his daughter to attend a nearby white school. The Supreme Court ruled on May, 17, 1954, that "separate facilities are inherently unequal." A year later, the court ordered desegregation of public schools to begin "with all deliberate speed." Though the South resisted integration

for years, the *Brown* decision proved to be a major legal victory for the civil rights movement.

1955 The Montgomery Bus Boycott

Life in racially segregated Montgomery, Alabama, was radically altered in December 1955 when Rosa Parks, a seamstress and NAACP secretary, refused to move from the "whites-only" section of a public bus. Parks' defiance led to her arrest and unified the city's black community. African Americans began a campaign to boycott the public bus system. The boycott reduced the bus system's gross revenue by 65 percent. Meanwhile, the NAACP tested the legality of bus segregation, and in 1956 the Supreme Court ruled it unconstitutional. This victory gave strength to a broader civil rights movement, and Martin Luther King, Jr., emerged as a leading spokesperson for civil rights.

1960 Kennedy-Nixon Debate on Television

In the first televised presidential debate, Democratic candidate John F. Kennedy debated Republican candidate Richard Nixon. Kennedy took advantage of the power of television, projecting a charismatic, vigorous image. Polls showed that those who listened to the debate on the radio thought Nixon had won, while those who watched the debate on television believed Kennedy had triumphed. In future political elections, candidates' television images would be groomed as carefully as their stands on issues.

1962 The Cuban Missile Crisis

In 1962 Cuban leader Fidel Castro secretly secured Soviet aid to install Soviet-made nuclear missiles in Cuba, well within striking distance of the United States. American officials learned of the missiles when American spy planes took pictures of the missile sites. After considering options that included a military attack on Cuba, President Kennedy set up a blockade around the island. Kennedy's strong stance placed the United States at the very brink of war with the Soviet Union. The Soviets however, pulled back, agreeing to remove the missiles. The event intensified the cold war and the arms race between the United States and Soviet Union.

1963 The Assassination of President John F. Kennedy

On November 22, 1963, President John F. Kennedy was struck by an assassin's bullets while riding through the streets of Dallas, Texas. The wounds were fatal and the stunned nation was plunged into mourning. Authorities arrested and charged Lee Harvey Oswald with the assassination, but two days later nightclub owner Jack Ruby murdered Oswald. Despite the official government report of the Warren Commission that Oswald had acted alone in the assassination, many Americans continued to believe that the murder was the product of a conspiracy of some sort. The assassination of President Kennedy, who had invigorated the nation with his youth and enthusiasm, inflicted a serious blow to the spirit of the nation.

1964 The Civil Rights Act

The 1964 Civil Rights Act outlawed discrimination in public places and in employment practices, and empowered the attorney general to bring suit against offenders. The Supreme Court upheld the legislation. The American government finally had taken strong action toward guaranteeing African Americans their civil rights.

1964 *The Gulf of Tonkin Resolution*

President Lyndon B. Johnson was determined not to allow South Vietnam to fall under the control of communist North Vietnam. Toward this end, he sought a way to strengthen the United States commitment to South Vietnam. Johnson saw his opportunity when American ships, in North Vietnamese waters to aid South Vietnamese raids, were attacked by North Vietnamese torpedo boats. Johnson described the incident as a confirmed example of North Vietnamese aggression. He persuaded Congress to pass the Gulf of Tonkin Resolution, which gave him broad powers in applying military force. Johnson eventually would use the resolution to send more than 500,000 troops to Vietnam.

1965 *The Voting Rights Act*

The Civil Rights Act of 1964 had gaps that made possible the continued disenfranchisement of African Americans by southern states. Further peaceful protest by civil rights activists helped force the federal government to address this issue. Congress passed the Voting Rights Act in 1965. The act outlawed devices, such as literacy tests, used to deny African Americans the vote. It also empowered the federal government to oversee elections. By 1968 one million African Americans had registered to vote, a force that would come to have a strong impact upon elections.

1969 *The Moon Landing*

The Soviet advantage in space technology in the early 1960s spurred President John F. Kennedy to invest heavily in an American space program. Throughout the 1960s the space program made rapid progress. On July 20, 1969, the Apollo 11 lunar module landed on the moon. The nation watched as Commander Neil Armstrong took the first steps outside the spacecraft. Humankind had made a giant stride in the exploration of space, the last great frontier.

1972–1974 *The Watergate Scandal*

The Committee to Re-Elect the President (CREEP) was determined to win the 1972 reelection of President Richard Nixon. Toward this goal, a group of men tried to break into the Democratic National Headquarters in the Watergate building in order to install a listening device. The break-in led to the burglars' arrest. President Nixon claimed to have had no prior knowledge of the break-in, but he did participate in a cover-up of the incident. Though Nixon was overwhelmingly reelected, the investigation of Watergate continued, and it became clear the President was involved. Facing certain impeachment, Nixon became the first President to resign from office.

1973 Roe v. Wade

The National Organization for Women (NOW) made changing abortion laws a priority in the early 1970s. Existing laws made it diffi-

cult for women to obtain abortions, and the procedure was illegal in many states. NOW argued that the individual woman, not the state, should have the right to decide if abortion was appropriate. The issue went before the Supreme Court, which held that a woman's right to privacy gave her the right to obtain an abortion and that the state could regulate abortions only after a certain point in the pregnancy. This decision was a major victory for women's rights activists, but it inspired strong opposition by antiabortion groups. In the years after *Roe* v. *Wade,* the abortion debate has become a leading political issue.

1981 *The Appointment of Sandra Day O'Connor to the Supreme Court*

President Ronald Reagan appointed Sandra Day O'Connor to the Supreme Court in 1981. Following her confirmation by the Senate, she became the first woman to sit on the Supreme Court. Her appointment marked an important symbolic achievement for American women, who continued to make gains in their access to leadership positions at all levels of government. In 1993 O'Connor was joined on the Supreme Court bench by Ruth Bader Ginsberg, who was appointed by President Bill Clinton.

1981 *The Discovery of the AIDS Virus*

In 1981 medical researchers discovered a fatal new disease, known as acquired immunodeficiency syndrome (AIDS). The disease, scientists learned, was caused by a virus that damages the body's ability to fight infection. Research also showed that the disease is transmitted through sexual contact with an infected person or by the sharing of contaminated intravenous needles. As yet, no cure for the disease nor means of immunization against the virus has been found. By March 1994, about 200,000 Americans had died of AIDS-related complications.

1991 *The Collapse of the Soviet Union*

Mikhail Gorbachev could not control the forces he had unleashed in the Soviet Union through his democratic, *perestroika* reforms. In the closing days of 1991, the Soviet Union dissolved, and the republics that once made up the Soviet Union became independent countries. In 1991, Boris Yeltsin leader of the Russian republic, declared a final end to the cold war, which had dominated American and Soviet foreign policy for over forty years.

1992 *The World Wide Web*

In the 1990s, a new term was added to our vocabulary—the Web. It refers to the World Wide Web, released in 1992 by CERN, the European Laboratory for Particle Physics in Switzerland. Originally designed to give members of the physics community a simple way to access information from different sources, the Web quickly grew, with a dramatic rise in its number of users beginning in 1993 and 1994. The Web itself is a group of electronic documents (often called Web pages) and links that lead from one document to another. Documents can contain text, pictures, audio clips and even video clips. Today, the Web holds documents on every subject imaginable and is the most popular way of using the Internet, a global computer network. Millions of people all over the world now read and add to the Web every day in a number of languages.

Glossary

This Glossary defines all key terms listed in section previews. The page number at the end of each entry indicates the text page on which the term appears in boldface. Key people are defined in the Biographical Dictionary on pages 1145–1151.

abolition Movement to ban, or abolish, slavery; began in the early 1800s and continued through the Civil War (p. 249)

acquired immunodeficiency syndrome (AIDS) Incurable, fatal disease that appeared in 1981; transmitted through the bodily fluid of an infected individual (p. 946)

Adams-Onís Treaty Agreement signed in 1819 in which Spain gave control of Florida to the United States (p. 189)

administration A President's term in office, or the group of officials that makes up the executive branch, including the President (p. 149)

AFDC Aid to Families with Dependent Children, the largest federal welfare program (p. 1007)

affirmative action Policy whereby employers try to make up for past discrimination by giving special consideration to the hiring of women and people from minority groups (p. 936)

agribusiness Method of producing agricultural goods in which corporations run large farms using high-tech machinery (p. 745)

Albany Movement Largely unsuccessful protests against racial inequality in Albany, Georgia, in 1961 and 1962; led by Martin Luther King, Jr. (p. 806)

Alien and Sedition Acts of 1798 Acts passed by Federalists giving the government power to imprison or deport foreign citizens and prosecute critics of the government (p. 162)

Allies The combination of Russia, France, Great Britain, and later the United States in World War I; opponents of the Central Powers (p. 550)

American Expeditionary Force (AEF) United States troops in World War I, including draftees, volunteers, and the National Guard (p. 559)

American Indian Movement (AIM) Native American rights group organized in 1968; organized protests and participated in the occupation at Wounded Knee in 1973 (p. 837)

American party Political party organized in 1854 by nativists to work against Catholics and immigrants; also called "Know Nothings" (p. 307)

American Revolution The war and the social and political changes that accompanied the creation of the United States of America (p. 98)

American System Economic policy proposed in 1825 by John Q. Adams and others under which the federal government would support business by passing protective tariffs and making internal improvements such as roads and canals (p. 227)

amnesty General pardon for those guilty of a certain crime; granted by President Jimmy Carter to draft evaders during Vietnam War (p. 926)

Anaconda Plan Civil War plan formed by the North to blockade the South and cut off its foreign trade (p. 328)

anarchist Political radical who opposes all government because it limits individual liberty and serves the wealthy, ruling classes (p. 406)

Anglo A white, non-Latino, English-speaking American (p. 832)

annexation Addition of a new territory to an existing country (p. 496)

Anti-Federalist Those who opposed the new Constitution between 1787 and 1789 on the grounds that the central government it would create would be too powerful (p. 144)

anti-Semitism Hostility toward or discrimination against Jews (p. 665)

apartheid Systematic separation and inequality of races in South Africa enforced by whites during the 1900s (p. 967)

appeasement Act of giving in to someone's demands in order to keep the peace; unsuccessful policy of England and France toward Nazi Germany before World War II (p. 666)

arbitration Process of settling disputes in which both sides accept the legally binding decision of an impartial third party; often used in labor conflicts (p. 529)

armistice Cease-fire during a war, particularly at the end of World War I in 1918 (p. 563)

Articles of Confederation Agreement establishing a form of government among the states in 1781 (p. 128)

assimilation Process by which people of one culture merge into, and become indistinguishable from, the people of another culture (p. 175)

autocrat Ruler with unlimited governing power (p. 552)

automation Using machines instead of human labor in farming, mining, and manufacturing (p. 1038)

baby boom Increase in birth rate that began in World War II and continued into the 1950s (p. 745)

balance of trade Difference in value between a country's imports and exports over a given period of time (p. 72)

banana republic A Central American country in the early 1900s that depended upon banana exports and whose politics and economy were dominated by American business (p. 498)

barrio City neighborhood inhabited by Spanish speakers (p. 832)

Battle of New Orleans Battle fought January 8, 1815, in which forces of the United States under Andrew Jackson defeated British troops in the War of 1812 (p. 179)

Battle of the Bulge Battle fought from December 16, 1944 to January 16, 1945, between the Allies and Nazi forces in Belgium (p. 675)

Battle of Tippecanoe Battle fought November 7, 1811, in which forces of the United States under William Henry Harrison defeated Native Americans led by Tenskwatawa (p. 177)

beatnik Member of the "Beat Generation" in the 1950s who protested the pressure to conform through writing, art, and unconventional living (p. 751)

Berlin airlift The emergency program undertaken by the United States to deliver supplies to West Berlin in 1948 and 1949 after the Soviet Union blocked other access routes (p. 725)

Berlin Wall Barrier built by the Soviets in 1961 to keep people of East Berlin from escaping to the West; symbol of the cold war; torn down in 1989 (p. 788)

bicameral legislature Two houses or groups of representatives, as in the United States Congress (p. 130)

bilingual education Education in which students with little knowledge of English are taught in both their native language and in English (p. 990)

Bill of Rights The first ten amendments to the Constitution, which guarantee freedom of speech, religion, and other basic rights (p. 146)

Black Power An African American movement seeking unity, self-determination, and economic and political power (p. 818)

black codes Laws intended to keep African Americans under white authority, especially following the Civil War (p. 190)

blitzkrieg "Lightning war"; German tactic employed at the beginning of World War II, based upon overwhelming the enemy with a series of sudden attacks by land and air (p. 670)

block grants Lump sums of money the federal government gives to a state to fund welfare as the state sees fit (p. 1012)

blue laws Laws that regulate work, business, or entertainment on Sunday (p. 443)

bonanza farms Large farms owned by big businesses and managed by professionals (p. 423)

Bonus Army Group of World War I veterans who marched to Washington in 1932 asking to receive their pension bonus early (p. 630)

boomer Person wanting to settle in the West in the late 1880s, especially one of those who pressured Congress in 1889 to take over Native American land for this purpose (p. 421)

bootlegging Supplying liquor illegally during prohibition (1920–1933) by producing or smuggling it (p. 600)

Boston Tea Party Demonstration in 1773 in which American colonists threw tea from ships into Boston Harbor to protest British taxes (p. 106)

boycott A means of protest based on refusing to buy products or use services (p. 103)

bracero Spanish term for "worker," particularly applied to the thousands of Mexican farm workers who migrated into the United States during World War II, most of whom were sent back after the war (p. 708)

Brooklyn Bridge Bridge completed in 1883 that connects Manhattan and Brooklyn (p. 391)

Bull Moose party Name for the Progressive party, organized to run Theodore Roosevelt for President in 1912 (p. 535)

busing Program begun in the 1960s to end racial segregation in schools by redistributing students (p. 890)

buy on margin Practice of buying stocks by paying 10 to 50 percent of the full price and borrowing the rest; common in the 1920s before the stock market crash of 1929 (p. 612)

cabinet Heads of the major departments of the United States government who advise the President (p. 148)

Camp David Accords Framework for peace between Israel and Egypt; signed in 1978 (p. 918)

canister Projectile used in a cannon that opens up after firing and sprays bullet-sized shot (p. 328)

capital Supply of wealth used to produce goods and profits (p. 215)

capitalism Economic system in which manufacturing is controlled by private corporations and individuals competing for profits (p. 215)

capitalist Person using capital to produce goods or services for profit (p. 220)

cartel Loose association of businesses supplying the same product, often formed secretly; its members agree to limit supplies to keep prices high (p. 395)

cash crop Crop raised and sold for money, as opposed to a crop raised to supply food to the grower (p. 423)

Central Powers Combination of Germany and Austria-Hungary in World War I; opponents of the Allies (p. 550)

centralize To locate tasks or responsibilities so that they all happen in one place (p. 216)

Civil Rights Act of 1964 Law prohibiting discrimination in public accommodations and job opportunities (p. 812)

Civil War Armed conflict between the northern and southern states between 1861 and 1865 (p. 298)

clan Type of kinship network; consists of a group of families descended from a common ancestor (p. 17)

coalition Union of several groups who work together toward a common political, social, or economic goal (p. 935)

cold war Condition of indirect conflict that existed between the United States and the Soviet Union from World War II through the late 1980s (p. 718)

collateral Something pledged as security for a loan that can be claimed by the lender if the loan is not repaid (p. 617)

collective bargaining Negotiation between employers and workers, usually through a labor union (p. 404)

colonization Generally, the founding of a colony; in the abolition movement, a proposal in the early 1800s to return free and formerly enslaved African Americans to Africa (p. 249)

colony An area settled by immigrants who continue their ties with the parent country (p. 41)

Columbian Exchange The encounter and exchange among the people of the Americas, Africa, and Europe that began in 1492 (p. 32)

commodity Something that can be bought and sold (p. 215)

communist Economic system in which manufacturing is controlled by the workers (p. 581)

Compromise of 1850 Agreement reached between northern and southern states in an effort to end dispute over the extension of slavery to the western territories (p. 304)

compulsory education System of education in the United States in which children are required to attend school until a certain age (p. 245)

confederation An alliance of states formed to coordinate defense and their relations with foreign governments (p. 128)

congregacion Spanish colonial village where Native Americans were forced to worship as European Catholics and to farm (p. 43)

Congress of Industrial Organizations (CIO) Labor group that split off from the American Federation of Labor in 1938 and organized unskilled steel, auto, and other workers (p. 654)

Congress of Racial Equality (CORE) Civil rights organization started in 1942; active in sit-ins and demonstrations during the 1950s and 1960s (p. 797)

conquistador Spanish term for "conqueror" in North and South America during the period of conquest after the opening of the Atlantic World (p. 40)

conscientious objector Person who opposes fighting in a war on moral or religious grounds (p. 860)

Constitutional Union party Political party formed of moderates from the South and the border states in the election of 1860 (p. 319)

containment Cold war policy of the United States intended to prevent communist power from expanding beyond its geographical boundaries after World War II (p. 723)

contra Rebel fighting the Marxist Sandinista government of Nicaragua in the 1980s (p. 947)

contraband Property of the enemy seized during wartime; applied during the Civil War to enslaved African Americans set free by the Union army (p. 337)

Copperhead A Democrat during the Civil War who worked against the war and the antislavery policies of the Republicans (p. 336)

cost-plus system System devised during World War II to allow profits from war production, in which the government paid for basic manufacturing costs, plus a percentage for profit (p. 693)

counterculture A cultural movement in the 1960s formed mostly of young people who rejected conventions and experimented with new practices in dress, sexual relationships, and drug use (p. 863)

cousinocracy The approximately one hundred families of the landowning gentry who ran Virginia in colonial times (p. 80)

Crédit Mobilier A dummy corporation created by the stockholders of the Union Pacific Railroad, which allowed them to pay themselves with federal grants to build the railroad (p. 377)

Cuban missile crisis Dispute between the United States and the Soviet Union in 1962 over Soviet missile bases in Cuba (p. 789)

cult of domesticity The widespread belief in the early to mid-1800s in the importance of women's work in the home (p. 257)

currency policy The federal government's plan for the makeup and quantity of the nation's money supply (p. 429)

de facto discrimination Discrimination caused by conditions rather than by law; common in the North for African Americans after the Civil War (p. 478)

de facto segregation Segregation in the North and elsewhere caused by ghetto conditions rather than by law (p. 815)

de jure segregation Segregation enforced by laws; common in the South through the 1960s (p. 815)

debt peonage Labor system common in the South after the Civil War in which debt was used to keep farm workers on the land (p. 373)

Declaration of Independence Document published in 1776 declaring the independence of the United States from British rule (p. 111)

deficit spending Economic policy in which the government spends more than it receives in taxes, making up the difference by borrowing money (p. 695)

deflation Period of gradually dropping prices, generally brought on by the decrease in the supply of available money (p. 429)

demagogue Charismatic leader who manipulates people with half-truths, false promises, and scare tactics (p. 650)

Democratic party Political party descended from Jeffersonian Democrat-Republicans and Jacksonian Democrats (p. 306)

denomination Subgroup of the Christian religion with its own set of beliefs and style of worship (p. 202)

depression Severe economic slump during which stock values, business activity, and employment decline severely or remain at very low levels (p. 102)

deregulation Policy of reducing or removing government controls on industry (p. 926)

détente Relaxation of strained relations between nations, especially among the United States, the Soviet Union, and China in the 1970s and late 1980s (p. 893)

direct primary Election system in which voters rather than political bosses select nominees for elections (p. 528)

dissident An opponent of the established government, especially in the Soviet Union (p. 919)

diversified conglomerate Extremely large corporation formed of other corporations of many types (p. 742)

division of labor The way that tasks are assigned within a culture (p. 18)

dollar diplomacy Policy of increasing United States investments abroad to keep foreign societies stable; adopted by President William Howard Taft in the early 1900s (p. 511)

domino theory Political theory common during the cold war that if one country fell to communism, countries nearby would also quickly become communist (p. 730)

"Double V" campaign Civil rights movement by African Americans during World War II, calling for victory both in the war and in the struggle for equality at home (p. 707)

doughboy Nickname for an infantryman in World War I (p. 560)

Dow Jones industrial average An average of the prices of the stock of leading industries that gauges the health of the stock market (p. 614)

downsizing Process by which companies lay off workers in order to cut costs (p. 952)

draft Legal means of forcing people to serve in the armed forces (p. 333)

Dred Scott* v. *Sandford Supreme court case in 1857 that refused to recognize African Americans as citizens and overturned the Missouri Compromise (p. 312)

e-mail Electronic mail (p. 1035)

economic sanction Coercive trade restriction taken by a nation or group of nations to enforce demands (p. 967)

economy of scale Producing or buying an item on a very large scale so the price per item goes down (p. 397)

Electoral College Body of electors chosen by voters in each state to elect the President and Vice President (p. 141)

Emancipation Proclamation Declaration by President Abraham Lincoln that as of January 1, 1863, all enslaved people in areas in rebellion against the Union would be considered free by the North (p. 336)

emancipation The freeing of enslaved people (p. 249)

Embargo of 1807 Period during which President Thomas Jefferson stopped American trade with Britain and France because of their warlike acts (p. 170)

embargo A policy of restricting trade with a nation (p. 888)

enclosure movement Practice begun in the late 1500s in Great Britain of forcing tenants off the land in order to enclose it for raising sheep (p. 50)

***encomienda* system** Social system in which Native Americans were required to work for an individual Spaniard, who was supposed to care for their well-being in return (p. 41)

entitlement Government program such as Social Security, for which spending rises automatically each year (p. 948)

entrepreneur Businessperson who takes risks for the sake of large profits (p. 215)

Environmental Protection Agency (EPA) Government agency established in 1970 to curb air and water pollution; now also regulates solid waste disposal, pesticides, and toxic substances (p. 842)

Equal Rights Amendment (ERA) Constitutional amendment to ensure equal rights for women; passed by Congress in 1972 but never ratified by the required number of states (p. 828)

escalation An increase or expansion, especially of war (p. 852)

evangelical movement Christian religious movement that emphasizes preaching instead of rituals, and stresses that salvation is possible only for those who believe in Christ (p. 202)

excise Tax on an item manufactured within a country (p. 157)

executive branch The part of a government that executes, or carries out, laws (p. 129)

Exoduster Member of a group of southern African Americans who participated in an exodus, or mass migration, to western lands in the late 1870s (p. 415)

faction Separate subgroup within a political system (p. 144)

Fall Line An imaginary line east of the Appalachian Mountains where coastal plateaus meet inland hills; marked by waterfalls where rivers descend from the hills (p. 75)

fascism A political philosophy that values the nation or race over the individual, autocratic over democratic rule, and rigid control of society and the economy over a free society and market (p. 664)

federal deficit The amount by which the federal government's spending exceeds its income in a given year (p. 942)

Federalist Supporter of the new United States Constitution in the 1780s; also a member of a party that favored a strong federal government in the 1790s and early 1800s (p. 144)

feminism Theory of political, economic, and social equality of men and women (p. 824)

feminist Person who advocates the political, economic, and social equality of men and women (p. 824)

feudalism A system of duties and exchanges among members of European medieval society, based on land, war, and tradition (p. 22)

Fifteenth Amendment Constitutional amendment of 1870 guaranteeing all citizens the right to vote (p. 370)

first American party system Earliest political party system in the United States; composed of Jeffersonian Republicans and Federalists (p. 156)

flapper A type of young woman having a straight, slim silhouette and a fondness for dancing and brash actions; a symbol of the Jazz Age (p. 592)

Fourteen Points Peace program proposed by President Woodrow Wilson in 1918, intended to prevent wars like World War I (p. 568)

Fourteenth Amendment Constitutional amendment of 1868 that guarantees civil rights and equal protection of laws to all citizens (p. 368)

franchise The right to open a restaurant or other business using a system developed by and a name owned by a parent company (p. 742)

free soiler Settler in Kansas in the 1850s committed to an antislavery policy (p. 311)

free trade Trade between states or nations without tariffs (p. 1016)

Freedmen's Bureau Federal bureau in operation after the Civil War that helped former enslaved people and war refugees with food, medical, and other aid as well as schooling (p. 366)

Freedom Rides Campaign by African American and white civil rights workers in 1961 to protest segregated southern bus facilities by riding through the Lower South on buses (p. 804)

French and Indian War War fought by the British and their colonists against the French and their Native American allies from 1754 to 1763 (p. 99)

French Revolution Series of conflicts between 1789 and 1799 in which the monarchy of France was overthrown and a democratic government established (p. 158)

Fugitive Slave Act Part of the Compromise of 1850 requiring all states to return runaway slaves (p. 304)

fundamentalism Christian religious movement based on pamphlets issued between 1909 and 1914; holds that every word in the Bible was inspired by God (p. 601)

Gadsden Purchase United States purchase of southern New Mexico and Arizona from Mexico for $10 million in 1853 (p. 288)

gag rule Rule passed in 1836 by southern representatives in Congress that prevented antislavery petitions from being considered by the House for eight years (p. 253)

general strike A strike in which many unions participate in order to show worker unity (p. 581)

gentry People, generally landowners, wealthy enough to afford others to work for them (p. 79)

Gettysburg Address Speech by President Abraham Lincoln at a Gettysburg cemetery dedication in 1863; redefined the meaning of the United States (p. 348)

ghetto Section of a city where de facto segregation limits residents to a certain ethnic or racial group (p. 456)

GI Bill Common name for Servicemen's Readjustment Act of 1944, which provided veterans' benefits such as low-interest mortgages (p. 745)

GI United States soldier serving during World War II (p. 677)

Gilded Age The period between 1877 and 1900; also called the Tragic Era and the Dreadful Decades (p. 442)

globalization Trend of increasing international interdependence among nations and businesses (p. 1033)

Good Neighbor Policy Policy promoted by President Franklin Roosevelt which encouraged trade with Latin America by lowering tariffs and loaning money to Latin American governments (p. 1020)

grandfather clause A part of a law that exempts a group from the law if they met certain conditions before the law was passed; used in the South in the late 1800s and early 1900s to ensure that white voting rights were not affected by literacy tests intended to screen out African American voters (p. 474)

Grange Farmer's group, also known as the Patrons of Husbandry, most popular during the 1860s and 1870s; formed farmers' cooperatives for buying large quantities of goods and pressured legislators to regulate railroads (p. 429)

Great Awakening Religious revival in the American colonies, 1730s–1740s (p. 90)

Great Compromise Agreement of 1787 that created a bicameral legislature in the Constitution; it established that representation in one house was to be proportional to population in one house and equal among states in the other (p. 138)

Great Migration Wave of migrants from England during the 1600s; sought a better economic situation, a different form of society, and freedom from religious persecution (p. 56)

Great Society The legislative program proposed by President Lyndon Johnson in the 1960s; included civil rights laws, federal aid to education, elderly medical care, and poverty programs (p. 778)

green cards Cards that allow foreigners to legally live and work in the United States (p. 985)

greenback Paper money established during the Civil War; named for its color (p. 335)

Gross National Product (GNP) Total amount of goods and services a nation produces; used to gauge economic strength (p. 616)

guerrilla Soldier who fights irregular warfare, especially one using surprise tactics to harass and sabotage the enemy (p. 501)

Gulf of Tonkin Resolution Resolution passed by Congress in 1964 that gave the President authority to use "necessary" military force in Vietnam (p. 852)

gunboat Type of steam-driven boat used during the Civil War that was fitted with cannons and, sometimes, iron armor; it was able to navigate shallow rivers (p. 329)

Harlem Renaissance Period in the early 1900s during which the literary, musical, and artistic expression of African Americans blossomed in Harlem (p. 589)

Hartford Convention Meeting in 1814 at which New Englanders considered leaving the United States because of losses they were sustaining during the War of 1812 (p. 179)

Hawley-Smoot tariff Import tax levied in 1930, the highest in United States history; produced the opposite of its intended effect when international trade slowed (p. 629)

Helms-Burton Act Federal law passed in 1996 that penalized foreign companies that do business with Cuba (p. 1018)

Helsinki Accords Agreement reached in the 1970s by a group of nations, including the United States and the Soviet Union, to cooperate economically and promote human rights (p. 912)

hidalgo Young Spanish gentleman who fought in the *reconquista* or conquered the Americas in the 1500s (p. 40)

hierarchy Social system of many levels in which each level has power over the levels beneath it (p. 22)

hippie A member of the counterculture during the 1960s (p. 863)

holding company A corporation that controls other companies by holding their stocks (p. 530)

holocaust Nazi execution of six million Jews and five million others during World War II in extermination camps (p. 675)

home rule Municipal reforms in the late 1800s and early 1900s that gave cities limited self-rule, rather than state rule (p. 523)

Homestead Act Law passed in 1862 that offered certain settlers 160 acres of land if they built a house and farmed for five years (p. 414)

homicide Murder (p. 993)

Hooverville Towns of makeshift houses built by homeless people during the Great Depression (p. 620)

horizontal consolidation Process of creating one giant business by bringing together smaller firms in the same field (p. 397)

House Un-American Activities Committee (HUAC) Committee of the House of Representatives active during the 1940s and 1950s that investigated supposed communist influence in the film and other industries (p. 734)

household economy Economic system common before the 1800s in which people's business consisted of maintaining households by growing food and making clothes and other necessities (p. 215)

hundred days First one hundred days of President Franklin D. Roosevelt's term of office (p. 640)

Immigration Act of 1965 A law that changed quotas favoring northern and western Europeans and expanded the number of people allowed to immigrate (p. 780)

impeach To formally charge a public official with misconduct; brought by the lower house in a legislative body (p. 369)

imperial presidency The type of presidency sought by President Richard Nixon, in which the executive branch would gain more power than allowed by the Constitution (p. 887)

imperialism A policy by which stronger nations attempt to create empires by dominating weaker nations economically, politically, or military; also called expansionism (p. 496)

indentured servant Person who contracts to work for another for a period of time (usually seven years), especially in return for travel costs or food and shelter (p. 50)

Industrial Revolution A period of major economic change that began during the late 1700s with the introduction of machines using sources of power other than humans or animals (p. 195)

Industrial Workers of the World (IWW) Radical labor organization of the early 1900s that sought the overthrow of the capitalist system; also known as the Wobblies (p. 566)

inflation A steady increase in prices and loss of value of currency that reduces people's ability to buy goods; usually results from an increase in the amount of money and credit available (p. 120)

installment buying A method of paying for an expensive item over many months in installments and including interest (p. 612)

Interim Committee Group of government leaders and scientists who studied the question of using the atomic bomb to force Japan's surrender during World War II (p. 683)

Intermediate-Range Nuclear Forces (INF) Treaty Nuclear arms reduction treaty signed by President Ronald Reagan and Soviet president Mikhail Gorbachev in 1987 (p. 947)

Internal Revenue Act of 1862 Law that created the Internal Revenue Service to manage collection of taxes (p. 335)

Internet Worldwide computer network (p. 976)

internment camp A camp in which people are confined or isolated, especially during a time of war (p. 710)

interracial Including two or more racial groups (p. 796)

Interstate Commerce Act Law passed in 1887 to curb rate-setting abuses by railroads and regulate other interstate business (p. 445)

Intolerable Acts Colonists' name for the Coercive Acts of 1774, passed by the British Parliament and meant to punish the colony of Massachusetts (p. 107)

Iran-contra affair A scandal during the administration of President Ronald Reagan in which money from illegal Iran arms sales was given to Nicaraguan contras to fight Sandinistas (p. 947)

iron curtain The imaginary line separating communist countries allied with the Soviet Union in eastern Europe and the allies of the United States in western Europe during the cold war (p. 721)

Islam Religion that began in the early 600s, based on the teachings of the prophet Muhammad (p. 23)

Jacksonian Democrats Name given to the Democratic party during the period from the 1820s to the 1850s; supported Andrew Jackson's policy of discouraging federal involvement in the United States economy (p. 228)

Japanese American Citizens League Organization that helped Japanese Americans after World War II (p. 834)

Jazz Age Term for the 1920s, a period marked by the great popularity of jazz music, which was linked to changes in manners, morals, and fashions (p. 591)

jazz Music that grew out of "raggy" rhythms and call-and-response forms for singers and instruments in New Orleans in the 1890s (p. 475)

Jeffersonian Republicans Name given to the Democratic party in the first American party system by historians seeking to distinguish it from the modern-day Republican party (p. 156)

Jim Crow System of laws in the late 1800s that segregated African Americans and forced them to use separate, inferior facilities (p. 477)

jingoism The swelling of national pride and desire for an aggressive foreign policy in late 1800s and early 1900s; resulted in the Spanish-American War and other expansionist activity (p. 501)

joint-stock company Company of investors who contribute to the cost of a venture and receive a share of the profits (p. 47)

judicial branch The part of a government that decides if laws have been broken (p. 129)

judicial review The power of federal courts to review laws passed by Congress and state legislatures to decide if they are constitutional (p. 169)

Kansas-Nebraska Act Act of 1854 establishing that the people of a territory should decide whether slavery would be allowed there (p. 308)

kinship network Type of social organization consisting of relatives, or kin, such as parents, children, grandparents, aunts, uncles, cousins, and those who marry into the family (p. 17)

Know Nothings The American party, a nativist political party active in the 1850s (p. 307)

Koran Holy book of the religion of Islam (p. 29)

Ku Klux Klan Organization formed in the South in 1866, which used lynching and violence to intimidate and control African Americans and others (p. 374)

laissez-faire Economic policy under which government takes a hands-off approach to economic matters and plays a limited role in business (p. 442)

Latino People whose roots lie in Spanish-speaking lands to the south of the United States, including Mexico, Central and South America, and many islands of the Caribbean (p. 831)

League of Nations Organization proposed by President Woodrow Wilson after World War I in the hopes of joining nations together for peace and security (p. 569)

Lecompton constitution Proslavery Kansas constitution of 1857 (p. 313)

legislative branch The part of a government that makes the laws (p. 129)

Lend-Lease Act Law allowing United States loans to Great Britain early in World War II, without specified time of payment; helped Britain resist attacks before the United States entered the war (p. 668)

liberal consensus View widely held in the 1950s and 1960s that capitalism was the best economic system and that the United States was threatened more by communism abroad than by domestic issues like poverty (p. 772)

Liberty Bonds Certificates issued by the United States to raise money to loan to the Allies during World War I (p. 564)

Limited Test Ban Treaty Agreement reached by the United States and the Soviet Union in 1963 banning nuclear testing above ground (p. 790)

lineage Kinship network in which the members trace their descent from a common ancestor (p. 27)

literacy tests Tests in which would-be voters have to demonstrate certain knowledge before they can vote; once used in several states to prevent certain groups from voting (p. 477)

long drive Practice of moving cattle from distant grazing ranges to railroad centers for shipment; common in the West from the 1860s to the 1880s (p. 425)

Louisiana Purchase Purchase from France of New Orleans and a vast area of land west of the Mississippi River in 1803 (p. 170)

low country Seaboard region of South Carolina and Georgia, excellent for growing rice and indigo (p. 86)

Loyalists American colonists who remained loyal to Britain during the American Revolution (p. 115)

Lusitania British passenger ship sunk by German U-boats in 1915 (p. 555)

lynching The illegal capture and execution of a person by a mob (p. 478)

mandate Wishes of constituents, as expressed in the election of a candidate by a large majority of voters (p. 773)

Manhattan Project Secret project that created the first atomic bomb in 1945 for use in World War II (p. 682)

manifest destiny Belief that the United States has a divine right to expand its territory; used to support imperialist expansion in the late 1800s (p. 286)

maquiladoras Factories along the Mexico-United States border that assemble imported parts (p. 1021)

Marbury v. *Madison* Court case of 1803 in which the Supreme Court first ruled a law unconstitutional; established the power of judicial review by federal courts (p. 169)

March on Washington Civil rights demonstration in Washington, D.C., led by Martin Luther King, Jr., in 1963 (p. 811)

Market Revolution Shift in the United States economy from home-based to market-based industries (p. 214)

Marshall Plan Program of European economic recovery after World War II, financed by the United States (p. 724)

Maysville Road Veto President Jackson's veto of a bill providing federal funding for road construction in Kentucky; demonstrated Jackson's view of the role of the federal government (p. 230)

McCulloch v. *Maryland* Supreme Court case of 1819 in which Chief Justice John Marshall invoked the "necessary and proper" clause of the Constitution, establishing that the federal government has powers beyond those specifically outlined in the Constitution (p. 231)

Medicare Public health-care plan that funds medical care for the elderly (p. 779)

mercantilism European economic theory of the 1600s whereby a nation's economy can be strengthened by the use of protective tariffs, trade monopolies, and a balance of exports over imports (p. 72)

Middle Passage Section of the triangular trade from Africa to the Americas that transported enslaved persons (p. 84)

midnight judges Federal judges hastily appointed by President John Q. Adams in the hours before he left office in 1801 (p. 165)

migratory farm workers Laborers who move from farm to farm planting, cultivating, and harvesting crops (p. 832)

Military Reconstruction Act of 1867 Legislation that divided the post–Civil War South into military districts governed by the North (p. 369)

militias Armies made up of people who are not professional soldiers (p. 995)

minstrel show Theatrical show of the late 1800s in which white actors wore blackface and parodied African American music, dance, and humor (p. 474)

minutemen Colonists who fought British forces in the American Revolution; pledged to volunteer military service at a minute's notice (p. 98)

Missouri Compromise Agreement of 1820 that admitted Missouri into the Union as a slave state and Maine as a free state; set a precedent that continued until the Civil War (p. 181)

modem A device that transmits data from one computer to another over telephone lines (p. 1035)

modern republicanism President Eisenhower's term for an approach to government that was "conservative when it comes to money, liberal when it comes to human beings" (p. 757)

monopoly Control of a commodity or service extending to the elimination of competition and the fixing of prices (p. 395)

Monroe Doctrine Policy of President James Monroe stating that the United States would consider any European interference in the nations of the Americas as an unfriendly act (p. 226)

Morrill Land-Grant Act Federal grant of 1862 that gave 140 million acres of western land to state governments, which then could sell the land to fund agricultural colleges (p. 414)

most-favored nation Trade status granting a nation the same trading privileges as other nations (p. 497)

mountain man Fur trapper and trader in the West in the early 1800s (p. 281)

muckraker Journalist of the late 1800s to early 1900s who tried to alert the public to alleged wrongdoing by politicians and big business (p. 525)

multiculturalism Social and educational movement that tries to embrace rather than exclude minority cultures (p. 974)

My Lai massacre The slaughter of more than a hundred unarmed Vietnamese peasants in March 1968 by United States forces during the Vietnam War (p. 857)

NAFTA North American Free Trade Agreement; international agreement in 1993 between Mexico, Canada, and the United States designed to promote free trade (p. 971)

Nation of Islam African American religious group founded in 1933 that believes in the religion of Islam, self-sufficiency, self-discipline, and the creation of a black nation (p. 816)

National Association for the Advancement of Colored People (NAACP) African American civil rights organization founded in 1910; fought for civil rights through demonstrations, lawsuits, and other means throughout the 1900s (p. 479)

national debt Total debt of the federal government (p. 653)

National Organization for Women (NOW) Feminist group founded in 1966 to pursue equal rights for women (p. 826)

National Republicans Political party of the 1820s that favored strong federal government and a national bank; supported John Q. Adams and opposed the Jacksonian Democrats (p. 228)

National Rifle Association (NRA) Organization that works to uphold the right of all Americans to bear arms (p. 996)

Nationalist Member of a 1780s political group advocating strong national government to control the states (p. 130)

nativism Practice of favoring native-born citizens over immigrants (p. 307)

NATO North Atlantic Treaty Organization; alliance of ten European nations, the United States, and Canada that pledged mutual assistance in the event of an attack on any member nation (p. 725)

natural rights Theory that human rights are intrinsic and are not granted by a monarch or government; incorporated into the Declaration of Independence by Thomas Jefferson (p. 110)

naturalization Process resulting in the citizenship of immigrants (p. 307)

Nazi party National Socialist Workers party; fascist political party that controlled Germany from 1933 until it was abolished in 1945; led by German dictator Adolf Hitler (p. 665)

New Deal Proposals and programs adopted by President Franklin Roosevelt in response to the Great Depression; included social and economic programs and changes in government regulation (p. 640)

new federalism Replacement of federal programs by federal grants to cities and states (p. 940)

New Freedom Political platform of Woodrow Wilson in the 1912 presidential election that criticized both big business and big government (p. 536)

New Frontier President John F. Kennedy's reform programs; included economic measures, aid to the poor, and the space program (p. 773)

New Jersey Plan Constitutional Convention proposal for a federal government having a unicameral legislature with equal representation for each state regardless of population (p. 138)

New Left Political movement of the 1960s advocating the need for radical change to solve the social problems of the United States (p. 859)

New Right Alliance of conservative special-interest groups in the Republican party from the 1960s to the 1990s (p. 936)

New Nationalism Program of progressive reforms proposed by President Theodore Roosevelt in 1910; included more regulation of business, welfare legislation, and other measures (p. 535)

nomad Person who migrates continually rather than living permanently in one place (p. 273)

NSC-68 National Security Council document of the cold war that suggested tripling the defense budget in an effort to contain communism (p. 726)

Nuclear Regulatory Commission Agency overseeing the operation of nuclear power plants in the United States (p. 925)

nullification A state's refusal to recognize or uphold a federal law (p. 232)

Open Door policy United States efforts to develop a trade relationship with China in the late 1800s to early 1900s; urged European nations with spheres of influence in China to not restrict trade in those areas (p. 505)

oral tradition Method of relaying history and beliefs from generation to generation by word of mouth (p. 19)

Organization of Petroleum Exporting Countries (OPEC) Group of Arab nations controlling prices and production of oil for export (p. 888)

Pacific Railroad Act of 1862 Legislation that allowed the federal government to offer public land and money to companies for construction of a transcontinental railroad (p. 335)

pan-Indian movement Native American movement developed to halt the expansion of the United States in the early 1800s by achieving spiritual and political unity between Native American groups (p. 176)

Panic of 1819 First great depression in United States history; London banks demanded payment from United States banks, who in turn demanded repayment of loans from their customers (p. 180)

Panic of 1837 Severe economic depression partly caused by the end of the national bank (p. 233)

Panic of 1857 Economic depression that struck the North particularly hard before the Civil War and helped persuade the South to cut economic and political ties with the North (p. 315)

paradox of power Combination of contradictory attitudes toward a powerful country (p. 517)

pardon Official forgiveness of a person for a crime (p. 366)

Patriots American fighting forces in the War for Independence (p. 115)

patronage Practice of elected officials appointing friends and supporters to government jobs (p. 230)

Peace Corps Federal program that trains and sends volunteers to aid people of developing countries (p. 785)

Pendleton Act Legislation of 1883 that established a Civil Service Commission to control government hiring, ending the patronage system (p. 445)

Pentagon Papers Secret study by the Defense Department on the Vietnam War; leaked to the *New York Times* in 1971 (p. 898)

per capita income Average income per person; used to compare income of states, countries, etc. (p. 742)

perjury Lying under oath (p. 899)

Persian Gulf War War between Iraq and United Nations forces led by the United States over Iraq's annexation of oil-rich Kuwait in 1991 (p. 951)

persisters Small groups of families during the late 1700s to early 1800s who settled permanently in an area while others continued to migrate farther west or south (p. 189)

Pickett's Charge Confederate attack led by General George Pickett at the Battle of Gettysburg in 1863 that resulted in severe Confederate losses; demonstrated the destructive powers of the new battle tactics and technology (p. 344)

piecework Work paid according to the number of finished units a worker produces (p. 399)

Pinkertons Private police force of the late 1800s and early 1900s; hired by companies to break strikes (p. 406)

Plumbers Secret White House group under President Richard M. Nixon; created to stop security leaks to the press (p. 897)

political asylum Protection the government of one country gives to a political refugee from another country (p. 985)

political boss Leader of a political machine (p. 458)

political left Those who wish to change the current social and political system or power structure (p. 649)

political machine Unofficial city organization designed to keep a particular party or group in power (p. 458)

political party Group actively involved in the political process; seeks to elect candidates to public office in order to control government policies (p. 156)

political right Those who wish to preserve the current social and political system or power structure (p. 648)

poll tax A tax (now unconstitutional) paid in some states before a person was allowed to vote (p. 477)

Pontiac's Rebellion Native American revolt against British policies in the Great Lakes region in the 1760s; named after the Ottawa sachem Pontiac (p. 103)

Poor People's Campaign Movement organized in 1968 by civil rights leader Martin Luther King, Jr., to attack economic injustice (p. 881)

popular sovereignty Belief that people can and should govern themselves (p. 111)

Populists Followers of the People's party of 1892 who sought radical reforms in United States economic and social policies; supported a silver standard, increased money supply, and a graduated income tax (p. 431)

precedent Custom arising from previous practice rather than a written law (p. 160)

presidio Spanish fort built in the American southwest to protect Spanish holdings and missions (p. 43)

Proclamation of 1763 Act of the British Parliament that prohibited American colonists from settling west of the Appalachian Mountains (p. 103)

productivity The amount a worker produces in a given period of time (p. 1038)

progressivism Political and social reform movement of the late 1800s and early 1900s; included socialism, the labor movement, municipal reform, prohibitionism, the settlement house movement, and other reform movements (p. 523)

prohibition Banning by law of the manufacture, transportation, sale, and possession of alcoholic beverages; enacted by the Eighteenth Amendment from 1920 to 1933 (p. 244)

proletariat Members of the working class (p. 719)

psychedelic drug Drug that produces hallucinations and other altered perceptions of reality (p. 864)

public works programs Government-funded projects to build public facilities; central to President Franklin Roosevelt's New Deal job programs (p. 641)

Puritans Members of the Protestant Church of England of the 1600s and 1700s who wanted to reform, or purify, the church; some migrated to New England in the 1600s (p. 56)

Radical Republicans Wing of the Republican party of the 1860s made up of abolitionists and others hostile to the South; forced harsh Reconstruction laws through Congress (p. 336)

ragtime Style of music consisting of complex syncopated rhythms played over a steady beat; developed by African American musicians in the 1880s (p. 474)

ratify To formally approve a suggested action (p. 145)

rationing Distribution of goods in a limited amount in times of scarcity (p. 698)

real wages Value of income adjusted to account for inflation; used to compare wages in different time periods (p. 610)

real purchasing power Value of money adjusted to account for inflation; used to compare economic conditions in different time periods (p. 742)

realpolitik Foreign policy theory based on efficiency rather than ethics; from the German term for "practical politics" (p. 892)

Reconstruction Period from 1865 to 1877 when the states of the Confederacy were controlled by the federal government before being readmitted to the Union (p. 360)

Reconstruction Finance Corporation Government corporation set up by President Herbert Hoover in 1932 that gave government loans to banks (p. 629)

red scare Fear of communism, socialism, or other so-called extreme ideas (p. 581)

Reformation Religious movement in Western Europe in the 1500s originally aimed at reforming the Roman Catholic church; resulted in the formation of Protestant churches (p. 46)

religious toleration Idea that people of different religions should live together in peace (p. 57)

Renaissance Great rebirth of learning and creativity in Europe that began during the 1300s (p. 24)

reparations Payments for economic injury exacted from a defeated enemy (p. 569)

republican women Women educated and trained to serve the United States as mothers, wives, and teachers in the early 1800s (p. 194)

Republican party Political party organized in the 1850s to oppose southern interests; gave rise to today's Republican party (p. 308)

reservation Land set aside by the federal government where Native Americans were forced to live after losing their homelands (p. 175)

Roosevelt Corollary Extension of the Monroe Doctrine by President Theodore Roosevelt whereby the United States would use force to prevent other foreign powers from intervening in the affairs of Western Hemisphere countries (p. 509)

Rosie the Riveter Fictional defense plant worker portrayed in government propaganda films and posters to attract women to the work force during World War II (p. 700)

S & L Savings and loan bank (p. 946)

sachem Leader of a Native American culture group (p. 60)

salutary neglect Great Britain's colonial policy of not interfering in colonial politics and economy as long as such neglect served Britain's economic interests (p. 74)

Sandinistas Marxist Nicaraguan revolutionaries who took control of the Nicaraguan government in 1979 (p. 947)

satellite nation Country controlled politically and economically by a powerful nation, especially by the Soviet Union during the cold war (p. 727)

scab Slang for a person hired to replace a striking worker (p. 406)

scalawag Southern white who became a Republican during Reconstruction to profit from unstable social conditions in that area (p. 372)

Scopes trial Tennessee trial of 1925 that challenged the law against teaching evolution in public schools (p. 601)

Scottsboro Boys Nine African American youths accused and unfairly tried and convicted of raping two white women in Alabama in 1931; gained national support and received new trials by order of the Supreme Court (p. 623)

secede Formally withdraw from a political organization; southern states seceded from the United States to form the Confederacy in late 1860 and early 1861 (p. 232)

secessionist Southerner who wanted the South to secede from the Union before the Civil War (p. 319)

Second Amendment Amendment to the Constitution that protects individuals' right to "keep and bear arms" (p. 995)

second American party system The political parties that developed out of the election of 1828; the National Republicans and Jacksonian Democrats (p. 228)

Second Great Awakening Wave of religious revivals in the United States during the early 1800s (p. 202)

section Region distinguished from others in United States geography by economic and cultural differences (p. 218)

secularize Transfer control from the church to the state (p. 278)

self-determination Freedom of a group of people to determine their own political status; proposed by President Wilson for ethnic groups in Austria-Hungary after World War I (p. 568)

separation of powers Constitutional provision that separates the powers of the federal government into legislative, executive, and judicial branches (p. 140)

17th parallel Latitude line established after World War II that divided North Vietnam from South Vietnam (p. 731)

sharecropper Farmer who grows crops on land owned by someone else and gives a share of the crops produced to the landowner in return for use of the land and supplies (p. 374)

shell Hollow cannon ball that explodes in the air or as it hits; developed during the Civil War (p. 327)

shuttle diplomacy Diplomatic negotiations conducted by an official mediator traveling frequently to the nations involved; used by Henry Kissinger in the 1970s to promote peace in the Middle East (p. 917)

siege Prolonged attack in which a city is surrounded and starved into surrender; used in the Civil War by General Ulysses S. Grant to capture Vicksburg, Mississippi (p. 344)

sit-down strike Work stoppage in which workers refuse to leave the premises until their demands are considered or met (p. 654)

sit-in Organized demonstration in which protesters seat themselves in segregated establishments to protest racial discrimination; became a common practice for many civil rights groups during the 1960s (p. 803)

Slave Power Name for the South used by opponents in the North before the Civil War (p. 308)

social Darwinism Application of Charles Darwin's "survival of the fittest" theory to human society; used by the great industrialists of the late 1800s to discourage government interference in business (p. 395)

social welfare program Government program that helps ensure a basic standard of living; includes unemployment, accident, and health insurance and social security programs (p. 524)

social contract Agreement between those who govern and those who are governed, defining the rights and limits of each (p. 110)

social gospel movement Social movement of the early 1900s that applied the Christian gospel to social problems (p. 462)

Social Security Act Legislation of 1935 that established a social welfare system funded by employee and worker contributions; included old-age pensions, survivor's benefits for victims of industrial accidents, and unemployment insurance (p. 646)

socialism The economic and political philosophy that advocates collective ownership of factories and property (p. 402)

socialist A person who advocates the principles of socialism (p. 627)

software Instructions or programs that tell a computer what to do (p. 1036)

sooner Person who settled land in the newly opened Indian Territory before it was officially made available in 1889 (p. 421)

Southern Christian Leadership Conference (SCLC) Civil rights organization founded in 1957 by Martin Luther King, Jr.; employed nonviolent means of protest and helped shift the focus of the civil rights movement to the South (p. 797)

speakeasy Establishment that illegally sold and served liquor during prohibition (p. 600)

speculation Undertaking risk on stocks or real estate for the chance of profit (p. 612)

speculator Person who buys large areas of land hoping to sell it later for a profit (p. 414)

sphere of influence Area of economic control exerted by a foreign power, especially in China during the late 1800s (p. 505)

spoils system Patronage system under President Andrew Jackson (p. 230)

Sputnik First artificial satellite to circle Earth; launched by the Soviet Union in 1957, beginning the space race (p. 759)

squatter Person occupying public land in order to gain title to it (p. 421)

stagflation Slow economic growth coupled with high rates of inflation and unemployment (p. 910)

Stamp Act British tax of 1765 requiring all printed materials in the American colonies to bear a stamp purchased from the government; sparked protests and a boycott of British goods (p. 103)

states' rights Theory that each state has the right to nullify acts of the federal government; advocated by 19th-century statesman John C. Calhoun to protect slavery and keep the North from gaining control of the federal government (p. 305)

steerage Large open area beneath a ship's deck where immigrants could travel cheaply but with few amenities (p. 448)

Strategic Arms Limitation Talks (SALT) Negotiations between the United States and the Soviet Union from 1971 to 1973 to limit offensive nuclear weapons (p. 896)

Strategic Arms Reduction Treaty (START) 1991 treaty between the United States and the Soviet Union that reduced the two nations' supply of long-range nuclear weapons (p. 951)

Strategic Defense Initiative (SDI) Satellite-operated defense system proposed by President Ronald Reagan in 1983; popularly called "Star Wars" (p. 940)

Student Nonviolent Coordinating Committee (SNCC) Student civil rights organization begun in 1960 to address the concerns of young African Americans; originally part of the Southern Christian Leadership Conference (p. 799)

Students for a Democratic Society (SDS) New Left political group organized in 1960 to work for radical change in United States society; heavily involved in Vietnam War protests (p. 858)

suburb Residential community on the outskirts of a city (p. 454)

suffrage The right to vote (p. 256)

supply-side economics Theory that the economy can be stimulated by increasing the availability of money for investments, achieved by reducing taxes on the rich; called "Reaganomics" in the 1980s (p. 938)

system of checks and balances United States system of government in which the power of each of the three branches of government is limited by that of the others (p. 141)

system of interchangeable parts System by which all parts of a product are made to an exact standard (p. 196)

Taft-Hartley Act Legislation of 1947 that allows a President to order striking workers in crucial industries back to work while the government investigates the dispute (p. 755)

Tammany Hall Political machine controlling New York City politics from the 1860s to the 1920s (p. 458)

tariff Tax on imports or exports (p. 157)

Tariff of Abominations Southern name for the Tariff of 1828, a high tax on imports that was intended to aid northern manufacturers (p. 232)

teach-in Extended lecture on a controversial issue; arose in the 1960s to protest the Vietnam War (p. 860)

Teapot Dome Scandal during the administration of President Warren G. Harding involving the lease of public oil reserves to private companies in exchange for illegal payments (p. 589)

telecommunications Electronically sending information over long distances (p. 1036)

televangelism Television broadcasts conducted by evangelists; often used to raise money and support for churches and political movements (p. 936)

temperance movement Campaign against alcohol consumption; began as part of the middle-class reform movements of the 1800s (p. 244)

tenant farmer Farmer who pays cash for rental of land (p. 374)

termination policy United States government policy of the 1950s to eliminate reservations and assimilate Native Americans into mainstream American life (p. 763)

Tet Offensive Attack by the Viet Cong in South Vietnam in 1968 during Tet, the Vietnamese lunar new year; turned the United States public against United States involvement in the Vietnam War (p. 853)

Thirteenth Amendment Constitutional amendment of 1865 outlawing slavery in the United States (p. 350)

Three-fifths Compromise Constitutional Convention agreement to count three fifths of a state's enslaved population when establishing state populations for representation in the House of Representatives (p. 139)

38th parallel Latitude line established after World War II that divided North Korea, which was allied with the Soviet Union, from South Korea, which was allied with the United States (p. 728)

Tories Majority party in the British Parliament during the American Revolution; also the name for American colonists still loyal to the crown (p. 115)

total war Warfare in which opponents attack civilians and the economic system of the enemy in addition to its soldiers (p. 345)

totalitarian Relating to a form of dictatorship or central government that has total control over all aspects of life and that suppresses all political and cultural expression of opposition (p. 719)

trade deficit Situation in which one country buys more products from another country than it sells to the other country (p. 1016)

trade surplus Situation in which one country sells more products to another country than it buys from the other country (p. 1017)

Trail of Tears Forced march of 15,000 Cherokee from their homes in the southeast to western reservations from 1837 to 1838 (p. 233)

Transcendentalism Intellectual and philosophical movement of the mid-1800s asserting that the nature of reality can be learned only by intuition rather than through experience (p. 243)

transcontinental railroad Railroad spanning North American continent; completed in 1869 (p. 388)

Treaty of Paris Agreement of 1783 that ended the War for Independence (p. 120)

Treaty of Ghent Agreement of 1814 that ended the War of 1812 (p. 179)

triangular trade Trade between the Americas, Europe, and Africa in the 1700s; supported New England economies (p. 77)

Truman Doctrine Cold war policy, established by President Harry S Truman, pledging United States support for "free peoples" resisting communism (p. 724)

trust Combination of companies that turn over their assets to a board of trustees to control prices and competition in a particular industry (p. 396)

Twenty-first Amendment Constitutional amendment of 1933 repealing the Eighteenth Amendment, thus ending prohibition (p. 627)

U-boat Submarine of the German navy; introduced during World War I (p. 555)

underground railroad Network of people who helped fugitives from slavery escape into the North and Canada (p. 252)

undocumented immigrants Immigrants living in the United States illegally (p. 985)

unicameral legislature Government having a single legislative house (p. 130)

Union United States of America as a national unit, especially during the Civil War; the North and its forces in the Civil War (p. 298)

United Farm Workers (UFW) Group organized in the early 1960s to help migratory farm workers gain better pay and working conditions (p. 832)

United Nations International organization formed in 1945 to promote peace, security, and economic development among nations (p. 723)

United States Sanitary Commission Northern women's group in the Civil War that provided aid to soldiers (p. 378)

utopian communities Small societies whose members seek perfect social and political conditions (p. 247)

vaudeville Theatrical performances of the late 1800s characterized by slapstick and song-and-dance routines (p. 473)

Versailles Treaty Agreement in 1919 ending World War I; included huge war reparations to be paid by Germany (p. 569)

vertical consolidation Control of all phases of a product's development, from raw materials to delivery of the finished products (p. 397)

veto Overturn a law or decision by using the constitutionally granted power of one branch of government to block legislation made by another; the President can veto a bill passed by Congress (p. 138)

Victorianism Moral ideas associated with Britain's Queen Victoria in the nineteenth century; characterized by strict moral codes (p. 475)

Viet Cong Communist guerrillas of South Vietnam during the Vietnam War (p. 851)

Vietnamization Nixon's Vietnam War policy to replace United States troops in Vietnam with South Vietnamese troops (p. 868)

Virginia Plan Constitutional Convention proposal for a federal government having a bicameral legislature with representation based on population (p. 138)

Volunteers in Service to America (VISTA) Federal program that sends volunteers to aid poor communities in the United States (p. 778)

Voting Rights Act of 1965 Legislation that gave the federal government the power to register voters in areas where local officials prevented African Americans from voting (p. 814)

WAC Women's Army Corps; organization of women who volunteered for military service in World War II; a member of the Women's Army Corps (p. 678)

Wagner Act National Labor Relations Act of 1935; legalized union practices such as collective bargaining and the closed shop and outlawed certain antiunion practices such as blacklisting (p. 646)

War for Independence War fought between American colonists and Great Britain from 1775 to 1783, resulting in an independent United States of America (p. 98)

war of attrition Warfare in which a weaker army inflicts small but continuous losses of soldiers and material that gradually add up to an unbearable burden for the enemy (p. 328)

Warsaw Pact Group of Eastern European nations that were allied with one another and with the Soviet Union on the communist side of the cold war (p. 1029)

Warren Commission Group headed by Chief Justice Earl Warren; formed to investigate President John Kennedy's assassination (p. 775)

Watergate Scandal of President Richard M. Nixon's administration that began in 1972 when leading Nixon supporters burglarized Democratic National Party Headquarters at the Watergate office building in Washington, D.C. (p. 897)

welfare capitalism Industrial policy of meeting workers' needs with increased pay and benefits for the purpose of preventing labor union organization (p. 611)

Whigs Name adopted by the National Republicans in the 1832 presidential election to oppose the Jacksonian Democrats; named after the 1700s British party opposed to the Tories (p. 231)

Whiskey Rebellion Pennsylvanian revolt against a whiskey tax in 1794; demonstrated that the federal government would use force to make citizens obey federal law (p. 159)

wildcat strike A workers' strike not authorized by their union (p. 695)

Wilmot Proviso Proposal of 1846 that slavery not be allowed in territory acquired from the Mexican War; defeated by Congress, but opened debate between the North and South on slavery in the western territories (p. 289)

woman question Wide-ranging debate of the early 1900s on the social role of women (p. 482)

Woodstock Rock music festival of 1969 that became a symbol of counterculture music and behavior (p. 865)

work ethic Idea that hard work will bring success (p. 1004)

World Wide Web A group of electronic documents and links that lead from one document to another (p. 1039)

writ of *habeas corpus* Court order requiring proof that a prisoner is being justly held (p. 334)

XYZ affair Incident of the late 1790s in which French secret agents demanded a bribe and a loan to France in lieu of negotiating a dispute over the Jay Treaty and other issues (p. 162)

yellow journalism Newspaper coverage that sensationalizes stories to increase circulation; inflamed anti-Spanish sentiment in the United States before and during the Spanish-American War (p. 474)

Zimmerman note Telegram intercepted from a German official proposing an alliance with Mexico and offering to help Mexico regain Texas, New Mexico, and Arizona if the United States entered World War I; increased pressure on the United States to enter the war (p. 557)

Biographical Dictionary

The Biographical Dictionary identifies key people listed in section previews. The page number at the end of each entry indicates the text page on which the name appears in boldface.

Pronunciations given here are based on those given in *Webster's Biographical Dictionary*. To determine the pronunciation of the symbols used, compare them with the following examples.

ā	fāte		ī	īce
ă	chăotic		ĭ	ĭll
â	câre		ĭ	dĭrect
ă	făt		ĸ	like *ch* in German *ich*
ă	ăccount		ō	ōld
ä	ärm		ŏ	ŏbey
à	àsk		ô	ôrb
à	sofà		ŏ	ŏdd
ē	ēve		oo	food
ē	ēvent		oŏ	foŏt
e	end		th	then
e	silent		ŭ	ŭp

´ accent

• syllable break

Adams, Abigail First Lady, 1797–1801; as the wife of Patriot John Adams, she urged him to promote women's rights at the beginning of the American Revolution (p. 113)

Adams, John Quincy Sixth President of the United States, 1825–1829; proposed greater federal involvement in the economy through tariffs and improvements such as roads, bridges, and canals (p. 226)

Adams, John Second President of the United States, 1797–1801; worked to relieve increasing tensions with France; lost reelection bid to Jefferson in 1800 as the country moved away from Federalist policies (p. 160)

Addams, Jane Cofounder of Hull House, the first settlement house, in 1889; remained active in social causes through the early 1900s (p. 463)

Agnew, Spiro Vice President under President Richard Nixon until forced to resign in 1973 for crimes committed before taking office; known for his harsh campaign attacks (p. 883)

Allen, Richard African American religious leader; founded the African Methodist Episcopal Church (AME) in 1816 (p. 204)

Arthur, Chester A. Twenty-first President of the United States,

1881–1885; signed 1883 Pendleton Act, which instituted the Civil Service (p. 444)

Askia Muhammad (ăsk´ē•à moo•häm´ măd) Ruler of the African empire of Songhai, 1493–1528; promoted Islamic culture (p. 28)

Austin, Stephen Leader of first American group of Texas settlers in 1822; worked for Texan independence (p. 279)

Stephen Austin

Bakke, Alan Student who won a suit against the University of California in 1978 on the grounds that the affirmative action program had kept him out (p. 927)

Baldwin, James African American author and spokesperson for the civil rights movement during the 1960s (p. 815)

Banks, Dennis Native American leader in 1960s and 1970s; helped organize American Indian Movement (AIM) and the 1973 Wounded Knee occupation (p. 836)

Beecher, Catharine Author whose 1841 book *Treatise on Domestic Economy* supported the cult of domesticity (p. 256)

Beecher, Lyman Revivalist during the Second Great Awakening; feared the rise of individualism in the United States (p. 243)

Begin, Menachem (bě•gēn´, mä•nä´hěm) Israeli leader during the 1970s; began the Middle East peace process by reaching the 1978 Camp David Accords with Egypt (p. 918)

Bell, Alexander Graham Inventor; developed the telephone in 1876; one of the founders of American Telephone & Telegraph (AT&T) in 1884 (p. 390)

Bellamy, Edward Author of the novel *Looking Backward* (1888), which proposed nationalizing trusts to eliminate social problems (p. 522)

Bethune, Mary McLeod African American educator, New Deal worker; founded Bethune Cookman College in the 1920s, advised the National Youth Administration (p. 644)

Beveridge, Albert J. Indiana senator in the early 1900s; saw United States imperialism as a duty owed to "primitive" societies (p. 499)

Booth, John Wilkes Southern actor who assassinated President Abraham Lincoln in 1865 (p. 350)

Brady, James Press Secretary to President Reagan who was paralyzed by a gunshot during a 1981 assassination attempt; the 1994 law requiring a five-day waiting period before purchase of a gun was named for Mr. Brady. (p. 996)

Breckinridge, John C. Presidential candidate of the southern wing of the Democratic party in 1860 (p. 318)

Brown, John Abolitionist crusader who massacred proslavery settlers in Kansas before the Civil War; hoped to inspire slave revolt with 1859 attack on Virginia arsenal; executed for treason against the state of Virginia (p. 311)

Bryan, William Jennings Advocate of silver standard and proponent of Democratic and Populist views from the 1890s through the 1910s; Democratic candidate for President in 1896, 1900, and 1908 (p. 432)

Buchanan, James Fifteenth President of the United States, 1857–1861; supported by the South; attempted to moderate fierce disagreement over expansion of slavery (p. 309)

Bush, George H. W. Forty-first President of the United States, 1989–1993; continued Reagan's conservative policies; brought together United Nations coalition to fight the Persian Gulf War (p. 949)

Byrd, William Wealthy plantation owner in colonial Virginia whose diary gives a vivid picture of colonial life (p. 80)

Calhoun, John C. Statesman from South Carolina who held many offices in the federal government; supported slavery, cotton exports, states' rights; in 1850 foresaw future conflicts over slavery (p. 226)

Carnegie, Andrew Industrialist who made a fortune in steel in the late 1800s through vertical consolidation; as a philanthropist, he gave away over $350 million (p. 393)

Carson, Rachel Marine biologist, author of *Silent Spring* (1962), which exposed harmful effects of pesticides and inspired concern for the environment (p. 841)

Carter, James Earl, Jr. Thirty-ninth President of the United States, 1977–1981; advocated concern for human rights in foreign policy; assisted in mediating the Camp David Accords (p. 913)

Castro, Fidel (käs′trō, fē•thĕl′) Revolutionary leader who took control of Cuba in 1959; ally of Soviet Union through the 1980s (p. 732)

Catt, Carrie Chapman Woman suffrage leader in the early 1900s; helped secure passage of Nineteenth Amendment in 1920; headed National American Woman Suffrage Association (p. 541)

Champlain, Samuel de French explorer who founded the city of Quebec in 1608 (p. 54)

Christopher Columbus

Chávez, César (chä′vāz, sā′sär) Latino leader from 1962 to his death in 1993; organized the United Farm Workers (UFW) to help migratory farm workers gain better pay and working conditions (p. 832)

Churchill, Winston Leader of Great Britain before and during World War II; powerful speechmaker who rallied Allied morale during the war (p. 668)

Clark, William Leader, with Meriwether Lewis, of expedition through the West in 1804; brought back scientific samples, maps, and information on Native Americans (p. 272)

Clay, Henry Senator from Kentucky; accused by Jackson of giving votes to John Q. Adams in return for post as secretary of state; endorsed the American

System to promote economic growth; advocate of Compromise of 1850 (p. 227)

Cleveland, Grover Twenty-second and twenty-fourth President of the United States, 1885–1889, 1893–1897; supported railroad regulation and a return to the gold standard (p. 445)

Clinton, Bill Forty-second President of the United States, 1993–; defeated George Bush after overcoming numerous political obstacles; advocated economic and health-care reform (p. 960)

Columbus, Christopher Explorer whose voyage for Spain to North America in 1492 opened the Atlantic World (p. 31)

Coolidge, Calvin Thirtieth President of the United States, 1923–1929; promoted big business and opposed social aid (p. 589)

Coughlin, Father Charles E. "Radio Priest" who supported and then attacked President Franklin Roosevelt's New Deal; prevented by the Catholic church from broadcasting after he praised Hitler (p. 650)

Coxey, Jacob S. Populist who led Coxey's Army in a march on Washington, D.C., in 1894 to seek government jobs for the unemployed (p. 446)

Custer, George Armstrong General who directed army attacks against Native Americans in the 1870s; commanded army forces killed in 1876 at Little Bighorn in Montana (p. 419)

Davis, Jefferson President of the Confederate States of America; ordered attack on Fort Sumter, the first battle of the Civil War (p. 320)

Dewey, George Officer in United States Navy, 1861–1917; led a surprise attack in the Philippines during the Spanish-American War that destroyed the entire Spanish fleet (p. 502)

Dinh Diem, Ngo (dĭn′zē′ĕm, nō′) Leader of South Vietnam, 1954–1963; supported by United States, but not by Vietnamese Buddhist majority; assassinated in 1963 (p. 850)

Dix, Dorothea Advocate of prison reform and of special institutions for the insane in Massachusetts before the Civil War (p. 246)

Dole, Robert Senator from Kansas, 1969–1996; challenged Bill Clinton for the Presidency in 1996 (p. 964)

Douglas, Stephen Illinois senator who introduced the Kansas-Nebraska Act, which allowed new territories to choose their own position on slavery; debated Abraham Lincoln on slavery issues in 1858 (p. 307)

Douglass, Frederick African American abolitionist leader who spoke eloquently for abolition in the United States and Britain before the Civil War (p. 251)

Du Bois, W.E.B. (dōō•bois′) African American scholar and leader in early 1900s; encouraged African Americans to attend colleges to develop leadership skills (p. 471)

Edison, Thomas A. Inventor; developed the light bulb, the phonograph, and hundreds of other inventions in the late 1800s and early 1900s (p. 387)

Ehrlichman, John Adviser on domestic policy to President Richard Nixon; deeply involved in Watergate (p. 887)

Einstein, Albert Physicist whose theory of relativity led to harnessing nuclear energy; proposed development of the atomic bomb in 1939 (p. 682)

Eisenhower, Dwight D. Thirty-fourth President of the United States, 1953–1961; leader of Allied forces in World War II; as

President, he promoted business and continued social programs (p. 673)

Eliot, T. S. Poet; his work "The Waste Land" described the struggle of youth in the 1920s (p. 603)

Ellsberg, Daniel Defense Department official; leaked Pentagon Papers to the *New York Times* in 1971, showing government lies to public about Vietnam (p. 897)

Father Divine African American minister; his Harlem soup kitchens fed the hungry during the Great Depression (p. 622)

Fillmore, Millard Thirteenth President of the United States, 1850–1853; promoted the Compromise of 1850 to smooth over disagreements about slavery in new territories (p. 304)

Finney, Charles Grandison Revivalist during the Second Great Awakening; emphasized religious conversion and personal choice (p. 243)

Fitzgerald, F. Scott Novelist who depicted the United States and the world during the 1920s in novels such as *The Great Gatsby* (p. 603)

Fitzhugh, George Southern author who criticized northern industrialists for exploiting workers in his 1857 book *Cannibals All!* (p. 300)

Ford, Gerald R. Thirty-eighth President of the United States, 1974–1977; succeeded and pardoned Nixon; failed to establish strong leadership (p. 908)

Ford, Henry Manufacturer from the 1910s through the 1940s; made affordable cars for the masses using assembly line and other production techniques (p. 598)

Franklin, Benjamin Colonial inventor, printer, writer, statesman; contributed to the Declaration of Independence and the Constitution (p. 80)

Frémont, John C. Explorer, military officer, and politician; led United States troops in 1846 Bear Flag Revolt when the United States took California from Mexico; ran for President as a Republican in 1856 (p. 287)

Friedan, Betty Feminist author; criticized limited roles for women in her 1963 book *The Feminine Mystique* (p. 750)

Garfield, James A. Twentieth President of the United States, 1881; his assassination by a disappointed office seeker led to the reform of the spoils system (p. 444)

Garrison, William Lloyd White leader of radical abolition movement based in Boston; founded *The Liberator* in 1831 to work for an immediate end to slavery (p. 250)

Garvey, Marcus African American leader from 1919 to 1926 who urged African Americans to return to "motherland" of Africa; provided early inspiration for "black pride" movements (p. 589)

George III King of England during American Revolution (p. 102)

George, Henry Author of *Progress and Poverty* (1879) linking land

Mikhail Gorbachev with Ronald Reagan

speculation and poverty; proposed a single tax based on land value (p. 522)

Gingrich, Newt Representative from Georgia, 1979–; called on Republican congressional candidates in 1994 elections to endorse "Contract with America" (p. 963)

Gorbachev, Mikhail (gôr′bǎ•chěv, myǐ•кǔ•ēl′) Soviet leader whose bold reforms led to the breakup of the Soviet Union in the late 1980s (p. 1029)

Gore, Al Senator from Tennessee; Vice President under President Bill Clinton, 1993– (p. 961)

Grant, Ulysses S. Eighteenth President of the United States, 1869–1877; commander of Union forces who accepted Lee's surrender in 1865 (p. 329)

Haldeman, H. R. Chief of staff under President Richard Nixon; deeply involved in Watergate (p. 887)

Hamilton, Alexander Officer in the War for Independence: delegate to the Constitutional Convention; Federalist and first secretary of treasury (p. 149)

Handsome Lake Leader of Seneca in late 1700s; encouraged return to Native American traditions (p. 175)

Harding, Warren G. Twenty-ninth President of the United States, 1921–1923; presided over a short administration marked by corruption (p. 589)

Harrington, Michael Author; wrote *The Other America* in 1962, which described areas of poverty in the otherwise prosperous United States (p. 1010)

Harrison, Benjamin Twenty-third President of the United States, 1889–1893; signed 1890 Sherman Antitrust Act later used to regulate big business (p. 446)

Harrison, William Henry Ninth President of the United States, 1841; died of pneumonia after only a month in office (p. 233)

Hayes, Rutherford B. Nineteenth President of the United States, 1877–1881; promised to withdraw Union troops from the South in order to end dispute over his election; attacked spoils system (p. 376)

Hearst, William Randolph Newspaper publisher from 1887 until his death in 1951; used "yellow journalism" in the 1890s to stir up sentiment in favor of the Spanish-American War (p. 501)

Hiss, Alger Former State Department official investigated as a possible communist spy by House Un-American Activities Committee after World War II; convicted of perjury in 1950 (p. 735)

Hitler, Adolf German leader of National Socialist (Nazi) party 1933–1945; rose to power by promoting racist and nationalist views (p. 665)

Ho Chi Minh (hō′ chē′ mǐn′) Leader of the Communist party in Indochina after World War II; led Vietnamese against the French, then North Vietnamese against the United States in the Vietnam War (p. 730)

Hollerith, Herman 1890 census agent who devised a machine that used punch cards to tabulate data (p. 1038)

Hoover, Herbert Thirty-first President of the United States, 1929–1933; worked to aid Europeans during World War I; responded ineffectively to 1929 stock market crash and Great Depression (p. 590)

Houston, Sam Leader of Texas troops in war for independence from Mexico in 1836; elected first governor of independent Texas (p. 280)

Humphrey, Hubert Democratic presidential candidate in 1968; lost narrowly to Nixon in an election bid hurt by support for the Vietnam War and by third-party candidate George Wallace (p. 882)

Isabella Ruler of Spanish Christian kingdoms with Ferdinand in late 1400s; sponsored Columbus's voyage to North America (p. 26)

Jackson, Andrew Seventh President of the United States, 1829–1837; supported minimal government and the spoils system; vetoed rechartering of the national bank; pursued harsh policy toward Native Americans (p. 178)

Jackson, Stonewall Confederate general known for his swift strikes against Union forces; earned nickname Stonewall by holding his forces steady under extreme pressure at the First Battle of Manassas (p. 327)

Jefferson, Thomas Third President of the United States, 1801–1809; main author of the Declaration of Independence; a firm believer in the people and decentralized power; reduced the federal government (p. 110)

Chief Joseph

Johnson, Andrew Seventeenth President of the United States, 1865–1869; clashed with Radical Republicans on Reconstruction programs; was impeached, then acquitted, in 1868 (p. 367)

Johnson, Lyndon B. Thirty-sixth President of the United States, 1963–1969; expanded social assistance with his Great Society program; increased United States commitment during Vietnam War (p. 777)

Joseph, Chief Leader of Nez Percé; forced to give up his home by United States army, fled toward Canada; captured in 1877 (p. 420)

Kamiakin Yakima chief who led Native Americans in 1855 war against Northwest settlers (p. 291)

Kelley, Florence Progressive reformer active from 1886 to 1920; worked in state and federal government for laws on child labor, workplace safety, and consumer protection (p. 525)

Kennedy, John F. Thirty-fifth President of the United States, 1961–1963; seen as youthful and inspiring; known for his firm handling of the Cuban missile crisis; assassinated in 1963 (p. 772)

Kennedy, Robert F. Attorney general under his brother, President John Kennedy, in the early 1960s; supported civil rights; assassinated while running for President in 1968 (p. 881)

Keynes, John Maynard British economist who believed that government spending could help a faltering economy; his theories helped shape New Deal legislation (p. 630)

Khomeini, Ayatollah Ruholla (kō•mā′nē, ĭ•yä′tŏl′lä rōō•hŏl′lä) Islamic fundamentalist leader of Iran after the 1979 overthrow of the Shah; approved holding of American hostages (p. 920)

King, Martin Luther, Jr. African American civil rights leader from the mid-1950s until his assassination in 1968; used nonviolent means such as marches, boycotts, and legal challenges to win civil rights (p. 762)

Kissinger, Henry Secretary of state under Presidents Richard Nixon and Gerald Ford; used *realpolitik* to open relations with China, to end the Vietnam War, and to moderate Middle East conflict (p. 887)

Khrushchev, Nikita (krōōsh′chôf, nyǐ•kyē′tǚ) Soviet leader from 1953 to 1964; opposed President Kennedy in the Cuban missile crisis (p. 787)

Lafayette, Marquis de (lä′fi•ĕt′, mär•ke′dě′) French officer who assisted American forces in the War for Independence (p. 119)

Lee, Jason First Methodist missionary to Oregon Country in 1834; built a mission school in Willamette Valley (p. 281)

Lee, Robert E. Brilliant general of Confederate forces during the Civil War (p. 331)

Lenin, Vladimir I. Revolutionary leader in Russia; established a communist government in 1917 (p. 580)

Levitt, William J. Built new communities in the suburbs after World War II, using mass-production techniques (p. 745)

Lewis, John L. Head of United Mine Workers through World War II; used strikes during the war to win pay raises (p. 695)

Lewis, Meriwether Leader with William Clark of expedition through the West in 1804; brought back scientific samples, maps, and information on Native Americans (p. 272)

Lincoln, Abraham Sixteenth President of the United States, 1861–1865; known for his effective leadership during the Civil War and his Emancipation Proclamation declaring the end of slavery in Confederate-held territory (p. 314)

Lindbergh, Charles A. Aviator who became an international hero when he made the first solo flight across the Atlantic Ocean in 1927 (p. 597)

Little Turtle Native American leader of the late 1700s; adopted policy of accommodation (p. 174)

Lodge, Henry Cabot Massachusetts senator of early 1900s; supported United States imperialism (p. 499)

Long, Huey Louisiana politician in 1930s called the Kingfish; suggested redistributing large fortunes by means of grants to families; assassinated in 1935 (p. 650)

Low, Juliette Founder of American Girl Scouts in 1912 (p. 517)

MacArthur, Douglas United States general during World War II and Korean War; forced to resign by Truman in 1951 (p. 671)

Madison, James Fourth President of the United States, 1809–1817; called the Father of the Constitution for his leadership at the Constitutional Convention (p. 136)

Mahan, Alfred T. Author who argued in 1890 that the economic future of the United States rested on new overseas markets protected by a larger navy (p. 498)

Malcolm X African American leader during the 1950s and 1960s; eloquent spokesperson for African American self-sufficiency; assassinated in 1965 (p. 816)

Mann, Horace School reformer and supporter of public education before the Civil War; devised an educational system in Massachusetts later copied by many states (p. 245)

Mao Zedong (mou′ dzǔ′ dŏŏng′) Leader of communists who took over China in 1949; remained in power until his death in 1976 (p. 725)

Marshall, George C. Secretary of state under President Harry Truman; assisted economic recovery in Europe after World War II and established strong allies for the United States through his Marshall Plan (p. 724)

Marshall, John Chief Justice of the Supreme Court appointed by John Adams; set precedents that established vital powers of the federal courts (p. 168)

Marshall, Thurgood First African American Supreme Court justice; as a lawyer, won landmark school desegregation case *Brown* v. *Board of Education* in 1954 (p. 762)

McCarthy, Eugene Candidate in the 1968 Democratic presidential race who opposed the Vietnam War; convinced President Lyndon Johnson not to run again through his strong showing in the primaries (p. 881)

McCarthy, Joseph R. Republican senator from Wisconsin in the late 1940s and early 1950s; led a crusade to investigate officials he claimed were communists; discredited in 1954 (p. 735)

McClellan, George Early Union army leader in the Civil War; careful organizer and planner who moved too slowly for northern politicians; ran against President Abraham Lincoln in the election of 1864 (p. 329)

McKinley, William Twenty-fifth President of the United States, 1897–1901; supported tariffs and a gold standard; expanded the United States by waging the Spanish-American War (p. 447)

Meade, George G. Union commander at Battle of Gettysburg in 1863; defended the high ground and forced Confederate army to attack, causing great casualties (p. 343)

Means, Russell Native American leader of 1960s and 1970s; helped organize American Indian Movement (AIM) and 1973 Wounded Knee occupation (p. 839)

Metacom Leader of Pokanokets in Massachusetts; also known by his English name, King Philip; led Native Americans in King Philip's War, 1675–1676 (p. 60)

Mitchell, John Attorney general under President Richard Nixon; deeply involved in Watergate scandal (p. 887)

Mohammad Reza Pahlavi, Shah Leader of Iran, from 1941 until his overthrow in 1979; supported by the United States; brought modernization to his country along with repression and corruption (p. 920)

Monroe, James Fifth President of the United States, 1817–1825; acquired Florida from Spain; declared Monroe Doctrine to keep foreign powers out of the Americas (p. 226)

Morse, Samuel F. B. Artist and inventor; developed telegraph and Morse code in the 1830s (p. 264)

Mott, Lucretia Women's rights leader; helped organize first women's convention in Seneca Falls, New York, in 1848 (p. 259)

Mussolini, Benito (moo͞'sô•le͞'ne͞, ba͞•ne͞'tö) Italian fascist leader from 1925 through 1945; called *Il Duce* — "the leader"; known for his brutal policies (p. 664)

Nader, Ralph Consumer advocate; published *Unsafe at Any Speed* in 1965 criticizing auto safety and inspiring new safety laws (p. 843)

Nimitz, Chester Leader of United States troops in World War II battle of Midway Island, during which much of the Japanese navy was destroyed (p. 673)

Nixon, Richard M. Thirty-seventh President, 1969–1974; known for his foreign policy toward the Soviet Union and China and for illegal acts he committed in the Watergate affair that forced his resignation (p. 756)

O'Connor, Sandra Day First woman Supreme Court justice; appointed by Reagan in 1981 (p. 946)

Oppenheimer, J. Robert Physicist; headed Manhattan Project in World War II to develop first atomic bomb (p. 683)

Paine, Thomas Author of political pamphlets during 1770s and 1780s; wrote *Common Sense* in 1776 (p. 109)

Paul, Alice Woman suffrage leader of early 1900s; her Congressional Union used aggressive tactics to push the Nineteenth Amendment (p. 541)

Penn, William English Quaker who founded the colony of Pennsylvania in 1681 (p. 987)

Perkins, Frances Secretary of labor 1933–1945 under President Franklin Delano Roosevelt; first woman cabinet member (p. 643)

Sandra Day O'Connor

Perot, H. Ross Billionaire businessman who challenged Bill Clinton and George Bush for the Presidency in 1992; strong opponent of NAFTA (p. 961)

Pierce, Franklin Fourteenth President of the United States, 1853–1857; signed the Kansas-Nebraska Act, which renewed conflicts over slavery in the territories (p. 306)

Pinckney, Eliza Lucas South Carolina plantation manager in the 1740s; promoted indigo as a staple crop (p. 82)

Polk, James K. Eleventh President of the United States, 1845–1849; led expansion of United States to southwest through war against Mexico (p. 286)

Polo, Marco Venetian traveler to China in the late 1200s; his book about the journey helped make Europeans aware of trade opportunities in eastern Asia (p. 23)

Popé (pō•pā') Medicine man who led Pueblos and Apaches against Spanish rule in the Revolt of 1680 (p. 44)

Powhatan Native American leader of Pamunkey people in Chesapeake Bay region of Virginia in late 1500s and early 1600s (p. 48)

Prosser, Gabriel Led a slave revolt in Virginia in 1800; captured and executed after revolt failed (p. 163)

Pulitzer, Joseph Early 1900s newspaper publisher; used "yellow journalism" to stir up public sentiment in favor of the Spanish-American War (p. 501)

Randolph, A. Philip Civil rights activist from the 1930s to the 1950s; planned the Washington march that pressured President Franklin Delano Roosevelt into opening World War II defense jobs to African Americans (p. 708)

Jackie Robinson

Reagan, Ronald Fortieth President of the United States, 1981–1989; popular conservative leader who promoted supply-side economics and created huge budget deficits (p. 934)

Robinson, Jackie Athlete who in 1947 became the first African American to play baseball in the major leagues (p. 760)

Rockefeller, Nelson Vice President appointed by President Gerald Ford in 1974; the nation's only nonelected Vice President to serve with a non-elected President (p. 909)

Roosevelt, Eleanor First Lady 1933–1945; tireless worker for social causes, including women's rights and civil rights for African Americans and other groups (p. 631)

Roosevelt, Franklin D. Thirty-second President of the United States, 1933–1945; fought the Great Depression through his New Deal social programs; battled Congress over Supreme Court control; proved a strong leader during World War II (p. 631)

Roosevelt, Theodore Twenty-sixth President of the United States, 1901–1909; fought trusts, aided progressive reforms, built Panama Canal, and increased United States influence overseas (p. 507)

Rosenberg, Julius and Ethel Husband and wife convicted and executed in 1953 for passing atomic secrets to the Soviet Union; their guilt is still debated (p. 735)

Rowson, Susanna Haswell Author of *Charlotte Temple* (1794), a popular moralizing novel that encouraged women to look beyond appearances when choosing a husband (p. 199)

Sacajawea (săk´å•jå•wē•å) Shoshone woman who served as guide and translator for Lewis and Clark on their exploratory journey through the West in the early 1800s (p. 272)

Sacco, Nicola (säk´kō, nĕ•kō´lä) Immigrant and anarchist executed for a 1920 murder at a Massachusetts factory, though believed to be innocent by many (p. 582)

Sadat, Anwar el- (så•dat´, ăn•wär´ ĕl) Egyptian leader in the 1970s; began the Middle East peace process by reaching the 1978 Camp David Accords with Egypt (p. 918)

Salinger, J. D. Author of 1951 novel *The Catcher in the Rye*, which criticized 1950s pressure to conform (p. 751)

Santa Anna, Antonio López de Mexican dictator who led government and troops in war against Texas; won the battle of the Alamo (p. 279)

Schlafly, Phyllis Conservative activist; led campaign during the 1960s and 1970s to block the Equal Rights Amendment (p. 829)

Seward, William Henry Republican antislavery leader during the 1860s; acquired Alaska in 1867 as secretary of state (p. 318)

Sheridan, Philip Union general in the Civil War who worked with Grant to cut off the retreat of Confederate forces after the fall of Richmond in 1865 (p. 350)

Sherman, William Tecumseh Union general in the Civil War; known for his destructive march from Atlanta to Savannah in 1864 (p. 342)

Sirica, John J. Washington judge who presided over the Watergate investigation in the 1970s; gave tough sentences to convicted participants and ordered President Richard Nixon to release secret tapes (p. 899)

Sitting Bull Chief Leader of Sioux in clashes with United States Army in Black Hills in 1870s (p. 419)

Slater, Samuel English textile worker who brought the Industrial Revolution to the United States in 1789 by duplicating British textile machinery from memory (p. 195)

Smith, John Leader of the Jamestown, Virginia, colony in the early 1600s (p. 49)

Smith, Joseph Founder of Church of Jesus Christ of Latter-day Saints, or Mormons, in New York in 1830; killed by a mob in Illinois in 1844 (p. 289)

Spock, Benjamin Pediatrician and author of *Common Sense Book of Baby and Child Care* (1946), which encouraged mothers to stay home with their children rather than work (p. 750)

Stalin, Joseph Leader of the Soviet Union from 1924–1953; worked with Roosevelt and Churchill during World War II but afterwards became an aggressive participant in the cold war (p. 674)

Stanton, Elizabeth Cady Women's rights leader in the 1800s; helped organize first women's convention; wrote the *Declaration of Sentiments* on women's rights in 1848 (p. 259)

Starr, Ellen Gates Cofounder of Chicago's Hull House, the first settlement house, in 1889 (p. 463)

Steinem, Gloria Journalist, women's rights leader since 1960s; founded *Ms.* magazine in 1972 to cover women's issues (p. 827)

Stevenson, Adlai Senator from Illinois and Democratic candidate for President in 1952 and 1956 against Eisenhower (p. 756)

Stowe, Harriet Beecher Author of the novel *Uncle Tom's Cabin* (1852), which contributed significantly to antisouthern feelings among northerners before the Civil War (p. 299)

Sumner, Charles Abolitionist and senator from Massachusetts; beaten badly in the Senate by a southern congressman after making an antislavery speech (p. 311)

Taft, William Howard Twenty-seventh President of the United States, 1909–1913; continued progressive reforms of President Theodore Roosevelt; promoted "dollar diplomacy" to expand foreign investments (p. 511)

Taney, Roger Chief Justice of the Supreme Court who wrote an opinion in the 1857 *Dred Scott* case that declared the Missouri Compromise unconstitutional (p. 313)

Taylor, Zachary Twelfth President of the United States, 1849–1850; tried to avoid slavery issues (p. 287)

Tecumseh Native American leader in the late 1700s and early 1800s; led a pan-Indian movement that tried to unite several groups despite their differences (p. 176)

Tenskwatawa (tĕn•skwä´tä•wä) Native American leader of the late 1700s known as the Prophet; he called for a return to traditional ways and rejection of white values (p. 175)

Thomas, Clarence Conservative African American Supreme Court justice appointed in 1991; during his confirmation hearings he was charged with sexual harassment (p. 952)

Thomas, Norman Socialist party leader and candidate for President in the 1920 and 1930s; won 2 percent of the vote in 1932 (p. 627)

Thoreau, Henry David Transcendentalist author known for his work *Walden* (1854) and other writings (p. 243)

Travis, William Leader in Texas's bid for independence from Mexico in 1836; died at the Alamo after appealing to the United States for help (p. 279)

Truman, Harry S Thirty-third President of the United States, 1945–1953; authorized use of atomic bomb; signed Marshall Plan to rebuild Europe (p. 684)

Truth, Sojourner Abolitionist and women's rights advocate before the Civil War; as a formerly enslaved person, she spoke effectively and authentically to white audiences on abolition issues (p. 260)

Tubman, Harriet "Conductor" on the underground railroad that helped enslaved persons escape to freedom before the Civil War (p. 252)

Turner, Frederick Jackson Historian who wrote an essay in 1893 emphasizing the western frontier as a powerful force in the formation of the American character (p. 434)

Sojourner Truth

Turner, Nat African American preacher who led a slave revolt in 1831; captured and hanged after the revolt failed (p. 224)

Tweed, William Marcy Boss of Tammany Hall political machine in New York City; convicted of forgery and larceny in 1873 and died in jail in 1878 (p. 458)

Tyler, John Tenth President of the United States, 1841–1845; accomplished little due to quarrels between Whigs and Jacksonian Democrats (p. 233)

Van Buren, Martin Eighth President of the United States, 1837–1841; Jacksonian Democrat; was voted out of the executive office after the Panic of 1837 brought widespread unemployment and poverty (p. 233)

Vance, Cyrus Secretary of state under President Jimmy Carter; invited Israelis and Egyptians to Camp David in 1978 to begin Middle East peace process (p. 918)

Vanzetti, Bartolomeo (văn•zĕt´ĭ, bär´tō•lōmâ´ō) Immigrant and anarchist executed for a 1920 murder at a Massachusetts factory, though believed to be innocent by many (p. 582)

Vesey, Denmark African American who planned 1822 South Carolina slave revolt; captured and hanged after revolt failed (p. 224)

von Steuben, Baron Prussian officer who trained Washington's troops in the winter at Valley Forge (p. 119)

Walker, David African American author of *Appeal to the Colored Citizens of the World* (1829), which called for an immediate end to slavery (p. 250)

Walker, Madam C. J. African American leader and businesswoman in the early 1900s; she spoke out against lynching (p. 480)

Wallace, George C. Third-party candidate for President in 1968; focused his campaign on issues of blue-collar anger in the North and racial tension (p. 883)

Warren, Earl Chief Justice of Supreme Court 1953–1968; led in many decisions that protected civil rights, rights of the accused, and right to privacy (p. 775)

Washington, Booker T. African American leader from the late 1800s until his death in 1915; founded Tuskegee Institute in Alabama; encouraged African Americans to learn trades (p. 471)

Washington, George First President of the United States, 1789–1797; led American forces in the War for Independence; set several federal precedents, including the two-term maximum for presidential office (p. 99)

Webster, Noah Author of the best-known American dictionary in the early 1800s; promoted a standard national language and public support for education (p. 194)

Whitman, Narcissa Prentiss Missionary; one of the first white women to cross the Rocky Mountains to Oregon in 1836; killed in 1847 in violence between whites and Native Americans (p. 281)

Whitney, Eli Inventor; developed the cotton gin in 1793, which rapidly increased cotton production in the South and led to a greater need for slave labor (p. 195)

Wilhelm, Kaiser (vĭl´hĕlm, kī´zêr) Emperor of Germany during World War I; symbol to the United States of German militarism and severe efficiency (p. 552)

Wilson, Pete Governor of California 1991– who, in 1994, declared a state of emergency in his state caused by money spent on illegal immigrants (p. 989)

Wilson, Woodrow Twenty-eighth President of the United States, 1913–1921; tried to keep the United States out of World War I; proposed League of Nations (p. 535)

Yeltsin, Boris (yĕlt´sĭn, bŭ•ryēs´) Leader of Russia in late 1980s and early 1990s; took over from Mikhail Gorbachev as reforms continued and Communist party control ended (p. 966)

Young, Brigham Mormon leader who supervised migration to Utah beginning in the 1840s; first governor when Utah became a United States territory (p. 289)

Index

Entries with a page number followed by a *c* indicate a chart or graph on that page; *m* indicates a map; and *p* indicates a picture.

The following index is designed as an at-a-glance topical reference. It combines appropriate **Student Edition** entries with **Teacher's Edition** activities and **In-depth** notes. It also lists the appropriate **Teaching Resources** folders. Page numbers refer to your Teacher's Edition page and the Teaching Resources folder. For example, 154; ALP 69; U2:32 means Teacher's Edition, page 154; Alternate Lesson Plan, page 69; Unit 2 folder, page 32.

Abbreviations Key

- ◆ **ALP= Alternate Lesson Plan**
- ◆ **LH = Local History**
- ◆ **TT = Teacher-to-Teacher Activity Network**
- ◆ **UI = Using the Internet**
- ◆ **U = Unit**

INDEX

INDEX

Acknowledgments

Cover Design Martucci Studio, Alison Anholt-White, and Bruce Bond

Front Cover Engraving "The Brooklyn Bridge," engraving by the Shugg Brothers after the original by R. Schwartz, 1883. Museum of the City of New York.

Back Cover Photo Richard Falco/Black Star

Book Design DECODE, Inc.

Epilogue and Prologue Design Paul Gagnon and Alan Lee

Picture Research Pembroke Herbert and Sandi Rygiel/Picture Research Consultants, Inc.

Time & Place Contributing Writers Carol Barrett, Department of Geography, University of Wisconsin at River Falls, River Falls, WI; Tom Baerwald, Program Director of Geography and Regional Science, National Science Foundation, Washington, D.C.; Peter Hugill, Department of Geography, Texas A&M University, College Station, TX

Maps

GEO Systems, A Unit of R.R. Donnelly & Sons, Co.: 70, 173, 250, 255, 280, 283, 287, 329, 331, 351, 497, 506, 509, 513, 543, 551, 562, 570, 643, 834, 1006, 1010, 1011, 1013, 1014-1015, 1016-1017

Horizon Design/Sanderson Associates: 16, 20, 29, 41, 42, 50, 62, 77, 78, 93, 99, 103, 118, 181, 191, 192, 197, 312, 320, 368, 375, 376, 389, 392, 419, 427, 431, 457, 502, 510, 515, 530, 587, 619, 633, 666, 667, 671, 672, 711, 720, 726, 729, 731, 732, 753, 787, 791,805, 815, 889, 914, 947, 968, 969

Illustration

Peter Brooks: 104-105,900

Function Thru Form: 34, 88, 129, 140, 171, 187, 220, 242, 244, 246, 265, 396, 398,406, 422, 434, 443, 469, 470, 479, 498, 552, 581, 596, 602, 612, 615, 616, 617, 654, 694, 695, 696, 702, 704, 745, 750, 774, 779, 780, 812, 825, 828, 888, 911, 937, 940, 943, 950, 963, 973, 976, 1007, 1008-1009, 1012, 1013, 1018

Paul Gagnon: 34, 67, 76, 76, 95, 123, 147, 153, 158, 183, 207, 228, 229, 237, 269, 291, 293, 304, 309, 323, 328, 355, 370, 381, 411, 439, 459, 465, 478, 489, 501, 519, 528, 531, 536, 538, 547, 573, 605, 637, 659, 689, 713, 739, 767, 793, 813, 821, 845, 847, 905, 931, 953, 964, 971, 977, 979

Matthew Pippin: 17, 24, 196, 219, 343, 391, 598-599, 758, 925

Photography

Abbreviation Key- LOC = Library of Congress; C/B = Corbis-Bettmann Archive; RH/LS = photo by Rob Huntley/Lightstream; NA = National Archives; PRC = Picture Research Consultants, Inc.; FRENT = Collection of David J. and Janice L. Frent; BB = Brown Brothers; CP = Culver Pictures; WW = Wide World Photos; GL = Gamma Liaison; WC = Woodfin Camp & Associates; C&G = Chermayeff & Geismar/MetaForm photo by Karen Yamauchi; BS = Black Star; MP = Magnum Photos

Prologue Page 2, CP; **3 T**, Harper's Weekly, May 26, 1883; **3 B**, C/B; **4 TL**, B, Rensselaer Polytechnic Institute; **4 M**, The Metropolitan Museum of Art. The Edward W.C. Arnold Collection of New York Prints, Maps and Pictures. Bequest of Edward W.C. Arnold.; **6 T**, WW; **6 INSET**, Andy Levin/Photo Researchers; **7**, RMIP/Richard Haynes; **8 T**, Missouri Historical Society. Block Brothers photograph; **8 INSET**, © Fredericks/The Image Works; **9**, Museum of Modern Art Film Still Archive.

Unit Openers Pages **10-11**, "Europeans Encountering Indians" artist unknown, ca 1700. (detail) Joslyn Art Museum, Omaha, Nebraska; **124-125**, "Election Day in Philadelphia" by John Lewis Krimmel, 1815. (detail) Courtesy, Winterthur Museum; **210-211**, "View of the Upper Village of Lockport Niagara Company, N.Y.", 1836. (detail) LOC. Hand-colored by Sandi Rygiel/Picture Research Consultants; **294-295**, Ruins of Richmond, Virginia, April 1865, Brady Studio. (detail) LOC. **382-383**, "Excursion Parties at Devil's Gate Bridge, Utah" by A. J. Russell. (detail) Courtesy of the Oakland Museum History Department; **492-493**, New York & Cuba Mail Steamship Company Dock scene. (detail) C/B; **576-577**, "Mother and Child" by Dorothea Lange (detail). LOC; **660-661**, New York & Cuba Mail Steamship Company Dock scene. (detail) C/B; **768-769**, "Selma March" March 1965 (detail by James H. Karales; **876-877**, Clinton Inauguration, January 1993 (detail) C/B.

American Album

Abbreviation Key: SI = Smithsonian Institution; OPPS = Office of Printing and Photographic Services, Smithsonian Institution. NPS = Courtesy of the National Park Service

First Encounters BOWL, Eric Long, SI, courtesy of the Museum of Indian Arts and Culture, Laboratory of Anthropology Collection, Santa Fe.; JAR, Eric Long, SI, courtesy of the Philbrook Arts Center, Tulsa, Oklahoma.; ARCHANGEL, Diane Nordeck, SI, courtesy of Zuni Pueblo; BELL, Laurie Minor-Penland, SI; BLANKET, Jeff Tinsley, SI; ROCK PAINTING, Courtesy of the Texas Memorial Museum, Austin; PUEBLO, Courtesy of the National Anthropological Archives, SI

After the Revolution JUG, Eric Long, SI;GRIDIRON, OPPS; SAMPLER, Eric Long, SI; SUIT, Eric Long, SI; RESPECT, LOC; TOYS, OPPS; DAIRYING, Courtesy of Princeton University Library, Dept of Rare Books and Special Collections; ANVIL & HAMMER, Eric Long, SI; GRAVESTONES, Dane Penland, SI

Engines of Change JOHN BULL, **Courtesy Harry Abrams**; REVOLVER, LOCK, VISE, GOODS, HARVESTING MACHINE, all by Rick Vargas, SI; SAFE, Eric Long, SI; REAPER, State Historical Society of Wisconsin

Life at War SHOULDER PLATE, KNIFE, TINS, CUTLERY, HARD TACK, all by Rick Vargas and Richard Strauss, SI; UNIFORM, Dane Penland, SI; FLAG, Alfred Harrell and Andrew Wynn, SI; QUININE, Dane Penland, SI; FIELD HOSPITAL, OPPS; MUSKETT, Rick Vargas, SI

The Growth of Sports FOOTBALL PLAYER, BASEBALL MUSIC, Larry Gates, SI; SKIING, FOOTBALL PANTS, BASEBALL, all by Rick Vargas, SI; SKATING, Jim Wallace, SI; BICYCLE, Alfred Harrell, SI; CYCLIST, Collection of Sally Fox

From Field to Factory RECORD BOOK, Dane Penland, SI; DOLL, Eric Long, SI; PLOW, Jeff Tinsley, SI; SUITCASE, Eric Long, SI; SOLDIERS, Courtesy of the National Archives and Records Administration; HOME SCHOOLING, LOC; JOBS, Jeff Tinsley, SI

The Jazz Age DUKE, Courtesy of John Hasse; RADIO, Dane Penland, SI; HYMIE, Danny Thompson, SI; SAXOPHONE, Dane Penland, SI; DRESS, Jeff Tinsley, SI; CLARINET, Dane Penland, SI; TRUMPET, Jeffrey Ploskonka, SI; BAND, Missouri Historical Society, Block Brothers Photo

Bringing the War Home Jeff Tinsley, SI all with the exception of; PROPAGANDA POSTERS, Richard Strauss, SI

Personal Legacy BOOTS, HELMUT, LETTER, WATCH, LETTER TO GARY, Eric Long, SI, NPS; DOGTAGS, Rick Vargas, SI, NPS; STUFFED ANIMALS, Richard Strauss, SI, NPS; VIETMAN MEMORIAL, Sandra Rogers, SI

The Information Age STAELLITE, OPPS; WATERGATE, Margaret McCullough, SI, courtesy of the National Archives and Records Administration; LASER HEAD, OPPS, SI; GRACE HOPPER, Danny Thompson, SI; HAND HELD COMPUTER, Courtesy of Apple Computer, Inc.; EARLY COMPUTER, Eric Long, SI; BAR CODES, MAD's UPC symbol cover is © E.C. Publications, Inc., 1978. Used with permission from MAD Magazine.; CHIP, Copyright of Motorola, Inc. Used by permission. FIBER-OPTIC, Courtesy of Intel Corporation; Jeff Tinsley, SI.

Chapter 1 Page **12 L**, Peabody Museum, Harvard University; **12 R**, National Maritime Museum, Greenwich, England; **13T**, National Museum of the American Indian; **13 MR**, Giraudon/Art Resource, NY; **13 ML**, "Arrival at Tomboctou from Barth", from *Travels in Central Africa*, 1857. Rare Book and Manuscripts Division, The New York Public Library, Astor, Lenox and Tilden Foundations; **13 B**, The Metropolitan Museum of Art, Gift of J. Pierpont Morgan, 1900. (00.18.2); **14 INSET**, National Museum of the American Indian; **15**, Courtesy The Edward E. Ayer Collection, The Newberry Library; **17 T**, Richard Alexander Cooke III; **18 L**, LOC; **20**, Etowah Indian Mounds Historic Site; **20 INSET**, Richard Alexander Cooke III; **21**, Werner Forman/Art Resource, NY; **22**, The Bridgeman Art Library; **23**, Giraudon/Art Resource, NY; **24**, Nimatallah/Art Resource, NY; **25**, Giraudon/Art Resource, NY; **26**, Palacio de la Alhambra, Granada; **27**, **28**, Photograph by Jeffrey Ploskonka, National Museum of African Art, Eliot Elisofon Archive, SI; **29**, Aldo Tutino; **30**, "Arrival at Tomboctou from Barth", from *Travels in Central Africa*, 1857. Rare Book and Manuscripts Division, The New York Public Library, Astor, Lenox and Tilden Foundations; **31**, The Metropolitan Museum of Art, Gift of J. Pierpont Morgan, 1900. (00.18.2); **32**, "Portuguese Caravels" from *America* by Theodore De Bry 1594. (detail) Rare Book and Manuscript Division, The New York Public Library, Astor, Lenox and Tilden Foundations; **33 TR**, Aztec drawing of smallpox victim from the Flortine Codex, v. 4, Book 12 (detail). Courtesy of biblioteca Medicea Laurenziana, Florence. Photo by Alberto Scardigli; **33 BL**, Courtesy of Magellan Systems Corporation; **33 BR**, London Science Museum. Photo © Michael Holford.

Chapter 2 **38 L**, Collection of Mass. Fish & Wildlife Commission. Courtesy of Peabody & Essex Museum. Photo by Mark Sexton; **38 R**, Courtesy of the Pilgrim Society, Plymouth, MA; **40**, Courtesy of South Florida Science Museum, Photo by Randy Smith; **43**, "Mother Maria de Jesus de Agreda Preaching to Chichime Indians in New Mexico" 1631 woodcut. Nettie Lee Benson Latin American Collection, Univ. of Texas at Austin, General Libraries; **44 R**, Anthony Richardson; **44 L**, Bureau of American Ethnology, SI, Washington, D.C. #34188-G; **45**, *Milicia y descripcion de lasindias*, *1599;* **46**, Photograph courtesy of Flowerdew Hundred Foundation, Hopewell, VA. Excavation 44PG65; **47**, "Jamestown, 1614" by Sidney King. Colonial National Historical Park; **49**, "European View of American Wealth" from *Twee Scheps-Togton* by Smith, 1707. pl facing p. 14. Rare Books and Manuscripts Division, The New York Public Library, Astor, Lenox and Tilden Foundations; **50**, From *Tobacco: Its History*, by Fairholt. Vol 2 pl opp. p. 310. (detail) Rare Books and Manuscripts Division, The New York Public Library, Astor, Lenox and Tilden Foundations; **51**, Sir Nathaniel Bacon, self portrait. LOC; **52**, "Landing of Negroes at Jamestown, 1619" Free Library of Philadelphia; **54**, Courtesy Plimoth Plantation, Plymouth, MA; **55**, Peabody & Essex Museum. Photo by Mark Sexton; **56**, "New Amsterdam" 1650-1653. Museum of the City of New York. The J. Clarence Davies Collection; **57 T**, "The Mason Children: David, Joanna, and Abigail" 1670 attributed to the Freake-Gibbs painter. Fine Arts Museums of San Francisco, Gift of Mr. & Mrs. John D. Rockefeller 3rd; **57 B**, Peabody Essex Museum. Photo by Mark Sexton; **58**, CP; **60**, Courtesy of Museum of the American Indian, SI, #4662, #4663; **61**, Princeton University Library, Department of Rare Books and Special Collections; **63**, "General Goffe Repulsing the Indians at Hadley." LOC; **64 BL**, "Philip King of Mount Hope" by Paul Revere American Antiquarian Society; **64 BR**, "Paul Revere," artist unknown, Private Collection; **65 BL**, "King Philip" by Thomas Hart Benton. Rev. Andrew J. Kelly Collection, Saint Joseph College, West Hartford, CT; **65 BR**, Dan Dudnik/WC; **65 M**, Cheyenne Ledger Drawings "Warrior Chasing Soldier on Horseback" (detail). Addison Doty Morning Star Gallery, Santa FE, NM.

Chapter 3 **70 L**, Lexington Historical Society. RH/LS; **70 R**, Museum of Early Southern Decorative Arts; **72**, Norwich textile sample book. Courtesy, The Winterthur Library: Joseph Downs Collection of Manuscripts and Printed Ephemera; **73**, LOC; **74**, James II from the Dominion of New England Charter, 1686. Mass. State Archives; **75**, LOC; **79 L**, John Lewis Stage; **79 B**, Colonial Williamsburg Foundation; **80**, Library Company of Philadelphia; **81**, "The First, Second, and Last Scenes of Mortality" by Prudence Punderson ca. 1783, Connecticut Historical Society; **82**, Breton Littlehales ©National Geographic Society; **83 R**, Wethersfield Historical Society; **83 INSET**, Wenham Museum, Wenham, MA; **84**, Collection of Roddy and Sally Moore; **85 T**, "The Slave Deck" by Godfrey Meynall, (detail) 1846. National Maritime Museum; **85 B**, Mass. Historical Society; **86**, "The Old Plantation" artist unknown 1795. Abby Aldrich Rockefeller Foundation, Colonial Williamsburg; **87**, Courtesy of The Mount Vernon Ladies' Association; **88**, The Stagville Center, Division of Archives and History, North Carolina Dept. of Cultural Resources; **89**, Courtesy of the Pilgrim Society, Plymouth; **91 T**, "Rev. George Whitefield" by J. Wollaston, 1742. Courtesy of the National Portrait Gallery, London; **91 B**, LOC.

Chapter 4 96 TL, BL, Nichipor Collection, Courtesy of Minuteman National Historical Park. RH/LS; **96 R**, Lexington Historical Society. RH/LS; **98**, LOC; **100**, Mass. Historical Society; **101**, LOC; **102**, Colonial Williamsburg Foundation; **103**, "Pontiac's War Prisoner Exchange" from Smith, *Historical Account, 1766*. Rare Book Division, New York Public Library, Astor, Lenox and Tilden Foundations; **104 TL**, The Bostonian Society/Old State House; **104 BR**, North Wind Picture Archives; **104 B**, LOC, **106 INSET**, "Boston Massacre" engraving by Paul Revere. LOC; **109**, SI, Division of Political History, Washington, D.C. #83-4869; **110 BR**, C/B; **110 INSET**, Independence National Historic Park, Philadelphia; **112**, US Dept of State; **113**, Mass. Historical Society; **114**, Library Company of Philadelphia; **115**, Lexington Historical Society. RH/LS; **116**, Courtesy Minuteman National Historical Park, RH/LS; **117**, "Attack on Bunker Hill, with the Burning of Charlestown" unknown artist. Gift of Edgar William and Bernice Chrysler Garbisch, ©1994, National Gallery of Art, Washington, D.C.; **118 BOTH**, Courtesy Minuteman National Historical Park, RH/LS; **119**, "Tarleton's Cavalrymen after the Battle of Cowpens" by William Ranney. Collection of the State of South Carolina. Photo by Hunter Clarkeson, Alt Lee, Inc.; **120**, New York Historical Society; **121 T**, LOC; **121 B**, Independence National Historical Park, Philadelphia.

Chapter 5 126 BR, Independence National Historic Park, Philadelphia; **126 TR**, National Archive. RH/LS; **128**, Yale University Art Gallery, Mabel Brady Garven Collection; **129**, "General Washington's Resignation" by Alonzo Chappel, Chicago Historical Society; **130**, Eric P. Newman Numismatic Education Society. RH/LS; **131**, *A Popular History of the United States* by William Cullen Bryant, 1881 p. 98. LOC; **133**, CP; **134**, *The National Archives of the United States* by Herman Viola. Publisher, Harry N. Abrams, Inc. Photograph by Jonathan Wallen; **136**, Independence National Historic Park, Phildelphia (detail); **137**, "James Madison: by Charles Willson Peale, 1783. LOC; **138**, "Independence Hall" by William Birch, 1790. Rare Book Department, Free Library of Philadelphia; **139**, "Signing of the Constitution" by Thomas Prichard Rossiter, 1872. Independence National Historic Park, Philadelphia; **142**, "Washington at Verplancke's Point" by John Trumbull, 1790. Courtesy, Winterthur Museum; **144**, "The Federal Ship Union" from AMERICAN MUSEUM, 1787, Philadelphia. Vol 4, p. 61. American Antiquarian Society; **146 B**, American Antiquarian Society; **146 T**, "The Federal Procession in N.Y., 1788" from Labm's History of the City of N.Y. American Antiquarian Society; **148**, Museum of American Political Life; **149**, "Washington Taking the Oath" by H.A. Odgen. LOC; **150 T**, "The Republican Court" 1861 by Daniel Huntington. (detail) The Brooklyn Museum 39.536.1, Gift of the Crescent-Hamilton Athletic Club; **150 B**, Museum of American Political Life; **151 TL**, LOC; **151 TR**, Fred J. Maroon

Chapter 6 154 L, Shelburne Museum; **154 R**, "Bust of Thomas Jefferson" by Jean Antoine Houdon, 1789. Gilder Lehrman Collection; **154 M**, New York State Museum; **156**, Columbiana Collection, Columbia University; **157**, "The Times: A Political Portrait" unidentified artist, 1795. The New York Historical Society; **158 TL**, "Alexander Hamilton" by John Trumbull. Yale University Art Gallery, Trumbull Collection; **158 TR**, "Jefferson" by Rembrandt Peale ©White House Historical Association/Photo by National Geographic Society; **159 BL**, "An Exciseman" (detail) Atwater Kent Museum; **159 T**, "Western Army at Fort Cumberland the 18th of October 1794" by Kemmelmeyer. Courtesy, Winterthur Museum; **162**, Henry Ford Museum and Greenfield Village; **163**, Valentine Museum; **164 T**, "The Providential Detection" American Antiquarian Society; **164 B**, "John Adams" by John Trumbull, 1793. National Portrait Gallery, SI, Washington, D.C./Art Resource, NY; **165**, C/B; **166 BL**, "Mad Tom in a Rage" 1801, Houghton Library, Harvard University; **166 BOTH**, Museum of American Political Life, Photo by Sally Anderson-Bruce; **167 BOTH**, C/B; **168**, Our Country by Benson J. Losing, 1877; **169**, "John Marshall" by Fevret de Saint Memin, 1801 Duke University Archives; **171**, "Ograbme" New York Historical Society; **174**, Pocumtuck Valley Memorial Association; **175**, *The National Archives of the United States* by Herman Viola. Publisher, Harry N. Abrams, Inc. Photo by Jonathan Wallen; **176**, "Shawnee Chief Prophet". National Portrait Gallery, SI, Washington, D.C.; **177 TL**, "Tecumseh" Field Museum of Natural History FNMH New # A993851; **177 TR**, Government of Canada: Fort Malden National Historical Park. Photo by Vern Harvey; **178**, Division of Political History, SI, Washington, D.C.; **180**, "Andrew Jackson at the Battle of New Orleans" by Dennis M. Carter. The Historic New Orleans Collection.

Chapter 7 184 L, West Virginia State Museum, photo by Michael Keller; **184 TR**, Museum of Art, Rhode Island School of Design, Gift of Miss Lucy T. Aldrich; **184 BR**, Old Sturbridge Village; **186**, Peabody & Essex Museum; **187 TR**, Collection of The Bostonian Society. Photo by J. David Bohl; **187 TL**, Collection of Dr. Juliet E.K. Walker; **189**, LOC; **190**, "Slave Trader Sold to Tennessee" by Lewis Miller 1853. Colonial Williamsburg Foundation; **193 TR**, National Museum of American History, SI, Washington, D.C. Photo by Charles Philips; **193 BR**, Private Collection; **194**, "Scenes from a Seminary for Young Ladies" (detail) unknown artist, 1810-1820. The St Louis Art Museum; **197**, The New York Historical Society; **198**, Pocumtuck Vallery Memorial Association; **199**, National Museum of American History, SI, Washington, D.C.; **200**, "The Courtship" by Eunice Pinney. Private Collection; **201**, "Country Wedding" by John Lewis Krimmel, 1819. Pennsylvania Academy of the Fine Arts; **202**, Dukes County Historical Society, photo by Robert Schellhammer; **203**, "Religious Camp Meeting" 1839, watercolor by J. Maze Burbank. New Bedford Whaling Museum; **204**, "Richard Allen" by G.W. Hobbs 1785. Moorland-Spingarn Research Center, Howard University; **205**, "The Presentation of a Gold Snuff Box of the Rev. R.T. Breckenridge" Bethel Church, Baltimore, December 18, 1845. LOC.

Chapter 8 212 TR, Collection of Don Duer. Photo by Wiley & Flynn; **212 BR**, Eric P. Newman Numismatic Education Society; **212 L**, Museum of American Textile History. RH/LS; **214**, Lowell Historical Society; **215**, CP; **217**, Old Sturbridge Village; **218**, Museum of American Textile History. RH/LS; **220**, Collection of Mr. & Mrs. Screven Lorillord; **222**, The American Numismatic Society; **223, 225**, LOC; **226**, FRENT; **227**, The New York Historical Society; **230**, Museum of the City of New York; **231**, The New York Historical Society; **232**, "Webster's Reply to Haynes" by G.P.A. Healy. City of Boston Art Commission; **233**, FRENT; **234**, "Trail of Tears" by Robert Lindneaux. Woolaroc Museum, Bartlesville, OK.

Chapter 9 240 R, Collection of Sue and Lars Hotham. RH/LS; **240 L**, New York State Historical Association; **242**, Collection of Sue and Lars Hotham. RH/LS; **243**, "A Philadelphia Anabaptist Immersion During a Storm." Metropolitan Museum of Art, Rogers Fund, 1942.; **245**, "Daguerreotype of Emerson School" 1855 by Southworth and Hawes. The Metropolitan Museum of Art. Gift of I.N. Phelps Stokes, Edward S. Hawes, Alice Mary Hawes, Marion Agusta Hawes, 1937; **247**, "Brook Farm" by J. Wolcott, 1844. Mass. Historical Society; **249**, Mass. Historical Society; **251**, National Portrait Gallery, SI, Washington D.C./Art Resource, NY; **252**, Sophia Smith Archives, Garrison Collection; **253**, Mass. Historical Society; **254**, ©Louis Psihoyos/Contact Press Images; **256**, American Antiquarian Society; **257**, Schlesinger Library, Radcliffe College; **258**, "Elizabeth Cady Stanton" by Harriet Stanton de Forest, 1860. Courtesy National Woman's Party, Washington, D.C. Photo by Jeff Mathewson; **259**, Senaca Falls Historical Society. RH/LS; **260**, Women's Rights Collection, Sophia Smith Archives; **261**, Courtesy of Special Collections, Vassar College Libraries; **262 BL**, Chicago Historical Society; **262 M**, LOC; **262 BR**, C/B; **263 BL**, Courtesy of The Oakland Museum History Department; **263 BR**, C/B; **264**, LOC; **266 T**, "Bare Knuckles" by George A Hayes. Gift of Edgar William and Bernice Chrysler Garbisch, ©1994 National Gallery of Art, Washington, D.C.; **266 B**, "Colonel and Mrs. James A. Whiteside, Son Charles and Servants" by James Cameron. Hunter Museum of Art, Chattanooga, TN. Gift of Mr. and Mrs. Thomas B. Whitside.

Chapter 10 270 R, ©Henry Groskinsky; **270 TL**, National Museum of American History, SI, Washington, D.C. #73-2348; **270 BL**, Southwest Museum; **272 L**, Roberta Campbell Lawson Collection, Philbrook Museum of Art, Tulsa, OK; **273 B**, Rare Books and Manuscript Division, The New York Public Library, Astor, Lenox and Tilden Foundations; **273**, © Jerry Jacka; **274**, "Migration of the Pawnees" by Alfred Jacob Miller, 1837. Collection of Western Americana, Beinecke Rare Book and Manuscript Library, Yale University; **275**, "Buffalo Chase, A Single Death" by George Catlin. National Museum of American Art, SI. Gift of Mrs. Joseph Harrison, Jr./Art Resource NY; **276**, Courtesy of the Oakland Museum History Dept.; **277 BL**, "Mission San Carlos Borremeo de Carmelo" by Oriana Day. Society of California Pioneers; **277 INSET**, Courtesy of the Texas Memorial Museum, Univ. of Texas at Austin, #41VV343; **278 TL**, Courtesy Museum of New Mexico, neg. #11329; **278 TR**, Lowell Georgia Photography; **279**, "Stephen F. Austin" by Brand. Archives Div.-Texas State Library; **280**, Courtesy of Texas Memorial Museum, Univer. of Texas at Austin; **281, 282 BL**, Boot Hill Collection, photo by Henry Groskinsky; **282 TR**, Oregon Historical Society; **284**, Utah State Historical Society; **286**, Courtesy of the Costume Dept. Chicago Historical Society; 1920.38; **290**, p 1983.20 California Forty-Niner c 1850, 1/4 plate daguerreotype with applied color. Amon Carter Museum, Fort Forth, TX.

Chapter 11 296 L, Museum of American Political Life; **296 R**, FRENT; **298 TL**, Museum of American Textile History. RH/LS; **298 TR**, Grant Heilman; **299 T**, LOC; **299 B**, The Stow-Day Foundation, photo by Steve Laschevere; **300 BL**, Chicago Historical Society; **301**, "Lazell, Perkins and Co., Bridgwater, Ma" 1858 by J.P. Newell. The Corcoran Gallery of Art, Mary E. Maxwell, Fund; **302 TL**, Collection of PRC; **302 TR**, Grant Heilman; **303**, Ontario County Historical Society; **304**, "The United States Senate, A/D. 1850" by R. Whitechurch. LOC; **305**, LOC; **307**, Milwaukee County Historical Society; **308**, "The Little Giant-in the Character of the Gladiator" 1858. Chicago Historical Society; **311**, Courtesy of the Decorative and Industrial Arts Collection, Chicago Historical Society; **313**, "Arguments of Chivalry" by Winslow Homer. LOC; **314**, LOC; **315**, Boston Athenaeum; **316**, "Dred Scott" by Louis Schultze, 1881. Missouri Historical Society; **318**, LOC; **321**, "Bombardment of Sumter" Harpers Weekly, 1861. LOC.

Chapter 12 324 TL, Museum of the Confederacy; **324**, Confederate Memorial Hall, New Orleans. From ECHOES OF GLORY; ARMS & EQUIPMENT OF THE CONFEDERACY. Photo by Larry Sherer ©1991 Time-Life Books, Inc.; **324 TR**, SI. From THE CIVIL WAR; TWENTY MILLION YANKEES. Photo by Larry Sherer ©1985 Time-Life Books, Inc.; **324 BR**, C. Paul Loane Collection, From ECHOES OF GLORY; ARMS & EQUIPMENT OF THE CONFEDERACY. Photo by Larry Sherer ©1991 Time-Life Books, Inc.; **326**, Collection of David & Kevin Kyle; **329**, Collection of Michael J. McAfee. Courtesy William Gladstone. Photo Seth Goltzer; **330**, LOC; **332**, "Last Meeting of Lee and Jackson" by Everett B.D. Julio. Museum of the Confederacy; **333**, West Point Museum Collections. Courtesy William Gladstone. Photo by Seth Goltzer; **334, 336, 337 T**, LOC; **337 INSET**, Collection of William Gladstone. Photo by Seth Goltzer; **338**, Moorland-Spingarn Research Center; **339**, Collection of William Gladstone. Photo by Seth Goltzer; **341**, SI, From THE CIVIL WAR; WAR ON THE MISSISSIPPI. Photo by Larry Sherer © 1985 Time-Life Books, Inc.; **342**, The Beverly R. Robinson Collection, U.S. Naval Academy Museum; **344**, "Five Them Cold Steel" painting by Don Troiani. Photo courtesy Historical Art Prints, Southbury, CT 06488; **346 TL**, West Point Museum Collections. Courtesy of William Gladstone. Photo by Seth Goltzer; **346 BL, BR** C/B; **346 TR**, LOC; **347**, **BL** P.J. Griffiths/MP; **347 M**, BR, Noel Quidu, Chip Hires/both GL; **348**, N.Y. State Dept of Military and Naval Affairs, Capitol Collection, Albany, NY. From ECHOES OF GLORY; ARMS & EQUIPMENT OF THE UNION. Photo by Larry Sherer ©1991 Time-Life Books, Inc.; **350**, "Sherman's March to the Sea" engraving after F.O.C.Darley. Photo by Ben Lourie. Collection of David M. Sherman, Washington, D.C.

Chapter 13 358 L, LOC; **358 TR, BR, 360, 361, 362**, Collection of William Gladstone. Photo by Seth Goltzer; **364 BL**, Courtesy of the Arnold Rogers Collection; **364 INSET**, Drawing by Frederick Law Olmsted from *A Journey in the Seaboard States, 1856*; **365**, Collection of William Gladstone. Photo by Seth Goltzer; **366**, FRENT; **367 TL, TR**, Collection of William Gladstone; **371**, Collection of Nancy Gewitz, Antique Textile Resource, Bethesda, MD; **372, 373 TL**, LOC; **373 TR**, "Commercial Center of Atlanta, Georgia" by Horace Bradley. Courtesy Robert M. Hinklin Jr., Inc., Spartanburg, SC (detail); **374 BL**, Collection of State Historical Museum/Mississippi Department of Archives and History; **374 TL**, LOC, **377**, Courtesy of the Decorative and Industrial Arts Collection of the Chicago Historical Society; Acc No. 1920.53; Photographer: John Alderson; **378**, Collection of William Gladstone. Photo by Seth Goltzer; **379**, LOC.

Chapter 14 384 L, Division of Community Life, SI; **384 R**, National Museum of American History, SI. Photo by H. Brooks Walker; **386**, Division of Political History, SI, #89-6626; **387**, Division of Community Life, SI; **388**, Division of Community Life, SI, #86-2200; **389**, Lightfoot Collection; **390 BL**, Div. of Political History, SI, #75-2343; **390 BR**, Courtesy Picture Tel; **393**, Museum of American Textile History; **394**, LOC; **395**, "The Protectors of our Industries." Puck. Feb. 7, 1883. LOC; **398**, LOC; **399**, "The Gun Foundry" by John Weir. Putman County Historical Society, Cold Spring, NY; **400**, Urban Archives, Temple Univ.; **401**, LOC; **402**, Collection of Ralph J. Brunke; **403 TR**, PRC; **403 TL**, "Underground Lodging for the Poor" by Paul Frenzeny. Harper's Weekly, Feb. 20, 1869. LOC; **406**, Haymarket Riot May 4, 1886" by Thure De Thulstrup. (detail) Harper's Weekly, May 15, 1886. LOC; **407**, BB; **408 BR**, Minnesota Historical Society/St. Paul Daily News; **408 BL**, LOC, **408 M**, Franklin D. Roosevelt Presidential Library; **409 BL**, C/B; **409 BR**, Courtesy International Brotherhood of Teamsters.

Chapter 15 412 R, Courtesy of the Panhandle-Plains Historical Society, Canyon, TX; **412 L**, ©Justin Kerr, 1989; **414**, The Oakland Museum History Department; **415**, Denver Public Library, Western History Dept; **418**, Addison Doty, Morning Star Gallery, Santa Fe, NM; **420**, LOC; **422**, The Oakland Museum History Department; **423 BR** State Historical Society of Wisconsin; **423 TL**, Solomon D. Butcher Collection, Nebraska State Historical Society; **423**, Grant Heilman; **424**, Western

History Division, Denver Public Library; **425 TL,** "Jerked Down" by Charles Russell. Thomas Gilcrease Institute of American History & Art; **425 TR,** North Wind Picture Archives; **428,** The Oakland Museum History Dept.; **430 B,** Kansas State Historical Society; **430 T,** East Carolina Manuscript Collection, J.Y. Joyner Library, East Carolina Univ.; **432,** LOC; **434,** Boot Hill Museum, photo by Henry Grosinsky; **435,** "The Cowboy" by Remington, 1902. Amon Carter Museum of Western Art; **436,** Buffalo Bill Historical Center, Cody, WY; **437,** Theodore Roosevelt Collection, Harvard College Library.

Chapter 16 440 TL, C&G; **440 BL,** Collection of PRC RH/LS; **440 R,** Museum of American Political Life. Photo by Sally Anderson-Bruce; **442,** Division of Political History, SI, #93-3020; **444 BL, 444 INSET, 446, 447,** LOC; **448,** National Park Service, Gift of Angelo Forgione; **449, BB; 450,** LOC; **452 BOTH, 453 INSET,** C&G; **453 T,** California Dept of Parks and Recreation, courtesy Fred Wasserman; **454,** Collection of PRC RH/LS; **455,** LOC; **456,** BB; **458,** FRENT; **460 BR,** Division of Political History, SI, #88-8676; **460 TL,** Collection of PRC RH/LS; **461,** C&G; **462, 463 TR,** LOC; **463 INSET,** California Museum of Photography WX5266.

Chapter 17 466 BL, Collection of John Craig. RH/LS; **466 TL,** Radcliffe College Archives, Schlesinger Library; **466 R,** Museum of the City of New York, Gift of Aaron & Abby Shroeder; **468,** Collection of Sue and Lars Hotham; **469,** Nebraska State Historical Society; **470,** Sophia Smith Collection; **471 BOTH,** BB; **472,** Collection of Sally Fox; **473 TR,** LOC; **473 INSET,** California Museum of Photography #X55458; **474 TL,** Chicago Historical Society; **474 B,** C/B; **474 INSET,** Artwork from Wood River Gallery, Mill Valley, CA; **475 BL,** LOC; **475 BR,** Peter Menzel/Stock, Boston; **476,** Chicago Historical Society; **477,** Old Court House Museum, Vicksburg, Mississippi; **479,** C/B; **480,** The Walker Collection of A'Lelia Perry Bundles, Alexandria, VA; **481,** Museum of American Political Life; **482, 483 T,** Collection of PRC RH/LS; **483 INSET,** Courtesy Maytag Co.; **484 TR,** Kansas Historical Society; **484 INSET,** State Historical Society of Wisconsin; **491,** Collection of Sally Fox.

Chapter 18 494 TR, Granger Collection; **494 BR,** Museum of American Political Life. Photo by Sally Anderson-Bruce; **494 L,** Courtesy Deere & Company; **496,** Oakland Museum History Dept.; **498, 499,** LOC; **500,** Collection of PRC Photo by Lightstream; **502 TL,** Chicago Historical Society; **502 INSET,** CP; **503,** NA; **504,** California Museum of Photography; **505,** Courtesy of the Liliuokalani Trust and the Bishop Museum (detail); **507,** Museum of American Political Life; **508 TL,** LOC; **508 INSET,** BB; **510,** "The World's Constable" by Dolrymple, JUDGE 1905, LOC; **511,** "William Howard Taft" (detail) White House Historical Assoc.; **512,** C/B; **514,** "Goddess of Liberty Weathervane" by L.W. Cushing, 1870. Courtesy of Fred and Kathryn Giampietro; **517 BOTH,** Courtesy Archives of Girl Scouts of the U.S.A.

Chapter 19 520 L, Division of Political History, SI, #79-1002; **520 R,** Collection of PRC RH/LS; **522,** Boston Athenaeum; **523,** Labor-Management Documentation Center, Cornell University; **524 B,** International Museum of Photography, George Eastman House; **524 INSET,** LOC; **525,** CP; **526,** C/B; **527,** Courtesy of the Decorative & Industrial Arts Collection of the Chicago Historical Society: 1978.154.4; photo by John Alderson; **529 TL,** CP; **529 TR,** Bob Daemmrich/Stock, Boston; **532 BR,** Museum of the City of New York; **532 INSET,** Stock Montage, Inc.; **534,** Museum of American Political Life; **535,** "Goodness Gracious I Must Have Been Doxing" by Joseph Keppler from PUCK. Theodore Roosevelt Collection, Harvard College Library; **536, 537, 539,** FRENT; **540,** Courtesy of the League of Women's Voters of the US; **542 T,** Sophia Smith College Archives; **542 B,** LOC; **544 BL,** Radcliffe College Archives, Schlesinger Library; **544 BR,** The New York Historical Society; **544 M,** NA #44-2A-229; **545 TB,** Collection of Bettye Lane; **545 BR,** C/B.

Chapter 20 544 TL, Collection of PRC RH/LS; **545 BL,** Collection of Sue and Lars Hotham. RH/LS; **546 TR, 548 ALL; 550 T,** Collection of Colonel Stuart S. Corning, Jr. RH/LS; **550 B,** CP; **552,** Bayerisches Hauptstaatsarchiv; **553,** CP; **555,**, Granger Collection; **556 TR,** Boston Athenaeum; **556 TL,** LOC; **557,** "Wilson" by Edmund Charles Tarbell, 1921, National Portrait Gallery, SI/Art Resource, NY; **558,** C/B; **559,** Collection of Colonel Stuart S. Corning, Jr. RH/LS; **560, 561 T,** NA #111-SC-25026, #111-SC-14129; **561 INSET, 562,** Collection of Colonel Stuart S. Corning, Jr. RH/LS; **564,** LOC; **565,** Collection of PRC; **566,** C/B; **567,** Wayne State University, Archives of Labor and Urban Affairs; **568,** The Michael Barson Collection/Past Perfect. RH/LS; **571,** NA #111-SC-25026.

Chapter 21 578 TL, FRENT; **578 R,** Courtesy Ford Archives; **578 BL,** Collection of Col. Stuart S. Corning, Jr. Photo by Lightstream; **580,** FRENT; **581,** Archives of Labor and Urban Affairs, Wayne State Univ.; **582 BL,** FRENT; **582 TL,** C/B; **583,** C&G; **584, 586 BR,** LOC; **586 TL,** Collection of Frank Driggs; **588 B, 588 INSET,** C/B; **588 R INSET,** Beinecke Library, Yale University; **588 L INSET,** Cartier Bresson/MP; **589,** FRENT; **590 TL,** LIFE Magazine December 10, 1925; **591 BR,** Nipper's Choice Phonograph, Keene, NH. Photo by Wright Studio; **591 TR,** LOC; **592, 593,** C/B; **594,** Collection of PRC RH/LS; **595,** Saturday Evening Post, June 30, 1928, Curtis Archives; **596,** Nancy Gewirz, Antique Textile Resource, Bethesda, MD. RH/LS. Collection of Joseph Benjamin Shuff; **597,** C/B; **599,** Courtesy Ford Archives; **600,** Michael Barson Collection/Past Perfect RH/LS; **602,** C&G; **607,** Missouri Historical Society, Block Brothers photo.

Chapter 22 608 TL, BL, FRENT; **608 R,** Detroit News; **610,** Courtesy of Speigel; Artwork from Wood River Gallery, Mill Valley, CA; **612,** Boston Athenaeum; **613,** C/B; **614,** LOC; **615 B,** C/B; **615 BL,** Copyright © 1929 by The New York Times Company; **620,** C/B; **621 T,** Museum of the City of New York. Photograph by Bernice Abbott, Federal Arts Project; **623,** C/B; **624 TL,** LOC; **627 T, 628 T,** C/B; **627 B,** CP; **629,** FRENT; **630,** Reprinted from the Albany Evening News 6/7/31, with permission of the Times Union, Albany, N.Y.; **631 T,** C/B; **631 B,** CP; **633,** FDR Library; **634 BL, TR; 634 TL,** FRENT; **635 TL,** Nixon Presidential Materials; **636 BL,** Lyndon Baines Johnson Presidential Library; **637 TR, BR,** Roy Roper and Diana Walker/GL.

Chapter 23 638 ALL, FRENT; **640,** LOC; **641,** FDR Library; **642 T,** US Forest Service; **642 B,** C/B; **643, 644,** "Mary McLeod Bethune" by Betsy G. Reyneau (detail). National Portrait Gallery, SI/Art Resource NY; **646,** LOC; **647,** FRENT; **648,** Margaret Bourke-White LIFE Magazine © Time Warner; **649,** FDR Library; **650,** C/B; **653,** The Oakland Museum History Dept.; **654 B, 655,** LOC; **656,** Museum of Modern Art Film Still Archive; **657,** James Prigoff.

Chapter 24 662 TL, Collection of Chester Stott RH/LS; **662 BL,** Nancy Gewirz, Antique Textile Resource, Bethesda, MD RH/LS; **662 R,** Collection of Col. Stuart S. Corning Jr. RH/LS; **664,** US Holocaust Memorial Museum; **665 TL,** Bilderdienst Suddeutscher Verlag; **665 TR,** NA #242-HMA-2773; **666 INSET, 667,** NA, *War & Conflict*, #993, #1131; **668 T,** Herbert Hoover Presidential Library; **668 B,** Collection of Col. Stuart S. Corning, Jr. RH/LS; **669 TR,** US Navy; **669 INSET,** NA #179-WP-936; **670,** Collection of Major General George S. Patton RH/LS; **671, 672,** C/B; **673,** Collection of Col. Stuart S. Corning, Jr. RH/LS; **676,** US Holocaust Memorial Museum; **677 B,** Collection of

Chester H. Stott, RH/LS; **677 T,** US Dept of Defense; **678, 679 B,** NA #127-PX-227672, #127-GR-137; **679 T,** Peter Stackpole © Time Warner; **681,** C/B; **682,** NA; **683,** HIROSHIMA SERIES, 1983. No. 2: "The Family". Gouache on paper 23"x17 1/2". Courtesy of Jacob Lawrence and Francine Seders Gallery Ltd.; **685 TR, 686 TR,** C/B; **686 BL,** LOC; **686 BR,** Archive Photos; **687 TL,** Department of Energy; **687 M, BR,** Leif Skoogfors, Howard Sochurek/WC

Chapter 25 690 BL, Collection of Chester Stott RH/LS; **690 TL,** Collection of Picture Research Consultants, Inc RH/LS; **690 R,** Collection of Jeff Ikler RH/LS; **691 TR,** NA *War & Conflict* #830; **692 T,** Private Collection RH/LS; **692 B, 694, 695,** NA, #127-GR-137, #208-MP-1-DDD-5, #44-PA-124; **696,** National Museum of American History, SI; **697 T,** C/B; **697 B,** LOC; **698 BR,** Michael Barson Collection/Past Perfect © 1943, DC Comics RH/LS; **698 BL,** Courtesy Hershey Foods Corp.; **698 T,** WW; **699,** Collection of Jeff Ikler RH/LS; **700,** Collection of Col. Stuart S. Corning, Jr. RH/LS; **701,** LOC; **702,** NA #208-NP-1-HHH-5; **703,** Rosie the Riveter Revisited Project, Oral History Program, California State Univer. Long Beach; **704,** Ellen Kaiper Collection, Oakland; **705,** Courtesy of the Norman Rockwell Family Trust and Curtis Archives; **706, 707 T, 708, 709,** LOC; **707 B,** Collection of Jeff Ikler RH/LS; **711,** NA #210-GC-160.

Chapter 26 716 ALL, 718, 719, 721 B, The Michael Barson Collection/Past Perfect RH/LS; **721 TR,** C/B; **721 TL,** Courtesy of the J.N. Ding Darling Foundation; **723,** C/B; **724 T, B,** Harry S Truman Presidential Library; **727 INSET,** Copyright © 1956 by The New York Times Company; **727 T,** ©Stern/BS; **728,** © 1959 Newsweek Inc. All rights reserved. Reprinted by permission; **729 INSET, 730 BR,** NA; **730 INSET,** NA #210-GC-160; **730 T,** C/B; **733, 734 TL & INSET,** The Michael Barson Collection/Past Perfect RH/LS; **735,** BB; **736,** C/B; **737,** Elliot Erwitt/MP.

Chapter 27 740, Collection of PRC RH/LS; **740 R,** Bill Ray LIFE Magazine © Time Warner; **742,** Collection of Robert and Bonnie Pope RH/LS; **743,** McDonald's Corp.; **744 TL,** Courtesy IBM Archives; **744 TR,** "Big Computers in Little Packages" ©1993 by Consumers Union of U.S. Inc., Yonkers, NY 10703-1057. Reprinted by permission from Consumer Reports, November 1993; **744 BL** National Museum of American History, SI. #90-15751; **744 INSET,** Photofest; **744 BR,** Courtesy Campbell Soup Company; **745,** J.R. Eyerman LIFE Magazine © Time Warner; **747,** Collection of PRC RH/LS; **748 T,** The Michael Barson Collection/Past Perfect RH/LS; **748 B,** Collection of Nancy Gewirz, Antique Textile Resource, Bethesda, MD RH/LS; **749 T,** Ralph Morse LIFE © Time Warner; **749 B,** Dan Weiner, Courtesy Sandra Weiner; **750,** Curtis Archives; **751,** The Michael Barson Collection/Past Perfect RH/LS; **754,** Museum of American Political Life, photo by Steve Laschever; **755 T,** FRENT; **755 B, 756,** C/B; **755 INSET, 757 T,** FRENT; **757 B,** Division of Political History, SI, #91-13778; **759 TR,** The Michael Barson Collection/Past Perfect RH/LS; **759 B,** Copyright © 1957 by The New York Times Company; **760 T,** Bob Adelman/MP; **760 INSET,** FRENT; **761 TL,** The Michael Barson Collection/Past Perfect RH/LS; **761 INSET,** Carl Iwasake LIFE Magazine © Time Warner; **761 BR,** WW; **762,** Grey Vielet LIFE Magazine © Time Warner; **763,** WW; **764 ALL,** C/B.

Chapter 28 770 TL, BL, R, 772, FRENT; **773,** JFK Presidential Library; **775 T,** © Charles Harbutt/Actuality Inc.; **775 INSET,** LIFE Magazine Cover December 6, 1963. Photo by Fred Ward/BS; **777,** Lyndon Baines Johnson Presidential Library. Photo by Henry Groskinsky; **778 BOTH,** FRENT; **779,** © Bob Daemmrich; **781,** Lyndon Baines Johnson Presidential Library; **782,** NASA; **784,** Courtesy Boeing Defense & Space Group; **785 T & INSET,** Courtesy of the Peace Corps; **785 B,** Fred W. McDarrah; **788,** C/B; **790 T,** FRENT; **790 B,** WW.

Chapter 29 794 L, Dan Budnick/WC; **794 R, 796,** Art and Artifacts Division, Schomburg Center for Research in Black Culture, The New York Public Library, Astor, Lenox and Tilden Foundations; **797, 799,** C/B; **800 T,** Steve Shapiro/BS; **800 B,** FRENT; **801,** Dial Juvenile Books, 1968, a Division of Penguin Books USA, Inc.; **803,** Don Uhrbrock LIFE Magazine © Time Warner; **804,** State Historical Society of Wisconsin; **805,** C/B; **806, 808 BL,** Charles Moore/BS; **808 BR,** Jack O'Connell/The Boston Globe; **809 M,** Nancy Pierce/BS; **809 BL,** Steve Northrup/TIME Magazine; **809 BR,** © Largo Int./Shooting Star International; **810,** Robert Phillips LIFE Magazine ©Time Warner; **811 T,** Fred Ward, **811 INSET,** Steve Schapiro, both BS; **812,** Eve Arnold/MP; **813,** FRENT; **814,** C/B; **815 TR,** WW; **817,** Eve Arnold/MP; **818,** C/B; **819,** Co Rentmeester LIFE Magazine © Time Warner.

Chapter 30 822 L, Museum of American Political Life. Photo by Sally Anderson-Bruce; **822 TR,** M. Abramson/BS; **822 BR,** Collection of Michael McCloskey; **824, 825 TR,** Al Freni LIFE Magazine © Time Warner; **825 B,** © 1993 Jill Krementz; **825 INSET,** FRENT; **826 T,** © Bettye Lane; **826 B,** Radcliffe College Archives, Schlesinger Library; **827 INSET,** Courtesy Lang Communications; **827 TR,** © Bettye Lane; **828,** Collection of PRC; **829 TR & BR,** Al Freni LIFE Magazine © Time Warner; **831 T & B,** FRENT; **832,** Paul Fusco/MP; **833,** Craig Aurness/WC; **835 TL,** George Bacon Collection, Hawaii State Archives; **835 TR,** WW; **836,** Eddie Adams/TIME Magazine; **838 B & BL,** Dirck Halstead/TIME Magazine; **839 T,** Rick Smolan/Against All Odds; **839 B,** FRENT; **840,** C/B; **841,** FRENT; **842 INSET,** Collection of PRC; **842 TR,** Alfred Eisenstaedt LIFE Magazine © Time Warner; **843 TR,** Ken Regan/Camera 5.

Chapter 31 848 R, Forest McMullin/BS; **848 L,** The Image Works Archive; **850 TL,** Courtesy United Nations. RH/LS; **851 TL,** Howard Sorhurek LIFE Magazine © Time Warner; **851 TR,** C/B; **852,** WW; **854 INSET,** Philip Jones Griffiths/MP; **854 L,** Zenith Electronics Corporation; **855 TL,** Catherine Leroy/AP, print courtesy Time Inc. Picture Collection; **856 INSET,** Larry Burrows LIFE Magazine © Time Warner; **857,** Courtesy of Le Ly Hayslip; **858,** FRENT; **859,** The Bancroft Library, University of California; **861,** © Lisa Law/The Image Works; **863 TL & TR,** The Oakland Museum History Department; **864,** © Lisa Law/The Image Works; **865 BL,** Frank Driggs Collection/MP; **865 BR,** Elliott Landy/MP; **866,** © Fredericks/The Image Works; **867,** Brad Markel/GL; **871,** Thai Khad. Chuon/C/B.

Chapter 32 878 T & B, FRENT; **880,** "The Time Machine" by Leslie Illingworth. Sept. 13, 1967 in *Punch*. Courtesy of the Lyndon B. Johnson Presidential Library; **881,** Joseph Louw LIFE Magazine © Time Warner; **882,** Bill Eppridge LIFE Magazine © Time Warner; **883 B (ALL),** FRENT; **883 T,** C/B; **884 BR,** Jean Louis Atlan/Sygma; **884 BL,** Arthur Grace/Sygma; **885 R,** J. Langevin/Sygma; **885 M,** C/B; **885 BL,** Jim Pickerell; **886 TL,** Richard Nixon Library. Photo © Henry Groskinsky; **886 BR,** Roddey E. Mims/C/B; **887,** Nixon Presidential Materials Project; **888,** Courtesy Draper Hill, Memphis, Tenn © The Commercial Appeal, Memphis; **891,** Ted Cowell/BS; **892,** Courtesy National Zoological Park, photo by Jessie Cohen; **893,** Gerald R. Ford Presidential Library; **894,** Nixon Presidential Materials Project; **895,** John Dominis LIFE Magazine © Time Warner; **896,** J.P. Laffont/Sygma; **897 INSET,** FRENT; **897 TR,** Nixon Presidential Materials Project; **898,** Dennis Brack/BS; **899,** C/B; **900 T,** Fred Ward/BS; **900 M,** "Watergate" by Tony Auth, 1973. Reprinted by permission of the Chicago Tribune-New York News Syndicate; **901,** "Nixon Caught in a Web of Tapes" by Robert Pryor. Courtesy of John Locke Studios, Inc.; **902,** Nixon Presidential Materials Project.

Chapter 33 **906 L**, Gerald R. Ford Presidential Library. Photo by Henry Groskinsky; **906 R**, Jimmy Carter Presidential Library. Photo by Henry Groskinsky; **908**, Courtesy Gerald R. Ford Presidential Library; **909 TR, WW**; **909 INSET**, Copyright © 1974 by The New York Times Company; **910**, "Inflation" by Frank Interlandi. Courtesy Gerald R. Ford Presidential Library; **912**, Matthew Naythons/GL; **913, 914 BL & BR, FRENT**; **915**, Jimmy Carter Presidential Library; **916**, Dennis Brack/BS; **917, FRENT**; **918**, Jimmy Carter Presidential Library; **919**, Alex Webb/MP; **920**, C/B; **921 TR**, Peter Marlow/MP; **921 TL**, Alain Mingam/GL; **923, 924 L & R**, Dennis Brack/BS; **927**, C/B; **928**, WW.

Chapter 34 **932 L & R, FRENT**; **933T**, C/B; **933ML, FRENT**; **933MR**, J.P. Laffont/Sygma; **933B**, R. Bossu/Sygma; **934, FRENT**; **935**, Fred Ward/BS; **936**, Diana Walker/Time Magazine; **937**, Les Schofer/Sygma; **938, FRENT**; **939**, Bob Daemmrich/Uniphoto; **941**, Randy Taylor/Sygma; **943**, Reagan Library; **944**, J.P. Laffont/Sygma; **946**, White House Photo/BS; **947**, WW; **949**, C/B; **950 L**, C/B; **950 R**, R. Bossu/Sygma; **952**, Rick Reinhart/Impact Visuals.

Chapter 35 **958 L**, Ira Wyman/Sygma; **958 R**; **959 T**; **959 M**, Les Stone/Sygma; **959 B**, JB Pictures Ltd.; **960**, John C. Sykes Jr.; **961 INSET**, John C. Sykes Jr.; **961**, Ira Wyman/Sygma; **962**, Jeffrey Markowitz/Sygma; **963**, John Harrington/BS; **964**, ©Walt Handelsman-Times Picayune; **965 L**, ©Bob Woodward All rights reserved. Simon & Schuster; **965R**.; **966**, Reuters/C/B; **967**, Les Stone/Sygma; **969 L**, AFP Photo; **969 R**, Leonard Freed/MP; **970**, Int'l Brotherhood of Teamsters; **972**, JB Pictures Ltd.; **976**, Rick Maiman/Sygma.

Chapter 36 **984 T**, C&G; **984 B**, Rebecca Cooney/NYT Pictures; **985**, Davies & Starr; **986 T**, Division of Political History, SI. #88-8676; **986 B**, BB; **987**, LOC; **988**, David Butow; **989**, ©1993 Time Inc. Reprinted by permission; **990 T**, Elsa Peterson/Stock, Boston; **990 B**, National Park Service, Gift of Angelo Forgione.

Chapter 37 **992 T**, New York Historical Society; **992 B**, David J. Sams/Stock, Boston; **993**, Boot Hill Museum, photo by Henry Grosinsky; **994**, North Carolina Museum of Art, Raleigh, Purchased with funds from the State of North Carolina; **995**, "The Cowboy" by Remington, 1902. Amon Carter Museum of Western Art; **996**, David Woo/GL; **997**, Dennis Brack/BS.

Chapter 38 **999 B**, John Zoiner/Uniphoto; **1000**, CP; **1001 TL & 1001 INSET**, Stock Montage, Inc.; **1001 B**, Museum of the City of New York; **1002 T, FRENT**; **1002 B**, LOC; **1003**, Bob Daemmrich/Tony Stone Images; **1004**, Barney Taxel/NYT Pictures.

Chapter 39 **1006 T**, PRC Archive; **1006 B**, Brooks Kraft/Sygma; **1007**, David Hurn/MP; **1008**, Brooks Kraft/Sygma; **1009 BL**, "Mother and Child" by Dorothea Lange (detail). LOC; **1009 TL & TR**, PRC Archive; **1010 T, FRENT**; **1010 B**, Kingsport Press, Inc.; **1011**, J. Pat Carter/GL; **1012**, ©Liederman/Rothco; **1013**, Michael Heron.

Chapter 40 **1015 T**, Courtesy of the Costume Dept. Chicago Historical Society; 1920.38; **1015 B**, Lisa Quinones/BS; **1016**, Matthew McVay/Tony Stone Images; **1017 T**, William Campbell/Sygma; **1018 T**, NA; **1018 B**, LOC; **1019 TL**, BB; **1019 TR**, Museum of American Political Life; **1019 B**, "The World's Constable" by Dolrymple, JUDGE 1905, LOC; **1020 T**, Collection of PRC Photo by Lightstream; **1020 BL, FRENT**; **1022**, Int'l Brotherhood of Teamsters.

Chapter 41 **1024 T**, "Goddess of Liberty Weathervane" by L.W. Cushing, 1870. Courtesy of Fred and Kathryn Giampietro; **1024 B**, Herman Kokojan/BS; **1025 T**, Christopher Morris/BS; **1025 B**, © 1992 Klaus Reisinger/BS; **1026 ALL**, Collection of Colonel Stuart S. Corning, Jr. RH/LS; **1027 T**, NA #179-WP-936; **1027 B**, WW, **1028 T**, ©1959 Newseek, Inc. All rights reserved. Reprinted by permission; **1028 B**, Brad Markel/GL; **1029**, R. Bossu/Sygma; **1030**, JEFF STAHLER reprinted by permission of Newspaper Enterprise Assn., Inc.

Chapter 42 **1032 T**, David Chambers/Tony Stone Images; **1032 B**, ©David Young Wolff/Tony Stone Images; **1033 T**, Borgman-Cincinnati Enquirer. Reprinted with special permission of Kings Features Syndicate; **1033 BL**, Courtesy Picture Tel; **1033 BR & 1034 BR**, Div. of Political History, SI, #75-2343; **1035 BL**, Nipper's Choice Phonograph, Keene, NH. Photo by Wright Studio; **1035 BM**, Courtesy Ford Archives; **1035 MR**, NASA; **1036 T**, National Center for Supercomputing Applications at the University of Illinois; **1036 B**, Division of Community Life, SI; **1037 B**, Artwork from Wood River Gallery, Mill Valley, CA; **1038 T**, Kansas Historical Society; **1038 B**, LOC; **1039**, C/B; **1041 L**, Courtesy IBM Archives; **1041 R**, "Big Computers in Little Packages" ©1993 by Consumers Union of U.S. Inc., Yonkers, NY 10703-1057. Reprinted by permission from Consumer Reports, November 1993; **1042**, Steve Dunwell/The Image Bank.

Epilogue **1044-1045**, Stock connection ©1996 Joe Schm/Chromoschm.

Source Readings **1050**, New York Historical Society; **1051**, "Independence Hall" by William Birch, 1790. Rare Book Department, Free Library of Philadelphia; **1053 T**, National Portrait Gallery, SI/Art Resource, NY; **1053 B**, Architect of Capitol; **1054**, Independence National Historic Park, Philadelphia (detail); 1055, American Antiquarian Society; **1057**, PA Academy of the Fine Arts, Philadelphia, General Fun; **1058**, "Lazell, Perkins and Co., Bridgwater, Ma" 1858 by J.P. Newell. The Corcoran Gallery of Art, Mary E. Maxwell, Fund; **1060**, LOC, **1061**, National Park Service, Gift of Angelo Forgione; **1064 & 1066**, C/B; **1068**, Bayerisches Haupstaatsarchiv; **1069**, BB; **1070**, Nipper's Choice Phonograph, Keene, NH. Photo by Wright Studio; **1072**, Detroit News; **1075**, The Michael Barson Collection/Past Perfect RH/LS; **1077**, Kennedy Library; **1079**, C/B; **1080**, WW; **1081**, Eddie Adams/TIME Magazine; **1083**, Reagan Library; **1084**, Paul Conklin; **1085**, Stock Connection ©1995 Joe Schm/Chromoschm; **1086-1087**, "From Sea to Shing Sea" Quilt by Jacqueline Paton. Photo from the Museum of American Folk Art.

Primary Source Bibliography

Chapter 1 **Father Joseph Lafitau:** *Customs of the American Indians Compared with the Customs of Primitive Times.* The Champlain Society, 1977, p. 184; **Chief Joseph:** McLuhan, T. C. *Touch the Earth: A Self-Portrait of Indian Existence.* Simon and Schuster, 1971, p. 54; **John Winthrop:** Morgan, Edmund. *The Puritan Dilemma.* Little Brown, 1958, p. 88; **anonymous poet:** Furnivall, F. J., ed. *Ballads from Manuscripts, Vol. 1, 1868–1872. Ballad Society Series,* 1873; **Duarte Pacheco Pereira:** Boahen, A. Adu. *Kingdoms of West Africa: American Heritage History of Africa.* American Heritage, 1971, p. 183; **Leo Africanus:** Bennett, Jr., Lerone. *Before the Mayflower: A History of the Negro in America.* Johnson Publishing Company, 1966, p. 18; **Christopher Columbus:** Morison, Samuel Eliot. *Admiral of the Ocean Sea: A Life of Christopher Columbus.* Little Brown, 1942, p. 231; **Inca Garcilaso:** Garcilaso de la Vega, El Inca. *The Royal Commentaries of Peru, La Florida Del Inca.* Fondo de Cultura Económica, 1956, pp. 220, 229.

Chapter 2 **Fray Alonso de Benavides:** Kupperman, Karen Ordahl. *Major Problems in American Colonial*
History: Documents and Essays. D.C. Heath, 1993, p. 43; **Popé:** Gutiérrez, Ramón A. *When Jesus Came, the Corn Mothers Went Away.* Stanford University Press, 1991, p. 131; **Antonio de Otermín:** Kupperman, p. 46; **John Smith:** Lankford, John, ed. *Captain John Smith's America: Selections from His Writings.* Harper Torchbooks, Harper and Row, 1967, p. 105; **Richard Frethorne:** Kupperman, p. 93; **Adriaen Van der Donck:** Jennings, Francis. *The Ambiguous Iroquois Empire.* W.W. Norton & Company, 1984, p. 47; **Samuel Maverick:** Cronon, William. *Changes in the Land: Indians, Colonists, and the Ecology of New England.* Hill and Wang, 1983, p. 139; **John Winthrop:** "A Modell of Christian Charity." *Collections of the Massachusetts Historical Society,* 3rd series, vol. 7, 1838, pp. 33–34, 44–48; **Miantonomo:** Cronon, p. 162; **Metacom:** Bourne, Russell. *The Red King's Rebellion.* Atheneum, 1990, p. 107; **Native Americans:** Bourne, p. 176. **Cotton Mather:** Howe, George. "The Tragedy of King Philip and the Destruction of the New England Indians," *American Heritage.* December 1958, Vol. 10, No. 1. American Heritage Publishing Company, 1958, p. 77.

Chapter 3 **Thomas Mun:** Bruchey, Stuart, ed. *The Colonial Merchant: Sources and Readings.* Harcourt, Brace & World, 1966, p. 52; **The Reverend Mr. Devereux Jarratt:** Issac, Rhys. *The Transformation of Virginia, 1740–1790.* University of North Carolina Press, 1982, p. 43; **William Blackstone:** Ulrich, Laurel Thatcher. *Good Wives.* Oxford University Press, 1982, p. 7; **Eliza Pinckney:** Ravenel, Harriott Horry. *Eliza Pinckney.* Charles Scribner's Sons, 1896, p. 6; **Olaudah Equiano:** Edwards, Paul, ed. *Equiano's Travels.* Heinemann Educational Books, 1967, p. 25; **Equiano:** Edwards, p. 32; **Charles Ball:** Bayliss, John F., ed. *Black Slave Narratives.* Macmillan, 1970, p. 52; **Jonathan Edwards:** Kupperman, Karen Ordahl, ed. *Major Problems in American Colonial History: Documents and Essays.* D.C. Heath, 1993, p. 369; **George Whitefield:** Gaustad, Edwin Scott. *The Great Awakening in New England.* Quadrangle Books, 1957, p. 27.

Chapter 4 **Caleb Rea:** Anderson, Fred. *A People's Army: Massachusetts Soldiers and Society in the Seven Years' War.* University of North Carolina Press, 1984, p. 202; **Lord Loudon:** Kupperman, Karen Ordahl. *Major Problems in American Colonial History: Documents and Essays.* D.C. Heath, 1993, pp. 495–497; **anonymous French traveler:** Ransel, David, ed. "American Historical Review," Vol. 26. American Historical Association, 1921, pp. 745–46; **Stamp Act Congress:** Morgan, Edmund S., ed. *Prologue to Revolution: Sources and Documents on the Stamp Act Crisis, 1764–1766.* University of North Carolina Press, 1959, pp. 62–63; **John Dickinson:** Greene, Jack P., ed. *Colonies to Nation, 1763–1789.* W.W. Norton & Company, 1975, p. 13; **Peter Bestes et al.:** Brown, Richard D., ed. *Major Problems in the Era of the American Revolution, 1760–1791: Documents and Essays.* D. C. Heath, 1992, p. 308; **Declaration of Independence; Abigail Adams:** Brown, p. 302; **John Adams:** Brown, p. 302; **Judith Sargent Murray:** "On the Equality of the Sexes," *The Massachusetts Magazine,* March 1790, pp. 132–135; April 1790, pp. 223–226; **anonymous Englishman:** Wallace, Willard M. *Appeal to Arms: A Military History of the American Revolution.* Quadrangle/The New York Times Book Co., 1975, p. 43; **Michael Graham:** Dann, John C., ed. *The Revolution Remembered: Eyewitness Accounts of the War for Independence.* The University of Chicago Press, 1980, p. 50; **Thomas Paine:** Foot, Michael and Isaac Kramnick, eds. *Thomas Paine Reader.* Penguin Books, 1987, p. 116; **Sarah Osborn:** Dann, p. 245; **Joseph Plumb Martin:** Brown, pp. 223–224.

Chapter 5 **Fisher Ames:** Wood, Gordon S. *The Creation of the American Republic, 1776–1787.* W. W. Norton & Company, 1969, p. 411; **Richard Price:** Wood, p. 396; **Benjamin Rush:** Wood, p. 466; **United States Constitution; United States Constitution; Thomas Jefferson:** Kammen, Michael, ed. *The Origins of the American Constitution: A Documentary History.* Penguin, 1986, p. 91; **French ambassador:** Harwell, Richard. *Washington.* Charles Scribner's Sons, 1968, p. 567; **Convention member:** Parton, James. *Life of Thomas Jefferson.* Da Capo, 1971, quoted in Barbash, Fred. *The Founding: A Dramatic Account of the Writing of the Constitution.* Simon and Schuster, 1987, p. 77.

Chapter 6 **Alexander Hamilton:** Miller, John C. *The Federalist Era: 1789–1801.* Harper and Row, 1960, p. 81; **Margaret Bayard Smith:** Morris, Richard B. and James Woodress. *Voices from America's Past, Vol. 1: The Colonies and the New Nation.* E. P. Dutton, 1963, p. 194; **Thomas Jefferson:** Peterson, Merrill D., ed. *Thomas Jefferson.* Library of America, 1984, p. 494; **Handsome Lake:** Wallace, Anthony F. C. *The Death and Rebirth of the Seneca.* Vintage Books, 1972, p. 268; **Tenkswatawa:** Edmunds, David R. *The Shawnee Prophet.* University of Nebraska Press, 1983, p. 38; **Tecumseh:** Esarey, Logan, ed. *Governor's Messages and Letters: Messages and Letters of William Henry Harrison, Vol. 1, 1800–1811.* Indiana Historical Commission, 1922, p. 466; **Tecumseh:** Edmunds, David R. *Tecumseh and the Quest for Indian Leadership.* Little Brown and Company, 1984, p. 205; **The Star Spangled Banner; Thomas Jefferson:** Peterson, 1984.

Chapter 7 **Morris Birkbeck:** Birkbeck, Morris. "Notes on a Journey in America from the Coasts of Virginia to the Territory of Illinois." Philadelphia, 1817, p. 34; **James Graham:** Rohrbough, Malcolm J. *The Trans-Appalachian Frontier.* Oxford University Press, 1978, p. 196; **Charles Willson Peale:** Wood, Gordon S. *The Rising Glory of America, 1760–1820.* Northeastern University Press, 1990, p. 202; **Noah Webster:** Wood, p. 169; **Massachusetts legislature:** Butts, Freeman R. *Public Education in the United States: From Revolution to Reform.* Holt Rinehart and Winston, 1978, pp. 51–52; **Miss P. W. Jackson:** Kerber, Linda K. *Women of the Republic: Intellect and Ideology in Revolutionary America.* University of North Carolina Press, 1980, p. 229; **William Bentley:** Brown, Richard D. *Knowledge Is Power: The Diffusion of Information in Early America, 1700–1865.* Oxford University Press, 1989, p. 215; **Susanna Rowson:** Rowson, Susanna Haswell. *Charlotte Temple.* Oxford University Press, 1986, p. 5; **Zadoc Long:** Rothman, Ellen K. *Hands and Hearts: A History of Courtship in America.* Harvard University Press, 1984; **William Thacher:** Gorn, Elliot J., et al. *Constructing the American Past: A Source Book of a People's History.* HarperCollins, 1991, p. 185; **John Thompson:** Hatch, Nathan O. *The Democratization of American Christianity.* Yale University Press, 1989; **Richard Allen:** Hatch, p. 107.

Chapter 8 **Mason Weems:** Weems, Mason. *The Life of George Washington.* The Belknap Press of Harvard University Press, 1962, p. xv; **From *The Life of Washington* :** Weems, p. 12; **millworker:** Larcom, Lucy. *A New England Girlhood.* Corinth Books, 1961, pp. 145–156; **Methodist women:** Davis, David Byron. *Antebellum American Culture: An Interpretive Anthology.* D. C. Heath, 1979, p. 267; **craftworkers:** Wilentz, Sean, ed. *Major Problems in the Early Republic, 1878–1848.* D. C. Heath, 1992, p. 342; **Harriet Robinson:** Davis, pp. 87–88; **Moses Grandy:** *Narrative of the Life of Moses Grandy Late a Slave in the United States of America.* Oliver Johnson Publishing Company, 1844, p. 11, quoted in Lerner, Gerda. *Black Women in White America, A Documentary History.* Vintage Books, 1973, p. 9; **Denmark Vesey:** Freehling, William W. *Prelude to the Civil War: The Nullification Controversy in South Carolina, 1816–1836.* Harper and Row, 1966, p. 54; **Edwin C. Holland:** Freehling, p. 59; **John Quincy Adams:** Wilentz, p. 341; **President Jackson:** Wilentz, p. 388. **Cherokee:** Van Every, Dale. *Disinherited: The Lost Birthright of the American Indian.* William Morrow and Company, 1966, pp. 135–136.

Chapter 9 **Abraham Lincoln:** Davis, David Brion. *Antebellum American Culture: An Interpretive Anthology.* D. C. Heath, 1979, p. 407; **William Lloyd Garrison:** Wilentz, Sean, ed. *Major Problems in the Early Republic, 1787–1848.* D. C. Heath, 1992, p. 477; **Martin Delany:** Wilentz, p. 514; **Catharine Beecher:** *A Treatise on Domestic Economy.* T. H. Webb, 1842, pp. 26–34, 36–38; **Elizabeth Cady Stanton:** Stanton, Elizabeth Cady, et al. *History of Woman Suffrage, Vol. 1.* Fowler and Wells, 1889, pp. 58–59; **Sojourner Truth:** *Anti-Slavery Bugle,* Salem, Ohio, June 21, 1851, 4: p. 81–82; **Sojourner Truth:** Ripley, Peter, ed. *Witness for Freedom: African Voices on Race, Slavery, and Emancipation.* University of North Carolina Press, 1993, p. 102; **Herman Melville:** Gilfolyle, Timothy J. *City of Eros.* W.W. Norton, 1992. p. 89.

Chapter 10 **President Jefferson:** Brown, Richard C., ed. *The Human Side of History.* Ginn and Co., 1970, p. 73; **James R. Walker:** Walker, James R. *Lakota Society.* University of Nebraska Press, 1982, p. 74; **Wilkis:** Grinnell, George Bird. *When Buffalo Ran.* University of Oklahoma Press, 1966, p. 46;

George Catlin: Thornton, Russell. *American Indian Holocaust and Survival: A Population History Since 1492.*

University of Oklahoma Press 1942, p. 98; **William Travis:** Ramsdell, Charles. "The Storming of the Alamo," *American Heritage*, Vol. XII, p. 2, February 1961, p. 91; **anonymous:** Unruh, John D., Jr. *The Plains Across.* University of Illinois Press, 79, p. 414; **Brigham Young:** Ricks, Joel Edward. *Forms and Methods of Early Mormon Settlement in the Surrounding Region, 1847 to 1877.* Utah State University Press, 1964, p. 47; **Reverend Walter Colton:** *The Years in California.* S.A. Rollo, 1850, pp. 242–253; **Richard Henry Dana:** Dana, R.H., Jr. *Two Years Before the Mast and Twenty- Four Years After.* P. F. Collier, 1909, p. 394.

Chapter 11 **Harriet Beecher Stowe:** *Uncle Tom's Cabin.* New American Library, 1981, p. 32; **Harriet Beecher Stowe:** p. 93; **George Fitzhugh:** Gorn, Elliot J., et al. *Constructing the American Past: A Source Book of a People's History, Vol.* HarperCollins, 1991, p. 259; **John C. Calhoun:** Thomas, John L. *John C. Calhoun: A Profile.* Hill and Wang, 68, p. vii; **John C. Calhoun:** Wiltse, Charles M. *John C. Calhoun: Sectionalist, 1840–1850.* The Bobbs-Merrill Company, 1951, p. 461; **John C. Calhoun:** Heffner, Richard D. *A Documentary History of the United States.* New American Library, 1965, pp. 119–120; **John C. Calhoun:** Heffner, p. 127; **Rutherford B. Hayes:** Holt, Michael F. *The Political Crises of the 1850's.* John Wiley and Sons, 1978, p. 120; **Know Nothings:** Holt, p. 163; **Stephen Douglas:** Holt, p. 145; **Charles Sumner:** Donald, David. *Charles Sumner and the Coming the Civil War.* Alfred A. Knopf, 1960, p. 285; **Preston Brooks:** Donald, p. 294; **New York Evening Post:** Gienapp, William E. *The Origins of the Republican Party, 1852–1856.* Oxford University Press, 1987, p. 301; **Roger Taney:** Heffner, Richard D. *A Documentary History of the United States.* New American Library, 1976, p. 147; **Abraham Lincoln:** Angle, Paul M. *Created Equal? The Complete Lincoln-Douglas Debates of 1858.* The University of Chicago Press, 1958, p. 42; **Abraham Lincoln:** *Selected Speeches and Writings.* The Library of America, 1992, p. 131; **John Brown:** Oates, Stephen B. *To Purge This Land with Blood: A Biography of John Brown.* Harper Torchbooks, 1970, p. 351; **Republican:** Holt, p. 212; **newspaper editor:** Holt, Michael F. *The Political Crisis of the 1850's.* John Wiley and Sons, 1978, p. 241.

Chapter 12 **editor of *Richmond Examiner*:** *Richmond Examiner*, September 27, 1861; **Tennessee soldier:** McPherson, James. *Battle Cry of Freedom: The Civil War Era.* Oxford University Press, 1988, p. 413; **Mary Boykin Chesnut:** Woodward, C.Vann et al., eds. *Mary Chesnut's Civil War.* Yale University Press, 1981, pp. 326, 327, 330, 333, 339; **William Seward:** Bensel, Richard Franklin. *Yankee Leviathan: The Origins of Central State Authority in America, 1859–1877.* Cambridge University Press, 1990, p. 141; **Abraham Lincoln:** *Selected Speeches and Writings.* First Vintage Books, Library of America, 1992, p. 364; ***New York Herald* reporter:** *New York Herald*, July 18, 1863; **Frederick Douglass:** *Douglass' Monthly*, August, 1863; **Henry Harmon:** Redkey, Edwin S. *A Grand Army of Men: Letters from African-American Soldiers in the Union Army, 1861–1865.* Cambridge University Press, 1992, pp. 34–35; **Union officer:** Wheeler, Richard. *The Siege of Vicksburg.* Thomas Y. Crowell, 1978, p. xii; **James Autry:** Walker, Peter F. *Vicksburg, A People at War, 1860–1865.* The University of North Carolina Press, 1960, p. 91; **Grant's fellow officer:** Ketchum, Richard M. et al., eds. *The American Heritage Picture History of the Civil War.* American Heritage Publishing Company, Doubleday, 1960, p. 308; **Emma Balfour:** Walker, p. 135; **Josiah Gorgas:** McPherson, p. 665; **Abraham Lincoln's Gettysburg Address; Second Inaugural Address:** Lincoln, pp. 449–450; **William Sherman:** Foote, Shelby. *Civil War: A Narrative, Vol. 3.* Random House, 1974, p. 613.

Chapter 13 **A. J. Lewis:** Foner, Eric. *Reconstruction: America's Unfinished Revolution 1863–1877.* Harper and Row, 1988, p. 12; **African American/anonymous:** Foner, p. 80; **Charlotte Forten:** "Life on the Sea Islands," *Atlantic Monthly*, Vol. 13 (May and June) 1864, pp. 588–589, 591–594, 666–667; **white northerner:** Foner, Eric, p. 109; **Thomas Arnold:** Hoffmann, Charles and Tess. *North by South: The Two Lives of Richard James Arnold.* The University of Georgia Press, 1988, p. 256; **Fourteenth Amendment:** United States Constitution; **African American state convention:** Levine, Bruce et al, eds. *Who Built America? Working People and the Nation's Economy, Politics, Culture, and Society.* Pantheon Books, 1989, p. 477; **DeBow's Review:** *DeBow's Review*, Vol. V (February 1868), p. 136; **Thomas Allen:** Gorn, Elliott J. et al. *Constructing the American Past: A Source Book of a People's History.* HarperCollins Publishers, 1991, p. 321; **Lydia Child:** Foner, Eric, p. 473; **Ira Steward:** Levine, Bruce et al., p. 539.

Chapter 14 **Cornelia Adair:** Adair, Cornelia. *My Diary. August 30th to November 5th 1874.* University of Texas Press, 1965, pp. 105, 117; **From the folk tale "Railroads Ain't No Good":** Randolph, Vance, ed. "Railroads Ain't No Good" from *Sticks in the Knapsack and Other Folktales.* Columbia University Press, 1958, p. 84; **Finley Peter Dunne:** Filler, Louis, ed. *Mr. Dooley: Now and Forever.* Academic Reprints, 1954, p. 221; **Andrew Carnegie:** Carnegie, Andrew. *The Empire of Business.* Doubleday, 1902, pp. 138–140, quoted in Kirkland, Edward Chase. *Dream and Thought in the Business Community, 1860–1900.* Cornell, 1956, p. 156–157; **resident of Lynn, Massachusetts:** Bureau of Labor, *Fourth Annual Report*, 1873, p. 306; **Frederick Winslow Taylor:** Taylor, Frederick W. *The Principles of Scientific Management.* W.W. Norton and Company, 1911, p. 39; **factory manager:** Massachusetts Bureau of the Statistics of Labor. *Thirteenth Annual Report*, 1883; **Jacob Riis:** Riis, Jacob. *Children of the Poor.* Ayer Company Publishers, 1971; **Samuel Gompers:** Gompers, Samuel. *Labor and the Employer.* Ayer Company Publishers, 1971, p. 118; **George Baer:** Roy, Andrew. *A History of Coal Miners of the U.S.* J.L. Trauger, 1906, p. 424; **August Spies:** Kogan, B.R. "The Chicago Haymarket Riot," 1959 (a reproduction of the circular in the Chicago Historical Society collection).

Chapter 15 **Dakota brochure:** Billington, Ray. *Westward Expansion: A History of the American Frontier.* Macmillan, 1982, p. 647; **preacher from Georgia:** Painter, Nell I. *Exodusters: Black Migration to Kansas After Reconstruction.* Knopf, 1977, p. 83; **Ruede, Howard:** *Sod-House Days. Letters from a Kansas Homesteader, 1877–1878.* Columbia University Press, 1937, p. 28; **Elinore Pruitt Stewart:** *Letters of a Woman Homesteader.* University of Nebraska Press, 1961, pp. 214–215; **Chief Joseph:** Utley, Robert M. *The Indian Frontier of the American West, 1846–1890.* University of New Mexico Press, 1984, p. 193; **newspaper reporter:** Fite, Gilbert, *The Farmer's Frontier, 1865–1900.* University of New Mexico Press, 1974, p. 205; **newspaper report:** "Commercial and Financial Chronicle," September 21, 1879, quoted in Fite, p. 82; **Henry George:** *Progress and Poverty.* Phoenix Publishing, 1979; **rhyme:** Hicks, John D. *The Populist Revolt: A History of the Farmer's Alliance & the People's Party.* Greenwood, 1981, p. 204; **Tom Watson:** Woodward, C. Vann. *Tom Watson, Agrarian Rebel.* Oxford University Press, 1963, p. 220; **William Jennings Bryan:** Billington, p. 680; **Frederick Jackson Turner:** Billington, Ray, ed. *Frontier and Section: Selected Essays of Frederick Jackson Turner.* Prentice Hall, 1961, p. 61; **Edward L. Wheeler:** *Deadwood Dick, The Prince of the Road.* Garland, 1979, p. 16.

Chapter 16 **anonymous:** Kutler, Stanley I. *Looking for America: The People's History*, Vol. 2. W.W. Norton & Company, 1979, p. 178; **Fiorello LaGuardia:** *The Making of an Insurgent.* J.B. Lippincott Co., 1948, pp. 64–65; **newspaper reporter:** Swinton, John. *The New Issue: The Chinese American Question.* American News Co., 1870; **Sadie Frowne:** Adapted from "The Story of a Sweatshop Girl: Sadie Frowne," Katzman and Tuttle. *Plain Folk: The Life Stories of Undistinguished Americans.* Illinois, University of Illinois Press, 1982; **Take:** Nakan, Mei T. *Japanese American Women: Three Generations, 1890–1990.* Mina Press Publishing, 1990, pp. 75–95; **Eleanor McMain:** "Behind the Yellow Fever in Little Palermo: Housing Conditions Which New Orleans Should Shake Itself Free From Along with the Summer's Scourge," *Charities and the Commons*, Vol. 15, 1905, pp. 152–159; **Emily Dinwiddie:** "Some Aspects of Italian Housing and Social Conditions in Philadelphia," *Charities and the Commons*, Vol. 12, 1904, p. 490; **Martin Lomasney:** *Boston Globe*, December 2, 1923, quoted in Zink, Harold. *City Bosses in the United States. A Study of Twenty Municipal Bosses.* Duke University Press, 1930, p. 83.

Chapter 17 **Pauli Murray:** *Proud Shoes.* Harper and Row, 1956, pp. 269–270; **notice to performers:** Royle, Edwin Milton. "The Vaudeville Theatre," *Scribner's Magazine*, Vol. XXVI, October 1899, pp. 485–495;

Madam C. J. Walker: Hine, Darlene Clark et al., eds. *Black Women in America. An Historical Encyclopedia*, Vol. 2. Carlson Publishing, 1993, pp. 1209–1214; **Edward H. Clarke:** *Sex in Education; or a Fair Chance for the Girls.* Ayer Co. Publishers, 1972 (reproduction of the 1873 edition).

Chapter 18 **James G. Blaine:** LaFeber, Walter. *The New Empire: An Interpretation of American Expansion, 1860–1898.* Cornell University Press, 1963, p. 165; **Albert J. Beveridge:** *The Meaning of the Times and Other Speeches.* Books for Libraries Press, 1908, pp. 84–85; **Hearst newspaper:** LaFeber, p. 230; **Theodore Roosevelt:** Hart, Albert Bushnell and Herbert Ronald Ferleger, eds. *Theodore Roosevelt Cyclopedia.* Roosevelt Memorial Association, 1941, p. 407; **Lucia Mead:** Crapol, Edward P., ed. *Women and American Foreign Policy: Lobbyists, Critics, and Insiders.* Greenwood Press, 1987, p. 72; **Carl Schurz:** "The Policy of Imperialism," 1899 address by Carl Schurz to Anti-Imperialist Conference in Chicago, October 17, 1899; **Bishop Alexander Walters:** "Wisconsin Weekly Advocate," August 17, 1899, quoted in Gatewood, Willard B., Jr. *Black Americans and the White Man's Burden, 1898–1903.* University of Illinois Press, 1975, p. 200; **Carl Schurz:** Lasch, Christopher. "The Anti-Imperialists, the Philippines, and the Inequality of Man," *Journal of Southern History*, August 1958, p. 115.

Chapter 19 **Edward Bellamy:** *Looking Backward.* River City Press, 1888, p. 56; **Jane Addams:** "Why Women Should Vote." *Ladies Home Journal*, Vol. XXVII, January 1910, pp. 21–22; **Upton Sinclair:** *The Jungle.* Doubleday, 1906, pp. 96–97; **Justice David J. Brewer:** *Muller v. Oregon*, quoted in Kerber, Linda J., and Jane De Hart, eds. *Women's America: Refocusing the Past.* Oxford University Press, 1987, p. 541; **Elizabeth Cady Stanton:** Flexner, Eleanor. *Century of Struggle: The Woman's Rights Movement in the United States.* The Belknap Press of Harvard University Press, 1975, p. 177; **Carrie Chapman Catt:** Flexner, p. 176.

Chapter 20 **Richard Harding Davis:** New York *Tribune*, August 1914; **Arthur Zimmerman:** Leckie, Robert. *The Wars of America.* Harper and Row, 1968, p. 628; **Woodrow Wilson:** Cooper, John Milton, Jr. *Pivotal Decades: The United States, 1900–1920.* W.W. Norton and Company, 1990, p. 265; **Mary Gladwin:** Dock, Lavinia L., et al. *A History of American Red Cross Nursing.* Macmillan, 1922, p. 179; **Corporal Elmer Sherwood:** Berger, Dorothy and Josef, eds. *Diary of America.* Simon and Schuster, 1957, p. 536; **Herbert Hoover:** "Gospel of the Clean Plate." *Ladies Home Journal*, August 1917, p. 25; **Alice Lord O'Brian:** *No Glory: Letters from France, 1917–1919.* Airport Publishers, 1936, pp. 8, 141, 152–153.

Chapter 21 **Bart Vanzetti:** Stong, Phil, "The Last Days of Sacco and Vanzetti," in Leighton, Isabel. ed. *The Aspirin Age, 1919–1941.* Simon and Schuster, 1949, p. 188; **Albert Johnson:** Daniels, Roger. *Coming to America: A History of Immigration and Ethnicity in America.* HarperCollins, 1990, p. 284; **New Orleans citizen:** "Additional Letters of Negro Migrants of 1916–1918." *Journal of Negro History*, April 4, 1919, p. 451; **Edna St. Vincent Millay:** "First Fig." *Edna St. Vincent Millay: Selected Poems.* HarperCollins, 1991, p. 19; **Preston Slosson:** *The Great Crusade and After, 1914–1928.* Macmillan, 1929, p. 157; **New York Sun:** Ward, John William. "The Meaning of Lindbergh's Flight." *American Quarterly*, Vol. X (Spring 1958), p. 1; **Henry Ford:** *My Life and Work.* Doubleday, 1923, p. 251; **Billy Sunday:** Sinclair, Andrew. *Era of Excess: A Social History of the Prohibition Movement.* Harper and Row, 1964, p. 248.

Chapter 22 **Lincoln Steffens:** Leuchtenberg, William. *The Perils of Prosperity, 1914–1932.* University of Chicago Press, 1958, p. 202; **Arthur Crew Inman:** Aaron, Daniel, ed. *The Inman Diary: A Public and Private Confession.* Harvard University Press, 1985, p. 401; **Broadway show tune:** Words by E. Y. Harburg, music by Jay Gorney. Harms, Inc., 1932. Renewed, permission from Warner Brothers Music. **Oklahoma woman:** Terkel, Studs. *Hard Times: An Oral History of the Great Depression.* Pantheon Books, 1970, p. 50; **Woody Guthrie:** *Bound for Glory.* E. P. Dutton, 1968, p. 189; **boy tramp:** Minehan, Thomas. *Boy and Girl Tramps of America.* Holt, Rinehart, and Winston, 1934, pp. 21–23, 53–54, 62–64; **Gordon Parks:** *Voices in the Mirror: An Autobiography.* Doubleday, 1990; **Wilson Ledford:** "How I Lived During the Depression." Interview taped and transcribed by Reuben Hiatt, November 7, 1982. Quoted in Snell, William R. ed., *Hard Times Remembered: Bradley County and the Great Depression.* Bradley County Historical Society, 1983, pp. 117–121; **Gerald W. Johnson:** "The Average American and the Depression." *Current History*, February 1932; **Kitty McCulloch:** Terkel, Studs. *Hard Times: An Oral History of the Great Depression.* Pantheon Books, 1970; **William Saroyan:** *Inhale and Exhale.* Random House, 1936, p. 81; **The 1932nd Psalm:** E. J. Sullivan. Quoted in McElvaine, Robert S., ed. *Down and Out in the Great Depression: Letters from the Forgotten Man.* University of North Carolina Press, 1983, p. 34; **Herbert Hoover:** Myers, William S., ed. *The State Papers and Other Public Writings of Herbert Hoover.* Doubleday, Doran and Company, Inc., Vol. II, 1934, pp. 408–413; **Franklin D. Roosevelt:** *New York Times*, September 24, 1932; **Roosevelt:** Inaugural Address, March 4, 1933.

Chapter 23 **Harry Hopkins:** Dawley, Alan. *Struggles for Justice: Social Responsibility and the Liberal State.* Harvard University Press, 1991, p. 367; **Mary McLeod Bethune:** "Faith That Moved a Dump Heap." *Who, The Magazine About People*, January 3, 1941, pp. 31–35, 54; **Letters to Roosevelt:** *This Fabulous Century: Sixty Years of American Life, 1930–1949.* Time Life Books, Vol. IV, 1969, p. 136; **federal official:** Markowitz, Gerald, and David Rosner, eds. "Slaves of the Depression." *Workers' Letters About Life on the Job.* Cornell, 1987, p. 154; **Walter White:** *A Man Called White: The Autobiography of Walter White.* Viking Press, 1948, pp. 179–180; **Sam E. Roberts:** Duram, James C. and Eleanor A. "Congressman Clifford Hope's Correspondence With his Constituents: A Conservative View of the Court-Packing Fight of 1937." *Kansas Historical Quarterly* 37/1 (Spring 1971), p. 71; **Hiram W. Johnson:** Barnes, William R., and A. W. Littlefield. *The Supreme Court Issue and the Constitution, Comments Pro and Con by Distinguished Men.* Barnes & Noble, 1937, p. 49; **Walter Reuther:** Madison, Charles A. *American Labor Leaders, Personalities and Forces in the Labor Movement.* Ungar, 1950, p. 382; **Mrs. Renee Lohrback:** Blackwelder, Julia Kirk. *Women of the Depression: Caste and Culture in San Antonio, 1929–1939.* Texas A&M Press, 1984.

Chapter 24 **Karl Alexander von Müller:** Flood, Charles Bracelen. *Hitler: The Path to Power.* Houghton Mifflin Company, 1989, p. 493; **Dellie Hahne:** Harris, Mark Jonathan, et al. *The Homefront: America During World War II.* G. P. Putnam's Sons, 1984, p. 27; **Dick Winters:** Ambrose, Stephan. *Band of Brothers: E. Company, 506th Regiment, 101st Airborne: From Normandy to Hitler's Eagle's Nest.* Simon & Schuster, 1992, p. 270; **Ernie Pyle:** Nichols, David. *Ernie's War: The Best of Ernie Pyle's World War II Dispatches.* Random House, 1986, p. 141; **Art Rittenberg:** Lidz, Richard. *Many Kinds of Courage: An Oral History of World War II.* G. P. Putnam's Sons, 1980, p. 243; **Eisenhower:** Carroll, James. "The monster that adds a chill to the August air." *The Boston Globe*, August 17, 1993; **Tatsue Urata:** Winkler, Allan M. *Life Under a Cloud, American Anxiety About the Atom.* Oxford University Press, 1993, p. 23.

Chapter 25 **Leonard Williamson:** Hoopes, Roy. *Americans Remember the Home Front: An Oral Narrative.* Hawthorn Books, 1977, p. 115; **Want ad:** *Sporting News*, February 25, 1943; **Wanita Allen:** Frank, Miriam, Marilyn Ziebarth, and Connie Field. *The Life and Times of Rosie the Riveter.* Clarity Educational Productions, 1982, p. 57; **Beatrice Clifton:** Gluck, Sherna Berger. *Rosie the Riveter Revisited: Women, the War, and Social Change.* Twayne Publishers, 1987, pp. 211, 219; **from the film *Women of Steel*:** Frank, Miriam, et al. *The Life and Times of Rosie the Riveter.* Clarity Educational Productions, 1982, p. 100; **Margaret Wright:** Frank et al., p. 94; **Roosevelt:** Columbus Day speech, 1942; **Lloyd Brown:** Blum, John Morton. *V Was for Victory: Politics and American Culture During World War II.* Harcourt Brace Jovanovich, 1976, p. 191; **Henry Murakami:** Harris, Mark Jonathan, et al. *The Homefront: America During World War II.* G. P. Putnam's Sons, 1984, p. 113.

Chapter 26 **Joseph Goulden:** *The Best Years, 1945–1950.* Atheneum, 1976; **Joseph Stalin:** Truman, Harry S. *Memoirs, Volume I: Year of Decisions.* Doubleday & Company, Inc., 1955, p. 86; **Harry Truman:** Truman, p. 289; **Truman:** Truman, *Memoirs, Volume I*; **MacArthur:** Phillips, Cabell. *The Truman Presidency: The History of a Triumphant Succession.* The Macmillan Company, 1966, p. 348; **Joseph Welch:** Lately, Thomas.

When Even Angels Wept: The Senator Joseph McCarthy Affair—A Story Without a Hero. William Morrow & Company, Inc., 1973, pp. 587–588.

Chapter 27 Walt Disney: Winkler, Allan M. *Life Under a Cloud: American Anxiety About the Atom.* Oxford University Press, 1993, p. 140; **Malvina Reynolds:** Winkler, Allan M. *Modern America: The United States from World War II to the Present.* HarperCollins, 1985, p. 86; **Eisenhower:** *Mandate for Change, 1953–1956.* Doubleday and Company, Inc., 1963, p. 548; **Betty Friedan:** *The Feminine Mystique.* Norton, 1963; **Harry Truman:** Winkler, p. 70; **Richard Nixon:** Wicker, Tom. *One of Us: Richard Nixon and the American Dream.* Random House, 1991, p. 98; **Eisenhower:** Holbo, Paul S., and Robert W. Sellen, eds. *The Eisenhower Era.* Dryden Press, 1974, p. 113; **Jackie Robinson:** Henderson, Edwin B. *The Black Athlete: Emergence and Arrival.* Publisher's Agency under the auspices of the Association for the Study of Afro-American Life and History, 1976, p. xii; **Martin Luther King, Jr.:** Sitkoff, Harvard. *The Struggle for Black Equality: 1954–1980.* Hill and Wang, 1981, p. 50; **Martin Luther King, Jr.:** *Stride Toward Freedom: The Montgomery Story.* Harper and Row, 1958, pp. 53–55; **Seminole petition to Eisenhower:** Josephy, Alvin M., Jr. *Now That the Buffalo's Gone: A Study of Today's American Indians.* Alfred A. Knopf, 1982, p. 28.

Chapter 28 John F. Kennedy: Inaugural Address. January 20, 1961; **John Kenneth Galbraith:** Winkler, Allan M. *Modern America: The United States from World War II to the Present.* HarperCollins, 1985, p. 125; **Lyndon B. Johnson:** Speech at the University of Michigan, May 1964; **Tom Hayden:** Winkler, Allan M. *The Recent Past: Readings on America Since World War II.* Harper and Row, 1989, p. 164; **John F. Kennedy:** Address to Latin American diplomats, March 13, 1961; **Arthur M. Schlesinger, Jr.:** Nash, Gary. *The American People. Volume Two, Since 1865: Creating a Nation and a Society.* Harper and Row, 1986, p. 963; **Paul Cowan:** *The Making of an Un-American: A Dialogue with Experience.* Viking Press, 1970, dedication page; **Senator J. William Fulbright:** Schlesinger, Arthur M. *A Thousand Days: John F. Kennedy in the White House.* Houghton Mifflin, 1965, p. 251; **Dean Acheson:** Winkler, Allan M. *Life Under a Cloud: American Anxiety About the Atom.* Oxford University Press, 1993, pp. 173–174.

Chapter 29 W. E. B. DuBois: Aptheker, Herbert, ed. *Pamphlets and Leaflets by W. E. B . DuBois.* Kraus-Thomason Organization Limited, 1986, p. 116; **Southern Christian Leadership Conference:** Sitkoff, Harvard. *The Struggle for Black Equality.* Hill and Wang, 1981, p. 65; **SCLC leaflet:** Sitkoff, p. 59; **Martin Luther King, Jr.:** Sitkoff, p. 92; **Todd Gitlin:** *The Sixties: Years of Hope, Days of Rage.* Bantam Books, 1987, pp. 148–149; **Anne Moody:** *Coming of Age in Mississippi.* Dell, 1968; **John Lewis:** Hampton, Henry, et al. *Voices of Freedom: An Oral History of the Civil Rights Movement from the 1950's Through the 1980's.* Bantam Books, 1990, p. 58; **James Farmer:** Hampton, p. 78; **Martin Luther King, Jr.:** "Letter From a Birmingham Jail." *Essay Series.* A. J. Muste Memorial Institute, p. 18; **John F. Kennedy:** Radio and Television Report to the American People on Civil Rights, June 11, 1963; **Martin Luther King, Jr.:** "I Have a Dream." Speech in Washington, D.C., August 1963. In Winkler, Allan M. *The Recent Past: Readings on America Since World War II.* Harper and Row, 1989, p. 275; **Fannie Lou Hamer:** Harley, Sharon, et al. *The African American Experience: A History.* Globe Book Company, 1992, p. 336; **James Baldwin:** *The Fire Next Time.* Dial Press, 1963, p. 132; **Malcolm X:** *The Autobiography of Malcolm X.* Ballantine Books, 1990, pp. 245–246; **Stokely Carmichael:** Nash, Gary B., et al., eds. *The American People.* Harper and Row, 1986, p. 1001; **Barbara Jordan:** Harley, et al , p. 343.

Chapter 30 Cathy Cade: Evans, Sara. *Personal Politics: The Roots of Women's Liberation in the Civil Rights Movement and the New Left.* Alfred A. Knopf, 1979, p. 205; **Mimi Feingold:** Evans, p. 204; **Helen Reddy:** "I Am Woman." Words by Helen Reddy, music by Ray Burton. Irving Music, Inc. and Buggerlugs Music Co., 1971; **Equal Rights Amendment to the Constitution, 1972; Marabel Morgan:** *The Total Woman.* Simon and Schuster, 1973, pp. 96–97; **Phyllis Schlafly:** Nash, Gary B. *The American People: Creating a Nation and a Society.* Harper and Row, 1986, p. 1008; **Rodolfo Gonzales:** Hammerback, John C., Richard J. Jensen and Jose Angel Gutierrez. *A War of Words: Chicano Protest in the 1960's and 1970's.* Greenwood Press, 1985, p. 59; **César Chávez:** Levy, Jacques E. *César Chávez: Autobiography of La Causa.* W.W. Norton, 1975; **César Chávez:** Levy, p. 293; **David Sanchez:** Vigil, Maurilio. *Chicano Politics.* University Press of America, 1977, p. 173; **Dennis Banks:** Zimmerman, Bill. *Airlift to Wounded Knee.* Swallow Press, 1976, p. 117; **Dennis Banks:** Dewing, Rolland. *Wounded Knee: The Meaning and Significance of the Second Incident.* Irvington Publishers, Inc., 1985, p. 41; **Vine Deloria, Jr.:** "This Country Was a Lot Better Off When the Indians Were Running It." *New York Times Magazine,* March 8, 1970; **Onondaga Chief Oren Lyons:** *Voices from Wounded Knee: The People Are Standing Up.* Akwesasne Notes, 1974, p. 96; **a Taos representative:** Debo, Angie. *A History of the Indians of the United States.* University of Oklahoma Press, 1977, p. 419; **Rachel Carson:** *Silent Spring.* Houghton Mifflin, 1962, p. 6; **Ralph Nader:** *Unsafe at Any Speed: The Designed-in Dangers of the American Automobile.* Grossman Publishers, 1972, preface.

Chapter 31 Lyndon B. Johnson: Kearns, Doris. *Lyndon Johnson and the American Dream.* Harper and Row, 1976, p. 316; **Angel Qunitana:** Maurer, Harry. *Strange Ground: Americans in Vietnam, 1945–1975, An Oral History.* Henry Holt and Company, 1989, p. 171; **Le Thanh:** Chanoff, David, and Van Toai Doan. *Portrait of the Enemy.* Random House, 1986, pp. 62–63; **Vietnamese peasant:** Trullinger, James Walker, Jr. *Village at War: An Account of Revolution in Vietnam.* Longman, 1980, p. 118. **Private Paul Meadlo:** *New York Times,* November 25, 1969, p. 16; **Bob Dylan:** "The Times They Are A-Changin.' " Words and music by Bob Dylan. Warner Brothers, 1963; **Tom Hayden:** Students for a Democratic Society, *Port Huron Statement.* Quoted in Winkler, Allan. *The Recent Past: Readings on America Since World War II.* Harper and Row, 1989, pp. 218–219; **Mario Savio:** Winkler, Allan M. *Modern America: The United States from World War II to the Present.* HarperCollins, 1985, p. 153; **Bo Burlingham:** Obst, Lynda Rosen, ed. *The Sixties: The Decade Remembered Now by the People Who Lived It Then.* Random House Rolling Stone Press, 1977, p. 300; **Lynn Ferrin:** Morrison, Joan and Robert K. *From Camelot to Kent State: The Sixties Experience in the Words of Those Who Lived It.* Times Books, 1987, p. 176; **Tom Law:** Makower, Joel. *Woodstock: The Oral History.* Doubleday, 1989, p. 333; **Richard Nixon:** Address to the Nation on the Situation in Southeast Asia. April 30, 1970; **Tom Grace:** Morrison, et al., pp. 332–333; **Ron Kovic:** *Born on the Fourth of July.* Pocket Books, 1989.

Chapter 32 Martin Luther King, Jr.: Kaiser, Charles. *1968 in America: Music, Politics, Chaos, Counterculture, and the Shaping of a Generation.* Weidenfeld and Nicolson, 1988, p. 144; **John Lewis:** Morrison, Joan, and Robert K. *From Camelot to Kent State: The Sixties Experience in the Words of Those Who Lived It.* Times Books, 1987, pp. 34–35; **Todd Gitlin:** Obst, Lynda Rosen ed. *The Sixties: The Decade Remembered Now by the People Who Lived It Then.* Random House Rolling Stone Press, 1977; **Richard Nixon:** Wicker, Tom. *One of Us: Richard Nixon and the American Dream.* Random House, 1991, p. 9; **Lawrence O'Brien:** Siegal, Frederick F. *Troubled Journey: From Pearl Harbor to Ronald Reagan.* Hill and Wang, 1984; **Richard Nixon:** Ambrose, Stephen E. *Nixon: Volume Two: The Triumph of a Politician, 1962–1972.* Simon and Schuster, 1989, p. 376; **Henry Kissinger:** *White House Years.* Little, Brown and Company, 1979, p. 45; **Richard Nixon:** *The Memoirs of Richard Nixon.* Grosset and Dunlap, 1978, p. 545; **Richard Nixon:** *Public Papers of the Presidents of the United States: Richard Nixon.* United States Government Printing Office, 1972, p. 237; **Richard Nixon:** *Public Papers of the Presidents of the United States: Richard Nixon,* p. 320; **John J. Sirica:** Bernstein, Carl and Bob Woodward. *All the President's Men.* Warner Paperback Books, 1975, p. 268; **M. Caldwell Butler:** Burns, James MacGregor. *The Crosswinds of Freedom.* Alfred A. Knopf, 1989, p. 507.

Chapter 33 Richard Rovere: Reeves, Richard. *A Ford, Not a Lincoln.* Harcourt Brace Jovanovich, 1975; **Gerald Ford:** *A Time to Heal: The Autobiography of Gerald R. Ford.* Harper and Row, 1979, pp. 177–178; **Jerold F. terHorst:** "How Good a President?" *Newsweek,* October 18, 1976, p. 31; **Jimmy Carter:** *Keeping Faith:*

Memoirs of a President. Bantam Books, 1982, p. 65; **Patrick Caddell:** Wooten, Jas. *Dasher: The Roots and the Rising of Jimmy Carter.* Weidenfeld and Nicolson, 1978, 356; **Alistair Cooke:** "On Language." *New York Times Magazine,* July 19, 1981; **Jimmy Carter:** Carter, pp. 1–143; **Cyrus Vance:** *Hard Choices: Critical Years in America's Foreign Policy.* Simon and Schuster, 1983, pp. 2–229; **Kathryn Koob:** *Guest of the Revolution.* Thomas Nelson Publishers, 1982, pp. 57, 64, 73; **Jimmy Cter:** Jordan, Hamilton. *Crisis: The Last Year of the Carter Presidency.* G. P. Putnam's Sons, 1982, p. 54;

Robert J. Samuelson: "Good People, but Not Very Good Government." *The Eugen Register-Guard,* January 19, 1981; **Jimmy Carter:** Public address; **Jimmy Carter:** Carter, p. 22; **Robert J. amuelson:** Samuelson, January 19, 1981.

Chapter 34 Ronald Reagan: Inaugural Address: "Putting America Back to Wo" January 20, 1981. *Vital Speeches of the Day,* Vol. XLVII, No. 9, February 15, 1981. **Kevin Phillips:** "Reagan's erica: A Capital Offense." *New York Times Magazine,* June 24, 1990; **George Bush:** "Open Letter to College Stunts on the Persian Gulf Crisis," January 9, 1991.

Chapter 35 Bill Clinton: Address to Congress and the Nation on Health Care Rem. September, 1993; **Jaimie S. Wurzel:** *Toward Multiculturalism: A Reader in Multicultural Education.* Intultural Press, Inc. 1988, p. 10.

Source Readings Acknowledgments

Unit 1 **The Captivity of Mary Rowlandson:** Lang, Amy Schrager, ed. "A True History of the Captivity and Restoration of Mary Rowlandson" in Andrews, William L., Sargent Bus Jr., Annette Kolodny, Amy Schrager Lang, and Daniel B. Shea, eds. JOURNEYS IN NEW AMERICAN WOMEN'S NARRATIVES. ©1990. (Madison: The University of Wisnsin Press.) Reprinted by permission of the University of Wisconsin Press. **A Young Woma's War-Time Diary:** From *Root of Bitterness: Documents of the Social History of American Women,* edited t Nancy F. Cott. ©1972 by Nancy F. Cott. Reprinted with the permission of Northeastern Univerty Press.

Unit 2 **Miracle at Philadelphia:** From *Miracle at Philadelphia* by Catherine Drinr Bowen. Copyright 1966 by Catherine Drinker Bowen. By permission of Little, Brown, and Co.; **Benmin Franklin Campaigns for the Constitution:** Reprinted by permission from the Putnam Publishg Group from DEBATES OF THE CONSTITUTIONAL CONVENTION 1787 edited by Gaillard Hur Copyright ©1903.

Unit 3 **Incidents in the Life of a Slave Girl:** Harriet Ann Jacobs, *Incidents in th Life of a Slave Girl: Written by Herself.* (Cambridge, MA: Harvard University Press, 1987); **"To a Locootive in Winter":** Walt Whitman. "To a Locomotive in Winter" in *Walt Whitman Complete Poetry and ollected Prose.* (New York, NY: Literary Classics of the United States, Inc., 1982).

Unit 4 **Diary of a Southern Woman:** Mary Boykin Chesnut. *A Diary from Dixie,* eited by Ben Ames Williams. (Boston: Houghton Mifflin, 1945); **The Gettysburg Address:** Abraham incoln. Gettysburg Address, in Henry Steele Commager, ed. *Documents of American History,* 8th ed. (Nw York: Appleton-Century-Crofts, 1968).

Unit 5 **Where Is America?:** Anzia Yezierska. *Hungry Hearts.* Permission granted y Ayer Company Publishers. **Separate but Equal:** *Plessy* v. *Ferguson,* 163 U.S. 537 (1896).

Unit 6 **The United States Looking Outward:** Adapted from Alfred T. Mahan, "Th United States Looking Outward," Boston, MA: *Atlantic Monthly,* December 1890; **All Quiet on the Western Front:** *All Quiet on the Western Front* by Erich Maria Remarque. "Im Westen Nichts Neues," ©1928 by Ullstein A.G.; ©renewed 1956 by Erich Maria Remarque. "All Quiet on the Western Front," ©1929, 1930 by Little, Brown, and Co.; © renewed 1957, 1958 by Erich Maria Remarque. All rights eserved.

Unit 7 **The Rich Boy:** Excerpted with permission of Scribner, a Division of Simon Schuster, from THE SHORT STORIES OF F. SCOTT FITZGERALD, edited by Matthew J. Bruccoli. ©925, 1926 Consolidated Magazines Corporation. Copyrights renewed 1953, 1954 by Frances Scott Fitzgerald Lanahan; **Letters from the Forgotten Man:** From DOWN AND OUT IN THE GREAT DEPRESSION by Robert S. McElvaine. Copyright ©1983 by the University of North Carolina Press. Usd by permission of the publisher.

Unit 8 **Survivors of the Holocaust Remember:** From *Shoah: An Oral History of the Holocaust,* by Claude Lanzmann. ©1985 by Claude Lanzmann. Reprinted by permission of Georges orchardt, Inc. for the author. **A Londoner Describes Life During the Blitz:** Studs Terkel. From *The God War: An Oral History of World War II* by Studs Terkel. Reprinted by permission of Donadio & Ashworth, Inc. Copyright 1984, Studs Terkel. **1984:** Excerpt from NINETEEN EIGHTY-FOUR by George Orwell, copyright 1949 by Harcourt Brace & Company and renewed 1977 by Sonia Brownell Orwell, reprinted by permission of the publisher.

Unit 9 **President Kennedy's Inaugural Address:** Department of State Bulletin, February 6, 1961. (Washington, D.C.: Office of Public Communication, Bureau of Public Affairs); **Letter from Birmingham Jail:** Reprinted by arrangement with The Heirs to the Estate of Martin Luther King, Jr., c/o Writers House, Inc. as agent for the proprietor. Copyright 1963 by Martin Luther King, Jr., copyright renewed 1991 by Coretta Scott King; **Letter Home from Vietnam:** From *Dear America: Letters Home from Vietnam,* edited by Bernard Edelman for the New York Vietnam Veterans Memorial Commission. Reprinted by permission.

Unit 10 **"These Are the Boys of Point du Hoc":** *Public Papers of the Presidents of the United States: Ronald Reagan,* 1984, p. 817; **An Oval Room with a View:** Bill Clinton. From *Vanity Fair,* February 1996.

Unit 11 **My American Journey:** From MY AMERICAN JOURNEY by Colin Powell with Joseph E. Persico. Copyright ©1995 by Colin L. Powell. Reprinted by permission of Random House, Inc.; **"Reclaiming the Dream":** From DIVIDED WE FALL: Gambling With History in the Nineties by Haynes Johnson. Copyright ©1994 by Haynes Johnson. Reprinted by permission of W. W. Norton & Company, Inc.

DATE DUE

APR 28 2000			
2-18-02			
MAR 18 2002			
FEB 13 2006			
APR 29 2008			
MAY 30 2009			
MAR 30 2009			
JUN 30 2010			
GAYLORD			PRINTED IN U.S.A